D1491846

THE OXFORD COMPANION TO
SHIPS AND THE SEA

THE OXFORD COMPANION TO

SHIPS & THE SEA

EDITED BY PETER KEMP

Oxford University Press · London · New York · Melbourne

Oxford University Press, Walton Street, Oxford OX2 6DP

OXFORD LONDON GLASGOW
NEW YORK TORONTO MELBOURNE WELLINGTON
KUALA LUMPUR SINGAPORE JAKARTA HONG KONG TOKYO
DELHI BOMBAY CALCUTTA MADRAS KARACHI
IBADAN NAIROBI DAR ES SALAAM CAPE TOWN

First published 1976
Reprinted with corrections 1979

Line drawings by Peter Milne and the OUP drawing office

Photographic credits are listed on page 972

Title page—The Spanish Armada in 1588;
engraving by J. Pine after a tapestry by H. C. Vroom

British Library Cataloguing Publication Data

Oxford companion to ships & the sea.
ISBN 0-19-211553-7
1. Kemp, Peter Kemp.
623.82′003   V23
Ships-Dictionaries

Filmset in Photon Times 9 pt. by
Richard Clay (The Chaucer Press), Ltd., Bungay, Suffolk
and printed in Great Britain by
Fletcher & Son Ltd., Norwich

Preface

The world's oceans cover a little more than seven-tenths of the earth's surface. Until the explosion of air passenger traffic during the last 30 years they were the only open highway which joined the nations of the world, and even now most of the world's trade is carried by sea. It is not surprising, therefore, that over a span of some 5,000 years, from the days when man first ventured on the waters in his crude canoe to the modern age of the nuclear submarine, the hydrofoil, and the ultra large crude carrier of half a million tons, much of the world's history has been written on the oceans. It is the purpose of this *Companion* to bring together in readily accessible form a range of marine information which can otherwise be gleaned only with the help of an extensive library. The field to be covered is immense, ranging from the ships and the men who first opened up the world with their voyages into the unknown, through the struggles of nations as they developed and recognized that power and prosperity depended on the exercise of sea power, to those who wrote about, and painted, the sea scene. And within that wide compass lie all sorts of maritime specialities, the changing designs of ships to meet particular developing needs, the huge growth of yachting as modern man and woman more and more finds delight, relaxation, and challenge in the wide spaces of the sea, and the modern developments in navigation which so greatly simplify the art of finding the way at sea. These, and a host of similar subjects, have their place in this *Companion*.

The rich language of the sea, exotic perhaps to the landman, is another field for the *Companion* to cover. It has developed through the centuries into a well-recognized and accepted *lingua franca* which binds together the seamen of many countries and makes them a breed of men whose colourful language quickly identifies their trade. As Smyth quotes in his *Sailor's Word-Book*, 'How could the whereabouts of an aching tooth be better pointed out to an operative dentist than Jack's "'Tis the aftermost grinder aloft, on the starboard quarter".' A great many household words also have been taken to sea and their shore meanings adapted to a completely new environment. Thus, in a sailing ship, may be found an apron, a bonnet, braces, a cap, and a shoe; a cot, a cradle, and a crib; a horse, bridle, saddle, stirrup, martingale, coach, carriage, whip, and hounds; a dog, fox, mouse, and rabbit (though the sailor, in his idiosyncratic way, spells it as rabbet). Definitions, and the derivation where known, are given for most of the words and terms used every day at sea; those which have fallen into disuse through technological development, as for example by the substitution of the power-driven merchant vessel for the older square-rigged ship, are also included because they appear so frequently in the literature of the sea. In this particular case a small problem of tenses arose; in general the present tense has been used in the *Companion* since many of these lovely old ships, including at least one four-masted barque, are still operational as sail training ships and others are being restored and opened to the public in many seafaring nations of the world as living examples of the great days of sail.

'I beg my dear', wrote Admiral Boscawen to his wife in 1756, 'will not be uneasy at my staying out so long. To be sure I lose the fruits of the earth, but then I am gathering the flowers of the sea.' It is to assist some others also to gather the flowers of the sea that this *Companion*, in part, exists. Some of the enjoyment of reading the classics of the sea, such as Richard Hakluyt's *Principal Navigations* or the works of Captain Marryat, is inevitably lost when the technical terms, with which they abound, are not fully understood. This *Companion* makes them clear. If, too, it can serve perhaps as an introduction to further voyages of exploration in sea literature, then there are still flowers to be plucked and enjoyed.

Fairly early on in the planning of *The Oxford Companion to Ships and the Sea* it became apparent that the subject was so vast that some arbitrary limitations would need to be imposed. One of the first casualties was in the world of the dinghy sailor, both cruising and racing. Their interests were it was felt amply catered for by a wealth of readily available literature which this *Companion* could not hope to rival in price or topicality. Another sad, but necessary, sacrifice lay in the huge field of oceanography, particularly in the flora and fauna of the sea. Yet even here one or two exceptions had to be made, for so much of man's endeavour at sea has been connected with the whale that a *Companion* such as this would have been incomplete without some account of the hunting, almost to extinction in some cases, of this gentle mammal. The seal, too, occupies almost as important a place as the whale in the sea's history, for the wide demand of sealskin for personal adornment led directly to new discoveries of the continent of Antarctica. So although some limits had to be imposed, the lines were drawn with a reasonable degree of flexibility.

In a subject so all-embracing as ships and the sea, it becomes particularly difficult to weigh up the relative importance of, say, one man as against another, to decide which of two ships or two battles should be included when there is space for only one. In the end, all such decisions must be dependent on the editor's own preferences and on his personal sense of values. Every such editor is conscious that his decisions may not accord with those of individual readers; he can only hope that his judgement in these cases is not too much at fault in the eyes of his readers. Since *Companions*, by their very nature, need periodically to be brought up to date by subsequent editions, it is to be hoped that readers who discover any such omissions will make their views known. Similarly, no book of this wide compass can hope to be free of all error. Although several eyes have read through the text, it is probable that some mistakes have escaped the net. The expertise has, it is hoped, reduced them to a minimum. Apologies are offered for those that occur, but again it is hoped that readers who discover them will make them known, so that they can be corrected in future editions.

A great many standard works have been consulted in the compilation of this *Companion*, but three have been outstandingly useful in the search for the meanings of seafaring words no longer in current use. Sir Henry Mainwaring's *The Sea-Man's Dictionary*, the first marine dictionary to be published in the English language (1644), was invaluable in this respect, as also was Falconer's classic *Marine Dictionary*, published just over a century later. Another century on, and Admiral W. H. Smyth produced his invaluable *The Sailor's Word-Book*, a mine of information. Of modern dictionaries and manuals there is an embarrassment of riches, but it would be ungracious not to mention the three volumes each of the *Admiralty Manual of Seamanship* and the *Admiralty Manual of Navigation*. Both these authoritative publications have provided the answers to a host of queries.

A large number of line drawings and diagrams have been included to amplify and clarify the text, particularly in the case of knots and splices, navigational definitions, cartography, types of ship rig, and the various oddities and implements of seamanship. Many distinguished contributors, listed on p. viii, helped with the compilation of this *Companion*, and while some attempts to edit their contributions into a uniform style have been made, in general it has been thought advisable to allow them to retain as far as possible their own individual styles. To them all, experts in their own fields, deep thanks are due not only for their willingness to contribute during the course of busy careers but also for the quality and knowledge shown in their work.

To others, personal thanks are due. Chief among these is the late Geoffrey Hunt, who was closely associated with this *Companion* from its first days and whose advice and encouragement throughout was outstanding and inspiring. After his untimely death, Michael Devenish stepped into the breach, and again thanks are due to him for much wise advice and stimulation when the spirit showed signs of flagging or of becoming overawed at the huge volume of text. He was one of those who read through the entire text to its great advantage, as also did Betty Palmer. Their help was immense. Another who did so, as well as contributing most of the yachting and some other articles, was Maurice Griffiths, and to him too a deep debt of gratitude is due. To Susan le Roux fell the overall task of arranging for the illustrations to be drawn, to Susan Stenderup that of hunting down the photographs, and to Olivia Brooks the layout. Acknowledgement and many thanks are due to Terence Armstrong and the staff of the Scott Polar Research Institute of Cambridge, to Rear Admiral Peter Buckley and the staff of the Naval Historical Library of the Ministry of Defence, and to Basil Greenhill and the staff of the National Maritime Museum at Greenwich for dealing so efficiently and patiently with a multitude of questions. Finally, Professor Arthur Marder's constant encouragement from afar kept the *Companion* moving steadily ahead, even through the stormiest of waters. The editor's debt to all these is immense, one that is freely acknowledged but which can be repaid only by his gratitude and amazement that they gave their time and knowledge so freely and unstintingly.

PETER KEMP
Maldon, Essex.
July 1975.

Publisher's Note

* Words are asterisked in the text when they or their close derivatives are the subject of a separate article which it may help the reader to refer to at that point. Cross-references to major topics of relevance are given in small capitals at the foot of many articles.

Metrification has presented something of a dilemma, for while the thickness of modern armament reads naturally in millimetres, to quote the length of an Elizabethan ship in metres seems absurd. In the event both imperial and metric units have been used as seemed appropriate, a conversion table for the two systems being included as Appendix 5 at the back of the book. Similarly with the measurement of time, convenience has been preferred to consistency, and this book follows the British Admiralty in adopting the 24-hour clock only from 1924 onwards, times before that date being quoted as a.m. or p.m.

The publisher would like to thank Mrs. Mary Pera and the staff of the Royal Ocean Racing Club for checking many of the yachting figures, the members of the Royal Thames Yacht Club for the hospitality of their library, and Mr. Christopher Thornhill, Jane Kimber, and Mr. John Clothier for much wise and kindly advice.

Contributors

Terence Armstrong, Captain Geoffrey Bennett, Miss Evelyn Berckman, Captain Charles H. Cotter, the late Captain John Creswell, the late Vice Admiral Sir Archibald Day, Ernest S. Dodge, Major J. de C. Glover, Vice Admiral Sir Peter Gretton, Maurice Griffiths, Miss Vivienne Heath, Rear Admiral John B. Heffernan, U.S.N., Richard Hough, Peter Kemp, H. G. R. King, Professor Christopher Lloyd, Captain Donald Macintyre, Professor Arthur J. Marder, Rear Admiral Samuel E. Morison, U.S.N.R., Peter Padfield, Rear Admiral G. S. Ritchie, the late Commander W. B. Rowbotham, Vice Admiral Brian B. Schofield, the late R. A. Skelton, Commander Gilbert A. Titterton, Oliver Warner, David Woodward.

A

A.B., the abbreviated title for the *rating of able seaman, a man able to perform all the duties of a seaman on board ship. In the old sailing ship days it was a man able to *hand, *reef, and *steer, but today, to be an able seaman a man must have many more maritime skills than that. By some, the initials were thought to refer to an 'able-bodied' seaman but this is not the case; they are merely the first two letters of 'able'.

AALESUND, a seaport on the Norwegian coast about 140 miles north of *Bergen. The town is built on two islands which enclose a magnificent harbour. The port was founded in 1824 as one of the principal centres of the North Sea herring fishery, but added to its importance by becoming a port of call for shipping between Bergen, Trondheim, Newcastle, Hull, and Hamburg. It is also celebrated as having in its neighbourhood the ruins of the castle reputed to be the birthplace of Rollo, founder of the dynasty of the dukes of Normandy, of whom one, William, became king of England by conquest in 1066. The original town was built of wood, and in January 1904 was destroyed by fire when a fierce gale fanned the flames. The town was later rebuilt and enlarged, and the port developed to include small shipbuilding and repair yards. It was occupied by the Germans in 1940 during the course of the Second World War and for a short period was the objective of a British counter-attack from troops landed further north at Aandalsnes, but it was an attack that never materialized, being overtaken by the speed of the German advance.

A-ARCS, in a warship, the limits to which the gun turrets and, when fitted, the secondary batteries can be trained. To open A-Arcs, to alter course in relation to the *bearing of an enemy so as to bring all the turret guns to bear on her.

AARHUS, a seaport on the east coast of Jutland and, after Copenhagen, Denmark's most important port, linked by rail with all parts of the country and thus handling a considerable import and export trade. In its cathedral it boasts the largest church in Denmark. It is one of the many ports in the district whose wealth was originally built on the vast herring shoals which abounded in the area before moving westward across the

North Sea in the 15th–16th centuries. Today it is a main export centre for agricultural produce.

AARON MANBY, the first steamship to be built of iron, was fitted with an engine designed by Henry *Bell. She made her first voyage in 1820 from London, carrying passengers across the English Channel and up the River Seine to Paris at an average speed of between eight and nine knots. After a few regular passenger trips on this run she was purchased in Paris by a group of French shipowners who used her for several more years in running pleasure trips up and down the Seine. The use of iron plates for her hull in place of the more conventional wood proved a landmark in the science of shipbuilding, and was widely copied during the next twenty to thirty years.

ABACK, the situation of the sails of a square-rigged ship when the *yards are trimmed to bring the wind to bear on their forward side. Sails are laid aback when this is done purposely to stop a ship's way through the water or to assist her in *tacking; they are taken aback when the ship is inadvertently brought to by an unexpected change of wind or by lack of attention by the helmsman.

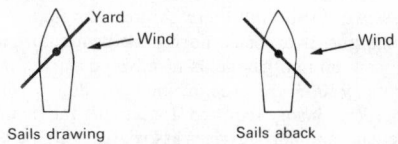

Sails drawing   Sails aback

'Lay all flat aback', the order in square-rigged ships to lay all sails aback in order to stop the ship and give her sternway. When lying to a single *anchor such ships normally spread a *mizen topsail laid aback to prevent the vessel surging to the anchor and fouling it with her *cable.

ABAFT, towards the *stern of a ship, relative to some other object or position. Abaft the *beam, any *bearing or direction between the beam of a ship and her stern. See also AFT; but 'abaft' is always relative, e.g., abaft the mainmast (*opposite to* before); 'aft' is general (*opposite to* forward).

ABANDON SHIP, the order given when a ship is in danger of sinking or on fire for the entire crew to take to the boats and * liferafts.

ABANDONMENT, a term used in marine insurance indicating the surrender of ship and cargo to the insurers in the case of a * constructive total loss.

ABATEMENT OF FALSE LIGHTS, a right, under the authority of the Merchant Shipping Acts, by which the * lighthouse authority in Britain may order the extinction or screening of any light visible to seaward which could be mistaken for that emanating from a lighthouse.

ABBOTT, LEMUEL (1760–1803), British portrait painter, is chiefly remembered for the many portraits of Lord * Nelson which he painted. The best known and most frequently reproduced of them was painted in October 1797, just after Nelson had lost his right arm, and of it Lady Nelson wrote: 'The likeness is great; I am well satisfied with Abbott.' The original of this painting is now in the National Portrait Gallery in London, but many copies are known to exist.

ABEAM, on a * bearing or direction at right angles to the fore-and-aft line of a ship. See also ABREAST.

ABERDEEN, the main seaport in the north of Scotland at the mouth of the rivers Don and Dee, about 130 miles north-east of Edinburgh. It is one of the chief Scottish centres for the deep-sea fishery, which was given a tremendous impetus by the introduction of the beam * trawl in 1882 and steam line fishing seven years later. Many of the famous British tea * clippers were also built at Aberdeen during the 19th century, and small vessels are still built there. A great development of the port is expected during the near future as the new oil and gas fields discovered during the years 1970–3 are brought into production with Aberdeen being required to handle the many ancillary shipping services associated with the oil industry, including the servicing of drilling rigs, etc.

ABIEL ABBOT LOW, the first small internal-combustion-engined boat to cross the Atlantic under power. She was a canoe-sterned single-screw cabin launch of 38 feet length overall with a draught of only 3·7 feet, built for the New York Kerosene Company to demonstrate the reliability at sea of their 10 h.p. kerosene (paraffin) marine motor. Named after the Company's president, she successfully made the crossing in July–August 1902 from New York to Falmouth, 3,100 miles, in thirty-six days without any serious engine trouble.

ÅBO, an important seaport in Finland in the Gulf of Bothnia. It was the seat of government of the country between 1809 and 1819, when it lost this function to the city of Helsinki (originally Helsingfors). It is now the second largest seaport in Finland, trading mainly in timber and agricultural produce. It also has a flourishing shipbuilding and yacht-building trade. A disastrous fire in 1827 destroyed most of the city, including its university with its famous library of more than 30,000 volumes. The 12th-century cathedral was extensively damaged but restored to its original design during the subsequent rebuilding. The port was also redeveloped to include extensive sawmills.

ABOARD, in or on board a ship. The word is also widely used in other maritime meanings; thus for one ship to fall aboard of another is for her to fall foul of another; in the days of sailing navies, to lay an enemy aboard was to sail alongside an enemy with the intention of * carrying her by * boarding; in square-rigged ships, to haul the * tacks aboard was to * brace the * yards round for sailing * close-hauled.

ABOUKIR, a village on the Mediterranean coast of Egypt at the head of the large bay of Aboukir where, in 1798, the battle of the * Nile was fought between a British fleet commanded by Rear Admiral * Nelson and a French fleet commanded by Vice Admiral * Brueys. The battle of the Nile is often referred to as the battle of Aboukir.

ABOUKIR, **H.M.S.,** an elderly armoured cruiser (launched 1900) of the British Navy at the opening of the First World War (1914–18) which, with her sister ships *Cressy* and *Hogue*, was torpedoed and sunk by the German submarine *U.9* on 22 September 1914 while on patrol in the southern North Sea 30 miles west of Ymuiden. The loss of life in the three cruisers was very heavy, over 1,400 being drowned and only just over 800 being saved.

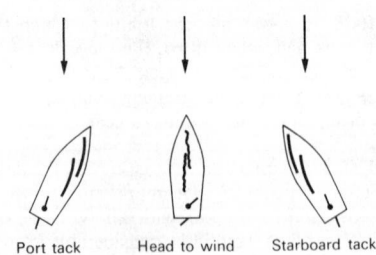

Port tack   Head to wind   Starboard tack

Three stages in going about

ABOUT, a term used in sailing, meaning across the wind in relation to the * bow of a sailing vessel. Thus, when a ship *tacks across the wind to bring it from one side of the ship to the other, she is said to go about. 'Ready about', the order given in a sailing ship to tack across the wind, the actual moment of the *helm being put down being signified by the order 'About ship'. In yachts and smaller craft, this order is usually 'Lee-oh', indicating that the helm is being put down to leeward.

ABOVE-BOARD, above the deck and therefore open and visible, which gave rise to the term used to denote open and fair dealing.

ABOX, an old sailing ship expression of the days of masts and *yards. To lay the head-yards abox in a square-rigged sailing vessel was to lay them square to the foremast in order to *heave-to. This brought the ship more under command if it was subsequently required to *wear or to *stay the vessel. But to *brace abox is to brace the head-yards flat *aback to the wind, not square to the mast, in order to ensure that the wind acts on the sails so that the bows of the ship *cast the required way.

A-BRACKET, the triangular bracket, often also known as a sole-piece or sole-bracket, which extends from the hull of a steam or motor vessel to give support to the *propeller shafts where they extend beyond the hull. See also SHIPBUILD- ING.

ABREAST, a position of a ship in relation to another or to a recognizable mark or place, being directly opposite to the ship, mark, or place. Thus when a vessel is abreast, say, a *lightship, then the lightship is *abeam of her. Line abreast, a naval fleet formation in which ships steam in position abeam of the *flagship, forming a line at right angles to the *course they are steering.

ABRUZZI, LUIGI AMADEO GIUSEPPE MARIO FERNANDO FRANCESCO DE SAVOIA-AOSTA, Duca di (1873–1933), Italian admiral and explorer, was born in Madrid. After entering the Italian Navy he led an expedition to the Arctic in 1899 which was to attempt the North pole from a base set up in Franz Josef Land. One of the team, Lieutenant Umberto *Cagni, with a sledge party, reached a point 207 miles short of the pole, at that time the nearest approach and improving on Fridtjof *Nansen's attempt in 1895 by 20 miles.

Subsequently he commanded a squadron of the Italian Navy during the Italian–Turkish war of 1912, and in 1913 was appointed commander-in-chief of the Navy, holding this position until 1917, when he quarrelled with his staff and retired. He was perhaps somewhat less than enterprising while holding the chief naval com-

mand during these years of the First World War (1914–18).

ABSALON (c. 1128–1201), Danish archbishop, made a great name for himself as self-appointed admiral of the Danish fleet in its operations against the Wendish pirates in the Baltic. His first expedition set out in 1160, but it was not until eight years later that he captured Arkona, on the island of Rügen, the chief stronghold of the Wends. From there he captured the Wendish political centre at Garz, destroyed their seven-headed god Rügievit, and established Danish suzerainty and the Christian religion. The capture of Garz enabled Absalon to dominate the western Baltic. His last naval success was in 1184 when, off Stralsund, he annihilated a Pomeranian fleet which was attacking Rügen. Although his main claim to fame rests on his efforts for and devotion to Christianity, he was also a formidable fighter and an inspired maritime leader. He was also renowned as being the finest swimmer in the Danish fleet.

A-BURTON, a term used in the stowage of casks in the *hold of a ship when they are laid *athwartships, in line with the deck *beams. In the older days of seafaring all ships had to take a great number of casks on board, as they were the only means of carrying fresh water and provisions, such as beef and pork pickled in brine, for the crew. The method of their stowage in the hold was therefore a matter of great importance, both to accommodate the greatest number in the smallest possible space and to make sure that they were easily accessible when required.

ACAPULCO, a port on the Pacific coast of Mexico, about 190 miles south-south-west of Mexico City. It is almost completely landlocked, with deep water up to the shore line, and thus the best and most secure harbour on this coast. From the earliest days of Spanish involvement in the Pacific until 1822, when Mexico achieved independence, it was the eastern terminus of the trans-Pacific trade from the Spanish East Indian colonies. To Acapulco in the 16th, 17th, and 18th centuries sailed the treasure *galleons from the East Indies for overland transport of the riches they carried across the Isthmus of Darien and a final voyage by sea to Spain. These rich galleons were a powerful magnet to many *privateering attackers, and in their time Sir Francis *Drake, Thomas *Cavendish, Woodes *Rogers, and Commodore George *Anson each captured a laden Acapulco galleon after a sharp action, returning safely home with immense treasure in their holds.

ACCOMMODATION, an older term for a *cabin when fitted for the use of passengers. It is also the word used when referring to steps in a ship, and thus a flight of steps leading from deck to deck in a ship for convenience of access and egress is properly known as an accommodation ladder.

ACCOMMODATION PLAN, a naval architect's set of drawings for the building of a new ship showing the layout below decks of cabins and berths for passengers, officers, and crew, together with the dining room, lounges, and other passenger spaces. The plan is normally drawn to a scale of 1:96 or 1:48 in feet (or 1:100 or 1:50 in metres) according to the size and complexity of the ship. Yacht designers usually term their accommodation drawing the General Arrangement plan, which shows in detail the principal features of the accommodation lay-out—berths, lockers, cupboards, toilet or shower, galley, navigator's space, etc.—both in elevation and in plan. In addition there may be a number of cross sections, or half sections, show-ing the accommodation arrangement relative to the curving inside of the hull. This plan is nor-mally drawn to a scale between 1:32 and 1:12 (or 1:30 and 1:10 in metres).

ACCOUNT, to go on the, an old term used by *buccaneers to describe their somewhat ir-regular way of life at sea and to give it an appar-ently more respectable backing than in fact it had. The dividing line between a buccaneer and a *pirate was very shadowy indeed; 'to go on the account' perhaps sounded a little better to some ears than 'to turn pirate'. But it may well be that the origin of the term lay in the meaning of account as responsibility for conduct, that if caught and charged with illegal practices they would be able to account for their actions as within the law.

ACCRA, a seaport on the Gulf of Guinea and formerly capital of the British colony of Gold Coast (now the independent nation of Ghana). Originally the centre of three trading stations, one British, one Dutch, and one Danish, it became entirely British in 1871 when the Dutch station was ceded to Britain. The Danish station had been ceded twenty years earlier. Strictly speaking, Accra is not a harbour, ships having to lie off the land because of the shallow water around those coasts and passengers and cargo having to be transhipped to reach the shore. A large part of the town of Accra was destroyed by fire in 1894, providing the opportunity to replace the original native huts by substantial buildings. The principal trade of Accra is cocoa, although with Ghana still a developing country, a large volume of machinery and machine tools are im-ported through Accra.

ACHENBACH, ANDREAS (1815–1910), German land- and seascape painter, was born at Kassel. As a boy he showed an undoubted flair for drawing and at the age of 12 began to study art at the Academy in St. Petersburg (now Leningrad) where his father was then living. In 1832 he visited Holland and was much influenced by the Dutch masters. After a visit to Norway and Sweden he painted two seascapes, 'A Storm off the Norwegian Coast' and 'A Wreck in Hardanger Fiord', which stamped him as a marine artist of considerable ability when they were exhibited in 1835. He spent the next ten years travelling, including two years on the island of Capri, but is mainly remembered for his pictures of the North Sea coast. He was specially noted for his estuarine works.

A-COCKBILL, orig. **A-COCKBELL,** a term used to describe an anchor when it hangs by its ring at the *cathead or from the *hawsehole ready for letting go. In the case of stockless anchors which are let go from the hawsehole, a few feet of cable are *veered so that the *shank hangs clear vertically.

ACORN, the small ornamental piece of wood, usually in the shape of either an acorn or a cone, which was fixed on the top of the spindle on the masthead of a sailing vessel which carried the *vane. Its purpose was to prevent the vane, which has a very loose-fitting sleeve, from being blown off the spindle. Although it was a standard fitting on all ships under sail, vanes are today rarely used even in those large sailing vessels still in commission, their place being taken by modern instruments to measure the strength and direction of the wind more accurately than ever could be done by means of a vane.

ACOUSTIC MINE, see MINES AND MINE WAR-FARE.

ACROSTOLIUM, the symbolical ornament, usually in the form of a shield or helmet, which ancient Greek or Roman ships carried on their *prows either to seek favour with the sea gods or to ward off evil. It was the forerunner of the *figurehead with which more modern ships were, and some still are, decorated.

ACTING, a prefix used in navies and merchant navies, as in other similar services, to denote that a higher rank is being temporarily held. Payment is, of course, at the full rate for the acting rank or rating.

ACTIUM, the old name of a promontory on the coast of Greece, at the entrance to what is now the Gulf of Arta on the southern side of the strait. It was the site of Mark Antony's camp and gave its name to the battle fought on 2 December, 31 B.C., between the Roman fleet of Octavian and the Egyptian fleet of Mark Antony. The two fleets, each of over 200 vessels, met outside the gulf, but the heavier ships of Antony's fleet were no match for the lighter and faster ships which made up Octavian's fleet. During the battle Cleopatra, queen of Egypt, who commanded one squadron of the Egyptian fleet, withdrew, and Antony slipped away with her to return to Egypt. Their defection went unnoticed by the remainder of the fleet until too late, when superior numbers sealed the fate of the battle and the Egyptian fleet was annihilated and put to the torch.

ACTIVE LIST, the list of officers of a navy or a merchant navy who, as in all similar services, are actually serving or are liable to be called upon for active service at any time. Officers on the retired list may also be liable to recall to active service if below a certain age.

ACTUAIRE (French), an open transport for troops, propelled both by oars and sails, of the 18th and early 19th centuries.

ACTUAIROLE (French), a small *galley propelled by oars and used for the transport of troops up and down the coast in the 18th and early 19th centuries.

ACUMBA, another term for *oakum. It was originally the Anglo-Saxon word for the coarse part of flax, and thus received its association with oakum as a suitable material for the purpose of *caulking a *seam.

ACUÑA, CHRISTOVAL DE (1597–c. 1676). Spanish missionary and explorer, was born at Burgos, Spain. He was sent on mission work to Chile and Peru in 1629, where his interest in exploration so exceeded his Christian zeal that for long periods he abandoned his mission in order to chart the then unknown coasts of western South America. His main claim to fame, however, rests on his exploration of the Amazon, in conjunction with Pedro Texiera, in 1639. The Spanish government attempted to suppress his narrative and charts of this exploration on the grounds that they would assist the Portuguese, who had recently revolted from Spain and re-achieved their independence, to colonize the area. The attempted suppression was unsuccessful, the book *Nuevo Descubrimiento del Gran Rio de las Amazonas* being published in 1641, with French and English translations appearing in 1682 and 1698 respectively.

ADAIR, JOHN (d. 1722), Scottish surveyor, is best known for his *Description of the Sea Coasts and Islands of Scotland*, Part I, published in 1703 for the use of seamen. He began this work in 1686, and was made a Fellow of the Royal Society two years later. He did not live long enough to complete Part II. Many of his original surveys are preserved in the King's Library of the British Museum and the Advocates' Library in Edinburgh.

He was paid for his surveying work by two Acts of Tonnage, passed by the Privy Council of Scotland in 1695 and 1705, under which part of the harbour dues paid by vessels using specified Scottish ports were made over to him, but they produced insufficient cash to cover his costs and he died in great want.

ADAMANT, an old name for the *lodestone. In its true meaning it was the name for any very hard stone and became finally the name for a diamond. According to contemporary seamen there were two explanations to account for its connection with the lodestone, one that the Latin derivation of the word was *ad-amare*, to take a liking to, to have an attraction for, which suggested a lodestone or magnet; the other that it was the name of a mythical rock with magic properties, of which one was the power of attraction. The association of the name with a lodestone came to an end in the 17th century when it became totally associated with a diamond.

ADAMS, WILLIAM (d. 1620), English navigator, served for a short time in the English Navy before joining the Company of Barbary Merchants as a pilot and navigator. In 1598, attracted by the Dutch trade to India, he sailed with a small squadron of five ships from the Texel, bound for India via the Straits of Magellan. Adams's ship was the *Charity*, and was the sole survivor of the expedition, finally reaching Kyushu, in Japan, with a crew of sick and dying men. His knowledge of ships and pilotage, as well as of shipbuilding, made him a valuable man in the eyes of the Japanese rulers who, although refusing him permission to return to England, presented him with an estate near Yokosuka and a Japanese wife. In 1612 he heard news of an English trading station which had been set up at Bantam, and after getting into communication with it, was visited a year later by an English ship from there. She was the *Clove*, commanded by Captain John Saris, and Adams assisted him in obtaining trading concessions from the Shogun of Japan in favour of the British *East India Company. He took a leading part in the company's organization in the Far East and, having now obtained permission to leave Japan, made many voyages to Siam and Cochin China on behalf of the company. He always, however, returned to Japan, where he died.

ADDEL or **ADDLE,** the name by which drinking water was described on board ship after it had gone stale and putrid in a cask. In the days before metal tanks and evaporating machinery, all drinking water in ships had to be carried in casks and lost its purity and freshness in a very few days, hence the constant need for ships on long voyages to make the shore to refill their casks with fresh water.

ADELAER, Count, see SIVERTSEN, Kurt.

ADEN, a seaport in the new nation of South Yemen. Originally it was the focus of the entrepôt trade between Europe and Asia, and was known to the Romans, who captured it in 24 B.C. In A.D. 1513 *Albuquerque unsuccessfully attacked it; it was captured by Turkey in 1538, becoming independent in 1735. A British ship was wrecked there in 1837, plundered by the natives, and the passengers and crew woefully maltreated. The sultan, in compensation for the outrage, agreed to sell the town and port to the British, and Captain Haines, of the Indian Navy, was sent from Bombay to take possession. The sultan's son refused to fulfil his father's promises, and a naval and military force was therefore sent to capture Aden, which was annexed to British India in January 1839.

Aden had by this time been reduced to a place of no importance as a seaport, for it was too far off the route to India around the Cape of Good Hope to serve any useful purpose. But with the British occupation and the development of trade between East Africa, the Red Sea ports, and Arabia and beyond, the port soon grew in use and importance, especially after it was developed as a coaling station by the *P and O Steamship Company. The opening of the *Suez Canal added vastly to its importance, and the volume of trade handled in the port, and the number of ships using it as a port of call, grew immeasurably. As the importance of coal as a fuel for shipping declined, the oil of the Middle East took its place, and this again added to the value of Aden to ships as a fuelling port, especially after the building and operation of oil refineries there. In recent years, however, since the termination of British protection, the volume of trade handled in the port has declined, and the closure of the Suez Canal after the Israeli–Egyptian hostilities of 1967 accentuated the decline. With the reopening of the Canal to traffic in 1975 following the clearance operations begun in 1974, Aden could well recover much of its lost trade, though the current development of the modern super-tanker, container ship, and bulk carrier, all with too deep a *draught to use the Canal unless it is drastically widened and deepened, would be certain to delay any rapid return to the port's original volume of trade.

ADMIRAL, in all maritime nations the title of the commander of a fleet or of a subdivision of it. The word certainly comes from the Arabic word *amir,* prince or leader, and in the Mediterranean, as early as the 12th century, the leader of the Moslem fleets had the title *amir-al-bahr,* commander of the sea. The substantive *amir* and the article *al* were combined by other maritime nations in the Mediterranean as they developed to form the title *amiral* (French) and *almirante* (Spanish). The title reached Britain and other north European nations probably as a result of the Crusades, but became confused with the Roman *admirabilis.*

As well as signifying the chief commander of the fleet, the title was also applied to his ship, and in many of the Elizabethan descriptions of voyages published in England the word almost invariably applied to the ship; the commander himself frequently being described as 'general' or 'captain', or a combination of the two.

The four active ranks, or flag ranks as they are known, are admiral of the fleet, admiral, vice admiral, and rear admiral, in descending order. These ranks are found in most navies though in different forms and spellings. For a table of equivalent ranks see APPENDIX 1.

The exclusively male tenure of the rank of admiral was first breached in 1972 when the United States Navy promoted a lady, Miss Alene Duerk, to flag rank as head of the Navy Nurse Corps. See also ADMIRAL OF THE FLEET.

ADMIRAL GRAF SPEE, a German *pocket-battleship of 11,900 tons, armed with six 11-inch and eight 5·9-inch guns and designed for commerce raiding. Launched on 30 June 1934, she had a very short career in the Second World War, ending when she was scuttled off Montevideo on 17 December 1939 after being in action with three British *cruisers in what is known as the battle of the *River Plate. See also HARWOOD, Sir Henry.

ADMIRAL OF THE FLEET, from the earliest days the senior *admiral in the British Navy, whose presence at sea was originally signified by the Royal Standard flown from the mainmast head, replaced at the end of the 17th century by the Union flag. The admiral of the fleet held his post until death. In 1693 he was paid £6 a day with no allowance for servants, but in 1700 his daily pay was reduced to £5 and he was allowed fifty servants for whom he drew £1,014 a year.

Until 1863 the rank was held only by the senior admiral on the list although one or two special exceptions were made. Admiral Lord St.

The Russian circular battleship Novgorod

Vincent (see JERVIS, Sir John) was made an additional admiral of the fleet in 1821 by King George IV because Lord Wellington had been made a field marshal by the army. And in 1830, to celebrate his accession to the throne, *William IV, the 'sailor king', made two more admirals of the fleet. All these, however, lapsed on the death of the holders, reducing the number again to one. Between 1854 and 1857 there was no admiral of the fleet in the British Navy. The admiral on the top of the list by seniority, and therefore the one to be made admiral of the fleet, was Thomas Gosselin, but as he had not been to sea for forty-five years and was also mentally deranged, he was not considered fit for promotion to so exalted a rank. When he died in 1857 the next admiral in seniority, Sir Charles *Ogle, was promoted.

In 1863, the army now having six field marshals, it was decided to allow the navy three admirals of the fleet. In 1870 new regulations were introduced to the effect that admirals of the fleet should retire at the age of 70, leaving vacancies for three always on the *active list. Promotions to this rank during and after the First World War (1914–18) increased the numbers both on the active and retired lists, and although they were reduced by deaths during the twenty years between the two world wars, the numbers were increased again as a result of promotions made during and after the Second World War. In 1940 all admirals of the fleet on the retired list were replaced on the active list in order to conform with the army practice in respect of field marshals, who never retired, and it was laid down that all future admirals of the fleet would remain on the active list for life. Equivalent ranks in other navies are fleet admiral (U.S.A.), Grossadmiral (Germany), and Grande Ammiraglio (Italy).

ADMIRAL POPOV, a Russian warship built at Nicolaev in 1875 to a design by, and named after, Vice Admiral Popov. She was a vessel of 3,553 tons, entirely circular, a design meant to provide a steady platform for her guns irrespective of the state of the sea. She was armed with two 12-inch guns mounted in a rotating circular *barbette in the centre of the ship and was powered by eight engines driving six propellers. A second ship, named the *Novgorod*, was later built to the same design. They were reasonably robust for so revolutionary a design, but suffered from two considerable drawbacks; they proceeded *awash in the slightest seaway and their flat bottoms pounded badly, and although when used in rivers they steered well when going upstream, they were unmanageable coming downstream and revolved continuously. See also LIVADIA.

ADMIRAL'S CUP, a perpetual challenge award established in 1957 by the *Royal Ocean Racing Club, London, for biennial international team racing for yachts originally limited to between 30 and 60 feet (9·1–18·2 m) in waterline length. The 'admiral' in the title was Sir Myles Wyatt, who in 1957 was 'admiral' of the Royal Ocean Racing Club. The series of races consists of two inshore races of 30 miles each and the two offshore races, to include the *Fastnet race, totalling some 830 miles. The limiting size of entrants was later modified to between 25 and 70 feet (7·6–21·3 m) R.O.R.C. rating. The cup was won by Great Britain the first year, by the Netherlands in 1959, by the U.S.A. in 1961, by Britain in 1963 and again in 1965, by Australia in 1967, by the U.S.A. in 1969, and was regained by Great Britain in 1971 by a team led by the then Prime Minister, the Rt. Hon. Edward Heath. The winner in 1973 was the West German team led by Hans-Otto Schumann. The Cup was again regained by Britain in 1975 and retained in 1977. The Admiral's Cup is now recognized as the most important international competition in the ocean racing world. See also YACHTING.

ADMIRALTY, the generic international term for jurisdiction over maritime causes, with authority to establish courts presided over by a judge of Admiralty. (See ADMIRALTY, HIGH COURT OF.) It did not, in times past, indicate military command of naval forces, which would normally be specifically conferred by a sovereign or other ruler on an individual who was sometimes called captain-general until the term *admiral came gradually to replace it during the late 13th and early 14th centuries.

At the same time, in Britain, Admiralty came also to be applied to the office of the *Lord High Admiral in its military and administrative aspects with regard to the Royal Navy, and the officials executing the office of the Lord High Admiral when that office was put into commission were known as *Lords Commissioners of the Admiralty and their committee as the Board of Admiralty. This system continued in Britain until 1964 when the office of Admiralty was absorbed with those of the army and the air force into a Ministry of Defence. As a concession to long tradition those within the Ministry of Defence charged with the overall direction of naval affairs are collectively called the Admiralty Board but are no longer Lords Commissioners. In other maritime nations the overall direction of their naval affairs is usually conducted by a Ministry of Marine or a Navy Department.

ADMIRALTY, BLACK BOOK OF THE, see BLACK BOOK OF THE ADMIRALTY.

ADMIRALTY, HIGH COURT OF, was a particularly British institution, dealing with maritime causes, such as piracy and *prize, which provided the *Lord High Admiral, one of the great officers of state, with the majority of his income. According to the *Black Book of the Admiralty, this court of jurisdiction was founded in the reign of Edward I (1272–1307), but a more probable date is during the reign of Edward III (1336–60). It was regulated by statutes passed in 1391 and 1392, and its jurisdiction founded on the laws of *Oleron. At first separate 'admirals' were appointed for the north, south, and west, each responsible for maritime law in their areas, but they were merged into a single high court in the early years of the 15th century. This court was empowered to try all cases arising from prize, and of crimes committed on board ships at sea or 'being and hovering in the main stream of great rivers only beneath [below] the bridges of the same rivers nigh to the sea'.

The judge of the High Court of Admiralty was appointed by Letters Patent under the Crown, and the Patent was usually all-embracing to cover anything that could possibly happen at sea. The Patent of the last judge, appointed in 1867, gave him the power to take cognizance of 'all causes civil and maritime, also all contracts, complaints, offences or suspected offences, crimes, pleas, debts, exchanges, accounts, policies of assurance, loading of ships, and all other matters and contracts which relate to *freight due for the use of ships, transportation, money or *bottomry ... to arrest ... all ships, persons, things, goods, wares, and merchandise, to enquire by the oaths of honest and lawful men of all things which ought to be enquired after, and to mulct, arrest, punish, chastise, and reform....' He also had jurisdiction to 'reform nets too straight and other unlawful engines and instruments whatsoever for the catching of fishes'.

But the great work of the Admiralty Court, particularly during the 18th and first part of the 19th centuries, was in the condemnation of prize. Admiralty court practice in respect of prize was universally recognized, and to deal with the immense volume of cases which came before it, and many from foreign stations, vice-admiralty courts were set up to sit in certain colonial centres. The volume of such cases during years of hostilities often ran into 1,000 a year, and in some years more than 2,000 were brought before the Court.

In 1875, by the operation of the Judicature Acts of 1873 and 1875, the High Court of Admiralty was merged with the other High Courts of England into the High Court of Justice, thus finally severing the connection of the High Court of Admiralty with the office of

Lord High Admiral. The badge of the Admiralty Court was a *silver oar, in the shape of a mace, which was carried in procession and laid on the table in court in front of the judge whenever a case was heard; it is now the badge of office of the Admiralty Marshal, who is an officer of the Court, though still placed before the President of the Probate, Divorce, and Admiralty Division of the High Court when he sits on a maritime cause.

In the U.S.A., the source of admiralty jurisdiction is Article 3, para. 2, of the U.S. Constitution, and in addition to the high seas embraces the great lakes and navigable rivers. When it was a British colony, vice-admiralty courts exercised maritime jurisdiction on a local basis, but after the Declaration of Independence, such local jurisdiction was transferred to the federal government. The extent of admiralty jurisdiction exercised by the U.S.A. has been defined as 'that defined by the Statutes of Richard II, under the construction given to them by contemporary or immediately subsequent courts of admiralty'. Thus the U.S. admiralty jurisdiction embraces all maritime contracts, torts, injuries, or offences.

In France, admiralty jurisdiction is exercised by the civil courts and based on the Code Napoléon, although there are some special commercial tribunals which deal particularly with shipping matters. Spain, Portugal, Belgium, Italy, and Greece have also adopted codes based on the Code Napoléon in which admiralty jurisdiction is exercised by the civil courts. Germany also has no admiralty court as such, but commercial courts have power to give judgement in appropriate shipping causes. In Holland, maritime cases are tried by the ordinary civil tribunals.

The Scandinavian nations (Sweden in 1891, Denmark in 1892, and Norway in 1893) adopted a maritime code which, although intended to apply equally in each nation, differs slightly in each. Maritime causes in Norway come before permanent maritime courts set up in the larger towns; in Denmark and Sweden they come before local courts set up temporarily when required. In each nation appeals from the lower courts lie to the supreme court.

ADMIRALTY MIDSHIPMAN, a term used in the British Navy during the 18th and 19th centuries to describe a *midshipman, who had served his time (six years) and passed his examination, appointed to a ship by Admiralty order as compared to those rated by the captain and appointed by an admiral.

ADORNINGS, a general name often used to describe the *gingerbread work on the *stern

and *quarter galleries of the old sailing ships, particularly naval, from about the 15th to the 19th centuries.

ADRIFT, a term denoting floating at random, as of a boat or ship broken away from her moorings and at the mercy of wind and waves. To cast adrift, of a ship, to abandon her at sea; of persons, to place them in a ship's boat or raft and leave them. The word is also used to describe a seaman absent from his watch, or his work, or failing in his prompt and due return from leave.

ADVANCE, the amount of wages paid to a seaman when signing on for a new voyage. In the Royal Navy, before the introduction of continuous service, the advance was two months' wages; in many merchant ships it was one month's wages, the clearing off of which was known as 'working off the *dead horse'.

ADVANTAGE, the term used to describe the method of *reeving a *tackle in order to gain the maximum increase in power. The power increase in a tackle is equal, if friction is disregarded, to the number of parts of the *fall at the moving block, and a tackle is rove to advantage when the hauling part of the fall leads from the moving block. Where a tackle is rigged so that the hauling part leads from the standing part, the power gained is less and the tackle is said to be rove to disadvantage. See also PURCHASE.

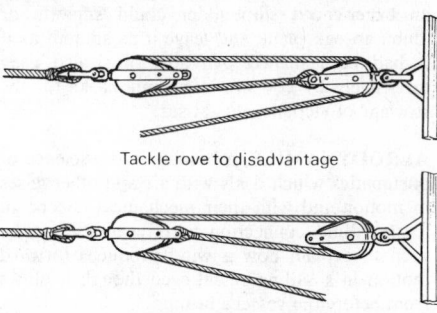

Tackle rove to disadvantage

Tackle rove to advantage

ADVENTURE, a commercial term recognized in maritime law to denote consignments of cargo sent abroad in a ship to be sold or bartered by the master to best advantage, hence cargo carried without fixed destination but to be sold when opportunity offers. A BILL OF ADVENTURE, one signed by a merchant in which he takes the chances of the voyage. It is now obsolete except perhaps in remote parts of the world. In French maritime law a BILL OF GROSS ADVENTURE is an instrument making a loan on a maritime security.

ADVENTURE, H.M.S., of fifteen ships bearing this name in the Royal Navy, the first was a 3rd *rate in 1594–1645 and the last a *cruiser minelayer, 1926–47. The second, a 4th rate, was active in the Dutch wars and in 1771 a famous holder of the name was a Whitby *collier or *cat, the *Marquis of Rockingham*, purchased for £2,103 and renamed for Captain *Cook's second voyage of discovery, 1772–6. The next *Adventure* was one of the first ships to be commissioned especially for surveying, being previously the transport *Aid*, which worked under W. H. *Smyth in the Mediterranean from 1817 to 1824 and charted Adventure Bank. The name was next used in 1833 for a sealing *schooner bought for £1,300 by Robert *Fitzroy when he needed a second ship to assist the *Beagle* in the Magellan Strait surveys, but lacking Admiralty support he had to sell her in 1834.

ADVICE-BOAT, a small vessel used during the period of sailing navies to carry orders or dispatches to and from fleets and single ships at sea. They were of no particular size or rig, the only criterion of their employment being speed.

ADZE, sometimes written as **ADDES** in old books on the shipbuilder's art, the principal tool of the old-time shipbuilder in the days of wooden ships, resembling a garden mattock but with a longer and sharper blade slightly curved inwards towards the handle. It was always considered a most difficult tool to use, but with it an experienced shipbuilder could smooth, or 'dub', an oak plank and leave it as smooth as if it had been planed. An adze was also used extensively by coopers in making casks for the stowage of victuals, etc., at sea.

AERODYNAMICS, a branch of the science of pneumatics which deals with air and other gases in motion and with their mechanical effects. In its maritime connection aerodynamics can be used to explain how a wind produces forward motion in a sailing vessel even though it blows from before the vessel's beam.

When a wind strikes a surface, its force can be resolved into two components, one acting at right angles to the surface and the other along the surface. If this surface is the sail of a boat, the component blowing along the sail can be disregarded, as it is providing no force on the sail, but the component at right angles to the sail does exert a force. That component can now similarly be resolved into two more components, not in relation to the angle of the sail but to the fore and aft line of the boat. The larger of these two components exerts a force which tries to blow the boat directly to leeward, and the smaller of them, blowing along the fore

Components of the wind

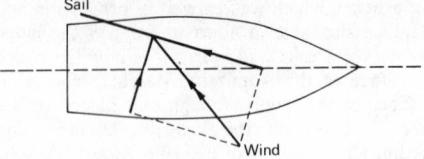

Wind resolved in relation to angle of sail

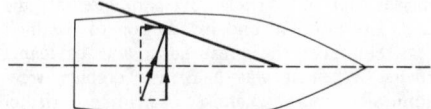

Part of wind resolved in relation to fore and aft line

and aft line, is all that is left of the wind to drive the boat forward. It is at this point that the *keel of the boat, or the *centreboard in the case of *dinghies, comes into play. It provides a lateral grip on the water which offers considerable resistance to the larger component and very little resistance to the smaller, so that the boat moves forward and makes only a small amount of leeway.

There is another element which gives forward movement to a sailing boat when the wind acts on her sail. In the resolution of forces considered above, the sail has been considered as a flat surface on which the wind strikes at an angle. In fact a sail has a parabolic curve fore and aft, of which the steepest part of the curve is at the *luff. When an airstream meets a curve at an acute angle it creates a partial vacuum as it flows over the steepest part of the curve, and in a sailing boat this partial vacuum acts to pull her forward and reinforce the small component of the wind that is driving her forward.

The greater the speed of the airflow over the steepest part of the curve, the more effective the partial vacuum, and so a modern sail design increases the speed of the airflow by creating a slot, or 'funnel', along the luff of the mainsail by setting a headsail forward of the mainsail. In cases where the *clew of the headsail overlaps the luff of the mainsail the wind is funnelled with even greater speed over the steepest part of the curve and so increases even more the partial vacuum.

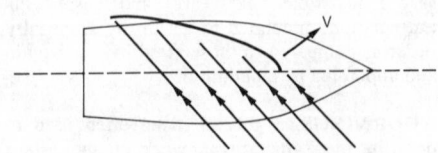

When a sailing vessel is close-hauled, with the wind blowing over the bow, she can thus move forward against the direction of the wind, first because of the small component of the wind which gives her forward motion, secondly because of the partial vacuum caused by the wind flowing over the curve at her luff which pulls her forward, and thirdly because of her keel which provides effective lateral resistance to the larger component of the wind and prevents her being blown down to leeward at right angles to her desired course.

AFER, the old Latin name for the south-west wind, to be found in some of the old accounts of early voyages. See WIND NAVIGATION.

AFFLECK, the name of two brothers who both became admirals in the British Navy. EDMUND (1724–88) was captain of the *Bedford*, the first ship to sight the Spanish fleet during Lord *Rodney's relief of *Gibraltar in 1780, resulting in the 'moonlight battle' in which Rodney heavily defeated de Langara's ships. He was on the American station during the latter part of the War of American Independence (1775–82) and played a considerable part in the battle of the *Saints in 1782, being made a baronet for his gallantry. He ended his naval service as rear admiral of the *Blue and member of parliament for Colchester. His brother PHILIP (1726–99) was with Admiral *Boscawen at the capture of Louisburg in 1758, served in American waters during the War of American Independence, and was commander-in-chief of the West Indies station from 1790 to 1793. On his return he was appointed a Lord Commissioner of the Admiralty until 1796 when he retired with the rank of admiral of the Blue.

AFFREIGHTMENT, CONTRACT OF, the legal term to describe the contract between a shipowner and a merchant under which the former contracts to carry the goods of the latter to a certain destination on the payment of a sum of money known as the *freight. The law which deals with contracts of affreightment is a branch of the general law of contracts. It should not be confused with a *charter party, under which a ship is hired by a merchant to carry his goods and who then takes temporary possession and control of her, or with a *bill of lading, which is the actual document signed by the *master of a ship acknowledging the shipment of goods.

AFLOAT, the condition of a vessel when she is wholly supported by the water and clear of the ground. The word is also often used in a more general sense to mean at sea, or of life at sea. AFLOAT SUPPORT, a term used in navies to indicate the provision at sea of auxiliary and supply ships to enable a fleet of warships to replenish with essential stores, fuel, etc., to enable it to operate for long periods at sea without recourse to shore bases. See also FLEET TRAIN.

AFT, at or towards the stern or after part of a ship, as a word either of position or motion. A gun may be mounted aft (an expression of position) and seamen sent aft to man it (an expression of motion). Fore and aft, from stem to stern. It is a contraction of *abaft, though used in a general, not a relative, sense. The adjective is AFTER, e.g., the after part of a ship, as above.

AFTERBODY, that part of a ship's hull which lies *aft of the midship section. It embraces the whole of the after half of the hull from upper deck to *keel, and on the designed shape of the afterbody depends the *run of the ship.

AFTERGUARD, seamen whose station in the days of sail was on the *poop or *quarterdeck to work the after gear of the ship. Also a term often used in yachting to denote the owner and his guests; in yacht racing, the helmsman and his advisers.

AFTERTURN, the twist given to *rope, when the *strands are laid up to form it, in the opposite direction to the twist of the strands. See also FORETURN.

***AGAMEMNON,* H.M.S.,** a ship's name used five times in the British Navy. The first of the name, a 64-gun ship launched at Buckler's Hard in 1781, had Horatio *Nelson as her captain in 1793–4 in the Mediterranean and later saw a good deal of action including the battles of *Copenhagen and *Trafalgar before she was wrecked in the Rio de la Plata in June 1809. The next *Agamemnon*, launched at Woolwich in 1852, can claim to be the first large warship specifically designed from the start as a single-screw *battleship as opposed to those which had an engine fitted in them after building. She assisted in the laying of the first Atlantic cable in 1858.

AGE OF THE MOON, the number of days that have elapsed since the day of new or change of the moon. A lunation, which is the interval between the times of successive new moons, is $29\frac{1}{2}$ days, so that the age of the moon at first quarter is 7 days; at full moon, 15 days; and at third quarter, 22 days.

AGRICOLA, GNAEUS JULIUS (A.D. 37–93), Roman governor of Britain and father-in-law of the historian Tacitus, was the first man to prove that Britain was an island by sending his fleet to sail round it.

AGRIPPA, MARCUS VIPSANIUS (63 B.C.–12 B.C.), Roman statesman and general, trained and commanded the fleet which defeated that of Sextus Pompeius at the battles of Mylae and Naulochus in 36 B.C. and won for Rome command of the sea around the coasts of Italy. For his services he received the honour of a naval crown, the highest Roman award for valour.

AGROUND, said of a ship when she is resting on the bottom. When put there purposely, a ship takes the ground, when by accident, she runs aground, or is * stranded.

AHEAD, a word (*opposite to* * astern) used in two senses at sea. Referring to direction, it means any distance directly in front of a ship on her current heading; referring to movement, it means the passage of a ship through the water in the direction in which her bows are pointing. It is a word much associated with the orders to work the engines of a ship, the usual engine room telegraph having the words 'ahead', 'astern', and 'stop' printed on the dial with a manually operated pointer to indicate slow, half, and full speed ahead or astern.

'AHOY!', the normal hail to a ship or boat to attract attention.

A-HULL, or **LYING A-HULL,** the condition of a ship drifting under * bare poles with her * helm * a-lee, or hove-to (see HEAVE-TO, TO) at sea under stress of weather. The term is also frequently applied to a ship which has been abandoned at sea.

AIRCRAFT CARRIERS, major warships capable of operating aircraft. The idea of operating aircraft from the decks of warships originated very soon after the flying machine became a practical proposition. In 1911 the American aviator Eugene Ely both took off and alighted on platforms erected on * cruisers. A few months later Commander Samson, of the British Navy, took off in a Short biplane from a similar platform on the * forecastle of the * battleship H.M.S. *Africa*. Though aircraft were regularly flown off numerous British warships during the First World War (1914–18) and, in 1917, a Sopwith 'Pup' aircraft was landed on the flight deck superimposed on the forecastle of H.M.S. *Furious*, it was not until that ship had a landing deck built * abaft her bridge superstructure that regular attempts to land on were made.

These were in the main a failure and it was not until a ship with an unobstructed deck over her whole length was completed in 1918 that the problem of landing on was satisfactorily solved. This was H.M.S. *Argus* which dispensed with any superstructure or funnel by incorporating a hydraulically raised and lowered bridge and by discharging her boiler smoke and gases over the stern.

She was followed by H.M.S. *Eagle* in 1920, converted from an uncompleted battleship, which had a superstructure and funnels offset on the starboard side of an otherwise unobstructed flight deck, as did H.M.S. *Hermes*, completed three years later and the first ship to be built as a carrier from the keel up. These were known as 'island' carriers. The *Furious* emerged in her final form in 1925, a flush-deck carrier like the *Argus*.

The U.S. and Japanese Navies had meanwhile commissioned their first small carriers in 1922, the *Langley* and *Hosho* respectively. These were flush-decked with funnels to one side which could be lowered horizontally during flying operations. No further carriers were built until after the conclusion of the Washington Treaty, when the U.S. and Japanese Navies each selected for conversion two capital ships due to be scrapped, the * battle-cruisers *Lexington* and *Saratoga* for the former, the battle-cruiser *Akagi* and the battleship *Kaga* for the latter. These were all island carriers (i.e., carriers with the bridge structure offset to the side) of some 36,000 tons, though the superstructure in the Japanese ships was comparatively small as it did not incorporate the funnels which, instead, projected horizontally over the side, a feature common to the majority of their carriers. The British selected the smaller ships *Courageous* and *Glorious*, originally sister ships of the *Furious*, for conversion to island carriers.

Subsequent carriers built for the three major navies, and the *Béarn*, converted from a battleship by the French, adopted the island design which thenceforward became standard. From 1937, however, when the British laid down the first of their post-Washington Treaty carriers, H.M.S. *Illustrious*, British design differed from that of other navies in the incorporation of armoured flight decks and hangar sides. This greatly improved their resistance to bomb attack but reduced the number of aircraft they could operate. War experience bore out the necessity for such increased protection and both the Americans and the Japanese adopted it for fleet carriers laid down after the battle of * Midway in 1942.

Carriers built up to the end of the Second World War (1945) were of three main types— large fleet carriers operating up to 100 aircraft,

H.M.S. Eagle, *an aircraft carrier launched in 1946*

light fleet carriers operating about 40, and escort carriers, ships of moderate speed and originally converted from merchant ships, to operate between 20 and 35 aircraft. None of the last type remain in service. The majority of light fleet carriers still in service have been relegated to auxiliary roles such as commando ships operating helicopters. Fleet carriers are now called attack carriers in the U.S. Navy, the only navy which still operates them in considerable numbers. The largest of these in existence is the U.S.S. *Nimitz,* displacing 95,000 tons and operating about 100 aircraft. She was commissioned in 1975 and has a crew of 5,700 officers and men. Like the U.S.S. *Enterprise* (75,700 tons) before her, she is nuclear-powered. Two more carriers in this class are planned, the *Eisenhower,* due to be launched in 1977, and the *Vinson,* 1980.

AIRFLOW, see AERODYNAMICS.

AIR–SEA RESCUE, a service introduced initially by the Royal Air Force in 1940 as a means of rescuing pilots and aircrew of aircraft ditched or shot down at sea as a result of enemy action. It was operated by high-speed launches based at a number of convenient points round the coastline of Britain, particularly along the Channel and North Sea coasts where the major-

ity of air action took place. Inflatable dinghies carried in aircraft were fitted with automatic wireless transmitters on which the launches could home. Since the war, the development of the helicopter has revolutionized air–sea rescue, and many countries, including Britain, operate them as a life-saving service at sea in addition to the *lifeboat services.

ALABAMA, an American Confederate *cruiser built by the Laird Company of Birkenhead in 1862 under a contract with Commander James Bulloch of the Confederate Navy. She was a three-masted *schooner with auxiliary steam power. The British government, which had declared its neutrality in the American Civil War, issued an order of detention on the vessel under construction, as yet unnamed but known as No. 290, but before the enforcement officers could reach Birkenhead the ship, now named *Eurica,* steamed down the Mersey without clearance but with a party of ladies and musicians on board ostensibly to carry out steaming trials. In the open sea she headed for Holyhead, landed her passengers, and easily eluding the pursuing Federal *frigate *Tuscaloosa,* made for the Azores where she picked up her armament which had been brought from Liverpool in two British ships. Under the command of Captain Raphael

*Semmes, she swept the seas of Federal shipping for two years until she was sunk in the English Channel off Cherbourg by U.S.S. *Kearsarge* on 19 June 1864.

After a long period of arbitration, based on the lack of proper diligence in her duty as a neutral, Britain agreed to pay damages of $15·5 m. (£3·25 m.) to the U.S.A. in compensation for the direct losses attributed to the *Alabama* and two other Confederate cruisers built in Britain, the *Florida* and the *Shenandoah*.

ALAMOTTIE, a sailor's name for *Procellaria pelagica*, the storm petrel. See also MOTHER CAREY'S CHICKENS.

ÅLANDS SJÖFARTSMUSEUM, Mariehamn, Finland, was originally a private museum established in 1935 on the initiative of Captain Carl Holmquist but was opened to the public in 1954. Its theme is the sea history of the Åland Islands and it includes among its exhibits the four-masted *barque *Pommern*, built in 1903, the captain's *cabin and *quarterdeck of the four-masted barque *Herzogin Cecilie*, and the gangway of the barque *L'Avenir*, together with name plates, ships' bells, shipbuilders' tools, nautical instruments, and a few pictures and engravings.

ALARCÓN, HERNANDO DE (*fl.* 1540–1), a Spanish navigator of the 16th century who led an expedition to the Californian coast in 1540 and was the first to establish that California was a peninsula and not an island. He surveyed the coast in great detail. The map he produced on his return to Spain in 1541 was so accurate that it remained the definitive map of California for close on two centuries.

'ALBANY BEEF', a slang name among British seamen during the War of American Independence (1775–82) for the sturgeon caught in the Hudson River. The term caught on among seafaring men and remained in general circulation for nearly a century.

ALBATROSS, a very large and long-winged seabird of the genus *Diomedea*, found almost entirely in the southern hemisphere. Examples (*D. exulans*) have been reported with a wing span of 15 feet, and they are capable of very long-sustained flights. Originally it was believed among seamen that albatrosses embodied the souls of dead sailors, and it was always considered most unlucky to kill one. This theme was immortalized by Samuel Taylor Coleridge in 1798 in his 'Rime of the *Ancient Mariner'. At sea in the southern oceans albatrosses will often follow a ship for weeks at a time.

ALBEMARLE, Duke of, see MONCK, George.

ALBEMARLE, C.S.S., was an *ironclad ship built as a *ram in the Roanoke River at Edwards Ferry, North Carolina, in 1863–4 under the supervision of Commander J. W. Cooke of the Confederate States Navy, formerly of the U.S.N. Her construction, far from any shipyard, reflected considerable credit on Cooke and his assistants who scoured the surrounding country for iron, and from the miscellaneous materials gathered together constructed this vessel. She was commissioned on 17 April 1864 and two days later at Plymouth, North Carolina, she rammed and sank the U.S.S. *Southfield* while forcing three other Federal vessels to withdraw. The immediate effect was to yield the town of Plymouth to Confederate forces. On 5 May the *Albemarle*, accompanied by a converted vessel captured from the Federal Army, attacked Union vessels below Plymouth, suffering slight damage. She was taken back up the river and there was torpedoed and sunk with a *spar torpedo by Lieutenant W. B. *Cushing, U.S.N., who had ascended the river in darkness in an improvised torpedoboat on the night of 27–8 October 1864. The *Albemarle* became famous partly because of the manner in which material for her construction was collected, partly because of the damage and fright caused to the Union Navy, and finally because of her dramatic end in the exploit of Cushing.

Albatross

Alfonso d'Albuquerque

ALBUQUERQUE, ALFONSO D' (1453–1515), Portuguese explorer and conqueror, was connected illegitimately with the royal family of Portugal, a fact which was sufficient to give him a good start in life by his appointment as chief equerry to King John II. He set out on an expedition to the east in 1503, reaching Cochin after rounding the Cape of Good Hope and setting up a fort there, from which sprang the Portuguese empire in the east. Returning home, he was given command of a squadron in the fleet led by Tristan da Cunha which in 1506 successfully attacked many Arab cities on the eastern coast of Africa. Parting company with da Cunha, Albuquerque attacked the island of Ormuz in the Persian Gulf, but was unable to retain possession of it for long. He then sailed for the Malabar coast, captured Goa, and fought a successful campaign for the possession of Malacca, where he remained for a year consolidating Portuguese power. On his return to Goa his ship, the *Flor de la Mar*, was wrecked, and in her Albuquerque lost the immense personal treasure he had gathered during his operations. While in Goa he received instructions from Lisbon to lead an expedition into the Red Sea, and in 1513 unsuccessfully attacked Aden,

later penetrating the Red Sea, the first European ever to do so, but without achieving any real successes. On his return voyage to Goa in 1515 he again attacked Ormuz, this time capturing it without difficulty.

As he was entering Goa harbour he was met by a ship from Portugal carrying orders from the king that he was to be superseded by his enemies at court. The shock was too much for him and he died at sea, his body being brought to Goa and buried there in the Church of Our Lady.

ALBURKAH, a small, iron, paddle-wheel steamer of 55 tons, designed by Macgregor *Laird, which was the first iron ship to make an ocean voyage. In 1832 she left Liverpool for the Niger, with her designer on board, returning to Liverpool in 1834 with only nine of her original crew of forty-eight, the remainder having died of fever.

ALDIS LAMP, a hand-held electric lamp fitted with a finger-operated shutter used for the sending of *signals at sea.

ALDRICH, PELHAM (1844–1930), British admiral, was with Sir George *Nares in both the *Challenger* expedition of 1872–6 and the Arctic expedition of 1875–6. Thereafter as a naval surveyor he commanded the *Sylvia* in Japanese waters, 1877–80, the *Fawn* in the Red Sea and on the east coast of Africa, 1881–3, the *Sylvia* again, now in South African waters and the Mediterranean, 1884–6, and the *Egeria*, 1887–8. In the *Egeria*, en route to the Pacific for a deep-sea sounding cruise concerned with the projected telegraph cable to connect Canada and Australasia, he visited Christmas Island in the Indian Ocean. Earlier in the same year, this uninhabited island had been the subject of a report by Maclean in the *Flying Fish* which was of particular interest to geologists because of the steepness of the slope that he found in coral formations. Accordingly the *Egeria* carried a naturalist by arrangement with the Royal Society, and another valuable report resulted. Christmas Island was annexed by Britain in 1888. This deep-sea cruise made history at the time by recording a depth of 4,000 fathoms, the deepest sounding yet attained.

In 1889 Aldrich commanded the *Research in home waters until 1891 when he returned to naval general service. But he was again to be associated with hydrography when, in 1903, as Admiral Superintendent at Portsmouth, he expedited the fitting out of the *Terra Nova* as a relief ship for *Scott's *Discovery* which was beset in Antarctic ice.

ALECTO, H.M.S., a *frigate of 880 tons, fitted by the British Admiralty in 1845 with a pair of paddle-wheels (see PADDLE STEAMER) driven by an engine of 200 nominal horsepower specifically to test the efficiency of paddle-wheels against that of a screw *propeller. An exactly similar frigate, H.M.S. *Rattler, was fitted with an engine of similar power driving a screw propeller, and in tests carried out between the two ships in March 1845 demonstrated that screw propulsion was superior to paddle-wheels in both speed and power.

A-LEE, the position of the *helm of a vessel when it has been pushed down to leeward in order to tack a sailing vessel or to bring her bows up into the wind. 'HELM'S A-LEE', the response of the helmsman after putting the helm down on the order to *tack. When a vessel *heaves-to under storm canvas in rough weather, the helm is lashed a-lee so that the bows are continuously forced up towards the wind, in which position the vessel lies more easily.

ALERT, **H.M.S.,** a four-gun screw *sloop of the British Navy launched at Pembroke Dock in 1856. She displaced 1,340 tons and was fitted with a 310 h.p. steam engine. In May 1875 under the command of Captain G. *Nares and in company with the *Discovery she formed part of an expedition which set out in an attempt to reach the North pole. Although the expedition got no further than latitude 82° N., it returned in the autumn of 1876 with a great deal of valuable scientific information. Between 1879 and 1882, under Captain J. F. L. Maclear, she was employed on a voyage of scientific discovery in various parts of the world. In 1884 she was presented to the U.S.A. for service with the Greely relief expedition.

ALFRED, known as THE GREAT (848–c. 900), king of England, is often said to be the founder of the English Navy. There is no real validity in this claim (a) because naval actions against the Danes had been fought before Alfred began to build warships, and (b) because for long periods after his reign, there was no navy in England. In the year 897 Alfred certainly designed and built ships of war to hold in check the Danish invaders whom he had defeated on land in a campaign which had begun in 893, but from such records as exist, the ships designed by him seemed to founder in rough weather with unhappy frequency.

ALGERINE PIRATES, Mediterranean *corsairs who owed allegiance to the Dey of Algiers and operated from that port in the 14th to 19th centuries. See also BARBARY PIRATES.

ALGOA BAY, a large shallow bay 436 miles east of the Cape of Good Hope, where Bartholomew *Diaz made his second landing in South Africa in 1488. It was also the first landing place of British emigrants to Cape Colony in 1820, where they founded the town of Port Elizabeth.

'ALL HANDS', an order on board ship for the seamen of all watches to muster on deck immediately. It is an order usually given either in an emergency or for performing an evolution which requires the use of all available seamen. The full order is 'ALL HANDS ON DECK', but it is normally shortened to 'ALL HANDS'.

ALL IN THE WIND, an expression used to describe the situation when a sailing vessel, while going about, is head to wind and all her sails are shivering.

ALL STANDING, a ship is said to be brought up all standing when she lets go her anchor with too much way on and so is brought suddenly to a stop as the anchor bites. In earlier sailing ship days, all standing was an expression sometimes used to denote that a ship was fully equipped.

ALL-A-TAUNT-O, the condition of a square-rigged sailing vessel where all the running rigging is hauled taut and *belayed and all her *yards are crossed on the masts, i.e., have not been sent down. In general it refers more to ships with very tall masts than to more rugged ships with shorter masts. See also TAUNT.

ALLCOT, JOHN (1889–   ), Australian marine painter, went to sea in sail at the age of 18 where he spent the next ten years, followed by fourteen years in steam. On leaving the sea he settled in Sydney, N.S.W., and devoted himself to painting pictures of sailing ships and life at sea. He is one of the best known of contemporary ship portraitists.

ALLEYWAY, the name usually given in merchant vessels to a passage-way along the decks below the upper deck, giving access to *cabins or other parts of the ship.

ALLIANCE, a frigate of the *Continental (U.S.) Navy, was built at Salisbury, Mass., and launched in April 1778. In 1779 she sailed for Brest from Boston, commanded by Pierre *Landais. She was part of the squadron of John Paul *Jones which sailed from France in August 1779 and was present at the action when the *Bonhomme Richard captured H.M.S. Serapis off Flamborough Head on 23 September.

In 1781, under the command of John

*Barry, she sailed from Boston with a member of President Washington's staff on board to ask for the dispatch of a French fleet to American waters to support the revolution. Later she made several minor captures and was used for escort purposes. She became the last remaining vessel of the Continental Navy and was sold on 1 August 1785.

ALLSTON, WASHINGTON (1779–1843), American landscape, portrait, and marine painter, was born at Waccamaw, South Carolina. He studied at Harvard University but decided to become an artist and with this end in view went to live at Charleston. After long travels abroad, he returned to Boston for good in 1818 and although regarded mainly as a painter of portraits and mythological subjects, he also painted a number of marine pictures which are as outstanding as the rest of his work. He was much influenced by Joseph *Vernet, particularly in his storm scenes, and his 'Rising of a Thunderstorm at Sea' has been described as 'the first major statement of the romantic seascape in American art' (Wilmerding). He has also been called the American Titian, whose rich colouring he sought to emulate.

ALMANACCO NAVALE, an Italian compendium of warship data published biennially under the auspices of La *Rivista Marittima, an influential maritime magazine. It was founded at the beginning of the 20th century by the Italian Navy League and had close connections with the German Weyer's Flottentaschenbuch in so far as technical information was concerned. It sought, however, more to emulate the style of *Brassey's Naval Annual in the quality of its articles on a wide range of naval matters.

Production ceased temporarily after the publication of the 1926 edition, but in the mid-1930s an enthusiastic navalist, Luigi Accorsi, managed to obtain the approval of the Italian naval authorities for publication to be restarted. Thereafter it appeared annually until 1943 when it became an official publication of the Royal Italian Navy, but was again discontinued with the signing of the armistice in 1944.

In 1960 two navalists, Giorgio Giorgerini and Augusto Nani, applied to the director of the Rivista Marittima, Admiral Aldo Cocchia, for help in resuscitating the Almanacco Navale. This was forthcoming and in November 1962 it reappeared in its present form and has been published biennially ever since. Today its production is the work of the above-mentioned authors in collaboration with Admiral Bazan and Rear Admiral Bertini. It always contains a review of the current naval situation in Italian, English, Spanish, and French, followed by ship details in tabular form with silhouettes, photo-

graphs, and line drawings of a high standard. At the end are sections dealing with maritime aircraft and missiles. A unique feature of the publication is the reproduction of the naval and marine *ensigns of all nations in colour.

ALMAYER'S FOLLY, the first novel written by Joseph *Conrad, published in 1895. Set in the Malay Archipelago, it shows the influence of the author's experiences as mate of the trading vessel S.S. Vidar in 1886–8.

ALOFT, above, overhead, also anywhere about the upper *yards, *masts, and rigging of ships. 'AWAY ALOFT', the command for *topmen to take up their stations on the masts and yards. 'GONE ALOFT', a sailor's phrase for a seaman who has died.

ALOOF, an old expression meaning 'keep your *luff', or sail as close to the wind as possible. Sometimes, in old books of voyages, written as 'ALUFFE'. The expression was most often used when a ship was sailing along a *lee shore, the order to 'keep aloof' meaning to keep the ship's head nearer to the wind to prevent her being driven closer to the shore.

ALOW, the opposite to *aloft, meaning on or near the deck of a ship. When a vessel is carrying all sail alow and aloft, she has all her sails, including *studdingsails, set and all *reefs shaken out.

ALTERNATING LIGHT, a navigational light displayed by a *lighthouse, *lightship, or lighted *buoy in which two colours are shown alternately, with or without a period of darkness separating them. See CHARACTERISTICS.

ALTITUDE, from the Latin altitudo, height, the angle between the centre of a celestial body and the rational *horizon as measured from the centre of the earth. It is one of the three sides of the astronomical triangle, through the solution of which a position line can be plotted on a chart. In the case of altitudes of stars, most of which are infinitely distant, the observer's horizon can be accepted as the rational horizon without any loss of accuracy, but in an observation for navigational purposes of the sun or moon, which are both much closer to the earth, a correction, known as semi-diameter, must be applied to the observed altitude to allow for the distance between the centre of the sun or moon and their lower limb, which is the point of observation, and for the distance between the observer's position on the earth's surface and the centre of the earth, which is the point from which the true altitude must be measured for astronomical calculations. See NAVIGATION, Celestial, and for illus. ZENITH DISTANCE.

ALTMARK, a German naval *tanker of 8,053 tons, was tender to the *pocket-battleship *Admiral Graf Spee* during the latter's operations as a commerce raider in the South Atlantic during the Second World War. On her way back to Germany with 299 British prisoners on board after the *Graf Spee* had been sunk, she was intercepted on 16 February 1940 by the British *destroyer *Cossack* in Jössing Fjord (Norwegian territorial waters), the prisoners rescued, and the ship left, as she was not then a warship. Later she became a supply ship for German surface raiders under the name of *Uckermark* and was accidentally destroyed at *Yokohama on 30 November 1942. See also VIAN, Sir Philip.

ALTONAER MUSEUM, Hamburg, West Germany, a well-known museum depicting the history of German shipbuilding. It was opened in 1901 but the building was destroyed during the Second World War and rebuilt after 1954. It contains approximately 200 models of merchant ships, fishing boats, and other craft, together with *figureheads and ship's decorations. There are dioramas showing methods of fishing, and workshops illustrating blockmaking, ropework, sailmaking, etc. Among the exhibits are some 100 nautical instruments and also examples of *scrimshaw, knots, and fancy work. The museum contains several hundred paintings, engravings, drawings, and photographs as well as a library of about 700 books, plans, and manuscripts.

AMAIN, an old maritime word meaning 'immediately', as 'let go amain', let go the *anchor at once. Another old naval expression of the 15th and 16th centuries was 'WAVING AMAIN', which was a direction by a warship to a merchant vessel, encountered in the waters claimed by a sovereign state, to strike her *topsails in salute. The actual waving was done with swords or pikes to indicate the warlike nature of the ship demanding the salute. In the same context, the merchant ship would 'STRIKE AMAIN', i.e., let fall her topsails immediately.

AMBERGRIS, from the French *ambre gris*, grey amber, a light, inflammable fatty substance sometimes found in the intestines of sperm whales (*Physeteridae*) or floating in tropical seas. It occurs in lumps from a few ounces to several hundred pounds and is used extensively in the preparation of perfumes. See also WHALING.

AMERICA, a *schooner yacht of 170 tons measurement built in New York in 1851 for John *Stevens, commodore of the *New York Yacht Club, by George Steers specially to race in English waters. On 22 August 1851, in a race round the Isle of Wight, she finished first of sixteen starters to win a cup presented by the *Royal Yacht Squadron, and known ever since as the *America*'s Cup. At the end of the season she was sold and later laid up at Cowes, Isle of Wight, and in 1858 largely rebuilt of English oak and renamed *Camilla*. In 1861 she was in Savannah and during the Civil War in America was used for various purposes on the Confederate side, including at one period having guns mounted on her deck for employment as a blockade runner. She was discovered and chased by the Federal Navy, and was eventually scuttled in the St. John's River, Florida, to escape capture. Raised later, she was commissioned into the Federal Navy under the name *Memphis*, later changed back to *America*, and took part in the blockade of Charleston. After the civil war she was sent to *Annapolis as a training vessel for midshipmen, but in 1870 she was recommissioned as a yacht and on 8 August 1870, on the occasion of the first British challenge for the *America*'s Cup, she was one of the twenty-three defenders, finishing fourth and beating the British challenger, James Ashbury's *Cambria*, by 13 minutes. She was sold in 1873 to General Butler and for many years was used as a cruising yacht, with an occasional entry into racing, until she was sold again in 1917, when her lead keel was stripped and used for war material. In 1921 she was presented to the Eastern Yacht Club at Marblehead and was sold by the club, for the sum of one dollar, to Admiral Henry Wilson for preservation at Annapolis. In March 1942 her timbers were crushed beyond repair when the roof of her shed fell in during a heavy snow storm.

AMERICAN NEPTUNE, THE, a quarterly journal established in 1941 concerned mainly with the American merchant marine from a historical point of view and widely recognized for the scholarship of its articles. It is published by the *Peabody Museum.

AMERICA'S **CUP,** a trophy, known at the time as the 'hundred guinea cup', originally presented by the *Royal Yacht Squadron in 1851 for a yacht race round the Isle of Wight and won by the 170-ton *schooner *America* on behalf of the *New York Yacht Club against a competing British fleet of fifteen yachts. It was lodged in the keeping of the New York Yacht Club and, now known as the *America*'s Cup, is held as a challenge trophy for a match of seven races between a yacht of the challenging club and a yacht of the New York Yacht Club. The first such challenge race was held in 1870, and in all 23 challenges have been made, 16 from Britain, 2 from

The schooner yacht America

America's Cup—challenging yachts, owners, and defenders

1870	*Cambria*, sch., James Ashbury	*Magic*, sch.
1871	*Livonia*, sch., James Ashbury	*Columbia* and *Sappho*, schs.
1876	*Countess of Dufferin*, sch., R. Canadian Y.C. syndicate	*Madeleine*, sch.
1881	*Atalanta*, sl., Alex Cuthbert	*Mischief*, cut.
1885	*Genesta*, cut., Sir Richard Sutton	*Puritan*, cut.
1886	*Galatea*, cut., Lt. William Henn	*Mayflower*, cut
1887	*Thistle*, cut., James Bell	*Volunteer*, cut.
1893	*Valkyrie II*, cut., Earl of Dunraven	*Vigilant*, cut.
1895	*Valkyrie III*, cut., Earl of Dunraven	*Defender*, cut.
1899	*Shamrock I*, cut., Sir Thomas Lipton	*Columbia*, cut.
1901	*Shamrock II*, cut., Sir Thomas Lipton	*Columbia*, cut.
1903	*Shamrock III*, cut., Sir Thomas Lipton	*Reliance*, cut.
1920	*Shamrock IV*, cut., Sir Thomas Lipton	*Resolute*, cut.
1930	*Shamrock V*, sl., Sir Thomas Lipton	*Enterprise*, sl.
1934	*Endeavour I*, sl., T. O. M. Sopwith	*Rainbow*, sl.
1937	*Endeavour II*, sl., T. O. M. Sopwith	*Ranger*, sl.
1958	*Sceptre*, 12-m, U.K. syndicate	*Columbia*, 12-m
1962	*Gretel*, 12-m, Australian syndicate	*Weatherly*, 12-m
1964	*Sovereign*, 12-m, U.K. syndicate	*Constellation*, 12-m
1967	*Dame Pattie*, 12-m, Australian syndicate	*Intrepid*, 12-m
1970	*Gretel II*, 12-m, Australian syndicate	*Intrepid*, 12-m
1974	*Southern Cross*, 12-m, Australian syndicate	*Courageous*, 12-m
1977	*Australia*, 12-m, Australian syndicate	*Courageous*, 12-m

sch. = schooner.   cut. = cutter.   sl. = sloop.   12-m = International 12-metre class.

Canada, and 5 from Australia. Until 1937 the matches were sailed between racing yachts of the largest class, but since the Second World War the yachts concerned have been built to the International 12-metre (39-ft) class, the match being the best of seven races. No challenger has yet been successful in winning the *America*'s Cup from the New York Yacht Club. The attempts made, with the names of the respective challenging yachts, their owners, and the defenders, were as listed on p. 19.

AMETHYST, H.M.S., a * sloop, commanded by Lieutenant-Commander J. S. Kerans, which, after being in action with the communists in the Yangtze river in April 1949, was held there by the enemy but made her escape in a gallant dash of 130 miles to the sea in July of that year.

AMIDSHIPS, in the middle of the ship, whether longitudinally or laterally. It is more usually known as a *helm order, normally shortened to 'MIDSHIPS, to centre the helm in the line of the keel.

AMPLITUDE, the angle between the point at which the sun rises and sets and the true east and west points of the horizon. In earlier days, amplitudes were used to find the * variation of the compass, the difference of either the morning or evening amplitude from the mean giving the variation. This was first suggested by Francisco Faleiro in his *Tractado de Esphera y del Arte del Marear*, published in 1535. In 1595 Thomas Hariot produced a table of amplitudes which saved the navigator the trouble of working them out; it is published in the introduction to the *Instructions for Raleigh's Voyage to Guiana*, now in the British Museum. This method of discovering the variation was liable to error because of the considerable refraction of the sun at sunrise and sunset. See also AZIMUTH.

AMSTERDAM, a city and seaport of Holland on the River Amstel, used to lie on an arm of the Zuider Zee, now being reclaimed, and is connected to the North Sea at Ijmuiden by the North Sea Canal constructed in 1876. It is also connected to Dutch and north German inland waterways by the series of canals on which Amsterdam itself was originally built, which gave it its one-time description of 'the Venice of the North'. It is a large and important seaport with a wide and growing trade, but now takes second place to * Rotterdam among Dutch ports in the volume and profitability of the trade handled.

Amsterdam was no more than a fishing village until 1240 when a dam was constructed to keep out the sea by Giesebrecht III of Amstel. It began to grow as a port from then onwards, became a

walled city in 1482, and in 1648, under the terms of the treaty of Westphalia which closed the River Scheldt to seaborne trade, it leapt into prominence and wealth as the most important port of the Low Countries. It is famous for the magnificence of its buildings, particularly the Nieuwe Kerk, dating from 1408, in which the sovereigns of Holland are crowned and which contains a fine monument to Holland's most famous admiral, Michiel de * Ruyter. In the Oude Kerk, which dates from 1300, are monuments to Admirals Jacob van * Heemskerk, Sweers, and van der Hulst. In Amsterdam also is the * Nederlandsch Historisch Scheepvaart Museum, an important museum which illustrates the history of Dutch shipping and shipbuilding from its earliest beginnings to the present time. In the Rijksmuseum in Amsterdam is a magnificent collection of marine paintings by famous Dutch artists.

AMUNDSEN, ROALD (1872–1928), Polar explorer, was born at Borgo, southern Norway. Inspired as a boy by the exploits of Sir John * Franklin he determined to explore the polar regions himself and abandoned a career in medicine in order to serve as a seaman in Arctic waters and to obtain his *mate's certificate. In 1897 he secured the position of first mate on de * Gerlache's * Belgica expedition to the Antarctic and was one of the first human beings to spend an involuntary winter in these regions when the ship became trapped in the ice. On his return in 1899 Amundsen obtained his * master's certificate. Thus equipped with a first-hand knowledge of ice navigation and survival techniques he resolved to lead an expedition of his own to traverse the * North-West passage and attain the North magnetic pole.

Encouraged by the veteran explorer Fridtjof * Nansen, Amundsen purchased an old 50-ton fishing-smack, the *Gjøa*, fitted with an auxiliary motor engine. Financial difficulties beset him but he succeeded in eluding his creditors by slipping away in June 1903 with six companions. Crossing to Greenland the expedition followed Franklin's track and for two years remained on the shore of King William Island, in the Canadian Arctic archipelago, making magnetic recordings and studying the local Eskimo. In August 1905 the *Gjøa* continued her voyage, finally reaching the Pacific and thereby becoming the first vessel to accomplish the North-West passage. Two years of successful lecturing enabled Amundsen to pay off his debts and to lay plans for a fresh enterprise—the achievement of the North pole by emulating Nansen's drift in the * *Fram*. The Norwegian government gave him the ship and preparations were in hand when the news of * Peary's success in the autumn of 1909 brought the scheme to a halt. Inspired by

Roald Amundsen

* Shackleton's attempt to reach the South pole in 1907–9, Amundsen decided to switch his plans to the south and by June 1910 the *Fram* was equipped and ready. While the world thought he was making for the Arctic, Amundsen was on his way to Madeira where he made known his intentions to place the Norwegian flag on the South pole. At the same time he cabled Captain * Scott, then in New Zealand en route to the Antarctic, notifying him of his intentions. The race for the South pole was on. Amundsen's plans went like clockwork. Carefully avoiding Scott's planned route to the polar plateau up the Beardmore glacier, Amundsen and four companions, using dogs and sledges, achieved their goal by a new and untried route, reaching the pole on 14 December 1911. The return journey was equally successful. Not a single member of the expedition suffered from * scurvy.

After the First World War (1914–18) Amundsen used a considerable personal fortune to build the *Maud*, a polar ship to replace the *Fram*. With her he planned to follow the * North-East passage to Bering Strait and then, after entering the pack ice, to drift with the polar current to Spitsbergen and Greenland. In August 1919 the *Maud*, after wintering near Cape Chelyuskin, reached Nome in Alaska. With a crew reduced to four, Amundsen prepared for drifting in the ice. Unluckily a broken propeller

forced him to winter off Siberia and then to return to Seattle for repairs in 1921.

By now Amundsen was convinced that the Arctic Ocean could best be explored from the air. An attempt to fly a Junkers aircraft from Wainwright, Alaska, to Spitsbergen in 1922 was a failure but in 1925 he succeeded, in the company of the American aviator, Lincoln Ellsworth, in achieving lat. 87° 43′ N., inside the Arctic Ocean, with a Dornier flying boat. This was the first long Arctic flight. In 1926 Amundsen flew the airship *Norge* from King's Bay, Spitsbergen, over the North pole to Telfer, Alaska, a distance of 3,390 miles. It was to be his last expedition. In June 1928 he flew by seaplane to effect the rescue of the Italian airship *Italia*, commanded by Umberto Nobile, wrecked off North East Land, Spitsbergen. He was never seen again. The plane probably crashed in the sea off the Norwegian coast. It was a fitting end for a great voyager who had achieved both poles, introduced successful aviation into polar travel, and made new contributions to science and surveying.

C. Turley, *Roald Amundsen Explorer* (1935).

ANCHOR, a large and heavy instrument designed to hold a ship in any desired locality and prevent her from drifting at the mercy of wind, tide, or current. This is achieved by her anchor, attached to the ship by a * cable, digging itself into the sea bed and holding the ship fast.

The earliest forms of anchor were large stones, or baskets filled with stones, and these were used by the ancient Greeks. As ships grew larger, more efficient anchors were required to hold them, and iron hooks, designed to dig themselves into the sea bed as any strain came upon them, were introduced. Their invention has been credited variously to King Midas of Phrygia and to the seamen of Tuscany. A second arm to the hook, making them double-headed, was added shortly afterwards, and the anchor thus took the general shape which we know today. An early improvement was the addition of a * stock, or horizontal arm, at the top of the * shank of the anchor and set at right-angles to the hooks, or * flukes, the purpose being to ensure that the flukes lay vertically on the sea bed and thus dug themselves in to provide maximum holding power.

This basic anchor, known as the fisherman's anchor, with two flukes and the stock at right-angles, remained the standard pattern of anchor for centuries, but in the early part of the 19th century a further improvement was made by curving the arms, which provided added strength in a period when welding was still an imperfect art. A persistent drawback to this type of anchor was the difficulty of stowage, but this was obviated later in the century by the invention of the Martin close-stowing anchor, in which the stock was in the same plane as the arms, which themselves canted about a pivot in the crown of the anchor and thus forced the flukes downwards into the sea bed to provide holding power. These anchors were stowed flat on an anchor-bed when not in use. It was a short step from the close-stowing to the stockless anchor, which had the advantages of making anchor beds unnecessary, of simplicity in working with a resulting saving of time and labour, and still greater ease of stowage.

For smaller craft, such as yachts, a further development of the stockless anchor has resulted in simpler and more efficient designs, such as the *CQR, or ploughshare (known in the U.S.A. as a plow anchor) and mushroom anchors and others similar in operation. While for their small size they provide better and more secure holding even than the stockless, they are unsuitable for seagoing ships of any size, since, when built large enough for this purpose, they present unacceptable problems of efficient stowage on board. But they are frequently used in cases where permanent anchoring is required, as in the case of *lightships, oil rigs at sea, and *moorings.

The most modern development is an anchor with particularly deep flukes which pivot round a stock at the bottom of the shank. For big ships it is the Meon anchor, and for small vessels the *Danforth. This development combines the advantages of both main types of anchor, as although it has a stock to turn the flukes into the ground, it can still be stowed in the *hawsepipe like a stockless anchor.

Efficiency factors of the different types of anchor have been worked out but are apt to be misleading as so much depends on the type of ground in which the anchor beds itself. In terms of resistance to drag, the CQR anchor is generally recognized as best, with the Danforth and Meon coming a close second. Least efficient is the fisherman's anchor.

TO ANCHOR, to let go the anchor. See also A-COCKBILL, APEAK, ATRIP, AWEIGH, BACK, to, BOWER, CATHEAD, CAT PENDANT, DRAG, to, FISH, to, KEDGE, SEA-ANCHOR, SHEET, SHOE, STREAM, WEIGH, to.

Fisherman's

Fluke — Bill — Ring — Cotter pin — Shank — Stock — Arm — Gravity band — Crown

CQR

Lug for anchor buoy — Fluke, or plough

Danforth

Tripping palm — Stock

Stockless

Gravity band

Four types of anchor

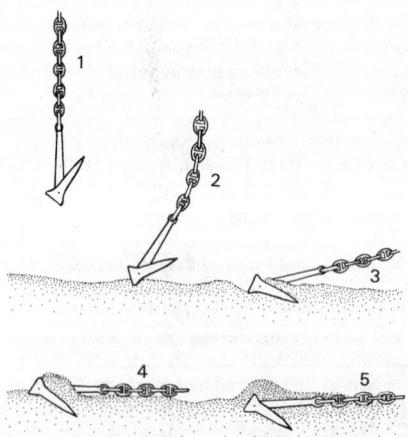

Stockless anchor digging in

ANCHOR BUOY, a buoy used to mark the position of a ship's anchor when it is on the bottom. With small anchors, such as those of yachts or fishing vessels, the buoy rope is usually attached to the * crown of the anchor with a turn round one of the * flukes so that it can be used to weigh the anchor if the flukes are caught in rocks or stones; in large anchors it is normally attached with a short length of rigging chain to the gravity band or the crown to avoid damage by chafing on the bottom. The length of the buoy-rope is of course adjusted to the depth of water in which the anchor lies, allowing for the fact that the buoy must be able to watch (rise without tightening the rope) at high water. When using an anchor buoy it is always streamed before the anchor is let go to avoid any danger of the buoy rope becoming entangled with the cable and being dragged under water as the cable runs out.

ANCHOR LIGHT, another name for a * riding light. For details of all navigational lights, see APPENDIX 3.

ANCHOR WARP, the name given to a hawser or rope when it is attached to an anchor and used as a temporary * cable.

ANCHOR WATCH, a precaution taken on board ship when lying to an anchor in bad weather with a danger of the anchor * dragging. The watch normally consists of an officer on the ship's bridge, who by frequent compass bearings of shore objects can detect whether an anchor is dragging, and a small party on the * forecastle ready to watch and work the cable. A dragging anchor can often be detected by feeling vibration in the cable; another sign is when the cable slackens and tautens alternately in a marked manner.

ANCHORAGE, an area off the coast where the ground is suitable for ships to lie to an anchor, giving a good and secure holding. These areas are marked on a chart with the symbol of an anchor. In older days it was also the name given to a royal duty levied on vessels coming to a port or roadstead for shelter.

ANCIENT, see ENSIGN.

'ANCIENT MARINER, THE RIME OF THE', was written by Samuel Taylor Coleridge (1772–1834) and was first published in *Lyrical Ballads* in 1798. The poem was almost certainly inspired to some extent by a remark made by William Wordsworth to Coleridge during a walk over the Quantock Hills in the summer of 1797 that he had been reading George * Shelvocke's *A Voyage Round the World* and had been struck by the passage in the book describing the shooting of an albatross after passing through the Straits of Le Maire by Simon Hatley, second captain of the *Success*, of which Shelvocke was captain. Other suggestions of its origin were a dream said to have been told to Coleridge by his friend George Cruickshank after reading Thomas * James's *Strange and Dangerous Voyage*, published in 1633, and a letter of St. Paulinus, Bishop of York (d. 644), to Macarius telling of the shipwreck of an old man and how, with only one remaining member of the crew, the ship was navigated by angels and steered by the 'pilot of the world'. However, the most likely source of the poem is unquestionably Shelvocke's account of his voyage.

ANDERSON, JOHN R. (1912–), British yachtsman and author, was leader of the expedition sponsored by the *Guardian* newspaper in 1969 to follow the Viking voyages to * Vinland. In the *Griffin*, a 44-foot cutter yacht, the party sailed by the old route via the Faeroes, Iceland, and Greenland to the Atlantic coast of North America at Martha's Vinyard, at the time thought to be the Norseman's colony in Vinland. More recent research places Vinland as more probably in northern Newfoundland.

ANDERSON, WILLIAM (1757–1837), Scottish shipwright, foresook his trade to seek his fortune in London as a marine painter. He began by painting river scenes and marine subjects in small format and these are considered to be his best work, revealing as they do his clear, bright colouring and a full understanding of perspective. Later he increased the size of his canvases, as in, for example, his picture of the 'Battle of the Nile' which he painted for Trinity House, Hull.

'ANDREW', a slang name among sailors for the Royal Navy. It is said to have been derived from an 18th-century press-gang officer named Andrew Miller who impressed so many men into naval service during the Revolutionary (1793–1801) and Napoleonic (1803–15) Wars that he was said to own the Royal Navy.

ANEMOMETER, an instrument for measuring the velocity of the wind. It consists of a number of wind-driven cups connected to a vertical spindle which, as it rotates, moves a pointer on a scale marked in * knots or miles an hour. In large ships it is mounted in any position where the wind is not blanketed by part of the superstructure, frequently at the masthead; hand-held models are sometimes used in smaller vessels although they are rapidly becoming permanent fittings in many small sailing yachts. In another type of anemometer, known as a ventimeter, the wind enters the bottom of a glass cylinder and pushes a disc up a vertical rod against the force of gravity, the wind strengths being marked up the side of the cylinder and indicated by the height reached by the disc. Of the two types, the wind-cup model is the more accurate and reliable.

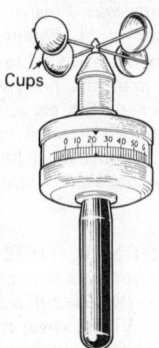

Cups

Hand-held anemometer of the wind-cup type

AN-END, a wooden mast is said to be an-end when it is cracked perpendicularly to the plane of the deck, or in the case of a topmast, to the plane of the *top. The expression is virtually obsolete as few vessels, even the smallest, have wooden masts today.

ANGARY, RIGHT OF, the claim by a belligerent power to seize the ships of a neutral country for its own use when under stress of necessity. It is a right recognized in maritime law but entails eventual restoration and the payment of indemnities for their use. A legitimate reason for the exercise of the right of angary is the prevention of the use of such ships by an enemy.

ANGEL-SHOT, another name used during the days of sailing navies for *chain shot, in which a cannon-ball was cut into two and the halves joined by a short length of chain. When fired from a cannon, the force of discharge caused the shot to rotate at great speed so that it cut a swathe through whatever it hit. It was designed for use against the rigging of enemy ships, but was also employed as an anti-personnel weapon against men working on the upper deck. It was no doubt in this role that it obtained its second name through its ability to send many men to join the angels at a single discharge. See also SHOT.

ANGLE OF CUT, in navigation, the smaller angle at which two position lines on a chart intersect. The reliability of a *fix obtained by intersecting position lines depends on the angle of cut. When fixing a ship's position by cross bearings of two marks, the prudent navigator aims to select marks whose bearings differ by not less than about 30°, recognizing that the nearer is the difference of bearings to 90°, and other factors being equal, the more reliable will be the resulting fix. See also NAVIGATION.

ANKER, JOHAN (d. 1940), Norwegian yacht designer, builder, and international racing yachtsman, was noted for his beautifully proportioned, slender, and successful racing yachts. He was the creator of the numerous *International Dragon class of 29-ft *sloops, of which some hundreds have been built in different European countries. His largest design was the 74-ft fast cruising *yawl *Rollo IV,* ex-*Magda XIII,* built by Anker and Jensen, the firm of which he was a senior partner, in 1938. He was at one time a pupil of the celebrated American designer Nathaniel *Herreschoff, and over the years many of his craft were shipped to the U.S.A. and to the Bermudas.

ANNAPOLIS, the capital of the State of Maryland in the U.S.A., a seaport, the shore-based headquarters of the U.S. Atlantic Fleet, and the seat of the U.S. Naval Academy, the establishment in which officers destined for service in the U.S. Navy receive their first training. The U.S. Naval Academy Museum contains several historic ships, which are preserved in their original state.

Annapolis was originally known as Providence and was settled by Puritan exiles from Virginia in 1649. It received its present name in 1694 in honour of Princess Anne, at the time heir to the throne of England.

ANNE (1665–1714), queen of Great Britain, served for twenty-nine days as *Lord High Admiral of Britain in 1708 following the death of her husband, Prince George of Denmark, who had held that office since 1702. This was not an honorary title and she performed the day-to-day duties of the position. She is the only woman actively to have held the office. Queen Elizabeth II, on the merging of the British Admiralty into the Ministry of Defence in 1964, assumed the title though not the office of Lord High Admiral, and it carries today no executive duties as it did when held by Queen Anne.

ANNUAL VARIATION, see VARIATION.

ANSON, GEORGE, Lord (1697–1762), British admiral of the fleet, circumnavigator, and administrator, was one of the founders of the naval profession as it became known to later generations. As a young man he had a variety of service including a spell in the Baltic under Admiral *Norris, and he made extended cruises in American, West Indian, and African waters.

Anson's first great opportunity came as a post-captain in 1740 at the beginning of the war with Spain and France. He was given charge of a small squadron of six ships with the rank of commodore and ordered to the Pacific where he was to harry Spanish possessions and if possible to capture one of the treasure ships which sailed yearly from * Acapulco in Mexico across the Pacific to Manila.

Anson's squadron was manned largely with pensioners from Greenwich Hospital. He met with much bad weather in the South Atlantic, mortality from * scurvy was unduly high, and the ships dispersed. But Anson pressed on, reaching the rendezvous at Juan Fernandez Island in his ship, the * Centurion, with no more than thirty men fit for duty. Two more of the squadron reached him later, two were wrecked rounding Cape Horn, and one returned to England. With such of his men as survived their earlier trials, he did considerable damage and took some booty in the Spanish settlements ashore, alarming the enemy far and wide.

By June 1743 misadventure had reduced Anson's force to a single ship, the Centurion. She, however, was by now well-armed and manned with veterans trained to cope with every eventuality, so that when a treasure ship was encountered off the Philippines on 20 June, the Spaniard struck her flag after a 90-minute engagement, in which, from the opening shot, the issue was never in doubt. Her name was the Nuestra Señora de Covadonga and her treasure was so enormous that it made Anson wealthy for life. The treasure which he brought home was valued at more than £500,000, and was paraded in triumph through the city of London in a procession of thirty-two wagons. After a bad start, Anson's had proved to be the most successful voyage of its kind since * Drake's circumnavigation in the * Golden Hind (1577–81). Unlike Drake (whose journal disappeared), Anson was able to supervise an account, which appeared under the name of his chaplain, Richard * Walter, which does justice to his achievement. Some idea of the mortality to be expected from such a voyage may be learnt from the fact that of the six ships' companies which were with Anson at the outset, only four men died from enemy action but over 1,300 from disease, mainly scurvy.

Anson returned home in 1744 and the rest of his career was an uninterrupted success story. He was given his flag in 1745, and two years later, when cruising off * Cape Finisterre, he defeated a French squadron, commanded by Admiral de la * Jonquière, which was protecting an outward-bound convoy to Canada. He captured four ships of the line and two frigates, and took seven merchantmen, thus adding considerably to his wealth by his share of the * prize money. He was made a peer, and in 1748 married Lady Elizabeth Yorke, daughter of the Lord Chancellor. Henceforward, Anson moved freely in the corridors of power, enjoying two separate spells as First Lord of the Admiralty, the first of them in Pelham's administration, and the second, shortly after the opening of the Seven Years War, in that of the elder Pitt who, with Anson, became one of the architects of victory.

Anson was very much a man of his age. His predominant characteristic was a rational calm which no adverse circumstance could shake. Until the very end of his famous voyage there was risk that misfortune might overcome him—for instance, on the last leg, only fog prevented the Centurion from being overwhelmed by a French fleet, into the midst of which she had inadvertently run. Anson was unmoved by peril.

At the Admiralty, he proved a determined reformer, notably improving the dockyards, which for generations had been a source of waste, inefficiency, and corruption; breaking the existing marine regiments and replacing them with a corps of marines, and drawing up a new code of the * articles of war. The officers he trained, among them Philip Saumarez, Piercy * Brett, Charles * Saunders, and Augustus * Keppel, were some of the most notable of their era. It was in Anson's time that a regular uniform was laid down for naval officers, though it was many years before the bulk of them readily conformed to it. Shugborough, his Staffordshire estate, which is now open to the public, is in some sort a memorial to his voyage, and Anson has a lasting claim upon remembrance for his improvements in the general standards of the navy. It was under his regime that men-of-war were * 'rated' on an established system and, although he did not live to see the triumphant conclusion of the Seven Years War, when he died he was not only head of his profession, but that profession had no rival in the world. For his biography see Sir John * Barrow's Life of George Lord Anson (1839).

ANSWERING PENDANT, a red and white vertically striped * pendant hoisted when answering a flag signal at sea to indicate that it has been understood. Until the signal has been fully understood, the answering pendant is hoisted at the dip, i.e., only half way up the signal * halyards. The same pendant is used both in the naval signal code and in the * International Code of Signals for merchant ships.

ANTARCTIC, a wooden sealer of 226 tons built in Norway in 1871 as the Cap Nor. She was used on Henrik J. * Bull's Norwegian Antarctic expedition of 1894–5 and later employed on Otto * Nordenskjöld's Swedish Antarctic expedition of 1901–3 when she was crushed and lost in the pack ice of the Weddell Sea in February 1903.

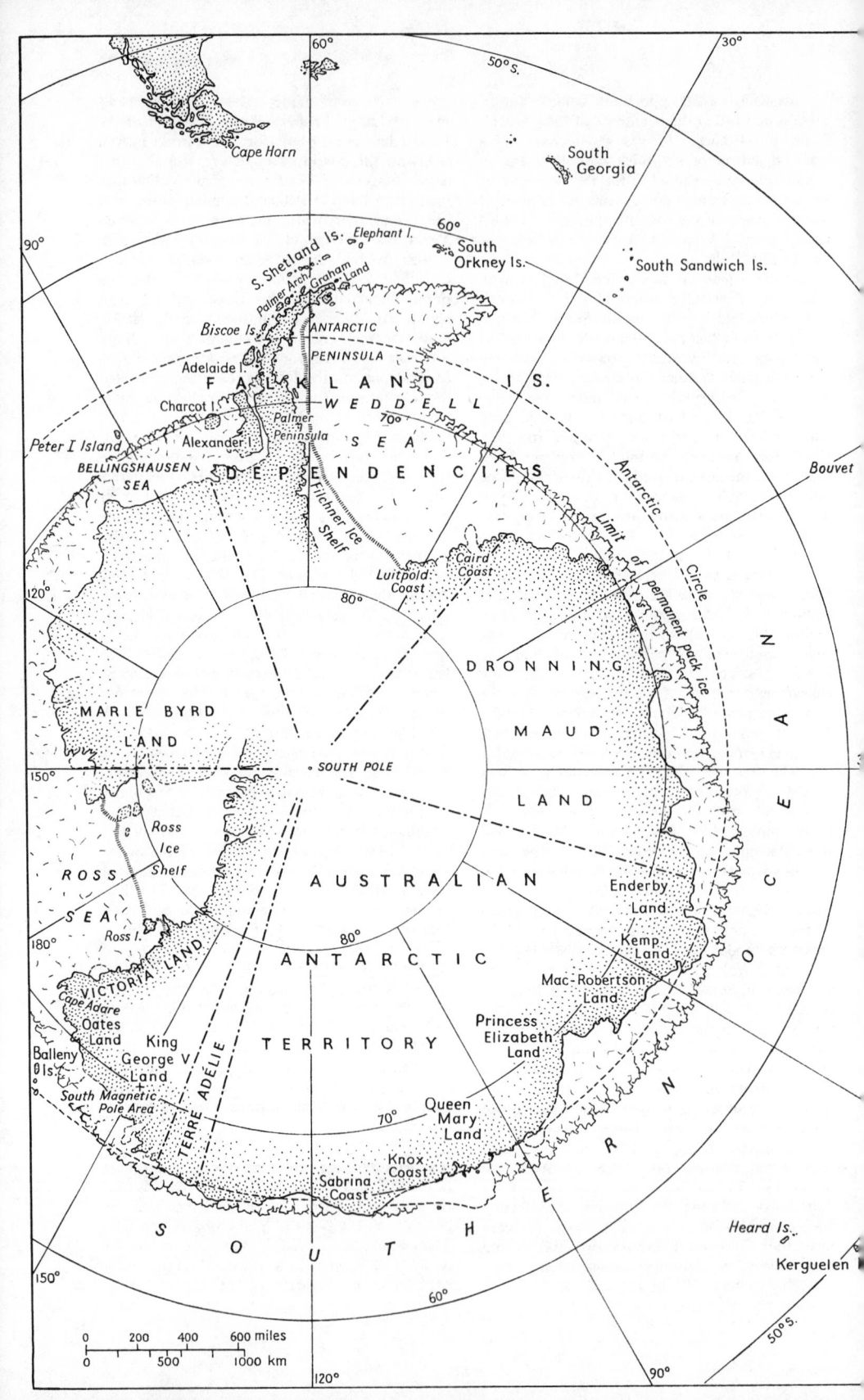

50° S.

Cape Horn

South Georgia

South Sandwich Is.

S. Shetland Is. · Elephant I. · 60°
South Orkney Is. ·

Palmer Arch. · Graham
Land
Biscoe Is. ANTARCTIC
PENINSULA
Adelaide I. F A L K L A N D I S.
W E D D E L L 70°
Charcot I. Palmer
Peninsula S E A
Peter I Island Alexander I.
BELLINGSHAUSEN D E P E N D E N C I E S
SEA
Filchner Ice
Shelf

Antarctic
Limit of permanent pack ice
Circle

Bouvet

Luitpold
Coast Caird
Coast

D R O N N I N G

M A U D

L A N D

80°
MARIE BYRD
LAND
·SOUTH POLE

O
C
E
A
N

Ross
Ice
Shelf A U S T R A L I A N Enderby
Land
R O S S
S E A Ross I. Kemp
Land
180° 80° Mac-Robertson
Land
VICTORIA LAND A N T A R C T I C
Cape Adare Princess
Oates Elizabeth
Land King Land
George V T E R R I T O R Y
Balleny ± Land
Is. Queen
South Magnetic Mary
Pole Area 70° Land

TERRE ADÉLIE
Knox
Coast
Sabrina
Coast

Heard Is.

Kerguelen

S O U T H

150°
60°

50° S.

120°

90°

ANTARCTIC CONVERGENCE, a boundary in the southern oceans along which cold, poorly saline Antarctic surface water, flowing north from Antarctica, sinks beneath warmer southward-flowing sub-Antarctic water. The zone in which this takes place lies in about lat. 50° S. across most of the Atlantic and Indian Ocean sectors and is located between latitudes 55° and 62° in the Pacific sector. It is accompanied by a fall in surface temperature from about 5° C to 3° C in summer and from 3° C to 1° C in winter. The Antarctic convergence marks not only a change in the ocean's surface temperature but also a change in chemical composition. There are also marked biological differences on either side of the convergence both with respect to life in the ocean and to bird life. Finally, the convergence influences the climatic characteristics of various sub-Antarctic islands whose shores are washed by its cold upwelling waters.

ANTARCTIC EXPLORATION. The idea of a frozen land mass in the southern hemisphere may be attributed to the Greeks of classical antiquity whose geography required such a region to balance the ice-covered region of ocean which they believed to exist under the constellation of Arktos, the Bear. During the early Middle Ages, when a flat-earth theory was supported by the Church, the concept of a southern hemisphere became anathema. But with the questing for a sea route to the Far East which began with *Henry the Navigator in 1418 the age of speculation gave place to the age of exploration. The rounding of Africa by *Diaz in 1487 and of South America by *Magellan in 1520 revealed the possibility of a land to the south of these continents. Some cartographers of the day, anxious to fill the void, portrayed a new continent centred on the south geographical pole and stretching in the Pacific Ocean sector to the north of the equator. The search for this great south land, or *Terra Australis Incognita, preoccupied many of the 16th and 17th century explorers, for it was believed to be a rich and fertile region populated with natives anxious to trade. As voyagers penetrated further southwards the imaginary continent was gradually whittled away. With the discovery in 1739 by Lozier Bouvet of the ice-covered island that now bears his name and *Kerguelen's discovery of the inhospitable Isles de Kerguelen in 1771, the way was open for Captain *Cook to demonstrate the true nature of the Antarctic.

Antarctic exploration proper can be said to begin with Cook's expedition of 1772–5 fitted out by the British Admiralty with the express intention of discovering or disproving the existence of the supposed southern continent. In the course of three cruises Cook circumnavigated the world in high southern latitudes crossing the

Antarctic Circle for the first recorded occasion in history and achieving a southern latitude of 71° 10′ S. in longitude 106° 54′ W. but without sighting land. His only discoveries of truly Antarctic land, South Georgia and part of the South Sandwich Island group, convinced him that if an Antarctic continent did exist it would be uninhabitable and of no economic importance. But South Georgia's plentiful stocks of fur seals were of great commercial value and attracted numerous British and American sealers to the region south of Cape Horn. This 'fur rush' was to result in the near extinction of the fur seals but it led directly to the first Antarctic landfalls. In 1819 the South Shetland Islands were discovered by a British sealer, William *Smith, and in 1820 mountains in the northern tip of the Antarctic Peninsula were sighted by Edward *Bransfield and the American Nathaniel *Palmer. In 1821–2 the South Orkney Islands were discovered and charted by George Powell, a British sealer acting jointly with Palmer. Contemporary with these discoveries was the Russian *Bellingshausen's circumnavigation of the Antarctic continent complementing that of Cook and leading to the discovery of Peter I Island and Alexander Island in 1821. Other voyages designed to open up new sealing and whaling grounds followed, some of which were to add significantly to the map of Antarctica. In 1823 James *Weddell entered the sea that carries his name today and achieved a record high latitude of 74° 15′ S. in longitude 34° 17′ W. In 1830 John *Biscoe, a sealing captain in the employ of Messrs. Samuel Enderby of London, circumnavigated the Antarctic continent, discovering Enderby Land in the present Australian sector as well as Adelaide Island, the Biscoe Islands, and Graham Land on the west side of the Antarctic Peninsula. Concluding these combined voyages of sealing and discovery were those of Peter *Kemp, commanding the *Magnet*, who in 1833–4 discovered Heard Island and Kemp Land, and of John *Balleny who with the *Eliza Scott* and *Sabrina* discovered the Balleny Islands and Sabrina Coast.

During the 1830s the prediction of the earth's south magnetic pole in the Antarctic by the magnetician Gauss added a scientific to the existing commercial motive for southern exploration, to which could also be added an element of national rivalry. Between 1837 and 1843 three nationally sponsored expeditions entered the field. The first, a French enterprise under the leadership of J.-S.-C. *Dumont d'Urville, attempted in 1838 to penetrate as far south as possible in the Weddell Sea but without success. Early in 1840 Dumont d'Urville returned to the Antarctic, this time with the intention of locating the south magnetic pole. In this, too, he failed but discovered instead a new Antarctic land which he named Terre

Adélie, to this day the traditional region of French activity in Antarctica. This discovery coincided in place and time with a U.S. exploring expedition authorized by Congress and led by Lieutenant Charles *Wilkes. Its aims in Antarctic waters were to follow Weddell's route, to visit Cook's farthest south, and to penetrate the Antarctic in the sector south of Tasmania. Like Dumont d'Urville, Wilkes failed to navigate the Weddell Sea but one of his squadrons succeeded in reaching 70° S. in latitude 105° W. In 1839 Wilkes sailed along the ice barrier towards Biscoe's Enderby Land and reported land at various points along the present Knox and Sabrina Coasts of Australian Antarctic Territory. The expedition equipped by the British Admiralty in 1839 was intended primarily to explore and to carry out a magnetic survey. Its leader, Captain James Clark *Ross, in command of two vessels, the *Erebus and *Terror, both specially strengthened for ice navigation, attempted to reach a high southern latitude to the east of the sector explored by Dumont d'Urville and Wilkes. Forcing a way through the pack ice of the present Ross Sea he discovered, in January 1841, the coastline of Victoria Land which he claimed for Britain. He also discovered the cliff-like front of the Ross Ice Shelf to which he returned on a second cruise in 1842, only to find his way to the south barred at latitude 78° 4′ S. A third cruise early in 1843 made little progress into the Weddell Sea but resulted in some discoveries off the northern tip of the Antarctic Peninsula. Ross's voyage south of New Zealand not only added significantly to the map of Antarctica but also pointed the way to the most accessible and the shortest route to the South pole.

No major additions were to be made to the map of Antarctica for a further fifty years but important evidence in favour of its continentality was derived from the deep-sea dredging of H.M.S. *Challenger, first steam vessel to cross the Antarctic Circle, during her circumnavigation of the world in 1874. During the last decade of the 19th century the possibility of developing a whaling industry in Antarctic waters engaged the attention of some commercial interests. A Scottish expedition from Dundee and a series of Norwegian expeditions under Captain Carl Anton *Larsen reconnoitred the Graham Land region between 1892 and 1894 though without making a profitable catch. Larsen, however, succeeded in exploring the usually inaccessible Weddell Sea coast of the Antarctic Peninsula to latitude 68° 10′ S. The area of the Ross Sea proved equally unprofitable when a Norwegian whaling expedition, led by Henrik J. *Bull, made the first landing on Victoria Land, at Cape Adare, in 1895. An additional stimulus to Antarctic exploration was given by the Sixth International Geographical Congress of 1895

when it urged the scientific institutions of the world to give priority to the task of Antarctic discovery. The challenge did not go unheeded. During the twenty years that followed, a series of expeditions took place which not only added considerably to knowledge of the Peninsula region but in the Ross Sea sector were to blaze a trail leading to the achievement of the South pole itself. This was the so-called 'heroic' period of Antarctic exploration of which only the barest summary can be given here. These expeditions are characterized not only by the fresh geographical discoveries which they made but also by the important scientific data which they brought home.

In the region of the Antarctic Peninsula a Belgian expedition led by Adrien de *Gerlache de Gomery mapped Gerlache Strait and Danco Coast, named Palmer Archipelago, and sighted Alexander Island. The expedition's ship *Belgica was beset and compelled to winter in the Antarctic, the first ship to do so. Between 1901 and 1904 the first sledging journeys along the peninsula's Weddell Sea coast were made by a Swede, Otto *Nordenskjöld, while during this same period the Scottish oceanographer, William Spiers *Bruce, discovered part of the Caird Coast and carried out deep-sea soundings in the Scotia and Weddell Seas. On the west, or Bellingshausen Sea, coast of the peninsula the Frenchman Jean-Baptiste *Charcot charted the waters as far south as Adelaide Island and Alexander Island and discovered Charcot Land, all during the course of two expeditions in 1903–5 and 1908–10. Further discoveries in the Weddell Sea were made by a German, Wilhelm *Filchner, who between 1910 and 1912 discovered the Luitpold Coast and the Filchner Ice Shelf. All these discoveries were eclipsed in the public esteem by the far more dramatic events in the Ross Sea area. Here, in 1898–1900, an expedition sponsored by the newspaper magnate Sir George Newnes and led by C. E. Borchgrevink, had spent the first winter in Antarctica at Cape Adare, Victoria Land. Following this, in 1901–4, Captain Robert Falcon *Scott, wintering in his ship *Discovery at Hut Point, Ross Island, made the first great sledge journeys southwards, achieving in latitude 77° 59′ S. the foot of the great glacier system leading up to the polar plateau. In 1907–9 Sir Ernest *Shackleton's British Antarctic Expedition sledged to within 97 miles of the South pole itself, discovering 500 miles of new mountain ranges flanking the Ross Ice Shelf. Early in 1911 Scott returned to Ross Island in the *Terra Nova determined to achieve the pole. En route he learned that a rival, the Norwegian Roald *Amundsen, was also in the field southward bound in the *Fram. The tragic sequel is an epic of history; Scott and his four companions achieved the South pole on 17 January 1912 to find themselves forestalled by Amundsen's party a month previously. On the return journey all perished, leaving their bodies and their diaries to tell the tale. In spite of this great tragedy, much scientific work and geographical discovery, including the addition of Oates Land to the map, was achieved by the remainder of the expedition. Contemporaneous with Scott's last expedition was Douglas Mawson's Australian expedition which discovered and claimed for Britain King George V Land and Queen Mary Land as well as exploring Terre Adélie. Shackleton's ill-fated Imperial Trans-Antarctic Expedition of 1914–17 can be said to mark the close of the 'heroic' period. His attempt to cross Antarctica from the Weddell to the Ross Seas collapsed when the ship *Endurance* was crushed by the ice. The escape of the crew to Elephant Island, Shackleton's hazardous journey in the *James Caird* to South Georgia, accompanied by Frank *Worsley and four of the men, and the eventual rescue of the main party with the help of the Chilean vessel *Yelcho*, are events which testify to Shackleton's extraordinary powers of leadership and dogged refusal to admit defeat.

With Shackleton's death on the *Quest* expedition of 1921–2 Antarctic exploration entered a new phase characterized by a series of spasmodic surveys carried out by a number of nations but lacking any cohesive overall plan. The introduction of aircraft to the Antarctic by Hubert *Wilkins and Richard E. Byrd and the development of radio communications were to hasten the hitherto slow unveiling of the continent. During the years between the two world wars the remaining large gaps in Antarctica's continental outline were filled and large new expanses of the interior ice sheet were revealed, in particular the sector known as Marie Byrd Land, discovered by Byrd's United States Antarctic Expedition of 1928–30. In Australian Antarctic Territory, Mac-Robertson Land, and Princess Elizabeth Land were discovered and annexed by Sir Douglas Mawson, while in the peninsula area important discoveries to the south were made by the British Graham Land Expedition of 1934–7 and extended by Byrd's expedition of 1939–41. Between 1925 and 1939 a series of survey cruises, the *Discovery* Investigations, circumnavigated the Southern Ocean while carrying out observations in oceanography and marine biology. During this same period the Norwegians promoted a number of sealing and whaling voyages in Antarctic waters which culminated in a claim to Dronning Maud Land.

The years following the end of the Second World War have seen nearly all Antarctica's major geographical features placed on the map. Scientific has replaced geographical discovery. Technological advances, particularly in the field of load-carrying aircraft, have made expeditions rather less dependent on icebreakers and ice-strengthened cargo ships for the transportation of food and equipment. Problems of navigating the pack during the short summer season are being eased by the evolution of orbiting satellites transmitting photographic reports of ice distribution at daily intervals. Meanwhile, politically, Antarctica, by virtue of an international treaty signed at Washington in December 1959, enjoys the unique status of an open territory free for peaceful scientific investigation by all nations.

ANTHONISSEN, HENDRICK VAN (c. 1606–c. 1654–60). Flemish marine painter, was born at Antwerp and was a brother-in-law of Jan *Porcellis. His paintings, typical of the Dutch school of the period, have a rich colour and a lively action which are at their best and most vivid in his battle scenes. He lived in *Rotterdam during the latter part of his life and many of his best works were painted there, based on his acute observations of the shipping in that bustling port.

ANTHONISZ, CORNELIS (c. 1499–c. 1560), Dutch painter and etcher, worked as a cartographer in the service of Emperor Charles V. His famous painted map of the city of Amsterdam is perhaps typical of his cartographical work, most delicately executed throughout. It can still be seen in the Weigh House in Amsterdam.

ANTI-AIRCRAFT (A/A) CRUISER, a small and obsolescent *cruiser with some of her main-armament guns removed and replaced with high-angle anti-aircraft batteries, used in the British Navy during the early years of the Second World War. Their function when thus converted was the defence of other ships from attack by aircraft. About eight of these cruisers, drawn from the 4,200-ton 'C'-class cruisers of 1917–19, served with the British fleets during the Second World War. With the rapid growth in sophistication of aircraft attack during the war, particularly in the sphere of rocket armament and consequent low-level attack, these cruisers became no longer viable in their anti-aircraft role and were gradually phased out of service from 1942 onwards.

ANTICYCLONE, an area of high barometric pressure around which the wind circulates in a clockwise direction in the northern hemisphere and anti-clockwise in the southern. Anticyclones are always fair-weather systems, usually slow moving, and with the strength of the wind never more than moderate. See also METEOROLOGY.

ANTIFOULING PAINT, a composition which includes poisons, usually based on copper or mercury, applied to the bottoms and sides, below the waterline, of all vessels to inhibit the growth of weed and *barnacles and, in the case of wooden vessels, attack by worm such as the *teredo. The paint forms a toxic solution in the water immediately around the vessel and is so mixed that the release of the poisons is gradual, lasting as long as the paint itself.

ANTI-GALLICANS, a pair of additional *backstays temporarily rigged to provide extra support to the masts of square-rigged ships when running before the trade winds. They were used only in merchant ships, as men-of-war were always more heavily stayed than merchant vessels and did not, in the general run of naval service, spend days on end running a fixed course before a following trade wind. It was this continuous strain, often lasting for many days and always in the same direction, which made additional support for the masts desirable. The origin of the term is obscure; certainly it had nothing to do with the French, as the name might suggest.

'ANTI-GUGGLER', a straw or tube feloniously entered into a cask or bottle to suck out the contents. It was a popular and relatively easy access to extra nourishment in hot climates during the 18th and 19th centuries when captains of ships often put their private stocks of wine and spirits in a hanging safe outside their *cabins to keep them cool. Modern cooling methods have effectively removed this method of succumbing to temptation.

ANTI-ROLLING DEVICES, see SHIP STABILIZERS.

ANTUM, AERT VAN (*fl.* 1608–40), Dutch marine painter, was a typical artist of the Flemish school whose pictures of ships and battles at sea have all the lively colour and action of the best period of Dutch marine painting. He was also a notable teacher, and it was in his studio that van Ertvelt learned his art. His skill and technique in large part opened the way to the supreme period of Dutch marine art of the second half of the 17th century, exemplified by the school of Van de *Velde. Examples of his work are in most of the great maritime museums of the world as well as in the national collections of most of the great nations.

ANTWERP, the largest seaport in Belgium, situated on the right bank of the River Scheldt. It became significant as a port at the end of the 15th century following the decay of Bruges, but fell into disuse in 1585 when it was captured by the Duke of Parma at the head of a Spanish army. He decreed that the Scheldt should be closed to navigation as a punishment for the spirited defence of the town, and for some hundreds of years following it was subject to the right of

Holland to exact a toll on all ships using the port. It was not until 1863 that it began to regain its original importance through the purchase by Belgium of the Dutch right to levy toll, and since then it has grown phenomenally into a port of the first importance. During the Second World War it was the scene of a major battle in 1944, its capture being essential as the only suitable port through which supplies to sustain the advance into Germany of the allied armies could be shipped. The dock area was substantially destroyed, and post-war rebuilding and redevelopment has made it one of the most modern and well-equipped ports in the world. Growing world trade, allied to its expanded dock area and modern methods of ship-handling to ensure rapid turn-round, now makes it one of the world's major seaports.

It is the home of the *Nationaal Scheepvaartmuseum, a maritime museum with a notable collection which illustrates the history of Belgian shipping.

APEAK, the position of the *anchor when the bows of a ship have been drawn directly above it during weighing, just before it is broken out of the ground. Originally the spelling was APEEK.

APOSTLES, the name given to the two large *bollards, fixed to the main deck near the bows in the larger square-rigged sailing vessels, around which hawsers or anchor cables were *belayed. In all the larger sailing vessels the anchor cables were brought inboard through the *hawseholes on the main deck level since it was on that deck that the main capstan was mounted. In some of the smaller merchant ships of the sailing era, where the anchor cables were brought in over the forecastle deck, the *knightheads, which supported the heel of the *bowsprit, were used as apostles when belaying the anchor cables.

APPAREL, see FURNITURE.

APPARENT WIND, the direction of the wind as it appears to those on board a sailing vessel. It differs from the true wind in speed and direction by an amount which can be worked out by a vector diagram: the vessel's speed through the water being represented by one leg of a triangle of which the true wind and the apparent wind form the other two sides. The difference between the apparent and true wind is most pronounced when the true wind blows from directly abeam, and is reduced as the vessel sails closer to, or further off, the true wind. It disappears completely with the wind from dead astern. It is to the apparent wind, not the true wind, that a sailing vessel trims her sails. In the diagram the strength of the wind has been taken as 12 knots and the speed of the vessel as four knots.

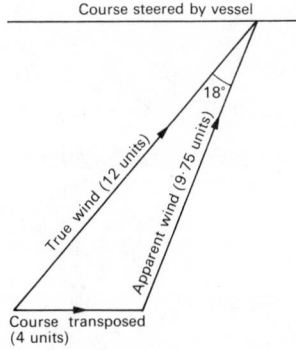

Course steered by vessel

18°

True wind (12 units)

Apparent wind (9.75 units)

Course transposed
(4 units)

True and apparent wind

APRAKSIN, FYODOR MATVEEVICH (1671–1728), Russian admiral and general, was a favourite of the Tsarevich Peter, later *Peter the Great, with whom he grew up and whom he served as a page. In 1700 he was appointed head of the Russian Admiralty and organized the building of fleets during the Russian wars against Charles XII of Sweden. He commanded in the Black Sea during the campaign of the Pruth in 1711, in the Baltic for the conquest of Finland in 1713, and in 1719–20 conducted the descents upon Sweden which ended in the favourable peace of Nyborg by which the Baltic States were ceded to Russia. For these services he was made admiral-general of the Empire.

APRON, (1) a strengthening timber behind the lower part of the *stem and above the foremost end of the *keel of a wooden ship. It takes the fastenings of the *fore-hoods or planking of the bow, and was also sometimes known as a stomach-piece. **(2)** APRON of a gun, a piece of lead sheet which was laid over the touch-hole to protect the vent from damp. **(3)** APRON of a *dock, the platform rising where the gates are closed and on which the *sill is fastened.

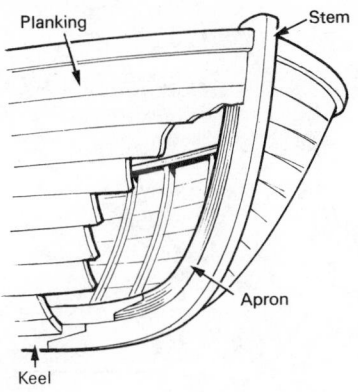

Planking

Stem

Apron

Keel

Apron

AQUALUNG, a device invented in France in 1943 by Captain Jacques-Yves *Cousteau and Emile Gagnan to enable a diver to operate under water independently of an air supply from the surface. It consists of three small cylinders secured on the back of the diver, filled with air compressed to a very high pressure and connected to an air regulator. Two tubes are led from the air regulator to a mouthpiece, and air is supplied to the mouthpiece by the regulator at the pressure exerted by the depth of water reached by the diver. Nose and eyes are enclosed in a rubber mask fitted with a glass front, and the diving dress is completed with rubber foot fins or flippers.

The safe depth to which a free diver wearing an aqualung can operate is about 100 feet, though experienced divers have operated successfully at depths greater than this. See also DIVING (3).

ARBUTHNOT, MARRIOT (1711–94), British admiral, was captain of the 50-gun 4th rate *Portland* in Sir Edward *Hawke's fleet at the battle of *Quiberon Bay in November 1759. She was one of the inshore squadron watching the movements of the French fleet when Hawke was driven off the coast by gales. As a 4th rate, and thus not officially a *ship of the line, the *Portland* took no part in the general action, but on the following morning she was sent in to destroy the French flagship *Soleil Royal* and the *Héro* which had been driven ashore. Both were burned. Arbuthnot's next service was with Admiral *Pocock at the capture of Havana in 1762, with which the Seven Years War (1756–63) was brought to a successful conclusion.

During the War of American Independence (1775–82) he was appointed commander-in-chief of the North American station. In 1779, in conjunction with a military force commanded by Sir Henry Clinton, he laid siege to, and finally captured, the port of Charleston in South Carolina, an action for which he received the thanks of both Houses of the British Parliament. He commanded the squadron which, in March 1781, fought an indecisive action against a French fleet under Commodore des Touches off *Chesapeake Bay, a battle for which he was severely criticized. It was again the old story of the rigidity of the British *Fighting Instructions* stifling all independence of individual action. Having gained the weather *gage of the enemy, Arbuthnot kept the signal for the *line of battle flying in his flagship instead of ordering close action, thus requiring the British captains to maintain their position in the line instead of using their superior speed and gun power against the French ships individually. It was said after the battle that Arbuthnot was so busy trying to fight his own ship that he forgot he was commanding a fleet. He was called home and never employed again.

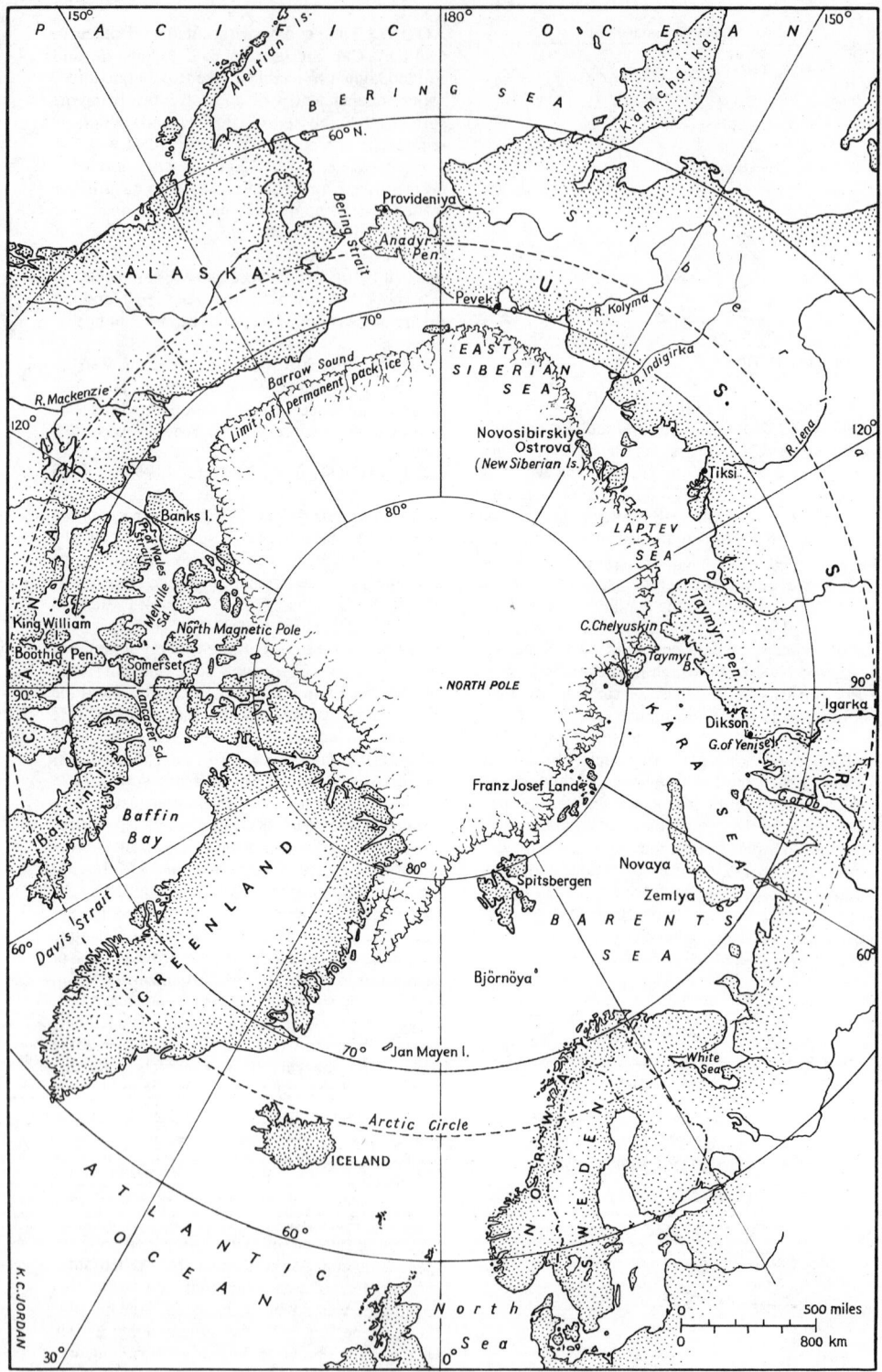

The Arctic

ARCANO DEL MARE, a magnificent work published in Italy in three volumes in 1645–6, by Robert *Dudley, self-styled Duke of Northumberland and Earl of Warwick. In addition to a superb collection of charts it contains details of all known navigational instruments, examples of contemporary shipwrightry, and a plan for the division of a naval force into ships of five *rates.

ARCHDEACON, WILLIAM EDWIN (1842–93), staff captain in the British Navy who exemplified the life of a naval surveyor, being continuously employed afloat for thirty-six years from 1857 to 1893. He first saw surveying service in the Bay of Fundy for nine years and in 1866 joined the Cape of Good Hope survey, taking charge of it the following year until its conclusion in 1872 when he and his party moved to Western Australia. In 1880 the *schooner *Meda* was ready for this survey and Archdeacon sailed her from England to the Swan river in six months. From 1882 he was in charge of the west coast of England survey, which included work on the Welsh, Irish, and Scottish coasts, with a diversion in 1887 to Heligoland and the Goodwin Sands.

ARCTIC EXPLORATION. The Arctic regions comprise vast tracts of land, sea, and ice covering an area of some 8,000,000 square miles. Within the Arctic circle, latitude 66° 33′ N., 3,300 miles in diameter, lie the northern fringes of the land masses of Europe, Asia, and North America, and numerous islands, the largest of which is Greenland. The Arctic Ocean has an area of approximately 5,400,000 square miles and it is 1,500 fathoms (2,743 m) deep at the North pole, though greater depths exist elsewhere. It is covered with sea ice which varies in thickness and extent according to the season, from 5 to 30 feet (1·5–9·0 m). In the winter it is a solid mass, but in the summer it breaks up into floes of varying size between which are channels known as leads. Under the influence of the wind the ice floes tend to pile up on one another to produce hummocks, and enormous pressures are thereby created sufficient to crush the most sturdily built ship. The general drift of the sea ice is north-westwards from the middle of the Siberian coast towards the north-eastern tip of Greenland. The water circulation is much influenced by the incursion of the warm *Gulf Stream flowing northwards between Greenland and Norway which, after cooling, sinks to the bottom and returns southwards through the Davis Strait bearing the icebergs which are such a danger to North Atlantic shipping.

The first explorer of the Arctic region of whom we have knowledge was the Greek navigator Pytheas who, according to Pliny, in 320 B.C. discovered an island in the northern ocean six days' sail from the Orcades (Orkney Is.) which he called Thule and which may have been either Iceland or Greenland. There is reason to believe that some time during the 4th and 5th centuries A.D. Russian explorers were active in the vicinity of the White Sea. In A.D. 800 Irish monks established themselves in Iceland, and nearly 200 years later the Norsemen, *Eric the Red and Ottar, discovered the White Sea and visited Greenland which, together with Iceland, they colonized in the 9th and 10th centuries. Thereafter, for almost six centuries, little appears to have been accomplished in the way of Arctic exploration. The motive which caused a revival of interest in it was the desire to find a shorter way for trade with the Orient than that round southern Africa or through the Magellan Strait. In 1551 a company of Merchant Adventurers was formed in London and in 1553 they sponsored an expedition comprising three ships under Sir Hugh *Willoughby to search for a *North-East passage to Cathay (China). Willoughby and two of the ships were lost, but his second-in-command, Richard *Chancellor, reached the White Sea and entered into negotiations with the Tsar which led to the formation of the Muscovy Company in 1555. During the next twenty years several voyages were undertaken in the furtherance of trade with Russia by such men as the *Borough brothers and Jenkinson; then in 1576 Martin *Frobisher made the first of three voyages in a north-westerly direction, visiting Greenland and discovering the bay named after him off the Baffin Islands. He brought back samples of iron pyrites, mistakenly believing them to be gold, and returned in 1577 and 1578 in an unsuccessful attempt to exploit this discovery. John *Davis's three voyages between 1585 and 1587 made a valuable contribution to our knowledge of the Arctic. On the first he thoroughly explored the Greenland coast and on the next two he passed through Davis Strait into unexplored Baffin Bay in his search for a *North-West passage to China.

In 1594 a Dutchman, William *Barents, returning to the search for a North-East passage, explored the west coast of Novaya Zemlya and discovered the straits leading into the Kara Sea. Two years later, on another voyage he discovered Björnöya (Bear Island) and Spitsbergen.

During the first decade of the 17th century, three unsuccessful attempts were made to find a North-West passage, but the next most important discovery was that made by Henry *Hudson during the last of his four voyages, when in 1610 he sailed into the great inland sea in northern Canada which bears his name. During a previous voyage in 1607 he had reached a latitude of 80° 23′ N., a record at that time, and on his return he discovered the island now known as Jan Mayen. The year after Hudson's tragic death at the hands of a mutinous crew, the English navigator, William * Baffin, undertook the first of five voyages to the Arctic, during the last of which, in company with Robert Bylot, he discovered the bay named for him as well as the sounds giving access to the North pole and the North-West passage. At the same time Thomas Batton was exploring the west coast of Hudson's Bay, the work being continued between 1619 and 1632 by Jens * Munk, Luke * Fox, and Thomas * James. As a result of their efforts, in 1670, the Hudson's Bay Company was formed, marking the beginning of northern Canada's development.

In 1648 the Russian explorer, Semyon * Dezhnev, navigated round the north-eastern tip of Siberia and through the strait which, in 1725, was rediscovered by Vitus * Bering in the service of the Imperial Russian Navy. Bering also charted Kamchatka and the Anadyr peninsula, besides landing in Alaska and visiting the Aleutian islands. Between 1733 and 1743 another Russian expedition, known as the 'Great Northern', mapped the greater part of the Siberian coast. One of its members, Fyodor Menin, sailed up the west coast of Taymyr as far as 75° N. and another, Khariton * Laptev, explored the east coast, leaving a gap of 500 miles unexplored between them, although the most northerly point, Cape Chelyuskin, was reached on foot by another member of the expedition, Semyon Chelyuskin, who gave it his name, indirectly through the explorer N. * Nordenskiöld, who was the next to visit it over 100 years later. During the reign of Catherine the Great (1762–96), Russian explorers were active in the waters beyond the River Ob.

The first expedition to be launched with the aim of reaching the North pole was that undertaken by Commodore C. J. * Phipps in 1773 when, with the ships Racehorse and Carcass, in the last named of which the young Horatio * Nelson was serving as a midshipman, latitude 80° 40′ N. was reached, further progress being impeded by ice. The next attempt on the pole was made in 1818 by Captains Buchan and * Franklin, also without success. About this time there was a revival of British interest in Arctic exploration, due mainly to the support given by the Secretary of the Admiralty, John * Barrow. Also in 1818 Captain John * Ross undertook a fruitless voyage to discover a North-West passage. His second voyage, ten years later, was more productive and resulted in the discovery of the North magnetic pole by his nephew James C. * Ross. Three further attempts to discover a North-West passage were made by William * Parry in 1819–20, 1821–3, and 1824–5. The first of these was the most successful when he managed to reach a point 600 miles west of his

departure in Baffin Bay, but each time ice barred further progress. Parry's fourth voyage in 1827 was an attempt to reach the North pole across the ice from Spitsbergen. He reached latitude 82° 45′ N., the highest yet attained. During the periods 1819–22 and 1825–7, Captain John Franklin was busy exploring and surveying the then unknown North American coastline, but the desire to find the elusive North-West passage remained uppermost in everyone's mind.

In 1836, Captain George * Back, who had already contributed much to the discovery of the northern territory of the North American continent, led an expedition with this objective, and in 1845, Sir John Franklin, now in his 60th year, left on the same errand, from which he was destined never to return. The disappearance of the entire expedition and its two ships led to the dispatch of no less than thirty-nine relief expeditions to search for news of its fate, and these made a major contribution to our knowledge of the geography of the area. The first of them, in 1848, under Sir James C. Ross in the ships Enterprise and Investigator, penetrated Lancaster Sound and succeeded in mapping Somerset Island. An extensive but unsuccessful search organized in 1850 and comprising five ships, under the command of Captains Penny, * Austin, and * Ommaney, succeeded in linking the Prince of Wales Strait and Melville Sound, while Sir John Ross in the Felix and Captain * Kennedy with Lieutenant * Bellot in the Prince Albert carried out an independent search later at the behest of Lady Franklin. Two American-sponsored expeditions in 1850 and 1853, the first under Henry Grinnell and the second under Elisha * Kane, discovered new territory but no traces of Franklin and his men. A further British government sponsored expedition under Rear Admiral Sir Edward * Belcher, comprising five ships, sailed in 1852 and, although not succeeding in its main object, accomplished the timely rescue of Captain Robert * McClure and his men who had been forced to abandon their ship off Banks Island, after having been the first to discover the existence of a North-West passage. The first traces of the Franklin expedition were found by Dr. John * Rae of the Hudson's Bay Company near the mouth of the Great Fish (later Back) River during his survey of some 700 miles of the Arctic coastline. Two more expeditions under Captain Edward * Inglefield in 1852 and in 1853–4 went in search of Franklin, but the mystery was not solved until that organized by Lady Franklin and commanded by Captain F. L. * McClintock in 1859 discovered a record of the last weeks of the ill-fated expedition in a cairn at Point Victoria, King William Island. This and other relics subsequently discovered by Captain Charles * Hall and Lieutenant * Schwatka of the U.S. Army in 1864 confirmed that all members of the Franklin expedition had perished after losing their ships.

During the latter half of the century greater attention was paid to the attainment of the pole itself by explorers of many nationalities. In 1871, Captain * Hall, on his third Arctic expedition, reached a point 412 miles from the pole in his ship *Polaris*. Four years later, Lieutenant Markham, serving with the British Arctic Expedition under Captain George * Nares, reached latitude 83° 20′ N., a record which remained unbeaten until the American expedition under Major-General Adolphus Greely in 1881–4. Meanwhile in 1879 another American expedition under G. W. * deLong, in the *Jeanette*, attempted to reach the pole but lost their ship when she was crushed in the ice off the New Siberian islands. Some years later her remains were found off the south-east coast of Greenland, providing evidence of the north polar drift referred to earlier. But it was the distinguished Norwegian explorer, Fridjtof * Nansen, who conclusively proved it when, in 1893, on his second polar voyage, he sailed his specially strengthened ship * *Fram* into the pack ice near where the *Jeanette* had been lost. After nearly three years drifting across the polar ice field, she emerged safely north-west of Spitsbergen. Nansen himself left the ship in April 1895 and sledged to within 227 miles of the pole. Four years later his record was bettered by 20 miles by a member of an Italian team under the Duke of * Abruzzi.

Soon after the turn of the century, in 1906, Roald * Amundsen in the sloop *Gjøa* succeeded in navigating the North-West passage, being the first man to do so. In 1909 Captain Robert * Peary, after six previous expeditions to North Greenland, made a dash for the pole, which he claimed to have reached on 6 April of that year. Controversy still surrounds that claim. Another contestant for the honour of being the first to reach the pole was F. A. * Cook who made the attempt in 1908, but his claim was subsequently disallowed for lack of evidence.

In the years preceding the First World War (1914–18), almost all the remaining unknown territory in the Arctic was discovered. Between 1906 and 1912, the north-west corner of Greenland was charted by the Danish explorers * Mikkelsen and * Rasmussen, who also explored the interior. Canadian Arctic expeditions under * Stefansson and Anderson in 1908–12 and 1913–17 to northern Canada added considerably to our knowledge of that territory and of the native Eskimos.

The advancing study of aeronautics had its impact on Arctic exploration. It began with an unsuccessful attempt in 1897 by the Swedish scientist Andrée to reach the pole in a balloon, which cost him his life and that of his companion. Amundsen and Ellsworth, in 1925, were the first to use a powered aircraft when, with two Dornier flying boats, they reached a point 120 miles from the pole. In May of the following year, a retired American naval officer, Richard E. Byrd, flew to the pole and back from his base in Spitsbergen and only two days later the Italian aeronaut Umberto Nobile crossed the North pole in his airship *Norge* from Spitsbergen to Alaska. In 1928 the Australian Hubert * Wilkins flew in an aircraft across the pole from Point Barrow in Alaska to Spitsbergen.

SCIENTIFIC OBSERVATION

Between the two world wars pioneer exploration in the Arctic virtually came to an end and was succeeded by scientific observation and the gathering of meteorological and other data, together with the production of more accurate maps. In all this Russia began to play an increasingly important part in keeping with her position as the occupier of the largest amount of Arctic territory. In 1932 a government department known as *Glavsevmorput* was set up to administer the northern sea route, and a party of Soviet scientists in the *Sibiryakov* navigated the whole length of the route, a feat accomplished only once previously by the Swedish explorer Nordenskiöld in 1878–9. It took four years to buoy and survey the route and to assemble the necessary ice-breakers, but in 1935 two ships were passed through in each direction. During the first full year of operation, 1936, over 100 ships successfully navigated various portions of it. In 1940 the German raider *Komet* passed from the North Sea to the Pacific by this means while the new ice-breaker *Joseph Stalin* managed to complete the double journey during this season.

In 1937 another memorable drift across the Arctic was begun by the Russian ship *Georgiy Sedov*, 3,056 tons, from Ostrov Belkovsky, ending three years later at a point 135 miles west of Spitsbergen, during which much valuable scientific data was obtained. The development of the submarine introduced a new dimension into Arctic exploration by making it possible to penetrate beneath the polar ice-cap. Sir Hubert Wilkins was the first explorer to use a vessel of this type, the specially-equipped *Nautilus*, but he was obliged to turn back on account of defects. The development of the nuclear-powered submarine with its ability to remain submerged for very long periods, yet steam at high speed, enabled the first transpolar voyage to be accomplished. This was successfully completed by U.S.S. * *Nautilus*, Commander W. R. Anderson, U.S.N., in August 1958. On 17 March of the following year, the nuclear-powered submarine U.S.S. * *Skate* also made history when she broke through the ice to surface at the North pole, being the first ship ever to do so. In August 1960 U.S.S. *Seadragon*, a sister ship of the *Skate*, navigated the North-West passage from the Atlantic to the Pacific via Lancaster Sound, Barrow, and McClure Straits. Russian submarines have also navigated under the polar ice-cap, so that the Arctic Ocean has now assumed a position of considerable strategic importance.

A great feat of Arctic travel was accomplished between February 1968 and May 1969 by the British Trans-Arctic Expedition under W. Herbert. The team of four men with dogs and sledges successfully crossed the polar ice-cap from Point Barrow, Alaska, over the North pole to Spitsbergen, a distance of over 3,000 miles which took them 476 days, during which they were supplied from the air. They were recovered from a rocky island off the north shore of Spitsbergen by H.M.S. *Endurance* on 11 June 1969.

In an effort to make greater use of the northern sea route, Russia is building larger and more powerful ice-breakers in which nuclear power is employed. The first of such ships, the *Lenin, 16,000 tons, was completed in September 1959 and two more of the 'Artika' class, 25,000 tons, are under construction.

It is appropriate that this brief survey of Arctic exploration should end where it began, with the North-West passage. The discovery of oil in large quantities in northern Alaska has once again brought the navigation of this route into prominence. It was navigated in August 1969 by the 150,000-ton specially constructed tanker *Manhattan, which had been fitted with an ice-breaking bow. On the return journey she suffered damage from an ice formation estimated to have been 140 ft (36·5 m) deep, and as a direct result of this it has been decided to transport the Alaskan oil by a pipeline overland to the southern shore of Alaska. Nevertheless, the commercial possibilities of the discovery are too great for efforts not to be continued to overcome this great natural hazard, which for centuries has been a challenge to explorers and navigators of the Arctic regions.

ARCTIC SEA ROUTE, see NORTH-EAST PASSAGE.

ARETHUSA, H.M.S., a ship's name used seven times in the Royal Navy. The second of these ships was a 5th *rate *frigate of thirty-eight guns, the 'Saucy Arethusa' of Prince Hoare's song, built at *Bristol in 1781. The fourth was a 4th rate of fifty guns, built at Pembroke in 1849. She was lent in 1873 to the Baroness Burdett-Coutts as a training ship for destitute boys and continued in this service, managed latterly by the Shaftesbury Homes, until replaced in 1932. She was broken up in 1933.

ARGO, according to legend the ship in which the *Argonauts sailed from Greece in search of the Golden Fleece. She was, in the Greek mythological story, built by Argos, the son of Phrixus and a famous shipbuilder of his time, of pines cut from Mount Pelion, supposed to have the property of never rotting. She was pierced for fifty oars, one for each of the fifty Greek heroes who manned her, and so perhaps would qualify to be considered as the first *longship ever to sail the seas. It was recorded that the construction of the ship was supervised by the goddess Athena, who inserted a piece of the holy oak from Dodona into the prow so that the ship would never lose her way. Her bows were painted vermilion. At the time of her building the *Argo* was said to be the largest ship in the world. Perhaps the best-known modern version of the old story is that by Charles Kingsley in his book *The Heroes* (1856).

ARGONAUTS, in Greek legend a band of heroes who undertook an expedition in the ship *Argo* under the command of Jason to bring back the Golden Fleece from Colchis on the farther shore of the Euxine (Black) Sea, a task imposed upon Jason by his uncle Pelias. The crew consisted of fifty of the noblest heroes of Greece. The voyage of the Argonauts is one of the best known and oldest of mythological tales, but may well have an element of truth about it as a voyage to open up the Euxine Sea to Greek trade and colonization. Certainly there were Greek trading settlements on the southern shores of the Euxine Sea as early as the 6th century B.C. The legend of the Golden Fleece may also possibly have a basis in fact because of the practice of the inhabitants of Colchis of pegging down the skins of sheep in the rivers to catch the particles of gold in the wool as they were washed down by the force of the streams.

Among the more notable of the Argonauts under Jason's command were Asclepius (Aesculapius), son of Apollo and doctor to the crew, *Castor and Pollux, twin sons of Zeus (Jupiter), their brother Heracles (Hercules), Orpheus, to charm the crew with his lute, and Tiphys, the pilot. Also among the crew was Atalanta, daughter of Schoeneus, disguised in a man's dress.

ARGOSTOLI, the capital of Cephalonia, in the Ionian islands, with a fine natural harbour. It is notable for a curious stream on the west side of the harbour which flows *from* the sea before losing itself in caverns inland. By arrangement with Greece, it was often used as a fleet anchorage and exercise area by the British Mediterranean fleet in the years preceding the Second World War.

The clipper ship Ariel

ARGOSY, the medieval name for a trading * carrack, principally in the Mediterranean. According to some, the name is derived from Ragusa, the original name of the modern Dubrovnik; others consider that the derivation is from the *Argo*, Jason's famous ship.

> 'Your mind is tossing on the ocean;
> There, where your argosies with portly sail,
> Like signiors and rich burghers of the flood,
> Do overpeer the petty traffickers.'
> Shakespeare, *The Merchant of Venice*

In 1588, twelve of the best ships from Ragusa, with the generic name of argosies, were included in the Spanish fleet known as the 'Invincible * Armada' and assembled for a planned invasion of England. All twelve were lost in the expedition.

ARIEL, one of the fastest and best-known British tea * clippers, was built by Robert * Steele of Greenock in 1865. The *Ariel* took part, in 1866, in a famous tea clipper race from the Pagoda Anchorage at Foochow, China, to the London Docks, 16,000 miles, with the * *Taeping, Serica,* * *Fiery Cross*, and *Taitsin*. The first three to finish, the *Taeping, Ariel,* and *Serica,* arrived in the Thames on the same tide and docked in London within two hours of each other. Their total passage time was ninety-nine days, a record that was never beaten by sailing ships. The other two both reached London two days later.

ARK, a word commonly used to mean a box or chest, but in a maritime sense used to describe the vessel said to have been constructed by * Noah to accommodate his family and representatives of each kind of animal to save them from the great flood (Genesis chs. 6–9). Its dimensions are given in the biblical account as 300 cubits long, 50 cubits broad, and 30 cubits high (1 cubit = 18–22 in. or 46–56 cm) and it was made of 'gopher' wood, which has been variously identified with cypress, cedar, and pine. It used to be an exercise of 'rationalist' theologians and others in the early 19th century to try to show that the stated dimensions of the ark were impossible in relation to the number of species of animals which needed to be housed and fed on board for the duration of the flood, and some extraordinary theories were produced, one authority calculating that the ark would have needed to cover an area of half an acre, another that it must have had a * tonnage of 81,062. More recent historians have been less inclined to take the story literally, and some have put forward the theory that the ark of Noah could not have had a wooden hull at all, but could only have been a large raft, of the measurements given, made from bundles of papyrus reeds, with only the animals' stalls and the family's shelter constructed of timber. Smaller rafts of this type were at that time in normal use in the Euphrates–Tigris basin, where all timber suitable for boat building was scarce.

In the U.S.A. the term was also used to describe the large flat-bottomed vessels used for the carriage of produce down the major rivers.

ARK ROYAL, H.M.S., was Lord *Howard of Effingham's flagship in the fight against the Spanish *Armada in 1588; she was the first of her name in the Royal Navy and was originally the *Ark Ralegh*, having been built by Sir Walter *Raleigh. Her name was changed to *Ark Royal* when she was bought by Queen Elizabeth I. She was built at Deptford in 1587 and carried fifty-five guns. Rebuilt in 1608 with forty-four guns, she was then renamed the *Anne Royal*.

The Royal Navy's other three ships of this name have all been *aircraft carriers. The first of them was built in 1914 and renamed *Pegasus* in 1934 in order to leave the name free for a new aircraft carrier launched in 1937. This was the ship which the Germans repeatedly claimed to have sunk in the Second World War. They finally did torpedo her in the Mediterranean and she sank in November 1941, while in tow. The third carrier of the name (launched in 1950) is still in service (1976) with the Royal Navy.

ARM, to, the process of placing tallow in the cavity and over the base of the lead when taking a *sounding by *lead line, in order to discover the nature of the bottom (sand, shingle, mud, rock, etc.) by what adheres to the tallow when the lead strikes bottom.

ARMADA, THE SPANISH, called by the Spaniards before it sailed the *felicissima*, most fortunate, and *invencible*, invincible, was a great fleet assembled by Philip II of Spain to force the English Channel, pick up the army of the Prince of Parma then operating in the Low Countries, and invade England. The fleet, consisting of 130 ships large and small, was commanded by the Duke of *Medina Sidonia and left Lisbon on 28 May 1588 but made such poor headway because of heavy weather that twenty days later it put in to Corunna for repairs, water, and provisions. It was another month before it again set sail, bound for England.

The English fleet was divided between Plymouth, where Lord *Howard of Effingham commanded a mixed squadron of ninety-four ships, and Dover, where Lord Henry Seymour with thirty-five ships was watching Calais for the arrival of Parma's army. The western squadron sailed from Plymouth as soon as the Armada was sighted off the Lizard on 19 July, an event which gave rise to the well-known story of Sir Francis *Drake and his game of bowls on Plymouth Hoe. The first shots of the battle were fired off the Eddystone on 21 July.

The Spanish fleet was sailing in a crescent-shaped formation, too strong for the English ships to attack in formation but, being generally smaller and more weatherly, they attacked singly at the full range of their guns to keep the Spanish ships on the move. During the next four days the Armada was thus continually attacked, losing two ships, and by the evening of the 25th the two fleets were abreast the Isle of Wight. By this time the English ships were running short of ammunition and Howard, when reporting this, stated his intention not to attack again until he had obtained a further supply from the shore.

Meanwhile the Armada continued its slow progress up Channel losing an occasional straggler to the English ships but in general keeping its crescent-shaped formation intact. It anchored off Calais on the evening of 27 July to await Parma's troops for the planned invasion. As it dropped its anchors, so also did Howard's squadron, which was promptly reinforced by Seymour's thirty-five ships.

With the wind at south-west, the English fleet was now anchored about half a mile to windward of the Spanish ships, very well placed for an attack with *fireships. Eight of these were sent down on the following night, causing much consternation and confusion among the tightly packed Spaniards. There was nothing they could do but cut their cables and make sail before the wind to escape the threatened holocaust. They were followed by the whole English fleet and a major action developed off Gravelines, in which Medina Sidonia lost three of his best ships and found himself being driven by the wind and the English towards the Dutch shoals. At the last moment, the wind *backed into the south-east and enabled the Spanish ships to *claw off the dangerous shallows.

Without Parma's troops on board, and with invasion now impossible, Medina Sidonia had no option but to make his way back to Spain as best he could. Short of ammunition and provisions, he could not fight his way back down Channel through the English fleet, and the only way left for him was around the north of Scotland and west of Ireland. Leaving Seymour and his squadron to guard the Channel and maintain a watch for any movement by Parma and his troops, Howard pursued the retreating Armada up the North Sea as far as the latitude of the Firth of Forth. There, running short of supplies himself, he decided to abandon the chase, though a few English *pinnaces continued to follow the Spaniards until they were past the Orkney Islands, and thus committed to a return to Spain by the west of Ireland. The weather, which had been rough in the North Sea, deteriorated further as the Armada ploughed its long way homewards and many of its ships were wrecked on the rocky coasts of Scotland and Ireland, where they were pillaged and their crews slaughtered. Of the 130 Spanish ships which had left Lisbon, only sixty-seven returned.

The contemporary English naval documents of the Armada campaign have been published by the Navy Records Society in J. K. Laughton,

Engraving of 1650 showing an armillary sphere, with an astrolabe lying on the table

State Papers relating to the defeat of the Spanish Armada (N.R.S., 1895); the contemporary Spanish naval papers are in C. Fernandez Duro, *La Armada Invencible*, 2 vols (Madrid, 1885). One of the best modern accounts of the campaign is that of Garrett Mattingly, *The Defeat of the Spanish Armada* (1959). Some almost contemporary illustrations are an engraving by Augustine Ryther of a chart drawn by Robert Adams to illustrate an account written in 1590, and Hendrick Cornelisz *Vroom's designs for a series of tapestries ordered by Howard of Effingham, which hung in the House of Lords until destroyed by fire in 1834. A fine set of engravings of them was made by John *Pine and it is reproduced in *Lord Howard of Effingham and the Spanish Armada*, published for the Roxburghe Club in 1919.

ARMED MERCHANT CRUISER (A.M.C.), a passenger *liner or merchant vessel taken up during time of war by naval authorities, fitted with medium-sized guns, and used for naval purposes. They were frequently employed in patrolling sea areas and assisting to enforce a *blockade. Armed merchant cruisers were used extensively during the First World War (1914–18) for a variety of naval purposes, but their value, mainly because of their necessarily weak armament, lack of armoured protection, and large target area offered to enemy gunfire, grew progressively less during the Second World War and by 1942 most had been withdrawn from active naval service, finding other naval work in a largely auxiliary role. During both world wars,

armed merchant cruisers were extensively employed by the German Navy as raiders to attack allied seaborne trade. An action between armed merchant cruisers was fought on 14 September 1914 when the British *Carmania* sank the German *Cap Trafalgar* in the South Atlantic. Among the many well-known armed merchant cruisers of the Second World War were the British *Jervis Bay* which fought a notable convoy action in 1940 and the German *Atlantis* which steamed 102,000 miles and sank over 140,000 tons of allied shipping.

ARMILLARY SPHERE, a skeleton model of the celestial sphere, generally with the earth in the centre, showing the equator, poles, tropics, zodiac, etc., on the outer ring, with inner rings for the sun, moon, and planets. It was an instrument dating from the late 14th or early 15th century, designed to give the navigator a knowledge of the arrangement and motions of the heavenly bodies. It is recorded that a brass armillary sphere, costing £4.7s.6d., was supplied to Martin *Frobisher for his first expedition in search of the *North-West passage in 1576.

ARMOUR. The earliest known record of a proposal to apply armoured plates to the sides of ships for protective purposes was made by Sir William Congreve in 1805. This was a suggestion to build armoured floating batteries for the purpose of engaging batteries ashore. In 1812 John Stevens, of New Jersey in the United States, submitted a design to Congress for an armoured ship. Nothing, however, came of either of these proposals, and although from time to time further strong suggestions for the use of armour in ships were made, notably in 1841 by General Paixhans, the great expert on guns, and in 1845 by the French warship designer, *Dupuy de Lõme, it was not until the destruction of the wooden fleet of Turkey by Russian shellfire at *Sinope on 30 November 1853 that the proposal was taken seriously. As a result, armoured floating batteries were laid down by Britain, France, and the U.S.A. in 1854, using wrought iron $4\frac{1}{2}$ in. (11·5 cm) thick on a backing of 18 in. (46 cm) of teak, and the success of the French batteries against the Russian forts at Kinburn in 1855, in which the losses in personnel were trifling in spite of frequent direct hits, brought the use of armour for ships into full development.

The earliest armour used for ships was constructed from wrought iron, either in a single thickness or in layers interposed with wood or concrete. With the vast improvement of naval *guns during the period 1860–85, iron armour had to be increased in thickness until it reached as much as 24 in. (61 cm). Cast iron was introduced by Gruson, of Magdeburg, in 1868, but was never widely used in ships because of its liability to fracture on the impact of a shell. It was not until steel was introduced by Schneider in 1876 that the use of wrought iron went out of favour and the thickness of ships' armour could be reduced. This followed an important trial at La Spezia in that same year when test firings showed decisively that steel had far greater resistance to shellfire than wrought iron, although this early steel had a tendency to crack. It was this cracking tendency which led to the introduction of compound armour in 1877, in which a steel surface is cemented on to a wrought iron foundation, using molten steel as the bonding cement. Another process was to make armour by running molten steel on to a white-hot foundation sheet of iron. By this means, the armour was given a harder face than if the sheet had been made of steel throughout and also had the merit of an iron backing which did not possess the liability of steel to crack under impact.

Improvements in the process of making steel up to 1890 had brought into existence steel armour plates in which the cracking tendency had been eliminated, but the greatest step forward came in methods of case hardening the face of the steel plate to produce a considerably greater hardness of the surface. This was achieved by chilling the heated surface of the steel by jets of water under pressure, an improvement on the older method of plunging the plate into water, in which a layer of steam was invariably formed between the water and the white-hot surface of the plate, resulting in the steel not chilling fast enough.

The next step forward came fast on the heels of case hardening when H. A. Harvey, of Newark, New Jersey, introduced a new process whereby steel plates could be case-hardened without the necessity of using a wrought iron backing. By thus producing a plate of armour made of steel throughout with a hardened face, a great saving in weight was achieved since all-steel armour did not require the thickness of compound armour to provide equal resistance to penetration. This all-steel armour was introduced in 1891. Further improvements came the following year when nickel and chromium were added to steel to provide yet greater hardness and strength.

Alfred Krupp, of Essen in Germany, introduced a new process of manufacture in 1893 by which nickel-chrome steel, by means of special heat treatment, is given a considerably deeper hard face than the ordinary case hardening and is also much tougher in the back of the plate. The Krupp process, with minor variations by different makers, was widely adopted by most firms making armour, and its excellence has been demonstrated in many subsequent naval actions.

With the passing of the *battleship as the paramount ship of war, the use of heavy armour has diminished. Battleships normally used steel armour of from 12 to 15 in. (30 to 38 cm) in thickness to protect their guns and other vital spaces, but modern ships, being smaller, and facing more potent threats than surface gunfire, do not require such immense thicknesses. As naval warfare tends to move under water or into the air, the use of armour in future warship building is likely to decrease considerably.

'ARMSTRONG PATENT', a slang expression used in the big trading sailing ships around the end of the 19th and beginning of the 20th centuries to indicate that a ship was not fitted with any mechanical aids, and that all the work of the ship had to be done by human (crew) labour—in fact by their strong arms.

ARNAULD DE LA PERIÈRE, LOTHAR VON (1886–1941), German vice admiral, was a *U-boat commander during the First World War (1914–18) and the most successful submarine captain in history. His first command was *U.35,* in which, between November 1915 and March 1918, he sank 189 merchant ships, totalling 446,708 tons, and two gunboats, receiving in October 1916 the *Ordre pour la Mérite* for his exploits. From May to November 1918 he commanded the new cruiser–submarine *U.139,* and from February 1919 to October 1920 commanded a naval storm battalion during the civil troubles in Germany. He retired as a captain in September 1931 and from 1932 to 1938 was an instructor at the Turkish Naval Academy. On 1 September 1939 he rejoined the German Navy and was successively admiral commanding Belgium and Holland, Brittany, and Western France. In February 1941 he was appointed admiral commanding South-East Europe but was killed in an air crash at Le Bourget on his way to take up this appointment.

ARNOLD, BENEDICT (1741–1801), an American general during the war of American Independence (1775–82), commanded a naval force on *Lake Champlain and held up the British advance from Canada into the U.S.A. in 1776. General Washington sent Arnold with a small force to capture Quebec in 1775. After many hardships he and his men reached the St. Lawrence River, opposite Quebec, on 8 November, after the Canadian winter was upon them. In conjunction with General Richard Montgomery, he attempted to capture Quebec on 31 December in a blinding snowstorm, but in the action Montgomery was killed and the attack failed, Arnold being severely wounded.

He managed to hold on in Canada until June 1776, but was too weak to accomplish anything. When he retreated to Lake Champlain he found that Washington had collected a small force of boats for his use and he then gave attention to the building of additional miniature vessels.

The British flotilla on the lake was commanded by Commodore Pringle and consisted of the relatively large and well-armed *Inflexible* and twenty-four smaller craft, many of them very small indeed. Arnold had collected fifteen small craft, and on 11 October 1776 fought a 'fleet action' while at anchor off Valcour Island. After losing about sixty officers and men killed or wounded, and having expended three-quarters of his ammunition, Arnold decided to escape to the southward during the night, but by noon on the 13th the pursuing British vessels began to overhaul the straggling Americans. The galley *Washington* was captured and Arnold's flagship, the *Congress*, was so shattered after a running fight of two hours that he ran her ashore with four attending *gondolas and set the five vessels on fire. With the crews he made his way to Crown Point, a distance of about 10 miles through the woods. By his shipbuilding efforts between June and October, and in his naval battles on 11 and 13 October, Arnold succeeded in delaying the planned British invasion from Canada, the military authorities deciding that no campaign could be conducted successfully in the remaining months of 1776.

After this naval effort Arnold returned to land operations. By the early summer of 1780 he was in command of the post at West Point and entered into a correspondence with the British General Clinton with a view to handing over West Point to the British in exchange for a considerable sum of money and a commission in the British army. His treason was discovered by Washington and Arnold fled to New York. In December 1781 he sailed for England with his family and lived in London, except for four years spent in New Brunswick, until his death.

The action off Valcour Island is graphically described in Kenneth Roberts's novel *Rabble in Arms* (1939) in detail and with great accuracy.

ARROW OF GOLD, THE, a novel by Joseph *Conrad published in 1920. It tells in fictional form the story of Conrad's gun-running adventures in an attempt to help the Carlist rebels in Spain shortly after he left Poland and settled temporarily in Marseilles.

ARROWSMITH, the family name of two generations of English mapmakers. AARON (1750–1823) made himself famous in 1790 with the publication of his large chart of the world on *Mercator's projection, and in 1794 published a second large chart of the world on the *globular projection, accompanied by a book of explanation of the system. His two sons, AARON and SAMUEL, succeeded him in the business, Aaron becoming Hydrographer to the Prince of Wales. A nephew, JOHN ARROWSMITH (1790–1873), joined his cousins in the business and many of his maps and charts, elaborately and carefully executed, and particularly those of Australia, Africa, America, and India, are among the best produced in this period.

ARTEMON, the name given to a small square sail set on a *yard and carried below a sharply *steeved spar over the bows of Roman merchant vessels from about 200 B.C. to the decline of Roman shipping at the fall of the empire. Its function was largely as an aid to steering, while its spar or mast could be described as the forerunner of the *bowsprit. It was virtually identical with the *spritsail of the 14th–17th centuries A.D. The name was also used, somewhat loosely and erroneously, to describe the mainsail of ancient ships.

ARTEMON MAST, originally a *sprit or mast set up in the bows of many ships of the 12th to 15th centuries, before the introduction of the *bowsprit, as an aid to steering the vessel by stopping the bows coming up into the wind, a natural result of carrying insufficient canvas forward of the mast. Oddly enough, the French word for *mizen is *artimon*, and the mizen-mast is *mât d'artimon*, which is of course at the other end of the ship. It is from the French word, and not the original, that in later ships built with four or five masts during the 19th and early 20th centuries, the fourth mast was sometimes known as an artemon mast.

ARTICLES, the conditions of service which are signed by a seaman in the merchant service when joining a ship. They are also signed by the *master of the ship concerned and form a legal contract binding on both sides. Normally a ship's articles embody provisions governing rates of pay, scale of victuals, daily hours of work, etc., and in older days when the route round Cape Horn was the only way to reach the Pacific Ocean from the Atlantic and was widely used as a normal trade route, they specified the extremes of latitude beyond which a seaman was not to be called upon to serve. In many ships' articles a clause is usually included that in danger or distress the master may call on the seaman for exertions beyond the limitations expressed in the articles. Ship's discipline on board is based on the articles, and the master has authority to punish members of the crew who transgress the articles.

ARTICLES OF WAR, a British disciplinary code for the Royal Navy based on the ancient sea laws of Rhodes and *Oleron in which maritime crimes and punishments are specified, were first issued in 1653. In Tudor times most captains of ships supplemented the laws of Oleron, issued in England in 1336 in the *Black Book of the Admiralty, with their own rules based on their own ingenuity in inventing punishments to fit the crime. Many of these individual punishments are listed and described by Captain Nathaniel *Boteler in his *Six Dialogues about Sea Service* (1685). In order to provide a code of punishment which would apply throughout the navy and not depend on the whims of individual captains, the Articles of War were introduced. They were incorporated into the first English Naval Discipline Act of 1661, to which was added a preamble from the Navigation Act of the previous year which referred to the Royal Navy 'wherein under the good Providence of God, the Wealth, Safety, and Strength of this Kingdom is so much concerned'. It was under the 13th Article of this harsh Act that Admiral John *Byng was condemned to execution after his failure to relieve *Minorca in 1756. Some penalties (e.g., the maximum number of lashes with the *cat-o'-nine-tails to be 48) were reduced by the next important Naval Discipline Act of 1866. Whereas the Articles of War were omitted from the Army Act of 1955, they were retained in the Naval Discipline Act of 1956, which as before orders them to be displayed in some prominent place in every ship or establishment.

In addition to the crimes listed in the Articles, other disciplinary measures were printed in the *Regulations and Instructions Relating to His Majesty's Service at Sea*, first issued in 1731. By these the maximum sentence of flogging with the cat-o'-nine-tails, unless by sentence of a court martial, was limited to 12 lashes but few captains observed this limit and continued summarily to award larger sentences of flogging right up to the final suspension of the 'cat' in 1879.

Unlike the *articles signed by a merchant seaman on joining a ship, the naval Articles of War are entirely a disciplinary code, and, notwithstanding the word 'War' in the title, they apply in peace as well as during hostilities; as shown by their incorporation in the Naval Discipline Act, they are part of statute law.

ARTIFICIAL HORIZON, an aid to taking an astronomical sight with a *sextant when the sea horizon is obscured through haze, fog, or darkness. The problem was recognized by navigators long ago, and many attempts have been made to remedy it. John *Hadley, inventor of the reflecting *quadrant, was the first, using a simple spirit level attached to the frame of the quadrant, but neither this nor a more sophisticated bubble horizon designed by John Elton in 1732 proved successful. An interesting suggestion was made by Serson, and later by the celebrated engineer John *Smeaton, for a spinning top with a polished upper surface which by means of its gyroscopic inertia would provide a horizontal reflecting surface for use as an artificial horizon. The difficulty of applying such a solution to the deck of a ship at sea was, however, immense.

In 1838 Lieutenant A. B. *Becher R.N. invented an artificial horizon which consisted of a small pendulum with its bob suspended, for damping purposes, in a cistern of oil. This arrangement was fitted in line with the optical axis of the sextant telescope, and a slip of metal of which the upper edge was fixed at right angles to the pendulum, served as a horizon to which the observed celestial body was brought into coincidence. Many other attempts have been made to produce a satisfactory artificial horizon, including those by Admirals *Beechey and Fleurais, but none was really practical at sea. The most successful has been the Booth *bubble horizon which was designed specifically for air navigation and has since been adapted for use at sea.

The problem of providing an artificial horizon ashore is simply solved by the use of liquid, usually mercury, introduced by George Adams in 1738. The use of liquid on board ship, however, is useless, as the slightest movement of the ship causes tremors to form on the surface of the liquid and thus break the desired horizon. See also NAVIGATION.

ASDIC, the original name of the underwater sound-ranging apparatus for determining the range and bearing of a submerged submarine. The name was derived from the initial letters of the Allied Submarine Detection Investigation

Committee, which was set up as an Anglo-French project in 1918, immediately after the First World War (1914–18). The invention was mainly French in conception. It is now known as *sonar.

ASHORE, aground, on the land, as opposed to *aboard. A sailor goes ashore when he disembarks from a ship or boat and steps on land, either on duty or for a spell of leave. A ship runs ashore when she strikes the land, but runs aground if she strikes a submerged bank not connected with the shore. 'A RUN ASHORE', the seaman's name for a short period of *liberty.

ASIENTO, TREATY OF, the treaty by which Spain, on her defeat in the War of the Spanish Succession (1702–13), was forced to concede to the British government the monopoly of supplying African slaves to the Spanish West Indian colonies for thirty years following the signing of the treaty in 1713. Under its terms British ships were permitted to introduce 144,000 slaves at the rate of 4,800 per annum. A company, known as the South Sea Company, was formed to work this monopoly which was granted to it by the British government, but came to grief in a speculative fever which became known as the *South Sea Bubble. British merchant shipping prospered and increased prodigiously during the years of the Asiento treaty, particularly as many more than the authorized annual number of slaves were smuggled into the Spanish colonies together with a constant stream of goods attempting to evade the customs. Friction over the constant abuses by Britain of the Asiento treaty, combined with the violence of the Spanish *guarda-costas* (customs officers), led to the War of Jenkins's Ear between Britain and Spain in 1739 (see also JENKINS, Robert). The Asiento treaty was not renewed after this war.

ASPECT RATIO, the ratio between the length of the *luff and the *foot of a yacht's mainsail.
Whereas in the early days of the so-called Bermudian or Marconi mainsails the aspect ratio used to be as low as 2:1, in modern class racing yachts the luff-to-foot length ratio is generally between 3·5:1 and 4·0:1. Such a high aspect ratio means a tall and narrow sail which is like a glider's wing set up on end. It is highly efficient in sailing very close to the wind (as near as $3\frac{1}{2}$ points or about 39°) as there is negligible twist in the surface of the sail from foot to head, whereas the old broader mainsails suffered from a pronounced sag to leeward. To make up for the loss of driving power of these small modern mainsails, very large headsails, often of more than twice the area of the mainsail, must be carried under certain conditions.

ASSISTANCE, a vessel of 423 tons built of teak at Calcutta in 1835 and originally named *Baboo*. She was purchased by the British Admiralty in 1848 and commissioned as a two-gun *barque by Captain (later Admiral) H. T. *Austin for a polar expedition in search of Sir John *Franklin in 1850. She was also part of the squadron under Captain Sir Edward *Belcher which sailed on a similar mission in 1852, but was abandoned by him in the ice in 1854.

ASSMAN, KURT (1883–1962), German naval officer and author, joined the Imperial German Navy in 1901 and served for most of the First World War (1914–18) as senior officer of a torpedo-boat flotilla operating off the coast of Flanders. From April 1933 to June 1943 he was head of the naval historical branch of the German Admiralty and as such gave many lectures and wrote numerous articles. After the Second World War he spent some years in England and, at the invitation of the British and American naval authorities, wrote on specific naval aspects of that war. He is best known for his books *Wandlungen der Seekriegführung* (The Conduct of Leadership in Sea Warfare), *Deutsche Schicksaljahre* (Years of Germany's Destiny), and *Deutsche Seestrategie in zwei Weltkriegen* (German Sea Strategy in Two World Wars). He reached the rank of vice admiral.

ASSOCIATION, H.M.S., was Admiral Sir Clowdisley *Shovel's flagship which was wrecked off the Scilly Isles when returning home from the Mediterranean in October 1707. She was a 2nd *rate *ship of the line of ninety guns, built at Portsmouth in 1697. Shovel and almost the entire complement of the ship perished in the disaster. In 1968 her wreck was discovered by skin divers off the Bishop and Clerk rocks off the Scillies and a considerable quantity of bullion, guns, and silver plate recovered.

ASTERN, backwards, behind. It is a word employed in two senses in maritime use; in movement, that of a ship going backwards; in direction, directly behind a ship. As an order given to the engine-room of a ship for the movement of her engines, it indicates that they must be made to revolve in the reverse direction. See, e.g., AHEAD, and for illus. see RELATIVE BEARINGS.

ASTROLABE, from the Greek *astrêr*, star, and *labin*, to take. The word astrolabe has been employed for a variety of instruments used for solving astronomical problems relating to the sun, moon, and stars. A spherical astrolabe, often called an *armillary sphere, consists of a series of concentric rings each representing one of the principal *great circles of the celestial sphere.

Equatorial armillaries were designed for determining * declination of a celestial body, whereas zodiacal armillaries served to ascertain a heavenly body's celestial * latitude and celestial * longitude, without having to resort to tedious computations. Planispheric astrolabes, which were perfected by the astronomers of India, Persia, and Arabia during the 7th century A.D., were complex instruments employing brass plates on which were engraved stereographic projections of the celestial sphere, each for a particular latitude of the observer, used essentially for time-measuring by solar observations during the day and observations of one of a small number of stars by night.

The seaman's astrolabe, unlike the complex astronomer's instrument of the same name, is a very simple device used not for time-measuring but for measuring the * altitude of sun or star. It consists of a massive graduated ring of brass fitted with an alidade, or sighting rule, pivoted at the centre of the ring. The instrument was suspended by the thumb or by means of a thread from a shackle at the top of the ring so that it hung vertically. The alidade was then turned about its axis so that the sun or star could be sighted along it and the altitude read off on the ring.

According to Ramond Lull, the famous Majorcan astronomer, the seaman's astrolabe was in use among the pilots of Majorca as early as 1295, but Samuel * Purchas informs us that Martin * Behaim was the first to adapt the astrolabe to navigation in 1484.

The seaman's astrolabe, like the seaman's * quadrant, was of little use for observations from the heaving deck of a lively ship at sea. For fixing the approximate latitudes of new discoveries, however, in which observations were made ashore, it was an instrument simple in principle and use and well-adapted to the explorer's needs. See also NAVIGATION.

ASTRONOMICAL NAVIGATION, see NAVIGATION.

ATHENE, also known as Pallas Athene and (in Latin) Minerva, the Greek goddess of wisdom, war, and all the liberal arts, was the mythological patroness of shipbuilding and, according to legend, the first to build a ship. She is associated, also in legend, with the * Argonauts and their ship *Argo* and it was due to her care for them and her zeal for navigation that they reached the Euxine (Black) Sea in safety in their quest for the Golden Fleece. During the Trojan war and its aftermath she favoured the Greeks mainly because Paris awarded the prize for beauty to her rival Aphrodite (Venus) who thus became the protectress of the refugee Trojan prince Aeneas, who later founded Rome.

ATHENIA, a passenger liner of 13,581 tons, owned by the Donaldson Atlantic Line and bound for the U.S.A. with a full passenger list, mainly women and children being evacuated from Britain because of war risks, was torpedoed by the *U.30* (Leutnant Lemp) south of Rockall Bank in the Atlantic on the opening day of the Second World War, 3 September 1939. A total of 1,300 survivors were picked up by various ships, but 112 passengers and crew were lost. The attack was in contravention of current orders to German * U-boat commanders to conduct themselves in accordance with the rules laid down by the Hague Convention; but Lemp was considered by his superiors to have acted in good faith in believing that the *Athenia* was an * armed merchant cruiser. The British Admiralty accepted the sinking as evidence that Germany would pursue a policy of unrestricted submarine warfare as she had done during the First World War (1914–18) and as a result pressed ahead with the design and building of sufficient escort vessels for the long task of * convoy protection against the U-boat onslaught which later developed as expected.

ATHWART, a direction across the line of a ship's * course. ATHWART-HAWSE, the position of a ship or other vessel driven by wind or tide across the stem of another. ATHWARTSHIPS, from one side of the ship to the other. ATHWART THE TIDE, the position of a ship held by the force of the wind lying across the direction of the tide when at anchor. See also WIND-RODE.

ATLANTIC, BATTLE OF THE, the name given to the campaign fought during the Second World War against the German and Italian * U-boat attack against allied trade at sea (see 'WOLF PACK'). The overall name is generally held to include the similar campaign in Arctic and other waters. During this campaign, which lasted from the first day of war until the last, the U-boats sank 2,828 merchant ships of a total tonnage of 14,687,231, while 782 German and 85 Italian U-boats were destroyed. The turning point in this long and bitter campaign came in May 1943 when at long last sufficient aircraft, both shipborne and land-based, became available to supplement the surface escort of convoys throughout the whole of their passages across the Atlantic. Until that date, the loss of merchant shipping was so immense that the allied powers were never very far from ultimate defeat; after that date the U-boats were able to cause only very slight damage to shipping and the result of the campaign, and indeed of the war as a whole, was never again in any doubt.

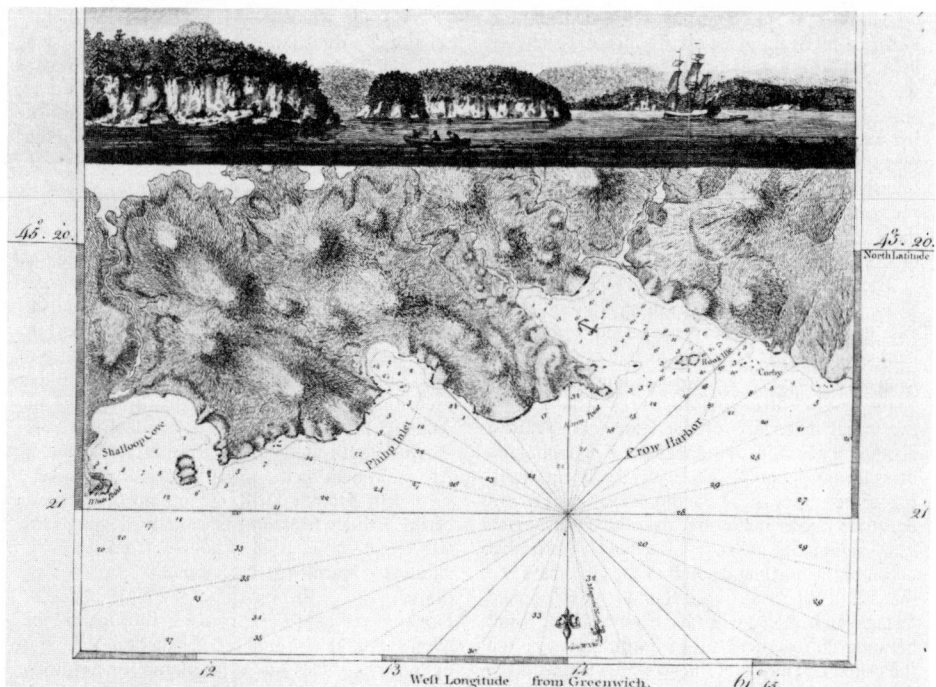

Detail and drawing from the Atlantic Neptune, *1777*

ATLANTIC NEPTUNE, a magnificent collection of charts of the eastern coast of North America issued by the British Admiralty for the use of the Royal Navy in 1777 from surveys made by J. F. W., *Des Barres, and others. Samuel Holland was the other chief surveyor engaged, and was in fact responsible for more of the surveys than Des Barres, but the series is made especially notable by the quality and beauty of the aquatints of views of ports and the coastline which were contributed by Des Barres.

The word *Neptune in the title was frequently used during the 18th century to describe collections of maps and charts, in much the same way as *Atlas.

ATLANTIC OCEAN, the expanse of sea which separates the western coasts of Europe and Africa and the eastern coasts of North and South America, bounded to the north by the Arctic Basin and to the south by the Great Southern or Antarctic Ocean, although for measurement purposes the north and south boundaries are taken as the Arctic and Antarctic circles, latitudes 66° 33′ N. and S. It received its name from *Atlas, the mythical god or Titan turned into a mountain to support the heavens and associated with the Atlas mountains at the western end of the Mediterranean. There is a Greek adjective *Atlantikos*, derived from this, referring to the

western exit from the Mediterranean. The great ocean lying beyond this, the end of the then known earth, fairly naturally was given the name Atlantic. Though as a whole known as the Atlantic Ocean, it is conveniently divided at its narrowest part, approximately at the equator, into the North Atlantic and South Atlantic Oceans.

For many centuries after the birth of Mediterranean civilization the Pillars of Hercules (*Gibraltar and the Atlas Mountains) were regarded both as the end of the earth, surrounded by the world-bounding ocean, and the gateway to the unknown, leading to the many myths of enchanted islands, such as the Greek Isles of the Blest, the Portuguese Isle of Seven Cities, the Welsh *Avalon, Hy *Brasil, *Lyonesse, and *Atlantis, in which the souls of the departed dwelt in permanent bliss. That the Pillars of Hercules were not the end of the earth but in fact the gateway to new and unknown lands was first demonstrated during the first millennium B.C., by the Phoenicians, who penetrated during this period both to the Azores and the Scilly Islands (see NAVIGATION). And that a new world did in fact lie across the ocean beyond the western shores of Europe and Africa was demonstrated by the voyages of the Norse *longships during the last two centuries of the first millennium A.D., when Iceland and Greenland were

colonized and *Leif Ericsson landed on the
North American coast at *Vinland (probably
northern Newfoundland). It was also being more
widely recognized that the earth was really a
sphere and not a flat plane and that a voyage to
the west must eventually reach land, believed at
that time to be India and China, which were well
known to lie to the eastward. The reality of this
recognition was proved in the voyages of such
navigators as *Columbus, *Cabral, *Cabot, and
others around the turn of the 15th century.

The voyage of Columbus in 1492 brought to
Spain the lordship of the western Atlantic and a
vast new empire of the newly discovered continent of America, bounded in the north by the
English discovery of Newfoundland and in the
south by the Portuguese discovery of Brazil. As
the initial discovery of the land was extended
north and south, proving that the American land
mass formed a complete barrier to ships proceeding direct into the *Pacific Ocean, great endeavours were made by the European maritime nations to discover sea routes into that
ocean to the north and south of the land mass. To
the south the way was found by Ferdinand
*Magellan in 1520 when he discovered the Strait
between the southern tip of South America and
the island of Tierra del Fuego which connects the
two oceans; to the north scores of voyages in the
search of a *North-West passage ended in failure
until the mid-19th century when Robert
*McClure first discovered the way.

The Atlantic Ocean is relatively free from
island groups, those of the British Isles, Azores,
Canaries, and the West Indies being the best
known. Individual islands, such as St. Helena,
Tristan da Cunha, and the two Falkland Islands
are few and widely scattered. The general wind
pattern is, in the south, anti-cyclonic in the central belt, giving rise to the traditional *trade
winds, but farther south, as the two bounding
continents, South Africa and South America,
taper off into narrow extremities leaving a vast
width of ocean unaffected by land masses, the
planetary circulation is left virtually unrestricted
and gives rise to steep pressure gradients which
result in continuously strong westerly winds,
known as the '*roaring forties'. In the North
Atlantic, where the land masses exert a greater
influence in temperature rise and fall, and where
the Arctic cold forms a permanent northern barrier, the tropical high pressure belt exists
throughout the year and the resulting anti-
cyclonic area is larger than in the south and the
movement of the air more vigorous. The need of
air constantly to fill the low pressure areas
produced by temperature rises of the land masses
causes generally cyclonic conditions in the
northern areas of the North Atlantic, so that
periodic gales produce some of the roughest seas
to be found in the world.

The trade winds generated either side of the
equator by the anti-cyclonic areas produce a
west-going current or drift, divided into the north
and south equatorial currents. The southern current, on reaching the South American coast,
splits into two parts, one moving south along the
coast as far south as about the mouth of the
River Plate; the other moving north, where it
joins the north equatorial current. The effect of
these two currents is appreciably to raise the
level of the sea at their ultimate destination in the
Caribbean Sea and Gulf of Mexico, and this rise
in level is relieved by a counter-current, known
as the *Gulf Stream, which flows up the coast of
North America (but separated from it by a cold
'wall' of water) to Newfoundland, where the
prevailing westerly wind takes it across the
Atlantic to Europe where it divides, one part
moving south along the north-western coast of
Africa, known as the Canary current, the other,
the North Atlantic Drift, moving north and west
of the British Isles and eventually flowing into
the Arctic Basin. It is, of course, from the comparatively warm water of the Gulf Stream that
the seaports of Britain and of the North Cape of
Norway are kept free from ice throughout the
winter months at a time when others in the same
or lower latitudes (as in the Baltic for example)
remain frozen.

Ignoring the enclosed seas contiguous with the
Atlantic Ocean, of which they are geographically
a part (Caribbean Sea, Gulf of Mexico, Gulf of
St. Lawrence, Hudson Bay, Baltic Sea, North
Sea, Mediterranean Sea, Black Sea), it has been
computed that the North Atlantic covers an area
of 10,588,000 square miles and the South
Atlantic an area of 12,627,000 square miles. The
greatest depth reached by sounding in the North
Atlantic is 5,049 fathoms obtained by U.S.S.
Milwaukee in the Puerto Rico trough off Guyana;
in the South Atlantic, 4,517 fathoms has been
reached in the South Sandwich trench. See also
CURRENT, METEOROLOGY.

ATLANTIS, a legendary island in the Atlantic
Ocean, was first mentioned by Plato in the
Timaeus, and a description of its supposed commonwealth is included in his *Critias*. It was supposed to have been engulfed by a tidal wave after
its armies had overrun most of western Europe,
only Athens successfully defying its assault.
Presumably it arose again from the sea, since it
was later identified with other well-known
mythical islands, particularly the Greek Isles of
the Blest, the Portuguese Isle of Seven Cities, the
Welsh *Avalon, Hy *Brasil, and others.

These islands were shown on the maps and
charts of the 14th and 15th centuries and formed
the objectives of several early voyages of
discovery, none of course successful. The actual
position of Atlantis itself was marked on many

charts of the Atlantic as a rock in 44° 48′ N., 26° 10′ W. at least as late as the mid-19th century when it was proved by detailed surveys not to exist.

ATLANTIS, a German *armed merchant raider of the Second World War which had the most successful career as a raider of either world war. She was also known as *Ship 16.* She was originally the *Goldenfels* of the Hansa Line, of 7,860 tons, launched in 1937 and in 1939 armed with six 5·9-inch guns. Her unfinished *voyage of 622 days, during which she steamed 102,000 miles in the Atlantic, Indian, and Pacific Oceans, and captured or sank twenty-two ships of 145,697 tons, began on 31 March 1940 and ended off Ascension Island on 21 November 1941 when she was sunk by the British cruiser *Devonshire.* Only seven members of her crew were lost, thanks to a rescue operation by 11 *U-boats organized by Admiral *Dönitz from his headquarters in France.

ATLAS, in Greek mythology a brother of Prometheus, was originally a marine god before Perseus showed him the Gorgon's head and turned him into a rocky mountain supporting the heavens. He was also known as one of the Titans. In the *Odyssey* (I. 52) he is described by Homer as 'one who knows the depths of the whole sea, and keeps the tall pillars which hold heaven and earth asunder'. In his famous book of maps, Gerardus *Mercator uses a picture of Atlas supporting the heavens as a frontispiece, and this use has led to the term atlas being used to describe a volume of maps.

ATOLL, probably from the Malayan *adal*, closing or uniting, a horseshoe-shaped or circular reef of coral enclosing a lagoon. The word itself is an acceptance into the English language of the Maldivian *atollon*, the native description of the Maldive Islands which are of this formation. It is formed usually on the tops of submerged volcanoes by coral polyps, kept alive on the outer edge of the reef by the continual surge of the sea which brings them their supply of food, but dying on the inside edge where the water of the lagoon is still and produces no nourishment. The outer edge of the reef continually expands as the polyps multiply, forming islands as the reef rises, while inside the reef the lagoon tends to get deeper as the originally live polyps die off from lack of food.

In 1971–2 an investigation into the growth of coral reefs revealed a threat to their formation through a significant increase in numbers of the Crown of Thorns starfish (*Acanthaster planci*) which feeds on coral polyps and thus causes the living reef to die. By an odd quirk of nature, coral polyps feed on the larvae of Crown of Thorns starfish but are unable to keep pace with the rise in their numbers. Attempts to control the increase of these starfish are being made by the introduction of predators, particularly the lump-headed wrasse (*Cheilinus undulatus*) and the painted shrimp (*Hymenocera elegans*) into areas where the starfish are particularly prevalent, and also by the application of a biochemical contraceptive during their breeding season between April and August.

A-TRIP. An anchor is said to be a-trip at the moment of *weighing when it is broken out of the ground by the pull of the *cable. In square-rigged ships topsails are a-trip when they are hoisted to their full extent and ready for sheeting home (see SHEET) and *yards are a-trip when they are *swayed up and their stops cut ready for crossing. A topmast or topgallant mast is a-trip when the *fid is loosened ready for it to be struck, or lowered.

AUBIN, GEORGES AMÉDÉS (1889–   ). French marine author, was born at Rezé (Loire-Atlantique). He went to sea at the age of 15 and later studied at the Hydrographic School at Nantes. On leaving in 1907 he was appointed third officer under Louis Paris *Lacroix in the sailing vessel *Geneviève Molinos* and eventually rose to command her on a voyage which forms the subject of his first book *L'Empreinte de la voile* (Shadow of the Sails) which, in 1954, gained him the *Grand Prix Littéraire* of the merchant navy. His second book *Nous les cap-horniers* (We the Cape Horners) is based on his experience with Lacroix in voyages round that formidable cape. He subsequently took to writing fiction in which he was equally successful, and also produced a *Dictionnaire de marine* which is still consulted.

AUCKLAND, one of the principal seaports of New Zealand, is on the east coast of North Island. It is one of the finest and most beautiful natural harbours in the Pacific, with sufficient depth of water to take the largest ships at any state of the tide, while the dry-docks and repair and servicing facilities in the port attract a growing seaborne trade. The city was founded in 1840 as capital of the colony by Governor Hobson and was named after Lord Auckland, who was president of the Board of Trade in Grenville's ministry of 'All the Talents'. It remained the seat of central government until 1865 when *Wellington took its place as the capital city of New Zealand.

AULIN, an Arctic gull, *Cataractes parasiticus*, with the unpleasant habit of making other sea-birds sick with fear by its fierce approach and then eating their vomit. Commonly called by fishermen, not unnaturally, 'dirty aulin'.

AURORA, a display of atmospheric lights visible in high latitudes, *Borealis* in northern latitudes and *Australis* in southern. They are caused by electrical discharges in the atmosphere, and when the displays are particularly bright, and movement of the light rapid, are almost invariably accompanied by severe electrical storms. There is also evidence that the frequency of display is generally similar to that of sun-spot activity, that in years of many sunspots there are more auroras than usual. Although the frequency of display varies from year to year, the largest number of displays in any year generally occur during the period of the equinoxes (March and September). Auroras take many forms, that of the corona being generally accepted as the most spectacular, although auroral curtains and bands are also magnificent spectacles. As the distance from the Arctic and Antarctic circles increase, the visible auroras generally take the form of the less exciting arcs and rays, while further away still the most frequent form is the diffused aurora.

AURORA, a 386-ton * barquentine-rigged Newfoundland sealer with auxiliary steam engines built in Dundee. She was used by Sir Douglas * Mawson on his Australasian Antarctic expedition 1911–14 and to transport Sir Ernest * Shackleton's Ross Sea party, 1914–17. On the latter occasion she was beset in the ice and drifted for nine months in the Ross Sea. In January 1917 she was used to rescue the surviving members of the Ross Sea party from Cape Evans.

AUSTER, the old Latin name for the south wind, used in some of the accounts of very early voyages. It was this meaning of south or southerly which gave the name * Terra Australis to the vast land mass which early geographers believed must exist in the southern hemisphere to balance the land mass which was known to exist in the northern hemisphere.

AUSTIN, SIR HORATIO THOMAS (1801–65), British vice admiral, entered the Royal Navy in 1813 on board the *Thisbe*, twenty-eight guns. The following year he joined the *Ramillies*, Captain Sir Thomas * Hardy, and in her took part in the war against the United States. In 1824, as first lieutenant of the * sloop * Fury, he sailed with Captain * Parry's third expedition in search of a * North-West passage, his ship being lost in the summer of 1825. There followed a scientific voyage to the South Atlantic and West Indies in the *Chanticleer* and in 1840, in command of the steamer *Cyclops* (six guns), he took part in operations against the Turks in the eastern Mediterranean. After a period of service in the * Royal Yachts, he was appointed in 1850 to

command an expedition to search for Sir John * Franklin. The force comprised the ships *Assistance, * Resolute, Pioneer,* and * *Intrepid* and sailed on 25 April of that year, returning in September of the following year without having accomplished its task. Austin was promoted to rear admiral in 1857 and served as Admiral Superintendent of * Deptford and Malta dockyards.

AUSTRALASIA, the name first given by de Brosses in his *Histoire des navigations aux terres australes* (1756) to that section of the Indian Ocean lying south of Asia. The name was coined from * Auster, the old name for the south wind, hence southern or to the south. William * Dampier, who landed in New Zealand, as it was then called although in fact it was Australia, in 1687 and described the aborigines he found living there in words which probably served Jonathan Swift for his description of the Yahoos in *Gulliver's Travels*, is believed to be the first man to give the name AUSTRALIA to the southern continent. See also BASS, George; COOK, James; FLINDERS, Matthew; QUIROS, Pedro Fernandez de; TASMAN, Abel; TERRA AUSTRALIS; TORRES, Luis Vaez de.

AUSTRALIS, TERRA, see TERRA AUSTRALIS.

AUTOMATIC HELMSMAN, a device fitted in many ships by which they are held on any desired course without the need of a man on the steering wheel. Any variation from the set course automatically supplies power to the steering engine so that the helm is put over and the vessel brought back to her course. In most systems the automatic helmsman is actuated by a gyroscopic * compass so that the course steered is a * true course. See SELF-STEERING GEAR.

AUXILIARY, (1) the name by which an engine is known when fitted for occasional use in a sailing yacht. **(2)** Machinery fitted in steam and motor vessels which is not a part of the main propelling machinery but used for ancillary purposes, such as pumps, capstan engines, air compressors, etc.

AVALON, in Welsh mythology an earthly paradise in the western seas. The Welsh name is YNYS YR AFALLON, or Isle of Apples, the apple, the largest fruit then known to the inhabitants of northern Europe, symbolizing the feasting which goes on in paradise. See also ATLANTIS.

AVAST, the order in any seamanship operation to stop or hold. It is generally thought to have been derived from the Italian *basta*, enough.

AVERAGE, see GENERAL AVERAGE.

AVERY, JOHN (*c.* 1665–97), pirate, alias Long Ben, was born in Devon and became the arch-pirate of his day. His most notable success came while he was operating from a base in Madagascar, when he captured the Mocha fleet, together with the daughter of the Great Mogul and her dowry. He disposed of some of the treasure in America before retiring to Bideford, Devon. Here he tried to sell the captured jewels to Bristol merchants, but they suspected that they were stolen goods and withheld payment. Avery died a pauper.

AVILÉS, PEDRO MENÉNDEZ DE (1519–74), Spanish seaman, ran away to sea at the age of 14, and for the next fifteen years enjoyed an adventurous life as a corsair. In 1549 he was commissioned by the Emperor Charles V of Spain to drive out French pirates who were operating on the north coast of Spain. He was so successful that the emperor appointed him in 1554 to command the **flota*, the convoy which carried the annual treasure to Spain from the New World. His appointment was vigorously opposed by the merchants since Avilés was known to be too honest a man to accept bribes for overlooking peculation, and they used all their powers to obstruct the appointment. His handling of the *flota* was brilliantly carried out, and he returned with a record amount of treasure, but on his reappointment for the *flota* of 1557 he asked for alternative employment because of the hostility of the merchants. He served in the Spanish Navy in the war against France until 1559, and commanded the fleet which brought Philip II back from the Low Countries. Again appointed to command the *flota*, he made voyages in 1560 and 1561 which were most successful, but in 1563 he was thrown into prison on false charges preferred by the merchants.

On his release from prison in 1565, he sailed again to the west under an arrangement with Philip II that he should be the proprietor of any colony he could found in Florida, where in fact French Huguenots were attempting to settle although the land was claimed by Spain through prior discovery. Avilés sailed with a small fleet and 1,500 men, reached the Bay of St. Augustine, and erected a fort there. A few weeks later he captured a body of Frenchmen, under their leader Jean Ribault, and slew them all. He justified this savage action because he regarded all Frenchmen as pirates and heretics, and in fact hung the bodies of those he had slaughtered on trees with the inscription, 'Not as Frenchmen but as Lutherans'. Three years later a French sea-captain, Dominique de Gourges, landed in Florida and, capturing the Spanish fort of San Mateo, hanged the entire garrison and displayed their bodies with the inscription, 'Not as Spaniards but as murderers'.

Avilés remained in Florida until 1567, returning to Spain in that year. He visited the colony once more, and died in Spain in 1574.

AWASH, the situation of an object almost submerged, as when seas wash over a wreck or shoal, or when a ship lies so low in the water that the seas wash over her. A falling *tide which exposes a rock or bank which is submerged at high water makes it awash.

A-WEIGH, or **AWEIGH,** the situation of the *anchor at the moment it is broken out of the ground when being weighed. See also A-TRIP. When the anchor is a-weigh the ship is no longer secured to the ground and will drift unless under sail or power. See also UNDER WAY.

AWNING, (1) a canvas canopy spread over a deck for protection from the sun. It is spread over a ridge rope in the centre line of the ship and secured to *stanchions erected for the purpose on either side of the deck. In small yachts, a sail spread across the *boom is often used for an awning. **(2)** In the older sailing vessels that part of the *poop deck which used to project beyond the doors of the poop cabins to form a shelter for the steering-wheel and *binnacle was also called the awning.

AXLE-TREES, (1) the name given to the two cross-pieces of a wooden gun carriage fixed under the fore and after parts of the cheeks and carrying the spindles of the wheels. **(2)** The iron spindle of the old-fashioned chain-pump used for pumping out the *bilges of ships was also known as an axle-tree.

'AYE AYE, SIR', the correct and seamanlike reply on board ship on receipt of an order. 'Aye-aye' is also the reply in the Royal Navy from a boat which has a commissioned officer below the rank of captain on board, when hailed from a ship. If no commissioned officer is on board, the reply is 'No No'; if a captain is on board the reply is the name of his ship, and if an admiral, the reply is 'flag'. Boats are hailed in this fashion so that watchkeepers on board ship may know the form of salute required when officers arrive on board.

AYLLON, LUCAS VASQUEZ DE (*c.* 1475–1526), Spanish adventurer, is best known as the man who introduced African slaves on to the mainland of North America. He had sailed with Nicolas Ovando to Hispaniola (Haiti) in 1502, and after prospering in various ventures, obtained from the Emperor Charles V an indefinite charter to found colonies. In 1526, with 500 colonists and 100 slaves, he landed on the mainland near the mouth of the Pedee river, but most of the colonists, including Ayllon, perished from fever. A second claim to fame is that, after the loss of one of his ships on the coast, he constructed a new one, this being considered the first example of shipbuilding in North America.

AYSCUE, Sir GEORGE (d. 1671), English admiral, was appointed admiral of the Irish Seas in 1649 and commanded the fleet at the relief of Dublin, at the time invested by forces still loyal to Charles I, who had been beheaded earlier that year. He also commanded the fleet sent to the West Indies in 1651 for the capture of Barbados, and with this mission safely accomplished, returned in time to take part in the First Dutch War (1652–4). Towards the end of the Commonwealth period, he was sent to Sweden as naval adviser, but returned to England at the restoration of Charles II in 1660. He served at sea in the Second Dutch War (1665–7), being rear admiral of the Blue at the battle of * Lowestoft (1665) and admiral of the White in the * Four Days Battle (1666), on the third day of which his flagship, the *Prince Royal*, was captured. Ayscue remained a prisoner in Holland until the end of the war. He did not serve at sea again.

AZIMUTH, from the Arabic *as sumat*, way or direction, a navigational term used to indicate the * bearing of a celestial body. Its navigational definition is the measure of the arc of the * horizon that lies between the elevated pole (north in northern hemisphere, south in southern) and the point where the celestial * great circle passing through the celestial body cuts the horizon. It can be measured by a ship's compass or, more usually, obtained from tables in the * Nautical Almanac. It is a vital factor in fixing a ship's position by astronomical navigation since it is along the azimuth of the celestial body that the * intercept obtained from an observation is laid off on a chart to obtain a position line. Azimuths are also frequently used as a means of checking

the * deviation of a magnetic compass, the difference between the compass azimuth and the true azimuth as obtained from the *Nautical Almanac* giving the compass deviation for the course on which the ship is sailing. See also NAVIGATION.

AZIMUTH COMPASS, see COMPASS.

AZORES, a group of islands lying in the north Atlantic about 900 miles due west of Lisbon, Portugal, and the scene of a battle which was fought on 31 August 1591 between an English squadron of seven sail commanded by Lord Thomas * Howard and a greatly superior Spanish fleet under Don Alonso de * Bazan. The English had been waiting at Flores to intercept the Spanish treasure fleet from America and were surprised by de Bazan who had come out from Spain to escort the fleet for the last portion of its homeward voyage. On the approach of the enemy Howard stood out to sea, hoping to gain the weather * gage, and became engaged in a running fight until nightfall when all except one ship managed to escape being cut off by the Spaniards. This ship was the * *Revenge*; her epic fight under Sir Richard * Grenville became the subject of Tennyson's famous poem 'The Last Fight of the *Revenge*'.

AZURARA, GOMES EANNES DE (d. 1474), Portuguese writer, was the author of *Chronica do Descobrimento e Conquista de Guiné*, the main authority for the early voyages of discovery made by the Portuguese down the African coast and into the Indian Ocean. Azurara was a great admirer of Prince * Henry the Navigator, and much of our present knowledge of Prince Henry comes from his writings. In 1454 he was made chief keeper of the archives and royal chronicler. The English version of his book on the early Portuguese voyages was published by the * Hakluyt Society in two volumes in 1896 and 1899.

B

BABOON WATCH, the unfortunate man detailed to remain on deck in harbour to watch over the ship's safety while the rest of the crew were off duty. The term was associated mainly with the big square-rigged sailing ships, and the 'baboon' was usually one of the apprentices carried on board.

BACK, Sir GEORGE (1796–1878), British admiral and Arctic explorer, was born at Stockport, Cheshire. He joined the Royal Navy in 1808 and saw active service in northern Spain during Wellington's campaign. Between 1818 and 1827 he served in three polar expeditions under Sir John *Franklin, in the second of which his courage and determination were instrumental in saving the lives of his companions. During the third voyage he was specially commended for his dealings with the Eskimos and promoted to captain by Order in Council. In 1833 he commanded an expedition sent to search for Sir John *Ross during which he discovered the Great Fish River, now named Back River after him, and Artillery Lake. On this expedition he was accompanied by Dr. Richard King who published an account of it. He continued his exploration of the North-West Territory in 1836–7 and his work was recognized by the award of two medals by the Royal Geographical Society. He was knighted in 1839 and was author of two books describing his work and voyages.

BACK, to, (1) the wind is said to back when it changes contrary to its normal pattern. In the northern hemisphere, north of the trade wind belt, the wind usually changes clockwise—from north through east, south, and west. When the change is anti-clockwise, the wind is backing. In the southern latitudes, the reverse is the general pattern of the winds. When the wind backs in either hemisphere it is generally taken as a sign that it will freshen. **(2)** To back a square sail is to *brace the *yards so that the wind presses on the forward side of the sail to take the way off the

ship. See also ABACK. **(3)** To back water is to push on the oars when rowing a boat, instead of pulling on them, in order to bring the boat to a stop. **(4)** To back an *anchor, the operation of laying out a smaller anchor, usually a *kedge or *stream anchor, ahead of the *bower anchor in order to provide additional holding power and to prevent the bower from *coming home.

BACK A STRAND, to, the operation, when making a *long splice, of filling the *score vacated when unlaying a strand with one of the opposite strands.

BACK SPLICE, a method of finishing off the end of a rope to prevent the strands unravelling by forming a *crown knot with the strands and then tucking them back two or three times each.

Back splice

BACKBOARD, a board across the *sternsheets of a boat just aft of the seats to form a support for passengers or for the helmsman if the boat is under sail.

BACKHUIZEN or **BACKHUYSEN,** see BAK-HUYSEN.

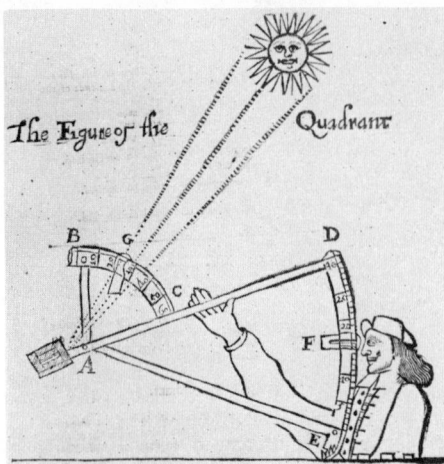

Back-staff also known as Davis's quadrant; from
Sturmy's Mariners Magazine, *1669*

BACK-STAFF, a navigational instrument for
measuring the *altitude of the sun, introduced
during the 16th century. It gained its name
because, unlike the *cross-staff which it
replaced, the user had the sun behind him when
taking an observation. It was virtually the same
instrument as the * Davis's quadrant.

BACKSTAY, a part of the standing *rigging of a
sailing vessel to support the strain on all upper
masts. In full-rigged sailing ships, backstays extend from all mastheads above the lower mast
and are brought back to both sides of the ship
and set up with *deadeyes and *lanyards to the
backstay plates. Their main purpose is to provide
additional support to the *shrouds when the
wind is abaft the beam. In particularly heavy
winds an additional backstay, known as a
*preventer, is frequently rigged temporarily. In
smaller sailing boats and yachts the backstays
are usually known as *runners, and the *lee one
is generally slacked off to allow further
movement forward of the *boom in order to
present a squarer aspect of the sail to the wind. In
*Bermuda-rigged yachts where the boom is short
enough to swing across inside the stern when
*tacking or *gybing, the normal two runners are
replaced by a single backstay or pair of fixed
backstays led from the masthead to the yacht's
*taffrail or *quarters. For illus., see RIGGING.

BACON, Sir REGINALD HUGH SPENCER
(1863–1947), British admiral, was named by
Admiral of the Fleet Lord *Fisher as one of his
seven 'brains' during the great naval reforms of
1904–10. Born at Wiggonholt Rectory, Sussex,
he entered the navy in January 1877 and as a
lieutenant specialized in *torpedo work. In 1897

he took part in the punitive expedition against the
city of Benin, being awarded the D.S.O. for his
services. While serving in the Mediterranean fleet
in 1899 he came under the notice of the
Commander-in-Chief, Admiral Sir John Fisher,
with whom his subsequent career became so
closely linked. Promoted captain in June 1900,
the following year he was charged with the construction and introduction of *submarines into
the Royal Navy. In 1904 he became naval assistant to the First Sea Lord (Fisher) and was
selected by him to command the first all-big-gun
battleship, H.M.S. *Dreadnought, with the
design of which he had been concerned. In
August 1907 he was appointed director of Naval
Ordnance and Torpedoes. Promoted to rear
admiral in July 1909, he retired four months
later to become managing director of the
Coventry Ordnance Works. He was recalled to
active duty in January 1915 and, after service in
France as officer commanding the Royal Marine
Siege Brigade, he was selected by Winston
*Churchill, then First Lord of the Admiralty, to
command the Dover Patrol forces. In 1917, at
the height of the German *U-boat campaign, his
handling of these forces aroused much criticism
in the British Admiralty because of the ease with
which U-boats managed to evade his forces and
slip through the extensive mine barriers laid
across the Channel. Although he maintained
firmly that no U-boats could get through without
detection, they did in fact do so in large numbers.
In January 1918 he was relieved of his command and was appointed controller of munitions
and inventions. Promoted to admiral in
September 1918 he finally retired in March
1919. He wrote several books, including a life of
his patron Lord Fisher and one of Admiral of the
Fleet Earl *Jellicoe, whom he staunchly supported throughout the *Jutland controversy. He
was a brilliant officer of the *matériel* school, an
expert on torpedoes, *mines, and submarines,
but was somewhat intolerant of his juniors and
not a man who would listen to advice or confide
his plans to his staff for discussion.

BADGE, originally an ornamental stern in
smaller sailing ships either framing a window of
the *cabin or giving a representation of a window. They were usually heavily decorated with
carvings of sea gods or other marine figures.
Today a ship's badge is normally a heraldic
device based on the ship's name or on some other
association which she may have. It is often
known as the ship's crest, and is usually
displayed on board in some prominent place.

BAFFIN, WILLIAM (1584–1622), English
navigator and discoverer, was believed to have
been a Londoner of humble origin but evidently

had a flair for mathematics which enabled him to establish himself as a navigator. In 1612 he was serving as chief pilot of an expedition seeking the *North-West passage to the Pacific. In 1615 he was pilot of the *Discovery in which detailed information on Hudson Strait was gathered; and in the following year he piloted the *Discovery* through the Davis Strait to discover the vast bay that bears his name, penetrating Lancaster and Jones Sounds and Smith Bay which he named after patrons of his voyages. His farthest north on that voyage (77° 45′) was not again reached in that sea until 1852 when an expedition searching for traces of the lost explorer Sir John *Franklin did so; nor were his discoveries confirmed until Captain *Ross's voyage in 1818.

Baffin next served with the recently formed *East India Company and, during a voyage to India in 1617–19, made valuable surveys in the Red Sea and the Persian Gulf. He sailed again to the east in 1620 where, following clashes with the Portuguese, the Company took reprisals by capturing the great trade centre of Ormuz at the entrance to the Persian Gulf. A necessary preliminary was the reduction of the fortress of Kishm, in the course of which action Baffin was killed.

BAG REEF, an additional fourth or lower row of *reef points on fore-and-aft sails which used to be fitted in the smaller sailing ships of the British Navy. They took in only a short reef to prevent large sails from bagging when *on the wind. In the American Navy it was the first reef of five in a topsail, again to prevent bagging when on the wind.

BAGGYWRINKLE, sómetimes written as **BAG-O'-WRINKLE,** a home-made substance to prevent chafe on sails from the *lifts, *stays, and *crosstrees during long periods of sailing. It is made by stretching two lengths of *marline at a convenient working height and cutting old *manila rope into lengths of about four inches which are then *stranded. These strands are then laid across the two lengths of marline, the ends bent over and brought up between the two lengths, pulled tight, and pushed up against other pieces similarly worked, to provide a long length of bushy material. This is then cut into suitable lengths and *served round wire and spars wherever there is a danger of the sails chafing.

BAGPIPE THE MIZEN, to, an order given to lay *aback a *lateen sail set on the mizen-mast by hauling up the *sheet to the mizen rigging, the purpose being to stop the way on a vessel or to slow her down. It was a quick and ready, if a little unseamanlike, means of bringing a ship to a halt.

BAIL, to, the process of emptying out the water from a boat or small vessel. The term implies that this is done by hand, not by mechanical means. Originally a boat was bailed out with a bail, an old term used to describe a small bucket, but the modern word is bailer, generally in the form of a scoop with a handle so that water in a boat can be thrown out more rapidly than with a bucket.

BAILY, EDWARD HODGES (1788–1867), British sculptor, executed the statue of Lord *Nelson which stands at the top of the Nelson Column in Trafalgar Square, London. His model for this statue is preserved in the entrance hall of the Old Admiralty Building in Whitehall. His father was a celebrated carver in wood, and was responsible for many of the carved figureheads of ships of the British Navy.

BAINBRIDGE, WILLIAM (1774–1833), American naval officer, was born in New Jersey and went to sea at the age of 15. He entered the U.S. Navy as a lieutenant in August 1798 and was given command of the *Retaliation* in the naval war with France. He was captured by French frigates and imprisoned for a time on Guadeloupe. In May 1803, Bainbridge took command of the frigate *Philadelphia* and sailed to join Commodore Edward *Preble in the Mediterranean. After taking several *Barbary pirate vessels and freeing some American prisoners, he headed for the coast of Tripoli.

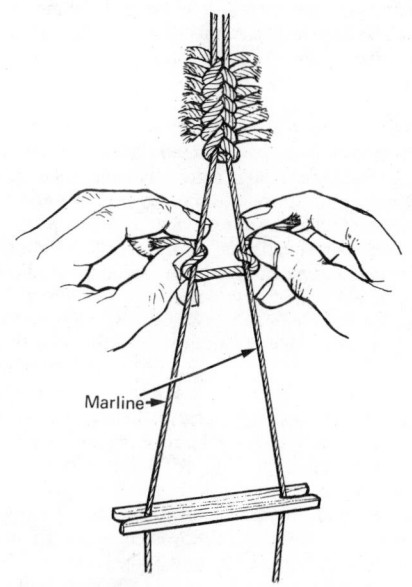

Marline→

Baggywrinkle in the making

While chasing a vessel the *Philadelphia* grounded on an uncharted reef. Efforts to lighten and refloat the ship failed, and after attempts to reduce her usefulness to the enemy, Bainbridge was forced to surrender, he and his crew becoming prisoners for about nineteen months.

His next active service was during the war of 1812 against Britain. After succeeding Isaac *Hull in command of the *Constitution*, he encountered H.M.S. *Java* off the coast of Brazil on 29 December 1812. Bainbridge was twice wounded in the bitter fight that followed, and the steering wheel of the *Constitution* was shot away after the first half hour. After about an hour of heavy action the *Java* lost her bowsprit and jib-boom, leaving her without headsails. Captain Lambert of the *Java*, recognizing that with her rigging cut to pieces the *Java* had little chance in a gun duel, decided that his best chance to win would be by boarding. As the *Java* was attempting to run alongside the *Constitution*, the fore-mast of the British frigate went overboard, and her main topsail was lost soon afterwards. About 30 minutes later, the *Java* lost her mizen-mast. Bainbridge then had little to fear from the dismasted British frigate, and he broke off the action to open the distance between the two ships and to repair the comparatively minor damage to the *Constitution*. When the American frigate returned to relatively close quarters, the *Java* surrendered. Captain Lambert had been killed, and the British loss was 22 dead, 102 wounded.

Later Bainbridge's reputation suffered for the part he played in a duel between James *Barron and Stephen *Decatur, Jr. Attempts were being made in the U.S.A. to stop duelling but Bainbridge insisted on acting as second to Decatur in spite of many protests by senior officers.

BAKHUYSEN (sometimes written as **BACK-HUYSEN** or **BACKHUIZEN**), **LUDOLF** (1631–1708), Dutch marine painter of German origin, was born in Emden but settled in Amsterdam at the age of 18 and studied painting under van Everdingen and Hendrik *Dubbels. He is also reputed to have studied in the studio of the two Van de *Veldes and he is often described as the most famous follower of the younger Van de Velde, although another opinion describes him as 'the last and in some ways the least of the great Dutch marine artists'. But it is certain that after Willem Van de Velde II left Holland to settle in England, Bakhuysen became the most popular marine painter in Holland and that his works were highly prized.

He used frequently to go to sea in stormy weather to observe the movement and behaviour of ships in high winds and rough seas, and his best pictures admirably capture the drama of the fight of ships against the elements. He preferred to paint large and in bold colours, and thus lacks some of the delicacy and feeling of so much of the Dutch school of marine painting. Nevertheless his work exerted a considerable influence on contemporary sea paintings, both Dutch and English, and even his most flamboyant storm pictures have a great charm. It is in his harbour and regatta scenes that he approaches most closely the poetic beauty of the work of Willem Van de Velde II.

BALANCE, to, a method of reducing canvas on a *lateen sail by lowering the *yard and rolling part of the *peak of the sail on to the yard, securing it to the yard about one-fifth of the way down. A BALANCE-REEF was a reefband which crossed a sail diagonally.

BALANCE FRAMES, those *frames of a ship's hull which are equal in area, one forward and one aft of the ship's *centre of gravity. Thus the aftermost balance frame of a wooden ship, to which the after *deadwood extends, is balanced by a similar frame of equal area in the *bows of the ship. See also SHIPBUILDING.

BALBOA, VASCO NUÑEZ DE (*c.* 1475–1517), known most widely as the discoverer of the Pacific Ocean, first arrived in the New World as a follower of Roderigo de Bastidas in his voyage of discovery in 1501. After an unsuccessful period as a plantation owner on Hispaniola (Haiti), he joined, and soon took the leadership of, an expedition that founded the town of Darien in the Gulf of Uraba in 1511. In the course of subjugating the hinterland he heard of an ocean beyond the mountains and of the gold of Peru.

On 1 September 1513 he led an expedition of 190 Spaniards, one of whom was Francisco Pizarro, the future conqueror of Peru, and 1,000 natives, which twenty-four days later reached the summit of the mountain barrier where the distant ocean came in sight. Reaching the coast on 29 September, Balboa formally took possession of the 'Great South Sea' in the name of King Ferdinand of Spain. After visiting the Pearl Islands in the Gulf of Panama, he made a triumphant return to Darien with much treasure.

When news of this discovery reached King Ferdinand, he named Balboa *Adelantado* (Admiral) of the South Sea and Governor of Panama and Coyba, and to take over the governorship of Darien itself he sent out Don Pedro Arias de Ávila.

Balboa was meanwhile having two small ships built with which he took possession of the Pearl Islands, and only adverse weather prevented him from anticipating Pizarro's descent on Peru. The new governor of Darien, jealous of Balboa's achievements and encouraged by Pizarro, now planned his ruin. Enticing him to Acla, near

Darien, he had him seized, tried, and, largely on the evidence of Pizarro, condemned for treasonable plans to throw off his allegiance to Spain. In 1517 Balboa was executed in the public square of Acla.

A. Strawn, *Golden Adventures of Balboa* (1929).

BALD-HEADED, a sailing term used to indicate a vessel under way without her headsails set. BALD-HEADED SCHOONER, see RAM SCHOONER.

BALEEN, the proper name for whalebone which consists of the plates in the mouth of the baleen whale (*Mystacoceti*) whose marginal bristles trap the small marine organisms which form the animal's food. During the 19th century baleen had considerable industrial value, particularly in corsetry, because of its flexibility, springiness, and strength.

BALINGER, a small, sea-going sailing vessel, without a forecastle and carrying either a square sail or a sail extended by a *sprit on a single mast, used in the 15th and 16th centuries mainly for coastal trade, but sometimes as transports carrying about forty soldiers.

BALK, an old term for naval timber, imported in roughly squared beams from Baltic countries. It is the origin of the present-day term 'baulk' used when describing timber.

BALL, Sir ALEXANDER JOHN (1757–1809), British rear admiral, was one of the 'band of brothers' which Admiral *Nelson formed around himself during the Mediterranean campaign of 1798–9. Ball was captain of the *ship of the line *Alexander* in this campaign and in May 1798 saved the fleet flagship, the *Vanguard*, from almost certain destruction by towing her to safety after she had been dismasted in a heavy storm and was being forced by the wind on rocks off the coast of Sardinia. During the battle of the *Nile the *Alexander* engaged the 120-gun French flagship *Orient*, and after that successful action Ball was sent by Nelson, with the *Audacious, Goliath*, and *Emerald* in company, to organize the blockade of *Malta and its subsequent capture. After the surrender of Malta he served for a short period as a navy commissioner at Gibraltar, returning to Malta to become its first British governor, a post he held until his death eight years later.

BALLAST, additional weight carried in a ship to give her stability and/or to provide a satisfactory trim fore and aft. In very small vessels the ballast is usually in the form of pigs of soft iron which are stowed as low as possible on the *floors; larger vessels either use water as ballast by flooding tanks on board or they take stone or gravel temporarily on board as ballast in the holds. IN BALLAST, the condition of a cargo vessel which has discharged her cargo and taken on ballast to stabilize and trim her while sailing empty, or light, to the port where she is next to take on cargo. Sailing vessels insufficiently ballasted are said to be *crank.

Most racing and cruising yachts carry ballast externally in the shape of lead or cast iron formed into a *keel. See BALLAST KEEL. Cruising yachts, however, may carry some ballast internally, in addition to the ballast keel, because by distributing the ballast, instead of concentrating it in a ballast keel, designers can obtain advantages such as an easier motion in a seaway.

BALLAST KEEL, the *keel of a yacht shaped from the ballast, usually lead or cast iron, which the yacht needs to carry to give her stability under sail. By this means her ballast is carried externally with its centre of gravity as low as possible and the inside of her hull left clear and unencumbered. Racing yachts especially rely on ballast keels rather than internal ballast to give them stability when carrying the maximum sail area.

BALLAST TANKS, external or internal tanks fitted in *submarines. They are of two types, main and auxiliary. Main ballast tanks, fitted either internally within the submarine's pressure hull, or externally in the form of blisters outside the main hull, when flooded with seawater, destroy the positive buoyancy of the vessel and thus enable it to submerge. When they are emptied, by blowing the seawater out by air pressure, positive buoyancy is restored and the submarine rises to the surface. Their only function is to destroy or restore the submarine's positive buoyancy so that she may dive or surface at will. They are normally completely full or completely empty, according to whether the submarine is submerged or on the surface, but in non-nuclear submarines in wartime, a submarine on the surface might have her main ballast tanks partially filled in order to reduce her silhouette and to enable her to dive more quickly if surprised on the surface. When in this condition, a submarine is said to be 'trimmed-down'.

Auxiliary ballast tanks are situated within the pressure hull of a submarine. Their function is to allow the submarine to be trimmed when submerged so that she is in a state of equilibrium with neither positive nor negative buoyancy. The weight of water in each of them is adjustable, either by admitting more from the sea or by pumping some out into the sea. As they are spaced longitudinally in the hull, a correct balance can be achieved to keep the submarine stable horizontally.

Most surface ships also have tanks distributed for use in a similar way to correct or alter the trim of the ship. They are, however, usually known as trimming tanks, not ballast tanks.

BALLENY, JOHN (*fl.* 1838–9), a British sealing captain who in 1838 was commissioned by Messrs. Samuel Enderby and other London merchants to search for new sealing grounds in Antarctic waters. Sailing with the cutter *Sabrina* and the schooner *Eliza Scott* he discovered in 1839 the Balleny Islands and the Sabrina coast of Antarctica, thus proving for the first time the existence of land within the Antarctic circle south of New Zealand.

BALSA, originally a raft or float used chiefly for fishing in coastal waters off the Pacific coast of South America. It consisted usually of two cylinders of a certain wood, which has great buoyancy, but there were some used which employed two inflated floats made of the skins of seawolves, with a platform between them. The wood, and the tree from which it comes (*Ochroma lagopus*), are known as 'balsa' from their use for this type of raft. A similarly constructed raft, colloquially known as a copperpunt, is still used in many dockyards for work on a ship's hull, particularly for painting in the waterline. Balsa wood was used for the well-known raft *Kon-Tiki*.

BALTIC SEA, in German and Swedish *Ostsee* and in Russian *Baltiyskoe Morye*, the inland sea lying to the north of Germany and Russia and the south of Finland and Sweden, approximately between the latitudes of 54° N. and 66° N. and the longitudes of 9° E. and 30° E. Its only connection with the outer seas is by three narrow channels between Sweden and the Danish islands, the Sound, the Great Belt, and the Little Belt, which lead into the Kattegat and Skagerrak and thus into the North Sea.

In early days the Baltic Sea owed its importance to the fact that it was the centre of the great European herring fishery, a state of affairs that existed until about the 14th–15th centuries when the herring migrated into the North Sea, possibly because of the lack of salinity in Baltic waters. Later, during the expansion of sail shipping in the 17th, 18th, and early 19th centuries, it became equally important as the world's main source of supply of masts, flax, and tar, used in shipbuilding and sail-making. Its importance as a trading centre died in this respect as the iron ship with steam propulsion replaced the sailing vessel as the means of ocean travel and trade.

Because of its narrow connection with the outer oceans and of the many rivers which drain into it, the water of the Baltic is much less salt than is normal seawater; and because it is cut off from the warm *Gulf Stream, large areas are frozen over every winter. Like the Mediterranean, and for the same reason, it is virtually tideless. It has been estimated that the area covered by the Baltic Sea is 166,397 square miles and its mean depth 36 fathoms, shallow in comparison with other seas of comparable size.

BALTIMORE, a major seaport on the east coast of the U.S.A., at the head of the tidal waters of the Patapsco river in the State of Maryland. The city was named after the Lords Baltimore, who founded the province of Maryland. It was here that Francis Scott Key composed the *Star Spangled Banner* in 1814 during an attack by British naval vessels on Fort McHenry, which guards the town. Its fine harbour handles an immense amount of traffic, mainly of manufactured goods, of which Baltimore itself is one of the main centres in the U.S.A.

During the late 18th century the port gave its name to the 'Baltimore *clippers', which were sail trading vessels although not now regarded as true clippers. Nevertheless the vessel which is often accepted as the first of the real clippers, the *Ann McKim* of 1832, was built at and traded from Baltimore.

BANCROFT, GEORGE (1800–91), American historian and diplomat, established the U.S. Naval Academy at Annapolis in 1845 while he was serving as Secretary of the Navy. Born in Worcester, Mass., he was educated at Harvard and in Germany, where he studied on a Harvard scholarship. He became the Secretary of the Navy in the cabinet of President Polk on 11 March 1845 and held that position until 9 September 1846. By 1850, he was generally recognized as the leading American historian.

BANDIERA, ATTILIO (1811–44) and **EMILIO** (1819–44), Italian brothers and patriots, were the sons of Admiral Baron Bandiera, and, like their father, were officers in the Austrian Navy. Being fervent supporters of Italian unity, they decided to make a raid on the Calabrian coast, being much encouraged by Mazzini, the great Italian liberator, and also by reports that the populace of the kingdom of Naples were ready to rise *en masse* at the first appearance of a leader. With twenty followers they landed at Cotrone on 16 June 1844, but were betrayed by one of their followers and also by some peasants who mistook them for Turkish pirates. They were captured and shot.

BANJO, the name given to the brass frame in which, in the early screw-driven ships, the *propeller worked. In those early days of steam propulsion no ship engaged on ocean passages carried enough *bunkers to accommodate all the fuel required for such a passage and had therefore to rely on her sails for the greater part of her voyage, her engine and screw acting only as an auxiliary means of propulsion when the wind failed. As a propeller would act as a drag stopping the ship's way through the water when under sail, it was fitted in a frame which could be hoisted within the hull when it was not required to drive the ship. This frame, the banjo, worked in a well between slides fixed to the inner and outer * sternposts. See also 'UP FUNNEL, DOWN SCREW'.

BANKER, the old name for a fishing vessel employed exclusively in the great cod-fishery on the * Grand Banks off Newfoundland.

BANKS, Sir JOSEPH (1743–1820), British naturalist, after inheriting an enormous fortune from his father, accompanied Captain James * Cook on his first voyage of circumnavigation, fitting out the * *Endeavour* at his own expense and taking with him a number of assistants, including Dr. Daniel Solander, to catalogue and delineate the flora and fauna discovered during the expedition. He had hoped to accompany Cook on his second voyage, but was unable to do so, though he had arranged for many of his assistants to be embarked. These now accompanied him in a voyage to Iceland. In 1778 he became President of the Royal Society.

BANTRY BAY, a small seaport in Co. Cork, Eire, was the scene of the French attempts to invade Ireland in 1689 and 1796 and of the landing of the troops of William of Orange in 1697. It was also to have been the destination of the unsuccessful attempt by Germany to run guns into Ireland in 1916 to support the Easter rising. Since the Second World War it has been developed as a major oil port.

BANYAN DAYS were meatless days in the diet of seamen in the English Navy, so called from the name of Hindu merchants noted for their abstinence from eating flesh. The custom was introduced during the reign of Queen Elizabeth I to economize on the cost of meat, fish or cheese being issued on banyan days in place of salt meat.

BARACUDA, sometimes written as **BARRACUDA,** a tropical fish, *Sphyraena baracuda*, particularly known for its fierceness and whose bite at certain times is poisonous. It is however eaten in the West Indies where its colloquial name is sea-salmon. It was also the name given to a carrier-borne bomber aircraft in the British Navy in the Second World War.

BARBAROSSA, the name by which the sons and grandson of Yakub of Mitylene, a coasting

Barbarossa

captain and trader, were generally known by Christians during the 16th century. Of his four sons, AROUJ, KHIZR, ELIAS, and ISAAK, the two former took to sea-roving and soon became feared throughout the Mediterranean for the ferocity of their attacks on both Christian shipping and the native African princes, being given the titles of 'admiral' among the * Barbary pirates. Both were heavily bearded with red hair, which probably accounts for the name Barbarossa, but Khizr was also known as Khair-ed-Din, a name which struck even greater terror in many Christian hearts though earning for him a reputation as a great hero throughout Islam. For about thirty-five years, from 1510 to 1545–6, the brothers engaged in almost continuous warfare, alternating their attacks on African states with descents on the Spanish or Italian coasts and the harrying of shipping in the Mediterranean. From time to time they owed allegiance to the Deys of Algiers and Tunis, but as often as not operated on their own account, burning, pillaging, and murdering as they went. Arouj was eventually killed by Spanish troops at the Rio Salado, but Khair-ed-Din lived until 1547, his last exploit being a plundering expedition to the coast of Italy in 1544. With his vast riches gained as a corsair he built a large palace at Constantinople, and was there when he died. His son HASSAN, also known as Barbarossa, was a corsair like his father, but he confined his operations mostly to the Levant and was not so terrifying a figure in Christian eyes, though his reputation as his father's son was often enough to suppress disorders along the North African coast as and when required.

BARBARY PIRATES, generations of * corsairs who operated from the coast of northern Africa, notorious for their ferocity and the skill with which they handled their piratical ventures. The name Barbary comes from the Berber tribes who occupied most of this coast. Originally under Turkish suzerainty, the African coastal towns from which the corsairs operated, mainly Tripoli, Tunis, Algiers, Bône, and Salli, broke free of Turkish rule in the mid-17th century and became military republics, choosing their own governors and living by plunder. Although piracy on this coast had existed more or less permanently from the time of the decline of Roman power, it reached its zenith in the years following the conquest of Granada by the Catholic forces of Spain, which drove many Moors living there into exile, and thus ever-ready to revenge themselves on Christianity in general and Spain in particular. Originally conducted in oared galleys rowed by slaves, this Mediterranean piracy reached a peak in the 17th century when a Flemish renegade, named Simon Danser, introduced to the corsairs the sailing ship, and so hugely increased the range of their operations. With such ships the Barbary pirates were able to stretch out into the Atlantic, and in fact were seen as far away as Iceland. In 1631 they sacked the town of Baltimore in Ireland and carried off most of the population who were sold in the slave market in Algiers. Indeed, the sale of slaves was one of the most lucrative aspects of this piracy, and during the first half of the 17th century more than 20,000 Christian slaves were sold in the market of Algiers alone, and as many more in Tunis.

This vast organization of piracy attracted many renegades from most European nations, dazzled by the ease with which fortunes could be made. One notorious such renegade was an Englishman named Verney, a member of the distinguished Buckinghamshire family of that name; another was a Fleming, who took the Arabic name of Murad Reis and became famous as one of the most successful and savage of the corsairs. It was he who led the pirates to Baltimore in 1631.

Piracy off the Barbary Coast declined during the 18th century, except for sporadic outbreaks, but was not completely eliminated until the French conquest of Algiers in 1830. Many naval expeditions against the pirate centres had been carried out by various European nations from the 17th century onwards, but none was completely successful in stamping it out for more than a year or two. The more notable of these were the British expedition under Admiral * Blake in 1655, several during the reign of Charles II (1660–85) in conjunction with the Dutch, two French expeditions in 1682 and 1683, American operations in 1801–5 and 1815, a combined British–Dutch expedition in 1816, and finally a successful French attack in 1830 in which Algiers was captured and Algeria annexed by France. See also BARBAROSSA.

BARBETTE, the inside fixed trunk of a modern gun-mounting in a warship on which the turret revolves. It contains the shell and cordite hoists from the * shell-room and * magazine. It was originally the name given to a raised platform on the deck of a warship protected by armour on the sides, on which heavy guns were mounted, firing over the armour.

BARCA-LONGA, from the Italian *barca*, a * skiff or * barge, a large fishing boat particular to Spain in the 17th to 19th centuries, with two or three masts each carrying a single * lugsail. They were built up to an overall length of about 70 feet (21·3 m) and had a keel of about 6 inches (0·15 m) extending the whole length of the hull. The word was also sometimes written as barqualonga or barcolongo.

BARCAROLLE or **BARCAROLE,** originally the name given to songs sung by the Venetian *barcaruoli* while rowing their gondolas, but the meaning has been extended to cover any song reminiscent of the original Venetian barcarolle, which normally had a slow tempo and most often a sad or doleful air.

BARCARUOLO, an Italian boatman, particularly attributed to Venice and its gondolas but the term was also sometimes used for boatmen plying for hire in other Italian ports. The word dates from the early 17th century.

BARCELONA, the principal seaport of Spain, situated on the eastern coast in the Mediterranean. The town, originally named Barcino, was according to tradition founded by the Carthaginian Hamilcar Barca in the 3rd century B.C. It was a Roman colony under the name of Julia Faventia. With the union of Catalonia and Aragon in 1149 it developed rapidly as one of the greatest ports in the Mediterranean, and in 1258 was accorded the singular honour of instituting a code of maritime law, known as the *Consulado del Mar*, or * *Consulate of the Sea*, which was widely recognized and accepted by many European nations. It also achieved fame in being one of the first seaports in Europe to introduce a system of marine insurance. Today it is a modern port with repair and shipbuilding yards, a port of call for many shipping lines, and handles a substantial volume of import and export traffic. Within the city is a famous school of navigation and also the * Museo Maritimo, particularly notable for a famous collection devoted to the history of navigation.

BARE BOAT CHARTER, sometimes known as BARE HULL or BARE POLE CHARTER, is one in which a ship is chartered without her crew and with a minimum of restrictions as to her employment by the charterer.

BARE POLES, the condition of a ship when, in a severe storm, all her canvas has had to be taken in because of the fierceness of the wind. A ship can attempt to *lie a-try under bare poles, though she will do so better under a *mizen *topsail or *trysail, or can *scud under bare poles before the wind, very often a hazardous undertaking if there is a high sea running.

BARENTS, WILLEM (c. 1550–97), Dutch navigator and explorer, was born about the middle of the 16th century on the island of Terschelling. A Spanish decree forbidding the Netherlands to trade with Portugal turned the eyes of the Dutch towards the discovery of a route to India to the north of Russia and in 1594 Barents, with two ships, sailed from Amsterdam with this object. He reached the coast of Novaya Zemlya and followed it northward until ice impeded further progress. The following year he repeated the attempt with seven ships but they failed to reach the Kara Sea, being held up by ice off Vaygach Island. On a third voyage undertaken with two ships in 1596 during which he sighted Spitsbergen and Bear Island, the two ships separated, Barents making for the north point of Novaya Zemlya, which this time he succeeded in rounding before being beset by ice and compelled to winter there. The following spring, as the ship was still held fast, it was decided to abandon her. This was done in two open boats, but Barents, already suffering from the hardships of an Arctic winter, died seven days later, on 20 June. Part of his journal was found four years later, but it was not until 1871 that his headquarters on Novaya Zemlya were discovered and the contents removed to The Hague. His name is perpetuated by the sea to the eastward of the North Cape which is named after him.

BARFLEUR, a naval battle of the War of the League of Augsburg, was fought between an Anglo-Dutch fleet and a French fleet on 19–22 May 1692, but was not finally brought to a successful conclusion until the 24th in the Bay of La Hougue. The action began in the morning of the 19th but the wind soon dropped. Fighting was hottest in the centre and the French flagship, the *Soleil Royal*, of 102 guns, was seen to be towing off to windward with her sails and rigging badly damaged. A thick fog came down two hours later which caused much confusion on both sides while it lasted, but when the weather cleared a partial renewal of the battle ensued

until the fog settled down again and both fleets anchored for the night. On the following morning the fog lifted and a *general chase was ordered by the allied commander. The wind, however, remained light and both fleets anchored when the tide turned against them.

The chase was continued on the 21st and the French admiral, the Comte de *Tourville, shifted his flag to the *Ambitieux* (92 guns) and the *Soleil Royal* eventually went ashore near Cherbourg. Towards evening a number of French ships were seen entering the Bay of La Hougue, and that night the allies anchored outside.

On the morning of the 22nd Vice Admiral Sir Ralph *Delavall, with ships of the English Red Squadron, attacked the French ships in Cherbourg Bay and burnt the *Soleil Royal*, *Triomphant* (74 guns), and *Admirable* (90 guns). The main body of the Anglo-Dutch fleet was occupied in working into the Bay of La Hougue, where the French ships had taken refuge. Twenty other French ships, chased by Admiral Sir John Ashby (Blue Squadron) and some Dutch ships, ran through the Race of Alderney and got safely into St. Malo; a few others also escaped to the eastward.

The following day Rear Admiral Sir Clowdisley *Shovel, leading the Red Squadron, had been ordered to destroy the ships at anchor at La Hougue, but he was incapacitated by a splinter wound in the thigh and his place was taken by Vice Admiral George *Rooke (Blue Squadron). The boats and fireships were sent in and six French ships were burnt that night. In places the English and Dutch boats were working in such shallow water that the French cavalry were able to ride right down among them, several of the troopers being pulled off their horses by the seamen with their boathooks. On the English side there was very little loss. The next morning the boats were sent in again and the remaining French men-of-war, as well as their transports and storeships, were all destroyed by fire.

BARGE, probably from the Latin *barca*, which would make it the equivalent of *bark or barque. In its oldest use, **(1)** this is probably the case as it was the name given to a small sea-going ship with sails, next in size above a *balinger. From about the 17th century onwards, the names barge and bark diverged into separate meanings.

(2) A ceremonial state vessel, richly decorated and propelled by rowers, used on state occasions and for river processions. Such was Cleopatra's barge described by Shakespeare in *Antony and Cleopatra* (Act II, sc. 2), which

... like a burnished throne
Burn'd on the water: the poop was beaten gold;
Purple the sails, and so perfumed, that

State barge of the Stationers' Company; etching by E. W. Cooke, 1829

The winds were love-sick with them: the oars
    were silver;
Which to the tune of flutes kept stroke, and
    made
The water, which they beat, to follow faster,
As amorous of their strokes . . .

Cleopatra's was probably carried a bit to extremes, but most state barges were immensely ornate even if their oars were not of silver but of wood. Shakespeare must have seen such barges on the Thames in Elizabethan times, and they continued in use down to the 19th century. A modern derivative of the barge in this meaning is an admiral's barge, originally a small steam boat, but today a motorboat used by flag officers for harbour transport.

(3) A large flat-bottomed coastal trading vessel having a large *spritsail and jib-headed topsail, a fore *staysail, and a very small *mizen; occasionally a jib is set on the *bowsprit. They are fitted with *leeboards in place of a keel so that they can operate without difficulty in shoal water. The absence of a keel permits them to operate effectively in shallow water and to remain upright when they are grounded. Normally the mast, which is *stepped on deck, is held in a *lutchet, a type of *tabernacle, so that it can be lowered to deck level when passing under bridges, etc. This type of barge is normally only found in the River Thames and on the south-east coast of England, and is used for the coastal transport of freight. A dumb barge is the hull of a barge, without means of self propulsion, used for the carriage of cargo from ship to shore or vice-versa in tow of a tug. It is more properly called a lighter.

(4) In past days, the second boat of a warship, a double-banked pulling boat with fourteen oars; more recently the largest boat of a battleship, with mast, sails, and a drop keel but also fitted for pulling fourteen oars.

(5) In the U.S.A., a double-decked vessel without sails or power, for carrying passengers and freight, towed by a steamboat. This is obsolete.

(6) The name given on board ship to the wooden dish in which bread or biscuit is placed on a mess table.

BARGEE, a man or boy who works as a hand on a trading *barge. Those who rowed the state barges were known as rowers, and never as bargees.

BARHAM, Admiral Lord, see MIDDLETON, Charles.

BARK, from the Latin *barca*, and now synonymous with *barque. Originally a general term to describe any small sailing ship of any rig. See also BARGE.

BARNACLE, a small shellfish, *Lepas anatifera*, which sticks by its pedicle to the bottoms of ships. They do no harm beyond slowing a ship down because of the additional friction caused by their irregularity. In the old days they were thought by many people to turn eventually into geese, hence the name barnacle goose, and in some papers published by the Royal Society of London in its early days, the process is actually described. The origin of this odd belief may lie in the fact that their foot is long and pectinated like a feather.

BARNEY, JOSHUA (1759–1818), American naval officer, was born in Baltimore, Maryland. He went to sea when he was 12 and showed exceptional ability when command of a merchantman devolved on him at the age of 15. He was the sailing master of the *Hornet*, in the squadron of Esek *Hopkins, and had a part in the capture of New Providence Island. He was commissioned a lieutenant in June 1776 and served in the sloops *Wasp* and *Sachem*. He was exchanged after being captured, and became first lieutenant of the *Virginia*, in which he was captured for the second time. He was first lieutenant of the *Saratoga* when captured for the third time, escaped once, was recaptured and sent to Mill Prison, near Plymouth, England. Escaping again he managed to get to France and finally reached Boston in December 1781.

When the Congress authorized the construction of six frigates, in 1794, as a consequence of Algerine seizures of American shipping, President Washington nominated Barney to be one of the original six captains of the U.S. Navy. He was ranked fourth among the nominees, but declined the appointment because of his jealousy of Silas Talbot who was ranked third. He then served for six years, 1796–1802, in the French Navy.

On the outbreak of the War of 1812, Barney sailed from Baltimore in the *privateer *Rossie*. In a period of ninety days he captured, sank, or otherwise destroyed eighteen enemy merchant vessels and took 217 prisoners. The value of the ships and cargoes captured and destroyed was about $1,500,000, but the expense of the cruise and the high duties on prize cargoes left relatively little *prize money for Barney or his officers and men. On 25 April 1814 he was given a captain's commission in the U.S. Navy. He was assigned to duty in Chesapeake Bay but his total force was only three gunboats and ten pulling barges, with about 500 men. He was compelled to burn these small vessels in the Patuxent River, near Upper Marlborough, to prevent them falling into the hands of the British, and he then marched towards Washington. He distinguished himself by his cool and determined stand at Bladensburg with his sailors and a small force of marines. The British troops advancing towards Washington were veterans who had served under Wellington in Spain, and they drove Barney from his position by outflanking him after the raw militia had fled, he himself being wounded and captured.

BARQUE, or **BARK,** a sailing vessel with three masts, square-rigged on the fore and main and

Four-masted barque

fore-and-aft rigged on the * mizen. (See diagrams of rigs, under RIG.) Until the mid-19th century, barques were relatively small sailing ships, but later were built up to about 3,000 tons, particularly for the grain and nitrate trade to South American ports round Cape Horn. Four-masted and even five-masted barques were later built for this trade, ranging up to about 5,000 tons. See also FRANCE, JACKASS-BARQUE. Barques are now obsolete as trading vessels, though there may be one or two small ones still used for inter-island trade in the Pacific, but several of the larger ones are still retained in commission as sail training ships while others have been preserved in many countries as museum ships and examples of the great days of sail. In the U.S.A. the term is always bark, never barque.

BARQUENTINE, occasionally **BARKEN-TEEN,** a vessel resembling a * barque but square-rigged on the foremast only, main and * mizen being fore-and-aft rigged. (See diagrams of rigs, under RIG.)

'BARRACK STANCHION', said of a naval officer or rating who spends long periods of his service in barracks or a shore establishment and seldom serves at sea.

BARRATRY, any fraudulent act on the part of the * master or crew of a ship committed to the prejudice of her owners or underwriters, such as deliberately casting her away, deserting her, selling her, or even diverting her from her proper course with evil intent.

BARRICADE, a rail supported by posts across the forward end of the * quarterdeck of a sailing man-of-war, the spaces between the posts being filled before going into action with rope mats or spare cable, and with nettings above the rail for the stowage of hammocks. The purpose of the barricade was to provide protection for those whose action station was on the quarterdeck from small arms fire from enemy ships.

BARRICADO, an old naval term of the 17th century for a tender, a small oared or sailing boat which attended warships in harbour as an odd-job boat. It was usually civilian or dockyard manned and not one of a warship's boats.

BARRICO (pron. breaker), a small cask which was designed for use in ships' boats, filled with fresh water and kept permanently in the boat for survival purposes in the event of the boat being used as a lifeboat in cases of shipwreck, etc. It is also known as a * breaker, but barrico is the more ancient word, having been in maritime use since the 16th century.

BARRIER REEF, a protective reef of coral formed offshore along a length of coast or encircling smaller islands, in each case being separated from the land by a channel of navigable water. The most notable example is the Great Barrier Reef which stretches for 1,200 miles along the north-east coast of Australia opposite Queensland; there are others in the Bermudas and other groups of islands mainly in tropical waters. They are caused by the rapid growth in seawater of coral which builds up into a ridge at sea level.

BARRON, JAMES (1768–1851), American naval officer, achieved a good deal of notoriety over the 'Chesapeake affair', one of the more publicized incidents which led to war between Britain and the U.S.A. in 1812.

He had entered the U.S. Navy as a lieutenant in 1798 and had served under John * Barry in the frigate * *United States*, being recommended for promotion. With the rank of captain he commanded the frigates * *Essex* and * *President* in the Mediterranean, but his conduct was called into question on the ground that he spent too much time in Italian ports. Nevertheless, in 1807 he was selected to command the Mediterranean Squadron and sailed from Hampton Roads in his flagship * *Chesapeake*. When east of Cape Henry he was stopped by the British frigate *Leopard* with a demand for the return of three alleged British deserters. On his refusal to hand the men over, the *Leopard* opened fire, and Barron, unable to clear the *Chesapeake* for action as her decks were still littered with stores, tried to surrender his ship. Any form of surrender was refused by the British ship, and the *Leopard* sailed away after removing a number of men alleged to be British deserters. The *Chesapeake*, slightly damaged as a result of the action, returned to Hampton Roads.

Barron was tried by court martial on a charge of cowardice, but was convicted only on the charge of neglecting to clear his ship for action. He had, in fact, reported her as ready for sea twenty-one days before she sailed. He was sentenced to be suspended for five years, during which time he served in the French Navy. On his return to the U.S.A. he applied for a new appointment at sea, but was refused. Barron then made charges that Stephen * Decatur, who was an officer junior to him, had borne false witness against him at his court martial, and challenged him to a duel. Unwisely Decatur was taunted into accepting the challenge against the advice of many senior officers. The duel took place at Bladensburg on 22 March 1820 and Decatur was mortally wounded by Barron, who himself suffered a wound in the thigh. See also BAINBRIDGE, William.

BARROW, Sir JOHN (1764–1848), British statesman and for forty years second secretary (the equivalent of today's permanent secretary) at the Admiralty, was born in the small Lancashire village of Dragley Beck, near Ulverston. His first employment was as superintending clerk in an iron foundry in Liverpool, but later he moved to Greenwich where he taught mathematics. Among his pupils was the son of Sir George Staunton, and through Staunton's interest he was attached to the British Embassy, which was being established in China, as comptroller of the Ambassador's (Lord Macartney's) household. He travelled widely throughout the country, learned the language, and became a recognized authority on China, frequently being consulted by the British government on Chinese affairs.

When Lord Macartney was sent to South Africa in 1797 to settle the government of the newly acquired colony of the Cape of Good Hope, he took Barrow with him as his personal secretary. The first task entrusted to him was the reconciliation of the Boers and Kaffirs. This took him the length and breadth of the new colony, and his reports on the state of the country were models of conciseness and wisdom. On his return to Cape Town he was appointed auditor-general. He was so taken with the new colony that he decided to settle there permanently, married the daughter (Anne Tzuter) of a Boer, and bought a house in Cape Town. His residence in the Cape, however, came to an abrupt end when, under the terms of the Peace of Amiens (1801), the Cape of Good Hope was returned to the Dutch.

On his return to England he was appointed second secretary of the Admiralty by Lord Melville and held the post for the next forty years, serving eleven First Lords throughout that period. He was greatly trusted by them all and his wise counsel did much to ease the strain caused in the Royal Navy by the rapid run-down of ships and men after the end of the Napoleonic War (1803–15). He retired in 1845.

During his Admiralty service he found time to become a biographer of considerable repute. He had already made something of a literary reputation in articles he contributed to the *Quarterly Review* during and after his visit to China; he now wrote lives of Lord Macartney, published in 1807, Admiral Lord * Howe (1837), and Admiral Lord *Anson (1839). Other notable books published during this period were accounts of his travels in China and South Africa.

While at the Admiralty he had taken a great interest in Arctic exploration and had promoted a number of voyages of discovery in these regions, including that of Sir John * Franklin. After his retirement he wrote a history of modern Arctic voyages which was published in 1846, followed by his autobiography in 1847.

He died full of honours. He had been elected a fellow of the Royal Society and Doctor of Literature at Edinburgh University in 1821. In 1835 he was made a baronet. He was particularly admired by King * William IV, whom he served when William, as Duke of Clarence, was appointed * Lord High Admiral in 1827–8, and on his accession to the throne William expressed his admiration of Barrow's long Admiralty service by many tokens of his personal esteem.

BARRY, JOHN (*c.* 1745–1803), American naval officer, was born in Co. Wexford, Ireland. Going to sea as a boy, he seems to have regarded Philadelphia as his home from 1760 onward. At the age of 21 he was a merchant shipmaster and in 1774 commanded the new ship *Black Prince* which was taken up by Congress on the outbreak of the war of American Independence and fitted out as a warship, renamed *Alfred*, and became the flagship of Esek * Hopkins.

On 14 March 1776 Barry was commissioned a captain and given command of the * Continental * brigantine *Lexington.* Off Cape Charles, Virginia, on 7 April, after a running fight lasting almost an hour, he captured the * sloop *Edward*, a tender to the British * frigate *Liverpool*, which became the first prize brought into the port of Philadelphia. After a short period ashore serving with the Pennsylvania militia, Barry was given command of the frigate *Raleigh*, but she was driven ashore and captured by the British ships *Experiment* and *Unicorn* in September 1778. His next command was the frigate * *Alliance* and in her, in September 1782, he learned from a captured prize that a homeward-bound British convoy of eighty-eight ships had been scattered by an exceptionally severe storm. He captured four ships from the convoy and being then in mid-Atlantic, short of water and filled with prisoners, determined to go to France. On his return to Martinique, he found orders to proceed to Havana to take in specie for Congress and return to Philadelphia. At Havana he joined forces with the converted vessel *Duc de Lauzun* with 72,000 Spanish dollars already on board, and the two ships sailed on 6 March 1783. Four days later, 90 miles south of Cape Canaveral, Barry sighted three British ships. Shots were exchanged at long range, but Barry was able to close the British frigate *Sybil* and his first broadside brought down her foretopmast. The *Alliance* continued firing as rapidly as possible and the *Sybil* drew off after 40 minutes. This was the last action of the Continental Navy before the declaration of peace.

On 4 June 1794 President Washington nominated six captains for the new U.S. Navy, and Barry was named as the senior. He superintended the construction of the frigate * *United*

States and commanded her during the naval war with France, 1798–1801. He died in 1803 having been the senior officer of the U.S. Navy since its inception.

W. Bell Clark, *Gallant John Barry* (1938).
J. Gurn, *Commodore John Barry* (New York, 1933).

BART, JEAN (1650–1702), French naval officer, was a native of Dunkirk and, like many seamen from that port, distinguished himself chiefly as a *corsair and commerce raider. Going to sea as a boy, he first served in 1666–7 under the Dutch admiral de *Ruyter and had his first experience of battle during the Second Dutch War (1665–7) before entering the French Navy. In 1689 he was captured by English ships while escorting a *convoy off the Casquets and was briefly imprisoned at Plymouth. He managed to escape and was promoted to captain on his return to France.

His most successful attack on commerce occurred in 1696 when he captured half of a large Dutch convoy. He had been ennobled by Louis XIV in 1694 and in 1697 was promoted *chef d'escadre*, the equivalent rank of commodore in other navies. His name has been commemorated in the French Navy by naming some of the largest and most important ships after him, including one of the last French battleships, of 35,000 tons, still incomplete at the time of the surrender of France to the Germans in 1940.

'BARTIMEUS', see RITCHIE, Sir Lewis.

BASILISK, an old name for the long 48-pounder gun used in the British Navy in the 17th, 18th, and early 19th centuries, so-called from the snakes and dragons which were sculptured on it in place of the more usual dolphins. Sir William *Monson describes the gun in his *Naval Tracts* and gives its range as 3,000 paces. See also GUNS, NAVAL.

BASQUE ROADS, THE BATTLE OF, was fought on 11–12 April 1809 between British and French squadrons during the Napoleonic War (1803–15). A French squadron of eight *ships of the line had slipped out of Brest and, evading a watching British force under Admiral Lord *Gambier, had anchored in Aix Roads preparing to sail for the West Indies. Captain Lord *Cochrane was selected by the Admiralty to lead a group of *fireships against them as they lay protected by a stout triangular boom; they were also anchored with *springs on their cables so as to present the smallest possible target. Cochrane led the attacking forces in on the night of 11 April. The first fireship succeeded in breaking the boom, whereupon the French ships cut their cables and all but two ran ashore. Gambier, with some show of reluctance, took his fleet into the Roads to complete the destruction, but only three of the French ships were taken and burned and a British East Indiaman was recaptured, though later it blew up. Cochrane opposed a Parliamentary vote of thanks to Lord Gambier because of the excessive caution he had shown, an action which did much to ruin his, Cochrane's, naval career.

BASS, GEORGE (1771–c. 1802), English naval surgeon, naturalist, and explorer, sailed in 1795 for New South Wales as surgeon in H.M.S. *Reliance* in which Matthew *Flinders was also serving as a midshipman. On arrival at Port Jackson (Sydney), the two young men got permission to undertake a coastal survey southwards in what is described as an 'eight-foot' boat, which they named *Tom Thumb*, with Bass's boy servant as crew. This first trip was of only eight days' duration but so successful was the resulting survey that in March 1796 the two men encouraged to make a second similar but longer voyage for which the same small boat was used. In spite of many perils and hardships, they were able to make remarkably accurate surveys of the coastline to the south of Port Jackson.

Bass's next nautical exploit was made without Flinders while the *Reliance* was being refitted. The excellence of his work was recognized by Governor Hunter of New South Wales who supplied him with a whaleboat in which, manned by six seamen from the *Reliance*, he sailed south from Port Jackson on 3 December 1797. Rounding Cape Howe, Bass explored the Australian coast as far as Western Port, which he discovered. From the evidence of the heavy swell from the west which he encountered, he deduced the existence of the strait between Van Diemen's Land (now Tasmania) and Australia which bears his name and which had previously been believed to be only a deep inlet.

Eight months later Flinders was given command by the Governor of the 25-ton sloop *Norfolk* and, in company with Bass, sailed along the north coast of Tasmania, reaching the northwest corner of the island on 9 December 1798 and then sailing on to complete its first circumnavigation. This was the first proof that Tasmania was an island, it having been previously thought to be a part of the mainland.

Bass returned to England sick in the following May and shortly afterwards left the naval service. He sailed again to Port Jackson at the end of 1800 but no records of his further existence have been discovered; he is believed to have died either in Peru or in the South Pacific in 1802.

BATCHELOR'S DELIGHT, the name given by a band of *buccaneers, led by John Cook, to a Danish ship of forty guns piratically captured in

1683 off the coast of Guinea. She was given her odd name presumably because the buccaneers exchanged their original ship at Sherbro, near Freetown, for sixty young black girls with whom they set sail for the Pacific. Cook died off the coast of Mexico and was succeeded in command by Edward Davis. After cruising unsuccessfully up and down the west coast of South America for several months, the buccaneers set off towards the East Indies, hoping to find more valuable prizes there. On the way they saw 'a small, low, sandy island and heard a great noise like that of the sea beating upon the shore right ahead of the ship'. Next morning they saw 'a range of high land, which we took to be islands'. It was this that was to be known as 'Davis's land', that William * Dampier thought 'might be the coast of * Terra Australis Incognita', and that Jacob * Roggeveen put forward as his objective in his voyage of discovery in 1721. There has never been any positive identification of 'Davis's land', but there is a possibility that it was in fact Easter Island.

BATEAU, sometimes **BATTEAU,** the French word for boat, but particularly the term used to describe the light river boats used by the French Canadians for transport on the Great Lakes and rivers. The term was also sometimes used to describe a * canoe.

BATELOE, a large wooden vessel with a crew of up to a dozen men, used on the river Madeira (widely known as the 'long cemetery') in Brazil to transport rubber from Bolivia to the Amazon, whence it is shipped abroad. They each carry about ten tons of latex, and are strongly constructed to withstand the dangers of the nineteen cataracts of the 250-mile stretch of the river between Guajare-Merim and San Antonio. Mortality among the crews of the bateloes was heavy, mainly from fevers.

BATHYSCAPHE, a small free moving submersible designed by Professor Auguste Piccard (1884–1962) for exploring the ocean depths. His first one, *F.R.N.S. I.* (Fonds/National à la Recherche Scientifique), was shaped like a balloon and consisted of a large tank containing petrol (sp. gr. 0·7) to provide buoyancy with an observation chamber suspended below it. The rate of descent and ascent was controlled by a number of iron pellets held in place by electromagnets. Slow movement in a horizontal direction was provided by electrically driven propellers. Defects which developed in the observation chamber during trials were rectified by the French Navy. A second bathyscaphe was subsequently constructed, named *F.R.N.S. II.* in which on 15 February 1954 Piccard reached a depth of 4,050 metres (13,284 ft). Meanwhile,

with Italian assistance, he had constructed another submersible named *Trieste I* in which the balloon shape was abandoned for that of a cylindrical tank beneath which was a spherical observation chamber. In 1958 the *Trieste I* was acquired by the U.S. Navy and, after extensive reconstruction, a depth of 11,000 metres (36,000 ft) was reached in the Guam Deep trench on 25 January 1960. The dimensions of the *Trieste* after reconstruction are, weight in air 84 tons, displacement 303 tons, length 23·9 m (78·6 ft), beam 4·6 m (15·3 ft). Propulsion is by three electrically-driven propellers to give a speed of two knots. Her complement is three.

BATHYSPHERE, a spherical steel vessel, 1·44 m (4 ft 9 in.) in diameter and 3·80 cm (1·5 in.) thick, weighing 2,270 kg (5,000 lb) and fitted with perspex windows, in which the designer, Charles William Beebe (1872–1962), an American zoologist, was lowered in 1934 to a depth of 923 m (3,028 ft), at that time a record for deep-sea diving. Subsequent developments in deep sea exploration resulted in the design of the * bathyscaphe.

BATTEN, (1) a thin iron bar which is used to secure the tarpaulin cover over a cargo hatch of a merchant ship. Several of them are used on each cover. When they have been placed in position and are held securely in place by wedges under the * batten-cleats, the hatches are said to be battened down. **(2)** A thin wooden or plastic strip which fits into a long, narrow pocket in the * leech of a * Bermuda mainsail in racing and cruising yachts to hold the leech out when sailing. The name is also given to the long, thin strips of bamboo which are inserted in * lateen sails to hold the form of the sail. These bamboo battens are also particularly used in the sails of * junks in Far Eastern waters.

BATTEN DOWN, to, the process of securing the openings in the * deck and sides of a vessel when heavy weather is forecast. A merchant vessel at sea will normally have the * hatches of her holds already battened down, though when exceptionally severe weather is expected these can be strengthened with strongbacks. In all ships when battening down, hatchways leading below deck, * scuttles, manholes, and other openings such as ventilators, etc., are all secured with steel covers either clipped down against a rubber watertight joint or, in the case of ventilation trunks, manholes, etc., usually with a circular plate screwed into the opening. In smaller craft, such as yachts, it is difficult to batten down effectively, except for fore hatches and scuttles, as the companionway to the saloon from the cockpit is normally closed only by wooden doors which cannot be made completely watertight.

The battle-cruiser H.M.S. Renown, *built 1916*

BATTENBERG, Prince LOUIS of, see MOUNT-BATTEN, Louis Alexander.

BATTEN-CLEATS, metal right-angled brackets welded on to the *coaming of cargo hatches in merchant vessels to hold the *battens which secure the watertight tarpaulin covering over the hatches. Wedges are driven in under the cleats to hold the battens firmly in position.

BATTLE HONOURS, the names of battles or individual ship actions in which a warship has taken part, usually displayed on a board in a prominent place in the ship as a source of pride in her name. Battle honours are hereditary, and a subsequent ship bearing the name usually displays the honours gained by her predecessors. This is a normal practice in all navies, though in the U.S. Navy they are known as battle stars.

BATTLE STARS, see BATTLE HONOURS.

BATTLE-CRUISER, a contemporary development of the *Dreadnought battleships pioneered in Britain. These ships were designed to function as advanced scouts of the battle-fleet, powerful enough to push home their reconnaissance even up to the battle-fleet of the enemy but also fast enough to outstrip it. They carried guns of the same size as the Dreadnought battleships but had a speed of some four knots faster, which was attained by cutting down the thickness of their armour protection. They were the brain-child of Admiral Sir John *Fisher, who was appointed First Sea Lord in the British Admiralty in 1904. He called them, in fact, fast armoured cruisers and it was some eight years later in 1912 that they were unhappily renamed generically as battle-cruisers, a description which may have tempted future fleet commanders to assume that they were designed to fight in the *line of battle in spite of their lack of protective armour. This assumption came about also in part as a result of Japanese practice; since Japan could not afford to build both battleships and battle-cruisers, their general battleship design became that of a glorified battle-cruiser, a hybrid vessel supposed to fulfil both roles.

The first battle-cruiser to be designed was H.M.S. *Invincible, a ship of 17,000 tons with a speed of $25\frac{1}{2}$ knots and carrying eight 12-inch guns; the first to be commissioned was her sister-ship the *Indomitable*, which in fact raced her down the launching *ways. Normal development once the type was established brought into being the *Lion*, flagship of Admiral *Beatty at

*Jutland and the best known of British battle-cruisers, and her sister-ship the *Tiger*, both of which had remarkable battle experience during the First World War (1914–18), and culminated shortly after that war in the building of the super-battle-cruiser *Hood*, of 42,000 tons and carrying eight 15-inch guns. She was eventually sunk in action against the German battleship *Bismarck* in 1941, a last bitter reminder that a thinly armoured ship is no match for one protected with adequate armour. The *Hood* was the last battle-cruiser built for the British Navy.

The fundamental weakness of the design was their lack of protective armour, particularly horizontal armour over the decks, and their inability to stand up to the punishment of heavy gunfire from battleships in spite of their carrying guns of equal calibre. The function designed for them by their 'onlie begetter', Sir John Fisher, was a valid one in the conditions of naval warfare of his day; their relative failure in action was the result of their misuse by subsequent fleet commanders. They ceased to have any relevance in naval battle when reconnaissance by naval aircraft, which could perform their task more economically and efficiently, became a reality between the two world wars.

BATTLESHIP, the modern equivalent of, and the name derived from, the older sailing *ship of the line of battle. In general terms it is taken to refer to capital ships of a navy subsequent to the transition from wood to iron, and later steel, as the material of which they were built. The first true battleship under this definition was the British 9,210-ton *Warrior*, launched in 1860, although the French *frigate *Gloire*, launched a year previously, had her wooden sides protected with iron plates. The transition from ship of the line to battleship was a comparatively gradual process, many of the old sailing first *rates being converted to iron protection on their hulls and lengthened to take steam propulsion, while the new iron ships retained the masts, sails, and gun batteries of the older wooden ships. It was only with the growth in reliability and radius of action of the steam engine, and the introduction of the breech-loading gun (see GUNS, NAVAL) and a more efficient propellant than black powder, that the battleship at last broke clear from her wooden predecessor and evolved as a type of her own. The first battleships which relied entirely on steam propulsion for movement were known as mastless ships. The first such ship was the 9,300-ton British *Devastation*, designed in 1869, which with a very low *freeboard and without *fore-castle or *poop was virtually a sea-going *monitor. Here, again, the two types overlapped considerably in time, the masted iron battleships lasting until nearly 1890.

Guns, armour, and steam machinery im-proved so rapidly during the period 1870–1900 that the battleship began to settle down into a recognizable type, with the main guns mounted in turrets, and most navies began to build them in classes instead of as single experimental ships. Displacement increased with each new ship, in Britain rising from the original 9,210 tons of the *Warrior* to the 15,000 tons of the *Majestic*, completed in 1896.

In 1904, when Admiral Sir John *Fisher came to the British Admiralty as First Sea Lord, he introduced a completely new type of battleship, known as the all-big-gun ship, which completely revolutionized battleship design. Every navy followed the British lead in this design. The first such ship was the *Dreadnought*, completed in 1906 and since then such ships were known as dreadnoughts and, subsequently, super-dreadnoughts. See also DREADNOUGHT BATTLE-SHIP.

BAWLEY, a small coastal fishing vessel or oyster dredger peculiar to Rochester and Whitstable, Kent, and to Leigh-on-Sea and Harwich, Essex, within the Thames Estuary area. They were *cutter-rigged craft with a short mast and topmast, and set a loose-footed mainsail (i.e., without a *boom) on a very long *gaff, a topsail,

The battleship H.M.S. Dreadnought, *1906*

and staysail. The Leigh-on-Sea bawley was used chiefly for shrimping. They are now very largely obsolescent, having been driven out of use by motorized fishing vessels, though one or two still exist as conversions to local cruising craft.

BAY, (1) the space between decks forward of the *bitts in sailing warships. They were often described as two separate spaces, the *starboard and *larboard bays; also, of course, **(2)** an indentation in the coastline between two headlands.

BAYAMO, a violent squall of wind off the land experienced on the southern coast of Cuba, especially in the Bight of Bayamo. They are accompanied by vivid flashes of lightning and usually end in heavy rain.

BAZAN, ALVARO DE, 1st Marquis of Santa Cruz (1526–88), Spanish admiral, was born at Granada. His father was general of the galleys, the equivalent of commander-in-chief of the naval forces of Spain in the Mediterranean, and Bazan followed his father and was given important commands while still a youth. He commanded the galleys which blockaded Tetuan in 1564 to suppress piracy, and in 1568 Philip II of Spain appointed him to command the galleys at Naples, an appointment which brought him into close relationship with Don John of Austria at the time of the formation of the Holy League against the Turks. This association resulted in Bazan commanding a division of the allied fleet at the battle of *Lepanto (1571), where his dash and skill averted a possible disaster when the Turkish admiral Uluch Ali broke through the division commanded by Andrea *Doria. He was again with Don John the following year at the capture of Tunis, and was raised to the peerage as Marquis of Santa Cruz as a result of his skill and gallantry on that occasion.

With Philip II enforcing his claim to Portugal in 1581–2, Santa Cruz was appointed as 'admiral of the ocean' to enforce the surrender of the Portuguese islands in the Atlantic, and in 1583 won a decisive victory off Terceira, in the Azores, which finally brought the islands under Spanish dominion. It was at this time that Philip II first began to plan his great campaign against England, and appointed Santa Cruz as commander-in-chief of the great *Armada which was to carry the invasion army. Financial difficulties and indecision on the part of Philip caused Santa Cruz to write critically to the king of the venture, and in an acrimonious correspondence each blamed the other for the delays in fitting out the Armada and getting the ships to sea. Santa Cruz was at Lisbon, unable to fit out the ships there for lack of supplies, when Sir Francis *Drake raided Cadiz and burnt the Spanish ships in the port in 1587, the episode known colloquially as 'singe-

ing the King of Spain's beard'. Santa Cruz died at Lisbon in February 1588, shortly before the Armada was ready to sail. In addition to his brilliance as a commander at sea he was a skilled naval architect and designed the great trade *galleons which brought the annual treasure from Vera Cruz in Mexico to Cadiz.

His son, ALONSO DE BAZAN, commanded the Spanish fleet at the battle of *Azores in 1591 in which the epic fight of Sir Richard *Grenville in his *Revenge took place.

BEACHCOMBER, originally a seaman who, not prepared to work, preferred to exist by hanging around ports and harbours and existing on the charity of others, but now more generally accepted to describe any loafer around the waterfront, particularly in the Pacific islands, who prefers a life of *dolce far niente* to work of any description.

BEACHY HEAD, a naval battle in the War of the League of Augsburg, was fought off Beachy Head in the English Channel on 30 June 1690 between an Anglo-Dutch fleet under Admiral the Earl of Torrington (see HERBERT, Arthur) and a French fleet commanded by Vice Admiral the Comte de *Tourville. Torrington at the time had only thirty-four *ships of the line with him; the Dutch, under Admiral Cornelis *Evertsen, 'the Youngest', provided twenty-two more. The French fleet, formed by the junction of the Brest and Toulon fleets, numbered sixty-eight ships of the line.

On 25 June the French were reported off the Isle of Wight. Torrington, who was then exercising his fleet a few miles to the eastward, did not intend to engage but to remain 'in being' and stood up Channel. Four days later, however, he received direct orders to give battle. The Anglo-Dutch attack was not well organized as a whole, the Dutch van and the English rear squadrons engaging more or less independently resulting in their being badly mauled. Torrington, in the centre, remained at long range to windward. In the afternoon the Dutch were being overpowered, when the wind fortunately dropped. The English ships anchored with all sail set, Torrington having first placed himself between the Dutch and the French, and a strong ebb tide carried the French ships out of gun range.

Casualties on both sides were heavy. The French lost no ship; the Anglo-Dutch fleet lost about eight. Torrington was tried by court martial for the ineffectiveness of his tactics and apparent reluctance to engage but was honourably acquitted.

BEACON, (1) a stake or other erection surmounted by a distinctive topmark erected over a shoal or sandbank as an aid to navigation. In many coastal estuaries without important shipping the low water level is marked by local beacons, often in the form of withies, as a guide to fishing craft and yachts using those particular waters. (2) A prominent erection on shore which indicates a safe line of approach to a harbour or a safe passage clear of an obstruction.

In older days fire beacons, on the tops of cliffs or hills, were used as a means of warning on the approach of danger. Thus, news of the arrival in English waters of the Spanish *Armada in 1588 was signalled from Plymouth to London by a chain of such fires each ignited as soon as the flames from the preceding fire was seen. In fact, the news of the Armada's arrival in the Channel was brought as far north as York within 12 hours by means of beacon fires.

BEAGLE, H.M.S., the best known of a number of ships that have borne this name was a four-gun *sloop of 235 tons built at Woolwich in 1820 and rigged as a *brig. Allocated to the surveying service in 1825 she was employed on a survey of the Magellan Strait under the command of Philip *King, and later Robert *Fitzroy, with whom, from 1831 to 1836, Charles *Darwin sailed on his world famous voyage, commemorated in his *The Voyage of the Beagle* (1839). Later the ship was engaged in surveys of Australian waters.

BEAGLEHOLE, JOHN CAWTE (1901–71), a New Zealand historian of great charm and modesty, was the leading authority on the life and voyages of Captain James *Cook and edited the journals which Cook kept of his three great voyages in a notable edition published by the *Hakluyt Society in four volumes (1955–67), widely recognized as a work of extreme scholarship. He was educated at Wellington College and Victoria University College, New Zealand, and at London University, and was historical adviser to the New Zealand Department of Internal Affairs from 1938 to 1952. Among the various books he wrote and edited, in addition to the Hakluyt edition of Cook's journals, were *The Exploration of the Pacific*, of which the best edition, greatly revised, was published in 1966, and *The Life of Captain James Cook*, published in 1974.

BEAK, the name sometimes given to the metal point or ram fixed on the bows of war *galleys and used to pierce the hulls, and thus to sink or disable enemy galleys.

BEAKHEAD, the space in a sailing ship of war immediately forward of the *forecastle. In the older ships of war the forecastle was built across the bows of the ship from *cathead to cathead, and the beakhead was open to the sea; there were short ladders down to it from the forecastle deck,

while doors from the forecastle itself led directly on to the beakhead. This space was used in warships as the seamen's lavatory, known as the 'heads'. In some later warship designs the beakhead was decked with gratings so that the sea, breaking through them, helped to keep the space clean. In the British Navy all lavatories on board warships are still known as 'heads'.

BEAM, (1) the transverse measurement of a ship in her widest part. It is also a term used in indicating direction in relation to a ship (see ABEAM), thus 'BEFORE THE BEAM', the arc of a semicircle extended to the horizon from one beam of the ship around the bows to the other beam; 'ABAFT THE BEAM', the similar semicircle extending round the stern of the ship. For illus. see RELATIVE BEARINGS. (2) The wooden or metal bar which spreads the mouth of a *trawl when used for fishing.

BEAM, one of the transverse members of a ship's frames on which the decks are laid. In vessels constructed of wood they are supported on the ship's sides by right-angled timbers known as *knees, in steel ships by steel brackets or *stringers. The depth of a beam is known as its *moulding, its width as its *siding. For illus. see SHIPBUILDING.

BEAM ENDS. A ship is 'on her beam ends' when she has heeled over to such an extent that her deck-*beams are nearly vertical and there is no righting moment left to bring her back to the normal upright position. See also METACENTRIC HEIGHT.

BEAN-COD, the English name, probably given in jest, of a small Portuguese vessel used for inshore and estuary fishing, having a sharp and very high curved bow, the curve being carried round inboard at the top. Single-masted, they spread a very large *lateen sail which extended the whole length of the vessel, making her remarkably weatherly.

BEAR, a heavy *coir mat loaded with sand and with ropes fixed at either end which is hauled to and fro across a wooden deck of a ship to scour it. See also HOLYSTONE.

BEAR, a wooden *barquentine of 703 tons built at Greenock, Scotland, as a sealer in 1874. In 1884 she was purchased by the U.S. government for the relief of the Greely Arctic expedition. After this she was transferred to the Coast Guard service and served on the Alaska patrol until 1929 when she became the property of the city of Oakland for use as a maritime museum. In 1933–5 she was used by Admiral Richard E. Byrd on his second Antarctic expedition and again on his U.S. Antarctic expedition of 1939–41. During the Second World War the *Bear* returned to coastguard duties. After being laid up for several years she eventually sank in a storm off Nova Scotia in March 1963.

BEAR, to, the direction of an object from the observer's position, usually expressed in terms of a * compass, e.g., the land bears NE. by N., the enemy bears 047 degrees, etc. In traditional seamen's language it was sometimes given with reference to the ship's head, e.g., the wreck bore 2 * points on the port bow. TO BEAR UP, in a sailing vessel, to sail closer to the wind; TO BEAR DOWN, to approach another ship from to windward; TO BEAR IN WITH, or TO BEAR OFF FROM, to approach nearer or to stand farther off, usually in connection with the land. See also BEARING.

BEARING, the horizontal angle between the direction of true north or south and that of the object of which the bearing is being taken. When the bearing is taken by a * magnetic compass, which is subject to * variation and * deviation, it has to be corrected by these before the true bearing is obtained. See also NAVIGATION.

BEAT, to, (1) the operation of sailing to windward by a series of alternate * tacks across the wind. **(2)** To beat to quarters, the order given to the drummers on board a sailing man-of-war to summon the crew to their stations for action against an enemy. In the British Navy the drums were beaten to the rhythm of 'Heart of Oak'.

BEATTY, DAVID, first Earl (1871–1936), British admiral of the fleet, was born of Irish fox-hunting stock and entered the Royal Navy at the usual age of 13. His strong personality, coupled with his exceptional dash and courage, were first shown during Kitchener's re-conquest of the Sudan (1896–8) when his service in command of a gunboat on the Nile gained him the D.S.O. and promotion to commander at the early age of 27. He was next executive officer of the battleship *Barfleur* on the China station where, though wounded while serving with the besieged Tientsin garrison during the Boxer Rebellion (1900), he led a naval detachment to extricate Admiral Seymour from Hsiku, which earned him promotion to captain at the age of 29 when the average age for this step was 43.

Beatty's time in command of several cruisers and of the pre-* dreadnought *Queen* was too short to qualify him for flag rank. To many he seemed more interested in hunting than in a naval career, of which marriage to a wealthy American lady had made him financially independent. Fortunately the British Admiralty realized how little they could afford to lose such an outstanding

officer and in 1910 he was promoted rear admiral by a special Order-in-Council shortly before his 39th birthday, an age without precedent for over a century. But he hazarded his future by declining the subordinate appointment of second-in-command of the Atlantic Fleet, which denied him further employment until, at a chance meeting in 1912, the First Lord of the Admiralty, Winston * Churchill, was sufficiently impressed by his wide understanding of the art and technique of war to appoint him his naval secretary.

Churchill next chose him, in spite of his lack of seniority, to command the battle-cruiser squadron which formed a part of the * Grand Fleet at the outbreak of the First World War (1914). The offensive panache with which, from H.M.S. *Lion*, he commanded what soon became the Battle-cruiser Fleet, based on Rosyth, was shown as early as 28 August 1914 when, by accepting the calculated risk of German minefields and a possible meeting with a superior force, his five battle-cruisers turned the potential defeat of an offensive raid by Commodore * Tyrwhitt's Harwich Force on German patrols in the * Heligoland Bight into a decisive victory. An error in signals, for which his flag lieutenant was responsible, spoiled his chance of bringing the German battle-cruisers to action after their bombardment of Hartlepool, Scarborough, and Whitby on 17 December. But he was slightly more successful on 24 January 1915, when Admiral * Hipper attempted a raid on the British * Dogger Bank patrols. Soon after 9 a.m. Beatty's squadron of five battle-cruisers was in action with four retiring German battle-cruisers although here again gunnery errors, which allowed the German ships to concentrate on the *Lion* and drive her out of the line, and a further signal error resulted in the British battle-cruisers concentrating on sinking the already disabled *Blücher* instead of continuing pursuit of the rest of Hipper's heavy ships, which were thus enabled to escape.

Beatty's handling of the Battle-cruiser Fleet at * Jutland on 31 May 1916 will always be questioned. His determination to ensure that Hipper did not again escape led him to seek action in the first stages of the battle without the decisive support of four 'Queen Elizabeth' class battleships attached to the battle-cruisers, which he subsequently hazarded under fire at too close a range from the German battle fleet. But he was wholly successful in spite of serious losses in discharging his chief duty, that of preventing Hipper from sighting the approaching British battle fleet, while at the same time leading the German battle fleet into a vulnerable position at the start of what was to be the only major naval action of the war.

Towards the end of 1916 Beatty succeeded Sir John * Jellicoe as commander-in-chief of the Grand Fleet. But the need to follow his predecessor's cautious strategy until the major defects in British capital ship and shell design, revealed by Jutland, had been remedied, and to give overriding priority to defeating the unrestricted * U-boat campaign, coupled with Germany's refusal to hazard the * High Seas Fleet again (except abortively in April 1918), denied him the chance of gaining the annihilating victory for which he longed. He had, however, the ultimate satisfaction of accepting the internment of the High Seas Fleet in British waters shortly after the Armistice in November 1918.

Promoted admiral of the fleet, created an earl and honoured with the Order of Merit, Beatty was First Sea Lord from 1919 to 1927, a longer period than any of his predecessors. He failed in his fight to regain control of the Fleet Air Arm, his arguments with the unbending Lord Trenchard being handicapped by his earlier ill-judged support for the absorption of the Royal Naval Air Service into the Royal Air Force in 1918. But he maintained an adequate post-war fleet against relentless American pressure and repeated Treasury demands for reductions in naval expenditure and opposition to new construction. To him the navy owed the battleships *Nelson* and *Rodney*, and the 'County' class cruisers which, in spite of the limitations imposed by the Washington Conference (1921) on the size and numbers of new warship construction, served the country so well in the Second World War.

Beatty's years of retirement, spent mostly in the hunting field, were short. Though suffering from influenza at the time he insisted on being a pall-bearer at Jellicoe's funeral in November 1935, an act of devotion to his war-time chief that cost him his own life four months later, when he too was honoured with a funeral in St. Paul's Cathedral. He is commemorated by a bronze bust in Trafalgar Square. For a biography see *The Life and Letters of David, Earl Beatty* by Rear Admiral W. S. Chalmers (1951).

BEAUFORT, Sir FRANCIS (1774–1857), British rear admiral, served from 1829 to 1855 as Hydrographer of the Navy with great distinction and for a longer period than any holder of the appointment before or since.

His active service began at the age of 13 and was full of incident, including the battle of the * Glorious First of June in 1794 and the expedition to Buenos Aires in 1806–7, when Beaufort made surveys in the River Plate. It concluded with the command of the * frigate *Fredericksteen* which was selected to survey the coast of Asia Minor from 1810 to 1812. Here Beaufort was badly wounded for the second time. In ensuing years he worked up his surveys for publication in chart form and published a distinguished account of them entitled *Karamania*. He continued his

scientific studies and built up many useful friendships in the world of * hydrography being a Fellow of the Geological Society from 1808 and of the Royal Society from 1814. He was a member of the Astronomical Society from its foundation in 1820 and was later a founder member of the Royal Geographical Society in 1830.

He had a prime interest in meteorology and kept a log from his earliest days at sea. Thus he developed his scale for wind and weather, although it has been said that Alexander * Dalrymple gave him the idea. It was to become internationally known and used. Another major interest was tidal theory in collaboration with Lubbock and Whewell at the Royal Society. Widespread and international tidal recordings were organized with practical benefit to navigators, such as the annual *Admiralty Tide Tables* first published in 1842.

Beaufort's period as Hydrographer saw the British Admiralty's introduction in 1831 of a scientific branch to include the Hydrographic Department, the Royal and Cape observatories, the Nautical Almanac, and the Chronometer offices. The Admiralty *Manual of Scientific Enquiry* to guide observers, especially medical officers afloat, appeared in 1849. In parallel there was the need for developing compasses and their correction because iron was being increasingly used in ship construction, and Beaufort set up a compass branch in 1842. Furthermore, the rapid spread of railways and the consequent coastal works led to the setting up of a harbour branch from 1846 which, to all intents and purposes, was responsible for the tidal waters of Britain until these duties were absorbed by the Board of Trade (now Department of Trade and Industry).

Surveys and chart production proceeded apace in so far as the Admiralty's sometimes niggardly allocation of ships, men, and money permitted, although Beaufort had the unwavering support in this work of Sir John * Barrow, then Secretary of the Admiralty. Surveys were world-wide, and the voluminous correspondence which Beaufort conducted with commanders-in-chief and the captains of his surveying ships has become a valuable historical record. At home there was the 'Grand Survey of the British Isles', tied to the Ordnance Survey triangulation where it existed. It owed much to John Walker, senior draughtsman in the Hydrographic Department, who had served Dalrymple and whose two sons carried on the family tradition until 1864. New charts were required to meet the needs of steam navigation and, to keep them up to date, the issue of * *Notices to Mariners* was begun in 1834, having been preceded by details given in the *Nautical Magazine*, first published in 1832 with the support of Beaufort and under the editorship of his principal naval assistant, Alexander * Becher.

BEAUFORT SCALE
Used to indicate the force of the wind.

Force on Beaufort Scale	Nautical miles per hr.	Description	Height of sea in ft	Deep sea criteria
0	0–1	Calm	—	Flat calm, mirror smooth
1	1–3	Light Airs	$\frac{1}{4}$	Small wavelets, no crests
2	4–6	Light Breeze	$\frac{1}{2}$	Small wavelets, crests glassy but do not break
3	7–10	Light Breeze	2	Large wavelets, crests begin to break
4	11–16	Moderate Breeze	$3\frac{1}{2}$	Small waves, becoming longer, crests break frequently
5	17–21	Fresh Breeze	6	Moderate waves, longer, breaking crests
6	22–27	Strong Breeze	$9\frac{1}{2}$	Large waves forming, crests break more frequently
7	28–33	Strong Wind	$13\frac{1}{2}$	Large waves, streaky foam
8	34–40	Near Gale	18	High waves of increasing length, crests form spindrift
9	41–47	Strong Gale	23	High waves, dense streaks of foam, crests roll over
10	48–55	Storm	29	Very high waves, long overhanging crests. Surface of sea white with foam
11	56–65	Violent Storm	37	Exceptionally high waves, sea completely covered with foam
12	above 65	Hurricane	—	The air filled with spray and visibility seriously affected

There were new and detailed general instructions for the conduct of surveys and particular ones for the officers in charge of them.

In Beaufort's last years the Crimean War broke out and he saw to it that surveying officers were attached to the fleets in the Black and Baltic Seas, where they did distinguished service in poorly charted waters. The war meant delaying the retirement which Beaufort had offered on account of failing faculties, but a year later, in January 1855, the Board of Admiralty released him.

BEAVOR-WEBB, JOHN (1849–1927), British yacht designer, was born in Ireland and intended for a career in civil engineering. But after owning and racing several yachts successfully at Kingstown he migrated to the Solent in 1871 where he became associated with the celebrated builder of Itchen Ferry boats, Dan Hatcher (1817–80), producing a number of winners in the racing classes. He was thereupon commissioned to design two *America*'s Cup challengers, producing the *Genesta*, 82-foot waterline *composite-built *cutter (1885), followed by the *Galatea*, 87-foot waterline steel-built cutter (1886). Both were outsailed by their respective defenders, the Edward *Burgess-designed *Puritan* and *Mayflower*. Following these races he married an American girl, settled in New York, and built up a highly successful yacht design

practice there. Among many racing and steam yachts he designed were two *Corsairs* for J. Pierpont Morgan and two *Intrepids* for Lloyd Phoenix, four of the largest steam yachts of their day.

BECALM, to, the act of blanketing a ship by cutting off the wind, either by the proximity of the shore or by another ship. A ship motionless through the absence of wind is said to be becalmed.

BÊCHE-DE-MER, the *Holothuria*, or sea-slug, much esteemed in China and the Far East as a gastronomic delicacy. Its eastern name is Trepang.

BECHER, ALEXANDER BRIDPORT (1796–1876), British rear admiral, was the first naval assistant to be appointed to the Hydrographic Department in 1823, where he remained until 1866 except for the surveying seasons of 1839 when he commanded the *Fairy* in the North Sea, and of 1847 commanding the *Mastiff* to complete the survey of the Orkney Islands. Previously he had had surveying experience on the Canadian Lakes in 1815–17; in the *Leven* working in the Azores; and in 1820–2 with Basil Hall in the *Conway*'s scientific cruise in the Pacific.

Becher's first task in the Hydrographic

Department was to classify and index the original documents, already numbering over 20,000. Thereafter, as additional naval officers joined, he was chief naval assistant to successive Hydrographers of the Navy in the persons of *Parry, *Beaufort, and Washington. In 1831 he was the first secretary of the Board of Visitors to the Royal Observatory, meeting under the royal warrant of William IV in 1830, and directed by the President of the Royal Society. In 1832 he became editor of the new *Nautical Magazine*, originally subsidized by the British Admiralty and having the dissemination of navigational information newly reported by mariners as its main purpose.

Becher was a Fellow of the Royal Astronomical Society and in 1854 received an award of £100 for a development of the *artificial horizon for taking sights of heavenly bodies when the ship's horizon is obscured. He published a number of papers on various subjects, including marine meteorology and compass correction.

BECKET, (1) a short length of rope whose ends have been spliced together to form a circle. **(2)** A short length of rope with an eyesplice in one end and a stopper knot in the other used to hold various articles (boarding pikes, cutlasses, etc.) together in their stowage. **(3)** A short rope with an eyesplice in each end used to hold the foot of a *sprit against the mast. **(4)** The eye at the base of a *block for making fast the standing end of a *fall.

BECUE, to, a method of making fast a rope to a boat's anchor for use on rocky ground. The rope is made fast to the *flukes of the anchor and then led to the ring, where it is secured by a light *seizing. If the flukes are caught in the rocks, a sharp jerk will break the seizing and the anchor will then *come home easily, being hoisted from the flukes.

BED, (1) a shaped piece of timber placed under the quarters of casks when stowed in a ship's hold so as to hold the *bilge, the central part of a cask where it swells, clear of the ship's floor. **(2)** Anchor bed, a flat space on either side of the bows of the ship on which, in the days before stockless anchors, the *bower and *sheet anchors were stowed after they had been *weighed and *catted. **(3)** Engine bed, the metal base on to which a ship's engines are bolted.

BEE, a ring or hoop of metal. BEES OF THE *BOWSPRIT, pieces of hard wood bolted to the outer end of the bowsprit of a sailing vessel through which are rove (see REEVE) the foretopmast *stays before they are brought in to the bows and secured.

BEE BLOCKS, wooden swells on each side of the after end of a *smack's or yacht's *boom, having sheaves through which to lead the *leech *reef *pendants or reefing *tackle.

BEECHEY, FREDERICK WILLIAM (1796–1856), British rear admiral, was well known for his work in surveying and geography. His interest was first aroused in 1818 when he was appointed to the *Trent*, commanded by Lieutenant (later Sir John) *Franklin for a voyage of discovery in the Arctic, of which he wrote an account. In the following year he was again in the Arctic, serving in the *Hecla* under W. E. *Parry. During 1821 he was with *Smyth in the *Adventure* and in 1822–3 he carried out a survey of the north coast of Africa. In 1825 Beechey commanded the *Blossom* in the Pacific, mainly on survey work and in trying to link up, through the Bering Straits, with the polar expeditions exploring that part of the world from the eastward. He wrote an account of this voyage which was published in 1831. Promoted captain in 1827, he sailed in the *Sulphur* to survey the coasts of South America but was forced to come home after a year on account of ill health. His next task was the survey of the Irish coasts, which occupied him ten years until 1847. For the remainder of his life he was in London continuing his geographical studies, being elected president of the Royal Geographical Society in 1855. But also from 1850 until his death he acted as the first naval officer for professional duties at the Board of Trade, a post instituted by the Mercantile Marine Act of 1850. Besides the two works mentioned above, Beechey also wrote many geographical papers for the Royal Society, of which he was a Fellow.

BEETLE, a heavy mallet used by shipwrights to drive *reeming irons into the *seams of wooden-planked sides and decks of vessels in order to open them up so that they can be *caulked with *oakum and pitch. See also HORSING-IRON.

BEFORE THE MAST, literally, the position of men whose living quarters on board are in the *forecastle, but a term more generally used to describe seamen as compared with officers, in phrases such as 'he sailed before the mast'. The days of men having their living quarters in the forecastle, which was their traditional home on board, are now largely past, most ships of any size now providing *cabins for their crews.

BEHAIM, MARTIN (c. 1436–1507), German navigator, emigrated to Portugal where he became a member of John II's council for the furtherance of navigation. He is said to have made some minor improvements in the navigational instruments of the period, notably the *cross-staff and *astrolabe, but his chief claim to fame probably rests with the terrestrial globe which he constructed at Nuremberg, still preserved there. Although of great beauty and antiquity, the globe is remarkably inaccurate and suggests that Behaim never in fact sailed to many of the places he claimed to have.

BEIRA, a seaport formerly of Portuguese East Africa, on the coast of the Indian Ocean and 490 miles north of Delagoa Bay. Originally an Arab settlement, the harbour was only developed into a major seaport following the building of a railway line from Rhodesia to the Pungwe river, at the mouth of which the port of Beira stands. It is also the terminal of an oil pipeline through which supplies to Rhodesia are pumped. Following the imposition of trade sanctions in 1965 by the United Nations after the unilateral declaration of independence by Rhodesia, the shipment of oil to Beira has been cut off by sea blockade, and much of the trade which formerly passed through the port, mainly to and from Rhodesia, has ceased.

BEITASS, the old Norse name for a *luff spar which was used in Viking ships, particularly the *knorr, to hold the luff of the sail taut, thus enabling the vessel to *claw off to windward. A step was fitted in the vessel just forward of the mast with one or two socket holes each side, and the end of the *beitass* was stepped in one of these when in use. See also FOREGIRT.

BELAY, to, the operation of making fast a rope by taking turns with it round a cleat or belaying pin. In general terms it refers only to the smaller ropes in a ship, particularly the running *rigging in sailing vessels, as larger ropes and cables are bitted, or brought to the *bitts, rather than belayed round them. It is also the general order to stop or cease.

BELAYING PINS, short lengths of wood, iron, or brass set up in racks in convenient places in the ship around which the running rigging can be secured or belayed.

BELCHER, Sir EDWARD (1799–1877), British admiral, was an indomitable and indefatigable man who attracted turbulent occasions, even during his surveying career, to an extent that Sir Francis *Beaufort, his chief as Hydrographer, was constrained to write in 1845 that 'the harvest he looked for from his [Belcher's] hands did not stretch beyond the reach of a deep sea line'. And a brother officer referred to him as a capital fellow for work but a devil incarnate with his officers. Some other sources do not justify so stringent a criticism.

His early naval service included the bombardment of Algiers in 1816, after which he was engaged on the west coast of Africa in operations against the slave trade. A period of invalidism ashore was devoted to study in science and languages, and various ingenious inventions were advanced by him. In the *Salisbury* at Bermuda he surveyed the intricate entrance channels and took leave to visit the U.S.A.

Next, in 1824, he joined Frederick *Beechey's expedition to the Pacific in the *Blossom*, twice visiting the Bering Straits in an endeavour to co-operate with the Arctic expeditions from the Atlantic under Sir John *Franklin and W. E. *Parry.

In 1830–3 he commanded the *Aetna* surveying on the African coast and became involved in the protection of British interests during the Portuguese hostilities on the river Douro. Then, after serving before Cartagena under Commodore Peyton, he continued his passage to the Pacific in the *Sulphur* and at once took an active part in the operations to capture Canton, making use of his surveying experience in negotiating the river. At home in 1842 he made a secret investigation of the Channel Islands and then sailed for Borneo in the *Samarang*. In Brunei he received the Sultan's offer of the island of Labuan, and in 1844 he was in successful conflict with pirates though receiving a serious wound. Other treaties with other Sultans were negotiated, and after surveys in the Philippines he returned home in the *Samarang* in 1847.

Belcher's last command was the *Assistance*, which with the *Resolute, North Star, Intrepid*, and *Pioneer* sailed in 1852 for the Arctic in search of Franklin and of the *Investigator (*McClure) and *Enterprise (Collinson) which vessels had entered the Arctic Sea through Bering Strait. Parties from the *Resolute* and *Investigator* made a historic meeting, thus completing knowledge of the *North-West passage. In April 1854 he had to abandon his ships and on his return to England a court martial acquitted him for so doing.

Belcher's principal publication was his *Treatise on Nautical Surveying* in 1835. It was a remarkable compilation discussing survey organization and instruments, to one of which, the *station pointer, Belcher made an important modification. *Hints to Travellers*, which was to have many revisions, was included. Belcher's obsession with the part surveyors could play in war received frequent mention. Until 1882 his book was accepted as the standard work, being then succeeded by *Wharton's *Hydrographical Surveying*.

BELFAST, the capital city of Northern Ireland, and one of the major seaports of the British Isles. It was in 1840 that the port really became of major importance, with the cutting of the Victoria channel leading to the open sea,

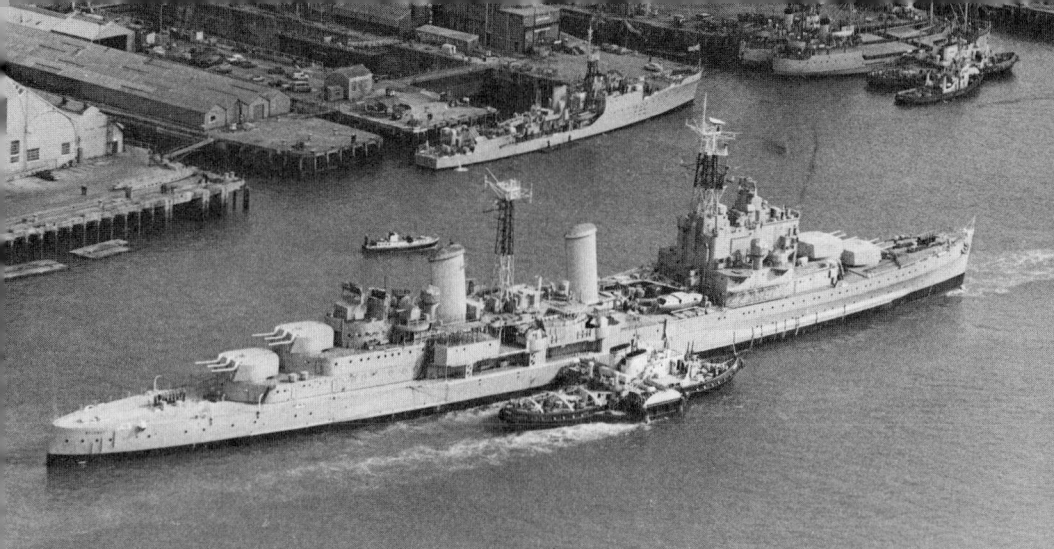

H.M.S. Belfast *leaving Portsmouth Dockyard, 1971*

although for more than two centuries it had carried much of the trade between Ireland and England. In 1791 a Scotsman, William Ritchie, introduced the trade of shipbuilding to Belfast, now grown to immense proportions. The famous shipbuilding firm of Harland and Wolff is now based in Belfast, and from their yards come some of the greatest ships in the world.

BELFAST, H.M.S., a *cruiser of 11,500 tons standard displacement with a main armament of twelve 6-inch guns in triple turrets, which has been preserved as a floating museum in the Thames in London and as an example of a type of ship now extinct in the Royal Navy. Built at Belfast and launched on 17 March 1938, she had a notable career during the Second World War, marred almost at its start by the explosion beneath her hull of an enemy magnetic *mine in the Firth of Forth on 21 November 1939 which broke her back and kept her out of service until 3 November 1942. She played an important part in the action off the *North Cape of Norway on 26 December 1943 in which the German *battle-cruiser *Scharnhorst* was sunk, was part of the bombarding force at the invasion operations on the Normandy coast in June 1944, and served in the Far East throughout the Korean War. She was finally paid off in 1971 when she was trans-ferred to the *Belfast* Trust for permanent preser-vation.

BELFRY, the small canopy or shelter supported on wooden brackets and often highly decorated with carvings and gold leaf, which used in older ships to be built over the ship's bell.

BELGICA, a Norwegian-built *barque-rigged sealer, formerly the *Patria*, of 244 tons em-ployed by A. de *Gerlache de Gomery for the Belgian Antarctic expedition of 1897–9.

Trapped in the pack ice of the Bellingshausen Sea, she was the first vessel to winter in the Antarctic. She was later acquired by the Duc d'Orléans for exploring voyages in the Greenland and Kara Seas.

BELIZE, the capital and principal seaport of British Honduras, in the Caribbean Sea. In the 17th century, large numbers of British logwood cutters, of whom one was William *Dampier, were employed to cut and ship the magnificent mahogany and other fine woods which grew in the neighbourhood in vast groves. This colony of logwood cutters was a favourite recruiting ground for the *buccaneers who flourished in the West Indies in the late 17th century. Fine timber still grows in British Honduras and still forms one of the principal trades through the port of Belize.

BELL, traditionally a ship's bell is made of brass with her name engraved on it. It is used for striking the bells which mark the passage of time, and is also used as a fog signal where no other form of audible warning, such as a foghorn or steam whistle, is carried on board. The fog signal is the ringing of the bell for five seconds every minute. When a ship is broken up her bell often becomes a highly prized memento of ser-vice in the ship and they frequently command very high prices when offered for sale. See also BELLS.

BELL, HENRY (1767–1830), Scottish engin-eer, was apprenticed to a shipyard in *Glasgow, and while there installed a small steam engine in a boat in 1800. He was able to study the opera-tion of *Symington's *Charlotte Dundas* and met Robert *Fulton when the latter was on a visit from America. It has been said that in 1803 Bell put forward proposals to the British

Admiralty for steam propulsion in warships, and a story has frequently been repeated that Lord * Nelson also harangued the Board of Admiralty on the merits of Bell's steamship designs, but it is unlikely that the story is true, particularly as Nelson never served as a Lord Commissioner of the Admiralty. Although Bell did not have the financial backing enjoyed by Symington, nevertheless he ordered from the yard of John Ward and Sons a small vessel which he named the *Comet*, and with her started a regular passenger and cargo service on the Clyde in 1812. The single cylinder engine, made to Bell's design by John Robertson, is preserved in the Science Museum in London. In 1819 Bell extended his service to Tarbert and Oban, in the Western Highlands, but while returning from Fort William during a gale in December 1820 the *Comet* was driven ashore and wrecked. Though he was to see great advances in steamship voyages in the next ten years, Bell was too poor, while living on a small pension provided by the River Clyde Trustees, to build another vessel, and he died almost penniless in Glasgow.

BELL BUOY, a * can, conical, or spherical buoy, normally unlighted, on which is mounted a bell with four clappers, hung inside an iron cage, which is rung by the motion of the sea and serves as a warning to shipping of shoal waters. See also BUOYAGE.

BELL ROCK, see INCHCAPE ROCK.

BELL ROPE, a short length of rope spliced into the eye of the clapper by which the ship's bell is struck. Traditionally the bell rope is finished with a double * wall knot * crowned in its end though why this should be so is obscure except perhaps that it is a neat knot which fits well into the palm of the hand.

BELLEROPHON, **H.M.S.,** the ship aboard which, on 15 July 1815, Napoleon surrendered to Captain Frederick Maitland in Basque Roads. Napoleon and his entourage remained in the *Bellerophon* until they were transferred to H.M.S. * *Northumberland* for passage to exile in St. Helena.

BELLIN, JACQUES NICHOLAS (1703–72), was the first engineer of the French Depôt des Cartes et Plans de la Marine, which was established in 1720 as headquarters of the French naval hydrographic service. He remained in charge of the office for over fifty years until his death. He became the first Ingénieur Hydrographe de la Marine in 1741 and later became a member of the Académie des Sciences in Paris. Bellin was in charge of a number of assistants and astronomers responsible for the making of charts from

data supplied by both naval and merchant seamen. During his long service France reached a peak of hydrographic eminence and her charts were used widely by both French and foreign navigators. His chart of the Mediterranean in three sheets published in 1737 and his *Le Petit Atlas maritime* of 1764 were of a standard of clarity and accuracy not previously achieved anywhere and mark him as an outstanding cartographer of his day.

BELLINGSHAUSEN, THADDEUS FABIAN VON (1779–1852), Russian naval officer, was born in Oesel, an island in the Gulf of Riga. He first saw service with the Imperial Russian Navy at the age of 25 as a junior officer with * Krusenstern on the latter's circumnavigation of the world in 1802–6. Thirteen years later Bellingshausen was put in command of an expedition promoted by Tsar Alexander I to circumnavigate the world, which was to complement rather than repeat the discoveries of Captain * Cook in 1772–5. The expedition sailed in July 1819 with Bellingshausen in command on board the *Mirny* and his second-in-command, Lieutenant Mikhail Lazarev, on board the * *Vostok*. In December they reached South Georgia and completed the coastal survey begun by Cook. From here the expedition proceeded to survey the South Sandwich Islands and showed they could not be part of any Antarctic land mass. (See ANTARCTIC EXPLORATION and map there.) Then followed a series of discoveries which brought the Russians within sight of the ice cliffs of present-day Dronning Maud Land in Antarctica, though no claim to any sighting of an Antarctic continent was ever made by Bellingshausen.

Continuing clockwise round the continent Bellingshausen's ships penetrated farther south than any previous expedition, reaching almost to Enderby Land, discovered over ten years later by John * Biscoe. After a cruise in the south and central Pacific Bellingshausen continued his Antarctic circumnavigation in November 1820, approaching the continent through the present Bellingshausen Sea. On 22 January 1821 Peter I Island was sighted, and soon after, Alexander I Island. Bellingshausen's final mission was a survey of the South Shetland Islands which he also demonstrated could not be part of the mainland. It was here that the celebrated meeting with the American sealer Nathaniel * Palmer took place. Bellingshausen's Antarctic discoveries received little or no recognition from his contemporaries but were to prove the basis of the Soviet Union's present-day interest in the region.

BELLOC, JOSEPH HILAIRE PIERRE (1870–1953), English author, was born at St. Cloud, near Paris, but was educated in England which he made his home. His works include novels, essays, verse, history, biography, and criticism, and among them are three which have long become favourites for their maritime associations, *Hills and the Sea* (1906), *The Cruise of the Nona* (1925), and *The Silence of the Sea and other stories* (1941).

BELLOT, JOSEPH RÉNÉ (1826–53), French naval officer and Arctic explorer, was born at Rochefort. He entered the naval academy at Brest at the age of 16 and distinguished himself on active service in Madagascar in 1845. In 1851 he volunteered to serve in an expedition being organized by Lady Franklin to search for her husband, and was appointed second-in-command to Captain W. Kennedy on board the *Prince Albert*. Although no trace of the *Franklin expedition was found, Bellot with a sledge party discovered the narrow strait between Somerset Island and the Boothia Peninsula which Kennedy agreed should be named after him. In June 1853 he joined another expedition to the Arctic under Captain *Inglefield, again in search of Franklin. While attempting to carry dispatches to Rear Admiral Sir Edward *Belcher, whose ships were beset in the ice at the western end of Lancaster Sound, Bellot and two sailors were carried away on an ice floe when a gale sprang up and were never seen again.

BELLS or **SHIP'S BELLS**, the strokes on the ship's bell to mark the passage of time on board ship. The day is divided into six *watches of four hours each, and the passage of time in each watch is marked by the bell every half-hour, one bell marking the end of the first half hour, and eight bells the end of each watch. In order to prevent the same men keeping the same watch each day, the watch between 1600 and 2000 is divided into two, known as the first and last dog watches, in order to produce an odd number of watches in each day. Thus the four bells struck at 1800 mark the end of the first dog watch; one bell at 1830 marks the end of the first half hour of the last dog watch; but eight bells instead of four are struck at 2000 to mark the end of the last dog watch.

Seamen, when reporting the time, traditionally refer to it as bells. Thus, for example, half-past three is seven bells, five minutes to one is five minutes to two bells, and so on.

BELLUM, the long canoe-shaped boat of the Shatt-al-Arab and adjacent waters in Iraq. They are paddled or poled, according to the depth of water, the larger ones being capable of carrying from fifteen to twenty-five men.

BELLY BAND, a strip of canvas sometimes sewn midway between the lower *reef points and the *foot of a square sail to strengthen it.

BENBOW, JOHN (1653–1702), British admiral, ran away to sea and served as a *master's mate in the Royal Navy until he was court-martialled for making disparaging remarks about his captain. He then left the navy and purchased his own ship for trading purposes, on one occasion defending her to such good purpose against an attack by Algerine *corsairs in the Mediterranean that he brought back the heads of thirteen Moors whom he had killed to substantiate his claim to be paid head-money. He rejoined the navy in 1689, becoming captain of the *Britannia* through the good offices of Arthur *Herbert, then First Lord of the Admiralty. He was master of the fleet at the battles of *Beachy Head (1690) and La Hougue (1692) (see BARFLEUR), and commanded a squadron in an attack on St. Malo (1693). His next appointment was master attendant at Deptford dockyard where he rented the house of John Evelyn, the diarist, which he later sublet to *Peter the Great of Russia, then on a visit to England to learn the arts of naval architecture.

In 1702, during the war of the Austrian Succession, he was appointed commander-in-chief in the West Indies. In an action against the French squadron there, his leg was shattered when his flagship, the *Breda*, was left deliberately unsupported, and he was forced to break off the action and retire to Jamaica, where he died of his wounds. As a result of the subsequent inquiry, two of the captains who failed to support him were condemned to death by shooting and others cashiered. Benbow was always fiery and outspoken in his conversation and it is said that his intemperate speech in criticism of his captains was the main cause of their dereliction of duty.

BEND, (1) the generic maritime name for a *knot which is used to join two ropes or

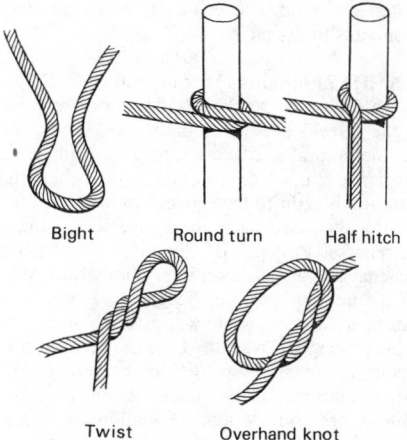

Bight   Round turn   Half hitch

Twist   Overhand knot

Some basic elements of bends

*hawsers together or to attach a rope or *cable to an object. In strict maritime meaning, a knot is one which entails unravelling the strands of a rope and tucking them over and under each other, such as in a stopper knot (*Turk's Head, *Matthew Walker, etc.) and is akin to a *splice in this respect. Bends, which are also known as *hitches, have a variety of different forms (*reef, *bowline, *clove hitch, etc.) designed to perform a particular function on board ship. (2) In sailing vessels, the chock of the *bowsprit.

BEND, to, (1) the operation in a ship of joining one rope to another or to some other object, originally with a *bend or *hitch. The term has continued in use even though more modern methods are in use; thus sails are still bent to the *yards of square-rigged ships and to *gaffs, *booms, and *stays in *fore-and-aft rig even though metal runners and spring-loaded *hanks may be used; a *cable is still bent to an *anchor even though it is joined to it by an iron *shackle. (2) To swing the body when pulling on an oar: 'bend to your oars', a term meaning to swing the oars farther forward at the beginning of a stroke.

BENDS, (1) a name sometimes applied to the thickest planks on the side of a wooden ship from the waterline or turn of the *bilge upwards. They are, however, more properly called *wales, and have the *beams and *knees of the hull structure bolted to them. (2) The colloquial name for *compression sickness. See also CAISSON DISEASE, DIVING.

BENEAPED, the situation of a vessel which has gone aground at the top of the *spring *tides and has to wait for up to a fortnight (during which the *neap tides occur) for the next tide high enough to float her off. Vessels beneaped at around the time of the *equinoxes when the highest spring tides occur may have to wait up to six months to get off.

BENGHAZI, a north African seaport in Libya, once a centre of the slave trade. It was founded by the Greeks and given the name Hesperides, and the natural gardens which grew with great luxuriance at the bottoms of large pits behind the town are thought to have given rise to the Greek myth of the Gardens of the Hesperides. During the reign of Ptolemy III the name of the town was changed to Berenice, in honour of his wife; but the modern name of Benghazi derives from that of a Moslem saint whose tomb is in the vicinity. Benghazi was the scene of much fighting during the Second World War, being captured and recaptured many times. As a port, its facilities are poor because of shallow water and the lack of protection in the outer harbour from the north and west.

'BENT ON A SPLICE', the sailor's term for being about to get married. The allusion is obvious, a splice being used to join two ropes together to make one.

BENTINCK, the name given to a small triangular *course for use in square-rigged ships, introduced by Captain Bentinck of the Royal Navy in the early years of the 19th century. Bentincks were superseded by storm *staysails, although in many American full-rigged ships they were retained throughout the century as *trysails. A Bentinck *boom was a spar often used to stretch the foot of a foresail in small square-rigged merchant vessels, thus dispensing with the *tack and *sheet, a *guy on the boom bringing the *leeches of the sail taut on the wind. Bentinck booms were widely used with a reefed foresail by whalers during the 19th century as it enabled them to see ahead under the sail when working in the ice.

BERESFORD, Lord CHARLES, first Baron of Metemmeh and Curraghmore (1846–1919), British admiral, became widely known throughout Britain as 'Charlie B' before his services in the Royal Navy, which he entered in 1859, and for the Conservative cause in Parliament, to which he was first returned in 1874, were rewarded with a barony in 1916. His courage and initiative at the bombardment of Alexandria (1882), at which he commanded H.M.S. *Condor*, first brought him into prominence. Promoted to captain, he next distinguished himself in command of the naval brigade that accompanied Sir Garnet Wolseley's abortive attempt to rescue General Gordon from Khartoum (1884–5), notably at the desert battles of Abu Klea and Metemmeh. As Junior Naval Lord (1886–8) he persuaded the Board of Admiralty to establish the Naval Intelligence Department, then resigned because his colleagues refused to build from this beginning an effective Naval Staff. Beresford's advocacy of a powerful fleet did much to persuade the British government to pass the Naval Defence Act of 1889 which converted a motley collection of old *ironclads into the balanced force, fit to challenge the combined fleets of France and Russia, that became the foundation on which Admiral Sir John *Fisher built the *dreadnought fleet that opposed Germany's *High Seas Fleet in the First World War (1914–18).

An ebullient sportsman of great charm, Beresford was, as a young man-about-town of many irresponsible escapades, a close friend of the Prince of Wales (later Edward VII), whose wise advice often dissuaded him from abandoning the navy for a whole-time parliamentary career. But in 1891 he lost the Prince's support after a bitter quarrel over Lady Brooke, later

Countess of Warwick, from whose charms Beresford was rescued by the determined wife he had married in 1878. Command of the cruiser *Undaunted* in the Mediterranean (1890–3) was followed by a mission to the Far East (1898–9), from which Beresford returned an ardent apostle of the 'open door' policy in China.

One of the most remarkable personalities of his generation and the best known sailor of his day, Beresford attained *flag rank in 1899, and went to the Mediterranean as second-in-command to Fisher (1900–2), whose many realistic reforms he greatly admired. But Fisher could not restrain his jealousy of Beresford's inherited wealth and aristocratic birth, nor Beresford circumscribe his contempt for Fisher's bourgeois upbringing, and the two were always at odds. When Beresford followed his two years as Vice Admiral Channel Squadron (1903–5) with a successful term as commander-in-chief in the Mediterranean (1905–6), Fisher, now First Sea Lord, though obliged to agree to Beresford going as commander-in-chief of the Channel Fleet in 1907, deliberately reduced the importance of this, the navy's chief command afloat, by hiving off a major part of it to form a separate Home Fleet. This provoked Beresford into an acrimonious dispute with the First Sea Lord over the production of war plans and developed into a fierce attack on Fisher's dictatorial methods with the inevitable result that Beresford was ordered to haul down his flag in 1909. His consequent letter to the Prime Minister arraigning the Admiralty obliged Asquith to conduct a formal inquiry which concluded that, while there was some justification for Beresford's charges, in particular in Fisher's refusal to create a Naval War Staff, both admirals were guilty of pursuing a bitter feud damaging to naval efficiency. Beresford's satisfaction at Fisher's resignation and retirement in 1910 was tempered by disappointment at being himself placed on the retired list instead of succeeding to this high office.

Unlike Fisher, Beresford did not serve again; he had to be content with his membership of Parliament where he was first an active supporter of Ulster's opposition to Home Rule for Ireland, and later a trenchant critic of the Admiralty's conduct of the First World War (1914–18) until his sudden death shortly after the armistice of 1918. Accorded the honour of a funeral in St. Paul's Cathedral, Beresford was one of a long line of naval officers whose outstanding merits gained him high rank, albeit without the chance to prove his capacity for command of a fleet in battle. For a full biography see *Charlie 'B'* by Geoffrey Bennett (1968).

BERGANTINA, a small Mediterranean rowing and sailing vessel of the 14th to 16th centuries, which could be considered as the Mediterranean counterpart of the English *pinnace of the same period. Bergantinas were built up to a maximum of about 40 feet in length and had from eight to sixteen rowing benches and a small superstructure aft for the captain and officers. They had one or two short masts, according to their length, to carry a single *lateen sail. They were essentially of light construction, relatively broad in the beam, and drew a maximum of about 18 inches. Their main function was as general purpose vessels for coastal and river work or for sailing to windward against a contrary current. They were in fact a member of the *galley family of vessels.

Like the English pinnace, bergantinas were carried 'knocked-down' in the holds of ships engaged in long voyages of exploration as they could be easily assembled on arrival at any coast where there was suitable wood for planking, and would prove useful for landing and surveying purposes. *Columbus carried bergantinas in the holds of his ships during his voyages to the New World, as did most other Spanish and Portuguese explorers of that period.

BERGEN, one of the principal seaports of Norway, lying at the head of the Byfjord. The town was founded by King Olaf Kyrre in 1070, and for a long period in the 15th, 16th, and 17th centuries was one of the trading centres of the Hansa merchants. It is today the centre of a considerable fishing industry and also has a flourishing shipbuilding industry. Like many Norwegian towns where timber is used extensively for building, it has seen many disastrous fires, those of 1702 and 1855 being particularly terrible. During the Second World War, after the occupation of Norway by Germany in 1940, it was used as a naval base by German warships.

BERING or **BEHRING,** VITUS (1681–1741), Danish explorer, was born at Horsem, Jutland. He entered the Russian Navy in 1704 and served in it during the war with Sweden. In 1725 *Peter the Great sent him to explore the north-east coast of Asia. He crossed Siberia to Kamchatka where he had several ships built and in 1728 he discovered the Bering Strait, the Big and Little Diamond Islands, St. Lawrence Island, and the Bering Sea. In 1730 he received a similar commission from the Empress Anna and founded the port of Petropavlovsk. In 1741 he sailed thence with two ships, the *St. Peter* and *St. Paul*, which became separated, but Bering carried on in the *St. Peter* to discover Alaska. On the return journey his ship was wrecked on Avatcha, the westernmost of the Aleutian Islands, now called after him and where he lies buried.

BERMUDA or **BERMUDIAN RIG,** a sail plan in which the main and/or mizen sail, or the foresail of a *schooner, is of triangular shape, very long in the *luff and set from a tall mast by slides running on a track or by the *luff rope fitting in a mast groove. The rig was commonly used by sailing craft in and around the West Indies from about 1800 and was introduced for small racing craft in Britain about 1911–12, spreading to larger racing yachts and cruising yachts in the twenty years between the two world wars. The rig is now almost universal in all modern yachts. The Bermuda rig is claimed to be more efficient to windward and also requires a smaller crew to handle it than the *gaff rig. See also RIG.

BERNOTTI, ROMEO (1877–1974), Italian admiral, entered the Royal Italian Navy as a midshipman in 1894 and after a distinguished career reached the rank of *ammiraglio di squadra* (rear admiral) in 1934. He took part in the Italo-Turkish war of 1911–12 and in the First World War (1914–18) and subsequently held the posts of deputy chief of the Naval Staff, 1927–9, admiral commanding the 2nd Naval Division, 1929–31, commandant of the Naval Academy, 1932–4, and commander-in-chief of the 2nd Naval Squadron, 1936–8, when he was made a senator of the realm, one of the highest honours which that country can offer. He was a dedicated student of naval history and published numerous books, among them *Sea Power in the Great War*, *Sea Warfare*, a critical study of its employment during the First World War, *The War at Sea*, *1939–45* (3 vols), and *The History of the War in the Mediterranean, 1940–43*.

BERRY, Sir EDWARD (1768–1831), British rear admiral, was one of Lord *Nelson's original 'band of brothers'. He became a lieutenant in 1794 as a reward for gallantry in leading a boarding party to capture a French man-of-war, and was first lieutenant of Nelson's ship, the *Captain*, at the battle of *Cape St. Vincent, 1797, where he again distinguished himself by leading the parties which boarded the Spanish ships *San Nicolas* and *San Josef*. He was captain of the *Vanguard*, Nelson's flagship at the *Nile, 1798, and after the battle was sent off with dispatches in the 50-gun *Leander* but had the misfortune to encounter the 74-gun *Généreux*, one of the two French *ships of the line which escaped from the battle. The odds against the *Leander* were too heavy and she was captured, but Berry was exchanged and reached England by the end of the year. As captain of the *Foud-royant* in the blockade of Malta during 1800 he was present at the capture of his old enemy, the *Généreux*, and also the *Guillaume Tell*, the other ship of the line which escaped from the Nile battle. He commanded the *Agamemnon* at *Trafalgar, the ship in which he had been first

lieutenant in 1796 when Nelson was her captain. He was knighted at the end of the war in 1815, and in 1821 was promoted to rear admiral but owing to ill health never hoisted his flag at sea.

BERTH, (1) a place in which to sleep on board ship, either in a *bunk or, formerly in naval ships, a place in which to sling a hammock. A snug berth, a situation of not too arduous labour on board a ship. **(2)** The place in harbour in which a ship rides to her anchor or is secured alongside. **(3)** A term used to indicate a clearance of danger, e.g., to give a wide berth to a rock, shoal, or a point of land, to steer a ship well clear of it.

BERTHON, EDWARD LYON (1813–99), British inventor, first studied for the medical profession but an interest in mechanical science turned his thoughts towards invention. He was one of the first men to try to adapt the principle of the Archimedes screw to steam propulsion at sea, but his two-bladed propeller, for which he took out a patent, was turned down by the British Admiralty, to whom he offered it, and he allowed the patent to lapse. A few years later he had the mortification of seeing Francis *Smith develop his idea to the stage of Admiralty acceptance. His next invention was known as 'Berthon's log', an invention by which the speed of a ship through the water was measured by the suction caused by the water streaming past the open end of a pipe projecting from the ship's bottom. This was recorded on a scale attached to a mercury column connected to the pipe. In its turn this invention, too, was rejected by the British Admiralty.

Some minor inventions for recording the *trim and roll of ships followed, but he is remembered mainly for his invention in 1849 of a folding boat, now universally known as a 'ber-thon boat'. Once again the British Admiralty showed no interest in his invention, but after much encouragement by Samuel *Plimsoll in 1873, who was mainly interested in its life-saving capabilities in connection with his campaign for better conditions for merchant seamen, he did further work on the design and received an Admiralty order for such boats to the value of £15,000. Some of his boats were supplied to General Gordon when he was besieged at Khartoum. They are still in wide use for a variety of purposes.

BERTHON BOAT, a folding or collapsible boat, of painted canvas stretched on a wooden frame, invented by Edward *Berthon. Their naval use was largely confined to destroyers and submarines as they could be folded away and stowed in a small space, but they also proved of great value for life-saving purposes and other similar uses.

BESSEMER, Sir HENRY (1813–98), a British engineer who, as well as his more famous invention of the Bessemer process in the manufacture of steel, designed a ship which was supposed to save its passengers from sea-sickness in rough seas. Within the hull her saloon was mounted so that, by the manipulation of hydraulic machinery, it would always remain level no matter to what degree the ship herself rolled or pitched. The hydraulic machinery was under the control of an engineer who regulated it with reference to a large spirit level fixed to the deck of the saloon. Such a ship, named the *Bessemer*, was built in 1875 and tried out on the cross-Channel service from Dover to Calais, but the idea failed to work as the engineer on duty could not produce counteracting movements of the hydraulic machinery fast enough to match the rolling of the ship. Not surprisingly, no more ships were built to this design.

BEST BOWER, the starboard of the two *anchors carried at the bow of a ship in the days of sail. That on the port side was known as the small bower, even though the two were identical in weight.

BETWEEN DECKS, the space contained between any two whole decks of a ship. The term has become widely associated with the *steerage of a passenger vessel, the space below decks in which passengers, and particularly emigrants, who could not afford *cabins, travelled, often enough in conditions of gross overcrowding and discomfort.

BETWEEN THE DEVIL AND THE DEEP BLUE SEA, see DEVIL.

'BETWIXT WIND AND WATER', on or near the line of immersion of a ship's hull. It was a term used largely in relation to cannon hits in naval battle, particularly with wooden warships, where a shothole in this position would give rise to a possibility of flooding through the influx of the sea. All wooden warships carried a variety of wooden plugs on board which the carpenter would attempt to drive into all holes made by cannon balls betwixt wind and water.

BEWPARS or **BEWPERS,** the old name for *bunting from which signal and other flags are made.

BEZAN or **BIZAN,** from the Dutch *bezaan*, a small yacht, usually *ketch rigged, of the 17th century. Charles II named one of his many yachts *Bezan*; she was of 35 tons *burthen and was given him by the Dutch in 1661. He had a second yacht, named *Isabella Bezan*, built for him by Phineas *Pett in 1680.

BIBBS, pieces of timber bolted to the *hounds of a mast of a square-rigged ship to support the *trestle-trees.

'BIBLE', the sailor's name for a small block of sandstone used for scrubbing the wooden decks of a ship, so called because seamen had to get down on to their knees to use them. The better known name is holystone, a name derived from the same source. Smaller blocks of sandstone used for scrubbing the deck in awkward places where the larger blocks would not go were known as prayer-books.

BIDDLE, NICHOLAS (1750–78), American naval officer, was born in Philadelphia. Going to sea at the age of 13, he became a midshipman in 1770 in the British Navy and served in H.M.S. *Portland*. He requested an appointment to the polar expedition of the Royal Geographical Society in 1772, but when his application was refused he waived his rank as a midshipman and served before the mast in a spirit of adventure. Another young man who enlisted for the same reasons was Horatio *Nelson, who served with Biddle. After his northern cruise, Biddle returned to America because of the strained relations between the colonies and England.

After entering the Pennsylvania State Navy, Biddle was chosen in December 1775 to command the brig *Andrew Doria* and was commissioned a captain in the *Continental Navy. In the squadron of Esek *Hopkins, he took part in the capture of Nassau, New Providence Island. He was fifth in the list of captains as fixed by the Continental Congress on 10 October 1776, and took command of the new frigate *Randolph*. He sailed from Charleston on 12 February 1778 with four vessels of the South Carolina State Navy in company, and a month later, near Barbados, sighted and engaged the British 64-gun ship *Yarmouth*. Biddle was wounded during the first 15 minutes of the engagement but his ship had suffered very little in the same period. He was directing the action from a chair on deck when the *Randolph* blew up. He was an officer of great promise and exceptional ability, and his death was a great loss to the Continental Navy.

BIDLINGMAIER, GERHARD (1907–71). German naval officer and naval historian, joined the navy in 1925 and served for over thirty years reaching the rank of Kapitän-zur-See. Early in his career he showed a great interest in naval history and his many years of study well fitted him for the post of lecturer in naval history at the college of Mürwik when he joined the Bundesmarine in 1956. While here he began work on his major undertaking, published under the title of *Seegeltung in der deutschen Geschichte* (Importance of the Sea in German

History). In 1963 he published another important work, *Der Einsatz der schweren Kriegsmarineeinheiten im ozeanischen Zufuhrkrieg* (Employment of Heavy Naval Ships in the War against Trade), subtitled *Strategische Konzeption und Führungsweise der Seekriegsleitung* (The Strategic Conception and Conduct of Sea Warfare). On completion of this work he was appointed head of the Department of Naval History at the Militärgeschichliches Forschungsamt at Freiburg-im-Breisgau, a post which he held until 1967. He was much in demand as a lecturer and wrote numerous articles on naval subjects.

BIERSTADT, ALBERT (1830–1902), German–American marine painter, was born at Soliegen, near Düsseldorf, but emigrated as a child with his family to New Bedford, Massachusetts. He started as a marine artist by painting ship portraits for local owners and sea captains, and followed this early beginning with more ambitious pictures in which his sense of the dramatic produced some notable results. A vivid feeling for colour and movement, particularly in his paintings of storm and disaster at sea, ranks him as one of the foremost American artists in this genre. He was elected a member of the National Academy in New York and was also made a Chevalier of the Legion of Honour by France in 1860.

BIGHT, (1) the name by which the loop of a rope is known when it is folded, or any part of a rope between its two ends when it lies or hangs in a curve or loop. **(2)** The area of sea lying between two promontories, being in general wider than a gulf and larger than a bay, is also known as a bight.

BIGOT DE MOROGUES, Vicomte de, see MOROGUES, Sebastien François Bigot, Vicomte de.

BILANDER or **BILLANDER,** from the Dutch *bijlander* and French *bilandre*, a small European merchant ship of the 17th and 18th centuries with two masts, occasionally used in the North Sea but more frequently to be seen in the Mediterranean. The mainmast was * lateen rigged but the foremast carried the conventional square * course and square topsail. They rarely reached a size of more than 100 tons.

BILBAO, one of the major seaports of Spain on the coast of the Bay of Biscay. From very early days it was famous for the quality of the steel blades forged there (the early English word *bilbo* (sword) was derived from the name of the town), and it is still the centre of the Basque steel and iron industries. It grew very rapidly in importance as a seaport during the second half of the 19th century when iron and steel formed the basis of so much of industrial growth, and it also handles a large export trade in wine and brandy. Shipbuilding is also carried out at Bilbao.

BILBOES, long bars or bolts, with a padlock on the end, on which iron shackles could slide, which were used on board ship to confine the legs of prisoners in a similar manner to the punishment of the stocks. It was a punishment usually known on board as putting a man in irons and continued in use, particularly in the American sailing ships, until the latter half of the 19th century. There are examples of bilboes in the Tower of London, taken out of ships of the Spanish * Armada. Thus Hamlet, musing on a forthcoming fight,

'That would not let me sleep; methought I lay
Worse than the mutines in the bilboes.'

The name originates from the steel which was forged at * Bilbao, at that time reckoned to be the finest in Europe.

BILGE, (1) that part of the * floors of a ship on either side of the * keel which approaches nearer to a horizontal than a vertical direction. It is where the floors and the second * futtocks unite, and upon which the ship would rest when she takes the ground. Hence, when a ship is holed in this part, she is said to be bilged. Being the lowest part of the ship inside the hull, it is naturally where any internal water would collect, and where the suction of the bilge pump is placed. These spaces on either side of the keel are collectively known as the bilges. **(2)** The largest circumference of a cask in the vicinity of its bung.

BILGE KEEL, also known as a docking keel, longitudinal projections fixed one on each side of a ship, parallel to the central * keel, at or just below the turn of the * bilge and protruding downwards. Their main purpose is to support the weight of the hull of the ship on the wooden * ways when * launching or on the lines of keel blocks when in dry-dock for cleaning or repairs. They are also of service to a ship in a seaway by providing additional resistance in the water when the vessel is rolling heavily, and in a sailing vessel provide a better grip on the water and thus allow her to hold a better wind. For illus. see KEEL.

BILGE PUMP, a small pump fitted in ships and designed to pump the * bilges clear of water which lies beyond the suction of the main pumps.

BILGE WATER, the water, either from rain or from seas breaking abroad, which runs down and collects in the * bilges of a ship and usually becomes foul and noxious. *Dana, in his *Two Years before the Mast*, talks of 'that inexpressibly sickening smell caused by the shaking-up of the bilge water in the hold'. In the older sailing vessels of the 17th and 18th centuries it was not unknown for men to be asphyxiated by the foul smells emitted from the bilges.

BILL OF HEALTH, a certificate properly authenticated by the consul or other recognized port authority certifying that a ship comes from a place where there is no contagious disease, and that none of her crew, at the time of her departure, was infected with such a disease. A certificate of this kind constitutes a clean bill of health; a foul bill of health indicates disease in the port of departure or among the crew.

BILL OF LADING, a memorandum by which the master of a ship acknowledges the receipt of goods specified on the bill and promises to deliver them in the same condition as received to the consignee or his order at the end of the voyage.

BILL OF SIGHT or **BILL OF VIEW,** a warrant for a custom-house officer to examine goods which had been shipped for foreign parts but not sold there.

BILL OF STORE, a licence, or custom-house permission, for re-importing unsold goods from foreign ports free of duty within a specified limit of time.

'BILLY BLUE', see CORNWALLIS, William.

'BILLY PITT'S MEN', see LORD MAYOR'S MEN, QUOTA ACTS.

BILLY TAYLOR, a character in a well-known, old comic song which was much sung on board ship during the 18th and early 19th centuries. The song tells the story of how he was taken by a *press gang for service in the British Navy and was followed to sea, unknown to him, by his sweetheart disguised as a seaman. When she discovered Billy Taylor being unfaithful to her she shot him, but retaining her disguise, rises to the rank of first lieutenant of the ship, the 'gallant *Thunderbomb*'.

BILLY-BOY or **BILLY-BOAT,** an east coast of England, bluff-bowed trading vessel of river-barge build, originally single-masted with a *trysail, and usually with the sails tanned. Later it took on a *ketch rig, with *gaff mainsail and mizen and square topsails on the mainmast. Billy-boys remained in general trading use along the Yorkshire coast and rivers at least to the beginning of the 20th century.

BINGE, to, the operation of rinsing out, or 'bulling' a cask to prepare it for new contents. Before the invention of metal tanks, casks were the main means of carrying on board the necessary amount of victuals, fresh water, etc., for the voyage, and were thus an important part of any ship's equipment; today modern methods of storage and preservation of victuals make casks obsolete for this purpose and their importance in the maritime sense has totally disappeared.

BINNACLE, formerly **BITTACLE,** the wooden housing of the mariner's *compass and its correctors and illuminating arrangements. The change from bittacle to binnacle came in about 1750, although the former name did not entirely disappear until the mid-19th century. The origin of the term would appear to be the Italian *abitacola*, little house or habitation, and was used by the early Portuguese navigators to describe the compass housing. The French word for binnacle is still *habittacle*.

In addition to the compass and a light, the binnacle in older ships was the proper stowage for the *traverse-board, the reel with the *logline and chip and the 28-second glass used for measuring a ship's speed. Charts in actual use, if any, were also properly stowed in the binnacle.

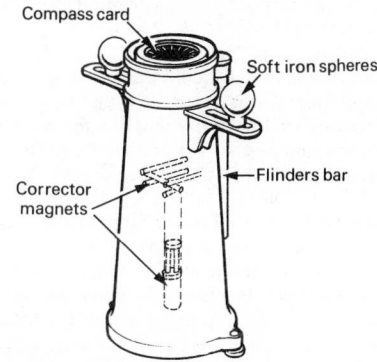

Binnacle

BIRCH, THOMAS (1779–1851), Anglo-American marine and landscape painter, was a son of William Russel Birch, an enamel painter and engraver of considerable competence who emigrated with his family from England to the U.S.A. in 1794. There Thomas studied art, being much influenced by the seascapes of Joseph *Vernet, and although he had little experience of the sea or ships, the majority of his paintings are of marine subjects. He had the ability to portray the liquidity of water to great effect, and there is a delicacy of treatment in his marine paintings that gives them a great charm. He strove always for perfection, and as a result usually painted several

Bireme; from an Assyrian sculpture of the time of Sennacherib, 700 B.C.

versions of the same subject, a course of action which in later years gave rise to much confusion in the correct attribution of his work. During the Anglo-American war of 1812 he painted a number of battle scenes, particularly of the famous *frigate actions, of which his pictures of those between the *Constitution and the *Guerrière*, the *United States and the *Macedonian*, and the *Wasp* and the *Frolic* are the best known today.

BIRD'S NEST, a small round *top, smaller than a crow's nest, which was placed right at the masthead to provide a greater range of vision from a ship at sea. It was chiefly used in the older *whalers as a look-out post for whales coming to the surface to *blow. With the modern whale factory ships and their fleet of catchers, all now equipped with *sonar and *radar, such old-fashioned means of locating whales are, of course, no longer used.

BIREME, a *galley having two banks of oars, used particularly for warlike purposes in the Mediterranean until the mid-17th century when sailing warships took their place. They were almost invariably fitted with a pointed metal *ram or *beak fixed to the bow at or below sea level for use against ships of an enemy, the traditional tactic of a galley being to sink enemy ships by ramming them. War galleys had three, sometimes four, rowers to each oar, and in biremes, the two banks were on different levels, one higher than the other. See also TRIREME.

BIRKENHEAD, a great seaport and shipbuilding centre on the river Mersey, in Cheshire, England, lying opposite the even greater seaport of Liverpool. It is of comparatively recent growth, the first docks not being opened until 1847, but since then its expansion has been phenomenal. It is best known, perhaps, for the great shipbuilding complex of Cammell Laird, one of the largest shipbuilding firms in Britain where many naval ships, including battleships, have been built. It is connected to Liverpool by the Mersey Tunnel, the two great ports together forming one of the largest seaports in the world.

BIRKENHEAD, an iron second-class *frigate and the first iron warship built for the British Navy. She was ordered by the Admiralty from John *Laird in 1843, but when she was ready for launching in 1845, second thoughts by the Admiralty resulted in orders to complete her as a *troopship. This decision was reached as the result of gun trials conducted against an iron hulk, the *Ruby*, in which the solid shot passed through her iron plates without difficulty. After a few trooping voyages in 1851, she sailed for South Africa on 7 January 1852 carrying a detachment of the 74th Highlanders (487 officers and men), reaching Simonstown on 23 February. Two days later she left for Cape Town. She struck a rock off Danger Point in Walker Bay in the early morning of 26 February and sank in shark-infested waters with a loss of 454 officers and men. The tragedy, ennobled by the discipline and calm of the soldiers who stood fast in their ranks on deck as the ship was sinking to enable the women and children on board to be got safely away, gave rise to many well-known poems and paintings. The rock on which she struck is today known as Birkenhead rock.

BIRLEY, Sir OSWALD HORNBY JOSEPH (1880–1952), British portrait painter, was commissioned by the British Admiralty after the Second World War to paint a series of portraits of the more famous of the admirals who served in the Royal Navy during that war for permanent exhibition in the Royal Naval College at * Greenwich, where they now hang.

BISCOE, JOHN (1794–1843), British discoverer, who had been an acting master in the Royal Navy, set sail in 1830 with the brig *Tula* and the cutter *Lively* under orders from Messrs. Samuel Enderby & Sons of London to seek new sealing and whaling grounds in Antarctic waters. He made a circumnavigation of Antarctica very similar to that of * Bellingshausen, discovering Enderby Land in February 1831, the first discovery of truly continental land in the Antarctic. Later, on the same voyage, Biscoe discovered Adelaide Island and the Biscoe Islands on the west side of the Antarctic peninsula and claimed Graham Land for Great Britain.

BISCUIT, the 'bread' which was supplied to ships, particularly naval, before bakeries were introduced on board. It was made with flour, mixed with the least possible quantity of water, and thoroughly kneaded into flat cakes and slowly baked. Good biscuit was supposed to be one-third heavier than the flour from which it was made. It was, before the days of tin-lined chests, packed in canvas or cloth bags and quickly became infested with black-headed weevils, a cause of much complaining by seamen. Ships' biscuit was issued until bakeries began to be fitted generally in ships at the beginning of the 20th century and bread became available even for long voyages, but even then large stocks of biscuit were held in naval victualling stores for issue to ships in wartime, and in many ships in the British Navy during the First World War (1914–18) and for some years after, biscuit was a victualling issue on board until the huge stocks were exhausted.

BISMARCK, German battleship of 45,000 tons, was completed at Kiel early in 1941 and sailed, accompanied by the heavy cruiser *Prinz Eugen*, from Gdynia on 18 May for operations against British convoys in the North Atlantic. She was reported as she passed through the Kattegat and sighted by air reconnaissance while in harbour near Bergen taking on additional fuel. Attempt-ing to break out into the Atlantic through the Denmark Strait between Iceland and Greenland, she was again sighted and reported by two British cruisers on patrol there, the *Suffolk* and *Norfolk*, which settled down to shadow her, reporting all her movements and alterations of course.

Meanwhile the British Home Fleet had sailed from * Scapa Flow. A northern squadron, consisting of the old battle-cruiser *Hood* and the newly commissioned but as yet unworked-up battleship *Prince of Wales*, was south of Iceland; the commander-in-chief in the battleship *King George V*, with the battle-cruiser *Repulse*, the aircraft carrier *Victorious*, three cruisers, and seven destroyers sailed on a more southerly course to cover outward and homeward bound convoys.

The *Hood* and the *Prince of Wales* made contact with the *Bismarck* and *Prinz Eugen* as they emerged from the Denmark Strait early on 24 May. In a brief action the *Hood* was sunk and the *Prince of Wales* damaged; the *Bismarck* was also hit three times, one shellburst isolating 1,000 tons of oil fuel stowed in tanks forward, a hit which had a considerable bearing on subsequent events. After the sinking of the *Hood*, the *Prince of Wales* joined the *Suffolk* and *Norfolk* and continued to shadow the German ships.

Later that day the British commander-in-chief detached the carrier *Victorious* to carry out an air attack with torpedoes on the *Bismarck*. One hit was obtained at about midnight, but did no damage to the *Bismarck*.

Meanwhile the British Admiralty had ordered Force H, consisting of the battle-cruiser *Renown*, the aircraft carrier * Ark Royal, and the cruiser *Sheffield*, normally stationed at Gibraltar, to sail to the northward, and the battleship *Rodney*, then some 550 miles to the north-eastward, to close the enemy. Early in the morning of the 25th, the *Bismarck* and *Prinz Eugen* parted company, the former steering south-eastward towards the coast of France, the latter southward into the mid-Atlantic. The reason for the *Bismarck* making for a port on the French coast was the loss of those 1,000 tons of oil fuel during the earlier action.

At about the same time the shadowing cruiser, the *Suffolk*, lost her radar contact with the *Bismarck*, and the German ship disappeared into the Atlantic. It was at first thought in the fleet that she had broken away to the north-westward, and both ships and aircraft searched in that direction. It was not until the evening that firm indications were received that she was in fact steaming towards a French port. By that time the British Home Fleet was about 150 miles astern of her.

All through the day of the 25th, and the night of the 25th/26th, the *Bismarck* was lost, and it was not until 1030 on the morning of the 26th that she was sighted by a shore-based aircraft flying a search patrol. Within a few minutes, naval aircraft from the carrier *Ark Royal* were also in touch, and they shadowed her throughout the day. Although the weather was deteriorating fast, naval air torpedo attacks were mounted from the *Ark Royal* during the evening of the 26th, and three hits on the *Bismarck* were obtained. Two did little damage, but the third torpedo hit her on her rudders, so that she was unable to steer. She came up into the wind, her speed reduced to six or seven knots.

A destroyer flotilla detached from a convoy made contact with her that night, keeping her always in sight and attacking with torpedoes. She was hit five more times. And throughout the night the *King George V* with the *Rodney* in company were closing for the kill. They sighted the stricken ship shortly after 0800 on the 27th and, opening fire with their heavy guns, reduced her to a shambles in a little less than an hour. She was finally sunk by torpedoes from the cruiser *Dorsetshire*. One hundred and ten survivors were picked up by the *Dorsetshire* and the destroyer *Maori*.

BITE, to, an *anchor is said to bite when the *flukes bed themselves into the ground and hold firm without *dragging.

BITT STOPPER, a length of rope, in the days when ships had hemp cables for their anchors, used to bind the cable more securely to the *bitts to prevent it slipping. When a ship anchored and enough cable was run out, it was brought to the bitts and secured by several turns round them. The bitt stopper was then passed round the turns to bind the cable in taut so that it could not render round the bitts. With the general substitution of chain for the older hemp cables, bitt stoppers no longer have any place in modern ships.

BITTER, the name given to any turn of the anchor *cable of a ship about the *bitts. Hence, a ship is 'brought up to a bitter' when the cable is allowed to run out to that turn around the bitts or to its modern equivalent which is a Blake slip stopper. See also BITTER END, CABLE STOPPERS.

BITTER END, that part of the anchor *cable of a vessel which is abaft the *bitts and thus remains within board when a ship is riding to her *anchor. To *pay a rope or chain out to the bitter end means that all has been paid out and no more remains to be let go. 'Bend to the bitter end' means to reverse a cable, to *bend the inboard end of it to the anchor so that the strain on the cable when a ship is anchored now comes on a part of it that has been less used and is therefore more trustworthy.

BITTS, in older ships, a frame composed of two strong pillars of straight oak timber, fixed upright in the fore part of the ship and bolted to the deck *beams, to which were secured the *cables when the ship rode to an anchor. Smaller bitts were fitted in square-rigged sailing vessels for securing other parts of the running *rigging, such as topsail-sheet bitts, paul-bitts, *carrick-bitts, *windlass-bitts, *gallows-bitts, *jeer-bitts, etc. They all served the same purpose, providing a convenient means of taking a securing turn with the *fall of whatever piece of rigging was involved.

BLACK BOOK OF THE ADMIRALTY, the English codification of the laws of *Oleron made in 1336 and containing also a list of the ancient customs and usages of the sea. The original book disappeared from the registry of the High Court of Admiralty at the beginning of the 19th century (it was last seen and consulted by Sir Christopher Robinson for his work *Collectania Maritima,* 1801). A few MS. copies of parts of it, some dating back to about 1420, exist, notably in the British Museum and Bodleian libraries. Sir Travers Twiss, H.M. Advocate-General, collated all known sources in his *Black Book of the Admiralty* (4 vols, 1871).

BLACK JACK, (1) the flag traditionally flown by pirate ships. Popular imagination gives this flag a white device of skull and crossed bones in the centre of the black field, but there is no real evidence to substantiate this. W. G. Perrin, an authority on ancient flags, gives the pirate flag as a black skeleton on a yellow field. It is more probable that individual pirate captains designed their own flags, if in fact they ever flew them, to their own taste of the moment. **(2)** The name popularly given by sailors to the bubonic plague, whose victims were said to turn black.

BLACK SHIP, a description used by British shipbuilders during the days of sail of a ship built in India of Burmese teak. The term presumably came from the colour of the men who built the ship rather than from the type of wood of which she was built, as teak is as light in colour as oak.

BLACK SQUALL, a sudden squall of wind, accompanied by lightning, encountered in the West Indies. It is usually caused by the heated state of the atmosphere near land where the warm expanded air is repelled by a colder medium to leeward and driven back with great force, frequently engendering electrical storms of great intensity.

BLACK STRAKE, a wide band of the planking along a ship's side, just above the *wales, which was painted during the 17th and 18th centuries with tar and lamp black as a preservative and also as a contrast between the white *boot-topping of the ship's bottom and the varnished wood of the sides. Oil paint was not used in ships, except very occasionally inboard, until the last quarter of the 18th century.

BLACKBIRD, an old sea term for an African slave. Hence the term blackbirding, said of ships which were engaged actively in the slave trade.

BLACK-DOWN, to, the operation of tarring and blacking the rigging, or of blacking the ship's side. The best mixture was said to be coal tar, vegetable tar, and salt water boiled together and laid on hot. In both cases the object was preservation against the action of salt water on hemp and wood.

During the 18th century some captains of British warships sent out to cruise independently against the enemy or his seaborne trade would black-down the entire hulls of their ships in the belief that a black ship appeared smaller at sea than she actually was and therefore might attract enemy ships, hopeful of an easy conquest, within range of her guns.

'BLACK'S THE WHITE OF MY EYE', a sailor's term indicating an indignant rebuttal of a charge of misdemeanour and that all he has just said is the truth, the whole truth, and nothing but the truth.

BLACKWALL FRIGATES, the generic name given to a series of sail trading ships built between 1837 and 1869 for the Indian trade following the expiration of the *East India Company's exclusive charter in 1833, which threw the trade to the East open to all comers. They got their name because many of them were built at Green and Wigram's yard at Blackwall, on the River Thames, and because they were said to be 'frigate-built', not from any resemblance in design to the typical naval *frigate but because they were built with a finer *run and were thus faster than the typical *East Indiaman and in this respect could be compared in performance much in the same way as could a frigate with a *ship of the line.

Three firms were concerned with the building of Blackwall frigates, Green and Wigram of Blackwall, T. and W. Smith of the Tyne, and Duncan Dunbar of Sunderland. The first of them was Green and Wigram's *Seringapatam*, a *packet-ship of 818 tons, built in 1837, which set up a new record of eighty-five days from London to Bombay. A large number of these Blackwall frigates were built, many of them at Moulmein of Burmese teak, and they dominated the trade to and from India until the opening of the *Suez Canal in 1869. Thereafter, though they continued to run successfully for a time in the wool trade from Australia, they were eclipsed by the revolutionary American-built *clipper ships.

BLACKWOOD, Sir HENRY (1770–1832), British vice admiral, was, after Thomas Masterman *Hardy, probably the best known of all Lord *Nelson's captains. He made a great name for himself in 1800 when, in command of the *frigate *Penelope*, he so harried the French *ship of the line *Guillaume Tell* when she tried to escape from Malta that she fell an easy prey to British forces the following day. In 1805, when Nelson and his fleet lay over the horizon off Cape Trafalgar waiting for the Franco-Spanish fleet to come out from Cadiz and fight, Blackwood in the *Euryalus* maintained a watch on them close inshore and, two days before the battle, reported to Nelson by *distant signal that the ships were *weighing their anchors. Thereafter he shadowed their movements, reporting every move to the British fleet, which remained beyond the horizon, until the morning of 21 October, when the two fleets were in sight of each other and the battle of *Trafalgar was imminent. The *Euryalus* was one of the repeating frigates during the battle, ensuring that all signals were passed on to those ships which might not be able to see them in the smoke of the battle.

He commanded the 80-gun ship *Ajax* in 1807 at the forcing of the *Dardanelles, was promoted rear admiral in 1814 and vice admiral in 1819, and ended his naval career as commander-in-chief at the *Nore, a post he held from 1827 to 1830.

BLAEU, WILLIAM JANSZOON (*fl.* 1608), Dutch publisher of maps and charts, followed Lucas *Wagenaer in the compilation of sea atlases. Little attempt had been made to keep Wagenaer's famous *Mariners Mirrour* (1585) up-to-date but in 1608 the house of Blaeu, which under Willem Blaeu had become the leading publishing house in Holland, brought out their *Licht de Zeevaerdt* (The Light of Navigation), an English version being published in 1612. Acknowledging the lead given by Wagenaer, Blaeu compiled much improved charts and the practice of exaggerating those parts of the coast where intricate pilotage was required was abandoned for true scale representation. The house of Blaeu built up an organization in Amsterdam which, by examining seamen's journals and questioning sailors, enabled the charts in *The Light of Navigation* to be kept up to date well into the 17th century. His atlases were beautiful examples of the contemporary cartographic art, decorated with cartouches of surprising loveliness, but nevertheless of great accuracy for their period.

BLAKE, ROBERT (1599–1657), British admiral and colonel, was born at Bridgewater and educated at Wadham College, Oxford. Nothing is known about him until he distinguished himself as a soldier in the defence of Bristol and Lyme during the Civil War. In 1649 he was appointed with *Deane and *Popham as a *'general-at-sea' to chase Prince *Rupert's squadron which had declared for the royalist cause, and in 1651 he captured the Scilly Islands which were still holding out for the royalists.

In 1652, at the start of the First Dutch War (1652–4), he commanded in the Channel, from which he evicted *Tromp and de *Ruyter, but was himself later defeated off Dungeness in an action from which the legend originated that Tromp lashed a broom to his masthead to indicate that he would sweep the English from the sea. He was also defeated by Tromp the next year off Portland, but at the subsequent battle of the *Gabbard forced him to retreat to the Texel.

In 1654 he commanded a fleet in the Mediterranean to bring to submission the *Barbary corsairs at the battle of *Porto Farina, Tunis. On the outbreak of the war with Spain in 1656 he was sent to operate off *Cadiz, where one of his captains, Richard Stayner, captured the treasure fleet. In April 1657 Blake intercepted another treasure fleet at *Santa Cruz, Tenerife, where, in spite of his wounds and the strong position of the enemy, he destroyed the escorting fleet. Ill health compelled him to return home and he died entering Plymouth Sound on 7 August 1657. His body lay in state at Greenwich before being buried in Westminster Abbey, whence it was exhumed and thrown into the Thames after the restoration of Charles II.

Blake laid the foundations of naval discipline and tactics in the British Navy by his introduction of the *Articles of War and the *Fighting Instructions. His short but brilliant career at sea fully entitled him to Lord Clarendon's tribute as 'the copy of naval courage'.

R. Beadon, *Robert Blake* (1935).
J. R. Powell, *Robert Blake* (1972).

BLAKE SLIP, see CABLE STOPPERS.

BLANE, Sir GILBERT (1749–1834), naval physician, took his degree at Glasgow and in 1779 accompanied Lord *Rodney as his personal physician to the West Indies, where Rodney made him physician of the fleet. In the War of American Independence (1775–82), and again when a commissioner of the Sick and Wounded Board from 1795 to 1802, Blane enforced the teachings of his predecessor, James *Lind, being a more influential though not so original thinker. During the peace he occupied a distinguished post at St. Thomas's Hospital and

was the personal physician of the Prince Regent. When he rejoined the naval service as a commissioner he was chiefly responsible for the introduction of lemon juice as a specific against *scurvy, as Lind had recommended forty years earlier.

After the war he led the way in the compilation of naval medical statistics and improved the status of the naval surgeon by founding the Blane Medal, which is still awarded for meritorious work in that branch. His most important books are his *Observations on the Diseases of Seamen* (1785) and his *Select Dissertations* (1822), in which he turned his attention to social medicine. He was a Fellow of the Royal Society and played a leading part in the affairs of the Royal College of Physicians.

BLEED, to, the operation of draining out of a *buoy any water which may have seeped inside after long use at sea. It was also a naval term in the British Navy to describe the surreptitious removal of *grog in transit between the point of issue from the grog-tub to the mess for which it was due. It was carried between these points in a tall *monkey, a wooden 'kid' or bucket wider at the bottom than at the top, and if a swig were taken en route, it was known as 'bleeding the monkey'. See also, similarly, SUCKING THE MONKEY.

BLIGH, WILLIAM (1754–1817), British vice admiral, proved himself as a navigator when he served as master of the *Resolution during Captain James *Cook's last voyage of circumnavigation in 1775–9. In 1787 he was appointed to command the armed transport *Bounty to take breadfruit seedlings from Tahiti to the West Indies. On 28 April 1789, when the ship was off Tofua in the Friendly Islands, a mutiny broke out under the leadership of Fletcher *Christian, Bligh's protégé: Bligh with eighteen others was turned adrift in the ship's launch, in which they made a remarkable open-boat voyage of 3,600 miles to reach Timor, near Java.

Bligh's severity as a commanding officer has been cited as the cause of the mutiny, but this is disputed (see BOUNTY). In his subsequent career he showed courage on many occasions, but a continuing difficulty in getting on with other people. He played a distinguished part as a captain at the battles of *Camperdown (1797) and *Copenhagen (1801), but when sent out as governor of New South Wales he quarrelled with his deputy over the rum traffic, was arrested by the local militia, and was sent home in 1808. He was promoted rear admiral in 1811 and rose to vice admiral three years later.

G. Mackaness, *Life of Vice Admiral William Bligh*, 2 vols (1931).

BLOCK, a wooden or metal case in which one or more sheaves are fitted. They are used for various purposes in a ship, either when as part of a *purchase to increase the mechanical power applied to ropes or to lead them to convenient positions for handling. Blocks are of various sizes and powers; a single block contains one sheave, a double block has two, and a threefold block has three, and so on. A fiddle block has two sheaves fitted one below the other.

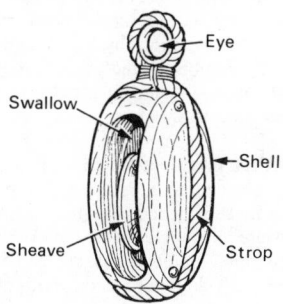

Single stropped block

Blocks consist of four parts: the shell, or outside wooden part, the sheave, on which the rope runs, the pin, on which the sheave turns, and the strop, which is of rope or wire spliced round the shell and by which the block can be attached wherever it is required to work. See also PURCHASE.

BLOCKADE, in maritime warfare a declaration published by a belligerent power forbidding seaborne trade with an enemy. Originally, in the days of the sailing warship and the short-range gun, blockade was virtually synonymous with investment, a squadron patrolling off an enemy port to prevent all movement in and out. With the invention of the long-range gun, the mine, and the torpedo, such close blockade became no longer a feasible operation of war, and a distant blockade took its place, in which seaborne trade with a declared enemy was intercepted many miles out at sea from the blockaded coast. Blockade is universally admitted to be a belligerent right to which neutral countries are bound to submit. It forms a part of international maritime law.

The declaration of a state of blockade was widely used, and abused, during the Napoleonic war, nations declaring what were known as 'paper blockades' without adequate naval power to enforce them. As a result, agreement was reached in 1826 and 1827, between Great Britain and the U.S.A., the main sufferers under the 'paper blockades', that for a blockade to be binding, especially with regard to neutral shipping, it must be effective, and it is on this basis that modern blockade is recognized.

An attempt to get international agreement on rules for blockade was made at the second Hague Conference in 1907 but had to be abandoned as, for some reason, it was not included on the agenda; but a conference of maritime powers was called by Great Britain in 1908 to formulate a set of rules covering all the branches of laws and customs of naval warfare, and among the subjects was that of blockade. Twenty-one articles setting out the rules under which blockade can be enforced were agreed, and these articles still constitute the law of naval blockade as we know it today.

If a ship breaks a blockade by escaping the blockading force she may, if taken in any part of a future voyage, be captured *in delicto* and subject to confiscation for the original running of the blockade.

BLOCKSHIP, a *hulk, or obsolete vessel, stripped of most of her internal fittings and filled with cement or other suitable material, and *scuttled in position either to block an entrance to a port or anchorage for war purposes or occasionally to fill a gap in a *breakwater or to provide other shelter to an exposed anchorage. Perhaps the best remembered use of blockships was during the First World War (1914–18) in the abortive British attempt in April 1918 to block the entrance to the Zeebrugge–Bruges Canal, used by German *U-boats as an exit from their shelters at Bruges into the North Sea. Another well-known example was the failure of a blockship to arrive in time to seal an entrance into the British naval anchorage at *Scapa Flow just after the start of the Second World War through which Günther *Prien, in *U.18*, entered the Flow and sank the British *battleship *Royal Oak* in October 1939. In this case the blockship arrived one day too late.

'BLOOD IS THICKER THAN WATER', a well-known saying attributed to Commodore Josiah *Tattnall, U.S.N., when justifying his intervention in the British attack on the Peiho forts in June 1859 during the Second China War (1856–9). He used his ship, the *Toeywan*, to tow the British boats from the shore with the survivors of the land attack, and is credited with using this expression in conversation with the British commander-in-chief, Sir James Hope, the following day.

'BLOODY FLAG', the colloquial description of the large square red flag which used to be hoisted at the mastheads of British warships to indicate that they were about to go into battle. Other nations also hoisted distinctive flags at the mastheads of their ships during battle. The main purpose for these flags was to serve as an aid to distinguishing friend from foe in the smoke of action. Today warships of all nations going into battle hoist their national *ensign, for this purpose known as a battle ensign, at the mastheads and other prominent positions in the ship.

BLOW, to, the action of a whale when it comes to the surface, or *breaches, and expels the seawater it has taken in while feeding. It blows out the seawater in a great spout several feet high, and it was this high spout of seawater which enabled the older whaling men, before the days of *radar and *sonar, to sight their prey and close for the kill. 'There she blows', the traditional hail of the look-out in a *whaler when he sights the spouting water thrown up by a whale.

'BLOWING GREAT GUNS AND SMALL ARMS', an old maritime term for a heavy gale or a hurricane.

'BLOWING THE GRAMPUS', a term used in older ships for waking a sailor asleep on watch by throwing a bucketful of cold water over him.

BLUE ENSIGN, originally denoted the rear admiral's squadron of the English fleet (see SQUADRONAL COLOURS). When the division of the fleet into red, white, and blue squadrons was abolished in 1864 the blue ensign was reserved for naval auxiliary vessels. Owners of yachts registered with certain clubs in Britain are granted permission by the British Admiralty to fly the blue ensign, but in all such cases the ensign must be defaced by the inclusion of some insignia or design in the *fly of the ensign.

BLUE LIGHT, a pyrotechnical preparation used for signalling in a fleet at night before the introduction of electric flashing lights and the *Morse code. It was also known as a Bengal light. Blue lights were used in conjunction with gunfire to express an admiral's wishes or for ships to make reports to him. By counting the number of guns fired and observing the blue lights shown, the captain of a ship could interpret through his night signal book the order which the admiral was making.

BLUE PETER, the signal that a ship is about to sail and that all persons concerned should report on board. The flag, which is hoisted at the foretopmasthead, or main-topmasthead in ships with only one mast, is a rectangular flag with a blue ground and a white rectangle in the centre. It is P flag in the *International Code of Signals.

'BLUE PIGEON', the sailor's name for the sounding *lead.

BLUE RIBAND (or RIBBON) OF THE ATLANTIC, a notional trophy for the fastest sea crossing of the Atlantic for which liners unofficially but none the less enthusiastically competed until the recent withdrawal of the last large and fast liners. One of the original *Cunard liners, the *Acadia* built in 1840, was the first to hold it; and her eastbound record was beaten in 1851 by the Collins liner *Pacific* with a speed of 13 *knots.

Ships of all the great transatlantic lines have held it since, with speeds rising progressively to 22·35 knots by the *Kaiser Wilhelm der Grosse* in 1897, to 27·4 knots by the *Mauretania* in 1907, over 30 knots by the *Queen Mary* and the *Normandie* in 1937, and finally 35·59 knots by the *United States* in 1952.

BLUEJACKET, a descriptive term used to describe the seaman of a British warship. It came into being in 1858 when rules for the uniform of seamen were promulgated in the *Navy List* of that year, which included a jacket 'to be made of navy blue cloth double-breasted, with stand and fall collar ... to reach the hips ... one inside breast-pocket and seven black horn crown and anchor buttons'. It was this jacket which brought the name bluejacket into use, the description used for this purpose before uniform was introduced being 'tar', short for tarpaulin, which seamen wore in wet and windy weather on board. See SAILORS' DRESS.

BLYTH, CHAY (1940–), British singlehanded yachtsman, assisted Captain John Ridgway, a fellow soldier in the Parachute Regiment, in rowing an open *dory, *English Rose III*, across the Atlantic from Cape Cod to the Aran Islands in 1966, taking ninety-two days. In 1968 he started a single-handed voyage round the world in *Dytiscus*, a 30-ft (9·1 m) *fibre glass sloop, but after sailing some 9,000 miles found the yacht unable to stand up to the seas in wild weather off the coast of Brazil and put into Port Elizabeth.

He was now determined to attempt to sail alone round the world 'the wrong way round' for sailing vessels, that is, westabout by way of Cape Horn, New Zealand, and the Cape of Good Hope. Under the sponsorship of the British Steel Corporation, he started from Hamble in November 1970 alone in the yacht *British Steel*, designed specially for this voyage by Robert *Clark and built of steel at Dartmouth. The circumnavigation was completed without undue trouble to yacht or gear when Blyth sailed back to Hamble in August 1971 in a record time for a single-hulled sailing vessel of 292 days. He is the author of *The Impossible Voyage*, and, with his wife Maureen Blyth, of *Innocent Aboard*.

H.M.S. Cossack *forcing her way alongside the German tanker* Altmark; *oil painting by Norman Wilkinson*

BOARD, a word much used at sea with a variety of meanings, but chiefly indicating the distances which a sailing vessel runs between *tacks when working to windward. Thus a ship tacking across the wind to reach a point to windward of her present position can make short or long boards according to the frequency of her tacks; the more frequently she tacks, the shorter the boards. To make a good board, to sail in a straight line when *close-hauled without making any *leeway; to make a stern board, to come up head to wind so that the vessel stops and makes way astern until she falls off on the opposite tack, often a very seamanlike operation when navigating in narrow channels; to board it up, a term often used by older seamen meaning to *beat up to windward.

Other meanings of the word are, to go on board, to go into a ship; to slip by the board, to desert a ship by escaping down the ship's side; by the board, close to the deck as when a mast is broken off close to the deck level, or goes by the board. See also BOARD, TO.

BOARD, to, an attempt to capture an enemy ship by going alongside and grappling her, and then assaulting her with a boarding party. This was a well-known practice in battle in the days of the sailing navies when ships engaged each other at a range of 'half-pistol-shot', or about 100 yards; it fell out of use as an operation of war when modern guns with a range of several miles were introduced into navies. Nevertheless, the last occasion of boarding in wartime occurred in February 1940 when H.M.S. *Cossack entered the Jossing Fjord in southern Norway and went alongside the German auxiliary *tanker *Altmark*, sending away a boarding party to rescue 299 British seamen who were held prisoner on board. See also CLOSE QUARTERS, CUTLASS, STINKPOT.

BOARD OF ADMIRALTY, see LORDS COMMISSIONERS FOR . . .

BOARD OF LONGITUDE, the general name by which the Commissioners for the Discovery of the Longitude at Sea were known. It was set up by Act of Parliament during the reign of Queen Anne in 1714. Its early history is closely associated with William Whiston, a dissenting clergyman who had been professor of mathematics in Cambridge University, and Humfrey Ditton, mathematics master at Christ's Hospital School. They published in 1713 a method of finding a ship's position at sea by using pyrotechnic and explosive signals, and although their proposals were impracticable, they engineered a petition to Parliament proposing that a reward be offered for a solution of the means of determining longitude at sea. The petition was received by the House and a committee appointed to examine it. Eminent mathematicians and astronomers, including Sir Isaac Newton and Edmund *Halley, were consulted, and on their recommendation the Board was set up.

It had long been recognized that accurate

longitude could be determined at sea if it were possible to know the exact time at Greenwich, from which all longitude east and west was measured, at the moment of local noon on the longitude on which the ship herself was, each 15° of longitude east or west equalling one hour in time earlier or later than the time at Greenwich. It was therefore on these lines that the probable solution lay, and most research was directed to the construction of a clock so reliable and accurate that it would record Greenwich time constantly throughout a ship's voyage. The Board offered a prize of £20,000 for a solution of the problem, stipulating an accuracy to within 30 miles, and it was awarded in 1765 to John *Harrison, the designer of several remarkable timepieces, the most accurate of which, during a voyage from Britain to Barbados and home, lost only 15 seconds in 156 days. Only half the prize money was paid at first, as some of the Commissioners expressed doubts as to the validity of Harrison's achievement, since the Act of Parliament called for a method to be generally applicable, and a single chronometer could hardly be classed as providing this. However, the balance of the prize money was paid to Harrison in 1773, although it was not until the mid-19th century that chronometers were readily available for all ocean-going vessels.

The Commissioners were also empowered to grant sums of money not exceeding £2,000 annually to assist *bona fide* investigators, and to award prizes for minor discoveries and improvements in relation to the longitude problem. The first such grant of money was made in 1737 and the last in 1815. The Board continued to operate until 1828, by which time the longitude problem ceased to attract attention. During its existence, the Board disbursed more than £100,000.

BOARDERS, sailors appointed to make an attack on an enemy ship by boarding, or to repel such attempts by an enemy. In the British Navy, four men from each gun's crew were generally allotted as boarders. Their duties, after the capture of the enemy ship, were to man the pumps, repair the rigging as much as possible to make the ship seaworthy, and trim the sails so that she could be sailed away as a *prize.

BOAT, the generic name for small open craft without any decking and usually propelled by oars or outboard engine, and sometimes by a small *lugsail on a short mast. Some exceptions to this general definition are fishing boats, sometimes decked or half-decked and propelled by sail and/or inboard diesel engine, and *submarines, which are generally known as boats irrespective of size. This oddity of nomenclature almost certainly derives from their original and universal description as submarine boats. The original torpedoboats, forerunners of the more modern *destroyers and *frigates, were also generally known in their time as boats although built up to a displacement of 250–300 tons. Another exception to the general rule is the modern fast patrol boat, successor to the *motor torpedoboats and *motor gunboats of the Second World War. Some yachts are also often known as boats.

Boat is a word frequently used by people ashore when they really mean ship, and such terms as packet boat, mail boat, etc., are in fairly general use. Railway companies also run boat trains to take passengers to a ship in which they are sailing for some destination. But a seaman will never call any sort of ship, packet, mail, or any other, a boat as the two terms are not synonymous and are to him quite distinct.

BOATSWAIN (pron. bo'sun), the officer, or warrant officer, in charge of sails, rigging, anchors, cables, etc. It is his responsibility that all these adjuncts of the ship work efficiently, and that sufficient stores are carried on board for their replacement when necessary. He has also direct charge of all work on deck under the general supervision of the officer of the deck or the executive officer and details the crew to carry out the day-to-day work of the ship. In spite of his title, the ships' boats do not normally come under his jurisdiction.

BOATSWAIN-BIRD, a tropical bird, *Phaeton oethereus,* so called because its cry has the sound of a boatswain's whistle. It is distinguished also by two long feathers in its tail, known by sailors as *marline-spikes.

BOATSWAIN'S CHAIR, a short board, secured in a *bridle, used to sway a man aloft for scraping or painting masts, and treating yards, rigging, etc.

BOATSWAIN'S PIPE, a peculiarly shaped whistle, of great antiquity, used by boatswain's mates of warships to pipe orders throughout the ship. A variety of tones can be produced on a pipe, and each order had its own particular call. Up to Tudor times in the English Navy, the pipe, or whistle, often set with jewels, was the personal insignia of the *Lord High Admiral, and was worn around the neck on a long gold chain. Since the advent of the Tannoy system of loudspeakers, boatswain's pipes are no longer in general use for promulgating orders and, in the British and some other navies, their only use today is for the ceremonial piping on board of visiting commanding officers and other dignitaries.

BOBSTAY, a chain or heavy wire rigging running from the end of the *bowsprit to the ship's *stem or *cutwater. Particularly heavy rigging was required in this position since the foretopmast in sailing vessels was *stayed to the bowsprit, exerting a strong upward pull when the sails were full of wind. The bowsprit was also secured by *shrouds from either bow of the ship. Very few sailing vessels are fitted with bowsprits today and in consequence the bobstay is rarely seen as a piece of rigging; the only ships still to use it being the square-rigged school ships which are operated by various nations for training purposes, and some yachts.

BODY PLAN, a drawing made during the design stages of a ship giving a view at right angles to the *sheer draught and showing the form of her principal or midship section. See also NAVAL ARCHITECTURE.

BOEIER or **BOIER,** a craft used on the inland waterways of the Netherlands, with apple-shaped bows and stern, rounded bottom, and broad fan-shaped *leeboards for sailing in very shallow waters. The boeier originated in the early part of the 16th century as a seagoing merchant vessel some 65 feet in length and 23 to 26 feet in breadth, rigged with either a *spritsail or a boomless mainsail having *brails and a standing *gaff, and often setting a square *topsail above. Some of the earliest and largest of the boeiers carried in addition a small *lateen mizen.

By the 19th century the boeier had changed to the present form of bluff-ended inland waterways type and been reduced in size, ranging generally from 40 feet to as little as 26 feet in length. The single mast, stepped in a *tabernacle for lowering at bridges, generally carried a boomed mainsail with the typical Dutch curved gaff, a foresail set on the forestay, and a jib which could be set on a running *bowsprit. Later examples were built of steel. The boeier became the most common type of *pavilionenjacht*, or pleasure craft with stateroom accommodation, until well into the 20th century.

BOLLARD, a vertical piece of timber or iron, fixed to the ground, to which a ship's mooring lines are made fast when alongside. They were also sometimes known as nigger-heads. In the old whaling days when *harpoons were launched by hand, the thick piece of wood fixed to the head of the whale-boat round which the harpooner took a turn of the line in order to veer it steadily after the whale had been struck was also known as a bollard. In many naval dockyards the old muzzle-loading ships' guns, planted breech end downwards, were used as bollards along the length of jetties, having been made redundant by the introduction of the breech-loading gun.

BOLSTER, a piece of wood fitted in various places in a ship to act as a preventive to chafe or

nip. They were more often to be found in wooden sailing vessels than they are in modern steel ships, although in the latter the pieces of oak timber often fixed to the deck around the *hawseholes to prevent the *cable from rubbing against the hawsehole cheeks are known as bolsters. In the older wooden sailing ships the pieces of soft wood, usually covered with canvas, which rested on the *trestle-trees to prevent them getting nipped by the rigging were also called bolsters.

BOLT, the standard measurement of length of canvas as supplied by the makers for use at sea. It is a piece, or roll, 39 yards (35·6 m) in length. There is no standard measurement of width, but normally it is supplied in widths varying from 22–30 inches (56–76 cm).

BOLT-ROPE, the name given to the rope which is sewn around the edges of a sail to keep the canvas from fraying. While the whole rope is known as the bolt-rope, it is subdivided in name according to the side of the sail on which it is sewn, as luff-rope, foot-rope, etc. Bolt-ropes are always placed slightly to the left of centre of the edge on which they are sewn to enable the seaman to orientate the sail by feel in the dark.

BOMB VESSEL or **BOMB KETCH,** a ship of the old sailing navies armed with one, or occasionally two, heavy howitzers or mortars and used for bombarding places ashore. Mostly the mortars were fitted in *ketches, either specially built or converted into such from a small three-masted vessel by the removal of her foremast to provide a good deck space forward for the mortars. When employed in bombardment, bomb vessels were moored in position with *springs on their cables so that the ships themselves were 'trained' for the mortars to fire on the desired bearing. Until 1804, in the British Navy, mortars in bomb vessels were manned and worked by the Royal Artillery; after that date by the newly formed Royal Marine Artillery. The development of naval guns which could be trained and elevated irrespective of the ship's course made all bomb vessels obsolete. Their modern naval counterpart could be said to be the *monitor.

During the latter part of the 18th and first half of the 19th centuries bomb ketches were also used extensively for exploration of the Arctic. They were always exceptionally strongly built and had had their decks stiffened with heavy beam bridges to support the shock of the recoil of the heavy mortars and thus were well suited to withstand the pressure of ice when frozen in or beset. They were generally vessels of 350–400 tons displacement with an average length of 110–20 feet and a beam of about 30 feet. See also FURY, H.M.S.; HECLA, H.M.S.; TERROR, H.M.S.

BOMBARD, ALAIN (1924–), French doctor of medicine and a pioneer of the art of survival at sea, was born in Paris and qualified at the Faculty of Medicine there before taking a hospital post at Boulogne. There he began to study the problems connected with survival at sea and in 1952, to prove his theory that it was possible for shipwrecked mariners to survive and exist solely on the resources of the sea, he set out to cross the Atlantic on an inflatable raft called L'Hérétique. The voyage was successful and he published an account of it under the title Histoire d'un naufragé voluntaire (History of a Voluntary Castaway). He built a sea laboratory for the study of the physiopathology of sailors in 1959, and subsequently became Délégué Général to the Fondation Scientifique Ricard which is sponsoring research into marine biology on the Île des Embiez, a few kilometres west of Toulon. He swam the Channel in 1951 and is a Chevalier of the Legion of Honour.

'BOMBARDON', see MULBERRY HARBOUR.

BOMBAY, the chief seaport of western India, is known all over the world by seamen as one of the most spacious and beautiful in the world, with a sheltered harbour of 70 square miles. Originally owned by Portugal, it passed to the British crown in 1661 through the marriage of Charles II with Princess Catherine of Braganza. In 1668 it was transferred by Charles to the *East India Company, who sent out a most enlightened man, Gerald Aungier, as its president. Under his rule, the town prospered exceedingly. Its seaport owes its existence to its development as a naval base during the British wars against France of 1744–8 and 1756–63. But what gave Bombay its greatest spur to development as a port was the great famine in China in 1770. More land there was, by government order, used for growing rice, and thus less land for growing cotton was available. The Bombay cotton mills were rapidly expanded to meet the demand from China for cotton cloth, and the whole cotton industry grew at a tremendous pace with Bombay becoming the chief port for its export. The opening of the *Suez Canal in 1869, with its considerable shortening of the route from India and the Far East to Western Europe, gave a further great impetus to the development of Bombay as a port.

The growth in size of modern shipping, particularly of bulk carriers and container ships, has brought problems to Bombay, where the depth of water inside the harbour is insufficient to take such large vessels. Plans are at present in existence to build a new deep water port on the opposite side of the estuary at Nhava-Sheva, where adequate berths for these large ships could be provided.

BONAVENTURE, an additional *mizen sail, *lateen in shape, which used to be carried on a fourth mast, known as a bonaventure mizen, in the older sailing ships. It went out of use during the 17th century, when the standard three masts was adopted as the most efficient rig for ships. Bonaventure was also a ship's name much in favour for merchant vessels in England, usually coupled with a christian name of the owner, during the reign of Elizabeth I (1558–1603). She herself owned a ship named Elizabeth Bonaventure. A possible reason for its popularity as a name was because all goods shipped abroad at this period in the way of opening up seaborne trade were carried under a *bill of adventure, with perhaps the French adjective bon attached to bring good fortune.

BONE, the white feather of water under the bow of a ship when she is under way. A ship moving fast through the water and throwing up an appreciable feather is said to have a bone in her mouth, or in her teeth.

BONE, Sir DAVID (1874–1959), was a member of a Scots family with notable artistic gifts. He went to sea as an apprentice in sail, his initiation being described in The Brassbounder (1910), which is of its particular sort a minor classic. He served the Anchor Line, in which he rose to become commodore, and by the time of the First World War (1914–18) was entrusted with the command of major vessels. His experiences were described in Merchantman-at-Arms (1919) which was illustrated by his artist brother, Sir Muirhead *Bone. At the outbreak of the Second World War in 1939 Bone, though in his fiftieth year at sea, was still commanding big ships. In these he served in many parts of the world, including some of the major landings on the Italian mainland. His later adventures were described in Merchantman Re-armed (1949) when once again he had the advantage of Muirhead Bone's illustrations. David Bone's career was most unusual, and the quality of his writing fully matched his adventures.

BONE, Sir MUIRHEAD (1876–1953), British artist, was born in Glasgow and studied art there before settling in London in 1901. He was noted particularly for the excellence of his drawing and he served as an official war artist with the British Navy in both the First World War (1914–18) and the Second (1939–45). The boldness of his line and his feeling for atmosphere and the sea made his drawings outstandingly powerful, never better exemplified than in the series of drawings he produced of the *Grand Fleet in *Scapa Flow during the First World War. His work has been compared with that of the great Italian artist Giovanni Piranesi (1720–78). He was the brother of Sir David *Bone, whose books were greatly enhanced by his illustrations.

'BONE', to, a naval term meaning to scrounge or pilfer. The term derives from a boatswain named Bone who served in the flagship of Admiral *Cornwallis during the Revolutionary War (1793–1801) and was adept at acquiring ship's stores from other ships to make good his deficits or build up a surplus. At the end of the commission Cornwallis is said to have remarked, 'I trust, Mr. Bone, that you will leave me my *bower anchors.'

BONHOMME RICHARD, the *frigate in which John Paul *Jones made his famous privateering cruise round Britain in 1779. She was originally the East Indiaman *Duc de Duras*, built in 1766, of about 900 tons and mounting forty guns. Her name was changed to *Bonhomme Richard* after she had been purchased for Jones by the French government. She sank after the well-known action with H.M.S. *Serapis* off Flamborough Head on 23 September 1779.

BONINGTON, RICHARD PARKES (1801–28), a British marine and landscape painter who in his twenty-seven years of life achieved great distinction. Born at Arnolf, near Nottingham, he accompanied his father to France at the age of 16 and after a period of study at the Louvre and the École des Beaux Arts, joined the studio of Baron Gros. To his teacher F. L. T. Francia belongs the credit for recognizing and encouraging his remarkable talent, and he quickly achieved fame. In 1824 he won a gold medal at the Salon and painted a number of beach scenes which are still greatly admired. One of his best, 'Sea-piece', which depicts a *cutter getting under way, can be seen in the Wallace collection in London.

BONNET, (1) an additional strip of canvas laced originally to the foot of fore-and-aft sails and *courses in small ships to increase the area exposed to the wind. In the 19th century bonnets were also used to secure the foot of an uppertopsail to a lower-topsail yard. 'Bonnets are those which are laced and eeked to the sayles to enlarge them; with reference thereto the mayne course, missen course, fore course is understood of those sayles without their bonnets.' *Henry Hudson the Navigator*, Hakluyt Soc., 1860. See also DRABLER. **(2)** The name given to the covering fixed to the top of a *navel pipe to prevent water escaping from the deck of a ship down into the cable lockers. They can be permanently fixed or portable, and are normally made of light steel with the opening for the cable facing aft. A slotted cover, which fits over a link of the cable, makes the opening reasonably watertight. For illus. see CABLE HOLDER.

BONNY, ANNE (*fl.* 1720), a female pirate of Irish birth who went to the West Indies with her father, a respectable attorney. While there she secretly married the pirate John Rackham, also known as 'Calico Jack', and joined his ship in man's clothing. She proved a redoubtable fighter but in the end was captured with Rackham and her friend Mary *Read (also a female pirate) at Jamaica in 1720. After the trial, when Rackham was about to be executed, she told him she was 'sorry to see him there, but if he had fought like a man, he need not have been hanged like a dog'. She herself was reprieved because she was pregnant.

BOOBY, a well-known tropical sea-bird, *Sula fusca*, of the family Pelecanidae. It prefers to rest out of water at night, often perching on the yards of ships. The name is derived from the ease with which it allows itself to be caught after it has settled. 'One of the Saylers espying a Bird fitly called a Booby, he mounted to the topmast and took her. The quality of which Bird is to sit still, not valuing danger.' Sir T. Herbert, *Travels*, 1634.

BOOBY-HATCH, (1) a small opening in the deck of a vessel used as an additional *companion to facilitate movement. **(2)** A name sometimes given to the sliding hatch on the raised cabin top of small cruising yachts.

BOOM, (1) a *spar used to extend the foot of a sail: thus (*a*) in square rig, *studdingsails are set on studdingsail booms extended from the ends of the yardarms; such booms (including booms temporarily rigged at deck level to extend the *clews of the lower sails) would normally be rigged only when it was required to make the most of a light wind which would not otherwise fill the sails. Thus a ship was said to come booming forward when carrying all the sail that she could make. (*b*) In fore-and-aft rig, however, (i) the boom is usually a permanent and important spar, at the foot of the mainsail, and also of the foresail of a *schooner and the mizen of a schooner, *ketch, or *yawl; it is pivoted at the fore end to the mast by a *gooseneck, and controlled by a *sheet at or near the after end, by which the sail is trimmed. A *spritsail has neither boom nor *gaff, and a gaff sail may be boomless (loose-footed), but for efficient sailing a boom is used in most types of fore-and-aft rig. The sail may be secured to it only at the *tack and clew, but is more often laced to it, or has a foot-rope which slides in a groove on top of the boom.

Traditionally a boom is a solid round wooden spar, tapering slightly towards the ends, or of uniform cross-section; in modern practice it may be of hollow glued wooden construction, or a metal tube, both serving to combine strength

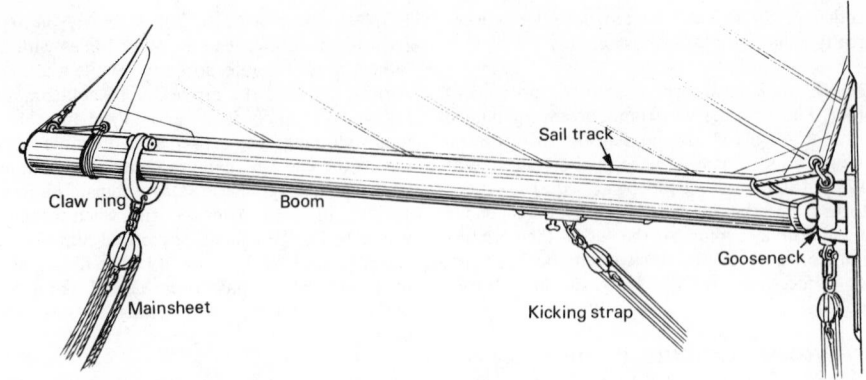

Typical yacht boom

with lightness; as greater stiffness is required in the vertical than in the horizontal plane it may be oblong or oval in section. In 19th/20th century racing yachts before the introduction of *Bermudian rig, main booms were often extremely long, overhanging the *taffrail at the stern, just as the same rig often included a long *bowsprit and a *jackyard topsail, to obtain a very large total sail area. Modern sail plans tend to favour height, generally in the form of a Bermudian mainsail, and a large fore-triangle without a bowsprit, obtained by stepping the mast well aft from the bows: the boom is kept short and its end may be well inboard, in which case the sheet is led straight down from the boom-end to the *horse or sheet block. In some large *J-class and similar Bermudian cutters, the boom was flat-topped and unusually wide at its widest part (and hence called a *Park Avenue boom, after the street in New York); the object was to obtain the best aerodynamic shape for the foot of the sail; but this peculiarity did not last. The purpose of any boom, however, is to enable the sail to set well, as near flat as necessary, without undue 'belly' or sagging of the upper part of the sail to leeward when close hauled. To increase flatness, in racing dinghies and smaller yachts, the boom is sometimes prevented from rising when it swings outwards by a *'kicking-strap' (as it is called by dinghy sailors) or *martingale, between a point on the boom and the foot of the mast. (ii) Also in fore-and-aft rig, the *spinnaker is normally set on a boom, which is a light spar used only when the spinnaker is set, in order to extend the foot of the sail. (iii) A fore-staysail may also be set on a boom, which is pivoted to, or just abaft, the forestay. This is not usual, and has the drawback that the staysail cannot then overlap the mast.

(2) A boom is also a spar rigged outboard from a ship's side horizontally at deck level or between the deck and the waterline, to which boats are secured in harbour or when at anchor in calm weather; the boats thus lie clear of the ship's side and ready for use.

(3) A boom is also the name of a barrier, usually floating, at water level across a harbour entrance or river to obstruct the entrance of an enemy or the passage of boats. Originally perhaps of floating logs (German *Baum*, Dutch *boom*, a tree) secured together, it may also be of chain or cable, buoyed to float. Its use in this connection has been extended to logging operations, and the size of log rafts floated down rivers is often controlled by booms of this nature.

(4) To boom off, to shove a boat or vessel away with spars.

BOOM BOAT, the larger sizes of ship's boats which are hoisted inboard and stowed in crutches on the skid *booms normally between the ship's fore and main masts. The smaller sizes of ship's boat are usually hoisted and secured at *davits.

BOOM CRUTCH, originally **CROTCH,** a temporary receptacle mounted on the *counter of small *fore-and-aft rigged sailing vessels on which the main *boom is stowed and held secure when anchored or lying on a mooring. It normally takes one of two forms, a metal shaft with semi-circular arms on top into which the boom fits, or a small folding wooden structure in the form of an X, the two feet held firm in slots on the counter with the end of the boom resting in the space between the upper arms. See also GALLOWS, GALLOWS-BITTS.

BOOM-IRONS, metal rings fitted on the yard-arms of square-rigged sailing ships through which the *studdingsail booms are traversed in cases where extra advantage is to be taken from a following wind by setting the studdingsails.

BOOMS, the space in the larger sailing vessels, usually between the foremast and mainmast, where the spare spars were stowed on board. The larger ship's boats were carried on the booms when the ship was at sea, either in crutches or between the spare yards themselves.

BOOT-TOPPING, a mixture of tallow, sulphur or lime, and rosin which was used to cover the bottoms of ships, partly as a deterrent against weed and *barnacles and partly to give the bottom of the ship a smooth surface to reduce friction through the water when sailing. The combined act of *breaming and covering the bottom was sometimes described as boot-topping. Today the various *antifouling compositions take the place of the older mixture though the original term is still used.

BOOTY, a form of *prize which, when a ship was captured at sea, was permitted to be distributed among the captors at once. In an old definition it was everything that could be picked up by hand above the main deck, all else in the ship having to be legally condemned by a prize court before its value could be distributed among the captors. As may be imagined, it was a custom which allowed of much abuse. This form of prize 'pickings' was abolished at the end of the Napoleonic War (1803–15).

BORA, a violent easterly squall experienced in the upper part of the Adriatic Sea. It is caused by the weight of the cold air from the mountains accelerating its flow to the sea.

BORE, or eagre, a sudden and rapid flow of tide in certain rivers and estuaries which rolls up in the form of a wave. Bores are caused either by the meeting of two tides, where the excess of water results in a rapid rise, or by a tide rushing up a narrowing estuary where the closeness of the banks or a shelving bottom encloses the tide so that it is forced to rise rapidly to accommodate the volume of water coming in.

The most impressive bore is probably that in the Hooghli River, known as *bahu* by the natives, which comes in with the noise of thunder. A bore also occurs in the River Severn, where it reaches a height of about six feet. The Bay of Fundy has a famous bore, especially in the River Petticodiac, where there is a rise of tide of seventy-six feet.

Although the two terms are virtually synonymous, each locality uses one of the two exclusively, thus in England the River Severn has a bore, the River Trent an eagre.

'BORN WITH A SILVER SPOON', an old naval saying to indicate those young gentlemen who, through birth or connection, were able to enter the Royal Navy without examination and whose subsequent promotion was assured. They were said to enter the navy through the *cabin windows in distinction from those others, said to

have been born with a wooden ladle, who rose by merit and were said to enter the navy through the *hawseholes.

BOROUGH (or BURROWE or BORROWS), STEPHEN (1525–84), British navigator, who as master of the *Edward Bonaventure* accompanied Sir Richard *Chancellor on his voyage in 1553 with Sir Hugh *Willoughby in search of a *North-East passage to China. He was the first Englishman to sight and name the North Cape and to reach the White Sea. On a second voyage in 1556 in the *Searchthrift* 'he discovered the Kara Straits south of Novaya Zemlya. In about 1558 he visited Spain and was instrumental in having Cortes's work, the *Arte of Navigation*, translated into English by Richard *Eden. In 1561, in the *Swallow*, he again visited Russia. Two years later he was made chief pilot of the Queen's ships in the Medway. His brother WILLIAM (1536–99) accompanied Stephen as an ordinary seaman on board the *Edward Bonaventure* during the voyage to Russia in 1553, but finally sought service under the Crown. In 1570 he fought an action against pirates in the Gulf of Finland. He commanded the ship *Lion* during Sir Francis *Drake's expedition against *Cadiz, but daring to question the wisdom of the attack on Lagos, fell into disfavour. In the battle against the Spanish *Armada in 1588 he commanded the *Bonavolia*. He was the author of *Instructions for the Discovery of Cathay* and *A Discourse on the Variation of the Compass*.

BOSCAWEN, The Hon. EDWARD (1711–61), British admiral, third son of 1st Viscount Falmouth, was through his mother a grandson of Arabella Churchill, sister of the Duke of Marlborough. He joined the navy in 1726 as a *king's letter boy and his first three years were spent in the West Indies with *Hosier's tragic fleet. He was promoted lieutenant in 1732 and captain in 1737, and was again in the West Indies in 1739 when *Vernon arrived to undertake reprisals against Spanish warlike acts. He was at the capture of *Porto Bello in 1739 and at the assault against Cartagena in 1741, on both occasions distinguishing himself in leading assault parties on shore.

Back in England in 1742 he took command of the *Dreadnought* (60 guns), and in her sighted two large French ships one night in the Bay of Biscay. His endeavour to engage them brought him his first nickname of 'Old Dreadnought'. In 1747 he commanded the *Namur* (74 guns), in the decisive victory over the French at Cape Finisterre, at which he was severely wounded in the neck, giving his head a permanent list to starboard. This earned him his second nickname of 'Wry-neck'd Dick'. In recognition of his services in this action the list of promotions to flag rank was specially extended to include his name.

In 1751 Boscawen was made a *lord commissioner of the Admiralty, and four years later appointed to command a squadron ordered to North America to attempt to stop a large French reinforcement for Canada. His orders were to attack the French squadron if he found them at sea, an unprecedented order in time of peace. In the fogs off the Canadian coast, Boscawen sighted only three of the French squadron and captured two of them. In the words of Hardwicke, the Lord Chancellor, it was at once 'too little or too much'; too little to cause any real distress to French arms, too much to be glossed over as an act not precipitating war.

In the succeeding Seven Years War Boscawen commanded squadrons in the Channel, off Brest, and in the Bay of Biscay. He was shocked beyond measure at the behaviour of *Byng at Minorca in 1756, remembering that as a young lieutenant Byng had used his father's influence to leave his ship when it was ordered on dangerous service. As a lord commissioner Boscawen signed the order for Byng's court martial, and as commander-in-chief at Portsmouth he also signed the order for his execution.

Promoted admiral of the Blue in 1758, Boscawen commanded the fleet which carried General Amherst and Colonel Wolfe for the siege and capture of Louisburg, which in turn led to the capture of *Quebec in 1759 and all Canada the following year. His selection for this duty was at the insistence of William Pitt, the Prime Minister, who always referred to him as 'my great admiral'.

In 1759 Boscawen was sworn a privy councillor and appointed to command in the Mediterranean. His main task was to prevent a French fleet under de la *Clue, then lying at Toulon, from joining the main fleet at Brest, intended to cover an invasion of England. All efforts to tempt de la Clue out of Toulon failed, and Boscawen withdrew his fleet to Gibraltar to refit and take on water. While he was there, the French fleet slipped through the straits. Within a couple of hours Boscawen was in chase. Overtaking and overpowering the rear French ship, which put up a magnificent defence for three hours, he chased de la Clue and four of his ships into *Lagos Bay. Ignoring Portuguese neutrality, the British fleet entered the bay, set two ships on fire, and brought out the other two, the *Modeste* and *Téméraire*, as prizes. The scattered remnants of the French fleet took refuge at Cadiz, where they were closely blockaded.

During most of 1760 Boscawen commanded the fleet in *Quiberon Bay, blockading the French ships in their harbours. He took possession of a small French island off the mouth of the

River Vannes, having it cultivated for the provision of fresh vegetables for his fleet. Throughout his career he had always shown concern for the health and comfort of his seamen and, though naval hygiene was still much of a closed book during his years of service, did much to improve the health of the men under his command.

Early in 1761, at Hatchlands, Surrey, a mansion he had built from the *prize money he had received, he died of typhoid fever contracted during his last period of service afloat.

BOSS, the swell of the ship's hull around the propeller shaft and also the rounded hub of the propeller.

BOSTON, the capital of the state of Massachusetts, and a major seaport on the east coast of the U.S.A. It is the home of the Charlestown Navy Yard, where the famous *frigates *Constitution* (1797) and *Independence* (1814) were built. It was also, in 1773, the scene of the Boston Tea Party, when 340 cases of tea shipped to Boston by the firm of Davison, Newman and Co., of London, were tipped overboard into the harbour as a protest against the taxation levied on the American colonies by the British government in London. In 1840, Boston was the American terminus of the *Cunard Line, the first regular transatlantic steamer line, but the connection with Cunard did not last. Expansion of the port was remarkably rapid around the end of the 19th century, mainly through the great growth of manufacturing industries in the neighbourhood, but partly also because Boston had among the largest wool and fish markets in the U.S.A.

BO'SUN, see BOATSWAIN.

BOTANY BAY, an inlet on the Australian coast, six miles south of the city of *Sydney, New South Wales. It was first discovered by Captain James *Cook in 1770 during his voyage of circumnavigation, and was named by Joseph *Banks, the official botanist of the expedition, on account of the variety of plants he found growing there. When, after the war of American Independence, those territories were no longer available for the transportation of convicts from Britain, the attention of the British government was drawn, through the descriptions of Cook and Banks, to the possibility of using Botany Bay as an alternative convict settlement. A squadron, known as the *'First Fleet', commanded by Captain Arthur *Phillip, sailed in 1787 to found a penal colony there. On arrival at Botany Bay Phillip considered the place unsuitable, and moved northward along the coast until he reached the site on which now stands the city of

Sydney, and it was here that the penal colony was established. Convicts were transported to Australia until 1840, when the practice ceased.

In recent years Botany Bay has been developed as a major oil *tanker port.

BOTARGO, a name sometimes used in the British Navy during the 16th and 17th centuries to describe the dried fish issued to crews at sea in lieu of salt meat on *banyan, or meatless, days. It is really the name for the dried roes of fish, but was adopted in the navy to embrace the whole fish.

BOTELER, NATHANIEL (*c.* 1577–*c.* 1643), British seaman, administrator, and historian. Nothing is known of his life prior to 1619, when he is mentioned as a member of the Virginia Company. In 1625 he was given the command of the *Jonathan* in Sir Edward Cecil's unsuccessful expedition against *Cadiz. Two years later he commanded the *Patient Adventure* in the attack on the Île de Ré and the following year (1626) commanded the *Nonsuch* in the expedition for the relief of La Rochelle. He is chiefly remembered for his manuscript *A Dialogicall Discourse* begun in 1621, but only issued in 1634. There are six dialogues in all and in them an admiral and a captain discuss a large variety of subjects connected with ships and the sea. They provide an interesting insight into the terms and customs of the British Navy at that time, and were reproduced by the Navy Records Society in its volume published in 1929. Boteler's real name was Butler, but an earlier spelling of the family name was used for the publication of his book *Six Dialogues about Sea Service* in 1685, and it is by this name that he is generally known today.

BOTTER, originally a Dutch fishing boat based normally between Volendam and Haderwijk in the South Zuider Zee. About 45 feet (13·8 m) long and 13 feet (4·0 m) in breadth, it is flat bottomed with curved sides and a high curved *stem with a low narrow *stern. The *leeboards are long and narrow, sword shaped, for use in rough waters for offshore fishing. Fishing botters had a free flooding fishwell amidships for keeping the catch alive. Many botters were converted into yachts, the large amount of space below decks providing comfortable and reasonably spacious accommodation, and many Dutch cruising yachts are still built on general botter lines.

'BOTTLE', a naval term for a reproof or criticism. It is said to have been derived from an old naval saying, 'a dose from the foretopman's bottle', which was a purgative given in all cases of sickness, or alternatively from a 'bottle of acid', corrosive and painful.

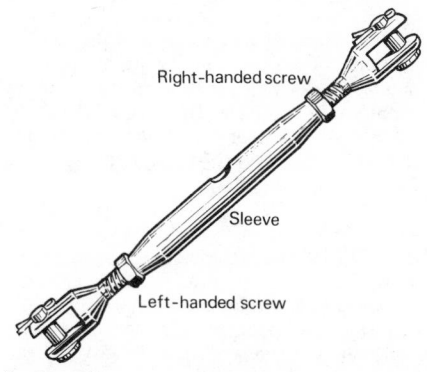
Bottlescrew

BOTTLESCREW or **TURNBUCKLE,** a rigging screw used to adjust any rigging equipment for length or tension, the correct maritime term being to 'set up' the rigging. A bottlescrew consists of an internally threaded sleeve into which a right-handed screw takes at one end and a left-handed screw at the other. As the sleeve is revolved, the two contra-threaded screws are drawn together, thus increasing the tension of those parts of the rigging to which they are attached. Bottlescrews are largely used for setting up the *shrouds of sailing vessels and the *guardrails and *davit guys fitted in ships. A large bottlescrew is also used in a screw slip (see CABLE STOPPERS) for securing an anchor in a *hawsepipe by screwing it home until the anchor *flukes are hard up against the rim of the hawsepipe so that it cannot move when the ship pitches in heavy seas.

BOTTOMRY, a mortgage on a ship executed by a *master who is out of touch with his owners and needs to raise money for repairs or to complete a voyage. If money is raised on the cargo, it is known as a *respondentia bond. Money raised by bottomry must be used only for the exact purpose stated and is always primarily for the purpose of getting a ship back to her port of registry. A bottomry bond takes priority over all other mortgages but if the ship is lost at sea before the voyage is completed, the lender loses his bond. Samuel Pepys (*Diary*, 30 Nov. 1663) has the word as bottomaryne; another variant spelling (Malynes, *Ancient Law-Merchandise*, 1622) is bottomarie.

BOUDIN, EUGÈNE LOUIS (1825–98), French marine painter, was the son of a pilot and born at Honfleur. He grew up with a close acquaintance with the sea and when he took to painting was unrivalled in his rendering of its atmosphere and movement. He was particularly successful in capturing the grey skies which predominate in Brittany, Normandy, and

Holland where most of his pictures were painted. In 1889 he gained a gold medal at the Salon in Paris and three years later was awarded the Grand Cross of the Legion of Honour. Among his best works are 'The Harbour at Deauville', and 'The Thunderstorm at Camaret'. His pictures were not so well appreciated during his lifetime as they are today.

BOUGAINVILLE, Comte LOUIS ANTOINE DE (1729–1811), is best known as a French naval officer and navigator although he was a professional soldier until the age of 37. In the latter capacity he served with distinction under Montcalm in Canada during the Seven Years War (1756–63). After the peace, however, his ambitions turned seawards. At his own expense he established a colonizing settlement in the Falkland Islands. This met with objections by Spain and, when Bougainville sailed in December 1766 in command of the frigate *La Boudeuse* and accompanied by the store ship *L'Étoile*, his first task was the evacuation of the colony.

This completed, the expedition passed through the Straits of Magellan and crossed the Pacific in the trade wind belt to Tahiti, which Bougainville formally annexed, though it had been discovered eight months previously by the British Captain *Wallis. The Frenchman's eulogistic description of the island and its inhabitants gave support to the contemporary cult of 'the noble savage'. Sailing on westwards, rediscovering *Quiros's Espiritu Santo, Bougainville found his way barred by the Great Barrier Reef in latitude 15° S. To withdraw from this area of perilous lee shores, he beat his way to windward until he could weather the eastern tip of New Guinea.

Passing through the Solomon Islands, one of which today bears his name, and visiting New Britain, the Moluccas, and Batavia, he completed his circumnavigation at St. Malo in March 1769, having lost only seven men out of the two hundred of his company, an achievement remarkable for the times.

During the War of American Independence (1775–82) Bougainville commanded a division of de *Grasse's fleet at the battle of the *Saints in 1782, blame for the disaster of which was, in part, justifiably laid at his door by de Grasse. During the French Revolution he narrowly escaped becoming a victim of the 'terror', and later gained the favour of Napoleon who made him a count of the Empire, a senator, and a member of the Legion of Honour. The flamboyant climbing plant *Bougainvillaea* is named after him.

BOUGUER, PIERRE (1698–1758), French scientist, was a distinguished hydrographer and also an authority on masts and masting, being awarded a prize presented by the Académie des Sciences in 1727 for his treatise on this subject.

He later become professor of *hydrography at Le Havre and wrote a number of scientific works. He is also remembered for his accurate measurement of one degree of longitude during a visit to Peru in 1735, his observations on this occasion leading to the publication in 1749 of *La Figure de la terre déterminée*.

BOUNTY, money paid at recruiting centres to encourage volunteers for service in the British Navy in time of war. State or royal bounties amounted to 30 shillings for an able seaman and 25 shillings for an ordinary seaman at the beginning of the 18th century, rising to four or five guineas later. There were additional municipal bounties to encourage local recruitment, ranging from £2 to as much as £40. Thus in 1795 the City of London offered a supplementary bounty of ten guineas for able seamen, eight for ordinary, six for *landsmen, and one or two for boys according to their height. The payment of recruitment bounties disappeared in Britain with the passage of the naval Continuous Service Act in 1857. In general, volunteers for naval service brought in by the bounties were objects of scorn to those in the navy who considered themselves real seamen. It was a system which also encouraged a good deal of deceit; men who had volunteered in one town for the bounty offered would tend to desert from the ship to which they had been drafted and then re-volunteer under a different name in a different town in order to receive a second bounty.

BOUNTY, originally a merchant ship, the *Bethia*, built at Hull in 1784, which was bought, renamed, and fitted out as an armed transport for a voyage in 1788 to carry breadfruit seedlings from Tahiti to the West Indies, a scheme designed to acclimatize these plants there as a cheap source of food for the slaves working on the sugar plantations. On 28 April 1789, under the leadership of Fletcher *Christian, part of the crew of forty-five men mutinied. Opinions differ regarding the cause of the mutiny, the most common being that the commanding officer William *Bligh was an unduly stern disciplinarian who brutalized the *Bounty*'s crew by the severity of his punishments; but a more likely cause was the attractions to Christian and others like him of the women and way of life of the South Sea Islands, so different from service on board a British man-of-war.

At the time of the mutiny the ship was near Tofua, in the Tonga group of islands. Bligh and eighteen men who remained loyal to him were cast adrift in the ship's launch and eventually reached safety at Timor after an epic open-boat voyage of 3,600 miles. The mutineers returned in the ship to Tahiti, then Christian and eight followers, accompanied by some islanders and

Mutiny in the Bounty; *after the painting by R. Dodd*

several women, sailed to Pitcairn Island where the *Bounty* was run ashore and burnt. The British Admiralty, when they received news of the mutiny after the return of Bligh, sent H.M.S. *Pandora* to Tahiti to bring back the mutineers for trial. Fourteen were secured at Tahiti, but four of these were drowned when the *Pandora* was wrecked on the Great Barrier Reef. The surviving ten were brought back to Portsmouth and court-martialled, three of them being hanged.

The copy of Captain James *Cook's three volumes describing his third voyage of circumnavigation, completed by Captain King and now in the Naval Library, Ministry of Defence, London, belonged to Bligh; he took it with him in the *Bounty*, making many notes in the margins. It was taken after the mutiny by Christian to Pitcairn Island and was recovered about forty years later when a British frigate visited the island. The last survivor of the mutineers, Seaman Adams, was still living there and exchanged the three volumes for a supply of pencils and paper. It says much for the new spirit of humanitarianism growing in the British Navy in the early 19th century that Adams was not brought home for trial on a charge of mutiny but allowed to remain to live out his life in peace.

BOUVET, FRANÇOIS JOSEPH (1753–1832), French admiral, began his sea service with the French *East India Company. He transferred to

the navy while in the East Indies and was with *Suffren's fleet in the famous campaign of 1781–3. On the outbreak of the French revolution, with the murder or removal of many senior officers of the fleet, his promotion was rapid. By 1793 he was a rear admiral, and commanded a division of the French fleet at the battle of the *Glorious First of June in 1794. In December 1796 he was selected to command the van division of the fleet which was to land General Hoche with an expeditionary force in southern Ireland, but stormy weather scattered the fleet. Bouvet made his way to *Bantry Bay, meeting the rest of the fleet and most of the transports on the way, but once again heavy weather disrupted the attempt to land troops, and Bouvet's flagship was blown out to sea. Convinced that no ship could remain on that coast in the prevailing weather, Bouvet made his way back to Brest, but discovered on his return that some of the French ships had been able to retain their anchorage in Bantry Bay. He was dismissed from his command for leaving them unprotected. He was re-employed for a short period during the peace of Amiens, commanding the squadron sent to re-occupy Guadeloupe, but that was the end of his naval service, and the rest of his life was passed in obscurity.

BOUVET, a French battleship, named after Admiral *Bouvet. She took part in the Anglo-French attack on the *Dardanelles during the

First World War (1914–18) but was sunk by a mine in March 1915 when returning from the second bombardment of Turkish forts on the peninsula.

BOW, the foremost end of a ship, the opposite of * stern. From bow to stern, the whole length of a ship. The word is frequently used in the plural, as 'the bows of a ship'. It is also used to give an approximate * bearing of an object in relation to the fore-and-aft line of the ship, as, e.g., 'the buoy bears 15 degrees on the port bow' or 'two * points on the starboard bow', as the case may be. On the bow, within an arc of four points (45 degrees) extending either side of the bow. It is the position in the ship where the * hawseholes for the * anchors are situated and where the * jack-staff is stepped.

BOW-CHASERS, two long guns mounted forward in the bow-ports of sailing warships to fire directly ahead. They were always of small bore in relation to their length in order to carry their shot for a greater distance. They were used particularly when chasing an enemy, to attempt to slow her down by shooting away her sails and rigging. See also CHASE.

BOWDITCH, NATHANIEL (1773–1838), was the author of the *American Practical Navigator*, for many years looked upon as the standard work on practical navigation among American seamen.

BOWEN, ABEL (1790–1850), American engraver and lithographer, was born at Sandlake village, Greenbush, N.Y. He worked in * Boston where he became known as the leading engraver. In 1816 he published *The Naval Monument*, which included many engravings of scenes from the War of 1812.

BOWER ANCHORS, the two largest * anchors in a ship carried permanently attached to their * cables, one on either * bow with the cables running through the * hawseholes so that the anchors are always ready for letting go in an emergency. They were originally known as * best bower and small bower, not from any difference in their size since they were the same weight, but from the bow on which they are placed, the best bower being the one on the starboard side and the small bower on the port. Today they are known purely as the starboard and port bower.

BOW-GRACE, the name given to old * junk cable or chain hung over the * bow of a wooden ship in very cold weather in a tideway to protect it from the edges of thin drift ice which can produce a cutting action serious enough to damage the bow.

BOWERS, HENRY ROBERTSON (1883–1912), a Royal Navy lieutenant who achieved immortality as a member of Captain R. F. * Scott's last expedition to the Antarctic, 1910–13. As officer in charge of stores, Bowers became one of Scott's most trusted men. He was chosen, along with Wilson, Oates, and * Evans, to accompany Scott to the South pole and died with them during the return journey in March 1912.

BOWLINE (pron. bōlin), **(1)** a knot tied in such a way as to produce an * eye, or loop, in the end of a rope. It is a knot with many uses at sea, whether to join two large hawsers together, with one bowline tied with its eye inside the eye of the other, or tied in the end of a hawser to provide a loop for dropping over a * bollard. It is a knot

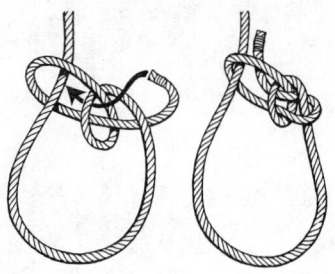

Running bowline

which will never slip and cannot jam. Variants of this knot are a running bowline, where the knot is tied around a bight of the rope to form a noose, and a bowline on the bight, where the knot is made with the bight of the rope to produce two eyes. This variant is often used to form a temporary * boatswain's chair when a man is needed to work aloft. **(2)** The name of the rope attached with a bowline to, and leading forward from, a bridle between * cringles on the * leeches of sails in a square-rigged ship. Its purpose, when hauled hard in, is to keep the weather edge of the sail taut and steady when the ship is * close-hauled to the wind. Thus a square-rigged ship is said to 'sail on a bowline', or 'stand on a taut bowline', when she is being sailed as close to the wind as possible. For illus. see RIGGING.

BOWSE, to, the act of hauling with a * tackle in order to produce an additional measure of tautness; thus the * tack of a * lugsail is bowsed down with a tackle after the sail has been hoisted so that the * luff is drawn tauter than can be achieved merely by hauling on the * halyards in hoisting. 'Bowse away', the order for all men on the hauling part of a tackle to haul away together.

BOWSPRIT (pron. bō-), orig. **BOLTSPRIT,** a large spar projecting over the * stem of large sailing vessels to provide the means of staying a

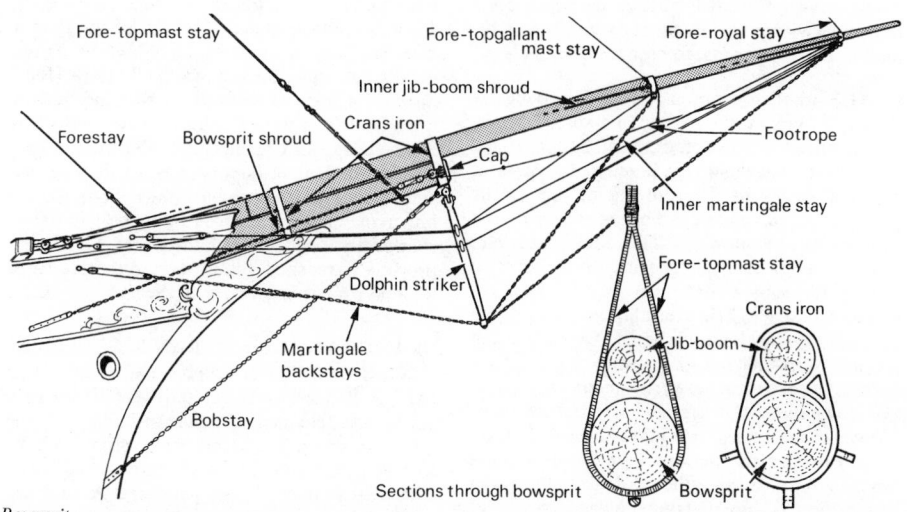

Bowsprit

fore-topmast and from which the *jibs are set. When a fore-topgallant mast is set, the bowsprit is extended by a *jib-boom, to the end of which is led the fore-topgallant mast stay on which the flying jibs are set. The bowsprit itself is held rigidly in place by *shrouds led to each bow of the vessel and by a *bobstay led from its outer end to the stem of the vessel just above the waterline. In some smaller *cutter-rigged sailing vessels the bowsprit was often fitted so that it could be run in, or furled, by sliding inboard and was known as a running bowsprit as opposed to a standing one.

With the wide adoption of the *Bermuda rig for most modern sailing craft and yachts, the bowsprit has virtually disappeared except in the few big sailing vessels still retained as school or training ships, and in the growing number of these ships which are being preserved for historical and museum purposes. In some yachts a small *bumpkin is fitted to the stemhead in the nature of a bowsprit.

BOX OFF, to, the act of hauling the head-sheets to windward and laying the head-yards flat *aback in a square-rigged ship to *pay the ship's head out of the wind when *tacking, when the action of the helm by itself is insufficient to produce that result. It is a means of ensuring that the ship does not miss stays, that is, remain head to wind and unable to pay off on either *tack. In *fore-and-aft rigged ships the same result can be achieved when the vessel hangs head to wind by hauling out the *clew of the *jib to windward.

BOX-HAUL, to, a method of *wearing a square-rigged ship in rough weather when the

force of the waves makes it impractical for her to *tack. The procedure is to put the helm *a-lee (1), as in tacking, to bring the bows up into the wind, when the strength of the waves as they strike the weather bow will force the bows down to *leeward (2). With the helm reversed, this movement is accelerated, and at the same time the aftermost sails are *brailed up to spill the wind out of them in order to give the foremost sails an added turning moment. As the stern of the ship crosses the wind the aftermost sails are braced to catch the wind (3) and increase the rate of turn until the wind is forward of the beam and the yards can again be braced (4). Box-hauling, as well as being a rough weather tactic, was also used when ships were too near the shore to *wear in the usual way.

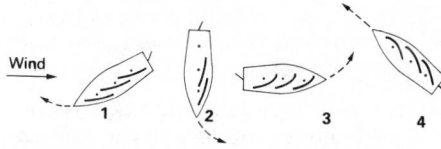

Box-hauling

BOX THE COMPASS, to, to know and to be able to recite the *points and quarter points of the magnetic compass from north through south to north again, both clockwise and anti-clockwise. In these days of the gyroscopic compass and hyperbolic navigation, the ability to box the compass is very nearly a lost art. It was never a particularly easy thing to do because of the rule that quarter points were never read from a point beginning and ending with the same letter. Thus, for example, boxing the compass clockwise, the quarter point next to, say, ENE.

would not be ENE. $\frac{1}{4}$ E., but is taken from the next clockwise point, E. by N., with the quarter points read backwards, to become E. by N. $\frac{3}{4}$ N.

BRACE, to, the operation of swinging round, by means of *braces, the *yards of a square-rigged ship to present a more efficient sail surface to the direction of the wind. By bracing the yards at different angles to the fore-and-aft line of the ship, the best advantage can be taken of any wind which may be blowing. Thus, the yards are braced *ABACK to bring the winds on the forward side of the sails to take the way off her, are braced *ABOUT to bring the ship on the opposite tack when going about, are braced *ABOX to bring the headyards aback to stop the ship, are braced *BY to bring the yards in contrary directions on different masts to *lie the ship to or *heave-to, are braced IN to lay the yards squarer to the fore and aft line for a *free wind, and are braced SHARP to bring the yards round to make the smallest possible angle with the fore-and-aft line when sailing *close-hauled.

'BRACE OF SHAKES, A', originally a maritime term which has found its way into everyday language. It denoted a moment of time which could be measured by the shaking of a sail as a ship comes into the wind: 'I will be with you before the sail can shake twice.'

BRACES, ropes or wire ropes rove to the ends of all *yards in a square-rigged ship by which the yards are *braced, or swung, at different angles to the fore-and-aft line of the ship to make the most of the wind. For illus. see YARD.

BRACKETS, (1) small shaped timbers or plates to connect two or more parts of a ship, but known as *knees when joining a deck *beam to a *frame in a wooden vessel. **(2)** The vertical sidepieces of the old-fashioned wooden gun carriage which support the gun by its trunnions, though a more usual name for these gun carriage brackets was *cheeks.

BRAILS, ropes leading from the *leech on both sides of a fore-and-aft loose-footed sail and through leading *blocks secured on the mast *hoops of the sail to deck level. Their use is to gather in the sail close to the mast so that it is temporarily *furled when coming up to a mooring or as required. The old-fashioned whaler rig in which the mainsail was loose-footed was always fitted with brails. TO BRAIL IN, to haul on the brails and bring the leech of the sail up to the mast.

BRAKE, the handle or lever by which the common ship's pump was worked before the days of auxiliary machinery. In ships of any size the pump was manned by up to six men working on the brake in short spells.

BRANCH, the certificate or diploma given by *Trinity House, England, to a pilot qualified to take navigational control of a ship in British waters. A full branch from Trinity House qualifies a pilot to navigate without any restrictions in British waters, which include the whole of the English Channel and all other waters around the British Isles even when they lie outside *territorial waters; a limited branch gives him a qualification to act as a pilot only in waters specifically named in the branch, having previously satisfied Trinity House that he has a full and proper knowledge of them.

BRANGWYN, Sir FRANK WILLIAM (1867–1956), Welsh painter and etcher, was born at Bruges, Belgium, and went to sea as a young man. He made a number of voyages to the Far East, an early influence which stimulated the love of rich colour and bold design which characterized so many of his paintings. A later apprenticeship with William Morris produced a sentimentality in his work which was not to everyone's taste. During the First World War (1914–18) he was appointed an official war artist, and his marine paintings of this period are among his best work, crisp, colourful, and accurate. One of his best known pictures in this genre is his water-colour of the training ship H.M.S. *Implacable.*

Brangwyn was a versatile artist who, in addition to his marine paintings, produced murals, decorative panels, frescoes, and designs for books, pottery, tapestry, and furniture. He had a reputation, amply deserved, for superb draughtsmanship, and this is strongly evident in his marine work.

BRANSFIELD, EDWARD (c. 1783–1852), a *master in the Royal Navy, visited the South Shetland Islands in 1820 in the company of William *Smith who had discovered them the previous year. Bransfield made a rough survey of the islands and on 30 January 1820 discovered Trinity Land, the north-western tip of the Antarctic peninsula. Shortly afterwards he claimed King George and Clarence Islands for Britain. Bransfield was the first to chart a portion of the Antarctic mainland.

BRASIL or **BRAZIL,** or **HY BRAZIL,** a legendary island in the Atlantic Ocean. It was one of the *Insulae Purpuraricae* described by Pliny, and so convinced were the early geographers of its existence that they included it in their maps, sometimes attaching it to the Azores group but more often showing it in mid-ocean some hundreds of miles due west of Ireland. Its existence was shown on some charts published as late as 1853. See also ATLANTIS, AVALON.

BRASSBOUNDER, a name used to describe an officer apprentice in a merchant shipping line, possibly because in most companies of ship-owners the apprentices wore caps with a thin gold *lace binding round them. The apprentice-ship system was often much abused in some shipping companies, youths buying an appren-ticeship and then frequently serving as unpaid deck-hands under *masters and *mates who did little or nothing to teach them their trade. This was, perhaps, particularly the case in the big trading *barques in the late 19th and early 20th centuries, a period when these ships were strug-gling for their existence against the competition of the tramp steamer and as a result were largely undermanned to save overhead costs.

BRASSBOUNDER, THE, the title of a book written by Sir David *Bone in which he de-scribes his experiences as an apprentice in sail. It was published in 1910 and is regarded as a minor classic of the sea.

BRASSEY, THOMAS, Earl (1836–1918), naval expert and author, first acquired an interest in nautical matters as a yachtsman, being elected to the *Royal Yacht Squadron a year after leaving Oxford University. Called to the Bar in 1866, he forsook the law for politics and was Member of Parliament for Hastings 1868–86. He con-tributed much to reforms in naval administration and policy during the era of transition from sail to steam, and from 1880 to 1884 was Civil Lord of the Admiralty in Gladstone's second admini-stration and from then until 1885 was Parliamentary Secretary.

He was raised to the peerage as Baron Brassey of Bulkely in 1886, and in that year there ap-peared under his editorship the first of the famous *Naval Annuals* still published today under the title *Armed Forces Annual*. From 1895 to 1900, Lord Brassey was governor of the colony of Victoria. As President of the Institute of Naval Architects from 1893 to 1896, and incessantly in the House of Lords, he expressed strong, though not always wise, views on naval administration. Made Lord Warden of the *Cinque Ports from 1908 to 1913, he was created an earl in 1911. He made a number of notable voyages in his yacht *Sunbeam*, includ-ing a voyage round the world described by Lady Brassey in *The Voyage in the 'Sunbeam'* (1878). He was the author of *British Seamen* (1877) and *The British Navy* (5 vols, 1882–3) which had a considerable success.

BRASSEY'S NAVAL ANNUAL, a well-known series of yearly publications on maritime affairs, first started by Lord *Brassey in 1886 and edited by him for many years. It contained articles on various maritime interests written with great authority by experts in their particular subjects, and also embraced a reference section of statis-tics and details of the world's navies. It is still in existence under the title *Armed Forces Annual* and now contains articles pertaining to armies and air forces as well as to navies.

BREACH, to, the breaking in of the sea, either in a ship or a coastal defence such as a sea wall. A sea which breaks completely across a ship is called a clean breach. Breaching, when applied to whales, is the act of leaping clean out of the water.

BREAD, the name euphemistically given, in the days before ships were fitted with bakeries, to ships' *biscuit, baked especially hard to preserve it for long periods. BREAD-ROOM, the compart-ment below decks in older ships in which the biscuit was stored in canvas cases.

'BREAD-ROOM JACK', the name given in the British Navy to a purser's assistant who used to issue the daily ration of *biscuit to the various messes on board. See also JACK OF THE DUST.

BREAK, the sudden rise or fall of the *deck when not flush, e.g., the break of the *forecastle, break of the *poop, etc.

BREAK BULK, to, to open up the *holds of a ship and start unloading cargo at the conclusion of her voyage.

BREAK GROUND, to, the act of *weighing a ship's anchor at the moment when the *cable lifts it off the bottom and breaks it out of the ground into which its *flukes have *bitten.

BREAK OF THE POOP, the forward end of a ship's after superstructure, where the *poop deck descends to the upper deck. It was the place where, in merchant ships, the crew were traditionally summoned to be addressed or harangued by the *master, according to his mood.

BREAK SHEER, to, when a ship lying to her anchor is forced, perhaps by wind or current, to swing across her anchor so as to risk fouling it with her own cable, she is said to break sheer. When she swings clear the other way, she is said to keep her sheer.

BREAKER, (1) a small barrel or cask kept per-manently in ships' boats for the stowage of drink-ing water for use for survival purposes in case of shipwreck. It is synonymous with *barrico, which is the older word. It is thought possibly to be the anglicized version of the Spanish *bareca*, a small keg, as, no doubt, is also barrico, **(2)** in the plural, waves breaking over rocks or shoals, and often a useful warning to ships off their course that they are standing into danger.

BREAKWATER, (1) an artificially placed construction in or around a harbour designed to break the force of the sea and to provide shelter for vessels lying within. **(2)** A low *bulkhead across the *forecastle deck of a ship which prevents seas which break over the bows or through the *hawseholes from running aft along the deck. It diverts the water into the *scuppers where it is drained overboard.

BREAM, to, the old method of cleaning a ship's bottom by burning off the weed, *barnacles, etc., which had grown there through long immersion. The operation was performed either in dock or by *careening the ship on a sloping shore so that the ebbing tide would expose one side of her bottom. Fires of furze or brushwood were then lit beneath her to burn off all growth. It was an operation not unattended by danger, and many a wooden ship in olden days has been set on fire and destroyed by breaming. Nevertheless it was a necessary and frequent operation, for voyages under sail were of long duration and weed on a ship's bottom grows quickly. *Boot-topping did something to inhibit the growth of weed and barnacles, but it was not until the introduction of copper-bottoming, of special *antifouling paints, and the increase in voyage speed when steam superseded sail, as well as the wide provision of docking facilities all round the world that breaming finally became a thing of the past. See also BROOM (2).

BREAST BACKSTAYS, a pair of *stays led from the head of a topmast or a topgallant mast in a square-rigged ship to *chain-plates forward of the standing *backstays to provide support for the upper masts from to windward. They formed part of the standing rigging of the ship. See also RIGGING.

BREAST HOOK, (1) a steel plate, or in a wooden ship, a timber in the form of ə *knee, secured internally across the *stem of a ship to give added strength to the *bows and to take the strain exerted by the *cables on the *hawsepieces when a ship lies to her *anchors. **(2)** A hook fitted internally on either bow of a dipping-*lug *cutter to which the *tack of the foresail was hooked when the wind came from abaft the beam. By shifting the tack to the breast hook, the foresail was given additional belly to make the most of the favourable wind.

BREECH OF A BLOCK, the part of a *block opposite the *swallow, which is where the rope enters.

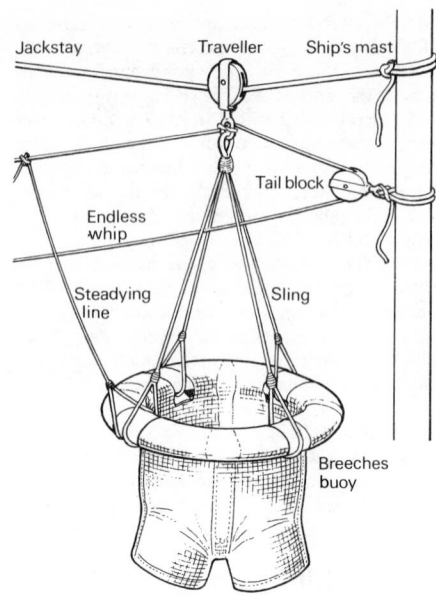

Breeches buoy

BREECHES BUOY, a ring lifebuoy fitted with canvas breeches and used for life-saving when a ship has run aground on a coast and is in danger of breaking-up or sinking. Contact with the wrecked ship is made from the shore by means of a line fired from a rocket gun, a *jackstay is then rigged between ship and shore, and the breeches buoy, supported in a sling attached to a traveller, is hauled back and forth between ship and shore by an endless *whip along the jackstay, the seaman being rescued having his legs through the breeches to give him support as he is hauled ashore. The breeches buoy is then hauled back empty to the ship for the next man to be rescued. See also COSTAIN GUN.

BREECHING, the name given to the thick rope which was used to secure the carriages of cannons in warships in the days of sail, and also to absorb the force of the recoil. The centre of the breeching was passed through a *thimble stropped to the cascable (the knob on the breech end of the gun) and the ends led through ringbolts on the sides or *cheeks of the gun carriage and secured by *clench-knotting to other ringbolts in the ship's sides. It was of sufficient length to allow the muzzle of the gun to be brought back far enough inboard so that it could be loaded and the shot rammed home, and also for housing and lashing the gun carriages inboard when the ship was on passage.

The strain on a gun breeching was tremendous, and one of the greatest dangers on board a wooden warship occurred when a breeching parted and the gun and its carriage took charge, sometimes during action through the force of the recoil or through damage caused by enemy shot, sometimes in very rough weather when the ship was rolling heavily. A 42-pounder gun and its carriage weighed several tons, and the scene on the gundeck when one or more of these broke loose and took charge can be imagined.

BREEZE, SEA OR LAND, a coastal wind which blows regularly in warmer climates from the sea in daytime and from the land at night. It is caused by the action of the sun in raising the temperature of the land during the day faster than that of the sea so that the warm air rises, thus drawing in a breeze from the sea. The process is reversed at night as the land cools more quickly than the sea, which retains its temperature, so that the cooler air from the land flows seaward to replace the warmer sea air, which rises. See also METEOROLOGY.

BREMEN, a major German port, including in its port complex Bremerhaven and Vegesack, built on both banks of the river Weser about 45 miles from the North Sea. It was one of the * Hanseatic towns and for some centuries has been a well-known centre of shipbuilding and other industries connected with the sea and navigation. Perhaps its best claim to fame is that it is the home port of many shipping lines, including the important. Norddeutscher-Lloyd, which was founded at Bremen in 1856.

BREMEN, a German transatlantic liner, flagship of the German Norddeutscher-Lloyd Line, which was caught in New York at the outbreak of the Second World War in 1939. She slipped out of harbour a few days after the declaration of war and the British Home Fleet searched for her in the hope of taking her in * prize. By steering a very northerly course she evaded the searching * cruisers and reached the Russian port of Murmansk safely. Some weeks later she sailed for Germany but was sighted by a British submarine on patrol in the Heligoland Bight. As, however, the *Bremen* was a merchant ship and, under the rules of the * Hague Convention, could not be attacked without prior warning, she was able to break clear and reach home in safety.

BRENDAN (*c.* 484–578), Irish saint, the hero of a (possibly) legendary voyage in the Atlantic. He is held by some to have been the first discoverer of America, on the basis of the text of *Navigatio Sancti Brendani Abbatis*, of which many manuscript copies exist, at least three dating from the 11th century. He is supposed to have made a voyage which occupied the years 565–73, accompanied by seventeen monks, but the many remarkable adventures recounted almost certainly place it within the realm of legend, particularly as they also appear in the pagan Irish saga of Maeldune and in Scandinavian mythology.

For many years St. Brendan's Island was marked on charts of the Atlantic. In his journal * Columbus records that the inhabitants of Madeira had seen it to the westward, and on his Nuremberg globe Martin * Behaim shows it west of the Canaries. A great many voyages were undertaken to locate the island, so persistent was the belief in its existence, but it was never found. In 1859 it was accepted as having been a mirage.

It is virtually impossible that St. Brendan could have reached America. If the voyage actually took place at all it is possible that it was to the northward to Iceland, and just possible that the monks then sailed southward to the Azores.

BRENTON, Sir JAHLEEL (1770–1844), British admiral, was born in the U.S.A., the eldest son of Rear Admiral Jahleel Brenton, who was a loyalist during the American Revolution and had all his property sequestrated. Brenton went to sea with his father in 1781, passed his examination for lieutenant, and served in the Swedish Navy against the Russians. With the outbreak of war against France in 1793 he received quick promotion, being made * post-captain in 1800. He made a name for himself as a frigate captain during the war but in 1803 was wrecked on the coast of France and taken prisoner. He was exchanged after about a year and continued to serve with distinction, being made a baronet in 1812. He reached flag rank in 1830. His younger brother, EDWARD PELHAM BRENTON (1774–1839), also served in the navy, reaching the rank of post-captain. He is best remembered for his books *Naval History of Great Britain from 1783 to 1822* (1823) and *Life and Correspondence of John, Earl of St. Vincent* (1838).

BREST, a French seaport and naval base on the northern Biscay coast on the peninsula of Finisterre. The advantages of Brest, with its magnificent land-locked harbour, as a naval base were first recognized by Cardinal Richelieu, who in 1631 had wooden wharves built to protect it from the westerly gales. The wooden wharves were replaced by masonry by * Colbert, and in 1680–8, the great Vauban constructed fortifications. The naval port of Brest includes a large dockyard and shipbuilding establishment, naval barracks, and the *École Navale*, which is to France what Dartmouth is to Britain and Annapolis to the U.S.A.

During the Second World War, the port of Brest was occupied by the German Navy and used as the base for their Atlantic squadron, consisting of the *battle-cruisers *Scharnhorst and *Gneisenau* and the heavy cruiser *Prinz Eugen*. These ships were, however, the objective of many heavy raids by British bombers and were severely damaged, the dockyard and town of Brest also suffering heavily from the bombing. The three German ships were eventually brought back to Germany in February 1942 without having been able to operate in the Atlantic because of the frequent damage they received. After the war the dockyard and town was largely rebuilt and quickly regained its maritime importance.

BRETHREN OF THE COAST, see BUCCANEERS.

BRETT, Sir PIERCY (1709–81), British admiral, was a lieutenant serving under Commodore Georgè *Anson during the latter's famous voyage of circumnavigation of 1740–4. During the voyage Anson promoted him into a vacancy as *post-captain, but on his return the British Admiralty refused to recognize the promotion on the grounds that Anson was not a commander-in-chief, who alone had power to make promotions at sea. It was only when Anson threatened to resign that Brett's promotion was acknowledged.

In 1745 Brett was in command of the 60-gun ship *Lion* when she fell in with the French *Elizabeth*, of sixty-four guns, which was escorting a small *schooner which was taking Prince Charles Edward, the Young Pretender, to Scotland. The *Lion* and *Elizabeth* were hotly engaged for five hours, and both so damaged at the end that they each had to make their way to port for repairs. Unfortunately for the Young Pretender, who made his way independently to Scotland, the *Elizabeth* was carrying the arms, stores, and money designed to nourish the Stuart rebellion, and he was thus deprived of the material support he had hoped to receive.

Brett was promoted rear admiral in 1762, vice admiral in 1770, and admiral in 1778. Admiral *Boscawen, under whom he served in 1756, found him 'stuck-up, humourless and tiresome' and he appears to have been an officer who always stood very firmly on his dignity.

'BRICK', the naval seaman's name for a projectile fired from a gun.

BRIDGE, an elevated platform built above the upper deck of a mechanically propelled ship and usually running *athwartships (except in the case of some fishing and similar vessels where it may be in the form of a wheelhouse), from which a ship is normally navigated and from where all activities on deck can be seen and controlled by the captain or officer of the watch. The bridge of a modern ship is normally totally enclosed by glass screens or windows to give protection from the weather, but in earlier vessels the bridge was usually open and protected from the weather only by a canvas *dodger and, in very hot weather, from the sun by a canvas *awning. The main magnetic compass and a repeater from the gyroscopic compass are normally situated on the bridge together with the steering wheel, a chart table for chart work, and radar scanners where fitted. In very large ships, such as ocean liners, etc., the bridge structure may contain two or even more bridges extending the full width of the ship.

In the days of sail, ships were controlled from the *quarterdeck, with the steering wheel in the after part of the *waist, but as steam propulsion was developed, first in the shape of paddle-wheels, it was discovered that the platform between the two paddle-boxes, known at the time as a bridge, gave a much better all-round view of operations on deck. When the propeller replaced the paddle-wheel the elevated structure amidships was retained as the navigational control position, and as further development took place, particularly in the number of boilers required to produce steam in sufficient quantity, this central bridge was moved forward and raised to keep it clear of the funnel smoke. The modern tendency in larger ships, particularly *tankers, is to construct the bridge well aft in the ship, mainly in order to keep the upper deck as clear as possible of such obstructions as a midships bridge structure, to give an uninterrupted view from the bridge of the whole of the upper deck, and to provide easier and more economical working conditions at sea and in harbour. This is made possible by the modern design of bulk carrier in which the propulsion machinery is placed as far aft as possible, with funnels or diesel exhausts, which affect the position of the bridge in the ship, close to the stern.

BRIDLE, (1) a length of rope, wire, or chain secured at both ends to a spar or other object, to the *bight of which a *purchase can be hooked on. The purpose is to provide a better balance in an unhandy object for lifting purposes. (2) The upper end of fixed *moorings laid in harbours and anchorages. When a ship lies to moorings, it is to the bridle, or the *buoy at the end of it, to which she is secured.

BRIDLE-PORT, a square port cut in the bows on either side of the stem of wooden ships on main deck level through which mooring *bridles were led. The same ports were used in warships for guns, moved up from the gunport next abaft, when it was required to fire as nearly ahead as possible, as when chasing. When used at sea for this purpose they were sometimes known as main deck *chase-ports instead of bridle-ports.

BRIDPORT, a small seaport on the coast of Dorset, England, where one of the best-known naval * ropewalks of the 17th and 18th centuries was situated. The finest * hemp was grown in the neighbourhood and by instructions from the * Navy Board in London, all anchor * cables for British warships had to be made at Bridport from the local hemp. This rule lasted until the great expansion of the navy during the Revolutionary (1793–1801) and Napoleonic (1803–15) wars against France, when the demand completely swamped the local supply. So excellent was this Bridport rope that all cables used for anchor work were known in the British Navy as Bridports. Rope is manufactured at Bridport to this day.

Originally the town appears to have been known as Buryport and it is under this name that it appears in the Armada map of the English Channel engraved by A. Ryther in 1590.

BRIDPORT, Lord, see HOOD, Alexander.

BRIERLY, Sir OSWALD WALTER (1817–94), British marine artist, was appointed marine painter to Queen Victoria and was an artist with very close connections with the Royal Navy. Born at Chester, he attended art school in London and studied naval architecture at Plymouth, and in 1839 he exhibited some drawings of ships at the Royal Academy. Later he travelled extensively, spending ten years in New Zealand. At the invitation of Captain Owen * Stanley, R.N., he accompanied him on board the * Rattlesnake during a survey of the north and north-east coasts of Australia together with the adjacent islands, T. H. Huxley being assistant surgeon of the ship. He next made a voyage in the Meander at the invitation of Captain (later Admiral Sir) Henry Keppel round New Zealand and to the Friendly Isles, an account of which he illustrated. For this, and the notes and sketches made on the previous voyage, he was made a Fellow of the Royal Geographical Society. He was again Keppel's guest on board the St. Jean d'Acre with the allied fleet in the Baltic and subsequently in the Black Sea during the Crimean War (1854–56). His sketches were published in the Illustrated London News. After that war he was commanded by the Queen to make sketches from the Royal Yacht of the naval review at Spithead in 1856. He was under the constant patronage of the Royal Family and on the death of J. C. * Schetky in 1874 was appointed marine painter to the Queen.

Brierly was a versatile artist, and the sketches and paintings he produced during his two voyages in Australian waters, his visits to the fleet during the Crimean War, and at the 1856 naval review all show a keen observation and a lively attention to maritime detail. He was less happy

when he turned his attention to historical painting and battle scenes, his bold treatment of line and colour hardly compensating for his lack of knowledge of ships of past centuries and how they fought.

BRIG, originally an abbreviation of * brigantine, but later a type of ship in her own right after some modifications in the original rig. The true brig is a two-masted vessel square-rigged on both fore and main masts. A * hermaphrodite brig, sometimes called a brig-schooner, has the usual brig's square-rigged foremast and a * schooner's mainmast, with * fore-and-aft mainsail and square topsails. Brigs were widely used in the days of sail for short and coastal trading voyages, and there are still a few to be found today employed in local trades. They were also used widely in several navies as training ships for boys destined to become naval seamen, and in many navies were retained for this purpose long after sail had disappeared in them for good. In the British Navy the training brigs for boys lasted into the first decade of the 20th century. For illus. see RIG.

BRIGANTINE, a two-masted vessel, as a * brig, but square-rigged on the foremast and * fore-and-aft rigged on the mainmast. The name comes from the fact that these ships were favourite vessels of the sea brigands, particularly in the Mediterranean, although in their case the vessel they used was more of the * galley type used with oars. But as sea brigandage spread to the more tempestuous waters of the Atlantic and North Sea, the ships used by these new brigands took the Mediterranean name even though the type of ship changed. For illus. see RIG.

BRIN, BENEDETTO (1833–98), Italian naval administrator, could probably be justly called the 'father' of the Italian Navy when it was formed after the unification of the country in 1870. A naval engineer, he was appointed under-secretary of state of the Ministry of Marine by the minister, Admiral Saint-Bon. These two men worked very closely together, and where Saint-Bon thought out the type of ships best suited for a navy such as Italy's, Brin drew the plans and superintended their construction. In 1876 he was appointed minister and continued to develop the fleet as an organic whole. The large battleships Dandolo and Italia were of his design, as were the smaller ships of the Garibaldi class. He also directed his attention to the operation of shipbuilding firms, dockyards, and gun foundries. He held the Ministry of Marine for eleven years in all, and when he was finally promoted to minister for foreign affairs, he left behind him an Italian Navy which was both strong and efficient, and well backed up by manufacturing and shipbuilding capacity.

BRINE, or PICKLE, the salted liquor in which beef or pork was preserved in casks for use in ships before the days of tinned or frozen meat.

BRING UP, to, the act of bringing a ship to an anchor or a *mooring. The normal practice, particularly in small ships or vessels under sail, is to bring up head to tide; at the periods of slack water when there is little or no tide, a vessel would bring up head to wind.

BRING-TO, to, to bring a sailing vessel to a stop with her sails still set. In the case of square-rigged ships this was achieved by *bracing the yards on her foremast *aback to counter the effect of those that were still drawing; in the case of a *fore-and-aft rigged vessel it is achieved by bringing her head to wind so that no sail will draw. The term is also often used when forcing another vessel to stop by firing a shot across her bows. (See also HEAVE-TO, TO.) When anchoring, the correct term is to bring a ship to an anchor, because in the days of sail it was usual to bring-to for anchoring by laying the foresails aback to take off the ship's way.

BRISTOL, a seaport on the Severn Estuary in south-west England. It owed much of its early importance to the development of the wool trade with Ireland, expanding this trade to the Baltic as the excellence of English wool became more widely known. Looms were set up in Bristol in 1337 by Thomas Blanket (hence the name still given to bedclothes) and the export of woven cloth became so great that Bristol in 1553 was made one of the Staple towns. One of the greatest cloth merchants in Bristol was William Canyng (1399–1474), five times mayor of the town, and it was during his mayoral administration that the Society of Merchant Venturers was founded, one of its first acts being the provision of ships for the voyages of John and Sebastian *Cabot. Other voyages of exploration followed, and trade grew apace, particularly that in African slaves during the 17th century. The abolition of the slave trade in the 19th century struck a great blow to the port of Bristol, particularly as Liverpool, with better port facilities and a great manufacturing complex in its near neighbourhood, was growing fast in importance as the major seaport on the west coast of England. For a short period in the 19th century Bristol regained its importance as the terminal port for the new steamship transport to the western world, inaugurated by the sailing of the *Great Western from Bristol to New York in 1838. This trade, however, was later moved to *Southampton. During the 20th century, a variety of trade has been built up and developed, and great improvements in the docks and warehousing has led to new and rapid expansion.

Bristol was, for centuries, a great shipbuilding port and it was there, in 1843, that the *Great Britain*, the first iron ship to be built as a transatlantic liner and the first ocean-going ship with screw propulsion, was launched. In 1970, 127 years later, she was salved and refloated in the Falkland Islands and towed back to Bristol where she is now preserved as an example of the very early days of iron shipbuilding.

BRISTOL FASHION, everything neat and seamanlike. The expression had its origin when Bristol was the major west coast port of Britain before the growth of *Liverpool brought competition, and during the palmy days when all its shipping was maintained in proper good order. The full expression is shipshape and Bristol fashion.

BRITANNIA, a 212-ton British racing yacht ordered in 1892 by the Prince of Wales, later Edward VII, and after his death owned by George V. Designed by G. L. *Watson, she was built on the Clyde of wood on steel frames, $121\frac{1}{2}$ feet overall, and in her original *gaff rig spread 10,327 square feet of canvas. Launched in 1893, her early racing years were remarkably successful, but after the introduction of time handicaps which allowed very much smaller yachts to race against the big ones, the Prince of Wales grew tired of the sport and in 1897 sold the *Britannia*. He bought her back four years later and fitted her out for cruising only. In 1921, in order to start big class racing again, her new owner, George V, fitted her out for racing, and for the first few seasons she had great success, though as the years progressed she was more and more unable to hold her own with the bigger *J-class racing yachts of more modern rig. Although converted to *Bermuda rig in 1931, she was still unable to match the newer yachts, and in 1935 she was withdrawn from racing, having sailed a total of 635 races, winning 231 first prizes and 129 second and third. After the death of George V in 1936 she was towed out into the English Channel and sunk in deep water off the Isle of Wight.

BRITANNIA, H.M.S., a ship's name associated with the Royal Navy since 1682, when the first of this name was built at Chatham.

This ship has a tenuous connection with one of Charles II's famous ladies. By his instructions Frances Stuart, Duchess of Richmond, sat as a model for Britannia to replace the Roman figure, seated on the shore of Britain, which Claudius (41–54) had used to commemorate his seizure of southern Britain. Charles was so pleased with the result that he ordered one of his new naval ships to be given the name *Britannia*.

The fifth ship of the name was allocated to the training of naval cadets in 1859 and was finally moored in the River Dart for this purpose. The subsequent college built there was also known as H.M.S. *Britannia*, but in 1953 a new *Royal Yacht was given the name *Britannia*, the college becoming known as the Britannia Royal Naval College.

BRITANNIA, R.M.S., the best known of the four ships with which Samuel *Cunard formed the Cunard Line of steamships in 1840. Like her sister ships *Acadia*, *Caledonia*, and *Columbia*, she was a wooden paddle steamer of 1,156 tons and an overall length of 207 feet. On her return from Boston to Liverpool in her first transatlantic voyage she carried sixty-three passengers and made the passage in fifteen days. On one occasion she was iced in at Boston when she was due to sail, and rather than delay her sailing the people of Boston cut a seven-mile channel through the ice to enable her to reach the open sea.

BRITISH STEEL, the yacht in which Chay *Blyth sailed single-handed round the world westabout in 292 days from November 1970 to August 1971. She was built of steel at Dartmouth and her design was by Robert *Clark. Of 15 tons displacement, with an overall length of 59 feet (18 m), she had a racing hull and was rigged as a *Bermuda *ketch with a masthead *jib and forestaysail working on a *boom. She was flush-decked with a small, low, steel deckhouse.

BRITOMART, more properly Britomartis, a Cretan goddess who is the patroness of hunters, fishermen, and sailors. She was a nymph, the daughter of Zeus and Carme, and when pursued by Minos, king of Crete, who was desirous of ravishing her, she sprang into the sea but was saved from drowning by the nets of some fishermen.

'BRITONS, STRIKE HOME', the title of a naval song much in favour in the 18th century and played on board British ships as they were sailing into battle. It was even more popular for this purpose than the equally well-known song *·Rule, Britannia'. The song comes from Purcell's opera *Bonduca* of 1695. A pamphlet printed in 1757 with the title *A faithful Narrative of the cruel Sufferings of Captain Death and his Crew*, written by Samuel Stoakes, includes the following: 'The master-at-arms had one of his arms and part of his body torn away: in this bloody condition he was carried down to the surgeon, who saying it was impossible to save his life, and the poor man finding himself dying, bravely in his last moments sang the song of "Britons, strike home", and expired with the words in his mouth.'

Broaching-to

BROACH-TO, to, the tendency of a sailing vessel to fly up into the wind when *running free or with the wind blowing strongly from the *quarter. In square-rigged ships the chief danger of broaching-to arose from the habit of many skippers of driving their ships too hard, keeping aloft too large a press of canvas to make the most of strong winds, particularly on main and *mizenmasts. In extreme cases of broaching-to, the sails could be caught flat *aback, in which situation the masts were likely to go *by the board, and the ship might even *founder stern first. *Foreand-aft rigged ships are less likely to suffer from broaching-to, though it does remain a major danger, particularly when sailing with a *spinnaker set. See also POOP, TO.

BROAD PENDANT, a swallow-tailed pendant, flown from the masthead, and in most navies the distinguishing flag of a *commodore. In Britain, until 1864, there were three qualities of broad pendants, red, white, and blue, indicating commodores of the first, second, and third class and corresponding to the organization of the British Navy into red, white, and blue squadrons. On the abolition of *squadronal colours in 1864, all commodores' broad pendants in the Royal Navy became white with a red St. George's cross.

BROADSIDE, the full weight of metal which can be fired simultaneously from the guns which bear on one side of a warship. Broadside on, sideways, the opposite of end on.

BROKE or **BROKEN,** the sentence of a court martial which deprived an officer of his commission. The full wording of the sentence in British courts martial was 'to be broke and rendered unfit to serve His Majesty at sea'. The modern equivalent is to be dismissed the Service.

BROKE, Sir PHILIP BOWES VERE (1776–1841), British rear admiral, served under *Nelson and St. Vincent (see JERVIS) and was promoted captain in 1801. In 1806 he was appointed to the command of the 38-gun *frigate *Shannon* and by hard training of her crew brought her to a high standard of efficiency, especially in gunnery. On 1 June 1813, during the war against the U.S.A., when off Boston, Massachusetts, he challenged Captain James *Lawrence of the U.S. frigate *Chesapeake* to fight. In disobedience of his orders, and with an untrained crew, Lawrence sailed out to do battle. After two destructive *broadsides, Broke led a boarding party and captured the *Chesapeake*, the whole action being over in a quarter of an hour. Since Britain had recently suffered many humiliating defeats in such frigate actions, this success made Broke extremely popular in Britain and also had a salutary effect on naval gunnery and training which were largely remodelled on his methods. Broke was made a baronet, but a wound suffered in the action prevented any further service at sea. He was promoted rear admiral in 1830.

BROOKING, CHARLES (1723–59), British marine painter, grew up in Deptford Dockyard, London, and was thus connected at an early age with ships and the sea. He began painting when young and was strongly influenced by the work of the two Van de *Veldes, who were working in Britain between 1672 and 1707, and many of his sea pieces have all the charm and serenity of the work of those two great masters. Another of the great Dutch marine artists whose work he followed was Simon de *Vlieger. Samuel *Scott, one of the great English marine painters of the period, had a very high regard for his work. Brooking befriended Dominic *Serres when he was brought to England after the capture of his ship in 1752 and taught him to paint, the pupil eventually becoming as great a marine painter as his master. Brooking's poverty was unfortunately exploited by unscrupulous art dealers who quickly appreciated the distinction of his work, and as a result his weak constitution became sadly undermined through overwork, leading to an early death at the age of 36. A representative collection of his paintings can be seen at the *National Maritime Museum, London.

BROOM, (1) an old custom of indicating that a ship was for sale was to hoist a besom at the masthead. Some have held that the old story of *Tromp hoisting a broom at his masthead 'to sweep the English seas' really arose from an earlier derisory English statement that he had the broom at his masthead to denote that his fleet was for sale as it was so inefficient. There would

however appear to be very little truth in either version of the story. **(2)** The shrub of that name was cut and used widely for the purpose of *breaming a ship, or burning off the weed and *barnacles which grew on the bottom. Brooming was often used as a synonym for breaming.

BROW, (1) the *gangway for the use of passengers and crew from ship to shore when a ship is lying alongside a wharf or quay in harbour, **(2)** that hinged part of the *bow of a landing craft or *ferry which is lowered to form a landing platform when the craft is run bows on to the shore. This is also known as a ramp. In modern large car ferries, the brow or ramp is usually fitted at the *stern.

BROWN, Sir JOHN (1816–69), British manufacturer, introduced *armour plating into the British Navy. In 1859, on behalf of his firm, Earl Horton and Co., he inspected the French armoured frigate *Gloire*, in which hammered plate was used, and came to the conclusion that it was possible to produce satisfactory armour by a better method. He experimented successfully with a rolling process and the British Admiralty was so impressed with the result that it placed an order with him to produce enough armour to protect three-quarters of the then existing navy.

BROWN ON RESOLUTION, the title of a novel by C. S. *Forester, published in 1929, which tells of the exploits of a British petty officer stranded on Resolution Island when it was being attacked from the sea by Germans during the First World War (1914–18).

BROWNSON, WILLARD HERBERT (1845–1935), American naval officer, graduated from the Naval Academy in 1865 and had the usual assignments of sea and shore duty. He served as commandant of *midshipmen at the Naval Academy 1896–8, was superintendent of the Academy 1902–5, and commanded the Asiatic fleet from October 1906 to April 1907. When he reached retiring age in July 1907 President Theodore *Roosevelt appointed him as Chief of the Bureau of Naval Personnel. In that appointment Brownson, who was an exceptionally able officer at all times, distinguished himself especially by his response to the President's intention to appoint a naval medical officer as captain of a hospital ship. Politely but firmly Brownson pointed out to the President that the commanding officer of a ship should be responsible for handling his vessel in matters of seamanship, navigation, and in battle, and that this was not necessarily a qualification of medical officers. Roosevelt insisted, and after making the appointment, Brownson resigned his post with the remark that the President should have a personnel adviser in whom he could have complete confidence. Although Brownson received some adverse comment in certain newspapers, most responsible naval officers applauded him for his action.

BRUCE, ERROLL (1913–   ), British naval officer and yachtsman, cruised and raced from an early age in a variety of craft from dinghies and naval whalers to *J-class yachts. He also raced in many offshore events in his ocean-racing yachts *Samuel Pepys*, *Belmore*, and *Figaro*, including the transatlantic and Bermuda races of 1950, 1952, and 1960. From 1961 to 1967 he was editor of *Motor Boat and Yachting* and is a British delegate to the Union of International Motorboating. He is also a member of the Royal Yachting Association Council and various committees, and a director of the Nautical Publishing Company. Among his books on yachting are *Deep Sea Sailing*, *When the Crew Matter Most*, *Local Knowledge*, and *Challenge to Poseidon*.

BRUCE, WILLIAM SPIERS (1867–1921), Scottish polar explorer and oceanographer, abandoned his medical studies to sail to the South Shetland Islands and Graham Land aboard the Dundee whaler *Balaena* in 1892–3. After a number of short expeditions to Novaya Zemlya, the Barents Sea, and Spitsbergen, he led his own Scottish National Antarctic expedition to the Weddell Sea area of the Antarctic in 1902–4, sailing in the *Scotia*. Here he carried out important oceanographic surveys and research on marine biology. In 1904 in the course of this voyage Coats Land, Antarctica, was discovered and a weather station set up in the South Orkney Islands which is still operating (1976). Several small expeditions to Spitsbergen followed but plans for a second Antarctic expedition failed. In 1907 Bruce founded the Scottish Oceanographical Laboratory in Edinburgh which he maintained until 1920.

BRUEYS D'AIGUÏLLIERS, FRANÇOIS PAUL (1753–98), French admiral, known as Brueys, served as a lieutenant during the American War of Independence (1775–82). Discharged from the Republican Navy as a royalist in 1793, he was reinstated under Napoleon's régime in 1795 and promoted to rear admiral. In 1798, as vice admiral, he commanded the fleet which escorted Napoleon's transports to Egypt, capturing Malta *en route*.

After the capture of Alexandria, Brueys took his fighting ships to *Aboukir Bay where he anchored his thirteen ships of the line parallel to a line of shoals inshore of them. There, after a long and frustrating hunt, Rear Admiral Sir Horatio *Nelson with fourteen ships of the line discovered them on the afternoon of 1 August

1798. The battle of the *Nile, the first of Nelson's three famous victories, ensued. The whole French fleet, with the exception of two ships of the line and two frigates which managed to set sail and escape in the early morning of 2 August, was destroyed or captured: Brueys himself was mortally wounded early in the action. See also CASABIANCA.

BRUNEL, ISAMBARD KINGDOM (1806–59), engineer and ship designer of British birth and nationality but French origin, began his engineering career in 1823 when he entered the office of his father, Marc Isambard *Brunel; he was his father's assistant engineer in the construction of the Blackwall Tunnel under the River Thames. In 1833 he was appointed engineer of the projected Great Western Railway, the design of which was mainly his work.

In addition to his railway work, Brunel took a keen interest in the development of ocean steam navigation and in 1835 suggested to the directors of the Great Western Railway that the line

Isambard Kingdom Brunel in front of the Great Eastern

should be extended to 'have a steamboat to go from Bristol to New York and call it the *Great Western*'. His proposal was accepted and he designed and built the *Great Western* at Bristol, a wooden *paddle steamer larger than any steamer of the day. She was the first steamship built to make regular crossings of the Atlantic and proved a most successful vessel, her first voyage to New York and back being made in 1838. Brunel went on to design an even larger ship, the *Great Britain*, which was the world's first large iron steamship, the largest ship afloat at the time, and the first big ship in which a screw *propeller was fitted. Launched in 1843, she made her first Atlantic crossing to New York in 1845, but the following year was carelessly run aground on the rocks in Dundrum Bay, Ireland. It was nearly a year before she was refloated but she was so little damaged that she was able to be used for many years in the Australian trade, a great tribute to the strength of Brunel's design.

This connection with the Australian trade fired Brunel to envisage a 'great ship' large enough to carry in her bunkers all the coal required for a voyage to Australia without the need of calling at a coaling station on the way and, if no coal was available at her port of destination, enough coal as well for the return voyage. He took his designs for his 'great ship' to the directors of the Eastern Steam Navigation Company, who accepted them and appointed him as their engineer for the project. In collaboration with J. Scott *Russell, Brunel's *Great Eastern was laid down in December 1853, but many difficulties were experienced during the course of construction and in the launching, and she did not finally get afloat until the end of January 1858. She was by far the largest ship ever built up to that time, with a length of 680 feet and displacing 18,915 tons. She had both screw and paddle propulsion. Brunel did not see her leave on her first voyage; two days before she was due to sail he suffered a severe stroke and died ten days later.

In addition to his designs for ocean-going steamships, Brunel was the engineer in charge of the construction of many docks and piers, particularly at Bristol, Plymouth, and Milford Haven, and in 1854, during the Crimean War, he designed a floating gun-carriage for the naval attack on Kronstadt. It is a measure of his versatility that he also designed and constructed a hospital on the shores of the Dardanelles at Erenkeni. But he is remembered mainly for his work on iron steamships, and many of the elements of his designs, as for example the construction of *double bottoms in the *Great Britain*, remain standard practice in shipbuilding today.

L. T. C. Rolt, *Isambard Kingdom Brunel* (1970).

BRUNEL, Sir MARC ISAMBARD (1769–1849), British inventor and engineer, was the father of I. K. *Brunel. He was born at Hacqueville, in Normandy, and as a youth served in the French Navy for six years. His pronounced royalist sympathies forced him to leave France during the French Revolution, and after a few years in America he came to England to settle. He had invented a method of making *blocks for ships and was able to interest the British Admiralty in the method, being instructed to set up his machinery in *Portsmouth dockyard. His machines, constructed by Henry Maudslay, were among the earliest examples of a range of machine tools which each performed one essential part in the making of a block. All blocks for use in ships had until then been made by hand; Brunel's machines not only produced a greatly improved article but made them quicker and cheaper, the annual saving when his machines were in full production being estimated at £24,000. Following this success, he invented machines for sawing and bending timber, and these were erected at Woolwich and *Chatham dockyard, where the handling of ship timber was completely reorganized on lines laid down by Brunel.

At this time he began to interest himself in the possibilities of steam navigation and in 1814 persuaded the Admiralty to experiment with steam tugs to tow the sailing men-of-war out of harbour. A few months later the Admiralty cancelled his contract on the grounds that his idea was 'too chimerical to be seriously entertained', but Brunel went ahead with it at his own expense. 'Chimerical' it may have been, but by 1822 the Admiralty owned two steam tugs, the *Comet* and *Monkey*, expressly for towing sailing men-of-war out of harbour.

His later career, as an engineer, with the exception of designing floating landing stages for the port of Liverpool, was not concerned with ships or the sea, and in this stage of his career he is perhaps best remembered for his construction of the Blackwall Tunnel under the River Thames.

BRUNSBÜTTEL, a German seaport on the North Sea coast, the western terminal of the *Kiel Canal where it leads into the North Sea.

BUBBLE HORIZON, an attachment which can be screwed to the frame of a *sextant immediately in front of the horizon glass to provide an artificial true horizon in weather conditions, or at night, when the real horizon is indistinct or invisible. When taking an *altitude of a celestial body, the navigator's line of sight through the telescope passes through the clear part of the horizon glass and enters the attachment where, by means of mirrors and a lens, the rays of light from a bubble inside the attachment are projected in a true horizontal direction. This

Bucentaur, *the doge's state galley*

provides an artificial true horizon, and when the reflected image of the body, seen in the silvered part of the horizon glass, is brought down to the artificial horizon, its altitude can be read off on the sextant scale.

BUCCANEERS, known among themselves by the romantic title of 'brethren of the coast', were seamen of all nationalities who cruised on their own account on the Spanish Main and in the Pacific in the 17th century. They styled themselves *privateers, but since they seldom carried valid commissions, they differed from pirates only by virtue of the fact that they did not prey on ships of their own nation. The word itself is derived from the French *boucan*, or grill, for cooking dried meat. It came into use after the publication of *Esquemeling's classic *Bucaniers of America*, 1678 (Eng. trans., 1684). Buccaneers were called by the Dutch *zee-rovers*, by the Spanish *corsarios*, and by the French *flibustiers*. They were inspired by the tradition of the Elizabethan privateers and became prominent for their marauding activities in the Caribbean after the capture of Jamaica in 1655, and later in the Pacific. Early bands were composed of adventurers of all sorts, whom Sir Henry *Morgan welded into an efficient force to capture Panama in 1671. They were excellent seamen and included several remarkable characters, such as Bartholomew *Sharp, William *Dampier, Alexander *Selkirk (the original of *Robinson Crusoe), Basil *Ringrose, and Lionel *Wafer. Their adventures and books enjoyed wide

popularity and have inspired writers such as *Defoe, *Stevenson, and *Masefield. Many of them made remarkable voyages around the world (see, e.g., COWLEY, DAMPIER). The outbreak of a European war in 1689 brought buccaneering to an end, the freebooters then being transformed into legitimate privateers.

BUCENTAUR, the traditional name of the state *galley of the doges of *Venice, from the Italian *buzino d'oro*, golden *bark. The name was also given to any great and sumptuous galley. The last and finest of the Venetian *Bucentaurs* was built in 1729 and, like all its predecessors, was used in the annual procession for the traditional symbolic ceremony of the wedding of the sea by the doge on Ascension Day, a ceremony which commemorates the victory of the Doge Pietro Orseolo II over the Dalmatian pirates in the year 1000. This *Bucentaur* was destroyed by the French for its golden decorations during their invasion of the Italian states in 1798. Its remains are in the Museo Civico Correr in Venice, and there is a fine model of it in the arsenal there.

The name, in the form *Bucentaure*, was used as a warship name in the French Navy in the 17th and 18th centuries, and it was in a ship of this name that Admiral *Villeneuve flew his commander-in-chief's flag at the battle of *Trafalgar.

BUCHANAN, FRANKLIN (1800–74), American naval officer and, later, an officer in the *Confederate States Navy, became a midshipman in 1815. As a commander, he was the first Superintendent of the U.S. Naval Academy at Annapolis. He was flag captain and chief of staff to Commodore Matthew C. *Perry during the latter's command of the East India Squadron and had an important part in the negotiations with the Japanese which Commodore Perry conducted in Japanese waters in 1853 and 1854.

He was in command of the Washington Navy Yard when Abraham Lincoln became President in 1861. After the surrender of the Pensacola Navy Yard, earlier in 1861, Buchanan had made plans for the defence of the Washington Navy Yard. Ten days after the attack on Fort Sumter he submitted his resignation as a captain in the U.S. Navy, acting on the belief that Maryland, his native state, would secede from the Union. In fact Maryland did not secede, but Buchanan's subsequent request to withdraw his resignation was refused and he was dismissed. He then went to Richmond and became a captain in the Confederate Navy on 3 September 1861. Initially he headed the personnel bureau of the C.S.N.

In February 1862 Buchanan was given command of a squadron of six vessels in the James River, the most important ship being the converted *ironclad *Virginia*, formerly the frigate *Merrimack*. In the *Virginia*, Buchanan left the Norfolk Navy Yard on 8 March 1862 and went down the Elizabeth River to Hampton Roads. His plan was to sink the Federal frigate *Congress* and the sloop *Cumberland*, which were stationed off Newport News, by ramming them in order to save ammunition. Insufficient depth of water alongside the *Congress* made it impossible to ram her and she had to be destroyed by gunfire, in the exchange of which Buchanan was wounded. Next morning he was urged to act on his doctor's advice and go ashore to the hospital for treatment, thus missing commanding the *Virginia* during her historic duel with the *Monitor*.

Buchanan was promoted to the rank of admiral for his successes on 8 March and after his wound was healed was ordered to Mobile, Alabama, to organize a naval defence of *Mobile Bay. He hoisted his flag in the C.S.S. *Tennessee* in February 1864, and was present at the battle of Mobile Bay on 6 August 1864 in which his opponent was Admiral *Farragut.

'BUCKO' MATE, the term applied to the *mate of a sail trading ship of the late 19th and early 20th centuries who drove his crew by the power of his fists, and generally by his brutality made life a hell on board for the crew. 'Bucko' mates were notably prevalent in the American square-rigged ships on the New York or Boston to California run after the discovery of the gold-fields there and before the railway to California

was built. The competition to make a quick passage round Cape Horn was always very fierce among these ships, and many owners appointed captains and mates to their ships on whom they could rely to drive the crews to exhaustion, and sometimes beyond, in their search for speed. These captains and mates did not spare their voices, fists, or rope's-ends to keep their crews at work whatever the Cape Horn weather, and many seamen in these ships went to their deaths in the Cape Horn seas mainly because exhaustion from being driven too hard caused them to miss their footing on the *yards when working the sails in a gale.

BUDGE-BARREL, the small barrel of gunpowder which in the days before powder was made up into cartridges, used to be brought on deck to serve the guns. It held a hundredweight of powder and the top end was fitted with a leather flap or bag drawn tight by a string which, when the barrel was brought to the guns, covered the open end to lessen the danger of accidental firing. After the introduction of cartridges which dates from about 1580, budge-barrels were generally used only in harbour for the purpose of firing salutes. Sir Henry *Mainwaring (*The Seaman's Dictionary*, 1644) says that cartridges were made of canvas, 'which is reasonable good', carefully measured to contain exactly the amount of powder required for the size of gun; 'this is wondrous necessary for our great ordnance and also for saving the powder which is in danger to be fired if in fight we should use a ladle and carry a budge-barrel about the ship'.

BUENOS AIRES, the capital city and major seaport of Argentina on the southern bank of the River Plate, and the home of the *Museo Naval, a naval museum of importance.

BUGEYE, a later and larger development of the *skipjack, used for offshore fishing and general cargo carrying in the Chesapeake Bay area of the U.S.A. Built originally as work boats and later copied as shallow draught yachts, bugeyes ranged from 40 to about 75 feet in length and were generally *ketch-rigged with jib-headed sails set on masts raking aft.

BUGGALOW or **BUGALILO,** the Marathi name for the trading *dhows which used to work on the Malabar coast of India and in the Persian Gulf.

BUGIA, BATTLE OF, an operation against the *Algerine pirates, fought on 8 May 1671 between an English squadron of six ships commanded by Vice Admiral Sir Edward *Spragge, and an Algerine fleet at Bugia (Port de Bougie). After a previous failure on the night of 2 May, a second attempt was made, this time in broad daylight. Shortly after 2 p.m. the English squadron anchored close in and bombarded the Algerine ships and fortifications for the space of two hours. Three boats were then sent in to cut the *boom across the entrance, which was done under a heavy fire, and the *Little Victory*, *fireship, entered and succeeded in setting fire to the whole of the Algerine fleet (seven warships and three prizes), which was completely destroyed. As Spragge wrote in his dispatch, 'the castles and town (were) miserably torn, with an infinite number of the inhabitants killed and wounded. Old Treky, their admiral, is likewise wounded.' The English loss was 17 killed and 41 wounded; the Algerines confessed to upwards of 360 killed.

BUILDERS OLD MEASUREMENT, a formula adopted in Britain by Act of Parliament passed in 1773 to calculate the *tonnage of a ship as a figure on which port and harbour dues, etc., could be based. The formula was

$$\frac{(L - \frac{3}{5}B) \times B \times \frac{1}{2}B}{94},$$

where L equals the length of the ship measured along the *rabbet of her keel and B equals her maximum beam, the result giving her measurement in *tons. This formula remained in force until the mid-19th century when the introduction of iron as the most efficient material for shipbuilding and steam as the means of propulsion resulted in the design of ships with longer, fine-lined hulls, to which the older measurement rule no longer applied.

BULB KEEL, a deep fin with a large bulb of lead on the bottom, widely used in racing yachts during the late 19th and early 20th centuries. Its purpose was to achieve the maximum resistance to the excessive heel of racing yachts, produced by the vast areas of sail they carried, by placing the centre of gravity as low as possible. Its use led eventually to the development of extreme and unseaworthy yachts, and was discouraged by the adoption of *rating rules which severely penalized yachts built in this fashion. See also KEEL.

BULGE, often used in the same sense as *bilge. A ship which is bulged (or bilged) is one whose bottom has been holed. It is also an expression to indicate that additional width has been built into a ship below the waterline by the construction of outer compartments in order to provide greater stability or, in the case of warships, greater protection from underwater attack.

BULKHEAD, a vertical partition, either fore and aft or *athwartships, dividing the hull into separate compartments. Main bulkheads, running athwartships, are normally made watertight, with watertight doors fitted where access through the bulkhead is required, to prevent extensive flooding if a ship is holed. A collision bulkhead is a watertight bulkhead situated near the bows of a ship to prevent flooding in the event of a collision at sea.

BULL, HENRIK J. (*fl.* 1894–5), a Norwegian sailor who promoted an expedition to the Antarctic for the purpose of establishing a southern whaling industry there. The expedition ship, *Antarctic*, reached the Antarctic continent in January 1895 and made the first landing in Victoria Land, at Cape Adare, on 24 January 1895. The expedition was an economic failure but one of its members, C. Borchgrevink, found lichen growing, the first evidence of plant life within the Antarctic circle.

BULL ROPE, (1) a rope used for hoisting a topmast or topgallant mast in a square-rigged ship. It is rove from the *cap of the lower mast, through a sheave in the *heel of the topmast, and then back through a *block on the lower masthead, with the hauling part led to the deck. When a topmast is hoisted, a pull on the hauling part of the bull rope sends the topmast up to the

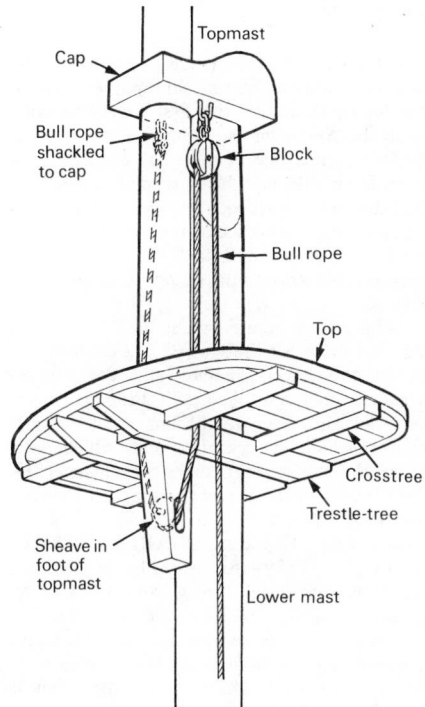

Bull rope

height where the *fid, which holds it securely in place, can be inserted. The reverse operation lowers the topmast. (But see also TRIPPING LINE.) (2) A line rove temporarily through a *bullseye on the end of a yacht's *bowsprit and secured to a mooring-buoy, designed to hold the buoy well clear of the yacht's bows and prevent it striking or rubbing against the hull.

BULLEN, FRANK THOMAS (1857–1915), British marine author, was born in London and went to sea at the age of 12 as a cabin boy on board his uncle's ship *Arabella*. Six years later he signed articles on board the whaler *Cachalot* at New Bedford, Massachusetts. This ship provided the material for his book *The Cruise of the Cachalot* (1898) which is considered to be his best work. In 1884 he became a clerk in the Meteorological Office and began writing in earnest, producing in all some thirty-six books, the best of which, including the one already mentioned, are *Idylls of the Sea* (1899), *Our Heritage the Sea* (1906), *From Wheel and Outlook* (1913).

'BULLOCK', a name given by sailors in the British Navy to a member of the Royal Marine Artillery before their amalgamation with the Royal Marine Light Infantry to form the Royal Marines. They were also known as Grabbies, Jollies, or Turkeys.

BULLOCK, FREDERICK (1787–1874), British admiral and marine surveyor, entered the navy in 1804 and in his first surveying command, the *Snap*, on the Newfoundland station, 1823–7, earned one of the early awards of the Polar Medal. It had been specially struck in 1827 and was awarded to people of every rank and class who distinguished themselves in Arctic expeditions from 1818 to 1855. Bullock had rendered assistance to the *Griper* (Captain Lyon) in 1824.

On his return from Newfoundland he began in 1827 his principal life's work in a detailed survey of the River Thames and the Thames Estuary, which continued until 1853. His name was originally given to the important entrance channel which he charted and which later became known as the Edinburgh Channel. He was a Fellow of the Royal Geographical Society from 1830.

His son, Captain CHARLES JAMES BULLOCK (1829–78), was also a surveyor throughout his naval career from 1844 to his retirement because of ill health in 1873. The greater part of his service was on the China Station, starting with a survey of Palawom passage in 1850–4. In 1855, during the Crimean War, he was with *Sulivan in the Baltic but next year returned to China where, when Captain

Bate was killed in the assault on Canton, Bullock took command of the *Dove*, working until 1861 off North China and Japan. After completing the resulting charts and sailing directions in England he was back on the China station for a final four years, 1865–9, commanding the *Swallow*.

BULLSEYE, (1) a circular piece of *lignum vitae*, hollowed in the centre to take a rope and grooved round the outside to accommodate a *strop which enables it to be fixed in position where required. Its main purpose is to change the lead, or direction, of a rope in cases where a *block for this purpose is not required. **(2)** It is also the name given to a piece of thick glass set flush in the deck of a ship to admit light to the deck below. **(3)** The small expanse of blue sky seen in the centre of a tropical storm is also known by many seamen as the bullseye.

BULLY BEEF, originally the seaman's name for salt beef from which all the fat and substance has been boiled away by the cook to enrich his grease tub, which was one of his perquisites. The name comes from the French *boeuf bouilli*. It has been cited as one of the causes of the mutiny in the *Bounty* in 1787, but in fact was not one of the reasons why the men rebelled. It was later also the name given by sailors of the Royal Navy to the first tinned meat issued on board ship in 1813, supplied by Messrs. Donkin and Hall from a process invented by a French chef, Nicholas Appert, which was marketed under the name *boeuf bouilli*. See also FANNY ADAMS.

BULWARK, the planking or woodwork, or steel plating in the case of steel ships, along the sides of a ship above her upper deck to prevent seas washing over the gunwales and also persons on board inadvertently falling or being washed overboard in rough weather. In sailing ships which used to round Cape Horn in the course of their voyages, nets were frequently rigged above the bulwarks to provide an added security against hands being washed overboard in the furious weather frequently experienced in that area.

BULWARK, H.M.S., a British battleship which was accidentally blown up at Sheerness in November 1914 during the First World War (1914–18) when she was taking on board ammunition. Only twelve of her crew of 750 survived the explosion. For a time foul play was suspected, but it was later established at a court of inquiry that the explosion was due to the instability of the cordite being embarked.

BUMBOAT, a small boat used for carrying vegetables, fruit, and provisions to ships lying in harbour. The term possibly derives from the Dutch *boomboot*, a broad-beamed fishing boat, but also possibly from *bumbay*, an old Suffolk word meaning quagmire. The word first appears in England in the by-laws of *Trinity House in 1685 under which scavenging boats attending ships in the Thames were regulated. These boats were employed to remove 'filth' from ships, and also to carry vegetables for sale on board. Apparently hygiene was not highly regarded by Trinity House in 1685.

BUMMAREE, a word synonymous with *bottomry. It is also a term applied to fish salesmen or porters in fish markets ashore.

BUMPKIN or **BUMKIN,** originally a short *boom projecting forward on either side of the bows of a sailing ship which was used to extend the *clew of the foresail to windward. It had a *block fixed to the outer end through which the *tack was rove and hauled aboard. Similarly, it was the name of a short boom which extended from each quarter of a sailing vessel to carry the main *brace blocks. In its modern meaning it is a short *spar extending directly over the stern of a sailing vessel to *sheet the *mizen sail in those cases where the mizen-mast is stepped so far aft that there is not enough room inboard to bring down the sheet and trim the sail. The name is also used, in some modern yachts, to describe a short spar extending from the *stemhead in place of a *bowsprit.

'BUNDLEMAN', a sailor's name, used in the British Navy, for another who is married. The term is derived from the days when men were allowed to purchase naval provisions at a cheap rate for their families, and a married man would be recognized by the bundle of provisions he carried when going ashore.

BUNG UP AND BILGE FREE, the method of stowing casks so that the bung stave is uppermost and with the bottom tier of casks resting on skids or beds so that the *bilge of the cask, which is the thickest part in the middle, is clear of the deck.

BUNK, a built-in wooden bed on board ship. In the main cabin of some sailing vessels engaged in trade during the 18th and 19th centuries the sides were lined with bunks fitted with sliding panels to provide privacy, since the captain, *mates, and any lady passengers, or the captain's wife, were all accommodated in the cabin. Generally, except in very large or expensive ships, bunks are erected in tiers one above the other, to obtain the maximum sleeping accommodation within the minimum space.

BUNKERS, compartments on board ship, most usually placed along the sides and bottom, for the stowage of fuel, whether coal or oil. The operation of filling or replenishing a ship's bunker with fuel is known as bunkering.

BUNT, the middle section of a square sail where it is cut full to form a belly. It applied more especially to topsails, cut to form a bag to gather more wind, than to lower sails which were generally cut square with only small allowance for bunt. In a full-rigged ship the bunt of the topsails was frequently so heavy and voluminous that a BUNT-JIGGER was fitted to the sails to assist the men on the yards in *furling them. This was a small *tackle of two single blocks by means of which the bunt of the sail was hauled up to the yard so that the *gaskets could be secured. BUNTLINES, ropes attached to the footropes of the square sails, were also fitted in the larger sailing vessels and led up through blocks attached to the yards. When hauled up they spilled the wind out of the sails for reefing or hoisted them right up to the yards for furling. BUNTERS, the topmen working in the centre of the yards who gather in the bunt when furling sails. BUNT-FAIR, said of a square-rigged ship when sailing before the wind. For illus. see SAIL.

BUNTING, a thin cloth of woven wool supplied in various colours from which are made signal and other coloured flags. Originally the name for bunting was *bewpars. It is the most satisfactory material for flags as it is light enough to be well spread even in a gentle wind, making the colours of the flags readily visible, and yet is more resistant to fraying in a hard wind than many heavier materials. In 1664 Samuel *Pepys, although at the time an official of the *Navy Board, entered into the business of supplying flags for the English fleet, buying coloured calicoes from wholesale drapers and having them made into flags which he then sold to the Navy Board in defiance of the rule which forebade officials to enter into trade with the navy. But his venture did not profit him much as calico proved an unsatisfactory substitute for bunting, being too heavy to fly well in the wind and at the same time fraying more rapidly when the flags flapped. The navy very quickly turned back to bunting for this purpose and Pepys was left with a large stock of calico which he had to use up in dresses for his wife and servant girls.

BUNTLINE BAND, a strip of canvas *tabled on to the forward side of a square sail to prevent the buntlines (see BUNT) from chafing the sail.

BUOY, a floating mark used mainly for navigational purposes to mark a channel, bank, *spoil ground, or similar area of which the navigator of a ship needs to know. Buoys came generally into use in European waters in the late 15th or early 16th century; in Britain they were

regulated under a charter given by Henry VIII to
*Trinity House in 1514. Buoys to assist pilotage
in the River Thames were first laid about 1538,
and most of the principal ports and harbours had
buoys to mark the entrance channels very shortly
afterwards. Rocks and shoals around the coast
were similarly marked with buoys. At first all
buoys consisted of baulks of timber usually surmounted by a staff or pole and moored in position, and it was only when iron ships generally
replaced wooden ones that metal buoys, more
efficient than wooden ones, came into use.
Navigational buoys are generally of four distinct
shapes, *can, conical, spherical, or *spar; mooring buoys for large vessels are usually cylindrical
in shape. One almost universal rule for the identification of a buoy is that its shape should be
considered more important than its colour, and
this can normally be established by reference to
the system of *buoyage in force in the waters
concerned, which is always given in detail in the
*Sailing Directions appropriate to those waters.

Buoys have other uses besides navigational,
such as *watch buoys to enable a *lightship to
check that she is not drifting off her station,
buoys to mark the position of telegraph cables or
submarine mining grounds, sewer outfalls, etc.
All these can have distinctive shapes and colours,
of which details are marked on navigational
*charts. Admiralty Chart 5011, issued by the
British Admiralty, which lists all the symbols
and abbreviations used on charts, has a section
which deals with buoys and beacons.

Some buoys, particularly those marking main
navigational channels, are lighted for identification at night, cylinders of compressed gas being
used for the purpose; others may be fitted with a
whistle operated by compressed air or with a bell
activated by the movement of the waves or by
other means to assist in their location in thick
weather. Since the wide introduction of *radar in
ships, many buoys are now fitted with reflectors
to facilitate their detection by this means and to
overcome the problem of sea-clutter.

Navigational buoys are attached to the seabed
by means of a chain cable or pendant secured to
ground tackle which varies according to the
nature of the bottom, the size of the buoy, and
the depth of water. In some harbours, in order to
make the best use of the available berthing space,
special mooring buoys are laid to which ships
can secure instead of having to lie to their own
*anchors, thus requiring room to swing with
the tide. They are classified according to the size
of ships for which they are suitable, and the
weight of the ground tackle. The use of buoys in
place of lightships has been made possible by
recent developments in construction and equipment. Known as Lanby (Large Automatic
Navigational) buoys, they are some 12 metres
(40 ft) in diameter, and 2·5 metres (8 ft) deep and

are equipped with a lattice mast carrying a light
12 metres (40 ft) above sea level with a range of
16 miles, as well as a powerful fog signal and
radar beacon. These buoys can be moored in
depths of up to 90 metres (300 ft) and they are
designed to operate for six months without attention, but their performance is constantly monitored by a shore station. The cost of maintaining
one of these buoys is about one-tenth that of
a lightship. See also BLEED, TO; BUOYAGE,
SYSTEMS OF; and APPENDIX 4.

BUOY ROPE, the rope which attaches a small
buoy to an *anchor when it is on the bottom to
mark its position. In length it needs to be slightly
more than the depth of water at high tide where
the anchor lies, and in normal practice it is of
sufficient strength to lift the anchor in the event
of the cable parting. Anchor buoys are generally
used when anchoring on a rocky bottom, and the
buoy rope is bent on to the *crown of the anchor
with a running *eye over one *fluke and with a
hitch taken over the other arm. If the anchor is
jammed in the rocks and cannot be weighed
normally by the cable, the buoy rope can then be
used to break out the flukes by hoisting the
anchor bottom upwards.

BUOYAGE, SYSTEMS OF, codes of practice,
adopted multinationally or nationally, under
which *buoys of various shapes and colours are

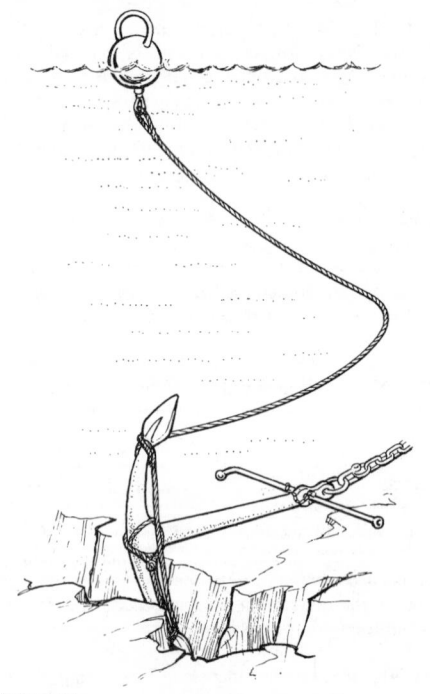

Buoy rope

used for the same navigational purpose. In 1882, in an attempt to get international agreement for a uniform system of buoyage, *Trinity House, the British authority responsible for buoys, called a conference of all other national authorities concerned. This eventually took the form of an international marine conference at Washington, D.C., in 1889 at which a uniform system of buoyage was one of the subjects discussed. Most of the maritime nations in the world attended, and the conference recommended the adoption of a lateral, or side-marking, system based partly on shape but primarily on colour. Thus it was agreed that buoys marking the *starboard side of a channel, defined as that on the right hand of a ship entering from seaward or going with the main *flood tidal stream, should be coloured black and be conical in shape. Those marking the *port side should be red or checkered, and can, or truncated cone, in shape. No agreement was reached on the marking of the middle grounds, which in Britain was always done with spherical buoys.

Another international marine conference was called at St. Petersburg (now Leningrad) in 1912 and an attempt made to reverse the Washington decision, but the proposal to do so was supported only by Spain, Italy, and southern Russia. But later some countries, particularly those bordering the Baltic Sea, found the lateral system not entirely suitable for their waters, and adopted a new system known as the cardinal, or directional, in which a combination of shape, colour, and topmark is used to indicate the compass quadrant in which the buoy is moored relative to the danger it marks. Countries exclusively using the cardinal system are Norway, Sweden, and Russia; Germany, Italy, and Turkey also use it either in addition to or in combination with the lateral system. Important changes to the colour of buoys in E.E.C. waters are under discussion (1976). The system of buoyage in use in any particular country is given in full detail in the *Sailing Directions appropriate to those waters. See APPENDIX 4.

BURGEE, a broad, tapering pendant, normally with a swallow tail but occasionally without. Burgees of yacht clubs are normally triangular, of a length twice that of the depth at the hoist, and carry on them the particular insignia of the club concerned. *Commodores of yacht clubs usually fly swallow-tailed burgees again carrying the insignia of the club. Burgees, without a swallow tail, are used as the substitute flags in the *International Code of Signals.

BURGESS, ARTHUR JAMES WEATHER-ALL (1879–1957), Australian marine painter, was born at Bombala, New South Wales, the son of a naval officer. He came to England in 1901 and soon earned recognition by his paintings, such as the well-known 'The Wash of the Next Ahead', 'Crossing the Bar', and 'The Entrance to Sydney Harbour'. During the First World War (1914–18) he was official war artist to the Royal Australian Navy. For a time he was art editor of *Brassey's Naval Annual.

BURGESS, EDWARD (1848–91), American yacht designer, was born in Boston, Massachusetts. On a visit with his family to England in 1883 he saw much of English yachting at Torquay and in the Solent, and when he returned to Boston and found the family merchandise business failing he opened a yacht broker's office and set up in practice as a self-taught designer. His first commission of note was from General Charles J. Paine to design a defender of the *America's Cup against the British challenger Genesta in 1885. This was the 80-ft waterline *cutter Puritan which soundly beat the British cutter. Again in 1886 Burgess designed the successful Cup defender Mayflower, and the following year the Volunteer, earning national acclaim as three times saviour of the Cup through the brilliance of his designs. His design practice grew rapidly and in a period of only seven years he produced designs for 137 different vessels which included, in addition to yachts, pilot boats, fishing craft, and steamers. In 1887 he was selected by the Secretary of the Navy as one of a special board to choose designs for the new American fleet, resulting in the construction of the battleships Maine and Texas. He died at the early age of 43 as the result of a fever brought on by his intensive naval work.

BURGOO, an old seafaring dish mainly of the days of sail, a sort of porridge or gruel made of boiled oatmeal seasoned with salt, sugar, and butter. It had the merit of being easily prepared in the *galley during very rough weather and was sustaining enough for seamen to perform the heavy work of the ship. But, like all things easy, it was apt to be overdone, and in many ships it became the daily evening meal of the crew because the cook was too lazy to prepare anything more elaborate, or the owner too mean to provide alternative rations. It thus became an object of dislike and derision among seamen. See also LOBSCOUSE, SKILLY.

BURKE, ARLEIGH ALBERT (1901–), American admiral, first distinguished himself while in command of a destroyer squadron in South Pacific waters during the Second World War. After providing gunfire support for the initial assault on Bougainville in November 1943, he and his destroyers fought in twenty-two separate actions during the following four months. They were credited with the destruction of 1 Japanese cruiser, 9 destroyers, and 1 submarine, in addition to several smaller vessels and nearly 30 aircraft. On a number of occasions, Burke responded to reports of enemy locations by radio messages that he was proceeding to the scene at 31 knots, and in that manner acquired the nickname '31-knot Burke'. His outstanding abilities were recognized by his appointment in March 1944 as chief of staff to Admiral Mark * Mitscher, Commander Fast Carrier Task Force 58 in the Pacific, and he added to his excellent reputation in that post. After commanding a cruiser division in the Korean War, and the destroyer force of the Atlantic fleet, he became Chief of Naval Operations in August 1955, retiring in 1961. His character, ability, and pleasing personality gained the respect and affection, as well as the admiration, of fellow naval officers and almost all who knew him.

BURNEY, JAMES (1750–1821), British mariner, was a member of the crew of the * Resolution during Captain * Cook's second voyage (1772–5) and subsequently a lieutenant on board the * Discovery during the third voyage (1777–80) of which he kept a journal, now in the Public Record Office, London. He was transferred back to the Resolution on the death of Cook's successor, Captain Charles Clerke. He was the author of a major work in five volumes, A Chronological History of the Discoveries in the South Sea or Pacific Ocean (1803–17) and also of a smaller work, A Chronological History of North-Eastern Voyages of Discovery (1819).

BURNS, SIR GEORGE (1795–1890), British shipowner, ran a line of small sailing ships between Glasgow and Liverpool. In 1838, in conjunction with Samuel * Cunard and others, he founded the Cunard Line of Atlantic steamships on the strength of obtaining the British government contract for the carriage of mails to North America. He was succeeded as head of the Cunard Line by his son, JOHN, who in his turn was succeeded by his son, GEORGE.

BURTHEN, the older term used to express a ship's * tonnage or carrying capacity. It was based on the number of * tuns of wine that a ship could carry in her holds, the total number giving her burthen. The term remained as an expression of a ship's size until the end of the 18th century but gradually fell into disuse after a new system of measurement of ships, known as the * Builders Old Measurement, was adopted by Act of Parliament in 1773.

BURTON or SPANISH BURTON, a special * purchase using three single * blocks, or two single blocks and a hook, in which one * whip is used to haul on the * fall of the other, thus multiplying the power gained. In sailing ship days it was used mainly to set up the * shrouds of the masts so as to get them as taut as possible, but today burtons are rarely used except where a strong haul is required in a restricted space.

BUSCH, FRITZ OTTO (1890–   ), German naval officer, one of that country's leading authors of popular works on naval history, particularly of the Second World War. Among his many works are Narvik, an account of the German naval occupation of that port and of the two battles of * Narvik in 1940; Die Aktion Dänemark–Norwegen, which described the German invasion and occupation of Denmark and Norway in April 1940; Tragödie am Nordkap, the sinking of the * battle-cruiser * Scharnhorst off North Cape in December 1943; Akten des Seekrieges, an account of the main actions of the war at sea during the Second World War; So war der U-bootskrieg, the U-boat campaign in the Atlantic, Mediterranean, and Arctic Ocean; and Kampf um Norwegens Fjörde, the sea war along the coast of Norway.

BUSHNELL, DAVID (c. 1742–1824), American inventor, was one of the fathers of the submarine. Graduating from Yale in 1775, the year of the first skirmish between British troops in America and the colonists, he had bitter feelings against Britain and determined to put his engineering abilities to use in aid of the American colonies in revolt. He designed and built a small 'submarine', shaped like an egg, which floated upright in the water and could be trimmed down until the * conning tower was * awash by admitting water to two small internal tanks. She carried a detachable charge of 150 lb of gunpowder which could be fixed to the bottom of an enemy ship by means of a screw. In 1776, when the British fleet was lying off New York, Bushnell launched his submarine with a sergeant in the American army, Ezra Lee, operating it. Lee managed to force it under the hull of H.M.S. Eagle, flying the flag of Lord * Howe, but was unable to screw the charge home as Bushnell had not made allowance for the fact that the bottoms of British warships at that time were sheathed with copper. This, and two more attempts which were made later, were unsuccessful. At the end of the war in 1782, Bushnell gave up his submarine experiments and assuming another name became a successful doctor. See also FULTON, Robert.

BUSKING, an old term, long obsolete, for a ship beating to windward along a coastline. It was also a term used when describing pirate vessels cruising in search of victims to attack.

BUSS, a 17th- and 18th-century fishing vessel, mainly used in the herring fishery, broad in the beam with two, and sometimes three, masts with a single square sail on each and usually of from 50 to 70 tons. The term, though known throughout Europe, was mainly used to signify Dutch and English fishing vessels in the North Sea. By some the origin of the term is thought to be the old French *busse*, a cask. The development of the *ketch with its handier rig gradually put the older fishing busses out of action.

'BUTCHER'S BILL', old naval slang term for the dead and wounded on board after battle.

BUTT, (1) the squared end of a plank used on the side of a wooden vessel where it is secured to the *timbers. It is also the name given to the space between the two squared ends of adjoining planks in a ship's side, which has to be caulked. Similarly, the ends of plates used in the sides of iron or steel ships are also known as butts. To start a butt is the condition when the end of a plank springs clear or loosens from its fastening to the timbers through the labouring of a ship in a heavy sea. **(2)** A cask containing 126 gallons.

BUTTER-BOX, a derisory name used by British naval seamen during the First (1652–4) and Second (1665–7) Anglo-Dutch Wars to describe Dutch seamen. As a sea song written to commemorate the victory over the Dutch at the St. James's Day battle, 25 July 1666, during the Second Anglo-Dutch War, has it:

'The cannons from the Tower did roar,
When this good news did come to shore,
The bells did ring and bone-fires shine,
And healths carrous'd in beer and wine,
God bless King Charles and all our fleet,
And grant true friends may safely meet,
Then Butter-boxes brag no more,
For now we have beaten you or'e and or'e.'

BUTTERSWORTH, JAMES E. (1817–94), Anglo-American marine artist, was famous for his paintings of *clipper ships at sea. Born in the Isle of Wight, he emigrated to the U.S.A. in 1845 and took a studio in Hoboken, N.J. He became one of Currier's best artists and it is said that he had an unrivalled knowledge of rigging and sails. His pictures are noted for their freshness and individuality.

BUTTOCK, the breadth of a ship where the *hull rounds down to the stern. A ship is said to have a broad or a narrow buttock according to the convexity of her hull below the *counter.

BUTTOCK LINES, longitudinal sections of a ship's hull parallel to the *keel. It is a term used in ship designing.

BUTTON or **BATTON,** THOMAS (*c.* 1577– 1634), British naval officer and explorer, entered the navy in 1589. In 1612 he was appointed to

command the *Resolution* in an expedition to search for the *North-West passage. Accompanied by the pinnace *Discovery*, he thoroughly explored the west coast of Hudson Bay and proved that there was no outlet to the north-west along it· He named Nelson river, New Wales, and Button's Bay. Later he commanded ships in Irish waters in the suppression of *piracy.

BUYS BALLOT LAW, a rough and ready method of discovering the direction of the centre of a circular storm. If an observer faces the direction of the true wind, the centre of low pressure will be between eight and twelve points (90°–135°) on his right hand in the northern hemisphere, and on his left hand in the southern. It takes its name from C. H. D. Buys Ballot, Dutch meteorologist, who published it in his *Comtes Rendus* (1857).

BY, in relation to the wind, to sail a vessel BY THE WIND is to sail her on or close to the wind with the *sheets hardened in. FULL AND BY, to sail on the wind keeping the sails full of wind without their *luffs lifting or shivering. BY AND LARGE, to sail a vessel near the wind but not fully on it, i.e., about five *points off the wind with the fore-and-aft rig and about seven points with square rig. BY THE LEE, the situation when a ship is *running free and the wind, either through a shift of direction or through careless steering, comes across the stern and blows on the *lee side of the sails, thus laying them *aback on the other tack and usually causing an involuntary *gybe. In small sailing ships it is a frequent cause of *capsizing or dismasting. See also BROACH-TO, TO.

BY GUESS AND BY GOD, a form of navigation under which a ship's *master or navigator relied more on his experience or powers of guessing to bring his vessel safely to her destination than on the proper processes of navigation by *compass and observation. Many of the older fishing skippers used to navigate their craft in this somewhat haphazard method, using the experience of past fishing trips to estimate their position. The term had particular application to the early *submarines, where the facilities for accurate navigation were limited, particularly when the submarine was dived, which limited visual observation, and where the magnetic

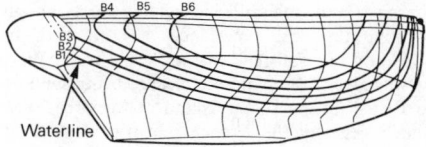

Buttock lines

compass, being entirely surrounded by steel in a confined space, was liable to erratic behaviour on account of the vessel's latent magnetism. In such cases, navigation had to be dependent to some extent on guesswork as to the strength and direction of tidal streams below the surface, of irregularities in the sea bed, on the performance of the compass, etc., and the hope on board was that God would exercise his divine powers to bring the submarine safely to her destination at the end. It could perhaps be said to be a form of navigation akin to * dead reckoning.

BY THE BOARD, close to the deck or over the ship's side. When a mast carries away it is said to have gone by the * board.

BY THE HEAD, a ship is said to be by the head when she draws more than her normal depth of water forward, with her bows lying deeper than her stern. Similarly, a ship is said to be BY THE STERN when she is drawing more than her normal depth of water aft. It is a result of the faulty trimming of her internal * ballast or a bad stowage of cargo, and can be corrected by transferring ballast from forward to aft, or aft to forward, as the case may be.

BY THE STERN, see BY THE HEAD.

BYNG, GEORGE, Viscount TORRINGTON (1663–1733), British admiral of the fleet, entered the navy in 1678 and for a time also served in the army. In 1688 William of Orange made him his agent in the British Navy to try to persuade British naval captains of his right to the throne of England on the flight of James II, and after William had become king, Byng's advancement was rapid. As a rear admiral he took part in the capture of * Gibraltar in 1704 and its defence at the subsequent battle of Velez Malaga. In 1715 he was employed in preventing supplies reaching the Jacobite rebels during the operations of the Old Pretender. In 1718, as admiral of the fleet, he decisively defeated a Spanish fleet off Cape * Passaro in Sicily and was raised to the peerage as Viscount Torrington. He was First Lord of the Admiralty from 1727 until his death.

BYNG, JOHN (1704–57), British admiral, was the fourth son of George * Byng, Viscount Torrington and admiral of the fleet. With his father's influence to help him he rose rapidly in the navy and quickly reached flag rank though without any real experience of command. In 1756, on the outbreak of the Seven Years War, he was given command of a fleet to bring support to British forces in the island of Minorca, then under siege by the French. He was delayed at * Gibraltar by arguments with the Governor, and on arrival off * Minorca found the island in the possession of the French but with the English garrison holding out in Port Mahon. He fought an indecisive action against a French fleet which was covering the invasion, but four days later, after a council of war, returned to Gibraltar and left Port Mahon to its fate. He was arrested and brought back to England, where he was court-martialled on a charge of failing to do his utmost to save Minorca. He was found guilty and sentenced to death. A recommendation for mercy was refused probably because the government needed a political scapegoat for the defeat. He was shot on the quarter-deck of H.M.S. * Monarch on 14 March 1757 and his execution inspired Voltaire's remark in Candide that in England it was sometimes necessary to shoot an admiral 'pour encourager les autres'.

BYRON, JOHN (1723–86), British admiral, known as 'Foul Weather Jack' on account of his unlucky experiences at sea, was the grandfather of Lord Byron the poet. As a midshipman in the Wager during Commodore * Anson's voyage round the world (1740–4) he was wrecked off the coast of Chile in 1740, returning home six years later after incredible hardships. In 1764, as captain of the * Dolphin, he made a rapid but fruitless circumnavigation of the globe in search of * Terra Australis Incognita, the mythical southern continent in the Pacific. In 1779, now promoted vice admiral, he was sent in command of a fleet to relieve British forces in North America during the War of American Independence (1775–82). After experiencing a most destructive gale on the passage out, he fought an indecisive action against the French admiral d'* Estaing off Grenada and was thus unable to provide the support for which his fleet was intended. He returned to England where ill health prevented him from serving again at sea.

BYWATER, HECTOR CHARLES (1884–1940), Anglo-American journalist and marine author, was born in London. He emigrated to Canada in 1898 and travelled extensively in the U.S.A. and Europe. Before the outbreak of the First World War (1914–18) he was correspondent in Germany for the British Navy League and during the war was attached to the Naval Intelligence Division in the British Admiralty. After the war he became naval correspondent of the Daily News, the Observer (1923–8), and the Baltimore Sun (1921–30). He wrote several books, among them Fleets at War, with Sir Archibald * Hurd (1915), Sea Power in the Pacific (1921), The Great Pacific War (1925), Navies and Nations (1927), Dramas and Mysteries of the Naval War (1932), A Searchlight on the Navy (1934), and Cruisers in Battle (1939). He was an associate of the Institute of Naval Architects and a gold medallist of the U.S. Naval Institute.

C

'CQD', the original wireless distress call made by a ship requiring assistance. It was introduced in January 1904, and stood for CQ, the signal for all stations, and D for distress, but became widely known as 'Come Quickly, Danger'. It still remained in operation for a number of years after *SOS was agreed internationally as the recognized distress call in 1908. When the White Star liner * *Titanic* sank in 1912 she sent out both CQD and SOS calls. See also 'MAYDAY'.

C.S.S., Confederate States Ship, the prefix used for the warships of the States of the Confederacy (South) during the American Civil War between North and South (1861–5) to distinguish them from the warships of the Union or Federal States (North) which used the prefix *U.S.S.

CABIN (possibly from the Latin *Capanna*, little house), a room or space in a ship partitioned off by *bulkheads to provide a private apartment for officers, passengers, and crew members for sleeping and/or eating. The first cabin as such was probably the *carosse, an open space under the *poop deck in a *galley where the admiral or captain had his bed. In later ships, the same space was enclosed by bulkheads to provide the 'great cabin', which was the admiral's or captain's living quarters, often divided into sleeping cabin and day cabin, where he kept his 'table', served by his private cook and servants. Forward of the great cabin, in larger ships, was another cabin known as the *coach where in flagships the flag-captain lived. As sailing ships, particularly warships, grew larger, with additional decks, there were two coaches, upper and lower, to provide additional cabins for officers. From about the early 17th century to mid-19th century, most officers of ships below the rank of captain were allowed temporary cabins, closed in by canvas screens or removable wooden bulkheads, in which a cot for sleeping and a chest in which clothes were kept occupied most of the available space, quickly dismantled in cases of need, such as battle, fire, etc.

The use of iron, and later steel, as the main building material for ships, combined with the 19th century expansion of travel and trade, brought about the construction in ships of permanent cabins for officers, and in passenger ships for some of the higher-paying passengers, although during this period a majority of passengers still travelled in the *steerage, a space in which they lived communally throughout the voyage. The continuing growth of travel led inevitably to the provision of cabins for all passengers, except in ships engaged only in short passages of a few hours, such as ferries, and during recent years the practice has been continued to provide cabins for each member of a ship's crew. See also HUDDOCK, STATEROOM, STEERAGE.

CABIN SOLE, a yachting term to describe the floorboards of the cabin accommodation, or cabin deck space. The planks rest on sole bearers which are carried athwartships beneath the *floor.

CABLE, (1) basically any very large hemp or wire rope, but normally associated with the *anchor of a ship, and thus the means by which the ship is attached to the anchor as it lies on the bottom or is stowed in the *hawsepipe or inboard. Originally, all such cables were of hemp, and in the Royal Navy of *Bridport hemp only, and an early definition of a cable, *c.* 1740, was a hemp rope of 20 inches in circumference containing 1,943 yarns, although the term was rapidly revised downwards to include any rope of 10 inches or more in circumference. By 1780 the general rule for the size of an anchor cable was half an inch in circumference for every foot in *beam of the ship; thus a ship with a beam of 60 feet had a cable 30 inches in circumference. Such a size of cable was that normally supplied to a first-*rate ship of war; it was tested to a breaking strain of 65 tons, and weighed $12\frac{1}{2}$ tons per 100 fathoms. Chain cable first made an appearance in about 1800 (*Nelson's attack on the French invasion vessels anchored in Boulogne in 1801 was frustrated by the use of chain cables by the French ships); in its larger sizes the links are studded across the middle to prevent them kinking. The size of chain cable is measured by the diameter of the links. The length of a rope cable is 100 to 115 fathoms, a *hawser-laid cable 130 fathoms. Chain cable is measured for length in *shackles of $12\frac{1}{2}$ fathoms, eight shackles being considered as a cable length. **(2)** A measure of distance at sea, 100 fathoms or 200 yards (183 m).

CABLE SHIP, a vessel fitted for the laying and repairing of submarine telegraph and telephone cables. One of the earliest and best-known cable ships was the *Great Eastern*, so used after she had failed as a passenger liner. A distinctive feature of modern cable ships is the large roller built out over the bows of the ship for paying out or underrunning cable.

CABLE STOPPERS, usually known as slips, are used to hold the cable when a ship lies to an anchor, either as a preventer, or stand-by, when the cable is held by the brake of the *cable-holder, or to hold the cable temporarily so that the inboard part of it can be handled. There are four types of stopper normally used for cable work in large ships, all tested to half the proof load of the cable.

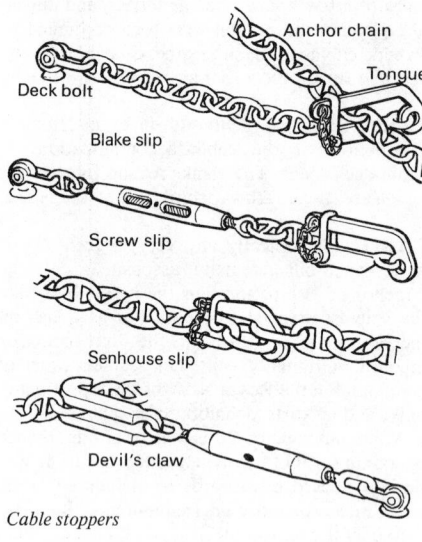

Anchor chain

Tongue

Deck bolt

Blake slip

Screw slip

Senhouse slip

Devil's claw

Cable stoppers

BLAKE SLIP, a general purpose slip, in which the tongue passes over a link of the cable, consists of a short length of studded chain shackled to a deck bolt close to the line of the cable between the cable-holder and the *hawsehole, with the slip attached to the end of the chain. Its main use is as a preventer when the ship lies to her anchor but it is also used to hold the cable if work is necessary on its inboard end.

SCREW SLIP, a Blake slip with a bottlescrew incorporated in the length of chain. It is used when securing an anchor for sea, the bottlescrew being turned to bring the *flukes of the anchor hard home in the hawsepipe.

RIDING SLIP, again a Blake slip, usually shackled to a deck bolt immediately above each cable locker, though occasionally on the upper deck between the cable-holder and the *navel pipe. When a ship is lying to an anchor and is riding to the brake on the cable-holder, the riding slip is put on as a preventer in case the brake *renders (slips).

SENHOUSE SLIP, a slip designed to secure the end of a cable. In this slip the tongue passes through the end link of the cable, which is studless, and not across a link as in the other slips. Its normal place in a ship used to be in the cable lockers where the inboard end of the cable is secured, but in several modern ships the end of the cable is shackled on to a deck bolt in the locker, no Senhouse slip being used. Smaller Senhouse slips are used in many smaller vessels and yachts to hold the ends of the *guardrails to the *stanchions. In these cases the tongue passes through an eye in the end of the guardrail.

In many merchant vessels the cable is stoppered with a Devil's Claw in place of a slip. Here there is no tongue, its place being taken by a fitting in the shape of two claws, the gap between them being the diameter of a cable link. The claws are passed across a link that lies horizontally on the deck and hold the link next to it, which must lie vertically.

CABLE-HOLDERS, two capstan-like fittings mounted on the *forecastle deck of larger ships by which the two *bower anchors are *weighed or *veered. They are set either side of the centre-line of the ship in the line of the bower cables, and the chain links of the cables fit into cavities round the drum of the cable-holders so that they are held firmly. When a bower anchor is being weighed, its cable-holder is geared into the capstan engine so that the anchor is hove in mechanically; when the anchor is being let go or veered, the cable-holder is unclutched from the capstan engine and can run freely, its speed being controlled by a friction brake, which is also used to hold the cable when the ship lies to her anchor. In very large ships which carry a *sheet anchor in addition to two bower anchors, a third cable-holder is not fitted, the sheet anchor cable being brought to the capstan for weighing and veering.

In smaller vessels a *windlass takes the place of capstan and cable-holders, with *gypsies, fitted to take the links of the bower cables, mounted inboard of each warping drum.

CABLE-LAID ROPE, a very thick and strong rope used only for the heaviest work on board ship and for the towing cables of tugs. It is made by laying-up (twisting) together three ordinary ropes, which have themselves been made by laying up three strands. Whereas in ordinary rope, known as *hawser-laid rope, the three strands are laid up from left to right, in cable-laid rope the three hawsers must be laid up from right to left; otherwise the strands in the hawser would become untwisted and lose much of their strength and durability. If three hawser-laid ropes of 120 fathoms in length each are laid up

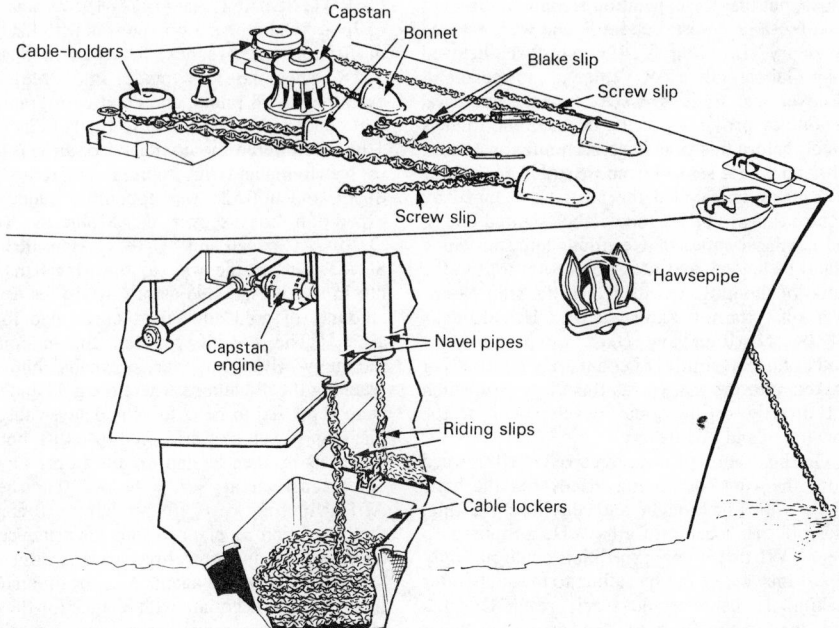

Cable-holders

in this way, they will make a cable-laid rope of 100 fathoms.

Cable-laid rope is sometimes known as cablet, and also as water-laid rope, because it absorbs less water than hawser-laid rope.

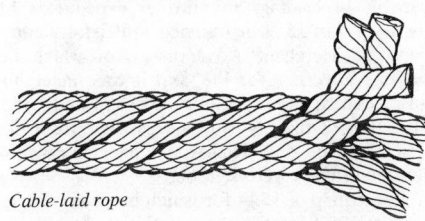

Cable-laid rope

CABOOSE, a name frequently used to describe the *galley, or cook-house, of a small vessel, normally on deck and not between decks, and in shape much resembling a sentry-box. It was originally a wooden box or covering of the galley chimney where it came through the deck, hence probably its association with cooking. The name applied only in the case of smaller merchant ships, such as coasters, fishing vessels, and the like, all larger ships having space for a galley between decks. The term is now largely obsolescent, and began to die out with the introduction of mechanical means of propulsion and the descent, even in the smallest craft, of the cooking arrangements to a position below the upper deck, although in some small craft the word is retained, possibly for sentimental reasons.

CABOT, JOHN, the Anglicized form of **CABOTO,** GIOVANNI (*c.* 1450–98), Italian navigator. Very little is known of his early life but it is believed that he was born in Genoa and as a boy went to Venice where he was naturalized as a Venetian citizen. He appears to have commanded a merchant ship which traded to the Levant and on one of these voyages is said to have visited Mecca where he was amazed by the market there in spices, silk, and jewels. Being told that they came overland by caravan from Asia, and knowing that the earth was a sphere, he was seized with the idea that it would be quicker to bring them to Europe by sea if he could reach * Cathay (China) and * Cipangu (Japan) by crossing the western ocean. Filled with this belief, but unable to convince the European courts to the extent of equipping an expedition, Cabot brought his family to London in 1484, and tried to persuade the more important merchants of Bristol that an attempt should be made to reach Cathay by sea. They agreed to take the risk of such a voyage but stipulated that he should first go by way of Hy *Brazil and the Isle of the Seven Cities, those mythical islands which were shown on all the medieval maps of the western ocean.

Before the expedition could be organized and dispatched, news was received in England that Christopher *Columbus had sailed to the west and reached the Indies. The British merchants now decided that time should not be spent either searching for Hy Brazil or the Isle of the Seven

Cities, but that the expedition should go direct to Asia by sailing west. Letters Patent were granted by Henry VII in March 1496 to his 'well-beloved John Gabote, citizen of Venice ... to seeke out, discover and finde whatsoever isles, countries, regions or provinces of the heathen and infidels which before this time have been unknown to all Christians'. He set sail from Bristol in May 1497 in a small ship called the *Mathew*, manned by eighteen men. On 24 June Cabot sighted one of the northern capes of Newfoundland, on which island he landed, and took possession of it in the name of the king. On its return the ship passed over what are now known as the *Grand Banks off the Newfoundland coast where the crew caught huge quantities of cod merely by lowering baskets into the sea. It was this discovery which led directly to the great development of the Newfoundland cod fishery.

On his return Cabot received £10 reward from the king for having discovered the 'new island' which he thought, and convinced the king, was off the coast of Cathay. He proposed to Henry VII that a new expedition could not only repeat the voyage but by sailing to the south after making the coast would surely reach Cipangu and thus make London the greatest trading centre in the world for the products of the east. Cabot, after the King's promise of a second expedition, made a visit to Seville and Lisbon in an effort to recruit men who had sailed with Columbus, but appears to have had little success. Henry VII issued new Letters Patent on 3 February 1498 giving Cabot the power to 'impress' six English ships for the voyage. Only five ships were, however, taken up; they were victualled for a year, and in accord with the King's licence, Cabot, proceeding westward from his last discovery until he reached the coast of Cipangu, was to set up a trading factory there for spices and silks.

This second expedition, of five ships and 300 men, sailed from Bristol in May 1498 and was never heard of again. For some 450 years it got somehow mixed up with a voyage made in 1500 by Jão Fernandez, known as Llavrador (farmer), to the east coast of Greenland, which was mistakenly named Labrador (after Fernandez) in the belief that it was a new discovery, and another in 1501 by Caspar Corte Real, which seems to have visited Newfoundland or the mainland of America thereabouts. These two voyages seem to have become amalgamated and were held by some authorities to constitute Cabot's second voyage, from which they have him returning safely to Bristol and dying there shortly after.

The best account of the Cabot voyages is in James A. Williamson's *The Cabot Voyages and Bristol Discovery under Henry VII* (Hakluyt Society, 1962). For a biography see H. Harisse, *John Cabot* (1896).

CABOT, SEBASTIAN (1476–1557), was a son of John *Cabot. As a boy he was with his father in Bristol, but was next heard of in Spain in 1518 when he was made Pilot Major, or examiner of all pilots, and chief cartographer of that country. During a visit to England in 1520–1 he was offered the command of an expedition to Newfoundland but refused. He returned to Spain, and in 1525 was appointed leader of an expedition 'to discover the Moluccas, Tarsis, Orphir, *Cipangu and *Cathay'. He sailed from Seville, but on the way to the Magellan Strait put in to La Plata, led astray by stories of large amounts of gold and silver to be had for the asking. The hostility of the Indians on the Paraguay River, however, prevented him from reaching the mountains where the gold and silver were supposed to be. After the delays caused by this vain search he was forced to return home to Spain, as by then he had exhausted his supplies. On his arrival at Seville he was banished to Africa for four years for his failure to conduct the expedition as planned, but his sentence was later remitted and after three years he returned to become Pilot Major again. Attempts he made at this period to negotiate with Venice for the command of a voyage of discovery were unavailing.

He then returned to Bristol, England, and for the next ten years tried to get a licence from Henry VIII to lead a new expedition of discovery but it was not until Henry was succeeded by his son Edward VI in 1547 that he received both encouragement and reward. By then, however, he was too old to lead, even if he was ever really capable of leading, any further expeditions of discovery. In 1551 he founded, at Bristol, a company of Merchant Adventurers, of which he became governor for life, and it was under his auspices that the expeditions of 1554 and 1555 in search of the *North-East passage, from the first of which only Richard *Chancellor's ship returned safely, were sent out.

In the map of 1544 for which he was certainly responsible, Sebastian claims joint credit with his father for the discoveries of 1497 but he is not a reliable witness.

CABOTAGE, the French name for the coasting trade. Many people believe that it is derived from *cabo*, Spanish for cape, as coasting ships generally sailed from cape to cape, but a more likely derivation is the French word *cabot*, a small vessel.

CABRAL, PEDRO ALVAREZ DE GOUVEA (*c.* 1467–1530), Portuguese navigator, commanded the expedition of some thirteen or fourteen ships which left Lisbon for India on 9 March 1500, following the return of Vasco da *Gama in August 1499 from his epoch-making voyage. On the advice of da Gama, Cabral steered south-south-west from the Cape Verde Islands to take advantage of the south-east trade winds; these carried him across the Atlantic and, on 22 April, he made landfall on the coast of South America in 17° South. This is commonly accounted the discovery of Brazil, though in fact the Spaniard Vicente Yañez *Pinzon had reached it nearly three months earlier.

After coasting north to Porto Segura (Baia Cabralia) in 16° 20′ South, where Cabral erected the usual wooden cross that denoted a claim to Portuguese sovereignty, the expedition continued its passage to India, during which a number of ships, including that of Bartholomew *Diaz, foundered. The remainder reached Calicut (now Kozhikode) with the aid of Gujerati pilots on 30 August 1500, where a factory (storehouse and residence for factors) was erected while cargoes of spices were negotiated. On 17 December this factory was treacherously attacked and all inmates killed or wounded. Cabral retaliated by burning ten Arab vessels and bombarding the town before moving on to Cochin where he completed loading.

Scattered by storms during the voyage home, the survivors straggled back to Lisbon at the end of July 1501. Cabral was appointed to command a second voyage but jealousies intervened; Vasco da Gama was given the command in his place and Cabral retired to enjoy his wealth.

J. R. McClymont, *Pedralvarez Cabral* (1914).

CADAMOSTO, ALVISE DA (1432–77), Venetian navigator, explorer, and author, was enlisted by Prince *Henry the Navigator to command two expeditions to explore the west coast of Africa. In his first voyage in 1455 he visited Madeira and the Canary Islands and, making the coast of Africa, sailed as far south as the Gambia River. In his second voyage in 1456 he reached Cape Blanco (21° S.) and was driven out to sea by a storm, to make the first known discovery of the Cape Verde Islands. After exploring the islands he returned to the coast of Africa and sailed south as far as Conakry before returning to Portugal.

Cadamosto wrote detailed accounts of both voyages and of the habits, customs, and trade of the natives he encountered, and drew a chart of his explorations. He also wrote a narrative of Pedro de Cintra's later voyage (1461) to the Gold Coast. All these were first printed in the Vicenza collection of voyages (*Paesi novamente retrovata et novo mondo de Alberico Vesputio Florentino*) of 1507, since reprinted and translated many times. Cadamosto's first voyage is also remarkable for the famous letter (12 December 1455), written by Antonio Uso di Mare, claiming during this voyage to have met at the Gambia River the last surviving descendant of the Genoese expedition of 1291 to West Africa.

Uso di Mare accompanied Cadamosto on his first voyage.

CADIZ, one of the principal seaports of southern Spain, facing the Atlantic Ocean. It was probably founded by the Phoenicians in about 1000 B.C., and became a great trading centre for amber and tin. It was occupied by the Romans, and in 49 B.C. Julius Caesar conferred Roman citizenship on its inhabitants. It achieved great fame throughout the Roman world for its cookery and its dancing girls, and even today, in Spain, it is known as *Cadiz la Joyosa*, Cadiz the Joyous. Its Roman name was Gades.

The town was destroyed by the Visigoths in the 5th century, and was under the dominion of the Moors until 1262 when they were driven out by Alphonso X. But with the discovery of America in 1492, Cadiz became the wealthiest port in Europe, for it was to Cadiz that all the Spanish treasure fleets from America sailed. As such it became a favourite target of attack, both by the *Barbary corsairs and also, towards the end of the 16th century, by English fleets. It was at Cadiz that Sir Francis *Drake 'singed the king of Spain's beard' in 1587, burning all the shipping in the harbour. Nine years later the Earl of Essex and Lord *Howard of Effingham, in command of an English squadron, put Cadiz to the sack after capturing and sinking most of the shipping in the harbour. The cost to Spain in ships and cargoes alone was put at 12 million ducats. Further attempts by English forces were made by the Duke of Buckingham in 1626 and by Sir George *Rooke in 1702. But in spite of these attacks, the wealth of Cadiz grew prodigiously.

Cadiz continued its chequered career in the Revolutionary and Napoleonic wars. It was blockaded by Lord St. Vincent (see JERVIS, John) in 1797, it was bombarded by Sir Horatio *Nelson in 1800, and in 1805 it was the port from which the Franco-Spanish fleet, commanded by Admiral *Villeneuve, sailed to meet its destruction at the battle of *Trafalgar. It was besieged by Napoleon between 1810 and 1812, and during these two years served as capital of all Spain.

Although Cadiz today is not numbered among the major ports of the world, it thrives on a big export trade of wine, fruit, and cork. It has a large shipbuilding capability and is used as a port by many liners, particularly cruise liners, for whom the fine old city and beautiful natural harbour are great attractions.

Until the year 1600, Cadiz was known in England as Cales.

CAGNI, UMBERTO (*c.* 1863–1932), Italian naval officer and explorer was joint leader with the Duke of *Abruzzi of a polar expedition in

1899 during which he led a sledge party to a point within 207 miles of the pole. Later he led an expedition to inquire into the failure of General Nobile's airship flight to the North pole in 1928 in which Roald * Amundsen and others lost their lives. It was as a result of this inquiry that Nobile was blamed for the disaster.

CAIQUE, from the Turkish *kaik*, a boat or skiff. (1) In its strict meaning it refers to the light boats propelled by one or two oars and used in Turkish waters, particularly the Bosporus, but it was also used as a term for the Sultan's ceremonial barge when he went by water to a mosque or to his harem. The word has since been loosely applied to most small rowing boats and skiffs in the Levant. (2) A small Levantine sailing vessel, usually with a * lateen rig, but here again the name has been loosely expanded to include a variety of modern sailing and motorized vessels, used mainly for island trade, as far west as Greece and Corfu.

CAISSON, from the French *caisson*, large chest, pronounced by the cognoscenti căssŏŏn but widely known as cayson, basically an enclosed space below water-level with means of flooding with or pumping out water. (1) A fixed enclosure reaching to the bottom from which the water can be pumped out, or alternatively filled with air under pressure, in order to give access to under-water areas for engineering works, such as the building of piers for bridges, breakwaters, etc. (2) The gate or movable structure which closes the entrance to a dock or dry-dock. (3) A floating platform or tank which can be submerged by the admission of water, and when in position under a wreck or other obstruction, pumped out in order to use the resulting buoyancy as a lifting force, and in this connection also known as a * camel. The use of caissons, or camels, for raising sunken ships is perhaps best exemplified by the raising of the German * High Seas fleet which was scuttled in * Scapa Flow in June 1919. It is common practice where conditions of depth, tide, position and condition of the wreck, etc., do not allow of other more direct methods of lifting. See also SALVAGE.

CAISSON DISEASE, alternative colloquial name for the * bends, properly * compression sickness. All three terms refer to the painful condition in which bubbles of nitrogen form in the body tissues when a diver makes a rapid return to normal atmospheric pressure after subjection to greater than normal pressure. Thus workers emerging from a * caisson (1), where the air pressure must be kept high to exclude water, must take the same precautionary measures as deep-sea divers returning to the surface. See also DIVING.

CALASHEE (or COOLASHI) WATCH, a watch on deck in a full-rigged ship in which all hands, including the * watch below, must stand by for a call. They were most frequently required when a sailing ship was * tacking in narrow waters or in a particularly heavy sea. The word came apparently from the Hindustani *khalasi*, sailor, as the system on board native ships was to work their watches in this fashion.

CALCUTTA, a major Indian seaport on the banks of the Hugli (Hooghli) River. It is also close to the mouths of the great river systems of the Brahmaputra and Ganges, and is thus the natural recipient of the produce of those two great fertile valleys. It is to this advantageous geographical position that it owes its great expansion as a port, one of the busiest in the world. Calcutta was founded in 1690 when Job Chernock, of the British * East India Company, settled finally at the village of Sutanati, having been driven from the company's factory further up the river by the Mogul. Sutanati became Calcutta, and although it had a chequered career of attack and counter-attack for the next sixty years, it was finally secured after the battle of Plassey in 1757. Today, one of the principal commodities handled in the port is jute, but a great industrial trade also keeps the port of Calcutta fully occupied.

CALDER, Sir ROBERT (1745–1818), British admiral, was born at Elgin, Scotland. He became rich when, as a lieutenant, he took part in the capture of the Spanish treasure ship *Hermione* in 1756 for which his share of the * prize money was £13,000. He was knighted for his services as captain of the fleet at the battle of * Cape St. Vincent and in 1804, as a rear admiral, he joined Admiral * Cornwallis in the blockade of * Brest. In 1805 he was detached to intercept the Franco-Spanish fleet commanded by the Comte de * Villeneuve on its return from the West Indies in case it intended to put into * Ferrol. On 22 July Villeneuve's fleet passed him in a thick fog on the way to Vigo and Calder only succeeded in cutting off two ships. He then fell back on the main fleet off Brest in case Villeneuve should turn north to join Admiral * Ganteaume at Brest, but was detached again on 22 August, by which date Villeneuve's fleet had turned south to * Cadiz. On taking command of the British fleet off Cadiz in September 1805 * Nelson's first unpleasant duty was to provide a ship for Calder to return to England to face a court martial, much to Calder's surprise and indignation as he considered he had done well in the action against Villeneuve. Possibly Nelson thought so too, as instead of providing a frigate for this duty, he sent Calder home in his own ship, the three-decker *Prince of Wales*, thereby weakening his own fleet on the eve of *Trafalgar. At the court martial Calder was severely reprimanded for not persevering in his action against Villeneuve. It was the end of his naval career.

CALES, the name by which *Cadiz was known in England up to the year 1600.

CALF, (1) the name by which the young of marine mammalia, such as the whale, are known. **(2)** In the Arctic and Antarctic regions, a mass of floe ice which when subjected to pressure breaks off from the main body and rises to the surface is known as a calf and the process is known as calving. **(3)** The term is also used to describe small islets which lie off larger islands, such as the Calf of Mull, or the Calf of Man.

CALIBRE, a term used for the measurement of guns. It is employed in two senses, but its strict meaning is the length of the gun expressed as a multiple of the bore or internal diameter measured at the muzzle; e.g., a 12-inch gun 30 feet long would be a 12-inch gun of 30 calibres. In its second sense the word expresses the bore of the gun, again measured at the muzzle, such as 6-inch calibre, 12-inch calibre, etc.

CALIFORNIAN, a 6,233-ton Leyland liner whose captain, Stanley Lord, was blamed by two inquiries into the loss of the *Titanic* on 14/15 April 1912 for failing to come to the rescue of the liner's passengers and crew although within eight to ten miles of the sinking ship and in sight of her distress rockets. This is based on ship's lights seen from the sinking *Titanic* at 1 a.m. and rockets seen from the *Californian* at about the same time. However the evidence from both inquiries is clear that the 'mystery' lights moved first towards and then away from the *Titanic*, and the *Californian* did not move her engines all night as there was an ice barrier ahead which Captain Lord did not want to negotiate in darkness. The alleged rockets seen by her watch officers were low in the sky, did not make the detonations usually associated with distress rockets or shells, and were not regarded as distress signals until after the news of the *Titanic*'s loss; company recognition lights and flares were common at the time. It is probable, from all log-book evidence, that the *Californian* was 19 miles from the sinking liner, and it is certain that her radio operator was off watch. Many think that the late Captain Lord was made the scapegoat for the *Titanic* disaster for he never received a fair hearing, appearing at both inquiries only as a witness with no charges against him, and thus unable to defend himself against the accusations finally levelled by the courts of inquiry.

CALL, (1) another name for the silver *pipe or whistle used by the *boatswain and his mates on board naval ships to call attention to orders. In Britain, in the early days of the navy, it was also the official badge of the *Lord High Admiral when exercising his command at sea, worn round the neck on a long silver chain. **(2)** The various cadences produced by a pipe are also known as calls; each order being piped has its own particular call by which it can easily be recognized.

With the technological advances of recent years by which orders can be broadcast simultaneously in every part of the ship the call has lost its function, though it is retained for ceremonial occasions when piping dignitaries and foreign naval officers aboard.

CALL SIGN, a particular group of letters or numbers in the *Morse Code used for identification. Radio beacons, used by vessels fitted with *radio direction finders for obtaining navigational *bearings, have individual call signs, or characteristics, by which they can be immediately identified.

CALLAO, the principal seaport of Peru, lies about 8 miles west of the capital city of Lima. It was founded in 1537, shortly after Francisco Pizarro had marked out the site of Lima, and as the only port on the western coast of South America below Panama it grew rapidly in importance. Sir Francis *Drake attacked Callao in 1578 during his voyage of circumnavigation, and a Dutch squadron made a similar attempt in 1624. The entire city was destroyed by an earthquake in 1746. In 1880 Callao was captured by a Chilean naval force, all the ships of the Peruvian Navy being scuttled in the harbour to prevent capture. The Peruvian copper mines today provide Callao with a flourishing trade; it is also the centre of the coasting trade and a port of call of several steamship lines.

CALLENDER, Sir GEOFFREY ARTHUR ROMAINE (1875–1946), British naval historian and founder of the *National Maritime Museum, Greenwich, was born at Didsbury, Cheshire, and gained 2nd class Honours in Modern History at Oxford in 1897. In January 1905 he joined the staff of the newly opened Royal Naval College at Osborne, Isle of Wight, as a teacher of history, and it was there that naval history became the main interest in his life. To encourage his pupils he wrote the three volumes entitled *Sea Kings of Britain*. In 1921 he moved to the Royal Naval College, Dartmouth, as Head of the History Department and on the establishment of a Chair of History at the Royal Naval College at Greenwich in 1922 he became the first holder of the post. While there he wrote his best known work *The Naval Side of British History*

(1924). As honorary secretary and treasurer of the *Society for Nautical Research he was largely responsible for the success of the appeal to save and restore H.M.S. *Victory as a national monument.

CALLIOPE, H.M.S., the third ship of the name in the Royal Navy, was the 3rd-class cruiser of 2,770 tons launched in 1884 at Portsmouth, which became famous as the only survivor of seven men-of-war (six of them belonging to other nations) and several merchant ships lying in the harbour at Apia Bay, Samoa, when a terrific hurricane struck on 15 March 1889. Her captain at the time was Captain Henry Coey Kane. In his report he said that the *Calliope*'s escape was due to the admirable order in which her engines and boilers had been kept by his engineering staff under Staff-Engineer H. G. Bourke, who was promoted as a result. A special medal was struck by the British Admiralty to commemorate the fine seamanship which made possible the survival of the ship in such tempestuous conditions and issued to every officer and man on board.

In 1907 the *Calliope* was placed on the sales list but was removed and converted to be the drill ship of the Tyneside Division of the Royal Naval Volunteer Reserve at Newcastle. In 1915 her name was changed to *Helicon*, the name *Calliope* being required for a new light cruiser launched in 1914 and present at the battle of *Jutland in 1916. When she was sold in 1931 the *Helicon* was again given the name *Calliope*. When she was finally sold for breaking up in 1951 a sloop, the *Falmouth*, was renamed *Calliope* and took her place as R.N.V.R. drill ship at Newcastle.

CAM or **CAO, DIOGO** (*fl.* 1482–6), Portuguese navigator, was the first European to explore the west African coast beyond the equator as far south as Walvis Bay. He reached the mouth of the Congo River in August 1482, returning to this coast in a second voyage in 1485–6. During his two voyages he set up stone pillars, engraved with details of his voyages, at Shark Point, on the Congo River, Cape Santa Maria, Monte Negro, and Cape Cross, and these pillars still stood until the early 20th century. The one at Shark Point is still in existence, though only in fragments; of the other three, two are in the museum of the Lisbon Geographical Society and one at Kiel.

CAMBER, (1) the athwartships curve of a ship's deck, usually giving a fall towards the sides of a quarter of an inch to each foot. **(2)** A small enclosed dock in a dockyard in which timber for masts and yards was kept to weather and pickle in salt water, and used also to provide a shelter for small boats.

CAMEL, (1) originally a wooden case made in two halves to fit on either side of a ship's *keel. They were filled with water and fitted to the keel by divers, being subsequently pumped out to provide extra buoyancy if a ship had to pass over a shoal. From this was evolved the tank which, sunk by being filled with water, could be placed under a wreck to provide lifting power when the water was pumped out. See also CAISSON. **(2)** A strong wooden stage sometimes used as a *fender when a ship lies alongside a wharf.

CAMOUFLAGE, a method of disguising the size, outline, course, and speed of a ship in wartime by painting her hull and upperworks in contrasting shapes and colours arranged in irregular patterns. See also DAZZLE-PAINTING.

CAMPERDOWN, a naval battle fought off Camperdown, on the coast of Holland, on 11 October 1797 between a British fleet commanded by Admiral Adam *Duncan with fourteen *ships of the line, and a Dutch fleet commanded by Vice Admiral Jan de *Winter, with eleven ships of the line, when the Dutch fleet was decisively defeated. The United Provinces (Netherlands) had been forced by Napoleon to become an ally of France in 1795, and for the next two years the close *blockade instituted by Admiral Duncan had kept the Dutch fleet shut up in the Texel. In the beginning of October 1797 Duncan had gone to Yarmouth Roads to refit, leaving only five ships to watch the Texel.

On the 9th the hired *lugger *Speculator* appeared at the back of the sands, flying the signal that the Dutch were out, and by noon Duncan had sailed with the rest of his ships for his old station. The Dutch fleet was sighted to leeward shortly after 9 a.m. on the 11th. The British bore down without waiting to form a strict *line of battle, and the action began at about 12.30 p.m., when Vice Admiral Richard Onslow in the *Monarch* broke through the enemy's line and engaged the Dutch second flagship, the *Jupiter*, from to leeward. A furious battle, reminiscent of the actions of the 17th-century Dutch wars, was maintained by both sides and was only brought to a close at 3 p.m. with the surrender of the two Dutch flagships, both of which were completely dismasted. By that time the British had captured seven ships of the line, two fourth-*rates, and two *frigates.

CAMPERDOWN, H.M.S., a twin-screw, armour-plated *barbette ship of 10,600 tons, launched at Portsmouth in 1885. She was re-rated as a battleship in 1887, and in 1893, while serving as the temporary flagship of Rear Admiral A. H. Markham during the manoeuvres of the combined Mediterranean Fleet, she collided with and sank the *Victoria*, flagship of

Vice Admiral Sir George *Tryon, Commander-in-Chief, Mediterranean, off Tripoli. Twenty-two of the *Victoria*'s officers, including the commander-in-chief, were lost in the catastrophe, together with 339 seamen of her company. A notable survivor was Commander J. R. *Jellicoe, later Commander-in-Chief, Grand Fleet, 1914–16. The subsequent court martial on the loss of the *Victoria* found that she was lost by a collision with the *Camperdown*, and 'with the deepest sorrow and regret' that this collision was due to an order given by the then commander-in-chief to the two divisions in which the fleet was formed to turn sixteen points inwards, the leaders first and the others in succession, the columns at that time being only six *cables apart.

CAMSHIP, a merchant ship fitted in the Second World War with a catapult with which to launch a fighter aircraft. They sailed in the ordinary way with a convoy and their purpose was to provide anti-aircraft protection against attack from the air. The camship was intended principally as an answer to the German long-range Focke-Wulf aircraft based in western France which could attack and shadow convoys a long way out in the Atlantic. The fighter from the camship could not, of course, land on board again after being catapulted, and the pilot saved himself by ditching his aircraft as close as possible to a merchant ship so that he could be picked up, the aircraft being abandoned. The name came from the initial letters of catapult aircraft merchant ship. See also MACSHIP.

CAN BUOY, a *buoy in the form of a truncated cone, normally painted in red or red and white chequers and numbered with an even number, used to indicate the port hand side of a channel when entering with the flood tide. The starboard hand side of the channel is marked with *conical buoys. See BUOYAGE, SYSTEMS OF, APPENDIX 4.

CAN HOOKS, a pair of flat hooks joined by a length of chain or rope and used for hoisting casks by fitting the hooks under the *chines, the projecting ends of the staves.

CANARIS, WILHELM (1887–1945), German admiral, was head of the *Abwehr* (intelligence service of the Wehrmacht) from 1935 to 1945, and one of the principal plotters against Hitler. He was a lieutenant in the light cruiser *Dresden* at the start of the First World War (1914–18) and was interned by the Chilean authorities when this ship was sunk on 14 March 1915. He escaped to Germany by rowing boat, by horseback over the Andes, and then by Dutch passenger ship and U-boat, and became a submarine commander in the Mediterranean in 1918. During 1918–20 he served with the naval free corps (Löwenfeld brigade), but returned to regular naval service in

1920, and in 1934 retired with the rank of rear admiral. In January 1935 he was appointed head of the *Abwehr*. He was never an enthusiastic Nazi and it would seem that by the end of 1937 his eyes were fully opened to the nature of the regime. He was soon aware of much of the plotting afoot, but was never sanguine as to its outcome. Nevertheless, until February 1944, when he was transferred to a minor post, he intervened constantly to sabotage the plans of Nazi organizations, so that, after the conspiracy of 20 July 1944, it was easy for the Gestapo to discover his complicity in a range of anti-Nazi plots. He was arrested on 23 July and executed at Flossenburg concentration camp on 9 April 1945.

CANOE, a small open boat originally by definition used by primitive nations. This description was generally extended to embrace similar craft, in which paddles were the motive force, all over the world as it was opened up by the great geographical discoveries of the 17th and 18th centuries. Some of these craft designated as canoes, particularly among the Pacific islands, were remarkably large vessels in which two banks of paddlers, up to twenty or thirty a side, were used. Today, the term embraces any very light craft propelled by a paddle, and in recent years the number of canoes in use has increased immensely since canoeing has been developed as an inland water sport, the modern canoe being made either of very light wooden construction or of canvas stretched across a light wooden frame. See also KAYAK, UMIAK.

CANT, (1) a cut made in a whale between the neck and the fins to which the purchase, known as a cant purchase, is secured in order to turn the animal round during the operation of *flensing. (2) The name given to those *timbers in a ship towards the *bow and the *stern which are sharply angled (or canted) from the *keel. See also CAST, TO.

CANT, to, the operation of turning a ship's head one way or the other, according to the requirement at the time, when weighing *anchor or slipping from a *mooring. It may, for example, be necessary to cant the ship's head to *port (or *starboard) in order to avoid other shipping or navigational hazards in the immediate vicinity.

CANT ROPE, an old name for four-stranded rope laid up without a central core. See also SHROUD-LAID ROPE, WATER-LAID ROPE.

CANUTE or **CNUT** (*c*. 995–1035), the king of Denmark and England who sat on the bank of the Thames at Westminster and ordered the tide to go back. He did this, in fact, to demonstrate to his courtiers that there were forces in the world greater than war, and to prepare them for his submission to the Holy See in Rome. Among his many qualities he was a great leader and commanded fleets at sea, defeating the Swedish fleet at Stangebjerg and the combined Norwegian–Swedish fleet at the mouth of the Helgeaa, both in 1028.

CANVAS, a cloth properly woven from hemp. (The word 'canvas' derives from *kannabis*, the Greek for hemp.) It is used at sea mainly for sails, *awnings, etc. It is numbered according to the thickness and weave, the lowest number being the coarsest and strongest, the highest number being the lightest. It is also a synonym for sails, a ship under sail being said to be under canvas. See also BOLT.

CAP, the wooden block on the top of a mast through which the mast above is drawn when being *stepped or lowered when being struck. It has two holes, one of them square which is fixed firmly to the top of the lower mast, the other circular through which the topmast is hoisted, until its *heel is nearly level with the base of the cap, in which position it is then secured with a *fid and sometimes also with a *parrel lashing, being held upright by *shrouds and *stays. In ships where *topgallant masts were stepped, there were similar caps on the tops of the topmasts. A *bowsprit cap serves a similar service for the *jib-boom. See also BULL ROPE.

CAPE ESPERANCE, BATTLE OF, a naval action fought in the Pacific during the Second World War, was a night surface action between American and Japanese forces in the approaches to Guadalcanal. It occurred during the night 11/12 October 1942 when the heavy cruisers *San Francisco* and *Salt Lake City*, the light cruisers *Boise* and *Helena*, and five destroyers intercepted a Japanese force steering to deliver a night bombardment of the airfield on Guadalcanal. The Japanese squadron under Rear Admiral Goto was composed of the heavy cruisers *Aoba*, *Kinugasa*, and *Furutaka*, and two destroyers.

The American squadron, steaming in single line ahead with three destroyers leading the cruisers and two following, enjoyed the vital advantage of an efficient surface warning radar in the *Helena*. When she detected Goto's ships at 14 miles distance shortly before midnight, however, she delayed for 15 minutes to pass this information to the admiral. Meanwhile a complicated reversal of course had been begun and had not been completed when Rear Admiral Scott, commanding the American squadron, learned that the enemy was only four miles distant.

Confusion still reigned when the enemy came in sight; but the Japanese, untypically, had been taken by surprise; the *Aoba* and *Furutaka* had their turrets still trained fore and aft when struck by a storm of shell which caused severe damage and killed Goto; the destroyer *Fubuki* was sunk.

The *Kinugasa*, in the rear, and the destroyer *Hatsuyuki*, turning away, escaped this punishment and engaged the destroyer *Duncan* which, in the mêlée, was shelled also by her own side and later sank. A confused chase of the retiring Japanese followed in which, although the *Furutaka* was sunk, Japanese night-fighting superiority re-asserted itself. The *Boise*, avoiding a flurry of torpedoes which only narrowly missed, was almost fatally shattered by Japanese gunfire and the destroyer *Farenholt* was crippled by misdirected American fire. The final outcome of the action was thus a moderate material success for the Americans though at the time it was wrongly believed to have been much more, with four enemy cruisers and four destroyers thought to have been sunk.

CAPE FINISTERRE, the most westerly cape of northern Spain, about 50 miles north-north-west of *Vigo, and famous in the prose and poetry of the sea. It should not be confused with Finisterre, or Finistère, the extreme north-western *département* of France in which is situated the great seaport of *Brest.

Cape Finisterre was the scene of a naval battle of the War of the Austrian Succession (1739–48), fought on 3 May 1747, about 70 miles north by west of the Cape, between a British fleet of fourteen ships of the line commanded by Admiral Sir George *Anson and two French squadrons which had not yet parted company to proceed to their separate destinations. One was making for North America for the recovery of Cape Breton Island; the other, together with a convoy, was intended to operate against British settlements on the Coromandel coast of India. There were thirty-eight French ships in all.

The French fleet was sighted at 9.30 a.m., and at noon nine of the French ships were seen to be forming a *line of battle while the rest made all sail away. At 3 p.m., Anson hoisted the signal for a *general chase, and by 4 o'clock the first British ship was up with the rearmost of the French. A running fight then ensued, the other British ships joining in as they got up. By 7 p.m., all the ships that had remained in the French line had struck their colours. The main body of the British fleet then brought-to, and three ships were detached to pursue the convoy, of which about six were captured as well as two small vessels of the escort. Night saved the rest. Specie to the value of £300,000 was taken with the prizes and Anson was rewarded with a peerage.

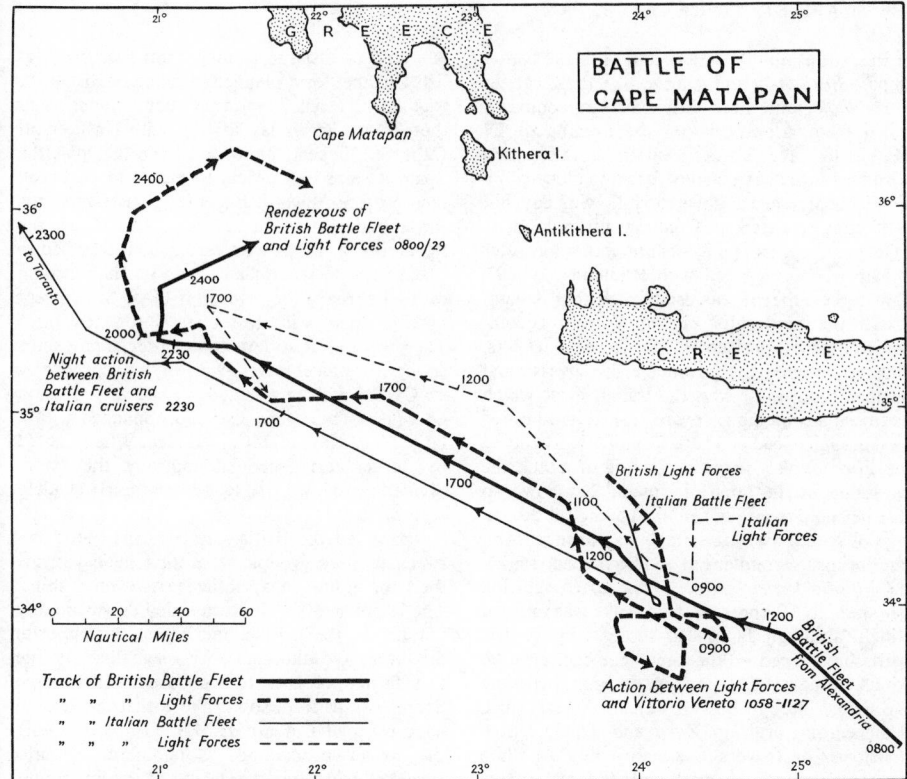

BATTLE OF
CAPE MATAPAN

G R E E C E

Cape Matapan

Kithera I.

Antikithera I.

2400

2300

to Taranto

Rendezvous of
British Battle Fleet
and Light Forces 0800/29

2400
1700

2000

Night action
between British
Battle Fleet and
Italian cruisers 2230

2230

C R E T E

1700
1200

1700

1700

1700

British Light Forces

Italian Battle Fleet

Italian
Light Forces

1100

1200

0900

1200

0900

0 20 40 60
Nautical Miles

Track of British Battle Fleet ————
    "   "   "   Light Forces — — —
    "   " Italian Battle Fleet ————
    "   "   "   Light Forces — — — —

Action between Light Forces
and Vittorio Veneto 1058-1127

British Battle Fleet from Alexandria

0800

CAPE HORN FEVER, an imaginary disease from which malingerers at sea are supposed to suffer when they plead illness. Its origin lay in the reluctance of many seaman to sign *articles in a ship engaged in making a passage of Cape Horn from east to west under sail, the contrary winds and heavy seas frequently entailing almost non-stop work on the yards in numbing conditions.

CAPE HORNERS, originally the American full-rigged ships which used to run regularly from the east to the west coast of America around Cape Horn during the 19th century. Comparatively few ships made this passage before 1847, but the discovery of gold in California in that year gave rise to the famous Californian *clipper ships which instituted a regular service. Commanded for the most case by hard-case captains and *'bucko' mates, they set many records and were driven unmercifully through the huge seas south of the Horn, frequently with loss of lives and *spars. This merciless driving quickly 'broke the heart' of these magnificent ships and few survived for more than five years at the most. The building of a railway across the isthmus of Panama in 1857 was the signal for their decline and ultimate withdrawal from this trade. By extension, the term Cape Horner has also been applied to all big sailing ships which regularly used the Cape

Horn route, particularly those carrying cargo from Europe or Africa westward to South American ports around the Horn and returning eastward with grain, nitrates, guano, or hides. This used to be a regular trade until well into the first decades of the 20th century, but was virtually killed by the opening of the *Panama Canal in 1914.

More recently the term has been adopted by societies of men who have rounded Cape Horn under sail and who meet to dine together and talk about their experiences.

CAPE MATAPAN, BATTLE OF, was fought on 28 March 1941 during the Second World War between the British Mediterranean fleet under Admiral Sir Andrew *Cunningham and an Italian battle group under Admiral Iachino, in which the British inflicted severe loss on their adversary without suffering damage or casualties.

News of an intended sortie by Italian naval forces against British convoys bound for the Piraeus prompted Cunningham to dispatch a force comprising four cruisers and four destroyers under Vice Admiral Pridham-Wippell to a position south of the island of Crete, where five more destroyers were to join him at daylight on 28 March. Meanwhile Cunningham with his flag in the battleship *Warspite and with the battle-ships *Barham* and *Valiant*, the carrier *Formidable*, and nine destroyers in company, sailed from Alexandria on the evening of 27 March to take up a position covering the advanced forces. An enemy force was located by air reconnaissance at dawn the following day, but conflicting reports kept Cunningham in doubt as to its composition and it was not until noon, after it had become engaged with Pridham-Wippell's light forces, that it was established that it comprised the battleship *Vittorio Veneto* accompanied by eight cruisers and fourteen destroyers. Having forfeited the advantage of surprise and being without air cover, the Italian force which had been advancing eastward turned and headed west at high speed at 1130. Cunningham ordered the *Formidable*'s torpedo aircraft to attack the battleship in the hope of slowing her down so that he could overtake her, she having the advantage of speed. The first attack was unsuccessful, but during a second one at 1515 a torpedo struck the *Vittorio Veneto* on the port quarter reducing her speed to 19 knots. A third strike was ordered which, although failing to score a hit on the battleship, torpedoed the 8-inch gun cruiser *Pola*, which brought her to a stop. Iachino, believing the British fleet to be still well to the eastward, detached the cruisers *Zara* and *Fiume* and a division of destroyers to stand by the *Pola* while he continued to the west with the rest of his force. Just after 2100 the cruisers in the van of Cunningham's pursuing fleet reported passing a stopped and darkened ship and Cunningham led his battleships towards her at 20 knots. Having reached the desired range he was about to give the order to open fire when two more darkened ships were sighted crossing his bows from starboard to port. Swinging his battleships to starboard to bring their guns to bear on the new targets—the cruisers *Zara* and *Fiume*—he opened fire on them at almost point-blank range. The two ships were immediately crippled and burst into flames. Two of their accompanying destroyers were also sunk. The original target, the *Pola*, was sunk later during the night by destroyers, many of the crew being rescued.

Cunningham was disappointed the following morning at not renewing contact with the damaged enemy battleship but he had achieved a substantial victory which was to stand him in good stead during the trials which lay ahead.

CAPE ST. VINCENT, BATTLE OF, was
fought on 14 February 1797, between a British fleet of fifteen *ships of the line under the command of Admiral Sir John *Jervis and a Spanish fleet of twenty-seven ships of the line commanded by Admiral Don José de Cordova. The Spanish ships had sailed from Cartagena bound for Brest to join the combined fleets of France and Hol-land and to assist in gaining control of the English Channel for a planned invasion of Britain. It was Jervis's task to prevent such a junction of these fleets. Jervis lay in wait with his fleet off Cape St. Vincent, unaware of the fact that the Spanish ships had orders to put in to Cadiz on their way northward. But strong easterly winds through the Strait of Gibraltar had blown the Spaniards far to the westward so that they had to *beat back to reach Cadiz, and on the morning of 14 February they were off Cape St. Vincent making their wind-tossed way towards port. They were in considerable disorder, many ships trying to make their own way independently to Cadiz, and as a result lacked all cohesion as a fleet. They were also badly manned with a large proportion of untrained men. When sighted by Jervis early on that morning they were divided into two loose groups fairly widely separated.

Jervis led the British fleet in line ahead between the two groups, separating them yet further, and at first engaged the lee division of ships. The larger weather division sailed down roughly parallel to the British line but in the opposite direction, and although Jervis signalled his line to tack in succession to bring them to action the Spanish ships were so far ahead that they would have escaped had not H.M.S. *Captain*, flying the broad pendant of Commodore Horatio *Nelson, worn (see WEAR) out of the line to cut across the escaping Spanish division. In the circumstances this was a bold decision as no signal was yet flying from the flagship that ships might act independently, and in the conditions of the current *Fighting Instructions* few men would have had the temerity to ignore them no matter how obvious the need. Nelson sailed the *Captain*

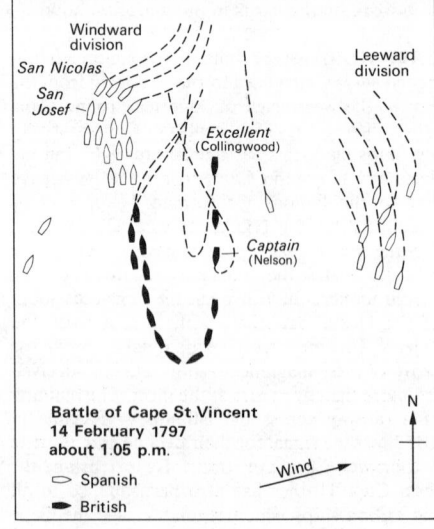

Windward division

San Nicolas

San Josef

Leeward division

Excellent (Collingwood)

Captain (Nelson)

Battle of Cape St. Vincent
14 February 1797
about 1.05 p.m.

Spanish

British

N

Wind

across the bows of the Spanish squadron followed by the *Excellent (Cuthbert *Collingwood) which had followed her round. Under a very heavy fire, with her foremast gone by the *board and her wheel shot away, the Captain succeeded in placing herself alongside the 80-gun Spanish San Nicolas, which had herself fallen foul of the 112-gun first-*rate San Josef. Nelson at once called for a boarding party and the San Nicolas was quickly overpowered. The boarding party also met with little resistance when they swept on from her deck to the San Josef, and she too surrendered. Both Spanish ships had been under a heavy fire from H.M.S. Prince George right up to the time the Captain boarded them, and no doubt their surrender was speeded up by the punishment they had already received. It was this occasion which Nelson later described as his 'patent bridge for capturing enemies'.

By this time the Spanish lee division, which had been only lightly engaged at the start of the action, were coming up in support of their hard-pressed companions, and Jervis decided that in the shattered state of some of his ships, it would be wiser to consolidate the victory than to risk a further encounter with fresh vessels. He flew the signal for the fleet to bring to in order to cover the prizes and his disabled ships. Four Spanish ships of the line had been captured; the remainder, demoralized and in no fleet order, made the best way they could towards safety. It was a good victory but could well have been better had Jervis pursued the Spaniards throughout the night. For his services in this action Jervis was made Earl St. Vincent; Nelson was rewarded with a knighthood.

CAPE TOWN, the principal seaport of South Africa, was founded in 1652 by Dutch settlers led by Jan van Riebeek. It was captured by British forces in 1806, and its magnificent Table Bay, in addition to its commanding geographical position at the junction of the Atlantic and Indian oceans, ensured it pre-eminence as a port of the first importance. Cape Town is the natural terminal point of many steamship lines trading to South Africa, notably the Union Castle line, and most of the production inland of gold and diamonds is exported to the world through the port. It also has extensive dock and ship-repair facilities. The adjacent naval dockyard is at *Simonstown.

CAPER, from the Frisian kapen, to steal, rob, plunder, a lightly armed ship of the 17th century used by the Dutch as a *privateer or corsair. The word was, by extension, also used to designate the captain of a privateer.

CAPPELLE, JAN VAN DE (c. 1624–79), Dutch marine painter, lived in Amsterdam where he was a wealthy dyer. He taught himself to paint in his spare time, though some sources give him as a pupil of Simon de *Vlieger, whose influence is certainly very apparent in Cappelle's seascapes. He has been described as 'the wizard of atmospheric painting' and is best known for his pictures of calm seas and limp sails against a background of still and windless skies, which with their grey and silver monochrome tones place them among the greatest maritime paintings of the period. He was a close friend of Rembrandt, of whose drawings he collected some 500, and had his portrait painted both by him and by Franz Hals.

CAPITAL SHIP, a term used in navies to denote the most important type of warship in the national fleet. For centuries throughout the era of sailing navies it was the *ship of the line, but after the introduction of iron, and later steel, construction, the *battleship, *dreadnought, and super-dreadnought were the capital ships of the world's navies. The development of ship-borne air power during and after the Second World War, which rendered the battleship virtually obsolete, for a time made the *aircraft carrier into the capital ship of most navies, but this type of warship in its turn has suffered from the development of its own original source of power into modern airborne, long-range weapons which have made the carrier into too vulnerable a target to be classed any longer as the capital ship of a navy. Many people would now consider that the nuclear missile-firing *submarine (see POLARIS, POSEIDON) is the true capital ship of present-day navies.

CAPPING, a strip of wood, usually of Canadian elm, fitted to the top of the *gunwale or *washstrake of wooden boats to strengthen it. In boats fitted to take oars, it is pierced at intervals to take *crutches or *thole pins, or cut away to form *rowlocks.

CAPSIZE, to, to upset or overturn in connection with a vessel at sea or in harbour. In general the term is normally related to natural causes, such as high winds or heavy seas, but refers also to human error in such cases as faulty stowage of cargo which may cause a ship to become unstable and thus overturn. One of the more notable cases of a ship capsizing through human error was that of H.M.S. *Royal George, which was being deliberately heeled over in Portsmouth harbour in 1782 for repairs to be made to an underwater fitting. The angle of heel became so great that the sea entered through her open gunports and she turned over and sank with a great loss of life. See also CAPTAIN, H.M.S., as an example of a ship capsizing through stress of weather.

CAPSTAN, a cylindrical barrel fitted in larger ships on the *forecastle deck and used for heavy lifting work, particularly when working anchors and cables. It is normally placed on the centre-line of the ship and is driven mechanically either by steam or electricity. The barrel is lined vertically with *whelps in order to provide a grip for hawsers or cables when they are being hove in, and above the barrel there used to a *drum-head with square pigeon holes in which wooden capstan bars, made of ash or hickory, were inserted when it was required to work the cap-stan by hand. A modern capstan does not nor-mally have a drumhead as present-day machin-ery is sufficiently reliable to make working a capstan by hand unnecessary. Below the barrel a series of *pawls is attached which work over a pawl-ring to prevent the capstan running back under a particularly heavy strain. In ships which are fitted with a capstan, two *cable-holders are normally geared into the capstan engine so that the *bower anchors can be weighed direct with-out their cables having to be led to the capstan barrel.

Before the days of mechanically driven aux-iliary machinery, the capstan was always found on the main deck of the ship and used for heavy lifting work, both for weighing an anchor and *swaying up a *yard (but see also JEERS). It was always worked by manpower through the use of capstan bars, connected at the ends with a *swifter to provide additional space for men to heave. In particularly heavy work a *messenger was rigged in addition to the swifter so that yet more men could be used on the capstan.

Smaller ships do not normally have capstans and separate cable-holders although in some smaller warships a combined capstan/cable-holder is fitted on the forecastle deck. But in most smaller ships the function of the capstan is taken over by a *windlass, the two bower cables being led round *gypsies which are attached to the spindle of the windlass.

The difference between a capstan and a windlass lies mainly in the fact that the spindle on which the barrel of a capstan is mounted is vertical, while that on which the drums and gyp-sies of a windlass are mounted is horizontal. For illus. see also CABLE-HOLDER, NIPPER.

CAPTAIN, in all navies the commissioned rank next below that of rear admiral; also by custom the title of the commanding officer of any naval ship irrespective of his commissioned rank. In the merchant navy, the *master of a merchant ship. By extension, captain is also the title of the senior rating in charge of a group of seamen engaged in particular duties, e.g., captain of the hold, captain of the maintop, etc. French, *capitaine de vaisseau*; German, *Kapitän-zur-See*. See also POST-CAPTAIN, and APPENDIX 1.

CAPTAIN, H.M.S., a ship's name famous in the British Navy. Of the seven ships thus named, the best known are the third, of seventy-four guns, in which *Nelson flew his commodore's pendant at the battle of *Cape St. Vincent in 1797, and the sixth, a turret ship designed by Captain Cowper *Coles which proved to be unstable and capsized in a squall off Finisterre in 1870.

CAPTAINS COURAGEOUS, a novel of the *Grand Banks cod fishery and the fishing *schooners of Gloucester, Massachusetts, which exploited them, written by Rudyard *Kipling and first published in 1897. It is a story of a young American boy, rich, spoilt, and arrogant, who falls overboard from an Atlantic liner and is picked up and befriended by the crew of a fishing schooner. His life among the fishermen until the schooner returns to harbour transforms him into a boy of modesty, good manners, and compassion.

CAPTAIN'S SERVANT, the name given to boys entering the Royal Navy at about the age of 12 before they became midshipmen. The custom of allowing captains to take such 'servants' into their ships derives from the older apprenticeship system. Such servants or followers did no menial work since they were aspiring officers. They were accommodated in the *gunroom under the general supervision of the gunner before graduating to the midshipmen's mess in the *cockpit, and thence on promotion to the lieu-tenant's *wardroom. The name was changed in 1796 to Volunteer, First Class, boys of the second and third classes not aspiring to the rank of commissioned officers. Unlike volunteers-per-order and *King's letter boys, who were

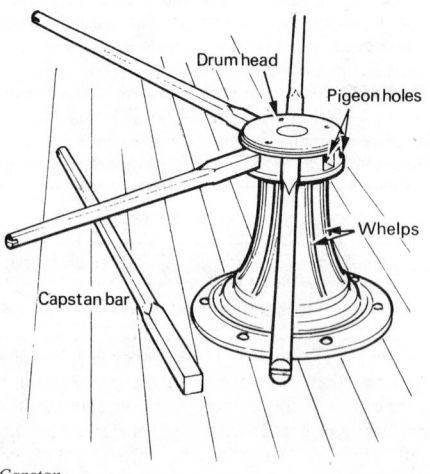

Capstan

Drum head

Pigeon holes

Whelps

Capstan bar

nominated by the Admiralty, a captain's servant was a personal follower of a *post-captain, taken on board to oblige relatives or friends. Lord *Nelson and most officers of his day joined the Navy in this way.

CARACCIOLO, Prince FRANCESCO (1732–99), Neapolitan admiral, learned his seamanship in the British Navy and served with distinction in the War of American Independence (1775–82) and in operations against the *Barbary pirates. When Naples was captured by the French in 1798, he escorted the Neapolitan king and queen to Sicily, and returned to Naples, becoming something of a convert to French republicanism. On the recapture of Naples in 1799, Caracciolo was captured and brought on board H.M.S. *Foudroyant, Lord Nelson's flagship, where a Neapolitan court martial condemned him to death by a majority verdict. Largely because of the declared enmity of the queen of Naples against Caracciolo, Nelson ordered the execution to take place on the following morning, and Caracciolo was hanged from the yardarm of the Minerva without being allowed the normal 24 hours for confession and prayers. Nelson's attitude in this affair has been widely criticized, and there can be little doubt that his infatuation for Lady *Hamilton, an intimate of Queen Mary Caroline of Naples and bearer to him of the queen's desire for Caracciolo's execution, caused him to act less than honourably in this matter.

CARAVEL, the relatively small trading vessel of the Mediterranean of the 14th–17th centuries, later (16th century) taken up by the Spanish and Portuguese authorities for voyages of exploration as well as for trade. They were developed as a large boat, having no *beakhead or stern castle but a simple curved *stem and a plain *transom stern. Originally they were *lateen-rigged on two masts (caravela latina), but the inconvenience of this rig for longer ocean voyages resulted in their development into three-masted ships with square *rig on the two forward masts and a lateen-rigged mizen (caravela rotunda). This provided a better balance of sail power and avoided to a great extent the main disability of the lateen sail, the immense length of the *yard on which the sail was set and the need when tacking to lower the sail in order to bring the yard to the other side of the mast. The average overall length of a three-masted caravel was 75–80 feet, although a few were built with an overall length of up to 100 feet. The *Santa Maria, a caravel and flagship of Christopher *Columbus's small squadron of exploration in 1492, was one of the larger type with a length of 95 feet. The other two caravels, the *Pinta and *Niña, were smaller than usual, being 58 feet and 56 feet overall respectively. When they left Spain the Niña was a caravela latina, but the rig was found so unsatisfactory out in the Atlantic that she was converted to the caravela rotunda rig in the Canary Islands. The ship in which Bartholomew *Diaz rounded the Cape of Good Hope in 1488 was also a caravel, as were the ships with which Ferdinand *Magellan set out on his circumnavigation of the world in 1519–22.

CARCASS, an incendiary ship-to-ship weapon used in battle in the days of sail, consisting of an iron shell filled with a composition of saltpetre, sulphur, resin, turpentine, antimony, and tallow. It had three vents for the flame and was often additionally fitted with pistol barrels which discharged their bullets at random. Carcasses were first introduced in the British Navy towards the end of the 17th century and lasted until the early years of the 19th. Similar weapons of this general type were developed by most other navies of the days of sail, their main purpose being to set on fire the sails and rigging of an opponent. They were never very successful and they were used more and more rarely as the years went by. In the case of shore-to-ship gun actions, the incendiary weapon was the cannon ball heated in a brazier to red heat before being fired normally from a gun.

CARDINAL POINTS, the four *points of north, south, east, and west on a magnetic compass card. The points halfway between these—north-east, south-east, south-west, and north-west—are known as half-cardinal points.

CARDINAL SYSTEM, see BUOYS, BUOYAGE.

CAREEN, to, the operation in older days of heaving a ship down on one side in order to expose the other for the purposes of cleaning the bottom of weeds and *barnacles or of repair. The vessel was laid ashore, preferably on a steeply sloping beach, parallel to the shore-line and hove down by means of *tackles attached to the mastheads. *Relieving tackles, running under the ship's *keel, were secured to convenient points on the exposed side, so that the angle of *heel could be controlled and the vessel brought back to an even keel after the side had been cleaned or the repairs made. After one side had been cleaned, the ship was floated off on the tide, turned round to face the other way, and careened again so that the opposite side could be cleaned. Small craft are still occasionally careened for cleaning on suitable beaches, but the cleaning of larger vessels is always now done in a *dry-dock.

Where it was unnecessary to expose the whole of the bottom for cleaning or repair, but only a few feet, the ship was given a *Parliamentary heel by shifting *ballast, guns, etc., from one side to the other in order to give her sufficient list to expose the side to the amount required. H.M.S. *Royal George* was capsized at Spithead in 1782 with a great loss of life when undergoing a Parliamentary heel to expose a few feet of her side for repairs. See also BREAM, TO.

CAREENAGE, a suitable beach with a steep, sandy shore-line, where ships could be * careened for cleaning their bottoms of weed and * barnacles or for repair.

CARGO JACK, a large screw jack which was used in the stowage of cargo, especially in the case of cotton and hides which were always jacked into a * hold, in order to compress them into the smallest possible space so as to be able to stow the maximum quantity. Charles * Dana, in his * Two Years Before the Mast, describes the process of jacking hides into a hold.

CARGO NET, a large square net made of rope in which to sling cased or packaged cargo into and out of a ship's * hold. While modern methods of loading and unloading ships, such as containerization and drive-on, drive-off facilities, are rapidly making obsolete these older methods of handling cargoes, there are still many smaller merchant ships for which they remain the only means of loading and unloading.

CARGO PALLET, a flat wooden tray with a *bridle at each end used for hoisting small cargo in and out of the * hold of a ship by means of cargo slings. Containerization, a quicker and more efficient means of stowing cargo in a ship, is replacing all these older methods.

CARLEY FLOAT, a life-raft capable of supporting a large number of persons—up to fifty in the biggest—both in and out of the water. It is in the form of a large oval ring of canvas painted to make it watertight and stuffed with kapok or granulated cork, with a light wooden grid inside the oval and hand lines on the outer circumference. It was supplied mainly to warships but has now been largely superseded by inflatable rubber life-rafts.

CARLINGS or **CARLINES,** pieces of squared timber fitted fore and aft between the deck * beams of a wooden ship. Their purpose is to provide support for the deck planking; in ships built of steel the usual practice is to lay a steel deck direct on the beams with planking, where necessary, laid on the steel. In yacht and small wooden vessel construction, carlings carry the half-beams in the way of * hatches and other deck openings, supporting the * coamings of the hatches or the * coachroof above them. See also SHIPBUILDING.

CARMANIA, **R.M.S.,** the first * Cunard transatlantic * liner to be fitted with * turbines in place of triple-expansion reciprocating engines. In September 1914, having been taken over by the British Navy as an * armed merchant cruiser, she fought a duel in the South Atlantic against the German armed merchant cruiser *Cap Trafalgar,* sinking her after a spirited action. In commemoration of her action the British Navy League presented the ship with a silver plate from Lord * Nelson's dinner service.

CARMICHAEL, JAMES WILSON (*c.* 1800–68), British marine painter, was born at Newcastle upon Tyne and found his early inspiration for painting along the coast of his native Northumberland. In 1854 he went with the British fleet to the Baltic at the start of the Crimean War to make sketches of the naval activities for the *Illustrated London News,* a series of some historical value as a record of naval life on board in the mid-19th century. He had previously travelled to Italy and there painted seascapes of great merit and charm. He was also the author of two books on marine painting, one dealing with the use of oil as a medium and the other with water-colour.

CARNEGIE, WILLIAM, Earl of Northesk (1758–1831), British admiral, became a captain in 1782. He was in command of the * Monmouth in 1796, one of the ships involved in the great naval mutiny at the * Nore in 1797. After much argument Northesk was asked by the mutineers to lay their demands directly before the king but when they were rejected as totally unreasonable Northesk remained in London, shortly afterwards resigning his command of the *Monmouth.*

On the outbreak of the Napoleonic War with France in 1803 he was appointed to the *Britannia,* a three-* decker, being promoted to rear admiral the next year and hoisting his flag in that ship. At the battle of * Trafalgar he was third in command of the fleet, his ship being fourth in the * weather line led by * Nelson. He was made a Knight of the Bath for his services in the action and was promoted to vice admiral in 1808 and admiral in 1814. From 1827 to 1830 he was commander-in-chief at Plymouth.

CAROSSE, the open space under the poop deck of a * galley where the admiral or captain had his bed. It could perhaps be taken as the original form of the * cabin.

CAROUS, a sort of gallery or bridge, pivoted in the centre and fitted in ancient warships, such as * galleys, as a means of * boarding an enemy. On forcing a way alongside an enemy it was hoisted up by a *tackle and swung round until it projected over, or into, the enemy vessel, forming a means of access for boarders. The introduction of the gun mounted in ships and firing a solid shot quickly put an end to this means of capturing ships as it was an unwieldy piece of equipment which even the most inexperienced of gunners could hardly miss.

CARPENTER, a senior rating in ships in charge of all the wood-work on board. In the days of sailing navies the carpenter was a warrant officer responsible for the condition of the hull, masts, spars, and boats of the ship. His duty in and after battle was to plug all shotholes with wooden plugs carried on board for the purpose, to *fish all masts and *yards damaged by shot, and continually to sound the *well to ascertain whether the ship was making water.

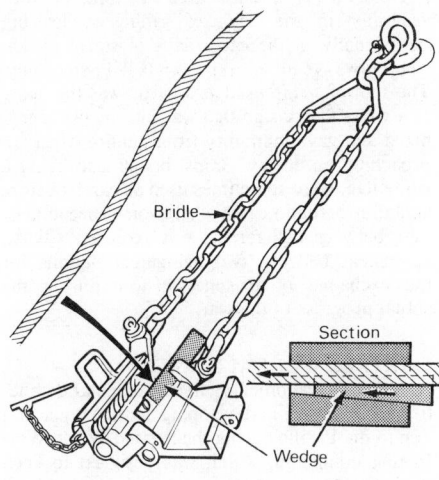

Carpenter's stopper

CARPENTER'S STOPPER, a metal stopper designed for holding a wire rope temporarily when it is under strain. It consists of a thick metal box of which the top is hinged and both ends are left open. One side of the box is grooved to take the *lay of the wire rope, the other, which is inclined to the lead of the wire, holds a wedge-shaped piece of metal similarly grooved. When using the stopper the wire is laid in the box against the grooved side and the top is closed. The wedge is then inserted and pushed home as far as it will go. As the pull comes on the wire the wedge is drawn down further into the box until it jams the wire. The box itself is fitted with a chain *bridle which is shackled to an eyeplate or deck-bolt so that it is anchored to the deck while holding the wire.

CARR, FRANK GEORGE GRIFFITH (1903–   ), British yachtsman and author, was assistant librarian of the House of Lords (1929–47) and succeeded Sir Geoffrey *Callender as director of the *National Maritime Museum, Greenwich (1947–66). He is an authority on pilot cutters, Thames *spritsail *barges, deep water cruising, and nautical history, and among the well-known yachts he has owned is *Cariad*, a 25-ton ex-Bristol Channel pilot *cutter. While at Greenwich he was instrumental in preserving the *clipper ship *Cutty Sark* and Sir Francis *Chichester's yacht *Gipsy Moth IV*, both of which are now exhibited there. *Cariad*, the ex-pilot cutter, is preserved at the Exeter Maritime Museum. He is the author of *Sailing Barges* (1931), *Vanishing Craft* (1934), *A Yachtsman's Log* (1935), *The Yachtsman's England* (1936), and *The Yachtsman's Guide* (1940).

CARRACK, the larger type of trading vessel of northern and southern Europe of the 14th–17th centuries, developed as a compromise between the typical square *rig of the northern European nations and the *lateen rig of the Mediterranean. They were very similar in rig to the later three-masted development of the *caravel (*caravela rotunda*) though larger, beamier, and generally more robust, with very high fore and after castles. The carrack was the forerunner, and first example, of the larger three-masted ship which dominated naval architecture until the general introduction of steam propulsion in the mid-19th century. They were square-rigged on fore- and

17th century carrack; engraving by F. H. Breughel

mainmasts and lateen-rigged on the mizen, and the largest carracks were built up to a tonnage of about 1,200. During the 16th and early 17th centuries, almost all the Spanish and Portuguese trading voyages to India, China, and America were performed in carracks. The carrack was superseded during the 17th century by the more efficient *galleon, designed by Sir John *Hawkins, which by eliminating the high forward castle produced a much more weatherly performance when sailing near the wind.

CARRICK BEND, a round knot used to join two rope *hawsers when they are required to go round the barrel of a *capstan, the need for such a special knot being that any other, such as a *reef knot which is flat, could get jammed between the *whelps of the capstan barrel.

Carrick bend

CARRONADE, see GUNS, NAVAL.

CARRY, to, in its naval meaning, to capture a ship by coming alongside her in battle, or laying her aboard in the idiom of the age, and taking possession of her by means of boarding parties.

CARRY AWAY, to, the breaking, or parting, of objects on board ship, particularly applicable in the case of *masts and *yards. It is an expression used also in the case of ropes and *hawsers when they break as a result of sudden violence, such as a particularly heavy gust of wind or a ship with too much way on her when attempting to secure alongside.

CARTARET, Sir GEORGE (c. 1609–80), commanded several ships of the Royal Navy in the reign of Charles I, and in 1639 was appointed comptroller of the navy. After the execution of Charles, he held the island of Jersey for the royalists until 1651. With the restoration of Charles II in 1660, he became treasurer of the navy, and held that post throughout the Second Dutch War (1665–7), using his own personal credit with bankers to finance the navy during these years. In 1667 he became deputy-treasurer of Ireland, and in 1673, when the Test Act debarred the Duke of York (see James) from holding the position of *Lord High Admiral, he was appointed one of the *Lords Commissioners of the Admiralty. He was a member of the committee of trade and plantations and was assigned the land between the Hudson and Delaware rivers, which was called, in honour of Cartaret, New Jersey to commemorate his defence of the island of Jersey for the king.

CARTARET, PHILIP (c. 1738–96), British rear admiral, was a lieutenant in H.M.S. *Dolphin during Captain John *Byron's voyage round the world, 1764–6. On his return he was appointed to command the *Swallow* which, with the *Dolphin* commanded by Captain Samuel *Wallis, was ordered to perform a second voyage of circumnavigation. The *Swallow* separated from the *Dolphin* after passing through the Straits of Magellan, and Cartaret completed the voyage alone, discovering hitherto unknown islands in the Polynesian and Melanesian groups, and making valuable surveys in the Philippine Islands. He returned to England in 1769, and his many discoveries entitle him to be considered as one of the greatest explorers of his period. In 1779 he served with Lord *Rodney in the West Indies, and he retired in 1794 with the rank of rear admiral.

CARTEL, (1) a ship used in time of war, generally in the days of sailing navies but occasionally in the early days of steam navies, when it was required to negotiate with an enemy. The sign of a ship used as a cartel was the flying of a white flag, a sign that was universally recognized and gave immunity from gunfire when approaching an enemy. Ships' boats, also flying a white flag, were sometimes used as cartels before and after battle in cases where some special message between belligerents was required. **(2)** An agreement between two belligerent nations for the exchange of prisoners-of-war during the actual progress of the war.

CARTER, WORRALL REED (1885–1975), American naval officer, gained particular distinction for his work in developing Service Squadron Ten in the Pacific during the Second World War. In that command, which was designed to keep the main fleets operational during prolonged cruises out of reach of shore support, his performance was outstanding. After the war ended he was recalled to active duty to prepare a history of the mobile services to the fleet. This work appeared in two volumes entitled *Beans, Bullets, and Black Oil*, published in 1952, and *Ships, Salvage, and Sinews of War*, written in conjunction with Rear Admiral Elmer E. Duvall and published in 1954. These excellent histories added to the distinction he had gained in service to the fleet. See also FLEET TRAIN.

CARTIER, JACQUES (1491–1557), French navigator, was the discoverer of the St. Lawrence River in Canada. In 1534 he commanded an expedition of two ships and sixty-one men with the aim of discovering a North-West passage to China. He reached Newfoundland and entered the Belle Isle Strait, but finding the prospect uninviting to the westward, sailed down and round the Newfoundland coast, reaching Anticosti Island and thus discovering the mouth of the great river. He returned to France, but set sail again with three ships in 1536, passed through the Belle Isle Strait, and anchored opposite Anticosti, naming his anchorage the bay of St. Lawrence. He sailed up the river as far as the Île d'Orléans, which he named in honour of the French royal family, and left his ships in the St. Charles River while he continued westward in the longboats, reaching the Indian village of Hochelaga, the site of the present Montreal. From the top of Mont Royal he was able to see the St. Lawrence River stretching to the west. His expedition returned to St. Malo in 1537.

His third voyage, with five ships, sailed from St. Malo in 1541 to make contact with the seigneur de Roberval, who was being sent from France with a regiment of soldiers to conquer the country. There were delays in getting the soldiers on their way, and Cartier, having waited in vain and now returning to France, met them off Newfoundland in the spring of 1542. He was sent once again to the St. Lawrence in 1543 to embark Roberval and his men, whose mission had failed, since the rich country of 'Saguenay' which they had been sent to conquer did not exist.

After returning to France with the soldiers in 1544, Cartier spent the remainder of his life at St. Malo.

CARTOGRAPHY, the science and practice of projecting an area of the earth's surface on to a flat plane, as a sheet of paper. There are a number of methods of projection, all of them with some advantages and some drawbacks. See, for example, GLOBULAR PROJECTION, MERCATOR'S PROJECTION. For a short history of the science of charts, see CHARTMAKING. For early cartographers, see, e.g., MARINUS OF TYRE; MERCATOR, Gerardus; PTOLEMY.

CARVEL, (1) a small *lateen-rigged vessel of the Mediterranean, normally with two masts, used for the carriage of small cargoes. Its period was the late middle ages, though it is thought by some to be a synonym for *caravel, a ship of the 14th–17th centuries. **(2)** A form of sea-blubber, consisting of jelly-fish, small molluscs, and the like, which form one of the main sources of food of the turtle.

CARVEL CONSTRUCTION or **CARVEL-BUILT,** a wooden vessel or boat in which the side planks are all flush, the edges laid close and *caulked to make a smooth finish, as compared with *clinker-built, in which the side planks overlap.

CASABIANCA, LOUIS DE (1762–98), French naval officer, was in 1798 captain of the 120-gun *ship of the line *Orient, flagship of Vice Admiral de *Brueys at the battle of the *Nile in *Aboukir Bay. She was first engaged by the *Bellerophon (Captain George Darby) whom she dismasted, set on fire, and drove from the action. The Bellerophon's place was then taken by the Swiftsure (Captain Benjamin *Hallowell) while on the Orient's other side, she was simultaneously engaged by the Alexander (Captain Alexander *Ball).

The French flagship, in which de Brueys had been mortally wounded, had earlier been painting her side, and the paint buckets had been left on deck. The wet paint in the buckets was set on fire by the British guns, and the flames spread quickly throughout the length of the ship eventually reaching her magazine. She blew up with a tremendous explosion just after 10 p.m. All but about seventy-five of her crew perished when she blew up, including Captain Casabianca. The heroism of his 10-year-old son Jacques who refused to leave his father's side to save himself is the subject of the well-known ballad by Mrs. Felicia Hemans:

> The boy stood on the burning deck
> Whence all but he had fled.

CASCO, the local name given to a flat-bottomed, square-ended boat of the Philippine Islands, used as a lighter for ferrying cargo from ship to shore and vice-versa.

CASE-SHOT, 'any kind of old iron, stones, musket-bullets or the like which we put into cases to shoot out of our great ordnance. These are of great use and do much execution amongst men . . . upon the upper deck when we come near or lie board by board.' Thus Sir Henry *Mainwaring (The Seaman's Dictionary, 1644). The cases in which the old iron, etc., was stuffed were normally made of wood although occasionally canvas bags were used if wooden cases were not

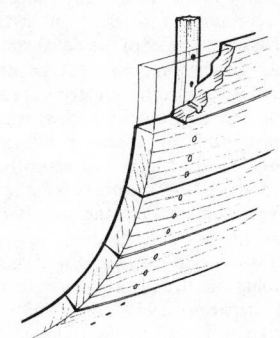

Carvel construction

readily available. But there was a danger with canvas bags that they might get caught and torn open by projections and irregularities inside the barrel of the gun with consequent damage to the bore, and wooden cases were always preferred.

CAST, to, the action of bringing the bows of a sailing ship on to the required *tack, just as the anchor is leaving the ground on being *weighed, by hauling on the sheet of a headsail so that the wind will force the bows off in the required direction. When there is insufficient wind to cast with a headsail but a *tide is running, it is often possible to cast on to the required tack by putting the helm over and letting the force of the tide act on the rudder to turn the bows.

CAST OF THE LEAD, the act of heaving the *lead and line to ascertain the depth of water. At each cast, the leadsman calls out the depth in fathoms of the water alongside the ship according to the *marks or *deeps of the line.

CAST OFF, to, the operation of letting go a *cable or rope securing a ship to a *buoy, *wharf, *mole, or alongside another ship, so that she may move away and proceed to sea or to another berth in harbour.

CASTAWAY, a shipwrecked sailor as compared with one who has been *marooned, or deliberately put ashore as the ship sails. In many maritime countries 'Castaway Clubs' have been formed for sailors who have been shipwrecked to meet together for social purposes.

CASTEX, RAOUL VICTOR (1878–1968), French admiral and strategist, was born at St. Omer, Pas de Calais, and entered the navy in 1896, reaching the rank of *capitaine de frégate* (commander) in 1918. From 1919 to 1922 he served in and completely reorganized the Historical Section of the Ministry of Marine. Promoted to *capitaine de vaisseau* (captain) in 1923, he was three years later appointed director of higher naval studies in strategy and tactics. He became a rear admiral in 1925, and in 1926 was appointed assistant chief of the naval staff, taking up in 1932 another appointment as director of the war college where he greatly impressed the students by the high quality of his lectures. He became port admiral at Brest in 1935, but returned to the war college as director the following year and on the outbreak of the Second World War commanded the northern naval forces. Ill health obliged him to retire in November 1939. He was a historian and writer of exceptional merit and his *Strategic Theories*, published between 1929 and 1939 in five volumes, is considered to be a classic work on the subject.

CASTOR, twin brother of Pollux, was by legend the son of Zeus by Leda, wife of Tyndarus, king of Sparta, though in another mythological context only Pollux was the son of the god, Castor's father being Tyndarus. Nevertheless, they were treated as twins and were removed from their mother immediately after birth by Mercury and carried away to Pallena, where they were brought up. As soon as they reached maturity they joined *Jason in his quest for the Golden Fleece and greatly distinguished themselves, Castor in the management of horses and Pollux by overcoming and killing Amycus in the combat of the cestus. During the expedition of the *Argonauts, while a violent storm was raging, two flames were seen to play around the heads of the twin brothers and at once the storm ceased and the sea became calm. Because of this occurrence, great faith was thereafter placed in the power of the twins to protect sailors; and the two flames, a phenomenon often seen in storms and known as *St. Elmo's Fire or *Corposant, are still widely known by sailors as 'Castor and Pollux'.

When they returned from Colchis, the brothers cleared the Hellespont and the neighbouring seas of pirates, from which service they have always been considered the friends of navigation. Sailors in a storm used to pray to them for safety, sacrificing a white lamb to their memory. After an eventful life, Castor was killed by Idas in revenge for the killing of his brother Lynceus. Pollux then killed Idas, to avenge the death of his twin, and as he himself was immortal (being as many thought the son of Zeus) and dearly loved his brother, he begged Zeus either to restore Castor to life or else to deprive him (Pollux) of his immortality. Zeus permitted Pollux to spend alternate days with his brother in the infernal regions, the other days being spent with the gods.

Another fable credits the god with celebrating their love for each other by placing them together in the sky in the constellation known today as Gemini. A variation of this legend is that they were placed in the sky as the morning and evening stars, the one rising in the sky as the other sets.

CAT, (1) the name of the purchase by which a ship's *anchor, before the days of the stockless anchor, was hoisted to the *cathead in preparation for stowing or for letting go. **(2)** A sailing collier, very strongly built, to carry about 600 tons of coal, widespread through northern Europe until the mid-19th century. They were built to a Norwegian model with a canoe stern with projecting quarters and a deep waist, and were particularly noticeable by the fact that they carried no *figurehead in days when even the humblest craft carried some sort of decoration

Catamaran

on their bows. For his voyages of discovery, Captain James *Cook selected Northumbrian cats as the ships best suited to his purpose. (3) The short name by which the *cat-o'-nine-tails was known. (4) A small open sailing boat in the U.S.A., more accurately known as a *cat-boat.

CAT, to, the process of hoisting an anchor by its ring so that it hangs at the *cathead either in readiness for letting go or, after it has been weighed, in preparation for securing it on the anchor bed. Anchors were catted by means of a two-fold or three-fold *purchase according to the size and weight of the anchor, either the fixed block of the purchase being secured to the end of the cathead or, more usually, the sheaves being incorporated permanently in the cathead itself. The whole process of catting an anchor was necessary only with anchors fitted with *stocks; the invention and almost universal adoption of the stockless anchor made the process of catting the anchor in preparation for letting go obsolete in all modern vessels. But when a large modern ship lies to a mooring buoy by her cable, the anchor is brought to a clump cathead on the forecastle, where it is secured so that the cable can be disconnected and brought to the ring of the mooring buoy to be *shackled on. While the cable is thus used, the anchor remains hanging from the clump cathead.

CAT RIG, see UNA RIG.

CATAMARAN, from the Tamil *katta*, to tie, *maram*, wood, **(1)** A sort of raft consisting of two or more logs or tree-trunks lashed together and used as a surf boat in the East and West Indies. The term is also used to describe the much larger rafts, made normally from the trunks of *balsa trees, of the western coast of South America. **(2)** A raft used in the St. Lawrence River, made by lashing two boats together. **(3)** A British naval invention of the autumn of 1804 specially designed to attack the French invasion flotilla as it lay in harbour at Boulogne. It consisted of a lead-lined chest about 21 ft long by 3 ft 3 in. broad with flat top and bottom and wedge-shaped ends. Within were about forty kegs of gunpowder and various combustibles, sufficient ballast to float it with the top at water-level, and a clock-work firing mechanism, which was started by withdrawing a peg and ran from four to six minutes before firing a pistol to explode the charge. The outside was caulked, covered with canvas, and well tarred, and was also fitted with a buoyed grappling iron to hook into an enemy's cable. The great weakness of the machine was that it had to be towed to reach the enemy, having no motive power of its own. Catamarans were first used at Boulogne in October 1804 but did virtually no damage beyond raising a clamour that Britain, by using them, had returned to barbarism. The French quickly made their use unprofitable by protecting their ships in harbour by booms and chain cables. **(4)** A small rectangular raft used in dockyards to protect the hulls of large ships from damage when lying alongside a mole or jetty. (5) A twin-hulled sailing *yacht, normally used for racing but also recently developed for cruising purposes. The twin hulls are connected by an above-water deck which carries mast and rigging, cockpit, and cabin. Normally rigged with *Bermuda mainsail and jib, catamarans can by reason of their low immersion area attain speeds considerably in excess of conventionally hulled sailing boats. See also MULTI-HULLS, TRIMARAN.

CAT-BOAT, a type of sailing boat which originated in the middle of the 19th century in the Cape Cod region of America, primarily for fishing in shallow waters but later adopted as a favourite type of *sandbagger for racing, as well as for coastal cruising. The cat-boat was very shallow and of great beam (some measured only two beams to the length) with a large weighted *centreboard of wood and a barndoor-like rudder. The mast, carrying a *gaff and *boom sail, was stepped right in the bows, close to the *stem. One, the $16\frac{1}{2}$-ft *Una*, was shipped to Cowes in 1852 and gave her name in English waters to this mast-in-bow, one-sail rig (see UNA RIG). Later some of the racing cat-boats set a foresail in addition on a long bowsprit.

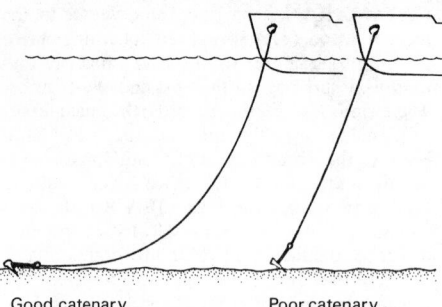

Good catenary   Poor catenary

CATENARY, the curve of an anchor *cable as it lies between the *anchor on the sea bottom and the vessel which lies to it. The deeper the curve, the more the catenary. A good catenary is essential for two reasons, the first being that the eventual pull on the anchor is horizontal, which tends to bury the anchor *flukes deeper into the ground; the second being that with the elasticity provided by a deep curve in the cable a vessel is prevented from *snubbing to her anchor as she rides to a sea. It is for this reason that most anchor cables, except in the very smallest of craft, are made of chain, where the weight of the chain tends to form a natural catenary.

CATHARPINGS, short ropes under the *tops at the lower end of the *futtock shrouds in square-rigged vessels, used to brace in the shrouds more tightly and thus give space to brace the *yards at a sharper angle to the fore-and-aft line when a ship sails *close-hauled. For illus. see FUTTOCK SHROUDS.

CATHAY, the name by which China was known during the Mongol dynasty and thus in European nations during the early years of discovery in the 15th, 16th, and 17th centuries. The discovery of America, first by Christopher *Columbus and then by John *Cabot, occurred because both these navigators were convinced that they could reach Cathay and India by sailing west across the Atlantic Ocean.

CATHEAD, a heavy piece of curved timber projecting from each bow of a ship for the purpose of holding *anchors which were fitted with a *stock in position for letting-go or for securing them on their beds after weighing. It holds the upper sheaves of the *cat purchase which is used to draw the anchor up to the cathead, a process known as catting the anchor. Since the invention of the stockless anchor, which is now almost universal in its use except in the few square-rigged ships still in commission, ships no longer have these large catheads, or need to cat their anchors before letting them go. But when a large ship secures to a mooring buoy with her cable, she first secures her anchor to a clump cathead where it remains hanging while the cable is in use to hold the ship to the buoy.

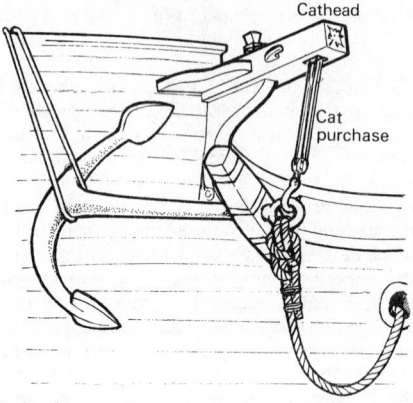

Cathead

CATHOLES, two small circular holes cut in the stern of the sailing men-of-war above the gunroom ports and on the same level as the *capstan. They were used for leading in a stern *hawser to the capstan when it was required to heave the ship astern. The gunroom ports, being cut on a lower plane than the capstan, would have been subjected to great strain had the stern hawsers been led in through them.

CAT-O'-NINE-TAILS, an instrument of punishment with which seamen were flogged on their bare backs in past days. It was made of nine lengths of cord, each about 18 inches long and with three knots in each, fixed to the end of a larger rope which was used as a handle. It was used in almost every navy in the world as a means of punishment during the days of sail. In the British Navy a captain was limited by regulations to a maximum of twelve lashes for any crime, but few captains abided by this rule. Sentences entailing a greater number of lashes could in theory only be awarded by sentence of court martial. The use of the cat-o'-nine-tails was suspended as a means of punishment in the Royal Navy in 1879 but had been falling into disuse long before that. See also FLOGGING ROUND THE FLEET, THIEVES' CAT.

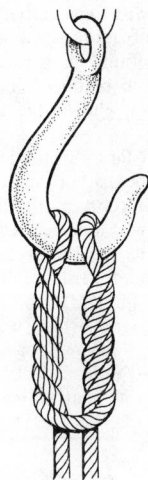

Catspaw

CATSPAW, (1) a twisting hitch made in the bight of a rope to form two eyes, through which the hook of a tackle is passed for hoisting purposes. **(2)** The name given to a ruffle on the water indicating a breath of wind during a calm. Old sailors, on seeing a catspaw on the surface of the water, would frequently rub the ship's backstay (as though fondling a cat) and whistle to induce the wind to come to the ship.

CATWALK, an elevated fore and aft passage way connecting the midships *bridge structure, in the older design of merchant vessels and some warships, with the *forecastle and *poop decks in order to provide safe and relatively dry access forward and aft from the bridge. In modern ship design, with the exception of some *tankers, catwalks are no longer built as the whole deck

forward of the bridge is normally flush, and protection on deck in heavy weather is provided by *lifelines.

CAUL, the membrane in which the heads of some babies are encompassed at birth. They were much esteemed by superstitious seamen as a guarantee against drowning and are still eagerly sought after by some mariners. See also SUPERSTITIONS OF SAILORS.

CAULK, to, the operation of driving, with a caulking iron, *oakum or rope *junk into the *seams of a ship's wooden deck or sides in order to render them impervious to water. After the oakum is driven in hard, the gap between the planks is filled with hot pitch or some other composition to prevent the oakum from rotting through contact with water.

CAVENDISH or **CANDISH,** THOMAS (1555–92), British circumnavigator, after having squandered a fortune inherited from his father, determined to make another by a life at sea. He purchased a ship and commanded her in the voyage made by Sir Richard *Grenville to attempt to colonize Virginia in the U.S.A. On his return he planned a voyage of circumnavigation similar to that carried out by Sir Francis *Drake eight years earlier. With three small ships, the largest of 140 tons, Cavendish sailed from London in 1586, reached the Pacific in February 1587, and sailed up the South American coast, burning and pillaging. In November of that year he had the good fortune to fall in with the annual Spanish treasure ship from Manila to *Acapulco, captured her after a hard fight of six hours, and loaded up his own ships with gold and treasure taken from her before setting her on fire. He returned to England by the Philippine Islands, Cape of Good Hope, and St. Helena, being the first man to discover that island. He arrived in English waters a few days after the defeat of the Spanish Armada in 1588.

On his return he attached himself to the court of Elizabeth I, quickly spent the money acquired during his voyage, and fitted out a second expedition to follow the lines of his first, in which he was joined by John *Davis as navigator. His ships reached the Straits of Magellan in March 1592, but were unable to get through because of the stormy weather. After two months, Cavendish abandoned the expedition and giving his other ships the slip during the night, attempted to return home alone via the Island of Ascension. He died during the voyage home.

CAVETA, see COVE (3).

CAVITATION, the loss of effective propeller thrust caused by the blades of a propeller cutting across the column of water sucked along by the propeller instead of working in it. It can be caused by a propeller being too small, or too near the surface for the head of water pressure to supply a solid stream for the propeller to work in, by poor streamlining of the blades or of the after *run of the hull form, or by too thick a leading blade on the propeller itself. The head of water is the pressure which forces the water into the propeller blades, and amounts to normal atmospheric pressure plus 0·434 lb per square inch for every foot below the surface that the propeller is submerged. The effect of cavitation, besides loss of thrust, is heavy vibration of the ship.

CAY, see KEY.

CEILING, the inside planking or plating in the *holds of a merchant vessel, laid across the *floors and carried up the sides of the holds to the level of the *beams.

CELESTIAL NAVIGATION, see NAVIGATION.

CELESTIAL SPHERE, the imaginary sphere on to which the heavenly bodies appear to be projected. For astronomical purposes the radius of the celestial sphere is considered to be infinite. For some purposes the sun is regarded as occupying the central position, but for others the earth's centre or the observer's eye is considered to lie at the centre. Systems of great circles on the celestial sphere, particularly the *horizon system, the *equinoctial system, and the *ecliptic system, have been devised to facilitate the solution of mathematical astronomical problems, especially those related to nautical astronomy. For illus. see ECLIPTIC.

CENTRE OF BUOYANCY, a point through which the resultant of all buoyant forces on an immersed hull are assumed to act. It is about this point that a vessel afloat could be said to be poised. It is also sometimes known as the centre of displacement, of cavity, or of flotation.

CENTRE OF EFFORT, a point of the sail plan of a sailing vessel through which the resultant of all wind forces is assumed to act. In a sail plan of a vessel each sail is assumed to have its centre of effort at its geometric centre, and on a drawing of a vessel's sail plan the resultant of these forces is assumed to be the centre of effort of the whole sail plan. In practice, however, the sails are never completely flat as shown on the plan, and the actual centre of effort moves at every fresh trimming of the sheets.

CENTRE OF LATERAL RESISTANCE, a point assumed to lie at the geometric centre of a sailing vessel's underwater profile. On a vessel's design plans this is indicated with the hull floating upright on its designed waterline. In practice, however, with sailing vessels heeled under a press of canvas and lifting and pitching over seas, the actual centre of lateral resistance is constantly shifting.

CENTREBOARD, a device which is raised or lowered it increases the vessel's lateral area and *keel of a boat of shallow draught, so that when lowered its increases the vessel's lateral area and its resistance to *leeway. Although it is accepted that certain Chinese river *junks were the first to employ a wooden drop, or sliding, keel which was raised and lowered on *tackles through a watertight case whose top came above the deck, the invention of the centreboard for small craft is generally attributed to America during colonial times. The need to be able to sail to windward, *close-hauled, with an entirely flat-bottomed work boat arose from the great stretches of very shallow waters found in Chesapeake Bay and along the Atlantic seaboard from Long Island Sound to Florida, and so the centreboard was born.

In 1774 Lord Percy introduced the device to England when he had a small vessel built at Boston, Massachusetts, on the lines of the local boats and fitted with one centreboard which was almost as long as the boat's keel, and had the boat shipped home for trials. Fifteen years later a larger boat was built at Deptford having three separate centreboards which were each narrow and deep, like a *dagger board, and could be raised or lowered independently to aid steering and balance of the boat under varying sailing conditions.

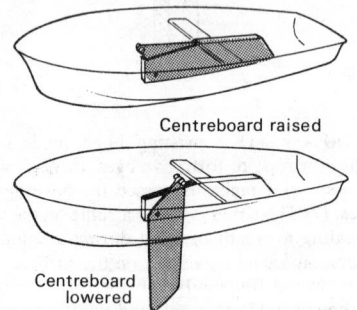

Centreboard raised

Centreboard lowered

In 1790 the British Admiralty built a revenue *cutter, the *Trial*, 68 feet on deck, which was fitted with three centreboards working on the same principle. The success of this experiment led to the building of a 60-ton *brig, the *Lady Nelson*, in 1798 with three similar centreboards expressly for a voyage of survey and discovery to New South Wales. Under the command of Lieutenant James Grant, R.N., this little vessel made a fast voyage out and was the first vessel to sail round Tasmania and discover that it was an island. The favourable reports on her voyage and the ease with which she could navigate in very shallow waters resulted in other vessels, including some merchantmen and work boats for the Teign and other shallow estuaries, being constructed on the same principle. About 1803 Commodore Taylor of the Cumberland Sailing Society had a yacht which he named *Cumberland* built on the Thames with five centreboards, which he raced with some success. The lines and a contemporary model of the hull of this yacht are preserved in the archives of the *Royal Thames Yacht Club.

By altering the shape of the centreboard and hanging it on a pivot at the fore end, Captain Shuldham of the Royal Navy introduced a distinct improvement in 1809 which became the most common form of the centreboard today. In the U.S.A. a number of local types of work boat such as *scows, *skipjacks, *bugeyes, *catboats, oyster *sloops and trading *schooners up to 150 feet in length, as well as many yachts, were built with pivoted centreboards. In the larger vessels the centreboard is generally built up from wooden planks, weighted to make it sink; schooners over 80 feet in length sometimes had two such centreboards. While centreboards and dagger plates are normally used in sailing and racing dinghies and yachts of shallow draught, metal centreplates, usually of bronze, have been fitted within the lead *ballast keels of some racing yachts in recent years. With their use the yacht can gain a little over a similar fixed keel competitor by increasing the lateral resistance to leeway when sailing on a wind (*closehauled), and when the course brings the wind free the plate is raised and the amount of wetted surface friction is accordingly reduced, allowing the yacht a little extra speed down wind. See also DROP KEEL.

CENTRING CHAINS, chains stretched across the entrance to and the head of a *dry-dock with a red and white disc inserted in them which indicate the line of the *keel blocks on which the vessel must rest when the dock is pumped out.

CENTURION, H.M.S., a 4th *rate of fifty guns, launched at Portsmouth in 1732, and selected as Commodore *Anson's flagship in his voyage round the world in 1740–4. She captured the treasure ship *Nuestra Señora de Covadonga*, a 56-gun ship belonging to Spain, off the Philippine Islands in 1743, with specie valued at £340,000 on board. She was also present at the battles of *Cape Finisterre (1747), *Quebec (1759), and the capture of Havana (1762); and was finally broken up in 1769. A later *Centurion* was the *battleship of 1911, which fought at *Jutland in 1916 and in 1941 was converted as an imitation of the new battleship *Anson* for

decoy purposes. She was finally sunk as part of one of the *Mulberry harbours used in the allied landings in Normandy in 1944. See also FIGUREHEAD.

CERVERA, PASCUAL CERVERA Y TOPETE (1839–1909), Spanish admiral, saw much active service during his rise to flag rank, and won many decorations for gallantry. He became minister of marine in 1892 but resigned from the cabinet when he found that the reforms he wanted to make were being blocked for political reasons and his naval estimates reduced. On the outbreak of the Spanish–American war in 1898 he was selected to command a squadron of four *cruisers (*Maria Theresa*, *Vizcaya*, *Oquendo*, and *Columbus*) and destroyers, which was ordered to Cuba, although Cervera pointed out that the ships had insufficient coal, provisions, and ammunition, and that some of the ships even lacked their guns. After coaling at the Cape Verde Islands he reached Santiago da Cuba, and on the approach of a vastly superior American fleet, was ordered to meet them at sea, again on political grounds and with no thought to the inevitable outcome of the battle. The squadron was totally destroyed and Cervera, with some 1,800 of his men, was taken prisoner. After the war he was tried by the supreme naval court of Spain but honourably acquitted. He became chief of staff of the Spanish Navy in 1903.

CESSER CLAUSE, that clause in a *charter party under which the charterer's liability ceases when the ship is loaded and the master has a lien on the cargo for *freight and *demurrage.

CHACK, PAUL (1876–1945), French naval officer and author, entered the navy in 1893 and in 1905 joined the hydrographic section of the Ministry of Marine. After the First World War (1914–18) he became head of the Service Historique de la Marine and thereafter devoted himself to historical studies, publishing a number of books of which the best known are a study on cruiser warfare, published in 1923, and one on sea warfare, published in 1926. His most important work, written in collaboration with Claude *Farrère, was a penetrating study of selected actions fought at sea, published in 1942. He retired in 1936.

In 1940 he volunteered for war service but after the fall of France later that year joined the collaborationist newspaper *Aujourd'hui*. On the liberation of France in 1944 he was accused of co-operation with the enemy, condemned to death, and executed.

CHAFE, see BAGGYWRINKLE.

CHAIN, see CABLE.

CHAIN, or **CABLE, LOCKER,** a compartment below decks in which a ship's *cable is stowed when the *anchor has been weighed and secured and the cable is all inboard. A ship has as many chain lockers as she has *bower and *sheet anchors. Originally the inboard end of a cable was secured by a Senhouse slip to a ringbolt high up on the side of the chain locker, so that in an emergency it could be knocked off with a cable still in the locker and the cable allowed to run out freely without being brought up to a *bitter end. Such an emergency might well have been when a ship at anchor was dragging her anchor rapidly on to a *lee shore and needed to slip her cable quickly to win free of the danger. The modern practice is to *shackle the end of the cable to a cable *clench at the bottom of the locker and, when the anchor is let go and the required length of cable *veered, to secure it with a riding slip at the top of the chain locker. It acts as a preventer should the brake of the *cable-holder fail to hold the cable while the vessel swings to it.

CHAIN SHOT, two cannon balls, connected together by either a chain or an iron bar, which when fired from a gun rotated at great speed through the air. It was designed to destroy the spars and rigging of an enemy ship and to clear the upper deck of men during an action.

CHAIN-PLATES, strips of iron or bronze with their lower ends bolted to the ship's side under the *channels of sailing vessels. They carry the *deadeyes or rigging screws to which the standing rigging is secured. In the older sailing ships these deadeyes were attached to short lengths of chain secured to the ship's side, and the name remained when chains were superseded by a plate. For illus. see RIGGING.

CHAINS, a small platform on either side of a ship from which the *leadsman heaves the lead when taking a *sounding to ascertain the depth of water. They are so called because originally, in the old sailing vessels, the leadsman cast his lead standing between the *shrouds, which were attached to the *chain-plates or, earlier still, to lengths of chain attached to the ship's side. The name has been retained, and is still apposite as a small chain is threaded through *stanchions at waist height rigged round the platform to prevent the leadsman from falling overboard as he makes a cast. In these days of *echo-sounders, the leadsman is no longer required and few ships today have chains for sounding. See also LEAD LINE, MARK, DEEP.

CHAIN-WALES, sometimes known as **CHAINS,** wooden projections from the sides of square-rigged ships abreast each mast to carry the *chain-plates clear of the *gunwale to give the *shrouds a wider base and spread from which to support the masts and also to hold them clear of the gunwale capping to prevent chafe. They are secured to the ship's side by *knees and bolts, each mast having its pair of chain-wales, one on each side of the ship. The name originated from the lengths of chain which preceded chain-plates as the fitting to which the *deadeyes of shrouds were secured.

CHALLENGE, an American *clipper ship of about 800 tons built in 1850 by William H. Webb of New York. She was commanded by the murderous 'Bully' Waterman, with the equally notorious *'bucko' mate Douglas, and she held the record for many years for the fastest passages from New York to California around Cape Horn. See also CAPE HORNERS.

CHALLENGER, H.M.S., a familiar ship's name among international oceanographers, remembered for the world cruise of 1872–6 when this *screw steam *corvette of 1,500 tons, built in 1858 at Woolwich, was commanded by George *Nares, with Wyville Thomson embarked as the senior scientist. The voyage was made at the instigation of the Royal Society with whom G. H. Richards, then Hydrographer of the Navy, closely collaborated in drawing up instructions. A second surveying ship of this name was in active and eventful service from 1931 through the Second World War until in 1949 she also executed a worldwide oceanographic cruise under the command of Captain Ritchie, later Hydrographer of the Navy, with T. Gaskell

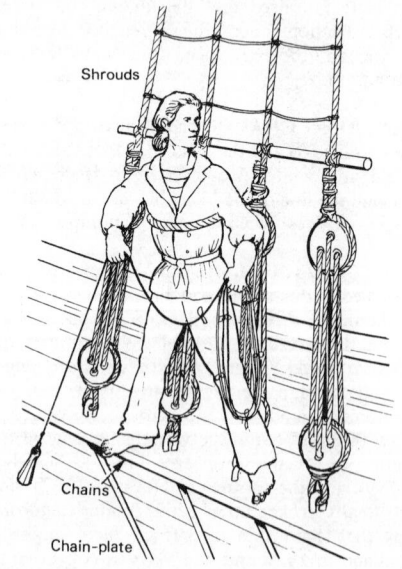

Old-fashioned chains

aboard as the senior scientist. Much scientific work continued until 1953 when the ship was sold for scrap.

CHAMBER, the name given to a small piece or ordnance during the 16th and 17th centuries from which gun salutes at sea were fired.

CHAMBERS, an old legal term used to describe those areas of sea which lay between headlands but beyond the strict * three-mile limit. In 1634, for example, the Lords of the English Admiralty instructed the judge of the * Admiralty Court and the Attorney-General 'to compose a reglement whereby his Majesty's ancient right in the * Narrow Seas, and in his chambers and ports, might be preserved'.

CHAMBERS, GEORGE (1803–40), Yorkshire artist who during his short life made a great name for himself as a marine painter. The second son of a Whitby seaman, he went to sea at the age of 10 and while apprenticed to Captain Storr of the brig *Equity* began to draw and paint. When the ship's owner saw his work he cancelled the remaining two years of his indentures to allow him to devote himself to art, albeit under conditions of great poverty. After three years he went to London and was employed as a scene painter. Befriended by a fellow townsman, the landlord of 'The Waterman's Arms' (later 'The Prospect of Whitby'), Chambers painted for him a picture of their native town which put him on the road to success. Two of his pictures exhibited in a shop window were noticed by Rear Admiral Thomas Capel, who introduced the young artist to his friends and fellow admirals. Through one of them he was presented to * William IV who commissioned some pictures from him. But now his health began to fail, although he managed to complete several paintings for the Painted Hall at * Greenwich. One of his best-known pictures is 'The Bombardment of Algiers, 27 August 1816', which hung for many years in the office of the First Lord of the Admiralty. His son GEORGE (1831–90) followed his father as an artist and it is not always easy to distinguish the works of one from the other.

CHAMPLAIN, SAMUEL DE (1567–1635), French explorer, was the son of a sea captain and himself a skilled seaman. He served first in the army of Henry IV of France but was given command of a ship in an expedition which sailed from Cadiz for the West Indies in 1599. He made his first voyage to Canada, with which his name is indissolubly linked, in 1603 as the agent of the Seigneur de Chastes, to whom the king of France had granted a monopoly of the fur trade and, following in the footsteps of Jacques * Cartier, explored the St. Lawrence River as far

as Montreal and above. On the death of de Chastes, the Canadian monopoly was taken over by the Sieur de Monts, and Champlain on his behalf returned to Canada for further exploration, the making of charts and surveys, and the finding of a site for a new settlement. He finally settled on a place in Acadia to plant the new settlement.

Disputes over the monopoly forced Champlain to return to France with the proposed colonists, but after these difficulties had been settled, he sailed again with two ships, one to colonize, the other to trade. He proceeded up the St. Lawrence River to the site of the present Quebec, and founded the first white settlement there in 1608, giving it its present name. In the company of Indians he discovered, the following year, the lake to which he gave his own name. He became embroiled in various tribal quarrels among the Indians, but on his return to France he prevailed upon the king to give him the appointment of lieutenant-governor. He remained convinced that there was a sea route through Canada to the east, up the St. Lawrence, across the great lakes, and down a river which flowed from the western end of the lakes to the Pacific, but in the end had to abandon his search through lack of success. He now devoted himself to the advancement of his town of Quebec, and each year returned to France to gain interest and support. In 1629 he was captured and taken to England when three ships, acting under * letters of marque, sailed up the St. Lawrence and forced Quebec to surrender. On the return of Canada to France in 1633 he returned to Quebec, dying there two years later.

CHANCE, a novel by Joseph * Conrad, published in 1913. It is the story of the captain of the ship *Ferndale* (probably based on the ship *Riversdale* in which Conrad sailed as second * mate) and the daughter of a financier who had been convicted of fraud and sentenced to prison.

CHANCELLOR, RICHARD (d. 1556), British navigator, was in 1553 appointed captain and pilot major of an expedition under Sir Hugh * Willoughby to find a * North-East passage to India. With Willoughby in the *Bona Esperanza* and himself in the 160-ton * *Edward Bonaventure*, and accompanied by the *Bona Confidentia*, the three ships were towed down the Thames on 22 May 1553 and past the Royal Palace of Greenwich, the ship's companies being dressed in sky-blue cloth and saluting the king as they passed. However the final departure from England was delayed until July, the ships reaching the Lofoten Islands in August where, after a stay of three days, they continued their northward voyage. As they prepared to round the North Cape, they encountered a severe storm and became separated. After waiting seven days at the rendezvous Chancellor went on alone and reached the White Sea where he landed and visited Ivan the Terrible in Moscow. This led to the founding of the Muscovy Company designed to stimulate trade between England and Russia. During a second voyage in 1555 he called at Arzina where Willoughby and his men had succumbed to an Arctic winter and collected the body of his former chief, together with his papers and goods. Returning from a third voyage in 1556 during which he had embarked a Russian ambassador to England, his ship was wrecked off Petsligo, Aberdeen, and Chancellor was drowned together with most of his crew.

'CHANNEL FEVER', the seaman's name for the excitement on board ship as she approaches her destination with the prospect for the crew of a spell of * liberty ashore. The longer the voyage, the greater the degree of channel fever.

CHANTEY or **CHANTY**, see SHANTY.

CHAPELLE, HOWARD IRVING (1900–75), American naval architect and author, served as apprentice and draughtsman with firms of naval architects in New York from 1920 onwards. In 1936 he started in business on his own as a naval architect and surveyor, and produced in all some 120 different designs for fishing craft, yachts, and sailing boats. During the Second World War he served in the U.S. Army in charge of ship- and boat-building programmes, and in 1956 went to Turkey as adviser on the construction and equipping of their fishing fleets. On his return to the U.S.A. he was appointed maritime historian at the Smithsonian Institution in Washington and was awarded the Smithsonian gold medal for distinguished service to the Institution. He was also chairman of the committee for the restoration of U.S.S. *Niagara*, flagship of Oliver Hazard * Perry at the battle of * Lake Erie. Among the many books he has written are *The Baltimore Clipper*, *History of the American Sailing Ships*, *Yacht Design and Planning*, *History of the American Sailing Navy*, *Bark Canoes and Skin Boats of North America*, *American Small Sailing Craft*, *American Sailing Craft*, and *The American Fishing Schooners*.

CHAPELLED, a ship was said to be chapelled, or to build a chapel, when, after losing her * way through the water in a light or baffling wind, she turns completely round or, when * close-hauled, goes * about without bracing her head-yards and then comes back on to the same tack as before. It can be caused either by the inattention of the helmsman or by a quick change in direction of the wind.

CHAPELS, the name given to the grooves in a built-up, or 'made', wooden * mast in which several pieces of timber are used to fashion it. In large sailing ships the lower masts were all 'made' * spars, the * topmasts and * topgallant masts were whole spars. The chapels occurred where the various pieces of which the mast was made were joined together.

CHAPMAN, FREDERIK HENDRIK AF (1721–1808), Swedish naval architect, was the son of Yorkshire-born Thomas Chapman who emigrated to Sweden in 1715 and was appointed a captain in the Swedish Navy. Frederik Hendrik grew up as a shipbuilder and built his first small Baltic trading * cutter when he was only 19. In 1741 he visited England and worked for a time in Deptford Dockyard, gaining valuable experience of warship construction. Three years later he started his own shipbuilding yard in Gothenburg, later laying aside the practical work of building to study naval architecture and new building methods at shipyards in France, the Netherlands, and England. He was appointed chief constructor of the Swedish Navy until his retirement on full pay in 1793, after which he continued work on his studies and writing until his death.

As part of his studies in naval architecture he built and used a tank for the testing of ship models which were drawn along by means of an ingenious system of drop weights. These tests and his writings on the form of ships' hulls, their construction, behaviour at sea, and speed through the water, made a long-lasting impact on the future of naval architecture and dockyard practice. He was the author of *Architectura Navalis Mercatoria* (1768), *A Treatise on Ship Building* (1775), *On Ships' Sails* (1793), *On Handling Ships* (1794), and *On War Ships* (1804). His published works not only described the designing and building of ships in detail, but introduced for the first time books containing superbly drawn plans shown in perspective with the ships at varying angles of heel. These fine steel engravings were drawn like works of art and set a high standard of marine draughtsmanship. See also CHARNOCK, John.

CHAPPELL, REUBEN (1870–1940), British marine artist, was born at Goole, the son of a master joiner and cabinet maker. At an early age he showed an interest in painting ship portraits and by the time he reached manhood he had established a reputation as a marine painter among the seafaring population of his native town. His patrons were mostly merchant seamen trading in and out of the port and in this he had something in common with the Roux family of Marseilles. He worked mainly in water-colour, only employing oil when his customers could afford the extra cost. His output was prodigious and during his working life he is reputed to have painted some 12,000 marine pictures, mainly ship portraits. These constitute an important record of the change from sail to steam, but it is only recently that their value in this respect has come to be appreciated. In middle life poor health obliged him to move to the Cornish port of Par where he lived until his death.

CHARACTERISTIC, the distinguishing qualities of a navigational light, whether from a *lighthouse, *lightship, or lighted *buoy, by which the navigator of a ship can easily identify it. In addition to their colours, white, red, or green, individual lights can be recognized by whether they are alternating, fixed, flashing, fixed and flashing, or occulting, and by the number or group of exposures in each cycle.

An alternating light is one in which two colours are used, exposed alternately in each cycle of the light and always in the same order. The colours are sometimes separated by periods of darkness, and sometimes alternate continuously. A fixed light shows a steady beam with no period of darkness, and thus has no cycle; a fixed and flashing light is one which shows a steady beam varied at regular intervals with a flash of brighter intensity. A flashing light is one in which the period in which the light is visible is less than the period of darkness between flashes in each cycle; an occulting light one in which the period of darkness is less than the period of light in each cycle.

These five main types are further varied for recognition purposes by what is known as grouping, in which a series of flashes or a series of eclipses (occulting) is separated by intervals of darkness or light. Thus in a group flashing light a series of two or more flashes are visible at regular intervals in each cycle; in a group occulting light there are two or more short intervals of darkness in each cycle. As an example, a light indicated on a chart as a group flashing light with four flashes every 15 seconds (Gp.Fl.(4)15 sec.) would show to the navigator four bright flashes with an interval of a second or so between them followed by a period of darkness occupying the rest of the 15 seconds. The 15 seconds is the period, or cycle, of the light, and is measured from the first flash in one group to the first flash in the next succeeding group.

Another differentiation of characteristics, introduced since the Second World War, is the quick flashing light, which is a modification of the flashing and group flashing systems. This comprises a light which displays rapid flashes at a greater rate than once every second. These quick flashing lights can be divided into three characteristics, quick flashing (Qk.Fl.) in which the flashes are continuous, interrupted quick flashing (Int.Qk.Fl.), in which a number of quick flashes are separated by an interval of darkness, and group interrupted quick flashing (Gp.Int.Qk.Fl.), in which a group of quick flashes, each separated by a short interval of darkness, is itself separated from the succeeding group by a longer interval of darkness.

The characteristics of every light, though not every lighted buoy, are clearly marked on all charts and are also listed, with the exception of lighted buoys and wreck-marking vessels, in the *Admiralty List of Lights*. Details of lighted buoys are listed in the * *Sailing Directions* appropriate to the waters in which they are situated and are also marked on the largest scale chart of each area.

CHARCOT, JEAN-BAPTISTE (1867–1936), French Polar explorer and man of science, made his first voyage to the Antarctic in 1903–5 in the *Français* with the intention of relieving the Swedish expedition under *Nordenskjöld, whose ship had been lost in the Weddell Sea. Finding that Nordenskjöld had already been rescued, Charcot devoted two seasons to exploring the west coast of Graham Land as far south as Alexander Island. In 1909 he again returned to the Antarctic Peninsula region, this time in the * *Pourquoi Pas?*. He explored Marguerite Bay and in January 1910 sighted new land to the south-west of Alexander Island which he named Charcot Land after his father. After the First World War (1914–18) Charcot resumed his work of exploration and research, this time in such places as Greenland and Rockall. He was drowned in September 1936 when the *Pourquoi Pas?* was wrecked off the coast of Iceland.

CHARIOT, the name given to the British type of manned *torpedo introduced during the Second World War. It was the same size as a normal 21-inch torpedo but was fitted with an electric motor capable of driving it at a speed of 2·9 knots for six hours and a ballast tank to adjust its trim. The warhead was detachable and incorporated magnets which could hold it to the hull of a ship under water. Two men in *frogmen's outfits controlled it, riding astride on saddles. They were usually taken to the vicinity of their target on board a *submarine, and after launching they were on their own, relying on being taken prisoners-of-war after the attack.

The originators of the concept were the Italians who used an early version to sink the Austrian dreadnought *Viribus Unitis* in Pola (Pula) harbour at the end of the First World War (1914–18). They revived this form of attack during the Second World War with considerable success, both against shipping off Gibraltar when they operated from a depot ship moored in neutral Spanish waters off Algeciras; and against the

The Charlotte Dundas

British Mediterranean fleet when, using submarine transport, they succeeded in crippling the battleships *Queen Elizabeth* and *Valiant* in Alexandria harbour in December 1941. The Germans also developed two types of manned torpedo called *Neger* and *Marder* which had some minor successes against shipping off the Normandy invasion beaches in 1944.

British successes with chariots during the war included the sinking of the Italian *cruiser *Ulpio Traiano* in Palermo harbour in January 1943.

CHARLES XIII (1748–1818), king of Sweden and Norway, served with great distinction as admiral of the fleet during the Russo-Swedish war of 1788, particularly at the battles of Hogland (17 June 1788) and Öland (26 July 1789), where his personal skill would have secured overwhelming victories had he been better supported by his second-in-command, Admiral Liljehorn.

CHARLEY NOBLE, originally the name of the chimney fitted when the *galley fires were lit to take the smoke above decks. The name was later extended to cover all portable chimneys fitted to the deck, i.e., for coal fires in admirals' and captains' cabins, wardrooms, etc.

CHARLOTTE DUNDAS, the first vessel in the world to use steam propulsion commercially. She was a small wooden ship, with a steam engine designed by William Symington, and built on the River Clyde to the order of Lord Dundas, a governor of the Forth and Clyde canal, the ship being named after his daughter. The engine drove a single paddle-wheel fitted in the stern and she made her first voyage in 1802 when she covered a distance of 20 miles on the canal with two *lighters in tow.

CHARNOCK, JOHN (1756–1807), British naval biographer and naval architect, was born at Barbados, West Indies, and was educated in England at Winchester and Merton College, Oxford. After graduating he entered the navy as a volunteer but returned to civil life after inheriting a considerable fortune, which he quickly lost in a life of dissipation. Thereafter he had to rely on his pen for a living. One of his great interests was naval architecture, which he studied assiduously, and he was among the first to employ models of ships towed in a trough or tank and to record their behaviour and performance in relation to full-sized vessels at sea. He was a contemporary of Frederik H. af *Chapman and, like him, wrote an elaborate book on the subject of naval architecture, *History of Marine Architecture*, beautifully illustrated and published in three large volumes in 1801. Again like Chapman, his studies and written works had considerable influence on contemporary ship design. On the biographical side his most important work was his *Biographia Navalis*, a biographical dictionary of all officers serving in the Royal Navy, but it suffered through many of the subjects being asked to contribute their own short biographies. He also wrote a *Life of Nelson*, published in 1806, not now considered as one of the better biographies of the admiral. The rewards of his writings, however, were unable to keep pace with his debts and he was committed to the King's Bench prison where he died.

CHART, a representation on a plane surface (paper) of an area of a spherical surface (the earth) for use for navigational purposes. In general terms, two types of charts are produced for use navigationally, a straightforward navigational chart, on the *Mercator or equivalent projection, in which *rhumb line courses appear as straight lines, and *gnomonic charts, on which great circle bearings appear as straight lines. In general navigation terms, ships steaming from one place to another across the sea steer rhumb line courses; charts on the gnomonic projection are used when wireless and direction-finding bearings, which travel in great circles, need to be plotted. A modern development, following the wide introduction of radio aids to navigation such as *Decca, *Loran, etc., is the combination of these two charts into one by the superimposition of hyperbolic graticules in colour on the navigational detail of the ordinary chart.

A chart is essentially a map of a sea area, showing on it any coastlines, rocks, etc., within the area covered, the positions of buoys, lighthouses, and other prominent features, the *characteristics of all lights, and depths of water below the *chart datum. A compass rose on every chart shows the direction and annual rate of increase or decrease of *variation. See also CHARTMAKING.

R. A. Skelton, 'Early Atlases', *The Geographical Magazine* (April, 1960); A. H. W. Robinson, *Marine Cartography in Great Britain* (1962); G. S. Ritchie, *The Admiralty Chart* (1967); A. Cortesão, *Junta de Investigacoes do Ultramar* (Lisbon, 1969).

CHART DATUM, the level below which depths indicated on a chart are measured and above which heights of the *tide are expressed in *tide tables. The level is essentially one below which the sea surface seldom falls. It is normally the mean level of low water at ordinary *spring tide (M.L.W.O.S.). The datum used is usually expressed on the chart, always if a different datum from M.L.W.O.S. is used.

CHARTER, the contract for the employment of a merchant ship. Charters are of two main types, a time charter, in which the owners of the ship provide the crew and all other requirements for operating the ship; and bare hull, or bare pole,

charter, in which the charterer provides the crew and all other requirements. In addition to the mercantile aspect, yachts are frequently chartered for short periods for holiday purposes, with or without a crew. See also FREIGHT.

CHARTER PARTY, the written deed or contract for the hiring for *freight of the whole or part of a merchant vessel either for specific voyages or on a time basis.

CHARTMAKING. Homer, who probably lived between 950 and 750 B.C., may not himself have conceived the idea of the known world as a disc surrounded by a mighty flowing river, but he certainly developed this theme in his poems, naming the river Okeanus. The earliest known map, moulded in clay, now in the British Museum and dated as 7th or 6th century B.C., shows this concept with Babylon at the centre of the disc.

The early Greek world maps followed this idea but with Delphi at the centre. By the 3rd century B.C. it seemed to mapmakers that the known world was longer in the east–west than in the north–south direction, and Dicaerchus's map shows an oblong representation of the Mediterranean and the Middle East based on a simple diaphragm of two lines, north–south and east–west, with Rhodes, the maritime centre of the world, at the point of intersection.

Pythagoras (*c.* 580 B.C.) had first realized that the earth was spherical, but his ideas were long in being accepted; even today there is a society for those who believe in a flat earth. A Greek from Cyrene in Libya, *Eratosthenes, keeper of the great library then maintained in Alexandria, accepted Pythagoras's spherical earth concept and set out in *c.* 200 B.C. to measure the circumference of the earth by a simple but elegant method. He worked out the north/south distance from Aswan to Alexandria by using the cadastral surveys which were already available of the fertile lands of the Nile valley and found this to be approximately 5,000 stadia. Aswan lies in the Tropic of Cancer and here no shadow was thrown by a gnomon set up at the time of summer solstice, while the length of a shadow thrown by a similar gnomon at Alexandria on the same day enabled Eratosthenes to work out that an angle of 7° 12' at the earth's centre subtended the arc on the earth's surface of 5,000 stadia. The total circumference of the earth derived from this method differs by only about four per cent from modern measurements.

Eratosthenes then constructed a map of the known world following on the lines of that of Dicaerchus with a grid of parallels and meridians based on Rhodes, but both these were unequally spaced in order to pass through known places of importance, such as the Pillars of Hercules at the

Sardinia and Sicily; map from Ptolemy's Geography *by Mercator, 1584*

western end of the Mediterranean and Meroe, the furthest known southern point in Ethiopia.

The first man to draw charts for seamen was probably *Marinus of Tyre in the 1st century A.D., who followed Eratosthenes's lead in providing meridians and parallels. His were equally spaced, although still based on the primary meridian and parallel of Rhodes.

Following closely on Marinus in the long story of maps and charts comes perhaps the greatest cartographer of all, *Ptolemy. He was born in Alexandria and became both mathematician and astronomer. He was the first man to devise a projection whereby a portion of the surface of the spherical earth could be depicted on a plane surface. His first conical projection, covering the known world in 180° from west to east, had meridians every 10° converging on the pole, the point of contact of the cone providing a curved parallel through Rhodes centred on the pole, while two similar parallels passed through Meroe and Thule, the furthest known southerly and northerly places respectively.

Ptolemy developed a second projection giving curvature to all meridians except the centre one while the parallels also remained curved. On this projection he drew a world map showing the Mediterranean with some accuracy, and England, Scotland, and Thule in the north. Africa appears as a vast continent stretching across the south of the Indian Ocean and continuing northward to join Asia.

The Romans had little interest in world maps, confining their cartography to the making of route maps covering the great highways which they built across their empire, and Ptolemy's projections and maps were forgotten for a thousand years.

Renaissance chartmaking. The *windrose and the *magnetic compass were known to the 13th century Mediterranean seaman, added to which he carried a *portolano, or manuscript pilot book, giving him seamanlike guidance along the coasts. At the end of the 13th century what is now called the *portulan chart appeared; sometimes they are known as 'compass charts' because magnetic compass roses, together with *rhumb lines of direction extended from them, were set down at frequent intervals over the parchment area. The rhumb lines were used by the cartographer to measure bearings when laying down the coastline, and by the navigator for setting his course by pricking off from a rhumb line with dividers and a straight edge.

The first portulan charts were drawn by cartographers of Venice and Genoa, the prominence of these two states in marine trading providing the commercial demand which has motivated chartmakers throughout history. Little hinterland detail is shown on the portulan chart, the land area being available for the insertion of numerous names, the flags and banners of the coastal states, and sketches of the main cities and ports.

From now on the ever-changing and improving skills of the chartmakers moved on from one country to another as each in turn required good charts to support its ascendancy in marine trading and overseas exploration. The kingdom of Aragon, which included the ports of Palma, Barcelona, and Valentia, as well as those in Sicily, had become an important maritime state by the early part of the 14th century and the Catalan portulan charts drawn by cartographers in Palma had a distinct Catalan style including scales of 'Portulan miles' which approximate to the length of a Catalan league of 6,000 metres.

During the course of the 15th century Portugal began to take the ascendancy in chartmaking largely spurred on by Prince * Henry the Navigator, the third son of John I of Portugal and his English queen Philippa. From 1415, after taking a distinguished part in the capture of Ceuta from the Moors, Prince Henry devoted the rest of his life until 1460 to preparing for the great explorations of the west coast of Africa and India, for which both navigating instruments and ocean charts were needed if the new discoveries were to be assigned to their correct position on the globe. Among those whom Henry brought to Sagres to pass on his skills as a chartmaker was Jafuda * Cresques, a leader of the Catalan school in Palma.

By the end of the 15th century Vasco da * Gama had discovered India for Portugal (1498) and * Columbus had discovered the West Indies for Spain (1492). The impetus that these and associated explorations had given to chartmaking in these two countries was great, and although few of their charts from before 1500 exist today a great number of beautiful Spanish and Portuguese portulan charts compiled in the early 16th century still survive.

Around 1500 both Portugal and Spain established offices for controlling trade and exploration, the Casa da India in Lisbon and the Casa de Contrataçion in Seville respectively, where up-to-date charts were kept and ocean pilots examined. In 1530 the King of Portugal appointed Pedro * Nuñes, a skilled cosmographer, as his Hidrofmor (chief hydrographer) in the Casa da India, and it was to him that Portuguese navigators turned for a solution to the problem they found when trying to plot ocean courses on a plane portulan chart. Nuñes realized, and published the fact, that meridians in reality converge towards the poles and that a course which crosses the meridians at a constant angle is in fact a spiral rhumb line leading to the pole.

In 1400 the works of Ptolemy, including his projections, had been discovered in Constantinople, brought to Florence, and translated from classical Greek into Latin. Many learned men came to Italy during the ensuing century to make translations of Ptolemy's works for their own

countries so that during the 16th century many cartographers in Europe were aware of the Ptolemy world map and were trying to fit into it the new discoveries; the development of printing and engraving made increasingly possible the wide publication of such maps.

Northern chartmakers. Meanwhile the focus of map and chartmaking had moved to the Netherlands where, in 1570, Abraham * Ortelius published in Antwerp his atlas *Theatrum Orbis Terrarum* which, among others, contained a significant world map. Using the prime meridian through the Canary Islands, the world is drawn in a projection developed directly from that of Ptolemy, but showing the full 180° both to the west and to the east of the prime meridian. All the new discoveries are shown, giving a good picture of the land masses of the world in general but with a vast continent encircling the southern portion of the world and named 'Australis Nondum Cognita', a vestige of Ptolemy's concept; it was to elude explorers for another two hundred years until James * Cook disproved its existence.

The previous year Gerardus * Mercator, working in Duisburg and described by Ortelius as the 'greatest geographer since Ptolemy', had published his world map in eighteen sheets which, although little noticed by seamen at the time, was to solve their problem of steering ocean courses which Nuñes had described forty years earlier.

Mercator's map used a rectangular latitude and longitude grid system with a proportional misplacement introduced into the spacing between the parallels of latitude on the chart as they move away from the equator, enabling rhumb lines cutting each meridian at the same angle to become straight lines. However, it was not until the end of the sixteenth century that an Englishman, Edward * Wright, made clear to the seaman the benefits to be gained by adopting Mercator's method. He described it in his book *Certaine Errors of Navigation* with the aid of a diagram of great clarity.

The northern navigators had never felt the need of a chart, relying upon courses between one cape and another handed down to them by their fathers, and on the use of the lead and line to warn them of dangers. However Lucas Janszoon * Wagenaer, a Dutch seaman, impressed by Ortelius's maps and having seen the portulan charts carried by Portuguese traders on their voyages to Flanders for wool, decided to publish an atlas of sea charts or *paskaerten*, as opposed to the *leeskaerten* (sailing directions) already in use by the Netherlanders. Wagenaer's sea atlas *Spieghel der Zeevaerdt* which was published in two parts in 1584–5 covered navigation from the Baltic to Cadiz.

Western Europe; map from Ashley's translation of Wagenaer's The Mariner's
Mirrour, *1588*

Wagenaer's charts still owed much to the portulan chart, but began to take on a more seamanlike look with soundings reduced to a mean level
datum shown in anchorages and over harbour
bars, and with sketches to assist recognition of
the coast. Standard symbols were introduced to
show safe anchorages, buoys, and submerged
rocks, and have survived on charts to the present
day. However, even on the small scale chart
covering the whole area from North Cape to the
Canaries, no use was made of Mercator's projection.

An English edition of the atlas, *The Mariner's
Mirrour*, made its appearance in London in
1588; its success with British seamen was immediate and long lasting, so that similar collections of charts were called *Waggoners by
sailors for a century or more to come.

It was clear that the Dutch knew more about
the English coasts than British seamen did themselves, and, after nearly 100 years of reliance on
the charts of Wagenaer and his successor *Blaeu,
Samuel *Pepys, Secretary of the Admiralty,
issued an Admiralty Order in 1681 assigning a
naval officer, Captain Greenvile *Collins, to the
task of surveying the British coasts and har-

bours. This was an enormous labour as there was
no national triangulation network at that time on
which to base the surveys, and Collins worked
with only a measuring chain, a compass, and a
*lead line for seven years until the work was
complete. In 1693 his *Great Britain's Coasting
Pilot* was published containing forty-eight harbour and coastal charts.

Collins's charts were still plane charts showing no cognizance of Mercator's work. The
charts were clear-cut and concise; added to the
soundings and other nautical information in the
style of the Dutch charts were excellent views to
illustrate leading and clearing lines by which
vessels could safely enter harbour. Widely used
by British seamen, and running into twelve
editions in the 18th century, *Great Britain's
Coasting Pilot* was nevertheless adversely
criticized in official circles on first publication
and compared unfavourably with *Le Neptune
françois* published by order of Louis XIV of
France in the same year.

Aided by his sea-minded Secretary of State
*Colbert, Louis had been fostering a scientific
revolution in the latter part of the 17th century
during which the Observatoire de Paris had been

established to bring about a better understanding of the celestial sphere. Here a method of finding longitude by the observation of Jupiter's satellites was devised, and, once the position of the observatory had been fixed in latitude and longitude, a triangulated survey of the whole of France was made, relating stations along the whole coastline to the prime meridian of Paris.

The charts in *Le Neptune françois* based as they were on this triangulated survey and also employing the Mercator projection for the smaller scales, were beautifully engraved. They showed a distinct advance over both the Netherlands and British charts and gave France a clear lead in chartmaking for seamen.

The Depôt des Cartes et Plans de la Marine was established in 1720 and through this office during the 18th century further editions of *Le Neptune* were published, culminating in 1764 with the official publication of *Le Petit Atlas maritime* under the direction of J. N. *Bellin; beautiful, clear-cut marine charts covering the greater part of the navigable world made up this cartographic masterpiece.

But longitude could still not be simply measured at sea, and thus newly discovered lands were plotted on the charts with little east/west positional accuracy. John *Harrison solved this final problem when, after many years and four attempts, he provided an elegant timepiece having no need of a pendulum and capable of carrying time across the sea from *Greenwich, the position of which had been established by workers at the Royal Observatory founded by Charles II. Captain Cook carried an early copy of Harrison's No. 4 chronometer, Kendall's No. 1, on his second Pacific voyage in 1772 and Cook (who better?) testified to its excellence in carrying time, hence longitude, at sea.

The use of a measured baseline from which a shore triangulation of fixed stations could be extended had reached Britain from the continent by the middle of the 18th century and was used by Murdoch *Mackenzie senior for his coastal surveys of the Orkneys, the west coasts of Scotland and Wales, and of Ireland, which he carried out for the British Admiralty. In retirement, and when his nephew of the same name had taken over the coastal surveys, he devised an instrument, subsequently named the *station pointer, for plotting the position of a ship or boat with reference to three triangulated points onshore, the two angles between them having been observed simultaneously by two men on board. In those days these angles were taken with the Hadley *quadrant used horizontally; subsequently displaced by the *sextant, this method of station pointer fixing has lasted into the present day and accounts for the rapidly increasing number of soundings appearing on sea surveys throughout the 19th century.

Contemporaneously with the work of the Murdoch Mackenzies, *Des Barres and others working in support of the British Army in North America were making detailed coastal surveys of the east coast which resulted in the publication by the British Admiralty of the atlas *Atlantic Neptune. Beautifully engraved, using an increasing number of symbols, and having extensive sounding coverage, this magnificent collection of charts recaptured from the French in the 1770s the ascendancy they had held since the beginning of the century. This atlas served as the primary source for most North American charts for fifty years after the birth of the U.S.A. in 1783.

By 1800, virtually the whole of the inhabited world appeared on charts and world maps. Cook had disproved finally the supposed existence of the great southern continent, first drawn in by Ptolemy about 1,500 years earlier, and had put New Zealand on the map; *Flinders had laid down the coasts of Australia; and *Vancouver and Broughton had delineated both shores of the North Pacific. Theirs were coastal running surveys; largely laid down from shipboard observations; the 19th century was devoted to detailed charting of bays and anchorages, passages, and approaches along every distant coastline and in this work the surveying service of the Royal Navy was to take a giant's share.

Admiralty surveys. The first chart produced by the British Admiralty from its own surveys was published in 1801. The need which inspired other maritime nations to set up national agencies for producing navigational charts and the way in which the needs of mariners were previously met appears under the entry for HYDROGRAPHY.

There have always been three steps before publication of a chart: a drawing based on a surveyor's work or a foreign chart; its engraving or inscription on copper or lithographic stone, and latterly other media; and printing. Following publication there are the arrangements for issues and sales to the maritime public and the need to promulgate corrections for later information. Similar steps are necessary for ancillary publications, such as *Sailing Directions, to convert original information into a suitable form to amplify but never conflict with the primary chart.

The chart is the navigator's working document, so the objective must be clarity, and there has been continuing development in the avoidance of encumbering the chart with detail that is not essential to its navigational purpose. In recent times increasing consultation has been made in this regard with chart users. Thus in 1961 an advisory panel, including representatives of forty-five major shipping companies, was set up. But from its beginning the organiza-

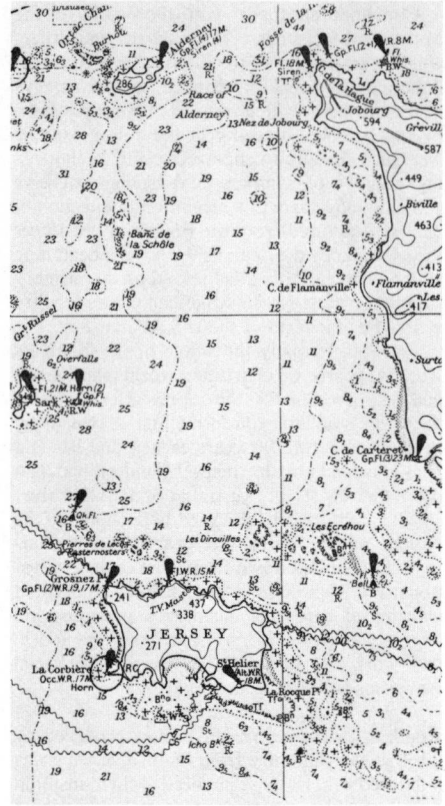

Portion of Admiralty chart, published 1955

tion of the British Admiralty's Hydrographic Department, and others, has taken care of this important aspect by choosing hydrographers from experienced seamen-surveyors and their naval assistants either from the same branch or from the ranks of navigating officers.

Alexander *Dalrymple, the first British Hydrographer of the Navy appointed in 1795, was one such and he established the association between those experienced in navigation and the civilians who made the chart drawings from the surveyor's originals. Dalrymple was perhaps over-meticulous in what he accepted as fit for publication but by him were set the high standards of integrity and accuracy for which British Admiralty charts are esteemed to this day.

Meanwhile some devolution of the Hydrographer's responsibility for the detailed work of the Chart Branch of the Hydrographer's department at the Admiralty saw the appointment of the first naval superintendent in 1862. Since then the post has been filled by senior naval surveying officers between appointments afloat, thus bringing up-to-date sea experience to the office. The

'life-blood' of the Admiralty Chart Branch is its store of original documents, numerous enough even in Dalrymple's day to make indexing a problem. These departmental records are incomparable and priceless, containing as they do original surveys mainly of British origin dating back to Captain James *Cook and old copies of Admiralty charts as well as latest copies of foreign charts.

From the old copies may be seen the various developments of the cartographic art and the continuous changes that have been made in the waterwork, in the representation of land features, in abbreviations, graduations, scales, compass roses, and so on, some of which, since the formation of the International Hydrographic Bureau in 1921, have been to conform with international standards.

For a short period in the early 19th century, when surveys were largely exploratory, surveyors were encouraged to send in drawings of their work fit for direct engraving, but soon it became ever more necessary not to circumscribe the surveyor and to make the office responsible for converting his detailed work into the navigator's needs, including the choice of scale for publication. Scale is subject to the dimensions of the projected chart and there has always been pressure for a standard size of chart which would be practical in use, convenient for chart tables and folio covers, and simplify the printing from, and the handling of, chart plates. A size of 38 × 25 in. (965 × 635 mm), known in the paper trade as double elephant, has been the most used, halved for smaller charts.

A chart was formerly judged for accuracy by the number and spacing of the soundings shown upon it, but a modern chart relies increasingly on depth contours or fathom lines with fewer supporting depths and makes more use of colours for depth differentiation. Fathom lines, too, have been simplified to speed reproduction stages.

The representation of land features has shown its greatest change in the hill-work which has gone through stages of hachuring, perhaps accompanied by 'smoke shading', to the present use of contours as on a land map. One reason has been the introduction of radar, and another simplicity in reproduction.

Since 1939 the development of radio navigational aids has called for a new family of charts in which hyperbolic graticules are superimposed in colour on the navigational detail for the users of *Loran, *Decca, and the like. Among other problems they have involved are the adaptation of reproduction processes in order to ensure the accurate registration of the various printing plates. And now, as shown in his annual report for 1967, the British Hydrographer of the Navy, the greatest producer of navigational charts in the world, has accepted the need for metrification. Depths originally shown in fathoms will gradually be replaced by metres.

Of the many British Admiralty committees set up from time to time to consider departmental organization, three were particularly important for chart work. The first was asked for by Dalrymple in 1807 to advise him on the use of material of which he had no personal knowledge. The second sat in 1905 to recommend special measures to avoid arrears in chart work owing to the increase of incoming foreign information; and the third sat in 1912 when it was realized that Admiralty charts had always been published on an *ad hoc* basis so that there was much unnecessary duplication and maintenance work. Integrated chart scheming was accordingly put in hand and from a peak figure of 3,650 the number of Admiralty navigational charts of the world fell gradually to around 3,500, its present number, although a reduction will undoubtedly be made as further duplication is gradually eliminated.

The promulgation of new information to keep charts up to date was begun in the *Nautical Magazine* in 1832. Two years later began the issue of *Notices to Mariners* for urgent items and today there are some 3,000 notices per annum which must be entered on existing charts to take account of changes and new coastline developments, etc. In 1907, to facilitate manuscript corrections afloat and in shore depots, paste-on reproductions of affected portions of a chart known as 'block notices' were issued, the Japanese being credited with their first use in 1904. There have been various schemes to lessen the load of manuscript corrections in chart depots and since the adoption of printing machines which are economical for short runs even with several colour plates the depots can carry smaller stocks with the consequent reduction in the labour of making corrections. For the basic chart plate copper had such advantages in longevity, safe preservation, and correctional facility that it is only now being replaced by plastic. The first chart based on an enamelled zinc appeared in 1942.

CHARYBDIS, see SCYLLA AND CHARYBDIS.

CHASE, when used as a noun, (1) the name given to a vessel being chased. (2) The names of the guns mounted on the upper deck in the bows and on the *poop deck astern of a sailing man-of-war and fixed to fire directly ahead or astern. They were known as the bow chase, to fire at a vessel being chased, and the stern chase, to fire at a vessel chasing. But see also CHASE GUNS.

CHASE, to, to pursue a vessel in wartime with a view to her destruction or capture, or to acquire information from her.

CHASE GUNS, guns which were temporarily moved from the normal *broadside gun tiers of a sailing man-of-war for use through chase ports cut on the gundeck level in the bows of a ship, i.e., they were not permanently mounted to fire ahead, as were the bow *chases, and were fired from the gundeck level and not from the upper deck.

CHASSE-MARÉE, the French name for a coasting vessel, one which works the tides. In the 16th century the typical French and other coasters were three-masted, normally rigged with square main and foresails, a *lateen mizen, a main topsail, and a *spritsail carried below the *bowsprit. During the 18th century many coasters adopted the *lug rig, based on a design of fishing vessel, and during the Revolutionary and Napoleonic wars (1793–1815) these *luggers, still known as chasse-marées, were used by the French largely for smuggling and privateering, the rig being refined to the highest possible pitch to provide a good turn of speed. This was achieved by adopting a large sail plan on three masts, all three raked aft, the mizen being stepped hard up against the vessel's *transom. A long bowsprit and *bumpkin enabled a greater area of canvas to be spread. All three masts carried a standing lugsail, with a jib to complete the rig, thus producing a very weatherly vessel. Some of the larger chasse-marées could also set a lug topsail on the mainmast. The need for the long bumpkin was to sheet the overhanging mizen. One drawback of the chasse-marée in her role as a privateer was the comparatively large crew required to handle the considerable area of sail and also provide gun crews; another was that when running before the wind they could be overtaken relatively easily by a ship with normal square rig.

CHATEAU-RENAULT, FRANÇOIS LOUIS DE ROUSSELET, Marquis de (1637–1716), French admiral, joined the army in 1658 but was transferred to the navy three years later. He was promoted to the rank of captain after the phenomenally short service of only five years in junior ranks. He was commanding at Brest at the outbreak of war with England in 1688 and was in charge of the *troopships which were carrying support to James II in Ireland. He commanded a squadron of the fleet led by the Comte de *Tourville at the indecisive battle of *Beachy Head in 1690, and on Tourville's death in 1701 he succeeded him as vice admiral of France.

In 1702 he was given the delicate task of convoying across the Atlantic the Spanish treasure fleet from America. Secret French instructions were for him to try to bring the Spanish *galleons into a French port, a difficult task in view of the fact that some Spanish officers were serving in his ships. Added difficulties were caused by reports of a strong Anglo-Dutch fleet cruising off the coast of Spain. Chateau-Renault managed to bring the treasure fleet safely into Vigo harbour, which he then fortified against attack. On 22 October 1702 Sir George * Rooke, commanding the Anglo-Dutch fleet, attacked Vigo, breaking the *boom which Chateau-Renault had erected across the harbour mouth, capturing or destroying every ship in the harbour, and sailing away with a vast amount of treasure. Chateau-Renault was not again employed at sea, although he was not blamed for the disaster at Vigo. He was made a marshal of France in 1703.

CHATFIELD, ALFRED ERNLE MONTACUTE, 1st Baron (1873–1967), British admiral of the fleet, was a gunnery specialist. He reached the rank of captain in 1909 and was flag captain to Vice Admiral Sir David * Beatty in the battle-cruiser * Lion during the first two years of the First World War (1914–18).

He commanded this famous ship during the actions of the * Heligoland Bight and the * Dogger Bank and also at the battle of * Jutland on 31 May 1916. He remained as flag captain when Beatty was appointed commander-in-chief of the * Grand Fleet and finished the war in command of H.M.S. * Queen Elizabeth. In 1919, when Beatty became First Sea Lord, Chatfield went with him to the Admiralty as Fourth Sea Lord and in 1920, on promotion to rear admiral, as Assistant Chief of the Naval Staff, in which appointment he was one of the British representatives at the Washington Naval Conference of 1922. From 1929 to 1932 he was commander-in-chief first of the Home Fleet and then of the Mediterranean Fleet, and in January 1933 returned to the Admiralty as First Sea Lord. He held this position until 1938, the years during which the growing threat of German naval rearmament under Hitler made it necessary to rebuild and modernize the British fleet. Being a gunnery specialist he concentrated much of the naval rebuilding on the construction of new battleships, a course of action which brought him a good deal of criticism from many of the younger naval officers who considered that the money available would be better spent on * flotilla craft and * submarines. The experience of the Second World War proved the younger officers to be largely correct in their view, the employment of battleships being limited by the newer weapons of the torpedo and seaborne air power.

His term of office as First Sea Lord ended in 1938 and a few months later he was appointed Minister for the Co-ordination of Defence with, after the outbreak of the Second World War, a seat in the War Cabinet. This venture into the political affairs of the nation was not a success, partly because of the strong views he held on the political administration of national defence and partly due to an inability to appreciate views and opinions contrary to his own. His ministerial office was abolished in 1940.

Chatfield was an aloof personality, austere in his habits and sometimes difficult to approach. He held his views on the big naval gun as being the supreme weapon at sea to the bitter end, even in the face of all the evidence of the Second World War which proved the supremacy at sea of the torpedo and the aeroplane. Yet he was greatly admired throughout the navy as a man of strict integrity and honour, with a strong sense of justice in all his dealings. He wrote two autobiographical books in which his strong opinions were forcibly expressed, *The Navy and Defence* (1942) and *It Might Happen Again* (1947).

CHATHAM, a port in Kent, England, on the banks of the River Medway, and for centuries a principal base of the British Navy. It is also one of the three royal dockyards of England. In the survey conducted for the Domesday Book, Chatham was recorded as in the possession of Odo, Bishop of Bayeux. It came into existence as a naval base during the reign of Henry VIII (1509–47) when he established the navy on a permanent footing and began building a dockyard there. The dockyard was much enlarged by Elizabeth I, and altered and improved by Charles II.

Many famous naval names are associated with Chatham, among the more notable being Sir John * Hawkins and Sir Francis * Drake, who built almshouses there for 'decayed seamen and shipwrights' and founded the naval charity known as the * Chatham Chest, and the Dutch admiral de * Ruyter, who led a Dutch fleet into the Medway in 1667 and destroyed many naval ships lying there. Until recently it was one of the three manning ports of the navy, * Portsmouth and * Devonport being the others. It has one of the best-equipped and most modern of the naval dockyards in England, and until the command was abolished in 1966 was the headquarters of the commander-in-chief, * Nore.

CHATHAM CHEST, THE, was a contributory benevolent fund for the English Navy established by Sir Francis * Drake, Sir John * Hawkins, and Lord * Howard of Effingham in 1590, to which seamen paid sixpence a month from their pay for the benefit of the wounded and the widows of those killed in action. To avoid peculation, the original Chatham Chest (which is preserved in the * National Maritime Museum at Greenwich, London) was fitted with seven locks, the seven keys to which were held by different individuals so that all had to be present when the chest was opened. In spite of this precaution, large sums were regularly illegally abstracted from the chest. The funds of the Chatham Chest were amalgamated with those of * Greenwich Royal Hospital in 1814.

CHATTERTON, EDWARD KEBLE (1878–1944), British naval officer and marine author, was born at Sheffield and educated at Oxford. He began working as an assistant dramatic critic, but is best remembered for his many books on ships and the sea. During the First World War (1914–18) he served as a lieutenant-commander in the R.N.V.R. He was a prolific writer and among his best-known works are *Sailing Ships* (1909), *Steamships and their Story* (1910), *Old East Indiamen* (1914), *Q-Ships and their Story* (1922), *Seamen All* (1924), *On the High Seas* (1929), and *The Commerce Raiders* (1943).

CHAZELLES, JEAN MATHIEU DE (1657–1710), French hydrographer, was appointed professor of hydrography at Marseilles in 1685 and was responsible for many coastal surveys in the Mediterranean. In 1693 he was commissioned to produce a second volume of the famous maritime atlas *Le Neptune françois*, to be devoted to the Mediterranean, and conducted a number of excellent surveys to this purpose.

CHEARLY, an old sea expression meaning heartily or quickly. 'Row chearly in the boats', row heartily.

CHECK, to, (1) the operation of easing away slowly, particularly in connection with a * purchase such as the * falls of a * lifeboat or the * sheets or sails, **(2)** the operation of bringing a vessel to a stop, by letting go an * anchor, by a mooring wire made fast to a wharf, or by going astern on the engines.

CHEEKS, (1) pieces of timber bolted to the mast of a sailing ship below the masthead to support the * trestle-trees, **(2)** the two sidepieces of the wooden gun-carriages in sailing warships, **(3)** the two sides of a * block, **(4)** the rounded portions of the bows of the old wooden men-of-war when they were extended by the erection of the * forecastle above the * beakhead, a feature of warship design introduced in the 15th century.

CHEESE DOWN, to, a method of coiling down the tail of a rope on deck to present a neat appearance. The end of the tail is in the centre and the remainder coiled flat round it in a tight spiral, each * fake touching those on either side of it so that the finished coil looks like a spiral rope mat laying on the deck. When a fall has been cheesed down, the final result is itself called a cheese. The end of a rope should never be cheesed down if it is required to * render quickly through a * block, as the tight coiling which forms a cheese is apt to make the rope kink when uncoiled quickly and thus to jam in the block.

CHERBOURG, a French naval base and commercial port on the southern shore of the English Channel at the tip of the Cotentin peninsula.

Although some doubts have been expressed, the site of the port is believed to have been the Roman station Coriallum, the present name deriving from Caesaris Burgus (Caesar's borough). Certainly when Duke William of Normandy, later William the Conqueror, built a church and hospital there during the 11th century, its name was Carusbur. Cherbourg was pillaged by an English fleet in 1295, suffered heavily in the many Anglo-French wars of the 14th century, and in 1418 was besieged by English forces, eventually surrendering after being cut off from all outside aid or relief for four months. It was recaptured for France by Charles VII in 1450, but was again extensively damaged by the British in an assault attack in 1758 during the Seven Years War (1756–63).

The naval harbour, which is distinct from the commercial, has an extensive dockyard and naval shipbuilding yards at which the largest warships can be constructed. It is also the site of a naval school, and is well protected by extensive fortifications planned in 1686 by the famous engineer Vauban but not completed until 1858. The commercial harbour is a port of call for many of the transatlantic passenger steamship lines and is a ferry port for cross-Channel car and train ferries. After the German occupation in 1940 it was recaptured by the allies on 26 June 1944.

CHESAPEAKE, U.S.S., was one of the * 'six original frigates' authorized in 1794 to form the U.S. Navy. She was intended to be a 44-gun ship but her completion was delayed as a consequence of a peace with Algeria and she was actually built as a 36-gun * frigate. She figured in the 'Chesapeake Incident' in 1807 when commanded by James * Barron, and she was under the command of James * Lawrence when he unwisely departed from good strategy and went out from Boston on 1 June 1813 to fight the British frigate * Shannon, lying offshore, as a result of a challenge to come out and do battle. Lawrence was killed and the *Chesapeake*, short of officers and with an untrained crew, was surrendered to Captain * Broke of the *Shannon* after an action that lasted only 15 minutes, one of the best-known frigate actions in naval history. She was taken to Halifax after her capture and later to Britain.

CHESAPEAKE BAY, a very large inlet on the east coast of North America, was the scene of two actions fought in 1781, during the War of

American Independence (1775–82), between the fleets of Britain and France. Both encounters took place in the Chesapeake Bay area and were closely connected with the attempt to prevent French aid from reaching the American land forces.

The first action was fought on 16 March, about 40 miles north-east of Cape Henry, when Vice Admiral Marriot *Arbuthnot with eight *ships of the line engaged an equal number of French ships under Commodore des Touches. The weather was hazy and squally, and it was not until 2 p.m. that the leading British ship opened fire; the van and centre got into action half an hour later, and at 3 p.m. the French line broke and stood out away from the land. Arbuthnot followed, but his two headmost ships, which had borne the brunt of the action, were disabled aloft; others also had damaged spars, and at 4.30 p.m. the enemy was lost in the thick haze. At 7 p.m. the British brought-to, anchoring later in Lynn Haven Roads and thus regaining command of the Chesapeake Bay area.

The second action was fought on 5 September, about 12 miles east of Cape Henry. Yorktown, which was held by the British Army under the Earl of Cornwallis, was being closely invested by American and French land forces and was gradually being reduced by starvation. Aid to both sides, however, was on the way. At anchor just inside the entrance to Chesapeake Bay was Vice Admiral the Comte de *Grasse with twenty-four ships of the line, and that morning there appeared on the scene Rear Admiral Thomas *Graves with nineteen sail of the line, who was bringing supplies to the British Army at Yorktown.

The French ships weighed anchor at 12.30 p.m. and came out as soon as the tide served; but nearly four hours elapsed before the British van and centre opened fire and their rear never got into action at all. This was owing to the faulty tactics adopted by Graves who approached at an angle, thus repeating Admiral John *Byng's tactical blunder off Minorca in 1756. The result was indecisive and all firing ceased at 6.30 p.m.

Although the two fleets remained in sight of each other for the next four days the French, who were in superior force, showed no inclination to re-engage. De Grasse's primary objective had been to reinforce the American besieging army, and on the 11th he re-entered Chesapeake Bay, thus preventing Graves from effecting the succour of Cornwallis.

Most of the British van ships had been more or less crippled and several were in want of bread and of water. A Council of War, held on board the *London* on the 13th, therefore resolved that the only possible course of action was to return to New York to refit, which left Cornwallis no option but to surrender on 18 September.

CHESSTREES, two pieces of oak secured to the *topsides of a square-rigged sailing ship at the point where the curve of the bow began to straighten out for the run aft, one on each side of the ship. Normally they had a hole through them in the centre, but occasionally they were fitted with a sheave. The *bowlines with which the main *tacks were hauled down were led through the hole or the sheave in the chesstrees to give the crew a clear haul. See also VEER AND HAUL. In the older warships and *East Indiamen, the chesstrees provided an opportunity for some highly decorative carving, in the form usually of a sun in splendour or a human or animal face, with the bowline being led through the mouth.

CHICHESTER, Sir FRANCIS CHARLES (1901–72), British deep sea yachtsman, was born in North Devon. He was intended for the Indian Civil Service but left school and at the age of 19 worked his passage to New Zealand with only £10 in his pocket. He held various jobs and speculated successfully, and by the age of 26 was making a large income in forestry and real estate dealings. In 1929 he returned to England, took flying lessons, bought a Gipsy Moth light aeroplane, and in December of that year flew the aircraft solo to Australia, the second man to achieve this flight.

His many flights made him an expert on air navigation and on the outbreak of the Second World War in 1939 he returned again to England to join the Royal Air Force, but was chagrined to be turned down as too old at 37. He was, however, able to produce numerous textbooks and introduce new techniques in astro-navigation for use in R.A.F. fighters and bombers throughout the war.

After the war he started his own business in London as a map publisher. Turning to sailing as a recreation, he bought *Gipsy Moth II*, a 17-year-old 34-ft (10·5 m) *sloop, in 1955 and won sixteen Royal Ocean Racing Club races during 1956 and 1957. In 1959 he became ill from diagnosed lung cancer, but with encouragement from his wife and great personal determination, made a good recovery. With a new yacht, *Gipsy Moth III*, a 39-ft (12 m) sloop, he won the first single-handed transatlantic race in 1960 in a time of just over 40 days. He crossed the Atlantic again alone in 1962, setting a record of 33 days 15 hours, and returned to Plymouth from Cape Cod in just under 27 days. In the next transatlantic race in 1964 he finished second to Eric *Tabarly, who was sailing a longer and faster yacht, in a time of 29 days.

Chichester was now determined to carry out a plan he had long been nursing, to equal or beat single-handed the average passage time of the old *clipper ships which sailed fully manned on the England to Australia passage. With a new yacht,

Gipsy Moth IV

Gipsy Moth IV, a 53-ft (16·3 m) *ketch, he sailed single-handed in 1966 from Plymouth nonstop to Sydney in 107 days, celebrating his 65th birthday during the voyage. From Sydney he went on to complete the circumnavigation back to Plymouth in an astonishing overall time of 274 days, of which 48 had been spent at Sydney. Sailing his yacht up the Thames to Greenwich, he was knighted by the Queen who used the same sword with which Elizabeth I had knighted Sir Francis *Drake aboard his ship *Golden Hind at Deptford in 1581. *Gipsy Moth IV* has been preserved at Greenwich close to the clipper ship *Cutty Sark*.

In 1969 Sir Francis had another yacht built, *Gipsy Moth V*, a 57-ft (17·5 m) ketch, and the following January he set himself a new challenge, an attempt to put up a single-handed record under sail of 4,000 miles in 20 days, and failed by a small margin of just over a day. After another serious illness and against medical advice he started in the 1972 single-handed transatlantic race, but was forced to return through ill health, and died in hospital in Plymouth later in the year.

Among many awards for his exploits at sea, he received the Blue Water medal of the Cruising Club of America in 1960 and 1967, the Institute of Navigation gold medal in 1961, the Yacht Club de France centenary award, and the Royal Geographical Society's gold medal. He was the author of *Seaplane Solo* (1933), *Alone over the Tasman Sea*, *Alone across the Atlantic*, *Along the Clipper Way*, *Atlantic Adventure*, '*Gipsy Moth' Circles the World*, and *The Lonely Sea and the Sky*.

CHILDERS, ROBERT ERSKINE (1870–1922), Irish author and politician, was born in London and educated at Trinity College, Cambridge, where he studied law. He was clerk to the House of Commons from 1895 to 1910 except while serving in the South African war in 1899. His chief hobby was sailing and he spent his holidays cruising in the North Sea and the Baltic in a 7-ton converted lifeboat named *Vixen*. As a result of these experiences he wrote *The Riddle of the Sands*, a novel the theme of which was German preparations for an invasion of

England in the event of war. Published in 1903 at a time when the air was full of rumours of the possibility of a German invasion, the book achieved immense popularity and quickly became a classic of the sea. On the outbreak of war in 1914 his knowledge of the German coast proved of great value and he was commissioned as a lieutenant in the R.N.V.R., serving first in the seaplane carrier *Engadine* and later in the Intelligence Division of the Admiralty. He was several times mentioned in dispatches and awarded the D.S.C. After the war he devoted himself to the furtherance of Irish independence and joined the Irish Republican Army, but was captured during a gun-running exploit in his yacht *Asgard* and shot by Free State soldiers on 24 November 1922 at his old home Glendalough House, Wicklow.

CHILOÉ, a province of southern Chile (derived from *Chile* and *hué*, 'port'), a name which occurs frequently in English books of voyages of the 16th to 18th centuries. It was the first sight of land—and therefore vastly welcome—to mariners as they entered the Pacific either round Cape Horn or through the Strait of Magellan. Chiloé is also an island, part of the province of the same name.

CHINE, (1) the angle where the bottom *strakes of a boat meet the sides. In a hard-chined boat this angle is pronounced; in a soft-chined boat it is rounded off gradually. **(2)** That part of the waterway along the edges of the upper deck of a wooden vessel which projects above the deck-plank so that the lower seams of *spirketting can more conveniently be caulked. **(3)** The ends of the staves of a cask which project beyond the top and bottom. When casks are stowed end to end in the *hold of a ship they are said to be stowed chine-and-chine.

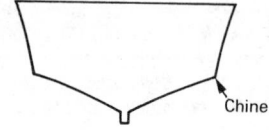
Chine

CHINESE GYBE, a type of wild and unpremeditated *gybe which occurs in a sailing vessel when the main *boom lifts over to the *lee side of the vessel while the *gaff does not follow. It is so called because of its prevalence with the Chinese *junk rig with its light bamboo *battens and no boom to hold the *foot of the mainsail steady.

CHINSE, orig. CHINCH, to, the operation of pressing *oakum into a *seam with a knife or chisel as a temporary measure until the seam can

be properly *caulked. The full expression is that the oakum is chinched in. It is also used to denote the light caulking of a seam in places where the ship's structure cannot withstand the full force of caulking with a *caulking iron and heavy hammer.

CHIOS, a small island on the west coast of Asia Minor which comes briefly into the maritime story as a place in which the Genoese trading company known as the Giustiniani had set up a factory. It was visited by Christopher *Columbus during his Mediterranean voyages and it was on this factory that he modelled his plans for a similar establishment when he reached *Cipangu (Japan). Previously Chios had been occupied by the Persians and its fleet of 100 ships had been forced to serve in the Persian fleet at the battle of *Salamis in 480 B.C.

CHIP LOG, see LOG.

CHIPS, the pieces cut off timber in the *Royal dockyards in Britain during the days of wooden ships when the dockyard carpenters shaped planks, etc., for shipbuilding and repairs. They were by tradition the perquisites of the carpenters and shipwrights, and could be carried out of the dockyard without penalty. It was a system which lent itself to considerable abuse, and whole planks and other timber were often carried out on the grounds that they were chips. There were many cases, particularly during the 17th century, when dockyard officials were found to have built whole houses and much of their furniture out of the 'chips' they had taken out of the dockyards.

CHOCK, to, an expression used by seamen to indicate the securing of articles stowed on deck in a ship to prevent their taking charge in rough weather when the vessel is rolling excessively.

CHOCK-A-BLOCK, the position when two *blocks of a *tackle come together so that no further movement is possible. It is also known as 'two blocks'.

CHOCOLATE GALE, the sailor's name for the brisk north-west wind which is the prevalent wind in the West Indies and off the Spanish Main.

CHOISEUL, ÉTIENNE FRANÇOIS, Duc de (1719–85), became Louis XV's great minister of marine in 1758, during the Seven Years War (1756–63). He put in hand many measures to increase the efficiency of the French Navy but was unable to undo all the mischief of previous administration before France had gone down to defeat in 1763. During the following years he reconstructed the French Navy and, building on the tactical doctrine of Bigot de * Morogues, raised it to a new pitch of efficiency with a view to starting a new war of revenge against Britain and regaining the vast territories of Canada and India. By 1770 his plans were reaching maturity and he was plotting with Spain to find a pretext for declaring war when his intrigues were discovered by the king and he was dismissed.

CHOKE THE LUFF, to, a quick and ready method of temporarily stopping all movement of a rope through a * block by placing the hauling part across the * sheave of the block, where it jams the sheave and holds it tight. A pull on the hauling part releases the sheave.

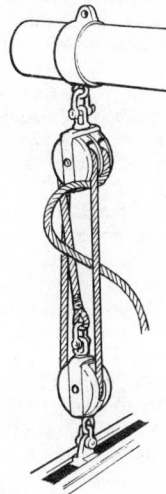

Choking the luff

CHOPS, the area where tides meet to cause an irregular sea, or where a channel meets the sea. 'Chops of the Channel', the western entrance of the English Channel when approaching from the Atlantic.

CHRISTIAN, FLETCHER (1764–93), a Cumberland man of Manx origin, was launched on a sea profession by William * Bligh and promoted by him from master's mate to acting lieutenant in the * *Bounty* for her voyage to Tahiti in 1788. Relations between the two deteriorated, however, and after a petty dispute Christian made preparations to desert, using a makeshift raft, when passing the Tonga Islands. Discontented members of the crew discovered this and persuaded him to lead a general mutiny (see BOUNTY, H.M.S.). His fate is uncertain. Though he probably died on Pitcairn Island, killed in a rising by the Tahitians, some slight evidence has been offered that he escaped from the island and returned clandestinely to England.

CHRONOMETER, in the words of the *Admiralty Manual of Navigation*, '. . . simply an enlarged watch . . . and its mechanism is by no means complicated although its construction demands the most accurate workmanship, and its adjustment requires a high degree of skill'. The * longitude of a ship at sea may readily be found by comparing the local time and the corresponding * Greenwich mean time. It is a relatively simple matter to compute local time by an astronomical observation, but until the advent of an accurate marine timekeeper it was by no means an easy matter to ascertain Greenwich time for the purpose of finding longitude. It was not until the 19th century that the mechanical construction of marine timepieces had reached a sufficiently high standard of efficiency; improvements in manufacture at the same time were accompanied by a sharp reduction in the cost of production and thus brought chronometers within reach of every navigator.

The essential feature of the traditional type of chronometer is the contrivance known as the compensated balance. This is a bimetallic device which compensates for temperature changes. Without a compensated balance an increase in temperature causes the rate of a timekeeper to be retarded; conversely, a decrease causes an accelerated rate. The object of the compensated balance is to correct this defect. But since the advent of radio time signals, the need for expensive chronometers no longer exists. It is an irony of navigational history that now that the need for a chronometer is almost non-existent a new type of marine chronometer which is reputed to have an accuracy of one part in a million has been produced. This degree of accuracy means that its * rate is within a little more than a second per month. See also BOARD OF LONGITUDE, HARRISON, John.

CHUBASCO, the name by which the violent easterly squall which blows on the western coast of Nicaragua and in the mouth of the Orinoco River is known to mariners.

CHURCHILL, Sir WINSTON LEONARD SPENCER (1874–1965), British statesman, was twice First Lord of the Admiralty, on each occasion at the outbreak of a world war.

Admiral Sir John * Fisher, the First Sea Lord, in 1907 first aroused Churchill's interest in the Royal Navy. Before this he had supported the navy in the House of Commons when he was attacking the plans of the Secretary of State for War, Brodrick, to retain a large standing army after the Boer War, but he had made no deep study of maritime affairs. Fisher was horrified when Churchill turned down the offer of the Admiralty in April 1908 in favour of the Board of Trade, but he continued to keep him well informed on naval matters until they parted company in 1911 over the controversy on *battleships, when Churchill and Lloyd George, determined on their expensive social reforms, bitterly attacked the increasing naval estimates. During the Agadir crisis in the late summer of 1911 Churchill's interest and vision again became apparent to the Prime Minister. After some indecision as to whether to appoint him or Haldane to the post, Churchill was made First Lord of the Admiralty on 23 October 1911, and 'the four most memorable years of my life' (words written in 1920) began.

In the public eye Churchill's main achievement at the Admiralty was to increase the size of the navy in preparation for the war with Germany. There is no doubt that he helped powerfully to do this, but his other achievements were in many respects more important. Firstly, he introduced a naval staff to control operations at the Admiralty and to assist the commanders at sea. Secondly, he encouraged aviation and indeed all the many technical advances which were then becoming important. Thirdly, and this is not particularly well known, he engaged in a great fight to improve the lot of the sailor; pay, discipline, and conditions of life generally were subjected to his intense investigation. He often had to work against the obstruction of some senior officers and civil servants but he showed a deep compassion for the lot of the lower deck and did much to bring about improvements.

His wartime achievements are better known though the tragedy of the *Dardanelles has been allowed to mask the considerable success he achieved elsewhere. With the help of the then First Sea Lord, Prince Louis of Battenberg (see MOUNTBATTEN, Louis Alexander) he ensured that the fleet was ready at its war stations when the time came in 1914. The operations at Antwerp, for which he was much blamed, were in fact successful in delaying the German advance and allowing a stable front line to be reached in Flanders. If his advice had been taken, the disaster of the sinkings of the *cruisers Hogue, Cressy, and *Aboukir in September 1914 would have been avoided.

The concept of the operations at Gallipoli (Dardanelles) was far-seeing and sound, but the execution of the senior officers on the spot was faulty. After a serious quarrel with Lord Fisher, whom he had recalled as First Sea Lord, Churchill was dismissed from office in May 1915 and given the sinecure post of Chancellor of the Duchy of Lancaster—a post which he retained for only a few months.

For the next twenty years his dealings with the navy were few, although when he was recalled to office as Minister of Munitions in 1917 he helped to dig the grave of the Royal Naval Air Service which he had done so much to create.

Between the wars his role was still equivocal. As Chancellor of the Exchequer he was responsible for the 'ten-year rule' which by postulating no major war for ten years, hamstrung the defence estimates between the two world wars. He maintained a faithful support for the Royal Air Force which, during the 1920s, was under attack by the two other Services. And, also as Chancellor of the Exchequer, he cut the navy mercilessly and, in particular, refused the cruisers which were so badly needed. Only in 1937, when he reckoned that the Royal Air Force was firmly secure, did he support the formation of the Fleet Air Arm as a separate naval flying service, though here again he failed to insist on the transfer of the control of operations of long range aircraft over the sea to the Admiralty. Thus, when he was appointed First Lord by Neville Chamberlain at the outbreak of war in September 1939, it seems surprising that the navy's welcome was so warm. But it was genuine, for in spite of the trials of the years between the wars the navy knew that he was a man with energy and ideas who would never weaken in his support.

As First Lord, Churchill brought some badly needed fresh air to the corridors of the Admiralty and he made certain that the reforms which he had initiated nearly thirty years before were continued. Again he was indefatigable in his encouragement of new technical advances, in radar in particular. He at once appreciated the defencelessness of *Scapa Flow and the blockship which he sent to Scapa to plug a gap in the defences arrived the day after the battleship Royal Oak was sunk by a *U-boat. When the solution to the problem of the magnetic *mine was found, he galvanized the energy of the shipbuilding industry and soon most warships and merchant ships were safe. Not all his energies were so well directed. He was still not fully aware of the danger to surface ships from air attack, particularly in narrow waters or close to enemy coasts. He wasted much time on an abortive plan to send a large expedition to the Baltic with the object, among other things, of stopping the flow of iron ore from the Swedish mines; and the expedition to Norway, which he strongly supported, failed, mainly because of the lack of appreciation by all concerned of the dangers from the German Air Force. But he was a most successful First Lord during the first months of the 'phoney' war and he succeeded in giving the navy confidence in itself and the nation confidence in the navy.

As Prime Minister he continued to take a close interest in naval operations and acted almost as though he were still First Lord. While he made mistakes—the dispatch of the Prince of Wales and the Repulse to Singapore without an aircraft-carrier as escort was the worst—his influence generally was sound and strong. It was he who first appreciated the dangers of the battle of the *Atlantic and who by his personal exertions succeeded in welding the naval and air forces concerned into a formidable defence; while in the ports and harbours he brought a new sense of urgency both to the loading and unloading and to the building and repair of ships. Later in the war he pressed the U.S.A. to allow the British fleet to take a significant part in the Pacific operations in spite of opposition from Admiral Ernest *King, the American Chief of Naval Operations. This assistance was fully appreciated at the time of the *kamikaze suicide attacks on warships.

After the Second World War Churchill's interests were shared with the Royal Air Force. He was at first mesmerized by the nuclear bomb and seemed to think that the days of navies were over. But the war in Korea changed his opinion and he strove to allow the Royal Navy to achieve the position it merited in the new North Atlantic Treaty Organization.

c.i.f., a term used in a commercial quotation for goods to be shipped overseas to indicate that the quoted price includes cost, insurance, and *freight.

CILLS, see SILLS.

CIMON (*c.* 507–449 B.C.), Athenian admiral (*strategos*) and general, was the son of Miltiades. He was in joint command with Themistocles of the Athenian squadron of the Greek fleet at the start of the battle of *Salamis in 480 B.C., but before the action was ended he virtually commanded the whole fleet and was the man most responsible for that notable victory and the subsequent expulsion of the Persian garrisons from the entire Thracian coast. For the next fourteen years he was variously engaged on land and sea against the Persians and finally defeated them in a combined naval and military battle at the mouth of the Eurymedon River in 466 B.C. It seems probable that his great naval and military successes and his subsequent popularity in Athens went to his head and he became the leading figure in the Athenian campaign to unify all the states which made up Greece. An attempt to coerce Sparta, then fighting her own war against the Helots, ended in failure and Cimon was ostracized and banished from Athens. He returned to favour in 453 B.C., and was placed in command of an amphibious expedition against Cyprus, dying before the walls of Citium during the siege of that town.

CINQUE PORTS, an association of towns on the Channel coast of England, mainly for juridical purposes, originally composed of five ports, Dover, Hastings, Romney, Hythe, and Sandwich, to which were later added the 'ancient towns' of Rye and Winchelsea. The date of the original formation is unknown, but the oldest charter still in existence is dated 1278. Until the 16th century the Cinque Ports were charged with furnishing ships and men for the service of the crown in wartime, thus constituting the medieval equivalent of a navy, in return for charters guaranteeing them certain privileges in tolls and fishing and in maritime jurisdiction in the waters of the eastern English Channel. Their importance declined with the growth of oceanic voyages and of the western ports of Plymouth and Bristol and, of course, with the institution of a permanent English Navy by Henry VII and his son Henry VIII.

CIPANGU, the name by which Japan was known in the early years of discovery in the 15th–17th centuries.

CIRRUS, a type of cloud formation. See METEOROLOGY.

CIVICO MUSEO NAVALE, Genoa, Italy, is a small museum founded in 1928 to illustrate the progress in the development of shipping between the 15th and 20th centuries. It is housed in the Villa Doria, a 16th-century building and occupies twenty-eight rooms. The collection includes models of war, merchant, fishing, and pleasure shipping, dugout canoes and exotic craft, figureheads, nautical instruments, and weapons. There is also a collection of paintings, drawings, and photographs.

CLAMPS, (1) pieces of timber fixed longitudinally to the *masts or *yards of square-rigged ships to strengthen them if they showed signs of weakness or bursting under strain. See also FISH, TO. **(2)** Planks laid fore and aft under the *beams of the *orlop and lower decks in wooden ships and *fayed to the timbers to add strength to the ship's structure. **(3)** *Strakes fastened to the inside of wooden ships' sides to form a support on which the ends of the deck beams can rest, the *knees being bolted or fastened with *treenails or bolts to the clamps.

CLAP ON, to, the seaman's expression when something is added temporarily to an existing part. Thus, a *purchase is clapped on to a *guy or *fall when additional hauling power is required. Some masters of sailing vessels used to order additional sails to be clapped on to take advantage of a fair wind. A *whipping is clapped on to the end of a rope, particularly in the case of a *West Country whipping where the two ends are brought up and changed from hand to hand, with an overhand knot at top and bottom.

CLARK, ROBERT (1904–   ), British yacht designer, is noted for the design of many successful racing yachts of various sizes with graceful lines and light construction. He was a successful competitor in many offshore races in yachts of his own design, winning the *Royal Ocean Racing Club championship in 1937 with his 48-ft (14·8 m) *cutter *Ortac*, and the same club's Class I championships in 1951, 1953, 1954, and 1957. Among his better known designs are *Gipsy Moth V*, Sir Francis *Chichester's 57-ft (17·5 m) *ketch, *Sir Thomas Lipton*, a 59-ft (18·1 m) ketch, *Carita*, a three-masted 485-ton *schooner, and *Captain Scott*, a 400-ton three-masted topsail schooner built for adventure training expeditions.

CLASS or **CLASSIFICATION,** the degree of seaworthiness of a ship as determined by a survey based upon her construction and the size, or *scantlings, of the materials used in her building. A vessel is classed in this way for a definite period of years, and on its expiry she must be resurveyed if she wishes to retain her original classification. In addition, after any disaster such as fire or shipwreck, a ship has to be resurveyed to re-establish her classification.

The body which issues such classifications is *Lloyd's Register of Shipbuilding, which has committees representing it in all maritime nations in the world. The modern Lloyd's classification is 100 A, with the figure 1 following the A if the survey includes her anchors and cables. The famous old classification, A1 at Lloyd's, is used now only for ships that operate in local waters, such as rivers, estuaries, etc.

CLAW OFF, to, the operation of beating to windward in a sailing vessel to avoid being driven on to a *lee shore. The expression implies danger of shipwreck because of a combination of a rough sea and a strong onshore wind.

CLAW RING, a fitting on the main *boom of a yacht to take the main sheet where roller reefing is fitted. A short preventer connected to the swivel band on the boom stops the claw ring from sliding too far forward when in use.

CLEAN, a term which refers to the lines of a vessel's hull when they give a fine and unobstructed *run from bow to stern so that she moves through the water smoothly without undue turbulence. A clean entrance, a clear run of the hull from a ship's bows so that she goes through the water without the swell of her bow creating undue resistance and turbulence in the water. A clean run aft, the same conditions at the ship's stern, a smooth tapering of the hull lines into the stern so that no *cavitation or drag is produced at the stern as the vessel moves through the water.

CLEAN BILL, the description of a ship when all the ship's company are in good health. A ship's *bill of health is a certificate signed by a consul or other port authority that no contagious disease existed in her port of departure and that none of the crew was infected with a notifiable disease at the time of sailing. Such a bill of health properly authenticated is a clean bill; where it cannot be so authenticated because of infection in the port of departure, it is a foul bill.

CLEAN SLATE, a, originally a log-slate, on which the *courses steered by a ship and the distances run as indicated on a *log were entered during the course of a *watch. At the end of the watch, the information on the slate was entered in the deck-log and the slate wiped clean so that the officer keeping the next watch could enter on it the courses and distances made good during his watch. The term has entered the English language as an expression meaning that past actions and occurrences are forgotten (wiped off the slate) and a new start can be made.

CLEAR, to, a ship is cleared to sail when all the formalities in connection with the ship's papers at the custom house before sailing from a port have been observed. The word has many other maritime meanings, such as to escape from, to unload, to empty, to prepare, etc. 'Clear for action', to prepare for battle by securing everything on board, testing all communications in connection with the ship's armament, rigging fire hoses, piping the ship's company to their action stations, etc. In wooden sailing warships the order entailed also the rigging of additional chain *slings to the *yards as a precaution against their being shot away by gunfire, the dismantling of officers' *cabins, formed by moveable wooden partitions or canvas screens, the *striking of all cabin furniture below decks, the hoisting out of all boats, which were towed astern during the battle, and the rigging of protective nets above the upper deck to safeguard men working on deck against falling masts and spars.

The term is also used in a navigational sense as, for example, to *lay a ship's *course so that she will clear a headland, a rock ledge, etc.

CLEAR HAWSE, a, the situation when a ship is at anchor with both her anchors down and the cables *growing clear of each other without crossing. Frequently, when a ship thus anchored is swung by the tide, she turns a complete circle and the two cables become crossed, a condition known as a *foul hawse. If she needs to weigh her anchors when her hawse is foul, she will have great difficulty in preventing the *flukes of the anchor being weighed from becoming entangled in the other cable. The term is also used to indicate that there is no obstruction, such as another ship's anchors or cables, between her and her anchor.

CLEAR LOWER DECK, a naval order for all hands on board to muster on the upper deck. The only men exempt from such an order are those on watch in the machinery spaces where the machinery is actually running.

CLEARANCE, the document giving permission to sail by the custom house in a port to the *master of a vessel going foreign. It is given after inspection of the ship's registry, her crew list, and *articles, receipts for port charges, the *bill of health, and the *manifest. The accuracy of all these papers has to be sworn by the master before clearance can be given. See also CLEAR, TO.

CLEAR-VIEW SCREEN, a circular disc of plate glass, which is revolved at high speed by an electric motor, incorporated in the glass screen of the navigating bridge. The centrifugal motion throws off all rain, sleet, or snow and gives the navigating officer a clear view ahead.

CLEAT, (1) a piece of wood or metal with two arms placed at convenient stations on board ship to which ropes or *falls can be made fast by taking two or three turns under and over the arms. **(2)** Small wedges of elm or oak fastened to the *yards of square-rigged sailing ships to prevent ropes or the *earings of the sails from slipping off the yard.

CLENCH, to, the operation of making a permanent join. Thus a clenched *shackle, with which the end of a chain *cable, for example, is secured to the bottom of the *chain locker, has its bolt hammered over so that it cannot be removed, thus closing the shackle permanently. See also CLINCH, TO.

CLERK OF ELDIN, JOHN (1728–1812), British writer on naval tactics and laird of an estate near Edinburgh, had no experience of seafaring other than sailing small boats in the Firth of Forth, but as a result of reading accounts of sea battles he held the view that British naval officers had no knowledge of tactics and that they had won their battles merely by hard fighting. He therefore conceived it his mission in life to teach them.

This he attempted to do, so it seems, solely through his own reasoning powers, for he makes no acknowledgement to the notable French works on the subject which had already been translated into English, those of the Abbé *Hoste (1697) and Bigot de *Morogues (1762), translated in 1762 and 1767 respectively. His claim that the publication of his *Essay on Naval Tactics* (Part 1 in 1790; Parts 2, 3, and 4 in 1797) contributed sub-

stantially to the great victories of this period is without direct foundation, but his endeavours undoubtedly interested serving officers and may well have led to more consideration of tactical problems than would otherwise have been given.

Clerk's work fell into some disrepute after the battle of *Trafalgar, when Lord *Nelson's tactics, specifically singled out by Clerk as suicidal, led to such a shattering success. When asked his opinion in 1806, Lord St. Vincent (see JERVIS, Sir John) wrote, 'upon the whole, his tactics are certainly ingenious, and worthy the study of all young and inexperienced officers. But the great talent is to take prompt advantage of disorder in the fleet of the enemy, by shifts of wind, accidents, and their deficiency in practical seamanship, to the superior knowledge of which much of our success is to be attributed, and I trust it will never be sacrificed to frippery and gimcrack.'

Most modern historians would endorse this view, which is as applicable in naval action today as it was in the days when Clerk of Eldin wrote his *Essay on Naval Tactics*.

CLERMONT, the name of the first steam vessel built in the U.S.A. and the world's first commercially successful steamboat in service. Her designer was the engineer Robert *Fulton but the engine used in her was made in Britain by Boulton and Watt of Birmingham, as no engineers in the U.S.A. had at that time sufficient experience to build steam engines suitable for ship propulsion. Her engine was a single vertical cylinder, 24 in. in diameter with a stroke of 48 in., which drove a pair of 15-ft paddle-wheels, one on each side of her hull, through bell cranks and spur gearing. The *Clermont* had an overall length of 133 feet and a *displacement of 100 tons and was built on the East Hudson River. On her initial trip in 1807 she steamed up the river to Albany and back, a distance of approximately 240 miles, in 62 hours. See also LIVINGSTON, Robert, PADDLE STEAMER.

CLEVELY, JOHN (1745–86), marine artist, was born in London and brought up near the naval dockyard at Deptford. He studied art under Paul Sandby and became a naval draughtsman. He was with Captain *Phipps, later Lord Mulgrave, in H.M.S. *Racehorse* during the polar expedition of 1773, in which Horatio *Nelson, as a midshipman in the *Carcass*, took part, and his sketches of that expedition are lively examples of his art as well as providing a useful historical record. He was a frequent exhibitor at the Royal Academy, much of his work being in water-colour. His twin brother ROBERT was a sailor but later studied art, painting many scenes of naval battles. John was appointed marine painter to the Prince of Wales, later George IV. He died as the result of falling over a cliff at Dover.

CLEW or **CLUE, (1)** in a fore-and-aft sail, the lower aftermost corner; in a square sail, the two lower corners. In cases where fore-and-aft sails are not normally *laced to a *boom, such as *jibs, *staysails, etc., it is the corner of the sail to which the *sheet, by which the sail is trimmed, is secured; in fore-and-aft sails which normally are laced to a boom, the clew is usually fitted with an *out-haul so that the *foot of the sail can be stretched tautly along the boom. For illus. see SAIL. **(2)** The *lanyards and *nettles by which a naval *hammock is slung from hooks in a deck *beam. The hammock clews, one at each end of the hammock, consist of a rope lanyard with a ring *spliced into the end from which originally twenty-two nettles were secured into the same number of eyelet holes in each end of the hammock. Later the number of nettles was reduced to eight, though they were doubled through the ring providing in effect sixteen nettles which were secured to sixteen eyelet holes in the two ends of the hammocks. See also DOUBLE CLEWS.

CLEW, or **CLUE, CRINGLE,** a spectacle iron (i.e., with two or more eyes) stitched into the *clews of a square sail so that two or more ropes or *tackles may be hooked into the eyes and led in different directions. They are used to give a greater movement to the *yards of a square-rigged ship when they are being *braced to the wind.

CLEW, or **CLUE, GARNET,** the clew line or *tackle of a lower square sail in a full-rigged ship, by means of which the clews are hauled up to the *yard and trussed when the sail needs to be furled or *goose-winged. In such a situation the sail is said to be clewed (or clued) up. Clew garnets are used only on the *courses of square-rigged ships, clew lines being used for all the smaller sails.

CLINCH, to, (1) a method of fastening or knotting large ropes to heavy objects by a half hitch with the end stopped back on its own part by a seizing. Thus a hemp *cable or *hawser would be clinched to the ring of a *kedge *anchor when required for use with, in older days, the inboard end clinched to the mainmast as a stopper. Thus, to run a cable out to the clinch means that there is no more to *veer. With the substitution of chain cable for older hemp cables, combined with the use of *shackles for joining the cable to the anchor and a Senhouse slip or cable clench to secure the inboard end, clinch-knotting is no longer used in modern ships in anchor work. But see also CLENCH, TO. **(2)** The simple method of fastening the hull planking of small craft to the *frames or *timbers by turning over, or clinching, the ends of the copper nails in place of riveting them.

CLINKER-, or **CLINCH-, BUILT,** a method of boat building in which the lower edge of each side plank overlaps the upper edge of the one below it. It is a method normally used only in small boat building as in larger vessels the added wetted surface produced by the overlapping planks would cause additional skin friction as the vessel progresses through the water. In the U.S.A., this method of building is known as lap-strake. For a comparison, see CARVEL CONSTRUCTION.

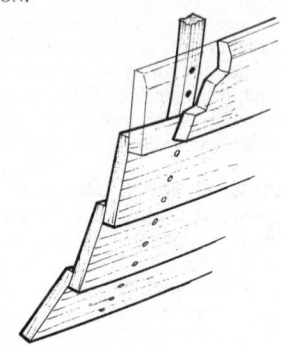

Clinker construction

CLIPHOOKS, two hooks of similar shape facing in opposite directions and attached to the same *thimble. They have a flat inner side so that they can lie together to form an *eye and are much used in small tackles where an ordinary hook might jump out.

CLIPPER, the generic name used very loosely to describe types of very fast sailing ships. It was applied first to the speedy *schooners built in Virginia and Maryland, known as the Baltimore clippers (though in fact they were not really clippers) which became famous during the War of 1812 as blockade runners and *privateers, and subsequently notorious as slave ships carrying human cargoes from Africa to the U.S.A. Their hull design, long and low, with a draught deeper aft than forward, a very sharp-raked *stem (the true mark of the clipper), and an inclined, overhanging *counter stern, thus reducing the area of hull in contact with the water, was later combined with the three-masted square rig in the beautiful clipper ships of the mid-19th century, the finest productions of the age of sail.

As early as 1832 an enlarged Baltimore clipper, the *Ann McKim*, had been given square rig; but the first true clipper ship is generally held to have been the *Rainbow* built in 1845 at New York. The discovery of gold in California in 1848 and in Australia in 1850, raising a demand for the fastest passages to both, and the repeal of the British Navigation Acts in 1849, opening the tea trade from China to London to foreign ships, gave a tremendous fillip to the production of

American clippers in which the shipbuilder Donald * Mackay, of Boston, took the lead.

His *Flying Fish* and *Flying Cloud* were perhaps the most famous of Mackay's clippers, though the *Lightning*, *Champion of the Seas*, *James Baines*, and *Donald Mackay*, which he built for James Baines's Black Ball Line of Liverpool, were equally successful. The American clipper ship * *Sovereign of the Seas* made the all-time record for a sailing ship for the voyage from New York to Liverpool of 13 days 14 hours, being credited with a speed of 22 knots at times. Another American flyer which broke records was the * *Challenge*. The Black Ball * liner *Marco Polo*, built at St. John's, New Brunswick, broke all records for passages to and from Australia in 1852–3.

This foreign competition, almost entirely from the U.S.A., now spurred British shipowners and shipbuilders who up to this time had been mainly content with improving the sailing quality of the * Blackwall frigates, though * schooner-rigged ships had been built since 1839 by Alexander Hall & Sons of Aberdeen for the England to Scotland passenger trade and one of them, the *Scottish Maid*, had reached London from Leith in 33 hours. The same firm now built the first small British clippers, the *Stornoway* and *Chrysolite*, for the tea trade, while R. & H. Green of Blackwall produced the *Challenger*.

Other British yards, chiefly Scottish, also began to build clipper ships, notably Robert * Steele & Co. of Greenock, who between 1855 and 1859 completed a number of small but very successful ships. The financial depression of 1857 and the American Civil War (1861–5) resulted in a decline in American commercial shipbuilding and in its place led to a revival in Britain which was to result in the golden age of the tea-clipper. Tea from China was a very profitable cargo in those days and several clippers were specially built for the trade. The first arrivals in London of the new crop each year commanded the highest prices.

Robert * Steele built such famous ships for this trade as the * *Taeping*, * *Ariel*, and * *Sir Lancelot*. In 1866 occurred the most famous of all the annual tea-clipper races when the * *Fiery Cross* left Foochow on 29 May, the *Ariel*, *Taeping*, and *Serica* on the 30th, and the *Taitsing* on the 31st. The *Taeping* docked in London at 9.45 p.m. on 6 September, the *Ariel* half an hour later, and the *Serica* at 11.45 p.m., after having sailed the 16,000 miles from Foochow. The *Fiery Cross* and *Taitsing* both reached London two days later. Two other tea-clippers featured in another famous race from Foochow in 1872. They were the * *Thermopylae* and the * *Cutty Sark*, both completed in 1868, which were lying approximately level when the latter lost her rudder in a gale off Cape Province, South Africa.

Handling sail on the yard of a clipper

The opening of the Suez Canal in 1869 struck at the *raison d'être* of the tea-clippers, making the long trip round the Cape of Good Hope unprofitable for their specialized freight. The ships transferred to carrying wool from Australia for a time, but were soon outmoded in a trade in which large cargoes, small crews, and less speed were more economical; these were better provided by the large, steel-hulled, four- and five-masted * barques with which the age of sail came finally to an end.

The term itself is said to have been coined because these very fast ships could clip the time taken on passage by the regular * packet ships, themselves very fast in their day.

J. Jobé, ed., *The Great Age of Sail* (1967); B. W. Battie, *Seven Centuries of Sea Travel* (1972); F. Knight, *The Clipper Ship* (1973).

CLOSE-HAULED, a condition of sailing when a vessel trims her sails so that she proceeds as close to the wind as possible with all her sails full and not shivering. In a square-rigged sailing ship this condition is achieved when her * yards are * braced as near to the fore-and-aft line as possible so that the wind, coming over the bow, fills the sails and drives the ship forward. When close-hauled, the square-rigged ship could get as near as about six * points off the wind. In ships with a fore-and-aft rig, to sail close-hauled is to harden in the *sheets as much as possible to bring the sails in flatter so that the wind strikes them at an acute angle. With this rig a vessel can keep her sails full without shivering when about four points off the wind, although with the modern high and narrow *Bermuda rig it is sometimes possible to sail even a little closer to the wind. See POINTS OF SAILING.

CLOSE-QUARTERS, strong barriers of wood erected across the decks of merchant ships in the days of sail, with loopholes through which muskets could be fired to resist boarding attacks from enemy *privateers. 'We have known an English merchant-ship of 16 guns, and properly fitted with close-quarters, defeat the united efforts of three French privateers who boarded her in the late war . . . The French sailors were, after boarding, so much exposed to the continued fire of musquetry, and coehorns charged with grenadoes, that a dreadful scene of carnage ensued . . .' Falconer, *Marine Dictionary*, 1771.

CLOSE-REEFED, the description of a square-rigged ship when all the *reefs of the topsails had been taken in.

CLOTHES, see SAILORS' DRESS.

CLOTHING, the name by which the various pieces of rigging which hold a *bowsprit in position are known. The comparable name in the case of masts is *apparel. See FURNITURE.

CLOTHS, the strips of *canvas or other cloth which are *seamed together to form a *sail. They are normally the width of the *bolt from which they are cut in order that they may be seamed along the selvedges, which are considerably stronger than a cut edge.

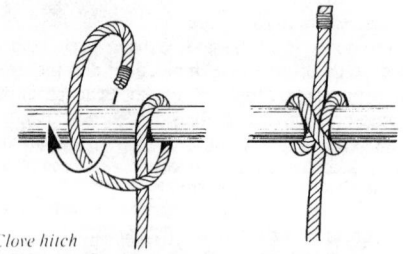

Clove hitch

CLOVE HITCH, a *bend formed by two half hitches, the second reversed so that the standing part is between the hitches, used at sea for making a line fast to a spar or a smaller line fast to a larger rope. It is also used when securing the *painter of a dinghy to a *bollard. It will not slip because the second half hitch rides over the standing part of the rope.

CLOWES, Sir WILLIAM LAIRD (1856–1905), British naval writer, was born at Hampstead and educated at King's College, London. In 1879 he took up journalism and gained his first insight into naval affairs while serving on the staff of the *Army and Navy Gazette*. He was naval correspondent successively of the *Daily News* (1885), *Standard* (1887–90), and *The Times* (1890–5). Under the pseudonym 'Nauticus' he wrote articles on a variety of naval subjects, but gave up journalism in order to study naval history. Between 1897 and 1903 he compiled *The Royal Navy, its History from the Earliest Times*, a work of seven volumes, in the preparation of which he was assisted by several well-known historians including Captain A. T. *Mahan and Sir Clements *Markham. In 1902 he received a knighthood but ill health obliged him to move to Davos, Switzerland. In 1892 he was awarded the gold medal of the U.S. Naval Institute. Besides his great historical work he wrote several stories of the sea.

CLUB HAUL, to, a method of tacking a square-rigged ship in a narrow space by letting go the *lee anchor from the bow, though with the hawser led aft and stopped on the quarter, as soon as the wind is out of the foresails. As the ship gathered sternway the pull of the anchor brought her head round on the other tack and the anchor hawser was cut. This method was only used in an emergency in heavy weather and when the ship was embayed. The most famous example of club hauling a ship was in 1814 when Captain Hayes extricated H.M.S. *Magnificent*, a *ship of the line, from almost certain capture by the French at the Basque Roads. It was blowing a full gale and, with lower yards and topmasts struck, Hayes found himself trapped between two reefs. He got to sea again by club hauling the ship, and was known as 'Magnificent Hayes' from that day on. It is not applicable to a fore-and-aft rigged vessel, which does not normally gather sternway when head to wind while tacking.

CLUE, see CLEW.

CLUE SABRAN, M. DE LA, more usually known as de la Clue (*c.* 1703–59), French admiral, was a *chef d'escadre* (commodore) at the battle of *Minorca in 1756 in which a British fleet commanded by the Hon. John *Byng was prevented from bringing relief to the British garrison besieged on the island. As a result the garrison was forced to surrender and the island was captured. Promoted to vice admiral shortly afterwards, de la Clue was placed in command of the fleet at Toulon and in 1759, in the course of French preparations for an invasion of Britain, was ordered to proceed out of the Mediterranean and join up with the fleet at Brest to obtain temporary command of the English Channel for the passage of the invasion forces.

The French Mediterranean fleet was at the time being blockaded in Toulon by British ships commanded by Admiral *Boscawen, but when he had to withdraw to Gibraltar to refit and revictual, de la Clue seized his chance, slipped out of Toulon, and passed through the Straits of Gibraltar into the Atlantic. Boscawen's ships, some with their *yards sent down, were still in dockyard hands at Gibraltar, but by extraordinary exertions managed to get to sea and set off in chase. During the night de la Clue's fleet was separated into two parts, one of which found refuge in Cadiz where they were securely blockaded by the British; the other, which included de la Clue's flagship, the *Ocean*, was brought to action off *Lagos in a running fight. To escape the fury of the battle de la Clue, with four of his largest ships, ran into the bay of Lagos which, being Portuguese, was neutral water. The *Ocean* and the *Redoubtable* were run ashore with such force that all their masts went by the board, the *Téméraire* and the *Modeste* anchored under the guns of a Portuguese fort. Notwithstanding Portuguese neutrality, Boscawen followed them in, burned the *Ocean* and *Redoubtable*, and captured the *Téméraire* and *Modeste*, which were added to the British Navy.

De la Clue was wounded in the action and was carried ashore at Lagos before his ship was burned, but later died there of his wound.

CLUMP BLOCK, a large single block with a wide *swallow, used for a variety of daily purposes on board ships. They are made with a thicker case than the usual run of blocks carried in a ship so as to provide added strength to the *purchases in which they are used.

COACH, a term used between the mid-17th and mid-18th centuries, originally to describe the forward part of the *cabin space under the poop deck and later the fore-cabin under the quarter-deck, just forward of the great cabin. About halfway through this period the term was used for both, the 'great coach or steerage' for the lower and the 'upper coach or *round-house' for the upper. The origin of the word may have been the ancient *'carosse' of the galley, the space under the poop deck where the captain or admiral had his bed. When the admiral had his quarters in the great cabin, his flag-captain occupied the coach; in private ships, i.e., those with no admiral on board, the captain occupied the great cabin and the *master (navigator) the coach.

'COACH HORSES', the name given in the old Royal Navy to the men who rowed the admiral's *barge or captain's *galley. The name also spread from the navy to embrace the crews of state barges when they rowed with their livery.

COACH-ROOF, the name by which the cabin top in older yachts is known.

COACHWHIPPING, a form of decorative square *sinnet work worked with an even number of strands to form a herring-bone pattern. It was used occasionally in the decorative *pointing of a rope but more usually for covering *stanchions with a patterned sinnet to make a ship look smart and *tiddley. The making of sinnets, officially the duty of the *boatswain and his mates, was a favourite pastime of sailors during long voyages, but such fancy rope and knot work is very rarely seen at sea today.

COAK, originally a wooden dowel, but the meaning has been extended to describe the small brass bearing in the centre of the sheave of a *block to keep it from splitting and to prevent wear by the pin on which it turns. Coaks, or dowels, used often to be fitted into the upper face of the wooden *knees to engage in corresponding holes in the *beams of ships to prevent them slipping. A spar is coaked when it has been broken and the two pieces joined together by making a hollow in one broken end and a projection in the other which fits it exactly. In a properly coaked spar the friction between the two butt ends prevents the two parts of the spar from drawing apart.

COAMING, the name given to the raised lip, usually about six to nine inches high, with which openings in the upper deck, such as *hatchways leading to the deck below, are framed to prevent any water on deck from running down the opening into the space below. They also serve as a framework for the cargo hatches of merchant vessels, though in this case somewhat higher, to which the strongbacks and hatch covers can be fitted and *battened down and to which the tarpaulin covers can be secured. In yachts, coamings are the vertical sides of the coach-roof or hatches above the deck.

COASTAL MOTOR BOAT (C.M.B.), a type of small warship used in the British Navy during the First World War (1914–18). They were designed by Tom I. *Thornycroft and constructed of wood with a single-stepped hydroplane hull, propelled by petrol motors, and were built in two sizes, 40-ft and 55-ft, with speeds of 30 and 42 knots respectively. They carried either *mines or *torpedoes, or *depth-charges when employed in an anti-submarine role. A few 70-ft coastal motor boats were also built as *mine-layers only. When armed with torpedoes the 40-ft boats carried one and the 55-ft boats two.

COASTAL NAVIGATION, see NAVIGATION.

COAT, canvas painted with thick tar and secured around a mast or *bowsprit where it passes through a deck or is bedded down over the *stem of a vessel to prevent water on deck running down the sides of a mast into the hold, or along the bowsprit between decks. A coat was also secured round the rudder head where it passed through the *counter of the ship. In most modern vessels the coats are made of rubber.

COBBING, an unofficial form of punishment in the British Navy, often inflicted as summary justice by the crew of a ship against a member who had transgressed the lower deck code of honour. It was also often used for the same purpose in the midshipmen's mess. Originally it was administered with a flat piece of wood called a cobbing-board, the offender being tied down as the punishment was inflicted on his breech. Later, in the 19th century, it became a much more vicious punishment, the instrument used being a hammock *clew which, with its then twenty-two *nettles, became in effect a 'cat o' 22 tails'. It was forbidden by the Admiralty towards the end of the 19th century.

COBLE, (1) a flat-bottomed, *clinker-built fishing boat used in coastal waters, particularly on the north-east coast of England, with a mast and *lug-sail, and occasionally a *jib on a temporary *bowsprit, and fitted for rowing with three pairs of oars. A feature of the coble is the rudder which extends four feet or more below the keel. The *forefoot is also made slightly deeper than the keel, partly to balance the rudder and partly to give a better grip to windward. The particular design allows the boat to be launched from a beach with her bows to seaward, the deep forefoot helping to keep the coble straight and steady. The rudder is shipped when sufficient depth of water is reached. On landing on a beach the bows are still kept to seaward, the coble being kept bows on to the waves as it is backed in with the oars or brought in with the waves. It was in a coble that Grace *Darling and her father rowed out to the rescue of the crew of the *Forfarshire* when she went aground off the Outer Farne Island light in 1838 during a storm. **(2)** A short, flat-bottomed boat propelled only by oars and used in salmon fishing and netting in the mouths of rivers and estuaries.

COCHRANE, THOMAS, 10th earl of Dundonald (1775–1860), British admiral, was the eldest son of the 9th earl whose eccentricity and inventiveness he inherited. While still a child he held commissions in both the army and navy, going to sea in 1793 in a ship commanded by his uncle, Alexander Cochrane. He made his name in command of the *sloop *Speedy* in 1800 when he captured the Spanish *frigate *El Gamo*. His commands of the *Pallas* and *Imperieuse* off the coast of Spain were equally brilliant, his exploits being immortalized in *Peter Simple* by Frederick *Marryat, then a midshipman on board.

His stormy political career as a radical began when he was elected Member of Parliament for Honiton in 1806 and the next year for Westminster. He combined attacks on the government with service in the navy until, after leading the *fireship attack in the battle of *Basque Roads, his demands for the court martial of his admiral, Lord *Gambier, and for reforms in general led to a refusal by the Admiralty to give him further naval employment. In 1814 he was involved in a fraud on the Stock Exchange which led to his expulsion from Parliament and the navy.

He accepted in 1817 an invitation from Chile to command their fleet in the war of independence against Spain. His capture of the enemy flagship *Esmeralda* at Lima led to the eventual freeing of Peru and Chile from Spanish domination. He transferred his services to Brazil in their war of independence against Portugal in 1823 but, as so often before, quarrelled with his employers. On his return to Europe he commanded the Greek Navy in the war of independence against Turkey in 1827.

He was reinstated in the Royal Navy in 1832 and, with the rank of admiral, commanded the American and West Indies Station from 1848 to 1851. He was disappointed when, as senior admiral, he was refused a command in the Crimean War (1854–6) at the age of 80.

Always interested in surprise attacks and novel methods of warfare, Cochrane introduced steamships as fighting vessels, though they were never engaged in action. He invented improvements in gas lighting, tubular boilers, steam propulsion, etc., and introduced the use of gas and smoke screens as early as 1812, his plans for which remained secret until 1914. His turbulent career is well described in his *Autobiography of a Seaman*, which appeared in 1860, the year of his death. A supreme egoist, he cannot be denied the highest praise for brilliance as a tactician and ingenuity as an inventor. For a biography see Christopher Lloyd's *Lord Cochrane* (1947).

COCK, the maritime term for what is called a tap on shore. Many of the essential pipes used in a ship or boat have their outlet to the sea, and it is necessary to fit a cock at the outboard end to prevent seawater coming in and flooding through the pipe.

COCKBILL or **A-COCKBILL, (1)** the situation of the *anchor, in the days when ships carried anchors with *stocks, when it has been lifted clear of its anchor bed, its cable bent on, and hangs 'up and down' at the *cathead ready for letting go. Similarly, when brought to the cathead after weighing in preparation for being secured on the anchor bed, it hangs a-cockbill. (2) The yards of a square-rigged sailing ship are a-cockbill when they are trimmed by topping them up with one *lift so that they lie at an angle to the deck. Yards a-cockbill used to be a sign of mourning for the death of a member of the crew.

COCKBURN, Sir GEORGE (1772–1853), British admiral of the fleet, was one of those fortunate young gentlemen in the Royal Navy who had relatives and friends in high political and naval circles. He was a protégé of Admiral Lord *Hood, and lacked neither appointments at sea nor rapid promotion. In 1782, although he was still at school, his name was entered on the books of a *frigate commanded by Captain Rowley, an intimate friend of the family; this was to ensure that he gained enough seniority for his later promotion to lieutenant. In 1792 he passed his examination for lieutenant and was appointed by Lord Chatham, First Lord of the Admiralty and another family friend, to the Mediterranean, where Lord Hood was to take over as commander-in-chief on the outbreak of the French Revolutionary War in 1793. Within a year Cockburn was a *post-captain and his future assured. He served under Horatio *Nelson in the operations of 1796 off the Italian coast, and commanded the frigate *Minerva*, with Nelson on board as commodore, at the evacuation of Elba in 1797. Being always a man of action and a skilled seaman, he had a most successful war, capturing many French and Spanish ships and amassing a fortune in *prize money.

He was made a rear admiral in 1812, commanded the British squadron off Cadiz, and was later sent to American waters to take over command of the British squadron operating in the Chesapeake. It was here that he performed the feat for which he is chiefly remembered, the destruction of military stores at Washington valued at about £3,000,000 and the burning of the White House. He returned home in 1815 and was appointed to command the squadron which took Napoleon to captivity in St. Helena, remaining as Governor of the island until 1816 when he was relieved by Sir Hudson Lowe. He had two spells of duty on the Board of Admiralty, as a junior lord from 1818 to 1830 and as first naval lord from 1846 to 1850. He became *admiral of the fleet in 1851.

COCKED HAT, the small triangular space usually found at the intersection of position lines on a chart when a ship's position is determined by plotting three bearings. With perfect observation and plotting, the three position lines should intersect at a common point; if they do not, a 'cocked hat' is formed. This provides sure proof of error in the process of fixing the ship, often caused by a small error in the *compass, and, in general, the larger the cocked hat, the greater the error. Navigators normally take the centre of the cocked hat, when it is not large, as the position of the ship.

COCKPIT, (1) the well of a yacht or small sailing vessel where the steering wheel or *tiller is located. It normally gives access to the saloon, but in some modern yachts a separate central cockpit is incorporated where the steering wheel and navigational instruments are situated. **(2)** In the old sailing navies the space near the after *hatchway and below the lower gundeck allotted originally to the senior *midshipmen of the ship and later to the surgeon and his mates for their messes. In action it became the operating theatre to which men who had been wounded were carried for the treatment of their wounds. During the battle of *Trafalgar in 1805 it was to the cockpit of H.M.S. *Victory* that Lord *Nelson was carried after he had been wounded on deck, and where he died.

COCKSCOMB, the name of a serrated *cleat often fitted to the ends of the *yards in square-rigged ships to which the *reef earings are hauled out and lashed when a sail is being reefed.

COD, (1) one of the best known and, in fishery terms, most important fish of the sea, *Gadus morrhua*, generally prevalent in the North Atlantic and its adjacent seas and particularly around Iceland and the *Grand Banks off Newfoundland. **(2)** The narrow pocket, also known as the cod-end, at the end of a *trawl in which the fish caught up in the trawl are collected. When the trawl is hauled in the cod-end is hoisted up on deck and the end opened so that the fish fall on to the deck. **(3)** The centre of a deep bay, a meaning which has now very largely fallen into disuse.

COD-BANGER, a name in use during the mid-19th century to describe a vessel used in fishing for cod. It applied particularly to those vessels which used lines, as opposed to *trawls, for catching the fish.

CODLINE, small line laid up with eighteen threads. It was originally the line used in fishing for *cod, but has also a variety of uses on board ship for purposes where small rope would be too large and clumsy.

CODRINGTON, Sir EDWARD (1770–1851), British admiral, received his early training under *Howe and, later serving under *Nelson, lived to command the fleet in the last considerable action fought wholly under sail. As a young man of 23 he was taken up by Lord Howe, made a lieutenant, and served in the *Queen Charlotte*, the flagship of the Channel Fleet, where he was directly under Howe's eye, serving as his aide. He was present at the battle of the * Glorious First of June in 1794 and prospered thenceforward. He was promoted to commander soon after the battle, and by 1805 was a * post-captain senior enough to command a ship of the line, H.M.S. * Orion, at * Trafalgar.

By the end of the long war with France, Codrington was a rear admiral and a Knight of the Bath, with experience in the Channel, the North Sea, and the Mediterranean, where he served for nearly three years. In 1827 he returned to the Mediterranean as commander-in-chief, in circumstances when great diplomacy was needed if war involving various powers was to be avoided.

At this time the Greeks were in active revolt against Turkish rule in the Morea and elsewhere. Great Britain, though not formally at war with Turkey, was in active sympathy with the Greeks; Byron had died at Missolonghi in their cause, * Cochrane was employing his talents on their behalf at sea, and there were French and Russian squadrons off the Morea ready to act against the Porte if given a lead by Britain.

Codrington had been in treaty with Ibrahim Pasha, the Turkish admiral, for a suspension of hostilities, but they reached no satisfactory conclusion. One episode led to another to raise tension further until on 20 October 1827 Codrington entered the Bay of Navarino, where the Turkish fleet was at anchor, with French and Russian ships of war in support. The original hope of the various commanders, and particularly of their governments, had been to intimidate Ibrahim Pasha, not to fight a battle, but the Turks were rash enough to fire first and in the space of a few hours their fleet was annihilated by opponents not only better trained but also much superior in strength.

After the battle, Codrington was recalled, as he realized he would be, for the fullest inquiry. Somewhat reluctantly he was cleared of blame for fighting the action. In 1831 he was appointed to command the Channel Squadron, and from 1839 to 1842 was commander-in-chief at Plymouth.

COFFERDAM, (1) a temporary structure in the form of an enclosed dam which can be erected on the seabed or the bed of a river and pumped dry to enable men to work within it below water level without having to wear diving suits. They are used largely in harbour works and for the construction of the piers of bridges. See also CAISSON (1). **(2)** Heavy transverse * bulkheads in large merchant vessels, particularly tankers, built as a safety measure between the holds or oil tanks. They consist of a double bulkhead with a narrow space between them, the space frequently being used for the carriage of oil fuel or water ballast.

COG, (1) a merchant ship of the 13th, 14th, and 15th centuries, * clinker built with a rounded bow and stern, fore and after castles, and very broad in the beam. It was particularly a North European ship, used widely in the Baltic, North Sea, and on the Atlantic coast of France and Spain. Though normally used for trade purposes, it was also occasionally used as a ship of war. At the battle of * Sluys (1340) Edward III led the English fleet in the cog *Thomas* against the French fleet off the Flemish coast. The * round ship of medieval times was virtually a cog. **(2)** A type of small sailing craft used for local commerce on the rivers Humber and Ouse in northeast England.

COIL, the normal method for the stowage of rope on board ship, laid up in circular turns known as * fakes. The direction in which the coils are laid up depends on the * lay of the rope; if it is laid-up right-handed the rope is coiled clockwise from left to right, if laid-up left-handed, it is coiled anti-clockwise from right to left. The reason for this is that the correct direction of coiling keeps the lay of the rope tight. Hemp rope is always coiled clockwise since it is always laid up right-handed. A range of fakes in the same plane is known as a tier, and a complete coil of rope consists of several tiers each consisting of several fakes. Wire rope is almost invariably coiled on a drum, though still consisting of fakes and tiers, as if not coiled on a drum it will not hold its shape as will rope made from fibres.

A Flemish coil, or cheese, is rope coiled flat on the deck in concentric turns forming only one tier, with the end of the rope in the centre. Its purpose is to give a neat, or * tiddley, finish to the * falls of * running rigging, etc., when a vessel is anchored or secured to moorings and at rest.

COIR, rope made from the husks of the coconut, light enough to float but with only about one-quarter the strength of * manila rope. It has many uses, particularly when bringing assistance to a ship in distress at sea when coir rope can be floated down across her bows enabling her to haul in a heavier cable for towing purposes. In a small sailing vessel running before a following wind and sea, a coir rope towed astern steadies the vessel down and allows the seas to pass under her. See also GRASS-LINE.

COLBERT, JEAN BAPTISTE (1619–83), French statesman, was the restorer of the navy of Louis XIV to its greatest level of excellence,

Mediterranean cog: painting of 'The Miracle of St. Nicholas' by the school of Gentile da Fabriano, early 15th century

becoming minister of marine in 1669. The king's interest lay only in military glory, and it was left to Colbert to champion the cause of the navy. He reconstructed the French naval port of Toulon, established the new naval base of Rochefort, and set up naval schools at Rochefort, St. Malo, and Dieppe. He re-equipped the navy with fine new ships, and to man them introduced a system of classes under which every seaman, according to his class, served for six months every three, four, or five years. He also introduced a scheme of lower-deck pensions, which made service in the navy popular. Yet at the same time he manned the French *galleys in a most brutal manner. He issued orders to magistrates to sentence every criminal and beggar to labour at the oar, and French settlers in Canada were instructed to capture Indians for the same purpose.

COLD FRONT, the line in a typical depression where the cold air coming in to fill the low pressure area meets with warm air and pushes it up in a wave-shaped bulge. This line is known as a cold front, and always follows a *warm front, which is the line in front of the bulge where the warm air has not yet been overtaken by the cold. As a cold front always travels faster than a warm front, it eventually catches it up and pushes underneath the warm air to fill up the *depression, a process known as occlusion. See DEPRESSION for illus., and METEOROLOGY.

COLES, COWPER PHIPPS (1819–70), British naval officer and ship designer, was the first man

to develop the idea of a warship with low *freeboard and carrying a few heavy guns in armoured, revolving turrets in place of the fixed gun batteries of former days. His designs for such a ship, the *Captain*, provided with a full rig of sails as well as steam propulsion, were submitted to the Admiralty in 1886 and caused fierce controversy but were finally approved by the First Lord of the Admiralty, H. C. E. Childers, in spite of doubts expressed by the *Controller of the Navy as to her stability and seaworthiness. The ship was built by Messrs. Laird of Birkenhead, and when launched in 1870 her freeboard proved to be two feet less than the eight feet which Coles had calculated. Caught by a squall during the night of 7 September 1870 with all her sails spread, she capsized and sank with almost all hands, including both Captain Coles, who was a passenger on board, and Childers's son, whom he (Childers) had appointed to her as a midshipman to demonstrate his faith in Coles's design.

COLES, KAINES ADLARD (1901–), British yachtsman and author, was winner of the *Royal Ocean Racing Club Class III championships in 1947, 1957, and 1963. He was also a member of the British team in the *One Ton Cup series of 1965. He is a prolific writer of books on sailing, of which the best known are *Heavy Weather Sailing, Creeks and Harbours of the Solent, Channel Harbours and Anchorages, Brittany Harbours and Anchorages, Biscay Harbours and Anchorages* (two volumes), *'Mary*

Anne' among Ten Thousand Islands, *Sailing and Cruising, North Atlantic*, *More Sailing Days*, *Close-Hauled*, and *Broken Waters*.

COLLAR, (1) a name given originally to the lower end of the principal *stays of a mast in a square-rigged ship, but later to the rope, with a *deadeye in its end, to which the stay was secured at its lower end. Thus, the collar of the forestay was the short length of rope attached to the stem of the ship to which the stay was set up and secured. **(2)** The *eye in the upper end of a stay or in the *bight of the *shrouds which is threaded over the masthead before being set up taut to hold the mast secure. **(3)** The neck of a ring bolt.

COLLIER, a vessel carrying a cargo of coal in bulk. In the 17th and 18th centuries 'sea coal' was carried in collier *brigs from the northern east-coast ports of Britain to London, and from other ports to other destinations. Loading and discharging arrangements were both primitive and the amount of coal carried was very small, though it sufficed for domestic requirements during the sailing era. A typical collier brig could carry about 300–400 tons of coal, unloading it into *lighters moored alongside, by a system known as 'coal-whipping'. Many of the Northumbrian collier brigs were known as *'cats' or 'cat-built', and it was these vessels which Captain James *Cook selected for his three great voyages of exploration in 1768–80. He had been first apprenticed to the sea in Northumbrian collier brigs and well knew their great strength of construction and hard weather qualities.

The advent of steam propulsion for ocean-going ships in the mid-19th century and the consequent necessity for establishing coal depots abroad for refuelling purposes, as well as growing industrial needs, gave rise to a requirement for vessels of much greater cargo-carrying capacity, and this was met by steam-driven ships with capacious holds which could carry at least 6,000 tons of coal in bulk. This world-wide trade in coal flourished for a century until the growth in use of oil as a fuel, coupled with the increasing use of diesel engines for ship propulsion, severely curtailed its extent. Nevertheless, many industrial purposes still call for the use of large quantities of coal, and this, allied to a wide domestic use for heating, still provides a worthwhile trade for ships fitted for the carriage of coal. Modern colliers are built to carry 25,000 tons or more as a single cargo.

COLLINGWOOD, CUTHBERT, 1st Baron Collingwood (1748–1810), British vice admiral, is recalled most often through his association with Lord *Nelson, but he was remarkable in his own right. Born in Newastle upon Tyne, he rose slowly in the navy for he had no influence behind him, and he won his commission as lieutenant at the battle of Bunker Hill during the American War of Independence for gallantry in supplying the soldiers engaged ashore.

Collingwood's next opportunity came in 1777 when he was serving in the West Indies with Nelson, who was ten years his junior. He succeeded his young friend in command of the *Badger* *brig, after which he was appointed to a *frigate, which gave him *post-captain's rank at the age of 32. There his luck ended, for in 1781, when commanding the *Pelican*, he was wrecked in a hurricane and he had no opportunity for distinction during the rest of the war.

During the two wars against France (1793–1801 and 1803–15) Collingwood was almost permanently at sea until his death. He took part in three major fleet engagements, *Howe's victory of the *Glorious First of June in 1794; at *Cape St. Vincent nearly three years later; and at *Trafalgar in 1805, when he was Nelson's second-in-command. On each occasion he distinguished himself by his personal gallantry, though in 1794 he was not among the captains who received the King's gold medal in spite of the fact that he had fought the *Barfleur* with credit after his admiral, George Bowyer, had been severely wounded and carried below. This omission, however, was remedied in 1797, when Collingwood commanded H.M.S. *Excellent* in Sir John *Jervis's action against a superior Spanish fleet. He did so well that it is hard to decide whether he, or Nelson in H.M.S. *Captain*, did more to ensure victory. On this occasion no invidious distinction was made in the distribution of awards, for all flag-officers and captains were included, and the Admiralty sent Collingwood a second gold medal for his part in Howe's victory.

In the preliminaries to Trafalgar it was Collingwood, flying his vice admiral's flag in H.M.S. *Dreadnought*, who watched *Villeneuve's combined Franco-Spanish fleet as it entered Cadiz shortly after an inconclusive action off Finisterre with Sir Robert *Calder. Properly reinforced, he remained stationed off that port until Nelson's arrival in September 1805 to take charge of operations as commander-in-chief.

On 21 October, the day Trafalgar was fought, Collingwood had charge of the lee column. He flew his flag in the *Royal Sovereign*, fresh from dock, and he was closely engaged long before the rest of his squadron. 'See how that noble fellow Collingwood takes his ship into action,' exclaimed Nelson from the deck of the *Victory*. Before the end of the day Collingwood received word of the mortal wound of his friend, and command of the fleet devolved upon him. He has been criticized for failing to anchor the fleet after the battle in view of the heavy storm which blew up, an order which in fact Nelson had given before the action opened. Many of the prizes taken in the battle were thereby lost by wreck or escape into Cadiz, but it is impossible to say that they would not have been lost even if Collingwood had given the order to anchor. For his share of the victory he was raised to the peerage.

With the death of Nelson, Collingwood succeeded to the chief command in the Mediterranean and found himself in charge of the naval strategy of a station stretching from the Dardanelles to western Spain, during a great war and at a time when Britain had few friends. His dispositions were never questioned by those at home, and his pleas to return were refused. He died early in 1810 off Minorca, sad that the peerage which had been granted him after Trafalgar was not allowed to descend through his two daughters. He lies buried in St. Paul's, close to Nelson.

G. Murray, *Life of Admiral Collingwood* (1936); O. Warner, *Life and Letters of Vice Admiral Lord Collingwood* (1968).

COLLINS, GREENVILE (d. 1694), English naval officer, sailed from 1669 to 1671 with Sir John *Narborough as *master in his expedition into the Pacific and was employed on hydrographic work during that voyage. But the continuing reliance of British seamen on Dutch charts for the navigation of their own shores led Samuel *Pepys, Secretary of the Admiralty, to appoint Collins in June 1681 'to make a survey of the sea coast of the Kingdom', the king granting him the title of Hydrographer to the King.

With inadequate funds and equipment Collins prepared 120 plans of harbours and stretches of open coast, forty-eight of which were engraved and issued in *Great Britain's Coasting Pilot*, first published in 1693. This was the first comprehensive survey of the British coast ever made, and although the work came under official criticism for its inadequacies, it ran into twelve editions in the 18th century and was widely used by British seamen.

COLLINSON, Sir RICHARD (1811–83), British admiral, was born at Gateshead. He entered the navy in December 1823 and served under Captain Forester in the *Chanticleer* while employed on a survey of South America. After service in China, he was promoted to *postcaptain in 1842 and in 1847 was appointed in command of the *Enterprise* in an expedition for the relief of Sir John *Franklin via the Bering Strait. Accompanied by Robert *McClure in the *Investigator*, he left Plymouth on 20 January 1850 but the two ships became separated off Cape Horn and proceeded independently northwards. The *Investigator* successfully rounded

Point Barrow, but ice prevented the *Enterprise* from doing so until the following year, and the expedition failed in its object of finding and bringing relief to Sir John Franklin. Collinson then spent three winters in the Arctic and added considerably to the geographical knowledge of the region. Although he discovered a *NorthWest passage, McClure had successfully made such a discovery first. After his return in 1858 he was awarded the gold medal of the Royal Geographical Society and in 1875 was appointed Deputy Master of Trinity House.

COLLISION BULKHEAD, an extra stout watertight transverse bulkhead built in the fore part of a ship to prevent the flow of water aft if the bow of the ship is damaged in a collision.

COLLISION MAT, a large square of very stout canvas roped and fitted with hogging lines at each corner to allow it to be drawn under the hull of a ship. The canvas is thrummed with small stuff or *oakum to act as a sealing agent. When drawn over a damaged part of the hull, the pressure of the seawater forces it tight against the ship's side and limits the inflow to little more than a trickle. The mat was invented in the mid-19th century by Rear Admiral the Hon. A. A. L. P. Cochrane of the British Navy. See also FOTHERING.

COLOMB, PHILIP HOWARD (1831–99), British rear admiral, and his brother Sir JOHN (1838–1909) played an important part in the higher education of the British Navy by their work as historians, tacticians, and strategists. As a naval officer, Philip Colomb served in many parts of the world and on the anti-slavery patrol in the Indian Ocean, of which he wrote a valuable account. His new system of signals and his research into the causes of collision at sea were widely accepted. In his most important book, *Naval Warfare* (1891), he came to many conclusions which were shortly to be more publicized by Captain A. T. *Mahan. Sir John Colomb's career was in the Royal Marines and in Parliament. He is best known for his books on imperial defence, *The Defence of Greater Britain* (1879) and *Imperial Federation: Naval and Military* (1886), which were written at a time when the question of the contribution of the colonies to the defence of the empire was first raised.

COLOMBO, the principal seaport of Sri Lanka. Originally an Arab settlement, it was taken by the Portuguese in 1517, captured by the Dutch in 1656, and surrendered to the British in 1796, by whom it was used as a naval base until Ceylon became independent. The vast trade of Sri Lanka in tea and coffee passes almost entirely through the port of Colombo.

COLOSSUS, a term often applied to statues of great size. The only such statue of maritime interest was the bronze statue of the sun-god Helios, one of the seven wonders of the world, which stood near the harbour at Rhodes. It was made by Chares of Lindus from the spoils of war left by Demetrius Poliorcetes when he raised the siege of Rhodes in 304 B.C. The statue, reported to be 70 cubits (110 ft) high, took twelve years to complete. Legend has it that the statue held in its hand a light to act as a beacon to shipping and that it stood across the entrance of the harbour, ships passing between its legs, but this is unlikely. The statue was overthrown by an earthquake in, it is believed, 224 B.C., the pieces lying where they fell for ten or eleven centuries, when they were purchased for conversion into weapons. It was also a name used for warships in various navies, a *ship of the line of this name being in the British fleet at the battle of *Trafalgar.

COLOURS, the name by which the national flag flown by a ship at sea is known. 'What colours does she fly?' What is her nationality? In British naval ships the colours are the jack flown on the jackstaff in the bows and the White Ensign flown at the yardarm when at sea or from an ensign staff at the stern in harbour. The colours of a British merchant ship is the *Red Ensign. Most other maritime nations use their national flag for the colours of their merchant marine, though in most such nations naval warships fly a special ensign in addition to the national flag.

The term also signifies the naval ceremony of the daily hoisting and lowering of national flags. In the Royal Navy the colours are hoisted at 0800 from 25 March to 20 September and at 0900 for the rest of the year. On foreign stations the time of hoisting is at the decision of the commander-in-chief. Colours are always lowered at sunset.

COLPOYS, Sir JOHN (1742–1821), British admiral, entered the navy in 1756 and saw active service at the capture of Louisburg in 1758, and of Martinique in 1762. After nearly forty years service he was made rear admiral in 1794 and hoisted his flag in the *London,* in the Channel fleet under Lord *Howe. Promoted vice admiral, he was present at *Spithead when the great mutiny in the Channel fleet broke out in 1797. At one point, owing to a misunderstanding, he came near to being hanged by the seamen. The Admiralty ordered him to strike his flag but it was made clear to him that this was not a reprimand. In 1803 he was appointed as commander-in-chief at *Plymouth, having meanwhile been promoted admiral. He did not serve at sea again, but in 1804 became a Lord Commissioner of the Admiralty; his last appointment was in 1816 as governor of *Greenwich Hospital.

COLT, in the old days of the Royal Navy a short piece of rope with a knot in the end used by petty officers, with varying degrees of brutality, to urge men on to work. Its use was officially forbidden by the Admiralty in 1809, though it persisted in some ships for a few years longer. See also START, TO.

COLUMBIA, a *cutter yacht of 102 tons displacement and spreading 13,100 sq ft of canvas designed by Nat *Herreschoff and built by the Herreschoff Manufacturing Company at Bristol, Rhode Island, in 1899 for a syndicate of American yachtsmen headed by J. Pierpont Morgan, to defend the *America's Cup against the first challenge made by Sir Thomas *Lipton with *Shamrock I.* Her hull had manganese bronze plating up to the waterline with steel plating for the topsides up to the deck. In the 1899 series of races *Columbia* successfully defended the cup. Two years later, in 1901, when Sir Thomas challenged again with a new yacht, *Shamrock II,* the American syndicate asked Herreschoff to design and build another contestant, named *Constitution.* In the eliminating trials the old defender, *Columbia,* still proved the faster of the two, and for the second time, in the capable hands of her skipper, Charles Barr, she successfully defended the cup against the British challenger, winning three races in a row by a narrow margin of 1 min. 20 sec., 3 min. 35 secs., and 41 sec.

Another *Columbia* was an American 12-metre (39-ft) *sloop designed by Olin *Stephens for a syndicate to defend the *America's Cup against the British challenger *Sceptre* in 1958, in which she proved more than a match for the British boat.

COLUMBUS, CHRISTOPHER (1451–1506), discoverer of America, was born in Genoa between 25 August and 31 October 1451 to a family of wool weavers named Colombo, and christened Cristoforo. Later, in Spain, he was known as Cristobal Colón; the latinized version was adopted by English writers. He grew up illiterate, helping his father Domenico at the loom, went to sea as a young lad, and made several voyages in the Mediterranean. In 1476, when serving as a seaman in a Genoese vessel which was attacked and sunk by a French fleet off Lagos, he swam ashore and made his way to Lisbon, joining his younger brother Bartholomew in chartmaking. The following year, in a Portuguese ship, he made a voyage to the north of Iceland and back, and in 1478, as *master or *supercargo, he engaged in a trading voyage from Madeira to Genoa. He married Felipa Perestrello, daughter of the hereditary captain of Porto Santo in the Madeiras in 1479 and the young couple settled at Funchal, whence

Columbus made a voyage to the Portuguese factory of São Jorge da Mina on the Gold Coast as master or pilot of a Portuguese ship.

Instead of following these promising beginnings as a professional mariner, Columbus now moved to Lisbon to promote his 'Enterprise of the Indies', as he called it. This was simply to sail west to the Orient, as an easier and shorter route than around the Cape of Good Hope, which the Portuguese were pursuing and were shortly to attain. In preparation, Columbus learned Portuguese, Castilian, and Latin, read widely, and annotated significantly books such as Marco *Polo's *Book*, Pierre d'Ailly's *Imago Mundi*, and the *Historia Rerum* of Pope Pius II, in which he found support for his conviction that the Atlantic was relatively narrow and that the Eurasian continent lapped most of the way around the world. The vulgar notion that Columbus was trying to prove the world to be round is baseless; all educated Europeans then regarded the world as a sphere. The main reasons why Columbus found it difficult to gain support were first, his gross underestimate of the distance to be covered (2,400 nautical miles from the Canary Islands to Japan, the correct distance being about 10,600), and second, his unprecedented demands: three vessels and their crews to be provided, and, in the event of success, ennoblement, admiralty jurisdiction, and viceroyalty over any new lands discovered, plus a ten per cent cut on all trade.

For over a decade Columbus sustained 'a terrible, continued, painful and prolonged battle' to get his 'Enterprise' adopted. John II of Portugal, Henry VII of England, and Charles VIII of France refused to back it; Ferdinand and Isabella, joint sovereigns of Spain, did so twice; but in 1492 they accepted, and signed 'capitulations' which gave him everything he asked for, not only for the voyage but for his future power, status, and profit, and that of his descendants.

He planned to drop down to the Canary Islands where the easterly trade winds began, and follow the centuries-old technique of latitude sailing, along latitude 28° N., which, according to existing geographical ideas, would hit either Japan or an island south of Japan such as Okinawa. There he proposed to set up a trading factory comparable to those he had seen at *Chios and in Africa, where products of the East and the West could be profitably exchanged. Following a royal command, the *Pinzón family of Palos, local merchant-ship owners, fitted out, manned, and commanded the *caravels *Pinta and *Niña for the Enterprise. The flagship *Santa Maria*, a Galician *nao* (ship) under her master-owner Juan de la Cosa, was chartered by Columbus; she had a crew of northern Spaniards.

On 3 August 1492 the three vessels dropped down the Rio Tinto from Palos on the morning ebb. After effecting repairs at Las Palmas,

Columbus arriving in the New World; illustration from an edition of Columbus's letters, 1493

Canary Islands, and completing with water and provisions at Gomera, they sailed thence on 6 September. Columbus shaped his course due west, and during his first ten days made 1,163 nautical miles. On the 25th, after a false landfall, the wind turned so light and the sea so calm that the men began talking about forcing a premature return, but on 2 October the easterly trades again blew full force. Columbus, after consulting with the two captains Pinzón, ordered the course of the fleet to be changed to WSW., because great flocks of birds were observed flying in that direction. On the 10th mutiny flared up among the men, who were only persuaded to desist by Columbus promising to turn back if no land were sighted within three days. On 11 October 1492, at 10 p.m., as the fleet plunged westward at seven knots, Columbus and several men thought they saw a dim light ahead. It disappeared; but at 2 a.m. on the 12th they made the real landfall, grey coral cliffs illuminated by a moon just past full.

This was the Bahamian island called Guanahaní by the natives and named San Salvador by Columbus. Columbus sailed around the southern cape, approached the lee shore through a gap in the barrier reef, and there landed with banners and took possession *por Castilla y por León*. The gentle Arawak natives, who received him and his people as 'men from the

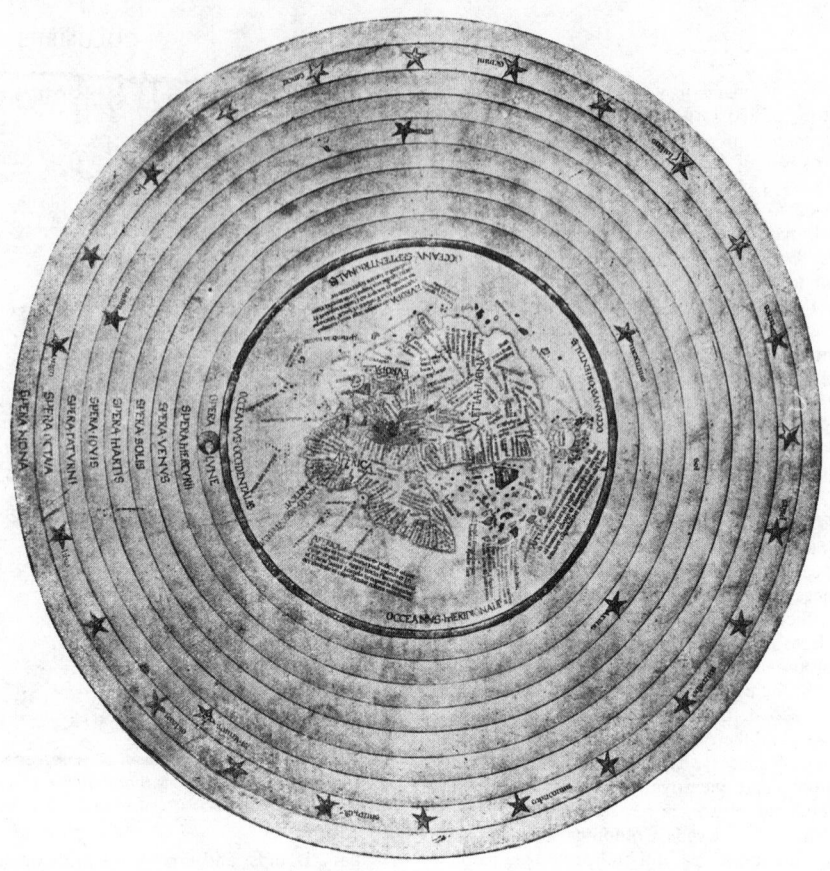

Representation of the world according to Columbus

sky', he called Indians, since this was exactly where he expected to find the Indies.

In quest of Japan, Columbus now sailed south-westerly with an Arawak pilot, discovering more Bahamian Islands. On 28 October he entered a harbour on the north coast of a big island that his pilot called Cuba. It looked so unlike Marco Polo's description of Japan that Columbus jumped to the conclusion that it must be an outlying promontory of China; he even sent an 'embassy' inland from Puerto Gibara to Holguín, hoping there to find *El Gran Can*, the emperor. On the way back to the sea this party passed natives smoking *tobacos*, as they called cigars; not the least valuable of Columbus's discoveries.

During November 1492 Columbus explored the north coast of Cuba from Puerto Padre to Cape Maisi, which he named Cape Alpha and Omega because he believed it to be the terminus of the Eurasian continent, corresponding to Cape St. Vincent in Europe. On 5 December he crossed the Windward Passage, discovered and named Hispaniola (Haiti), passed through Tortuga Channel, greeted everywhere with enthusiasm by the native Arawaks, and entered Caracol Bay, Haiti, on Christmas Eve. There the *Santa Maria*

ran hard and fast on a coral reef. The local cacique being friendly, Columbus decided to build a fort there, man it with volunteers who would search for a gold mine, and return home in the *Niña*. The Admiral (as his men called him after the discovery) set sail from Navidad (as he named the fort) in the *Niña* on 4 January 1493. The *Pinta*, which had parted from him in Cuba, shortly rejoined. They explored the north coast of Hispaniola eastward to Samaná Bay, and on 16 January took off for the homeward passage.

The two caravels, keeping as near the wind as possible, steered north-easterly to about latitude 32° N., longitude 51° 60′ W. On 1 February they caught the westerlies; and after passing latitude 35° N., the Admiral turned due east. Eleven days later they ran into really dirty weather, scudded under bare poles through the dangerous seas of a severe cyclonic disturbance, and parted company. On 15 February the *Niña* sighted Santa Maria in the Azores, but three days more were required to reach a good anchorage off the village of Anjos. There Columbus sent half the *Niña*'s crew ashore to visit the local chapel and fulfil the vows they had made during the recent tempest The acting captain of the island, assuming that they had been poaching on Portuguese Guinea, arrested them; and Columbus could only obtain their release by threatening to bombard the town.

On 24 February the *Niña* made a fresh start eastward. She was soon overtaken by a fresh tempest, with terrifying cross seas. At 7 p.m. on 3 March, when under bare poles, Columbus sighted the Rock of Sintra. He set the one sail that had not been blown to ribbons, * clawed off, and at 9 a.m. on the 4th anchored off Belem, four miles below Lisbon.

After being received by the king of Portugal and convincing him, by exhibiting his captive Indians, that he really had been in 'the Indies', Columbus resumed his course home, and at midday on 15 March 1493 anchored off Palos, whence he had departed thirty-two weeks earlier. Later the same day the *Pinta*, which had missed the Azores but made Bayona in northern Spain, entered and anchored alongside.

Columbus's greatest moments followed shortly. On Easter Sunday, at Seville, he received a letter from Ferdinand and Isabella confirming all his titles and privileges, and ordering him to come to the Court at Barcelona. He made the long overland journey on horseback, accompanied by a few of his men, several Indians, caged parrots, and gold artefacts from Hispaniola. The sovereigns received him honourably and gave him charge of preparations for a a second voyage, intended to establish a string of Spanish trading factories on the coast of Hispaniola and to make further explorations of 'the Indies'. Seventeen vessels (including the *Niña*) were assembled at Seville and Cadiz, provisioned for 1,200 to 1,500 men, most of them to be colonists, and also with horses, seeds, and plants, and a few priests to convert the natives, whom the sovereigns ordered to be treated 'lovingly'.

This fleet sailed from Cadiz on 25 September 1493, topped up with provisions and cattle at Gomera, and on 13 October took its departure from Ferro in the Canaries. Columbus shaped his course W. by S. in the hope of finding the Lesser Antilles, as directed by his captive Indians. The voyage, before the * trade winds, was uneventful. On the morning of Sunday 3 November the lookouts raised a high island which Columbus appropriately named Dominica; and, finding no harbour, anchored in a roadstead off the round island which he named Mariagalante after his flagship. The fleet then spent six days off an island which Columbus named Santa Maria de Guadalupe, there encountering the man-eating Caribs. In succession, Columbus passed and named each of the Leeward Islands, St. Croix (where his men had their first fight with the Caribs), the Virgin Islands, and Puerto Rico. He made a brief landing at Añasco Bay, Puerto Rico, on 22 November crossed the Mona Passage, coasted the north shore of Hispaniola, and on the 27th anchored off Caracol Bay, Haiti. Columbus there expected to be greeted by the garrison of Navidad, but not a man was alive. The Spaniards, after quarrelling over gold and women, had formed a gang which penetrated the interior where they encountered a tough cacique named Caonabó who had killed them all.

Navidad was ruled out as the seat of the first settlement. That was made at Isabela on the north coast, which the fleet reached on 2 January 1494 after a long beat to windward. It was a bad site from any point of view. Within a week 300 to 400 of the men were ill. Alonso de Ojeda explored the interior and brought back such big gold nuggets that no Spaniard would attend to fishing or planting crops. On 2 February 1494 Columbus sent home twelve of his seventeen sail, with these big nuggets, specimens of what he thought to be oriental spices, and twenty-five captured Indians. In person he led an exploring expedition into the Vega Real, the interior plateau of Hispaniola, and built a small fort there.

Leaving Isabela in charge of a council headed by his younger brother Diego, the Admiral spent the next five months cruising to the westward in the *Niña* and two smaller caravels, hoping to prove Cuba to be a peninsula of China. Although he made a number of discoveries, including Jamaica, he turned back before reaching the western cape of Cuba and reached Isabela, still convinced that he had discovered a promontory of China. At Isabela he found all in disorder. Diego Colón had proved incapable of handling hundreds of greedy, gold-seeking Spaniards, and his brother Bartholomew, who had just arrived from Spain with supplies, had as yet no authority. Many Spaniards spent their time roving about the interior, despoiling the natives. One group seized the caravels which Bartholomew brought out, and sailed for home with their ill-gotten gold. In 1495 the Columbus brothers were mainly occupied in subduing Hispaniola, whose native caciques, now thoroughly aroused by the Spaniards' cruelty and cupidity, attempted ineffectively to resist. The Admiral himself started the Indian slave trade by shipping 500 captives home. More than half perished during the passage; the remainder were sold at the slave market in Seville, and most of them languished and died.

Deciding it was time for him to go home and attend to his political fortunes, Columbus set sail in the *Niña*, accompanied by a second caravel, on 10 March 1496. They were badly overcrowded with 225 Spaniards and thirty Indian slaves. He tried sailing the reverse course of his outward passage of 1493. Taking departure from

Guadeloupe on 20 April, the caravels made slow progress against head winds in the *horse latitudes. By 8 June, when they made landfall some 35 miles north of Cape St. Vincent, provisions had fallen so short that there was talk of eating the Indian captives. Three days later they anchored off Cadiz.

Assuming that his troubles were caused by an excess of pride, Columbus now assumed the humble garb of a Minorite friar. The sovereigns invited him to court, but it was obvious that their enthusiasm for 'the Indies' was waning, and that complaints against the rule of the Columbus brothers in Hispaniola were taking effect. Although the Admiral had plenty of gold artefacts to present and lost no time in making proposals for a third voyage, two years elapsed before a new expedition was fitted out. His object was to explore south of his former landfall in the Lesser Antilles in the hope of finding a continent.

Columbus's third voyage began on 30 May 1498 at Sanlúcar de Barrameda. He had three vessels, the ship *Santa Maria de Guia* and two caravels. After calling at Funchal and Gomera, they dropped down to the Cape Verde Islands and took departure from Santiago on 4 July. Steering south-west to latitude 10° N., which Columbus thought he could follow to the expected southern continent, he was becalmed for nine days, then caught a south-east wind which took him on 31 July to a landfall of three hills, on an island which he named Trinidad. Entering the Gulf of Paria by the Boca del Sierpe, Columbus explored it fairly thoroughly, and went ashore on 5 August at Ensenada Yacua on the Paria Peninsula of what is now Venezuela. This was the first European landing on the American continent, assuming that John *Cabot in 1497 did not sail beyond Newfoundland and that the site of *Vinland, briefly colonized by *Thorfinn Karlsefni, is also in Newfoundland.

After leaving the Gulf of Paria by one of the Bocas del Dragon on 13 August, Columbus reached the conclusion, based on the vast volume of water coming down the Orinoco, that this land was continental; an *otro mundo* (other world) unknown to the ancients. That did not alter his conviction that he was in the Indies. He believed that this *otro*, or *nuevo*, *mundo* was a land mass with the same relationship to continental Asia as the big islands of Indonesia.

Passing and naming Margarita, and getting word of the pearl fisheries at Cubagua, Columbus crossed the Caribbean to Alta Vela, Hispaniola, and beat up to Santo Domingo which in his absence had replaced Isabela as the capital. Here the third voyage terminated on 31 August 1498.

The Admiral found Hispaniola in turmoil. One Roldán had raised the flag of rebellion against Bartholomew, and had not been subdued.

So few Spaniards remained loyal to the Columbus régime that the Admiral had to make a humiliating peace with Roldán, largely at the expense of the Indians, who were rapidly dying as a result of forced labour. Royal discontent with Columbian rule, and the small returns in gold caused the Spanish sovereigns to send Francisco de Bobadilla to Santo Domingo to reduce the island to order. Bobadilla took the part of the defeated rebels, clapped the Admiral and his brothers in jail, and shipped all three back to Spain in fetters. They reached Cadiz in October 1500.

After six weeks Ferdinand and Isabella ordered them to be released, and invited them to court; but instead of recalling Bobadilla in disgrace and restoring Columbus to his vice-royalty as he naturally expected, they appointed Nicolás de Ovando as Governor of the Indies, sending him out in a fleet of thirty sail carrying 2,500 more colonists. Columbus they paid off by allowing him to fit out a fourth voyage at their expense.

His objective on this *alto viaje* (high voyage) as he called it, owing to the many adventures and difficulties he encountered, was to explore the Gulf of Mexico and find a strait or passage through to the Indian Ocean. This time he had four caravels, *La Capitana* (the flagship) and three smaller ones. His brother Bartholomew captained one, and an old Genoese friend named Fieschi another; his 14-year-old son Ferdinand came too. The fleet sailed from Cadiz on 11 May 1502 and took its departure from Ferro on the 26th. After a quick trans-atlantic passage of twenty-one days he reached Martinique on 15 June, coasted along the Lesser Antilles, anchored in the roadstead off Santo Domingo on 29 May, and sent one of his captains ashore to ask Ovando's permission to enter harbour for shelter from a hurricane that he sensed to be brewing. Ovando rudely refused, mocked at Columbus's weather forecast, and sent thirty ships to sea forthwith. The hurricane caught them in the Mona Passage; only one ship reached Spain and only three others escaped total destruction. In the meantime, Columbus's good seamanship caused his four caravels to weather the typhoon with slight damage.

From Cayo Largo off Cuba, Columbus crossed the Caribbean to Bonacca, one of the Bay Islands off Honduras, and thence proceeded to the mainland, where the city of Trujillo was later founded. On about 10 August 1502, hoping to find a strait, he began a twenty-eight-day beat to windward along the mainland, finally rounding the cape that he appropriately named Gracias à Dios. Now, with sheets started, he skirted the coasts of Nicaragua and Costa Rica, entered Chiriqui Lagoon on 6 October, disappointed that it was not a way through; but he did gather from the Indians that another ocean was not far away.

From 17 October 1502 to New Year's Day 1503 the fleet switched back and forth, buffeted by storms, the people hungry and miserable, between El Escudo de Veragua and Puerto Escribanos, east of Nombre de Dios, Panama. Weary and beaten, the men kept Christmas as best they could off what is now the northern entrance to the Panama Canal, never suspecting that the Pacific Ocean lay but a few miles distant. Sailing thence, they anchored on 6 January 1503 off a river of Veragua, which Columbus named Belén. A bar off its mouth and the lagoon inside made so sheltered an anchorage, and signs of gold in the vicinity were so abundant, that Columbus began to build a trading factory. A local cacique called the Quibián, reacting as Indians usually did to Europeans who gave signs of settling down, decided to attack Belén and, after a brisk fight, drove the Spaniards out. One worm-eaten caravel was abandoned in the harbour, and the other three vessels set sail on 16 April 1503.

Columbus's plan was to push easterly along the coast until he reached the meridian of Hispaniola, and to call there before returning to Spain. One caravel, riddled with *teredos, had to be abandoned at Porto Bello, and the two remaining, *La Capitana* and *Santiago*, were in so bad a way that Columbus left the mainland at Cape Tiburón where the present boundary between Panama and Colombia touches the sea. He passed between the Cayman Islands, anchored during a week of stormy weather at Cayo Bretón, and after vainly trying to beat to Hispaniola stood towards Jamaica on the port tack, all hands pumping and baling for dear life. On 25 June, with main decks almost awash, they entered St. Ann's Bay, Jamaica.

There the two caravels were run aground, and there Columbus and his men remained for a full year. The amiable natives furnished them with food, and when the supply slackened off, Columbus scared them into resuming it with an opportune total eclipse of the moon. Mutiny was fomented by the Porras brothers whom Columbus had been forced by the government to take along. Two of the Admiral's most loyal officers, Diego Méndez and Fieschi the Genoese, crossed the Windward Passage in dugout canoes to get help, but Ovando kept them waiting for nine months before he would allow a small caravel to be sent out on 29 June 1504, at Columbus's expense, to rescue him and his men. At Santo Domingo Columbus chartered another vessel, in which he, his son and brother, and some of his men departed for Spain on 12 September, arriving at Sanlúcar on 7 November 1504.

He had less than eighteen months to live, most of that time in misery from arthritis, and from his sense of outrage at the ingratitude of the crown. The queen, his benefactor, died, and Ferdinand, who had never cared for Columbus, would do nothing for him. Painfully the Admiral followed the court to Valladolid where he died on 20 May 1506. The court chronicle did not even notice his death, and years elapsed before his ashes were given honourable burial in the cathedral of Santo Domingo.

Columbus died in sorrow and frustration. He had not found the Strait, he had not met Chinese or Japanese potentates, nor had he converted any large number of heathen. Although, as he well stated in a famous letter, 'By divine will I have placed under the sovereignty of the King and Queen an Other World, whereby Spain, which was reckoned poor, is become the richest of countries,' the same Sovereign had not only failed to honour him with a title but had stripped him of his legal prerogatives.

Four and a half centuries after Columbus's death there can be no reasonable doubt of his having been one of the greatest navigators in modern history. Although his celestial navigation was not remarkable, his dead reckoning, always right when his pilots called it wrong, was impeccable. His first voyage was the effective discovery of America, in spite of his mistaken identification; and the other three enlarged the area of discovery to include the entire Caribbean except the Gulf coasts of Mexico and the U.S.A. *Magellan is the only navigator in history to have discovered more islands and a greater extent of coast than did Columbus. As a colonial administrator Columbus failed; but as an Italian attempting to govern Spaniards he was hindered from the start; and as Oviedo wrote, any early governor of Hispaniola, to have been a success, must have been 'angelic indeed and superhuman'.

The standard biographies of Columbus are Professor Samuel Eliot Morison's *Admiral of the Ocean Sea* (Boston 1942), the same author's *Christopher Columbus, Mariner* (Boston 1955), and B. Landstrom's *Columbus* (1967).

'COMB THE CAT', to, the habit of a *boatswain's mate, during the flogging of a seaman, of running his fingers through the tails of a *cat-o'-nine-tails after each stroke in order to separate them in preparation for the next. After several strokes, when the victim's back had begun to bleed, the tails of the cat were apt to become coated with blood and to stick together, and a stroke with the tails matted together could inflict serious and permanent damage to the man undergoing punishment. It was necessary therefore, in the victim's own interests, to separate the tails before inflicting the next stroke.

COME, to, a verb with many maritime meanings. When a helmsman in a sailing vessel receives an order to come no nearer, he is to hold the vessel as close as she already is to the wind and not attempt to sail her any closer. A ship comes to an *anchor when she lets it go. 'Come up the *capstan', an order to walk the *cable back to take off the strain or to *veer some of the cable; 'come up the *tackle', an order to let go the *fall.

COME HOME, to, an *anchor is said to come home, or be coming home, when its *flukes are not holding in the ground and it *drags.

COMMANDER, (1) the naval rank next below that of *captain; in a large warship he is the executive officer and second in command. In the various branches of naval service (engineering, supply, medicine, etc.) the head of each branch on board a large ship would usually be of commander's rank. In smaller warships, such as *frigates, *submarines, etc., the commanding officer would normally be of commander's or lieutenant-commander's rank.

Originally, in the British Navy, promotion to commander meant promotion to the command of a ship smaller than a 'post' ship, i.e., not a *rated ship. The officer thus promoted had the title of captain but not the actual full rank, only achieving this when he was posted to a rated ship. (See also POST-CAPTAIN.) In some European navies this nomenclature is still retained for the equivalent rank of commander, e.g., the French *capitaine de frégate*, the German *fregatten-kapitän*, etc. For a table of equivalent ranks, see APPENDIX 1. **(2)** The name given to a large wooden-headed mallet used for heavy work on board ship.

COMMISSION, (1) the documents by which naval officers hold their status as accredited officers in the navy in which they serve. It is normally issued when an officer reaches the rank of sub-lieutenant or its equivalent in other navies. In the case of 'Royal' navies it is usually issued by the sovereign, and in the cases of 'republican' navies by either the President or the national naval authority. **(2)** The period in which a warship, with a full complement of officers and men, is allocated to particular duties which may be in any part of the world. After she has been commissioned she continues in that state until she returns to her home, or occasionally another, port to *pay off, when her company disperses. Commissions are usually for a fixed term, which may vary according to the part of the world in which the ship serves. At the end of a commission a ship may recommission immediately with a new complement, may remain temporarily out of commission during a major dockyard refit, or if at the end of her active life may be laid up in reserve or pending sale or breaking up. The *commissioning pendant flown at the masthead is the sign that a ship is in commission. **(3)** The instrument, now abolished, under which a privately owned vessel was permitted to carry arms and to cruise in time of war or *reprisal against the ships of another nation as a *privateer. This particular commission, issued by the national naval authority, was known as a *letter of marque or mart.

COMMISSIONING PENDANT, the long, narrow pendant flown at the masthead of warships commanded by commissioned officers. In the British Navy it is white with a red cross, and is flown permanently, by night as well as by day, so long as the ship remains in *commission.

COMMODORE, an intermediate rank between captain and rear admiral, often held by a senior captain when appointed to certain commands and posts of extra responsibility. It is not a step in the ladder of promotion (a captain is normally promoted direct to rear admiral) but pertains only to the responsibility of the job. A commodore flies a *broad pendant as the sign of his rank. In merchant navies the senior captain of a commercial shipping line is usually known as the commodore of the line. In a yacht club the commodore is the senior officer of the club by election of its members; he is normally assisted in his duties by a vice-commodore and rear-commodore, also elected to those posts by the members of the club. See APPENDIX 1.

COMMON LOG, see LOG.

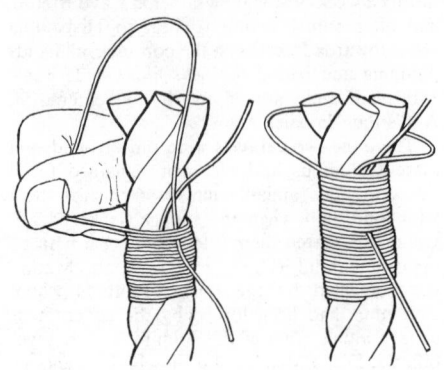

Common whipping

COMMON WHIPPING, a whipping widely used to prevent the strands at the end of a rope from unlaying or fraying. The end of the whipping twine is laid along the rope towards its end and a number of turns of the twine passed round the rope against its *lay, each turn being hauled taut. At about half the length of the required whipping, the other end of the twine is laid along the rope in the opposite direction and the whipping continued with the bight of the twine, taking the bight over the end of the rope with each turn. When the bight becomes too small to pass over the end of the rope, the second end of the twine is hauled through the turns until the whole whipping is taut. The two ends are then cut off. See also SAILMAKER'S WHIPPING, WEST COUNTRY WHIPPING.

COMPANION, in the days of sail the framing and sash lights on the * quarterdeck and of the * coach through which daylight entered to the cabins below. More recently it is the covering over an upper deck hatchway which leads to the companion-way, or staircase, to the deck below. The word is also loosely used today in place of companion-way and is generally understood to mean the stairs themselves.

COMPANION LADDER, the ladders leading down from the * quarterdeck to the upper deck, one on each side of the ship, in the sailing warships and merchant vessels which had a raised quarterdeck.

COMPANY, the whole crew of a ship, including all officers, men, and boys.

COMPARTMENTS, (1) the spaces between the transverse * bulkheads of a ship. Some of the seagoing * junks met with in the China Sea during early voyages in the 16th and 17th centuries were found to be divided by watertight bulkheads, but the first wooden ships to be fitted with transverse bulkheads in the western hemisphere were the * *Erebus* and * *Terror*, which sailed in 1835 with Commander Edward * Belcher for an Arctic exploration. H.M.S. *Terror*, holed aft by the ice, was saved by her after bulkhead, reaching home with her after section completely full of water. With the introduction of iron, and later steel, as the material used for shipbuilding, transverse bulkheads, and thus division into watertight compartments, became the normal practice in ship construction. **(2)** An old name for those areas of sea contained between the headlands of a nation's coastline and claimed as territorial waters although lying beyond the strict three-mile limit. See also CHAMBERS.

COMPASS, the instrument by which a ship may be steered on a pre-selected course and by which * bearings of visible objects may be taken to fix a ship's position on a chart. There are two types of compass in use at sea, the magnetic compass, of which the north mark points to the magnetic north pole, and the gyroscopic, or gyro, compass, of which the north mark points to the true north pole.

Magnetic compass, a compass which depends for its action on the horizontal component of the earth's magnetic field. It is not known by whom the magnetic compass was invented. Knowledge of the attractive property of the * lodestone is of great antiquity but knowledge of its directional property, fundamental to the magnetic compass, came relatively late in the history of science and technology. The forerunner of the modern magnetic compass consisted of a magnetized needle thrust into a straw or piece of cork which floated freely in a basin of water. On settling, the marked end of the needle indicated the direction of magnetic north. In later times a primitive pivoted needle or needle system was used to serve the same purpose, and later still a compass card, on which the points of the compass were drawn, was attached to a magnetized needle, and the whole was enclosed in a suitable bowl to afford protection, the bowl in turn being mounted in * gimbals in a * binnacle. Magnetic compasses of a rudimentary type were in use in the Mediterranean at least as early as the 12th century.

The magnetic compass was an imperfect instrument until after the time when the first iron ship appeared. The magnetism inherent in an iron ship's structure caused considerable difficulty in the early days, to such an extent that it was suggested seriously that such ships would never be successful for they would be quite unsafe in the absence of well-behaved compasses.

On wooden vessels the directive power of a magnetic compass is dependent, apart from relatively minor effects of ironwork fittings in its vicinity, on the earth's magnetism. Nevertheless, as far back as the beginning of the 19th century, Matthew * Flinders discovered that the compass needle may be deviated from the direction of magnetic north as a result of local attraction, as it was termed, of the ship's iron. He demonstrated that this * deviation was at a maximum with ships' * courses of east or west by compass and disappeared when a ship steered north or south. He also showed how the ship's magnetic effect could be neutralized by means of an unmagnetized rod of iron placed vertically near the compass. This form of corrector is still universally used and is named a Flinders' Bar.

With the advent of iron and steel ships, a great deal of study was directed to the nature of ship magnetism with the object of devising a method of neutralizing it at the compass position. Among those who engaged themselves in this important work was the Astronomer Royal, Sir G. B. Airy, who had the iron steamer *Rainbow* placed at his disposal in 1838. From his careful examination of the vessel's magnetic condition, he introduced a method of neutralizing a ship's magnetism by placing magnets and pieces of unmagnetized iron in the vicinity of the compass.

A perfectly pivoted and properly protected compass is a perfect model of Nature's compass

Compass; from a 16th-century MS

when the effect of the ship's magnetism at its position is neutralized by the compass correctors. The present-day 'dry-card' compass owes its character to Lord Kelvin (see THOMSON, William). It was generally thought, before Kelvin studied the problems of the mariner's compass, that steadiness depended upon the weight acting on the pivot rather than on the natural period of vibration of the compass card with its attached needle system. Kelvin introduced a card light in weight but having a large amount of inertia about its vibration, which was, therefore, a steady card. He achieved this by fitting an aluminium ring at the circumference of the card, above which the card, made of thin rice paper, is supported by fine silk threads secured to the ring. The needle system is slung by silk threads from the ring, and a jewelled cap is set in a small aluminium boss to which the threads supporting the card and the needle system are secured. The jewelled cap is supported on the fine bearing point of an iridium-tipped pivot to keep frictional effects to a minimum.

An alternative method of reducing friction at the compass pivot is to employ a liquid compass. The card, in this case, is immersed in liquid, and it is provided with a flotation chamber which makes the buoyancy of the card and needle system only slightly less than their combined weight. The liquid in the compass bowl also has the effect of damping down the swing of the card. Liquid compasses, on account of their greater steadiness, are used in most ships, and particularly in small craft and lifeboats, as well as in aircraft.

Azimuth compass, a compass designed to observe the amount of magnetic *variation. Many of the early navigators had no knowledge of the existence of variation, and it was not until the 15th century that it was first discovered that the compass needle did not point to true north. It has often been said that it was *Columbus in his first voyage who discovered the existence of variation, but this is not true. The first recorded description of an azimuth compass occurs in João de Lisboa's *Livro de Marinharia*, published in 1514, and for the next two centuries various types of compasses were constructed for the purpose of observing the current value of the variation. Most were completely separate compasses from that used for steering a course, but all had the same basic objective; to take a compass bearing of the sun, the moon, or a star so that a comparison could be made with the calculated bearing, the difference between the two being the variation. One of the great drawbacks to all these compasses was that they required two operators, one to align the sight with the sun or star, the other to take the reading on the compass scale.

The first real improvement in the azimuth compass came in 1812 when Schmalcalder fitted a prism to the sight, by which the compass scale was reflected on to the sight, so that one person could align the sight and simultaneously read off the bearing on the compass scale. Schmalcalder's invention was improved in 1876 by Sir William *Thomson, later Lord Kelvin, using a prism and a lens.

Azimuth compasses are no longer in use, as an azimuth ring, which fits over the top of the standard compass and can rotate around it, enables an azimuth bearing to be taken simply and easily. A magnifying prism is the only sight required. Today there is no need to observe the amount of variation anywhere in the world, since it is recorded on every chart, and azimuth rings are used mainly when swinging ship to discover the individual ship's *deviation, or to take bearings of shore and other objects in the normal course of navigation.

Gyroscopic compass, an electrically driven compass which points to the true north pole as opposed to the magnetic pole to which a compass activated by magnets points. It owes its directional properties to a spinning wheel. Every spinning body has the property whereby it tends to maintain its axis and plane of rotation relative to space, known as gyroscopic inertia. Another property of all spinning bodies is that known as precession, a seemingly paradoxical motion of the spinning body's axis of rotation when an external couple or turning force is applied to it.

A metal wheel mounted within a framework so that its axis of spin may be set to any desired direction, and having friction at all bearings reduced to an absolute minimum, constitutes the basis of a gyroscopic compass. Such a wheel made to spin at very high revolutions by electrical means would tend to maintain its axis of spin in a fixed direction in space. Because of the earth's rotation, such a direction is not fixed relative to the planes of the *meridian and the *horizon at any terrestrial position. It follows that if the direction of the spin axis of the wheel is to serve to indicate a definite compass direction, the apparent movements of the axis relative to the planes of the horizon and the meridian must be controlled in some way.

In a gyroscopic compass the case within which the spinning wheel is housed is fitted with a compass card which, being a model of the natural compass, must remain horizontal at all times with its north–south radial lines always in the plane of the meridian. This is achieved by a device known as a gravity control which is fitted to the sensitive element of the compass. The essence of this control is a mass which, when acted upon by the force of gravity, precesses the wheel axis against its tendency to drift away from the vertical plane of the meridian at exactly the right rate to keep it in the plane of the meridian.

The first successful gyroscopic compass, which was introduced in 1908, was invented by the German engineer Dr. Anschutz. In 1911 Dr. Elmer *Sperry of the U.S.A. patented his gyroscopic compass, and some five years later the British scientist and inventor S. G. Brown introduced his similar compass.

The usefulness of a gyroscopic compass is not confined only to its directional property. The 'master' compass may be used to operate repeater compasses in different parts of the ship, a course recorder, and, most important of all, an *automatic helmsman.

COMPASS ERROR, the combination of *variation and *deviation, is the horizontal angle between the direction indicated by the north point of a magnetic compass card and the true north. It is named east or west according to whether the compass points to the right or to the

left of the true direction. It must be applied to all true *courses taken from a chart in order to ascertain the corresponding compass courses. Likewise it must be applied to compass *bearings in order to find the corresponding true bearings for laying down on a navigational chart.

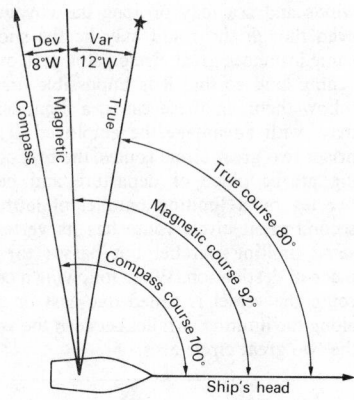

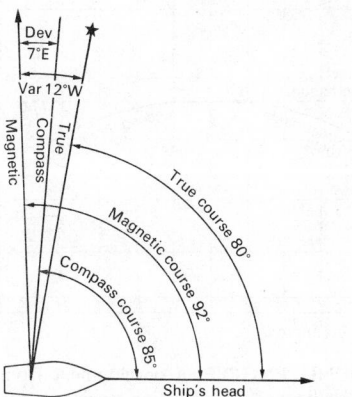

Compass error with westerly (above) and easterly (below) deviation

COMPASS TIMBER, the name given to shipbuilding timber which has been steamed and curved to take up the desired shape when building the hull of a wooden ship.

COMPOSITE BUILT, a ship which is planked with wood on an iron or steel frame. A great many of the *clipper ships of the mid-19th century were composite built, as also were many yachts up to about the beginning of the 20th century.

COMPOSITE GREAT CIRCLE SAILING, a method of sailing between two positions along the shortest route possible without crossing to the poleward side of a parallel of specified *latitude. A feature of *great circle sailing is that a great circle route, unless it be along a *meridian, lies on the poleward side of the corresponding *rhumb line route. In many oceanic routes, especially those of the South Pacific, a vessel following a great circle route would be carried into very high latitudes where adverse winds and sea may prolong the voyage unduly even though the route may be the shortest. In some instances great circle paths pass over intervening land so that it is impossible for ships to follow them. In these cases, a composite route may, with advantage, be employed. This comprises two great circle routes, the first commencing at the place of departure and having its *vertex on a limiting parallel of latitude. The second great circle route has its vertex on the same limiting parallel but passes through the place of destination. When following a composite route the vessel is sailed due east or due west along the limiting parallel between the vertices of the two great circle arcs.

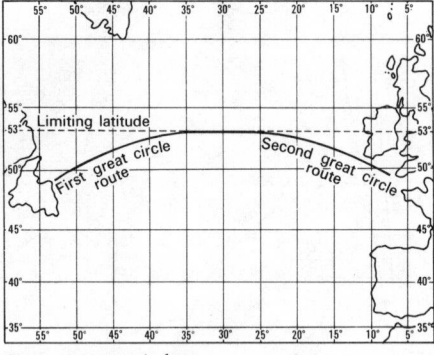

Composite great circle

COMPOUND ENGINE, a development from the single cylinder *reciprocating marine engine in which the steam, after leaving the first cylinder, was passed through a second low-pressure cylinder of larger diameter before being drawn off to a *condenser to be changed back to boiler feed water. This second use of the steam added to the thrust produced by the engine results in a higher engine efficiency for the same amount of steam. Although the principle of compounding an engine was patented as early as 1781 by Jonathan Hornblower, a contemporary of James Watt, it was not until the decade 1860–70, when higher boiler pressures were introduced in marine boilers, that compounding became practicable at sea. See also TRIPLE EXPANSION ENGINE.

COMPRADOR, the equivalent in the Far East of a ship-chandler. The word entered the English language largely through the novels and stories of Joseph *Conrad and Somerset Maugham, who both wrote about the East, and whose tales

attracted a wide public. Originally it was a Portuguese word introduced in the East to denote a house steward and was later adopted by business houses, and particularly those dealing with sea business, as the title of the chief native representative or manager.

COMPRESSION SICKNESS, a disease to which divers are subject if the reduction of pressure in their diving suits is too rapid. Air is a mixture of oxygen and nitrogen, and at normal atmospheric pressure the human blood can absorb both the oxen being used up and the nitrogen lying inert in the tissues of the body. When a diver under water receives this mixture at a pressure equal to that exerted by the water, which at 20 fathoms (36 m) is approximately the pressure of three atmospheres, he can still breathe it without difficulty.

It is when he rises again to the surface, and the pressure of the air he breathes is correspondingly reduced, that he is subject to compression sickness, known among divers as the 'bends'. It is caused by the nitrogen which he has breathed in while under pressure, which forms bubbles when the pressure is suddenly reduced. As these bubbles try to force their way out of his tissues they cause a violent pain in the diver's muscles and joints, which can ultimately result in death if remedial action is not taken.

The remedial action is relatively simple. If the diver's ascent has been too rapid and he is suffering from compression sickness, he can at once be put under pressure again, when the nitrogen is forced back into solution. If the pressure is now released gradually, enabling the body tissues to get rid of the nitrogen without it forming bubbles, the danger of compression sickness is eliminated.

This gradual decompression is normally achieved in one of two ways. The first is to arrange the ascent of the diver in stages, making him pause for various periods of time at various depths as he comes up. A great deal of research on the problems of compression sickness was carried out by Dr. J. B. S. Haldane of the British Admiralty in the first decade of the present century, and he, in conjunction with a scientific committee, produced a table giving the lengths of stoppages at various depths and the total time of ascent. Thus, if a diver has been working for 15 minutes at a depth of 20 fathoms (36 m), he must stop in his ascent at 5, $3\frac{1}{2}$, and $1\frac{1}{2}$ fathoms, and must take not less than 17 minutes over his ascent. If he has been working at this depth for over 90 minutes, he must stop at $8\frac{1}{2}$, $6\frac{1}{2}$, 5, $3\frac{1}{2}$, and $1\frac{1}{2}$ fathoms and must take not less than 163 minutes over his ascent.

The other method of arranging decompression is to make the diver enter a decompression chamber during the course of his ascent. This chamber acts initially on the principle of a diving bell while it is lowered, and the diver enters the chamber through the bottom, the air within it being at the equivalent pressure of the surrounding water. When he is inside the chamber, the door at the bottom through which he entered is closed, and the pressure within is maintained while it is hoisted to the surface. The diver remains in it while on the surface until the specified time of ascent has elapsed, the pressure inside the chamber being gradually reduced corresponding to the ascent stages at which the diver should have paused on his way up.

The maximum depth at which a diver, wearing the normal helmet and rubber suit and breathing compressed air, can work is about 42–5 fathoms (77–82 m), and at that depth only for very short periods. In recent years, with the need to reach far greater depths, considerable research has been carried out in using a mixture of oxygen and helium in place of the normal air mixture of oxygen and nitrogen. It has been discovered that, using this oxygen/helium mixture, there is virtually no known depth limit for deep diving, the only limiting factor being the decompression time, which can be very considerable for a diver working at a great depth. For example, if a diver has been working for 5 minutes at a depth of 100 fathoms (182 m), his decompression time is 5 hours and 38 minutes. See also DIVING.

COMPRESSOR or COMPRESSOR STOPPER, a device for holding the chain *cable attached to an *anchor against the side of the *navel pipe by choking it to prevent it running out. In some larger vessels separate compressors are mounted on the forecastle in the line of the cables, which are then led directly through them. In such cases the cables are held on the compressors after anchoring until they can be permanently secured by the *slips. A more usual practice, however, is to hold them for this purpose by a brake on the *cable-holders. In the older sailing ships, when hemp cables were used instead of chain, the compressor was a curved iron bar, pivoted at one end, with a handle to give leverage which could be applied to the cable where it passed over a block of wood mounted on deck in the line of the run of the cable, either to check the speed at which it was running out or to bring it to a stop altogether and hold it until the cable could be *bitted and secured.

CON, COND or CUN, to, from the Anglo-Saxon *connan*, to know, to be skilful, or possibly from the Latin *conducere*, to lead or conduct, the giving of the necessary orders to the helmsman to steer a ship in a required direction, usually in channels or in sight of land where it is not always necessary or desirable to steer by the *compass. The term is not very frequently used today except in the U.S.A. where it is used as a noun meaning the navigational direction of the ship: 'to take the con', to take over the navigational duties on the *bridge of a ship. The naval *conning tower also derives from the verb, being in its original meaning the armoured tower from which a warship was controlled navigationally in battle.

CONCLUDING LINE, a small line rove through the centre of the wooden steps of a *Jacob's ladder or a stern ladder. It is used for hauling up the ladder for stowage, when each step collapses on top of the step below it.

CONDEMN, to, a legal term in *prize law by which the cargo of a ship, or a ship herself, may in wartime, after the declaration by a belligerent of a *blockade, be declared as contraband and confiscated by a Court of Admiralty. See also CONTINUOUS VOYAGE.

CONDENSER, a piece of equipment in a ship's engine room by which the steam, after use in the main engines, is reconverted into feed water for the boilers. The earliest form of condenser was the jet condenser which was introduced by James Watt for his marine engines. In this, the exhaust steam emitted from the cylinder entered an iron or brass chamber where it was condensed back into fresh water by encountering a jet of cold seawater. The condensed steam, or condensate, was drawn off into the hot well for re-use in the ship's boiler. An improvement on the jet condenser was the surface condenser, introduced around 1845, which is virtually the same type as that used in steamships today. The principle is the same as the jet condenser, but the exhaust steam on entering the condenser chamber passes over a battery of small-bore pipes through which a continuous flow of cold seawater is led, and the condensate is then pumped as before to the supply tanks for re-use in the boilers. In all modern ships an oil separator is used to extract the cylinder lubricating oil which has become mixed with the exhaust steam and would otherwise cause foaming or serious priming of the water in the boilers. An additional effect of the condenser is to produce a partial vacuum which takes the steam from the engines after use and thus increases their efficiency by providing the incoming steam with a greater relative pressure.

CONFEDERATE STATES NAVY (C.S.N.), the navy of the southern states of the U.S.A. which seceded from the Union and brought about the American Civil War of 1861–5. The navy achieved very little of note during its four years of existence, its main success coming on 8 March 1862 when the converted *ironclad *Virginia*, formerly the Federal *frigate *Merrimack*, sank the Federal frigate *Congress and the *sloop *Cumberland* at *Newport News. The captain of the *Virginia* on that occasion was Franklin *Buchanan, who was wounded in the engagement and was thus unable to command the ship during her historic duel next day with the *Monitor*. He was promoted to admiral after sinking the *Congress* and sent to command the main naval forces at Mobile, Alabama, and organize the defence of *Mobile Bay. His force was, however, virtually wiped out in the battle fought at Mobile Bay on 6 August 1864, the Federal squadron being commanded on that occasion by Admiral *Farragut. With the surrender of the southern army in 1865 the Confederate States Navy came to an end, such useful warships as remained to it being absorbed into the U.S. Navy.

CONFLANS, HUBERT DE BRIENNE, Comte de (1690–1777), French admiral, served with distinction as a captain in the West Indies against the British during the War of Austrian Succession (1739–48) and in 1746 successfully fought a West Indies *convoy through to its destination against considerable odds. By the time of the Seven Years War (1756–63) he had been made a marshal of France as a result of fifty-three years of naval service, and was appointed vice admiral in command of the Brest fleet. By 1759, France had come to realize that only a successful invasion of Britain could stave off defeat in the war. The part to be played by the Brest fleet was to escort a French army from Vannes round the west of Ireland and land it in the Clyde estuary, then to proceed north of Scotland to Ostend, pick up a second French army, and land it on the Essex coast in the Crouch and Blackwater estuaries. Conflans, for all his success during the Austrian Succession War, was no longer the man for the job. Even as a young officer he had always stood firmly on his dignity as an aristocrat, and this made him haughty and unapproachable in his new command. Now he had been set a task which demanded all the energies of a young man and qualities of inspiring leadership which he had never possessed.

Brest, in 1759, was being *blockaded by the British Western Squadron commanded by Sir Edward *Hawke. But Hawke was temporarily blown off station by a westerly gale in November 1759, and Conflans took his chance to put to sea in order to attack the British inshore squadron under Captain Robert Duff which was watching the invasion transports lying in *Quiberon Bay in the Morbihan estuary. As he chased the squadron seawards on 20 November, he was confronted by Hawke's returning fleet. In a gale of wind from the north-west, both fleets crowded on sail, the French to escape and the British in chase, into the rock- and shoal-strewn

waters of Quiberon Bay. In the pell-mell rush of French ships to escape, Conflans lost all control of his fleet.

In a furious, confused fight which continued into the following day, seven French *ships of the line, including the flagship, the *Soleil Royal*, were taken, wrecked, foundered, or beached and burned. Five, trapped in the Morbihan, managed to bump their way over the bar of the River Vilaine into waters which no ship of their size had ever penetrated before. Most of them broke their backs on crossing the bar and were never again fit for service. Conflans never served at sea again, spending the rest of his life in retirement.

CONGRESS, U.S.S., was one of the *'six original frigates' with which the U.S. Navy was originally formed by Act of Congress in 1794. She was broken up in 1834 because of the deterioration of her hull. A second *Congress* was launched in 1841. She was a sailing *frigate and during the American Civil War (1861–5) was set on fire in Hampton Roads on 8 March 1862 by the C.S.S. *Virginia* (ex-*Merrimack*), under the command of Franklin *Buchanan, the day before the historic duel between the two *ironclads *Monitor* and *Virginia*.

CONICAL BUOY, a *buoy in the shape of a cone used to mark the *starboard hand side of a channel when entering with the flood tide. They are generally painted black or some other solid colour and are usually marked with odd numbers. The *port hand side of a channel is indicated with *can buoys, marked with even numbers. See BUOYAGE, SYSTEMS OF, APPENDIX 4.

CONNARD, PHILIP (1875–1958), British painter, began his working life as a house painter, but won a scholarship to the Royal College of Art and later a British Institution prize which took him to Paris for a period of study. During the First World War (1914–18) he was appointed an official war artist with the British Navy and painted a number of pictures of naval life and of the fleet which were outstanding in their quality and realism, making Connard one of the foremost marine artists of the day. He was elected A.R.A. in 1918, R.A. in 1925, and was appointed Keeper of the Royal Academy in 1945.

CONNING TOWER, (1) the armoured control centre of a major warship after the change from wood to iron and steel from which, originally, the ship was navigated in battle. Later, with the increasing sophistication of weapons and their control, it became additionally the centre of communications with the guns and torpedo tubes; and all information in relation to a ship's fighting requirements, such as *radar plots and ranges, fall of shot observation, alteration of enemy's *courses, etc., is fed into it. It is occupied only in battle: on all other occasions navigation and weapon control is exercised from the *bridge. **(2)** The connecting structure between the bridge and the pressure hull of a *submarine, in older submarines no more than a trunk with an internal ladder, sealed at both ends by watertight hatches which are closed when the submarine is submerged. In the larger modern submarines the conning tower provides space for equipment and the captain's *cabin, and is usually known as the 'sail'.

CONOLLY, RICHARD L. (1892–1962), American admiral, served with distinction in *destroyers in the eastern Atlantic during the First World War (1914–18) and was in command of a destroyer squadron in the Pacific when the Japanese attack on *Pearl Harbor took place on 7 December 1941. In April 1942 he was appointed to the staff of Admiral Ernest *King, commander-in-chief U.S. Fleet, and in March 1943 became Commander Landing Craft and Bases, North-West African Waters, and later commanded amphibious forces in attack landings on the shores of Sicily and Italy. Assigned to the Amphibious Forces, Pacific Fleet, in October 1943, he participated in a series of landings at Kwajalein, Wake, Marcus, Guam, Leyte, and Lingayen Gulf, and in each instance the force under his command displayed outstanding efficiency. For a period after the end of the Second World War he served as deputy chief of Naval Operations and in September 1946 was selected to command the U.S. naval forces in Europe and continued in that post until September 1950. His last appointment was as president of the Naval War College at Newport, Rhode Island. His performance of his duties in Europe was characterized by quiet leadership which won the esteem of naval officers of all countries, as well as of the officers and men serving under him. He and his wife were killed in an air crash.

CONRAD, JOSEPH (Josef Teodor Nalecz Korzeniowski) (1857–1924), seaman and novelist, was born in Poland when that country was part of the Russian Empire. His parents, both of good family, were Polish patriots who longed for national independence, and his father, Apollo Korzeniowski, was exiled to Russia for subversive activities, whither his wife and only son accompanied him. Conrad's mother died when he was 7 and his father when he was 11, and he was placed in the care of his uncle, Thaddeus Bobrowski, who long befriended and advised him. As a child he was a great reader in Polish and in French, but at school at Cracow he was unhappy and expressed the wish to go to sea. Through family connections in Marseilles he was

Joseph Conrad

enabled to migrate there and began his sea experience in French ships, visiting Mauritius once and the West Indies twice. He was involved in a gun-running adventure to help Spanish rebels, described later in *The Arrow of Gold* (1920), but being still legally a Russian citizen, he felt insecure in France.

His uncle urged him to aim at British naturalization, and he joined the crew of a British ship, the *Mavis*, from which he first landed in England, at Lowestoft in 1878. It was only at the age of 20 that he began to learn English. After serving briefly in a coaster between Lowestoft and Newcastle, he joined the full-rigged ship *Duke of Sutherland* for a voyage from London to Sydney and back in 1879. After a voyage to the Mediterranean he passed his examination for second *mate in London, and sailed as a junior officer in the *Loch Etive* to Australia, returning in 1881.

Now began a series of voyages to eastern, especially Malayan, waters which deeply influenced his later thought and writing. He was second mate of the *Palestine*, 425 tons, with a cargo of coal for Bangkok, when her cargo was found to be on fire and she was abandoned off Java Head in 1883; the basis for his story 'Youth' (1902). He returned home from Singapore as a passenger in a steamer, and the same year sailed as second mate in the *Riversdale* from Britain to Madras; he went to Bombay and returned as second mate of the *Narcissus*, the name and some features of which he used in *The Nigger of the 'Narcissus'* (1898). His third voyage to the east was in the *Tilkhurst*, 1,500 tons, to Singapore and Calcutta. He had obtained his first mate's certificate in 1884 and now obtained his certificate as a *master, and also British naturalization (1886). He sailed again as mate of the *Highland Forest*, 1,000 tons, from Amsterdam to Semarang, where he fell ill. On recovery he became mate of the S.S. *Vidar*, 800 tons, trading from Singapore through the archipelago to Borneo and Celebes. It was in this service that he came into close contact with the rivers and *campongs* of the islands, European and Eurasian traders, and Malays of various types, and heard the names, and made the acquaintance, of men like Almayer (in fact Olmeijer) and Tom Lingard, about whom he later wrote, mingling fact with imagination. Early in 1888 Conrad was sent from Singapore to Bangkok to take command of the *barque *Otago*, whose master had died at sea; an experience described in *The Shadow Line* (1916), which is almost pure autobiography. The new master and the steward, the only two fit men among a fever-stricken crew, brought the ship through calms at last to Singapore. Leaving Malay waters (in fact never to return) Conrad (still known as Captain Korzeniowski) took the *Otago* to Sydney and Mauritius, whence he returned to Europe.

In a restless spirit he went in 1889 to the Congo, having been promised the command of a river steamer under the Belgian colonial authorities, but the command never materialized. He was disgusted by the oppression of Africans that he witnessed, and he returned home disillusioned, though with material that he afterwards used in *Heart of Darkness* (1899). He was already writing his first novel, *Almayer's Folly* (1895), but still considered himself a seaman and in 1891–2 and 1892–3 he made two further voyages as first mate of the *Torrens*, 1,276 tons, a fine *clipper ship, from London to Australia. On the second return voyage he met the future novelist John Galsworthy and his friend Edward Sanderson, who were passengers. He settled in London with the ambition of publishing his novel, but took one more berth on a ship, the *Adowa*, due to sail from Rouen to Canada. The sailing was delayed, while Conrad sat writing in his cabin at Rouen, and eventually cancelled. This was his last ship, and though he later made tentative efforts to obtain a berth as master or mate, he had ceased to be—if he ever was—interested in a career in the merchant service.

Almayer's Folly was published in 1895 under the name Joseph Conrad which he used thenceforth, followed by *An Outcast of the Islands* (1896), similar in theme and setting. Considering that he was brought up speaking Polish and then

French, his command of English in these books is remarkable, but it is not seamen's English, his style being based rather on wide reading of English as well as French books (he acknowledged a debt to Balzac and de Maupassant). With his next books, *The Nigger of the 'Narcissus'* and *Lord Jim* (1900) he developed a freer and more individual style. He wrote later: 'In the *Nigger* I give the psychology of a group of men and render certain aspects of nature. But the problem that faces them is not a problem of the sea, it is merely a problem that has arisen on board a ship where the conditions of complete isolation from all land entanglements make it stand out with a particular force and colouring.' This is typical of Conrad's attitude to the sea, which he regarded as the great testing and proving experience. In some men, and frequently among Conrad's characters, a fatal flaw or weakness leads to self-betrayal, as in *Lord Jim* when Jim, against his better instincts, joins the other white men in abandoning the *Patna*, leaving a shipload of Malayan pilgrims to their fate—though ironically she did not founder and Jim could have stayed on board; or as in the case of Captain Brierly, whose suicide on a calm night, with his ship in perfect order, is also related in *Lord Jim*. *Typhoon and Other Stories* (1902) contains in the title story a classic of sea literature in which Captain MacWhirr, unimaginative and somewhat unintelligent, ignoring the precepts of sound seamanship to heed weather forecasts and avoid the eye of a *typhoon, takes his steamship through the heart of a typhoon as if it were all in a day's work. In *The Mirror of the Sea* (1906) Conrad brought together a collection of shorter writings which includes some of his best work on sea subjects.

In 1904 he published his great novel *Nostromo*, and others which followed were *The Secret Agent* (1907), *Under Western Eyes* (1911), *Chance* (1913), *Victory* (1915), and *Within the Tides*, a collection of four stories (1915), all of them of a rare quality although *The Secret Agent*, *Under Western Eyes*, and *Victory* are less concerned with sea life, as also is *Romance*, a novel written in conjunction with F. M. Hueffer. His last complete novel was *The Rescue*, published in 1920, begun long previously and left unfinished, in which he returned to the eastern background and Tom Lingard, a study of the conflict of loyalties with, as in *Lord Jim*, the fatal flaw in Lingard leaving him broken in spirit.

Conrad died in 1924 before he could finish a new novel, *Suspense*, on which he was engaged. His remarkable personal experience at sea and in the east, and his unique ability to render it in works of literature in a language not his mother tongue make him unchallengeable among English writers on the sea.

CONSOL, a *hyperbolic navigational aid by means of which the *great circle bearing of a Consol transmitting station may be found, when conditions are favourable, with a high degree of accuracy for ranges of up to 1,000 miles. A Consol transmitting station employs an array of three aerials which produce audible signals at a receiver tuned to the frequency of transmission. By counting the numbers of dots and dashes during a transmission cycle the navigator is able to determine, either from a Consol lattice chart or from specially designed Consol tables, the great circle bearing of the station. An observation from each of two Consol stations produces a fix at the intersection of two great circle position lines. See also NAVIGATION.

CONSTELLATION, U.S.S., was one of the *'six original frigates' authorized by the U.S.A. in 1794. She was built in Baltimore, and was the first of the six *frigates to go to sea, in June 1798, at the beginning of the undeclared naval war with France. When the stars and stripes became the national flag of the U.S.A., the white stars on a blue field were called 'a new constellation', from which the name of the frigate was derived. Under the command of Thomas *Truxtun the ship captured one French frigate and fought another one in a night action until the French captain attempted to surrender. The *Constellation* had a long record of active service, and was in the Mediterranean during the American Civil War (1861–5). In 1871 she was laid up in Baltimore to be retained there as a historical exhibit. She has had various rebuildings over the years, but efforts have been made to restore her to her original condition.

CONSTITUTION, U.S.S., one of the *'six original frigates' authorized by the U.S. Congress in 1794, is generally regarded by Americans as the most famous ship in the history of the U.S. Navy. She was launched in 1797 and served in the quasi-war with France. Her length was 204 ft, beam $43\frac{1}{2}$ ft, depth of hold 14 ft 3 in., displacement 2,200 tons, and she carried forty-four guns. In the war with Tripoli (1801–5) she served as the flagship of Commodore Edward *Preble. It was in the war of 1812 against Great Britain that she established her enduring reputation. Congress declared war on 18 June 1812 although no plans and no preparations had been made. The U.S. Navy then consisted of eight frigates and eight smaller vessels. Morale in the U.S.A. was low after an initial setback, when news came in that the U.S.S. *Constitution* had defeated and destroyed the British *frigate *Guerrière* of forty-eight guns on 19 August 1812. Tradition has it that much of the British shot failed to penetrate the side of the *Constitution*, and that as a result her own sailors gave

her the name 'Old Ironsides'. Captain Isaac *Hull commanded her in that victory. On 29 December 1812, under the command of Captain William *Bainbridge, she captured and destroyed the frigate *Java*. On 20 February 1815, the *Constitution*, commanded by Charles *Stewart, captured two smaller British vessels, the *Cyane* (thirty-two guns) and *Levant* (twenty guns), in a battle lasting about four hours.

The *Constitution* was condemned as unseaworthy in 1828, and it was recommended that she be broken up. In his poem 'Old Ironsides' Oliver Wendell Holmes aroused public sentiment for the preservation of the old vessel and so far as possible the ship has been restored to her original appearance and characteristics. After restoration in 1927–31, she called at ninety ports in the U.S.A. and was visited by about 4,500,000 people. She returned to Boston in 1934, where she had been built, and she is berthed in the Navy Yard there where she is open to visitors.

CONSTRUCTIVE TOTAL LOSS, a marine insurance term indicating that the cost of repairing damage to a ship will exceed the total value of the vessel. In such a case the insurance payment is the overall sum in which she has been insured, and not the estimated cost of repairs.

CONSULATE OF THE SEA, a famous collection of maritime customs and laws published in Barcelona in the second half of the 15th century. Its Catalan title is *Lo Libro de Consolat*, and the edition of 1494, of which the only known copy is in the National Library in Paris, is considered as the first printed edition, though manuscript copies exist which date back at least to 1436 and possibly even to the previous century. The laws and customs in the *Consulate of the Sea* follow closely the more famous sea laws of *Oleron.

CONTAINER SHIP, a cargo vessel specially designed and built for the carriage of cargo prepacked in containers. With a standardized size of container, holding 18 tons of cargo, holds and deck spaces can be designed exactly to accommodate containers, leading to greater ease and efficiency in stowage and the eradication of much of the danger of the cargo shifting during heavy weather at sea. Nevertheless, the modern practice of carrying additional containers stowed on deck, sometimes as many as three deep, does introduce an element of danger by the reduction of the *metacentric height of the vessel below the safety level, particularly during the course of a voyage when the consumption of fuel may, in itself, cause the metacentric height to diminish.

CONTINENTAL NAVY, the name by which the navy of the U.S.A. was known between the Declaration of Independence in 1776 and the resolution passed by Congress in 1794 providing for the foundation of a U.S. Navy. See also 'SIX ORIGINAL FRIGATES'.

CONTINENTAL SHELF, the area of sea around a land mass where the depth increases gradually before it plunges into the deeps of the ocean. Definition of the shelf has become important only during relatively recent years since exploitation of the mineral wealth of the seabed, particularly of oil deposits, has become technically possible. Ownership of the continental shelf is accepted internationally as being vested in the state bordering the shelf, but there are some cases where this doctrine can cause a clash of national interests, as for example in the Celtic Sea west of Britain and north of France, where the continental shelf is common to both countries. Some confusion can also be caused in the case of outlying islands, sovereignty of which is exercised by an adjacent nation. Ownership of the continental shelf is a subject which has exercised the Law of the Sea Conference for many recent sessions, and it still awaits a solution.

CONTINUOUS VOYAGE, the legal doctrine in which the cargo of a ship may be * condemned in * prize even though it is consigned to a neutral port provided that it can be shown that the ultimate onward destination of the cargo is a belligerent. It is a doctrine which applies only after a declaration of * blockade by a belligerent in time of war.

CONTLINE, the modern name for the spiral grooves between the * strands of a rope after it has been * laid up. It is, perhaps, a less suggestive and more refined name for these grooves than the original term * cunting.

CONTRABAND, goods which have been prohibited from entering a belligerent state by the declaration of a * blockade. Contraband is of two kinds, absolute contraband, which includes munitions, weapons, and other commodities which can be directly attributable to the prosecution of war, and conditional contraband, declared by the blockader, which is ancillary to the prosecution of war. Thus imports of food by a belligerent can be claimed by a blockader as conditional contraband since no army or navy can fight without it, irrespective of what effect the lack of such imports may have on a civilian population.

CONTROLLER, the Third Sea Lord who sits on the British Admiralty Board and is responsible for the design and building of naval ships. His full title is Third Sea Lord and Controller of the Navy, but he is normally known only as the Controller. See also COLES, Cowper Phipps.

'CONUNDRUM', see PLUTO.

CONVOY, one or more merchant ships sailing in company to the same general destination under the protection of naval ships. Convoy has a very ancient history and specific cases of ships proceeding in groups under naval protection have been traced back to the 12th century. It is probable that the general principle existed even long before this, mainly as a protection against piracy, although in such cases the reason for ships sailing in company was more likely to be mutual protection rather than naval protection, as most merchant vessels in those days carried their own armament.

The history of naval warfare has always shown an immense loss in merchant shipping, in the older days at the hands of * privateers and * corsairs; in the more recent wars since the international banning of privateering, at the hands of their modern counterparts, * armed merchant raiders and * submarines. The only naval method of minimizing such loss is by the institution of convoy, in which adequate naval protection can usually deter enemy attacks on trade. During the Revolutionary and Napoleonic wars against France (1793–1801 and 1803–15) losses of British merchant shipping were so immense that no merchant ship was allowed to sail out of convoy, and the owners and * masters of those which attempted to do so were liable to a fine of £100.

In the two world wars of the 20th century, immense losses of merchant shipping were again experienced, almost entirely at the hands of submarines. In the First World War (1914–18) the principle of ocean convoy was not introduced until 1917, a failure in established and proved naval practice that very nearly lost the war for the allied nations. In the Second World War convoy was instituted at the outbreak of war but a lack of sufficient escort vessels resulted in under-protection of convoys and once again tremendous merchant ship losses were experienced until an adequate strength in escort vessels was built up. Once this strength had been reached, losses fell away to negligible proportions and the road to ultimate victory was cleared. During this war the influence of air power on naval operations was most clearly demonstrated in the field of convoy protection, and it was not until all convoys were provided with air escort in addition to surface escort that convoys were able to cross the oceans in almost complete safety.

Many of the great sea battles of naval history have been fought as a result of convoy protection, notably those of the Spanish * Armada in 1588, where the Spanish fleet was proceeding up Channel to escort an invasion convoy to England, the * Glorious First of June in 1794, where the French fleet was caught at sea protecting a convoy, and the great Mediterranean sea battles of the Second World War fought around the convoys taking supplies to the besieged island of Malta.

CONYNGHAM, GUSTAVUS (*c.* 1744–1819), Irish–American naval officer, emigrated from Ireland to Philadelphia and learned navigation in a cousin's ship. At the outbreak of the War of American Independence (1775–82) he was stranded in Europe but Benjamin Franklin, the American representative in France, issued him with a captain's commission in the *Continental Navy and he sailed from Dunkirk in the *lugger *Surprise*. He took several prizes and brought them to French ports, but after strong protests from the British ambassador, France released the prizes, seized the *Surprise*, and arrested Conyngham with his crew. Franklin managed to have him released, and he went to sea in the *cutter *Revenge*. His cruise in the North Sea and the Irish Sea caused considerable alarm and he took many prizes. In 1778 he cruised from Spanish ports with much success. More prizes were taken by his skill and daring when he went to the West Indies, and he arrived in Philadelphia in February 1779 having captured sixty ships in the preceding 18 months.

Cruising off New York harbour entrance, the *Revenge* was captured by H.M.S. *Galatea* and Conyngham was sent to England as a prisoner. On his third attempt he escaped from prison and, with help from friends in London, made his way to the Netherlands where he joined the *Alliance* (John Paul *Jones). He left the *Alliance* in Corunna and sailed for America in the *Experiment*. Captured again, he was returned to Mill Prison, near Plymouth, England, for a year, then exchanged. He was at Nantes, preparing for a new cruise, when the war ended. He was a member of the Philadelphia City Council during the war of 1812 and assisted with plans for the defence of the city.

COOK, FREDERICK ALBERT (1865–1940), American doctor of medicine and explorer, was born at Callicoon Depot, New York. He studied medicine at New York University and in 1891 was appointed surgeon to the Arctic expedition led by Captain Robert E. *Peary, U.S.N., which visited northern Greenland. In 1897–9 he served in a similar capacity with a Belgian expedition to the Antarctic. In 1909 after another expedition to the Arctic, Cook claimed to have reached the North pole, but the claim was disallowed by Copenhagen University to which he submitted his data. He was later imprisoned for fraud in connection with stock promotion, but in May 1940 was granted a pardon by President Roosevelt, dying three months later.

COOK, JAMES (1728–79), captain in the British Navy, was the son of a day labourer of Marton, in Yorkshire. He was taught reading, writing, and basic arithmetic at a 'dame' school there, but was otherwise self-educated. In 1746 John Walker, head of a shipping firm mainly engaged in the east coast coal trade, accepted him as a sea-apprentice. By a natural aptitude for mathematics, James Cook quickly became skilful as a navigator as well as a seaman and became mate of a Walker ship in 1752.

By 1755 Cook had decided that the merchant navy lacked scope for his ambitions and, though he had been offered his first command, he declined it and volunteered for the Royal Navy as an able seaman. Drafted to the 60-gun ship *Eagle*, his qualities quickly brought him advancement to the warrant rank of *boatswain. In July 1757 he was promoted *master of the *Solebay* and later of the *Pembroke*, in which he sailed in 1758 with the expedition for the capture of *Louisburg and subsequently *Quebec.

Masters were responsible for their ship's navigation and pilotage, the latter including any survey required of uncharted water. Cook attracted notice for his efficiency during the survey of the St. Lawrence River and particularly the intricate Traverse, which enabled the big ships of the fleet to ascend it—the first ever to do so—and so to play a decisive part in the capture of Quebec and the conquest of Canada. Following this he was appointed master of the flagship of the squadron remaining in North American waters and for three summer seasons was engaged in further surveys of the St. Lawrence and on the Nova Scotia and Newfoundland coasts.

At the end of the Seven Years War in 1763, Cook returned to Newfoundland where, for the next five years, he was engaged in surveying the coast in his own independent command, the *schooner *Grenville*. His observations of an eclipse of the sun visible in Newfoundland in 1766 and the accompanying calculations communicated to the Royal Society brought him to the favourable attention of that influential body. This made him acceptable as one of their official observers for an expedition planned to go to Tahiti to record observations of the transit of the planet Venus across the face of the sun; and when the Society's own choice for a commander, Alexander *Dalrymple, who was a civilian, was vetoed by the British Admiralty, Cook was the obvious alternative.

The scientific expedition became part of a more extensive voyage of discovery when the Admiralty decided that when the observations at Tahiti had been completed, Cook was to sail south to search for the southern continent, *Terra Australis Incognita, believed by geographers to exist. He was also to explore the coast of New Zealand, discovered by *Tasman in 1642, but still thought to be part of some such land mass, before returning home by Cape Horn or the Cape of Good Hope at his own discretion.

On the advice of Cook, by this time promoted to lieutenant, a full-rigged *cat-built Whitby *collier of the type which he knew so well was chosen for the expedition, being re-named H.M.S. *Endeavour. The Endeavour left Plymouth on 25 August 1768, called at Madeira and Rio de Janeiro, rounded Cape Horn with exceptional ease in fair weather, and reached Tahiti on 10 April 1769. She arrived with not one man suffering from *scurvy, that scourge of voyages in the sail era, a state of affairs almost unheard of at the time. This was a result of Cook's tireless and intelligent attention to the cleanliness of the ship below decks and to the food of the ship's company, which included experimental anti-scorbutic articles of diet, such as 'sour krout' (pickled cabbage), 'portable' (dried) soup, malt, and the juice of oranges and lemons, as well as 'scurvy grass' gathered ashore whenever possible.

Cook had no chronometer with him on this voyage though the first reliable example of such an instrument had just been produced by John *Harrison; Cook and the astronomer Green, the other official observer, were able, however, to calculate the *longitude of their points of call to within a close degree of accuracy by means of *lunar observations which involved the measurement of the angular distance between the moon and a fixed star. At a temporary observatory set up ashore, the transit of Venus was duly observed and recorded on 3 June 1769 and in mid-July the Endeavour weighed anchor to carry out the second part of the Admiralty's instructions. The stay at Tahiti among the friendly Polynesians, examples in the minds of contemporary philosophers of 'the noble savage', had been a halcyon experience, marred only by the thieving, particularly of any iron objects, which was the universal pastime of the stone-age natives. This was to be a recurrent problem and was to lead eventually to tragedy.

Sailing south from Tahiti as instructed, amid increasingly bad weather, Cook reached 40° S. *latitude without sighting land; furthermore the long southerly swell showed that open sea must persist in that direction. He accordingly turned west and on 7 October 1769 made landfall on the east coast of New Zealand at approximately 39° S. Rounding its northern cape, he sailed south down the west coast and through the Strait between the North and South Islands that has since borne his name and thence round the South Island, disproving the long accepted belief that New Zealand was a northerly promontory of a southern continent.

Cook was now free to return home either by Cape Horn or the Cape of Good Hope. He chose the latter in order to find and explore the east coast of New Holland (Australia) before making his way to Batavia where the Endeavour might have a much-needed refit. Sailing west from New Zealand, Cook hoped to make a landfall on the east coast of Van Diemen's Land, as Tasmania was then known, which was thought to be connected to Australia; southerly gales forced him northwards and on 21 April 1770 he reached the south-easterly corner of Australia (Point Hicks) and turned north. Following the coast and always carrying on a running survey, he anchored in *Botany Bay where the first aborigines were encountered, primitive, hostile, and implacable. Sailing on northwards he eventually found himself being hemmed in by the converging Great Barrier Reef, with obstacles in his path multiplying until during the night of 11/12 July the Endeavour struck and remained fast on a coral reef.

By good fortune and skilful seamanship she was refloated and worked into the mouth of a river—now Endeavour River—where she could be beached and repaired. Getting under way again on 6 August, Cook first took the Endeavour outside the Barrier Reef only to escape by a hair's breadth being wrecked on it when becalmed. Saved by the arrival of a breeze, Cook decided that the perils outside the reef were greater than inside; he passed through it by an opening in the coral and thereafter continued cautiously coasting to the tip of Cape York.

Having thus reached the end of Australia's east coast, Cook decided that he must confirm the separation of Australia from New Guinea to the north which only the Portuguese de *Torres had previously claimed to have demonstrated 164 years before by passing through the strait since given his name. Cook took the Endeavour through the maze of shoals and reefs between Cape York and its off-lying islands to discover and chart the Endeavour Strait, before turning north for New Guinea and the East Indies.

Tragically, Batavia, which he reached on 10 October 1770, proved deadly, spreading malaria and dysentery among the men whose health Cook had so well preserved till then. Before the ship sailed again a number had died; more were to do so on the way to the Cape; the dead included Green the astronomer, Lieutenant Hicks, the Endeavour's master, Molyneux, and her surgeon Monkhouse.

The Endeavour anchored in English waters on 12 July 1771, but her voyage had not yet disproved the possible existence of Terra Australis Incognita. Vast areas south of 40° S. longitude still remained unexplored. If a southern continent did exist the British government wished to claim possession before the French or Spanish could do so, and in consequence a new

'The Reception of Captain Cook in Hapaee'; engraving from Cook's Voyages, *late 18th century*

voyage was planned and Cook, promoted to commander, was given two other Whitby 'cats', renamed * *Resolution* and * *Adventure*, to replace the worn-out *Endeavour*. With Tobias Furneaux in command of the *Adventure* the two ships set out on 13 July 1772. In the *Resolution* went a copy, by Larcum Kendall, of Harrison's prize-winning chronometer.

From the Cape of Good Hope, Cook first steered south-east in search of the land discovered by the Frenchman Bouvet in 1739 and believed by him to be the tip of a southern continent. Cook proved it could only be an island by criss-crossing its longitude well to the south of its reported latitude. Slanting thence southwards and eastwards amidst ever-increasing ice, cold, and storms, he became, in mid-January 1773, the first navigator ever to cross the Antarctic circle. Forced to retreat northwards by the ice, he searched unsuccessfully for the islands discovered in the Indian Ocean by * Kerguelen and Crozet before again striking south-east to 60° S. and thence eastwards to the longitude of the east coast of Australia. That no southern continent existed in the one-third of the earth's circumference he had sailed over at an average southern latitude of 60° had now been clearly proved; and on 16 March 1773 he set course for Queen Charlotte's Sound, New Zealand, to rendezvous with the *Adventure* which had lost touch in gale and fog in February. There in mid-May the two ships were reunited.

After refitting, Cook spent the mid-winter months in making a similar negative proof by sailing eastwards from New Zealand between latitudes 41° and 46° S., never before covered, nearly to the meridian of Pitcairn Island, before swinging north and west for a period of rest and refreshment at Tahiti which he reached on 16 July.

From Tahiti he steered west to locate the Tonga or, as he named them, the Friendly Islands, previously visited by Tasman in 1643, before turning south for New Zealand, on the way to another penetration of the Antarctic. The *Adventure* once again lost touch; the two ships missed one another at Queen Charlotte's Sound by a few days and thenceforward cruised separately. Furneaux left New Zealand at the end of December 1773 and, sailing eastwards in latitudes between 56° and 61° S., passed 400 miles south of Cape Horn and returned home via the Cape of Good Hope, the first commander to complete a circumnavigation of the globe in an easterly direction.

Meanwhile, the *Resolution* had again taken an easterly zig-zag course in high latitudes, twice crossing the Antarctic circle and on the second occasion reaching 71° 10′ S. on 30 January 1774 before being turned back by an impenetrable field of ice. That there could be no great habitable continent in the South Pacific had now been definitely proved, and Cook would have been justified in returning home in the wake of Furneaux.

But his ship was still sound and his crew in good health; this was enough to persuade him to undertake a third season of exploration of the still largely unknown Pacific. The wide circling sweep north and then westward which he now

'Cook and his men shooting "Sea Horses" for food'; engraving from Cook's Voyages, late 18th century

made between 40° and 10° S. made no new discoveries but enabled Cook accurately to chart *Roggeveen's Easter Island and the Marquesas Islands, not seen since their discovery by *Mendaña 170 years earlier. After a month's rest at Tahiti, Cook was off again in mid-May to visit and chart the remainder of the Society Group, the Friendly Isles, de *Quiros's Australia del Espiritu Santo, and the remainder of the group to which it belonged which he named the New Hebrides, and to discover and name New Caledonia, the Isle of Pines, and Norfolk Island, before sailing once again to Queen Charlotte's Sound for a final refit.

On 11 November 1774 he started for home, crossing the Pacific again on a latitude between 54° and 55° S., rounding Cape Horn at the turn of the year, and traversing the South Atlantic, rediscovering South Georgia and discovering the South Sandwich Islands, before turning north for the Cape of Good Hope. The last possibility for the existence of Terra Australis Incognita had been finally disproved. The *Resolution* reached Portsmouth on 29 July 1775.

Cook was now promoted *post-captain and elected a Fellow of the Royal Society which awarded him the Copley Gold Medal. Within a year he was off again with instructions to go via Cape Town, the French Indian Ocean islands, Marion, Crozet, and Kerguelen, and on to Tahiti, whence he was to make for the west coast of North America and coast northwards in search of the Pacific end of that will-o'-the-wisp of the age of discovery, the *North-West passage.

From the start this third voyage was blighted. Cook was given the *Resolution* once again and was accompanied by another Whitby 'cat', the *Discovery*, commanded by Charles Clerke. The refit of both ships was shamefully skimped and continuous defects, particularly in the rigging of the *Resolution*, were to occur.

The two ships touched at Tasmania and Queen Charlotte's Sound, discovering the Cook and Palmerston Islands before making Tahiti, where a native brought to England on the previous voyage by Furneaux was returned and a gift from George III of live cattle and poultry was delivered. In December they set out again and on 18 January 1778 discovered the Polynesian-inhabited Hawaiian group, to which Cook gave the name Sandwich Islands in honour of the then First Lord of the Admiralty, the Earl of Sandwich. After a brief stay for replenishment of fresh provisions and water they sailed on, sighting the North American coast at latitude 45° N. on 7 March. A lee shore made any close approach unwise and Cook steered north well to seaward until he found the deep inlet of Nootka Sound which he entered in order to give the *Resolution* an urgently needed refit and renew her rigging.

From there the two ships coasted north again making only the sketchiest survey. But at about 60° N. the shore line swung westwards and along this southern coast of Alaska Cook made a more detailed survey, penetrating far up one deep sound, and in constant danger in the uncharted, rocky waters in recurrent thick fog.

Rounding the south-western extremity of the Alaskan peninsula and passing through the Aleutian Islands chain, Cook sailed on through the Bering Strait to reach $70\frac{1}{2}°$ N. before an impenetrable ice wall forced a return southwards. By the end of November Cook was back at the Sandwich Islands and surveying the coast of Hawaii in spite of constant trouble with the *Resolution*'s masts and spars. Finally on 17 January 1779 the two ships anchored in Kealakekua Bay and set about refitting.

Here Cook went ashore to find himself greeted with prostrations and solemn ceremonies which mystified him: he did not realize that he was being accepted as a Polynesian god whose return to the islands in a 'large island with trees', bringing gifts including swine and dogs, was prophesied in Polynesian legends. To welcome him adequately the priests and chiefs called upon the people to make contributions which strained their resources to the limit. By the time the two ships sailed again on 4 February 1779 their departure was hailed with heartfelt relief. It was disastrous therefore that two days later the *Resolution* sprung her foremast, forcing the two ships to return.

On this occasion the natives' welcome had turned to sullenness. Relations were strained and it required only a spark to set the fires of hostility blazing. This occurred as a result of thefts culminating in that of a large ship's boat. As he had done on many occasions previously with success, Cook went ashore to bring a chief off to the ship as a hostage for its return. On the previous day, 13 February, there had been an affray from which some sailors of a watering party had narrowly escaped with their lives. The prestige of the white strangers had suffered a fatal blow, and now a large mob of natives armed with stones and knives gathered to resist the arrest of their chief. Attacked by one of them, Cook fired one barrel of his double-barrelled shot gun which was loaded only with small shot. These bounced harmlessly off a warrior's matting armour and, though the solid shot from the second barrel was effective, a general attack was started in which Cook was overwhelmed and stabbed to death before his guard of marines were able to drive the mob off.

Captain Clerke, though dying of consumption, now took over the command, completed the refit, and sailed for the second season's northerly exploration via Petropavlovsk to the Asiatic side of the Bering Sea. Ice conditions were even worse than in the previous year and little was achieved before the expedition finally turned south at the end of July. Clerke died a month later, his place being taken by Lieutenant Gore of the *Resolution* who brought the ships home via Canton and the Cape of Good Hope, reaching the Thames in October 1780.

Between 1955 and 1967 the *Hakluyt Society of Britain produced in four volumes *The Journals of Captain Cook*, edited by J. C. *Beaglehole, which give a useful memoir of Cook himself, descriptions of his ships and crews, and a complete text of the journals he kept during his three voyages of discovery. In addition to editing the journals, Beaglehole wrote *The Life of Captain Cook*, published in 1974. A previous biography is J. R. Muir's *Captain James Cook* (1939).

COOKE, EDWARD WILLIAM (1811–80), British marine painter, was born in London, the son of an engraver. One of his earlier works was a series of sixty-five etched plates of shipping and coastal craft, still accepted as a contemporary record for its textual accuracy of hull shapes and rigging. Later he devoted himself entirely to oil painting, though still retaining the acute observation which distinguished his earlier engravings. He was elected to the Royal Academy in 1863.

COOKE, FRANCIS BERNARD (1872–1975), British yachtsman and author, founded the Fambridge Yacht Club in 1898 and was secretary for forty-four years of the East Coast Mutual Yacht Insurance Association. For over half a century he owned and sailed a variety of small yachts and boats in the waters around Essex and Kent, all of which were based at Fambridge on the River Crouch. He wrote some thirty books on yachting, of which the best known are *Cruising Hints* (1904), *The Singlehanded Yachtsman* (1909), *Yacht Racing for Amateurs* (1911), *In Tidal Waters* (1919), *Weekend Cruising* (1933), *Small Yacht Cruising* (1937), and *Yachting with Economy* (1961).

COOPER, JAMES FENIMORE (1789–1851), American novelist, was born at Burlington, New Jersey, and educated at Yale, from which he was expelled. In 1808 he entered the U.S. Navy and was employed on the Great Lakes patrol, but retired three years later to take up writing as a profession. Several of his works were influenced by his early naval experience, among the best known being *The Pilot* (1823), *The Two Admirals* (1842), and *History of the Navy* (1839). As an author he exhibited remarkable powers of description and narrative and although he is chiefly remembered for his tales of the Red Indians of whose woodcraft and lore he had an intimate knowledge, his books about the sea stamp him as a maritime writer of considerable ability.

CO-ORDINATES, the definition of the exact position of a point on the surface of the globe in relation to two lines, *latitude and *longitude, which intersect at right angles. The system was

The battle of Copenhagen, 1801; oil painting by Nicholas Pocock

introduced by the French philosopher René Descartes (1596–1650), and is known as the Cartesian system of co-ordinates. To define a position on the surface of a sphere an extension of the Cartesian system is employed. In this case the two spherical distances of the point from each of two *great circles which are mutually perpendicular, are the spherical co-ordinates of the point. Terrestrial positions are most commonly described in terms of two spherical distances, one northwards or southwards from the equator (latitude) and the other eastwards or westwards from a great circle secondary to the equator known as the *prime meridian (longitude). Positions on the *celestial sphere, for the purposes of navigation, are usually stated using co-ordinates of the *ecliptic system, the *equinoctial system, or the *horizon system.

COPENHAGEN, the capital and principal seaport of Denmark, is on the east coast of the island of Zealand at the southern end of the Sound. In addition to the commercial harbour, it has a naval dockyard and shipbuilding establishment. Copenhagen has a chequered history of capture and recapture as various Baltic, German, and Swedish principalities battled for its possession; it has twice been laid waste by fire and twice by bombardment. It was the scene of two major battles, both fought to protect the flow of Britain's naval supplies from the Baltic countries during the Revolutionary and Napoleonic wars, and her general trade with that area.

In 1801, inspired by Paul I of Russia, the northern powers began to form an armed coali-

tion which could have become a serious threat to British interests. Paul I was assassinated in Russia before the coalition proved to be effective and his policy was reversed by his son, Alexander I, but before this happened a British fleet had been sent to the Baltic under Admiral Sir Hyde *Parker, with *Nelson as his second-in-command, to disrupt the coalition.

Nelson convinced Parker that, failing a direct attack on the Russian fleet, the best initial step would be an assault on the Danish fleet at Copenhagen. This he was allowed to lead in person, on 2 April 1801, with ships of suitable draught. The Danish ships, forts, and floating batteries resisted so stubbornly that Parker, at the most critical time of the engagement and apprehensive of heavy British losses, signalled for the action to be broken off. Nelson disregarded the order for, as he said, he had a right to be blind sometimes since he had a sightless eye. His ships at last overcame the Danish defences, and he himself then negotiated an armistice with the Danish Prince Regent. Shortly afterwards, Parker was recalled, and Nelson became commander-in-chief in his place.

Nelson considered that, in spite of her sharp lesson, Denmark would soon come wholly within the French orbit, and his surmise was justified by the result. Six years later, in 1807, the Danes were again seen to be disposed to further French interests, and the threat to the flow of Baltic sea traffic had become so acute that a further northern expedition had to be mounted. This time troops were employed under Lord Cathcart (with whom the future Duke of

Wellington served), together with a fleet under Lord *Gambier. Copenhagen was first invested and then bombarded. Considerable damage was done and fires were started which grew so serious that the Hanoverian commandant agreed to a cease-fire. Under the terms of the resultant armistice, most of the major units of the Danish fleet were removed to British ports and an immediate threat was averted.

Neither expedition, in spite of their apparent success, achieved the long-term object of neutralizing Denmark. Her shipyards continued to build *privateers and gunboats for the service of France, which were used to harass sea traffic in the Sound, the Kattegat, and elsewhere until the very end of the war. Denmark then paid a stiff price for her services to France by forfeiting Norway, whose crown had been united with her own since the Middle Ages, to the Swedish king, for Sweden found herself at the end of hostilities on the winning side and benefited accordingly.

There are a number of maritime museums in Copenhagen, the most important of them being the *Orlogsmuseet, which illustrates the development of the Royal Danish Navy from 1500.

COPPER PUNT, see BALSA.

COPPERED, the hull of a wooden ship sheathed below the waterline with thin sheets of copper to prevent the *teredo worm eating into the planks and also to limit weed and barnacles building up on the ship's bottom. Originally lead was used for this purpose as far back as the 17th century but was found to be unsatisfactory (a) because of its weight, (b) because it was difficult to fasten securely to the ship's bottom and thus frequently dropped off, and (c) because it was too soft and frequently tore off in a heavy sea. For a period the only defence against the teredo was a layer of canvas impregnated with tar laid between the two layers of plank forming the hull.

Copper sheathing was first introduced in the British Navy in 1761 when the frigate *Alarm* was thus treated. Although the protection afforded was satisfactory, few other ships were coppered at the time because of the galvanic action set up between the copper sheets and the iron bolts by which the hull planking was secured to the timbers. In 1783 orders went out that copper bolts should replace iron bolts in naval ship construction, and copper sheathing then became general. Other navies introduced it at about the same time as the result of British experience.

COPPER-BOTTOMED, the slang term for secure, to be trusted, cannot fail, was derived from the coppering of ships. See also SHEATHING.

CORACLE, from the Welsh *corwgl*, carcass, or Irish *curach*, boat, a small boat, occasionally circular but more often rectangular with rounded corners, constructed of wickerwork and made watertight originally with animal hides but more recently with pitch or some other watertight material, used for river and coastal transport by the ancient Britons, and still used by fishermen, mainly for salmon, on the rivers and lakes of Wales and Ireland. It is light enough to be carried easily on a man's back.

CORAL, the hard calcareous skeleton of many species of marine zoophytes. These coral-producing animals abound in vast numbers in tropical seas, forming by the aggregate growth of countless generations reefs, barriers, and islands. The red coral, *Corallium rubrum*, of the Mediterranean is highly prized for decorative purposes. See also ATOLL.

CORAL SEA, BATTLE OF THE, a naval action in the Pacific during the Second World War fought between U.S. and Japanese carrier forces. The ease with which the Japanese had secured their initial war objective, the so-called southern resources area, led them to plan an expansion of their gains to include Midway in the east and the Solomon Islands and Port Moresby (on the south-eastern coast of Papua) in the south, whence Australia and its communications with America could be threatened.

The first operation aimed at the latter objective was initiated at the beginning of May 1942 with the dispatch of a small expedition to seize Tulagi in the Solomons consisting of a troop convoy covered by the light *aircraft carrier *Shoho* and four cruisers, routed round the eastern end of Papua for Port Moresby. In the belief that surprise could be achieved, a main covering force of only the two fleet carriers *Shokaku* and *Zuikaku* was deployed in the Coral Sea. The Americans, however, were able to read Japanese enciphered signals which enabled the U.S. commander-in-chief in the Pacific to deploy the carriers *Lexington* and *Yorktown* and the Australian–American cruiser force in time to oppose the Japanese operation.

In the battle which resulted, each of the carrier forces began operations with a tactical error. The American Rear Admiral Fletcher, believing that the convoy covering force located early on 7 May by his scout planes was the main Japanese carrier group, launched virtually his whole air strength, including the majority of his fighters, to the attack. Though this succeeded in sinking the *Shoho*, it left his own carriers almost defenceless. Fortunately the Japanese similarly mistook an American *tanker for a carrier and expended their striking power in sinking it and its destroyer escort.

By the end of the day Fletcher was still without knowledge of his main opponent's position, whereas his own position had been reported by a

Japanese reconnaissance plane. The Japanese launched a striking force of twenty-seven aircraft in heavy weather conditions. Not only did they fail to locate the American carriers but, intercepted by American fighters, a number were shot down; others failed to find their ships in the gathering darkness and only seven finally landed back on board.

On the 8th each side simultaneously launched an air strike in which the *Shokaku* and *Lexington* were both heavily damaged, the former to limp home for repairs; the latter, however, swept by petrol fires, had to be abandoned and sunk. The *Yorktown* also suffered bomb damage but was not put entirely out of action. It was a tactical victory for the Japanese, though this was offset by their much heavier losses of trained aircrew. Strategically, not only were the Japanese forced to abandon their amphibious expedition against Port Moresby but the damage to the *Shokaku* and their aircrew losses were to deprive them of the use of both the *Shokaku* and *Zuikaku* in the decisive battle of *Midway soon to be fought.

CORBETT, Sir JULIAN (1854–1922), British naval historian, was born at Thames Ditton, Surrey, and educated at Trinity College, Cambridge, where he gained a 1st class in Law tripos in 1875. Called to the Bar in 1879, he abandoned it three years later and travelled extensively. He began by writing fiction but turned to biography with a life of George *Monck published in 1889. This was followed by one of Sir Francis *Drake; then for a while he reverted to fiction, but in 1898 he produced his first serious contribution to historical literature, *Drake and the Tudor Navy*. He joined the newly founded *Navy Records Society, for which he edited several volumes. In 1900 he wrote *The Successors of Drake* and two years later he was appointed lecturer in history at the Royal Naval College, Greenwich. In 1903 he delivered the Ford lectures at Oxford and the following year his book *England in the Mediterranean 1603–1714* was published. This was followed in 1907 by *England in the Seven Years War*, which showed the important part played by naval power in national policy. In 1910 he published *The Campaign of Trafalgar* and the following year *Some Principles of Maritime Strategy*. On the outbreak of war in 1914 he offered his services to the Admiralty and was employed collecting material for the official history of the war at sea of which he wrote the first three volumes. He was knighted in 1917.

He was a personal friend of Admiral Sir John *Fisher when the latter was First Sea Lord in 1904–10 and had a large, though unofficial, hand in many of the revolutionary naval papers which emanated from that dynamic officer. He wrote the introduction to the secret British war plans of 1907 and his hand can be detected in many more of the confidential Admiralty papers of the day which Fisher used to send him in draft for his comments and corrections.

CORBIE'S AUNT, a term sometimes used by fishermen in the north-east of Scotland to describe *St. Elmo's Fire or *Corposant.

CORBITA, the merchant ship of imperial Rome, a large, full-bodied vessel massively built and capable of carrying as much as 400 tons of cargo. They set a single large squaresail on a mast amidships, sometimes with two *raffee topsails above the yard, and a small squaresail on an *artemon mast over the bows. During the 1st century A.D., Roman corbitas made regular voyages between ports in the Red Sea and the west coast of India as well as normal Mediterranean passages.

CORD, small laid-up rope of an inch or less in circumference, more often referred to in ships as 'line'. It is about half-way between twine and rope, and is used on board for a variety of purposes where rope would be too large and clumsy. It is also widely described as *codline.

CORINTHIAN, a 19th and early 20th century term for an amateur yachtsman who sails his own yacht, i.e., without the aid of a professional skipper. The term originated in the U.S.A. in the mid-19th century to describe a rich amateur sportsman, and spread to Britain mainly in its yachting connotation. The *Royal Corinthian Yacht Club, now at Burnham-on-Crouch, Essex, was formed in 1872, at a time when many owners of racing yachts employed professional skippers, exclusively to provide regular yacht racing for owners who steered their own yachts.

CORIOLIS FORCE, the name given, in commemoration of the 19th century French mathematician Gustave Coriolis, to an inertial force generated in a rotating frame and acting on the basic Newtonian laws of motion of bodies. The Coriolis force has a significant effect in *meteorology and *oceanography, since the earth is a rotating frame of reference, and surface motions over the earth are therefore subject to accelerations from the force. It affects the prevailing winds and the rotation of storms and, in the sea itself, the rotation of whirlpools. In counterclockwise rotation, the Coriolis force acts to the right of the direction of body motion, in clockwise rotation, to the left.

CORNWALLIS, Sir WILLIAM (1744–1819), British admiral, commonly known as 'Billy Blue' from his fondness for flying the Blue Peter flag to make sail, or as 'Coachee' or 'Mr. Whip' from his florid complexion, was a lifelong friend of Horatio *Nelson. He became a *post-captain at the early age of 22 and served throughout the War of American Independence (1775–82). In 1788 he was sent out to India where his brother was governor-general. In 1795, as a vice admiral, he conducted a masterly retreat from a greatly superior French force under Admiral *Villaret de Joyeuse when cruising off Brest. He succeeded Lord St. Vincent (see JERVIS, John) in the command of the Channel Fleet blockading Brest in 1801 and adopted the same tactics of close blockade from Ushant, the hinge upon which the whole anti-invasion strategy turned. By preventing Admiral *Ganteaume from coming out of Brest with his squadron to join the remainder of the French fleet under Admiral *Villeneuve in the West Indies, he defeated Napoleon's strategy for the invasion of Britain in the year of *Trafalgar.

When Cornwallis sent Sir Robert *Calder to intercept Villeneuve on his return from the West Indiès to *Ferrol, he was criticized by Napoleon for dividing his force, but the irresolution of the French admiral justified the risk. No great battle is associated with the name of Cornwallis, but the determination shown in his rigorous blockade of Brest entitles him to the highest honours. In spite of his reserve and lack of glamour and, also, of his reputation as a severe disciplinarian, he was popular with the men under his command because of his consideration of their needs in the long dull years of blockading duty. He retired in 1806 to live in Hampshire until his death.

CORONEL, a naval battle of the First World War (1914–18), was fought on 1 November 1914 between British and German cruiser forces off the coast of Chile, in which the latter gained a decisive victory. Obliged to evacuate Chinese waters because of British and Japanese superiority in the area, the German Vice Admiral Graf von *Spee led his force, comprising the armoured cruisers *Scharnhorst and Gneisenau, and the light cruisers Nürnberg and Leipzig, across the Pacific to the South American coast, where he was joined by the light cruiser Dresden. Off Coronel he was brought to action by an ill-assorted British force under Rear Admiral Sir Christopher *Cradock consisting of the old armoured cruiser Good Hope (flagship), the cruiser Monmouth, the light cruiser Glasgow, and the armed merchant cruiser Otranto. The old battleship Canopus, intended to provide heavy support for Cradock's force but unable to keep up, was some 300 miles to the south. When contact was made between the two forces in the late afternoon on 1 November, each side believed that only a single enemy ship was present, but when Cradock was informed by the Glasgow of

the enemy's strength he believed it to be his duty to engage although he could have escaped to the southward. Von Spee held off until he had the British ships silhouetted against the setting sun, and when his ship opened fire at 11,200 m (12,300 yards) range their gunnery was so superior that the British ships were overwhelmed, particularly as the heavy sea and swell prevented them from using their secondary guns. After a short action the Good Hope was sunk, followed soon afterwards by the Monmouth; there were no survivors from either ship. The Glasgow and the Otranto escaped. Von Spee's squadron subsequently rounded Cape Horn and was decisively defeated at the battle of the *Falkland Islands five weeks later.

CORPOSANT, from the Italian corpo santo, the fiery balls or brushes which appear at the masthead or at the yardarms of ships when the air is surcharged with electricity. See ST. ELMO'S FIRE.

CORSAIR, a private ship fitted out by an owner to operate under licence by the government against the merchant shipping of an enemy. The word is particularly applicable to Mediterranean waters and is most often associated with the privateering cruisers which operated off the Barbary (Saracen) coasts of North Africa as late as 1825 and preyed on the merchant ships of Christian states. Although many people regarded these corsairs as pirates, they were usually legitimate *privateers licenced by the Turkish government at Constantinople. The word is also used to describe the men who manned these ships. See also LETTER OF MARQUE.

CORVETTE, a flush-decked warship of the 17th–18th centuries with a single tier of guns, smaller than a *frigate but ship-rigged on three masts. The design was originally French and was a development of the *lateen-rigged *galley, with virtually the same hull form being taken for the corvette. Proving fast and weatherly, the design was adopted in the British Navy, the best British corvettes being those built of cedar wood in Bermuda. They were found particularly suitable for service in hot climates as the flush deck construction admitted a free circulation of air.

The type name was re-adopted during the Second World War to describe a class of escort vessels used in the battle of the *Atlantic against *U-boats. First ordered in 1939 as a quick production to fill the gap in anti-submarine escorts, the original design was based on that of the *whale catcher and they were fitted with a 4-cylinder triple-expansion steam engine, the only design quickly available, driving a single centre-line propeller. This original design proved unsatisfactory in Atlantic winter weather because of their excessive rolling. The original corvettes were the 'Flower' class, named after flowers, but they were succeeded by new and better designs, the 'Castle', 'River', and 'Loch' classes coming forward in large numbers as the war progressed. These corvettes, smaller than the anti-submarine frigates and armed with one or more 4-inch guns and *depth-charges, provided the bulk of the British anti-submarine escorts of the Second World War and, in their later designs, proved remarkably successful in sinking U-boats around the *convoys they were protecting.

COSSACK, H.M.S., a British *destroyer of the Tribal class, built in 1938, with a *displacement of 1,870 tons and armed with eight 4·7-inch guns and four *torpedo tubes. She was the ship in which Captain Philip *Vian entered Jossing Fjord in Norwegian *territorial waters in February 1940 to rescue 299 British merchant seamen, who had been captured during the war cruise of the German *pocket-battleship *Admiral Graf Spee, from the German *tanker *Altmark. She was damaged in the second battle of *Narvik in April 1940 and was at the sinking of the German *battleship *Bismarck in May 1941, attacking her with torpedoes throughout the night of 26 May and keeping her in sight until the ships of the British Home Fleet arrived the following morning to sink her. In October 1943 she was sunk by the German *U-boat *U.563* west of Gibraltar.

COSTAIN GUN, an early line-throwing gun which fired a small rocket projectile to which a thin line was attached. It was used mainly for life-saving purposes in conjunction with a *breeches buoy, the line being used to haul over a *jackstay secured between the life-saving station ashore and the ship requiring rescue, with the breeches buoy being hauled back and forth along the jackstay. It has many other similar maritime uses such as when it is required to pass a line between two vessels at sea. It can throw a line up to 80 fathoms (480 ft or 146 m) in distance.

COT, the wooden bed frame, enclosed in canvas and slung by its four corners from deck beams, in which officers of ships used to sleep before the introduction of permanent bunks in cabins. They were about 6 feet long, 2 feet wide, and 1 foot deep, with a mattress laid in the bottom.

COTMAN, JOHN SELL (1782–1842), British artist, was a member of the Norwich school of painters and, after John Crome (1768–1821), its most important representative. He studied art in London under Rudolph Ackermann, whose influence can be seen in the architectural features of many of his oil paintings and water-colours. Although he is chiefly recognized as a landscape artist he painted a number of seascapes and

marine pictures, bringing a fresh approach to this branch of the art with his vivid feeling for colour and movement, particularly in his treatment of choppy and confused seas, where the structural strength of his painting is impressive. Although during his lifetime he was subject to fits of depression brought about by the lack of public appreciation of his work, he is recognized today as one of the foremost artists of his time, and nowhere more so than in his marine paintings.

COUNTER, the arch forming the overhanging *stern of a vessel above the waterline, its top, or crown, being formed by the aftermost deck beams and its lower ends terminating in the wing *transoms and *buttocks. The term is also loosely used to indicate the small area of deck abaft the sternpost or rudder-head. Most large ships today are built without a counter, the after end terminating in a *transom or a rounded or cruiser stern, but *tugs are always built with a pronounced counter, mainly to keep their towing hawsers, when they fall into the water, clear of the propellers. Most yachts, too, are built with

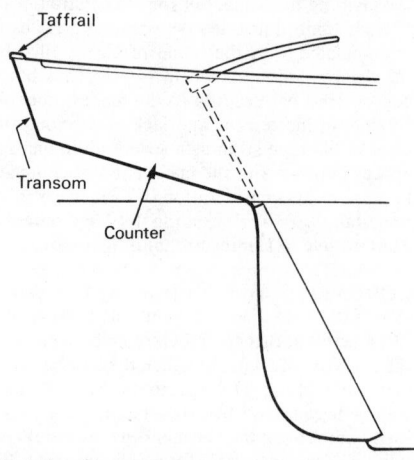

Typical yacht counter

counter sterns, particularly racing yachts where the counter is often pronounced, with a long overhang. COUNTER STERN, the overhang of the stern abaft the rudder used in the sense of describing a type of stern. SAWN-OFF COUNTER, as above, but with the aftermost part terminating abruptly in a vertical end instead of being carried on in the normal line of the hull form.

COUNTER BRACE, to, the operation of *bracing the head-*yards one way and the after-yards the other when going *about, or lying to the wind, in a square-rigged ship. The counter brace is the *lee brace of the fore topsail yard at the time of going about. When the fore topsail begins to shake as the ship is brought up into the wind, the lee brace is hauled in hard to flatten the sail against the lee side of the topmast to force the ship's head across the wind. Counter bracing was also the old term used in a square-rigged ship to make her lie-to in a wind by taking the way off her, in order to lower a boat, to speak to another vessel, or for any purpose which required the ship to be stopped. The modern term for bringing a ship to a stop is to *heave-to.

COUNTER CURRENT, that part of the water which is diverted from the main stream of a current by an obstruction or by the formation of the land and which as a result flows in the opposite direction. It is also the term given to the reverse movement of water caused by many of the big ocean currents, such as the Humboldt, Gulf Stream, etc., which have their own counter currents just outside the limits of their main stream where the water flows in the opposite direction as a compensatory movement.

COURSE, the horizontal angle contained between the direction of north or south and that of the fore-and-aft line of a vessel extended ahead. The angles between true, magnetic, and *compass norths and souths and the path of a vessel are known respectively as true course, magnetic course, and compass course. The angular difference between the true and magnetic course is known as *variation, and that between magnetic and compass course as *deviation. The combination of variation and deviation is the *compass error.

The course of a ship is usually today denoted in three-figure notation from 000° to 359°; 000° corresponding to due north; 090° to due east; 180° to due south; and 270° to due west. These are true courses, read from a gyroscopic compass which is not subject to variation or deviation, and is now the usual compass fitted in all ships of any size. In older days, when the magnetic compass was the normal compass used in ships, the *points of the compass were invariably used in specifying a ship's course. See also GREAT CIRCLE, LAY A COURSE, RHUMB LINE.

COURSE, in theory, the sails set upon the lower *yards of a square-rigged ship to which *bonnets could be attached. The original spelling for these sails was corps or corse. But the original definition of 'course' was extended to all sails set on the lower yards irrespective of whether they were adapted to carry bonnets, and they were designated by the name of the mast on which they were set, as fore course, main course, and mizen course. Gradually staysails set on lower masts and the main staysails of *brigs and *schooners also became known as courses. A ship which set only foresail, mainsail, and mizen was said to be under her courses. For illus. see SAIL.

COURTAULD, AUGUSTINE (1904–59), British explorer and deep-sea yachtsman, was president of the Cruising Association from 1957 until his death. His keen interest in the proper training of youth resulted in his yacht *Duet*, a 22-ton *yawl built in 1912, becoming one of the sail training yachts of the Ocean Youth Club with headquarters on the Essex coast.

COUSTEAU, JACQUES-YVES (1910–), French naval officer, explorer, and oceanographer, was born at St. André-de-Cubzac in the Gironde, and has achieved worldwide fame both as a free diver (see DIVING (3)) and as an explorer of the sea bed. He invented the automatic diver and diving saucer and, with Emile Gagnan, the *aqualung, which makes possible free diving down to a depth of 150–180 feet (48–55 m). He also developed a camera sled to facilitate photography of the sea bed in the greatest depths of the oceans. He has written a number of books of his experiences, among the best known in English translations being *To a Depth of 18 Metres*, *The Silent World*, *The Voyage of the 'Calypso'*, and *Sharks, Coral, and Pollution*, and has made two full-length films, *Le Monde du Silence* (*The World of Silence*), produced in 1956, and *Monde sans Soleil* (*World without Sun*), produced in 1964, as well as several television series. Since 1957 he has been director of the Oceanographic Museum at Monaco, and has within the last few years been carrying out experiments in living on the sea bed for long periods of up to a week or ten days. He was awarded the Gold Medal of the National Geographic Society in 1961. To him, more than to any other man, is due the vast development of the sport of free diving in recent years.

COVE, (1) a small coastal inlet frequently protected from the worst of the prevailing winds by high cliffs or promontories. (2) The wooden roof of the stern *gallery in the old sailing warships and *East Indiamen. (3) A thin, hollowed line cut along a yacht's sheer strake below deck level, and traditionally gilded. It is also known as a caveta.

COVERING BOARD, the name given, particularly in yacht construction, to the outermost plank of the main deck, which is usually wider than the other deck planks. In larger wooden ships it is more usually called the *plank sheer.

COWAN, Sir WALTER (1871–1956), British admiral, saw early service in the Royal Navy at the Brass River expedition (1895), the capture of Benin (1897), in a *gunboat on the River Nile for Lord Kitchener's reconquest of the Sudan (1898), and on Lord Roberts's staff for the first part of the South African War in 1899.

Promoted captain in 1907, he spent the First World War (1914–18) with the *Grand Fleet, first in command of the pre-dreadnought *Zealandia*, then of the *battle-cruiser *Princess Royal* in which he was present at the battle of *Jutland, and finally as *commodore of the First Light Cruiser Squadron, which he led with dash and distinction in the inconclusive action fought off *Heligoland on 17 November 1917.

Having hoisted his flag as a rear admiral shortly before the armistice in 1918, Cowan spent the first post-war year in command of the British naval force supporting the Baltic States in their resistance against Bolshevik domination. On 17 August 1919 his *coastal motor boats immobilized the Russian Red Fleet by a daring raid on its Kronstadt base. By the time he returned to England in 1920, the sovereign independence of Estonia, Latvia, and Lithuania, as well as of Finland, had been secured. He subsequently commanded the battle-cruiser squadron of the Atlantic Fleet before serving as Flag Officer in Command, Coast of Scotland, followed by an appointment as commander-in-chief, North America and West Indies, and retirement in 1929.

Though nearly 70 at the outbreak of the Second World War Cowan insisted on serving again in the rank of commander. Being too old to be employed at sea his war service was ashore, first with the Commando Brigade, then with the Indian Division in North Africa with which he was in action; he was taken prisoner by the Italian Army at Bir Hakim in the Western Desert in March 1941. Although released and repatriated because of his age, he rejoined the commandos in Italy and was actively engaged in the Adriatic in the support of the Yugoslav resistance fighters for which in 1944 he was awarded a bar to the D.S.O. which he had gained on the Nile forty-two years earlier. Cowan's reputation for being the strictest of martinets (which resulted in his being involved in three naval mutinies) was matched by an insatiable appetite for action. For a biography see Captain Lionel Dawson's *Sound of the Guns* (1949).

COWES, a small port in the Isle of Wight, England; the headquarters of the *Royal Yacht Squadron, the premier yacht club of Great Britain, and a number of other yacht clubs. It has extensive building yards, for both small ships and yachts. The first week in August each year, known in yachting circles as Cowes Week, is one of the greatest festivals of yachting in Britain, with racing provided daily for a multitude of yachts of all classes and designs.

COW-HITCH, any *bend or *hitch which slips as a result of being improperly tied; or a 'homemade' knot which is not a recognized maritime knot as used at sea. The great majority of knots used on board a ship have recognized purposes and each has stood the test of time as the best and most efficient knot for its purpose, and if a different knot is made up or 'invented' for such a purpose, it would qualify to be called a cow-hitch.

COWL, (1) a ship's ventilator with a bell-shaped top, which can be swivelled on deck to catch the wind and force it below. **(2)** The cover of a ship's funnel as used in harbour, and also the vertical projection at the forward end of a funnel to direct the smoke aft and away from the *bridge.

COWLEY, WILLIAM AMBROSE (*fl.* 1683–6), English mathematician and navigator, comes briefly into the maritime story through a remarkable journal he kept during an involuntary voyage round the world. After obtaining a M.A. degree at Cambridge he went to Virginia, where in 1683 he was persuaded by John Cook, a well-known *buccaneer, to navigate his ship, the *Revenge*, to Hispaniola (Haiti). Cowley agreed, and the ship sailed on 23 April 1683, not for Hispaniola but for a buccaneering voyage to the South Seas. Cowley was not informed of this until the *Revenge* was well out to sea. They crossed the Atlantic to Sierra Leone where they captured a Danish ship of forty guns (an act of pure *piracy), and apparently exchanged their own ship for sixty Negro girls, renaming the Danish ship, aptly, *Batchelor's Delight*. From Sierra Leone they sailed round Cape Horn and into the South Pacific, where the first ship they encountered was another English buccaneering vessel, the *Nicholas*, commanded by Captain John Eaton. The two ships cruised in company with remarkable lack of success and the usual buccaneering quarrels, until they decided to part company on 2 September 1684, Cowley electing to join the *Nicholas* as her navigator to make for Guam, which was reached after a voyage of 104 days, much beset with *scurvy. After replenishing on the island they sailed via the Ladrones to Canton, where they found many rich pickings and all became comparatively wealthy. The ship then visited Borneo, the Celebes, the Moluccas, and finally reached Timor, where more quarrels broke out and the crew split up. Cowley, with nine companions, bought a small boat and reached Java and then, in a yet smaller boat, sailed to Batavia, where he finally parted company with the remaining buccaneers and signed on as navigator in a Dutch ship bound for Holland. After a brief stay at the Cape of Good Hope Cowley navigated the Dutch ship up the Atlantic, round the north of Scotland in a thick fog, and brought her safely to an anchor at Brill on 28 September 1686, returning in a yacht to London, which he reached on 14 October.

Cowley, as a man of some education, attempted to preserve his anonymity throughout, and hid his name as author of his journal under the pseudonym 'an ingenious Englishman'. It is through his journal that the details of this comparatively early circumnavigation became known. He lost the first half of his journal on the island of Gorgona; the second half is now in the British Museum (Sloane MSS 54). Later he reconstructed the first half from memory, and the whole was published in William *Hack's *Collection of Voyages* in 1699, still under Cowley's original pseudonym. Hack's MS copy is preserved in the Naval Library, Ministry of Defence, London (MSS 4).

COXSWAIN, orig. **COCKSWAIN** (pron. coxun), **(1)** the helmsman of a ship's boat and the senior member of its crew who has permanent charge of it. Originally all boats carried on board a ship were known as cockboats, or 'cocks', which gives the origin of the term. **(2)** The senior petty officer on board small naval craft such as *destroyers, *submarines, etc. As these craft were originally known in navies as boats rather than ships (torpedo boat, submarine boat, etc.), the term was applied to the senior petty officer on board in the same way as it would be to the senior rating of a ship's boat.

CQR, a type of *anchor introduced for small vessels and yachts shortly before the Second World War. The *fluke is roughly in the form of two plough shares set back to back and is held to the *shank by a pin about which it can pivot to some extent. The CQR anchor has no *stock, but when it reaches the bottom, any pull on it automatically turns it over so that the point of the fluke digs into the ground. It has considerably greater holding power than a fisherman's anchor of comparable weight and, having no stock, cannot be fouled by the anchor cable. The CQR is not suitable as an anchor for large vessels because of the difficulty of stowing it on board, but it has proved admirably efficient for small craft, such as yachts, and is deservedly popular.

It was designed by Sir Geoffrey Taylor who originally proposed to name it the 'Secure' anchor, but decided that the letters CQR, which give approximately the same sound, would be better remembered. In the U.S.A. it is usually known as a plow anchor. See also DANFORTH ANCHOR, and for illus., ANCHOR.

CRAB, a *capstan but without a *drumhead, and in which the bars are inserted right through the top of the barrel instead of into pigeon-holes in the upper perimeter (drumhead) as in a capstan proper; the holes for the bars in a crab being in different planes. It was used for any heavy lifting work on board in exactly the same way as a capstan but sometimes extemporized for use in positions where the *fall of the purchase used for lifting a weight could not be led to an existing *winch or capstan. With the wide extension of auxiliary power in ships, the need for these hand-worked appliances no longer exists in larger vessels except, perhaps, in very awkward positions where a powered pull cannot be obtained.

CRADLE, (1) the timber frame which is constructed round the hull of a ship while she is on the launching *ways in the course of being built. When launched, the cradle slides down the ways with the ship. **(2)** In general, any device which supports another when at rest, such as cargo booms, ship's boats, etc., which may have cradles for their permanent stowage on board.

CRADOCK, Sir CHRISTOPHER (1862–1914), British rear admiral, entered the Royal Navy in 1875 and served at the British occupation of Crete (1878) and with the naval brigade in Upper Egypt (1884), subsequently displaying outstanding courage at the storming of the Taku forts and the relief of Tientsin during the Boxer Rebellion (1900). In his several commands as a captain he proved an outstanding leader, with a strong belief in unswerving devotion to duty and unquestioning obedience, tempered by good comradeship between officers and men. Promoted to flag rank in 1910, he was knighted for his part in rescuing the Duke of Fife and the Princess Royal after the stranding of the P & O liner *Delhi* on the coast of Morocco in 1911.

Having assumed command of the North America and West Indies Station in 1913, Cradock had the misfortune just to miss destroying the German light *cruiser *Karlsruhe* shortly after the outbreak of the First World War (1914–18). But he cleared the North Atlantic trade routes by driving her and the cruiser *Dresden* into the South Atlantic. Ordered to make the Falkland Islands his base for the task of countering the possible appearance of Admiral von *Spee's powerful East Asiatic Squadron in South American waters, Cradock was determined not to be branded for failing to engage the enemy (as Rear Admiral Troubridge had been during the first week of the war for calling off his pursuit of the *Goeben) in spite of the Admiralty's inability to provide him with an adequate force. This impelled him to stand and fight when, on 1 November 1914, after rounding Cape Horn into the South Pacific in search of the enemy he located von Spee's squadron off *Coronel. A mistaken but undeniably gallant belief that his ships might do enough damage to compel his stronger opponent to seek internment in a neutral port was ended by the destruction of the armoured cruisers *Good Hope* and *Monmouth* in a defeat that cost Cradock his life.

CRAFT, in the 15th, 16th, and 17th centuries a term which denoted any kind of net, line, or hook used for catching fish. Fishing vessels, such as *hoys, *ketches, *busses, were in consequence usually described as small craft. The term has now been expanded to include all small vessels whether they are fishing vessels or not.

CRAMP, CHARLES HENRY (1828–1912), American shipbuilder, learned his trade in the shipyards of his father, one of the pioneers of American shipbuilding. He specialized in naval architecture and design, and built many ships for the U.S. Navy, first the *New Ironsides in 1862, the *battleships *Indiana, Iowa, Massachusetts, Alabama,* and *Maine* in the great reconstruction of the navy in the years from 1887 onwards, and many *cruisers. He was in the forefront of the technological development of naval ships in their progress from sail to steam, and his reputation was such that many foreign admiralties came to him for the design and construction of their ships. He was equally successful with commercial designs and built many passenger liners and merchant ships.

CRAN, a unit of measurement for herrings, being as many fresh or green unsalted herrings as will fill a barrel.

CRANCE, CRANS, or **CRANZE, (1)** an iron band on the outer end of a *bowsprit fitted with eyes to take the bowsprit *shrouds and the *bobstay. In larger sailing vessels where a *jib-boom is rigged the crance carries an additional opening through which the jib-boom is traversed, serving also to hold its heel firmly in place on the bowsprit. It is sometimes known as crans-iron.

CRANE LINES, (1) small ropes which were set up to keep the *lee *backstays from chafing against the *yards of a square-rigged ship when running with a quartering wind. **(2)** The lines which were rove from the *spritsail topmast to the centre of the *forestay to steady the former, acting somewhat in the manner of a backstay. With the spritsail topmast set up on the *bowsprit, there was no way of staying it except by such temporary means.

CRANK, a sailing ship which either by her construction or the stowage of her *ballast or cargo heels too far to the wind, or one which through lack of ballast or cargo cannot carry sail without the danger of overturning, is said to be crank. Ships which are built excessively deep in relation to their breadth are notoriously crank. 'Crank by the ground', a ship whose *floor is so narrow that she cannot be put ashore for cleaning or repair without danger of overturning unless supported by *legs.

CRAS, HERVÉ PIERRE (1910–   ), French naval medical officer and historian, joined the French Navy as a surgeon in 1928. During the Second World War he distinguished himself at the evacuation of *Dunkirk in 1940, where he was severely wounded. He later served in North Africa on the staff of Admiral Auphan, and after the war took to the writing of naval history, eventually joining the Service Historique de la Marine and later becoming its head. Written under the *nom de plume* Jacques Mordal, his books have attracted wide attention for their accuracy and clear exposition of naval strategy and thought. His first book, *Dieppe, the Dawn of Decision,* based on his experiences at Dunkirk and published in 1948, won awards by both the Naval Academy and the Académie française. He then wrote, in collaboration with Auphan, a history of the French Navy during the Second World War which won the second Grand Prix d'Histoire awarded by the Académie française. Among his other works, the best known is *Vingt-cinq Siècles de guerre sur mer* (Twenty-five Centuries of Sea Warfare), published in 1959.

He was promoted to Médécin Ier Classe (the equivalent rank of surgeon-captain in the Royal Navy) in July 1957.

CREEPER, another name for the small four-hooked *grapnel used to recover articles dropped on the sea bed by dragging for them. In clear water a white plate or dish dropped overboard immediately after the object falls gives a useful guide to where to use the creeper.

CRÉPIN, LOUIS PHILIPPE (1772–1851), French marine and landscape painter, was born in Paris and studied art under Joseph *Vernet. His output of marine paintings was considerable, mainly pictures of naval battles between British and French ships; he almost invariably had the habit of showing the French ships fighting at a disadvantage. He painted a notable picture of the British attack on Boulogne in 1801 in an attempt to destroy the French *flotilla assembled there for the invasion of Britain, one of the few naval actions in which Lord *Nelson was worsted.

CRESQUES, ABRAHAM (d. 1387), Jewish cartographer, was a member of the Catalan school of *portulan chartmakers working in Majorca in the 14th century. There are several references to the king of Aragon ordering special *mappamundi* from Abraham Cresques. In 1420 *Henry the Navigator, gathering round him at Sagres a number of cosmographers and chartmakers, sent for 'Master James of Majorca' who is believed to have been Abraham's son

JAFUDA. As persecution of the Jews was increasing in the kingdom of Aragon, Jafuda was glad to come to Sagres, bringing with him his skills as a chartmaker to found the Portuguese school of cartography which reached such heights in the 16th century.

CRESSY, H.M.S., see ABOUKIR, H.M.S.

CRIB, the name widely used during the early 19th century to describe the small permanent sleeping berths in *packet ships. Its meaning has since been expanded by many writers to cover any small sleeping berth in a small vessel.

CRIMP, one who makes it his business to persuade seamen to desert from a ship in order to sell them to another or to deliver them to the *press gang on payment of head money. Most of them operated as keepers of seamen's lodging houses or taverns in ports with a busy turn-round of ships, and the usual method of delivering seamen to a ship in need of hands was to make them drunk and deliver them on board, while still insensible, an hour or two before the ship's departure. The word is first noted in this sense in 1638. Although the practice was widespread around the world the most notorious port in which crimps flourished was San Francisco in the late 19th and early 20th centuries, when the rate for seamen delivered to a ship about to sail reached $30 a head plus expenses. Often crimps also claimed the first month's pay of the men they thus delivered. In Britain, crimping was an indictable offence leading to a prison sentence.

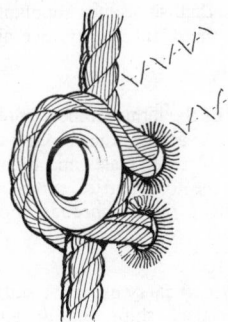

Cringle

CRINGLE, a short piece of rope worked *grommet fashion into the *boltrope of a sail and containing a metal thimble. They are used to hook in the tack and sheet tackles when they have to be moved up when a sail is reefed. In the days of square-rigged ships, cringles were used on the sails for extending the *leech of the sail by means of bowline *bridles for extra driving

power on a side wind. The word is derived from the old English *crencled*, meaning a circle, or circularly formed.

CROSS LASHING, a method of lashing with a rope in which the consecutive turns, instead of lying close up against each other in the same direction, are crossed diagonally. This type of lashing, by binding in upon itself with each turn, is less liable to give or *render.

CROSS SEA, a sea running in a contrary direction to the wind. During a gale in which the direction of the wind changes rapidly, such as during a cyclonic storm, the direction of the sea, whipped up by the wind, lasts for some hours after the wind has changed, throwing up a confused and irregular wave pattern which can be dangerous for ships caught in such a gale.

'CROSS THE T', to, a favourite manoeuvre in naval battle with fleets sailing in the normal battle disposition of line ahead. If a fleet in this disposition, either by a superiority of speed or by approaching at an angle, can cross ahead of the enemy's line approximately at right angles, it has a considerable tactical advantage in that all its guns can be fired on the broadside while the enemy can reply only with those guns which can fire ahead. It is also a tactical situation which forces an enemy to turn away, and in the resulting loss of speed during the turn and the difficulty of keeping guns bearing on an enemy while turning, the fleet 'crossing the T' has a considerable gunnery advantage. See, e.g., JUTLAND, BATTLE OF.

CROSSING THE LINE, a ceremony performed on board ships when members of passengers or crew are crossing the equator for the first time during a voyage. Usually all members of a ship's company who have not previously crossed the Line are initiated at a special ceremony held to mark the occasion. On the day the equator is crossed one of the ship's company appears on the forecastle suitably attired as King Neptune, encrusted with barnacles, wearing a golden crown and flowing beard, and clasping a *trident. He is accompanied by his wife, Queen Amphitrite, an evil-looking barber, a surgeon of equally villainous appearance, some fierce-looking guards, and as many 'nymphs' and 'bears' as the occasion may demand. After parading round the ship, court is held on a platform erected beside a large canvas bath filled with sea-water. After bestowing awards on distinguished veterans, King Neptune summons the novices one by one who, after receiving the attentions of both surgeon and barber, are tipped backwards into the bath, where the bears ensure that they receive a good ducking. This procedure earns them a certificate which exempts them from a repetition of the treatment on any future crossing of the Line that they may undertake.

The ceremony undoubtedly owes its origin to ancient pagan rites connected with the propitiation of the sea god *Poseidon or *Neptune. Before ocean navigation began in earnest in the middle of the 16th century, it was the custom to mark the successful rounding of prominent headlands by making a sacrifice to the appropriate deity, many of whom had temples erected in their honour on such points. With the spread of Christianity many of the vows and oblations paid to the heathen gods were transferred to the saints. In 1529 the French instituted an order of knighthood called *Les Chevaliers de la Mer* in which novices were given the accolade when rounding certain capes.

The earliest accounts of visits to ships from an imaginary King Neptune appear in Aubin's *Dictionnaire Nautique* (1702) and in Woodes *Rogers's book *A Cruising Voyage round the World* (1712), in which is described the performance of a ceremony on passing the tropic of Cancer which is similar to that performed today on crossing the equator. *Jal, in his *Glossaire nautique*, claims that in the middle of the 17th century it was the custom in French ships on crossing the Line for the second mate to impersonate Neptune and initiate all novices on board with a stout blow from a wooden sword followed by a dousing from a bucket of sea-water.

CROSS-JACK (pron. crojeck) **YARD,** the lower *yard on the mizen-mast of a square-rigged ship, to the arms of which the *clews of the mizen topsail are extended. In some sailing ships a sail, called a cross-jack, used to be set on this yard.

The term is also applied to any fore-and-aft rigged ship which sets a square sail below the lower *crosstrees.

CROSS-STAFF, an early navigational instrument for measuring the *altitude of a heavenly body. It was also often called a fore-staff and, erroneously, Jacob's staff. The Jacob's staff was first described in writing by Levi ben Gerson (1238–1344), a Jew of Provence, although its invention is usually ascribed to Jacob ben Makir who flourished during the same period. It consists of a square-sectioned staff graduated with tangential parts fitted with a sliding transom or cross-piece set at right angles to the staff. One end of the staff is held at the observer's eye and the upper and lower edges of the transom are made to coincide respectively with the observed body and the horizon vertically beneath it. The point where the transom cuts the scale is noted and converted by reference to a table into degrees and minutes.

The principle of the Jacob's staff and of the later cross-staff is the same as that of the *kamal. Although the Jacob's staff was invented as early as the 13th century for astronomical use, it was not used by mariners. In the early 16th century the cross-staff, probably adapted from the kamal by Portuguese navigators, was brought into use at sea. It was similar to the Jacob's staff except that the scale was divided off into degrees and minutes and the staff was shorter (about 3 feet in length) to facilitate handling on board ship. Martin Cortes, in his *Arte de Navegar,* first published in 1551, described the cross-staff's use at sea and gave his readers instructions for making the instrument, but the earliest reference is *c.* 1514. In the latter half of the 16th century it became customary to provide the cross-staff with three or even four crosses or transoms, designated the 10°, 15°, 30°, and 60° transoms respectively. Each transom was used in conjunction with one altitude scale engraved on the sides of the staff for measuring small, medium, and large altitudes respectively. It could also be reversed and used as a back-staff to measure the angle of the shadow cast by the sun.

The cross-staff was superior to the seaman's *quadrant or *astrolabe for certain observations, for it was more suitable for use on board a ship in a seaway and its larger scale enabled angles to read off more accurately. It was not, however, an easy instrument to use on account of the difficulty of scanning the arc between the observed body and the horizon below it—it would not be used when this arc was greater than about 55°. Nevertheless it continued in use among Dutch seamen into the 19th century. The *back-staff or *Davis quadrant supplemented it from the 1590s and among English seamen supplanted it almost entirely in the 17th century. See also HADLEY, John.

CROSSTREES, light timber spreaders fixed *athwartships across the *trestle-trees at the upper ends of lower masts and topmasts to give support to the tops and to spread the topmast and topgallant mast *shrouds. For illus. see also RIGGING.

CROWD, to, to carry excessive sail particularly in square-rigged ships, or to approach too closely another ship which has the right of way (see RULE OF THE ROAD).

CROWN, (1) a knot formed by tucking the strands of a rope's end over and under each other to lock them and prevent them unravelling. A crown knot made on top of a *wall knot is the basis on which a manrope knot is formed. **(2)** The lower part of an anchor where the arms are fixed to the *shank.

CROW'S FOOT, the name given to the method of attaching *reef points to a sail. The points are cut to the required length and each end *whipped. A crow's foot is then formed in the middle by twisting against the lay so that the individual strands are separated, pulling each one out and letting it twist up on itself. The crow's foot is then sewn to the starboard side of the sail (if possible on a seam) after the reef point has been drawn through the sail.

CROW'S NEST, a small shelter on the foremast for the masthead lookout, originally made from a cask. It was used extensively in *whalers to watch for the blow of a whale, and for navigation in ice-bound waters to distinguish the channels. See also BIRD'S NEST.

CROZIER, FRANCIS RAWDON MOIRA (c. 1796–1848), British naval officer, was born in Ireland and entered the navy in 1810. He accompanied Captain W. E. *Parry on his three voyages to the Arctic between 1821 and 1827. After a voyage to the Davis Straits and Baffin Bay with Captain J. C. *Ross in 1836, he was appointed to the command of the *Terror in 1839 and, again in company with Ross, visited the Antarctic. Promoted to captain in 1841, he was reappointed in command of the *Terror* and accompanied Sir John *Franklin in the *Erebus* on

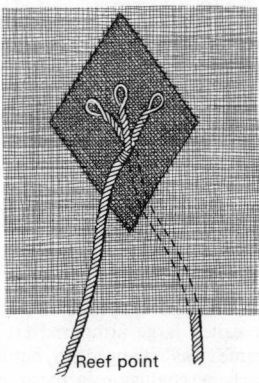

Reef point

Crow's foot

his ill-fated expedition to discover the *North-West passage. The first news of Crozier's fate came with the discovery in 1859 of a record on King William Island dated 1848 stating that the explorers under Crozier's command were about to start for the Great Fish River, a journey they failed to complete.

CRUISER, orig. **CRUIZER,** in the days of sailing navies a ship, usually a fourth *rate or large *frigate, detached from a fleet to cruise independently in search of the enemy with the duty of falling back on the fleet to report on sighting a strange fleet. Frigates and smaller warships engaged in the protection of trade or in the *guerre de course* were also usually known as cruisers. The one essential characteristic of any ship detached for duty as a cruiser was a good sailing speed, superior to that of the enemy she was seeking.

   With the introduction of steam propulsion and iron armour in the mid-19th century the cruiser gradually became a generic type of warship in her own right, being built in three or four categories ranging from armoured cruisers which were large ships of up to 15,000–16,000 tons displacement, through belted cruisers (those protected only by a waterline belt of armour), second class cruisers with only light armour, and light cruisers with virtually no armour but with particularly high speed. In Britain the needs of empire protection, requiring fleets and squadrons stationed permanently overseas, called for large numbers of cruisers of the various types, which on many of the more distant overseas stations formed the backbone of the local fleet or squadron. In a fleet the primary duties of cruisers remained, like that of their predecessors under sail, that of reconnaissance, though differing slightly in that they were not detached from the fleet but remained in visual touch. During battle their primary task was to station themselves in such positions relative to the main action that

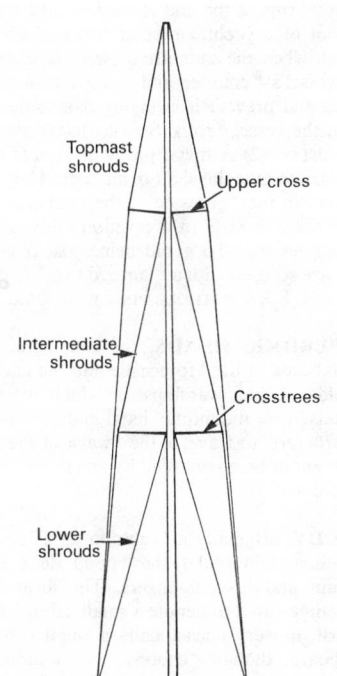

Topmast shrouds

Upper cross

Intermediate shrouds

Crosstrees

Lower shrouds

Crosstrees

they could see and report the movements of the enemy fleet in the event of the admiral being unable to see enemy movements himself by reason of smoke or poor visibility. Other duties included attack by guns or * torpedoes as occasion offered, and protection of the fleet by driving off attacks by light craft.

The role of the cruiser was complicated during the first decade of the 20th century by the development of the * battle-cruiser, a lightly armoured ship of comparable size to the * battleship and carrying guns of the same * calibre, but with an appreciably higher speed. Originally called large armoured cruisers their generic name was changed to battle-cruisers, causing perhaps confusion in the interpretation of their correct role in battle.

After the First World War (1914–18), all nations abandoned the various different types of cruiser which had proliferated during the past fifty years, the main reason being the increasing use of aircraft to carry out reconnaissance, the primary duty of all cruisers. Instead, a single category of ship, called simply a cruiser, was included in a fleet, size being indicated by the size of guns mounted, e.g., 8-inch cruiser, 6-inch cruiser, etc. Since reconnaissance for the fleet was no longer her primary duty in action, she assumed other subsidiary duties such as trade protection, amphibious support, etc. Like most other warships, modern cruisers are usually armed with missiles in place of guns, and a future naval role envisaged for them is as miniature * aircraft carriers in conjunction with vertical take-off aircraft.

The term is also used to describe a great many sailing and power yachts designed or adapted for short- or long-distance cruising. Small yachts without cabin accommodation are frequently known as day cruisers, returning to their home port after each day's sailing, but all other yachts except racing yachts come under the generic name of cruiser. Before the days of modern yacht construction, a favourite type of cruiser was a converted fishing smack or pilot * cutter, stoutly built craft able to sail anywhere in the world and live in heavy seas. Notable examples of such converted craft were the Havre pilot cutter * Jolie Brise, owned by E. G. * Martin, in which in 1926 he sailed some 10,000 miles across the Atlantic and back, and the West Country fishing smack Moonraker, owned by Dr. E. A. * Pye, which he and his wife sailed across the Atlantic, through the Panama Canal, and up to British Columbia and back.

While a great many of these elderly yachts are still in commission and actively engaged in cruising, modern construction methods, using * ferro-cement, * fibre glass, and bonded plywoods, have enabled yacht designers and builders to produce standard hulls, finished to their owners' requirements for internal accommodation, thus allowing for series production with worthwhile saving in initial cost. This has led, since the Second World War, to an immense increase in the number of cruising yachts around the world, while the construction of yachting * marinas in a great many countries has added yet another impetus to the sport. See also YACHTING (Cruising).

CRUISING ASSOCIATION, THE, a British institution to assist cruising yachtsmen, was formed in 1908 with a central office in London where its members could obtain the latest information on charts and sailing directions for cruising between the Skaw (Denmark) and the Spanish coast. At its headquarters it houses an extensive nautical reference library of over 10,000 volumes; it publishes a comprehensive *Handbook* containing chart-plans of harbours and anchorages with sailing directions for the whole of the British Isles and home waters. Local boatmen representing the Cruising Association are employed at nearly every yacht harbour round the coast of Britain.

'CRUSHER', a slang term on the lower deck for a member of the ship's police, or regulating petty officer, in a warship.

CRUTCH, (1) a * stanchion with two short, curved arms at the end shaped to take the main * boom of a yacht, or other fore-and-aft rigged vessel, when the sails are stowed. It is fitted on the vessel's * counter and is used to secure the boom and prevent it swinging from side to side when the vessel * rolls. See also GALLOWS, GALLOW-BITTS. **(2)** A metal pin with jaws at the top of a size to take the shaft of an * oar. They fit into sockets in the * gunwale of the boat placed just abaft the * thwarts in a position convenient for pulling an oar. To avoid being lost overboard, they are secured with a * lanyard to a * stringer in the boat. See also THOLE PINS, ROWLOCK.

CUBBRIDGE HEADS, the old name of the * bulkheads of the * forecastle and the half-decks in older sailing warships, in which were fitted sockets for mounting hand-guns, known as * murderers, to traverse the * waist of the ship in the event of being boarded by an enemy. See also PASSARADO.

CUDDY, originally a * cabin in the after part of a sailing ship under the * poop deck for the captain and his passengers. The term is also sometimes used to denote a small cabin on board a boat, or very occasionally a small cookhouse on board, though * caboose was a more usual word for this. In larger ships the cuddy was the compartment where the officers had their meals.

CULVERIN, see GUNS, NAVAL.

CUMBERLAND FLEET, see ROYAL THAMES YACHT CLUB.

CUMULUS, a type of cloud formation. See METEOROLOGY.

CUNARD, Sir SAMUEL (1787–1865), British shipowner, was a successful merchant of Halifax, Nova Scotia, who owned a number of sailing ships. When the British government in 1838 invited tenders for a service of steamships to replace the transatlantic mail *brigs, Cunard travelled to Britain, joined forces with Robert Napier, one of the best-known marine engineers of the day, and put in a tender for the mail service. In the terms of his tender he agreed that he would build four ships and would guarantee to operate two voyages to America and back every month, winter and summer. With his tender for the service accepted, Cunard formed a company with the shipowners George *Burns of Glasgow and David MacIver of Liverpool, placed orders for four wooden paddle steamers, and began transatlantic operations in 1840, sailing from Liverpool to Boston. The passenger and mail service which he created has held a leading position in the transatlantic passenger trade from that day to the present. Cunard was created a baronet in 1859 for his outstanding services to the British shipping industry.

CUNARD LINE, a transatlantic steamship line founded in 1840 by Samuel *Cunard, of Halifax, Nova Scotia, in conjunction with George *Burns and others, to operate regular steamship sailings across the Atlantic for the carriage of passengers and mail. The line was founded on the basis of a successful tender for the carriage of British mails made by Cunard in 1838, and the first regular voyages between Liverpool and Boston were begun in the summer of 1840.

The first ships of the Cunard Line, of which the best known is the *Britannia, were wooden paddle steamers which made the transatlantic crossing in an average time of fifteen days. The first iron Cunarder was the *Persia*, commissioned in 1856. As the transatlantic trade developed, the Cunard ships increased in both size and numbers, the line always retaining its position as the foremost transatlantic passenger service against whatever opposition offered. Many famous ships have sailed under its house flag, of which the best known in their day were the *Umbria* of 1884, the *Campania* of 1893, the *Mauretania* and *Lusitania* of 1907, and the famous *Queen Mary* of 1936 and *Queen Elizabeth*, launched in 1938, both of them generally considered to be the greatest *liners ever built. In 1934, before the last two were built, the

The Queen Elizabeth *in 1954*

Cunard Line had merged with the *White Star Line of transatlantic passenger liners to form a single company to build and operate these magnificent ships.

Following the Second World War, during which most of the Cunard White Star liners served as troopships and *armed merchant cruisers, the competition of air travel led to a marked and rapid reduction in sea passenger traffic. The two 'Queens' were sold, and by 1969 the line had been reduced to a single liner in the top flight, the much smaller *Queen Elizabeth II*, which alternates her transatlantic service with holiday cruises. Other Cunard ships today operate purely as cruise liners, virtually the only profitable employment left to these great ships.

CUNDALL, CHARLES ERNEST (1890–), British painter, was born at Stretford and studied at the Royal College of Art and the Slade School in London, and subsequently in Paris. During the Second World War he was an official war artist serving with the Royal Navy. His painting of the evacuation of the British Expeditionary Force from *Dunkirk in 1940, now in the *Imperial War Museum, London, is a notably strong example of his power of expression of a swiftly moving battle.

CUNNINGHAM, ANDREW BROWNE, first Viscount Cunningham of Hyndhope (1883–1963), British admiral of the fleet, known throughout the Royal Navy as 'A.B.C.', was the foremost British naval commander of the Second World War. He was born in Dublin of Scots parents, entered the navy by way of H.M.S. * *Britannia*, and first saw active service with the Naval Brigade during the South African War of 1899–1902. He was given his first independent command in 1908 while still a lieutenant when he was appointed to H.M. Torpedo Boat No. 14. For most of the next ten years he was first and foremost a * destroyer man. A succession of commands included that of H.M.S. *Scorpion*, a coal-burner in which he served for seven years, including a large part of the First World War (1914–18). In 1914 he took part in shadowing the German * battle-cruiser * *Goeben* and light cruiser *Breslau* and was later sent to the * Dardanelles. While serving there he was promoted commander and awarded the D.S.O. Later he joined the Dover Patrol and was present in support of Admiral * Keyes's raid on * Zeebrugge in April 1918. He was given a bar to his D.S.O. in 1919 and a second bar the following year for his services when his ship, then H.M.S. *Seafire*, was in the Baltic with a squadron under Admiral Sir Walter * Cowan. He was promoted captain in 1920.

Between the wars Cunningham held various destroyer commands. He was flag-captain to Cowan on the America and West Indies Station 1926–8 and later commanded the * battleship *Rodney*. Shortly before the opening of the Second World War he was for some months at the Admiralty, in the rank of vice admiral, as deputy chief of the naval staff. When war broke out he was in command of the Mediterranean Fleet.

After Italy entered the conflict in 1940, just before the collapse of France, the Mediterranean became an area of increasing tension. Cunningham, always with inferior numbers, dominated the Mediterranean, winning spectacular successes in a naval air attack on * Taranto in November 1940 and by his destruction of a cruiser squadron in the battle of * Cape Matapan in March 1941. German intervention in the Middle East, and their successes in Greece and Crete from which British expeditionary forces had to be withdrawn in the face of overwhelming air superiority, caused Cunningham such loss in ships and men as might have broken the spirit of a less buoyant leader. Misfortune continued well beyond the entry of the U.S.A. into the war in December 1941.

In 1942 Cunningham was sent to Washington as head of the British Admiralty Delegation. He returned to the Mediterranean in November as commander-in-chief of all naval forces, under the supreme direction of General Dwight D. Eisenhower, during the landings in French North Africa and in the later invasions of Sicily and the Italian mainland. In July 1943 he had the satisfaction of accepting the surrender of the Italian fleet, and in October of the same year he succeeded Admiral of the Fleet Sir Dudley * Pound as First Sea Lord, thus becoming professional head of the navy and a member of the Chiefs of Staff committee, responsible, under the guidance of Winston * Churchill, for British maritime strategy.

Cunningham was present at summit meetings of the allied heads of state at Quebec, Yalta, and Potsdam, and he continued as First Sea Lord until after the conclusion of peace with Japan, when he retired. In 1945 he had been created a Knight of the Thistle, the only man to be thus honoured for services at sea, and in the following year he became a viscount.

Cunningham, like Lord * Nelson, was a prince among delegators. Having once proved a subordinate, he trusted him thenceforward, and the response he received from this trust was magnificent. He was valiant in action and in facing adversity. He was staunchly loyal to his superiors and generous to his equals. It is fitting that, although Cunningham was buried at sea, he should be commemorated, with other great commanders in the crypt of St. Paul's, and that his bust should be seen in Trafalgar Square. The best biography is his own autobiography *A Sailor's Odyssey* (1951).

CUNNINGHAM HOLE, a semi-circular space cut near the bottom of the * luff of a mainsail in a racing yacht to enable the luff to be set up more tautly while racing. In many racing classes there are restrictions against hoisting the mainsail higher than a particular mark on the mast or lowering the inboard end of the boom below a similar mark. A Cunningham hole allows a * tackle to be attached so that the luff of the sail above can be tensioned as necessary.

CUNT SPLICE, the old name for what is now known as a * cut splice.

CUNTING, an old nautical word to describe the hollows or grooves that lie spirally between strands when they are twisted up into rope. '* Worm the cable in the cunting', lay a small rope or line spirally in the hollows between strands in preparation for * parcelling and * serving. See also CONTLINE.

CURRACH or **CURRAGH,** a boat peculiar to Ireland, especially its western coast, used for local traffic. It is of great antiquity, contemporary with, and very similar to, the * coracle, being originally constructed of animal skins attached to

Aran Island currach

a wicker frame, often nearly circular in shape and operated by paddles. Currachs of today are constructed of two skins of calico or canvas, tarred to make them watertight, most frequently stretched over an interlaced framework of elm laths, although other woods are used when elm is not easily available. They are now of conventional boat shape and have been constructed for use with as many as eight oars, though they are normally of rather smaller size. A small mast and square sail is usually carried for use when the wind is favourable. The currach is particularly associated with the Aran Islands, off the west coast of Ireland, where it is used for the transport not only of people and goods but also of cattle.

CURRENT, the flowing of the sea in one direction. Currents may be periodic in relation to the tides, seasonal in relation to a prevailing wind which blows only at certain times of the year, or permanent in relation to the main rotational winds (i.e., winds affected by the earth's rotation, such as the *trade winds) which blow over the wide ocean surfaces. Differences in water temperatures also affect the formation of currents, in very much the same way as differences in air temperatures affect the force and direction of winds.

Atmospheric circulation over the oceans, where the wide uninterrupted surfaces give stability and permanence to air flows such as the recognized trade winds, is the most effective producer of the drift movements of the surface waters which we know as currents. Thus, in the Atlantic Ocean, the two patterns of trade winds on either side of the equator, the north-east and south-east trades, give rise to two westward-moving drifts, known as the equatorial currents, which themselves generate between them a compensatory counter-current flowing in the opposite direction along the equatorial belt. When the southern equatorial current reaches the coast of South America at about Cape St. Roque it divides into two parts. One branch, the Brazil current, flows south following the coast as far as the River Plate, where it comes under the influence of the strong westerly winds known as the *'Roaring Forties'. It then flows eastward across the South Atlantic as far as the Cape of Good Hope, part continuing into the Indian Ocean, part being deflected northward by the African land mass to become the Benguella current, eventually reaching and joining the South Atlantic drift. The other part of the southern equatorial current flows north and joins the northern equatorial current. These two drifts, blocked by the shape of the land, escape into the Caribbean Sea and Gulf of Mexico where, unable to continue their drift westward because of the total land block formed by the Isthmus of Panama, they raise the level of the sea. This congestion of water must escape, and the only direction available is north-east up the coast of North America. This is the *Gulf Stream. It is deflected off the coast of Newfoundland by the south-flowing Labrador current (see below) and flows eastward across the North Atlantic until it is blocked by the coast of Europe, where it divides. The southern part becomes the Canaries current and eventually rejoins the northern equatorial drift; the northern part divides into three branches, one flowing west of Britain to Norway and into the Arctic basin, the second, known as the Irminger stream, passing up the western side of Iceland, the third flowing up the Davis Strait to Baffin Bay. These three branches are separated by south-flowing compensatory currents from the Arctic basin, known as the Greenland current and the Labrador current, and it is the latter which deflects the Gulf Stream eastward off Newfoundland.

In the Indian Ocean, north of the equator, the dominant factor in the creation of currents is the *monsoon winds. The currents in the open sea change with them, forming north-east and south-west drifts. During the summer the south-west monsoon sets up a strong north-easterly drift in the Arabian Sea, and the water which this draws from the African coast is replaced by cold water rising from below. South of the equator the dominant factor is the powerful Equatorial current which flows westwards between the approximate latitudes of 7° and 20° S. This sets up an eastward-flowing counter current, known as the Indian counter current, which follows approximately the line of the equator. When the Equatorial current meets the coast of Africa it divides into two parts, the smaller, north-flowing, following the coastline until it meets and is absorbed by the Indian counter current. The larger part flows south to form the Mozambique current, which becomes the Agulhas current south of Cape Corrientes and is one of the most powerful currents in the world at times flowing at a rate of 4–5 knots. As soon as it reaches open water south of the Cape of Good Hope it meets the west wind drift caused by the 'Roaring Forties' and joins it to form a strong east-flowing stream. On reaching Australia, a part of this is diverted northward by the continental land mass to form the West Australia current until it reaches and merges with the Equatorial current.

The Pacific currents are, in general, less pronounced than those of of the Atlantic and Indian Oceans. The North Equatorial current, a westerly stream caused by the action of the north-east trade winds, splits into two parts when it meets the Philippine Islands, one part flowing north and repeating very much the characteristic pattern of the Gulf Stream in the Atlantic. It is known as the Kuro Siwo, or Black, Stream and it feeds a drift circulation influenced by the North Pacific winds, becoming the Californian current when it meets the North American coast. This follows the coastline until it divides, one part continuing down the coast to form the Mexican current, the other rejoining the North Equatorial current.

Further south, the South Equatorial current is the dominant feature. It is produced by the south-east trades. It divides when it reaches the western Pacific, part flowing southwards to the east of New Zealand and Australia and known as the East Australian current, and part northwards. Most of this joins the Equatorial counter current, which flows eastward between the North and South Equatorial currents, but during the north-east monsoon some of this northern drift makes its way through the China Sea to the Indian Ocean. During the south-west monsoon period it is reversed and joins the Kuro Siwo. Between the Kuro Siwo and the Asiatic coast, a band of cold water known as the Oya Siwo flows southward following the coastline.

Still further south, the surface movement of the waters again comes under the influence of the 'Roaring Forties' to form an east-flowing stream. When it reaches South America, the southern portion continues past Cape Horn but the part that meets the coast is diverted northwards to form the Humboldt, or Peruvian, current, which eventually joins the South Equatorial current.

The setting, or direction, of a current is that point of the compass towards which it flows, the drift of a current is the rate in *knots at which it runs. Information on currents is given in the *Current Atlas of the World* and is also included in the appropriate * *Sailing Directions*.

CURRIE, Sir DONALD (1825–1909), British shipowner, founded the Union Castle Line of steamships to South Africa. He started his career with the *Cunard Line but in 1862 decided to start out on his own. His first venture was the Castle Line of sailing ships, operating between Liverpool and Calcutta, and in 1872, by now based in London, he founded the Castle Line of steamships to South Africa, dividing the government mail contract with the already existing Union Line. The two, under Currie's direction, were amalgamated as the Union Castle Line in 1900. In 1880 he began a compaign in Parliament to persuade the British Admiralty to utilize fast merchant ships in wartime as auxiliary, or *armed merchant, cruisers, and their subsequent employment in that role was largely due to Currie's advocacy.

CURRY, MANFRED (1900–53), American doctor and yachtsman, was a pioneer exponent of the study of aerodynamics in yachts' rig and racing, leading to great changes in yacht racing tactics. He spent most of his working life in Europe and took his medical degree in Munich where he engaged in medical research work and in 1935 founded an American bioclimatic institute, now the Manfred Curry Institut in Riederan. Yacht racing, boat designing, and writing were his other interests. To yachtsmen he is best known for his books *Yacht Racing: Aerodynamics of Sails and Racing Tactics* (1928) and *Racing Tactics* (1949). See also AERO-DYNAMICS.

CURVE OF CONSTANT BEARING, a line on the earth joining points at which the *great circle bearing of a *radio beacon is constant.

CUSHING, WILLIAM BARKER (1842–74), American naval officer, distinguished himself in the American Civil War (1861–5) and had the most brilliant record of any officer except the senior commanders. He was born in Wisconsin and entered the Naval Academy in 1857. After brilliant service in the blockading fleet off the North Carolina coast he made plans to fit out a *torpedoboat to destroy the formidable Confederate *ram *Albemarle* which had recently been completed and was lying at Plymouth, North Carolina, eight miles up the Roanoke River. With fifteen volunteers Cushing made his way up river on 27 October 1864 and in spite of dense small arms fire succeeded in exploding his *spar torpedo under the *Albemarle*, destroying her.

In the capture of Fort Fisher in January 1865 he commanded a company of sailors and marines which led the assault. He was probably under fire more often than any other officer of the Union Navy but was never wounded. He served in the Pacific and Asiatic squadrons after the war.

CUSTANCE, Sir REGINALD NEVILLE (1847–1935), British admiral, was born at Belfast and entered the Royal Navy through H.M.S. *Britannia* in 1860. After a period as assistant director of Naval Intelligence he was appointed in 1890 to command the cruiser *Phaeton* and in 1895 the battleship *Barfleur*, having in the interval served as naval attaché in Washington and Paris. From 1899 to 1902 he was Director of Naval Intelligence and on promotion to rear admiral commanded a squadron in the Mediterranean Fleet. Promoted to vice admiral in 1906, he was appointed second-in-command of the Channel Fleet and two years later reached the rank of admiral. A lifelong student of naval warfare, and one of the most brilliant brains in the British Navy, he fell foul of Admiral Sir John *Fisher towards the end of the latter's period as First Sea Lord in 1910, and his outspoken criticism of Admiralty policy led to his premature retirement in 1912. He was the author of *Naval Policy* (1907), *The Ship of the Line in Battle* (1912), and *War at Sea* (1919).

CUT AND RUN, to, an expression often thought to imply the cutting of a hemp *cable with an axe, thus abandoning an *anchor, when a ship needed to get quickly under way in an emer-gency. The more accurate origin of the saying was the custom of square-rigged ships, when at anchor in an open roadstead, of furling their sails with them stopped to the yards with ropeyarns, so that the yarns could be cut and the sails let fall when the need to get under way quickly was urgent.

CUT OF HIS (HER) JIB, the, a saying that has taken its place in the English language as the recognition of a person by, originally, the shape of his or her nose, but now probably extended to embrace other recognizable characteristics. The term originated in the sailing navies of the mid-18th century, when the nationality of warships sighted at sea could be accurately determined by the shape of their *jib long before the national flag could be seen. Spanish ships, for instance, had only a very small jib or none at all; French ships very often had two jibs when other ships had only one; moreover, the French jib was cut much shorter on the *luff than English jibs, giving a distinctly more acute angle in the *clew.

CUT SPLICE, two ropes spliced together to form an *eye. The splice is not made with the two ropes end to end, as in a short splice, but overlapping to the extent required to form the eye, the end of each rope being spliced into the body of the other rope and the splices then *whipped.

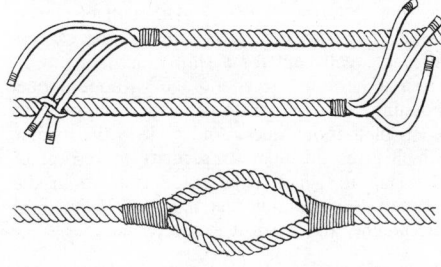

Cut splice

CUTCH, a preservative dressing used to prolong the life of canvas sails. It consists of broken up gum catechu boiled in fresh water in the proportion of 5 lb of gum to eight gallons of water. See also TAN, TO.

CUTTER, a term which embraces a variety of small vessels. **(1)** In its older meaning it referred to a small, decked ship with one mast and *bowsprit, with a *gaff mainsail on a *boom, a square yard and topsail, and two *jibs or a jib and a *staysail. The rig was introduced in about 1740. These vessels were relatively fast on a wind and were employed mainly as auxiliaries to the war fleets and in the preventive service against smugglers. They were armed with up to ten 4-pounder guns. Later they were widely used in the *Trinity House pilot service, and Trinity House still class their steam/diesel light tenders and pilot vessels as cutters. (2) A *clinker-built ship's boat, length 24–32 feet, pulling eight to fourteen oars and rigged originally with two masts with a dipping *lug foresail and a standing lug mainsail, giving way in the 20th century to a single mast with a *de Horsey rig of a loose-footed gaff mainsail and fore staysail. (3) A sailing yacht with, in much of the world, a mainsail and two foresails; but in the U.S.A. such vessels are called *sloops, and the term cutter refers only to the old-fashioned rig where such vessels had a very long bowsprit. Modern cutters are almost invariably *Bermuda-rigged though there are still some older boats gaff-rigged with a jib-headed topsail. (4) A steam vessel of about 2,000 tons in the U.S. Navy, used largely in the coastguard, ice patrol, and weather patrol services.

'CUTTING HIS PAINTER', an expression meaning, in terms of a ship in harbour, to make a clandestine departure, but also, in seaman's language and in terms of an individual, to depart this life. Ship's boats are secured alongside by means of their *painters, and a silent or clandestine departure can only be made by cutting the painter and allowing the boat to drift silently away from the ship until it is out of earshot of those on board. Although of course larger ships do not have painters, the expression is equally apt for a ship which slips away from a harbour or anchorage without notice, possibly to avoid customs inspection or payment of harbour dues. And as it is the painter which gives the boat its security in respect of the ship to which it is made fast, so in the seaman's imagination his personal 'painter' is his lifeline, and when it is severed he dies.

CUTLASS, originally a sabre with a curved blade, but generally recognized to mean the short swords issued to seamen in warships for use when boarding, cutting-out, or fighting ashore. Cutlasses were carried on board major warships of the Royal Navy up to the second decade of the 20th century, but were discarded when such hand-to-hand fighting as these weapons involved was made unlikely both by modern small arms firepower ashore and the extreme unlikelihood of the boarding of enemy ships ever again becoming an operation of naval war. (Nevertheless, there was an occasion of boarding an enemy vessel during the Second World War when H.M.S. *Cossack, on 16 February 1940, entered Jössing Fjord on the coast of Norway and boarded the German tanker *Altmark to set free 299 British seamen who had been captured by the *Admiral Graf Spee during a cruise in the South Atlantic and South Indian oceans against British merchant shipping. The boarders were armed with rifles on that occasion, not with cutlasses.)

CUTTY SARK, the only survivor of the British tea *clippers, is now preserved as a museum ship and example of the great days of sail at *Greenwich, London. She was built to the order of Captain Jock Willis, son of the Captain Willis who was known as 'Old Stormy' and immortalized in the sea *shanty 'Stormalong'. She was built expressly as a challenge to the great British clipper *Thermopylae and the two ships were almost identical in size, with a length of 212 feet, a *beam of 36 feet, and a depth of 21 feet. The Cutty Sark was designed by Hercules Linton and built partly by the firm of Linton and Scott and partly by William Denny and Brothers, as the price quoted by Linton and Scott was too low and they were forced into liquidation during construction of the ship. She was launched at Dumbarton in November 1869, and the following year took part in the annual tea race from China to London. But by then the *Suez Canal had been opened, and the trade was being lost to steamships which could use the shorter Canal route. The Cutty Sark made eight voyages in the tea trade but never matched the times put up by the earlier clippers, her best being in 1871 when she sailed from Shanghai to the North Foreland in 107 days. Only once did she race home in company with the Thermopylae, but on that occasion lost her rudder during heavy weather in the Indian Ocean when she had worked out a lead of 400 miles.

When the sailing clippers finally had to abandon the tea trade to the competition of the steamers, the Cutty Sark was forced to look for cargoes wherever they were to be had, but in 1883 she began regular voyages in the wool trade from Australia and made some remarkably fast passages, seventy-three days from Sydney to the Downs in 1885 and sixty-nine days from Newcastle, New South Wales, to the Lizard in 1887–8. From 1885 until the end of her wool-carrying days she was commanded by Captain Richard Woodgett, a fine seaman who knew how to drive a square-rigged ship. Her last wool voyage from Australia was in 1894–5, and on arrival in London she was sold to the Portuguese. She operated under the Portuguese flag for twenty-seven years, for many of them re-rigged as a *barquentine.

In 1922, after a refit in London, she was forced to put into Falmouth in a Channel gale while on her way back to Lisbon. There she was seen by Captain Wilfred Downman, who bought her and restored and re-rigged her to her original clipper rig. On his death in 1936 his widow

The Cutty Sark; *oil painting by D. Sherrin*

presented her to the Thames Nautical Training College and she was towed to Greenhithe for use as a boys' training ship. In 1949, no longer required for this service, she was offered to the *National Maritime Museum which was unable to accept her, but, largely through the hard work and enthusiasm of Mr. Frank *Carr, the London County Council sponsored a scheme for her permanent preservation in a specially constructed dock at Greenwich. She entered the dock in 1954, work on her hull and rigging was completed in 1957, and she was then opened to the public.

Her name comes from Robert Burns's poem 'Tam O' Shanter', which tells the story of a Scottish farmer who was chased by the young witch Nannie, who wore only:

> Her cutty sark, o' Paisley harn
> That while a lassie she had worn
> In longitude tho' sorely scanty
> It was her best, and she was vauntie.

The *Cutty Sark*'s *figurehead is a representation of the witch Nannie in her cutty sark (short shift), with her left arm outstretched to catch the tail of the farmer's grey mare on which he was trying to escape.

CUTWATER, the forward curve of the *stem of a ship. It was also sometimes known as the *knee of the head or *beakhead.

CYCLONE, see TROPICAL STORMS.

D

DD, (1) the letters used in the naval *muster-books in the British Navy to indicate that a member of the crew had died on board or had been killed and that his pay ceased from that date. The letters stood for Discharged Dead. **(2)** The code letters used to indicate a 'swimming' tank developed during the Second World War for use in amphibious assault landings. They were launched from the ramp of an *L.C.T. or *L.S.T. a short distance offshore and 'swam' to the assault beach under their own power, being given sufficient buoyancy for the purpose by a canvas screen, or skirt, erected round the tank.

d.w.t. see DEADWEIGHT.

DAGGER, a steel bar which plays an essential part in the launching mechanism of a ship. When the *dog shore is knocked out, the dagger acts as a trigger which releases the vessel and starts her down the launching *ways. Although in modern ship launches the whole operation is performed by power, and men with sledge hammers no longer knock out the dog shores, the principle and mechanics of a launch remain unaltered.

DAGGER-BOARD, a drop *keel, or sliding *centreboard of wood or metal which can be raised or lowered inside a case through a slot in a shallow draught boat's keel, to increase the effective draught and thereby reduce *leeway when sailing *close-hauled. It was one of the earliest types of sliding keel and originally used by the Chinese in some of their river *junks. It is so called because it is generally narrow in proportion to its length and, not being pivoted like a true centreboard, slides down from its case like a dagger from a sheath.

DAHABEEYAH or **DAHABIAH,** from the Arabic *dahabiyah*, golden, a large river sailing vessel with high *lateen sails associated with the River Nile. Originally the term applied to the gilded state *barges of Egyptian rulers, hence its derivation.

DAHLGREN GUN, a modification of the Paixhan gun, introduced into the U.S. Navy in 1859 by Commander (later Admiral) J. A. Dahlgren. His guns were 'the first practical applica-tion of results obtained by experimental determinations of pressure at different points along the bore', and as a result of their curve of pressure they looked like and were given the name of 'ginger-beer bottles' as they were exceptionally thick for two-thirds of their length and then narrowed down to a comparatively thin muzzle. They were produced in two sizes, a 9-inch shell gun and a 50-pounder firing solid shot, and were cast in iron with smooth bores. The extreme thickness of the barrel at the breech end made them unwieldy in action and although they performed reasonably successfully during the American Civil War (1861–5) they were gradually replaced in the U.S. Navy with guns of more conventional shape.

DALE, RICHARD (1756–1826), American naval officer, was born in Norfolk County, Va. He went to sea at the age of 12 and was in the loyalist sloop *Lady Susan* when she was captured by the *Lexington (John *Barry) in 1776. Dale became a master's mate in the *Continental Navy on the day of his capture after a talk with Barry, but was captured by the British and confined in Mill Prison, near Plymouth. He escaped and made his way to France where he became first lieutenant of the *Bonhomme Richard (John Paul *Jones). In the famous action off Flamborough Head he was the first to board H.M.S. *Serapis*, where he was severely wounded. He served also with Jones in the *Alliance*, and returned to America with him in the *Ariel*.

In 1794 Dale was appointed a captain in the new U.S. Navy by President Washington, but a mistake by the new Navy Department caused President Adams to resubmit the name of Silas *Talbot and Dale for confirmation as captains in the U.S. Navy. Thomas *Truxtun chose to consider that this error made him senior to both Talbot and Dale, and the latter therefore declined to continue on active duty. The question of relative rank was finally decided by President Adams, who held that neither Talbot nor Dale had done anything to justify an alteration in their status. Dale served in the Mediterranean as the commander of a squadron of five naval vessels, 1801–2, and during the War of 1812 he was a member of the Philadelphia committee for the protection of the city.

Dahabeeyahs on the Nile

DALLMANN, EDUARD (*fl.* 1873), a German sealing captain who visited the South Shetland Islands in 1873 at the instigation of the German Society for Polar Navigation to investigate the possibilities of reviving the southern sealing industry, then moribund. His ship, the *Grönland*, was the first steam *whaler to visit Antarctic waters. Dallmann charted and named Bismarck Strait, south of the Palmer Archipelago, and roughly charted the adjacent mainland and islands.

DALRYMPLE, ALEXANDER (1737–1808), was the first Hydrographer of the Navy when the Hydrographic Department of the British Admiralty was established in 1795. He had made his career in the *East India Company which he joined as a writer in 1752, going first to Madras. His absorbing and lifelong interest in geography and discovery was given rein when in 1762 he made a voyage via Palembang and Sulu to Canton, seeking routes for East Indiamen.

There followed a period in England from 1765 to 1776 when he published a number of charts of the East Indies and, in 1771, an essay on nautical surveying. Concurrently he took a prominent part in discussions about the 'Great

Southern Continent', or *Terra Australis Incognita, and its development, and when in 1766 the Royal Society proposed an expedition to observe the transit of Venus in the South Pacific, Dalrymple was in their mind as leader. The Admiralty, however, insisted that the expedition be led by a naval officer and it was James *Cook who in 1768 sailed in command of what was to be the first of his three great voyages of discovery.

After a brief return to East India Company's service at Madras in 1776, Dalrymple was appointed in 1779 as the first East India hydrographer, being prolific in the preparation of charts, plans, and directions, and he continued to hold this appointment during his service as Hydrographer to the Admiralty from 1795 to 1808.

At the Admiralty he was faced with the immense task of sorting and classifying the accumulated original documents. As he was hesitant to publish material of which he was in doubt or of which he had no personal knowledge, the output of charts for the fleet was slow, and he sought in 1807 the help of a naval chart committee with whom, however, as with the Admiralty Board, his relations were uneasy. Eventually in

1808 his age and the ill health which had dogged him for some years led to his enforced retirement and within three weeks he died of 'mortification' (gangrene). But under his direction the Hydrographic Department of the Admiralty had been well founded on high standards of accuracy and integrity, and there was a nucleus of engraved plates from which Admiralty charts could be printed within the Admiralty with a consequent reduction in reliance on purchases from other publishers. Through his sound initiative the Hydrographer had become, and was to remain, the Admiralty's sole adviser on all navigational matters.

DAMELOPRE, a Dutch sailing barge or coaster in which the mast is stepped in a *tabernacle so that it can be lowered for passing under a bridge. With the almost universal substitution of power propulsion in place of sail in such vessels, the name is now virtually obsolete.

DAMPIER, WILLIAM (1652–1715), British *buccaneer, navigator, and surveyor, was born at East Coker, Somerset. He became an orphan when still a boy and at the age of 18 was apprenticed to a ship's captain with whom he made a voyage to the Newfoundland fisheries. With his apprenticeship served, he joined an *East Indiaman as an able seaman and sailed in her to Java, a part of the world which gave him instant delight and to which he was to return many times. He returned from this voyage in 1672 and, at the outbreak of the Third Dutch War (1672–4), enlisted in the Royal Navy, serving on board the *Royal Prince*, flagship of Sir Edward Spragge. He was present at the two battles of Schooneveld but was invalided at the end of the war.

Offered employment as manager of a sugar plantation in Jamaica, Dampier discovered on arrival that he was expected to work in the refinery on menial jobs. After nine months he was discharged as unsatisfactory with a month's wages which he spent in a drunken debauch. He joined a ship bound for the Bay of Campeachy and found employment with the logwood-cutters there, spending the next year (1675–6) in that arduous labour.

Campeachy was the nursery of the English buccaneers at that time, and Dampier found himself attracted to that life, not so much, perhaps, at the hope of riches as for the opportunity it presented of sailing to new places. He joined a band of buccaneers led by Captain Bartholomew *Sharp and marched with them across the Isthmus of Darien for an attack on the Spanish town of Panama. Seizing some canoes on reaching the Pacific coast, the buccaneers attacked and captured a Spanish warship and in her ravaged the Spanish settlements along the Peruvian coast.

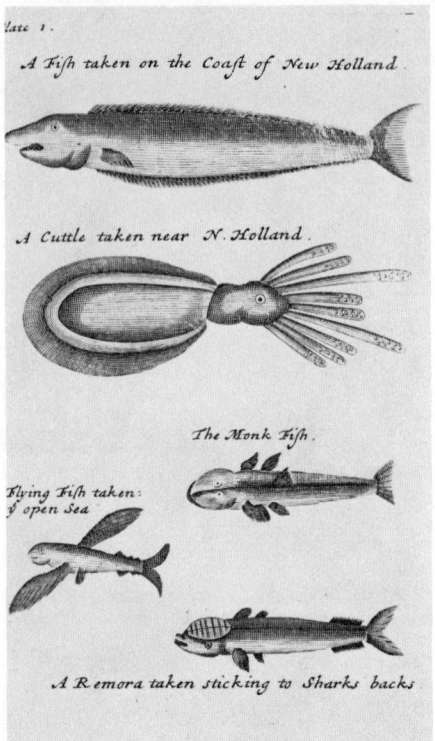

Illustration from Dampier's A Voyage to New Holland *in 1699, 1709*

In 1680 he, with about fifty other buccaneers, quarrelled with Sharp and made their way back to Panama in small boats, crossing the isthmus again to the Atlantic shore (see also WAFER, Lionel). Here Dampier engaged in aimless, and largely unsuccessful, buccaneering cruises in the Gulf of Mexico. He finally joined a new band, led by Captain Cook, which in 1683 set out on a piratical voyage to the South Seas which was eventually to take Dampier round the world. At this time he was keeping a journal, which he carried for safety in a joint of bamboo sealed at both ends with wax, later (1697) to be published as *A New Voyage Round the World*, a work of great charm which has been reprinted at intervals ever since. It is notable not so much as an account of his voyage as for his observations on the winds and tides, and the flora and fauna of the places visited.

The voyage was a mixture of periods of hardship (on one occasion the starving men decided to kill and eat the officers, starting with a Captain Swan who was 'lusty and fleshy') and long periods of drunkenness and debauchery at the various islands at which the ship anchored. Eventually tiring of this life, Dampier and some of the crew broke away in the Philippines and set off on their own account, sailing to China and then to the Spice Islands and New Holland (the Australian mainland). After a number of cruises up and down these waters, pillaging such few merchant ships as crossed their path, Dampier was marooned with two others and half a dozen Malays on the Nicobar Islands. There they found a canoe which Dampier managed to navigate to Sumatra, where he found employment in various dubious local cruises, on one occasion with a contraband cargo of opium. Necessity at last forced him to take the post of gunner at the British fort at Bencoolen, but he succeeded in deserting and signed on as a seaman in a British ship homeward bound to England, which he reached in 1691.

The success of *A New Voyage Round the World*, published six years later, brought him to the notice of the British Admiralty and in 1699 he was sent out as captain of H.M.S. *Roebuck* on a voyage of discovery around Australia. He made a careful survey of much of the west coast of the continent, but the lack of suitable harbours or inlets along that coast in which to refit his ship, and of fresh water and provisions ashore, forced him to abandon the cruise and sail to Timor to refit the *Roebuck*. From Timor he sailed to New Guinea where, after a brief period of surveying, his crew mutinied as a result of his harsh treatment of them. Returning to Timor, he sailed for home but the *Roebuck* foundered off Ascension Island and Dampier and his men had to return in an East Indiaman which they were fortunate enough to attract to the island by their signals of distress. On his return to England in 1701 Dampier was brought before a court martial for his behaviour on board the *Roebuck* and was fined the whole of his pay for the voyage. He was also declared unfit for any further employment in the Royal Navy.

Although by this voyage Dampier had proved that he was too unreliable successfully to command a ship, his reputation as a navigator was unimpaired. In 1703, he learned of an expedition of two ships fitting out for a privateering voyage in the Pacific and applied to join it. He was able to talk the owners into giving him command of the expedition by promises of fantastic profits which his knowledge of those waters could guarantee. He sailed as captain of the *St. George*, but the voyage was a disaster from the start, largely owing to Dampier's autocratic behaviour to his officers and his indecision in attacking possible targets where the rewards might have been considerable. Eventually the two ships parted company, each to go her own way, and a mutiny in the *St. George* removed most of the crew, who embarked in a captured ship and left Dampier with only twenty-seven men. However, he managed to bring them back to England by way of the East Indies and the Cape of Good Hope, not in the *St. George* whose bottom fell out in the Gulf of Panama but in a small Spanish ship which they captured. Dampier reached England in 1707, thus completing his second voyage round the world. This voyage is remembered as the occasion on which Alexander *Selkirk, whose story inspired Daniel *Defoe to write his novel *Robinson Crusoe*, was marooned on Juan Fernandez Island.

Within a year of his return Dampier set out again on a privateering voyage to the Pacific, this time not in command but as navigator. The expedition was commanded by Captain Woodes *Rogers and was a great financial success, and on its return to England in 1711, Dampier had completed his third voyage round the world. However he died in London before he could receive his full share of the profits. One incident of this voyage was the rescue from Juan Fernandez Island of Alexander Selkirk after living alone there for four years.

The standard editions of Dampier's voyages are those edited by John Masefield in 1906 and the later limited edition published by the Argonaut Press, *A New Voyage Round the World*, edited by Sir Albert Gray (1927); *Voyage to Campeachy*, edited by C. Wilkinson (1931); *Voyage to New Holland*, edited by J. A. Williamson (1939). The best biographies are C. Wilkinson, *William Dampier* (1922), and C. Lloyd, *William Dampier* (1966).

DAN BUOY, a small, temporary *buoy used for marking a position at sea. It consists of a float, made of cork or similar substance, with a staff passing through it, to the top of which a small flag is attached for ease in recognition, and it is anchored on the bottom by a weight and lines. Dan buoys are used extensively for marking the position of fishermen's nets, for marking wrecks until permanent wreck buoys can be moored in position, and in all such similar cases at sea. Dan buoys are also required equipment for yachts racing under I.Y.R.U. rules, to mark the position if any member of the crew should fall overboard.

DANA, RICHARD HENRY (1815–82), was born at Cambridge, Massachusetts. His family had been lawyers for generations, and Richard was sent to Harvard to study for the same profession, but an attack of measles during a period when he was rusticated from the university so affected his eyes that he was unable to continue his studies. He had the idea that a sea voyage and work on board a ship would cure his eye troubles, and he signed on as a paid hand in the *brig *Pilgrim* of Boston for a trading voyage round Cape Horn and up the Pacific seaboard. The brig sailed from Boston in August 1834, and Dana stepped ashore again in Boston in

September 1836 with the eye weakness permanently cured, having returned in a larger ship, the *Alert*, which he joined halfway through the voyage to escape the brutalities of the captain of the *Pilgrim*.

He kept a log throughout the two years of his spell at sea, and during the intervals of his law studies prepared the log for publication under the title *Two Years Before the Mast*. As with so many masterpieces, no New York publisher would look at it until eventually Harper's was persuaded to give it a trial. They bought all rights in the manuscript for 250 dollars, and the book was published in 1840. It at once went into several editions, as it did in England too where it was published in 1841. The simple, direct style of writing, the 'voice from the forecastle' as Dana himself described the book, stamped it as one of the great masterpieces of the sea.

Dana became an authority on maritime law, and was also something of a politician, but public office in this field always just evaded him. Nor, in his writing, did he ever again reach the heights of his first book. He wrote a *Seaman's Manual* (1841) that went into four editions, and *A Voyage to Cuba and Back* (1859), which has none of the freshness and delightful simplicity of *Two Years Before the Mast*. He died in Rome before he could complete the book on international maritime law on which he was engaged.

DANCE, Sir NATHANIEL (1748–1827), British master mariner, entered the service of the *East India Company in 1759 and received his first command of one of their ships in 1787. In 1804 he was the senior *master, and therefore *commodore, of an unescorted convoy of sixteen East Indiamen and twelve independent or 'country' ships homeward bound from Canton which, on 14 February, was intercepted off the southern entrance to the Malacca Strait by the French Rear Admiral Linois with a squadron composed of one *ship of the line, three heavy *frigates, and an armed *brig. Though all ships of the convoy were armed to some degree, none could be considered a match even for a frigate man-of-war. The situation was thus perilous for the convoy; and, indeed, in the opinion of the French historian Chevalier, had Linois determined to attack, he could have captured the greater part of the convoy.

Defiant manoeuvres by Dance deceived Linois into thinking that three British ships of the line were among the convoy; after a brief, half-hearted, and ineffective attack the French admiral hauled his wind and fled, chased for two hours by the merchantmen before they resumed their course for the Strait of Malacca. On the safe arrival of the convoy in England, Dance was knighted, and received a sword of honour as well as the service of plate and sum of money usually presented to merchant officers who had saved their ships.

DANDOLO, the name of one of the most illustrious Venetian families, which provided four doges of *Venice. The first of these, Enrico Dandolo (*c.* 1120–1205), extended the maritime power of Venice far and wide in the Mediterranean. He commanded the fleet which subdued a Dalmatian revolt, and in conjunction with the Crusaders of the Fourth Crusade, at the age of 83, led the attack with his fleet on the city of Constantinople, which finally fell after a second attack. Among the vast booty obtained by the Venetians after this capture were the four bronze horses which now stand in St. Mark's square in Venice. Dandolo proved himself a brilliant leader at sea, and during his life Venetian sea power in the Mediterranean was paramount. A later member of this family was Girolamo Dandolo, the last admiral of the republic of Venice. He died in 1847. One of the large Italian battleships designed by Benedetto *Brin in 1881 was named after the family.

DANDY-RIG, another name for the *ketch and *yawl rigs, but sometimes used to describe the rig when the mizen-sail is about one-third the size of the mainsail, the true ketch rig having a mizen-sail about half the size of the mainsail and the true yawl rig having its mizen-sail a quarter or less. In some English west country (Devon and Cornwall) craft the mizen-mast was stepped just forward of the *transom stern either to one side of the *tiller or with an iron tiller crooked around the mast. The sail, of triangular or 'leg o' mutton' shape, sheeted to an *outrigger or *bumpkin, was called the dandy, and a boat so rigged, such as the Falmouth Quay punt, was called dandy-rigged. The term is very rarely used today.

DANFORTH ANCHOR, an American-designed anchor in which the two pivoting *flukes are placed close together with the *shank between them. The *stock is across the crown of the anchor instead of in the more usual place at the top of the shank, and this makes it impossible for the anchor to be fouled by the cable. It has great holding power for its weight, though slightly less than that of the *CQR anchor, but has the advantage that it stows flatter on deck. It is deservedly popular for small craft such as yachts. For illus. see ANCHOR.

DANZIG, see GDANSK.

DARDANELLES, the narrow strait which separates Turkey in Europe from Turkey in Asia, and connects the Mediterranean with the Sea of Marmara. It was the scene in 1915 of a bitter campaign of the First World War (1914–18), initiated when the British Mediterranean Fleet bombarded the Turkish forts in the Dardanelles in an attempt to force a passage to Constantinople and put Turkey out of the war. The fleet was unsuccessful because of lines of moored *mines laid across the straits, and the campaign developed into an amphibious one with large military forces landed, with great loss in the face of fierce Turkish opposition, on the Gallipoli peninsula. The whole British campaign ended in failure, the only bright aspect being the successful withdrawal of the troops without loss in December 1915 and January 1916.

DARLAN, JEAN LOUIS XAVIER FRANÇOIS (1881–1942), French admiral and minister, was an officer of exceptional ability and strong personality. Born at Nérac (Lot et Garonne), he entered the Naval Academy in 1899 and became a specialist in gunnery. During the First World War (1914–18) he commanded a battery on the Western Front and for a short time in Greece, and was cited for his distinguished service. Promoted to commander in 1920 and to captain in 1926, he attained flag rank in 1929 and was commended for exceptional service during the London Naval Conference of 1930. He commanded the 1st Light Cruiser Division, and after promotion to vice admiral in 1932 commanded the Atlantic Squadron. He was appointed Chief of the Naval Staff at the end of 1936, and on 6 June 1939 was promoted admiral, becoming commander-in-chief of the French Navy later that year. After the fall of France in June 1940 he became secretary of state for the navy and, in February 1941, vice-president of the Council of Ministers. In 1942 he was made commander-in-chief of all French military forces and on 12 November of that year relinquished his ministerial post to become High Commissioner for France in North Africa. He was in Algeria when the Anglo-American invasion took place on 8 November 1942 and he ordered all opposition to the allied forces to cease. A victim of political intrigue, he was assassinated on 24 December 1942 in Algiers.

DARLING, GRACE HORSLEY (1815–42), British lighthouse-keeper's daughter, achieved great fame for the rescues she made with her father when the merchant vessel *Forfarshire*, bound from Hull to Dundee, was wrecked on the Farne Islands on 7 September 1838. Grace's father, William Darling, was keeper of the Longstone lighthouse on the islands, and observing the wreck determined with his daughter to try to reach the survivors. In a tremendous sea, and knowing they would be unable to return unless helped by survivors, they set out in a *coble and reached the wreck, bringing back four men and a woman. William Darling and two of the survivors then returned, and brought back four more men. They were the sole survivors, the remaining forty-three members of the crew being drowned. Grace and her father each received the gold medal of the Royal Humane Society for their courage during these rescues. Of a delicate constitution all her life, Grace Darling died of consumption at the age of 27.

DART, **H.M.S.,** was notable among the many surveying ships of the Royal Navy employed on Australasian coasts during the 19th and into the 20th centuries, when Australian ships took up the task. Originally a steam screw yacht, the *Dart* began surveying duties in 1882 and so continued for eighteen years. Besides working in the New Hebrides and the Solomon Islands she spent many years on the Barrier Reef's inner route and her crews successfully planted coconuts on the low-lying adjacent islands both to aid navigation and to supply shipwrecked mariners. Among her commanding officers were no less than three future Hydrographers of the Navy, A. M. Field, C. Purey-Cust, and J. F. *Parry.

DARTMOUTH, see *Britannia,* H.M.S.

DARWIN, CHARLES ROBERT (1809–82), English naturalist, comes briefly into the maritime story for his connection with the voyage of the *Beagle* (Robert *Fitzroy) from 1831 to 1836. His work on the geology and fauna of the places visited during this long voyage was recorded in many books and papers; his observations on this voyage, and particularly in the Galapagos Islands, started him off on his thoughts about the transmutation and origin of species. In 1839 he published his *Journal of Researches into the Geology and Natural History of the various countries visited by H.M.S. Beagle.*

DAVELUY, RENÉ (1863–1939), French vice admiral, was born at Etampes. He entered the navy in 1880 and subsequently was appointed to the experimental submarine *Gymnote* where, with some assistance, he succeeded in making the first effective periscope. He was soon putting forward new and sensational views in which he found himself at odds with current thought in the French Navy. He advocated the construction of large sea-going *destroyers instead of the numerous *torpedoboats then in favour and was also an ardent supporter of naval aviation. In 1911, when in command of the *Foudre,* he carried out trials with the launching of an aircraft from a platform on board that ship. Promoted to rear admiral in 1916, he was given command of a cruiser division in the Mediterranean, but involvement in the political difficulties which arose over Greece led to his being relieved and he retired in 1920. He was the author of several books on naval strategy and an amusing series of memoirs published in *La * Revue maritime.*

'DAVID', the name given to a series of small *submarines, built by the *Confederate States Navy of the U.S.A. during the Civil War (1861–5). They were in fact not true submarines, but submersibles, and were driven by steam propulsion. They carried a *spar torpedo over their *bows. The steam 'Davids' were not designed to dive fully, but were trimmed down so that they proceeded awash. One, commanded by Lieutenant Glassell, attacked the Federal ship *New Ironsides* at Charleston on 5 October 1863, but her spar torpedo was not exploded deep enough against the *New Ironsides* to do significant damage. The 'David' herself was swamped by the waves set up by the explosion and sank.

Another form of 'David' was propelled by hand-power, eight men inside the boat turning a propeller by means of a series of cranks and a ninth man steering. On 7 February 1864 a hand-driven 'David' attacked the Federal ship *Housatonic* and sank her with a spar torpedo just as she was about to get under way. Some years later, when divers were sent down to examine the wreck of the *Housatonic*, they found the 'David' lying on the bottom alongside her, with the remains of the crew of nine men still on board.

DAVIS, CHARLES HENRY (1807–77), American naval officer, served with distinction in the American Civil War (1861–5). He was a prime mover in establishing *The American Ephemeris and Nautical Almanac* and was one of the founders of the National Academy of Sciences in 1863.

DAVIS or **DAVYS, JOHN** (*c.* 1550–1605), English navigator and explorer, was one of the greatest of the Elizabethan seamen. He went to sea as a boy, and being a west-country man (he was born near Dartmouth, in Devon) was friendly with the two great seafaring families of that neighbourhood, the *Gilberts and the *Raleighs, who between them did much to rouse and nourish his enthusiasm for maritime exploration.

In 1583 he became convinced that navigation was possible between Europe and the Far East around the north of America (the *North-West passage) and two years later he had persuaded the English authorities to fit out an expedition under his command to explore the northern seas west of Greenland. In all he made three voyages in search of the passage (1585, 1586, and 1587) and though he penetrated as far north and west as Baffin's Bay, he just missed, as had Martin *Frobisher before him, discovering Hudson's Bay, though he did apparently sight Hudson's Strait. Many of the names still on the map of the Arctic are memorials to his endeavours; the great strait which bears his own name, Exeter Sound, Cape Walsingham, Cumberland Sound, etc.

He was home in time from his last expedition to command the *Black Dog* in the battle of the Spanish *Armada in 1588 and in 1589 was in the Earl of Cumberland's fleet operating off the Azores. He was taken on as pilot and navigator by Thomas *Cavendish in his second privateering expedition round the world in 1591, which proved a fiasco. Davis's participation in this doubtful venture arose partly it appears from Cavendish's suggestion that a search might be made for the North-West passage from the western end rather than from the eastern. When Cavendish deserted his little fleet at the entrance to the Strait of Magellan, Davis went on alone with his own ship to attempt the passage of the Strait but was driven back by storms. On his way home to England, he discovered the Falkland Islands.

Davis was more than a skilled navigator; he was also author of two excellent books on navigation (*The Seaman's Secrets* in 1594 and *The World's Hydrographical Description* in 1595) and the inventor of the back-staff and double quadrant, known as *Davis's quadrant, which remained a principal instrument of navigation until the reflecting quadrant was introduced by *Hadley in 1731.

The remainder of Davis's life was spent mainly in voyaging, particularly to the Far East. He was master (navigator) of Raleigh's flagship in the expedition to Cadiz and the Azores, 1596–7; went as pilot of a Dutch expedition to the East Indies (1598–1600) in which he only just avoided being killed by treachery in Sumatra; he was first pilot to Sir James *Lancaster in 1601–3 in his voyage to the east on behalf of the *East India Company; and in 1604 sailed in the same situation with Sir Edward Michelborne, but was killed the following year by Japanese pirates near Sumatra.

For a biography see *Voyages and Works of John Davis*, edited by A. H. Markham, Hakluyt Society, 1880.

DAVIS, JOHN KING (1884–1967), was one of the greatest Antarctic seamen. He first went south with Sir Ernest *Shackleton as first officer of the *Nimrod* in 1907 and afterwards was second-in-command of Sir Douglas *Mawson's *Aurora* during the Australasian Antarctic expedition, 1911–14. In 1917 he again commanded the *Aurora* as leader of the relief expedition which rescued the Ross Sea shore party of Shackleton's Imperial trans-Antarctic expedition of 1914–17.

DAVIS'S QUADRANT, sometimes called the back-staff and, by the French, the English quadrant. John *Davis, the famous English navigator and explorer of Elizabethan times, invented a simple instrument for measuring the altitude of the sun which obviated the need of sighting the sun direct. It consisted of a graduated staff on which was fitted a half transom in the form of an arc of a circle which could be slid along the staff. At the fore end of the staff was a horizon vane with a slit through which the horizon could be observed. In use the staff was held horizontally, the observer having his back to the sun. The half transom was then moved along the staff to a position at which the edge of its shadow struck the horizon vane and coincided with the horizon viewed through the slit in the vane. The staff of this simple instrument was graduated to 45 degrees and the instrument was useful for measuring altitudes of the sun of less than about 45 degrees. For measuring greater altitudes Davis invented another form of back-staff called the 90° back-staff to distinguish it from the 45° back-staff described above.

The 90° back-staff employed two half transoms, one straight and the other an arc. The straight half transom was fitted perpendicularly to and stood vertically above the staff when the instrument was in use. It was designed to slide along the staff. The arcuate half transom was fixed to the lower side of the staff and provided with a sighting vane. The fore end of the staff was fitted with a horizon vane through which the horizon could be sighted.

To take a sight with the 90° back-staff the straight half transom was set at a graduation on the staff corresponding to a few degrees less than the sun's altitude. The instrument was then held in the vertical plane and the observer, with his back to the sun and his eye at the sighting vane, slid the latter to a position on the arc so that he was able to see the horizon through the slit in the horizon vane coincident with the shadow of a shadow vane fitted at the top of the straight half transom. The sun's altitude was the sum of the angles indicated on the staff and arc respectively.

With the passage of time the 90° back-staff was modified. Before the end of the 17th century it had all but replaced the simple *quadrant, the *astrolabe, and the *cross-staff; and it was not superseded for sea use until the middle of the 18th century when *Hadley's reflecting quadrant was introduced.

The Davis quadrant in common use during the first half of the 18th century employed two arcuate transoms, both of which formed integral parts of the instrument. The upper arc, known as the greater arch, contained 65°, and the lower or lesser arch contained 25°. The greater arch was divided to degrees, and the lesser to minutes, of arc by means of a diagonal scale. The horizon,

sight, and shade vanes provided with the instrument were all portable.

The quadrant was not capable of adjustment and it was therefore necessary for the user to ascertain in advance its instrumental error. This was usually done by making meridian altitude observations at places of known latitude. Having thus discovered the error, the observer applied it to all altitudes measured with it. According to whether the error tended to increase or decrease the ship's northerly latitude the quadrant was said to be northerly or southerly.

DAVIT, small cast-iron cranes, fitted with hoisting and lowering gear in the form of blocks and tackles and placed along both sides of the upper deck of passenger *liners and *ferries, from which a ship's *lifeboats are slung. The older-fashioned radial davits were manoeuvrable by twisting in their base sockets so that, when hoisted, the boats could be swung inboard so that they did not project beyond the side of the ship. Many modern davits, known as luffing davits, have a geared quadrant fitted to their inboard end so that boats can now hang at the davits inboard of the ship's side though still suspended to seaward of the davits, a great saving of time and labour if the boats have to be used in an emergency. In another modern pattern, known as gravity-type, the davit consists of two parts, the upper, which holds the lifeboat on its *falls, being mounted on rollers on the lower part. When the lifeboat is not in use, the upper part is hauled up by a wire and the lifeboat lies inboard. When it is to be used, the wire is released and the

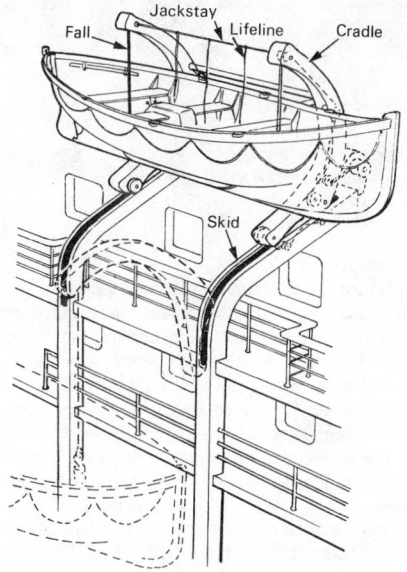

Lifeboat on gravity-type davit

upper part slides down the lower part, bringing the lifeboat level with the deck and ready for lowering directly into the sea.

Most vessels carry at least one or more of their boats at davits, either along their sides or, in the case of very small vessels, over the * stern.

DAVY JONES, in nautical slang the spirit of the sea, usually cast in the form of a sea devil. 'This same Davy Jones, according to the mythology of sailors, is the fiend that presides over all the evil spirits of the deep,' Tobias Smollett, *Peregrine Pickle* (1751), Ch. XIII. Thus also, Davy Jones's Locker, the bottom of the sea, the final resting place of sunken ships, of articles lost or thrown overboard, of men buried at sea. Thus it has become also a seaman's phrase for death, as in the saying 'He's gone to Davy Jones's Locker' when referring to anyone who has been buried at sea. The term is often shortened to Davy.

Davy Jones; engraving by G. Cruickshank from Smollett's Peregrine Pickle

DAWSON, MONTAGUE J. (1895–1973), British marine painter, was born at Chiswick, the son of a captain in the Merchant Navy, but spent much of his childhood on Southampton Water where his love of ships developed. During the First World War (1914–18) he served in the Royal Naval Volunteer Reserve in * destroyers and * Q-ships, and illustrated a number of events for *The Sphere*, culminating in the internment of the German * High Seas Fleet in 1918, to which a whole issue of that periodical was devoted. After the war he became well known to many prominent yachtsmen on account of his paintings of their vessels, in which he incorporated much accurate detail; but his greatest claim to fame

arose through the many beautiful pictures of * clipper ships under full sail which he painted, recognized for the accuracy of the rigging and sails to an extent where they are accepted both as a record of and reference to the great days of the sailing era. During the Second World War he again served in the Royal Navy in * aircraft carriers, sketching and painting whenever opportunity offered. Prints of his pictures are deservedly popular and are widely sold, while his original paintings now command very high prices.

DAY, THOMAS FLEMING (1861–1927), American yachtsman and editor, designed and built for himself a * yawl, *Seabird*, in 1902. A keen advocate of the seaworthiness of any small well-designed and well-found cruising yacht, he set out from Providence, Rhode Island, with two friends in June 1911 to sail to Rome. Except for riding out a hard gale to a * sea anchor, they had no troubles with navigation or gear, and made a quick passage to Fayal in the Azores in $19\frac{1}{2}$ days. They sailed on to Gibraltar, some 1,220 miles in 12 days, and concluded a cruise in the Mediterranean with a visit to Rome.

The next year Day was chosen to skipper a 35-ft motor cruiser, the *Detroit*, across the Atlantic under power. Built by the Scripps Motor Company of Detroit to demonstrate the reliability of their gasoline (petrol) marine engine, the boat made the passage from New Rochelle to Queenstown, County Cork, during July–August 1912, 2,760 miles in 28 days. Day continued the demonstration voyage up Channel to the Kiel Canal, calling at various ports on the way, and as far as St. Petersburg (now Leningrad).

As editor of the boating magazine *Rudder* he took a leading part in encouraging both sailing and power boat racing and cruising offshore, and was the driving force behind the first race from Brooklyn to Bermuda, which was organized jointly by the Brooklyn Yacht Club and Royal Bermuda Y.C. in 1906. Day also promoted offshore power boat races to Bermuda and Havana before the First World War (1914–18). He was author of *Across the Atlantic in 'Seabird'* (1912), *The Voyage of the 'Detroit'* (1919), and *Hints for Young Skippers*.

DAZZLE-PAINTING, a method of deceiving an enemy as to the size, outline, course, and speed of a ship by painting her sides and upperworks in contrasting colours and shapes arranged in irregular patterns. It was widely used in the two world wars to make it difficult for the gunnery control officers of enemy ships and the captains of * U-boats accurately to plot a victim's movements when manoeuvring for an attack. A ship scientifically disguised by dazzle-painting could be made to look at a distance smaller than she actually was, faster than she was actually steaming, and steering an entirely different course from the one she was actually on, thus throwing out calculations of the correct deflection to allow when firing at her by gun or * torpedo. Dazzle-painting, later called * camouflage, was originated by Norman * Wilkinson, a British marine artist.

DE GRASSE, FRANÇOIS-JOSEPH PAUL, Comte, see GRASSE, François-Joseph Paul, Comte de.

DE HORSEY RIG, a sail rig for use in the larger pulling boats carried by British warships, such as * launches, * pinnaces, and * cutters, introduced by Admiral de Horsey in the early 20th century. It consisted of a single mast stepped in a * tabernacle and carrying a * gaff mainsail with a loose foot, i.e., without a * boom, and a single fore staysail.

DE ROBECK, Sir JOHN MICHAEL (1862–1928), British admiral of the fleet, went to sea in 1877 and had a varied career at home and abroad before being promoted to commander in June 1897. For the next nine years he was senior officer of destroyer flotillas based on the Nore and, after promotion to captain in January 1902, of flotillas based on Portsmouth and in the Mediterranean. After subsequent commands of the armoured cruiser *Carnarvon* and the battleship *Dominion*, he was promoted to rear admiral in December 1911. In this rank he served as Admiral of Patrols, 1912–14, and for the first six months of the First World War (1914–18) was Flag Officer, Cape Verde–Canaries station. In January 1915 he was appointed second-in-command of the naval forces at the * Dardanelles under Vice Admiral Carden.

With his flag in the *Vengeance* he played a prominent part in the successful bombardment operations to silence the outer forts at the end of February; and in the failure to penetrate the minefields across the Narrows in the first half of March. When Carden's health broke down De Robeck succeeded him in command in the rank of acting vice admiral on 17 March 1915; on the following day he launched the great assault by the Anglo-French fleet of eighteen battleships which was so disastrously repulsed with the loss of the *Bouvet, Irresistible,* and *Ocean,* and serious damage to the *Inflexible,* on an undiscovered line of mines.

As a result of this, De Robeck became convinced that the Dardanelles could never be forced by naval strength alone and his recommendation that attempts to do so should be suspended until the planned combined operations on the Gallipoli peninsula were ready was accepted. But the damage had already been done,

the naval bombardments having alerted the Turkish forces to the probability of assault landings on the peninsula. De Robeck remained in command of the naval element of these Gallipoli operations, and it was he who urged the use of British and French submarines against Turkish supply routes in the Sea of Marmara, but no purely naval operations could avert or break the military stalemate on the Gallipoli peninsula. After the successful withdrawal of the soldiers in December 1915/January 1916, a superbly successful operation, De Robeck served for the rest of the war in home waters, commanding first the 3rd and then the 2nd Battle Squadrons of the * Grand Fleet. After the war he was commander-in-chief in the Mediterranean from 1919 to 1922 and in the Atlantic from 1922 to 1924. This was his last appointment. He was promoted admiral of the fleet in November 1925.

De Robeck was one of the more promising younger British admirals of the outbreak of the First World War. Tall, broad-shouldered, handsome, and charming, he was described by one of his contemporaries as 'an exceptionally strong-minded, talented, and popular officer of great dignity and charm'. He was greatly admired throughout the Royal Navy, as much by seamen as by officers.

DE RUYTER, MICHIEL ADRIENSZOON, see RUYTER, Michiel Adrienszoon de.

DE WINTER, JAN WILLEM, see WINTER, Jan Willem de.

DE WITH, WITTE CORNELIS, see WITH, Witte Cornelis de.

DEACON, Sir GEORGE EDWARD RAVEN (1906–), British oceanographer, was a member of the * *Discovery* Committee Investigation. He came to specialize in the physical characteristics of the Southern Ocean and became Director of the National Institute of Oceanography in 1949.

DEAD FREIGHT, the * freight charges for which a merchant is liable when he fails to ship cargo on board a merchant vessel for which he has reserved space in the holds.

DEAD HORSE, the term used by seamen to describe the period of work on board ship for which they have been paid in advance when signing on, usually a month's wages. In merchant ships there used to be a custom of celebrating having worked off the dead horse by parading an effigy of a horse stuffed with straw around the decks, to the song 'Old man, your horse must die', then hoisting it to the * yardarm and cutting it adrift to fall into the sea. In ships where passengers were carried, the stuffed horse was often put up to auction among them before being cut adrift, the money being divided among the crew. To flog a dead horse, to expect, vainly, to get extra work out of a ship's crew while they are working off the dead horse.

DEAD MARINE, an empty wine bottle after its contents have been drunk. The aphorism is supposed to have been first employed by * William IV when Duke of Clarence at a dinner on board one of his ships when he ordered the steward to remove the 'dead marines'. On expostulation by a marine officer, he remarked that he had used the expression in the sense that, like the marines, it had done its duty nobly and was ready to do it again.

DEAD MEN, * reef and * gasket ends left flapping instead of being tucked in out of sight when a sail has been furled. See also IRISH PENNANTS.

DEAD RECKONING POSITION, usually abbreviated to D.R., a position which is obtained by applying * courses and distances made through the water from the last known observed position. The origin of the term, which has been used for at least four centuries, is obscure, although it has been suggested by some that it is a corruption of ded. reckoning, deduced from the reckoning. In view of its very long period of use, however, this origin of the term is improbable; it has too much of a modern ring about it. Possibly the term originally came into use from the much older custom of seamen of describing unknown seas as 'dead' seas, in the sense that there was no body of knowledge about the extent, or even of the actual existence, of these seas, shown by many early geographers on their world maps.

Dead reckoning, as a system of navigation, implies charting the position of a ship without the use of any astronomical observation whatever; merely arriving at the ship's position by laying off on the chart courses steered and distances run, with due allowance for currents, tidal streams, and * leeway, from the last fixed position. Before the days of modern navigational aids, such as the * hyperbolic systems of navigation, there were always likely to be periods of storm and overcast during a voyage during which the navigator was unable to see sun, moon, or stars, and his only means of reckoning his ship's position was by dead reckoning. When at last he did see the sun or stars again and was able to take an observation, he had to use his D.R. position as the basis for working out his sight, having no position more accurate on which to work.

In the great days of discovery, particularly before the perfection of the ship's * chronometer

and thus the accurate determination of * longitude, dead reckoning was the main method of navigation, though it was fairly early on refined slightly by the introduction of the * traverse board, which converted the day's run of the ship into difference of * latitude (d.lat.) and * departure (easily converted into d.long.), which enable the navigator to plot his new dead reckoning position by measuring off the day's differences on the longitude and latitude scales of his chart.

Dead reckoning is still a useful adjunct of navigation, though with the number of modern navigational aids available, such as radio direction finding aerials, depth recorders, it is becoming less important. But it remains a useful guide to a vessel's position between fixes and also serves as a permanent check on the reliability of bearings obtained by direction finders, which can be erratic; particularly around dawn and dusk. The Inertial Navigation System (see NAVIGATION) gives virtually a continuous dead reckoning position, as each movement measured is automatically resolved into its co-ordinates and translated into speeds and distances to be applied to the initial position, which is the basis of all dead reckoning.

DEAD SHARES, an additional allowance of pay enjoyed by the officers and warrant officers of the British Navy of the 16th and 17th centuries and achieved by the entry in the ship's muster book of fictitious names, for whom sea pay and victuals were drawn and the proceeds divided among the officers of the ship. The scale of payment ranged from fifty shares for an admiral to half a share for the cook's mate. It was introduced during the reign of Henry VIII (1509–47) and remained in force until 1733, though from 1695 the proceeds were diverted from the officers and given to * Greenwich Royal Hospital for the provision of pensions to the widows of seamen killed in action. See also WIDOWS' MEN.

DEAD WATER, the eddy formed under the * counter of a ship by the angle of her * run aft as she passes through the water. It is so called because it passes away more slowly than the water along her sides. See also CAVITATION, to which it is closely allied in its effect on the vessel's way.

DEAD WORK, an old maritime expression meaning all that part of a ship above the waterline when she is fully laden. It is what we would today call the ship's * freeboard.

DEADEYE, orig. **DEAD-MAN'S-EYE,** a circular block usually of * lignum vitae, though sometimes of elm, grooved around the circumference and pierced with three holes. In older sailing vessels they were used in pairs to secure the end of a *shroud to the *chain plate. A lanyard was threaded through the holes in the deadeyes and by this means a *purchase was created whereby the shroud could be set up taut. The triangular block of wood with a single large hole in the centre and known as a *heart, which was used to set up a *stay, was also at one time called a dead-eye.

Officially the term 'dead' was used because although deadeyes perform the function of triple *blocks, they have no revolving sheaves, though no doubt the original name of dead-man's-eye arose from the remarkable resemblance of these blocks with their three holes to a human skull.

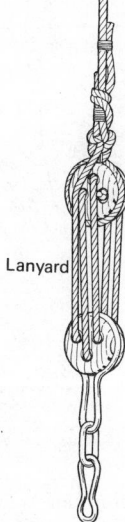

Lanyard

Deadeye

DEADLIGHT, a metal plate, today usually of brass but originally of wood or iron, which is hinged inboard above a *scuttle or *port and can be let down and secured by a butterfly nut to protect the glass of the scuttle in heavy weather. An additional use of deadlights in warships was to darken ship at night in wartime so that no light was visible to an enemy.

DEADWEIGHT, a measurement of a ship's *tonnage which indicates the actual carrying capacity of a merchant ship expressed in tons weight. The figure is arrived at by calculating the amount of water displaced by a ship when she is unloaded, but with her fuel tanks full and stores on board, and the amount of water similarly displaced when she is fully loaded with her cargo holds full. The difference expressed in tons (35 cubic ft of seawater = one ton) gives the ship's deadweight tonnage. It is usually expressed in shortened form as d.w.t.

DEADWOOD, the solid timbering in *bow and *stern of a sailing vessel just above the *keel where the lines narrow down to such an extent that the separate side timbers cannot each be accommodated. Generally the fore deadwood extends from the *stem to the foremost *frame, the after deadwood from the sternpost to the after *balance frame. Both deadwoods are firmly fixed to the keel to add strength to the ship's structure.

DEANE, RICHARD (1610–53), English *general-at-sea, spent his early career in the army during the Civil War in England (1642–9), and as one of the commissioners for the trial of Charles I signed the warrant for his execution.

From the army he went to the navy as a commissioner of the office of *Lord High Admiral, with the title of general-at-sea. He shared command of the fleet with Robert *Blake at the battle of *Portland against the Dutch in 1653. He was killed later that year at the battle of the North Foreland, and was buried in Westminster Abbey. After the restoration of Charles II in 1660, his body was disinterred and burned in a pit of quicklime, a fate suffered by all the regicides fortunate enough to have died before the restoration of the king. Those still living at that time were hanged, drawn, and quartered. Samuel *Pepys went to watch one of the executions, that of Major-General Harrison (*Diary*, 13 October 1660).

DECATUR, STEPHEN, Jr. (1779–1820), American naval officer, was born in Maryland. During the operations against the *Barbary pirates in 1803–4, Decatur was commanding the *schooner *Enterprise* off Tripoli and conceived the idea of slipping into the harbour and destroying the American frigate *Philadelphia* which the Tripolitans had captured. He had captured the Tripolitan *ketch *Mastiko*, and, after renaming her *Intrepid* and manning her with volunteers, he entered the harbour on the night of 16 August 1804 and took the *Intrepid* alongside the *Philadelphia* with the excuse of a broken rudder. The Americans then appeared from below decks, swarmed aboard the frigate, and burned her, making their escape with only one man wounded. Decatur was promoted to captain for this exploit and continued to distinguish himself in close combat throughout the Tripolitan war.

When war against Britain began in 1812 Decatur, in command of the frigate *United States*, went to sea and on 25 October near Madeira captured H.M.S. *Macedonian*. The *United States* was more heavily gunned and Decatur skilfully manoeuvred to exploit this advantage. In May 1813 the *United States* was driven into New London by a superior blockading force and forced to remain there until the end of the war.

Decatur and his crew transferred to the *President in New York, and in January 1815, in a north-easterly gale, he attempted to take her out to sea. The ship grounded and was pounding heavily for about two hours before floating again. Next morning she was sighted and chased by a British *razee and three frigates. In spite of the reduction in speed caused by her grounding, the President outdistanced her pursuers with the exception of the frigate, Endymion. Knowing that he had superior gun-power, Decatur turned on the Endymion and damaged her considerably but in the process he himself was painfully wounded and his crew suffered severely. When the other British ships came up he surrendered. He was killed in a duel with James *Barron who had accused him of malicious persecution during the court martial following the *Chesapeake–Leopard affair.

DECCA NAVIGATION SYSTEM, a method of fixing a ship's position which is of great accuracy and of particular value when coasting or when making a landfall, particularly when low visibility makes it difficult to distinguish navigational marks ashore. Whereas celestial navigation depends on the angles between rays of light, which are straight lines, and the intersection of lines, which are arcs of circles, on the earth's surface, the *hyperbolic systems, of which Decca is one, depend on a pattern of curves known mathematically as hyperbolae, plotted on the earth's surface and defined by the inter-relation of systems of radio waves broadcast from a chain of land-based stations. In this system there is a master station and three 'slave' stations, designated red, green, and purple respectively. A ship carries a Decca receiver and three Decometers (red, green, and purple), together with a Decca lattice chart on which the systems of hyperbolae are shown. Because radio waves do not travel instantaneously, but at a speed of 300,000 kilometres a second, waves leaving two stations on shore simultaneously, and covering different distances, may be either 'in phase' or to varying degrees 'out of phase' on reaching the ship. The Decometer is an electronic instrument which can determine accurately the phase difference, expressed as any interval from 0° to 360°, between the waves from the master and from one of the slave stations. This figure enables the user to fix his position as somewhere on a curved line or narrow curved band on the Decca chart. A similar comparison between the master and a different slave station fixes another curved line or narrow band on the chart. Where these intersect, in a point if the lines are definite, or else in a *diamond of error, is the ship's position. Three slave stations are provided as in some positions the intersection of position lines from two would be at too acute an angle or

otherwise unsuitable, and the most suitable pair of lines can always be used. The degree of accuracy of a Decca fix varies within the coverage area. It also depends to some extent on the time of day, being less accurate during the hours of darkness because of distortion of wireless waves than during daylight, but the system is of course unaffected by fog or bad visibility and operates continuously throughout the 24 hours, enabling a fix to be obtained at any time. In ideal circumstances the ship's position may be pinpointed with an accuracy of a few yards. Most ships fitted with Decca would, however, also have *radar and would use the latter to detect the coastline and other shipping at close range, relying on Decca for general navigation in the areas covered. These extend several hundred miles from the British Isles. See also CONSOL, LORAN.

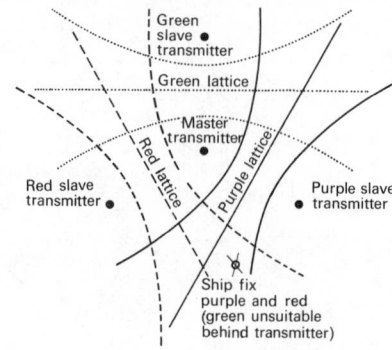

Decca chain; a normal layout with master transmitter and three slave transmitters

DECK, the horizontal platforms in ships which correspond to floors in houses. Starting from the bottom, the decks in an average large ship are the *orlop, lower (though the two are now sometimes combined in a single deck known as the lower), main, upper, shelter, *bridge, and boat. These, however, may vary considerably from ship to ship according to her function. Smaller ships, of course, have fewer decks; larger vessels have more, the *Cunard liner Queen Elizabeth II having as many as thirteen. In some types of ships, these decks have other names; in large liners, for example, the shelter deck is frequently known as the promenade deck and other names are coined to denote different decks according to their main purpose, such as hurricane deck, cabin deck, etc. In the days of the sailing navy, the upper deck was often known as the spar deck, and the main deck as a gundeck. (But see also DECKER for warships with more than one gundeck.)

Properly speaking, a deck is only one which extends the full length of the ship, but in cases where they do not extend the full length, the word is still used, if improperly, to describe the built-up portions forward and aft of a ship, the fore portion being known as the *forecastle deck and the after portion as the *poop deck. That portion of the upper deck which lies between forecastle and poop is often known in merchant ships as the well deck, and in many other types of ship as the *waist.

The origin of the term is obscure but probably comes from the old Dutch *dec*, a covering, cloak, or horse-cloth, although in its nautical meaning the word was in use in England at least a century and a half earlier than in Holland.

DECK HOUSE, a square or oblong *cabin erected on the deck of a ship. In the sailing warships of the Royal Navy it was known, in a perverse sort of way, as the 'round house' because one could walk round it. Originally, in the 17th and 18th centuries, it was the name given to the upper *coach but by the end of the 18th century the term round house was used to describe the lavatory fitted in the sick bay of warships for men who were unable because of illness or wounds to get forward to the normal place in the head of the ship.

In many merchant vessels, particularly sailing ships in the days of the *clipper ships and the later big trading *barques, a large deck house was erected just abaft the foremast to house the *galley and to provide quarters for the watch-keeping crew, while a smaller deck house abaft the mainmast provided accommodation for the daymen and apprentices.

DECKER, a term used in the old sailing navies to describe the number of gundecks, and there-fore the size, of warships, such as a two-decker, three-decker, etc. It referred only to the decks on which batteries of guns were mounted and not to the total number of decks in the ship. The gun-decks of a three-decker, in ascending order, were the lower gundeck, main gundeck, and upper gundeck, even though this upper gundeck was on the deck next below the upper deck.

DECLARATION OF PARIS, a statement of the principles of international law relating to mari-time war which was adopted on 16 April 1856 at the Treaty of Paris. It was this declaration which brought to an end the *guerre de course*, or *privateering. The nations which signed the declaration were Britain, France, Austria, Prussia, Russia, Sardinia, and Turkey. The U.S.A. refused to sign the declaration, and as a result suffered severely from this form of war against trade throughout the Civil War of 1861–5. The principles of the Declaration of Paris were reaffirmed at the *Hague Conference of 1907, but a new door was opened towards the waging of a *guerre de course* when a majority of the maritime nations endorsed the use of *armed merchant cruisers, and in the two world wars waged since that date, maritime attack on trade has proved a major weapon.

DECLINATION, a term used in celestial *navigation to indicate the angular distance of a celestial body north or south of the equator measured from the centre of the earth. It corre-sponds, therefore, to the geographical latitude of the body. Tables of declination for those bodies used by navigators in working out positions by celestial navigation are included in *nautical almanacs.

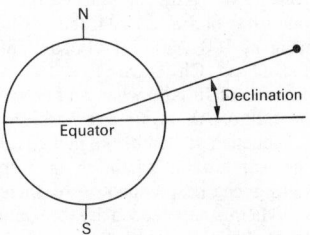

DECOY, an old stratagem in sea warfare to induce a small ship to chase a larger one and thus to separate her from her friends with the intent of capturing her when she had been drawn far enough from the support of her own fleet. This was done by painting the sides and stern to represent a much smaller war vessel, usually by painting out one of the rows of gunports, and to hoist an extra large sail as though crowding on sail to escape, at the same time altering the *trim of the ship in order to lose way by sailing badly. At night decoys were used to attempt to escape from a superior fleet by casting overboard a cask of lighted pitch, altering course at the same time, in the hope that the enemy would try to follow the light and thus lose sight of the ship.

DEEP, a position in the oceans, often also known as a trench, where the water is of exceptional depth in comparison with adjacent areas. Depths of over 3,000 fathoms in the oceans are given the generic name of deeps. See also ATLANTIC, INDIAN, PACIFIC OCEANS.

DEEP, a point on a *lead line which corresponds to a *sounding in *fathoms but has no distin-guishing mark on the line. The hand lead line, with which soundings are taken from a ship in relatively shallow water, has different distin-guishing *marks, recognizable both by sight and touch, at 2, 3, 5, 7, 10, 13, 15, 17, and 20 fathoms, and when one of these marks is on the sea level after the lead is hove as the line is vertical, the leadsman knows exactly the depth of water he is getting. If, however, after heaving the lead, there is no distinguishing mark on the sea level, he must estimate the depth of water by the nearest distinguishing mark that he can see above the level of the water. This is known as a deep, and he will call the depth of water with the words 'Deep —', by which the navigator will know that he has not got an exact depth by means of a mark on the line. The use of a lead and line for sounding is now virtually obsolete as most vessels, even the smallest, are today fitted with *echosounders.

DEFENCE, H.M.S., a name used for six ships of the Royal Navy. The first was a third *rate of seventy-four guns, launched at *Plymouth in 1763. She took part in the battles of the *Glorious First of June, 1794, the *Nile, 1798, *Copenhagen, 1801, and *Trafalgar, 1805. She was wrecked on Christmas Eve 1811 on the southern coast of Jutland when on her way home from the Baltic. An armoured *cruiser named *Defence*, launched at Pembroke in 1907, was the last large warship in Britain to be fitted with reciprocating engines, which were then in the process of being superseded by *turbines. She was sunk at the battle of *Jutland in 1916 when serving with the 1st Cruiser Squadron.

DEFOE, DANIEL (*c.* 1660–1731), English political pamphleteer, journalist, and novelist, was born in London, the son of a butcher. He had an early escape from disaster after joining the Duke of Monmouth's rebellion in 1685, but lay low until the arrival of William III from Holland whose army he joined on the abdication of James II. He began writing political pamphlets in 1701, and in 1703 was fined, sent to prison, and sentenced to the pillory for a pamphlet he had written the previous year. Embittered and impoverished, he started a newspaper, wrote further pamphlets, and sold his services as a secret agent to the Whig faction in Parliament.

It is as the author of *Robinson Crusoe* that he enters the maritime story. Originally published in 1719, it is based on a short pamphlet written by Alexander *Selkirk (or perhaps by a ghost writer), in which he described the four years he spent on the deserted island of Juan Fernandez in the Pacific, having been marooned there by Captain Stradling of the ship *Cinque Ports*. The book was a success from the start and has remained a favourite ever since, and Defoe followed it with a series of novels of which *Captain Singleton, Moll Flanders*, and *A Journal of the Plague Year* are the best known today. In 1724 he published *A New Voyage Round the World*, unsigned but now known to have been written by Defoe, a book which foxed maritime historians for many years. It is of course pure fiction, but at the time was accepted as genuine and for long afterwards was widely quoted in various books of voyages. This was followed in 1726 by *The Four Voyages of Capt. George Roberts*, but this was a work which was accepted as fiction from the start.

But it is on *Robinson Crusoe* that Defoe's fame is firmly established. It was translated into many languages and has been republished again and again in countless editions. With its basis in truth, it remains a convincing account of a shipwreck (which in Selkirk's case did not happen) and of Crusoe's success in adapting himself to a solitary island life (which did happen).

DEGAUSS, to, or **DEGAUSSING,** an operation of the Second World War by which ships were enabled largely to ignore the presence of magnetic *mines laid in the waters through which they needed to pass. The magnetic field created by the hull of a steel vessel was enough to activate a magnetic mine over which she passed, but it was a relatively simple matter, once the polarity of the mine was known, to counteract or reverse the ship's magnetic field by passing a current through an electric cable encircling her hull. The polarity of the German magnetic mines was discovered when one was dropped by an aircraft, through indifferent navigation, into the mud off Shoeburyness in the Thames Estuary. It was recovered and dismantled and it was found that it was fired by a change of magnetism in the vertical field. With this knowledge, the degaussing of all ships was able to be put in hand. This did not lessen the need for all such mines to be swept, which was eventually achieved by the development of the *LL Sweep, as degaussing could not guarantee complete immunity, but it considerably reduced the risk of detonating the mines and also increased the confidence of the crews of merchant vessels when they sailed through waters known to be mined.

DEGREE, a unit of measurement applied to the surface of the earth, the length subtended at the equator by one degree of *longitude. This form of measurement owes its origin to Pythagoras (6th century B.C.), the Greek mathematician who first set out the theory that the earth was a sphere and not a flat surface, and its implementation to *Eratosthenes, the first man to make a calculation of the circumference of the earth based on accurate measurement of the length of shadows cast simultaneously by the sun at two points a known distance apart.

DEL CANO, JUAN SEBASTIAN (*c.* 1486–1526) was a pilot embarked by Ferdinand *Magellan for the first circumnavigation of the world in 1519–22. He was also one of the ringleaders of the serious mutiny against Magellan's leadership which broke out at Port St. Julian, in Patagonia, but was too valuable as a pilot to suffer execution with the other ringleaders and his life was thereby spared. By chance he was placed in command of the *caravel *Vittoria, which was the only ship of the expedition to survive and return to Seville, and as a result was honoured, faute de mieux, by the King of Spain with a coat of arms and a life pension. A statue to him was erected in Guipozoa and still stands there, a signal honour for a mutineer.

DeLANY, WALTER STANLEY (1891–   ), American vice admiral, was born in Pennsylvania and graduated from the Naval Academy in 1912. He was serving as assistant chief of staff and operations officer on the staff of the Commander-in-Chief, Pacific Fleet, at the time of the Japanese air attack on Pearl Harbor in 1941, and commanded the *cruiser New Orleans in the *Guadalcanal campaign in 1942. Later that year he was ordered to Washington as assistant chief of staff (operations) to Admiral Ernest J. *King, Commander-in-Chief, U.S. Fleet. He remained in staff appointments for the remainder of the Second World War and headed the postwar naval training policy board.

After his retirement he was appointed by President Eisenhower as deputy administrator of the Mutual Defence Assistance Control Act, continuing in that post until March 1961. Since then he has worked voluntarily for the Naval Historical Foundation, of which he became president in 1967.

DELAVALL or **DELAVAL, Sir RALPH** (c. 1642–1707), British admiral, served in the Royal Navy through the Second (1665–7) and Third (1672–4) Dutch Wars, reaching the rank of *post-captain by the end of the Second. In 1689 he was the officer selected to declare to William and Mary the loyalty of the fleet on their assumption of the throne of England after the abdication of James II in 1688, and was knighted and promoted to the rank of vice admiral. He commanded the rear (Blue) squadron of the fleet at the indecisive battle of *Beachy Head in 1690 against the French fleet, and in 1692 was third in command of the centre (Red) squadron at the battle of *Barfleur, again against the French. After that battle, with the French fleet in flight, Delavall entered the port of Cherbourg in chase of the French flagship Soleil Royal and burnt her to the waterline.

His next naval task was to cover the huge convoy to Smyrna of 400 ships which sailed from England in 1693. Sir George *Rooke, commanding the close escort, proposed to look into Brest to make sure that the French fleet had not sailed but was overruled by a Council of War at which Delavall led the opposition. But, sure enough, the French fleet had sailed, and later fell upon the convoy, capturing over 100 ships worth nearly £1,500,000. Delavall, quite rightly, was held mainly responsible for the disaster and

relieved of his command of the Channel Fleet, but William III, remembering how he had brought him the loyalty of the navy on his accession, was able to mitigate his dismissal with an appointment as one of the *Lords Commissioners of the Admiralty, his last naval duty and one which he held for a year.

DeLONG, GEORGE WASHINGTON (1844–81), American naval officer and Arctic explorer, graduated from the Naval Academy in 1865. He had been appointed to the Juniata in 1873 when that vessel was sent to the Arctic to search for the missing steamer Polaris. This experience interested him in Arctic research and he in turn interested James Gordon Bennett, the newspaper publisher.

After careful planning a steamer was purchased and fitted out for Arctic exploration. In this vessel, renamed Jeanette, DeLong sailed from San Francisco on 8 July 1879 in an attempt to reach the North pole via the Bering Strait. The ship was caught in the ice on 5 September, drifted north-west for more than twenty-one months, and was finally crushed by ice and sank on 13 June 1881. It took the crew two months of struggling over frozen sea, with boats and provisions, before they reached open water, where they embarked in three boats for the Lena Delta in Siberia in September. One boat, commanded by Lieutenant Chipp, was never heard of again, but the other two, under DeLong and Engineer Melville, reached shore. Although Melville and his boat's crew landed safely, DeLong's boat put ashore in uninhabited country with only a few days' provisions left. DeLong led his men southward until all were exhausted and, towards the end of October, the men died one by one of starvation and exposure. The following spring Melville led a search party back to the area, where the bodies of DeLong and his crew were discovered. The expedition did establish, however, the existence of a north-westward polar drift, determined the size of Wrangel Island, and discovered a small group of hitherto unknown islands which are now called the DeLong Islands.

DEMURRAGE, the compensation payable to a shipowner when his ship is held up in port beyond the time specified in the *charter-party in cases where it is the fault of the consignee through non-arrival of the cargo for which space in the holds has been reserved. It is also legally liable when, in time of war, a vessel has been detained in *prize but later is not *condemned by the prize court.

DENHAM, Sir HENRY MANGLES (1800–87), British admiral, is probably best remembered for his work as a naval surveyor on the River Mersey. He had by then already made a survey of the Bristol Channel in 1832, in itself a notable event as being the first British Admiralty survey for which a steam vessel was used. After seven years' work in the River Mersey he published, in 1840, his *Mersey and Dee Navigation*, in which he set down principles for preserving the régime of the estuary and its approach channels, which proved of great advantage to the port of Liverpool, which at that time was growing into one of the most important ports of Britain. In 1839 he was made a Fellow of the Royal Society.

His next duty was a survey of the Bight of Benin, on the west coast of Africa, and he followed this with seven important years (1852–9) in the Pacific in command of H.M.S. *Herald*. The main objective of this large-scale survey was the opening up of communications between the Australian colonies and western America, and Denham, in the course of it, covered large areas of the western Pacific Ocean. He surveyed, for example, in Tonga, Fiji, and the New Hebrides groups, and then concentrated his attention on the Coral Sea with its many isolated reefs, through which the charting of a safe route was of high importance.

His task completed, Denham sailed home via the Torres Strait in 1860 but not before he had furthered his consultations with the Australian authorities, leaving behind him an Australian determination to organize local surveying efforts in the coastal waters of the various states, a task which was admirably carried through largely as a result of Denham's enthusiasm, example, and encouragement. He was knighted in 1867.

DEPARTURE, (1) the last position on a * chart, when a ship is leaving the land, fixed from observations of shore stations. Thus a ship, when starting on a voyage, takes her departure not from the port from which she sails but from the position where the last * bearings of points ashore intersect on the chart. It is the correlative of * landfall at the end of the voyage. **(2)** The number of * nautical miles that one place is eastwards or westwards of another. Where the two places are on the same parallel of * latitude the departure between them is equivalent to the difference of * longitude in minutes of arc multiplied by the cosine of the latitude. In the 16th, 17th, and early 18th centuries, the general system of navigation over long voyages was to convert the various * courses sailed during a day into their two components of difference of latitude and difference of longitude, converting the departure by means of a * traverse table, and thus to plot the ship's new position after her day's run by measuring off so many miles north or south and so many miles east or west from the previous position. A well-known contemporary example of this navigational system exists in the manuscript log of Bartholomew * Sharp, the * buccaneer, now in

the Naval Library of the Ministry of Defence, London (MSS 4). It contains pages of these calculations made during Sharp's voyage from the Pacific, round Cape Horn, and to the West Indies in 1681, the whole voyage being made without sight of land. See also DEAD RECKONING, NAVIGATION.

DEPRESSION, an area of low barometric pressure around which the wind circulates in an anti-clockwise direction in the northern hemisphere and clockwise in the southern. Depressions are basically bad-weather systems in which the strength of the wind increases considerably towards the centre of low pressure, frequently giving gales and storms, often with heavy rain. They are relatively fast moving, the average rate being about 25 miles an hour. See also METEOROLOGY.

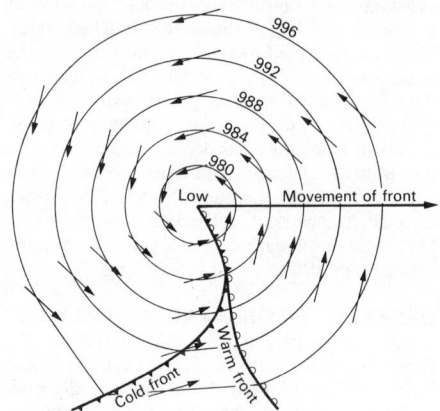

Depression with associated fronts

DEPTFORD, a London borough on the south bank of the River Thames, adjoining that of * Greenwich, and one of the earliest of the naval * dockyards of England. It probably preceded * Portsmouth as a harbourage and repair establishment for the 'king's ships', as the English Navy in those days was known. It was a naval dockyard in the reign of Henry VII (1485–1509) but its first naval dock was not constructed until about 1542, some two years later than the dock at Portsmouth. A considerable improvement in its facilities was put in hand during the last years of the reign of Henry VIII (1509–47), and by the later Stuart period (1660–88) it was the most important of the English naval dockyards, closely associated with the name of the * Pett family, master shipwrights, who designed many famous warships of the period. Deptford was also the headquarters of the * Victualling Board, which built extensive warehousing to store the food, clothing, rum, and other stores required for the naval service of Britain. This activity remained at Deptford after the work of the

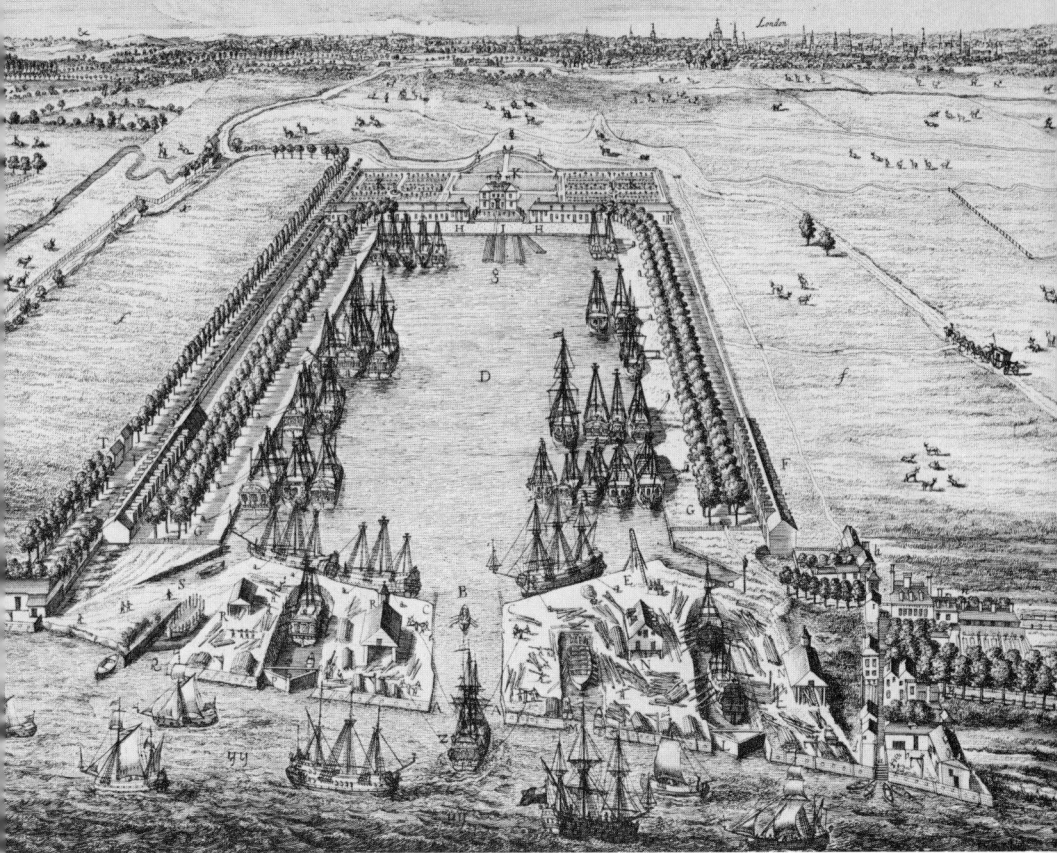

Howland's Great Dock, Deptford; engraving by J. Kip

Deptford yard was transferred to * Chatham and Sheerness dockyards in 1869, much of the site being then converted into the Royal Victualling Yard for the manufacture and storage of naval requirements of all kinds in the nature of food, drink, clothing, and furniture. It remained in use for this purpose until 1965 when the whole area was vacated by the Royal Navy. Many of the old victualling warehouses are still in existence though now converted to other uses. It was to Deptford that the * *Golden Hind* was brought in 1581 after her circumnavigation of the world, and there that Sir Francis * Drake was knighted by Elizabeth I for that exploit.

Deptford was also the place where * Trinity House was founded in 1517, in the parish church of St. Clement, and where for many years it maintained a hospital for master mariners. It is also associated with * Peter the Great, who stayed in Deptford in 1698 while studying naval shipbuilding in the dockyard there.

DEPTH-CHARGE, a weapon designed during the First World War (1914–18) for use against submerged * U-boats. It consists of a canister filled with explosive and fitted with a hydro-

statically controlled pistol which detonates the explosive at a pre-selected depth. The hydrostatic valve operates by the pressure of the water against a spring, and the tension of the spring is varied to correspond to the depth at which the charge is required to explode. Until the development of the * squid towards the end of the Second World War, which was a weapon firing depthcharges ahead of the ship, depth-charges could only be released over the stern of the attacking ship or fired on either beam from a depth-charge thrower, which entailed the attacking vessel passing over the submerged U-boat before the charges could be released. Another development of the depth-charge during the Second World War was the * hedgehog, an ahead-firing mortar which discharged twenty-four small charges which exploded on contact. Also during that war, depth-charges with a shallow setting of 30 feet were developed for use by aircraft against U-boats sighted on the surface.

Modern developments in the depth-charge include a nuclear explosive to widen the lethal area of explosion and the introduction of an active homing device to attract it to the close vicinity of the target before it explodes.

DERELICT, any vessel abandoned at sea. When a ship is abandoned, whether by consent, compulsion, or stress of weather, she is a derelict, although legally if any live domestic animal, such as a cat or dog, is on board when found, the owner may recover the ship within a year and a day by paying *salvage if he so wishes. See also WRECK.

DERRICK, a large single spar fixed on board ship pivoted at the lower or inboard end and fitted with *stays and *guy pendants, and to which a *topping-lift and a *purchase is attached, used like a crane for hoisting boats, cargo, and other heavy weights. It is controlled laterally by the guy pendants, which allow it to swing through a wide arc, and vertically by the topping-lift, by means of which the hook of the purchase can be positioned directly over the object to be lifted. With the development of

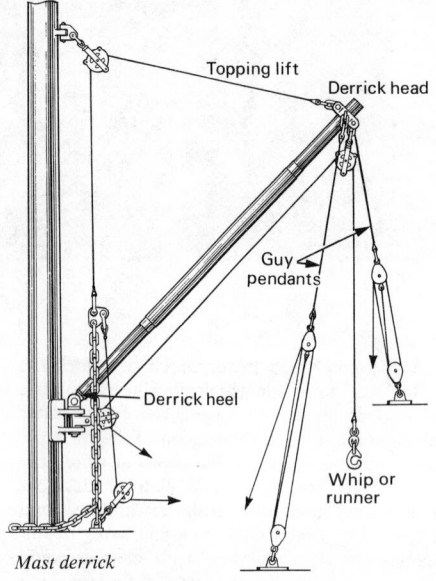

Mast derrick

modern cargo handling methods, the derrick as a principal lifting agent on board ship is now rarely fitted. The name comes from a 17th century hangman named Derrick who was employed in his grisly trade at Tyburn, London, presumably because in both cases weights dangle from the ends of ropes.

DERROTERRO, the Spanish version of a *rutter or sailing directions, incorporating views of the coast from seaward and forming, as the pages are turned, a complete picture of the coastline in the general area covered by the derroterro. A notable example of a derroterro, with the coastline painted in its natural colours, is in the Naval Library, Ministry of Defence, London,

being the original taken by Bartholomew *Sharp out of the captured Spanish ship *Rosario* during his *buccaneering voyage in the South Pacific, 1680–1.

DES BARRES, JOSEPH FREDERICK WALLET (or WALSH) (1721–1824), British cartographer and marine engraver, is best remembered for his portfolio of charts of the north-east coast of North America, known as the *Atlantic Neptune,* and today considered as one of the gems of the cartographer's art. He himself undertook some of the original surveys on which the charts are based, though the collection as a whole is the work of several surveyors. It was published in 1777 for the use of the British Navy. One of the most charming features of these beautiful charts is the series of sketches of landfalls and views of harbours which he painted and engraved on the charts. He was at the same time a considerable marine artist and one of his best-known pictures is an aquatint which shows the frigates *Phoenix* and *Rose* engaged by enemy *fireships and *galleys.

According to a memoir written by J. C. Webster, des Barres was within a month of being 103 years old when he died, which would make the year of his birth 1721 and not 1722 as usually stated.

d'ESTAING, JEAN-BAPTISTE CHARLES HENRI HECTOR THÉODAT, Comte, see ESTAING, Jean-Baptiste, etc., Comte d'.

D'ESTRÉES, JEAN, see ESTRÉES, Jean d'.

DESTROYER, originally torpedoboat destroyer, a light, fast warship developed in the last decade of the 19th century as a counter to the fast *torpedoboats which had become a significant weapon in most fleets, and originally known as torpedoboat catchers. The first two were launched in Britain in 1886, but both they and their immediate successors proved insufficiently fast to fulfil their primary task efficiently. It was not until 1893 that orders were placed in Britain for two ships of a new design, to be known as torpedoboat destroyers, with Mr., later Sir, Alfred *Yarrow, and H.M.S. *Havock* and H.M.S. *Hornet* were launched later that year, the first true destroyers in the world. With a speed of 27 knots and a combined gun/torpedo armament, they were able successfully to demonstrate their superiority over the existing torpedoboats, and indeed quickly assumed the torpedoboat role in modern naval warfare in addition to proving to be their antidote.

The introduction, first, of the marine *turbine in place of the triple-expansion engine, and, secondly, of oil instead of coal as fuel, revolutionized the design of destroyers throughout the world, giving them greater flexibility and

H.M.S. Cavalier, *a C-class destroyer*

speed and a significant economy in manpower. By the time of the First World War (1914–18), the displacement of destroyers had increased from around 250 tons to 2,000 or more, and this increase in size enabled the destroyer not only to acquire an increased endurance at sea but also a wider variety of tasks in the overall spectrum of naval warfare.

The development of the submarine during the first decades of the 20th century added appreciably to the traditional tasks of the destroyer in war. It already had the dual role in battle of attacking an enemy battle-line with salvoes of torpedoes launched from above-water torpedo tubes and of beating back similar attacks on the fleet made by enemy destroyers. To this was now added the task of screening the fleet against possible submarine attack on every occasion of putting to sea. The menace of the German *U-boat campaign of 1914–18 brought yet further tasks to this ubiquitous class of warship, first in the unprofitable attempt to patrol areas of sea through which merchant ships, the prime targets of the U-boats, were to pass, and from 1917

onwards the escorting of *convoys across the oceans. During this war, too, many destroyers were fitted as *minelayers to operate in areas close to the enemy coasts.

Developments between the two world wars and during the Second World War brought yet further fleet responsibilities. The big expansion in naval air techniques necessitated some destroyers to be fitted as air-direction ships to control the activities of carrier-borne and shore-based aircraft. The development of the *asdic, later known as *sonar, gave them improved anti-submarine capability and brought added responsibilities in this role, particularly when allied to the new anti-submarine weapons such as the *hedgehog and the *squid.

Since the Second World War, destroyers as such have been largely relieved of their anti-submarine tasks by the development of the modern *frigate but modern techniques in guided missiles have brought new tasks in naval warfare, and these have, in general, been responsible in the growth of the destroyer from an average tonnage of 2,000 to 5,000 and above.

DEUTSCHES MUSEUM VON MEISTER-WERKEN DER NATURWISSENSCHAFT UND TECHNIK, Munich, West Germany. Founded in 1903 and opened in 1906, the marine section of the museum is only part of the whole collection, which was designed by Gabriel von Seidl. It contains 160 ship models of various types, also many kinds of *canoes. Of particular interest are the first motorboat, dating from 1886, and the first *U-boat (*U.1*). Propelling machinery is well represented by engines of various types, paddle-wheels, *propellers, etc.; there are cutaway models of ships showing a 17th-century gundeck, passenger and crew accommodation, a large collection of nautical instruments, among them the first gyroscopic *compass by Herman Anschütz-Kaempfe (1907) and the first echo-sounder by Alexander Behm (1912), and a remarkable wave testing tank. Among the weapons are *torpedoes, *mines, and *depth-charges, and the photographic collection numbers 20,000, including 12,000 portraits. The library, which is open to the public, contains 460,000 books, 1,800 reviews and plans, and 61,560 manuscripts.

DEUTSCHLAND, the name of the first of the three *pocket-battleships built by Germany as commerce raiders between the two world wars. She was an armoured ship of 10,000 tons nominal with two triple 11-inch turrets and eight 5·9-inch guns, and was propelled by diesel machinery. After the sinking of her sister-ship, the *Admiral Graf Spee*, in December 1939, her name was changed to *Lützow*; because, it is said, if she too were sunk by the British Navy, the effect in Germany of losing a ship with such a prestigious name would be traumatic. In May 1945 she was scuttled at Swinemünde after being damaged by the Royal Air Force. A possibly more worthy *Deutschland* was the sailing vessel, formerly the *Bjørn*, built in Norway in 1905 for polar navigation. She was purchased by Wilhelm * Filchner for the German Antarctic expedition of 1910–12 which discovered Luitpold Land and the Filchner Ice Shelf. She was beset in the ice during the voyage and drifted for nine months in the Weddell Sea.

DEVEREUX, ROBERT, 2nd earl of Essex (1567–1601), Earl Marshal of England and a favourite of Elizabeth I, was born at Netherwood, Herefordshire. He was educated at Cambridge and presented at court, but seeking a more active life took part in the Earl of Leicester's expedition to Holland in 1585 to assist the States General. In 1589 he accompanied Sir Francis * Drake on his ill-fated expedition to Portugal. He personally superintended the fitting-out of an expedition which resulted in the capture of * Cadiz in 1596 and in which he commanded the land forces. The following year, in command of an expedition comprising twenty ships, he sailed for the Azores, but returned with very little booty. From this time dates his decline in royal favour attributed largely to the influence of Sir Walter * Raleigh. In 1599 he was appointed Governor-General of Ireland, but failed to take adequate measures to suppress a rebellion and on his return to England was imprisoned, but subsequently released.

He tried in vain to regain the Queen's favour and in desperation organized a rebellion in London, an action which led to his arrest. Accused of high treason he was condemned to death, but as a result of Elizabeth's reluctance to sign the warrant for his execution, this was deferred until 25 February 1601.

DEVIATION, an error of a magnetic * compass caused by a ship's own residual magnetism. If a ship had no residual magnetism, the needle of her magnetic compass would point direct towards the north magnetic pole, but as every modern ship has metal fittings which affect the compass, there is always some error. Deviation varies according to the heading of the ship because as a ship changes course, the metal in her changes its position in relation to the compass as the ship swings round. Deviation is therefore read off for every quarter * point (about 4°) as the ship is swung through 360° and is tabulated on a deviation card so that it can be applied, together with * variation, to every compass course or bearing to convert them to * true courses or bearings. It can rarely be completely eliminated in a ship's magnetic compass though it can be very con-

siderably reduced by the use of soft iron balls mounted on each side of the compass and by bar magnets, known as Flinders bars, hung in the * binnacle below the compass bowl. See also FLINDERS, Matthew.

DEVIL, the caulker's name for the * seam in the upper deck planking next to a ship's waterways. No doubt they gave it that name as there was very little space to get at this seam with a caulking iron, making it a particularly difficult and awkward job. This is the origin of the saying 'Between the devil and the deep blue sea', since there is only the thickness of the ship's hull planking between this seam and the sea.

It is also the name given by caulkers to the * garboard seam, which was always, when a ship was * careened, not only the most awkward to get at but usually the wettest and most difficult to keep above water and caulk. See also CAULK, TO, 'DEVIL TO PAY'.

'DEVIL TO PAY', an old seafaring term meaning something very difficult or awkward. It originates from the name given by caulkers to the * garboard * seam in a ship's hull, which was universally known as the * devil, as it was difficult to * pay in the * oakum and hammer it home. 'Devil to pay and no pitch hot', a situation so difficult that no means of solving it is immediately apparant. See CAULK, TO.

DEVIL'S CLAW, see CABLE STOPPERS.

DEVONPORT, one of the four * Royal dockyards of England and a main naval base, it forms a part of Plymouth Sound. The naval dockyard was established in 1689 as Plymouth Dockyard, and was known by this name until 1824, when the town around it, contiguous with * Plymouth, was named Devonport. As well as containing various naval technical schools, Devonport is the home of the Royal Naval Engineering College, which was opened at Keyham in 1880, the culmination of a great expansion begun in 1850 to bring the dockyard up to date to be able to cope with the changeover in the navy from sail to steam. A second big expansion took place in 1905 to construct the large docks and refitting berths required for the new * dreadnought type battleships introduced by Admiral Sir John * Fisher. A third large expansion is currently under way to make Devonport an operational and refitting base for nuclear fleet submarines.

DEWEY, GEORGE (1827–1917), American admiral, graduated at the Naval Academy in 1858. He was a lieutenant in the steam sloop *Mississippi* during * Farragut's passage of the forts below New Orleans in April 1862 during the American Civil War, and also served with distinction in the fighting below Donaldsonville in 1863. In the steam gunboat *Agawam* he was engaged in the North Atlantic blockade of the South and was in the attacks on Fort Fisher at the end of 1864 and beginning of 1865, in which year he was promoted lieutenant-commander. After service in European waters in 1866–7 he became an instructor in the Naval Academy for a two-year spell and then twice commanded the *Narragansett*, in 1870–1 and 1872–5.

For the next twenty years he served ashore, for many years in the lighthouse service of which, in 1893–5, he was a member of the board, and after an appointment as president of the board of inspection and survey, had reached the rank of commodore. He then sent in a request to be returned to sea service and was appointed to command the American squadron in Asiatic waters. While lying at Hong Kong in April 1898 he received the news that war had been declared between the U.S.A. and Spain and that his duty was to capture or destroy the Spanish fleet, then in Philippine waters. He reached Manila Bay, where the Spanish fleet of eight ships under Admiral Montojo was lying, and annihilated it on 1 May 1898 without the loss of a single man in the American squadron. For this action he received the thanks of Congress and a sword of honour, and medals were struck for presentation to every officer and man present at the action.

Promotion to rear admiral followed the action and in August Dewey and his squadron assisted in the capture of Manila. While still there maintaining control he received, by special Act of Congress, the rank of admiral of the navy, previously borne only by Farragut and David *Porter. On his return to New York he was given a hero's welcome and there were some moves to try to persuade him to accept nomination as Democratic candidate for President. He resisted all such pleas, preferring to live quietly in retirement except for serving on one or two commissions and Courts of Inquiry.

Healy & Kutner, *The Admiral* (New York, 1944).

DEZHNEV, SEMYON IVANOV (*c.* 1605–73), Russian explorer, made the first recorded transit of Bering Strait. Born in north Russia, he served as a cossack in Siberia, where he travelled much in the north between 1638 and 1670. He sailed along the north coast of eastern Siberia from the Lena River to Bering Strait, though not in a single voyage. His most famous voyage, in 1648–9, was from the Kolyma River eastwards, through Bering Strait from north to south, and on to Anadyr. By this voyage he demonstrated the separation of Asia and America, but his report lay forgotten in the archives at Yakutsk until 1736, by which time Vitus *Bering had been sent to make this discovery. The north-east tip of Asia is now called Cape Dezhnev (Mys Dezhneva) in belated recognition of his discovery.

DGHAISA, a Maltese passenger boat, used in harbours and around the coast, propelled by one or two men with oars to which they stand and push instead of sit and pull. They are characterized by very high vertical bow and stern projections somewhat similar to the Venetian *gondola, but straight up and down and not curved. Many of them, particularly those used in Grand Harbour, Valletta, are highly decorated with coloured paintwork and are a source of great pride to their owners.

DHOW, in its strict meaning a trading vessel of 150 to 200 tons, *lateen-rigged on a single mast, and indigenous to the Red Sea, Persian Gulf, and Indian Ocean, but the name has been extended to embrace any trading vessel of similar size in those waters, irrespective of the number of masts rigged. Some modern dhows are fitted with diesel engine propulsion. They were formerly used extensively in the slave trade from East Africa to the Arabian countries.

DIAGONAL BUILT, a method of planking the sides of a wooden vessel in which the *strakes are laid diagonally instead of horizontally. A diagonal built vessel is normally double-skinned, with the inner skin fastened diagonally in one direction on the *timbers and the outer skin laid diagonally in the opposite direction. The main purpose of diagonal planking is to give the hull of a vessel additional strength. It is a system of construction used for small naval vessels of the *motor-torpedoboat and *motor-gunboat types, some yachts, and also in sailing *dinghies in the glued plywood method of construction, such as the Fairey Firefly class. It is normally too expensive a method of construction to be used for commercial wooden vessels.

DIAMOND KNOT, a stopper knot made in a length of rope, the *strands being unlaid, the knot formed by tucking the strands through the bights of each other, and laying up the rope

Single diamond knot

again. A double diamond knot is made by tucking the strands twice. The purpose of a stopper knot is to prevent a rope from running through an eye, for example the foot-rope of a *jib-boom, and also for certain ornamental work.

DIAMOND OF ERROR, in hyperbolic systems of navigation, such as *Loran or *Decca, the concept of a position band instead of a position line is of importance. The width of a position band is proportional to the degree of accuracy of the observed hyperbolic position line. Two position bands intersect to form a diamond of error. See also COCKED HAT.

DIAMOND SHROUDS, masthead stays in the rigging of some yachts, made of steel wire or rod and carried in pairs over short struts to a lower position on the mast, thereby forming a diamond outline to support the upper part of a yacht's mast. They are used only with the *Bermuda rig, and not necessarily in all yachts so rigged.

DIAPHONE, a type of sound signal emitted from lighthouses and light vessels in fog, characterized by a powerful low note ending with a sharply descending tone known as the grunt.

DIAZ DE NOVAES, BARTHOLOMEW (c. 1455–1500), Portuguese explorer and discoverer of the Cape of Good Hope, was first heard of in 1481 when he commanded one of the vessels of an expedition to the Gold Coast. By 1487 he had achieved distinction as a navigator and was placed in command of an expedition of three ships to extend Portuguese exploration of the African west coast beyond the existing point of 21° 50′ S. which had been reached by Diogo *Cam.

Diaz had sailed his ships as far south as the point which today bears his name (latitude 26° 38′ S.) where he erected a commemorative pillar, when he was swept to the southward for thirteen days by strong gales. Steering west as soon as a moderation of the weather permitted and finding no land after several days, he turned north and made a landfall in February 1488 at Mossel Bay on the south coast of Cape Colony. From there he coasted eastwards, reaching the mouth of the Great Fish River before his officers and men, alarmed by this venturing into the unknown, forced him to return. By this time, however, the north-easterly trend of the coast made it clear that the southernmost point of Africa had been rounded.

On his return passage he first named this southernmost cape the Cape of Storms (*Cabo Tormentoso*), but either he or King John of Portugal later renamed it Cape of Good Hope (*Cabo da Bona Esperanza*). Diaz received little or no reward for his discovery and on his next

voyage in 1500 was only second-in-command to Pedro *Cabral on his voyage to India during which his ships first made a landfall on the coast of Brazil. It was on this same voyage that Diaz perished in a great tempest off his own Cape of Storms.

DIBDIN, CHARLES (1745–1814), British actor, dramatist, and song writer, was born at Southampton. He was a chorister in Winchester Cathedral in 1756 and made his first appearance as an actor in London in 1762. He was a prolific composer of songs which he himself sang in public, many of them becoming lasting favourites. In 1789 he produced a variety show, 'Oddities', in which he introduced some nautical songs, the best known being 'Tom Bowling', 'Saturday Night at Sea', and 'The Good Ship "Rover"'. With their lilting airs these won him great acclaim and were even credited with having had a beneficial effect on naval recruiting by making the navy popular. It is by these sea songs that he is remembered today and 'Tom Bowling' is still a regular favourite. The song was written as a portrait in words of his brother Captain Thomas Dibdin, and was so well known and well loved that a stanza of it is carved on his tombstone.

The 'Rogue's March', which was beaten on drums during the course of the naval punishment of *flogging round the fleet, was based on Dibdin's 'Right Little, Tight Little Island'.

DICKIES, the two small seats in large square-sterned rowing boats, such as naval *cutters, fitted in the angles between the *transom and *gunwale, on which the *coxswain sits when the boat is under oars.

DIEMEN, ANTHONY VAN (1593–1645), Dutch admiral, rose rapidly in rank in the service of the Dutch *East India Company. In 1636 he was made governor-general in the Dutch East Indies, extending Dutch possessions in that area by capture from the Portuguese and opening up new avenues of trade with China and Japan. He was responsible for organizing the voyages of exploration in 1636 and 1642 of Abel *Tasman, who named after him, as Van Diemen's Land, the island now known as Tasmania.

DIGBY, Sir KENELM (1603–65), English naval commander, was better known as an author and scientist than for his exploits at sea. In 1627 he used his influence with James I to be appointed commander of an expedition against French and Venetian ships in the Levant, but because of the opposition of the Duke of Buckingham, the then *Lord High Admiral, Digby's voyage had to be made under a *letter of marque as a private adventurer. Sailing with two ships from Deal at the end of 1627, he captured a number of French and Venetian ships at Scanderoon after a fierce engagement, and reached England in 1628 with considerable * prize money on board.

DILKE, Sir THOMAS (1667–1707), English rear admiral, commanded the * *Adventure*, of 50 guns, at the battle of * Barfleur and La Hogue in 1692. He was sent to the West Indies in the *Rupert* (sixty guns) in 1696, and with the death of the vice admiral, rear admiral, and most of the senior captains on the station, found himself in command of the squadron. He was in the fleet under the command of Sir George * Rooke during the attack on * Vigo in 1702, and being shortly afterwards promoted rear admiral, commanded a squadron in the Channel which captured or destroyed a French convoy of 45 ships escorted by three * frigates. He commanded the * White squadron at the battle of * Malaga (1704), being knighted by Queen Anne for his services, and was with Sir John * Leake at Gibraltar in 1705 when a French squadron was captured or destroyed, and in 1707 was second-in-command to Sir Clowdisley * Shovel in the Mediterranean. He remained in the Mediterranean as commander-in-chief when Shovel returned to England, and thus escaped the disaster when Shovel and four naval ships were wrecked in the Scilly Isles. He died of fever while on a naval visit to Leghorn.

DINGHY, from the Hindi *ḍeṅgi* or *ḍiṅgi*, a small boat used on rivers, originally a small open rowing boat, pulling one pair of oars, usually * clinker-built, and used as a general work-boat in warships and merchant vessels or as a tender to a yacht. By about the end of the 19th century some dinghies were being built partly decked and were used for racing under sail in many parts of the world, but it was not until after the First World War (1914–18) that dinghy racing began to take a major part in the sport, particularly after the introduction of the International 14-ft and National 12-ft classes. With the enormous growth of all kinds of pleasure boating that took place after the Second World War racing dinghies and dinghy classes proliferated, and in Britain alone there are over 300 different racing classes of dinghies. Both national and international racing events for dinghy championships are held in all yachting countries.

DIP of the horizon, the allowance which must be made when observing the * altitude of any heavenly body with a * sextant for (*a*) the refraction of light passing through the atmosphere from the horizon to the observer, and (*b*) the height of the observer's eye above the level of the sea. The effect of these two is to increase the observed altitude and the correction is made by subtracting from the observed angle the angular distance of dip, which is calculated and given in dip tables included in all compilations of nautical tables. The result is known as the apparent altitude. For illus. see HORIZON.

DIPPING LUG, a rig in which the forward end of the * yard carrying a * lugsail projects forward of the mast of a sailing vessel, entailing lowering the sail two or three feet and dipping the yard round the mast whenever the vessel goes * about and rehoisting the sail on the other tack. For this purpose dipping lines are secured to the end of the yard, one on either side of the sail, by which the yard is pulled down and dipped round the mast as the sail is lowered.

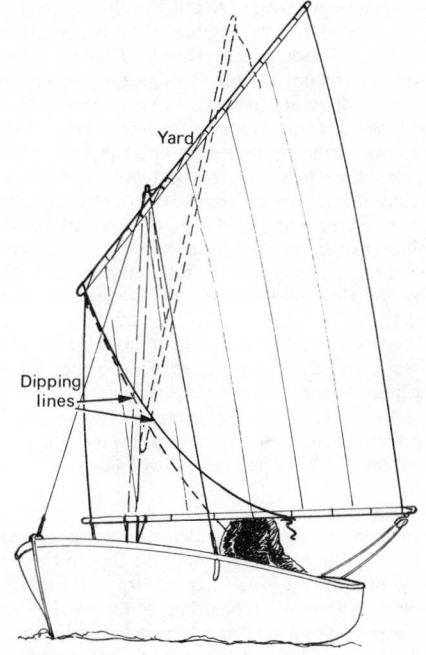

Dipping lug

DIRECTOR SIGHT, a means of directing and controlling the gunfire of warships introduced into the British Navy in 1912 following much research and experiment by Admiral Sir Percy * Scott, one of the greatest gunnery experts in the Royal Navy of those years. Guns had originally been laid and fired individually by a gunlayer at each gun, but in the heat of firing it was always difficult to make sure that each gunlayer in a ship was firing at the same target. Funnel smoke, cordite smoke, and mist and haze were additional hazards militating against accurate gunnery. Scott's system involved a single telescopic sight mounted in the fore-*top of the warships, well above funnel and cordite smoke, and connected electrically to the sights of each gun, so that individual gunlayers had only to line up their gunsights with a pointer on a dial to ensure that all fired at the target selected by the director sight with the same elevation and allowance for deflection. The guns were all fired simultaneously by electric contact by the single gunlayer in the fore-top so that their shells always fell together and were thus easier to spot.

Scott perfected his new director system in 1910 but there was considerable opposition in the navy to his idea, the argument being that if the electrical communications from the director sight in the ship's fore-top broke down or were damaged by gunfire, the ship's gunnery would be ineffective as a result of the lack of training of individual gunlayers. A full *calibre firing test was arranged in November 1912 between two similar *dreadnoughts, H.M.S. *Thunderer* and her sister-ship H.M.S. *Orion*, the *Thunderer* using a director sight, the *Orion* relying on her individual gunlayers at each gun. After three minutes firing by each ship at a range of 9,000 yards, the *Thunderer* emerged with six times as many hits as the *Orion*. By the outbreak of the First World War (1914–18), eight British battleships had been fitted with director sight firing; under the spur of war the rate was increased and by the time of the battle of *Jutland in May 1916, all but two of the *capital ships in the *Grand Fleet had the system installed. It was later adopted also for the secondary armament of capital ships.

As a result of the success of the British system, most of the world's navies introduced a similar system of gun control and firing.

DIRK, the small naval sword worn by *midshipmen or their equivalents in most navies, when in full dress uniform. In the British Navy it was originally a naval dagger worn, and used, by junior officers when boarding an enemy ship but gradually developed as a ceremonial adjunct to the uniform worn on board. As a naval weapon it dates from the late 17th or early 18th century, the name probably coming from the Scottish dirk, or durk, a short sword worn by Highlanders.

DISADVANTAGE, see ADVANTAGE.

DISCOVERY, a ship's name famous in the history of exploration. The first *Discovery*, belonging to the *East India Company, explored the newly discovered Hudson Strait under the command of Captain George Weymouth in 1602. In April 1610 Henry *Hudson set out on his fourth and last voyage in the same *Discovery* in search of a *North-West passage. In 1774 the British

Admiralty fitted out a small Yorkshire collier, or *cat, built at Whitby as the *Bloodhound*, as H.M.S. *Discovery* which accompanied Captain James *Cook's *Resolution* on his third and last voyage. In 1791–5 Captain George *Vancouver circumnavigated the world in another converted collier also named *Discovery*. In 1875–6 an ice-strengthened H.M.S. *Discovery*, a converted 1,274-ton whaler, accompanied Sir George *Nares's *Alert* on a naval expedition towards the North pole, and this ship was the prototype of the polar vessel *Discovery* which Captain R. F. *Scott commanded on his first Antarctic expedition of 1901–4. With a registered *tonnage of 485, she was made of wood with an immensely strengthened frame and bows to withstand the polar pack. Her subsequent career was a chequered one; after service with the Hudson's Bay Company as a store ship she was used by the *Discovery* Investigations Committee to carry out oceanographical surveys in the Antarctic whaling grounds in 1925–7. In 1929–31 Sir Douglas *Mawson used her to survey Australian Antarctic territory. She was then replaced by a new research ship, the *Discovery II*, and laid up. Today she is permanently moored off the Thames Embankment in London where she serves as a training ship and Antarctic museum.

DISCOVERY INVESTIGATIONS, a programme of continuous research into the oceanic resources of the Antarctic with the particular object of providing a scientific foundation for the whaling industry. The body responsible for these investigations was the *Discovery* Committee, named from Captain R. F. *Scott's ship of that name, set up in 1923 on the recommendation of an inter-departmental committee on research and development in the Dependencies of the Falkland Islands. The committee's main tasks were to provide information on the life histories of whales with a view to the proper regulation of their catch, and to make accurate charts of the Falkland Islands Dependencies. During a total of 12 commissions, between 1925 and 1939, the crews of the research ships *Discovery* (replaced in 1929 by the *Discovery II*) and *William Scoresby* carried out thousands of routine oceanographic observations, completed a number of whale-marking cruises, and made accurate charts of South Georgia, the South Sandwich, the South Orkney, and the South Shetland Islands. Two circumnavigations of the Antarctic continent were completed and the approximate position of the *Antarctic Convergence plotted. After the Second World War the work of the *Discovery* Committee was carried on by the National Institute of Oceanography and the Falkland Islands Dependencies Survey. The results of the investigations are published in the series known as the *Discovery Reports*.

DISMAST, to, the process of losing a mast. It is used most often in the past tense; a vessel is dismasted when her mast goes by the *board.

DISPLACEMENT, the weight of the water which a ship displaces when she is floating with her fuel tanks or bunkers full and with all stores on board. This, at the rate of 35 cubic feet per ton, is the actual weight of the ship, since a floating body displaces its own weight in water. Naval vessels are usually measured in terms of displacement, merchant ships in terms of registered or *deadweight *tonnage calculated on cubic capacity. The size of yachts is usually expressed by their waterline length but where tonnage is mentioned, it is calculated by the *Thames Measurement Rule.

DISTANT SIGNALS, objects, such as balls, cones, etc., which were hoisted instead of flags when the distance at which they were to be read was too great to distinguish the colours of the flags. Before the battle of *Trafalgar in 1805, information of the sailing of the Franco-Spanish fleet from Cadiz was transmitted to Lord *Nelson some 40 miles away and below the horizon by distant signals through a relay of three ships, reaching him in less than ten minutes. In these days of wireless and radio telephones, distant signals at sea have little relevance except in the case of small craft in distress or distinguishing signs to indicate vessels engaged in fishing, laying telegraph cables, towing, etc., although from shore stations distant signals in the form of cones are still hoisted to indicate forecasts of gales. At sea, a vessel not under control hoists a signal of two balls vertically six feet apart to warn other ships to keep clear of her, though more for the purpose of easy recognition than as a true distant signal. See also DISTRESS SIGNALS.

DISTRESS SIGNALS, a means of calling for help or assistance at sea. In the very early days they were probably made by smoke or flames by burning pitch or tar on board, but when gunpowder came into general use during the 15th century the firing of cannon became the usual signal of distress. Although at that period there was no internationally agreed code, there are many instances of ships drifting ashore and summoning help by firing off their guns.

In 1857 an *International Code of Signals was established and a special flag was allocated for distress; other signals which came into use during the 19th century were a square flag with a ball above it, a cone point upwards with a ball above or below it, continuous sounding on *foghorns and, for night use, flames or shells or rockets throwing stars of any colour. It was not until 1954 that agreement was reached that distress rockets had to be red.

The most profound change in distress signalling was brought about by the invention of wireless and the formation of the Marconi International Marine Communication Company in 1900. Several passenger liners were fitted with Marconi equipment the same year, as also was the Borkum Light Vessel, whose crew were probably the first lives to be saved by a wireless call after their ship broke adrift in a gale. In January 1904 the Marconi Company issued a circular stating that the call 'to be given by ships in distress or in any way requiring assistance shall be "CQD" '; this was the general call 'CQ' (all stations) followed by 'D' for distress, although it became widely known as 'Come Quickly, Danger'.

The first time wireless signals played a part in a major disaster was in January 1909 when the White Star liner *Republic* was struck by the Italian liner *Florida* in dense fog off Nantucket. Jack Binns, radio officer of the *Republic*, which sank later, called the White Star liner *Baltic* (via a shore station) to the rescue of the damaged liners and then guided the *Baltic* in through the fog by direct wireless communication. Binns used the 'CQD' call although 'SOS' had come into force as the international wireless distress call on 1 July 1908. 'SOS' was chosen because it was easy to read in morse (three dots, three dashes, three dots) and was unlikely to occur in normal messages; it did not stand for 'Save Our Souls' as legend soon had it. The first recorded use of 'SOS' was by the American steamer *Arapahoe* disabled by a broken propeller shaft off Cape Hatteras in August 1909.

When the *Titanic* sank in 1912 she sent both 'CQD' and 'SOS' calls; the fact that a nearby ship, the *Californian*, received none of these because her single radio operator was off duty led to an Act of Parliament of 1919 requiring British ships with 200 or more persons on board to have sufficient radio operators to keep a 24-hour watch. Experiments were also made with auto-alarms actuated by wireless distress calls, and in 1927 the British government approved such a device and exempted any ship fitted with one from carrying the two additional radio officers otherwise necessary for a continuous watch. In 1933 wireless installations became compulsory on all passenger ships and on cargo ships of 1,600 tons upwards, and since 1954 it has been internationally compulsory for all such ships to keep a continuous watch on the distress frequency, either with a radio officer or an auto-alarm. The distress call to actuate the auto-alarm is twelve 4-second dashes with one second between each.

DITTY BOX, a small wooden box in which a sailor kept his valuables, such as letters from home, photographs, etc.

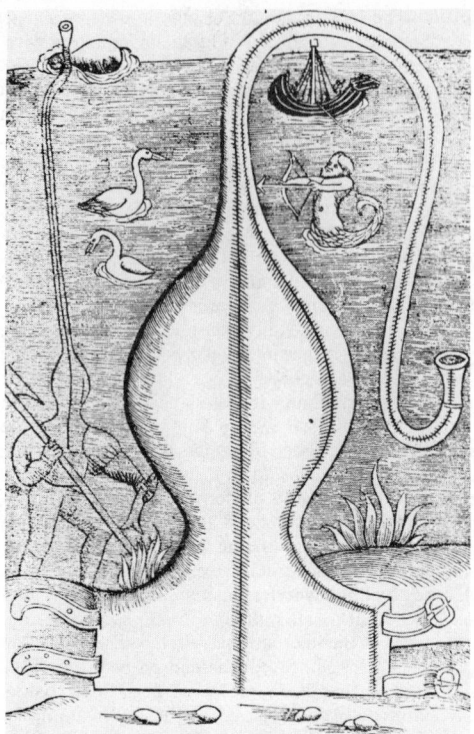

Diving helmet; engraving from Vegetius's De Re Militari, *edition of 1553*

Diving suit designed by C. H. Kleingert, 1797; early 19th-century engraving

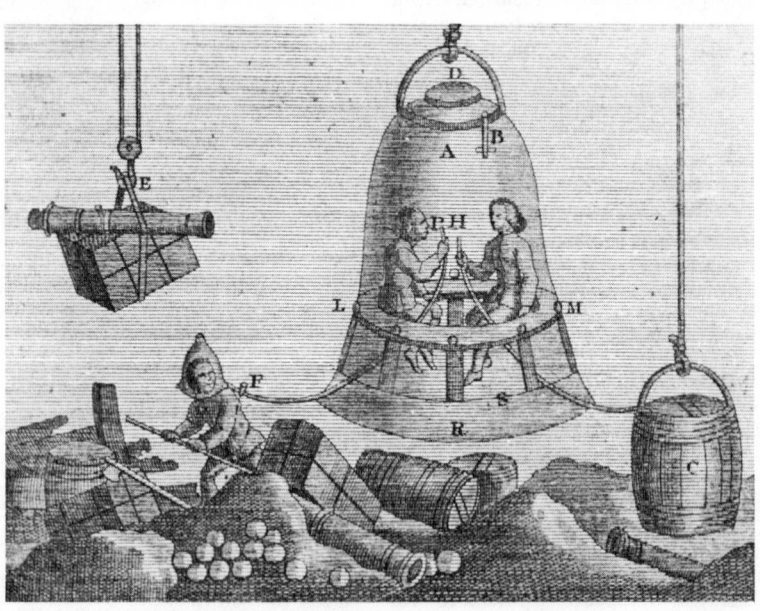

Halley's diving bell and helmet; late 18th-century engraving

DIVING, the process by which a human body, either unassisted or assisted by special machinery or clothing and the provision of compressed air, proceeds below the surface of the sea for purposes of salvage, repair, or exploration of the depths. That the practice of diving dates back many centuries before the Christian era can perhaps best be proved by the words of Homer in the *Iliad*, when Patroclus, having slain Cebrion, Hector's charioteer, on the plains of Troy, exclaims:

'Good heavens! what active feats yon artist shows.
What skilful divers are our Phrygian foes!
Mark with what ease they sink into the sand!
Pity, that all their practice is by land!'

If we can accept the words of Homer, the art of diving was not unknown 1,000 years before the birth of Christ. Nor was Homer the only one of the ancient writers to mention it. During the siege of Syracuse (734 B.C.) Thucydides records that divers were employed to saw down the wooden barriers which had been erected under water in the harbour entrance to obstruct the Greek warships attempting to enter. That divers were also employed commercially for salvage purposes is recorded by Livy, who wrote that in the reign of Perseus a large quantity of treasure was recovered from sunken ships. In the Rhodian laws of the sea, the forerunner of the better known Laws of *Oleron, a scale of reward for divers was laid down. For treasure recovered from ships lying at a depth of 8 cubits (2 fathoms or 4 m), the diver was entitled to one-third of the value recovered; from ships lying at a depth of 16 cubits (4 fathoms or 8 m), his share was one-half.

1. Unassisted diving. All this, of course, was what is known as free, or unassisted, diving, in which the diver has no mechanical assistance and relies entirely on the volume and power of respiration of his lungs. Under such conditions the time spent underwater is a maximum of about two minutes and the depth to which an unassisted diver can descend is limited to about 6 fathoms (10–12 m). In some parts of the world unassisted diving is still practised, as in the Ceylon pearl fisheries and the Mediterranean sponge fisheries, though both of these are succumbing rapidly to mechanical means of bringing oysters and sponge to the surface. Some exceptionally deep dives of up to 10 fathoms (20 m) have been recorded by Arab divers for pearls and sponges, but these are rare. The general practice for unassisted diving in the search for sponge or pearl oysters is to lower a large stone, with a hole in the centre to which a rope is attached, from the diving boat as a guide to the diver of the area he is to search. When he reaches the bottom of the sea he recovers as much sponge or as many oysters as he can reach in his limited time and then signals by a pull on the rope that he is ready to be hauled up.

There is, of course, great danger to the human system in this type of unassisted diving. The pressure of water increases with the depth, each 30 feet (9 m) in depth approximately equalling one atmosphere in pressure, so that the strain on lungs and eardrums when diving is intense. Exhaustion and bleeding frequently follow a prolonged spell of unassisted diving at depths of 30 feet (9 m) or more.

2. Assisted diving. The history of assisted diving is nearly as old as that of unassisted. Aristotle, without describing the method, mentions divers being provided with breathing apparatus by which they can draw air from the surface of the water, probably some sort of metal tube, suggested, no doubt, by the elephant which can breathe through its trunk when the rest of it is submerged. In another work he describes a metal vessel which is let down to a diver and retains air within it, obviously an early application of the principle of the diving bell.

The earliest known mention of a diving helmet occurs in *De Re Militari*, by Vegetius, published in 1511, in which he illustrates a diver wearing a tight-fitting helmet to which is attached a long leather pipe with a bell mouth supported above the surface by a bladder. The engraving shows no method of allowing for the escape of foul air after exhalation, and so probably was little more than an idea which occurred to Vegetius, but which he did not work out to a proper conclusion.

The first big step forward from the ancient methods of a pipe with one end supported on the surface came in 1679, when G. A. Borelli brought out a diving apparatus using air forced down to the diver by means of a bellows, a method which allowed considerably greater depths to be reached. John Lethbridge, of Devonshire in England, was the next man to take a hand in the evolution of diving methods; in 1715 he invented a watertight leather case in which the whole person of the diver was encased, but with leather arms and legs to allow for normal movement on the bottom of the sea. This leather suit was capable of holding half a hogshead of air, and was used extensively for purposes of salvage from ships lying on the bottom at depths up to about 30 feet (9 m). Lethbridge is said to have made a large fortune from this invention, the half-hogshead of air being sufficient to sustain a diver working on the bottom for up to 30 minutes.

The German inventor Kleingert produced a diving dress in 1797 which embodied many of the features of the modern dress, though in one respect it was retrograde, discarding the forced air principle introduced by Borelli. His diver wore a leather jacket with tight-fitting arms and leather drawers with tight-fitting legs. He then was fixed into a domed metal cylinder which went over his head and reached down to his hips, leaving his arms free, and was fixed to his dress so that it was both watertight and airtight. Air was drawn into the metal cylinder through a pipe supported on the surface by a bladder, in the same manner as that illustrated by Vegetius in 1511, but a considerable innovation was a second pipe, also supported by a bladder on the surface, to allow the escape of foul air. The first pipe was held by the diver in his mouth, an ivory mouthpiece at the end being held between his teeth. He breathed in through his mouth, and out through his nose, and the expansion of his chest as he inhaled forced out the foul air in the cylinder. A glass window in the metal cylinder allowed for vision. Lead weights hooked into the cylinder took him down to the required depth; when he wished to ascend he released one or more of the weights which he then attached to a rope which he held in his hand when ascending, the weights being hauled up to the surface after he had reached the top.

In 1819 the father of modern assisted diving, Augustus *Siebe, introduced his 'open' diving dress, which worked in conjunction with a pump which forced air down to the diver at a pressure depending on the depth at which the diver was working. The main feature of the dress was a metal helmet and breastplate which was attached to a loose watertight jacket. Under the jacket the diver wore a combination suit which reached to his armpits. To the helmet was attached a flexible metal tube, working through an air inlet valve, which kept him supplied with a constant stream of fresh air from the pump on the surface. This constant stream of air escaped between the jacket and the combination suit, very much in the manner of a diving bell, the pressure at which the air was supplied preventing the water from entering the jacket from below.

This was an admirable system so long as the diver was able to remain upright on his feet, but if he stumbled and fell his 'open' dress soon filled with water and he drowned unless he could be very quickly brought to the surface. Yet, with this one drawback, it was by far the most successful dress yet invented, and for the first time enabled divers successfully to undertake a variety of work at considerable depths.

Aware of this danger of his 'open' dress, Siebe carried out a number of diving experiments over the next few years and in 1830 introduced his 'closed' dress, in which an air regulating outlet valve was incorporated into the helmet, so that the closed suit was supplied, as in the open suit, with a constant stream of fresh air which was able to escape through the outlet valve in the helmet. It did not now matter if the diver did

stumble and fall, for his suit remained fully watertight and filled with air. Boots weighted with leaden soles, and chest and back weights attached to his dress, took the diver down to the required depth.

In its essentials, this is the modern diving dress, although later refinements, particularly in the form of armoured and articulated diving dress, do allow divers to work at greater depths. Yet, even before these modern adaptations, a great deal of underwater work was carried out in the Siebe dress at depths of up to as much as 200 feet (61 m). In dock and pier construction, in underwater repair work, in salvage, and in sponge and pearl fishery, the Siebe closed dress opened a new era in the history of diving. In general, it can be said that for all underwater work up to about 200 feet below the surface, the Siebe dress is still that used and favoured by divers. (For the effect of air supplied at pressure on lungs and blood, see COMPRESSION SICKNESS.)

The diving bell works on the principle of lowering an inverted container with an open bottom into the water. As it descends, so the air inside it is compressed in relation to the depth reached. If, however, air from the surface is pumped into the top of the container at a pressure equal to that exerted by the water at the depth reached, the container will be exactly full of air, the water being pressed down inside the container to its lower edge, any excess pressure of air escaping into the sea under the lower edge of the bell.

The invention of the diving bell is sometimes attributed to Roger Bacon in the mid-13th century, but there is no firm evidence on which this statement can be fully justified. An experiment at Toledo in Spain, in 1538, in which two Greek divers were lowered into the water in a large inverted 'kettle' is fairly well authenticated as it was conducted by John Taisnier in the presence of the Emperor Charles V and a large crowd of spectators. Although it can be said that this experiment was successful in demonstrating the principle of the diving bell, it was not followed up by any useful application of enabling divers to work for long periods submerged.

Francis Bacon, in his *Novum Organum*, describes a diving bell made of metal which could be lowered to the bottom of the sea. It stood on three feet, each about $4\frac{1}{2}$ feet (1·4 m) long, and was, in theory, designed to allow divers to work on the bottom and to refill their lungs with air when they could no longer hold their breath. This could, of course, be applicable only to working in comparatively shallow depths, as at any deeper depth the air in the bell would be compressed to an extent where it was out of reach of the diver standing on the sea bottom.

The first really practical diving bell was undoubtedly that invented by Dr. Edmund *Halley, who was secretary of the Royal Society of England, in 1717. His diving bell was constructed of wood in the form of a truncated cone and sheathed with lead both to give it the necessary weight to sink it to the bottom and to keep it upright in the water. His bell was $4\frac{1}{2}$ feet (1·4 m) diameter at the bottom, 3 feet (0·9 m) at the top, and nearly 9 feet (2·7 m) in height. In the top a glass lens was inserted to provide light for the diver, together with a hand-operated tap to let foul air escape.

Halley provided a most ingenious means of supplying fresh air to his diving bell. He had two barrels lined with lead, each with a bung-hole in the top and bottom. To the top bung-hole was attached a leather pipe which was led into the diving bell, but this pipe was so weighted that it hung down in the water below the level of the bottom bung-hole so that no air could escape. When the diver in the bell required a fresh supply of air, he raised the leather pipe so that the pressure of the water in the bottom of the barrel forced the air out into the bell. As the air from one barrel was exhausted, the second one was lowered, and by thus using the two barrels alternately, a constant supply of fresh air was assured. Halley claimed that he, with four others, was able to remain at the bottom of the sea at a depth of 60 feet (18 m) for an hour and a half at a time without any trouble or inconvenience.

Halley's diving bell was improved by the celebrated engineer John *Smeaton, who in 1778 introduced, in place of Halley's weighted barrels, a pump to force air under pressure into the bell when it was submerged. He used a diving bell of this nature when consulted about repairs to the foundations of Hexham Bridge in Durham, England, and designed a new one ten years later when placed in charged of the construction of Ramsgate Harbour, in Kent. This bell was rectangular instead of cone shaped, and being $4\frac{1}{2}$ feet (1·4 m) long by 3 feet (0·9 m) wide, gave sufficient room inside it for two men to work side by side. It weighed $2\frac{1}{2}$ tons, sufficient to cause it to sink under its own weight, and was supplied by an air pump worked from a boat on the surface.

Although diving bells were used widely for underwater construction, such as the piers of bridges and the building of moles and breakwaters in harbour works, steady improvement in the dress of the assisted diver gradually made their use uneconomic. For about a century from 1780 onwards diving bells proved their value in many major developments on the civil engineering side connected with harbours and bridges, but the growing efficiency of the diving dress, and the ability of the assisted diver to work at ever-increasing depths, coupled with the relatively high cost of construction of the diving bell, has made their use since about the year 1900 very spasmodic.

Salvage worker wearing Augustus Siebe's diving suit; engraving c. 1885

The largest diving bells used in recent years were those constructed in connection with the building of the new harbour at Dover, England, during the first decade of the 20th century. Four of them were used simultaneously, each measuring 17 feet (5·1 m) in length and 10 feet (3·0 m) in width, giving working accommodation for six men in each. Each weighed 35 tons, and they were lit by electric light and connected to the surface by telephone. The depth at which the concrete foundations for the breakwater were laid was 70 feet (21 m).

Armoured articulated shells are used for dives at depths which are below the range of the normal diving suit. When the Peninsular and Orient Company's liner *Egypt* was sunk in 1922 off *Ushant after a collision with a French ship, she lay in 65 fathoms (390 feet or 119 m) of water, well below the maximum depth at which divers wearing a normal diving helmet and rubber suit could operate at that time. Since she was carrying at the time of her loss about 5 tons of gold and 10 tons of silver, the salvage of this treasure was an attractive proposition. It was organized and operated by the Italian firm of Sorima, who had considerable experience of salvage at great depths, and their divers worked from the small, specially fitted salvage ship *Artiglio*. Since the conventional diving suit was quite useless in the case of the *Egypt*, they used armoured shells designed by the German firm of Neufeldt and Kuhnke, fitted with articulated joints to allow a certain degree of movement to the diver.

One of the basic principles of the normal diving suit is that air must be pumped into it at the same pressure as that exerted by the sea at the depth at which the diver is working. This means,

Free diving using aqualungs

naturally, that the diver works under pressure, which both limits the time that he can spend working on the sea bottom and also calls for a long period of decompression before he can be allowed to regain the natural atmospheric pressure. The armoured shells used for the recovery of the gold and silver bullion from the *Egypt* suffered from no such disadvantage. They were strong enough to resist the pressure of the water at depths up to 100 fathoms (180 m), and inside them a diver could work at the ordinary atmospheric pressure, and thus for very much longer periods than with a conventional suit. Nor could he be subject to compression sickness, or the 'bends' as it is known. But a diver enclosed in such a suit lacks mobility, for although the arms and legs are jointed, the necessity for keeping such joints watertight under heavy pressure puts a limit on their movement; nor can he use his hands—all he can do is to manipulate a pair of pincers extending from the end of the arms of his armoured suit through watertight ball joints.

Air inside the armoured shell is used many times, thus making a supply pipe from the sur-face unnecessary. The diver wears a mask which covers nose and mouth, connected to a chamber containing caustic soda or caustic potash. As the diver breathes out, the used air is passed through the caustic soda, which removes the carbonic acid, or carbon dioxide. Oxygen, contained in bottles under pressure, is then released to re-oxygenate the air cleaned by the caustic soda, thus providing a constant supply of pure air inside the armoured shell. See also SALVAGE.

3. Free diving is diving in which the diver operates independently of an air supply from the surface. Before the development of the *aqualung, the free diver wore the normal diving dress of metal helmet and rubber suit, and carried down on his back cylinders of oxygen compressed to a pressure of 120 atmospheres, with which he could rejuvenate the air trapped in his helmet. As the diver exhaled through a canister of caustic soda, the carbon dioxide in the used air was absorbed, and oxygen released from the cylinders on his back made this cleaned air suitable for breathing again.

Free diving, combined with a redesigned dress of skin-tight rubber or neoprene and an oxygen mask, with flippers on the feet to give rapid movement under water, received a great impetus during the Second World War, when it made possible a number of operations of war of a clandestine nature. The great possibilities of this new type of underwater warfare was first demonstrated by divers of the Italian Navy who, with rare courage, penetrated the British naval base at Alexandria in December 1941 and fixed delayed-action mines to the hulls of the British battleships * Queen Elizabeth and Valiant. As a result of the explosions, both ships were seriously damaged and incapacitated for many months. These men, known as 'human torpedoes' (see also CHARIOT), were in fact launched from a submarine off the entrance to Alexandria, and their success in this operation led to further developments in the art of free diving as the exigencies of war called for other tasks in this field.

The Italian 'human torpedoes' were copied by other navies, especially that of Britain, and many notable operations directed against hostile ships were mounted. They led also to the development of the * 'frogman', the individual free diver in his close-fitting rubber suit and flippers, whose main value lay in beach reconnaissance and the underwater clearance of mines and obstacles. In all the great amphibious landings of the later stages of the war, frogmen played an invaluable role in measuring beach gradients, establishing the nature of the beach foundations, and locating and removing seaward defences.

The aqualung was first developed in France in 1943. It consists of three small cylinders, filled with air compressed to a pressure of 150 atmospheres, connected to an air regulator. Two tubes join the regulator to a mouthpiece, and air is supplied to the mouthpiece at the pressure exerted by the depth of water reached by the diver. The nose and eyes are enclosed in a watertight rubber mask with a glass front, and rubber foot fins, or flippers, completed the original dress.

With the aqualung apparatus, the depth limit to which the free diver can safely descend is around 30 fathoms (54 m). To venture to a greater depth is, in the words of a diving expert, 'to have one foot on a tightrope between mortality and oblivion'. French aqualung divers, who are the acknowledged experts in its use, say that the 'fatal limit' is 40 fathoms (73 m), and that only specialists should attempt such a depth.

Perhaps the greatest exponent of aqualung diving, and the inventor, with Emile Gagnan, of the aqualung, is Captain Jacques-Yves * Cousteau, who introduced aqualung diving as a new sport after the Second World War. Today it is a pastime enjoyed by thousands, introducing into man's experience the mysteries and beauties of an entirely new and unknown world. It also has its commercial uses, particularly since the development of offshore oil and gas wells, in the laying of underwater oil and gas mains from the wells to the processing stations ashore. See also BATHYSCAPHE, BATHYSPHERE.

DIXON, GEORGE (c. 1755–1800), British navigator, sailed with Captain James * Cook in his third voyage of discovery, and was made a * post-captain in the British Navy on his return. In 1785 he sailed on a commercial venture in the ship Queen Charlotte to the coasts of British Columbia, partly to develop the fur trade and partly for exploration. Among his discoveries were Queen Charlotte's Island, Port Mulgrave, Norfolk Bay, and Dixon's Archipelago. On his return to England he became a teacher of navigation at Gosport, near Portsmouth, and was the author of The Navigator's Assistant, published in 1791.

DOCK, the area of water in a port or harbour totally enclosed by piers or wharves. Some sailors refer to the wharves themselves as the dock, but in the strict meaning of the term it is the area of water in between. In the U.S.A., however, the word is always used to mean the wharf or pier and does not refer to the enclosed water. See also DRY-DOCK, FLOATING DOCK.

DOCKING KEELS, also known as * bilge keels, are small subsidiary * keels projecting downwards from the * hull of a ship at about the turn of the * bilge, and run parallel with the main keel. They support the weight of the ship on the launching * ways when she is ready to take the water after building, and also assist in supporting the weight of a ship when she is lying on the blocks in * dry-dock. Additionally, they provide extra hull resistance when a ship is rolling in a heavy sea. But see also in this respect, SHIP STABILIZERS.

DOCKYARD, in its naval sense an establishment in a strategic position ashore which serves not only as a base for warships but also provides all services they can require, such as repair, refit, replenishment, etc. Most naval dockyards of any size also have building slips for the construction of warships, and * dry-docks for their servicing. In Britain the naval dockyards are known as the * Royal dockyards, probably an abbreviation of Royal Naval dockyards. Civilian dockyards exist around the world to provide the same services for merchant ships, though often without the building facilities, being geared more to the repair and refit of ships than to their construction. Yet all building yards, where ships are built, normally have their own dockyards where the ships they launch are completed with machinery, necessary fittings, etc.

The world's first true naval dockyard, where ships were laid down, built, and repaired, was at *Deptford, near London. It became a dockyard during the reign of Henry VII (1485–1509) and preceded the naval dockyard at *Portsmouth by a few years, though the first naval dock was constructed at Portsmouth two years before a similar dock was installed at Deptford. Both these dockyards were earlier than the highly organized dockyards at *Venice and *Genoa set up in those places for their *galley fleets.

DODD, ROBERT (1748–1815), British painter and engraver, was primarily a marine painter in oils, but was also a very competent engraver in line and aquatint. In 1779 he went to live at Wapping, where there also resided another artist, Ralph Dodd, who may have been his brother, and their works are sometimes difficult to distinguish. Robert's paintings of naval battles were much admired and he made aquatints and engravings of them. He first exhibited at the Royal Academy in 1780 and continued to do so until 1800. He produced a remarkable set of pictures depicting the great storm encountered by Admiral *Graves's squadron on 16 September 1782 when returning to England from the West Indies with a convoy of *prizes, of which many of the prizes and two *ships of the line were lost. He also painted pictures of the battles of *Cape St. Vincent and the *Nile, Hyde Parker's action off the *Dogger Bank in 1781, Lord *Rodney's victory at the *Saints in 1782, and the battle of *Trafalgar.

DODGER, a painted canvas screen erected at chest height around the forward side and wing ends of a ship's *bridge as a protection against the weather before the days of glass-enclosed bridges. All small steamships, and indeed some large ones, used dodgers for protection up to the 1920s, when strengthened glass was introduced which would not shatter under the weight of water thrown up by the motion of the ship in rough weather. The totally protected bridge did not come into general use in small vessels, such as fishing *trawlers and *drifters, *tugs, etc., until after the Second World War and some older passenger ferries plying in sheltered waters still have open bridges protected by dodgers.

DOG, to, the operation of backing the tail of a block with several turns around a *stay or *shroud, with the tail going with the lay of the rope. This is one way of *clapping on a *purchase where additional hauling power is required.

DOG SHORES, two blocks of timber which support either side of a ship on the launching *ways when she is being built and which prevent the ship from starting down the ways when the keel blocks, on which she rests while building, are being removed ready for launching. When they are knocked out, the ship begins to slide down the ways into the water. See also DAGGER.

DOG VANE, a small temporary *vane, often of cork and feathers threaded on a thin line and attached to a short staff, fixed on the weather *gunwale of sailing ships to enable the helmsman to judge the direction of the wind.

'The Dog-vane staff the Quartermaster moves,
 The wind upon the larboard quarter proves.'
H. B. Gascoigne, *The Navigator's Fame*, 1825.

DOG WATCHES, the two half *watches of two hours each into which the period from 4 p.m. to 8 p.m. is divided. The purpose of dividing this watch into two is to produce an uneven number of watches in the 24 hours, seven instead of six, thereby ensuring that watchkeepers in ships, whether organized in two or three watches, do not keep the same watches every day. These two watches are known as the First Dog and Last Dog, and *never*, except by landlubbers, as First Dog and Second Dog. How they came by these names is not known; they were certainly in use by the 17th century. One suggestion that they were called dog watches because they were curtailed, though ingenious, does not appear to have any foundation in fact.

DOGGER, a development of the original *ketch, square-rigged on the main and carrying a *lugsail on the *mizen, with two *jibs on a long *bowsprit. Short, wide-beamed, and small, she was a fishing vessel engaged in *trawling or lining on the *Dogger Bank in the North Sea, hence her name. The name dates from the early 17th century, but was virtually synonymous with ketch until the latter began to increase in size (over about 50 tons) in the mid-17th century.

The Dutch *dogger*, a fishing vessel operating a trawl, gave its name to the Dogger Bank, and in its turn the Dogger Bank gave its name to the fishing vessel above.

DOGGER BANK, an extensive shoal in the North Sea about 60 miles east of the coast of Northumberland. It has a minimum depth over it of about 6 fathoms, but large portions of it lie at depths varying from 10 to 20 fathoms. It is particularly well known as a rich fishing ground, and it owes its name to this fact, being derived from the Dutch word *dogger*, meaning a *trawler. A battle was fought in 1781 between the Dutch fleet and the British fleet off the southern end of the bank, but a more famous encounter occurred during the night of 21 October 1904 when the Russian Baltic fleet commanded by Admiral *Rozhestvensky, *en route* to the Far East during the Russo-Japanese war (1904–5), fired on the Hull fishing fleet, sinking one trawler and damaging others, in the belief that they were Japanese *torpedoboats. This nearly led to war between Britain and Russia, but the affair was referred to an international commission of five admirals, and was finally settled by Russian apologies and payment of damages.

During the First World War (1914–18), a *battle-cruiser action between the British Battle-cruiser Force and the German First Scouting Group was fought on 24 January 1915. The German ships left their anchorage in the Jade on 23 January with the object of attacking British patrols and fishing vessels in the area of the Dogger Bank. Forewarned of the move by Intelligence sources, the British Admiralty was able to make dispositions to intercept the German force. The battle-cruisers *Lion* (flagship of Rear Admiral David *Beatty), *Tiger*, *Princess Royal*, *New Zealand* (flagship of Rear Admiral Arthur Moore), and *Indomitable*, accompanied by the 1st Light Cruiser Squadron were ordered to rendezvous with the Harwich *cruiser and *destroyer force under Commodore R. Y. *Tyrwhitt, to the north-east of the Dogger Bank at dawn on 24 January. Soon afterwards the German force consisting of the battle-cruisers *Seydlitz* (flagship of Rear Admiral Franz von *Hipper), *Moltke*, *Derfflinger*, and the armoured cruiser *Blücher*, accompanied by four light cruisers and two destroyer flotillas, were sighted heading westward at high speed. Rather than risk an engagement with what he believed was a superior force, Hipper turned for home but was overhauled by the fast division of Beatty's battle-cruisers which opened fire at extreme range. A running fight ensued during which the *Lion* received severe damage which reduced her speed and forced her to drop astern. On the German side both the *Seydlitz* and the *Blücher* were severely damaged but the former managed to keep her speed, the *Blücher* slowing down. Moore, now in command of the British force and misinterpreting Beatty's signalled intentions which were to pursue the fleeing enemy and leave the slower *Indomitable* to finish off the *Blücher*, broke off the chase. By the time Beatty had transferred his flag to a destroyer and rejoined, it was too late. The *Blücher* was sunk, 189 of her crew being rescued by British destroyers, but the remaining German ships all escaped. The crippled *Lion* was towed back to base by the *Indomitable*. Total British casualties were 15 killed and 80 wounded, while the German total was 954 killed and 80 wounded. From the damaged *Seydlitz* the Germans learned a lesson which stood them in good stead at the battle of *Jutland, which was that magazines were vulnerable to the flash of bursting shells and burning cordite. Their ships were rendered safe by fitting anti-flash arrangements in the ammunition trunks; the British did not learn this lesson until Jutland, when five good ships were lost through unprotected magazines.

'DOGGER BANK ITCH', the fisherman's name for the skin abrasions suffered on hands, wrists, and arms caused by freezing salt water when working with *trawl nets and *warps. The expression is also used by yachtsmen suffering same salt water abrasions when working the gear in yachts.

DOGHOUSE, a yachting term introduced from the U.S.A. to denote the short *deckhouse or main hatchway which is raised above the level of the cabin top or coachroof.

DOGS, (1) the metal hand clips fitted to *bulkheads and decks around watertight doors, small hatch covers, etc., which when turned, force the rubber gasket lining the doors and hatches hard up against the sealing to ensure a watertight seal. **(2)** Metal bars, with their ends turned down and ending in a point, are also known as dogs. They were used for holding a baulk of timber steady while carpenters shaped it with an *adze. They are, of course, still in use for temporarily securing timber against unwanted movement, as much ashore as at sea.

DOG-STOPPER, a heavy rope, secured round the mainmast of a sailing ship and used to back up the deck *stopper on the *anchor cable when the ship rode in a heavy sea in the days before chain cable and *cable-holders. It was not in any way a permanent fitting and was used only as an additional safety measure to secure the ship when anchored in very rough weather.

DOLDRUMS, the belt of calm which lies inside the *trade winds of the northern and southern hemisphere. This area, which lies close to the equator except in the western Pacific where it is south of the equator, had great significance during those years when the trade of the world was carried by sailing ships; today they are of no significance except, perhaps, for occasional yachts. The areas immediately north and south of the trade winds also used to be known as doldrums but are now known as variables. The term is also used to signify a state of depression or stagnation, an analogy of the general depression of the crews of ships lying motionless while in the areas of the doldrums, unable to find wind to fill their sails.

DOLLY, a timber similar to a single *bollard which is set horizontally in the *bulwarks of a ship and used as a convenient means for securing temporarily the *fall of a *purchase by taking a jamming turn round it when there was no *cleat conveniently placed. With the growing mechanization of modern ship handling and the simpler rigging plan following the decline of the square rig, dollies are rarely to be found in ships today.

DOLPHIN, (1) a sea mammal of the genus *Delphinus*, small cetaceous animals resembling porpoises which inhabit the warmer seas and have the engaging and spectacular habit of leaping clean out of the water. Brass castings in the form of a dolphin standing on its head have for centuries been a favourite form of naval decoration, and by some are held to be a symbol of *admiralty. Admirals' *barges, in the Royal and some other navies, always had these brass castings as supporters of the canopy in the *sternsheets. **(2)** A large wooden pile, or collection of piles, serving as a *mooring post for ships, or occasionally as a beacon. **(3)** Small brass guns carried in a ship and fitted with two lifting handles over the trunnions. They were used mainly as anti-personnel guns during the 15th, 16th, and early 17th centuries, much like a *murderer or *robinet. **(4)** The plaited rope strap (also known as dolphin of the mast) round the mast of a square-rigged ship to prevent nip between the lower *yard and the mast and at the same time to secure the *puddening round the mast which prevented the lower yard falling to the deck if the *jeers and *slings were both shot away. **(5)** A small light rowing boat of ancient times. It was from this name that arose the story recounted by Pliny of a boy going daily to school across the Lake of Lucerne on a dolphin.

DOLPHIN, H.M.S., now the name of the British submarine headquarters at Fort Blockhouse, Gosport. There have been some 22 ships of the name in the Navy, the twentieth being a sloop launched in 1882 which in 1912 became the first submarine depot ship at Fort Blockhouse. She was sold in 1925, her place being taken by the *Pandora*, which was then renamed *Dolphin*. Since then, although the base is entirely housed in buildings on shore, various small craft have borne the name *Dolphin* as name ships for the submarine base. An earlier *Dolphin*, a 6th *rate of 511 tons and twenty-four guns, was launched at Woolwich in 1751. After seeing action in the fighting off *Minorca in May 1756, she took part in two circumnavigations of the world, those of Commodore the Hon. John *Byron in 1764, and Captain Samuel *Wallis in 1766–8. She was broken up at Woolwich in 1777.

DOLPHIN STRIKER, a short perpendicular spar under the *cap of the *bowsprit of a sailing vessel used for holding down or guying the *jib-boom by means of *martingales. It was a necessary spar to support the rigging needed to counteract the upward pull on the jib-boom of the fore top-gallant stay. The name, of course, comes from the position of the spar—pointing vertically downwards towards the sea just beyond the *bows of the vessel, i.e., it would strike a *dolphin were one to leap out of the water just beneath it. For illus. see BOWSPRIT.

DONEGAL, a county in the north-west of Ireland, in the waters off which a naval battle was fought on 12 October 1798 when a French attempt to land troops in Ireland in order to take advantage of the unrest in that country during the Revolutionary War, was frustrated by Commodore Sir John *Warren with three *ships of the line and five *frigates. The invading force comprised the French ship of the line *Hoche* and eight frigates, all crowded with troops, under the command of Commodore Jean Bompard. The French ships were first sighted in bad weather off Tory Island at noon on 11 October and a *general chase was ordered. The invaders were overhauled early the following morning, and an action ensued, both squadrons being in rather straggling order.

The *Hoche*, which had already lost her main topmast in the gale on the previous day, struck her colours at 11 a.m. and was taken as a *prize, and by 12.30 p.m. three of the French frigates had also hauled down their colours and prize crews placed on board. The others escaped, though three more were captured a few days later. The remaining two frigates, despairing of being able to land any of their troops in Ireland, returned to France.

DÖNITZ, KARL (1891–   ), German grand admiral and last Chancellor of the German Third Reich, was, on the outbreak of the First World War (1914–18), a lieutenant in the light *cruiser *Breslau* when, with the *_Goeben_, she escaped to the Dardanelles after giving the slip to the British Mediterranean Fleet. In 1918 he commanded the submarine *U.68*, sunk by the British merchant ship *Queensland* on 4 October 1918 while operating with *U.48* against a convoy in the Mediterranean. This was one of the earliest examples of *U-boats working together against a convoy, a method of attack to which Dönitz had given much thought although he was not the first to use it. After having been a prisoner-of-war in Britain, he was released in the summer of 1919 on grounds of ill health and returned to naval service in Germany, believing that U-boats, banned under the treaty of Versailles, would soon be once again part of the German Navy. In fact he was obliged to wait sixteen years. In the early 1930s he built up the anti-submarine school, training officers and men who were to form the nucleus of the new U-boat arm which came into existence officially in June 1935 and which Dönitz was appointed to command on 1 January 1936.

When the Second World War began, Germany possessed only fifty-seven U-boats. Dönitz, however, calculated that at least 300 would be needed for an effective *blockade of Britain. After a year of war the total number of U-boats in service was still only fifty-seven, losses and new construction having balanced each other exactly. In spite of the few boats available, the period of the U-boat war between October 1940 and March 1941 was known afterwards by the Germans as the 'happy time'. Frequently there were no more than three to six boats in contact with allied shipping at a time, but in October 1940 eight U-boats sank sixty-three ships totalling 352,407 tons during the month. Much of this success could be attributed to the shortage of British escort vessels, but Dönitz had trained some brilliant young captains and he introduced novel forms of warfare which were henceforward to be essential features of the U-boat battle. Dönitz began with the problem of finding the enemy. Hitherto a submarine had been sent to an area and remained there waiting for an enemy to come in sight. Dönitz arranged that the U-boats should be continuously in touch with each other by wireless and distributed over a great area, through some part of which enemy shipping might be expected to pass. When a submarine spotted the enemy it called other boats to the scene to join in the attack, forming a *'wolf pack' which, when possible, attacked on the surface at night. This was the second great novelty introduced by Dönitz, exploiting the facts that when on the surface a U-boat could not be detected by *asdic (as *sonar was then known), that her surface speed was much greater than when submerged, and that on the surface at night a U-boat presented a very small silhouette and target and was virtually invisible to the defending escort vessels.

Throughout the war, even in the early stages when there were so few U-boats available, Dönitz always held back a large proportion of them, often as much as half, for training and trials purposes. He never believed in a short war and always resisted the temptation to throw all his forces into the battle at once, leaving no reserves.

The year 1941 saw the continuation of the hard struggle in the North Atlantic. Dönitz realized that here the whole outcome of the war was to be decided, and he was always very loth to detach more than a few boats from this main theatre of war. When he did so it was usually for political reasons, for example, the dispatch of boats at the end of 1941 to support the Italians in the Mediterranean, or when special opportunities offered, such as the entry of the U.S.A. into the war, when the tanker traffic off the Atlantic seaboard and in the Caribbean Sea offered an extraordinarily rich target until the Americans were able to organize a *convoy system and an effective coastal blackout.

At the beginning of 1943, Admiral Erich *Raeder having resigned as a protest against Hitler's orders to place the remaining German heavy surface ships out of commission, Dönitz was appointed to succeed him and began his career as commander-in-chief by persuading Hitler to cancel his order to pay off the big ships. March 1943 saw the highest point, in the loss rate of allied shipping, of the U-boat war and, in May, when the pendulum swung heavily towards allied defence measures, came the first admission of how heavy the losses in U-boats had been. As a result Dönitz ordered a suspension of attacks on Atlantic convoys while new offensive measures were being worked out (see also ATLANTIC, BATTLE OF THE).

As commander-in-chief of the navy, Dönitz was responsible for the naval element of all anti-invasion measures. Both he and Hitler appreciated that the Atlantic was the first line of defence in the west; Dönitz saw, however, that U-boats would never be able to stop an invasion but could only hamper it. After the invasion of Western Europe had begun in June 1944, the defeats of the German Army on both the western and eastern fronts, together with the bomb plot against Hitler on 20 July 1944, severely restricted the number of generals in whose ability and loyalty Hitler still had confidence. Dönitz, on the other hand, had always been an ardent adherent of the Nazi party, to the annoyance of many of his own officers, and in the last days of the Third Reich he came to be almost the only senior officer on whom Hitler could rely. Dönitz continued to be optimistic about a successful intensification of the U-boat war and as late as 28 March 1945 was making plans for the post-war German Navy.

On 30 April 1945 Hitler committed suicide in Berlin, having appointed Dönitz as his successor. In the few days left to the Reich, Dönitz tried to get as many troops and civilians as possible out of the area being overrun by the Russians, but the mass surrenders of the Germans began at Lüneberg Heath on 3 May leaving him too little time. The Dönitz government continued to function in Flensburg until its members were arrested by the British on 23 May. Dönitz was placed on trial before the International Military Tribunal at Nüremberg. Sentenced to ten years imprisonment for war crimes, he was released in 1956.

DONKEY ENGINE, a small auxiliary steam engine with its own small boiler, used for furnishing power for a variety of smaller mechanical duties on board a vessel in harbour for which it would be uneconomic to produce steam from the main boilers.

DONKEY FRIGATE, a class of small ships built for the Royal Navy at the end of the 18th and beginning of the 19th centuries. They carried twenty-eight guns and were, more accurately, ship-rigged * sloops built * frigate-fashion, having guns protected by the upper deck, i.e., on a single gundeck, with additional guns on * forecastle and * quarterdeck.

DONKEY-HOUSE, the name of the structure on deck in which the * donkey engine is contained. It is only in smaller merchant ships that such an engine-house is fitted as in all larger steamships there is normally enough auxiliary machinery requiring steam to warrant firing up one of the ship's main boilers.

DONKEY'S BREAKFAST, the merchant seaman's name for his mattress in the days when it was normally stuffed with straw. Such rudimentary conditions for seamen existed right up into the 20th century in a majority of ships and it was mainly the growth in power of trade unions of seamen, aided by the passage of Merchant Shipping Acts or their equivalents in the various maritime countries, which led to an improvement in the conditions on board, making such ship-board economies as straw-filled mattresses things of the past. Straw-filled mattresses pertained only to the wooden bunks, lining the * forecastle or * deckhouse, in which merchant seamen were accommodated; they were not used in the hammocks in which naval seamen slept, these having a thin tick stuffed with horsehair as mattress.

DORIA, ANDREA (1466–1560), Genoese admiral, was in command of the Genoese fleet in operations against the Turks and the * Barbary pirates between 1510 and 1520. For some years in the service of France after the French occupation of Genoa, he became disgruntled as a result of French meanness over his pay and sailed for home, driving the French occupiers out of Genoa and setting up a republican state, of which he became chief censor. He commanded the Genoese fleet again in various actions against the Turks, and was present at the capture of Tunis in 1535. He remained in active command of the fleet until the age of 89, commanding it in expeditions against the Barbary pirates in 1550 and against the French in Corsica in 1553–5. Even in his old age he was a man of indomitable energy and courage.

His name was given to a 23,600-ton Italian battleship which was surrendered to the British Mediterranean Fleet in September 1943 after the defeat of Italy in the Second World War. It was also the name of an Italian transatlantic liner which was sunk off New York in July 1956 after a collision with the Swedish liner *Stockholm*.

DORLING, HENRY TAPPRELL (1883–1968), British naval captain, author of sea stories and broadcaster, wrote a great many well-known books under the pseudonym 'Taffrail'. Born at Duns, Berwickshire, he joined H.M.S. * *Britannia* as a naval cadet in 1897 and saw active service in South Africa and China, taking part in the relief of Peking in 1900. During the First World War (1914–18) he commanded destroyers of the Harwich Force, receiving the D.S.O. for his services. He retired in 1929 by which time he had established himself as a writer of popular stories of the sea. His first novel, *Pincher Martin O.D.*, was a considerable success and he followed it with many others including *Pirates* (1929), *Endless Story* (1931), *Seventy North* (1934), and *Mid-Atlantic* (1936).

Recalled to duty during the Second World War, he served in the Ministry of Information and after the landing in North Africa in 1942 joined the staff of Admiral Sir Andrew * Cunningham, commander-in-chief in the Mediterranean, as press liaison officer. At the end of the war he was appointed naval correspondent of the *Observer*. His post-war books included *The Battle of the Atlantic* (1946), *Western Mediterranean 1942–45* (1948), and *Arctic Convoy* (1956). His authoritative work *Ribbons and Medals*, first published in 1916, was brought up-to-date and republished in 1956/7. His literary work was remarkable not only for its historical accuracy but also for the vivid way in which he recaptured actual day-to-day work at sea.

DORY, (1) a small flat-bottomed boat associated with the coast of New England and used widely for line fishing on the * Grand Banks off the coast of Newfoundland. One of their great advantages for this purpose was that they could be stacked on board fishing craft one within the other, the collective noun being a nest of dories. **(2)** A fish, *Zeus faber*, known as a John Dory. This name comes from the French *jaune d'orée*, by which name it was known to the French fishermen of the Banks on account of its golden-coloured scales. **(3)** More recently the name given to a type of hard-* chine dinghy with flared sides, suitable for an outboard motor and widely used by yachtsmen and amateur fishermen, being properly considered as a useful weight-carrying work-boat.

DOUBLE, to, or **DOUBLING,** the operation of covering a ship with extra planking or plates when the original skin is weak or worn. In wooden ships the term was only used when the new planking was more than two inches in thickness. To double a cape or other point of land, to sail a vessel round it so that on completion the land is between the ship and her original position.

DOUBLE BOTTOM, the space between the outer skin on the bottom of a ship and the watertight plating over the *floors. A double bottom serves two purposes, first as a protection against disaster when the outer bottom is holed by running aground or striking some object in the sea, and second as a convenient stowage for liquid ballast. The construction of double bottoms is now standard design practice in the building of all ships of any size. The first ship in which double bottoms were incorporated in the original design was the *Great Eastern*, I. K. *Brunel's great ship launched in 1858. See SHIPBUILDING.

DOUBLE CAPSTAN, two *capstan *barrels on the same central shaft designed to provide a capstan on two adjacent *decks. In the old sailing *ships of the line double capstans were almost always fitted to provide lifting power on an upper and a lower deck with a single installation.

DOUBLE CLEWS or **CLUES,** an old sea term for getting married. *Clews, with their *nettles, are the cords which support a seaman's *hammock and thus a double set of clews, in seamen's humour, would be required to support the weight of two people, a man and his wife, in the same hammock. Double clews were also supposed to give a wider spread to a hammock and the extra width thus obtained may also have had something to do with the origin of this seaman's term. A seaman entered, or embarked, in double clews when he got married.

DOUBLED-CLEWED JIB, a sail introduced in 1934 by Mr. (later Sir) Thomas *Sopwith for the *America's Cup races in that year between his yacht *Endeavour* and the American *Rainbow* with Mr. Harold *Vanderbilt at the helm. The sail consisted virtually of an extra large *jib with the clew cut off to form a four-sided foresail *sheeted with two sheets. The new fourth side, corresponding to the *leech of a normal foursided fore-and-aft sail, was either loose or laced to a small boom sheeted at either end. It proved to be a powerful sail and was thought during the *Endeavour's* trial races to be more efficient than the normal triangular jib, but in the first of the Cup races the *Rainbow* set a single *Genoa jib in place of the normal jib and *staysail and more than held her own against Mr. Sopwith's new rig. The double-clewed jib was given the slang name 'Greta Garbo'. It never caught on as a racing sail.

DOUBLING, the name given to that portion of the mast of a large sailing vessel where an upper mast overlaps the lower, as a topmast with a lower mast, a *topgallant mast with a topmast. It is a word more often used in the plural than in the singular, as in normal square-rig each mast will have two doublings.

DOUGHTY, THOMAS, executed for mutiny at Port St. Julian in 1578, see DRAKE, Sir Francis.

DOUGLAS, Sir CHARLES (*c.* 1725–89), British rear admiral, was known for his gunnery improvements. As Lord *Rodney's flag captain at the battle of the *Saints in 1782, it was Douglas who was credited with advising Rodney to break through and disrupt the French line of battle at the height of the action, a tactic which revolutionized the old sterility of naval battle in line ahead. His enthusiasm for gunnery came near to fanaticism. When commanding the 98-gun *Duke* (1779–81) he increased the rate of fire by constant drill and by inventions and sheer gadgetry financed by himself, and he also increased the angles through which the guns could be trained. When Rodney chose him for his staff in his flagship *Formidable* in 1781 he adapted her guns in the same way. At the battle of the Saints the improvements, many of which had been copied by other ships in the fleet, paid handsome dividends and the French, by confession of their own officers, were completely outgunned. To judge by their subsequent adoption throughout the Royal Navy the most important changes Douglas brought about were goose-quill tubes instead of loose powder for the vents of cannon, flannel-bottom cartridges which left no debris in the bore, and the reintroduction of flint-locks in place of the slow match for instantaneous discharge.

Earlier in his career he had seen service in the Seven Years War (1756–63) with Admiral Sir Charles *Saunders at the capture of *Quebec in 1759, commanding the small 16-gun ship *Boscawen*, and in the spring of 1776 during the War of American Independence (1775–82), commanding the 50-gun *Isis*, he had reached Quebec through the ice on the St. Lawrence to relieve it from the siege of the American forces under General Montgomery. In the same year he was in charge of the construction of a British squadron on *Lake Champlain, required to support a British capture of Port Ticonderoga. Many delays, however, caused in the main by the enterprise and exertions of Benedict *Arnold, the American defender, and his home-built squadron of *galleys and *gondolas, made the capture of Ticonderoga in 1776 impossible for the British. This delay was perhaps the main reason for the British failure in the campaign which ended in American independence from colonial rule.

DOVER, an English seaport at the eastern end of the English Channel, and one of the *Cinque Ports of England. Originally it became a port for Roman ships during the Roman occupation of Britain because the sand and shingle bank formed by the outfall of the River Dour provided well-sheltered water behind it. It was the scene, in 1217, of a famous naval battle between the ships of the Cinque Ports and a French fleet led by Eustace the Monk, and again, in 1652, of the action between a British fleet under the command of Robert *Blake and a Dutch fleet commanded by Marten *Tromp. This battle was the first action of the First Anglo-Dutch war (1652–4) and was fought for what was known then as 'the honour of the flag', a requirement that all foreign ships should salute the English flag when it was encountered at sea in English waters by lowering topsails and dipping the flag. Tromp's ships were sheltering from bad weather under the South Foreland, and when Tromp sighted Blake's ships he weighed and stood over towards Calais to avoid making the necessary salute. But receiving information from another Dutch ship of an English attack on a Dutch convoy off Start Point a week earlier, he reversed his course and steered close to the English ships. On coming within hail, the Dutchman's topsails were in process of being lowered, but there was some delay in striking Tromp's flag. Blake thereupon opened fire and a general action ensued. The result was in favour of the English, the Dutch losing two ships. One of these, however, was recovered later, having been abandoned by the *prize crew who thought that she was sinking.

At the end of the 19th century, Dover was selected by the British Admiralty as a useful halfway naval base between the *chops of the Channel and the North Sea, a move forced upon it by the German naval rearmament before the start of the First World War (1914–18). This selection of Dover as a minor naval base was the cause of the building of the great *mole, with an eastern and western entrance, which today forms Dover harbour.

For centuries Dover, as the British end of the shortest sea route to France across the English Channel, has been the principal port for passenger traffic between the two countries, and today is a terminal port for an extensive system of car ferries and *hovercraft to the European continent. Dover castle, built on the cliffs overlooking the port, is the official residence of the holder of the historic title Warden of the Cinque Ports.

Dover is one of the standard ports for which the times and heights of high and low water are predicted for every day of the year and printed in the annual *Tide Tables.*

DOWNES, JOHN (1784–1854), American naval officer, was born in Massachusetts. Appointed midshipman in June 1802, he served in the Mediterranean during the war with Tripoli, where he was commended for his gallantry and promoted to lieutenant in 1807. He was first lieutenant of the *Essex,* under Captain David *Porter, when she sailed in October 1812 from the Delaware capes on her famous cruise to the Pacific. In April 1813 Downes, in the boats of the *Essex,* captured two British vessels. He fitted one of these (*Georgiana*) as a *cruiser, and in June captured three more ships, one of which was an 11-gun *privateer. Meanwhile, Porter had captured the *Atlantic* and renamed her *Essex Junior.* Downes then took command of the *Essex Junior,* and cruised in her for several months, sometimes alone and sometimes in company with Porter. When, in March 1814, the two ships tried to run out of Valparaiso, Chile, where they were blockaded by H.M.S. *Phoebe* and *Cherub,* Downes played a gallant part in the battle that ensued. After a fierce struggle of nearly two and a half hours the Americans were forced to surrender to the superior long-range guns of the British.

Downes next commanded the *Epervier* in *Decatur's squadron during operations against Algiers in May 1815, and was promoted into the *Guerrière* after the capture of the Algerian flagship *Mashuda* on 17 June 1815. His last active service was command of the *frigate *Potomac* and of the Pacific station. With orders to obtain satisfaction for an outrage that the Malays had committed on an American merchant ship, Downes stormed the town of Quallah Batoo, Sumatra, and destroyed the greater part of it.

DOWNHAUL, (1) a single rope fitted in large sailing ships for hauling down a *jib or *staysail when shortening sail. It was led up along a stay and through the *cringles of the sail and then made fast to the upper corner of the sail. Downhauls were also rigged for similar use with *studding-sails, being led through blocks on the outer *clews of the sails to the outer yardarms of the studding-sail. But in general, any rope fitted for the purpose of hauling down a sail would be called a downhaul. In racing yachts, the rope attached to a spinnaker pole to hold it down is known as a downhaul, and frequently the boom *vang is also called a downhaul. **(2)** A term sometimes used in small craft for a greatcoat, but the origin of this curious bit of seaman's language is obscure.

DOWNS, the anchorage on the east coast of England which lies inside the *Goodwin Sands and between the North and South *Foreland. The Goodwin provides shelter from all easterly winds, the land shelter from the west. It was a particularly busy anchorage during the days of sail, as it was there that incoming merchant vessels picked up their pilot for the Thames and outgoing merchant vessels dropped theirs. This was always done while at anchor, unlike today when ships need not stop to embark a pilot. The

Downs was also a convoy assembly area in wartime and a convenient naval anchorage for ships operating in the southern North Sea during the days of sailing navies.

DRABLER or **DRABBLER**, an additional length of canvas laced on to the foot of the *bonnet of a sail in a square-rigged ship to give it a greater area when *running free in light winds. 'As the bonnet is to the *course, so in all respects is the drabler to the bonnet.' Nathaniel Boteler, *Six Dialogues about Sea-Services*, 1685.

DRAG, the amount by which a ship floats lower *aft than *forward. Almost all ships are designed, when in proper trim, to draw slightly more effect in turning the ship. In sailing ship *propellers a better grip on the water and thus avoid creating *cavitation and partly to give the *rudder a slightly deeper immersion and thus more effect in turning the ship. In sailing ship days a hard-headed ship with a tendency to *gripe and carry excessive *weather helm was eased by being trimmed down *aft to give her more drag; similarly a light-headed ship with a tendency to *pay off, needing *lee helm to correct, could be improved by giving her less drag through being trimmed down forward.

DRAG, to, an expression used to indicate that the *flukes of a ship's *anchor are not holding in the ground. It is the anchor itself which drags when the flukes do not hold; the ship drags her anchor, although colloquially the last two words are frequently omitted, e.g., 'the ship is dragging', meaning in fact that the anchor is dragging, or the ship is dragging her anchor. See also COME HOME, TO.

DRAG CHAINS, lengths of chain shackled to weighted drags which act as a brake and bring a ship to a halt after she has been launched into the water down the *ways. They are mostly used when the building slip is in a narrow waterway where there is not sufficient room for the ship to be launched without stopping her, for fear of her running ashore on the opposite bank.

DRAGON, see INTERNATIONAL DRAGON CLASS.

DRAKAR, the Danish *longship, used by the Danes in their many assaults against England, the first in the year 787 when three drakars raided the southern coast of Wessex. These raids from the sea continued for over 100 years and only ended when *Canute, the greatest of the Danish kings, was accepted as king of England. Drakars were almost identical with the Viking longships in build, size, and rig. The name almost certainly comes from the custom in Danish, as well as Norwegian, longships of decorating the stemhead with a carving of a dragon or serpent, the carving being continued, in the more important vessels of a fleet, the whole length of the longship with the tail carved at the sternpost.

DRAKE, Sir FRANCIS (*c*. 1543–96), English admiral, was born at Crowndale, near Tavistock, Devon, though the date of his birth is uncertain. Nor is anything known about his early years beyond the assumption that, after his father became a preacher at Chatham, he served his apprenticeship in the Thames coastal trade. Drake was a cousin of John *Hawkins of Plymouth and after a voyage to the west coast of Africa with John Lovell in 1566 he was given the command of the 50-ton *Judith* on Hawkins's third slave-trading voyage in 1567. This voyage was not a financial success, only the ships commanded by Hawkins and Drake returning safely after being attacked by the Spaniards at San Juan de Ulloa on the coast of Mexico. Having inherited strong Protestant convictions from his father, Drake thenceforward combined them with a passionate desire for revenge on the Spaniards for what he regarded as their treachery on this occasion.

The next few years were spent in *privateering raids on the Spanish Main, of which many romantic stories are told, particularly about his attack on Nombre de Dios in 1572, his interception of the mule trains transporting silver across the Isthmus of Panama, and his first sight of the Pacific, when he prayed that he might be the first 'to sail an English ship in those seas'.

His opportunity came in 1577 when he was engaged by a syndicate headed by Elizabeth I to make the first circumnavigation of the world by an Englishman. Many details of this famous voyage are obscure because they were suppressed at the time for reasons of state, since much of the voyage was to be through seas claimed exclusively by Spain. We do not know if any official commission was ever issued, or if Drake himself kept a log. One of the declared objects of the voyage was to discover the legendary continent of *Terra Australis Incognita, another to return through the *North-West passage, but these were undoubtedly put out to disguise the real object, which was plunder. In the event it became an exceedingly successful privateering expedition, which not only paid £47 for every £1 invested but also put England on the map as a rising sea power.

Drake sailed from Plymouth on 13 December 1577 in command of the 100-ton *Pelican* (renamed *Golden Hind* in the Pacific), together with four smaller ships and about 160 men. Since he had no charts, a Portuguese pilot was kidnapped and later put on shore when they reached the Pacific. At Plymouth, in a mixed

Sir Francis Drake; the 'Jewel' portrait

crew of experienced seamen and gentlemen of the court who had attached themselves to the expedition as representatives of the Royal syndicate, Drake had also signed on two of his closest friends, the brothers Thomas and John Doughty. The whole undertaking had been planned in great secrecy between Elizabeth and her syndicate and Drake, so as to keep it unknown to Spain. Thomas Doughty, to whom Drake had explained the true nature of the voyage in confidence, revealed the secret to Lord Burleigh, the Lord Treasurer of England, who, aghast at the effect of such a voyage on English relations with Spain, already exacerbated by Drake's previous voyages, did all in his power to prevent the expedition taking place, and apparently persuaded Doughty to disrupt it should it succeed in getting away.

Almost as soon as the ships had cleared the Channel, Doughty began making trouble and inciting the crews to mutiny. After a long and difficult passage, in the course of which Drake accused Doughty of being a sorcerer and creating contrary winds and storms, the expedition reached Port St. Julian, close to the entrance of the Magellan Straits. It was at this spot that Ferdinand *Magellan had quelled a mutiny in his

own circumnavigation, and the remains of the gallows on which he had hanged his mutineers were found by Drake and his men. With the fate of the whole expedition hanging in the balance, Drake realized that it was time to strike at the discord which was bedevilling his ships. He had Thomas Doughty arrested, convened a 'court of law' complete with a jury of twelve men, and charged Doughty with treason and mutiny. He was acquitted on the charge of treason but found guilty on that of mutiny, and on the following day was beheaded.

The next four weeks were spent in Port St. Julian refitting the ships for the adventure into the Pacific, but the execution of Doughty had not succeeded in removing the discord between the professional crews and the gentlemen of the court. Drake was forced to act again if the expedition was to succeed. At the end of the month he mustered the entire expedition and made it the occasion of a remarkable speech to the men, one of the best known of any ever made at sea. After reminding the men of the desperate nature of their voyage into unknown waters and of the recent mutinous troubles, he continued: 'For by the life of God, it doth even take my wits from me to think on it. Here is such controversy between the sailors and the gentlemen, and such stomaching between the gentlemen and sailors, it doth make me mad to hear it. But, my masters, I must have it left. For I must have the gentleman to haul and draw with the mariner, and the mariner with the gentleman. What! let us show ourselves all to be of a company and let us not give occasion to the enemy to rejoice at our decay and overthrow. I would know him that would refuse to set his hand to a rope, but I know there is not any such here . . . .'

Having sailed through the Straits of Magellan, he was driven south by a storm to about latitude 57° S. thus proving that Tierra del Fuego was an island and not a part of the great southern continent or Terra Australis Incognita as it was becoming known. The smaller ships had already left him, and during the storm he was separated from his only remaining consort, the *Elizabeth* commanded by William Wynter, who decided to return home when he could find no trace of Drake and the *Golden Hind*. The *Golden Hind* thus entered the South Seas alone, but as the Spanish settlements were unguarded, Drake made several successful raids up the coast of South America, sacking towns and plundering shipping, his richest prize being the treasure ship *Cacafuego* taken off Lima.

He continued north as far as latitude 48° N. where he turned south again to land at New Albion, near San Francisco. From there he sailed across the Pacific to the Moluccas, where he took six tons of cloves and, for disciplinary reasons, dismissed his preacher, Francis Fletcher, who wrote the best account of the voyage. He returned to Plymouth on 26 September 1580, anxiously inquiring if the queen were still alive to protect him against Spanish charges of piracy. His treasure, estimated at half a million pounds in Elizabethan currency, was taken by land to the Tower of London while he sailed the *Golden Hind* round to *Deptford. There he was knighted by the queen, though she handed the sword to a courtier for the actual accolade.

With his share of the plunder Drake purchased Buckland Abbey, near Plymouth, which is today the Drake family museum. His ship was laid up in dry-dock as a memorial, but the only surviving timbers are a chair at the Bodleian Library, Oxford, and a table in the Middle Temple Hall, London.

In 1585 he was given the command of an amphibious expedition which was the first act of open war with Spain. On this 'descent of the Indies' he proved himself a master of combined operations, sacking San Domingo, Cartagena, St. Augustine in Florida, and then taking off the first Virginian colonists. He returned to England to hear news of the preparations for the Spanish *Armada, some ships of which he proceeded to

destroy at Cadiz in April 1587 in the operation known as 'the singeing of the King of Spain's beard'. Soon afterwards he captured his greatest prize, the Portuguese carrack *San Felipe* laden with goods from the East Indies valued at £114,000. The so-called Drake's Prayer which he is supposed to have composed off Cadiz is in fact a compilation made in 1941 from his letters to the government.

When the Spanish Armada sailed in 1588 Drake was appointed vice admiral of the English fleet at Plymouth under Lord *Howard of Effingham. There, on Plymouth Hoe, the first news of the Armada's appearance off the Lizard was received on 19 July (29 July new style) when, it is said, a game of bowls was being played. Drake is reputed to have remarked, 'There's time to finish the game and beat the Spaniards too', but as the English fleet was embayed, and as the remark is first recorded in 1736, it is doubtful if he made it, though the game of bowls is quite possible.

His own part in the campaign, in command of the *Revenge, was that of leader of the fleet during the first night of the week-long chase up Channel, when he took the opportunity to capture the *Rosario* galleon which he sent into Dartmouth. He may well have suggested the *fireship attack at Calais, and he certainly took the leading part in the gun battle off Gravelines on 29 July. He continued the chase north until 2 August when he returned with the fleet to the Thames.

In 1589 it was decided to destroy the remnants of the Armada on the north coast of Spain. Drake was put in command of the ships and Sir John Norreys in command of the troops, which were landed at Corunna and Lisbon. They failed to achieve anything and disease soon decimated their numbers. Elizabeth was so displeased at this failure that Drake was not employed again for five years, during which time he became mayor of Plymouth and represented the city in Parliament.

In 1595 he and Hawkins were sent in command of another descent on the Indies, but by this time the Spanish settlements were so well fortified that nothing was achieved. An attempt on Puerto Rico failed, Hawkins dying of dysentery off the island before the attack. Nombre de Dios and other places on the mainland were sacked, but no treasure was found and Drake himself fell a victim of yellow fever. On 28 January 1596 he died off Porto Bello and was buried at sea.

Drake's fame became legendary in his own day. Though he spent comparatively few years in the service of the state, he was a founder of the British naval tradition because of the heroic quality of his exploits. He was the first captain to take his own ship round the world, and he was the greatest privateer of all time. In appearance he was short, stocky, and red-haired. Essentially a man of action, he was a brilliant tactician both at sea and on land, but he was less successful as an administrator. He may have been ruthless, ambitious, and boastful, but he was also generous, cheerful, and an ideal leader of men.

The best account of Drake and his career is Sir Julian Corbett's *Drake and the Tudor Navy*, two vols (1898), and an excellent shorter biography is the same author's *Sir Francis Drake* in the 'English Men of Action' series (1890). Two recent biographies are N. Williams's *Francis Drake* (1973) and G. M. Thomson's *Sir Francis Drake* (1972).

DRAKE'S DRUM, a drum said to have been in the possession of Sir Francis *Drake and carried by him on board his ships to beat the crews to quarters, and now at Buckland Abbey, Devon, Drake's old home. According to legend, the drum gives a drumbeat whenever England is in danger of invasion from the sea. Some doubts have been cast on its authenticity.

'DRAKE'S DRUM', a famous poem of the sea written by Sir Henry *Newbolt and first published in the *St. James's Gazette* in 1897. It is included in the collection of 12 naval poems published in 1898 under the title *Admirals All* and was later set to music by Vaughan Williams.

DRAUGHT, (1) sometimes written as draft, the depth of water which a ship draws, which of course varies with the state of her loading. Her maximum draught, known as her deep load draught, occurs when she is fully loaded down to her *Plimsoll line. Normally a ship has draught marks painted on her sides both on the *stem and the *sternpost from which the depth of water she draws forward and aft at the time can be read. Draught marks are normally painted in roman figures, one to each foot of draught, the depth of water a ship is drawing being indicated by the lower end of the painted figures. **(2)** The drawings or lines, prepared by a marine architect in the design of a vessel, from which the shipbuilder works.

DRAW, to, (1) the condition of a sail when it is full of wind, the sail being said to be drawing. To let draw, to trim the *jib of a small sailing vessel with the *lee *sheet after it has been held to *windward by the *weather sheet in order to assist in forcing the *bows across the wind when *tacking. In very light winds, where the vessel may not have sufficient way to make tacking easy, the jib is held out to windward when the vessel is head to wind to assist the bows across. As soon as this is achieved, the order to let draw

ensures the jib being sheeted normally on the new tack. After a ship is hove-to (see HEAVE-TO, TO) at sea, in which condition the jib is permanently sheeted to windward, the order to let draw gets her sailing again. **(2)** Said of a ship to indicate her *draught, e.g., 'the ship draws, or is drawing, so many feet *forward and so many *aft'.

DREADNOUGHT, H.M.S., a name used nine times in the Royal Navy. The first *Dreadnought* fought against the Spanish *Armada in 1588, and the fifth, after fighting at *Trafalgar, became in 1830 a seamen's hospital at *Greenwich before being finally broken up in 1857. The sixth *Dreadnought* was originally the *Caledonia*, but was renamed when she became hospital ship at Greenwich in 1857. The seamen's hospital was transferred on shore in 1870, but is still known as the Dreadnought Seamen's Hospital. The best known ship of the name was the eighth, a 17,900-ton *battleship built at Portsmouth and launched in February 1906. She was the first 'all big gun' battleship in the world, a design which revolutionized battleship construction at that time, superior in both fire power and speed to any other capital warship then afloat, and also the first battleship in the world to be fitted with *turbines. She was the conception of Admiral Sir John *Fisher who described her as 'the hardboiled egg—because she cannot be beat', and she gave her name to the type of capital ship which succeeded her. She served throughout the First World War (1914–18) and in 1915 rammed and sank the German submarine *U.29* in the North Sea. She was sold for breaking-up in 1920. The Royal Navy's present *Dreadnought* is a nuclear submarine, built at Barrow-in-Furness by Vickers-Armstrong and launched by Elizabeth II on Trafalgar Day, 21 October 1960.

DREADNOUGHT BATTLESHIP, a 20th century capital ship combining high speed, adequate protection, and a main armament comprising large guns of uniform calibre; otherwise, the 'all-big-gun' *battleship.

The introduction into naval warfare during the 1840s and 1850s of the high-explosive shell, the rifled gun, armour plate, and steam propulsion of acceptable reliability, made obsolete the traditional three-*decker wooden *ship of the line, which for three centuries had remained basically unchanged in hull configuration, rig, speed, and offensive power.

The first seagoing *'ironclad', precursor to the 20th century battleship, was the French *Gloire* (1858). The British answered with the *Warrior* (1859) of 9,200 tons. Though classed as *frigates, these 13-knot men-of-war, powered by engines of over 3,000 horsepower but also carrying a full sailing rig, could overtake and

The two forward turrets of 15-inch guns in H.M.S. Warspite, *1937*

overwhelm any contemporary three-decker ship of the line.

Lacking the technical impetus and tactical lessons of a major naval war, the ironclad battleship, derived from these frigates, passed through a series of compromise phases, each the result of theoretical hypotheses or of new discoveries in armour plate metallurgy, gun construction and mounting, shell propellants, and hull and machinery design.

By the time of the first German Naval Law (1896), every permutation of large and small guns, high and moderate speed, thick and thin armour plate, had seemingly been exhausted, and naval architects had settled on a basic specification for the battleship (the term 'ironclad' had been dropped). This combined an armament of four big guns, about ten guns of various smaller calibres, and a large number of quick-firers to deal with the new threat to the battleship, the *torpedoboat. Displacement was in the region of 10,000 tons, and speed about 16 knots. After an unduly prolonged extension of their useful life, sails had at last been discarded. But another anachronism, the *ram bow, intended to sink the enemy by direct impact, emphasized the tactical

importance still attached to close-range action. The value of the ram in the calculations of theoreticians, was seemingly confirmed by the results of the second battle of *Lissa, where it did considerable execution, and by accidental collisions, such as the sinking in 1893 of the *Victoria, flagship of the Royal Navy's Mediterranean Fleet.

The impulses which created the long overdue revolution in battleship design in the early years of the 20th century were German naval rearmament, combined with imperial and mercantile expansion and the new imbalances of power these brought about; the tactical lessons of the Russo-Japanese war (1904–5) at sea; and the new technological revolution, which was simultaneously perfecting the *torpedo, the *submarine, wireless telegraphy, and the internal combustion and diesel engines. The aeroplane was already a practical probability.

Single-calibre armament had been tried unsuccessfully in freak Italian and British battleships in the 1870s. But the inefficiency of mixed heavy armament, to which designers soon reverted, was finally and fully revealed in the Russo-Japanese naval engagements in 1904 and 1905. Mixed batteries in the Russian and Japanese battleships complicated ranging and spotting the 'splash' of the shells in action. Moreover, to universal astonishment, accurate firing at almost 20,000 yards with the heaviest guns was demonstrated by both protagonists. The lesson was clear. By concentrating an overwhelming weight of the heaviest shell at extreme range, an enemy could be sunk or put out of action before his medium calibre guns and his torpedoes could become effective.

Even before the decisive battle of * Tsushima (May 1905), the Japanese had laid down the first-ever 'all-big-gun' battleship, the *Aki*. Only a precarious national economy and delivery difficulties with the guns prevented her completion as the first pure 'dreadnought'. The Russian Admiralty and the Board of Construction of the U.S. Navy had also seen the light and were projecting 'all-big-gun' battleships as early as 1904.

But it is to the Royal Navy that credit must be given for the completion, years before its rivals, of the battleship whose generic name, 'dreadnought', and broad outline of design, was to endure for some 40 years. In 1903 *Fighting Ships*, the distinguished naval annual, edited by Fred T. * Jane, carried an article by the distinguished Italian naval architect, Vittorio Cuniberti, entitled 'An Ideal Battleship for the British Fleet', calling for a vessel combining an armament of twelve 12-inch guns, 12-inch armour plate, and a speed of 24 knots—an unprecedented combination of qualities. H.M.S. * *Dreadnought*, launched in 1906, overturned all the long-established principles of naval architectural compromise, made every other battleship in the world obsolete, created a furore in Britain as well as abroad, and only marginally fell short of Cuniberti's ideal.

H.M.S. *Dreadnought* was a many-parented brain-child. Its leading progenitors were the Constructor, William H. Gard, Sir Philip Watts, the Director of Naval Construction, and the members of the Admiralty Committee on Designs, convened in November 1904 for the consideration of future warships for the Royal Navy. This committee included such officers of future eminence as Captains John R. * Jellicoe, Henry B. * Jackson, and R. H. S. * Bacon, and Rear Admiral Prince Louis of Battenberg (see MOUNTBATTEN, Louis Alexander). But history justly gives the first credit to Admiral Sir John * Fisher, the brilliant new First Sea Lord; and less justly gives little credit to the wise Lord Selborne, the First Lord of the Admiralty, who politically supported Fisher on this and so many more of his radical *matériel* and administrative reforms.

The *Dreadnought* was laid down at Portsmouth on 2 October 1905, launched by Edward VII (the most powerful of Fisher's supporters) on 10 February 1906, and was steaming on her trials eight months later. The record speed of her construction was due to the galvanizing influence of Fisher. With her armament of ten 12-inch guns, displacement of 17,900 tons, and maximum speed of 21 knots, her superiority to any other fighting ship was so manifest that no naval power could afford to build to any other pattern. Moreover, she was powered by * turbine machinery which offered greatly superior dependability, simplicity, and cleanliness: an advantage that was not imitated by foreign designers for several years.

While causing acute anxiety and imitation abroad, H.M.S. *Dreadnought* had a mixed reception at home. Controversy raged about many aspects of her specification, not least her high cost. It was undeniable that she made the rest of the British battle fleet, the most powerful and numerous in the world by a wide margin, as out of date as that of her most likely enemy, Germany. But the revolution in design was bound to come, and by building first, and fast, Britain had stolen a march on every rival. Before Germany had completed her first class of four 'dreadnoughts', Britain had seven in commission. In addition, by then the Royal Navy possessed three equally radical * battle-cruisers, which were faster, less heavily armed and protected cousins to the *Dreadnought*.

The 'dreadnought race', as it came to be called, continued at a steadily increasing tempo over the following fifteen years. Germany, Britain's greatest rival at sea, dropped out in the later stages of the First World War (1914–18), preferring to divert her resources to submarine construction, but the competition between the U.S.A. and Japan continued until the Washington treaty on the limitation of naval armament was signed in 1921. Britain completed forty-eight 'dreadnoughts' up to 1918, Germany twenty-six. France, Italy, and Russia all commissioned these new and expensive symbols of power; even South American republics ordered a brace or two.

The most formidable battleships during this phase of construction were British, American, and Japanese. Guns of 16-inch * calibre had become commonplace, armour plate, internal protection, propellants, and shells were all improved. H.M.S. * *Hood*, the biggest capital ship serving between the world wars, displaced 41,200 tons, carried a main armament of eight 15-inch guns, and could steam at 31 knots.

The British and German 'dreadnought' battle fleets fought only one brief and inconclusive engagement, at * Jutland (31 May 1916), during the First World War. The abortive nature of this action confirmed the reluctance of commanders-in-chief to commit their capital ships in the face of determined torpedo attack; for by now the value of the *matériel* had seemingly become of such crucial importance, by contrast with the Napoleonic wars, that the preservation of the fleet was judged to be of paramount importance.

Twenty years later, with new naval rearmament, the threat of the aerial bomb had been added to that of underwater weapons. In spite of the prophecies of the advocates of air power, like General 'Billy' Mitchell in the U.S.A., Air Marshal Sir Hugh Trenchard in Britain, and General Giulio Douhet in Italy, all the major powers laid down new battleships in the last few years before another world war was to break out in 1939. Without exception they conformed to the *Dreadnought*'s basic design formula of high speed, elaborate protection, and all-big-gun armament, although batteries of anti-aircraft guns replaced the anti-torpedoboat quick-firers of pre-1914 battleships, and greater emphasis was laid on horizontal protection. Many battleships surviving from the First World War, now modified and re-equipped, did useful service in 1939–45.

Early lessons of the Second World War, at *Taranto in 1940 where the Italian fleet was crippled by a handful of obsolescent British *Fleet Air Arm aircraft, and at the U.S. Naval base of *Pearl Harbor in 1941, suggested that the battleship was an obsolete and expensive anachronism. But the day of the battleship was not yet over. Its new batteries of light anti-aircraft guns served to protect the navy's new capital ships, the *aircraft carriers; its old heavy guns, built for fleet action against the enemy line as in Lord *Nelson's day, proved invaluable for shore bombardment. The battleship continued to be effective in this role during the Korean War.

The flexibility of the battleship exploded the theories of many astute military thinkers. When friendly shore- or carrier-based aircraft controlled the skies above its decks, the sturdy battleship was regarded as the least vulnerable warship in the fleet. But, as the British learned with the destruction by the Japanese air force of the new battleship *Prince of Wales* and the older battle-cruiser *Repulse* in the South China Sea in December 1941, and the Japanese themselves discovered in their turn, no battleship could successfully defend itself without air support against determined assault by torpedo- and bomb-carrying aircraft.

The biggest battleships ever built were the Japanese *Yamato* and *Musashi*, completed in 1941 and 1942. They displaced over 63,720 tons, carried nine 18·1-inch guns, and could steam at 27 knots. But in spite of elaborate protection against bombs and torpedoes, they were both sunk at small cost after sustained attacks by U.S. aircraft.

The Royal Navy's last battleship, the *Vanguard*, was scrapped in 1960. The last battleship to see action was the U.S.S. *New Jersey*, reconditioned and recommissioned in 1967–8 for bombardment service off Vietnam, where its 16-inch guns proved highly effective more than 60 years after the launching of H.M.S. *Dreadnought*.

W. Hovgaard, *Modern History of Warships* (1920); R. Hough, *Dreadnought, A History of the Modern Battleship* (1965); O. Parkes, *British Battleships* (rev. edn. 1966).

DREDGE, an iron wedge-shaped contrivance with a small net in the fashion of a *trawl attached, by means of which oysters and other molluscs are brought up from their beds. Towed along the bottom by a *smack, the iron wedge loosens the hold of the shellfish and guides them into the net.

DREDGER, a self-propelled vessel fitted with mechanical means for deepening harbours or clearing the entrances to rivers by removing part of the bottom. The commonest form of dredger is fitted with an endless chain of buckets which scoops up the bottom and discharges the contents of the buckets into *lighters secured alongside. The endless chain, driven by machinery, normally operates through a central well so that the area of the bottom being dredged is immediately below the vessel, although side and stern dredges are not unknown. Where the area to be dredged consists of silt or soft mud, a suction dredger can be used, the bottom being removed by means of a vacuum pipe which sucks up the silt or mud and similarly discharges it either into a lighter or *hopper, or alternatively into tanks on board. Some modern suction

Dredger

dredgers employ cutters to loosen the bottom which can then be sucked up. The *hovercraft principle has also recently been developed for small dredgers of up to 150 tons for use in very shallow waters and along the banks of rivers and estuaries.

One of the earliest steam bucket dredgers was constructed in 1806 by Richard Trevithick at Penydaren and mounted on a wooden hulk. It was used in excavating boulder clay at the entrance to the East India Dock, London.

DRESS, see SAILORS' DRESS.

DRESS SHIP, to, the operation of decorating a ship with flags on occasions of national or local celebration, and in the case of yachts on the day when their club holds its annual regatta. A ship is dressed when she flies flags at her mastheads; she is dressed overall when she displays a continuous array of flags from her *jackstaff via the mastheads to her *ensign staff. On naval occasions when ships are dressed overall the order in which the flags are displayed is, in most navies, laid down in regulations and is never haphazard; in merchant vessels and yachts there is a recommended order in which flags of the *International Code of Signals are displayed.

DREYER, Sir FREDERIC CHARLES (1878–1956), British admiral, was in his time one of the greatest gunnery experts in the Royal Navy. As a lieutenant he passed out of H.M.S. *Excellent, the naval gunnery school, with honours. He was the first gunnery specialist appointed to H.M.S. *Dreadnought, first of the all-big-gun battleships, in 1907, and, after service in her, concentrated on the invention and design of a fire control table, submitting his combined 'time and range' and 'time and bearing' machine to the Admiralty. He was set to work to perfect it in competition with other fire control methods, notably Arthur *Pollen's 'true' plot, the final result being the Dreyer fire control table officially adopted in 1913 and used in ships of the Royal Navy throughout the First World War (1914–18).

In October 1915 he was appointed flag captain to Admiral Sir John *Jellicoe, commander-in-chief of the *Grand Fleet, and was present in that capacity at the battle of *Jutland (31 May 1916). After the battle he was head of the fleet committee which inquired into the gunnery failures, particularly the poor performance of British armour-piercing shells, and when Jellicoe went to the Admiralty as First Sea Lord in 1916, Dreyer accompanied him to take up the post of director of naval ordnance. After the war he remained with Jellicoe during his tour of the Dominions to inquire into, and make recommendations for, the future development and composition of the Dominion navies.

Dreyer's promising career was halted by the naval mutinies at *Invergordon in 1931; at the time he was Assistant Chief of Naval Staff on the Board of Admiralty, and thus shared in the collective responsibility of the Board for this breakdown of naval discipline and was placed on the retired list. He was re-employed in the Second World War, first as a *commodore of *convoys, and later as inspector of merchant ship gunnery, later still as deputy director of air equipment, in which post he raised a loud voice for the diversion of more long-range aircraft from the bombing of enemy territory in order to protect merchant convoys in the Atlantic. The subsequent experience of the battle of the *Atlantic proved him as correct in this view as he had been in his views on the proper development of naval gunnery four decades earlier.

Dreyer was a mixture of great intellectual power, tremendous personal drive and organization, and intolerance of juniors, no matter how brilliant in their own specializations. He was a man who was impelled to do everything himself and to distrust initiative in others. Lacking the gift of leadership, he was never popular.

DRIFT, (1) the distance a vessel makes to *leeward, by the action of either the tide or the wind. **(2)** The term used to indicate the rate in knots of ocean currents, as for example the 'west wind drift' which circles the globe in southern latitudes under the influence of the *Roaring Forties. **(3)** The distance a shell fired from a rifled barrel deviates from its aimed trajectory because of the rotation imparted to it by the rifling, a matter of considerable importance in the long ranges at which big naval guns are fired at sea. **(4)** The accumulation of pieces of wood, trunks of trees, etc., or of small ice broken away from the edges of icefields, collected together by the action of wind or current and lying on the surface in a mass. See also DRIFT NET.

DRIFT NET or, more correctly, a **DRIFT OF NETS,** a long shallow net or series of nets buoyed on the top edge with cork or with glass or plastic balls and weighted along the bottom edge with pieces of lead so that it hangs vertically downward in the sea from the surface and catches surface shoaling fish, such as herring, mackerel, and pilchard, by the gills as they swim into the mesh. See also DRIFTER.

DRIFTER, a type of fishing vessel, originally fitted with sails but today more commonly using steam or diesel engines, employed to catch fish which normally swim near the surface in shoals, as opposed to bottom-lying fish which are caught in a *trawl. A drifter shoots its nets, of which the top edges are supported on the surface by cork or hollow glass or plastic balls and the bottoms weighted with lead, and which then hang vertically downward across the estimated path of the shoals. The drifter then lies to *leeward of the net, drifting with it, until it is time to haul it in with the *capstan; the fish which swim into the net are caught and held in the meshes by their gills.

Drifters are essentially fishing vessels which operate in home waters, their main catch being herring, though pilchard and similar surface shoaling fish are also caught. They are mainly to be found in the North Sea and around the coasts of Scotland and Ireland where the herring congregate in vast numbers, but are also common in other parts of the world where surface fish are prevalent. See also FISHERIES, RING NET.

DRIFT-ICE, the small débris of the pack which has broken away by action of the wind or sea, or by approach to warmer water. It presents little problem to ships except in conditions of extreme cold when it can quickly re-form into pack ice. See also BOW-GRACE, DRIFT.

DRIVE, to, a ship drives when her *anchor fails to hold the ground and she is at the mercy of wind and tide. In the case of a sailing vessel, a ship drives to *leeward when the force of the wind is so great that she cannot be controlled by sails or rudder. In a full gale, too violent for the sails to be hoisted, she drives under bare poles before the wind (see also SCUD, TO). Similarly, a steam vessel will drive before the wind if her engines are broken down or not powerful enough to hold her against the wind. One of the best known examples of ships driving before the wind was during a hurricane at Apia, Samoa, in 1889, when only one ship, H.M.S. *Calliope, escaped, six other warships and several merchant vessels driving ashore before the wind. The word is often connected with maritime disaster, as of ships driven by storms on to rocks, etc.

She drove in the dark to leeward,
  She struck, not a reef or a rock,
But the combs of a smother of sand. Night drew her
  Dead to the Kentish Knock.
G. M. Hopkins, 'The Wreck of the "Deutschland" '

DRIVER, an additional sail hoisted in the form of a *studdingsail to take advantage of a following wind. Introduced about 1700, its original form was as a high narrow square sail, hoisted to the *mizen *peak on a short *jackyard, with its *clews brought down to a *boom fixed *athwartships at the after end of the *poop. It developed in the mid-18th century into a larger form of the old *lateen-mizen, set on the same yard but with its foot extended by a boom which projected over the ship's stern. In its final form it

became known as a *spanker, this name for it beginning to come into use in 1790, when the sail was regularly bent to the *gaff and not hoisted up as a form of studdingsail.

DROGUE, usually an improvised contraption by which a sailing vessel is slowed down in a following sea to prevent her from being *pooped by waves coming up astern. It can vary from a long *warp towed astern in small sailing craft to a spar with a weighted sail in larger sailing ships. A drogue is very widely confused with a *sea anchor, but in fact the two serve different purposes. Sir Francis *Drake used a drogue comprised of wineskins in the *Golden Hind when chasing the treasure ship *Cacafuego* in the Pacific as he did not wish to alarm her by coming up with her too fast.

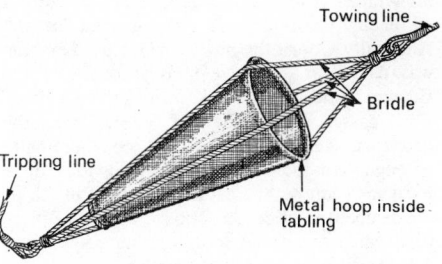

A drogue

An extremely efficient drogue is made by many sailmakers for use in yachts, etc. It consists of a hollow cone of canvas with a line attached to a *bridle at the base of the cone and another line attached to the top. With the cone towed from the bridle and the top line loose, it forms an efficient drogue to slow the yacht down; when this is no longer required, a pull on the line connected to the top of the cone collapses it so that it no longer acts as a drogue.

When an open boat approaches the shore through lines of breakers, a *grass line over the stern acts as an efficient drogue, both slowing the boat down and holding it steady so that the waves do not turn it broadside to the beach and upset it or wash it ashore.

DROITS OF ADMIRALTY, that part of the *prize fund which in Britain accrued by right to the *Lord High Admiral and from which, in early days, he derived his income. These rights consisted of ships improperly brought in for adjudication in a prize court before the declaration of war or *reprisal, ships brought in by those operating without a lawful commission or *Letter of Marque, and ships forced into a British port by stress of weather or wrecked on the coast through faulty navigation. Civil droits were those which accrued in times of peace. They arose from wrecks, *flotsam, *jetsam, *lagan, royal fishes (see FISHES ROYAL), *derelicts, and the goods of pirates, traitors, felons, and fugitives captured at sea. When the office of the Lord High Admiral was placed in commission, the droits of Admiralty were paid into the Consolidated Fund as some offset against the salaries of the Commissioners. The prize fund in Britain came to an end in 1945, though most other maritime nations had abolished prize long before, and droits of Admiralty, together with *droits of the Crown, became things of the past.

DROITS OF THE CROWN, that part of the *prize fund which in Britain accrued by right to the sovereign. They consisted of all ships captured on the high seas or sent in under a prize crew under suspicion of *contraband, or cut out of enemy harbours. If *condemned in the Admiralty Court, the money raised by their sale was paid into the prize fund as droits of the Crown. Under what was known as the 'Cruizers' Act', passed in the reign of Queen Anne, the droits of the Crown, though still nominally belonging to the sovereign, were divided on a fixed scale among the actual captors of the ships condemned in prize. In Britain, the naval prize fund came to an end in December 1945, long after most other maritime countries.

DROMON or **DROMOND,** a large vessel of the Mediterranean which operated between the 9th and 15th centuries. Byzantine in origin, the name was at first used to denote a royal ship, but came into general use as describing any very large ship propelled by many oars and with a single mast and a large square sail. They were used principally for trade or as transports in war. Most of the Christian armies used in the Crusades were transported in dromons, which also carried the horses of the cavalry.

DROP KEEL, (1) a portion of the *keel in early *submarines which could be detached in emergency to give additional buoyancy. By releasing this portion of the keel, usually weighing up to about 20 tons, a submerged submarine had a chance of returning to the surface if she could not regain positive buoyancy by any other means. It was released by a mechanism within the pressure hull. As the submarine developed into more reliable forms, the original drop keel was omitted from the design. **(2)** A term often used, though erroneously, to describe a *centreboard or *dagger plate.

DROWN THE MILLER, to, an old expression much used by sailors in the Royal Navy to indicate that more than the statutory amount of water was being mixed with the rum in the daily ration of *grog. The statutory mixture was three parts of water to one part of rum, but in the days of the sailing navy some *pursers were tempted to 'drown the miller' to make the rum go further, pocketing the difference in value.

DRUMHEAD, the top part of the barrel of a *capstan, in which are the square pigeon-holes to take the ends of the capstan bars when an *anchor has to be weighed, or a heavy weight lifted, by hand. In modern ships with plenty of auxiliary power and relatively small crews, the operation of weighing an anchor by hand is virtually a thing of the past.

DRY-DOCK, a watertight basin, with one end, which can be closed and sealed by a *caisson, open to the sea, in which ships can be docked for repair, examination, or cleaning of the underwater body. When a ship is to enter a dry-dock, the dock is flooded, the caisson withdrawn, and the ship floated in and held in position so that her *keel and *docking keels are immediately above the lines of blocks prearranged on the floor of the dock. The caisson is replaced and the water in the dock pumped out, the ship's keels settling on the blocks as the water level falls to support the weight of her hull. After her repair or cleaning, the dock is flooded up, lifting her off the blocks, the caisson withdrawn, and she is floated out. See also FLOATING DOCK, GRAVING DOCK.

DRYGALSKI, ERICH VON (1865–1949), German geographer, led an expedition to the Antarctic in 1901–3 aboard the *Gauss, exploring part of Wilkes Land and naming Kaiser Wilhelm II Land. Drygalski himself made an important contribution to present knowledge of the relation of the surrounding oceans to the Antarctic continent and demonstrated the existence of what was later termed the *Antarctic Convergence.

DUBB, to, the operation of smoothing away a plank with an *adze to make it suitable for use in planking the sides or deck of a wooden vessel. An experienced carpenter could dubb a plank with an adze and leave it as though it had been planed. The operation of taking a thin cut with an adze on the side planking of an existing ship in order to examine the condition of the wood was also known as dubbing. With powered saws and modern planing machines, the art of using an adze is rapidly dying out in the boatbuilding trade and is rarely seen today.

DUBBELS, HENDRIK JACCBSZ (c. 1620–76), Dutch marine painter, was born in Amsterdam. Although a most competent marine artist in his own right, much in the style of the elder Van de * Velde of whom he was a contemporary, he is perhaps more widely known as the teacher of Ludolf * Bakhuysen, after the two Van de Veldes the most accomplished of the marine painters of the Dutch school. As a painter Dubbels had a lively sense of colour and movement, and examples of his work can be seen in most of the major galleries of Europe.

DUCK UP, to, an order used in the sailing navies to haul on the * clew-garnets and clew lines of the mainsail and foresail so that the man on the helm or at the wheel could see where the ship was going. The same term was used in the case of a * spritsail when a warship was chasing an enemy and wished to fire her forward * chase guns, as the spritsail would obscure the line of sight. 'Duck up the clew lines', hoist the clews (bottom corners) of the lower sails to provide a clear view forward.

DUCKING AT THE YARDARM, an early form of naval punishment said to be first instituted by the French for blasphemy, sedition, or desertion. 'The ducking at the main * yard-arm is when a malefactor, by having a rope fastened under his arms and about his middle and under his breech, is thus hoisted up to the end of the yard and from thence is violently let fall into the sea, sometimes three several times one after another, and if the offence be very foul, he is also drawn under the keel of the ship, which is termed keel-raking. And while he is thus under water a great gun is fired right over his head, the which is done as well to astonish him so much the more with the thunder of the shot, as to give warning unto all others of the fleet to look out and be wary by his harms.' Thus Captain Nathaniel * Boteler, writing in 1634 in *A Dialogicall Discourse concerning Marine Affaires*. See also KEEL-HAULING. These forms of punishment went out of fashion in most navies at about the end of the 17th century, being superseded by the less elaborate but more brutal form of punishment with the * cat-o'-nine-tails.

DUDLEY, Sir ROBERT (1573–1649), English seaman and cartographer, was the natural son of Robert Dudley, Earl of Leicester, and Lady Douglas Sheffield, daughter of Lord * Howard of Effingham. He is first heard of in the maritime field as taking part in a voyage to the West Indies in 1594, and he was knighted after * Drake's expedition to Cadiz in 1596, in which he served with distinction. His first wife was a sister of Thomas * Cavendish (or Candish), the second Englishman to sail round the world. As a young man he inherited two large fortunes, that of his father in 1588 and that of his uncle, Ambrose Dudley, Earl of Warwick, in 1589.

After the death of Elizabeth I he attempted to obtain a declaration of legitimacy so that he could inherit the titles of his father and his uncle, but without avail. He left England in 1605 in company with Miss Elizabeth Southwell, a young lady of great beauty, smuggling her out of the country dressed as his page. He failed to obey an order to return home and was outlawed. On the strength of a warrant given him by the Holy Roman Emperor Ferdinand II he called himself Earl of Warwick, and also Duke of Northumberland, a title which had been held by his grandfather until his execution by Mary Tudor.

Robert Dudley after leaving England settled in Florence in 1606 and entered the service of Cosimo II, grand-duke of Tuscany, serving his new master well. He directed the draining of the marshes behind Leghorn and the construction of that port. He also took part in operations against the * Barbary pirates. But his chief claim to fame and remembrance in the maritime world lies in his wonderful *Arcano del Mare*, published in three volumes in 1645–6 at Florence. As well as a superb collection of 130 charts, admirably drawn, the first comprehensive series drawn on the * Mercator projection, it contains details of all known navigational instruments of the age, many mounted in volvelles, i.e., discs mounted centrally which can be revolved to show how the instruments worked, examples of shipwrightry, and a plan for a naval force with five rates of ship, all written and described in Italian by Dudley himself. He died at Florence, leaving a large family of sons and daughters, the offspring of Elizabeth Southwell.

DUFEK, GEORGE JOHN (1903–77), American rear admiral, had a various and distinguished career as a polar navigator. He was in command of the * Bear during Admiral Richard Byrd's Antarctic expedition of 1939–41, and in 1946 was again in the Antarctic with Byrd in an expedition known as 'Operation Highjump'. In 1955 he was appointed in command of Task Force 43, the first of a series of Antarctic expeditions, code-named 'Deep Freeze', in support of the American scientific effort on the Antarctic continent during the International Geophysical Year, 1957–8, a post he held until he retired in 1959.

DUFF, ROBERT (c. 1720–87), British vice admiral, is remembered mainly for his share, although his ships were not actually engaged in the fighting, in Sir Edward * Hawke's great victory at * Quiberon Bay. He had previously made a name for himself as a captain in the amphibious operations against St. Malo and Cherbourg in 1758, and commanded the * frigate squadron which was watching the French fleet in Brest during Hawke's * blockade of that coast in 1759.

When heavy gales drove Hawke off the coast and back to England in November 1759, Duff was left with his inshore squadron of frigates to maintain the watch on the French ships. He remained on his station, beating up and down throughout the gales, until the French admiral, the Comte de * Conflans, took advantage of Hawke's absence to put to sea. Duff's frigates shadowed him until they were driven off, and then spread all sail to warn Hawke of the French break-out. They met Hawke's fleet returning from England, gave him the news, and there followed the great and victorious battle.

Later Duff became commander-in-chief on the Newfoundland station in 1775 and in the Mediterranean in 1777, reaching the rank of vice admiral in 1778.

DUG-OUT, the primitive form of a * canoe consisting of a tree-trunk hollowed out by burning or other means. The two ends were sometimes roughly pointed. They were propelled in the earliest days presumably by the hands of the occupant, later by paddles when these were developed during the third millennium B.C. Such primitive canoes were in existence in some of the islands of the South Pacific until quite recent years, and may well still be used by some of the less-developed riverine peoples of central South America.

DUGUAY-TROUIN, RENÉ (1673–1736), French seaman, was a native of St. Malo, one of the great cradles of French privateering. In the war which broke out against England in 1689 he served in a * privateer with great success, and proved himself possessed of such courage and resource that in 1691 his family gave him a vessel of fourteen guns to command. After varied successes his ship was captured and he was imprisoned in Plymouth Castle, but escaped with the help of a pretty girl who sold provisions to the prisoners. Given command of a vessel of forty-eight guns, he continued his run of successes against English and Dutch merchant ships, so much so that he was given a commission as *capitaine de frégate* in the French Navy. Quick promotion followed his capture of the larger part of an English convoy off the Lizard, and in 1711 he achieved even greater fame by capturing Rio de Janeiro and holding it to ransom. By 1728 he had reached the rank of vice admiral and his last naval duty was the protection of French commerce in the eastern Mediterranean. He is considered by many to be one of the two most outstanding naval leaders of France, the other being the Bailli de * Suffren.

DUGUAY-TROUIN, a French 80-gun ship, flagship of Rear Admiral Dumanoir-le-Pelley at the action off * Ferrol in 1805 in which the remnants of the French fleet which had escaped from the battle of * Trafalgar were engaged and captured by a British squadron commanded by Sir Richard * Strachan. She was taken into the British Navy and renamed H.M.S. * *Implacable* and, with the exception of H.M.S. * *Victory*, was the last surviving wooden * ship of the line until she was sunk in the English Channel in 1949, her timbers having then rotted beyond repair.

DUILLIUS NEPOS, GAIUS, Roman consul, was the first man to obtain a victory over the naval power of Carthage, in 260 B.C. at * Mylae. He captured fifty of the Carthaginian ships and was honoured with a naval triumph, the first that was ever held in Rome. Medals were struck in commemoration of this victory and there still exists in Rome a column which was erected on the occasion.

DUKE OF YORK, JAMES, see JAMES, Duke of York.

DUKW, the code letters used for a military amphibious vehicle developed during the Second World War capable of being driven normally on land and across rivers and estuaries. Its official description was Amphibian Vehicle All-Wheel Drive Dual Rear Axle.

DULCIBELLA, the name of the small yacht in Erskine * Childers's classic novel *The Riddle of the Sands* (1903). She was a converted lifeboat.

DUMAS, VITO (1900–   ), Argentinian single-handed sailor, was the first to make a solo circumnavigation of the world round Cape Horn by an east to west route—the contrary way round for all sailing vessels—in the remarkably short time of thirteen months. In 1931 he bought a 20-year-old converted * yawl, *Titave*, which had raced consistently in France in the * International 8-metre class, renamed her *Legh*, and sailed 6,300 miles in her alone from Arcachon to his native Argentina, reaching Buenos Aires early in 1932.

For a time he worked on the pampas as a farmer, but the call of the sea proved stronger than the plough and he again sailed alone on ocean voyages, logging nonstop passages of 103 days and 117 days. With a new boat, *Legh II*, a * Bermuda * ketch, he set off from Buenos Aires in June 1942 during the Second World War, and sailed her alone round the world by the southern route from east to west, arriving back at Buenos Aires in August 1943. During this voyage, made by the so-called 'impossible route', an east–west passage of the Horn, he completed four great passages in between landfalls of 7,200 miles in 104 days, 5,400 miles in 72 days, 4,200 miles in 58 days, and finally 3,000 miles in 70 days.

During part of the time he was severely handicapped by a septic arm. At that date this voyage was the fastest circumnavigation accomplished by one man.

DUMONT D'URVILLE, JULES-SÉBASTIEN-CÉSAR (1790–1842), French naval officer and explorer, joined the navy at the age of 16 and showed an early predilection for the study of travels and voyages of exploration and an interest in various fields of science, especially ethnology. While serving in the Mediterranean in 1820 he visited the island of Melos where he reported the discovery of an ancient Greek statue of outstanding beauty. On his recommendation it was secured for the Louvre and later became famous as the Venus de Milo. Returning to Paris, Dumont d'Urville helped to found the Paris Geographical Society and began to draw up plans for a scientific voyage of circumnavigation through the south Pacific Ocean which duly received the approval of the Ministry of Marine. From 1822 to 1825 Dumont d'Urville was at sea on board the *Coquille* carrying out studies in *hydrography and natural history. He returned dissatisfied with the scientific work and planned a second voyage to remedy it. This, too, was to receive official approval but he was further required to look for traces of the expedition of *La Pérouse which had come to grief in 1788 at Vanikoro in New Caledonia.

Between 1826 and 1829 Dumont d'Urville was again at sea in command of the *Coquille*, now rechristened *Astrolabe* in commemoration of La Pérouse's vessel. The results of this expedition were entirely successful; the Australian continent had been coasted from King George's Sound to Port Jackson and visits made to various parts of New Zealand, the Fiji Islands, the Loyalty Islands, New Caledonia, New Guinea, Van Diemen's Land, the Caroline Islands, Celebes, and Mauritius. The wreck of La Pérouse's ship was also discovered. Dumont d'Urville was occupied with the task of compiling the narrative of the voyage when the revolution of 1830 took place and he was called upon to escort Charles X into exile. For some reason he seems to have incurred the hostility of the new monarch, Louis Philippe, and spent the next few years in eclipse and poverty. But his enthusiasm for the study of the Pacific islands and their ethnology remained unabated and at last he was able to get his plans for an anthropological expedition submitted to the king. Louis Philippe approved but proposed, possibly at the suggestion of Baron von *Humboldt, a preliminary trip into Antarctic waters to surpass James *Weddell's record in these high southern latitudes.

Dumont d'Urville accepted this added task without enthusiasm; neither his own ship, the *Astrolabe*, nor its companion the *Zelée* under the command of Captain Jacquinot, was suitable for navigation in ice. The expedition set sail in September 1837 and in January 1838 entered the pack ice but failed to penetrate far south of the Antarctic circle. Concluding that Weddell was a liar, Dumont d'Urville turned north and after discovering a group of islands north of the Antarctic Peninsula, sailed for the Pacific to pursue the main objectives of the expedition. Two years later he made one more attempt to penetrate the Antarctic ice south of latitude 60° S. between *longitudes 120°–160° E. in the hope of discovering the South Magnetic Pole. As he frankly admitted, he was spurred by the known presence in these waters of a British expedition under James Clark *Ross and an American under Charles *Wilkes. On this occasion his perseverance was rewarded by the discovery of continental land in the region which he named after his wife, Terre Adélie, on 20 January 1840. Shortly afterwards, the *Astrolabe* hailed a passing vessel which failed to communicate; it was Wilkes's *brig *Porpoise*. Dumont d'Urville continued to follow the ice barrier until ill health compelled him to return to the Pacific. On his return to France in November 1840 he settled down to the task of editing the expedition's records. The following year he was promoted rear admiral and appointed president of the Council of the Paris Geographical Society. In May 1842 he was killed, with his wife and son, in a railway accident.

DUNCAN, ADAM, first Viscount Duncan (1731–1804), British admiral, commanded the fleet in the North Sea which in 1797 won a decisive victory over a Dutch fleet off *Camperdown on the Dutch coast. As a midshipman he had served in the *Centurion* with Augustus *Keppel, an inspiring leader who fired the boy's ambition to become a naval hero, and fifteen years later it was Keppel who promoted him to *post-captain to command his flagship in the expedition to Belleisle during the Seven Years War (1756–63) and the attack on Havana.

He commanded the *Monarch* in the 'moonlight battle' of 1780 when a fleet commanded by Sir George *Rodney roundly defeated a Spanish fleet under Vice Admiral de Langara during an operation to bring supplies to Gibraltar, at the time under heavy siege. He was with Lord *Howe at the next relief of Gibraltar in 1782 and was engaged in the long-range and indecisive action against a French fleet trying to bar the way. He was made rear admiral in 1787 and vice admiral in 1793, but although the Revolutionary War with France was declared in that year, it was not until 1795 that he was recalled to active service and appointed commander-in-chief in the North Sea, with his principal objective the Dutch fleet in the Texel, at the time allied to France.

In 1797, the year of the great naval mutinies at *Spithead and the *Nore, the trouble spread to Duncan's fleet which was then lying in Yarmouth Roads. Duncan himself was a remarkably handsome Scot of towering build, great personal strength, and impressive presence and when the first signs of mutiny appeared in the *Venerable*, his flagship, he quickly isolated the six ringleaders and by force of character won the remainder of the crew to his side. He dealt with a mutiny in the *Adamant* in similar fashion. When one of the men came forward to dispute his authority he seized him by the collar and with one arm held him suspended over the side while he addressed the crew: 'My lads, look at this fellow—he dares to deprive me of the command of the fleet.' His words were greeted with cheers, and the *Adamant*, like the *Venerable*, had done with mutiny.

Hoping that the whole fleet would now follow him, he took it to sea bound for the Texel, but one by one the ships deserted him and sailed back to England until only the *Venerable* and *Adamant* were left. On arrival off the Texel Duncan, by the signals he kept making, convinced the Dutch that he was communicating with a fleet just over the horizon and they remained in harbour. For the next five months he maintained a close blockade of the Texel, the ships of his fleet returning one by one to their duty, but eventually he had to take them all back to Yarmouth to revictual, leaving only a small observation squadron to keep an eye on the Dutch. While he was at Yarmouth one of this squadron appeared flying a signal to say that the enemy fleet was out. Duncan was at once on his way and on 11 October sighted the Dutch fleet of fifteen *ships of the line seven miles off shore and making for the shoal water off the coast to escape action. Duncan ferociously engaged them without waiting to form a *line of battle and a fierce action was fought in the shallows in which nine Dutch ships of the line and two *frigates were finally captured. After the battle he brought out his fleet and the Dutch prizes from the perils of a lee shore in the face of an onshore gale.

He was a man not only of great personal courage but also of great benevolence and humanity. When dealing with the mutiny in his fleet he did not exercise the disciplinary rigours at his disposal against the ringleaders but realized that there were some aspects of lower deck social life which could drive men to extremes, and so was merciful in his judgements. He died a rich man, full of honours. He had proved that in the British Navy discipline did not need to be maintained by the *cat-o'-nine-tails, and he had earned the love and admiration of his crews.

For a biography see the Earl of Camperdown, *Admiral Duncan* (1898).

DUNCAN, EDWARD (1803–82), British engraver, etcher, and lithographer, was born in London and was later a landscape artist in watercolours. Among his prints are a number of naval subjects which he engraved from pictures painted by William *Huggins. When he abandoned engraving for water-colour painting, in which he was also successful, his work in this medium included a number of marine pictures as well as landscapes.

DUNKIRK, a seaport of major importance on the northern coast of France and the birthplace of Jean *Bart, the famous French *privateer captain. The large roadstead off the port is well sheltered to the north by the great range of sandbanks which lie off the coasts of north-east France, Belgium, and Holland, and the port itself is capacious and able to take large vessels. It is well equipped with docks, repair, and shipbuilding facilities, and has recently been developed as a ferry port operating roll-on, roll-off ferries.

For a short period Dunkirk was in the possession of England, but was sold back to the French by Charles II in 1667 when he was in financial difficulties. It sprang into fame during the Second World War as the scene of the evacuation of the British Expeditionary Force after the German break-through into France in 1940 when an armada of small vessels of all types, largely manned by amateurs, coupled with destroyers of the British fleet, succeeded in bringing back to England a total of 338,226 men who had been pinned down on the coast by the German Army. The operation lasted nine days.

DUNNAGE, loose wood or wooden blocks used in the *holds of a merchant ship to secure the cargo above the *floors and away from the sides to protect it from any sweating of the plates and also to wedge it firmly so that it does not get thrown about by the motion of the ship at sea. See also FARDAGE.

DUPONT, SAMUEL FRANCIS (1803–65), American naval officer, had an important share in the basic planning for the Federal blockade of the Confederate seaports during the American Civil War (1861–5). He was born at Bergen Point, New Jersey, and became a *midshipman in 1815. His service before 1861 was outstanding, especially in command of the *sloop-of-war *Cyane* on the Pacific coast during the Mexican War, in the Gulf of California, and around San Diego. He became commandant of the Philadelphia Navy Yard in December 1860 and in that position he facilitated the passage of militia units to Annapolis and Washington via Chesapeake Bay. He was the senior member of a board which studied the Confederate coast from Alexandria, Virginia, to the Rio Grande. In

The evacuation from Dunkirk, 1940; oil painting by Richard Eurich

command of the South Atlantic Blockading Squadron, he was brilliantly successful in the capture of Port Royal Sound and the occupation of other ports of South Carolina and Georgia.

Had he been permitted to do so, he could have conducted the blockade of his portion of the sea coast more effectively than was possible under the constant interference from the Navy Department. The Secretary of the Navy, Gideon *Welles, did not believe in the blockade and advised President Lincoln that it should be dropped. At the same time the Assistant Secretary of the Navy, G. V. Fox, advised Lincoln that the navy could capture Charleston without military support and that such a capture would bring the Civil War to an end. Dupont protested against this, both by letter and in a personal visit to Welles and Fox in Washington, but was overruled. When the attack failed to accomplish the capture of the city and the *monitors under Dupont suffered unexpectedly heavy damage, Welles publicly blamed Dupont and he was relieved of his command. Many historians have accepted the unjustified abuse of Dupont in which Welles indulged, but the official records clearly indicate that Dupont had been wise and accurate in the information and advice he had given to Welles and Fox.

DUPUY DE LÔME, STANISLAS CHARLES HENRI LAURENT (1816–85), French naval architect, was a pioneer in the introduction of the iron warship. He was sent to England in 1842 to study iron shipbuilding, and directed the construction of the first iron ships in France. In 1848 he designed and built the first steam-driven *ship of the line in the French Navy, the *Napoléon*, and in 1859 his armoured *frigate *Gloire* led the world by incorporating side armour in her construction. He was made inspector-general of naval *matériel* in 1861. Later he turned his inventive talents in other directions, and during the Franco-Prussian war was engaged with plans for a steerable balloon with which to escape from the siege of Paris, but the city capitulated before the balloon was ready. He also drew up plans in 1875 for a train ferry to operate between Calais and Dover which he exhibited at the Academy of Sciences in conjunction with plans for improvements to the port.

DUQUESNE, ABRAHAM, Marquis (1610–88), French naval officer, spent his early maritime life in the merchant service, but when his father was killed in action against the Spaniards, he entered the navy and joined fiercely in the war against Spain, showing great courage in the battles of Guetaria (1638), Corunna (1639), Tarragona (1641), Barcelona (1643), and the Cabo de Gata (1643). On the decline of the French Navy he offered his services to Sweden, and as a vice admiral of that nation defeated the Danish fleet in two decisive battles. After his return to France the revolt at Bordeaux in 1650, supported by arms from Spain, gave him another chance of having a smack at the hated Spaniards. He fitted out a squadron of ships at his own expense and blockaded the Gironde, compelling the town of Bordeaux to surrender.

After a few years in the Mediterranean in operations against pirates, the revolt at Messina against Spanish domination once again brought the chance of battle against Spain. After a series of minor actions he met the combined Spanish–Dutch fleet, commanded by no less an admiral than Michiel de *Ruyter, near Catania and won an overwhelming victory in which de Ruyter was mortally wounded. For this success he was made a marquis by Louis XIV. His last naval actions were the bombardment of Algiers in 1682 and 1683, and of Genoa in 1684.

DURAND, COUPPEL DE SAINT-FRONT MARIN-MARIE-PAUL, best known as Marin-Marie (1901–   ), French yachtsman, painter, and author, made many notable single-handed cruises, including two crossings of the Atlantic, from New York to Le Havre in his yacht *Arielle* in 1936 and from Brest to New York in his *Winibelle* in 1938. As a painter he was appointed official artist to the Ministry of Marine in France and with his sense of design and colour, allied to an acute personal knowledge of the detail of ships and sailing craft, produced some pictures and seascapes that have rarely been excelled in modern times. His best-known book was *Wind Aloft and Wind Below* (1939).

DUTCHMAN'S LOG, see LOG.

DUTTON, THOMAS (*c.* 1816–78), British lithographer, worked in London from 1845 until the year of his death, devoting himself mainly to nautical subjects and particularly to sailing vessels, of which he acquired considerable technical knowledge, making great use of it in the detail of his drawings. It is because of this technical knowledge, allied to the excellence of his colour and design, that original prints by him have today become so highly prized by collectors.

'DYNASHIP', a project under current (1976) examination in Germany designed to return to the use of the winds as the main motive power for merchant vessels in modern trading conditions. Basically, the proposition is to reintroduce square-rigged ships as bulk carriers with an aerodynamically designed sail plan allied to mechanical means of sail handling. It has been estimated that this could produce an improvement of up to 60 per cent in wind energy directly used for propulsion in comparison with that used in the conventional square rig. Although the proposed vessels will still be square-rigged, the sails are attached to the *yards on runners and operated much as a curtain operates on a runner; they are controlled by one man on the *bridge by electro-hydraulic means, making it possible to set or reef all sails and trim all yards without the necessity of sending a single man up on the yards to handle the sails. A small auxiliary engine in each vessel provides the electric power required and also has the ability to take the ship out of calms and into areas where winds are forecast. Bulk carriers of up to 17,000 tons are envisaged in the 'Dynaship' project.

The main impetus behind this new project lies, first, in the ever-increasing cost of bunker fuel for ships and the possibility of the world's supply of oil being again used as a political weapon as happened during the Arab–Israeli war of 1973, and, second, in the improvements in forecasting which have evolved since the use of satellites in observing weather patterns on the earth. Predictions based on these observations should indicate areas of strong and steady winds to which the 'Dynaship' could be moved under her auxiliary engine and in which she could operate at her maximum efficiency.

E

EAGLE, H.M.S., a ship's name used more than twenty times in the Royal Navy. The best known are probably the aircraft carriers. The first of these was laid down as a battleship for the Chilean Navy and named *Almirante Cochrane*, but was taken over by the Royal Navy during the First World War (1914–18) and launched as an aircraft carrier on 8 June 1918 with the name *Eagle*. She was sunk by a *U-boat in the Mediterranean on 11 August 1942. The second aircraft carrier *Eagle* was launched on 19 March 1946 by Harland & Wolff of Belfast, and reconstructed in Devonport Dockyard in 1959–64. In view of current British naval policy of abandoning the big aircraft carriers as ships of war, the present *Eagle* is unlikely to be followed at the end of her useful life by another vessel of the same name and type.

EAGRE, see BORE.

EARING, a small rope used to fasten the upper corners of a square sail to its *yard. The outer turns of the earings, after being passed through the head *cringles on the sail, are then passed beyond the *lifts and rigging on the yardarm and are designed to stretch the head of the sail tight along the yard, while the remaining turns, known as inner turns, draw the sail close up to the yard and are passed within the lifts. Below the earings are the *reef earings, by which the reef cringles are similarly made fast to the yard when the sail is reefed.

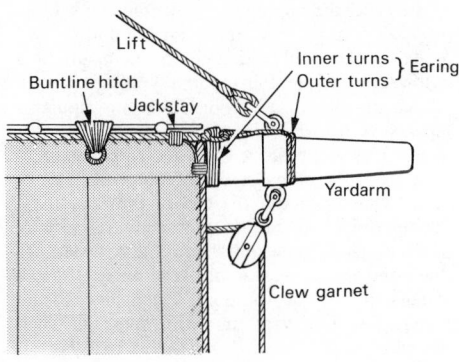

Earing

EASE, to, or **EASY,** a good maritime term meaning, in general, to take the pressure off. A sailing ship, on the order 'ease her', is *luffed, or brought closer into the wind in order to reduce the wind pressure on her sails in a heavy blow; the *helm in a steamship is eased by reducing the angle previously ordered, in order to slow down the rate of swing; and so on. Similarly, in sailing yachts, the sheets are eased, sometimes to take the pressure off the sail to reduce the angle of heel, at others to produce a squarer aspect of the sail to the wind.

EAST INDIA COMPANY, the name of several incorporated companies for the exploitation of trade in India, the East Indies, and the Far East. In all, there were eight East India companies, set up by England, Holland, France, Denmark, Scotland, Spain, Austria, and Sweden, but only two of these, those of England and Holland, were of importance.

The English East India Company, known as the Honourable East India Company, was founded towards the end of the 16th century and was incorporated by Elizabeth I by royal charter on 31 December 1600. It was set up with a capital of £72,000 subscribed by 125 shareholders. The first governor was Sir Thomas Smythe. The early voyages, known as 'separate' voyages, were made by individual shareholders who bore the cost and took the profit from them, but from 1612 onwards all voyages were made by the company as a whole. During these years the company's ships reached as far as Japan, where friendly relations were established. At the same time factories (trading centres) were established at Masulipatam and Pettapoli on the mainland of India.

These initial trading moves were vigorously opposed by the newly incorporated Dutch East India Company, and a state of virtual war existed between the two. In 1619 an agreement was reached to stop these disputes, but it lasted for only one hour, recriminations and fighting breaking out as soon as the smoke from the saluting guns had cleared. This period of fighting reached its peak in 1623 with the massacre at Amboyna, where the English merchants were tortured and killed by the Dutch governor while protected by a flag of truce.

In 1609 the English East India Company

The sale room at India House; aquatint from Ackermann's Microcosm of London

built its own dockyard at *Deptford, on the River Thames, and it was there that the magnificent ships which formed the company's fleet were built. Not only were they the best and largest merchant ships of their time, they were also armed as warships both to guard against the piracy which was rife in the Malay States and to hold their own against similarly armed merchantmen of the Dutch, Portuguese, and French companies. These ships—*East Indiamen as they were called—were the aristocrats of the shipping world.

The English East India Company was successful from the start, and was given further impetus by Charles II, who enlarged its charter by the right to acquire territory, exercise civil and criminal jurisdiction, make treaties, wage war, command armies, and issue its own money. With its already established position in India, with three 'presidencies' in Bombay, Madras, and Bengal, it was but a matter of time before the whole of India was subdued and the various native rulers brought under the control of the company. Its very success in this respect caused the English government to look again at the charter. When Robert Clive won the battle of Plassey

in 1757 to make the company all-powerful in India, the British government was virtually forced to accept some responsibility for the territory thus acquired. This was done by making the top company appointments subject to government approval, and gradually through this means political, financial, and military control of India passed from the company to the government in London.

In 1813 the monopoly of all trade with India was taken away from the company and thrown open to the public, though the company was allowed to retain the monopoly of trade with China. In 1833, trade with China was similarly opened to all who wished to venture in it. This opening of the eastern trade routes to competition from the ships of other companies and of individuals spelt out the end of the East India Company as a trading monopoly. Gradually their ships disappeared from these waters as the competition increased, particularly with the extension of the original Peninsular Steam Navigation Company into the Peninsular and Oriental S. N. Co. (*P & O) in 1842. Nevertheless, because the East India Company already had all the machinery of government in operation in India, the London government, as a matter of administrative convenience, decided to leave the operation of civil government entirely in the hands of the company, and this continued until 1857 and the outbreak of the Indian Mutiny at Meerut. The excesses of the mutiny and the severity of the subsequent punishments forced the London government to step in and take over responsibility for the internal government of India, replacing many of the company's officials with men appointed direct from London and taking others into direct employment. The East India Company was then officially dissolved in 1858.

The Dutch East India Company was founded by charter from the States-General in 1602 to regulate and amalgamate all the various trading ventures to the East Indies already in existence. It was directed in Holland by local boards for each province of the States-General acting under a main directorate of seventeen members elected by the local boards. It was granted a monopoly of the East Indian trade, exempted from import taxes, and authorized to maintain armed forces by sea and land, erect forts, make war or peace, and coin its own money.

Its early history is mainly a history of warfare, driving out of the East Indies first the Portuguese and then the English. It established its main capital in Batavia, with subsidiary capitals in the Malay Archipelago, Ceylon, Java, Malacca, Amboyna, and Ternate, with a fortified post at the Cape of Good Hope to ensure the safety of the route to and from Holland.

At the height of its success, which lasted for most of the 17th century, the company possessed 40 warships, 150 merchant ships, and 10,000 soldiers. But it held in its own success the seeds of its ultimate decline. Its policy in the East Indies was complete monopoly of trade, maintained by force of arms where required, and this inevitably led to rivalry and hostility with the English and French interests in the area. The Dutch, by the early 18th century, had been driven from the mainland of Asia and Ceylon, and disappearing profits, combined with a big increase in military costs, brought eventual bankruptcy. When Holland was invaded by the French revolutionary armies in 1798 the company was officially wound up. See also JOHN COMPANY.

EAST INDIAMEN, the name given to the ships of the various *East India companies. The great national importance of these companies, particularly those of England and Holland, coupled with the rich returns of their monopoly of trade in the east, resulted in the building of proud and magnificent ships, as much for national and company prestige as for the actual trade. Ships of these companies, as large as any built in the world, were highly gilded and decorated with

carving, and were finished internally as much for comfort and luxury for captain, officers, and passengers as for cargo capacity. They were always armed as warships for protection against pirates and against the warships of other nations (see, e.g., DANCE, Nathaniel). Both the English and Dutch companies equipped their own private dockyards where their ships were built, and it was only in the 19th century, when the monopoly of eastern trade began to be eroded by private competition, that the British company began to put out its shipbuilding to outside interests, the greater part of it to the Blackwall yard of Green and Wigram.

Throughout the long histories of the individual companies, East Indiamen were regarded as the *ne plus ultra* of the shipping world. For more than two centuries these stately, magnificent ships were generally acknowledged to be the lords of the ocean.

EASTERN SOLOMONS, BATTLE OF THE, a naval action fought in the Pacific during the Second World War between fleets of U.S. and Japanese ships and naval aircraft. In order to cover the delivery of reinforcements to their army on Guadalcanal, the Japanese combined fleet was deployed in an area north of the Solomon Islands, divided into several groups. A carrier striking force was composed of the *aircraft carriers *Zuikaku* and *Shokaku* under Admiral *Nagumo with a vanguard group of two *battleships and three heavy *cruisers stationed in close support, while an advance force of six cruisers and the seaplane carrier *Chitose* scouted far ahead; finally, as a diversionary group to decoy the American carrier strikes, the small carrier *Ryujo*, with a cruiser and two *destroyers as escort, was detached from the main body.

To oppose this fleet, an American task force comprising the aircraft carriers *Saratoga*, *Enterprise*, and *Wasp*, with a battleship, cruisers, and destroyers under Rear Admiral Fletcher, advanced north of the Eastern Solomon Islands, and early on 23 August 1942, had information via a shore-based reconnaissance seaplane of a small Japanese troop convoy. Strike aircraft took off from Guadalcanal as well as from the carriers, but in the rain and low cloud they failed to find their target and all returned to spend the night on Guadalcanal.

Meanwhile Fletcher, suspecting a ruse, had detached the *Wasp* to refuel 240 miles to the south; so that when a report of a Japanese carrier group 300 miles to the north was received, he found himself committed to battle with only two-thirds of his available strength. The enemy discovered was, in fact, the decoy *Ryujo* which was overwhelmed and sunk by the strike planes from the *Enterprise* and *Saratoga*, while at the same time a large bomber force was being flown off the *Shokaku* and *Zuikaku*. Fletcher, profiting from previous experience, had retained a strong fighter defence; its direction was not altogether effective, however, and though no Japanese torpedo planes got through, their dive-bombers arrived over the target unopposed. A majority were shot down by the ships' gunfire, or by fighters after the attack, but the *Enterprise* was extensively damaged by three bombs.

A second wave of strike planes which had flown off from the *Enterprise* and *Saratoga* before the enemy attack had developed failed to find Nagumo's carriers and succeeded only in seriously damaging the *Chitose*. The Japanese troop convoy had meanwhile been attacked by marine dive-bombers from Guadalcanal which sank two of the ships and forced the remainder to turn back.

The outcome of the battle must be assessed tactically as inconclusive, but very heavy Japanese aircrew losses were to make it another step towards Japan's eventual defeat in the Pacific.

EBB, the flow of the tidal stream as it recedes, from the ending of the period of *slack water at high tide to the start of the period of slack water at low tide. Its period is about 6 hours, which is approximately divided into three parts, the first 2 hours being known as the first of the ebb, the middle 2 hours as the strength of the ebb, and the last 2 hours as the last of the ebb. See also FLOOD.

E-BOAT, the British and American name in the Second World War for the *Schnellboot*, the German *motor-torpedoboat. Built in great numbers, they had a waterline length of 106 feet and carried two torpedo tubes and two small anti-aircraft guns. They were capable of a maximum speed of 39 knots, and in general performance were considered superior to their British counterparts.

ECHO SOUNDER, an instrument based on the principle of *sonar by which the depth of water can be measured. By using a vertical sonar pulse and measuring the time taken between emission of the signal and the receipt of the echo off the bottom, the depth of water can be accurately calculated. Echo sounding was developed shortly after the end of the First World War when the Anglo-French *asdic was introduced as a means of locating the positions of submerged submarines, and was quickly adapted for use in marine surveys for recording soundings without the labour of the hand and deep sea *lead line. It is also quicker and more accurate in recording a sounding than a *sounding machine. It has since been developed for use in all types of vessels, modern echo sounders producing a continuous

trace which shows the contour of the bottom beneath the vessel. Small sets, run off a battery, have been developed for use in yachts, and are claimed to be able to record a depth of as little as one fathom.

ECLIPTIC, from the Greek *ekleipsis*, disappearance, is the *great circle on the *celestial sphere traced out by the sun in the course of a year. It is so called because for an eclipse of the sun or moon to occur, the moon must lie on or near the ecliptic. The ecliptic intersects the celestial equator, or *equinoctial, twice during the year at dates known as the equinoxes; on 21 March at the 'first point of Aries', which is 0° Right Ascension, and on 23 September at the 'first point of Libra', at 180° Right Ascension, and is furthest from the equator (23° 23′ N. or S.) at the points marking the summer *solstice (June) and winter solstice (December).

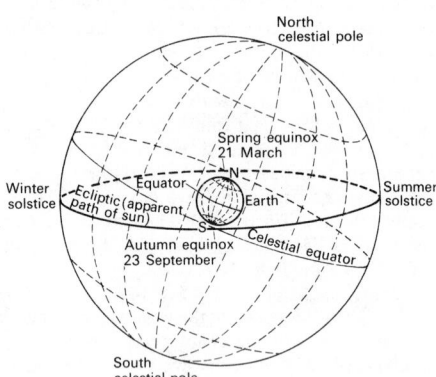

Ecliptic

EDDY, a small local current in the sea usually caused by tidal streams as they ebb and flow round or against objects fixed or moored to the sea bed. A pier or jetty will produce eddies according to the direction of the tidal stream, as also will a buoy moored in tidal waters. Points of land or other similar obstructions produce their eddies. They can also be formed by particular winds, particularly on mountainous coastlines where the wind can be deflected or accelerated by the contours of the coast and act on the surface water of the sea to give it a temporary eddy. An eddy flows in a different, often opposing, direction to the main current.

EDEN, RICHARD (*c.* 1512–76), English translator, is chiefly remembered for his translation from the Spanish of Martin Cortes's *Breve Compendio de la Sphera y de la Arte de Navegar*, published in 1551, to which he was encouraged by Stephen *Borough. At that time the knowledge in England of navigational practice was almost non-existent, and the translation of this Spanish textbook on the art proved to be a tremendous fillip to English voyages of exploration. It was published in England in 1561. Eden had already shown his interest in the sea by two previous translations, in 1553 of Münster's *Cosmography* and in 1555 of Peter Martyr's *Decades of the Newe Worlde or West India*. He has been described as a forerunner of the great Richard *Hakluyt in his efforts to make known information about the early voyages of navigation and discovery.

A probably more famous treatise on navigation than that of Martin Cortes was the *Arte de Navegar* of Pedro de Medina, written in 1545. Because of the similarity of title (Cortes's book frequently having its title shortened to *Arte de Navegar*) it is often thought that it was Medina's book which was translated by Eden. This book, translated into English by John Frampton, did not appear until 1581 and had nothing like the success in England that was gained by the earlier publication.

EDGELL, Sir JOHN AUGUSTINE (1880–1962), British vice admiral, was Hydrographer of the Navy in 1932–45, his appointment being extended beyond the normal five years to cover the Second World War during which his leadership ashore and afloat was outstanding. Having joined the navy in 1893 he began a surveying career in 1902 in H.M.S. *Triton* on the east coast of England. He then had experience in the *Egeria* in British Columbia, in the *Rambler* on the China coast and Borneo, in the *Merlin* in the Red Sea and Malaya, and in the *Sealark* off Ceylon and the Queensland coast of Australia. His first command in 1912 was the *Mutine* on the west coast of Africa and in this ship he believed he was the last naval officer to leave harbour with the *yards manned (see also SALUTE). In 1914 he was in the *Hearty* on North Sea surveys and the following year took the *Endeavour* with printing equipment installed to support the Mediterranean Fleet at the *Dardanelles by being able to produce on the spot detailed diagrams and surveys of those waters. In 1917–20 he was at the Admiralty and in 1920–1 surveyed the vicinity of the then projected *Singapore naval base. Periods in the Hydrographic Department were varied by the command of the Australian surveying ship *Moresby* during 1925–8, a time when senior British officers were being lent to the young Australian Navy, and of the *Endeavour* in the Rea Sea and on the Palestinian coast in 1930–1.

During the Second World War the Hydrographic Department was evacuated from London to Bath and chart printing was inaugurated at a Taunton establishment. The latter was planned by Edgell to house eventually the whole department, though this was only to come about in 1968. Rotary offset machines were available in time for the peak years when some 7,000,000 charts were needed to provide, *inter alia*, for the Normandy landing fleets. A large variety of special charts had to be compiled and the total staff of the Hydrographic Department rose to 1,600.

Internationally, Edgell was widely respected and he regularly attended international hydrographic conferences. In scientific fields he saw a naval meteorological service become part of his department in 1937 and in the same year a start was made on the construction of the non-magnetic ship *Research. But war intervened, and though nearly completed, the ship had regrettably to be abandoned for financial reasons. At the Royal Society, of which he was made a Fellow in 1943, he initiated a movement which ended with the formation of the National Institute of Oceanography in 1951.

EDWARD BONAVENTURE, a ship of 160 tons *burthen in which Richard *Chancellor made his first voyage to Arctic Russia in 1553. She was wrecked off Petsligo, Aberdeen, in 1556 on her way back from Chancellor's third voyage on behalf of the Muscovy Company.

EGERIA, H.M.S., a ship's name well known in the British hydrographic service. The first of the name was a screw *sloop of four guns and 894 tons which worked as a surveying ship from 1886 to 1910. Her first eight years were spent in the Far East, including a deep-sea cruise in 1889 from Australia to Canada to make soundings in connection with the trans-Pacific cable, finally laid in 1901. Her main task was however surveying in British Columbia waters from 1897 to 1911, when she was sold on the station. A new *Egeria* of 160 tons displacement came into service for inshore surveys in British waters in 1959. The name is also familiar in hydrographic circles for its application to a type of floating beacon which was standard equipment over many years.

EGYPT, a 7,940-ton *P & O passenger liner, outward bound with over £1,000,000 of gold, which was rammed and sunk 22 miles south-west of Ushant on 20 May 1922. She was steaming through fog patches with engines on 'stand-by' when a whistle was heard to *port; her engines were stopped. Four minutes later a small steamer, later identified as the French *Seine*, was seen through the fog to port on a collision course and moments afterwards she struck the *Egypt* abreast No. 3 hatch, damaging the watertight bulkheads at both ends of the hold. The liner took an immediate heavy list and sank in 20 minutes. Six lifeboats were got away safely and 252 persons were saved; eighty-six lives were lost, including fifteen passengers.

In 1929 the Italian salvage firm Sorima started operations to locate her wreck with a view to recovering the gold. They found her in 1930 in 400 feet of water. A diver in an armoured diving suit was lowered to her, the greatest depth to which any diver had been to that date, and the task of cutting away three decks above the strong room began. The diver was connected by telephone to the salvage ship above and he directed the lowering of explosives and the positioning of them to blow the decks open; afterwards remote-control grabs were lowered to remove the torn metal. In June 1932, after daunting setbacks, the first gold bars were lifted. Operations to recover the remainder continued until 1935 when almost all the bullion on board had been lifted, an epic story of courage, endurance, and patience. See DIVING, SALVAGE.

EJECTAMENTA MARIS, products of the sea thrown up on a beach when officially they become, in Britain, one of the * droits of Admiralty except in the case of * 'Fishes Royal' (whales, dolphins, and sturgeons). Since 1971, when royal ownership was renounced by Act of Parliament, such fish are allocated to museums for study purposes.

ELPHINSTONE, GEORGE KEITH, first Viscount Keith (1746–1823), British admiral, was born near Stirling, entered the navy in 1761, and distinguished himself at the capture of Charleston, S. Carolina, in 1780. At the beginning of the French Revolutionary War (1793–1801) he was promoted rear admiral, took part in the capture of Toulon, and in 1796 defeated a Dutch squadron at Saldanha Bay, S.W. Africa, after which troops were landed to occupy the Cape of Good Hope.

He helped to suppress the great naval mutinies of 1797 and was appointed second-in-command of the Mediterranean Fleet under Lord St. Vincent (see JERVIS, John). The fleet failed to intercept the French admiral Bruix on his passage from Brest to Toulon, but subsequent French inactivity in the Mediterranean caused no embarrassment to British arms. On St. Vincent's recall to London Elphinstone became commander-in-chief in the Mediterranean, an appointment which caused much annoyance to Lord * Nelson who was operating independently off Naples and Sicily. With his fleet Keith blockaded the Genoa coast until Napoleon's victory at Marengo forced him to withdraw his ships. In 1801 he and General Sir Ralph Abercromby conducted the first successful amphibious expedition of the war when they defeated the remnants of the French Army in Egypt.

From 1803 to 1807, during the Napoleonic War (1803–15), in command of the North Sea station, Keith was primarily responsible for defence against invasion. In 1812–15 he commanded the Channel Fleet, and it was to the * Bellerophon, a ship under his command, that Napoleon surrendered off Rochefort in 1815.

Though never associated with any major battle, and without achieving either popularity or renown, Keith rose to the top of his profession by his gift of administration; he also became a very rich man through the acquisition of * prize money. He married twice, his second wife being Hester Thrale (Dr. Johnson's 'Queenie'), and his daughter married Napoleon's aide-de-camp, the Comte de Flahault.

EMBARGO, a temporary arrest or injunction laid on ships or cargo to prevent their arrival or departure in time of war. An embargo can be general, affecting all ships of whatever nationality, or partial, in which only ships of certain nationalities are affected. Originally embargoes could be declared in anticipation of a declaration of war, a method used by many nations to detain ships of the enemy which might be in port. However, in the Hague Convention of 1907, a clause laid down that it was desirable that ships in an enemy port on the outbreak of war should be allowed to depart freely but did not make it binding on the belligerent. A ship stopped by embargo may not be confiscated but only detained without compensation, and must be restored to her owners after the war. It is customary today to give a respite to enemy merchant ships to leave port on the outbreak of war so that neither ship nor cargo is subject to embargo.

EMBARK, to, a verb with three meanings: **(1)** to put on board a vessel, **(2)** to go on board a vessel, **(3)** of a ship, to receive on board. EMBARKATION, the process or action of embarking.

EMDEN, S.M.S., a German light * cruiser of 3,600 tons, was the best-known surface raider of the First World War (1914–18). In a cruise lasting from the outbreak of war until 9 November 1914, she captured or sank twenty-three merchant ships totalling 101,182 tons. After leaving Admiral von * Spee's force in the Pacific she entered the Indian Ocean and began operations off Rangoon. For fear of the Emden the port was closed for a fortnight and the marine insurance market disrupted. On 22 September the Emden shelled the oil installations at Madras, and was then narrowly missed by British and Japanese cruisers. She then headed south towards Ceylon and as a result the sailings of troop convoys were held up from Australia and New Zealand. Between 25 and 27 September she cap-

The Emden *on the rocks at Keeling Island, November 1914*

tured six ships and then went off to Diego Garcia in the British Maldive Islands where she carried out repairs. For lack of wireless the inhabitants of these islands were ignorant of the outbreak of war and her self-refit passed off without notice.

She returned to the Bay of Bengal, entered Penang harbour, sank the Russian light cruiser *Zhemchug* and the French *destroyer *Mousquet*, and disappeared again. Her next and final move was an attack on the cable station at Cocos Keeling Island. While a landing party was engaged in trying to cut the cables the Australian light cruiser *Sydney* appeared and in a short engagement shattered her beyond repair and drove her ashore as a total wreck, securing the surrender of her survivors. The landing party which was to cut the cables escaped in a small *schooner and eventually, after a daring trip lasting seven months, arrived at Constantinople via southern Arabia. Throughout the *Emden*'s cruise her captain, Karl von Müller, had taken the greatest possible care to avoid casualties and to look after his prisoners and his memory is held high as one of the great seamen of the age.

EMPRESS AUGUSTA BAY, BATTLE OF, was a night surface action of the Second World War, fought in the Pacific between an American force of four 6-inch *cruisers, *Montpelier* (flag of Rear Admiral Merrill), *Cleveland*, *Columbia*, and *Denver*, and eight *destroyers, covering an amphibious force effecting a landing on Bougainville Island, and a Japanese force of two heavy cruisers, *Myoko* (flag of Rear Admiral Omori) and *Haguro*, the light cruisers *Sendai* and *Agano*, and six destroyers.

The main feature of the battle, which took place on the night of 1/2 November 1943, was Merrill's newly conceived tactics of manoeuvring his cruiser line to deny it to the Japanese as an easy target for their long-range, high-speed *torpedoes, and of freeing his destroyer divisions to act independently in attacking the enemy with torpedoes. After an initial success in which the concentrated, *radar-controlled fire of Merrill's sixty 6-inch guns destroyed the *Sendai*, the battle became a confused mêlée, except in the American cruiser line which, though it failed to cause much damage to the enemy, was, for the first time in one of these encounters, kept clear of the Japanese torpedoes.

At the end of the battle the Japanese retired. They had lost the *Sendai* and one destroyer and had suffered minor damage to their cruisers, in return for having slightly damaged the *Denver* and sunk the destroyer *Foote* which had by chance crossed the path of the torpedoes aimed at the American cruisers.

ENDEAVOUR, the name of two yachts built for Mr. (later Sir Thomas) T. O. M. *Sopwith with which he challenged for the *America*'s Cup.

The Endeavour *being repaired after grounding on the Great Barrier Reef; engraving from Cook's* Voyages, *late 18th century*

The first was a *J-Class yacht of 143 tons *displacement and setting 7,560 sq ft (724 sq m) of sail, designed by Charles E. *Nicholson and built by Camper and Nicholson at Gosport, Hampshire, in 1933. She was considered the best yacht of her day in the J-Class, and at the Cup races in 1934, when she came very close to defeating the American defender *Rainbow*, she set for the first time in the history of these matches a *double-clewed jib which had been designed by her owner, who also skippered his yacht during the series. While she was on tuning-up trials in the Solent, however, her novel jib with its double *sheets had been spotted by astute American observers in time for the defender to be equipped with a similar type of sail, so that Sopwith's aerodynamic advantage was largely nullified.

The second *Endeavour* was also a J-Class yacht and again designed by Charles E. Nicholson and built by Camper and Nicholson at Gosport in 1936 for Sopwith's second attempt to win back the *America's* Cup the following year. Displacing 163 tons and carrying 7,540 sq ft (722 sq m) of canvas, she was built to the maximum waterline length allowed by the Cup rules, namely 87·0 ft (26·52 m). Trials in the Solent indicated that *Endeavour II* was demonstrably faster than her predecessor of 1934, but she was to find herself pitted against a defender whose design owed much to the joint work of W. Starling Burgess and a brilliant new designer of large racing yachts, 29-year-old Olin J. *Stephens. In the series of 1937 the American *Ranger* proved

beyond doubt the faster of the two, and it was to be said later that she was the fastest J-Class yacht ever produced.

The first *Endeavour* is in the process of being restored to her original rig for permanent display at Cowes, Isle of Wight.

ENDEAVOUR, H.M.S., a ship's name made famous by Captain James *Cook's first voyage in her in 1768–71. She was originally a *cat-built *collier, specially selected by Cook for her strong construction, and renamed *Endeavour* after her purchase at Whitby. Her naval description was a *barque of 366 tons with ten carriage guns (4-pounders) and twelve swivels.

The name was used for a number of minor vessels from 1652 to 1813 and again in 1913 for a ship of 1,280 tons specially built for ocean-going surveying at a time when anti-fouling composition replaced copper sheathing and wireless telegraphy was new equipment. Moreover, in the First World War (1914–18) she was the first surveying ship to carry chart production equipment (see also EDGELL, Sir John), principally for the *Dardanelles campaign. In 1937 she began an extensive programme in New Zealand coastal waters, but the Second World War intervened and in 1943 she was paid off at Suez after more than thirty years service.

ENDURANCE, the name given by Sir Ernest *Shackleton to a Norwegian sealer of 350 tons which he purchased in 1914 to accompany his Imperial Trans-Antarctic expedition. Her origi-

nal name was *Polaris*. In January 1915, while
in the Antarctic, she was beset in the ice of the
Weddell Sea, abandoned, and drifted until the
following November when she was finally
crushed and sank.

ENIWETOK ATOLL, an amphibious operation
in the Pacific during the Second World War
undertaken to complete the occupation of the
Marshall Islands by American forces during the
war against Japan. The Eniwetok group of
islands consists of three main islands rising from
the circular coral reef surrounding a lagoon some
21 miles long by 17 miles wide—Eniwetok and
Parry in the south-east, Engebi at the northern
end. A fleet of ten transports, nine *L.S.T.s, and
six *L.C.I.s, with ten escorting *destroyers,
carried the assault force of 5,700 marines of the
22nd U.S. Marine Regiment and 4,509 soldiers
of the 10th Infantry Regiment. A group of three
battleships, three heavy *cruisers, and seven destroyers provided fire support; three small *aircraft carriers gave air support.

D-day was 17 February 1944. Between 31
January and 6 February, again between 10 and
12 February, and on the 16th, continuous air
strikes on Eniwetok and Engebi were kept up by
aircraft from a supporting fast carrier group.
Engebi was the first to be assaulted on D + 1 day
after the entrance to the lagoon had been swept
for *mines on D-day and artillery landed on
satellite islets. By the afternoon of D + 1 the
Japanese garrison of some 1,200 had been
liquidated and the island secured.

On D + 2 it was Eniwetok's turn, with landings made under cover of a heavy bombardment.
Though losses at the beach were light, it was not
until 21 February that the island was finally
secured. The landing on Parry was therefore
postponed until the 22nd, the island being kept
meanwhile under harassing bombardment. A
similar plan to that for Engebi was successfully
followed, but through a tragic mistake three
L.C.I.s came under fire from an American destroyer and suffered heavy casualties. Resistance
by the garrison of some 1,300 Japanese was
stubborn but had been overcome by nightfall.

ENSIGN, (1) the national flag as worn by the
ships of a nation. Many countries which have
navies as well as merchant ships use two ensigns,
one for naval ships and one for merchant vessels.
For British ships three ensigns are used, the
White Ensign flown by a ship or naval shore
establishment indicates a unit of the Royal Navy,
the Blue Ensign is flown by naval auxiliary vessels, and the Red Ensign by vessels of the merchant navy. But see also ROYAL YACHT SQUAD-
RON, whose yachts above a certain tonnage may
fly the White Ensign. Many yacht clubs also have
approval for their yachts to fly the Blue Ensign

defaced with the badge of the club in the *fly.
Any British vessel not naval may fly the Red
Ensign, but again many yacht clubs have permission to fly this ensign defaced as above. See also
SQUADRONAL COLOURS, FLAGS OF CONVENIENCE.
In earlier days an ensign was often called an
ancient. **(2)** A naval rank in the U.S. and some
other navies equivalent to that of *midshipman
or sub-lieutenant. See Appendix 1.

ENTER, to, (1) the act of a man who signed on
voluntarily for service in the British Navy in the
days of *impressment. It has been fairly reliably
estimated that from about one-third to one-half
of the seamen enrolled during these years entered
voluntarily, the remainder being supplied by the
*press gangs and the *Quota Acts. The number
varied widely from ship to ship, according to the
popularity or otherwise of her captain and the
nature of the service to which she was ordered. It
varied, too, according to current naval successes
in battle, a notable victory being frequently followed by a surge in voluntary recruitment. **(2)**
The act of boarding an enemy ship. A boarding
party enters the enemy, his deck having first been
cleared as much as possible with fire or *stinkpots. 'It happens many times that there are
more men lost in a minute by entering than in
long fight board by board.' Mainwaring, *The
Seaman's Dictionary* (1644). **(3)** Entering ladder, the wooden steps fixed up the side of a
sailing warship level with the *waist and leading
to the entering ports which were cut down on the
middle gundeck of the old three-decker *ships of
the line, by which seamen came on board from a
boat lying alongside, or a rope ladder hung over
the *gallery in cases where it was too rough for a
boat to lie safely alongside. **(4)** Entering rope, a
rope which hung down the ship's side alongside
the entering ladder to assist men coming on
board. **(5)** Entering or entered, a term which
indicates that the *master of a ship which has
arrived from a foreign port has sworn the contents of his ship's papers before the customs
authorities.

ENTERPRISE, a 128-ton American yacht
designed by W. Starling Burgess in 1929 to the
order of Harold S. *Vanderbilt to defend the
**America's* Cup against the fifth and last chal-
lenge made by Sir Thomas *Lipton with *Shamrock V*. Three other possible defenders were built
for the occasion by different syndicates, *Weeta-
moe*, *Yankee*, and *Whirlwind*, but at the eliminating trials *Enterprise* proved to be the fastest
yacht and was selected as the defender. Like the
challenger she was designed to the *J-Class
Universal rule of America, built with equivalent
strength of hull to *Lloyd's rules, and rigged
with a jib-headed or *Bermuda mainsail with
three working headsails, jib, jib topsail, and fore-

staysail without a *bowsprit. She won the first four races of the seven-race contest and so retained the *America*'s Cup for the *New York Y.C.

ENTERPRISE, a ship of 470 tons, fitted with a steam engine, which in 1821 made a passage of 103 days from London to Calcutta during which she covered 11,450 miles. During her voyage she used her engine, driving a pair of paddle-wheels, on 64 days, the remainder of the passage being made under sail. Her voyage is noteworthy as the first long passage on which steam propulsion was used to a significant extent.

ENTERPRISE, H.M.S., a *sloop of 471 tons purchased by the Admiralty in 1848 for £24,545 and fitted out, together with the *Investigator*, for Captain James C. *Ross's expedition to the Arctic in search of Sir John *Franklin in 1848–9. She was employed on a similar mission in the *Collinson–*McClure expedition of 1850–5. In 1860 she was lent to the Commissioners for Northern Lights and used as a coal hulk at Oban, and in 1889 lent to the Board of Trade. She was finally sold for breaking up in 1903.

ENTERPRISE, U.S.S., the first ship of this name in Continental service was captured from the British on *Lake Champlain on 18 May 1775. The second, third, and fourth *Enterprises* were *schooners, the third seeing service in the Mediterranean and in the War of 1812. Andrew Sterrett and Stephen *Decatur, Jr., made their reputations in this *Enterprise* in operations against Tripoli. The fifth *Enterprise* was a screw *sloop launched in June 1874. Later she was a training vessel at the Naval Academy and was used by the Massachusetts State Nautical School. The seventh *Enterprise* was the *aircraft carrier, known as 'Big E', launched on 12 May 1938. She earned twenty battle stars (see BATTLE HONOURS) in the Second World War and was decommissioned in February 1947. This *Enterprise* was hit and damaged by Japanese *kamikaze bombers on three different occasions, also once by a horizontal bomber, and twice by dive bombing planes. Apart from these six occasions on which she suffered damage from enemy action, she was in the battles of *Midway and of the *Philippine Sea as well as eighteen other actions against the enemy. She was followed by the present *Enterprise*, a nuclear-powered carrier of 75,700 tons operating about 100 aircraft.

ENTREPÔT, a description often used for the particular type of trade of a port. The strict meaning of the word is a place to which goods are brought for distribution to other parts of the world, and when used in connection with a port is generally taken to mean the centre to which

local manufactures or produce is brought for export. It is frequently used, however, to indicate trade in the opposite direction; a port is said to be an entrepôt for the goods imported from overseas for distribution in its immediate neighbourhood.

ENTRY, the form of the fore-body of a ship under the load line as it thrusts through the sea. A ship with a slim bow is said to have a fine entry. It is in many ways the complement of *run, which is the shape of the after-body of a ship in relation to the resistance it causes as it moves through the water. See also SHIPBUILDING.

ENTRY PORT, a large *port cut in the sides of the larger sailing warships through which men entered on board the ship. They gave the opportunity to many contemporary ship designers to include elaborate carvings to embellish the port.

EPHEMERIS, from the Greek, a diary, an astronomical almanac in which are tabulated the predicted celestial positions of the heavenly bodies on the *equinoctial system against a standard time, usually *Greenwich Mean Time. The *Nautical Almanac includes ephemerides of the sun, moon, and navigational planets, as well as other information of use to the nautical astronomer.

EQUINOCTIAL, from the Latin *aequus*, equal, and *nox*, night, the *great circle on the *celestial sphere in the plane of the earth's equator, sometimes called the celestial equator. The sun is on the equinoctial on two occasions each year, these occurring on 21 March and 23 September, days known as the equinoxes. On these days the sun rises at 6 a.m., and sets at 6 p.m. (local time) at every place on earth. The two points of intersection of the equinoctial with the *ecliptic are called the spring and autumnal equinoctial points respectively, or more usually the First Points of Aries and Libra for the spring and autumnal equinoxes.

The word is also used as an adjective to describe phenomena happening at or about the time of the equinox, e.g., equinoctial gales, equinoctial rains, etc.

ERATOSTHENES (*c.* 276–194 B.C.) was a Greek man of science from Cyene in Libya. While keeper of the famous library at Alexandria he accepted Pythagoras's theory that the earth was spherical and made the first measurement of the circumference of the earth by working out the north–south distance from Aswan to Alexandria using existing surveys and measuring the length of the shadow cast by the sun of a gnomon simultaneously at the two places. From this he deduced that the distance between Aswan and Alexandria (about 5,000 stadia) subtended an angle of 7° 12′ at the earth's centre, which of course gave him the circumference of the earth by simple mathematics (see also CARTOGRAPHY, CHARTMAKING). His measurement was only about four per cent in excess of modern determinations of the mean circumference of the earth and has led to his being regarded by many as the founder of geodesy.

He compiled a map of the inhabited world based on a diaphragm centred on *Rhodes and with unequally spaced parallels and *meridians designed to pass through known places from the Pillars of Hercules in the west to the Ganges in the east and from Taprobane (? Ceylon) in the south to Borysthenes (? mouth of the Danube) in the north.

EREBUS, H.M.S., a bomb *ketch of 372 tons built at Pembroke and launched in 1826. She carried ten guns and her complement was sixty. After service in the Mediterranean in 1827–30 and nine years in the reserve, she was selected to take part in Captain James C. *Ross's expedition to the Antarctic in 1839 from which she returned in 1843. In 1845 she was fitted with a steam engine and screw propeller to sail under Sir John *Franklin's command on his last voyage to the Arctic. She was abandoned in the ice in April 1848. Her name is always associated with that of H.M.S. *Terror which accompanied her on both these expeditions and suffered the same fate in the second.

ERIC THE RED (*fl.* 985), so-called from the colour of his hair, Norse explorer, was forced to leave Norway, probably in the year 984, to escape trial for murder or manslaughter, and fled to Iceland. He was quickly again in trouble in Iceland and, hearing that another trader had sighted new land to the westward, decided to investigate. He verified its existence, gave it the name of Greenland, and returned to Iceland to persuade a group of people to join him in colonizing the new land. He returned to Greenland in the summer of 985 with a band of colonists, rounded Cape Farewell, and landed in Eriksfjord (near the present Julianehaab) where he founded the settlement of Brattahlid.

ERICSSON, JOHN (1803–89), was born in Sweden and served in the Swedish Army where he achieved considerable recognition from his proficiency in mechanical drawing. At the age of 24 he came to London and in 1829 a steam locomotive designed by him was entered in the railway competition at Rainhill, the first prize of which was won by Robert Stephenson's famous 'Rocket'. Turning his attention to marine engines, and after building many small steam-driven ships, he took out a patent for a screw

*propeller, for which he was awarded one-fifth of a prize of £20,000 offered by the British Admiralty for the successful development of this method of propulsion.

Ericsson left England for America in 1839 where he set up in business as an engineer and constructor of iron ships, eventually becoming a U.S. citizen in 1848. He also interested himself in the development of *armour for naval ships. When, during the American Civil War (1861–5), the northern states learned that the southern states were converting the wooden ship *Merrimack into an *ironclad, the Navy Department in Washington was forced to design and build a ship capable of meeting her in battle. Ericsson was quick to submit such a design which was accepted and in 1862 his famous armoured turret ship *Monitor was launched, and two months later engaged the *Merrimack* (by then renamed *Virginia*) in an action which decisively vindicated his ideas on ship armour and the turreted gun. This famous action established both armour and the gun turret as standard equipment in all navies in the world. After his death in New York his body was taken back for burial in his native Sweden.

ERICSSON, LEIF, see LEIF ERICSSON.

ESCORT VESSEL, the generic name for ships of various types whose main employment at sea in wartime is the protection of single ships or *convoys against attack by submarines, aircraft, or surface warships. The name embraces such various types of ships as *trawlers fitted for anti-submarine duties, *sloops, *cutters, *frigates, etc.

ESNECCA or **SNEKKJA,** a long *galley or *longship, propelled by oar or sail, used by Scandinavian seamen as a warship probably between the 5th and 11th centuries. It is generally described as having twenty rowing benches, but occasionally up to thirty were fitted. The Scandinavian meaning of the word was snake, probably in reference to its extra length in comparison with the normal longship. No illustration of an esnecca is known to exist though it has been suggested that the ship incorporated in the seal of the city of Monmouth may be one.

Later, the word was used in England to describe a vessel belonging personally to the king in which he made voyages of state. Both Henry I and Henry II are recorded as having esneccas during the 12th century. It was the then equivalent of a *Royal Yacht.

ESQUEMELING or **OEXMELIN, JOHN** (*c.* 1660–1700), was the author of *The Bucaniers of America*, from which writers from *Defoe to *Masefield have drawn information about

Sir Henry *Morgan and other *buccaneers. Esquemeling appears to have been a French surgeon serving with the buccaneers from 1666 to 1674. His book was first printed in Dutch in 1678 and translated into many languages, the English version of 1684 being taken from the Spanish and hence containing a libellous account of Morgan. Some think that his real name was Smeeks, the author of a Dutch romance which has something in common with *Robinson Crusoe*, but both names appear on the roll of the Dutch Surgeons' Guild.

ESSEX, Earl of, see DEVEREUX, Robert.

ESSEX, U.S.S., was a *frigate launched on 30 September 1799 at Salem, Massachusetts. She was built by contributions raised by the citizens of Salem and the surrounding area and presented to the government. Edward *Preble took command of her and sailed, with the U.S.S. *Congress* in company, in January 1800 to round the Cape of Good Hope and go to the Far East to protect American commerce against French *privateers. The *Congress* was dismasted in a gale and Preble continued alone in the *Essex*. In the war of 1812 against Britain the *Essex* was commanded by David *Porter and she again went into the Pacific. Porter had protested that his vessel should have long guns instead of carronades (see GUNS, NAVAL) but he managed to take a great many British *prizes in the Pacific until his ship was captured by the British frigates *Phoebe* and *Cherub* in Chilean territorial waters after an action lasting $2\frac{1}{2}$ hours.

ESTABLISHMENT OF A PORT, the interval between the time of meridian passage of the new or the full moon and the time of the following high tide. This interval is constant for a given port and is sometimes known as the High Water Full and Change Constant (H.W.F. & C. Constant). Because the tides are governed largely by the moon, and because the time of meridian passage of the moon is later each day to the extent of about 50 minutes, it follows that if the *age of the moon and the establishment of the port are known, the approximate times of high and low waters on any day may be found. If, for example, the H.W.F. & C. Constant for a given port is 3 hours 45 minutes and the age of the moon is three days, the time of the a.m. high water at the port will be 0615 approximately, i.e., 0345 + (3 × 50) min. = 0615.

ESTAING, JEAN-BAPTISTE CHARLES HENRI HECTOR THÉODAT, Comte d' (1729–94), French admiral, started life as a soldier and served in the East Indies, where he also had some experience in command of ships. He was twice captured by the British and by 1767

had reached the rank of lieutenant-general. In 1777 he was made a vice admiral and commanded a French fleet which, in 1778, sailed to America to assist the revolutionary states in their fight against Britain for independence. Although he had a considerable superiority of force in those waters, his actions were generally somewhat half-hearted though he captured the West Indian islands of St. Vincent and Grenada from the British. An indecisive action was fought against Admiral John *Byron in the West Indies in 1779, but his attempt to raise the siege of Savannah with American support failed with heavy losses. On his return to France in 1780 he entered politics, later embracing the principles of the French Revolution though without condoning its excesses, but his deposition in favour of Marie Antoinette cost him his life.

ESTRÉES, JEAN D' (1624–1707), Marshal of France and vice admiral, was born at the family estate of Estrées, near Arras, and served in the army as a volunteer, distinguishing himself in Mazarin's war with Spain and rising to the rank of general. On the conclusion of the Flanders campaign of 1668 he transferred to the navy and on the outbreak of the Third Anglo-Dutch War (1672–4) commanded the French squadron in a combined Anglo-French fleet, taking part in the battle of *Solebay on 28 May 1672, the first and second battles of the Schoonveldt on 28 May and 4 June 1673, and that of the *Texel on 11 August of the same year. His actions were much criticized by his second-in-command, *Duquesne, and also by the English admirals who suspected him of 'backwardness'. In 1676 he was sent to the West Indies to continue the French war against the Dutch but after recapturing Cayenne his fleet of seventeen ships was wrecked on the isle of Aves, 150 miles west of Dominica. Family influence prevented this setback from affecting his further career. In 1681 he was created a Marshal of France and in 1688 became governor of Brittany.

EUDOXUS OF CYZICUS (*fl.* 130 B.C.), Greek navigator, commanded a fleet sent by Ptolemy Euergetes to explore the seas of Arabia, making two voyages which considerably extended Egyptian knowledge of these waters. Following these voyages Eudoxus left Egyptian service and travelled to Gades (Cadiz) with the intention of leading further expeditions designed to explore the western coast of Africa. He made at least two voyages southward down this coast, but the distance to the south that he reached is not known. His explorations first in the Arabian seas and later on the west African coast have led some to claim that he was the first man to sail round the coast of Africa from the Red Sea to the Pillars of Hercules (Gibraltar), but no evidence exists to substantiate this claim and it would appear, in view of the stage of development of shipping at that date, highly unlikely that such a prolonged expedition would have been possible.

EUGENIE, the name given to a woollen cap worn by seamen in the late 19th century in Arctic and Antarctic waters. The name originates from the caps presented by the ex-Empress Eugénie of France to every officer and man on board the *Alert* and *Discovery* during the Royal Navy's Arctic expedition of 1875.

EURICH, RICHARD ERNST (1903–), British marine painter, was born at Bradford and from his early youth had a natural inclination towards the painting of maritime subjects. He studied at the Bradford School of Arts and the Slade School in London, and gained practical experience of the sea in all its moods while sailing with friends, a knowledge he was able to express on canvas with a brilliance few have exceeded. Although he was recognized as a marine artist of exceptional merit during the 1930s, it is his work as an official war artist in the Second World War which is better known today. In 1940 he was commissioned by the War Artists Advisory Committee to paint a picture of the evacuation of the British Expeditionary Force from *Dunkirk, subsequently purchased by the Canadian government, and was later appointed an official war artist to the British Admiralty being given a commission as a captain in the Royal *Marines. After the war he was again commissioned by the Admiralty to paint a picture of the last British battleship, H.M.S. *Vanguard, being towed out of Portsmouth harbour to be broken up. Collections of his paintings can be seen in the Tate Gallery, the *National Maritime Museum at *Greenwich, and the *Imperial War Museum.

EVANS, EDGAR (d. 1912), British naval petty officer, served in Captain R. F. *Scott's two Antarctic expeditions of 1901–4 and 1910–13. A man of exceptional vigour and endurance and a ready sense of humour, he was described by Scott as a tower of strength. Along with Wilson, Bowers, and Oates he accompanied Scott to the South pole which they reached on 18 January 1912, only to find that Roald *Amundsen had beaten them to it. On the return journey he was the first to show sign of weakness and died, after a number of falls, on 17 February 1912.

EVANS, EDWARD RADCLIFFE GARTH RUSSELL, 1st Baron Mountevans (1880–1957), British admiral, entered the Royal Navy from the training ship *Worcester* in 1895. In 1902 he was selected as second officer of the whaler *Morning*, and sent to the Antarctic to aid Commander

(later Captain) R. F. *Scott's ship *Discovery which had been trapped in the ice. Returning to naval service he qualified in navigation, and in June 1910 returned to the Antarctic as navigator and second-in-command to Scott in the *Terra Nova from which the latter made his successful dash to the South pole, but from which he failed to return.

After promotion to commander Evans commanded the *destroyers *Mohawk, Viking,* and *Broke.* In the last-named, during the First World War (1914–18), in company with H.M.S. *Swift,* on the night of 20/21 April 1917 he fought a spirited and successful action against six German destroyers in the Straits of Dover, in which two of the enemy ships were sunk. He was thereafter known as 'Evans of the *Broke'.* He ended the war with the rank of captain in command of the *cruiser *Active.* Promoted rear admiral in 1928, he commanded the Australian squadron in 1929–31 and subsequently held the posts of Commander-in-Chief, South Africa, and Commander-in-Chief, Nore. During the Second World War he was appointed regional commissioner for civil defence in the London area, a post to which he brought 'the directness and dash of the sailor, a power of leadership that in the difficult days to come inspired and sustained men and women all over London' (Sir H. Scott). He was raised to the peerage in 1945 as 1st Baron Mountevans.

EVANS, Sir FREDERICK JOHN OWEN (1815–85), British naval captain, entered the navy as a second-class volunteer in 1828 and rose to be Hydrographer of the Navy from 1874 to 1884, having already achieved in 1862 an international reputation and become a Fellow of the Royal Society for his work in problems of terrestrial magnetism and the *deviation of the compass in iron ships.

Evans's first appointment to a surveying ship was in 1833 for a three-year commission as *master's assistant in the *Thunder* on the West Indies station. The next was in the *Fly* in 1842–5 on an outstanding cruise in Australasia. Then in 1845–51 he was in the *Acheron* on the New Zealand coasts, having as a brother officer Richards, his predecessor as Hydrographer. During the Crimean War (1854–6) he served under B. J. *Sulivan in the *Lightning,* attached to the Baltic fleet, and achieved notice for his pilotage of various men-of-war, sometimes under enemy fire.

In 1855 Evans began his long service ashore, first as superintendent of the compass branch of the Hydrographic Department of the Admiralty, then at Woolwich. He compiled a world *variation chart for 1858 and his *Admiralty Manual for Deviations of the Compass* appeared in 1862, owing much to the collaboration of the mathematician Archibald Smith. This was followed by his *Elementary Manual* in 1870 for the practical use of seamen. Evans was also chief naval assistant to the Hydrographer from 1866, a post carrying with it the secretaryship of the Board of Visitors of the Royal Observatory. An early publication of his was an *Ice Chart of the Southern Hemisphere*, compiled from many sources, including Captain James *Cook's voyages, which exemplified Evans's keen interest in ocean meteorology.

As Hydrographer Evans saw the completion of the *Challenger* expedition in 1876 and he was concerned in the publication of its results with Wyville Thomson and T. H. *Tizard. He also advised on the scientific objectives of the *Alert* and *Discovery* expedition to the Arctic under Sir George *Nares in 1875–6. His surveying ships, seven of which usually worked abroad, were largely employed in colonial waters, but there was also one in Japanese waters until 1882. Much work was also done in Oceania. The arrangements for Indian surveys came under review during Evans's term of office and in 1880 a director of the Indian Marine was appointed.

A notable paper was prepared by Evans for the 50th anniversary of the British Association for the Advancement of Science in 1881 entitled *Oceanic or Maritime Discovery, Exploration, and Research in the Half Century*. In the Hydrographic office Evans coped with the customary administrative problems and was successful in the ever-difficult task of persuading the Admiralty to agree to the necessary increases of staff to meet the ever-growing commitments. With his background as a master he was also able usefully to advise on the future of *navigation in the fleet, although in 1878 he was perhaps unduly cautious about the value of the new *Thomson's *sounding machine in enabling ships to proceed at speed in fog. He was a member of the Meteorological Council.

Evans earned special promotion to staff captain in 1867 and was, exceptionally, transferred to the executive captain's list on his naval retirement in 1872 at a period when staff captains, being specialists, were not eligible for executive posts in the naval service. His death was hastened by his attendance as a British representative to the Prime Meridian conference at Washington, D.C., when he was already in failing health.

EVEN KEEL, a vessel is said to be on an even keel when she floats exactly upright in the water without any *list to either side.

EVERETT, JOHN (1876–1949), British marine painter, was the son of a Dorset vicar and studied art at the Slade School in London. His enthusiasm for marine art was stimulated by a voyage in 1898–9 in which he sailed round the world as a *boatswain, painting pictures in his spare time. Later he made something of a speciality of painting Edwardian yachting scenes, period pictures by which he is best known today. During the First World War (1914–18) he produced a series of paintings of *dazzle-painted merchant ships which were used by the Ministry of Information in educating the public in the realities of seaborne trade in a major war.

EVERTSEN, the name of one of the Netherlands' most distinguished naval families, five of whom became admirals. The four most famous were:

Evertsen, Jan (1600–66), born at Flushing, was the eldest son of Commodore Jan Evertsen (c. 1572–1617). He commanded his first ship at the age of 23 and took part in Marten *Tromp's defeat of the Spanish fleet off Dover on 18 September 1639. He commanded the reserve squadron at the battle of the *Kentish Knock on 28 September 1652, during the First Anglo-Dutch war (1652–4) and was present at the battle of Dungeness on 29 November of that year, the battle off *Portland on 18 February, and flew his flag in the *Brederode* at the battle of the *Texel on 29 July 1653, on which occasion he took over command when Tromp was killed. He accompanied De *With to the Baltic in October 1658, and in the Second Anglo-Dutch war (1665–7) took part in the battle of *Lowestoft on 3 June 1665, and was killed at the St. James's Day battle on 25 July 1666.

Evertsen, Cornelis (The Old) (1610–66), his brother, was born at Flushing, the second son of Commodore Jan Evertsen with whom he went to sea at an early age. He took part in the battle of the Kentish Knock and that off the Texel during the First Anglo-Dutch war during which he was taken prisoner. He played an important part in the battle of Lowestoft in the Second Anglo-Dutch war and again in the *Four Days battle on 1–4 June 1666 during which he was killed.

Evertsen, Cornelis (The Younger) (1628–79), was born at Flushing, son of Jan Evertsen, and was captain of his father's flagship, the *Brederode*, at the battle off the Texel in 1653 in which he was severely wounded. He became a vice admiral in de *Ruyter's fleet and took part in the raid on the Medway on 9–13 June 1667, being entrusted with taking the captured *Royal Charles* back to Holland. He stoutly defended a convoy he was escorting when attacked, before the outbreak of the Third Dutch war (1672–4), by an English force under Sir Robert *Holmes in March 1672. He took part in the battle of *Solebay on 28 May of that year and the battle off the Texel on 11 August 1673. He was the first of the Evertsen admirals to die in his bed.

Evertsen, Cornelis (The Youngest) (1642–1706), known as 'Devil' Evertsen, was born at Flushing, the eldest son of 'The Old' Evertsen, and saw service under de Ruyter during the raid on the Medway in 1667 and with his cousin ('The Younger') during the convoy action in March 1672. He was present at the battle of Solebay; and he commanded a squadron under Jacob Binckes in the West Indies, capturing the island of St. Eustatius in June 1673. Later that year he took part in a successful attack on forty English merchantmen in the James River, Virginia, and on 30 July, off New York, destroyed eighty ships and captured the city, renaming it Nieuw Amsterdam. He commanded the fleet which escorted William of Orange to England until relieved by Admiral *Herbert, under whose command he took part in the battle against the French fleet off *Beachy Head on 30 June 1690.

EXCELLENT, H.M.S., the ship name of the Royal Navy's gunnery training establishment at Portsmouth. The first ship of this name was a 3rd *rate of seventy-five guns, built at Harwich in 1787. After an active naval career, which included the battle of *Cape St. Vincent in 1797, the naval gunnery establishment was formed on board her at Portsmouth in the early 1830s and, although the ship herself no longer exists, the name persists as the headquarters of all modern British thought and experiment in naval gunnery in all its branches, including today that of ship-launched missiles.

EXECUTION DOCK, the place on the bank of the River Thames near Wapping in London where, traditionally, men convicted of *piracy at sea were executed. Originally the method of execution was to peg them down at low water below the high water mark on the river bank, so that the rising tide would drown them slowly, but by the 16th century the method of execution was changed to being hanged in chains at a tall gallows, with the body remaining exposed on the gallows until it decomposed or was eaten by seagulls, as a warning to others of the fate meted out to pirates. See also KIDD, Captain William.

EXMOUTH, Lord, see PELLEW, Edward.

EXPLOSION VESSEL, an *ad hoc* weapon at sea used for destroying or crippling objects with which it could be brought into contact. It was usually an old or obsolescent ship with its own means of propulsion, filled with explosive, and run alongside the object to be destroyed, when the charge was exploded, either by slow-match or a time fuse, the crew making its escape by boat. Examples of its use were, e.g., in 1809 when H.M.S. *Mediator*, an old 4th *rate ship, was run alongside the *boom at the *Basque Roads and used to blow an entrance through the boom; the dockyard craft *Fly* used similarly against fortifications in Algiers harbour in 1816; and the old

destroyer *Campbeltown* which was used to ram the dock *caissons at St. Nazaire in 1942 and subsequently exploded, wrecking the dock mechanisms.

EYE, properly speaking, the circular loop in a *shroud or *stay where it passes over a mast at the *hounds. It is formed by *splicing the ends of two ropes or wires into each other to form a loop to fit over the mast. But by extension it has come to mean any loop spliced or *whipped at the end of a rope or wire, usually round a *thimble. A Flemish eye was a method of making the eye in a shroud or stay by dividing the *strands, knotting each part separately and then *parcelling and *serving. This method, though very neat, was frowned upon by all good seamen as it lacked strength where, for the safety of the ship, it was most needed.

The word has other nautical meanings. The eye of the wind, or wind's eye, is a term used to describe the exact direction from which it blows, or dead to windward. The eyes of the ship, or 'eyes of her' is used to describe the extreme forward end of a ship, the term being derived from the old eastern and Mediterranean custom of painting an eye on each bow so that the vessel could see where she was going. By some it is considered that the *hawseholes are equivalent to the eyes in a modern ship, but this is a somewhat doubtful attempt to fit the physical fact of more modern ship construction to an older derivation. The eye of a tropical storm, the area in the centre where all is still.

EYE SPLICE, a loop or *eye made in the end of a rope or wire by turning the end back and splicing it through the standing part, usually around a *thimble, with the length of the *splice *served to prevent fraying and to make a neater job.

Eye splice

EYEBOLTS, metal bolts with an *eye in the end secured in various convenient places on board ship to which the *blocks of *purchases can be hooked or other lines secured.

F

FAG OUT, to, the tendency of the *strands of a rope to fray out at the ends. It is stopped either by holding them securely in place with a small whipping, by a *back splice, or by pointing the rope. See WHIP, TO.

FAG-END, the end of any rope, but particularly applied to the end of a rope where the strands have become unlayed and have frayed out.

FAGGOTS, a name given in the British Navy to men who, for a small fee, could be persuaded to answer to the names of those absent from a ship when the crew were mustered by a *muster-master in a naval dockyard. A man who failed to answer his name at a muster was liable to have R, for 'run', entered against his name, which automatically labelled him as a deserter and subject to very heavy penalties if apprehended; and he was moreover unable to draw his pay when the ship eventually became due for payment. There was thus always a temptation to find someone who would stand in and answer 'Aye' when an absentee's name was called. More efficient methods of naval book-keeping introduced during the 19th century not only made the monthly muster of a ship's company unnecessary but also put an effective end to this fraudulent practice.

FAIR, a term applied to the direction of the wind when it is favourable to the *course being steered in a sailing vessel. It is more comprehensive than *large, which indicates a wind which blows from the beam or abaft it, while a fair wind can blow from about four points on the bow to right astern. Any wind which will enable a sailing vessel to *fetch a desired point without *tacking or *pinching is a fair wind.

FAIRLEAD, a means of leading a rope in the most convenient direction for working, perhaps with a leading *block to alter its direction or with *eyes or *cringles to keep it clear of obstructions.
  In some older ships, a board with holes in it, through which various parts of the running rigging were rove, was used to provide fairleads. Similarly in these ships, the *chesstrees were fairleads for the *bowlines with which the main *tacks were hauled down.

FAIRWAY, the navigable channel of a harbour for ships entering or leaving. It is, in all harbours of any size, marked by *port and *starboard hand *buoys, and usually in the smaller harbours by withies or similar marks. Obstructions in a fairway, such as a *middle ground, are also marked by buoys.

FAKE, a complete turn of a rope when it has been coiled either on deck or on a drum. When a rope has been properly faked down, it is clear for running, each fake running out without fouling those below it. The word is used as both a noun and a verb.

FALCONER, WILLIAM (1732–69), Scottish poet and lexicographer, was born in Edinburgh and became a sailor. As a result of his experiences he wrote a poem in three cantos entitled 'The Shipwreck' published in 1762. Although a work of variable quality, it enjoyed a considerable vogue in its day and gained him the patronage of the Duke of York through whose influence he was appointed *purser in various ships of war. In addition to other poems of little merit, he compiled *An Universal Dictionary of the Marine*, by which he is now chiefly remembered and which is accepted today as an accurate record of 18th-century seamanship practice. It proved a popular and successful work, several editions being published from 1768 onwards. It was the first English marine dictionary to give the French equivalents to all the entries. He was drowned when the *frigate *Aurora*, in which he was serving, foundered off Cape Town in December 1769.

FALKLAND ISLANDS, a group of islands belonging to Great Britain in the South Atlantic Ocean about 200 miles east of the nearest part of South America in Patagonia. The first European to sight them was John *Davis in 1592; two years later they were again sighted by Sir Richard *Hawkins. A Dutch seaman named Sebald de Wert visited them in 1598 and named them the Sebald Islands, but they were renamed Falkland Islands in 1693 by Captain Strong, of the British Navy, after Lord Falkland, then First Lord of the Admiralty. They were visited by Comte Louis de *Bougainville in 1764 during his voyage of circumnavigation, who claimed possession of them for France, and a year later by Captain John *Byron in his circumnavigation who reclaimed possession for Britain. At that period the islands were of little strategic value, and these alternating claims of possession were not taken very seriously.

After a doubtful cession of them by France to Spain they finally became British in 1771 by a convention signed with Spain. It was not until the steam era of navigation that they became of strategic importance, Port Stanley being developed as a coaling station to support the British naval squadron maintained in the South Atlantic station. There is a long-standing claim to their possession by Argentina, diplomatically important in the present day because of the possibility of considerable oil deposits in the surrounding sea.

They were the scene of a naval action on 8 December 1914 during the First World War (1914–18) between British and German detached *cruiser forces, at which the earlier British defeat of *Coronel was avenged. After defeating Admiral *Cradock's squadron off the Chilean coast, the German Admiral Graf von *Spee took his squadron, consisting of the two armoured *cruisers *Scharnhorst and Gneisenau, and the three light cruisers Nürnberg, Leipzig, and Dresden round Cape Horn and into the Atlantic, hoping to break through to Germany. The British Admiralty, meanwhile, had dispatched the *battle-cruisers Invincible and Inflexible under Rear Admiral Sir Doveton *Sturdee to the Falkland Islands, where they were joined by the cruisers Kent, Cornwall, and Glasgow. The battle-cruisers reached their destination on 7 December and were engaged in coaling when the German squadron was sighted off the harbour. Realizing that he was confronted by superior forces—the British battle-cruisers each carried eight 12-inch guns while the German armoured cruisers mounted eight 8·2-inch guns each—von Spee made off to the south-east at high speed, but the British ships quickly got under way and set off in pursuit. After a long-range action lasting 4 hours the Gneisenau was sunk, followed 1¾ hours later by the Scharnhorst.

Of the remaining ships of the German squadron, the Nürnberg and Leipzig were also sunk, but the Dresden escaped, only to blow herself up three months later when discovered by the cruisers Kent and Glasgow in the port of Mas à Fuera. British casualties during the action were minimal, but the German losses amounted to almost 2,000.

FALL, the handling end of a *tackle, the end of the rope, rove through *blocks, on which the pull is exerted in order to achieve power. When used in the plural the term refers to the complete tackles by which a ship's boat or lifeboat is hoisted in or lowered from the *davits.

FALL OFF, to, a ship falls off when she sags away to *leeward or further off the wind. It is the opposite to *griping, and similarly requires the movement of ballast inside the vessel to correct the tendency. The shifting of ballast forward to trim the vessel by the head gives a greater grip of the water in the bows and thus less tendency to sag away from the wind.

FALSE FIRE, a method of night signalling in most navies before the invention of electric light signals or wireless telegraphy. A composition which burned with a blue flame was packed into a wooden tube and when ignited would burn for several minutes. As well as being used for night signals, false fires were sometimes employed to deceive an enemy, either by setting one alight in a drifting boat for the enemy to follow or by burning one on board a fast *frigate to draw the enemy away on a false course.

FALSE KEEL, an additional *keel secured outside the main keel of a wooden ship, usually as a protection should the ship take the ground but sometimes also to increase her *draught in order to improve her sailing qualities. In modern shipbuilding double bottoms provide the same protection to the hull when running aground as the false keel did for the older sailing ships.

'FAMISHING FIFTY', see 'HUNGRY HUNDRED'.

FANCY LINE, (1) a line rove through a block at the jaws of a *gaff and used as a *downhaul when lowering the sail. It was only necessary in larger vessels setting a gaff-rigged sail. (2) A line used for cross-hauling the lee *topping-lift to hold it clear of the sail to leeward so that it would not beat or rub against the canvas or reduce the sail's aerodynamic properties by creating a ridge in the sail when it stands *taut.

FANNING, EDMUND (1769–c. 1835), American navigator, began a career at sea at the age of 14 and in 1797 sailed in command of the *brig Betsey from New York for the South Pacific with the object of obtaining sealskins to sell in the China market. Rounding Cape Horn, he proceeded via Mas à Fuera Island, where a cargo of skins was obtained, to the Marquesa Islands. From there he shaped a course for Canton which led to his discovery of the Line group of islands which he named New York, Fanning, Washington, and Palmyra Islands. From Canton the Betsey completed a circumnavigation of the world, returning to New York via the Cape of Good Hope. Fanning again made a circumnavigation of the globe in the *corvette Aspasia.

FANNY ADAMS, an old Royal Navy lower deck slang term for tinned meat. The origin of this term lay in the murder in 1820 of a seven-year-old girl named Fanny Adams by a solicitor's clerk who disembowelled and cut up his victim. Tinned meat had recently been introduced into the British Navy, and a sailor finding a button in a tin of meat and suggesting to his messmates that it came from the murdered girl's clothing led to the use of the name as descriptive of this article of diet. Its later meaning, absolutely nothing, has no maritime derivation.

FANTAIL, the overhanging part of a ship's *stern, a term used particularly in the case of large yachts and passenger liners. Although the correct word for the stern overhang of all ships, it is not often used in this connection except in the U.S.A. It has not quite the same meaning as *counter, but comes very close to it.

FARDAGE, loose wood or other substance used in the stowage of bulk cargoes to prevent them shifting in the holds of a ship in a seaway. See also DUNNAGE.

FARRAGUT, DAVID GLASGOW (1801–70), U.S. admiral who won fame in the American Civil War (1861–5), was born near Knoxville, Tenn. Taking Farragut to sea with him as a *midshipman in the *Essex in 1811, David *Porter supervised his education and training while seizing every opportunity to throw responsibility on the boy. Farragut commanded a *prize at the age of 12 and was in the *Essex during her action with H.M.S *Phoebe*.

Farragut was a student afloat and ashore. He became fluent in French, Italian, and Spanish during service in the Mediterranean, and also had a knowledge of Arabic. He served under Porter again in operations against West Indian pirates, 1823–4.

Although listed as a citizen of Tennessee, and living in Norfolk, Virginia, Farragut moved his wife and son to the north immediately after the attack on Fort Sumter and the outbreak of the Civil War. When consulted concerning a possible attempt to capture New Orleans, his advice was that ships should run past the forts on the lower Mississippi River and proceed up to the city. He was familiar with the area and emphasized that supplies and ammunition could be brought to ships in the river via various waterways if the capture of the city were delayed. Commanding the operation, and in spite of unexpected difficulties, Farragut passed the forts on 24 April 1862; fought off the Confederate armed steamers above the forts; and on the 25th appeared off New Orleans, which capitulated on the 26th. It was this operation, performed with great

skill and dash, that earned him his nickname of 'Old Salamander'.

If permitted to follow the policy he had recommended, Farragut would have made battle repairs and then attacked the forts at the entrance to Mobile Bay. Instead, orders from Washington compelled him to ascend the Mississippi River to attack Vicksburg, but he was forced to withdraw, learning once again the lesson that warships are no match for fortifications ashore. In 1863, however, when at last Vicksburg fell to General Grant after a long siege, part of the success was due to Farragut who on his own initiative had gone up river and stopped the flow of supplies to Vicksburg and Port Hudson.

With the clearing of the river it was at last possible to attack Mobile, which since the fall of New Orleans had become the principal southern port in the area. Farragut was kept waiting for seven months for *ironclad ships with which to match the Southern ironclads in the port, but having received them, he forced the passage into Mobile Bay on 5 August 1869, losing his leading ship, the *Tecumseh*, on a *mine, then known as a *torpedo. In the ensuing action he captured or destroyed all the ships of the enemy, including the flagship of the Southern Admiral *Buchanan, the *ram *Tennessee*. It was on this occasion that Farragut is supposed to have used the words by which he is so often remembered: 'Damn the torpedoes, full speed ahead.'

Farragut returned to New York to a hero's welcome and Congress instituted the rank of vice admiral especially for him; there had previously been no rank beyond that of rear admiral in the U.S. Navy. Two years later the rank of admiral was created, and Farragut was promoted to it. In 1867 he paid a visit to the principal European nations flying his flag in the *Franklin*, an occasion of no naval or political import but an opportunity to exchange international courtesies between the various European navies and the great American admiral.

A useful biography is that by Captain A. T. *Mahan, *Admiral Farragut* (1892).

FARRÈRE, CLAUDE (1876–1957), French naval officer and historian, was born at Lyons and entered the navy in 1894, taking part in the 1897–9 campaign in Indo-China. Subsequently he served on board the French guardship *Vantour* at Constantinople, of which Julien Viaud (better known as Pierre *Loti) was in command. During the First World War (1914–18) he was, like many other French naval officers, seconded to the army to take part in tank warfare on the Western Front. He retired, on promotion to *capitaine de corvette* (lieutenant-commander) in 1918, to devote himself to writing. His works of fiction, many of which concern the sea, have achieved little lasting fame, but his works of history are of a high standard, particularly his *History of the French Navy* published in 1935. Other outstanding historical works from his pen are *The Battle of Tsushima* and *Combats and Battles at Sea*, which he wrote in collaboration with Paul *Chack.

FARTHELL, to, an old nautical term meaning to *furl, using *gaskets at the *bunt of the sails but rope yarns at the yardarms as the weight of the sail there was not so great. The word referred only to the mainsail, foresail, and spritsail of square-rigged ships. FARTHELLING LINES, small lines on the topsails and *topgallant sails leading to the yardarms to furl those sails. The bunts of topsails required no line or gasket for furling as they were laid on the *top and secured to the head of the mast. It is an oddity of old-time maritime phraseology that although topsails and topgallants were always described as furled and not farthelled, they were fitted with farthelling lines.

FASHION PIECES, the aftermost *timbers in the *run, or underwater body, of a ship which form the shape of the *stern.

FAST, in terms of a ship, secured, attached, fixed. Thus, to make something fast is to secure it firmly; e.g., a ship alongside a *mole or jetty, a boat to a *boom, etc. It is also a word used to designate the lines or hawsers which secure a ship to a wharf or pier, generally indicated by the position in which they are used in relation to the ship, as bow-fast, breast-fast, stern-fast, etc. These particular terms are, however, very rarely used today.

FAST PATROL BOAT, a development, post-Second World War, of the *motor torpedoboat or *motor gunboat into an all-purpose small vessel for naval warfare in coastal waters. In most navies the original two or three petrol engines which produced speeds of 38–40 *knots have now given way to gas turbines, and the *torpedo tubes or small guns to small guided missiles with a range of 80–100 miles.

FASTNET, the name of a rock off the south-west coast of Eire (Ireland), on which a *lighthouse was erected in 1854. It is one of the main weather-reporting stations in the chain around the British Isles.

The rock has given its name to the most important of the ocean races organized by the *Royal Ocean Racing Club, held biennially and alternating with the Long Island–Bermuda ocean race. It was first sailed in 1925 as a result of a suggestion by E. G. *Martin, who organized the race and won it in his Le Havre pilot cutter *Jolie Brise*. The race, for which yachts start at

Ryde, Isle of Wight, sail round the Fastnet rock, and finish at Plymouth, Devon, covers a distance of 605 miles and is one of the races included in the international competition for the *Admiral's Cup. See also YACHTING, Offshore racing.

FATHOM, the unit of measurement in most maritime countries for the depths of the sea or the lengths of rope and *cables. The word comes from the old English *faedm*, to embrace, and is a measurement across the outstretched arms of a man, approximately 6 feet in a man of average size; the length of a nautical fathom is therefore 6 feet. The term is becoming obsolete with the growing tendency in most countries to adopt a metric system of measurement.

In most British *charts the *soundings are still shown in fathoms though gradually they are being replaced by soundings in metres. It is a process which will obviously take many years to complete on account of the great number of charts which must be altered. A fathom is equal to 1·8256 metres.

When used as a measurement of ropes and cables, the length of a *hawser-laid cable is 130 fathoms. As a measurement of distance a cable is 100 fathoms, and a chain anchor cable, made up of eight *shackles, is the same length, although of course in large ships many more than eight shackles of cable are attached to the *bower anchors.

FAY, to, the operation of fitting together two pieces of timber in ship- and boat-building so that they lie close to each other with no perceptible space between them.

FEATHER, to, (1) the operation of altering the angle of the blades of a *propeller so that they lie with the leading edge more or less in the line of advance of the vessel, normally a sailing vessel, to which they are fitted. The object of feathering a propeller is to reduce the drag when the vessel is under sail alone. (2) The turning of the blade of an *oar from the vertical to the horizontal while it is being taken back for the next rowing stroke, performed by dropping the wrists at the end of the stroke. The object of feathering an oar is twofold: it lessens the effort by reducing the windage of the blade on the backstroke and it does not take the way off the boat if it hits the water during the backstroke, which may easily occur when rowing in a choppy sea. Feathering an oar is, however, much more practised in inland waters than at sea, and few seamen, when *pulling an oar, bother to feather it.

FEAZE, to, an old word meaning to unlay old tarred rope and, by teasing it, convert it into *oakum for use in caulking the sides and decks of wooden vessels. See CAULK, TO.

A felucca on the Nile

FELUCCA, a small sailing or rowing vessel of the Mediterranean, used for coastal transport or trading. The larger feluccas were narrow, decked, *galley-built vessels, with *lateen sails carried on one or two masts, occasionally also with a small *mizen. Smaller feluccas were propelled with six or eight oars, though some of the smaller sailing feluccas used oars and sail simultaneously. The sea-going type has almost completely died out, but they are still in use on many Eastern Mediterranean rivers, particularly the Nile.

FEND OFF, to, the operation of bearing a vessel off, by a spar, boathook, or *fender, in order to prevent violent contact when coming alongside.

FENDER, an appliance let down between the side of a ship and a wharf or other ship to prevent chafing when ships are lying alongside or to take the shock of a bump when going alongside. They come in many shapes and sizes, such as large bundles of withies lashed together, large bags of granulated cork, the ends of large coir cables, or even old rubber motor tyres. Boats' fenders used for the same purpose were traditionally made of canvas stuffed with granulated cork but are now more often formed of rubber or synthetic moulding. But see also RUB-BING STRAKE.

FENTON, EDWARD (d. 1603), English navigator, commanded the *Gabriel* in Martin *Frobisher's second voyage in search of the *North-West passage in 1577, and in the following year was second-in-command of the third expedition for the same purpose, sailing in the *Judith.* In 1582 he was selected to command a trading expedition into the Indian Ocean and eventually to China, with instructions to discover, if possible, a western entrance to the North-West passage. This expedition got no further than Brazil because of quarrels among the officers, and in fact returned to England with many of them in irons. In the battle of the Spanish *Armada in 1588, Fenton commanded the English ship *Mary Rose.*

FERNANDEZ, ALVARO (*fl.* 1440), was one of the early Portuguese discoverers who flourished under Prince *Henry the Navigator, having started life as a page to the prince. His uncle, João Gonzalez Zarco, was a governor of Madeira, which island he had re-discovered while in the service of Prince Henry. In the great expedition down the coast of Africa in 1445 he gave his nephew command of the finest *caravel in the fleet and charged him especially to devote all his energies to discovery. Fernandez performed these duties in exemplary fashion, reaching 'Cabo dos Matos' (probably between

Cape Verde and the Gambia River), the farthest point south yet attained. The following year he pushed still farther south, reaching a point just short of Sierra Leone. Here he was wounded by a poisoned arrow in a brush with the natives, which forced him to return to Portugal, to remain in Prince Henry's suite as one of its most distinguished explorers.

FERNANDEZ, JUAN (*fl.* 1560), Spanish navigator, discovered the island in the Pacific Ocean which bears his name and which is still associated with the story of *Robinson Crusoe. He was the first sailor to appreciate that the contrary winds which made passage up the western coast of South America so difficult and tedious might not blow farther out to sea, and proved the correctness of his theory by encountering the trade winds at sea and making a passage from Chile to Callao in thirty days, a feat which earned him arrest on a charge of sorcery. He discovered the Juan Fernandez group of islands in 1563 during a voyage from Lima to Valdivia, and was granted by the Spanish government a concession to develop them, but the colony he set up there failed to flourish. The goats which he took with the colony did, however, establish themselves, and it was some of their descendants which were caught by Alexander *Selkirk (Robinson Crusoe) and later still by Commodore *Anson in his voyage of circumnavigation (1740–4). Juan Fernandez is still credited with the first sighting of Easter Island and he claimed also to have sighted a 'continent' which, if true, must have been either Australia or New Zealand.

FERROCEMENT, or cement-mesh or ferro-crete, a form of construction of small craft. The method employs several layers of wire mesh, generally of the welded type, which are wired to the intersections of steel rods and tubes forming a close-knitted framework of the vessel's hull. The whole fabric when complete is rendered waterproof by an application, simultaneously from both inside the hull and outside, of a semi-liquid mortar mix. The mortar is composed of cement and very fine sand, which may include pozzolano or volcanic ash as used in ancient Roman mortar for its adhesive properties, and when cured and set over a period of a week or more, the resulting surface of the hull is smooth, hard, and resilient. A ferrocement hull might be likened to a steel mesh reinforced plastic, and is far removed from the popular notion of concrete, as in harbour piling, buildings, or even the early concrete ships introduced during the First World War (1914–18).

The rod and wire mesh method of construction with cement mix was first introduced in Italy in 1943 by Professor Luigi Nervi, whose firm used it successfully to make the spring diving boards for the Olympic Games, as well as for buildings and the shell-shaped roofs of the Sydney Opera House. Thousands of yachts, harbour launches, and other small craft up to 80 feet or so in length have been constructed in ferro-cement, and the production of the traditional wooden *sampans in China has been virtually stopped in favour of mass production of similar boats in ferrocement.

FERROL, a seaport in north-west Spain, with one of the finest natural harbours in Europe. It has a naval dockyard and is a base of the Spanish Navy, but is also one of the principal shipbuilding yards in Spain, and in 1972 there was launched at Ferrol the largest tanker yet built in Europe, the 327,000 d.w.t. *Arteaga*. The approaches to Ferrol was the scene, in July 1805, of an indecisive naval action between a British squadron of fourteen ships commanded by Rear Admiral Sir Robert *Calder, and the French fleet under Admiral *Villeneuve which was returning to France after being chased to the West Indies by the British Mediterranean Fleet. On 22 July, in poor visibility, Calder sighted Villeneuve's fleet of twenty French and five Spanish ships, the latter bringing up his rear. After capturing two Spanish ships and inflicting more damage on the French than he received, Calder broke off the action and failed to renew it the following day, thereby enabling Villeneuve to escape into Vigo harbour. Much to his surprise, Calder was censured for his failure to inflict crippling damage on his opponent. This action proved to be the prelude to the battle of *Trafalgar, Villeneuve slipping out of Vigo to take refuge in Cadiz harbour, from which he sailed on 19 October to meet Lord *Nelson off Cape Trafalgar.

These waters were also the scene of an action in November 1805 between a British squadron, commanded by Captain Sir Richard *Strachan, and the remnant of the French fleet which had escaped from the battle of Trafalgar, all of which were forced to strike their colours.

FERRY, a vessel designed for the transport of persons and goods from one place to another on a regular schedule of sailings. They can vary from small boats used as ferries across rivers and estuaries, sometimes with a chain across the bottom by which they are hauled over either by hand or with the chain operated around a winch, to large specially built ships with roll-on, roll-off facilities for cars, lorries, and trains.

FETCH, to, to reach, or arrive at, some place or point, particularly in conditions of an adverse wind or tide. The word is used only in relation to sailing vessels when *close-hauled or *on a wind, and implies being able to arrive at the desired point without having to *tack to windward. As a noun the word signifies the distance of open water traversed by waves before they reach a given point, such as a ship's position or a stretch of coast. The longer the fetch, the higher generally are the waves, and the more strongly the *swell will run after the wind has dropped. It is also used to indicate the distance a vessel must sail to reach open water, thus a yacht can anchor in an inlet on a coast, and have a fetch of so many miles to reach the open sea.

FIBRE GLASS, or glass reinforced plastic (GRP), as used for the moulding of boat hulls, decks, superstructures, and other parts, consists of very fine fibres of glass made up into strands or in chopped mat formation, to which is applied a polyester resin in liquid form when the necessary thickness of glass fibres or mat is laid over the pre-formed mould. A catalyst, such as methyl ethyl ketone peroxide, together with a hardener is applied as a liquid which will cause the glass fibre to set hard at normal workshop temperature (about 15° C) and form a plastic shell. On the hull of a GRP vessel the outside is normally given a finishing coat, known as a gel coat, producing a smooth, shiny, and exceedingly hard surface.

Once a suitable mould or pattern has been constructed, hulls can be reproduced from it in large numbers. At first, immediately after the Second World War only *dinghies and small boats were produced in GRP, but as demand grew and techniques improved, yacht hulls were moulded in ever-increasing sizes. Manufacturers with premises far inland could produce the shells of hulls in quantity for the boatyards to complete and fit-out to customers' requirements, and much time in building new yachts was thereby saved. Advantages claimed for fibre glass, such as its freedom from rust and corrosion, wet or dry rot, and shipworm, its lightness in relation to its proved strength, its resilience to knocks and minor collisions, and the additional space given inside by the thin shell, encouraged many boatbuilding yards to give up wooden construction altogether in favour of plastics. As a result, in America, Holland, France, and Great Britain, some 90 per cent of dinghies, yachts, and small craft up to about 75 feet (22·8 m) in length are produced in GRP, the remainder being of wood, steel, or *ferrocement. Small craft for the American Lifesaving Service, and all boats and harbour craft under 32 feet (9·7 m) in length for the Royal Navy, have for many years been moulded in GRP, and recent naval *minesweepers (or mine hunters) have been a further development in plastics construction, the particular advantage of this type of minesweeper hull being its non-magnetic property.

FID, (1) a square bar of wood or iron, with a wider shoulder at one end, which takes the weight of a topmast when *stepped on a lower mast. The topmast is hoisted up through a guide hole in the *cap of the lower mast until a square hole in its *heel is in line with a similar hole in the head of the lower mast, when the fid is driven through both and the hoisting *tackles slacked away until the fid is bearing the weight. The two masts are then generally secured firmly together with a *parrel lashing. Similarly a fid would support the weight of a topgallant mast at the head of a topmast. **(2)** A circular pin of hard wood, usually *lignum vitae, tapering to a point and used for opening the strands of large cordage for splicing. It has a groove down one side used for feeding in the strand being tucked. **(3)** In the days of muzzle-loading guns the piece of *oakum used to plug the vent to prevent it getting blocked when the gun was not in use was called a fid.

FIDDLE, a rack fixed to mess tables on board ships in rough weather to prevent crockery, glasses, knives and forks, etc., from sliding to the deck as the ship rolls and pitches. The simplest fiddles were merely battens fixed to the edges of the tables and projecting about an inch above the table level so that if the plates, etc., slid, they were brought up by the battens, but more elaborate fiddles, used in liners and other expensive ships, usually fitted the tables exactly and had compartments in them to hold each item firmly in position so that they were unable to move whatever the ship's motion.

FIDDLE BLOCK, a double *block in which the two *sheaves lie in one plane one below the other instead of being mounted on the same central pin as in more normal double blocks. The upper sheave is larger than the lower so that it vaguely resembles a violin in shape. They were used chiefly for the lower-yard *tackles of square-rigged ships as they lay flatter to the *yards.

FIDDLEHEAD BOW, the stemhead of a vessel finished off with a scroll turning aft or inwards, as at the top of a violin. This form of stemhead was originally adopted in small sailing warships which had no *figureheads as a piece of simple bow decoration; the term has remained to describe the termination of a *clipper bow which has this inward-turning decorative ending.

FIDDLER'S GREEN, a sailor's paradise, where public houses, dance halls, and other similar amusements are plentiful and the ladies are accommodating. It really had only a celestial and not a terrestrial connotation in the sailor's mind, a sort of permanent sensual Elysium or sailor's heaven but still vaguely related to the delights enjoyed by sailors ashore in such well-known places as Wapping, in the east end of London, and Portsmouth Point, in the naval harbour of Portsmouth, and indeed in most other ports in the world which catered for the sailor who came ashore with money in his pockets. A sailor who died, and was known to have enjoyed such pleasures in his life, was often said to have gone aloft to Fiddler's Green.

FIDDLEY, a raised grating on the decks of small steam or diesel vessels fixed over the hatches above the engine and boiler rooms to let the hot air and fumes escape. Fresh air enters the engine room through the ventilators and forces the hot air out through the fiddleys. In rough weather they are made watertight by tarpaulins spread over them and secured by *battens.

FIELDING, ANTHONY VANDYKE COPLEY (1787–1855), British marine and landscape painter, was born at East Sowerby. He studied art under John Varley and in 1824 gained a gold metal at the Salon in Paris. He soon became one of the 19th century's more notable artists and, like *Bonington and others, was well known for the forceful manner in which he depicted the beauty of nature as he saw it. He is renowned for his seascapes and his numerous pictures are widely distributed among the galleries of Europe and the United States. He was at one time President of the Society of Water Colour Artists.

FIERY CROSS, a famous British tea *clipper, was the second ship of her name, and was designed by Rennie and built by Chaloner of Liverpool in 1860. She was four times the winner of the premium for the first ship home with the season's tea crop from China.

FIFE, WILLIAM (1822–1902), British naval architect, was the son of a wheelwright, also William Fife, who took to boatbuilding and founded a small yard at Fairlie, Ayrshire, in about 1800 where he built fishing boats. The business grew rapidly and in 1814 the yard built the *Industry*, a small river *paddle steamer which ran until she became the oldest steamboat afloat in Scotland. William was apprenticed to his father's yard at the age of 13 when the yard was beginning to specialize in building yachts for the gentry. Before he was 21 he was given full control of the yacht side of the business, and began to produce the designs and beautiful hulls which were to make Fifes of Fairlie celebrated. His first notable yacht was the *Stella* of 1848, and after her a long line of successful racing and cruising yachts emerged from the yard, including such vessels as *Cymba, Fiona, Cythera, Cuckoo, Bloodhound, Foxhound,* and *Neptune. Cymba* was remarkable at the time (1852) in having a

*ballast keel of some three tons bolted to the underside of her wooden keel, a practice which was in due time to become universal among racing yachts.

William Fife's son, also WILLIAM, began his career in the family yard but to gain wider experience entered the shipbuilding yard of J. Fullerton & Company at Paisley. From there he was appointed manager of a yacht building yard owned by the Marquis of Ailsa on his estate at Culzean. Here in 1884 he designed and built the 20-tonner *Clara* which finished top in her class in all the regattas that season. Under new ownership next year she was sailed across the Atlantic to New York and proved more than a match for all the American 55-footers. This third William Fife's designs of racing yachts retained all the beauty inherited from his father's vessels and among the great yachts which came from his board were *Shamrock I*, challenger for the *America*'s Cup in 1899, and *Shamrock III* which similarly challenged in 1903.

FIFE RAILS, (1) the rails erected on the *bulwarks which bounded the *poop and *quarterdeck of the old sailing men-of-war, *East Indiamen, and the larger merchant vessels. As well as being decorative, they were useful in providing a convenient means of securing the *clew lines of the sails when under sail. **(2)** The circular or semi-circular rail around the base of a mast of a sailing vessel which holds the *belaying pins to which the *halyards of the sails are secured. The masts of modern yachts do not normally have fife rails as the halyards are brought down inside the hollow mast and secured below deck to avoid creating windage.

FIGHTING INSTRUCTIONS, a code of tactical signals in the early days of the British Navy first issued by *Blake, *Deane, and *Monck in 1653. The instructions, twenty-one in number, established the *line of battle and imposed some sort of tactical discipline on the fleet. Later admirals, from *James, Duke of York, and Prince *Rupert to *Vernon, *Anson, and *Hawke, issued additional instructions for use in the fleets they commanded, some of which were incorporated in the permanent or printed instructions, which first appeared in 1672 as the *Sailing and Fighting Instructions.* Similar French *Ordres et signaux généraux* date from 1690, but in France more theoretical treatises on the subject were written, from Père *Hoste's *L'Art des armées navales* (1697) to those of *Morogues, Pavillon, and others in the middle of the 18th century.

Partly as a result of reading these French works, *Howe and *Kempenfelt improved the old system of signalling between 1776 and 1782 under which an instruction was conveyed to the fleet by the position of a particular flag. By the numerary method adopted from the French, numbered flags from 0 to 9 gave a commander more flexibility in handling his ships. Their *Signal Book for the Ships of War* (1780, 1782, 1790) issued officially by the Admiralty in 1799 thus distinguished between the old fighting instructions and modern methods of flag signalling, which were greatly extended by Sir Home *Popham's *Marine Vocabulary* (1800, 1803), with its twenty-five letter flags and a dictionary of 1,000 words. *Nelson's famous Trafalgar signal was made by the three-flag hoists of this method, the word 'duty' having to be spelled out because it was not in the list of words.

The old *Fighting Instructions*, before the work of Howe, Kempenfelt, and Popham did so much to add flexibility to fleet movement, were unduly rigid in the tactical doctrine they laid down, but many British admirals felt themselves bound to follow them when confronted by an enemy fleet. Notable among the naval actions which had calamitous results as a result of rigid adherence to them were *Byng's action off *Minorca in 1756, which lost the British fleet the useful base of *Port Mahon, and *Graves's action at *Chesapeake Bay in 1781 which resulted in the loss of the American colonies. Some admirals, however, were more venturesome in battle and fought many successful actions by ignoring the *Instructions* or modifying them with their own additional instructions. See, e.g., GENERAL CHASE.

FIGHTS, an old name for the waist-cloths rigged above the *bulwarks along the *waists of sailing men-of-war before going into action to conceal the seamen working on deck from sharpshooters in the *tops of enemy ships. The use of waist-cloths lasted only a very few years beyond the 17th century because of the additional hazard presented by them of fire on board during battle.

FIGURE OF EIGHT KNOT, a knot made in the end of a rope by passing the end of the rope over and round the standing part, over its own part and through the bight. Its purpose is to prevent a rope from unreeving when passed through a block.

Figure of eight knot

FIGUREHEAD, more accurately written figure head, an ornamental carved and painted figure erected originally on the *beakhead of a vessel but later on the continuation of the *stem below the *bowsprit as a decorative emblem generally expressing some aspect of the ship's name or function. The origin of the figurehead in the early days of seagoing was probably twofold, a mixture of religious symbolism and the treatment of a ship as a living thing. On the one hand, some propitiatory emblem was carried on board to claim the protection of a sea deity while the vessel was at sea; on the other hand, there was a widely felt belief that a ship needed to find her own way across the waters, and could only do so if she had eyes. The Ancient Egyptians drew on their extensive pantheon to provide both protection and eyes by mounting figures of the holy birds on the prows; the Phoenicians used the heads of horses to symbolize both vision and swiftness; Greek ships had a boar's head for both its quick sight and ferocious reaction; Roman ships often carried a carving of a centurion to indicate their prime fighting quality. William the Conqueror's ship pictured in the Bayeux Tapestry had a lion's head carved on the top of her stem; by the 13th century one of the favourite figureheads for ships was the head and neck of a swan, possibly in the hope that the ship would thereby possess the same mobility and stability as that bird upon the water.

In northern Europe the favourite decoration for the high stem of the longship was a serpent, though there were variations. Some Danish ships of the period had dolphins or bulls as figureheads; *Sweyn's longship in A.D. 1004 was decorated in the form of a dragon, its head forming the figurehead and its tail the *sternpost. All these figureheads were carved on to, or mounted on, the beakhead.

The figurehead as we know it today was an effect of the change in the design of the ship which came about in the 14th, 15th, and 16th centuries. The examples mentioned above were mounted on, or carved directly on to, the actual beakhead or stem of the ship, but with the development of the *carrack type of ship, and her successor the *galleon, forecastles were built above and beyond the ship's stem, so that the position of the figurehead had to be moved. In the early stages of these designs there was no place for the figurehead, and although Henry VIII's ship *Holigost* of 1514 is recorded as being fitted with carvings of a swan and an antelope at a cost of £4. 13s. 4d., they were probably placed on the quarterdeck or stern gallery. In these early designs the beakhead was nearly horizontal, and figures of some sort could be placed on top of them; the earliest ships known to carry them, the *Salamander* and *Unicorn* of 1546, had carvings representing their names.

In the century between approximately 1540 and 1640, the long beakhead developed into the rounded bow by the addition of *cheeks, and the position and stance of the figurehead consequently changed. At the beginning of the period

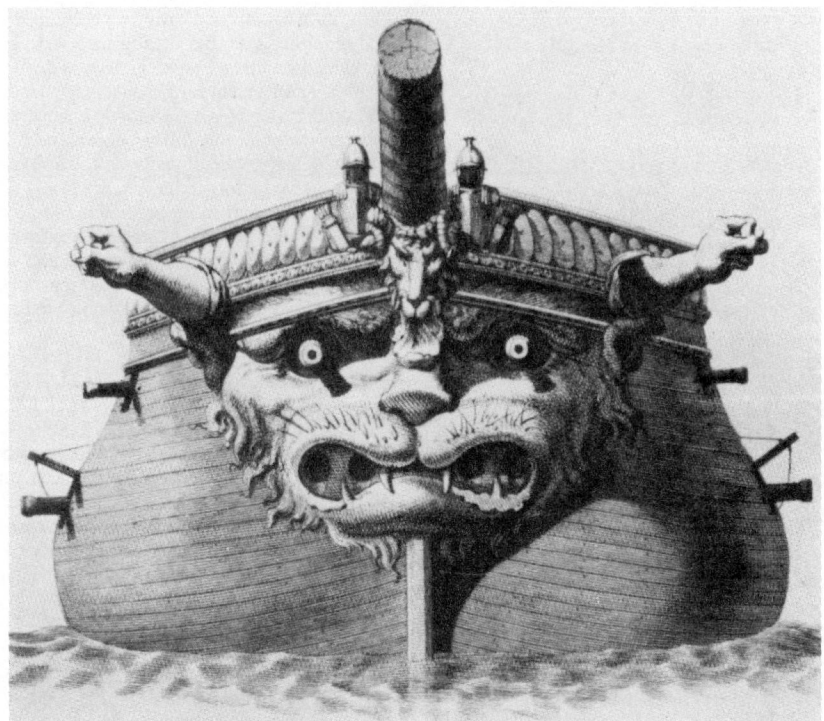

Figurehead of a ship of the line; design by P. Ozanne, c. 1800

the figurehead, nearly always an animal such as a lion or leopard, was virtually horizontal, but as the beakhead gradually disappeared into the bow it became more upright, finally reaching the perpendicular by about 1700 and then leaning farther and farther backwards, puffing out its chest, through most of the 18th century. In smaller ships, with little space available for a rounded figure, some form of heraldic carving frequently took its place. Of the larger ships which formed the navy of Elizabeth I, five had a figurehead of a lion (*Charles, Defiance, Repulse, Rainbow, Garland*), five had a dragon (*Bonaventure, Adventure, Dreadnought, Nonpareil, Hope*), the *Mary Rose a unicorn, the *Swiftsure* a tiger, and the *White Bear* had a figure of Jupiter sitting on an eagle. Most Dutch ships of the period also had a lion as their figurehead, as did many of the ships of Spain. French ships carried, in general, more elaborate figureheads, such as Neptune driving a pair of sea horses or, a general favourite, Jupiter sitting on his eagle.

The lion remained the favourite figurehead for warships of most nations throughout the 17th century, though some of the larger and more important ships had more elaborate designs. The English *Prince Royal* of 1610 had a representation of St. George slaying the dragon, and the *Sovereign of the Seas* of 1637 had as her figure-

head King Edgar on horseback trampling upon seven kings. The *Naseby*, one of the great ships of Oliver Cromwell's Commonwealth Navy of 1649–60, had, according to the diarist Evelyn, 'Oliver on horseback trampling six nations under foot: a Scot, Irishman, Dutchman, Frenchman, Spaniard, and English, as was easily made out by their several habits'.

The lion finally went out of fashion as a figurehead for warships in the second half of the 18th century, being replaced by carvings usually indicating the name of the ship. Thus the *Edgar* of 1774 had a carving of King Edgar for her figurehead; the *Egmont* of 1768 and the *Bedford* of 1775 had figures of statesmen, presumably the First Lords of the Admiralty after whom they were named. The *Brunswick*, which fought in the battle of the **Glorious First of June* in 1794, had a figure of the duke of that name wearing a cocked hat and a kilt. The cocked hat was shot away during the battle while she was engaging the *Vengeur*, an accident which so concerned her crew that Captain Harvey gave them his own cocked hat and the carpenter nailed it on to the Duke of Brunswick's head.

Lord Sandwich, First Lord of the Admiralty, 1771–82, introduced many classical names into the British Navy, a great opportunity for the carvers to let their imaginations loose.

Modern figurehead of the merchant ship Baldrian, *Fred Olsen Line*

British naval figureheads of the 19th century were generally uninteresting owing mainly to an Admiralty order restricting the amount of money which could be spent on such appendages. Yet when the new system of training for shipwright apprentices was initiated at Portsmouth early in the century, J. C. *Schetky was appointed as drawing master to train them in the carving of figureheads. He was a considerable artist and for a few years the carving of figureheads flourished under his tuition although his designs were so elaborate that they were almost invariably vetoed by the Admiralty on account of expense.

French warships, which never took to the standard lion figure as did those of other nations, were much more uninhibited in their designs. Frequently it was a single figure, carved by an artist of repute, and generally much more graceful and appropriate than the figureheads of other nations. Occasionally ships had group figures, particularly during the reign of Louis XVI, when he was often depicted seated on his throne, sword in hand, with Fame or Victory about to place a wreath of laurel on his head, or riding in a triumphal chariot with chained captives on either side. But mostly they were single figures representing Fame, Victory, Glory, and the like. The Revolution produced a few curiosities, such as the frigate *Carmagnole* which had a model of the guillotine for her figurehead.

Spanish ships relied mostly on the lion except in ships named after saints, which usually had a carving of the saint in question. The *Santissima Trinidad* had a group figurehead representing the Trinity. One of the best known and finest American naval figureheads was that of the *Constitution*, which had a whole figure of President Jackson.

Merchant ships, up to about 1800, followed naval practice fairly closely, and most vessels of the various *East India companies used lions as figureheads. With the advent of the *clipper ship, with her graceful lines, the figurehead blossomed, usually into a single figure, either full length or half length. Women were, if anything, rather more popular than men, and very often reflected a superstition of seamen by having one or both breasts bared. Women in general were thought to be unlucky on board ship, but a naked woman was supposed to be able to calm a storm at sea.

The 19th century technological changes of sail to steam and wood to iron spelled out the gradual end of the naval figurehead. The first two *ironclad warships built in Britain, the *Warrior* and *Black Prince*, did indeed have figureheads; later ships with their straight iron stems had no more than a medallion or shield, with supporters on either side. Figureheads for the larger warships were finally abolished in Britain in 1894 but some smaller ships kept them until the First World War (1914–18).

In merchant ships, as in warships, the figurehead began to disappear when steam replaced sail, the loss of the bowsprit, under which the figurehead was traditionally placed, being the main reason for its disappearance. In some modern shipping lines a form of figurehead is today being revived for decorative purposes, particularly in the ships of the Fred Olsen Line, all of which carry one. See also ACROSTOLIUM.

J. Carr Laughton, *Old Ship Figure-heads & Sterns* (1925); G. Frere-Cook, ed., *The Decorative Arts of the Mariner* (1966).

FILCHNER, WILHELM (1877–1957), German explorer, led two expeditions to the polar regions. The first was to Spitsbergen in 1910; the second, and more important, was to Antarctica in 1911 with the intention of crossing the continent. He was the first man to reach the head of the Weddell Sea, discovering Vahsel Bay in the process. His ship, the *Deutschland*, was beset in the ice and drifted for nine months before reaching open water, but the scientific investigations made in these then unknown waters proved to be exceedingly valuable and important. Later Filchner became a notable explorer of central Asia and Tibet.

FILIBUSTER, a name under which *buccaneers were originally known in Britain. It owes its derivation from the Dutch *vrybuiter* (freebooter), translated into French as *flibustier*, and from there into English as *filibuster*.

FILL, to, to *trim the sails of a fore-and-aft rigged ship, or to *brace the yards of a square-rigged ship, so that the wind can fill the sails. In square-rigged ships it was possible to move ahead, to stop, or to move astern all on the same wind by bracing the yards so that the sails could fill, shiver, or *back with the wind, i.e., with the wind blowing on the front of the sail.

FIN-KEEL, see KEEL.

FIORAVANZO, GIUSEPPE (1891–   ), Italian admiral, entered the Royal Italian Navy as a *midshipman in 1912 and after a distinguished career attained the rank of *ammiraglio di squadra* in 1952. During the Second World War he commanded successively two battleship divisions and a cruiser squadron. He was director of the Naval Historical Section 1950–60, and from 1958 he combined this duty with that of editor of the *Rivista Marittima*. A prolific writer, he has published some 600 articles and 50 books, many of which have been translated into foreign languages. Almost all of them deal with the history of the Italian Navy or with the strategic aspects of war at sea.

'FIRE AND LIGHTS', an old name on the lower deck in the British Navy for the master-at-arms. Its origin arose from the nightly duty of the master-at-arms, exercised through the ship's corporals, to make frequent inspections below decks throughout the night to ensure that all fires were drawn and all lights extinguished, a very necessary precaution in the days of wooden ships.

FIRECREST, Alain *Gerbault's 39-ft (11·8 m) cutter yacht in which he sailed single-handed round the world in 1924–9.

FIRESHIP, a small vessel, usually of little particular value, filled with combustibles and fitted with special ventilating ducts in order to ensure rapid combustion. The charge was ignited by a slow match and train of powder, set to fire after a predetermined interval, and an armament of usually around eight small guns was provided for defence when not about to be used as a fireship. Their role in battle, or when attacking enemy ships at anchor, was to sail down as near to their victim as possible, lash the helm so that the fireship continued on her course, secure her to her victim with grappling irons, and at the last moment ignite the slow match, the captain and crew escaping in a boat towed astern or alongside.

A successful attack by a fireship in which an enemy vessel of forty guns or over was destroyed was, in the British Navy, rewarded by the captain receiving £100 or a gold chain and medal of the same value at his choice 'to remain as a Token of Honour to him and his Posterity', and by each

Launch of the English fireships against the Armada, 1588; oil painting by an unknown artist

other member of the crew receiving £10. If it were the enemy flagship that was so destroyed, the rewards were doubled.

Fireships were used with great success at the battle of the Spanish *Armada in 1588 when six English fireships were employed in a night attack against the Spanish fleet at anchor off Calais, forcing the ships to cut their cables and make their way out to sea, where they were attacked by the English fleet. They were also used extensively at sea in the battles of the three Anglo-Dutch wars in the 17th century. The last occasion on which fireships were employed in the British Navy was during the British attack on French warships at anchor in the Basque Roads in 1811.

FIREWORKS, an old naval term which embraced any means of setting fire to an enemy ship during battle. They included fire-pots, fire-balls (in which cannon balls were heated to red heat in a brazier before being fired), fire-pikes (boarding pikes with burning tow attached which were thrown, javelin-fashion, on board an enemy), arrows similarly tipped, etc. *Fireships were not included in this general description, although their contents were.

FIRST FLEET, the name given to the squadron which, under the command of Captain Arthur *Phillip, set sail on 13 May 1787 with the first 700 convicts destined for *Botany Bay. The fleet consisted of the frigate *Sirius*, the tender *Supply*, three storeships, and six transports.

FISGIG or **FISHGIG,** a four-pronged *harpoon used for spearing fish by hand, often from a *dinghy in shallow water but sometimes in connection with free *diving techniques as an underwater sport. Frequently they used to be weighted with lead at the end in order to turn the fish over after it had been struck.

FISH, a long piece of wood, concave on one side and convex on the other, used to strengthen a mast or a *yard of a sailing vessel that has been sprung or otherwise damaged. Two such fish are placed one on each side of the weak point and secured either with metal bands or with a strong lashing known as a *woolding. See also FISH, TO.

FISH, to, (1) the operation of strengthening a yard or a mast in a sailing vessel by binding on *fish with a lashing known as a *woolding in those places where it has been sprung or otherwise damaged. Broken spars can also be temporarily repaired with fish in cases where no spare yard is carried. **(2)** To fish an *anchor, the operation of drawing up the *flukes of a *stocked anchor to the *cat davit preparatory to its being stowed on an anchor bed. The modern stockless anchors have no need to be fished as their permanent stowage when weighed is in the *hawse-holes and not on anchor beds.

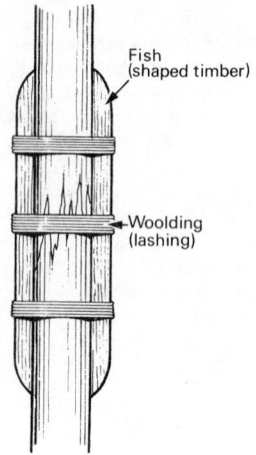

A fished spar

FISHER, JOHN ARBUTHNOT (1841–1920), first Baron Fisher of Kilverstone, British admiral of the fleet, the greatest administrator the Royal Navy has produced since Lord Barham (see MIDDLETON, Charles) and whose name will always be connected with the navy at the apex of its power. He went afloat in 1854, when only 13 years old, 'penniless, friendless, and forlorn', as he later wrote. By the early 1870s he had a reputation as an extremely able officer and an ardent apostle of progress who appreciated the significance of the emerging age of steam, *armour, electricity, machinery, and *torpedoes.

The more important phase of his career began with his appointment to the command of H.M.S. *Inflexible* (1881), the greatest *battleship of the day, which played a prominent role in the bombardment of the Alexandria forts by the Mediterranean Fleet in 1882. There followed a succession of shore appointments: captain of H.M.S. *Excellent*, the navy's gunnery school (1883–5), Director of Naval Ordnance and Torpedoes (1886–91), Admiral Superintendent at Portsmouth Dockyard (1891–2), and Third Sea Lord and Controller (1892–7). Fisher excelled in all these appointments. As Controller he was responsible for the adoption of the *destroyer and the water-tube boiler, and played a large role in the 'navy scare' of 1893 which resulted in the Cabinet's adoption of a big five-year construction programme. He was promoted rear admiral in 1890 and vice admiral in 1896, and made K.C.B. in 1894.

Fisher returned to sea in 1897; an uneventful command of the North America and West Indies station. In 1899 he was recalled to serve as the British naval delegate at the First Hague Peace

Conference, where his intemperate remarks about preserving peace by making war too horrible to contemplate shocked the other delegates. In spite of his performance at The Hague and his well-publicized apothegms 'moderation in war is imbecility' and 'war is the essence of violence', Fisher was in reality a man of peace. It was his conviction that once war, the greatest idiocy of life, broke out, the British fleet must 'hit first, hit hard, and keep on hitting', so as to destroy the enemy and spare Britain the horrors of a prolonged conflict.

In the years 1899–1902 Fisher served as commander-in-chief of the Mediterranean Fleet, becoming a full admiral in 1901. The navy was in a very backward state, being still in the 'spit and polish' era, when strategy, the higher training of officers, and * gunnery were neglected and the torpedo was undervalued. It was also a time when British sea power was scattered over the world and the welfare of the lower deck commanded little attention. Around Fisher there formed a little band of ardent reformers, mainly captains, inspired by Fisher and his ideas and dedicated to his goals of the efficiency of the fleet and its instant readiness for war. The Fisher system vastly improved the efficiency of the Mediterranean Fleet and paved the way for the great reform era of 1904–10.

The principal fruit of Fisher's tenure as Second Sea Lord (1902–3) was the 'Selborne Scheme' of entry and training (named after the First Lord of the Admiralty) of 1902, an attempt to introduce unity and harmony in the officer corps and to ensure that in an age of mechanization all officers would have some familiarity with engines. Its main feature was common entry and training of officers at colleges at Osborne and Dartmouth and in the following four or five years at sea. The common training included for all officers the seamanship necessary for executive duties and a practical acquaintance with engineering. In 1903–4 Fisher was commander-in-chief at Portsmouth, from which position he could superintend the establishment of the Royal Naval College at Osborne, where newly entered cadets received their initial naval training. He also served on the Esher Committee (1903–4), whose reports, accepted by the Cabinet, called for a reorganization of the War Office on the lines of the Board of Admiralty and a revamped Committee of Imperial Defence.

When Fisher became First Sea Lord in October 1904, he was 63, 'but still the youngest man of the navy in brain and heart and energy'. His most pronounced characteristics were a phenomenal energy, tenacity of purpose, high spirits, a sparkling wit, and an extraordinary charm and capacity for work. Kind, warm, generous, and loyal, he made and held friends easily; but in his official dealings he could be arrogant,

stern, and vindictive. His two great hobbies were dancing and listening to sermons. He had a quite exceptional knowledge of the Bible and would draw on it and on naval history (which otherwise he considered without value) for arguments to prove a case or fell an opponent. He was as vigorous and exuberant a writer as he was a talker, making use of vivid phrases and apt illustrations in his correspondence. He was made an admiral of the fleet and received the Order of Merit in 1905.

Fisher's five years as First Sea Lord were an unparalleled era of reform. The genesis of the reforms lay in the emergence of Germany as a first-class naval power, and with it Fisher's certainty that a war with her was inevitable and would be provoked when the German fleet could catch the Royal Navy unprepared. Given this challenge, the war readiness of the British fleet was essential. (One must not take his 'plans' to 'Copenhagen' the German fleet too seriously; he himself never did.) The other consideration for Fisher was economy, which he regarded as essential in view of the grumbling in Parliament and the country about the constantly rising navy estimates. Under him the estimates did drop for three years running, and without a reduction in the fighting efficiency of the fleet. But naval efficiency was the main thrust of Fisher's administration. He is chiefly remembered for these reforms: (1) The introduction of the all-big-gun type of capital ship in H.M.S. * *Dreadnought* (laid down in October 1905, completed in December 1906), whose main battery of ten 12-inch guns represented a great advance over the mixed 9·2- and 12-inch primary armaments of the last pre-dreadnought classes. At the same time a new and larger type of armoured * cruiser, with medium armour protection, 25 knots speed, and an all-big-gun armament—* battle-cruisers as they came to be called—was built (H.M.S. * *Invincible*). Their principal duty was to act as super-scouting cruisers—ships fast and powerful enough to push home a reconnaissance in the face of an enemy's big armoured cruisers. (2) The nucleus crew system, which Fisher rightly called 'the keystone of our preparedness for war'. Its purpose was to render the Fleet Reserve ships as nearly efficient as possible to the fleet in commission by providing them with a two-fifths complement, the most important ranks and ratings, who lived on board and became thoroughly familiar with the ship. When mobilization was ordered, the crews could be completed quickly from the shore barracks and instructional establishments. To get the personnel for the new system, as well as to concentrate their strength into ships of undoubted fighting value, (3) Fisher reduced the seagoing fleet by a ruthless scrapping of ships of comparatively small fighting power. (4) To meet strategic ('and not sentimental') requirements, there was a wholesale redistribution of the fleet, thus concentrating its main strength in home waters instead of in the Mediterranean. To these major innovations must be added the gunnery renaissance, fathered by Captain Percy *Scott and promoted by Fisher. By 1908 most ships were making much better shooting at 6,000 and 7,000 yards than they had done at 2,000 yards a few years earlier. To Fisher the navy owed the beginning of the substitution of oil for coal as boiler fuel and the introduction and improvement of the submarine. He was among the first to foresee the offensive possibilities of the submarine.

Fisher's interests were not entirely in *matériel*. Thus, he defied the class prejudices of the officer corps when he urged that naval careers be thrown open to talent, no matter from what class in society, on the grounds of democratic principle and fleet efficiency, by the abolition of fees at the Osborne and Dartmouth colleges. His campaign bore fruit in later years. Always keenly interested in the welfare of the lower deck, Fisher removed many of the old grievances of the men as regards food, quarters, discipline, and professional prospects.

Particularly from the summer and autumn of 1906 a formidable and vociferous opposition inside and outside the navy (the 'Syndicate of Discontent' or 'Adullamites' were Fisher's pet terms for them) attempted to discredit the whole policy of the Admiralty. Much of the antagonism towards Fisher was due to the ingrained conservatism of the navy and to his unorthodox methods: his alleged personal rule and espionage in the fleet, his unblushing use of the press, promotion of those officers who agreed with his methods (they were known as 'in the *Fishpond'), and harassment of independent officers. Of the major reforms, only the nucleus crew system was generally well received. The opposition to the Selborne Scheme, hitherto muted, assumed (incorrectly) that the principle of 'interchangeability' intended to make one and the same officer qualify for service as an expert in many different capacities; the scrapping policy was assailed for denuding distant stations of police forces, lowering British prestige through the disappearance of the flag, and depriving the fleet of ships which would have been useful in wartime for trade protection. Fisher did make due provision for such police purposes as were still necessary, and believed that an attack on trade in war would be carried out by powerful cruiser squadrons, against which small ships would be ineffective. The dreadnought policy was derided on technical grounds (as was the battle-cruiser type), and on the ground that by rendering all existing battleships obsolete, it swept away Britain's overwhelming preponderance in capital ships (about three to one over

Germany) and gave Germany a nearly level start in the competition for naval supremacy. Fisher had made the plunge in the certainty that the all-big-gun battleship was inevitable on both technical grounds (e.g., long-range hitting had become practicable), and on intelligence of what the U.S.A. and Japan in particular were planning.

Admiral Lord Charles *Beresford was the acknowledged leader of the anti-Fisherites—an officer of engaging personality though of mediocre intellectual and professional attainments. As Commander-in-Chief, Channel Fleet, from April 1907, he adopted an attitude of sharp antagonism to Admiralty policy that was often tactless and insubordinate in manner. His most serious grievance was over the new Home Fleet (October 1906), which he described as a 'fraud upon the public and a danger to the Empire', because it was not under the Channel commander-in-chief's immediate and direct command, though it would be so in war, and a large proportion of its vessels had only a nucleus crew on board. (Fisher's idea in establishing a Home Fleet was to concentrate the strength of the navy in home waters by slow degrees and unostentatiously.) Beresford pressed for an increase of strength to his own Channel Fleet. Another major criticism was that the Admiralty would not send him their war plans. This was true enough: it was traditional policy to provide the commander-in-chief with brief 'War Orders', which contained only 'the general intentions of the Admiralty' as regards actual war strategy and indicated the reinforcements that would be sent out in specified contingencies. On the basis of the War Orders the commander-in-chief was expected to draw up his own detailed war plans and to have them approved by the Admiralty.

By early 1908 the Beresford–Fisher feud had split the upper ranks of the navy into two corps of warring partisans. The row intensified following various incidents during the year. One by-product of the 1909 naval scare of accelerated German building was the strengthening of the anti-Fisher campaign, and he was attacked for having been caught 'napping'. Beresford, who had been ordered to haul his flag down in March 1909, put pressure on the Asquith government to appoint a sub-committee of the Committee of Imperial Defence (April 1909) to investigate his charges that the naval situation was perilous owing to faulty strategic distribution of the fleet (the dispersion of the fleets for the defence of home waters under separate commands), the great destroyer and cruiser deficiency, and the non-existent Admiralty war plans. The committee's report in August did not sustain the general indictment, but it loosed another barrage of invective against Fisher. Profoundly hurt by the failure of the Cabinet to give him solid backing against the attacks of the Beresford clique, anxious to ensure the succession of Admiral Sir A. K. Wilson as First Sea Lord while the latter was still of age (he could be depended on to continue Fisher's policies), and aware that the inquiry had weakened his position, Fisher resigned, effective on 25 January 1910, his 69th birthday. On 9 November 1909 he was raised to the peerage, one of the few naval officers so honoured except for actual services in war.

Fisher did well to leave Whitehall when he did. The navy badly needed an end to the vendetta for which he was partly responsible and which had shattered the spirit of unity. Also, new problems were coming to the fore which could best be solved by a naval general staff, and here Fisher, who took a dim view of a naval staff, was a major obstacle. Again, relations with the army were bad; in this, Fisher was far from blameless. By 1910 his work had been done. He had given the lethargic Royal Navy of the turn of the century a thorough shake-up, producing in the process a stronger and better organized one. Winston *Churchill, no uncritical admirer of Fisher, afterwards wrote: 'There is no doubt whatever that Fisher was right in nine-tenths of what he fought for. His great reforms sustained the power of the Royal Navy at the most critical period in its history.'

Churchill, when he became First Lord in October 1911, relied on Fisher's advice. Fisher was closely associated with the fundamental Churchill decisions in the realm of *matériel* in 1912: to build a fast division of battleships armed with 15-inch guns and driven by oil fuel (the famous 'Queen Elizabeth' class). Oil was now adopted for the smaller ships of war as well. To solve the procurement and technical problems involved in the adoption of oil, Churchill appointed a royal commission on fuel oil chaired by Fisher. Its work was finished by early 1913, and in July 1913 Churchill was able to inform Parliament that oil would gradually replace coal as the basis of the navy's motive power.

On 29 October 1914 Churchill brought Fisher back as First Sea Lord. Sensing the war would be of long duration, Fisher spent much of his energy in the task of constructing a vast armada, some 600 ships of every type, which proved a godsend when the Germans, in 1917, launched their unrestricted submarine attack on commerce. Fisher played a vital part in the development of small non-rigid airships, the 'S.S.' (submarine scout) airships (or 'blimps' as they were later called), to combat the *U-boat menace. He derived great satisfaction from the annihilation of Admiral von *Spee's squadron at the *Falkland Islands on 8 December 1914, 'the only "substantial victory" of ours in the War' and a vindication of the battle-cruiser type. It was his bold stroke in detaching two battle-

Lord Fisher of Kilverstone as a rear admiral

cruisers from the *Grand Fleet that had ensured the victory. He revived his pre-war 'Baltic Scheme', proposing now to land Russian troops on Germany's Pomeranian coast, at a point some 90 miles from Berlin, meanwhile denying the North Sea to the German *High Seas Fleet by sowing it with mines on a vast scale. He never worked out the details for a project which most expert opinion would have considered too hazardous in view of the development of the submarine, mine, and torpedo.

Fisher at first worked amicably and, on the whole, successfully with Churchill; but incompatibility of temperament and outlook prevented them from working in harmony for very long, and Churchill's regular interventions in purely expert matters increasingly irked Fisher. The *Dardanelles campaign brought matters to a head. Fisher had reluctantly, Churchill enthusiastically, supported the operation, but as time went on Fisher saw the danger of continuing to draw heavily on home resources for the operation. He feared a German move in the North Sea and he wanted the ships for his Baltic scheme. When on 15 May 1915 Churchill called for sizeable fresh reinforcements for the Dardanelles considerably in excess of what had been apparently agreed upon with Fisher the night before, Fisher resigned almost immediately.

He was brought back in July 1915 to serve as chairman of the newly established advisory Board of Invention and Research, whose task it was to apply science to the war requirements of the navy. Four months of managing a 'chemist's shop' were quite enough for his restless spirit, and thereafter, with considerable support in the country, he worked to return to the Admiralty as First Sea Lord, First Lord, or in any other capacity. He did not succeed, the final crushing blow to his hopes coming in February 1917 when Admiral Sir John *Jellicoe, the new First Sea Lord, turned down his offer to serve under him as Third Sea Lord and Controller. His temper was not improved by the ineffectiveness of the Board of Invention and Research and 'apathy' and 'want of vision' at the Admiralty; above all, its supposed passive strategy angered him. One result of his disgust with higher authority was his growing political radicalism as early as 1917: anti-monarchy, pro-Labour Party, etc. After the war, in 1919, he wrote two volumes of vivid memoirs, *Memories* and *Records*, a combination of autobiography, prophecy, and rambling reflections, and he speculated on the war of the future (air fighting was to be the dominant feature) in many letters to the press.

For biographies see Richard Hough's *First Sea Lord* (London, 1969) and R. Mackay's *Fisher of Kilverstone* (1973). Fisher's correspondence was admirably edited by Professor Arthur J. Marder in *Fear God and Dread Nought* (3 vols., 1952–9). His First Sea Lord papers were edited for the Navy Records Society in two volumes in 1960 and 1964.

FISHERIES, a general term used to denote all the activities concerned with the catching of fish, whether by line, net, or other means. Until about 1900, the taking of fish was largely unregularized, and haphazard fishing resulted in certain areas being fished out. Since that date the importance of the fisheries in terms of national industries and as a source of food has been widely recognized internationally, resulting in international conventions to preserve the supply, such as close seasons during breeding and national quotas in certain types of fish.

The art of taking fish from the sea has been widely expanded during the 20th century, partly through the development of more efficient fishing craft and their gear, partly through the use of modern technological developments, such as *sonar, to discover the whereabouts of shoals, and partly through a great increase internationally in the study of oceanography, which can indicate the most prolific breeding grounds and the subsequent directions of the migrations of fish. Other modern developments have been improvements in the retention of fish on board by means of efficient refrigeration, thereby allowing fishing craft to remain for longer periods on the fishing grounds, and the provision of fish factory ships to process the catches at sea and to provide maintenance and support for a fleet of fishing vessels, again extending the period of time during which fishing can be continued.

In very general terms, fisheries can be divided into three main categories according to method of capture. (1) *Drift net fishing, employed mainly in relatively shallow waters, is the means of taking fish which do not normally lie on the bottom, of which the more usual types are herring, mackerel, and pilchard. Operated by a *drifter, the net is supported on the surface of the sea by pieces of cork or by glass or plastic balls and hangs vertically downwards to a depth of 40–50 feet. The net is shot by the drifter which then lies at the leeward end of the net, drifting with it, until it is time to haul the net in. Fish are caught and held in the meshes of the net by their gills. A variant of drift net fishing is *ring net fishing. When a shoal of surface swimming fish is seen, a purse net is shot in a wide circle around it and the bottom of the net drawn in; the whole is then brought alongside the fishing vessel and the fish scooped out, or the net is hoisted up and emptied on deck. In many areas where the normal weather conditions allow, such as the Mediterranean, etc., ring netting is employed at night in conjunction with bright electric lights to attract the fish into shoals before the net is shot.

In (2) line fishing, hooks are attached at about three- or four-foot intervals to a long line, baited, and then laid in an area where fish are believed to abound. This method is used for bottom-lying fish and was the common method used for cod on the *Grand Banks off the Newfoundland coast, the lines being shot from *dories attached to the *schooners which operated from the Massachusetts fishing ports. As the numbers of *trawlers increased through the years, so the incidence of line fishing decreased.

The more usual and more prolific method employed for bottom-lying fish is the (3) *trawl, operated by a trawler. In its essentials a trawl is a large bag of net which is towed slowly along the bottom of the sea. Its mouth is held open as it is towed and the fish, disturbed as it approaches, swim into it and are concentrated in the end of the trawl, known as the *cod or cod end, where they are held in a sort of pocket until the trawl is hoisted up by a winch. When brought on board, the net forming the cod end is released and the fish are deposited in the well of the trawler for sorting and cleaning. For the whale fishery, see WHALES AND WHALING.

FISHERMAN'S BEND, a knot very similar to a *round turn and two half hitches, differing from it only in that the first of the two half hitches is made through the round turn and round the standing part of the rope instead of round the standing part only. It is the recognized knot with which a hawser is bent to the ring of an anchor, and when used for this purpose the end of the rope, after the knot has been formed, is usually *seized to the standing part with two or three turns of *marline as a safety measure.

Fisherman's bend

FISHERY, LAWS OF. The international and national regulation of fishery dates back many hundreds of years, but as a generally accepted rule it can be said that on the high seas outside territorial waters, a common right to catch fish exists for all people of all nations. In earlier centuries claims used to be made to restrict various areas of ocean to the fishermen of a single nation, as for example in the 16th century when Denmark claimed the exclusive right to fish in the North Sea, in that area of the high seas which lay between herself and her possessions of Norway and Iceland. This claim was strongly challenged by Elizabeth I of England in 1602 in a remonstrance to Denmark quoting 'the law of nations which alloweth of fishing in the sea everywhere ...', and Denmark's claim was disallowed throughout Europe. The general law can be modified by conventions or agreements between nations with regard to fishing in certain areas of sea, either in respect of custom (ancient rights of fishery) or of type of fish (e.g., lobsters). Other fishing conventions agreed between nations may restrict the universal right of fishing in respect of seasons (e.g., the breeding seasons of whales, seals, etc.). This ancient universal right to fish in the high seas has also been challenged in recent years, and currently, by the unilateral extension of territorial waters and on claims to preserve fish breeding grounds. Within territorial waters it has been universally agreed that the right of fishery belongs exclusively to the subjects of the nation owning such waters unless modified by treaty or convention.

An anomaly of this general law is the lack of general agreement between nations on the limits of territorial waters. In theory, there is no international legislative rule to stop an individual nation announcing whatever limit it likes, and cases have occurred of nations claiming a territorial limit of 200 miles, though such enlarged claims are often ignored by other nations and are difficult for the nation making the claim to enforce. There has also been a growing tendency on the part of many nations to divorce the control of fishery from the long accepted rule of territorial waters, and to declare a new fishery limit, irrespective of the territorial waters limit, on the grounds of over-fishing of recognized offshore breeding grounds. This is an aspect of international maritime law which is discussed at successive Law of the Sea conferences but so far without agreement internationally. The present generally agreed limit is 12 miles, a figure which was reached by the European Fishery Limits Convention of 1964, based on the consensus which emerged from the U.N. Law of the Sea Conference of a few years earlier.

Within the territorial waters of almost all nations, the general law of fishery is that it is a right to be enjoyed by all subjects of that nation. It is legally held to be a right pertaining to the soil covered by tidal waters, and as the owner of such soil is the nation, or in some cases the crown, though perhaps devolved for administrative purposes to counties or boroughs, it follows that the subjects of such states or crowns have the right to fish in such waters. Most nations of which fishery is a major industry place the regulation of the fishery within their territorial waters in the hands of a department of state, which is given the legal power to enforce its rules, such as the imposition of close seasons for certain types of fish, the size of mesh of nets to prevent undersize fish being taken, and so on. Such a department also has the right to require the registration of fishing craft above a certain size and to enforce rules on manning such craft, conditions of service, lights to be carried at night, etc.

Irrespective of the general right of the citizens of a nation to fish freely in its territorial waters, certain areas of sea bed are frequently reserved in many countries exclusively for fishing by certain individuals, such as designated oyster fisheries, and also mussels, cockles, lobsters, and crabs. The taking of salmon from the sea shore by nets is also regulated in most countries by legislative acts.

FISHES ROYAL, whales, dolphins, and sturgeon which are stranded on the shores of Great Britain. By a statute of 1324, *De praerogative regis*, such fish were claimed as royal and were the exclusive property of the sovereign. Many of the museums in Britain owe their collections of casts to these 'fishes royal', released to them by the sovereign for study and observation. The royal right to these fish was renounced by the Crown in 1971 and legislation passed in Parliament to put this decision into effect. In fact, under this legislation, cetaceans stranded on British shores will still go to museums and marine biological institutions for study, as required, but they are now no longer royal and are dealt with by the authority responsible for the shoreline on which they are stranded. See also EJECTAMENTA MARIS.

FISHING FLEET, (1) a collective term used to describe the fishing vessels owned by one individual or firm, or operating out of one port. It is also sometimes used, more loosely, to describe all the fishing vessels of one nation. Another use is to describe the fishing vessels of one type, e.g., the trawler fleet. **(2)** A term used, particularly in the British Navy during the years when fleets and squadrons were maintained on foreign stations, to describe the unmarried young ladies who, usually with their families, sailed out to these stations in the hope of finding an eligible young officer who could be hooked in marriage.

'FISHPOND', the name given to those officers of the British Navy who during the period 1900–10 were strong adherents of Admiral Sir John *Fisher and backed him in his revolutionary reforms in the training of naval personnel and the development of new types of fighting ships. Such officers were said to be 'in the Fishpond' and, with Fisher in high naval office during these years, virtually monopolized the promotions and appointments to the more important naval commands.

FITCH, JOHN (1743–98), American pioneer of steam navigation. After an adventurous career in which he made and lost a fortune, he formed a company in 1786 to exploit the use of steam ferries on the largest American rivers, and a ferry of his design operated on the Delaware River in 1787, though without much success. He claimed to have invented steam navigation, but this was disputed, in particular by James Rumsey of Virginia. After the collapse of his company he committed suicide.

FITTING-OUT, the general preparation of a ship to make her in all respects ready for sea. In a shipyard where a vessel has been newly constructed and launched the ship will be given a berth alongside the yard quay in the fitting-out dock basin, where the remainder of her machinery with its ancillary equipment, the electrical installations and wiring, the fresh and salt water systems and plumbing throughout the ship, the masts and *derricks or cranes with their *rigging, the deck *winches, *lifeboats and their launching gear, anchors and cables, and a host of other items of the vessel's equipment will be installed. The hull, decks, and superstructure will be painted or varnished in accordance with the specifications, and the officers' and crews' quarters, and passenger accommodation if any, as well as the galley and refrigeration equipment, prepared for service. With fitting-out advanced to this stage inclination trials will follow under the direction of the shipyard and the ship's designer, or naval architect, to prove the vessel's stability—her ability to return to an even keel after being heeled by shifting weights first to one side then the other—under varying conditions of loading. After these inclining tests the ship, now almost ready for sea, is taken out of the basin for her first steaming trials with the owners or their representatives in attendance. These are generally referred to as the acceptance trials, for if the speed attained and fuel consumption are satisfactory the vessel is then handed over to her owners, completely fitted-out and ready for service.

In the case of a vessel which has been out of service or laid up for a considerable period, a major refit may be necessary and will call for dry-docking to inspect the underwater part of the hull, the rudder fittings and propeller(s), and to coat the bottom with *antifouling composition. All ballast, fuel, and water tanks may need inspection, and the main engines, boilers and bunkers (if any), auxiliary machinery and electrical gear, deck winches, lifeboats, masts and rigging, and such items checked and repaired if necessary, the paintwork chipped and cleaned, and bright work varnished where necessary.

To the yachtsman who takes care of his boat himself, fitting-out entails a period of hard work shortly before the sailing season opens. All last season's varnish is scraped off, rubbed down, and a new coat applied, the topsides are repainted, and the vessel's bottom scrubbed and an antifouling composition painted on. All the wire and mild steel standing *rigging is inspected and overhauled, and the rope running rigging, *warps, *hawsers, *blocks, *tackles, etc., are checked and tested, being replaced where necessary. The anchor and chain cable are cleaned and placed on board, the *wardrobe of sails inspected, and the engine, batteries, fuel tank, and all other auxiliary equipment checked to be in good working order. After the mast is hoisted in and stepped, the standing rigging set up, and the running rigging rove, the yacht is ready for launching.

In the case of a wooden-hulled yacht, it is usual to leave her on her mooring for a short period before sailing so that the planking may 'take-up', or swell, in order to close up all seams.

FITZROY, ROBERT (1805–65), British rear admiral, is best remembered for the voyage of the *Beagle, 1831–6, in which he was accompanied by the naturalist Charles *Darwin. He was first appointed to command the 240-ton *brig *Beagle* in 1829 and was engaged in surveying the Straits of Magellan and adjacent areas until 1830, when he brought the ship home. He recommissioned the ship for further service on the same station in 1831, and then followed the world voyage with Darwin which concluded Fitzroy's career at sea. After completing the survey of the Magellan Straits the voyage was continued westwards across the Pacific to New Zealand and Australia via Tahiti and then home to England via the Cape of Good Hope and Brazil.

After working up the mass of data collected on the voyage, completing the charts based on his surveys, and writing an account of the circumnavigation, Fitzroy was elected a Member of Parliament and introduced a Bill for the improvement of conditions in the merchant navy. Although the Bill was defeated, it was the means of bringing about the introduction of voluntary certificates for *masters and *mates by the Board of Trade in 1845. Many other ideas embodied in Fitzroy's Bill were included in the Mercantile Marine Act of 1850. He was appointed Governor of New Zealand 1843–5.

In 1850 he asked to be retired from the navy on account of his health and pressure of private affairs. During his service afloat he had always been interested in meteorology and weather prediction and when the government decided in 1854 to set up a meteorological department of the Board of Trade, Fitzroy was chosen as its first superintendent. He was the first man to draw *synoptic charts for forecasting weather patterns based on observations at sea, and was also the first man in England to realize the need of using the newly invented electric telegraph to give warnings of imminent gales at various ports in the United Kingdom, a system already introduced in the U.S.A. In connection with this need of early warning of imminent storms, he instituted in 1861 the visual warning system of storm cones hoisted at conspicuous places in many ports and harbours. Although his work at the Meteorological Office was demanding, he also found time to carry out the duties of secretary of the Lifeboat Institution. By 1865 he was feeling the strain of overwork but refused to rest, and in a fit of depression took his own life.

Fitzroy, throughout his life, was highly strung, but he was a tireless worker who always had the welfare of seamen at heart. Much of his work at the Meteorological Office was actuated by this desire to safeguard the lives of seamen by providing early warnings of storms, and he felt frustrated when the observations at sea, on which his forecasting depended, failed to reach him in

time. It was said after his death that it was an incorrect forecast which caused him to commit suicide. For a biography of this remarkable man see H. E. L. Mellersh, *Fitzroy of the 'Beagle'* (1968).

FIX, to, the process of ascertaining the position of a ship from observations of *land- or *seamarks or by astronomical, radio, or electronic methods of navigation. The word 'fix' is often used as a noun to denote a position obtained from observations and is synonymous with the term 'observed position'.

FIXED AND FLASHING LIGHT, a navigational light in which a steady beam constantly visible is varied at fixed intervals by a flash of brighter intensity. See CHARACTERISTICS.

FIXED LIGHT, a navigational light displayed by a *lighthouse, *lightship, or lighted *buoy in which the light exposed is a steady *beam with no intervals of darkness. See CHARACTERISTICS.

FLAG OFFICER, a general term to embrace all officers of all navies of the rank of rear admiral or its equivalent and above, i.e., any officer who denotes his presence in command at sea by flying a flag, in distinction to *commodores who fly *broad pendants. 'He has got his flag', he has been promoted to flag rank. For 'FLAG' as a boat's reply to a hail, see under 'AYE AYE, SIR'.

FLAGS, see SIGNALS AT SEA, and Appendix 2.

FLAGS OF CONVENIENCE, in some countries known as flags of necessity, a term applied to ships registered in certain small countries, notably Liberia and Panama, by owners who are not nationals of the countries, thus flying flags which do not represent their true origin. The practice started in the shipping slump of 1920–30 when a few owners sought to evade the inspections and regulations imposed by traditional maritime countries, but the real growth of the practice occurred after the Second World War when mainly Greek and Italian owners bought up war surplus tonnage, often with U.S. finance, and registered it in Panama, Liberia, Honduras, or Costa Rica, thus evading state inspections of ships and crews, collective agreements with crews, currency restrictions, and all but nominal taxes. Up to 1950–60 these fleets were considered sub-standard, but freedom from taxes on profits soon allowed the old vessels to be replaced by large, modern ships as good as any in the world. At the same time Liberia particularly attracted what the U.S.A. called 'flag of necessity' ships; these were a product of the huge U.S. stake in the international oil industry and her inability to compete in the oil carrying trade because of the high wages and conditions of U.S. sailors; a U.S. tanker crew cost five times a Greek or Spanish crew. Besides commercial necessity, the U.S.A., as the world's greatest naval power, had a strategic necessity to maintain a tanker fleet and a cargo fleet on important supply routes, recognizing that the backbone of sea power was the merchant ship. For all these reasons 'flag of convenience' tonnage soared and overtook British merchant tonnage during the decade 1960–70. While the real ownership of such ships is shrouded in mystery it is probable that some half is U.S.-owned, and much of the rest U.S.-financed. All the U.S.-owned tonnage is guaranteed to the U.S. government in emergency. Nominal ownership of merchant ships according to the national flags flown is shown in * Lloyd's Register of Shipping.

FLAGS OF NECESSITY, see FLAGS OF CONVENIENCE.

FLAGSHIP, in navies, the ship that carries an * admiral's flag, or in mercantile shipping lines, the ship of the * commodore or senior captain of the line.

FLAKE, an old maritime name for a cradle or stage, suspended over a ship's side, on which men could work in recaulking or repairing the ship's side.

FLAKE, to, the operation of laying out the chain anchor * cable of a ship on the * forecastle deck for examination. It is hove up out of the cable lockers and ranged up and down the deck so that any weak or worn links can be located and the * shackle of cable in which such a link occurs can be taken out of the cable and replaced with a new one.

FLAMSTEED, the Revd. JOHN (1646–1719), English astronomer, was appointed by Charles II in 1675 as his 'astronomical observator', the equivalent of today's Astronomer Royal, to correct the tables of all heavenly bodies 'for the use of his seamen'. At the observatory at * Greenwich he had constructed at his own expense a mural arc, by the aid of which he observed the moon and stars, which resulted in the publication in 1712, under the editorship of Edmund * Halley, of the *Historia coelestis*, which included the Greenwich star catalogue. This work was denounced by Flamsteed as only a partial publication of the observations he had made, and he spent the rest of his life in perfecting his great *Historia coelestis Britannica*, which was posthumously published in three volumes in 1725. Although some of his observations and calculations were later shown to contain errors, this important work was the basis of a great advance in the navigation of ships by celestial observation. The old observatory in Greenwich Park is today known as Flamsteed House in memory of the great astronomer.

FLANNEL, an article of clothing forming part of the traditional rig of seamen in most navies. It is worn under the jumper, in cold weather over a vest, in warm weather next to the skin. It is usually bordered on the top with a narrow strip of dark blue material, and is about thigh length, tucking into the trousers below the waist. Before the days of pyjamas, it also formed the normal night wear of seamen. See SAILORS' DRESS.

FLARE, (1) the outward curve of the bows of a ship, which is designed to throw the water outwards when meeting a head sea, instead of letting it come straight up over the bows. **(2)** A signal, often to indicate distress, used in ships at night. A proposal to use rockets or flares of different colours to indicate various other requirements or conditions of a ship, such as her position or the need for a pilot, has been put forward for international agreement but no firm decision has yet been reached. See also ROCKET.

FLASHING LIGHT, a navigational light displayed by a * lighthouse, * lightship, or lighted * buoy in which the period of light is shorter than the period of darkness separating the flashes. See CHARACTERISTICS.

FLATBOAT, a large flat-bottomed pulling boat supplied during the 18th and early 19th centuries to warships which were to be engaged in amphibious operations and used for landing troops on open beaches. They carried up to thirty men and light field guns.

FLEET, (1) a company of vessels sailing together. The use of the word is sometimes expanded to embrace the whole of a national navy or all the ships owned by a shipping company. It is also used to describe fishing vessels, those owned by one company, those operating out of the same port, or occasionally those linked by function, e.g., the trawler fleet. In its naval use it can be used to describe either the whole of a national navy, e.g., the British fleet, Russian fleet, U.S. fleet, or a homogeneous assembly of some of the entirety of warships, such as the Home Fleet (British), 7th Fleet (U.S.), Black Sea Fleet (Russian), etc. It is also sometimes used to describe all warships of one nation with the same general function, such as * U-boat fleet (German), etc. See also FIRST FLEET. **(2)** A creek or ditch which is tidal.

FLEET, to, a verb with a number of different meanings, but generally used to describe a means of obtaining a better haul on a rope, purchase, or cable. To fleet a rope is the operation of coming up on it to get a more convenient haul. When a *tackle is approaching *two blocks so that no more movement is possible, the moving block is fleeted along to give a more advantageous haul. When *shrouds become stretched in sailing vessels so that the *deadeyes come too close together, the upper set of deadeyes is fleeted further up the shroud so that there is room to haul it tauter. When an *anchor was weighed by hand, the *swifter was fleeted round the ends of the *capstan bars to provide space for additional men to be used on the capstan.

Fleet used as a verb is also a colloquial expression of fishermen describing a vessel's first movement when she drags her keel along the ground as the rising *flood tide is just beginning to float her off.

FLEET AIR ARM, since 1924 the name under which the air wing of the British Navy has been known. Naval aviation in Britain dates from 1912 when the naval wing of the Royal Flying Corps broke away from the parent body to become a separate air force operated and controlled directly by the Royal Navy under the title *Royal Naval Air Service, but on 1 April 1918, following the recommendation of a government committee under the chairmanship of General J. C. Smuts, the R.N.A.S. and the Royal Flying Corps of the Army were amalgamated into one independent Service under the title of Royal Air Force, and on this date all aircraft, air stations, and the entire flying personnel, air and ground staff, of the R.N.A.S. were transferred *en bloc* to the new service. Thereafter, until 1937, all naval flying and procurement of aircraft was controlled by the Royal Air Force, a state of affairs which proved a constant source of naval discontent as naval flying took second place in the councils of the Air Ministry to the heavy bombing policy adopted by the Royal Air Force, resulting in indifferent training of pilots and observers and the provision of aircraft basically unsuitable for specialized operations at sea. In an attempt to remedy this state of discontent the Air Ministry in 1924 set up a branch of the Royal Air Force with the title Fleet Air Arm of the Royal Air Force. A proportion of naval officers trained as specialized pilots and observers for purely naval duties, amounting eventually to 70 per cent of the total flying personnel. Administrative difficulties and discontent continued, however, and eventually, in 1937, this branch of the Royal Air Force was severed completely from its parent body and placed under the direct control of the Admiralty as an integral part of the navy, retaining the title Fleet Air Arm. It has remained so ever since.

See also AIRCRAFT CARRIERS, SWORDFISH, TARANTO, Battle of.

FLEET TRAIN, the generic term used during the Second World War to describe an assembly of auxiliary vessels, such as oilers, repair ships, ammunition ships, replenishment *aircraft carriers, provision and store ships, etc., which accompanied the fighting fleet to sea on operations and enabled it to remain operational at sea for long periods without having to return to port to replenish. The term now usually employed for this function is afloat support.

FLEMISH HORSE, the short foot rope at the end of a *yard used by the man at the outer corner of a square sail when *reefing or *furling. The outer end of the Flemish horse is normally spliced round the *gooseneck of the *studdingsail boom iron and the inner end secured inside the *braces.

FLENSE, to, the process of stripping the blubber from a whale when it has been caught and hauled up on the deck of a whale factory ship. The operation is performed by the use of flensing irons to cut the blubber loose and by *tackles brought to the *winches to haul it away from the carcass. The deck on which the operation is performed is known as the flensing deck.

FLINDERS, MATTHEW (1774–1814), British navigator and explorer, entered the Royal Navy in 1789, served at the battle of the *Glorious First of June in 1794 and in the following year sailed as a *midshipman in the *Reliance* to New South Wales. He struck up a close friendship with the surgeon on board, George *Bass, with whom he shared an enthusiasm for exploration. Individually and in company, the two made several surveys which culminated in the passage through the Strait which bears Bass's name in the *sloop *Norfolk* in September 1798 to prove that Tasmania was an island.

Returning to England, Flinders was appointed in command of the sloop *Investigator* in which he sailed in July 1801 to South-West Australia where, between December 1801 and May 1802, he surveyed much of the Great Bight, including St. Vincent's Gulf (the present site of Adelaide), Bass's Strait, and Port Phillip (site of Melbourne), before reaching Port Jackson (Sydney). In July 1802 he continued the circumnavigation of Australia in the worn-out and leaky *Investigator*, surveying parts of the Great Barrier Reef and the shores of the Gulf of Carpentaria, finally sailing west and south-west of Australia to return again to Port Jackson on 9 June 1803 after great sufferings from privation and *scurvy which resulted in the loss of many of his ship's company and damage to his own health.

Besides his extensive surveys, Flinders made many scientific studies, particularly with regard to *deviation of the compass caused by the iron

The Bermuda floating dock; engraving from the Illustrated London News, *July 1869*

components of the ship, which were to prove of the greatest importance. The compensating bars around a magnetic compass are still named after him. With the massive collection of material and papers arising out of his voyages, he set off for England as a passenger, first in H.M.S. *Porpoise*, which was wrecked on the Barrier Reef, and then in the *schooner *Cumberland*. Putting in at the French island of Mauritius in December 1803, he was made a prisoner-of-war in spite of a French passport which, unfortunately, was made out specifically for the *Investigator*.

Flinders's health further deteriorated during his captivity which lasted until 1811. On his return to England he nevertheless set himself to compile his splendid account, *A Voyage to Terra Australis*, which was published on the day he died.

E. Scott, *Life of Matthew Flinders* (1914).

FLINT, FRANCIS RUSSELL (1915–77), British marine artist, is the son of Sir W. Russell Flint, who served in the *R.N.V.R. in the First World War (1914–18). In this respect, as well as in vocation, the son followed the father and served in the R.N.V.R. in the Second World War, and his experiences there served as the subject of many important pictures, a collection of which is now in the *Imperial War Museum. His pictures have a vivid sense of movement and design which give them an important place in contemporary marine art.

FLIP, a once favourite drink at sea introduced, it is said, by Admiral Sir Clowdisley *Shovel in the late 17th century. It is a mixture of beer, spirits, and sugar heated with a red-hot iron.

FLOATING BATTERY, originally a *razeed sailing warship with guns on board for bombarding installations ashore, but in its better-known connotation, the first attempt to use protective iron plates in warships. They evolved from the abortive attack by British and French wooden *ships of the line against the Russian naval base of Sebastopol in 1854 during the Crimean War, when the attack had to be hurriedly abandoned because of the damage the ships were receiving. Floating batteries, with their hulls protected by iron plates to the waterline and with a small steam engine installed, were constructed in Britain and France and reached the Crimea in 1855. Their first action was the bombardment of the Kinburn forts, where they created a great impression, inflicting great damage on the forts and receiving very little themselves. The ultimate development of the floating battery was the *monitor.

FLOATING DOCK, a dock constructed in the main of watertight tanks. When these are flooded, the dock is immersed in the sea to a depth where it can receive the hull of a ship. As the tanks are then pumped out, the dock rises bringing the ship with it, until the hull is above water. The great value of a floating dock, *vis-à-vis* a *graving dock which is a permanent structure, is that it can be towed to any place where its services are required.

FLOG A DEAD HORSE, to, see DEAD HORSE.

FLOG THE GLASS, to, an expression used on board ship to indicate attempts to speed up the passage of a * watch in the days when watches were timed by the half-hour sand glass. The run of the sand was supposed to be quickened by vibrating the glass, and when weary watch-keepers towards the end of their watches shook the glass to make the sand run out more quickly, they were said to flog the glass. See also WARMING THE BELL.

FLOGGING ROUND THE FLEET, a form of punishment in the old days of the British Navy for the more serious crimes committed on board. It could be awarded only by sentence of a court martial. The man undergoing sentence was placed in a boat in which a ship's grating had been lashed upright across the * thwarts, and rowed alongside each ship lying in harbour, where he was given twelve strokes with a * cat-o'-nine-tails by a boatswain's mate of the ship off which the boat was lying. After each infliction of a dozen strokes a blanket was thrown across his back while he was being rowed to the next ship. A naval doctor was always in attendance in the boat to make certain that the man undergoing punishment was fit to receive further instalments of his sentence as he came alongside each ship. In each ship visited the crew were mustered on deck and in the rigging to witness the punishment, drums on board beating out the * 'Rogue's March' as the boat approached.

FLOOD, the flow of the tidal stream as it rises from the ending of the period of * slack water at low tide to the start of the period of slack water at high tide. Its period is about six hours which is divided into three parts of about two hours each, the first two hours being known as the young flood, the middle two hours as the main flood, and the last two as the last of the flood. An approximate rule both for the amount of the rise and the speed of the flow of a flood tide for each of the six hours of the period of tide is $\frac{1}{12}$ for the first hour, $\frac{2}{12}$ for the second, $\frac{3}{12}$ for the third and fourth, $\frac{2}{12}$ for the fifth, and $\frac{1}{12}$ for the sixth.

FLOOR, the lower part of a transverse * frame of a ship running each side of the * keelson to the * bilges. In the general run of shipbuilding, this part of the frame is usually approximately horizontal, so that the floor of a vessel, i.e., the lower section of its transverse frames, is a virtually horizontal platform extending to the ship's sides at the point where they begin to turn up towards the vertical. See also SHIPBUILDING.

FLOTA, the name given to the annual * convoys of merchant vessels which brought treasure from America and the Indies to Spain during the 16th and 17th centuries. See also GALIZABRA.

FLOTILLA, from the Spanish diminutive of *flota*, a fleet, *flotilla*, a little fleet, a squadron of small ships, and a name more especially connected in navies with * destroyers, * submarines, and smaller warships. It was occasionally used in naval circles as a collective noun for all small surface craft, such as destroyers and * torpedoboats, but the more general meaning was restricted to the ships which made up one group under the command of a captain, the individual ships in a flotilla being commanded by lieutenant-commanders or lieutenants.

In the British Navy the word has today almost completely died out, having been replaced by 'squadron'.

FLOTILLA LEADER, a small warship of the * destroyer type which carried the senior officer in command of a destroyer * flotilla. They were built rather larger than the other ships of the flotilla since they carried a larger complement associated with command, such as additional signalmen and officers responsible for the efficiency of all ships in the flotilla in their specialist skills: gunnery, torpedo, signals, engineering, etc. In most cases flotilla leaders also carried a larger armament of 4·7-inch guns in place of the usual 4-inch and also had a greater speed by two or three knots. The flotilla leader was introduced into most navies around 1908 when destroyers were being built in great numbers and were still relatively small warships of around 1,000 tons displacement, but disappeared as a distinctive type in the period 1930–40 when the displacement of destroyers increased to 2,000 tons or more.

During the First World War (1914–18), some of the flotilla leaders in the British * Grand Fleet were light * cruisers.

FLOTSAM, (1) any part of the wreckage of a ship or her cargo which is found floating on the surface of the sea. It was originally in Britain a part of the perquisites of the * Lord High Admiral, but is today considered as * derelict property and goes to the finder or salvor. To be flotsam, however, it must be floating and not on the bottom of the sea, when other questions of ownership arise. See also JETSAM, LAGAN. **(2)** The spat, or spawn, of the oyster is sometimes known as flotsam.

FLOTTES DE COMBAT, LES, a well-known French reference book, often considered as the counterpart in France of the English * *Jane's Fighting Ships*, published every two years and containing details of the warships, naval aircraft, and missiles of all countries. It was founded in

1892 by Lieutenant the Marquis Testu de Balincourt of the French Navy with the title of *Études sur les navires d'aujourd'hui*, the printers being the Imprimerie Noisette of Paris. In 1897 the title was changed to *Les Flottes de combat étrangères* and the publication was taken over by Berger Levrault, the format being altered to the well-known oblong shape. In 1903 ships of the French Navy were included for the first time and the title was again altered, to *Les Flottes de combat*. Publication was prevented during the years 1901–2, 1905, 1913, and 1916 owing to the absence of the editor on active service abroad.

In 1917 de Balincourt retired and publication was not resumed until 1925 when it reappeared under the auspices of the French Naval Staff. In 1929 Captain Vincent Bréchignac of the French Navy was appointed editor on his retirement from the active list and held the post until his death in 1943. He was succeeded by the present editor, M. Henri * le Masson, who had been working as his assistant. He in turn is being assisted by M. Jean Labayle-Couhat, a leading expert in warship construction. Over the years many improvements have been made in its scope, accuracy, and presentation of naval information.

FLOWER OF THE WINDS, an old expression for the engraving of the *wind-rose on the earliest charts and maps, and extended after the introduction of the magnetic *compass to include the compass rose on charts.

FLOWING, (1) the situation of the *sheets of a sail in fore-and-aft rigged ships when they are eased off as the wind comes from broad on or abaft the beam, and the *yards of a square-rigged ship when they are braced more squarely to the mast. A ship is said to have a flowing sheet when the wind crosses her beam and the sails are trimmed to take the greatest advantage of it. **(2)** A term used in connection with the *tide, a synonym of flooding. See FLOOD.

FLUKE, (1) the triangular shape at the end of each arm of an *anchor immediately below the bill or point which, by digging into the ground when any strain or pull comes on it, gives an anchor its holding power. They are also sometimes called *palms. Many seamen do not sound the 'k', pronouncing it as 'flue'. For illus., see ANCHOR. **(2)** The two triangular parts which make up the tail of a whale. It was this which gave the old whale fishers the expression of 'fluking' when their whalers, in those days under sail power only, were *running free with a following wind with the foresail boomed out, or *goose-winged, on the opposite side to the mainsail.

FLUKY, a description of a wind at sea when it is light and variable in direction and has not settled down to blow steadily from any one quarter. It is a term used more often in connection with sailing vessels than with other type of craft.

FLUSH DECK, a continuous deck of a ship laid from fore to aft without any break. Strictly speaking, the only true decks of a ship are those which continue from forward to aft without a break, the remainder being only part decks, but the generally accepted meaning of the word has been expanded to include every deck, whether whole or part. The term flush deck is also frequently used to denote a type of ship which has no *forecastle or *poop.

FLUSHING, in Dutch, Vlissingen, a seaport in the province of Zeeland at the mouth of the western Scheldt. It was, up to the mid-19th century, an important naval base of the Dutch Navy but was later developed considerably as a commercial port, with extensive docks and shipbuilding industries. Although the Dutch government backed its expansion as a commercial port after it had lost its naval significance, it was never able to compete with *Rotterdam or *Antwerp.

FLÛTE, (1) a French word used widely in the days of the sailing navies to indicate a ship which has had some of her guns taken out of her or struck down into her hold in order to provide additional accommodation for troops or stores. Strictly, the expression is *en flûte*. **(2)** The anglicized version of the Dutch *fluyt*, a small supply vessel with a rounded stern rigged as a *pink, i.e., ship-rigged on three masts.

FLY, (1) the old maritime word for the *compass card from the time it was pivoted in the compass bowl and thus able to revolve freely. **(2)** The part of a flag or pendant farthest from the staff or *halyard on which it is hoisted, i.e., the part which flutters in the wind.

FLY-BOAT, a 16th–19th century flat-bottomed Dutch vessel with a very high and ornate stern with broad *buttocks, and with one or two masts either square-rigged on both or with a *spritsail on the mainmast. They were of about 600 tons, and used mainly for local coastal traffic.

FLY-BY-NIGHT, the name given to an additional sail which acted as a sort of *studding-sail set by naval *sloops which were not issued with such sails, during the 18th and early 19th centuries. It was normally a square sail set on a temporary *yard when the wind came from directly astern, but was occasionally a spare *jib set from the topmast head and sheeted by *tack and *clew to the upper yardarms.

FLYING DUTCHMAN, The, perhaps the most famous of all legends of the sea. There are several variations of it. The most usual story is that of a Dutch skipper, Captain Vanderdecken, who on a voyage home from Batavia and faced with a howling gale, swore by *Donner* and *Blitzen* that he would beat into Table Bay in spite of God's wrath. His ship foundered as he had this oath on his lips, and he was condemned to go on sailing until eternity in his attempt to reach Table Bay. The spectre of his ship is supposed to haunt the waters round the Cape of Good Hope and a strong superstition among sailors is that anyone who sets eyes upon her will die by shipwreck. A German legend concerns a Herr von Falkenberg condemned to sail for ever around the North Sea in a ship without *helm or helmsman and playing dice with the devil for his soul. A similar Dutch legend equates the Flying Dutchman with the ghost of the Dutch seaman van Straaten.

The theme of the Flying Dutchman has been used by novelists, poets, and dramatists, the best known being Captain *Marryat in his book *The Phantom Ship*, Scott in his poem 'Rokeby', and Wagner in his opera *Der fliegende Holländer*. In the opera the captain, Vanderdecken, is allowed ashore once every seven years to find a woman whose love alone can redeem him.

The origin of the legend is uncertain but it is possibly derived from a Norse saga which tells of the Viking Stöte who, having stolen a ring from the gods, was found later as a skeleton in a robe of fire seated on the mainmast of a black spectral ship.

f.o.b., a mercantile abbreviation in connection with the shipment of cargo, standing for free on board, and meaning that all charges of freight, insurance, etc., have been paid up to the time of arrival on board.

FOG SIGNALS, a series of sound signals in fog laid down in the international regulations for preventing collisions at sea. A steamship under way sounds one prolonged blast on her steam whistle or foghorn every two minutes, a vessel under way but stopped sounds two prolonged blasts, and a vessel towing, a cable ship at work, a fishing vessel engaged in fishing, or a vessel not under command sounds one prolonged and two short blasts. Ships at anchor ring a bell rapidly for five seconds every minute. Sailing ships give blasts on their foghorn every minute, one blast meaning that she is under way on the starboard tack, two blasts on the port tack, and three blasts running with the wind abaft the beam. Short blasts are used to indicate changes of course, one blast meaning altering course to starboard, two to port, and three going astern.

In the old days of sailing navies, fog signals consisted of firing a gun at intervals, beating drums, and ringing the ship's bell.

FOG-BUOY, a small buoy towed astern at the end of a long *grass-line by naval vessels when steaming in line ahead in thick fog to give an indication to the next ship astern of the distance away of the ship next ahead in the line, thus providing a means of retaining formation. By keeping the fog-buoy of the next ahead in sight and close to the *stem of the next following ship, there is no danger of collision in the fog. When fog-buoys are in use, they are said to be streamed.

FOGHORN, a sounding appliance fitted in ships, or a portable horn carried on board small craft, used for giving warning of a vessel's presence in fog. Smaller ships may be fitted with a steam whistle in place of a foghorn, but use the same signals. *Fog signals are also made by *lighthouses and by *lightships when they are in their correct position.

FOOT, the bottom side of a sail, whether triangular or four-sided. Thus, also, footrope, that part of a *bolt rope, to which the sides of a sail are sewn, which bounds the foot of the sail. For illus. see SAIL.

'FOOT IT IN', to, an order given to the men *furling the *bunt of a square sail when it was required to stow the sail especially snugly. It entailed the topmen stamping this part of the sail in as hard as they could, supporting themselves by hanging on to a topsail *tye. It was a process also known as 'dancing it in'.

FOOTROPES, the ropes in square-rigged ships, supported at intervals by ropes from the yard known as *stirrups, which hang below a *yard and on which the *topmen stand when aloft *furling or *reefing sail. They were sometimes also known as horses of the yard, possibly because of the connection with stirrups. For illus. see YARD.

FORBES, Sir CHARLES MORTON (1881–1960), British admiral of the fleet, commanded the British Home Fleet at the outbreak of the Second World War. He had specialized in gunnery and, having been promoted to commander at the end of 1912, became in November 1914 the first executive officer of the new battleship *Queen Elizabeth* until, in October 1915, he joined Admiral Sir John *Jellicoe's war staff in the flagship *Iron Duke*, in which capacity he took part in the battle of *Jutland.

Promoted to captain in 1917, Forbes commanded both these battleships in the Atlantic and

Mediterranean fleets respectively and served as Director of Naval Ordnance before promotion to rear admiral in 1928. He served as rear admiral in command of destroyers in the Mediterranean Fleet, sat on the Board of Admiralty as Third Sea Lord and Controller, and acted as second-in-command in the Mediterranean. He was promoted to admiral in 1936 and became commander-in-chief of the Home Fleet in April 1938, a post he held for the first thirteen months of the Second World War.

The most important fleet operations he conducted during this period were the opening moves of the Norwegian campaign in April 1940. A failure to get the Home Fleet to sea promptly because of doubts, shared by the Admiralty, as to the credibility of intelligence warnings of the opening German moves permitted the enemy to carry out his initial plan unmolested, for which Forbes did not escape criticism. He was, nevertheless, promoted to admiral of the fleet and had the rare distinction of flying his Union Flag at sea from May to October 1940 when he was relieved by Admiral Sir John * Tovey.

During the last three months of his command of the Home Fleet, Forbes was in disagreement with the Admiralty over the latter's transfer of * cruisers and * destroyers to the southern commands to guard against a threatened German invasion after the conquest of France, a transfer which almost immobilized the Home Fleet and left the Western Approaches Command almost bereft of escorts for the ocean * convoys. Forbes stoutly maintained that invasion by sea was not to be feared unless and until the German air force had gained air supremacy over the English Channel and Britain, and although both the Admiralty and the government expressed similar views, their disposition of the available naval forces belied them and was, in Forbes's opinion, as dangerous as it was faulty.

His last appointment was as commander-in-chief at Plymouth from May 1941 to June 1943.

FORBIN, CLAUDE DE (1656–1733), French seaman, ran away to sea as a boy, joined the navy, and served with such great gallantry in campaigns under d'* Estrées and * Duquesne that his promotion was rapid. In 1686 he was selected to accompany a French embassy to Siam, but when the embassy returned Forbin was persuaded to stay in the service of the King of Siam as grand admiral of the fleet, general of the armies, and governor of Bangkok. Two years of this was enough for him, and he returned to France, serving in a * privateer ship with Jean * Bart, with whom he was captured, confined at Plymouth, and later escaped. After further service in the war against Spain, he was selected to command the squadron which was to land the

Old Pretender (son of James II) in Scotland in 1708, but found the coast so effectively guarded that the squadron had to return to France with its mission unfulfilled. This was his last service and he retired to the country to write his memoirs.

FORE-AND-AFT RIG, (1) the arrangement of sails in a sailing vessel so that the * luffs of the sails abut the masts or are attached to * stays, the sails except in the case of * jibs and * staysails being usually extended by a * boom. See RIG. **(2)** The expression FORE-AND-AFT is also used to describe the seaman's uniform which consists of a jacket and peaked cap.

FOREBITTER, the sailors' songs sung in the * forecastle when the men of a watch were off duty. They were not in any way * shanties, which were always working songs, but songs sung for recreation or entertainment. It is almost certain that the name arose because the sailors gathered around the fore * bitts on the forecastle to sing them. In fact these songs were also known, more prosaically, as fo'c'sle songs.

FORECASTLE, pronounced fo'c'sle, the space beneath the short raised deck forward, known in sailing ships as the * topgallant forecastle, to be seen usually in smaller ships. The origin of the name lies in the castle built up over the * bows of the oldest fighting ships in which archers were stationed to attack the crews of enemy vessels or to repulse boarders * entering in the * waist of the ship. It used also to be the generic term to indicate the living space of the crew for many years in the forward end of the ship below the forecastle deck but this meaning has gradually died out as better living conditions for crews have made their way into all modern ships. In this connection, it was also the name given to the deckhouse on the upper deck of large sailing ships in which the seamen had their living quarters.

FOREFOOT, the point in a ship where the * stem is joined to the forward end of the * keel.

FORE-GANGER, (1) a length of 15 fathoms of chain, slightly heavier than the anchor cable, which in some ships used to be inserted in the cable between the anchor and the first * shackle to take the additional wear on the cable as it lay in the * hawsepipe when the anchors were secured for sea. **(2)** In whaling, a short piece of rope connecting the line with the shank of the * harpoon when spanned for killing.

FOREGIRT or **FARGOOD,** a short wooden spar lashed to the mast and used to boom out the leading edge, or * luff, of a * lugsail. It was sometimes known as a 'wooden bowline', as it served the same purpose of keeping the leading edge of the sail as far forward as possible when sailing *on a wind. It was chiefly used in small French and English fishing craft from about the middle of the 19th century, being probably an importation from a similar spar sometimes used in North American waters.

The foregirt may have been a late descendant of the early Norwegian *beitass, a luff spar used in Viking ships, particularly the *knorr, which held the luff taut, thus enabling the vessel to *claw to windward. These ships had a step with one or two socket holes each side just forward of the mast into one of which the end of the beitass was stepped.

FOREGUY, a rope leading forward from the end of a mainsail *boom to the *bitts to prevent the boom from swinging inboard when broad-reaching or running before a following wind which is patchy in force or direction. It applies mainly to *gaff-rigged vessels.

FORE-HOODS, the foremost outer and inner planks of a wooden-hulled vessel, those whose ends are *rabbeted into the *stem. See also HOOD-ENDS.

FORELAND, NORTH and **SOUTH,** two famous headlands on the eastern coast of Kent, the South Foreland being three miles north-east of Dover and the North Foreland marking the southern end of the entry to the Thames estuary. Both appear widely in both prose and poetry of the sea. The battles of *Dover and the *Kentish Knock, in the First Anglo-Dutch War (1652-4), were both fought in the vicinity of the South Foreland; the *Gabbard, sometimes known as the battle of North Foreland in the First Anglo-Dutch War, and the St. James's Day battle, in the Second Anglo-Dutch War (1665-7) were both fought off the North Foreland.

FORELOCK, a flat wedge or pin driven through the hole in an anchor *shackle to secure the shackle pin, much in the nature of a cotter pin. They were usually held in place by a pellet of lead which, when struck with a sledge hammer, expanded to fill the cavity behind the head, but a more modern method is to insert a lead ring which fits into a cavity and holds the pin in position until removed with a shearing punch.

FORE-REACH, the distance a sailing vessel will shoot up to windward when brought head to wind in the act of tacking. If a vessel has a good fore-reach, which is a function of her underbody design and her sailing speed at the time, it can sometimes be useful to make this distance to windward while remaining on the same *tack, e.g., in those cases where it might mean rounding a mark or fetching a point without having to go

*about on the opposite tack. The term can also be used as a verb to indicate that a vessel can make progress to windward when coming about or hove-to. See also FETCH, TO; PINCH, TO.

FORE-SHEETS, the forward part of a boat, right in the bows, the opposite end of the *stern-sheets. It has often been suggested that the origin of the term came from the fact that it was in that part of the boat that the sheets of the foresails, when spread, are handled, but, while this is true of stern-sheets, the sheets of foresails are almost invariably handled amidships or aft. It is more probable that because the after part of a boat is called the stern-sheets, someone decided that the forward part should be called by the opposite name.

FORESTER, CECIL SCOTT (1899-1965), novelist and creator of the character of Horatio Hornblower, was brought up in London and was originally destined for the medical profession. Failing his anatomy examinations, he took to authorship in a way described in a fragment of autobiography, *Long Before Forty* (1967), which was published posthumously. His best-known maritime stories include *Brown on Resolution* (1929), an imaginary episode of the First World War (1914-18), *The Ship* (1943), in which the story centres on the second battle of *Sirte in the Mediterranean during the Second World War, and the long and detailed Hornblower series of six full novels and a number of shorter stories, the evolution of which he described in *The Hornblower Companion* (1964). Forester's hobby was sailing; he also saw something of maritime warfare in the Second World War; and his books succeed through convincing veri-similitude, a detailed knowledge of square-rig seamanship soundly based on considerable study and research, and an uncommonly strong narrative gift. Hornblower's adventures during the long wars with France (1793-1815) are as graphic as anything imagined by his predecessor, Frederick *Marryat, and Forester's range of interest was very wide indeed. He was invalided from the *R.N.V.R. during the Second World War and spent his later years in California.

FORE-TRIANGLE, in yachts, the area formed between the masthead, the base of the mast at deck level, and the lower end of the fore masthead *stay, whether it reaches the stemhead or the fore end of a *bowsprit. In the rating rules for offshore racing the size and area of the fore-triangle plays an important part in making it possible to increase a yacht's sail area forward of the mast without incurring a handicap penalty; this has resulted in the modern sail plan in which yachts are rigged with small mainsails and correspondingly large headsails.

FORETURN, the twist given to the *strands of which *rope is made, before they are laid up into rope. See also AFTERTURN.

FORGE OVER, to, a ship forges over a shoal or sandbank when she is forced over by the wind acting on a great press of sail. If the wind was fair it was often possible to free a ship which had been caught on a shoal by setting additional sails and using the wind to push or forge her over.

FORMER, a cylindrical piece of wood used for making the cartridges with which a naval gun was loaded in the days of sailing navies. It was slightly less than the diameter of the bore of the gun for which cartridges were to be made and paper or linen was wrapped round it as a container for the gunpowder required to fire the ball. It was of a size to take exactly the amount of powder required for the charge.

***FORMIDABLE,* H.M.S.,** a name which was introduced into the Royal Navy in 1759, when the French ship *Formidable* was captured at the battle of *Quiberon Bay and added to the Royal Navy under her own name. Her immediate successor in the Royal Navy was a 2nd *rate of ninety guns launched at Chatham in 1777. This ship took part in Admiral Augustus *Keppel's action of July 1778 off *Ushant, and served as the flagship of Admiral Sir George *Rodney at the battle of the *Saints in April 1782. The fifth and latest of her name in the Royal Navy was the aircraft carrier launched in 1939. During the Second World War she was present at the battle of *Cape Matapan and took part in the evacuation of Greece and Crete in 1941, and in the Salerno landings in 1943. Later in the war she was in the British Pacific Fleet and was present at the first Anglo-American attack on the Japanese mainland. She was broken up in 1953.

FORTUNUS, originally a Roman god to whom sacrifices were made in Rome in honour of naval victories. However, the emperor *Agrippa (63– 12 B.C.) dedicated a temple to *Neptune in the Campus Martius in 31 B.C., in honour of the naval victory of *Actium, thus confirming Neptune as the Roman god of the sea. See also POSEIDON.

FORWARD (pron. forrard), towards the bows of a ship, or in the fore part of a ship. It has no particular boundary line in the ship, being used more in a relative or directional sense than as a definition of any area.

FOSTER, HENRY (1796–1831), naval surveyor and astronomer, entered the Royal Navy in 1812. In 1820 he accompanied Captain Basil Hall to South America and assisted him with his pendulum investigations. He built on this experience during three visits to the Arctic; in 1823 with Clavering in the *Griper*, and in 1824–5 and 1827 with Sir William *Parry with whom he served as astronomer, making various observations on the diurnal *variation and intensity of the magnetic needle and other subjects connected with terrestrial magnetism and astronomical refractions. In 1827 he was appointed to command the *Chanticleer*, a *sloop sent to the South Seas at the suggestion of the Royal Society (of which Foster was a Fellow) to determine the ellipticity of the earth by a series of pendulum experiments and to carry out other scientific investigations. During the course of this voyage Foster visited the South Shetland Islands where he carried out pendulum experiments on Deception Island. He was drowned while trying to determine the meridian distance between Chagres and Panama.

FOTHERING, a method of stopping a leak at sea. The old practice was to fill a basket with ashes and chopped ropeyarns and cover it loosely with canvas. The basket was then fixed to the end of a long pole and plunged repeatedly into the sea as near as possible to the leak. As the ropeyarns were gradually shaken through the sides of the basket or over the top, they were drawn into the leak with the water entering it, and so choked it. A more efficient method, developed later, was to draw a sail or similar piece of canvas, closely thrummed with yarns, under the bottom of the ship in the area of the leak, the pressure of water holding it close to the ship's side and thus stopping the leak. This is the same principle as that on which the *collision mat works, but is used in smaller vessels in which proper collision mats are not carried.

***FOUDROYANT,* H.M.S.,** a French ship of eighty-eight guns, captured by H.M.S. *Monmouth* in 1758, was the first of the name in the Royal Navy. She took part in the expedition against Martinique under Rear Admiral George Brydges *Rodney in 1762, and in Admiral *Keppel's action off *Ushant in July 1778. In April 1782, commanded by Captain John *Jervis, she captured a newly launched French ship, the 74-gun *Pégase*. She was taken to pieces in 1787. The next *Foudroyant*, launched at Plymouth in 1798, had been selected by Horatio *Nelson as his flagship in 1797 while still on the stocks, but because she was not ready in time Nelson took the *Vanguard instead, the *Foudroyant* thus narrowly missing being the fleet flagship at the battle of the *Nile. In June 1799, at Palermo, Lord Nelson transferred his flag to her from the *Vanguard* and she remained his flagship until his return to England in 1800. After a refit she became the flagship of Lord

*Keith and in this capacity was present at the capitulation of the French at Alexandria in 1801. After the war she was laid up at Devonport until 1872, when she became an instructional vessel for gun drill. She was placed on the sale list in 1891 and was initially bought by a German firm, but was purchased from them by Mr. Wheatley Cobb, who restored her as she had been in her fighting days. She was unfortunately destroyed by fire at Blackpool in June 1897, and in order to carry on the name Mr. Cobb bought another old warship, the *Trincomalee*, a 5th *rate built at Bombay in 1817. She had been fitted as a training ship for naval reserves in 1860 and served in that capacity until 1895. Mr. Cobb renamed her *Foudroyant* and on his death his widow handed her to the Society for Nautical Research. She is now used as a holiday training ship for boys and girls in Portsmouth harbour.

FOUL, an adjective with various nautical meanings, generally indicative of something wrong or difficult. Thus a foul *hawse is the expression used when a ship lying to two *anchors gets her *cables crossed; a foul bottom is the condition of a ship's underwater hull when weeds and barnacles restrict her way through the water; a foul wind is one which, being too much ahead, prevents a sailing ship from laying her desired course. When used as a verb it indicates much the same thing. One vessel can foul another when she drifts down on her, or can foul a ship's hawse by letting go an anchor and cable across that of the other. In a yacht race, one can foul another by bumping into her.

FOUL, or **FOULED, ANCHOR,** an *anchor which has become hooked in some impediment on the ground or, on weighing, has its *cable wound round the *stock or *flukes. The fouled anchor is also the official seal of the *Lord High Admiral of Britain and another version of it is the decorative device on his flag, which until the office of Admiralty was merged into the Ministry of Defence in 1964, was flown day and night from the Admiralty building in London. It is now the personal flag of the Queen, who assumed the title of Lord High Admiral in 1964. This flag, in conjunction with the Royal Standard and the Union flag, is traditionally flown when the sovereign of Britain proceeds to sea, indicating that it is from the sovereign that the office of Lord High Admiral derives. The only other occasion on which it is flown is at the launch of a British warship, being hoisted on a flagstaff on the hull as it goes down the launching *ways.

Its adoption as the official seal of the Lord High Admiral of England dates from the end of the 16th century when it was incorporated as part of the arms of Lord *Howard of Effingham, then Lord High Admiral. A form of it, however,

had been in use by the Lord High Admiral of Scotland about a century earlier.

The use of the foul, or fouled, anchor, an abomination to seamen when it occurs in practice, as the seal of the highest office of maritime administration is purely on the grounds of its decorative effect, the rope cable around the shank of the anchor giving a pleasing finish to the stark design of an anchor on its own.

Foul anchor

FOUL HAWSE, see HAWSE.

FOUNDER, to, the act of a ship which sinks at sea, generally understood to be by the flooding of her hull either through springing a leak or through striking a rock. Other causes of a ship sinking, such as explosion, etc., are not usually associated with the word.

FOUR DAYS BATTLE, the, an action of the Second Anglo-Dutch War (1665–7), was fought on 1–4 June 1666 in the southern North Sea between an English fleet of fifty-six ships under the command of the Duke of Albemarle (see MONCK, George) and a Dutch fleet of eighty-five ships commanded by Admiral de *Ruyter. The English fleet was below strength, Prince *Rupert, with the White squadron, having been ordered by Charles II to proceed to the westward to meet a supposed French fleet which did not materialize. Albemarle attacked shortly after noon on the first day and a hot action ensued till 10 p.m., but the high sea running prevented the English, who were to windward, from using their lower deck guns. Each side lost two or three ships. At the end of the day Albemarle stood off to the westward, repairing damage, and the Dutch were in no condition to pursue. The following morning the English returned to resume the fight, having now forty-four ships against about eighty. The fleets engaged each other on opposite tacks, and at one time the Dutch van was thrown into confusion by the insubordinate tactics of two junior flag officers who quitted the line, but the English were too weak to press home this advantage. The day ended with Albemarle once more hauling off to the westward, in fact in full retreat. Each side again lost about three ships.

On the third day the wind was still easterly and Albemarle continued his retreat, maintaining good order, sending his most damaged ships ahead and covering them with the twenty-eight ships which were still fairly sound. Three of his hopelessly mauled ships were abandoned and burnt. The Dutch pursued but did not molest him. During the day a fleet of twenty sail was sighted to the westward. This was Prince Rupert's squadron, and towards nightfall he effected a junction. The English then had about sixty sail fit for action against de Ruyter's seventy-eight. On the final day the wind shifted, blowing fresh from the south-west. The action was resumed all along the line and continued for two hours, during which time two Dutch vessels were burnt. Although hotly contested, the fighting gradually became more ragged, until at last the English gained the weather position and comparative safety. Both sides were by now completely exhausted, and the battle finally came to an end. The Dutch had about six or seven ships sunk or burnt, and 2,000 officers and men killed and wounded. The English casualties were much greater.

FOX, an old name for a strand or fastening formed by twisting several ropeyarns together by hand for use as a * seizing or for weaving a * paunch mat.

FOX, the name of the small screw yacht fitted out for service in the Arctic by Lady Franklin in 1856 in the continuing search for her husband's Sir John * Franklin) expedition. The *Fox* was commanded by Captain F. L. * McClintock.

FOX or FOXE, LUKE (1586–1636), British navigator, was born at Hull. He went to sea at an early age and in 1606 offered his services for a voyage to Greenland, but was turned down. However, he had set his heart on Arctic exploration and in 1629 he petitioned the king for money to finance an expedition to discover a * North-West passage to the * South Seas. He set out from Bristol in 1631 in the * pinnace *Charles*, provided by the Admiralty together with a crew of twenty-two, reaching Frobisher Bay and then working his way along the north shore of the Hudson Strait until he reached Coates Island, where he began his search for the passage. He made many observations along the channel which bears his name but with the winter ice closing in he decided it was time to return home without having succeeded in his object.

FOX, UFFA (1898–1972), naval architect, was the first British yachtsman to win the New York Canoe International Trophy. During the First World War (1914–18) he served in the * Royal Naval Air Service, working on flying boats and seaplanes, and the experience he gained there served him well when he returned to boat designing. Realizing that a ∨-shaped hull would enable a

boat to ride over its own bow wave, and thus greatly increase its speed, he designed the 14-ft *Avenger*, which in 1928 out of fifty-seven racing starts won fifty-two first prizes, two second, and three third. His most notable successes with these planing boats were in the National 12-ft and International 14-ft dinghy classes, and with his planing * keel boats such as the 'Flying Fifteen' series. He also designed a number of cruising and ocean racing yachts, deservedly achieving a high reputation as one of the leading naval architects in the yachting world.

During the Second World War he designed for the Royal Air Force an airborne lifeboat which saved many hundreds of lives. Based on his hard * chine dinghy design it was a 20-ft plywood boat carried folded in all aircraft, and opening automatically as it was dropped by parachute. It was self-bailing and self-righting, carried all necessary survival gear, and could be sailed or rowed to safety.

Fox was an endearing personality, an extrovert with a love of laughter and living. Born and bred in Cowes, Isle of Wight, he never lost his broad Hampshire accent. His second marriage was to a French lady, and at the end of his life he lived largely in France. Among the many books he wrote were *Sailing, Seamanship and Yacht Construction*; *Sail and Power*; *Racing, Cruising and Design*; *The Crest of the Wave*; and *Joys of Living*.

FRAM, a three-masted * schooner of 402 tons with auxiliary steam power, was the first vessel designed to winter in the polar pack ice, her hull being so shaped that no matter how strong the pressure of the ice she would be lifted free of it. The brain child of the Norwegian polar explorer, Fridtjof * Nansen, she was first employed on his famous drift across the Arctic Ocean in 1893–6. In 1898–1902 Otto Sverdrup used her to explore the islands north-west of Greenland. In 1910 the *Fram* was taken by Roald * Amundsen to the Antarctic where he and four companions successfully reached the South pole.

Today the *Fram* is preserved as a national monument in a building specially constructed for her near Oslo.

FRAME, a * timber or rib of a ship, running from the * keel to the side rail. A ship's frames form the shape of the hull and provide the skeleton on which the hull planking or plating is secured. In a wooden ship the frames are built up of sections called * futtocks, in steel ships they are normally of angle iron bent to the desired shape. A ship with her frames set up and ready for planking or plating is said to be 'in frame'. For illus. see SHIPBUILDING.

FRANÇAIS, an exploration vessel built in France for J.-B. *Charcot's Antarctic expedition of 1903–5. She was later sold to the Argentine government and renamed *Austral*, but sank in the Rio de la Plata soon afterwards.

FRANCE, a five-masted steel *barque owned by the A. D. Bordes line and built by Henderson & Son of Glasgow in 1890. She was the largest sailing vessel in the world in her time, of 5,900 deadweight tons, and traded mainly round Cape Horn to Chile in the nitrate trade, making some notably fast passages, the best being sixty-three days. In March 1901 she was struck by a *pampero off the coast of South America and took a list of 45° when her cargo shifted, in the course of which she sprang a serious leak. Although she staggered on for two months, she was in the end unable to keep pace with the leak and was eventually abandoned, her crew being rescued by the German four-masted barque *Hebe*. She was followed by the *France II*, another five-masted steel *barque, larger than the *France* and, at 8,000 deadweight tons, the largest sailing ship ever built. She was launched in 1911 by Chantiers de la Gironde, Bordeaux, for the Société des Navires Mixtres. In July 1922 she was drifting in the Pacific because of lack of wind and went ashore on a coral reef near Noumea, where she was abandoned by her crew. Although

her salvage was a possibility, the depressed state of the *freight market made her owners reluctant to face the cost and her hull was sold for breaking-up for £2,000.

FRANKLIN, Sir JOHN (1786–1847), British naval officer and Arctic explorer, was born at Spilsby, Lincs. He entered the navy and was present on board the *Polyphemus* at the battle of *Copenhagen in 1801. Later he served under his cousin, Captain *Flinders, in the *Investigator* where he showed his ability as a surveyor. He was present at the battle of *Trafalgar as signal officer in the *Bellerophon* in 1805. In 1818 he was chosen to command the *Trent* in which, with the *Isabella*, *Alexander*, and *Dorothea*, he accompanied Captain Buchan on the first of three voyages to the Arctic. The squadron, often under conditions of the greatest hardship, surveyed many thousands of miles of the North American coastline as well as exploring the Mackenzie River.

In 1821 he was promoted *post-captain and elected a Fellow of the Royal Society, and in 1825 set out on another expedition to the North-West Territory which proved even more successful and certainly less arduous than the previous one. In 1829 he was knighted and from 1836 to 1843 was Governor of Tasmania. On 19 May 1845, in command of the *Erebus*, with Captain

The Fram

Francis *Crozier in the *Terror, he set out to discover a *North-West passage from the Atlantic to the Pacific. After being sighted on 26 July at the head of Baffin Bay, the two ships were never heard of again. Thirty-nine expeditions were dispatched in search of the missing vessels but it was not until 1859 that a cairn was found by Captain *McClintock in the steam yacht *Fox containing the log of the expedition up to 25 April 1848. It showed that just as the ships were on the point of discovering a passage through Peel Sound, they became fast in the ice near King William Island and after eighteen months they were abandoned and the party tried to march to safety, but none survived.

G. F. Lamb, *Franklin* (1956).

FRAP, to, the operation of binding together to increase tension or to prevent from blowing loose. Thus *shrouds, if they have worked loose, are frapped together to increase their tension; a sail is frapped with turns of rope round it to prevent it from flapping in the wind. Frapping lines are passed across the tops of *awnings to hold them secure in a high wind. In older days, ships' hulls were sometimes frapped by passing four or five turns of cable-laid rope round them when it was thought that they might not be strong enough to resist the violence of the sea.

FRASER, BRUCE AUSTIN, first Baron Fraser of North Cape (1888–   ), British admiral of the fleet, joined H.M.S. *Britannia* as a cadet in 1902 and, on passing out in 1904, served in the Home Fleet and in the Mediterranean before being selected to specialize in gunnery in 1911. A marked talent for mathematics and a naturally scientific turn of mind led to an advanced gunnery course and his return to the gunnery school at H.M.S. *Excellent* on the staff before appointment as gunnery officer of H.M.S. *Minerva* in 1914. After a further spell at the gunnery school, he became gunnery officer of the battleship *Resolution* and, on promotion to commander at the end of 1918, he remained in her as executive officer during operations in the Black Sea in support of White Russian forces.

While ashore at Baku on a secret mission he was arrested by the Bolsheviks and imprisoned there for eight months before being released. He then rejoined the gunnery school on the senior staff, an appointment followed by one to the Admiralty in 1920, where he served in the Directorate of Naval Ordnance and played a leading part in the development of a new fire control system.

Appointed fleet gunnery officer in the Mediterranean in 1924, he was promoted captain in 1926 and returned to the Admiralty, with alternating periods of service ashore and afloat until January 1938 when he was promoted rear admiral and served as chief of staff to Admiral Sir Dudley *Pound in the Mediterranean. In 1939 he became Third Sea Lord and Controller, being promoted vice admiral in May 1940 and knighted the following year.

Sir Bruce Fraser hoisted his flag in H.M.S. *Anson* in 1942 as second-in-command of the Home Fleet and in May 1943 became commander-in-chief with the acting rank of admiral. At Christmas that year he commanded in the operations which culminated in the destruction of the German *battle-cruiser *Scharnhorst* in the battle of the *North Cape. Promoted admiral in 1944, he relieved Admiral *Somerville in command of the Eastern Fleet in August of that year and, three months later, was appointed to command the yet unformed British Pacific Fleet, in which capacity he reported for duty at Pearl Harbor in January 1945. There, his principal and most difficult task was to persuade the U.S. commander-in-chief, Admiral *Nimitz, and through him the Chief of Naval Operations in Washington, Fleet Admiral Ernest *King, to agree to the British serving alongside the Americans in the main theatre of operations against the Japanese instead of being relegated to a back area. In this he was successful.

Being too senior to command at sea, he left his second-in-command to do so while he set up his headquarters at Sydney, N.S.W. At the end of the war he was raised to the peerage as Baron Fraser of North Cape. He served as commander-in-chief at Portsmouth from 1947 to 1948 and, after promotion to admiral of the fleet in 1948, was First Sea Lord until 1951.

FREE, a ship is said to be SAILING FREE when her sheets are eased, and RUNNING FREE when the wind is blowing from astern. 'To free the sheets', to ease them off to present a squarer aspect of the sails to the wind. For illus. see POINTS OF SAILING.

FREEBOARD, the distance, measured in the *waist, or centre, of a ship, from the waterline to the upper deck level.

FREEING PORTS, square ports cut in the *bulwarks of a ship to allow seawater which has been shipped on deck to run away over the side. The doors on these ports are normally hinged on the top edge and situated outboard so that they can be forced open by the pressure of water on deck but held tightly closed against the bulwarks by the pressure of the sea if the ship rolls to an extent where they are under water. See also SCUPPERS.

FREETOWN, capital and principal seaport of Sierra Leone. It was known as the 'White Man's Grave' because of its unhealthiness, but new drainage and the reclamation of the adjacent marshes which were a breeding centre for mosquitoes, undertaken at the beginning of the 20th century, has brought a vast improvement. It has a large harbour which, in the days when Sierra Leone was a British colony, was used as a base and fuelling station for the British Navy. Today it has a flourishing trade and is a port of call for all steamship lines operating on the west coast of Africa.

FREEZING, a term sometimes used to describe the ornamental painting around the bows, stern, and quarters of the old sailing ships, most often in the form of arms and armour or maritime emblems. There can be little doubt that this was the contemporary shipwright's method of spelling friezing, from frieze, a band of ornament.

FREIGHT, goods transported in a ship, or the money paid for the transport of such goods. Freight, in its meaning of goods transported, is specified in the *bill of lading and when shipped *c.i.f., remains the property of the consignor until delivery is taken by the consignee at the port of unloading. Where freight is shipped *f.o.b., the goods become the property of the consignee immediately they arrive on board and he is responsible for the payment of insurance and freight charges.

In older forms of commerce the shipowner often owned the goods loaded in his ship and carried them to foreign ports to sell to the best advantage, replacing them when sold with goods purchased abroad and brought home for sale at a profit. In this case there were of course no actual freight charges as such, this element of the cost coming from the overall profit from the sales of outward bound and inward bound goods. An alternative to this general pattern was for a merchant to charter a ship to carry his goods to foreign ports for the *master, or an agent known as a *supercargo or *husband, to sell to the best advantage. In this case the actual freight charges would not be specifically determined but would be a part of the sum paid in chartering the ship.

With the introduction of the steamship, and of more rapid means of communication such as undersea cables and, more recently, wireless, the telephone, and air mail, the old pattern of freight changed. Instead of a shipload of goods being adventured abroad to be sold to the best advantage at ports visited, sales of specific goods were arranged direct between merchants, and the freight was arranged with a shipowner or shipping line trading regularly to the port nearest to the consignee.

As the overall volume of world trade expanded from the late 19th century, the pattern of freight again changed, especially in the design of ships to carry one particular product, such as coal, grain, oil, etc. The increasing volume of trade, taken in conjunction with the profits to be made from freight charges in handling larger cargoes, has resulted in the building of bulk carriers of increasing tonnage, ships designed to carry only containerized cargo, and very large *tankers to carry hundreds of thousands of tons of crude oil in a single voyage. See ADVENTURE, CONTAINER SHIP, U.L.C.C., V.L.C.C.

FREMANTLE, capital and principal seaport of the state of Western Australia, at the mouth of the Swan River. It is a port of call for the chief steamship lines serving Australia and is also the centre of a shipbuilding industry.

FREMANTLE, Sir THOMAS FRANCIS (1765–1819), British vice admiral, served in his early years in home waters and the West Indies, being promoted to captain in 1793. He was with Horatio *Nelson in Corsica in 1794, and in 1797 commanded the *Seahorse* in the boat attack on Tenerife, where both he and Nelson were badly wounded, the latter losing his right arm. He was appointed to the *Ganges* in 1800 and took part in the battle of *Copenhagen in 1801. He commanded the first-*rate ship *Neptune* at *Trafalgar, being the third ship in the weather line. In 1810 he was promoted rear admiral and in 1812 commanded a squadron of ships in the Adriatic, being present at the capture of Fiume (Rijeka) and Trieste. For these services he was knighted and made a baron of the Austrian States. He became commander-in-chief in the Mediterranean in 1818 and died at Naples in 1819. He married, in 1797, Betsy Wynne, whose entertaining diaries were later published under the title *The Wynne Diaries*. His grandson, Sir Edmund Robert Fremantle (1836–1929), and great-grandson, Sir Sydney Robert Fremantle (1867–1958), both reached the rank of full admiral in the Royal Navy.

Frenchman

FRENCHMAN, the name given to a left-handed loop when coiling down wire rope right-handed. Wire rope, especially in long lengths, does not absorb turns as easily as fibre rope, and if the wire being coiled is not free to revolve during coiling, it will become twisted. An occasional left-handed loop introduced into the coil will counteract the twists.

'**FRESHEN HIS HAWSE, to**', an expression used by the old seamen, particularly in the square-rigged ship days, to describe the action of officers who would take two or three nips of rum or whisky after a long spell on deck in stormy weather to regain their activity in running the ship.

FRESHES, the name given to the fresh water which drains off the land after a period of heavy rain and increases the flow of the ebb tide as it recedes from estuaries and the mouths of large tidal rivers, carrying the land silt to a considerable distance out to sea and discolouring the water. Thus, the freshes of the Nile are well known for carrying sand many miles to seaward, turning the water yellow, and other rivers whose freshes are notorious for the distance they discolour the water are the Congo, Mississippi, Indus, Ganges, and Rhône. In the earlier days of navigation, these freshes were often used as a useful indication of a ship's position, the navigator knowing, when he sailed into discoloured water, that his ship was off the mouth of a large river.

FREYCINET, LOUIS-CLAUDE DESAULSES DE (1779–1842), French navigator, joined the expedition under Captain Baudin which sailed in 1800 with the two ships *Naturaliste* and *Géographe*, in which his elder brother was serving, to explore the south and south-west coasts of Australia. Most of this coast had already been explored by Matthew *Flinders, and in Freycinet's account of the expedition some doubtful credit was taken for discoveries which had already been made and charted. In 1817 Freycinet sailed again in command of the *Uranie* to Rio de Janeiro for scientific observations in geography, astronomy, terrestrial magnetism, and meteorology, and then, accompanied by the *corvette *Physicienne*, cruised for three years in the Pacific, visiting Australia and many of the island groups. After rounding Cape Horn the *Uranie* was wrecked in command of the Falkland Islands during the return to France. Under Freycinet's direction an account of this voyage was published in thirteen volumes, with four more volumes of charts and plates, between the years 1824 and 1844. This magnificent production is one of the finest and most detailed accounts of a voyage ever published.

FRIEDRICH, CASPAR DAVID (1774–1840), German painter of the Romantic school, painted a number of pictures of the sea and ships in which his feeling for design, his use of space evocative of silence and eeriness, and his immaculate technique and use of colour are impressive. He was born in Greifswald, a small Baltic

The frigates Shannon *and* Chesapeake *off Boston on 1 June 1813; lithograph after J. C. Schetky*

Frigates in line ahead, 1970

harbour town; a series of pictures painted there show the tall forms of sailing ships at anchor or becalmed, sometimes silhouetted against the evening light, sometimes seen through mist, and have an almost religious feeling as have his other well-known pictures of Gothic churches and cathedrals lying in ruins and in silence. A picture of shipwreck in the Arctic, one of his best known paintings, expresses most vividly not only the ship and her surroundings but the innate cruelty of these barren waters. Friedrich's paintings are few and scattered—many were destroyed by fire during an exhibition of his work in Berlin—but their sense of loneliness and mystery, nowhere better expressed than in his series of ship pictures, is remarkable.

FRIENDSHIP SLOOP, originally a type of fishing boat working offshore out of the port of Friendship on the coast of Maine, U.S.A. With fixed keel and deep draught, a wide beam and *fiddlehead bow, and a broad *counter stern, Friendship sloops have been built in sizes from about 20 up to 35 feet in length. Yachts have copied the workboats, and a Friendship Sloop Association is in existence.

FRIGATE, a class of ship in the navies of all countries. During the sailing era frigates were three-masted ships, fully rigged on each mast, and armed with from twenty-four to thirty-eight guns carried on a single gundeck. In navies where ships were *rated according to the number of guns they carried, they were 5th- or 6th-rate ships, and thus not expected to lie in the line of battle. Possessing superior sailing qualities to the larger *ships of the line, they were used with the fleet as look-outs and, in battle, as repeating ships to fly the admiral's signals so that other ships in the line which might be blanketed from the admiral by the smoke of gunfire could read his signals. Alternatively, frigates worked independently of the fleet, cruising in search of privateers or as escort ships for convoys, in which case they were generally given the generic name of *cruisers. There was a convention in the days of sailing navies that larger ships did not engage frigates during fleet battles unless the latter opened fire first, though it was not unknown for frigates occasionally to engage ships of the line. This convention only applied in fixed battle and did not hold good if a frigate were met at sea unaccompanied by a fleet.

During the wars against France (1793–1815) a class of 44-gun frigates, rated as 4th rates, was introduced in Britain, carrying guns on two decks. They had little success as a class, being both too small to lie in the battle line and inferior in sailing qualities to the single-decked frigates. Among many famous frigate names of the sailing navy are the American *Constitution* (Captain Isaac *Hull), which fought a notable action

against the British frigate *Java*; the British
* *Shannon*, which defeated the American
* *Chesapeake* in an action which lasted only 15
minutes; the British *Euryalus*, in which Captain
* Blackwood shadowed and reported the Franco-
Spanish fleet during the two days and nights
which preceded the battle of * Trafalgar, and the
British *Pallas*, commanded by Lord * Cochrane,
which captured a number of very valuable prizes
and, in 1805, made something of a stir by sailing
into Plymouth with three five-foot silver candle-
sticks, taken out of a rich prize, lashed to the
trucks of her three masts.

During the Second World War the term
frigate was revived for a class of medium-speed
anti-submarine vessels used on convoy escort
work. Since then it has become the generic term
for smaller warships in all navies with an anti-
submarine, anti-aircraft, aircraft-direction, or
general purpose capability.

FROBISHER or **FORBISHER**, Sir MARTIN
(*c.* 1535–94), English navigator and explorer,
was one of the ablest of the great seamen of the
Elizabethan age, endowed equally with courage,
resource, and seamanship. However, he made
himself unpopular with his subordinates by the
strict discipline he expected, and captains of ships
were sometimes unwilling to serve under him.

He first gained fame as leader of three expeditions in search of the * North-West passage to
* Cathay (China). The first of these, consisting of
two little ships, *Gabriel* (25 tons) and *Michael*
(20 tons), set out in 1576. In the course of it
Frobisher, in the *Gabriel*, crossed what was later
named the Davis Strait and discovered the Strait
which has borne his own name ever since.

The glitter of mica in some stones he brought
back encouraged a belief in the presence of gold
and brought support for a second voyage in
the following year when Elizabeth I lent him
the Royal Navy ship *Aid* of 200 tons to accompany the *Gabriel* and *Michael*. Though this voyage only achieved a more detailed survey of
Frobisher Strait, the continuing lure of gold led
to a third and larger expedition of fifteen vessels
sailing under Frobisher's command in 1578. The
voyage was of considerable navigational interest
but brought no commercial profit and the discovery meanwhile that the glittering stones were
valueless brought the series to an end. In 1585
Frobisher commanded the *Primrose* as vice
admiral in Sir Francis * Drake's expedition to the
West Indies.

During the operations against the Spanish
* Armada in 1588 Frobisher, in the *Triumph* of
1,100 tons, largest of the English men-of-war,
distinguished himself in the fighting and, together
with several others, was knighted on board the
* *Ark Royal* by the * Lord High Admiral, Lord
* Howard of Effingham.

Sir Martin Frobisher; oil painting by C. Ketel

In 1590 and again in 1592, Frobisher commanded squadrons stationed off the Spanish
coast to intercept treasure ships from the Indies,
in which he was not successful though he dis-
located the Spanish treasure convoy system.

Frobisher's last expedition was in 1594 when
he was given command of a royal squadron to
assist Henri IV of France to defeat a Spanish
attempt to fortify the peninsula of Camaret and
threaten the port of Brest. The assault from land
and sea was successful but at the cost of heavy
casualties of whom Frobisher was one. Though
he brought his squadron back to Plymouth, he
survived his wound only a few weeks. Accounts
of Frobisher's voyages are in Richard Hakluyt's
Principal Navigations (1589) and in the Hakluyt
Society's *Three Voyages of Frobisher* (1867).

F. Jones, *Life of Frobisher* (1878); W. McFee, *Sir
Martin Frobisher* (1928).

FROGMAN, the name given, a little loosely, to any free diver using an *aqualung or equivalent device. The name came into general use during the Second World War when free divers were widely used by many navies for a variety of purposes, including underwater location of mines and beach obstacles, reconnaissance of beach gradients and formations in preparation for assault landings, and attacks on enemy vessels in conjunction with *chariots and midget submarines. The frogman normally wears a skin-tight neoprene suit, flippers to give speed and control under water, and an aqualung or equivalent which enables him to breathe under water.

FROUDE, JAMES ANTHONY (1818–94), British historian, was born at Dartington, Devon, and educated at Westminster and Oxford. Between 1856 and 1870 he wrote his great twelve-volume work *The History of England from the fall of Wolsey to the Spanish Armada*, and this was followed by a short study published under the title *The Spanish Story of the Armada*. He became Thomas Carlyle's literary executor, writing his biography. He subsequently visited Australia and the West Indies, following these travels with the publication of *Oceana* (1886) and *The English in the West Indies* (1888). In 1892 he was appointed Regius Professor of Modern History at Oxford University, and it was from a series of lectures delivered there that he wrote the book by which his marine interests are best remembered, *English Seamen in the Sixteenth Century*, which was published posthumously in 1895.

FROUDE, WILLIAM (1810–79), British engineer, naval architect, and mathematician, was the elder brother of J. A. *Froude. He was born at Dartington, Devon, and in 1837 became assistant to I. K. *Brunel in his work on railway engineering. He left this work after nine years to devote himself to the study of ship behaviour and hydrodynamics, for which he later became famous and in which his work greatly influenced naval design techniques.

In 1868 he served on a committee appointed by the British Association to study ship design, and, against the current beliefs held by his colleagues, he advocated a more thorough investigation into the laws governing the relationship between scale models and full-size ships in their performance in *pitching, *rolling, resistance, and engine power. An invitation to explain his proposals to the British Admiralty in 1870 led to a grant to build a ship-model testing tank at his home near Torquay. This was the forerunner of the numerous sophisticated ship test tanks employed today by the navies and merchant marines of all principal countries.

Froude discovered that the principal causes of resistance to a ship's motion were hull surface, or skin friction, and eddy- and wavemaking. From this he propounded his famous *wave line theory which has influenced naval design ever since. His last work was the construction of a dynamometer for recording the power developed by ships' engines. He was elected a Fellow of the Royal Society in 1870 and received its medal in 1876. His many published papers were reprinted in one volume by the Institution of Naval Architects in 1955.

FULL AND BY, the condition of a sailing vessel when she is held as close to the wind as possible with the sails full and not shivering. See also BY.

'FULL SEA', an old term, *temp.* 15th–16th centuries, used to describe the state of high water at the top of the flood *tide in a port or harbour.

FULTON, ROBERT (1765–1815), American engineer, was first apprenticed to a jeweller, then took up portrait and landscape painting as a profession, and finally, during a visit to England in 1794, decided that engineering was to be his career. His initial energies were devoted to canal engineering and he took out a British patent for superseding canal locks by inclined planes, an invention which failed to attract much attention. In 1797 he settled in Paris and after a great many setbacks managed to persuade Napoleon in 1801 that the French answer to British sea power lay in the possession of a fleet of *submarines. He received a grant of 10,000 francs with which to construct a prototype and built the *Nautilus*, ellipsoid in shape with a length of 21 feet and a diameter of 7 feet, and enabled to submerge by the flooding of internal tanks. She was driven under water by a propeller turned by hand and on the surface by a collapsible mast and sail. At a demonstration at Brest Fulton succeeded in blowing up an old *schooner, moored in the centre of the harbour as a target, by diving the *Nautilus* beneath her and attaching to her bottom an explosive charge carried externally. In spite of this success the French ministry of marine remained unimpressed and Fulton then crossed to England to demonstrate his submarine to a committee set up by the British Admiralty. It, too, was uninterested and Fulton then took his plans back to America, where he and his submarine were equally ignored.

He was much more successful with his ventures into the steam propulsion of ships and as early as 1803 demonstrated a small boat driven by steam power on the River Seine in Paris. On his return to America he built the *Clermont*, using an engine made by Boulton and Watt, of Birmingham, England, a steam vessel which, in 1807, plied on the Hudson River between Albany and New York. In 1815 he constructed, for the American Navy Department, a 38-ton steam vessel with central paddle-wheels, which was named *Fulton* and was the first steam-driven warship in any of the world's navies. Other inventions with which his name is connected were in rope-making, flax-spinning, and the cutting and polishing of marble. See TURTLE-BOAT.

FURL, to, the operation of taking in the sails of a vessel and securing them with *gaskets; in the case of square-rigged ships by hauling in on the *clew-lines and *buntlines and rolling them up to the *yards; in the case of fore-and-aft rig, by lowering *gaff-rigged sails and similarly securing them to the *booms or rolling up triangular sails and securing them to the *stays on which they are set. To take off the sails of a ship and stow them in sail lockers below decks is not, strictly, furling although the final result in respect of the ship is the same. To furl in a body, a method of furling sail in square-rigged ships occasionally practised when the ship is expected to remain for some time in harbour. It entailed gathering the sail into the *top at the heel of the topmast by releasing the *earings at the *yard-arms so that the sail could be drawn in towards the centre of the yard.

FURNITURE, the whole movable equipment of a ship—rigging, sails, spars, anchors, boats, and everything with which she is fitted out to operate her, but not including her consumable stores, such as fuel and victuals.

FURRING, an old term in shipwrightry meaning to replank a vessel to give her more beam and freeboard. 'There are two kinds of furring, the one is after a ship is built, to lay on another plank upon the side of her (which is called plank upon plank). The other, which is more eminent, and more properly furring, is to rip off the first planks and to put other timbers upon the first, and so to put on the planks upon these timbers. The occasion of it is to make a ship bear a better sail, for when a ship is too narrow, and the bearing [freeboard] either not laid out enough, or too low, then they must make her broader, and lay out her bearing higher.' *Mainwaring, *Seaman's Dictionary* (1644). Mainwaring's strictures refer to errors in the original design of ships in that they were being built too narrow in the beam and with insufficient freeboard to carry the amount of sail for which they were designed.

FURY, **H.M.S.,** a bomb *ketch (see BOMB VESSEL) of 377 tons built at Rochester in 1814. Together with H.M.S. *Hecla* she took part in the first three of Sir Edward *Parry's expeditions in search of a *North-West passage, being commanded by him during the second one. During the third voyage in 1825, the *Fury* was wrecked. These bomb ketches, because of their exceptionally strong construction, were especially suitable for Arctic exploration. Originally designed as three-masted vessels, they later had their foremast removed to make room for the mortars (known at the time as bombs), the deck beneath being stiffened with sturdy beam bridges to support the shock of their recoil. Other vessels of this type employed on Arctic expeditions were the *Carcass,* *Racehorse,* *Erebus,* and *Terror.*

FUTTOCK, the separate pieces of timber which form a *frame or rib in a wooden ship. There are normally four, or occasionally five, futtocks to a rib in a ship of moderate size, the one nearest the *keel being known as a ground or naval futtock, the remainder being called upper futtocks.

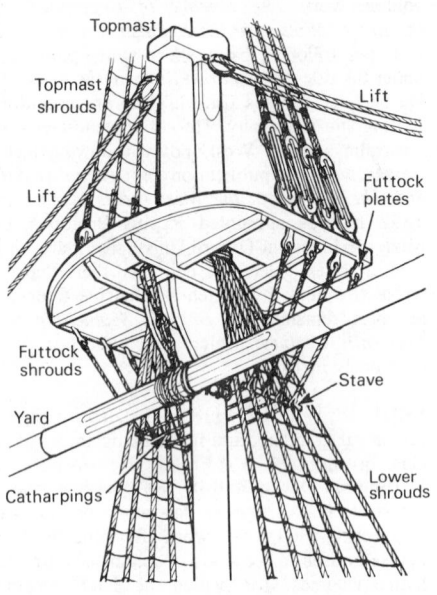

Futtock shrouds

FUTTOCK SHROUDS, originally short *shrouds of chain or large hemp, but later metal rods, which give support to the *top on a lower mast. They run from the futtock plates, secured to the sides of the top, downwards and inwards towards the lower mast being secured either to a stave in the lower shrouds close under the top, from which the catharpings (see HARPINGS) are led to the mast, or to a futtock band round the mast itself. The futtock plates, to which the upper ends of the futtock shrouds are secured, carry the futtock chain plates to which the topmast shrouds are set up. The word would appear to be seaman's pronunciation of foothook.

G

G.R.P., see FIBRE GLASS.

G.R.T., gross register tonnage, see TONNAGE.

GABBARD, The, a sandbank lying off the coast of Suffolk, England, to seaward of Orfordness, and the name given to a battle of the First Anglo-Dutch War (1652–4), fought on 2–3 June 1653 between an English fleet of 100 ships and five *fireships commanded by the *generals-at-sea George *Monck and Richard *Deane, and a Dutch fleet of ninety-eight ships and six fireships under the command of Admiral Marten *Tromp. The Dutch fleet was sighted at daylight on 2 June but owing to the lightness of the wind it was 11 a.m. before action was joined. Deane was killed at the very beginning of the action. Fighting continued until 6 p.m. when the enemy hauled off with the loss of three or four ships. During the night the English were reinforced by a squadron of about eighteen fresh ships commanded by Robert *Blake, and in the morning they steered to cut off the Dutch from their home ports. The wind still remained light and it was not until noon that fire was opened. By 4 p.m. the Dutch fleet was in a state of great confusion and in full retreat, being hotly pursued until it was too dark to see. In all eleven ships of the Dutch fleet were captured and nine were destroyed, 1,360 prisoners being taken. In the English fleet no ship was lost or even seriously damaged, the total casualties being 126 killed and 236 wounded.

The action is also sometimes known as the battle of North Foreland, as it was off this point that most of the decisive fighting took place. The Gabbard was the place where the Dutch fleet was first sighted by the English.

GABRIELE, MARCIANO (1927–), Italian professor of naval history, was born at Firenzuolo D'Arda, Piacenza, and since 1960 has taught naval history and policy at the University of Rome, also carrying out similar duties at the University of Naples in 1962 and 1967. He is considered a great expert on naval and maritime history in its politico-military and economic aspects, and is adviser to the Italian government on the economic realities of sea and air transport. A well known international lecturer on his subjects, he is also the author of several books, of which the best known are *Italian Naval Policy from the Union to the Eve of * Lissa* and *The Naval Agreements of the Triple Alliance.*

GADES, the name by which *Cadiz was known during the period of its occupation by the Romans. The name occurs in the many histories and accounts of the port up to the 14th century.

GAFF, a spar to which the *head of a four-sided *fore-and-aft sail is laced and hoisted on the after side of a mast. The forward end, against the mast, is built up laterally to form *jaws, or pivoted to a wrought iron saddle, to fit round the mast. To hold the gaff against the mast in all conditions,

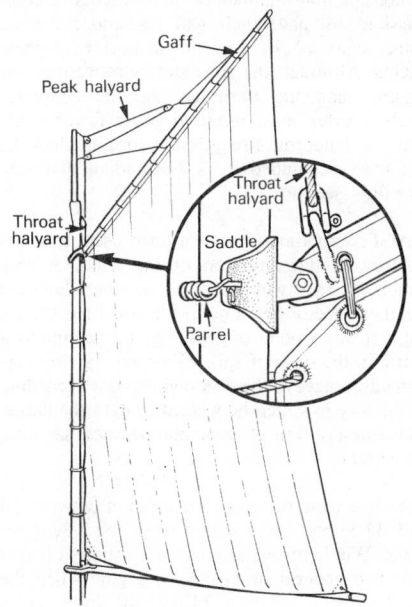

A typical gaff

the gaff jaws are usually joined by a stout jaw rope on which are threaded wooden balls known as *trucks or *parrels to allow the gaff to slide easily up and down the mast. Two sets of *halyards are used to hoist a gaff sail, *throat halyards at the mast end and *peak halyards at the outer end, but on many traditional types of Dutch craft the gaff is a very short spar, usually cut into an arched curve, and only a single halyard, attached to a span on the gaff, is used to hoist it.

The gaff *rig is a development of the earlier *spritsail rig and was, according to pictorial evidence, in existence in Sweden as early as 1525, although it is generally believed to have originated some years earlier in Holland. For the first hundred years or so of its existence the gaff itself was known as a half-sprit. It was the logical development of the earlier sprit, serving the same purpose of spreading the sail, but with much greater efficiency and with considerably lighter and handier spars.

For some centuries, up to the introduction of mechanical power, it was the sailing rig of the great majority of small craft, including *trawlers and *drifters, with the exception perhaps of those plying in eastern waters and the Mediterranean where the *lateen rig predominated. It remained as such until the gradual introduction, in the first two decades of the 20th century, of the *Bermuda rig for small yachts, extended after the First World War (1914–18) to the larger ocean-going and racing yachts (see also J-CLASS). A considerable number of older yachts in commission still have their gaff rig, and there are some signs of its revival in purely cruising yachts. Although the rig requires more running rigging than the Bermuda rig, the comparatively shorter mast required poses fewer problems in structural strength and support than the tall mast demanded by a Bermudian mainsail. For illus. see RIG.

GAGE, sometimes gauge, a term used at sea in relation to the direction of the wind. A ship which is to *windward of another has the weather gage of her; one to *leeward has the lee gage. It was a point of great significance in naval battle in the days of sail, either gage giving certain advantages to the fleet commander according to the way in which he wished to fight the battle. For a description of these manoeuvres, see LINE OF BATTLE.

GALE, a wind blowing at a speed of between 34 and 47 knots, force 8 and 9 on the *Beaufort Scale. Winds of this strength are usually divided into two general descriptions, a gale when the wind speed is between 34 and 40 knots and a strong gale when it blows between 40 and 47 knots.

Gales are associated with *depressions, and when the *synoptic evidence indicates an approaching depression deep enough to produce gale force winds, gale warnings are broadcast to shipping giving the probable area and strength. Although winds of above 47 knots are officially designated as *storms, they are usually still broadcast as gale warnings of force 10 or above.

An indication of gale strength winds is also provided by the state of the sea. When the waves are high and the crests begin to break into spindrift, a gale is blowing. Crests beginning to topple and roll over, with dense streaks of foam along the direction of the wind, are signs of a strong gale. See METEOROLOGY.

GALISSONNIÈRE, ROLAND-MICHEL BARRIN, Marquis de la (1693–1756), entered the French Navy in 1710, reaching the rank of *post-captain in 1739. Governor of Canada, 1745–9, he was promoted *commodore (chef d'escadre) on his return to France. In 1756, with the rank of lieutenant-general, he commanded the fleet from Toulon which covered the French expedition against *Minorca. He fought an indecisive battle with a British fleet of equal strength commanded by Admiral John *Byng, sent from England to relieve the English garrison of Minorca. The outcome of the action was the loss of Minorca to the French. Ill health forced de la Galissonnière to resign his command shortly afterwards and he died in October of the same year.

GALIZABRA, a particular design of ship used by the Spanish in the 17th and 18th centuries. Galizabras were of similar size to a *frigate, fast, weatherly, and very heavily armed. Their purpose was to bring the treasure over from America and the Indies to Spain, sailing independently and relying on their speed and gun power to avoid capture, thus saving the long, slow, and costly process of using the fleet to escort the annual *flota.

GALLEASS or **GALLEASSE,** a compromise between the oared *galley and the *galleon, in which oars were retained to provide free movement irrespective of the direction of the wind although masts and sails were also carried. In order to accommodate the masts and *rigging, galleasses had to be built with a greater *beam and a deeper *draught than the galley. They were *lateen rigged on two or three masts, but suffered from the inevitable defects of compromise, being unable to carry the more effective square rig of the sailing ship because of the modified galley hull form and also, for the same reason, being unable to retain the speed and manoeuvrability of the true galley. Six galleasses were included in the Spanish fleet for the *Armada campaign of 1588 but were unable to accomplish anything in the stormier waters of the English Channel and North Sea. The type died a fairly rapid death as warships.

The name was also used to describe the oared sailing vessels of the Mediterranean, widely used for the carriage of *freight during the 16th and

17th centuries. These were large vessels of up to 150 feet in length with a beam of 25 feet, two- or three-masted with a lateen rig and a single bank of oars, and designed for the longer trade voyages. During the summer months they were frequently to be seen as far away from the Mediterranean as the ports of north Europe, laden with produce from India and China which had been taken on board at *Genoa or *Venice.

GALLEON or **GALEON,** a development of the *carrack following the successful experiments of Sir John *Hawkins in 1570 in eliminating the high *forecastle with which all large ships were then built. In his three round voyages to Africa and the West Indies, he had discovered that the high-built forecastle always caught the wind, forcing the bows of the ship down to *leeward so that she was unable to hold her course to *windward. With its elimination a ship became much more weatherly and manoeuvrable. This new design reached Spain about seventeen years after its introduction in England and resulted in the development of the galleon, originally as a warship but over the course of the next thirty to forty years also taking the place of the carrack as the principal type of trading ship. Although the design was essentially English, the actual name was never adopted in England or among the north European nations.

The Griffin, *galleon of 200 tons; engraving by Visscher*

GALLERY, the walk built out from the admiral's or captain's cabin in larger sailing warships and extending beyond the stern. They were often highly decorated with carved work, gilded or painted, and were covered in with a wooden roof, known as a *cove, and protected from the weather with elaborate glassed windows. First- and second-*rate men-of-war normally had three galleries, a large stern gallery with smaller galleries on either quarter. In these ships the galleries extended over two *decks, thus giving six individual galleries. See also STERNWALK.

GALLERY, DANIEL VINCENT, Jr. (1901–), American rear admiral, distinguished himself by capturing a German submarine during the Second World War while he was in command of the small aircraft carrier *Guadalcanal* in the Atlantic. As a consequence of his careful planning the German submarine, *U.505*, was captured in June 1944 and brought into port successfully. Afterwards this *U-boat was taken to Chicago and installed in concrete cradles alongside the Museum of Science and Industry in that city. Gallery was in command of the carrier *Hancock* at the time of the Japanese surrender ceremonies in Tokyo Bay in 1945. He is the author of *We Captured a U-Boat* (1957).

GALLEY, (1) the oared fighting ship of the Mediterranean dating from about 3000 B.C., and lasting into the 18th century A.D. Originally propelled by oars arranged on a single level, galleys were developed with oars arranged in banks, or different levels, known as *biremes (two banks) and *triremes (three banks). Galleys are mentioned in ancient writings with more banks of oars than three—quadreremes, quinqueremes, and in fact up to seventeen banks—but obviously this cannot refer to banks of oars arranged on different levels, and some other method of classification must have been adopted, though no records exist of the method today. In multibank galleys, up to the trireme, the length of oars differed according to the bank on which they were mounted, and it is generally thought that the length of oar in the upper bank was about 14 feet, in the middle bank about 10 ft 6 in., and in the lower bank 7 ft 6 in. The number of rowers in each bank also varied, and in a typical Greek trireme with an overall length of 130 feet and a beam of 18–19 feet, there would be thirty-one oars each side in the upper bank (known as thranites), and twenty-seven oars each side in the middle (zygites) and lower (thalamites) banks.

The weapon of the galley was the *ram, a pointed spur fixed to the bow of the galley on or just below the waterline. In the 16th and 17th centuries guns were mounted on a platform in the bows of galleys, but they could not be trained and had to fire only directly ahead.

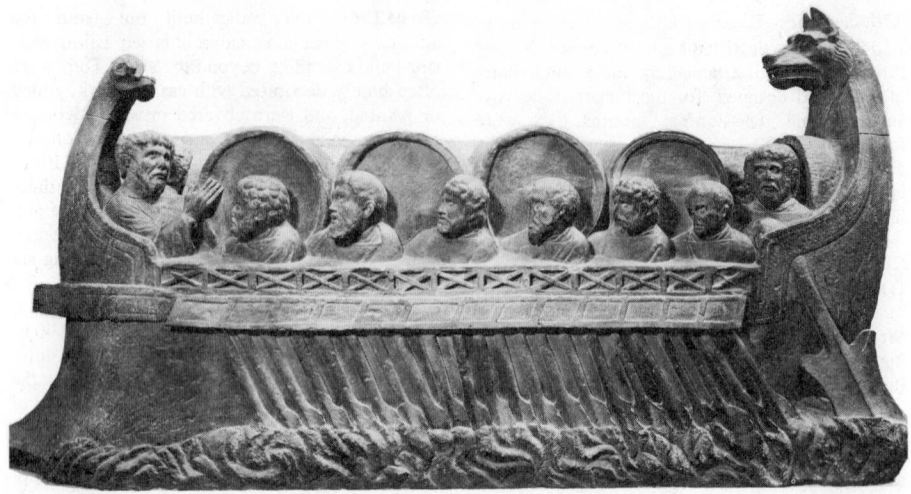

Roman galley of the 3rd century A.D.

The galley was basically an unstable vessel, suitable only for use in calm waters. They were capable of sailing before the wind and had one or two masts, depending on their length, carrying in their early days one square sail on each mast but in later periods of their existence *lateen sails. Masts and sails were used only for passage-making and were always lowered and stowed away before action, to ensure that the great man-oeuvrability given by the oars was always available in battle. A trireme, with all three banks of oars operating, was estimated to be capable of a speed of between eight and nine *knots, but only for a short period depending on the stamina and strength of the rowers. The last naval action in which Mediterranean galleys took part was fought in 1717; in the Baltic, galleys were still employed in warfare as late as the Russo-Swedish war of 1809.

(2) (*a*) An open rowing boat, with six or eight oars, used largely by customs officers in the 18th and 19th centuries, and in the British Navy, by *press gangs visiting ships afloat in search of recruits. (*b*) A warship's boat, originally *clinker-built but more recently of *carvel construction, rowing six oars and usually reserved for the use of the captain. Two masts, carrying lateen or *lug sails, could be stepped for sailing.

(3) The ship's kitchen, sometimes also called in smaller merchant vessels the *caboose.

GALLEY FRIGATE, a *frigate of a type built for the English Navy in the time of Charles II (1660–85) to take oars or sweeps as well as sails. Very few were built and, being generally ineffi-cient, they were quickly discarded.

GALLEY PEPPER, the sailor's name for the soot and ashes which used on occasions to fall accidentally into the victuals while they were being cooked.

GALLEY SLAVE, a prisoner sold in the slave market and condemned to serve in the war *galleys, where he pulled one of the oars, being secured to his rowing bench by a fetter round his ankle chained to an iron bar at deck level.

GALLIGASKINS, the wide breeches worn by seamen in the old sailing warship days, also known as petticoat-trousers. They were most prevalent in the 16th and 17th centuries, but did not finally disappear in warships until the begin-ning of the 19th century. Being made of canvas, the wide apron-like front was a protection for the men lying out on the *yards when the weather was wet. See SAILORS' DRESS, SLOPS, TARRY-BREEKS.

GALLIOT, originally a small *galley, rowed by sixteen or twenty oars, with a single mast and sail, used in the 17th and 18th centuries to chase and capture enemy ships by boarding in wartime, the entire crew being armed to form a boarding party. During the 18th century it became the accepted term for a small Dutch trading vessel, the hull built *barge fashion with a bluff, rounded bow, fitted with *leeboards, and fore-and-aft rigged on a single mast, often with a *sprit. They are still used in Holland and North Germany almost entirely for local coastal traffic in much the same way as barges in Britain.

GALLOWS, (1) a raised wooden frame consisting of two uprights and a cross-piece on which the spare *booms and spars in a square-rigged ship rested. These booms ran from near the *forecastle along the *waist of the ship and were used for the stowage of the ship's boats, giving rise to the name 'booms' as the proper place for the stowage of boats on board. **(2)** A temporary wooden structure erected on the *counter of small *fore-and-aft rigged sailing craft on which the main boom is stowed and secured when the vessel is at anchor or lying on a mooring. See also BOOM CRUTCH. **(3)** Inverted U-shaped iron or steel frames fitted in pairs on one or both sides of a steam or diesel *trawler and carrying a large sheave to take the trawl *warps. They are colloquially known as 'the galluses'. **(4)** Gallow-bitts, a wooden frame fitted in the days when fishing *drifters operated under sail and lowered their masts to rest on these *bitts when lying to their nets in order to ease the strain on the *warp by which the nets were secured to the drifter.

GAMA, VASCO DA (*c.* 1460–1524), Portuguese navigator, conquistador, and the first European to discover the sea route to India, fought as a soldier before becoming a seaman. In 1497 he was selected by the king of Portugal to command a squadron of four ships to follow up the discovery by Bartholomew *Diaz, nine years earlier, that there was a great ocean to the east of the Cape of Good Hope across which a route to the Orient might well exist.

Rounding the Cape of Good Hope successfully, Vasco da Gama followed the east coast of Africa to Malindi whence, under the direction of a Gujerati pilot, he crossed the Indian Ocean, reaching Calicut on the Malabar Coast on 20 May 1498. There he set up the marble pillar by which Portuguese navigators marked any new discovery and claimed possession of it for Portugal. Owing to the rivalry of the established Arab traders who incited the native Hindus against him, he was unable to establish a trading post or 'factory' there. He was able, however, to satisfy himself of the great resources of this new land and to load a full cargo of spices with which he returned home in September 1499, the voyage showing a profit of 600 per cent, while da Gama himself was given honours and awards by King Manoel.

In order to exploit da Gama's discoveries, a second Portuguese expedition was dispatched to India led by Pedro *Cabral, who by sailing too far to the westward on the first part of the voyage accidentally discovered Brazil. He was able to establish a factory at Calicut, but it was later treacherously attacked and its occupants all killed or wounded, again at the instigation of the Arab traders. To avenge this slaughter a fleet of ten ships was fitted out in Portugal and the command given to da Gama, with the title of Admiral of India. He arrived off Calicut in 1502 and at once bombarded the town, treating the inhabitants with merciless cruelty before sailing on to Cochin where he obtained an immensely rich cargo for his ships.

On his return to Portugal he was created Count of Vidigueira and granted other honours and privileges, and retired to enjoy his great wealth. Meanwhile Portuguese possessions in India greatly expanded under a succession of viceroys. Abuses crept into the administration, and in 1524 da Gama was recalled by John III and nominated as viceroy, charged with putting through a thorough reform. He arrived at Goa in September 1524 but had hardly begun his task before he fell ill and died at Cochin on 24 December. His body was brought home to Portugal in 1538 and buried at Vidigueira, but in 1880 it was exhumed and reburied in the church of Santa Maria de Belem in Lisbon.

GAMBIER, JAMES, Lord Gambier (1756–1833), British admiral of the fleet, first distinguished himself as captain of H.M.S. *Defiance* in the battle of the *Glorious First of June, when his ship was the first to break through the French *line of battle. He was promoted rear admiral in 1795 and for the next six years was one of the lords commissioners of the Admiralty. After two years as governor and commander-in-chief in Newfoundland, he returned to the Admiralty. In 1807 he was put in command of the fleet sent to the Baltic to compel the surrender of the Danish Navy. After a three-day bombardment of *Copenhagen, the city surrendered and all the seaworthy ships of the Danish Navy were taken to England. He was in command of the Channel Fleet during the attempt to destroy the French fleet in the *Basque Roads in 1809, where his orders of withdrawal to Captain Thomas *Cochrane, who commanded the inshore squadron of *fireships and other modern weapons and whom he personally disliked, ensured that the attack was only partially successful. He was tried by court martial but the Admiralty, which of course had responsibility for his appointment, made sure that he would be honourably acquitted by assembling a court friendly to Gambier. He remained in command of the Channel Fleet until 1811, his last appointment.

GAMMON IRON, a circular iron band used to hold a *bowsprit to the stem of a sailing vessel. When a bowsprit is fitted in a yacht, the gammon iron has two metal sheaves fixed on either side which act as fairleads for the anchor cable.

GAMMON LASHING or **GAMMONING,** seven or eight turns of a rope lashing passed alternately over the *bowsprit and through a hole in the *stem of a sailing vessel to secure the bowsprit at the *knightheads. Good gammoning was a skilled operation, and when properly performed made a *cross lashing. Nowadays a *gammon iron replaces the old gammon lashing.

GANG, an old name used to describe the full set of standing rigging used to set up a mast in a square-rigged sailing vessel.

GANGES, **H.M.S.,** a ship's name in the British Navy frequently given to warships built of teak in India or Burma. The second ship of this name in the Royal Navy was the last sailing *ship of the line built for Britain. She was built of teak at Bombay in 1821 and was paid off in 1861, being converted in 1866 into a training ship for boys at Falmouth. She was not broken up until 1929, after 108 years of useful existence. The name was subsequently given to the boys' naval training establishment at Shotley, Suffolk, where boys from the age of 14 learned to become seamen.

GANGWAY, originally the name given to the platforms on either side of the *skids in the *waist of a ship, on which her boats were stowed, connecting the *quarter-deck to the *forecastle. It provided a convenient means of walking from one to the other without descending to the deck level of the waist. By extension it has today come to mean the movable passage way operated from the shore by which passengers and crews can enter or leave a ship when she lies alongside a wharf or pier. It is also widely used to describe the *companion ladders, which are rigged down a ship's side when she lies to an anchor, for embarking or disembarking with boats or launches communicating with the shore.

GANTEAUME, Comte HONORÉ-JOSEPH-ANTONIN, (1755–1815), Vice Admiral of France, served as a young man in the merchant marine and was employed as a reserve officer in the French Navy during the War of American Independence (1775–82), serving under Admirals d'*Estaing and *Suffren. After a short time as a prisoner-of-war in England and further service in the merchant marine, he rejoined the navy as a lieutenant in 1793 and in the following year was made *post-captain. He was wounded three times during the battle of the *Glorious First of June in which he commanded the *Trente-et-un-Mai*. Serving as chief of staff to Admiral *Brueys at the battle of the *Nile, he had a miraculous escape from the disaster that overtook the flagship l'*Orient*. He was promoted rear admiral on Napoleon's recommendation and served as his naval commander throughout his campaign in Egypt. Later he became a member of the Council of State entrusted with naval affairs, and for the next four

years commanded a squadron operating from Toulon and trying unsuccessfully to carry reinforcements to Egypt. Promoted vice admiral and made a count of the Empire, Ganteaume was in command during the *Trafalgar campaign of the Brest fleet which, because of the close British blockade, was unable to break out to join the Toulon fleet commanded by Vice Admiral *Villeneuve. When Napoleon was banished to Elba, Ganteaume transferred his loyalty to the restored Bourbon king and adhered to him during the 'hundred days' between Napoleon's return to France and his final defeat at Waterloo in 1815.

GANTLINE, the modern corruption of girtline, a single *whip originally used to hoist to the masthead or *hounds the standing *rigging which was to be secured there while the ship was *fitting-out, and also to hoist the *riggers, in *boatswain's chairs, to do the work. The gantline was also used for hoisting sails in square-rigged ships from the deck when required to be bent on to their *yards, as they were far too heavy to be carried up the rigging by the *topmen.

GANTLOPE or **GAUNTLOPE** (pron. gantlet), a form of punishment employed in the British Navy in the late 17th, 18th, and early 19th centuries which involved the whole crew of the ship. In the most serious cases the man under punishment was drawn in a sawn-down cask through a double line of the ship's company, each man armed with a knotted cord known as a *nettle or knittle, and lashed as he passed. For minor offences the man under punishment ran through the double line up to three times. Originally it was a punishment for stealing from messmates, but it was occasionally awarded for the more serious forms of naval crime. It was known as 'running the gantlope', and was abolished by order of the British Admiralty in 1806. It has given its name to the expression 'running the gauntlet', usually used today in reference to sustained criticism.

GARBOARD or **GARBOARD STRAKE,** the first plank on the outer hull of a wooden vessel next to the *keel, into which it is *rabbeted. It runs from the *stem to the *sternpost, and is similarly rabbeted into those timbers. The term was also used in wooden ships to describe the first *seam nearest the keel, the most difficult of all to *caulk. 'Here is the most dangerous place in all the ship to spring a leak, for it is almost impossible to come to it withinboard' (Mainwaring, *Seaman's Dictionary*, 1644). Similarly, in steel ship construction, the plates next to the keel are known as the garboard plates. It seems to have been a garbled version of 'gathering-board' and came into the English language from the Dutch *gaarboord*, itself derived from *gadaren*, to gather, and *boord*, board.

GARLAND, a sea term with many meanings. **(1)** A collar of rope round a mast to support the standing *rigging and prevent it from chafing the mast. In the early sailing days when ships only had single pole masts, the *tops were circular or semi-circular platforms built round the masts, and that part of the pole mast above the top was known as the topmast. The only mark on the mast above the top was the garland which supported the *stays, and that part of the pole mast above the garland was known as the 'top-garland' mast, which may have become *topgallant. **(2)** The wreath of carved wood, most often in the form of foliage, which for decorative purposes surrounded the circular *ports cut in the sides of the *forecastle and *quarter-deck of warships for the upper deck guns. **(3)** The racks between the gun carriages and around the hatches on the gundecks of wooden warships, with holes cut for the stowage of shot, were known as shot garlands. **(4)** A small circular net extended by a wooden hoop slung from the beam above each mess in a warship in which seamen could stow their provisions to keep them beyond the reach of cats, cockroaches, rats, etc. It would also take a can of beer, rum, or *flip since as it swung with the movement of the ship there was no danger of spillage. See also WEDDING GARLAND.

GARNERAY, AMBROISE-LOUIS (1783–1857), French marine painter, was born in Paris, the eldest son of the artist Jean François Garneray. He joined the French Navy at the age of 14 and took part in numerous actions in the East Indies. In 1806, during the Napoleonic War (1803–15), he was taken prisoner by the British and spent the rest of the war in captivity. On his return to France he studied art under his father and in 1817 was appointed marine painter to the Duc d'Angoulême, Admiral of France. From then on he became a regular exhibitor at the Salon in Paris. His best-known painting is perhaps his 'Battle of Navarino', now in the *Musée de la Marine, Paris.

GARNET, a *tackle used in a square-rigged ship for hoisting in casks and provisions. It was rigged from a *guy or pendant made fast to the mainmast head with a block *seized to the mainstay over the hatchway. In some merchant ships the tackle was large enough to be used for loading and unloading cargo as well as provisions. See also CLEW-GARNET.

'GARTERS', seamen's slang for the *bilboes, or *irons, which were used to secure men under punishment by leg-irons shackled to a long bar.

GASKET, a rope, plaited cord, or strip of canvas used to secure a sail, when *furled, to a *yard or *boom of a vessel. In large square-rigged ships gaskets were passed with three or four turns round both sail and yard, with the turns spaced well out. The *bunt gasket, which had to hold the bunt or heaviest part of a square sail when furled, was sometimes made of strong netting. In the old seamanship manuals of the 17th and early 18th centuries the word is sometimes written as caskets. The modern term, used in yachts, is 'tier'.

GATE VESSEL, a small ship, often a *trawler or similar vessel, which operates the central section of an anti-submarine *boom, consisting of submarine nets, across the entrance to a harbour or anchorage in time of war. There are two such ships, one at each end of the central section, and they lower this section of the net to the bottom when required to enable ships to pass through the boom, rehoisting it and thus closing the boom when the ship has passed.

GAUSS, a wooden sailing vessel of 721 tons, rigged as a three-masted *schooner with auxiliary steam engines, used by Erich von *Drygalski's German Antarctic expedition of 1901–3. She was the second vessel ever to winter in the Antarctic. See also BELGICA.

GAUSSIN ERROR, a magnetic *compass error temporarily induced through the soft iron in a ship when she has been steering one *course for a long time, or has been lying in one direction alongside a pier or wharf. It can be counteracted by the temporary adjustment of the compass correctors mounted close to the compass.

GDANSK, formerly Danzig, a seaport and naval base on the Baltic coast of Poland, built on the left bank of the mouth of the River Vistula. It has had a chequered career, being at one time one of the four chief towns of the *Hanseatic League. It has also, in the course of its career, belonged to Pomerania, Poland, Brandenburg, Denmark, the order of Teutonic Knights, Russia, Prussia, and was for a short period a free town. It has a first-class dockyard and a large shipbuilding industry.

GDYNIA, a seaport on the Baltic coast of Poland, and home of the *Muzeum Marynarki Wojenne, a maritime museum which illustrates Polish naval history from the 10th century to the present time.

GEARY, Sir FRANCIS (1709–96), British admiral, started his naval career with a stroke of good fortune during the war of the Austrian Succession (1739–48) when in 1743 he captured a French ship chartered by Spanish merchants and having on board sixty-five chests of silver, each containing 3,000 *pieces of eight, fifty-seven bales of indigo, five of cochineal, and one of vanilla. His share of the *prize money was immense and within a year he had captured a French *frigate, having on board 24,000 dollars, and eight French West Indiamen, all richly laden. As if this were not enough he came ashore and married a Kentish lady of immense fortune.

At the start of the Seven Years War (1756–63) he was with Admiral *Boscawen on the passage to Canada which captured two French *ships of the line, on board which was the money (£80,000) to pay the French troops in Canada—yet more prize money in his pocket. On his return to England he was a member of the court martial that condemned Admiral John *Byng to death. He was with Sir Edward *Hawke in 1759 but missed taking part in the great battle of *Quiberon Bay because of a sprung topmast. He was promoted rear admiral in this year, was port admiral at Portsmouth from 1760 to 1762, his last appointment during this war.

In 1780, during the War of American Independence (1775–82) Geary, now a full admiral, was appointed commander-in-chief of the Channel Fleet. In a cruise off Brest the fleet cut off twelve ships out of a French convoy of twenty-four; all would have been taken had not thick fog come down just as they were being overtaken. But by now Geary's health was failing, and in 1781 he was forced to haul down his flag and go ashore.

GELLYWATTE, a very old seaman's term for the boat used by the captain of a ship when he went ashore. By some it is thought to be the original name by which the *jolly-boat, which first came into use in the 18th century, was known.

GENERAL AVERAGE, a term in marine insurance for the adjustment of a loss when cargo on board a ship belonging to one or more owners has been sacrificed for the safety of the whole, whereby the amount of the loss is shared by all who have shipped cargo in the vessel. A case for general average would occur, for example, if the deck cargo of a ship had to be jettisoned to safeguard the ship in rough weather. There are strict rules which bind a claim for general average; the loss must have been voluntary and not accidental, must not have been caused by any fault on the part of the owner claiming general average, must have been necessary and successful in saving the remainder of the cargo, and must have been made by order of the *master of the ship.

GENERAL CHASE, a naval signal introduced into the British Navy in the mid-18th century in an attempt to circumvent the rigid *line of battle laid down for naval action by the current *Fighting Instructions. Few admirals were prepared to risk their reputations by departing from the tactical rules in the *Fighting Instructions*, one of which was that battle could not be joined with an enemy fleet until the line had been formed and was directly opposite the enemy's line. As a result of this order naval battles were somewhat formal affairs in which each ship fought its opposite number in the enemy's line while remaining rigidly in station in its own line. In order to break this sterility the general chase signal was introduced, in which each ship of war made all sail towards the enemy and engaged the nearest ship as she came up, even though it was not the ship she should have engaged in a line battle, succeeding ships coming up, passing her on her disengaged side, and engaging the next enemy ship within reach. It was a signal which restored initiative to the naval commander and flexibility to the line of battle and, when employed, produced some notable victories. The battles of *Cape Finisterre (1747) and *Quiberon Bay (1759) are fine examples of naval battles fought with the signal for a general chase flying.

GENERAL-AT-SEA, the title given in England during the Protectorate of Oliver Cromwell, 1649–60, to those men appointed by Parliament to lead the English fleet in battle. Some of them, e.g., Robert *Blake and George *Monck, were appointed direct from the army. They were, of course, the equivalent of admirals.

GENOA, Ital. Genova, one of the largest and most important seaports of Italy, on the Ligurian coast. With its fine natural harbour it has been a seaport from the earliest days, being well known by Greeks, Romans, and Carthaginians. During the dark ages it was one of the Italian principalities and had its own navy, which grew to quite considerable proportions during a long period of warfare against the Saracens. The port grew rich during the years of the crusades, absorbing all the carrying trade which those campaigns generated.

Genoa can claim, as one of its citizens and most distinguished navigators, Christopher *Columbus, and might well have become heir to the riches of the new world had the city-state provided him with the ships and men he demanded for his dream of discovering a new route to China. Another famous seaman of Genoa was Andrea *Doria.

The modern port is extensive, with fine docks and an important shipbuilding industry from which some of the largest vessels are launched. The best known of the shipbuilding firms at Genoa is Ansaldo, which has built many famous ships for the Italian Navy. With the exception of *Marseilles, it is the largest seaport in the western Mediterranean, and through it passes nearly a half of all Italian trade. In the Villa Doria in the town of Genoa is the *Civico Museo Navale, a small maritime museum of considerable interest.

GENOA JIB, a large *jib or foresail used in racing and cruising yachts, almost invariably in conjunction with a *Bermuda mainsail. Its features are (a) its size, considerably larger than a standard jib and often larger than the mainsail, and (b) its shape, with the *clew extended much farther aft than in an ordinary jib, overlapping the mainsail by an appreciable amount, its *foot often parallel with the deck sheer. In effect, it combines jib and fore staysail in a single large sail. As well as transferring the main driving power of a yacht's sails to the *fore triangle, it also, by the sheeting of its clew well abaft the mast, increases the speed of the airflow over the *luff of the mainsail and thus increases the partial vacuum there which helps to pull the yacht forward. See AERODYNAMICS for an analysis of this forward pull.

GENTLEMEN CAPTAINS, court favourites of the Tudor and Stuart kings and queens of England who were appointed to command ships in the English Navy without having had to work their way up by promotion from lower ranks. Very often they had no knowledge of the sea or the ways of a ship, but solicited these appointments for the opportunities of plunder and *prize money which they offered. Such captains were disliked by the crews of the ships they commanded and particularly by captains who had reached their rank by the normal methods of promotion, known as *tarpaulin captains. Equally disgusted by this backstairs method of appointment was Samuel *Pepys who, as Secretary of the Admiralty, 1673–9 and 1684–9, made the lives of gentlemen captains a misery by insisting that they remained on board their ships unless given official leave and also by requiring them to forward logs for their ships punctually every month to the Navy Office. Under this strict régime few courtiers found it worth while to solicit appointments to command ships and the practice was effectively stamped out.

GERBAULT, ALAIN (1896–1941), French yachtsman and author, spent his early years at Dinard where he learned to handle boats and acquired a love of the sea aboard his father's yacht and among the Breton fishermen. He spent the First World War (1914–18) in the Flying Corps but after the war was unable to settle to any steady occupation though he showed his athletic qualities by becoming a tennis champion.

With the help of a friend who had spent years sailing the seas in his little ship Gerbault found in 1921 a 39-ft *cutter yacht built in 1892 to designs by Dixon *Kemp, called *Firecrest*. After buying her and fitting her out he sailed her by way of the Bay of Biscay to the Mediterranean and spent more than a year learning to cruise single-handed before setting off on a voyage he had long planned.

In April 1924 he left Cannes, reached Gibraltar a week later, and in June sailed alone on the direct route for New York, taking 101 days over the passage, during which many days were lost through repairs to worn-out sails and rigging. His was nevertheless the first middle-route passage east–west to America made single-handed; the first man to have made the northern passage east–west being an American, John Buckley in a *gaff *ketch-rigged converted ship's lifeboat, *City of Ragusa*, fifty-four years earlier. Gerbault wrote of his experiences in *The Fight of the 'Firecrest'*.

While in New York he altered his yacht's rig to *Bermuda cutter, and proceeded to make a round-the-world voyage in the *Firecrest*, arriving back in Le Havre in July 1929, after almost four and a half years. He received a great ovation, was acclaimed as a national hero, and was awarded the Légion d'Honneur on board a French *destroyer. Meanwhile the *Firecrest*, while being towed too fast by a naval vessel, was pulled under and lost. Gerbault's second book, *In Quest of the Sun*, described the circumnavigation.

During the time he had spent among the Pacific islands he had developed a passionate concern for the future of their natives, and with few interests left in his own country he planned to design and build a better, modern vessel and to return to work for their betterment. In a new 38-ft cutter which he designed on Norwegian *redningskoite* (lifeboat) lines and named *Alain Gerbault* he sailed alone once more to his beloved South Seas in 1932. He settled among the natives on Bora Bora, but on the outbreak of war in 1939 tried to return to his native France. He met many difficulties and fell ill when he reached Timor on his way to Madagascar, dying there in 1941, only a few hours before the Japanese invasion of the island.

GERLACHE DE GOMERY, ADRIEN DE (1866–1934), Belgian naval officer, inspired and led the Belgian Antarctic expedition of 1898–1900. After exploring the north-west coast of the Antarctic Peninsula the expedition's ship, *Belgica*, was beset in the ice and its crew forced to winter on board, the first to do so in the Antarctic. Between 1905 and 1909 Gerlache de Gomery made a number of oceanographic cruises in the Greenland, Barents, and Kara Seas. See ANTARCTIC EXPLORATION.

GERMAN MILE, a sea measurement used mainly by Dutch navigators in the 17th and early 18th centuries. It was equal in length to 4 *nautical miles.

GET SPLICED, to, see SPLICED, TO GET.

GHORMLEY, ROBERT LEE (1883–1958), American admiral, was born in Oregon and graduated from the Naval Academy in 1906. He was sent to London by President Roosevelt in August 1940 as a special naval observer at the American Embassy where his acute observation of the naval operations and procedure in the early years of the Second World War, and the many friendships he made with British naval officers, did much to make easy the naval co-operation of the two countries when the U.S.A. entered the war in 1941. He later distinguished himself by his service in the south Pacific area in 1942 and then served on the staff of the commander-in-chief, U.S. Fleet, and in the Navy Department before becoming Commandant of the 14th Naval District and Commander of the Hawaiian Sea Frontier in 1942 and 1943.

GHOST, to, the art of making headway in a sailing ship without any apparent wind to fill her sails. By taking advantage of such breaths of wind as may occur, a well-trimmed sailing vessel can often make quite an appreciable way through the water, appearing to move, or ghost, even in a flat calm.

GHOSTER, a light-weather sail set in yachts *hanked to the topmast *stay for use in very light winds. It is very similar in shape to either a *genoa or a *yankee, according to choice, but with its *luff extending the whole length of the stay instead of short of the masthead as is often the case with a genoa or yankee. It is made of much lighter cloth, usually 6-oz Terylene, than a genoa and is suitable for use in winds of up to force 2 on the *Beaufort Scale.

GIBRALTAR, a rocky promontory which guards the western entrance to the Mediterranean Sea. It takes its name from Jebel Tariq, the mount of Tariq, which commemorates its capture by Tariq ben Zaid in 711. It was he who ordered fortifications to be constructed on the rock, and these have been enlarged and improved throughout the centuries as Gibraltar became the scene of attack and defence. Gibraltar was captured by British forces under the command of Admiral Sir George *Rooke in 1704, almost as an afterthought and in theory in the interests of the Archduke Charles of Austria, but after its capture Rooke hoisted the British flag over the fort. Since that year Gibraltar has been the subject of many sieges, the best known

being that of 1779–83, when its defence was conducted by General Sir George Elliot with great skill and fortitude.

After its capture in 1704, Gibraltar was developed as a principal naval base for use by the British Navy, a purpose which it still serves. It has a naval repair yard and dry-docks, and though not truly a port in the context of trade, is used as a port of call and fuelling port by many commercial steamship lines.

GIG, a light, narrow ship's boat, built for speed, originally *clinker-built but within more recent years frequently of *carvel construction, rowing four or six oars single-banked. It had *steps or *tabernacles for two short masts which could be shipped when required, setting two *lug or *lateen sails. Such ship's boats are a rarity today, the small petrol or diesel engine having largely superseded oars and sails. Some six-oared gigs, originally used for salvage work in the Scilly Isles, are beautifully preserved there and are still used for inter-island races.

GILBERT, Sir HUMPHREY (*c.* 1539–83), English navigator, of Compton, near Dartmouth, was a half-brother of Sir Walter *Raleigh. In early life he followed a military career, soldiering in France, in Ireland where he was knighted for his services, and in the Netherlands.

He had a lifelong ambition, however, to voyage in search of the *North-West passage to *Cathay and in 1576 published a famous *Discourse* on the subject. He was eventually granted a charter in 1578 by Elizabeth I for such a voyage, as well as to plant a colony in Newfoundland of which he was to be the Governor. His first expedition, which set off that year, suffered from divided councils from the start. It got no farther than Cape Verde where it met disaster at the hands of the Spaniards.

Money and credit exhausted, Gilbert returned for a while to soldiering; but in 1583 he was able with Raleigh's help and, as he himself put it, by 'selling the clothes off my wife's back', to raise enough money to get another expedition together. He sailed in June 1583 from Plymouth in the *Delight*, together with the *Ark Raleigh* (see also ARK ROYAL) furnished by Sir Walter and the biggest vessel of the flotilla, the *Golden Hind*, *Swallow*, and the little 10-ton *Squirrel*.

The *Ark Raleigh* soon deserted the expedition and returned on the pretext of sickness on board. The remainder continued and reached St. John's, Newfoundland, where, having taken possession of the territory in the queen's name, Gilbert set up the first English colony in North America on 5 August 1583.

Patriotic, pious, and learned, Gilbert was no leader of men. He found the task of imposing discipline and law on the new colony beyond him. Having dispatched the *Swallow*, carrying the sick and disaffected, to England, he embarked in the *Squirrel* and led the remainder southwards to explore the coast. The *Delight* ran aground and was lost on 29 August. Two days later the *Golden Hind* and the *Squirrel* shaped course for home.

Fierce storms were met off the Azores. During a clearance following one of them, Gilbert was seen from the *Golden Hind* sitting calmly in the stern of the *Squirrel*, book in hand; when the two ships came within earshot he called out cheerfully, 'We are as near to heaven by sea as by land.'

In his report, Captain Hayes of the *Golden Hind* described how the little *Squirrel* was lost that night. 'The same Monday night, about twelve, the frigate [*Squirrel*] being ahead of us in the *Golden Hind*, suddenly her lights were out ... in that moment the frigate was devoured and swallowed up of the sea.' There were no survivors.

GILES, JOHN LAURENT (1901–69), British naval architect, was a versatile designer of ocean racers, cruising yachts, and motor yachts. He introduced the retroussé (forward sloping) * transom stern for racing yachts, the * hogged or reverse sheer, and other features which were widely adopted for yachts of all kinds. He also pioneered model tank and wind tunnel tests for new * International Metre Class designs, and adapted new methods of weight-saving in wooden yacht hull construction. He was a leader in the design of light displacement, high performance, cruising yachts with diesel engines of adequate power to give maximum hull speed—the advanced motor-sailer type—and his technical knowledge of design was widely used by the * Royal Ocean Racing Club on many of their Committees for over twenty years.

GIMBALS, two concentric metal rings which form the mounting and suspension for * compasses, and * chronometers on board ship. The rings are mounted on knife edges, the bearings of one being fixed fore and aft in the ship's line and the other athwartships, thus allowing the compass or chronometer to remain level irrespective of the rolling or pitching of the ship. Gimbals are also used to mount table lamps, cooking stoves, etc., in small vessels. The earliest description of a gimbal mounting dates from the beginning of the 17th century.

GIMBLET, to, or **GIMBLETING,** the action of turning an anchor around on its * fluke in the days before stockless anchors and when they were stowed at sea on a bed. It was a necessary operation in order to get the anchor into position

so that it would lie flat on its bed before being secured for sea. The origin of the term appears to be that the action of turning the anchor by rotating the * stock resembled that of turning a gimlet by hand.

GIN BLOCK, a sheave in a metal cruciform frame used as a * whip for general purposes, such as shifting cargo. They are usually used with a chain rather than with rope.

GINGERBREAD or **GINGERBREAD-WORK,** the gilded scroll work and carving with which the * hulls of large ships, particularly warships and * East Indiamen of the 15th to 18th centuries, were decorated. 'To take some of the gilt off the gingerbread', an act which diminishes the full enjoyment of the whole. For illus. see STERN.

GIPSY MOTH, the name of five yachts owned by Sir Francis * Chichester in which he made many long ocean voyages, including a single-handed circumnavigation in 1966–7.

GIRD, to, to haul in or to bind something together with the object of securing more space. It is an expression used particularly in regard to * rigging and more especially to the rigging of a square-rigged ship, where extra space was needed to * brace the lower * yards round when sailing * close-hauled. The standing rigging of a mast when it reached the * hounds often formed a limit to the degree a lower yard could be braced round; if this rigging could be girded in to the mast, extra space for the yard was made and it could be braced sharper. See also CATHARPINGS.

GIRDLE, an additional thickness of planking secured along the * wales, or bends, of a wooden ship about her waterline for the purpose of giving her more stability in the water. It was a common practice in the 16th and 17th centuries, when the art of shipwrightry was still largely experimental, to build ships too narrow in the * beam to carry their sail. This was particularly the case when topmasts and * topgallant masts became a commonplace and the amount of sail carried increased accordingly. The word was used both as a noun and a verb; a ship was girdled when she was fitted with a girdle. See also FURRING.

GIRT, a ship is girt when she is moored with two anchors out with both cables hauled in so taut that they prevent her swinging to wind or tide. The cables as they * grow out tautly to the anchors catch her * forefoot as she attempts to swing and prevent any such movement. It is a situation easily corrected by * veering one of the cables slightly.

GIRTLINE, the old, and more correct, word for
*gantline.

GLAS, GEORGE (1725–65), Scottish seaman
and adventurer, commanded a ship which traded
between north-west Africa and Brazil, and during one of his voyages in 1763 he discovered a
navigable river which led some way inland from
the African coast, possibly at Gueder. By arrangement with the Board of Trade in London,
he was granted £15,000 if he could obtain cession to the British crown of the area he proposed
to develop. To this purpose he made a treaty with
the Moors, and named his settlement Port
Hillsborough.

In November 1764, on a visit to Lauzarote to
buy a small *barque for river work, he and his
companions were seized by the Spaniards and
imprisoned at Santa Cruz. While he was in
prison his settlement was attacked by natives,
and the survivors, including his wife and small
daughter, fled to Tenerife. After representations
by the government in London, Glas was released
from prison and, with his wife and child, took
passage to England in the barque *Earl of
Sandwich*. On the voyage the Portuguese and
Spanish members of the crew mutinied because it
was rumoured that there was much bullion on
board, killed the captain and slaughtered the
crew. George Glas was stabbed to death and his
wife and daughter flung overboard. The ship was
later recaptured and the mutineers were hanged
on arrival at Dublin.

GLASGOW, a city of Scotland and a major
seaport, situated on the River Clyde. For many
years Glasgow suffered as a port through
inadequate depth of water, but by narrowing the
river to increase the scour and by an extensive
scheme of dredging during the 19th century,
Glasgow was enabled to grow as a port at a
prodigious rate. Its early prosperity was founded
on the cotton and tobacco trade, and later maintained and magnified by the great iron-founding
industry which grew upon the discovery of the
value of the local blackband ironstone for smelt-
ing into pig iron. Another enormous industry is
shipbuilding, and some of the most famous shipbuilding yards were situated on the banks of the
Clyde including that of John Brown which built
most of the great *Cunard liners. During the
closing years of the 19th century and the first
three decades of the 20th, the Clyde was the
home of the most famous yacht designers of the
period, G. L. *Watson and William *Fife.

GLASS, the seaman's name for a telescope, a
barometer, and—before clocks suitable for use
on board ship were developed—a sand-glass.
Although the word telescope is as old as the

instrument itself, being used by Galileo in 1611
to describe his invention, the name did not take
on in maritime circles until very much later. In
1619 there is a reference to it in England under
the name trunke-spectacle, but the first naval
use of the name was in 1744 by Murdoch
*Mackenzie in his treatise on surveying. In gen-
eral maritime use was the name glass, an abbreviation of long-glass or spy-glass, and Captain
*Marryat was using that name in his naval
novels at least as late as 1844.

The barometer was, and is, almost invariably
known as a glass, even when in the form of a
barograph. 'The glass is high, low, rising, falling'
being the usual description of the movements of
the barometer.

The *sand-glass, used in the measurement of
time, was always known as a glass from the
earliest times. Thus Richard *Hakluyt, in his
Principal Voyages (1599, II, p. 126), 'We laye
six glasses *ahull tarying for the pinesse (*pinnace).'

GLASS REINFORCED PLASTIC, see FIBRE
GLASS.

GLOBE, a depiction, in the form of a revolving
sphere mounted at the poles, of the earth or the
constellations of the heavens. They are known as
terrestrial (earth) and celestial (heavens) globes.
Although ancient globes, many of them very
beautiful and rare works of art, were often
designed as furniture for libraries, there is
evidence that they were used, especially during
the 16th century, as instruments of navigation.
In the days before the invention of logarithms
and the true *Mercator principle, the problems
of nautical astronomy could be solved only
by prolix mathematics which, in general, were
foreign to navigators. Globes, however, offered
the means of solving many of these problems
instrumentally by inspection. Finding the *latitude from two *altitude observations of the sun
or a pair of stars, finding the true *azimuth of a
heavenly body, or finding the *rhumb line
*course and distance from one position to
another were problems easy of solution by means
of a celestial or terrestrial globe.

An important treatise on the use of globes,
including navigation, was written by Robert
Hues and published in Latin in 1592. It was
'made English for the benefit of the Unlearned'
by Edmund Chilmead in 1638. In the eyes of the
original author, the most important part of the
treatise was that dealing with the practical uses to
which globes could be put by the navigator.

With the advent of the Mercator chart and
arithmetical navigation, facilitated by the use of
logarithms, the fragile, cumbersome, and costly
globes fell into disuse so far as ship navigation
was concerned. See NAVIGATION.

French prizes captured at the Glorious First of June arriving at Portsmouth; water-colour by T. Rowlandson, 1794

GLOBULAR PROJECTION, a form of map-making in which the central meridian and the periphery are arbitrarily marked off in equal parts for lines of *latitude to be drawn, and the equator equally divided up to accommodate the meridians of *longitude. The resultant map shows less distortion of land areas than other methods of projection, but is useless for plotting distances or directions. See also ARROWSMITH, Aaron; GNOMONIC CHART; MERCATOR, Gerardus.

GLOIRE, a *frigate of the French Navy, designed by Stanislas *Dupuy de Lôme and launched in 1859, was the first truly sea-going *ironclad warship in the world, making her appearance a year before the British *Warrior, the first ironclad *battleship in the world. With a displacement of 5,600 tons, she was built of oak and had a belt of iron armour 4·7 in. thick along her sides. She had, as in all warships of this period, a full rig of masts and sails, with steam propulsion which gave her a speed of 13½ knots. She carried a single tier of thirty-six guns of a new design of 66-pounder, breech-loading with rifled barrels and firing shells.

The introduction of armour protection for warships was the result of the Turkish experience at *Sinope in 1853 when a squadron of wooden warships was burnt down to the waterline by the shells of a Russian squadron. That, and the

punishment received by British and French wooden *ships of the line at the bombardment of Sebastopol in 1854 during the Crimean War (1854–6), spelt the end of the wooden man-of-war.

GLORIOUS FIRST OF JUNE, The: 1794, a battle in the North Atlantic between the British and French fleets commanded respectively by Admirals Lord *Howe and *Villaret de Joyeuse. It was the first major sea encounter of the Revolutionary War (1793–1801). Tactically it was a success for Howe, since he took six *prizes and sank a seventh French *ship of the line without the loss of a single British unit. Strategically, however, there is no doubt that the French came off best, since the reason for the French being at sea was to give cover to a large convoy, chiefly of grain ships, which had sailed from America for the relief of starving France. Although Howe made dispositions to intercept and destroy or capture the merchantmen, his plans failed. The ships reached France safely amid national rejoicings.

The action itself was the culmination of a series of general or partial engagements extending over several days. On 1 June Howe, who had by then obtained the *windward position, intended to break through the French line at all points and to attack from to *leeward. Not many of his admirals and captains fully appreciated his intentions, and penetration of the French line of battle was far from complete. It was always held that had Howe followed up his victory, he could have captured the convoy after defeating the French, but four days of fighting, at the age of 68, had exhausted him. Nevertheless, the action was hailed in Britain as a great victory and Howe returned to a hero's welcome.

GLUT, (1) a strengthening piece of canvas sewn into large square sails at the *bunt, with an eyelet hole in the middle, for the bunt *jigger to go through when the sail was being *furled. These big sails were too heavy for the men working on the yard to lift by hand, and so a small purchase (jigger) was used to haul up the foot of the sail, hence the need to strengthen the canvas where the jigger was hooked on. **(2)** A word, used as a verb, to denote the prevention of slipping; e.g., a *messenger was glutted by *nippers to prevent it slipping on the cable to which it was nipped; a *tackle is glutted (or choked) by the *fall drawn across the *sheave of a *block to stop the rope rendering through the block.

GNEISENAU, a German armoured *cruiser of the First World War (1914–18) and a *battle-cruiser of the Second World War. See SCHARN-HORST AND GNEISENAU.

The German battle-cruiser Gneisenau

GNOMONIC CHART, a chart of great utility in *great circle sailing based on the gnomonic projection. This is a perspective projection in which part of a spherical surface is projected from the centre of the sphere on to a plane surface tangential to the sphere's surface. The principal property of this projection is that great circle arcs are projected as straight lines.

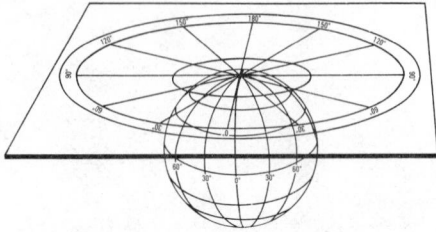

Projection of a gnomonic chart

In order to draw a great circle on a *Mercator chart—the projection being a relatively complex curve always concave to the equator—the route is first drawn on a gnomonic chart by connecting the plotted positions of the places of departure and destination with a straight line. Positions of a series of points on this line are taken from the gnomonic chart and marked on the Mercator chart. A fair curve is then drawn through these points, this being the required projection of the great circle route on the Mercator chart.

The gnomonic chart became popular with the publication by Hugh Godfray in 1858 of two polar gnomonic charts covering the greater part of the world, one for the northern, and the other for the southern hemisphere. Although it was generally believed that Godfray was the original inventor of this method of great circle sailing, it is interesting to note that a complete explanation of the construction of a polar gnomonic chart, with a detailed example of a great circle route from the Lizard to the Bermudas, appeared in Samuel Sturmey's *Mariners' Mirror,* of 1669.

Gnomonic charts are also used navigationally for the plotting of wireless directional bearings which follow a great circle route.

'GOBBIE', the sailor's name for a coastguard. Its origin is obscure, but until 1923 the coastguard service in Britain was administered by the Admiralty and manned by naval pensioners, and the term was probably a slang name for a pensioner.

GOEBEN, S.M.S., a German *battle-cruiser of 23,000 tons with ten 11-in. guns, launched in 1912, was the centre of a celebrated British court martial during the First World War (1914–18), when Rear Admiral *Troubridge, commanding a squadron of four *cruisers in the Mediterranean in 1914, failed to bring her to action because of orders to avoid being drawn into battle with a force of superior power. In company with the light cruiser *Breslau* the *Goeben* had shelled the Algerian ports of Bône and Phillipeville early in the morning of 4 August 1914 in order to interrupt the transport of troops to France. A few hours later, before the expiration of the British ultimatum to Germany, the *Goeben* was shadowed by the two British battle-cruisers *Indomitable* and *Indefatigable* but was too fast for them and contact was lost. The two German ships coaled at Messina (Italy being then neutral) and then headed for the * Dardanelles, an alliance having been concluded on the outbreak of war between Germany and Turkey. British arrangements to intercept the two ships and bring them to action failed to stop them because of the order mentioned above, and on arrival at Constantinople the two German ships were nominally sold to Turkey though they retained their German crews.

On 29 October 1914, without warning, the two ships bombarded the Russian ports of Sebastopol and Novorossisk, and war between Turkey and the allied powers followed. Until 1918 the *Goeben* and *Breslau* were based on Constantinople and on 20 January 1918 they made a brief sortie into the Mediterranean during which they sank two small British * monitors. On the way home the *Breslau* struck seven mines and sank at once, while the *Goeben*, also mined, ran aground off Nagara Point and remained there for a week, the target for British aircraft which dropped some 500 bombs but secured only two hits.

After the conclusion of the war the *Goeben*, renamed *Yawuz*, remained for many years the principal ship of the Turkish Navy but was sold in 1973 for breaking up.

'GOFFER', the sailor's name for mineral water or a non-alcoholic fruit drink.

GOKE, an old name, *temp.* 17th century, for the heart, or core, around which four-stranded rope is normally laid up.

GOLDEN HIND, the ship in which, in 1577–80, Francis * Drake circumnavigated the globe. She was originally the *Pelican*, but as Drake entered the Magellan Straits he changed her name to *Golden Hind* in honour of his patron Sir Christopher Hatton, whose crest was a hind *passant or*. The *Golden Hind*, alone of the five ships which originally set out on the expedition, completed the circumnavigation and finally dropped anchor in Plymouth Sound again on 26 September 1580. After landing the treasure she had brought home, she was berthed at Deptford where, at a banquet held on board six months after his return, Elizabeth I knighted Francis

Drake. Soon afterwards, the *Golden Hind* was placed in a special dock at Deptford where the public were admitted to view her on payment of a small sum, the money going to charities.

Another *Golden Hind* was one of the five ships which accompanied Sir Humphrey * Gilbert when he sailed from Cawsand Bay in June 1583 to form a colony in Newfoundland. One of the ships, the *Ark Raleigh*, returned home because of sickness on board. Sir Humphrey Gilbert landed in Newfoundland in August, and, after sending one ship home and losing another, returned soon afterwards to England in the *Squirrel*, accompanied by the *Golden Hind*. The *Squirrel* was unfortunately lost with all hands, but the *Golden Hind* arrived safely at Falmouth on 22 September.

A third *Golden Hind*, of 50 tons (Captain Thomas Flemyng), was on scouting duty off the Lizard in July 1588 when she sighted the first ship of the Spanish * Armada making for England. Her captain brought the news in to Plymouth on 19 July and the English fleet put to sea at once. During the action off Portland on 22 July the *San Salvador*, a 958-ton Spanish ship, blew up and was abandoned by the Spaniards. On the following day she was brought in to Weymouth by the little *Golden Hind*.

GOLOVNIN, VASILY MIKHAILOVICH (1776–1831), Russian vice admiral, first served as a volunteer in the British Navy. In 1807 the Russian Admiralty commissioned him to make a survey of Kamchatka and the Kurile Islands, but while he was surveying the coast of Kunashiri he was seized by the Japanese and imprisoned for three years. On his return to Russia he was given command of a ship with instructions to sail round the world. He left Russia in September 1817, rounded Cape Horn, visited Kamchatka, and returned to Russia via the Cape of Good Hope, reaching home in September 1819. He wrote several important books describing his voyages.

GOMEZ, DIOGO (d. 1482), Portuguese explorer, was a seaman in the service of Prince * Henry the Navigator. His first voyage in 1445, in command of three * caravels, was along the West African coast, hoping to reach India by this route; but strong currents south of Cape Verde caused delays and many of his officers and men refused to sail any further, believing that they were reaching the edge of the ocean. Returning to the Gambia, Gomez explored the river and the surrounding countryside before returning to Portugal. His second voyage in 1462 resulted in the rediscovery of the Cape Verde Islands. His main claim to remembrance, however, is a manuscript which he wrote detailing the life and discoveries of his patron, Prince Henry.

Traditional beak of a gondola

GONDOLA, (1) a light pleasure boat, much ornamented, with a high rising and curving stem and sternpost used on the canals of Venice and propelled by one man with a single oar, standing near the stern. The high stem is surmounted by the *ferro*, a bright metal beak in the shape of the ancient *rostrum tridens*. The origin of the gondola is unknown (it is certainly mentioned in contemporary writings as early as 1094) although surprisingly the hull form embodies the principles of the *wave line theory of modern shipbuilding. **(2)** A small boat of passage on the coasts of Italy, rowed by six or eight oars. **(3)** A small wooden warship, carrying a single gun in the bows and propelled by oars, built in some numbers on Lake Champlain under the direction of Benedict *Arnold in conjunction with other vessels with which he held up for a year the British advance from Canada into the American colonies in 1776 at the start of the War of American Independence (1775–82). Although Arnold described them as gondolas, it is probable that he really meant to designate them as *gundalows.

GOOCH, Sir DANIEL (1816–89), British engineer, was the man who laid the first electric telegraph cable across the Atlantic. Although mainly a railway engineer, he chartered the steamship *Great Eastern*, adapted her for cable laying, and in 1865 supervised the attempt, but the cable broke in mid-ocean. In the following year he made a second attempt, in which he was not only successful but also managed to pick up the two ends of the broken cable and splice them together, thus providing two complete cables. In all, he laid four cables across the Atlantic using the *Great Eastern*.

GOOD HOPE, CAPE OF, the southern extremity of the continent of Africa, which marks the dividing line between the South Atlantic and Indian Oceans. It was discovered in 1488 by Bartholomew *Diaz de Novaes. He had been sent on an expedition by John III of Portugal to prolong to the southward the earlier discoveries of Diogo *Cam. After reaching Diaz Point (lat. 26° 38′ S.) he was driven by strong winds to the southward for thirteen days, finally running into a severe storm. Steering east, the Portuguese ships found an empty sea, and altering course to the north, finally reached the land in South Africa at what is today Mossel Bay. After coasting eastward as far as the Great Fish River, Diaz was forced to turn for home because of a near mutiny among his ships, but he had gone far enough to make certain that he had discovered the way round Africa by sea. He established on his return voyage that the Cape of Good Hope was the most southerly point of the continent of Africa and gave it the name of Cabo Tormentoso (Cape of Storms) in memory of the great storm he had experienced after being driven to the southward. On his return he reported his discoveries to the king, who promptly renamed the cape Cabo da Bona Esperança (Cape of Good Hope) because of the promise it held out of a sea route to India and China, a hope made good some ten years later when Vasco da *Gama rounded it and reached the coast of India.

GOODWIN SANDS, The, a large bank of shoal sands, which are partially exposed at low water, lying about 6 miles east off the coast of Kent near the entrance to the English Channel from the North Sea. The sands are shifting and attempts in the past to erect a *lighthouse on them to mark the danger have always failed. Today they are marked by *lightships.

The shoal forms the eastern shelter of the anchorage known as the *Downs and is traditionally the site of an island known as Lomea, which were part of the lands of Earl Godwine. The island is said to have submerged during the 11th century when Godwine diverted the money earmarked for its protection to building the steeple of Tenterden Church. The present name is derived from Godwine.

The sands, because of their shifting habit, are particularly dangerous to shipping, and many good ships have met their end on them. During the great storm of 1703, thirteen British warships anchored in the Downs, together with several merchant vessels, were driven on to the

Goodwin Sands and all were lost, perhaps the most terrible of the many disasters associated with the Sands.

'GOOSEBERRY', see MULBERRY HARBOUR.

GOOSENECK, a metal fitting on the inboard end of a *boom of a sailing vessel by which it is connected to a metal ring round the base of the mast on which the sail, spread by the boom, is set. It has reference only to the fore-and-aft sailing *rig or to the *spanker of a square-rigged ship. The fitting allows for the swing of the boom sideways and is also hinged to allow the boom upward movement. It is a device of some antiquity, being known to *Falconer and included in his *Marine Dictionary* of 1771.

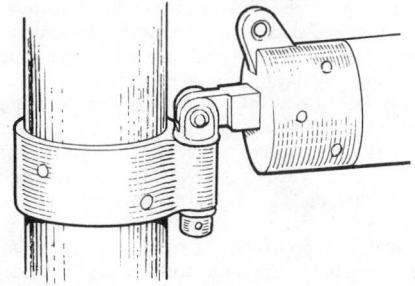

Gooseneck

GOOSE-WINGS, originally the *clews of a *course or topsail of a square-rigged ship used to *scud under when the wind was too strong for the whole sail, fully reefed, to be used. With the *bunt of the sail hauled up to the *yard, only the clews would remain spread. More recently, as goose-winged, a term applied in *fore-and-aft rigged sailing craft to indicate the *jib or *staysail being *boomed out on the opposite side to the mainsail in a following wind to present the largest possible area of sail to the wind. The assumption in such a case is that the vessel concerned does not carry, or does not wish to set, a *spinnaker, which is the most efficient means of getting the most out of a following wind in fore-and-aft rig.

GORES, (1) *cloths of canvas which are cut on an angle to increase the breadth or depth of a square sail or to shape the *leech of a fore-and-aft sail. In a four-sided fore-and-aft sail, the leech is always longer than the *luff, and some cloths must be cut on an angle whether they are *seamed vertically or horizontally. **(2)** Angular pieces of plank in a wooden vessel inserted to fill up the planking at any part requiring it.

GOSNOLD, BARTHOLOMEW (d. 1607), English navigator, commanded the *Concord*, which had been chartered by Sir Walter

*Raleigh in 1602, and sailed across the Atlantic on a trading voyage. Reaching the coast of Maine he sailed northward, landing at Cape Cod and Martha's Vineyard and giving them both their present names. He returned with a cargo of furs obtained in trade with the Indians, and promoted the colonization of this area, contributing, through the interest he aroused, to the charters granted to the London and Plymouth companies in 1606. In 1607, in company with Christopher Newport, he returned with three ships carrying the first Jamestown colonists to Virginia. He took an active part in the affairs of the colony, but died of swamp fever later in the year.

GOTHENBURG (Göteborg), a port in Sweden on the shore of the Kattegat and the home of the *Sjøfartsmuseet i Göteborg, a maritime museum of importance which illustrates the maritime history of Sweden from its earliest days.

GRAB, a coasting vessel used along the coasts of India during the 18th and 19th centuries. They ranged from about 150 to 300 tons and normally were *lateen rigged on two masts, though some of the smaller ones had only a single mast with a lateen sail. These smaller ones also had *sweeps for rowing when the wind failed.

GRAF SPEE, German *pocket-battleship, see ADMIRAL GRAF SPEE.

GRAIN, a five-pronged harpoon attached to a line and carried on board many ships in the days of sail for fishing, particularly for catching dolphins. The fisherman usually climbed out on to the *jib-boom or the *bumpkin and drove the grain into the dolphin as it flashed beneath him. See also FISGIG.

GRAND BANKS, The, an extensive shallow patch in the North Atlantic Ocean lying south and east of Newfoundland, a prolific breeding ground of *Gadus morrhua*, the cod. It is also known as the Newfoundland Bank. It was first discovered by John *Cabot in 1497 on his return from his voyage of discovery in which he reached Cape Breton Island. When passing over the bank, the crew of his ship caught immense quantities of cod merely by lowering baskets into the sea. It was this discovery which led to the great cod fishery, with at first vessels from Britain, France, and Holland making the long transatlantic crossing to return full of fish. Later, fishing vessels from Spain joined in, but, with the fish proving virtually inexhaustible, there was only occasional friction between the fishing fleets of the various nations.

As North America became developed and populated, the Grand Banks proved an irresistible source of fish and a number of ports were developed along the coast, chiefly of Massachusetts and Maine, to handle the trade, of which Gloucester, Mass., was probably the largest and most important. These ports each had fleets of *schooners with which they exploited the great banks. They engaged almost entirely in line fishing from *dories carried on board.

The Grand Banks, the cod fishing, and the Gloucester schooners were immortalized by Rudyard *Kipling in *Captains Courageous*.

GRAND FLEET, the name given on two occasions in the naval history of Britain to the principal fleet gathered together for prosecuting the war. The first occasion was during the two wars against France, the Revolutionary (1793–1801) and the Napoleonic (1803–15); the second was during the First World War (1914–18). See also HIGH SEAS FLEET. The Japanese fleet, commanded by Admiral *Togo at the battle of *Tsushima in 1905, was also known at that time as the 'grand fleet'.

GRAPNEL, sometimes **GRAPPLE,** a small four-pronged anchor often used as such in dinghies and similar small boats. Grapnels were also used in the sailing navy days to hold a ship alongside an enemy for the purpose of boarding her by hooking them in the rigging or over the *gunwale, and particularly by *fireships when attaching themselves to their victims, but when used for this purpose the four arms were barbed like fishhooks. A grapnel can also be used for dragging the bottom for articles lost overboard.

GRASSE, FRANÇOIS-JOSEPH PAUL, Comte de, Marquis de Tilly (1722–88), was a distinguished French admiral of commanding presence who earned the gratitude of George Washington for the part he played in the War of American Independence (1775–82). Born at Château du Bar, near Grasse, he began his naval service in 1738 and took part in numerous engagements during the War of the Austrian Succession (1739–48) in which he was wounded and taken prisoner, and in the Seven Years War (1756–63). He was promoted to captain in 1762 and was serving in the West Indies when the American colonists rebelled in 1775 but returned to France to take command of the *ship of the line *Intrépide*. When in 1778 France lent her support to the American cause, he was commanding the *Robuste* with the rank of *commodore and took part in the indecisive battle off *Ushant on 27 July of that year. In February 1781 he was nominated commander-in-chief of the Atlantic Fleet with the rank of lieutenant-general and sailed on 23 March for the West Indies. On 5 September off *Chesapeake Bay, he outmanoeuvred a British fleet under Admiral *Graves,

thereby preventing the British relief of Yorktown and ensuring its fall, a decisive action in the context of the war as a whole. But on 12 April 1782, at the battle of the *Saints between his fleet and a British one under Sir George *Rodney, the French were decisively beaten and his flagship, the *Ville de Paris* of 104 guns, was captured. De Grasse was taken prisoner but was returned to France later that year under a *cartel. His efforts to exculpate himself for his defeat were in vain and led to his banishment from court and his retirement from the navy.

GRASS-LINE, a rope made of sisal, not particularly strong but with the property of floating on the surface of the water. It has several uses at sea, particularly in cases of rescue and salvage, when a grass-line floated down across the bows of a disabled ship in rough weather can be easily picked up and used to haul across a towing cable. It is used by naval ships when streaming a *fogbuoy. It is also of value in small sailing or rowing vessels in a following sea; when a length of grass-line is towed astern it acts as a *drogue and steadies the vessel down so that the seas pass under her and do not carry her along dangerously on the crests of the waves. Similarly, when a small boat approaches a shore on which waves are breaking, a grass-line towed astern provides an extra grip on the water and helps to prevent the boat being turned broadside on to the breakers, rolled over, and capsized.

GRATICULE, (1) the network of projected parallels of *latitude and *meridians on a map or chart. **(2)** The scale, traditionally made from filament spun by spiders, inserted into *submarine *periscopes, rangefinders, and marine binoculars.

GRAVE, to, (1) the operation of burning off the accumulated weed growing on a ship's bottom after she has been some time in the water and *paying over her cleaned bottom with tar. Graving a ship was synonymous with *breaming. The word has also given its name to a graving dock, in older days a *dry-dock in which ships were graved. **(2)** The operation of inserting a new piece of timber, known as a graving piece, in place of timber which has rotted in the hull of a wooden vessel.

GRAVES, THOMAS, 1st Baron (1725–1802), British admiral, was the man whose indecisive action with a French fleet off *Chesapeake Bay in 1781 led directly to the final American victory in the War of Independence (1775–82). Born at Thankes, Cornwall, he entered the navy at an early age and saw much action as a junior officer. He reached flag rank in 1779 and in 1781, on the return of Vice Admiral *Arbuthnot, took command of the fleet blockading the east coast of North America during the War of Independence.

One of the functions of this command was to support and succour the British land forces at Yorktown, and Graves left New York in August 1781 with nineteen *ships of the line of this force to keep open communications by sea with this force. But in the meantime a French fleet of twenty-four ships of the line, under command of Admiral de *Grasse, had arrived from France and had reached Chesapeake Bay, effectively preventing all communication with the British Army ashore. When Graves arrived off Chesapeake Bay on 5 September 1781 with his fleet, de Grasse weighed anchor and put to sea. Graves had a chance to engage the French van and centre individually as they came out but hesitated to do so as his fleet had not yet formed a *line of battle as enjoined by the official *Fighting Instructions, a lack of initiative which was to cost Britain dear. After a partial action with little loss or damage on either side, Graves retired four days later with his ships to New York while de Grasse returned to re-occupy Chesapeake Bay. Cut off from all hope of succour from the sea, the British forces at Yorktown were forced to surrender and Britain lost her American colonies.

Graves commanded the *van of the British fleet under Admiral Lord *Howe at the battle of the *Glorious First of June in 1794 in which he distinguished himself and was wounded. For his services on that occasion he was created a peer.

GRAVES, THOMAS (*c.* 1800–53), British naval captain, was a marine surveyor of great distinction. He made many surveys in the Aegean Islands from 1832 to 1850, which were particularly notable for the attention he paid to numerous archaeological sites. His ships during these years were the *Mastiff*, *Beacon*, *Volage*, and lastly the *Spitfire*, and in the *Beacon* he had the help of the naturalist Edward Forbes. Their reports and the artistry of Graves attracted much attention and many fine original documents from his pen are still in the Hydrographic Department's records at the British Admiralty. He was made a Fellow of the Royal Society and of the Royal Geographical Society.

Earlier in his career he had been in the Mediterranean, serving in the *Adventure*, and in 1825–30 was surveying in the Magellan Straits under Philip *King. His final appointment was as port superintendent at Malta where he was assassinated by a local boatman.

GRAVING DOCK, a permanent dock with walls usually constructed of stone or concrete, and sealed in the normal way with a *caisson. The term originates from the old practice of graving a ship's bottom, i.e., burning off the accumulated weed and paying it over with tar. For this purpose, ships were either laid aground at the top of the tide and graved as the tide fell, or docked for graving, in a permanent dock which could be closed after the ship had entered, and pumped dry, the ship's hull resting on a line of *keel blocks. See also BREAM, TO. Today, a graving dock is synonymous with a *dry-dock.

GREAT BRITAIN, the first large iron ship built as a transatlantic liner and the first to be screw-propelled. She was designed by Isambard King-

dom *Brunel and launched at Bristol in 1843. She was 322 feet in length, with a displacement of 3,270 tons, and engines that developed 1,500 horse-power and gave her a speed of 12 knots. As originally designed she had six masts and her hull was divided into six compartments by watertight bulkheads, the first ship to use watertight subdivision as a safety measure. She was also built with *bilge keels and had a chain drive for her *propeller. On her first voyage to New York in 1845 she carried sixty first-class passengers in single staterooms, as well as a full complement of *steerage passengers and 600 tons of cargo. After this crossing she ran ashore on rocks in Dundrum Bay where she lay stranded for eleven months. Her still excellent condition when she was finally salvaged was a convincing tribute to her design and iron construction. Later she was used as a cargo and passenger ship to Australia, on one voyage carrying more than 600 passengers. Finally, after nearly forty years in service, she was damaged in a severe gale off Cape Horn and was beached at Port Stanley, Falkland Islands, and used as a coal hulk.

In 1970 she was raised and placed on a pontoon which was towed first to Montevideo and then to Bristol, where she was successfully placed in the very dock in which she was built and from which she was floated 127 years previously. She is being restored to her original condition and rig as a national monument and an example of iron shipbuilding in its earliest days. See also SHIP.

GREAT CIRCLE, the largest circle which can be inscribed on the surface of a sphere. In terms of the earth, the *equator, and all the *meridians of longitude, since they pass through both poles, are great circles, i.e., the centres of all these circles lie at the centre of the earth. It follows therefore that any circle inscribed around the earth which has its centre at the centre of the earth is a great circle.

These circles are of great importance in the art of *navigation. The shortest distance between any two points on the earth's surface lies along the great circle which passes through them both. Wireless signals, and hence wireless direction-finding bearings, follow the path of great circles. In these connections, see also GNOMONIC CHART, MERCATOR PROJECTION.

GREAT CIRCLE SAILING, a method of navigating a ship along the shortest distance between the point of departure and the point of arrival, subject of course to no land or other navigational hazard lying between the two points. On any sphere, the shortest distance between any two points is the circumference of the circle which joins them and whose centre is at the centre of the sphere. In terms of the earth, this is a *great circle, and if it were possible for a ship to sail along the great circle connecting her point of departure with her point of arrival, she would sail the shortest distance between the two. But unless both these points lie on the equator, which is of course a great circle, and along which she can steer a steady *course due east or west, she cannot do this unless she sails a continuing curve, permanently altering course to keep herself on the great circle.

The theory of great circle sailing has been known and understood almost from the days when it was realized that the earth was a sphere, and it is described in many of the early books written about the art of navigation. But it was of little use to a ship which depended on the wind and her sails to get from one place to another. It was quite impossible for any such ship to adhere to a predetermined course, and she had to make the best of her way according to the vagaries of the wind. But when, during the 19th century, steam began to take the place of sails as the means of ship propulsion and enabled a ship to steer a course irrespective of the wind, the economies of great circle sailing in terms of fuel consumption and time on voyage were quickly appreciated.

One of the properties of a *gnomonic chart is that a great circle appears on it as a straight line, and a ship's navigator, if he wants to plot a great circle track on a *Mercator chart, which he uses for navigation, needs to join his point of departure and his point of arrival by a straight line drawn on a gnomonic chart and then to transfer a series of positions on this straight line, read off in *latitude and *longitude, on to his Mercator chart. These positions will then lie on a curve, which he can sketch in. Although he will not be able to steer his ship along this exact curve, he can approximate to it with a number of short, straight courses, known as *rhumb lines, which are chords of the great circle and which appear as straight lines on a Mercator chart. If he keeps his ship on these straight courses, always altering course to the next one when necessary, he will be keeping his ship as close as conveniently possible to the great circle joining the two points. By this means he is sailing the shortest reasonable course between them, thus saving fuel and time. See NAVIGATION and for illus. see MERCATOR PROJECTION.

GREAT EASTERN, the third of Isambard Kingdom *Brunel's great shipbuilding masterpieces, the others being the *Great Western and *Great Britain, was a ship far in advance of her day. Laid down in 1854 and launched in 1858, at a time when the largest ships afloat were of under 5,000 tons, the Great Eastern had a designed tonnage of 18,914.

The launch of the Great Eastern

Brunel designed her to carry 4,000 passengers (or 10,000 soldiers if used as a troopship) as well as 6,000 tons of cargo to India or Australia without recoaling. An oscillating engine drove a pair of paddle-wheels and a horizontal direct-acting engine drove a propeller. With a length of 692 feet and a beam of 82 feet, she had a top speed of 15 knots. She was the first ship to incorporate a steering engine and also the first to be fitted with a cellular double bottom. This, and her very strong construction, was demonstrated when she escaped with minor damage after running on to a rock.

Construction difficulties and launching delays ruined Brunel's collaborator, John Scott *Russell, in whose yard the ship was built, and caused a breakdown in Brunel's own health from which he died before the *Great Eastern* was able to make her maiden trip. Although Brunel designed her for the Australia or India run, in view of the large numbers of settlers or soldiers going to these countries, she was mistakenly used on the transatlantic run where she proved a failure. She was later converted to a cable carrier and employed in laying four cables across the Atlantic and one from Aden to Bombay.

She was finally beached at New Ferry, Cheshire, in 1888 for breaking up. See also GOOCH, Sir Daniel.

GREAT HARRY, see HENRY GRACE À DIEU.

GREAT WESTERN, the first steamship to ply regularly across the Atlantic, was specially designed by Isambard Kingdom *Brunel for transatlantic operation. On her maiden voyage she arrived at New York on 23 April 1838, fifteen days out from Bristol, having made an average speed of eight knots. Built of wood, she was 236 feet long and of 1,321 tons *burthen. Half her interior space was taken up by her four boilers and the two-cylinder Maudslay side-lever engine which drove paddle-wheels. On this trip twenty-four first-class passengers paid a fare of 35 guineas each. The most important aspect of her passage was that she still had 200 tons of coal remaining in her *bunkers when she reached New York, proving that the old problem of carrying sufficient fuel for long voyages was easy of solution with proper ship design.

GREEK FIRE, a liquid charge made largely from naphtha and thrown from mortars as an offensive weapon against ships, acting as a flaming torch against masts and sails. It was developed in the Byzantine Empire during the 7th century A.D., and came into general use after it was employed with conspicuous success against the Arab fleet which attacked Constantinople in 678, launched from the walls and towers of the city defences. It was then widely adopted as a naval weapon by most of the maritime countries of the Mediterranean, but fell into disuse after the

A galley using greek fire from a blow-tube; detail from a Byzantine MS

introduction of guns as naval weapons, the consequent increase in range at which battles at sea were fought making it useless, since the charge always burned out before it was able to reach its target.

GREEN MEN, the five supernumerary hands which British *whalers fishing in Arctic waters had, by British regulations, to sign on to qualify for the government bounty on *tonnage. A condition of qualification for the bounty was that none of the five had previously been on a voyage to the Arctic. The regulation was in force between approximately 1820 and 1880, a period of fairly intense Arctic exploration, and its purpose was to create a pool of men who had experienced the rigours of an Arctic voyage from which the many expeditions could be manned.

GREENWICH, a metropolitan borough of London, lying a few miles south-east of the city on the River Thames, and the home of the Royal Naval Staff College and the *National Maritime Museum. Greenwich is full of the history of the British Navy. The partially erected royal palace built there by Charles II was assigned by William and Mary to some of the great officers of state for conversion to a hospital for seamen wounded in battle, and to the original block of buildings three others were added to form *Greenwich Royal Hospital, which was opened in 1705.

In the King William block is the great painted hall, now the dining hall of the naval college but formerly a naval picture gallery. In this hall the body of Lord *Nelson lay in state when it

was brought home after the battle of *Trafalgar. Across the road from the college are the buildings which house the National Maritime Museum, part of which was formerly 'Queen's House', built by Charles I for his queen, Henrietta Maria. Behind the museum stretches Greenwich Park, notable for the erection in 1675 of the Royal Observatory at the top of the hill, designed for the advancement of navigation and nautical astronomy (see FLAMSTEED). On the removal of the Royal Observatory to Hurstmonceux, Sussex, in 1965, the building was incorporated into the National Maritime Museum. Through this building passes the *meridian of 0°, from which British and all other foreign geographers reckon the measurement of *longitude.

GREENWICH MEAN TIME (G.M.T.), the present basis of all navigational measurement of time by which the results of observations of heavenly bodies are worked out and the position of a ship fixed at sea. It was not until 1880 that international agreement was reached to accept the *longitude of *Greenwich as the *prime meridian from which all time at sea should be measured; until that year many maritime nations had their own prime meridians, resulting in a variety of navigational times according to the nationality of the particular ship whose position was being fixed. That of France, for example, was the meridian of Paris, that of Spain the Azores. Greenwich Mean Time, therefore, now means the exact time which is being recorded at Greenwich at any moment of local time around the earth. This exact Greenwich time is discoverable on board ship by means of *chronometers, in conjunction with their known *rate of change, and/or by the many periodical time signals broadcast by wireless from a multitude of stations all round the earth.

GREENWICH ROYAL HOSPITAL was built by Wren, Vanbrugh, and Hawksmoor on the site of the old royal palace at Greenwich after a charter had been granted by William and Mary in 1695 to found a hospital for seamen who had been injured or grown old in the service of the crown, as Chelsea Hospital had been instituted for soldiers by Charles II. In practice this meant naval seamen, who contributed sixpence a month from their pay towards the upkeep of the hospital, but merchant seamen also had to contribute sixpence because at that time there was no real distinction between the two navies. See also SIXPENNY OFFICE.

The first pensioners arrived in 1705. By the end of the century they numbered 2,700, but in the 19th century it was found preferable to pay out-pensions, so that the hospital closed in 1869, the buildings being converted to the use of the Royal Naval College, which opened there in 1873.

The buildings are composed of the painted hall (decorated by Sir James Thornhill), the chapel (designed by Stuart), the infirmary (also by Stuart, now the *Dreadnought* Seamen's Hospital), and the blocks built by Wren and his associates known as King William, Queen Mary, Queen Anne, and King Charles (the last built previously by Webb as part of another projected palace and converted by Wren).

The Royal Hospital School, associated with Greenwich Hospital and founded for the education of sons of seamen, was built in the hospital grounds but in 1934 was moved to Holbrook, in Suffolk, when its old premises were converted to the use of the *National Maritime Museum. The Greenwich Hospital Charity continues to make grants to the school from rents received from its widespread properties. See also CHATHAM CHEST.

GREGALE, a Mediterranean wind blowing from the north-east, usually in sudden squalls and particularly associated with Malta and Sicily.

GREIF, a German *armed merchant cruiser of the First World War (1914–18), was formerly the *Guben* of 4,963 tons. She left the River Elbe on 27 February 1916 on a commerce raiding mission in the North Atlantic disguised as the Norwegian *Rena*.

Two days later, about 120 miles west of Sognefjord in Norway, she was stopped by the British armed merchant cruiser *Alcantara* and

opened fire with guns and torpedoes at about 1,200 yards. The *Alcantara* replied and at that range neither could miss. The *Alcantara* was torpedoed and began to sink but kept up her fire so that the *Greif* herself was also soon sinking. The *Andes*, another British armed merchant cruiser, reached the scene, finished off the *Greif*, and picked up 220 survivors of her crew of 306. The *Alcantara*'s crew was rescued by the British destroyer *Munster*.

GRENVILLE, Sir RICHARD (1542–91), English gentleman and property owner whose name is associated with the last fight of the warship *Revenge*, was born at Buckland Abbey, Devon. Little is known of his early life except that he killed a man in a duel, was admitted a student of the Inner Temple in 1559, elected a Member of Parliament in 1563, and took part in the Emperor Maximilian II's campaign against the Turks in 1567. In 1576 he was made sheriff of Cornwall and knighted, and in 1585 he made the first of two voyages to Virginia to further the development of a colony there. By now a wealthy shipowner, he contributed three ships to the fleet being assembled at Plymouth in 1588 under Lord *Howard of Effingham to resist the Spanish *Armada and, after the enemy had been routed in the North Sea, he commanded a small naval force in Irish waters hoping to pick up one or two of the Spanish ships as prizes.

These were the years when the lure of Spanish gold was an irresistible urge to Englishmen to take to the seas, and in 1591, Grenville got himself appointed as vice admiral and second-in-command of a naval force under Lord Thomas Howard which was dispatched to the Azores to lie in wait for a homeward bound Spanish treasure fleet. While awaiting its arrival, the ships' companies became seriously depleted through sickness, Grenville's flagship the *Revenge* being obliged to land over half her crew of 250.

Unknown to the English, a strong Spanish force had been sent out to escort the treasure convoy and when on 30 August the Spanish fleet was reported in the offing, Howard's force was much too weak to give battle. There was just time to embark the sick and escape from the clutches of a greatly superior force. The *Revenge*, having most men ashore, was the last to leave and she was cut off from her consorts. She tried to fight her way through the Spanish fleet but was surrounded. For 15 hours she did battle against the Spaniards, sinking one ship and driving off another with heavy damage. But the odds against her were too great and in the end she was forced to strike her *colours to prevent further slaughter. Grenville, mortally wounded, was taken on board the Spanish flagship *San Pablo* and died three days later; the *Revenge*, shattered in the

Sir Richard Grenville; oil painting by an unknown artist

fight, sank in a gale before she could be taken as a *prize to Spain. The action is immortalized in Tennyson's 'The Last Fight of the *Revenge*', first published in his *Ballads and other Poems* (1880).

A. L. Rowse, *Sir Richard Grenville* (1937).

'GRETA GARBO', the slang name which was given to a quadrilateral or *double-clewed jib used in a few large racing yachts around the years 1934 and 1935. See also AMERICA'S CUP, ENDEAVOUR.

GRID or **GRIDIRON**, a stage usually in a boat-builder's yard on the water's edge, formed by cross beams, which is above water at low tide. Flat-bottomed vessels, particularly *barges and the like, are floated over it at high water and secured, and as the tide ebbs the vessel rests on the grid where, at low water, her bottom is exposed for repairs or cleaning.

GRIFFITHS, MAURICE WALTER (1902–), British yacht designer, editor, and author, was born in London and became a journalist after spending two years with a firm of estate agents. He was editor of *Yacht Sales and Charters*, 1925–6, and of *Yachting Monthly* from 1926 until his retirement in 1967. He started designing yachts in 1928, mainly of a sturdy cruising type ranging from 5 to 30 tons, but specialized in shoal draught *centreboarders. He was one of the pioneer designers from 1950 onwards in developing the twin *bilge keel type, and among other designs produced, in conjunction with the *Yachting Monthly*, the 24-ft (7·3 m) and 26-ft (7·9 m) *Eventide* and 30-ft (9·1 m) *Waterwitch* bilge keel classes, of which more than 700 boats have been built. He served in the *R.N.V.R. during the Second World War and was decorated for the clearance of magnetic *mines. He is the author of *Yachting on a Small Income* (1924), *The Magic of the Swatchways* (1932), *Ten Small Yachts* (1933), *Little Ships and Shoal Waters* (1937), *Post-War Yachting* (1946), *Dream Ships* (1949), *Every Man's Yachting* (1952), *Sailing* (1966), *Swatchways and Little Ships* (1971), together with novels *Dempster and Son* (1938), *No Southern Gentleman* (1939), and *Sands of Sylt* (1945).

GRIPE, to, the tendency of a sailing vessel to come up into the wind when sailing *close-hauled, and thus to carry too much weather *helm to correct this tendency. It is sometimes an effect of the overall *trim of the vessel and if so can be reduced by lightening the vessel forward or trimming down aft to make her stern draw deeper into the water. This is of course normally done by the movement of *ballast from forward to aft. But more usually it is the effect of an ill-balanced *hull, too bluff a bow causing an excessive bow-wave, a short *run aft causing *drag or turbulence. An unbalanced rig can also cause a vessel to gripe, which can be corrected by reducing the fore canvas. In cases where griping is more or less built into the design, there is little that can be done to remove it.

GRIPES, broad plaited bands of small rope used to secure boats on deck when at sea and to hold a ship's lifeboats steady against the *davits. For boats normally stowed on deck the gripes are secured to ringbolts on the deck, passed over the boat, and set up on the other side by lanyards. When securing a lifeboat, the gripes are made fast to the tops of the davits and crossed diagonally outside the boat before being secured to the bottom of the other davit.

GROG, a dilution of rum with water. In 1687, following the conquest of Jamaica, rum was introduced into the Royal Navy in place of brandy as a daily ration. By an order from Admiral *Vernon in 1740, with a view to reducing the incidence of drunkenness in his fleet, the ration of one pint of neat rum a day for men and half a pint for boys was diluted by adding a quart of water. This was issued in two halves, to the tune of 'Nancy Dawson', at a *scuttle butt at noon and 6.0 p.m. daily. Vernon's nickname in the fleet was 'Old Grogram', from the material of which his boat cloak was made, and the watered-down rum was speedily given the name 'grog'. The word groggy is derived from the effects of too large an intake of the spirit. The evening issue of grog was abolished in the Royal Navy in 1824 and the daily ration reduced to one gill in 1850. The issue of rum to officers was stopped in 1881, the popularity of gin having replaced that of rum among them. The issue to warrant officers ceased in 1918. Chief and *petty officers drew their rum undiluted. For all other ratings the grog ration was one and a half gills of water to half a gill of rum until 1970, when the issue of rum was totally discontinued in the British Navy.

'GROG-BLOSSOM', the sailor's name for a red nose or an inflamed pimple.

GROG-TUB, a *scuttle-butt, or cut-down cask, traditionally used in the British Navy for the daily issue of the watered-down rum, or *grog, ration to seamen. The mixture of three parts of water to one part of rum in order to form grog was always made in the presence of an officer to protect seamen from being given a short allowance of rum by adding too much water, a practice by which some of the old-time *pursers used to enrich themselves. The words God Save the King (or Queen) were traditionally fixed to the grog-tub in large brass letters. Any grog left over was, by order, poured into the *scuppers so that it should run overboard and not be used to supplement the daily ration or consumed by persons who did not qualify for the daily issue.

GROMET or **GRUMMETT,** from the Low Latin *gromettus*, a youth or servant in the British Navy. Gromets ranked above ship's boys and below ordinary seamen. They formed a regular part of a ship's company until in the 18th century they were rated as volunteers, 2nd class. In the days of the *Cinque Ports navies until about 1500, gromets were the boys who tended the ships while in harbour.

GROMMET (pron. grummet), a ring formed by laying up a single *strand of rope three times, and used originally to fasten the upper edge or *luff of a sail to its stay. Its place for this purpose has been taken by the modern spring-loaded *hank or clip-hook. Grommets have various other uses on board ship and, when the two sides of one are brought together by a *serving, it forms a couple of connected *eyes, always a useful article to have available on deck. In boat-work grommets are used to hold the oars to *thole pins when rowing.

GRÖNER, ERICH (1901–65), German marine archaeologist and author, volunteered for service with the naval air arm in 1918. Subsequently he studied political economy. He also became interested in warship and merchant-ship construction and the information obtainable from photographs of them. When the German Navy and air force were being reformed during 1929–30, both made much use of his specialized knowledge, and in 1931 he collaborated with Alexander Bredt in the production of a book entitled *Die Deutsches Kriegsschiffe* (German Warships). When Bredt became editor of Weyer's *Flottentaschenbuch* in 1932 Gröner developed his technique for the production of scale drawings and silhouettes of warships for this book of reference and his system was subsequently adopted for recognition handbooks in the navy and air force. During the Second World War several editions were produced of his invaluable handbook *Die Handelsflotten der Welt* (Merchant Fleets of the World), for use by *U-boats and other ships in identifying their victims. In 1945 his collection of photographs fell into Russian hands, but he later managed largely to reconstitute it. He served on the staff of the *Marine Rundschau* where his expert knowledge was of great value. He had brought *Die Deutsches Kriegsschiffe* up to date before his death and his friends, appreciating its historical value, arranged for its publication in two volumes, now universally recognized as very reliable reference books.

GROOS, OTTO (1882–1970), German naval officer and naval historian, joined the Imperial German Navy in 1900. He served throughout the First World War (1914–18), being navigating officer of the *battle-cruiser *Von der Tann* at the battle of *Jutland. In 1917 he was appointed to the staff of the 4th Scouting Group. After the war he was chosen to write the official history of the war in the North Sea. Between 1922 and 1925 he produced five volumes covering the period from August 1914 to June 1916 which earned him a doctorate of philology. Later he commanded the cadet training *cruiser *Hamburg* during a world cruise. In 1929 he published a book on naval strategy entitled *Seekriegslehren in Lichte des Weltkrieges* (Lessons of Sea Warfare in the Light of the World War) to which Grand Admiral von *Tirpitz contributed an introduction and which is highly regarded. He became an instructor at the newly formed Wehrmacht Academy in 1935 and during the Second World War he was head of a special staff set up to deal with economic warfare.

GROSS REGISTER TONNAGE, see TONNAGE.

GROUND TACKLE, a general term embracing all the gear (*anchors, *cables, etc.) carried by a ship to enable her to anchor or to *moor. By some it is also held to include permanent moorings for ships and smaller vessels including *trots, but more usually the term refers only to a vessel's own means of anchoring.

GROUND TIER, the lowest tier of casks stowed in the holds of a ship. Before the days of refrigeration and fresh water tanks, most of the provisions carried for a voyage (beef, pork, flour, etc., and particularly fresh water) had to be carried in casks, and in view of the very long periods during which a ship under sail alone might remain at sea in those days, sufficient provisions for six months were usually carried. Several tiers of casks were necessary to carry this amount, and they were known as ground, second, third, etc., to the top tier.

GROUP, a navigational term which indicates the number of exposures of a fixed navigational light, whether from *lighthouse, *lightship, or lighted *buoy, in each cycle of operation. See CHARACTERISTICS.

GROW, to, the term used of an *anchor *cable referring to the direction in which it lies in relation to the ship when a ship is at anchor, e.g., 'the cable grow?', a frequent question from the bridge forward on the starboard side. 'How does the cable grow?, a frequent question from the bridge of a ship to the officer in charge of the *forecastle when weighing anchor, for a ship pulls herself up to her anchor when it is being weighed and it is necessary for the navigator or pilot to know where her bows will be when the anchor is *a-trip.

GROWLER, a piece of low-lying ice floating in the sea in high northern or southern *latitudes which is difficult to see from a ship approaching it because of its dark colour. Growlers are formed of blocks of ice which have broken away from the ice pack or from icebergs, and have been blown or have drifted clear.

GUADALCANAL, BATTLE OF, one of the decisive naval engagements of the Second World War, took place in the south-west Pacific Ocean at the crisis of the struggle for the island of that name in the Solomons group, when American surface forces clashed with Japanese squadrons advancing through the night to bombard Henderson Airfield, held by the Americans, and to cover the landing of military reinforcements. With American aircraft taking on the opposition during daylight, the battle continued intermittently from soon after midnight on 12/13 November 1942, when the first of the night surface actions developed, until the morning of the 15th.

In the first of these surface actions an American force of cruisers and destroyers, which had successfully escorted a convoy of troopships to and from Guadalcanal, was steaming through the night in single line ahead when a surface warning *radar indicated the approach of a Japanese force at a range of some fifteen miles. This was composed of two *battleships, one cruiser, and fourteen destroyers, disposed in small groups as a screen. Lacking radar, their first intimation of the presence of an enemy was when the leading destroyers on either side came into sight of one another and altered course to avoid collision. The Americans, however, failed to profit by their radar advantage. Japanese night-fighting skill brought the American ships under a storm of fire and their destroyers launched a mass torpedo attack before the first American gun opened fire. The action therefore resolved itself into a confused mêlée in which four American destroyers were sunk and two others severely damaged, as also were all the cruisers of which one was later scuttled. On the Japanese side two destroyers were sunk and three damaged, and one battleship was so crippled that daylight revealed her limping slowly away to the north of Savo Island where, after suffering numerous air attacks, she was scuttled.

The next Japanese bombardment force of cruisers and destroyers arrived unopposed off Henderson Field during the night of 13/14 November; their gunfire failed to wreck the airstrip and at daylight aircraft from the field as well as from the aircraft carrier *Enterprise*, operating south of the island, sank one and damaged three of the cruisers. During that day aircraft also continuously harassed a Japanese convoy of eleven transports making for Guadalcanal, destroying seven of them; the remaining four, however, pressed doggedly on.

Meanwhile a further Japanese bombardment force had been assembled. As it steamed through the night of 14/15 November bound for Guadalcanal, it sighted and manoeuvred to engage an American squadron which had been deployed in opposition. When the American destroyers in the van clashed with their Japanese opposite numbers, two of the American destroyers were quickly sunk and another two crippled; of the Japanese force one destroyer was so damaged that she had later to be scuttled.

The Japanese force now entered the scene at the moment that one of the American battleships, with an electric failure, sheered blindly out of the line. As many as thirty-four torpedoes were fired at her without securing a hit, but she was taken under a punishing fire by the Japanese heavy ships. Rescue came when another American battleship's radar-controlled main armament of 16-inch guns smothered one of the Japanese battleships, reducing her to a motionless wreck eventually to be scuttled.

The Japanese survivors retired, abandoning their planned bombardment. Massed air attacks on the four surviving Japanese transports which were unloading on the beaches caused fearful slaughter, destroyed most of the stores and ammunition landed, and brought the long-drawn battle to an end on the morning of 15 November. In spite of the heavy losses suffered by the Americans, the long battle had, in fact, finally secured their hold on the island and its vital air strip.

GUARDA-COSTA, the Spanish name for their coastguard vessels in the West Indies during the 17th century charged with preventing all foreign trade to the islands, at that time part of the Spanish empire and preserved as a trading monopoly by Spain. They were held in great detestation by ships of other nations attempting to open up a trade to the islands, not so much for their role of attempting to stop the trade as for the extreme cruelty with which their officers treated all foreign seamen who fell into their hands. It was the action of Spanish guarda-costa officers against the captain of a British merchant ship which was the ostensible reason for the outbreak of the War of Jenkins's Ear in 1739 between Britain and Spain, which developed into the War of the Austrian Succession (1739–48). See also ASIENTO in regard to the trade in slaves from Africa to the West Indies during this period.

GUARDRAIL, the upper deck rail along both sides of a vessel to prevent anyone on board from falling overboard. In smaller ships they are usually of wire, supported at intervals by *stanchions and secured at each end to the foremost and aftermost stanchion by small Senhouse slips. In larger vessels they are usually solid metal bars supported by the stanchions. Ships with *bulwarks do not need a guardrail as the bulwark takes its place.

GUARD-SHIP, a warship stationed at a port to act as a guard; in earlier days in the British Navy it was the ship in which men brought in by the *press were received. It was usually the flagship of the port admiral. A guard-boat is a boat which goes the round of the fleet at night to ensure that a proper watch is kept on all ships. As it approaches each ship it is hailed by the watch on deck; failure to do so indicates a slack watch and trouble usually follows.

GUDGEON, orig. **GOOGING,** the metal plate carrying an eye bolted on to the *sternpost of a vessel which takes the *pintle of the *rudder to allow it free movement in either direction in those vessels in which the rudder is hung either from the sternpost or the *transom. Normally two gudgeons and two pintles are fitted to hold a rudder steady. In almost all ships today, even the smallest, a balanced rudder is fitted and so pintles and gudgeons are not required, since the rudder is fixed to a rudder post which rises through the vessel's *counter. Gudgeons and pintles are today used only in boats and very small yachts. The main value of this fitting, apart from its simplicity, is that the rudder can be easily unshipped when not in use.

GUDIN, JEAN ANTOINE THÉODORE, Baron (1802–80), French marine painter, was born in Paris and studied at the École des Beaux Arts. He was commissioned by the Royal household to paint a series of ninety marine pictures for the galleries of the Palace of Versailles, and this was followed by a further commission from the Duc d'Orléans. Many of his marine pictures were of battle scenes or storms at sea, and he is represented in the Wallace Collection in London by his picture 'Tempête', an example of his best period.

GUERRE DE COURSE, a term originally accepted in international maritime law to indicate the practice of *privateering, or the right in wartime of individual owners of ships to arm them and proceed against the merchant ships of an enemy power when licensed to do so by an official *letter of marque. In all maritime wars up to the mid-19th century, the merchant shipping of belligerent powers suffered severe losses under the *guerre de course*, and it was brought to an end by international agreement at the *Declaration of Paris in 1856, only the U.S.A. refusing to sign the declaration. U.S. merchant shipping, as a result, suffered severe loss from the *guerre de course* during the Civil War, 1861–5.

A form of *guerre de course* was reinstated at the *Hague Convention of 1907 when it was agreed among the signatories of the Convention that merchant ships of a belligerent power could be taken up for war service and fitted out with guns and *torpedoes as *armed merchant cruisers. This differed from the proper meaning of the term in that such ships had to be manned by the navy of the belligerent power and fly the naval *ensign. It was not a return to privateering and the letter of marque, under which private owners of ships were licensed to operate their vessels as warships for private gain. Nevertheless, the result was much the same in so far as commerce-raiding was concerned.

The term was revived in this later sense in British discussions of her naval policy before the First World War (1914–18) for possible commerce-raiding by enemy warships which, it was urged, the Royal Navy ought to be equipped to defeat in contrast to the fleet actions towards which most naval policy seemed to be directed. It remained a term of theory and was not applied to actual commerce-raiding operations.

GUEST-ROPE, a rope thrown to a boat from a ship, either to tow her or to enable her to make fast alongside; it is also sometimes known as a guess-rope or gift-rope.

GUEYDON, LOUIS HENRI, Comte de (1809–86), French naval officer, was born at Granville and entered the navy in 1825. He was present at the capture of St. Jean d'Ulloa, was governor of Martinique from 1853 to 1855 and governor-general of Algeria in 1871–2. He was a student of naval warfare and wrote a number of penetrating books on the subject, of which the best known today are *The Truth about the Navy* (1849) and *Naval Tactics* (1868).

GUFAH or **GOPHER,** a *coracle, shaped like a cauldron and constructed of dried reeds coated with bitumen, indigenous to the River Tigris. They vary in size from 4 to 12 feet in diameter. In Genesis 6:14, Noah is told to make an *ark of gopher wood in which to escape the coming flood. This may be a mistranslation from the original Hebrew and should possibly read 'an ark gopher of wood'. No wooden vessel, even an ark, is likely to be built of only one species of wood, and a gopher is a type of vessel which might well have been used as the basic design of the ark.

GUICHEN, LUC-URBAIN DU BOUËXIC, Comte de (1712–90), French admiral, entered the navy in 1730 and was recognized as a coming man when, in command of the *frigate *Sirène* in 1748, he captured a number of English *privateers off San Domingo. In 1755 he took part in the expedition to Canada of which Admiral *Boscawen captured two ships, an act of aggression which virtually started the Seven Years War (1756–63), and he commanded a division of the French fleet at the battle of *Ushant on 27 July 1778. In February 1780, with sixteen *ships of the line, he escorted a convoy of eighty-three merchant ships with 4,000 troops embarked to the West Indies, where he was joined by the fleet under Admiral de *Grasse. After a fierce but indecisive encounter with a British fleet under Admiral *Rodney off Martinique on 17 April, followed by two equally indecisive skirmishes, he returned with his fleet to Europe. In 1781 he again sailed for America, escorting a large convoy, but fell in with a British squadron under Admiral *Kempenfelt which captured twenty ships of the convoy and scattered the rest. His last naval action was the attempt in 1782 to prevent a large British convoy, escorted by Lord *Howe, reaching Gibraltar, which had been under siege for three years, but in this, too, he was unsuccessful.

GULF STREAM, The, sometimes also known as the North Equatorial Current. It starts in the Caribbean Sea where the water, expanded by the heat, escapes into the Gulf of Mexico. Here it is warmed still further and expands to a vast bulk, escaping through the Florida Straits and to the eastward of the *Grand Banks off Newfoundland, continuing in great depth across the North Atlantic to northern Europe. Its warmth ensures a temperate climate in all countries which lie in its path. Its velocity is calculated at about 80 miles a day. A counter current flows to the south of it westward across the Atlantic to the Caribbean Sea. See also CURRENT.

GULL, to, the action of the pin of a *block when it wears away the *sheave, round which the rope of a tackle revolves. When the sheave begins to wobble in the block because of wear by the pin, it is called gulling. Similarly, when the *yards of a square-rigged ship rubbed up against the mast, they were said to gull the mast.

GUN TACKLE, a *tackle comprising a rope rove through two single *blocks with the standing part of the rope made fast to the *strop of one of the blocks. It multiplies the power exerted on the fall of the tackle by three when rove to *advantage. Its original use was to run out a gun after it had been loaded so that the muzzle projected through the gunport ready for firing, but being a useful tackle for many purposes it is still widely used in ships and yachts. See also PURCHASE.

GUNBOAT, a small lightly armed vessel used in most navies for a variety of war or policing duties, particularly in rivers and on shallow coasts which precluded the use of larger warships. Many of the older river gunboats, used for police duties in such places as the Yangtse River and the Persian Gulf, were built with stern-wheels in place of propellers so that they could operate in areas where the depth of water only exceeded the *draught of the vessel by an inch or two. See also STERN-WHEELER. During the First World War (1914–18), old, shallow-draught vessels armed with one medium-*calibre gun were employed as gunboats to bombard shore positions, and in the Second World War *motor gunboats, driven by three 12-cylinder petrol engines, often with a stepped hull to enable a high speed to be obtained and armed with Oerlikon guns, were used to operate against enemy convoys proceeding close inshore, or against similar enemy craft. Although gunboats have today no place in the world's larger navies they are included in some of the smaller navies, particularly those with policing responsibilities in a largely riverine coastline.

GUNDALOW or **GUNDELO,** a form of river *barge, now obsolete, in the U.S.A. with a high curved bow and a large *lateen mainsail set on a short, stumpy mast. The lateen yard was very high in the peak and the lower end was heavily weighted and balanced so that it could easily be lowered on deck. The small offshore fishing *schooners of Maine, with characteristic high sterns, were also known as gundalows. They, too, are now obsolete.

GUNNER'S DAUGHTER, the name of the gun to which the boys serving in a warship of the British Navy were 'married', or tied, when receiving punishment. Captain *Boteler, in his *Six Dialogues about Sea Services*, published in 1685, notes that 'the waggery and idleness of the ship's boys is paid by the *Boatswain with a rod. And commonly this execution is done upon the

Monday mornings, and is so frequently in use that mere seamen and sailors believe in good earnest that they shall not have a fair wind until the poor boys be duly brought to the chest; that is, be whipped every Monday morning.'

GUNNERY, NAVAL, the art of firing to the greatest effect with guns mounted in ships. Until about 1850, the naval gun in almost universal use was the cannon, a muzzle-loading smooth bore which fired a solid ball with a charge of gunpowder for a maximum distance of about a mile, though the effective range, at which most ships preferred to fight, was known as half pistol shot, or about 100 yards. The method of fire in battle was preferably the broadside, as this threw out the greatest weight of shot in a simultaneous discharge and was best calculated to inflict the maximum damage to an enemy ship. There were minor improvements made from time to time in the art of gunnery, such as the provision of hand-spikes in ships with which to train the gun carriages through a few degrees of arc, though always very approximately; the invention of the goose-quill tube by Sir Charles *Douglas to replace the loose powder in the vents of cannon as a more reliable means of firing the gun; and so on. For the remainder, it was constant gun drill which bore the responsibility for the increase in efficiency.

The technical advances of the half-century 1850–1900 revolutionized the art of naval gunnery, particularly the changes from solid shot to explosive shell, from smooth bore to rifled bore, from muzzle-loading to breech-loading with the interrupted thread breech block, and from the charge of gunpowder to that of cordite. Yet the great advances which were made possible by these technological advances, and particularly by radical improvements in the mounting of guns, in general failed to materialize. The cause of this, particularly in the British Navy, was the feeling of security engendered by the long years of peace of the 19th century which produced a pronounced lack of incentive to improve gunnery techniques. There was also a strong feeling throughout the British Navy that 'what was good enough for *Nelson is good enough for us', which bred apathy in regard to new techniques and reluctance to take them seriously. A result of this feeling was that all gunnery drills and practices were woefully scamped. Among the few men of this period who worked for improvements in this field were Captain Cowper *Coles, with his passionate advocacy of the turret ship as the supreme mistress of the seas, and the two great gunnery enthusiasts of the end of the century, Admiral Sir John *Fisher and Captain Percy *Scott who, by their insistence on adequate training in gunnery, increased within ten years the range of accurate naval gunnery

Gunnery practice on board H.M.S. Britannia; *engraving from the* Illustrated London News, *1859*

from 2,000 to 10,000 yards and the speed of firing from one round in three minutes to two rounds in one minute with the heaviest guns.

The launch of the *Dreadnought in 1906, the first all-big-gun *battleship with her implied reliance on pure gunnery as the supreme naval weapon of destruction, quickened the pace of improvement. Arthur *Pollen and Captain Frederic *Dreyer took it a great step further with their range and speed plotting machines, and the invention of the *director sight, by which all the guns of a ship were laid, trained, and fired from a single observation position placed high above funnel and gun smoke, brought a new accuracy in firing until this, in its turn, was superseded by the invention of *radar, with its ability to detect ranges far more exactly than the most accurate rangefinder, at night or in fog as well as in daylight. From there it was but a step to the fully automatic gun of today which loads, trains, lays, and fires itself with supreme accuracy. See also GUNS, NAVAL.

GUNPORT, the square hole cut in the side of wooden men-of-war during the years of sail through which the broadside guns were fired. Each gun had its own port, and they lined the gundecks at the height of the muzzle of the gun, being closed with a port-lid, hinged on the top, when not in use. Until about the Revolutionary War with France (1793–1801) the outside of the port-lid in the British Navy was painted the same colour as the outside of the ship; the inside was red, as also were the sides of the ship and, in a few cases, a strip of the gundecks in the vicinity

of the guns as well; the reason, it was said, being that any blood spilled in action would not show against the red paint and thus have a depressing effect on the gun crews. During the Napoleonic War (1803–15) the fashion changed, and port-lids were painted in contrasting colours on the outside, usually black against the white or yellow *wales level with the gundecks. This was known in the British Navy as 'Nelson fashion', and was introduced around the period of the battle of *Trafalgar, giving the familiar chequer pattern of British *ships of the line. At about the same time, the inside colour was changed to yellow.

GUNROOM, originally a compartment on the lower gundeck of a sailing man-of-war which was used as a mess by the junior *midshipmen. In more modern warships the gunroom, while still the mess of sub-lieutenants and midshipmen, was no longer located in the deep bowels of the ship but brought up to the main deck. In the British Navy ships no longer carry a sufficient number of midshipmen to justify the maintenance of a gunroom as a junior mess such as used to exist in *battleships, *cruisers, etc.

GUNS, NAVAL. Authorities differ regarding the date at which cannon were first mounted on board ships, confusion often arising from differences of interpretation of medieval Latin phrases used by scholars and historians with no personal knowledge of weapons. The first veritable record is probably that which states that guns made in Tournai were aboard the ships that Louis de Mâle sent to attack Antwerp in 1336.

The early guns were either cast in bronze—a technique long known and used for making church bells—or were made of wrought iron. The latter were built up from bars of iron welded into crude tubes and strengthened by hoops shrunk on to the outside. A bronze cylinder might be inserted at the breech end to serve as a powder chamber. Cast iron, however, replaced wrought iron for all but the largest pieces during the 16th century, bronze being too expensive when guns were manufactured in thousands.

A great many sizes and types of gun were made in a process of continuous development during the 15th and 16th centuries, ranging from the 'whole' cannon firing a ball of more than 70 lb weight down to the 'smeriglio' or * 'robinet', firing a shot of between $\frac{1}{2}$ and 1 lb. A multiplicity of names which were sometimes transferred from one type of gun to another were used, such as base, * basilisk, bombard, culverin, perier, drake, falcon, * murderer, minion, saker, passavolante, * serpentine, sling, mortar, trabucchio, and others.

The guns of the 15th and 16th centuries can be broadly grouped into four classes:

a, *the cannon.* This was of large calibre and medium length and range. Its two principal subtypes were the 'whole' cannon, of approximately 7-in. calibre, 11 ft in length, and firing a 50-lb ball; and the 'demi-cannon' of much the same length, but of 6-in. calibre and firing a 32-lb shot.

b, *the culverin.* This was of smaller calibre relative to its length and therefore of greater range. It was subdivided into:

(i) the culverin, a typical example of which would be of 5-in. calibre and firing a 17-lb shot; its length might vary greatly between 13 ft for a bow chaser and 8 or 9 ft for a broadside gun.

(ii) the demi-culverin, a 9-pounder of 4-in. calibre and up to 11 ft in length.

(iii) the saker, a 5-pounder of 3-in. calibre and some 9 ft long.

(iv) the minion, a 4-pounder of 3-in. calibre and also some 9 ft in length.

(v) the falcon and falconet, which were 2- to 3-pounders and 1- to 2-pounders respectively.

c, *the perier or cannon-perier.* This was a short-barrelled gun firing a medium-sized stone shot for a comparatively short distance. A typical example would have been an 8-in. gun, only 5 ft long, firing a 24-lb stone shot to a maximum range of some 1,600 yards, as compared to about 2,500 yards of the culverin and 1,700 yards of the demi-cannon.

d, *the mortar.* This was an even shorter gun, the original type of which was of conical bore, resembling an apothecary's mortar. Ship-borne mortars of this date fired quantities of small pieces of iron or stone or bullets, either loose or made up in linen or leather bags, their target being would-be boarders on the enemy's deck.

The culverin type of gun was preferred for arming ships during the 16th century rather than the heavy and comparatively unwieldy cannon and demi-cannon. The steady improvement in the quality and power of gunpowder and quicker combustion, together with increasing accuracy in the manufacture of the guns themselves, permitted smaller charges to be used and the length of the culverin to be reduced. At the same time naval guns were mounted on the low wooden carriages running on small, solid, wooden wheels or trucks which they were to retain thereafter, in place of the two or four-wheeled, higher carriages or, sometimes, timber scaffolds on which they were mounted in the early Tudor ships.

The development in the late 16th century by the English and the Dutch of the * galleon, with sides pierced for gunports, brought about a new form of naval warfare, relying upon comparatively long-range broadside fire instead of boarding. Its effectiveness was first notably demonstrated in the defeat by the English fleet of the Spanish *Armada in 1588.

With further improvement in the quality of powder during the 17th century, guns were again shortened, permitting greater calibres for the same weight. Even such large pieces as the 'cannon-royal', weighing some 8,000 lb and firing a 66-lb shot, were sometimes mounted. By the end of the period, however, the usual sizes were the 42-pounder on the lower decks and the 24-pounder on the upper gundecks. The medieval names were now abandoned and the guns identified simply by the weight of the shot they fired.

Except for the addition of the carronade about 1779, naval guns changed very little from this time until the industrial revolution, though refinements were made in the arrangements for absorbing the recoil, and the flint-lock was introduced in place of the slowmatch and linstock.

The carronade, so named after the Carron Iron Founding and Shipping Company where it was invented, was a very short, light carriage gun making use of a small propellant charge to fire a relatively heavy shot for a limited range. It commended itself to the Royal Navy during the French wars of the late 18th and early 19th centuries as an auxiliary to the main armament for use in the yard-arm to yard-arm type of fight the British always aspired to bring about. It first proved itself in Lord * Rodney's victory of the * Saints in 1782 and soon became a regular feature of all British men-of-war, being later copied by the French. It was known in the British Navy as a 'smasher'.

When the British lost sight of its original purpose as an auxiliary weapon, however, and took to equipping ships with it as their primary armament, its inherent weakness of lack of range was revealed in combat with American ships in the war of 1812, leading to a number of humiliating British defeats.

The introduction of *armour to warships and the development of explosive shells in the middle of the 19th century brought about the first major changes to the naval gun since Tudor times. Bigger guns, able to penetrate the early wrought-iron armour, were answered by thicker armour. A continuous process of competition between the means of attack and defence developed, culminating by 1876 in iron armour 20 inches thick, and rifled guns of 17·7 inches calibre, weighing 110 tons.

The development of face-hardened, steel armour plate on the one hand and, on the other, of improved propellants, higher muzzle velocity, and armour-piercing shells enabled the dimensions of both armour and guns to be reduced, though the competition between the two began again and continued until the self-propelled missile came largely to supersede the big gun. By that time, guns of 18·1-in. calibre, capable of firing shells weighing more than a ton for over 16 sea miles, had been mounted in *battleships, and the thickness of armour had again increased to 16 inches or more.

It was not mainly in their size, however, that guns were transformed during the 19th century. Rifling of barrels and the substitution of improved propellants such as cordite vastly increased their range and accuracy. The invention of efficient breech-loading mechanisms, employing the interrupted thread breech-block or the sliding wedge, improved their rate of fire, particularly when quick-firing breech mechanisms were invented, enabling the breech to be opened or shut by the single motion of a lever.

Smaller guns varying in bore from 3 inches to 8 inches formed the armament of smaller ships such as *cruisers and *destroyers and were mounted in battleships as secondary armament for protection against destroyers delivering *torpedo attacks or, on high-angle mountings, against attacking aircraft.

Guns of both main and secondary armaments were hydraulically or electrically operated and mounted in revolving turret-barbettes. In more recent times guns up to 8-in. calibre have been made fully automatic, being loaded, aimed, and fired entirely mechanically without the aid of any crew.

The further development of the guided missile seems certain soon to supersede guns of all calibres in men-of-war; but this has not yet entirely come about. See also GUNNERY, Naval.

GUNTER RIG, a development of the *lugsail rig in which the sail is cut with a very short *luff and very long *leech. The *head of the sail is laced to a *yard, which when fully hoisted, and with the *tack of the sail *bowsed hard down,

lies virtually as an extension of the mast, making the sail in effect very similar to a *Bermuda sail. It is a rig which is included in the generic term of *standing lug.

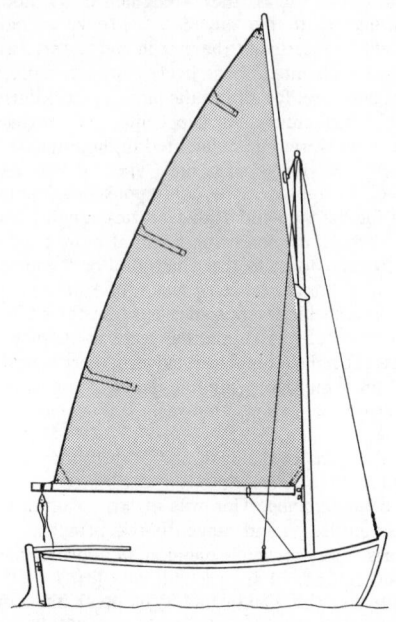

Typical gunter rig

GUNWALE (pron. gunnel), **(1)** a piece of timber going round the upper *sheer strake of a boat to bind in the top work. **(2)** The plank which covers the heads of the *timbers in a wooden ship. **(3)** In modern terms, the projection above the upper deck level of the two sides of a small vessel as a means of preventing the influx of seawater when the vessel heels over.

GUY, (1) a rope or *tackle used to control the lateral movement of a *derrick. Normally four guys are attached to the moving end of a main derrick, two to direct it forward on the port or starboard side, known as the port fore and starboard fore guys, and two to direct it aft on the port or starboard sides, known as the port after and starboard after guys. **(2)** A rope or wire led forward from a *boom as part of the *running rigging of a fore-and-aft rigged vessel. In sailing yachts a guy, called a boom guy, may be rigged between the end of the boom and a point well forward when running before the wind, particularly in light winds or when the yacht is *rolling in a swell, to prevent the *sheet from going slack and the boom swinging excessively; a *spinnaker boom nearly always needs a boom guy (or spinnaker guy) because this sail is less under control by the sheet than a mainsail.

'**GUZ'**, the slang name in the British Navy for the naval base of Devonport at Plymouth, Devon. The origin of the name is not easy to establish, but is said to come from the fact that men from the West Country districts of England are great eaters, or guzzlers. According to another theory it is called GUZ because these were the prefix letters of the Devonport Barracks radio call sign.

GUZZWELL, JOHN (*c.* 1930–   ), British yachtsman, was taken by his parents, while still an infant, to South Africa in *Our Boy*, a 52-ft (15·8 m) *ketch which his father had had built for ocean cruising. He emigrated as a young man to British Columbia, and saved enough money to build a small boat for ocean cruising. The result was *Trekka*, a 20-ft (6·1 m) *yawl with a reverse or hogged *sheer, which he built himself in 1954–5 to designs prepared for him by Laurent *Giles. In this tiny yawl he left Victoria, British Columbia, in July 1955 and sailed alone to Hawaii, Russell in New Zealand, Thursday Island off the Queensland coast, Mauritius, Durban, the Panama Canal, Hawaii again, and back to Victoria in just over four years. *Trekka*, only 18½ ft (5·6 m) on the waterline, was the smallest boat of any kind to have sailed round the world.

During the voyage, in 1957, he met Miles and Beryl *Smeeton and their young daughter Clio in *Tzu Hang*, and agreed to leave *Trekka* in port for the time being and help crew the Smeetons on their way round Cape Horn from west to east. He was aboard, therefore, when *Tzu Hang* was rolled over and dismasted off the pitch of the Horn by giant seas, and by superb seamanship they managed to get a jury rig set and eventually reached a Chilean port. For this feat he was awarded jointly with the Smeetons the Royal Cruising Club's Seamanship Medal. In 1965–8 he built a larger yacht, *Treasure*, a 40-ft *cutter, in which he sailed with his wife and children to Sydney, New South Wales. He is the author of *Trekka Round the World*.

GYASSI or **GAIASSA**, the traditional sail trading vessel of the upper Nile. They were not unlike the *nugger of the lower Nile but mostly had only one mast and spread a very large *lateen sail on a yard twice as long as the mast and as long as or longer than the vessel herself. Some of the larger gyassis carried two masts with normal lateen sails. They were all flat-bottomed with broad, square sterns and large *rudders like barn doors.

GYBE, or **JIBE, to,** the action when *wearing a sailing vessel at the moment when the *boom of the mainsail swings across as the wind crosses the stern. The word can also be used as a noun, e.g., a ship can make a gybe.

The stronger the wind, and the greater the area of the mainsail and weight of the main boom, the more strain a gybe will put on gear and crew, but if properly sailed a *fore-and-aft rigged vessel should be able to gybe in any strength of wind in which she can carry normal canvas. The force of the gybe is broken by hauling in the main sheet before the boom is allowed to swing across, thus considerably reducing the strain as the gybe takes place. If the wind is so strong that a gybe would be dangerous, this may be a reason for setting a *trysail, smaller in area and with no boom, in place of the mainsail. An involuntary gybe, caused by running *by the lee through bad steering, or by a sudden squall from an unexpected quarter, is always dangerous.

If the vessel is not fitted with a permanent *backstay, the operation of gybing requires the setting up of the weather (when the vessel is on her new *tack) *runner before the boom swings across the stern and the *overhauling of the lee runner to allow the boom to swing forward as the wind takes it. To gybe without attending the runners, or to do so involuntarily, is known as to 'gybe all-standing', and is dangerous. See also CHINESE GYBE.

GYN, a form of temporary derrick used on board ship which consists of three spars with their heels splayed out and their heads lashed together to form a tripod. A gyn can lift heavier weights than *sheer legs but can be used only for a straight lift and cannot be traversed as can sheer legs.

GYPSY, an attachment to a ship's *windlass shaped to take the links of a chain cable for anchor work in a small ship where no *capstan or cable holders are fitted. Normally two gypsies are fitted, one each end of the horizontal shaft of the windlass inside the warping drums, in order to work the two *bower anchors which a ship normally carries in her *hawseholes. They can be disconnected from the windlass shaft by means of clutches when they are required to run freely, as when letting go an anchor. They take the place of the cable-holders of larger ships.

GYROSCOPIC, or **GYRO, COMPASS,** see COMPASS.

H

H. L. HUNLEY, C.S.S., a Confederate *submarine privately built in the spring of 1863 in Mobile, Alabama, by officers of an Alabama volunteer regiment from plans furnished by Horace L. Hunley, James R. McClintock, and Baxter Watson. She was fashioned from a cylindrical iron steam boiler as the main centre section, with tapered ends added, and was built for propulsion by hand power. Of her crew of nine, eight were to turn the hand-cranked *propeller and one was to steer. She was equipped with ballast tanks at each tapered end which could be flooded or pumped dry and carried a *spar torpedo. She was brought to Charleston, South Carolina, from Mobile Bay by rail, with the initial intention of torpedoing the U.S.S. *New Ironsides*, but that vessel was anchored in water too shallow for the *H. L. Hunley* to pass below her *keel. After being accidentally sunk in Charleston harbour, the *H. L. Hunley* was raised and reconditioned and on the night of 17 February 1864 she destroyed the U.S.S. *Housatonic*, a Federal *sloop which was anchored in about 27 feet of water off the channel entrance to Charleston. By the time the lookouts on board the *Housatonic* decided that she was not a log or some other harmless object, the guns of the ship could not be depressed enough to hit the *H. L. Hunley*, but she came under small arms fire as she approached. The *Housatonic* slipped her *cable and tried to back away but the *Hunley*'s spar torpedo struck home under water and the *Housatonic* sank rapidly. Five of the *Housatonic*'s crew were killed or drowned but all the remainder scrambled to safety in the rigging. The *H. L. Hunley* failed to return from this exploit and she may have been carried down beneath the hull of the *Housatonic*. She was the first submarine to sink a warship in combat.

H.M.S., the prefix placed before the name of a warship of the British Navy to indicate that she is Her (His) Majesty's ship. The abbreviation came into use from about 1790, the custom before this date being to indicate a ship of the Royal Navy in the form 'His Maties Ship'. The earliest example of the use of H.M.S. as an abbreviation is a reference to H.M.S. *Phoenix* in 1789.

H.M.S. PINAFORE, the title of a light opera, with words by Sir William Gilbert and music by Sir Arthur Sullivan, first performed in the Opera Comique in London in 1878. It is a lighthearted and mildly satirical comment on life in the Royal Navy in Victorian days, and for nearly a century has provided almost uninterrupted popular enjoyment.

HACK, WILLIAM (*fl.* 1680–1700), thought to have been a *buccaneer in his youth, had by 1680 settled at Wapping, near London, as a copyist, transcribing the journals of notable voyages of the time, particularly those of the buccaneers. He was also a skilled copier of maps. It is certain that Bartholomew *Sharp, on the completion of his buccaneering voyage in the Pacific, 1680–1, brought to Hack both his journal and the book of maps, in the form of a *derroterro, which he had captured from a Spanish ship he had attacked. Hack had the sailing directions translated from the Spanish by Philip Dassigny and produced an English version of the book, redrawing and colouring the maps, which under the title *Wagoner of the Great South Sea*, was in 1682 presented to Charles II by Sharp after he had been acquitted on a charge of piracy. These were the first reasonably accurate navigational charts of the Pacific to be seen in England, and were thus of great importance to a maritime nation about to expand across the world. No manuscript collection of charts can equal Hack's *Wagoner* (now in the British Museum) for its richness of colouring and the magnificence of its heraldic emblems. Hack produced a second copy in 1685 which was dedicated to *James, Duke of York.

Hack's *Collection of Original Voyages*, edited from the journals which he copied, was published in 1699. It contains among others the voyages of Sharp, Ambrose *Cowley, and Sir John *Narborough. See also WAGGONER.

HACK WATCH, a chronometer watch used on deck when taking astronomical sights for navigational purposes. Its accuracy is ascertained by daily comparison with the *chronometer. It is a convenient means of taking a sight since the chronometer itself is normally retained in a fixed position in a ship and slung in *gimbals to keep it level, and can hardly be brought up on deck for use whenever a navigator wishes to take a sight.

HACKLE, to, a process in rope-making in which the fibres are drawn through hackle-boards, blocks of wood or steel studded with steel prongs, in order to get them all lying straight in preparation for spinning into *strands. See also ROPEWALK.

HADLEY, JOHN (1682–1744), English mathematician and scientist, was the inventor of the reflecting *quadrant which in 1731 replaced the far less accurate quadrant invented by John *Davis, until then the main instrument for taking navigational sights at sea. Before turning his attention to his quadrant Hadley had been engaged in making improvements in reflecting telescopes used in astronomy and his successes in this field brought him a fellowship of the Royal Society and, from 1728, its vice-presidency.

Hadley's quadrant was in fact an *octant, but as the principle of double reflection made one degree of arc of the octant represent two degrees between the observed objects, it was given the name of quadrant. The incorporation of a spirit level in 1734 made it possible to take a *meridional altitude at sea without the *horizon being visible.

After details of Hadley's new invention had been announced in the Royal Society in 1731 the British Admiralty ordered a series of observations to be made to test the instrument, and it was as a result of these observations that his quadrant was widely accepted at sea as a vastly improved aid to *navigation.

HAGS, or **HAKES, TEETH,** the name given to those parts of a woven *paunch mat, or *pointing, inexpertly tucked so that they are irregularly spaced or project above the proper level.

HAGUE CONVENTION, a peace conference held at The Hague, Holland, in 1907, one of its objectives being the limiting of armaments, particularly naval, and of restraining the naval building race then in progress by most maritime powers. A previous peace conference held at the Hague in 1899 had achieved little; that in 1907 was held initially on a Russian proposal for the revision of international law in naval and military procedures in wartime. Limitation of naval armaments foundered at the Conference on the refusal of Germany even to discuss the subject, but some progress was made in the maritime law aspects governing the capture or sinking of the merchant vessels of a belligerent or neutral power, laying down that such a vessel must be visited and searched if suspected of carrying *contraband, and adequate arrangements made for the safety of her crew, if she were found to be carrying contraband, before she could be sunk. The Convention also amended international maritime law to the effect that a declaration of war must be accompanied by an adequate period of notice or ultimatum, an amendment caused by the unannounced attack by the Japanese fleet on the Russians at Port Arthur in 1904 which began the Russo-Japanese war of 1904–5. An attempt

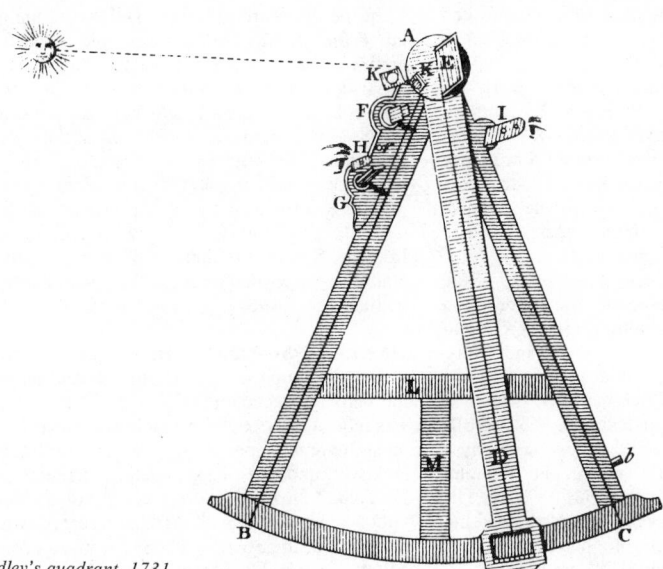

Hadley's quadrant, 1731

was made by some neutral countries to get the Convention to abolish the right of the capture and detention of neutral merchant vessels carrying contraband after a declaration of a *blockade, but this failed in the face of the opposition of all the naval powers.

In one respect the Hague Convention took an apparently retrograde step. Privateering and the *guerre de course had been abolished by the *Declaration of Paris in 1856, but the use by belligerents of *armed merchant cruisers in wartime was legitimized by the Convention, precipitating a revival of a form of the traditional guerre de course, which again flourished so grievously in the world wars of 1914–18 and 1939–45.

HAKLUYT, RICHARD (pron. Hacklit) (1552/3–1616), English collector and editor of travel narratives, was born of a Herefordshire family. He was sent to Westminster School where he found delight in reading books of travel. One of his cousins, on a visit to the Temple, showed him an old map of the world and this so fired the boy that he resolved 'by good assistance, to prosecute that knowledge and kind of literature'. As a scholar of Christ Church, Oxford, he learned five or six languages to assist him in reading books of voyages in various languages and in talking to seamen of other nationalities. Also while at Oxford he studied navigation and the art of map-making, and by reading as many of the original journals kept by mariners as he could lay his hands on he compiled a collection of voyages to America and the West Indies which was published in 1582 as Divers Voyages touching upon the Discovery of America.

On leaving Oxford he took Holy Orders and in 1583 went to Paris as chaplain to the English ambassador. During the six years he remained in that post he compiled the great work for which he is famous, The Principall Navigations, Voiages, Traffiques and Discoveries of the English Nation, of which a first edition in one folio volume was published in 1589, the year after the defeat by England of the Spanish *Armada, and a second and enlarged edition in three folio volumes ten years later.

This was one of the really great books of the English language, and probably the greatest and best loved of all in the realm of maritime literature. Hakluyt was a superb editor and translator, and his prose reads like poetry. His life, too, was dedicated to the maritime cause of England, and he believed that many of the ills of poverty in England could be overcome by a life in the New World where, he thought, Englishmen had a particular part to play. His love of England equalled his love of the sea and acted as a perpetual spur to his never-ending labour of reading manuscript descriptions of

voyages and searching out mariners who had something to tell him of their experiences and voyages. He himself tells, in his 'Epistle Dedicatorie' to the three-volume edition, how 'the ardent love of my country devoured all difficulties, and as it were with a sharp goad provoked me and thrust me forward into this most troublesome and painfull action. And after great charges and infinite cares, after many watchings, toiles, and travels, and wearying out of my weake body; at length I have collected three severall Volumes of the English Navigations, Traffiques, and Discoveries, to strange, remote, and farre distant countreys.'

After the publication of the first edition of his Principal Navigations Hakluyt became rector of Wetheringsett in Suffolk in 1590, and in 1602 was made prebendary of Westminster, later becoming archdeacon. Ten years later he became rector of Gedney, Lincolnshire, and died there in 1616. He was buried in Westminster Abbey.

Throughout his life, even after the publication of Principal Navigations, he continued to collect, read, copy, and make notes of every account of a voyage he could find, often travelling long distances to copy original sea journals or to talk with a seaman who had made a long or difficult voyage. He assembled a huge collection of manuscripts, many more than appear in his Principal Navigations, and he was working on them until his death. They were then acquired by Samuel *Purchas, who published them in the five volumes of his Pilgrimes in 1625, but, sadly, Purchas was no editor of the stamp and dedication of Hakluyt, and many of the accounts of voyages which Purchas edited are garbled and truncated.

In the literature of the sea Hakluyt is immortal. Principal Navigations is an epic work, now approaching its quatercentenary, which remains as vivid, lovely, and inspiring as on the day it was first published. It has been frequently reprinted in modern editions. The original editions were printed in black letter, not always easy to read to the modern eye; the best of the recent editions are those produced by Robert Maclehose and Co., Glasgow (1903) and Everyman's Library (J. M. Dent & Sons, London, 1907). A biography of Hakluyt was written by Sir C. R. *Markham and published in 1896.

HAKLUYT SOCIETY, THE, a learned society in Britain, founded in 1847, to edit and publish the texts and accounts of voyages. The Society was named after Richard *Hakluyt, editor of the most famous book of voyages in the English language, and one of its founding members was Sir John *Barrow, who edited one of the early volumes. Sir Clements *Markham, secretary and president of the Society, 1858–87, was a prolific editor, responsible for no fewer than eighteen volumes. The first series of volumes published, numbering 100, was completed in 1899, and a second series was begun in the same year, some 120 volumes in this series having been produced to date. An extra series, which includes Hakluyt's *Principal Navigations* in twelve volumes, Samuel *Purchas's *Pilgrimes* in twenty volumes, and James *Cook's *Journals* in four volumes, has also been produced.

All the Society's publications are remarkable for their fidelity to the original texts and the scholarship with which they have been edited.

HALF BEAMS, short beams which extend from a ship's side to the *coamings of the *hatchways. Normally a beam extends the whole distance across the ship from side to side, but where a hatchway, leading to the cargo holds, intervenes, only half beams can be used as the whole space enclosed by the hatchway has to be left clear for loading and unloading cargo.

HALF HITCH, a single turn of a rope around a spar or other object with the end of the rope being led back through the *bight. It is the basis on which many knots used at sea are constructed.

'HALF SEAS OVER', the condition of a ship stranded on a *reef or rock when the seas break over her deck. In this condition she is usually unable to take any action to ease her situation. The expression has passed into the English language to describe the situation of a person incapacitated by drink and incapable of steering a steady *course.

HALF-BREADTH PLAN, a drawing made during the design stages of a ship showing the deck lines from *stem to *stern for half the breadth of the hull. Only half the breadth is shown, as the other half is the same. See also SHIPBUILDING.

HALF-DECK, traditionally the apartment or structure on the upper deck of a merchant vessel in which the apprentices were berthed. It was usually in the *waist of the vessel, but could vary in individual ships from below the *poop deck to below the *topgallant forecastle. In its stricter definition it was the space between the foremost *bulkhead of the *steerage and the forward part of the quarterdeck.

In the modern designs of flush-deck merchant ships, the *bridge structure right aft would house the equivalent of the old half-deck. By modern extension, the name has been given to any deck which extends over only part of the ship, but this is a misuse of the original term.

HALF-MUSKET SHOT, the traditional range at which British *ships of the line preferred to fight their battles during the days of the sailing navies.

The maximum killing range of a musket was around 200 yards and, in general, British fleets on engaging an enemy fleet would withhold their fire until they had approached to about 100 yards, when every shot fired would tell. It was for this reason that British naval gunners concentrated their fire on the hulls of enemy ships, while those of most other navies, which usually opened fire in battle at a rather longer range, concentrated their fire on masts and *yards to cripple British ships before they could close in to what was virtually point-blank range.

HALF-SPRIT, see GAFF.

HALIFAX, the capital of the province of Nova Scotia and a major Canadian seaport. It was founded in 1749 by the Hon. Edward Cornwallis as a rival to the French port of *Louisburg, in Cape Breton, and was named after the second Lord Halifax. Until 1905 it was the base of the British North American naval squadron of the Royal Navy; since then it has been an important base for the Royal Canadian Navy. It has an extensive dockyard and is an important centre for the fishing industry. During the Second World War it was a major assembly port for convoys to and fro across the Atlantic between Britain and Canada. The *Maritime Museum of Canada, founded in 1948, was housed in the Citadel of Halifax, but currently is stored in a warehouse pending the construction of a new building in the town.

HALL, CHARLES FRANCIS (1821–71), American Arctic explorer, began life as a blacksmith. An enthusiasm for Arctic exploration led him in 1859 to volunteer to search for Sir John *Franklin, and with money raised by public subscription he set out in the *whaler *George Henry* to the north of Hudson Bay, where, becoming icebound, he lived with the Eskimos of Baffin Land for two years. Although not discovering any clues to the fate of Franklin, he did find relics of the voyages of Martin *Frobisher made in the 16th century. He returned to the Arctic in 1864 and obtained several Franklin relics and information about the fate of seventy-six of the crew during a five-year stay with the Eskimos. In 1870 he was granted $50,000 by the U.S. Congress and in 1871 was given command of a north polar expedition sent out by the U.S. government. Sailing in the *Polaris*, he reached the latitude of 82° 11′ N., the highest attained until the British expedition of five years later. After going into winter quarters Hall fell ill and died at Thank God Harbour, Greenland. The *Polaris* was subsequently lost but her crew was rescued. Hall wrote books about his life with the Eskimos which received considerable attention among polar explorers.

HALL, JAMES (d. 1612), British navigator, is thought to have been born at Hull in Yorkshire, but most of his maritime life was spent in the service of Denmark. Between 1605 and 1611 he acted as chief pilot in three expeditions to Greenland, during the first of which he set off in a *pinnace and explored the coast to the northward. During this exploration he thought he had found a source of silver ore which he later determined to exploit. After the completion of his three Danish voyages he organized a fourth expedition and in 1612 sailed with two ships, the *Patience* and *Heartsease*, to further his discovery and return with the silver ore. Before he could find it he was killed during a quarrel with Eskimos.

HALL, Sir WILLIAM REGINALD (1870–1943), widely known as 'Blinker' Hall for his habit of rapidly blinking his eyes while talking, was a British admiral who established a brilliant reputation as Director of Naval Intelligence during the First World War (1914–18). A specialist in gunnery, he was promoted to captain in 1905 and commanded the training *cruiser *Cornwall*, the cruiser *Natal*, and the *battle-cruiser *Queen Mary*. It was in this latter command that he introduced a number of lower deck reforms with far-reaching effects, of which the abolition of the ship's police was the most notable and had the greatest effect on the everyday life of the sailor. Ill health obliged him to relinquish command of the *Queen Mary* in November 1914 but fortunately the office of Director of Naval Intelligence fell vacant and Hall was appointed to it. He took a very broad view of his duties and soon built up a brilliant organization which was expanded to include a Trade Intelligence department. One of his most successful coups was the exposure of the 'Zimmermann telegram' which disclosed German plans for persuading Mexico to declare war against the U.S.A. should the latter declare war on Germany. Publication of this telegram induced the U.S. government to do just this in 1917. After the war Hall entered politics and represented the West Derby Division of Liverpool in Parliament, and later Eastbourne. In the 1929 election he did not seek re-election but continued to take an active interest in public affairs. He was a man of exceptional talent and unflinching courage and the ultimate allied victory over Germany in 1918 owed much to the touches of sheer brilliance which characterized his services while he was responsible for naval intelligence. For a biography see Admiral Sir William James, *The Eyes of the Navy* (1955).

HALLEY, EDMUND (1656–1742), English astronomer, had many connections with the sea. At the age of 17 he published observations on the

was connected with the *East India Company on the recommendation of Charles II; and in 1682 began a long series of lunar observations with a view to discovering a better method of fixing *longitude at sea. In 1698 he was appointed captain of the *Paramour* for the purpose of observing the conditions of terrestrial magnetism, and after a voyage of two years published, in 1701, a *General Chart of the Variations of the Compass*, the first world chart to incorporate *isogonic lines and a landmark in the history of *navigation. He was secretary of the Royal Society from 1713 to 1721, and in 1720 succeeded John *Flamsteed as Astronomer Royal, retaining that position until his death.

HALLOWELL, Sir BENJAMIN (1760–1834), British admiral, was with Horatio *Nelson in Corsica in 1794, and was one of the famous 'band of brothers'. As captain of the *Swiftsure*, he played a considerable part in the battle of the *Nile in 1798 and it was he who, after the action, presented Nelson with a coffin made from the mainmast of the French flagship *L'*Orient*, destroyed in the battle, in which in fact Nelson was buried in 1806. For the next two years he remained in command of the *Swiftsure* in the Mediterranean, but had the misfortune to be captured by a strong French squadron.

A few years later Hallowell again served with Nelson off Toulon and his ship was in the chase to the West Indies in 1805 to search for Admiral *Villeneuve, later joining Cuthbert *Collingwood in the watch on Cadiz where the French fleet under Villeneuve had taken shelter. His ship was detached to Gibraltar for stores and water just before the battle of *Trafalgar, which he thus missed. He was promoted rear admiral in 1811 and vice admiral in 1819. In 1829, under the terms of a will, he assumed the name and arms of Carew, and for the rest of his life was known as Benjamin Hallowell-Carew. He reached the rank of admiral in 1831.

HALSEY, WILLIAM FREDERICK, Jr. (1882–1959), American fleet admiral, was born in Elizabeth, New Jersey, and graduated from the Naval Academy in 1904. Much of his early career was spent in destroyers and he was recognized as an exceptionally competent authority on destroyer tactics and strategy. After flight training at Pensacola, Florida, he qualified as a naval aviator in 1935. During the Second World War, at the time of the Japanese attack on *Pearl Harbor in 1941, he commanded the *aircraft carriers of the Pacific Fleet, which were exercising at sea when the Japanese planes arrived and so escaped the holocaust. From early 1942 Halsey participated in nearly every operation in the *Pacific which included aircraft carriers.

in the victory of *Santa Cruz Islands on 26 October 1942, and in the series of battles around *Guadalcanal, which began in November 1942. He held various titles before June 1944 when he was appointed as Commander Third Fleet. His recommendation led to the attack on the enemy in *Leyte Gulf earlier than had been planned.

In connection with the return of American forces to the Philippines, Halsey had an important part in the preparatory campaign which included air strikes in the Palaus, on the Philippine Islands themselves, on Formosa, on Okinawa, and in the South China Sea. He was in direct command of the force which inflicted very severe damage on the Japanese Navy in the battle off Cape Engano on 25 October 1944. Halsey's Third Fleet participated in the latter stages of the Okinawa campaign, and in attacks on Japan in February and March 1945. He was present in Tokyo Bay when the formal surrender of Japan was received. In November 1945 he was relieved as commander-in-chief of the Third Fleet and was assigned to duty in the office of the Secretary of the Navy. He retired in 1947.

HALYARDS, HALLIARDS, or **HAUL-YARDS,** the ropes, wires, or *tackles used to hoist or lower sails, either to their *yards in square-rigged ships with the exception of the fore, main, and mizen *course or on their *gaffs or by their peaks in fore-and-aft rigged ships. The courses, which are very heavy sails, are hoisted by the jeers.

HAMBRO, or **HAMBER, LINE,** also widely known as cod line, a three-stranded small size rope tightly laid up and used for lacing sails and for lashings where strength is essential. It is normally supplied in hanks whereas smaller stuff (twine, *marline, etc.) is usually supplied in balls.

HAMBURG, a German seaport on the North Sea coast at the mouth of the River Elbe, one of the greatest ports in the world. In the 13th century it became one of the principal ports of the Hanseatic League, and as such its sea trade expanded enormously. Another great opportunity for expansion came in 1783 when the U.S.A. became an independent nation and Hamburg became not only the chief trading link between Europe and the new nation but also a centre for European emigration to America.

A great shipbuilding complex is centred on Hamburg, mainly at Altona, capable of constructing the largest ships, and an extensive dockyard handles all types of maritime repairs and services. It is the home port of the Hamburg–Amerika and Norddeutscher–Lloyd transatlantic shipping lines. It is also the home of the Altonaer Museum, one of the more important maritime museums in the world.

HAMELIN, FRANÇOIS ALPHONSE (1796–1864), French admiral, began his seafaring life as a cabin boy in the *frigate *Venus*, which was captured in the Indian Ocean by the British *Boadicea* in 1810, Hamelin becoming a prisoner. He was fortunate, unlike the majority of officers, in being retained in the French Navy after the conclusion of the Napoleonic War in 1815, and his advance was rapid. He was captain of the frigate *Actéon* in 1828 during operations off Algiers and was present at its capture in 1830. As a flag officer he commanded in the Pacific, was promoted vice admiral in 1848, and commanded the French fleet in the Black Sea during the Crimean War (1854–6), co-operating with the British admiral, Dundas, in the bombardment of Sebastopol in 1854. Promoted admiral, he returned to France to become minister of marine, and it was due to his encouragement of the designer *Dupuy de Lôme that the first seagoing ironclad warship, the frigate *Gloire*, was launched in 1859, setting an example which was followed by all other navies in the world.

HAMILTON, EMMA, Lady (c. 1765–1815), was the wife of Sir William Hamilton, British ambassador at Naples during the Revolutionary War (1793–1801), and the mistress of Lord *Nelson. She was the daughter of a blacksmith named Lyon, and was christened Amy. Her mother changed her name to Hart after the death of her husband and brought Amy, now renamed Emma, to London where Emma began to work for a somewhat disreputable quack doctor called Graham in what was probably a high-class brothel. From there she became the mistress of Sir Harry Featherstonehaugh who, however, turned her adrift after she had become pregnant.

In her distress she appealed to the Hon. Charles Greville, whom she had met earlier. He arranged for the birth of her child, which was farmed out to foster-parents, and took her as his mistress, with her mother, who had now changed her name to Cadogan, as housekeeper. They lived together in great happiness and Greville introduced her to the painter Romney who recorded her great beauty on canvas in many famous portraits. Greville, however, was deeply in debt, and in 1786 sent Emma on a visit to his uncle, Sir William Hamilton, in Naples on the understanding that she should become Sir William's mistress while the uncle paid Greville's debts. She was married to Sir William in 1791. She became a great success in Naples and the close friend and confidante of the queen of Naples, and it was this friendship which enabled the British fleet in the Mediterranean in 1798, commanded by Nelson, to take in water and provisions in the Neapolitan ports of Naples and Syracuse when all other ports in the Mediterranean were closed to it by French sea

Emma Hamilton; oil painting by G. Romney, c. 1785

power. As a result of this sustenance, the fleet was enabled to hunt down the French fleet and annihilate it at the battle of the *Nile.

On his return to Naples after the Nile, Nelson fell deeply under the spell of Emma and she became his mistress. She bore his daughter, Horatia, in 1801. After Nelson's death at *Trafalgar in 1805 many attempts were made to procure her a government pension for the services she had rendered to the British fleet in the Mediterranean but all were met with refusal by the government. Much addicted to gambling, she was imprisoned for debt in 1811, and on her release a year later went to Calais to escape her creditors. She died there in want.

HAMMOCK, from the Carib *hamorca*, a type of native bed, and the bed of the naval seaman for hundreds of years, but now no longer, as the seaman sleeps in a bunk. The hammock was invented, it is said, by Alcibiades, but its introduction in ships dates from the time of Christopher *Columbus who noted that the natives of the Carib islands used them slung between trees. The maritime version is made of canvas with a row of small eyelet holes at each end through which are rove *nettles which spread from a ring, the nettles as a whole being known as the *clews of the hammock. When used on board, hammocks were slung from hooks in the deck *beams. When not in use they were lashed up, with the blankets inside them, by nine turns of a rope; and in the event of shipwreck or disaster in battle, a properly lashed hammock was capable of supporting the weight of a man in the water for a considerable time. See also HAMMOCK NETTINGS.

HAMMOCK NETTINGS, the stowage space for *hammocks when they have been lashed up after use. In the days of sailing warships hammock nettings were placed along the sides of the upper deck and along the break of the *poop so that the hammocks could act as a protection from musket fire from an enemy ship during battle. They were also thus stowed so that they would float free, if the ship were sunk, for use as a form of *lifebuoy for seamen in the water.

HANCE, a step where the rail of a ship drops to a lower level in cases where a *deck is not continuous, as from *poop to upper deck, etc. As such a step, if unfilled, is square and unsightly they were, in the days when most wooden ships were highly decorated with carved work, filled by hancing pieces, usually combined with long drop carvings often in the form of a human figure, to produce a curved instead of a square step. The elaborately carved hancing pieces of the Tudor and Stuart periods (1550–1690) gave way to a more restrained and simplified design in the 18th century as an economy measure. They are not applicable in the modern days of steel ships.

HAND, to, (1) the term used to describe the act of furling the square sails of a ship to the *yards. In a strong wind the two *leeches of the sail were first brought to the yard since if the leeches were left to belly or fill with wind, it would be impossible for the men on the yard to get the sail in. The order given in a square-rigged ship was 'HAND IN THE LEECH'. **(2)** As a noun, a member of the ship's crew. 'ALL HANDS', the order for all seamen to come on deck either in an emergency or to assist in some operation which is beyond the capacity of the watch on deck. **(3)** HAND-OVER-HAND, to haul rapidly on a rope or *tackle by men passing their hands alternately one before the other and thus keeping the hauling part in motion. A seaman was said to go hand-over-hand when he went up the mast by means of a *stay or *shroud without using the *ratlines. The expression also means rapidly, as, e.g., 'we are coming up with the ship ahead hand-over-hand'.

HANDELS OG SJØFARTMUSEUM PÅ KRONBORG, Helsingør, Denmark, a private museum supported by the government and housed in the ancient castle of Kronborg of which, since 1922, it occupies more than half. It was opened in 1915 and the exhibits portray the history of Danish shipping from the earliest times to the present day. It contains models of ships of the Viking period, the Middle Ages, 16th, 17th, and 18th centuries, sailing ships of Schleswig and Holstein of the 19th century, ferries, and ice-breakers, also nautical instruments and charts. There are some 400 paintings and drawings on display, together with 200 portraits of prominent shipowners and seamen. The library, which is open to students, contains some 14,000 books and over 1,000 plans.

HANDSOMELY, the order given when it is required to ease off a line or *tackle gradually and carefully. 'Lower away handsomely', the order when lowering a *seaboat or a *lifeboat from the *davits of a ship so that she may go evenly down the ship's side and be kept level during the process.

HANDY BILLY, the name of a small *jigger purchase or watch *tackle, used on board ship for a variety of purposes, especially in handling cargo in the holds. It is rove with one double and one single block and multiplies the power by four when rove to *advantage.

HANK, (1) a small ring or hoop of metal by which the *luff of a *jib or *staysail is *bent to the *stays of a sailing vessel. Modern hanks are usually spring-loaded so that they can easily be slipped on or off the stays as desired. **(2)** A skein of small line or twine, used on board for small work such as *whipping the ends of ropes, passing a *seizing, etc.

HANSEATIC LEAGUE, a trading confederation of north German towns dating from about 1240. The League, mainly operating maritime trade, led to a huge expansion in merchant shipping especially during the 14th and early 15th centuries when it was at the height of its powers, almost the whole of the trade of Germany and Flanders, both inwards and outwards, being channelled through its ports. The first two Hansa ports were Lübeck and *Hamburg, later joined by Lüneburg, Wismar, Rostock, Stralsund, and Danzig. It eventually united the merchants of over thirty German towns, and set up 'hansas', or trading guildhalls, in foreign cities, including London, King's Lynn, Boston, York, Hull, Yarmouth, and Bristol, in England, and Bergen in Norway.

At the height of its power the League could claim and operate a monopoly in seaborne trade, but industrial growth throughout Europe, particularly in England with the formation of companies of merchant adventurers, quickly produced a challenge to the monopoly which the League was unable to withstand and in the late 15th century its power began to fail. Over a period of about twenty years, approximately 1480–1500, so many merchants challenged the trade monopoly that the League no longer existed in its former monopolistic shape and soon began to disintegrate under the growing liberation of trade. It was virtually dead by 1600, and although an attempt was made to revive it at a general assembly held in 1669, it was unsuccessful.

The trade of shipbuilding and the development of ships, both in size and reliability, flourished exceedingly under the Hanseatic League. North Sea and Baltic fishing, too, was one of the monopolies it claimed, and great progress in fishing methods and equipment was made during its years of power.

HANWAY, JONAS (1712–86), British philanthropist, founded the *Marine Society in 1756 with the twofold object of saving destitute boys from the streets of London and helping to man the British Navy with them when saved. Boys from this source were much appreciated by naval captains as they compared favourably with the men brought in by the *press gangs. In 1762 Hanway was appointed a commissioner for victualling the navy, holding the post for twenty-one years. Other, non-maritime, claims to remembrance were that he was the first Londoner to carry an umbrella and was a champion and protector of the small boys employed to sweep chimneys.

HARBOUR DUES, the amount of money the owner of a ship has to pay to a harbour authority for the use of the harbour and its facilities. It is usually quoted as a charge per ton based on a ship's gross registered *tonnage, or in the case of yachts, per foot of their overall length. In many ports, the bare harbour dues are increased by an additional charge for the use of navigational beacons and lights.

HARBOURMASTER, an official of a port who is responsible for seeing that the port regulations are enforced, particularly in respect of *moorings and the proper berthing of ships. Queen's, or King's, Harbourmaster, an official post in the British Navy, usually filled by a captain, responsible for all the navigational regulations and requirements of a naval base or port, again including moorings and berthing.

HARD UP IN A CLINCH AND NO KNIFE TO CUT THE SEIZING, a sailor's saying indicating that he is overtaken by misfortune and can see no way of winning clear of it.

HARDEN-IN, to, the operation of hauling in the *sheets of a sailing vessel to present the sails at a more acute angle to the wind.

HARDING, SETH (1743–1814), American naval officer, was born in Eastham, Mass. After commanding merchant ships, he took over command of the Connecticut State *brig Defence on the outbreak of the War of American Independence (1775–82). He captured two armed transports in a single action on 16 June 1776, and took another transport on the following day. Following this, Harding commanded two other vessels of the Connecticut State Navy, a second Defence and the Oliver Cromwell. He made a number of valuable *prizes while in the two latter vessels.

He was selected to command the Continental *frigate Confederacy, then being built at Norwich, in 1778, and a year later sailed for France carrying John Jay, who was to be the minister to Spain, and M. Gérard, the French envoy to the Continental Congress. When off Newfoundland the Confederacy was dismasted in a severe gale but Harding's excellent seamanship enabled him to take her to Martinique in her damaged condition. The ship was refitted and Harding operated against British shipping in the West Indies until the Confederacy was captured by the British frigates Roebuck and Orpheus on 14 October 1781.

After being exchanged in 1782, Harding commanded the *privateer Diana until he was captured a second time. Again obtaining his freedom he joined the *Alliance, then commanded by John *Barry. While serving in her he was wounded in an action with the British frigate Sybil, one of the last engagements of the Revolutionary War.

HARDY, THOMAS BUSH (1842–97), British marine artist, was born at Sheffield and was a prolific painter of sea pictures, particularly in watercolour. Their great delicacy of colour and design, together with accuracy of detail in sail and rigging, make them very considerable collectors' pieces. He travelled widely in Holland and Italy, and his shipping scenes in those countries are among his best work.

HARDY, Sir THOMAS MASTERMAN (1769–1839), British admiral, was a member of the well-known Dorset family and the only officer of rank to have been present at all three of Lord *Nelson's great victories, the *Nile, *Copenhagen, and *Trafalgar. As a lieutenant he was sent with a boarding-party to take charge of the Spanish *frigate La Sabina after her capture by Nelson as the result of a sharp action in the Mediterranean in December 1796. The frigate was later retaken, and Hardy with her, but was exchanged shortly afterwards, only to have another narrow escape from capture when, in the presence of the enemy, he took charge of a boat to go to the rescue of a seaman who had fallen overboard. 'By God,' Nelson exclaimed, 'I'll not lose Hardy. Back the mizen topsail.' The Spaniards, who were bearing down on the boat, were so surprised at Nelson's manoeuvre that they stood off. Hardy was rescued, and was thus able to be present at the battle of *Cape St. Vincent a few weeks later.

Hardy's first command was the Mutine, *brig, a *prize which he himself cut out in broad daylight while serving under Nelson at *Santa Cruz. The Mutine was the only light vessel to be with Nelson's squadron at the Nile, where she helped to tow off the Culloden, which had stranded at the entrance to *Aboukir Bay. After the action the Mutine was sent away with dispatches, Hardy himself being transferred to the *Vanguard as Nelson's flag-captain. For the rest of Nelson's life the pair were rarely separated, for Hardy's discipline and attention to detail suited Nelson, giving him freedom to dispatch the enormous volume of business which fell to him as a commander-in-chief.

When Nelson went to the Baltic in 1801, Hardy had command of the *St. George*, which was of too deep a draught to take part in the attack on the Danish fleet at Copenhagen. But he accompanied Nelson as a volunteer on board the * *Elephant* and the night before the battle distinguished himself by taking soundings of the depth of water available in the channel which Nelson proposed to use next day.

When war was resumed with France in 1803, and Nelson went to the Mediterranean as commander-in-chief, Hardy once more became his flag-captain. He took part in the long watch on Toulon and the entire campaign of Trafalgar, and was pacing the deck by Nelson's side when the admiral was mortally wounded. As soon as it was clear that the commander-in-chief could not live, Hardy warned Admiral *Collingwood, second-in-command, of the burden he would have to assume. He was created a baronet for his services, which included those of chief of staff, for at Trafalgar Nelson had no captain of the fleet, the officer in question, George Murray, having been left behind in England.

As promotion to flag rank was then by rule of seniority, Hardy had many years to wait before he was given his flag. It was in the rank of *commodore that he became commander-in-chief on the South American station, 1819–24, at a time when the former Spanish colonies were completing the process of winning their independence and where his services in maintaining a situation at sea where the insurgents might prosper won him a high regard among the new South American nations.

Hardy became a rear admiral in 1825 at the age of 56. Five years later he became senior lord (First Sea Lord) of the Admiralty, a post which he held until 1834. The last years of his life were spent as governor of *Greenwich Hospital. For a biography see Broadley and Bartelot, *Nelson's Hardy, his Life, Letters and Friends* (1909).

HARMATTAN, an easterly wind which occasionally blows during the dry season (December, January, February) on the west coast of Africa, coming off the land instead of the more normal wind which blows off the sea. It is a very dry wind, usually accompanied by dust storms which the wind has picked up from the desert. It is sometimes also known as the 'doctor', as it is cooler than the normal temperatures of the coast.

HARNESS. 'One hand for the ship, the other for yourself' has been the seaman's adage through the ages, but aboard a small yacht battling through the seas in an offshore race, both hands may have to be used in an emergency and it is

then all too easy for a member of the crew to fall overboard and be lost astern. With the intention of preventing such accidents the *Royal Ocean Racing Club, together with other associations connected with offshore yacht racing, introduced a rule that safety harness must be worn at night and in very heavy weather by the watch on deck when racing. The Royal Society for the Prevention of Accidents has encouraged this precaution among all who go to sea in small boats. It is an unwise skipper who permits any of his crew to work on deck at night without some form of harness, attached to part of the yacht. The harness is usually of strong webbing which passes round the chest and over both shoulders, with a length of line having a metal clip on its end for easy attachment to a handy *stanchion, one of the *shrouds, or any really strong object, leaving the wearer free to use both hands.

HARNESS CASK, a large cask usually kept on deck in the days of sail which contained the salted provisions for immediate use. Salt pork and salt beef were usually known among sailors as salt horse because the meat was so hard and unsavoury, and the harness cask was where the horse without its harness was stabled.

HARPINGS or **HARPENS, (1)** the forward parts of the *wales at the *bows of a wooden ship where they are fixed into the *stem. They are normally thicker than the after part of the wales in order to provide additional strength at the bows, where most of the strain on a ship falls. **(2)** Lengths or ribbands of timber used to bind in the *frames at bow and stern of a wooden ship until the ship is planked. **(3)** Catharpings are the cross pieces at the end of the *futtock staves used for *girding, or hauling in, the standing *rigging to allow the lower *yards of a square-rigged ship to be *braced sharp up. By holding the standing rigging as close in to the mast as possible, there is more room for the lower yards to be braced at a sharper angle to the fore-and-aft line of the vessel and thus enable her to carry a better wind when sailing *close-hauled.

HARPOON, a spear with a barbed head and with a line attached used for catching and securing a whale. In the early days of the whale fishery, harpoons were launched by hand by a harpooner standing in the bows of a boat rowed by members of the crew of a *whaler; today they are fired from a harpoon-gun mounted in the bows of a *whale-catcher. Modern harpoons are of two types, electric or explosive; in each case the whale is quickly killed when it is hit.

HARPOON GUN, the modern method of launching a harpoon in whale fishing, developed by Sven Foyn in Norway in 1860–70 to replace the

Harrison's chronometer made in 1728–35, which was taken on board H.M.S. Centurion *in 1736*

hand-launched harpoon. Smaller mechanical harpoon guns have been developed for use in connection with free diving techniques for underwater fishing. See also FISGIG.

HARRISON, JOHN (1693–1776), a carpenter and self-taught mathematician and clockmaker who constructed the first sea-going timepiece or *chronometer of sufficient reliability to enable *longitude to be calculated at sea.

Born at Foulby, Yorkshire, it was while employed as an estate carpenter and living at Barrow-on-Humber, Lincolnshire, that John and his younger brother James constructed, between 1713 and 1726, a number of remarkably accurate long-case clocks incorporating many unique features, including the first bimetallic pendulum to overcome errors due to temperature variations.

By an Act of Parliament of 1714 a *Board of Longitude had been set up to encourage means of accurately determining longitude at sea. The Board offered a prize of £20,000, and to win the full amount, the invention would have to achieve an accuracy of within 30 miles after the usual six-weeks' voyage to the West Indies. With his eye on this prize, John Harrison completed four time-keepers between 1735 and 1760, the first a massive mechanism of brass and wood weighing

72 lb, the last a watch about twice the size of a pocket watch which, in two trials made in 1762 and 1764, easily fulfilled the requirements to win the award. Only £10,000 was paid to him, however, the remainder being withheld until the Board of Longitude was satisfied with fresh proof of the 'general utility at sea' of his watch. Harrison's last years were embittered by the long struggle to obtain his just dues, and it was not until 1773 that these were finally granted by Parliament.

A copy of Harrison's watch, by Larcum Kendall, was used by Captain *Cook on his second voyage of Pacific exploration and gave an error of less than 8 miles in calculated longitude when Cook made his final landfall at Plymouth on 29 July 1775 after circumnavigating the world.

The four chronometers made by Harrison are now preserved in working order at the *National Maritime Museum, London.

HARTFORD, U.S.S., a ship-rigged *sloop with auxiliary steam power launched at the Boston Navy Yard in November 1858 and completed in June 1859. In 1862 she mounted twenty 9-in. Dahlgren guns and two 20-pounder Parrott rifles. She became famous as Admiral

*Farragut's flagship during the American Civil War (1861–5), particularly during the battle of *Mobile Bay.

HARVEY TORPEDO, a primitive type of towed *mine, at that date known as a *torpedo, introduced into the British Navy in 1871. It was the joint invention of Captain John Harvey and Commander Frederick Harvey, and consisted of a copper canister, not unlike an oblong chest in shape, which was towed behind a vessel at the end of 150 yards of wire. It contained, in the large size, 76 lb of black powder or guncotton or, in the smaller, 27 lb of the same explosive. It was fired by a bolt, driven in by impact when a ship was hit, which fractured a glass tube filled with sulphuric acid.

The *otter principle was built into the torpedo so that when it was towed at any speed, it swung out at an angle of about 45° from the *course of the towing vessel. The object was to tow it across the *bows of an enemy ship so that when the towing wire came up against the bow, or the *cable if the enemy was at *anchor, the torpedo would, with its speed through the water, swing up against the side of the enemy and explode.

Harvey torpedoes were never used in action, being quickly overtaken by the development of the locomotive torpedo.

HARWOOD, Sir HENRY (1888–1950), British admiral, was a *torpedo specialist of considerable intellectual attainments which led to his selection, in the intervals between sea appointments, for every available staff and war course, the course at the Imperial Defence College and, in 1934–6, as instructor at the Naval War College.

The outbreak of the Second World War found him with the rank of *commodore commanding the British squadron on the South American station, and he was soon engaged in the hunt for the elusive German commerce-raiding *pocket-battleship *Admiral Graf Spee. Early in December 1939 Harwood correctly forecast that the German raider was about to attack shipping off the *River Plate and, on the 12th, he concentrated his flagship, the *cruiser Ajax, her sister-ship H.M.N.Z.S. Achilles, and the 8-inch cruiser H.M.S. Exeter in that area. Early the next morning the Graf Spee was sighted and, unwisely, steamed in to the attack.

In the action which followed Harwood divided his out-gunned and lightly armoured ships into two divisions, thereby forcing the enemy to divide his fire. Although the Exeter was soon crippled and driven out of the action, the two other cruisers kept up their fire; though both were hit, they were able to damage the Graf Spee sufficiently to force her to make for the neutral port of Montevideo for repairs. When the limit of stay in a neutral port

permitted under international law was reached, her captain, bluffed into believing that an overwhelming British force awaited him in the offing, steamed slowly out into the Plate estuary and *scuttled his ship. Two days later he committed suicide. Harwood was specially promoted to rear admiral on the day following the action, and knighted for his brilliant leadership in the battle.

After service at the Admiralty as an assistant chief of naval staff, he was selected to relieve Admiral Sir Andrew *Cunningham in April 1942 as commander-in-chief in the Mediterranean, but ill health caused him to relinquish this command less than a year later. In the final months of the war he commanded the Orkneys and Shetlands station, but was invalided from the navy with the rank of admiral in October 1945.

HASLAR, a creek in *Portsmouth Harbour. It is particularly well known for the naval hospital there, founded in 1746. Designed by John Turner, it was built on three sides of a quadrangle, and when completed was not only the largest naval hospital in the world but also the largest building constructed of brick in Europe. The first physician appointed in charge of the hospital was James *Lind, the father of nautical medicine and the author, in 1753, of Treatise of the *Scurvy, the first English book to prove that oranges and lemons were an adequate specific against this distressing maritime disease. He held this post from 1758 to 1783, when he was succeeded by his son. Other famous naval physicians in charge were Sir Gilbert *Blane and Thomas *Trotter. The hospital buildings were extensively damaged by bombing during the Second World War but have been rebuilt and redesigned. Also at Haslar is Fort Blockhouse which, as H.M.S. Dolphin, is the headquarters of the British submarine service.

HASLER, H. G. (1914–   ), British marine consultant, inventor, and designer of Chinese rigs, played a leading part in originating the first single-handed transatlantic race in 1960, and the Round-Britain race in 1966. He experimented with a Chinese *junk rig on his 25-ft (7·6 m) Folkboat Jester, in which he was second in the 1960 and fifth in the 1964 single-handed transatlantic races. He also invented the pendulum-servo system of *vane self-steering gear for offshore yachts. He has cruised extensively round the British Isles, and to Rockall and the Brittany coast over many years, and is author of Harbours and Anchorages of the North Coast of Brittany.

HATCH, an opening in the ship's deck for ingress and egress of either persons or cargo. The cover that closes it is known as a hatch cover, though many seamen call this also a hatch. The term hatchway is generally taken to mean the vertical space through a series of hatches, one below the other, through the decks of a vessel. In large hatches leading to the cargo *holds, a removable hatch-beam is fitted fore-and-aft to serve as a support for the hatch covers when they are *battened down. Hatch battens are strips of steel wedged to the sides of the hatch *coaming so that the waterproof tarpaulin cover can be secured over the hatches.

In many modern cargo ships the hatch covers are of steel, pivoted in sections which allow the covers to be rolled back, folding together in cantilever fashion at either end of the hatch opening.

HAUL, to, the seaman's word meaning to pull. Virtually every rope that needs a pull to perform its function, such as the *falls of *tackles, the *sheets which trim a sail, *hawsers which secure a vessel to a wharf, are hauled at sea, never pulled. 'Mainsail-haul', the order given in a square-rigged ship to haul round the after *yards when she is nearly head to wind when *tacking. A ship also hauls her wind when she is brought nearer to it after having been running with the wind free.

HAWKE, EDWARD, 1st Baron (1705–81), British admiral of the fleet, was brought up by his uncle, Martin Bladen, Comptroller of the Mint and a strong supporter of the Prime Minister, Sir Robert Walpole. With this influence behind him, Hawke's promotion was rapid and he was made a *post-captain at the age of 29.

Hawke early showed his mettle. He was the only captain to emerge with credit from an inconclusive action fought against a Franco-Spanish fleet off Toulon in 1744, his ship, the *Berwick*, driving a Spanish ship out of the *line of battle. She was the only *prize taken, and Hawke secured her because he had the courage to disregard the rigid *Fighting Instructions and leave the line of battle to do so. Because he was not censured for this action, as he might well have been, he developed the *general chase tactics which were to play so great and successful a part in future naval battles.

He was promoted rear admiral in 1746, George II insisting, the story goes, that he be retained on the active list when there was some question whether he might not be superannuated. The King's confidence was soon vindicated when, commanding a squadron off *Ushant in 1747, Hawke defeated and captured the greater part of a French squadron escorting a convoy to La Rochelle. His success was achieved as the result of a chase action, confirming Hawke in his belief that this was the best way of achieving victory at sea.

Early in the Seven Years War (1756–63)

Hawke was sent as commander-in-chief in the Mediterranean to try to retrieve the disastrous situation there following Admiral *Byng's failure to relieve *Minorca in the face of a French attack. But matters in the Mediterranean were by then past redemption, and on his return to home waters he was appointed to command, with General Sir John Mordaunt, an amphibious force to capture Rochefort. The attempt proved abortive, and in a fit of pique Hawke hauled down his commander-in-chief's flag and came ashore. He was superseded by Lord *Anson, but agreed to serve under him until his offence was expiated.

In 1759 he was appointed to command the blockading force which was watching the French fleet in Brest under Admiral *Conflans. French troopships gathered in the Morbihan were awaiting escort by the Brest fleet for a planned invasion of Britain but, with Hawke outside, Conflans could not get to sea. In the face of great difficulties, particularly the lack of regular supplies of fresh food and water, Hawke maintained his watch unbroken from May to November when, early in the month, a westerly gale blew him off station and allowed Conflans to escape. Hawke's ships struggled back to Torbay, repaired the gale damage at top speed, and were at sea again within a day or two to resume their watch on Brest. The gale was still blowing when the British fleet reached the French coast, where Hawke received the news of the French fleet's escape. They were sighted off *Quiberon Bay and Hawke hoisted the signal for a general chase. With every ship crowding on sail, they chased the French into the bay as darkness was falling, using the enemy ships as their pilots to keep clear of the many rocks and shoals. In the short action before complete darkness fell, six French ships of the line were taken, burnt, or wrecked; the rest fled up the Rivers Vilaine and Charente but most of them broke their backs in the shallow water. Two British ships were wrecked during the night, their crews being taken off in the morning.

It was a shattering victory, and the culmination of Hawke's active career. He came ashore for good in 1762, and in 1766 was made First Lord of the Admiralty, a post he resigned in 1768. He was made a baron in 1776.

Hawke's coat-of-arms bore the motto 'Strike' beneath it, and this perhaps sums up the man to perfection. He could be patience itself while waiting for his chance, as his blockade of Brest exemplifies, but when the chance for action came, he lost not a moment in forcing battle on his opponent. Where he led in developing the chase action, succeeding British admirals followed with devastating success.

The standard biography of Hawke was written by Montagu Burrows and published in a review edition in 1896; a good modern biography is Ruddock Mackay's *Admiral Hawke* (1965).

HAWKINS, Sir JOHN (1532–95), English admiral, was the son of William Hawkins, mayor of Plymouth, and the cousin of Sir Francis *Drake. The Hawkins family had traded with West Africa for some years before John, on his first voyage to Hispaniola (Haiti) in 1562, extended the trade to the transport of slaves between Africa and the Spanish West Indies. As the first English slave trader, he antagonized not only the Portuguese, whose practice he was adopting, but also the Spanish, who did not want their monopoly in the Caribbean infringed. However, backed by a syndicate of merchants and by Elizabeth I, who lent him a royal ship for his second voyage in 1564–5, he succeeded in selling slaves to the Spanish colonists at a great profit. His third voyage of 1567–8 was, however, disastrous: the queen's ship, the *Jesus of Lubeck*, was captured at San Juan de Ulloa in Mexico and only those commanded by Drake and himself returned home safely. This affair marks the beginning of the long quarrel with Spain which later led to open war.

Having married the daughter of Benjamin Gonson, treasurer of the navy, Hawkins became involved in naval administration, in addition to intelligence work in which he discovered the connection between Spain and the cause of Mary, Queen of Scots. In 1577 he succeeded Gonson as treasurer, adding the post of comptroller in 1589, the two most important posts on the *Navy Board, which was responsible for the manning, design, and maintenance of royal ships. He was thus virtually responsible for the Elizabethan Navy, designing and building new ships to replace the old ones inherited by Elizabeth from Henry VIII. His new 'low-charged' ships were faster and more weatherly, and also carried more guns. He was also responsible for improving the pay and conditions of the seamen, and in 1590, with Lord *Howard of Effingham and Drake, he founded the *Chatham Chest fund for their relief.

In the campaign of the Spanish *Armada in 1588 he commanded the *Victory* and was knighted by the *Lord High Admiral, Howard of Effingham, off the Isle of Wight on 25 July 1588 during the actual battle. In succeeding years he evolved the strategic idea of a blockade of Spain from the Azores, but the plan was much in advance of his time because as yet ships could not keep at sea long enough.

In 1595 he and Drake were appointed to the joint command of an expedition to the West Indies, but there was dissension from the start, Hawkins at the age of 63 being undoubtedly too old for a sea command. Off Puerto Rico on 12 November 1595 he succumbed to dysentery and was buried at sea.

Hawkins was the architect of the Elizabethan Navy. Though his financial honesty was im-

pugned on occasion, he defended himself convincingly and maintained a comparatively high standard of administrative integrity. He is well remembered for his ship's order: 'Serve God daily, love one another, preserve your victuals, beware of fire, and keep good company.'

For a biography see J. A. Williamson, *Hawkins of Plymouth* (1949).

HAWKINS, Sir RICHARD (1562–1622), English admiral, was the only son of Sir John *Hawkins. Having sailed to the West Indies in 1582, he commanded a small ship in *Drake's expedition to the Indies in 1585. In the campaign of the Spanish *Armada in 1588 he commanded the *Swallow*, a royal ship, and on his father's voyage to the Azores in 1590 he was captain of the *Dainty*, a private ship.

In this 300-ton ship he proposed to follow the example of Drake and *Cavendish by making a voyage round the world, and in June 1593 sailed in her from Plymouth. He rediscovered the Falkland Islands, sighted by John *Davis two years before, which he named 'Hawkins His Maidenland'. He passed through the Straits of Magellan, attacked Valparaiso, and fought his way up the coast until he was forced to surrender after a three-day fight off Paita on 22 June 1594. He was imprisoned, first at Lima and then in Spain, until in 1602 he was ransomed for £3,000. He was knighted on his return to England and represented Plymouth in Parliament. In 1620 he sailed with Sir Robert *Mansell on an unsuccessful naval expedition against the *Barbary corsairs. He died in 1622, it was said because of his anger at the delay in paying his men.

He wrote in 1603–4 an account of his voyage to the Pacific, though it was not published until the year of his death, under the title *The Observations of Sir Richard Hawkins, Knight, in his Vojage into the South Sea*, a work which has become a classic of the sea. His remarks about the conditions in ships at sea at that time provide the best and most authentic picture we have.

HAWSE, strictly, that part of a ship's *bow where the *hawseholes and hawsepipes are situated through which the anchor *cables pass. But it is by extension and in its most generally accepted meaning also the distance between the ship's head and her anchor as it lies on the bottom. Thus another vessel which crosses this space is said to cross the hawse. When a ship lies to two anchors, she has a clear hawse when the two cables *grow from the ship without crossing; when they do cross, the ship has a *foul hawse. The normal practice in ships when they lie to two anchors is to insert a *mooring swivel between the two cables so that the ship swings in a restricted circle without the cables becoming crossed.

HAWSE BAG, a canvas bag stuffed with *oakum which was used in older days in heavy seas to stuff into the *hawseholes so that sea water was prevented from coming inboard through them. That was in the days when *anchors were stowed on an anchor bed and the hawsehole, normally cut in the ship's side near the *bow on the main deck level, had no *cable running through it when at sea. The same service is performed today by a hawse block or a hawse buckler, a wooden or a metal plug respectively, shaped to fit round the links of the cable at the inboard end of the hawsehole. In the U.S. Navy hawse bags were known as *jackasses.

HAWSEHOLE, the hole in the forecastle deck, or upper deck in the case of vessels without a forecastle, right forward in the bows of a ship, through which the *anchor cable passes. The hawseholes form the entries to the *hawsepipes which lead the cables from the deck to the outside of the ship's hull. Large ships are usually fitted with three hawseholes, one each side of the *stemhead through which are led the cables for the port and starboard *bower anchors, and a third just aft of the starboard bower through which is led the cable for the *sheet anchor.

Originally, in most wooden ships of any size and also in the early iron ships, the *capstan was fitted on the main deck and the cables worked from there, so that the hawsehole was no more than a hole cut in the ship's side close to the *stem on the main deck level. Those were the days before the invention of the stockless anchor, and when a ship was at sea, her anchors were secured on anchor beds, the cables being unbent and stowed inboard. The hawseholes were stopped with *hawse bags so that no seawater could enter through them in rough weather.

HAWSE-PIECES, in a wooden ship the timbers which form the *bow, usually parallel to the *stem and through which the *hawseholes are cut; in a steel ship, the plates similarly placed. They are strengthened in the general construction of the ship by the *breast hooks.

HAWSEPIPE, the inclined pipe or tube which leads from the *hawsehole of a ship, on the deck close to the *bows, to the outside of the vessel. The anchor *cable is led through the hawsepipe and the *anchor, bent to its end with a shackle, lies with its *shank in the hawsepipe when it is hove up close and secured for sea.

HAWSER, a heavy rope or small *cable with a circumference of 5 inches or more. They are used for a variety of purposes on board ship which require a strong and heavy rope, as, e.g., a *warp for a *kedge anchor, and for breastropes and *springs when a ship is secured along-side a wharf. In smaller vessels, such as yachts which have no chain cable, the rope used as an anchor warp is sometimes called a hawser, even though less than the size normally accepted as the minimum to qualify for the name.

HAWSER-LAID ROPE, the description given to rope in which three *strands are laid up against the *twist to form the rope. It is the normal form of rope used for most purposes at sea. In Britain, most hawser-laid rope is laid up right-handed, or anti-clockwise, but left-handed ropes are sometimes found. Three strands each of 150 *fathoms in length will make a hawser-laid rope of 120 fathoms. See also CABLE-LAID ROPE and for illus. see S-TWIST.

HAYES, ISAAC ISRAEL (1832–81), American Arctic explorer, was a doctor of medicine and was appointed as surgeon to Elisha K. *Kane's second Arctic expedition in 1853. He believed firmly in the existence of an open polar sea, and in 1860–1 made an attempt to reach the North pole in the ship *United States* but was unable to reach further north than latitude 80° 14′, being stopped by the ice. He made a third voyage to the Arctic in 1869, spending some months in exploring northern Greenland, a visit which he described in his book *The Land of Desolation* (1871). He had previously written two books about the Arctic, *An Arctic Boat Journey* (1860) and *The Open Polar Sea* (1867).

HAYET, ARMAND (1882–1969), French author, spent much of his sea life in rescuing from oblivion the sea *shanties and folk lore of the days of sail. All his seafaring was done in sailing ships, of which he had a deep love, and he waged an incessant war against the incorrect use of words in matters concerning ships and the sea. In 1927 he published the first edition of a collection of shanties, meticulously and painstakingly researched, under the title *Chansons de Bord*, which contained the French versions of many of the English and American shanties sung by seamen. Because, for the sake of decency, the words of some of them had to be bowdlerized, he also published a limited unexpurgated edition, *Chansons de la Voile, sans voile*, under the name Jean Marie le Bihor, who was one of his sailors. Another of his books concerned the customs of the sea, translated into English as *Ways and Customs of Deep Sea Sailors* (1953) which is recognized as a masterpiece of its kind.

While these are the books by which Hayet will be chiefly remembered, he wrote also a number of authentic stories of the sea and sea life, of which the best known is *Le Prince Matelot*. He was awarded a medal by the Marine Academy of Paris in 1939 for his work.

HAZE, to, to make life on board a ship as uncomfortable as possible for the crew by keeping them hard at work at all hours of the day and night, often unnecessarily so. It was the practice of some captains, particularly in the big sail trading ships and *barques of the 19th century, to try to assert their authority by hazing their crews unmercifully, even to the extent of inventing work to deprive the *watch below of the legitimate hours of rest. Richard Henry *Dana, in his *Two Years Before the Mast*, describes how Captain Thompson used to haze the crew of the *brig *Pilgrim* by turning out the watch below, rain or fine, making them stand round the deck far enough apart to be unable to speak to each other, picking *oakum. See also 'BUCKO' MATE.

HEAD, a much used maritime word meaning the top or forward part. The top edge of a four-sided sail is called the head, the top of the mast is the masthead, the head of a ship is the bows (but the ship's head means the compass direction in which she is pointing). Headsails are the *jibs and *staysails hoisted at the forward end of a sailing vessel; a headboard is the small wooden insertion at the top of a *Bermuda mainsail. The word is also used as a verb in very much the same sense; a sailing vessel is headed by the wind when it swings round towards the vessel's bows so that the original course can no longer be laid.

By the head, a ship which is drawing more water forward than aft.

HEAD ROPE, that part of the *boltrope of a sail which lies along the head of a four-sided sail. Triangular sails, of course, have no head and therefore no head rope.

HEADBOARD, of a *Bermuda mainsail, see HEAD.

HEADS, the name given to that part of the older sailing ships forward of the *forecastle and around the *beak which was used by the crew as their lavatory. It was always used in the plural to indicate the weather and lee sides, seamen being expected to use the lee side so that all effluent should fall clear into the sea. They were floored with gratings so that the sea could assist in washing them clean, though there was always a small working party told off from each *watch to clean the heads, never a very popular task and one usually reserved as a punishment for small misdemeanours.

The name has been largely retained among seamen, even in these days of lavatory bowls and modern flushing arrangements. See also BEAK-HEAD.

HEARNE, SAMUEL (1745–92), British explorer, entered the British Navy in 1756 and served in the Seven Years War (1756–63), at the end of which he joined the Hudson's Bay Company. His first task was to examine parts of the Bay with the object of improving the cod fishery, the next to discover copper mines which had been described by Indians. He made three expeditions to the north-west for this purpose: the first in 1769 failed because the Indians he took with him deserted; the second failed early in 1770 because he broke his *quadrant; but the third, at the end of 1770, was successful in his discovery of the basin of the Coppermine River. He also traced the river to the Arctic Ocean, being the first white man to cross overland from Hudson Bay to that ocean. In 1775 he was made governor of Fort Prince of Wales but was captured by Jean-François *La Pérouse in 1782 and taken to France as a prisoner, being released in 1787.

HEART, a form of *deadeye which was used for setting up the *stays of a square-rigged ship in the same way as deadeyes were used for setting up the *shrouds. It was in the form of a triangular block of wood, sometimes cut heart-shaped, with a single large hole in the middle grooved for the rope or lanyard (according to the size of ship) to provide a degree of purchase when setting the stay up taut.

'HEART OF OAK', a patriotic song written by David Garrick and beginning:

'Come cheer up, my lads, 'tis to glory we steer,
To add something more to this wonderful year,'

It was set to music by William Boyce in 1759, and first performed in the pantomime *Harlequin's Invasion*. It commemorated the achievements of 1759, the year of victories, 'this wonderful year' as the song has it, during the Seven Years War (1756–63), when the army had triumphed at Minden, the navy at *Lagos and *Quiberon Bay, and both together at the capture of *Quebec. The song was later traditionally played on board British *ships of the line when they sailed into battle (though see also 'BRITONS STRIKE HOME'), and when the drums on board beat to *quarters, they did so to the rhythm of 'Heart of Oak'.

HEAVE-TO, to, to lay a sailing ship on the wind with her helm *a-lee and her sails shortened and so trimmed that as she comes up to the wind she will fall off again on the same tack and thus make no headway. Vessels normally heave-to when the weather is too rough and the wind too strong to make normal sailing practicable. A steamship can similarly heave-to in stormy weather by heading up to the sea and using her engines just enough to hold her up in position. The whole idea in heaving-to is to bring the wind on to the weather bow and hold the ship in that position, where she rides most safely and easily.

HEAVING LINE, a light line with a small weighted bag at the end used for heaving from the ship to shore when coming alongside; a heavier wire rope or hawser is attached which can then be hauled over by the heaving line.

HECKSTALL-SMITH, BROOKE (1869–1944), British yachting writer, succeeded Dixon *Kemp as secretary of the Yacht Racing Association (see ROYAL YACHTING ASSOCIATION) in 1898. He was yachting editor of *The Field*, 1920–8, yachting correspondent of the *Daily Telegraph*, and until the Second World War on the editorial staff of the journal *Yachting World*. In 1904 he proposed through the Yacht Club de France an international agreement on all yacht racing rules, as a result of which the International Yacht Racing Union, representing twenty-four nations, was formed in Paris in 1907, and he was appointed its secretary. He was also secretary of various international yachting conferences between 1906 and 1937, when identical rules of yacht measurement and racing were universally adopted by Great Britain, the U.S.A., and all other yachting nations.

Brooke Heckstall-Smith was a popular and jovial personality and a well known figure in the big yacht racing scene. He was an expert helmsman, and among his many racing successes was to steer *Noresca* to win the King's Cup at the Royal Ulster Yacht Club's regatta 1924. Among his best-known books were *Manual of Yacht and Boat Sailing, All Hands on the Mainsheet, The Complete Yachtsman, Yacht Racing*, and *The 'Britannia' and her Contemporaries*. His brother was Malden Heckstall-Smith who was an authority on yacht rating rules and editor of the *Yachting Monthly* for six years following the death of its founder-editor, Herbert Reiach, in 1921.

HECLA, H.M.S., a *bomb *ketch of 375 tons launched at North Barton in 1815. In 1819 she was commanded by Lieutenant W. E. *Parry during his first expedition to discover a *North-West passage. In 1821 under the command of Lieutenant G. F. Lyon she took part in Parry's second expedition, the latter then commanding the *Fury*. Parry again took command of the *Hecla* during his third and fourth expeditions, during the last of which he reached latitude 82° 45′ N. She was sold out of the Royal Navy in April 1831.

HEDGEHOG, a development during the Second World War of the *depth-charge weapon against *U-boats. It consisted of a 24-barrelled mortar

mounted on the forecastle of an escort vessel and it fired simultaneously that number of small 35-lb charges over a pre-determined spread which exploded on impact against a U-boat's hull. The advantage of an ahead-firing weapon was that *sonar contact with the U-boat could be held up to the moment of firing whereas in the case of the conventional depth-charge dropped over the stern of the hunting vessel, sonar contact was lost as the ship passed directly over the submerged U-boat.

Although a great improvement on the original depth-charge dropping gear, one drawback of the hedgehog was that it needed one of the charges to hit a submerged U-boat to sink her. It was quickly overtaken by the *squid, a much more formidable ahead-firing weapon against U-boats.

HEEL, (1) the after end of a ship's *keel and the lower end of the *sternpost, to which it is connected. **(2)** The lower end of a mast, *boom, or *bowsprit in a sailing vessel. The heel of a mast is normally squared off and is lowered through a hole in the decks until it fits into a square step cut in the *keelson of the ship, or alternatively is held in a *tabernacle on deck in the case of masts which can be lowered, or raised, at will.

HEEL, to, in relation to a ship, to lean over to one side. It is not a permanent leaning over, as with a *list, or spasmodic, as when a vessel *rolls in a sea, but somewhere between the two. Thus a sailing vessel will heel over when the wind catches her sails, unless she has the wind directly astern, and she will retain that heel until she alters course by coming nearer the wind or bearing away or the wind changes in strength or direction; a steamship will heel outwards, when turning at speed, through her centrifugal force, returning to the upright when the turn is over. When used as a noun, the word refers to the amount, or angle, to which a vessel is heeled. See also BREAM, TO, PARLIAMENT HEEL.

HEELING ERROR, an error in a yacht's magnetic *compass which can be caused when she *heels. Whereas most ships' compasses are stabilized and corrected with small magnets to prevent errors when the vessel is rolling or takes a slight list, the compass of a sailing yacht is more liable to become affected when the yacht heels sharply under the pressure of the wind on her sails. The cause is usually due to the shifting positions of adjacent ferrous metal objects in relation to the compass card, which remains level to the horizon by means of its gimbals. While any error in the compass may have been corrected by magnets when the yacht was upright, this correcting influence can be upset as soon as the yacht heels to port or to starboard, and the iron, steel, or electrical objects causing the error move above or below the compass card. A separate correction card for compass error at different angles of heel may have to be made out, or, if the error is excessive at certain angles of heel, it may become necessary to relocate the compass.

HEEMSKERK, JACOB VAN (1567–1607), Dutch seaman and explorer, was born at Amsterdam. He went to sea in the *Greyhound* in 1595 with William * Barents, on a voyage to the Arctic aimed at finding a passage to China. The expedition was obliged to return because of ice, but set out again in 1596. On this occasion the ships were beset in the ice and only twelve members of the expedition returned, their survival being mainly due to Heemskerk's courage and skill. He was one of the * Sea Beggars during the years of Dutch revolt against Spanish occupation, and in 1607 he set sail with a fleet of twenty-six ships to intercept a Spanish fleet reported to be on its way to attack the Dutch East Indian settlements. He found the Spaniards in Gibraltar Bay on 25 April, destroyed their fleet which included ten * galleons, but died of wounds received during the action. He was buried in the Oude Kerk at Amsterdam.

He is one of the great naval heroes of Holland, and many ships in the Dutch Navy have borne his name.

HELIGOLAND, Germ. Helgoland, an island in the North Sea off the west German coast, was taken by Britain from Denmark in 1807, during the Napoleonic War (1803–15), and used as a base for smugglers to beat Napoleon's continental * blockade of Britain. It was formally ceded to Britain in 1814, but exchanged in 1890 for the German African colonies of Zanzibar and Uganda, a bargain described in the German press as the 'surrender of the keys of Africa for a trouser button'. Before the First World War (1914–18) it was fortified by Germany as a protection for the western end of the * Kiel Canal. The fortifications were dismantled in 1919 under the terms of the treaty of Versailles, but were rebuilt in 1935 when Germany renounced that treaty. They were finally blown up in 1947 following the defeat of Germany in the Second World War.

HELIGOLAND BIGHT, BATTLE OF, was fought on 28 August 1914 between British and German light forces. It was planned as a raid on German patrols in the Heligoland Bight, the position and movements of which had been reported by British submarines stationed there. The Harwich Force, comprising the light * cruisers *Arethusa* and *Fearless* accompanied by two flotillas of * destroyers under the command of Commodore R. Y. * Tyrwhitt, covered by the Battle-Cruiser Force and the 1st Light Cruiser Squadron under the command of Rear Admiral David * Beatty and Commodore W. E. Goodenough respectively, entered the Bight at dawn on 28 August and the action began at 7 a.m. when Tyrwhitt's cruisers sighted two patrolling enemy * torpedoboats, one of which they sank. The German light cruisers *Stettin* and *Frauenlob* moved to support the torpedoboats and were joined by the *Mainz*, and later by the *Köln* (Rear Admiral Maas), *Stralsund*, and *Ariadne*. Heavily outgunned, the Harwich Force was obliged to withdraw but was saved from disaster by the timely support rendered by Beatty's * battle-cruisers. The German ships then withdrew under cover of mist, but not before losing the light cruisers *Mainz*, *Köln*, and *Ariadne* at a cost to the British forces of one cruiser and one destroyer damaged, both of which reached port. British casualties were thirty-five killed and forty wounded, those of the Germans over 1,200 killed, wounded, and taken prisoner.

HELLESPONT, the ancient name for the * Dardanelles, the strait which separates Turkey in Europe from Turkey in Asia and which connects the north-eastern corner of the Mediterranean with the Sea of Marmara.

HELM, another name for the * tiller, by which the * rudder of small vessels, such as yachts, dinghies, etc., is swung, and also the general term associated with orders connected with the steering of a ship. Steering by tiller was the general form of steering for all ships, after the replacement of the original * steering oar by the rudder, and although the tiller gave way long ago to the steering wheel in all ships of any size, the original helm orders (applicable to the tiller) remained in operation. The steering wheel is connected to the rudder so that the direction of turn is the same as the movement of the rudder, i.e., when the wheel is put over to * starboard, the rudder moves to starboard and the ship's head swings the same way. The reverse is the case with the tiller which moves in the opposite way to the rudder; when the tiller is put to starboard the rudder moves to * port and the ship's head swings also to port.

For some three centuries all helm orders given in ships remained applicable to the tiller, and an order from the navigator of a ship to a helmsman of, for example, 'port 20' meant that the helmsman put the wheel over 20° to starboard, the equivalent direction of moving the tiller 20° to port, and the rudder and the ship's head moved to starboard.

This practice was universal until after the First World War (1914–18), when some nations began to adopt the practice of relating helm orders to the rudder and no longer to the tiller, so that an order of, for instance, 'starboard 20' meant turning the wheel, the rudder, and the ship's head all to starboard. By the mid-1930s all maritime nations had adopted this practice, which removed the anomaly of a navigator giving the order 'port' when he wanted to turn the ship to starboard, and vice-versa.

HELSINKI, formerly **HELSINGFORS,** capital of Finland and the major seaport of that country. It is a centre of the shipping trade inside the Baltic and also with the rest of the world. The fine natural harbour is protected by the fortress island of Sveaborg, which was briefly occupied by British naval forces during the Crimean War (1854–6).

HEMP, the plant *Cannabis sativa,* from the fibres of which the best natural rope is made. Hemp rope is usually tarred as a preservative against perishing, but when not so treated is known as white rope. Although for centuries regarded as the best kind of rope for use in ships, it is today being rapidly replaced by rope made from synthetic or man-made fibres, which are impervious to weather, do not shrink when wet, and size for size are of greater strength, if sometimes less kind to a seaman's hand and apt to slip when knotted.

HENGST, a typical Dutch fishing vessel of south Holland with a flat bottom, two *chines a side, a rounded low stern, narrow *leeboards, and straight *stem at about 45° *rake. They are small craft with an average overall length of 30–35 feet with the traditional Dutch rig of a foresail set on the stemhead *forestay and a tall, narrow, loose-footed mainsail with a short *boom and curved *gaff. Later fishing hengsts, and those converted into private yachts, were fitted with auxiliary petrol or diesel engines. Like the somewhat larger *hoogaarts they are decked forward of the mast.

HENRY, Prince of Portugal (1394–1460), known as the Navigator, was the third son of John I of Portugal and grandson of John of Gaunt. He gained military renown at the capture of Ceuta in 1415 and in other Moroccan campaigns in 1436 and 1458, but is best remembered for his inspiration and patronage of a long succession of Portuguese seamen who made voyages of discovery among the Atlantic islands and down the west coast of Africa which led, after his death, to the discovery of the Cape of *Good Hope and the sea route to India.

As governor of the Algarve he lived for the last twenty-two years of his life at Sagres where he established a naval arsenal to which he attracted Arab, Jewish, and other mathematicians to teach *navigation, astronomy, and cartography to his captains and pilots; he himself was an ardent student of geography. The Prince also constructed a notable observatory, the first in Portugal.

Voyages inspired by Prince Henry rediscovered the Madeira group and the Azores in 1420 and 1427 respectively and led to their colonization and cultivation. In 1434 one of his ships commanded by Gil Eannes first rounded Cape Bojador; eight years later, Nuno Tristam passed Cape Blanco to explore the coast beyond, whence there came to Portugal the first Negro slaves as well as gold-dust.

Exploration had thus become profitable and therefore popular, leading to a burst of maritime activity: more than thirty ships with the Prince's licence sailed to Guinea between 1444 and 1446. Senegal was reached by several navigators in 1445; Cape Verde was rounded by Diniz Diaz and, in the following year, Alvaro *Fernandez pushed on almost to Sierra Leone. Although the kidnapping of slaves was forbidden in 1456, slaving voyages continued unchecked. Prince Henry's enthusiasm continued to be an inspiration of explorers even after his death.

R. H. Major, *Prince Henry of Portugal* (1868).

HENRY GRÂCE À DIEU, in her day the largest warship in the world, was launched at Erith, in Kent, England, in June 1514. She was in her time, and still is, widely known under the name *Great Harry.* She was built by William Bond, master shipwright, directed by Robert Brygandine, clerk of the ships, at the command of Henry VIII, and was probably of 1,000, although some contemporary accounts give the figure of 1,500, tons. She had four pole masts, each, except the *bonaventure *mizen, with two circular *tops, and set three square sails on fore and main masts and *lateen sails on mizen and bonaventure mizen. Her sails, at least on state occasions, were of cloth of gold damasked. She had a complement of 700 men and she was armed with twenty-one heavy guns of 'brass', which in those days meant bronze, and a light armament of 231 weapons of various types, but mainly *murderers. She was accidentally destroyed by fire at Woolwich in August 1553.

A picture, painted by Volpe, showing the *Henry Grâce à Dieu* at the embarkation of Henry VIII at Dover in May 1520 for Boulogne is at Hampton Court, and the well-known coloured drawing of her in the contemporary Anthony Roll is in the Pepysian collection of manuscripts at Magdalene College, Cambridge.

HENTY, GEORGE ALFRED (1832–1902), English author, yachtsman, and war correspondent, was born at Trumpington, near Cambridge, England. He served in the Crimean War (1854–6) then drifted into journalism. He was war correspondent of the London *Standard* for the

Austro-Italian War of 1866, followed Garibaldi in the war in the Tyrol, was with Lord Napier in the Magdala campaign and with Lord Wolseley at Kumassi, a service which brought extremes of mountainous passes and malarial swamps. He then reported the Franco-German war of 1870 for the *Standard*, being caught in Paris in the siege of the Commune and nearly starving to death, and was later with the Carlist insurrection through the Pyrenees. His next assignment for his newspaper was in Asiatic Russia with the Khiva expedition and he then reported the war of liberation in Serbia, being caught up in some of the violent hand-to-hand fighting.

He returned to London to edit the *Union Jack*, a magazine for boys, and perhaps then found his true vocation in life. Some serial stories which he wrote for the *Union Jack* proved so successful that he settled down to write adventure books for boys, almost all with a historical naval or military flavour, of which *Under Drake's Flag* was perhaps a typical example. He wrote some eighty of these books, and his name became synonymous with high adventure and moral excellence among his many thousands of young readers. He was also a keen yachtsman and spent some six months of every year sailing around the coasts of Britain. In November 1902 he was found dead on board his yacht as she lay at anchor in Weymouth Harbour.

HERBERT, ARTHUR, first Earl of Torrington (1647–1716), British admiral of the fleet, served in the Second Dutch War (1665–7) and against the * Barbary corsairs in the Mediterranean. Promoted admiral in 1680, he was dismissed in 1687 in consequence of refusing, as a Member of Parliament, to vote for the repeal of the Test Act. He went to Holland and placed his services at the disposal of William of Orange, who appointed him to command the fleet covering William's successful invasion of England in 1688. As a reward he was made First Lord of the Admiralty and commanded the fleet which failed to prevent the French landing at * Bantry Bay, Ireland, in 1689. In 1690 he commanded an Anglo-Dutch fleet in the Channel against the French admiral de * Tourville, but was worsted in the engagement off * Beachy Head and compelled to retire into the Thames. He was acquitted at a court martial by contending that he had maintained his 'fleet in being', so that no invasion could be safely attempted. Torrington never served again at sea, though until his death he regularly attended the House of Lords and frequently spoke in naval debates.

HERMAPHRODITE BRIG, sometimes known as a brig-schooner, a two-masted sailing ship rigged on the foremast as a * brig with square sails set on * yards, and as a * schooner on the mainmast, with a square topsail set above a * gaff

The Henry Grâce à Dieu; *contemporary drawing in the Anthony Roll*

mainsail. She differed from a *brigantine by the square topsail set on the mainmast, brigantines being fully fore-and-aft rigged on the main.

HERMIONE, H.M.S., the ship built at Bristol in 1782, in which, in 1797, 'the bloodiest mutiny that ever occurred in a ship of the Royal Navy' took place. The mutiny was the result of the tyrannical behaviour of her captain, Hugh Pigot, who was murdered by the mutineers, together with nine of his officers. The men then sailed the ship to the Spanish Main and handed her over to the Spaniards. During the succeeding ten years, more than twenty of the mutineers were hunted down and hanged at the yardarm by the Royal Navy. The *Hermione* herself was recaptured in October 1799 by the boats of H.M.S. *Surprise*, under Captain Sir Edward Hamilton, who cut her out from Porto Gabello harbour.

HERRESCHOFF, NATHANIEL GREENE (1848–1938), U.S. marine architect, was born near Bristol, Rhode Island, on the shores of Narragansett Bay, and was one of the gifted family of six sons and three daughters of Charles and Sarah Herreschoff. His elder brother, John Brown Herreschoff (b. 1841), from the first showed a flair for boat building and marine engineering and encouraged Nathaniel in the same interests. Before the latter was 12 years old the two boys designed and built a 22-ft sailing boat, *Sprite*, which was not only a consistent winner for a number of years at local regattas but also had a very long life and is now preserved at the Ford Museum, Dearborn, Michigan.

Following a course in mechanical engineering, the nearest subject to naval architecture then available, at the Massachusetts Institute of Technology in 1866, Nathaniel spent the next nine years with the Corliss Steam Engine Company at Providence, largely on the design side. His own genius for boat design resulted in 1876 in his producing a 30-ft racing *catamaran, Amaryllis*, an innovation to Narragansett waters, which soundly beat all the local *sandbagger yachts and gave a number of twin-hulled imitators of his design a brief triumph until catamarans were outlawed by changes in the racing rules.

With the formation of the family business, the Herreschoff Manufacturing Company at Bristol, Nathaniel turned his talents to the design of steam yachts and launches and their machinery, while continuing to design a succession of beautiful racing yachts. Although by this time his brother John, inheriting a Herreschoff family weakness of the eyes, had gone blind, he was an equally active partner and was the inventor of a new type of coil boiler used for high speed yachts and naval torpedoboats, for which the firm became famous. After 1891 the Herreschoff Com-

pany turned back from building steam vessels as the new gasoline (petrol) internal combustion engine began to replace engines and boilers in pleasure craft, and concentrated on the building of sailing yachts of various types. While Nathaniel drew the lines of the various yachts on his board, his blind brother John checked the hulls with unerring accuracy using only his hands. From the Herreschoff yard emerged yachts of outstanding performance in the American racing world, among them the New York Yacht Club 30-, 40-, 50-, 65-, and 70-footer one-design classes, in which all the yachts of a class were built exactly to the same plans. At this time, too, the Herreschoff brothers introduced what was then a novel labour-saving method of erecting the hulls of identical yachts with the keel uppermost before turning them over to have the deck and interior arrangements fitted, thereby introducing what were to become normal quantity production methods in yacht building.

Among the more celebrated sailing yachts designed and built by the firm were the successful *America*'s Cup defenders *Vigilant* (1893), *Defender* (1895), *Columbia* (1899 and 1901), *Reliance* (1903), and *Resolute* (1920). Afflicted in his latter years with inherited blindness Nathaniel died at Newport, Rhode Island, in his 91st year. Models of 220 of his designs have been brought together in the Herreschoff Model Room, Rhode Island.

HERVEY, the Hon. AUGUSTUS JOHN, later third Earl of Bristol (1724–79), British admiral, took part in Admiral *Byng's indecisive action off *Minorca in 1756, being ordered home after the action to give evidence at Byng's trial. In 1759, flying the broad pennant of a *commodore and in command of the inshore squadron, he kept a close watch on the French fleet in Brest, earning high praise from Sir Edward *Hawke for the way he conducted this part of the blockade. In the autumn of 1761 he was ordered to the West Indies to join Sir George *Rodney's fleet where, with a small squadron, he captured the island of St. Lucia and later, with *Keppel, captured the Havannah after heavy casualties. For a short while, in 1763, he was commander-in-chief in the Mediterranean, and in 1771 he became a lord of the Admiralty. While serving as a captain Hervey kept a journal which is now recognized as a minor classic of the sea. Edited by David Erskine it was published in 1953 under the title *Augustus Hervey's Journal.*

HERZOGIN CECILIE, a four-masted *barque built at Bremerhaven for the Norddeutscher-Lloyd steamship company as a sail training ship carrying seventy-five cadets. With an overall length of 337 feet, she set *royals over double *topgallants, with a double *spanker, and was used for trading all over the world. She was dismasted off Cape Horn on her maiden voyage, but proved to be a very fast ship and in 1909 made the passage from Bremen to Mejillones, Chile, in sixty-eight days, returning from that port to the Scilly Islands in sixty-three days, with a further five days from there to Rotterdam. She also made a very fast passage of eighty-one days from Geelong, Australia, to Falmouth, England, with a cargo of wool. The outbreak of the First World War (1914–18) found her at Coquimbo, Chile, where she was interned, being allocated to France after the war and sold by that country to Gustav Erikson of Mariehamn, Finland, one of the best-known operators of trading sail ships. He used her for trading voyages wherever there were cargoes to be carried, and in 1931 she was recorded as having covered 365 miles in twenty-four hours, with a maximum speed of 20¾ *knots at one period. She was wrecked on Bolt Head, on the south Devon coast of England, in 1936, a few hours after leaving Falmouth.

HEWITT, HENRY KENT (1887–1972), American admiral, distinguished himself in command of the operations on the coast of Morocco and then in the Mediterranean during the Second World War. During the invasion of North Africa in November 1942 Hewitt's amphibious force established itself in Morocco on the first day of the assault. In February 1943 he established his headquarters in Algiers and from that port began to operate in conjunction with British naval forces under Admiral Sir Andrew *Cunningham. On 10 July 1943, he commanded the American half of the invasion of Sicily and two months later supported the allied landings in Salerno, Italy. In February 1944 he commanded the assault landing at Anzio and in August directed the operations which established American and allied troops on the south coast of France. Promoted to admiral in April 1945 he became, in August of that year, Commander, U.S. Forces in Europe.

HEYERDAHL, THOR (1914–   ), Norwegian scientist and adventurer, was born at Larvik and educated at Oslo University. One of his interests at the university was the study of the early civilizations and movements of oceanic peoples, and in 1937, after much preparation, he set out on an expedition to the Marquesas Islands in the Pacific to continue his studies at first hand. It was there that he first began to suspect that the Polynesian civilization may have had its roots in an earlier migration of South American Indians, though it seemed impossible to conceive how the long ocean voyage could have been made without ships, unknown in the Pacific at that time, and with no knowledge of navigation and ocean currents. Heyerdahl returned to Norway in 1938 to continue his studies and came to the conclusion that if his theories about the emigration were correct, it could only have come about by drifting across the ocean on rafts.

The Second World War, in which he served in the Norwegian Army and Air Force, interfered with his plan of putting his theories to the test by attempting to make the ocean crossing by raft, but by 1947 he was ready for the venture. In the face of much opposition, and with the help of five companions, he constructed a raft from the trunks of the indigenous *Ochroma lagopus* trees (also known as 'balsa'), using only such fastenings to bind the trunks together as would have been available to the Indians at the time of their supposed migration. The raft was rigged with a short mast and single square sail, and Heyerdahl set off to drift and sail across the Pacific with his five companions, leaving Callao, Peru, on 28 April 1947. The raft, 45 ft long and 18 ft beam, was named *Kon-Tiki* after the legendary sun king of the South American Indians. It was finally beached on Raroia Reef, in the Tuamotos, on 7 August after having drifted 4,300 miles in 101 days, proving that his theory about the colonization of the Polynesian islands was a physical possibility even in the earliest days of Pacific sea travel. The story of the voyage is related in his book *The Kon-Tiki Expedition*, published in 1948.

Still attracted to the Pacific islands and the mysteries surrounding the genesis of the Polynesian civilization, he visited the Galapagos Islands in 1953 and in 1955–6 led a Norwegian expedition to Easter Island to make a study of the origins of the great statues found there. An account of the expedition and its findings was given in his book *Aku-Aku, The Secret of Easter Island*, published in 1958.

Heyerdahl's next field of interest lay in the many ancient accounts of very early Egyptian navigations, and he determined to attempt, as he had done with the *Kon-Tiki*, an ocean passage in the type of vessel which the ancient Egyptians would have used. He considered that the most likely material available in Egypt at that time was the papyrus reed, and he constructed a vessel made of reeds, which he named *Ra*, after the sun god of ancient Egypt. In it he set sail with a party of companions to attempt to cross the Atlantic, but the boat disintegrated in heavy seas when nearing the West Indies. Undaunted by this mishap, Heyerdahl constructed a second papyrus boat, *Ra II*, and in 1970 successfully made the Atlantic crossing from Safi, Morocco, to Bridgetown, Barbados, thus demonstrating that oceanic voyages by the ancient Egyptians were well within the bounds of possibility.

In addition to the popular accounts of his voyages, Heyerdahl has written a number of scientific works.

HEYN, PIETER PIETERZOON (1578–1629), Dutch admiral, started life as a fisherman. He was taken prisoner by the Spaniards as a youth and forced to row in the *galleys. After four years he was released and became a successful merchant skipper, making a modest fortune from his trade.

He was a director of the Rotterdam branch of the Dutch *East India Company, frequently acting in command or second-in-command of their fleets for various voyages, and in 1628 achieved great fame, and a vast fortune for his company, by capturing the Spanish treasure fleet, valued at 4,000,000 ducats. During the last year of his life he was selected to command the naval forces of Holland and clear the Channel and North Sea of Dunkirkers, pirates or *privateers operating out of the port of Dunkirk, who were acting for the king of Spain in the Netherlands. He brought them to action in June 1629 and severely defeated them, but was himself killed by a cannon ball early in the battle. Known as Piet Heyn, he is one of the great Dutch naval heroes.

HIGH SEAS, in international law all the area of sea not under the sovereignty of states with a seaboard. For many years various claims had been made by different states on the extent of their *territorial waters, some choosing an arbitrary figure such as 100 miles, others the range of visibility, and so on. As the interests of navigation and trade grew, it was universally accepted that the dictum *terrae dominium finitur ubi finitus armorum vis* applied to the definition of territorial waters, and so the utmost range of a cannon-shot, accepted as 3 miles, was taken as the limit of sea which could be claimed nationally. All sea outside this limit was high seas and open to all without hindrance.

In recent years this limit of territorial waters has been challenged by many seafaring nations, mainly to preserve to themselves their inshore fishing grounds, and the limit has been gradually extended, with most nations now accepting 12 miles as marking territorial waters. But this, too, presents great difficulties with some nations claiming an extended limit ostensibly to preserve their fish breeding grounds, and in view of the growing exploitation of the seabed in drilling for oil and natural gas. A current suggestion, as yet unaccepted by all maritime states, is that territorial waters should extend to the limit of the continental shelf, normally represented by the 100-fathom line. More recently, proposals have been made by some maritime states for a territorial limit of 200 miles. Successive international conferences on the Law of the Sea have debated the subject but without as yet (1976) reaching any agreement.

HIGH SEAS FLEET, the principal fleet of the German Navy, 1907–18. In August 1914, under the command of Admiral von Ingenohl (flagship *Friedrich der Grosse*) it comprised 15 *dreadnought *battleships, four *battle-cruisers, 32 pre-dreadnought battleships and coast defence vessels (obsolete or semi-obsolete), 9 armoured *cruisers, 12 light cruisers, 88 *destroyers and torpedoboats. In October 1918, commanded by Admiral von *Hipper (flagship *Baden*) the fleet numbered 18 dreadnought battleships, 5 battle-cruisers, 14 light cruisers, and 60 destroyers. For the most part the obsolete battleships and cruisers had been paid off to provide officers and crews for *U-boats, an indication of how the emphasis changed from surface ships to submarines during 1914–17.

When war began the Kaiser, who intervened in naval matters far more than in military, decided that the fleet should be exposed to as little risk as possible. He envisaged a speedy victory on land over France and Russia, to be followed by a peace conference at which Germany, with an undamaged battle fleet, would be in a position to obtain greater concessions from Britain than would otherwise be possible. After the British raid into the *Heligoland Bight on 28 August 1914, a limited freedom of action was given the High Seas Fleet, whose battle-cruisers, commanded by Rear Admiral Hipper, bombarded Yarmouth (3 November 1914) and West Hartlepool, Scarborough, and Whitby (16 December 1914). On the way back from covering the latter operation the High Seas Fleet had an excellent opportunity to cut off an isolated British battle squadron, an opportunity missed because of Ingenohl's meticulous adherence to the letter of his orders. A month later Hipper was at sea again and narrowly escaped disaster at the hands of Admiral *Beatty and his battle-cruisers at the battle of the *Dogger Bank. After this Ingenohl was replaced by the even more cautious Admiral von Pohl, who had been Chief of the Naval Staff and it was not until he fell ill and was replaced by Admiral *Scheer that the High Seas Fleet was again seriously engaged, Scheer's policy leading up to the action at *Jutland on 31 May 1916. After Jutland the High Seas Fleet came out into the North Sea only on three further occasions, 19 August and 18/19 October 1916, and 23–25 April 1918.

After the introduction of unrestricted U-boat warfare on 1 February 1917, Scheer considered that the principal duty of the High Seas Fleet was to facilitate that campaign by protecting the *minesweepers which kept open the channels through the North Sea minefields by which the U-boats passed on their way to and from their operational areas. In the summer of 1917 disorders took place in the big ships of the fleet, owing to a mixture of boredom, left-wing propaganda, poor food, and unimaginative handling of the men. Two of the mutineers were executed. During the winter of 1917–18 destroyers and light cruisers of the High Seas Fleet raided allied convoy routes in the North Sea and the Straits of Dover with some success in support of the U-boat war, and the High Seas Fleet itself, in its sortie of April 1918, reached the latitude of Bergen, missing two convoys because it failed to use available intelligence concerning British shipping movements. In August 1918 Hipper succeeded Scheer as commander-in-chief, but at the end of October, when he planned to take the fleet to sea to cover raids on the mouth of the Thames and the Straits of Dover, mutinies broke out in several of the big ships, first at Wilhelmshaven and then at Kiel, and the High Seas Fleet came to an end as an organized fighting force. See also GRAND FLEET.

HIGH-CHARGED SHIPS, warships of the sailing navies up to about 1585 built with high castles at bow and stern from which archers, and later musketeers operating a variety of small hand guns, were the principal fighters on board. These were the days when warships were manned by mariners who sailed and navigated the ship and soldiers who fought the battles at sea. The universal tactic of battle at sea was to mass the ships of a fleet in as closely packed a formation as possible, swamp the enemy personnel with concentrated flights of arrows or musketry, and then to get in among the enemy ships and carry them by boarding to put them to the torch.

High-charged ships were most unhandy and difficult to control, as the high castle built up on the bow presented so large an area to the wind that the ship's bows were continually blown down to *leeward. See also HAWKINS, Sir John; LOW-CHARGED SHIPS; NAVY.

HIGHFIELD LEVER, a form of hand-operated lever used aboard sailing yachts as a rapid method of setting up or tautening running backstays or forestays. It was invented about 1930 by J. S. Highfield, then rear-commodore of the Royal Thames Y.C., for trial aboard his 15-metre racing yacht *Dorina*. Casting off the *lee runners (or *backstays) and setting up the weather ones every time the yacht changed tacks showed up the degree of smartness or otherwise of a racing yacht's crew. With the advent of the *Bermuda rig with its lofty mast and taut rigging in the 1920s, the *blocks and *purchase of the old-fashioned backstays were no longer swift or taut enough, and the Highfield lever solved the difficulty. The end of the backstay wire is led to a block which slides along a lever pivoted above deck so that the lever works in a fore-and-aft direction. When the lever is turned aft and its end pressed down on to the deck, the block holding

the backstay wire comes below the line of the pivot bolt, thus holding the stay taut. To slacken the stay, the end of the lever merely has to be tripped up, and the stay is immediately released. Forestays can also be set up and released in the same manner. Variations and improved designs of the Highfield lever are to be found aboard yachts in all parts of the world.

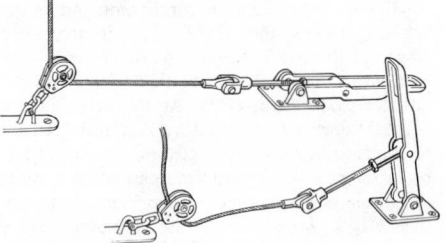

Highfield lever

HINDOSTAN, an all-wooden *paddle steamer and one of the first ships built for passengers rather than cargo. She sailed for India in 1842 and won the Indian mail contract for the *P & O Line.

HIPPER, FRANZ RITTER VON (1863–1932), German admiral, was born in Bavaria and therefore had no links with the sea, but early made up his mind to become a naval officer. His widowed mother, to discourage him, gave him Captain *Marryat's books to read, but this only strengthened his resolve and he entered the Naval Academy with the class of 1881. After some foreign service he returned home in 1890 and spent the rest of his career in home waters. This apparently was his own choice; for him the battle fleet was the be-all and end-all of the German Navy. After taking a course in *torpedoes he commanded a torpedoboat division and was promoted lieutenant-commander in 1895. Thenceforward he was almost continuously associated with the reconnaissance forces of the *High Seas Fleet and at the outbreak of war in 1914 was in command of all the scouting groups of that body with his flag in the *battle-cruiser *Seydlitz*. He is described by those who served under him as having a cheerful, light-hearted disposition and a great dislike of paper work. His career was unusual for a flag officer in that he never served either in the German Admiralty or at the Staff College. Admiral *Raeder, who was his chief-of-staff during most of the war, described him as 'an improvised leader'.

Operating within the limits imposed by the dead hand of the higher direction of the German war at sea, he twice led his scouting forces with dash and skill against the English coast in 1914. On 24 January 1915, however, he was intercepted while on a scouting foray to the *Dogger Bank by Admiral *Beatty's superior force and withdrew at high speed. His flagship, the *Seydlitz*, was badly damaged by an enemy shell that caused a huge ammunition fire, as the result of which the ship came near to blowing up, two of her turrets being out of action. As the battle went on, the last ship in the German line, the armoured *cruiser *Blücher*, was shot to pieces and sank.

Hipper continued as admiral commanding the scouting forces and at *Jutland, in the early stages of the battle, his five battle-cruisers sank two out of the six British battle-cruisers without any losses to themselves. At the crisis of the battle Hipper was ordered by Admiral *Scheer to protect the withdrawal of the High Seas Fleet by leading his battle-cruisers in an attack against the whole of the British *Grand Fleet. Although this attack lasted only four minutes before another order was substituted, it nevertheless became a famous incident in the battle, the utility of which was doubted by Hipper, who found himself at the end of it with his flagship *Lützow* sinking. Hipper transferred himself and his staff to a *destroyer but was unable to hoist his flag in another battle-cruiser (*Moltke*) for another two hours, as two out of the four were virtually out of action though still able to steam.

Hipper's conduct in the battle has been highly praised ever since. In August 1918 he was appointed to succeed Scheer as commander-in-chief of the High Seas Fleet and held that post until the end of the war.

The mutinies in the fleet at Wilhelmshaven in October and November 1918 completely overwhelmed him and he retired to a lonely village in Lower Saxony where he spent the rest of his life.

HISCOCK, ERIC CHARLES (1908–   ), British deep sea yachtsman and author, began cruising under sail at an early age in Solent waters. With his wife Susan he made a tentative cruise from Lymington to the Azores and back in his 24-ft (7·3 m) *cutter *Wanderer II*. This encouraged them to plan a world cruise in a larger yacht and *Wanderer III*, a 30-ft (9·1 m) *sloop of 8 tons, was built at Burnham-on-Crouch to a John Laurent *Giles design in 1952. In this yacht the Hiscocks by themselves sailed round the world in 1952–5 by way of the Cape of Good Hope, for which they were awarded the Royal Cruising Club's Challenge Cup and the Cruising Club of America Blue Water medal. Between 1959 and 1962 the Hiscocks completed a second circumnavigation by way of the Suez Canal. Other cruises to the West Indies and the Pacific coast of North America followed. In 1968 *Wanderer III* was sold to make way for *Wanderer IV*, a 49-ft (14·9 m) steel *ketch built in Holland, in which they continued their life afloat, voyaging to the Pacific and on to New Zealand. Among his many books the best known are *Wandering Under Sail, Voyaging Under Sail, Cruising Under Sail, Around the World in 'Wanderer III', Beyond the West Horizon*, and *Atlantic Cruise in 'Wanderer III'*.

HISPANIOLA, the old name by which Haiti was known. Although called Haiti (mountainous country) by the original natives, it was given the name of Espagnola (little Spain) by *Columbus when he landed there in 1492, the name subsequently being latinized into Hispaniola. After considerable conflict in 1801–3 against France, which had acquired the island from Spain, accompanied by acts of unexampled barbarity, the insurgents, led by the Negro Jean Jacques Dessalines (1758–1806), obtained independence in 1804 and renamed the island Haiti. This name has remained ever since.

HITCH, a series of knots by which one rope is joined to another or made fast to some object, such as a spar. There are many types of hitches used for various purposes, such as a *half hitch, a *rolling hitch, a *clove hitch, a running hitch, etc. They come within the overall genus of *bends, which include all the more common knots in use at sea.

HOBART, the capital of Tasmania and the main seaport of the island, built on the shores of a deep inlet in the south-east corner. It is a regular port of call for several shipping lines, its deep harbour being not only capable of taking the largest ships without difficulty but also sheltered from all possible winds.

HOBART PASHA, AUGUSTUS CHARLES HOBART-HAMPDEN (1822–86), British naval officer and Turkish admiral, saw his first naval service as a *midshipman in the suppression of the slave trade. In the Crimean War (1854–6) he commanded H.M.S. *Driver* in the Baltic and was present at the capture of Bomarsund in 1855. Bored with peacetime service he retired from the navy in 1862 in order to command a blockade-runner in the American Civil War (1861–5) and successfully evaded the Federal blockade eighteen times, running war materials into Charleston and returning with cargoes of cotton.

After the conclusion of that war he entered the service of Turkey in 1867 as a rear admiral and was almost at once employed in suppressing the insurrection in Crete, for which service the Sultan awarded him the title of Pasha. On the outbreak of the Russo-Turkish war he was given command of the Turkish fleet in the Black Sea, which he dominated so completely that no Russian warship was able to move. In 1881 the Sultan promoted him to the rank of *Mushir*, or marshal, the first Christian ever to hold so exalted an office.

HODGES, WILLIAM (1744–97), British artist and draughtsman, began life as an errand boy in the Shipley School of Drawing where he learned to draw. He accompanied Captain James *Cook on his second voyage of discovery (1772–5) and was subsequently employed by the British Admiralty to finish the sketches he made during the expedition and to supervise their engraving. On completion of his work at the Admiralty in 1778 he went to India under the patronage of Warren Hastings, where he painted landscapes 'of strange beauty and brilliance'. In 1786 he was elected A.R.A. and in 1795, on retiring as an artist, he opened a bank at Dartmouth which, however, failed. His pictures of Cook's voyage are now mainly divided between Admiralty House in London and the *National Maritime Museum.

HOG, an old-fashioned device for cleaning the dirt and weed off a ship's bottom. It was formed by enclosing a number of birch twigs between two planks, binding them together securely. The tops of the twigs were then cut off to form a stiff broom. The hog was guided under the ship's bottom by a long staff attached to the hog and drawn upwards by two ropes, one at each end of the hog, which was held hard against the ship's side by the staff. This operation was usually conducted from one of the ship's boats. HOGGING LINES, the lines attached to the corners of a *collision mat to manoeuvre it into position under the ship's bottom.

HOG, to, the condition of a ship in which the bow and stern have drooped, when she is said to be hogged. A vessel whose midship section is supported on a wave crest and whose bow and stern are poised over the trough either side of the wave is said to be subject to a hogging stress. It is the reverse of *sagging, in which the bow and stern are supported on succeeding wave crests with the midship section over the trough between the two waves.

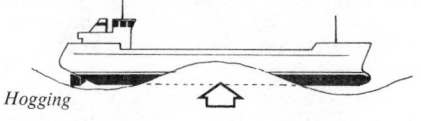

Hogging

HOGUE, H.M.S., see ABOUKIR, H.M.S.

HOGUE, LA, BATTLE OF, see BARFLEUR, BATTLE OF.

HOIST, (1) the name given to the *luff of a *fore-and-aft sail; the distance which it must be hoisted to get a taut luff. In a square sail it is the depth of the sail measured from its mid point. **(2)** That part of a flag or ensign which lies along the flagstaff and to which the *halyards are bent.

HOIST, to, the operation of hauling something up, particularly a sail or a flag, though the word is used in connection with most things which have to be lifted. An exception is a *yard of a square-rigged ship which is *swayed up, never hoisted.

HOLD, a large compartment below decks in a ship mainly for the stowage of cargo but also, in earlier days, for stowing provisions for a voyage, and often ship's gear. Sailing warships had holds for the stowage of casks containing salt beef and pork, beer, rum, or fresh water, other victualling supplies, slop clothing, and similar articles, but their holds were relatively small and confined to the space between the *orlop and lower decks. In the merchant ship of those days the holds were generally as large as could be fitted on board for the carriage of as much cargo as possible, as the more cargo stowed in the holds, the bigger the return in the *freight charges.

In modern times the holds of the average merchant ship extend right down the depth of the ship to the *floors and access to them is by large square hatches on the upper deck, *battened down at sea to make them watertight. In modern bulk carriers and *container ships, the stowage of cargo is scientifically controlled to prevent the danger of the cargo shifting at sea, but in many smaller ships cargo-stowing is an art of fitting in the various pieces and wedging them securely so that they do not take charge in a high sea. In particular, loose cargoes of coal or grain are apt to shift at sea when a ship rolls heavily, piling up on one side to give the ship a dangerous *list, but the risk of this can be reduced considerably by the erection of temporary wooden *bulkheads, known as *shifting boards, to divide and control the loose cargo. The modern large cargo vessel may well have twelve or more holds, each separated from the next by watertight *bulkheads to form a series of watertight compartments to lessen the danger of the ship sinking if she is holed in any one of these holds.

Vessels employed in the fresh food trade, such as meat, fruit, etc., have special refrigerated holds to preserve the produce; other specialized carriers at sea have their holds designed for the particular cargo they will be carrying. Most modern *trawlers have refrigerated holds for the stowage and preservation of the fish they catch.

HOLIDAY, a gap unintentionally left uncovered when painting or varnishing on board ship and applying equally to a ship herself or to her *masts and spars. It is also a gap left, equally unintentionally, in *paying a deck seam with *oakum and pitch.

HOLLAND–AMERICA LINE, one of the famous North Atlantic liner companies, was founded in 1871 by two young men in Rotterdam as Plate, Reuchlin & Co. Ltd.; the following year they began a monthly service to New York with two new ships of 1,700 tons. In 1873 the company was absorbed into a larger organization formed to raise capital for expansion; this was the Netherlands–American Steam Navigation Co., which before the end of the century had become internationally known as the Holland–America Line. An expansion of services to South America and via the Panama Canal to the Pacific coasts of Canada and the U.S.A. occurred after the First World War (1914–18), and in spite of crippling losses to the Germans in the Second World War the line was rebuilt afterwards and now runs a modern fleet mainly of cargo liners. The flagship is the striking passenger liner *Rotterdam*, 38,645 tons.

HOLLOND, JOHN (*c.* 1612–*c.* 1675), British naval administrator, was the author of two *Discourses on the Navy* (1638 and 1659), which are of great historical interest. Nothing is known of his place and date of birth, but he entered the naval service as a clerk to Captain Joshua Downing, assistant to the navy commissioners at Chatham, about 1624 and was subsequently employed in the Admiralty. In 1635 he became paymaster of the navy and three years later wrote the first of his *Discourses on the Navy*, which dealt with the many abuses which were prevalent at that time. During the Civil War he was one of the Commissioners for the Navy but resigned in 1645/6. In 1648/9 he was a member of a new commission appointed to regulate the Navy and Customs and in his second *Discourse* comments unfavourably upon its transactions. The commission was dissolved in 1654 and he then settled in Deptford and engaged in the timber trade. He trimmed his sails to the political wind, but little is known of the latter part of his life. His two discourses, edited by J. R. Tanner, were printed by the *Navy Records Society in 1896.

HOLMAN, FRANCIS (*fl.* towards the end of the 18th century), a British marine painter about whom little is known. He is said to have lived at Shadwell, Wapping, and to have been the master of Thomas *Luny. He painted numerous pictures of storms and naval engagements as well as scenes in the dockyards bordering the Thames. He was a successful ship portraitist and the studies which he made of the sturdy ships in which Captain James *Cook made his voyages of discovery are of great interest. He is also noted for his pictures of *East Indiamen. Among his exhibits at the Royal Academy was one of the yacht *Augusta* with George III on board reviewing the fleet at *Spithead.

HOLMES, JAMES WILLIAM (1855–1932), British master mariner and self-taught artist, was born at Deal where from an early age he watched the famous tea *clippers passing through the Downs. Attracted by their grace and beauty, he started to draw them, his first recorded painting being one of Captain Marryat's *Ariadne*. At the age of 14 he was apprenticed in sail and for the next fifty-four years served in sailing ships, the last twenty-nine in command. Whenever opportunity offered he made accurate, detailed, and attractive water-colour paintings of the ships in which he sailed and of many others with which he came in contact. His collection is a unique record of the last years in sail.

HOLMES, Sir ROBERT (1622–92), British admiral, first came into prominence in 1663 when as a captain he sailed in command of a small squadron to protect English interests on the west coast of Africa where the Dutch had seized some English trading stations. At first he tried to regain them by peaceful persuasion but in the end had to use force, and for good measure occupied some Dutch settlements as well. In 1664 he crossed the Atlantic and occupied the Dutch settlement in America of Nieuw Amsterdam, renaming it New York in honour of *James, Duke of York, then Lord High Admiral of England. During the Second Dutch War (1665–7) he commanded the *Revenge* at the battle of *Lowestoft. He was knighted in 1666 and took a prominent part in the *Four Days Battle. After the successful St. James's Day battle in 1666 Holmes operated with his squadron off the Dutch coast following the defeat of the Dutch fleet, burning and destroying. Some 170 merchant ships were discovered at anchor in the Vlie River and were put to the torch by boats of the English fleet, the conflagration being known in history as 'Sir Robert Holmes, his bonefire'. The loss to the Dutch was estimated at £1,200,000, a prodigious sum in those days. During the Third Dutch War (1672–4), Holmes flew his admiral's flag in the *St. Michael* at the battle of *Solebay, his last naval activity. He spent the remaining twenty years of his life as governor of the Isle of Wight and a Member of Parliament.

HOLYSTONE, a piece of sandstone used for scrubbing wooden decks on board ship. Opinions differ as to how it received its name, whether because it was used originally for scrubbing the decks on Sundays, because the easiest method of supply was by robbing churchyards of their tombstones, or because seamen had to use holystones on hands and knees to get a good result. Large holystones were known among seamen as 'bibles', smaller ones for use in difficult corners were 'prayer books', and these names certainly came into use because seamen had to get down on their knees when using them. A deck scoured by holystones and then washed down with salt water quickly takes a smooth, even surface and the wood becomes almost white.

HOMER (*c.* 810–730 B.C.), the Greek poet to whom is attributed the authorship of the *Iliad* and the *Odyssey*. Little is known of his early life, and seven cities have been suggested as his birthplace. He is supposed to have been blind. The *Iliad* is an epic poem in twenty-four books and deals with the tragic consequences of the siege of Troy; the *Odyssey* records the adventures of *Odysseus on his voyage home from Troy. Since Greece is a sea-girt nation it is not surprising that both these poems are interspersed with many memorable phrases describing the sea, such as 'wine dark', 'with many voices', 'unharvested', etc., and in consequence they are considered to rank with some of the finest sea literature ever written. Homer, it is said, did not write them down but, as was the custom in those days, they were repeated by word of mouth. A century later, under Solon's prompting, Pisistratus committed them to writing. Both poems were recited in their entirety at the Athenian festival of Panathenaea held in the late summer each year.

HONDIUS, LODOCUS (Joos or Josse de Hondt) (1563–1611), Flemish map-maker, was educated at Ghent and followed the family profession of engraver from an early age. The siege of Ghent (1584) during the revolt of the Netherlands against Spanish occupation forced him to take refuge in London where he set up as a type-founder, an engraver of maps and charts, and a maker of globes, celestial and terrestrial, larger than any known before.

Hondius engraved some of the earliest maps of England and other countries. Charts drawn by him were used to illustrate accounts of the circumnavigations of Francis *Drake and Thomas *Cavendish, embellished by portraits of the two navigators and of Elizabeth I, Henry IV of France, and Gerardus *Mercator. On the death of Mercator in 1594 he removed to Amsterdam where he published an improved version of Mercator's *Atlas* in 1606, adding fifty more plates to the original. He also published a treatise on the construction and use of globes. His is one of the greatest names in the early history of cartography.

HONG KONG, one of the great seaports of the world, is situated on an island off the south-east coast of China. The island was first ceded to Britain in 1841 and confirmed by the treaty of Nanking in 1842. Under the Peking treaty of 1860 the Kowloon peninsula was added, and in 1898 the territory behind the peninsula up to a line from Mirs Bay to Deep Bay was leased for a period of ninety-nine years. There are two large natural harbours at Hong Kong, Deep Water Bay and Tytam Bay, and an immense trade passes through them. Hong Kong is a free port. It was captured by the Japanese during the Second World War but reoccupied by Britain in 1945.

HOOD, the canvas cover set up over a *companion-hatch or a skylight to give protection from sun and rain and, in older sailing ships, the tarred canvas covering the *eyes of the standing rigging to keep water out and thus preventing the rope from rotting. It was also the name given to the top of the galley chimney, which was made to turn round so that the galley smoke might go down to *leeward.

HOOD, the name of a family of British naval officers, most of whom achieved flag rank in the navy. Because of the same christian names they are sometimes confused. In chronological order, the most eminent of the family have been:

(1) SAMUEL, Viscount Hood (1724–1816);
(2) ALEXANDER, Viscount Bridport (1726–1814), brother of the above;
(3) Captain ALEXANDER Hood (1758–98);
(4) Vice Admiral Sir SAMUEL Hood (1762–1814), his brother and both cousins of the first two;
(5) Rear Admiral the Hon. Sir HORACE Hood (1870–1916), a descendant of Viscount Hood.

(1) Viscount Hood was the son of a country parson and reached the rank of *post-captain in 1756. Three years later he captured the French *frigate *Bellona*, thirty-two guns. From 1763 to 1767 he was in charge of the North American station, flying a *commodore's broad pendant. Promoted rear admiral in 1780, he handled his squadron with great skill when outnumbered by French forces under Vice Admiral de *Grasse during operations in the West Indies in the War of American Independence (1775–82). He was second-in-command at Sir George *Rodney's great victory off Dominica in 1782, but was critical that the success was not better followed up. On his return to England he was given a peerage as Lord Hood. He held the Portsmouth Command, 1786–9 and 1791–3, and he served on the Board of Admiralty, 1788–95.

At the outbreak of war with France in 1793, Hood was appointed to the Mediterranean command, and for a time, in co-operation with the Spaniards, his forces occupied Toulon. Driven therefrom, he then made plans to secure Corsica as a naval base. He was recalled in 1794, and two years later became governor of *Greenwich Hospital, a post he held until his death at over

90. Lord *Nelson ranked him as among the greatest of admirals, and without doubt he was the greatest of his family.

(2) Viscount Bridport, although two years younger than his brother, was made a post-captain six weeks before him, and held a succession of valuable appointments, including the treasurership of Greenwich Hospital. He was promoted rear admiral in 1780 and two years later took part in Lord *Howe's relief of Gibraltar. He served as one of Howe's admirals at the battle of the *Glorious First of June in 1794, as a result of which he received a peerage as Lord Bridport, and later took operational command of the Channel Fleet, the appointment being regularly confirmed in 1797, owing to Howe's continued illhealth.

During this year occurred the great naval mutiny at *Spithead. He succeeded in pacifying the men of his flagship, but when the mutiny broke out again a few days later he was unable to control it, and Lord Howe had to be called in to persuade the men to return to their duty. Bridport took the fleet to sea when the mutiny was over and for two years, 1798–1800, directed the blockade of Brest, being relieved by Lord St. Vincent (see JERVIS, John). He retired in that year after fifty-nine years service.

(3) Captain Alexander Hood, son of a naval purser, benefited with his brother Samuel from the patronage of their distinguished cousins. As a boy of 14, Alexander was taken into the *Resolution, commanded by James *Cook, and was in the explorer's second circumnavigation. An island in the Marquesas was named after him since he was the first to sight the group in 1777. Later he served in the West Indies and on the North American station, and had risen to post-captain's rank by the age of 23. In 1798, while commanding the *Mars*, he was killed during the course of a most creditable action with the French ship *Hercule*, which surrendered off the Bec du Raz, Brittany.

(4) Vice Admiral Sir Samuel Hood, when young, served under both his cousins and was present at Rodney's victory of the *Saints of 1782. He became a post-captain at the age of 26, and in 1793 was sent to the Mediterranean with Lord Hood's fleet. Later he became associated with Nelson. He was at *Santa Cruz in the *Theseus* in 1797, and in the following year had a great part in the battle of the *Nile, when he took his ship inshore of the French.

In 1803 Hood was given command of the Leeward Islands station in the rank of commodore, and he captured St. Lucia and Tobago from the French. In 1805 he lost an arm during an action in which he captured some French frigates. Two years later he was with Lord *Gambier in operations against *Copenhagen,

and also saw service in the Baltic as a rear admiral under Sir James *Saumarez.

Hood was made a baronet for his services off Corunna in 1809 during the withdrawal of Sir John Moore's army. As a vice admiral he went to the East Indies as commander-in-chief, and died of fever at Madras. Sir Samuel, with his notable service under Rodney, Nelson, Gambier, Saumarez, and others, probably ranks next to his cousin, Lord Hood, in the variety and success of his activities, and had he survived he would undoubtedly have reached the highest ranks in the navy.

(5) Rear Admiral the Hon. Sir Horace Hood, had a career of such achievement as to hold promise that he would rise to the head of his profession. As a young officer in H.M.S. *Calliope* he endured the tremendous hurricane which wrecked all other men-of-war then at Apia, Samoa. He was promoted commander for distinguished service in the Nile campaign of 1897–8, in which David *Beatty and Winston *Churchill also fought. He was made a captain at the age of 33 and won the D.S.O. on active service ashore in Somaliland in 1904. He was promoted rear admiral in 1913, and served for a time as Naval Secretary to the First Lord of the Admiralty, then Winston Churchill, a post which had previously been held by Beatty.

In May 1915 Hood flew his flag in the *battle-cruiser *Invincible*, and a year later was with the *Grand Fleet at the preliminaries to the battle of *Jutland on 31 May. Racing ahead of the *battleships to join Beatty and the main battle-cruiser force, his ship was soon engaged. She shot splendidly until, at 6.33 p.m., she herself was hit on 'Q' turret by a salvo from the *Derfflinger*. This blew the *Invincible* in half, and only six men survived. 'You should have seen him bring his squadron into action,' said Beatty to a fellow admiral: 'it would have done your heart good. No one could have died a more glorious death.'

The best biography of the first four of these admirals is *The Admirals Hood* by Dorothy Hood (1941).

HOOD, H.M.S., a *battle-cruiser of 41,000 tons, laid down during the First World War (1914–18) and completed in 1923, was in her time the largest warship in the world. During the Second World War she was sunk in action with the German *battleship *Bismarck* in May 1941, her *magazine exploding when she was hit by a salvo of shells. She was named after Admiral Lord *Hood.

HOOD-ENDS, the ends of those planks in the hull structure of a wooden vessel which fit into the *rabbets of the *stem and *sternpost. See also FORE-HOODS.

View of H.M.S. Hood

HOOKER, a development of the original *ketch, a short, tubby little vessel with main and mizen-masts, originally square-rigged on the main and with a small topsail above a fore-and-aft sail hoisted on a *gaff on the mizen. She usually set two jibs on a high-*steeved *bowsprit. She was a fishing vessel, and probably, as her name suggests, was used mainly for line fishing. She became a distinct type of vessel in her own right, as opposed to the generic ketch, early in the 18th century. The rig was much favoured by Dutch fishing craft.

The name is also used, slightly contemptuously, for any vessel when she grows old and has lost her early bloom, or perhaps has come down a bit in the maritime world.

HOOP, (1) in older *gaff-rigged sailing craft the *luff of the mainsail was secured to the mast by wooden hoops which slid up or down the mast as the sail was hoisted or lowered. **(2)** Although square in form, the metal bands which held the *stock of the old-fashioned anchors to the *shank were called hoops. **(3)** The name given to an old form of naval punishment for two men accused of fighting each other below decks. They were stripped to the waist, their left hands bound to a wooden hoop, and with a knotted cord in their right hand had to lash each other until one of them gave in. The loser knew that he would usually also receive a few lashes with the *cat-o'-nine-tails, a means of ensuring that both men laid on with a will while undergoing this punishment.

HOORN, originally a small seaport in north Holland with three claims to be remembered. It was at Hoorn in 1416 that the first 'great' net was made for the herring fishery; it was the birthplace of Jacob *le Maire who, with Willem *Schouten, discovered and rounded Cape *Horn in 1616 and named it after Hoorn; and it was also well known to Abel Janszoon *Tasman, the discoverer of Tasmania. It is now a small inland port on the Ijselmeer (late Zuider Zee).

'HOPE-IN-HEAVENS', a seamen's slang name for the small, light sails set above the *royals in square-rigged ships in very light winds. They were also sometimes known as 'Trust-in-Gods'.

HOPKINS, ESEK (1718–1802), commander-in-chief of the fleet created by the Continental Congress in 1775, was born in Scituate, Rhode Island. He went to sea as a young man and commanded *privateers during the Seven Years War (1756–63). On the declaration of independence his elder brother became chairman of the Naval Committee of the Congress and Hopkins was nominated to be the fleet commander. At the time he owned a number of merchant vessels and was as well qualified for the fleet command as any other colonial.

Various matters delayed the fitting out of the fleet and Hopkins was not able to sail from the Delaware Capes until February 1776. Three days earlier he had directed his commanding officers to remain in company with him; if they became separated they were to rendezvous in the Bahamas. This indicated that he had decided to disregard the orders which directed him to enter Chesapeake Bay and attack the vessels operating there under Lord Dunmore, which were manned in part by officers and men of the Royal Navy.

Hopkins reached the Bahamas with six of his eight vessels: the *Alfred*, *Columbus*, *Andrew Doria*, *Cabot*, *Providence*, and *Wasp*. Although he landed a party to surprise the port of Nassau he failed to blockade the port and returned with only a small portion of the military stores he had set out to capture. Shortly after his return Hopkins received a formal vote of censure from the Congress and in the following year was suspended from his command, being formally dismissed a few months later.

HOPKINS, JOHN BURROUGHS (1742–96), American naval officer, was born in Providence, R.I., eldest of the ten children of Esek *Hopkins. He sailed in the fleet under the command of his father in 1776 in command of the brig *Cabot*. In 1776 he was listed 13th in the seniority list of Continental Navy captains adopted by the Congress and was given command of the new *frigate *Warren* when she was blockaded in the Providence River. Choosing a bitter cold night in March 1778, he slipped through the blockade. He sailed from Boston in March 1779 with the *Queen of France* and *Ranger* in company and cruised for about six weeks off the Virginia Capes. The Marine Committee initially praised Hopkins for this cruise, but a later inquiry conducted by the Committee led to his suspension and he had no further naval command.

HOPPER, a dumb *lighter (i.e., without means of self-propulsion) used in conjunction with a *dredger for receiving the spoil brought up in the buckets, or for the carriage of sewage or similar material for disposal. When full, hoppers are towed to a *spoil ground (an area of sea where spoil may be deposited). At the bottom of the watertight *holds in which the dredged spoil or sludge is carried, hinged doors are opened on arrival at the spoil ground and the spoil allowed to fall out on to the sea bed. These doors are operated by chains suspended from large pulleys hung on a fore-and-aft girder. Some larger hoppers today are self-propelled with steam or diesel engines.

HOPSONN, Sir THOMAS (1642–1717), British vice admiral, is remembered for the part he played in the successful attack on *Vigo in 1702 at the start of the War of the Spanish Succession (1702–13) when an Anglo-Dutch fleet commanded by Sir George *Rooke, of which Hopsonn was second-in-command, discovered the Franco-Spanish fleet, which had

been escorting the Spanish treasure ships from the West Indies, at anchor there.

They were in the inner harbour, the entrance to which was closed by a *boom of 30 feet in girth composed of *masts, *yards, *cables, top chains, etc. At each end of the boom was a 70-gun ship, with five others anchored inside the boom with *springs on their cables so that they presented their broadside to any attacker. Hopsonn, with his rear admiral's flag in the *Torbay*, led the assault on the boom and partially broke through it but was wedged in by the wreckage and unable to move. His ship came under such heavy fire that she was reduced almost to a wreck, and to complete her destruction the French admiral, *Chateau-Renault, hastily improvised one of the merchant ships in harbour as a *fireship and sent her down on the *Torbay*. She set the *Torbay* on fire and, when her powder train reached the explosive charges, blew up. But she had been laden with a large cargo of snuff which was scattered far and wide. It acted as a very efficient fire extinguisher and put out the fires in the *Torbay*; and it so affected the crews of the French warships that many of them had to dive into the sea for relief from the pain of having inhaled the snuff in large quantities. Moreover, the explosion of the fireship completed the work of breaking the boom, and Rooke sailed in with his ships. The French and Spanish ships were doomed, and though Chateau-Renault ordered them to be scuttled, Rooke was too quick for him. Thirteen *ships of the line were taken and a number of Spanish treasure *galleons.

It was estimated that the treasure captured at Vigo was worth over £2,000,000, and, as a measure of the British government's appreciation of the success of the exploit, all the gold coins minted in England in 1703 from the captured gold were struck with the word Vigo on them. As a reward for his gallantry Hopsonn was knighted and promoted to vice admiral.

HORATIO HORNBLOWER, the hero of a number of novels and short stories about the British Navy, written by C. S. *Forester, which cover the period of the Revolutionary and Napoleonic Wars (1793–1815). Immensely popular, the novels and stories describe the adventures of Hornblower in his rise from midshipman to admiral and, no matter how spectacular these fictional adventures may be, they have the ring of truth about them because of the meticulous knowledge of contemporary seamanship with which Forester describes the various ship actions. It is generally thought that the fictitious Hornblower is largely based, at least in the earlier part of his career, on Thomas *Cochrane, who was as dashing a young captain in real life as was Horatio Hornblower in Forester's novels. They have inevitably been compared with the naval novels of Frederick *Marryat and are considered by many as at least as graphic as any of those classic stories. Forester has described the evolution of the Hornblower series in *The Hornblower Companion*, published in 1964.

HORIZON, from Greek *horos*, 'a boundary', *horizo*, 'form a boundary', 'limit'. **(1)** The line which limits an observer's view of the surface of the earth and of the visible heavens. In astronomical navigation three meanings must be distinguished: (*a*) the visible horizon, that which is actually seen. This however is affected by the *dip of the horizon which depends on the refraction of light by the atmosphere and the observer's height above the sea; (*b*) the sensible horizon, the true horizon at sea level at the observer's position on the earth's surface, corrected for dip; it is the projection on the celestial sphere of a plane tangential to the earth's surface at that point; (*c*) the rational horizon, this is the projection on the celestial sphere of a plane parallel to the sensible horizon but passing through the centre of the

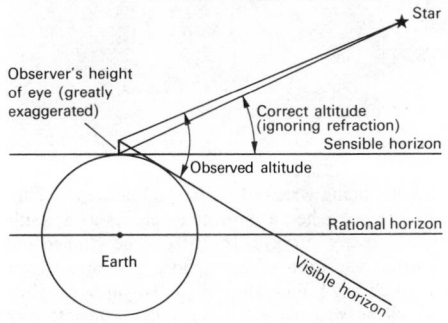

Horizon

earth instead of tangential to its surface. In measuring the *altitude of a heavenly body considered as infinitely distant, the radius of the earth is insignificant, and normally the sensible and rational horizons coincide. For some purposes, however, they must be distinguished. **(2)** The broad ring, most frequently of wood, in which a globe of the earth is fixed. The upper surface of the ring, level with the centre of the globe, represents the plane of the rational horizon. See also BUBBLE HORIZON.

HORIZONTAL SEXTANT ANGLE, the angle in the horizontal plane between two *land- or *sea-marks. By measuring such an angle the navigator is able to plot a position circle on his chart somewhere on which his ship may be fixed. A second position circle obtained in the same way, or a straight position line, which intersects the first position circle indicates the ship's position at the point of intersection. See also NAVIGATION.

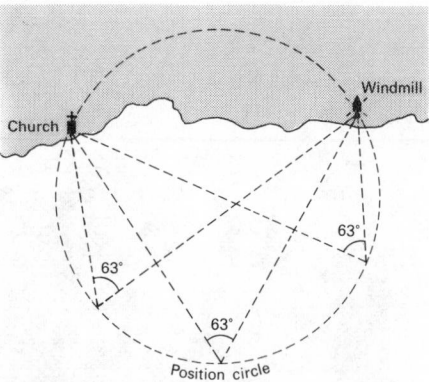

Horizontal sextant angle

HORN, CAPE, the southernmost point on the group of islets which lie off the southern tip of Chile in *latitude 56° S. Sir Francis *Drake claimed to have landed on Cape Horn during his voyage of circumnavigation in 1577 and although there is some doubt whether in fact he did so, he was at least the first man to discover that there was sea beyond the southern end of South America and that it was not joined, as all geographers then believed, to the great southern continent of *Terra Australis Incognita. When his ship, the *Golden Hind*, was driven far south by a storm after he had made the passage of the Straits of Magellan, he discovered, according to his journal, that 'the Atlantic Ocean and the South Sea meet in a large and free scope'. It was these words of Drake's which inspired a Dutch merchant, Isaac le Maire, to form a new company to trade in the Pacific by discovering a new route to that ocean, the only known way (by the Straits of Magellan) being barred to him by the monopoly of the Dutch *East India Company. He fitted out two ships under the command of his son Jacob *le Maire and Willem *Schouten to discover the truth of Drake's remark. The two ships sailed from the Texel in June 1615, and on the morning of 25 January 1616 passed through the junction of the two oceans 'in a large and free scope', naming it the Straits of le Maire. Four days later they sailed past a grim and forbidding cape which they recognized as the most southerly tip of the South American continent. They named it Cape Hoorn, after the home town of the chief financial backer of the expedition. The name, as Cape Horn, has remained to this day.

HORNPIPE, in its maritime sense a dance once popular with seamen. It was originally an old solo dance, three-in-a-measure, danced to the Celtic instrument known as a hornpipe but by the beginning of the 18th century, when its

British sailors dancing the hornpipe at Constantinople; engraving, 1878

maritime popularity began, it was changed to two-in-a-measure. Its adoption as a dance for sailors was purely fortuitous, as it previously had no maritime associations.

HORNS, (1) the points of the jaws of a *boom or *gaff in a sailing vessel where they embrace the mast. Normally a boom is attached to the mast with a *gooseneck, but in some cases jaws were used instead, as jaws allow a spar to slide up and down the mast, while a gooseneck is fixed in position. A gaff always has jaws. **(2)** The name by which the outer ends of the *crosstrees of a mast are known. **(3)** Two projecting bars sometimes bolted to the after part of a *rudder from which chains can be led as an alternative method of working the rudder should the rudder-head be damaged or broken off.

HORSBURGH, JAMES (1762–1836), an officer of the British *East India Company and compiler of the *East India Directory*, for which he is justly renowned. It was published in 1810, the year in which he succeeded Alexander *Dalrymple as Hydrographer at the East India office in London, and is full of accurate and invaluable navigational information of East Indian waters. From 1784 until this appointment Horsburgh was continuously voyaging in eastern

waters, being wrecked on Diego Garcia in 1786, and he published a number of charts as a result of his many surveys. In 1802–4 he studied the diurnal variation of barometric pressure which resulted in a publication by the Royal Society, of which he was made a Fellow in 1806. He was a founder member of the Royal Geographical Society in 1830 and he continued in the East India Office as Hydrographer until his death. Horsburgh Lighthouse in Singapore Strait is a fitting memorial to his work in those waters.

HORSE, (1) the footrope of a *yard in a square-rigged sailing ship on which seamen stand when they are working aloft on the sails. It is supported at intervals from the yard by *stirrups. **(2)** An elevated rod, fixed at both ends and parallel with the deck of a sailing vessel to which the *sheets of sails can be led, lateral movement of the sheet being made possible by means of a *traveller which can slide from side to side of the horse according to the trim of the sail. Before the evolution of the modern high, narrow sail plan with the foresail overlapping the main, a horse was fitted mainly for use with headsails. In smaller sailing craft, the mainsail sheet is almost invariably led to a small horse fitted on the *counter or *taffrail of the vessel. See also FLEMISH HORSE.

HORSE LATITUDES, the areas of the ocean which lie between the generally westerly winds of the higher latitudes and the *trade winds, usually areas of prolonged calms. The name is said to come from the throwing overboard of the *'dead horse', most ships on long voyages in the older days of sail taking about two months out of England to win clear of the horse latitudes, by which time the seamen had worked off their advance of pay on signing on.

HORSING IRON, a *caulking iron attached to a wooden handle so that it can be held in position along a deck *seam while another man drives it in hard with a *beetle to consolidate the *oakum. HORSING UP, to harden up the oakum in the deck seams by means of a horsing iron.

HORTEN, a Norwegian seaport near the mouth of the Oslo Fjord in the south of Norway, and the home of the *Marinemuseet, one of the world's more important maritime museums.

HORTON, Sir MAX KENNEDY (1883–1951), British admiral, was born in Anglesey and educated in H.M.S. *Britannia (Dartmouth), where he showed a bent for engineering and mechanics. He was soon drawn to the infant *submarine service and was appointed as a sub-lieutenant in October 1904 to the depot ship *Thames* for training. A year later, as a lieutenant of 22, he received his first command, the submarine *A.1*. Except for an interval of two years, 1910–12, he remained in command of submarines for the next fifteen years.

During the First World War (1914–18) he established a reputation as one of the foremost British submarine commanders, and was the first to sink an enemy warship, the German *cruiser *Hela* in the Heligoland Bight. He subsequently commanded the British submarine flotilla operating in the Baltic with such success that the enemy put a price on his head and ruefully referred to the Baltic as 'Horton's Sea'. Command of the submarine *J.1* and of the submarine monitor *M.1.* which mounted a 12-in. gun followed; and at the end of the war he went back to the Baltic in command of the submarine flotilla in the British squadron operating against the Bolsheviks. In June 1920 he was promoted captain.

Between the wars he held varied command and staff appointments, rising to the rank of vice admiral. He was commanding the Reserve Fleet when the Second World War broke out. After a few months in command of the Northern Patrol, he stepped into the eminently suitable post of Vice Admiral Submarines. He remained there for nearly three years, his personality, reputation, and grasp of the problems facing the submarine crews combining to inspire the men of that most dangerous branch of the navy.

In November 1942 he took over from Admiral Sir Percy Noble as Commander-in-Chief Western Approaches at the most critical phase of the Battle of the *Atlantic. Though the groundwork had been laid by his predecessor, much of the credit for the victory gained six months later on the North Atlantic convoy routes must be ascribed to the improvements he made in training methods for the escorts, the measures he set afoot to improve the air cover given to the convoys, and the establishment of support groups centred on escort *aircraft carriers.

At the end of the war he had the satisfaction of formally taking the surrender of a group of German *U-boats at Londonderry. He was awarded the Grand Cross of the Order of the Bath, in which Order he had been made a Knight Commander in 1939, and was appointed to the American Legion of Merit in its highest degree—that of Chief Commander.

He struck his flag for the last time on 15 August 1945 and went on the retired list. He was given a State funeral at Liverpool, of which he had been made a freeman, the scene of his great days as Commander-in-Chief Western Approaches. For a biography see Rear Admiral W. S. Chalmers, *Max Horton and the Western Approaches*, 1954.

HOSIER, FRANCIS (1673–1727), British vice admiral, became a captain in 1696 when he commanded the *Winchelsea*. In 1707, in command of the *Salisbury*, he brought home the body of Sir Clowdisley *Shovel after the wreck of the *Association* in the Scilly Isles. He was promoted vice admiral in 1723, and in 1726 was appointed to command a squadron of sixteen ships in the West Indies with orders to prevent the sailing of Spanish treasure ships without engaging in hostilities, a requirement impossible of achievement. Hosier began by blockading *Porto Bello but the British seamen suffered severely from yellow fever which eventually caused well over 4,000 deaths, including those of two admirals, eight captains, and fifty lieutenants. Hosier himself was one of the victims, his body being buried in the *bilges of his ship and later brought home for permanent burial. Twelve years later the poet Richard Glover wrote a famous ballad, 'Admiral Hosier's Ghost'. Hosier's orders not to engage in hostilities against the Spaniards are blamed for the disaster on the odd grounds that the excitement of battle would have kept the fever at bay.

HOSTE, PAUL, properly l'HOSTE (1652–1700), a Jesuit mathematician who served for twelve years at sea under three French admirals. He was with the third of these, de *Tourville, at the battles of *Beachy Head (1690) and

*Barfleur (1692) and in 1697 he published L'Art des armées navales. Briefly, his analysis comprises a description of the 'orders' in which a fleet may need to be disposed—the order of battle, five different orders of sailing, and the order of retreat. Of these the order of battle is naturally the most important. It is, of course, in a *line ahead, aimed at engaging the enemy fleet in a similar line, and there is emphasis on the view that the line should be close-hauled (six points from the wind), a view which was presumably held by de Tourville although there were some French admirals who preferred to form their line with the wind abeam. Each order of sailing was so designed as to form the fleet in a compact body until the enemy was in sight when it could be changed to the order of battle quickly and smoothly in whatever direction was needed.

The problems of manoeuvring once a battle is imminent are discussed in the section entitled 'On the Movements of a Fleet without Touching the Orders'. In his preface to this section Hoste writes: 'It is in this that the art of war at sea properly consists. I feel that I have not the necessary lights to give rules on a subject of so much importance, and so do not propose to give precepts for admirals of fleets, but content myself with proposing to them examples ...' This diffidence, however, did not deter him from much deep thinking and clear reasoning. One manoeuvre, familiar in the Dutch wars and taken up by the British Navy nearly a century later, namely passing through the enemy's line, is described as 'equally delicate and bold'. Hoste does not think it is greatly to be feared by the enemy and suggests it should not be attempted unless to avoid a greater evil, or if the enemy leaves a great space in the centre of his line, or if it is necessary to extricate some ships that have been cut off.

The most important parts of Hoste's treatise were translated into English in 1762. Its reputation was so enduring that an extensively subscribed translation of the complete work was published in 1834.

HOSTE, Sir WILLIAM (1780–1828), British naval officer, entered the Royal Navy in 1793 under the auspices of Lord *Nelson, who had a great affection for the boy. He was present at the battle of the *Nile as a lieutenant in the *Theseus*, and was appointed by Nelson as commander of the *Mutine* after the battle. From 1808 to 1814 he commanded a squadron of *frigates in the Adriatic with great skill, making many amphibious attacks on French posts ashore and frequently engaging French ships whenever he came across them. In 1811 he fought a brilliant action off the island of Lissa, capturing two and driving ashore one of a force of ten French and Venetian frigates which had attacked his squadron of four frigates. Rear Admiral Dubourdieu,

commanding the French–Venetian force, was killed in the action. After the end of the war in 1815 Hoste returned to England and did not go to sea again.

'HOT CHASE', a so-called principle of naval warfare with no valid basis in law, sometimes quoted by admirals in their own defence after committing a breach of international law. The principle of 'hot chase' is that a flying enemy may be followed into neutral waters and destroyed there if the chase began in international waters. The best known example of 'hot chase' occurred at the battle of *Lagos in 1759 when four French *ships of the line tried to escape from Admiral *Boscawen's fleet by taking shelter in neutral Portuguese waters in Lagos Bay. Boscawen, who had been chasing them all night, followed them in, captured two of them, and burned a third. The fourth, the French flagship, was in so great a hurry to get in that she ran ashore under full sail, her three masts going by the *board. She was set on fire by her own crew as they scrambled ashore. On this occasion the Portuguese authorities accepted the principle of 'hot chase', possibly because the French were not popular in Portugal at that time. Boscawen, after claiming the principle of 'hot chase', added in his report to the Admiralty that it was better to destroy the ships first and argue the principle later.

HOT PRESS, the name given to a condition of *impressment when the need for men to man British warships in time of war was so acute that the *press gangs were given instructions to *press men for the navy regardless of any *protections they might carry. When news of a hot press in any district got around, all likely men usually went into hiding until the danger was past.

HOUGUE, LA, BATTLE OF, see BARFLEUR, BATTLE OF.

HOUNDS, wooden shoulders bolted below the masthead to either side of a wooden mast of a sailing vessel which originally supported the *trestle-trees. In smaller vessels without trestle-trees, hounds are used to support the *shrouds by which the mast is stayed laterally. In the days of large sailing ships the hounds of the lower masts were more properly known as *cheeks.

HOUSE, to, in general terms a word meaning to secure or make secure. Thus a topmast or *topgallant mast is housed by being lowered until its top is level with the top of the mast next below it and its *heel secured to the lower mast by a *parrel lashing or a *frapping line so that its rigging does not chafe or rest on the *cap. Topmasts and/or topgallant masts were normally

Cross-channel hovercraft

housed when it was expected that the wind would increase into a gale of such force that the upper masts would be in danger. In gales of exceptional severity, topmasts and topgallant masts were struck down to the deck. Guns of the old sailing warships were housed when not in use by being run in from the gunports and secured by *tackles, muzzle lashings, and *breechings so that they would not take charge if the ship rolled in a seaway. See also STRIKE DOWN, TO.

HOUSTON, a seaport in Texas, U.S.A., is the third largest, after New York and New Orleans, in that country. Houston itself is said to be a 'town that built a port that built a city', a true enough description of the immense growth of both port and city within a relatively short period. The development of the port dates from the early years of the 20th century when the shallow, twisting 25-mile bayou that connected the town with Galveston Bay was dredged into a channel deep enough to take all but the largest ships. A second 25-mile channel was dredged through the coastal shallows into the deeper water of Galveston Bay.

This access to the deep water of Galveston Bay, together with the boom in oil fuel, has mainly accounted for the staggering growth of the port. Allied to a very extensive *barge distribution system and a modern railway and road development which links Houston with much of the south-western U.S.A., the port today handles something above 70,000,000 tons of shipborne

trade annually. Active plans for the construction of offshore terminals to handle the modern super-*tankers, *container ships, and barge-carrying vessels, which at present are too large for the dredged channel, would appear likely to sustain the phenomenal growth of the port over the next few decades.

HOVERCRAFT, a vehicle which rides on a cushion of air under pressure between it and the surface over which it is travelling. The principle was first considered in 1875 in the Netherlands, but constructional difficulties prevented its practical realization until 1950 when the British engineer Sir Christopher Cockrell evolved a practicable design. In 1958 he persuaded the British government to sponsor the project, and after several years of experiment the first commercial hovercraft, SRN-4, went into service in 1968. With a weight of 165 tons, a length of 130 ft 2 in. (39·7 m), a beam of 76 ft 10 in. (23·5 m), and an overall height when resting on its landing pads of 42 ft 5 in. (13·0 m), it carries either 610 passengers or 256 passengers and 30 motor cars. The hull is divided into twenty-four watertight compartments giving a reserve buoyancy of 250 per cent. Power is provided by four Proteus gas turbines which drive four variable pitch air screws and also four twelve-bladed centrifugal fans which provide the cushion of air beneath the hull. This is prevented from escaping by a neoprene skirt 7 ft (2·1 m) deep, which enables the vessel to ride successfully in waves up to between 4 and 5 ft high. The cruising speed is 55 knots with a maximum speed of 65 knots. The military uses of the hovercraft are under active study both ashore and afloat and it appears to offer considerable possibilities in the field of amphibious warfare.

By 1972 hovercraft were in regular service as vehicle and passenger ferries on several routes linking England with the Isle of Wight and, across the Straits of Dover, with north-eastern France.

HOVGAARD, GEORGE WILLIAM (1857–1950), Danish naval officer, was born at Aarhus. He entered the Danish Navy in 1875 and later qualified as a naval architect. In 1895 he was seconded from the navy to take up a position with the shipbuilding firm of Burmester and Wain, Copenhagen, but two years later returned to naval service. In 1901 he was offered the position of professor of warship construction at the Massachusetts Institute of Technology and during the First World War (1914–18) was employed by the U.S. Navy Department, becoming a naturalized American. He retired in 1934. He wrote a number of technical works of considerable merit on ship construction and also *Voyages of the Norsemen to America*, an account of the earliest transatlantic voyages made by the Viking *longships. In 1917 he was awarded the gold medal of the British Institution of Naval Architects and in 1927 was made a commander of the Order of Dannebrog.

HOWARD, CHARLES, second Lord Howard of Effingham and first Earl of Nottingham (1536–1624), *Lord High Admiral of England, is chiefly remembered as commander-in-chief of the English fleet against the Spanish *Armada in 1588. His father was Lord Admiral before him under the Catholic Queen Mary; it is said that Charles served at sea under his father at this time. His adult experience before his appointment as Lord High Admiral in 1585, while extending to brief periods of command of a squadron of ships and of soldiers, was mainly as courtier, diplomat, and trusted servant of Elizabeth I. His portrait in later years shows a grave face with a strong nose; he comes down to us as an elegant, handsome man, not sufficiently dashing perhaps to win Elizabeth's heart, but cautious, steady, strong, and a good Protestant. In December 1587, with the threat of a Spanish invasion, he was commissioned as 'lieutenant-general and commander-in-chief of the navy and army prepared to the seas against Spain', a mark of Elizabeth's great confidence in him.

The confidence was not misplaced; he was diligent in examining every vessel in his fleet—'I have been aboard of every ship that goeth out with me, and in any place where any man may creep'—and in seeing to the comfort and victualling of his crews, even to the extent of dipping into his own pocket, which was never overfull. That the organization for the supply of ammunition and the men's wages broke down later is no reflection on Howard, rather on the unprecedented scale of the 1588 mobilization; no Englishman had experience of such a vast fleet and there was no administrative backing to cope with its demands. Howard constantly risked Elizabeth's displeasure on behalf of the men who fought for her.

Before the Armada reached the Channel Howard had been convinced by his second-in-command, Sir Francis *Drake, that the Spaniards could best be defeated on their own coast, but Elizabeth's hesitation and then contrary winds forced him into a defensive posture which was probably more in keeping with his character. During the progress of the Spanish fleet up Channel the English refused to play into the enemy's hands by engaging in a close mêlée where the seasoned, disciplined soldiers aboard the Spanish ships could have decided the contest as in a land fight; they held off and played at 'long bowls'. This again suited Howard's temperament, but it is certain that his most experienced seamen commanders like Drake and Sir John *Hawkins approved and probably suggested the policy. Howard's achievement should be assessed as a diplomatic and administrative one in keeping together, more or less, such a band of disparate individualists as Drake, Hawkins, and *Frobisher. For this, for his care of his men, and for the prudent tactics which resulted in the eventual failure of the Armada, Howard deserves recognition as one of England's most successful fleet admirals as well as her first commander-in-chief of a major fleet.

After the Armada campaign Howard continued to serve as Lord High Admiral in major expeditions afloat, notably that which destroyed Spanish shipping in Cadiz in 1596, but mainly in an administrative role ashore; he did not retire until 1618 when a commission investigating naval administration reported adversely. Although always conscientious, Howard had held his high office too long and was, at the age of 82, not vigorous enough to check the abuses flourishing under him.

R. W. Kenny, *Elizabeth's Admiral* (Johns Hopkins Univ., 1970).

HOWE, RICHARD, Earl Howe (1726–99), British admiral of the fleet, was the pattern of an 18th century naval commander. Lord St. Vincent (see JERVIS, John) said that he 'liked to follow his example even in his dress', and Lord *Nelson once described him as 'our great master in naval tactics and bravery'. Howe came of an aristocratic family which had benefited through the

Lord Howe at the Glorious First of June; oil painting by Mather Brown

Hanoverian dynasty—he himself had German blood. He became the favourite officer of George III, who in later years called him 'Earl Richard' and never felt quite at ease while anyone else commanded the Channel Fleet.

He was made a *post-captain at the age of 20 and saw considerable service in the War of Austrian Succession (1739–48) with France and Spain. By the beginning of the Seven Years War (1756–63), he had established his reputation. In *Hawke's great victory of 1759 at *Quiberon Bay, when the French fleet under de *Conflans was defeated, Howe led the line in the *Magnanime*. Hawke once said of him: 'I have tried my Lord Howe on most important occasions. He never asked me how he was to execute any service entrusted to his charge, but always went straight forward and performed it.' He had also shown his abilities as a *commodore in charge of combined operations.

While still a captain, Howe served as a member of the Board of Admiralty 1762–5, after which he became treasurer of the navy which at that time was a political rather than an administrative office. He was given his flag in 1770 and during the earlier stages of the War of American Independence (1775–82) he co-operated with his brother, General Sir William Howe, who commanded ashore. In times of difficulty, with a fleet outnumbered by the French who had allied themselves with the colonists, Howe always showed great resource.

He resigned his command in 1778 owing to disagreement with Lord North's administration. He was ashore for some four years but when, upon a change of ministry in 1782, he accepted command of the Channel Fleet, much was hoped of him and expectations were fulfilled. At that time the war in America was in its concluding stages, but Gibraltar was enduring a protracted siege and relief in the way of troops and supplies was essential. Sir George *Rodney had brought help to the garrison in 1780, George Darby in the following year. When the task fell to Howe he also had charge of an immense outward-bound convoy, whose safety he had to ensure in spite of the fact that he would be operating in the face of a numerically stronger Franco-Spanish fleet. Howe himself considered that the task was the most difficult he had ever undertaken but it was successfully completed. Gibraltar was relieved, and although the enemy appeared in strength, they were content with a long range and partial action. Lord Heathfield, in command of Gibraltar, was enabled triumphantly to sustain every assault of the enemy.

In 1783 Howe was made First Lord of the Admiralty during the first administration of the younger Pitt. Howe was thus one of the few men who were closely associated both with Pitt's father, the Earl of Chatham, architect of victory in the Seven Years War, and with the young politician who was to dominate Parliament until his death at the height of the struggle with Napoleonic France. Howe, being an Irish peer, sat in the House of Commons during his term of office. He was created an earl in the peerage of the United Kingdom in 1788, when he was superseded at the Admiralty by Pitt's elder brother.

Howe was not long in eclipse. In 1790 he was again given command of the Channel Fleet, though as it was a time of peace there was no occasion for his services. Three years later, when war with France broke out, the king begged him, in spite of his considerable age and uncertain health, to take up the principal command. The appointment was justified by the victory in the Atlantic of the *Glorious First of June in 1794 when, with an equal fleet, Howe defeated the French admiral Louis *Villaret de Joyeuse, taking six *prizes. Although the battle was a tactical triumph, strategically the French succeeded in their object of safeguarding a large grain convoy from America destined for the relief of a starving country.

During the year following the encounter Howe was forced by ill health to go ashore, and it was at Bath, in 1797, that he began to receive warnings of much discontent among the sailors in the Channel Fleet that eventually led to mutiny. Howe was out of touch, but so also was the Board of Admiralty, and when the ships' companies at *Spithead refused to weigh anchor, serious trouble began.

After concessions had been exacted, Howe visited each ship in turn, though the effort nearly killed him. It was largely due to his mediation, allied to his immense popularity among the seamen in the fleet, that the mutiny was settled on honourable terms with no subsequent victimization of the mutineers. Howe had no further naval service, but in 1797 he was made a Knight of the Garter, the first occasion when this most senior of orders had been given for services purely naval in character.

Howe cared nothing for popularity, but much for principle. He once told Sir Edward *Codrington: 'I have observed throughout life that the test of a man's honour is money, and the test of his courage is responsibility.' He himself was one of the most responsible commanders of his age. He liked to keep strict control of his fleet up to the moment of battle, when he knew that everything must depend on the behaviour of individual captains. Devoted to his wife and daughters, he had few close friends in a Service in which he was revered rather than beloved. It was in great measure due to him that improved methods of

signalling (see SIGNALS AT SEA) were introduced, Howe adopting a system long advocated by such officers as Richard *Kempenfelt, who realized the need for clearer and fuller communication at sea.

The standard biography is *The Life of Earl Howe* by Sir John Barrow, published in 1838.

HOY, a small coasting sailing vessel of up to about 60 tons, in England usually with a single mast and *fore-and-aft sail, sometimes with a *boom and sometimes loose-footed and used largely for carrying passengers from port to port. Hoys in Holland mainly had two masts, usually *lug-rigged on both. The hoy had no definite characteristics as such, being any small coasting vessel which might, in other places, be called a *sloop or a *smack.

A hoy becalmed; engraving by W. Harvey

HOYT, CHARLES SHERMAN (1879–1961), American naval architect and yachting journalist, began sailing as a boy and raced his own sailboat with success at the age of 14. He studied naval architecture at Brown (U.S.A.) and Glasgow Universities and was employed as a draughtsman for a time at John Brown's shipyard on the Clyde. During both the world wars he was engaged in supervising construction for the U.S. Navy. He became internationally famous as a crew, sail trimmer, and successful tactician in top class yacht racing and took part in the International 6-metre (20-ft) team races at Oyster Bay, on the Clyde, and in the Solent in the decade 1920–30. He also designed several successful 6-metre yachts. In 1924 he sailed in *Memory* to win the Bermuda Race and later crewed in famous ocean racers which included **Jolie Brise*, *Niña*, *Dorade*, *Vamarie*, and *Mistress*, which he designed. He was a member of the *afterguard in the *America's Cup defenders *Enterprise and *Rainbow* when they beat *Shamrock V and *Endeavour respectively in 1930 and 1934. Their success was largely due to his advice and skill as a racing tactician.

HUASCAR, a Peruvian ironclad turret ship or *monitor, designed in 1864 by Captain Cowper *Coles, which in 1877 mutinied and attempted to interfere with British merchant shipping, an intolerable insult in British eyes at that date. She was brought to action by the unarmoured British *frigate *Shah* and the unarmoured *corvette *Amethyst*, but although she was hit some sixty to seventy times by the British ships, she escaped serious damage. At one period the range was reduced to 400 yards and the *Shah* fired a *torpedo, the first ever used in action, but the *Huascar* was able to steam away faster than the torpedo could run through the water. She eventually escaped by anchoring in shallow water where the British ships could not penetrate because of their greater *draught. Two years later the *Huascar* was in action again during the war against Chile. She was caught, when engaged in raids on the Chilean coast, by the Chilean ships *Encelada* and *Almirante Cochrane*. She was overwhelmed by the Chilean gunfire, and after considerable slaughter, was surrendered by her crew who ran on deck waving white towels while her sole surviving officer was intending to *scuttle her.

HUBATSCH, WALTER (1915–   ), German historian and professor of history at Bonn University, was born at Königsberg and studied history, philology, and geography at the universities of Königsberg, Munich, Hamburg, and Göttingen. He served in the army during the Second World War and subsequently became a reserve officer in the Bundesmarine. Since the war he has become one of the foremost naval historians in West Germany, and his books include *Die Ära Tirpitz*, *Der Admiralstab und die obersten Marinebehörden in Deutschland 1848–1945*, *Weserübung, die deutsche Besetzung von Norwegen und Dänemark 1940*, and *Hitler's Weisungen für Kriegführung* (edited). He has also contributed articles to numerous periodicals.

HUDDOCK, the name by which in older days the cabin on board a sailing *collier was known.

'Twas between Ebbron and Yarrow,
There cam' on a bluidy strong gale.
The skipper luicked out o' th' huddock,
Crying "Smash, man, lower the sail." '

Anon.

HUDSON, HENRY (d. 1611), English navigator and explorer, was first heard of in 1607 when he made the first of two voyages for the English Muscovy Company seeking a route to China initially by way of the North pole but when that proved impossible, by way of the *North-East passage. Following the east coast of Greenland northwards, he was met by the ice barrier which he sailed along as far as Spitsbergen. On his homeward passage he discovered the island later called Jan Mayen.

On his second voyage he followed the track of the Dutch navigator Willem *Barents, again seeking a North-East passage, but failed to find any way through the ice in the Barents Sea. At the end of 1608 he was invited to undertake a similar search on behalf of the Dutch *East India Company for a passage to China either by the north-west or north-east; and in April 1609 he sailed from the Texel in the *Half Moon*, reaching the Barents Sea again by 5 May. Frustrated once more by impenetrable ice, Hudson persuaded his mutinous crew to follow an alternative proposal to cross the Atlantic to North Virginia and seek the westerly passage, believed by some to exist in latitude 40° N.

Reaching the Virginia shore on 28 August, he coasted north, entered New York Bay, and sailed 150 miles up the river that now bears his name and, from his observations, proved that it could be no strait. Returning to Europe, the *Half Moon* put in at Dartmouth where Hudson was forbidden to give his services any further to the Dutch.

Still confident in the existence of a *North-West passage, Hudson sailed again on 17 April 1610 in the 55-ton *Discovery*, reaching the Strait since known by his name and sailing on to enter Hudson Bay on 3 August. After three months spent examining the eastern shore of the Bay, the *Discovery* went into winter quarters in the south-west corner of James Bay, remaining frozen in until the spring. Hardship and privation led to discontent and finally to' a mutiny under Hudson's worthless protégé Henry Greene, who had Hudson and some others, some of them sick, put ashore before sailing for England on 22 June 1611.

Greene and several others were killed in a fight with Eskimos; some of the crew died before the ship reached England in September, and the survivors were imprisoned. No evidence of Hudson's fate has ever been discovered.

G. M. Asher, *Henry Hudson the Navigator* (1860); L. Powys, *Henry Hudson* (1927).

HUÉ, JEAN FRANÇOIS (1751–1823), French marine artist, was born at St. Arnould-en-Yvelines, Seine et Oise, and studied in the studio of Joseph *Vernet. He painted a number of pictures of historical events but was happiest and at his best when he painted sea scenes, naval battle pictures, wreck scenes, and views of seaports. He completed the notable series of pictures of French ports begun by Vernet, was made an Academician in 1782, and was a regular exhibitor at the Salon.

HUGGINS, WILLIAM JOHN (1781–1845), marine painter, entered the service of the *East India Company early in life but later devoted himself to the study of marine painting, becoming one of the most eminent sea painters of his day. Both George IV and William IV appointed him marine painter to the court. Many of his finest pictures were of *East Indiamen, of which most were superbly engraved in aquatint by C. Rosenberg and E. *Duncan.

HUGHES, Sir EDWARD (c. 1720–94), British admiral, had a naval career full of action. He was with Admiral *Vernon at *Porto Bello in 1739, at Cartagena in 1741, and he was a lieutenant at the battle of *Toulon in 1744. He was promoted captain after a spirited action with the Spanish *Glorioso*, was with Admiral *Boscawen at *Louisburg in 1758, and with Admiral *Saunders at the capture of *Quebec in 1759. During the War of American Independence (1775–82) he commanded the British fleet in the East Indies and in 1782 captured the French base at Trincomalee. He fought five fierce naval battles in those waters against a French fleet commanded by the great Admiral *Suffren, probably the best admiral ever produced by France, and when the war ended he still held the command of the seas in that part of the world.

HULK, (1) originally a large ship used either as a transport or for carrying merchandise, particularly in the Mediterranean where hulks ranged up to about 400 tons. It was contemporary with the *carrack and occasionally described as such. In general, any large and unwieldy ship of simple construction with a rounded bow and stern was described as a hulk. **(2)** Another name for the *hull of a ship, but this use of the word had fallen into disuse by the end of the 18th century. **(3)** An old ship converted for some use which did not require it to move. Early hulks were used as floating storehouses, as the temporary abode of naval seamen awaiting draft to a sea-going ship, and particularly for quarantine purposes. Some were also fitted out for use in *stepping or lifting out masts in sea-going ships. Later, particularly in the late 18th and early 19th centuries, they were used as prisons. 'It was as a

means of devising a severe mode of punishment short of death that the Hulks on the Thames were introduced in 1776,' Chambers' *Books of Days*, Vol. II, p. 67.

HULL, probably from the German *hulla* or *hulle*, a cloak or covering, the main body of a ship apart from her masts, rigging, and all internal fittings, including boilers, engines, etc. It consists virtually of the upper deck, sides, and bottom of a ship. HULL-DOWN, a ship so far distant that only her masts and/or sails, funnels, etc., are visible above the *horizon.

HULL, to, a ship is said to be hulling when she drives to and fro without rudder or sail or engine movement. To hull a ship, to penetrate her hull with a shot from a gun. To strike hull, in a sailing vessel, to take in all sail in a storm and to lie with the *helm lashed *a-lee. This is also known as lying a-hull, or to lie a-hull.

HULL, ISAAC (1773–1843), American naval officer, was born in Connecticut and commanded a merchant vessel before he was 21. Becoming a lieutenant in the new U.S. Navy in March 1798 he served in the *frigate *Constitution during the naval war with France. During the war with Tripoli he commanded the *Enterprise and later the *Argos.

When war was declared against Great Britain in 1812, Hull left Chesapeake Bay in the *Constitution* on 12 July. At sea he encountered five British men-of-war and was chased for nearly three days, managing to escape capture by outstanding seamanship. Going to sea again, Hull encountered the British frigate *Guerrière* on 19 August. Again Hull displayed outstanding seamanship in manoeuvring the *Constitution* to minimize the effect of the *Guerrière*'s rapid gunfire while closing the range to pistol shot distance before opening fire himself. About 30 minutes after the *Constitution*'s first broadside the *Guerrière* was dismasted and so badly shattered that she was forced to surrender, but had to be burned as she was too much damaged to be brought into port. Hull's victory was the first of the frigate actions which greatly raised American morale, though in fact they had little effect on the greatly superior British naval strength.

HULLOCK, an old maritime term for a small piece of a sail loosed (spread) in heavy weather when it is impossible to spread more because of the strength of the wind. The term referred only to two sails, either the mizen *course, when a hullock was loosed at the mizen yardarm to keep the ship's head to the sea, or the foresail, to lay her head the other way. The correct nautical term used with hullock was to loose, 'let loose a hullock'.

HUMBOLDT, FRIEDRICH HEINRICH ALEXANDER, Baron von (1769–1859), a Prussian naturalist and scientific explorer, is best known for his journey in South America in 1799–1803 in company with the Frenchman Bonpland, during which they explored the Orinoco to its source, proved its connection with the Amazon, ascended the Magdalena, and crossed the frozen Cordilleras to descend on the other side to Quito, whence they visited the sources of the Amazon. After a year in Mexico and a visit to the U.S.A., Humboldt returned to Europe and spent twenty years digesting and describing the notable scientific results of the journey.

Humboldt also made valuable investigations into terrestrial magnetism and finally, in the fourteen years before his death in 1859, composed his *Kosmos*, a summary and exposition of the laws and conditions of the universe. His name has been given to the constant north-running, cold * current that is a dominant feature of the Pacific off the west coast of South America.

'HUNGRY HUNDRED', an epithet used in the British Navy to describe 100 Royal Naval Reserve officers from the merchant navy who in 1895 were offered and accepted permanent commissions as lieutenants in the Royal Navy to meet the shortage of officers of that rank. A condition of the offer was that these officers were not eligible for promotion beyond the rank of lieutenant except for war service. The epithet stemmed from the fact that most merchant navy officers still had no permanent career structure, having to sign on for each new voyage, while naval officers were on a permanent salary.

Three years later, with the shortage of lieutenants continuing in the Royal Navy, a further fifty Royal Naval Reserve officers were given similar permanent commissions. They were inevitably known as the 'Famishing Fifty'.

HURD, Sir ARCHIBALD (1869–1959), British naval architect and writer, joined the editorial staff of the *Daily Telegraph* in 1899 and for six years was also joint editor of * *Brassey's Naval Annual*. He was the author chosen after the First World War to write the official war history of the merchant navy, which was published in three volumes, 1921–9. During the Second World War he served as a member of the Council of the Institution of Naval Architects. A prolific writer, he was a pungent critic of British naval policy between the two world wars, criticism based on a lifetime's knowledge of ships and the sea.

HURD, THOMAS (1753–1823), British naval captain, the first of an unbroken line of senior naval officers with surveying experience to act as Hydrographer of the Navy. In his early naval service he assisted in surveys of Newfoundland and Nova Scotia under * des Barres and Holland and after active naval service as a lieutenant in the American War of Independence (1775–82) he spent nearly nine years making a highly detailed survey of the Bermudas, from which the British fleet was to benefit during the succeeding wars against France. Having completed the fair drawings of this work in the Hydrographic Office of the British Admiralty, he made a survey off Brest in 1804 and then joined the Chart Committee set up in 1807 to assist Alexander * Dalrymple, whom he succeeded as Hydrographer of the Navy in the following year.

Hurd was then successfully concerned with organizing the British surveying service as a naval one, both in ships and men. H.M.S. * *Investigator* was specially built in 1811 as a survey ship and a corps of naval surveying officers with special rates of pay was established by the Admiralty in 1817. Surveys at home and overseas became the responsibility of the Hydrographer. Chart production and supplies to the fleet proceeded apace with small increases of staff, and in 1819 Hurd obtained long-sought permission for the sale of Admiralty charts to the mercantile marine.

He was secretary to the * Board of Longitude, 1810–19, and in 1818, when on a Royal Society proposal the Admiralty accepted the administration of the Royal Observatory at * Greenwich, responsibility for its operation was placed on Hurd's shoulders; the management of it continuing to be part of the Hydrographer's duty until 1965, when the new Science Research Council took over.

Hurd died while still serving as Hydrographer.

HURRICANE, see TROPICAL STORMS.

HUSBAND or **SHIP'S HUSBAND,** before the days of high-speed communications, was the title given to an agent appointed by deed, executed by all the owners of freight carried on board, with the power to advance and lend money, to make all necessary payments in regard to the freight carried and to receive all money obtained from the sale of any freight, being accountable to the owners for all his transactions. See also SUPERCARGO, another name for the cargo-owner's agent on board a merchant ship.

HUYGENS, CHRISTIAAN (1629–95), Dutch astronomer and physicist, comes into the maritime story through his work on telescopes and their lenses and through his horological inventions. In 1665 he developed a new method of grinding and polishing lenses which provided much clearer vision than was possible with any then existing and, although these were developed mainly with astronomy in view, they were adapted to the maritime telescope with much improved results.

His horological work was probably of considerably greater importance in marine affairs, though there is some mystery attached to it. He was certainly responsible for the application of the pendulum to regulate the movement of clocks, which sprang from his need of a more exact measure of time for his work in observing the heavens; he also invented the spiral watch-spring. It is these inventions which have given rise to claims that he may have been the first man, rather than John * Harrison to whom the credit is usually given, to have solved the problem of discovering * longitude by the time method. There are reports that in 1662 he made two 'watches for the Longitude' which were brought to England for trial in a naval ship. The result of the trial was reported back to Huygens as unsatisfactory but it has been suggested that the result was falsified to put the Dutch off the scent and reserve the solution of the longitude problem for the benefit of British navigation. It seems an unlikely suggestion since it was another full century before the problem was finally solved with Harrison's * chronometer. Some possible credence is given to the suggestion by the fact that Huygens was elected a member of the Royal Society during a visit to England in 1663, but it is probable that this honour came to him more for his astronomical work, in which he was a world figure, than as a consolation for stealing the design of his 'watch for the Longitude'.

Huygens published his horological discoveries in 1673 in *Horologium Oscillatorium*, the most important of his published works. He bequeathed all his manuscripts to the University at Leiden, where they remain.

HYDRA, H.M.S., a steam * sloop of 818 tons, employed as a surveying ship, 1864–8, was one of several ships that carried this name. Her most notable task was a deep-sea cruise in 1867–8 in the Mediterranean and in the Atlantic Ocean. There was at the time a new emphasis on ocean soundings which came from the requirements for laying trans-ocean cables. A great advance in the procedure of deep-water sounding was evolved in the *Hydra* by the use of a * lead from which weights were automatically detached on striking the bottom, so that the labour of heaving-in was greatly reduced. The *Hydra*'s blacksmith received an award for this invention although some years earlier an American * ensign named Brooke, under the encouragement of the distinguished oceanographer * Maury, had produced a similar device.

In 1965 another *Hydra* joined her sister ships *Hecate* and *Heda* in a new class of 2,800-ton vessels equipped for ocean survey work, the need this time stemming from the operation of British * Polaris submarines.

HYDRODYNAMICS, a branch of physics concerned with pressures and behaviour of fluids, is closely connected with the study of the design of ships and sailing yachts. When it was discovered by William * Froude that the behaviour characteristics of scale models of ships towed at scale speeds through water along a testing tank varied exactly in accordance with their full size prototypes, he was able to propound his law of comparison, which later became more widely termed the Law of Mechanical Similitude. Froude showed that the behaviour of water as it flowed past a moving hull could be measured in terms of resistance and drag on the hull, and could be applied with reference to a full-size ship of identical design. It was clearly demonstrated that scale models, therefore, could be used to determine in advance the seagoing and performance characteristics of any new design of ship, in smooth water and in waves and rough weather conditions, and so to discover more accurately the ship's resistance and the engine power needed to give the requisite service speed. Running model tests was less time-consuming and considerably less costly than building the ship first and making modifications afterwards.

Study of the movements of liquids in the allied subject of hydrokinetics also resulted in the discovery of what came to be termed the stream-line form, which presents the lowest resistance to a liquid flowing past the object. For example, if a floating rectangular box is towed through water, or is anchored and the water is allowed to flow past, a wave will build up against the front face of the box, forming an area of pressure. The disturbed water then flows round both sides and underneath the box, producing friction drag along the surface of the box. Behind the flat rear end the water flow endeavours to close in upon itself, and does so with a series of eddies and whirlpools which break up the flow, producing a disturbed wake for some distance downstream. This disturbance forms a distinct suction at the rear of the box that, added to the pressure at the forward end and friction along the sides, creates a considerable amount of drag (Diagram 1).

If a block of ice is cut into a rectangular shape similar in plan to the box, and it is held fast in a moving stream of slightly warmer water, the edges of the ice will begin to melt. The water flowing both round and under the ice will steadily erode it until the ice assumes a sleekly curved form which reduces the overall drag to a minimum. This naturally moulded teardrop shape, fuller at the front than at the tail end, offers minimal resistance to the flow of the water, and is said to be streamlined. Whatever shape the ice might be to begin with, its erosion by melting will inevitably reduce it to a curved shape approximating to Diagram 2: approximating, because the exact form and relation between the length and the breadth will depend upon the rate of the stream, i.e., the speed of the water past the ice. The greater the speed of flow the narrower and sleeker the figure will become in proportion to its length.

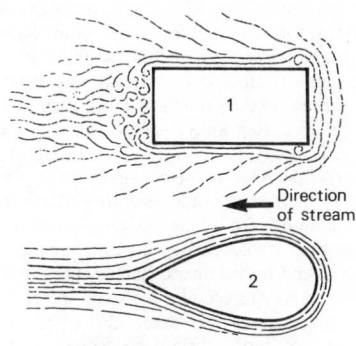

1 Box in flowing stream
2 Sheet of ice in flowing stream

Streamlined flow

It might be thought that such a streamline form would be eminently suitable for the design of a ship's hull, for like a fish it seems ideal for offering the minimum amount of resistance to the ship's forward progress. During the 18th and 19th centuries shipbuilders did in fact copy a modified 'cod's head and mackerel tail' form of hull below the waterline in sailing ships, small coasters, pilot boats, and revenue *cutters. These excessively full bows with a very fine run aft were normal over a period from about 1700 to 1850, and many yachts were built on the same principle, until a more balanced form was introduced, leading to modern designs. Other considerations in commercial ship design make such a fully streamlined hull impracticable: the full bow causes high resistance, if not damage to the ship herself, when driven into a head sea, while the very fine lines aft create a condition of 'squatting', or settling by the stern, which is aggravated by the suction of the *propeller(s). Consideration of cargo carrying, passenger accommodation, and machinery space also rules out any fully streamlined vessel in favour of the conventional straight-sided ship with suitably designed bow and stern. A more recent development of the streamline principle, designed to minimize the bow waves and to reduce pressures of water along the ship's hull and so reduce drag and wash, is to be seen in the bulbous bow fitted below the waterline to many fast ships and giant tankers.

The fact that liquids are virtually incompressible makes it possible for a suitably shaped object which attains sufficient speed to rise above the water and skate along the surface, like a small flat stone skimmed by a child. When only steam machinery was available its weight in relation to the power it developed (i.e., the power/weight ratio) rendered it impracticable to drive a boat fast enough for it to begin to skim over the surface, and it was only when development in internal combustion engine design and lightweight boat construction produced a more advantageous power/weight ratio that boats could be made to plane, or skim along the water.

For this purpose the old conception of the fast launch with a fine entrance forward, narrow beam, and a fine run to the stern, so as to make as few waves as possible, went by the board. A new type of hull was designed on the principle of a water sledge which would rise on to the surface at high speed and plane, with only its after part, rudder, and propeller in the water. The design was found to need a broad flat stern to prevent squatting at speed, and sharply V'd sections at the bow. At velocities of 40 knots and over water can be treated as though it were almost solid, and to assist boats to start planing in the early days of power boating many boats were built with one, two, or more steps on the underside of the hull, on which the boat was designed to ride like a sledge.

Based on the same principle as this stepped hull is a further development with some commercial uses—the *hydrofoil. In this craft a series of curved vanes or hydrofins is fitted to a leg attached to each side of the hull forward, and similar vanes to another pair of legs fitted aft. As soon as the speed reaches a certain point the vessel rides up until its hull is completely clear of the water, and so runs on only the hydrofins. Hydrofoil craft operate as fast (50- to 60-knot) ferries in different parts of the world, particularly in the Mediterranean and on Russian rivers.

To be able to start planing under sail power alone it is essential for a conventional boat to be of exceedingly light construction with V'd bow sections and a flat bottom at the stern like the engine-powered speedboat, together with a highly efficient rig to supply the necessary drive. Although some light displacement yachts, such as Half-Ton Cup competitors and some multihull racers, can sail down wind with short bursts of speed in a state bordering on planing, true planing—riding along the surface at high speed for considerable periods—is normally achieved only by certain classes of high performance racing dinghies.

Making use of this property of water the *hovercraft is able to lift itself just clear of the surface by maintaining a cushion of air at low pressure which is more or less imprisoned within the skirt surrounding the vessel's bottom. Here the water acts almost like a solid surface, and only a small amount of surface water is dissipated in spray while the vehicle is hovering. See also HOVERCRAFT, PLANING, FROUDE, William, WAVE LINE THEORY.

HYDROFOIL, a type of craft beneath which planes or foils are fitted which lift the *hull of the vessel clear of the water when travelling at high speed. Research in this field began in 1891 and trials took place on Lake Maggiore in 1906 with a craft designed by Enrico Forlanini, which was fitted with ladder-type foils, and reached a speed of 38 *knots. Three years later the U.S.A. conducted successful experiments with submerged foils and in 1927 German engineers evolved what is known as a surface-piercing foil. In 1956 the first commercial hydrofoil went into operation between Sicily and Italy and, the following year, the first passenger-carrying hydrofoil craft was launched in the Soviet Union at Krasnoye Sormovo shipyard.

Today there are basically two types of hydrofoil craft, those fitted with the 'canard' type foil in which 30 per cent of the boat's weight is supported by the forward foil and 70 per cent by the after foil, and the conventional type in which the weight distribution is reversed. With the former the boat rides clear of the water on a cushion of air above the surface-piercing foils, whereas with the latter, though the hull is lifted clear of the water, the foils remain submerged, giving greater stability though not such high speed.

The naval uses of hydrofoil craft for antisubmarine warfare are under active development in the U.S.A. and Canada, and they are also being considered for *minesweeping. Their commercial use as ferries is now widespread, particularly in the Soviet Union for river transport.

HYDROGRAPHY, the science of marine surveying and of determining the position of points and objects on the surface of the globe, depths of the sea, etc. It is an art which has no historical beginning, the requirement gradually arising, so far as surveys at sea are concerned, with the slow expansion of seaborne trade. It is said that as early as 1600 B.C. Chinese mariners were aware of the property of the *lodestone, and therefore had some form of *compass, but there are no records to suggest that such a compass was combined with linear measurement, or that compass angles were combined with distances to form any sort of maritime chart. In the third century B.C., the Greeks are credited with measurement of distances at sea by means of a *log-line during their trading voyages along the coast from the Indus to the Persian Gulf, but they had no compass with which to measure angles, however roughly.

The earliest charts of which any knowledge exists were based on astronomical observations and determinations, but, with the crude measuring instruments then in use, were wildly inaccurate. It is with the Arabs in medieval times that the art of nautical surveying can be said to begin. They had the *astrolabe and the compass and thus could, and did, make charts of the coastlines which they visited. Vasco da *Gama in 1498 records that he saw a chart of the coastline of India, and many of his eastern voyages were dependent for their success on the Arab charts he was able to consult during his travels.

As ships pushed out east and west into the unknown world the growth of nautical surveying, and thus cartography, grew slowly, being recorded mainly in the form of *rutters, *portolanos, *derroterros, etc., and, later, *waggoners, which were crude maritime atlases, their name coming from the Dutch cartographer *Wagenaer whose work in this sphere was highly prized by mariners. Each nation guarded its own surveying results as state secrets, and thus knowledge of the shape and trend of the coastlines of more distant parts was slow to reach the world at large. The work of such cartographers as *Mercator, *Hondius, *Ortelius, and others, though still showing many inaccuracies, did much to break down this attitude of secrecy. The invention of more precise instruments of measurement, particularly of the *quadrant and its later development the *sextant, naturally brought a vast increase in cartographical accuracy, and by the 17th century the art of maritime survey had reached a remarkably high degree of precision. Greenvile *Collins, Seller, and a host of others used these new means of measurement to produce accurate navigational charts of coastal waters, and the simultaneous development of astronomical measurement methods of calculating *longitude brought about a far clearer knowledge of ocean distances and the true positions of continents and islands. By the mid-18th century the art of nautical surveying and cartography had reached a stage which brought a new exactitude in the navigation of ships which enabled them to make their ocean passages with far more certainty and knowledge. The two arts of navigation and cartography progressed towards a new understanding and a new appreciation of the world's geography, amply demonstrated in the surveys and voyages of James *Cook.

Most of the world's hydrographic knowledge and practice has come from the operations of the world's navies. A general requirement, before the birth of the various national hydrographic departments, was for the *masters (navigators) of the naval ships of all nations to observe, survey, and report to their respective admiralties on all possible occasions. Towards the end of the

18th century most maritime nations had thus collected large volumes of mainly uncollated hydrographic information, and most of them appointed official hydrographers during the course of the next half century to organize this mass of knowledge and to publish it for the benefit of seamen of all nations. A Hydrographer's department was established in Great Britain in 1795. France had been the first to set one up in 1720, followed by Denmark in 1784, Spain in 1800, the U.S. Coast and Geodetic Survey in 1816 and the U.S. Hydrographic Office in 1830, and Russia in 1827. Offices were later set up in Germany (1861), Japan (1871), Italy and Sweden (1872), Norway, Netherlands, and Chile (1874). Others have followed and the founding of an international organization in 1921 is mentioned below.

The extent of its overseas possessions or trade initially governed each maritime country's source of information and its ability as well as its need to produce charts for its own naval or merchant shipping. France soon built up and has since maintained an extensive coverage. The U.S. Hydrographic Office, now the Oceanographic Office, with its considerable resources has done likewise, with the U.S. Coast and Geodetic Survey charting their extensive home waters.

Britain, however, has provided the most complete coverage of the world's seas, with its Admiralty *charts. The 19th century period of the 'Pax Britannica' with its doctrine of freedom of the seas required a British naval presence in every ocean of the world, and therefore the navy's need for charts was world-wide. But it was also appreciated that, once established, a closely integrated set of charts, sailing directions, and other navigational publications, subject as it must be to continuous maintenance for new information, would have an inestimable value to all mariners, not only British.

THE BRITISH HYDROGRAPHIC SERVICE

The framework on which the organization, responsibility, and output of the British Hydrographic Department is presently based was largely established between 1795 and 1855. It is, perhaps, typical of the contemporary development of most other national hydrographic offices, and its description here can be taken as the pattern of other maritime nations. In the early 19th century the Hydrographer to the Admiralty was more personally involved than subsequently, when the volume of work and the number of staff increased. Thus, early developments are customarily related to the individuals appointed as Hydrographer, of whom Alexander *Dalrymple, 1795–1808, was the first. Assisted by at most two engravers and two draughtsmen, he sorted the store of documents and published in 1801 the first Admiralty chart. Dalrymple was

succeeded by Thomas *Hurd, 1808–23, the first of a long line of naval officers who have since held the post of Hydrographer of the Navy. Perhaps his greatest service to the science of hydrography was to persuade the Admiralty that charts should be on sale to the maritime public world-wide, a major change from the days when national security or the interests of the individual surveyor were considered paramount. Of almost equal importance was his demonstration that *surveys at sea, as and when required, would best be conducted by H.M. ships. He thus originated the naval surveying service with officers of executive rank graduating by experience both to command the ships and conduct their surveys, an organization which was largely adopted by other national hydrographic services. Hurd and his successors were also accepted as the Admiralty's advisers on scientific matters and, in particular, the administration of the Royal *Greenwich Observatory, until in 1965 it was taken over by the newly formed Science Research Council.

An additional facility to navigators was introduced between 1823 and 1829 when both *Sailing Directions and *Light Lists were published by the British Hydrographic Office. The increasing volume of work led to the appointment of naval assistants, who have continued to provide superintendence of civilian staff in the various branches of the department. At about the same time the exchange of information with other national hydrographic offices was fostered. *Tide Tables were initiated in 1833 and *Notices to Mariners, for promulgating new information, in 1834, a previous means of so doing being the Nautical Magazine begun in 1832. The number of charts published by the British Admiralty reached 2,000 at this period.

Surveys in home waters were conducted more scientifically and were based on ordnance triangulation. Overseas activity was stimulated by the Chinese and Crimean wars in which the involvement of the surveying service in naval operations emphasized the value of its naval basis, an argument to be used more than once throughout the department's history when, for example, naval retrenchment in peacetime has occasioned suggestions for its civilianization.

Steam propulsion and the use of iron in shipbuilding led to the foundation of a committee to improve *compasses and in 1842 a compass branch, with an observatory at Woolwich, was set up. The Hydrographer of the Navy retained this responsibility until 1911. Tidal theory and marine meteorology were also developed, Sir Francis *Beaufort's contribution in 1840–50 with his wind and weather scale being well known. Climatological observations over the oceans, resulting in synoptic charts, were introduced, with the famous American hydrographer

Matthew *Maury playing a prominent part in this while in charge of the Depot of Charts, later the Naval Observatory, Washington, from 1841 until the Civil War of 1861. Collaboration with the Royal Society in geophysical matters was fostered and became traditional so that up to 1945 Hydrographers of the British Navy were honoured with fellowships.

The production of charts and accompanying books proceeded vigorously as British overseas interests built up. There was the development of deep sea sounding in the *Atlantic, in association with Matthew Maury, for the laying of the first telegraph cable between Britain and America and the interest thus stimulated in oceanography crystallized when the *Challenger sailed on her world voyage, 1872–6, with George *Nares in command and Wyville Thomson as senior scientist. In navigation the most important advance was the *sounding machine enabling soundings to be taken from ships under way.

The last twenty years of the 19th century saw Britain's overseas responsibilities increase yet further with steamships opening up new routes and ports in the East and Australasia, and also in Africa, following its European colonization. There was much international activity in polar regions, including the 1901 British National Expedition in the *Discovery under Captain R. F. *Scott. There was Marconi's invention of wireless in 1902 leading to publication of the Admiralty List of Wireless Signals in 1922 and facilitating world-wide determinations of accurate longitude hitherto accomplished by carrying time by *chronometer.

BRITISH COLONIAL DEVELOPMENT

A lessening of responsibility for the surveying and charting of colonial waters came up for renewed consideration in 1904, the year in which Canada set up a hydrographic service. There had been a reconstituted Marine Survey of India from 1874, and by 1906 one of the Indian officers had sufficient experience to take charge in place of an officer lent from Britain. Shared costs had begun in Australia as early as 1860 and there has been a natural extension of self-sufficiency to the present day as one-time colonies have become independent. Close relations have, however, been maintained throughout with the British Hydrographic Department.

War brought its special problems. Importantly for hydrography, it led through anti-submarine warfare to a keener appreciation of applied oceanography and the eventual development of *echo sounding. In 1918 the British hydrographer chaired an interdepartmental committee on uniformity in time-keeping at sea so that civil and astronomical days were brought into line and *zone times introduced. He had the support of the French hydrographer Renaud and it was

these two who in 1919 organized the International Hydrographic Conference in London, attended by twenty-four countries. There followed in 1921 the inauguration of the International Hydrographic Bureau at Monaco where it had the encouragement of Prince Albert, an oceanographer in his own right. The objective was to promote rapid and informed exchange of hydrographic information in standardized terms between the member states. A convention has been drafted to give the bureau inter-governmental status in order to facilitate its important tasks.

TECHNICAL DEVELOPMENTS

The 1930s saw the introduction of echo sounding and the first major development in surveying equipment since the sextant. The station pointer also came into use. At the same time the introduction of rotary offset printing made possible the issue of the millions of charts which would be required during the coming war.

The International Geophysical Year, 1957–8, a subsequent special oceanographic committee of the International Council of Scientific Unions, and the inter-governmental Oceanographic Commission have all attracted the attention of international hydrography. Underwater defence developments have increased the need for oceanographical data, and many maritime countries now co-operate in the vast areas of the oceans.

Developments that aided hydrography in the Second World War were radar and radio aids and their subsequent technological advances. These, combined with modern work studies, are revolutionizing methods ashore and afloat. Thus can be met the ever increasing demands for greater accuracy in surveying and charting exemplified by mammoth *tankers, maritime traffic separation, and sea bed exploitation.

National hydrographic offices have been relieved to some extent by various commercial and major harbour hydrographic services that have developed since the Second World War. Nevertheless international maritime mobility owes much to the integrated world-wide chart coverage with ancillary publications which for historical reasons the Royal Navy has built up and continues to maintain. And it is, perhaps, a continuing tribute to the Royal Navy's work in this field that the Admiralty chart still retains its name though the Admiralty itself was swallowed up in the Ministry of Defence in 1964.

U.S. Coast & Geodetic Survey (Washington, 1963); A. L. Shalowitz, Shore and Sea Boundaries, 2 vols (1963); Admiralty Manual of Hydrographic Surveying (1965); A. Day, The Admiralty Hydrographic Service, 1795–1919 (1967).

HYPERBOLIC NAVIGATION, see NAVIGATION.

The Russian nuclear ice-breaker Lenin

I

ICEBERG, a floating island of ice. Icebergs in the northern hemisphere almost all originate in Disko Bay in Greenland. The mountains of northern Greenland are covered by a vast ice-cap which moves slowly down the valleys until it reaches the sea, where great sections break away in a process known as calving. They float out to sea and are then carried southward by the Labrador Current. Their usual life-span is about two years, the second summer finding them at their most southerly point in the region of the *Grand Banks off Newfoundland. Small portions which break away from the main icebergs and are still large enough to constitute a danger to navigation are known as growlers. Only one-ninth of the total mass of an iceberg is visible above water level.

They are, of course, a considerable hazard to shipping, especially in the summer months in the North Atlantic when most transatlantic shipping lines route their ships farther to the northward to make a shorter passage (see, in this connection, GREAT CIRCLE SAILING). The best remembered disaster at sea caused by an iceberg was when the White Star liner *Titanic* sank on 14 April 1912 after striking an iceberg near the Grand Banks off Newfoundland with a loss of 1,589 lives.

Today an ice patrol, directed from Halifax, is maintained in the North Atlantic to observe the position of all icebergs, the rate and direction of their drift, and to report them so that all shipping can be warned of their presence. In many cases the warning comes to a ship in the form of a chart transmitted by wireless, so that the navigator has a copy of the actual chart in front of him when plotting his course.

ICE-BREAKER, a vessel specially designed with a reinforced bow and *forefoot and with extremely powerful engines to force a way through pack ice in extreme northern *latitudes. The largest and best-known of modern ice-breakers is probably the Russian *Lenin*, a nuclear-powered ship of 16,000 tons. Her engines develop 44,000 horse power and give her a maximum speed of 18 knots. She is said to be able to clear a channel 100 feet wide through pack ice eight feet thick at a speed of four knots. Larger nuclear-powered ice-breakers, able to clear a passage through even thicker ice, are reported to be under construction in Russia.

The *Lenin* and other Russian ice-breakers are used to clear a shipping lane in the 'Northern Sea Route', which connects the Atlantic with the Pacific Ocean north of Russia and Siberia (see also NORTH-EAST PASSAGE). Similar attempts have been made to open the *North-West passage, which runs north of Canada, especially in connection with the discovery of immense oil deposits in Alaska and the surrounding area. Many other ports which are frozen up in winter employ ice-breakers to clear a passage for ships.

IDLERS, the name which used to be given to those members of a ship's crew who, by reason of their employment, do not stand the normal *watches. The *carpenter, cook, sailmaker, *boatswain, painter were the usual members of the *round house mess where idlers were accommodated. The name has now largely fallen into disuse, but was widespread in navies and merchant navies during the days of sail.

IDRISI or **EDRISI** (1099–1154), Arab geographer, was a member of an Arabian princely house, his full name being Abu Abdallah Muhammad Ibn Muhammad Ibn Abdallah Ibn Idrisi. He was born in Ceuta, during the Moorish occupation of southern Spain, and at some period between 1125 and 1150 was invited to the court of Roger II of Sicily, who presented him with a large amount of silver from which to make a terrestrial and celestial sphere. Although this absorbed only one-third of the silver, Roger presented Idrisi with the balance, plus 100,000 pieces of silver money, and the rich cargo of a ship recently arrived from Barcelona. Idrisi was next commissioned by Roger to produce a new description of the inhabited world, and for this purpose seamen and travellers were sent to all parts to collect information. The result was a famous work published in 1154 under the title *Al Rojari*, which contained a full description of the known world. It is not a particularly accurate work except in so far as the coast of Africa is concerned, but it has been suggested that it was Idrisi's descriptions of this coast that stimulated the great voyages sent there under the auspices of Prince *Henry the Navigator some three centuries later. In spite of its inaccuracies, Idrisi's world map places him well at the summit of Muslim cartography of the Middle Ages.

ILLINGWORTH, JOHN HOLDEN (1903–), British naval officer and yacht designer, learned to sail at the age of 8 on Malham Tarn, near his home in Yorkshire. He entered the engineering branch of the Royal Navy and specialized in *submarines and their design. His first yacht was the *Queen Bee*, a 28-ft (8·4 m) Albert *Strange *yawl which he raced in Hong Kong waters in 1927, showing his coming flair for improving the rigs of racing boats by re-rigging her on novel lines. He took up offshore racing seriously in 1937 when, in collaboration with Laurent *Giles, he planned his first ocean racer, *Maid of Malham*, a 48-ft (14·6 m) *cutter. With this yacht he won a number of *Royal Ocean Racing Club races.

After the Second World War he built his most outstanding racer, the *Myth of Malham*, a 38-ft (11·6 m) cutter, again in collaboration with Laurent Giles who drew the lines of the hull while Illingworth designed the rigging and other details. The *Myth* proved a consistent winner in Royal Ocean Racing Club events, including the *Fastnet races, between 1947 and 1959, and with her design he pioneered a new conception of light displacement, a fin-keeled yacht with short overhangs at bow and stern for offshore racing. His early introduction of masthead jibs, which at first was regarded with disapproval by designers and sailmakers alike, became accepted practice throughout the yacht-racing field. Other yachts of the same type in principle which followed included his *Minx of Malham*, a 31-ft (9·5 m) cutter which was adopted as the Royal Naval Sailing Association 24-ft (7·3 m) class; *Mite of Malham*, *Wista*, and *Merle of Malham*, Class V junior offshore group cutters; and *Monk of Malham*, a Class II R.O.R.C. cutter. He was *commodore of the Royal Ocean Racing Club and the Royal Naval Sailing Association, 1950–4, chairman of the *Royal Yachting Association council, 1949–51, and President of the *Junior Offshore Group, 1953–68. His influence on the design and rigs of ocean racers and on the technique of racing in small offshore yachts was considerable. Among the books on yachting which he has written are *Offshore*, *Further Offshore*, *Where Seconds Count*, and *Twenty Challenges for the America's Cup*.

IMPERIAL WAR MUSEUM, The, London, was established by Act of Parliament in July 1920 as a memorial and record of all aspects of the First World War (1914–18) but now covers the Second World War and subsequent campaigns as well. The naval section contains models of warships of almost every class, dioramas of special operations, guns, *torpedoes, *mines, uniforms, and medals, as well as relics and trophies of famous actions and of the ships which took part in them. A large collection of paintings and portraits is housed in the basement, and the photographic library contains some 3,000,000 pictures covering every aspect of the wars. The library contains over 60,000 books and manuscripts covering the period from 1914.

IMPLACABLE, H.M.S., was originally a 74-gun French ship, the *Duguay-Trouin*, one of those which escaped from *Trafalgar but was captured in November 1805 and added to the Royal Navy as the *Implacable*. After seeing action in the Baltic and on the coast of Syria she became, in 1855, a training ship for boys at Devonport. In 1912 she was lent to Mr. Wheatley Cobb and moored at Portsmouth as a training ship for sea scouts and similar oganizations, in conjunction with the *Foudroyant*. Used as a store depot by the Admiralty during the Second World War, she was taken out to sea and sunk in December 1949 as her timbers had rotted beyond repair.

The press gang; water-colour by T. Rowlandson

IMPRESSMENT, the name given in Britain for the state authority to require the service of a subject for the defence of the country. Although universally known as 'press' or 'impress', the origin of the word is 'prest', a sum of money advanced to a man in the form of conduct money to reach an appointed * rendezvous.

Impressment was a general and recognized method of recruitment in most countries of the world, and applied equally to service ashore and afloat. In England, for example, the famous 'New Model' army of Oliver Cromwell was largely recruited by impressment. But because service in the navy was always unpopular, and the demand for seamen always so great, it is the naval element of impressment on which most attention has been focused.

The parliamentary legality of impressment in Britain, as opposed to the previous royal prerogative, was first laid down in an Act of Mary Tudor (1556) in which a claim by Thames watermen to be exempt from impressment was not allowed. In an Act of Elizabeth I (1563) 'touching politick considerations for the maintenance of the Navy', fishermen and mariners were protected from the press for service on land but liable to be pressed for service at sea in the navy. This Act was renewed every few years until in the reign of Charles I (1631) it was made permanent. Under Elizabeth I's Vagrancy Act (1597), disreputable characters could be drafted

for service at sea. Apprentices were exempted from impressment below the age of 18 by an Act of Queen Anne (1703) 'for the increase of Seamen ... and the protection of the Coal Trade', many apprentices being engaged in this trade. Men over 55 years of age were exempted by an Act of George II (1740), and Thames watermen employed by fire insurance companies, the * masters and * mates of merchant vessels, and a proportion of men in each * collier were protected from pressing by an Act of 1774.

All other 'seamen' and 'mariners' were liable to impressment, but naturally enough, in the chronic and persistent need of naval manpower, no authority questioned closely whether a man brought in by the press was necessarily a seaman or a mariner. The most prolific source of recruitment came under the various Vagrancy Acts, which encouraged local justices to clear their gaols and get rid of their worst characters by drafting them into the navy, and the later * Quota Acts, under which each town and county was given a quota of men to be provided for service at sea.

The operations of the impressment service were widespread throughout Britain, and were employed as well at sea, where homeward bound merchant ships could be stopped and a proportion of the crew taken off, essential men being replaced (in theory) by less efficient men from the pressing ship (see MEN-IN-LIEU). Although this method of impressing men for the navy was limited to homeward bound ships, outward bound vessels frequently suffered the same fate; by the time any complaint of such treatment from an outward bound ship reached the authorities in London, the incident would be too far in the past to command any action. This pressing at sea, which the men concerned could not evade as they could ashore, was the subject of much abuse. In 1802, for example, an *East Indiaman bringing home a valuable cargo was stopped in the Bay of Biscay and so many seamen pressed out of her that she was unable to offer any resistance when encountered later by a French *privateer and was forced to surrender.

The impressment service operated only in time of war. It was last employed in Britain during the Napoleonic War of 1803–15, although the right to operate a press was still retained. Under an Act of 1835, men who had once been pressed for service and had served five years were exempted from further pressing. But with the introduction of continuous service in the navy in 1853, under which seamen could make service in the navy a career with a pension after a fixed number of years, the need for impressment faded. When, again, large numbers of men were required, as in the two world wars of the 20th century, Acts of compulsory national service were passed and men were drafted into the various fighting services in a more fair and orderly fashion than under the haphazard method of the press. See also PRESS GANG, TENDER, HOT PRESS.

IN SOUNDINGS, a vessel is said to be in soundings when she is being navigated in water sufficiently shallow for soundings (see SOUND, TO) to be made and used as a means for ascertaining the approximate position of the ship. Traditionally a ship is reckoned to be in soundings when she is within the 100-fathom line, this *isobath being taken as marking the edge of the *continental shelf.

IN STAYS, a sailing vessel is said to be in stays when she is head to wind and temporarily unable to pay off on either *tack, though in its original meaning the term was used to indicate the act of tacking.

INCHCAPE ROCK, sometimes known as Bell Rock, a sandstone reef off the Angus coast of Scotland, about 11 miles south-east of Arbroath. The reef extends about 700 yards and is covered at high water, a few feet of it being exposed at low water. It was the scene of a multiple shipwreck during the great gale of 1799, no fewer than seventy vessels being wrecked on it, including the *York,* a 74-gun *ship of the line of the British Navy. As a result of this disaster a 100-foot tower, designed by Robert Stevenson,

was erected on the reef, being completed in 1812 at a cost of £61,300.

According to local tradition, the rock had previously been marked by a bell, activated by the waves, erected on it by an abbot of Aberbrothock, or Arbroath in the modern spelling, so that it should serve as a perpetual warning to mariners. This bell was removed by a sea rover whose ship was later wrecked on the reef on his return from his piratical ventures, and he and his whole crew were drowned. This event was made the subject of his 'Ballad of the Inchcape Rock' by Robert Southey.

INDIAN OCEAN, the great area of sea bounded on the north by Persia and India, on the east by the East Indian islands and western Australia, on the south by the Antarctic circle, and on the west by Africa. It was thought by the early geographers to be a vast inland lake, and on their maps they drew Africa bending round to the eastward eventually to join up with China. It was not until 1488, when Bartholomew *Diaz, sailing from Portugal down the western coast of Africa, rounded the Cape of Good Hope and reported an ocean beyond it, that geographers began to include an ocean there on their maps.

Nine years after Diaz reported the new ocean, King Manõel of Portugal selected the conquistador Vasco da *Gama to command a squadron of exploration in order to follow up the discovery and, if possible, to find a sea route to India. He rounded the Cape of Good Hope in 1497 and sailed up the east coast of Africa as far as Malindi where he had the good fortune to discover a Gujerati pilot. With his aid he crossed the ocean and reached the Malabar coast of India at Calicut, where he erected the usual marble pillar with which Portuguese navigators claimed possession of new territories for Portugal. Although he was unable to set up a trading post at Calicut because of the rivalry of Arab traders and the hostility of the Hindus, he was able to observe the riches of the new country and load a cargo of spices before returning home.

The next Portuguese navigator to cross the Indian Ocean was Pedro *Cabral who succeeded in establishing a 'factory', or trading post, at Calicut. A few months later it was attacked by Arab traders and put to the sword. When the news of this assault reached Portugal another expedition, led by da Gama, was dispatched. He reached Calicut in 1502, bombarded the town from his ships, and took vengeance on the inhabitants, treating them with merciless cruelty. He then sailed down the Indian coast, setting up new trading stations at Cochin and Goa.

Although in the early days of discovery newly found territories were treated as state secrets, news of the wealth of these lands spread through Europe. Expeditions, first from England, then from Holland and France, were sent to open up the country and establish trading factories, and so vast were the rewards that *East India Companies were set up by the various nations and given monopolies of this eastern trade. More and more expeditions were fitted out by these companies both to expand their interests and to defend their monopolies, by which means increasing knowledge of the new ocean and its navigational hazards was obtained.

Another source of exploration which helped to expand knowledge of the Indian Ocean was the search for the mythical *Terra Australis, a great land mass believed by geographers to exist in the southern hemisphere to balance the land mass in the northern. This, and the gradually increasing number of circumnavigations, brought a much more exact definition of the Indian Ocean which was reflected in a greater cartographical accuracy, both on the part of the various East India Companies which appointed their own hydrographers and by national hydrographical departments which correlated and expanded the information gained through individual voyages.

The total area of the Indian Ocean, including the Persian Gulf and the Red Sea, has been calculated as over 17,000,000 square miles. It contains three great islands, Madagascar, Socotra, and Sri Lanka (Ceylon), and a number of smaller ones of which the Maldive, Chagos, and Cocos groups are of typical coral formation while Mauritius, the St. Paul's, and Crozet groups are of volcanic origin. The main current is the great Equatorial Current which flows westward across the ocean between the parallels of 7° and 20° S. A compensatory current, the Indian Countercurrent, flows eastward along the equator.

INERTIAL NAVIGATION, see NAVIGATION.

INMAN, the Rev. JAMES (1776–1859), mathematician, was principal of the naval school at Portsmouth and professor of nautical mathematics. He published, in 1821, his *Navigation and Nautical Astronomy for Seamen*, the nautical tables of which have been used by generations of seamen for working out navigational problems connected with observations of the sun, moon, and stars.

INTERCEPT, the difference, measured in nautical miles, which the navigator obtains when he works a *sight of an astronomical object. It is the difference between his estimate of the ship's position by *dead reckoning and the position obtained from his *altitude observations. He transfers this to the *chart by measuring the length of his intercept along the *azimuth of the observed object and drawing his position line at that point at right angles to the azimuth. See also MARCQ ST. HILAIRE METHOD.

INTERNATIONAL CODE OF SIGNALS, a series of signal flags and *pendants, one flag for each letter of the alphabet and one pendant for each number between 0 and 9, with three additional pendants for substitutes and four for special meanings, which has been agreed and adopted by all maritime countries for communication between ship and ship, and ship and shore. It was founded in 1817 on Captain F. *Marryat's code of signals and consisted originally of only fifteen flags and pendants. By 1855 it was being widely challenged by codes developed in France by Captain Reynold de Chauvaucy, in Great Britain by Rohde (1836) and Watson (1842), and in the U.S.A. by Rogers, but an international committee was set up in 1856 to try to reach agreement on a single code for universal use. Its final recommendation was based almost entirely on Marryat's original flags and it published a *Commercial Code of Signals* which received universal recognition. In 1887 the existing code ran into difficulties because of the adoption of the four-letter group for ship identification. Additional coloured flags and pendants were incorporated into the code, making a total of forty in all. The revised code, universally agreed in 1900, was brought into use in 1902. See SIGNALS AT SEA, and APPENDIX 2.

INTERNATIONAL CONVENTION FOR THE SAFETY OF LIFE AT SEA, the official body, composed of government representatives of all maritime nations, which among other responsibilities draws up the International Regulations for Preventing Collisions at Sea, more widely known as the *Rule of the Road. The Convention is called together from time to time by member governments to review the existing rules and to propose amendments when required. The existing regulations were last approved in full by the Convention in 1960; the most recent meeting was held in London in 1972 when two modifications to the existing regulations were proposed. The first suggests the introduction of one-way traffic for ships in congested waters; the second the adoption of special distinguishing marks for extra large ships, such as very large crude carriers, to warn all other ships to keep clear of them in shallow waters where their ability to manoeuvre is limited. These amendments are intended to come into force in 1976, but in order to become part of the international regulations they need first to be ratified by a minimum of fifteen nations representing between them not less than 65 per cent of the world's merchant tonnage.

INTERNATIONAL DATELINE, a line running mainly along the *longitude of 180° but with adjustments to avoid the division of certain island groups which lie astride that longitude, the Aleutian Islands in the north and the Fiji, Tonga, and Kermadoc groups, with New Zealand, in the south. It is on this international dateline that the *zone times of +12 hours and −12 hours meet and the date changes. If a traveller round the world sets out from *Greenwich, on 0° longitude, and travels eastward, he puts his clock forward by one hour as he crosses each 15° of longitude, so that by the time he reaches the longitude of 180°, he has put his clock forward by one hour twelve times. If he continues his journey eastward, he will still have to put his clock forward by one hour as he crosses each 15° of longitude, so that by the time he reaches Greenwich again, his clock has been put forward by 24 hours and he is one day ahead in date. To correct this anomaly, he changes the date when he crosses the international dateline, subtracting one day when he crosses it eastward and adding one day when he crosses it westward. Thus in the former case the same calender date is used for two successive periods of 24 hours; in the latter case one calender date is omitted altogether. The time apparently gained or lost is compensated for by the separate hours gained or lost by the adjustments to the clock at 15° intervals in the rest of the circumnavigation, or of course by recrossing the international dateline in the other direction.

INTERNATIONAL DRAGON CLASS, a *one-design keel *sloop 29·2 ft (8·88 m) in overall length, designed by Johan *Anker and introduced in Norway in 1928. The class became

International Dragon Class yacht, 1965

an international one when it was adopted by other countries throughout the world, while the rules governing it continued to be rigidly controlled by the country of its origin. The essential simplicity of its hull construction and rigging, together with all the advantages of a small cabin, appealed for many years to yachtsmen who looked for a first-class racing yacht which was at the time comparatively inexpensive to operate. Its popularity, however, as a racing class of yacht has recently been on the wane since many less expensive classes have been introduced.

INTERNATIONAL METRE CLASS YACHTS, yachts designed under the International Yacht Racing Union rules to rate as 12, 10, 8, 6, or 5·5 metres, according to the rule restrictions of their respective class. The 8-, 10-, and 12-metre classes were introduced to meet the need for thoroughbred racing yachts equipped with acceptable cabin accommodation for making coastal passages from regatta to regatta, and were appreciably less costly to build and maintain than the *J-class and similar big racing yachts.

The metre yachts of the same class are not all identical, as in a *one-design class, but bear the characteristics of the individual designer and his interpretation of the formula. The rating is calculated by a formula which takes into account such measurements as the yacht's length overall, length on waterline, breadths at different points between bow and stern, depths inside the hull, *draught, total displacement, and the measurements of various sails including the overall height of the rig. In each yacht in its class these measurements can differ, but when applied to the rating formula the resultant figure must produce the class rating of 12-metres, 8-metres, and so on.

Because of the greatly increased costs of racing a J-class yacht after the Second World War, 12-metres were selected for the *America's Cup challenges from 1958 onwards. In Scandinavia, and notably in Sweden, towards the end of the 1920s two new classes were introduced as lighter, faster, and less expensive racing boats than the English 6-metres. Both the 22 sq metre (236 sq ft) and the 30 sq metre (322 sq ft) class have cabin accommodation although both are of lighter displacement than the normal cabinless 6-metre. These, nevertheless, have remained essentially a continental type, not much favoured in British waters.

INTERNATIONAL OCEANOGRAPHIC COMMISSION, an agency of the United Nations based in Paris, with the object of collating and collecting oceanographical observations for the use of shipping of all nations. A pilot scheme, in which the information gathered by four nations (Great Britain, U.S.A., Canada, and

West Germany) is collated and exchanged, is in operation and is expected to develop into the Integrated Global Ocean Stations Systems to form the oceanographical equivalent of the World Weather Watch, in which forecasts based on bathythermograph data would be distributed worldwide to shipping. The data at present being collected consists of the ocean temperature at the surface, at the depth of the surface layer (i.e., the depth at which the first considerable drop in temperature occurs), the temperature at the depth of 200 metres (109 fathoms), and the bottom temperature.

INTERNATIONAL REGULATIONS FOR PREVENTING COLLISIONS AT SEA, the official title of the internationally agreed rules by which ships at sea keep clear of each other, more generally known as the *Rule of the Road. They are drawn up and approved by the *International Convention for the Safety of Life at Sea, which meets from time to time to review the existing regulations and propose amendments when required. The regulations are binding on all ships using the sea and govern every case in which a danger of collision may arise when ships meet at sea or congregate in narrow waters. But the fact that a strict interpretation of the rules may give the right of way to one of two vessels where there is a risk of collision if they both continue on their present *course, does not absolve the *master of the vessel with the right of way from taking the necessary action if a collision appears imminent. For example, although the regulations lay down that in all cases of danger of collision a vessel under steam power gives way to a vessel under sail, it would be unreasonable to expect a giant *tanker navigating in narrow waters to give way to a yacht under sail. It is for reasons such as these that the regulations lay down on all masters of vessels, whether they have the official right of way or not, a duty to avoid a collision by taking whatever action is necessary.

The steering and sailing rules currently in force, with the rules governing sound signals in fog, are set out under RULE OF THE ROAD.

INTERNATIONAL   YACHT   RACING UNION, see YACHTING, Racing rules.

INTREPID, H.M.S., a screw *sloop of 342 tons originally a merchant vessel named *Free Trade* and purchased by the British Admiralty in 1850 for service in the Arctic. She was commissioned as a *tender to H.M.S. *Assistance* for the *Austin–*Ommaney expedition of 1850–1 in search of Sir John *Franklin, under the command of Lieutenant J. B. Cator R.N. During Captain Sir Edward *Belcher's expedition of 1852–4 for the same purpose she was tender to H.M.S. *Resolute* and commanded by

Commander F. L. *McClintock. Some of the ships of the expedition, including the *Intrepid* and the *Resolute*, were beset in the ice in 1853 and abandoned, the crews making their way to safety. McClintock and other captains of the ships involved were exonerated over the loss of their ships. See also INVESTIGATOR, H.M.S.; KELLETT, Sir Henry.

INVERGORDON, a fleet anchorage of the Royal Navy at the mouth of the Cromarty Firth, on the north-east coast of Scotland, and the scene in September 1931 of an outbreak of indiscipline by seamen of the Royal Navy. The Invergordon *mutiny, as it is generally known, occurred when the seamen refused to take the ships of the Atlantic Fleet to sea as ordered. This refusal was caused by the inept handling of the Board of Admiralty of a decision to reduce the pay of seamen by 10 per cent in the face of the world financial depression of 1929–31. No preliminary announcement of the proposed cut was made and the first notification received by the seamen was an order pinned on ships' notice boards that the reduction in pay would take place immediately. With the rates of pay then in force, such a reduction was certain to demand sacrifices which were too heavy for some ratings to bear, and, in the words of the First Lord of the Admiralty, the cause of the outbreak was that 'many decent men were driven to distraction by anxiety about their homes; that they were swept off their feet by this anxiety'.

Be that as it may, there was a very wide feeling of discontent throughout the Atlantic Fleet, partly because of the suddenness of the announcement and partly because men of the other armed forces, Army and Royal Air Force, had not been asked to face similar cuts in pay. This resentment was stimulated by the speeches of a few seamen both on board ship and in the canteen ashore, and showed itself by a mass refusal to weigh anchor when the Fleet was ordered to sea. When the order for the cuts in pay was retracted by the Admiralty a day or two later, the mutiny subsided. The men considered by the Admiralty to be responsible for fanning the original discontent into open mutiny were dismissed from the Royal Navy.

INVESTIGATOR, H.M.S., the first ship of the name in the British Navy was a vessel of 334 tons, bought and armed with twelve guns for use by Matthew *Flinders during his Australian surveys in 1801–3. The name was next used in 1811 for the first naval surveying ship to be specially built for the purpose. Of 121 tons, she was built in four months at Deptford and was commanded by G. Thomas, *master, throughout the whole of her twenty-five years service in U.K. home waters. In 1848–50 Sir Robert

*McClure's ship with the Arctic expedition under Captain James *Ross in the search for Sir John *Franklin was also named *Investigator*. She was abandoned in Mercy Bay in June 1853 when McClure's party were rescued by Captain *Kellet in the *Resolute*. Since 1885 the name has been continuously used by the Indian Marine; a predecessor was an Honourable *East India Company ship, 1807–40.

INVINCIBLE, H.M.S., a ship's name used by many navies for their larger warships, and in the Royal Navy used five times for important ships. The first British ship *Invincible* was a French third-*rate of seventy-four guns, of the same name, captured by Vice Admiral Sir George *Anson at the battle of *Cape Finisterre in 1747. She was wrecked on the Dean Sands, St. Helen's, in 1758. She was followed by four other *Invincibles*, three of which saw a good deal of action and were all finally sunk.

The first was launched in 1765, took part in Lord *Howe's action of the *Glorious First of June in 1794, and was wrecked in 1801 off the Norfolk coast, her captain John Rennie and about 400 of her crew being drowned. The next, launched in 1869, was the *flagship of Admiral Sir F. B. Seymour, commander-in-chief in the Mediterranean at the bombardment of Alexandria in the Egyptian War of 1882, and provided a contingent for Lord Charles *Beresford's Naval Brigade which took part in the battles of Abu Klea, Metemmeh, and Wad Habeshi in 1884. She was later renamed *Erebus* for use as a torpedoboat *destroyer base at Portsmouth, and again renamed *Fisgard II* (as part of the Boy Artificers' Training Establishment). She finally foundered off Portland while under tow on 16 September 1914. The third was the *battle-cruiser launched in 1907 as the prototype of this class of warship. She took part in the action of the *Heligoland Bight on 28 August 1914, and was Admiral Sir F. C. D. *Sturdee's flagship at the battle of the *Falkland Islands in December of the same year. On 31 May 1916, during the battle of *Jutland, she blew up after being hit by German shells with the loss of Rear Admiral H. L. A. *Hood and all but six of her complement.

The first of the Royal Navy's new design of *cruiser, capable of operating aircraft and due for completion in 1980, has provisionally been named *Invincible*.

IRISH HORSE, the sailor's name in the old days for salt beef which was tougher than usual, probably based on the belief in those days that the Irish, being so poor, worked their horses much harder and longer than the English. There was a sailor's song of the 18th century in which he addressed his ration of salt beef:

'Salt horse, salt horse, what brought you here?
You've carried turf for many a year.
From Dublin quay to Ballyack
You've carried turf upon your back.'

IRISH HURRICANE, a sailor's name for a flat calm, when no wind blows. It was also sometimes referred to by seamen as a Paddy's hurricane.

IRISH PENNANTS, the seaman's name for loose ends of twine or ropes left hanging over a ship's side or from the rigging, a sure sign of a slovenly crew. Similarly, the name given to the ends of *gaskets and *reef points left flapping on the *yard when the sail is furled in a square-rigged ship. See also DEAD MEN.

IRON DUKE, H.M.S., a *dreadnought battleship of the British Navy, named after the first Duke of Wellington, was launched in October 1912 by the Duchess of Wellington, wife of the fourth Duke. The ship was present as fleet *flagship flying the flag of Sir John *Jellicoe at the battle of *Jutland fought on 31 May 1916 but saw no further action in the First World War (1914–18). After the war she went to the Mediterranean as fleet flagship and returned home in 1926 to become flagship of the 3rd Battle Squadron. She was guard ship at *Scapa Flow in 1939, and in 1940 was damaged by bombing. She was paid off for scrapping in 1945.

IRONCLAD, the early name for warships built of iron, or whose wooden hulls were protected by iron plates. The name was adopted as a generic description for such warships after the action at *Sinope in 1853 in which a Turkish squadron of wooden ships was set on fire and utterly destroyed by Russian shellfire. It was this event which influenced all navies in the world to adopt iron as the main shipbuilding material. The world's first true ironclad warship was the French *frigate *Gloire* launched in 1859. She was followed in 1860 by the first *battleship built entirely of iron, the British *Warrior* of 9,210 tons.

The name continued as a generic description of iron or steel warships until the advent of H.M.S. *Dreadnought* in 1906 when it was largely dropped, subsequent ships of the type being known as dreadnoughts and earlier ones being vaguely reclassed as pre-dreadnoughts.

IRONS, (1) a sailing ship is in irons when, by carelessness or through a fickle wind, she has been allowed to come up into the wind and lose her way through the water so that she will not pay off again on either *tack. It is in the process of tacking, which entails a vessel coming up head to wind and bringing the wind on the other side, that the most frequent cause of a ship being in irons occurs. **(2)** Another word for the *bilboes, a punishment on board ship in which men had their legs shackled to a long iron bar, somewhat in the nature of the punishment of the stocks ashore. A man was said to be put in irons, or ironed, when undergoing this punishment. It was a punishment fairly common in ships of all nations, both warships and merchant vessels, and is said to have been introduced into England from Spain, the *Armada ships all having them on board. Some of the irons fitted in the Armada ships are still to be seen in the Tower of London.

IRRADIATION, an optical phenomenon whereby bright objects viewed against a darker background appear to be bigger than they are; and dark objects viewed against a lighter background appear to be smaller. The sun viewed against the darker background of the sky, and the sky viewed against the normally darker background of the sea, result in irradiation effects for which an allowance should be made when correcting the observed *altitude of the sun in astronomical navigation. The same conditions apply to moon altitude observations. An interesting effect of irradiation of the moon is often to be seen when the moon is cresent-shaped and the remainder of the moon's surface is faintly illuminated by reflected earth-shine. When the moon is young—not more than three or four days after new moon—this phenomenon is referred to as 'the old moon in the new moon's arms'.

ISMAY, THOMAS HENRY (1837–99), British shipowner, was one of the founders of the *White Star shipping line. After an apprenticeship with a firm of shipowners and brokers he travelled extensively and, on his return to Liverpool, took over, in 1867, the White Star line of Australian *clippers. In the following year he realized the vast future in trade and travel which steam navigation would bring, and founded the Oceanic Steam Navigation Company, which later became the White Star Line. In 1870 his first steamship, the *Oceanic* of 3,807 tons, was launched from the yard of Harland and Wolff in Belfast, a ship that was to set a new pattern in North Atlantic travel. During the Russo-Turkish war of 1878, when for a time it looked as though Britain might become engaged, he offered the British Admiralty the whole of the White Star fleet as transports.

ISOBATH, from the Greek *iso*, equal, and *bathos*, depth, a line on a *chart linking points of equal depth, sometimes called a depth contour.

ISOBATHYTHERM, a line connecting points in vertical sections of the sea which have the same temperature.

ISOGONIC LINES, lines drawn on a *chart which connect points of equal *variation of the compass. The first world chart to incorporate isogonic lines was published by Edmund *Halley in 1701, a notable landmark in the history and development of cartography and *navigation.

ISOHALSINE LINES, lines on a chart joining parts of the sea which have an equal salinity.

IWO JIMA, one of the Volcano group of islands lying 650 miles south of Tokyo, which was of vital importance to the Japanese during the Second World War as a staging post for aircraft from Japan to the Philippines and the South-West Pacific. Its capture by the Americans in February 1945 was an equally essential preliminary to the projected final assault on Japan as it enabled fighter escort to accompany raids by heavy bombers.

For seven months, from 15 June 1944, Iwo Jima was repeatedly bombed and bombarded with little effect on the defences which included systems of immensely strong, interconnected underground shelters and mutually supporting blockhouses built to withstand naval gunfire. A Japanese garrison of more than 21,000 troops defended the 10 square miles of the island.

The force assembled to assault it on 19 February 1945 comprised a total of some 900 ships and 70,000 U.S. *marines and was divided into a number of task forces and groups, the attack force of transports and landing ships, the amphibious force which included the gunfire and covering force of *battleships, *cruisers, and *destroyers and a support carrier group of eleven escort *aircraft carriers, the logistic support group, a service squadron of 250 vessels from which support equivalent to that obtainable from a *dockyard was supplied, and a search and reconnaissance group of some 147 shore-based aircraft. During 16 and 17 February, while preliminary softening-up bombardments covered the necessary minesweeping off the Iwo Jima beaches, the fast carrier task force delivered massive air strikes on airfields and aircraft plants in the Tokyo area during which 364 Japanese aircraft were shot down and another 209 destroyed on the ground.

The attack force arrived off the Iwo Jima beaches before dawn on 19 February. Naval gunfire support was maintained for about two hours with short breaks for air strikes until the first wave of landing craft reached the shore. The unsuitable nature of the beaches caused a catastrophic destruction of landing craft and a confusion which was to remain acute for the next five days. Suffering heavy casualties, the marines made very slow progress inland and a month of bitter fighting was to ensue before the last organized Japanese resistance ceased on 16 March, when the defenders had died almost to a man. American casualties on and around the island totalled 20,845 killed and wounded.

J

JACK, (1) the national flag which is flown from a *jackstaff on the *stem of naval ships when at anchor. **(2)** Pilot Jack, originally the name given to the flag, which was a Union flag surrounded by a white border, flown by ships in need of a pilot. This requirement is now met by 'G' flag in the *International Code of Signals, yellow and blue vertical stripes. **(3)** Cargo jack, sometimes also known as a jack screw, an appliance used in the *holds of merchant ships for moving heavy pieces of cargo and for compressing cargo such as cotton, hides, etc., into as small a space as possible to increase the carrying capacity.

JACK or **JACK TAR,** the familiar name for a British naval seaman. Tar is the shortened version of tarpaulin, the tarred canvas which

The Sailor's Progress; *engraving by G. Cruikshank*

seamen, and especially *topmen, used to wear as protection against the weather. Originally the name was applied only to able seamen and men whose station in the ship was on the masts and *yards of square-rigged warships, but it has been extended to cover all British naval seamen.

JACK ADAMS, a name given in the British Navy to men who become argumentative in somewhat stupid situations. 'A proper Jack Adams', a stubborn fool.

JACK IN THE BASKET, the name given to a mark in coastal waters, consisting usually of a wooden box or basket on the top of a pole, to show the edge of a sandbank or other obstruction.

JACK OF THE DUST, a colloquial term in the old days of the British Navy for the *purser's assistant who was employed in the bread room, where the flour issued as part of the daily victuals was stowed. In the Royal Navy of today the equivalent rating dealing with victualling stores is usually called Jack Dusty.

JACK WITH A LANTERN, the description sometimes used by English seamen to describe *St. Elmo's Fire.

JACKANAPES COAT, see MONKEY JACKET.

JACKASS, (1) the name used in the U.S. Navy for a *hawse-bag in the days when such appliances were commonly used to stop seawater being forced up the *hawsepipes and over the *forecastle deck in rough weather. Today, more efficient metal collars or plugs perform the same purpose. **(2)** A type of heavily built open boat used in Newfoundland.

JACKASS-BARQUE, a four-masted sailing ship square-rigged on the two foremost masts and fore-and-aft rigged on the two after masts. A number of these jackass-barques were used in the late 19th and early 20th century nitrate trade around Cape Horn to the Chilean ports, many owners and skippers considering them to be more efficient in the particularly stormy weather so frequently experienced around the Horn.

JACKSON, FREDERICK GEORGE (1860–1938), British explorer, was born at Alcester, Warwick. In 1893–4 he made a sledge journey in Siberia from Kharbarovsk to Kirkenes in preparation for an attempt to reach the North pole. He led the Jackson–Harmsworth expedition to Franz Josef Land in 1894–7 in the ship *Windward*, fortuitously encountered Fridtjof *Nansen, and brought him back. He served in the army during the Boer War (1899–1902) and also during the First World War (1914–18). He was made a Fellow of the Royal Geographical Society and published several books on his experiences, among them *A Thousand Days in the Arctic* (1899).

JACKSON, Sir HENRY BRADWARDINE (1855–1929), British admiral of the fleet, was born at Barnsley, Yorkshire, and pioneered the introduction of radio telegraphy in the Royal Navy. He entered the navy through H.M.S. *Britannia* in 1868, and as a lieutenant specialized first in *navigation and later in *torpedo work. Promoted to commander in January 1890 he began experimenting with radio waves and eventually succeeded in transmitting signals over a distance of several hundred yards. Soon after promotion to captain in June 1896 he met Marconi and discovered that they had both been working along similar lines.

In 1900 Jackson's efforts were rewarded when the Admiralty placed contracts for the supply of Marconi radio equipment to ships of the Royal Navy, and in 1901 he was elected a Fellow of the Royal Society in recognition of his work in this field. After serving as captain of H.M.S. *Vernon*, the torpedo school ship, in 1904, he was appointed Third Sea Lord and Controller in the new Board of Admiralty in which Sir John *Fisher was First Sea Lord, and thus became responsible for the construction of H.M.S. *Dreadnought*, the world's first all-big-gun *battleship. After commanding a *cruiser squadron and representing the Admiralty at the International Conference on aerial navigation in 1911, he was appointed to command the newly created War College at Portsmouth. In February 1913 he returned to the Admiralty as Chief of the War Staff, a post he held until shortly before the outbreak of the First World War (1914–18).

On the resignation of Lord Fisher in May 1915, Jackson took his place as First Sea Lord, but was himself superseded by Admiral Sir John *Jellicoe in December 1916, and appointed President of the Royal Naval College, *Greenwich. In July 1919 he was promoted to admiral of the fleet and the following year became chairman of the Radio Research Board of the Department of Scientific and Industrial Research.

JACKSTAFF, a short pole mast erected perpendicularly on the *stem of a modern ship, or at the end of the *bowsprit in the days of large sailing vessels, on which the national flag is hoisted in naval ships when at anchor. In many ships the jackstaff has a piece of gilded decoration, a crown or some other symbol, at the top.

JACKSTAY, a wire or hemp rope or pendant secured firmly between two points and used as a support. Thus, when using a *breeches buoy for saving life from a ship aground, a jackstay is rigged between ship and shore along which the breeches buoy is hauled to and from the ship; when refuelling at sea, the oil hosepipe is suspended between the tanker and the ship being refuelled on a jackstay. When an awning is spread over a deck in hot weather as protection from the sun, it is supported centrally on a jackstay, though in this particular case the jackstay is often called a ridge-rope.

Jackstays are rigged with a minimum safety factor of four, i.e., the load supported by a jackstay including its own weight should not be more than one-quarter the breaking strain of the wire or rope used.

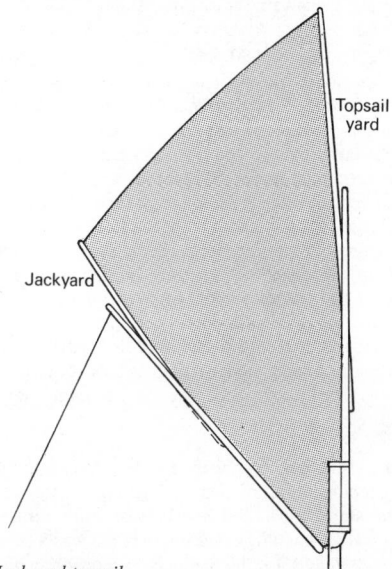

Jackyard topsail

JACKYARD TOPSAIL, a triangular topsail set above the mainsail in a gaff-rigged vessel, setting a larger area of sail than a *jib-headed topsail as both the *luff and the *foot of the topsail are laced to jackyards which extend beyond the top of the mast and the *peak of the *gaff.

JACOBS, WILLIAM WYMARK (1863–1943), British author, was born at Wapping, London, where the arrivals and departures of ships were part of daily life. Educated at Birkbeck College he entered the Civil Service at the age of 16. Success as a writer came slowly, his first book, *Many Cargoes*, a collection of short stories, being published in 1896. Two years later he resigned from the Civil Service to devote himself to writing. His work has three aspects, the misadventures of sailors ashore, country village life, and tales of the macabre, but in all of them seafaring absurdities are cleverly introduced. He was a master of the humorous short story and enjoyed a well-deserved and wide popularity. He also wrote a number of plays. His last book, *Night Watches*, was published in 1914 when he gave up writing.

JACOB'S LADDER, (1) formerly a ladder, with rope sides and steps, fitted on the after side of a * topgallant mast where there are no * ratlines for ascending the rigging. **(2)** A term also used to describe the shakes and short fractures, rising one above another, in a defective single-tree spar. **(3)** More recently, the name of the rope ladder which hangs from the lower * boom of a warship to which ships' boats are made fast in harbour.

JACOB'S STAFF, see CROSS-STAFF.

JAEGT, the typical sailing boat of the Norwegian coast, now virtually obsolete. The true jaegt is the direct descendant of the Viking * longship, with the same high * stern and * stem and a large square sail carried on a single mast; they remained in use from about the 14th to the 19th century. Their main use was to bring down to Bergen the fish catch from the Lofoten Islands, the centre of the Norwegian cod fishery, returning up the coast with, it was said, mainly elm boards for coffins which were off-loaded at the various ports of call. They were also frequently in demand for traditional wedding parties, the bride and bridegroom sitting in an arbour built up on the * poop while the guests made merry below.

JAL, AUGUSTE (1795–1875), French naval archaeologist and historian, began his career as a naval student, 1811–15, before devoting himself to naval archaeology and history. He was a press correspondent in the French expedition which captured Algiers in 1830, of which he wrote the official marine history, and was one of the founders of the study of naval archaeology and the author of some important works on the subject which are still frequently consulted. But the work for which he is best known, and indeed famous, is his *Glossaire nautique*, published in 1848. This great dictionary is still considered one of the main authorities on the seamanship of the period, ranking with, and in some respects surpassing, that of William * Falconer.

JAMAICA DISCIPLINE, a code of laws adopted by the * buccaneers respecting the division of * prize captured by them. It was operative in the late 17th and early 18th centuries. Under the rules, the captain of a buccaneer ship received two shares, officers one and a half shares, and seamen one share each in all captures. In some ships additional rules were adopted dealing with women on board and drinking hours.

JAMES, DUKE OF YORK (1633–1701), * Lord High Admiral of England, was the second son of Charles I. During the civil war in England he fell into the hands of the Parliamentary Commissioners where he remained until April 1648 when he escaped in women's clothes from St. James's Palace, London, to the Netherlands.

During his twelve years of exile on the continent he followed a military career, serving in the army of Marshall Turenne from 1652 to 1655, rising to the rank of lieutenant-general. Forbidden by his brother (Charles II) to continue in French service, he served for a time under the Spanish crown in 1657.

At the Restoration (1660) he was appointed Lord High Admiral and was enthusiastically received by the British fleet when it arrived off Scheveningen to escort home the returning Charles II. The administration of the navy and, indeed, all things nautical became an absorbing interest in which he was greatly aided by Samuel * Pepys. The * Navy Board was reconstituted and enlarged under James's administration and his general instructions for its conduct remained largely in force until the reorganization of the Admiralty in 1832.

On the outbreak of the Second Dutch War 1665–7, James went to sea in command of the fleet which won a hard-fought victory off * Lowestoft on 3 June; but he failed to take full advantage of it through breaking off the pursuit prematurely. He was forbidden by the king to risk his life at sea in the other battles of the war since he was heir to the throne, but he remained Lord High Admiral. As such he must bear some of the blame for the laying-up of the fleet while peace negotiations were still unresolved, an event which allowed de * Ruyter to make his famous incursion into the Thames and Medway in 1667 to attack the defenceless ships and to threaten London.

Always in his heart a Roman Catholic, James accepted full and open conversion to the faith in 1672, a move which aroused fierce passions in Protestant England, and though he commanded the fleet at the drawn battle of * Solebay at the beginning of the Third Dutch War (1672–4), the passing by Parliament in March 1673 of the Test Act banning all Catholics from holding public office forced him to resign all his offices.

By 1684 the growing popularity of Charles II enabled James to regain his position as Lord High Admiral and on ascending the throne as James II in February 1685 he retained the post in his own hands. As such, ably seconded by Pepys, he was able to introduce several important reforms in the administration of the navy. But growing unpopularity because of his religious views cost him not only the loyalty of the fleet but his throne as well which was quietly transferred to William of Orange.

JAMES, THOMAS (c. 1593–1635), British navigator, of whom the first mention is in 1628 when he was granted a * letter of marque for the *Dragon of Bristol* of which he was owner and * master. In 1631, with the King's approval, he was given command of an expedition to discover a * North-West passage into the South Sea. He left Bristol in the *Henrietta Maria* and reached Hudson Bay early in August where he met Luke * Fox. He then proceeded to James Bay, giving the name Cape Henrietta Maria to the north-western point of the bay, and finally arrived off Charlton Island where he decided to winter. He spent nearly a year in an examination of the coast but failed to find the passage and returned to Bristol in 1632. He was obliged to decline further employment owing to ill health. An account of his last voyage, published in 1633, has been suggested by some as the source of 'The Rime of the *Ancient Mariner' by the poet Coleridge, though a more probable source is George * Shelvocke's voyage of 1719.

JAMES, WILLIAM (d. 1827), British naval historian, was the author of *Naval History of Great Britain from the Declaration of War by France in 1793 to the Accession of George IV*, first published in five volumes, 1822–4, and reprinted in six volumes in 1826. From 1801 to 1813 he was a proctor in the Vice-Admiralty Court of Jamaica, and, being in the U.S.A. when war was declared against Britain in 1812, was taken prisoner but escaped to Halifax. His work is a monument of accuracy but so full of detail that it is less a work of history than a chronicle of unconnected incidents. In an effort to decry the long series of successful * frigate actions enjoyed by U.S. ships against British vessels, he went to great pains to prove that, ship for ship, the American frigates were more heavily armed and carried larger crews, and some of his work is suspect on this account. Nevertheless, it has stood the test of time and remains the best account of the naval side of the Revolutionary and Napoleonic Wars (1793–1801, 1803–15).

JAMES, Sir WILLIAM MILBOURNE (1881–1973), British admiral and author, joined the Royal Navy and rose steadily to reach flag rank in 1929. During the First World War (1914–18) he was flag commander to Vice Admiral Sir Doveton * Sturdee in the * Grand Fleet and later was appointed to the Naval Intelligence Division where he was placed in charge of the famous * Room 40 in which the German naval codes were deciphered and the information passed to the fleet. He commanded the * Battle-Cruiser Squadron in the Atlantic Fleet, 1932–4, and on the outbreak of the Second World War was commander-in-chief at Portsmouth, a post he held until 1942. He was subsequently Chief of Naval Information and from 1943 to 1945 represented North Portsmouth in Parliament. As a small boy he was the model for the well-known painting 'Bubbles' by his grandfather, Sir John Millais. His publications include *The British Navy in Adversity* (1926), *Blue Water and Green Fields* (1939), *The Life of Admiral Sir William Fisher* (1943), *Portsmouth Letters* (1946), *The British Navies in the Second World War* (1946), *The Durable Monument* (a biography of * Nelson) (1948), *Old Oak* (a biography of Lord St. Vincent) (1950), *The Eyes of the Navy* (a biography of Admiral Sir William * Hall) (1955), and *A Great Seaman* (a biography of Admiral of the Fleet Sir Henry * Oliver) (1956).

JANE, FREDERICK THOMAS (1865–1916), British journalist and novelist and founder of the famous annual *All the World's Fighting Ships*, was born at Upottery, Devon. At the age of 15 he started to make pen and ink sketches of warships and thus in the course of time compiled an album containing pictures and details of the ships of most of the world's navies. This, after some additions and revision, became the original on which his world famous annual was founded.

The first edition, published early in 1898, comprised 215 pages and included details and sketches of nearly 1,000 warships. His interest in the strategical and tactical problems of naval warfare led to the production of a naval war game which was used by several navies for instructional purposes. The 1902 edition of * *Jane's Fighting Ships* contained a hint regarding the possible employment of aircraft for reconnaissance duties with the fleet and in 1910 the first edition of *All the World's Aircraft* was published. He was naval correspondent of the *Engineer, Standard*, and *Scientific American*, and his death at the age of 50 was a great loss in the field of technical naval journalism.

JANE'S FIGHTING SHIPS, an annual British publication which is generally regarded as the standard reference book for information regarding the warships of all nations and their auxiliaries, as well as of naval aircraft and missiles. It was first published in 1897 under the title of *All the World's Fighting Ships*, the compiler being the British journalist and author Frederick T. *Jane who had been working on the project for fifteen years. The wide acclaim with which the first edition was received led to the publication of a second in 1898, since when it has appeared annually without interruption. The illustrations in the early editions were pen and ink drawings beautifully executed by Jane himself, but in 1900 he agreed to use photographs of the more important warships. At first the text accompanying the illustrations was confined to statistics of the ship's year of launch, length, armament, main protection, and speed, with notes of any differences between sister ships and some occasional remarks. Gradually these particulars were extended until today they cover in addition, displacement, beam, draught, type of machinery, boilers, horse power, fuel capacity, name of builder, dates of keel laying and completion, and complement. Plans and elevation drawings of the most important vessels are included.

In 1901 several important changes were made in the layout, the ships of each country being rearranged according to their fighting value. It was in the 1902 edition that the idea of an all-big-gun *battleship, later known as the *dreadnought type, was first proposed by the Italian Colonel Vittorio Cuniberti. He followed it up in the 1903 edition with an article entitled 'An Ideal Warship for the British Fleet', on which Admiral *Fisher is said to have based the design of the British *Dreadnought*, and that year the contents were rearranged, the eight leading naval powers being placed first in order of strength. Five years later ships of the various categories in each navy were listed according to their age, a procedure still followed. The growth of the Imperial German Navy was reflected in the 1909 and subsequent editions, and in the 1910 edition naval aviation was discussed for the first time. Jane died in March 1916 but a succession of distinguished editors has kept the publication in the forefront of the world's naval reference books.

Perhaps one of the most notable features of *Jane's Fighting Ships* over the last twenty years is the way in which the editor's foreword has reflected the policies of the major powers with regard to such forces, and effectively mirrored their failures as well as their achievements.

JAUNTY, sometimes written **JONTY,** the slang name for the *master-at-arms in a British warship. Being responsible for the good observance of rules and regulations on board ship, and as head of the ship's police, many seamen used to view him with suspicion and, sometimes, fear.

JAURÉGUIBERRY, JEAN BERNARD (1815–87), French admiral, saw active service in many parts of the world, including the Crimea.

During the Franco-German war of 1870 he came ashore to fight for his country, being present at the actions at Coulmiers, Villépion, and Loigny-Poupry, where he commanded a division, and at Le Mans where he was a corps commander. He was without question the most distinguished of the many naval officers who came ashore to fight in that war. Later he commanded the fleet at Toulon and in 1876 commanded the experimental squadron of the French Navy charged with determining the most efficient steam tactics for battle and the most desirable advances in *matériel*. He was twice minister of marine, in 1879 and 1880, and was later elected a senator for life.

JAVA SEA, BATTLE OF THE, a naval action fought in the Pacific during the Second World War between an Anglo–U.S.–Dutch naval force and a Japanese force, both of *cruisers and *destroyers. Following the initial southward thrusts by Japanese invasion forces in December 1941 and January 1942 which led to their conquest of Malaya, Singapore, Borneo, the Philippines, the Moluccas, and the Bismarck Archipelago, a multi-pronged amphibious operation to capture Sumatra and Java was launched in February. To oppose them, an Anglo–U.S.–Netherlands naval force had been assembled under the Dutch Rear Admiral Karel Doorman. On paper it was a formidable force; but its heterogeneous and polyglot composition, together with the absence of an agreed signalling system, greatly reduced its effectiveness. Furthermore it had to operate under a sky totally dominated by the enemy's air force which, by 26 February, had put out of action one American and one Dutch cruiser and disabled the after turret of the remaining American cruiser *Houston*.

In these circumstances Doorman had been unable to oppose the landing at Palembang, Sumatra; but when the invasion force for Java was reported as approaching, he led his force to sea from Sourabaya on 27 February 1942: the Dutch light cruisers *De Ruyter* and *Java*, the heavy cruisers U.S.S. *Houston* and H.M.S. *Exeter*, the light cruiser H.M.A.S. *Perth*, three British, two Dutch, and four American destroyers. The true fighting value of this force is perhaps best indicated by the fact that the Japanese, though they had a battle fleet and a carrier striking force available, contented themselves by opposing it with a covering force composed of the two heavy cruisers *Nachi* and *Haguro*, the two light cruisers *Naka* and *Jintsu*, and fourteen destroyers.

The two forces met that afternoon. In a long-range gunnery duel interspersed with massed torpedo attacks by Japanese flotillas and counter-attacks by their opponents, the *Exeter* suffered shell damage that drove her out of the action and

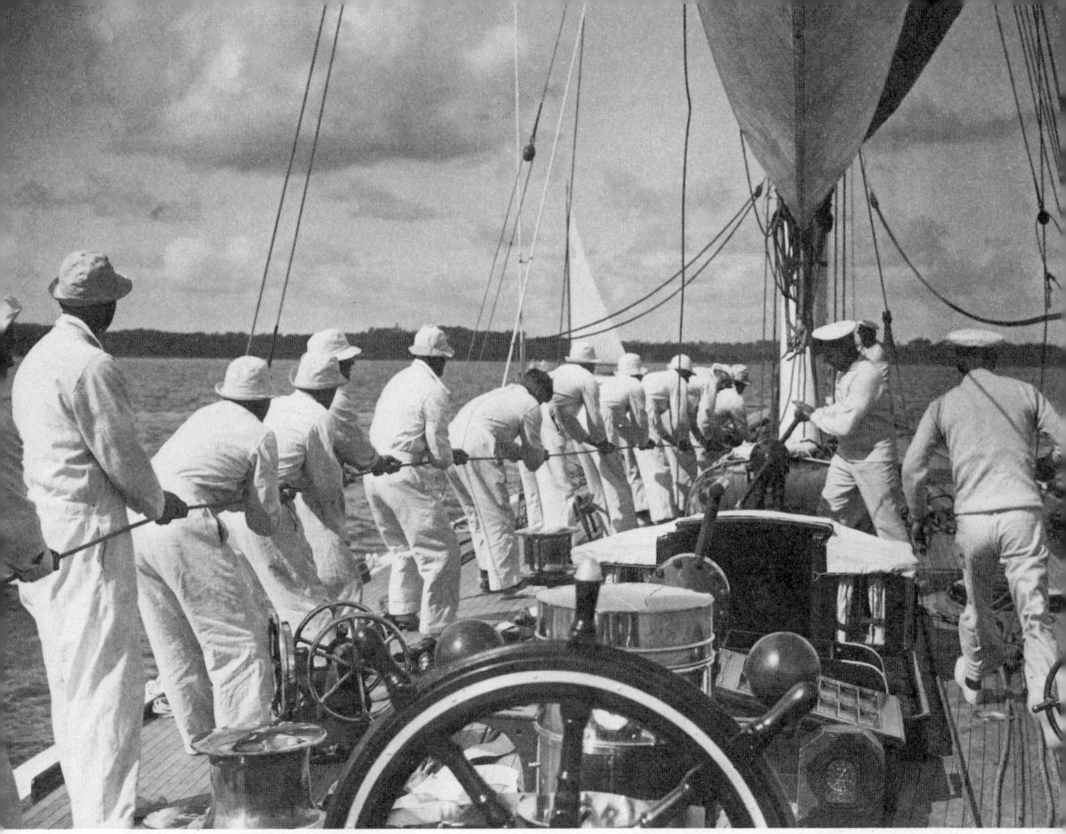

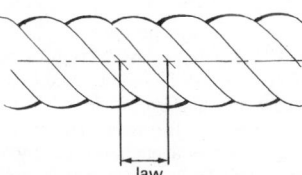

Hoisting the mainsail on board Endeavour II

the British destroyer *Electra* and the Dutch *Kortenaer* were sunk, against one Japanese destroyer seriously damaged by shell fire. Doorman therefore broke off the action with the object of circling round the enemy to get at his troop convoy under cover of darkness.

The four American destroyers, having expended all their torpedoes, were ordered back to harbour; the British destroyer *Jupiter* was lost when she struck a mine. The remainder were confronted after dark by the two Japanese heavy cruisers which torpedoed and sank the *De Ruyter* and *Java*, whereupon the *Perth*, in accordance with a last order from Doorman, withdrew the surviving ships. The following night the *Perth*, *Houston*, and *Exeter*, with the destroyers H.M.S. *Encounter* and U.S.S. *Pope*, were all sunk as they tried to pass through the Sunda Strait to reach safety.

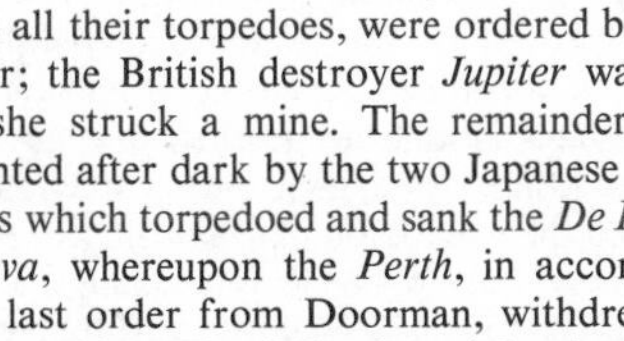

JAW, the distance between adjacent *strands on a rope. It gives a measure of the hardness or tightness of the *lay—the shorter the distance,

the harder the lay. When a rope has been much used and the lay has become slack, the rope is said to be long-jawed or slack-jawed.

J-CLASS YACHTS, the largest class of racing yachts built under the 1925 international rating rule, sometimes known as the universal rule, with a waterline length varying from 75 to 87 feet (23–6 m). Several yachts were built in the U.S.A. under this rule, notably the three *America*'s Cup defenders *Enterprise*, *Rainbow*, and *Ranger*, while in Britain equally well known yachts such as *Shamrock V*, *Endeavour*, and *Endeavour II* were constructed under the rule as challengers for the cup.

The J-class yachts are often regarded as the peak of yacht-racing history and the peak of extravagance in pleasure sailing. As a class they were remarkably short-lived in comparison with other, healthier, classes of racing yacht, no doubt because they were the playthings of only the very rich. With a professional skipper and crew of up to twenty-four men, with new sails and new equipment always being tried to improve their sailing qualities, as for example the *Park Avenue boom, the costs of keeping such a yacht in racing commission were prodigious.

During the summer yachting season they raced at the major yacht club regattas round the coasts, from, in Britain, Harwich to the Clyde, taking in French regattas at Le Havre and the Irish regattas, and in the U.S.A., along the length of the East coast. But, apart from the *America's* Cup races, the J-class yachts of the U.S.A. and Britain, with the exception of one season when the American yacht *Yankee* crossed the Atlantic in 1935 to compete in British regattas, never raced together. They were essentially light weather craft and could not stand up to winds above about force 5. It used to be said of this class of yacht, rather cruelly, that the owners would put a lighted candle on their booms at night, and if it was still burning in the morning would decide that there was not enough wind for racing, and if it was out, that there was too much wind to race.

Rising costs of construction, maintenance, and professional crews brought the J-class, as a racing class, to an end in 1936 though some of the existing yachts in the class had their rig cut down and were used as cruisers.

JEERS, a heavy *tackle with double or treble *blocks used for hoisting the lower *yards in square-rigged sailing ships, an operation known as *swaying up the yards. A jeer *capstan was one fitted between the fore and main masts used for heaving on the jeers, and was also the usual place of punishment in naval ships where men sentenced to flogging were strung up, on gratings, to receive their lashes from a *cat-o'-nine-tails. In the square-rigged ships of today, mainly used as school ships, auxiliary power is normally used in place of the jeer capstan.

JELLICOE, JOHN RUSHWORTH, first Earl (1859–1935), British admiral of the fleet, was the son of a master mariner and entered the Royal Navy in 1872. He passed out of the training ship H.M.S. *Britannia* top of his term. As a young lieutenant he showed courage of a high order during Arabi Pasha's rebellion in Egypt (1882), adopting native disguise to carry secret dispatches to Sir Garnet Wolseley through a hostile horde. Having qualified as a gunnery specialist with distinction in H.M.S. *Excellent*, he served as gunnery officer of the turret ship *Monarch* (1885) before joining the new *battleship *Colossus* (1886). A period on the experimental staff of H.M.S. *Excellent* was followed by his first Admiralty appointment, to help the Director of Naval Ordnance, Captain J. A. *Fisher, in implementing the Naval Defence Act 1889. It was an association that was to have a profound effect on his subsequent career.

Promoted commander in 1891, Jellicoe was executive officer of the Mediterranean flagship *Victoria* when, during manoeuvres off the Levant coast, she was rammed and sunk by the *Camperdown* with considerable loss of life,

including that of the commander-in-chief, Admiral *Tryon. Though ill with Malta fever at the time, Jellicoe survived this disaster to become executive officer of the new flagship, H.M.S. *Ramillies*, until his promotion to captain in 1897. After a year on the Ordnance Committee, he went out to China as flag captain in the *Centurion*. Accompanying the commander-in-chief, Admiral Seymour, on his abortive attempt to lead an international naval brigade to the relief of the legations in Peking during the Boxer Rebellion (1900), Jellicoe again narrowly escaped with his life after a bullet pierced his lung. His command of the *cruiser *Drake* was soon terminated by Fisher's appointment as First Sea Lord: this dynamic reformer needed an officer with Jellicoe's exceptional brain, capacity for hard work, and talent for administration to be his Director of Naval Ordnance, and to serve on the committee charged with producing the first all-big-gun battleship, H.M.S. *Dreadnought*.

Promoted rear admiral in 1907, Jellicoe first hoisted his flag as second-in-command of the Atlantic Fleet. A year later he became Controller and Third Sea Lord, to give Fisher invaluable help in ensuring that the Royal Navy maintained an adequate lead in dreadnought construction over Germany. In command of the Atlantic Fleet, and subsequently of the Second Division of the Home Fleet, Jellicoe gained the experience needed for the task for which Fisher had earmarked him, 'admiralissimo when Armageddon comes'. His appointment as Second Sea Lord was cut short by the imminence of the First World War (1914–18); at the end of July 1914, he was ordered north to *Scapa Flow to assume command of the *Grand Fleet, flying his flag in the super-dreadnought *Iron Duke*.

Jellicoe's outstanding qualities were abundantly proved by the standard of fighting efficiency to which he trained the Grand Fleet, and by the high morale he instilled in many thousands of officers and men during the years that followed the realization that, contrary to expectation, there was to be no immediate clash with Germany's *High Seas Fleet. So, too, with his strategy; the Grand Fleet's prime task of maintaining command of the sea by a distant *blockade of Germany's ports was not to be hazarded by needlessly exposing it to attrition in German minefields and by *U-boat attack. His tactics will, however, always be questioned. When, on 31 May 1916, he brought the High Seas Fleet to battle off the coast of *Jutland, his skilful deployment placed his superior battle fleet between the enemy and its base. But his belief that an action should be fought as a gunnery duel by a rigidly controlled single line of battle was ill-suited to an engagement in which the battle fleets did not come into contact until the daylight of a misty day was already beginning to fade. His unfounded

Admiral Sir John Jellicoe on board H.M.S. Iron Duke

conviction that the Germans would use *mines and *submarines in a fleet action, coupled with an exaggerated fear of *torpedo attack, were likewise ill-suited to maintaining contact with an enemy bent on avoiding destruction in visibility that seldom exceeded 12,000 yards. And his hopes of a day-long decisive action on the following day were dashed by the enemy's success in crossing his rear, through his *destroyer flotillas, during the night. It was his misfortune that priceless information obtained from the deciphering of German codes giving the course of the German fleet's retreat was not sent him because of administrative carelessness in the Admiralty. (See also ROOM 40 O.B.)

Germany's decision, consequent on this narrow escape, to stake all on an unrestricted U-boat blockade, for which the British were ill-prepared to prevent a near catastrophic loss of merchant shipping, led to Jellicoe's appointment as First Sea Lord in December 1916. There, after the entry of the U.S.A. into the war in 1917 had made available the necessary additional destroyers, he introduced, though with reluctance, the *convoy system which in 1918 effectively defeated the U-boats. He also reorganized the Naval Staff to a pattern that survived the test of the Second World War. But the pessimistic caution with which he viewed the conduct of the war at sea was so ill-matched to the volatile courage of the Prime Minister, David Lloyd George, that he was abruptly dismissed at the end of 1917,

almost a year before the navy garnered the fruit of its long blockade, the internment in British waters of the High Seas Fleet, with all its U-boats, in November 1918.

In 1919–20 Jellicoe visited India, Australia, New Zealand, and Canada to advise their governments on how they could best contribute to the naval defence of the Empire, from which the most important outcome was the construction of a major base at *Singapore, albeit without the strong fleet in the Pacific he intended it to serve. Created a viscount, honoured with the Order of Merit, and promoted to admiral of the fleet, Jellicoe was governor-general of New Zealand, 1920–4, for which service he was rewarded with an earldom. He devoted the years of his retirement to an active interest in such organizations as the British Legion, of which he was president, the National Rifle Association, and the Scout movement. Throughout his life he was served by officers and men with a love and devotion which very few other leaders have enjoyed. He is commemorated by a bronze bust in Trafalgar Square. He wrote *The Grand Fleet 1914–1916* (1919), *The Crisis of the Naval War* (1920), and *The Submarine Peril* (1934). For full biographies see *The Life of John Rushworth, Earl Jellicoe* by Admiral Bacon (1936) and *Jellicoe: a Biography* by A. Temple Patterson (1969). His papers have been edited and published by the *Navy Records Society (Vols 108 and 111).

JENKINS, ROBERT (*fl.* 1731–45), British merchant ship captain, was the begetter of the so-called 'War of Jenkins's Ear' in 1739, which later developed into the War of the Austrian Succession (1739–48). When in command of the *brig *Rebecca* in 1731 he alleged that he was boarded in West Indian waters by a Spanish *guarda-costa, his cargo rifled, and one of his ears cut off. On his return to England he complained of this treatment, but although the British commander-in-chief in the West Indies confirmed his report, little notice was taken of his complaint. Seven years later, when anger against Spanish intransigence was widespread in England, Jenkins repeated his story before a committee of the House of Commons in London, reputedly producing the ear that had been cut off. Indignation was so widespread that it finally resulted in a declaration of war. (See also ASIENTO, TREATY OF.)

After losing his ear, Jenkins entered the service of the *East India Company and commanded one of their ships. For a time he was acting governor of St. Helena, at that time a station of the East India Company on the route to the east. He is also credited with a successful action against a pirate ship, but details are lacking.

It has been suggested that, rather than having had his ear cut off by a guarda-costa, he lost it when standing in the pillory as a result of a drunken debauch. It is difficult to believe that the ear he produced in Parliament in 1738 was the same as that allegedly cut off in 1731.

He was the author of *Spanish Insolence Corrected by English Bravery* (1739).

JERVIS, JOHN, 1st Earl St. Vincent (1735–1823), British admiral of the fleet, was born at Meaford, Staffordshire. His parents moved to Greenwich and he went to school there, but promptly ran away from home, hid in a docked ship for three days, and shortly thereafter, on his immovable demand for a naval career, entered the navy at the age of 13. A little over eleven years later, at 25, he was promoted *post-captain and served under Sir Charles *Saunders at the capture of *Quebec in 1759, his ship standing in the channel under heavy French fire while taking the transports with General Wolfe's troops on board above Quebec before the landing at the Anse du Foulon.

From 1761, for fourteen years, his career hung fire. He used the interval in getting a firm grip on the French language and in taking cheap voyages to Swedish and Russian waters, making his own charts and discovering by this means some of the lethal errors so prevalent in contemporary charts. On the outbreak of the War of American Independence (1775–82) Jervis could again breathe his native air of ships and combat. In 1782, when in command of the *Foudroyant*, came his first great stroke of fortune, his spectacular capture of the French first-*rate ship *Pégase*, with not one of his men killed and himself suffering nothing worse than two black eyes. He was made a baronet as a reward. More opportunities came his way in the Revolutionary War with France (1793–1801). As a vice admiral he commanded the successful expedition to the West Indies for the capture of Martinique, St. Lucia, and Guadaloupe. Yet all this was mere preamble to the crowning achievement of his career when in 1795, at the age of 60 and as commander-in-chief, he opened the towering epic of the Mediterranean campaign. Here, in the teeth of constant shortages of ships, men, and every essential supply, he was responsible for two considerable victories. In the first, with his fifteen ships numbering about one-half of those of the enemy, he lay in wait off *Cape St. Vincent in 1797 for the Spanish fleet which was to reinforce the French fleet at Brest for a joint invasion of England. His ships damaged it severely, captured four ships of the line as *prizes, and permanently prevented their rendezvous with the French. Jervis was created Lord St. Vincent, Earl and Viscount, the name of St. Vincent being adopted at George III's suggestion.

His second great achievement was the battle of the *Nile, when he took the perilous step of cutting his own inadequate force into two squadrons, giving Rear Admiral Horatio *Nelson command of the stronger one, and sending him out with orders to find Napoleon's fleet. Of this victory too—except that he was not personally on the scene of battle—he was the sole creator, not least by his choice of Nelson as the chief instrument, against the protests of Admirals *Parker and *Orde who claimed (and in fact possessed) seniority over Nelson.

In 1799 he suffered a total breakdown in health and returned to England. He recovered brilliantly, becoming First Lord of the Admiralty in 1800. *Prize money and his £2,000 annual pension from the Cape St. Vincent victory had made him a rich man, and he entertained lavishly at his country home in Essex, the house (Rochetts) still standing today.

In his quiet breadth of vision, his great humanity, his never-ending quest for naval efficiency, St. Vincent is unequalled as the pattern of all that was best in the 18th century naval officer. The first great formative influence of his character, if only by default, was his father, Swynfen Jervis, a solicitor and later treasurer and auditor of *Greenwich Hospital. The minutes of the Hospital Board of Governors show him as dilatory, inefficient, constantly embroiled with his colleagues, and ruinously irregular in his attendance at Board meetings. His action in dishonouring a £20 draft which his son had drawn on him in 1751 helped to lay a momentous foundation in the future St. Vincent's character, upon which rose up grandly the fabric of his whole life. A 16-year-old without a penny, he managed to pay back the sum shilling by shilling in three years, but its immediate consequence instantly and sharply changed his life on the level of social recognition. Unable to pay mess expenses he left his mess at once and no longer ate with the other *midshipmen. Unable to afford to dress decently—he once made himself a pair of trousers out of his bedding—he no longer associated with them except during hours of instruction or duty. Debarred from his natural companionship, and all his life he was intensely companionable, he was driven to find friendship aboard among the warrant officers of his ships, admirable men of great practical competence, though often half-literate, and, from his enforced long-term intimate association with the lesser naval hierarchy he came to know the British seaman in all his aspects—his needs, his virtues, and his failings, the awful wrongs that were done to him, the poor food, the savage punishments, the inadequate medical care—as perhaps no other naval officer of the time had known them. Out of those three years of below-decks friendships, also, he evolved his secret of leadership.

The second great faculty developed by his unusual apprenticeship was a power of judgement almost clairvoyant, displayed in a manner also peculiar to himself, of divining in men comparatively or totally unknown those talents which as yet they had had little chance to demonstrate. This flair led him, during the Mediterranean campaign, to Dr. Andrew Baird, an undistinguished naval surgeon by no means young. These two men together made perhaps the most formidable team that has ever worked to improve and stabilize the health of the navy. In ships in which *scurvy and typhus were still rampant, they were pioneers of new and drastic procedures, such as ship and hospital regulations for obligatory daily rations of lemon juice. Where this was applied, scurvy and unhealing wounds vanished. In ships swarming with the typhus louse they introduced an enforced rigid cleanliness and adequate ventilation. Baird, a merciless inspector of badly run naval hospitals, introduced the use of a separate room for operations, previously performed in the open ward in pre-anaesthetic days, where the patients could see and hear the struggles and screams of the men under the surgeon's knife.

But the crowning example of this flair of St. Vincent's is found in his immediate sponsorship of the man who reported to him in his flagship on 14 January 1795. Horatio Nelson was at that time a disgruntled and unhappy naval captain, filling his letters to his wife with lamentations over his treatment during his previous two years service in the Mediterranean: 'Every other man has got some place or other ... I, only I, am without reward.' His whole life changed from the moment St. Vincent laid eyes on him. From that moment occurred the fusion of a perfect working association between two strangers united by professional compatibility and divided by every other quality of personality or temperament. This pattern is so unchanging throughout their whole association that it must be mentioned at the outset.

St. Vincent almost at once promoted Nelson to the rank of *commodore and, for the next thirteen months of the sweeping French advance, positioned him in the hottest centres of combat at Genoa, Leghorn, Corsica, Elba, and Bastia. He had utter confidence in him: 'The moment I knew of your arrival, I felt perfectly at ease.' In another four months—on 14 February 1797—came the battle of Cape St. Vincent. The classic high point of the engagement was the moment at 12.51 when Nelson took the revolutionary step of *wearing his ship from her appointed station in the *line of battle, a straight court-martial offence, and running on board and then capturing two Spanish first-rates separated, with other ships, from their fleet and trying to rejoin it. This spectacular action has diverted the limelight of

victory from St. Vincent, the commander-in-chief, and focused it on his subordinate officer, Nelson. But a comparison of the logs of St. Vincent's and Nelson's ships brings to light the true facts:

Log, H.M.S. *Victory* (St. Vincent) 14 February 1797	Log. H.M.S. *Captain* (Nelson) 14 February 1797
12.51. p.m. General signal: Take out Suitable Stations *and Engage Enemy as Arriving up in succesion.*	12.50. p.m. The Commodore ordered the ship to be wore when she was immediately engaged with the *Santissima Trinidad* and 2 other 3-decked ships.

In other words, at exactly the same moment that St. Vincent was ordering all ships to leave their regular stations and attack where they could, Nelson, not waiting for orders, was leaving his station and driving at the Spaniards. Here is the proof of the two men's unanimity of mind, the electric spark that passed from one to the other without need of formal communication.

Yet at all stages of their acquaintance St. Vincent had had harsh things to say of Nelson, 'He is a partisan devoured with vanity ... his sole merit animal courage, his private character most disgraceful', while Nelson was not behindhand in confiding to Emma *Hamilton similar sentiments about his chief. But St. Vincent's bitter words are redeemed by his 'God bless you, no man loves and esteems you more truly', and Nelson's by his, 'Without you, I am nothing.'

St. Vincent, in his old age, faced ceaseless appeals from starving old shipmates and their families, and he helped or tried to help them all, his attitude movingly expressed: 'I never yet have forsaken any man who served well under me.'

He was not of the type to become a public idol like Nelson, though contemporaries describe his presence as splendid and even dramatic, intimidating at will or irresistibly genial and amusing. His greatness never rested upon the noise and glare of popularity, but on his total devotion to the British Navy. The standard biography, *Memoirs of Earl St. Vincent*, was written by Jedediah Tucker, the son of St. Vincent's private secretary, and published in 1844; the best recent biography is Berckman, *Nelson's Dear Lord* (1962).

JERVIS BAY, H.M.S., an *armed merchant cruiser of the Second World War in the British Navy which fought a notable action in 1940 against the German *pocket-battleship *Admiral Scheer*. She was originally a 14,000-ton passenger *liner built in 1922–3 with a speed of some 15 knots and was converted to an armed merchant cruiser by the mounting on deck of seven old 6-inch guns. The majority of her officers remained in her with commissions in the Royal Naval Reserve; in command of her was Acting-Captain E. S. Fogarty Fegen, R.N.

On the evening of 5 November 1940 the *Jervis Bay* was the sole escort of a 37-ship homeward-bound Atlantic convoy which was intercepted by the *Admiral Scheer*. Ordering the convoy to scatter under cover of smoke, Fegen steered to engage the German ship, a suicidal action in face of the *Scheer*'s main armament of six 11-inch guns, but it achieved his gallant object of distracting and delaying the enemy while the convoy scattered. It took the *Admiral Scheer* half-an-hour to destroy the *Jervis Bay*, and as a result only six of the convoy were caught and sunk. The tanker * *San Demetrio* was immobilized and abandoned but was afterwards reboarded by a portion of her crew and steamed under immense difficulties to England. Another of the convoy, the Swedish *Stüreholm*, returned after dark to pick up survivors of the *Jervis Bay*. Captain Fegen was not among them and he was posthumously awarded the Victoria Cross for his gallant sacrifice.

JETSAM, the legal term for goods or equipment thrown overboard from a ship at sea, differing from *flotsam in that the goods are deliberately thrown overboard from a ship, for instance to lighten her if she is in danger, while flotsam covers goods accidentally lost overboard or which may float up from the hull of a wrecked ship. In the strict and original legal sense, jetsam is the place where such goods are thrown overboard, and not necessarily the goods themselves, and also implies total abandonment of such goods to a later finder.

JETTISON, to, the act of throwing goods or equipment overboard to lighten a ship in stress of weather or other danger. See also JETSAM.

JETTY, normally considered to be a solid structure built out, usually into the sea but in some cases along the shore as part of a port or *dockyard alongside which ships can lie for loading or discharging cargo, repair, etc. But in its modern connection, some jetties, as for example jetties alongside which *tankers may lie to load or discharge oil, are built out on piles in the fashion of a *pier.

JEWEL BLOCKS, the blocks attached to *eye-bolts on those *yards (lower and topsail yards) on which *studdingsails were set in square-rigged ships and through which the studdingsail *halyards are rove. They were also used for the more lugubrious purpose of reeving the rope by which men sentenced to death were hanged at the yardarm in naval ships.

JEW'S HARP, a name sometimes given to the *shackle with which a chain *cable is attached to an *anchor. It is always secured with the bow of the shackle outboard so that, when the anchor is let go, the lugs of the shackle do not catch up on the rim of the *hawsehole.

JIB, a triangular sail set by sailing vessels on the stays of the foremast. The largest square-rigged sailing vessels of the late 19th century and early 20th century carried as many as six jibs, named, from aft forward, storm, inner, outer, flying, spindle, and jib-of-jibs. Smaller sailing vessels, particularly those *fore-and-aft rigged, normally set only one jib, other triangular sails set before the foremast being known as *staysails. In the older design of the fore-and-aft rig, where a *bowsprit carried a fore topmast stay beyond the *stem of the vessel to give additional support to the mast, it was on this stay that the jib was carried, with a staysail set on the forestay. In the modern rig design, where no bowsprit, or only a very short bowsprit, is fitted, the single forestay is set up on, or even inboard of, the *stemhead and this usually only carries one large jib, no staysail being set. These large jibs, of which the *clew extends well abaft the mast, are known as *Genoa or *yankee jibs, and for a period during the decade 1930–40, some of the larger racing yachts set a four-sided jib, known as a *double-clewed jib, or 'Greta Garbo', which was virtually a Genoa jib with its after corner cut off. It proved, however, a fashion which never caught on and was quickly abandoned.

In most modern sailing vessels of any size, the jib is sheeted to winches to trim the sail instead of being done by manpower, which was the normal means of trimming up to only a few years ago. Jibs vary in size according to the strength of the wind, ranging from the Genoa, made of light cloth for use in winds of up to about force 4 on the *Beaufort scale, to the storm jib, made of heavy duty canvas, for heavy blows.

The jib and *jib-boom were introduced in 1705 for smaller ships as a replacement for the older *spritsail and spritsail topmast, and by 1719 had been also adopted by the largest ships then built. From its inception it proved a great step forward in the efficiency of a sailing vessel on a wind and was, as William *Falconer (*Marine Dictionary*, 1771) says, 'a sail of great command on a side wind, and particularly when sailing *close-hauled'. This is an opinion with which few modern sailors would disagree.

'JIBBER THE KIBBER', to, an old term for the act of decoying a ship ashore by means of false lights. The art was to tie a lantern to a horse's neck and hobble one of its legs to give a motion very similar to that of a ship's light at sea.

JIB-BOOM, a continuation of the *bowsprit in large ships by means of a spar run out forward to extend the *foot of the outer *jib and the *stay of the fore *topgallant mast. Flying jib-boom, a further extension with yet another spar to the end of which the *tack of the flying jib is hauled out and the fore *royal stay secured. For illus. see RIGGING.

JIBE, to, see GYBE, TO.

JIB-HEADED TOPSAIL, a triangular topsail set above the mainsail in a gaff-rigged vessel. The *peak of the topsail is hoisted to the masthead and the foot is stretched along the top of the *gaff, so that the sail just fills the triangle formed by the masthead, the peak of the gaff, and the *jaws of the gaff. See also JACKYARD TOPSAIL.

JIB-OF-JIBS, a sixth *jib set as a jib topsail on the fore *royal stay in a square-rigged ship. It is a light weather sail only set in a gentle breeze when sailing *on the wind.

JIGGER, (1) a light *tackle consisting of a double and single *block, multiplying the power by four when rove to *advantage and used for many small purposes on board ship. Originally it was designed to hold on to the *cable as it was being hove on board in the form of a temporary stopper when *anchors were weighed by hand, but in fore-and-aft rigged ships (see RIG) a jigger was also often used on the standing part of the *throat and *peak *halyards to give them the final *sweating up. A boom jigger was one used to rig the *studdingsail booms in and out from the lower and topsail yards of square-rigged ships. It is in effect a *luff tackle used with a rope of smaller size. (See also PURCHASE.) **(2)** The name given to the small sail set on a *jigger-mast.

JIGGER-MAST, a small mast set right aft in some smaller sailing craft, and a name frequently given to the after mast of a small *yawl, though this is more properly called a *mizen, and to the small mast set right aft in some *spritsail *barges. It is also the name given to the fourth mast in a five- or six-masted *schooner.

JOCKEY POLE, a metal *spar used to prevent the *spinnaker guy rope fouling the *stanchions on a modern yacht of beamy design. The jockey pole runs athwartship from the mast to the guy and is rigged only when the spinnaker boom is trimmed well forward, close to the forestay.

JOGGLE SHACKLE, a long, slightly curved *shackle used in anchor work to haul the *cable of one *anchor round the bows of a ship when *mooring to two anchors. The occasion of its use is when a mooring swivel is inserted into the two cables to prevent a *foul hawse with two anchors on the ground.

'JOHN COMPANY', a colloquial name widely used to describe the British *East India Company.

JOLIE BRISE, a French pilot *cutter of 44 tons *Thames Measurement built at Le Havre in 1913 and converted to a yacht. Under the ownership of Commander E. G. *Martin in 1925, she won the first race from Ryde round the *Fastnet rock to Plymouth, 615 miles, and earned Martin the Blue Water medal of the Cruising Club of America when the following year he made a 10,000-mile voyage to New York, won in his class in the Bermuda race, and returned to Plymouth. Under the ownership of Robert Somerset she won the Fastnet race again in 1929 and 1930. In 1932 she again crossed the Atlantic to compete in the Bermuda race, when during the race Somerset put his cutter alongside an American yacht, *Adriana,* which had caught fire, and rescued her crew. By now outclassed in ocean racing, this massively built pilot boat continued to make long distance cruises to Portugal and the Mediterranean, and was based for a number of years at Lisbon.

'JOLLIES', a nickname for the Royal *Marines in the British Navy. Originally all soldiers carried on board a British warship were known as jollies, a 'tame jolly' being a militiaman and a 'royal jolly' a marine, but the name today is applied only to marines.

"'E was scrapin' the paint from off of 'er plates an' I sez to 'im, " 'Oo are you?"
'Sez 'e, "I'm a Jolly—'Er Majesty's Jolly—soldier an' sailor too!" '

R. Kipling, *Barrack-Room Ballads,* 1896.

JOLLY ROGER, the name popularly given to a flag flown by pirate ships as seen by the eyes of writers of pirate stories. It was supposed to be a white skull on a black ground, sometimes with crossed bones below the skull. There is, however, no evidence that such a flag was ever flown by a pirate ship at sea, and if there ever were a general flag which might be recognized as a pirate flag, it would probably be the plain black flag which some such ships were occasionally reported as flying from their main masthead. Another version of a pirate flag was said to be a black skeleton on a yellow field, but this may have arisen from a mistaken impression of the imperial flag of Austria, which was a black double-headed eagle on a yellow field. During the 18th century a number of *privateers sailed under Austrian *letters of marque, which were much easier to obtain than those of other nations, and as many privateers, flying the imperial flag of Austria, behaved little better than pirates, the impression may well have gained ground that this was in fact the pirate flag.

JOLLY-BOAT, possibly from the Dutch and German *jolle*, Swedish *jol*, a small *bark or boat, though this may be the derivation of the English *yawl, or possibly a perversion of *gellywatte, a small ship's boat, generally of the 18th and 19th centuries, used for a variety of purposes, such as going round a ship to see that the *yards were square, taking the steward ashore to purchase fresh provisions, etc. It was *clinker-built, propelled by oars, and was normally hoisted on a *davit at the stern of the ship. When it was included as part of a warship's outfit of ship's boats, it pulled six oars on three *thwarts. Its equivalent in a ship of today would probably be a *skiff.

JONAH, one of the minor prophets of the Old Testament who, after being instructed by Jehovah to go to Nineveh to preach repentance of sins, attempted to avoid his task by running away by sea to Tarshish. During the voyage a great storm arose and the mariners, suspecting Jonah to be the cause of it, threw him overboard. He was swallowed by a whale, but was spewed up three days later when, chastened by his experience, he proceeded in execution of his previous orders. His name has survived in maritime circles as the description of a man who brings ill-fortune to a ship, and has spread from its original maritime use to become a part of the English language as a person who brings ill-fortune to all with whom he comes into contact.

When the development of *whaling and of zoological science showed that most, or all, species of whales have throats too small to swallow a man, much controversy arose about the factual basis of the story, but it is now generally agreed to be legendary or allegorical. No actual species of whale but only a mythical sea monster is implied by the original Hebrew.

JONES, JOHN PAUL (1747–92), American naval officer, was born at Kirkbean, Galloway, son of John Paul, gardener on the Arbigland estate. Between 1761 and 1773 he served in the British merchant marine, making voyages as *master from the Solway Firth, London, and Africa to the West Indies and Virginia, where an elder brother had settled as a tailor. Having killed at Tobago, in self-defence, a mutinous seaman who was a popular local character, he changed his name to John Jones and fled to Virginia in 1773. When fighting broke out between England and the Thirteen Colonies, and Congress built the *Continental Navy, John Paul

Jones (as he now called himself) was commissioned as first lieutenant.

After promotion to captain, he was appointed in 1777 to command the sloop *Ranger*, then fitting out at Portsmouth, New Hampshire. After reaching Nantes on 2 December 1777, Jones visited Paris, where Benjamin Franklin, commissioner of the American colonies in France, sized him up as a great fighter and became his protector. Receiving orders to cruise about the British Isles to 'distress' the enemy, Jones's main efforts were shore raids. On the night of 22/23 April 1778, he raided Whitehaven, hoping to destroy with incendiaries the large number of ships in harbour. The landing was bungled and little destruction was effected, but the moral effect was immense.

On the morning of 23 April Jones landed with a boat's crew on St. Mary's Isle, intending to abduct the owner, the fourth Earl of Selkirk. His purpose was to use the Earl as a hostage to obtain the release of American sailors, several hundred of whom, captured in naval actions, were in English gaols with indictments for treason hanging over them. The Earl being absent, Jones's men, who disliked profitless raids, seized the family silver. Jones afterwards apologized, bought the silver back from his men, and returned it to the Selkirks. A more satisfactory exploit, on 24 April, was the *Ranger*'s battle with H.M.S. *Drake*, off Belfast Lough. The two were approximately equal in *burthen and armament. After a close action lasting an hour, and after the *Drake*'s rigging had been cut to pieces and her commanding officer killed, the British master surrendered. Jones, first towing his *prize, then sailing her under *jury rig, got her safely into Brest, together with 200 prisoners-of-war, who were exchanged for American sailors in English prisons.

Jones's next command was a squadron built around an old 900-ton *East Indiaman which the French government purchased for him and renamed *Bonhomme Richard* as a compliment to Franklin. The rest of the squadron consisted of the new U.S.S. *Alliance*, commanded by a half-mad Frenchman in the American Service named Pierre *Landais, the French *frigate *Pallas*, and a French *corvette and *cutter, all flying the American ensign. With infinite difficulty Jones got the *Richard* converted, gunned, equipped, and manned. The squadron sailed from Lorient on 14 August 1779. The French cutter got lost off the Skelligs and never rejoined. The *Alliance* went off prize-taking on her own account for most of the voyage. Jones, passing between the Orkneys and the Shetlands, shaped his course south, planning to place Edinburgh under contribution, but the plan miscarried. Continuing south, Jones intercepted a Baltic convoy of forty-four sail escorted by H.M.S. *Serapis* (Captain

John Paul Jones; 19th-century engraving

Richard Pearson) and H.M.S. *Countess of Scarborough*. There ensued one of the most bitter naval contests of the century, the battle of Flamborough Head, 23 September 1779. Pearson's first concern was for the safety of his convoy, and he covered it as it escaped to the north, holding the American squadron at bay. Having made sure of its safety he turned to engage the *Bonhomme Richard* while the *Countess of Scarborough* gave battle to the much larger *Pallas*. After raking the *Bonhomme Richard* the *Serapis* grappled her for boarding, but was unable, because of the hot fire, to get a party aboard. The two ships fought muzzle to muzzle for two hours, and the *Bonhomme Richard* had all her guns knocked out except two when fire broke out on board the *Serapis* and Pearson was forced to surrender.

The *Bonhomme Richard* was, however, in worse shape than the *Serapis*. In spite of all efforts to save her, she sank two days later, Jones transferring to the captured *Serapis*. The losses in each ship were high, 128 killed and wounded in the *Serapis*, 150 in the *Bonhomme Richard*.

Jones, accompanied by the rest of his squadron, took refuge in the Texel on 3 October. Delayed by repairs, neutrality complications, and a British *blockade, the squadron remained there until 27 December, Jones flying his pendant in the *Alliance*. He cruised to Corunna and then back to Lorient which he reached on 19 February 1780. In mid-April Jones proceeded to Paris where he found himself the hero of the year. After some weeks of dalliance he returned to America in the sloop *Ariel*. Congress now gave Jones command of the *America*, the only U.S. 74-gun ship, then about half-built at Portsmouth, New Hampshire. For a year Jones worked hard getting the *America* completed, launched, and rigged, only to lose her in 1782 because Congress, unwilling to support a peacetime navy, presented her to France.

Jones spent a good part of the rest of his life in France, going through the tiresome business of collecting *prize money due to his squadron, and endeavouring without success to obtain a command in the French Navy. At last, in the Imperial Russian Navy, he obtained flag rank as rear admiral commanding a squadron of nine frigates on the Liman of the Dnieper, where Russia was trying to capture Ochakov from the Turks. The Russian Black Sea Fleet was a scratch collection of shoal draft vessels manned by impressed serfs, Cossacks, Volga boatmen, and Levantine pirates, officered in part by adventurers of six or seven nations. The Empress Catherine felt that only an outstanding naval officer from another country could weld this motley collection into a real fighting force. Possibly Jones could have done so had he not got into the ill graces of Prince Potemkin, the commander-in-chief, who resented having another foreign flag officer on his hands. In spite of all intrigues, Jones fought the Turks and won the two battles of the Liman on 6 and 17 June 1788—shoal water fights in a narrow estuary with little space to deploy and manoeuvre between mudflats. Prince Nassau-Siegen, commander of the light flotilla (corresponding to modern landing or beaching craft), got all the credit from Potemkin, and Jones was left out of the post-battle list of honours. He won the respect and loyalty of the Russian naval officers under him, but that did not help him with the commander-in-chief who relieved Jones and sent him to St. Petersburg to await orders.

Jones waited there through the winter of 1788–9. In the spring an important personage, probably Nassau-Siegen, arranged to have him charged on a false accusation of rape; shortly after the same adventurer, who had charmed the Empress, received command of her Baltic fleet, which post Jones had been led to anticipate for himself. He left Russia, and after travelling through central Europe, settled down in May 1790 in a pleasant apartment at 19 rue de Tournon, Paris. He spent most of his time writing letters to every influential person of his acquaintance, looking for a naval or diplomatic job; and his importunity was finally rewarded by two commissions from President Washington of 1 and 2 June 1792 appointing him American consul in Algeria and plenipotentiary to negotiate with the Dey for the release of American prisoners. It was too late. On 18 July, weeks before these commissions reached France, Jones died from an attack of bronchial pneumonia, on top of jaundice and nephritis.

The Assemblée Legislative gave him a state funeral, and he was buried in the Protestant cemetery on rue Granges-aux-Belles. In 1905 the lead coffin was exhumed, the body identified and carried to Annapolis in an American cruiser, escorted by three others, and met off Nantucket Shoals by seven battleships. At Annapolis John Paul Jones's body finally came to rest, in a marble sarcophagus in the crypt of the Naval Academy chapel.

Jones's fame rests not only on his superb fighting qualities and impeccable seamanship but on ideas expressed in many letters on naval education, training, tactics, and strategy. He was an early and ardent believer in sea power. 'Without a Respectable Navy—alas America!' he wrote to Robert Morris. Despising the *guerre de course* to which circumstances and his people's greed for prize money compelled him, he longed to command a fleet and engage an enemy in line of battle. Perfectionism, fault-finding, and occasional explosions of rage made him unpopular in his own navy; his care of prisoners and generosity to impressed pilots made him a kind of a Robin Hood to the English. There are a dozen ballads and at least forty English chapbooks with such titles as, *The Life, Voyages and Sea Battles of that Celebrated Seaman, Commodore Paul Jones*. Although he never had an opportunity to implement his strategic ideas, Jones showed his greatness on the tactical level by making the right decisions in the heat of battle, and his refusal to admit the possibility of defeat in the battle of Flamborough Head, emerging victorious from the most desperate circumstances, is an inspiration to every sailor. For a biography, see *John Paul Jones* by Samuel Eliot Morison (1959).

JONQUIÈRE, JACQUES DE TAFFANEL, Marquis de la (1680–1752), French commodore, took part in *Duguay-Trouin's expedition against Rio de Janeiro in 1711. During the War of Austrian Succession (1739–48), he was promoted *commodore (*chef d'escadre*) and was in command of a *squadron of seven *ships of the line, escorting a military convoy, which was intercepted off Cape Finisterre by a squadron of 14 British ships of the line commanded by Admiral Lord *Anson on 3 May 1747. Jonquière offered battle with his warships and six armed ships of the French *East India Company from the convoy. Anson made the signal for a *general chase and in the ensuing battle captured all but one of the French force and another ship of the convoy. Jonquière was taken to England as a prisoner-of-war. On his release two years later he was appointed governor of Canada by the French and it was there that he died.

JUGLE or **JOGGLE,** a notch cut in the edge of a plank to admit the narrow butt of another when planking up a wooden vessel. Its purpose is to make a more watertight joint and also to make it less likely for the butt of the plank to start or *spring.

'JUMBO', the name often used for the fore *staysail in a *fore-and-aft rigged ship. It is the largest of the foresails, which perhaps explains the name, and in general terms corresponds to the *Genoa jib of the modern yacht rig.

JUMPER, a chain or wire *stay which leads down from the outer end of the *jib-boom to the *dolphin striker in a square-rigged ship. It provides support for the jib-boom in staying the fore *topgallant mast, countering the upward pull of the fore topgallant stay. JUMPER STAY, a truss stay which leads from the root of the lower crosstrees in a sailing vessel to the fore side of the masthead, given additional spread at the top by means of a *jumper strut.

JUMPER STRUT, a short metal or wooden strut on a yacht's mast canted forward at an angle of about 45° which spreads the effective angle of a short masthead or jumper *stay. Its purpose is to add stiffness and support to the long mast used in *Bermuda rig.

Chinese junk; photograph, 1870–71

JUMPING, or **JUMPER, WIRE,** a serrated wire leading from the stemhead of a *submarine to the forward edge of the *bridge casing above the *conning-tower, and from the after edge of the bridge casing to the stern, used for cutting a way through defensive nets when submerged. Wire nets, buoyed along the top edge and suspended across the entrances to harbours and narrow straits, were used extensively during the First World War (1914–18) as defences against submarines, but when fitted with a jumping wire a submarine could force her way through.

JUNIOR OFFSHORE GROUP, an organization formed in 1950 to provide ocean races for owners of smaller and less costly yachts than those which normally race in the main *Royal Ocean Racing Club's series of races. The yachts racing in this group are limited to between 16 and 24 ft (5 to 7 m) in waterline length and compete in races of up to 250 miles. The group was formed largely through the efforts of Captain J. H. *Illingworth, Commodore of the R.O.R.C. in that year. In the U.S.A., the Midget Ocean Racing Club caters for a similar demand.

JUNK, (1) a native sailing vessel common to Far Eastern seas, especially used by the Chinese and Javanese. It is a flat-bottomed, high-sterned vessel with square bows, with two or three masts carrying *lugsails often made of matting stif-

fened with horizontal battens. The name comes from the Portuguese *junco*, adapted from the Javanese *djong*, ship. It is a very old design, with the maximum beam about one-third of the length of the ship from aft, the bow having no recognized *stem but being chamfered off. It has no *keel, is very full at the stern, and carries a very large *rudder which, when at sea, is lowered below the depth of the bottom. The largest junks were built at least to the size of a square-rigged ship of the 18th–19th centuries, around 3,000–4,000 tons deadweight, and were oceangoing trading vessels from China throughout the western Pacific at least as far south as the Philippine Islands. It was also, for many years, the general warship of the Chinese, being armed with guns on deck. **(2)** Old and condemned rope cut into short lengths and used for making swabs, mats, *fenders, *oakum, etc. **(3)** The word applied colloquially by seamen to the salt beef and pork used on board, presumably to imply that it was old and ripe to be condemned as in the other meaning (2) of junk.

JURIEN DE LA GRAVIÈRE, JEAN-PIERRE BAPTISTE EDMOND (1812–92), French hydrographer and admiral, was the son of Admiral Jurien de la Gravière who served through the Revolutionary (1793–1801) and Napoleonic (1803–15) wars. His service in the French Navy started in China where he became interested in hydrography and carried out some useful surveys. He commanded a ship in the Black Sea during the Crimean War (1854–6) and conducted the *blockade of the Austrian ports in the Adriatic in 1859. In 1861–2 he commanded the French squadron in the expedition against Mexico, and during the Franco-Prussian war of 1870 was commander-in-chief in the Mediterranean. In 1871 he became director of the Hydrographic Department of the French Navy and was responsible for organizing many surveys of French colonial waters, a task which had become somewhat neglected by his predecessors. He wrote several books on naval subjects, the best known being *Souvenirs d'un amiral* (1860); a memoir of his father, *La Marine d'autrefois* (1865); and *La Marine d'aujourd'hui* (1872).

JURY, a temporary makeshift to bring a disabled vessel back to harbour. A jury mast is one erected to take the place of a mast which has been *carried away; jury rig is the contrivance of masts and sails to get a ship under way after she has been disabled; jury *rudder is a makeshift arrangement to give a ship the ability to steer when she has lost her rudder.

JUTLAND, BATTLE OF, known in Germany as the battle of the Skagerrak, was the greatest naval engagement of the First World War, fought between the main fleets of Britain and Germany on 31 May 1916. Both fleets were divided into two distinct bodies, advance forces of *battle-cruisers, *cruisers, and *destroyers commanded respectively on the two sides by Vice Admiral Sir David *Beatty and Vice Admiral Franz von *Hipper, and the main fleets of *battleships, cruisers, and destroyers commanded by Admiral Sir John *Jellicoe and Vice Admiral Reinhard *Scheer.

The battle arose from an initial German plan to station *U-boats off the entrances of the main British fleet bases and then proceed to sea with the fleet up the Danish coast towards the Skagerrak, hoping that this would tempt the British fleet to put to sea, when the U-boats could attack it with torpedoes. The plan miscarried, mainly because of the weather, and it was only on the very last day of the U-boats' patrols (30 May) that the weather made it possible to take the German fleet to sea. The object now was limited to a raid on allied shipping in the Skagerrak and on the Norwegian coast, all thoughts of tempting the British ships over the U-boats having been abandoned. First to sail was Hipper's advanced force; the main *High Seas Fleet followed some 60 miles astern.

Indications that German ships were putting to sea were received in London when signals were deciphered in the Admiralty (see ROOM 40, O.B.),

and although it was not known how many ships were involved, the *Grand Fleet was ordered to sail. It, too, put to sea with the battle-cruiser force forming up some 60 miles ahead of the main force.

Neither fleet had any definite knowledge of the other as they steamed across the North Sea, and as the day of 31 May wore on with no sightings on either side, all four admirals, two British and two German, had thoughts of returning to their respective bases after yet another fruitless sortie. The actual contact between the fleets came almost by accident. On the port wing of the advanced screen of British light cruisers H.M.S. *Galatea* sighted a Swedish merchant ship stopped and blowing off steam. Almost simultaneously the same ship was sighted by the port wing ship of the German advanced screen. Both turned to investigate, and in a few more moments signals of 'Enemy in sight' were flashed back to both fleets.

Beatty, with his six battle-cruisers and not waiting for a division of four fast battleships attached to his force to join him, worked up to maximum speed southward as the *Galatea*, continuing her reconnaissance, reported sighting German battle-cruisers. The two forces were soon in action, Hipper altering round to the south to lead the British ships into the grasp of Scheer's battleships some 60 miles south of him. With a superiority of six to five in battle-cruisers, Beatty forced the engagement to the utmost, but faulty British ship design, particularly in anti-flash arrangements, and a failure in the correct distribution of gunfire, led to two British battle-cruisers, the *Indefatigable* and *Queen Mary*, being hit and sunk. Meanwhile Scheer was steaming north at maximum speed and Beatty, with no knowledge that the main High Seas Fleet was at sea (the British Admiralty had previously signalled that it was still in harbour), was suddenly faced with the sight of the main German fleet steaming towards him. He at once reversed his course with the intention of playing on Hipper and Scheer the same game that had been played on him, that of leading the enemy into the hands of the British Grand Fleet, still many miles to the northward. An error in signalling, one of many in the battle, failed to make his intentions clear to the battleships attached to his force and they were heavily engaged by the German main fleet before they, too, could turn northward. Scheer and Hipper, both unaware that the British main fleet was at sea, continued the chase of Beatty's ships believing that they were the only opposition and hoping to use their present vast superiority in numbers and weight of gunfire to annihilate them.

The two main fleets came into contact just after 6 p.m. about 80 miles west of the coast of the Jutland peninsula. Further errors in signals,

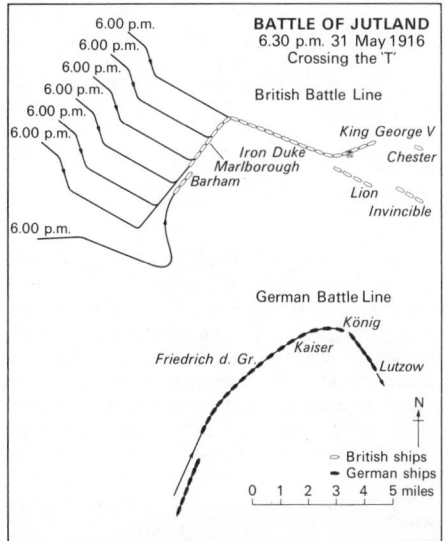

BATTLE OF JUTLAND
6.30 p.m. 31 May 1916
Crossing the 'T'

6.00 p.m.
6.00 p.m.
6.00 p.m.
6.00 p.m.
6.00 p.m.
6.00 p.m.
6.00 p.m.

British Battle Line

King George V
Iron Duke   Chester
Marlborough
Barham
Lion
Invincible

German Battle Line
König
Kaiser
Friedrich d. Gr.
Lutzow

N

○ British ships
● German ships

0   1   2   3   4   5 miles

or the lack of them, combined with navigational errors, had left Jellicoe in ignorance of the exact position of Scheer's ships and until the very last moment he was unable to decide the best means of deployment of the fleet to cut the enemy off from his bases in Germany. In the end Jellicoe deployed the fleet into line of battle on the port wing column, a masterly tactical stroke which not only placed the Grand Fleet across the German line of retreat but also *'crossed the T' of the German line of battle.

The scene was now set for a substantial British naval victory although the lateness of the day and the typical misty North Sea conditions made gunnery difficult. Twice Scheer, in desperation, tried to force his way down towards the safety of his bases only to find on both occasions the overwhelming strength of the Grand Fleet blocking the way, and twice he had to extricate his ships by an emergency turn away, the second time under cover of a suicidal order to his already battered battle-cruisers to 'charge the enemy'.

In the enveloping mist and approaching darkness, the two fleets lost touch before the tactical advantage obtained by Jellicoe's deployment could be brought to fruition. Both settled down in night-steaming formation on a south-easterly course towards the German home ports with the British fleet in the inside position between the German ships and the safety of their bases. They steamed steadily down the North Sea, Jellicoe confident that the action could be continued the following morning, Scheer with the knowledge that unless somehow he could force his ships through the British fleet they were doomed to destruction.

If Scheer tactically had lost the day battle, he won that of the night. While Jellicoe's fleet, in compact night-steaming formation, ploughed steadily on with his destroyer *flotillas stationed astern, Scheer's ships crossed astern of the British fleet. They ran foul of the destroyer flotillas while doing so and lost one old battleship, the *Pommern*, in a series of isolated encounters, but finally reached the security of the German minefields in the Heligoland Bight. When day broke on the morning of 1 June, Jellicoe found himself patrolling an empty North Sea.

There were many reasons why the battle of Jutland was not the overwhelming British victory that it had promised to be. During the night German signals deciphered in the Admiralty indicated beyond question that Scheer was making for the most northerly of the three routes through the German minefields, but this information was not signalled to Jellicoe, who had thought that Scheer would use one of the southern routes. If that information had reached Jellicoe, the battle could have been resumed in the morning of 1 June with, probably, decisive results. There were yet further signal failures in the British fleet, none of the many ships which were engaged in or witnessed the night destroyer actions informing Jellicoe that Scheer was crossing the stern of the Grand Fleet with the whole of the High Seas Fleet. Faulty ship design was directly responsible for the loss of three British battle-cruisers and three armoured cruisers, and faulty shell design resulted in British armour-piercing shells breaking up on impact instead of exploding inside the enemy ships. British losses in the battle were three battle-cruisers, three armoured cruisers, and eight destroyers; German losses, one old pre-dreadnought battleship, one battle-cruiser, four light cruisers, and five destroyers.

Yet in the context of the war as a whole, Jutland was a British strategic victory of great importance. Never again in the war did the German fleet challenge, or even question, British dominance of the North Sea. In terms of the sea blockade Germany, without the rigorous use of her fleet, could no longer avoid eventual economic strangulation. Another of the end results of Jutland were the mutinies of 1917 and 1918 in the High Seas Fleet which were the signals for the final German collapse.

JYLSON, or **JILLSON, BLOCK,** a heavy sheave fitted on the foremast of fishing vessels and used to hoist the *trawl off the deck before the *cod-end, the bag containing the catch, is opened.

K

KAMAL, from the Arabic word meaning guide, a navigational instrument of great antiquity, used by Arab seamen in the Red Sea and the Indian Ocean for at least six centuries for measuring the *altitude of a celestial body. The instrument became known to European navigators through Vasco da *Gama after he had rounded the African continent from the Atlantic to the Indian Ocean in 1497. The principle of the kamal, which is the same as that of the *cross-staff, depends upon the geometrical properties of similar triangles. The simplest form of kamal consisted of a rectangular board or tablet of wood, to the centre of which was secured a knotted cord. The tablet was held so that the upper and lower edges coincided respectively with the observed body and the *horizon vertically below it. In this position the cord was stretched taut to the observer's eye, and the ratio between the fixed length of the tablet and the variable length of the cord between tablet and eye, being a function of the altitude of the observed body, gave the measurement. The positions of the knots on the cord were related to the meridian altitudes of a given star appropriate to the *latitudes of headlands and harbours along the route. The ancient kamal in a modified form is used even today by the Arab navigators of the *dhows often to be seen in the Red Sea and off the East African coast.

KAMIKAZE, the 'Divine Wind' which in 1281 sprang up in the Sea of Japan and destroyed the invasion fleet of Kublai Khan, was the name given by the Japanese to their 'special attack units', bomb-loaded aircraft the pilots of which were dedicated to crashing suicidally into enemy ships, with which, during the Second World War, they hoped to turn the tide of the sea war in the Pacific in 1944.

The organization was initiated by Vice Admiral Takijiro Ohnishi when he took command of the 1st Air Fleet in the Philippine Islands in October 1944. When he took over he quickly realized how attenuated its force had become and how little support it would be able to give to the fleet, using orthodox tactics, in the great battle for *Leyte Gulf about to begin. He put his suicide attack idea to some of his pilots and found enough volunteers to try out the new tactic at Leyte Gulf, choosing the .American

*aircraft carriers as the main targets. The success he obtained encouraged him to develop the organization which grew, now with compulsory participants, until massed kamikaze attacks, known as *kikusui*, became the main form of attack on the U.S. fleet during the assault on Okinawa early in 1945. In the largest of these attacks, 355 kamikaze and 341 other planes took part. The number of ships sunk or seriously damaged by suicide attacks on this occasion came very near to forcing a withdrawal of the American and British carrier fleets.

KANE, ELISHA KENT (1820–57), American Arctic explorer, was born at Philadelphia. After qualifying as a doctor of medicine at the University of Pennsylvania in 1842, he was appointed surgeon to the American mission to China, western India, Egypt, and Europe, returning to the U.S.A. in 1846. After taking part in a survey of Mexico, he was appointed in 1850 senior medical officer of an expedition dispatched to search for Sir John *Franklin. It left New York in May of that year in the ships *Advance* and *Rescue*, but was unsuccessful. Three years later, in command of the *Advance*, Kane again sailed from New York to resume the search, and proceeded up Baffin Bay through Smith Sound to latitude 78° 43′ N. where his ship was beset in the ice for twenty-one months and finally had to be abandoned when provisions began to run out and *scurvy made its appearance. He led his crew to the safety of Danish settlements in Greenland after a perilous ten-week journey of 1,300 miles during which only one man was lost. Kane was awarded a Congressional Gold Medal, and also that of the Royal Geographical Society, for this feat.

KAPAL, a square-rigged trading vessel, usually two-masted but very occasionally with three, used in Far Eastern waters, particularly in Malaya, for inter-island trade. It is rapidly becoming obsolete under competition from the diesel engine.

KARACHI, the principal seaport of Pakistan, at the extreme western end of the Indus delta. Its birth as a port began with the silting up of Shahbandar, the ancient port of Sind, during the 18th century, and its development grew under

A Japanese kamikaze attack on H.M.S. Formidable, *1945*

the rule of the Kalhora princes, and also under that of the Talpur Mirs, who captured the town in 1795 and built a fort at the entrance to the harbour. Karachi province became British in 1843, and considerable port development followed this acquisition, making it into the third largest seaport in India. It became Pakistani at the partition of India in 1947.

KARLSKRONA, a seaport of Sweden on the Baltic coast and a principal base of the Swedish Navy, was founded as a naval headquarters by Charles IX in 1680. The Swedish Naval Academy is there, as well as other naval technical schools, and a substantial *dockyard in which the dry-docks are cut out of solid granite. Karlskrona has a large and secure harbour protected by two forts on the islands of Aspö and Kungsholm. It is also the home of the *Marinmuseum och Modelkammaren, a maritime museum and model room of significant importance.

KAUPSKIP, the general name of the Norse trading vessels of the 10th and 11th centuries, in which the Viking expeditions to Iceland and Greenland, and the discovery of *Vinland, were made. These were *keel ships, with mast and square sail and with provision for the use of oars forward and aft, the waist section being reserved for the carriage of cargo. They were almost certainly undecked.

KAYAK, an Eskimo word for a light, covered-in, *canoe-type boat used for fishing, in common use in northern waters from Greenland to Alaska. It is made by covering a wooden framework with sealskin, with a hole in the centre of the top of the boat into which the kayaker, also dressed in sealskin, laces himself to prevent the entry of water. It is propelled by a double-bladed paddle. The word kayak, in its strict meaning, applies only to one of the boats when it is occupied by a man; if a woman uses one, it is called a umiak. It is thought by some people that the origin of the word is from the Arabic *caique, the name being given to these native boats when they were first seen by the early explorers and subsequently taken into the Eskimo language, but this seems unlikely as the name is the same in all Eskimo and Greenland dialects. In recent years kayaks have been widely used for recreational purposes on inland waters in many other parts of the world.

K-CLASS SUBMARINE, a revolutionary *submarine design produced by the British Navy during the First World War (1914–18). The basis of its design was the requirement in the British *Grand Fleet for a submarine fast enough on the surface to accompany the fleet in its searches for the German *High Seas Fleet and to dive and attack the enemy fleet with *torpedoes when contact had been made. Since the normal diesel submarine propulsion could not produce the required surface speed, a steam turbine was the only answer, and steam requires a boiler to produce it.

Two prototype steam-driven submarines, named *Nautilus* and *Swordfish*, were produced in 1916 but neither was a success. From these two boats a new class of submarine, named the K-class, was produced. They needed to be very large in order to accommodate boiler, fuel tanks, and turbine for surface propulsion, coupled with electric batteries and motors for submerged propulsion. They were, therefore, 338 feet in overall length with a submerged *displacement of 2,500 tons. They had two collapsible funnels to carry away the boiler fumes, and these were shut down, and the boiler room completely sealed off, when the submarine dived. Their surface speed was 24 *knots and their submerged speed 10 knots, and they were fitted with ten torpedo tubes.

They were, however, a failure, mainly because of their initial high diving speed. The steam generated while on the surface lasted for about 15 minutes after the boiler room was sealed off, and so they dived on their turbines. At least two K-class submarines were unable to pull out of their initial dive and continued down until their hulls were crushed by the pressure of the sea. They were also difficult to steer on the surface and were liable to mechanical failures, another cause of accident by which some K-boats were lost at sea. Yet in their use of steam for propulsion, they were in a way the forerunners of today's nuclear submarines, which are also propelled by steam and have a speed even higher than that of the K-boats on the surface.

KEARSARGE, U.S.S., was one of the sloops of war built during the early years of the American Civil War (1861–5). A screw steamer of 1,031 tons, she was armed with one 28-pounder rifle, two 11-inch Dahlgren smooth-bore shell guns, and four 32-pounder guns. Her most notable action was when she sank the Confederate *cruiser *Alabama* off Cherbourg on 19 June 1864. She ran aground and was wrecked on 10 February 1894.

KEATS, Sir RICHARD GOODWIN (1757–1834), British admiral, became a captain in 1789. In the naval mutiny in the Channel Fleet at *Spithead in 1797 he was put on shore by the seamen, but in June of that year again commanded a ship at sea. His most notable success came in 1801 during the Revolutionary War with France (1793–1801) when in command of the *Superb*, during an action off Algeciras, when a small English squadron under Sir James *Saumarez was shadowing a Franco-Spanish fleet. The *Superb* was sent ahead in the dark to harass and delay the enemy, and by midnight was close astern of the *Real Carlos*, a first-*rate *ship of the line of 112 guns. Keats let go his port broadside, some shots of which struck another three-decked ship of the line which in the darkness assumed the *Real Carlos* to be an enemy. The two ships then became hotly engaged and blew each other up; meanwhile the *Superb* was capturing a French ship.

Keats was promoted to rear admiral in 1807 and vice admiral in 1811, when he joined Sir Edward *Pellew off Toulon with his flag in the *Hibernia*. Owing to ill health he resigned his command in 1812, and was given a shore appointment as governor and commander-in-chief of Newfoundland, returning to England in 1815. He was appointed governor of *Greenwich Hospital in 1821, and was promoted to admiral in 1825.

KECKLE, to, the operation of covering a hemp cable spirally with old rope to protect it from chafing in the *hawsehole, a necessary precaution in the days before chain *anchor cables. In the days of large sailing vessels, anchors and cables were normally worked on the main deck, the hawsehole being cut in the ship's side close to the *stem. As there was no hawsehole as such in the modern sense of a sloping pipe, the wear through the hawsehole on an unprotected hemp cable as a ship swung to her anchor was prodigious, hence the need for keckling it. Chain cable was not generally adopted for anchor cables until the third or fourth decade of the 19th century.

KEDGE, a small ship's *anchor formerly carried on board to *warp a ship from one harbour berth to another or to haul her off into deeper water after grounding; also the name by which the spare anchor normally carried in yachts is known.

The original name was *cagger*, an early derivation from *catch* (i.e., to catch the ground) and dates back certainly to the 14th century, but it had developed into kedge at least by the end of the 16th century. In addition to its main uses as a means of hauling off a ship after grounding or shifting berth in calm waters, it was also frequently used in harbour by sailing vessels as the main anchor to which the ship lay in order to save labour when the time came to weigh it for departure. In the days of sail a kedge was also sometimes used to back up the *bower anchor when a ship was anchored in bad holding ground or when heavy weather was expected. In modern ships, with their more efficient ground tackle and powerful engines, the kedge anchor has lost much of its former usefulness and is rarely carried on board larger ships.

A kedge anchor is part of the standard ground tackle of yachts, and the name embraces whatever type of spare anchor is carried; e.g., fisherman's, stockless, mushroom, *CQR, etc. It is frequently used to hold a yacht against an adverse tide when there is insufficient wind to make headway against it, and also for anchoring a yacht in water too deep for the cable of the main anchor. See also TIDING OVER.

KEEL, (1) the lowest and principal *timber of a wooden ship, or the lowest continuous line of plates of a steel or iron ship, which extends the whole length of the vessel and to which the *stem, *sternpost, and *ribs or *timbers of the vessel are attached. It could be called the backbone of the ship and is its strongest single member. In the sailing *barges of the Thames the keel is a continuous run of oak 16 inches square, an indication of the great strength required in the keel of any ship.

In large steel ships, two additional keels, known as *bilge keels, are fitted to the hull either side of and parallel to the central keel, running along the turn of the *bilge approximately along the length of the hull where the sides are parallel. Their main purpose is to support the weight of the hull on the launching *ways in a building slip or on blocks on the floor of a *dry-dock when the ship is docked for cleaning or repairs, but they serve a subsidiary purpose in a seaway by providing additional resistance to the ship's rolling. Some modern small yachts are built with twin bilge keels, which in this case are appendages fitted under the turn of the bilge to *port and *starboard and approximately at right angles to the hull at this point, which act in the same way as a normal centreline *ballast keel. The first recorded yacht to have two keels abreast in this fashion was the *Iris*, a 60-ft (18·3 m) long by 12 ft 6 in. (3·8 m) beam *ketch built in Dublin Bay in 1894, whose draught upright was only 3 ft 6 in (1 m). In 1924 the Hon. R. A. Balfour designed a 23-ft *sloop *Bluebird* with twin keels fitted to the bilges, and cruised extensively in her. The advantages of twin bilge keels are that they enable a yacht with shallow draught to sail to windward as well as any similar *centreboard boat, to sit upright when on level ground, and to be self-supporting without the need for shoring-up on *slipways or road trailers. These advantages were recognized after the Second World War when deep water anchorages became congested and yachts had to accept more and more

mooring sites where they must take the ground at low water. Cruising yachts with twin bilge keels in addition to a centreline ballast keel were built in large numbers from 1950 onwards to designs by Robert Tucker and Maurice *Griffiths, pioneer designers of this type of yacht, and numerous *fibre glass production yachts of twin bilge keel type have since been manufactured in the U.K.

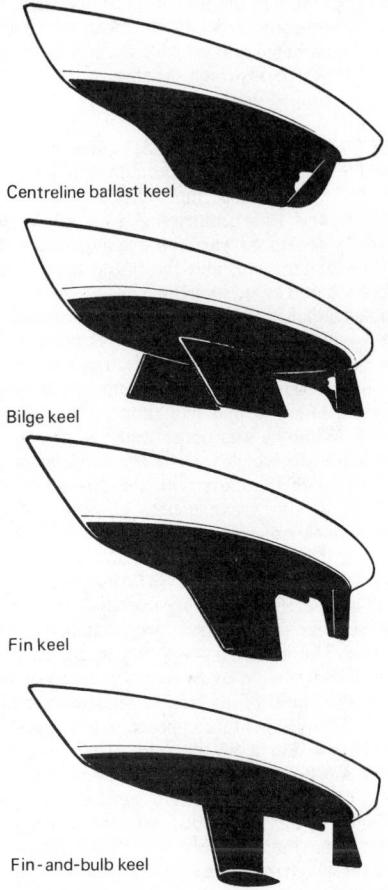

Centreline ballast keel

Bilge keel

Fin keel

Fin-and-bulb keel

Types of yacht keel

An additional type of keel used in yachts, particularly for racing, is the fin keel. It is a comparatively deep and narrow keel short in the fore-and-aft line, and fitted about amidships. Like a lowered centreboard it presents a long leading edge to give sufficient 'bite' to the water for working to windward, while its short fore-and-aft length makes the boat quick on the helm and very handy to steer. A fin keel can be built up in wood with a cast iron or lead base for ballast, or it can be a steel plate with bulb-shaped cast ballast at its base. This latter type is known as a fin-and-bulb keel.

(2) The name of a flat-bottomed vessel used

extensively in north-eastern England for loading *colliers before modern mechanical methods of handling coal were introduced. They approximated very closely to the modern *lighter and have been immortalized in the song 'We'el may the keel row that my laddie's in', first published in *Tyneside Songs* in 1863.

KEEL BLOCKS, the line of blocks on the floor of a building slip on which the *keel of the ship to be constructed is laid. Also the line of blocks in a *dry-dock on which the ship rests when the dock is pumped dry.

KEEL-HAULING, a naval punishment on board ship said to have been invented by the Dutch, but introduced into other navies around the 15th and 16th centuries. A rope was rigged from *yardarm to yardarm passing under the bottom of the ship, and the unfortunate delinquent secured to it, sometimes with lead or iron weights attached to his legs. He was hoisted up to one yardarm and then dropped suddenly into the sea, hauled underneath the ship, and hoisted up to the opposite yardarm, the punishment being repeated after he had had time to recover his breath. While he was under water, a 'great gun' was fired, 'the which is done as well to astonish him so much the more with the thunder of the shot, as to give warning unto all others of the fleet to look out and to be wary by his harms' (Captain Nathaniel *Boteler, *A Dialogicall Discourse*, 1634). *Falconer (*Marine Dictionary*, 1711), apparently believing that the punishment was peculiar to the Dutch, was suitably ironic. 'In truth,' he wrote, 'a temporary insensibility to his sufferings ought by no means to be construed into a disrespect of his judges, when we consider that this punishment is supposed to have peculiar propriety in the depth of winter, while the flakes of ice are floating on the stream; and that it is continued until the culprit is almost suffocated for want of air, benumbed with the cold of the water, or stunned with the blows his head received by striking the ship's bottom.'

Keel-hauling went out of fashion in most navies at the beginning of the 18th century, being generally replaced with the more sinister *cat-o'-nine-tails. See also DUCKING AT THE YARDARM.

KEEL-RAKING, see DUCKING AT THE YARD-ARM, KEEL-HAULING.

KEEL-ROPE, another name for the *limber-rope which is threaded through the *limbers alongside the *keel of a vessel to clear the *bilges.

KEELSON or **KELSON,** an internal *keel in the form of a *stringer bolted on to the keel, to provide additional strength and to support the *floors.

KEITH, Lord, see ELPHINSTONE, George.

KELLETT, Sir HENRY (1806–75), British vice admiral, exemplified the part played by naval surveyors in the Chinese wars. In 1841 he was with Sir Edward *Belcher in the attacks on Canton and in 1843 was with Sir Richard *Collinson surveying the channel to Woosung, later leading the commander-in-chief's ship to Nanking. Previously, after joining the navy in 1822, Kellett had been on the west coast of Africa with the *Eden* under W. F. *Owen. In 1837 he sailed the *Starling*, a *cutter of 105 tons, round Cape Horn and surveyed the coast of some Pacific islands en route to China.

In February 1845 he had command of the *Herald* in the Pacific and made three voyages in 1848–9 to the Arctic regions through the Bering Strait in search of Sir John *Franklin. In 1851 he was given command of the *Resolute*, one of Belcher's squadron for the Arctic search which ended in the ships being abandoned in 1853, though their captains were exonerated.

Kellett's career continued as *commodore in command at Jamaica, superintendent of Malta Dockyard, and finally as commander-in-chief of the China station, 1868–72.

KELPIE, a sea spirit said to haunt the northern British Isles. Local mythology attributed several shapes to the kelpie, but it is mostly depicted as a horse. It was a malignant spirit whose chief delight was drowning seamen and travellers.

KELVIN, Lord, see THOMSON, William.

KEMP, DIXON (1839–99), British yachting journalist and designer, was born at Ryde, Isle of Wight, and was expected to follow his father's profession as an architect, but an early love for sailing boats in the Solent led him into reporting yacht races for the *Isle of Wight Observer*, and later to becoming its editor. In 1863 he was appointed editor of the yachting pages of the *Field* in London, and in 1875 he was one of the organizers of the Yacht Racing Association (later to become the *Royal Yachting Association). He learned the art of yacht designing by taking off the lines of every yacht for which he could obtain permission to do so, and studying all the plans closely. His first self-taught design was an 18-ft boat, *Boojum*, built in 1871, which had a long and useful life. He became a versatile designer, his creations ranging from highly successful lightweight up-river racing boats of the fin-keel, skimming-dish type to 30-tonners and fine cruising yachts. His books *Yacht Designing* (1876), *A Manual of Yacht and Boat Sailing* (1878), *Yacht Architecture*, and *An Exposition of Racing Rules* (1898) remained standard works of reference for many years.

KEMP, PETER (d. 1834), a British sealer in the service of Messrs. Daniel Bennett and Son of London who, while in command of the *snow *Magnet*, on 26 December 1833 discovered land in *latitude 66° 35′ S., *longitude 59° E., a part of the Antarctic continent now known as Kemp Land. On the return journey he fell overboard and was drowned.

KEMPENFELT, RICHARD (1718–82), British rear admiral, was a successful commander and a thoughtful student of war. His family was Swedish but his father, the original of Captain Sentry in the *Coverley Papers*, spent his life in British military service. Richard Kempenfelt's experience was wide but his rise in the navy was slow. He served under Admiral *Vernon at the capture of *Porto Bello in 1739. Much later, he served in the Far East, being flag-captain to Admiral Cornish when he captured Manila at the end of the Seven Years War (1756–63).

Kempenfelt had to wait until he was nearing 60 before he received his flag. During the War of American Independence (1775–82) he made himself invaluable as chief-of-staff to Sir Charles Hardy, Sir Francis *Geary, and George Darby, who were given charge of the Home Fleet at a time when few officers of first-rate ability were willing to serve an unpopular administration.

His own great chance came in 1781 when, flying his flag in the *Victory*, he snapped up a French convoy, destined for America, under the nose of a superior escort under Admiral de *Guichen. It was his last opportunity of service. In the summer of 1782 he was to have taken part in the operations under Lord *Howe which were to relieve Gibraltar. His flag was then flying in the *Royal George*, which had been Sir Edward *Hawke's flagship at the victory of *Quiberon Bay in 1759. While undergoing a temporary repair at Spithead which involved heeling the ship over on her side, she flooded through her gunports. Part of her structure collapsed and she turned right over, taking Kempenfelt and many of her company with her to the bottom.

Kempenfelt was a scientific officer far in advance of his time, who had studied the leading writers on naval affairs, many of whom were French (see, e.g., HOSTE, Paul). They also included *Bigot de Morogues, an expert on tactics, M. de la Bourdonnais, who wrote on signals and whom Kempenfelt credited as the real inventor of the numerical code which he recommended, and Bourde de Villehuet, part of whose work he translated for the benefit of Sir Charles *Middleton, later Lord Barham, who was then Comptroller of the Navy. Kempenfelt was fortunate enough to engage the interest of Lord Howe in an improvement of the signal code and was responsible for many important innovations, and the subjects of his letters to Middleton (published in the *Barham Papers*, N.R.S., 1906, 1909, 1910) range over strategy, gunnery, the proper use of various types of vessel, fleet dispositions, tactical principles, health, and, above all, internal discipline. These reasoned letters show him to have been one of the most prescient officers in the entire history of the Royal Navy. Kempenfelt advocated, in particular, the system of *divisions by which officers were to be directly responsible for the discipline and welfare of their men. It is typical of his whole attitude to his profession that a portrait of him by Tilly Kettle (1735–86) shows him holding an octagonal telescope of an improved kind.

Kempenfelt was deeply religious, belonging to the 'evangelical' school of which Middleton, *Gambier, and others were members. He wrote some remarkable verse, published under the pseudonym of 'Philotheorus' in 1777. His tragic death in the loss of a famous vessel inspired the poem 'Toll for the Brave' by William Cowper, more notable for feeling than for sense.

KENNEDY, WILLIAM (1813–90), British pioneer, joined the Hudson's Bay Company as a young man, serving eight years in Labrador before resigning his post in 1851 to assist with the search for the Sir John *Franklin expedition. He was given command of the 90-ton vessel *Prince Albert* which had been chartered by Lady Franklin and his second-in-command was Lieutenant Joseph *Bellot of the French Navy, who had volunteered his services. Although no trace of Franklin was found, Kennedy and Bellot discovered the narrow channel which separates Somerset Island from the Boothia peninsula and which was named Bellot Strait. Kennedy returned to England in 1852 and subsequently settled in Canada.

KENNET, see KEVEL.

KENTISH KNOCK, The, a naval battle of the First Anglo-Dutch War (1652–4), was fought near the sandbank of that name in the southern North Sea on 28 September 1652, when an English fleet of sixty-eight ships commanded by Robert *Blake defeated a Dutch fleet of fifty-nine ships under Vice Admiral Witte Corneliszoon de *With. The Dutch were sighted about noon, 18 miles to the eastward of the North *Foreland, but action was not joined until about 5 p.m., when Blake and his vice admiral, William *Penn, engaged with the *van and centre divisions, followed shortly by the rear division. Darkness put an end to the conflict. Two Dutch ships were captured and many others were badly damaged with great loss of men. The English loss was very small.

KENTLEDGE, the pigs of iron cast as *ballast and laid over the *keelson plates to provide additional stability to a vessel. If they are laid in the *limbers, they are known as limber-kentledge. Following this reasoning, heavy items of cargo stowed low in the *holds of a ship as an addition to ballasting during a voyage are sometimes known as kentledge-goods.

KEPPEL, AUGUSTUS, 1st Viscount Keppel (1725–86), British admiral, joined the navy at the age of ten, and five years later distinguished himself during Commodore *Anson's round-the-world voyage in the *Centurion, being promoted lieutenant. When only 24, he commanded a small naval squadron sent into the Mediterranean to discipline the piratical Dey of Algiers, whose ships had been preying on British merchant shipping. During the Seven Years War (1756–63) Keppel commanded the 74-gun *ship of the line Torbay and took a gallant part in Sir Edward *Hawke's great victory in *Quiberon Bay in 1759. He was then given command of an expedition to capture the heavily fortified island of Belleisle in the Bay of Biscay, in which he was brilliantly successful. He was rewarded with an appointment as second-in-command to Sir George Pocock of the naval element of the expedition to capture Havana in 1762, receiving on its successful conclusion his rear admiral's flag and *prize money of nearly £25,000.

On the outbreak of the War of American Independence (1775–82) Keppel, as a committed Whig politician and like others of his persuasion, refused to serve at sea in what he considered an unjust war, but when France came into the war he was offered and accepted the command of the Channel Fleet. On 27 July 1778, during the indecisive second battle of *Ushant, he was poorly supported by his second-in-command, Sir Hugh *Palliser, who was a convinced Tory; and though Keppel made no accusations the story reached the newspapers, drawing contentious accusations of Keppel's misconduct from Palliser in reply. Both admirals were tried by court martial and both were acquitted, but while Keppel's reputation was enhanced, the court martial added a censure to Palliser's acquittal.

On the fall of Lord North's Tory government in 1782, Keppel became First Lord of the Admiralty and was raised to the peerage. He retired from office at the end of the war.

KERGUELEN-TREMAREC, YVES JOSEPH DE (fl. 1771–4), French navigator, was a nobleman at the French court and by instruction of the king was placed in command of an expedition to discover *Terra Australis Incognita and to enter into commercial relations with its inhabitants. Rounding the Cape of Good Hope at the end of 1771 and standing to the southward to reach the fabled continent, he discovered and took possession of a group of desolate and sub-Antarctic islands in February 1772 to which he gave the name Îles de Kerguelen. Thinking that these might be outlying islands of the continent he continued the search but was unable with his ships to penetrate the ice barrier. He returned to the Kerguelen islands in a second voyage in 1774 and came to the conclusion that they could not possibly form any part of any southern continent, and in fact that the existence of this continent, so confidently displayed in contemporary maps of the world, was unlikely.

KERHALLET, CHARLES MARIE DE (1809–63), French naval hydrographer, was born at Rennes, entered the navy in 1825, and took part in campaigns in the West Indies and off Brazil. He specialized in hydrography and in 1846 was attached to the chart section of the Ministry of Marine. After surveying off the coast of Senegal he published a manual of navigation of the west coast of Africa and this was followed by other publications of a similar nature. Promoted to captain in 1854, he was again employed on survey work in the vicinity of Gibraltar and on his return to the Hydrographic Department of the Ministry of Marine he published a similar description of the coast of Morocco. His work is considered as a model of clarity and accuracy in the hydrographic field.

KERSAINT, ARMAND GUY SIMON DE COETNEMPREN, Comte de (1742–93), French admiral, served with distinction in the Seven Years War (1756–63), and had reached the rank of captain by 1782. At that time the officers of the French Navy were divided into two parties, the 'reds', or those of noble birth, and the 'blues', those of plebeian origin. Although by birth a red, Kersaint's sympathies lay with the blues, and he made no secret of his support for their principles. On the eve of the French Revolution he submitted a scheme for the reorganization of the navy on republican lines, and after he had been elected to the Constituent Assembly, worked consistently for his scheme.

Realizing that such reform was impossible until the power of the monarchy in making naval appointments had been curbed, he voted in 1792 in favour of the deposition of Louis XVI. Still with the object of furthering his schemes of naval reform, he succeeded in getting accepted the formation of a committee of defence, which later developed into the notorious Committee of Public Safety. He was promoted vice admiral at the beginning of 1793, but although he went a long way in his sympathy with the new revolutionary ideas in France, he would not vote in favour of the execution of Louis XVI, and later denounced the September massacres. He

The ketch H. F. Bolt *built at Bideford in 1876*

was arrested, taken before the Revolutionary Tribunal for trial, and sentenced to death. He perished on the guillotine.

KETCH, a sailing vessel with two masts, the recognized description being that the *mizen is stepped before the rudder-head, while in a *yawl it is stepped abaft it. This, however, is not an exact definition, the true difference between the two rigs depending more on the size of the mizen-sail; if the difference depended on the position of the mizen-mast, most of the yawl-rigged beach boats, including the well-known Norfolk yawls, would be ketches. The original name in England was 'catch', but although this suggests that they were used primarily for fishing, their main use was in fact as small coastal trading vessels. Suggestions have also been made that the name indicated vessels used to chase or pursue others in time of war, but this appears to be negatived by a description by Glanville in 1625 that 'catches, being short and round built, be very apt to turn up and down, and useful to go to and fro, and to carry messages between ship and shore almost with any wind'. They were small vessels, originally of 50 tons or less, but they roughly doubled in size during the reign of Charles II (1660–85), who used the ketch design for his royal yachts. They were square-rigged

on both masts to the full ship rig, and were often described as 'a ship without a foremast', the reference being to sail rig and not to the vessel as a type.

Large numbers of small ketches were built by the English, French, and Dutch navies during the wars of the late 17th and early 18th centuries to act as tenders to the fleets, and the design was also adopted by the English to serve as *bomb vessels, the large open space forward of the mainmast being ideal for the accommodation of a large mortar, by which the bombs were fired. For this particular use the size of the average ketch was increased through adding to her length, and as a result they became fast and weatherly, and a new use for them was developed as *packet vessels. From the ketch rig was also developed the *hooker and the *dogger.

With the wide naval use of bomb vessels dying out in the mid-19th century, the naval value of the ketch diminished and it largely resumed its original use as a coastal trading vessel until, with the growing popularity of *yachting during the 19th century, the advantages of the rig again became apparent. The substitution of *fore-and-aft rig for the older square rig during the 19th century enhanced their weatherliness and greatly increased their popularity among yachtsmen. See also DANDY-RIG.

KEVEL, sometimes known as **KENNET,** a large *cleat formed of two upright pieces of wood usually fitted on the *gunwale of a sailing vessel and used for *belaying ropes. Kevel-heads are the ends of a vessel's top *timbers projected beyond the level of the gunwale and similarly used for belaying ropes.

KEY or **CAY,** from the Spanish *cayos*, rocks, a small islet in the West Indies covered with scrub or sparse vegetation. The name was introduced into the English language by the *buccaneers who infested that area of the sea in the late 17th and early 18th centuries. They are sometimes coral formations, sometimes outcrops of sand and rock.

KEYES, ROGER JOHN BROWNLOW, first Baron Keyes of Zeebrugge (1872–1945), British admiral of the fleet, entered H.M.S. *Britannia* as a cadet in 1885 where he had an undistinguished career before passing out in 1887 and going to sea as a *midshipman in the full-rigged steam *frigate *Raleigh*, flagship on the Cape station, returning home in 1890. He remained academically unremarkable, his talents lying rather in the realm of action and sport, particularly any form of horsemanship. In command of the *destroyer *Fame* on the China station during 1900 he had his first opportunity to display his qualities of personal daring. During the operations connected with the Boxer Rising he captured four Chinese destroyers at Tongku by boarding and, at the head of a landing party, secured the key fort on the river route to Tientsin. Chafing at inaction after these exploits, he contrived to have himself appointed *aide-de-camp* to the general commanding the British relief column for the Peking Legation, in which expedition he played a dashing part. He incurred the strong disapproval of his commander-in-chief for thus abandoning his command, but succeeded in overcoming it by a personal confrontation and, at the end of 1900, was promoted commander.

After further service in destroyers and two years as naval attaché in Rome, Keyes became the youngest captain in the navy in 1904 at the age of 32. The next landmark in his career was his appointment in 1910 to be Inspecting Captain of Submarines—head of the *submarine service—in which capacity, serving in the rank of *commodore, he found himself senior naval officer at Harwich at the beginning of the First World War (1914–18). His thirst for offensive action led him to propose and plan the successful *Heligoland Bight operation in August 1914 as a result of which three German *cruisers and a destroyer were sunk and three other cruisers damaged. In January 1915 Keyes was appointed chief-of-staff to Admiral Carden, and later to his successor Vice Admiral de *Robeck, in command of the *Dardanelles operations. He took a highly personal part in the naval attempts to force the Straits and continued to believe in its feasibility even after the initial failures and eventual abandonment.

In January 1918, with the rank of vice admiral, he superseded Vice Admiral Sir Reginald *Bacon in command of the Dover Patrol to implement the plan he had prepared for the blocking of *Zeebrugge and Ostend, exit ports for German *U-boats. This was carried out with great heroism, but without any success, on 23 April 1918. Among the numerous awards was a knighthood of the Bath for Keyes. At the end of the war he was made a baronet. In 1921 Keyes served in the Admiralty as deputy chief of naval staff; in 1925 was appointed commander-in-chief in the Mediterranean, and in 1929 became commander-in-chief at Portsmouth. He was raised to the rank of admiral of the fleet in 1930 and hauled down his flag in January 1931. In a by-election in February 1934 he was elected Member of Parliament for North Portsmouth, a seat he was to hold for the next nine years. At the outbreak of the Second World War, Keyes pressed to be given active employment. Unsuccessful at first in this, he used his intimacy with the First Sea Lord and Winston *Churchill to urge more offensive action in the Norwegian campaign and, in particular, a direct assault, using the Home Fleet, on Trondheim. This was officially judged unrealistic in the face of German air power and his persuasions failed.

In the political crisis which led to Mr. Chamberlain's resignation as Prime Minister Keyes, arrayed in naval uniform, delivered a notable speech in the House of Commons. In July 1940 the new Prime Minister, Churchill, found a suitable outlet for Keyes's martial spirit as director of combined operations. In this post he predictably proved an awkward subordinate to the Chiefs-of-Staff, especially in his urging of operations such as an attack on the Mediterranean island of Pantellaria which, like the earlier Trondheim scheme, was judged unrealistic. In October 1941 he was superseded by Lord Louis *Mountbatten. He returned to the House of Commons where he was active until January 1943 when he was created Baron Keyes of Zeebrugge and of Dover. His final service to the country was a goodwill mission to Australasia and the South-West Pacific in 1944. His papers, edited by Paul Halpern, are published by the *Navy Records Society, Vol. I in 1972, Vol. II still to appear. He wrote his memoirs (*The Naval Memoirs of Admiral of the Fleet Sir Roger Keyes*) in two volumes (1934–5). For a biography see C. F. Aspinall-Oglander, *Roger Keyes* (1951).

KHAIR-ED-DIN, see BARBAROSSA.

KHAMSIN or **KAMSIN,** a hot wind, usually from the south-west, which blows over Egypt and the eastern Mediterranean Sea, normally only in the months of March and April. It is a source of much discomfort, very similar to the *sirocco of the central Mediterranean. When blowing strongly it causes sandstorms, sometimes far out at sea. There is an ancient Arab saying, 'When the Khamsin has blown for three days a man is justified in killing his wife.'

KHIZR, the East Indian deity of the sea. Until quite recently he was propitiated in many small coastal communities by the burning of small wooden boats known as *beera*, either annually as a festival or before the start of long voyages.

KICKING-STRAP, the name usually given by helmsmen of racing *dinghies and yachts to the *martingale which prevents the *boom of the mainsail from rising when it swings outwards, thus presenting a flatter sail to the wind and increasing its driving power.

KIDD or **KID,** Captain WILLIAM (*c.* 1645–1701), English pirate, began his life at sea as a merchant seaman. Little is known of his early life, but if the many stories of his pirate treasure are true, he may have taken to *piracy before he received a commission in 1696 from the newly appointed colonial governor at Boston, Lord Bellomont, to apprehend pirates. He was placed in command of the *galley *Adventure* for the purpose. Maybe the temptations of his former activities were too strong, or the policy of setting a thief to catch a thief did not work, but when he returned to Boston in 1699 after a cruise in the Indian Ocean, he was arrested and sent to England to stand trial for piracy for his capture of the *Quedagh Merchant*, owned by the Great Mogul, and for the murder of his gunner, William Moore. Kidd claimed that he was entitled to take the *prize and that Moore's death was accidental when he knocked him down with a bucket for mutiny.

It seems certain that Lord Bellomont, who may have changed his original opinion about him, suppressed certain vital evidence in Kidd's favour, and as a result he was convicted and hanged at *Execution Dock, London, in 1701 and his effects, valued at £6,472, were given by Queen Anne to *Greenwich Hospital. Part of the money was used to purchase the property which is now the *National Maritime Museum. Kidd certainly buried other treasure when operating as a pirate in the West Indies and many later expeditions have been mounted in search of 'Kidd's treasure', though with little success. Some £14,000 of his treasure was reputedly found on Gardiner's Island, off the eastern end of Long Island, U.S.A., during the 19th century.

KIEL, the chief naval port of West Germany in the Baltic, lying at the head of the Kiel Fjord. It is one of the oldest seaports in Germany, being mentioned as early as the 10th century as a safe haven for ships. In 1284 it entered the *Hanseatic League, becoming prosperous through the growing trade which was handled during the great years of the League. In 1773 Kiel became a part of Denmark, but was ceded to Prussia with the rest of Schleswig-Holstein after the war of 1866. It has a magnificent harbour some 11 miles in length with an average depth of water of 40 feet. The great naval dockyard there was constructed in the early years of the 20th century to accommodate the large fleet built by Wilhelm II before the First World War (1914–18), and at Kiel, too, are the great shipbuilding firms of Germania and Howaldt. The naval academy and various naval specialist schools are all at Kiel. At Wik, $1\frac{1}{2}$ miles north of Kiel, is the eastern entrance of the Kaiser Wilhelm or *Kiel Canal.

KIEL CANAL, a ship canal across the isthmus of Schleswig-Holstein built in the early years of the 20th century to link the Baltic and North Seas. Known as the Kaiser Wilhelm Canal, its building was a strategic move by the German Emperor to link the principal German naval bases of *Kiel in the Baltic Sea and Wilhelmshaven in the North Sea, and it was constructed to take the largest *battleships then in existence. The design and launching in 1906 of the British *Dreadnought*, the first all-big-gun battleship in the world, cut across the strategic purpose of the canal, since all navies, including that of Germany, were forced to follow suit and build the new type, and the Kiel Canal had not been constructed wide enough to take these new ships. Work was then started on widening the canal to a width able to take the largest ships then envisaged, a task which was completed in 1914 on the eve of the First World War (1914–18). The Baltic entrance to the canal is at Wik, one and a half miles north of Kiel; the North Sea entrance is at *Brunsbüttel.

KILLICK or **KILLOCK,** (1) the name originally used to describe a small *anchor, or more usually a large stone at the end of a rope used as an anchor, carried by small craft. It lost its meaning in this sense when anchors were developed with *stocks to turn them over on the ground so that the *flukes would bite. Nevertheless, the word is still frequently used at sea by sailors as a slang term for anchor, no matter how large. (2) The seaman's name in the British Navy for the *rating of leading seaman, of which the badge is a *foul anchor sewn on the sleeve of the jumper. The foul anchor is the official seal of the *Lord High Admiral.

KIMMEL, HUSBAND EDWARD (1882–1968), American admiral, was commander-in-chief of the Pacific Fleet at *Pearl Harbor, Hawaii, at the time of the Japanese surprise attack on 7 December 1941 which brought the U.S.A. into the Second World War. He was born in Kentucky, graduated from the Naval Academy in 1904, and was gunnery officer on the staff of Admiral Rodman in 1917–18 with the *battleship division which served with the British *Grand Fleet at the end of the First World War (1914–18). After two years in command of a *cruiser division, as a rear admiral, he became commander-in-chief of the Pacific Fleet, with the rank of admiral, on 1 February 1941.

Although he was never officially charged with permitting the fleet to be surprised by the attack, and never brought to trial by a court martial, various newspapers and individuals worked hard to convince the American public that he was culpable in the matter. He was relieved of his command on 17 December 1941 and retired at his own request in March 1942. It appears that there was some prior warning of a possible Japanese attack through Intelligence sources, and a *radar interception of the attacking aircraft while they were still some way out to sea failed to get through to the authorities.

KING, CECIL GEORGE CHARLES (1881–1942), British marine painter and author, was a founder member of the Royal Society of Marine Artists, of which later he was a vice-president. He studied art in Paris, subsequently becoming interested in maritime affairs, and in 1914 he published his *History of British Flags*, a subject on which he became an acknowledged expert. During naval operations in the Baltic in 1918–19 he accompanied the British squadron and made numerous sketches of its activities there which are now in the *Imperial War Museum. The *Royal Thames Yacht Club appointed him its marine painter in 1932. He was a prolific illustrator of maritime books, in which his great knowledge of ships and of their construction and fittings stood him in good stead, and his mastery of detail was impressive. He also wrote three books all published between 1940 and 1943, the last posthumously.

KING, ERNEST JOSEPH (1878–1956), American fleet admiral, served first as commander-in-chief of the U.S. Atlantic Fleet and later as Chief of Naval Operations during the Second World War from 1941 to 1945. He was born in Lorain, Ohio, and graduated from the Naval Academy in 1901, serving in *destroyers, *submarines, *cruisers, and *battleships before taking flight training in 1927. He commanded the *aircraft carrier *Lexington*, 1930–2, completed the senior course at the Naval War College in April 1933, and then became Chief of the Bureau of Aeronautics in the Navy Department, as a rear admiral, holding that appointment until 1936. As a vice admiral he was Commander Aircraft, Battle Force, 1938–9, and in February 1941 took command of the Atlantic Fleet with the rank of admiral, at the end of that year moving up to the top naval command.

King was never popular with his fellow officers, but he had the respect of almost all, and he was never a 'yes man'. After the surprise at *Pearl Harbor, in December 1941, King recognized and resented the fact that reports from Washington were so managed as to lead the public to believe that the navy was responsible. Throughout the war he presented the facts as he saw them without distortion or exaggeration, and all his proposals for war plans were based on carefully considered naval strategy. In conversation with fellow officers he was usually frank, but not always tactful. A book, *Fleet Admiral King: A Naval Record* (1953), was written in the third person with the assistance of Walter Muir Whitehill, and it is an accurate exposition of the thoughts and opinions of King himself. Fellow naval officers believe that the book is objective in presenting the naval operations of the war, including the actions of King, but some readers regret that many important political decisions are passed over in silence even though some of them had an unfortunate effect on the conduct of the war and the postwar world.

Naval opinion generally agreed that King's wartime services were truly outstanding. He was the second of three officers advanced to the newly created rank of fleet admiral, U.S.N., in December 1944. The others were William D. *Leahy and Chester W. *Nimitz.

KING, PHILIP PARKER (1793–1856), British rear admiral, was born at Norfolk Island when his father was Governor of New South Wales. Having joined the navy in 1807, King's service was largely in the Mediterranean, but it was on the north and west coasts of Australia that he made his significant hydrographic contributions. There he made four voyages between 1817 and 1822 in continuation of Matthew *Flinders's discoveries, and among his more important surveys was that of Port Essington. He sailed in the cutter *Mermaid* and later the sloop *Bathurst*, extending his voyages briefly to Bass Strait and Tasmania to measure meridian distances.

He was then given command of the *Adventure*, accompanied by the *Beagle* (P. Stokes), for five years surveying in the Magellan Strait and this strenuous appointment was his last active one. His compilation on the geography of the extremity of southern America was read at the Royal Geographical Society in 1831. He was a Fellow of the Royal Society.

KING SPOKE, that spoke of the hand steering-wheel in a ship which is uppermost when the helm is amidships. It is often marked with a ring carved on it or by a *turk's head knot fixed round the spoke.

KINGSTON, WILLIAM HENRY GILES (1814–80), British author of books about the sea, spent most of his youth in Oporto where his father was a merchant. He went to sea on many voyages in his father's ships while still a boy, a fact which gave him not only an acute knowledge of the ways of a ship but also a deep sympathy with and understanding of seafaring men. As he grew up he became a man of parts and negotiated a commercial understanding with Portuguese traders which brought him a Portuguese knighthood.

He came to England when he was 36 and began to write stories of the sea for boys. His first book, *Peter the Whaler* (1851), was a great success and he wrote many more in the same vein, the best known being *The Three Midshipmen* (1862), *The Three Lieutenants* (1871), *The Three Commanders* (1875), and *The Three Admirals* (1877). All of them sold widely and were reprinted many times.

KINKAID, THOMAS CASSIN (1888–1972), American admiral, distinguished himself in a number of engagements in the Pacific during the Second World War; notably in battles around the Solomon Islands and the Santa Cruz Islands, in the battle of the *Coral Sea, the battle of *Santa Cruz, and a naval action south of *Guadalcanal, all fought during 1942. He commanded the campaign in the Aleutian Islands early in 1943 and in November of that year was appointed to command the Seventh Fleet in the south-west Pacific area. He commanded the naval forces which entered *Leyte Gulf and landed American troops in the Philippines.

KINGPOST, a short mast close to the cargo *hatches of merchant ships from which is worked the smaller cargo *derrick. Kingposts are used for loading and unloading cargoes into *lighters where normal port cranes are not available or there is no room for the ship to lie alongside a loading or unloading berth in a port.

KING'S LETTER BOY, the usual description in the British Navy given to the *rating of 'volunteer-per-order', a method of entry into the Royal Navy of 'young gentlemen' destined to become officers. The rating was introduced by Samuel *Pepys in 1676 and the recipient received a letter from the Crown which virtually guaranteed him promotion to commissioned rank after the specified training and passing the examination for lieutenant. The last of the King's Letter Boys

to enter the navy was George Brydges *Rodney in 1732, who as Lord Rodney was one of the great names in British naval history. King's Letter Boys were paid at the rate of £24 per annum. The purpose of this particular rating, as expressed in the letter from the Crown, was 'our Royal desire of giving encouragement to the families of better quality among our subjects to breed up their younger sons to the art and practice of navigation . . .'

Similar entry into the navy after the end of the King's Letter Boys was as *captain's servant, a fiction under which *post-captains were allowed so many 'servants' who were, in fact, young protégés to be trained for higher rank. This in its turn was followed by a system of nomination by admirals and the First Lord of the Admiralty, which finally gave way to entry by competitive examination.

KIPLING, JOSEPH RUDYARD (1865–1936), British author and poet, was born in Bombay, and after education at United Services College, Westward Ho!, Devon, returned to India where he worked as a journalist in 1882–3. Besides his many stories and poems with an Indian or army background, he wrote several books and poems in which the sea has a prominent place. In his second book of verse, *Barrack Room Ballads* (1892), there are three nautical poems and in *The Seven Seas* (1896) he has a great deal to say

An illustration from the first edition of Captains Courageous

about the sea, the collection including the well-known 'Anchor Song' and 'The Merchantman'. The following year his first wholly sea story, *Captains Courageous*, appeared, a stirring tale of the life of the fishermen of the *Grand Banks off Newfoundland. In 1898, being a guest in the Channel Fleet, he wrote *A Fleet in Being*, and in a collection of stories published under the title of *The Day's Work* (1898) three nautical ones are included, 'The Ship that found Herself', 'The Devil and the Deep Sea', and 'Bread upon the Waters'. In another book of verse, *The Five Nations* (1903), are five more sea poems, while in *Traffics and Discoveries* (1904) stories of sailors predominate. During the First World War (1914–18) he made good use of his descriptive powers and his *Fringes of the Fleet* (1915) and *Sea Warfare* (1916) not only caught the popular mood but were effective in bringing to the public notice the work of the Royal and merchant navies. Although he continued to write until a few years before his death in 1936, the flame of patriotism burned perhaps a little less brightly, but he is still remembered as 'the most patriotic, virile, and imaginative of writers'.

KITCHEN RUDDER, see RUDDER.

KITE, a fitting attached to a *hawser or wire which is being towed by a vessel, designed to hold it at a certain depth beneath the surface of the sea. It works on exactly the same principle as an *otter (illustrated), though in the vertical plane as opposed to the otter's horizontal plane. It consists of an inclined surface attached to the hawser or wire, the pressure of the water upon it as it is being towed forcing it down beneath the surface. The required depth is arranged by varying the distance from the point of tow at which it is attached to the hawser. It is used particularly in certain minesweeping techniques. See, e.g., OROPESA SWEEP.

KITES, a general name used to describe the additional light sails spread in a square-rigged ship to make the most of light following winds. Originally they included all sails set above the topsails but as the square rig was extended in the 18th and 19th centuries, and the *topgallant sail became standard, the term referred only to sails set above that sail, but included *studding-sails and jib-topsails.

KLIPPER, a larger type of Dutch cargo carrier or *barge, about 65 to 80 feet (20–24·5 m) in length, steel built with *leeboards and normally *ketch rigged when used under sail. These barges are recognizable by the upright stem curved at the top into a form of *clipper bow and a round *counter stern. Almost all klippers are today diesel driven with only a *derrick mast.

KNEE, a timber or metal bar fashioned into a right-angle to provide strengthening and support at the points of intersection of ship's *timbers in a wooden ship. They are of various kinds, such as a hanging knee, which fits vertically under a deck *beam and supports its ends; a lodging knee, which is fixed horizontally between the forward side of a beam and the ship's side; a bosom knee, which performs the same purpose on the after side of a beam; and a *carling knee, which strengthens the right-angle between a carling and a beam. Knees of ships' boats, which support the *thwarts, or in small sailing craft, which support the deck beams, are preferably fashioned from naturally grown timber in which the grain of the wood follows the right-angle round. Trees used to be artificially bent during growth to provide knee-timber for shipbuilding.

KNELL, WILLIAM ADOLPHUS (1805–75), British marine painter, was the senior and best known of three British marine painters of that name. He painted a number of battle scenes of great merit, of which his picture of Sir John *Jervis's action off *Cape St. Vincent is perhaps the best known. He was commissioned by Queen Victoria to record in painting the arrival of Prince Albert at Dover before his marriage to the queen and also the royal review of the British fleet at Spithead in 1853. But the pictures for which he is best remembered are of the North Sea coasts, painted with a lively feeling for the restless movement of the sea in tidal waters.

KNIGHT, EDWARD FREDERICK (1852–1925), British yachtsman and author, was born in Cumberland and brought up in France where his father, a retired army officer, lived. Fluent in French, he tried to enlist in 1870 to fight in the Franco-Prussian War but was rejected because of his nationality. Undeterred, he marched with French troops into the Sahara, and when exploring the desert on his own was arrested as a spy. Returning to England he went to Cambridge where he read law, and during vacations, spent again in France, he learned to sail a small boat on the River Seine from which he developed a love for ships and the sea. Although called to the Bar he never practised, his restless energy leading him into more exciting schemes. When his father died he inherited some money which made him partly independent and enabled him to buy his first cruising yacht, the *Ripple*, a 6-ton *yawl. With this boat he learned the art of single-handed cruising and small boat navigation during cruises in the English Channel and along the Normandy and Brittany coasts.

At the age of 28, with a partner, he bought a 28-ton yawl, named *Falcon*, and with two other amateur sailors and a ship's boy sailed to the

Amazon and spent almost two years exploring the South American rivers and coastline. His book on the venture, *Cruise of the Falcon* (1884), proved an immediate success and its royalties encouraged him to travel widely and record his adventures as a writer.

In 1887 he bought an old ship's lifeboat, had her converted at a Thames-side boatyard, and named her also *Falcon*. With only a young lad as crew he sailed her to Copenhagen by way of Harwich, Rotterdam, the Zuider Zee, the East Frisian Islands, Töning, and the Schleswig-Holstein Canal (the *Kiel Canal having not yet been built), bringing her back to the Thames the following year. The resulting book, *The Falcon in the Baltic* (1888), was to become a favourite book of reference for generations of amateur cruising yachtsmen.

Fired by a belief in a hidden treasure in Trinidad, he joined a syndicate of nine adventurers with a paid crew aboard the 56-ton yawl *Alerte* in 1888. He returned empty-handed, but with material for another adventure book, *Cruise of the 'Alerte'*, which again became popular reading. He became a war correspondent for *The Times* and later for the *Morning Post*, reporting many wars, civil wars, and revolts all over the world. Of his two books on sailing for the beginner, *Small Boat Sailing* proved the best known and many yachtsmen owed their introduction to sailing to its pages.

KNIGHTHEADS, the name given to two large timbers, one on each side of the *stem of a wooden ship, which rose above the deck and supported the heel of the *bowsprit between them. In older wooden merchant ships, the name was also frequently given to the two timber *frames abaft the foremast which supported the ends of the *windlasses. In some smaller vessels the knightheads of the bowsprit were also called *bitts, as with no space for separate bitts to be fixed to the deck, the anchor cable was brought to the knightheads for bitting.

KNOCK DOWN, to, the operation of knocking off the hoops of a cask when it is empty and gathering up the *staves for stowage until it is required to remake the cask. In the days of sailing ships, casks were a very important part of their equipment, as most food for the voyage and all drinking water were carried in them. All ships of any size in those days carried a cooper on board whose duty it was to maintain the casks in good condition, making new ones to replace any that had been *staved accidentally and retaining for future use all parts of casks which had been knocked down.

The term is also used to describe, in yachting, the action of a small vessel which is rolled over with her mast(s) and sails in the water by a sea breaking over her or by a violent squall.

KNORR, the name of the old Norse merchant ship of the time of the Vikings. It was modelled on the traditional *longship, with one mast and a single square sail set on a yard. When working to windward a *luff spar, known as a *beitass*, was fitted to hold the luff of the sail taut.

A knorr recently excavated from Roskilde Fjord, Denmark

KNOT, (1) the nautical measure of speed, one knot being a speed of one *nautical mile (6,080 feet) per hour. The term comes from the knots on the line of a chip *log which were spaced at a distance of 47 feet 3 inches. The number of these knots which ran out while a 28-second *sandglass emptied itself gave the speed of the ship in nautical miles per hour. As a measure of speed the term is always knots, and never knots an hour. **(2)** It is also a generally used term to describe a *bend or *hitch in ropes, but in its strict maritime sense only refers to a tucking knot in which the strands of a rope are tucked over and under each other to form a *stopper knot, or a knob or enlargement of the rope, such as a manrope knot, a Matthew Walker, a turk's head, etc., or a *splice, such as a long, short, back, or eye splice. In more general terms, a knot is meant to be permanent, a bend or hitch temporary. The term is very rarely used in this strict definition today and is widely employed to embrace every form of knot, bend, or hitch.

C. W. Ashley, *The Ashley Book of Knots* (1944); *Admiralty Manual of Seamanship*, Vol I (1972); G. R. Shaw, *Knots Useful and Ornamental* (1973).

KNOWLES, Sir CHARLES (*c.* 1704–77), British admiral, commanded the *frigate *Diamond* and was with Admiral *Vernon at the attack on Cartagena in 1741. He was promoted rear admiral in 1747, made commander-in-chief at Jamaica, and in October 1748 fell in with a Spanish *squadron of similar force to his own, but the subsequent action was badly mismanaged. Knowles was brought home to face a court martial and was reprimanded for the poor tactics he employed on that occasion. He was made governor of Jamaica in 1752 and on the outbreak of the Seven Years War (1756–63) returned to England, was promoted vice admiral, and was second-in-command to Sir Edward *Hawke at the abortive expedition against Rochefort. Public indignation at the failure of this expedition caused him to strike his flag, and though he was promoted admiral in 1758 he never served again at sea. In 1770 he resigned from the navy to accept a command under Catherine of Russia in the war against Turkey.

His son, Sir CHARLES HENRY Knowles (1754–1828), also an admiral, was born at Kingston, Jamaica, and served as a lieutenant and captain in the War of American Independence (1775–82). He commanded the *Porcupine* in the Mediterranean with considerable skill and success, and during the Revolutionary War with France (1793–1801) was again in the Mediterranean with Sir John *Jervis. He commanded the *Goliath* at the battle of *Cape St. Vincent, but this was his last service at sea though he was promoted to rear admiral, vice admiral, and admiral when his seniority brought

him to the head of the lists of captains, rear admirals, and vice admirals respectively.

Knowles was a man with a scientific mind, and he made many valuable suggestions for improving the art of naval signalling, many of them adopted by Lord *Howe in his signal reforms. He also wrote valuable treatises on the internal discipline in ships, shipbuilding, cordage, and *tonnage of ships.

KNOX, DUDLEY WRIGHT (1877–1960), American naval officer, served on the staff of Admiral W. S. *Sims in London during the First World War (1914–18), and earned an excellent reputation as a historian during the period when he headed the historical division in the Navy Department in Washington from 1921 to 1946. He graduated from the Naval Academy in 1896 and had an outstanding record in all duty assignments at sea. Knox was one of the officers who advocated the development of carefully considered tactical and strategical doctrines for each type of warship, and for effective naval planning and operations. His outstanding abilities were recognized, and when he was retired for physical disability (deafness), he was assigned to the history division as a retired officer on active duty. In addition to many published articles on naval and maritime questions, he was the author of *A History of the United States Navy* (New York, 1936) with a revised edition in 1948 which covered the Second World War.

KNOX-JOHNSTON, ROBIN (1939–), British master mariner, won the *Sunday Times* Golden Globe when his *ketch yacht *Suhaili* was the only boat of seven starters to finish the solo non-stop voyage round the world in 1968–9. The race was from Falmouth, England, back to Falmouth, eastabout by way of the Cape of Good Hope, New Zealand, and Cape Horn: Knox-Johnston covered the distance of 30,123 miles in 313 days. *Suhaili* was built in Bombay in 1964 with her owner taking part in her construction.

KOCHAB, or β Ursae Minoris, a star used by navigators from 1500 B.C. to about 300 A.D. as the Pole Star. See also POLARIS.

KOLOMBANGARA, BATTLE OF, a night action fought in the Pacific in 1943 during the Second World War between a force of American cruisers and destroyers which included one cruiser of the Royal New Zealand Navy, and a similar Japanese force. The action was brought about by the interception of the Japanese force which was escorting four destroyer-transports to Kolombangara Island in the Solomons, on the night 12/13 July 1943. Both sides were equipped with electronic detection apparatus, *radar on the American side, and radar intercept on the

Robin Knox-Johnston at the start of the round the world race in 1968

Japanese. Each was aware of the approach of the other through the dark night and both manoeuvred to launch *torpedoes, backed on the American side by the powerful 6-inch gun armament of the cruisers.

In the first exchange one Japanese torpedo hit and damaged the New Zealand cruiser *Leander*, forcing her to withdraw, while the Japanese cruiser *Jintsu* was overwhelmed by concentrated gunfire and later sunk by torpedoes. Four of the Japanese destroyers retired and, under cover of a rainstorm, reloaded their torpedo tubes. Returning to re-engage, they succeeded in blowing off the bows of the American cruiser *Honolulu* with one torpedo and sinking the destroyer *Gwin* without loss or damage to themselves.

KOMANDORSKI ISLANDS, BATTLE OF, was a day surface action fought during the Second World War between an American force of cruisers and destroyers blockading the Japanese-occupied Aleutian Islands of Kiska and Attu and a similar but more powerful Japanese force covering an attempt to break the *blockade by running supply vessels through to the islands. It began at first light on 26 March 1943 when the American force made radar and visual contact with the Japanese force to the northwards. The Americans were at first unaware of the composition of their opponents and the Japanese, unaware of the American presence, turned north to make a rendezvous with another transport. The

American admiral was following at a moderate speed while re-concentrating his force when, at 0810, the Japanese discovered his presence. Sending away their transports, they turned to engage. At about 0840 the two sides opened fire, the Japanese cruisers also launching torpedoes a few minutes later. A lengthy running fight ensued during which the Japanese cruiser *Nachi* was significantly and the cruiser *Tama* slightly damaged; in return, both the American cruiser *Salt Lake City* and the destroyer *Bailey* were badly mauled. Though the *Salt Lake City* was brought for a time to a standstill shortly before noon, the Japanese admiral decided at that time to break off the action and also to abandon the attempt to get the transports through with their vital supplies on account of information received of American air strikes on their way to attack him. The U.S. Army aircraft did not, in fact, get off the ground until 1330. Thus the Japanese missed an opportunity to achieve a notable victory; unwilling to fight their transports through, they were forced to evacuate Kiska three months later.

KON-TIKI, the name given by Thor *Heyerdahl to the raft made of *balsa wood on which he and five companions drifted 3,800 miles from Callao to Raroia Island, Polynesia, in 1947. The raft itself, 45 ft (13·7 m) long and 18 ft (5·5 m) beam, is now preserved in the *Kon-Tiki Museum, Oslo, Norway.

The Kon-Tiki *at the start of her voyage, 1947*

KON-TIKI MUSEUM, Oslo, Norway, was established in 1949 and the collection is founded on material brought back by Dr. Thor *Heyerdahl after his famous voyage on the raft *Kon-Tiki* from South America to Polynesia. Besides the raft itself, the exhibits include old and new models of exotic ships in wood, reed, stone, and ceramic; log rafts and boats from Peru and Polynesia; outrigger *canoes from Raivavae Island; fishing gear, hooks, etc., from Easter Island and the Marquesas Islands. A small library, not open to the public, contains books dealing with American and Polynesian archaeology and ethnology.

KOTZEBUE, OTTO VON (1787–1846), Russian navigator, accompanied Adam *Krusenstern on his voyage of circumnavigation (1803–6). On promotion to lieutenant in 1815 he was placed in command of an expedition to find a *North-East passage across the Arctic Ocean and explore the south-west Pacific. In command of the *brig *Rurik*, with a crew of only twenty-seven men, Kotzebue rounded Cape Horn, discovered the Romanzov, Rurik, and Krusenstern islands, and sailed up the west coast of America to Kamchatka, discovering and naming Kotzebue Gulf and Krusenstern Cape. He returned to Russia in 1818 through the Pacific and Atlantic oceans, unable because of ice to discover a passage through the Arctic. Five years later, by now promoted captain, he was placed in

command of two warships for the dual purpose of carrying reinforcements to Kamchatka and undertaking further scientific investigation. He returned home in 1826 with a great collection of previously unknown plants and geological specimens. He wrote accounts of both voyages which were published in 1821 and 1830.

KRAKEN, a mythical sea-monster of enormous size said to inhabit the waters off the coasts of Norway and Sweden. According to one legend the kraken lies sleeping on the sea bed battening on huge seaworms in its sleep; when the waters at the bottom of the sea grow warm from the fires of Hell, the monster will rise to the surface and die. Another legend has the monster rising from the sea and lying on the surface like an island, only to sink again to the bottom. It is sometimes depicted in the form of a giant octopus or squid.

Belief in its existence can be traced back at least to 1555 when Bishop Olaus Magnus of Sweden described the kraken as having a skin which looked like gravel on the seashore so that men were tempted when it appeared on the surface to think it was in fact an island and to land on it and light fires to cook their victuals. It was also reported that in 1700 Bartholimus, a Danish priest, celebrated Mass on its back. Bishop Pontoppidan of Norway (*The Natural History of Norway*, 1755) also describes the kraken as an enormous sea monster but pours scorn on its rising to the surface in the shape of an island.

KRETSCHMER, OTTO (1912–), German admiral, was the most successful of all German *U-boat commanders of the Second World War. During the first eighteen months of the war he sank a total of forty-four merchant ships totalling 266,629 tons. He commanded successively *U.23* and *U.99*, and at an early stage of the war introduced his own ideas of how *submarine warfare should be carried on. Initially, captains of the U-boats had been instructed that 3,000 yards was the best range for *torpedoes, which, it was added, should be fired in salvoes of four or six at a time in order to make certain of a hit. Kretschmer took the view that one torpedo should suffice for each target, although this meant coming much closer to the enemy and, if necessary, penetrating within the surface escort of the convoy usually by night and on the surface. He became the principal exponent of this type of attack which was not only phenomenally successful but also difficult to counter.

His most successful single coup was the torpedoing and sinking on 3 November 1940 of two British *armed merchant cruisers, the *Laurentic* (18,724 tons) and *Patroclus* (11,314 tons). In a three-day convoy battle, lasting from 15 to 17 March 1941, Kretschmer sank five ships and damaged another before his U-boat was sunk by the British *destroyer *Walker*, Kretschmer and thirty-nine of his crew being taken prisoner. Later he was sent as a prisoner-of-war to Bowmanville Camp, Ontario, where he organized a system for the transmission of intelligence to Germany in spite of the camp censorship. This method of communication was developed to such a degree that he was able to arrange for a U-boat to rendezvous at the mouth of the St. Lawrence River to pick up escaped German prisoners. The U-boat duly appeared but in the meantime the escaped prisoners had been recaptured. Kretschmer returned to Germany after the war and, when the Federal German Navy was founded, he joined it and became a flotilla admiral.

KRONBORG, an ancient castle at Helsingor in Denmark, on the shore of the Sound which separates Denmark and Sweden, in which is accommodated the *Handels og Sjøfartmuseum, a large private maritime museum which illustrates the history of Danish shipping from the earliest times to the present day.

KRONSTADT, a Russian naval base in the Baltic, on the island of Kotlin near the head of the Gulf of Finland. It was founded as a naval base by *Peter the Great in 1710 after the capture of the island from Sweden in 1703. It withstood a bombardment by an Anglo-French fleet during the Crimean War (1854–6), and was the first naval base in which the revolution of 1917 was proclaimed, the sailors rising against their officers and appointing seamen's Soviets on board each ship.

In March 1921 the Kronstadt Navy mutinied against the Soviet government and took possession of the fortress and two ironclads. After a bombardment lasting many days Soviet troops

An artist's impression of the kraken; late 18th-century engraving

Krupp's naval building yard

made a night attack across the ice and the revolt was crushed with much severity. As a port Kronstadt is closed by ice for five months of the winter.

KRUPP VON BOHLEN, the name of the German steel and armaments firm which produced the arms and armour for the *High Seas Fleet during the ten years preceding the First World War. The firm was founded by Alfred Krupp (1812–57) and carried on by his son Friedrich Alfred (1854–1902). Krupp armoured steel and Krupp guns had a reputation for excellence that became worldwide, and proved the basis of the vast family fortune built up over the years. Alfred's granddaughter Bertha married Dr. Gustav von Bohlen und Halbach in 1906, and under his management the firm changed its name to Krupp von Bohlen and prospered enormously with Germany's emergence as a major sea power during the early years of the 20th century, becoming during those years the largest steel and armaments firm in the world.

KRUSENSTERN, ADAM IVAN (1770–1846), Russian admiral and hydrographer, served in the British Navy from 1793 to 1797 and during those years visited America, India, and China.

He wrote a paper on the advantages of a direct route from Russia to China via Cape Horn, sent it to Alexander I, and was commissioned by him to make a voyage to demonstrate the possibility. Two ships were purchased in England, renamed *Nadezhda* and *Neva*, and accompanied by Otto von *Kotzebue and Yuri *Lisiansky, Krusenstern left Kronstadt in 1803 and proceeded to Kamchatka round Cape Horn and via the Sandwich Islands. After a prolonged series of exploratory voyages in the northern part of the Pacific, the expedition returned to Kronstadt by way of the Cape of Good Hope. Krusenstern thus became the first Russian circumnavigator and was received with many honours and promotion to admiral by Nicholas I. He became director of the Russian navy school and carried out considerable research on the best method of compensating compasses against the residual magnetism of iron ships. As a hydrographer he is best remembered for his *Atlas de l'Océan Pacifique*, published in 1824–7.

KULA GULF, a naval night action fought in the Pacific during the Second World War in July 1943 between an American squadron of three cruisers and four destroyers which was attempting to intercept and destroy a Japanese force of seven destroyer-transports, escorted by three unhampered destroyers, engaged in delivering troops and supplies to Vila on Kolombangara in the Solomon group of islands.

Three of the Japanese supply destroyers had been detached to deliver their cargoes from a position at the entrance of the Kula Gulf between Kolombangara and New Georgia at 0118 on 6 July 1943 and the other four had just been detached at 0147 when the American force in their usual single line, with destroyers in *van and rear and the cruisers in the middle, was sighted crossing ahead of the three Japanese escort destroyers. The latter increased speed to 30 knots and prepared to fire their high-speed, oxygen-fuelled 'Long Lance' *torpedoes.

The American cruisers, which had been in *radar contact since 0140, opened accurate radar-controlled fire on the *Niizuki*, the Japanese flagship, and quickly sank her. Two of the Japanese destroyers, however, launched their sixteen torpedoes, five of which hit and sank the American cruiser *Helena*. In reply, besides the destruction of the *Niizuki*, two Japanese destroyers were damaged in some confused skirmishes before their force retired, having completed their supply-running mission.

KURITA, TAKEO (1889–), Japanese vice admiral, spent most of his naval career in battleships and cruisers. Holding very conservative views on naval tactics, his part in the Second World War was virtually confined to providing a support role for the Japanese aircraft carriers until all their naval air power had been eliminated by American action. At the battle of *Midway, he commanded a cruiser squadron which lost half its number to American carrier planes after a collision between two of them had severely restricted their manoeuvrability. Nevertheless, he rose steadily in rank and, after the annihilation of Japanese naval air power, his formidable Second Fleet, which included the two huge battleships *Yamato and *Musashi*, became the only remaining naval striking force in the Japanese Navy.

As such it was cast for the principal part in the complex operations of the battle for *Leyte Gulf. Shaken by two days of almost incessant air attack from American naval aircraft, during the first of which the *Musashi* was destroyed, Kurita appeared to lose his nerve at the very moment when the opportunity to inflict shattering losses on the Americans arrived. That it would almost certainly have involved the eventual destruction of his own ships may have influenced his decision, though this was not in line with the usual Japanese attitude in such circumstances. His taciturnity under interrogation after the war did not help in providing an explanation of his conduct on that occasion.

KWAJALEIN, an *atoll in the Marshall Islands group in the Pacific which was the scene of an amphibious attack by American forces during the Second World War and was the principal feature in the seizure from the Japanese of the whole of the Marshall Islands. D-day for the assault was 31 January 1944.

Kwajalein atoll, which encircles a lagoon 66 miles in length, has two main island groups; in the north-east corner are the twin islands of Roi and Namur, joined by a causeway; in the south, Kwajalein itself. Each has several smaller satellite islands.

For several weeks prior to D-day all the atolls and islands of the Marshalls were subjected to intensive bombing and bombardment to soften up Kwajalein and Roi-Namur and to neutralize the other groups on which air bases existed. Two American attack forces were assembled and trained, a northern force for Roi-Namur, transporting 20,788 U.S. *marines of the 4th Marine Division, and a southern force for Kwajalein with 21,768 troops of the 7th U.S. Infantry Division.

Profiting from the lessons learned during the amphibious assault on *Tarawa in the Gilbert Islands two months previously, a plan was prepared which was carried out to the letter and was completely successful. The main assaults on the islands took place on 1 February. Air strikes on the islands were continuous until the assault troops were no more than 3,000 yards from the beaches, and they were followed by naval gunfire, rocket fire from landing craft, and gunfire from howitzers previously landed on unoccupied satellite islets which had been taken the previous day.

Roi Island, defended by 600 Japanese, was secured by dark; the 6,000 defenders of Namur resisted stoutly until killed almost to a man, the island being fully occupied by the afternoon of the next day. Kwajalein had been completely devastated by gunfire culminating on 31 January and the first assault wave in the morning of 1 February met little resistance. However, the dazed garrison, originally about 4,000 strong, recovered sufficiently after two hours to put up a stiff fight, and though 11,000 American troops had been landed by the evening of 1 February, all resistance on the island was not overcome until the last Japanese defenders were killed on the afternoon of the 4th. American casualties in the operation totalled more than 800.

'KYE', the lower deck slang name in the British Navy for hot cocoa, which is still a welcome drink for watchkeepers during night watches at sea. Cocoa in large slabs, from which the drink is made by adding boiling water and condensed milk, is an official victualling issue in the British Navy.

L

L, the 'three L's of navigation', much favoured by seamen in the days before nautical astronomy became widely adopted as a means of finding a ship's position at sea, provided a rough and ready means of ensuring the safety of a ship. They were usually regarded as *lead, *latitude, and look-out, though some seamen sometimes substituted *log for latitude. The fourth, and most desirable of the L's, was *longitude, and this was finally added in the late 18th century by the production of a reliable *chronometer. With this final dimension added, a ship was able to plot her position accurately on a *chart and thus know where she was.

L.C.A., the short title for Landing Craft Assault, small landing craft used during the Second World War in military or *marine assaults on enemy beaches.

L.C.I., an abbreviation for Landing Craft, Infantry, small craft used during the Second World War in which infantry carried in *L.S.I.s were put ashore on coasts for assault purposes. They were normally carried at the *davits of L.S.I.s and lowered into the water for the assault, being fitted with bow doors which were opened when the craft grounded.

L.C.P., Landing Craft Personnel, small wooden landing craft of the Second World War used for transporting personnel on assault operations.

L.C.S., the short title for Landing Craft Support, small landing craft armed with Oerlikon guns used as supporting vessels in assault operations in the Second World War.

L.C.T., an abbreviation for Landing Craft, Tank, small vessels used during the Second World War in which tanks carried in *L.S.T.s were landed on an assault beach. They were normally carried at the *davits of L.S.T.s and lowered into the water with their tanks on board, being fitted with bow doors and a ramp down which the tank was driven either to land dryshod direct on to a beach if conditions allowed or else to swim ashore if the L.C.T. grounded too far out to reach the beach herself. Larger L.C.T.s, carrying up to four tanks, were self-propelled and made passages to

the assault area independently, either grounding on the beach to launch the tanks dryshod or letting down the ramp offshore for the tanks to swim ashore.

L.S.I., an abbreviation for Landing Ship, Infantry, large vessels converted and used during the Second World War to carry infantry for assault purposes in amphibious operations. Either they carried small landing craft at their *davits in which the infantry were ferried to the beach under assault (see also L.C.I.) or, where beach conditions were suitable, they were grounded on the assault beach and the infantry landed directly through bow doors and down a ramp.

L.S.T., an abbreviation for Landing Ship, Tank, a large merchant ship converted to carry tanks and used during the Second World War for assault purposes in amphibious operations. They usually carried tank landing craft at their *davits in which the tanks were ferried close to the beach under assault, but where beach conditions were suitable they could be grounded close in and the tanks landed through bow doors and down a ramp, either directly on to the beach if the beach contours were suitable or swimming ashore.

LA BOURDONNAIS, BERTRAND FRANÇOIS, Comte Mahé de (1699–1753), French naval officer, began his maritime career with the French *East India Company and in 1724 was present at the capture of Mahé on the Malabar coast at which he acted with such gallantry that he was given the honour of adding the name of the town to his own. For a short time he was in the service of the Portuguese at Goa, but in 1735 was appointed governor of Madagascar and Mauritius. Returning to France at the outbreak of the War of the Austrian Succession (1739–48), he was placed in command of a fleet and sent to Indian waters, where he was successful in preventing the capture of Mahé by the British, relieved Pondicherry which was under siege, and took part in the blockade of Madras.

He was, in general, a stubborn and quarrelsome man, quick to imagine offence where none was offered, and unwisely he quarrelled with Dupleix, commander of the French forces in

India, who made several unjust accusations against him. Returning to Madagascar, he found another governor there in his place, appointed by Dupleix. In a fit of temper he sailed for France in a Dutch ship and was captured by the British and paroled. On his return to France he was arrested on a charge of peculation and maladministration and imprisoned in the Bastille. He was tried and acquitted two years later in 1751. Broken in health by his imprisonment, he died in Paris, maintaining to the end his accusations against Dupleix.

LA HOGUE or **LA HOUGUE, BATTLE OF,** see BARFLEUR, BATTLE OF.

LA PÉROUSE, JEAN-FRANÇOIS GALOUP, Comte de (1741–c. 1788), French navigator, joined the French Navy when a boy and, at the age of 18, was fortunate to survive the slaughter on board the *Formidable* when that ship was captured at the battle of * Quiberon Bay in 1759. He served with distinction during the War of American Independence (1775–82).

In 1785 he was given command of an expedition of exploration, sailing from Brest in the *Boussole*, accompanied by the *Astrolabe*, to seek initially for the Pacific end of the * North-West passage to China. He arrived on the coast of Alaska on 23 June 1783 but had made no discoveries of importance by the time his ships were driven off by bad weather six weeks later. He made for the Hawaiian group of islands where he discovered Necker Island before crossing the Pacific in accordance with his further instructions to explore the north-east coasts of Asia, the China and Japan Seas, the Solomon Islands, and Australia.

Touching at Quelpart Island, La Pérouse followed the Korean coast northward to reach De Castries Bay, near the modern Vladivostok, on 28 July 1787 before crossing the Sea of Japan to discover the strait dividing Japan from Sakhalin which today bears his name. He visited Petropavlovsk in Kamchatka, whence he sent home the records of his expedition to that date, and then sailed for the South Pacific, reaching Mauna in the Samoan group on 8 December. There the captain of the *Astrolabe* and ten of his crew were murdered.

From Samoa the expedition sailed via the Friendly Islands and Norfolk Island to the British settlement at * Botany Bay which was reached on 26 January 1788. After sailing from there soon after 7 February—the date of La Pérouse's last letter to the Ministry of Marine— the expedition disappeared, no trace of it being found until 1826 when wreckage discovered on the reefs of Vanikoro Island, one of the Santa Cruz group, was identified as the remains of the two French ships.

LA RONCIÈRE LE NOURY, CAMILLE, Baron de (1813–81), French admiral and author, entered the navy in 1829 and commanded a squadron of gun vessels which took part in the Baltic operations of 1855 during the Crimean War (1854–6). Promoted to rear admiral in 1861, he commanded in 1866 the battle squadron which was sent to end the action in progress against Mexico. Like many other naval officers he served ashore in a military role during the Franco-Prussian War of 1870 and commanded a division of * marines manning the forts of Paris, later returning to sea and being appointed as commander-in-chief of the French fleet in the Mediterranean. His main naval interests lay in the field of navigation and he was a member of the Bureau of * Longitude and for some years president of the Geographical Society of France. He wrote a number of books on subjects connected with the navy, some of which because of their erudition and authority deserved more attention than they received.

LA SPEZIA, see SPEZIA, LA.

LABOUR, to, the description of a ship when she rolls or pitches excessively in a rough sea. The expression, though applied to all ships, is most apt in its application to sailing ships since pronounced rolling produces a great strain on masts and rigging and may lead, in sailing vessels with wooden hull subjected to such a strain, to an opening of the * seams.

LACE, also known as gold lace or distinctive lace, the rings denoting rank worn on the sleeves of an officer's coat or on the shoulder-straps of tropical uniform and greatcoats.

LACE, to, the act of attaching, in a sailing vessel, a sail to a * gaff or * boom by passing a rope or cord alternately through eyelet holes and round the spar. In the case of a boom the eyelet holes are in the foot of the sail, in the case of a gaff they are in the head. The rope or cord itself is known as a lacing. Similarly, in square-rigged ships, a sail is laced to a * yard, a * bonnet to a * course, and a * drabler to a bonnet.

LACROIX, LOUIS PARIS (1877–1958), French sailor and author, was the last of a long line of sea captains in sail. At 18 he went to sea as an apprentice pilot and obtained his first command in sail at the age of 26. He soon gained a reputation as a hard but courageous * master, a fine seaman, and one who was humane and considerate in his treatment of his crew. In 1920, with the virtual disappearance of square-rigged sailing ships, he settled down to produce his great work *Les Derniers Grands Voiliers*. In all he wrote about a dozen books and in 1939 was awarded the prize of the Marine Academy and in 1945 that of the Académie française.

LADDER, (1) the general nautical term for what on shore would be called a staircase. Ladders leading from deck to deck are known as accommodation ladders; gangway ladders, rigged over the side when a ship is anchored or at a mooring, extend from a small platform level with the upper deck down to the level of the water for use when embarking or disembarking from small boats. **(2)** It is also a term used in the control of naval *gunnery when finding the range of an enemy vessel. Up or down ladders are fired according to the fall of shot; if a salvo of shells is seen to fall short by its splashes, the range is corrected upwards by steps of, say, 400 yards until the splashes caused by the fall of shot are seen to cross the target, thus forming an up ladder. Similarly, a down ladder is ordered when the splashes are seen initially beyond the target.

LADE, to, the older equivalent of to load, in relation to a ship and her cargo or a warship and her guns, the present participle being used as a noun to denote the whole of the cargo on board. There was an ancient superstition of sailors that if, while the cargo was being brought on board, the ship heeled to *port (or ladeboard) the voyage would be successful, if to *starboard (or steerboard), storms would blow up. LADEBOARD, an old term for the side of a vessel across which the cargo was carried on board. It was the left-hand, or port, side of the ship, as the *steering oar projected from the right-hand, or starboard, side and thus made it awkward to lie alongside a loading wharf starboard side to. Ladeboard, which developed into *larboard, was thus the old term for port in its meaning of left-hand side.

Guns were laded when the cartridge was rammed home, the wad and ball similarly rammed, and the cartridge pierced with a *priming iron to expose the powder ready for firing.

'LADY OF THE GUNROOM', the colloquial name given in the British Navy during the days of sailing warships to the gunner's mate placed in charge of the gunner's stores which were stowed in the *gunroom or in a small compartment just abaft of it. In ships so fitted, the separate compartment for the gunner's stores was known as the after-scuttle.

LAGAN, a term in maritime law for goods which are cast overboard from a ship with a *buoy and buoyrope attached so that they may be later recovered. It is a term also sometimes used to refer to articles still within a sunken ship as she lies on the bottom. The word comes from the old French *lagand*, lying. By extension, the term has now come to mean any goods lying on the bottom of the sea, whether buoyed, inside the hull of a ship, or loose on the bottom. See also FLOTSAM, JETSAM.

LAGOON, a stretch of water enclosed, or mainly enclosed, by coral islands, *atolls, and reefs. As the coral polyps flourish and die, they form reefs, which can eventually develop into islands, and as these grow, so an area of sea water becomes enclosed and forms a lagoon. The conditions of life of the polyps accentuate this tendency, as those on the inside, or sheltered, edge of a reef are brought no food by the action of the sea and thus die without breeding, while those on the outside edge, to which the sea brings food, continue to multiply and, as they die, build up the reef on its outer edge so that it continually grows higher, and extends further, thus forming a lagoon.

LAGOS, a seaport of southern Portugal, the centre of an important sardine and tunny fishery. It is well known for its connection with Prince *Henry the Navigator, who founded the town of Sagres at Lagos in 1421. It is also remembered for an important naval battle of the Seven Years War (1756–63) fought off Lagos in 1759 between a British fleet commanded by Admiral *Boscawen and a French fleet under Commodore de la *Clue Sabran. Boscawen with fifteen *ships of the line, was refitting at Gibraltar after having blockaded de la Clue in Toulon; and late one evening one of his look-out *frigates reported that fifteen sail of the enemy were out and standing to the westward along the Barbary shore.

By 10 p.m., in spite of many of the ships having their *yards struck down, the British fleet was clear of the bay and in full pursuit; but next morning only seven of the enemy were in sight, the rest (five of the line and three frigates) having parted company during the night and entered Cadiz. At 2.30 p.m., the French opened fire as the leading British ships came up and a running fight ensued, but the action was not general owing to the wind failing later in the afternoon. Boscawen's ship, the *Namur*, was disabled aloft and he therefore shifted his flag to the *Newark*; while transferring to the latter ship a round shot struck his boat and it started to sink, but he immediately plugged the hole with his wig. After about three and a half hours the French *Centaure*, of seventy-four guns, which had been engaged with every British ship in turn as she came up, was forced to strike, and as the wind rose again the French endeavoured to get away.

The pursuit was continued all night, during which two of the French ships escaped, and at daybreak the remaining four were sighted about 15 miles from Lagos. The French flagship ran ashore and struck her colours, and after her crew had been taken out she was set on fire. The other three anchored under the Portuguese batteries but, following the principle of *'hot chase', the *Téméraire* and *Modeste* were captured and brought out while the remaining ship, the *Redoutable*, was burnt. Commodore de la Clue died of his wounds at Lagos.

LAID, a term associated with rope-making, from *lay, meaning the twist of the rope. Single-laid rope is one *strand of rope, the strand consisting of fibres twisted up. *Hawser-laid rope consists of three strands twisted together into a rope against the lay of the strands; *cable-laid rope is three hawser-laid ropes twisted up together to form a cable. Cable-laid rope was also frequently known as water-laid rope.

LAIRD, MACGREGOR (1808–61), Scottish merchant, was with his brother a pioneer of the iron steamship. He designed a 55-ton *paddle steamer, the *Alburkah*, which in 1832 left Liverpool for the Niger River, the first iron ship to complete an ocean voyage. She returned to Liverpool in 1834, Laird, who sailed in her, having in the meantime explored the river mouth. In 1837 he was one of the promoters of the British and American Steam Navigation Company to run a line of steamships between Britain and America. In 1838 the company's ship *Sirius* was the first ship to cross the Atlantic from Britain to America entirely under steam.

Laird's elder brother JOHN (1805–74) was one of the first shipbuilders to use iron as a building material. He constructed in 1829 an iron lighter of 60 tons for use on canals, and in 1834 he built for a customer in Savannah, U.S.A., the paddle steamer *John Randolph*, the first iron ship to be seen in America. He also built an iron ship, the *Nemesis*, for the *East India Company in 1839, the first iron vessel in the world to carry guns, and was the designer of the transport *Birkenhead*, which was wrecked off the Cape of Good Hope in 1852.

LAKE CHAMPLAIN, a large lake in the northern U.S.A. between the states of New York and Vermont and the scene of two naval actions. The first, during the War of American Independence (1775–82), was fought for the control of communications on the lake on which the revolutionary American colonists had established themselves with a *flotilla of small craft under the command of Benedict *Arnold. It began on 11 October 1776 and was not finally concluded until the 13th, when the British obtained a complete victory.

The vessels engaged comprised a miscellaneous collection of small craft of various types, carrying such armament as they could accommodate. All had been built on the lake, the largest being the British *brig *sloop *Inflexible* of eighteen guns. The British flotilla was manned from ships on the station and by many volunteers,

aided by a detachment of Royal Artillery. It was commanded by Commander Thomas Pringle.

On the first day the Americans were attacked off Valcour Island. Owing to lack of wind the action was only partial and was not pressed, the Americans losing a 12-gun *schooner and a *gundalow; a second gundalow was also captured on the 12th. On the 13th the final attack took place off Crown Point. Except for four vessels which escaped to Ticonderoga, all the remaining American craft were captured or burnt. Nevertheless, the American ships on the lake had so delayed the British advance down the lake that further movement was impossible.

The second action on the lake was fought during the War of 1812–14 on 11 September 1814. British troops numbering more than 11,000 men had reached Plattsburg six days earlier after marching from Montreal. The governor-general, Sir George Prevost, commanded the troops but made no attempt to seize the bluffs and use artillery to drive the American vessels from their carefully chosen anchorages off Plattsburg, N.Y. Commodore Downie commanded the British vessels and the two squadrons were equal in the total weight of broadside fire though Downie had a superiority in long-range guns. Because of pressure from Prevost, Downie approached Plattsburg with his most formidable vessel, the *Confiance*, thirty-seven guns, unready for battle. The American commodore, Thomas *Macdonough, showed exceptional qualities of leadership and foresight in planning the battle and in conducting it. To offset the British advantage in long-range guns, he had anchored his vessels in carefully chosen positions, and rigged *springs on the anchor cables to enable his ships to turn at their anchors in order to bring into action the unengaged broadsides. The British vessels were compelled to approach bows on, thus permitting the Americans to *rake them. Even so, Downie had ordered a concentration on the U.S.S. *Saratoga*, Macdonough's flagship, and the first broadside from the *Confiance* killed or injured about one-fifth of the crew of that ship. Downie was killed some 15 minutes later, and the lack of training in the *Confiance* became apparent without his leadership. The battle lasted for about 2 hours. In addition to the *Confiance*, Commodore Downie had a *brig of 16 guns, 2 *sloops mounting 11 guns each, and 12 small gunboats. Macdonough had 26 guns in the *Saratoga*, another 44 mounted in 3 smaller vessels, and 10 row-galleys.

Losses on both sides were tremendous, but the failure of the British squadron to drive off the American vessels left the waters of Lake Champlain firmly in American hands and Prevost's troops were forced to withdraw from their proposed invasion.

LAKE ERIE, one of the Great Lakes of North America, bounded on the north by the Canadian province of Ontario and on the south by the American states of Ohio, Pennsylvania, and New York. It was the scene of a naval action fought on 10 September 1813, near the Bass Islands, during the British–U.S. War of 1812–14. Both fleets had been built on the lake and the crews of all vessels lacked training and experience. Commodore Barclay of the British squadron had sixty-three guns against fifty-five in the vessels of Oliver Hazard * Perry, U.S.N., but the weight of metal of the American broadside was greater.

In his flagship the *Lawrence* Perry advanced more rapidly than his other vessels in the light winds then blowing and in consequence Barclay's flagship, the *Detroit*, and his next most powerful unit, the *Queen Charlotte*, concentrated their fire on the *Lawrence*, causing extensive damage with their long guns before the Americans could reply effectively with their * carronades. Taking the brunt of the enemy action for two hours, Perry found his flagship unmanageable and his crew nearly all wounded. Using the one boat which had not been damaged, Perry had himself rowed to the *Niagara*. There Captain Elliott volunteered to bring the American * schooners into close action. In the *Niagara*, which had suffered little damage, Perry passed through the British line, raking five vessels. The *Queen Charlotte* surrendered, and the *Detroit* became unable to continue the action. The smaller American vessels then came into close action and the other British units surrendered.

LAMINAR FLOW, the pattern of motion of particles in a thin zone of water which a vessel of normal ship or yacht form draws along the surface of its hull. In this zone, which in the case of a smooth racing yacht's hull may be of the order of 3 mm in thickness, layers of water slide over each other in a direction parallel with the surface of the hull. Around rough hulls, pitted with rust or coated with weed or barnacles, this zone will be much thicker and will in consequence greatly increase the drag or resistance to the vessel's forward motion.

In the water immediately beyond and at a distance which depends on the size, shape, speed, and smoothness of the vessel's hull the laminar flow becomes disturbed and gives place to a much thicker zone of turbulently flowing water also drawn along with the hull. It is the drag induced by these layers which causes the resistance to rise so sharply as the speed of a vessel increases. See also WAVE LINE THEORY.

C. Marchaj, *Sailing Theory and Practice* (1964).

LAMINATED CONSTRUCTION, a method of construction of many parts of small wooden vessels when suitable planks and crooks, in which the grain of the wood follows the required curve, are not readily available. With this method such members of the hull as the * stem, the * sternpost, the * keel, fore-and-aft * stringers, * frames, * knees, deck * beams, etc., are formed of several thin layers of timber which are bound together with water-resistant glue into the various curves required. By means of prefabricated jigs or rigid patterns, various parts of the hull can thus be laminated in large numbers, enabling production of identical wooden hulls to be carried out with a reduction in time and labour costs. A familiar form of laminated construction is plywood which is formed of three or more thin layers or veneers of wood bonded together with glue.

LANBY BUOY, a special * buoy developed to take the place of a * lightship. It is a very large buoy with a diameter of 12 metres (40 ft) and a depth of 2·5 metres (8 ft), surmounted by a lattice mast which carries a * characteristic light at a height of 12 metres (40 ft) above sea level with a visibility of 16 miles in clear weather. In addition to the light, Lanby buoys are fitted with a sound fog signal and a * radar beacon. They can be moored in position in any depth of water up to 90 metres (300 ft) and are designed to operate for up to six months without attention. At all times their performance and position are monitored by a shore station. As they are unmanned, they can operate much more economically than a lightship, which normally has a crew of three or four, and it has been estimated that the ratio of cost of Lanby buoy to lightship is one-tenth. The name comes from the initials of large automatic navigational buoy.

LANCASTER, Sir JAMES (*c.* 1555–1618), English navigator, made three important voyages. In the first, 1591–4, he commanded the * *Edward Bonaventure* and reached Achin, in Sumatra, in September 1592. In his second voyage, 1594, he commanded a plundering expedition to Pernambuco. His third, 1601–3, was the most important, as he commanded the first * East India Company expedition of five ships to the Indies, taking John * Davis as his chief pilot. Reaching Achin in June 1602 he set up a factory, or trading post, returning to England the following year.

LAND BREEZE, an evening wind which blows from the land to seaward when the temperature of the land falls below that of the sea. As the sun sets, areas of land cool more quickly than the sea adjoining them, the air over the land thus becomes heavier and flows out to sea to establish an equilibrium with the lighter air over the sea.

LANDAIS, PIERRE (*c.* 1731–1820), a native of St. Malo, France, was an officer in the French

Navy before he went to America in 1777. At that time, during the War of American Independence (1775–82), it was fashionable to think well of France and of Frenchmen as a number of them were volunteering to help the colonial cause, and in disregard of the proven abilities of various Americans, Landais was given a commission in the *Continental Navy and command of the *frigate *Alliance. In her he sailed from Boston for Brest on 14 January 1779. He was present off the English coast on 23 September 1779, when John Paul *Jones in the *Bonhomme Richard captured H.M.S. Serapis in a famous frigate action. Landais in the Alliance fired into the two ships, doing more damage to the Bonhomme Richard than to the Serapis.

On his return to France, he was removed from command of the Alliance but still managed to put to sea in her. In crossing the Atlantic he behaved in a half-mad manner and was forcibly imprisoned in his cabin. Samuel Eliot *Morison, in John Paul Jones, A Sailor's Biography (1959), gives an account of the services of Landais, and Wm. Bell Clark, in Gallant John Barry (1938), tells of the court martial of Landais which resulted in his dismissal.

LANDMARK, any fixed object on the land whose position is marked on a *chart. Some, such as *lighthouses, beacons, leading-marks, are set up specifically as guides to navigation or warnings to seamen; others, such as prominent buildings or church towers, can be used as navigational guides if the chart in use shows their positions. Cross-*bearings of any landmarks will fix a ship's position in coastal waters with complete accuracy.

LANDSMEN or **LANDMEN,** a *rate given in the British Navy to men without any naval training who served on board warships. In theory they were volunteers since, because they did not use the sea as a profession, they enjoyed immunity from *impressment. But during the long series of naval wars of the 18th century the demand for men to man the ships of the fleet grew so prodigious that the operation of the press laws grew lax and virtually any man brought in by the *press gangs was accepted and rated on board as a landsman, being paid on a smaller scale than that of an ordinary seaman. The rating was abolished in 1862, to be replaced by that of ordinary seaman second class. The spelling 'landsman' for 'landman' begins to appear about 1800.

LANGREL or **LANGRACE,** a type of cannon shot much used at sea by *privateers when attacking merchant vessels during the 18th and early 19th centuries. It was made from a collection of various pieces of iron gathered together in a thin casing to fit the bore of the gun, scattering in a wide arc when fired. It was a villainous kind of shot as, although it was meant in theory to cut the sails and rigging of a ship, many privateer captains used it as an anti-personnel weapon. The pieces of iron from which it was made were usually jagged fragments which tore an ugly hole in each man hit, and the wide scatter of the shot was enough to decimate the men on the upper deck of merchant vessels attacked. It was a type of shot very rarely used in warships but almost entirely in ships operating under a *letter of marque.

LANTERN, the means by which the ships of a fleet could remain in company throughout the night during the early days of sailing navies. Most ships of war in these navies used to carry three great lanterns mounted on the *poop rail which at night were lit by large candles so that the next ship astern could keep station on them. Some of the larger ships carried as many as seven. In his diary for 17 January 1661, during a visit to the Royal Sovereign, Samuel *Pepys wrote: 'my Lady Sandwich, my Lady Jemimah, Mrs. Browne, Mrs. Grace, and Mary and the page, my lady's servants, and myself all went into the Lanthorne together'. According to James Howell (Epist. Ho-Elianae) the largest ships' lanterns would hold ten people.

LANYARD, a short length of rope or small stuff used for a variety of purposes on board. In sailing vessels, before the introduction of *bottle-screws and similar modern fittings, the *shrouds of all masts were set up taut by means of lanyards rove through the *deadeyes. A sailor carries his knife on a lanyard. And when flintlocks were introduced into navies as the firing mechanism of a warship's guns, they were fired with a lanyard which released the hammer.

LAPENOTIÈRE, JOHN RICHARDS (1770–1834), was the British naval officer who brought back to England the first news of the battle of *Trafalgar. Born at Ilfracombe, Devon, he went to sea in the merchant service at the age of 10 and joined the Royal Navy as a lieutenant in March 1794. In 1802 he was appointed to command the *schooner Pickle (ten guns) attached to Lord *Nelson's fleet and was present at the battle of Trafalgar. He was entrusted by Lord *Collingwood, after the death of Nelson, with the task of taking home his dispatches. When the Pickle arrived at Falmouth after the battle, Lapenotière hurried to London using relays of horses and arrived at the British Admiralty at midnight on 5 November to deliver the momentous news.

As was the usual custom, Lapenotière was rewarded by promotion to commander and a gift of £500.

LAPTEV, DMITRI YAKOVLEVICH (*fl.* 1733–43), Russian Arctic explorer, was a naval lieutenant and was appointed a member of the 'Great Northern Expedition' (1733–43), to survey a route from the Atlantic to the Pacific round the northern coasts of Russia and Siberia. He was placed in charge of a detachment from the main expedition with instructions to explore the Siberian coast eastwards from the Lena River. Between 1736 and 1741 he succeeded in sailing the 60-ft *cutter *Irkutsk* to Cape Bolshoy Baranov, a distance of about 1,000 statute miles, mapping the coast as he went—a notable feat of surveying. He finally reached the rank of vice admiral in the Russian Navy. The Laptev Sea is named in honour of him and of his cousin Lieutenant KHARITON PROKOFYEVICH Laptev (d. 1763), who explored the region to the west of the Lena River in 1739–42. See also NORTH-EAST PASSAGE.

LARBOARD, the old term for the left-hand side of a ship when facing *forward, now known as *port. During the early years of the 19th century the term larboard began to give way to port as a helm order in order to avoid confusion with the similar sounding *starboard, and the change was made official in 1844. Opinions differ as to how larboard originated as describing the left-hand side of a ship. The most favoured theory is that larboard derives from ladeboard, as many of the old merchant ships had a loading, or lading, port on their left-hand side. See LADE, TO.

LARBOLINS or **LARBOLIANS,** an old word to describe that part of the ship's company who formed the *port watch.

> 'Larbolins stout, you must turn out,
> And sleep no more within,
> For if you do, we'll cut your clue,
> And let *starbolins in.'

The clues are the *nettles which support a slung hammock.

LARGE, a point of sailing where the *sheets which control the sails in a sailing vessel can be eased well away to make the most of a quartering wind. In square-rigged ships it was the point where *studding-sails would draw if set. The term does not refer to a wind from dead astern but to one from abaft the beam. To sail large, to ease away the sheets and sail further *off the wind.

LARSEN, CARL ANTON (1860–1924), Norwegian whaler, was primarily responsible for opening up the first land-based Antarctic *whaling industry. During two Antarctic voyages between 1892 and 1894 in search of Right whales and seals, he made important discoveries along the Weddell Sea coast of the Antarctic Peninsula, discovering the King Oscar II and Foyn coasts and penetrating the Weddell Sea as far south as latitude 68° 10′. He was also the first man to make a collection of fossils from the Antarctic continent. In 1901 he accompanied Otto *Nordenskjöld's expedition as captain of the *Antarctic* which was lost in the Weddell Sea, the crew escaping over the ice. In 1904, with the support of Argentina, Larsen founded the Norwegian-managed Compañia Argentina de Pesca, based on Grytviken, South Georgia, the first attempt to exploit economically the Antarctic whales and one of the root causes of subsequent British political interest in the area. He obtained the British concession for whaling in the Ross Sea area of the Antarctic in 1923 and led a whaling expedition there in 1923–4 with the factory ship *Sir James Clark Ross.* He died on board in December 1924.

LASH, to, to secure anything with a rope or cord. Hammocks, with the bedclothes inside, are lashed up every morning before being stowed away; *Ulysses had himself lashed to the mast of his ship so that he could listen to the songs of the *sirens without being able to leap overboard to join them. Lash, as a noun, a stroke with the *cat-o'-nine-tails.

LASK, to, an old sailing term meaning to sail *large with a quartering wind. A ship was said to be lasking along when sailing with a wind over the quarter.

LASKETS, small cords sewn in loops to the *bonnets and *drablers of a square-rigged ship by which, when they are set, they are *laced to the *courses and bonnets respectively by means of a line threaded through the loops. They were also sometimes known as latchings.

LATEEN (from *latin,* meaning Mediterranean), a narrow, triangular sail set on a very long *yard of which the forward end is *bowsed well down so that it sets obliquely on the mast and produces a high *peak.

The lateen rig is one of great antiquity, believed to be pre-Christian and probably of Arab origin. The yard was formed of two or more pieces bound together so that the outer ends would whip more easily than the middle. Because no forestay could be fitted, the *mast usually had a pronounced *rake forward, and the yard was held to the mast by a form of easily released slip knot. Two bow *tackles were used to haul down the forward end of the yard, while the after end was checked by braces, thus producing a curve in the yard. The Arab version of the sail is not a true lateen but a seltee-lateen, having a short luff to the forward edge of the sail, thus making it a four-sided sail. The yard on which the sail is set is often longer than the ship herself, on occasions by as much as one-third. The rig is today virtually restricted to the Mediterranean, the upper Nile, and the northern waters of the Indian Ocean, being hazardous in any but calm waters. It is the typical sail of the Mediterranean * felucca and the Arabian * dhow.

LATERAL SYSTEM, see BUOYS, BUOYAGE.

LATITUDE, from the Latin *latitudo*, breadth. It is one of the spherical * co-ordinates used to describe a terrestrial position, the other being * longitude. Treating the earth as a perfect sphere the latitude of a point on its surface is the angular measure between the point and the plane of the * equator along the * meridian on which the point is located. This is equivalent to the corresponding angle at the earth's centre. The earth's shape, however, is not that of an exact sphere so that these two angles do not coincide exactly except for points on the equator (latitude 0°) or the poles of the earth (latitude 90°).

Geographical latitude, also called true latitude, is equivalent to the true * altitude of the elevated celestial pole at the place. This is always greater (except at latitude 0° or 90°) than the corresponding angle at the earth's centre, which latter angle is called the geocentric latitude of the place.

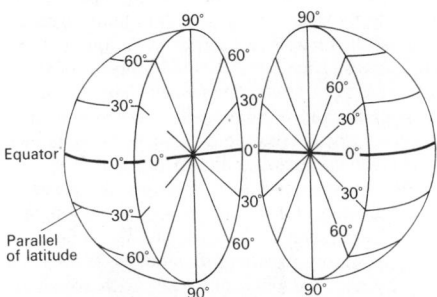

Parallels of latitude showing angular measurement

The latitude of a ship at sea may be found by observing the meridional altitude of the sun by day and, very approximately, of the pole star at night.

LAUGHTON, Sir JOHN KNOX (1830–1915), British naval historian, was born at Liverpool, the son of a master mariner. He joined the Royal Navy as an instructor and saw active service during the Crimean War (1854–6) and in China. In 1873 he was appointed head of the department of meteorology and marine surveying at the Royal Naval College, * Greenwich, and three years later delivered his first lecture on naval history, to which he subsequently devoted his life.

Although he retired from the navy in 1885 to become professor of modern history at King's College, University of London, it was very largely due to his initiative that the * Navy Records Society was formed in 1893. He became its first secretary, a post which he retained until 1912, and he also edited its first two volumes, *State Papers relating to the defeat of the Spanish Armada*. His first book, published in 1886, was *Nelson's Letters and Despatches* which was followed in 1887 by *Studies in Naval History* and in 1889 by *Memoirs relating to Lord Torrington*. He was also a prolific writer of shorter studies on naval history, many of which appeared in books later edited by him. Most of the short naval biographies in the *Dictionary of National Biography* came from his pen, a monument of research and erudition which stamps him as one of the great historians of the age.

LAUNCH, (1) a type of vessel used as a * gunboat in the Mediterranean during the 18th and 19th centuries by the navies of France, Spain, the Italian States, and Turkey. They were largely flat-bottomed craft with comparatively little * freeboard and built long for their * beam, a design which gave them a poor performance under sail. Smaller craft of similar design, also called launches, were used under oars in shoal coastal waters for a variety of purposes, such as underrunning cables, laying out anchors, etc. **(2)** The largest ship's boat of a sailing man-of-war, also known as a * longboat. They were * carvel built and carried a mast and sails for short cruises independently of the ship which carried them. It was from this ship's boat that, in the steam * battleship era, the modern launch was developed, the largest sailing and pulling boat carried in warships of this size. They were 42 feet long and pulled eighteen oars, nine each side. * Diagonal built and later fitted with a paraffin engine and screw propeller, they were capable of laying out a * bower anchor, or mounting a light gun in the bows. They had one mast with a * de Horsey rig, * gaff mainsail without a * boom, and a fore * staysail. With the virtual disappearance from all navies of the battleship and large armoured cruiser, this particular ship's boat is now obsolete. **(3)** The generic name for the small steam or power boat carried as a tender in the larger cruising yachts. Although most of these were at first steam propelled, in present times the use of petrol engines, either inboard or outboard, or small diesels is virtually universal.

LAUNCH, to, the act of sending the completed * hull of a newly built vessel from its place of construction into the water. The hull of a ship is supported on * keel blocks while she is being built and held in position by wooden * shores. When the hull is completed, the deadweight is

The 14,500-ton Syrie *being launched at Sunderland, 1968*

gradually edged from the keel blocks to wooden cradles, or sliding * ways, which rest on * launching ways which lead down into the water. In the case of very large ships a softwood cushion is fitted under the cradle supporting the bow to soften the great load concentrated there at one point during the launch when the vessel's after end is supported by the water and the forward end is still on the ways. When the hull is ready to be launched, the launching ways are covered with thick grease, the keel blocks are removed, and the weight of the ship is taken wholly on the cradles, being held stationary by mechanical triggers which in modern launching techniques take the place of the earlier * dog-shores. The wooden shores holding her steady are then knocked away and the hull is ready for launching. In the case of very large ships hydraulic rams are erected to start the hull down the ways if it does not go when the triggers are released, and heavy drag chains are attached to the hull to slow it down and bring it to a stop when fully waterborne.

Ships are launched according to the state of the tide, and the time of launching has to be adjusted to the moment when the tide is exactly right. If launched when the tide is too low, there is a tendency for the stern to droop before it is supported by the water; if too high, hull distortion may occur when the stern gets waterborne with the weight of the remainder of the hull still taken on the ways. Ships are always launched stern first so that the rudder and propellers are not damaged by the drag chains as the hull enters the water.

Smaller vessels are sometimes launched sideways, particularly in cases where there is a restricted area of water into which the launch can be made. The general procedure, however, is the same.

The launch of any ship is normally made the occasion of the naming ceremony, in which the sponsor of the vessel generally uses a time-honoured phrase, 'I name this ship ... May God bless her and all who sail in her.' A lever on the launching platform is then pulled by the sponsor, a bottle of wine is broken on the vessel's bow, the triggers are released, and the vessel, slowly at first but quickly gathering speed, slides down the ways into the water.

LAUNCHING WAYS, the beds of timber blocks, sloping gradually down towards the water, on which the * bilge-keels of a ship rest after she has been constructed in a building slip, sometimes also known as bilgeways. When a vessel is * launched they support the sliding ways, a sort of cradle which goes down with the ship into the water. See also DOG-SHORES, LAUNCH, TO.

LAURIA, LORIA, or **LURIA,** ROGER DE (d. 1305), Aragonese and Sicilian admiral, was quite the most remarkable naval commander of his age. Taken to Spain by his mother as a boy he was brought up in the court of Aragon, and at the time of the Sicilian Vespers (the famous revolt against the misrule of Charles of Anjou) in 1282 was a close friend and devoted follower of Peter III of Aragon. He accompanied Peter III in the campaign against Sicily and Naples, and after Peter had been crowned as King of Sicily Lauria was given command of the fleet.

For the next twenty years, until the peace of Calatabellota in 1303, Roger de Lauria fought a series of campaigns in which he was always victorious, not by reason of the number of his ships but by the discipline and skill with which he handled them. The French maritime forces of Charles of Anjou relied on the traditional naval fighting method of capturing enemy ships by running alongside and boarding them; Lauria trained his crews in the use of the * ram and the cross-bow, both the small cross-bows used by hand and the large ones mounted on the * bulwarks in the manner of ships' guns. He achieved his first naval victory in 1283, the year of his appointment, when he defeated a French fleet in the service of Charles of Anjou off Malta.

Two years later he conducted a brilliant naval campaign off the coast of Catalonia which was a shining example of the correct use of sea power in a largely land campaign. Catalonia had been invaded by the French king, Philippe le Hardi, in order to support Charles of Anjou, his cousin, and the Pope had given his blessing to this assault, ranking it as a holy crusade. The campaign ashore was fought with great bitterness, the excesses of the French invaders stimulating the Catalans to defend their country town by town and mountain pass by mountain pass. Lauria, recalled by Peter III from Sicily, saw that the invasion was being entirely supported by sea, all supplies and reinforcements coming from France under the protection of French squadrons, stationed at intervals along the Catalan coast. He realized that if he could defeat the centre squadron, he could roll up the two flanks without difficulty, even though the overall strength of the French was greatly in excess of his own.

He fell upon the central squadron near the Homiga islands, deciding to fight a night action and handling his fleet with superb skill. He doubled on the head of the French line, bringing the leading ships under fire from both sides, and cleared the French decks with cross-bow fire before going in with the ram. The victory was complete and decisive, and followed by the usual massacre. He then fell upon the French squadron at Rosas, using the French flag to tempt it out to sea, and defeated it with equal completeness. Deprived of supplies and facing starvation, the French forces ashore were forced to retreat and were virtually annihilated in the mountains by Catalan irregulars. This superb campaign ruined the naval power of France, and stands out as one of the most brilliant in the whole history of naval warfare.

Lauria's beloved master, Peter III, died in 1286, and his son Alphonso in the following year. The throne of Aragon descended to James, brother of Alphonso, who sought to make peace with Anjou by giving up Sicily. James's younger brother Frederick had, however, different ideas and held out in Sicily, of which he had himself crowned king, and thus landed himself with two wars, the current one against Anjou and a new one against his brother of Aragon. For a time Lauria gave his services to Frederick, but the two men were incompatible in temper and after a year or two Lauria returned to his original allegiance to Aragon. Frederick thereupon confiscated Lauria's estates in Sicily and had one of his nephews tried on a charge of treason and put to death. Lauria was not slow to react, and in two ferocious sea battles swept the Sicilian forces off the sea.

This bitter, bloody war was ended in 1303 at the peace of Calatabellota and Lauria, his work at an end, retired to his estate at Valencia. He died two years later and, at his request, his body was buried at the feet of his old lord and master, Peter III.

LAUVERGNE, BARTHÉLEMY (1805–71), French marine painter, was born at Toulon. He was the official draughtsman appointed to record scenes of interest during the voyage of exploration between 1830 and 1832 of *La Favorite*, and later served in a similar appointment on board *La Bonite* during her voyage of exploration. The accounts of these two voyages are largely illustrated with his work.

LAWRENCE, JAMES (1781–1813), American naval officer, became a *midshipman in September 1798 and in 1812 commanded the *Hornet*. In company with William *Bainbridge, he sailed to the south Atlantic where he *blockaded the British *sloop *Citoyenne* in Bahia, Brazil, until driven into port by H.M.S. *Montague*. Escaping in darkness, Lawrence fell in with the British *brig *Peacock* off British Guiana. In a brief, close action the *Hornet*, with her superior gun power, damaged the *Peacock* to such an extent that she could not be kept afloat after her surrender. In March 1813 Lawrence returned to New York and learned that he had been promoted to the rank of captain. He was ordered to command the *frigate *Chesapeake*, then at Boston, with instructions to intercept British vessels on their way to Canada.

Lawrence was an officer of considerable ability with a real fighting temperament, but in the events which followed he displayed very poor judgement. Without any sound reasons to back such an opinion, he had formed the idea that officers of the British Navy were overrated. In the *Chesapeake* he had an inexperienced crew and was short of his officer complement; nevertheless he decided to attack the British frigate *Shannon* which was then lying off the port of Boston. He sailed out of Boston on 1 June 1813 and headed for the *Shannon*. In less than 15 minutes after the first gun was fired Lawrence was mortally wounded, the *Chesapeake* was a shambles, and 146 men had been killed and wounded to 85 killed and wounded in the *Shannon*. As he was carried below in a dying condition, Lawrence is said to have repeated, 'Don't give up the ship.' At the time he was hailed as a hero, but sober and sensible consideration of all the facts leads to the conclusion that if he had not been killed he should have been brought to a court martial. The *Chesapeake* was taken as a *prize and sailed back to England.

LAWS OF OLERON, THE, see OLERON, THE LAWS OF.

LAWSON, Sir JOHN (c. 1605–65), British admiral, fought under Robert *Blake in the battles of *Dover and *Kentish Knock in 1652 during the First Anglo-Dutch War (1652–4). He commanded the *Fairfax* in the successful battle of *Portland in 1653 and as a rear admiral was in command of the *Blue (rear) division of the fleet in the battles of the *Gabbard and *Scheveningen. In 1660, with the final collapse of the Parliamentary government of England, he declared for the return of the monarchy and was selected to command the fleet which went to Holland to bring back Charles II, a service for which he was knighted. After serving in the Mediterranean in operations against the Algerine pirates, Lawson was recalled in 1664 and placed in command of the *Red (centre) squadron of the fleet in the Second Dutch War (1665–7), but was mortally wounded in the opening battle off *Lowestoft.

LAY, (1) the twist given to the strands of a rope, **(2)** a share in the profits of a whaling or fishing voyage.

LAY, to, a verb much used by seamen with a variety of meanings. A sailing vessel lays her *course when, if *close-hauled, she can reach her objective without *tacking; a ship lays-to when she is hove-to; *topmen lay out on the *yards in square-rigged ships when handling the sails; a ship is laid up when she is placed out of commission. To lay aft or forward, an order to seamen to move in the direction indicated.

LAY DAYS, the name given to the days which are allowed for the loading or discharging of the cargo of a merchant ship while she lies in port. On the expiration of the lay days, *demurrage becomes chargeable.

LAZARETTO, (1) a compartment set aside in smaller ships for the stowage of provisions and stores. It was frequently in the stern of the ship, under the direct eye and control of the *master to make pilfering more difficult, but was by no means unknown at the fore part of the 'tween decks. In modern days, with ships spending less time over a voyage and much better conditions of messing, both in quantity and variety, this type of lazaretto in a ship no longer exists. **(2)** An isolation hospital for men who may have infections or contagious diseases from ships which have been placed in quarantine.

LAZY GUY, a small *tackle or rope used to prevent the *boom of a sail swinging unduly when a sailing vessel is rolling heavily.

LAZY PAINTER, (1) a small rope for securing a boat lying alongside a ship in fine weather when her own painter is unnecessarily large for the job. **(2)** A rope or wire with a *thimble in the end hanging vertically from a lower *boom rigged out from a ship's side to which her boats are made fast when in harbour, the boat's own painter being rove through the thimble and brought back inboard and secured. This form of lazy

painter is necessary since the boom is rigged several feet above the level of the water and out of reach from a boat.

LE GOUAZ, YVES MARIE (1742–1816), French engraver, was born at Brest. He married Marie Jeanne Ozanne and helped her to engrave the pictures of Nicolas *Ozanne illustrating the campaigns of Admiral *Duguay-Trouin. He and his wife specialized in the engraving of maritime pictures, particularly those of his two brothers-in-law Nicolas and Pierre. Le Gouaz was as distinguished an engraver in his own right as the members of the famous family into which he married.

LE HAVRE, a seaport of north-west France and French terminal port of much of the cross-Channel traffic from England, and of some trans-atlantic shipping lines. The town contains the 16th century church Notre-Dame de Grâce, a true sailors' church which contains many votive offerings from seamen desiring success in their voyages, and to which Le Havre owes its other name of Havre de Grâce, conferred on it by Francis I. In 1762 it was one of the main home ports of the French *East India Company.

LE MAIRE, JACOB (1585–1616), Dutch navigator, was the son of Isaac le Maire, a director of the Dutch *East India Company who eventually quarrelled with the company and succeeded in breaking its monopoly of trade to the East. This powerful company had prevailed upon the States General to grant it the monopoly of eastern trade by both the route around the Cape of Good Hope and that through the Magellan Strait. These, it was thought at the time, were the only routes to the East since all the geographers of the period showed the land south of the Magellan Strait as part of the great continent of *Terra Australis Incognita, a solid land mass extending without a break to the South pole.

Isaac le Maire, however, was not convinced that no other route existed. He consulted Henry *Hudson about the feasibility of a *North-West passage but later discovered a more promising possibility. He read Richard *Hakluyt's *Principal Navigations* and came across the remarks of Sir Francis *Drake during his voyage of cir-cumnavigation after being blown to the southward in the second great gale following his passage of the Magellan Strait. On that occasion Drake had reported Tierra del Fuego as an island, south of which 'the Atlantic and the South Sea meet in a large and free scope'.

With this report of another route into the Pacific, Isaac le Maire consulted Willem Cornelisz *Schouten, one of the best of the East India Company's captains, to receive the reply,

'There is great reason it might be found.' He applied for, and was granted, a licence by the States General to make four voyages to any places discovered in the South Sea by means of 'new passages'. He then fitted out two ships, the *Eendracht* of 220 tons and the *Hoorn* of 110, and gave his son Jacob the title of merchant and president of the venture and Schouten that of master mariner. The two ships left the Texel on 14 June 1615, but the *Hoorn* was lost by fire at Port Desire while she was being *breamed for the removal of weed and barnacles. The *Eendracht* proceeded on her own and in January 1616 sailed through a channel ten miles long to the south of Tierra del Fuego, discovering another island to the southward. To this they gave the name of Staaten Island, in honour of the States General, and they named the channel Le Maire Strait, names by which they are both known to this day. Four days later, after weathering a severe gale, the look-outs in the *Eendracht* sighted a dark shape that towered up into the sky, and as the sea to the westward was open it was recognized as a vast cape marking the end of the land. To this cape le Maire and Schouten gave the name Hoorn after the town in Holland which was the home of the principal backers of the expedition. The *Eendracht* rounded it at 8.0 p.m., on 29 January 1616. The cape is still known as Cape *Horn.

On the ship's arrival at Ternate, the Dutch governor of the East Indies Company there refused to recognize Le Maire's claim to have discovered a new route into the Pacific and branded the ship's log as a forgery. In the words of Captain Burney, 'this was a most cruel requital for men to meet with from their own countrymen in return for having, with superior sagacity and spirit, undertaken and accomplished an enterprise so hazardous and reputable, the lustre of which continues to this day to reflect honour on their country'.

LE MASSON, HENRI JOSEPH (1900–), French marine author and editor of *Les *Flottes de Combat*, was born in Paris and educated at Paris University. He graduated in law and political science. Poor eyesight prevented him from joining the navy during the First World War (1914–18) though he subsequently became a signals officer and interpreter in the naval reserve. On the outbreak of the Second World War he was one of the liaison officers of the French Navy attached to the Admiralty in London and from 1944–5 served in the French naval intelligence division.

He originally took up maritime journalism as a hobby, but in 1943 became editor of the *Flottes de Combat*, the equivalent in France of *Jane's Fighting Ships* in Britain, and has published over 800 papers on naval history and maritime affairs

as well as a large number of books. Among these last may be mentioned *Forces sur mer* (1945), *Le Deuxième Conflit mondiale* (1946–7), *De la 'Gloire' au 'Richelieu'* (1946), *La Marine de Guerre moderne* (1951), *Histoire du Torpilleur en France 1872–1940* (1966), and *Du 'Nautilus' au 'Redoutable'* (1969). He was President of the Académie de la Marine, 1968–9.

LEAD LINE, a means of finding the depth of water near coasts and probably the earliest of the devices used by coastal navigators to facilitate safe navigation, especially in thick or hazy weather. It consists of a hemp line to which is attached, by means of a leather *becket or a rope *strop, a lead weight or plummet of about seven pounds. The lower end of the plummet is cup-shaped to accommodate the arming of the lead, this being a lump of tallow pressed into the hollow at the base of the lead to indicate the nature of the bottom deposits. Sand, mud, shingle, etc., adheres to the tallow and tells the leadsman the type of bottom he is finding; when the tallow comes up clean, he is finding rock.

The hand lead line of about 25 fathoms is used in shallow water and an experienced and skilful leadsman is able to measure depths of as much as 20 fathoms with a ship making moderate headway of about 10 knots by heaving the lead ahead of the ship so that when it reaches the bottom it will be vertically beneath him. The line is marked in a traditional way with pieces of leather at 2 (two strips), 3 (three strips), and 10 (a square piece with a hole in it) fathoms; white duck at 5 and 15 fathoms; red bunting at 7 and 17; and blue serge at 13 fathoms. The mark at 20 fathoms is a piece of cord with two knots in it. The unmarked fathoms between the marks of the lead line are called *deeps. When sounding with the lead line in darkness, the leadsman can still tell the depth by feeling the number of leather strips or the type of cloth.

For measuring depths greater than is possible with a hand lead line, the deep sea lead line is used. By its use depths of up to about 100 fathoms may be measured. The lead, in this case, is about 14 lb in weight and the line is marked at each multiple of 10 fathoms with cord having a number of knots equal to the number of tens of fathoms. Each intermediate fifth fathom is marked with a piece of cord having a single knot.

The lead is always cast from the weather side of the ship, in the case of the hand lead from a platform called the *chains, and the depths are reported to the officer of the watch by singing them loudly in a traditional manner. In earlier days when taking a cast with the deep sea lead line, the vessel was hove to and the lead carried forward. The line was then passed aft to the *poop clear of the weather rigging and other obstructions. Seamen stationed at intervals along the weather side held a small coil of the line in their hands, and at the order 'heave', the heavy lead was cast into the sea, the leadsman warning the seaman next abaft that the weight was about to come on his hand, by the call 'watch there, watch'. This seaman, on letting go his coil, after first ensuring that the lead had not yet reached bottom, gave the same warning to the hand next abaft him; and so on until the lead was felt to reach the bottom.

LEADING BLOCK, a single block, frequently a *snatch block, used as a *fairlead to bring the hauling part of a rope or the *fall of a *tackle into a more convenient direction, or to lead it on to the barrel of a winch. In the case of a tackle, the fall is known, after it has been led through a leading block, as the leading part.

LEADING LIGHT, see LEADING MARK.

LEADING MARK, a mark sometimes set up on shore or fixed on the bottom in shallow water which, when brought into line with another mark or prominent object ashore, will lead a ship clear of a local danger, such as a rock or shoal, when approaching the shore. They are sometimes lighted at night, displaying the light to seaward, for the same purpose.

LEADING WIND, the description given to a wind which is blowing *free in relation to the desired *course of a sailing vessel; i.e., any wind which enables the *sheets of a sail to be eased off to present a square aspect of the sail to the wind.

LEAGUE, a measurement of distance, long out of use. A league at sea measured 3·18 *nautical miles, the equivalent of four Roman miles, but those on land had different values according to the country, ranging from a minimum of 2·4 to a maximum of 4·6 statute miles. Usually at sea, for practical purposes, the league was taken as three nautical miles, the odd fraction being omitted.

LEAHY, WILLIAM DANIEL (1875–1959), American fleet admiral, was born in Hampton, Iowa, and graduated from the Naval Academy in 1897. He was in the *Oregon* in the battle off Santiago, Cuba, on 3 July 1898 and was serving on the Asiatic station at the time of the Boxer Rebellion in China, and the Philippine insurrection. After promotion to rear admiral he was appointed chief of the Bureau of Ordnance (1927–31) and from 1933 to 1935 was chief of the Bureau of Navigation. As a vice admiral he commanded the battleships of the Battle Force and in 1936, when he was promoted admiral, he was appointed commander Battle Force. He served as Chief of Naval Operations from 1937 to 1939, when he retired.

President Roosevelt, recognizing his great qualities, appointed him to serve as governor of Puerto Rico immediately after his retirement, and in 1940 sent him as U.S. ambassador to France. He was recalled to active duty in the navy in July 1942 and became Chief of Staff to the president. At the same time he became a member of the Joint Chiefs of Staff (U.S.) and of the Combined Chiefs of Staff (U.S. and G.B.), and reached the highest naval rank of fleet admiral in 1944.

Leahy held very definite views on all important problems, which were happily combined with exceptional tact in bringing out the opinions of officers of all ranks. Perhaps above all was his ability to ask pertinent questions and the patience to listen to the replies.

LEAKE, Sir JOHN (1656–1720), British admiral of the fleet, served at sea in both the navy and the merchant service. His first command in the navy was the *fireship *Firedrake* in 1689, and he was present at the two actions against the French at *Bantry Bay. His next command was the *Dartmouth*, a 40-gun ship in which in July 1689 he forced the *boom at Londonderry in a notable action and reached the beleaguered city with two victualling ships. He commanded the *Eagle* at the battle of *Barfleur in 1692 and in 1702 he was made governor and commander-in-chief of Newfoundland. After service in the Mediterranean at the start of the War of the Spanish Succession (1702–13) Leake joined Sir George *Rooke and had a part in the capture of Gibraltar and the immediately following battle of Malaga in 1704, and for the next two years he was much concerned with the defence of Gibraltar.

Early in 1708, following the death by shipwreck of Sir Clowdisley *Shovel in 1707, Leake was promoted to admiral of the *White and appointed commander-in-chief in the Mediterranean. On his passage out to that station he captured a large fleet of French victualling ships which he took in to Barcelona, at that time nearing starvation after a long siege by the French. He waged a most successful campaign at sea and finally returned home after the capture of Sardinia and *Minorca, becoming one of the naval lords of the Admiralty.

LEBRETON, LOUIS (d. 1866), French marine painter, was appointed official artist in the voyage of discovery to the Pacific islands and the Antarctic led by Admiral *Dumont d'Urville in the *corvettes *Astrolabe* and *Zelée*; his illustrations are a distinguished feature of the official account of this voyage. One of his better known works is his picture of the *Astrolabe* in the pack ice which was exhibited in the Salon in Paris in 1841.

LEE, probably from the Dutch *lij*, shelter, or the old English *hléo* with the same meaning, though some authorities quote the Scandinavian *loe* or *laa*, sea, as the derivation; the side of a ship, promontory, or other object away from the wind. Thus the lee side of a ship is that side which does not have the wind blowing on it, lee *helm, the helm of a vessel put down towards her lee side to bring the bows up into the wind. Yet a lee shore is a coastline on to which the wind blows directly, i.e., it is down wind from any ship in the offing, and thus can be dangerous as the wind tends to force a sailing vessel down on it. The lee of a rock or promontory, that side sheltered from the wind. The word can be used both as a noun and as an adjective.

LEE, SAMUEL PHILLIPPS (1812–97), American naval officer, was a member of the Lee family of Virginia, born in Fairfax County. He became a *midshipman in 1825 and in 1851, in command of the *Dolphin*, he cruised in the Atlantic making soundings and charting currents, and his reports assisted Matthew *Maury in the latter's oceanographic work.

Lee was at the Cape of Good Hope *en route* to the East Indies in command of the *Vandalia* when he learned of the Confederate attack on Fort Sumter which initiated the American Civil War (1861–5). Without orders, he returned to the U.S.A. and was sent to join the *blockade. In command of the *gunboat *Oneida*, under David *Farragut, he was sent ahead with two other gunboats to destroy Confederate ships above the Mississippi forts. He drove off Confederate *rams that had attacked a Union ship and received the surrender of the Confederate steamer *Governor Moore*. He became a captain in September 1862, and as acting rear admiral took command of the North Atlantic Blockading Squadron off the coasts of Virginia and North Carolina. Later during the war he commanded the Mississippi Squadron. He became a rear admiral in 1870 and commanded the North Atlantic Squadron, 1870–2.

LEEBOARD, (1) an early type of drop *keel, usually made of wood and pivoted at its forward end on each side of a flat-bottomed or shallow draught sailing vessel. They were first introduced in Europe, notably in the Low Countries, during the first half of the 15th century. When the board on the *lee side is lowered it increases the effective *draught, thereby reducing the *leeway made when sailing *close-hauled. When the vessel has to turn through the wind to change from one *tack to the other, the board on the lee side is lowered as the sails fill on the new tack while the board on the *weather side is hauled up. According to the Dutch *Dictionnaire de la Marine* (1702), leeboards were made of 'three boards laid one over another and cut to a shape of a sole of a shoe', but in fact they normally vary slightly in shape according to the waters in which the vessel sails. In those which use inland waters and canals the leeboards are generally very broad in relation to their length, in shape not unlike an opened fan, so as to present the greatest practicable area to resist leeway within the limits of depth of water. In those which work in coastal waters, where rough seas can blow up with great rapidity, the leeboards are usually long and narrow, more like *dagger plates, and a 40-ft fishing vessel, for example, would carry leeboards made up of five or six planks of oak, bound and clad with galvanized sheet iron, about nine feet long with a width of little more than two feet at the lower, and wider, end. These boards are normally cut so as to be concave on the inboard side and slightly hollowed on the outboard side, giving them a flattened aerofoil shape for greater efficiency. Mounted with a slight 'toe-in', or squint, by means of angled *wales attached to the vessel's sides, they are highly effective in reducing leeway when sailing on a wind. **(2)** A board or other preventive fitted to the side of a *bunk on board ship to keep the occupant from rolling out of it when the vessel is lively in a rough sea.

LEECH, the *after side, or lee edge, of a fore-and-aft sail and the outer edges of a square sail; in the case of square sails they are known as *port and *starboard leeches according to which side of the ship they are nearest. The leechrope is that part of the *boltrope which borders the leech of a sail. For illus. see SAIL.

LEE-FANG, the older name for a *vang. It was 'a rope which is reeved into the *cringles of the *courses when we would haul in the bottom of the sail to lace on the *bonnet' (Mainwaring, *Seaman's Dictionary*, 1644), and was also used in *fore-and-aft rigged ships, after Mainwaring's time, to prevent the *peak of a *gaff sagging away to *leeward when sailing *close-hauled.

LEE-LARCHES, an old sea term for the occasional violent rolls to *leeward made by a sailing vessel in a high sea when a particularly heavy wave strikes her on her windward side. The term is now quite obsolete.

LEESKAERTAN, literally 'reading chart', was the Flemish name for a *rutter, the old-time equivalent of the modern *Sailing Directions* and the forerunner of the navigational *chart. It consisted of continuing views of the coastline as seen from seawards together with such instructions as were necessary for safe *navigation, details of anchorages, *tides, rocks, shallows, etc. When the navigational chart was subsequently developed, it was known in Flemish as a *paskaertan*.

LEEWARD (pron. loo'ard), a term denoting a direction at sea in relation to the wind, i.e., down wind as opposed to windward, up wind.

LEEWAY, the distance a ship is set down to *leeward of her *course by the action of wind or tide. A vessel can make a lot of leeway if a strong cross *tide is running or if her *keel is not long enough or deep enough to give her a good grip of the water and hold her up to the wind. The word has also a colloquial meaning as having fallen behind in something: 'He has a lot of leeway to catch up' to reach the required position or standard.

LEG, the seaman's term for the run or distance made on a single *tack by a sailing vessel. Thus, when making for a point directly to windward, a sailing vessel will sail legs of equal length on each tack alternately; if the required *course is not directly to windward but still higher than she can *fetch on a single tack, she will sail by means of long and short legs alternately.

LEGHORN, Ital. Livorno, a major seaport and naval base in Tuscany, Italy, and the home of the Italian Naval Academy. The town itself dates from 891, but it was not until the 14th century that its development as a port began, though only on a very small scale. In 1407 the king of Spain sold it to the Genoese for 26,000 ducats; the Genoese in turn sold it to Florence in 1421. This brought it, in the 16th century, under the control of the powerful Medici family who improved the harbour considerably and provided inducements for business men of all nationalities to settle and trade there. Leghorn became free and neutral in 1691, and although this status was temporarily abused by Napoleon in 1796 when he seized all the hostile ships lying in the port, it remained so until 1867 when it was incorporated into the newly formed nation of Italy. Leghorn is now among the three or four greatest seaports of Italy, and is the home of the great Orlando shipbuilding yard.

LEGS, wooden supports lashed each side of a deep-keeled vessel, such as a yacht, to hold her upright when she takes the ground either for cleaning or repair. They extend to the depth of the keel. See also CRANK BY THE GROUND.

LEIF ERICSSON (*fl.* 999–1001), Norse explorer, a son of *Eric the Red and founder of the Scandinavian colony in Greenland, in 999 visited the court of Olaf Tryggvason in Norway, returning the following year with a commission from the king to proclaim Christianity in Greenland. According to some of the Norse sagas (particularly the *Flatey Book*) a Norse trader named Biarni Heriulfsson had in the year 986 been blown off course on his voyage to Greenland and had sighted land to the south-west but had not investigated it. Leif Ericsson, on his return from Norway in 1000, decided to investigate this report and, probably in 1001, duly discovered this land, landing at Helluland (now believed to be Baffin Island), Markland (probably Labrador), and *Vinland (Newfoundland), at which place he discovered self-sown wheat, vines, and 'mösur' wood. These have recently been tentatively identified by Professor S. E. Morison as Lyme grass (*Elymus arenarius*, var. *villosus*), the wild red currant or mountain cranberry, and the white or canoe birch.

This voyage firmly establishes Leif Ericsson and his crew as the first Europeans to set foot on the American continent, and if one can believe the saga of the *Flatey Book*, it also establishes Biarni Heriulfsson as the first European to sight that continent. See also THORFINN KARLSEFNI.

LEM, to, or **LEMMING,** the process of cutting the meat from the carcass of a whale after the removal of the blubber by *flensing.

LEMONNIER, ANDRÉ (1896–   ), French vice admiral and author, entered the navy in 1913 and saw service in *submarines during the First World War (1914–18). Promoted to captain in 1939 he was in charge of the anti-aircraft defences of Paris. He was in command of the *cruiser *Georges Leygues* which, with two others, reached Dakar in advance of an allied force dispatched to secure it on behalf of the Free French. Promoted to rear admiral in 1942 he joined the Free French forces at the time of the allied assault on north-west Africa and became Chief of the Naval Staff and of the navy at Algiers in 1943. In 1944 he was in command of the French cruisers supporting the invasion of southern France and was promoted to vice admiral.

He became director of the Institute of Higher National Defence Studies and in 1950 founded the NATO Defence College. In 1951 he was attached to the staff of General Eisenhower at Supreme Headquarters Allied Powers in Europe (SHAPE) and retired in 1956. He is the author of several books on maritime affairs.

LEMSTERAAK, a Dutch cargo carrier originating in the Friesland town of Lemmer. They are built with a round bottom, and are generally similar in shape to the *boeier but run up to 55 feet in length. Some lemsteraaks have been built as yachts, others converted into yachts. The traditional rig was a *loose-footed mainsail having a curved *gaff and a large foresail set on the forestay to the *stemhead, with the mast *stepped in the usual *tabernacle to facilitate lowering when required.

The battle of Lepanto; detail from an oil painting by Vasari and Sabbatini

LENIN, the name of a Russian nuclear-powered
*ice-breaker with a displacement of 16,000
tons, and the world's first surface ship to be
so powered. Built at Kirov Elektriria Works,
Leningrad, she was commissioned on 15
September 1959. Her three pressurized water-
cooled reactors provide heat for her boilers, the
steam raised driving three *turbines which
develop 44,000 s.h.p., to give a maximum speed
of 18 *knots. She carries two helicopters and has
a complement of 230. She is employed as an ice-
breaker on the *Northern Sea Route between
Novaya Zemlya and the Bering Sea and it is
claimed that she can clear a channel 100 feet
wide through pack ice eight feet thick at a speed
of between three and four knots.

LEOTYCHIDES (491–469 B.C.), a king of
Sparta, was in chief command of the Greek fleet
of 110 ships at Aegina and Delos in 479 B.C. and
later that year won the resounding battle of
Mycale on the coast of Asia Minor opposite
Samos, annihilating the Persian fleet and inflicting a crushing defeat on the army, thus bringing
the Persian war to an end. In 476 B.C. he conducted a successful land campaign in Thessaly
but accepted a bribe from the enemy to bring
operations to a close. For this he was sentenced
to exile, his son succeeding him as king of
Sparta.

LEPANTO, a great naval battle fought on 7
October 1571 between a combined fleet of the
Christian nations bordering the Mediterranean
and a Turkish fleet which embraced squadrons
drawn from Tunis and Algiers. The battle is
notable as the last example of a naval action
fought between *galleys manned by oarsmen and
as the last 'crusade' against the Turks which
broke for ever their command of the sea in the
eastern Mediterranean.

The Christian fleet was the outward expression of a holy league promoted by Pope Pius V,
with Venice and Spain providing the majority
of the force, to face the situation caused in
the Mediterranean by the Turkish capture of
Cyprus. The commander-in-chief was Don John
of Austria, natural brother of King Philip of
Spain, with local squadrons commanded by local
admirals. The Turkish fleet was commanded by
Ali Pasha, with Chulouk Bey of Alexandria and
Uluch Ali of Algiers as squadron commanders.
The two fleets met south of Cape Scropha, near
the Gulf of Patras, drawn up in long lines
abreast, 200 Christian galleys facing 273
Turkish. The issue of the battle was long in doubt
once the fighting began, but the more robust
Christian galleys in the end outweighed the
numerical superiority of the lighter Turkish craft
and gave Don John the ultimate victory. The
Turkish fleet was finally crushed with immense

loss of ships, and an estimate of those slain during the battle gave the Turkish losses at 20,000 and the Christian at 8,000.

The battle was of great political importance, a combined stand by many Christian states against the very real and increasing threat of a Turkish domination of the Mediterranean. It is said that among the Christian fleet there was at least one representative of every noble house in Italy and Spain, and that when calls for boarders were made during the battle, each boarding party had a prince at its head. Among the English volunteers to fight in the Christian fleet is said to have been Sir Richard * Grenville, the hero of the fight of the * Revenge off the Azores in 1591. Among the Spanish contingent was Don Miguel de Cervantes Saavedra (c. 1547–1616), the author of the famous novel Don Quixote. He lost an arm in the action.

Lepanto is commemorated in a poem of the same name by G. K. Chesterton.

LEPOTIER, ADOLPHE (1898–   ), French naval officer, was born at Nantes, studied at the naval college there, and gained a diploma in radio techniques at the school of electricity. During the Second World War he commanded, first, the * destroyers Trompe and Tempête and, later, the * cruiser Montcalm. After the war he served in the Ministry of Marine until 1948. He is perhaps better known as an author of many maritime books, among which the best known are La Victoire vint à la mer (1945), La Guerre Moderne dans les trois dimensions (1949), Sous la Banquise (1961), and Les Fusiliers Marins (1962). He has also written histories of the naval ports of Brest and Lorient.

LESSEPS, FERDINAND DE (1805–94), French diplomatist, is remembered in the maritime field as the creator of the * Suez Canal and the leading member of the abortive * Panama Canal project of 1879 which landed him in deep political controversy and condemnation when it failed. The permanent monument to his greatness, however, is the Suez Canal, which links the Mediterranean to the Indian Ocean, of which he turned the first sod at Port Said on 25 April 1859, remaining as chief engineer and director until it was formally opened by the Khedive, Ismail Pacha, on 17 November 1869.

LESTOCK, RICHARD (c. 1679–1746), British admiral, was second captain of the Barfleur, * flagship of Sir George * Byng at the battle of Cape Passaro in 1718. After various appointments at home and abroad he commanded the Boyne in the West Indies in 1740 and flew a broad pendant as * commodore and third in command under Vice Admiral * Vernon, taking part in the operations off Cartagena in 1741.

He was promoted rear admiral in March 1742 when in the Mediterranean, and there then followed a period of strained relations between him and the commander-in-chief, Vice Admiral Thomas * Mathews. This clash of personalities had serious consequences in an action against the French fleet off Toulon in February 1744 when Lestock failed to support Mathews. After the action Mathews sent Lestock home where he was court-martialled for failing to do his utmost to engage the enemy. He was acquitted on a technicality arising out of the rigidity of the * Fighting Instructions. After the trial he was promoted admiral and commanded a squadron in an expedition against Lorient in 1745 which ended in failure.

LET FLY, to, the action of letting go the * sheets of a sailing vessel so that the sails flap directly down wind and lose all their forward driving force. It is a means, though possibly an unseamanlike one, of losing the way quickly off a boat under sail when bringing her alongside a pier or wharf or picking up a * mooring buoy. In the Royal Navy it was also the form of salute in a boat under sail when passing a senior officer.

'LET GO AND HAUL' or **'AFORE HAUL',** one of the orders given during the process of * tacking a square-rigged ship, being given when the bow of the ship has just passed across the wind and is about to * pay off. 'Let go' refers to the fore * bowline and what are now, after crossing the wind, the weather * braces, and 'haul' refers to the lee braces.

LETTER OF MARQUE or **MART,** a commission issued in Britain by the * Lord High Admiral, or Commissioners executing his office, and by the equivalent authorities in other countries, licensing the commander of a privately owned ship to cruise in search of enemy merchant vessels, either as * reprisal for injuries suffered or as acts of war. The ships so licensed were also themselves sometimes referred to as letters of marque, though more usually called * privateers. The earliest mention of such a letter is in 1293 and they continued to be issued in time of war or of reprisal until privateering was abolished at the * Convention of Paris in 1856.

A letter of marque or reprisal normally describes the ship, her owners and officers, the amount of surety which has been deposited, and stresses the necessity of having all * prizes condemned and valued at a * Vice Admiralty Court for the payment of * prize money. The practice of licensing privateers by special commissions was very often a highly profitable affair and many owners were anxious to equip their ships with guns in wartime to prey on such merchant shipping as they could come across. In spite of the official commissions they carried, many of them were not too particular about the nationality of the ships they attacked, acting more as pirates than as licensed privateers. It was a form of warfare much criticized by all navies, as the rewards of a successful privateering voyage were often so great that they attracted seamen away from service in regular warships.

LEVANTER, a strong, raw wind from the east or north-east which blows in the Mediterranean.

LEVIATHAN, in its scriptural meaning a gigantic sea animal, the maritime equivalent of the behemoth ashore. It has been described in the Bible as a crocodile (Job xli. 15) and a sea dragon or serpent (Isaiah xxvii. 1). In modern usage it is mostly taken to mean a whale and, by extension, a very large ship. When used as an actual ship's name, however, the vessels concerned have not all been unduly large. It was the name given to a British armoured *cruiser of 14,100 tons launched in 1901, and was also the name given by the Americans to the German *liner *Vaterland*, built in 1913, when they took her over after the First World War (1914–18) after she had been interned in New York for the duration of that war. The *Great Eastern*, designed by I. K. *Brunel, was also known as *Leviathan* until her name was changed on her launching in 1858.

LEWIS, MICHAEL ARTHUR (1890–1970), British naval historian, was educated at Uppingham and Trinity College, Cambridge. In 1913 he was appointed assistant master at the Royal Naval College, Osborne. During the First World War (1914–18) he served in the Royal Marine Artillery, returning to Osborne as a term master in 1917. In 1919 he went to the Royal Naval College at Dartmouth as assistant head of the history and English department. From 1934 to 1955 he was professor of history and English at the Royal Naval College, *Greenwich. During the Second World War he worked on various projects centred on Dartmouth. His publications include light verse and novels but his real love was naval history. Among his many books on this last subject are *England's Sea Officers* (1939), *The Navy of Britain* (1948), *History of the British Navy* (1957), *A Study of the Spanish Armada* (1960), *Napoleon and his British captives* (1962), *A Social History of the Navy 1793–1815* (1960), *The Navy in Transition* (1965). For a great many years he served on the council and as vice-president of the *Navy Records Society and the *Society for Nautical Research.

LEXINGTON, U.S.S., a ship's name used seven times in the U.S. Navy. The first was the *brigantine *Wild Duck* purchased by Congress and renamed *Lexington* in 1776. Under the command of John *Barry she avoided the British *frigate *Roebuck* which was just inside the entrance to Delaware Bay and succeeded in reaching the open sea. Off Cape Charles, Virginia, she captured the *sloop *Edward*, a tender of the British frigate *Liverpool*, manned by a crew of twenty-nine men of the British Navy. There was another *Lexington* in the navy in 1825 and she had some part in the Mexican War. Three others were used in various ways during the Civil War (1861–5), one a side-wheel converted river steamer purchased by John *Rodgers.

One of the two ships initially designed as *battle-cruisers and completed as *aircraft carriers was the *Lexington*. She was sunk in the battle of the *Coral Sea on 7 May 1942. Another *Lexington*, also a carrier, began service on 17 February 1943 and earned eleven battle stars during the fighting of the Second World War.

LEYTE GULF, BATTLE OF, a naval action fought on 23–26 October 1944, during the Second World War, between the main fleet of Japan and the Third and Seventh Fleets of the U.S.A. In terms of the size of the opposing forces and the area over which it ranged, it was the biggest naval battle in history.

From 20 October a huge amphibious expedition was being established by the Americans in the Gulf of Leyte in the Philippines. The Japanese launched a counter-attack with their Combined Fleet divided into four sections. Two groups came from Singapore via Brunei: Vice Admiral *Kurita's Force 'A', composed of the giant battleships *Yamato* and *Musashi*, the older battleships *Nagato*, *Kongo*, and *Haruna*, ten heavy cruisers, two light cruisers, and fifteen destroyers, and Vice Admiral Shoji Nishimura's Force 'C', the battleships *Yamashiro* and *Fuso*, the cruiser *Mogami*, and four destroyers. Force 'A' was to pass through the Sibuyan Sea and the San Bernardino Strait to approach Leyte Gulf from the north on the morning of 25 October, while Force 'C' was to debouch at the same time into the Gulf through the Surigao Strait to the south. Nishimura was to be followed by the 2nd Striking Force under Vice Admiral Kiyohide Shima, advancing from the Ryukyus, composed of two heavy cruisers, a light cruiser, and four destroyers. Directly from Japan came the aircraft carrier force under Vice Admiral Jisaburo *Ozawa: the carriers *Zuikaku* (flag), *Chitose*, *Chiyoda*, and *Zuiho*, the *hermaphrodite battleship-carriers *Hyuga* and *Ise*, three light cruisers, and eight destroyers. The carrier force had only a handful of aircraft flown by half-trained pilots, and it was given the role of decoy to draw out of Kurita's path the U.S. carrier Task Force 37—

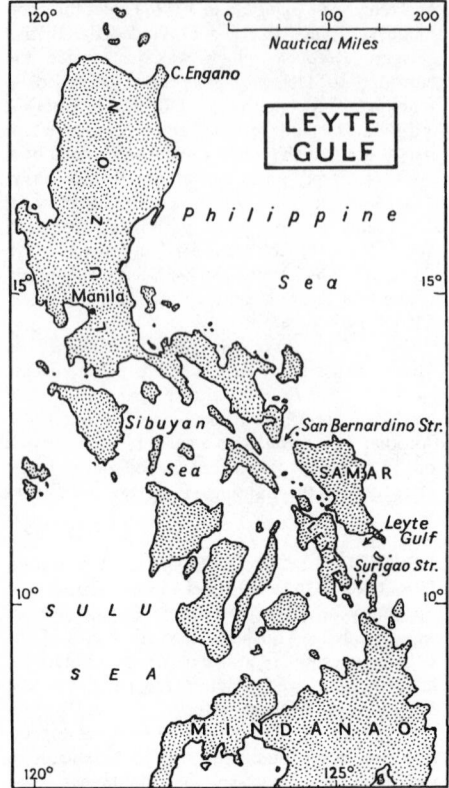

eight fleet and eight light carriers in four task groups, each with a battleship, cruiser, and destroyer screen—of Admiral William *Halsey's Third Fleet which was operating in the Philippine Sea. Other American forces in the area were Task Group 77.4 of Admiral Thomas *Kinkaid's Seventh Fleet—sixteen escort carriers in four task units operating to the east of Samar and Mindanao Islands in support of the landings in Leyte Gulf—and the bombardment and fire support group of six old battleships, four heavy and four light cruisers, and twenty-one destroyers organized into a battle force under Rear Admiral J. B. Oldendorf.

At dawn on 23 October the U.S. submarines *Darter* and *Dace* sank the heavy cruisers *Atago* (Kurita's flagship) and *Maya* and crippled the *Takao*. Aircraft from Task Force 37, commanded by Vice Admiral Marc *Mitscher, discovered Kurita's force early on the 24th as it was entering the Sibuyan Sea. The Japanese plan allowed for air cover at this point to be supplied by shore-based naval aircraft controlled by Vice Admiral Shigeru Fukudome. He decided that the best way of protecting Force 'A' was by attacking the American Third Fleet carriers rather than by giving fighter cover. The carrier Task Group 38.3 commanded by Rear Admiral F. C.

*Sherman bore the brunt of these attacks. Its fighter planes drove off most of the Japanese aircraft, but a single dive-bomber scored a hit which set the light carrier *Princeton* uncontrollably ablaze so that she had eventually to be *scuttled. In reply, repeated air strikes were launched against Kurita throughout the day; and the *Musashi* eventually sank. Although his other ships suffered little damage, Kurita was delayed so that early on the 25th, when he should have been off Leyte Gulf, he was only just emerging from the San Bernardino Strait.

Oldendorf's support group had been ordered to block the exit from the Surigao Strait against Nishimura's and Shima's squadrons which were reported approaching on the 24th. During the night of 24/25 October it sank the battleships *Yamashiro* and *Fuso* and three destroyers and severely damaged the heavy cruiser *Mogami* (eventually scuttled), a light cruiser, and another destroyer, as first Nishimura and then Shima attempted to break through into Leyte Gulf.

At dawn on the 25th, soon after entering the Philippine Sea, Kurita sighted the most northerly of the four task units of Task Group 77.4, six escort carriers with three destroyers and three destroyer-escorts under Rear Admiral Clifton Sprague. Sprague at once flew off every available aircraft to attack as best they could while near misses from enemy gunfire were shaking his flagship *Fanshaw Bay*, then under cover of a rain squall altered course towards Leyte Gulf, hoping for help from Oldendorf's ships. The *Gambier Bay* was sunk while planes from Task Group 77.4 and the escorts of Sprague's unit fought a brilliant rearguard action in which, at the cost of two destroyers and one destroyer-escort sunk and others damaged, they sank three of Kurita's heavy cruisers and heavily damaged another before Kurita abandoned both the chase and the part allotted to him in the battle plan, instead turning to retire through the San Bernardino Strait.

The desperate tactic of *kamikaze suicide attacks was meanwhile being directed against Task Unit 77.4.1, commanded by Rear Admiral T. L. Sprague. At 0740 on 25 October one of these aircraft dived through the flight deck of the escort carrier *Santee*, but she survived both this and a torpedo from a Japanese submarine. The *Suwannee* also survived being struck by a kamikaze. Soon after its unexpected escape from Kurita, Task Unit 77.4.3 was also subjected to kamikaze attacks. The majority were shot down, but one hit the escort carrier *St. Lo* which blew up and sank and another heavily damaged the *Kalinin Bay*.

The Seventh Fleet's near-disastrous exposure to Kurita's battleships had come about because Kinkaid had understood that Halsey was leaving his battleships to cover the exit from the Strait:

he had in fact taken his whole force north to attack Ozawa's aircraft carrier force. Off Cape Engano during the 25th, all the Japanese carriers, the light cruiser *Tama*, and two destroyers were sunk. The rest escaped owing, in the view of Halsey, to his decision, under pressure from the Commander-in-Chief Pacific, to send back his battleship force to Kinkaid's support. This, in the event, arrived too late to affect the issue or to engage Kurita before he re-entered the San Bernardino Strait. He was harried by U.S. naval and military aircraft as he retired during the 26th, but lost only one more ship, the light-cruiser *Noshiro*.

Including mopping-up operations which occupied a few days more, the total Japanese losses in the battle for Leyte Gulf were three battleships, four aircraft carriers, six heavy and four light cruisers, and nine destroyers as against American losses of one light carrier, two escort carriers, two destroyers, and one destroyer-escort. Furthermore nearly every major Japanese unit was damaged, some seriously. From that time, the Japanese Imperial Navy was reduced to an auxiliary role in their war effort.

LIBERTY, the sailor's name for short leave from his ship. Sailors with permission to go ashore for the day or night are known as liberty men.

LIBERTY SHIPS, mass-produced, prefabricated merchant vessels with all-welded hulls produced in U.S. shipyards between 1941 and 1945 to replace tonnage sunk by German, Italian, and Japanese *U-boats during the Second World War. A total of 2,770 Liberty ships amounting to 29,292,000 d.w.t. (see TONNAGE) were built, including 24 equipped as *colliers, 8 as tank carrier ships, 36 as aircraft transports, and 62 as *tankers. The original design was produced by the Sunderland Company, Newcastle upon Tyne, England, as long ago as 1879 and these plans were adopted by the Americans because they incorporated simplicity of design and operation, rapidity of construction, large cargo-carrying capacity, and a remarkable ability to withstand war damage. As the entire U.S. capacity for *turbines and diesel engines was earmarked for naval and other essential construction, Liberty ships were fitted with *triple-expansion steam engines and steam-driven auxiliary machinery. Of a *deadweight tonnage of 10,500, they had an overall speed of 11 knots.

The construction of Liberty ships throughout the U.S.A. was organized and directed by Mr. Henry Kaiser, whose original idea it was. Though never previously having run a shipyard, he laid down the procedure for quantity production on a massive scale and oversaw the entire processes of this massive experiment in rapid and vast shipbuilding. See also VICTORY SHIPS.

LIE A-TRY, to, the operation of a sailing vessel in a very high sea to lie head to the wind, or as near to it as possible, keeping a slight forward motion in order to remain within a trough of the waves. It involves taking in all sails except, perhaps, a *mizen topsail or *trysail, though it is also a possibility under *bare poles. See also TRY, TO.

LIE-TO, to, a sailing ship lies-to when, in a gale, she keeps her head as steady as possible about six points off the wind, making a little way ahead as she falls off away from the wind to avoid drifting down to *leeward. For this purpose just enough sail is set to give her forward motion as she falls away from the wind, bringing her back up to it. The main objective in lying-to is to keep the vessel in such a position with the wind on the bow that heavy seas do not break aboard. See also DRIFT, TO, HEAVE-TO, TO.

LIEUTENANT, the rank in virtually every navy in the world next below that of lieutenant-commander or its equivalent. Originally there was no such rank as lieutenant-commander, lieutenants being promoted direct to *captain, in those days captain being the equivalent rank of the commander of today, and *post-captain that of today's captain. In the Italian and Spanish Navies, and most South American Navies, the prefix is omitted and the rank is *tenente* or *teniente*. In almost all navies there are two grades of lieutenant, in the British Navy sub-lieutenant and lieutenant, in the U.S.A. lieutenant, junior grade (j.g.), and lieutenant; in Germany *leutnant zur See* and *ober-leutnant zur See*; in France *enseigne de vaisseau* and *lieutenant de vaisseau*.

The origin of the term comes from the French *lieu*, place, and *tenant*, holder, one who holds his authority from a senior officer. The word is pronounced 'leftenant' in English, but follows the spelling in other countries ('lootenant' in the U.S.A.). It would appear that the English pronunciation derives from the old French form of *luef* for *lieu*. See APPENDIX 1.

LIFEBOAT and LIFE-SAVING. A reasonable definition of a lifeboat would be a boat specifically designed for saving life at sea, although ordinary ships' boats are called lifeboats when engaged in saving life. They are normally known as seaboats when employed for other purposes. Britain enjoys the reputation of being the first nation in the world to adopt a comprehensive organization for saving life at sea. Admiral *Graves is credited with building a lifeboat in about 1760, but a better claim for being the real initiator is usually given to Lionel Lukin, a coachbuilder, who in 1785 converted a Norwegian *yawl by giving her a projecting cork *gunwale, air-chambers at bow and stern, and a false *keel of iron, to provide buoyancy and

Greathead's lifeboat; early 19th-century engraving

Arun class 54-ft lifeboat

stability. This he called his 'insubmergible boat', but although he took out a patent for it, the invention had no success. He did, however, design an 'unimmergible' *coble for use at Bamborough, Yorkshire, which saved many lives.

It took the disaster of the *Adventure* in 1798 to dispel public apathy in saving life at sea. This ship was wrecked in rough seas off Newcastle, only 300 yards from the shore while a large crowd watched helplessly as her crew, one by one, dropped to their death in the fierce seas. A public meeting was held and money raised for the best design of a lifeboat. A design by Henry Greathead, boatbuilder of South Shields, was selected as the best, and the lifeboats he built did sterling service.

The year 1823 is the next milestone in the history of lifeboats and life-saving, when Sir William Hillary, of the Isle of Man, who had himself taken part in the saving of over 300 lives from ships wrecked on the coast, succeeded in getting the question discussed in Parliament. He founded in 1824 the Royal National Institution for the Preservation of Life from Shipwreck, which became the Royal National Lifeboat Institution. This institution, which has authority over all life-saving stations in Britain, did noble work up and down the coasts of Britain, but at first was always hampered by lack of money. When the Duke of Northumberland became president in 1851, he successfully aroused public enthusiasm, money flowed in, and the committee of management advertised a prize of 100 guineas to the designer of a self-emptying, self-righting lifeboat. The prize was won by Mr. James Beeching of Great Yarmouth, and many examples of his boat were built.

Since then the design of lifeboats has been under constant review and experiment, and immense advances made in stability, buoyancy, speed, and robustness of construction. The modern shore-based lifeboat is fitted with two-way wireless communication, searchlights, and medical supplies for treating and maintaining life in cases of injury. Powerful motors give them good mobility in even the roughest conditions of sea. In Britain, the Royal National Lifeboat Institution is run on an entirely voluntary basis.

At most life-saving stations around the coast, *breeches-buoy equipment is kept ready for use in cases where it can be usefully employed. The equipment consists of a line-throwing gun, by which means a light rope can be fired from a position ashore to a ship which has gone ashore. This line is then used to haul across a wire *jackstay which is secured between ship and shore and along which a breeches-buoy travels on a *sheave. Men from the wrecked ship are then hauled ashore one by one in the breeches-buoy.

In the U.S.A. the first government life-saving stations were set up in New Jersey in 1848, although one or two local organizations had been operating along the coast since the pioneer Massachusetts Humane Society had been inaugurated in 1789. In 1871 Mr. S. Kimball was appointed as head of the Revenue Cutter Service, which was the governing body of the various life-saving stations in existence, and he undertook a thorough and most efficient reorganization of the entire life-saving service which lifted it into one of the finest such services in the world.

The life-saving service in Belgium was established in 1838, that of Denmark in 1848, Sweden in 1856, France in 1865, Germany in 1885, Turkey in 1868, Russia in 1872, Italy in 1879, Spain in 1880.

Since about 1960, the emphasis on life-saving at sea has been progressively attached to the helicopter, which has a distinct advantage over the lifeboat in speed, manoeuvrability, and stability. In most advanced nations today, the coastline is divided into sectors, with a helicopter service, normally provided by the armed services, on call in emergency. Although lifeboats still provide the backbone of the normal life-saving service, it seems probable over the next few years that the use of helicopters for this service will continue to expand.

At sea, ships carry their own lifeboats and *carley floats or their equivalent, sufficient to accommodate the entire crew and all passengers. These lifeboats are always kept at their *davits, ready for lowering in an emergency, and always fully stocked with food, water, and medical supplies. Rubber self-inflatable dinghies, with hoods as protection against weather, are growing in popularity, both for the safety and protection they afford and for their ease in stowage.

O. Warner, *A History of the Royal National Lifeboat Institution* (1974).

LIFEBUOY or **LIFEBELT**, a buoy designed to support a human body in the water. The majority of lifebuoys are circular rings of cork covered with canvas, but some are cruciform, made of copper, and fitted with a calcium flare which burns for 20 minutes when it comes in contact with seawater. These lifebuoys can support the weight of two men in water. At one period in the history of the British Navy these lifebuoys, which were carried one on each quarter of the ship on a sloping platform ready for instantaneous letting go, were also fitted with a container holding one gill of brandy, but the temptation was found to be too great even for those who did not fall overboard. In most small craft, including many yachts, one lifebuoy is attached to the vessel by a line to make it easier to haul back on board when supporting a man overboard. In many racing yachts, international rules require, in addition, a * dan buoy to be carried to mark the position when a member of the crew falls overboard.

LIFE-JACKET, a short jacket worn across the chest and back for saving life at sea by holding a body upright in the water. The old-fashioned type, still in wide use today, consists of sections of cork enclosed in canvas and fashioned to slip over the head, being secured by tapes tied round the waist. Under Board of Trade regulations every British ship must carry one for every person on board and similar regulations are enforced in the ships of other nations by their national authorities. A more modern design of life-jacket is the inflatable type, where air is held between layers of the jacket sufficient to support a body in the water. They are often inflated automatically by a carbon dioxide cylinder.

LIFELINES, ropes or wires stretched fore and * aft along the * decks of a ship in rough weather, so that men can hang on to them in heavy seas as a safety measure against being washed overboard. In yachts, they are the lines rigged fore and aft on to which * harnesses are clipped.

LIFERAFT, originally any raft made on board ship from any available timber and used for saving life in shipwreck or other calamity. More recently, many ships carry inflatable rubber rafts for the same purpose.

LIFTS, the hemp ropes, later replaced by wire ropes or chains, which in square-rigged ships are led from the various mastheads to the two ends of the corresponding * yards to support them. In the days of sailing navies ships going into battle used to supplement these rope lifts with chain lifts as a precaution against the yards being shot away by * chain or bar shot.

LIGHT TO, to, an order, when * belaying a hawser round a * bollard and the first turn has been made, to * fleet the hawser back along the deck to provide enough slack for additional turns round the bollard to be made. When there is tension on the hawser, the first turn round a bollard will hold it momentarily, but additional turns are then required to make it secure, and enough rope to make these additional turns is provided by the order 'Light to'.

LIGHT LISTS, a periodical publication, in two volumes, of the British Hydrographic Department of the Navy, giving the position and characteristics of every navigational light, whether from * lighthouse, * lightship, or lighted * buoy, in the world. It supplements the information shown on charts, which remain of course the primary navigational documents.

LIGHTER, a dumb vessel (i.e., one without its own means of propulsion), usually of * barge or similar build, used for the conveyance of cargo from ship to shore, or vice versa. They are towed by tugs. A variant, known as an X-lighter, was used by the British naval forces during the First World War (1914–18) for amphibious operations, carrying troops and field guns from a ship to an open beach. They were fitted with a ramp over the bows and were propelled by a small diesel engine. They were used in the landings at Gallipoli in 1915.

LIGHTHOUSE, a building or other construction erected to display a * characteristic light as a warning of danger at sea and an aid to navigation.

The lighthouse has a long history, and no doubt owes its origin to the beacon fires which were maintained by priests in ancient Egypt. There is a description of a lighthouse at Sigeum (the present Cape Inchisari) in the writings of the poet Lesches in 660 B.C. The most famous of the older lighthouses is undoubtedly the Pharos of Alexandria, which was built in the reign of Ptolemy II (283–247 B.C.) by Sostratus of Cnidus. This was well authenticated as one of the wonders of the world. Contemporary claims that the tower, which carried the light at the top, was 600 feet high are, however, open to some doubt.

The oldest lighthouses in western Europe are said to be those erected by the Romans at Dover and Boulogne, in the 1st or 2nd century A.D. There were famous lighthouses in Italy in the 1st century, those at Ostia, Ravenna, and Messina being the best known. The light exhibited at Cordouan, a rock in the sea in the Gironde estuary, is recognized as the first example of a lighthouse built out at sea. The earliest of the Cordouan towers dates from about A.D. 800.

With the growth of seaborne trade and the consequent expansion of shipping, the need for lighthouses grew. This development has continued to the extent that where there is any reasonable volume of traffic passing through coastal waters, no ship at sea is ever out of range of a light of some sort.

The first lighthouses were lit by braziers in which wood or coal fires were burnt. By the end of the 18th century this haphazard means of illumination was being replaced by oil lights reflected off parabolic mirrors, the first example of such a light being set up in 1763 in the Mersey by Mr. Hutchinson, dockmaster at Liverpool. This is known as the catoptric system, light being reflected only from the faces of incidence, which may be plane, parabolic, or spherical. Some twenty years later a dioptric system, in which the light rays pass through optical glass and are thus refracted, was used at Portland, England, the invention of T. Rogers. The catadioptric system,

Winstanley's lighthouse on the Eddystone Rock, 1699; engraving after a contemporary drawing

which combines these two, was first installed in the Chassiron lighthouse, France, in 1827. In areas where fog or mist are prevalent, the tendency has been to place the lighthouse as near sea level as possible in order to achieve maximum visibility in these conditions.

Individual lights are recognized by their characteristics, which can vary from a fixed light visible all round or in a certain advertised sector, to *flashing, *occulting, or *fixed and flashing lights. The pure mechanics of such lights can be simply achieved by revolving the assembly of lenses, prisms, and mirrors around the light. A flashing light is one in which the period of light displayed is less than the period of darkness between flashes; an occulting light is one in which the period of light is more than the period of darkness. Further variations in characteristics can be reached by arranging the flashes in a flashing light in groups of two or more; the same can be done, of course, with an occulting light. A

fixed light can have flashes incorporated in it to make it a fixed and flashing light.

Lighthouses come under the control of the national authorities on whom has been placed the responsibility for all coastal lights and navigational marks. See, e.g., TRINITY HOUSE.

LIGHTNING, H.M.S., later renamed Torpedo-boat No. 1, was the first warship in the world equipped to launch a locomotive *torpedo. Of 19 tons displacement, she was launched in 1876 and on her trials reached the then impressive speed of 19 knots. Originally designed to carry *spar torpedoes, she was modified in 1879 by the addition of two above-water tubes for the discharge of *Whitehead torpedoes. Her success led to an order from the British Admiralty for twelve similar torpedoboats from various builders, and two of them, Nos. 17 and 18, built by *Yarrow, reached the unbelievable speed for that time of 21·9 knots.

The Smith's Knoll lightship in the North Sea

LIGHTSHIP, normally a dumb vessel (i.e., non-navigable) though in some countries lightships are fitted with diesel engines for self-propulsion, moored over a shoal or bank where, because of the distance from the shore or constructional difficulties, a *lighthouse is impracticable. Its purpose is exactly the same as that of a lighthouse, a warning to seamen of danger and an aid to navigation. Like lighthouses they display at night a *characteristic light, carried on a tripod mast, and by day a special mark, both easily identifiable and marked on every chart which covers the waters in which they are moored. They are also equipped with fog and submarine signalling equipment and *radar beacons. Again like lighthouses they come under the control of the national authorities on whom has been placed the responsibility for all coastal lights or navigational marks, in English waters, Trinity House, in Scottish waters the Commissioners of Northern Lights. In British and many other waters, lightships are always painted red.

Lightships, which normally carry crews of three or four men, are gradually being replaced, on grounds of economy, with *Lanby buoys, which are unmanned but provide the same service for navigators.

LIGNUM VITAE, the hard smooth wood of the guaiacum tree, grown in the West Indies and often thought in older days to have medicinal qualities, also widely used for the manufacture of drinking vessels. It had many maritime uses, particularly for the *deadeyes and *chesstrees of sailing vessels and the sheaves of wooden *blocks, its hardness standing up well to wear caused by ropes and its smoothness allowing a rope to render through it easily. One principal marine use during the 19th century was as a seawater self-lubricating bush for the stern tubes of early *screw steamships. It was first introduced for this purpose by John Penn, marine engine builder, in 1854, and until the introduction of more modern metallic packings, solved the serious problem of leaking stern bearings for some forty years.

LIMBERS, holes cut in the floor *timbers of wooden ships on either side of the *keelson to allow a free passage for the *bilge water to run down to the pump well. In the larger ships a small chain or rope, known as a limber-rope, was threaded through the limbers extending the whole length of the bottom; by pulling it backward and forwards any blockages of the limbers by dirt or other obstructions was cleared. As bilgewater normally stank and was often a breeder of disease, it was most important to keep the limber-ways clear so that the bilges would drain themselves of an accumulation of water. Smaller ships which had no limber-rope were fitted with limber-boards, which were short removable boards, part of the lining of a ship's *floor close to the keelson and directly above the limbers so that they could be freed of dirt when required.

'LIMEY', a name originally used by Americans when referring to a British seaman, though now frequently enlarged to embrace all British people. It originated from the British regulation that all ships registered in the U.K. were to carry a stock of lime juice on board for issue to the crew as a preventive against *scurvy. For the same reason, British ships were known in the U.S.A. as 'lime-juicers'.

LIND, JAMES (1716–94), British naval surgeon and the father of nautical medicine, entered the British Navy as a surgeon in 1739 and took his physician's degree at Edinburgh University in 1748. The previous year, as surgeon in H.M.S. *Salisbury* and shocked at the huge casualties from *scurvy which had occurred during Commodore *Anson's voyage round the world in 1740–4, he had made the first controlled dietary experiment in history, discovering that the juice of oranges and lemons was a sure specific against the disease. He made known his findings in his *Treatise of the Scurvy*, published in 1753, but administrative apathy prevented the knowledge becoming widespread and it was not until 1795, and then at the instance of one of Lind's followers, Sir Gilbert *Blane, that the issue of lemon juice was officially adopted in the Royal Navy. Shortly after this date, lime juice was substituted for lemon juice as a specific against scurvy although it has little anti-scorbutic properties. The reason for the change was that limes were grown in the British West Indian colonies while lemons had to be imported from Mediterranean countries (see also LIMEY).

Lind wrote two books on hygiene which were more immediately effective than his *Treatise of the Scurvy*, the first, *An Essay on the Most Effectual Means of Preserving the Health of Seamen*, being published in 1757, and the second, *An Essay on Diseases Incidental to Europeans in Hot Climates* (1768), being the first handbook ever produced on tropical medicine. In 1758 he was appointed physician in charge of the new naval hospital built at *Haslar, Portsmouth, a post in which he remained until 1783 when he was succeeded by his son John.

It is a sad commentary on Lind's discoveries in relation to the control and cure of scurvy that it took more than forty years and tens of thousands of deaths from the disease before his findings were implemented and the disease virtually stamped out at sea.

LINE, a fleet formation used by warships for cruising or battle. Since most warships armed with guns produce their maximum weight of fire on the *beam, the normal formation for battle is line ahead, each ship following in the wake of the ship ahead of her. This was particularly the case in the days of sailing warships where the guns were mounted on *carriages and could only fire broadside on through the *gunports cut in the ship's side. In more modern warships, with guns mounted in turrets which can be trained through an arc either side of the centre line, the line ahead formation is not so essential, and ships disposed in quarter-line are usually able to bring all their guns to bear. LINE *ABREAST, ships formed in a line abeam of each other; LINE OF BEARING, ships disposed in a line on any particular bearing from the flagship. See also LINE OF BATTLE, A-ARCS.

LINE OF BATTLE, the line formed by ships of a fleet before joining battle with an enemy fleet. Since most conventional warships can bring the maximum weight of gunfire to bear only when they fire on the beam or quarter, the usual line of battle is either line ahead of quarter-line. Wind direction, the position of the sun, visibility, and so on, are always factors which will influence a fleet commander in his choice of where and how he forms his line of battle.

In the days of sailing warships, only the wind had to be taken into account, according to whether the admiral wanted to be to *windward or to *leeward of the enemy line when battle was joined. With fleet actions normally fought at a range of 100 yards or less, visibility, position of the sun, etc., were of less importance. Both windward and leeward positions had advantages. The fleet to windward was less affected by smoke from the guns and could see signals hoisted by the repeating *frigates without difficulty. The windward position also enabled an admiral, if his line overlapped that of an enemy, to order ships of his *van or rear to double (come up on the other side of) the enemy line. In the early days when *fireships were important weapons of attack, the fleet to windward could employ them, the fleet to leeward could not.

The advantages of the leeward position were that disabled enemy ships would be driven down by the wind on to the ships to leeward and thus captured; ships damaged in the leeward line could bear away before the wind, leaving room for ships not already in action to take their place; ships to leeward could also keep their lower gunports open in a seaway much longer than ships to windward, and thus bring a heavier weight of gunfire to bear longer; and, most important, an admiral in the leeward position could force an enemy fleet to fight if its admiral had ideas of declining battle.

LINE SQUALL, a squally wind heralded by a dark cloud stretched across the horizon, sometimes arched in form. It is caused by a narrow area of low pressure passing across the sea with an area of high pressure following close behind it. Where the differences of pressure are considerable, a heavy squall blows up accompanied by a distinct drop in temperature.

LINER, (1) a ship belonging to a shipping company which carries passengers on scheduled routes. The older sailing * packet ships were occasionally known as liners, but the name generally came into wider circulation with the change from sail to steam, roughly about 1840. With the recent rapid growth of air traffic and its consequent competition with liners for the available passengers, the number of liners in commission today has been considerably reduced, and many of them can only make a profit for their owners by becoming cruise liners catering for holiday traffic. A cargo liner is a cargo-carrying vessel with accommodation for a few passengers. **(2)** A word often used in the days of sailing warships to describe a * ship of the line. **(3)** A fishing vessel engaged in fishing at sea with lines. Before the use of * trawls or * purse seine netting in sea-fishing, cod and ling were almost entirely caught by line with baited hooks.

LINES, the designer's drawings of a ship. Normally they consist of three plans: the sheer plan which shows the longitudinal vertical section of the ship; the body plan which shows the vertical cross-sections; and the half-breadth plan which shows the longitudinal transverse section at the deck line and waterline and other stations in the same plane. See also DRAUGHT, SHIPBUILDING.

LININGS, additional pieces of canvas sewn to a sail to prevent chafe. They are used mainly in such places as the reef-bands, buntlines, etc., and are generally only to be seen in the sails of square-rigged ships where the chances of chafing are much greater, due to the multiplicity of rigging, than in * fore-and-aft rigged ships.

LINSCHOTEN, JAN HUYGEN VAN (1563–1611), Dutch explorer, was born at Haarlem. In 1576 he joined his brothers in business at Seville, Spain, and in 1583 sailed for India where he remained until 1590, being wrecked at Terceira on the voyage home. He remained for two years in the Azores and wrote a well-known account of the last fight of the * *Revenge*. In 1594, in company with Willem * Barents, he sailed with a

squadron of three ships from the Texel on a voyage to discover a * North-East passage to China. While Barents explored the west coast of Novaya Zemlya, the other two ships reached the Kara Sea and reported open water to the northward. On his return Linschoten convinced the States-General that a northern route to China and India had been discovered, and the following year seven vessels were dispatched in which he was one of the chief commissioners, but this time ice prevented them from reaching the Kara Sea. He wrote an account of his voyages that was to be an inspiration for the later Dutch and English penetration of the East Indies. His fame today rests mainly on his great collection of accounts of voyages published under the title *Itinerario*.

LION, H.M.S., was a famous British * battlecruiser built at Devonport and launched in 1910. She was the flagship of Vice Admiral Sir David * Beatty, commanding the Battle-Cruiser Fleet at the actions of the * Heligoland Bight (August 1914), the * Dogger Bank (January 1915), and the battle of * Jutland (May 1916), at which she was very nearly sunk when a shell fired by the German battle-cruiser *Derfflinger* penetrated one of her gun turrets and burst inside. She was only saved by the quick action of Major Harvey, a Royal Marine officer in command of the turret, in flooding the magazine before flames from the explosion could reach it. He had had his legs blown off by the explosion and was posthumously awarded the Victoria Cross after the battle. In November 1916, when Beatty was appointed commander-in-chief of the * Grand Fleet, Rear Admiral William C. Pakenham hoisted his flag in her as Rear Admiral Commanding Battle-Cruiser Force. She was sold for breaking-up in 1924.

The name *Lion* has been used for ships of the Royal Navy since the 16th century, the first battle honour being that for the * Armada in 1588. In that battle the *Lion* was commanded by Lord Thomas Howard.

LIPTON, Sir THOMAS JOHNSTONE (1850–1934), British merchant and yachtsman, was born in Glasgow of Irish parentage in poor circumstances. He started his commercial life as an errand boy at the age of ten, later becoming a cabin boy aboard a steamer on the Glasgow–Belfast run. At the age of 15 he took a * steerage passage to America, landing with a few shillings in his pocket, and had various jobs working on a tobacco plantation in Virginia, a rice plantation in South Carolina, as driver of a horse car in New Orleans, and as a grocery clerk in New York. Returning home to Glasgow he opened, on his 21st birthday, a small grocery store of his own. This store developed into a chain of stores throughout Britain, and in time expanded to ownership of tea, coffee, and cocoa plantations in

The battle of Lissa, 1866; lithograph by F. Kollarz

Ceylon and packing houses in Chicago and Omaha. Lipton's tea became world famous. His generosity for the less fortunate became proverbial and included gifts of £25,000 for London's poor on the occasion of Queen Victoria's jubilee, and other large amounts to provide poor peoples' eating houses and for famine relief in India and elsewhere. For his services he was created a knight in 1898 and a baronet three years later.

It was not until he was nearing 50 that he started his yachting career by purchasing one of the largest steam yachts in the world, the 1,240-ton *Aegusa* which he renamed *Erin*. He decided then that, as both the English and the Scots had failed to win back the *America's* Cup, it was time an Irishman should 'lift that ould mug' with a green yacht to be called *Shamrock*. This 89-ft waterline *cutter, built for him by William *Fife, sailed to the U.S.A. in August 1899, and was defeated by the Cup defender *Columbia.

Lipton went to G. L. *Watson for his next challenger, *Shamrock II*, in 1901 but was beaten by a very narrow margin by the same defender, *Columbia*. Undeterred, he had *Shamrock III* built by Fife and in the 1903 series for the Cup was easily beaten by the defender *Reliance*. Lipton challenged again in 1914 with *Shamrock IV*, built by Camper and Nicholson, but the First World War intervened and the races did not take place until 1920, when the American yacht, *Resolute*, narrowly defended the Cup.

In 1930, now aged 80, he made his last challenge with *Shamrock V*, a *J-class cutter built again by Nicholson, but was decisively beaten by the defender *Enterprise*. By now his health was failing, and his long expressed desire to be elected a member of the Royal Yacht Squadron was at last granted, but the honour no longer meant much to him. He had been a great sportsman and a generous philanthropist.

LISBON, the capital city of Portugal and a major seaport at the mouth of the River Tagus. It is also a main base of the Portuguese Navy. The *Museu de Marinha, which illustrates the maritime history of Portugal, is in Lisbon and is one of the finest such museums in the world.

LISIANSKY, YURI (1773–1837), Russian explorer and circumnavigator, was appointed by Alexander I to accompany Adam *Krusenstern in his voyage to Kamchatka in the *Nadezhda* and *Neva* in 1803–6. The outward voyage was by way of Cape Horn, and after much time spent in exploring the north Pacific, the two ships returned to Russia, rounding the Cape of Good Hope and thus completing the first Russian circumnavigation of the world.

LISSA, an island in the eastern Adriatic off the coast of Yugoslavia, now known as Vis, and the scene of two naval battles. The first was fought on 13 March 1811 between a squadron of four British *frigates under the command of Captain William *Hoste and a Franco-Venetian force of six frigates and four smaller ships under Commodore Dubourdieu, which had been ordered to capture the British-held island of Lissa. After a hotly contested engagement during which Dubourdieu's flagship ran aground and three of his frigates were captured, the remnants of his force fled. The action is considered one of the most creditable in British naval history. British casualties numbered 190, but those of the enemy were much larger.

The second battle of Lissa was fought on 20 July 1866 between an Austrian fleet under Rear Admiral Wilhelm von *Tegetthoff and an Italian fleet under Admiral Count Carlo di Persano. It is remembered as being the first encounter between armoured ships and for the ramming tactics employed. On 17 July a powerful Italian fleet comprising twelve *ironclads, fourteen wooden vessels, five scouts, and three *transports began an attack on the Austrian-held island of Lissa with a view to capturing it. During the morning of 20 July the Italian ships were engaged by an Austrian fleet comprising seven ironclads, seven wooden vessels, and four scouts, and a fierce engagement ensued. Tegetthoff ordered his ironclads to ram their opponents and in the mêlée which followed the Austrian flagship *Erzherzog Ferdinand Maximilian* struck the Italian *Re d'Italia*, which was stopped at the time, causing such damage that she quickly sank. About noon Persano tried to reform his scattered fleet, but Tegetthoff had succeeded in getting between the Italian fleet and the island, so the latter withdrew. The Italians lost two armoured ships together with 612 officers and men, while the Austrians had only one wooden ship severely damaged and their losses in men amounted to thirty-eight. It is generally considered that the defeat of the Italian fleet, in spite of its numerical superiority, was due to the timidity of Admiral Persano and the pusillanimity of his tactics. The Austrian victory had a marked influence on the design of warships during the next forty years, the *ram becoming a prominent feature.

LIST, the inclining of a ship to one side or the other due usually to a shift in the cargo or the flooding of some part of the *hull. It is a more permanent situation than a *heel, which is more often due to the pressure of the wind and lasts only as long as a ship's course relative to the wind is held without alteration.

LITERATURE, see MARINE LITERATURE.

LITTLE BELT, a British naval *sloop of twenty guns which on 16 May 1811 was engaged, before a declaration of war, by the U.S. *frigate *President*, Commodore John *Rodgers, mounting fifty-two guns. The *Little Belt* was cruising off Cape Henry when the *President* ran down to her, but when hailed by the British ship, failed to answer. The time was just after 8 p.m. and it was dusk. A gun was fired, probably by accident, but there was a conflict of evidence as to which ship fired it. The captain and officers of the *Little Belt* declared that the American ship fired first and two British seamen on board the American frigate, who later deserted and made their way to Halifax, also gave evidence that it was fired accidentally by the *President*. The American officers were equally insistent that it was the *Little Belt* which fired first. The two ships were heavily engaged for half an hour, in which the *Little Belt*, greatly out-gunned by her adversary, suffered severe damage and thirty-two casualties; one seaman was slightly wounded on board the *President*.

The two ships lay off for the rest of the night repairing damage, and at daylight on the 17th the *President* again closed with the *Little Belt*. A boat was sent over from the American frigate with a message to the effect that Commodore Rodgers regretted engaging so small an adversary but that he had mistaken the sloop for a frigate. And since, as he maintained, the *Little Belt* had fired the first gun, he had been forced to retaliate.

LITTLE SHIP CLUB, THE, a London-based British yacht club, was founded in London in 1926 to establish a centre in the City where cruising men, with or without boats of their own, could gather periodically and swop yarns over a meal. From a rented room in a public house, the club rapidly expanded until, with its library of nautical books, it occupied part of Beaver Hall, headquarters of the Hudson's Bay Company. Monthly lectures were held and classes given in seamanship, navigation, signalling, first aid, and other subjects. Port officers, representing the members' interests, were appointed at most yachting centres round the coast. Since the Second World War, with a membership reaching almost 4,000, the club can claim to be the largest of its kind in the world, and a new clubhouse was built on the bank of the Thames near London Bridge.

LIVADIA, a Russian *royal yacht built in Scotland by John Elder and Company in 1880. Tsar Alexander II, after a visit he paid to the *Admiral Popov*, a circular warship built in 1875, ordered a new royal yacht to be built on similar lines since he suffered much from sea-sickness and believed that such a ship could neither pitch nor roll. He commissioned Vice Admiral Popov, who was responsible for the design of the warship, to design his yacht but with the stipulation that the finished result should look like a yacht. Admiral Popov, in conjunction with the builders, solved this problem by retaining a nearly circular, or turbot-shaped, hull under water and placing a conventional yacht hull on top of it, with engines and boilers in the lower part and the royal cabins and staterooms on top. The *Livadia* had a tonnage of 3,900, a length of 235 feet, and an underwater beam of 153 feet. She had a speed of 17 knots, produced by three engines each driving a propeller 16 feet in diameter. She had five masts, two pairs being placed athwartship and the fifth on the centreline aft, and three funnels placed abreast. She proved to be a very comfortable and successful yacht and was broken up in 1926 after forty-six years of service.

LIVELY LADY, the 9-ton * cutter yacht in which Sir Alec * Rose sailed single-handed round the world in 1967–8.

LIVERPOOL, one of the greatest seaports of Britain, on the coast of Lancashire at the mouth of the River Mersey. It was originally colonized by Norsemen in the 8th century, and its present name is said to come from the Norse *Hlitharpollr*, 'pool of the slopes'. Its history as a seaport began in 1229 with a charter from Henry III for the formation of a guild of merchants, but it did not flourish until Liverpool shipowners discovered in the early 18th century the profits to be made from the African slave trade. The first Liverpool slaver, a ship of 30 tons, sailed from the port in 1709 and carried fifteen slaves across the Atlantic for sale in the West Indies. One hundred years later 185 slave ships operated out of Liverpool, carrying 49,213 slaves, returning with cargoes of rum and sugar, and Liverpool had overtaken * Bristol in this valuable trade. During the Seven Years War (1756–63) and the War of American Independence (1775–82) Liverpool was a great centre for * privateering, in 1778 no fewer than 120 privateers carrying 1,986 guns and crewed by 8,754 men being fitted out in the port.

The great development of trade with America, particularly in raw cotton to feed the huge cotton industry of Lancashire, was the solid foundation on which Liverpool was built up into one of the great ports of the world. The fact that it is the natural outlet for the huge manufacturing area of Lancashire and Yorkshire was another. It is also a terminus of several steamship lines. Across the river, on the southern bank, lies the port of * Birkenhead, which adds to its importance.

During the Second World War Liverpool was the headquarters of the Western Approaches Command of the British Navy which conducted the successful campaign, known as the Battle of the *Atlantic, against German * U-boats.

LIVERPOOL PENNANTS, originally the name given to rope yarns used in place of buttons on a sailor's coat, and now occasionally used to describe the beckets and wooden toggles with which duffel coats are fastened.

LIVINGSTON, ROBERT (1746–1813), American statesman, was an associate of Robert * Fulton in the introduction of steam navigation in France and the U.S.A. Although best known to history as the negotiator of the Louisiana purchase from France, he had also received from the state of New York a monopoly of steam navigation on all waters within the state boundaries. He met Fulton while he was in Paris negotiating the Louisiana purchase and joined him in the trials of a paddle-wheel steamboat on the River Seine in 1802. The * *Clermont*, to designs by Fulton and built in 1807 on the East Hudson River, was a joint venture by the two men and was named after Clermont, N.Y., Livingston's home.

LIZARD, a short length of rope with a * thimble spliced into the end, used for various purposes on board ship; in square-rigged ships as a * fairlead for the * buntlines, for example. The length of wire rope, also with a thimble in the end, which hangs from the lower * boom of a ship at anchor and to which her boats can be made fast is also known as a lizard.

LL SWEEP, a method of exploding magnetic * mines at a safe distance behind a pair of minesweepers working abreast of each other by producing the required strength of magnetic field to actuate the firing mechanism of the mine. It was introduced by the British Admiralty in 1940 to combat the German magnetic ground mines which were being laid in large numbers in British coastal waters. The magnetic field required to explode the mines was achieved by each minesweeper of the pair towing two buoyant cables with electrodes at the end, one cable being 750 yards (685 m) long and the other 175 yards (160 m) long. A current generated in the towing ship passes through the cables and the water between the two pairs and creates a magnetic field of sufficient intensity to explode the mines. As most minesweepers were incapable of producing a continuous electric current of sufficient ampèrage to maintain a permanent magnetic field, the current was pulsed and each pulse created a field which was large enough to explode all mines lying within it. As the longer cables passed out of the end of the magnetic field, another pulse was passed to create a new magnetic field contiguous with the first, so that a continuous passage was swept. By using two minesweepers working abreast, this swept passage was wide enough to provide a safe lane for ships through the minefield. When only one mine-sweeper was used, known as the L Sweep, the path was a narrow one, insufficient for the safe navigation of, say, a *convoy through the mine-field.

LLEWELLYN, MARTIN (c. 1565–1634), probably the first English cartographer, spent the last thirty-five years of his life as steward of St. Bartholomew's Hospital, London. The discovery in 1975 of a large folio of 16 charts drawn by him, covering the sea area from the Cape of Good Hope to the Far East, including Japan and the western Pacific down to the north-western part of New Guinea, stamps him as the earliest English chartmaker yet known, earlier by over half a century than Greenvile *Collins and other Stuart cartographers. His sixteen charts are drawn on sheets of vellum, each measuring about 36 in. by 26 in., and are in black ink and four colours.

Substantial evidence of his life and activities while at St. Bartholomew's Hospital points to a voyage made by him to the Far East before 1599, as there is no period of his later life unaccounted for during which he could have made such a voyage. A note accompanying the charts, written by one of his sons in 1634, states that they were 'drawn in his own hand and according to his own observations'. The only voyage to the Far East completed before 1599, apart from those of Portuguese navigators who claimed the whole of that part of the world as their private possession, was that of the Dutchman Cornelis de Houtman, who returned to Holland in 1597 after a two-year trading voyage into those waters. Llewellyn's charts include a number of names given by the Dutch to islands discovered by them, and consequently it appears certain that he must have been a member of that expedition, of which it is known that at least eighty survivors returned to Holland.

The newly discovered sea atlas bears strong evidence of having been drawn during the last decade of the 16th century, and an actual date of 1598 has been postulated before the International Conference on the History of Cartography, held at Greenwich in 1975. It certainly contains the earliest known English charts of the Far East, as the Oriental volume of the *English Pilot*, hitherto considered to be the first English charts of those waters, was not published until a century later.

LLOYD'S, an association of underwriters which traces its origin to daily meetings of London merchants in Edward Lloyd's Coffee House in the City of London. It has a continuous history of marine underwriting from 1601. As well as its main business of marine and other insurance, it is also a centre of maritime intelligence of the daily movements of merchant ships, marine casualties, etc. Lloyd's is also the leading international authority on the specification of ships in relation to the strength of building and cargo capacity, and in this respect its specifications are acknowledged and accepted by every maritime country of the world. *Lloyd's List* is a daily publication of shipping movements, and *Lloyd's Register of Shipping* is an annual publication giving a list of all merchant ships, with details of their tonnage, engine power, and owners, which have been built to the specifications laid down by *Lloyd's Register of Shipping, the society which publishes the annual of the same name. *Lloyd's Register of Yachts* does the same for the world's yachts.

LLOYD'S PATRIOTIC FUND, a charity founded officially in 1803 by J. J. Angerstein, chairman of *Lloyd's, 'to assuage the anguish of the wounded, to palliate in some degree the more weighty misfortune of the loss of limbs, to alleviate the distresses of the widows and orphans, and to soothe the brow of sorrow for the fall of dearest relatives, the props of unhappy indigence or helpless age, and to hand out every encouragement to our fellow subjects who may be in any way instrumental in repelling or annoying our implacable foe, and to prove to them that we are ready to drain both our purses and our veins in the great cause which imperiously calls on us to unite the duties of loyalty and patriotism with the strongest efforts of zealous exertion'.

The charity had its origin in 1782 when £6,000 was raised by subscribers of Lloyd's for the widows and orphans of seamen drowned in the loss of the *Royal George*. In 1794 £21,281 was raised after the battle of the *Glorious First of June for distribution among the widows and orphans of men killed and the wounded seamen, and in 1797 £2,614 was subscribed after the battle of *Cape St. Vincent and £53,000 after *Camperdown. The *Nile brought in £38,000 in 1798 and the battle of *Copenhagen £15,500 in 1801. After its official incorporation as a permanent charity in 1803, no less than £123,600 was raised on 5 December 1805 at divine services held throughout the country in thanksgiving for the battle of *Trafalgar. In all, Lloyd's Patriotic Fund has raised well over a million pounds for widows, orphans, and men wounded in action.

LLOYD'S REGISTER OF SHIPPING, a society formed in the 18th century to draw up rules regarding the construction of merchant ships. It originated in 1760 when a number of merchants engaged in marine insurance and underwriting at *Lloyd's formed an association to protect their interests. From this small beginning grew the leading and widely known classification society of today called Lloyd's Register of

Shipping. The society lays down rules regarding the *scantlings used in a ship's structure, depending on her length, *beam, *draught, depth, and the nature of the cargo she is intended to carry. A list of the ships built according to these rules is published annually in *Lloyd's Register of Shipping* and they are accorded the classification 100A. If the *anchors, *cables, and *hawsers are also in accordance with the standard laid down, the figure '1' is added and the classification becomes 100A1. In the case of ships other than those designed to carry dry cargo for which certain additional requirements have to be met, a descriptive phrase is added, e.g., 100A1 oil tanker, or 100A1 ore carrier, as the case may be. The old and famous classification A1 is now reserved for ships trading within sheltered waters such as estuaries. Additional specifications are laid down for ships liable to navigate where ice conditions may be encountered, and with fire being a recognized hazard in ships, particularly in those which carry combustible cargoes, Lloyd's Register lays down rules regarding the fire-fighting equipment which they must carry.

The Society is managed by a committee composed of shipowners, shipbuilders, marine underwriters, marine engineers, shippers, naval architects, and steel merchants. There is also a technical committee with international affiliations which assists the general committee, as well as national committees formed in various foreign countries. Some 11,000 marine surveyors working on behalf of the Society are distributed round the world to assist with the classification of new ships and to carry out periodical surveys of ship's hulls, boilers, machinery, refrigeration plants, etc.

LOADSTONE, see LODESTONE.

LOBLOLLY BOY, the name by which, during the days of sailing navies, a surgeon's assistant was known in a British warship. The origin of the name is the old country word *loblolly*, a kind of porridge or gruel, which was adopted in the navy to describe the surgeon's potions for the sick on board. Tobias *Smollett, who served as a surgeon's mate in H.M.S. *Chichester* during the attack on Cartagena in 1741, notes in his novel *The Adventures of Roderick Random* that 'among the sailors I was known as the Loblolly Boy', although as a surgeon's mate, and not a surgeon's assistant, in fact he was not.

LOBSCOUSE, a well-known dish at sea, particularly among the crews of sailing ships, in the days before refrigeration. It was a mixture of salt meat cut small, broken biscuit, potatoes, onions, and such spices as were available, boiled up into a stew. See also SKILLYGALEE.

LOBSTER, the traditional name by which a British naval seaman describes a British soldier. The name dates from the 18th century, and the expansion during that century of the British empire, when large numbers of British soldiers were dispatched to various parts of the world to fight in the various wars of expansion. They were transported in naval ships, often joining with the navy in combined operations for the capture of colonial territories of France and Spain, the traditional enemies. Since the soldiers always wore red coats, the name was apposite. *Marines, who also wore red coats, were also widely known as lobsters. But see also JOLLIES.

LOCKWOOD, CHARLES ANDREWS (1890–1967), American naval officer, graduated from the Naval Academy in 1912 and particularly distinguished himself by his service in command of the *submarines in the Pacific from 1942 to the end of the Second World War. His first problem in the Pacific was the ineffectiveness of the American *torpedoes in the early part of the war when many commanding officers of submarines had the frustrating experience of seeing torpedoes pass under targets without exploding. Lockwood made his own investigations and determined beyond doubt that the torpedoes were running very much deeper than they were supposed to, and that the magnetic pistols (exploding mechanisms) were not operating properly. With the facts presented by Lockwood, Admiral *Nimitz managed to force the necessary changes in design and manufacture.

Later in the war Lockwood gave evidence of his exceptional efficiency in the handling of submarines as scouts to report on the movements of Japanese *aircraft carriers, *cruisers, and *destroyers. Under his command the submarines of the Pacific Fleet played a vitally important role from February 1943 to the end of the war. At a cost of 47 submarines in the western Pacific area, 174 Japanese warships of 493,981 tons and 877 merchant vessels totalling 3,489,741 tons were sunk. Towards the end of the war against Japan Lockwood used many of his submarines as rescue craft for bomber crews forced down into the sea after raids on Japanese-held positions, and hundreds of aviators were saved by them.

LODEMAN, from the Old English *lad*, a leader or guide, and thus occasionally used at sea to mean a pilot. In the Laws of *Oleron (see also BLACK BOOK OF THE ADMIRALTY) it was laid down, 'If a ship is lost by default of the lodeman, the maryners may ... bring the lodeman to the windlass or any other place and cut off his head.'

LODEMANAGE, an old word based on the Old English *lad*, a leader or guide, meaning pilotage or the hire of a pilot. It was first used in this sense of pilotage in the Laws of *Oleron. There was a Court of Lodemanage which sat at Dover during the days of the *Cinque Ports for the examination and appointment of pilots in the brotherhood of the ports. Of his ship's captain Chaucer, in the Prologue to the *Canterbury Tales*, wrote:

'His herborough, his moone, and his lode-
    manage,
There was none such from Hull to Cartage.'

The term lasted into the 18th century and an Act of Parliament (3 Geo. I, cap 13) of 1716 laid down: 'A very useful Society or Fellowship of Pilots of the *Trinity House of Dover who have always had the sole Piloting and Load-manage of all Ships and Vessels from the said Places up the Rivers of Thames and Medway ... Every Person must appear at a Court of Load-manage and be publicly examined touching his Skill and Abilities in Pilotage before he is admitted a member of the said Society.'

LODESTAR, a sailor's name for *Polaris or α Ursae Minoris, the north star or Pole star. The origin of the name presumably comes from the same old English source as *lodeman, *lode-manage, *lodestone, to give a meaning as 'guiding star'. For all practical purposes the star Polaris remains fixed above the North pole and thus bears north from all points of observation in the northern hemisphere, making it a true guide to mariners. See also KOCHAB.

LODESTONE or **LOADSTONE,** the seaman's name for magnetic oxide of iron. It is said that the ancient Chinese discovered that, when freely suspended, it would point to the north, and therefore used it to form the earliest crude magnetic compass. Recent research suggests that this was not the case, although the Chinese were probably aware that a soft-iron bar, stroked with a lodestone, acquired a directional north–south property. There was, however, a long way to go before mariners were able to harness this directional property to a compass card. Presumably it was given its name from the old English *lad*, a leader or guide, as the 'guiding stone' for mariners.

LOG, (1) the name given to any device for measuring the speed of a vessel through the water or the distance she has sailed in a given time, **(2)** the short name by which the *log book or deck log is generally known.

All the various early types of measuring device to give a vessel's speed through the water were based on the same principle.
Common Log. This was first described in print in *A Regiment for the Sea* written by William Bourne, and published in 1574. In its earliest form it consisted of a wooden board attached to a log-line and hove from the stern of the vessel. The log-line was allowed to run out for a specified period of time and, on the assumption that the board remained stationary in the water, the length of line which had run out in a specified time indicated the distance sailed by the vessel through the water in that time, from which her speed could be easily calculated.

With the introduction in the 15th century of the *nautical mile as the unit of distance measurement at sea came the marking of the log-line by knots (and later by knotted cords worked into the log-line) spaced uniformly at a distance proportional to a mile as was the running time of the sand in a log-glass to an hour. The log-glass of that time had a running time of 30 seconds and so the spacing of the knotted cords was 7 fathoms (42 ft). With the log-line marked in this way, the common log thus became a direct-reading instrument. At that time it was believed

A 17th-century pilot's lodestone

that a nautical mile measured 5,000 feet, and this was the basis of the 7 fathom spacing of the knots on the log-line. But after measuring a meridian arc between London and York for the purpose of ascertaining the exact dimension of the earth, Richard Norwood in his *The Seaman's Practice*, first published in 1637, advised seamen to remark their log-lines on the basis of 6,120 feet per nautical mile. The length of a nautical mile is, in fact, 6,080 feet, and the marking of the log-line before it became obsolete at the beginning of the 20th century should have been a spacing of 47 feet 3 inches for a log-glass whose running time was 28 seconds, the proportion of 47 feet 3 inches to 6,080 feet being the same as 28 seconds to one hour. Most navigators, however, used 48 feet, this being 8 fathoms and thus easier to measure, one fathom being taken as the span of a man's arms.

An early development of the first common log, introduced in about 1600, was the chip log, in which the original board was replaced by a wooden quadrant weighted with lead on the circular rim to make it float upright. This was designed to give it more resistance in the water to the drag of the log-line as it ran out, thus providing a more accurate reading.

Dutchman's Log. On much the same principle as the common log, the Dutchman's log was the method of estimating speed at sea favoured by Dutch mariners during the 17th and 18th centuries. The means of calculating the speed using this log involved measuring the time during which a chip of wood, dropped into the sea level with the bow, travelled between two marks cut on the * gunwale of the vessel. Knowing the distance between the marks, it was a simple arithmetical matter to find the rate of sailing, for, as a contemporary account puts it:

'As the time given is to an hour,
So the way made, to an hour's way.'

Patent, or **Self-recording, Log.** With the growth of seaborne trade in the 17th and 18th centuries the need for a more accurate measurement of a ship's speed became widespread, and many inventors turned to a rotator towed by a ship as a means of measuring speed. The earliest invention in this line was Robert Hooke's 'way-wiser', demonstrated to the Royal Society in 1683, but there is no record of whether it was tested in a ship. Henry de Saumarez made an instrument which he called a 'marine surveyor', consisting of a simple rotator towed by a line attached to the spindle of a wheel mounted on the stern of the towing vessel, which recorded the number of revolutions of the rotator. In experiments conducted between 1715 and 1729, his invention was tested in English, French, and Dutch ships, but the weight of the rotator, needing a heavy line to tow it and a large wheel to record the revolu-

tions, introduced so much friction that the readings were valueless.

John * Smeaton was the next to take a hand in the development of a patent log, producing a lightweight rotator in 1754, and at about the same time similar inventions came from William Russell, Joseph Gillmore, Gottlieb of Germany, Benjamin Martin, James Guérimand, and Pierre * Bouguer. There were several others, but they all suffered from the same drawback, that the wheel-work at the inboard end could not be made free of an unacceptable degree of friction which falsified the readings. A partial solution came in 1792 when Richard Gower fitted his rotator in a wooden cylinder which also contained the registering dials. Although this largely eliminated the friction, it entailed hauling in the log every time the ship changed course as well as when the watch changed. In 1802 Edward Massey produced a log which began to resemble a modern patent log. A streamlined rotator was attached to a case containing the dials by four lengths of cane jointed together, the whole being towed at the end of a log-line. It still involved hauling in the log to take a reading, but the results proved impressively accurate and it was the Massey log which was extensively used at sea throughout the 19th century.

Massey's nephew was Thomas Walker, a name widely associated with the modern development of the patent log. His 'Harpoon' log, similar to Massey's but with the dials incorporated in the outer casing of the rotator, was patented in 1861, and his famous 'Cherub' log was introduced in 1884. By this time, engineering development had reached the stage where revolutions of the rotator astern could be transmitted accurately to a register inboard without distortion by friction.

Bottom Logs. Other types of patent log are known as bottom logs, in that they are not towed astern but protrude from the ship's bottom. There are three basic types, known as the pitometer, the Chernikeef, and the electromagnetic. The pitometer log is based on an invention by Henry Pitot in 1730 using an open L-shaped glass tube to measure current flow. If the foot of the L is placed facing forward beneath a ship, water is forced up the tube as the ship proceeds to a distance depending on the speed of the ship. A number of experiments were made with this device, and improvements introduced, but it was not until the 20th century that reliable logs on the Pitot principle were evolved.

The Chernikeef system relies on a small rotator in a retractable tube carried a few feet below the hull of a ship. It was originally developed by Captain B. Chernikeef of the Russian Navy in 1917 and has since been developed and is widely used.

The most recent development is the electromagnetic log, in which the potential difference generated in water by its movement relative to a magnetic field is sensed by two electrodes lowered beneath the hull. The magnetic field is produced by an electro-magnet. After many trials, this method of measuring ship's speed has been found to be accurate, economic, and simple, and is widely fitted in ships today. For smaller vessels, such as yachts, an electronic log, in which a small impeller fixed externally to the keel is connected electrically with the main instrument inboard, gives accurate readings of speed and distance run.

LOG BOOK, usually referred to as a log, a compulsory document which must be kept by all ships in which is recorded information relating to the navigation of the ship, the organization of her crew, and all other relevant activities on board. It is a *watch-to-watch record of meteorological conditions, courses and speeds, punishments, deaths, etc. Log books kept by British naval ships are sent monthly to the Ministry of Defence, those kept by British merchant ships to the Superintendent of the Mercantile Marine office before whom the ship's crew is paid off and discharged and from him to the Registrar-General of Shipping and Seamen, a department of the Ministry of the Environment. The log books kept by ships of other nations are sent to their appropriate authorities. The usual practice is to write up this official log book from the day-to-day deck and engine-room log books.

LOGGERHEAD, (1) the wooden *bitt in the stern of a whaling boat around which the *harpoon line was controlled as it ran out after striking a whale in the days when harpoons were launched by hand. **(2)** A ball of iron attached to a long handle used for the melting of tar or pitch. The ball was heated in a fire to red heat and then plunged into the tar or pitch bucket.

LOG-LINE, a specially woven line of contra-laid cotton used for towing a patent log from the *taffrail of a ship. The reason for the special weaving is to prevent twist, so that it will faithfully repeat the number of revolutions made by the patent log as it is towed through the water.

LOLL, a term used to describe the state of a ship which is unstable when upright and as a result floats at an angle of *heel on one side or the other. It is caused usually by a large area of free-surface water inside the hull, as for instance a ship with flooded compartments, but can also be caused by too much weight carried high up in the ship. It is not the same as *list, which is caused by quite different conditions. Loll in a ship can be reduced by removing top weight, adding to bottom weight, or by reducing the area, and particularly the width, of the free-surface water in the ship.

François l'Ollonois; engraving from Esquemeling's The Bucaniers of America, *1684–5*

L'OLLONOIS or **NAU** (d. 1668), French buccaneer, so called because he was born at Les Sables d'Olonne. He joined the buccaneers at Hispaniola (Haiti) about 1665 and became the most bloodthirsty of them all. He was credited with tearing out and eating the hearts of his captives. He was eventually caught and lynched by Indians on his way to the sack of Cartagena.

LONDON, capital city of Great Britain and one of the greatest seaports in the world. It has an ancient history, certainly being a port by the time the Romans landed in England in 55 B.C. There were by then imports of ivory, glass, necklaces, and amber, and exports of fighting dogs, gold, iron, tin, and lead. The first *dock was constructed during the reign of *Alfred the Great (848–c. 900) when he gave land on the river bank to Ethelred to develop into a dock. Named Ethelredhithe, it was renamed Queenhithe when the land was given to Matilda, queen of Henry I. It still retains this name.

The growth of the modern port dates from about 1800, when the prevalence of river thieves, known as 'mudlarks', forced shipowners to build enclosed docks where ships could be loaded and unloaded in secure conditions. It was estimated that in the early years of the 19th century there were as many as 11,000 of these 'mudlarks' operating in the river. The first of the enclosed docks to be built were the West India Docks at the Isle of Dogs, followed by the East India Docks, St. Katherine's Dock, Royal Victoria Docks, Millwall Dock, Royal Albert Docks, Tilbury Docks, and the Surrey Commercial Docks.

West India Docks; lithograph by W. Parrott, 1841

Halfway through the 19th century, as ships grew rapidly larger and required a greater depth of water, a river authority, the Thames Conservancy, was set up with the duty of keeping the river dredged and the various navigable reaches clear. Later, with the need of a more powerful and purposeful central authority, a new body known as the *Port of London Authority was set up in 1908, with responsibility for the condition of the river bed from Teddington, to the west of London, to Yantlet Creek, at the mouth of the River Thames. It also owns all the various areas of the port within those limits, including wet and dry-docks, quays, and warehouses. Tilbury, part of the complex of the port of London, is the passenger terminus for several big steamship lines and has also recently been developed as a major container port.

The major operations of the port of London are gradually moving down river, so that some of the docks within the city are now being closed.

LONDON, H.M.S., a ship's name which has been used nine times in the Royal Navy. The first was one of Charles I's *ship money fleet, originally a merchantman, converted in 1636 to a 40-gun man-of-war. She declared for the Parliament at the rebellion in the fleet in July 1642 and later, during the First Dutch War (1652–4), took part in the battle off the *Kentish Knock (1652) and the battles of the *Gabbard and the Texel (1653). The next *London*, a 2nd *rate of sixty-four guns, launched in 1657, was one of the squadron which in 1660 brought over Charles II at his restoration as king of England.

The eighth *London* was a *cruiser, built at Portsmouth and launched in 1927. She served with distinction throughout the Second World War and in September 1941 she conveyed the British and American mission to Russia for a three-power conference in Moscow. In September 1945 the Japanese surrender was accepted at Sabang by Commodore A. L. Poland in the *London*. She was scrapped in 1950. The latest ship of the name is a guided missile *destroyer.

LONDONDERRY, an important city and port in Northern Ireland. It was held by the Protestants during the attempt by James II to regain his throne in 1689. It had been besieged by the Jacobite forces for more than three months, and the relieving force under General Piercy Kirke was slow in coming to its relief. Meanwhile the city was faced with starvation and could not hope to be able to hold out for much longer.

Succour by land having failed, two of the victuallers of the relieving force, the *Mountjoy* and *Phoenix*, volunteered to try to force their way up the River Foyle to the beleaguered city, and on 28 July 1689 they proceeded under escort of the *frigate *Dartmouth*, commanded by Captain John *Leake. On coming up to the *boom placed across the river the victuallers tried to break through, but there was insufficient wind to give them the necessary speed. The *Dartmouth* then set her boats to cut the boom with axes. This was done and the *Phoenix* was hauled through, being followed shortly afterwards by the *Mountjoy*. Captain Leake continued to engage the enemy batteries until the victuallers were safely in and alongside Derry quay, which they reached at about 10 p.m. Londonderry was thus relieved, and during the night of the 31st the Jacobites burnt their camp and raised the siege, which had lasted for 111 days.

During the Second World War Londonderry was a main base of the British Navy, used for escort forces engaged in the *Atlantic battle against German *U-boats.

LONG CLOTHES, the seaman's name, during the 18th and early 19th centuries, for the clothes worn by men ashore. It was a wise precaution for a British merchant seaman to have a suit of long clothes on board as an aid to avoiding *impressment into the navy when his ship reached a home port after a voyage. Thus John Nicol, in *The Life and Adventures of John Nicol, Mariner* (1822): 'When the (press) boat left the vessel we crept from our hiding hole, and not long after, a custom-house officer came on board. When we cast anchor, as I had a suit of long clothes in my chest, I put them on immediately and gave the custom-house officer half a guinea for the loan of his cocked hat and powdered wig. I got a waterman to put me on shore. I am confident that my own father, had he been alive, could not have known me. All these precautions were necessary. Had the waterman suspected me to be a sailor, he would have informed the press-gang in one minute.' See SAILORS' DRESS.

LONG SPLICE, a method of splicing two ropes by unlaying the ends to a distance of eight times the circumference of the rope and then laying up the strands in the space left where the opposite strand has been unlayed. By this means

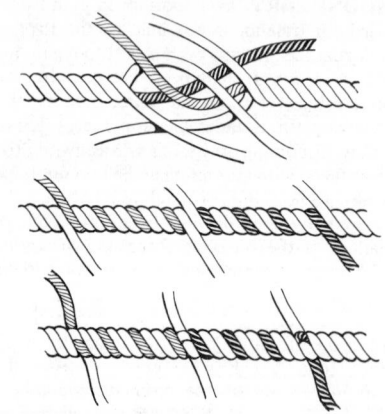

Long splice

the two ropes are joined without increasing the thickness over the area of the splice. A long splice is used where the rope is required, to *reeve through a *block after it has been spliced.

LONG STAY, see STAY.

LONGBOAT, the largest boat carried on board a full-rigged ship, particularly in warships of the 18th century. It was *carvel built with a full bow and high sides, and furnished with a mast and sails for short cruises where required. A ship's gun could also be mounted in the bows. Its principal uses on board were to transport heavy stores to and from the ship and to take empty water casks ashore to be refilled whenever fresh drinking water was required. It was also the principal lifeboat carried on board and was kept fully provisioned for use in any case of emergency. It was from the longboat that the *launch was developed as the major warship's boat during the 19th and early 20th centuries.

LONGITUDE, from the Latin *longitudo*, length. It is one of the spherical *co-ordinates used to describe a terrestrial position, the other being *latitude. It is the arc of the equator or the angle at either pole between the planes of the *prime meridian and the *meridian of the places measured eastwards or westwards from the prime meridian. The longitude of a ship at sea may be found from the methods of nautical astronomy or by calculating the local time of noon on the longitude of *Greenwich, the difference in time giving the longitude east or west of Greenwich. Because the earth rotates uniformly on its polar axis, the longitude of a place is proportional to the time the earth takes to rotate through the angle contained between the planes of the prime meridian and the meridian of the place, and thus the measurement of this time is bound to give the longitude. Originally this was done by a ship's *chronometer, but it is today more easily achieved by means of the many time checks broadcast throughout the day and night by radio stations. See also BOARD OF LONGITUDE, LUNAR OBSERVATION.

LONG-JAWED, the term used to describe rope which, through much use, had had the twist, or *lay, in its strands straightened or pulled out and has no longer the resilience to resume its normal tightness of lay after use.

LONGSHIP, a Norse or Viking *galley, used mainly for raiding and for war purposes approximately between the years A.D. 600 to A.D. 1000. The largest longships pulled up to eighty oars, the smallest about forty or fifty. They also carried a mast, housed in a *step, which was always lowered aft when under oars. A single square sail was hoisted on a *yard, and by the use of *bowlines and bearing-out spars, known as beitass, to *brace the yard, it was possible to use the sail for working to windward as well as for running. As longships had neither deck nor

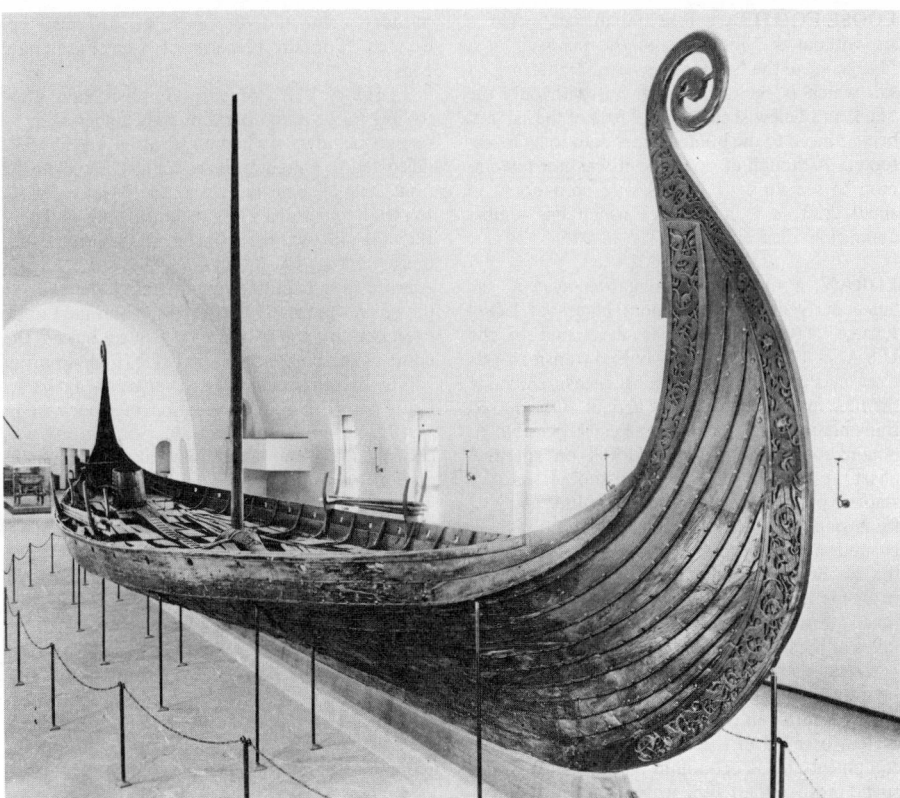

The Oseberg longship

*keel, they gave no protection to their crews and also were poor seaboats, and normally did not operate in the winter when rough seas might be expected. The usual practice was to haul them up on shore during the autumn for launching again in the following spring. Yet they made many remarkable voyages, as far west as Iceland and Greenland, as far south as the Mediterranean Sea.

LOOF, (1) the after part of the bow of a square-rigged ship just before the *chesstrees, at the point where the side planking—or, when iron or steel was used for the *hulls of large sailing ships, the plates—begins to curve in towards the *stem of the ship. The term is now almost completely obsolete, and was never applied to ships propelled otherwise than by sail. **(2)** The old word, sometimes also written as loofe, meaning *luff.

LOOM, (1) the inboard end of an *oar, that part of it which lies inside the boat from the *crutch or *rowlock when the oar is shipped for rowing,

including the grip. **(2)** An effect of refraction in a light fog at sea which makes objects look larger than they are. 'That ship looms large', the dim outline of a vessel seen through fog and appearing larger than she in fact is. The same effect is often observed when the land is seen through a fog from seaward, cliffs frequently appearing much higher than they really are. **(3)** Also an effect of reflection on low cloud in the case of the light from a *lighthouse or *lightship, when the light itself cannot be seen directly although its reflection is visible.

LOOSE, to, a term applicable to the sails of a square-rigged ship when the *gaskets, or stops, of a *furled sail are cast loose so that the sail may be set.

The term refers only to sails set on *yards, and only when they are furled on the yards, implying the actual casting loose of the gaskets. Thus, if additional canvas such as a *royal is sent up in fair weather, it is set, not loosed, as it was not already in position furled on the yard with gaskets.

LOOSE-FOOTED, a fore-and-aft sail which is set without a *boom, as in the mainsail of a *barge, or in the *de Horsey naval *cutter rig. A sail which is set on a boom but with only the *tack and *clew secured, the *foot of the sail not being *laced to the boom, is also said to be loose-footed. Although at one time it was not uncommon to see sails set in this way on a boom in small craft, it is a practice which has almost completely died out.

LORAN, a hyperbolic navigation system, the name derived from the initial letters of LOng RAnge Navigation. It was developed in the U.S.A. in 1940–3 and uses pulsed transmissions from master and slave stations. Measurement of the time interval between the arrival of the pulsed transmissions at the ship makes it possible to obtain a position line and plot it on a lattice chart. A second reading from another pair of stations produces a second position line, and so a fix is obtained. The low frequency used gives a groundwave coverage of about 700 miles over the sea in the day, and the skywave reflections from the ionosphere, provided skywave corrections are applied, increase the range to 1,400 miles at night.

Loran covers much of the eastern Pacific and western Atlantic, and is used mainly by U.S. ships operating in those waters. It is an expensive system because of the high cost of the receiver equipment and is economic only in ships which spend most of their time at sea within the Loran coverage area. It is unlikely to be extended to other areas, since the Omega system is planned to give worldwide cover and can do so with far fewer stations than Loran. See also NAVIGATION.

LORCHA, a sailing vessel with a European-shaped *hull and a Chinese *junk rig. They are believed to have originated at Macao when it was first settled by the Portuguese. The typical *lateen rig of the Mediterranean, with its somewhat eastern look, led to many ships so rigged being wrongly called lorchas.

LORD HIGH ADMIRAL OF ENGLAND, an office first established in 1391 when Edward, Earl of Rutland, was appointed Admiral of England, uniting the offices of Admiral of the North and Admiral of the South, instituted some ninety years earlier. Subsequently the titles 'High Admiral' and 'Lord Admiral' were indiscriminately used in the wording of the Letters Patent, crystallizing eventually as 'Lord High Admiral', ninth of the nine great officers of state of the Crown.

The title of *Admiral did not originally confer command at sea, but jurisdiction in maritime affairs and authority to establish courts of *Admiralty. To give the Lord High Admiral military command, however, he was also appointed 'Captain General of Our Fleets and Seas'.

In Henry VIII's reign the English Navy grew too big for its administration to be undertaken by one man, and its civil administration was in 1532 delegated to a committee which, by Elizabeth I's time, had become known as the *Navy Board. In 1628 the Lord High Admiral, the Duke of Buckingham, was assassinated and *Lords Commissioners for Executing the Office of Lord High Admiral assumed his administrative duties over the navy. Admiralty jurisdiction continued to be exercised by the Admiralty Court, but in the name of the king, not of the Lord High Admiral.

This arrangement was reverted to intermittently until, after the execution of Charles I in 1649, the office of Lord High Admiral was abolished by the Commonwealth government and an Admiralty Commission appointed in which the *generals-at-sea, who commanded afloat, were included as members.

At the Restoration in 1660, the office of Lord High Admiral was revived in the person of *James, Duke of York, who commanded the fleet with distinction in the victory over the Dutch off *Lowestoft in 1665. James was, however, deprived of his office in 1673 as a result of the anti-Catholic Test Act and Charles II appointed a Committee of the Navy over which he himself presided. Six years later he was forced to appoint a Board composed of members of the House of Commons; but in 1684 was able to revoke its commission.

When the Duke of York came to the throne as James II, he resumed the office of Lord High Admiral and, with the assistance of Samuel *Pepys as Secretary, presided over Admiralty affairs until his abdication in 1688.

From that day, except for brief periods, the office was maintained in commission until 1964 when the three separate Service ministries were brought together into a single Ministry of Defence. The title, though not the office, of Lord High Admiral was then resumed by the Crown in the person of Elizabeth II.

LORD JIM, a novel by Joseph *Conrad, published in 1900, and thought by many to be his most outstanding novel. It tells the story of a man, a junior officer making his first voyage, with a fatal flaw which leads to self-betrayal, but which he redeems by an honourable death.

LORD MAYOR'S MEN, originally *landsmen who were induced to join the British Navy to avoid debts or disgrace, or were given the option by city magistrates to serve in the navy under the *Quota Acts of 1795 in place of a gaol sentence for misdemeanours. Later, in the Napoleonic

War (1803–15), the phrase was unofficially applied to any landsman who joined the navy in order to qualify for a *bounty. They were held in great derision and contempt by professional seamen from whom they were easily distinguished by the clothes they wore on joining a ship.

LORDS COMMISSIONERS FOR EXECUTING THE OFFICE OF LORD HIGH ADMIRAL, the full title of the officials in Britain who were more generally known as the Lords Commissioners of the Admiralty or the Board of Admiralty. Commissioners were first appointed in 1628 by Letters Patent on the assassination of George Villiers, Duke of Buckingham, the then *Lord High Admiral, and were selected from the Lords of the Council and headed by the Lord Treasurer, who was First Commissioner. The continuing title of Lords Commissioners in later years stemmed from this fact, and the First Commissioner was known as the First Lord.

The duties of the Lord High Admiral's office were, in fact, of two kinds—juridical in maritime causes and administrative over the Royal Navy. When the office was put into commission, Admiralty jurisdiction continued to be exercised by the Admiralty Court, with Vice Admiralty Courts in outlying stations, but in the name of the king, not of the Lord High Admiral. Administration of the navy, on the other hand, including the civil administration which since Tudor times had been delegated to the *Navy Board, remained the responsibility of the Board of Admiralty.

With intermissions when a Lord High Admiral was again appointed, arrangements mainly similar to these held good over the next two centuries (1628–1832). Many of the successive First Lords were serving naval officers; all were Members of Parliament, either of the House of Lords or of the Commons, and were thus responsible to Parliament as well as to the sovereign for all aspects of naval command and administration. Other members of the Board had no particular departmental duties and acted in a purely advisory capacity. The donkey work of administration was performed by the Navy Board with its subsidiary *Victualling Board and, later, Sick and Hurt Board.

In 1832 this unsatisfactory system of divided control was abolished, the surviving Commissioners of the erstwhile Navy and subsidiary Boards each coming under the direction of one of the Lords Commissioners of the Admiralty. Further reforms in 1868 and 1872 finally set the pattern for the Board of Admiralty for the next ninety-two years. Service members of the Board were Naval Lords (in later years Sea Lords) with a (parliamentary) Civil Lord responsible for dockyards and a Parliamentary Secretary for finance.

The Lords Commissioners ceased to exist in 1964 when the three separate armed services were brought together in a single Ministry of Defence.

LORIENT, a naval base, seaport, and *dockyard in western France on the coast of the Bay of Biscay. Originally the port was the small town of Port Louis, but development on the opposite bank of the river to Port Louis attracted merchants trading to India, and when the French *East India Company based itself there, the new port was developed to an extent where it took the whole of the trade from Port Louis. This new port was named Lorient by the East India Company, or *Compagnie des Indes Orientales*. Extensive shipbuilding facilities exist at Lorient, and many vessels for the French Navy are constructed there.

During the Second World War many German *U-boats, engaged in the Battle of the *Atlantic, were based there. This cut the distance to and from their patrol areas, compared with a base in Germany, by many thousands of miles, allowing them to spend a considerably longer time on patrol in their areas. It was heavily and frequently bombed during the war, but massive concrete shelters built in the dockyard, in which the U-boats lay when in harbour, successfully withstood even the heaviest hits.

As well as being a great naval base, Lorient is renowned for its oysters.

'LOSE THE NUMBER OF HIS MESS, to', a naval saying implying death. It can be used in both the past and future tenses: 'he's lost the number of his mess', meaning that a man has died, been killed, or drowned, or 'he will be losing the number of his mess' if he continues to act in a reckless way. It was a term more applicable in warships, where the seamen's messes are numbered, than in merchant vessels, where the subdivision of seamen into small messes is not the usual practice.

'LOSS OF THE ROYAL GEORGE, THE', the title of the well-known poem,

> 'Toll for the brave,
> The brave that are no more....'

written by William Cowper (1731–1800) to commemorate the oversetting of H.M.S. *Royal George* at Spithead on 29 August 1782 with the loss of Rear Admiral *Kempenfelt and the majority of her complement. Its lack of historical accuracy is perhaps more than counterbalanced by the poem's dramatic treatment of this sad event.

LOTI, PIERRE, pen name of a French naval officer, Louis Marie Julien Viaud (1850–1923). He was born at Rochefort and at the age of 17 entered the naval school of Le Borda. He saw much service around the coasts of South America, in the Pacific, the coast of Senegal, and in the eastern Mediterranean. He is said to have been an extremely shy man, and his pseudonym comes from the fact that his messmates gave him the nickname of *le loti*, an Indian flower that prefers to bloom unseen. His first novel, *Aziyadé*, was published in 1879, a curious story of Constantinople where he had been serving, but it was with the publication in 1883 of *Mon frère Yves*, a novel based on the experiences of a French * bluejacket serving around the world, that he achieved wide recognition. Its publication coincided with a series of critical articles which he wrote on the French war in Indo-China, particularly of the excesses after the capture of Hué, for which he was recalled to France and suspended from the navy for a year. In the wide public discussion of these articles, Loti finally emerged with great credit.

In 1886 appeared the work for which he is probably best remembered, *Pêcheur d'Islande*, a novel of life among the Breton fishermen, and this was succeeded in 1887 by *Propos d'exil*, a semi-autobiographical series of studies of life in exotic places, a series of great charm and merit which deserved far more attention than it received. In 1892 he was elected a member of the Académie française.

Meanwhile his naval career continued with service in China and Japan, but in 1898 he retired from the navy, only to rejoin two years later to serve on the staff of the French China Command during the Boxer rebellion. He subsequently commanded the guardship at Constantinople, retired for a second time in 1910 with the rank of captain, and was recalled for service during the First World War (1914–18).

Pierre Loti, at his best, was one of the finest descriptive writers of his day. His greatest successes came from an ethereal mixture of fact and fiction, written almost in a spirit of confession and with great depth of feeling. He was a good draughtsman and musician as well as a talented author. He left an important and intimate journal which has yet to be published.

LOUISBURG, a port on the southern coast of Cape Breton Island off the coast of Canada which was captured from the French on 26 July 1758 by a British combined force under Admiral the Hon. Edward * Boscawen and Major-General Jeffery Amherst. It was the opening move in a campaign to capture * Quebec and the whole of Canada. The expedition, which had left England in the previous February, assembled at Halifax, whence it sailed on 28 May, the total number of warships and transports amounting to 157 sail. Louisburg was reached on 2 June; but for several days the heavy surf prevented the troops being landed, and it was not until the 8th that they could be put on shore under a heavy fire from the defences. Regular siege operations were begun five days later, but the inclement weather continued to cause many casualties among the boats landing guns, ammunition, and provisions, and during the next fortnight 100 boats were lost in the surf. On 26 June, 200 marines were landed, and next day the bombarding batteries were reinforced by guns landed from the ships. After successful operations ashore which cut the land approaches to Louisburg, the boats of the fleet entered the harbour on the night of 25/26 July and cut out the *Bienfaisant* and burnt the *Prudent*, the last two remaining French * ships of the line that had been in the harbour, three others having been destroyed by fire on the 21st. The town surrendered on the following day. With Louisburg fell the whole of the island of Cape Breton and also St. John (Prince Edward) Island, and opened the way to the capture of Quebec in 1759 and the whole of Canada in 1760.

LOUTHERBOURG, JACQUES PHILIPPE DE (1740–1812), Anglo-Swiss landscape and marine painter, was born at Basle, the son of a miniature painter who moved first to Strasburg and then, in 1755, to Paris. There de Loutherbourg studied painting under Claude-Joseph * Vernet, having a picture exhibited at the Salon at the age of 22 and being elected a member of the French Academy in 1767. He moved to London in 1771 where he became a naturalized British subject and spent the rest of his life, being elected as a Royal Academician in 1781. At first he painted English landscapes, but on the outbreak of war with France in 1793 he took to painting scenes of naval and military engagements with considerable success. He also made a series of drawings, now in the British Museum, of the men of the lower deck who fought with Adam * Duncan at the battle of * Camperdown and with Horatio * Nelson at the battle of * Cape St. Vincent. These are unique records of their kind, superb examples of draughtsmanship and full of character.

LOW AND ALOFT, a nautical expression describing a sailing ship with sail spread from deck to truck; every stitch that she can carry. Many people are inclined to think that the phrase is an abbreviation of alow and aloft, but it is in fact the other way round, alow and aloft being an expansion of the correct term.

LOW-CHARGED SHIPS, warships of the sailing navies from about 1585, when the high castle built on the bows of warships was abandoned and replaced by a *beakhead. The design was introduced by Sir John *Hawkins, Treasurer of the Navy of England in the days of Elizabeth I, as a result of voyages made earlier by him. He had found that the traditional castle forward made his ships very unhandy when sailing *on a wind as the area presented to the wind was so large that the bows of his ships were always blown down to *leeward. By this time, too, the normal tactics of naval battle had changed as a result of ship-mounted cannon in place of the archers and musketeers of earlier days, and the elimination of the high castle forward brought much better sailing qualities to the ships so that they were faster, more manoeuvrable, and able to hold a much better *course to windward. See also HIGH-CHARGED SHIPS, NAVY.

LOWER DECK, the *deck of a ship next above the *orlop deck. It is also a term frequently used to indicate the ratings of naval ships, e.g., officers belong to the *quarterdeck, ratings to the lower deck. This expression possibly comes from the order *'Clear lower deck', given when all seamen are required on the upper deck for some purpose, either in an emergency or to hear some important announcement by the captain.

LOWESTOFT, a small fishing port on the coast of Suffolk, England, and the scene of a battle of the Second Anglo-Dutch War (1665–7) fought on 3 June 1665 between an English fleet of 109 ships, commanded by *James, Duke of York, and a Dutch fleet of 103 ships under Jacob van *Wassenaer. The scene of the action, which began at 4 a.m., was about forty miles south-east of Lowestoft. The two forces at first fought passing each other on opposite tacks, but order gradually broke down on both sides and the battle degenerated into a gigantic mêlée. The two flagships were hotly engaged until the Dutch ship, the *Eendracht*, blew up, only five men being saved. By 8 p.m., the enemy was in full flight, during which time seven ships, at two different spots, fouled one another, caught fire, and were all destroyed.

The total Dutch loss was about thirty-two sail but only nine *prizes were brought in; their casualties amounted to about 4,000 killed and 2,000 taken prisoner. The English loss was slight in comparison, 283 killed and 440 wounded; their only ship lost was the *Charity* which was captured early in the fight.

LUARD, WILLIAM BLAINE (1897–   ), British naval officer and yachtsman, was educated at the Royal Naval Colleges Osborne and *Dartmouth but was invalided out of the navy in 1917. He invented various navigational devices and contributed to numerous publications on maritime affairs. After leaving the navy

he became a well-known deep sea yachtsman and competed in many offshore races, including the transatlantic race to Plymouth in 1930. He was president of the *Little Ship Club (1944–54), and chairman of the Cornwall Sea Fisheries Committee. Among his many books are *A Celtic Hurly Burly* (1931), *All Hands* (1933), *Conquering Seas* (1935), *The A.B.C. of Blue Water Navigation* (1936), *Little Ship Navigation* (1950).

LUBBER'S HOLE, an opening in the floor of the *tops on the fore, main, and *mizen-mast of square-rigged ships, just abaft the heads of the lower masts, to give access to the tops from below. It was so termed because timid climbers up the rigging preferred to go through this hole to reach the top rather than over the *futtock shrouds, the way the experienced sailor went.

LUBBER'S LINE or **POINT,** the black vertical line or mark on the inside of a *compass bowl which represents the *bow of the ship and thus enables a *course to be steered by bringing the lubber's line to the point on the compass card which shows the desired course.

LUBBOCK, BASIL (1876–1944), British marine author, was an authority on *clipper ships. He was educated at Eton and then went to Canada during the Klondyke gold rush of 1896–7, returning home by signing on as an ordinary seaman in a *barque which rounded Cape Horn. He volunteered for service in the Royal Navy during the South African War (1899–1901) and also in the First World War (1914–18). He was a prolific writer: among his many books are *Round the Horn before the Mast*, *The China Clippers* (1914), *The Colonial Clippers* (1921), *The Blackwall Frigates* (1922), *The Log of the *Cutty Sark* (1924), *The Down Easters* (1929), *The Nitrate Clippers* (1933), and *The Arctic Whalers* (1937). They are notable for their accuracy and detail and are authoritative records of a type of ship which has now virtually disappeared.

LUCE, STEPHEN BLEECKER (1827–1917), American naval officer, was born in Albany, New York, and became a *midshipman in 1841. He had service at the Naval Academy, at that time at Newport, during the Civil War (1861–5), and published a textbook on seamanship in 1863. As commanding officer of the *Pontiac* in 1865 he co-operated with General Sherman in the vicinity of Charleston, South Carolina. After the Civil War he was commandant of midshipmen at the Naval Academy, which had by then returned to *Annapolis. He was an exceptionally inspiring leader who acted vigorously and unselfishly to improve conditions in the navy, particularly those under which the seamen had to work. He also became an ardent advocate of an institution for advanced studies for naval officers and he was the logical choice to be the first president of the Naval War College, established at Newport, Rhode Island, in October 1884. Luce chose Captain Alfred *Mahan as a lecturer on naval history at the War College, which became a pattern for similar institutions abroad. He was promoted rear admiral in 1886 and retired in 1889.

LUCKNER, Graf FELIX VON (1881–1966), German naval officer, was captain of the *armed merchant cruiser *Seeadler*, a square-rigged sailing vessel with an auxiliary engine which operated in the Atlantic and Pacific Oceans in 1916–17 during the First World War.

Having run away from home when aged 13 and shipped *before the mast in a Russian sailing ship, he returned home at the age of 21, stating that he had been a member of the Salvation Army, a dishwasher, a soldier in the Mexican Army, and the keeper of a monkey house. He obtained a *master's ticket and, entering the German Navy, was commissioned during the First World War and served at the battle of *Jutland in the *battleship *Kronprinz Wilhelm*. He was appointed to the *Seeadler* because he was the only officer of the regular German Navy (i.e., not a reservist) who had served in sailing ships.

His cruise lasted from 21 December 1916 to 2 August 1917, when the ship was wrecked on Mopelia in the Society Islands, having sunk fourteen allied merchant ships, eleven of them sailing vessels. After the shipwreck Luckner was taken prisoner by the New Zealand authorities. When the war was over he sailed the world in his own four-masted *schooner *Vaterland* until she was destroyed by fire in 1935. He then acquired a small two-masted schooner in which he continued his voyaging.

In the closing stages of the Second World War he was living in retirement near Erfurt which was being defended by a fanatical National Socialist. The commander of the approaching American force, General Allen, presented an ultimatum which was refused and the Americans prepared to bomb and shell the town. Luckner intervened and succeeded in securing the surrender of the town intact.

LUFF, the leading edge of a *fore-and-aft sail. (For illus. see SAIL.) 'Hold your luff', an order to the helmsman of a sailing vessel to keep her sailing as close to the wind as possible and not allow her to sag down to *leeward. In many of the older books on seamanship the spelling of the term is loof or loofe.

When used as a verb, 'luff', or luff her', is an order to the helmsman to bring the ship's head up closer to the wind by putting the helm down, or to leeward. In yacht racing to luff an opponent is to come up closer to the wind, or even head to wind if necessary, to prevent her overtaking to *windward, a legitimate procedure under the rules of yacht racing.

LUFF TACKLE, a *purchase which has a single and a double *block, the standing part of the rope being secured to the *strop of the single block, and the hauling part coming from the double block. It increases the power by four times when rove to *advantage. It was originally used for hauling down the *tack of a fore-and-aft sail to tauten the *luff, but the term is now used to describe any tackle rove through a single and a double block in which the size of the rope is 3 inches in circumference or greater. LUFF UPON LUFF, one luff tackle hooked on to the fall of another in order to double the increase in power. See PURCHASE.

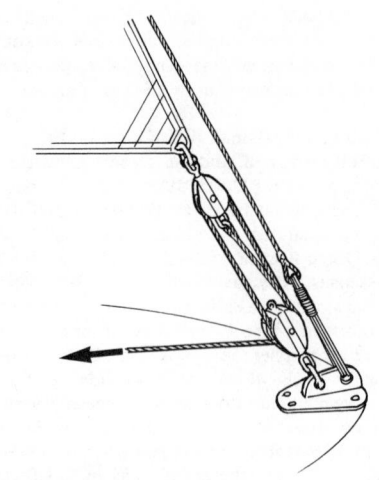

Luff tackle rove to disadvantage

LUG, (1) the name, rarely used, of the *yard on which a *lugsail is set but more often employed to describe the sail of a small boat (see LUGSAIL). **(2)** A projection on a mast or *bowsprit fitting with an *eye to take a *shackle of a *stay or *shroud.

LUGGER, a sailing vessel with a *lugsail rig, normally two-masted except when they were used for smuggling or as *privateers, when a mizen was stepped right aft. The lug rig came in during the late 17th or early 18th century, particularly for fishing and for the coastal trade where its increased weatherliness over the square *rig gave considerable advantages when working the *tides. See also CHASSE-MARÉE.

LUGSAIL, a four-sided sail set on a *lug or *yard, used mainly in small craft. The sail is very similar to a *gaff sail but with a wider throat, and depends on its *luff for its stability. The yard, or lug, by which the sail is hoisted is normally two-thirds the length of the *foot of the sail and carries a *strop one-fourth of the way from *throat to *peak. This strop is hooked to a *traveller on the mast and is hoisted in the normal way until the luff is as taut as possible.

The earliest known drawing, by a Dutch artist, of what may have been a lugsail is dated 1584, but the name itself does not appear for another hundred years. Suggestions that it is of much more ancient origin and first appeared in the Mediterranean in Egyptian and Phoenician craft around the first century B.C., are not borne out by any evidence and probably arose through confusing the *lateen rig with the true lug rig. The original lugsails were set on *dipping lugs which, when the vessel went *about, entailed lowering the sail sufficiently to enable the forward end of the lug, together with the *tack of the sail, to be passed round abaft the mast to the (new) *lee side as the vessel came head to wind.

The *standing lugsail, in which the forward end of the lug is *bowsed down so that it becomes virtually an extension of the mast, came in very much later and never became viable except for a short period for small racing yachts. It is more usually known as the *gunter rig, or gunter lug. The balanced lugsail is laced to a *boom which extends a short way forward of the mast, and set flat by a tack *tackle.

It is said to have been a Western adaptation of the short-boomed Chinese lugsail, and became popular in the West around the end of the 19th century.

LUNAR OBSERVATION, the observation of a lunar distance for finding *longitude at sea before *chronometers were perfected. The moon has a relatively rapid motion across the heavens in relation to the fixed stars, so that the angular distance between the moon and any fixed star which lies in the moon's path changes comparatively rapidly. The earlier Nautical Almanacs provided the navigator with tables of predicted lunar distances (the angles between the moon and certain fixed stars, as well as the sun) against *Greenwich time. By observing a lunar distance it was possible to ascertain, by interpolation between tabulated values of lunar distances against Greenwich time, the precise Greenwich time of the observation. By comparing this with the local time of the observation, the longitude of the ship could be ascertained. The introduction of the chronometer, bringing Greenwich time permanently on board, made lunar observations no longer necessary for the accurate determination of longitude.

LUNY, THOMAS (1758–1837), British marine artist, was trained in the workshop of Francis *Holman and was a regular exhibitor at the Royal Academy between 1780 and 1802. His pictures are chiefly remarkable for their atmosphere of natural light and the perfect finish of important detail. He is best known for his marine paintings which, though apt to be sombre, are masterpieces of technique and execution with a real feeling for atmosphere and the reflection of light off water. He painted many pictures of naval actions but those which show the quiet serenity of ships at anchor, and his harbour scenes, are generally considered to be among his best.

LUSITANIA, R.M.S., a ship of the *Cunard Line of 31,500 tons, was built in 1906, a quadruple screw express *liner. She captured the Atlantic *'blue riband' in 1907 by crossing from Liverpool to New York at a speed of 23·99 knots. She continued monthly sailings from Liverpool to New York and back after the outbreak of war in 1914.

Before she left New York on 1 May 1915 the German authorities in the U.S.A. published warnings that she would be attacked by submarines, and advised passengers not to sail. The warnings were not regarded as serious, and it appears that warnings of German *U-boat activity in the area were not signalled to her by the British Admiralty on 6 May 1915 as she approached southern Ireland on a return passage from New York. According to her sailing orders she should have been steering a zig-zag course and had been instructed to keep away from landfalls, but these instructions were ignored and she approached the Old Head of Kinsale on a steady course at a reduced speed of 21 knots when at 2.15 p.m. on 7 May two torpedoes struck her starboard side, fired from the German submarine *U.20*. Great loss of life was caused by the rapidity with which she sank—she went under in 20 minutes—and because she was listing so heavily and was at so steep an angle bows down when she sank that it was difficult to get her lifeboats away. The number of passengers and crew lost was 1,198. According to one theory by apologists for the brutal manner in which she was attacked without warning, she was struck by only one torpedo and the second explosion was caused by the detonation of contraband cargo; it was also averred that she was deliberately ordered into the path of the submarine by Winston *Churchill, then First Lord of the Admiralty, and by Sir John *Fisher, First Sea Lord, as an attempt to bring the U.S.A. into the war. There is no apparent basis for either of these allegations.

It was said, however, that the outrage felt in the U.S.A. was a factor in bringing America into

R.M.S. Lusitania, *a Cunard liner of 31,500 tons*

the war in 1917: in the words of Theodore Roosevelt at the time it was 'piracy on a vaster scale than the worst pirates of history'. But this was an overstatement probably made under stress of the fact that 124 American citizens were among those lost. The Germans claimed that the *Lusitania* was an *armed merchant cruiser carrying troops from Canada, but at the time it was stated in London that she carried no troops and no guns, and that her only war cargo was 5,000 cases of cartridges. Later evidence suggests that included in her cargo was a small quantity of fulminate of mercury fuses in addition to the ammunition.

Nevertheless, since she had no guns mounted and was not an armed merchant cruiser, it was contrary to the rules laid down at the *Hague Convention of 1907 for such a vessel to be sunk without first visiting her to establish the fact that she was carrying *contraband and then making provision for the safety of her passengers and crew.

LUTCHET, a mast fitting in the form of a *tabernacle used in *spritsail *barges and *wherries to enable the mast to be lowered to deck level when passing under bridges, etc. The mast, stepped on deck, is held in place by the lutchet, the after side of which is left open to allow free passage of the mast when it is lowered. It differs from a tabernacle, whose forward side is

left open, in that with a lutchet the mast is pivoted at the base and not at the top of the fitting.

LUTINE BELL, the bell of H.M.S. *Lutine* which was recovered after she sank in a heavy gale off the mouth of the Zuider Zee in October 1799. She was carrying a large amount of coin and bullion, and since this was private and not government money the burden of the loss fell on the underwriters who had insured her cargo. The bell was brought to the surface during salvage operations and, since the underwriters who had borne the loss were members of *Lloyd's of London, it was taken to Lloyd's where it now hangs. It is rung whenever there is an important announcement to be made to the underwriters.

LÜTKE (LITKE), Count FEDOR PETRO-VICH (1797–1882), Russian naval officer and Arctic explorer, was born in St. Petersburg (now Leningrad) of a German grandfather. He joined the Russian Navy at the age of 15 and sailed round the world in the *Kamchatka* (Captain V. M. *Golovnin) in 1817–19. In the summers of 1821–4 he was in charge of an expedition which made important explorations of Novaya Zemlya. In 1826–9 he commanded the sloop *Senyavin* on her voyage round the world, and did survey and scientific work in the western Pacific and the Bering Strait region. He was tutor to the second son of Nicholas I, was first

President of the Imperial Russian Geographical Society, and President of the Academy of Sciences. In 1850–7 he was admiral in command of the ports of Reval and Kronstadt in the Baltic Sea.

LYNCH, PATRICIO (1825–86), Chilean rear admiral, was born at Valparaiso, the son of an Irish merchant who had settled there. He entered the navy at the age of 12 and was engaged in the operations which ended in the overthrow of the dictator Santa Cruz. For a brief period he served as a midshipman in the British Navy on board the frigate *Calliope* during the China War of 1840. During the Spanish War of 1865 he became a colonel of the National Guards, maritime prefect of Valparaiso, and minister of marine, and it was largely under his direction that the Chilean Navy was enlarged and properly trained. During the war between Chile and Peru (1879–82) he commanded brilliantly both at sea and on land, was specially promoted for his distinguished services, and was rewarded by being placed in command of the army of occupation in Peru. As a rear admiral he represented Chile as minister at Madrid. He is one of the great naval heroes of Chile.

LYONESSE, a legendary country supposed to lie off the southern coast of Cornwall, England, which is frequently mentioned in the various legends associated with King Arthur and his Knights of the Round Table. The country, including its sudden and unexplained disappearance beneath the sea, is described in great detail in several of the early English chronicles, such as that of Florence of Worcester, who died in 1118.

LYONS, EDMUND, 1st Baron Lyons (1790–1858), British admiral, served at sea in the Napoleonic War (1803–15) and reached the rank of post-captain in 1814. He commanded one of the British ships at the battle of *Navarino in 1827. For thirteen years from 1840 he was in the diplomatic service as minister to Greece, Sweden, and Switzerland, but was recalled to the navy on the outbreak of the Crimean War (1854–6) and was second-in-command, and later commander-in-chief, of the British Black Sea Fleet.

On the purely military side he is best remembered, perhaps, for the way he took his flagship, the *Agamemnon*, in to bombard the forts of *Sebastopol, but more important was the considerable part he played in the planning and overall direction of the whole campaign in the Crimea, working very closely and intimately with Lord Raglan, who commanded the armies ashore.

LYSANDER (*fl.* 407 B.C.), Spartan general-at-sea during the Peloponnesian War. His early history is obscure, but by 407 B.C. he had become leader of the Spartan fleet, and won a considerable naval victory at Notium in the following year. He also won the decisive victory of Aegospotami and took a leading part in the siege of Athens. He gave himself the task of building up a Spartan empire of which he would be head, but his initial successes aroused so much jealousy that he was recalled from his triumphs and his influence at Sparta was eroded. Later he appears to have commanded armies in the field, and was killed during an attack he mounted on the town of Haliartus.

M

M.G.B., the abbreviation for *motor gunboat in the British Navy in the Second World War.

M.T.B., the abbreviation for *motor torpedoboat in the British Navy in the Second World War.

M.V., the prefix placed before the name of a ship to indicate that she is a motor (diesel) vessel.

M.Y., a prefix used before the name of a yacht to designate a motor yacht.

MACARONI LUG, an obsolete name for the *standing lug rig.

MACARONI MATE, a man signed on as *mate in a merchant vessel though without the required qualifications and without pay. The origin of the term, and the practice, is believed to have arisen at the time of the Napoleonic occupation of Genoa and Leghorn in 1796 when many of the sons and favourite employees of the English merchants there were thus signed on in American merchant ships with the object of escaping both capture and imprisonment by French troops and possible *impressment at sea if the ship were stopped by British *cruisers.

Impressment at sea by the British Navy was permissible in the case of British nationals serving in foreign ships, but it was thought that British naval officers would be unlikely to question the nationality of a man serving as mate, or second-in-command, of an American ship. Such a rank automatically implied American nationality and it was not difficult for an Englishman to assume an American accent, if questioned, with a good chance of getting away with it.

McCLINTOCK, Sir FRANCIS LEOPOLD (1819–1907), British admiral and Arctic explorer, was born at Dundalk, Ireland. He entered the navy in 1831 and first saw service in the Arctic under Captain Sir James C. *Ross in H.M.S. *Enterprise*. In February 1852 he was appointed to command the auxiliary sloop *Intrepid* as tender to H.M.S. *Resolute*, commanded by Captain Henry *Kellett during an Arctic expedition under Captain Sir Edward *Belcher. He made a sledge journey of 1,210 miles in 105 days and charted the west coast of Prince Patrick Island and adjacent waters.

In 1857, while commanding the yacht *Fox purchased by Lady Franklin and fitted out at her expense, he discovered the diaries and log book of the Sir John *Franklin expedition. These included a letter written in 1848 by Lieutenant Gore which established the date of Franklin's death and the tragic fate of the expedition. An account of this discovery appeared in McClintock's book *The Voyage of the Fox*, published in 1859. He was knighted the following year and subsequently served in the Mediterranean, Channel, and West Indies, his last appointment being commander-in-chief of the West Indies station.

McCLUER, JOHN (d. c. 1794), was a commander in the Bombay Marine and a noted hydrographer. He surveyed the Persian Gulf and the waters around Bombay with such accuracy that he was sent on similar work to the Pelew Islands and New Guinea. He was apparently so taken with the beauty of the women of the Pelew Islands that he suddenly decided to resign, making over command of the expedition to his first lieutenant in breach of all naval discipline. After fifteen months with his 'family', he sailed for China in a native boat without any navigational instruments and with no provisions beyond coconuts and water, reaching Macao safely. There he purchased a ship with a bill of exchange drawn on the Bombay Marine, returned to the Pelew Islands and embarked his wives, men servants, and women servants, and sailed for Calcutta. He was never heard of again.

McCLURE, Sir ROBERT JOHN LE MESURIER (1807–73), British vice admiral, was the discoverer of the *North-West passage in 1850. He commanded H.M.S. *Investigator* and, having sailed through the Straits of Magellan and the Bering Strait, penetrated both the Prince of Wales and McClure Straits to prove the existence of the North-West passage. His ship was abandoned in Mercy Bay in June 1853, McClure and his company suffering from *scurvy. They were rescued by Captain Henry *Kellett in H.M.S. *Resolute* and brought back to England, which they reached in 1854.

MACDONOUGH, THOMAS (1783–1825), American naval officer, distinguished himself by building and equipping a small squadron with which he defeated a British squadron under Commodore George Downie on *Lake Champlain in September 1814. He was born in Delaware and became a midshipman in 1800. He served in the naval war with France and again in the war with Tripoli.

Arriving on Lake Champlain in October 1812 he had the task of creating a small squadron for operations on the lake. By the time the ice had melted and navigation had become possible on Lake Champlain in the spring of 1814, Macdonough had assembled thirteen small vessels and, for the time being, achieved naval superiority over the British squadron although Downie was building a powerful 37-gun ship, H.M.S. *Confiance*, and its completion would have given the British a decisive advantage. Macdonough wisely chose to fight from a well-planned disposition at anchor in Plattsburgh Bay. He was helped in this plan by the knowledge that the Governor-General of Canada, Sir George Prevost, who had marched an army of veteran troops to Plattsburgh, had exerted pressure on Downie to sail before the British vessels were ready for action.

Macdonough had taken the precaution of placing anchors and *springs in position before the action, and after 90 minutes of fighting in which both squadrons suffered severely, he hauled his ship round on her spring to bring his disengaged broadside to bear on the *Confiance*, which was by then too severely damaged to match this manoeuvre. Downie was compelled to surrender, and as soon as General Prevost saw the result he marched his veteran troops back to Canada.

Macdonough served later in the Mediterranean and commanded a squadron there.

MacGREGOR, JOHN (1825–92), Scottish canoeist, is generally accepted as the pioneer of the sport of canoeing in Britain. He was a great traveller and a well-known researcher into the methods and history of marine propulsion. In his canoe *Rob Roy* he travelled many thousands of miles, across the North Sea and English Channel as well as on inland waterways, and his accounts of these travels, published from 1866, were widely read and were the chief means of introducing the sport to other followers.

MACKAY, DONALD (1810–80), American shipbuilder, was born at Shellburne, Nova Scotia, and is generally considered to have been the greatest builder of American sailing ships and perhaps of sailing ships of any nation. After an early career in New York in the yard of Isaac Webb, and at Newburyport as a partner in Currier's yard, he moved to Boston in 1840, setting up in partnership with the American shipowner Enoch Train. There, after building a number of splendid Western Ocean ships for

Train, he produced the revolutionary *Staghound*, the first of a long line of world-famous Mackay *clippers. These made record passages to California from New York, the best known being the *Staghound, Flying Cloud, Flying Fish*, and * *Sovereign of the Seas*. Others, built by Mackay for the English Black Ball Line for use in the Australian emigrant traffic, were equally famous. The best known of these were the *Lightning, James Baines, Champion of the Seas*, and *Donald Mackay*.

MACKENZIE, Sir ALEXANDER (c. 1755–1820), Canadian fur trader and explorer, made many travels in the North-West Territories of Canada to open up knowledge of that area. In 1789 he voyaged from the Great Slave Lake down the Mackenzie River (named after him) to the Arctic Ocean, surveying the area. He wrote an account of these travels in *Voyages on the River St. Lawrence and through the Continent of North America to the Frozen and Pacific Oceans*, which was published in 1810.

MACKENZIE, MURDOCH (b. 1712), was a grandson of the Bishop of Orkney and as a young mathematician was appointed in 1742 to make a geographic and hydrographic survey of the Orkneys. The *Navy Board lent him a theodolite, a plane-table, and a measuring chain for the work.

Mackenzie adopted new scientific principles by measuring a base line over three miles on a frozen lake and observing its direction relative to a magnetic needle. Then with the theodolite he took angles to intersect beacons established on the surrounding hills from either end of the base line, and subsequently extended this network through the islands by a series of observed triangles. He finally checked the scale of the survey by observing *latitude by *meridian altitude of the sun, using Rowley's *quadrant, on North Ronaldsay and at Kirkwall. From a boat he then delineated the coastline and off-lying rocks by taking intersecting compass bearings to two or more of his triangulated beacons ashore. In May 1750 the results of his work were published in the atlas *Orcades*.

He was then commissioned by the British Admiralty for surveys along the west coast of Britain and round the whole of Ireland. Twenty years later, in 1770, with Ireland and the British coast as far south as Pembroke completed, Mackenzie retired. In 1774 his book *Treatise on Maritim Surveying* was published wherein a mechanical method of plotting a position of a boat or ship by a resection method using three fixed marks onshore is envisaged.

His nephew, also MURDOCH, was a lieutenant in the British Navy and took up the survey for the Admiralty where his uncle had given up, moving through the Bristol Channel and on south-west to Land's End and thence east to Plymouth. From here he was ordered by the Admiralty to proceed with surveys in the Thames Estuary; the first being that of a new channel off Margate. Here in 1775 Mackenzie and his assistant Graeme Spence were clearly using the resection method advised in his uncle's *Treatise on Maritim Surveying*, and may even have made an early form of mechanical *station pointer to plot the boat's position by simultaneously observing two angles by *Hadley's quadrant between three fixed marks onshore. The abundance of soundings on this and subsequent surveys by these two men can only be explained if this was so.

Ten years later Graeme Spence demonstrated a station pointer to the First Lord of the Admiralty who ordered a number of such instruments to be made by Troughton, after which it rapidly became an indispensable part of the marine surveyor's equipment.

McMULLEN, RICHARD TURRELL (1830–91), a pioneer of single-handed cruising, was an instigator of *Corinthian sailing as opposed to 'Cowes yachting'. Living at Greenhithe, Kent, he was frequently accompanied by his wife on his cruises in yachts which were based nearby on the lower Thames. During this time he met and inspired a younger amateur sailor, Claud *Worth. He owned a number of small craft built to his requirements. His cruises were mostly made single-handed, from Greenhithe down Channel to the Scilly Isles and the French coast, and his book *Down Channel*, a yachting classic, was a model of modest descriptive writing that helped others for generations to learn boat handling and cruising alone. In June 1891 he left his moorings on the Thames alone in his *lugger *Perseus* and was later picked up off Eastbourne by French fishermen who found him dead at the tiller while his lugger was sailing herself on course down Channel. The autopsy revealed that he had been dead for twenty-four hours.

McMURTRIE, FRANCIS EDWIN (1884–1949), British marine journalist and author, was prevented by ill health from joining the British Navy, on which he had set his heart, and began work as a journalist, but his interest in ships and the sea dominated his life. In 1904 he became a regular contributor to *Jane's Fighting Ships* in co-operation with its founder, Fred *Jane, and from 1923 to 1929 he was joint editor of this publication with Dr. Oscar *Parkes, succeeding him as editor in 1935, a post which he held until his death. He was also a regular contributor to *Brassey's Naval Annual* and many other publications. He was at one time naval and shipping correspondent of the *News Chronicle*, and later of the *Daily Telegraph* and *Sunday Express*. He founded the Anchorites dining club to foster international co-operation among all those connected with the sea.

McPHERSON, ARTHUR GEORGE HOLDSWORTH (1873–1942), British cruising yachtsman, took up offshore cruising in small yachts only late in life. He also assembled a famous collection of nautical prints, acquired later by Sir James Caird for the *National Maritime Museum at Greenwich. In 1930 he had a 39-ft (12 m) *cutter yacht of 13 tons built by Camper and Nicholson at Gosport, named *Driac* (Caird reversed), and with companions the following year sailed to the Mediterranean and back, being awarded the *Royal Cruising Club's challenge cup. Finding *Driac* too large for his purpose he had *Driac II*, a 32-ft (9·6 m) cutter of eight tons, built in 1932 at Portsmouth, and cruised with her to the Azores and back. The next year, accompanied by Bill Leng, his paid hand, he took her to Iceland and the Gulf of Finland.

These cruises were followed by others to the West Indies (1934), Gibraltar and Haifa (1935), and again to the eastern Mediterranean (1936). The following year, also with Bill Leng as crew, he sailed down the Red Sea to Singapore, the East Indies, and Darwin, thence westward again to South Africa. In Durban, after completing 45,000 miles at sea, ill health forced him to give up ocean sailing, and he gave *Driac II* to Bill Leng. McPherson did not publish any book describing his extensive cruises, but logs of all were recorded in the *Journal* of the Royal Cruising Club between 1931 and 1938.

MACSHIP, a merchant vessel, usually a tanker or grain ship, fitted during the Second World War with a temporary flying deck above her superstructure from which, initially, land-based fighter aircraft could be flown off and landed on. The requirement for such ships arose from the attacks on *convoys in the *Atlantic made during the first three years of the war by German long-range Focke-Wulf aircraft which could operate up to 700 miles out to sea. With fighter protection provided within the convoy, these aircraft could be shot down or driven off before making their attacks or reporting the convoy's position to waiting *U-boats.

After these Focke-Wulf attacks had ceased, macships were used in an anti-submarine role with naval *Swordfish aircraft, modified to carry *depth-charges, embarked; but by this stage of the war the small escort *aircraft carriers were being built in large numbers to take over this role until the very long range shore-based aircraft were released for convoy escort. The name comes from the initial letters of merchant aircraft carrier. See also CAMSHIP.

MADDEN, Sir CHARLES EDWARD (1862–1935), British admiral of the fleet, was born at Gillingham, Kent, and saw his first active service as a sub-lieutenant during the Egyptian war of 1882. In 1901 he was promoted to captain and appointed to command the armoured cruiser *Good Hope*, and in 1905 was at the Admiralty as naval assistant to the Third Sea Lord. He had by this time been selected by Admiral Sir John *Fisher as one of his 'brains', and became Fisher's naval assistant in the office of the First Sea Lord. He left the Admiralty in 1907 to become captain of the *Dreadnought*, the world's first all-big-gun *battleship and Fisher's brain-child, and returned to the Admiralty in 1908 as naval secretary to Mr. R. McKenna, First Lord of the Admiralty, a post of great influence. He remained in the Admiralty until 1911, as Fourth Sea Lord for the last two years, being promoted to rear admiral during this service.

At the outbreak of the First World War (1914–18) he became Sir John *Jellicoe's chief of staff in the *Iron Duke*, flagship of the *Grand Fleet. He was Jellicoe's brother-in-law, their wives being sisters, and there was a great bond of friendship between the two which promised well for the top command of the fleet. Where Jellicoe had been a brilliant gunnery specialist, Madden had been equally brilliant as a *torpedo officer, and both were tacticians of genius. He was present at the battle of *Jutland, and when Jellicoe left the Grand Fleet to become First Sea Lord, he strongly recommended Madden to succeed him as commander-in-chief. The choice, however, fell upon Sir David *Beatty and Madden became second-in-command, a position he filled with distinction and in which he proved of great assistance to his new chief.

After the war he commanded the Atlantic Fleet and in 1927 succeeded Beatty as First Sea Lord. His three years in this supreme naval office were particularly difficult ones, coinciding with the pressure for naval disarmament and extreme financial stringency and ending with the London Naval Conference of 1930 by which the Royal Navy was greatly reduced in strength and efficiency.

MADOC, a Welsh sailor, probably legendary, who in the 12th century is said to have dreamed of a new continent beyond the western horizon and to have sailed in search of it, discovering America nearly 350 years before *Columbus reached it in 1492 and spending the remainder of his life with the Indians. The story was widely believed in Wales, and its acceptance grew with reports filtering back into Wales of hunters and traders in the new continent having met Indians who spoke Welsh. It received a tremendous boost in 1669 when the Rev. Morgan Jones returned from a missionary tour through North Carolina with a story of how he and some companions were captured by Indians who threatened to kill them. When Jones turned to his companions and told them, in Welsh, to prepare themselves for death, the Indians were said to have understood Jones's remark, welcomed them as cousins, and set them free. But more than a century later John Evans, another Welsh preacher, explored the valleys of the Mississippi, Missouri, and Ohio rivers between 1792 and 1797 in search of Welsh-speaking Indians but was unable to find a single one. There is general acceptance today that the story of Madoc's discovery is a complete myth and that Columbus can remain unchallenged in his claim to fame so far as Madoc is concerned.

MADRAS, a major seaport on the eastern coast of India. Its foundation dates from 1640 when Francis Day, of the British *East India Company, obtained from the local ruler a grant of land on the site of the present city on which to build a fort, which he named St. George because it was completed on St. George's Day, 1640. Under the trading monopoly of the East India Company the town built around the fort prospered, and in 1653 the area was recognized as an independent presidency of the company. It was captured by the French in 1746, restored to British possession by the Treaty of Aix-la-Chapelle in 1748, besieged again by the French in 1758, and relieved by the arrival of a British fleet two months later. Madras today enjoys a great and growing entrepôt trade, with cotton, coffee, hides, and machine manufactures being the principal exports.

MADRID, the capital city of Spain and the home of one of the great maritime museums of the world, the *Museo Naval.

MAE WEST, (1) a large parachute *spinnaker used in yacht racing, so called from the large swelling curve it takes up when filled with wind, reminding yachtsmen, perhaps, of the film actress of that name who delighted large audiences with her feminine curves in the years between 1932 and 1940 when she made several successful films. **(2)** A slang term, used largely by the Royal Air Force during the Second World War, for an inflatable life-jacket carried by aircrews for survival purposes if shot down over the sea. In this case the large curves of the life-jacket were attached to the human chest, an even apter reason for the term.

MAELDUIN, THE VOYAGE OF, a well-known Irish romance which dates back to the 8th century and records the travels of Maelduin, the foster-son of an Irish queen, who sailed with seventeen companions in search of his father's murderer. The account of their voyage is given in considerable detail in the manuscript *Imram Curaig Mailduin*, preserved in the Royal Irish Academy in Dublin. It has a distinct resemblance to the account of the voyage of St. *Brendan, and is no doubt based to some extent on the older stories of *Jason's and *Ulysses' wanderings.

MAELSTROM, a term commonly accepted as meaning a whirlpool, but in fact referring to a strong current which rips past the southern end of the island of Moskenaes in the Lofoten group off the west coast of Norway. It is also known as the Maskenstrom. It is marked on the map of the area which appears in *Mercator's *Atlas* of 1595. The word would appear to come from the Dutch *malen*, to grind, and *strom*, stream or current.

MAGELLAN, FERDINAND (Fernão de Magalhaes) (*c.* 1480–1521), Portuguese navigator, was born at Villa de Sabrosa in Trasos-Montes and was the inspirer and commander of the first voyage of circumnavigation of the globe. After passing his early years as a page and attendant at the Portuguese court of John II, he enlisted as a volunteer for the voyage to India of Francisco d'Almeida, first Portuguese viceroy of the East, in 1505. In 1509 he joined Diogo Lopes de Sequeira for his voyage from Cochin to the Spice Islands, during which the expedition only narrowly escaped destruction as a result of Malay treachery at Malacca. He was promoted to the rank of captain for his skill and courage on this occasion, and in 1511 joined the expedition under *Albuquerque which attacked and captured Malacca. His next employment was with the expedition under Antonio d'Abreu to explore the Spice Islands (Moluccas) which reached Amboyna and Banda, where they found so many spices that the expedition proceeded no further.

In 1512 Magellan returned to Portugal where

he was raised to the noble rank of *fidalgo escudeiro*. He was lamed for life during the attack on the Moroccan town of Azamur in 1513, but was accused of trading with the enemy and fell into disfavour. Renouncing his nationality, he proceeded to Spain in October 1517 and gained the ear of the Emperor Charles V with a scheme to reach the Spice Islands by steering westward, sailing south of the New World into the great *South Sea discovered four years earlier by *Balboa. With the support of many influential friends he persuaded Charles V to grant permission for the voyage, and an agreement was signed by which Magellan and his backers were to receive one-twentieth of the profits, and for the government of all new lands discovered to be vested in them and their heirs.

As captain-general of a squadron of five ships with his flag in the *Trinidad*, he led it across the Atlantic in September 1519, making a landfall near Pernambuco, whence he coasted south to the River Plate estuary which he examined in the hope of finding a strait before sailing on to reach Port St. Julian (49° 20′ S.) on 31 March 1520. There, after crushing a dangerous mutiny, he settled down to pass the winter. He named the natives of the place Patagonians (big feet) because of their great size.

Sailing again in August 1520, he discovered the long and tortuous strait that today bears his name on 21 October 1520. Thirty-eight days later his squadron, with the exception of one ship which had deserted, emerged into the ocean which, from the gentle weather with which it received him, he named the Pacific. Ninety-eight days of appalling hardship from starvation and *scurvy followed before an island, probably Guam, was reached. After three days of rest and refreshment there, the ships sailed on to reach Cebu in the Philippines on 9 March 1521.

Here Magellan made friends with the native ruler, who embraced the Catholic faith the better to endear himself to his Spanish visitors. On the

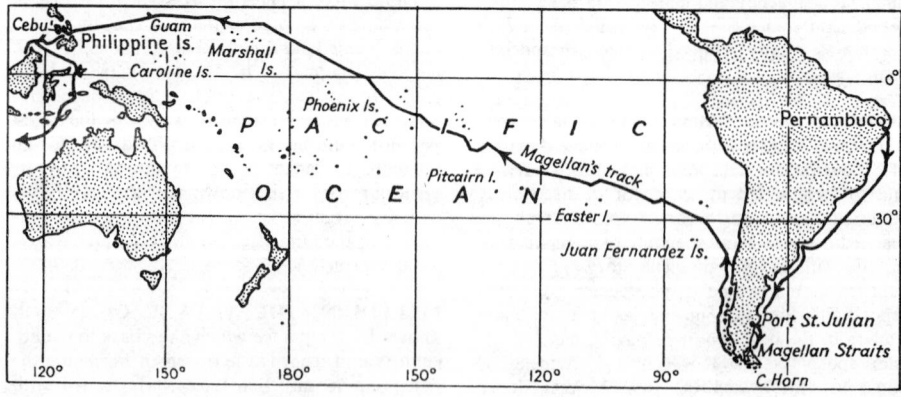

Magellan's track across the Pacific

Ferdinand Magellan; engraving by J. Stradanus, 1522

pretext of conquering the island of Mactan for Catholicism, he persuaded Magellan to lead an expedition against it. Magellan was killed in the fight against the islanders (27 April 1521) and the ruler of Cebu then proceeded to murder many of the remaining leaders of the expedition. Two ships, the *Trinidad* and * *Vittoria*, got away but the *Trinidad*, being leaky and undermanned, remained with her crew in Borneo while the *Vittoria*, under Juan Sebastian * del Cano, made her way home by way of the Cape of Good Hope. Her troubles were by no means over for her crew suffered badly from scurvy and starvation before reaching the Cape, and when she called at Cape Verde Islands on the last lap of her voyage, thirteen of her crew were taken prisoner by the Portuguese. She finally reached Seville at the end of July 1522, with only thirty-one of the 270 men who had set out on the expedition, to complete the first circumnavigation of the world.

One of the thirty-one who returned in the *Vittoria* was Antonio * Pigafetta, an Italian gentleman of Magellan's suite, who wrote an account of the voyage. It is published in *The First Voyage Round the World by Magellan, translated from Pigafetta*, edited by Lord Stanley of Alderly for the Hakluyt Society (London, 1874).

MAGELLANIC CLOUDS, a popular name for the two *nebiculae*, or cloudy-looking areas in the southern sky, which consist of a great number of small stars much resembling the Milky Way. They were named after Ferdinand * Magellan.

MAGNETIC COMPASS, see COMPASS.

MAGNETIC MINE, see MINES AND MINE WARFARE.

MAGNETIC POLE, the point on the earth's surface to which the needle of a magnetic * compass points. It is not at the North pole but some distance away in the Canadian Arctic, nor is it in a fixed position, but wanders according to the vagaries of terrestrial magnetism. Although its approximate location had been known for many years, it was not until 1831 that Sir James Clark * Ross discovered that it was on the west side of the Boothia Peninsula. The angular difference between the magnetic pole and the North pole at the point of a magnetic compass is known as * variation, and must be applied to a magnetic * course or * bearing to obtain the true course or bearing.

MAGNITUDE, as it applies to nautical astronomy, refers to the apparent brightness or luminosity of any of the navigational stars or planets. First to classify stars according to their apparent brightness was Hipparchus, the prince of ancient astronomers. His system comprised six magnitude classes, the small group of some fourteen of the brighter stars forming those described as being of the first magnitude, and the relatively large number of faint stars just visible to the unaided eye forming the group of sixth magnitude stars. This rough and ready classification was improved during the 19th century with the introduction of a decimal scale of magnitudes and the extension of the magnitude scale to include telescopic stars, whose magnitude numbers are more than six, and fractional and negative magnitudes. Sir John Herschel, son of the astronomer Sir William Herschel, is credited with having suggested that a star of magnitude 1·0 should be regarded as being 100 times as bright as a star of magnitude 6·0.

Nautical almanacs include tables providing for the navigational use of selected stars of the first and second magnitude, but those of lower magnitudes are never used for observation although they may form part of the constellations which enable the navigational stars to be identified. With the use of these tables, a navigator can obtain a position line of his ship on a *chart after taking an *observation of a navigational star.

MAHAN, ALFRED THAYER (1840–1914), U.S. rear admiral and naval historian, was born at West Point. He inherited an aptitude for study from his father and, after two years at Columbia College (now Columbia University), New York, made a brilliant showing in an entrance examination for the Naval Academy and was permitted to join the class which had completed one year at Annapolis. Graduating from the Naval Academy in June 1859, he served afloat until May 1870, except for eight months at the Naval Academy in 1862. He had no opportunity to make a name for himself during the Civil War (1861–5), but he served in blockading vessels and on the staff of Rear Admiral John A. Dahlgren.

After varied duty following 1870, Mahan became a captain in September 1885. He had commanded the *Wasp* on the South Atlantic station, served in the Boston and Brooklyn navy yards, been head of the Department of Ordnance and Gunnery at the Naval Academy, and commanded the *Wachusett* in the Pacific. He published a Civil War volume, *The Gulf and Inland Waters*, in 1883.

Mahan had served under Stephen B. *Luce at the Naval Academy in 1862 and had been chosen by him as executive officer of the *frigate *Macedonian*. When planning for the formation of a Naval War College which he had suggested, Luce turned to Mahan again and invited him to lecture on history at the college. Mahan accepted and devoted all possible time to reading history during the final year of his service in the *Wachusett*. He succeeded Luce as president of the Naval War College in 1886.

After various rejections, *The Influence of Sea Power upon History, 1660–1783*, based on his initial lectures at the Naval War College, was published in Boston in May 1890. Two years later *The Influence of Sea Power upon the French Revolution and Empire, 1793–1812* was published in two volumes, and in this same year he published a biography of Admiral *Farragut.

One of the first Americans to applaud Mahan on the appearance of *The Influence of Sea Power* was Theodore Roosevelt, then a civil service commissioner in Washington, who wrote that he had read the book through in two days, and later wrote a glowing review of it for the *Atlantic Monthly*. It has often been said that the many enthusiastic readers of these two works were mainly officers of foreign navies, but in fact a considerable number of officers of the U.S. Navy also read and appreciated these works on the influence of sea power. One reader who was intensely influenced by Mahan's theories of sea power was Wilhelm II of Germany, who decided after reading these books that Germany must become a maritime nation of the first magnitude. The German Navy Law of 1898, which started Germany on a naval building race with Britain and led in part to the outbreak of the First World War (1914–18), was a result of the Kaiser's enthusiasm for Mahan's naval doctrines.

In 1893 Mahan was appointed to command the cruiser *Chicago*, flagship of the European station. As representatives of the U.S.A., the admiral and the captain of the *Chicago* were extended many official and unofficial courtesies, but Mahan's well-earned reputation caused many people to seek his acquaintance in each port visited, and the cruise became a series of tributes to Mahan the historian. The *Chicago* was at Gravesend for the London season, May and June 1894, and Mahan received honorary degrees from Cambridge University on 18 June and from Oxford University on 20 June. At this time he had not received similar honours from any American university.

The *Chicago* returned to New York in March 1895 and Mahan retired the following year. In 1898 he was recalled to active duty and made a member of the Naval War Board. Writing in 1901, he recorded that he had been an 'anti-imperialist' before 1885. He declared that his studies had altered his views and he began to advocate 'guardianship' of the Hawaiian Islands in 1893. In Washington, in 1898, he advocated the transfer of the Philippine Islands to the U.S.A., a proposal which created a sharp conflict of political opinion, both in that year and in the presidential elections of 1900.

Mahan was one of five American delegates to the first Hague Conference of 1899. During the following years he wrote many articles on naval history, strategy, and foreign policy for various periodicals at home and abroad. His foreign policy articles were also related to history, but many of them touched also on questions in the political field, offending a number of his fellow countrymen who held that political controversy was not the proper field for a historian.

In addition to the four works published before 1895, mentioned above, Mahan published three other excellent histories: *The Life of Nelson*; *The Embodiment of the Sea Power of Great Britain* (2 vols, 1897), *Sea Power in its Relations to the War of 1812* (1905), and *The Major Operations of the Navies in the War of American Independence* (1913).

The American Historical Association recognized Mahan's achievements by making him president for the year 1902. His naval rank was advanced, on the retired list, from captain to rear admiral in 1906 in accordance with an Act of Congress which applied to certain Civil War veterans.

It would be difficult to overestimate the influence of Mahan's work on the navies of most maritime nations. His books were closely studied at most naval staff colleges and war colleges and his arguments were brought forward in many nations to divert a larger proportion of national income to the building of larger and more balanced navies. He was a strong believer in the theory of 'a fleet in being', the premise that even a small fleet held in a position of potential threat, even if permanently inactive, will lock up a greater fleet and render it virtually impotent. This was in fact the British experience in the First World War when a smaller German *High Seas Fleet in its base at Wilhelmshaven to all intents and purposes immobilized the British *Grand Fleet.

MAINSAIL, the principal sail of a sailing vessel. On a square-rigged vessel this is the lowermost (and largest) sail carried on the mainmast, and is usually termed the main *course. The earliest known mainsails in European waters, as depicted on Roman pottery and mosaics of the 3rd century A.D., were set with a *sprit. This rig held good in the Netherlands and North Sea ports until about the 15th century, when the sprit was superseded by the *gaff and *boom, while in the eastern Mediterranean it became the *lateen. Thames sailing barges, however, are still rigged with sprit mainsails for ease of handling with a crew of two.

On *smacks in the past the gaff and boom mainsail was loose-footed, i.e., the *foot was not laced to the boom, but attached only at the *tack and the *clew. On certain types of fishing craft, such as the Thames hatch boat, the cockle bawley, the Plymouth hooker, the mainsail had an extra long gaff and no boom, the mainsheet being led from two or more points on the leech of the sail to blocks on the stern *horse. In Bermuda from the late 18th century a simple form of

triangular or jib-headed mainsail was used on local *sloop-rigged boats, which was set on a sharply raked mast having a long boom but no gaff. In this early version the boom was almost as long as the *luff of the sail. A more sophisticated application of this type of sail was introduced to racing yachts in Europe in the early part of the present century. Developed in time into a very tall and narrow sail with a luff-to-foot proportion (*aspect ratio) of about 4 : 1, this so-called Bermudian mainsail is now almost universal on both racing and cruising yachts throughout the world.

'MAINSAIL HAUL', the order given during the *tacking of a square-rigged ship to *brace round the after *yards. The timing of the order is vital during the operation if the ship is not to be caught in *stays. The moment comes after the sails on the foremast have been *backed and the ship is very nearly exactly head to wind.

MAINWARING, Sir HENRY (1587–1653), English vice admiral, was the grandson of Sir William More, Vice Admiral of Sussex, and as a boy listened to his grandfather telling him tales of the Elizabethan sea-dogs which aroused in him the infatuation for ships and the sea which so coloured his later life. He matriculated at Brasenose College, Oxford, at the unusually early age of 12 and received his degree of Bachelor of Arts three years later in 1602. He had some experience of war, probably as a soldier in the Low Countries during the years 1608–10, and in 1611 received a commission from the *Lord High Admiral to proceed against the pirates who were operating in the Bristol Channel.

It was at this time that he met Sir Robert Shirley, a colourful, swashbuckling adventurer sent to the court of James I by the Shah of Persia to solicit English help against the Turks. The young Mainwaring, attracted by Shirley to the adventurous life, had little difficulty in acquiring from the Lord High Admiral a *letter of marque to operate as a *privateer against Spanish ships. He purchased and fitted out a small ship of about 160 tons, the *Resistance*, and sailed to the Mediterranean, making his base at Mamora at the mouth of the Sebu River on the Barbary coast, where he quickly proved himself a born leader of men, becoming one of the most successful pirates in that sea so noted for the skill and ferocity of its corsairs. Unlike most of his comrades, however, he retained throughout his love and respect for the English flag, never capturing an English ship, and on one occasion, when he stopped two ships from Lübeck and Calais trading to Spain and took out of them merchandise worth over £3,000, he refunded the full amount when he discovered that the ships were carrying goods consigned by an English trader to his factor in Spain. After making a considerable fortune by his acts of piracy against the ships of Spain he returned to England in 1618, was pardoned for his acts of piracy by James I, and appointed a gentleman of the royal bedchamber, being knighted by the king.

Still fired by the spirit of adventure, he played a considerable part in frustrating the infamous Spanish plot against Venice in 1618, proceeding secretly overland to Venice in spite of the European network of Spanish agents who had been warned of his journey and instructed to stop him at all costs. He had hoped to be placed in command of the Venetian squadron being gathered to resist the Spanish fleet, but Spain abandoned the plot when it was learned that an English fleet was being fitted out for the Mediterranean. On his return from Venice Mainwaring was appointed Lieutenant of Dover Castle and Deputy Warden of the *Cinque Ports as a reward for his Venetian endeavours.

The appointment of the Duke of Buckingham as Lord High Admiral placed Mainwaring firmly on the ladder of naval service. He was, in 1626–7, a member of the special commission which inquired into naval abuses, and in the latter year was made a brother of *Trinity House. He equipped and surveyed the fleet dispatched to the Île de Rhé in 1627 and took a notable part in the reorganization of the navy when Charles I succeeded his father as king of England. He served in the *ship-money fleets sent out by Charles annually between 1636 and 1641, being promoted to the rank of vice admiral. On the outbreak of the Civil War in 1641 Mainwaring followed the royalist cause and was with Prince Charles, later Charles II, when Charles I was executed. He returned to England in 1651, made a composition with the committee for compounding the estates of royalists, and died two years later.

Mainwaring, however, has a greater claim to fame than his colourful career at sea. When he received the royal pardon for his acts of piracy he wrote, and presented to James I, a treatise on the practices and suppression of piracy, which is a model of sound common sense. And while he was at Dover Castle, 1620–3, he wrote *The Seaman's Dictionary*, the first authoritative English work on seamanship. Although it was not printed until 1644, he made several manuscript copies which were presented to and used by many influential naval commanders. He wrote it for the use of what were known as the *gentlemen captains of the day; very few of whom 'though they be called seamen do fully and wholly understand what belongs to their profession'. For a biography see G. E. Mainwaring (with W. G. Perrin in Vol. II), *The Life and Works of Sir Henry Mainwaring* (N.R.S., 1920, 1922).

MAKE AND MEND, a half-day's holiday on board ship. The term originates from the custom of relieving men from ship's duties on one afternoon each week to give them a chance to make and mend their clothing.

MAKE HER NUMBER, to, see SIGNAL LETTERS.

MALAGA, after *Barcelona the most important seaport in Spain, faces the Mediterranean on the coastal edge of the plain of Malaga. It was important as a seaport in Carthaginian days, and also used as such by the Romans and Visigoths. It was a Moorish city during the 700 years of occupation of southern Spain, and in 1487 it was captured and put to the sack by the forces of Ferdinand and Isabella. It was sacked a second time in 1811 by French troops under General Sebastiani. It is today a thriving port handling a great variety of trade.

MALLOWS, the old English name for the French port of St. Malo, often to be found in English books of the sea of the 15th–17th centuries. Samuel *Pepys uses this version in his famous diary, as does Richard *Hakluyt in his *Principal Navigations*.

MALMÖ, a seaport of Sweden facing the Sound, was of great commercial importance during the period of the *Hanseatic League, its prosperity depending to a large extent on the Baltic herring fishery. During the 16th and 17th centuries, when the herrings migrated from the Baltic to the North Sea, its importance and trade declined rapidly. It is remembered in Britain, however, for its citadel in which the Earl of Bothwell, third husband of Mary Queen of Scots, was imprisoned after he fled from Scotland in 1567.

MALTA, a strategically placed island in the central Mediterranean Sea commanding the relatively narrow channel between the southern extremity of Europe and the northern extremity of Africa. The island, in consequence of its strategic position, has had a chequered history of war and capture. It was at one time occupied by the Phoenicians; the Carthaginians were there in the 6th century B.C.; and it later became a Roman colony. Hannibal was born in Malta, and St. Paul was shipwrecked on the island in A.D. 58. On the break-up of the Roman empire, Malta passed to Constantinople in A.D. 395. It was next conquered by the Normans in 1090, became a vassal state of Aragon in 1282, and in 1530 was granted to the knights of St. John, who had been driven by the Turks from Rhodes, for the annual tribute of a falcon. Malta was besieged by the Turks in 1565 in one of the most famous sieges

Tugs round the stricken tanker Ohio *in Grand Harbour, Valletta, 1942*

in history. In 1798 Napoleon occupied Malta as a result of treachery and it was captured by the British in 1799 and confirmed as under British rule in the Treaty of Paris in 1814. It became an independent nation in 1963.

In the maritime field Malta owes its fame to the magnificent deep-water harbour of Valletta, named after one of the most famous grand masters of the Order of St. John, Jehan Parisot de la Valette. Important as a central trading station in the Mediterranean from the earliest days, it became even more so as a naval base because of its commanding position within that great inland sea. For a century and a half it was the main naval base of the British Mediterranean Fleet, and after the Second World War, in which Valletta suffered severely from air attack by Germany and Italy, became a base of the NATO navies. It has an extensive dockyard and is an important fuelling base. See also OHIO.

MAN THE YARDS, to, or **MAN SHIP, to,** a form of ceremonial salute in a warship with masts and *yards in the days of sail to honour the visit of a high official. The yards were lined by men standing upon them supported by lifelines rigged between the *lifts and the masts and with one man, known as the button-man, standing on the *truck of each *topgallant mast.

This form of salute continued in the British Navy until about 1885, when sail finally gave way to steam. But the practice is still occasionally seen in square-rigged sail training ships and in shore training establishments which have a mast crossed with yards.

MANDEVILLE, Sir JOHN, a pseudonym for the unknown compiler of a famous book of travels, partly fictitious and partly made up of accounts of voyages by other writers, *The Voiage and Travaile of Sir John Maundervile, Kt* . . ., originally published in French between 1357 and 1371. The author is usually identified with a physician who practised in Liège, Jehen de Bourgogne or Jehen à la Barbe (d. 1372). The work was first published in England by Wynkyn de Worde in 1499 and enjoyed great popularity, with 'Mandeville' being described as the 'father of English prose', a belief which existed until 1725 when the French origin was established. The best modern edition is that produced by Macmillan in the Library of English Classics in 1900 which reproduces the Cotton manuscript in the British Museum, the earliest known text, edited by A. W. Pollard. Another early manuscript text in the British Museum, in the Egerton papers, was published by the Roxburghe Club in 1889, edited by G. F. Warner.

MANFRONI, CAMILLO (1863–1935), Italian professor, taught history at the Naval Academy at Leghorn and at the Universities of Genoa, Padua, and Rome. He was a great exponent of the works of Rear Admiral A. T. *Mahan and a founder member of the Italian Navy League. Among his best-known works are *A History of the Italian Navy* (3 vols) and *The History of the Italian Navy during the World War* (*1915–18*).

MANGER, a small space in the bows of a ship immediately abaft the *hawsepipes and bounded on the after side by a low *coaming called a manger-board. Its purpose was to prevent any water from running aft along the deck should it enter through the hawsepipes. It applied principally to sailing ships and the early steamships when the hawsepipes were on the maindeck level. In modern ships, where the hawsepipes are on the forecastle deck level, the same purpose is achieved by an athwartships breakwater abaft the *cable-holders.

MANHATTAN, a *tanker of 150,000 tons owned by the U.S.A., and the largest ship yet to transit the *North-West passage from east to west and vice versa. The discovery of oil in considerable quantity in northern Alaska posed the problem of how best to transport it. In an effort to overcome the difficulties presented by ice in the approaches to the area it was decided to fit the *Manhattan* with a 125-ft spoon-handled bow weighing over 5,000 tons and a protective steel belt 9 feet thick, 30 feet deep, and 670 feet long. Her twin propellers were replaced by specially strengthened ones and her two rudders reinforced with steel plating. Sailing from the Delaware River on 24 August 1969 she reached Thule, Greenland, on 4 September and, assisted by extensive air reconnaissance and two ice-breakers, successfully forced her way through Lancaster Sound, Barrow Strait, and Viscount Melville Sound until brought to a halt by heavy pack ice in McClure Strait in approximately the same position as that in which the *Investigator* was beset 116 years earlier. After freeing herself with the aid of the Canadian ice-breaker *John A. MacDonald*, she headed down Prince of Wales Strait, reaching Prudhoe Bay, Alaska, on 19 September, having covered 4,600 miles in twenty-eight days. On the return journey she suffered severe ice damage to her side plating and had to be docked for repairs. Not long afterwards the Swedish vessel *Trojoland* (6,000 d.w.t.) made the passage to and from Bathurst Island with drilling equipment without mishap.

The difficulties of navigating the North-West passage with tankers of a size sufficient to handle the great quantities of oil in the area are so great that an overland oil pipeline to an ice-free port in southern Alaska is being built.

MANIFEST, a document carried by all merchant ships which gives the name of the ship and her port of registry, her *tonnage and the name of her *master, full details of her cargo with the names of shippers and consignees, and all other relevant information about the ship, her crew and passengers, and all she carries on board. A ship cannot enter or clear a port unless her manifest has been passed at the custom-house.

MANILA, the capital and principal seaport of the Philippine Islands. It was founded by the Spanish in 1571 and became a centre for the collection of treasure and other rich cargoes which were shipped across the Pacific by *galleon to Acapulco on the coast of Mexico, for final transit to Spain. This lucrative trade, however, withered in the 17th and 18th centuries as Dutch power in the East Indies grew through the operations of the *East Indies Company. Manila was captured by a British fleet in 1762, during the Seven Years War (1756–63), but returned to Spain after the war; and it was the site of a naval battle in 1898 during the war between the U.S.A. and Spain when an American *squadron under the command of Commodore *Dewey destroyed the Spanish fleet anchored there. Manila is the centre of the *hemp trade, and also has a great entrepôt trade in a part of the world which is growing and developing at a great rate.

MANILA, a type of rope much used at sea before the introduction of man-made fibres. It is made from the fibre of the wild banana plant, grown in the Philippine Islands, and takes its name from the capital of those islands, Manila. Rope made from these fibres does not need to be tarred, as does rope made from *hemp fibres which will rot when exposed to seawater unless preserved with tar.

MANLEY, JOHN (*c.* 1734–93), American naval officer, was a merchant captain who in 1775 was commissioned by President George Washington to command one of the seven ships which comprised what was then known· as 'Washington's fleet', *privateers designed to capture British merchantmen. Manley proved the most successful of the seven captains, being made commodore of the fleet by Washington. On the formation of the *Continental Navy in 1776, congress gave him the rank of captain and graded him second in the seniority list.

He was given command of the *frigate *Hancock* and in June 1777, in company with the Continental frigate *Boston*, he captured the British frigate *Fox*, which he retained with him with a *prize crew on board. A month later the three ships fell in with a small British force of two frigates and a 10-gun *brig, and after a short action Manley surrendered the *Hancock* and the

Fox was quickly retaken. After a year as a prisoner-of-war Manley was exchanged under a cartel and on his return to America was tried by court martial for the loss of the *Hancock*, but was acquitted.

With no ship of the Continental Navy available for him to command, he returned to privateering but was again captured in 1779 when the *Cumberland*, which he was commanding, was taken by H.M.S. *Pomona*. He escaped from prison in Barbados, made his way back to Boston, and took over command of the privateer *Jason*, but was captured yet again by the British. This time he was taken back to England and was confined in the Mill prison, near Plymouth. He was held there for two years before being exchanged. On his return he was appointed to command the Continental frigate *Hague*, and in 1782 only just managed to escape capture for a fourth time when by brilliant seamanship he gave the slip to a superior British naval force. His ship captured the last valuable British prize of the war when he took the merchant ship *Baille* in January 1783.

MANSELL, Sir ROBERT (1573–1656), British admiral, is chiefly remembered for his command in 1620–1 of a fleet sent to the Mediterranean to halt the activities of Algerine pirates. It was perhaps one of the more inglorious exploits of the English Navy, achieving nothing beyond the release of forty English merchant-captains offered him as a sop by the Dey of Algiers. While Mansell and his fleet lay off the town, pirate vessels with their captures came into harbour with impunity. An attempt by Mansell to burn the shipping in port with *fireships was a failure because of the half-hearted way in which it was mounted, and the activities of the pirates, operating as far afield as the English Channel, the River Thames, and even against the English fishing fleet on the Newfoundland *Grand Banks, continued unabated.

Mansell is remembered too for the years 1604–18 in which he held the appointment of Treasurer of the Navy, years in which naval administration sank to a very low ebb and Mansell's private fortune increased prodigiously. He was a close friend of James I, which may explain his immunity from prosecution as a venal naval administrator and a half-hearted naval commander.

MARCQ ST. HILAIRE METHOD, a means of finding a ship's position by nautical astronomy known to the French as the *méthode du point rapproché*, and to British navigators as the *intercept method. It was introduced in 1875 in a paper published in the *Revue Maritime* by a French naval officer, Captain (later Admiral) Marcq St. Hilaire. The basis of the method rests on the fact that for every heavenly body at a given time there is a spot on the earth's surface (its 'geographical position') where it is at the *zenith. For other places, its observed *altitude, subtracted from 90°, gives its *zenith distance, and this determines a circle on the globe, called a 'circle of equal altitude', with its centre at the geographical position of the body; somewhere on this circle the observer's position must be. The navigator, however, is concerned only with the small segment of this circle which runs near his estimated position, and, because the circle is very large compared to the length of the segment in question, this may be plotted on a *chart as a straight line; it is known as a *position line. To obtain such a line, the navigator decides his estimated position by *dead reckoning or other means, and from the *nautical almanac he obtains by calculation the altitude of a convenient navigational star or other heavenly body (usually the sun), as it would be observed from the estimated position at the time of observation. The bearing or *azimuth of the selected heavenly body is also obtained. Its altitude is observed and this probably differs by a small amount from the calculated altitude, the true position of the ship not being identical with her estimated position. The difference in minutes of arc is known as the intercept, and is set out on the chart either towards, or away from, the bearing of the heavenly body, according to whether the observed altitude is greater or less than calculated. From the end of the intercept a position line is drawn at right angles, and the ship's position at the time of observation is somewhere on this line. By carrying this line forward according to *course and distance run, and obtaining another position line, the ship's position is found by the intersection of the two lines.

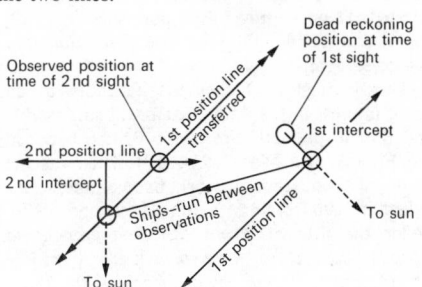

A Marcq St. Hilaire fix

It will be seen that this method does not depend on a noon altitude of the sun, but it does involve the use of a reliable *chronometer or means of knowing the exact time of observation, and the existence of good nautical almanacs; it was therefore not available till a fairly late stage in the history of navigation, but modern navigators find it generally useful except in so far as astronomical navigation has been replaced by *hyperbolic navigational systems such as *Decca or *Loran, or by a ship's inertial navigation system. See also NAVIGATION.

MARDER, ARTHUR JACOB (1910–), American historian, was born in Boston. He graduated from Harvard University in 1931 and obtained his Ph.D. five years later. His interests were diverted during this period towards British naval history, a subject to which he has devoted his main activities ever since. He was assistant professor at the University of Oregon, 1936–8, and research associate at Harvard and Radcliffe, 1939–41. When the U.S.A. entered the Second World War at the end of 1941, he was appointed a research analyst in the Office of Strategic Studies in Washington, learning Japanese for the purpose, but had to relinquish the post because of ill health. After appointments on the professional staff at Hamilton College and University of Hawaii, he became professor of history at the University of California, Irvine, in 1964.

During these years he laid the foundations of a reputation as the foremost exponent of British naval history of his day. This reputation was based on his two earliest books, *The Anatomy of British Sea Power* (1940) and *Portrait of an Admiral*, a biography of Admiral Sir Herbert *Richmond, based on his diaries and papers, published in 1952. Both showed a remarkable degree of scholarship and insight into the period in which his main interest lay, from about 1896 to 1920. He had, during his research for these books, fallen to some degree under the spell of that remarkable naval officer, Sir John *Fisher, and it was natural that his next major work should be three volumes devoted to the correspondence of Fisher, superbly edited and annotated. These volumes were published in 1952, 1956, and 1959 under the title *Fear God and Dread Nought*.

This interest in Fisher led naturally to an equal interest in his immediate naval successors, and thus to the activities of the British Navy in the First World War (1914–18). This was the theme of his next major work, five volumes, published in 1961, 1965, 1966, 1969, and 1970, under the title of *From the Dreadnought to Scapa Flow*. It is a work which is widely regarded as a classic naval history of the years 1904–19, and one likely to remain as a permanent monument to Marder's skill, industry, and integrity as an historian of the first water. This work was recognized in Britain by the award of an honorary C.B.E. in 1970; in 1968 he received the Chesney Gold Medal of the Royal United Services Institution, awarded periodically to historians of outstanding merit. Among his subsequent publications are *From the Dardanelles to Oran* (1974) and *Operation 'Menace'* (1976).

MARE CLAUSUM, or 'Closed Sea', a term in international law which was used in connection with the claim by certain maritime nations to exclusive ownership of areas of open sea or ocean. Spain, in the 15th and 16th centuries, claimed dominion of whole oceans; Britain, in the 17th century, similarly claimed dominion of all the seas surrounding her. The obvious difficulties of such a doctrine, particularly in the sphere of navigation and trade, fishery, etc., led to attempts to modify these outrageous claims among the nations concerned.

In 1609 Grotius wrote his *Mare Liberum*, or 'free sea', in which he advocated the unrestricted right of all ships to use all waters. This was answered in 1631 by John *Selden who wrote *Mare Clausum* in an attempt to sustain the older point of view that seas could become the exclusive property of nations in exactly the same way as land.

The final compromise was suggested by Bynkershoek in his *De dominio maris*, published in 1702, that dominion over the sea should be restricted to the range at which it could be protected from the adjacent land, i.e., the maximum range of a cannon, which was agreed among the nations at that time to be three miles. Hence the *three-mile limit.

MARE LIBERUM, see MARE CLAUSUM.

MARIEHAMN, a Finnish port in the Åland Islands, at the mouth of the Gulf of Bothnia, and well known for many years as the last home of the 'windjammers', square-rigged ships used for trading and training in sail, which fought a largely losing battle against the steel steamship up to about the outbreak of the Second World War in 1939. It is the home of the *Ålands Sjöfartsmuseum.

MARINA, a term said to have originated since the Second World War in the U.S.A. to describe the modern sophisticated harbour designed specially for the safe berthing of yachts. Variously called yacht station, harbour, haven, or basin, the marina is essentially a complex of floating piers and jetties at which yachts can lie, together with the facilities demanded by the modern yacht owner and his family. These include fresh water, fuel and electric power laid on, shipwright and engineering services, a yacht chandler's store, laundry services, a clubhouse with bar and showers, grocery stores, a car park and good access roads. Elaborate yacht harbours or marinas are being constructed in almost all countries throughout the world where yachting is an accepted way of life and range generally from the small harbour holding 100 berths or so to giant marinas in Florida and California where 2,000 and more yachts are regularly based.

MARINE LITERATURE. 'The history of the world,' wrote Thomas Carlyle, 'is but the biography of great men' and the same can be said of the history of ships and the sea. It is through the biographies and literature of the men who have lived and fought on the sea, and who have voyaged across it in search of new lands, that we are able to chart its influence on events. The literature of the sea is comparable in its extent with the oceans themselves. Some idea of its compass can be obtained from the fact that the Naval Library of the Ministry of Defence in London contains over 5,000 books dealing with voyages and travel, over 6,000 biographical works, and the names of 21,000 marine authors, and this is not by any means the whole story. All the nations with a seafaring history can boast of similar collections, so that in sum there is a wealth of evidence of man's abiding interest in an element which, until the coming of the space age, provided him with his greatest challenge.

Although the Phoenicians and the Egyptians were among the earliest known users of the sea, the Greeks were the first to write about it. Homer's heroic epics, the *Iliad* and the *Odyssey*, committed to writing about 600 B.C., provide some of the earliest examples of sea literature we possess. The Romans, less romantic and more practical mariners, wrote comparatively little about it. Virgil, who studied Greek, appears to have borrowed some of Homer's nautical genius for expression when writing about ships and the sea, but the inspiration which led Catullus (c. 84–54 B.C.) to write in such moving terms about the laying up of an old ship is exceptional.

Those doughty seamen the Norsemen were men of action rather than of literature and the eddas and sagas which they have left us are more in the nature of mythological stories of war and adventure than historical records. There followed almost 500 years during which very little contribution was made to the literature of the sea. It had little attraction for the monastic scholars, but with the introduction of printing and the dawning of the great age of discovery in the 16th century, a new impulse was imparted to it.

In 1516 Sir Thomas More published *Utopia* which, for all its limited scope, manages to include the drama of seafaring. The early seamen knew little of the art of writing and their accounts of their voyages deal less with the hardships of their passages across the oceans than with the wonders they discovered at their journey's end. The first records of such discoveries come from Portuguese and Spanish sources and these accounts provoked the English seamen to emulate them. Such were *De Orbe Novo* by Peter Martyr Anglerius, published about 1511, and Giovanni Batista Ramusio's collection of voyages which began to appear in 1550. The doyen of English sea literature is Richard *Eden, not as

an author so much as an anthologist and the forerunner of Richard *Hakluyt. Eden's *Arte of Navigation*, translated from the Spanish and published in 1561, was undoubtedly designed to stir up British merchants and seamen to follow the example of their foreign rivals. One of the most notable narratives of this period is the account of his voyages by Sir John *Hawkins which contains many astute observations. Hakluyt's diligence has preserved for us a memorable piece of narrative literature in the account of Sir Humphrey *Gilbert's last voyage in the *Squirrel* when, on his way home from founding the colony of Newfoundland, the little ship capsized in a storm and sank. Another notable contribution to the literature of discovery was made by Sir John Hawkins's son Richard in *The Observations of Sir Richard Hawkins, Knight, in his Voiage into the South Sea, anno Domini 1593*.

The debt we owe to Richard Hakluyt is immense. He rummaged through extant accounts of voyages, examining the papers of shipowners, merchants, and travellers, and was ably assisted in his work by Sir Walter *Raleigh. It was characteristic of him to include in his great anthology the first piece of naval propaganda of which we have knowledge, the anonymous 15th-century poem 'Libelle of Englysshe Policie'. His successor, though not so gifted, was Samuel *Purchas, a number of whose narratives cover the adventures of English travellers in the Far East including those of William *Adams, the first Englishman to set foot in Japan and the father of Japanese shipbuilding. Also worthy of mention are Pedro Fernandez de *Quiros's letter 'Terra Australis incognita etc.' (1617) and Richard Boothby's *Description of the most famous island of Madagascar* (1646).

In the later part of the 17th century we find greater notice being taken of personnel problems and the manning and working of ships. Typical of these is Captain John Smith's *An Accidence or the Path-way to Experience necessary for all young Seamen, or those that are desirous to go to Sea* (1626) reprinted in 1653 as *The Sea-man's Grammar*. The search for the *North-West passage produced a literature of its own in which men like Luke *Fox and Captain Thomas James figure prominently. When during the reign of Charles I the British Navy was allowed to run down, attempts were made by writers like Sir Henry *Mainwaring and Captain Nathaniel *Boteler to remind their countrymen of its abiding importance. The last-named, in his *Six Dialogues about the Sea Services* (1685), emphasizes the high standing of a sea captain. In 1689 appeared what might be called the first attempt at a Navy List under the title of *Gloria Britannica, or the Boast of the British Seas* which included a statistical summary of the Royal Navy of England.

Meanwhile a wealth of folk lore and superstition connected with the sea had accumulated over the centuries and these began to appear in literature, as in Chaucer's 'Nun's Priest's Tale' and, a century or so later, in the plays of William Shakespeare who seems to have been very well acquainted with them. His most nautical play is, of course, *The Tempest*, for which he is said to have derived the inspiration from the wreck of Sir George Somers's ship *Sea Venture* on the Bermudas in 1609. Generally speaking, however, there are comparatively few plays with a marine setting, until we come to Gilbert and Sullivan's lighthearted naval satire *H.M.S. Pinafore*, first produced in 1878.

The influence of the sea is also revealed in early poetry, such as that of Edmund Spenser (1552–99) and John Donne (1572–1631); later it is most apparent in song from the sea *shanties of the sailing ship days through the patriotic age of Sir Henry *Newbolt and Rudyard *Kipling to the work of the sea poet *par excellence* John *Masefield.

Tobias George *Smollett has been described as the first novelist of the navy and the literary father of the 'British tar', but it was not until the first half of the 19th century that the sea novelist proper appeared in the person of Captain Frederick *Marryat. It is necessary to distinguish between authors whose books deal with adventures at sea and those who treat of the sea itself, like Herman *Melville in his famous novel *Moby-Dick*. Joseph *Conrad followed along the course set by these pioneers in the realm of sea fiction, though he preferred to think of himself as a writer and not merely a marine novelist. His contemporary W. W. *Jacobs, on the other hand, created for his readers a world peopled with short-sea sailors of a markedly humorous type.

The naval historian is of comparatively recent origin, though Herodotus (484–424 B.C.) includes in the wide sweep of his histories descriptions of naval actions such as the battle of *Salamis. The great diarist Samuel *Pepys, whose record of naval administration during his period of office is unique, does not fall into this category either; in fact no attempt seems to have been made to separate naval history from the general chronicle of events until the French writers the Comte de *Gueydon and Eugène *Sue attempted to do so. The American Rear Admiral *Mahan set the pattern which others were to follow in not only chronicling naval history but expounding the lessons to be learned from a study of it. His successors were such well-known historians as Sir John *Laughton, Sir Herbert *Richmond, Sir Julian *Corbett, Sir Geoffrey *Callender, and Michael *Lewis, to name but a few.

Finally we have the literature of the technical experts who wrote of the way in which ships were built, of their rigging and armament. The earliest of these date from the first half of the 17th century and they have numerous followers during later years. One of the most remarkable of them was Frederik Hendrik af *Chapman. He was employed in the Swedish Royal Dockyards, and in 1768 he published his *Architectura Navalis Mercatoria* which contained drawings of a great variety of 18th-century ships. He followed it up with his *Tractat om Skepps Byggeriet* published in 1775 which contained explanatory notes relating to the drawings in the first volume, the two together being regarded as having laid the foundation of modern naval architecture and as providing a key to the scientific design of ships. Also worthy of mention is Auguste *Jal whose *Glossaire Nautique* (1848) is a mine of technical information about the sailing-ship era. *The Naval and Shipping Annual* founded by Earl *Brassey in 1889 carried information of this kind into the 20th century, its place being ultimately taken by the works of other technical authors, the best known of whom is F. T. *Jane who founded the famous annual *Fighting Ships*. This last now has its rivals in France, Germany, Italy, and the U.S.A.

MARINE MUSEUM OF THE CITY OF NEW YORK, New York, U.S.A., although not the largest of the eight maritime museums located in New York city and state, is of interest as having been established in 1928 by the New York Ship Model Society. The collection includes ship models and half models, *figureheads, whaling tackle, *scrimshaw, paintings, engravings, photographs, and dioramas. The other maritime museums of New York are the Franklin D. Roosevelt Library in Hyde Park with 100 ship models, the Marine Museum of the Seaman's Church Institute of New York with 250 models, the New York Yacht Club, the New York Historical Society, the Seaman's Bank for Savings, with 140 ship models and 250 paintings, the Canal Museum, and the Skenesborough Museum.

MARINE PAINTING. The earliest known pictures of ships and boats are those which decorate Egyptian pottery of the period around 3200 B.C. Wall paintings and reliefs of the two periods of Egyptian ascendancy, 2500–2300 B.C. and 1500–1085 B.C., are often of such clarity and detail that contemporary methods of shipbuilding and rig are made clear. The methods and weapons of sea battle can be seen in a wall painting in the temple of Medinet Habu to the west of Thebes on the upper Nile. It depicts the victory of the Egyptian fleet of Rameses III (1198–1166 B.C.) over the combined fleets of sea-raiders from Crete, Cyprus, Philistia, and Libya.

Portuguese carracks; oil painting by C. Anthonisz, c. 1553

Of the periods of Greek and Roman sea power, no true paintings exist beyond some pottery decoration. A Greek vase dating from 540 B.C., now in the British Museum, has a painting of a Greek merchant vessel being pursued by a pirate * galley, and a carving in relief from the Temple of Fortune at Praesneste, now preserved in the Vatican, shows one of the Roman warships at the battle of * Actium in 31 B.C. There are also, of course, the coloured representations of French ships of 1066 in the Bayeux tapestry, which again provide details of contemporary building and rig.

Although representations of the sea and ships appear in many paintings of the early Renaissance (Botticelli's 'The Birth of Venus' is a typical example), true marine painting, as a direct expression of sea and ships, is of comparatively recent growth. Volpe's painting of Henry VIII leaving Dover on his way to the Field of the Cloth of Gold in 1520 shows his great ship * *Henry Grâce à Dieu* in considerable detail and accuracy, though the sea in which she floats bears little or no resemblance to reality. Similarly the equally well known picture of Portuguese * carracks by Cornelis * Anthonisz, while detailing the features and build of these ships with great skill and attention, lacks any verisimilitude in representing the sea around them. These famous pictures are in no way seascapes, but merely portraits of ships.

The true birth of marine painting, which may be taken as portraying the sea itself as well as the ships that sailed on it, occurred in Holland in the second half of the 16th century, coinciding with the rise to maritime power of the Dutch Republic. The first of the Dutch painters to specialize in seascape as such was Cornelisz Hendriks * Vroom who, if best known in Britain for his designs for the * Armada tapestries which used to hang in the House of Lords in London (see also PINE, John), painted a picture of Dutch ships running into the port of Flushing in the teeth of a gale. It is his finest picture and shows a rare feeling for both ships battling against a high wind at sea and the anger and force of a rough sea, and was the first true seascape in that it directly related the sea conditions with the behaviour of ships affected by them. He began a school of painting which was carried on by such Dutch artists as Andries van Ertvelt, Jan * Porcellis, and Abraham * Storck, reaching its greatest heights with the two Van de * Veldes, father and son. They raised the standard of marine painting to its greatest heights, in both fidelity of detail in the ships they painted, based on meticulous initial drawings, and the skill with which they painted the surrounding sea in all its moods. Another Dutch master of seascape, a contemporary of the Van de Veldes, was Ludolf * Bakhuysen, who made a speciality of storm scenes at sea.

The two Van de Veldes came to England during the winter of 1672–3 to become marine

The Dutch fleet off Sheerness during the attack on the Medway; grisaille by W. Van de Velde I, 1667

painters to Charles II. The period of their later life in Britain corresponded with the rise of British sea power to a dominant position in the world, and the influence of their meticulous style can be seen in the early paintings of the British school of marine painting which grew up around these years. Peter *Monamy, Charles *Brooking, and Samuel *Scott, if not exactly slavish copiers of the Van de Veldes, owed much of their style and detail to these great masters.

The great period of British marine painting should have been the 18th century, the years of overwhelming British naval supremacy at sea and studded with a series of great naval battles. But in general the British marine painters of that century did not quite live up to the heroic nature of their subject, though such artists as Nicholas *Pocock, Thomas *Luny, and Jacques Philippe de *Loutherbourg painted some pictures well above the general level in their fidelity to seas and ships and the stress of a battle. Another French painter to adorn the British marine scene at this period was Dominic *Serres, the master of a French merchantman captured at sea. Ironically, he was to become probably the best of the marine painters of the English school of this period.

In France, marine painting received so little encouragement that it never really prospered to the extent that it did in Holland and Britain.

Ambroise-Louis *Garneray, who began to paint when he was a naval prisoner-of-war in the prison *hulks in Portsmouth harbour during the Napoleonic War (1803–15), was the most notable painter in this genre, though an earlier artist, Claude Gellée, had painted some marine pictures which compared not unfavourably with some of the Dutch marine paintings of his day. In the U.S.A., Fritz Hugh Lane was the first painter to specialize in seascapes.

During the 19th century the birth of Impressionism, so frequently attributed to French painters but in fact generated in England, brought a new dimension to marine painting. J. M. W. *Turner, the real father of Impressionism, was the outstanding landscape painter of his generation but his seascapes, though not many in numbers, are of remarkable beauty in both atmosphere and colouring. He was not in any way an accurate portraitist of ships, as had been the Van de Veldes and others of the traditional Dutch and English schools, but he introduced a particular luminosity and drama in his studies which lifted them to new heights of pure artistry. Some of his sketches in oils of the River Thames and its shipping, though violently attacked by the art critics of the time for their lack of formal organization, brought a new dimension to the art of seascape.

This was the century when the sailing ship

Fishing boats off Yarmouth; oil painting by J. S. Cotman

Sketch for East Cowes Castle, the Regatta beating to Windward; oil painting by J. M. W. Turner

reached its perfection of design and the century which saw the introduction of the iron steamship. The many great English painters of the lovely sailing ships which graced the 19th century are best represented by George *Chambers, Clarkson *Stanfield, and Sir Oswald *Brierly. Of this period, the pure seascape as such, not depending on the ship as its central theme, flourished under the brushes of Richard Parkes *Bonington and John Sell *Cotman, both of whom, though better known as landscape artists, produced seascapes of exquisite quality and atmosphere. The transition from sail to steam is best represented in the work of W. L. *Wyllie, a prolific artist whose water-colours of great delicacy and beauty are as much appreciated as many of his more stirring and dramatic oil paintings.

The two world wars of the 20th century produced a plethora of marine artists, in both Britain and the U.S.A., as a result of naval appointments of painters as official artists to record scenes of naval activity. Sir Muirhead *Bone spanned both world wars as an official artist, and his drawings and etchings were powerful and evocative. Some others who have made names in this particular field of marine painting are Frank Mason, Norman *Wilkinson, and Charles *Pears.

Historically, at least up to the 20th century when the camera became available as an instrument of record, the overall volume of marine painting, of whatever country of origin, remains of great importance as a source of knowledge of ship construction and design, of sails and rigging, of ship decoration, and of the transitional age when iron superseded wood as the material of construction and steam superseded sail as the means of propulsion. It is a record, too, of naval operations throughout the great sea campaigns of the 16th, 17th, and 18th centuries. Of this historical value it is possible to speak with great certainty; of the aesthetic value of marine painting in the overall field of art, and of its inspirational value in focusing the endeavour and activity of man in his conquest of the sea, there can hardly be less doubt.

For works by A.-L. Garneray see NAVARINO, battle of; by C. Pears see TIRPITZ; by N. Pocock see COPENHAGEN, battle of, TRAFALGAR, battle of; by D. Serres see SAILORS' DRESS; by A. Storck see TEXEL, the; by C. Vroom see title-page; by N. Wilkinson see BOARD, TO, DUNKIRK.

MARINE RUNDSCHAU, the leading German naval periodical which, except for the interruptions caused by the First and Second World Wars, has been published regularly since 1890. It was originally a product of the News Bureau of the German Admiralty and continued as such during the period that Grand Admiral Alfred von *Tirpitz held office. Publication ceased in August 1914 but was resumed in 1921, and shortly afterwards it was taken over by the Army Department of the Defence Ministry. In 1930 Rear Admiral D. Gadow was appointed editor and held the position until 1943 when he was relieved by Rear Admiral Lützow. Meanwhile, in 1938, the publication once more became the responsibility of the German Navy and continued until September 1944 with the publication of Volume 49. Production was not resumed until 1953 under the editorship of Erich *Gröner, an expert in naval architecture, the publishers being E. S. Mittler und Sohn, first at Darmstadt and subsequently at Frankfurt-am-Main. Gröner died in 1964 and his place was taken by Admiral Erich Forster who was followed in 1970 by the present editor, Dr. Jurgen *Rohwer, who had joined the staff in 1954 as production manager. Originally a monthly publication, it was produced on a two-monthly basis between 1953 and 1970 but monthly publication was resumed that year. Each issue averages about sixty pages and the contents include essays on both historical and current maritime affairs, news regarding the Bundesmarine and foreign navies, and also on merchant shipping.

MARINE SOCIETY, THE, was founded in London in 1756 by Jonas *Hanway, a governor of the Foundling Hospital and a commissioner of the *Victualling Board, who with the assistance of Sir John Fielding, the Bow Street magistrate, provided poor boys and vagrants willing to go to sea with a full outfit of clothes, bedding, etc., and placed them on board ships with strict arrangements for their humane treatment. The society was supported by public subscription. Thousands of recruits were thus gained for the British Navy and employment provided for them in the merchant service in peacetime. One of the conditions of the society was that boys accepted for help in this way must be 'stout and well made and have no disorders upon them further than the itch'. The Society's work still continues.

MARINEMUSEET, Horten, Norway, a museum founded in 1853 and now housed in an old warehouse, which illustrates through its exhibits the history of the Royal Norwegian Navy. It contains some 1,200 items which include models of war and merchant ships, a *torpedoboat of 1873, two *submarines, *figureheads, ship's engines, weapons, King Haakon's and other naval uniforms, medals, and flags. There is also a small collection of paintings, drawings, engravings, and photographs.

MARINER'S MIRROR, THE, (1) a quarterly journal (monthly from January 1911 to September 1914) published by the *Society for

Title page of Anthony Ashley's The Mariner's Mirrour, *1588*

Nautical Research, at Greenwich. It is recognized throughout the world as one of the most scholarly of maritime journals with a range of interests that embraces every aspect of nautical life and history.

(2) A sea atlas, compiled by Lucas * Wagenaer, first published in Holland in 1585 under the title of *Spieghel der Zeevaerdt*, of which a translation by Anthony Ashley, under the title *The Mariner's Mirrour*, was produced in England in 1588. It was one of the most famous collections of charts of its time and was widely used by British seamen for the next hundred years. The area covered by the atlas included the Baltic and North Sea coasts, the English Channel, and the Atlantic coasts of France and Spain. See CHART-MAKING.

MARINERS MUSEUM, Newport News, Virginia, U.S.A., was founded in 1930 and opened four years later; it houses the most important collection of marine artefacts in the U.S.A. Its scope is wide and embraces man's conquest of the sea, the culture of the sea, and its influence on civilization. Among a large number of ship models, the Crabtree collection of miniature ship models is notable. Over eighty-five * figureheads are on display as well as billet-heads, stern ornaments, and miscellaneous ship embellishments. The shipbuilding models number 230 and there are over 2,500 other exhibits

including nautical instruments, weapons, uniforms, * scrimshaw, medals, flags, etc. Also displayed are fittings from British warships sunk in the York River in 1781 during the War of American Independence (1775–82). The collection of paintings, drawings, and engravings numbers over 5,000, together with 100,000 photographs. The library, which is open to the public, contains 45,000 books. A diorama depicts the first engagement between * ironclads, that between the * *Merrimack* and the * *Monitor* on 9 March 1862.

MARINES, soldiers specially trained and adapted for maritime warfare. Most naval nations have marine corps but in very few cases, except in Britain and the U.S.A., do they actually serve at sea.

The origin of the British marine force was an Order-in-Council of 1664 directing that 1,200 soldiers be raised to be 'distributed in His Majesty's fleete prepared for sea service'. They were originally known as the 'Lord Admiral's regiment'. For some years after that, these marines were raised and disbanded according to the requirements of war and peace, but from 1755 a radical reorganization away from the regimental system on which they had previously been raised was brought into effect, under which marines became a permanent naval force, serving on board all warships of any size as an integral part of the complement. During what might be called the steam * battleship era, marines manned one of the gun turrets, provided sentries where required, and formed the ship's band, as well as providing the nucleus of any armed landing parties required in the course of operations. For many years British marines were organized into two branches, the Royal Marine Light Infantry (R.M.L.I.) and Royal Marine Artillery (R.M.A.), but in 1923 this distinction was abolished, both branches amalgamating into a single corps known as the Royal Marines. During the Second World War, Royal Marines were trained in Commando tactics, and this is still their major role today. See also JOLLIES.

In the U.S.A. the Marine Corps was formed in 1775, the same date as the U.S. Navy. It is a completely separate military body, though under the control of the Navy Department. Its development has been remarkably similar to that of the British Marine Corps in organization and experience.

In both countries, the reputation of the marines for courage, discipline, and fighting skill is unsurpassed by any other branch of the fighting services.

MARIN-MARIE, see DURAND, Couppel de Saint-Front Marin-Marie-Paul.

**MARINMUSEUM och MODELKAM-
MAREN,** Karlskrona, Sweden, was founded in
1752 to house the models of ships designed by
the famous Swedish naval architect Frederik
Hendrik af *Chapman. In 1954 the collection was moved to its present site in the
Amiralitetsslätten, where it occupies forty rooms
on three floors. In addition to the models, the
exhibits include *figureheads, ship's carvings,
technical models of engines and harbours, a large
selection of tools, nautical instruments, weapons,
firearms, uniforms, medals, seals, and flags. The
library contains 10,000 books, besides maps,
plans, archives, manuscripts, and photographs.

MARINUS OF TYRE (c. 70–130) was probably of Greek extraction and born at Tyre where
he worked on an early form of sea *chart. He
used an equidistant-cylindrical projection forming a grid of parallels and *meridians, the mid-
parallel and prime meridian passing through
Rhodes, the then maritime centre of the known
world. His proportion of the distances between
parallels and meridians was four to five, giving
an elongated appearance to the Mediterranean.
*Ptolemy pays tribute to him in his *Geographia*
and acknowledges his indebtedness to him in his
own great work on the same subject.

**MARION-DUFRESNE,   NICHOLAS
THOMAS** (1729–72), French naval officer,
discovered the Prince Edward Islands and Îles
Crozet in January 1772 while on a voyage from
Mauritius to the south-west Pacific. He mistakenly
believed these latter islands to be off-shore islands
of a southern continent, thus prolonging the belief
in the existence of *Terra Australis Incognita.
While refitting his ships in New Zealand in March
1772 he and several members of his crew were
murdered and eaten by natives.

MARITIME LAW, that branch of international
law which concerns maritime matters and causes.
It was originally derived chiefly from the ancient
codes of laws of the sea, particularly those of
*Oleron, but it is, of course, continually
amended and expanded as modern experience
brings in new examples and conditions requiring
international legislation. It covers such subjects
as *Rule of the Road at sea, territorial and international waters, ocean *fishery, *contraband,
*blockade, belligerent rights, etc. The usual
means of change and modernization are international conferences and conventions, at present
held under the auspices of the United Nations.
Judgement, on the international scale, is exercised by the International Court at The Hague.

All maritime nations have also their own
corpus of maritime law dealing with their own
maritime requirements within their own territorial waters.

MARITIME MUSEUM OF CANADA, Halifax, Nova Scotia, was founded in 1948 and was
formerly accommodated in the Citadel at Halifax, N.S., but pending the construction of a new
building the exhibits have been stored in a warehouse. They portray the maritime history of Canada, and especially Nova Scotia, and include a
number of models of ships of various types, tools,
fishing tackle, nautical instruments, weapons,
paintings, and photographs. There is a library of
about 400 books, also some maps and plans.

MARITIME MUSEUMS. Interest in maritime
archaeology and the preservation of marine
artefacts has grown enormously during the
present century. In the U.S.A., for instance, there
are over 130 maritime museums, while in France
there are 32, and in Great Britain 58. Inevitably
some collections are large and important, others
less so, and the list opposite is restricted mainly
to the former. Details of these will be found
under their individual names.

MARITIME TERRITORY, a term in international *maritime law to denote coastal waters
which, although not within the strict *territorial
waters limit, are in direct contact with the open
sea. There is no limitation over the dominion of
maritime territory. A bay or gulf, no matter how
large, that cannot be held to be part of an open
ocean highway is considered to be the maritime
territory of the nation which occupies its shores,
as, for example, the Gulf of St. Lawrence would
be the maritime territory of Canada. A strait, of
which both shores are within a national boundary, is also considered to be maritime territory,
and the passage of foreign ships through it can be
forbidden. But where the two shores of a strait
are held by different countries, as for example
Britain and France in the case of the Straits of
Dover, the water between the shores cannot be
claimed as maritime territory by either nation
but is an international ocean highway.

MARK, the fathoms of a *lead line which have
a distinguishing mark; those unmarked being
called *deeps. The marks on a hand lead line,
which is normally 25 fathoms in length, are:

Depth in fathoms	Mark
2	Two strips of leather
3	Three strips of leather
5	Piece of white duck
7	Piece of red bunting
10	Piece of leather with a hole in it
13	Piece of blue serge
15	Piece of white duck
17	Piece of red bunting
20	Two knots

When using a line longer than 25 fathoms, the
line is marked with one knot at each five fathoms

MARITIME MUSEUMS

Name	Place	Country
Ålands Sjöfartsmuseum	Mariehamn	Finland
Altonaer Museum	Hamburg	W. Germany
Civico Museo Navale	Genoa	Italy
Deutsches Museum von Meisterwerken der Naturwissenschaft und Technik	Munich	W. Germany
Handels og Sjøfartmuseum på Kronborg	Helsingør	Denmark
Imperial War Museum	London	Great Britain
Kon-Tiki Museum	Oslo	Norway
Marinemuseet	Horten	Norway
Marine Museum of the City of New York	New York	U.S.A.
Mariners Museum	Newport News, Va.	U.S.A.
Marinmuseum och Modelkammaren	Karlskrona	Sweden
Maritime Museum of Canada	Halifax, N.S.	Canada
Musée de la Chambre de Commerce	Marseilles	France
Musée de la Marine	Paris	France
Museo Maritimo	Barcelona	Spain
Museo Naval	Buenos Aires	Argentina
Museo Naval	Madrid	Spain
Museo Storico Navale	Venice	Italy
Museu de Marinha	Lisbon	Portugal
Muzeum Marynarki Wojenne	Gdynia	Poland
Nantucket Whaling Museum	Nantucket, Mass.	U.S.A.
Nationaal Scheepvaartmuseum	Antwerp	Belgium
National Maritime Museum	Greenwich	Great Britain
Nederlandsch Historisch Scheepvaart Museum	Amsterdam	Netherlands
Nelson Museum	English Harbour, Antigua	West Indies
Newport Historical Society	Newport, R.I.	U.S.A.
Norsk Sjøfartsmuseum	Oslo	Norway
Old State House, Bostonian Society	Boston, Mass.	U.S.A.
Orlogsmuseet	Copenhagen	Denmark
Peabody Museum of Salem	Salem, Mass.	U.S.A.
Penobscot Marine Museum	Searsport, Maine	U.S.A.
Philadelphia Maritime Museum	Philadelphia, Penn.	U.S.A.
Port Adelaide Nautical Museum	Port Adelaide	Australia
Portsmouth Naval Shipyard Museum	Portsmouth, Va.	U.S.A.
Sandefjord Sjøfartsmuseum	Sandefjord	Norway
San Francisco Maritime Museum	San Francisco, Cal.	U.S.A.
Sjøfartsmuseum i Göteborg	Göteborg	Sweden
Smithsonian Institution	Washington, D.C.	U.S.A.
Søfartssamlingerne ved Svendborgsund	Troense, Taasinge	Denmark
Statens Sjöhistoriska Museum	Stockholm	Sweden
Submarine Library and Museum	Groton, Conn.	U.S.A.
U.S. Naval Academy Museum	Annapolis, Md.	U.S.A.
Vikingskiphuset	Oslo	Norway
Vojenno-Marskoi Moezjei	Leningrad	U.S.S.R.

---

and with three, four, five knots at 30, 40, and 50 fathoms.

When a seaman takes a *sounding with a hand lead line he calls out the depth of water according to the mark on the line which is on or near the surface of the sea when the *lead reaches the bottom beneath him. If he sees, for example, that the first piece of red bunting is on the surface after his cast, he calls out, 'By the mark, seven.' If he sees that it is approximately six feet above the surface after his cast, he calls out, 'Deep, six.'

For England when, with favouring gale,
Our gallant ship up Channel steered,
And, scudding under every sail,
The high blue western land appeared
To heave the lead the seaman sprung
And to the pilot cheerly sung,
'By the deep nine'.

W. Pearce (c. 1793)

MARKHAM, Sir CLEMENTS ROBERT (1830–1916), British naval officer, traveller, and explorer, was born at Stillingfleet, Yorkshire. He joined the navy in 1844 and served on board the *Assistance* during the Arctic expedition of 1850–1 in search of Sir John *Franklin. He retired from the navy in 1852 to devote himself to travel and horticulture and in 1853 entered the Civil Service. Among his chief horticultural activities were the introduction of the Peruvian quinine-bearing tree into India and the Brazilian rubber tree into Malaya.

He was assistant secretary in charge of geographical work at the India Office, 1867–77, secretary of the Royal Geographical Society, 1863–88, and secretary and president of the *Hakluyt Society, 1858–87 and 1893–1905. He took an active part in the revival of Arctic exploration and in 1875 accompanied Sir George *Nares to Greenland. He also interested himself in the Antarctic and selected Commander (later Captain) R. F. *Scott as leader of the successful expeditions to those regions in the *Discovery* in 1901–4. His literary output was prodigious, amounting to over fifty volumes, and included biographies of *Columbus and John *Davis.

MARL, or **MARLE, to,** the operation of putting on a *serving by which the *worming and *parcelling of a rope is secured. Ropes are frequently wormed and parcelled in places where heavy use may fray or gall them or where it is desired to make them impervious to water. An old rhyme instructs us to

> 'worm and parcel with the lay,
> turn and serve the other way.'

The serving is secured on each turn by a *marling hitch, hence its name.

MARLINE, a small light line used for a variety of purposes on board ship. It is two-stranded, loosely twisted, and was originally used for bending light sails to their *yards or *stays. It is usually supplied both tarred and untarred.

MARLINE SPIKE, a steel spike pointed at one end and used for lifting the strands of a rope to make room for another to be tucked in when splicing.

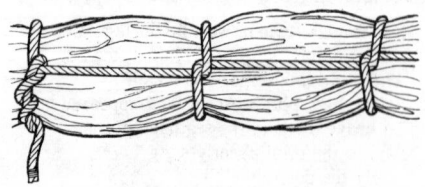

Marling hitch

MARLING HITCH, a series of round turns in which the end is passed over the standing part and under the bight and pulled taut on each turn. Unless there is an *eye in the end of the rope a marling hitch is usually started with a *timber hitch and is used for lashing up sails, *awnings, hammocks, etc.

MAROON, to, deliberately to put ashore a sailor and leave him there when the ship sails away. The action usually implies being left, or marooned, in some relatively inaccessible place. Perhaps the best-known case of a marooned seaman was that of Alexander *Selkirk.

MARR, JAMES WILLIAM SLESSER (1902–65), British marine biologist, carried out extensive research on the life-cycle of krill (*Euphausia superba*), the chief food of Antarctic baleen whales. As Scout Marr he accompanied the *Shackleton–Rowett expedition of 1921–2 to the Antarctic. In 1925 he sailed with F. A. *Worsley's British Arctic Expedition to Spitsbergen and Franz Josef Land, and later joined the *Discovery* Investigations, accompanying a number of oceanographic surveys in Antarctic waters. During the Second World War he organized and commanded British land bases in the Grahamland area of the Antarctic, forerunners of the present British Antarctic Survey scientific stations.

MARRY, to, the operation of bringing two ropes together, such as the *falls of a boat to be hoisted at the *davits of a ship, so that the haul on them can be combined and the boat is hoisted level. The term is also used in other maritime contexts where two ropes, or other objects, are brought together and laid side by side.

MARRYAT, FREDERICK (1792–1848), British naval officer and novelist, was born at Westminster, London, the son of Joseph Marryat, who was agent for Grenada in the Windward Islands group of the West Indies and who wrote pamphlets in defence of the Slave Trade, and grandson of Thomas Marryat, a physician, author, and poet. As a boy he frequently ran away to sea and finally entered the Royal Navy in 1806.

His first ship was the frigate *Imperieuse*, commanded by Captain Lord *Cochrane, an introduction to naval life which stood him in good stead for his later career as a novelist. During the two years and a half he served in the *Imperieuse* he took part in more than fifty engagements, ranging from the attack on French ships at the *Basque Roads in 1809 to the expedition to Walcheren in the same year.

He was promoted commander in 1815 and four years later commanded the sloop *Beaver*, guardship at St. Helena until the death of Napoleon in 1821. His next appointment was captain of the *Larne* in the East Indies, and he was senior naval officer at Rangoon in 1824 during the Burmese War. He commanded the expedition in 1825 which ascended the Bassein River and captured the town of that name, together with the stores collected there for the Burmese Army.

He was a naval officer of quite remarkable achievement ranging from the award of the medal of the Humane Society for 'a dozen or more' life-saving rescues to the compilation of a code of signals, based on those of Sir Home *Popham, for the mercantile marine, which became the basis of the *International Code of Signals. He was made a Fellow of the Royal Society in 1819 for his code of signals, and a Chevalier of the Legion of Honour by Louis Philippe in 1833.

He was promoted to captain in 1830 and resigned from the navy in order to devote himself to writing novels. *Frank Mildmay*, his first book, had been published while he was still serving, and his second, *The King's Own*, came out in the year of his retirement. *Frank Mildmay*, which some readers, wrongly, thought was in part autobiographical, was received coolly on publication though it was in such contrast to the general run of historical romance that discerning readers prophesied a bright future for the captain turned novelist; this mixture of adventure, high-spirited fun, distress and hardship, heroic action, friendship, and hatred was like a breath of fresh air to the contemporary novel, and with the publication of *The King's Own*, any lingering doubts about the quality of this new author in the field of adventure were set at rest.

The book was a great success, and was followed in quick succession by *Newton Foster* (1832), *Peter Simple* (1834), *Jacob Faithful* (1834), *The Pacha of Many Tales* (1835), *Japhet in Search of a Father* (1836), *The Pirate and the Three Cutters* (1836), and, in the same year, *Mr. Midshipman Easy*, the best known of his many stories. Much of the naval adventure with which these books were packed were based on his experiences in the *Imperieuse* with Cochrane, and to all of them he brought the authentic smell of the sea and an intimate knowledge of the way of a ship at sea. He had a gift for characterization that suited his adventurous heroes admirably, and in 'Equality Jack' in *Mr. Midshipman Easy* he created, perhaps, the perfect hero in the realms of naval adventure stories, a man whom most readers have identified with the dashing figure of Lord Cochrane.

If *Mr. Midshipman Easy* is today his best-known story, the one which followed it, *The Dog Fiend or Snarleyyow* (1837), is in a purely literary sense the real masterpiece of his literary output, in which his skill in characterization and construction, coupled with his sense of the truly dramatic, reached its peak. The novel is set in 1699, at the period when William of Orange still sat precariously on the British throne amid an atmosphere of plot and conspiracy. Marryat, who had a romantic attachment to the Jacobites and was equally attracted to the novelistic and adventurous aspect of smuggling, brought these two together in a story that can still tingle the blood.

Around this time Marryat devoted many of his talents to writing books for boys, of which *Masterman Ready* (1841) and *The Children of the New Forest* (1847) are the two best known. But many other books still in the nature of his earlier successes continued to flow from his pen. *The Phantom Ship*, a tale woven round the story of the *Flying Dutchman, and *Poor Jack*, set in Greenwich and around its great hospital for naval pensioners, are the best of this period, but show that Marryat had probably passed his peak as a storyteller. One of the reasons for the decline was that to keep up the flow of royalties he was trying to write for two markets simultaneously, the magazine serial market and the book market, and many of these later books bear the stamp of previous serialization and suffer thereby. It needed the skill of a Dickens, which Marryat did not have, to combine the two effectively.

He continued writing almost up to his death, leaving an uncompleted novel, *Valerie*, and another, *The Little Savage*, to be published posthumously. During a visit to the U.S.A. in 1837 he wrote a play, *The Ocean Waif*, which was not a success. He bought an estate in Norfolk in 1843 and with the substantial royalties earned by his books took to farming in an experimental and costly way. He fell ill in 1848 and when he learned of the death of his son in a shipwreck, the shock and despair proved fatal.

MARSEILLES, a city and seaport of France on the Mediterranean coast, the greatest of the French ports and also the largest in the Mediterranean, was founded as the Greek colony of Massalia in 600 B.C. It is possible that the Phoenicians were established as traders there before the arrival of the Greeks, and some reports of naval conflict in those waters about that time may be an indication that the Greek colony was not established without a fight. The settlement broke away from Greece after the Persians had captured the Greek cities of Asia Minor in 542 B.C., and over the years colonized the adjacent coastal strip from Monaco down to Cape St. Martin in Spain, but this expansion was halted and reversed when Massalia (or Massilia as it became in Roman times) chose to fight on the losing side in the war between Pompey the Great and Caesar; in A.D. 49 it became a free city under Roman protection with all her colonies stripped from her.

Great prosperity came to the port during the period of the crusades, and continued to grow steadily until the French Revolution, when the long wars of Napoleon dealt a heavy blow to French maritime commerce. The city which had given birth to the battle hymn of the Revolution, *La Marseillaise*, rejoiced at the downfall of Napoleon at the battle of Waterloo, and was a scene of much slaughter when those in the city suspected of imperialist views found themselves victims of the mob.

Two events during the 19th century vastly increased the development and prosperity of the port, the conquest of Algeria and the opening of the Suez Canal. Since then it has increased steadily to become one of the greatest seaports in the world. Being the centre of a considerable manufacturing area, and connected to the Rhône valley by a canal from Marseilles to Arles, its rich hinterland feeds the port with an ever-growing commerce.

Marseilles is known throughout the maritime world for many features. One is the majestic church of Notre Dame de la Garde, which crowns the ridge behind the city and is remarkable for the votive offerings of seamen for the protection of Our Lady extended to mariners. Another is the Rue Cannebière, running from the old harbour along the Joliette basin to the harbour railway station. It takes its name from the old *ropewalks which used to operate along its length, the Provençal word for *hemp, of which the ropes were manufactured, being *cannebe*. It is also known for the *Musée de la Chambre de Commerce, a maritime museum of importance with a fine library and a large collection of paintings, drawings, engravings, and plans. It is housed in the building originally constructed for the colonial exhibition of 1922.

MARSHALL, JOHN (*c*. 1784–1837), British naval officer, was the author of a remarkable naval biography. He went to sea at the age of nine and served throughout the later stages of the Napoleonic War (1803–15) mainly in *sloops and small craft. After promotion to lieutenant in 1815 he received no further employment. In 1823 he began the publication of his *Royal Naval Biography*, covering flag officers, *post-captains, and commanders on the Navy List of 1823. The work was completed in 1835 and occupies twelve volumes. Many of the biographies were contributed by the officers themselves, and are thus liable to be suspect, but among the valuable features of the work are the many official and private letters reproduced in it.

MARTIN, EVELYN GEORGE (1881–1945), British yachtsman and author, was a successful helmsman in small class racing boats until the outbreak of the First World War (1914–18), in which he served in the R.N.V.R. in *monitors and in the salvage tug service. In 1924 he found at Le Havre a pilot *cutter, *Jolie Brise*, 44 tons, which he converted into a sturdy cruising yacht. He was instrumental in organizing the first race round the *Fastnet rock in 1925, which he won in *Jolie Brise*.

In 1926 he sailed *Jolie Brise* some 10,000 miles to Long Island Sound, won in his class in the race to Bermuda, and returned to Plymouth, a voyage for which he was awarded the Blue Water medal of the Cruising Club of America. After selling *Jolie Brise* he bought a half share in the Thames *spritsail *barge *Memory* of Ipswich and sailed as *mate in her, trading up and down the East Coast until the outbreak of the Second World War, when he was again called up for service in the Royal Navy. His book *Sailorman* (1933) described his bargeing experiences. Other books by him are *Deep Water Cruising* (1929) and *Helmsmanship* (1934).

MARTINGALE, (1) the *stay which holds the *jib-boom down against the pull exerted by the fore *topgallant-mast stays in a square-rigged ship. It runs from the outer end of the jib-boom to the *dolphin-striker. Martingale *guys hold the dolphin-striker firm, being run from its end and secured on either bow of the ship. **(2)** A rope or strap which runs from a point on the *boom of a *dinghy's mainsail to the foot of the mast, designed to prevent the boom from rising when it swings outwards and thus to present a flatter sail surface to the wind. It is normally fitted only in racing dinghies, and is usually known as a *kicking-strap.

MARTINO, Chevalier EDUARDO DE (1838–1912), marine painter, was born at Meta, near Naples, and was official artist to the Emperor of Brazil, Pedro II, during that country's war with Paraguay (1868–9). He subsequently settled in England where he was made marine painter in ordinary to Queen Victoria, and later to Edward VII. His best-known pictures are those of warships, which he painted assiduously on such occasions as royal reviews of the fleet, naval manoeuvres, etc., and he also recorded on canvas scenes during visits and cruises made in the *royal yachts. He was an accomplished artist in this genre.

MARTNETS, a term no longer employed but one which was used in older days in square-rigged ships to describe the *leech-lines of a square sail. When these martnets were used to haul the leeches of the sail up to the *yard, for *furling or shortening sail, they were said to be topped.

MARY CELESTE, a *hermaphrodite brig of some 280 tons found abandoned in the Atlantic in November 1872. How she came to be in that condition remains one of the great mysteries of the sea.

She sailed from New York on 5 November with a cargo of 1,700 barrels of alcohol, bound for Genoa. She was under the command of Captain Benjamin Briggs, who had his wife and two-year-old daughter on board, and his crew consisted of a mate, second mate, cook, and four seamen. On 24 November he made the Azores, but ran into a wind of force 7 on the *Beaufort scale which forced him to shorten sail to two *jibs, upper and lower *topsails, foresail, and *staysail. On the morning of the 25th he sighted and sailed past the island of Santa Maria, leaving it to the southward and made a note to this effect on the deck slate so that it could later be entered into the ship's *log. Captain Briggs, his wife and small daughter, and the entire crew were never seen again.

Nine days later the *Mary Celeste* was sighted over 350 miles to the eastward of Santa Maria by the *brigantine *Dei Gratia*, also out of New York. The *Mary Celeste* was heading easterly on the port *tack in a light breeze, but with her reduced canvas, still shortened for the force 7 wind, set for the starboard tack. Obviously something was wrong and the mate of the *Dei Gratia*, Deveau, with one seaman, boarded her. They found the vessel abandoned, her only boat gone, and the remains of the boat's *painter (or perhaps the *peak *halyards used as a painter) hanging over the *Mary Celeste*'s stern. The side rails abreast of the boat's stowage on board were lying on the deck, an evident sign of a hasty abandonment, and by the deck pump was lying a sounding rod, with which the depth of water in the *bilges is measured. Aloft, the running *rigging was snarled up, the halyard to the main *gaff parted (the rest may have been used as the boat's painter) and the upper topsail and foresail blown out. The main *hatch and the cargo was secure but the small fore and after hatches were off, as was the *galley hatch, and the skylight above the main *cabin was open. There was $3\frac{1}{2}$ feet of water in her, but this was not excessive for such a ship.

A salvage crew from the *Dei Gratia* was put on board the *Mary Celeste* and she was sailed to Gibraltar, arriving there on 13 December 1872. On the way she had made very little water. On her arrival a court of inquiry was assembled to try to discover why she had been abandoned. An extensive survey on her arrival revealed virtually no internal or external damage beyond very minor injury to the hull planking on either *bow about three feet above the waterline.

Almost at once a number of theories were put forward, some of them assisted by the evident desire throughout the inquiry by the assessor at Gibraltar, Mr. Solly Flood, to prove foul play. He tried to make much out of the discovery of an old sword on board covered with bloodstains, but on analysis the bloodstains were found to be rust, and the theories of mutiny and murder which this discovery raised had to be abandoned. A collision with a giant squid was another theory, while the most popular suggestion for a long time was that there was collusion between Captain Briggs and the *master of the *Dei Gratia* so that salvage money could be claimed and later divided. The inquiry concentrated on this theory for many days but, somewhat regretfully, had to abandon it in the end.

There are two possible explanations of the mystery of why the *Mary Celeste*, a ship still in good order, was abandoned so suddenly. Nine of the casks of alcohol in her cargo were empty or damaged, and it has been suggested that a minor explosion of alcohol vapour may have led Briggs and the crew hurriedly to man the boat and pay her out astern on as long a painter as possible in case the rest of the cargo exploded, hoping to haul the boat back to the ship by the painter if nothing more happened. While the boat was lying astern of the ship, the painter may have parted and the ship sailed away faster than the boat could be pulled to catch her up. But against this theory is the fact that, on examination in Gibraltar, there was no sign of an explosion on board. Had there been, even if only a very small one, the deck *beams would surely have been blackened by flame or smoke.

The other possible explanation is that she was struck by a waterspout and that the steep water pressure gradients associated with waterspouts forced water up the pump well, giving the impression to those sounding the well that she was filling rapidly. The presence of the sounding rod lying on deck alongside the pump certainly indicates that the well was being sounded at the time, and the sight of water flowing out of the pump well on to the deck would certainly give the impression that the ship had a leak so large that the pump could never handle it. The same sequence then followed, the boat manned and veered well astern, the parting of the painter and the ship sailing away.

No satisfactory explanation of the mystery of the *Mary Celeste* has ever been found. Her subsequent career was unhappy. For thirteen years she went from owner to owner, seventeen in all, none being able to make her pay her way. Finally she was deliberately wrecked by her last owner on a reef off Haiti, in order to make a false insurance claim. She became a total loss.

MARY ROSE, H.M.S., a 'great ship' of 600 tons, having an armament of about twenty heavy and sixty light guns and a complement of 400, was built for Henry VIII and named in honour of his sister, Mary Tudor. This ship, the first of her name in the British Navy, took part in the first (1512–14) and second (1522–5) French wars of Henry VIII, always as the flagship of the *Lord High Admiral, her good sailing qualities making her a favourite as a flagship. In 1536 she was rebuilt to some extent and given a complete lower deck of guns—probably the first of the British Navy's ships to be so fitted. In 1544–5 she was active in Henry VIII's third French war, but when going out to engage the French fleet off Portsmouth on 19 July 1545 she was swamped through her lower deck *ports and sank in a very short space of time with the loss of nearly all her company, including her captain, Sir George Carew. In 1968 her hull was discovered by skin-divers and it is hoped eventually to raise her.

The second *Mary Rose*, of 500 tons and thirty-six guns, was built in 1556. She fought against the Spanish *Armada in 1588 and in 1590 was Sir John *Hawkins's flagship on the coast of Spain. In June 1596, under the command of another Captain Sir George Carew, she took part in the combined Dutch and English expedition against Cadiz. After further service, which included the 'Voyage to the Islands' in 1597, i.e., an unsuccessful attempt to waylay and capture the Spanish treasure fleet, and an expedition to the coast of Spain in 1602, her hull was brought alongside and filled to make a wharf at Chatham.

A later *Mary Rose* was originally the *Maidstone*, built at Woodbridge in 1654 and renamed in 1660. She took part in several battles of the Second Anglo-Dutch War (1665–7) including those of *Lowestoft, the *Four Days Battle, and the St. James' Day Fight. In December 1669, when commanded by Captain John Kempthorne, she saved a *convoy, after a severe action of four hours, from an Algerine pirate *squadron of seven ships which attacked them off Cadiz. She was much damaged and lost thirty men killed and wounded. Captain Kempthorne was knighted for this action. In the Third Anglo-Dutch War (1672–4) the *Mary Rose* was present at the battle of *Solebay (28 May 1672) and the first battle of the Schooneveld. In July 1691 she was captured by a French squadron when escorting a convoy to the West Indies.

The Royal Navy had no more ships named *Mary Rose* until the First World War (1914–18) when a *destroyer launched in 1915 was given the name. This ship took part in the battle of *Jutland in 1916 and was sunk in a gallant action in October 1917 while attempting to save a west-bound convoy from Norway which was attacked by the German cruisers *Bremse* and *Brummer*.

MASEFIELD, JOHN EDWARD (1878–1967), British poet, was educated as a cadet on board the training ship H.M.S. *Conway* and went to sea at the age of fifteen as an apprentice in a square-rigged ship in which he rounded Cape Horn. A few years later his health failed while his ship was in New York and he went ashore, supporting himself by taking any job, however humble, through which he could earn his keep. On his return to England he became a journalist and joined the staff of the *Manchester Guardian*.

He had already started to write poetry and was one of the pioneers in the revival of narrative poetry, of which his *Dauber*, published in 1913, was based in part on his early experience at sea. He settled in London during the first decade of the 20th century, and a volume of poems, *Salt Water Ballads*, came out in 1902, and was an instant success. Among the poems in it was 'Sea Fever', one of the best-loved ballads of the sea, which was later set to music by John Ireland. Another book of poetry, *Ballads and Poems*, followed in 1910. At the same time he was writing short stories of the sea, published in *A Mainsail Haul* (1905) and *A Tarpaulin Muster* (1907). He also wrote plays.

His first novel was *Captain Margaret*, published in 1908, and among the dozen or so that he wrote, the two most connected with the sea were *The Bird of Dawning* (1933), a gripping story of the tea *clippers, and *Victorious Troy* (1935), which tells the story of a sailing ship dismasted and officerless, but brought back to safety by an apprentice on board. He also wrote a not very successful naval history, *Sea Life in Nelson's Time* (1905).

It is, however, in his poetry that he is best remembered, by such nostalgic, and even sentimental, poems as 'Sea-Fever' ('I must down to the seas again, to the lonely sea and the sky') and by his many verses in praise of the merchant navy in which he spent his early years, perhaps exemplified by his 'Cargoes' ('Dirty British coaster') type of ballad. They were simple, direct, and held the true flavour of the sea.

Masefield was appointed Poet Laureate in 1930. During his later years he became intensely interested in the tragic loss of H.M.S. *Captain* in 1870 and contemplated making it the subject of a narrative poem, but never succeeded in bringing the idea to fruition.

MASKELYNE, NEVIL (1732–1811), British astronomer, introduced into the art of navigation the determination of *longitude by *lunar distances. He worked out this method of discovering a ship's longitude during a voyage in 1761 to St. Helena, where he was sent by the Royal Society to observe the transit of Venus. He became Astronomer Royal in 1765 and held the position until his death.

MASON, MICHAEL HENRY (1900–), British yachtsman and explorer, started an adventurous career by crossing the 300-mile Great Slave Lake in north-western Canada by sailing canoe at the age of 21. In 1929–30 he explored by boat the islands along the Chilean coast towards Cape Horn, and in 1936 explored over 4,000 miles of the Atlantic coast of Africa under sail. Taking up off-shore racing, he sailed to America in 1938 and took part in the Bermuda race for which he was awarded the Cruising Club of America's transatlantic pennant. He owned *Violetta*, an *International 8-metre (26 ft), and *Latifa*, a 70-ft (21·5 m) ocean racing *yawl of 53 tons designed and built for him by *Fife of Fairlie in 1936, and with them won many races, holding the Solent 8-metre (26 ft) championship in 1933 and 1934 and winning several offshore races, including the *Fastnet, Belle Île, Round Heligoland, and Channel races in 1936–8. He is the author of numerous books including *Where the River Runs Dry*, *Trivial Adventures*, *The Arctic Forests*, *Where the Tempests Blow*, and *Paradise of Fools*.

MAST, a vertical spar set in a ship. Its prime use was, of course, to carry sails, but in modern mechanically propelled ships the mast usually serves to carry such essentials as wireless aerials, radar arrays, etc., and is not necessarily a vertical spar, particularly in warships in which the masts are more usually of steel lattice. Flag signals at sea are hoisted on *halyards led to the mast, or to a *yard across it, in order to obtain the maximum visibility through the height of the hoist, and a mast also carries on it the compulsory *steaming lights which a vessel has to display when under way at night.

In sailing vessels the masts are normally taken through holes in the deck and their *heels, which are squared off, fitted into *steps in the *keelson of the ship. In the larger sailing vessels they are held firm in the deck holes with wedges, and are secured in place by *shrouds, running from the masthead or the *hounds to *chainplates on the ship's side, and by *stays, which run from the masthead to deck level forward and aft. In square-rigged ships the yards are crossed on the masts, from which they are held in position by *lifts, with the sails set on the yards; in fore-and-aft rigged vessels the sails are set on the masts themselves, either by means of slides working on a track fixed to the after side of the mast, by hoops which slide up and down the mast as the sail is hoisted or lowered, or in modern yachts by means of a mast groove within which the luff rope itself slides.

Originally, before the growth in size of ships which occurred during the 17th century, ships' masts were single spars, cut from the trunk of a fir tree, but as the size of sailing ships developed in the 17th and 18th centuries with the consequent addition of an increased number of sails and of upper masts, the original pole masts fashioned from a single trunk of a fir tree were not strong enough or tall enough to carry the larger *yards and sails, and so had to be made of several pieces of timber in order to get the required strength, circumference, and height and were thus called made masts. In most ships of the 17th century and later, the lower masts were all made masts, topmast and *topgallant masts being pole masts.

Today, only a few small *gaff-rigged craft and small dinghies have solid wooden masts, and only a minority of yachts still have hollow wooden masts, usually built up from spruce, *scarfed and glued. A majority of modern yachts and racing dinghies have masts and booms made from extruded aluminium tubes, the masts shaped aerodynamically in cross-section to reduce windage. For illus. see RIGGING.

MAST COAT, a covering either of painted canvas or of rubber, secured round the foot of a mast and to the deck around it, which prevents water running below through the opening in the deck where the mast of a vessel goes down to its *step in the *keelson. It is mainly used in sailing vessels where the masts have to be allowed a certain amount of play as they go through the openings in the deck in order to absorb the pressures of wind upon sails.

MAST SHIP, a vessel, of the period of sail, used for the transport of *masts. They were ships which had extensive square *ports cut in the *bows and *stern so that the larger timbers intended for the manufacture of lower masts and topmasts could be loaded inboard through them. The traditional countries of supply of suitable timbers for this purpose were those bordering the Baltic Sea, and the special mast ships carried on a flourishing trade through the centuries during which sail was the main motive power of all shipping. With the demand growing exceedingly throughout the 18th and early 19th centuries through the great expansion of shipping, and with the Baltic countries unable to meet the full demand, a second source of supply was discovered in North America, where the vast forests of firs proved an inexhaustible reservoir of suitable timber. So great was the demand, particularly for the ships of Britain, France, and Spain which had no indigenous sources of suitable timber, that attempts were made in Canada and North America to construct temporary mast ships made entirely of timber suitable for mast-making, by lashing them together in the rough shape of a ship's hull, setting up three masts and trying to sail them across the Atlantic, when they could be broken up into individual mast timbers on arrival. The attempt, however, was a failure as the lashings usually parted as the timbers worked in the sea, and the 'ship' disintegrated en route.

Mast ships continued in operation until iron and steel replaced timber.

MASTER, (1) originally an officer in a warship responsible solely for the navigation of the ship. In the British Navy, he was appointed by the commissioners of the *Navy Board, and his duties, in addition to a responsibility for all navigational problems, included working the ship into her proper station in the *line of battle. He ranked with the lieutenants but was subordinate to them in command although he was usually accommodated in a better cabin in the *coach. After 1814 masters in the navy ranked with commanders and the rank was known as master and commander, but this term lapsed towards the end of the 19th century when the study of navigation became a specialization within the executive hierarchy. **(2)** The usual name given to the captain of a merchant vessel, qualified to take command by passing a professional examination for a master's *ticket.

MASTER-AT-ARMS, the officer, appointed by warrant, who is responsible for police duties on board a naval ship. In the early days he was also responsible for exercising the crew in the use of small arms, but this duty was later taken by the junior lieutenant on board who was known as the lieutenant-at-arms. See also JAUNTY.

MASTER'S MATE, an old naval rate in all navies during the days when the *master of a warship was the officer responsible for her navigation. His mates were petty officers entered in the ship's muster list to assist him in his duties.

MATE, the rank in the merchant marine next below that of *master. They are divided into first, second, third, etc., to indicate their seniority on board, and in Britain and most other countries with a merchant navy have to pass an examination (in Britain known as a certificate or *ticket) to qualify for the rank, such examination being held under the control of the government department normally responsible for overseas trade. In fighting navies, mates originally held the rank of petty officer, being allocated to certain duties under the charge of a warrant officer, e.g., boatswain's mate, carpenter's mate, etc. Later, in the British Navy, a mate was an officer commissioned from the *lower deck and ranking with a sub-lieutenant. The tendency in the British merchant marine today, particularly in the larger steamship companies, is to substitute the word officer for mate, seniority being denoted by the prefixes first, second, third, etc.

MATHEWS, THOMAS (1676–1751), British admiral, is remembered chiefly as the victim of a notorious court martial in 1745 which followed an unsatisfactory action in the Mediterranean. He had served in command of the *Kent* in Sir George *Byng's great victory off Cape Passaro in 1718, and had risen by 1742 to the rank of vice admiral of the Red. He was appointed commander-in-chief in the Mediterranean in that year, taking over from Rear Admiral *Lestock who remained as his second-in-command, a situation which gave rise to much bad feeling on Lestock's part. In 1744 the British fleet met a combined *squadron of French and Spanish ships off Toulon which, although inferior in strength, was allowed to escape with only slight damage. The subsequent courts martial hinged on the interpretation of the current *Fighting Instructions.* Although Mathews was engaging the enemy with much courage, his signal to engage was ignored by Lestock because, at the same time, the signal for the *line of battle was still flying. Lestock's argument was that with this signal flying he could not follow his chief's action as the line had not been properly formed. Lestock was acquitted on this technicality in the instructions, Mathews was found guilty of closing in to attack before forming the line, even though it was shown that there was not sufficient time to form the line. Mathews was cashiered, a result which drew so much attention to the penalties to be expected if admirals and captains, in their eagerness to engage the enemy, went beyond the strict rules of the *Fighting Instructions* that it stultified almost all initiative in battle for the next twenty years.

MATTHEW WALKER KNOT, a *stopper knot near the end of a manrope or the end of a *lanyard to prevent it running through an *eye. It is made by forming a half hitch with each strand of the rope in the direction of the *lay and then tucking the strands over and under until the knot is formed. A finished Matthew Walker knot looks similar to other stopper knots. (See illus. of DIAMOND KNOT.)

MAURY, MATTHEW FONTAINE (1806–73), American naval officer, was born in Fredericksburg, Virginia, and became a *midshipman in 1825. He devoted his energies to the study of navigation and is best known for his work in oceanography, which brought him a world-wide reputation. He was appointed to the U.S.S. *Vincennes* for her circumnavigation of the world and while on leave after this voyage published a volume entitled *A New Theoretical and Practical Treatise on Navigation* which was highly successful.

He was made superintendent of the Depot of Charts and Instruments of the Navy Department in Washington in 1842, and given additional duty as Superintendent of the new Naval Observatory. His interest in hydrographic and meteorological work induced him to issue his 'Wind and Current Chart of the North Atlantic' in 1847. In the following year he issued *sailing directions for use with his chart under the title of *Abstract Log for the Use of American Navigators*, bringing out new editions of this work in 1850 and 1851. His charts and sailing directions made possible considerable savings in travel time and gained the enthusiasm of mariners from many nations. Many masters of ships co-operated with him by reporting their regular observations of winds and currents. His success led to the international conference on oceanography which was convened in Brussels in 1853, at which he represented the U.S.A. His uniform system of recording oceanographic data was adopted for all naval and merchant vessels.

Maury published *The Physical Geography of the Sea* in 1855, and prepared a chart representing the bottom profile of the Atlantic between Europe and America to demonstrate the practicability of a submarine cable across the ocean. Before the Civil War (1861–5) Maury had become internationally recognized for his work and was awarded many medals and honorary degrees.

Although he had opposed the idea of secession, Maury resigned from the U.S. Navy after Virginia had seceded, and accepted a commission as a commander in the *Confederate Navy. He experimented with electric *mines before being sent to England where his reputation was expected to aid him in securing vessels for the Confederate Navy, but he was not notably successful in that endeavour.

Maury was one of the Confederates specially excluded from the early amnesty proclamations after the Civil War and he did not return to the U.S.A. at once. He offered his services to the Emperor of Mexico and was made Imperial Commissioner of Immigration. After resigning that post he went to England for a time. At the urging of friends he returned to Virginia in 1868 and was made a professor at the Virginia Military Institute, Lexington. He passed the rest of his life there, and is buried in Hollywood Cemetery, Richmond, between the tombs of Presidents Monroe and Tyler.

'MAYDAY', an international distress signal made by voice radio on a wavelength of 2,182 kHz, a wave which is permanently watched ashore. It is said that the origin of the signal is the French *m'aidez*, help me.

MAYFLOWER, the ship in which, in 1620, the Pilgrim Fathers sailed from Plymouth, England, to establish the first permanent colony in New England. The original voyage, in company with the *Speedwell*, started from Southampton, England, but the *Speedwell* was found to be unseaworthy and the ships put into Plymouth, from which port the *Mayflower* sailed alone on 6 September. She was a ship of 180 tons, and carried 100 (or according to some reports 102) passengers. They reached Provincetown Harbor on 11 November 1620 and a small party, under the leadership of William Bradford, was sent ahead to choose a place for settlement. They landed at what is now Plymouth, Massachusetts, on 21 December.

MEASUREMENT, see BUILDERS' OLD MEASUREMENT, THAMES MEASUREMENT, TONNAGE.

MEDINA SIDONIA, DON ALONSO PEREZ DE GUZMAN EL BUENO, 7th Duke of (1550–1619), commander-in-chief of the Spanish *Armada against England in 1588, was born into one of the wealthiest and most illustrious families of Spain. He was by no means a proud man; his portrait suggests a sensitive and melancholy monk, but his many letters to the king, filled with whining demands for money, show him to be a man of mean spirit. When Philip II picked him as captain general of his Armada even before the death of the original commander, the Marquis of Santa Cruz (see BAZAN, ALVARO DE), in February 1588, his reply was a model of humility: 'The undertaking is so important that it would not be right for a person like myself, possessing no experience of seafaring or of war, to take charge of it . . .'. He was chosen for the task mainly because his exalted social station made it certain that none of the noble officers in the Armada would feel it a slight to serve under him, also because he was known to be a good administrator.

Although not an inspiring personality, Sidonia organized his fleet with great efficiency, its arms, supplies, signals, order of sailing and of battle, with the help of a carefully chosen staff of veteran officers, including a gunnery expert. When the Armada reached the English Channel his conduct can hardly be faulted, though a chance of success was lost when the English fleet was not attacked at Plymouth. The decision not to attack, however, was taken after a Council of War with his experienced commanders. After this his steady progress up Channel in a defensive crescent formation was a triumph for his captains' seamanship and discipline. Sidonia ensured that fleet discipline was strictly enforced, in one case by sending provost marshals aboard the ships of one squadron with instructions to hang any captain who left his station. His flagship was always the first to support vessels in distress, and after the panic caused by the English *fireships off Calais she was the first to anchor again. In the ensuing struggle off

Gravelines he kept her in the position of honour at the rear, nearest the pursuing English. Nothing can be said against Sidonia's personal courage, or his administrative ability, but he lacked both the professional knowledge and the dash to make a great commander. Although he blamed himself for the failure of his mission, Philip II, having read the reports, refused to do so and kept him in all his exalted positions.

After the return of the remains of the Armada to Spain, Medina Sidonia became the target of much abuse and contempt, and his handling of the defence of *Cadiz in 1596, when it was lost to a British and Dutch naval attack, was widely criticized. Yet the royal favour continued, and in 1606 he was in command of a Spanish squadron at Gibraltar which was destroyed by the Dutch mainly through his folly.

MEDITERRANEAN SEA, a sea almost enclosed by land lying approximately between the *latitudes of 32 °N. and 44° N. and the *longitudes of 5° W. and 35° E. connected in the west to the Atlantic Ocean by the narrow Strait of Gibraltar and in the east to the Red Sea by the Suez Canal. It was originally a vast ocean which stretched across half the globe but it shrank to its present size through the rise of surrounding land areas in the Oligocene era. It now has a total area of 1,145,830 square miles, a maximum depth of over 2,220 fathoms in the central eastern Mediterranean, and a mean depth of 782 fathoms. With its only direct access to the open sea being through the Gibraltar Straits, it is virtually tideless, as within the periodic *flow and *ebb of the tide of six hours insufficient water is able to flow through the narrow Gibraltar entrance to affect the whole area of the Mediterranean more than one inch or two. In this respect is resembles the *Baltic Sea.

Egyptian shipbuilding. The Mediterranean is traditionally the birthplace of western navigation, a period of maritime endeavour which is generally considered as spanning the three and a half millennia of about 2500 B.C. to A.D. 1000. Egypt was the first Mediterranean nation to acquire the art of shipbuilding, possibly from the Arab or Indian countries to the east, and the earliest known example of an Egyptian ship, excavated from the tomb of the Egyptian Pharaoh Cheops and dating from about 3500–3000 B.C., shows a remarkable degree of constructional skill. But this particular ship, built only for funerary purposes, was not capable of anything more than river travel and would have broken up if tested in the rigours of the sea. It is generally thought, from the evidence of wall paintings and pottery decoration, that the first tentative voyages into the Mediterranean Sea were made at around 2500 B.C. They were at first all-coastal voyages,

ships following the coast by day and anchoring by night, but gradually, as ships ventured further into the unknown sea, direct passages were made, in search of both trade and imperial power; and from the purely trading vessel was evolved the war vessel in the form of the rowed *galley. Egyptian merchant ships, under their protection, extended their voyages to cover most of the eastern basin of the Mediterranean, trading, colonizing, and exacting tribute as they went.

The Greek navigators. As the power of Egypt faded, a long struggle for supremacy of the sea developed between the ships of Crete, Persia, and the various Greek states, from which the Greeks emerged as the paramount sea power, still with the galley as the instrument through which it was wielded. As yet, civilization had not reached the nations bordering the western Mediterranean, and it was still only the eastern basin that was the scene of any real maritime activity although, as Greece extended her sphere of influence, she began to reach out towards the west. This expansion brought her eventually into conflict with Rome, to whom control of the sea passed after the disaster of *Mylae in 260 B.C. when the fleet of Carthage, at that time the most powerful of the Greek states in the maritime sphere, was utterly destroyed.

The Greeks, rather than the Egyptians before them or the Romans after, made navigation into an art rather than a desperate and fumbling venture into unknown waters. They were the first mapmakers and astronomers, producing rough sea charts as early as the 6th century A.D., a process which reached its peak in the work of *Ptolemy and *Marinus of Tyre in the first and second century A.D.

The Phoenician navigators. If the Greeks were the first mapmakers, the Phoenicians were the first true navigators. They built ships which, both for trade or war, excelled those of all other Mediterranean sea powers. Phoenicia, the southern Syria of today, was at first essentially a trading power through her ports of Tyre and Sidon and never a warlike one, and she built up a vast trade through the establishment of centres, or factories, all along the Mediterranean coasts and even beyond the Pillars of Hercules. They could relate the effect of prevailing winds and currents on the *courses they wished their ships to steer, and they understood the use of the stars (particularly *Polaris) as aids to accurate navigation. As early as the 7th century B.C. a Phoenician fleet was reported to have sailed round Africa, and the richest trading centre they established was in Tarsish (Tartessus in south-west Spain) where they found not only a most profitable fishery but also extensive silver mines. To exploit this trade they designed and built the great Tarsish ships, much larger than any others of the period and comparable to the magnificent *East Indiamen of later centuries. So rich was the trade that these ships, it was said, returned to Tyre with their anchors made of silver, their holds being already full of the metal, and still more waiting to be shipped. Outside the Mediterranean, their ships reached the Scilly Islands and returned laden with tin. But in the course of time Phoenicia developed her trading centres into colonies from whom she drew annual tribute, a condition from which, as they grew stronger and richer, they broke away into independence.

Renaissance sea powers. Inevitably, as the Greek and Roman civilizations spread westward, the centre of sea power moved westward too, with Spain and Portugal becoming dominant. Preferring to develop their trade with the newly discovered lands across the Atlantic and in the Indies, they allowed the Mediterranean to develop into something of a backwater, dominated by the lesser sea powers of Venice, and at times Genoa. But with few of the larger maritime nations still interested in protecting their Mediterranean trade, or perhaps because their navies had more pressing calls to defend the growing trans-oceanic trade, the Mediterranean became a temptation for the exploitation of organized *piracy that many could not resist. For 1,000 years the inland sea was a hotbed of maritime lawlessness, based largely on the Levant coast in the east and the north African coast in the south-west, whole nations living on the plunder from merchant ships and the sale of their passengers and crews in the slave markets (see also BARBARY PIRATES). It was a scourge that was not finally eradicated until the 19th century when Algiers, the last stronghold of organized piracy, was bombarded and set on fire by a British fleet in 1816.

Suez Canal. In 1869, when the dream of Ferdinand de *Lesseps came to fruition with the opening of the *Suez Canal, the Mediterranean became more than a vast maritime lake. This eastern exit into the Red Sea opened a direct seaway from the west to India and the Far East, saving thousands of miles around the southern tip of Africa which had until then been the only sea route from Europe to the East. It brought into the Mediterranean a huge increase in shipping, at the same time making it one of the most strategically important sea areas in the world as each maritime nation strove to maintain in those waters a fleet large enough to protect its trade passing through. Dominating this new and growing trade route was the small island of Malta, with its position astride the relatively narrow channel between the southern tip of Italy and the northern extremity of Africa, its magnificent deep-water harbour at Valletta, and its great naval *dockyard. This was constructed by the

British during the second half of the 19th century as a base to maintain the British Mediterranean Fleet; until the First World War (1914–18) the largest and most powerful of their many fleets around the world.

In 1967, during the 'Six Day War' between Israel and Egypt, the Suez Canal was closed to shipping, not to be reopened until 1975. This period saw the building of very large oil tankers and bulk cargo carriers to make economic the longer voyage round the Cape of Good Hope which closure of the canal involved. The Suez Canal is not deep enough to take ships of this size and in this situation the Mediterranean has inevitably lost some of its former strategic importance although, for other reasons, large naval forces are still maintained in that sea, principally those of NATO, the U.S.A., and Russia.

MEDWAY, a river in Kent, England, on which stands the naval base of *Chatham and the former naval base of Sheerness. It was the scene in 1667 of a major Dutch naval success during the Second Dutch War (1665–7) when Admiral de *Ruyter forced his way up the river and burned or captured several English warships. He was able to do so for two reasons, first that in the hope of successful peace negotiations, and because of a bankrupt Treasury, the English fleet had not been fitted out in the spring of 1667 and the ships were left in *ordinary (i.e., in reserve with their stores taken ashore) at Chatham, and secondly because a large number of English naval seamen, whose pay was months in arrears, had deserted to the Dutch fleet and, knowing the waters, were prepared to act as pilots in Dutch pay.

A strong *squadron of Dutch warships entered the Medway on 10 June and having successfully broken through a chain stretched across the river above Sheerness to form a *boom, attacked the English ships as they lay at anchor, virtually unmanned, above it. George *Monck, sent hurriedly by Charles II to Chatham to organize the defence, found everything in confusion and although he ordered all ships to be moved further up river, he was beaten in this by the speed of de Ruyter's advance. The loss to the English was five ships burned and two captured, with two more sunk by Monck's orders higher up the river to block it against any further Dutch advance.

The presence of the Dutch fleet in these English waters caused a panic in London. The banks suspended payment and many citizens loaded their goods and furniture on hastily purchased carts and set off for the country. Samuel *Pepys, the future secretary of the Admiralty and at the time a commissioner of the *Navy Board, made two copies of his will and sent his wife and father out of London with as much gold as they could carry to bury in the garden of his father's house in Huntingdonshire. After burning the English ships, de Ruyter remained in the Thames for a month and *blockaded London, so that the price of coal there rose from 10s. to £5 10s. a chaldron (1⅓ tons), and other goods normally brought in by sea rose in price in a similar proportion.

MEHEUT, MATHURIN (1882–1958), French marine painter and draughtsman, was born at Lamballe (Côte du Nord) and after studying at the École des Beaux Arts, settled down to paint mainly along the Brittany coast. He was appointed official artist to the Ministry of Marine in Paris, and also wrote a two-volume study of the sea.

MELBOURNE, capital of the state of Victoria, Australia, and a major seaport, is situated on Hobson's Bay at the north end of the huge harbour of Port Phillip. In the year 1835 it was a small village named Dootigala, but was renamed Melbourne in the same year after the Prime Minister of Great Britain, Lord Melbourne. Sheep farming brought many settlers to the neighbourhood, and during the second half of the 19th century the great wool trade drew many famous sailing ships to the harbour there, but the discovery of gold at Ballarat in 1851 resulted in a vast influx of inhabitants so that the town trebled its population in two years with a yet further growth in overseas trade. The actual port of Melbourne, originally called Sandridge, is today one of the great seaports of the world and a port of call of most of the big steamship lines which serve Australia.

MELVILL VAN CARNBEE, PIETER, Baron (1816–56), Dutch hydrographer, was the grandson of a Dutch admiral, and though himself destined for the navy, became so interested in cartography and hydrography that he devoted his life to it. He was engaged as a surveyor during his first voyage to the East Indies in 1835, and when there again in 1839, was attached to the hydrographical office at Batavia and produced in 1842 a detailed chart of Java complete with *sailing directions. On his return to Holland he served in the hydrographical department of the Dutch Navy and in 1850 returned to the East Indies as flag lieutenant to Vice Admiral van den Bosch, with overall responsibility for the production of new charts of the East Indies. Unfortunately he contracted fever and died before he could complete a new atlas of the Dutch East Indies.

MELVILLE, HERMAN (1819–91), American novelist of Scottish descent, was born in New York City and went to sea as a cabin boy at the age of eighteen, first in a transatlantic *packet ship running between New York and Liverpool. Four years later he signed on in the *whaler *Acushnet* and sailed in her round Cape Horn for the whaling grounds of the south Pacific. A year later, joined by another sailor of the *Acushnet*, he deserted the ship at Nukahira in the Marquesas Islands because of the living conditions on board and the harsh treatment by the captain and first *mate. They had intended to find temporary sanctuary with the Happar tribe, known to be friendly, but went to the wrong valley where they were taken and held in captivity by the Typee tribe of cannibals. A month later Melville and his companion were rescued by an American whaler which later transferred them to a U.S. naval *frigate. On returning home Melville married and settled down at Pittsfield, Massachusetts, where he formed a close friendship with Nathaniel Hawthorne which was to start him off as a writer. Later he moved back to New York City, spending the last thirty-five years of his life as a customs officer in the port of New York.

Melville began his literary career with the novel *Typee, a Peep at Polynesian Life* (1846), for which he drew upon his experiences when in captivity in the Marquesas. This was followed in 1847 by *Omoo, a Narrative of Adventures in the South Seas*, a continuation of his adventures after his rescue. Both books are, to some extent, autobiographical but embellished with adventures and experiences which did not in fact come Melville's way. Yet they are valuable for the vividness with which they describe the manners, conditions of life, and customs of the Polynesian tribes, at that time subject to the attempts of missionaries to convert them to Christianity. Melville's characters reveal the superficiality of this attempted conversion and while there is little of the 'noble savage' belief in his writing, he does bring out the quick reversion to tribal customs and beliefs as the thin veneer of conversion wears off.

His next books, both published in 1849, were *Redburn*, for which he drew on his earliest sea experiences as a cabin boy, and a philosophical romance, *Mardi, and a Voyage Thither*. But already he was working on the novel which was to make him famous; this was *Moby-Dick or the White Whale*, one of the true classics of the sea, which was published in 1851. For it he drew on his year's service in the *Acushnet* to get the authentic flavour of the whaling industry in the days of sail, when whales were *harpooned by hand from a boat under oars. The book is full of detail of whales, their habits and anatomy, and tells the story of the undying love/hate relationship between Captain Ahab, of the whaler *Pequod*, and Moby-Dick, an immense and ferocious white whale which in an earlier encounter had been responsible for the loss of one of

Ahab's legs. Ahab searches for the whale half-way round the world, sworn to kill it to avenge his lost leg. The two meet in the end, Moby-Dick is harpooned by Ahab, but in the last *sound of the dying whale the harpoon line catches round Ahab and drags him down with the whale.

Moby-Dick was an instantaneous success, much of which rubbed off on to *Typee* and *Omoo*, and all three became bestsellers. But Melville's sudden popularity as an author waned when, in 1852, he published another novel, *Pierre, or The Ambiguities*, a psychological novel of incestuous passion which alienated so many of his readers that the sales of his previous books dropped alarmingly. For the next years he devoted himself entirely to his duties as a customs officer, writing little more than occasional poems and articles. Nearly at the end of his life he published a volume of biography, *John Marr and Other Sailors* (1888), and shortly before he died he finished *Billy Budd*, which was published posthumously. In this book, a great and deserved success, he wove his story around the activities of the *press gang in Britain and the bitter cruelties and injustice of life in the navy during the period of the Napoleonic War (1803–15). The story of Billy Budd was later turned into an opera by Benjamin Britten.

MENDAÑA, ALVARO DE (d. 1596), Spanish navigator, who with Pedro Sarmiento de Gamboa fitted out two ships in Peru and sailed in 1567 to seek the 'southern continent' which they expected to find only 600 *leagues from the South American coast. They had, in fact, covered 120 degrees of *longitude close to the equator, sighting nothing, when they discovered a group of islands between 5° and 10° South which they believed to be the islands of King Solomon and named the group accordingly.

After six months exploring the islands, the expedition returned to Peru. Mendaña was anxious to exploit his discovery but it was not until 1595 that he was permitted to sail to colonize the islands and to discover the southern continent believed to lie beyond. He had, however, greatly underestimated the distance of his Solomon Islands. Having discovered and named the Marquesas Islands, a further long passage brought him to Santa Cruz which he likewise named and, in the face of increasing discontent and insubordination, he decided to found his colony there.

Fever carried Mendãna off; the lethargy of his men and their ill-treatment of the natives made colonization impossible. The chief pilot, Pedro Fernandez de *Quiros, led the survivors back to Manila.

The standard authority on these early explorers of the *Pacific is J. C. Beaglehole's *Exploration of the Pacific* (3rd edn. 1966).

MEN-IN-LIEU, seamen put on board a merchant vessel by the British naval *impressment service after prime seamen had been removed at sea, in order that the vessel could reach port in safety. It was legal in wartime for naval ships at sea to stop homeward bound merchant ships and press seamen out of them, though there were regulations which made it unlawful to take so many men that the ship could not navigate. But trained seamen were so valuable in the navy that many warships would wish to take more than they were allowed under the regulations; when this occurred they made up the merchant ship's crew by transferring some of their own men. It was a good way, from the naval point of view, of getting rid of some of their worst characters and of untrained men.

MERCATOR, GERARDUS (1512–94), Flemish geographer, used the latinized form of his name, which was really Gerhard Kremer. In 1534 he founded a geographical establishment in Louvain and three years later began producing his own maps. At the start of his career he was much influenced by the theories of *Ptolemy, and his first map of the world, in two hemispheres produced in 1538, shows this influence. His terrestrial globe was produced in 1541, and ten years later a celestial globe followed.

Mercator was threatened with religious persecution in 1544, having changed his Catholic religion to Protestantism, but escaped the severest penalties although he was tried for heresy. An invitation to occupy the chair of cosmography at the university of Duisburg offered him a means of escaping the religious intolerance of the day and he accepted eagerly. It was here that he did his greatest work, turning his back upon the Ptolemaic theories and introducing his own projection with parallels and *meridians at right angles. His first work embodying these new principles was published in 1569, the famous world map in 18 sheets. Several other maps followed, and in 1585 he issued the first part of his famous atlas in which he planned to bring together maps of all parts, to form an atlas of the world. He produced a world map on his projection in 1587 for inclusion in his atlas, and the final world atlas, which was accompanied by cosmographical essays, was produced in 1594, the year of his death.

It was some years after his death before the Mercator projection was accepted for navigational use at sea on any significant scale, but by about 1640, largely through the support of French seafarers, its use was widespread. See MERCATOR PROJECTION.

MERCATOR PROJECTION, the method adopted by Gerardus *Mercator of producing a sea *chart in which parallels of *latitude and

Double portrait of Mercator and Hondius; engraving from Volume I of Mercator's book of maps, 1538

*meridians of *longitude cut each other at right angles, and on which a *rhumb line, which is a line of constant *compass *bearing, will appear as a straight line. As ships normally steer rhumb line *courses, such a chart would obviously be of great navigational value.

Mercator introduced his new projection in 1569, but it was nearly another seventy years before its use became widespread at sea. His system depended on the principle that the convergence of meridians as they approached the North and South poles is in proportion to the cosine of the latitude, and that if a proportional misplacement is introduced in the spacing between the parallels of latitude on the chart as they move away north and south from the equator, then a rhumb line, which cuts all meridians at the same angle, must become a straight line.

In geometrical terms, Mercator's projection can be envisaged as a cylinder touching the globe at the equator, on to which the meridians and parallels are projected from the earth's centre, which is then developed (i.e., unwrapped) to form a flat chart. As the axis of the cylinder is the same as the polar axis of the globe, the projection of each pole will be at infinity and the polar regions therefore cannot be shown on Mercator's projection. The distortion is least in the region of the equator and increases progressively towards high latitudes. By 'distortion' is meant that the linear scale for north–south distances becomes more and more divergent from that for east–west distances, increasing with the latitude, though not in the same proportion. This means that in a chart covering an area with a considerable north–south dimension, such as North or South America, the regions in high latitudes, e.g., Baffin Land or Tierra del Fuego, appear exaggerated in size compared with tropical areas such as the Isthmus of Panama; they also appear distorted in shape, e.g., Greenland on Mercator's projection appears to stretch out almost indefinitely to the north because, as the Arctic is approached, the projection becomes less and less convenient. Nevertheless, for nautical purposes the projection has the unique advantage that rhumb lines always appear as straight lines.

In measuring distances on a Mercator chart,

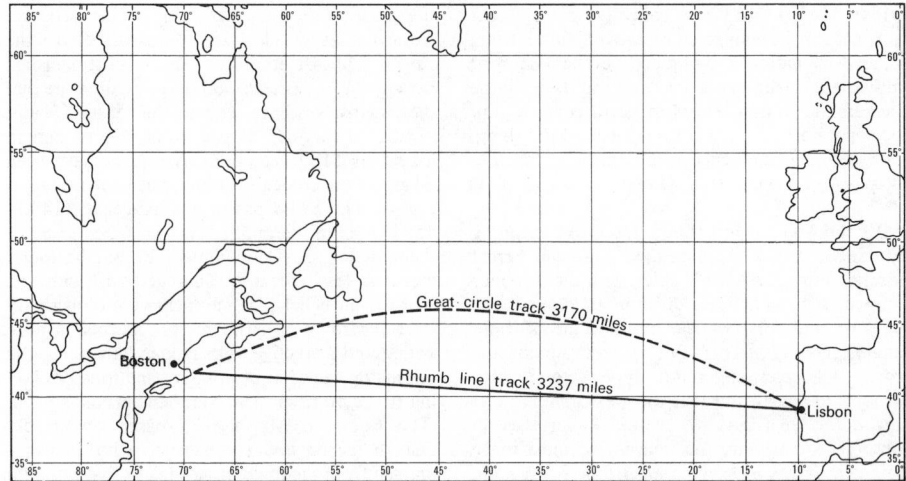

Mercator projection: rhumb lines appear straight

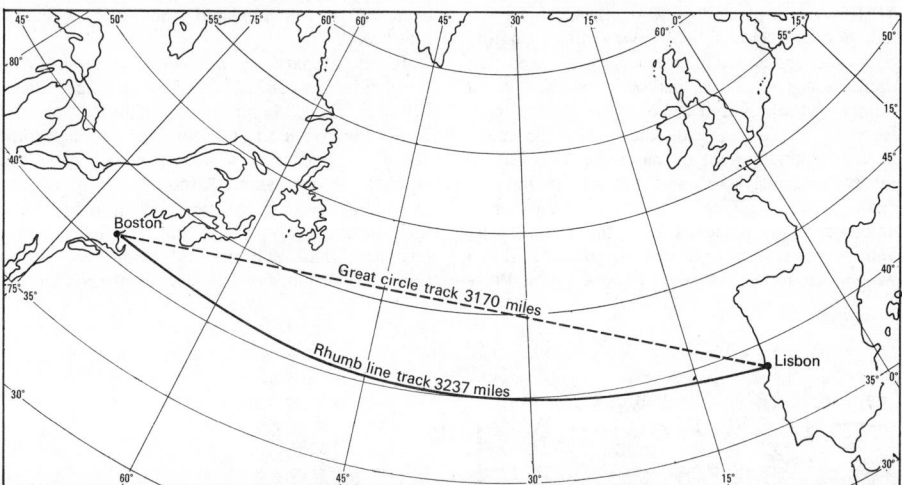

Gnomonic projection: great circles appear straight

therefore, it is essential to measure the span of degrees of latitude on the sides of the chart which lie on the same latitude as the distance being measured. These degrees will each represent sixty nautical miles for the measurement required. Degrees measured in other parts of the chart (i.e., not on the same latitude as the distance to be measured) will not, and of course the scale of degrees of longitude in the top and bottom margin is useless for measuring distances. For this reason no linear scale of miles can be included in any Mercator chart, except in the largest-scale plans showing a small area only. No linear scale could be drawn that would be accurate for different latitudes on a chart of any considerable area.

Mercator's projection can also be used with the axis of the cylinder not coinciding with the axis of the earth through the poles, and the resulting projections are known as Transverse Mercator (if the axis is at right-angles to the polar axis) or Oblique Mercator. The former results in the projection being least distorted along a given meridian, instead of along the equator, and is useful for mapping regions extending in a north–south direction, e.g., the British Isles on the Ordnance Survey. Oblique Mercator gives a line of least distortion which can be arranged to suit the area being mapped, running at an angle to both meridians and parallels of latitude. Both these varieties, however, are useless for navigation.

MERCHANT NAVY, a collective name to describe the merchant ships on the official registers of any one nation. It embraces merchant ships of all varieties, from passenger liners and very large tankers and bulk carriers to small coasters, but does not normally include vessels used in fishing. See also, e.g., CUNARD, P & O, LINER, TANKER, FLAGS OF CONVENIENCE, SHIPBUILDING.

MERIDIAN, from Latin *medius* meaning middle, and *dies* meaning day, is a semi-*great circle joining the earth's poles. Meridians, better known perhaps as lines of *longitude, cross the equator and all parallels of *latitude at right angles. Owing to the uniform rotation of the earth, all celestial bodies appear to revolve around the earth towards the west, making one revolution in a day. When the sun crosses an observer's meridian, the time is reckoned to be midday, that is to say the local time is 12 noon at the instant the sun is at meridian passage.

MERMAIDS, mythological denizens of the sea, half human and half fish, have a history dating back into antiquity. It is generally believed that there is a connection between the apsaras of Hindu mythology and the nymphs of the Greek legends. These last, together with Oceanids, nereids, naiads, and sirens, were believed to inhabit streams, lakes, and the sea. In the 3rd century B.C. the Greek historian Megasthenes, ambassador of Seleucus I to the Indian king Sandrocottus, reported that a creature like a woman inhabited the seas round Ceylon. Pliny the Elder (23 B.C.–A.D. 37) in his *Historia Naturalis* says, 'Nor are we to disbelieve the stories told of Nereids. ... Several distinguished persons of Equestrian rank have assured me that they themselves have seen off the coast of Gades [Cadiz] a merman whose body was of human form.' In 1187 a merman is said to have been taken off the coast of Suffolk, but he managed to escape. The Swiss physician Paracelsus (1493–1541) tells of mermaids 'who woo men to make them industrious and home-like', but he found mermen less friendly. This accords with the Norwegian belief that mermen were oldish with black beards and hair, whereas mermaids were young and attractive with golden hair. Icelandic mermaids were full of mischief and fond of playing tricks on fishermen. Matthew Arnold's poem 'The Forsaken Merman' is based on an old Danish legend about a merman who entices a maiden from the town of Aarhus to live with him at the bottom of the sea. The converse is the theme of Leyden's poem 'The Mermaid' who is deserted by her husband 'the lovely chief of Colonsay'.

From all parts of the world come tales of mermaids. In 1825 one said to have been brought from Japan was exhibited at the Bartholomew's Fair, London, but on inspection she was found to be a woman with a fish's tail stitched to her skin. Although many of the legends concerning mermen and mermaids have their origin in mythology, the reported encounters with these supernatural beings are sometimes too circumstantial to be dismissed as mere

Sea-virgin, sea-monkey, and sea-Turk; engraving from Cosmographia Universalis, *by S. Munster, 1555*

hallucinations. The explanation doubtless lies in the existence of two aquatic mammals, the manatee and the dugong, both of which bear a passable resemblance to the human face. The attitude of the female dugong when suckling her young takes on a particularly human appearance. Further the plantive cries of seals and sealions have often been likened to those of human children. There is, in fact, ample natural evidence to support the mermaid mythology.

MERRIMACK, U.S.S. (C.S.S. *VIRGINIA*), the name of the Confederate warship which on 9 March 1862, during the Civil War in America (1861–5), fought an inconclusive duel in Hampton Roads with the U.S.S. **Monitor*. Although the action was entirely indecisive, it has gone down in naval history as the first encounter in war between **ironclads. The *Merrimack* was one of six naval vessels authorized by Congress in 1854 and named after rivers. She displaced 4,650 tons, was 275 feet long with 51-feet beam, and a **draught of nearly 24 feet. Although often called a steam **frigate, she was really a sailing frigate with auxiliary steam power. She carried forty guns, including some Dahlgren 8-inch or 9-inch. During the Civil War she was **scuttled, fell into the hands of the Confederates, and was renamed *Virginia*, though in most accounts of this ship's encounter with the *Monitor*, she is usually referred to as the *Merrimack*. The Confederates, who raised the ship, overhauled her machinery, and converted her into an ironclad, deserve great credit for their achievement, but the *Monitor* is entitled to the chief credit for making her a truly 'famous' ship. If there had been no *Monitor* present on 9 March the *Virginia* might have sunk or seriously damaged the U.S.S. *Minnesota* on that date, but she could not have gone to sea with any hope of reaching New York or Boston. Her limitations would have been evident, the wild suggestions of her holding New York City to ransom to finance the Confederacy would have remained unfulfilled. She was destroyed by her own crew when the Confederates evacuated Norfolk. She had destroyed the sailing warships *Cumberland* and *Congress* on 8 March 1862 but that was the limit of her success.

MERROW, the name by which a **mermaid is called in Ireland.

MERRY DANCERS, the name often given to the streamers of coloured light associated with the **aurora borealis or northern lights.

MERRY MEN OF MAY, a name often given to the tide-rips formed during the **ebb in the Pentland Firth in the far north of Scotland.

MESSENGER, (1) an endless rope which was used in weighing the **anchor in the days before the introduction of steam power in ships and when the **capstan was worked by hand. As the hemp anchor **cables of those days were generally too thick and heavy to be brought themselves round the capstan direct, a messenger was used instead. It was led through two single blocks from the vicinity of the **hawseholes, along the main deck so that it ran close alongside and parallel with the cable, round the capstan, where three or four turns were taken round the barrel, and back along the main deck on the other side of the ship. As the capstan was turned, so the messenger moved with it, and the cable was bound fast to the messenger with **nippers so that it was hove in at the same rate as the messenger. See also VIOL, NIPPER for illus. **(2)** A small rope attached to the **eye of a **hawser and used to haul it out to the ring of a mooring **buoy is also called a messenger.

METACENTRE, the point of intersection of a vertical line, in relation to the ship's structure, drawn through the centre of gravity of a ship when she is lying upright and a vertical line drawn through the centre of buoyancy when the ship is heeled. To make certain that a ship is stable so that a righting moment comes into play when she is heeled, the metacentre must be above the centre of gravity. The theory of the metacentre in shipbuilding was first evolved by the Frenchman Pierre **Bouguer in the mid-18th century.

METACENTRIC HEIGHT, the vertical distance between the centre of gravity of a ship and her transverse **metacentre. It is an important element of the righting moment exerted to bring a ship back to the vertical when she **rolls under the influence of the sea or wind; the greater the metacentric height, the more the righting moment. At angles of roll of more than about 10°, the position of a ship's metacentre, and therefore her metacentric height, varies, and a designer must arrange the shape and dimensions of a ship's hull to provide not only reasonable initial stability at normal conditions of loading but also reasonable stability at the probable angles of heel to which a ship may roll in heavy weather. This becomes particularly important in the case of container ships where the stowage of containers on the upper deck, in addition to in the **holds, obviously raises the position of the vessel's centre of gravity and thus reduces her metacentric height.

METACENTRIC SHELF, a method of indicating the relative balance or imbalance between the forebody and afterbody of a vessel under varying angles of heel by plotting the metacentric positions of the * sections of the vessel's hull lines when heeled. The form of this plotted curve, which is termed the metacentric shelf, reveals any lack of balance or irregularities in the vessel's submerged form which, it is claimed, can be corrected before the final design draught is reached. This metacentric shelf method of checking a vessel's lines for balance when heeled was invented by Engineer Rear Admiral Alfred Turner, of the British Navy, in about 1935.

A lack of balance in the underwater body of a vessel will cause her to * gripe, and many of the older sailing vessels, built under the rule-of-thumb method, proved very badly unbalanced at sea when sailing under a press of canvas, and under certain conditions would take charge and fly up into the wind no matter how hard the helmsman struggled to control them and hold them on course. This was a cause of many collisions in the days of sail, particularly with ships working in close company in narrow channels or in fleet manoeuvres. With a well balanced hull a vessel will not gripe, and with the metacentric shelf system it is claimed that a balanced hull is obtainable by amending the draught before construction.

METEOROLOGY, the study of weather patterns with the object of predicting change in the weather. It is a complex and still inexact science, based on current weather reports over a large area, but it is of great importance to navigators, particularly to those of small vessels and yachts, in enabling them to avoid areas in which stormy weather is predicted.

Pressure. The basic cause of all weather change lies in the property of a gas to rise when heated. Air is a gas, and when it is warmed by the sun or by a large, hot area such as a desert, it rises, produces an area of low pressure, and colder air from the surrounding area of higher pressure flows in to take its place. This action causes variations in the atmospheric pressure at sea level. To the navigator, therefore, the atmospheric pressure in the vicinity of his position at sea is the most important guide he has to the likely behaviour of the weather in the immediate future.

Atmospheric pressure is measured by the height of a column of mercury in a tube sealed at the top and open at the bottom to the pressure of the atmosphere, as in the ordinary mercury barometer. The average pressure at sea level in winter is 29·9 inches and in summer is 30·0 inches, and variations above or below this level indicate areas of high or low pressure. Most maritime barometers are now marked in millibars rather than in inches, 3·4 millibars equalling one-tenth of an inch. Another method of measuring atmospheric pressure is with an aneroid barometer, in which a hermetically sealed chamber of thin metal is partly exhausted of air and thus susceptible to any change in external pressure, which can be read off by means of a pointer on a graduated scale. Aneroid barometers are also almost all marked to read pressure in millibars rather than in inches, and pressure on all modern weather charts are today given in millibars. Thus, the average atmospheric pressure at sea level in millibars is 1,013 in winter and 1,016 in summer. A refinement of the aneroid barometer, favoured by many navigators, is a barograph, in which a continuous curve reflecting the changes in atmospheric pressure is traced on a small chart mounted on a revolving clockwork drum which makes one complete revolution in a week. This trace gives an accurate and continuous picture of pressure changes, providing visible evidence from which forecasts can more easily be made. Most large ships, in addition to aneroid barometers and barographs, carry at least one mercury barometer because of their greater accuracy and sensitivity. This is read and entered in the ship's deck log every watch. Smaller ships and yachts, in which the movement in rough weather makes it difficult to accommodate a mercury barometer, normally only carry an aneroid barometer or barograph.

Weather systems. There are two main weather systems in the general weather patterns, * anticyclones and * depressions. In the northern hemisphere an anticyclone is a system of wind which circulates spirally in a clockwise direction around an area of high pressure, which can at times cover an area of immense size. In the southern hemisphere the anticyclonic wind circulates in an anti-clockwise direction, though still around a high pressure area. The stronger winds are found at the outer limits of the anticyclone, those nearer the centre being very light or at times non-existent. This is always a fair-weather system, with the air dry and the wind strength never more than moderate. Anticyclones are normally slow moving and sometimes stationary for quite long periods. The approach of an anticyclone can usually be predicted by a steadily rising barometer and a clearing sky.

In a depression, basically a bad-weather system, the wind blows in an anti-clockwise direction about a centre of low pressure in the northern hemisphere, and in a clockwise direction in the southern hemisphere. The winds are usually high, sometimes violent, often accompanied by heavy rain, and strongest near the centre of the low pressure area where the barometer gradient is steepest. Depressions usually move swiftly, at an average rate of about 25 miles an hour. A navigator needs to know where the centre of a depression is in relation to the position of his vessel, in order to avoid the

GOPAK®

First for Folding Tables

GOPAK - First for folding tabl[es]

NEW
Round table
Request further details to

IDEAL FOR BANQUETING

Easy to use

For banqueting & contract use

Available in laminate or plywood top

www.gopak.co.uk

area of highest wind, and can do so by applying the *Buys Ballot law. If he faces the wind in the northern hemisphere, the centre lies on his starboard hand just abaft the beam; if he does so in the southern hemisphere, it lies just abaft his port beam. The approach of a depression can be foretold by a falling barometer, a backing wind, and the appearance in the sky of high cirrus cloud, the 'mare's tail' sky of sailors. Further evidence of an approaching depression is a halo, or white luminous ring, around the sun or moon, and a banking up of low, heavy cloud. For illus. see DEPRESSION.

It does not necesarilly follow that every rise in barometric pressure foretells an anticyclone and that'every fall foretells a depression. Variations of three or four millibars up or down from the average, except in the tropics, are fairly normal and may produce little change in the current weather pattern; it is only when variations of five or more millibars from the normal occur that some predictions are possible. A barometer reading of five millibars below normal, with the barometer steady or still falling, is an indication of a period of unsettled weather; five millibars above and a steady or still rising barometer indicates settled weather with light or moderate winds. In the tropics, where variations of atmospheric pressure are generally limited to a small diurnal oscillation, a fall of three millibars below the average needs to be treated with suspicion, especially if it persists for two or three days, when it is a fairly sure indication of a *tropical storm somewhere within a radius of about 250 miles. In other areas, atmospheric pressure of less than 1,000 millibars, and the barometer falling rapidly at one millibar or more in an hour, is a sure indication of strong winds and rain; a barometer rising rapidly indicates a fine period of a day or two but likely to be followed by a fall in pressure and more unsettled weather. Other weather conditions that can be foretold by the behaviour of the barometer are best illustrated by two simple rhymes that every seaman should know:

'Long foretold, long last,
Short notice, soon past.'

This indicates that steady fall in pressure over a long period indicates a long period of bad weather, but that a rapid fall indicates that though the weather will be severe it will be of short duration.

'First rise after low
Foretells a stronger blow.'

The full force of a *gale at sea is frequently felt after the centre of a depression has passed, the first rise of the barometer of course indicating that the centre has passed. Gales with a rising barometer are invariably squally.

Cloud formation is also frequently a useful guide in weather prediction. There are four main types of cloud formation, *cirrus, cumulus, stratus*, and *nimbus*, but combinations of these main formations can also be indications of the type of weather ahead. *Cirrus*, the highest of the cloud formations, is cloud in the form of light wisps stretched across the sky. If these wisps are few in number and tend to disappear quickly, the probability is that fine weather will continue. If they are numerous and appear to group themselves in long streaks radiating from a common centre, a depression accompanied with strong winds is likely to be on the way. Sometimes *cirrus* takes the form of a thin film of cloud across the sky which, at night, produces a halo around the moon. This is almost certain evidence of violent weather.

Cumulus is the cloud which looks like masses of cotton wool billowing up in the sky. When *cumulus* comes on a summer day and disappears in the heat of the sun, the weather will remain fine and settled. If it appears to increase at the end of the day, a weather change is probable. When it builds itself up in pyramids and appears to topple over, it is a sure sign of thunder.

Stratus is the lowest of the cloud formations, and appears as a bank or pall of shapeless low-lying cloud, often forming in the evening and disappearing at dawn. Although it may at times look threatening, it has little message for the forecaster unless, towards dusk, its edges appear torn and twisted to windward. If then in its advance across the sky it meets *cumulus* cloud, a period of bad weather can be predicted.

Nimbus, the rain cloud, is the darkest of the clouds, often inky in appearance, and indicates rain. When it has a hard lower edge broken by vortex-like wisps and moving fast, it indicates a line squall approaching with the cloud.

As much, however, can generally be foretold from the nature of all these clouds as from their actual form. When any of them are soft-looking and reasonably low, then the weather will be fine with moderate breezes; when they are hard-edged and oily-looking, it is a sign of increasing wind; when they are small and inky-looking, rain is certain.

Clouds form when the temperature of the air falls below its saturation point. When air has been heated by passing over a warm land or sea area, it expands and rises, and as it mounts it expands still further because of the decrease in atmospheric pressure. This expansion causes it to cool, and if this cooling process continues beyond the point of saturation, the excess water condenses into the droplets which form clouds. The formation of mist and fog is fundamentally the same as that of cloud, except that the air is cooled below its saturation point at ground level. When warm, moist air is blown over a cold sea surface, by which the lower layers of the air are cooled, fog will form. Sea fogs are most common in spring and the early part of summer, seasons at which the sea is still cold, but adjacent land areas have warmed up. Sea fogs are also prevalent in the areas where cold ocean currents flow.

The difference between mist and fog is purely one of degree, and a generally accepted definition is that when the visibility exceeds 1,000 metres it is classed as mist, and when under 1,000 metres, it is classed as fog.

HISTORY

Meteorology as the basis of weather forecasting owes its birth to Admiral Robert *Fitzroy, who gained a worldwide reputation as a practical meteorologist as a result of his voyages in the brig *Beagle. When the British government decided to institute a meteorological department of the Board of Trade in 1854, Fitzroy was invited to become its first superintendent. He brought great energy and ability to this work and compiled the first *synoptic charts for forecasting weather changes. He also introduced in 1859 the system of visual gale warnings by cones hoisted at conspicuous places in many ports and harbours, a practice which has lasted to the present day. His books on weather forecasting, published in 1858, 1861, and 1863, were based on scientific research and remained as standard works on the subject for many years after his death in 1865.

Modern meteorology is served by a far greater volume of basic information than was available in Fitzroy's day. Weather ships in the oceans provide almost continuous reports of atmospheric pressures, wind velocities, air and sea temperatures, and conditions in the upper atmosphere obtained from balloon probes; and modern signalling methods bring all this information into the various meteorological offices of the world in a matter of seconds. Other reports come in from ice-reporting ships, lightships, shore stations, warships, and merchant ships, all of which contribute to the building-up of accurate synoptic charts. Today, a great deal of additional meteorological information is received from satellites which can monitor the conditions of the upper atmosphere and provide a continuous picture of cloud formations over huge areas from which much valid information for forecasting weather changes can be obtained. See also WEATHER LORE.

Admiralty Weather Manual (1938); H. R. Byers, *General Meteorology*, 3rd edn. (New York, 1959); A. Watts, *Weather Forecasting Ashore and Afloat* (1967).

METRE CLASS YACHTS, see INTERNATIONAL METRE CLASS YACHTS.

MIAOULIS, ANDREAS VOKOS (1768–1835), Greek vice admiral, was a successful merchant captain at the outbreak of the Greek War of Independence against Turkey in 1820, and was chosen to lead the naval forces of the Greek islands against the Turkish-held mainland. Under his direction the force of small vessels of all descriptions, which made up the Greek insurgent navy, caused many losses among Turkish warships, harried them to and fro around the coast (on one occasion by the use of *fireships), and in 1822 successfully raised the siege of Missolonghi. He also commanded the expedition which, in the same year, was dispatched to take revenge for the massacre at Chios by the Turks.

Until 1827, when the British admiral Lord Dundonald (see COCHRANE, Thomas) arrived to take command of the Greek naval forces, the whole direction of the naval war fell on Miaoulis's shoulders, a task he carried through with marked success considering the overwhelming strength in ships and men deployed by Turkey. After the winning of independence, he was again called upon to lead Greece out of the hands of the extremists of the Russian party who were trying to take over control of the country, and his naval victory at Poros in 1831 turned the scale. He was a member of the deputation which offered the throne of Greece to King Otho, by whom he was promoted to rear admiral and, later, vice admiral.

MIDDLE GROUND, an obstruction in the form of a sand or mud bank, or an outcrop of rock, in a *fairway. Its extremities are marked by *buoys so that vessels entering or leaving can pass either side of it in safety. See BUOYAGE.

MIDDLE PASSAGE, the second of the three legs of the old slaving voyages from England of the 16th, 17th, and 18th centuries. The first leg was from England to the west coast of Africa with a cargo of rum, brass goods, and firearms; these were exchanged on the west coast for slaves who were shipped on the middle passage to the West Indies or the southern states of America, and the money from the sale of the slaves invested in a cargo of cotton, sugar, or tobacco for the third and last leg of the voyage back to England. As each leg of the voyage was immensely profitable, the number of British ships attracted to the slave trade during these years was very great. The prosperity of *Bristol and *Liverpool as great seaports was built on these voyages.

MIDDLETON, CHARLES, first Lord Barham (1726–1813), British admiral, and First Lord. Although in early life he was some years at sea, he never served afloat in flag rank or made any particular mark. His gifts lay in administration.

From 1778, when he became Comptroller of the Navy, until his retirement in 1806 at the age of 80, he gave continuity to affairs at the *Navy Board and at the Admiralty, and the great mass of his papers, edited by Sir John *Laughton for the *Navy Records Society, shows beyond doubt how much the navy of the age of the long wars with France (1793–1815) owed to his grasp.

Middleton held the post of Comptroller, in which he was responsible for ship design and building, for twelve years (1778–90), during which time he reached flag rank and became Member of Parliament for Rochester. In 1794, soon after the outbreak of war with France, he was once more involved in sea affairs as a member of the Board of Admiralty. The greatest service he ever rendered his country was when, as the result of Lord Melville's resignation in May 1805 as First Lord owing to his impeachment on a charge of misappropriation of naval funds, Middleton took supreme charge of naval strategy and administration. This was at a crisis in the war, when Napoleon's plans for the invasion of Britain were being countered by *Cornwallis, *Nelson, *Collingwood, and other leading admirals then serving afloat. On taking office as First Lord, Middleton was given a peerage and it is as Lord Barham that he is known to history.

One of Barham's principles was that the key to Britain's naval strategy lay in a strong Western Squadron, not only to control the entrance to the Channel but also to watch the French Atlantic ports and to give cover to the immense flow of trade to and from the British Isles, upon which the prosperity of the country depended. The same idea had been strongly advocated by Admiral Edward *Vernon and it had been, in fact, a cardinal factor in the distribution of naval strength for several generations.

Barham had at first been critical of Nelson's abortive chase of Admiral *Villeneuve to the West Indies in the summer of 1805, and when Nelson returned home, he sent for the *Victory's journals. Mastering their contents, he decided that continued trust in Nelson's judgement was fully justified, and gave him a free hand in his final preparations for the movements which led to the battle of *Trafalgar. After the battle, and the consequent removal of every possible threat of invasion (Napoleon's Grand Army had left the shores of the Channel even before it was fought, and would never again return), Barham could retire, his work accomplished.

Barham was not a popular figure in the navy of his time for various reasons. The first was the comparative paucity of his service afloat. The second was his religion. He belonged to the Evangelicals, known to the irreverent as 'canting Methodists', as also did his friends such as *Kempenfelt in earlier days and *Gambier later.

He was, moreover, a 'political' admiral, though the politicians used him for his professional knowledge, not for his political sagacity or influence. None doubted, though, that he was devoted to the improvement of the navy, and in the course of a long life few men did more for its benefit.

No biography of Middleton has been written, but in the three volumes of his letters and papers, edited by Sir John Laughton, together with a long biographical introduction by the editor which precedes them, a very good picture of his life and achievements is presented. The volumes were published by the Navy Records Society in 1906, 1909, and 1910.

MIDDLETON, CHRISTOPHER (d. 1770), British navigator and scientist, joined the Hudson's Bay Company about 1720 where his considerable abilities were soon recognized. In 1737 he was elected a Fellow of the Royal Society for his researches on magnetic variation and methods of obtaining *longitude by astronomical observation. In 1741 he was prevailed upon to undertake a voyage in search of a *North-West passage and on 5 March of that year he was granted a commission as a commander in the Royal Navy and given command of the bomb *ketch *Furnace*. Two months later he sailed for the Arctic in company with the *sloop *Discovery*, commanded by Lieutenant Moor. They reached Churchill River, Hudson's Bay, on 9 August and decided the season was too far advanced to continue the voyage, so winter quarters were established there. The crews suffered severely from *scurvy, so the following July, after discovering Wager Inlet, the ships returned to England, arriving in the Thames on 2 October 1742. The failure of the expedition led to bitter controversy between the promoter of the voyage, the Hudson's Bay Company, and Middleton himself, who as a result, and in spite of the outbreak of war with France, was unemployed for almost two years after his return. In 1745 he was given command of the sloop *Shark*, but when peace was declared in 1748 he was placed on half pay until his death.

He wrote *A Vindication of the Conduct of Captain Christopher Middleton*, published in 1744, a curious and now very rare book.

MIDGET SUBMARINES, see X-CRAFT.

MIDSHIPMAN, a non-commissioned rank in all navies (Fr. *aspirant*, Ger. *Fähnrich*, It. *guardiamarina*) next below that of the equivalent in the British Navy of sub-lieutenant. The British midshipman was originally a petty officer under the immediate command of the *boatswain. At the restoration of Charles II in 1660, a system of sending volunteers—younger sons of the nobility and gentry—to sea with a 'letter of service' was adopted with a view to breeding up a new generation of naval officers. These volunteers received the pay of a midshipman. This system of officer entry was changed in 1729 when a school was opened at *Portsmouth through which all volunteers had to pass before going to sea as midshipmen. The school was reorganized in 1773 and again in 1806, until in 1859 the old *ship of the line *Britannia was taken over for this purpose, being finally established at Dartmouth and replaced by a college built ashore in 1903. All appointments as midshipmen were made after three years training in the Britannia or four years in the college when it replaced the ship.

The great majority of young men destined to become naval officers had, before the days of the Britannia, gone to sea as a *'captain's servant', or by nomination of the First Lord of the Admiralty, and were automatically rated midshipman after three years' service. They sat an examination for the rank of *lieutenant after a total of six years service. This method of entry, which depended so largely on family influence, came to an end with the introduction of the Britannia.

Present day service of midshipmen in a fleet is essentially one of training for higher command. They are placed in charge of a ship's boats, keep watch at sea and in harbour under the eye of a senior officer, and generally play a part, under supervision, in all the ship's activities. At the end of their midshipman's time they take an examination in seamanship for promotion to sub-lieutenant. See also KING'S LETTER BOY. For a table of equivalent ranks see APPENDIX 1.

MIDWAY, BATTLE OF, an action of the Second World War, proved to be a turning point in the Pacific naval war. On 3 June 1942 American aircraft based on Midway Island in the Hawaiian group located and attacked Japanese transports on their way for an invasion of the island, being then about 600 miles west of Midway. Next day aircraft from four Japanese *aircraft carriers struck the installations on Midway Island and inflicted heavy losses among the Marine Corps and Army aircraft based there. Aircraft from the three American carriers *Enterprise, Hornet, and Yorktown located the Japanese fleet and concentrated their attacks on the four Japanese carriers, sinking two of them that day and the other two on 5 June. Japanese carrier aircraft severely disabled the U.S.S. Yorktown. With knowledge of the loss of his four carriers, Admiral *Yamamoto abandoned his plans to invade Midway and retired westward. Admiral R. A. *Spruance, with the carriers Enterprise and Hornet, five heavy *cruisers, one light cruiser, and *destroyers, followed the Japanese fleet to the west but correctly surmised

that if he pursued the enemy too closely he might bring his two undamaged carriers under gunfire from Japanese *battleships and heavy cruisers. After carrier aircraft attacks on the retiring Japanese force on 5 and 6 June, Spruance turned eastward to refuel. One American destroyer and a Japanese heavy cruiser were sunk on 6 June. On the 7th the carrier Yorktown was torpedoed and sunk by a Japanese submarine while she was retiring in a damaged condition.

This battle proved to be one of the most decisive in naval history. In addition to the loss of four aircraft carriers, the Japanese also lost the major portion of their highly trained and battle-experienced carrier aircraft pilots. Although it is difficult to be certain on such a matter, it is believed that the Japanese never again attained such a high standard of trained carrier-based pilots.

The battle is of great interest in the terms of naval warfare as the first action fought at sea at the range of carrier-borne aircraft instead of at the range of ships' guns, and it spelled out the end of the battleship as the naval queen of the ocean. It was the first of a series of such battles fought in the Pacific in which the aircraft carrier demonstrated herself as the supreme weapon system of naval battle. Her reign as such, however, has proved to be short-lived; the great development of the guided missile has now to a large and growing extent taken the place of ship-borne aircraft as the most effective naval strike weapon.

MIKASA, a Japanese *battleship, laid down in 1899 and launched in 1902, was the flagship of Admiral Heihachiro *Togo at the battle of *Tsushima in May 1905 against the Russian Baltic Fleet commanded by Admiral *Rozhestvensky. She was fairly severely damaged during the action and later that year, in September, while in dockyard hands for repair, was accidentally blown up and sunk. She was later raised and repaired, and at the end of her useful naval life was preserved as a national monument at *Yokosuka dockyard. She survived the bombing of the Second World War and is still preserved at Yokosuka.

MIKKELSEN, EINAR (1880–1971), Danish explorer, was born at Copenhagen. He went to sea at the age of fourteen and six years later took part in an expedition to East Greenland and ultimately became an authority on this region. In 1901 he was a member of an unsuccessful U.S. expedition to reach the North pole. Five years later he returned to the Arctic in search of land believed to lie north of Alaska, and in 1909 led an expedition to north-east Greenland in search of the diaries and reports of the Danish expedition of 1906–8. He was successful in finding some of them, though a series of mishaps very nearly cost him his life. His book *Lost in the Arctic*, published in 1913, gives an account of his adventures. From 1932, for a period of eighteen years he was Inspector-General of East Greenland, and during the Second World War he was attached to the Danish Legation in Washington, D.C., as an adviser on questions concerning Greenland.

MILE, see NAUTICAL MILE.

MILLER, ROBERT CLYDE (1936–), Australian yacht designer, was born at Boggabri, New South Wales. He began life as a sailmaker and taught himself naval architecture, his first success, *Taipan*, an 18-ft (5·5 m) skiff, revolutionizing dinghy sailing in Australia. This led to his designing Flying Dutchman class boats which won the Interdominion (Australia–New Zealand) championships. On opening his own sail loft in Sydney, Miller started to design larger yachts. These included *Mercedes III*, 42 ft (13 m), which helped to win the Admiral's Cup for Australia in 1966, and *Apollo*, a 60-footer (18·5 m) for Alan Bond which later, in England, held the record for a single-hull yacht round the Isle of Wight. *Apollo II* and a sister ship *Ginko* dominated the Australian offshore scene in 1972–3, while *Ceil III*, 40 ft (12·4 m), won the Sydney–Hobart race that year. After designing the 80-ft (24·4 m) *Ballywho*, Miller designed a number of cup winners in class racing, as well as two 12-metre class yachts to challenge for the *America*'s Cup. As a racing helmsman he was twice chosen to represent Australia in Olympic Games yachting.

MILLIBAR, a unit of measurement of atmospheric pressure, 1,000 millibars equalling the atmospheric pressure required to raise a column of mercury in a vacuum tube to a height of 29·53 in. (750 mm). Lines drawn on a *synoptic chart connecting points of equal atmospheric pressure in millibars are known as isobars. See also METEOROLOGY.

MINELAYER, a warship built or converted to lay *mines. Mine warfare, in the modern meaning of the term, came into being during the Crimean War (1854–6) when moored mines were laid by the Russians to protect their harbours in the Baltic Sea. But it was not until the First World War (1914–18) that mines were laid in numbers sufficient to require ships specially designed or converted to lay them. Minelayers during this war were almost without exception ships converted for the purpose, fast passenger ships or *destroyers, fitted with rails along their decks on which mines, with their sinkers on wheels, were launched along the rails and over

the stern into the sea. Some *submarines were also converted for minelaying.

Mine warfare during this war had reached such great proportions that most navies then designed ships especially for the purpose. The first, the British H.M.S. *Adventure*, was designed to carry several hundred mines. At the same time, more thought was given to the design of submarine minelayers, and most nations constructed a number of such ships which, of course, had the advantage of laying mines in complete secrecy.

With the development, during the Second World War, of new types of mine, such as magnetic, acoustic, and pressure mines, a more efficient method of minelaying was by aircraft, and the surface minelayer, as such, was largely abandoned as a type by all navies, although all these types of mines can be laid by surface vessels without much conversion.

The main essential of the conventional minelayer was speed, for the ability to reach a desired area for mining and to lay the mines in the dark was a necessary procedure to keep the position of the mines secret. British minelayers of the Second World War, such as H.M.S. *Welshman* and H.M.S. *Manxman*, had a designed speed of 45 knots. See MINES AND MINE WARFARE.

MINERVA, see ATHENE.

MINES AND MINE WARFARE. The first man to devise a means of exploding gunpowder underwater was the American David *Bushnell who devoted himself to devising various means of attacking ships below the waterline during the American War of Independence (1775–82). His methods, one of which was the loosing of floating explosive kegs upstream of the British squadron in the Delaware, though primitive, were feasible and failed only owing to the vigilance of the British crews. Another American, Robert *Fulton, demonstrated methods of sinking ships with towed explosives to both the French and British naval authorities during the Revolutionary and Napoleonic Wars (1793–1815) and though neither side would make use of what they thought a barbarous weapon, the British unsuccessfully tried his concept of explosive *barges against the French fleet at Boulogne in 1804. Both Bushnell's and Fulton's weapons were, however, more in the nature of *torpedoes than of mines as we know them today.

Not until the Crimean War (1854–6) were naval mines resembling those of modern times used by the Russians in harbour defence. Invented by M. Jacobi, these were mechanically fired on contact by means of a chemical fuse, making use of sulphuric acid in a glass tube. One exploded under H.M.S. *Merlin*, but the amount of explosive was too small to do any damage.

The British ships H.M.S. Merlin *and H.M.S.* Firefly *struck by mines during the Crimean War; 19th-century engraving*

By this time mines, which were always moored and, by international agreement, were required automatically to become safe if they broke adrift, were of two main types: (*a*) 'observation' or 'controlled' mines fired electrically from the shore or (*b*) 'contact' mines actuated when struck by a ship. Various methods of detonating the latter were used, but most of them depended on the crushing of one of a number of protruding lead horns. These were the types mainly used during the First World War (1914–18), though a mine actuated by the magnetic field of a ship passing over it was developed by the British before the end of the war.

Counter-measures took the form of sweeping by means of a toughened wire towed by two *minesweepers, or by the use of a system adapted from the fisherman's *otterboard used to spread the mouth of a *trawl net; this was known as the *Oropesa Sweep. Another method, though not so much sweeping as such but to protect warships crossing a minefield, was the *paravane, towed from the bows of a ship on either side, which diverted a moored mine from the path of the ship and guided its mooring wire into a wire cutter incorporated in the paravane.

During the Second World War mines became much more effective and more widely used as a result of the development of influence types—

magnetic or acoustic—which could be either moored or laid on the sea bottom in relatively shallow water. In even shallower water mines actuated by the pressure wave of a ship passing overhead could also be laid on the bottom. They could all be laid by surface craft, *submarines, or aircraft.

Counter-measures were made more and more difficult by such anti-sweeping devices as explosive charges to destroy sweep wires, delaying mechanisms which made necessary a variable number of sweeps to actuate influence mines, and by the inclusion of several different types of mine in one minefield. Some types, particularly the pressure mines, were virtually unsweepable and the technique of mine-hunting, using *sonar to detect them and *frogmen to remove them, has had to be developed to deal with them.

M. F. Sueter, *The Evolution of the Submarine Boat, Mine and Torpedo* (1908); A. M. Low, *Mine and Countermine* (1940); J. S. Cowie, *Mines, Minelayers and Minelaying* (1949).

MINESWEEPER, a vessel designed or adapted to sweep or explode *mines laid at sea. In the early days of mines, these vessels were usually fishing *trawlers taken up in wartime and converted as minesweepers to tow an underwater sweep of serrated wire with cutters inserted at intervals designed to catch and cut the mooring wire of a mine so that it came to the surface where it could be destroyed. The normal practice was for two minesweepers to tow a sweep stretched between them in order to clear a wide path through a minefield. This was developed in 1919 into the *Oropesa Sweep in which a single minesweeper could do the original work of two by spreading the sweep wire with the use of a *kite and *otter.

The development between the two world wars and later of more sophisticated types of mine of the magnetic, acoustic, and pressure variety called for new types of minesweepers designed to explode mines of these types and of combinations of them. The *LL Sweep, which was introduced in 1940 to explode magnetic mines, naturally required wooden minesweepers, since a steel-hulled vessel would herself explode the mine before the sweep could do so. The wooden mine-sweeper is today being replaced by minesweeping vessels with hulls constructed of *fibre glass. Acoustic mines were destroyed by simulating the noise of a ship's propellers passing over them. The most difficult mine to sweep is the pressure mine, for which the minesweeper requires to be fitted with *sonar for location and to carry divers or frogmen for removal. See MINES AND MINE WARFARE.

MINORCA, an island in the western Mediterranean in the Balearic group, which was the scene of a naval action between British and French fleets fought in 1756. The island was held by the British at the beginning of the Seven Years War (1756–63) and as a result of the action was obliged to surrender to the French. Admiral the Hon. John *Byng had been sent out from Britain to relieve the garrison holding Port Mahon and had with him a weak and inefficient force of thirteen *ships of the line. On 20 May 1756 when about 30 miles south-east of Port Mahon, to which the British garrison had retired, he encountered a numerically equal French fleet under Admiral the Marquis de la *Galissonnière.

The British fleet bore down on the enemy but, owing to the angle of approach, the attack was not made simultaneously. The action was indecisive and the French drew off. But Byng made no attempt to interfere with the French ships that were covering and supplying their troops who had already been landed on the island, and a Council of War held on board his flagship decided to return to Gibraltar to await reinforcements from England. Byng framed the questions put to the Council of War very much with the idea of getting it to recommend abandonment of the attempt to relieve the garrison. There was no alternative to the British garrison in Port Mahon than to surrender, leaving the

Streaming an Oropesa Sweep

whole island in the hands of the French invaders. The British government, without waiting to receive Byng's dispatch and going merely by the French account, sent out Vice Admiral Sir Edward *Hawke to supersede him, to relieve the garrison, and recapture the island, but he arrived on the station too late to retrieve the situation.

MIRROR OF THE SEA, THE, a collection of shorter writings on the sea by Joseph *Conrad, published in 1906, which contains some of his finest work on this subject.

MISTRAL, a cold wind from the north-west which blows down the Rhône valley into the western Mediterranean Sea. In the Adriatic and eastern Mediterranean, a similar north-west wind is called the maestrale.

MITRE, the seam in a sail where cloths which run in two directions are joined. Triangular sails, such as *staysails and *jibs (and occasionally yachts' Bermudian mainsails), are normally made with the lines of the cloths running in two directions; for example, the upper cloths of a jib might run at right angles to the leech, and the lower cloths at right angles to the foot. The mitre seam usually forms a strengthened narrow cloth running diagonally from the clew to some point on the luff. Different sailmakers have their own ideas of the best method of setting the cloths and the mitre seam, but the latter is usually arranged to run more or less in line of the *sheet so as to distribute the strain of the sheet evenly throughout the sail cloths. For illus. see SAIL.

MITSCHER, MARK ANDREW (1887–1947), American admiral, graduated from the Naval Academy in 1910 and was one of the first officers in the U.S. Navy to receive a pilot's certificate. He commanded the new *aircraft carrier *Hornet* in the battle of *Midway on 4 June 1942, and in July was promoted rear admiral in command of a patrol wing before being sent to command a fleet operating from Noumea. From August 1943 to January 1944 he was in command of the naval air units on the west coast, after which he assumed command of Carrier Division Three. In March 1944 he took command of the First Carrier Task Force which became famous as Task Force 58, operating alternatively in the Pacific with the Second Carrier Task Force known as Task Force 38. From July 1945 until March 1946 he was Deputy Chief of Naval Operations for Air in the Navy Department. He was serving at sea as commander-in-chief of the Atlantic Fleet when he suffered a heart attack which caused his death.

MIZEN or **MIZZEN,** the name of the third, aftermost, mast of a square-rigged sailing ship or of a three-masted *schooner, or the small after mast of a *ketch or a *yawl (but see also JIGGER MAST). The word probably came into the English language either from the Italian *mezzana* or the French *misaine*, which in fact are the names in those languages for the foremast, but for some reason its position in the ship was changed round when the word was adopted in Britain. The French word for mizen is *artimon*, and *artemon was the name given in England to an additional mast in the forward end of a vessel, probably the forerunner of the *bowsprit.

MOBILE BAY, Alabama, the scene of a major battle during the American Civil War (1861–5), between an attacking Federal force commanded by Rear Admiral David *Farragut and a defending Confederate Force under Admiral Franklin *Buchanan.

At the entrance to Mobile Bay lies Fort Morgan, which Farragut had to pass before he could reach Buchanan's ships inside the bay. He disposed his eighteen ships in a column of four *monitors, led by U.S.S. *Tecumseh*, nearest the fort, with the remainder, which were wooden vessels, in a line formation of seven of the larger ships with the seven smaller ships lashed alongside them. The *Tecumseh* struck a *mine (which in those days went under the generic name of *torpedo) and sank, and the leading wooden vessel, the *Brooklyn*, stopped, partly because the three remaining monitors were crossing her path and partly because her captain sighted a line of small *buoys which he took to indicate the boundary of the minefield. The tide and the momentum of their advance brought the next two ships in the line, one of which was Farragut's flagship, the *Hartford*, close up to her. In this critical situation Farragut ordered the *Hartford* to alter course and make for the entrance to the bay, but his attention was directed to the line of buoys. It was at this moment that he is said to have made his famous remark, 'Damn the torpedoes, full speed ahead.' Whether he said it or not, he had already taken the action which implied it.

After anchoring his ships, Farragut was planning to attack the Confederate armoured *ram *Tennessee* when she was seen approaching. A mêlée followed as ships attempted to sink each other by ramming. Eventually the *Tennessee*, which apart from three small converted vessels was the only ship on the Confederate side, was overwhelmed and forced to surrender. As a result of the action, Fort Morgan, and other forts defending the bay, later fell into Union hands, ending all Confederate access to the port of Mobile.

MOBY-DICK, the name of the great white whale in Herman *Melville's famous classic of the same name.

MOCENIGO, the name of a noble Venetian family, many of whom became doges and admirals of the republic. Tommaso Mocenigo (1343–1423) was the admiral who commanded the crusaders' fleet in 1396, and was also successful in battle against the fleet of * Genoa. He also won a notable victory against the Turkish fleet at Gallipoli. Pietro Mocenigo, who was Doge of * Venice in 1474, was one of the greatest Venetian admirals, and restored the naval power of Venice, which had fallen to a very low pitch, to a new degree of excellence. He captured Smyrna in a naval campaign in 1472, and in 1476 inflicted a crushing defeat on the Turkish fleet which was besieging Scutari. Another Mocenigo, Luigi, Doge from 1570 to 1577, took an active part as a squadron commander in the battle of * Lepanto.

MOEWE, S.M.S., a German * armed merchant raider of the First World War (1914–18), was the ex-banana carrier *Pungo* (1915) of 4,788 tons. After the German commerce raiding warships and armed liners had been rounded up during the first year of the war, it was decided to equip as a raider a small, inconspicuous merchant ship with an economical coal consumption. The *Moewe*, commanded by Burggraf und Graf zu Dohna-Schlodien, sailed on 29 December 1915. Within four days she had laid a minefield off the Gironde in the Bay of Biscay and began a career of commerce raiding, chiefly in the central and southern Atlantic, which lasted until her return home on 4 March 1916, during which time she sank or captured twelve ships of 65,000 tons. On her second voyage, from 23 November 1916 to 22 March 1917, she sank twenty-seven ships of 119,600 tons. Her operations were directed principally against the grain trade in the North Atlantic and off the River Plate, but their effects were even more widespread. Thus, when she was reported to have stopped the Belgian relief steamer *Samland* in the South Atlantic on 7 December, the sailing of British troop transports was halted from ports as widely separated as Cape Town, Dakar, and Freetown.

MOIDORE, a Portuguese gold coin much beloved by writers of pirate stories, struck between the years 1640 and 1732, and with a sterling value of 13s. 5½d. The double moidore, worth 27s. in sterling, was struck in 1688. It, too, figures in many pirate stories.

MOITESSIER, BERNARD (1925–   ), French sea wanderer and solo circumnavigator, was born in Indo-China. With a small * junk, *Marie-Thérèse*, rigged as a * gaff * ketch, he made his first long distance voyage alone from Singapore in 1952, being wrecked on the Chagos Bank. Going to live in Mauritius, Moitessier, with native help, built a 28-ft ketch (8·5 m), *Marie-Thérèse II*, this time * Bermuda rigged. In 1955 he sailed her alone by way of the Cape of Good Hope, St. Helena, Ascension Island, and Fernando-Noronha to the Caribbean, where this boat, too, was wrecked. Returning to the south of France, he built, again largely with his own labour, a 39-ft (11·9 m) ketch, *Joshua*, with a steel hull and decks, in which he and his bride, Françoise, sailed 14,216 miles non-stop in 126 days from Moorea, in the Society Islands, round Cape Horn to Alicante, in Spain. Mme Moitessier was the first woman at that date to have sailed round Cape Horn in a small yacht.

Moitessier entered his ketch for the single-handed round the world race in 1968–9, and having almost completed the 31,000 mile course, abandoned the race and continued on round the world covering non-stop a record distance of 37,455 miles in ten months. He was awarded (with Mme Moitessier) the Blue Water medal of America, the Wren medal, and the Neptune d'Or. He is the author of *Cape Horn: The Logical Route* and *Sailing to the Reefs*.

MOLE, a long pier or breakwater forming part of the sea defences of a port. It can be built either in the form of a detached mole constructed entirely in the sea or with one end of it connected to the shore. The ports of * Dover and * Gibraltar, for example, are protected by three moles, two of them attached to the shore on the eastern and western boundaries of the harbour, with a detached mole to seaward, providing an entrance to the harbour at each end of it. In old days the word, sometimes written as mole-head, was also used, wrongly, to describe a harbour protected by a mole.

MOLLIE, (1) sometimes **MOLLYMAWK,** a sailor's name for *Diomedia melanophrys*, a species of small albatross found in the southern seas and particularly round the Cape of Good Hope. They are more dusky than the normal albatross and are known for their greed and for their skill in fishing. **(2)** A convivial gathering of captains of whalers in the * cabin of one of them while on the fishing grounds. Ostensibly for the purpose of discussing the fishing, they were usually the excuse for a night's carouse, though sometimes lasting for several days. The hoisting of a bucket at the * mizen * topgallant masthead was the invitation to hold a mollie on board. In these days of whale factory ships and mechanized whaling, the holding of mollies, and indeed the use of the word itself, has almost entirely died out.

MONAMY, PETER (1689–1749), British marine artist, was one of the foremost of the early 18th-century sea painters, basing his work very closely on the style of the two Van de * Veldes. He was born in Jersey, in the Channel Islands, and as a youth apprenticed to a house painter on London Bridge. He was self-taught and the Thames and its shipping gave him his inspiration and is featured in the great majority of his work. He was meticulous in style and never departed from what might be called the Van de Velde tradition in marine art, and as a result there is little variety in his paintings. He was one of the artists commissioned to paint the decorations at Vauxhall Gardens, a London centre for concerts and spectacular entertainments. His later paintings were dark and strong, lacking in some respects the light and delicacy of his earlier work. There are small collections of his work at the * National Maritime Museum and the Victoria and Albert Museum, both in London.

MONARCH, H.M.S., a ship's name of great distinction in the British Navy. The first of the name was a 3rd * rate * ship of the line of seventy-four guns taken from the French by Rear Admiral Sir Edward * Hawke in October 1747 at the battle of * Ushant and bought for the navy in 1748. She had the gloomy distinction of being the place of execution, on 14 March 1757, of Admiral John * Byng. The second *Monarch* had a long and distinguished career of forty-eight years. She was built at * Deptford in 1765 and was first engaged, as one of Augustus * Keppel's fleet, in the action against the French in the second battle of Ushant in July 1778. She was in Sir George * Rodney's action off St. Vincent in 1780; and her activities in the West Indies in 1781 included the capture, in company with the * frigates *Sibylle* and *Panther*, of the Dutch ship of the line *Mars* and her convoy. In 1782 she saw further action in West Indian waters against French fleets commanded by Admiral de * Grasse off St. Kitts and Dominique, and in 1790 she was fitted at * Chatham for the East Indies. As the flagship of the commander-in-chief, Vice Admiral Sir G. * Elphinstone (later Lord Keith), she led the expedition which in 1795 captured the Cape of Good Hope, and in 1796 forced the surrender of a Dutch squadron which had been sent out to recapture the Cape. In 1797, as the flagship of Vice Admiral Sir Richard * Onslow, she was the first ship to engage the enemy at the battle of * Camperdown, when she had 36 of her company killed and 100 wounded. She took a substantial part in the first battle of * Copenhagen in 1801, when she lost 56 killed (including her captain, James Robert Mosse) and 164 wounded, and in the autumn of 1806 she was one of Commodore Sir Samuel * Hood's squadron off Rochefort when, with the *Centaur* and *Mars*, she captured the French frigates *Armide*, *Minerve*, and *La Gloire*. She was eventually condemned and taken to pieces in 1813.

MONCK, GEORGE, 1st Duke of Albemarle (1608–70), British * 'general-at-sea' and military governor, was born in Devon. Seeking a life of adventure, his first taste of action was as a youth of 17 on an unsuccessful expedition to Cadiz. Becoming a professional soldier, he learnt his trade in that notable school of arms, the Netherlands, where Protestants fought Catholic Spain. By 1640 Monck was in England, and he served Charles I against the Scots in what was known as the 'Second Bishops' War', when the king was defeated. He was next employed in Ireland on Charles's behalf, returning to England with Irish troops to help the royalists in the Civil War (1642–8). In 1644 he was taken prisoner at Nantwich by the Parliamentary general, Fairfax. As a seasoned and senior military officer, Monck was important enough to be confined in the Tower of London where he composed a treatise, mainly for professional soldiers, which was published in 1671, after his death, as *Observations upon Military and Political Affairs*. It is full of practical sense but includes little about politics.

After the defeat of Charles I, Monck was persuaded to serve the Commonwealth. He crossed once more to Ireland, and later took a leading part in Cromwell's victory over the Scots at Dunbar in 1650, being left in charge in Scotland when Cromwell returned to London, and setting to work to pacify the Highlands. In 1652 when war against the Dutch broke out Monck, expert in artillery, was chosen to serve as a 'general-at-sea'. He fought with courage and distinction and with his colleagues, Robert * Blake and Richard * Deane, defeated Marten * Tromp off * Portland during a protracted engagement, on 18–20 February 1653. Later in the same year he met the Dutch in two more battles, off the * Gabbard (2–3 June) and off * Scheveningen (31 July), during the second of which Tromp was killed.

Monck returned to Scotland at the end of the war at sea, and remained there until after Cromwell's death in 1658. In the following year he moved south, pausing at the town of Coldstream, from which place his own regiment, now the Coldstream Guards, takes its name. Later, finding support from Fairfax and from many others, Monck marched to London, where he took a leading part in the restoration of a full Parliament, and thus in the re-establishment of the monarchy under Charles II. The king rewarded Monck with a dukedom and the Order of the Garter, the highest honour in Britain, and he became one of his main advisers on matters not involving politics.

After the outbreak of the Second Dutch War (1665–7) Monck again became active at sea. In 1666 he fought a stubborn action, protracted over four days (1–4 June), and known as the * Four Days Battle, in which his opponent was the great Dutch admiral de * Ruyter. The British

The Monitor *engaging The* Merrimack, *9 March 1862; engraving by Currier and Ives*

fleet had been divided, Monck was outnumbered, and it was only after Prince *Rupert had joined him on the last day that catastrophe was averted, though the battle ended in defeat. This was avenged off *Orfordness on 25 July when, at the cost of a single vessel, Monck and Rupert defeated de Ruyter, who lost twenty ships in the action. It was Monck's last service afloat, and even he could not save his country from humiliation in 1667 when the great ships were laid up and the Dutch boldly sailed up the River *Medway, burning the British ships and causing general alarm in London.

Although he had no qualifications purely as a seaman, Monck has been ranked high as a naval tactician by many authorities, including Captain A. T. *Mahan. He believed in surprise and in the value of artillery through the combined broadsides of ships fighting in close support of one another. Above all, he sought the mêlée in naval battle as being likely to lead to decision.

Increasing years and experience often breeds ultra-caution in commanders. It was not so with Monck, and when he held command jointly with Prince Rupert, who had an almost legendary reputation for dash, it was Monck who, as often as not, supported the bolder measures. Considering that by 1665 he had become heavy and indeed dropsical, an infirmity from which he died five years later, Monck's last battles at sea show him to have been a man possessed of exceptional

fire and resolution. Ashore, as military strategist, as governor of Scotland, as principal agent in the Restoration of Charles II, he was known for circumspection. At sea, it was otherwise. Had signals in his day been less elementary, his successes may have been even more considerable.

MONITOR, a low freeboard, shallow draft ship mounting one or two large guns for coastal bombardment purposes. The name comes from the original *Monitor, an *ironclad designed by John *Ericsson for the American Navy in 1862 during the Civil War (1861–5) and was chosen from a phrase in a letter to the Secretary of the Navy about his design which Ericsson wrote. 'The impregnable and aggressive character of this structure will admonish the leaders of the Southern Rebellion that the batteries on the banks of their rivers will no longer present barriers to the entrance of the Union forces. The ironclad intruder will thus prove a severe monitor to those leaders.... Downing Street will hardly view with indifference this last Yankee notion, this monitor.' Downing Street, in fact, viewed the *Monitor* with complete indifference, having two years earlier launched the *Warrior, which could have blown fifty *Monitors* out of the water. Nevertheless, monitors were built in large numbers during the First World War (1914–18) by the British Navy for coastal bombardment, and indeed were also used by Britain in the

Second World War. They have no place, as such, in modern navies owing to wide adoption of guided missiles in place of guns.

MONITOR, U.S.S., an *ironclad, shallow draft vessel mounting two guns in a revolving turret, was built in New York in early 1862 to a design by John *Ericsson. She arrived in Hampton Roads late on 8 March 1862, a few hours after the C.S.S. *Virginia* (ex-*Merrimack*) had rammed and sunk the *sloop *Cumberland* and burned the grounded sailing *frigate *Congress*. The first battle between ironclads was thus fought on 9 March 1862, between these two ships, but was completely inconclusive. Circumstances combined to make the appearance of the *Monitor* in Hampton Roads dramatic, and additional vessels of the same general type were ordered and rushed to completion in the north. The *Monitor* herself was capable of no more than about four knots speed, and it was reported that she was not seaworthy. She nearly sank twice in her passage from New York to Hampton Roads and finally foundered off Cape Hatteras on 31 December 1862. In spite of her serious limitations she gave her name to a whole class of naval vessels.

MONKEY, (1) the name of a small coastal trading vessel, single-masted with a square sail and, occasionally, a topsail set above it, of the 16th and 17th centuries. They ranged up to about 40–50 tons *burthen. **(2)** A name also given to a small wooden *kid or cask in which *grog was carried after issue from the *grog-tub to the seamen's messes in ships of the British Navy. The name lingered on beyond the days of small wooden casks for this purpose and was used for the metal mess kettles in which, in later days, the grog was carried. See also BLEEDING THE MONKEY. **(3)** The name given to a form of marine steam reciprocating engine where two engines, either single-cylinder or *compound, were used together in tandem on the same propeller shaft. They were installed on opposite sides of the crankshaft so that when one engine pulled, the other pushed.

MONKEY BLOCK, the name given to a small single *block stropped with a swivel, and used on board in places where it is awkward to get a straight haul. The name was also used in square-rigged ships to describe the blocks fastened to the *yards through which the *bunt-lines are rove.

MONKEY JACKET, originally a thick, close-fitting, serge jacket worn by seamen while keeping watch in ships at night or in stormy weather; now the usual jacket worn by officers and petty officers of ships for everyday wear. It was also sometimes known as a Jackanapes Coat.

'MONKEY-PUMP', the seaman's name for a straw or quill inserted through a gimlet hole in a cask of wine or spirits, combined with the necessary mouth suction to draw off some of the contents.

MONK'S SEAM, the seam made by a sailmaker after sewing the overlapping edges of *cloths together to make a sail. It is a line of stitches through the centre between the two rows of edging stitches. See also PRICK, TO.

MONSON, Sir WILLIAM (1568–1643), English admiral, is best remembered for the six books of *Naval Tracts*, which he wrote towards the end of his life. They are the first detailed and critical account of naval warfare written by a seaman who actually took part in it. It was first printed in 1682 and a fully edited version by M. Oppenheim was produced by the *Navy Records Society in five volumes (1902, 1912–14). The tracts provide a detailed and comprehensive account of the Elizabethan war with Spain between 1585 and 1603, and contain also many suggestions as to how England could best deploy to her own advantage the sea power won for her after the victory over Spain.

Monson was born in Lincolnshire, the third son of Sir John Monson. In 1581, after two years at Balliol College, Oxford, he ran away to sea, partly fired by the exploits of such men as Sir John *Hawkins and Sir Francis *Drake, at that time the current naval heroes, and partly, as he says, 'led thereunto by the wildness of my youth'. He was captain of a *privateer in 1587 and in the sea campaign of the Spanish *Armada in 1588 he served as a volunteer on board the *Charles*, a *pinnace belonging to Elizabeth I, an event which caused him to devote the rest of his seafaring life to the service of the Crown. He was with the Earl of Cumberland in the semi-royal expeditions against the Spanish treasure fleets of 1589 and 1591, when he was taken prisoner by Spain and sentenced to the *galleys, though he does not seem to have been put to the oar, the miserable fate of so many captives of that country. He was released in 1592, was with Cumberland again in 1593, and the following year remained ashore to take his M.A. degree at Oxford. In 1595 Monson quarrelled with Cumberland and transferred his loyalties to the Earl of Essex (see DEVEREUX, Robert) and commanded the *Rainbow* in the *Cadiz expedition of 1596 as flag-captain to Essex, a service for which he collected one of the many knighthoods so liberally bestowed by Essex and Lord *Howard of Effingham after that successful assault.

When Essex fell from royal favour, Monson attached himself to Howard of Effingham, and he was vice admiral, under Sir Richard Leveson, Effingham's son-in-law, of the expedition of 1602 which captured the immensely rich Spanish * carrack *St. Valentine* in Cezimbra Bay on the coast of Portugal. In 1604 he was appointed to the position of admiral of the Narrow Seas, the chief naval command in home waters below that of * Lord High Admiral. Like some others of the disreputable court of James I, he was in the pay of Spain, a circumstance which did not come to light until 1614 when Sir John Digby, the English ambassador in Madrid, managed to get hold of a list of the Spanish king's English pensioners. Compared with the others he was but a modest pensioner, and the money he received was only to induce him to observe a benevolent neutrality towards Spanish ships in English waters, a much less benevolent neutrality towards Dutch ships, and occasional assistance in smuggling a few Spanish priests into Britain. He was imprisoned in the Tower of London in 1616, but fortunately for him the king was anxious to hush up all suspicions of Spanish pensions, as he himself received a large one, and Monson was released six months later. In 1635 he was again employed at sea as vice admiral of the summer fleet (no ships were commissioned during the winter months), and later he served on one or two commissions of inquiry into various aspects of the naval service.

MONSOON, a seasonal wind caused by the summer heating and winter cooling of a large land mass. The most important monsoons occur in the Indian and western Pacific Oceans where the huge land mass of Asia is the dominant factor. Only in the western part of the Arabian Sea and the northern part of the China Sea does a monsoon wind reach gale force; for the most part the winds are no more than fresh, about force 5 on the * Beaufort Scale. There are three recognized monsoons, the South-West monsoon which blows from about May to September over the northern Indian Ocean and western North Pacific, the North-East monsoon which blows over the same areas from about October to April, and the North-West monsoon which blows from about November to March over parts of the Indian Ocean and western Pacific Ocean south of the equator. This last is in effect the North-East monsoon after it crosses the equator where the reversed effect of the earth's rotation changes it into a north-westerly wind.

MONTAGU or **MOUNTAGU,** EDWARD, 1st Earl of Sandwich (1625–72), English admiral, was originally a soldier, his sea career beginning in 1653 when he was made a * general-at-sea. He took a prominent part in the restoration of Charles II in 1660 and was raised to the peerage as Earl of Sandwich. He commanded a squadron of the English fleet during the Second Dutch War (1665–7) and was present at the battle of * Lowestoft in 1665. He became commander-in-chief later the same year but fell into trouble over the plundering of some rich prizes which he had captured and was removed from the navy. During the Third Dutch War (1672–4) he again commanded a squadron and was present at the battle off * Solebay where his ship, the *Royal George*, was set on fire and blown up, his body being recovered from the sea some days later. He was the patron of Samuel * Pepys, for whom he obtained his first Admiralty post, and is the 'My Lord' who appears so frequently in the famous diary.

MONTAGU, JOHN, 4th earl of Sandwich (1718–92), British statesman, entered politics at an early age and became a * Lord Commissioner of the Admiralty in 1744. He was First Lord from 1749 to 1752, and again in 1763, an ambivalent period of his life during which he showed a fair degree of administrative skill in naval affairs while at the same time earning considerable notoriety as a gambler, a rake, and a friend of John Wilkes, whom he subsequently betrayed in a prosecution for obscene libel, thereby acquiring the nickname of 'Jemmy Twitcher', the character in Gay's *The Beggar's Opera* who betrayed Captain Macheath, his friend. Sandwich was a member of the notorious Hellfire Club at Medmenham, and is remembered in naval circles as the only First Lord who kept a resident mistress at Admiralty House. This period of his life is also commemorated in the word 'sandwich', an invention of his by which supper need not interfere with his gambling.

He was again First Lord of the Admiralty between 1771 and 1782 when, as the Prime Minister's (Lord North) right-hand man, he suffered the disasters and humiliations of the American War of Independence (1775–82), a series of naval setbacks which were at least due as much to the incompetence of his admirals as to their distrust of him. Yet his abilities as an administrator and his services to the navy during these years were considerable.

It was due to his advocacy that the coppering of ships' bottoms was introduced, which greatly improved their sailing performance and inhibited the growth of weed and barnacles, and he was also responsible for the adoption of the carronade (see GUNS, NAVAL) into the armament of British warships. He had also a great interest in exploration, and in conjunction with the Royal Society promoted the three voyages of discovery of Captain James * Cook, the Hawaiian group of islands being named the Sandwich Islands by Cook in his honour.

In a minor sphere, it was he who introduced the 'classical' names for ships into the Royal Navy, many of which have become famous and are retained to this day.

MONTGERY, JACQUES MERIGNON DE (1782–1839), French naval officer and author, was an officer in the *squadron of Commodore Hoche in the attempted but unsuccessful French invasion of Ireland in 1796, and later served on the staff of Admiral Bruix. He was in Admiral *Villeneuve's fleet at the indecisive action off *Ferrol following the French fleet's return from the West Indies in 1805, and was also in the battle of *Trafalgar a few weeks later. He was an officer with thought and beliefs far in advance of his time, and startled naval opinion in France when he published in 1814 his *Memoir on Iron Ships*. He also wrote *The New Naval Force* (1822) in which he set out his ideas of a modern navy for France, which included the building of iron ships and the introduction of mechanical propulsion. He also wrote a treatise on rockets, in which he compared their performance favourably with that of guns. Although these writings attracted a large amount of interest in French naval circles, they became devalued when Montgery later lost his reason and had to be kept under surveillance.

MONTREAL, a city and seaport of Canada at the junction of the Ottawa and St. Lawrence rivers, nearly 1,000 miles inland. The opening within the last few years of the St. Lawrence Seaway gives all the year round access to the port of Montreal for the largest ships; before its opening Montreal was closed by ice during the four winter months. The present city is built on the site of a Red Indian village named Hochelaga. Jacques *Cartier was the first European to travel up the St. Lawrence as far as the present city, reaching it in 1535, and seventy-six years later, in 1611, the first governor of French Canada, Samuel de *Champlain, established a trading post on the site of Hochelaga. The building of the city was begun by Paul de Chomedey de Maisonneuve in 1642. In 1760 Montreal capitulated to the British in the face of attack by three British armies converging on the city from different directions while a British fleet held the great St. Lawrence waterway, and with its capitulation the whole of Canada fell from French into British control.

The wealth of Montreal as a great seaport was built on grain, grown in vast quantities on the Canadian prairies. Today the port handles a very considerable proportion of all the imports and exports of Canada.

'MOONLIGHT BATTLE', THE, see ST. VINCENT, BATTLE OF.

MOON-LORE. From the earliest times the phases of the moon have been of import to seamen, and the regularity of its movements provided a means for recording the passage of time. The moon was credited with considerable influence on the weather and Virgil (70–19 B.C.) summarized some of the popular beliefs concerning it in one of his Georgics. According to Pliny (A.D. 23–79) the fourth and fifth days of new moon were to be watched with particular care. A new moon with horns erect on the fourth day was believed to forecast great storms at sea. The Venerable Bede (673–735) in his *De Natura Rerum* says of the moon, 'If she looks like gold in her last quarter, there will be wind, if on top of the crescent black spots appear, it will be a rainy month, if in the middle, her full moon will be serene.' A star-dogged moon was regarded by sailors as a bad omen, and reference to this phenomenon is to be found in an old Scottish ballad of 1281, 'Sir Patrick Spens', and also in Samuel Taylor Coleridge's 'The Rime of the *Ancient Mariner'. In several of his plays, Shakespeare refers to the popular beliefs concerning the moon which, in *Hamlet*, he describes as 'The moist star upon whose influence Neptune's empire stands'.

While many of the superstitions regarding the moon are not supported by modern meteorology, the lunar haloes to which Varro (116–27 B.C.) refers as foretelling wind from the brightest quarter of the circle, with a double circle indicating a violent storm, are well authenticated as precursors of bad weather.

Although the Greek astronomer *Ptolemy, who lived at Alexandria during the 2nd century A.D., appreciated the connection between the movements of the moon and the *tides, it was not until Sir Isaac Newton (1642–1727) discovered the law of universal gravitation that this phenomenon was satisfactorily explained.

MOONRAKERS, names given to the small light sails set above the *skysails of square-rigged ships in very fine weather. They are also often called moonsails or *raffees. See also 'HOPE-IN-HEAVENS', 'PUFF-BALLS', 'SAVE-ALLS', 'TRUST-TO-GODS'.

MOOR, to, in its strict meaning the condition of a ship when she lies in a harbour or anchorage with two *anchors down and the ship middled between them. When a ship is moored in this fashion it is usual to bring both cables to a mooring swivel just below the *hawseholes so

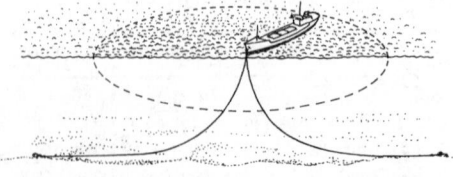

Ship moored

that the ship may swing to the tide without getting a *foul hawse; that is, without getting her cables crossed. The word is also loosely used to describe other ways of anchoring a ship using two anchors, e.g., when a ship has a stern anchor laid out she is said to be moored head and stern, and is today also widely used to describe a vessel which is secured head and stern to a quay or alongside another vessel, or which lies with the bow secured to a quay and an anchor laid out astern. See also MOORING.

MOORE, Sir ALAN HILARY (1882–1959), British maritime author, was one of the original founders of the *Society for Nautical Research and served on the committee formed by that society to restore H.M.S. *Victory* to the condition in which she was at the time of the battle of *Trafalgar. Among his many books the best-known are *The Last Days of Mast and Sail* (1925) and *Sailing Ships of War, 1800–60* (1926).

MOORING, a permanent position in harbours and estuaries to which ships can secure without using their own *anchors. For large ships, a mooring consists of two or three large anchors laid out on the bottom and connected with a chain *bridle, from the centre of which a length of chain *cable leads upward to a large mooring *buoy, to the ring of which a ship can lie in safety by shackling on her own cable. The vertical cable is short enough to ensure that the ship swings with the tide within her own length. Smaller moorings for smaller ships may require only one anchor or a block of concrete, with a chain rising to a small buoy. For yachts, a very small buoy, light enough to be lifted easily on board with a boathook, is attached by a length of rope to a light chain, itself attached to a concrete block, and the mooring is hauled up until the chain reaches the surface and the yacht secured with it. See also TROT.

MOORSOM'S RULE, a mathematical formula for determining the cubic capacity of ships. It came into force in 1849 on the recommendation of a committee under the chairmanship of Admiral Moorsom set up by the British Admiralty at the request of the Board of Trade to recommend rules for assessing the *tonnage of ships. By dividing the calculated cubic capacity of the entire British merchant fleet by the total of its registered tonnage, the figure of 98·22 was arrived at. Moorsom suggested that the figure of 100 cubic feet of capacity per gross ton should be adopted, and it is on this basis that the gross tonnage of ships is calculated.

MORDAL, JACQUES, the nom de plume of Hervé Pierre *Cras.

MOREELL, BEN (1892–   ), American admiral, was born in Utah and graduated from Washington University, St. Louis, in 1913 after a course in civil engineering. After the declaration of war against Germany in 1917 he entered the civil engineer corps of the U.S. Navy. He became chief of the Navy Department's Bureau of Yards and Docks in December 1937 and in that post formed the navy construction battalions which became known as 'Seabees'. These organizations of trained construction men and engineers went into the forward areas where they laid out roads, manned floating *dry-docks, and built the necessary facilities for advance bases. In addition they were taught to fight, which they did effectively on many occasions when enemy attacks developed. Moreell's services were so effective that he became the first officer belonging to a staff corps of the U.S. Navy who reached the rank of vice admiral. He was later advanced to the rank of admiral.

MOREL-FATIO, ANTOINE LÉON (1810–71), French marine painter, was born at Rouen. He was present as an official artist at the bombardment of Algiers by the French Navy in 1830, which finally brought to an end the *piracy endemic for centuries along the North African seaboard, and a picture which he painted of that attack brought him immediate recognition. He was again an official artist appointed to accompany an expedition to French Guinea in 1854, and was so well regarded that he became director of the important *Musée de la Marine in Paris, at that time housed in the Louvre, on the terrace of which Morel-Fatio died of an apoplectic fit. Under his direction the museum was greatly expanded, and a collection of his pictures can be seen there.

MORESBY, JOHN (1830–1922), British admiral, is remembered for his exploration of the coast of New Guinea, the siting of Port Moresby, and the finding of gold during a voyage from 1871 to 1874 in the *Basilisk*. Ostensibly the ship's purpose was to stop the exploitation of natives in the pearl fishery, and Moresby had to find an excuse for his other activities by instituting a search for a missing explorer. Thus he explored and surveyed 1,000 miles of coastline and off-lying islands, many of which he annexed in Queen Victoria's name. His surveys made possible a quicker route between Australia and China.

Moresby's career in the navy from 1842 had seen him in the Baltic under Bartholomew *Sulivan during the Crimean War (1854–6), and he commanded two ships on the China station between 1858 and 1864. After his voyage in the *Basilisk* he was captain in charge at Bermuda until his retirement as a rear admiral in 1881.

MORGAN, Sir HENRY (*c.* 1635–88), English
*buccaneer, was born at Llanrhymney in
Glamorganshire. His early life is obscure until he
emerged as the leader of a band of buccaneers at
Jamaica in 1662. His most notable exploit was in
1671 when he captured Porto Bello and Panama,
having led a band of buccaneers, among whom
was Bartholomew *Sharp, in the first land crossing of the Isthmus of Panama in force. Since
England was at peace with Spain at the time he
was recalled home under arrest, but with war
against Spain threatening once more, he was
knighted by Charles II and sent out to Jamaica as
deputy-governor. In this capacity he proved a
scourge to the buccaneers and an embarrassment
to successive governors of the island. He died a
rich landowner at Lawrencefield, Jamaica.

Morgan's character has been traduced ever
since the publication of *Esquemeling's
Bucaniers of America in 1684, though he won a
libel action against the printers. He was a fine
leader of men, no more cruel or rapacious than
others, and a good tactician.

MORGAN GILES, FRANCIS CHARLES
(1883–1964), British naval architect, was one of
the best known of the English yacht designers
and builders from the early years of the century.
At an early age he set up in business on his own
in London with a small boatyard at Hammer-
smith but moved to larger premises at Hythe,
Southampton, in 1908. He proved a highly successful designer of 6-metre class yachts and in
his own *Jonquil* he won forty-four first prizes in
one season.

During the First World War (1914–18) he
obtained a commission in the Royal Naval
Volunteer Reserve and served throughout the
war in command of motor patrol craft. Soon
after the end of the war he bought a near-derelict
shipyard at Teignmouth, Devon, and from its
slipways have come over 1,000 yachts and boats
of all descriptions noted for their fine design and
construction. In 1927 he represented Britain in
the International Seawanhaka Cup races in the
U.S.A. in his own designed 6-metre *English
Rose*, while he was also a leading figure in the
introduction of the 14-ft International dinghy
class. During the Second World War his yard
produced over one hundred *motor torpedoboats for the Admiralty. He remained an active
member of the firm he had founded until his death.

MORISON, SAMUEL ELIOT (1887–1976),
American naval historian, was born at Boston,
graduated from Harvard University with a Ph.D.
in 1912, and became a member of the faculty in
1915. During the First World War (1914–18)
he served in the U.S. Army, and was a delegate at
the Peace Conference in Paris in 1919. Returning to the academic life, he devoted his energies
to historical research, particularly in the sphere
of exploration and discovery by sea, and by his
energy in research and great gift in teaching
quickly made himself one of the foremost
American historians of his time, receiving wide
recognition with the award of an honorary M.A.
at Oxford in 1922 and a Litt.D. at Harvard in
1936.

With the entry in 1941 of the U.S.A. in the
Second World War, Morison was specially
selected by President Roosevelt as official historian of the U.S. Navy, and for this purpose was
commissioned as lieutenant-commander in the
U.S. Naval Reserve so that he could serve afloat
in all combat areas to gain first-hand knowledge
of naval operations during the war. During the
four and a half years of the war he rose in rank
to rear admiral, visited and served in all the naval
commands, and amassed a wealth of first-hand
material on which to base his official history.
This was published in fifteen volumes between
1947 and 1962, a massive, detailed work under
the title *History of U.S. Naval Operations in
World War II* which covered exhaustively every
aspect of the naval war in the Atlantic, Arctic,
Pacific, and Indian Oceans. The speed with
which the volumes were written and the extraordinary detail in which the complex naval
operations were described and analysed form a
lasting monument to Morison's capacity and
industry as a historian.

He had, before the war, already written three
exceptional maritime histories, two of which
were published before the American entry into
the war and the third during the war. They were
Portuguese Voyages to America (1940), *The
Maritime History of Massachusetts* (1941),
and *Admiral of the Ocean Sea: A Life of
Christopher Columbus* (1942), the last-named
recognized universally as the standard work on
this subject. He later wrote another book on
*Columbus, *Christopher Columbus, Mariner*
(1955), which in some ways amplified in a more
popular form his previous biography. Since the
war he has continued his vast programme of
historical research, and has had published many
outstanding books, among which the best known
are *John Paul Jones: A Sailor's Biography*
(1950), *By Land and By Sea* (1953), and *The
European Discovery of America* of which the first
volume, *The Northern Voyages*, was published
in 1971 and the second, *The Southern Voyages*,
in 1974. His biography of John Paul *Jones, like
that of Columbus, is generally accepted as the
standard work.

His historical work has been recognized by
many awards. He won the Pulitzer Prize twice,
for his biographies of Columbus and Paul Jones,
and in 1963 received the first Balzan Foundation
Award in History in a worldwide competition
against some fifty living historians. President

Lyndon Johnson presented him with the Presidential Medal of Freedom for his historical work, and he has also received the gold medal of the American Academy of Arts and Letters, the Emerson-Thoreau medal of the American Academy of Arts and Sciences, and the Francis Parkman medal of the Society of American Historians.

MOROGUES, SEBASTIEN FRANÇOIS BIGOT, Vicomte de (1705–81), transferred to the French Navy after an earlier career as an officer of artillery and became *chef d'escadre* (*commodore) in 1764. He had founded, in 1752, the Académie Marine at Brest, an establishment set up to study the art of manoeuvring fleets and of improving the code of signals then in force in the French Navy. He became intensely interested in this subject and published in 1763 his *Treatise on Evolutions and Signals*, a system far in advance of contemporary thinking on those subjects in the British Royal Navy. It was not until the British naval signal system was taken in hand by Lord *Howe and Rear Admiral *Kempenfelt towards the end of the 18th century that the British Navy was able to match the advances in the art created by Bigot de Morogues. See also SIGNALS AT SEA.

MORRELL, BENJAMIN (*fl.* 1820–30), American sealer, made a claim that in March 1823 he had penetrated the Weddell Sea in Antarctica to a position of 70° 14′ S., 40° 03′ W. The claim was made only a month after James Weddell's voyage to the same region and, if true, would predate Sir Ernest Shackleton's voyage to the same region by nearly a century. Morrell also claimed to have coasted along part of a land which he called New South Greenland, now thought to be non-existent. His reputation for hyperbole has tended to cast suspicion on both claims.

MORSE CODE, a method of signalling much used at sea. It was invented by Samuel Finley Breese Morse (1791–1872), who got the first ideas for his invention during a voyage on board the *packet ship *Sully*. He nearly starved to death while perfecting his invention, only to discover that most of the nations to whom he offered it refused to give him a patent for it. Eventually, however, the U.S. government gave him an appropriation to cover his costs, and the first Morse signals were passed between Washington and Baltimore on 24 May 1844. In 1858 most nations in Europe contributed 400,000 francs as payment to him for the use they had made of his invention. The Morse code was one of the best methods of signalling at sea until the introduction of the radio-telephone, its system of alphabetical and numerical symbols made up of dots and dashes making it as easy to transmit in sound, as by wireless; in light, as by *searchlight or *Aldis lamp; or by motion, with hand signal flags. It was a quick and easy code to master, and has proved invaluable for communication at sea. See APPENDIX 2.

MOSES, a very broad flat-bottomed boat which in the days of sailing ships was used in the Caribbean to bring hogsheads of sugar from the island beaches to shipping which had to lie off because of the shallowness of the water inshore. They were propelled by oars.

MOSQUITO CRAFT, a generic name, particularly in the U.S.A., to encompass all fast minor warships, driven by internal combustion engines, armed with guns, *torpedoes, or guided missiles.

MOTHER CAREY'S CHICKENS, the name given by sailors to small sea birds (*Procellaria pelagica*), the presence of which near a ship was supposed to indicate the approach of a storm. The name Mother Carey derives from the latin Mater Cara whose birds—*Aves Sanctae Mariae*—they were supposed to be. French sailors call them *les oiseaux de Notre Dame*. The bird is ordinarily known as the Storm Petrel, a corruption of the Italian Petrello or little Peter, a name bestowed on it because of its ability to run lightly over the surface of the sea, thus imitating St. Peter's achievement of walking on the water.

MOTOR GUNBOAT (M.G.B.), a small fast warship built in large numbers during the Second World War by several of the combatant navies, designed mainly for anti-shipping patrols in coastal waters. Those built for the British Navy, which may be taken as reasonably typical of all such craft, were of two sizes, the larger with a length of 110 feet, the smaller with a length of around 70 feet. They mounted one 2-pounder gun and four 0·5-inch anti-aircraft guns. The majority had two shafts, though some were built with three, and they were driven by 8- or 12-cylinder petrol engines at a speed of up to 40 knots.

MOTOR TORPEDOBOAT (M.T.B), a small warship propelled by internal combustion petrol engines and armed with two upper deck *torpedo tubes and one or two small anti-aircraft guns. They were built in large numbers by most of the combatant navies during the Second World War (known as *Schnellboote* in the German Navy and as Mosquito craft in the U.S.A.) for naval warfare, mainly in an anti-shipping role, in coastal waters. The British motor torpedoboats, which were somewhat smaller than those of most other navies, were about 70 feet long on average, and driven by three petrol internal combustion engines at a speed of up to 40 knots, or by two at around 28 knots. See also E-BOAT, FAST PATROL BOAT.

MOULDING, the shipbuilder's term to describe the depth of any member of a ship's construction, such as her *frames, *keelson, *keel, *stern, *sternpost, *beams, etc. The width measurement is known as the *siding.

MOULD-LOFT, a long building with a considerable floor area on which a *naval architect's draught, or lines, of various parts of the hull of a newly designed vessel can be laid off in their full dimensions. These full-dimensional drawings can then be moulded, with the aid of *moulds, to provide the patterns to which the steel angle frames, in the case of ships built of steel, or the *timbers, in the case of a wooden-hulled vessel, are bent or shaped. See also SHIPBUILDING.

MOULDS, the name given to the thin, flexible lengths of wood used on the floor of a *mould-loft to form a pattern of the various *frames used in the construction of the *hull of a vessel. Being flexible, the moulds can be easily bent to take up the required shape, and they form the pattern from which in the actual construction of the ship, the steel frames are shaped to the design of the naval architect. In a wooden-hulled vessel, they form the pattern to which the *timbers are to be shaped. See also SHIPBUILDING, modern developments.

MOUNTBATTEN, LOUIS ALEXANDER, 1st Marquess of Milford Haven (formerly Prince Louis Alexander of Battenberg) (1854–1921), British admiral of the fleet, was the eldest son of Prince Alexander of Hesse and the Rhine, and grandson of Louis II, Grand Duke of Hesse and the Rhine. He settled in England as a boy and became naturalized, entering the Royal Navy in 1868. His early career was one of distinction throughout and his promotion was rapid. In 1894, as a captain, he was made secretary of the naval and military committee on defence which later developed into the Committee of Imperial Defence. In 1900 he became assistant director of naval intelligence, and after a year's service in the Mediterranean, he returned to the Admiralty in 1902 as director. Admiral Sir John *Fisher, who came to the Admiralty as First Sea Lord in 1904, had already marked Battenberg for high command. On promotion to flag rank he was appointed to command a *cruiser squadron, and in 1907 became second-in-command of the Mediterranean Fleet. In 1908 he was selected as commander-in-chief of the Atlantic Fleet, and three years later joined the Admiralty Board as Second Sea Lord. On the retirement of Admiral

Sir Francis Bridgeman he was made First Sea Lord by the Prime Minister on nomination to that post by Mr. Winston *Churchill, then First Lord of the Admiralty.

It was in this appointment that, in July 1914, Battenberg was faced with the decision whether or not to keep the reserve fleet in commission on completion of the test mobilization in view of the threatening situation in Europe. Mr. Churchill was absent from the Admiralty during the critical days and the decision rested with Battenberg. It was due to his initiative and understanding of the situation that when the declaration of war came on 4 August the reserve ships and their crews were not dispersed.

Shortly after the outbreak of war a scurrilous press campaign was started, concentrating on Battenberg's German origins. His great patriotism and love for England led him to resign his position as First Sea Lord.

In 1917, at the request of the king, he relinquished his title as Prince of Battenberg and assumed the name of Mountbatten. He was created Marquess of Milford Haven in the same year. He married Princess Victoria of Hesse and the Rhine, the granddaughter of Queen Victoria.

During his career in the navy he was responsible for many improvements in naval techniques, particularly in gunnery and signals, and among his many inventions was the course indicator which bore his name. He was a founder member of the *Navy Records Society, later becoming its president, and was the author of the standard work on medals and decorations. He also wrote a useful little book on warship names in the Royal Navy.

MOUNTBATTEN, LOUIS FRANCIS ALBERT VICTOR NICHOLAS (1900–), Earl Mountbatten of Burma, British admiral of the fleet, was the younger son of Prince Louis of Battenberg (see MOUNTBATTEN, Louis Alexander) and a great-grandson of Queen Victoria. He joined the R.N. College Osborne as a cadet in 1913 and served during the First World War (1914–18) in Admiral *Beatty's flagships *Lion and *Queen Elizabeth as *midshipman; and was second-in-command of patrol-boat P.31 as a sub-lieutenant. After two terms at Christ's College, Cambridge, in 1919, he acted for the greater part of the next three years as A.D.C. to the Prince of Wales during his two Empire tours in H.M.S. Renown. Soon after his return he married Edwina Ashley, a considerable heiress.

Their wealth and brilliant social life led to Lord Louis being sometimes mistaken for a 'playboy'; whereas, in fact, he was a hard-working and highly efficient naval officer, particularly in the field of radio communications in which he specialized in 1924, holding several appointments as W/T officer on the staff before

Admiral of the Fleet Earl Mountbatten of Burma

becoming Fleet W/T officer in the Mediterranean in 1931 under Admiral Sir W. W. Fisher. In 1934 he obtained his first command, the new *destroyer *Daring*, shifting thence to H.M.S. *Wishart*. Experience of another branch of the navy came with his appointment in 1936 to the Naval Air Division of the Admiralty.

When the Second World War broke out, Mountbatten, recently promoted captain, was in command of H.M.S. *Kelly* and the 5th Destroyer Flotilla. Going to the assistance of a tanker which had been mined, the *Kelly* was herself mined and badly damaged. She was again put out of action in collision with H.M.S. *Mohawk* early in 1940, but was repaired in time to play an outstanding part in the evacuation of the allied force from Namsos after the German invasion of Norway in May 1940. Soon afterwards she was torpedoed by a German *motor torpedoboat off the Dutch coast. Mountbatten's successful salvage of the *Kelly* under incessant air attack made an epic story of courage and endurance.

His luck was still out, however, when he embarked in the *Javelin* to lead the flotilla against a German destroyer force in the Channel on 29 November 1940. The *Javelin* was torpedoed in the bow and stern and reached port only by a narrow margin. In April 1941 the 5th Flotilla

was ordered to Malta and on 21 May was thrown into the battle for the defence of Crete. There the *Kelly* was sunk by dive-bombers on the 23rd. This brought Mountbatten's destroyer career to an end. In October 1941 he was selected by the Prime Minister, Winston *Churchill, for the appointment of adviser on combined operations, with the rank of *commodore, which he held in 1941–2, becoming the chief of combined operations in April 1942 with the concurrent ranks of vice admiral, air marshal, and lieutenant-general. While he was at its head, this command brought off the brilliant raids on St. Nazaire, Vaagso, and Bruneval, but was also responsible to some degree for the disastrous operation at Dieppe. It played a large part in planning the landing operations in North Africa and Sicily, and much of the technology and planning for the invasion of Normandy in 1944 was set on foot under Mountbatten's aegis before, in October 1943, he was appointed Supreme Allied Commander, South-East Asia. There he set about raising the morale of the allied forces in Burma which had come to believe themselves a 'forgotten army'. The first major operations under Mountbatten's supreme command were the desperate defensive battles in the Arakan and, farther north, at Imphal and Kohima.

Hopes of outflanking the Japanese by combined operations on the coast foundered on the shortage of landing craft and other naval units, few of which could be spared from other theatres. It was thus largely by a frontal assault that the reconquest of Burma was finally achieved during 1945. The amphibious operation to capture Malaya and *Singapore which was planned for later that year had not been launched at the time of the surrender of the Japanese government, though it was later mounted against no opposition. On 12 September 1945, in the presence of representatives of all the allies, Mountbatten accepted the formal surrender of the Japanese expeditionary force, Southern Region, in the Municipal Building, Singapore.

In June 1946, after relinquishing the post of Supreme Commander, Mountbatten was raised to the peerage as Viscount Mountbatten of Burma. He then prepared to return to his naval career; but in February 1947 the Prime Minister, Clement Attlee, asked him to assume the post of Viceroy of India with the task of organizing the transference of sovereignty of India from the British crown to the people of India. His liberal views and the terms of friendship he established with Indian leaders made him ideally suitable for the post. Independence was achieved within five months of his arrival, though in the form of the two independent states of India and Pakistan and in the presence of widespread inter-communal massacres and riots in various parts of both territories.

Created Earl Mountbatten of Burma, he continued to serve as Governor-General of India under the new constitution until June 1948, when he returned home and reverted to the rank of rear admiral to command the First Cruiser Squadron in the Mediterranean. Subsequently he served as Fourth Sea Lord, 1950–2; commander-in-chief in the Mediterranean (concurrently holding the post of Commander-in-Chief Allied Forces Mediterranean), 1953–4; First Sea Lord, 1955–9; and Chief of the Defence Staff, 1959–64. Perhaps his most outstanding achievement in the last of these appointments was to be the moving spirit behind the reorganization of the three individual Service ministries into a single, co-ordinated Ministry of Defence in 1964.

MOUSE, a stop made of *spunyarn fixed to the collar of the *stays in a square-rigged ship to hold the running eye of the rigging from slipping down the stay. It is also a mark fixed on the *braces and other rigging of the *yards to indicate when they are square. In general, any small collar made with spunyarn round a wire or rope with the object of holding something in place, such as an *eye threaded on the rope, would be called a mouse.

MOUSE A HOOK, to, the operation of passing two or three turns of *spunyarn across the jaw of a hook to prevent it jumping out of a ringbolt or *eye into which it has been hooked, or to prevent a rope running across the hook from jumping clear.

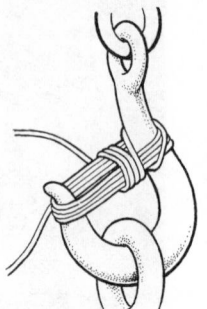

Hook half moused; to be finished with more turns and a reef knot

MUDHOOK, the sailor's slang name for an *anchor.

MULBERRY HARBOUR, an artificial harbour constructed during the Second World War off the coast of Normandy in 1944 to supply the allied invasion of northern France designed to liberate that country from its German occupation. The concept of artificial and prefabricated harbours was born after the abortive amphibious raid on Dieppe in 1942 of which the object was to discover whether a fortified harbour could be seized, without undue damage to its harbour facilities, and held against counter-attacks. The costly experience of Dieppe proved that this was not possible, and plans were therefore put in hand to provide artificial harbours and shelters through which the allied invading armies could be maintained and supplied until large well-equipped ports could be captured during the subsequent advance.

The original plan was to provide sheltered water off the five assault beaches by means of an artificial *breakwater composed of *blockships brought across the English Channel under their own steam and *scuttled in line. These five breakwaters were known as 'gooseberries' and were at Verreville, St. Laurent, Arromanches, Courseulles, and Ouistreham, the individual ships comprising them being known as 'corncobs'. Two obsolete *battleships, the *Centurion* (British) and *Courbet* (French), two old *cruisers, the *Durban* (British) and *Sumatra* (Dutch), and fifty-five merchant ships were used for this purpose. Two of the 'gooseberries', one off the British assault beaches and the other off the American, were then to be developed into artificial harbours by being prolonged and turned shorewards by sinking prefabricated *caissons of

The Mulberry harbour off the Normandy coast showing the prefabricated breakwater with a calm sea inside

steel and concrete, known as 'phoenix', to form two harbours each the size of *Dover harbour. In all, 213 caissons were required, of which the largest were 60 metres (200 ft) long, 17 metres (55 ft) wide, and 18 metres (60 ft) deep.

Inside these two harbours were floating piers, known as 'whales', consisting of articulated steel roadway supported on *pontoons, with specially designed pierheads, anchored to the ground with four legs to keep them in position but free to float up and down with the tide, so that unloading could take place at any state of the tide. These piers could deal with all shallow draught vessels engaged in supplying the armies. For larger ships an additional breakwater to seaward of the harbour was provided, composed of heavy steel floating structures known as 'bombardons', cruciform in section and each 200 feet (60 m) long and 25 feet (7·6 m) high.

The whole assembly was known as a 'Mulberry'. They were designed and built in Britain and in all amounted to a fraction short of 2,000,000 tons of concrete and steel. With the exception of the 'corncobs', which proceeded under their own steam, each section was towed across the Channel by tugs and fitted together on the far shore somewhat in the manner of a jig-saw puzzle. The 'Mulberry' off the British beaches at Arromanches became operational within two or three weeks of the initial assault landings, but that off the American beaches on the eastern side of the Cherbourg peninsula broke up in the exceptionally heavy weather

which followed the landings. All were dismantled after the end of the war.

MULGRAVE, 2nd Baron, see PHIPPS, Constantine John.

MULIER, PIETER (1615–70), Dutch marine painter, was born at Haarlem and became a member of the Guild of that city in 1640. Few details are known of his life beyond the fact that he was an artist of considerable merit who specialized in painting ships in stormy seas. His son PIETER (1637–1701), who was taught to paint in his father's studio, became known as 'Tempesta' Mulier because of his addiction to painting storm scenes. More is known of him than of his father, for he murdered his wife after falling in love with another girl. He was arrested and condemned to death, but his sentence was commuted to five years in prison. Although he lived for much of his life in Italy, the gentler Mediterranean scene never seduced him from his earlier love of the sea in its fiercer moods of storm and tempest.

MULTI-HULL, a type of vessel formed of two or more hulls or floats which is propelled by paddles, sails, or mechanical power. Sailing *catamarans (two identical hulls) and *trimarans (a central hull with twin floats) have been built during the 20th century in large numbers and increasing sizes for ocean voyaging and racing. Craft having more than one hull have been known in the Indian and Pacific Oceans for many hundreds of years but their use in the western

The trimaran Toria

hemisphere is of comparatively recent growth. In 1874 the London, Chatham, and Dover Railway built a twin-hulled ferry of 1,533 gross tons, named the *Castalia*, for their cross-Channel service, and followed her a few years later with the *Calais-Douvres* of 1,820 gross tons. Both these vessels were propelled by paddle-wheels working between the two identical hulls.

The advantages of a multi-hull design are lightness and stability, and therefore, when used as sailing craft, an increase in speed for a given sail area. In a moderate or fresh wind from the *beam or forward of the beam the catamaran is faster than the conventially rigged yachts and speeds of more than 20 knots have been recorded in quite small craft. But a disadvantage of a catamaran is that in a strong puff of wind or a squall she is likely to lift her weather hull out of the water, and beyond a certain point she

becomes unstable and capsizes. A trimaran cannot capsize, but if she is driven hard she can bury her bows in the sea and turn stern over bows. In both catamarans and trimarans, their stiffness (i.e., inability to *roll because of their basic design) imposes a considerable strain on hull and rigging, and in a seaway the structural stresses are considerable.

Many long voyages, however, including circumnavigations, have been made in multi-hulls.

MUNCASTER, CLAUD (1903–74), British landscape and marine painter and author, was born at West Chillington, Sussex, the son of a well-known landscape artist, Oliver Hall. He began his professional career as a landscape artist in 1919 and three years later took the nom de plume of Claud Muncaster to free himself from the shadow of his distinguished father. He became a regular exhibitor at the Royal Academy and held his first one-man exhibition in London in 1926. He travelled extensively by sea and in 1931 signed on as a seaman for the voyage of the *barque *Olivebank* from Melbourne to Britain via Cape Horn. During the Second World War he joined the Royal Navy as a navigator and later as adviser on camouflage until invalided in 1944. After the war he travelled widely, recording his travels in a series of vivid sea pictures in which his great knowledge of ships and the sea ensured accuracy of detail. He also painted a number of commissions for the Union Castle Steamship Company, and in 1967 commemorated Sir Francis *Chichester's memorable single-handed voyage round the world with a painting showing *Gipsy Moth IV* rounding Cape Horn. He estimated that in fifty years he had painted some 4,500 pictures.

MUNICH (München), West Germany, an inland town but notable as the home of the *Deutsches Museum von Meisterwerken der Naturwissenschaft und Technik, which has a considerable marine section of outstanding interest.

MUNK, JENS ERIKSON (1579–1628), Danish explorer and admiral, was born near Arendal, Norway, and at the age of 12 went to sea with his parents, who settled in Bahia, South America. He was back in Europe in 1601 and for four years was employed by a shipping firm trading in the Baltic, in which he learned seamanship and navigation. In 1605 he became a shipowner on his own account and in 1609 determined to try to discover a *North-East passage from Europe to the Far East to open up a trade with the rich countries known to exist there. He set sail with two ships to pass north of Novaya Zemlya, but his own vessel was wrecked off Kolguyer Island and he and his crew were rescued by his consort, which put into Archangel on the way home. On his return to Denmark he was able to interest Christian IV in his plans to open up a northern trade route to China and Japan, and the king placed him in command of another expedition to discover the passage. With two ships, the *Angelibrand* which he commanded, and the *Rytteren*, under the command of Knud Madsen, he set out for Novaya Zemlya in 1610, but got no further than Kildin Island where the ships were stopped by the ice.

In 1611 Sweden and Denmark declared war and Munk was commissioned as a captain in the Royal Danish Navy. When the war ended two years later, he returned to his original shipping interests, but disappointed in the two failures to find a North-East passage, determined to attempt the discovery of a *North-West passage and was again able to interest Christian IV in the project. He was appointed to the command of a naval expedition for this purpose consisting of the *frigate *Enhiornigen* and the *sloop *Lamprenen*. The two ships left Denmark in May 1619 and wintered in Hudson Bay, intending to find the long-sought-for passage the following summer. But during the long winter the crews of the two ships were ravaged by *scurvy and, greatly weakened, Munk was forced to return home.

The Thirty Years War, which had broken out in Europe in 1618, was beginning to involve the Scandinavian countries by 1625, and Christian IV once again called on Munk, giving him command of a squadron of six ships with the rank of admiral. He was sent on *blockade duties off the mouth of the River Weser but died three years later on board his flagship.

MURDERER, a small iron or brass hand gun fitted with an iron pin on the stock which was inserted into a socket so that the gun could be traversed easily by hand. Sockets for these guns were fitted in several places in a ship so that they could be rapidly taken where most needed at the time. They were purely anti-personnel guns, loaded with ball and small pieces of jagged iron for use against *boarders, and were more or less standard supply in all merchant ships up to the beginning of the 19th century, particularly for defence against *privateers in the *guerre de course*. Their use in navies went out during the early 18th century when *marines, or soldiers in lieu, became a permanent part of the warship's complement, these being employed in battle as marksmen to shoot down individuals in an enemy ship and boarders as they scrambled over the side, thus making murderers unnecessary.

MURRAY, Sir JOHN (1841–1914), British geographer, was appointed naturalist to the *Challenger* voyage in 1872, editing the reports and being co-author of the narrative of the cruise. He interested himself in the study of oceanography and published many valuable papers on the subject. In 1880–2, he carried out an extensive exploration of the Faeroe channel.

MUSÉE DE LA CHAMBRE DE COMMERCE, Marseilles, France, depicts the history of merchant shipping, with particular reference to the port of Marseilles and the Provence area. It contains a few models of ships and one of the harbour and its environs, together with some 600 nautical instruments, but the main attraction is the collection of some 8,000 paintings, drawings, engravings, and plans, and a library, open to the public, of 250,000 books.

MUSÉE DE LA MARINE, Paris, a famous collection which owes its origin to the one-time Minister of Marine, Jean Baptiste *Colbert. In 1679, with the approval of Louis XIV, he ordered the construction of scale models of French warships, which form an important part of the exhibits, together with the notable collection of paintings by *Vernet which were added in 1801. The exhibition's first home was in the Louvre where it was assembled in 1827 and opened to the public six years later. In 1943 it was moved to its present site in a wing of the Palais de Chaillot, situated on an eminence in the heart of Paris. Its theme is to portray French maritime history and it owes much for the variety and extent of its 8,700 exhibits to Admiral *Paris, curator from 1871 to 1893. Among the 450 models is one of the 44-gun *frigate Le Muiron in which Napoleon returned from Egypt to Toulon in October 1799 and which was made by his order in 1803. Also on exhibition is the Emperor's *barge built in 1811 and elaborately decorated by the sculptor van Petersen. Of more recent times is the *raft on which Dr. Alain *Bombard made his memorable drift across the Atlantic to demonstrate survival techniques.

There are a number of smaller maritime museums located at ports in France and affiliated to the Musée de la Marine in Paris, the most important of which are those at Bordeaux, Camaret (Finisterre), Dunkerque, Guidel (Morhiban), Le Croisic, Lorient, Port Louis, Saint Malo, Saint Tropez, and Toulon.

MUSEO MARITIMO, Barcelona, Spain, an important collection which is housed in an old building known as Las Atarazanas. It owes its origin to James I, King of Aragon and Count of Barcelona during the 13th century, but it was not until 1941 that it formally became a maritime museum open to the public. The exhibits display the history of navigation and the museum's towering entrance walls are ornamented with busts of Spanish naval heroes. Over 400 ship models are on display, together with tools, nautical instruments, medals, flags, paintings, drawings, engravings, and photographs. A full size replica of the Real, Don John of Austria's flagship at the battle of *Lepanto, has recently been added. A collection of some 2,500 charts and maps has a room of its own, and there is a large display of ships in bottles.

MUSEO NAVAL, Buenos Aires, Argentina, though founded in 1882, was not opened to the public until 1915. The collection is now housed in the arsenal of the Argentine Navy. It contains some fifty models of ships of various types and part of the hull of the *frigate 25 de Mayo, sunk in 1826 but recovered in 1933, as well as nautical instruments, medals, flags, paintings, drawings, engravings, and photographs. The library, which forms part of the Department of Historical Research, contains about 2,000 volumes, maps, and archives.

MUSEO NAVAL, Madrid, Spain. The museum owes its formation to Don Martin Fernandes de Navarrete (1765–1844) and was formally opened to the public in 1843 in the Palacio de los Consejos; it is now housed in a new building, a part of the Ministry of Marine. The exhibits include a collection of 238 model ships dating from the 16th century and over 500 marine paintings. The library contains 10,000 books and a collection of some 15,000 charts, maps, and plans; it is not open to the public.

Associated with the Museo Naval in Madrid is another smaller one known as the Palacio del Viso del Marques, which was formerly a private collection made by the Marques de Santa Cruz and presented by his family to the Spanish Navy in 1928. The collection is housed on two floors of the magnificent palace and contains pictures and archives relating to Spanish and Portuguese history.

Smaller maritime museums in Spain are to be found at Bueu (Pontevedra), Cartagena, Luanco, Palma de Mallorca, San Sebastian, and Seville. The last named is housed in La Torre del Oro dating from 1221 and contains a number of portraits of famous navigators, including Ferdinand *Magellan.

MUSEO STORICO NAVALE, Venice, Italy. This important collection was founded in 1919 and is now housed in the former granaries of the Venetian Republic, which date from the 16th century. It contains the major part of the collection of the former Venetian Admiralty and of the Italian Navy, and portrays Italian maritime history from the 16th century onwards. The ship models, some of which date from the 16th century, are mostly of men-of-war. Of special interest are the *port and *starboard sides of a 16th century *galley. Weapons predominate among the remaining exhibits. Also on view are a small number of paintings, drawings, and engravings, together with some 5,000 photographs.

There is another naval museum at La Spezia known as the Museo Tecnico Navale della Marina Militare, and items of naval interest are included among the collections of the Museo della Scienza e della Tecnica at Milan and the Museo del Mare at Trieste.

MUSEU DE MARINHA, Lisbon, Portugal, one of the more important maritime museums of Europe, was opened in 1863 in the Palacio das Laranjeiras. It aims to give a comprehensive review of Portuguese maritime history from the earliest days to the present time and contains, among many other items of great interest, a magnificent collection of charts, *derroterros, and atlases of the great days of Portuguese navigation and discovery in the 15th and 16th centuries.

MUSEUM SHIPS. A number of ships are being used as museums in various countries as shown in the list below.

Name	Type	Place	Country
Alabama, U.S.S.	Battleship	Mobile	U.S.A.
America	Replica schooner	Annapolis	U.S.A.
Aurora	Cruiser	Leningrad	U.S.S.R.
Banning, U.S.S.	Escort vessel	Hoodriver	U.S.A.
Belfast, H.M.S.	Cruiser	London	Great Britain
Belle of Louisville	Steamer	Louisville	U.S.A.
Burza	Destroyer	Gdynia	Poland
Cavalla, U.S.S.	Submarine	Galveston, Texas	U.SA.
Constitution, U.S.S.	Frigate	Boston, Mass.	U.S.A.
Cutty Sark	Clipper	Greenwich	Great Britain
Discovery	Research ship	London	Great Britain
Fram	Topsail schooner	Oslo	Norway
George M. Verity	Steamboat	Keokuk, Iowa	U.S.A.
Gjøa	Sloop	Oslo	Norway
Great Britain	Steamer	Bristol	Great Britain
Julius C. Wilkie	Steamboat	Winona, Minn.	U.S.A.
Keno	Steamer	Dawson City, Yukon	Canada
Lucy Evelyn	Schooner	Beach Haven, N.J.	U.S.A.
Lady Hopetoun	Steamer	Sydney, N.S.W.	Australia
Marion	Steamer	Mannum	S. Australia
Mark Twain	Steamer	Hannibal, Miss.	U.S.A.
Massachusetts, U.S.S.	Battleship	Fall River, Mass.	U.S.A.
Mayflower II	Replica of original	Plymouth, Mass.	U.S.A.
Medway Queen	Ferry steamer	Cowes, I.o.W.	Great Britain
Mikasa, I.J.N.S.	Battleship	Yokosuka	Japan
Nancy, H.M.S.	Lake steamer	Toronto, Ont.	Canada
Niagara	Brig	Pennsylvania	U.S.A.
North Carolina, U.S.S.	Battleship	Wilmington, N.C.	U.S.A.
Oregon	Brig	Portland, Or.	U.S.A.
Olympia, U.S.S.	Cruiser	Philadelphia, Pa.	U.S.A.
Passat	Barque	Lübeck	W. Germany
Philadelphia	Gunboat	Essex, N.Y.	U.S.A.
Rose, H.M.S.	Replica frigate	Newport, R.I.	U.S.A.
Santa Maria	Carrack	Barcelona	Spain
Sprague	Steamer	Vicksburg, Miss.	U.S.A.
Star of India	Barque	San Diego, Cal.	U.S.A.
Texas, U.S.S.	Battleship	San Jacinto, Texas	U.S.A.
Ticonderoga	Paddle steamer	Shelburne, Vermont	U.S.A.
Trafik	Steamer	Hjö	Sweden
Victory, H.M.S.	1st rate	Portsmouth	Great Britain
W. P. Snyder	Sternwheeler	Marietta, Ohio	U.S.A.

See also MARITIME MUSEUMS.

MUSTER, to, the operation of assembling the crew of a warship on deck and calling through a nominal list of the complement, to which men answered to their names. It was a necessary administrative action in earlier days before modern book-keeping and accounting methods were introduced in order to check that fictitious names, for whom pay and victuals were being drawn, had not been entered in the *muster-book. See also WIDOWS' MEN. It was on the evidence of the monthly muster that naval seamen became entitled to their pay and rations. In the early days of the British Navy there was widespread abuse of the system of pay and vic-

tuals by drawing larger amounts than were required and accounting for them by retaining on the muster-book the names of men who had died or deserted, and entering in the book fictitious names to whom other members of the crew answered when the names were called.

MUSTER-BOOK, the book kept on board a naval vessel in which was entered the names and ratings of all men serving in the ship, with the dates of their entry and final discharge against each name. It was the basis on which victuals were issued and payment was made, the *purser being responsible for the accounting of all victuals in accordance with the muster-book. All muster-books of the British Navy are held in the Public Records Office in London, thus preserving a nominal list of every man who has ever served in the Royal Navy.

MUSTER-MASTER, the dockyard official whose duty it was to carry out the monthly musters of naval vessels in port.

MUTINY, a resistance by force to recognized authority, an insurrection, but applied particularly to any form of sedition in any naval or military force of a nation. In its strict legal sense the term implies the use of force, but by long custom a refusal to obey a legal order of a superior officer is considered to be mutiny. It is not necessarily restricted to naval and military forces; a crew which rises against its officers or a crew member who strikes a superior officer or refuses to obey a legal order is just as guilty of mutiny in a merchant vessel as in a naval ship. Mutiny in a naval or military force is always tried before a court martial, in a merchant ship before a civil court.

During the days of sailing navies, the penalty for mutiny in all navies was invariably hanging at the *yardarm; when an entire ship's company mutinied, the ringleaders were hanged. But in the British naval mutiny at *Spithead in 1797, when all the ships of the Channel Fleet were in mutiny against the pay and conditions of naval service, there were no victims, and indeed no one was brought before a court martial as it was considered that the men were justified in their complaints. But in the mutiny at the *Nore which immediately followed that at Spithead, a number of the ringleaders were hanged, since all the demands of the seamen had already been met at Spithead and there was thus no justification for the mutiny. (See PARKER, Richard.)

One of the best known of all naval mutinies was that on board H.M.S. *Bounty in 1789; another was the mutiny in Germany's *High Seas Fleet in 1918, which led directly to the defeat of Germany in the First World War.

MUZEUM MARYNARKI WOJENNE, Gdynia, Poland, a maritime collection which displays Polish naval history from the 10th century up to the present time. It contains ship models from the former war museum in Warsaw, a large collection of weapons, some of which are relics of the Second World War, tools, nautical instruments, uniforms, medals, seals, flags, a few paintings and engravings, and about 6,000 photographs. The destroyer *Burza*, which played a prominent part in the Second World War, forms part of the museum.

There are four other museums in Poland which house marine artefacts, Muzeum Latarnictwa at Rozewie, Muzeum Morskie at Gdansk (Danzig), Muzeum Pomorza Zachndiego Dzial Morski at Szczecin (Stettin), and the Muzeum Techniki at Warsaw.

MYLAE, BATTLE OF, a naval engagement fought in 260 B.C. between a Roman fleet commanded by Gaius *Duillius and a Carthaginian fleet off Mylae on the northern coast of Sicily. Duillius, a general, was appointed to command the fleet when Cornelius Scipio Asina, its original commander, was captured by the Carthaginians. Duillius planned to attack the fleet of Carthage in as military a fashion as possible, and for this purpose designed grappling irons with which to bind his ships to those of the enemy and boarding bridges across which his fighting men could attack the Carthaginian crews. By these means he gained a brilliant and complete victory. Among the honours awarded him were a Roman triumph, and the attendance of a torchbearer and flute player whenever he walked the streets of Rome in the evening. A column, adorned with the *beakheads of the captured Carthaginian ships, was set up to commemorate his great victory.

MYLNE, ALFRED (1873–1951), British naval architect, was apprenticed to the Glasgow firm of G. L. *Watson and Company and set up in business for himself as A. Mylne & Co. in 1900. He rapidly achieved fame as a designer of successful racing yachts, which included the 19-metre (62 ft) *Octavia*, the 15-metre (49 ft) *Ma'oona*, *Veronica*, *Marina*, and *Jenetta*, all 12-metres (39 ft), *Freya* and *Severn II*, 8-metres (26 ft), and *Saskia*, *Volga*, *Vorsa*, and *Vrana*, 6-metres (20 ft). Altogether over 600 yachts were built to his designs and he was responsible in addition for over 260 different one-design classes.

MYNGS, Sir CHRISTOPHER (1625–66), British admiral, sprang into fame when, commanding the *Elizabeth* in 1653, he captured and brought in a Dutch *convoy of merchant ships escorted by two warships. He was appointed to the *Marston Moor* in 1655 to suppress a mutiny in the ship, and by firm measures brought the men back to a state of discipline. With the restoration of Charles II in 1660 he remained in naval favour, and during the Second Dutch War (1665–7) was vice admiral of the *White at the battle of *Lowestoft in 1665. He was killed in the *Four Days Battle in 1666, and Samuel *Pepys, attending his funeral, reports that a group of men from Myng's ship came to his coach and begged to be given a small *fireship, at that time the most dangerous form of naval service, so that they could go out to avenge their late captain against the Dutch. Myngs was, still according to Pepys, 'a man of great parts and most excellent tongue among ordinary men'. See also NARBOROUGH, Sir John.

N

NAGUMO, CHUICHI (1887–1944), Japanese vice admiral, commanded the *corps d'élite* of the Japanese Navy, the Fast Carrier Striking Force, for the first eleven months of the Second World War, though he was neither an aviation specialist nor the type of dashing, flamboyant character that the spectacular exploits of his force might seem to suggest. He had made his name as a * torpedo specialist and in command of * cruisers; he was never entirely happy as an admiral commanding * aircraft carriers. He had little faith in Admiral * Yamamoto's * Pearl Harbor strategy and, against the advice of his air staff, he left the task half completed. At the battle of * Midway, his fatal vacillation led to his carriers being caught with most of their aircraft on deck being fuelled and rearmed, resulting in the loss of all four carriers present. At the battles of the * Eastern Solomons and * Santa Cruz Island, a more thrusting commander might have followed up partial success to achieve resounding victories. Relieved of his command after the latter battle, he was relegated to the comparative backwater of the Marianas command where he committed suicide when it became clear that the American assault had succeeded.

'NAKED', the term used to describe the bottom of a sailing warship after the copper * sheathing had been removed, either by the action of rough seas or in dock for examination or replacements. Copper sheathing was used to cover the bottoms of warships both to prevent damage by the * teredo worm and to discourage the excessive growth of weed and barnacles.

NAKHIMOV, PAUL STEPANOVICH (1803–55), Russian admiral, sailed with Captain Lazareff as a junior officer in his circumnavigation of the world in 1820–1. He served in the Russian squadron which formed part of the allied fleet in the victory against the Turkish fleet at * Navarino in 1827, and during the Crimean War (1854–6) was commander-in-chief of the Russian Black Sea Fleet. In 1853, during the Russian hostilities against Turkey which preceded the Crimean War, he discovered the Turkish squadron commanded by Vice Admiral Osman Pasha at anchor off * Sinope and annihilated it on 30 November, an action which brought the era of the wooden warship to an abrupt end. He died of wounds received during the defence of Sebastopol against the Anglo-French attack which resulted in the capture of that port.

'NANCY DAWSON', the tune to which, by tradition, the daily issue of * grog was distributed in the British Navy. It was a popular song among seamen during the 18th century and may perhaps have become associated with the daily grog issues, as one of the effects of the spirit upon many men was to encourage them to burst into song. This pleasant little naval tradition died during the 19th century.

NANSEN, FRIDTJOF (1861–1930), the famous Norwegian explorer and scientist, was born near Oslo and educated at the university there. He was appointed assistant curator of the Natural History Museum at Bergen and in 1888–9 he crossed the Greenland ice sheet from east to west, a description of his journey being published in his book *First crossing of Greenland and Eskimo Life*. In 1893, in order to test his theory of the existence of a polar current flowing towards the east coast of Greenland, he set sail in the specially constructed wooden topsail * schooner * *Fram* which was allowed to drift with an ice floe towards the North pole. On reaching what he estimated would be its furthest north, he left the ship in charge of Captain Sverdrup and with a companion named Johansen sledged across the ice to reach latitude 86° 13′ N., thereby establishing a record for the furthest penetration to the north for that time. He then turned south to reach Franz Josef Land where he wintered, being picked up by the Jackson–Harmsworth expedition in 1896. From 1905 to 1908 Nansen was the first Norwegian ambassador to Great Britain, but resigned in order to carry out oceanographic research round Iceland and Spitsbergen and also in the Kara Sea. In 1919 he was appointed Norwegian representative to the League of Nations and in 1920 director of an organization for the repatriation of prisoners-of-war. He was awarded the 1923 Nobel Peace Prize and, in 1926, was made Lord Rector of St. Andrews University, Scotland.

The *Fram* is now preserved in its own museum at Oslo.

NANTUCKET WHALING MUSEUM, Nantucket, Massachusetts, U.S.A. Opened in 1930, the museum is devoted to a portrayal of the whaling industry which flourished there from about 1672 to 1869. The collection contains a few models, a full-sized whale boat, a selection of the tools used aboard whaling ships and in the workshops ashore, a sail loft, rigging loft, cooper's shop, spermaceti press, * try works afloat and ashore, nautical instruments, a large collection of * scrimshaw and models made from whalebone, together with a few paintings and engravings, books, maps, and old log books. Another museum devoted to whaling is that maintained at Cold Spring Harbor, New York, which commemorates the period between 1836 and 1862 when it was a thriving whaling port. Although small, the collection contains a number of interesting items. Other whaling museums in the U.S.A. are at: Beaufort, North Carolina (Alphonso); Chatham, Massachusetts (Whaling Museum); Sag Harbor, New York (Suffolk County Whaling Museum); Sharon, Massachusetts (Kendall Whaling Museum).

NAO, the Spanish word for a ship during the 13th–16th centuries. It was not any particular type of vessel, only the general word meaning ship. The three ships with which Christopher * Columbus sailed across the Atlantic in 1492, though * caravels in type, were all described as *naos* in contemporary Spanish records.

NAPIER, Sir CHARLES (1786–1860), British admiral, was known as 'Black Charley', or 'Mad Charlie'. He had reached the rank of * post-captain when the Napoleonic War (1803–15) ended, and having inherited a large fortune proceeded to live in France and Italy, finally settling in Paris where he lost his fortune in trying to run a service of steam vessels on the River Seine. Under the pseudonym of Carlo de Ponza he commanded the fleet of Doña Maria of Portugal during the Miguelite insurrection, defeating the Miguelite fleet off Cape St. Vincent and commanding the military forces ashore which captured Lisbon. He served in the Syrian campaign of 1840, making himself unpopular by not observing the orders of the commander-in-chief and also by signing a treaty with Mehemet Ali, thus bringing the war to an end, without reference to the government in London. On the outbreak of the Crimean War with Russia in 1854 he was appointed commander-in-chief of the British Baltic Fleet, but by this time he was 68 years old and losing his nerve, nor had he any conception of the proper use of steam * ships of the line, his ideas of naval warfare not having advanced since the days of * Nelson. His fleet did nothing during its stay in the Baltic, and on its return, Napier was ordered to strike his flag and

come ashore. He spent the remainder of his life quarrelling with the Admiralty. He was a man of considerable vanity, and his eccentric ways caused a good deal of offence to his brother officers. Although he insisted that his officers followed the uniform regulations in minute detail, he himself delighted in wearing the oddest clothes he could find.

NARBOROUGH, Sir JOHN (1640–88), English admiral, first went to sea in the navy as cabin-boy to his kinsman Christopher * Myngs, serving with him in this capacity in the West Indies. He was a lieutenant, still with Myngs, in the battle of * Lowestoft and the * Four Days Battle of the Second Dutch War (1665–7), and was beside him when Myngs was killed on the fourth day of that action. He was promoted captain on Myngs's death and commanded the *Assurance* in the West Indies, being wounded at the capture of Surinam.

In 1669 he was selected by Charles II to command an expedition into the South Seas (Pacific Ocean) to try to break down the Spanish monopoly of trade there. Sailing in command of the *Sweepstakes*, with the * pink *Bachelor* in company, he reached the Magellan Straits in the summer of 1670, the *Bachelor* deserting him there and returning to England with a report that the *Sweepstakes* had been lost. Narborough continued the voyage through the Straits alone and at the end of the year anchored off Valdivia, in Chile, attempting to open a trade with the Spaniards and Indians. Two of his officers and two men, sent ashore to negotiate with the Spanish government for the replenishment of fresh water, were detained in the fort, and Narborough, unable to secure their release and without sufficient strength to attack the fort, was forced to leave them there and return to England. With him as navigator on this voyage he had the famous hydrographer Greenvile * Collins. He was home in time for the Third Dutch War (1672–4) and commanded the *Prince*, flagship of * James, Duke of York, at the battle of * Solebay. With him also, as cabin boy and servant, was Clowdisley * Shovel, whose career in the navy he was forwarding, as Myngs had forwarded his. In the spring of 1673, returning from * Cadiz with the young Shovel on board, Narborough was within an ace of being wrecked off the Scilly Islands, and on the same Bishop and Clerk rocks which were to claim Shovel and most of the crews of the three ships lost on them in the disaster of 1707.

Narborough was promoted rear admiral after the war and spent the next three years as commander-in-chief in the Mediterranean where between 1674 and 1677 he waged a ceaseless war against the pirates of Algiers and Tripoli, finally obtaining the release of 128 British slaves and

80,000 dollars compensation for the capture of two British ships after the articles of peace had been signed. With the 80,000 dollars Narborough purchased the release of 'a great number of Christians of foreign nations who were in slavery there, and particularly several Knights of Malta'. During this campaign, Narborough also captured an Algerine warship of twenty-two guns named the *Orange Tree*, commanded by 'Bryam' (Ibrahim) 'Raise' (Reis = captain) who was known throughout the Mediterranean by the nickname of 'Bufflo Bill'.

On his return from the Mediterranean Narborough served as a *Lord Commissioner of the Admiralty from 1679 to 1687, and went into partnership with William *Phips, who in 1687 had found a wrecked Spanish treasure ship and recovered £300,000 from it. Narborough pleaded the case with James II and arranged to be sent as commander-in-chief to the West Indies to assist Phips in the recovery of further treasure, but died on board his ship at the end of an unsuccessful search.

NARES, Sir GEORGE STRONG (1829–1915), British rear admiral, is best remembered for his command of the *Challenger*'s deep sea voyage of 1872–5, which he left near its conclusion to lead the Arctic expedition of 1875–6.

Among other naval service, starting in 1845, Nares was in the Arctic with Sir Henry *Kellett in the *Resolute*, 1852–4, surveying on northern Australian coasts in the *Salamander*, 1864–6, and in taking deep sea soundings in the Mediterranean for telegraph cables in the *Newport*, in which ship he carried the Hydrographer of the Navy and the Admiralty Director of Engineering and Works for an inspection of the newly opened Suez Canal in 1870. A prominent rock in Suez Bay was named after him.

In 1871, en route for further surveys in the Red Sea in the *Shearwater*, he investigated the Gibraltar Strait currents with the assistance of Dr. Carpenter of the Royal Society. On the latter's instigation, the Royal Society's proposal for a world oceanographic voyage soon followed, and with Nares in command and Wyville Thomson as senior scientist, the *Challenger* set out in 1872.

The Arctic expedition led by Nares in the *Alert* and *Discovery* during 1875–6 succeeded in reaching further north than any predecessor, as well as making scientific studies. He concluded his sea service in the *Alert* in South America from 1878 to 1879, when he became Marine Adviser to the Board of Trade.

Nares's son, JOHN DODD Nares (1878–1957), vice admiral, was also a hydrographic surveyor serving from 1898 to his retirement in 1931 in a wide-ranging career afloat and ashore.

Soon after retirement he became President of the Directing Committee of the International Hydrographic Bureau at its headquarters in Monaco. He returned to England at the outbreak of the Second World War and worked in the Hydrographic Department of the British Admiralty. He then returned to the I.H.B., and served on the Directing Committee until his death.

NARROW SEAS, THE, those seas over which the King of England claimed sovereignty from the earliest days of England's emergence as a maritime power. They were the two seas which lay between (*a*) England and France (the English Channel) and (*b*) England and the Netherlands (the southern North Sea). Sovereignty of these seas implied the demanding of a salute, by the striking of topsails, from all foreign ships meeting an English warship in these waters, and also the right of regulating all fishing in those seas. One of the chief naval appointments of those days was that of Admiral of the Narrow Seas, two of whose chief duties were to enforce the salute and patrol the fisheries. The claim of English sovereignty over these seas was maintained until the adoption of the *three-mile limit limited national sovereignty over the seas and introduced the legal definition of international waters, free for all navigation, for all areas of sea lying beyond the various national three-mile limits.

NARVIK, a seaport of northern Norway at the head of the Ofotfjord and a main dispatch port for the great iron ore deposit of the region. It was the scene of two naval battles fought between British and German naval forces during the Second World War when a German force of ten *destroyers had been ordered to Narvik to capture the port at the time of the German invasion of that country on 8 April 1940. A force of five British destroyers under the command of Captain B. Warburton-Lee steamed up the fjord on the morning of 10 April, and three of them entered the harbour at 0430, sinking two German destroyers and damaging three others. German supply ships in the port were also sunk. But on the return passage down the Ofotfjord, five other German destroyers made their appearance, and bringing the British force under two simultaneous fires, two destroyers were sunk and another severely damaged, the German ships also suffering severe damage. Captain Warburton-Lee, killed in the action, was awarded a posthumous Victoria Cross.

The second battle of Narvik was fought three days later when the British *battleship *Warspite* and nine destroyers entered the fjord. The eight remaining German destroyers were all sunk, as well as a *U-boat which had taken shelter at the head of the fjord. The British force suffered no losses though two destroyers, including H.M.S. *Cossack*, were damaged.

NASMITH, Sir MARTIN ERIC DUNBAR (1883–1965), British admiral, entered the navy in 1896 and as a lieutenant volunteered for service in *submarines. In the first years of the First World War (1914–18) he commanded the submarine *E11* and early in 1915 was sent to operate off the *Dardanelles, at that time under attack by a combined British and French fleet. On his first patrol in those waters he succeeded in forcing his way up the Dardanelles through nets and minefields into the Sea of Marmara, harrying the Turkish seaborne supplies to their army in Gallipoli. On one occasion he proceeded up the Bosphorus and torpedoed a large transport as it was lying alongside a jetty in the harbour at Constantinople. Since these submarines could carry only a limited number of *torpedoes, he evolved a means of making every one of them tell by setting them to float at the end of their run and recovering all that did not hit their targets. This involved following up the track of the torpedo and, when close enough, swimming off to it and removing the firing pistol before manoeuvring it, tail first, through the rear torpedo tube back into the submarine, a particularly dangerous operation as a single false move in the removal of the pistol could detonate the warhead. It was typical of Nasmith that he always insisted on swimming off and removing the pistol himself when a torpedo was to be recovered. In all, he made three patrols, lasting three months, in the Sea of Marmara, and for his courage and initiative in such dangerous circumstances he was awarded the Victoria Cross.

Between the two world wars he held a number of important positions, being flag captain to the commander-in-chief in the Mediterranean, director of the Trade Division in the Admiralty, captain of the R.N. College *Dartmouth, Flag Officer Submarines, commander-in-chief in the East Indies, and Second Sea Lord. During the Second World War he was commander-in-chief at Plymouth and Western Approaches and Flag Officer in Charge, London. After retirement he served for six years as vice-chairman of the Imperial War Graves Commission.

Throughout his naval career Nasmith was a man of great courage, modesty, and integrity, the beau idéal of a naval officer.

NATIONAL MARITIME MUSEUM, Greenwich, London, was established by Act of Parliament in 1934 as a result of the initiative of Professor Sir Geoffrey *Callender who was its first director. It is housed in the Queen's House, formerly part of the old Royal Palace of Greenwich; it also occupies the old Royal Observatory buildings in Greenwich Park which include Flamsteed House. The collection, one of the finest in the world, covers all phases of maritime history with special emphasis on that of Great Britain, and includes nearly 1,000 ship models, several *barges and *galleys, 20 *figureheads, stern carvings, and ship fittings. Of particular note is the collection of 1,700 nautical instruments, 200 globes, and 60 *astrolabes, but that of 3,400 paintings and 28,000 drawings and prints is outstanding. The library, available to students, contains 45,000 books, 14,000 maps, and over 100,000 plans and manuscripts.

Smaller collections exist in the Maritime Museums of Cardiff (National Museum of Wales); Castletown, Isle of Man (Nautical Museum); Chatham (Dockyard Museum); Devonport (Devonport Museum); Dundee (Broughty Castle Museum); Edinburgh (Royal Scottish Museum and Scottish United Services Museum); Exeter (Maritime Museum); Falmouth (Maritime Museum); Grimsby (Doughty Museum); Hull (Maritime Museum); Isles of Scilly (Valhalla Museum); Liverpool (City Museum); London (Science Museum, South Kensington); Norwich (Bridewell Museum); Paisley (Paisley Museum); Plymouth (Buckland Abbey); Portsmouth (H.M.S. Victory Museum); Shoreham (Marlipins Museum); Sunderland (Sunderland Museum and Art Gallery); Whitby (Whitby Museum); Worthing (Worthing Museum and Art Gallery).

NATIONAAL SCHEEPVAARTMUSEUM, Antwerp, Belgium. Founded in 1926 as the Municipal Maritime Museum in the School of Commerce, the name was changed to Nationaal Scheepvaartmuseum (National Maritime Museum) in 1952, three years after the collection was moved to its present site in the Steen Castle, an ancient fortress built about A.D. 1000. It depicts the history of Belgian shipping and contains a fine selection of ship models, a Viking *figurehead, a 6th–9th century boat found at Bruges, scale models of shipbuilding techniques, fishing gear, tools, nautical instruments, weapons, uniforms, medals, flags, paintings, drawings, and engravings, together with some 20,000 photographs. The library contains 16,000 books, 20,000 plans, 5,000 maps and manuscripts.

Other Belgian museums with nautical artefacts are to be found at Brussels (Musée Royal de l'Armée et d'Histoire Militaire and the Musée Communal de la Ville); Ostend (Museum-Aquarium 'Paster Pype').

NAUTICAL ALMANAC, an annual publication which gives the navigator all the information he needs for working out his position by celestial navigation. For deep-sea sailing, the best nautical almanacs are those produced by the Hydrographic Department of the British Ministry of Defence (published by H.M. Stationery Office) and the U.S. Department of the Navy. In 1958 agreement was reached that each should be printed with a standard lay-out, so that both are now identical, and the information provided in the most convenient form for navigators. Reed's and Brown's nautical almanacs give the same information in a condensed form but, however, both include much additional information which is not found in the national publications, such as tide tables and tidal constants for British waters, lights, buoys, radio beacons, etc. This additional information makes them invaluable for the small boat sailor who, without them, would need also to carry on board copies of *The Admiralty Tide Tables*, *The Admiralty List of Lights*, and *The Admiralty List of Radio Signals*.

NAUTICAL MILE, the unit of distance used at sea, and differing considerably from the standard mile of 1,760 yards used on shore. A nautical mile is the distance on the earth's surface subtended by one minute of *latitude at the earth's centre. If the earth were a perfect sphere, one nautical mile would be equivalent to an arc length of one minute at all places and in all directions, but the earth is not exactly spherical, being an oblate spheroid flatter at the poles, with its axis of rotation having the least diameter.

Because of this shape, the length of the nautical mile varies slightly with the latitude, being shortest at the equator, where the curvature of the *meridians is greatest, and longest at the poles. The arithmetical mean of a nautical mile measured at the equator and one measured at the poles is 6,077 feet, but this figure is rounded off to 6,080 feet (1,852 m), which is the length of the 'standard' nautical mile. The errors of navigation arising from the use of a 'standard' nautical mile instead of its actual length for the latitude in which a ship is being navigated are obviously greatest at the equator, but they are of negligible proportions and are of no significance in practical navigation.

On a navigational *chart, except in large-scale plans where the differences in latitude are very small, it is impossible to incorporate a scale of miles because the projection of the chart (see, e.g., MERCATOR'S PROJECTION) distorts the latitude; the further north or south of the equator, the greater the degree of distortion on the chart. When measuring a distance on a chart, it is therefore essential that it is measured on the latitude scale, on the east and west borders of the chart, corresponding to the mean latitude in which the distance to be measured lies.

The origin of the nautical mile rests, of course, with the realization that the earth was spherical, and not flat as so many of the earliest map-makers believed. It was Pythagoras who first put forward the theory in *c.* 580 B.C., but his ideas were long in being accepted. Nearly 400 years later, in *c.* 200 B.C., *Eratosthenes set out to measure the circumference of the earth by the measurement of shadows cast by the sun of gnomons of equal length set up at Alexandria and Aswan. His measurement differed by no more than four per cent from modern measurement. It was from the general acceptance of Pythagoras's theory and from the measurement made by Eratosthenes that the nautical mile was born as the recognized unit of measurement at sea.

NAUTILUS, **(1)** the name given to a conventionally powered *submarine of 1,732 tons lent in 1931 to the Australian polar explorer Sir Hubert *Wilkins for an attempted voyage under the polar ice-cap which, however, failed on account of repeated breakdowns. **(2)** The name also of the world's first nuclear-powered submarine built by the General Dynamics (Electric Boat) Corporation for the U.S. Navy. Her keel was laid on 14 June 1952 and she was first commissioned for service on 30 September 1954. She has a displacement of 3,530 tons standard, 4,040 tons submerged, a length of 99 metres (324 ft) and a beam of 8·5 metres (28 ft). Her propulsion is by two steam *turbines developing 15,000 h.p. to give a submerged speed of over 20 knots, with a nuclear reactor providing the heat to produce steam. Her normal complement is ten officers and ninety-five men. In August 1958 she succeeded, where the earlier submarine of the name failed, in making the passage from the Pacific to the Atlantic under the polar ice-cap, and she reached the pole itself on 3 August. An important factor in the success of this voyage was the system of inertial *navigation with which she was fitted. **(3)** The name of the submarine in which Captain Nemo sailed 20,000 leagues under the sea in Jules *Verne's well-known novel of that name.

NAUTOPHONE, an electrically operated sound signal of high pitch used in fog, fitted on *buoys and unmanned *lightships.

NAVAL ARCHITECT, a person qualified to design ships, within whose brief comes responsibility for the strength and stability of the vessel, her internal and external fittings, and her suitability for the purpose for which she is designed. For a fuller description of the art, see SHIPBUILDING.

NAVAL ARCHITECTURE, the art and science of designing ships, submarines, floating docks, yachts, and other craft for use at sea. See SHIPBUILDING.

NAVAL AVIATION, a general term for air-craft, both seaborne and shore-based, which are controlled and administered by, and operate with, navies in attack and defence roles, *sub-marine detection and attack, *convoy protection, reconnaissance, and marine commando and as-sault operations. See also AIRCRAFT CARRIERS, FLEET AIR ARM, ROYAL NAVAL AIR SERVICE.

NAVAL CHRONICLE, THE, a journal which was published by Joyce Gold and was at one time edited by James Clarke and John M'Arthur, who collaborated in writing the official life of Lord *Nelson, was issued in six-monthly volumes between the years 1799 and 1818. The series is valuable historically in that it spans the greater part of the two long wars with France (1793–1801 and 1803–15). It was illustrated with prints, including portraits which are often good and sometimes excellent, and a large proportion of its matter was directly contributed by serving naval officers. For instance, after the battle of the *Nile, Nelson himself sent the editors, at their request, a characteristic 'Sketch of his Life', as did Lord *Collingwood after the battle of *Trafalgar. Collingwood's sketch, like many others, first appeared in an 'edited' version, and not to his great advantage, but after his death his original contribution was printed, and it is found to be as direct and remarkable as his let-ters.

While even good contemporary material often needs to be regarded with circumspection, *The Naval Chronicle* is generally accurate and re-mains a mine of detailed information not to be found elsewhere.

NAVAL HOODS or **WHOODS,** large pieces of thick timber which were used in the days of sailing navies to encircle the *hawseholes in order to take the wear caused by the heavy hemp *cables when a ship rode to her *anchors.

NAVARINO, THE BATTLE OF, was fought on 20 October 1827 between a combined British, French, and Russian fleet under Admiral Sir Edward *Codrington in support of Greek independence and a Turco-Egyptian fleet under Ibrahim Pasha which was endeavouring to restore Turkish hegemony over Greece. The British contingent comprised 4 *ships of the line, 3 *frigates, and 4 other vessels, the French, 4 ships of the line, 1 frigate, and 2 other ships, the Russian, 4 ships of the line and 4 frigates. The Turkish fleet comprised 7 ships of the line, 15 frigates, 26 *corvettes, and 17 other vessels. The Turco-Egyptian fleet was anchored in a semicir-cular formation in Navarino Bay and, to prevent it from sailing, Codrington ordered the allied fleet to anchor within the half circle formed by the enemy fleet. While this order was being

carried out, a Turkish ship opened fire, at first with musketry, to which the British replied with shot, so that in a short while the action became general. After an engagement lasting four hours the Turco-Egyptian fleet was decisively defeated, losing 1 ship of the line, 12 frigates, and 22 corvettes together with a number of smaller ves-sels, and with casualties estimated at some 4,000. Although, in terms of naval battle, the action was most successfully concluded, there is little doubt that Codrington took his ships into Navarino Bay with the intention of provoking the Turks to action even though his orders from the govern-ment were to avoid battle. The initial firing was directed at a boat from a British frigate ordering a Turkish ship to move her position as her guns commanded the entrance to the bay; the Turks on board, believing that the boat contained a boarding party, opened musketry fire on her. The frigate replied to the musketry fire with cannon shot.

After the action Codrington was recalled to London and, reluctantly, cleared of a charge of disobeying orders.

NAVE LINE or **NAVEL LINE,** a rope or small *tackle in square-rigged ships leading from the main and foremast heads and secured to the *parrels or *trusses of the *yards. Its purpose is to hold the parrels up while the yards are *swayed up, and exactly level with the yards so that they can be fully *braced.

NAVEL PIPE, the name of the pipe which leads from the *forecastle deck, or in the case of ear-lier warships when the *capstan was situated between decks, from the main deck, to the *chain or *cable lockers below and through which the cable passed. The origin of the term, it would appear, was anatomical, coming from the simi-larity of feeding the cable through a pipe into the chain locker with a mother feeding an unborn baby through the umbilical cord (not unlike a navel pipe) into its stomach.

NAVICERT, a certificate issued to a neutral merchant vessel by the representative of a block-ading power at her port of departure during wartime to allow her to pass through the blockaded zone without being brought in for examination. It was introduced by Great Britain during the First World War (1914–18) to take account of the factors which had changed since the last naval war had been fought. One of these was the very great increase in volume of sea-borne trade, for without something like a navicert system, the stopping and examining of all neutral trade would have been so great a task that ships would have been delayed for months before their cargo could be examined for *contraband. Another was the change from the earlier close

The battle of Navarino, 1827; water-colour by A.-L. Garneray

*blockade to the distant blockade used in modern war. The development of weapons during the 19th and early 20th century, particularly the long-range gun, the *mine, and the *torpedo, had made close blockade of an enemy's ports impossible in terms of modern warfare, and as a result, blockade had to be enforced much further out at sea. This meant that merchant vessels had to be intercepted often several hundred miles from the examination anchorages, and without some sort of pass, or navicert, innocent ships would be faced with greatly increased fuel consumption by being diverted to the nearest examination anchorage.

The system of navicerts worked well during the First World War (1914–18) and as a result was again brought into action for neutral shipping during the Second World War.

NAVIGATION, from the Latin *navis*, a ship, and *ago*, to drive, the art of conducting a vessel from one place on the earth's surface to another by sea safely, expeditiously, and efficiently.

OUTLINE HISTORY

Coastal navigation. So far as it is possible to reconstruct the distant past, all the earliest navigation was purely coastal, ships relying entirely on visual contact with the shore. For

several thousands of years after man first ventured to sail on the seas there were no aids to his navigation; no *compass or other navigational instrument, no *chart or map, no means of measuring distance at sea. The ships of this earliest period crept around the coasts, and if they were blown out to sea by storms, or hidden from the sight of the shore by fog, they were lost until again they sighted the coast.

Man has generally looked upon the Mediterranean Sea as the birthplace of navigation as we know it, but it is equally possible that, at the same time or even earlier, similar use of the sea was occurring in the older civilizations of the East, and particularly in the Persian Gulf, where there is some evidence from pottery decoration that the use of a sail for motive power was born. But be that as it may, the generally accepted date of the building of boats large enough to be used for the carriage of goods for trade is around 3,500 B.C., and it is that period which marks the beginning of navigation as we know it. Within the next thousand years or so, the *lead line or *sounding rod for measuring the depth of water appeared, but this was the only artificial aid to coastal navigation until the adoption of the *wind-rose, on which were depicted the directions of the eight principal winds, named after the countries from which they blew. Since, in the

Mediterranean, winds were on average steady and predictable, the use of such a rose could provide an approximate sense of direction, though this obviously required an ability to recognize the wind when out of sight of land, as perhaps in sailing from cape to cape, by its temperature, moisture content, or strength. Generally, however, during this very early period, ships normally only sailed by day and anchored at night. A possibly later development was the use of stars to steer a course by night, and certainly the Phoenicians during the first millennium B.C. could plot a course by the recognition of certain stars, particularly the constellation of the Little Bear which contains *Polaris, or the Pole Star; the stars could be related to the windrose, allowing the navigator to identify the current wind.

The property of the *lodestone to attract iron had been known from very early days, as also that a piece of iron touched by the lodestone would attract other pieces of iron. But the adaptation of this property into what we know as the magnetic compass took thousands of years, and the earliest form of compass, generally known as the mariner's compass, consisted of a needle of soft iron, magnetized by a lodestone, floating in a bowl of water with buoyancy given it by a reed or piece of straw, or even a small block of wood. This was of no use for steering a ship on a predetermined *course; its value resided in helping to recognize the current wind which was blowing, and thus by reference to the wind-rose, to give an approximate indication of direction.

The magnetic compass, which entailed the pivoting of the needle on a central point in a compass bowl, and the fixing to it of a compass card divided into *cardinal and half-cardinal points, came some hundreds of years later, possibly in the late 13th or early 14th century A.D. Its introduction as a new aid to more accurate navigation would inevitably be slow, partly on account of the prohibitive cost of the earliest models and partly by the slowness with which news of the invention spread from nation to nation. Its real value to the coastal mariner came with the growth of chartmaking, first in the form of the *portolano or *rutter, and only later in the form of a navigational chart, which to be effective had to await the solution of how to project on to a plane surface (the chart) an accurate representation of a curved surface (part of a sphere, or the earth). The portolano was, in effect, a list of coastal landmarks, harbours, anchorages, etc., in the order of their appearance to a seaman sailing along the coast, together with distances and *bearings and sailing directions in the form, perhaps, of depths of water, notes on tidal streams, and good holding ground for anchoring.

The new navigational aids which were invented during the years of the great expansion

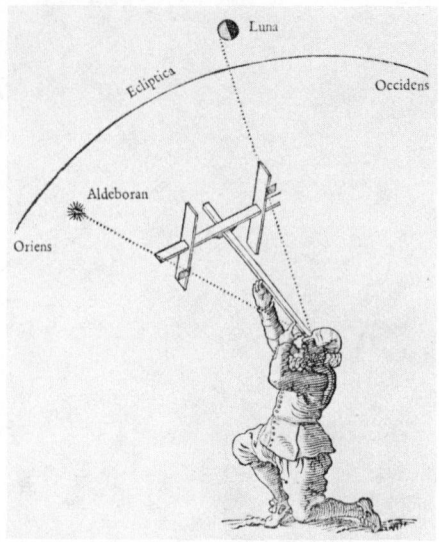

Measuring lunar distance using a form of cross-staff; engraving from Christian Longomontanus's Astronomica Danica, 1633

of seafaring, from about 1400 to 1800, such as the *back-staff, *cross-staff, *astrolabe, *quadrant, *sextant, etc., had little relevance in coastal navigation. More important to the coastal navigator was the growth of land and sea marks in the form of *lighthouses, *beacons, *buoys, *lightships, and so on. These enabled him to provide a constant check on his position by bearings and distances, or cross-bearings, of objects ashore whose position was known, and the great number of such marks today give to the coastal navigator an almost continual source of positional fixes.

Ocean navigation. The history of ocean navigation is, until the mid-18th century, very largely a story of 'hit and miss'. There is general acceptance that ocean navigation, that is, pre-planned voyages out of sight of land, was first brought into prominence by the Phoenicians during the first millennium B.C., though without doubt there were previous unplanned ocean voyages in which ships, blown off course or by error of captain or helmsman, disappeared out to sea and eventually made a landfall somewhere else. The voyage of St. Paul in A.D. 61 was such a case, for the planned voyage from Caesarea to Rome would largely be coastal, with only comparatively short stretches to be sailed beyond sight of land. The fact that a storm blew the ship to Malta and safety was fortuitous and by no means an example of planned navigation.

The Phoenicians are believed, in their voyages, to have sailed as far as the Azores and also to have reached the Scilly Islands, whither they came for tin. Their navigational guides, such as they were, were the wind-rose and the stars, and there is some reason to believe that they had a knowledge of the apparent movement of the sun to give them an approximate direction. Of their use of the stars, the Greek poet Aratus, writing of the Phoenician seamen in 275 B.C., says, 'By her guidance [the constellation of *Ursa minor*] the men of Sidon steer the straightest course.' It can hardly be a coincidence that *Ursa minor* contains the Pole Star.

The Scandinavian voyages of the first millennium A.D. also marked a notable extension of ocean navigation. The bones of deep-sea fish, found in an early Stone Age site on the Norwegian coast at Stavanger, indicates that they regularly ventured out to sea well beyond the sight of land, though this can hardly be classed as true ocean navigation. But the regular voyages to Iceland and Greenland of A.D. 900–1000, and the voyage to * Vinland in A.D. 1001, is proof of a high degree of skill in deep sea navigation, with only the wind and the sun and the stars as a guide.

The magnetic compass, the chart, and the astrolabe were the first real milestones along the road towards precision in ocean navigation. The magnetic compass, with the pivoted needle and the compass card, made its appearance in ships probably about the early 14th century or even earlier. The earliest form of chart, the portolano, or rutter, was being used in the Mediterranean at about the same time, but the navigational chart, which was originally a portolano drawn to scale, needed another century of development before it could become a useful tool in ocean navigation. All three were still very approximate in their contributions towards an improved navigation; the magnetic compass because as yet no one had any idea of the influence or amount of * variation; the chart partly because accurate measurement of distances at sea was still beyond the skill of contemporary cartographers, partly because the knowledge of geography itself was still in its infancy, and partly because of the difficulty of reproducing a spherical surface (the earth) accurately on a plane surface (a flat piece of paper); and the astrolabe because (a) it was at

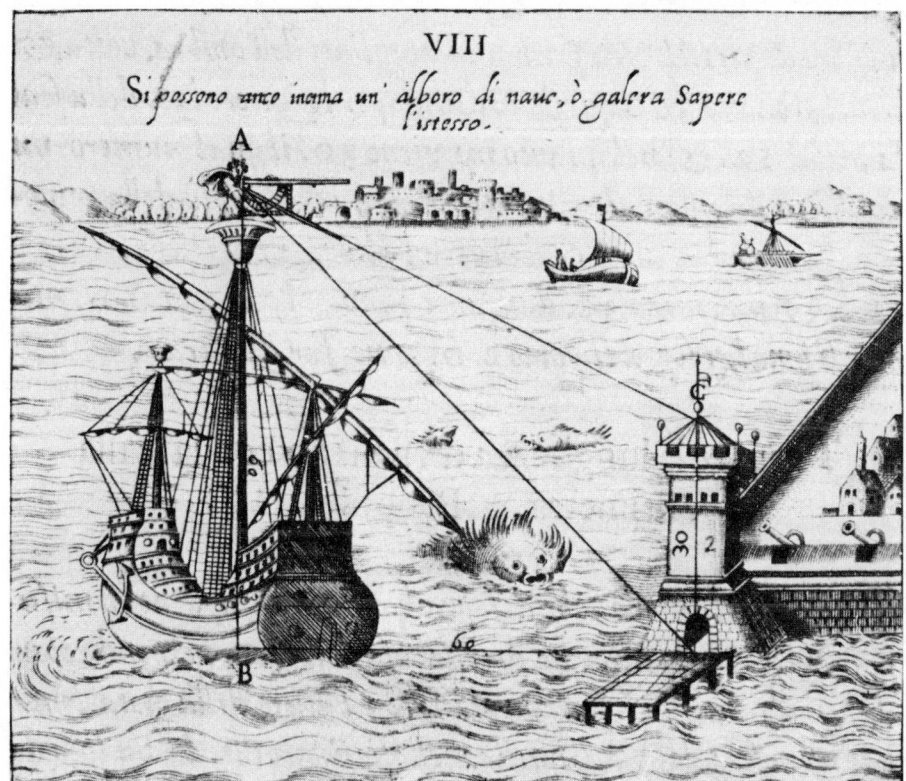

Measuring the distance from ship to shore using a quadrant; engraving from Ottavius Fabri's L'usa della squadra mobile, *1598*

best an inaccurate tool with which to measure *altitudes, and (b) because navigational knowledge of the heavens was still a considerable rarity among mariners.

All these improved during the 16th and 17th centuries, both navigational instruments and the knowledge of how to use them. The astrolabe gave way in turn to the back-staff, the quadrant, *octant, and sextant; a knowledge of the effect of variation made the magnetic compass a more precise instrument of navigation (the first world chart of magnetic variation was produced in 1701), and Gerardus *Mercator provided the first solution of reproducing an accurate representation of a spherical surface on to a plane surface. All ocean navigators knew that *latitude could be calculated accurately from a *meridian altitude of the sun or, in the northern hemisphere, by an *altitude of the star Polaris, and they knew, also, how to resolve a course steered by a ship into its two components of difference of latitude (north–south) and *departure (east–west) which enabled a system of navigation known as *dead reckoning to be applied to long voyages. Given all these, the task of the contemporary navigator was considerably lightened.

What still was beyond measurement, the final key to the solution of most navigational difficulties, was *longitude. All navigators knew that the sun reached its maximum altitude at local noon, no matter where their ship might be. If they could know, at the moment of their local noon, what was the exact time on the longitude of *Greenwich (0°), then they could very easily calculate the longitude of their present position by the difference of the two times (one hour equalling 15° of longitude). In Britain a prize of £20,000 was offered by an officially sponsored *Board of Longitude to anyone who could construct a clock that would retain an accuracy within three seconds per day over a period of six weeks; other nations offered smaller prizes for the same purpose. The British prize was won by John *Harrison with a chronometer accurate to one-tenth of a second per day, and in 1779, when James *Cook returned from his second voyage of circumnavigation during which longitude had been accurately measured throughout by a copy of Harrison's fourth chronometer made by Larcum Kendall, the seal of approval was given to this final piece in the navigational jig-saw. Until this time, it had been possible to calculate longitude accurately by means of *lunar observations (accurate lunar tables were first produced in 1767), but it needed a brilliant mathematician to work the calculations, and few deep sea navigators had that sort of mathematical skill. But although the new chronometer had provided the solution to the accurate determination of longitude, it was an instrument too rare and expensive for most merchant ships of the period, and many years were to pass before it became standard navigational equipment in all ocean-going ships.

For the next two centuries, the art of ocean navigation was a development of these known means, in the form of wider dissemination and more accurate measurement of variation, more sensitive compasses secured by the design of a better pivotal system for the card and needle, better *binnacles, and ultimately by the introduction of compass correctors (see also FLINDERS, Matthew), the development of the sextant into an instrument of supreme accuracy, the production of astronomical tables for the quick solution of astronomical observations (see, e.g., INMAN, the Revd. James), and above all by the great growth in surveying and cartography during the great period of world exploration between approximately 1750 and 1850.

The 20th century has been particularly rich in its aids to the ocean navigator, the first being the introduction by Elmer Ambrose *Sperry of the gyroscopic compass, which underwent its first sea trials in 1907. This compass, unaffected by the iron or steel of which modern ships are built, points to the true North pole, as compared to the magnetic north pole, which wanders slightly in position, to which the magnetic compass points. Thus variation and *deviation are not factors which affect the gyroscopic compass. The second great navigational aid of the 20th century was the development and growth of wireless telegraphy, by which means time signals were promulgated, first to provide daily checks on the accuracy of chronometers and later almost to make the chronometer no longer an essential factor in navigation. Since then, wireless has been developed into the *Decca Navigator, *Loran, *Consol, Omega, and similar systems to give their navigational positions to ships on demand by the intersection of position lines having the form of spherical hyperbolae. The term hyperbolic navigation has been used to denote these systems and their use. The Decca Navigator is an accurate short range system with ranges out to about 250 miles from the shore transmitting stations; Loran is a much longer range system covering about a quarter of the world's oceans, while Omega when finally completed will provide world-wide ocean cover.

Other navigational systems of an advanced nature have been developed within recent years to make still easier the ocean navigator's task. The use of artificial satellites has a navigational value, while a completely new system, based on the property of the gyroscope to point to a fixed position in space, by which all linear and rotational accelerations of a ship are detected and measured, has been developed and tested. It is known as inertial navigation.

COASTAL NAVIGATION

The difference between coastal navigation and *pilotage is narrow, but a general definition of the former would be the safe conduct of a ship where the navigator has the land on one side of his *course and the open sea on the other, even though he is in fact navigating in what is known as pilotage waters. When a ship is proceeding in sight of a coastline, her navigator need never be in doubt of her exact position, for the largest-scale *chart of the area will give him the exact position of all landmarks, lighthouses, lightships, buoys, etc., and by taking compass bearings of suitable objects on the shore and transferring these bearings on to the chart, the point of inter-section of the bearings, called a *fix, gives the ship's position. Since all courses and bearings laid down on a chart are *true, the bearings taken with the compass must be corrected before being drawn in on the chart, by the application of *variation and *deviation in the case of a mag-netic compass, and of any gyro error in the case of a gyroscopic compass.

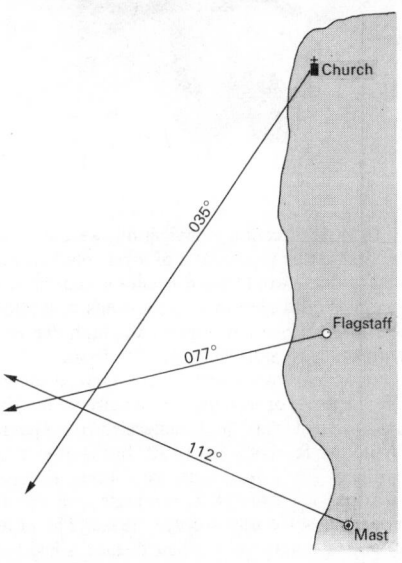

A fix

Where the chart shows only one conspicuous object in a long coastline, a position can be obtained by means of a running fix. A compass bearing of the object is transferred to the chart and, later, when the bearing of the object has altered sufficiently to give an adequate angle of cut which should preferably be around 90° and never less than 45°, a second bearing is taken and laid off on the chart. If the first bearing is transferred by parallel rulers by the distance the ship has run in the interval between the bearings along the course steered, making due allowance

for the distance and direction the ship has been carried by the tide, the point of intersection of the transferred bearing with the second bearing gives the ship's position.

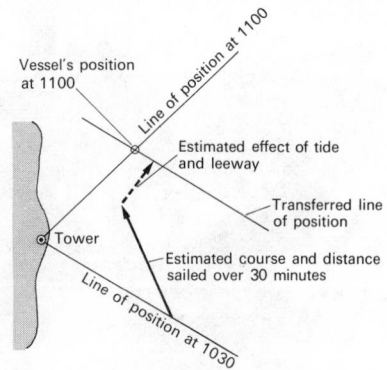

Running fix

Other methods of fixing a ship's position when in sight of land are by sextant angles. If the height above sea level of an object on land, such as a lighthouse or church tower, is known, a *vertical sextant angle, by means of simple mathe-matics, will give the distance between the ob-server and the object, and when combined with a compass bearing, provides a position on the chart by bearing and distance. A *horizontal sextant angle (illustrated) between two objects ashore will give a position line which is the arc of a circle on which the ship and the two objects both lie. A second horizontal sextant angle be-tween two other objects gives a similar position line, and again the ship's position is at the point of intersection of the two arcs.

Modern aids to navigation make the task of the coastal navigator even easier. *Radar is a means of providing the navigator with vital infor-mation in darkness or in fog, enabling him to 'see' the land and in many cases providing him with an accurate bearing and distance of land-marks which are marked on his chart. Hyper-bolic navigation (see below), such as the *Decca Navigator system, is another means of accurate fixing, using the principle of phase comparison of continuous wave radio signals.

A wise navigator, unless he has no alternative, does not use buoys as marks with which to fix his ship's position. Buoys can drag their moorings and thus be out of position and, being unmanned, can give no warning of any error. Lightships, however, are manned, and when they drag their moorings and are out of position, they indicate the fact by displaying the marks or lights laid down in the *Rule of the Road to show the navigator that they are not in the position as marked on the chart.

A modern sextant

CELESTIAL NAVIGATION

The astronomical methods of position-finding at sea used at the present time are the culmination of an evolutionary process which began even before the first Phoenician sea traders navigated their vessels in the waters of the western Mediterranean and along the Atlantic coast of north-west Europe some 3,000 years ago, using the heavenly bodies to guide them.

Perhaps the true origin of nautical astronomy was the realization that the star known today as *Polaris, or the Pole Star, always lay to the north. Certainly the Phoenicians knew this, and it is probable that this fact had not escaped the notice of earlier navigators. That an observation of Polaris, or of the midday sun, also gave the *latitude of the observer followed quickly and naturally, and this was the principle that has been used since the earliest navigations. But the problem of finding *longitude has not been nearly so simple, and it was one which exercised the attention of many brilliant astronomers right down to the middle of the 18th century, when ultimately it was solved.

There were two methods of discovering the longitude of an observer at sea, one by time and one by *lunar observation. Both, in the context of 14th–18th century navigation, were difficult; the first in the production of a reliable *chronometer which would keep accurate and constant time on board ship in all conditions of weather, heat and cold; the second by the high degree of mathematical skill required to work out the astronomical measurement of lunar distances. The method of calculating longitude by time measurement was first suggested by Gemma Frisius as far back as 1530, but it was to be another 250 years before John Harrison produced a chronometer accurate and reliable enough to solve this problem at sea. The means of finding longitude by lunar distances had been proposed many times since the 16th century onwards, but this method could not be adopted for use by navigators until accurate lunar tables became available.

The nautical astronomer, or navigator, relies on astronomical tables, or *ephemerides, to solve problems in spherical trigonometry before he can translate his observations of heavenly bodies into a position on a *chart. Important in the history of nautical astronomy is the year 1252, for this is the date of the first publication of a significant set of astronomical tables, known as the Alphonsine tables and published by order of the Castilian King Alphonso X. At about the same time, an important textbook on spherical trigonometry was written. This was the *Sphaera Mundi* by John Holywood, known as Sacrobosco, and it was to remain the standard textbook on the subject for many centuries.

The Alphonsine tables were improved by Purbach (1423–61) and Müller (1436–76) and printed by Walther (1430–1504), all three of them of Nuremberg. These were the tables which were to prove invaluable in the hands of the Portuguese navigators sent out by Prince *Henry the Navigator during the 15th and early 16th century to discover the way to India and China.

In England in 1674 Charles II established an observatory in *Greenwich Park for the benefit of navigation, and particularly for the making of careful observations of the motions of the moon so that accurate lunar tables might be devised specifically for navigational purposes. The Revd. John *Flamsteed was the first Astronomer Royal to be appointed in 1675, but his work on the compilation of lunar tables was a long-term project, and it was not for another fifty years that adequate lunar tables appeared. These were the work of Tobias Mayer, of Göttingen, and in 1765 they were adapted by the then Astronomer Royal at Greenwich, Nevil *Maskelyne, for the first *Nautical Almanac and Astronomical Ephemeris*, published that year but giving tables for the year 1767.

The *Nautical Almanac*, which is published annually, provides the navigator with all the necessary astronomical data which he needs for his nautical astronomical purposes. The main purpose of the early *Nautical Almanacs* was to facilitate the finding of longitude, for so long the bugbear of all navigators, by observations of lunar distances, and the lunar tables printed in them were their main feature. Yet within a few years the marine chronometer had been perfected and the lunar method of discovering longitude became obsolescent. Lunar tables were finally dropped from the British *Nautical Almanac* in 1906.

During the 19th century the finding of longitude at sea by the time method was simplified and systematized by the discoveries and ingenuities of Captain Thomas *Sumner and Admiral Marcq St. Hilaire, and their methods of obtaining a ship's position by observation of one or more heavenly bodies became the navigator's standard practice. The *sextant, the chronometer, the *Nautical Almanac*, and mathematical tables are the indispensable instruments of nautical astronomy, and with them a navigator can find his position on a chart anywhere in the world.

Until the compilation of new astronomical tables to assist the air navigator in obtaining a quick position by celestial observations, the solution of a sun, moon, or star sight, by which a position line on a chart could be obtained, required a knowledge of spherical trigonometry and the solving of what is known as the PZX triangle, where P is the position of the celestial pole, Z is the observer's *zenith (i.e., the point in the sky directly overhead), and X is the celestial body. The triangle is solved by calculations on the lines of the Cosine Theory and involve extensive use of mathematical tables. But the new air navigation tables, now in wide use by many navigators at sea, have made the solution very much simpler, and with these and a Nautical Almanac, a navigator can obtain his true position without the long calculations previously necessary.

From his observed altitude of the celestial body a navigator obtains from the tables the true zenith distance of the body and from the Nautical Almanac the zenith distance from his *dead reckoning or assumed position. The difference between these two distances is known as the *intercept, and shows the navigator how far his real position is from his assumed position in one direction. He finds this direction from the exact time at which he took his sight which, from the tables, gives him the Greenwich Hour Angle.

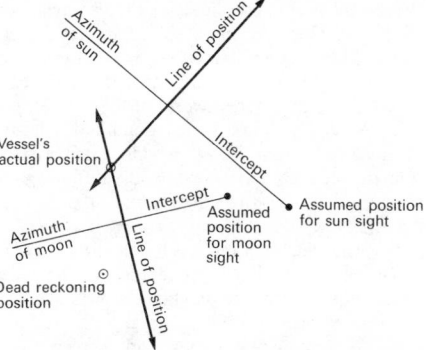

Celestial fix using simultaneous sights of sun and moon

His assumed *longitude then gives him the Local Hour Angle and, using the body's declination from the Nautical Almanac, the *azimuth, or bearing, is obtained. By drawing this bearing on the chart from his assumed position and measuring off the intercept, a line drawn through that point at right angles to the azimuth provides a position line. A similar sight taken at the same time of a second celestial body on a different bearing will provide a second position line and the observer's true position is at the point of intersection of these two position lines.

An alternative method for use during daylight hours when the sun is normally the only celestial body in sight is to take a second observation of the sun some 3 or 4 hours later when its azimuth has altered sufficiently to provide a satisfactory angle of cut, which should never be less than 45°. The solution of this second observation produces a position line in exactly the same way as the first. If, now, the first position line is transferred on the chart with a parallel ruler to take account of the distance run and the course steered during the time which has elapsed between the two observations, the point of intersection of the two position lines is the true position of the vessel. This is known as the *Marcq St. Hilaire method (illustrated).

The new tables, though much quicker and simpler to use, do not give quite the accuracy of the older method of calculation. Where the new tables will produce an observed position within about a nautical mile of the true position, navigators using the older method normally worked to a tenth of a nautical mile, or 200 yards, and would expect their sights, providing they were taken from a reasonably steady platform, to produce an observed position within this distance of the true position.

HYPERBOLIC NAVIGATION

The need to provide an accurate position-fixing system for British bombers flying over Germany in 1940 led to the development by Britain of a hyperbolic system of navigation known as 'Gee'. In the U.S.A. a similar system called *Loran was developed and in operation by 1942. During the next three or four years these aircraft systems were further developed for use by ships, and during the allied invasion of Europe in June 1944, which called for extremely accurate navigation in the difficult tidal conditions of the English Channel, the *Decca Navigator system, which was then known as 'QM', was successfully used for the first time. In 1946 an international conference to consider radio aids to marine navigation was held in Britain and specifications for radio navigational systems were worked out and agreed. This agreement resulted in the development of four hyperbolic systems which will eventually cover the whole area of the world, known as *Consol, Decca Navigator, Loran, and Omega. Each system varies slightly in its methods of using radio transmissions from master and slave transmitters and in the frequencies they adopt, high radio frequencies giving great ground wave accuracy for distances up to about 50 miles, very low frequencies having to be used where long range coverage is required. There are thus variations in accuracy according to whether the coverage is in coastal areas (high frequency) where continuous fixing of great accuracy is required, or in ocean areas (very low frequency) where such a degree of accuracy is not necessary but the ability to fix at long range is essential.

These systems are all based on the fact that radio waves emanating from transmissions travel in curves known mathematically as hyperbolae and navigationally as *great circles, and since they all travel at the same speed it is possible, by measuring the difference of time between the receipt on board of the signals from two of them, which depends on the difference in distance of the ship from the two stations, to plot the requisite curve on the chart. By repeating this process with another transmitting station in conjunction with one of the first two, usually known as the master, another curve can be plotted on the chart. Since the position of the ship must be somewhere on each curve, the point of intersection is her actual position.

In ships fitted for hyperbolic navigation, these operations are performed simultaneously and continuously by electronic receivers, and over-printed lattice charts or tables are used, so that the point of intersection can be determined quickly and accurately from the readings of the electronic receivers. For illus. see DECCA NAVIGATION SYSTEM.

INERTIAL NAVIGATION

This system of navigation, known as S.I.N.S. (Ship's Inertial Navigation System), was developed after the Second World War for use in nuclear submarines. It is a crucial part of the philosophy of modern nuclear submarine warfare that they should remain submerged for long periods, and some method of navigation needed to be evolved to make it unnecessary for them to come up to periscope depth to fix their position by hyperbolic or celestial methods, thus perhaps compromising their invisibility. The method also had to be completely free from outside detection and without any need for receiving aerials.

Inertial navigation is reasonably simple in concept although it requires a very high degree of engineering and electronic precision which makes it expensive. If a submarine's position is accurately plotted at the start of her voyage, and if all subsequent accelerations in their component directions can be measured, they can then be translated by calculation into speeds and distances which, when applied to the initial position, give the final position. By this means the navigator of a nuclear submarine fitted with the inertial navigation system has a continuous picture of his position, even though he may not have seen the sun, moon, or stars for weeks on end.

Inertial navigation is in fact an extremely sophisticated method of *dead reckoning, using accelerometers. The system can measure every acceleration due to speed and course changes, yet can eliminate the greater accelerations produced by gravitational attraction, pitching, rolling, etc. The final result gives positional data which is highly accurate. The first major demonstration of the extreme accuracy of this system was in 1958 when the U.S. nuclear submarines *Nautilus* and *Skate* navigated under the polar ice-cap. Since then nuclear submarines have made circumnavigations while remaining submerged, again relying on their inertial navigation systems. In its ability to make absolute measurements, a margin of error of not more than 100–200 metres is expected after a circumnavigation of the world, though in a voyage of that length, purely for the purpose of periodical checking on accuracy, the system does need occasional reference to a few positions fixed exactly by observations *en route*, since there is a certain amount of drift in inertial navigation.

In addition to most nuclear submarines, S.I.N.S. is fitted in certain surface ships, though its cost as yet makes it beyond the economic reach of most commercial vessels. The development of a simplified inertial system which would reduce the initial cost is under consideration.

W. R. Martin, *Naval and Nautical Astronomy* (1888); E. G. R. Taylor, *The Mathematical Practitioners of Tudor and Stuart England* (1954); *Admiralty Manual of Navigation*, 3 vols (1954–64); E. G. R. Taylor, *The Haven-Finding Art* (1956); D. W. Waters, *The Art of Navigation in Elizabethan and Early Stuart Times* (1958); E. W. Anderson, *Principles of Navigation* (1966); W. E. May, *History of Marine Navigation* (1973); C. Worth, *Yacht Navigation and Voyaging* 3rd edn. (1948).

NAVIGATION LAWS, enactments made by nations to protect the commerce of their own flag or to regulate navigation within their own territorial waters. In the second category, these are in the nature of local acts dealing with such things as regulations for the use of harbours, the licensing and employment of pilots, aids to navigation, etc.

It is in the first category that most interest normally lies, although the old-time Navigation Acts, which restricted the employment of foreign ships in a nation's external trade, are now almost entirely obsolete. The first British Navigation Acts were passed in 1381 and 1390, and these expressly forbade the carriage of any merchandise out of British ports except in a British ship. Later Navigation Acts, while retaining the requirement that exports must be carried in British ships, also restricted the carriage of imports either to British ships or to the ships of the country concerned. Much of the most profitable trade during the great period of expansion of the 17th–19th centuries came from India and China, countries which had no shipping of their own, and this limitation on the carriage of imports was, of course, of tremendous value to the *East India Company, an organization sufficiently powerful in its own right to demand the passing of such Acts. Almost all other nations engaged in the carriage of goods in ships passed similar acts, and these were renewed from time to time as individual nations strove to secure advantages for their own ships above those of other maritime nations. It took the great increase in world trade during the period of the industrial revolution to remove these national limitations on the freedom of ships to trade irrespective of their nationality; in Britain this was achieved by the passage of the Customs Consolidation Act of 1853, under which foreign ships were in the same position as British ships in relation to British trade. One provision of this Act, however, was that restrictions could be imposed on the ships of any nation in which British ships suffered similar restrictions. The British coasting trade, as was the coasting trade of most other nations, was until 1854 entirely restricted to British registered ships navigated by a *master who was a British subject; after that date the coastal trade was opened to ships of any nationality, which were in fact protected from unfair discrimination by regulations that they were not to be charged higher rates (harbour dues, etc.) than were British ships.

NAVIGATION LIGHTS, the lights which are laid down under the *International Regulations for Preventing Collisions at Sea which vessels must display when under way at sea at night. They include a white light on the mast (two lights if the vessel is over 150 feet in length with the second abaft of and higher than the first), red and green *sidelights to *port and *starboard respectively, and a white stern light. Their arcs of visibility are strictly laid down so that it is possible to judge the *course of a ship at night by studying the steaming lights which are visible to an observer. Other steaming lights are laid down to indicate various types of vessel at sea, such as fishing craft, tugs with vessels in tow, etc. Small sailing vessels are not required to carry the white light on the mast; red and green sidelights alone are necessary under the regulations. For details of all navigational lights, see APPENDIX 3.

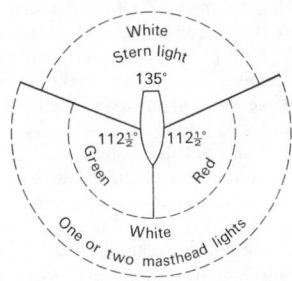

Navigation lights—arcs of visibility

NAVIGATOR, the officer on board responsible for the navigation of a ship, but in earlier centuries the term was applied to those in command of the great voyages of exploration into unknown oceans. The word is also responsible for the English term navvy, meaning a man who labours with his hands. This originated when the system of canals in England was being brought into existence during the 18th and 19th centuries. Canals were then generally called navigations, the men engaged to dig them being known as navigators, shortened to navvies. The term spread, and the workmen engaged on the construction of railway lines were frequently known as railway navigators. See also NAVIGATION.

NAVY, from the Latin *naves*, ships, in its original meaning the entire shipping of a nation, whether warships, merchant ships, or fishing vessels, referred to as a single entity. Today, however, the word used singly is generally understood to mean only that part of the overall body of a nation's shipping which is devoted to war, defence, maintenance of law, police, etc., including its auxiliaries and support ships. The term also, in its modern sense, includes the personnel employed both in the ships themselves and in their administration. Where merchant vessels are concerned, the whole body of ships which operate under a national flag are collectively known as that nation's merchant navy.

National navies. Navies have been described as instruments of national policy, and while this is an accurate enough general definition from about the middle ages onwards, many of the world's earlier navies were collections of vessels capable of warlike action and used for private gain in the raiding and harassing of weaker peoples. There were some, organized on a national basis, which were used to further national policies of conquest or defence, such as the early Mediterranean navies of Egypt, Persia, Greece, and Rome, but it was more usual to find squadrons of national ships in the hands of leaders licensed to use them in piratical acts. Typical of these were the Danish and Viking *longships which harried western Europe in the 8th, 9th, and 10th centuries.

By the time of the Crusades national navies were beginning to take the political shape of navies as we know them today, being employed in the execution of distinct policies of policing waters to stamp out individual piracy, to further national seaborne trade, and in wars of national aggrandizement. But it was not until the early years of discovery, in the late 15th and early 16th centuries, that national navies began to grow and to assume a shape and function akin to the navies of today. As the known world opened up with the discoveries of the sea routes to America, India, and China, the growing volume of lucrative trade with these new countries and the national competition which it invoked called for navies to control and defend these routes and

the trade monopolies claimed as a result of the prior right of discovery. This was the start of the national struggle for sea power on which so much of the wealth of the trading nations depended. From the start of the 15th to the early years of the 19th century, Spain, Holland, France, and England were more or less permanently engaged in maritime wars to win mastery of the oceans and control of their vital trade routes, with each nation in turn holding the supremacy.

At the beginning of the period Spain was the dominant naval power, but her supremacy, first challenged in the campaign of the Spanish *Armada, began to fall rapidly away and finally disappeared as a power on the world scale after the wars of the Spanish (1702–13) and Austrian (1739–48) Successions. Holland, during the 17th century, was one of the two or three greatest naval powers in the world, but her navy was shattered in the three Anglo-Dutch wars of 1652–4, 1665–7, and 1672–4. The navy of France, with that of Britain, disputed for a century the mastery of the seas with varying fortunes, that of France being temporarily eclipsed after the Seven Years War (1756–63) and finally destroyed in the Revolutionary (1793–1801) and Napoleonic (1803–15) wars, while that of Britain suffered great adversity, though by no means annihilation, in the War of American Independence (1775–82).

At the end of the 19th century three new navies emerged to challenge the maritime power which had been exercised by that of Britain as the result of the final victory over the naval power of France and Spain achieved at the battle of *Trafalgar in 1805. They were those of the U.S.A., Japan, and Germany. The two world wars of the 20th century radically changed the balance of naval power. The navy of Germany was annihilated as the result of the First World War (1914–18); that of the U.S.A. rose to parity with that of Britain, while the navy of Japan greatly increased in strength and dominated the western Pacific Ocean. As a result of the Second World War, the Japanese Navy was annihilated and that of the U.S.A. increased to surpass that of any other power. Since that war, however, a new navy to challenge that of the U.S.A. has emerged with a sustained build-up of naval power by Russia, and these two navies, approximately comparable in overall naval strength, far outstrip those of any other nation.

Types of warship. For the first two or three millennia, naval strength, centred in the Mediterranean, was based on the war *galley, a vessel propelled by banks of rowers pulling oars and armed with a pointed beak, or *ram, with which to pierce the hull of an adversary. Its subsidiary weapons were bows and arrows and *Greek Fire, and later a single cannon mounted on a platform in the bows. They remained the principal type of warship in the Mediterranean until the 18th century, but outside those relatively calm waters they were of little value in battle. The sail as the motive power for ships was coming in widely from the 8th century onwards, and the navies of those nations which did not border the Mediterranean had to develop the sailing vessel as their warship. For three or four centuries the sailing warship differed little from the sailing merchant ship except that the warship had high 'castles' built forward and aft from which archers, and later musketeers, fired at the enemy. These were all known as *high-charged ships. Naval warfare in those days was military warfare conducted at sea with seamen to navigate the ships and soldiers to fight. The universal tactic was to mass ships in as close a formation as possible, to overwhelm the enemy soldiers with arrows or musketry, and then to go in to board the enemy and put his ships to the torch. No prisoners were ever taken; all were put to the sword or thrown overboard.

The first change in the methods of sea warfare came in the early 16th century with the mounting of cannon on board and the cutting of *gunports in the sides of ships so that the cannon could be mounted on a gundeck below the upper deck. The English *Henry Grâce à Dieu, launched in 1514, carried twenty-one large guns which all fired through gunports cut in the sides and stern, and some Spanish *carracks of equivalent date also had gunports cut in their sides. It is from the mounting of cannon in ships that navies made a step forward from being ships to carry soldiers to fight, to become ships fought by their own crews. They still had the two large 'castles' forward and aft, manned in battle by musketeers using various types of hand gun, such as *serpentines and *robinets, and for a few more years the principal battle tactic was to carry an enemy ship by boarding, but the day of the soldier on board, except in his later form of *marine, was over.

Yet the greatest part of any national navy was still the merchant ship, taken up by the sovereign in time of war and hurriedly adapted for warlike practices. But all sovereigns of this period (1500–1600) had a nucleus of their own naval warships, designed and built specially for war, around which their wartime navies were built.

The next great advance in the development of navies was the introduction of the *low-charged ship, designed in 1585 by Sir John *Hawkins. This entailed the removal of the high 'castle' built in the bows of the ship which, by presenting a large area to the wind at the fore end of the ship, made it almost impossible to sail *on a wind. This new design made the ships both faster and much more weatherly, and for the next 300 years

formed the universal design of the sailing warship. The only change to be noted throughout these years was an increase in the overall size of warships, the introduction, with size, of a second, third, and even, though very rarely, a fourth gundeck, the heightening of the masts with topmasts and *topgallant masts, and a larger and more complex sail plan.

Iron and steel. Technological advances during the 19th century completely changed the fighting ship. Iron, and later steel, replaced wood as the material of which ships were constructed; steam replaced sail as the means of propulsion. The change was gradual, edging in slowly against the innate conservatism of the admiralties and naval officers of all navies, and finally emerging through the concepts of sailing warships with steam auxiliary power and steam warships with sail auxiliary power. The naval cannon, a muzzle-loader on a wooden carriage, was the subject of intense technological development during the second half of the 19th century, finally emerging as a big, long-range, breech-loading gun, at one stage being developed into a monstrous piece with a *calibre of 18·1 inches and a weight of 111 tons. But by the end of the century the normal big naval gun had a 12-inch calibre and an effective range of about eight *nautical miles. High-explosive shells replaced the round, solid shot of the older cannons. And with the new big guns with their high penetrative capability came thick steel armour to protect the ship against their shellfire. The old sailing *ship of the line had developed into the modern *battleship.

The pace of change grew greater in the 20th century. The mixed armament battleship of 1900 had become the all-big-gun *dreadnought of up to 20,000 tons by 1906 and rapidly developed into the super-dreadnought of up to 45,000 tons by 1940. Her reciprocating steam engines of 1900 had been replaced by high-speed turbines before the end of the first decade of the 20th century. Her guns increased from 12-inch to 15-inch calibre and new developments in propellants increased their range to 15 nautical miles or more. But an even more sinister naval vessel was beginning to make its appearance in the shape of the *submarine, firing the relatively new underwater weapon of a *torpedo while itself submerged and invisible. A few years later than the submarine came the ship-borne aircraft operating from *aircraft carriers, which increased the range at which fleets at sea could fight from a few miles to several hundreds.

Dominance of the submarine. The naval experience of the First (1914–18) and Second World Wars established the submarine as the dominant naval weapon of the 20th century. The post-Second World War development of nuclear propulsion for submarines, which has removed their former handicap of having to come to the surface at intervals to recharge their electric batteries, has made them even more formidable, and this, allied to their ability to carry long-range guided ballistic missiles armed with nuclear warheads which can be fired from below the surface, has made them the dominant weapon of all warfare, naval, military, and aerial. With the development of the submarine-fired missile has come the parallel development of the surface ship missile with an active or passive homing device, so that the naval gun is no longer the main armament of the surface ship.

A natural corollary of these modern developments is a great reduction in the size of the individual warship. No longer is it necessary to build battleships of 45,000 tons or more to mount a battery of ten or twelve 15-inch guns when a smaller ship with a guided missile can be certain of hitting her at a range to which her big guns will not reach. The big aircraft carrier too is becoming too expensive and vulnerable a target in a missile age. More and more it appears that modern navies will deploy their striking power under water, with the surface element concentrated in small, immensely versatile ships of less than 20,000 tons. See also SHIP.

NAVY BOARD, a board of commissioners set up by Henry VIII in 1546 responsible for the supply and administration of the British Navy under the control of the *Lord High Admiral, who was responsible for the operational control of the navy. The original commissioners were the Lieutenant of the Admiralty, who supervised all activities of the Board, the Treasurer, Comptroller, Surveyor, Clerk of the Ships, and Master of the Ordnance for the Ships. After a few years the post of Lieutenant of the Admiralty lapsed and the Treasurer became the chief administrative officer. The Clerk of the Ships became the Clerk of the Acts, or virtually Secretary. The Navy Board ran in parallel with the Board of Admiralty until 1832 when it was merged into the Admiralty to form a single organization responsible for every aspect of the naval affairs of the nation. See also PEPYS, Samuel.

NAVY RECORDS SOCIETY, a learned society in Britain which publishes annually volumes of original naval records, correspondence, and similar source material of British naval history. It was founded in 1893 largely on the initiative of Sir John *Laughton, Prince Louis of Battenberg (see MOUNTBATTEN, Louis Alexander), and other distinguished naval historians and is administered by a committee of councillors who are recognized as experts in this field. The Society is based at the *National Maritime Museum, Greenwich, London, S.E.10.

NEAL-TO, an old expression meaning steep-to when describing a bank of sand underwater or the shoreline itself. A bank is neal-to when the water shoals suddenly from deep to shallow as the bank is reached; the shore is neal-to when deep water exists right up to the shoreline.

NEAP TIDES, those tides which occur during the first and third quarters of the moon when the pull of the sun is at right angles to that of the moon. The effect of this counteraction is to make the high water lower and the low water higher than when the sun and moon both exert their pull in the same direction, a condition which causes *spring tides. TO BE NEAPED, the expression used of a vessel which goes aground on the spring tides and has to wait for the next springs before there is enough depth of water to float her off.

NECHO II, Pharaoh of Egypt, according to the Greek historian Herodotus, sent an expedition to sea in about 600 B.C. sailing south from the Red Sea with orders to continue as far south as possible while remaining in sight of land. Three years later the expedition reached the Mediterranean Sea through the Straits of Gibraltar, having in the meantime sailed all round Africa. Necho II was also the first man to attempt to construct a canal across the isthmus of Suez to connect the Mediterranean and Red Seas. This attempt, which was unsuccessful, has been dated 610 B.C., and it is said that no fewer than 12,000 slaves perished during the digging operations.

NEDERLANDSCH HISTORISCH SCHEEPVAART MUSEUM, Amsterdam, Netherlands, an important private collection opened to the public in 1922. The collection illustrates the history of Dutch shipping and shipbuilding with some 300 models of war, merchant, fishing, and other vessels, parts of ships, tools, nautical instruments, globes, weapons, medals, seals, and flags. Of particular interest are the 300 paintings, together with 2,000 engravings and 1,000 drawings. A department of the Rijksmuseum in Amsterdam is also devoted to Dutch national maritime history. In addition to models and other artefacts it contains works by many of the famous Dutch marine artists.

There are numerous smaller maritime museums in the Netherlands, among which may be mentioned those at Delfzijl (Stichting Museum); Den Helder (Helders Marine Museum); Dordrecht (Museum Meester Simon van Gijn); Elburg (Visserijmuseum); Enkhuizen (Rijksmuseum Zuiderzeemuseum); Groningen (Noordelijk Scheepvaartmuseum); Hoorn (West-Fries Museum); Rotterdam (Maritime Museum 'Prins Hendrik' and National Technisch Institut voor Scheepvaart en Luchtvaart); Vlaardingen (Museum voor de Nederlandse Zeevisserij).

The Burghley nef

NEF, a French ship of the 15th and 16th centuries, a development and enlargement of the *cog (in France known as *cogge*) up to 300–400 tons. They were three-masted with square mainsail and topsail on the mainmast and a single square sail on the fore and *mizen, with a *spritsail under the *bowsprit. Some of the larger nefs carried a *bonaventure mizen with a square sail in addition. They were of *carvel construction and were used for trade and war purposes alike. The word has come down to us today to describe the table ornaments, in the shape of a ship, which in those days decorated the dining tables of the nobility and in which was kept the salt, a costly commodity in medieval times. They were of very beautiful, intricate, and exquisite design, almost always of silver but very occasionally of crystal, and today are extremely rare and valuable.

NEGRO'S HOLIDAY, the old sailor's name for Sunday at sea. Although meant to be a day of rest, the work in a ship has to be done regardless of the day of the week. The origin of the term comes from the fact that the Negro slaves on the American plantations were made to work on Sundays as well as weekdays, and if Sunday was a 'holiday' on the plantations celebrated by a full day's work, so also was it at sea.

NELSON, HORATIO, first Viscount (1758–1805), British vice admiral, was born at Burnham Thorpe in Norfolk on 29 September 1758. He was the third surviving son of the Revd. Edmund Nelson, rector of the village, which lies close to the North Sea coast. What formal schooling he had was local, and at 12 years old he joined H.M.S. *Raisonnable*, commanded by his uncle, Captain Maurice *Suckling. In July 1771 he was sent in a merchantman on a cruise to the West Indies, his first extensive voyage.

Within a few years Nelson had accumulated a variety of sea experience. He had served in an Arctic expedition and spent nearly three years on the East Indies station. Shortly after returning home he was made an acting lieutenant, substantive rank being given him in 1777 at the age of 19. His first great opportunity came when he was sent across the Atlantic during the War of American Independence (1775–82). Admiral Sir Peter *Parker, the commander-in-chief at Jamaica, gave him his first command, the *Badger*, *brig, and later promoted him to a *frigate, so that, while still some months short of the age of 21, he became a *post-captain with an immediate chance to distinguish himself on active service.

Nelson was sent to Nicaragua as the senior officer in command of a joint expedition to attack the Spanish fort at San Juan, Spain having by this time joined the French in support of the American colonists. In spite of immense difficulties the fort was eventually captured, largely due to the initiative and leadership of Nelson, but at the end he was struck down by fever and had to return home to recover. Later he sailed for the North American station in command of H.M.S. *Albemarle*, in which he served until the end of hostilities.

In 1784 he began his only peacetime commission as a captain. He went to the West Indies in H.M.S. *Boreas*, a frigate, where he and his friend Cuthbert *Collingwood became active in suppressing illicit trade with the former American colonists, operations in which he made himself vastly unpopular with the local merchants who threatened legal actions. In 1787 he married Frances Nesbit, the widowed niece of the President of Nevis. He returned home a few months later but in the greatly reduced peacetime navy was unable to persuade the Admiralty to give him command of another ship. He was on half-pay for five years, living mainly in Norfolk with his wife and his stepson, Josiah.

In 1793 there began the war with Revolutionary and Napoleonic France which, with only one short break, was to extend over more than two decades. Nelson was given command of the *Agamemnon, of sixty guns, and appointed to Lord *Hood's fleet, which was destined for the Mediterranean. He was the most active captain in the fleet, serving on inshore and blockade duty, mainly off the coast of Italy, but also being present at the two indecisive actions fought against the French fleet.

His activities included one protracted spell ashore, helping the army to secure Corsica from the French. At the siege of Calvi, he was blinded in the right eye when an enemy shot struck the battery near which he was standing and drove sand and gravel into his chest and face.

Nelson took a distinguished part in the actions of 13–14 March and 13 July 1795 against the French fleet, one of the few captains to show initiative and a thirst for battle. He was promoted *commodore and left the *Agamemnon* for the larger, *Captain, but French successes ashore, combined with a renewal of hostilities with the Spaniards, compelled the British to leave the Mediterranean at the end of 1796. Among his last duties Nelson had to cover the withdrawal of the garrison and stores from Elba. Still flying his commodore's *broad pendant in H.M.S. *Captain*, he played a most distinguished part in the battle of *Cape St. Vincent, fought on 14 February 1797 between Sir John *Jervis's fleet of fifteen *ships of the line and a numerically superior but operationally much inferior Spanish fleet. It was largely due to Nelson's initiative in *wearing his ship out of the *line of battle and attacking a group of Spanish ships that four *prizes were taken during the battle. He himself joined a boarding party that captured two Spanish ships, and personally received the surrender of a number of Spanish officers. The two ships captured were the San Nicolas and San Josef, the latter being boarded from the deck of the former, a feat which was described at the time as 'Nelson's patent bridge for boarding first-rates'. He was promoted rear admiral of the *Blue, by seniority, six days after the battle (he had already been given the honorary rank of colonel of *marines) and his courage and skill in this battle brought him a knighthood in the Order of the Bath.

No success attended his efforts the following July when, with a small force, he attempted to capture a Spanish treasure ship at Santa Cruz, Tenerife, in the Canary Islands. His expedition was repulsed with loss, and Nelson himself was so seriously wounded in his right arm that the limb had to be amputated that evening in the *cockpit of H.M.S. *Theseus*, and he was invalided home. For some months the wound gave him immense pain, as during the hasty amputation a nerve had caught in the ligatures. He remained at home until April 1798 when, his health fully recovered and the nerve now freed from the ligatures, he was sent, with his flag in H.M.S. *Vanguard, to rejoin Jervis, now Earl St. Vincent, off the Portuguese coast. The commander-in-chief at once gave him command of a detached squadron, whose individual captains became collectively known as the 'band of brothers' to search for and destroy a French armament known to have been collected and about to sail from the French Mediterranean ports for an unknown destination. Napoleon Bonaparte was himself in charge of this expedition, and his first success was to capture and garrison *Malta soon after Nelson's arrival in the Mediterranean. He then proceeded to Egypt where he landed an army unopposed in preparation for an extended eastern campaign.

On the way to *Toulon to watch the movements of the French fleet, the *Vanguard* was dismasted in a severe gale off Sardinia and only just escaped being wrecked. In four days she was refitted with *jury masts but by the time Nelson arrived off Toulon the French fleet had sailed. His few frigates, believing the *Vanguard* so badly damaged that she must be repaired in a dockyard, returned to Gibraltar. Nelson, deprived of these 'eyes of the fleet', proceeded down the west coast of Italy in search of news of the French fleet, but found none. When news of the fall of Malta was received, Nelson was convinced that the French destination was Egypt, particularly as the wind had been blowing strongly from the west for some days. He therefore took his fleet to the eastern Mediterranean only to discover those waters bare of French warships. He had, in fact, passed the French fleet during the night just before they reached their destination. He then returned to Sicily to replenish with water and fresh meat and only in a second cast to the east did he find the French admiral, François Paul *Brueys, at anchor in *Aboukir Bay near the Rosetta mouth of the Nile. In the course of a night action on 1 August 1798, known as the battle of the *Nile, Nelson annihilated the entire enemy fleet with the exception of two *ships of the line and two frigates which, under Rear Admiral *Villeneuve, managed to escape in the morning of the following day, the British ships being too damaged in masts and rigging to pursue them.

Nelson himself, lightly wounded in the right temple during the action, took part of his *squadron to Naples after the battle, where he was hailed as the saviour of Italy and taken care of by Sir William Hamilton, the British Minister, and his wife, Emma, with whom Nelson fell deeply in love. Honours, a peerage included, were showered upon him, and he soon involved himself in the affairs of Naples, encouraging the

Horatio Nelson; oil painting by W. Beechey, 1800–1

king to act against the French. The advice led to disaster. Ferdinand of Naples was driven from the mainland of Italy and took flight to Sicily under Nelson's protection. It was at Syracuse that the liaison between Nelson and Emma *Hamilton developed into a permanent love affair, and it was during this period of his life that Nelson, under pressure from the Neapolitan court, committed the one mean and ungenerous action of his life, when on the court's brief return to Naples he was instrumental in the hanging of the republican Commodore Francesco *Caracciolo, who had been captured at the surrender of the Neapolitan republican forces. It was shortly after this episode that Nelson, whose presence in Italy could do no further good to his own country, was recalled. He travelled home across Europe by way of Trieste, Vienna, Prague, Dresden, and Hamburg, in company with the Hamiltons, taking four months over the journey and fêted everywhere as one of the rare commanders

who had enjoyed a decisive success against the all-conquering French.

Back in England, Nelson found his marriage in ruins, the notoriety of his association with Emma Hamilton having preceded his arrival. But he was almost at once re-employed, being appointed second-in-command to Admiral Sir Hyde *Parker on an expedition to the Baltic designed to defeat a coalition of- northern Powers, the mainspring of which was Paul I, Tsar of Russia.

The Tsar was assassinated and his policy reversed by his successor, Alexander I, but before the momentous news had become known, Nelson, with a detachment of ships of the fleet of comparatively light draught, attacked and defeated the Danish fleet at the hard-fought battle of *Copenhagen on 2 April 1801. At a critical stage of the action, Hyde Parker signalled to the engaged portion of the fleet to break off the action, an order that Nelson refused even to see since, as he remarked, he had a blind eye and sometimes had a right to use it. To have obeyed Hyde Parker's signal at that moment would have been to court disaster, so critical was the squadron's position in shoal waters.

Nelson himself arranged the terms of the resultant armistice with Denmark, and when the circumstances of the action were known at the Admiralty, Hyde Parker was recalled and Nelson made commander-in-chief in his place. He was also created a viscount.

As the northern coalition had by now been dissolved, there was no further occasion for Nelson's services in the Baltic, and he was allowed to return home. He landed at Great Yarmouth, and was appointed to command those inshore forces which were designed to protect the country from invasion.

Nelson showed his usual activity in preparing measures of defence, but an attack on the invasion vessels at Boulogne which he planned to take place in August 1801 was repulsed with heavy losses due mainly to the French use of chain anchor *cables in place of the more usual *hemp. No further opportunity for active service occurred before the brief Peace of Amiens. During the months of this uneasy truce, for it was scarcely more, Nelson lived at Merton, a modest country estate in Surrey which he had acquired, and which he shared with Sir William and Lady Hamilton.

Sir William Hamilton died in London on 6 April 1803 and on 16 May, Nelson, now a vice admiral of the Blue, was appointed to the command of the Mediterranean Fleet with his flag in H.M.S. *Victory. For the next two years his duty was to keep a close watch on Toulon to prevent the squadron in that port from getting out and joining forces with others from French and Spanish ports. Villeneuve, the French admiral, twice evaded Nelson's watch. On the first occasion he was driven back to port by stress of weather, but on the second, in April 1805, he got clean away and into the Atlantic before Nelson could be sure of his destination.

Napoleon, by now Emperor of the French, had ordered his admiral to the West Indies, where he was to take command of a combined fleet which was to assemble from various Mediterranean and Atlantic ports. This was designed to sweep aside the British western squadron, to secure temporary command of the English Channel, and to enable the French Army to cross for an assault on Great Britain.

Nelson, misled partly by false information and partly by the speed of Villeneuve's return when he heard of Nelson's arrival, missed the French fleet, which returned to Europe in haste before the other squadrons from Europe could join. Reaching the Bay of Biscay, Villeneuve's ships fought an inconclusive engagement off *Ferrol in

July with a squadron under the command of Sir Robert *Calder, and eventually took refuge at *Cadiz, joining forces with a Spanish squadron there. This combined fleet was blockaded in the port by Collingwood, whose small detachment was soon reinforced. Meanwhile Nelson, on hearing of Villeneuve's departure from the West Indies, followed him back to Europe and then, having satisfied himself that the French fleet had not returned to the Mediterranean, which was still his responsibility, himself sailed for home in the *Victory* for a few days of rest at Merton. He was there when the news of Villeneuve's arrival at Cadiz reached England, and he at once posted to the Admiralty to receive orders to return to the Mediterranean. He arrived off Cadiz at the end of September 1805 and at once began to plan in meticulous detail for the battle which he knew would come.

Villeneuve would have preferred to stay at anchor in Cadiz but Napoleon, his plan of invasion foiled and his army on the march elsewhere, ordered him to take the fleet into the Mediterranean. To make sure that he was obeyed, Napoleon sent another admiral to take over command of the fleet, a fact of which Villeneuve was aware. The humiliation was too much for him and he ordered his ships to weigh and to make for the Straits of Gibraltar. No move of the enemy ships eluded Nelson's inshore frigates and, within minutes, the news of the combined Franco-Spanish fleet's departure from Cadiz was on board the flagship. Once he had put to sea, Villeneuve had thoughts of getting back to Cadiz, but in the end he decided to face his great opponent. On 21 October 1805 the last great action of the days of sail was fought out in historic waters off Cape *Trafalgar—twenty-seven British ships of the line against thirty-three French and Spanish. Nelson won an annihilating victory, but fell in the hour of triumph, struck down by a bullet fired by a marksman in the fighting top of the French *Redoutable*. It was as the British fleet was sailing into action that Nelson gave to his signal officer, John *Pasco, instructions for hoisting the most famous signal in British naval history.

Nelson was fortunate in his opportunities, but he had his full share of failure and misfortune. While still a captain, an attack which he made on the French-held Turk's Island in the Bahamas during the War of American Independence proved an utter failure through lack of thoughtful preparation. More than once he was lucky not to have been killed in action, as in Corsica and at Santa Cruz, where his repulse would have disheartened a lesser man. His sojourn in Naples was almost wholly unfortunate, both professionally and personally, but his four brilliant successes, as a subordinate at Cape St. Vincent and Copenhagen, and as an independent commander at the

Nile and Trafalgar, stamp him as a master tactician, able to infuse his officers and men with his own ardour, and prepared to work to a low factor of safety. His successes were not due to rashness but to a shrewd knowledge of the forces ranged against him. This knowledge, gained in battle, was reinforced by study, for Nelson was not only a keen student of history but was alive to every new tactical development and idea.

He was a supreme example of a leader who could trust his captains, take them fully into his confidence, and leave them to exercise their own initiative. He received from them not only personal devotion but services in battle which very few other admirals have inspired.

As a man Nelson was deeply religious and affectionate, and although his marriage foundered as a result of his liaison with Emma Hamilton, this was the sole instance in his life when a long enduring tie was broken through a fault of his own.

For a man who died at the age of 47, Nelson left a wealth of letters, memoranda, and dispatches which show his fire, his brilliance, his capacity, his versatility, his loyalty, and generosity to companions in arms, and his kindness to all those (except, in his last years, his wife) who needed it.

'Nelson was the man to *love*,' exclaimed Sir Pulteney Malcolm, who came to know most of the principal commanders of a remarkable era. In spite of his faults, which included vanity, posterity has endorsed Sir Pulteney Malcolm's opinion. That is, perhaps, why his flagship at Portsmouth and his tomb in the crypt of St. Paul's Cathedral continue to be places of pilgrimage.

For biographies, see A. T. Mahan, *The Life of Nelson* (1897), Carola Oman, *Nelson* (1947), and A. Bryant, *Nelson* (1970). His letters and dispatches are in Sir N. H. Nicolas, *Despatches and Letters of Vice-Admiral Lord Nelson* (7 vols, 1844). The best description of the Trafalgar campaign is Sir Julian Corbett's *The Campaign of Trafalgar* (1910).

NELSON MUSEUM, THE, English Harbour, Antigua, W. Indies. The collection was begun in 1951 by the Friends of English Harbour and is housed in a wooden house built on the site of Commissioner's House in the old dockyard. It contains a model of the original dockyard of 1725, *figureheads, *anchors, tools, nautical instruments, a collection of uniform buttons, medals, seals, drawings, paintings, and engravings.

'NELSON TOUCH', THE, a phrase used by Admiral Lord *Nelson before the battle of *Trafalgar (1805) in explaining to his captains his plan of attack. ' . . . when I came to explain

to them the "Nelson touch", it was like an electric shock. Some shed tears, all approved . . .' Elsewhere he described the 'Nelson touch' as the fact that his *order of sailing was his order of battle, i.e., that no time need be wasted in bringing the enemy fleet to battle. The phrase is indeterminate, it could also have been his favourite battle tactic of concentrating his whole force on part of the enemy's *line of battle, to annihilate it before the rest of the line could *tack or *wear to come to its assistance. Or equally, it could have meant the magic of his name among officers and seamen of his fleet, which was always enough to inspire them to great deeds of heroism and endurance.

NELSON'S PRAYER, the last piece of writing by Vice Admiral Lord *Nelson, composed in his cabin on board H.M.S. *Victory on the morning of 21 October 1805 within an hour of the start of the battle of *Trafalgar, in which he was killed. The prayer runs, 'May the Great God, whom I worship, grant to my Country, and for the benefit of Europe in general, a great and glorious Victory; and may no misconduct in anyone tarnish it; and may humanity after Victory be the predominant feature in the British Fleet. For myself, individually, I commit my life to Him who made me, and may His blessing light upon my endeavours for serving my Country faithfully. To Him I resign myself and the just cause which is entrusted to me to defend. Amen. Amen. Amen.'

NEPTUNE, a Roman god of unknown origin but thought to have been associated with Salacia, the goddess of salt water. He was later, in 399 B.C., identified with the Greek god of the sea *Poseidon. It had been the god *Fortunus to whom sacrifices were made in Rome in honour of naval victories, but the Emperor Augustus's right-hand man, Marcus Vipsanius *Agrippa, changed that by dedicating a temple in the Campus Martius to Neptune in honour of the naval victory of *Actium.

NEPTUNE, H.M.S., a name used for seven major ships of the Royal Navy, all but one of which saw action in the naval wars of their day. The 90-gun *Neptune,* built at *Deptford in 1683, was present at the battle of *Barfleur in 1692, flying the flag of Vice Admiral George *Rooke. She was rebuilt twice; at Blackwall in 1710, and at Woolwich in 1730. In 1744 she was the flagship of Vice Admiral Richard *Lestock in the action of 11 February with the French and Spanish fleets off *Toulon. In 1749 she was reduced to a 74-gun ship and in 1750 her name was changed to *Torbay.* The next *Neptune,* also of ninety guns, was launched at *Portsmouth in December 1756 and in September of the next year she took part, as the flagship of Vice Admiral Charles * Knowles, in * Hawke's expedition against Rochefort. As flagship of Vice Admiral Charles * Saunders she was one of the ships at the capture of * Quebec, September 1759. She was broken up in 1816. The *Neptune* of ninety-eight guns, launched at Deptford in 1797, was the flagship of Rear Admiral * Gambier, third in command of the Channel Fleet, in 1801. At the battle of * Trafalgar, commanded by Captain Thomas F. * Fremantle, she had ten of her people killed and forty-four wounded. After the battle she towed the * *Victory* into Gibraltar. In January 1809, as the flagship of Rear Admiral the Hon. Alexander F. I. Cochrane, she was present at the capture of Martinique and in April of the same year she took part in the attack on a French squadron off Cape Roxo, Puerto Rico, which resulted in the capture of the French *d'Hautpoult* of seventy-four guns. In January 1810 she was employed in operations against Guadeloupe, and after further service as a prison ship she was broken up at * Plymouth in 1818. The 120-gun *Neptune* launched at Portsmouth in 1832 saw action in the Baltic campaign of 1854 as the flagship of Rear Admiral A. L. Corry, who was succeeded by Rear Admiral J. H. Plumridge. She was sold for breaking up in January 1875. The * battleship *Neptune*, of 19,900 tons, was built at Portsmouth and launched in September 1909. Commissioned in 1911, she was the flagship successively of Admiral Sir F. C. B. Bridgeman and Admiral Sir G. A. Callaghan as commanders-in-chief, Home Fleet. In 1914 she reverted to a private ship on the transfer of the flag to H.M.S. * *Iron Duke*. As one of the 1st Battle Squadron, * Grand Fleet, she took part in the battle of * Jutland and continued to serve in the Grand Fleet throughout the war. She went into reserve in 1919 and in 1921 was paid off, being sold in September 1922. The 7,175-ton cruiser *Neptune* was launched at Portsmouth in January 1933. She served in the Second World War until sunk by a mine off Tripoli while on duty with a Malta convoy in December 1941.

NEPTUNE'S SHEEP, another name for waves at sea breaking into foam, so frequently known as white horses.

NEREIDES, in Greek legend the fifty daughters of * Nereus and * Doris, all nymphs of the sea.

NEREUS, in Greek mythology the son of * Oceanus and Terra, and a deity of the sea. See also NEREIDES.

NET, lines rigged from the mast to the forestay of a racing yacht when running before the wind with a * spinnaker set. Their purpose is to

prevent the spinnaker wrapping itself round the forestay if it should collapse as a result of a lack of wind or an unexpected backdraught.

NET REGISTER TONNAGE, see TONNAGE.

NETTINGS, (1) spaces around the upper deck, * forecastle, * poop, and the break of the * quarterdeck in sailing warships in which the * hammocks in which the crew slept were stowed in the daytime. They served several purposes, one, that exposure to fresh air limited the number of lice they might contain; two, they served as a defence in battle against enemy musket-fire; three, they acted as liferafts in case of shipwreck: a properly lashed hammock would support a man in the water for six hours before it became waterlogged and sank. **(2)** A net formed of small ropes seized together with yarns and spread across the * waist of a ship in hot weather. Sails were laid on them to form an * awning to provide protection from the sun. They were also used in some merchant ships as a defence against boarders, since merchant vessels usually lay lower in the water than warships and boarders would have to drop down on to the deck. It proved, however, more dangerous than defensive, as boarders soon learnt the trick of cutting the netting down and enveloping the men beneath it. SPLINTER-NETTING, a stout rope netting rigged in battle in the days of sailing navies between the mainmast and * mizen-mast at a height of about 12 feet above the quarterdeck. Its purpose was to prevent those engaged there being injured if masts or spars were shot away during the action. It also served to break the fall of men in the * tops or on the * yards if they fell as a result of the enemy's gunfire.

NETTLE, sometimes written as **KNITTLE, (1)** small line often used for * seizing rope to form an * eye or to bind the tucks of an * eye splice, or in other similar places where a seizing may be required. **(2)** The small line used in the * clews of * hammocks, doubled round a ring and secured with a * half hitch in the eyelet holes at the head and foot of a hammock. See also GANTLOPE, RUNNING THE.

NEW IRONSIDES, U.S.S., a * monitor built of iron and launched in May 1862 at * Philadelphia. She was commissioned in August of the same year and first went to sea in January 1863. She flew the flag of Admiral * Dupont in the attempt to persuade the Confederates into surrendering the port of Charleston by a show of force of * ironclad vessels in Charleston harbour on 7 April 1863, and although she was hit some fifty times on that occasion she was not seriously damaged. She had been planned and built hurriedly on the lines of the * *Monitor* and the

Navy Department failed to supervise all details of the planning with the result that she was an unhandy and uncomfortable ship.

NEW ORLEANS, a city in the state of Louisiana, U.S.A., and a great seaport, situated at the head of the delta of the Mississippi River. It was founded by Jean Baptiste Lemoyne, sieur de Bienville, in 1718 and named in honour of the Duc d'Orleans, at that time regent of France. For nearly a century it was little more than a village or small town of ill-repute, inhabited in the main by gold prospectors, escaped or deported galley-slaves, prostitutes, and general riff-raff (the term employed in 1763 by Mayor Kerlerec to describe its inhabitants). Until its purchase by the U.S.A. in 1803 New Orleans was a small Franco-Spanish-American seaport, but development of its natural trade in sugar, cotton, and tobacco quickly raised it to a position of importance. It was unsuccessfully attacked by British forces in 1815, and in 1862, during the American Civil War (1861–5), was the scene of a long-drawn-out naval action by Union forces, under Captain D. G. *Farragut, which finally resulted in the capture of the town. As a seaport New Orleans suffered a considerable drop in trade for twenty years after the Civil War, but since about 1880 the trade handled in the port has grown at a prodigious rate.

NEW YORK, one of the greatest seaports in the world situated at the mouth of the Hudson River in the U.S.A. New York Bay and the Hudson River were first discovered by Giovanni da *Verrazzano in 1524, but it was nearly another century before any attempt was made to build a settlement there. This was in 1614, when a company of Dutch merchants established a trading post on Manhattan Island, there to deal in furs with the Indians. In 1623 the Dutch West India Company chose Manhattan Island as a centre for trade and three years later Peter Minuit, a director of the company, bought the whole of Manhattan Island for 60 guilders, the equivalent of 25 dollars or £5 sterling. The centre was given the name of Nieuw Amsterdam. But by 1664 the arbitrary rule of Peter Stuyvesant, the Dutch governor, had become so oppressive that when a British fleet arrived in that year to attempt the conquest of the province, most of the burgo-masters and prominent citizens threw in their lot with the British rather than suffer any more the oppressions of Stuyvesant, and Nieuw Amsterdam was surrendered without a fight on 8 September 1664. It was renamed New York in honour of *James, Duke of York, brother of Charles II and *Lord High Admiral of Britain.

The harbour of New York is one of the largest and most beautiful in the world, with piers stretching the length of both sides of the North and East rivers. Those of the main transatlantic passenger lines are on the North River. On the East River is the Brooklyn Navy Yard, a main base and shipbuilding centre of the U.S. Navy. In terms of volume of trade, New York as a port ranks with London and Rotterdam.

There are a number of maritime museums in New York, of which the most interesting is probably the *Marine Museum of the City of New York.

NEW YORK YACHT CLUB, THE, the principal yacht club in America, had its birthplace in the cabin of the 51-foot schooner *Gimcrack*, anchored in New York harbour in July 1844, when nine original members met on board to found the club. John C. *Stevens, owner of the *Gimcrack*, was voted *commodore and remained in this post for ten years. From the first the club encouraged members to handle their own yachts and held *Corinthian regattas to further this aim. Commodore Stevens in 1851 also headed the syndicate of six members who had the *schooner *America built. The 100-guinea cup, which she won at Cowes in that year, has been lodged, as the America's Cup, in the New York Yacht Club's strongroom ever since. As the senior yacht club in the U.S.A., the N.Y.Y.C. has done much to foster the best in yacht racing and cruising, and in its clubhouse on West 44th Street its collection of yacht models dating from its inception is famous throughout the yachting world.

NEWBOLT, Sir HENRY JOHN (1862–1938), British author and poet, was born at Bilston, Staffordshire, and educated at Clifton and Oxford. He studied law and was a barrister for twelve years, but all the while with a leaning for literature. In 1896 he wrote a famous poem, 'Drake's Drum', which appeared first in the *St. James's Gazette* and was included in a collection of twelve poems under the title *Admirals All*, published in 1897. The little book went into four editions in two weeks, and Newbolt, established as writer and poet, forsook the law. Similar books from his pen appeared at regular intervals until the outbreak of the First World War (1914–18). The best known were *Sailing of the Longships* (1902), *Songs of the Sea* (1904), *Year of Trafalgar* (1905), *Songs of the Fleet* (1910), and *Book of the Blue Sea* (1914).

During the First World War he worked in the Admiralty and the Foreign Office, and was knighted in 1915. After the war and on the death of Sir Julian *Corbett he was invited to complete Corbett's work as official historian of the war at sea, and the last two volumes of the five-volume *Naval Operations* came from his pen. They were published in 1922, and he was appointed a Companion of Honour.

NEWCOMB, SIMON (1835–1909), American astronomer, did much work in the compilation of the American *Nautical Almanac* of 1857, and twenty years later was appointed director of the office, a post he held until 1897. He was appointed professor of mathematics in the U.S. Navy, and in 1906, possibly as a move to correct this apparent anomaly, was by Act of Congress given the rank of rear admiral.

NEWPORT, a city and seaport of the U.S.A. on Rhode Island, and a great American east coast yachting centre. It has a magnificent inner and outer harbour, but in terms of volume of seaborne trade, does not now rank as one of the great American seaports, although at one time it was a greater port than *New York. It was founded, originally with the name Aquidneck, in 1639 but has a place in naval history for the destruction there of the British revenue *sloop *Liberty* in May 1769, one of the earliest acts of violence which eventually led to the War of American Independence (1775–82). The port was held by the British between 1776 and 1779, but was then evacuated and became a base for the French fleet, France having by then joined the war on the American side.

The city is the home of the Newport Historical Society, a museum founded in 1853 and with a separate marine room opened in 1930. It is devoted primarily to the history of Narragansett Bay and Rhode Island waters and contains some ship models, a harbour model, nautical instruments, weapons, dress, *scrimshaw, medals, seals, flags, paintings, drawings, and engravings. A small library open to the public contains about 400 books, maps, manuscripts, and archives. Also located on Rhode Island is the Herreschoff Model Room, opened in 1954, which houses almost the entire collection of 220 ship models from the workshop of Nathaniel Greene *Herreschoff, the marine architect. The Rhode Island Historical Society, located at Providence and founded in 1822, possesses items of interest relating to shipping in Long Island Sound and Narragansett Bay.

NEWPORT NEWS, a city and port of entry in Warwick County, Virginia, U.S.A., on the James River, and important both as a commercial port and as a great marine shipbuilding yard where large numbers of ships of all descriptions and sizes are built both for the U.S. Navy and for commercial purposes.

The site of the present city was first settled in 1621 by Irish planters brought over by Daniel Gookin, and the position was chosen on the advice of Sir William Newce and his brother, but the actual city was not laid out until the coming of the railway in 1882. The name is said to be in honour of Christopher Newport, who laid out the city, and Sir William Newce, the original selector of the site for the settlement.

It is the home of the *Mariners Museum, one of the most important maritime collections in the U.S.A.

NICHOLSON, CHARLES ERNEST (1868–1954), British designer and builder of yachts, joined the family firm of Camper and Nicholson, yacht and shipbuilders of Gosport and Southampton, at the age of 17, and the skill as a designer of beautiful racing and power yachts which he had inherited from his father brought the firm orders for fine yachts from many parts of the world. Charles Nicholson designed and built at that yard the *America's Cup challengers *Shamrock IV* in 1914 and *Shamrock V* in 1930 for Sir Thomas *Lipton, and *Endeavour* in 1934 and *Endeavour II* three years later for Sir Thomas *Sopwith. Among his largest steam yachts were *Sagitta*, of 756 tons, in 1908, *Miranda*, of 942 tons, in 1910, and *Marynthea*, of 900 tons, in 1911. He was also responsible for designing and building the first large diesel-engined yacht to be built in Great Britain. This was the *Pioneer* of 400 tons, launched in 1914, which was in naval service during the First World War (1914–18), and later saw many years of government service in the Pacific as the official yacht for the Governor of Fiji. His largest yacht, *Philante*, a 1,629-ton twin screw diesel vessel built for Sir Thomas Sopwith, launched in 1937, has since become the Norwegian royal yacht *Norge*. Charles Nicholson was a liveryman of the Worshipful Company of Shipwrights, chairman of Camper and Nicholson, and a prominent and active member of the *Royal Yachting Association until his death.

NIGGER HEADS, a name sometimes given to the *bollards which line a *quay or *wharf and to which ships lying alongside secure their *hawsers. This name may have its origin from the fact that bollards are usually painted black. It is particularly applied to the metal bollards which are so frequently found in British naval *dockyards consisting of an old ship's gun planted breech downwards and with a cannon ball slightly larger than the bore fixed in the muzzle of the gun. When breech-loading guns were introduced into the British Navy during the second half of the 19th century, vast numbers of the old muzzle-loading guns became surplus, and using them as bollards, etc., was a good way of disposing of them.

NIGGER OF THE NARCISSUS, THE, a novel written by Joseph *Conrad and published in 1898. Conrad served for a short time as second *mate of the *Narcissus*, an experience which gave him some of the features of the novel.

NILE, BATTLE OF THE, an action between British and French fleets fought in the Mediterranean in 1798. The French government, encouraged by Napoleon Bonaparte, had decided on an expedition to Egypt, with a view to further eastern conquests on an ambitious scale. These preparations became known in Great Britain, though the general destination remained uncertain. The Earl of St. Vincent (see JERVIS, John), whose fleet was then based on the Tagus, was ordered to send a detached *squadron into the Mediterranean to seek out, attack, and if possible destroy the French armament.

The officer chosen to lead this force was Horatio *Nelson, then a junior rear admiral, a fact which caused some jealousy in the fleet. At the outset, Nelson met with a series of setbacks. His flagship, H.M.S. *Vanguard, was dismasted and nearly wrecked off the island of Sardinia, his *frigates, due to a misunderstanding, rejoining the main fleet. Nevertheless, convinced that Napoleon's destination was Egypt, he took his fleet there only to find that there was no sign of the French ships. But on a second cast to the east he discovered François Paul *Brueys, the French admiral, on 1 August with his squadron anchored near the Rosetta mouth of the Nile, at *Aboukir Bay.

Nelson attacked at once. He had thoroughly briefed his captains as to his intentions, and they showed splendid initiative. The four leading ships, risking shoals, made their way inshore of the enemy line, the remainder attacking from seaward, thus bringing the French line under fire from both sides. During the night of heavy fighting, the huge *l'* Orient*, Brueys's flagship, was set on fire and, when the flames reached her *magazine, blew up with a huge explosion that scattered spars and wreckage a considerable distance. When morning came, the light fell upon a scene for which victory, as Nelson himself remarked, was scarcely an adequate word.

Nelson had with him thirteen *ships of the line, of which one was small and another grounded on the shoal on the way in to Aboukir Bay, and took no part in the battle. Two French ships of the line were destroyed and nine taken as *prizes, of which three were later burned as being too damaged to be of value. The remainder were added to the Royal Navy. Only two French ships of the line and two frigates under Rear Admiral *Villeneuve escaped to fight another day. The triumph brought new hope to Britain in her long struggle with France, brought Nelson a peerage and made his name a household word, and marooned the French Army in Egypt.

The flag-captain of the French flagship was the Comte de *Casa Bianca, who was dangerously wounded in the early stages of the fighting. He had taken his small son, aged 10, to sea with him.

The pathetic death of this small boy who 'stood on the burning deck' is commemorated in the poem 'Casabianca', written by Mrs. Hemans in 1829.

After the battle Captain Ben *Hallowell of H.M.S. *Swiftsure had a coffin made from timber cut from the Orient's mainmast by the Swiftsure's carpenter, which he presented to Nelson. It was this coffin, enclosed in the catafalque, in which he was buried in the crypt of St. Paul's Cathedral in London after his death at the battle of *Trafalgar.

The battle of the Nile brought Nelson even odder fame in the shape of a fourth verse to the National Anthem, said to have been written by Mr. Davenport, editor of the *Political Miscellany*, though a rival claim to its authorship has been put forward on behalf of Miss Cornelia Knight, who was staying with the British ambassador in Naples at the time. The verse ran:

> Join we in Great Nelson's name,
> First on the rolls of Fame,
> Him let us sing.
> Spread we his fame around,
> Honour of British ground,
> Who made Nile's shore resound,
> God save the King.

Emma *Hamilton, who was just beginning to fall in love with Nelson, wrote to him in even more heady terms. 'If I was King of England,' she wrote, 'I would make you the most noble present, Duke Nelson, Marquis Nile, Earl Aboukir, Viscount Pyramid, Baron Crocodile, and Prince Victory, that posterity might have you in all forms. Your statue ought to be made of pure gold and placed in the middle of London.'

NIMBUS, a type of cloud formation. See METEOROLOGY.

NIMITZ, CHESTER WILLIAM (1885–1966), American fleet admiral, commanded the U.S. Pacific Fleet and the Pacific Ocean Area for almost the whole period of the Second World War in which the Pacific Ocean was a theatre of naval operations. He was born in Fredericksburg, Texas, and graduated from the Naval Academy in 1905. His early naval duty was mainly in *submarines, and during the First World War (1914–18), he served as chief of staff to the commander of U.S. submarines in the Atlantic following the American entry into the war in 1917. After the war he was executive officer of a *battleship, commanded a submarine *squadron, and completed a course at the Naval War College, which was followed by another spell of staff duty in the U.S. fleet.

Nimitz established one of the first of the naval reserve officers training units at the University of California, taking part as an instructor. He was flag-captain in the heavy *cruiser *Augusta* in the Asiatic Fleet in 1933–4 and followed that with three years ashore as assistant chief of the Bureau of Navigation. Promoted rear admiral, he commanded a *cruiser division, followed by a battleship division, and in 1939 became chief of the Bureau of Navigation, retaining that post until December 1941 when, after the disaster of *Pearl Harbor, he was selected to command the U.S. Pacific Fleet in place of Admiral Husband *Kimmel. He hoisted his four-star admiral's flag in a submarine at Pearl Harbor on 31 December 1941.

It was a fortunate appointment, for after the Japanese attack on Pearl Harbor on 7 December 1941, morale in that stricken island and throughout the Pacific Fleet was low. Nimitz, with his pleasing personality, calm demeanour, and courteous speech, was quick to restore confidence among his officers and men, and he had the wisdom to wait through a lean period and to attempt nothing rash. Although his headquarters were ashore at Hawaii and he did not fly his flag operationally at sea, he had the gift of selecting his maritime commanders with skill for the particular tasks he demanded of them, and moreover realized that, to get the best out of them, he could not expect them all never to make a mistake. His philosophy for command selection was a belief that 'every dog should be allowed two bites', and it was only after two failures that he ever replaced a commander. It was a philosophy which not only did not sap an officer's confidence but also endeared him to all who worked under him.

The first measure of his sure touch as commander-in-chief came in the battle of *Midway, where his primary task was to try to neutralize the vast superiority of Japanese numbers, 162 Japanese warships against the American total of 76. He refused to be drawn by the Japanese subsidiary attack on the Aleutian Islands timed to take place four days before the attack on Midway, and with the aid of decoded intelligence, he was able to make exceptional tactical deployments to meet the advancing Japanese. He instructed his sea commanders to be prepared to take calculated risks in the coming battle, a policy amply justified by the sinking of four Japanese *aircraft carriers, and the whole of their fast carrier fleet, with only the *Yorktown* of the American carriers being sunk.

There followed the long and often painful campaign of *Guadalcanal, the campaigns of the Gilbert and Marshall Islands, the capture of New Guinea and the Mariana Islands, the battle of the *Philippine Sea, and finally the great naval action of *Leyte Gulf, which led to the reoccupation of the whole of the Philippine Islands, which had been lost to the U.S.A. at the beginning of the Pacific fighting. In all of these operations Nimitz showed the clear touch of the expert, his strategic sense equalling the tactical brilliance with which he had made so deep an impression at Midway. By now, under his guidance, a war that had once seemed to be virtually hopeless had been transformed into a triumphant advance that was finally to lead to the capture of Okinawa and the dramatic downfall of Japan herself. It was his intelligence and ability throughout the three and a half years of maritime battle which inexorably swept the Pacific clear of all Japanese ships.

Nimitz was promoted fleet admiral in December 1944 and on 2 September 1945, on board the battleship *Missouri* anchored in Tokyo Bay, accepted the formal surrender of Japan. On 15 December 1945 he succeeded Fleet Admiral Ernest *King as Chief of Naval Operations, serving two years in that post. Afterwards, he served as a special adviser to the Secretary of the Navy for Pacific and West Coast matters.

NIMROD, the name given by Sir Ernest *Shackleton to one of the ships selected to accompany him on his British Antarctic Expedition of 1907–9. She was built for work in Arctic and Antarctic waters as a sealer, and was a vessel of 200 tons deadweight.

NIÑA, a *caravel of 90 tons with a crew of eighteen men, which, with the *Santa Maria* and *Pinta*, sailed under the command of Christopher *Columbus in 1492 on the voyage which was to end with the first discovery of America. At the start of the expedition she was a three-masted *caravela latina*, with *lateen sails on all three masts, but at Las Palmas she was re-rigged with square sails 'that she might follow the other vessels with more tranquility and less danger'.

NIP, (1) the name given by seamen to a short turn or twist in a rope or *hawser (see also FRENCHMAN). **(2)** That part of a rope bound by a *seizing around a thimble or round the tucks of an *eye splice. Nip in the *hawse, a twist in a ship's *cable when lying to an *anchor, which can usually be cured by *veering a few feet more cable to an order to 'freshen the nip'.

NIP, to, a vessel is said to be nipped, or beset, when she is caught between two converging ice-floes in Arctic or Antarctic waters.

NIPPER, (1) a short length of rope, usually braided or *marled from end to end, which was used to bind the anchor *cable temporarily to the *viol, or *messenger, in those days when the anchor was weighed by hand round the *capstan. Several nippers were required in this operation as in older warships, up to the mid-19th century, cables were not brought up to the *forecastle

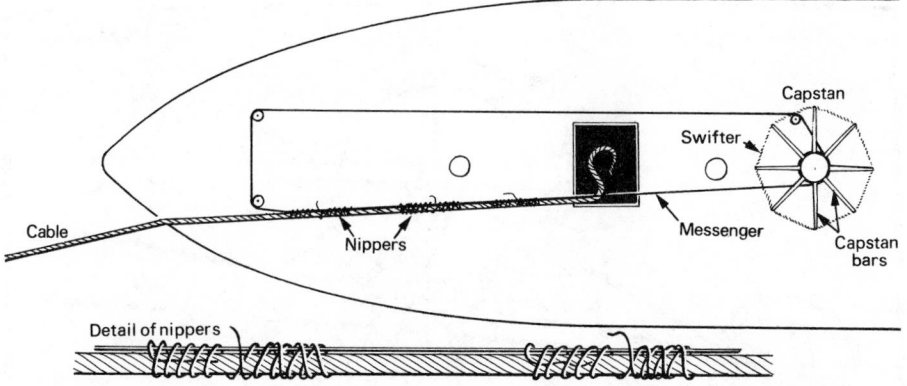

Weighing anchor

deck as today but were always worked on the main deck. As the *hemp cable itself was always very thick and heavy, and therefore unsuitable for use round the capstan direct, a smaller endless rope (viol or messenger) was passed with three or four turns round the capstan and led by *blocks forward so that it would run close alongside and in the line of the cable. As the capstan was turned, the cable was bound into the messenger with nippers and was thus hove in with it, the nippers being passed with two riding turns round the cable, then spirally around cable and messenger, with two final riding turns round the messenger. There were always six or eight boys or men with nippers and having secured a nipper near the *hawsehole, the boy or man would walk aft with it as the cable came in, binding the cable to the messenger and casting it off when he reached the main *hatchway to run forward and secure it again round the cable and messenger near the hawsehole. This was continued until the anchor was hove up high enough to be *catted. In most merchant ships of the period, cables were not so thick and heavy that they could not be taken round the capstan, and messengers were rarely necessary. (2) Boys or men who worked the nippers when the anchors were being weighed were themselves called nippers. (3) When the *yards of square-rigged ships were wet and slippery, nippers were often used to form slings for them when they were hoisted. (4) A *hammock lashed up with so little bedclothing in it that it would not stand on end in a hammock netting was also known as a nipper.

NO MAN'S LAND, the area between the after end of the *forecastle and the forward end of the *booms in square-rigged ships, where ropes, *blocks, and *tackles used on the forecastle are stowed. The term is obscure in origin, but arose possibly because it is neither on the forecastle nor in the *waist, nor on the *port or the *starboard side of the ship.

'NO, NO', see 'AYE, AYE, SIR'.

NOAH, one of the first recorded shipbuilders and builder of the *Ark, in which he and his family, together with male and female specimens of all living animals, escaped the deluge (Genesis, 6–9). Later research suggests that the Ark was not built of wood (it was in any case unlikely that there was enough wood in the entire Tigris–Euphrates region to build this great vessel entirely of timber) but followed the traditional local pattern of a raft built of reed (papyrus) roughly in the shape of a tea-tray of the size given in Genesis, with such local wood as available being used for the domestic quarters, cowsheds, pigsties, etc. This theory, however, does not remove from Noah his reputation as one of the earliest builders of a large waterborne vessel.

In addition to this watery claim to fame, Noah has another as the first man to plant a vineyard and to get tipsy on its produce.

NOCTURNAL, an early instrument designed essentially for measuring the time of night by means of *Polaris (the Pole Star) and either the 'pointers' of the Plough in the constellation *Ursa Major*, or the guards of the constellation *Ursa Minor*. It was first described in print by Michel Coignet in 1581. The earliest nocturnals consisted of two concentric circular plates of brass or wood. The circumference of the larger was divided into twelve equal parts corresponding to the months of the year and that of the smaller into twenty-four equal parts corresponding to the hours of the day. The larger plate carried a handle and the inner plate was fitted with a long index, one end of which was pivoted to the centre of the plate. To ascertain the time by the nocturnal a projecting tooth at the position corresponding to 12 o'clock on the smaller plate was turned to coincide with the date on the larger plate. The instrument was then held at arm's length and Polaris viewed through a small hole at

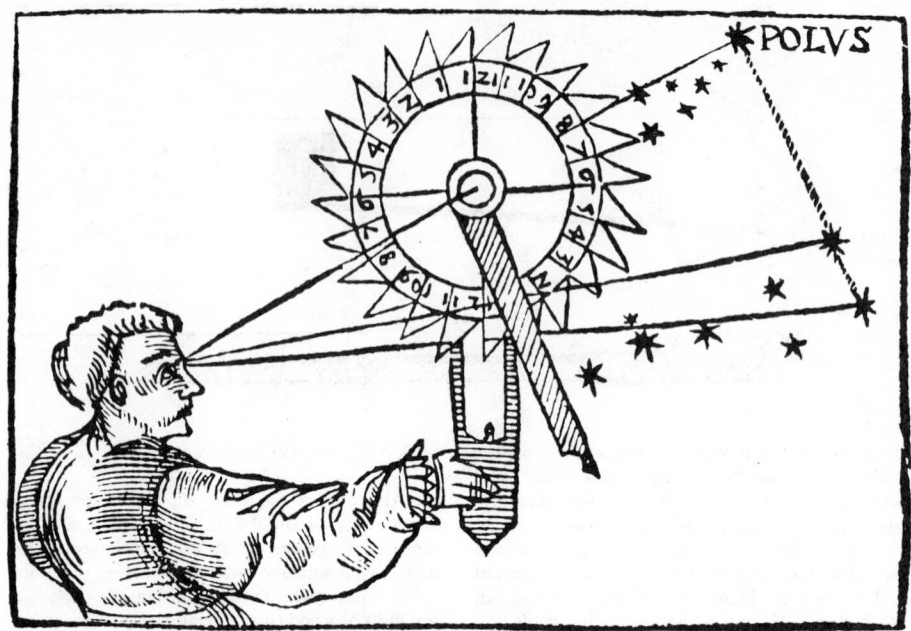

Nocturnal; engraving from Peter Apian's Cosmographia, *1539*

the centre of the instrument. The index arm was then turned until the bevelled edge coincided with the line joining the pointers or the guards, as the case might be, and the time of night was then read off the scale of hours on the smaller plate. Nocturnals were also used for working out the time of high water at a port for which the *establishment was known. It was not too difficult a matter to relate the time of the moon's southing and the *age of the moon by means of circular scales attached to the nocturnal. By applying the establishment of the port to the time of the moon's southing, the approximate time of high water, or 'full sea' as it was called, could readily be found.

NODAL, BARTHOLOMÉ and GONZALO DE, Spanish sea captains, were brothers who were commissioned by the Spanish government in 1618 to verify the discovery of a new route into the Pacific to the south of the Magellan Straits reported by Jacob *le Maire and Willem Cornelisz * Schouten in 1616. They sailed from Lisbon in 1618 in two *caravels of 80 tons each and verified the Dutch report by sailing through the Straits of le Maire in January 1619. After sighting Cape Horn they were driven to the southward by strong winds and the Cape Horn current, eventually sighting a small group of islands to which they gave the name of Diego Ramirez, whom they had with them as pilot and cosmographer. After fixing their position with

great accuracy they sailed up the western coast of Tierra del Fuego, surveying as they went, rounded Cape Desire, and proceeded eastward through the Magellan Straits to reach the Atlantic Ocean, whence they returned to Spain. Both brothers lost their lives in 1622 when their ships ran into a hurricane in the West Indies and foundered.

NOORT, OLIVIER VAN (*fl.* 1597–1600), the first Dutch circumnavigator, sailed with a small fleet from the Netherlands in 1597 and, with the riches of the East in view, passed through the Magellan Straits into the Pacific in 1598, twenty years after Francis *Drake and seventy years after Ferdinand *Magellan had made their passages. His dream of riches, however, proved a false one, though in 1590 he sacked the port of Valparaiso and held it to ransom. Tremendous gales and mutinous crews reduced his small fleet to a single ship, and though van Noort returned safely to Holland in her, the venture showed no profit.

NORDENSKIÖLD, NILS ADOLF ERIK, Baron (1832–1901), Swedish scientist and explorer, was born in Finland but later moved to Sweden because of political disagreements with the Russian authorities. Trained in geology, of which he soon became a professor, he took part in many expeditions to Spitsbergen and Greenland between 1858 and 1883. In 1867, in the iron steamer *Sofia*, he reached the highest northern *latitude (81° 42′) yet reached in the eastern hemisphere. This voyage concentrated his attention on Arctic exploration and the development of the sea route to northern Siberia.

In 1875 and 1876 he organized and took part in two successful pioneering voyages to the Yenisey, which led him to his most famous contribution to northern exploration, his circumnavigation of Europe and Asia in the *Vega (Lieutenant L. Palander) in 1878–9. The traverse of the *North-East passage with which the voyage started was the first made, and was very nearly accomplished in one season: the *Vega* was within 100 miles of Bering Strait when the new ice forming in September brought her to a halt. The voyage was concluded without incident the following year, Nordenskiöld being raised to the peerage as a baron on his return to Sweden. He published a detailed account of this expedition in five volumes, and also wrote a popular account of it in two volumes.

His last voyage was in 1883 when he sailed to the east coast of Greenland and navigated his ship through the great ice barrier, a feat which had eluded navigators for the past 300 years.

His contributions to knowledge in the field of historical geography were as great as those of Arctic discovery. In 1889 he published his *Facsimile Atlas*, which brought together in reproduction most of the more important geographical documents of the 15th and 16th centuries, but an even more important work was his *Periplus of 1897, a work of great and painstaking research into the history of early cartography and charts used by mariners during the Middle Ages.

NORDENSKJÖLD, OTTO (1870–1928), Swedish geographer and polar explorer, organized a scientific expedition to southern South America in 1895 and followed this with an expedition to Graham Land, in the Antarctic Peninsula, in 1901–3. From here he sledged along the east coast as far as latitude 66° S. In 1903 his ship *Antarctic* was crushed by the ice and the crew was forced to winter on Paulet Island, where they were later rescued by the Argentine vessel *Uruguay*. Nordenskjöld later paid a number of visits to the Arctic to study problems of geography and geology.

NORE, The, a sandbank at the mouth of the River Thames, England, lying off the entrance to the River Medway, and for a great number of years a naval anchorage which later gave its name to one of the chief commands of the British Navy. The first commander-in-chief appointed to the Nore Command was Rear Admiral John Campbell in 1778, and it included then the naval *dockyard at *Chatham. During the late 19th century a smaller dockyard was constructed at

Caricature of the mutiny at the Nore; engraving by G. Cruikshank

Sheerness, at the mouth of the River Medway, and this also became part of the Nore Command, the two forming, with *Portsmouth and *Plymouth, one of the three main home bases of the British fleet, with the commander-in-chief exercising naval operational control of the North Sea. In the post-Second World War naval reconstruction, Sheerness was abandoned as a naval dockyard and turned over to civilian purposes, and the Nore ceased to be an operational naval command although Chatham was retained as a naval dockyard.

The Nore was the scene in 1797 of a great naval mutiny which followed that at *Spithead, unnecessarily since the earlier mutiny had won for the seamen of the fleet the increase in pay and the better conditions of victualling and shore *liberty which they had demanded. It was led by Richard *Parker, of H.M.S. *Sandwich*, but after some initial success, including the persuasion of the great majority of Admiral Adam *Duncan's North Sea Fleet, then lying at Yarmouth, to join the mutiny, the ships one by one succeeded in breaking free of the mutineers' control and returning to their allegiance. Parker, during the mutiny, had drawn up the ships in two lines of battle, and those ships which first attempted to escape from his domination had to do so under the concentrated fire of the others. Within a few days the first trickle of returning ships became something of a torrent, and the mutiny collapsed. The ringleaders were brought before a court martial, and Parker and twenty-four seamen were hanged at the yardarm. They had achieved nothing and their lives ended in the contempt and ridicule of the men they had tried to lead.

NORIE, JOHN WILLIAM (1772–1843), mathematician and hydrographer, compiled a set of nautical tables which achieved deserved praise and widespread use among navigators. His *Epitome of Navigation* was for a great many years a standard work on the art. He was the original Norie in the publishing firm of Imray, Laurie, Norie, and Wilson, which in addition to publishing a large number of nautical books produced a set of coastal charts of Great Britain much in demand by yachtsmen.

NORMAN, (1) a short wooden bar which was thrust into one of the holes of a *windlass or *capstan and used to *veer a rope or to secure the *anchor cable if there was very little strain on it, **(2)** a preventer pin through the head of the *rudder to secure it against loss, **(3)** a metal pin placed in the *bitt crosspiece to prevent the cable falling off was also called a norman.

NORRIS, Sir JOHN (1660–1749), British admiral, was a lieutenant at the battle of *Beachy Head in 1690 and was promoted into the command of a *fireship as a result of his gallantry on that occasion. He commanded the frigate *Sheerness* as one of the escorts of the great Smyrna convoy of 1693, most of which was lost when the commander of the escort, Sir George *Rooke, fell into a trap set by the French and left the convoy unguarded. Norris, however, came out of this disaster with some credit, saving a number of the ships and bringing them together under the defence of the *Sheerness*.

With the rank of commodore he was sent in command of a squadron of eight ships to recover the British settlement in Hudson's Bay which had been overrun by the French, having on board a large number of troops for the purpose. Unfortunately, by his orders, he had to call a council of war before taking any warlike action, and when reports of a French squadron in the vicinity were received, the military officers of the council voted against attack on the grounds that the French were too strong. With the majority against him, Norris was unable to move against the French ships, but sent one of his frigates to investigate, only to receive, too late, the intelligence that the enemy squadron consisted of ships of small naval force which were returning to France laden with the plunder of the Spanish West Indies. There was a parliamentary inquiry when Norris returned home but he was held blameless in the failure to capture the French.

Norris, always a man of outspoken views and fiery temperament, had not endeared himself to his own officers by his remarks on this occasion, but his next effort, which took place during the expedition against *Cadiz in 1702, was more serious. During a visit to Rooke's flagship he quarrelled with the flag captain on the quarter-deck, struck him across the face, and drew his sword against him. This was quite unpardonable, but fortunately for Norris, Captain Ley, the aggrieved captain, died suddenly a few days after Norris had been placed under arrest, and the case against him was dropped.

In command of the *Orford* in 1704, Norris was second-in-command of the *van squadron of the British fleet at the battle of *Malaga. Commanding the squadron was Sir Clowdisley *Shovel, who was so impressed by Norris's fiery courage that he asked for him as his second-in-command on his appointment as commander-in-chief of the Mediterranean Fleet. Norris had been sent back to England with the dispatches after the capture of *Barcelona in 1705, had been knighted and presented with a purse of 1,000 guineas, was promoted rear admiral in 1706, and was with Shovel in the Mediterranean during the operations of 1706–7, only just escaping the disaster at the Scilly Islands in which Shovel lost his life.

Although he held a number of important appointments during the remainder of his life, including that of a seat on the Admiralty Board, the years of peace offered him little chance of adding to his renown, and by the time war came again, against Spain in 1739 as a result, initially, of Captain *Jenkins's ear, his fierce temper had caused his permanent retirement. He was, throughout his career, a remarkably able seaman, a superb fighter, and a negotiator of skill. Like Admiral John *Byron some sixty years later, he seemed to attract foul weather for his ships, and the seamen of the fleet always foretold a storm whenever he put to sea.

NORSK SJØFARTSMUSEUM, Oslo, Norway, a maritime museum in the form of a private collection assisted by government grants, which was founded in 1914 and moved to its present site in a new building in 1960. It contains some 250 ship models, and a similar number of half models, besides fishing gear, nautical instruments, *scrimshaw, tattooing designs, medals, flags, paintings, and photographs. The library contains some 12,000 books, plans, maps, archives, and manuscripts, also some phonographic records of seamen's memoirs. Smaller maritime collections in Norway are at Arendal (Aust–Agder Museet); Grimstad (Grimstad Bymuseum og Ibsenhuset); Haugesund (Museet for Haugesund og Bybdens); Kaupanger (Heibergske Samlinger, Sogn Folkmuseum); Kristiansand (Sjøfartsmuseum); Molde (Fiskerimuseet paa Hjertøya); Skien (Fylkesmuseet for Telemark og Grenland); and Trondheim (Trondhjems Sjøfartsmuseum).

NORTH CAPE, BATTLE OF, a naval action fought during the Second World War off the North Cape of Norway on 26 December 1943 between a squadron of the Home Fleet, under the command of Admiral Sir Bruce *Fraser, and a detached cruiser force, and a battle group of the German Navy commanded by Rear Admiral Erich Bey.

The action arose out of the passage of Convoy JW 55B with war supplies to North Russia. In addition to its close escort of destroyers and frigates, the convoy had a covering force of three cruisers (* *Belfast, Norfolk,* and *Sheffield*) and distant cover of a Home Fleet squadron, consisting of the battleship *Duke of York,* the cruiser *Jamaica,* and four destroyers. Opposition to its passage was expected, as the German battle-cruiser *Scharnhorst* with a flotilla of destroyers was known to be based in Altenfjord, at the northern extremity of occupied Norway. The German ships sailed in the evening of Christmas Day.

On the morning of 26 December the three cruisers covering the convoy picked up the *Scharnhorst* on their radar, closed her at full speed, and opened fire at a range of 13,500 yards

(12,500 m). They hit her with their first salvoes and, among other damage, destroyed her forward radar installation. Taken completely by surprise, the *Scharnhorst* turned away and was soon lost in the Arctic darkness, but Vice Admiral Burnett, commanding the three cruisers, expected her to make for the convoy and himself closed it to provide additional defence against the expected attack. Rear Admiral Bey, because of the wild Arctic weather, had ordered his destroyers to return independently to base, and so was alone, but still confident that his great ship was more than a match for the British cruisers. Two and a half hours later, as Admiral Burnett had expected, the *Scharnhorst* turned up close to the convoy, only to be confronted once again by the three British cruisers. In the ensuing gun duel the *Scharnhorst* was hit again and the *Norfolk* slightly damaged by two hits, but after 20 minutes the German battle-cruiser broke off the action and made off at high speed to the south-east, pursued and shadowed by Admiral Burnett's cruisers.

It was from this direction that Admiral Fraser, unknown to the *Scharnhorst*, was coming up with his squadron. Four hours later the *Duke of York* picked up the battle-cruiser on her radar at a range of 44,000 yards (40,740 m). The *Duke of York* and the *Jamaica* closed the range to 12,000 yards (11,111 m), illuminated the *Scharnhorst* with *starshell, and opened fire. Again the German battle-cruiser was heavily hit, this time by the 14-inch shells of the *Duke of York,* and, again taken completely by surprise, she turned away and made off to the east. She had a margin of four knots in speed over the *Duke of York,* but the hits she had received from her had caused underwater damage and flooding, and gradually her speed dropped, allowing Admiral Fraser's destroyers to catch her and slow her down yet further with torpedoes. The British ships closed in and under an intense fire from guns and torpedoes, she rolled over and disappeared. Only thirty-six of her total complement of nearly 2,000 were picked up.

NORTH STAR, a ship's name long associated with British Arctic exploration. A vessel of this name formed part of John *Davis's second expedition to Baffin Bay in 1586–7 in the elusive search for the *North-West passage.

A later one was a *frigate of 501 tons and twenty-eight guns built for the British Navy at Woolwich and launched in 1824. She was commissioned the following year and saw service in home waters, in China, and New Zealand before being used in the Arctic with Captain Sir Edward *Belcher's expedition of 1852–4 in search of Sir John *Franklin, during which she was used as a depot ship. She was broken up at Chatham in 1860.

NORTH-EAST PASSAGE, the name given to the sea route round the north of Europe and Asia. (For chart, see ARCTIC EXPLORATION.) Parts of it were possibly navigated by primitive inhabitants of the adjoining land masses from earliest times, but it first became known to western civilization from its Atlantic end. The first section, north of Scandinavia into what is now called the Barents Sea and the White Sea, was well known to Norsemen by the 10th century, and to the northward-thrusting men of Novgorod by the 12th. In the 14th century many Russian ships used this route to Norway. Some started at this time sailing eastwards out of the White Sea, towards the more ice-ridden and difficult Kara Sea. By the middle of the 16th century, some Russians, and probably some Norsemen, had very likely found their way into that sea; and Paolo Giovio records that in 1525 a Russian diplomat in Italy, Dmitriy Gerasimov, suggested that there might even be the possibility of a sea route along the coast to China. At about the same time (1527) in England Robert Thorne was making the suggestion that a north-about voyage might be the best way to reach *Cathay (China) and yet avoid the Spaniards and the Portuguese.

So now the concept of a North-East passage was born. The English were among the first to explore the idea. Voyages were made by Sir Hugh *Willoughby (1553), Richard *Chancellor (1553), Stephen *Borough (1556), James Bassendine (1568), Arthur Pet and Charles Jackman (1580), and Henry *Hudson (1607 and 1608). Between 1594 and 1597 the Dutch also sent out expeditions, on which William *Barents was the leading personality. Although each of these expeditions was remarkable, and some very sensational discoveries were made, none of the voyages came anywhere near to achieving the object of discovering a North-East passage; in fact none penetrated further east than the western part of the Kara Sea—or about one-eighth of the total distance between the White Sea and Bering Strait.

The early lack of success in finding the north-eastern route to Cathay led to fewer attempts being made. Two English vessels under Captain Wood and Captain Flawes tried in 1676, but did not pass Novaya Zemlya. A Russian expedition under V. Ya. Chichagov, undertaken in 1765 at the suggestion of the polymath Mikhail Lomonosov, got no further than Spitsbergen. Another in 1768 under F. Rozmyslov was stopped at Novaya Zemlya—where excellent work was done. Commander David Buchan and Lieutenant John *Franklin of the Royal Navy attempted to reach the Bering Strait by way of Spitsbergen in 1818, but ice forced them to return when still in the region of the latter. In 1872 the forcing of the North-East passage was one of several alternative objects of Weyprecht

and Payer's Austrian Arctic Expedition; but the ship was frozen into the ice north of Novaya Zemlya and drifted north-westwards to unknown land, which was named (Kaiser) Franz Josef Land.

All these failures to achieve the main objective did not, however, prevent the advance of knowledge in a more local context. The route through the south-west Kara Sea to the estuary of the Ob was much used by Russian traders in the late 16th and early 17th centuries. Archaeological evidence seems to indicate Russian voyages to points further east, even to the Laptev Sea, in the first quarter of the 17th century. But a Moscow decree of 1620 forbade trading by these routes, and trading vessels did not return to these waters until the 1870s.

Further east, however, the fur traders and Cossacks reached forward to the Arctic Ocean by way of the Lena, Indigirka, and Kolyma rivers. Descending these rivers by boat in the 1640s, they followed the coast to the mouth of the next river. The most notable of such voyages was that of Semen *Dezhnev in 1648–9, when he sailed eastwards out of the Kolyma and rounded the north-east tip of Asia (which now bears his name). His voyage was forgotten for a century, and the strait between Asia and America was named after *Bering, who reached it only in 1728.

In the 18th century a major effort was made by the Russian Navy to describe and map the whole northern coast of Russia (the early navigators in the Kara Sea had left no written guides). A large and remarkable organization called the Great Northern Expedition (also known as the Second Kamchatka Expedition) put a series of parties into the field between 1733 and 1743. Each party was responsible for a section of coast, and by the end of the period almost the whole of the north coast had been mapped, mostly from the seaward side—a result achieved only after overcoming great difficulties. It was now clear that a North-East passage existed, but the technology of the time could not fully overcome the ice problem. Another naval party, under the English-born Captain Joseph Billings, who had sailed with Captain James *Cook, made a determined but not very successful attempt in 1785–94 to improve knowledge of the far northeast.

Expeditions, largely naval, were mounted from time to time in the 19th century to clarify particular regions. Thus Baron von *Wrangell (in Russian Vrangel) and Lieutenant P. F. Anjou (Anzhu) charted the region east of the Kolyma in 1820–4, and the region of Novaya Zemlya was explored by Lieutenant F. P. *Lütke (Litke) in 1821–4, Lieutenant P. K. Pakhtusov in 1832–3, and Lieutenant A. K. Ciwolka (Tsivolka) in 1837–9.

In the 1860s the question of trading voyages into the Kara Sea was again raised by the Siberian merchants M. K. Sidorov and A. M. Sibiryakov. Interest was taken by two persons in particular: Captain Joseph *Wiggins of Sunderland, who went on to demonstrate, in a series of voyages between 1874 and 1895, the practicability of the undertaking; and Professor N. A. E. *Nordenskiöld, a Swedish Finn, who after successful voyages to the Yenisey in 1875 and 1876 performed the great feat of navigating the whole North-East passage aboard the *Vega in 1878–9. He could probably have completed the voyage in one season if he had not delayed to carry out the scientific work which was the main object of the expedition.

Once the *Vega* had demonstrated the practicability of making the passage, others followed. There were three important scientific expeditions, which did not, however, aim to repeat Nordenskiöld's achievement: the American G. W. *deLong drifted in the *Jeannette* across the northern part of the East Siberian Sea while trying to reach the pole (1879–81); Fridtjof *Nansen traversed the Kara and Laptev Seas in the *Fram* before allowing her to be frozen in and to drift across the Arctic Ocean (1893–6); and the Russian Baron E. *Toll followed Nansen's course as far as Novosibirskiye Ostrova in the *Zarya* (1900–2). Of these three, only Nansen survived. The passage itself was also attempted again by scientifically rather than economically motivated parties. In 1912 the Russians G. L. Brusilov in the *St. Anna* and V. A. Rusanov in the *Gerkules* both tried from the western end and met disaster without getting further than the Kara Sea. In 1914–15 a Russian hydrographic expedition under B. A. *Vilkitskiy in the *Taymyr* and *Vaygach* made the full traverse, this time from east to west, wintering off Taymyr. In 1918–20 Roald *Amundsen made the third traverse, from west to east, in the specially built *Maud*. This exploratory phase may be said to have ended in 1932, when the first traverse in one season was made by Otto Shmidt in the small Soviet ice-breaker *Sibiryakov* (launched in Glasgow in 1909 as *Bellaventure*).

Meanwhile trading voyages to the Ob and Yenisey grew in number, and in 1911 analogous voyages started from the Pacific end into the River Kolyma. The growth of this traffic, and the *Sibiryakov*'s achievement, were factors in causing the Soviet government to plan for major development of the northern sea route (as the North-East passage was called in the U.S.S.R.). The main object was to open up northern Siberia; the idea of the through route, from one end of the country to the other, was subsidiary. A new government department was formed— the Chief Administration of the Northern Sea Route—and its first Head was Otto *Shmidt, a professor of mathematics who led many Arctic expeditions both before and after his appointment. Large resources of money and skill were deployed in the attempt to make the northern sea route a 'normally working waterway'. Expeditions were put in the field, a network of 100 shore stations was completed, an ice-breaker fleet was built up, scientists at the Arctic Research Institute developed an ice reconnaissance and forecasting service. Ports were built or enlarged at Dikson, Igarka, Tiksi, Pevek, and Provideniya.

The navigation seasons of the 1930s were exciting and not always successful. A major disaster occurred in 1937 when twenty-six ships, including seven out of eight serviceable ice-breakers, were obliged to winter at sea. Among the repercussions was a violent shake-up in the Chief Administration, leading to the appointment of a new head, I. D. Papanin.

During the Second World War the route was mainly used to re-supply northern settlements. Lease–lend ships operating out of the American west coast passed through Bering Strait to ports along the north coast of Siberia. The Germans realized this, and there were some naval actions in the Kara Sea. There was also some military use of the through passage. In 1940 the Russians permitted the German merchant raider *Komet* to make the traverse from west to east, and Soviet naval vessels came through to reinforce the Atlantic Fleet after the Soviet entry into the war.

After the war there was an increase in activity on the route. No complete picture of any season's operations is issued in the Soviet press, but from occasional news releases the impression is gained that in the 1950s and 1960s probably 200 to 300 ships operated in these waters each summer, carrying between one and two million tons of freight. The biggest traffic is to and from the Yenisey River, where there are important nickel mines at Norilsk and a substantial timber industry at Igarka. After that comes traffic from the Pacific to Pevek and the Kolyma River, where again there are mines. There is not generally any significant through traffic—unless it is naval and therefore not reported. In 1967 the Soviet government offered to open the route to foreign shippers but none accepted the offer, which seems to have been tacitly withdrawn later. The ice is the biggest variable in all this, and it largely determines the success or failure of each season.

These operations are made possible by the existence of a fleet of about a dozen powerful (over 10,000 h.p.) ice-breakers, most of them Finnish-built. The flagship from 1960 to 1967 was the Soviet-built *Lenin, nuclear-propelled and with nearly twice the power (44,000 h.p.) of the next most powerful ice-breaker afloat. She performed some impressive feats but has been out of action for undeclared reasons since 1967. The ice-breaker fleet, together with the improved knowledge of ice distribution and behaviour stemming from a large scientific programme, has led to a lengthening of the season from about two and a half months in the early 1930s to four months, or four and a half in some places and seasons. At the time of writing no serious thought seems to have been given to the possibility of using * submarine freighters and ice-strengthened super-* tankers—two ideas thought promising in the western hemisphere. Probably the shallow waters of the continental shelf, over which almost the whole northern sea route runs, would make operation of both types of ship difficult. Quite a large fleet of ice-strengthened freighters of up to about 10,000 tons * deadweight has been built up over the years; particularly successful has been the *Ob*-class, 6,500 d.w.t., able to overcome moderately severe concentrations unescorted. Most important of all, however, is the body of highly trained and experienced men who operate the northern sea route and its ancillary services.

NORTHESK, Earl of, see CARNEGIE, William.

NORTHUMBERLAND, **H.M.S.,** a ship's name used six times in the Royal Navy, of which the most distinguished is undoubtedly the 74-gun 3rd * rate * ship of the line which was built on the Thames in 1798. She took part in Lord Keith's (see ELPHINSTONE, G. K.) expedition to Egypt in 1801, and in 1805 was the flagship of Rear Admiral the Hon. Alexander Cochrane with the squadron then engaged in watching for the enemy off * Ferrol and Corunna. In 1806 she took part in Vice Admiral Sir John Duckworth's action against a French fleet off St. Domingo when she had twenty-one killed and seventy-nine wounded, Cochrane being knighted for his part in the battle. In company with the *Growler* * brig, the *Northumberland* drove ashore and destroyed off Lorient the French 40-gun * frigates *Ariane* and *Andromaque* and the 16-gun brig *Mamelouck* in 1812, her casualties on this occasion being five killed and twenty-eight wounded. In 1815, flying the flag of Rear Admiral Sir George * Cockburn, she performed the service for which she is most generally known, the conveyance of Napoleon to his exile in St. Helena after he had surrendered to H.M.S. * *Bellerophon* following his flight from the field of Waterloo. Ultimately, after many years of service as a * lazaretto in Standgate Creek, she was taken to pieces at * Deptford in 1850.

NORTH-WEST PASSAGE, the name given to the sea route from the Atlantic to the Pacific to the north of Canada. (For chart, see ARCTIC EXPLORATION.) The search for this northern Arctic sea route has lured explorers since John * Cabot reached the new world at Newfoundland in 1497 and thought that it was the coast of Asia. He lost his life on a second and similar voyage the following year. But it soon became obvious to explorers that Asia still lay many thousands of miles further to the west and that the road to * Cathay was blocked by the North American continent. In 1535 the French navigator Jacques * Cartier thought the St. Lawrence River would prove to be the gateway to the Far East, but the North American wilderness closed in and there were only rapids before him.

The driving search for a northern sea route, especially by the English and Dutch in the 16th century, either by the north-east or the north-west, was brought about when, in the late 15th century, the Ottoman Turks completed their conquest of the eastern Mediterranean and the ancient overland caravan routes, over which spices and other products from the Orient had come to the European market for centuries, were effectively closed off. Northern Europeans were further frustrated, forty years after the Turks captured Constantinople, when Pope Alexander VI, in 1493, drew a line 370 * leagues west of Cape Verde and gave all newly discovered areas east of the line to Portugal and all parts to be found henceforth west of it to Spain. The agreement was confirmed the next year at the Treaty of Tordesillas. Thus, when the only two feasible sea routes to the Orient (around the Cape of * Good Hope and through the Straits of * Magellan) were discovered during the next thirty years, they were controlled by Spain and Portugal. The Dutch and the English were, therefore, sealed off from the lucrative trade which became ever more profitable with the increasing shortage of spices and consequent soaring prices. The Dutch sought to correct the situation by attempting to sail north round the top of Asia to China by a * North-East passage. The English, also making a few abortive attempts in this direction, turned their attention to finding a North-West passage through or over North America. They stubbornly continued in their search for about 350 years. Both Dutch and English were supported by wishful-thinking geographers who postulated an open polar sea.

The search for the North-West passage, which was always primarily an English undertaking, was concentrated in two periods. Sir Humphrey * Gilbert in a petition to Elizabeth I, in 1555, offered to undertake 'the discovering of a passage by the Northe, to go to Cataia [Cathay], & all other the east partes of the worlde' provided that he and his brothers were given a monopoly for trade through the passage. Nothing came of it, but Gilbert followed his petition with a letter to his brother, Sir John Gilbert, in 1566, entitled 'A discourse of a discoverie for a new passage to

Cataia'. This now famous document circulated in manuscript for ten years before it was published. Gilbert's confidence in the existence of a commercially feasible route to the east probably inspired to some extent the attempts to find a North-West passage which began in the last quarter of the 16th century. The principal expeditions during this first period began with the three voyages of Martin *Frobisher in 1576, 1577, and 1578 to Frobisher Bay. Until Charles F. Hall discovered in 1862 the site of Frobisher's activities, it was thought that he had reached southern Greenland. On Frobisher's last voyage, with a fleet of fifteen vessels, he hoped to bring back from Frobisher Bay cargoes of gold which he thought he had discovered on his second voyage, but the ore turned out to be worthless. The next important explorer, John *Davis, also made three voyages in 1585, 1586, and 1587. He discovered Davis Strait and invented the *backstaff known, in its refined form, as the Davis *quadrant. The next expeditions of consequence were those of Henry *Hudson who made four voyages between 1607 and 1611. On the third voyage, under Dutch colours, he discovered the Hudson River. On his last, when he discovered Hudson Bay, he was set adrift there with his son and loyal crew members by a mutinous crew. William *Baffin, sailing usually as pilot, made five voyages between 1612 and 1616, and penetrated to the northern end of the bay which bears his name. The last voyages of this early series were those of Luke *Fox and Thomas *James in 1631. Their expeditions proved conclusively that there was no passage through the continent from the western shores of Hudson Bay. Foxe Channel and Basin to the north of the Bay and James Bay on the south commemorate their endeavours. They brought to a close the first great period of Arctic exploration; a period that was distinguished by the failure of its primary purpose, to find a commercially practical passage to the Far East.

One result of their endeavours, however, was the formation in 1670 of the Hudson's Bay Company for the purpose of exploiting the trade in furs. During the 18th century the company came under extensive criticism for its lack of interest in attempting to find a North-West passage, which by its charter it was bound to do. For the sake of its public relations it began a rather erratic search, consisting of minor sea voyages around Hudson Bay and various land journeys up into the north. The most important of these was the overland expedition of Samuel *Hearne who, in 1771, discovered the long and winding Coppermine River. A few years later Sir Alexander *Mackenzie, in the employ of the North-West Company, discovered and reached the mouth of the still longer river now named after him. Thus, there were now two points of contact on the Arctic Ocean itself. When Captain James *Cook, on his third voyage of circumnavigation, explored much of western Alaska and, searching for a *Pacific entrance to the North-West passage, penetrated through Bering Strait to Icy Cape, the general outline of the North American continent began to assume its modern form. The most important voyages during the 18th century were those of Christopher *Middleton to Hudson Bay in 1741 and 1742, and William More and Francis Smith to the same place with the ships *Dobbs* and *California* in 1746 and 1747. These voyages were both sponsored by Arthur Dobbs, an inveterate believer in a practical North-West passage, who wanted to prove that the Hudson's Bay Company was withholding information about a navigable passage for its own benefit.

During the second great period of exploration for the passage in the 19th century, the goal was more to solve a geographical problem than to find a commercially feasible route to the Far East. The series of great British expeditions that were mounted during this period were first stimulated by the amendment of an Act that was passed by Parliament in 1745 offering a reward of £20,000 to any British subject, excepting those on naval vessels, who discovered a North-West passage through Hudson Strait. There were few takers. When the Act was amended, however, twenty years later, the naval restrictions were removed and the desired location was changed from Hudson Strait to north of *latitude 70° between the Atlantic and the Pacific. The Act was further altered in 1817 to provide a sliding scale of rewards for approaching the pole and for reaching certain *meridians of *longitude.

This was the Act that inspired the first of the great 19th century British Admiralty expeditions. Commodore John *Ross was dispatched in April 1818 in command of the ships *Isabella* and *Alexander*. His second in command in the *Alexander* was William Edward *Parry, and Ross's nephew, James Clark *Ross, was a *midshipman on the voyage. Ross penetrated Davis Strait and Baffin Bay as far as Lancaster Sound. His short penetration of the Sound, however, was stopped by what he considered a high range of hills, which he named Croker's Mountains. He turned back and was in England again in November. This expedition was followed by a long and acrimonious argument over whether or not any mountains, in fact, existed. Sir John *Barrow, Secretary of the Admiralty, was especially critical. Barrow decided to send out another expedition to Lancaster Sound the following year but he replaced Ross with his former lieutenant, William Edward Parry. This expedition in the ships *Hecla* and *Griper* departed in May 1819 and did not return until

October 1820. Not only was it the first to winter in those northern latitudes, it was also one of the most successful of the many expeditions, for Croker's Mountains vanished and Parry penetrated through Lancaster Sound, Barrow Strait, and Melville Sound to Melville Island, where he wintered. So sanguine were the hopes of sailing through the passage after Parry's tremendous effort that he was dispatched on a second expedition with the *Fury* and *Hecla* in 1821, and a third in 1824 and 1825 with the same vessels, when the *Fury* was wrecked. The same year Captain George Lyon made a voyage in the *Griper* and Frederick W. *Beechey was in the Pacific in H.M.S. *Blossom* hoping to join Parry by penetrating the Arctic through Bering Strait.

In 1829 John Ross was back on the scene with the *Victory* on a private expedition financed by Felix Booth. He did not return until 1833, spending four winters in the Arctic where his ship was wrecked on the Boothia Peninsula. During the enforced winterings his nephew and second-in-command, James Clark Ross, located and discovered on 1 June 1831 the magnetic north pole while on a sledging expedition. In 1836 George *Back made a voyage in the *Terror and spent one winter in the Arctic, returning in September of 1837.

The last of this series of voyages ended in the tragedy of Sir John *Franklin, who sailed in May 1845 in the *Erebus and Terror. He was last spoken to by a *whaler in Baffin Bay and was never seen again. His ships were wrecked on King William Island and every man on the expedition perished. When he did not return in 1848, James Clark Ross was sent out in the *Enterprise and *Investigator on the first of some forty search expeditions. It was these search expeditions that actually finally mapped the North-West passage. Robert *McClure, in 1850, discovered the passage's existence and Leopold *McClintock, in the *Fox in 1857, discovered the site of Franklin's tragedy.

No more exploration or attempts to sail through the North-West passage occurred for fifty years. Then, on 16 June 1903, Roald *Amundsen, in the Norwegian fishing boat *Gjøa*, successfully navigated the passage over a period of three years—arriving in Alaska on 31 August 1906. It was ironic that after all the expensive British Admiralty expeditions, with large ships and hundreds of men, Amundsen, with a small crew in a fishing *sloop, should be successful. There the matter rested until June 1940 when Henry Larson in the Royal Canadian police boat *St. Roch* sailed the North-West passage from east to west and did it again in 1944. Ten years later the Canadian ice-breaker *Labrador* made the voyage under Captain O. C. S. Robertson, and twice more under Captain T. C. Pullen in 1956 and 1957. The most dramatic

modern voyage occurred when Commander William Anderson, in command of U.S.S. *Nautilus, a nuclear submarine, sailed from the Pacific to the Atlantic via the North pole in 1958. That same year Commander James F. Calvert, in the nuclear submarine U.S.S. *Skate*, completed another voyage during which he scattered the remains of the Arctic explorer Sir Hubert *Wilkins at the North pole.

In 1969 the 350-year-old European dream of a commercially feasible North-West passage was at last realized when the Humble Oil Company's tanker *Manhattan* brought the first cargo of Alaskan crude oil to the refineries of the east coast, though at a heavy cost in damage from the ice.

NOSTROMO, a novel by Joseph *Conrad published in 1904. It is a story of the South American seaboard, and one of the books by which he is best remembered today.

NOTICES TO MARINERS, a periodical publication of the British Hydrographic Department of the Navy containing details of all alterations to British Admiralty *charts required to keep them permanently up to date. They were first issued in 1834. Previously, beginning in 1832, these corrections were published in the *Nautical Magazine*, a somewhat haphazard means of promulgation which was unlikely to reach all users of British Admiralty charts. Such details as changes in the characteristics of navigational lights, positions of *buoys, new work on ports and harbours, positions of wrecks, etc., are invariably included in *Notices to Mariners*. A feature of the modern issues of this publication is the reproduction of areas of the chart affected, showing the needed correction, on gummed paper which can be stuck directly on to the chart, saving much labour in making corrections. Similar publications are issued by other national authorities who produce navigational charts.

NOYES, ALFRED (1880–1958), British poet, was born at Wolverhampton and educated at Oxford. Much of his poetry is devoted to the sea, and his best-known work in this genre is his sea epic *Drake*, serialized in *Blackwood's Magazine* and published in 1906. This was followed a year later by *Forty Singing Seamen*. There is also much of a maritime flavour in the great work by which he is best remembered, *The Torch Bearers* (1922–30).

NUGGER or **NUGGAR**, the traditional sail trading vessel of the lower part of the River Nile. They were two-masted with a very large *lateen sail on the mainmast and a much smaller lateen on the *mizen. A distinctive feature of their construction was the very abrupt rise of the

A Nile nugger

* stem as a precaution against the broken water which is very quickly knocked up by a squall across the desert. They carried quite sizeable cargoes, mainly of grain grown in the south coming down river, and manufactured goods made in the north going up river. See also GYASSI.

NULL, see RADIO DIRECTION FINDER.

'NUMBER', the somewhat odd designation of a group of four letters assigned to every merchant ship for identification purposes. A ship makes her 'number' by hoisting the alphabetical flags in the *International Code of Signals which represent the four letters which have been assigned to her. The allocation of these distinguishing letters is done on an international scale, every maritime nation being given groups of letters from which they assign individual distinguishing letters for every ship registered in their country.

NUÑEZ, PEDRO (1492–1577), Portuguese geographer, was professor of mathematics at Coimbra and is chiefly remembered for his translation of much of *Ptolemy's works in 1537 and for his *De Arte Atque Ratione Navigandi* (1546) which was a famous treatise on the navigational instruments used by the Portuguese explorers.

NUÑEZ CABEZA DE VACA, ALVARO (*c.* 1490–*c.* 1564), Spanish explorer, sailed with Pamfilo de Narvaez in 1527 for the Gulf of Mexico. When Narvaez was lost by shipwreck, Nuñez Cabeza de Vaca succeeded in reaching the mainland somewhere to the west of the mouth of the Mississippi River and, with three companions, managed to make his way after much hardship and many privations to the city of Mexico, which he reached in 1536. He returned to Spain the following year and was appointed governor of Rio de la Plata, taking out a squadron of ships there in 1541. Sending his ships on to Buenos Aires, he set out with 150 men to relieve the Spanish garrison at Asunçion, but was nearly a year on the way mapping the coast. He was back in Spain in 1544, but in 1551 was banished to Africa for eight years. After only one year of his banishment he was recalled to Spain to become a judge in Seville and took no further part in exploration of the new world.

NUT, the ball on the end of the *stock of an Admiralty pattern *anchor. Its purpose is to prevent the stock from penetrating the ground, thus forcing it to lie flat on the bottom so that the *flukes, at right angles to the stock, are driven into the ground to provide good holding.

O

OAKUM, tarred hemp or manila (tow) fibres made from old and condemned ropes which have been unpicked, used for *caulking the *seams of the decks and sides of a wooden ship in order to make them watertight. It was rammed down between the seams with a caulking iron and a heavy hammer, and then held in position with hot pitch poured along the seams. The unpicking of oakum for naval use was the principal labour of the old workhouses to which the old and infirm were condemned when they were no longer able to support themselves by their labour. It was also an old naval punishment, every man condemned to cells on board ship having to unpick a pound of oakum daily. It was a tedious and slow process, and very hard on fingers and thumbs.

OAR, a wooden instrument which, working as a lever, is used to *pull a boat through the water. It has three parts: the blade, the part of the oar which enters the water; the shaft, the main body of the oar; and the *loom, the inboard end on which the rower pulls. The point of leverage is the *rowlock, *crutch, or *thole pin in the *gunwale of the boat. It is so basic an adjunct of the sea that, according to legend, *Ulysses/Odysseus was told, on his retirement from a life at sea, that he should journey inland carrying an oar over his shoulder until he should find a people who asked him what it was he was carrying. There, after making a sacrifice to *Neptune, he should build his house.

O'BRIEN, CONOR (1880–1952), Irish yachtsman and author, was born in County Limerick, Ireland, and trained as an architect but took to the sea at an early age, sailing in local *whalers and fishing boats. He bought *Kelpie*, a 26-ton *yawl, and with her smuggled guns during the insurrection in Ireland of 1915–16. Later, when sailing *Kelpie* single-handed and asleep below, he lost her by running her aground on the coast of Galloway. He then designed and built *Saoirse* (Erse for Freedom), a 42-ft (12·8 m) copy of an

Irish trading *ketch which he rigged for long distance voyaging as a staysail-*brigantine. In her, with various crews, he sailed round the world by way of Cape Horn in 1922–5.

The next year he skippered the 56-ft (17 m) ketch *Ilen* from Baltimore to the Falkland Islands, but remained faithful to *Saoirse* until forced to sell her after the Second World War. He was a keen and practical advocate of square rig for ocean voyaging and had an inventive mind for improving the rigging and gear of offshore yachts. Among the books he wrote were *Across Three Oceans*, *From Three Yachts*, *On Going to Sea in Yachts*, *Voyage and Discovery*, *Deep Water Yacht Rig*, *The Small Ocean Going Yacht*, and *Yacht Gear and Gadgets*.

O'BRIEN, RICHARD BARRY (1888–1969), British merchant navy captain and author, first went to sea in 1902 as an apprentice in the Glasgow wool *clipper *Loch Broom*. He joined the *White Star Line in 1912 and, after service in the First World War (1914–18) in an *armed merchant cruiser, was in the liners *Olympic* and *Majestic* between the two world wars. He was well known for a series of sea stories which were published in the *Wide World* magazine, and later issued in book form under the titles *Square Rigger Days*, *I Tell of the Seven Seas*, and *Epics of the Square Rigged Ships*.

O'BYRNE, WILLIAM RICHARD (1823–96), British author, conceived the idea, while he was still a young man, of compiling biographical details of every living British naval officer. The first fruits of his work, *Biographica Navalis*, were published in 1845 and the whole, comprising 1,400 pages, in 1849. In spite of its meticulous accuracy, the work has no great claims to literary merit and it was not a financial success for its author although the Royal United Service Institution presented him with a piece of plate and £400. A second edition of the work begun in 1859 was never finished. Like the naval

Oar

Blade — Shaft — Leather — Loom

biographical dictionary of John *Charnock, published about sixty years earlier, he invited serving officers to contribute their own biographical notices, so that it appears as something like a catalogue of naval paragons.

OCCULTING LIGHT, a navigational light displayed by a *lighthouse or *lightship in which the period of darkness is shorter than the period of light. See CHARACTERISTICS.

OCEAN, in its proper meaning, the whole body of water which encircles the globe with the exception of inland seas, lakes, and rivers. For more precise geographical purposes, the ocean is divided into five separate oceans—the *Atlantic (North and South), *Indian, *Pacific, Arctic, and Antarctic. It has been calculated that the oceans cover 71 per cent of the whole area of the globe.

OCEAN RACING, see YACHTING.

OCEAN RATING COUNCIL, an international body which supervises the rules under which racing yachts are rated. It is a complementary body to the International Yacht Racing Union (see YACHTING, Racing rules).

OCEANIA, a term sometimes used to describe the *South Seas but more accurately those south Pacific islands included in the area bounded by Hawaii in the north, Easter Island in the east, New Zealand in the south, and New Guinea in the west. This area is subdivided into Polynesia in the east, Micronesia in the north-west, and Melanesia in the south-west.

OCEANIDES or **OCEANITIDES,** the generic name given to the legendary sea nymphs, daughters of *Oceanus. Contemporary estimates of their number vary from 41 to 3,000. The Oceanides, like many of the rest of the inferior deities, were honoured with libations and sacrifices, in their case by seamen. Prayers were offered to them, and they were entreated to protect sailors from storms and dangerous tempests. The *Argonauts, before they proceeded on their expedition, made an offering of flour, honey, and oil on the seashore to all the deities of the sea, sacrificed bulls to them and entreated their protection throughout the voyage on which they were about to embark in the arduous quest for the Golden Fleece.

OCEANOGRAPHY, the science which deals with the phenomena common to the whole ocean. Attempts to particularize this science under the general name 'thalassography' have been resisted since it was first proposed by the Italian authorities at the end of the 19th century; similar attempts to align this science with the general title of *hydrography have similarly failed to find favour, since oceanography is a wider study than pure hydrography.

Oceanography, in its widest meaning, embraces every aspect of the oceans of the world, their flora and fauna, their winds and currents, the nature of the bottom, their salinity, depth, density, mean temperature, etc. It is based, in general, on the information contained in ships' scientific logs and in the multiplicity of observations made by research vessels. It is from this vast basic information that knowledge of the oceans is built up and particularized. The father of modern oceanography is probably the American Matthew Fontaine *Maury, whose methods and plans were accepted by international congresses held in Brussels in 1853 and London in 1873. Many millions of individual observations contained in ships' logs were tabulated to provide the basis of knowledge of the general phenomena of the oceans, and maritime nations have continued to pool this information for the ultimate benefit of all seafarers.

With Maury as the leading spirit bringing together the various national observations into an international body of knowledge of ocean phenomena, the voyage of H.M.S. *Challenger in 1872–6 is generally accepted as marking the start of oceanography as a science of precision. Following on the Maury/Challenger epoch, the institution in 1901 of the International Council for the Study of the Sea, sponsored by Norway, Sweden, Denmark, Great Britain, Finland, Russia, Holland, Belgium, and Germany, with its headquarters at Copenhagen and a central laboratory at Oslo, was the next great step forward. Although the immediately basic idea underlying the institution of this council was the study of the North Sea *fisheries, its interests quickly spread beyond this limited objective to embrace the study of all the world's oceans.

The laying of submarine cables during the second half of the 19th century gave a considerable fillip to the study of oceanography by the necessity for an accurate measurement of depth of ocean along the course of the proposed cables, and this stimulated the invention of new methods of sounding in great depths. With these new deep sounding methods went new inventions for bringing up samples of the floor of the ocean, so that studies of this nature were also made possible.

Most maritime nations have institutes of oceanography, or their equivalents, in which modern methods of study are directed towards increasing the knowledge of the subject, particularly by the interchange of observations on an international basis.

OCEANUS, an influential Greek deity of the sea, son of Coelus (the sky) and Terra (the earth). He married *Tethys, of whom was born most of the principal rivers together with a number of daughters who are called, from him, *Oceanides. According to Homer, he was the father of all the gods, and on that account received frequent visits from the rest of the deities. Oceanus is generally represented as an old man with a long flowing beard sitting upon the waves of the sea; he presided over every part of the sea, even the rivers being subject to his power. Mariners of the ancient world were deeply reverential in their worship of Oceanus, and served with great solemnity a deity to whose care they entrusted themselves when going on any voyage.

OCTANT, a reflecting navigational instrument for measuring the *altitude of heavenly bodies, having an arc of one-eighth of a circle, but because of its reflecting properties, capable of measuring altitudes of up to 90°. When John *Hadley invented his reflecting *quadrant in 1731, it was in fact an octant, but was still called a quadrant because that was the name by which all seamen called the existing common, or seaman's, quadrant, even though Hadley's reflecting, or double image, sector doubled the degree of altitude which could be measured. Octants remained in use by navigators up to the 19th century, *sextants, which were introduced during the second half of the 18th century, being generally used for *lunar observations in the calculation of *longitude. When the introduction of *chronometers made these involved lunar calculations no longer navigationally necessary, the sextant replaced the octant as the standard navigational instrument for the measurement of altitudes.

ODESSA, a principal seaport and naval base of southern Russia, in the north-west corner of the Black Sea. Originally it was a Greek settlement, but with the decay of Greek civilization in the 3rd and 4th centuries B.C., the settlements died away. The town was held by the Lithuanians from the 14th to 16th centuries when it was seized by the Tartars. The Turks occupied it during the early 18th century and in 1789 it was captured by Russian forces under French leadership, being finally ceded to Russia in 1791. It is from that date that development of Odessa as a major seaport and naval base was begun. During the Crimean War (1854–6) it was attacked unsuccessfully by an Anglo-French fleet; the Turks were equally unsuccessful during the Russo-Turkish War of 1876–7.

The massacre on the Richelieu steps, from the film The Battleship Potemkin

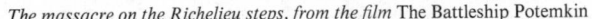

Odysseus and the Sirens; 5th-century B.C. *Attic vase*

One of the principal features of Odessa is the magnificent flight of 200 granite steps which lead from the Richelieu monument to the harbour. This was the scene in 1905 of a charge by Cossack cavalry, in which many hundreds of people were killed, during the famous * *Potemkin* mutiny.

ODO OF BAYEUX (*c.* 1036–1097), Norman bishop and English earl, comes briefly into maritime history as the man who provided the ships with which William of Normandy invaded Britain in 1066 and became king of England after the defeat of Harold at the battle of Hastings. In spite of his bishop's robes, Odo was a man of vast wealth gained by robbery and extortion, and he was thus able to acquire the necessary ships for the invasion, for which service, of course, he made sure of adequate recompense.

ODYSSEUS, according to Greek legend the son of Laertes and Anticleia and one of the most famous heroes of ancient Greece. After the capture of Troy, effected by his stratagem of the wooden horse, he set sail for Ithaca but un-

favourable winds carried him along the coast of North Africa and across unknown seas to Italy, where he braved the dangers of * Scylla and Charybdis. After many adventures he was, again according to legend, slain unknowingly in his old age by his son Telemachus.

Odysseus has been identified with * Poseidon, Hermes, and other legendary Greek gods by various subsequent writers and students of Greek mythology, but whoever he was he is generally accepted as the fount from which sprang the sailor-race whose voyages and adventures so influenced and educated the Hellenic race. He was the archetype of the true Greek when their sea power was stretching out across the Mediterranean from the Black Sea to the western basin. The Latin equivalent of Odysseus is Ulixes, more often written Ulysses. See also HOMER.

OEXMELIN, JOHN, see ESQUEMELING, John.

OFF SOUNDINGS, or **BEYOND SOUND-INGS,** a ship is off soundings when she is in waters which lie to seaward of the 100-fathom line. Before the days of * sounding machines and *echo-sounders, the deep sea *lead line could measure depths up to about 100 fathoms, so that this was in those days the limit of soundings, all greater depths being off, or beyond, soundings.

OFF THE WIND, said of a sailing ship when she is sailing with the *sheets well eased off with the wind coming *free or from broad on the *bow. When a vessel sails as close to the wind as she can, she is *on the wind.

OFFING, the distance that a ship at sea keeps away from the land because of navigational dangers, fog, or other hazards. The term is generally, though not necessarily, understood to mean that the ship remains in waters too deep for anchoring. To keep, or to make, a good offing, is to lay a *course which takes a ship well off the land and clear of all danger.

OHIO, an oil *tanker carrying fuel to Malta during the Second World War which was successfully fought through one of the bitterest *convoy battles of the war. She was an American tanker on loan to the British Ministry of War Transport, carried 11,500 tons of kerosene and oil fuel, was manned by a British crew under a British master, Captain D. W. Mason, and was the sole tanker in the vital relief convoy to Malta which entered the Mediterranean on 10 August 1942 as part of Operation 'Pedestal', the code name given to this convoy. During the first three days, in spite of repeated heavy air attacks, only one merchant ship was fatally crippled, though the *aircraft carrier *Eagle* was sunk by a *U-boat and a damaged *destroyer had to be *scuttled.

In the Sicilian Narrows, however, where the heavy ships of the escorting force could not accompany it, the convoy and its close escort were decimated by air, *submarine, and *motor torpedoboat attacks. The *Ohio* was torpedoed, set on fire and stopped, but was got under way again; an Italian bomber crashed on to her deck and numerous near misses brought her once more to a stop. Attempts to take her in tow were repeatedly interrupted by further bombing attacks which increased her damage.

Nevertheless, as a result of heroic efforts by her crew and those of her escorts, by the morning of 14 August she was got under way with a *minesweeper towing and destroyers lashed on either side; and she was brought in a sinking condition into Malta's Grand Harbour. The 10,000 tons of fuel salved from her were a decisive factor in enabling Malta to hold out against further Italian and German air attacks.

OIL BAG, a container from which oil is allowed to drip into the sea in rough weather to form a slick and prevent waves from breaking. It is used in cases of distress, when it is necessary to bring a boat alongside a ship in a heavy sea, or when it is necessary to try to prevent waves breaking over the deck of a ship.

OILSKIN, see SAILORS' DRESS.

OKTIABRSKY, SERGEI PHILIPPOVICH (1899–1969), Russian admiral, was born of a peasant family and entered the Soviet Navy in 1918. During the Second World War he was responsible for the defence and subsequent evacuation of Sebastopol during the advance of German forces into the Crimea, and later was in command of the naval operations which led to its recapture. He was awarded the title of Hero of the Soviet Union and eventually became deputy commander-in-chief of the Soviet Navy.

OLAF I, TRYGGVESSON (969–1000), Norwegian king, possibly began life by being sold as a slave in Estonia. He became a protégé of King Valdemar and after fighting in the service of the Emperor Otto III he married the daughter of the Wendish king Burislav, through whom he inherited a large fortune. On her death he became a typical Viking marauder, harrying the coasts of France and England. He was converted to Christianity by a hermit in the Scilly Islands and celebrated his conversion by marrying Gyda, sister of the king of Dublin, through whom he acquired a second fortune.

Hearing of the unpopularity of Earl Haakon, ruler of Norway, he sailed there and was accepted as king, with the avowed intention of converting the whole of Scandinavia to Christianity. He attempted to marry Sigrid, the widowed queen of Sweden, to amalgamate the two countries, but she refused to give up her heathen beliefs. He then married Thyre, sister of the king of Denmark, who had deserted her heathen husband. In an attempt to take possession of her estates he led a fleet of Norwegian *longships to the island of *Svolde, or Swold, near Rügen, where he was assailed by the combined fleets of Denmark and Sweden. Olaf fought to the bitter end against impossible odds, leaping overboard when his ship was overrun to escape capture. He was never seen again.

His ship was the *Long Serpent*, the mightiest longship in all the northern countries, and famous in Norse song and ballad. Olaf himself was one of the great heroes of Norway.

OLD STATE HOUSE, BOSTONIAN SOCIETY, Boston, Massachusetts, was opened in 1881, and became a marine museum in 1910. It illustrates the maritime history of the port of Boston from 1630 to the present day. The collection comprises ship models, *figureheads, tools, fishing gear, nautical instruments, medals, paintings, and engravings. Other museums in Boston with maritime connections are the Boston Marine Society, the Museum of Fine Arts, the Museum of Science, and the State Street Trust Company. The U.S.S. *Constitution* is moored in the Boston Navy Yard where she is used as a naval museum.

OLDSTER, in the old days of the British sailing navy a *midshipman of more than four years' seniority who, with the *master's mates, also known as oldsters, occupied the *cockpit of the ship. Junior midshipmen of less than four years' seniority were under the charge of the gunner in the *gunroom.

OLERON, THE LAWS OF, a code of maritime law enacted by Eleanor of Aquitaine, who married Henry II of England in 1152, and attributed by her to the Island of Oleron, part of her duchy and renowned for the skill and courage of its seafaring population. It is possible that they were based on the older Rhodian Law of the Mediterranean. The laws dealt mainly with the rights and responsibilities of ships' captains in relation to discipline, mutiny, pay, cargoes, sickness on board, pilotage, and similar matters.

The Laws of Oleron were introduced into England in about 1190 by Richard I, son of Henry and Eleanor of Aquitaine, and were codified in the *Black Book of the Admiralty* in 1336.

OLIVER, Sir HENRY FRANCIS (1865–1965), British admiral of the fleet, exercised a great influence on his country's naval policy during the First World War (1914–18). Born at Lockside, near Kelso, he entered the navy through H.M.S. *Britannia* in 1878. As a lieutenant he specialized in navigation and spent a considerable time on survey work. On reaching the rank of commander he put forward proposals for improving the organization and training of the navigation branch of the navy and was directed by the Second Sea Lord, then Sir John *Fisher, to implement them. He started a navigation school in the sloop *Harrier*, subsequently transferred to the old Naval College in Portsmouth Dockyard. He was promoted to captain in 1903 and as fleet navigator once led the entire Channel Fleet in formation into an anchorage on the southern coast of Ireland in a thick fog, the ships anchoring by signal. When the fog lifted the following day, every ship was in perfect position. In September 1908 he was appointed Naval Assistant to Fisher, now *First Sea Lord. His aversion to saying anything unnecessary, coupled with an unsmiling countenance, brought him his nickname of 'Dummy'.

In January 1912 he was appointed to command the new *battleship *Thunderer* and in August 1913 became Director of Naval Intelligence, being promoted to rear admiral in December of that year. On 5 November 1914, a week after Fisher's return to office as First Sea Lord, he was appointed Chief of the Admiralty War Staff in the acting rank of vice admiral. In the absence of a proper naval staff he had to deal almost single-handed with the many problems which the conduct of the war at sea presented, an unremitting task entailing long hours of work. In the spring of 1918 he was given command of the 1st Battle-Cruiser Squadron and in 1919 became vice admiral commanding the Reserve Fleet. From 1920 to 1924 he held the post of Second Sea Lord and from 1924 to 1927 that of commander-in-chief of the Home Fleet. He was advanced to admiral in November 1923 and to admiral of the fleet in January 1928.

Oliver had the reputation, throughout his naval service, of being the worst-dressed officer in the Royal Navy. His whole active life was spent in work; he rarely took any leave and was reputed to work fourteen hours a day, Sundays included. What he may have gained in wisdom, he sacrificed in largely failing to inspire and lead the officers and men he commanded.

OMMANEY, Sir ERASMUS (1814–1904), British admiral, was born in London, entered the navy at the age of 12 on board H.M.S. *Albion*, and was present at the destruction of the Turkish fleet at the battle of *Navarino in 1827. After promotion to lieutenant in 1835 he volunteered to serve under Captain James *Ross in an expedition to the Arctic to bring relief to some *whalers which were ice-bound in Baffin Bay, and was commended for his services on that occasion. Promoted to captain in 1846, he commanded two expeditions in search of Sir John *Franklin and was the first man to discover traces of the missing ships. His Arctic experience brought him the command of an expedition during the Crimean War (1854–6) to *blockade Russian ports in the White Sea, but this was so far removed from the main theatres of war that it was an exercise of singularly little value. His final naval service was as Senior Naval Officer at Gibraltar, and he retired from the navy in 1877.

'ON THE BEACH', said of a seaman who has retired from sea service. See also SWALLOW THE ANCHOR, TO.

ON THE WIND, said of a sailing vessel when she is sailing with her *sheets hauled as far aft as possible, or as close to the wind as the ship will go. See also OFF THE WIND.

ONE TON CUP, THE, an international challenge trophy put up by the Cercle de la Voile de Paris in 1965 to encourage offshore racing for

One tonners: Saracen *and* Gumboots

yachts built to the 22-ft (6·7 m) * Royal Ocean Racing Club rating. Originally the cup, first presented in 1907, had been used for a series of races by the International 6-metre (19·7 ft) class, but this racing had lapsed, and in the new style of contest each competing nation may enter three boats. The first contests comprised two races of 30 miles and one of 300 miles, but in 1968 these were amended to one race of about 300 miles in the middle of four day races, totalling some 775 miles in all. The rating for contestants was also altered to 27·5 ft (8·4 m), and the yachts raced without handicaps.

The first series, held off Le Havre in 1965, was won by Denmark with *Diana III*; the second, held in Danish waters in 1966, was won by the U.S.A. with *Tina*; in 1967 *Optimist* won the cup during races off Le Havre for Germany, and again the next year off Heligoland. In 1969 *Rainbow II* carried the trophy to New Zealand, where in 1971 it was won by Australia with *Stormy Petrel*. New Zealand won it back in 1972 with *Wai-Aniwa* in the series of races sailed off

Sydney. It was won by Britain in 1974 by *Gumboots*.

The success of this series, in which an average of eighteen boats had sailed in each race, encouraged similar contests to be organized between the different countries, resulting in Quarter Ton 5·5-metre (18·0 ft), Half Ton 6·6-metre (21·7 ft), and Three Quarter Ton 7·5-metre (24·5 ft) classes to be formed. The fact that many of the smaller boats can be transported by road on trailers has greatly stimulated the international popularity of this form of yacht racing.

The formulae for calculating the ratings of yachts to arrive at a figure of 1·0, 0·75, 0·50, and 0·25 (tons) are long and complicated.

ONE-DESIGN CLASS, a class of yachts or boats all of which have been built to one accepted design. In an attempt to give all yachts of a class an equal chance in racing, and to eliminate the complications of handicapping, one-designs are built and rigged so as to be as nearly identical one to another as is practicable. All the yachts of the class should, in theory, have precisely the same sailing performance, and the race results should depend therefore on the individual skills of the helmsmen and their crews. In practice, yachts reflect the amount of maintenance they receive and the care the owner gives to his boat's tuning-up and details of sails and gear, and the relative performance of one-designs can accordingly vary widely. The principle of the one-design, however, limits the advantage the wealthy owner can have over the less opulent, and on the whole racing in any one-design class tends to be very fair. For this reason, the majority of sailing clubs which organize races number at least one one-design class among their racing fleets, as for example the Royal Burnham and Royal Corinthian one-design classes, the Bembridge one-design class, etc., which race exclusively in those clubs. Other one-design classes can be international or national in character, such as the International Star class, the National Flying Fifteen class, etc.

ONION PATCH TROPHY, a series of yacht races between teams of three boats held in the U.S.A. on the same lines as the *Admiral's Cup in Britain. It is held every two years, alternating with the Admiral's Cup. Like the British series, it consists of two short races and two offshore races, the second offshore race being the biennial Newport–Bermuda race of 635 miles. The 1974 series was won by the U.S.A. team, with Britain and Canada equal second.

OPEN HAWSE, the condition of a ship when she is lying to two *anchors without the *cables becoming crossed. It is the opposite of a *foul hawse, in which the ship has swung with the tide to an extent where the two cables *grow across each other.

ORDE, Sir JOHN (1751–1824), British admiral, was a captain in 1778 and saw various service in the War of American Independence (1775–82). Shortly after the outbreak of the Revolutionary War with France (1793–1801) he was promoted rear admiral and joined the fleet of Lord St. Vincent (see JERVIS, Sir John) as third in command. The fleet at the time was watching *Cadiz, and when in 1798 intelligence of considerable French activity in the Mediterranean called for a British detached squadron to investigate the reason, Orde by reason of his seniority would normally have been placed in command of it. Instead, St. Vincent selected Horatio *Nelson, considerably Orde's junior, a choice which roused Orde to fury. He expressed his opinion forcefully to St. Vincent and to the Admiralty in London in a long series of letters, which resulted in his being sent home, to remain unemployed for the next six years.

He was in command of the squadron watching Cadiz in 1805 when Admiral *Villeneuve, escaping out of the Mediterranean, appeared off the port to join forces with the Spanish ships there. Orde withdrew his squadron to join his force with that of Lord Gardner off Brest in case Villeneuve should come north, but instead the Franco-Spanish fleet sailed to the West Indies, the long voyage which was to become the prelude to the battle of *Trafalgar. Orde was promoted admiral in 1805 but had no further service.

Orde, a proud and sensitive man, had nevertheless been a successful officer and one who had treated his crews with humanity in a period when many captains still relied upon the *cat-o'-nine-tails to maintain discipline on board. 'Sir John Orde ... carries himself high; he needed not great sensibility to feel indignities,' wrote Captain Cuthbert *Collingwood of him. Had he been less touchy over the Nelson episode, he might have made a good run-of-the-mill admiral. See also PARKER, Sir William.

ORDER OF SAILING, the disposition of a fleet of warships when sailing in company, or of a *convoy. It is from the order of sailing that the order of battle is formed when an enemy fleet is sighted. See also NELSON TOUCH, THE.

ORDINARY, an old naval term to indicate a ship laid up in a *dockyard or harbour. When ships were thus laid up their masts, rigging, sails, and guns were taken out and stored ashore and the upper deck temporarily roofed over with timber to keep them dry. The term was also sometimes used to indicate the men who remained on board ships laid up in ordinary, usually the warrant officers and their servants.

ORDINARY SEAMAN, the lowest man's rating on board British ships. Boys are rated ordinary seamen and begin their man's time on board at the age of 18, normally being rated *able (A.B.) at the age of 21. The abbreviation is O.D., probably derived from OrDinary.

OREGON, U.S.S., American battleship authorized by Congress in 1890. She was built at the Union Ironworks, San Francisco, and on the outbreak of the Spanish–American War of 1898, was ordered to join the American squadron *blockading Havana. Her passage round South America via Cape Horn was presented to the American public as a race against time, although in fact she arrived in time to be at the final action in which Admiral *Cervera's squadron of *cruisers was destroyed. President Theodore Roosevelt used her long passage from San Francisco to Cuba as a powerful argument in favour of building a *Panama Canal, pointing out the great delay which had occurred in a vital war situation by the lack of such a canal.

ORFORDNESS, a battle of the Second Anglo-Dutch War (1665–7), was fought on 25 July 1666 between an English fleet of 89 ships and 17 *fireships under the joint command of Prince *Rupert and the Duke of Albemarle (see MONCK, George) and a Dutch fleet of 88 ships, 20 fireships, and 10 dispatch vessels under Admiral de *Ruyter. The action began at about 10 a.m., in the broad part of the Thames Estuary, about 40 miles south-east of Orfordness, and was continued for two hours. Then Admiral Cornelis *Tromp, with the Dutch rear squadron, broke through the English line and engaged the British Blue squadron, both squadrons disappearing in a confused mêlée to the westward while the main battle was heading nearly due east. By 1 p.m., the Dutch *van was in full flight to the eastward, and three hours later their centre also gave way, but the English were too exhausted to take full advantage of it. Towards nightfall, however, they attacked once more, with de Ruyter maintaining a masterly retreat.

Desultory fighting continued throughout the night and became brisk again next morning; but a strong north-easterly wind was blowing and with the shoals off the Dutch coast being close at hand, the pursuit was at last discontinued. All this time the two rear squadrons had been closely engaged to the westward, but by the following morning the British ships were in close pursuit of Tromp, who eventually escaped behind the shoals. It was a brilliant English victory. The Dutch lost about 20 ships and had 4,000 killed and 3,000 wounded; the English lost only the *Resolution and relatively few men.

ORIENT, L', the 120-gun flagship of Vice Admiral *Brueys at the battle of the *Nile in 1798, which caught fire and blew up with heavy casualties, including Brueys, during the action. See also CASABIANCA.

ORION, H.M.S., a name used five times for ships of the Royal Navy, all of which saw action against the enemy of their day. The first, built on the Thames and launched on 1 June 1787, took part in Lord *Howe's action of the *Glorious First of June, 1794, Lord Bridport's (see HOOD, Alexander) action against Admiral *Villaret de Joyeuse off Île de Groix in June 1795, the battle of *Cape St. Vincent, 1797, the *Nile, 1798, *Trafalgar, 1805, *Copenhagen, 1807, and in the Baltic in 1808. She was broken up at *Plymouth in 1814.

It was not until 1854 that another *Orion* was launched, and she saw action as one of Admiral Dundas's fleet in the second Baltic campaign of 1855 during the Crimean War (1854–6). The third *Orion*, a twin-screw *ironclad of 4,830 tons, was originally laid down as the *Burjizafar* for Turkey, but was purchased for the Royal

Navy while building and was launched as the *Orion* in 1879. She took part in the Egyptian War of 1882 and contributed a detachment to the Naval Brigade in the actions of Tel-el-Mabuta and Tel-el-Kebir. Her name was changed to *Orontes* in 1910, when a new *battleship of 22,500 tons, launched at *Portsmouth in August 1910, was named *Orion*. This battleship commissioned in January 1912 as flagship of the 2nd Battle Squadron, Home Fleet, in which capacity she continued to serve throughout the First World War (1914–18). In 1916, flying the flag of Rear Admiral A. C. Leveson, she took part in the battle of *Jutland. In September 1920 she became the flagship of the Vice Admiral Commanding Reserve Fleet (Vice Admiral Sir R. F. Phillimore) and in June 1921 she was recommissioned as a *private ship, being paid off at Devonport in April 1922 and sold in December of the same year.

The cruiser *Orion*, of 7,215 tons, was launched at Devonport in 1932. She served throughout the Second World War and was at the battle of *Cape Matapan and at Crete in 1941, taking part also in the *Malta convoys of that year. In 1943 she was at the Sicily and Salerno, and in 1944 at the Anzio and Normandy, landings. In October 1944 she was made flagship for the operations leading to the liberation of Greece. She was sold for breaking up in 1949.

ORLOGSMUSEET, Copenhagen, Denmark. A private museum founded in 1857 and opened the following year. It contains an important collection of ship models dating from 1669 and illustrating the development of the Royal Danish Navy from 1500 onwards, also many *figureheads, nautical instruments, weapons, uniforms, seals, medals, and flags. Owing to lack of space some of the items are stored.

There are several smaller museums in Denmark which house marine artefacts, among which may be mentioned those at Aabenraa (Aabenraa Museum); Dragør (Dragør Museum); Esbjerg (Esbjerg Museum); Kerteminde (Ladbyskibet); Copenhagen (Burmeister og Wain Museet and Nyboders Mindestuer); Kolding (Museet paa Koldinghus); Marstal (Marstal og Omegns Museum); Svendborg (Svendborg Amts Museum); Roskilde (Vikingeskibshallen).

ORLOP, orig. **OVER-LOP,** the name given to the lowest deck in a ship. It was the platform laid over the *beams of a ship below the turn of the *bilge, and in the sailing men-of-war was the deck on which the *cables were coiled in their lockers when the *anchors were weighed and also the deck on which were found the powder magazines, the principal store-rooms, and the *cabins of junior officers. In merchant ships, the orlop deck forms the floors of the cargo *holds.

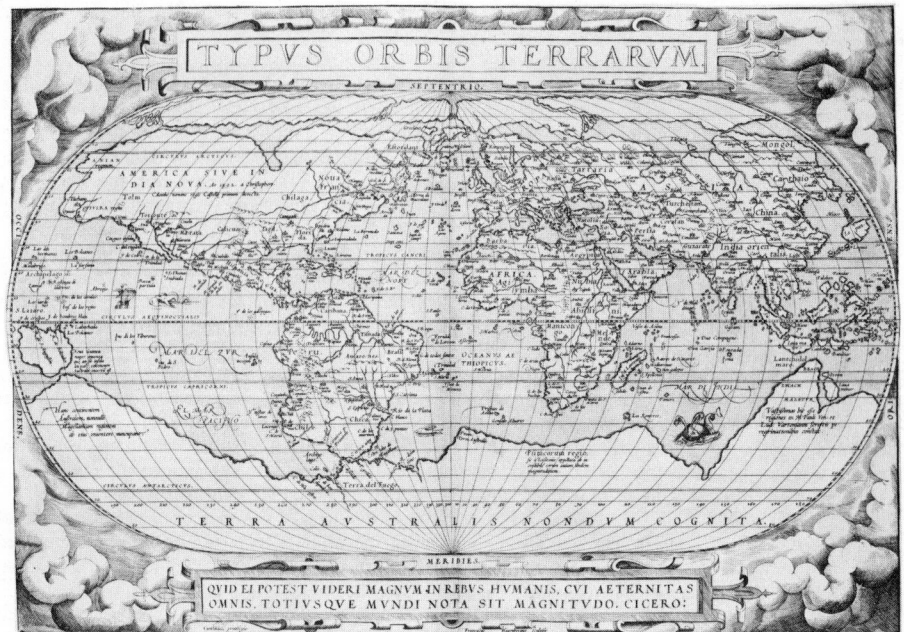

Ortelius's map of the world, 1570

OROPESA SWEEP, a method of sweeping moored *mines by a wire towed by a *minesweeper: it required only one minesweeper to operate it. It swept mines to the side of the minesweeper by means of a long wire fitted with wirecutters placed at intervals along the wire to cut the mine moorings. The wire was towed astern of the minesweeper with a *kite fitted to the wire a short distance from the point of tow to keep the wire down to a fixed depth below water. Near the end of the wire was an *otter which forced it outwards as it was towed through the water, and at the end was a float to hold the wire at its fixed depth and prevent it sinking to the bottom. As the wire came into contact with the mine mooring wires, they slid along it until meeting a cutter, when the mooring wire was severed and the mine floated to the surface, where it could be destroyed or sunk by rifle fire.

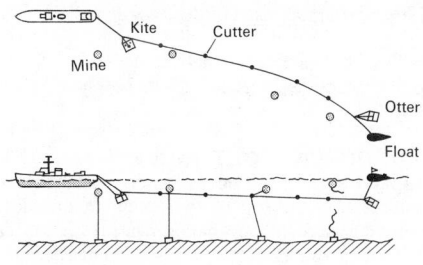

Oropesa Sweep

This form of sweep was first developed in 1919 in the minesweeper *Oropesa* during the clearance of the northern mine barrage laid during the First World War (1914–18) across the northern North Sea from the Orkney Islands to the Norwegian coast, and was improved between the two world wars by the substitution of multiplane otters for the earlier single otter used for spreading the sweep and by better designs of cutters.

ORTELIUS, ABRAHAM (1527–98), Belgian geographer of German origin, was, next to Gerardus *Mercator, the greatest geographer of his age. In his youth he travelled widely and was attracted to the science of geography by his friendship with Mercator who suggested to him the compilation of a world atlas, by which he became famous. This was his *Theatrum Orbis Terrarum*, consisting of fifty-three maps, which was first published at Antwerp in 1570. By the time of his death in 1598 no fewer than twenty-five editions had been produced, in addition to editions in Latin, Flemish, French, and German. This atlas was, admittedly, a compilation of the work of many cartographers, but in spite of many errors due to the contemporary lack of knowledge, it was with its accompanying text a masterpiece of erudition. Ortelius later published an additional seventeen maps as a supplement to his *Theatrum*. Philip II of Spain appointed him as his personal geographer in 1575.

During the remainder of his life Ortelius

brought out other cartographical publications, of which the more notable were *Nomenclator Ptolemaicus* (1584), *Parergon* (maps illustrating ancient history), and *Itinerarium per nonnullas Galliae Belgicae partes*, a series of large-scale maps of a journey made by him through Belgium and the Rhineland. At his death in Antwerp he was given a public funeral.

OSBORN, SHERARD (1822–75), British admiral and explorer, entered the navy in 1837 and was present at the operations in Malaya in 1838, at Canton in 1841, and at the capture of the Woosung batteries in 1842. In 1849 he led the demand for a new search for Sir John *Franklin and in 1850 commanded the *Pioneer* during the Arctic expeditions of Captain Austin and Sir Edward *Belcher, making in 1851 a famous journey by sledge to the western end of Prince of Wales Island.

He commanded H.M.S. *Medusa* in the Crimea during the war with Russia (1854–6) and served in the Second Chinese War, making a classic navigation of the Yangtze River to Hankow in H.M.S. *Furious*. He was in the troubles in the Gulf of Mexico in 1861, commanding the *Donegal*, and after a short period of service with the Chinese on anti-piracy duties, took command of H.M.S. *Royal Sovereign* in 1864 for trials of the turret system of mounting naval guns. He was promoted to rear admiral on the retired list in 1873 after having served for eight years as managing director of the Telegraph Construction and Maintenance Company, engaged in the laying of deep sea cables, and it was in this connection that the large deep in the Indian Ocean, north-west of Australia, was named the Sherard Osborn Deep.

Throughout his naval career he never lost his interest in Arctic exploration, and was the moving force behind Sir George *Nares's expedition of 1875–6. He wrote *Stray Leaves from an Arctic Journal* (1852) and *The Career, Last Voyage, and Fate of Sir John Franklin* (1860), and edited the journals of Sir Robert *McClure (1856).

OSLO, the capital city and a principal seaport of Norway, at the head of the Oslo Fjord, leading north from the Skagerrak. It is the home of the *Kon-Tiki Museum, the *Norsk Sjøfartsmuseum, and the *Vikingskiphuset.

OSTEND COMPANY, a trading company organized in 1717 by merchants and shipowners of Ostend, then in the Austrian Netherlands, on the lines of the *East India companies of other nations. Not surprisingly, it ran into fierce opposition from the Dutch and English East India companies whose monopolies of trade in the east were being threatened. The Dutch took their opposition to the lengths of seizing an Ostend Company ship with a rich cargo off the African coast

in 1719, whereupon the English did the same off Madagascar.

The Emperor of Austria, Charles VI, gave the Ostend Company in 1722 letters patent to trade for thirty years in the West and East Indies, and two trading stations were set up at Coblom on the Coromandel coast and at Bankibazar on the Ganges, and for a year or two the Company enjoyed a peaceful and prosperous trade. But in 1725 the English, Dutch, and Prussians signed a defensive league at Herrenhausen which was able to put such pressure on Charles VI that he was forced to withdraw his letters patent. Without this protection, the company withered and died.

OTTER, a board rigged with a line and bridle which, when towed underwater, stretches the line by reason of the outward angle at which the bridle holds it. It is used widely in fishing to spread out a net or to keep open the mouth of a *trawl. (When otter boards are used on a trawl they are normally called doors.) The name comes from the otter board used by salmon fishers to tauten their line or net as they towed it along the shore, the otter being a great predator of salmon.

The principle of the otter board was also used in minesweeping devices. See OROPESA SWEEP, PARAVANE.

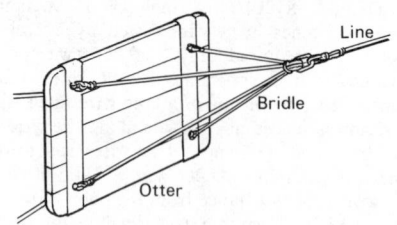

OUTCAST OF THE ISLANDS, AN, a novel by Joseph *Conrad, published in 1896 in which he uses his experiences in Malayan waters as a background for the story.

OUTHAUL, a line or purchase by which a sail is hauled outboard along a spar. Aboard a square-rigged ship the *studding-sails and their booms were hauled out along the yards by means of outhauls. On old-fashioned yachts with long *bowsprits, the *tack of the jib was hooked on to a traveller, a large iron ring running along the bowsprit, which was then hauled towards the outer (or crans iron) end of the bowsprit by the outhaul.

OUTLICKER, OUTLIGGER, or **OUTLEAGER,** a short boom which was extended astern from the top of the *poop in the older square-rigged ships to haul down (or 'lig-out' in the older phrase) the mizen sheet when the *mizenmast was stepped so far aft that there was

Fishing canoe with outrigger

no room to do so inboard. Most *carracks and four-masted *galleons fitted an outlicker. The modern equivalent is a *bumpkin.

OUTRIGGER, (1) an extension to each side of the *crosstrees of a sailing vessel to spread the *backstays, in a *schooner the topmast backstays, and in a full-rigged ship the *topgallant and *royal backstays. **(2)** A counterpoising log of wood rigged out from the side of a native canoe in the Pacific and Indian Oceans to provide additional stability when carrying sail in a stiff breeze. **(3)** The projecting beams rigged on the sides of sailing men-of-war to which additional *shrouds were led for extra support of the masts when the ship was *careened. A great strain was exerted on the mast during careening as the ship was hauled down on to her side by *tackles secured to the mastheads, hence the need for extra support by additional, temporary, shrouds.

'OVER THE BAY', an expression used by the old seamen, particularly in the days of square-rigged ships, to describe officers who had taken a few more nips of rum or whisky than necessary to *'freshen their hawse'.

OVERFALL, a condition of the sea when it falls into breaking waves caused by wind or current over an irregular bottom, or by currents meeting. *Tide-rips and *tide-races frequently cause overfalls.

OVERHAUL, to, (1) to increase the distance apart of the *blocks of a *tackle by running the rope back through the sheaves, **(2)** the expression used to describe the action of a ship when she overtakes, or is catching up with, another ship at sea, **(3)** an expression sometimes used in connection with the inspection, testing, and repair of a vessel's machinery, but the more correct nautical word in this respect is refit.

OVER-RAKED, a vessel is said to be over-raked when she is riding to her *anchor(s) in bad weather and the seas break continuously over her *bows. It is a condition which can often be ameliorated by increasing the *scope of the *cable through *veering an extra amount so that the vessel may lie more easily.

OVERTAKING LIGHT, a white light displayed at the *stern of a vessel under way at night, forming part of the compulsory *navigation lights which a ship must burn under the regulations laid down by the International Convention for Preventing Collisions at Sea. The overtaking light, also widely known as a sternlight, must have a visibility of two miles on a clear night and must show through an arc on either side of the vessel from right astern to two *points *abaft the *beam. For details of all navigational lights, see APPENDIX 3.

OWEN, WILLIAM FITZWILLIAM (1775–1858), British vice admiral, is best remembered for his surveys of the west African coasts. An expedition to the coast of Africa under his command was dispatched by the Admiralty in 1821 with the intention, it was said, of benefiting the whole civilized world by surveying those waters and also by assisting in the suppression of the slave trade. The principal ships were the *Leven* and *Barracouda*, and among the surveyors embarked was the future Vice Admiral *Vidal. Fever took an immense toll of the ships' companies so that, in a subsequent account to the Royal Geographical Society, the survey (prodigious in its scope) was said to have been drawn and coloured with drops of blood.

Soon after his return in 1826 Owen was sent in the *Eden* to establish a British settlement at Fernando Po, thought at home to be a more healthy area than the existing settlement at Sierra Leone. However, it was quickly shown that the health conditions there were no better, and the proposed settlement was abandoned. This was Owen's last active appointment; while at Fernando Po he was offered the post of Hydrographer of the Navy, only to learn in the same mail that Admiral Sir Francis *Beaufort had been selected.

Owen had entered the navy in 1788 and before his African surveys he saw much active service, including Lord *Howe's action of the *Glorious First of June in 1794. He commanded the *Nemesis* in Lord *Nelson's squadron based on Dover in 1801 as an anti-invasion measure. Thereafter he was in the East Indies and in 1808–10 was a fellow prisoner with Matthew *Flinders in Mauritius. In 1815–16 he began the surveys of the Canadian Lakes, and it was in Canada that Owen spent his retirement until his death.

OX-EYE, a name given to a small cloud which occasionally appears in the sky off the eastern coast of Africa and spreads quickly to cover the whole of the sky, presaging a severe storm accompanied by a violent wind. It gets its name from its resemblance, when first seen, to the eye of an ox.

OXTER PLATE, the name given to the outer plates of a ship's *hull which are riveted or welded to the *sternpost of a ship.

OZANNE, NICOLAS MARIE (1728–1811), a member of a famous family of French engravers, natives of the port of Brest. He was also an accomplished seaman and marine architect. When his father died in 1744, only Nicolas had learned the trade and he was obliged to support his mother, brother, and two sisters. Eventually the two boys and the two girls all became engravers. Nicolas became a pupil of Roblin, and in 1750 succeeded him as drawing master at the Naval College at Brest.

Among his many works are a series of twenty-three pictures illustrating the campaigns of Admiral *Duguay-Trouin which were engraved by his sister MARIE JEANNE Ozanne (1735–86) and her husband Yves *Le Gouaz. In 1756 he visited Toulon and made sketches of the squadron commanded by Admiral *Galissonnière under orders for Minorca, which earned him the post of draughtsman to the navy. Ten years later he designed the *frigate *Aurore* and drew up plans for the port of Ambleteuse, and in 1769 he was given the task of teaching the Dauphin's son ship construction and seamanship. He made several engravings of the ports of Brest, Toulon, Le Havre, and Marseilles.

His brother PIERRE (1737–1813), also born at Brest, joined the navy and rose to the rank of captain. During his service he painted several sea pictures and engraved a series of sixty drawings of ships.

OZAWA, JISIBURO (1886–1966), Japanese vice admiral, was the ablest strategic thinker among the Japanese admirals in the Second World War, a quality which no doubt accounted for his appointment as an instructor in the Naval Academy in 1935 and, after commanding a *cruiser and a *battleship, to the post of chief of staff to the Combined Fleet, 1937–8. Though not himself a specialist in naval aviation, he was among the first to appreciate the potential of the *aircraft carrier and he initiated the policy of using them offensively *en masse*. He was unlucky to have to wait until November 1942 to take over command of Admiral *Nagumo's Third Fleet, by which time the odds in carrier warfare were swinging rapidly in favour of the Americans following the heavy Japanese losses at *Midway and in the subsequent battles in the Solomon Islands. He was in supreme command of the fleet at the battle of the *Philippine Sea, and, forced by the situation to act offensively, his impeccable tactics foundered on the American superiority in quantity and quality of fighter aircraft and the lack of skilled Japanese naval pilots, their most highly trained men having all been lost in the previous actions.

In the final great sea battle of the Pacific War, *Leyte Gulf, with no trained carrier pilots remaining, he sailed out with almost empty carriers and played the part of sacrificial decoy imposed upon him with skill and fatalistic courage.

P

P & O, as the Peninsular and Oriental Steam Navigation Company is generally known, is the largest shipping group in the world with over 3,000,000 tons of ships. The parent line grew out of a shipping agency business run by two young men, Brodie Wilcox and Arthur Anderson, after the Napoleonic War (1803–15). In 1826 these two became London agents for one of the first successful coastal steamship companies, the City of Dublin Steam Packet Co., and began a steamship service to Portugal. In 1837 this service, which had prospered during the Portuguese and Spanish civil wars, secured a British government contract to carry the mails to the Iberian peninsula. This was the first overseas mail contract ever given to a commercial shipping company and may be said to have started the fashion in mail contracts which gave British shipping such an advantage in the mid-19th century. In 1840 the Peninsular Steam Navigation Co., as it was then called, was given a contract to carry mails to Egypt and India; 'Oriental' was added to the line's name and the U.K.–Egypt service was inaugurated by the S.S. *Oriental*, a 1,674-ton * paddle steamer, in the same year. In 1842 the company started the Suez–Calcutta link, and in 1852 added a Suez–Bombay mail service. In that year they also secured a mail contract to Australia; as they already ran ships to Singapore and Chinese ports they were now a powerful force in eastern waters.

The opening of the * Suez Canal in 1869 enabled them to run a through service from Britain with increased passenger comfort, for which they had always prided themselves. It is widely believed that the slang word * posh came from discriminating P & O passengers having their tickets stamped with the letters P.O.S.H., standing for port outwards, starboard home, thus securing for themselves not only the cooler side of the ship both ways but also that best protected from the glare of the sun on the sea; but this is an inherently unlikely derivation of the word. Life on board P & O ships was an extension of eastern life for the sahibs and memsahibs of the British 'Raj'; most of the stewards were from the Portuguese Indian colony of Goa, most of the sailors were Lascars, and the engine-room crew were also Indian. The ships themselves were black-hulled with buff upperworks and masts and black funnels; they were not fast like transatlantic * liners, but beamy and comfortable.

In 1914 the line amalgamated with another great eastern company, the British India Line, giving a combined total of over a million tons of ships. During the First World War (1914–18) other lines were acquired, notably the New Zealand Shipping Co., so that by the end of the war, in spite of having lost half a million tons of shipping to * U-boats and surface raiders, the group controlled over 1,500,000 tons of ships. The fleets were built up after the war, the parent company adding five new passenger liners whose names all began with the prefix Strath, which started a new tradition for the line by being painted all white with yellow funnels and masts. By 1939 the group had over two million tons of ships; during the Second World War they lost over half this total. During the years 1950–60 the group added * tanker operation to its cargo and passenger services, the latter being distinguished by fewer, but larger and faster, liners, notably the 45,000-ton *Canberra*. In 1965 the group, together with other British shipping groups, formed Overseas Containers Ltd., to operate * container cargo services. In 1969, after the Suez Canal had been closed for some years, thus adding some 5,000 miles to the India passage, P & O stopped the services to this subcontinent which it had maintained for 127 years.

PAASCH, HENRY (*c.* 1840–*c.* 1900), German marine architect and author, was born on the shores of the Baltic and went to sea with his father at the age of 10 in a coasting vessel. Three years later his father was drowned and, single-handed, the boy brought the vessel into port. At 15 he joined the German Navy and after the German–Danish war of 1864 transferred to the Danish Navy, but later served in the ships of various nations, becoming ultimately master of a Russian * East Indiaman. He left the sea in 1870 and settled in Antwerp where he held the post of Lloyd's Surveyor for Belgium. In 1885 he published his *Marine Dictionary*, followed by a similar book in 1890, *De La Quille à la Pomme du Mât* (From the Keel to the Masthead) which went into four editions and was translated into five languages. His international recognition as an expert on the subject is based on this book.

PACIFIC IRON, (1) the cast-iron cappings at the *yardarms of a square-rigged ship which support the *studdingsail *boom irons and to which a *Flemish horse is made fast. **(2)** The *gooseneck at the deck end of a cargo *derrick which permits movement of the derrick in any required direction is also known as a Pacific Iron.

PACIFIC OCEAN, the area of sea bounded on the east by the west coast of North and South America, on the west by the coast of Asia and the East Indian Islands, on the north by the Bering Strait, and on the south by the Antarctic Ocean and the northern coast of Australia.

The Pacific was the last of the five great oceans to be discovered by Europeans, and was not shown on the earliest world maps, geographers believing that the eastern coasts of Asia bordered the Atlantic Ocean in the west. That a great new ocean separated America and Asia became apparent shortly after it was established that the new land discovered by Christopher *Columbus in 1492 was not India and China, as he supposed, and that a great unexplained gap on the world's surface existed between the eastern coast of China, reached by the Portuguese in 1517, and the western coast of America, reached by the Spaniards shortly after the discovery of the mainland. It could be filled with nothing but ocean.

The first white man to sight the new ocean was Vasco Nuñez de *Balboa on 25 September 1513 when, on a journey across the Isthmus of Darien, he reached the top of the mountain range which runs down the isthmus. Looking westward from the peak he had reached he saw the great ocean and sent three of his men, of whom one was Francisco Pizarro, ahead to reconnoitre; he himself reached the coast on 29 September, formally taking possession of the 'Great *South Sea' in the name of King Ferdinand of Spain. The first white man actually to sail upon the Pacific Ocean was Alonzo Martin, one of the scouts sent ahead by Balboa with Pizarro.

For the next 200 years a precarious sovereignty over the Pacific was claimed and exercised by Spain, though breached many times by *privateering and piratical voyages made by men of other nations. The first full crossing of the Pacific was made by the expedition led by Ferdinand *Magellan during his circumnavigation of 1519–22, and it was crossed again in many subsequent circumnavigations, notably those of Francis *Drake (1577–80), Thomas *Cavendish (1586–8), and Olivier van *Noort (1598–1601), but those circumnavigations were made not so much with the object of gaining knowledge of the new ocean as of plundering the riches of Spain. The true voyages of exploration of this early period were those of Pedro

Fernandez de *Quiros and Luis Vaes de *Torres (1605–6), which discovered the Tuomotus and New Hebrides groups of islands and the Torres Strait, and the three voyages of Abel *Tasman in 1634, 1642, and 1644, discovering Australia. Yet it was the early circumnavigations, bent on plunder, which had set the pattern for the next hundred years, and a whole host of adventurers, virtually pirates but calling themselves *buccaneers or privateers, were let loose upon the Pacific, among whom the names of Bartholomew *Sharp, William *Dampier, Ambrose *Cowley, and Woodes *Rogers are notorious. From 1680 to 1720 they took a heavy toll of Spanish settlements and shipping in those waters, and between them they broke the Spanish monopoly which the declining sea power of Spain was unable to hold. They were followed by the expedition of Commodore George *Anson in 1740–4, during the War of the Austrian Succession (1739–48), which was the final nail in the coffin of Spanish sea power in this great ocean.

With the final extinction of the buccaneers in the first decades of the 18th century and the end of Spanish sovereignty, the Pacific was open for the systematic voyages of exploration of the mid and late 18th century by men of proved ability in marine *surveying, exemplified by such names as James *Cook, Louis Antoine de *Bougainville, Jean-François, Comte de *La Pérouse, Samuel Wallis, and many others who between them charted the great ocean and fixed the positions of the island groups they discovered. By the end of their era, which may be taken as around the year 1780, the general area of this vast ocean had been accurately captured on charts and opened to seamen of the world.

The name Pacific was given to this ocean by Magellan because of the general absence of storms, an observation made in the earliest days of Spanish occupation and exploitation and based in the main on the coastal waters which lap the American continents; and although the waters are lashed occasionally by typhoons of tremendous severity, in general the ocean answers to its name. And as a result of geopolicy, the name has been equally deserved until recent years in respect of warlike operations, the Pacific Ocean lying mainly outside the sphere of western international quarrels. On its western edge it was long a hotbed of local piracy, but it did not suffer from major wars, as have the Atlantic and Indian Oceans, until the Second World War when, from the end of 1941 onwards, it was the scene of bitter fighting between the fleets of Japan and those of the U.S.A., Great Britain, Holland, Australia, and New Zealand, that ended only with the collapse of Japan in August 1945.

The Pacific is the largest of the world's five oceans, covering an estimated area of

55,623,900 square miles, of which the great majority (39,621,550 square miles) lies at a depth of over 2,000 *fathoms. The greatest depth *sounded to date is in the Mindanão Trench, between Midway and Guam Islands, where a depth of over seven and a half miles (6,600 fathoms) has been reached. In 1960 the *bathyscaphe *Trieste I* reached a depth of 6,000 fathoms in the Guam Trench.

The southern half of the Pacific Ocean is studded with groups of islands, mainly coral in formation and many of them formed on the crests of extinct volcanoes on the sea bed. The main surface currents, which are caused by the prevailing winds, are the North and South Equatorial Currents, the North current flowing generally eastward and the South generally westward.

For a fuller account of the history of the Pacific Ocean, see J. C. Beaglehole's *Exploration of the Pacific* (1966).

PACKET, a shortened form of packet-boat, which was originally a vessel plying regularly between two ports for the carriage of mails, but available also for goods and passengers. In the 16th century, State letters and dispatches were known as 'the Packet', and a Treasury account of 1598 gave details of 'Postes towards Ireland, Hollyheade, allowance as well for serving the packett by lande as for entertaining a bark to carie over and return the packet, x pounds the moneth'. They were essentially mail boats, and were also known as *post-barks.

By the 18th century they were built with a finer hull than average in order to give extra speed; still designed primarily for the carriage of mails they were plying regularly as far from England as America, the West Indies, and India. They were armed with ten or twelve small guns for self defence in wartime, and carried, in addition to the mails, official passengers, and special cargo for important persons such as ambassaders, commanders-in-chief, etc. They lost their role as mail carriers when, with the introduction of steam propulsion and in order to promote the development of the merchant marine, many governments gave contracts for the carriage of mails to private owners of steamships during the mid-19th century. The name, however, in the form 'steam packet ship', remained for a few more years to describe those ships of a merchant line which made regular voyages between the same ports carrying passengers and cargo.

PADDLE STEAMER, a steam vessel in which propulsion is by a pair of paddle-wheels mounted amidships or a single paddle-wheel at the stern, driven by reciprocating engines.

Wheels fitted with various forms of paddles, blades, or floats for propelling small ceremonial craft and operated by men or animals were known to the Ancient Egyptians and the Chinese from an early date. With the development of the steam engine in the latter half of the 18th century steam-driven paddle-wheels were introduced in various forms, at first mounted between two hulls as in Patrick Miller's steamboat of 1788, or within the hull as in William Symington's *Charlotte Dundas* of 1802, but later vessels had a pair of wheels arranged amidships on a common shaft which was driven by the steam engine.

The earliest paddle-wheels carried six or more fixed floats, and some (e.g., those fitted to the P.S. *Savannah* in 1819, and to the British *frigate Galatea* in 1829) could be dismantled and carried on deck when not in use. By about 1840 most paddle-wheels were fitted with a feathering device in which radial rods mounted on an eccentric moved the floats in turn so that as they entered the water and left it they remained nearly upright, thereby gaining more propulsive power and causing less wash. In the early days of the century there were also many experiments in the arrangement and shape of the floats, from single paddles to multiple shutters, all aimed at increasing the wheel's efficiency and reducing the shocks as the floats struck the water: many variations of these ideas in model form can be seen in the Science Museum, South Kensington, London. Up to the end of the paddle-steamer era, however, the traditional wheel with feathering floats was almost universal.

For the first fifty years of steam propulsion at sea the paddle-wheel had few rivals. The first regular transatlantic *liners (see, e.g., GREAT WESTERN) relied on paddle-wheels, as did those of other regular steamship lines to the Iberian Peninsula, the Mediterranean, and other equally distant parts of the world. But shipowners were well aware of some of the disadvantages of this form of propulsion for oceangoing vessels, such as the danger of broken paddle shafts and damaged engines when the ship rolled heavily in bad weather, and the varying effect in speed and coal consumption between a cargo vessel deep laden with wheels deeply immersed, and in the light condition when the floats had little grip of the water. For warships, too, paddle-wheels proved far too vulnerable to enemy gunfire or collision, and attention was inevitably drawn to the advantages of the fully immersed screw *propeller (see SMITH, Sir Francis Pettit).

The Admiralty trials of 1845 (see ALECTO, H.M.S., and RATTLER, H.M.S.), and other tests carried out later, clearly demonstrated the superiority of screw propulsion over paddle-wheels for oceangoing ships. Yet I. K. *Brunel's monster *Great Eastern*, launched in 1858, was powered, in addition to a single 24-ft propeller, with a pair of the largest paddle-wheels, 56 feet in diameter, ever fitted to an ocean liner. So reluctant were

The race on the Mississippi between the paddle steamers Robert E. Lee *and* Natchez; *lithograph by Currier and Ives*

passengers of the day to trust themselves to the early screw-driven steamers that the *Cunard Company continued to build paddle steamers for their Atlantic services until as late as 1861, and their last paddler, the *Scotia*, was the most handsome ship on the Atlantic at that time and the ultimate in oceangoing paddle steamers. Her side lever engines, built by Robert Napier, had cylinders 100 inches in diameter with a 12-ft stroke —the size of a small room in a house—and developed 4,600 horsepower to give a service speed of 16 knots.

With the introduction within the next ten years of higher pressures in marine boilers, together with the introduction of the *compound engine and its greatly increased economy in coal and water consumption, the paddle-wheel was gradually swept from the high seas. But for passenger services on rivers and lakes and in inshore waters paddle steamers held their own until recent years. Unlike the screw, paddle-wheels exert virtually as much power going astern as ahead, and a paddle steamer can therefore come to a stop, or back away from a berth alongside a pier, far more smartly than can a similar screw steamer, and this faculty for quick manoeuvring has made paddle steamers popular and well adapted for excursion services all over the world.

For the same reason paddle tugs have been built for all kinds of service except ocean work. Furthermore, as they carry no passengers, they are permitted by law to be able to disconnect the

shaft and to work each wheel independently of the other. By varying the speed of the wheels, or by going ahead on one wheel and astern on the other, a paddle tug is said to be able to 'turn on a sixpence'. This nimbleness is particularly suitable in docks and other restricted spaces, and the British Admiralty has long favoured paddle tugs for this kind of service, to such an extent that following the Second World War new naval tugs have been built with paddle-wheels operated with a diesel-electric drive.

For rivers where numerous shoals and rapids had to be negotiated and the vessel's draught reduced to a minimum, flat-bottomed craft with a single paddle-wheel at the stern were developed (see STERN-WHEELER). The wheel, in this case usually of a simple type with fixed floats, was driven direct by two cylinders of long stroke placed on deck on a level with the paddle shaft and fed from a boiler, or boilers, mounted on the same deck right forward near the bows. Such stern-wheelers were to be found at work on countless shallow rivers in Africa, Egypt, Arabia, India, Australia, and other parts of the world.

In North America, although roughly 50 per cent of the river steamboats were stern-wheelers of this type, the larger and faster passenger river boats were almost all side-wheelers. Some Mississippi and Ohio steamboats were built as large as 5,000 tons gross with five or six decks rising above a flat hull in shape like a pointed tea tray. To turn their 40-ft paddle-wheels a form of walking beam engine was developed in which the moving beam, in full view above the top deck, was built up, together with the trusslike structure on which it was mounted, largely from timber and locally wrought iron supports. It was a type of paddle-steamer engine not to be found elsewhere in the world, a product of American ingenuity which proved ideal for its purpose, and in the great steamboat races of the 1870s, when boats like the *Robert E. Lee* and *Natchez* were immortalized in the colour prints of Currier and Ives, speeds of 18 and 19 knots were claimed between Natchez and New Orleans.

In naval history paddle steamers played their part on many occasions, from the China Opium War of 1842 and the Crimean campaign (1854–6) to the American Civil War (1861–5) when fast paddlers were built specially to run the *blockade of the Southern ports. During the First World War (1914–18) the Liverpool excursion paddle steamers *Daffodil* and *Iris* were at the blocking of *Zeebrugge in 1918, each being given the prefix *Royal* to their names after the action. There were a number of paddlers at the evacuation of the British Expeditionary Force from *Dunkirk in 1940 during the Second World War, while these vessels were extensively used later as *minesweepers, being powerful enough to tow a *LL Sweep at speed.

Although, with the exception of some harbour tugs, paddle steamers are no longer being built, there still remain a few in commission as ferries and excursion steamers.

PAINTER, a length of small rope in a boat used for securing it when alongside a pier or jetty or a ship, at the gangway, astern, or the lower *boom. The inboard end is usually spliced with a *thimble to a ringbolt in the stem of the boat, the outboard end being stopped from unravelling with a *whipping or, more fancifully, by being *pointed.

PAIR OF OARS, the name by which a large river-boat plying for hire on the River Thames in London was known during the 17th and 18th centuries. They were rowed by two men each pulling a pair of oars. In those days the Thames was one of the main highways of communication, and with only one bridge (London Bridge) across the river, a great number of boats plied for hire, both for crossing the river and for journeys up and down. Smaller river-boats, with a single boatman pulling a pair of oars, were known as *scullers.

PAKENHAM, the Hon. Sir THOMAS (1757–1836), British admiral, first came into prominence when he commanded the 74-gun *ship of the line *Invincible* at Lord *Howe's victory over

the French fleet known as the *Glorious First of June, at which he was largely responsible for the capture of the 84-gun *Juste*, into which he was appointed as captain in 1795, reaching flag rank in 1799. Thereafter he moved steadily up the promotion ladder by seniority, becoming a full admiral in 1810.

In his earlier service Pakenham became known for a remarkable *frigate action in 1781 in which, commanding the 28-gun *Crescent*, he fought the Dutch *Briel* of thirty-six guns in an action lasting two and a half hours, in which he lost his mainmast and had ninety-three men killed or wounded out of a total complement of 198. A remarkable feature of this action was that, in a relatively small and cramped ship, the surgeon performed forty-nine amputations on wounded seamen during and after the action, and all survived. Although Pakenham struck his colours to the *Briel*, she was driven off by another British frigate before she could take possession of the *Crescent*. Pakenham, because he had surrendered, refused to consider himself still captain of the *Crescent* and handed over command to his first lieutenant. He demanded a trial by court martial, but was acquitted and fulsomely praised by the court for the gallant way in which he had fought his small ship.

PALLETTING, a raised platform in the magazines of older warships on which the powder barrels were stored to keep them dry. With wooden ships liable to make water, and the magazines always located as low down as possible on the vessel's *floors, some form of keeping the gunpowder well above the level of water in the *bilges was obviously necessary. As a modern form of cargo handling, pallets, or palletting, has little relevance at sea, particularly in these days of *container ships.

PALLISER, Sir HUGH (1723–96), British admiral, is probably best remembered in history mainly because of the famous court martial of Admiral Augustus *Keppel after the battle of *Ushant in 1778. Palliser, as a vice admiral, had been appointed third-in-command of the Channel Fleet under Keppel, and in the indecisive action did not support Keppel as he could have done. He applied for and obtained a court martial on Keppel, urging that Keppel had in the first instance attacked before properly forming the *line of battle, a charge for which Admiral *Mathews had been earlier cashiered. A second charge was that Keppel had not done his utmost to 'take, sink, burn or destroy' the French fleet. The verdict of the court martial was to give Keppel a clear acquittal, announcing the charges as 'malicious and ill-founded'. Palliser then resigned his appointment and applied for a court martial on himself. The proceedings were in fact more those of a court of inquiry, since there were neither charges nor prosecutor. Briefly, the verdict was that Palliser was not 'chargeable with misconduct or misbehaviour'; he was therefore acquitted, though neither unanimously nor honourably.

He is, unhappily, much less remembered for his spell of duty as commander-in-chief and governor of Newfoundland following the Seven Years War (1756–63) during which he befriended and supervised James *Cook, later to become the famous navigator. Himself a skilled navigator, he taught Cook mathematics, navigation, and the principles of surveying, and without his interest and encouragement the world might well never have known its greatest navigator.

PALM, (1) the triangular face of the *fluke of an Admiralty pattern *anchor, **(2)** the sailmaker's thimble used in sewing canvas, consisting of a flat thimble in a canvas or leather strip with a thumb hole. The whole is worn across the palm of the hand, which gives it its name.

PALMER, NATHANIEL BROWN (1799–1877), a sealer from Stonington, Connecticut, visited the South Shetland Islands as second *mate of the *brig *Hersilia* in January 1820. In November of the same year he revisited the region in command of the *shallop *Hero* and reported land now known as the Palmer Coast of the Antarctic Peninsula. This was one of the first recorded sightings of the Antarctic mainland. In December 1821 he and a British sealer, George Powell, jointly discovered and charted the South Orkney Islands.

PAMPERO, a violent squall, accompanied by heavy rain, thunder, and lightning, which blows up with great suddenness on the pampas of the Rio de la Plata plain and frequently drifts out to sea where it blows with the force of a hurricane, the wind usually coming from the south-west. The great five-masted *barque *France* was struck by a pampero in 1901 and later foundered as a result of the damage she sustained.

PANAMA CANAL, the canal cut through the Isthmus of Panama connecting the Atlantic and Pacific Oceans and thus shortening by many thousands of miles the previous route round Cape Horn or through the Magellan Straits near the southern point of South America which was the only ice-free means of passing from one ocean to the other. (But see also NORTH-EAST PASSAGE, NORTH-WEST PASSAGE.)

The length of the canal is $42\frac{1}{4}$ miles (68 km), and its civil engineering problems were massive. Since the mean levels of the two oceans lie at different heights, it was necessary to raise the canal to a height of 85 feet (26 m) above sea level

and at places, Lake Gatun in particular, this necessitated, unlike the *Suez Canal where the relative levels are the same and the land is flat, a series of locks in the canal. The locks had to be large enough to take the largest oceangoing vessels. This also entailed, since ships in the locks were unable to use their propellers, the provision of electric locomotives along the sides of the locks to tow the ships within them.

Proposals for a canal across the Isthmus of Panama date back to 1523 when the Emperor Charles V, following reports from the various Spanish explorers who followed Christopher *Columbus, expressed interest in its desirability, but his plans came to nothing. Another strong proponent for a canal linking the two oceans was the geographer Baron von *Humboldt during the 19th century. After the successful opening of the Suez Canal in 1869, Ferdinand de *Lesseps formed a company to construct a canal across the Isthmus, but it came to grief after running out of money. A considerable fillip to its building came in 1898 when the American *battleship *Oregon*, built at San Francisco, was ordered to Cuba during the Spanish–American war of that year and took some weeks to get there round Cape Horn. This threw a bright light on the naval strategic value of such a canal to the U.S.A., then in the throes of building a navy large enough to control the two oceans which bounded her eastern and western shores. President Theodore *Roosevelt, always a strong advocate of a Panama Canal, used this occurrence to great advantage in his political campaign

At the bottom of Gatun Lock; drawing made during the construction of the Panama Canal

to sanction the construction of the canal and the acquisition of extra-territorial sovereignty of the necessary strip of land in Panama so that the canal should remain under the political and operational control of the U.S.A.

Preliminary work on the construction of the canal was begun in 1904, but it was not until 1908, when the construction was entrusted to the U.S. Corps of Army Engineers, that real progress was made. The work proceeded under great difficulties because of the unhealthy conditions, mainly yellow fever and malarial diseases, of the land through which it was cut, but all such difficulties were overcome and the canal was opened to navigation in 1914.

PANAMA PLATE, a metal plate bolted to the lugs of a *fairlead to close the gap between them when there is any risk of a *hawser or *warp jumping out, as for example when a ship is secured alongside a high quay and the hawser comes down through the fairlead at a steep angle. It originated in the Panama Canal where ships have to secure to the sides of the many locks at constantly varying heights as the level of the water in the locks is raised or lowered.

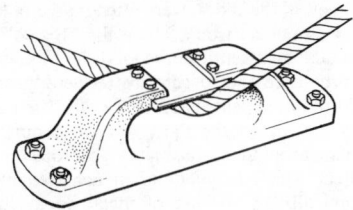

Panama plate on fairlead

PAPAGAYO, a gale from the north-east which occasionally blows with great force off the coast of Central America, often without any adequate signs to warn a navigator of its imminence.

PARALLAX, in its navigational meaning, an *altitude correction necessary to moon altitude observations, owing to the relative proximity of the moon to the earth. The true altitude of a heavenly body is a measure of an arc of a vertical circle contained between the celestial *horizon of an observer and the true direction of the body from the earth's centre. For all celestial bodies except the moon, their true directions from the earth's centre are regarded as being the same as from the observer located on the earth's surface. This is acceptable because of the great distances between the earth and these bodies compared with the radius of the earth, i.e., the distance between the earth's centre and an observer on its surface. For the moon, however, the angle subtended at the moon between lines which terminate respectively at the observer and at the earth's centre may be as much as nearly a degree

of arc. The parallax correction for moon sights depends upon the distance between the earth and moon, the *latitude of the observer, and the altitude of the moon. Tables of parallax for moon observations are normally included in all compilations of nautical tables.

Parallax can also refer to the margin of error in reading a *compass *course where the observer or helmsman stands to one side and there is an appreciable space between the graduated edge of the card and the *lubber's line. This of course can be eradicated by standing directly above the compass when reading off the course.

PARASELENE, sometimes known as a 'mock moon', a weakly coloured lunar halo, a result of refraction through ice crystals, identical in form and optical origin to the solar *parhelion, which is frequently observed in high *latitudes. It is often taken as a sign of approaching wet weather.

PARAVANE, a device invented during the First World War (1914–18) as a defence against moored *mines for ships *under way. The paravane is essentially a glorified wirecutter which is towed, one on each bow of a ship, at the end of a length of toughened wire. The paravane itself works on the *otter principle to keep it at a fixed depth, to stretch its towing wire taut, and to hold it at an obtuse angle to the ship's course. If a moored mine lies in the path of a ship, the bow wave pushes it aside and its mooring wire is deflected down the towing wire of the paravane into the wirecutter where it is severed. The mine then floats to the surface where it can be sunk by rifle fire. Paravanes, introduced into the Royal Navy in 1916, are used by the larger warships when any danger from moored mines may exist. It was invented by Commander Burney.

The paravane principle is also used in the *Oropesa method of sweeping mines.

PARBUCKLE, a means of hauling up or lowering a cask or other cylindrical object where it is not possible to use a *purchase. The middle of a

Parbuckling

length of rope is passed round a *bitt, *bollard, or any convenient post and the two ends are led under the two quarters of the object to be hoisted or lowered and are brought back over it. The cask is hoisted by hauling away on the ends or lowered by lowering away on them.

PARCEL, to, the operation of winding strips of tarred canvas round a rope after it has been *wormed and before it is *served or *marled. Parcelling, like worming, is always done with the lay of the rope, and serving against the lay. As the old seamanship rule has it:

'Worm and parcel with the lay,
Turn and serve the other way.'

The object of worming, parcelling, and serving a rope is to make it watertight, and thus prevent it from rotting in those parts which are continually subject to immersion.

PAREJA, a Spanish or Portuguese fishing vessel, very similar to a *trawler, used off the Atlantic coasts of those countries.

PARHELION, sometimes known as 'mock sun' or 'sun dog', either or both of two luminous spots having a reddish tinge on the inner edge, that appear on both sides of the sun, usually in high *latitudes. The effect is caused by the refraction of sunlight within hexagonal ice crystals whose axes are vertical. See also PARASELENE.

PARIS, the capital city of France about 100 miles up the River Seine from Le Havre. The river is navigable for small ships as far as the city, but its importance in the maritime world lies in the fact that it is the home of the *Musée de la Marine, one of the world's most important maritime museums with a magnificent collection of artefacts and pictures.

PARIS, FRANÇOIS EDMOND (1806–93), French vice admiral, author, and marine artist, was born at Brest and entered the naval college at Angoulême in 1820. His first experiences of naval service were three voyages of circumnavigation, with *Dumont-d'Urville in the *Astrolabe* in 1826–9, with Laplace in the *Favorite* in 1830–2, and in the *Artemise* in 1835–7. During these circumnavigations he made a number of paintings and drawings illustrating the three voyages; they have not been published but are exhibited in the *Musée de la Marine in Paris. He navigated the first steam vessel to make the voyage from Brest to the Chinese coast (Macao) in 1843, and after promotion to captain in 1846, served in the Crimean War (1854–6). He reached flag rank in 1858, was promoted to vice admiral in 1864, and his last naval service was as director of the chart department of the French Admiralty.

In 1871 he retired to become director of the Musée de la Marine, a post he held until his death, and one in which he immeasurably improved that superb collection of marine artefacts. As an author he wrote a number of important books on marine architecture and also, in collaboration with his father-in-law, a marine dictionary. He had two sons, both of whom became marine painters, ARMAND specializing in painting all types of sailing vessels and LÉON in scenes of life on board.

'PARISH-RIGGED', the seaman's term, in the days of square-rigged ships, for a vessel which, through the parsimony of its owner, had worn or bad gear aloft and meagre victuals below.

PARK AVENUE BOOM, a main *boom fitted for a period in *J-class racing yachts during the decade 1930–9 when these racing yachts were at their most exotic. It was triangular in section with a wide flat top, and was fitted with a series of transverse rails at short intervals along its length. Along the *foot of the *Bermuda mainsail were sewn metal slides which engaged in the transverse rails. Stops, which limited the movement of the slides, were fitted on the rails in such positions as would allow the *foot of the sail to take up a gentle curve, in order to prevent any turbulence and to get a better aerodynamic flow as the wind passed across the sail. The width across the top of the Park Avenue boom was sufficient to allow a reasonably generous curve, an effect which is today often achieved more economically by the use of metal booms with inbuilt flexibility.

Park Avenue booms proved no more than a passing phase in big yacht racing, the fractional gain in sail efficiency being probably at least counterbalanced by the loss caused through the additional windage of the over-large boom.

PARKER, the name of an East Anglian family which contributed a great many officers to the 18th century navy of Britain, two of whom served as commander-in-chief of a fleet. Sir HYDE Parker (1714–82) began his naval career under Commodore George *Anson, and as a young captain greatly distinguished himself by the number of French *privateers he captured during the early years of the Seven Years War (1756–63), incidentally amassing a tidy sum in *prize money. He commanded the *frigate *Brilliant* in Admiral *Rodney's squadron at the bombardment of Le Havre in 1759, when immense damage was inflicted on the town and harbour works, and on his promotion into a *ship of the line he was sent to the East Indies, being present at the siege of Pondicherry and, in 1762, at the capture of Manila. Here, again, he was able to add, perhaps fortuitously, to his prize money. Having been sent to search for a Spanish treasure ship bound from Acapulco to Manila, he sighted a strange sail, chased her, and after a hard-fought action forced her to surrender, only to discover that she was not the treasure ship *Philippina* he had been sent to intercept, but the 60-gun ship *Santissima Trinidad*. Nevertheless, she proved to be a rich * prize, being * condemned in the prize court for more than half a million pounds.

Shortly after the outbreak of the War of American Independence (1775–82), Parker was promoted rear admiral and second-in-command to Admiral * Byron ('Foul-weather Jack') in the squadron destined for the West Indies. The squadron was shattered in tremendous gales during the voyage across the Atlantic, but after a refit at New York, he was present at the series of indecisive engagements off Grenada with the French fleet commanded by d'* Estaing. When Byron returned home through ill health, Parker succeeded him as commander-in-chief, and promptly captured a French squadron of seven ships, which added considerably to his already comfortable fortune acquired through prize money. This run of good fortune continued, and a number of other prizes were captured during the desultory fighting in West Indian waters. Yet it would be unfair to dwell entirely on his remarkable propensity for capturing prizes; he was also a fine seaman and a brave officer. In what was almost his last action in the West Indies, when * blockaded at St. Lucia by a greatly superior French fleet under de * Guichen, he forced his way through the French ships and, by superior seamanship, saved a British * convoy with 3,000 troops on board from almost certain capture by the French.

On his return to England Parker was given command of the fleet in the North Sea designed to protect British shipping from the Dutch, who had joined the war on the side of France. His fleet comprised most of the oldest and decrepit ships of the navy, all that could be found after equipping the British fleets in American waters. In 1780 he escorted an outward bound convoy of 500 sail safely to the Baltic and, collecting the homeward-bound ships there, escorted them across the North Sea. He found a Dutch fleet, also escorting a convoy, off the * Dogger Bank. Both admirals, having detached * frigates to safeguard their merchant ships, squared up for battle, a typical Anglo-Dutch slogging match reminiscent of the Dutch wars of the 17th century. As Ralfe (*Naval Biography*, 1828) has it: 'When within pistol-shot of the enemy Admiral Parker made the signal to commence action, the cannonade immediately became general on both sides and continued with increasing fire for three hours and forty minutes, the destructive effects of which now became visible; the ships lay like

logs on the water, totally unmanageable.' The result might, perhaps, be fairly held to be a draw, though one Dutch ship of the line was so badly damaged that she sank before she could reach the safety of a Dutch harbour.

On his return to the * Nore Parker was surprised to find the king, the Prince of Wales, and the First Lord of the Admiralty come down in the * royal yacht to meet him and to escort his battered ships to their anchorage. But because he held different political beliefs from the First Lord, he refused all honours and, indeed, struck his flag. With a change in the administration in 1782, and in spite of his age of 68, he accepted a further appointment as commander-in-chief in the East Indies. He sailed for those waters in the 50-gun ship *Cato* but on arrival she was wrecked in the Malabar Islands. All the survivors, including the admiral, were murdered by the natives as they reached the shore.

His son, also Sir HYDE (1739–1807), was commander-in-chief of the British fleet at the first battle of * Copenhagen, and is chiefly remembered for the signal he hoisted during the battle to leave off action, the signal to which Lord * Nelson was said to have lifted his telescope to his blind eye. He had a varied and not unsuccessful naval career, mainly in North American waters during the War of American Independence (1775–82) and in the Mediterranean during the Revolutionary War with France (1793–1801).

PARKER, Sir PETER (1721–1811), British admiral of the fleet, was a close friend and patron of Horatio * Nelson when the latter was a young captain in the West Indies. He continued on terms of intimate friendship until Nelson's death at the battle of * Trafalgar in 1805, and was the chief mourner at his funeral at St. Paul's in 1806, being then 85 years old.

His naval career was spent largely in the Atlantic and West Indies, playing an active part as captain and rear admiral in the Seven Years War (1756–63) and the War of American Independence (1775–82). He was promoted vice admiral in 1779 while commander-in-chief at Jamaica and returned to England in 1782 bringing with him the Comte de * Grasse and other French officers as prisoners-of-war, following Admiral Lord * Rodney's victory at the battle of the * Saints. In 1793 he became commander-in-chief at Portsmouth, a post he held for six years, and he was promoted to admiral of the fleet in 1799.

PARKER, RICHARD (1767–97), British naval mutineer, was said to have been of gentle birth. He was rated * midshipman in the navy, and for a short period, it is said, served as acting lieutenant. According to one source, he picked up considerable * prize money in the American War of Independence (1775–82), came ashore, and spent it prodigally; according to another he challenged his captain to a duel and was thrown ashore. He was next heard of in Scotland, married and trying to make a living as a maker of golf balls and schoolmaster. At the outbreak of the Revolutionary War (1793–1801) with France, he volunteered for the navy again and again was rated midshipman. He quickly fell into trouble, was brought before a court martial, disrated, and finally discharged as unfit from rheumatism. He fell into debt and was thrown into prison in Edinburgh.

Rather than serve a long sentence he applied for a * bounty for joining the navy (at that time £30), was drafted in March 1797 to H.M.S. *Sandwich* in the * Nore under the * Quota Act, and was at once rated able seaman. Two months later he was the leader, with the self-styled title of admiral, of a widespread mutiny which affected all the ships at the Nore. This mutiny was, ostensibly, to procure better pay and treatment for seamen, but it immediately followed a similar mutiny at Spithead in which all these aims had already been achieved. One by one the affected ships renounced the mutiny until the *Sandwich* was isolated. The mutiny collapsed and Parker, with the other ringleaders, was hanged at the yardarm.

PARKER, Sir WILLIAM (1743–1802), British vice admiral, was a * midshipman at the capture of * Quebec in 1759. He commanded the *Audacious* in 1794 at the battle of the * Glorious First of June, and in 1797, as a rear admiral, took part in the battle of * Cape St. Vincent, engaging the 112-gun Spanish ship *San Josef* and damaging her so badly that Commodore * Nelson had little difficulty in boarding and capturing her in the well-known incident of 'Nelson's patent bridge for capturing Spanish firstrates'.

He was again with Lord St. Vincent (see JERVIS, Sir John) in 1798 in the fleet off * Cadiz at the time Nelson was detached in command of a squadron into the Mediterranean, resulting in the battle of the * Nile. Like Sir John * Orde, Parker was furiously angry at St. Vincent's selection of an officer junior to himself for this important appointment. For three months he bombarded the Admiralty with furious letters protesting at this affront to his seniority, but without effect. He finished his naval career as commander-inchief at Halifax, being eventually recalled for disobeying orders.

PARKES, Dr. OSCAR (1885–1958), medical practitioner, marine artist, and author, was born at Handsworth, Staffs., and educated at Berkhamsted and Birmingham University. During the First World War (1914–18) he served in the Royal Navy as a temporary surgeon lieutenant and in 1918 was attached to the Naval Intelligence Division in the Admiralty as a naval artist and director of the photographic section of the * Imperial War Museum. For five years after the war he was neurologist to the Ministry of Pensions and then took up general medical practice at Ringwood, Hampshire.

From his boyhood he had been fascinated with warships, particularly with aspects of their design and appearance, and through the years had amassed a vast and detailed knowledge of the warships of all nations. In 1918 he was invited to become joint editor of the famous * *Jane's Fighting Ships*, a post he held until 1935 (from 1923 in co-operation with Francis * McMurtrie). Many of his sketches of particulars of individual designs decorated the pages of *Fighting Ships* during these years. Although his knowledge covered all types of warship, his greatest enthusiasm was for the * battleship, and in 1954 he published *British Battleships*, a magnificently detailed and authoritative account of every British battleship from the *Warrior* of 1860 to the *Vanguard* of 100 years later. He also wrote and illustrated a great many articles on naval subjects.

PARLIAMENT, or **PARLIAMENTARY, HEEL,** a makeshift method of cleaning or repairing the sides of a British naval ship of the era of sail when there was neither time nor opportunity of of * careening her or placing her in a dock. She was heeled over by running the guns from one side of the ship over to the other side. Only the upper * strakes could be cleaned since the maximum angle of heel with the ship still afloat was limited by the level of the lower * gunports. According to an old belief, the name derived from the contempt in which parliamentary rule was held in the English Navy, implying that a half-done job was good enough to satisfy a parliamentarian, but the more likely derivation is from the period of its introduction, the term coming into the British Navy during the First Anglo-Dutch War (1652–4) when England was governed by Cromwell's Parliament and when this process was much used. It did not spread into general use beyond the English Navy.

When, in 1782, H.M.S. * *Royal George* capsized and sank at Spithead with a great loss of life, she was undergoing a Parliament heel to carry out underwater repairs and the angle of heel was great enough for the sea to enter her lower gunports. For an account of this well-known disaster, see LOSS OF THE ROYAL GEORGE, THE.

PARREL, originally a rope threaded with * trucks but later an iron collar by which the lower * yards of a square-rigged ship were held to the mast giving them freedom to be * braced round to the wind. The *topgallant and smaller yards were held to the mast with a parrel lashing, which was a length of rope with an *eye at each end. It was passed round the yard and round the after part of the mast, the ends being then brought back, one over and one under the yard, and the two eyes lashed together. As square-rigged ships, and of course their yards, grew larger with the years, these smaller yards were generally held to the mast with a parrel rather than with a parrel lashing. A parrel lashing was also a lashing which was sometimes used to secure the *heel of a topmast or topgallant mast to the head of a lower mast or topmast as an additional security for the *cap and *fid. For illus. see YARD.

PARRY, Sir JOHN FRANKLIN (1863–1926), British admiral, followed in the footsteps of his grandfather Sir William *Parry as Hydrographer of the Navy. Having entered the navy in 1877 he started his surveying career in 1884 under Thomas Henry *Tizard in H.M.S. *Triton* on the east coast of England, but was soon sent out to the *Rambler* for surveys on the coasts of China and Borneo. From 1890 to 1900 he was on the Australian station, first in the *Penguin* and then in the *Dart*, which he commanded from 1897. Surveys in H.M.S. *Dart* were mainly of the Queensland Inner Route where many islets were successfully planted by him with coconuts for the use of navigators and shipwrecked mariners. In 1903–5 he surveyed in the *Egeria* in British Columbia waters, returning there in 1908–10, having in 1906 commissioned a new ship, H.M.S. *Merlin*, for the China Station, only to contract dysentery in the Red Sea.

Four years as Assistant Hydrographer then preceded his appointment as Hydrographer of the Navy in London in 1914 and his brilliant leadership of the department throughout the First World War (1914–18) enabled it to meet the unprecedented demands of modern naval war. Staff of the Hydrographic Department increased from 61 to 367, many female clerks and draughtswomen breaching the Admiralty's hitherto male preserve. Many special operational charts were produced and the needs of the Royal and merchant navies increased chart printings from $1\frac{1}{2}$ million to $2\frac{1}{2}$ million by 1919. Afloat, surveying ships, much reduced in numbers, were employed on operational surveys and senior surveyors were attached to the fleets, often to apply surveying methods in bombardments of enemy coasts. A new venture was to equip H.M.S. *Endeavour* with chart-printing equipment, and she did valuable work during the *Dardanelles campaign.

After the war Parry reconstituted the surveying fleet, into which, as a result of wartime developments, *taut wire measuring gear and

later *echo sounding was introduced. He was also concerned with running down the department to a peacetime establishment which included planning for an Admiralty Chart Establishment.

In 1918 Parry chaired an Admiralty conference on uniformity of *time-keeping at sea which adopted the use of *zone times and the start of the astronomical day at midnight instead of at noon. In 1919 he was chairman of the International Conference of London which instituted the International Hydrographic Bureau. It was set up in Monaco in 1921 with Parry as its first presiding director, a post he filled until his death.

PARRY, Sir WILLIAM EDWARD (1790–1855), British rear admiral, is best remembered for his expeditions to the Arctic, but he was also Hydrographer of the Navy from 1823 to 1829.

As a young lieutenant in 1810 he had experience of northern waters and of chartmaking when he was appointed to H.M.S. *Alexandria*, protecting the Spitsbergen whale fishery, and later he continued his interest in navigational matters while serving in various ships on the North American station. In 1818 he volunteered for service under John *Ross in an Arctic expedition, commanding the *Alexander*. Another Arctic expedition the following year to discover the *North-West passage was led by Parry in H.M.S. *Hecla*, accompanied by Matthew Liddon in the *Griper*; and in 1821–3, in H.M.S. *Fury*, with George Lyon in the *Hecla*, Parry spent another two seasons in the Arctic.

Made Hydrographer of the Navy in succession to Sir Alexander *Hurd, he was soon in charge of yet another Arctic expedition in the *Fury* and *Hecla*, 1823–5, and in 1827 was absent again in the *Hecla* attempting a sledge journey to the North pole, which failed owing to unexpected ice conditions.

During his period as Hydrographer a major development was the institution of *Sailing Directions. *Light Lists were also inaugurated, and in 1829 a sole agent was appointed in London for the worldwide sale of British Admiralty charts. There was also begun interchange arrangements with other national hydrographic offices, which Parry's grandson, Sir John *Parry, was to regularize at the International Hydrographic Conference in London in 1919.

Surveys and chart production continued vigorously under Parry's rule, but such departmental work, especially as it was under the close supervision of J. W. Croker, Secretary to the Admiralty, to whom hydrography in all its aspects had a great appeal, had little interest for him and he resigned when not yet 40, having by then been knighted and made a Fellow of the Royal Societies of London and Edinburgh.

After five years in Australia as Commissioner of the Australian Agricultural Company, Parry came back to the Admiralty in 1837 to organize a new department as Comptroller of Steam Machinery. In 1847 he retired for health reasons, became captain superintendent of *Haslar Hospital and later lieutenant-governor of *Greenwich Hospital.

A. Parry, *Parry of the Arctic* (1963).

PARSONS, Sir CHARLES ALGERNON (1854–1931), British marine engineer, was the youngest son of the third Earl of Rosse, developed early talents as a mathematician, and was Eleventh Wrangler at Cambridge University in 1877, whence he was apprenticed for four years at the Elswick works of Sir William Armstrong. In 1884, as junior partner in Clarke, Chapman and Co., Gateshead, he invented the first steam *turbine-driven dynamo, a $7\frac{1}{2}$-kW machine of which some 200 were produced, mainly for ship lighting systems.

In 1889 Parsons founded the firm of C. A. Parsons at Heaton which produced the first turbo-dynamo machinery for a power station, and thereafter for many others. He next attacked the problem of marine propulsion at the separate Wallsend works of Parsons Marine Steam Turbine Co., where was constructed the first turbine-propelled vessel, the *Turbinia,* which, with a speed of over 30 knots, made such a sensation at the 1897 Naval Review at Spithead that two years later the British Admiralty entrusted Parsons with the construction of the first two turbine-driven *destroyers, H.M. ships *Viper* and *Cobra*. These attained a record speed of 37 knots; but their design made use of too light *scantlings, resulting in the loss of the *Cobra*, which broke her back in heavy weather. Nevertheless the principle of turbine drive had been proved successful and Parsons turbines were thereafter adopted for fast passenger *packets, *destroyers, *cruisers, and, finally, for the epoch-making *battleship *Dreadnought* in 1905. At the same time the *Cunard Company installed them in the *Lusitania* and in the *Mauretania* which held the Atlantic *Blue Riband for nearly twenty-five years. Parsons also developed the geared turbine, initially for merchant ships in 1909; and in 1918 the high pressure geared turbine-driven passenger vessel *King George V* was the pioneer of high pressure steam at sea.

Another interest of Sir Charles Parsons was optics in all its forms; Ross Ltd. and the firm of Sir Howard Grubb and Sons, which he controlled, were responsible for a large output of glass for optical purposes and many notable astronomical instruments.

Parsons was made Fellow of the Royal Society in 1898, being awarded their Rumford and Copley Gold Medals; he also received the Albert Medal of the Royal Society of Arts and the Faraday and Kelvin Medals of the Institution of Electrical Engineers. He has been acclaimed as the most original engineer Great Britain has produced since James Watt.

PART OF THE SHIP, the division of a ship into areas as an administrative convenience in bringing a greater flexibility in the division of the crew for daily work purposes. In large ships, particularly large warships, the crew, in addition to their division into watches (*port and *starboard in the two-watch system; red, white, and blue in the three-watch system), are further divided into parts of the ship, the normal number of divisions in the largest ships being four. In the British Navy, following the old navy pattern, these are the forecastle division, fore-top division, main-top division, and quarterdeck division. In smaller warships three parts of the ship (forecastle, topmen, quarterdeck) or two parts (forecastle, quarterdeck) are used. This method makes it simpler to detail men for the day-to-day work of the ship, as they can then be divided into large working parties by watches or smaller working parties by parts of the ship.

PARTNERS, a framework, consisting of stout plank, secured to the decks of wooden ships round the holes through which pass the masts or the spindle of the *capstan, thus strengthening the deck in these places to assist in taking the strain when the masts carry a press of sail or the capstan is heaving in some considerable weight.

PASCO, JOHN (1774–1853), British rear admiral, is remembered for his association with the most famous naval signal in British maritime history. Although the senior lieutenant of H.M.S. *Victory* at the battle of *Trafalgar in 1805, and thus first in line for promotion if success should follow the action, he willingly forbore to assert his seniority in order to continue to serve the commander-in-chief, Lord *Nelson, as his signal officer. As the British fleet was sailing into battle, Nelson turned to Pasco and said: 'Mr. Pasco, I wish to say to the fleet, England confides that every man will do his duty. You must be quick, for I have one more signal to make, which is for close action.' Pasco asked if he could substitute 'expects' for 'confides', as the former was in the vocabulary signal book (see POPHAM, Sir Home) and the latter would need eight separate hoists to spell it out. 'That will do; make it directly,' was Nelson's reply, and so the famous signal was hoisted. Pasco was severely wounded in the battle, was promoted to commander in December 1805 and to captain in 1811.

After the end of the Napoleonic War in 1815, Pasco was unemployed for thirty years; in 1846 he was appointed to command his old ship, H.M.S. *Victory*, at Portsmouth, and a year later was promoted to rear admiral.

PASSARADO, an old name for the rope used to haul down the * sheet blocks of the fore and main * courses of a square-rigged ship when they were hauled aft. This was done when it was required to sail the ship * large. The name may possibly have come from the Adriatic, where a 'passaro' was the lacing used to make fast the foot of a sail to the * yard of a * trabacolo.

PASSAREE, a rope used in square-rigged ships when running before the wind, with the lower * studding-sail * booms rigged, to haul out the clews of the foresail to the ends of those booms in order to get the maximum spread of that sail.

PASSARO, CAPE, a naval battle of the War of the Quadruple Alliance (1717–20), was fought on 31 July 1718 between a Spanish fleet which was intending to take Sicily from the French, to whom it had been ceded under the Treaty of Utrecht, and an English fleet which had been sent out to the Mediterranean especially to defeat this project. The English fleet of 21 ships under the command of Sir George * Byng met the Spanish fleet, commanded by Vice Admiral Don Antonio de Gastañeta, off Cape Passaro. The Spanish fleet comprised 11 * ships of the line, 13 * frigates, and 21 others, but having only recently been assembled was not in very good order. At about noon on 30 July the Spaniards were sighted but having no desire to engage a superior force, retreated. The four fastest British ships of the line were ordered to * chase.

There was little wind, and the Spanish ships were towed by their * galleys throughout the night. Nevertheless, at daylight next morning, the British ships were nearly up with the enemy, whose galleys and other small craft were then ordered to stand inshore. Seeing this, Byng ordered eight of his ships to chase them, Syracuse being given as the rendezvous after the action. The rest of the British fleet stood on after the main body of the enemy and the action became general as the British ships came up. By nightfall several of the enemy had been taken and the rest were in full flight, being still pursued by the British. In all, seven Spanish ships of the line and nine frigates were captured or burnt, besides several other smaller vessels. It was a complete victory for Sir George Byng, who was created Viscount Torrington for his services.

PASSAT, the old German name, dating from the mid-16th century, for the north-east * trade wind which blows in the north Atlantic. This was the wind which helped Christopher * Columbus in his first voyage to the West Indies in 1492. It was also the name given to one of the best-known of the big four-masted German trading * barques of the early 20th century.

PATENT LOG, see LOG.

PATERNOSTER, the framing of a chain * pump as fitted on board older sailing ships before the introduction of steam. It was by the paternoster that the two copper tubes, in which the chain with its washers worked, were held firmly in position.

PATRIMONIAL SEA, a legal term to denote those waters adjacent to a country over which it claims jurisdiction. The extent of this patrimonial sea is today a subject of international argument closely bound up with fishing rights to which various individual nations lay claim. See MARE CLAUSUM, TERRITORIAL WATERS.

PATTERSON, DANIEL TODD (1786–1839), American naval officer, served in the U.S.S. * Constellation in the second squadron sent to the Mediterranean in the war against Tripoli, and was captured on 31 October 1803 while on board the * Philadelphia, being imprisoned for more than nineteen months. He rendered conspicuous service in operations against pirates in the Caribbean and raided the base of the pirate Jean Lafitte, in Barataria Bay, Louisiana, where he captured six * schooners and other small vessels.

Patterson's greatest achievement lay in his accurate estimate of the situation in 1814 which enabled the Americans to arrange for the successful defence of New Orleans. General Andrew Jackson had been appointed by the President to defend the area against a British expedition which was known to be preparing in Jamaica for an attack on the American coast. At Patterson's suggestion, Jackson took the forces available to him to New Orleans, while Patterson mustered a small force of * gunboats in Lake Borgne. Although they were all finally captured by the Royal Navy they accomplished a decisive delay of nine days. By constant bombardment from the guns of Patterson's ships, and from the artillery which General Jackson had brought up, profiting by the nine days delay caused by Patterson's gunboats, the British attacking force was held and finally broken up, and the whole operation called off by the British.

Patterson received a vote of thanks from Congress and was promoted to captain. In 1824 he commanded the U.S.S. * Constitution, flagship of Commodore John * Rodgers in the Mediterranean Squadron, and in 1828 he became one of the Navy Commissioners. In 1832 he was assigned to command the Mediterranean Squadron. He died while in command of the Washington Navy Yard.

PAUNCH or **PANCH,** a thick mat made by weaving together twists of ropeyarns, known as * foxes, and forcing them home as close as possible. Paunch matting was used round * yards and rigging to prevent rubbing and wear when the ship was rolling heavily. See also BAGGY-WRINKLE.

PAVESSE, a wooden shield used on board warships of the Tudor Navy to line the fore and after castles. They were usually painted with the heraldic arms of the admiral, captain, or other noblemen on board, and in later Tudor times were extended to line the *waist of the ship as well as the fore and after castles. They were primarily intended as a protection for men on deck against small shot from enemy ships, and were made of poplar, which did not splinter when pierced. Later they became much more of a form of ship decoration than of protection in days when warships were highly carved, gilded, and painted. They were copied from the shield protection which lined the *gunwales of the Viking *longships.

PAWLS, a series of metal dogs, hinged at one end, at the bottom of the barrel of a *capstan, which drop into scores in a pawl-ring round the capstan at deck level and prevent it from taking charge and overrunning when being used for *weighing an *anchor or lifting a heavy load.

PAY, to, (1) to pour hot pitch into a deck or side *seam after it has been *caulked with *oakum, in order to prevent the oakum getting wet. **(2)** To dress a mast or yard in a sailing vessel with tar or varnish, or with tallow in the case of masts on which sails are frequently hoisted or lowered. **(3)** To cover the bottom of a vessel with, in older days, a mixture of sulphur, rosin, and tallow (see also BREAM, TO) or in modern days, an antifouling mixture.

PAY OFF, to, (1) a sailing vessel's head pays off when it falls further off the direction of the wind and drops to *leeward. It is a term used particularly in relation to *tacking when the bows of the ship have crossed the wind and she continues to turn away from the wind until she reaches the position when her sails are full and drawing. **(2)** To close the accounts of a naval ship when she reaches the end of a *commission and all officers and men receive the balance of all pay owing to them, or in the case of a merchant ship, to close the accounts at the end of a voyage.

PAY OUT, to, the act of slackening a cable or rope so that it can run out freely to a desired amount. It differs from casting off in that when a rope or cable is paid out it is re-secured in a new position, when it is *cast off it is let go completely.

PAYNE, ALAN (1921–), Australian yacht designer, was educated in Sydney, New South Wales. He began work in a shipyard in 1939, and gained qualifications in shipbuilding and design through the Sydney Technical College, leading to membership of the Royal Institution of Naval Architects. He began designing yachts in 1945 and produced a variety of racing and cruising types, of which the most widely known were the two Australian challengers for the *America's* Cup, *Gretel I* and *Gretel II* which raced in 1962 and 1970 respectively. He now specializes in yacht designs intended for quantity production methods.

PEABODY MUSEUM OF SALEM, see SALEM.

PEAK, (1) the upper, after corner of the four-sided fore-and-aft sail extended by a *gaff. The halyards used to hoist the outer end of a gaff sail are known as peak halyards. For illus. see SAIL. **(2)** The bill or end of the *palm of an *anchor; the 'k' is not pronounced when used in connection with an anchor and the word is often written as pea.

PEARL HARBOR, the naval base in Oahu Island, in the Hawaii group in mid-Pacific, of the U.S. Pacific Fleet in 1941. In the early morning of 7 December 1941 it was attacked without warning and without a prior declaration of war by a strong force of Japanese seaborne aircraft. Details of the attack had been worked out by Admiral *Yamamoto earlier in the year; the attacking force of six *aircraft carriers, with a support force of two *battleships and two heavy *cruisers, accompanied by screening *destroyers, *submarines, and supply *tankers, sailed from Japan in small detachments to avoid remark, met together at Tankan Bay in the Kurile Islands, and set out for Pearl Harbor on 26 November, the whole expedition being under the command of Vice Admiral Chuichi *Nagumo. It crossed the Pacific unobserved and arrived 500 miles to the north of Oahu after dark on the night of 6 December. The carriers turned south and early the following morning, when 275 miles off Pearl Harbor, flew off their first striking force of 40 torpedo-bombers, 49 high level bombers, 51 dive bombers, and 51 fighters. They arrived over Pearl Harbor at 0750. A second wave of bombers came in about an hour later.

Most of the U.S. Pacific Fleet, with the exception of the aircraft carriers which were at sea on a training exercise, were in harbour with a large proportion of their officers and crews ashore on week-end leave. The Japanese attack was devastatingly accurate and losses were very heavy: seven battleships and three destroyers were sunk or badly damaged, and more than half the American aircraft stationed on the island were destroyed.

The attack signalled the start of American involvement in the Second World War. When it was suggested in Washington that a medal should be struck to be issued to all who had been involved in the action, one of the surviving com-

The U.S. battleship California *under attack at Pearl Harbor, 1941*

batants from Pearl Harbor suggested that the ribbon should be made of black crape.

Admiral Husband *Kimmel, who commanded the U.S. Pacific Fleet based on Pearl Harbor, was relieved from active duty as a result of the attack, as also was the general commanding ashore. It was held against them that they had not reacted sufficiently firmly in holding Pearl Harbor in an advanced state of readiness in view of intelligence reports from Washington and passed to Pearl Harbor which indicated the probability of imminent Japanese attacks on unspecified targets which were certain to lead to war.

PEARS, CHARLES (1873–1958), British marine artist, was born at Pontefract and began his career in art as an illustrator of nautical books, in which he excelled in the clarity and detail with which he pictured the construction and fittings of ships of all types, historical as well as modern. In the First and Second World Wars he was appointed an official naval war artist, and a large collection of his work in this field can be seen in the *Imperial War Museum in London. His pictures always show a fearless use of colour, a fine sense of design, and vigorous brush work which gives them a feeling of movement and excitement.

PEARY, ROBERT EDWIN (1856–1920), American Arctic explorer, was born at Cresson, Pennsylvania, and was the first white man to reach the North pole.

He studied civil engineering at Bowdoin College, Maine; graduated in 1877 and joined the civil engineer corps of the U.S. Navy in 1881 with the rank of lieutenant. In 1886 he obtained leave of absence for a trip to Greenland, making a sledge journey inland along the northern icecap, and in 1891 organized an expedition to Greenland, wintering in Inglefield Gulf on the north-west coast. With a Norwegian companion, he crossed the ice-cap, proving for the first time that Greenland was an island. His wife accompanied him on the expedition as far as Inglefield Gulf, wintering there with the ship and becoming the first white woman to join an Arctic exploration.

Peary continued his explorations over the next few years, establishing that a polar ocean lay to the north of Greenland and in company with his Negro servant Matthew Henson and a party of Eskimos reaching a northerly *latitude of 84° 17′ 27″, the highest latitude reached to that date in the western hemisphere. In 1903 he supervised the construction of a vessel specially designed for Arctic exploration, the first such ship built in the U.S.A. She was named *Roosevelt* and, with Peary on board, she sailed from New York for Greenland in July 1905 with enough supplies for two years on board. Winter quarters were set up on the north coast of Grant Land and Peary set out with a party on sledges. Delays because of open water held the party back but in April 1906 they reached a latitude of 87° 6′ N., beating their previous record by nearly 170 miles. They made a safe return to the *Roosevelt* in the face of great difficulties as they were cut off by open water from some of the supply dumps laid down on the outward journey.

In August 1908 the *Roosevelt* set sail again for Greenland, wintering in Grant Land, and Peary, with a party, set off on sledges in March 1909. As supplies were consumed, so various members of the party were sent back to the *Roosevelt*, the last to do so leaving in 87° 48′ N., the highest northerly latitude then reached. Peary, with his servant and four Eskimos, continued and reached the North pole on 6 April 1909. They remained there for thirty hours, and when Peary made a *sounding through a fracture in the ice a few miles from the pole, he found no bottom at 1,500 *fathoms. One Eskimo was drowned on the return journey, but the remainder reached the *Roosevelt* in safety.

Less than a week earlier, Dr. Frederick *Cook, who had been surgeon with Peary's 1891 expedition, claimed that he had reached the North pole on 21 April 1908. He had accompanied an expedition towards the pole in 1907, but as nothing had been heard of him since, it was thought that he had perished. A bitter controversy followed these conflicting claims, but a scientific investigation later sustained Peary's claims and discredited those of Cook. Peary was thanked by the U.S. Congress for his work in the field of Arctic exploration and in 1911 was placed on the retired list of the civil engineer corps of the navy with the rank of rear admiral.

J. G. Hayes, *Robert Edwin Peary* (1929).

PEETERS, BONAVENTURA (1614–52), Flemish marine painter, was born at Antwerp but, after a quarrel with the Jesuits, went to live at Hoboken. He was one of the very few Flemish artists to specialize in marine painting, and was greatly influenced by the Dutch school in this branch of art, particularly by Simon de *Vlieger and the elder Van de *Velde, of both of whom he was a contemporary.

Like Van de Velde, he had served at sea, making many voyages and qualifying as a *master, an experience which gave him his knowledge of ships, their rigging, and their behaviour in a sea. His later pictures are not considered to be as good as his earlier ones, as in his later life he tended to elaborate his paintings with an exces-

sive use of bright colours and decoration. Examples of his work can be seen in many maritime museums, with a good representative collection at the *National Maritime Museum at Greenwich. He was also, with his brother, a mapmaker, but examples of his work in this field which have survived are not usually of very great merit.

PEGGY-MAST, sometimes written as pegy-, pygy-, or pege-mast, occasionally a short mast or, more usually, a *yard, to which a *pennon was attached in very early warships. It was current during the 15th century but had fallen into disuse by the mid-16th century with the growth in the size of ships and consequently in the number of places from which a pennon could be flown. In the accounts of the Lord High Treasurer for Scotland for 1496, there is an entry for 'one barel of pyk (pitch) and one pegy mast to the said schip'.

PELICAN, see GOLDEN HIND.

PELICAN HOOK, see SLIP HOOK.

PELLEW, Sir EDWARD, Viscount Exmouth (1757–1833), British admiral, entered the Royal Navy in 1770 and in 1777, as a *midshipman, was present with General Burgoyne at Saratoga, where he was captured. On his return to England in 1778 his promotion was rapid, to lieutenant that year, to commander in 1780, and to *postcaptain in 1782, in each case as a reward for gallantry. When the Revolutionary War (1793–1801) with France broke out, Pellew continued to distinguish himself by his valour and example. Commanding the 36-gun *frigate *Nymphe* he took the French *Cléopâtre*, the first frigate to be made a *prize in the war, and in her captured the French naval signal code. Three years later, in 1796, he was made a baronet in recognition of his exceptional bravery and resource in saving the crew and passengers of the *Dutton*, a troop *transport which had run ashore and which was rapidly breaking up in Plymouth Sound. In the same year, while commanding a squadron of frigates, he captured several important prizes, including a more heavily armed French frigate, the *Virginie*, forty-four guns, after a fifteen-hour chase which began off the Lizard and ended in a running fight.

Pellew's most famous exploit was the destruction of the 74-gun French *ship of the line *Droits de l'Homme* off the coast of her own country. His frigate, the *Indefatigable*, was in company with another, the *Amazon*, Captain R. C. Reynolds, when the enemy was sighted returning from an expedition to Bantry Bay. Action began at 5.30 p.m. on 13 February, in darkness and heavy weather, and it was continued almost throughout the night which followed, during the course of which all three ships nearly ran ashore. The *Indefatigable* alone escaped wreck on the Penmarch rocks, heavy loss of life from storm being added to the toll of battle.

Pellew entered Parliament as member for Barnstaple in 1802, and supported the Admiralty with spirit and success against hostile criticism, some of which was justified. Two years later, he was given his flag, and was sent to the East Indies as commander-in-chief. In the Far East he destroyed a Dutch fleet which would otherwise have been used in the cause of Napoleon.

Pellew returned to England in 1809 and during the following year was appointed to be commander-in-chief in the North Sea. But Lord * Collingwood, who had died on service in the Mediterranean, proved extremely difficult to replace and eventually it was Pellew on whom the choice fell. He retained this post, one of exceptional arduousness in view of the ever-changing European situation and involving control of an ever-increasing number of vessels, until after the conclusion of the war.

Even under peacetime conditions, there were various problems which remained unsettled, one of the most intractable being the refusal of the Dey of Algiers to abolish Christian slavery in the territory under his control. When all efforts at diplomacy had failed, Pellew, in August 1816, with five ships of the line and five frigates actively engaged, bombarded Algiers successfully and won his point by force. Six Dutch ships were present with his fleet.

Pellew was made a viscount for his services in the Mediterranean, taking the title of Lord Exmouth. In 1817 he was given the Plymouth command, which he held for four years. He had no further service. He had been, in his time, the *beau idéal* of a frigate captain, and as an admiral, officers were proud to be under his command.

C. N. Parkinson, *Edward Pellew* (1934).

PELLEW, Sir ISRAEL (1758–1832), British admiral, was the brother of Sir Edward * Pellew. After early service in the West Indies and on the North American station he was promoted commander in 1790 and was with his brother in the * frigate *Nymphe* in 1793 when she captured the French *Cléopâtre*, an action which brought him promotion to * post-captain. He had a fortunate escape from death when his frigate, the *Amphion*, blew up in Plymouth Sound in 1796 with heavy loss of life.

He was appointed to the *Conqueror*, of seventy-four guns, in 1804 and joined Lord * Nelson's fleet in the Mediterranean on watch off * Toulon, and in May 1805 he took part in the chase of the French fleet, under Admiral * Villeneuve, to the West Indies, returning to join Admiral * Collingwood's squadron which was blockading * Cadiz. He was still there in October and at the battle of * Trafalgar his ship was the fourth in the windward (Nelson's) column. It was to her that the French flagship, the *Bucentaure*, struck her colours, but as the *Conqueror* was subsequently engaged with the Spanish four-decker *Santissima Trinidad*, it was to the captain of the *Mars* that Villeneuve surrendered his sword. It is said that when Villeneuve, on surrendering his sword, learned that the *Conqueror* was commanded by Captain Pellew, he remarked that he felt 'glad to have struck to the fortunate Sir Edward Pellew'. On hearing that his captor was in fact Israel Pellew, the French admiral is said to have exclaimed, 'What—are there two of them? Hélas.'

Pellew was promoted to rear admiral in 1810, vice admiral in 1819, and admiral in 1830.

PELORUS, a circular ring fitted to the rim of a * compass bowl and carrying two sighting vanes, used for the taking of azimuths (* bearings) of celestial objects. The ring can be easily revolved and the compass bearing read off by sighting the vanes on the required object. Alternatively, the ring can be fitted to a 'dumb' compass which can be set by hand to the * course of the ship before taking a bearing.

The word comes from the name of Hannibal's pilot, probably a Greek who sided with the Carthaginians, and assisted Hannibal to get his troops across to Europe and kept him in touch with Carthage by sea.

PELORUS JACK, the name given to a dolphin which, at the end of the 19th and beginning of the 20th centuries, used regularly to accompany every ship which sailed through the French Pass, a narrow strait separating d'Urville Island from the mainland of South Island, New Zealand. The name came from Pelorus Sound, of which French Pass forms the westernmost part. A contemporary description gave Pelorus Jack a length of about 15 feet and a mainly white colour with brown stripes. He was so well known and so regular in his habit of accompanying every ship that used French Pass that his life was protected by the New Zealand government. It was said that there was one ship which Pelorus Jack invariably ignored whenever she appeared in those waters because on her first passage of the Pass a member of the crew had fired a shot at him.

PENDANT, (1) a * strop, or short length of rope or wire with a * thimble spliced into the end, fixed on each side of the main- and foremasts of a square-rigged ship just below the shrouds, and to which the main and fore * tackles were hooked. They received their name as they hung vertically downwards as low as the * catharpings. **(2)** Any length of rope or wire used in those places where it is required to transmit the power of a purchase to a distant object. Generally they have a thimble or a *block spliced into one end. They usually also have a qualifying name attached to indicate their use, as a *cat pendant, used in catting an *anchor, a mooring pendant, used to haul the end of a chain cable round the bows of a ship when two anchors are down and it is required to insert a mooring swivel.

PENDANT, sometimes written and always pronounced pennant, a narrow tapering flag used for signalling or to designate some particular purpose. There are ten numbered pendants and fourteen special pendants used in British naval signalling, and ten numbered pendants and an answering pendant in the *International Code of Signals. See also COMMISSIONING PENDANT.

PENINSULAR AND ORIENTAL, see P & O.

PENN, Sir WILLIAM (1621–70), British admiral, was brought up to the sea by his father, a merchant and seaman of Bristol. He fought on the parliamentary side in the Civil War, mainly in Irish waters, and in 1648 was made a rear admiral. At the outbreak of the First Dutch War (1652–4) he was made a vice admiral and second-in-command to Robert *Blake, and fought in all the naval actions of the war, becoming one of the parliamentary *generals-at-sea.

While he was a fine seaman, he was also unscrupulous and prepared always to serve him who paid him best. He offered to take the fleet over to Charles II (then in exile) in 1654, but withdrew the offer on being appointed to the command of the squadron sent to the West Indies to capture Jamaica, an operation which resulted in his being sent as a prisoner to the Tower of London on account of the repulse at San Domingo. After making a humble submission to the government he was released, retiring to the estates in Ireland which he had received after the dispossession of their royalist owners. Nevertheless, he was still in correspondence with the royalists and played some small part in the restoration of Charles II in 1660. His reward was to be appointed a commissioner of the navy, and he served as captain of the fleet at the battle of *Lowestoft (1665). He was partly responsible for the tactical code known as the Duke of York's Fighting Instructions.

He was the father of William Penn, the founder of Pennsylvania, and threatened to disinherit him on his conversion to Quakerism. He was, however, reconciled to him shortly before his death, after which the king granted William Penn lands in America in settlement of arrears of salary due to his father.

PENNANT, see PENDANT.

PENNELL, HARRY LEWIN LEE (1882–1916), British naval officer, was commander of Captain R. F. *Scott's ship, the *Terra Nova, on the British Antarctic Expedition of 1910–13. During this period he made three consecutive voyages from New Zealand to the Ross Sea. He discovered Roald *Amundsen's ship, the *Fram, in the Bay of Whales in January 1911 and afterwards explored the coast westwards, discovering Oates Land. After the expedition Pennell worked up the magnetic observations and *charts for publication. He went down with his ship when he was serving in the *battle-cruiser Queen Mary at the battle of *Jutland.

PENNON, a long, coloured streamer flown from the mastheads or *yardarms of warships in the 15th and 16th centuries on occasions of state or national importance. Although it is not particularly a naval word, naval pennons are very much longer than those flown ashore, being on occasions as much as 60–80 feet in length.

PENOBSCOT MARINE MUSEUM, a maritime museum at Searsport, Maine, devoted to the maritime history of the eastern part of the coast of Maine. It was opened to the public in 1937 and the collection is housed in six buildings and includes paintings, prints, ship models, builders' half models, shipbuilding tools, navigational instruments, nautical memorabilia, and small craft. The collection of log books covers the voyages of seventy-four sailing ships during the period 1788 to 1924.

PEPYS, SAMUEL (1633–1703), naval administrator and noted diarist, was born in London and educated at St. Paul's School and Trinity Hall, Cambridge, from which he later transferred to Magdalene. He was elected to college scholarships in 1651 and 1653, developed a taste for the Latin classics and an interest in mathematics, and learned Shelton's system of shorthand. Foremost among a wide range of interests was music, and he played the flute, the viol, and the flageolet.

Soon after obtaining his bachelor's degree, Pepys entered the service of his first cousin once removed, Edward *Montagu, Cromwellian statesman and one of the *generals-at-sea of the Commonwealth fleet, who also obtained for him a post as a clerk in the Exchequer. In December 1655 he married Elizabeth St. Michel, an Anglo-French (Huguenot) girl of 15 with whom he lived in Montagu's lodgings.

In the republican administration set up by the army generals after Cromwell's death, Montagu's sympathies began to turn towards the Royalist cause and he was driven from office, Pepys remaining in charge of his affairs in London and setting up his own household in Axe

Yard, Westminster. The political turmoil of the times was one of the factors which encouraged him to begin his famous diary on 1 January 1660.

At the Restoration Montagu was again in office as general-at-sea and he took Pepys to sea with him as his secretary. On the return of the fleet with Charles II from Holland, Montagu was created Earl of Sandwich and showered with honours, and he promised Pepys that the two of them should rise together. As a first step he obtained for him the post of Clerk of the Acts to the *Navy Board, the body responsible for the civil administration of the English Navy.

This made Pepys one of the 'Principal Officers' of the navy: he resigned his clerkship in the Exchequer and moved to the Clerk of the Navy's official lodgings in Seething Lane. The new Clerk of the Acts, by hard work and long hours of labour, soon became the leading member of the Board. His powers were to be tested to the full during the Second Dutch War (1665–7) when the Board's work was crippled by lack of money and only his efforts to drive his colleagues, clerks, and the contractors, and a campaign to root out the worst cases of corruption, prevented a complete breakdown of the system of supply of the fleet.

In June 1667, through the premature laying-up of the fleet while peace negotiations were still in progress, England suffered the humiliation of seeing the Dutch fleet in the Thames and the Medway where for a time they *blockaded London and destroyed a number of warships at Chatham. When attempts were later made to lay the blame on the Navy Board, Pepys addressed an elaborate and unanswerable memorandum to the Parliamentary Commission of Public Accounts justifying the conduct of the Navy Office throughout the war and made a memorable speech in Parliament proving that the blame for the disaster lay elsewhere. Eye strain and a belief that he was going blind led Pepys to end his diary in 1669.

In June 1673 Samuel Pepys left the Navy Board to become the first Secretary to the Admiralty or, more strictly, to the Commission that exercised the office of the *Lord High Admiral when the Duke of York (see JAMES, Duke of York) was forced from office by the Test Act. He now lodged at Derby House in Cannon Row, becoming one of the most important civil servants in the country. The Third Dutch War (1672–4) was drawing to a close and on its conclusion he launched a vigorous programme of recovery and reform. By 1678 he had developed the navy into a powerful, well-disciplined force and the previously unsystematic office of the Lord High Admiral into an efficient government department.

Pepys was Member of Parliament for Castle

Samuel Pepys, aged 33; oil painting by J. Hayls, 1666

Rising, 1673–8, and for Harwich in 1679, being accepted in the Commons as spokesman for the service he had created and the administrative machine which managed it. Disaster now struck, however, when his old master, the Duke of York, was accused of conspiracy to betray the country to France and he himself was accused of being a secret papist and of selling naval secrets to France. After six weeks as a prisoner in the Tower of London, the charges against him were dropped; but for the next five years he was out of office.

Meanwhile Admiralty business suffered under an inept Commission and in 1683—the year Pepys became President of the Royal Society—Charles II made him his Secretary for Admiralty Affairs, a post which he retained when the Duke of York came to the throne as James II. With the help of a special commission to perform most of the work of the Navy Board, set up in 1686, he set about a restoration of the good governance of the navy. Between 1685 and 1687 he was again Member of Parliament for Harwich and Master of the *Trinity House where he instituted many reforms.

At the dethronement of James II, however, Pepys was once again falsely accused of treasonable relations with the French and of secret Jacobitism and he was forced to resign. He now finally retired into private life. In 1700 his health began to break down and on 26 May 1703, after a long and painful illness, he died at the country home of his closest friend, William Hewer, at Clapham.

During his long service at the Navy Board and Admiralty, Pepys had an ambition to write an authoritative history of the British Navy, and for this purpose collected a great quantity of official and other papers, which passed on his death, together with his library of 3,000 books, to Magdalene College, Cambridge, where they are still preserved. In fact he never wrote his great history, but in 1690 he published his *Memoires Relating to the State of the Royal Navy*, a business-like account of the work of the Commission of 1686 in restoring the administration of the navy to a sound footing.

His famous diary, written in shorthand, is preserved with his library and some of his other papers at Magdalene College. An abbreviated version of the diary, heavily edited by Lord Braybrooke, was published in 1825. A more complete version, about four-fifths of the whole edited by the Revd. Mynos Bright, appeared in six volumes between 1875 and 1879. The next editor was Henry Wheatley whose eight volumes of text and commentary appeared between 1893 and 1896. He used most of the text, but suppressed some sections which he considered undesirable. In 1970 the first three volumes of a new and complete edition in eleven volumes, faithfully following and annotating the text and edited by Professor Latham of Cambridge and Professor Matthews of the University of California, were published, succeeding volumes being published at intervals. For a biography, see Arthur Bryant, *Samuel Pepys*, 3 vols: *The Man in the Making* (1933), *The Years of Peril* (1935), *The Saviour of the Navy* (1938).

PERIAGUA, another name occasionally used for the type of *canoe known as a *pirogue.

PERIPLUS or **PERIPLOUS,** literally a sailing around or circumnavigation, was the word used to denote the earliest form of *sailing directions. One of the earliest examples is *The Periplous of Scylax of Caryanda*, a comprehensive pilot book for the Mediterranean which, starting at the mouth of the Nile, guides the mariner from port to port in a clockwise direction. Written about 500 B.C., the book gave comprehensive directions for coastal navigation including details of safe anchorages, adverse currents, etc. *The Periplus of the Erythraean Sea*, written about A.D. 60, is a combination of seaman's pilot book and merchant's handbook which describes the trade to be expected in the ports in the area, that of the Red Sea and Arabian Gulf. In addition, details of sailing routes to the western coasts of India are given according to the monsoons prevailing.

Periplus was used by the distinguished Finnish polar explorer N. A. E. *Nordenskiöld as the title of his great work on the history of *charts and sailing directions published in Stockholm in 1897. This has sometimes caused confusion in the minds of students new to the history of sea chartmaking.

PERISCOPE, a long metal tube containing an arrangement of lenses and prisms which magnifies and deflects the light vertically downwards and into the eye of an observer below. Their naval use is particularly in *submarines, and their employment gives the ability to see above the surface when the submarine is submerged, the periscope being capable of being raised or lowered by hydraulic power as required. A periscope normally extends to a distance of about 40 feet above the hull of the submarine, and this governs the maximum depth (known as periscope depth) at which it can be used.

PERRY, MATTHEW CALBRAITH (1794–1858), American naval officer and diplomat, was born at Newport, R.I., and joined the navy in 1809, seeing action in the war of 1812. He served as a lieutenant in the Mediterranean and in the U.S. Africa Squadron, and in 1843–5 was commodore of the squadron concerned with the foundation and protection of the republic of Liberia. A strict disciplinarian, his gruff voice earned him the nickname 'Old Bruin', but his just dealings and concern for the health and welfare of his men made him beloved by the ratings.

Perry's chief claim to fame rests on his success in 'opening' Japan to the rest of the world. He was selected to command the U.S. East India Squadron specifically to make overtures to that isolated country to persuade it to permit a limited foreign trade and to repatriate shipwrecked seamen. In 1852 he made his first visit to Japan in the steam *frigates *Mississippi* and *Susquehanna*, calling first at Okinawa where, much against the will of the local authorities, he made a state visit to the Regent. He reached Sagami Bay, Japan, in June 1853 bearing a letter from the President to the Emperor, and refused to leave until the letter had been properly received and acknowledged. After five weeks of discussion, it was agreed that two high officials would receive the letter in a specially erected building near the village of Kurihama. On 14 July the two steam frigates anchored off the beach and trained their guns ashore, while Perry with some 250 *marines and bluejackets landed from the ships' boats. They were outnumbered on the spot by about forty to one, as the Shogun had ordered mobilization, and the Americans were confronted by archers, pikemen, cavalry, musketeers carrying ancient smoothbores, and earthworks armed with Dutch cannon. Excellent discipline on both sides prevented an explosion which might have touched off a war instead of a treaty. In silence Perry presented the engrossed presidential letter in its gold casket, remarked that he would be back next year to negotiate, and retired. He waited three days to complete his surveys of Tokyo Bay 'just in case', and sailed to Hong Kong via Okinawa.

On his return in February 1854 Perry anchored his squadron off Yokosuka. This time, satisfied that Perry's declarations of peaceable intentions were sincere, the Shogunate did not mobilize. It persuaded Perry to negotiate at the village of Yokohama instead of at the capital and after a ceremonious landing the negotiations began through a Dutch interpreter. In the meantime the Americans set up and operated their presents for the Emperor, of which a quarter-size steam railway and a telegraph instrument made the greatest impression.

On 31 March the Treaty of Kanagawa was signed. It opened Shimoda and Hakodate to American ships to obtain supplies, provided for the reciprocal return of castaways, and gave permission to set up an American consulate. Perry was careful to insist on nothing (such as a cession of land) which might humiliate Japan, the commissioners felt that they had preserved national honour, and the proceedings concluded with uproarious banquets on board and ashore, the Japanese relishing whisky and champagne as much as the Americans did *saké*.

The rest of Perry's life was largely devoted to preparing the official narrative of the expedition in three volumes, edited by F. L. Hawks. This has become a classic. He delivered several lectures, always praising the people of Japan and predicting that they would shortly become a great industrial nation. On his death he was given a State funeral. Japan has reciprocated his high regard by erecting monuments to him at Shimoda, Kurihama, and elsewhere.

PERRY, OLIVER HAZARD (1785–1819), American naval officer, was a brother of M. C. *Perry. He joined the navy in 1799 and during the war of 1812 was ordered to build a fleet on *Lake Erie to prevent a British advance into the U.S.A. At the same time Commander Robert Barclay was also constructing a British fleet on the lake to support the advance. Both fleets were built of wood from the adjacent forests; both faced similar difficulties in the transport of all ordnance, ship chandlery, and supplies for long distances over wilderness roads.

By August 1813 Perry had completed two 500-ton *brigs, U.S.S. *Lawrence* and *Niagara*, and several armed *schooners and *sloops; and Barclay had four small craft and two square-rigged, three-masted sloops, H.M.S. *Detroit* and *Queen Charlotte*, of similar burthen and gunpower to Perry's brigs. The battle of Lake Erie was fought principally by the four square-riggers, as most of the small craft were left behind owing to their inferior speed in light

wind. After getting his vessels out in the lake Perry sailed to the western bight of Lake Erie, anchored in Put-in Bay, and challenged Barclay to come out and fight. This the Englishman did on 9 September, for the compelling reason that the hordes of friendly Indians encamped round his base had consumed almost all his provisions.

At sunrise on 10 September, Perry's lookouts sighted the British fleet; he weighed, and as the two fleets approached each other in line of battle heading west, a light south-easterly wind gave the Americans the weather gage. Barclay's ships were armed largely with long guns, Perry's with carronades; Perry therefore held his fire for almost half an hour and began replying vigorously around 12.15 p.m. after he had closed the range. Commander Jesse D. Elliott, commanding the *Niagara*, refused to close, remaining safely out of British gun range, thus allowing the *Detroit, Queen Charlotte*, and a schooner to concentrate on the *Lawrence*. By 2.30 the American flagship was dead in the water, every gun silenced, her deck covered with dead and wounded. Leaving most of the surviving crew to repel boarders if necessary, Perry had himself rowed to the still unscathed *Niagara*, took command, and sent Elliott away to try to bring up the small craft. A lucky freshening of the wind enabled Perry to reach the British ships where he engaged the already well-mauled *Detroit, Queen Charlotte*, and the schooner so vigorously that around 4 p.m. Barclay struck his colours, surrendering his entire squadron.

The battle was decisive and Perry became at once a hero. He was promoted captain, given a medal and a bonus by Congress, and fêted; but his later years were embittered by the attempt of Elliott to make himself out as the real victor.

After a cruise to the Mediterranean, Perry planned to retire, but in response to an urgent appeal from the Secretary of the Navy, he accepted a difficult mission in 1819. This was to sail an armed schooner 300 miles up the Orinoco River to Angostura (now Ciudad Bolivar) in order to persuade the 'Liberator' to call off his semi-piratical *privateers. He found Bolivar absent, and while dealing with procrastinating officers, most of the crew including Perry went down with yellow fever. Not much could be done for him in the schooner's hot little cabin, and he survived only as far as the Gulf of Paria.

Perry won golden opinions in British circles by his humane and chivalrous treatment of prisoners and the British governor of Trinidad paid him the tribute of a military funeral. Seven years later his body was transferred from Port of Spain to Newport, R.I.

PETER I, called Peter the Great (1672–1725), Tsar of Russia, was the founder of the Russian Navy. One of his great interests as a boy was shipbuilding and sailing, and after the death of his mother in 1694 had made him Tsar in fact as well as name, he built, some with his own hands, a small squadron of ships in the White Sea.

His first move was to expand the kingdom of Russia northwards and southwards in order to reach the Baltic and Black Seas respectively. A new fleet of two warships, twenty-three *galleys, and four *fireships was built on the banks of the Don River, and under the command of Peter sailed down river to the Sea of Azov, then in the hands of Turkey, and successfully prevented the Turks from relieving the fortress of Azov by water while Russian troops captured the fort. Determined to consolidate this success, Peter constructed the naval base of Taganrog at the head of the Sea of Azov on which his new fleet was based.

Peter I next undertook a period of foreign travel to study western ideas on warfare. He studied gunnery at Königsberg, shipbuilding at Deptford, and navigation at Venice. Returning to Russia, his overriding ambition was now to acquire a Russian outlet to the Baltic. The 'Great Northern War', which was to achieve this ambition, opened in 1700 and lasted for twenty-one years. Although as a result of it Russia lost her gains in the Sea of Azov, she acquired instead the Baltic provinces which had belonged to Sweden, and Russia became, by this acquisition, at last a maritime power. In 1721 Peter I was acclaimed as emperor of the new Russia; one of his most enduring monuments is the great city of Leningrad, of which he laid the foundations in 1707, under the name of St. Petersburg.

C. de Grunwald, *Peter the Great* (1956).

PETER SIMPLE, a novel of life in the British Navy at the turn of the 18th–19th centuries written by Captain Frederick *Marryat and based on the exploits of Lord *Cochrane when he commanded the *frigates *Pallas* and *Imperieuse*, in which Marryat served as a *midshipman.

PETT, PHINEAS (1570–1647), British master shipwright, was the son of Peter Pett (d. 1589), master shipwright at Deptford, who had achieved a great reputation as a shipbuilder. Phineas was assistant master shipwright in the *Royal Dockyard at Chatham in 1603, and later master shipwright and a commissioner of the navy. He is best remembered, perhaps, for his design and building of the *Sovereign of the Seas* (see ROYAL SOVEREIGN), of 1,500 tons and, at the time, the largest warship in the world. He had three half-brothers who were master shipwrights; a nephew, PETER Pett (1592–1652), who was master shipwright at Deptford; a son, PETER (1610–72), who was navy commissioner at Chatham; another son, CHRISTOPHER

(1620–68), who was master shipwright at Woolwich and Deptford; and a grandson, PHINEAS (1628–78), who followed in his grandfather's footsteps by becoming master shipwright at Chatham.

PETTICOAT-TROUSERS, see GALLIGASKINS, SAILORS' DRESS.

PETTY OFFICER, the naval equivalent of the rank of sergeant in military forces. In the British Navy they are divided into two grades, chief petty officer and petty officer. The word petty comes from the French *petit*, small.

PETTY WARRANT, the scale of victualling allowed in the British Navy during the 16th, 17th, and 18th centuries to ships' companies when in port, generally at about two-thirds the scale allowed at sea. When victualling stores ran short at sea, because of either the length of a voyage or deterioration to the extent of condemnation as unfit for consumption, the issue was reduced to the scale of petty warrant, but was not called by that name, being known as 'six upon four', i.e., six men to exist upon the quantity allowed to four. When this occurred, an addition to the rate of pay, known as short allowance money, was credited to the men for the period during which the scale of 'six upon four' was issued.

PHILADELPHIA, one of the principal seaports on the eastern coast of the U.S.A. in the state of Pennsylvania on the right bank of the Delaware River as it widens into Delaware Bay. It was founded by William Penn, who was granted land in the American colonies in settlement of the debt owed by Charles II to his father, Admiral Sir William *Penn, and the name of the state enshrines his name. As well as being one of the great American seaports handling an ever-growing volume of trade, Philadelphia is a main base of the U.S. Navy and the site of a large naval *dockyard at which the largest warships can be built. The *Philadelphia Maritime Museum is one of the more important museums of this type in the U.S.A., and three other museums with maritime sections are maintained in the city.

PHILADELPHIA MARITIME MUSEUM, Philadelphia, Pennsylvania, was founded in 1951 and opened in 1961. It is devoted to American maritime history with special reference to the ports of the Delaware valley. The collection includes models of ships which brought early explorers and settlers to the Delaware valley, together with papers, personal effects, and portraits. Also shown are log books, *letters of marque, cargo lists, some of Robert *Fulton's letters, and many other items indicating the important role of shipping in the development of the city and the U.S.A. generally. Moored near by is the former Portuguese * Grand Banks fishing * barquentine *Gazela Primeiro* which forms part of the museum.

Other museums with marine sections in the city of Philadelphia are the Atwater Kent Museum, the Commercial Museum, and the Franklin Institute.

PHILIPPINE SEA, BATTLE OF THE, was fought in the Pacific during the Second World War between an American fleet commanded by Admiral * Spruance, with Admiral * Mitscher commanding the carrier fleet, and a Japanese fleet under the command of Vice Admiral * Ozawa. Spruance, with his fleet of 15 * aircraft carriers, 7 * battleships, 21 * cruisers, and 69 * destroyers, had been covering the amphibious landing on the island of Saipan, in the Marianas group, which had gone in on 15 June 1944. On the same day he received a report from U.S. * submarines that a force of Japanese carriers was steaming towards him from the San Bernardino Strait and another force from Surigao Strait, both in the Philippine Islands. The two forces combined to make a total of 9 aircraft carriers, 5 battleships, 13 cruisers, and 28 destroyers.

Action was joined on the morning of 19 June when Ozawa launched his carrier aircraft in a series of four raids on the American fleet, which was then about 100 miles south-west of Saipan. The raids were met by fighters from the American carriers, and were broken up with very heavy losses of Japanese aircraft and only slight damage to one or two of the American ships. Two Japanese carriers were sunk by American submarines. By the end of the day the Japanese had lost no fewer than 346 aircraft and 2 carriers, crippling losses in the light of their already overstrained naval air arm. The day has gone down in the history of the U.S. Navy as the 'Great Marianas Turkey Shoot'.

On the following day, 20 June, the American carrier groups set off to hunt the retreating Japanese. They were not found until 1540: this meant that an American air strike flown off to attack the ships would return to land on their carriers after darkness had fallen. Nevertheless, a total of 216 aircraft were sent out and sank one more Japanese carrier and two * tankers which had accompanied the fleet. Twenty of the 216 aircraft were shot down during the attack, but more were lost during the attempts to land on the carriers in darkness. The final score in air losses was 395 Japanese carrier aircraft, 31 of the battleship and cruiser float planes, and about 50 land-based bombers destroyed during a raid on Guam. American air losses were 130 carrier aircraft, but many of the aircrew of these were rescued, and the total aircrew loss was 76.

If the battle of * Midway can be considered as the turning point of the naval war in the Pacific, and the battle of * Leyte Gulf as the greatest in terms of number of ships engaged, the battle of the Philippine Sea was probably the most decisive. After the battle Spruance was criticized by some for holding his fleet too close to Saipan during the action, even though this was his primary responsibility, and Mitscher was criticized for his failure to send out searches for the Japanese fleet on the evening of 19 June, thus avoiding the long period on the 20th when Ozawa's position was not known. But in the final result neither of these criticisms was justified, and both the American admirals could be well satisfied with their victory. For the Japanese it was a crushing defeat, a final confirmation that the war as a whole had been lost.

PHILLIP, ARTHUR (1733–1814), British vice admiral and first governor of Australia, was born in London. He went to sea in 1755 and after seeing active service in the Mediterranean and West Indies during the Seven Years War (1756–63), was promoted to lieutenant in 1762. On peace being declared he retired to become a farmer and country gentleman, but on the outbreak of the War of American Independence (1775–82) he returned to active duty and in 1781 was promoted to post-captain.

In 1787 Phillip commanded a small fleet conveying the first contingent of convicts transported to Australia (see FIRST FLEET). His frigate *Sirius* having pressed on ahead, he reached * Botany Bay on 18 January 1788 and, considering the place unsuitable, he went on to Port Jackson where, on 27 January, he hoisted the British flag to mark the founding of the city of Sydney, which he named after Viscount Sydney, Under-Secretary of State for Home Affairs. After much privation and consequent unrest among the convicts and their guards the new settlement began to prosper, thanks in the main to Phillip's firmness and the manner in which he dispensed justice to both the convicts and the aborigines. Failing health obliged him to resign his office and he returned to England in December 1792. He was promoted to rear admiral in 1801 and vice admiral in 1810.

G. Mackaness, *Admiral Arthur Phillip* (Sydney, 1937).

PHIPPS, CONSTANTINE JOHN, 2nd Baron Mulgrave (1744–92), British naval officer, was * commodore of a small expedition sent in 1773 to try to find a * North-East passage to the Pacific. The two ships comprising the expedition were H.M.S. *Racehorse* and H.M.S. *Carcass*, in which Horatio * Nelson was serving as a * midshipman. The expedition was obliged to return when the ships sailed north from Spitsbergen and found the way barred by ice.

Phipps commanded the 74-gun *ship of the line *Courageux* at the inconclusive battle of *Ushant in 1778, from which arose the court martial of Admiral Augustus *Keppel on charges brought by Admiral Sir Hugh *Palliser. Phipps had supported Palliser in his charges, and when these were dismissed as irrelevant and spiteful, his career in the navy came to an end.

PHIPS, Sir WILLIAM (1651–95), governor of Massachusetts, began life as a shepherd, became a ship's carpenter, and opened a shipyard on the Sheepscot River in Maine, but had to abandon it because of Indian depredations. In 1684–6, he headed a search for a wrecked Spanish treasure ship; in the following year he found it but only received £16,000 as his share of the £300,000 recovered from it. He commanded two naval expeditions against French Canada in 1690, but the second ended in disaster. In 1692 he was appointed governor of Massachusetts, but was too quarrelsome a man to make much success in this role.

'PHOENIX', see MULBERRY HARBOUR.

PHORMIO (*c.* 481–428 B.C.), Athenian naval leader, commanded the ships of Athens during the early stages of the Peloponnesian War, and his naval operations in the Gulf of Corinth, with his ships based at Naupactus, were handled with great skill and dash. Unhappily, Phormio died only three years after the start of the first phase of the war (431–421 B.C.); had he been active during the final phase which ended in 403 B.C., Athens would have fared much better and the whole result of the war might have turned out very differently.

PHOSPHORESCENCE, a glowing condition of the sea when the surface is broken by a wave, the dipping of oars, the bow wave and wake of a ship, etc. The cause of phosphorescence is not completely established but is generally considered to be a secretion emitted by jellyfish and other similar dwellers in the sea when disturbed, which emits light through oxidization when the surface of the sea is broken. It is known that many deep sea fish can become phosphorescent when excited, and in some varieties of mollusc the secretion of a glandular organ not only glows through the transparent body but continues to glow after being ejected into the water.

PICAROON or **PICKAROON,** an old name, *temp.* 17th century, for a *pirate or *privateer. It comes from the Spanish *picarón*, pirate.

PICKLE, (1) the salt brine in which beef and pork was immersed in casks to preserve it for use as daily rations in the days of sail. (2) The salting

of naval timber for masts and yards in dockyards by letting it float in seawater in mast docks or mast ponds in order to improve its durability and strength. Occasionally chloride of zinc was used for this purpose.

PIDGEON, HARRY (1869–1954), American farmer and round-the-world yachtsman, was born on a farm in Iowa, a son of a family from Surrey, England, which had emigrated to America. He was eight years old before he first saw the ocean. With no taste for farming, he led a restless life. In Alaska he and another young farmer built themselves Indian-style canoes and explored the Yukon River, making fishing excursions on the lakes. Some years spent in the high sierras as a naturalist and photographer enabled him to save enough money to follow the dream he had long been nursing, to build himself a real seagoing boat and to sail the world in her.

At Los Angeles in 1917 he bought plans of the Fleming *Day 34-ft V-bottom *yawl *Sea Bird*, built her on a borrowed lot in some eighteen months, and named her *Islander*. After taking her for a cruise to Honolulu and back to gain experience and confidence at sea, he set off again single-handed in November 1921 across the Pacific to Thursday Island off the Queensland coast. Here his decision to carry on westward rather than return home to Los Angeles crystallized, and he sailed *Islander* through the East Indies, across the Indian Ocean to Durban, then across the South Atlantic to Panama, and arrived back in Los Angeles in October 1925, after circumnavigating the world in almost four years. He wrote an account of this voyage in *Around the World Single-handed* (1932).

For the next sixteen years he lived alone on board the *Islander*, spending only three nights ashore during that time, until he decided to sail around the world a second time in order, as he said, to look up many old friends.

On his return from this second circumnavigation and at the age of 75, he married, he and his wife setting off in *Islander* for a third circumnavigation of the world. The yawl was wrecked during a hurricane in the New Hebrides, and Pidgeon built himself another boat of similar design, but only 25 feet in length, which he named *Lakemba*. In this boat he made a home for himself and his wife until a month before his death.

PIECES OF EIGHT, Spanish coins much beloved by writers of pirate stories. They were the equivalent of a Spanish dollar of a value of eight reals. Such vast numbers of these coins were minted in Spain between the 17th and 19th centuries that they were accepted almost as a world currency during those years.

PIER, a structure, usually of timber and supported on wooden piles, built out into the sea at seaside resorts as an attraction for holidaymakers and for excursion steamers to come alongside. Some *jetties, which basically are solid structures, were named piers, particularly where two of them may form the arms embracing a small harbour, just as some piers, which basically are open structures, may be called jetties, as for example some jetties alongside which *tankers may lie to load or discharge oil.

PIERHEAD JUMP, an expression indicative of joining a ship at the last possible moment because of a sudden and unexpected appointment to her. Charles Powell, the central character in Joseph *Conrad's novel *Chance*, entered into a new world of experience with a totally unexpected pierhead jump into the ship *Ferndale*.

PIG, see BALLAST.

PIG YOKE, a name used by many old seamen when describing the *Davis quadrant in the days before it was replaced by the reflecting quadrants and *sextants.

PIGAFETTA, ANTONIO (*fl.* 1519–22), the chronicler taken by Ferdinand *Magellan in his circumnavigation of the world to record the events of this historic voyage and, fortunately, one of the few who survived the hardships of the voyage and returned to Spain in the * *Vittoria*. His original MS. was widely copied, the best and most accurate versions being the Ambrosiana MS., which is the text followed in the *Hakluyt Society volume describing this voyage (1st series, No. 52, 1874), and the Phillips MS., now in the library of Yale University, U.S.A. Following Pigafetta, a large number of anonymous narratives of the voyage made their appearance, but only his is known to be genuinely contemporary.

PILE-DRIVER, (1) a machine, normally worked by steam or compressed air, used to drive piles into the ground. Though by no means exclusively maritime, it has a considerable nautical use in dock and harbour construction, coastal defences against the sea, and for similar uses. **(2)** A name given to a ship which, by reason of her short length, cannot ride two consecutive waves and pitches violently into the second.

PILLAGE, by an ancient law of the sea, the right of the captors of a ship taken in *prize to take to themselves everything found above the main deck except the *furniture and guns of the vessel. It was a right which, not unnaturally, could lead to great abuse as, in the heat and excitement of capture, there were few to swear what was, or was not, found above the main deck. In many cases the holds of captured ships were broken open and the contents strewn on the upper deck, to be picked up a moment later and claimed as pillage.

PILLOW, a block of timber fixed to the deck of a sailing vessel just inside the *bow on which the inner end of the *bowsprit was supported. Its use was to take any wear on the deck caused by the working of the bowsprit.

PILOT, a qualified coastal navigator taken on board a ship at a particular place for the purpose of conducting her into and from a port or through a channel, river, or approaches to a port. In all maritime nations the jurisdiction over pilots is invested in national authorities who specify the conditions under which pilots must be taken on board and the pilotage fees to be charged. In many ports and navigable waterways, local regulations make it compulsory for ships over a certain size to embark a pilot.

Before ships were fitted with radio, pilots would wait near the points of entry into pilotage waters in pilot-*cutters, from which they could be picked up by incoming ships and into which they could be dropped by outgoing ships. For smaller ports, a ship would anchor off the entrance and hoist a signal, in a flag of the *International Code of Signals, for a pilot, and await his arrival in a launch which would be towed in to its destination by the ship with the pilot aboard. But today arrangements are normally made well in advance by ships requiring a pilot by means of radio requests, the pilot being picked up at a predetermined place.

*Masters of cross-Channel *ferries and other similar vessels which habitually navigate in pilotage waters are usually themselves qualified pilots, and so do not require to embark one for their passages. When a ship has a pilot on board, her master retains the responsibility for her safety, though the regulations require him to follow the pilot's instructions. When used as a verb, the word embraces the acts of a pilot in taking a ship through pilotage waters.

The word is also used as a loose or affectionate term for the navigating officer of a ship. The volumes of * *Sailing Directions* are also colloquially known as Pilots. See also PILOTAGE, TRINITY HOUSE.

PILOT JACK, see JACK.

PILOTAGE, from the Dutch *peillood*, sounding lead, the act of navigating a vessel coastwise, especially when the land is close aboard and the water shallow. The expert *pilot is able to navigate his vessel in and out of harbour using his local knowledge of the disposition of channels and shoals and their land- and sea-marks; and of *tides and currents and other factors which influence safe navigation. At most harbours licensed pilots are available, and the services of these expert craftsmen are invariably engaged by masters of vessels who are unfamiliar with local conditions.

PINCH, to, the operation of sailing a vessel so close to the wind that the *luffs of the sails are continually lifting. There are obviously some few occasions when it is desirable to pinch a sailing vessel, as for instance when it would be possible by pinching a little to *fetch a mark or other desired point of sailing without having to make a *tack, but in general a sailing vessel loses speed quite considerably when she is being pinched.

PINE, JOHN (1690–1756), British engraver, was born in London and is remembered as the engraver of the *Armada tapestries made to the order of Lord *Howard of Effingham from designs by Hendrick *Vroom. These were presented by Howard to the House of Lords in London and were hung there until they were destroyed by fire in 1834. The tapestries were contemporary impressions of the incidents in the great battle of 1588 against the Spanish fleet in the English Channel and North Sea, and it is only through Pine's engravings that the details shown in the originals are known today.

PINK, a small square-rigged ship with a narrow and overhanging *stern, often used for the carriage of masts. In the 15th and 16th centuries the name was loosely applied to all small ships with narrow sterns, a fairly common design in those days, and later was adopted by the Danish Navy to describe a small warship in which the stern was broadened out at upper deck level to accommodate quarter guns, though still remaining narrow below. Before the days of motor and steam herring drifters, the Dutch herring boats from Scheveningen were also called pinks.

PINKY, one of the oldest types of New England fishing and trading vessels. Built with a Baltic form of hull having a pointed *stern similar to the *bow, over which a false stern was carried out beyond the rudder like a square *counter, it resembled the North Sea and Danish pink of the early 18th century, from which it was named. These small craft, from 50 to 70 feet in length, were generally *schooner-rigged with or without a forestaysail or *jib.

Beaching a pink in heavy weather at Scheveningen; oil painting by E. W. Cooke

A pinnace; lithograph from Pleasure Boats and Boats of Lading *by E. Solvyns, c. 1795*

PINNACE, (1) a small vessel of about 20 tons dating from the 16th century, with two masts normally square-rigged on both but occasionally with a *lugsail on the main. Later the square rig was abandoned for a *schooner rig. They carried oars as well as sails and were used frequently as advice boats taking messages from a senior officer to other ships under his command. They were also used, perhaps a little recklessly, as small ships accompanying the early voyages of exploration, and although in his *Principal Navigations* *Hakluyt describes the small *Squirrel* in which Sir Humphrey *Gilbert lost his life on his return from Newfoundland in 1583 as a *frigate, she was more accurately a pinnace. See also FOX, Luke. **(2)** A ship's boat which, in the days of sailing ships, was rowed with eight oars but later was increased in length to accommodate sixteen oars. The larger variety were able to step a mast when required and set a *sloop rig. They were discarded as ships' boats when the small petrol or diesel engines were developed to provide motive power in place of oars and sails.

PINTA, a *caravel of 50 tons with a crew of eighteen men which, in company with the *Santa Maria* and *Niña*, sailed from Palos in 1492 under the command of Christopher *Columbus on his voyage to the westward.

PINTLE, a vertical metal pin attached to the leading edge of the *rudder of a small boat. Normally two pintles are fitted to such a rudder, and they drop into *gudgeons, or rings, fixed to the boat's *stern, when the rudder is placed, or hung, in position. This method of hanging a rudder allows it to be swung as desired through the use of the *tiller. An advantage of this form of hanging a rudder is that it can be unshipped when not required.

PINZON, MARTIN ALONZO, FRANCISCO, and VICENTE YAÑEZ, Spanish navigators, were three brothers of Palos, in Andalusia, who were all associated with Christopher *Columbus in the discovery of America in 1492. Martin Alonzo commanded the *Pinta*, of which ship Francisco was the *pilot, and Vicente Yañez commanded the smaller *Niña*. Of the three brothers, Vicente Yañez was the most adventurous. At the end of 1499 he sailed with four *caravels across the Atlantic on a south-westerly course to reach the continent of South America at Cape St. Agostinho, thus reaching Brazil some three months before Pedro *Cabral. During this cruise he also discovered the estuary of the River Amazon and Costa Rica. In 1507, with Juan Diaz de Solis, he again visited South America, reaching as far south as the La Plata estuary. The last mention of Vicente Yañez is in 1523, all trace of his later career as a navigator, if any, being lost.

PIPE, another name for the *boatswain's *whistle, on which, in naval ships, a *call was piped as a prelude to an order to the crew. Many orders had their own particular cadences on the pipe, by which they were identified. The pipe was of silver and worn by boatswain's mates on a long silver chain around their necks.

PIPE, to, the operation of making a *call on a *boatswain's *pipe or *whistle. In naval ships, a call on the pipe normally preceded any order given to the crew, usually with a particular cadence to identify particular orders.

PIPE COT, a hinged cot fitted in many yachts and small vessels where the space available does not permit the inclusion of a fixed *bunk. When not in use they are folded up and secured against the vessel's side.

PIPE DOWN, the *call on the *boatswain's *pipe, made last thing at night in a naval vessel, for the hands to turn in, for silence on the messdecks, and for the lights to be extinguished. It is also a term used by sailors when they want to stop a man talking or making a nuisance of himself.

Ann Bonny and Mary Read: women pirates; engraving c. *1720*

PIPING THE SIDE, the ceremonial call made on a *boatswain's *pipe or *whistle when a member of the Royal Family, foreign dignitaries and naval officers, admirals and captains, when making an official visit, arrive on board a ship of the British Navy. With its long-drawn-out low, high, and low notes, the call dates from the days when visiting officers at sea were hoisted in and out of a ship in a boatswain's chair at the end of a yardarm *whip. The actual notes were the orders by which the men manning the whip knew when to hoist and lower.

PIRACY, the act of taking a ship on the high seas from the possession or control of those lawfully entitled to it. The operative word in that definition is 'lawfully', as the international law of the sea accepts the declaration, by a belligerent power, of a state of *blockade as a legitimate reason for the detention of any ship, whether neutral or belligerent, suspected of carrying *contraband. Without that legal right, every such act would by definition rank as piracy.

Piracy was endemic among all seafaring nations until the birth of regular navies. Very early in maritime history it was recognized and agreed that the pirate was an enemy not of any particular state but of all mankind, and could thus be punished by the competent courts of any country. In the early days of maritime expansion, no seas were free from piracy, from the Japanese in the Far East to the *Barbary pirates in the Mediterranean and eastern Atlantic, and, after the discovery of America, to the hordes of pirates who flourished in the West Indies, the Gulf of Mexico, and along the western coast of South America. It was only when national navies began to develop as permanent institutions that a concerted stand against this scourge of the seas became possible.

Pirates have naturally operated throughout history from small, fast ships which could *overhaul their prey at sea, out of reach of interference by other ships, and capture it by *boarding. As gunnery developed, pirates also equipped their ships with naval *guns, usually captured from other ships, so that they resembled a small warship.

The oldest continuous history of piracy not unnaturally belongs to the Mediterranean, the cradle of maritime endeavour. It was common in the great days of Egypt, Greece, and Rome, and history records many expeditions to burn out and destroy the bases from which they operated. During the later Middle Ages and until the beginning of the 18th century it was highly organized on a national scale along the northern coast of Africa, with Tunis and Algiers as the main centres. It became the main basis of the national economies of the states which occupied that coast, and the Tunisian and Algerine corsairs operated as far afield as the English Channel in their search for ships to capture and crews to sell in the slave markets. Although the growing strength of national navies throughout the 18th century brought about a less vigorous campaign of piracy by Tunis and Algiers, it was not until the bombardment of the latter port in 1816 by an Anglo-Dutch fleet and the destruction of the pirate vessels in port, followed by the subsequent

French occupation of the whole of Algeria, that piracy in the Mediterranean was brought to an end.

In English waters, the seamen of Devon and Kent were notorious for their acts of piracy in the English Channel, with the seamen of Fife and Berwickshire equally violent in the waters of the Firth of Forth, and it was not until these seas were cleared by the navy of Henry VIII during the first half of the 16th century that ships could sail in them with any degree of safety.

The classic age of piracy was the late 17th and early 18th centuries, when many of the * privateers operating in the West Indies and Indian Ocean deteriorated into pirates. Their exploits achieved wide notoriety with the publication of Charles Johnson's *General History of the Robberies and Murders of the Most Notorious Pyrates*, which some believe to have been really written by Daniel * Defoe. It is from this source that R. L. * Stevenson and others have drawn for their adventure stories, because of its lively accounts of such pirate captains as John * Avery, who worked from a base in Madagascar, Edward * Teach, also known as 'Blackbeard', who worked the coasts of Carolina, Bartholomew * Roberts, who operated most successfully off the coasts of West Africa, Mary * Read and Anne * Bonny, the female pirates, and above all William * Kidd, who committed his many acts of piracy in waters as far apart as the West Indies and the Indian Ocean. All these, and most others of their kind, were finally extirpated by British naval * frigates sent specially to extinguish the evil.

Pirates must be distinguished from privateers and * buccaneers, though in the latter case the distinguishing line was often perilously thin. When captured, pirates were usually hanged in chains on prominent headlands, where they could be seen as a warning by passing ships or, in England, staked to the ground at * Execution Dock, Wapping, to be drowned by a rising tide. The last pirate was executed in England in 1840, in the U.S.A. in 1862.

It is an act of piracy if a ship is seized out of the control of her legal * master and crew by those who have boarded the vessel in disguise as passengers. Piracy by gangs of 'passengers' who came on board with concealed arms and revealed their true purpose when at sea was by no means uncommon in Chinese waters as late as the 20th century. Though the worst excesses of piracy have now been stamped out, there are still some areas of the world where it continues to exist on a relatively small scale. It is most prevalent today in the seas around Borneo and Indonesia, due perhaps partly to disputed claims of sovereignty and partly to the ease of concealment along the jungle coastline.

PIRAEUS, the port of Athens, in the eastern basin of the Mediterranean, is today a thriving seaport with a large * entrepôt trade and a growing tourist trade. It is one of the oldest of the world's ports, but was not of much naval or military importance until Themistocles (*c.* 528–462 B.C.) pointed to its natural strength. This was increased by the fortifications around the port built in 493 B.C. before the Persian wars, and its use in time of war was further secured by the construction in 460 B.C. of the Long Walls, which enclosed a fortified corridor linking it to Athens.

After the defeat of the Athenians at Aegospotami in 403 B.C. and the eclipse of Athenian naval power, the Spartan army of occupation destroyed the Long Walls and Piraeus lost most of its naval importance until modern times. But in the days of the Athenian empire it was a great naval centre, containing three docks, or slips, which housed 196, 94, and 82 * galleys respectively. In the later Greek (Hellenistic) period and under the Roman and Ottoman empires it was of lesser importance, though always the port of entry for Athens. Its importance increased after the independence of Greece (1821) and today it is one of the main bases of the Greek Navy.

PIROGUE or **PIRAGUA,** a seagoing * canoe formed out of the trunks of two trees, hollowed out and fastened together, usually of cedar or balsa wood. It was a common form of coastal transport in the Gulf of Mexico and on the west coast of South America during the 16th and 17th centuries and is frequently mentioned in the writings of European voyagers to those waters during that period. When the * buccaneer Bartholomew * Sharp and his party crossed the Isthmus of Darien in 1680 and reached the Pacific Ocean near Panama, their first act was to seize a number of local pirogues lying on the beach, from which they captured a Spanish ship and put to sea to harass the Spanish shipping.

PISANI, VETTOR (d. 1380), Venetian admiral, is remembered for his two victories over the Genoese fleet in 1378 and 1380. As a result of the first battle he recaptured Cattaro (now Kotor) and Sebenico (Sibenić), which had fallen to the Hungarians, who at the time were allies of Genoa. In the following year the Genoese fleet defeated him in a battle off Pola (Pula), and he was thrown into prison in Venice in disgrace. With the Genoese fleet following up their victory and threatening Venice itself, the inhabitants demanded that Pisani, in whom they had great confidence, be released and again put in command of the fleet. Although now an old man, he took the fleet to sea, inflicted a crushing defeat on the Genoese, and blockaded Genoa itself until that republic was forced to sue for peace.

PITCH, (1) a mixture of tar and coarse resin, fluid when heated and hard when cooled, used to cover the *oakum when caulking the *seams of a vessel's deck or sides. **(2)** Pitch of a propeller, the distance which a ship is moved forward in calm water by one revolution of her propeller.

PITCH, to, a ship pitches when a wave lifts her *bows and then, after passing down her length, subsequently lifts her *stern, giving her a fore-and-aft motion.

PITCHPOLE, to, the description of a vessel which is up-ended by heavy seas so that it turns over *stern over *bows. This is a fate which overtook the yacht *Tzu-Hang* when she was being sailed round Cape Horn in 1957 by Miles *Smeeton and his wife.

PLAIN SAILING, an expression which has come into the English language to mean anything that is straightforward and easy. The origin of the term arose from the plane charts of the 16th century which were drawn on the assumption that the earth was flat, even though by then all navigators knew that it was not. It was not until the first *Mercator chart was produced in 1569 that the solution to the chartmaking problem of how to draw *meridians as parallel lines without distorting the navigational process was solved, but for more than a century after Mercator, most navigators continued to use plane charts for their navigation, usually explaining their errors in *longitude calculation on an easily invented ocean current. The use of these charts was known as plane sailing, often written as plain sailing, and since the use of this type of chart did not involve any calculations to convert *departure into difference of longitude, it was obviously easier for the navigator.

PLANE, to, a term used to describe the action of a boat which attains sufficient speed to cause the forward part of the hull to rise and for the boat then to run along the surface of the water. In order to start planing the hull must be of a suitable form and very light in weight in relation to its sail area or power available. Power boats with a V-sectioned bow and a broad flat hull are noted for their ability to start to plane above a certain speed, and to skim along the surface with only the after part of the hull and the propeller and rudder in the water. Lightweight, high-performance racing dinghies, given suitable wind and sea conditions, can get up and plane for short or longer periods depending on the continuing strength of the wind and the skill of the helmsman. While planing, a boat's speed can rise to twice or even two and a half times the theoretical maximum sailing speed of a displacement (normal heavy) boat of the same length obtained from the speed formula 1·4 times the square root of the waterline length in feet ($1 \cdot 4 \sqrt{\text{LWL}}$ knots). Thus a dinghy with a waterline length of 16 ft has a theoretical maximum speed under sail of 5·6 knots if it cannot plane, but if it is of the planing type with a sufficiently high power/weight ratio, under the right wind and sea conditions its speed may rise to 8 or 9 knots, when it will surge along the surface with speed rising in bursts to 12 or even 14 knots. While the boat is poised on the surface thus, and the tiller feels almost rigid in the helmsman's hand, great skill must be displayed by the helmsman to prevent a violent sheer to one side or the other and a sudden capsize. The power-driven speedboat, on the other hand, is usually quite stable as the thrust driving the boat is beneath the water surface, and the flat form of the underwater body enables the boat to be steered in sharp turns without such a high chance of a capsize.

Planing requires a suitable shape and bow on a lightweight hull which, once it reaches a certain critical speed, suddenly encounters much less resistance as the fore part of the hull lifts above the surface. In these circumstances the bow no longer has to force the water aside, so that speed immediately rises dramatically. Early speedboat designs before and soon after the First World War (1914–18) experimented with steps on the underside of the hull, on which the boat was designed to ride at speed, and these eventually led to aerofoil appendages resulting in the high-speed hydrofoil ferry boats of today. See also HYDRODYNAMICS.

PLANK SHEER, the outermost deck plank covering the *gunwale of a wooden vessel or the plank covering the timber heads of the *frames when they are brought up above the level of the gunwale. Another name for the plank sheer, particularly in the construction of yachts, is *covering board.

PLANKTON, a name invented by Professor Victor Hensen for the drifting small fauna of the seas and oceans. In very general terms, plankton are divided into three classes according to the depth of water they inhabit, the epiplankton in waters to a depth of 100 fathoms, mesoplankton from 100 to 1,000 fathoms, and hypoplankton below 1,000 fathoms. The density of plankton in seawater varies with temperature and, to some extent, with light. They form the larger part of the diet of most species of fish, and it has been held that they can help to sustain human life in desperate situations of shipwreck, etc. Thor *Heyerdahl and his companions, in their exploratory voyage on the raft *Kon-Tiki*, secured plankton by towing a canvas bag astern of the raft and consumed it without any apparent ill effects.

PLAT, (1) from the verb, to plait or weave, braided rope which used to be made from *foxes and wound round the *cable where it lay in the *hawseholes to protect it from wear when the ship rode to her *anchor in a rough sea. This was, of course, before the days of chain cable and referred only to the hemp cables used in those days.

(2) From the verb to plot, in the sense of plotting a ship's *course or position on a *chart, an old name, c. 17th century, for a chart or map, usually, but not necessarily, engraved. 'Thence home, and took my Lord Sandwiches Draught of the Harbour of Portsmouth down to Ratcliffe to one Burston, to make a plat for the King and another for the Duke and another for himself—which will be very neat.' S. *Pepys, *Diary*, 18 February 1665.

PLATE, (1) the steel sheets used in the construction of a ship and riveted to the *frames and deck *beams to form the sides and decks. In most modern ship construction, the plates are welded together instead of being riveted. Armour plate, the thick plates of case-hardened steel used for side, deck, and turret armour in the construction of warships. **(2)** The name sometimes given to the *dagger- or *centreboard of a sailing boat. **(3)** A strip of bronze or iron bolted to the sides of a sailing vessel and carrying the lower *deadeyes of each pair of shrouds, if the standing *rigging is secured by deadeyes and *lanyards, or the lower ends of the *rigging screws if these are used. They are more generally known as *chain-plates.

PLEDGET, a string of *oakum rolled from the picked fibre and ready for use in the *caulking of a deck or side *seam of a wooden vessel. It is inserted into the seam after it has been opened with a *reeming iron, rammed hard home, and then *payed with *pitch to make a watertight joint between the planks.

PLIMSOLL, SAMUEL (1824–98), British politician, was early in life reduced to destitution through his failure as a coal merchant and for a time lived in common lodging houses, a fact which he claimed introduced him to the wretched conditions under which the poor lived. He directed his attention chiefly to what were widely known as 'coffin ships', vessels which were unseaworthy and overloaded, and heavily insured against loss, in which many shipowners, under the existing law, were permitted to risk their crews. Eventually successful in business, he entered Parliament in 1868 and tried to get a bill passed on this subject. Failing in this, he wrote a small book entitled *Our Seamen*, which aroused so much interest in the country that in 1873 he was able in Parliament to get a royal commission appointed to consider the matter. As a result of

its report, the government introduced a bill in 1875 but later abandoned it as a result, it was said, of political pressure by shipowners. Plimsoll lost his temper in the House of Commons, called the members 'villains', and shook his fist in the Speaker's face. He later apologized, but the depth of feeling in the country forced the government to reintroduce the bill which, in 1876, was passed as the Merchant Shipping Act, under which the Board of Trade was given strict powers of inspection and required a mark to be painted on a ship's side to indicate the depth beyond which she might not be loaded. This mark has always been known as the *Plimsoll Mark.

In later years Plimsoll became president of the Sailor's and Firemen's Union, and campaigned about conditions in the cattle ships.

PLIMSOLL MARK or **LINE,** a mark painted on the sides of British merchant ships which indicates the draught levels to which a ship may be loaded with cargo for varying conditions of season and location. The Plimsoll Mark shows six loading levels, those which may be used in tropical fresh water; fresh water; tropical sea water; summer, sea water; winter, sea water; and winter, North Atlantic, for vessels under 100 metres (330 ft) in length. This mark is accompanied by another, consisting of a circle bisected by a horizontal line with letters which indicate the registration society. In Britain, these are normally LR, indicating *Lloyd's Register. The horizontal line on the registration mark indicates the summer *freeboard and so is in line with the level marked S on the Plimsoll Mark.

The Plimsoll Mark was made compulsory in Britain under the conditions of the Merchant Shipping Act, 1876, passed after a long and bitter parliamentary struggle conducted by Samuel *Plimsoll, M.P., a champion of better conditions for seamen.

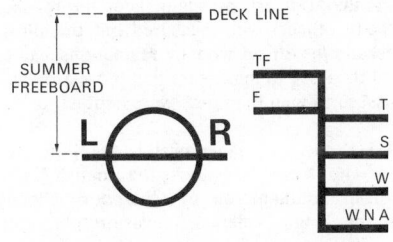

TF Tropical fresh water	WNA Winter, North Atlantic, for vessels under 100 metres (330 feet) in length
F Fresh water	
T Tropical sea water	
S Summer, sea water	LR These letters indicate the registration society, in this case Lloyd's Register.
W Winter, sea water	

Plimsoll mark and load line

PLOTTING SHEET, a sheet of plain or squared paper on which a navigator plots position lines obtained from nautical astronomical observations to facilitate finding his ship's position. Since the scale of most navigational ocean charts is too small to allow of accurate results when used for plotting position lines, navigators generally use a plotting sheet on which they can select the most convenient scale, say one inch to one mile, with which to plot their * intercepts and position lines. By using such a scale, either the differences of * longitude and * latitude or the bearing and distance between the ship's * dead reckoning and observed positions can be accurately measured off on the plotting sheet and then transferred direct to the chart.

PLUG, (1) a tapering piece of wood or a screwed metal stopper, used to stop the drain hole in the bottom of a small boat. Warships of the sailing navy carried a number of wooden plugs of varying sizes to stop the shot holes after battle, particularly those below the waterline. It was one of the * carpenter's duties after battle to inspect the hull for shot holes and hammer home the plugs. **(2)** The name given to the pattern, or male former, on which the hulls of small craft, such as yachts and harbour boats, are moulded in * fibre glass.

PLUSH, a naval term to describe the amount of * grog left over after the daily issue to the messes in a British warship. Official instructions were that any plush after the daily issue was to be poured into the * scuppers and allowed to run overboard to prevent anyone getting more than his ration, but seamen were adept at saving such waste. In its strictest connotation, plush was the amount of grog left over after its issue as a result of short measure given to the seamen; it was later surreptitiously divided between the cooks of the messes who came to the daily issue to collect the grog for their mess in their * monkeys. It involved a degree of conspiracy between the cooks, the * purser's assistant (later the regulating petty officer) who measured out the allowances, and the officer who, by regulations, had to attend the issue to make sure that more grog was not issued to men than they were entitled to.

'PLUTO', the code name given to the 'Pipe Line Under The Ocean' laid across the English Channel from Southampton to Cherbourg shortly after the Anglo-American invasion of northwest France on 6 June 1944 during the Second World War. It was an entirely British achievement designed to provide a continuous supply of petrol to sustain the allied armies as they drove the Germans eastwards. Further pipelines were laid as the allied armies advanced. As ports were liberated and reactivated during the advance, supplies of fuel were brought in by normal tankers and petrol carriers, and delivery by underwater pipeline was brought to an end.

The pipe through which the petrol flowed was wound on huge floating drums, known as 'conundrums', which were then towed across the Channel unwinding the pipe as they progressed. The operation was directed and controlled in its entirety by Captain John Fenwick Hutchings of the Royal Navy.

PLYMOUTH, a British seaport and naval base in the county of Devon, facing the western end of the English Channel. It was a port as early as 1311, and it was from Plymouth that many expeditions were launched against France in the 14th century. It sprang into great prominence after the discovery of America in 1492, and during the reign of Elizabeth I was the foremost port in the country, exceeding the port of London in the volume of trade handled. It has also a long connection with the history of exploration. A native of Plymouth, named Cockeram, sailed with John * Cabot in 1497, Sir John * Hawkins was a citizen of Plymouth, its port admiral, and, in 1571, its Member of Parliament. Sir Humphrey * Gilbert sailed from Plymouth on his second colonizing expedition to America in 1583; Sir Francis * Drake left Plymouth on his voyage round the world in 1577, and it was in Plymouth Sound that, in 1588, the English fleet awaited the sighting of the Spanish * Armada and sailed out to give it battle under the command of Lord * Howard of Effingham and Sir Francis Drake after the famous game of bowls on Plymouth Hoe. It was from Plymouth, too, that the * Mayflower sailed with the Pilgrim Fathers to America in 1620.

Around the corner from Plymouth lies * Devonport, one of the main bases of the British Navy, with its important * dockyard and shipbuilding facilities.

PLYMOUTH, a town and harbour in Massachusetts, U.S.A., notable as the place where the Pilgrim Fathers landed from the * Mayflower in 1620. On the harbour shore lies the famous Plymouth Rock, a granite boulder on which the Pilgrim Fathers first set foot. In Pilgrim Hall in the town are many relics of the original Pilgrim Fathers, including a portrait of Edward Winslow, Governor Bradford's bible, and Myles Standish's sword.

POCKET-BATTLESHIP, a type name given to three heavily armoured * cruisers built by Germany during the decade 1930–40. They were the * Admiral Graf Spee, * Deutschland (later renamed Lützow), and Admiral Scheer. Although of 10,000 tons * displacement, they were built in * battleship fashion and armed with six 11-inch guns in two triple turrets, eight 5·7-inch guns, and anti-aircraft guns. They had diesel propulsion which gave them a very considerable cruising endurance and range of action, and were built for commerce destruction in war. They were given the prefix 'pocket' on account of their small tonnage in comparison with conventional battleships of the period.

POCOCK, NICHOLAS (1741–1821), British marine painter, went to sea in his early life and rose to the command of merchant ships. He began to paint in oils in 1780 and settled in London nine years later, quickly becoming distinguished as a painter of naval battles. His drawings are of great accuracy and delicacy, details of masts and rigging being particularly fine, and his feeling for colour and design accentuate the quality of his work. He helped to found the Watercolour Society and was a frequent exhibitor there and in the Royal Academy. There is an important collection of his pictures in the *National Maritime Museum at Greenwich.

POD, the collective name for a group of whales or sea-elephants.

POINT, a division of the circumference of the magnetic compass card, which is divided into thirty-two points, each of 11° 15′. The compass card shows four cardinal points (N., S., E., W.) and four half cardinal points (NE., SE., SW., NW.), the remaining twenty-four divisions being full points. Each point on the card is subdivided into half and quarter points. When *boxing the compass, the points are always read from the cardinals and half-cardinals, and the points and their nomenclature, from north to east, in the first, or north-east, quadrant of the card, are N., N. by E., NNE., NE. by N., NE., NE. by E., ENE., E. by N., E., and so on for the other quadrants.

A point of the compass was, in the days of the older square-rigged ship, about the smallest

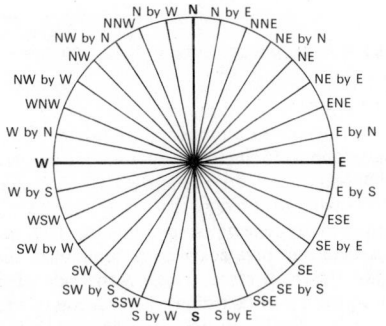

Points of the compass

division to which an average helmsman could steer by wheel, but with the growing efficiency in the rig of these vessels it was possible for a good helmsman to hold a *course between the points. This led to the introduction of half and quarter points, the half point measuring 5° 37·5′ and the quarter point 2° 48·75′.

The requirements of more efficient coastal navigation which came from the growing volume of shipping, and particularly with the realization of the effect of *variation and *deviation, on both the course steered by a ship and the accuracy of compass *bearings in fixing her position on a *chart, led to the abandonment of points as a means both of steering a vessel and of taking bearings and their substitution by degrees, each quadrant being divided into 90°. With the exception of due east and due west, all courses and bearings are read from the two cardinal points of north and south. Thus a ship with a magnetic compass which might formerly have steered a course of, say, NE. by E. would today steer a course of N. 56° E. Since both variation and deviation are always expressed in degrees east or west of north, this system of subdivision of the compass card makes it a simple matter to apply the corrections which are entailed in converting compass courses and bearings into true courses and bearings.

The term is still used, however, in expressing approximate bearings in relation to the ship's head. A lookout, on sighting another vessel at sea, may report its position to the *bridge of the ship as, for example, two points on the *starboard bow, or a point abaft the *port *beam, as the case may be. But even this use of the term is gradually dying out with the growing tendency to report such positions in relation to red (port side) and green (starboard side), and a report, for example, of a vessel bearing Green 45 is rapidly taking the place of its equivalent of four points on the starboard bow.

POINT, to, the operation of tapering the end of a rope to prevent it becoming *fagged out and also to make it more handy for reeving through a *block. The rope is unlayed for a short distance from the end and the *strands gradually thinned down until they finish in a point. The length of the pointing is then *whipped with a *West Country whipping to hold the strands together.

POINTS OF SAILING, the headings of a sailing vessel in relation to the wind. When a vessel is sailing as near to the wind as she can, she is said to be *close-hauled to the wind, i.e., with her sails sheeted (hardened) well in and just full of wind without any shivers in the sails. With a *Bermuda racing rig, a yacht can sail close-hauled about 3½ *points (39°) off the wind, a Bermuda cruising yacht about 4 points (45°), a gaff-rigged vessel about 4¾ points (50°–55°),

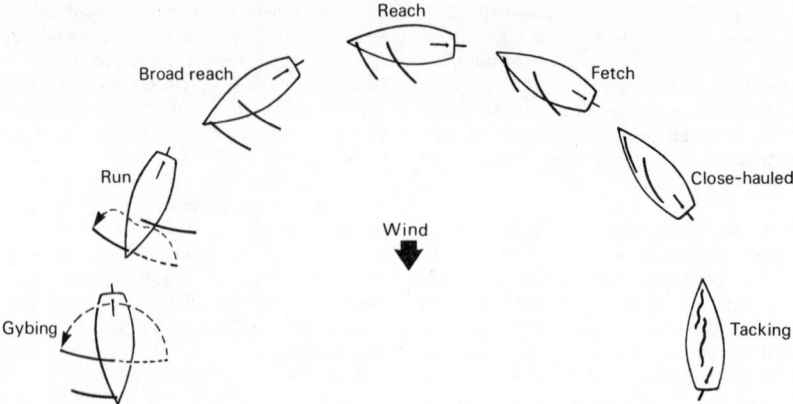

Points of sailing

and a square-rigged vessel about 6 points (70°). When her desired course takes her further off the wind, she is said to be sailing *free, i.e., she can begin to free her sheets to present a squarer aspect of her sails to the wind. When the wind is within the angle of about two points (22°) before the beam and four points (45°) abaft the wind, a vessel is said to be *reaching across the wind, and in many cases this is her fastest point of sailing, particularly when the wind is blowing from abaft the beam. On this point of sailing, her sheets are eased well away so that the angle of the main *boom is at a little less than a right angle to the direction of the wind.

When the wind is blowing within the angle of 4 points (45°) either side of the stern, the vessel is said to be running with the wind, and she has her sheets eased right away to allow the boom to take up the broadest possible angle to the wind direction. See also BY THE LEE, a condition of sailing which frequently arises when a vessel is running before the wind.

POLACRE, a ship or *brig peculiar to the Mediterranean. In the ship version, with three masts, they were usually *lateen-rigged on the fore and *mizen and square-rigged on the main, but occasionally square-rigged on all three. In the brig version they were normally square-rigged on both masts. A feature of their design was that the masts were formed from a single spar so that they had neither tops nor *crosstrees. There were no *footropes to the yards, the crew standing on the topsail *yards to loose or *furl the *topgallant sails and on the lower yards to loose, *reef, or furl the topsails, the yards themselves being lowered sufficiently for that purpose.

POLARIS or *α* **URSAE MINORIS,** the brightest star in the constellation of Ursa Minor, more commonly known as the Pole Star, and sometimes as Stella Maris, the seaman's star. It is a star of the 2nd magnitude, and by describing a circle of only 2° 25′ daily about the North pole, is of great service to navigators since it points, within a degree or two, to the true north. The *altitude of *Polaris* is also virtually equal to the *latitude of the observer. The Phoenicians are said to have been the first navigators to have recognized the value of this star in relation to many of the navigational problems of their day.

POLARIS, the name given to a nuclear weapons system which can be released underwater from submarines. It is basically one or more nuclear warheads mounted on a long-range rocket, which can be targeted on to distant objectives. The range of the Polaris rocket is some 2,500 miles, and the yield of the warhead is in the megaton range. Normally submarines fitted to fire Polaris weapons carry sixteen missiles.

Polaris is the name of a particular rocket system, mounted in submarines of the British and U.S. Navies. Other nations have similar rocket systems mounted in submarines under different names. See also POSEIDON.

POLE STAR, see POLARIS.

POLEAXE, a boarding weapon used by seamen in the days of sailing navies. It had a wooden handle about 15 inches long with an axe head which had a curved spike at the back. The blade of the axe was used to cut away the running rigging of an enemy ship after she had been *boarded, the spike at the back being often used to assist men in clambering up the side of the ship in the act of boarding when several of these axes would be driven into the side of the enemy ship one above the other to form a sort of ladder.

Mediterranean polacre; engraving from Recueil de veues etc. *by P. J. Gueroult de Pas, 1710*

POLLEN, ARTHUR HUNGERFORD (1866–1937), British business executive, was a pioneer of fire control in the Royal Navy. He showed an interest in naval affairs while at Oxford before being called to the Bar, and in 1901 became probably the first man scientifically to attack the new problems posed by long range naval gunfire; he had a brother in the navy at the time. Long range fire meant longer times of flight of shells, and some means had to be devised to find the relative position of a moving target ship at the time in the future when the shell would reach it. Pollen set out to make an apparatus which would produce a continuous 'true' plot of the enemy, and when he failed in 1905 due to inaccurate naval bearing and rangefinding instruments, he started again to design a gyroscopically controlled plotting table. Trials of what he called his 'aim correction' gear continued until 1913 when the British Admiralty chose a rival method devised by Lieutenant Frederic *Dreyer. There is no doubt, however, that the Dreyer system borrowed heavily from Pollen's, and this was recognized in an award in 1926 to Pollen of £30,000 for his 'great contribution to fire control'. He wrote books and articles on naval affairs and was a director of several well-known companies.

POLLUX, see CASTOR.

POLO, MARCO (c. 1254–1324), Venetian traveller, was famous for his overland journey to the court of Kublai Khan in Peking, his seventeen years in China in the Great Khan's service,

and his sea voyage thence to Persia on his way home. He was the son of Nicolo Polo who, with his brother Maffeo, had made an overland journey to Cambaluc (Peking) and returned to Venice in 1269, bringing letters from the Great Khan to the Pope requesting the dispatch of a body of educated men to teach Christianity and the liberal arts.

After a delay of two years owing to an interregnum following the death of Pope Clement IV, the two brothers set out again with a reply from Pope Gregory X, though without teachers. With them they took the young Marco and arrived at the Khan's court in September 1275. Kublai received them warmly and was much taken by Marco who set himself to acquire the many languages of the nationalities subject to the Mongol emperor. Kublai employed him in the public service in the course of which he travelled widely throughout the empire and, for three years, was governor of the city of Yangchow.

When the Polos had been in China more than ten years they became anxious to return home with the great wealth they had acquired. Kublai was unwilling to let them go, however, and it was not until their request was reinforced by the pleas of envoys from the Mongol king of Persia, the grandson of Kublai's brother Hulagu, that he relented. The envoys had arrived to escort a Mongol bride to their master. As, owing to the perils of the overland route, the journey would have to be made by sea, they begged that the Polos, particularly Marco, who had recently visited the Indies, might accompany them to give them the benefit of their experience. Reluctantly

An incident recorded by Marco Polo; illustration from the Livre de Merveilles de Marco Polo *by the Maître de Boucicault, 1410*

the Khan consented and, at the beginning of 1292, the expedition sailed from Zaitun (Chang-chow). The voyage, which involved a stay of some months in Sumatra while waiting for the seasonal shift of the monsoon winds, and a similar stay in southern India, took more than two years to reach Persia.

The Polos travelled on overland to Venice where they arrived towards the end of 1295. Three years later a maritime war between Genoa and Venice culminated in the great *galley battle of Curzola in which the former were completely victorious and more than sixty Venetian galleys destroyed. One of these had been commanded by Marco Polo who became one of the 7,000 prisoners carried off to Genoa.

There he was imprisoned for nearly a year during which he dictated the material for the book which described his experiences. Little is known of Marco Polo's history following his release. His will, now in St. Mark's Library, Venice, was made on 9 January 1324 and it is almost certain that he died in the same year.

POLYPHEMUS, H.M.S., a name first used for a ship of the Royal Navy in 1782, when it was given to a 3rd *rate of sixty-four guns, launched

at Sheerness. This ship took part in the battles of *Copenhagen (1801) and *Trafalgar. In 1807 she was Rear Admiral George Murray's flagship during the operations against Buenos Aires and in 1809 was present at the reduction of San Domingo. She became a hulk for the storage of gunpowder at *Chatham in 1813 and was broken up there in 1827. The next *Polyphemus*, built in 1881 at Chatham, was an experimental type of ship that soon proved herself a monstrosity. She was described as a *torpedo *ram and her leading features were a strong ram bow, a powerful underwater torpedo battery, and great speed and handiness. She had no guns at all, apart from a few light shell guns and machine-guns on the hurricane deck for the purpose of repelling boat or torpedo attack. The ram consisted of a very strong steel spur which projected 12 feet in advance of the *stem of the ship and was so placed that it would strike several feet below an enemy ship's armour belt. It was removable and could be unshipped when not required for active use. This type of ship was not repeated in the Royal Navy, as the long range gun and the torpedo soon rendered the ram obsolete. The *Polyphemus* was sold for scrap in 1903.

POMIGLION or **PUMMELION**, a name given by seamen to the cascable (the knob on the breech end) of a ship's gun in the days of solid shot and muzzle loading.

POMPEIUS, SEXTUS (*c.* 80–35 B.C.), the younger son of Pompey the Great, who, when his father was defeated by Julius Caesar, carried on a civil war in Spain as an outlaw, winning appreciable successes. After a settlement of his differences with the Senate he was appointed in 43 B.C. to command the fleet, but, outlawed once again, used his ships to occupy Sicily from which he raided and *blockaded the Italian coast. In 40 B.C. he supported Antony against Octavian and was given the governorship of Sicily and Sardinia by the treaty of Misenum, but when accused by Octavian of breaking the treaty, won the naval battles of Cumae and Messana in 38 B.C., beating back the forces which were attacking him. The attack against Pompeius was resumed in 36 B.C. and he was defeated by Agrippa at the battle off Mylae; after the final naval action of Naulochus, Pompeius escaped with some of his ships to Asia Minor, where in the following years he was captured and executed. It was said of him that he was so confident of naval success against all his enemies that he called himself the son of *Neptune and lord of the sea.

'POMPEY', the sailors' slang name for Portsmouth, the British naval base on the English Channel. It is not known how or when the name came into being, one theory being that it owes its origin to the fact that the local fire brigade, known as the Pompiers, used to exercise on Southsea Common, adjacent to the town of Portsmouth.

'PONGO', the sailor's name for a soldier. The term is said by some to have been borrowed from Africa where it is used to indicate a gorilla, or any other great ape.

PONTOON, (1) a flat-bottom boat often used as a *lighter or *ferry. **(2)** A boat of special design to support a temporary road or foot bridge across a river. **(3)** A hollow, watertight structure used in *salvage for its lifting power when the water it contains is pumped out. (See also CAISSON.) **(4)** A floating structure frequently used at the ends of fixed piers or alongside quays so that it rises and falls with the *tide to provide ease of access. **(5)** A low, flat vessel fitted with cranes, *tackles, and *capstans which was used in the days of sail to haul down, or *careen, ships for bottom cleaning or repair.

POOP, from the Latin *puppis*, stern, the name given to the short, aftermost deck raised above the *quarterdeck of a ship. In square-rigged ships it formed the roof of the *coach, or *round house, where the *master normally had his cabin. Only the larger sailing ships had poops, but the name has survived and is often used to describe any raised deck right aft in the ship. It is, in fact, sometimes wrongly used to describe that part of the deck which lies at the after end of a ship, regardless of whether raised or not. See also ROYAL.

POOP, to, a ship is pooped, or pooping, when a heavy sea breaks over her *stern or *quarter when she is *scudding before the wind in a gale. It is a situation of considerable danger, particularly in a ship heavily laden, as it usually comes about when the speed of the ship is approximately the same as the speed of the following sea, so that the *rudder has little or no grip on the sea. In such cases, a sea which poops a ship is very apt to swing her off course until she is broadside on the sea, with the danger of rolling over. It is dangerous also in smaller craft, such as yachts, as a pooping sea will bring a great weight of water inboard. The danger of being pooped in a heavy following sea can always be reduced by slowing down the ship's speed in relation to the speed of the sea by towing a *drogue.

A vessel pooped

POOP ROYAL, a short deck above the after end of the *poop seen in many French and Spanish warships during the days of sailing navies, where the *master or pilot had his cabin. It was known to English shipwrights as a topgallant poop, possibly because the gunports were usually decorated with *garlands, a typical English practice with regard to upper deck gunports. Some of the largest British warships incorporated this deck to accommodate the upper *coach.

POOR JOHN, the name given by seamen to salted and dried fish of the cheaper varieties, such as hake and cod, when supplied as part of the victualling allowance on board sailing warships of the

British Navy. Issues of fish occasionally replaced issues of salt beef or pork and were never popular on the lower deck.

POPHAM, Sir HOME RIGGS (1762–1820), British admiral, had several claims to fame, one of them perhaps being that he was his mother's 21st child. He entered the navy in 1778 and had a curious experience between 1787 and 1793 when he engaged in some sort of personal trading to India and the Far East, in which waters he carried out many surveys for the *East India Company. His ship was seized in 1793 by the East India Company on the ground that he was infringing their monopoly. He put his loss at £70,000, and after a protracted law action was awarded damages of £25,000 in 1805. He served ashore for a time with the Duke of York in Flanders as 'superintendent of inland navigation', and through the Duke's influence was promoted to captain, only to run foul of Lord St. Vincent (see JERVIS, Sir John), then First Lord of the Admiralty, for the cost of repairs to his ship which he had incurred at Calcutta after operations in the Red Sea. The Admiralty tried to charge these bills to him personally, implying dishonesty on Popham's part, but he brought his case before Parliament and not only proved his innocence but also maladministration on the Admiralty's part.

In 1806, in a combined operation with troops commanded by Sir David Baird, he seized the Cape of Good Hope from the Dutch, and then persuaded Baird that an attack on the Spaniards at Buenos Aires would be supported by the colonists. His squadron provided cover for a landing of 1,400 troops, but the Spanish colonists, instead of rising in support, took the soldiers prisoner. Popham was recalled to England and court-martialled for leaving his station in South Africa, but although he was censured the City of London presented him with a sword of honour for attempting to open new markets. He was promoted rear admiral in 1814.

One of his major contributions to the British Navy arose from his scientific interest in signalling, and in 1803 the Admiralty adopted his system of a vocabulary code which vastly extended the range of orders and instructions at the disposal of an admiral in directing his fleet. It was with Popham's code that Lord *Nelson was able to send his famous signal to the fleet at the start of the battle of *Trafalgar.

POPPET, a small squared piece of wood fitted inside the *gunwale or *washstrake of a boat which has *rowlocks to take the oars when the boat is being rowed. They are shaped to the rowlocks and provide support to the gunwale at these points. See also SHUTTER.

PORCELLIS, JAN (c. 1585–1680), Dutch marine artist, was born at Ghent, of Spanish descent, and has been described as the 'Raphael of sea painters'. He worked under Hendrik Vroom and became one of the foremost artists of the Dutch marine school. At one time he contracted with a dealer in Antwerp to paint, with the help of a pupil, forty marine pictures with ships in twenty weeks, two to be delivered each week. In 1617 he became Master of the Antwerp Guild and from 1622 to 1680 lived in Haarlem. His picture 'Ships in a gale', painted about 1650, is still considered one of the best storm scenes ever painted. He died at Soeterwoude, near Leiden. His son JULIUS (c. 1609–45), born at Leyerdorp, combined his father's talents with a rare aesthetic sense, although it is reasonably certain that he was not one of his pupils. Nevertheless he was influenced by his parent's style and technique to the extent that it is sometimes difficult to distinguish the work of one from the other, especially as they both signed their pictures with the initials 'J.P.'

PORT, (1) the name of the left-hand side of a vessel as viewed from aft. The name probably owes its derivation to the fact that the old-fashioned merchant ships had a loading, or *lading, port on their left-hand side, and the later sailing warships also had their *entry port on that side. Originally, the left-hand side of the ship was known as the *larboard side, but this was changed officially to port in 1844 to avoid any confusion with the similar sounding *starboard, or right-hand, side. But the word port had been used for this purpose very much earlier than this, and Rear Admiral Robert *Fitzroy is usually credited with its introduction into the British Navy in H.M.S. *Beagle in 1828. *Mainwaring, in his Seaman's Dictionary (1625), indicates the use of the word for *helm orders some 300 years earlier, and has: 'Port. Is a word used in *Conding the Ship . . . they will use the word steddy a-port, or Steddy a-Starboard.'

The theory that the word port was chosen to replace larboard because a vessel burns a red light—the colour of port wine—at night on her left-hand side is demonstrably false, as the word port was used in this connection long before ships burned navigation lights at night.

(2) A harbour with facilities for berthing ships, embarkation and disembarkation of passengers, and the loading and unloading of cargo.

PORT ADELAIDE NAUTICAL MUSEUM, Port Adelaide, South Australia, a small museum originally opened as a general museum, is now devoted to shipping and contains some eighty ship models, and other marine artefacts. There are the beginnings of other maritime museums in

Australia at Ehuca, Victoria; Mannum, South Australia; Melbourne, Victoria; and Sydney, New South Wales.

PORT ARTHUR, a Russian port at the southern tip of the Liao-tung peninsula on the Manchurian coast. It was the scene of much fighting around the turn of the 19th century, being a fortified Chinese naval base until it was captured and destroyed by Japan in 1894. Four years later it was leased to Russia, who built extensive new fortifications round the large and spacious harbour and made it the main base of their Asiatic fleet during the Russo-Japanese War of 1904–5. In Port Arthur occurred the total destruction of this fleet as the Japanese closed in towards the end of 1904, the town being surrendered on 1 January 1905. The Chinese name of Port Arthur was Lu-shun-k'ou, but it was Europeanized when leased to Russia.

PORT ELIZABETH, a seaport of the Union of South Africa on the southern side of Algoa Bay some 360 miles due east of *Cape Town. Bartholomew *Diaz landed a party at Algoa Bay in 1488, the first white men to set foot in southern Africa, and for 300 years the bay remained, for seamen, 'a landing place with fresh water'. Many of the early voyagers and discoverers put in there to replenish their casks with water.

It first began to develop as a port in 1820 when it was selected as a place of settlement for 4,000 British men and women. It received its name following a request from the acting governor of Cape Colony, Sir Rufane Donkin, that it should commemorate his young wife who had recently died, 'one of the most perfect human beings'.

Port Elizabeth is the third largest seaport in South Africa and growing fast, being developed for the handling of container ships. It enjoys the advantage of water deep enough without dredging to accommodate ships of up to 375,000 tons. It is a main distribution port for ore, citrus, wool, and hides, all produced in its immediate hinterland, and with the rapid growth of containerization is expected eventually to handle a wider range of imports and exports.

PORT GYBE, a *fore-and-aft rigged sailing vessel is sometimes said to be on the *port *gybe, instead of on the port *tack, when the wind comes from abaft the beam on the port side.

PORT MAHON, capital and principal seaport of the island of Minorca, in the Balearic Islands, is a port which has seen much fighting and bloodshed. It was captured by the Moors and recaptured from them by James I of Aragon in 1232. *Khair-ed-Din, son of *Barbarossa, besieged and captured it in 1535

and a corsair named Piali sacked it in 1558. Minorca was seized by the British in 1708 and Port Mahon was captured by France in 1756 after a heroic siege and the failure of Admiral John *Byng to relieve it. Restored to British rule in 1762, Port Mahon was lost again to France in 1782 after a long and painful siege. It was finally ceded to Spain in 1802.

PORT OF LONDON AUTHORITY (P.L.A.), a central authority created by Act of Parliament in 1908, which came into force in 1909. It owns all the docks, quays, warehouses, etc., within the area of the port of London, which extends from Teddington Lock, west of the city, to Yantlet Creek at the mouth of the River Thames. It has the responsibility of maintaining the navigable waterways within the limits of the port by dredging, removal of obstacles, etc. See also LONDON.

PORT SAID, an Egyptian seaport which marks the northern entrance to the *Suez Canal. Port Said was a fuelling port of importance and also a port of call for many steamship lines, but during the closure of the Suez Canal following the Israeli–Egyptian war of 1967 it virtually lost all its former importance. It was severely damaged during the 'Six Days' War' of 1973 but with the Suez Canal again opened for traffic is likely to regain its former importance.

PORT SILLS or **CILLS,** the name given to the lengths of timber used for lining the top and bottom edges of the *gunports in sailing men-of-war.

PORT TACK, the situation of a sailing vessel with her sails trimmed for a wind which comes over the *port side of the vessel. Although the verb 'to tack' postulates a vessel sailing *close-hauled, a vessel on any point of sailing is on the port tack if the wind comes over her port side. But see also PORT GYBE.

PORTER, DAVID (1780–1843), American naval officer, was born in Massachusetts and entered the navy in 1798. During the War of 1812 he was given command of the frigate *Essex and in 1813 took her into the Pacific where he raided the British whaling fleet, taking more than a dozen *prizes. One of these prizes was fitted out as a naval vessel and renamed *Essex Junior*, but the two ships were blockaded by H.M.S. *Phoebe* and H.M.S. *Cherub* for six weeks in Valparaiso. On attempting to leave harbour Porter lost his topmast in a squall, and after an action of two and a half hours the two American ships were compelled to surrender, having lost 155 men out of a total of 225.

After commanding the experimental steam vessel *Fulton*, in 1815, he became one of the naval commissioners in Washington and eight years later was promoted commander of the West Indies Squadron with the rank of *commodore. In that area he vigorously suppressed *piracy, but some of his actions aroused criticism and led to a court martial. Although the sentence against him was considered a light one he believed it unjust and resigned from the navy in 1826. He then accepted an appointment as commander-in-chief of the Mexican Navy where he served for three years, being granted land in payment at Tehuantepec which he hoped to develop for a canal between the Atlantic and Pacific. After his return to the U.S.A. he was appointed minister to Turkey and died twelve years later at Constantinople.

PORTER, DAVID DIXON (1813–91), American admiral, was born in Chester, Pa., the third of ten children of Commodore David *Porter. He went to sea with his father at the age of 10, and entered the Mexican Navy as a *midshipman three years later. He became a midshipman in the U.S. Navy in 1829.

At the start of the American Civil War (1861–5) Porter recommended that David *Farragut, whom his father had adopted, be chosen to command the naval force against New Orleans and he himself commanded the flotilla of mortar boats that supported Farragut's attack on the forts below New Orleans. Later, still in command of the mortar boats, he supported Farragut's larger ships when they ran past the batteries at Vicksburg in the Mississippi River. In October 1862 he was promoted acting rear admiral and given command of the Mississippi squadron. In the closing months of the Civil War, he was given command of the North Atlantic blockading squadron and directed the operations resulting in the capture of Fort Fisher, N.C., and the sealing of the entrances to the Cape Fear River which had been the principal refuge of *blockade runners. After the war he spent four years as superintendent of the Naval Academy at *Annapolis. He became a vice admiral in July 1866 and, on Farragut's death, was promoted admiral in August 1870.

PORTLAND, a battle of the First Anglo-Dutch War (1652–4), was fought in the English Channel on 18–20 February 1653. In the morning of the 18th, when some 20 miles south of Portland Bill, Admiral Marten *Tromp, with about eighty ships, escorting a homeward-bound *convoy of about 200 vessels, was intercepted by the English fleet under Robert *Blake and Richard *Deane. The English also had about eighty ships but the *White squadron, under General George *Monck, was about five miles to leeward.

At about 9.00 a.m., Tromp attacked the English *Red and *Blue squadrons, which bore the brunt

of the action until the White squadron was able to get up. Fighting in the van ceased at about 4.00 p.m., but to leeward it was continued until dark. Tromp, who had kept his convoy intact to windward, interposed his fighting ships between it and the English, and the Dutch continued their progress up Channel.

Next morning, the English were about ten miles south of the Isle of Wight, and at daylight sail was made after the Dutch; but owing to lack of wind they did not get up with the enemy until the afternoon, when a running fight was maintained until dark. By this time there was a serious shortage of ammunition in the Dutch fleet but the lightness of the wind and the short day prevented a decisive result from being obtained. Disorder began to manifest itself in the convoy as they gradually lost faith in their escort.

The battle was renewed at about 9.00 a.m., on the 20th, when the fleets were off Beachy Head. Tromp continued his retreat, making a running fight of it all the time, but his ships were in a bad way and the smaller English ships were let loose among the convoy. The action ceased at dusk, when the battered remainder of the Dutch fleet anchored off Calais. Blake also anchored for the night, intending to attack again next day; but in the morning not one enemy ship remained in sight. The Dutch losses are not known for certain but it seems that about six fighting ships were lost, as well as 30–50 of the convoy captured. The English lost only one ship.

PORT-LAST or **PORTOISE,** a word meaning level with the *gunwale, in connection with the *yards of a sailing vessel. An order to 'lower the yards a-port-last, or a-portoise' was to lower them down to the gunwale. For a ship to ride a-port-last or a-portoise was for her to ride out a gale with her lower yards struck down.

PORTO BELLO (PUERTO BELLO), a seaport of the 18th century on the north side of the Isthmus of Darien, and the scene in 1739 of the first action of the War of Jenkins's Ear, which developed into the War of Austrian Succession (1739–48). It was captured on 22 November of that year by a *squadron of six British *ships of the line under the command of Vice Admiral Edward *Vernon, who had been sent out to the West Indies in the previous July under a declaration of general *reprisal against Spain and with instructions to intercept the annual Spanish *flota of treasure ships before they left Mexico for Spain. The intelligence given to Vernon was that the treasure *galleons were to rendezvous at Cartagena after their voyage from Spain and then proceed to Porto Bello to unload their European cargoes and take on board in its place the annual treasure gained from the mines in Mexico and other places on the mainland.

Vernon reached Porto Bello on the night of 20 November and the next day bombarded the castle guarding the entrance to the harbour. It was stormed and captured by a landing party from the ships, men standing on each other's shoulders to climb into the embrasures. On the following day the town surrendered.

Ten thousand dollars of public money were taken and distributed by Vernon among his men; the civilian inhabitants were not molested. The total British casualties were no more than six killed and thirteen wounded. The fortifications were demolished during the next three weeks, the captured Spanish gunpowder being used for the purpose.

PORTO FARINA, BATTLE OF, was an assault on 4 April 1655 by an English fleet of twenty-four ships under Robert *Blake which had been sent out to the Mediterranean to conduct reprisals against the *Barbary pirates for the injuries done to English shipping. When his demands for redress were refused by the Dey of Tunis, he attacked the forts and the nine pirate vessels that were in Porto Farina, about 25 miles north of Tunis. Blake, with fifteen ships, sailed with a fair wind into the harbour and anchored, and soon all ships were heavily engaged with the forts. Under cover of the smoke the boats of the fleet boarded and set on fire all the Tunisian ships. The work was completed by noon and Blake then withdrew. Most of the English casualties occurred among the boats' crews, the total being twenty-five killed and about forty wounded or hurt.

PORTOLANO, a form of *sailing directions which was used in the Mediterranean between the 12th and 15th centuries as an aid to navigators. It described the coasts and ports, anchorages, rocks and shoals, and the facilities available for trade at the various ports. It was contemporary with, and backed up with additional information, the *portulan charts of the areas.

PORTS, square holes cut in the sides of the sailing ships of war through which the guns were fired, or for other purposes such as *bridle-ports in the bows, entry ports in the waist, and stern ports between the stern timbers. When not in use they were closed by port-lids which were hinged along the top edge. This term is often wrongly applied to the circular openings in the sides of modern ships with a hinged glass 'window' and an inner metal deadlight for use in heavy weather. The uninitiated often call these port-holes; the proper term is *scuttle.

PORTSMOUTH, a seaport and major naval base in Hampshire, England, facing the English Channel. The first naval *dock in Britain was built at Portsmouth in 1540 by Henry VIII, but the port was an important naval station long before that date, the king's ships being always accommodated there. The main *dockyard area was many times expanded during the 17th, 18th, and 19th centuries to make it the most important naval station in Britain. Portsmouth is the home of the naval gunnery establishment at H.M.S. *Excellent at Whale Island in the harbour, of the naval *torpedo establishment at H.M.S. *Vernon* alongside the dockyard, and the naval *submarine headquarters at H.M.S. *Dolphin on the opposite side of the dockyard across the harbour entrance.

Many famous naval ships have been built in the dockyard at Portsmouth, including H.M.S. *Dreadnought*, the world's first all-big-gun battleship, in 1906. H.M.S. *Victory*, flagship of Lord *Nelson at *Trafalgar, and the most venerated ship in the British Navy, is permanently preserved in her original state in a dry-dock in the dockyard.

PORTSMOUTH   NAVAL   SHIPYARD MUSEUM, Portsmouth, Virginia, U.S.A., was founded in 1949 in the naval shipyard but not opened until 1963. The collection is now housed in a modern building. It depicts the history of the American armed forces from 1607 to the present day, and contains a number of ship models, tools, weapons (including a *Polaris missile), small arms, uniforms, paintings, drawings, engravings, and photographs. The library contains about 3,000 books, some maps, plans, manuscripts, and archives.

PORTUGUESE   MAN-OF-WAR, a small jellyfish, *Physalis pelagica*, which floats on the water in tropical seas. The long tentacles which hang down from its body are poisonous to the touch. It is distinguished by a small fluted ridge on its body which projects above the water and is blown along by the breeze, often reflecting the colours of the water.

PORTULAN, or **PORTOLAN, CHART,** a form of *chart first made in the Mediterranean in the 13th century to meet the practical needs of seamen. These charts are typified by the extensive use of compass roses and extended *rhumb or direction lines closely covering the entire area of a goatskin or sheepskin used for the chart. A coastal outline with the positions of the cities and ports, together with their flags and banners, was shown, but no details of the hinterland were given. The portulan chart probably originated in Venice and Genoa, was further developed by the Catalan chartmakers, and reached its peak of

A Portuguese portulan chart of the Mediterranean and Atlantic coast of Europe made on a sheepskin; attributed to Sebastian Lopes

perfection in Portugal and Spain in the 16th century. It should not be confused with a *por-tolano.

POSEIDON, the Greek god of the sea, known to the Romans as *Neptune. In Greek mythology he was lord and ruler of the sea. He was the son of Cronos and Rhea, and his palace was believed to lie at the bottom of the sea off Aegea in Euboea. His wife Amphitrite was a grand-daughter of Titan (Ocean). He was credited with the power of gathering clouds, raising and calming the sea, letting loose storms, and granting safe voyages.

POSEIDON, a nuclear weapons system fitted in *submarines, consisting of several nuclear warheads mounted on a long range rocket and capable of being fired while the submarine carrying it remains submerged. It is a later development of *Polaris, but like Polaris has a range of approximately 2,500 miles. A submarine thus armed normally carries sixteen rockets. The Poseidon rocket system, entirely developed in the U.S.A., is mounted only in U.S. submarines.

POSH, a slang term for the wealthy, supposedly derived from the letters P.O.S.H. (Port Out Starboard Home) which used to be printed on the first-class tickets of passengers travelling on the *P & O Line rich enough to pay extra for cabins on the *port side of the ship going out and the *starboard side coming home in order to avoid the heat and glare of the sun in the Indian Ocean.

POSITION LINE, a line drawn on a *chart or *plotting sheet, as a result of a *bearing or *sight, on which the ship from which the bearing or sight is taken must lie. A position line is usually indicated by a single arrow head at each end, this serving to distinguish it from other lines on the chart or plotting sheet. For details of the part it plays in fixing a ship's position, see NAVIGATION.

POST-BARK, a name often used in the 16th and 17th centuries for what was also known as a *packet or packet-boat, a vessel specially designated for the carriage of mails overseas.

POST-CAPTAIN, the rank in the British Navy in sailing warship days which corresponds to that of captain today. There were in those days two grades of captain, depending on the size and quality of the ship to which the appointments were made. On promotion, *lieutenants were given the rank of captain and appointed to the command of a small ship (*sloop, *cutter, etc.). The equivalent rank today would be that of *commander. After sufficient experience in command of such a ship they were 'posted', i.e., given command of a rated ship, and took the rank of post-captain. For rated ship, see RATES.

POTEMKIN, GRIGORY ALEKSANDRO-VICH, Prince (1739–91), Russian statesman and lover of the Empress Catherine II, was a follower of *Peter the Great in making Russia a maritime power in the south, as Peter had made her a maritime power in the north. In 1784–5 he built a fleet in the Black Sea of fifteen *ships of the line and twenty-five smaller vessels which did good service in Catherine's second Turkish war of 1787–92, and under his direction the dockyard at Sevastopol and the naval arsenal at Kherson were contructed. He was a man of vast appetite for life in all its forms, and while he is credited with being a stupendous lover, it is also recorded that during four months in 1791 he spent over 850,000 roubles in banquets and entertainments. It is perhaps typical of the man that he is said to have died as a result of eating a whole goose at a sitting. He gave his name to the battleship *Potemkin, scene of a famous mutiny in the Russian Navy in 1905.

POTEMKIN, more properly *Kniaz Potemkin Tavricheski*, a Russian *battleship of the Black Sea Fleet which was the scene, in June 1905, of a famous mutiny. The ostensible reason for the mutiny was bad meat brought on board to be made into bortsch, which the men refused to eat. The ship's commander, Giliarovsky, considering this refusal amounted to mutiny and acting in accordance with an old Russian naval custom, ordered that a number of men should be selected at random, covered with a *tarpaulin, and shot. The men selected to do the shooting refused to fire their rifles. This account was later denied by officers of the ship who survived the mutiny, but one rating named Vakulinchuk was undoubtedly shot by Giliarovsky, whereupon he, the captain, the chaplain, and four other officers were killed by the crew. When the *Potemkin* returned to *Odessa, Vakulinchuk's body was exhibited to the crowd ashore and rioting followed, some five to six thousand people losing their lives mainly during the famous charge of mounted Cossacks down the Richelieu Steps. After meandering round the Black Sea in search of support the *Potemkin* was *scuttled by her crew in shallow water off Constanza, but was later raised and refitted. She was broken up after the First World War (1914–18). The mutiny forms the subject of the Soviet film *Bronenosets Potemkin* (*The Battleship Potemkin*) made in 1925 and famous in the history of the cinema, although the ending, showing the Russian fleet rallying to the *Potemkin*'s leadership, is pure fiction.

POUCHES, an old name for the small bulkheads, often temporary, erected in the *holds of a cargo ship when a shifting cargo, such as corn or coal, is taken on board, their purpose being to prevent movement of the cargo when the ship rolls or *pitches. In the older sailing days, pouches were fitted in warships before they were *careened for bottom cleaning so that the shingle ballast which most of them carried, shifted by hand to help heel the ship, should not run back to the centre line.

The battleship Potemkin

Admiral of the Fleet, Sir Dudley Pound, 1943

POUND, Sir ALFRED DUDLEY PICKMAN ROGERS (1877–1943), British admiral of the fleet, specialized in *torpedoes in the Royal Navy. His sea service prior to achieving flag rank was exclusively in *capital ships, the highlights being command of H.M.S. *Colossus* during the battle of *Jutland, of H.M.S. *Repulse* in the Atlantic Fleet, 1920–2, and as chief of staff to Admiral Sir Roger *Keyes when the latter commanded the Mediterranean Fleet, 1925–7. After promotion to rear admiral in March 1926, Pound alternated commands at sea with staff appointments in the Admiralty. He commanded the Battle-cruiser Squadron in the Atlantic Fleet from 1929 to 1931 and served as Second Sea Lord 1932 to 1935. Promoted admiral in January 1935, he was commander-in-chief in the Mediterranean from March 1936 to May 1939. Two months later, on the death of Admiral Sir Roger Backhouse, he became First Sea Lord and Chief of the Naval Staff with the rank of admiral of the fleet on the verge of the outbreak of the Second World War.

The appointment was something of a surprise to the fleet where, owing to his unsmiling manner and lack of *panache*, he was a little-known and not always popular figure. The return of so dynamic a person as Winston *Churchill to office as First Lord of the Admiralty in September 1939 might have been expected to reduce the quiet-mannered admiral to 'rubber stamp' status, but in the event he succeeded in impressing on Churchill the principle that the

First Sea Lord was the final arbiter in technical and professional matters. He was instrumental in restraining Churchill's enthusiasm for unsound naval adventures and his quiet wisdom did much to guide the Royal Navy successfully through the first difficult years of the war at sea.

If there is a criticism of Dudley Pound's tenure of the office of First Sea Lord during these anxious years, it lies in his tendency to give Admiralty instructions directly to sea commanders, by-passing normal channels even though Admiralty operational control is endemic in the British naval system. An unhappy example of this was his order in 1942 to Convoy *PQ 17, bound to Russia, to scatter in the face of an unconfirmed threat by a German squadron which included the battleship *Tirpitz*, over the head of and against the advice of the commander-in-chief of the Home Fleet, Sir John *Tovey. It resulted in catastrophe and the virtual annihilation of the convoy. Yet other characteristics there were, however, which made him a great wartime First Sea Lord; a willingness to accept the blame for disasters, to remain silent and undismayed in the face of uninformed press attacks, and to apply his notable organizational ability with a ceaseless energy. This last probably hastened his death while still in office owing to pain and exhaustion brought on by a tumour on the brain. By the time of his death the war at sea had virtually been won, due in no small measure to his wise overall guidance of the Royal Navy during the nation's years of peril.

POURQUOI PAS?, a *barque-rigged vessel with auxiliary steam engines built in France for J.-B. *Charcot's Second French Antarctic Expedition, 1908–10. She was subsequently employed on oceanographical work in the North Atlantic and the Mediterranean and on several expeditions to Greenland. She was lost, with Charcot, off Iceland in 1936.

POWDER MONKEY, a ship's boy in a warship whose duty when the crew was *piped to *quarters for battle was to carry powder from the *magazine to the gundecks during the days of sailing navies. They were assisted in this task by any women who might be on board; many of the larger ships carried three or four wives of trustworthy petty officers or seamen when at sea, particularly for their value in nursing the wounded after battle. The powder that they and the powder monkeys carried to the gundecks was weighed out into silk bags in the form of cartridges for the guns.

PQ 17, the code letters and numbers of a convoy carrying supplies to North Russia during the Second World War. It sailed from Iceland on 27 June 1942 with a close escort of six destroyers, four corvettes, and two anti-aircraft ships, a close support force of four cruisers and three de-stroyers, and distant cover by the British Home Fleet. The convoy consisted of thirty-five merchant ships and made good progress for the first seven days, passing north of Bear Island, between Spitsbergen and the North Cape of Norway, on 3 July. On this date the British Admiralty received intelligence that two German *pocket-battleships, the *Scheer* and *Lützow*, had sailed from Narvik bound for Altenfiord, a temporary base in the far north of Norway. Further intelligence came in the same day that the battleship *Tirpitz* and the heavy cruiser *Hipper* had sailed from Trondheim, bound for the northward. It appeared to the British Admiralty that these heavy ships could only be gathering in the far north for an attack on Convoy PQ 17, and a quick calculation indicated that they could reach the convoy during the night of 4 July.

U-boat and air attacks on the convoy began on 4 July, but were beaten off with the loss of three merchant ships. It was appreciated in the Admiralty that the distant cover of the Home Fleet was much too far to the westward to be able to intervene if the German surface ships attacked, and also that the close support ships and the close escort, four cruisers and nine de-stroyers, were no match for the guns of the *Tirpitz* and the pocket-battleships. On the assumption that these ships had already sailed, the

A PQ convoy under attack, 1942

Admiralty ordered the convoy to scatter and the close support force to withdraw to the westward as ordered. Unfortunately, the six destroyers of the escort force, believing from the Admiralty signal that an action with the German ships was imminent, accompanied the support force and also withdrew westward in the expectation of providing much needed support to the cruisers in the coming battle. Although no enemy appeared, they remained with the support force throughout the night.

In fact the *Tirpitz*, *Scheer*, and *Hipper* (the *Lützow* ran aground when leaving Narvik and was damaged) did not leave Altenfiord until shortly before noon on 5 July, but by then there was no task for them. The merchant ships, no longer a convoy for they had obeyed the order to scatter, were falling victim one by one to the torpedoes of U-boats and aircraft. Of the thirty-five that had sailed from Iceland, only eleven reached their destination in North Russia.

PRAAM, PRAM, or **PRAME, (1)** a small two- or three-masted ship used by the French for coast defence purposes during the Revolutionary and Napoleonic wars (1793–1815). They were flat-bottomed, drew very little water, and carried from ten to twenty guns, being used as floating batteries or gunboats as a defence against coastal raids or assaults. The majority were *ketch-rigged. **(2)** A *lighter used in Holland and in the Baltic for loading and unloading merchant vessels lying at anchor in the ports. They were first mentioned in this role as far back as the 14th century. **(3)** A small ship's boat of the 16th–18th centuries. **(4)** A *dinghy usually used as a small tender to a *yacht, frequently with a truncated or sawn-off bow.

PRATIQUE, a certificate given to a ship when she arrives from a foreign port when the port health officer of the port of arrival is satisfied that the health of all on board is good and that there are no cases of notifiable diseases in the ship. A ship remains in *quarantine on arrival in port until she has been granted her certificate of pratique.

PRAYER-BOOK, see BIBLE.

PREBLE, EDWARD (1761–1807), American naval officer, was born in Falmouth (now Portland), Maine. He began his sea service at the age of 16 in a *privateer and became a midshipman in the Massachusetts State Navy in 1779 in the *Proctor*, being captured by the British in 1781. After a time in a prison ship he was released and spent the remainder of the War of American Independence (1775–82) in the Massachusetts *cruiser *Winthrop*. After the war he had fifteen years of service in merchant vessels but in 1798 became a lieutenant in the new U.S. Navy and served in command of the *brig *Pickering* under Commodore John *Barry in the West Indies. He was promoted captain in 1799 in command of the new *frigate *Essex* and during *convoy duty she was the first American warship to go beyond the Cape of Good Hope.

Preble commanded the third squadron to be sent into the Mediterranean in the operations against *Barbary pirates, with his flag in the *Constitution*. His command included the frigate *Philadelphia*, but that vessel had been captured before he reached the eastern Mediterranean. With the *Constitution* and his five smaller vessels, he began an active *blockade of Tripoli, and also employed mortar boats and *gunboats procured from the kingdom of the Two Sicilies. With this force and two *prizes, he bombarded the city of Tripoli on 4 August 1804, inflicting severe damage on Tripolitan shipping.

At this early period in the history of the U.S. Navy the commanders in the Mediterranean were changed periodically without regard to the situation in that area. Under this unthinking policy Preble was superseded at a time when he had developed a high standard of duty and performance in his command.

PRESIDENT, U.S.S., one of the *'six original frigates', was delayed in her construction but was launched on 10 April 1800. She put to sea in August of that year under the command of Thomas *Truxtun. Eleven years later, when commanded by John *Rodgers, the *President* encountered the British *Little Belt* in May 1811, one of the series of incidents which eventually led to the Anglo-American war of 1812. In the beginning of that war Rodgers went to sea and successfully induced British naval vessels to go in search of him rather than to remain off the American ports to capture incoming American merchantmen still unaware of the declaration of war. Later, under the command of Stephen *Decatur, the *President* was blockaded in the port of New York for a time and when attempting to escape during bad weather, grounded on the entrance bar at New York and pounded heavily for several hours before freeing herself. On 15 January 1815 she surrendered to a force of four British vessels, the *Endymion*, *Majestic*, *Pomone*, and *Tenedos*.

PRESS GANG, the name given popularly to a group of naval seamen, under the command of an officer, employed in time of war to bring in seamen for service in the navy. Although connected by most people with the British Navy, other nations employed similar methods of recruitment for their navies and the *impressment of men for service in warships was widespread. In Britain these groups operated mainly in seaports, but occasionally visited inland towns to pick up seamen who may have been thought to reside or visit there. Men thus taken were, in the British Navy, entered in the ship's muster-book as pressed men, or *landsmen, and were paid at a lower rate than those who volunteered. See also IMPRESSMENT, RENDEZVOUS, TENDER.

PRESSURE MINE, see MINES AND MINE WARFARE.

PREVENTER, the name given to any additional rope or wire rigged temporarily to back up any standing *rigging in a ship in heavy wind and weather. It is most usually associated with sailing vessels, and particularly with the mast *stays of such ships.

PREVENTIVE SERVICE, the official name in Britain during the 17th, 18th, and 19th centuries of the establishment of coastguards and customs round the coasts for the prevention of smuggling. All other nations had, of course, similar establishments. It was in Britain both shore and sea based, revenue *cutters being used at sea to run down and examine vessels suspected of carrying and landing goods which had not paid the customs duties.

PRICK, to, (1) the operation of sewing an additional central seam between the two seams which are normally employed to join the *cloths of a sail. This was normally only done when the sails were worn and the original stitching weakened by long wear. See SAILMAKER'S STITCH. **(2)** Also the operation of rolling up leaf tobacco in canvas and *serving it with tarred twine to compress it as solidly as possible; when matured and cut with a knife it was a favourite smoke or chew of old *tars. Those prepared to sacrifice a portion of their rum ration in which to soak the tobacco before it was served always professed to enjoy it the more. A quantity of tobacco in its canvas and serving was known as a prick, qualified by the weight of leaf tobacco thus treated, as a half-pound prick, pound prick, etc.

PRIEN, GÜNTHER (1908–41) German *submarine commander, was born in humble circumstances. At 15 years of age he was helping his mother sell lace to the shops of Leipzig. He also acted as a courier to businessmen attending the Leipzig Fair during 1923, the year of the great inflation. One businessman paid Prien's salary in Swedish kronor; the rate of exchange was such that this comparatively small sum, exchanged into marks, paid Prien's fees at a nautical school in Hamburg. He passed out as a fourth officer but, after a short time, the depression closed in on German shipping and he was unemployed.

Eventually he was engaged at subsistence wages to work at one of the National Socialist *Landjahr Heime* for young boys. He entered the navy in 1932 as a warrant officer and was almost immediately commissioned in 1933. At the outbreak of the Second World War he commanded *U.47,* and with this boat entered *Scapa Flow and sank the British *battleship *Royal Oak* on 14 October 1939. Afterwards Prien became one of the most successful of German submarine commanders, sinking twenty-eight merchant ships with a total *tonnage of 164,953. On 8 March 1941 his boat was sunk with all hands by the British destroyer *Wolverine.* A brave officer and a fine ship-handler, Prien was less successful in his relations with his crew and his fellow officers. His much publicized statement: 'I get more pleasure out of a really good *convoy exercise than out of any leave' was a point of view which set him apart from other men.

PRIME, to, in general nautical terms, the operation of making ready in relation to immediate use. A *lead is primed before taking a *sounding by inserting a piece of tallow or soft soap into the cavity at the end so that as it strikes the bottom it will pick up sand, shells, or small stones to give a navigator information of the nature of the bottom. In the days of hand *pumps on board, the pump was primed by having water poured into the barrel so that the leather washers would take up firmly on the lining of the barrel. When muzzle-loading guns were used in warships, they were made ready for firing by being primed, with the cartridge pierced with a *priming iron to expose the powder and a pinch of gunpowder, or later a quill firing-tube, inserted in the vent hole. When used as an adjective in the term 'a prime seaman', it means one who is fully trained and able to *hand, *reef, and *steer.

PRIME MERIDIAN, from Latin *primus,* first, and *medius dies,* middle-day, the terrestrial *meridian from which *longitudes are measured eastwards or westwards. The longitude of the prime meridian is 0°.

The ancient navigators of the Mediterranean region used the meridian through the 'Fortunate Isles', now known as the Canaries, which were considered at that time to be the westernmost part of the habitable earth, as their first, or prime meridian from which all longitudes were measured eastwards. During the 15th and 16th centuries when the peoples of western Europe emerged as sea traders, almost every maritime nation used as a prime meridian a meridian passing through its own territory. The French, for example, used the meridian of Paris; the Dutch, that through Amsterdam; and the English the meridian through London. The inconvenience to navigators caused by the existence of a multitude of prime meridians, and thus a multitude of *charts with differing meridians east and west, was not resolved until the closing decade of the 19th century when it was decided by international agreement to adopt the meridian of *Greenwich as the prime meridian.

PRIMING IRON, a thin piece of iron with a point at one end and a wooden handle at the other which was thrust down the vent hole of a muzzle-loading cannon when loaded in order to pierce the cartridge and expose the powder so that when the quickmatch was put to the powder train or, later, the quill-tube inserted and fired, the powder in the cartridge would ignite.

PRINCIPALL NAVIGATIONS, VOYAGES, TRAFFIQUES AND DISCOVERIES OF THE ENGLISH NATION, THE, the famous book of voyages edited by Richard *Hakluyt and published (first edition) in one folio volume in London in 1589 and (second edition) in three folio volumes in 1599. Hakluyt, an ideal editor, went to enormous pains to discover accounts of as many early voyages as he could, and his work starts with the voyage of King Arthur to Iceland in the year 517. Just as his first edition was going to press, the account of Sir Francis *Drake's great voyage of circumnavigation of 1577–80, hitherto kept as a state secret, became available, and additional pages describing this great voyage were printed and inserted in some copies of the first edition. In order to avoid any mistakes in pagination, these additional pages were unnumbered.

The *Principal Navigations* is probably the best known of all maritime books, a long labour of love of its distinguished editor. It has been reprinted many times in modern editions, the best being those produced by Robert Maclehose and Co. of Glasgow in 1903 and by J. M. Dent and Sons of London in Everyman's Library in 1907. Another notable edition, but printed in limited numbers, was that of the *Hakluyt Society in twelve volumes (1903–5).

PRIVATE SHIP, the description given to a warship in commission which has no flag officer on board, and is thus not a *flagship.

PRIVATEER, a privately owned vessel armed with guns which operated in time of war against the trade of an enemy. The name has come to embrace both the ships and the men who sailed in her. Such vessels were commissioned by *letters of marque, which licensed them to take *prizes in time of war, and which served both as official letters of *reprisal and bonds of good behaviour. The first letter of marque was issued in England in 1293, but only from 1589 did they provide for prizes to be condemned at an Admiralty Court

and a division of their value made between the Crown and the owners. The division was usually on the basis of 10 per cent to the Crown and 90 per cent to the owner. All nations adopted this method of commerce destruction until privateering was abolished by the *Declaration of Paris in 1856. Thus Francis *Drake was essentially a privateer on his voyage round the world even though he did not have a letter of marque for the voyage, as also was Paul *Jones before he became a regular naval officer. By the time that national navies were established on a permanent basis, the authorities often disapproved of privateering because it drained off the best seamen, but it was such an efficient method of commerce destruction that the French, notably those from St. Malo and Dunkirk, such as Jean *Bart, and the Americans, made great use of it, to such an extent that all other nations were more or less forced to follow suit. In this way privateers may perhaps be considered as the strategic predecessors of *submarines, when used, as in the First and Second World Wars, in operations against the merchant shipping of an enemy state.

In English history the reign of Elizabeth I (1558–1603) was the golden age of privateering. French privateers were most active in the century following the War of the Spanish Succession (1702–13), and American privateers were far more numerous than naval ships in the War of American Independence (1775–82) and the war of 1812–14. In the American Civil War (1861–5) both sides preferred to arm merchantmen as regular warships than to commission privateers. By the *Hague Convention of 1907 it was agreed that such ships must be listed as warships (see ARMED MERCHANT CRUISER), though the right to arm merchantmen in self-defence is still admitted. See also GUERRE DE COURSE.

PRIZE, the name normally used to describe an enemy vessel captured at sea by a ship of war or a *privateer. The word is also used to describe a *contraband cargo taken from a merchant ship and *condemned in prize by a Court of Admiralty. In its strict and original legal definition, prize in Britain is entirely a right of the Crown, and no man may share in prize except through the gift of the Crown. Most other maritime nations had similar definitions of prize, limiting it by right to the ruling body from whom it issued by gift. With the growth of maritime trade throughout the years and thus the increase in value of prize, nations passed their own prize laws under which the taking and condemnation of prize cargoes was controlled. At the second *Hague Convention in 1907, international rules were adopted to regularize the capture of prize. See also PRIZE MONEY.

A navy agent refusing to pay prize money; aquatint by T. Rowlandson

PRIZE MONEY, the net proceeds from the sale of ships and goods captured in prize and condemned in an Admiralty Court. In Britain, all prize captured at sea is forfeit to the Crown, and known as *Droits of the Crown; all prize taken by shipwreck or from ships driven ashore pertains to the Lord High Admiral, or to the Commissioners for executing his office, and is known as *Droits of Admiralty. The High Court of Admiralty became the legal prize tribunal in 1589, with Vice-Admiralty Courts exercising local jurisdiction wherever they were set up. In 1692, with a view to making service in the British Navy more popular, the Crown waived its right to part of the Droits of the Crown, granting it to the actual captors in a scale of shares laid down by Royal proclamation. By an Act of Queen *Anne in 1708, known as the Cruisers Act, the whole of the Droits of the Crown were allocated to the captors, the value of the prize being divided into eighths, of which three went to the captain, one to the commander-in-chief, one to the officers, one to the warrant officers, and two to the crew. Any unclaimed prize money was allocated to *Greenwich Hospital.

Prize Acts lapse at the end of a war but are normally re-enacted at the start of the next. The last Prize Act in Great Britain came into force on the outbreak of the Second World War but when it lapsed after the end of the war it was announced that this was the last occasion on which prize money would be paid, thus bringing Britain into line with most other maritime countries, which had already abolished it. Each nation had, of course, its own prize law and decided its own method and scale of distribution.

Prize in British naval history was always a considerable incentive to recruitment and large numbers of men were tempted to join the navy for the chance of quick riches from this source. One of the most remarkable instances of prize distribution followed the capture in 1762 of the Spanish treasure ship *Hermione* by the *frigates *Active* and *Favourite*. She was condemned in prize for £519,705, and each of the two captains received £65,000, every lieutenant £13,000, and every seaman in the two ships £485. There were other captures as rich as this, but in most cases the numbers entitled to share in the distribution were considerably greater than the crews of two frigates, and thus the individual shares were proportionally smaller.

PROA (Malayan *prau*), in the Malay language the term for all types of ship or vessel, from *sampan to square-rigged *kapal, but generally looked upon by Westerners as the vessel used by pirates in eastern waters. They carried a very large triangular, usually *lateen, sail and an *outrigger to prevent excessive heel.

PROPELLER, the rotating screw of a steamship by which she is forced through the water. The first mechanical propulsion of a ship had been by means of sternwheels or paddle-wheels (see PADDLE STEAMER), but these were accompanied by considerable disadvantages as, when a ship so fitted rolled in a sea, one paddle would be lifted out of the water while the other was deeply submerged, thus putting a tremendous strain on the engine. It was this fact that led to efforts to design a means of propulsion which would be permanently submerged and thus capable of being driven without putting too varying a strain on the engine. The principle of the Archimedes screw was well enough known, and it was an adaptation of this principle which eventually produced the answer. Four engineers are usually credited with its invention, all at about the same period between 1833 and 1836. They were the Englishman Robert Wilson, the Frenchman Frédéric Sauvage, the Swede John *Ericsson, and another Englishman, Francis Pettit *Smith, whose invention was finally awarded a patent. His invention was eagerly taken up by most of the big steamship lines and by most navies in the world, and the propeller has developed through the years into a remarkably efficient means of transforming a ship's engine power into forward thrust through the water.

The first propellers fitted to ships had only two blades, very thin and long, and closely resembling the propellers fitted to early aircraft. H.M.S. *Warrior*, the world's first *ironclad *battleship, launched in 1860, had a single two-bladed propeller weighing 10 tons, and when it was raised on the occasions when the ship required to use her sails, it needed 600 men on the *falls of the *sheers rigged over the *stern to lift it clear of the water. Nevertheless, this single propeller, at its maximum revolutions of 56 per minute, gave the battleship a speed of 14·3 *knots.

From the original two-bladed propeller, the design of three- and four-bladed propellers proceeded reasonably rapidly and with generally increasing horsepower; and particularly with the development of the original reciprocating engine into the compound and triple-expansion engine, propellers increased in numbers from the single propeller driven by a shaft in the centreline of the ship, first to two, with one on each *quarter, and then, for the largest ships, to four, with two on each quarter, an arrangement which not only brought greater efficiency by providing a cleaner run of water to the propellers, but also gave additional control in steering and turning the ship. The introduction of the *turbine, bringing a great increase in engine revolutions, concentrated the attention of designers towards greater efficiency in the shape and *pitch of the propeller blades. Today, in order to absorb the ever-increasing power needed to propel single-screw super-tankers, five-bladed and six-bladed propellers have been introduced, their size closely approaching the 24-foot diameter of I. K. *Brunel's *Great Eastern*'s four-bladed propeller.

For sailing yachts with auxiliary power, propellers are usually made to fold, to *feather, or to rotate freely when the vessel is under sail, in order to minimize drag as the vessel goes through the water. Each type has its advantages, and it is usually a matter of personal choice as to which type is fitted. See also BANJO, 'UP FUNNEL, DOWN SCREW'.

PROTECTION, the name given to the certificate carried by certain classes of men which rendered them immune from *impressment for the navy in Britain. Those who by law could carry protections were *masters and *mates of merchant ships, seamen in outward bound but not homeward bound merchant ships (but see MEN-IN-LIEU), a proportion of the crews of colliers, men employed by the Customs Office, Salt Office, and Trinity House if laying *buoys, men employed in the Royal dockyards, the crews of *privateers, Thames watermen employed by fire insurance companies, those employed on the Woolwich ferry, and men in particular occupations, such as building *lighthouses, etc. Protections were also given to apprentices under 18 and men over 55, if they could prove their age. Harpooners in the Greenland fishery and fishermen on the east coast during the herring season were also exempt from the press and normally carried protections. In general, a man had to prove his trade, and show that it came in an exempt category, before he could be issued with an official protection.

PROTEST, (1) a formal document drawn up by the *master, first *mate, and a proportion of the crew of a merchant ship at the time of her arrival at a port, and sworn before a notary public, or a consul in a foreign port, that the weather conditions during a voyage were such that if the ship or cargo sustained damage it did not happen through neglect or misconduct on their part. It is a safeguard against the owners of the ship being held accountable for the damage, if any, if the cause of it was stress of wind and weather. One of the conditions of such a protest is that the cargo *hatches must not be removed until a survey has been carried out. **(2)** The method by which a racing yacht may object to a rival on the grounds of a breach of the racing rules. To signify a protest a flag or *burgee is flown from the *shrouds of the yacht immediately after the incident which has occasioned the protest. The grounds of the protest are heard after the race by a committee of the yacht club organizing the race, and can be upheld, if it is proved that a breach of the racing rules occurred, or dismissed if the grounds of the protest are held inadequate.

PROVISO, the old name for a stern *warp. When a ship lay to a single anchor in the stream with her stern held fast to the shore by a warp, she was said to be moored a-proviso.

PROW, a word used, though rarely by sailors, to describe the forward end of a vessel. It was also a term used in the 16th and 17th centuries to denote the fore gundeck of a naval vessel where the bow *chasers were mounted, and later, in the 17th and 18th centuries, as specifically indicating the *beak of a *felucca or a *xebec.

PTOLEMY (Claudius Ptolemaeus) (c. A.D. 90–168) was probably born in Egypt of Greek extraction and worked for most of his life in Alexandria. He was a mathematician and astronomer, wrote about the earlier cartographers, including *Marinus of Tyre, and himself built the very foundations of *cartography, inventing a number of projections whereby an area on the curved surface of the earth could be represented on a flat surface. Of his many works the most famous was his *Geographical Treatise* or *Guide to Geography*, written in eight books, including an atlas of the world as it was then known. The work is usually known simply as *Ptolemy's Geography* or *Geographia* and also includes a list of 8,000 places, the *latitudes and *longitudes of which are given, some from astronomical observations but many taken from earlier maps or extracted from travellers' tales.

Ptolemy's first projection was a simple conic projection (see CARTOGRAPHY, CHARTMAKING), while his second, more sophisticated equal-area projection has curved *meridians as well as

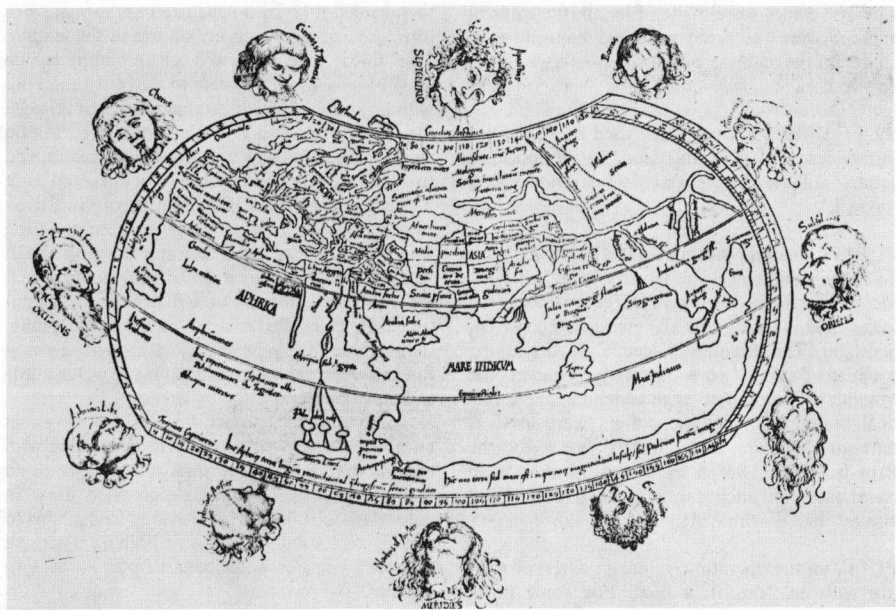

Ptolemy's map of the world

parallels, only the central meridian being a straight line. On this projection Ptolemy drew a map showing the world as contained within 180° of longitude from a *prime meridian through the Canary Islands in the west to Asia in the east. The Mediterranean is shown with some accuracy; the existence of England, Scotland, and Ireland is indicated; while Africa appears as a vast continent continuing across the south of the Indian Ocean and then northwards to join China. The Indian sub-continent is shown and the island of Ceylon, their relative sizes reversed; the Red Sea and the Persian Gulf are fairly accurately depicted.

With the fall of the Roman Empire and the dark ages of cartography, Ptolemy's great work was lost and it was only in 1400 that the Greek manuscript of a copy of *Geographia*, together with the maps and projections, came to light in Constantinople (now Istanbul). The work was translated in Italy into Latin at the beginning of the 15th century and Ptolemy's world maps then formed the basis for the mapping of all the new discoveries of the 15th and 16th centuries, the wide distribution of these world maps being made possible by the development of printing, particularly in Italy and Germany.

A considerable source of error in Ptolemy's maps arose through his acceptance of the measurement of Poseidonius (135–50 B.C.) of the earth's circumference as 18,000 miles instead of the earlier measurement of *Eratosthenes of 25,000 miles, which was a far more accurate

figure. This meant that the length of a degree of *latitude was 50 miles instead of its true length of 60 miles, and as a result most of the maps included in his *Geographia* were distorted. Nevertheless, it is almost impossible to overestimate Ptolemy's influence on world mapping.

PUDDENING, a thick matting made of yarns, *oakum, etc., which was used in places where there was a danger of chafing. Another form of puddening was fastened round the main and foremasts of square-rigged sailing warships directly below the *trusses of the *yards, both to guard against undue chafe and to prevent the yards from falling if the *lifts were shot away in battle. It was made by taking a length of rope twice the circumference of the mast and splicing the two ends together to form a *strop, thus doubling it in thickness. A *thimble was then *seized into each end and the doubled rope was *parcelled and *served to an extent where it was thickest in the middle, tapering to each end. With a *lanyard attached to one thimble it was held to the mast with both thimbles on the fore side of the mast and fixed firmly in position by *reeving the lanyard alternately through the thimbles and drawing the two ends together as tautly as possible. As an extra precaution to prevent it slipping under the weight of the yard if the lifts or slings were shot away, a *garland was passed over it to bind it even more securely to the mast.

In general, puddening is used in all places where undue chafe is likely. In the old days when anchor *cables were made of hemp, the rings of anchors were protected with puddening to stop chafe in the cables. See also BAGGYWRINKLE, PAUNCH.

'PUFF-BALL', a slang name used by seamen in sail to describe a *bonnet laced to the foot of a square sail. It was also sometimes known as a 'save-all'.

PUFFER, a small steam vessel with a capacious hold, built mainly on the River Clyde, Scotland, for the carriage of general cargoes among the lochs and islands of the western coast of Scotland. The engines, placed right aft at the rounded *stern, were normally tandem (or *monkey) *compound engines with a single vertical boiler. Many Clyde puffers were used as harbour *tenders and *liberty boats by the British fleet at *Scapa Flow and other Scottish naval bases and anchorages during both the First and Second World Wars.

PULL, to, the operation, in most navies, of rowing with an *oar in a boat. For some naval reason, boats are not rowed, they are pulled. Perhaps this may have come about because most naval seamen at the oars in a boat are not very much concerned with the finer points of rowing, such as *feathering the oar at the end of a stroke, but are more concerned with getting the blade square into the water and pulling it through with maximum force.

PULPIT, (1) a raised platform in the bows of the old-fashioned oared whaleboat from which the *harpoon was launched by hand. **(2)** A metal tubular frame, U-shaped in plan, at a yacht's stemhead or *bow, carrying the forward ends of the lifelines or guardrails for the safety of hands working on the foredeck. A similar frame mounted above a yacht's *taffrail or *stern and carrying the after ends of the guardrail is colloquially termed a pushpit.

PUMP, an essential piece of mechanism on board ship, used for emptying the *bilges of any water which may have collected in them. Three types of pumps were fitted in the old sailing vessels to clear the bilges. A small hand-pump, similar to those used ashore, was placed near the mainmast, used when there was only very little water in the bilge and a short spell of pumping would clear it. It was a slow and laborious method. Several ships, particularly those of Holland and Germany, additionally used a burr-pump, also known as a bilge-pump, in which a spar of wood about six feet long had a burred end to which a leather was fixed. Two men standing over the pump thrust the spar down into the box in which the bilge-water collected, and six men

then hauled it up by a rope fixed to the spar, thus lifting the water which lay on top of the leather. The third type was the chain-pump, which worked on a similar system to the burr-pump but with an endless motion so that there was no need for men to thrust it down into the bilge-box on each stroke. This was a most efficient pump, and two men working on it could lift a ton of water in 55 seconds. Modern pumps in ships are driven by either steam or electricity, capable of lifting some hundreds of tons of water an hour; most yachts are fitted with a centrifugal pump which for the same amount of effort can lift several times as much water as a plunger-type pump, though several also have a two-stroke hand-pump for use when only a small amount of water needs to be pumped out.

There are, of course, many other types of pump in modern ships used in connection with the internal machinery, such as fuel pumps to feed the boilers, circulating pumps to draw in cold seawater for the *condensers, feed pumps to return condensed steam to the boilers, trimming pumps to transfer water ballast from one tank to another, and so on.

PUNT, (1) a small flat-bottomed craft, built in the form of a floating platform or stage, used originally by seamen and artificers when *caulking a waterline seam, *breaming the side of a ship, or repairing the bottom. **(2)** A small wooden boat, with sharp pointed bows and stern and a very low freeboard, used by wildfowlers in estuaries and local waters for setting-up to ducks or geese, either with a punt-gun mounted in the bows or with hand-guns. It is propelled with small paddles fitted over the hands, the punter lying full length in the punt in order to remain hidden from the quarry. **(3)** A flat-bottomed pleasure boat with square ends and drawing very little water used on rivers and propelled by poling.

PURCHAS, SAMUEL (c. 1575–1626), English priest, was born at Thaxted, Essex, took Holy Orders, and was rector of St. Martin's Church, Ludgate, London. He was a friend of Richard *Hakluyt, whose vast collection of manuscripts, on which he was working up to the time of his death, came into Purchas's hands. Some of this great collection was published by Purchas in five folio volumes in 1626 under the title of *Hakluytus Posthumous, or Purchas his Pilgrimes*, but sadly they lack the perfection of editing which Hakluyt brought to his work. Purchas was an indifferent editor and he mutilated and garbled many of the accounts of voyages of which Hakluyt had collected the details. Some of the accounts were contracted to a degree which defies understanding, and some were accompanied with much foolish editorial comment. Nevertheless, the *Pilgrimes* do contain the first accounts of voyages and travels which cannot be found elsewhere, and as such have an important place in English maritime literature.

PURCHASE, a mechanical device to increase power or force, whether by means of levers, gears, or blocks or pulleys rove with a rope or chain. In its its maritime meaning it is only the last of these which is known as a purchase, a rope rove through one or more blocks by which the pull exerted on the hauling part of the rope is increased accordingly to the number of sheaves in the blocks over which it passes.

Where two or more blocks are involved in the purchase, it is generally known as a * tackle (pronounced taykle), though there are exceptions to this general rule when two double or two treble blocks are used, these being known as two-fold and three-fold purchases respectively. The blocks of a tackle are known as the standing block and moving block, the rope rove through them is known as the fall and is divided into three parts known as the standing, running, and hauling parts. The amount by which the pull on the hauling part is multiplied by the sheaves in the blocks is known as the mechanical * advantage.

The mechanical advantage of a purchase is reckoned by the number of parts of the fall at the moving block, and it follows therefore that any tackle, with one exception, can be rove to advantage or disadvantage according to which block of the tackle is made into the moving block. Where the two blocks concerned each have the same number of sheaves, if the block from which the hauling part comes is made the moving block, the tackle is rove to advantage; where the two blocks concerned have a different number of sheaves,

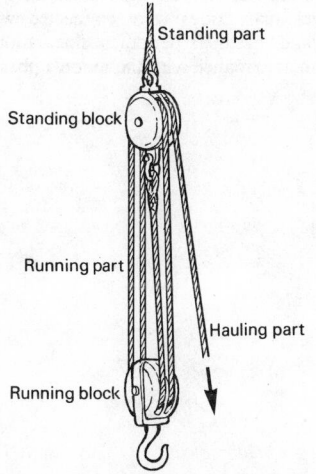

Two-fold purchase rove to disadvantage, mechanical gain 2·26

that which has the greater number should be made the moving block if advantage is to be gained.

There are several combinations of blocks in a tackle, each with a name that indicates its general use or size. Where one single block is used for a straight lift, it is known as a single whip and used where speed of hoisting is required. There is no mechanical advantage as the block does not move. When rove so that the block does move, as for example when hauling taut the backstays of a yacht, it is known as a * runner and the mechanical advantage, ignoring the loss due to friction, is 2, since there are two parts of the fall in the moving block. Double whips are tackles using two single blocks with the standing part of the fall secured to, or near to, the upper block. They are used for hoisting and the mechanical advantage is 2, again ignoring the loss due to friction. This is the one tackle which cannot be rove to advantage as the hauling part must come from the standing block.

The gun tackle also has two single blocks but is not used for hoisting and so cannot be called a double whip. When rove to advantage the mechanical gain is 3; to disadvantage it is 2. A * luff tackle has one double and one single block with the standing part of the fall made fast to the single block. It is used for general lifting or hauling and when rove to advantage gives a mechanical gain, ignoring the friction loss, of 4, and of 3 when rove to disadvantage. A luff tackle using smaller rope is usually known as a * jigger.

Two-fold and three-fold purchases are used only for heavy lifting, such as hoisting boats inboard. When rove to advantage, their theoretical mechanical gains are 5 and 7 respectively, when rove to disadvantage, the gains are 4 and 6, though in each case the loss due to friction of the sheaves is considerable since more sheaves are used. Allowing for average friction these gains are reduced to 4·37 and 3·57 when rove to advantage, and 2·26 and 3·75 when rove to disadvantage.

PURSE NET, a fishing net of which the bottom can be drawn together after shooting to form a purse so that the fish enclosed cannot escape. They are much used in * ring netting when fish congregate in schools or shoals, or are brought together by night by bright lights fitted in the fishing craft.

PURSER, (1) the old name by which the paymaster and officer responsible for provisions and clothing (see SLOPS), in both the British and U.S. Navies, was known. He was normally appointed by warrant, and in the old days before the reforms of the seaman's victuals, received his emolument partly by a small direct salary and partly by a commission on the issue of the daily victualling allowance. This was achieved by calculating the purser's pound (in weight) at 14 ounces while the victuals were drawn from store at a weight of 16 ounces to the pound. His commission, therefore, was the equivalent of $12\frac{1}{2}$ per cent. Many pursers became rich men under this rule, which was a perennial cause of unrest, and sometimes mutiny, in naval ships. (2) The rank of purser is still used in the merchant service and applies to the officer in charge of the financial side of administering a ship's company and, particularly, a ship's passengers.

'PUSSER'S MEDAL', the sailor's name for a food stain on clothing. The purser (usually known as 'pusser') was responsible for issuing all food in a ship according to the daily scale of rations laid down.

PYE, EDMUND ARTHUR (1902–66), British medical practitioner and yachtsman, bought for £25 a 30-ft (9 m) West Country fishing boat, which he and his wife Anne converted for deep sea cruising and renamed *Moonraker*. In 1948 he gave up his London medical practice, and with his wife and another man as crew started a series of lengthy cruises in *Moonraker*. These took the old *cutter to Spain, into the Baltic, across the Atlantic, and through the Panama Canal into the Pacific, and up the west coast to British Columbia; then back to England. Other cruises were northwards to the Baltic again and to Finland, and again across the Atlantic to Brazil and some distance up the River Amazon. After returning from a stormy cruise to Spain in 1966 Pye was taken ill and died in hospital soon after landing in England. He was for some years *commodore of the *Royal Cruising Club and author of *Red Mains'l* (1952), *The Sea is for Sailing* (1957), and *A Sail in a Forest* (1961).

His yacht *Moonraker* is preserved at the Exeter (Devon) National Maritime Museum.

PYTHEAS, Greek navigator and astronomer, lived in the Greek colony of Massilia (Marseilles). He is thought to be a contemporary of Alexander the Great, which would place him in the 4th century B.C. His actual writings have been lost, but there are sufficient quotations from them, particularly by Polybius and Strabo, for it to be certain that he made a long voyage round the western and northern coasts of Europe, during which he visited Britain and made a number of detailed observations. It is also certain that it was from him that the Greeks obtained their first definite information of the existence and extent of these lands.

Pytheas began his voyage from Gades (Cadiz) and proceeded round the coasts of Spain and France until he reached Britain, sailing up the east coast of England to Scotland and, possibly, even farther north as far as the Orkneys and Shetlands, to which he gave the name Thule. After leaving Britain he continued east along the northern European coast probably as far as the estuary of the Elbe, though some accounts state that he reached the Baltic Sea, at that time completely unknown to all Mediterranean geographers. It is, though, unlikely that he penetrated as far east as this, as there was apparently no mention in his account of the Danish peninsula, which he would have to have rounded to reach the eastern sea.

As well as being a navigator and geographer, Pytheas was a distinguished astronomer and was one of the first men who used observations of the sun's *altitude to fix the *latitude of places he visited. His observation of the latitude of Massilia, which he fixed with remarkable accuracy, was accepted by *Ptolemy and was the basis of the Ptolemaic map of the western Mediterranean. He was also the first Greek navigator to discover that *tides were connected with the moon and that their periodical fluctuations took place in accordance with the moon's phases.

Q

Q-SHIP, a small merchant ship, either steam or sailing, fitted with a concealed armament and used by the British Navy during the First World War (1914–18) in home waters and the Mediterranean as a lure for *U-boats. The holds of the vessels were usually filled with timber to provide additional buoyancy in the event of being torpedoed. The armament was concealed behind shutters, the officers and men wore plain clothes, and the ships sailed under the Red (or merchant) Ensign, the White (naval) Ensign being broken out when they revealed their true nature. Their method of carrying the war to the U-boats was to pose as defenceless merchant ships, small enough to tempt a U-boat to the surface to attack her by gunfire instead of wasting a *torpedo on her. When the U-boat closed on the surface and opened fire, the shutters concealing the guns were dropped and fire opened on the U-boat. Apart from a very few noteworthy exceptions, the Q-ship was not a success and in 1917, when the U-boats began their unrestricted warfare, they were withdrawn. The most successful of the Q-ship captains was Captain Gordon Campbell, who was awarded the Victoria Cross for his success in operations in 1916.

Q-ships were again tried at the beginning of the Second World War in spite of their lack of success in the First, though for security reasons they were known as 'freighters'. Six ships were fitted out with concealed armaments and sent out into the Atlantic to roam the Western Approaches, but their lack of success was even more dismal than in 1914–18. None of them even sighted a U-boat and two were sunk by U-boat torpedoes. They were all withdrawn in March 1941.

QUADRANT, from Latin *quadrans*, the fourth part. **(1)** The name given to a variety of nautical astronomical instruments including the *seaman's quadrant, *Davis's quadrant, and *Hadley's quadrant. **(2)** The quarters of the magnetic compass card are also known as quadrants when they are graduated by degrees instead of by *points. Such a compass card has 90° in each quadrant, measured from the north and south points and running to east and west. A compass card thus graduated is known as a quadrantal card. It is a method of graduation of the magnetic compass card which is rapidly becoming obsolete. See COMPASS.

QUADRUPLE EXPANSION ENGINE, see TRIPLE EXPANSION ENGINE.

QUARANTINE, a harbour restriction placed on a ship which has an infectious disease on board or has arrived from a port or country which is notoriously unhealthy. While under quarantine she must fly Q flag in the *International Code of Signals, a square yellow flag usually known as the yellow *jack, and her crew may not land until either the infectious period (a maximum of forty days in the case of plague) has elapsed or she is granted *pratique as free from disease. These quarantine laws originated in a Council of Health held in *Venice in the 14th century.

English quadrant, also known as a back-staff; detail of the tomb of Robert Smith (d. 1697) in Waltham Abbey, Essex

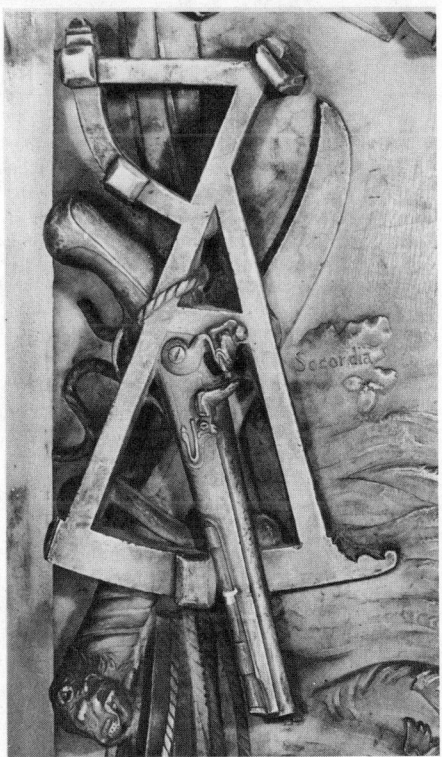

The stern of H.M.S. Asia, *showing quarter galleries; etching by E. W. Cooke, 1829*

QUARTER, the two after parts of the ship, one on each side of the centreline. Strictly, a ship's *port or *starboard quarter is on a bearing 45° from the *stern, but the term is more often rather loosely applied to any point approximately on that bearing. The term is also applied to the direction from which the wind is blowing if it looks like remaining there for some time, e.g., the wind is in the south-west quarter. For illus. see RELATIVE BEARINGS.

QUARTER GALLERY, a small *gallery on each *quarter of a ship, with balustrades in the larger ships, which communicated with the stern gallery. Like the large gallery in the stern, they were used to provide a private walking space for the occupant of the cabin with which they communicated. Also like the stern gallery, they were, in ships such as warships and *East Indiamen, highly decorated with carvings. Galleries and quarter galleries first made an appearance in the late 14th or early 15th century and were still in use in the larger warships in the form of a stern-walk until the second decade of the 20th century.

QUARTER-BILL, a nominal list of officers and men in a warship which gives the action station of every man on board when the ship goes into battle. It was the origin of the naval order to 'beat to quarters', the drummers beating a particular rhythm on their drums to indicate that action was imminent and that men must go to their battle stations. In the British Navy, the rhythm used was that of *'Heart of Oak'. Today, when drums are no longer used on board ship to beat to quarters, the usual order is 'Action Stations', when every man closes up to his station as indicated in the ship's quarter-bill. See also WATCH-BILL.

QUARTER-BLOCKS, two single blocks fitted on the quarters of a *yard of a square-rigged ship, one on each side of the point where the *lifts are secured, through which the topsail and *topgallant *sheets, and topsail and topgallant clewlines, are rove. Quarter-blocks on the main yard take the topsail sheets and clewlines, those on the topsail yard take the topgallant sheets and clewlines. (For illus. see YARD.) On board yachts, blocks on the deck at the quarters, on each side of the *stern, through which the main *sheets are rove are also known as quarter-blocks.

QUARTER-CLOTHS, strips of canvas, normally painted red, which were fixed on the outboard side of the quarter-*nettings, extending from the *quarter galleries to the gangways, in sailing warships of most navies. Their purpose was to protect the *hammocks, stowed by day in the nettings, from seas breaking aboard.

QUARTERDECK, that part of the upper deck of a ship which is abaft the mainmast, or approximately where the mainmast would be in the case of those ships without one. In medieval British warships, the religious shrine was set up at the break of the quarterdeck and was saluted by every man taking off his hat or cap as he passed it. This led to the habit in British warships of saluting on every occasion of entering the quarterdeck, a tradition which is still in existence in British ships of war.

In sailing ships it is the part of the ship from which she was commanded by the captain or *master, or by the officer of the watch, as there is no *bridge as a command post in a sailing ship. It was also traditionally the part of the ship where the captain used to walk, usually on the *starboard side, when he came on deck to take the air or oversee the conduct of the ship, and also from which the navigator took his *sights when *fixing the vessel's position. It was the custom in most ships that only officers might use the quarterdeck, ratings being allowed there only when detailed for specific duties. The *boatswain, carpenter, and other warrant officers or seamen in sailing vessels were called to the quarterdeck to receive orders, announcements, etc.

It is still, in most ships, that part of the deck where the officers take their walks and recreation, the seamen taking theirs on the *forecastle deck and *waist. For illus. see SHIP.

QUARTER-GUNNER, a petty officer in the days of sailing navies whose duty it was to assist the gunner of the ship in keeping the guns and their carriages in proper order, scaling the barrels when necessary, filling the cartridges with powder, etc. Quarter-gunners were appointed in each ship at the rate of one for every four guns.

QUARTERMASTER, originally a petty officer appointed to assist the *master of a ship and his *mates in such duties as stowing the hold, coiling the cables, etc., but now a term more generally applied to the senior helmsman who takes over when a ship is entering or leaving harbour. He is also concerned with the upkeep and use of much of the navigational equipment, such as *sounding machines, patent *log, *lead and lines, etc.

QUATUOR MARIA, an old term for the four British seas, those which surround Great Britain. The term dates from the time of Mary I (1553–8) when there was trouble with France over the salute demanded by English ships in the British seas. The four seas are now known as the North Sea, English Channel, Irish Sea, and the Atlantic Ocean bordering the Scottish west coast. Quatuor was the Tudor way of spelling quattuor, which is the better Latin.

QUAY, a projection, usually constructed of stone, along the boundaries of a harbour to provide accommodation for ships to lie alongside for the loading or unloading of cargo, embarkation and disembarkation of passengers, etc. When a quay is built out from the harbour boundary into the water, it is usually called a *mole. See also WHARF.

QUEBEC, a province of Canada and a major seaport which stands some 300 miles up the St. Lawrence River on the north bank. The first white man to penetrate so far up the St. Lawrence was the French explorer Jacques *Cartier in 1535, who found there the Indian village of Stadacona. Quebec itself was founded in 1608 by Samuel de *Champlain. It was captured by British forces commanded by Sir David Kirke in 1629 but returned to France in 1632 by the treaty of St. Germain-en-Laye. Further British attempts to capture the city were made by Sir William *Phips in 1690, an attempt defeated by the French governor, Frontenac, and by Admiral Sir Hovenden Walker in 1711, whose fleet was wrecked in the Gulf of St. Lawrence on its way up to the city.

It was successfully attacked and captured in 1759 by an amphibious British force commanded by Vice Admiral Charles *Saunders and Major-General James Wolfe. The expedition against Quebec was ordered in January 1759 and sailed from England on 16 February. The fleet and transports anchored off the Isle of Orleans, in the St. Lawrence River on 26 June, and next day the troops were landed at various places. All attacks on the city were repulsed and the situation seemed incapable of solution until, in a reconnaissance above the city, Wolfe noticed a possible path up the cliffs in the Anse de Foulon. On the night of 12 September, with about 5,000 men, Wolfe dropped down the river in the boats of the fleet and landed at the foot of the Anse. In silence the troops scaled the cliff and seamen of the fleet hauled up guns from the ships. By the morning of the 13th the British troops were formed up on the Plains of Abraham, where they were met by Lieutenant-General the Marquis de Montcalm, with about 10,000 men. After a very short engagement the French retreated in disorder and fell back on Quebec. Both Wolfe and Montcalm were killed. The French morale was poor and their troops became completely disorganized. On the 17th, while British bombarding batteries were being erected and the ships were taking up positions to cover them, the Governor of the city offered to surrender, and the articles of capitulation were signed in the morning of the 18th.

Brigadier-General George Townshend, who succeeded Wolfe in command of the troops on the latter's death, wrote in his dispatch, 'I should not do justice to the Admirals and the Naval Service if I neglected this occasion of acknowledging how much we are indebted for our success to the constant assistance and support received from them, and the perfect harmony and correspondence which has prevailed throughout all our operations in the uncommon difficulties which the nature of this country, in particular, presents to military operations of a great extent, and which no army can itself solely supply: the immense labour in artillery, stores and provisions; the long watchings and attendance in boats; the drawing up of our artillery by the seamen, even in the heat of action. It is my duty, short as my command has been, to acknowledge for that time how great a share the Navy has had in this successful campaign.'

QUEEN ANNE'S FREE GIFT, a sum of money which was granted annually to surgeons in the British Navy to augment their earnings. Surgeons in those days were paid at the rate of twopence per man per month for all men carried on board, a rate which led to only the most indifferent surgeons volunteering for service in the navy. This additional award was designed to attract a more competent type of man and to improve the rate of recruitment.

QUEEN ELIZABETH, H.M.S., the Royal Navy's only ship of the name, was a *battleship built at Portsmouth and launched in 1913. She was present at the *Dardanelles operations in 1915 and in 1917–18 was the *flagship of Admiral Sir David *Beatty, commander-in-chief of the *Grand Fleet. She was the ship in which the formal instrument of internment of the German *High Seas Fleet was signed in November 1918. After early service in the Second World War she was refitted and commissioned as flagship of the commander-in-chief of the Mediterranean Fleet, Sir Andrew *Cunningham. She was engaged in the operations off Crete in May 1941 and during the evacuation of the island, and on 19 December of that year was seriously damaged while in harbour at Alexandria by an Italian 'human torpedo' (see CHARIOT). After long repairs she was in action in the Pacific in 1945, and in 1946 was reduced to reserve at Portsmouth, being sold for breaking up in 1948.

QUEEN ELIZABETH, R.M.S., launched in September 1938 as a companion transatlantic *liner to the *Queen Mary, with a gross tonnage of 82,998, had not completed fitting out at John Brown's yard on the Clyde when the Second World War broke out. In February 1940 she steamed to New York and in November of that year to Singapore for fitting out as a *troopship with a carrying capacity of 8,200 troops. Between April 1941 and April 1943, based on Sydney, N.S.W., she was continuously employed troop-carrying on a world-wide scale. She then began a career lasting until the end of the war as a transatlantic troop ferry.

After the war she was fitted out for her original purpose and sailed from Southampton for New York on her first commercial voyage on 16 October 1946. She was finally withdrawn from service in 1969 and was sold to American speculators who moored her at Port Everglades, Florida, as a tourist attraction and convention centre. Difficulties arose, however, in respect of fire safety arrangements which could not be resolved and she was again sold for £1,300,000 to Mr. C. Y. Tung of Hong Kong, sailing in February 1971 for that port where she was intended to become the Seawise University. Defects developed on passage and, after refitting, the *Queen Elizabeth* reached Hong Kong on 7 January 1972, only to catch fire as a result of sabotage and finally to sink in the harbour.

QUEEN MARY, R.M.S., was the *Cunard Company's transatlantic *liner which, with the same company's *Queen Elizabeth, may be said to have constituted the ultimate in size, speed, and luxury of such vessels before the volume of shipborne transatlantic passenger traffic dwindled in the face of the competition of air travel.

The 81,237-ton *Queen Mary* was launched on 26 September 1934 and sailed on her maiden transatlantic voyage on 1 June 1936. In August 1938, having alternated for two years with the French Line's S.S. *Normandie* as holder of the *'Blue Riband' for the fastest round trip across the Atlantic, she emerged as the undisputed holder with average speeds of 30·99 knots westbound and 31·69 eastbound, a record which she was to retain until losing it after the Second World War to the U.S. liner *United States.*

At the outbreak of the Second World War, the *Queen Mary* was in New York harbour whence she sailed in March 1940 to Sydney, N.S.W., for conversion to a troopship. Based on Sydney, she operated world-wide until April 1943 with a troop-carrying capacity of some 8,200 troops. From this time onwards she operated continuously as a ferry across the Atlantic with her capacity increased to over 15,000 troops during the summer months and 12,000–13,000 in winter. By the end of the war she and the *Queen Elizabeth* had between them transported 320,000 out of the 865,000 American troops brought to the United Kingdom across the Western Ocean. On three occasions she had

The Cunard liner Queen Mary *of 81,237 tons*

Winston *Churchill and the British Chiefs of Staff as passengers.

The *Queen Mary* reverted to her passenger liner role after the war, but was finally withdrawn and sold in 1967 for £1,500,000 to an American company which has berthed her at Long Beach, California, as a tourist museum and hotel.

QUEST, the ship purchased by Sir Ernest *Shackleton for the Shackleton–Rowett Antarctic expedition of 1920–1. She was originally the 204-ton Norwegian *whaler *Foca I* and was converted and strengthened for use in Antarctic and Arctic waters. She was used in 1928 in the search for General Nobile and the crew of the Italian airship *Italia* after their attempt to fly over the North pole had failed, and she was in Arctic waters again in 1930–1 when she was chartered by the British Arctic Air Route expedition to Greenland. She was finally lost in the ice off Labrador on 5 May 1962.

QUIBERON BAY, a rock-strewn bay on the west coast of France in the department of Morbihan, about 100 miles south-east of Brest, and the scene of a naval battle of the Seven Years War (1756–63) which was fought on 20 November 1759 between a British fleet under the command of Admiral Sir Edward *Hawke and a French fleet commanded by Admiral the Comte de *Conflans, which had been blockaded in Brest by the British. For some time past a British inshore *squadron under Captain Robert *Duff had been watching Morbihan, where French troop transports were lying for a planned invasion of Ireland. A gale on 9 November drove Hawke and his fleet to Torbay, and on the 19th Conflans sailed from Brest to sweep Duff's ships aside and link up with the transports. Warned of his danger, Duff made sail and was chased by Conflans; he had almost been brought to action when Hawke's fleet appeared over the horizon on its return to the Brest blockade. Conflans's fleet was sighted by Hawke at 8.30 a.m. on the 20th, and Duff's squadron joined up with the main body of the British fleet at 11.00 a.m.

In spite of a westerly gale and the shortness of daylight, the British fleet under all sail chased the French into the dangerous and rock-strewn Quiberon Bay. The master of Hawke's flagship ventured to call the admiral's attention to the danger he was running, but the latter replied, 'You have done your duty in pointing out to me the danger; now lay me alongside the enemy's flagship.' The action began at 2.30 p.m., and lasted until dark, the result being a complete

The battle of Quiberon Bay; detail from the oil painting by R. Paton, 1760

victory for the British. Out of twenty-one French *ships of the line and four *frigates, six were taken, burnt, or wrecked, eleven escaped up the River Vilaine, and eight up the River Charente; of those that escaped, however, few were ever fit for service again, most of them breaking their backs on the bars across the mouths of the rivers. The number of British action casualties was remarkably small; but the *Resolution* and the *Essex* were both wrecked during the stormy weather on the following day.

QUICK FLASHING LIGHT, a navigational light displayed by a *lighthouse or *lightship in which quick flashes of less than one second duration are shown. See CHARACTERISTICS.

QUICKWORK, the planking of a ship's *bulwarks between the *ports in a sailing man-of-war, and also that part of the inner upperworks above the *covering board in a wooden ship. See also SPIRKETTING, with which quickwork is largely synonymous.

QUILTING, the name given to *paunch matting secured to the outer planking of a wooden-hulled vessel to protect it against drift ice.

QUINTANT, a reflecting navigational instrument, on the same general lines as a *quadrant or *sextant, and used specifically for making *lunar observations. Its arc subtended a fifth of a circle, or 72°, hence its name, and because of its reflecting property was able to measure angles of up to 144°.

QUIROS, PEDRO FERNANDEZ DE (1565–1615), Spanish navigator and explorer, was born in Evora, Portugal, but became Spanish by nationality when the two crowns were united in 1580 under Philip II. He had probably been serving for several years at sea when he emigrated to Peru where, in 1595, he was appointed chief pilot, or senior navigator, in the ship of Alvaro de *Mendaña, who was setting out with an expedition to colonize the Solomon Islands which he had discovered in the south-west Pacific Ocean thirty years earlier.

Mendaña failed to find his islands again and his expedition culminated at Santa Cruz Island, north of the New Hebrides group, where he died. His ships by then were in poor condition but Quiros navigated them to Manila in the Philippine Islands, discovering Ponape, in the Caroline Islands, on the way. By this time he had conceived his life-long ambition to discover and colonize for the Christian faith the great southern continent, or *Terra Australis, then still believed to exist.

It was not until the end of 1605 however that he was able to set out with two ships and a *launch from Callao, Peru, whence he steered west-south-west, with the intention of holding that course until reaching 30° S. *latitude. On reaching 26° S. however, and against the remonstrations of his second-in-command, Luis Vaez de *Torres, Quiros seemed to lose his nerve and altered course to west-north-west, thus losing the chance of discovering New Zealand, which he would have been bound to find had he continued as originally planned. Passing through the Tuamotus, and discovering the Duff group of the Santa Cruz Islands, the expedition, at the end of April 1606, then steered south to discover the New Hebrides group of islands, the largest of which Quiros believed to be continental, and a part of Terra Australis Incognita. He named it Australia del Espiritu Santo, and proposed to found the city of New Jerusalem there.

When the expedition sailed again to continue southwards to explore the supposed new continent, the crew of Quiros's ship mutinied and insisted on returning to Peru. The other two vessels, under Torres, continued the voyage to the south and, after passing through the strait between New Guinea and Australia, which was named after Torres, turned north and reached Manila via the Moluccas. Quiros, still determined to discover and colonize Terra Australis Incognita, spent the last years of his life seeking support for another voyage, only to die just when approval and the promise of ships and money for it had been secured.

QUOIN, a wedge used to elevate a ship's cannon in the days of the sailing navies in order to obtain a greater range. They were also used to separate casks of wine, spirits, or oil when stowed on board so that their *bilges should not rub against each other or get stove in during rough weather.

QUOTA ACTS, two Acts passed in the British Parliament in March 1795, under the stress of the Revolutionary War against France (1793–1801), to provide seamen for the Royal Navy. Under these Acts each county and borough was compelled to provide a quota of men for service in the navy, e.g., Devon 393 men; Dartmouth 394 men, etc. Since magistrates could seldom find sufficient volunteers to fill the quota, tramps, vagabonds, men who might be a burden on the parish, and petty criminals were drafted, being known in the navy as Billy Pitt's Men (after the Prime Minister, William Pitt the Younger, whose administration it was that introduced and passed the Acts), or *Lord Mayor's Men. The intake of men under these two Acts were largely responsible for the great naval mutinies of 1797, at *Spithead and the *Nore, and those brought into the navy under them were heartily despised by the professional seamen in the fleet.

All men drafted into the navy under the quota were entitled to the *bounty payable to attract volunteers, which at times of great stress and shortage of men, as when the Quota Acts were passed, could amount to as much as £70. Edward *Brenton, in his *Naval History of Great Britain* (1823), wrote: 'The seamen who voluntarily enlisted in 1793, and fought some of the most glorious of our battles, received the comparatively small bounty of £5. These brave fellows saw men, totally ignorant of the profession, the very refuse and outcasts of society, fleeing from justice and the vengeance of the law, come on board with bounty to the amount of £70. One of these objects, on coming on board a ship of war with £70 bounty, was seized by a boatswain's mate who, holding him up with one hand by the waistband of his trousers, humorously exclaimed, "Here's a fellow who cost a guinea a pound."'

R

R.M.S., the prefix, short for Royal Mail Ship, placed before the name of a British merchant ship with a licence to carry the Royal Mails. It was the granting of mail licences to commercial shipowners during the 19th century which gave so great a fillip to British shipbuilding and made possible the formation of the big steamship lines, *Cunard, *P & O, etc. Until that time the oversea mails had been carried in sailing *packets owned and operated by the Post Office, but with the introduction of steam propulsion it proved too great a financial burden on the Post Office to build new steamships, and thus the carriage of the mails was farmed out to commercial shipowners. Only the fastest ships, which were normally passenger *liners, received the licence and thus the right to use the prefix R.M.S.

R.N.R., Royal Naval Reserve, originally a volunteer force of officers and men of the merchant service prepared to serve in the Royal Navy during times of war or emergency. Since 1956 the R.N.R. has been reorganized to include all naval reserves, not only those raised from the merchant service. All maritime nations raise a force of naval reserves for service in their navies in time of war or emergency. See also HUNGRY HUNDRED, THE.

R.N.V.R., Royal Naval Volunteer Reserve, a volunteer force of officers and men raised for service, in time of war or emergency, in the Royal Navy. It differed from the *R.N.R. in that its members were not recruited from the merchant service. In 1956 the R.N.V.R. was absorbed into the R.N.R. to form a single reserve force.

RABBET, from the word rebate, an incision in a piece of timber to receive the ends or sides of planks which are to be secured to it. Thus the *keel of a wooden ship is rabbeted to receive the sides of the *garboard *strakes and the *stem and *sternpost similarly rabbeted to take the ends of the side strakes. The word is also used as a verb; a strake is rabbeted into a keel or stem and sternpost.

RACE, (1) the name generally used to describe strong and confused currents produced by the narrowness of channels, an uneven bottom producing *overfalls, or the crossing of two tides. **(2)** The contest of skill and seamanship when yachts take part in a race. See YACHTING.

RACE, to, the action of a ship's *propeller when the ship *pitches to an extent that the propeller is occasionally lifted out of the water. The lack of resistance from the water will cause the engine, and thus the propeller, to race, with a consequent strain on the engine.

RACEHORSE, H.M.S., a *bomb *ketch of 385 tons, was originally the French *privateer *Marquis de Vaudreuil*, which was captured during the Seven Years War (1756–63). In 1773, together with H.M.S. *Carcass*, she was fitted out for Arctic exploration in another search for the *North-East passage into the Pacific Ocean. The two ships, under the command of Captain Constantine *Phipps, sailed from the *Nore in June 1773, Horatio *Nelson, as a *midshipman, being appointed to the *Carcass*. The two ships reached Spitsbergen, but were iced in at the end of July. A fortunate change in the weather gave them the opportunity to break clear during August, when they returned to England.

During the War of American Independence (1775–82) the *Racehorse* was captured by the American ship *Andrea Doria* and taken into Delaware Bay, where she was later destroyed by the Royal Navy during an attack on 15 November 1777.

RACK, to, the operation of holding two ropes together temporarily with *marline or other small stuff to bind them firmly and prevent rendering or slipping. This is done by taking the marline under and over each rope alternately and crossing it between them two or three times, much in the fashion of a series of figures of eight. It is often used to prevent a *tackle slipping while the hauling part is being secured if the strain on it is so great that the tackle cannot be held with the hands without overrunning. If a more permanent junction of two ropes is required, this is done by passing a racking *seizing round them, as above but with more turns of the marline and the ends of it secured by tucking back under the turns.

RADAR, an abbreviation of 'RAdio Direction And Range', a method of detecting objects by sending out pulses of radio waves; if these strike anything they are reflected back and the time taken for these 'echoes' to return is measured in a cathode ray tube. As the speed of radio waves is known, this time can be automatically translated into the distance of the object. Direction is given by the direction in which the transmitting aerial points at the time. The information is presented to navigators in plan form on the face of the cathode ray tube. As the transmitting aerial revolves to 'scan' all round a ship, so a 'trace' revolves in exact synchronism with it on the fluorescent face of the tube, and each echo arriving back from an object brightens the trace at a distance from the centre of the tube corresponding to the distance of the object. Thus a complete picture of all surrounding radio-reflective objects is painted on the screen. The range is conditioned by the height of the aerial, but is seldom less than 25 miles on modern vessels.

The idea of radio detection is almost as old as radio, the first experiments being made by Herr Hulsmeyer of Dusseldorf in 1903. In 1922 Marconi himself suggested the idea, but it was not until the decade 1930–40 that serious development work was started in Britain, Germany, and France. Ancestors of modern radar aerials were fitted to the British * battle-cruiser *Repulse* and the German * pocket-battleship * *Admiral Graf Spee* in 1936, but both proved inaccurate, with a very short range, and cumbersome. Shortly afterwards the French transatlantic * liner *Normandie* was fitted, but again the maximum range, five miles, proved too short to be useful.

The breakthrough for shipborne radar occurred in 1940 with the British invention of the magnetron to produce very short wavelengths of under 10 centimetres; by 1943, 1·9 centimetre wavelength sets were capable of detecting * U-boats' * periscopes during the Second World War. By this time warships were using radar for shadowing an enemy and providing ranges for gunnery. Probably the first time gunnery radar was used in action was during the night of 26–27 May 1941 by the German * battleship * *Bismarck* against British * destroyer attacks.

After the war radar sets were installed in merchant ships as aids to navigation and for the prevention of collision in thick weather, becoming standard equipment shortly after 1950. At first it seemed that they would enable ships to travel at normal speeds through fog, but a series of what were termed 'radar-assisted' collisions occurred, which reduced the permissible speed in fog to below that of pre-radar days. This was because radar can detect other ships but cannot indicate on the cathode ray tube their * course or speed. This can only be calculated by plotting, and if the ship being plotted is altering course at the time, plotting will not give the correct answer, nor will it ever give a prediction of future courses. The most notorious 'radar-assisted' collision was that between the liners *Andrea Doria* and *Stockholm* off New York in July 1956. However it is probable that the term is misconceived as it is not radar but its interpretation or the action based on it that is always at fault. It has been argued with force that it is the use of radar in the context of collision regulations framed for the different capabilities of the human eye which is the true cause of these collisions. at sea.

In its earliest days, radar in Britain was known as RDF, the initial letters of radio direction finding, but the name was changed early in the Second World War to avoid confusion with H/F D/F, high frequency direction finding, a completely different process in which a radio bearing is taken of a wireless signal made on high frequency. See RADIO DIRECTION FINDER.

RADAR REFLECTOR, a metal plate or similar object fitted to buoys or other * sea-marks to reflect radar waves and give a positive identification on the cathode ray tube.

RADDLE, the name given to describe small stuff (* marline, * codline, etc.) interwoven to make flat * gaskets, or * gripes, for securing boats when hoisted on the * davits of a vessel.

RADFORD, ARTHUR WILLIAM (1896–1973), American admiral, was a specialist in naval aviation and was particularly known for the skill with which he directed the training of naval aviators before and during the Second World War. He became a naval pilot in November 1920 and served in all types of aviation duty, including the command of carrier air squadrons, executive officer and commanding officer of * aircraft carriers, commander of divisions of aircraft carriers in the Pacific operations of the Second World War, and finally commander-in-chief of the U.S. Pacific Fleet at the time of the Korean War (1950–2) in which naval aviation played the chief maritime part. He retired in August 1957 after four years as chairman of the Joint Chiefs of Staff in Washington, the first naval officer to serve as chairman.

Radford was made responsible for naval aviation training on 1 December 1941, a few days before the Japanese attack on * Pearl Harbor, and in addition to his other important duties he continued to direct the flight training throughout the war. He was especially successful in the training of night fighter pilots, but the high degree of skill and expertise achieved by American naval pilots and observers in all spheres of naval air warfare as the Pacific war progressed was in very large part entirely due to Radford's superb methods of training.

RADIO BEACON, a land-based radio station which transmits medium frequency signals, by means of which the navigator in a ship fitted with a *radio direction finder can obtain a radio bearing to give him a position line on his *chart. The necessary details relating to radio beacons can be found in the *List of Radio Signals*, a periodical publication issued by the British Admiralty and in some nautical almanacs. Radio beacons provide a radio aid to a navigator which is particularly valuable to a mariner making a *landfall, when navigating coastwise in thick weather, or when *landmarks or *sea-marks are not available. They are additional to, and in no way part of, hyperbolic systems of *navigation.

RADIO DIRECTION FINDER, a navigational instrument by which a *bearing of a radio beacon can be obtained and plotted on a chart. A wireless aerial in the form of a loop is directional, and if it is turned on its axis, there are two points, 180° apart, where the strength of the signal loses volume and fades away. These points are known navigationally as nulls, and they occur when the loop is trained at right angles to the transmitting station. The correct bearing is therefore at right angles to the plane of the loop when the null occurs.

Radio beacons transmit signals regularly on fixed frequencies, varying from 250–420 kHz, and each can be recognized by its frequency and type of signal. The signal is transmitted once every three or six minutes, and as beacons are frequently grouped so that a vessel can often be within the operating range of two or more beacons at the same time, a *fix by two or more position lines can be obtained. The strength of beacons varies considerably, but most of them have effective ranges of up to between 15 and 200 miles.

Bearings taken at or around sunrise and sunset are liable to distortion, and those which cross land, or cross the coast at a narrow angle, can give readings some degrees in error. A wise navigator, when taking a bearing by radio direction finder, avoids if he can the beacons which entail the signal crossing the land, particularly if the ground is high.

The first experiments in radio direction finding were conducted during the first decade of the 20th century; the first ship to be fitted with a radio receiver designed to take bearings was the Cunard liner *Mauretania* in 1911. See NAVIGATION.

RAE, JOHN (1813–93), British Arctic explorer, was a surgeon in the Hudson's Bay Company and in 1846 made a boat voyage to Repulse Bay, surveying 700 miles of unknown coastline between the surveys previously carried out by William *Parry and John *Ross. In 1848 he joined the expedition under Sir John Richardson which went out in search of Sir John *Franklin, and in 1851 made another Arctic journey to explore the coastline south of Victoria Land, for which he received the Founders Gold Medal of the Royal Geographical Society. He was back again in the Arctic in 1853 on a further surveying journey, and during the course of it obtained the first authentic information of the fate of Franklin, for which he received the £10,000 reward offered by the British Admiralty. Later journeys were made by him in Greenland and Iceland on surveys for routes for telegraph lines.

RAEDER, ERICH (1876–1960), German admiral, was the son of a teacher at Wandsbeck, Hamburg. Until 1914, Raeder had a varied career, with unusual emphasis on historical study, at the German Admiralty and at the Naval Academy at Kiel. He also learned Russian. At the outbreak of the First World War (1914–18) he was chief of staff to Admiral *Hipper, then flag officer commanding the Scouting Forces of the *High Seas Fleet. He remained in this post until the autumn of 1917, taking part in the battles of the *Dogger Bank and *Jutland. On 14 October 1918 he became chief of the Central Department of the Admiralty. When the first steps were taken to refound the Navy under the extremely stringent disarmament clauses of the Treaty of Versailles, Raeder was appointed to the Historical Section of the Admiralty and was responsible for the first two volumes of the official naval history of the First World War, dealing with *cruiser operations on the high seas.

Under the Weimar Republic Raeder rose rapidly in the service but was sometimes criticized for his pro-monarchist leanings. However, he avoided the fate of several senior politicians and officers, who were removed from office because of their attitude, and in October 1928 he was appointed commander-in-chief of the navy. By the time Hitler came to power, preparations had already been made to violate the disarmament clauses of the Treaty of Versailles and this process was begun, at first clandestinely, and then openly after 16 March 1935. Raeder realized that the new German Navy must eventually be prepared to take on the navy of Britain, and for this purpose he drew up his famous 'Z-plan' which provided for the construction by 1944–5 of six *battleships of 56,000 tons, four smaller battleships of between 31,000 and 42,000 tons, three *battle-cruisers of 31,000 tons, and two *aircraft carriers, as well as cruisers, *destroyers, and *submarines.

When the Second World War broke out, long before the date Raeder had anticipated, he found himself fighting a very different war, with only 4 *capital ships instead of 13, and with only 57 out of a planned grand total of 267 *U-boats, although it was certain that it would be upon them that the main brunt of the naval war would fall. To cope with this paucity of U-boats, Raeder advocated the use of the German Army to redress Germany's unfavourable position at sea. It was thus due largely to his requirements that the army was used to seize and occupy Norway and the Atlantic coast of France in 1940 in order to make the passage of the U-boats to the open Atlantic so much shorter and easier. Raeder considered the proposed invasion of Britain in 1940, which was given the code name of Operation Sealion, impracticable in view of the power of the British Navy, and after it had been postponed he urged military offensives in the Mediterranean against Gibraltar, Malta, and Suez, as well as, if possible, against the Canaries, the Azores, the Cape Verde Islands, Dakar, and Iceland. Thanks to the land campaign of General Rommel, Germany came within measurable distance of success as far as Suez was concerned, but shortly after the battle of Alamein and the North African landings towards the close of 1942, resulting in the loss of all the African gains, Raeder resigned his command. His resignation followed a violent attack by Hitler on the handling of the German surface ships, occasioned by the action of 31 December 1942 when a surface attack by the *pocket-battleship *Lützow* and the heavy cruiser *Admiral Hipper* on a British *convoy to North Russia was beaten off by a force of British destroyers.

Raeder was succeeded as commander-in-chief by Admiral Carl *Dönitz, who had commanded and planned all U-boat operations since the start of the war. After Germany's surrender Raeder was put on trial with the other major Nazi war criminals at Nuremberg and was sentenced to life imprisonment, but was released in 1955.

RAFFEE, another name for the sail in a square-rigged ship known as a *moonraker, set only in light weather. It comes within the general classification of all such sails as *kites.

RAFT, (1) a flat, floating framework of spars, planks, or other timber formerly used to carry goods or cargo from the shore to a ship lying off for loading on board. Similarly a temporary platform made on board as a substitute for a boat in cases where a ship was wrecked or otherwise totally disabled, being used for life-saving purposes. **(2)** Lumber, cut inland and floated down a river to the sea or an estuary, lashed together, is also known as a raft. **(3)** RAFT-PORT, a square *port cut through the *stern of *mast and timber ships under the *counter so that timber and plank could be received on board as cargo, the length of the timber making it impossible for it to be received on board in any other way. See also LIFERAFT.

RAKE, the angle, in relation to the perpendicular, of a ship's masts and funnels, which can be raked forward or aft. It is a word also sometimes used to describe the degree of overhang of her bow and stern.

RAKE, to, the operation of manoeuvring a warship so that she could fire her broadside guns down the length of an adversary, particularly during the days of sailing navies when a ship's guns were ranged to fire on the broadside only. Wooden *ships of the line were built immensely strong on their sides, with oak or teak planking to a thickness of 15 to 18 inches, and their weakest point was at the stern with its wide galleries and windows. If a warship could so manoeuvre as to cross the stern of an enemy at right angles, she could fire her guns through the stern, creating immense damage and slaughter, with virtually no enemy guns to fire back at her. Almost equally advantageous was to cross her bows at right angles, as this part of the ship of the line was also a weak point defensively. See also CROSS THE T, TO.

RALEIGH or **RALEGH** (almost certainly pronounced Rawley in Elizabethan days), Sir WALTER (*c*. 1552–1618), English adventurer and explorer, was born near Budleigh Salterton, Devon. After a brief education at Oriel College, Oxford, he went as a soldier to fight with the French Huguenots and was present at the battle of Jarnac (13 March 1569) and was also probably in Paris during the massacre of St. Bartholomew three years later.

Raleigh's half-brother was Sir Humphrey *Gilbert, who in 1578 obtained a patent from Queen Elizabeth I to 'discover and take possession of any remote, barbarous and heathen lands not possessed by any Christian prince or people'. This was the type of adventure which had long attracted the gentlemen of Devon, and Raleigh accompanied his half-brother and embarked on what developed into a piratical expedition against the Spaniards. Raleigh commanded the *Falcon* in the expedition, but it met with no success, being driven back after an engagement in the Atlantic with Spanish warships in which one of the expedition's ships was sunk. A second expedition the following year was equally disastrous. Raleigh was forced to look elsewhere for his livelihood and attached himself to the Court in London, obtaining employment as captain of a company of soldiers sent to Ireland to suppress the rebellion in Munster of the Desmonds. He played a significant, if somewhat unsavoury, part in the ruthless defeat of the rebels, resorting to massacre and assassination as a means of achieving the end.

He returned to England at the end of 1581, and immediately became a favourite of Queen

Elizabeth, who showered honours and rewards upon him. It is possible that he did lay his cloak over a puddle that the Queen might walk dry-shod over it, and equally possible that he did scribble a verse with a diamond on a pane of glass where he was sure the Queen would see it. These would be actions typical of Raleigh at this period of his life, but it is more probable that his tall and handsome presence was a more powerful reason for the Queen's favouritism. He grew exceedingly rich with the grants and monopolies received from the Queen, and there can be little doubt that he extorted the last penny out of all of them. Among his other grants from the Queen was 40,000 Irish acres of the land forfeited by the Desmonds after the rebellion; here he introduced the potato as a suitable crop, and attempted the cultivation of tobacco.

Sir Humphrey Gilbert's patent was due to run out in 1584, and in 1583 Raleigh, with much of his own money and with the help of some of the London merchants, financed him for the voyage in which he discovered Newfoundland and in which he lost his life. When the patent expired, Raleigh was able to get it renewed in his own favour, and used it to start a series of expeditions which in theory were designed to settle colonists in the new land of Virginia but in practice were an attempt to discover gold and silver mines. These expeditions were all unsuccessful and Raleigh claimed to have lost as much as £40,000 through them.

During 1588, the year of the Spanish *Armada, Raleigh was appointed vice admiral of Devon, a purely legal and administrative post, and took no part in the great campaign. His star at Court was now beginning to set with the rise of that of the Earl of Essex (see DEVEREUX, R.) as the Queen's prime favourite. In 1589 he took part in an expedition to the coast of Portugal to foster a revolt against Philip II of Spain, which failed miserably. In 1591 the Queen forbade him to accompany the Azores voyage against the Spanish treasure *flota, and his place was taken by his cousin, Sir Richard *Grenville, who perished gloriously in the last fight of the *Revenge. During the following year he started off on a similar expedition but was recalled by the Queen on the discovery that he had seduced Elizabeth Throgmorton, one of her maids of honour. He was thrown into the Tower of London, but was released on a passionate plea for clemency coupled with his marriage to Elizabeth, which took place in the Tower itself. It is pleasant to record that the marriage was a great success, husband and wife remaining devoted to each other for the rest of their lives.

On his release, Raleigh decided to retire with his wife to an estate in Dorset, but although he and Elizabeth had a son in 1594, retirement soon began to pall. He set out in 1595 on a voyage in search of gold to South America, attracted there by stories of the mines of El Dorado. He found no gold, but wrote an account of his voyage in *The Discoverie of Guiana* which, if more romantic than truthful, remains as one of the finest narratives of Elizabethan adventure. He was admiral in command of the triumphant expedition against *Cadiz in 1596, an early model of a successful naval and military combination in an amphibious assault role.

The death of Queen Elizabeth spelled the ruin of Raleigh. One by one his estates and privileges, granted by the Queen, were stripped from him. He was accused, falsely, of taking part in conspiracies against the life of James I, who succeeded Elizabeth in 1603, and was condemned to death, but instead of execution was confined in the Tower, where he remained for the next thirteen years.

He was released in 1616 under conditions as discreditable on the part of the King as they were despairing on the part of Raleigh. In return for his freedom, he promised to discover for the King a gold mine in Guiana without infringing any Spanish possession. This was inherently impossible, as Spain had many settlements already on that coast, and Gondomar, the Spanish ambassador in London, pointed this fact out to the King. James, chronically short of money and to whom a gold mine would be a godsend, promised Gondomar that on his return he would execute Raleigh if a clash with the Spaniards took place. He sent Raleigh off on an expedition which was ill-found and badly manned, and with him sailed Raleigh's eldest son Walter. The ships reached the mouth of the Orinoco at the end of 1617 but by then Raleigh was sick with fever and remained at Trinidad, sending five small vessels up the river under the command of Lawrence Keymis, his most trusted captain. Inevitably they found a Spanish settlement in the way and fighting broke out in which Raleigh's son was killed, as well as some Spaniards. After a fruitless search for a gold mine, the vessels returned with their dire news. Keymis, despairing after Raleigh's reproaches, committed suicide and the expedition returned sadly home. Raleigh was arrested and executed on 29 October 1618. He died, a brave man, with dignity and serenity.

During much of his life Raleigh was an unpopular man in England, particularly during his period of favouritism with Queen Elizabeth, mainly because of the grasping and extortionate means by which he built up his fortune. But with the death of the Queen the mood changed. He made no secret of his enmity against Spain, which endeared him to a public that was suspicious of James's close relations with that country, and the patent falsity of his trial in 1603 and his long years in captivity in the Tower made him a popular hero. His execution at the Spanish

Sir Walter Raleigh; miniature by N. Hilliard, c. 1585

ambassador's instigation and insistence enhanced his popularity, and through the centuries which have followed his death, he has remained in popular affection as one of the heroes of Elizabethan England, his name linked with those of men such as Sir Francis Drake, Sir John * Hawkins, and the others of that famous band of sea adventurers.

S. J. Greenblatt, *Sir Walter Raleigh* (Yale Univ. Press, (1973); M. Irwin, *That Great Lucifer* (1960).

RALPH THE ROVER, see INCHCAPE ROCK.

RAM, a strengthened or armoured projection from the bow of a warship for the purpose of disabling or sinking an enemy ship by ramming her. The old rowed war * galleys of the Mediterranean were fitted with a sharp spike in their bows for this purpose. The ram as a naval weapon disappeared during the age of sail but made its reappearance when steam was adopted

as a means of maritime propulsion, and most * ironclad warships built up to about 1910 were fitted with ram bows even though, in an age of relatively modern gunnery, no ship was likely to be able to get near enough to an enemy to use her ram. The best-known case of the ram being used successfully in battle was when the Austrian ironclad *Ferdinand Maximilian* rammed and sank the Italian battleship *Re d'Italia* at the battle of * Lissa in 1866. This success, allied to certain disasters in peacetime manoeuvres when ships were accidentally rammed and sunk— the * *Vanguard* and * *Iron Duke* in 1875 and the * *Victoria* and * *Camperdown* in 1893— prolonged the life of the ram as a naval weapon long beyond the date when it should have been obvious that its use in war was virtually impossible. The word was also used to describe a warship whose offensive power was centred mainly in its ram, types of warships which were extensively built by both sides in the American Civil War of 1861–5.

RAM, to, an operation of war by which an attempt to sink an opponent by ramming her is made. During the First and Second World Wars a number of ships, particularly *submarines, were sunk by being rammed. The word generally indicates a conscious act to sink an enemy, and although occasionally used for the purpose, does not properly cover the sinking of a vessel through an accidental collision in which a ship's bows may cut through the plating of another ship and cause her to sink.

RAM SCHOONER, the description of a *schooner which does not set *topmasts but is rigged with pole *masts only. It is also sometimes known as a bald-headed schooner.

RAMED, the state of a ship on the building slip when all her *frames are set up on her *keel, the *stem and *sternpost fixed in position, and the whole adjusted by the ramline, the line at deck level of the fore-and-aft line of the keel.

RAMILLIES, H.M.S., a name used four times in the Royal Navy, commemorating the Duke of Marlborough's great victory against the French in 1706. The first of the Royal Navy's ships of this name was originally the *Royal Katherine*, built in 1664 and renamed *Ramillies* in 1706. She was rebuilt in 1742 and re-launched in 1748. In 1756 she was Admiral John *Byng's flagship in his action off *Minorca in May of that year and in 1757, as the flagship of Admiral Sir Edward *Hawke, she led an abortive expedition against Rochefort. She was wrecked on Bolt Head in February 1760 with the loss of 700 lives. A second *Ramillies*, a 3rd *rate of seventy-four guns, was launched at Chatham in 1763. In July 1778 she took part in Admiral *Keppel's action against the French off *Ushant. In September 1782, flying the flag of Rear Admiral Thomas *Graves, who was in command of the squadron of *prizes sent home after Lord *Rodney's action at the *Saints in that year, the *Ramillies* foundered in a hurricane in the Atlantic. Her crew, however, were all taken off safely.

The third *Ramillies*, another 3rd rate of seventy-four guns, was launched on the Thames in 1785. She took part in Lord *Howe's action of the *Glorious First of June in 1794 and the blockade of Rochefort in 1799. In June of the following year she was one of the ships of the expedition under Captain Sir Edward *Pellew which sailed to Quiberon Bay to co-operate with the French Royalists. As one of Sir Hyde *Parker's division she went to the Baltic in 1801 and joined Vice Admiral Lord *Nelson at the close of the battle of *Copenhagen. During the succeeding fifty years she saw service in the Channel, the West Indies, and North America and was made a *lazaretto in 1832, being finally taken to pieces in 1850. A *battleship launched in 1916 was the Royal Navy's last *Ramillies*. She was not completed until 1917 and commissioned in May of that year when she joined the 1st Battle Squadron of the *Grand Fleet. In the Second World War she took part in the chase of the *Bismarck*, and she was broken up in 1948.

RAMSDEN, JESSE (1735–1800), British instrument maker, was considered to be the finest maker of navigational instruments of his day and supplied many of the scientific instruments taken by Captain James *Cook during his three voyages of circumnavigation. Among them was a brass 15-inch *sextant, now preserved in the National Maritime Museum, Greenwich, used by Cook during his second (1772–5) and third (1776–80) voyages.

RANDAN, a method of balancing three rowers in a boat so that equal thrust is generated on either side. Stroke and bow row one oar each while the man in the centre rows a pair of oars.

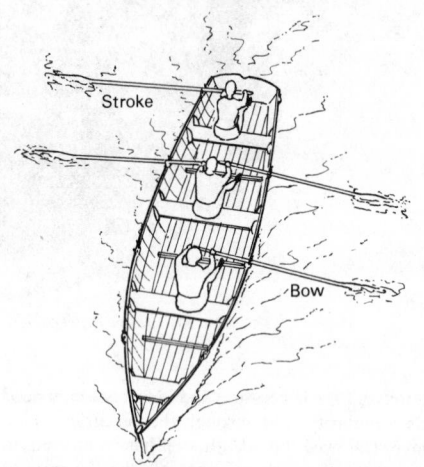

Randan

RANDOM RANGE, the usual description of the maximum range of a warship's muzzle-loading guns during the days of sailing navies. It was anything up to two miles, according to the bore of the gun, the length of the barrel, and the weight of the charge of powder used. It was called random, as a gunner was not expected to hit an enemy ship with a round shot from his gun at its maximum range, but might possibly do so with a lucky shot. Random range was rarely used in battle; ships usually preferring to get within *half-musket shot before firing their broadsides, but it was employed when *chasing or being chased in the hope that a lucky shot would damage a mast or rigging, thereby slowing down the vessel being chased or the vessel chasing, according to which achieved the lucky shot.

RANGE, to, the operation of heaving the *anchor *cable of ships up from the *chain lockers and laying (*faking) it out on deck for examination to discover the presence of weak links, if any. It is also done when it is necessary to chip the cable and treat it for rust, operations normally carried out when a ship is in *dry-dock and no emergency can arise requiring the sudden use of anchor and cable. In some small vessels which had an awkward run of cable between chain locker and *hawsehole, it used occasionally to be necessary to range sufficient cable on deck before anchoring to ensure that the anchor reached the bottom without being brought up by an obstruction, but this was a result of poor ship design and would be a most unlikely occurrence in the present state of the art. Some yachts, however, still range their cable before anchoring if they have no clear run from the cable locker over the foredeck.

RANGOON, the capital and principal seaport of Burma, whose wealth as a great trading port was firmly established on rice and teak. The city and port are 21 miles up the great Rangoon River, which is navigable for a further 900 miles above the city, thus making the port the main communications centre of a huge area. It began to become an important centre of trade in 1753 when the city was rebuilt by Alompra, founder of the ruling line of Burmese kings, and though it has been captured and recaptured many times in the course of its history, and once destroyed by fire in 1850, it has retained its great importance as one of the major seaports of the world. For nearly a century it was in the possession of Britain, but was captured by the Japanese in 1942 during the Second World War and recaptured by British forces in 1945, suffering much damage during the fighting. Its connection with Britain ceased in 1947 when Burma became an independent nation.

RANSOME, ARTHUR (1884–1967), British journalist and author, was a man of wide attainments, both in the literary field and as a fisherman and yachtsman. As a youth books, fishing, and sailing absorbed his interests, and his first job after leaving school was in a small publishing firm. From that he turned to journalism, contributed notes and articles on fishing to many journals, and between 1909 and 1912 wrote three books, *A History of Story-Telling*, *The Hoofmarks of the Fawn*, and a book on Oscar Wilde. This last landed him in a libel action brought by Lord Alfred Douglas, of which the verdict was that the words complained of were a libel but true. One of the significant documents in the case was the original manuscript of Wilde's *De Profundis*, of which the unpublished part did much to prove Ransome's case.

In 1913 he went to Russia to learn the language, being at the same time correspondent in Moscow of the *Daily News* and the *New York Times*. He was still there at the time of the revolution in 1917 and became, if not a supporter of, at least sympathetic to, Bolshevist aims. He was a member of the *Royal Cruising Club and while in the Baltic had a 13-ton *ketch built to his own specifications at Riga. This was *Racundra*, and the story of her voyages in the Baltic is told in *Racundra's First Cruise* (1923). Later he visited Egypt and China as correspondent of the *Manchester Guardian*, but a serious illness in the latter country cut short his visit and on his return to England he had to live carefully and quietly in the Lake District. It was during this period of convalescence that his mind turned towards writing the books which were to enshrine him in the hearts of a host of young readers of many nations. The first two, *Swallows and Amazons* (1930) and *Swallowdale* (1931), were only moderately successful, but the third, *Peter Duck* (1932), established his reputation which grew each year as book followed book. They were stories of children and boats and lakes and islands, with some seagoing adventures thrown in, but their great success came through the fact that Ransome did not write his books for 'juveniles' but was indeed an authentic children's novelist. He knew at first hand the ways of a boat in the water and he was able to impart that knowledge and lore in a way that was real to children, understanding them and always taking them seriously.

For much of his life he was a keen cruising yachtsman, and *Racundra* was followed in 1938 by *Selina King* and in 1946 by *Peter Duck*. For the latter part of his life he lived in Suffolk. *The Autobiography of Arthur Ransome* was posthumously published in 1976

RAP FULL, the point of sailing where a vessel keeps as close to the wind as she can without any shiver or lift in the *luffs of her sails; in other words her sails full without a wrinkle in them. It is another way of saying *full and by.

RASMUSSEN, KNUD JOHAN VICTOR (1879–1933), Danish Arctic explorer, was born at Jakobshavn, Greenland, his mother being of Eskimo descent. He was educated at Copenhagen University and in 1901 visited Lapland. The following year he accompanied an expedition to Cape York, Greenland, to study the Eskimo and in 1910 he established an Eskimo settlement at Thule. Subsequently he made numerous journeys to Greenland and in 1916 took part in the second Thule expedition to north-west Greenland, an account of which he published. From 1921 to 1924 he made a polar journey from the west of Baffin Island to the north-east corner of Siberia and in 1931 was engaged in a reconnaissance of Greenland in a small motor vessel, during which he covered over 2,500 miles.

RATE, (1) the six divisions into which warships of sailing navies were grouped according to the number of guns carried. Almost all navies of any size adopted this method of classification. The system was introduced in Britain by Admiral Lord *Anson during his first term as First Lord of the Admiralty (1751–6) but some naval writers have ante-dated it for the sake of convenience in describing earlier warships. Thus H.M.S. *Resolution*, launched in 1610, is frequently described as a first rate of 80 guns. What this means is that she was one of the largest ships of her time in the British Navy and could therefore be considered as a first rate. Later first rate ships were those which carried from 100 or 110 guns upwards, the change from 100 to 110 coming in 1810. Second rates carried from 84 (later 90) to 100 (110); third rates 70 (80) to 84 (90); fourth rates 50 (60) to 70 (80); fifth rates 32 to 50 (60); and sixth rates, any number of guns up to 32 if commanded by a *post-captain. Such ships when commanded by a commander were rated as *sloops. Only ships of the first three rates were considered to be sufficiently powerful to be in the *line of battle in actions between main fleets. Ships of the fifth and sixth rates were generally known as *frigates; fourth rate ships, of which very few were built, did not lie in the line of battle, except occasionally in the smaller fleets. Carronades (see GUNS, NAVAL), first introduced into the Royal Navy in 1779, were not included in the number of guns which decided the rating of a ship until 1817. (2) The rank held by a naval seamen is known as a rate. See RATING.

RATE OF CHANGE, a correction which is applied to the reading of a *chronometer when a navigator in a ship works out the *Greenwich Mean Time of an observation of a heavenly body which he has taken for the purpose of fixing his ship's position. Until very recently no man-made ship's chronometer could be exactly accurate in time-keeping, usually gaining or losing a second or two every day. If this rate of gain or loss, which is known as the chronometer's rate of change, is worked out through accurate daily observation of the chronometer over a period, it can then be applied to each reading of the chronometer to produce the exact time of the observation, and thus the exact reckoning of Greenwich Mean Time.

RATHBURNE, JOHN PECK (1746–82), American naval officer, was born in Exeter, R.I. He was commissioned a lieutenant in the *Continental Navy in December 1775, and served in the *sloop *Providence* under Esek *Hopkins in the expedition to Nassau in 1776. He remained in the *Providence* when John Paul *Jones commanded her, and moved to the *Alfred* when Jones became her captain. On 19 April 1777 he was given command of the *Providence*, and took a number of *prizes. He also planned to make another descent on Nassau, and surprised the garrison and residents by sailing in during the night of 27 January 1778. With his small vessel and small crew he seized the fort, raised the American flag, seized small arms, ammunition, and gunpowder, and sailed away after two days without having shed any blood. In recognition of his achievements, he was given command of the *frigate *Queen of France*, and in June 1779 sailed from Boston in company with the *Providence* and the *Ranger* to patrol the Newfoundland Banks. On 16 July, in a thick fog, the three American vessels found themselves with a Jamaica *convoy of about sixty sail bound for London. Remaining with the convoy and pretending to be escorting vessels, the three American ships captured ten vessels of the convoy in one day and then sailed them out of the convoy that night.

After being captured in Charleston in 1780 and released on parole, Rathburne returned to New England. There was no command available for him in the Continental Navy and he accepted the command of the Massachusetts *privateer *Wexford*. In that vessel he was captured by H.M.S. *Recovery* on 19 September 1781, and died in Mill Prison, near Plymouth.

RATING, a term used to describe a seaman in a warship, but more accurately the status of seamen, corresponding to rank in the case of officers. Men hold rates according to their abilities, the normal chain of lower deck promotion in the British Navy being ordinary seaman, able seaman, leading seaman, petty officer, chief petty officer, with similar steps in most other navies. The word is the present participle of the verb to rate: seamen are rated to the rate they hold. (For a table of equivalent rates, see APPENDIX 1.)

RATING, a calculation of a yacht's expected performance relative to another yacht around a racing course, based upon measurement of the yacht rather than observed performance. A rating rule is the rule of measurement and calculation by which a yacht's rating is produced. Ratings may be used, together with a time allowance formula, to permit yachts of different rating to race against each other with a handicap based on rating, and may also be used to control the size and proportion of yachts that can race against each other at a fixed rating without handicap.

There have been many rating rules over the years and they have varied in the factors that they have measured, how they have measured them, and in the formulae in which the factors have been combined. The common feature of all rating rules is that they have expressed the ratings in linear units of feet or metres. The earliest rating rules were intended to restrict the variations of proportions of yachts within classes that were to race without handicap. Examples of these rules were the rater classes of the late 19th century, a class of which is still sailing on the Thames at Kingston. Later examples of the same principle were the International classes of the International Yacht Racing Union where the actual rules differed in their values and limits in determining the 6-, 8-, 10-, 12-, 15-, and 23-metre classes. Of these rules the best known today is the 12-metre, which is still used for the *America*'s Cup contests. In the U.S.A., the Universal rule was used in the same way to control the R-, M-, and *J-classes. The J-class rule was used for the challenges of *Shamrock V*, *Endeavour I*, and *Endeavour II* for the *America*'s Cup.

In the years between the two world wars the advent of ocean racing required the use of rating rules under which cruising yachts of different types and sizes could race together. Of these the best known were the rules of the Cruising Club of America (the C.C.A. rule), and the *Royal Ocean Racing Club (the R.O.R.C. rule). After the Second World War efforts were made over the years to bring these two rules into line and progress was made in unifying the restrictions on rig and sail dimensions. The two rules were finally brought together in 1970 to become the International Offshore Rating Rule (I.O.R. Mk. II), the forerunner of I.O.R. Mk. III which is in operation worldwide today. This rule is used for handicap racing with time allowance systems in local races and such international events as the *Admiral's Cup. It is also used in the 'Ton Cup' classes for races at fixed ratings without handicap.

The principle underlying any rating rule is that a yacht's ultimate speed is proportional to the square root of its waterline length. However, these speeds are only reached in strong winds, and at lower speeds the amount of sail area that a yacht spreads, and also her displacement, will affect her performance. All rules therefore specify a measurement of length, which is usually some combination of the waterline length and the bow and stern overhangs. There will also be rules for the measurement of sail areas in the different parts of the rig. The displacement of the yacht will be included in some form, either by weighing or by measurement of the immersed depths of the hull at certain points. Corrections are also included for items such as beam, draft, freeboard, engines and propellers, centreboards and keels, all of which have some effect on a yacht's performance. Some measurement of stability or bal-

last ratio is also necessary to encourage adequate strength in the hull structure. These measurements have finally to be combined to arrive at a rating. As an example, in the I.O.R. Mk. III Rule:

$$RATING = \left(0.13 \frac{L \times \sqrt[2]{S}}{\sqrt[2]{B \times D}} \right.$$
$$\left. + 0.25 L + 0.2 \sqrt[2]{S} + DC + FC \right)$$
$$\times EPF \times CGF \times MAF,$$

where L is a measure of length, S is a measure of the sail area, B × D is a measure of beam × depth or bulk, DC and FC are draft and freeboard allowances, EPF is the engine and propeller factor, CGF is the stability factor, and MAF is a factor for movable keel surfaces.

RATLINE, one of a series of rope steps up the *shrouds of a mast, 15 to 16 inches apart, by which men working aloft in square-rigged ships reach the *yards via the *tops and *crosstrees. Ratlines normally are made of 18-thread tarred rope with an *eye in each end *seized to the outermost shrouds, being secured to each intermediate shroud by a *clove hitch.

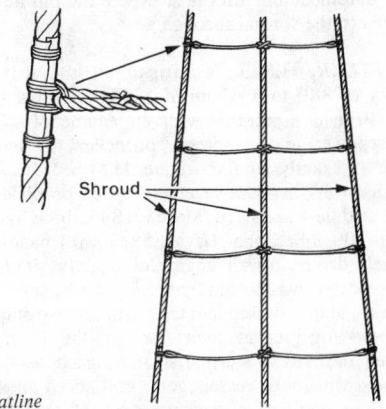

Ratline

RATSEY, THOMAS WHITE (1851–1935), British sailmaker and yacht designer, was born at Cowes, Isle of Wight, in the year the *schooner *America* came to the Solent and first won the '100-guinea cup' which later became known as the *America*'s Cup. From that time many British challengers for the Cup were to have sails made by Ratsey's firm, which had been established by his grandfather in 1790. Acquiring branches at Gosport, Gourock, and in New York, the firm made sails for yachts of almost all racing classes in the United Kingdom as well as overseas. Ratsey designed the *Dolly Varden*, a 28-ton *cutter, in 1872, won many prizes with her, and kept her in the family until his death. He was a founder member of the Island Sailing Club at Cowes and its *commodore for many years.

H.M.S. Rattler *towing H.M.S.* Alecto; *coloured lithograph, 1845*

RATTLE DOWN, to, the operation of securing the *ratlines to the *shrouds with a series of *clove hitches round each shroud except the forewardmost and aftermost, where the ratline is seized to the shroud through an *eye.

RATTLER, **H.M.S.,** a *frigate of the Royal Navy of 880 tons which in 1845 was fitted by the British Admiralty with an engine of 220 horsepower and a screw *propeller for tests with an exactly similar frigate, H.M.S. *Alecto, to discover the relative efficiency of propellers and paddle-wheels. In March 1845, in a race over 100 miles, the *Alecto,* fitted with paddle-wheels driven by an engine of exactly similar horsepower, was beaten by the *Rattler* by several miles, and in a subsequent test, with the two ships secured together at their *sterns, the *Rattler* towed the *Alecto* stern first at a speed of 2·7 *knots with both vessels going full speed ahead on their engines, a conclusive proof that the propeller not only drove a ship faster through the water than paddle-wheels, but also exerted considerably more power.

RATTLESNAKE, **H.M.S.,** a ship's name much associated with the surveying service of the Royal Navy. Of a number of ships bearing this name a 6th *rate of 503 tons and 20 guns earns mention for her two surveying cruises in 1848–50 in Australasia working in the northern part of the Inner Route, Torres Strait, and the Louisade Archipelago. She was commanded by Owen *Stanley and had H.M.S. *Bramble* in company. T. H. Huxley was carried as assistant surgeon, having been recommended by Sir John Richardson at the R.N. Hospital *Haslar, who had himself been surgeon-naturalist with Sir John

*Franklin in 1819–22 and 1825–7. With Charles *Darwin of the *Beagle* as a precedent, surveying ships frequently carried naturalists and in their absence scientific investigation and reports fell to the surgeon. The *Rattlesnake*'s cruises were exceptionally arduous and Stanley, wearied by the constant anxiety, ended his own life on her return to Sydney. To Huxley the cruises of the *Rattlesnake* were an introduction to a life spent in the service of science, much of it in fields where Darwin had contributed so much.

RAWALPINDI, **H.M.S.,** a British *armed merchant cruiser of the Second World War, was originally a *P & O *liner of 16,697 tons and was converted to an armed merchant cruiser by the mounting of eight old 6-inch guns. On 23 November 1939 she was at sea between Iceland and the Faeroe Islands as a unit of the Northern Patrol when she encountered the German *battlecruiser *Scharnhorst* which, in company with the *Gneisenau,* was attempting to break out into the Atlantic. In command of the *Rawalpindi* was Captain E. C. Kennedy who was able to pass a report to the commander-in-chief, Home Fleet, before engaging the enemy ship. She was overwhelmed and sunk by the vastly superior gunpower of the German ship, but the *Scharnhorst* and *Gneisenau* were forced to abandon their break-out to the North Atlantic trade routes and returned to their German base.

RAZEE or **RASEE,** a sailing *ship of the line which had her upper works taken off so that she was reduced by one deck; thus a razeed two-decker would become a heavy *frigate. The word was used both as noun and verb and was taken from the French *raser,* to cut.

REACH, (1) the *point of sailing of a vessel which can point her *course with the wind reasonably *free and her sails full throughout. A broad reach is the same but with the wind abeam or from slightly abaft the beam. For illus. see POINTS OF SAILING. **(2)** A straight, or nearly straight, stretch of a navigable river or estuary. Thus a vessel coming up the River Thames to the Port of London will, after passing Tilbury, navigate through Long Reach, Erith Reach, Halfway Reach, Barking Reach, Gallion's Reach, Woolwich Reach, Blackwall Reach, Greenwich Reach, and Limehouse Reach.

REACH, to, the act of sailing a vessel with the sails full and the wind free. A sailing vessel which overtakes another is sometimes said to reach ahead of her. It was also a word used to describe a sailing vessel when she was standing off and on, waiting perhaps to pick up a *pilot or for some other purpose. See also FORE-REACH, TO.

READ, MARY (*fl.* 1710–20), enlisted as a soldier during the War of the Spanish Succession (1702–13), but growing tired of military life turned to *piracy as a more exciting type of life. She signed on with John Rackham, also known as 'Calico Jack', who had married Anne *Bonny, another female pirate. They were all captured at Jamaica in 1720. Rackham was hanged as a pirate but both women escaped the death penalty, Anne Bonny because she was pregnant and Mary Read on account of her sex. She died in prison.

'READY ABOUT', the order in a sailing vessel to *tack. See also 'LEE-OH'.

RECEIVER OF WRECK, a port official to whom all objects recovered from the sea or from sunken ships must be delivered for adjudication as to ownership.

RECEIVING SHIP, an old, and usually decayed, warship permanently moored in a naval port in which new recruits for the navy, or men brought in through *impressment or under the *Quota Acts, were accommodated until they were drafted to seagoing ships. Receiving ships, which later became more widely known as *hulks, remained a feature of British naval dockyards as accommodation ships until they were finally replaced by barracks built ashore around the end of the 19th and beginning of the 20th centuries.

RECIPROCATING ENGINE, a form of steam engine in which a piston moves back and forth inside a cylinder, transmitting its motion by connecting rod and crank to a driving shaft. Reciprocating engines used at sea to drive a propeller shaft were usually installed so that the pistons

moved vertically up and down the cylinders, but in some cases were installed to give a horizontal movement. After the introduction of the *turbine the commonest form of ships' reciprocating engines, which had their cylinders in line above the crankshaft, were called by their crews the 'up and downers'. See also COMPOUND ENGINE, TRIPLE EXPANSION ENGINE.

RECKONING, the record of *courses steered and distances made good through the water since the time at which the ship's position was fixed by shore or astronomical observations. This record used usually to be kept on a log-slate on which times of altering course and distances made as indicated by the log on each course were chalked up on the slate. At the end of each watch the record was transferred to the *log book and the relieving officer-of-the-watch started his watch with a clean slate. By applying an allowance for current and *leeway to a *dead reckoning position the navigator arrives at an estimated position, this being his best estimation of his ship's position at any given time until new observations provide a *fix.

RED DUSTER, the colloquial name for the Red Ensign flown by all British merchant ships. The use of the name dates from the latter part of the 19th century when British merchant tonnage exceeded that of all other maritime nations put together and the Red Ensign was the one most frequently seen in all seas all round the world.

RED ENSIGN, the ensign originally used to denote the senior squadron of the English fleet (see SQUADRONAL COLOURS). When the division of the fleet into red, white, and blue squadrons was abolished in 1864, the Red Ensign, informally known as the *red duster, became the ensign of the British merchant fleet and is today flown by all British merchant vessels and also by many yachts belonging to yacht clubs which do not have a warrant to fly a *Blue Ensign defaced.

REEF, (1) the amount of sail taken in by securing one set of *reef-points. It is the means of shortening sail to the amount appropriate to an increase in the strength of wind. In square-rigged ships, sails up to the *topsails normally carried two rows of reef-points, enabling two reefs to be taken in; sails set above them usually had no reef-points as they would normally be *furled or sent down in a wind strong enough to require the sails to be reefed. In *fore-and-aft rigged ships, *gaff or *Bermuda sails usually have three sets of reef-points. Triangular sails normally have no reef-points, being reefed either with a patent reefing gear which enables them to be rolled up on the *luff or, more usually, by substitution of a smaller sail. In square-rig, the first reef is at the * head of the sail and is reefed up to the * yard; in fore-and-aft rig the first reef is at the * foot of the sail and is reefed down to the * boom. Another method of reefing a mainsail set on a boom, almost entirely restricted to yachts, is to roll the sail down by rotating the boom until the sail has been shortened sufficiently for the weather conditions. (2) A group or continuous line of rocks or coral, often, though not necessarily, near enough to the surface of the sea for waves occasionally to break over it but, generally speaking, at a depth shallow enough to present a danger to navigation.

REEF, to, the operation of shortening sail in a vessel by reducing the area exposed to the wind, an operation required when a vessel begins to labour because of the strength of the wind. To double reef, to tie down a second reef in a sail. See also REEF, SPANISH REEF.

REEF KNOT, a square knot formed of two half hitches in which the ends always fall in line with the outer parts. It is used when it is required to join two pieces of rope particularly if they are of an equal thickness and, of course, when tying * reef-points. It is one of the commonest and most useful knots used at sea.

Reef knot

REEF-BAND, a strip of extra canvas * tabled on to a sail of a square-rigged sailing vessel along the line of the * reef-points to support the strain on the points when the sail is reefed.

REEF-CRINGLES, * thimbles spliced into the * bolt-rope on the leeches of a square-rig sail at the ends of the * reef-bands. When the sail is to be reefed, the cringles are hauled up to the * yard and lashed to it. In fore-and-aft rig sails, the reef-cringles, similarly set in the lines of the * reef-points, become the new * tack and * clew of the sail when a reef is tied down.

REEF-POINTS, short lengths of small rope set in the * reef-bands of square-rig sails used to tie down a reef. In fore-and-aft rig, the reef-points are usually set direct on to the sail, reef-bands being unusual in these sails. In both cases, the reef-points are secured to the sail by a * crows-foot.

REEF-TACKLE, a * tackle which is hooked into the * reef-cringles of a square-rig sail to hoist it up the yard for reefing.

REEMING IRON, an iron wedge used by ship-wrights to open up the * seams of wooden-planked vessels so that they can be * caulked with * oakum and pitch. They are driven into the seams with a * beetle.

REEVE, to, the operation of passing the end of a rope through the * throat and thus on to the * sheave of a * block when forming a * tackle, or through an * eye, * thimble, or * cringle. Generally, when the end of a rope is passed through anything, it is said to be rove through it.

REFORMADO or REFORMADE, a 16th and 17th century name for a naval officer serving on board a ship without having obtained a commission from the Admiralty or ministry of marine of his country. This was frequently necessary, as in those days disease or battle casualties frequently carried off an officer, a state of affairs on board which required the temporary upgrading of * midshipmen or other * ratings so that the work and discipline of the ship might be maintained. Though they might act as lieutenants, they had as yet no official commission to do so, and were thus known as reformadoes.

The term originated in Tudor times, but was given a new impetus by Charles II, who encouraged the younger sons of the nobility and gentry to join the navy with a letter from him which entitled them to receive table-money and other encouragements. Although this was in no way an official commission, these young men frequently acted as lieutenants and, occasionally, captains. Later in the same reign, when Samuel * Pepys became Secretary of the Admiralty, this abuse was eradicated, and young men entering the navy with the king's letter had to serve their time as able seamen and midshipmen before they could receive a commission as lieutenant.

REFRACTION, the bending of light rays as they pass from one transparent medium to another of different optical density, an important consideration when using celestial bodies for fixing a ship's position. Light from an observed celestial body or from the observer's visible horizon suffers atmospheric refraction, that in the former case being called celestial refraction, and that from the horizon terrestrial refraction. The effect of atmospheric refraction is apparently to elevate celestial objects and the horizon, so that it is necessary to make allowance for this effect when converting observed * altitudes to true altitudes. The altitude correction known as mean refraction is defined as the angular measure along an arc of a vertical circle between the true and apparent directions of a celestial body, when atmospheric temperature, pressure, and humidity are normal. Abnormal refraction gives rise to effects such as * looming and mirage. Mean refraction varies from about 33 minutes of arc for objects on the horizon to nothing for objects at the zenith. See NAVIGATION, Celestial.

REGIME, a term used in *hydrography to describe the channels and tidal characteristics of a port or estuary. By the building of *moles, *jetties, and other port installations, the tidal flow, and thus the regime, of a port can be altered; alternatively, these constructions can be sited so as to give the tidal flow an extra scouring effect to deepen normal approach channels, etc., and thus maintain and improve the regime of the port.

REGISTER OF SEAMEN, a nominal list of men trained to the sea. For centuries in Britain it was a dream of all men responsible for the manning of ships of the Royal Navy; with such an instrument, they argued, it would be possible to find and draft into the ships sufficient men properly trained in their profession, thus replacing the largely second-rate men dredged up by the *press gangs and the undesirables produced by the *Quota Acts. The dream always foundered against the administrative difficulties of producing and maintaining such a list, as the nation was not then geared to such a degreee of control. Such a register was, however, set up by Act of Parliament, though on an incentive basis, in 1696, when only those naval seamen on the register, who contributed to the *Sixpenny Office, were allowed to benefit from the *Royal Hospital at Greenwich. This, however, proved an insufficient incentive to bring forward enough men and the register fell into disuse in 1710. In the case of merchant seamen, a register was successfully introduced in 1835, preventing the employment of seamen without a certificate, and still operates efficiently to this day.

France was more successful in introducing a register of seamen, *Colbert starting his *Inscription Maritime* in 1669. From it there grew the system of compulsory naval service which kept the French Navy adequately manned throughout the years, and from it also grew the naval hospitals, headed by Les Invalides in Paris, which were founded to provide medical attention to the conscripted seamen.

REGISTER SHIP, an old naval term to describe a Spanish treasure *galleon or plate ship. It originated from the requirement of the Spanish government that every Spanish ship trading to her American colonies required a licence to do so, those owners to whom licences were granted having their name entered on a register. It was a fairly widespread belief in England that every ship returning to Spain from America must be laden with treasure, and as these were always desirable ships to capture in time of war, they became widely known as register ships to distinguish them from Spanish ships trading to other parts of the world. See also FLOTA.

REGISTER TONNAGE, see TONNAGE.

REGULATING CAPTAIN, a captain of the British Navy, usually elderly and with no prospect of an appointment at sea, appointed during a war to administer a district under the *impressment service for the acquisition of men to man the navy. He was paid, in addition to his full pay, an allowance of £5 a month, later raised to £1 a day. He hired and paid the *press gangs who operated in his district.

REINEL, PEDRO and JORGE (*fl.* 1519–72), father and son, were both in their time Portuguese official cartographers. Pedro is the earliest of the Portuguese cartographers known by name and a number of his *portulan charts, many unsigned, exist today. In 1519 he was sent to Spain to bring back his son Jorge, who had fled there after being involved in a street brawl in Lisbon. He found Jorge making charts in preparation for Ferdinand *Magellan's voyage. Pedro was still living in 1542, and Jorge was living 'sick, old, and poor' in 1572. A very beautiful chart from his pen in portulan style, covering the area from Scotland down the west coast of Africa and nearly to the Cape of Good Hope, dated 1540, is in the private collection of Barone Ricasoli-Firidolfi in Florence.

RELATIVE BEARINGS, the *bearings of objects in relation to a ship's head. They can be expressed in two ways, as bearings on the port or starboard bow, beam, quarter, etc., with the expressions 'fine' or 'broad' to add further definition, or, more accurately, in degrees from ahead on each side of the vessel, with the prefix 'red' if on the port side and 'green' if on the starboard. When relative bearings are given in this way, the word 'degrees' is always omitted.

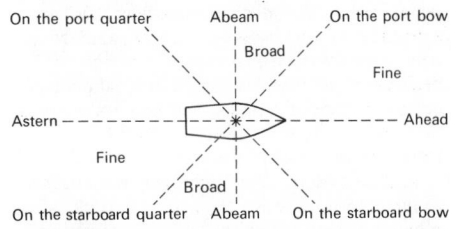
Relative bearings

RELIEVING TACKLES, (1) two strong *tackles (pron. tayckle) used in sailing men-of-war to provide a safeguard against a ship overturning when she was being *careened on a beach with little slope down to the water. *Guys were attached to the moving block of the tackle, led under the * keel of the ship, and hooked into the * sills of the lower * gunports on the side of the ship being exposed for cleaning. As the ship was hauled over to expose her bottom, the relieving tackles were eased away, but could be secured immediately to hold her if she showed a tendency to fall right over on her side. They were also used to assist in righting the ship after her bottom had been cleaned and the * boot-topping applied. (2) Purchases rigged on either side of the * tiller of a ship to ease the strain in heavy seas when the pressure on the * rudder is too great for steering with the wheel alone. They were made unnecessary when steering engines were introduced, in which movement of the steering wheel activates the engine, the tiller being thus put over by the engine and not by the wheel.

RENDER, to, (1) the act of easing away gently, such as by taking one or two turns with a rope or * hawser round a * bollard or * winch and easing it slowly to absorb a heavy pull upon it. **(2)** The action of a rope as it passes over the * sheave of a * block. A seaman talks of a rope rendering through a block, and never passing through it.

RENDEZVOUS, (1) a naval recruiting centre in Britain of the 18th and early 19th centuries usually set up in times of war in some tavern near the waterfront of seaport towns with a strong lock-up room, known as a press room, in which to hold the recruits until they could be dispatched to a * receiving ship in a home port. It was the centre of the local * impressment service administered by a * regulating captain whose duty it was to examine the men brought in by the * press gangs and to pay the official * bounty to those men who could be persuaded to volunteer. Those who did not volunteer nevertheless joined the navy as pressed men. It was colloquially known as a 'rondy'. **(2)** A position at sea where several ships are ordered to join company.

REPRISAL, originally a period of belligerency which preceded a declaration of war. Where a grievance existed against another country for acts committed, which might not rate a full declaration of war, the aggrieved nation could declare a state of reprisal, and undertake operations short of war until its grievances were settled. It was usually the signal to issue * letters of marque under which * privateers were licensed to take reprisal against the seaborne trade of the other nation. Needless to say, a declaration of reprisal almost invariably drifted into full scale war.

The question of reprisal was brought before the * Hague Convention of 1907, and strict limitations were agreed on the employment of force at sea for the recovery of contract debts.

RESCUE SHIP, a merchant vessel supplied with special stores, such as blankets, cots, clothing, medical supplies, etc., which accompanied * convoys during the Second World War and were charged with the rescue of survivors of ships that had been torpedoed or sunk by other means. Her position was always in the rear of a convoy.

RESCUE, THE, a novel by Joseph * Conrad published in 1920, his last complete novel. It is set in Malayan waters, as were many of Conrad's earlier works. It is a story of the conflict of loyalties and, as in * *Lord Jim*, the fatal flaw in a man's character which leaves him, in the end, broken in spirit.

RESEARCH, H.M.S., was commissioned in 1889 as a surveying ship of 500 tons and notably was the last of several paddle-wheelers, all employed in British home waters. The first had been the *Shearwater* in 1840, followed by the *Porcupine* which operated in the Baltic during the Crimean War (1854–6) and attended over 858 Atlantic telegraph cable-laying operations. Then, in 1882 the composite built *Triton* began her thirty-two-year-long career mostly on the coast of England, thus outlasting the *Research*. Her hull was still sound in 1967 when she went to the shipbreakers.

R.R.S. *Research*, a non-magnetic ship, was built for the Admiralty to replace the American *Carnegie* destroyed by an explosion off Samoa in 1925 after 25 years study of magnetic variation. Launched in 1939 at Dartmouth and all but completed, she was regrettably abandoned in 1945 as a post-war economy. A ship of the U.S.S.R. eventually took up her intended role.

RESOLUTE, H.M.S., a * barque originally built for the East India trade and named *Ptarmigan* but purchased by the British Admiralty for purposes of Arctic exploration in February 1850 for £10,777 from Messrs. Smith of Newcastle and renamed *Resolute*. She was one of the two ships which went to the Arctic with the * Austin–* Ommaney expedition of 1850–1 to search for Sir John * Franklin. She was also one of the squadron under the command of Captain Sir Edward * Belcher which was dispatched on a similar mission in 1852–5.

RESOLUTION, H.M.S., a ship's name of great antiquity and history in the British Navy. The first ship of the name was originally the *Prince*, or *Royal Prince*, a 1st * rate of eighty guns launched in 1610 at Woolwich. She was renamed *Resolution* in 1650 under the Commonwealth and saw service with the * 'generals-at-sea', Robert * Blake and Edward * Popham, being present at the battles, during the First Dutch War (1652–4), of the * Kentish Knock, the

*Gabbard, and *Scheveningen. After the restoration of Charles II in 1660, the *Resolution* was renamed *Royal Prince* and the name *Resolution* given to the *Tredagh*, a 3rd rate of sixty guns, launched in 1654. This second *Resolution* took part in the battles of *Lowestoft, the *Four Days Battle, and the St. James's Day Fight during the Second Dutch War (1665–7). In the latter action she was destroyed by a *fireship.

The Royal Navy's next five ships named *Resolution* were all 3rd rates of seventy or seventy-four guns. The first of these, launched at Harwich in 1667, served throughout the Third Dutch War (1672–4) and was present at the battle of *Solebay, the first and second battles of Schooneveld, and the battle of the *Texel. She was also at *Barfleur and La Hogue in 1692 in the war against the French following the accession of William of Orange to the English throne. The following year, in January, she went to the West Indies station and before the end of the year had taken part in the expedition against Martinique and the attack on St. Pierre (Newfoundland). She was rebuilt at Chatham in 1697–8 and saw further service both at home and in the West Indies before being lost off the Sussex coast in the great storm of 27 November 1703.

In 1770 a *collier of 562 tons was launched at Whitby and given the name *Marquis of Granby*. Four months after her launching an Admiralty order was made to purchase this ship and name her *Drake*, and in December 1771 another Admiralty order was issued that she was to be renamed *Resolution*. From then until 1779 she was one of Captain James *Cook's ships, taking part in both his second and third voyages round the world. In 1781 she was fitted as an armed transport and while serving in that capacity was captured by a French squadron under Admiral de *Suffren in the East Indies.

Between then and 1816 the name *Resolution* was kept alive in the Royal Navy by two *cutters and a *lugger, but in 1892 a first-class *battleship of 14,150 tons was launched at Jarrow and named *Resolution*. This ship had an uneventful career and was sold in 1914, the name being passed on to another battleship, of 25,750 tons, which was launched at Jarrow in 1915. During the First World War (1914–18) she served with the 1st Battle Squadron of the *Grand Fleet and in the Second World War she was in the Home Fleet until 1942 and in the Eastern Fleet in the Indian Ocean until she was paid off in 1943 to become part of the Stokers' Training Establishment, H.M.S. *Imperieuse*, at Portsmouth. She was scrapped in 1948. The name has since been revived for a nuclear *submarine.

RESPONDENTIA, a loan made upon the goods laden in a ship for which the borrower is personally responsible. This is very similar to *bottomry, the difference being that in bottomry the ship and her tackle are security for the loan, in respondentia it is the goods alone.

REUTER, LUDWIG VON (1869–1943), German admiral, was captain of the *battle-cruiser *Derfflinger* at the start of the First World War (1914–18), and he and his ship took part in the bombardment of Scarborough and the battle of the *Dogger Bank. Promoted *commodore in 1915, he commanded the Fourth Scouting Group of light *cruisers at the battle of *Jutland and, later, the Second Scouting Group, comprising the most modern light cruisers, in the Baltic during the attack on Dago and Oesel in October 1917 and at the second battle of Heligoland in November 1917. On 17 August 1918 he succeeded Admiral *Hipper in command of the scouting forces.

In November 1918 he was appointed to take to the United Kingdom the ships to be interned at *Scapa Flow under the terms of the Armistice (eleven *battleships, five battle-cruisers, eight light cruisers, and fifty *destroyers). From the beginning of the internment he realized that he might have to order the *scuttling of this fleet rather than let it fall into the hands of the allies against the wishes of the German government. His first task was to restore discipline among his crews, affected by the mutinies of October and November 1918 at *Wilhelmshaven and *Kiel. This he managed to do by sending home the most notorious trouble-makers and shifting his flag from the semi-mutinous battleship *Friedrich der Grosse* to the better-behaved light cruiser *Emden*. In fact, the German government did agree to surrender the ships, but Reuter was not informed of this and, owing to a misunderstanding as to the date on which the allied ultimatum expired (it had been extended by two days unknown to Reuter), he ordered the scuttling which took place on 21 June 1919. Reuter and his crew were held as prisoners-of-war in England until January 1920 when they were repatriated.

REVENGE, H.M.S., one of the best-known ship's names of the British Navy. The first ship of the name must surely be one of the most widely known ships which ever sailed because of Lord Tennyson's poem which tells of her last fight in 1591. She was a thirty-four-gun ship of 441 tons, launched at Deptford in 1577, and was Sir Francis *Drake's flagship in the battle against the Spanish *Armada in 1588. In the following year, again commanded by Sir Francis Drake, she was one of the expedition which sailed from Plymouth to attack the Spaniards in Portugal. In 1590, under Sir Martin *Frobisher, the *Revenge* was engaged in an expedition to the coast of Spain, undertaken in the hope of intercepting the

Spanish treasure ships returning from the Indies. It was in August 1591, 'at Flores, in the Azores', that the *Revenge*, flagship of Sir Richard * Grenville, fought her last fight, which lasted for 15 hours, against overwhelming odds. When there was no further hope of fighting her, Grenville ordered her to be sunk. His surviving officers, however, would not agree to this and terms of surrender were made with the Spaniards on the understanding that the lives and liberties of the ship's company should be spared. Grenville, who had been wounded three times during the action, was carefully conveyed on board the ship of the Spanish admiral but died two days later. Five days after the battle the *Revenge* foundered in a storm off St. Michael's, taking with her 200 Spaniards who had been put on board.

The sixth ship of the name in the Royal Navy was a 3rd * rate of seventy-four guns launched at Chatham in April 1805, thus being in time for the battle of * Trafalgar in October of that year. In April 1809 the *Revenge* took part in Captain Lord * Cochrane's action in Basque Roads. In 1814 she was paid off, but commissioned again in 1823 and continued an active career until 1842, when she was finally paid off, being taken to pieces in 1849.

A 14,150-ton * battleship was launched at Jarrow in 1892 and named *Revenge*. Shortly after the outbreak of war in 1914 she commissioned for the 5th Battle Squadron, * Grand Fleet, and in November she became flagship of the Dover Patrol and was present at the bombardment of * Zeebrugge. In 1915 her name was changed to *Redoubtable*, when the new battleship launched in 1915, which had been laid down as the *Renown*, had her name changed to *Revenge*. This ship, the ninth of her name in the Royal Navy, was present at the battle of * Jutland in 1916 and in 1917–21 was flagship of the 1st Battle Squadron, Grand Fleet (known from 1919 as the Atlantic Fleet). She paid off at Devonport in 1921. Thereafter, until the outbreak of the Second World War in 1939, she served with the 1st Battle Squadron, being flagship of the commander-in-chief, Atlantic Fleet, in 1924–7. In 1941–3 she was with the Eastern Fleet in the Indian Ocean and in 1944 she became one of the ships of the Stokers' Training Establishment, H.M.S. *Imperieuse*. She was scrapped in 1948. The name has since been revived for a nuclear * submarine.

REVENUE CUTTER, a single-masted * cutter with fine lines built expressly for the prevention of smuggling and the enforcement of customs regulations. Their greatest period of activity was during the late 18th and early 19th centuries when high import duties made the running of selected dutiable goods a highly profitable business and the lack of adequate coastguard stations presented smugglers with plenty of unguarded coastline to which to run their cargoes. This made it desirable to catch the smugglers at sea and led to the special design of these cutters to provide a margin of speed over the smugglers. They carried up to ten guns, usually 'long 9's', nine-pounder guns with extra long barrels to provide a greater range.

REVUE MARITIME, LA, for nearly a century and a half one of the best-known maritime journals in the world. Founded in 1816 by Louis Marie Barjot, a civilian member of the staff of the French Ministry of Marine, with the original title of *Annales Maritimes et Coloniales*, it was only moderately successful although of a remarkably high standard, and the editor was obliged on occasions to meet an annual deficit out of his own pocket. On his death in 1860 the journal was combined with other publications to form a new monthly review under the auspices of the ministry with the title of *La Revue Maritime*. The post of editor was held throughout by a French naval officer, the last being Capitaine de Frégate J. Demerliac who was appointed in 1962. In 1971 the Minister of Defence decided that the journal must make way for one produced on a tri-Service basis and the final issue of *La Revue Maritime* appeared in December of that year. It will always be remembered for the high standard of its articles and illustrations covering every aspect of maritime affairs and for its consistent advocacy of the important part played by the sea in national affairs.

RHODES, the largest island in the Dodecanese group in the eastern Mediterranean, and in the earliest days of western navigation considered to be the central point of the known world, on which the ancient charts were based. Thus * Eratosthenes, who lived in the third century B.C., constructed his map of the known world centred on Rhodes with unequally spaced parallels of * latitude and * meridians of * longitude passing through those places whose positions were known. The port of Rhodes, in the northeastern corner of the island, was famous for its 'colossus', an immense statue which was said to have been mounted astride the entrance to the port and to have carried a light to guide ships into harbour during the night. But in maritime circles, its fame must more surely rest on the Rhodian law of the sea, on which the laws of * Oleron are said to have been originally based.

RHUMB LINE, from the old French *rumb*, a compass * point, is a line on the earth's surface which intersects all * meridians at the same angle. Meridians and parallels of * latitude are rhumb lines, the angle of intersection being respectively 0° and 90°. Rhumb lines which cut meridians at oblique angles are called loxodromic curves from the Greek *loxos*, meaning oblique, and *dromus*, meaning running. The radial lines on a *compass card are also called rhumbs, and the term 'sailing on a rhumb' was often used in the 16th to 19th centuries to indicate a particular compass heading. The extension of the radial line of the compass card through the fore-and-aft line of ship ahead clearly will cut all the meridians the ship crosses at a constant angle, this being equivalent to the *course angle. It is easy to see, therefore, that a line of constant course is a rhumb line. On a plane surface, this would be the shortest distance between two points, and over relatively short distances where the curvature of the earth is negligible, it can be considered so, and a rhumb is thus used for plotting a ship's course. Over longer distances at sea, and especially ocean passages, *great circle sailing provides a more direct course, but even so, the inconvenience of having to change course continually when following the path of a great circle between the points of departure and destination of a voyage makes rhumb-line sailing the popular method of navigation. In other words, navigators are content in general to sacrifice distance for convenience.

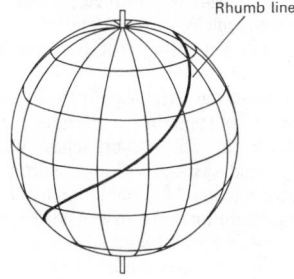

Rhumb line

Because of the importance of rhumb-line sailing, the principal requirement of a navigator in relation to his *chart is that it should be constructed on a projection on which rhumb lines are projected as straight lines. Such a chart is the Mercator chart which is based on the *Mercator projection.

RIBAULT, JEAN (*c.* 1520–65), French navigator, was appointed in 1562 to prepare a settlement for French Protestants in America. Sailing with two ships on 18 February, he landed in Florida at St. John's River on 1 May, settled his colonists and built a fort for them there, and then returned to France to find the country embroiled in civil war. A relief expedition under René de Laudonnière was dispatched from France in 1564, but on arrival discovered that the colony had disintegrated and most of the settlers had attempted to return to France in a

small boat. (Fortunately they were picked up by an English ship when on the point of starvation.) In 1565 Ribault was sent out again to discover how Laudonnière's settlement was progressing, but his ships were attacked by Spaniards while lying at anchor in the mouth of St. John's River. In an attempt to do battle with the Spanish fleet, Ribault's ships were lost in a storm and the survivors set out to return to the French settlement by land. On arrival they discovered that the fort had been overrun by Spaniards and the colonists put to the sword. Ribault and his men had been given a safe conduct to the fort by the Spaniards, but were duly slaughtered on arrival. A sad but typical 16th century story, though justice (or revenge) triumphed in the end when the massacre was avenged two years later by a French force under Dominique de Gourgues which left not a single Spaniard in the place alive.

RIBBAND, in *naval architecture the long flexible lengths of fir fixed temporarily to the outsides of the *ribs of a wooden vessel and to the *stem and *sternpost to hold the *timbers together in *frame, until the deck *beams and *stringers are fitted. It is also a term used in connection with wooden boat construction, for which see RIBBAND CARVEL.

RIBBAND CARVEL, sometimes colloquially termed ribbon *carvel, a form of construction of a lightweight wooden vessel, such as an upriver racing yacht, in which, in place of the more usual athwartship *frames, *timbers, or *ribs, a number of *stringers, splines, or ribbands are laid fore and aft from stem to stern at approximately even spacing, covering the inside seams of the fore-and-aft laid carvel planking.

RIBS, another name for the *frames or *timbers of a ship as they rise from the *keel to form the shape of the hull. See also FUTTOCK.

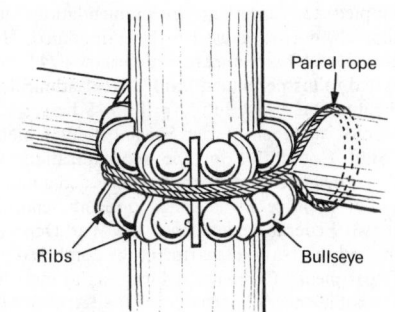

Ribs of a parrel

RIBS OF A PARREL, an old form of a *parrel in square-rigged ships, in which the wooden ribs forming it were separated by *bullseyes.

The ribs had two holes in them, through which the two parts of the parrel rope were rove with the bullseye between. The bullseyes and the smooth inner edge of the ribs bore up against the mast so that the *yard to which the parrel was applied would slide easily up and down when it was *swayed up or *struck down. The bullseyes also provided an easier turn when the yard was *braced to the wind.

RICHARDSON, JAMES OTTO (1878–1974), American admiral, was born in Paris, Texas, and graduated from the Naval Academy in 1902. On his own initiative he studied the problem of fuel oil supplies for the future needs of the navy, and he made suggestions to the Navy Department which led to the creation of the Navy Fuel Oil Board, of which he became a member. He served as navigator and then executive officer of the battleship *Nevada* in 1917 and in 1919 became head of a department at the Naval Academy.

After a three-year period as assistant chief of the Bureau of Ordnance in the Navy Department, Richardson commanded a destroyer division in Europe. After promotion to rear admiral in 1934, he commanded a cruiser division, briefly, before being appointed chief of staff to the Commander-in-Chief, U.S. Fleet.

He was made Commander-in-Chief, U.S. Fleet, with the acting rank of admiral on 6 January 1940. After the annual manoeuvres of the fleet in the area of the Hawaiian Islands Richardson was informed that the fleet would remain there until further notice as a deterrent to Japanese ambitions in the East Indies. Richardson, who had learned enough in his varied assignments to know that *Pearl Harbor was not suitable as a base for fleet training over a period of months, represented the problems to the Chief of Naval Operations and, on at least two occasions, discussed the facts with President Roosevelt. He was informed that in all probability he would lose his command if he attempted to repeat his recommendations to Roosevelt, but he refused to be intimidated. He was relieved of his command in February 1941 and reverted to his permanent rank of rear admiral.

From June 1944 until April 1945 he served as senior member of the Special Joint Chiefs of Staff Committee on the reorganization of national defence. The committee included a number of army officers who joined in recommending that two Federal departments, the War Department and the Navy Department, be combined in a Department of Defense, which was to include also another new department of the (Army) Air Force. Richardson opposed them in a minority report. Throughout his career, Richardson was an officer of outstanding ability and strong character. His performance of duty and judgement were always excellent and he was removed from his command of the U.S. Fleet because he gave advice which was not wanted. When Japanese aircraft attacked Pearl Harbor, Hawaii, on 7 December 1941, Richardson's successor as U.S. Fleet Commander and the Chief of Naval Operations in Washington were both removed from their posts.

RICHMOND, Sir HERBERT WILLIAM (1871–1946), British admiral, entered the Royal Navy in 1885 and was an early specialist in torpedoes. From his earliest service he was always critical of the navy's preoccupation with *matériel* and its neglect of the study of strategy and tactics, an understanding of which, he maintained, could only come through the study of history. The energy with which he conducted his beliefs brought him into conflict with many of his superiors, but some of his ideas on naval education were accepted by Admiral Sir John *Fisher when, as Second Sea Lord, he introduced the reforms known as the Selborne Scheme (named after Lord Selborne, the then First Lord of the Admiralty) in 1902. Where he came into sharp antagonism with Fisher was in his reiterated clamour for the formation of a naval staff at the Admiralty, an anathema to Fisher. When, in 1912, such a staff was formed shortly after the appointment of Winston *Churchill as First Lord, it was but fitting that Richmond should become one of its original members.

Throughout the First World War (1914–18), Richmond's constant and vociferous criticism of its conduct in all its branches made him unpopular and suspect with his seniors. He was the complete iconoclast, campaigning ceaselessly for the substitution of a new navy based on an officer corps who had studied naval warfare in terms of strategy and tactics for a navy which relied on *matériel* almost to the exclusion of knowing how best to use such vast strength. While there was much wisdom in his strictures, he tended to gather around him a small group of similar vociferous critics, appearing at times to higher authority almost to be trying to form a cabal to challenge the naval leadership during a desperate war. He was appointed away from the Admiralty in 1915 as liaison officer with the Italian fleet, and in 1916 as captain of the old *battleship H.M.S. *Commonwealth*, one of the so-called *'wobbly eight'.

Richmond's strong and dissentient views continued after the end of the war, but he was too brilliant an officer to be entirely discarded. He was given a relatively minor command (1923–5) as commander-in-chief of the East Indies station, and ended his naval career as first commandant of the newly formed Imperial Defence College in 1926. Realizing he could go no further up the ladder of promotion, he retired at his own request in 1931. In 1934 he was elected as the first Vere Harmsworth Professor of Imperial and Naval History at Cambridge University, and in 1936 became Master of Downing College, Cambridge, a position he held until his death.

One of his best claims to fame is as the leading spirit in the creation of the quarterly *Naval Review*, an influential journal with a closed circulation among naval officers designed to further the spread of thought and study among young officers to fit them for higher command in the mould which he so ardently desired and typified. He wrote two studious and brilliantly researched books on naval history, *The Navy in the War of 1739–48* (1920) and *The Navy in India, 1763–83* (1931), but his most influential historical work was *Statesmen and Sea Power* (1946), a book which he was later developing into a two-volume work under the title *The Navy as an Instrument of Policy*. He did not live to complete this work, and the first volume was published posthumously in 1953.

RICKERS, the name used to describe the short, light spars supplied for the masts of small ships' boats, boat-hook staves, bearing-off spars, etc.

RICKOVER, HYMAN (1900–   ), American admiral, was responsible for the construction of the world's first nuclear-powered submarine, the U.S.S. * *Nautilus*, first commissioned in 1954. A man of great energy and drive, he forced the project through with great efficiency and success, or, according to some, with great ruthlessness. As a result of his initial success with the *Nautilus* he was put in charge of the U.S. nuclear propulsion programme and developed the submerged missile-firing submarines of the * Polaris programme.

RIDDLE OF THE SANDS, THE, the famous spy novel of the North Sea and German islands written by Erskine * Childers and published in 1903. It was based on his own cruises in those waters in a converted * lifeboat, the 7-ton *Vixen*.

RIDE, to, a verb with many maritime uses. A ship rides to her * anchor when it is on the bottom and is holding her. When she is at anchor she can ride easily or hard, according to the state of the sea and the * scope of her cable, or * apeak or * athwart, according to the direction in which the anchor and * cable * grows. When at anchor she can ride to the tide or to the wind, or ride out a gale, which she can also do to a * sea anchor in the open sea or, indeed, without a sea anchor by remaining head to the gale. In a square-rigged ship a seaman on the * yards who * foots-in the * bunt of a sail is riding it down (see also DANCE IT IN, TO). A rope round a * capstan or * windlass rides when the turn with the strain overlies and jams the following turn.

RIDERS, (1) the name given to timbers secured between the * keelson of a wooden ship and the * orlop * beams to give her additional strength if she has been weakened by * stranding or other such cause. They are normally only used when the floors or timbers have been broken or damaged in order to give the vessel enough strength to enable her to reach a port for repairs. They are also sometimes known as lower or middle * futtock-riders according to the position in which they are required. **(2)** The name given to the upper tiers of casks stowed in a ship's hold.

RIDGE ROPE, the name given to the * jackstay on which an * awning over the deck of a ship is spread.

RIDING LIGHT, a navigational light displayed by a ship at night when she is lying to her anchor. For details of all navigational lights, see APPENDIX 3.

RIDING SLIP, see CABLE STOPPERS.

RIG, a term used in most navies and many shipping lines to describe the various sets of uniform worn by officers and men, such as No. 1 rig, working rig, etc.

RIG, a general term which embraces those characteristics of a sailing vessel in relation to her masts and sails by which her type is determined, such as * cutter, * yawl, * schooner, * barque, * brig, etc.

Square rig, the arrangement of sails in a vessel where the main driving sails are laced to yards which lie square to the mast. It is a rig of the greatest antiquity, originating with the single square sail set on a short mast to take advantage of a following wind. The discovery that it was possible to sail a square-rigged vessel to windward by * bracing the * yard so that it made a pronounced angle to the fore-and-aft line of the vessel is said to have been made by the Scandinavian * longships around the 10th century A.D., and this facility, combined with a marked increase in the size of vessel built, quickly led to a much greater versatility in the rig. As ships grew in size, the single mast was replaced by two masts, and later by three, each at first carrying a single square sail. Further growth in hull size was followed by lengthening the mast with the addition of a topmast and increasing the number of sails set on each mast, first with * topsails and later, by adding a * topgallant mast, with topgallant sails. As in the case of the fore-and-aft rig, local conditions of sea and weather dictated to some extent the type of ship developed, the Mediterranean nations pinning their faith largely to * caravels and * carracks, built with very high

Longship

Sixteenth century rig with spritsail

Barque

Barquentine

Brig

*poops, the north European nations developing the *galleon from the *high-charged ship by eliminating the high forecastle in order to provide a more weatherly ship for the rougher waters of the north.

The general picture of square rig by the 15th and 16th centuries was a two- or three-masted vessel, carrying three square sails (*course, topsail, topgallant sail) on each mast, with a *spritsail carried below the bowsprit and an additional lateen or spritsail on the mizen-mast.

The introduction of staysails into the square rig came about the mid-17th century, and the jib replaced the spritsail below the bowsprit about fifty years later. What is known as the ship rig (square sails on all masts) remained more or less standard practice until the end of the 18th century. But with the great development of world trade during the 19th century and the consequent large increase in hull size to carry it, new sail plans incorporating some features of fore-and-aft rig were developed, the barque and *barquentine for the larger three-masted ships and the *brig or *brigantine for the two-masted. These were found to be as efficient under sail as the ship-rigged vessels and had an advantage, in terms of trade, of requiring a smaller crew through the replacement of square sails by fore-and-aft sails on the mizen-mast.

A further development during the 19th century was the introduction of the *clipper ship, though this was less a development of square rig

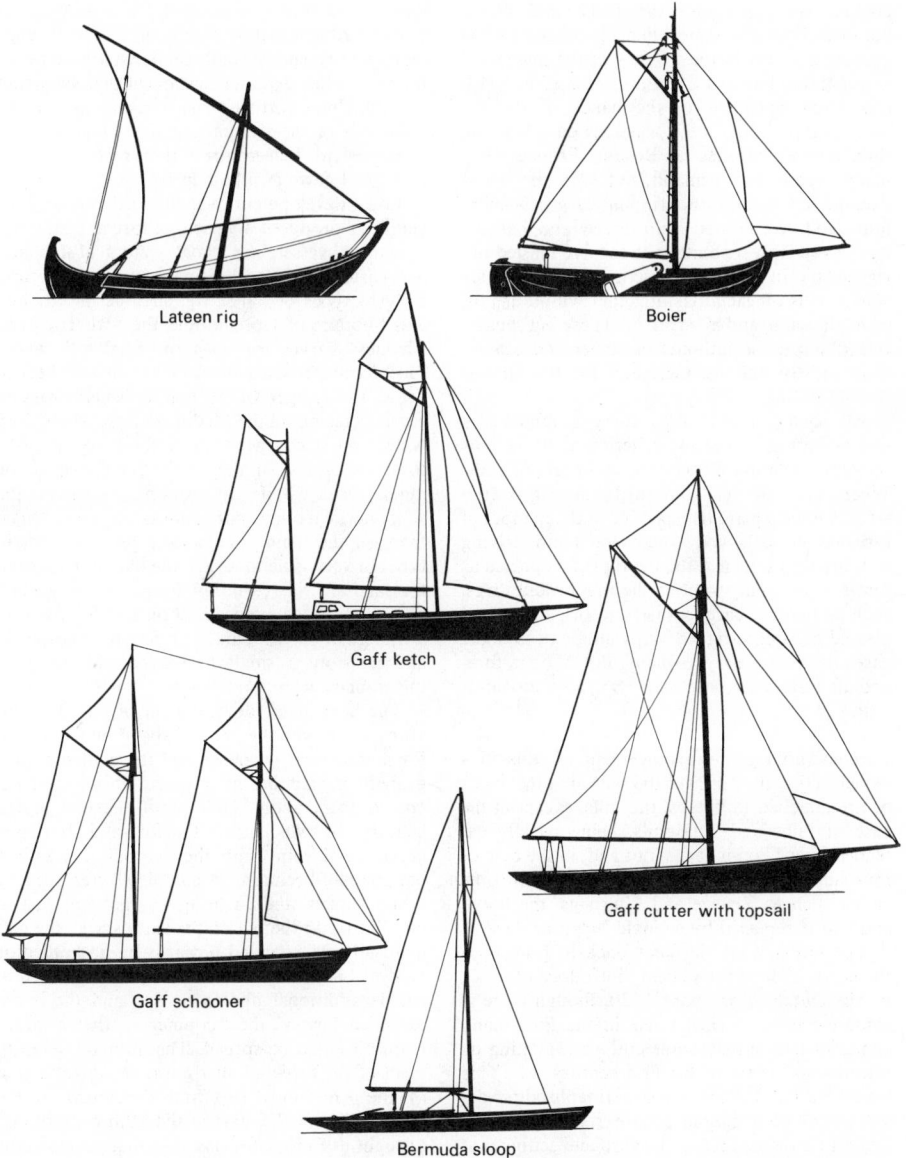

Lateen rig

Boier

Gaff ketch

Gaff cutter with topsail

Gaff schooner

Bermuda sloop

than one of hull form. In the competition for trade during the early years of the century, the choice was between a hull designed to carry a large amount of cargo at a relatively slow speed or one to carry a small cargo at a relatively high speed. The clipper hull was developed in the U.S.A., where speed was accepted as the criterion, the remainder of the trading world largely opting for the deeper, broader hull and larger cargoes. Nevertheless, there were some specialized cargoes, particularly tea and wool, on which a

premium was placed on speed, and some famous clippers were built in Europe with these cargoes in view.

The final development of the square rig came as late as the early 20th century to take advantage of the last of the great trade routes still open to sailing vessels, the route around Cape *Horn for the Chilean nitrate trade. Whereas the steamship had effectively killed the sailing ship on all other routes, she could not compete in the waters south of Cape Horn, partly because of the lack of coaling stations along the route and partly because of the mechanical damage inherent when propellers raced in the troughs of the huge seas, and until the Panama Canal was opened in 1914, this trade remained in the hands of the big sailing ships. Much of it was carried in the big three-masted barques of Britain, France, Germany, Spain, and Finland, but with the world demand for nitrates outstripping cargo capacity, four- and five-masted ship-rigged and barque-rigged vessels were built, with the five-masted full rigged ship in fine weather setting as many as six square sails on each mast together with four jibs, eight staysails, and a * spanker. These big square-rigged ships, the ultimate in power and beauty, were mostly built in Germany for the famous 'Flying P' line.

All square-rigged ships carry a number of fore-and-aft sails, but the criterion as to the correct nomenclature rests on the main driving sails. Where they are set from yards, the rig is considered to be square irrespective of the number of fore-and-aft sails set; where the main driving sails are set by their luffs, the rig is recognized as fore-and-aft. The various hermaphrodite rigs, such as barque, barquentine, and brigantine, are classed as square-rigged ships although in some cases they may carry as many, if not more, fore-and-aft sails as square sails. See also RIGGING, SAIL.

Fore-and-aft rig, the arrangement of sails in a vessel so that the * luffs of the sails abut the masts or are attached to * stays, the sails, except in the case of * jibs and * staysails, being usually extended by a * boom at the foot and, in the case of four-sided sails, by a * gaff at the head. In some cases, such as * barge and * lug rigs, the boom and gaff is replaced by a single * sprit or yard.

The fore-and-aft rig dates back in Europe to the early 15th century, being introduced largely by the Dutch in or about 1420, though there is some evidence of earlier use in the East many centuries before that, some authorities dating its introduction there to the first century A.D. This would be the * lateen rig, a hermaphroditic development of a simple square rig into a fore-and-aft rig by elongating the yard and setting it at a pronounced angle to the mast along the fore-and-aft line. It is probable that, so far as Europe is concerned, the earliest form of fore-and-aft rig was a four-sided mainsail set on a sprit, and that the fore * staysail, a triangular sail set on the forestay, was introduced to provide a better sailing balance and prevent excessive * weather helm.

The invention of the gaff and boom came about a century later, the first known example being found in a picture of Dutch ships painted in 1523. Probably it developed naturally as vessels grew in size, for the larger the ship, the longer and heavier the sprit. A massive sprit would well be worth replacing on weight grounds alone by two smaller and handier spars, and even more so when experience showed that such substitution increased in large measure the overall efficiency of the rig, particularly when working to windward. Indeed, for a great many years the gaff was known as a half-sprit.

Local development over the next two or three centuries produced a variety of fore-and aft types of sailing vessel, the shoal waters of Holland and eastern England lending themselves particularly to types of barge rig, such as the * boiers and * botters of Holland and the * wherries and Thames barges of eastern England, where * leeboards are used in place of a fixed * keel to avoid the danger of grounding when crossing sandbanks, etc. In the Mediterranean, where deep water and steady winds were the governing factors, variations on the lateen rig provided the main types, while in American waters the schooner, carrying more canvas on the foremast than on the main, was widely used as a main type. In very general terms, the overall pattern of fore-and-aft rig, certainly in European waters, was a four-sided mainsail set on a gaff and boom, a triangular staysail, and a jib set on a * bowsprit, and possibly a small four-sided sail set on a mizen-mast, as in * ketches and yawls.

The next major development of the fore-and-aft rig came with the gradual abandonment of sail for commercial purposes and the contemporary growth of yachting as a sport. This period extended from about 1850 until the end of the century, by which time the fore-and-aft rigged commercial ship (with the exception of sailing barges) had been almost completely replaced by steam vessels, and yachting was growing fast in popularity. In the search for extra speed, the gaff mainsail was extended upwards by jib-headed or jackyard topsails, the bowsprit was lengthened to enable additional jibs to be set, and the boom extended beyond the * counter so that a larger mainsail could be spread. The ultimate development of the fore-and-aft rig was the introduction of the * Bermuda rig, first developed in the West Indies at the start of the 19th century and brought to Europe for use in sailing yachts in the years just preceding the First World War (1914–18). It is now the most widely used rig in all sailing yachts, and during the last twenty years has been significantly developed on aerodynamic principles to provide greater driving power with a smaller overall sail area.

The main emphasis of this aerodynamic development is the progressive transfer of the driving power of the wind from the main to the fore triangle, by shortening the foot of the mainsail to present a taller and narrower sail area to the wind and by increasing the size of the jib or staysail by extending the luff to the masthead and sheeting the clew abaft the mast. Apart from thus increasing the area of the fore triangle, this has brought an added dividend by funnelling the wind over the luff of the mainsail and increasing the partial vacuum in the lee of the mainsail luff which provides some of the forward pull when sailing close to the wind. See AERODYNAMICS.

A majority of today's racing and cruising yachts use a *sloop or *cutter rig, but *ketches, *yawls, and *schooners are also popular for cruising.

R. C. Leslie, *Old Sea Wings, Ways and Words* (1930); M. Vocino, *Ships Through the Ages* (Milan, 1951); *Admiralty Manual of Seamanship*, 3 vols (1964–72); B. W. Battie, *Seven Centuries of Sea Travel* (1972); F. Knight, *The Clipper Ship* (1973).

RIG, to, the operation in a sailing vessel of setting up the standing rigging, sending up the *yards, and *reeving the running rigging; in a steam vessel of setting up the standing rigging only, there being no running rigging. The word is also used to describe many other operations on board ship, such as to rig an *awning, to rig a *boom, to rig the *falls of a *seaboat, etc.

RIGAUD, JACQUES (*c.* 1681–*c.* 1754), French draughtsman and engraver of great virtuosity, was born at Marseilles. As a draughtsman he was employed on the design of *galleys and he appears to have lived in the Marseilles region until about 1720 when he moved to Paris and established himself as an engraver and printseller. Among his works are two well-known folios each containing six drawings, one entitled 'Marine (pictures) wherein are reproduced various matters connected with galleys', presented to Mgr. Le Chevalier d'Orléans, Grand Prior and General of the Galleys of France; the other also entitled 'Marine (pictures) and continuation of the Galleys', dedicated to M. Philippeaux.

RIGAUD, JOHN FRANCIS (1742–1810), French portrait painter who lived and worked in England, was born in Geneva and came to England as a young man and settled in London. He is chiefly remembered as having painted the first portrait of Horatio *Nelson. It was begun in 1777 but not completed until 1781, Nelson having to cut short his sittings when his ship was ordered to the West Indies. It is a fine portrait of Nelson at the age of 18½ when he was second lieutenant of the *frigate *Lowestoffe*. It now hangs in Trafalgar House in the collection of Earl Nelson.

RIGGER, a man employed on board ships or in shipyards to fit or dismantle the standing and running *rigging of ships. His duties include all the stretching, *splicing, *serving, and *seizing required before setting up a ship's rigging.

RIGGING, the term which embraces all ropes, wires, or chains used in ships and smaller vessels to support the masts and *yards and for hoisting, lowering, or trimming sails to the wind. All rigging used in the support of masts and yards, and a *bowsprit when fitted, is known as standing rigging.

In a square-rigged ship this is both extensive and complex, as the number of masts involved varies from two to four in the case of sail training ships still in commission and operational; and in the 19th century heyday of sail trading, there were occasionally as many as six. Each mast consisted of at least three separate parts, and occasionally four when a *royal mast was added, each of which needed its own support. In addition each mast had up to six yards crossed on it and each of these, too, had its own standing rigging to support it.

Athwartship Support. A mast is supported athwartships by *shrouds, which run from the *hounds, or a *stayband where this is fitted in their place, a short distance below the top of the mast to the *chain-plates on the outer side of the hull opposite the mast. Originally made from special four-stranded rope, they are today normally made of steel wire rope or, in most modern yachts, of mild steel bars. When made of rope or wire, the lower ends allow for torsioning, originally by means of lanyards threaded through *deadeyes but today by *bottlescrews or similar forms of rigging screws, so that any temporary slackness in the shrouds can be taken up. In the large square-rigged ships, multiple shrouds spaced about 2 feet apart at the chain-plate are required to take the heavy strain on the mast exerted by large sails, and these are secured laterally by *ratlines which not only assist in maintaining and equalizing the tension in each shroud but also form a rope ladder by which men ascended the mast to work on the yards.

In sailing ships where topmasts and *topgallant masts are fitted, the supporting shrouds are led from their hounds or staybands to the *top of the mast below, this top being a platform which rests on the *crosstrees and *trestle-trees, and provides an adequate span to spread the shrouds so that the topmast or topgallant mast is held rigidly in place laterally. The trestle-trees are held in place by *cheeks, bolted to each side of the mast, and the tops themselves, besides being secured to the crosstrees and trestle-trees, are further supported by *futtock shrouds, which are led from the outer ends of the top downwards to a futtock stave secured to the shrouds or to a stayband round the mast. Individual shrouds are designated by the mast they support as, for example, fore shrouds, main topmast shrouds, mizen topgallant shrouds, etc.

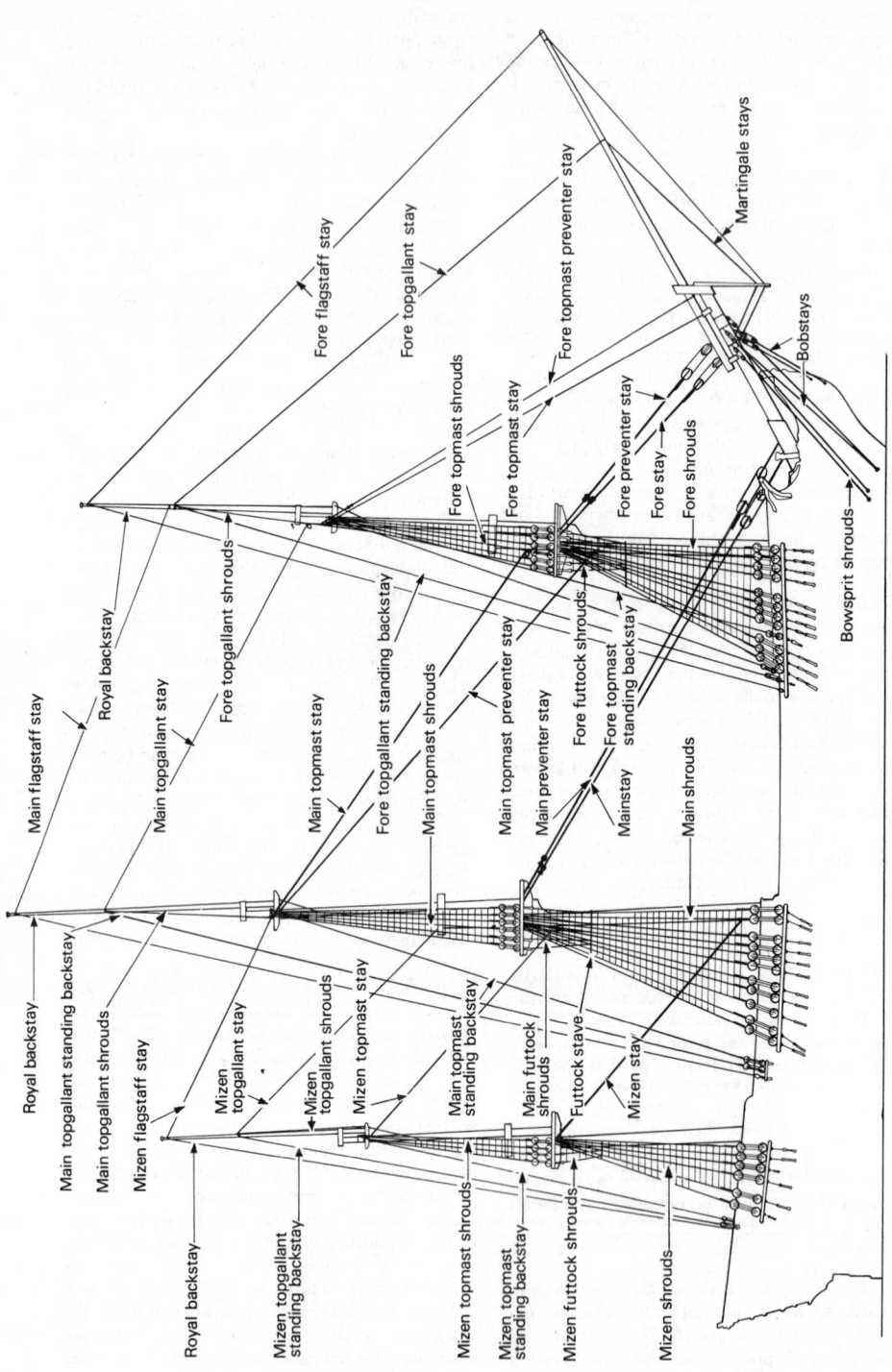

Principal elements of a ship's standing rigging

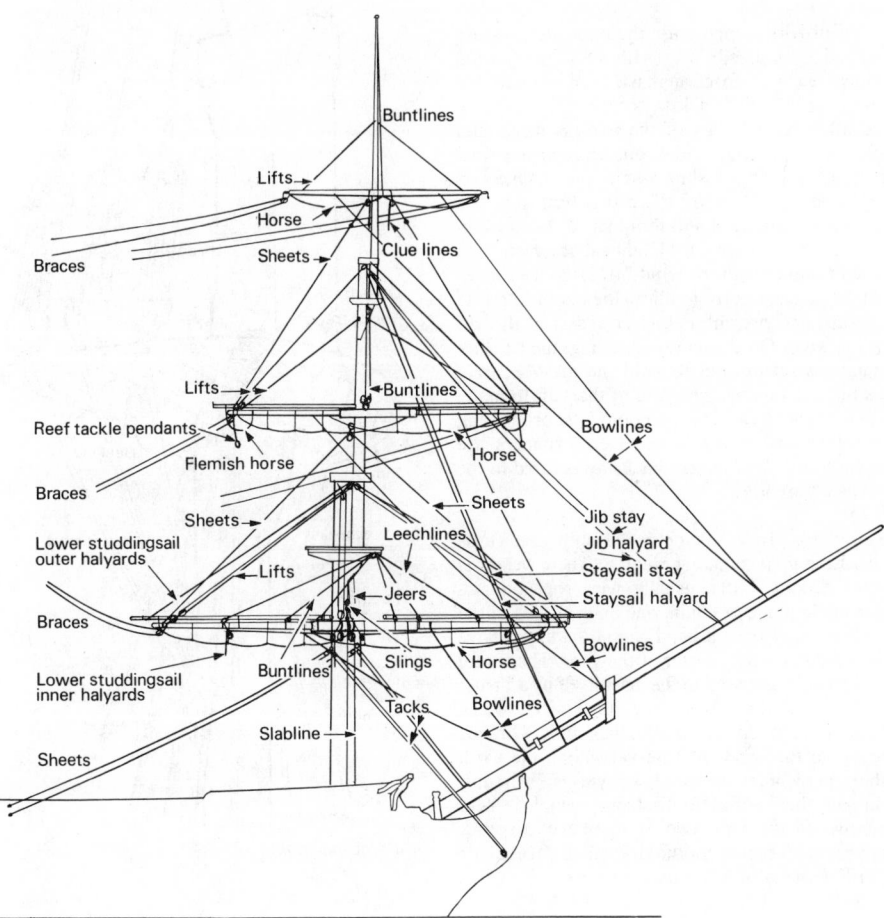

Buntlines

Lifts

Horse

Sheets

Braces

Clue lines

Lifts

Reef tackle pendants

Buntlines

Bowlines

Flemish horse

Horse

Braces

Sheets

Jib stay

Sheets

Jib halyard

Leechlines

Lower studdingsail
outer halyards

Staysail stay

Lifts

Jeers

Staysail halyard

Braces

Bowlines

Lower studdingsail
inner halyards

Buntlines

Slings

Horse

Tacks

Bowlines

Sheets

Slabline

Foremast showing the principal elements of a ship's running rigging

Longitudinal Support. To hold a mast firmly in the fore-and-aft direction, *stays are used. In the case of a foremast, particularly when extended with a topmast and topgallant mast, the support base is extended by a *bowsprit, with further extension by a *jib-boom. The bowsprit and jib-boom must of course be themselves supported before they can be used to hold the foremast, and this is done laterally by pairs of shrouds led from the end of the bowsprit and the jib-boom and secured to plates at the widest part of the bows. Longitudinal support is provided by a *bobstay led from the end of the bowsprit to a fitting on the vessel's stem near the waterline, and by *martingales led from the end of the jib-boom and similarly secured to the stem. In order to give a wider angle of support, a *dolphin striker is fitted to lead the martingales down at a less acute angle than would otherwise be possible. A foremast is held by a forestay secured at its bottom end to the *stem, or sometimes to the deck just inside the stem, and at its top end to the stayband. A fore topmast is stayed from the bowsprit end to the fore topmast stayband, and a fore topgallant mast from the end of the jib-boom to its stayband. These stays support their masts against pressures exerted by the sails which would tend to force the mast over towards the stern of the ship. Main- and mizen-masts are similarly supported in this direction by stays led from the mast ahead of them; a mainmast, for example, by stays from the tops of the three masts which make up the foremast, and so also for the mizen-mast. A stay which extends from masthead to masthead is also known as a *triatic stay.

To provide support for the opposite pressure exerted by the sails, i.e., with a following wind which tends to force a mast over towards the bows of the ship, *backstays are fitted. These are led aft from the tops of the various masts and secured to the ship's sides, one on each side. In a fore-and-aft rigged ship where the mainsail is extended by a *boom, these two backstays are known as *runners, and terminate at the deck in a single *purchase or *Highfield lever so that, when running with the wind *free, the lee runner can be slacked away to allow the boom to swing forward and present a squarer aspect of the sail to the wind. On this point of sailing, the weather runner is set up taut to hold the mast securely against the forward pressure of the sail. In many modern yachts, where the boom is short enough to swing across inside the stern, runners are replaced by a permanent backstay secured to the yacht's *counter.

The Yards. In a square-rigged ship, the yards also have their standing rigging. Their weight is supported by *lifts, usually wire rope but occasionally made of chain, one on each side of the mast running from a band round the mast above the yard to each *quarter of the yard. The centre of the yard is secured to the mast itself by a *truss or *parrel, which is loose enough to allow the yard to turn on the mast when it is *braced round to the wind. At intervals along the yard, short perpendicular ropes, known as *stirrups, support the *horse, or footrope, which is held parallel to the yard two or three feet below it to provide a secure foothold for men *reefing or *furling the sails. For illus. see YARD.

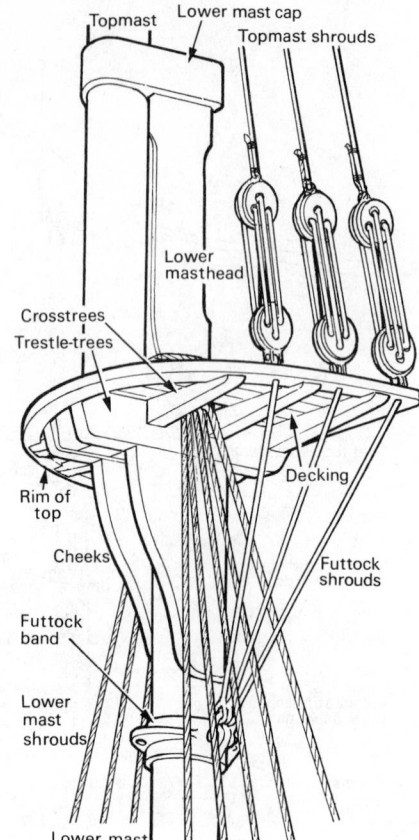

Mast top and fittings

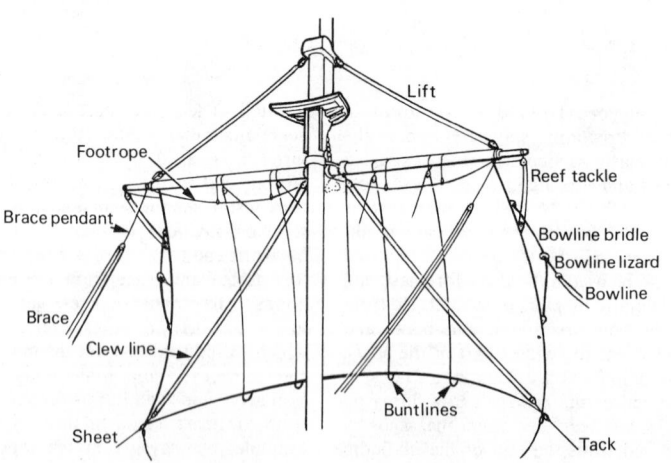

Elements of square sail running rigging

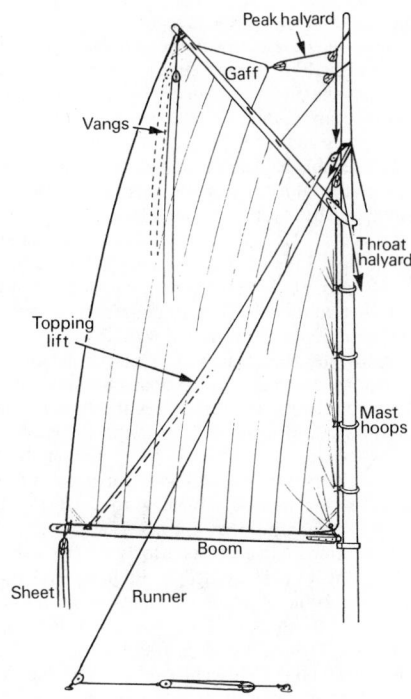

Gaff mainsail—an example of fore-and-aft rig

Running Rigging. All rigging used in hoisting, lowering, or trimming the sails of a vessel, or hoisting or *striking the yards of a square-rigged ship, is known as running rigging. Purchases used for hoisting sails are known as *halyards, those for hoisting the yards as *jeers. In square-rigged ships, only the triangular sails—jibs and staysails—have halyards; the square sails are hoisted up to their yards in bundles by *jiggers and then laced to the yards ready for spreading when required. Since they are very heavy sails, they have small lines or purchases, known as *buntlines, leading down from the yard to the foot of the sail to assist in gathering them up when reefing or furling. As with the standing rigging, individual halyards take the name of the mast they serve, as fore halyards, main halyards, etc. In the case of *jibs, they are known as jib halyards.

Fore-and-aft rigged ships have all their sails hoisted by halyards, originally of hemp but today mainly of flexible wire rope, frequently with a Terylene, or occasionally hemp, tail for ease of handling where sails are hoisted by hand. In the case of *gaff rig, the sails have two halyards, one for the *throat and another for the *peak of the sail. *Topping lifts are also fitted to the booms to take their weight and ensure a better set of the

sail, while gaff-rig mainsails frequently have *vangs fitted to the peak of the gaff to prevent it sagging away to leeward.

Fore-and-aft sails are trimmed to the wind by *sheets, rove with a purchase except in the case of very small sails where a single rope is adequate. Square sails are not directly trimmed to the wind; the yards are trimmed by *braces attached to each yardarm and led aft, and the sail, laced to the yard along the whole of its length, must therefore take up the same angle. But when a square-rigged ship is *close-hauled to the wind, the individual sails can be trimmed in a little harder by the *bowlines, which are attached to *bridles on the *leeches of the sail, and led forward towards the ship's bows. When the bowlines on the *weather leeches are hauled hard in, they keep the leech taut to the wind so that a better leading edge is obtained. In addition, a tack (led forward) and a sheet (led aft) is attached to the clews of all square sails in order to get a better trim of the sail.

Other running rigging in a ship are, for example, the *guys of *spinnakers and of *derricks, as well as purchases used permanently when working a crane or derrick. But in general any moving rope or wire used in the everyday running of a vessel, with the exception of such specialized articles as anchor *warps, mooring ropes, and wires, etc., is considered as running rigging. See also RIG.

J. Fincham, *A Treatise on Masting Ships*, 3rd edn. (1854); J. Irving, *Cruising and Ocean Racing* (1933); *Admiralty Manual of Seamanship*, 3 vols (1964–72).

RIGGING SCREW, a screw clamp for bringing together the two parts of a wire rope and holding them steady while they are *spliced. See also BOTTLESCREW.

RIGOL, a curved, semi-circular steel strip riveted to a ship's side over a *scuttle with the object of deflecting any water which runs down the side of the ship and preventing it from entering the scuttle when it is open.

RIJEKA, orig. **FIUME,** a principal seaport of Yugoslavia in the northern Adriatic. It is the centre of a large shipbuilding industry and a port of call for many shipping lines. Originally the Ligurian port of Tersatica, it has been fought over many times, and at various periods has belonged to France, Austria, Hungary, and Italy. Under Italian and Austrian ownership it was known as Fiume; today it belongs to Yugoslavia and takes its new name from the small River Rjecina on which it stands.

RING NET, a means of catching surface fish at sea in cases where a shoal of fish is visible or where they can be attracted into a small area by the use of powerful lights. In the operation of ring netting, a *purse net is paid out, usually from the *sternsheets of a rowing boat, around the shoal, the *warps from each end of the net being brought on board the fishing vessel. The bottom warps are hauled in to close the purse underneath the shoal and then, with the fish firmly enclosed, the whole net is hauled alongside and the fish within ladled out into the well of the fishing craft with a large scoop operated by the vessel's *derrick. When the majority of the fish are out, and no danger of the net breaking under the weight of the fish remains, the entire net is lifted by the derrick over the well, the bottom warps let go, and the remainder of the fish fall into the well.

RINGROSE, BASIL (d. 1686), British *buccaneer, was a surgeon who joined the buccaneering band led by Bartholomew *Sharp in 1679, in which also were William *Dampier and Lionel *Wafer. The band crossed the Isthmus of Darien to attack Panama, seized a ship, and cruised in the Pacific. As so often in these buccaneering bands, quarrels divided the men and the leadership was disputed, but when Dampier and others returned across the Isthmus, Ringrose continued with Sharp round Cape Horn to Antigua and thence to Dartmouth, England, in 1681. His account of this remarkable voyage was published in 1685 as a supplement to *Esquemeling's book, *The Bucaniers of America*. Meanwhile Ringrose had returned to the Pacific on another buccaneering voyage with Captain Swan in the *Cygnet*, but was killed in the attack on Santiago, Mexico. In his *Voyage Round the World*, Dampier calls him 'my ingenious friend'.

RINGTAIL, (1) an extension fitted to the *leech of a *fore-and-aft mainsail to provide a greater area of canvas to spread before a following wind. In earlier days it was rectangular and was attached to the leech of the *spanker and extended by a ringtail *boom attached to the main boom. Later it became triangular with the peak secured to the end of the *gaff and the foot forming an extension of the mainsail. **(2)** A small triangular sail set on a short mast stepped on the stern of a vessel and extended by a small boom overhanging the stern, used only in light and favourable winds. Ringtails are today used in yachts making single-handed voyages to form a self-steering device. See also VANE SELF-STEERING GEAR.

RINTELEN, FRANZ VON (1884–1949), German naval officer and saboteur, was serving on the Naval Staff in Berlin on the outbreak of the First World War (1914–18) and was sent in 1915 to the U.S.A. His first mission was to buy and dispatch war materials to Germany, but finding this impossible because of the British *blockade, he attempted the sabotage of allied merchant ships sailing from New York. He posed as the director of an import–export agency and recruited his collaborators from Irish-Americans and from German seamen. With their help he smuggled explosive devices aboard ships sailing for allied ports and also succeeded in damaging by explosion the Black Tom pier at New York. He founded an American Trade Union called the Labour National Peace Council which protested against the shipping of war materials to the allies and organized dock strikes to the detriment of the allied war effort.

Returning to Germany in October 1915 disguised as a Swiss businessman, he was intercepted by the British authorities at Falmouth and interned as a prisoner-of-war. After the entry of the U.S.A. into the war in 1917 he was sent back to New York for trial and was sentenced to four years imprisonment, returning to Germany in 1921. Considering that Germany was not sufficiently appreciative of his efforts on her behalf during the war, he settled in England in 1926. His first book of memoirs, *The Dark Invader* (1933), was an immediate best-seller but subsequent investigation has proved its unreliability. His second book, *The Return of the Dark Invader* (1935), sold less well. It was mostly concerned with his complaints of Germany's ingratitude to him. During the Second World War he was interned in Britain from 1940 to 1945, and died suddenly on 30 May 1949 in London.

He described himself as Captain von Rintelen, but the highest rank he held was Kapitänleutnant, the equivalent of lieutenant-commander.

RIO DE JANEIRO, former capital city of Brazil and a major seaport, was discovered by André Gonçalves, a Portuguese navigator, who reached the bay on 1 January 1502 and, believing it to be the mouth of a great river, named it Rio de Janeiro (river of January). The first settlement there was by French Huguenots under Nicholas Villegaignon, but in 1560 and 1567 the French settlements were destroyed by a Portuguese expedition under Mem de Sá. A French expedition sent in 1710 to capture the town was defeated; another in 1711 under the command of René *Duguay-Trouin was successful, but the town was given up on payment of a large ransom.

As a great seaport, the wealth of Rio de Janeiro was founded on the discovery of gold in Minas Geraes at the end of the 17th century, and grew vastly during the 19th century with the increasing popularity of coffee as a domestic beverage. The huge deep-water bay is large enough to accommodate a vast number of ships at any one time, and Rio de Janeiro is one of the principal bases of the Brazilian Navy and the home of the Naval Academy.

RIOU, EDWARD (c. 1758–1801), British naval officer, was in his time one of the best-known *frigate captains in the Royal Navy. Two outstanding events marked his career. The first occurred during his command of H.M.S. *Guardian* during a voyage from England to Sydney, Australia, with stores, cattle, and convicts. In December 1789, when some 1,200 miles southeast of the Cape of Good Hope and over 5,000 miles from Botany Bay, the *Guardian* approached a large iceberg in order to replenish with fresh water but grounded on a submerged spur of ice. Riou got the ship off but found her badly holed. He put as many of her crew as possible into boats with orders to make independently for the Cape, which they eventually reached. Those remaining on board the *Guardian* manned the pumps while Riou shaped *course for the Cape where he arrived after five weeks of anxious sailing. While lying in False Bay under repair the *Guardian* was unfortunately wrecked during a hurricane.

The second act of distinction occurred when he commanded the frigate *Amazon* at the battle of *Copenhagen in 1801. Two days before the action Riou took the commander-in-chief, Admiral Sir Hyde *Parker, and Lord *Nelson to examine closely the defences of Copenhagen and on the following day led the bombarding squadron through the narrow channel from the north to their battle positions. During the night of 1/2 April, Riou was in constant attendance on Nelson, who placed all the frigates and small craft under his orders. During the battle the *Amazon* found herself unsupported in face of the powerful Tre Kroner battery but was giving a good account of herself when Riou saw the signal to break off the action flying from Hyde Parker's flagship. Not realizing that Nelson was ignoring the signal, Riou weighed anchor and while withdrawing was cut in half by a round shot from the battery. A monument to his memory was erected in St. Paul's Cathedral.

RISING, a narrow *strake secured to the inside of the *frames of a small rowing boat to support the *thwarts. Risings are often used for this purpose in place of *knees in the smaller rowing boats.

RITCHIE (RICCI), Sir LEWIS ANSELM DA COSTA (1886–1967), British naval officer, was the author of many fictional stories of naval life which he published under the pseudonym of 'Bartimeus'. He joined the Royal Navy through the training ship H.M.S. *Britannia* in 1901 and served for a short while in ships in home waters before being obliged to transfer to the paymaster branch on account of bad eyesight. During the First World War (1914–18) he served on the staff of the commander-in-chief of the *Grand Fleet, Admiral Sir John *Jellicoe, and followed him to the Admiralty in 1916 where he spent the rest of the war. In 1932 he was appointed to the *Royal Yacht *Victoria and Albert* and was serving in her when the Second World War broke out in 1939. He joined the Naval Intelligence Division at the Admiralty and later the Ministry of Information, and was present as an eyewitness at the withdrawal from *Dunkirk and many other important naval occasions, which formed the subject of articles and broadcasts. In June 1944 he was appointed Press Secretary to George VI and held the post until 1947. His first book, published during the First World War, was *Naval Occasions* (1916). It was followed by *The Long Trick* (1917), *The Navy Eternal* (1918), *An Awfully Big Adventure* (1920), *The Bartimeus Omnibus* (1933), *A Make and Mend* (1934), and *Steady as You Go* (1942). His highly sentimental style achieved great popularity during the First World War and the immediately succeeding years, but proved less to the taste of later generations.

RIVER PLATE, BATTLE OF THE, the first naval action of the Second World War, was fought on 13 December 1939 between the British *cruisers *Exeter*, *Ajax*, and *Achilles* under the command of Commodore H. *Harwood and the German *pocket-battleship *Admiral Graf Spee* (Captain H. Langsdorff) off the entrance of the River Plate, on the east coast of South America. Harwood's cruiser force was one of several searching for the *Graf Spee* in the South Atlantic when news was received of two British merchant ships sunk in the St. Helena area on 2 and 3 December. Realizing that they were almost certainly the victims of the *Graf Spee* and that the area of their sinking pointed to her next appearance in the waters off the River Plate where she might expect to find many possible victims, Harwood ordered the cruisers *Exeter* and *Achilles* to rendezvous in that area with his own ship, H.M.S. *Ajax*, on 12 December. His intuition proved correct and at dawn on 13 December the *Graf Spee* was sighted on the horizon. She closed at full speed to give battle. The German ship had an armament of six 11-inch and eight 5·9-inch guns compared with the *Exeter's* six 8-inch and the other two cruisers' eight 6-inch guns, but by dividing his force with the *Exeter* to starboard and the other two ships to port of the enemy ship, Harwood obliged Langsdorff to choose between dividing his main armament or concentrating on one group to the advantage of the other. Langsdorff first concentrated his heavy guns on the *Exeter* and after 25 minutes succeeded in knocking out all but one of her guns and causing such heavy damage that she was obliged to withdraw. Meanwhile the *Ajax* and *Achilles* had been closing in and had scored a number of hits on the *Graf Spee* with their smaller guns. Both sides

The German pocket-battleship Admiral Graf Spee *being scuttled off Montevideo*

fired *torpedoes but no hits were obtained. The *Graf Spee* then turned her 11-inch guns on the *Ajax*, causing considerable damage to both her hull and her gun turrets. As a result Harwood broke off the engagement and retired under cover of a smoke screen. But contrary to expectations, since she had not been seriously damaged and her fighting efficiency was still virtually unimpaired, the *Graf Spee* did not pursue the British ships but set course for the neutral port of Montevideo, in the estuary of the River Plate, where she arrived shortly after midnight on 13/14 December, being shadowed to her destination by the *Ajax* and *Achilles*. Trapped into believing that a superior British force was awaiting his departure by reports put out that more British warships had concentrated off the Plate, Langsdorff consulted naval headquarters in Berlin as to his best course of action, landed most of his crew and the prisoners taken from ships he had sunk, and on the evening of 17 December took his ship out of harbour. On reaching the *three mile limit, he *scuttled her. Three days later Langsdorff committed suicide.

RIVISTA MARITTIMA, LA, an old-established and well-known Italian naval publication of international repute. It was first issued in Florence in April 1868, only seven years after the individual Italian states were brought together to form a single nation, with the encouragement of the then minister of marine, Rear Admiral Augusto Riboty, who thought that the publication of such a journal would help to consolidate the new nation. With many of the individual states having a keen interest in maritime affairs, and some with their own navies, a cultural magazine devoted to naval matters was reasonably certain of a warm welcome. Its first editor was Commander Carlo de Anezaga.

It was not long before the magazine achieved an international reputation for its professional standard, the accuracy of the information published, and the range of maritime interests covered. It is still recognized as an authoritative journal both on technical and professional subjects and many experts in particular fields of nautical interest contribute regularly. The present editor is Admiral Antonio Mondaini.

ROACH, the curve in the side or *foot of a sail. Square sails have a hollow roach in their foot to keep them clear of the mast *stays when the *yards on which they are set are *braced up, and this is known as a foot roach. When sails are roached on their sides, as in the *leech of a *gaff mainsail, they are known as leech roaches.

ROARING FORTIES, the area in the South Indian Ocean between the latitudes of 40° and 50° S. where the prevailing wind blows strongly from the west. Sailing ships in the Australian trade used to make for this area after rounding the Cape of Good Hope, as they could then rely on the westerly gales to lift them along their way. This was known as *running the easting down', and some of the *clippers reported exceptional daily runs in this area. The expression is also frequently used to describe the very rough parts of the oceans in the northern hemisphere between the latitudes of 40° and 50° N., particularly in the North Atlantic.

ROBANDS, orig. **ROPE-BANDS,** small, sometimes plaited, lines rove through the eyelet holes in a sail with a running eye by which the *head of the sail is brought to be *laced to a *yard or *jackstay after the *earings have been secured. They have reference only to the sails of square-rigged ships.

ROBECK, Sir JOHN MICHAEL DE, see DE ROBECK, Sir John Michael.

ROBERTS, BARTHOLOMEW (1682–1722), British pirate, was probably the most successful pirate in history. He never drank anything stronger than tea, went to bed early, was a strict Sabbatarian, and never gambled. He operated off the coast of Guinea and in the West Indies, where he is said to have captured as many as 400 vessels. He was killed in an action after Captain Chaloner *Ogle had been sent out by the British Admiralty to clear the west coast of Africa of pirates in 1722, having lived what he himself called 'a merry life and a short one'.

ROBERTSON, ARCHIBALD (c. 1745–1813), British naval officer, served in the navy throughout the War of American Independence (1775–82) and made a number of brilliant sketches of the various American ports he visited and engagements at which he was present, which form a particularly valuable archive of the naval side of this war. The collection of these sketches is in the New York Public Library, a part of the larger Spencer Collection.

ROBINET, a small ship's hand-gun of the 15th and 16th centuries. It had a calibre of one inch and fired an eight-ounce ball with a charge of the same weight of 'cannon corn' or 'meal' powder. The maximum, or random, range was 1,000 paces. When the powder used was 'fine corn', the same quality as that used in muskets, the charge used was reduced by one-quarter. Robinets were upper deck or 'castle' guns and were used purely in an anti-personnel role. See also GUNS, NAVAL; SERPENTINE.

ROBINSON, CHARLES NAPIER (1849–1936), British naval officer, joined the Royal Navy in 1861 and saw service in the suppression of the slave trade operating off the east coast of Africa and in operations against Malayan pirates. He retired from the navy in 1882 with the rank of commander to start a new career in journalism, and in 1884 was appointed assistant editor of the *Army and Navy Gazette*, at the same time being the naval correspondent for Europe of the *New York Herald*. In 1895 he joined the staff of *The Times* as its naval correspondent, a post which brought him great influence in the discussion of British naval policy which followed the passing of the German Navy Laws of 1898 and 1900 and set Germany on the path of naval rearmament. He was a close friend and confidant of Admiral Sir John *Fisher during his period as First Sea Lord (1904–10), and did much to explain and popularize Fisher's radical naval reforms of those years. From 1929 until his death he was editor of *Brassey's Naval Annual*.

In addition to his journalistic activities Robinson was a naval historian of distinction. One of his hobbies was collecting naval prints, and using these as illustrations he wrote two historical works of great merit, *The British Fleet* (1894), which was largely a study of the development of *matériel* and naval administration, and *The British Tar in Fact and Fiction* (1909), a valuable social history of the lower deck. Other publications were *The Sea Services* (1891) and *Old Naval Prints* (1924). He was a founder member of the *Navy Records Society and of the *Society for Nautical Research. In 1933 he was awarded the Chesney Gold Medal of the Royal United Service Institution for his outstanding contributions to naval literature.

ROBINSON CRUSOE, the castaway hero of Daniel *Defoe's novel of the same name published in 1719. The story is based on the experiences of Alexander *Selkirk, who was marooned on Juan Fernandez Island in 1704 by Captain Stradling, the *buccaneer, from the vessel *Cinque Ports*, in which Selkirk was serving as first mate. Selkirk, rescued by Woodes *Rogers fifty-two months later, wrote a short account of his adventures, and it is from this account that Defoe got the inspiration for his novel.

Robinson Crusoe saving his goods from the wreck; engraving from the 1st edition, 1719

ROCKET, a pyrotechnic device used at sea mainly as a signal of distress, but with other meanings when used for naval purposes, such as the executive order to start a particular manoeuvre, etc. Rockets have also been used as recognition signals (see, e.g., TITANIC) between vessels of the same shipping line, but this practice has been discouraged as leading to confusion in the meaning of rocket signals at sea, which remain basically signals of distress calling for assistance. Proposals have been made for an international code of rocket signals based on the colour of the rocket fired, such as, for example, red for distress, white to indicate position, blue to call for a pilot, and so on, but as yet no international agreement has been negotiated on this subject. See also VERY LIGHTS.

RODGERS, JOHN (1773–1838), American naval officer, was born in Harford County, Maryland. He had completed eleven years in the merchant service when he entered the navy as a lieutenant and became executive officer of the *frigate *Constellation* in 1798 under the command of Thomas *Truxtun. When the *Constellation* defeated and captured the French frigate *L'Insurgente* on 9 February 1799 Rodgers took command of the *prize with Midshipman David *Porter and eleven men. He served in the Mediterranean for much of the time between 1802 and 1806 in the war against Tripoli. In command of the frigate *John Adams*, he captured the Tripolitan ship *Meshuda* without a fight in May 1803, when she was attempting to enter the port of Tripoli under Moroccan colours.

He was appointed to command the *President in 1810. On 6 May 1811, east of Cape Henry, a ship was sighted and chased, darkness having made any identification difficult. After an exchange of hails both vessels opened fire, each claiming afterward that the other had fired first. In the U.S. naval Court of Inquiry, Rodgers proved that his officers had been cautioned in advance against opening fire without orders, but there was some evidence in a British inquiry from one of the members of the *President*'s crew that a gun had been fired accidentally in the *President*. Both ships, after the firing, remained in the vicinity, showing lights and repairing damage. At daybreak the *President* sent a boat, to discover that the ship she had engaged was the British *sloop *Little Belt* of twenty guns, less than one-third the size of the *President*. The smaller vessel had eleven killed and twenty-one wounded in the action, and suffered considerable damage to her masts, rigging, and hull.

The U.S.A. declared war on Great Britain on 8 June 1812 and three days later Rodgers sailed from New York with a squadron of five ships and headed north-east in the hope of intercepting a *convoy bound to England from Jamaica. The British frigate *Belvidera* was chased but escaped into Halifax after inflicting considerable damage on the *President*. Her arrival in Halifax with the news that she had been chased and fired upon was the first intimation to the British in those waters that war had been declared.

Rodgers's next duty was the defence of Baltimore, then threatened by a British military force supported by frigates and smaller craft. He was tireless in organizing the defence of the city and successfully blocked the river approach by sinking *hulks in the channel. The attack was eventually driven off. On 28 February 1815, Rodgers became the senior member of the new Board of Navy Commissioners. The two other members who took office at the same time were Isaac *Hull and David *Porter. Rodgers retained his position until December 1824 when he was appointed to command the Mediterranean Squadron. He became a Navy Commissioner again after his return from the Mediterranean, and resigned the position in May 1837 because of poor health.

RODING, the old name for the anchor *warp or *cable of a coasting *schooner. The term is said to be derived from roadstead, the place where such craft normally anchored.

RODNEY, GEORGE BRYDGES, first Baron (1719–92), British admiral, entered the Royal Navy in 1732. Because of influential connections his promotion was rapid; he was a lieutenant at 19 and a *post-captain at 23. He commanded H.M.S. *Eagle* in Sir Edward *Hawke's successful battle of *Cape Finisterre against the French in 1747, and in the following year became governor of Newfoundland, an appointment he held for nearly four years.

He was promoted rear admiral in 1759, during the Seven Years War (1756–63), and at once made his mark by the successful *blockade and bombardment of Le Havre to forestall any attempt at invasion from that port. Later he was made commander-in-chief of the Leeward Islands station, reducing Martinique and taking possession of the islands of St. Lucia, Grenada, and St. Vincent from the French.

Rodney became governor of *Greenwich Hospital in 1765, relinquishing the post for the command in Jamaica, but at the same time quarrelling with Lord Sandwich, First Lord of the Admiralty, that he was not allowed to employ a deputy in order to continue to enjoy the emoluments of the Greenwich Hospital appointment. Between 1775 and 1779 he lived in Paris to escape his many creditors and was able to return to England only through the kindness of the French Marshal Biron, who made him a loan in spite of the fact that Rodney's and the Marshal's countries were at war. At that time Lord

George Brydges Rodney as a young captain; oil painting after Sir J. Reynolds

Sandwich was having difficulty in finding naval commanders of calibre who were willing to serve an administration which was losing the confidence of the country, and Rodney's return at that time was more than welcome.

He signalized his return in 1780 by the successful relief of Gibraltar, then undergoing protracted siege. In the course of this operation he intercepted a Spanish squadron of nine ships near Cape *St. Vincent, and in a moonlit battle fought on 16 January in conditions of storm and close to a lee shore, he sank one and captured six of the enemy without loss to himself. His achievement was recognized by his appointment to a knighthood of the Bath.

After the relief of Gibraltar Rodney proceeded to the West Indies as commander-in-chief where he had an able second in Samuel *Hood. His financial straits always made him avaricious for *prize money, and this failing was confirmed by the attention he gave to the seizure of the Dutch island of St. Eustatius as soon as he arrived on the station. The treasure concerned was immense, but the capture brought nothing but trouble since British mercantile interests were

involved and lawsuits followed, remaining unsettled for years. After a brief period of ill health at home in 1781, he rejoined Hood in the following year, and crowned his career by a victory over Admiral de *Grasse off Dominica (see SAINTS, BATTLE OF THE), on 12 April, when a sudden change of wind enabled his fleet to break through the French line in two places. Among the four enemy ships captured was the flagship *Ville de Paris*, which surrendered to Hood in the *Barfleur*. The victory was decisive, but could have been greater had it been followed up through the evening and night. The Admiralty, uncertain both of Rodney's stamina and his ardour for more aggressive operations of war, had sent out a relief for him before they knew of the success, which enabled Britain to make a better peace with France than had at one time been thought possible. Rodney was created a peer, and in the ten more years before his death in 1792 was able to enjoy the enlarged circumstances and the social life which he found congenial.

Rodney was a man who invited no confidences, and was feared rather than liked by his subordinates, of whom, as a whole, he formed a poor opinion. It was for them to obey his orders; but when he attempted to introduce new tactics, such as attacking part of an enemy fleet with his whole force instead of engaging ship to ship in the old formal fashion, his instructions met with incomplete understanding because he had never taken his subordinates into his confidence.

Of the value to Great Britain's morale of his victories of 1780 and 1782 there was never any question. An overstretched navy was engaged in a difficult and protracted war, about which public opinion was sharply divided. There was much dissension even within the navy, and the Admiralty was fortunate to find in Rodney a commander of experience and resolution, able to command obedience if he did not inspire devotion.

D. Spinney, *Rodney* (1969).

ROGERS, WOODES (d. 1732), British *privateer, was engaged by a syndicate of British merchants during the War of the Spanish Succession (1702–13) to lead a privateering expedition under a *letter of marque to the *South Seas (South Pacific) in the ships *Duke* and *Duchess*, described in his journal as *'frigates' of twenty and twenty-six guns respectively. With Rogers in the *Duke* was William *Dampier, enlisted as navigator of the expedition. They sailed from Bristol in 1708, took a few *prizes of little worth in the voyage to the south, rounded Cape Horn, and set a course for the island of Juan Fernandez to rest, and to take in fresh water and such provisions as they could find. Here they discovered Alexander *Selkirk, who four years earlier had been *marooned on the island by Captain Stradling of the *Cinque Ports*. (See also ROBINSON CRUSOE.)

The two privateers had the good fortune off the coast of Mexico to intercept the Spanish *galleon *Nuestra Señora de la Encarnación Desengano*, which struck her colours after a short engagement, Rogers being wounded in the action. She was richly laden with silks, bullion, and precious stones, and after transferring her cargo to the *Duke* and *Duchess* it was decided to cross the Pacific to Guam, as it was unlikely that many more Spanish ships would be at sea after the alarm caused by the presence of British ships in those waters. The voyage home round the Cape of Good Hope was uneventful and the two ships anchored in the Thames in 1711. The prize goods taken during the voyage were sold for the then considerable sum of £148,000.

Rogers wrote an entertaining account of his circumnavigation in *A Cruising Voyage Round the World* (1712) and in 1718 was appointed governor of the Bahamas with a mandate to stamp out piracy. His first tour of duty there ended in 1721 and he was appointed for a second term in 1729, dying there three years later.

ROGGEVEEN, JACOB (1659–1729), Dutch navigator, led an expedition of discovery into the South Pacific in 1721. His father, Arend Roggeveen, had been an instructor in mathematics, astronomy, and navigational theory, and it was from him that Jacob learned to be a navigator. In 1675 Arend had put forward a proposition to the States-General of Holland for a voyage of discovery into the Pacific with the object of developing Dutch trade, but had been unable to get sufficient financial backing for such an expedition. Jacob revived his father's proposal in 1721, applying to the Dutch West India Company for support. The company agreed to equip three ships, retaining for themselves nine-tenths of any profits, with one-tenth to Jacob.

There had been, since Arend's original application, a reported discovery of a large island in the Pacific which, in the words of William *Dampier in his *A New Voyage Round the World* (1697), 'might be the coast of *Terra Australis Incognita', the great continent which all geographers still believed existed in the southern hemisphere to balance the land mass in the northern hemisphere. The 'discoverer' had been the *buccaneer Edward Davis during the cruise in 1687 of the ship *Batchelor's Delight* in the Pacific, in which Dampier had been present. Jacob Roggeveen, in his application to the Dutch West India Company, proposed steering west from the coast of Chile along the *latitude of 27° S. until he came to 'Davis's Land', which he confidently expected to prove to be Terra Australis Incognita. He set out in 1721 with the ships *Den Arend*, *Thienhoven*, and *De Africaansche Galey*, and made his first landfall in the Pacific on Easter Sunday, 1722, discovering an island which he named Paasch Eyland (Easter Island). During the visit of his ships there, the thieving proclivities of the natives led to a tragic affray in which some 12–15 of them were shot and killed as a result of a panic among some of Roggeveen's sailors. However, a state of peaceful co-existence had been restored by the time the three ships left Easter Island. Proceeding westward, Roggeveen reached the Society group of islands and Samoa, but after a further vain search for the great southern continent, returned to Holland.

ROGUE KNOT, the seaman's name for a *reef knot tied 'upside down', the two short ends appearing on opposite sides of the knot after tying instead of on the same side. It is the knot which ashore would be called a 'granny' and is very apt to slip when it takes a strain.

ROGUE'S MARCH, a particular cadence beaten on the drum when a man of bad character was dismissed the naval service in Britain for an offence committed on board ship. It was also used when a man was sentenced to a *flogging round the fleet, the boat in which he was taken alongside each ship and in which he received twelve strokes with a *cat-o'-nine-tails being greeted on arrival alongside with the rogue's march. It appears to have been introduced into the British Navy during the latter half of the 18th century, obviously designed to attract the attention of seamen to the severe penalties inflicted for offences committed on board ship, and its use lasted for about eighty to ninety years. It was probably introduced in the navy in imitation of the practice in the army when soldiers convicted of serious crimes were drummed out of their regiments.

ROGUE'S YARN, a coloured yarn of jute laid up in a strand of rope to identify the materials from which it is made. Commercially made *manila rope is marked with a black rogue's yarn, naval manila rope with red in each of two strands. Commercial *sisal rope has a red rogue's yarn, naval sisal has yellow in each of two strands. Commercial *hemp has no rogue's yarn, naval hemp has red in all three strands. *Coir rope is marked with a yellow rogue's yarn in one strand only. Originally, rogue's yarns were used only in naval rope and indicated from their colour the ropeyard in which they were made. They were introduced to stop thieving by making the rope easily recognizable, as in the days of sailing navies naval rope was considered far superior to all other and there was a great temptation to smuggle it out of the dockyards and sell it to owners or captains of merchant vessels.

Rogue's yarns of different colours are also used in the running *rigging of yachts to identify the individual *halyards, *sheets, etc.

ROHWER, JÜRGEN (1924–), German naval officer, served in the German Navy throughout the Second World War and subsequently studied at Hamburg University. From 1954 to 1959 he was publications manager of the Arbeitskreis für Wehrforschung and then became head of the Bibliotek für Zeitgeschichte in Stuttgart and editor of the official naval journal *Marine Rundschau, to which he also contributed. He is a leading authority on *U-boat warfare and his analyses of *convoy battles have received wide acclaim.

His works include *Entscheidungsschlachten des zweiten Weltkrieges* in collaboration with Dr. H. A. Jacobsen and *Chronik des Seekrieges 1939–1945* in collaboration with Dr. Gerhard Hümmelchen, an excellent reference book. As a result of twenty years research he published *Die U-Boot-Erfolge des Achsenmächte 1939–1945*, which was followed by *U-Boote: ein Chronik in Bildern*.

ROLLING HITCH, a hitch used on board ship for *bending a rope to a *spar. The end of the rope is passed round the spar and then passed a second time round so that it rides over the standing part; it is then carried across and up through the *bight. A rolling hitch properly tied will never slip.

Rolling hitch

ROMME, CHARLES (1744–1805), French geographer and professor of mathematics and navigation, was the author of several important scientific works on masts and sails, and also on the determination of *longitude. In 1792 he brought out his authoritative *Dictionnaire de la Marine Française*, which was followed by his *Science du Marin* (1800). In addition he produced a table of winds, tides, and currents throughout the world.

ROOKE or **ROOK,** Sir GEORGE (1650–1709), British admiral of the fleet, was born near Canterbury, the second son of an influential and wealthy family. He entered the navy as a volunteer and was present at some of the actions of the Second Dutch War (1665–7), fierce battles with heavy casualties on both sides, generally conducted as a disorganized mêlée, which may have had some bearing on the rigid battle tactics on which he insisted later in his career. After promotion to *post-captain he commanded the *Deptford* at the battle of *Bantry Bay in 1689 and at the subsequent relief at *Londonderry, at which he did not appear to appreciate the desperate state of the garrison and the need for a quick relief. He lay inactive for six weeks while the garrison starved, and it has been said that the final breaking of the *boom and relief of the garrison by Captain Leake in the *Dartmouth* was done more with Rooke's permission than by his orders.

He received his flag as a rear admiral in 1690, was a junior admiral at the inconclusive battle of *Beachy Head, and third-in-command of the English fleet at *Barfleur in 1692, when he also commanded the subsequent boat attack on the French ships which had taken shelter at La Hogue, burning thirteen *ships of the line and many transports, part of the French expedition designed to reinstate James II on the throne of England. This was a gallant and highly successful operation which won Rooke a knighthood and brought him into the limelight as one of the great naval commanders, a reputation which he never quite lived up to in his further career. He was in charge of the escort of the great Smyrna *convoy of 400 ships in 1693 with the duty of taking them safely to the Levant past the French squadrons based at *Brest and *Toulon. The convoy was waylaid by the combined French squadrons off Cape St. Vincent and many of the ships captured, resulting in a loss to British and Dutch merchants estimated at £6,000,000. Rooke was not blamed for the disaster; indeed, he came out of it with some credit in that the loss might have been yet greater; yet later analysis shows that to some extent he fell into a trap engineered by the French admiral and, moreover, was too much reliant on the deliberations of a Council of War, that perennial inhibition of swift and decisive action.

During the War of the Spanish Succession (1702–13) Rooke was commander-in-chief of the combined Anglo-Dutch fleet, and it is during this war that his greatest successes came. In 1702, after a miserable failure to capture *Cadiz, a fortuitous descent upon *Vigo was a pronounced success, resulting in a considerable destruction of Spanish ships and the capture of a good proportion of treasure which had recently arrived in the annual *flota from the west. Two years later, commanding in the Mediterranean, Rooke's attempt to capture *Barcelona was an even more ignominious failure than that on Cadiz in 1702, but was redeemed by a sudden decision to capture *Gibraltar, then believed to be in a weak state of defence. Gibraltar fell to a heavy bombardment and an effective landing by seamen and marines of the fleet, and was retained at the battle of *Velez Malaga three weeks later when a French fleet under the command of the Comte de *Toulouse failed to dislodge the ships under Rooke's command and in the end relinquished the field of battle, and Gibraltar, to the English.

The capture of Gibraltar was, ironically, the signal for the dismissal of Rooke. His Tory friends in Parliament put it about that the capture of Gibraltar was a greater victory than had been the land battle of Blenheim, fought a few weeks earlier, and that Rooke as a leader was as distinguished as, if not more distinguished than, the Duke of Marlborough. This claim so infuriated the Whig party of Marlborough, then in political power, that Rooke was firmly put on the shelf, never again to be employed.

Rooke was, no doubt, the greatest seaman of his age, of any nationality, but throughout his naval career lacked any flexibility of tactical thought. He fought his naval battles in rigid lines, and reprimanded any captain who tried to achieve a tactical advantage by departing from them. But if he was too rigid in his tactical thought, too much dependent on the advice of Councils of War, at least in an age of great venality he was throughout his career an honest man. 'I do not leave much,' he said on his deathbed, 'but what I leave was honestly gotten. It never cost a sailor a tear, or the nation a farthing.'

A memoir of Sir George Rooke, by Rear Admiral C. C. Penrose Fitzgerald, is included in *From Howard to Nelson*, edited by Sir John *Laughton (1899). His private journal was published by the *Navy Records Society (Vol. IX, 1897).

ROOM 40 O.B., the room in the British Admiralty during the First World War (1914–18) where German naval signals and other messages were deciphered. It was set up early in the war by the Director of Naval Intelligence, Admiral Sir William *Hall, and its team of cryptographers was brought together and trained by Sir Alfred Ewing, who had been Director of Naval Education in the Admiralty. It was in this room that the signals made to and from the German *High Seas Fleet during the battle of *Jutland in 1916 were deciphered and passed to Admiral Sir John *Jellicoe, commanding the *Grand Fleet, though during the night some vital signals were not sent out as their importance was not recognized. After that battle Commander (later Admiral) W. M. *James took charge of the room and it had many notable successes. Perhaps the most dramatic of them was the interception and deciphering of the famous Zimmerman telegram which, when revealed to the President of the U.S.A., was the main reason for American entry into the war. The initials O.B. stand for Old Building, the eastern block of the quadrangle which formed the Admiralty.

ROOSEVELT, THEODORE (1858–1919), 26th president of the U.S.A., was assistant secretary of the navy at the beginning of the Spanish–American War of 1898, and author of *The Naval War of 1812* (1882). He resigned his post in the Navy Department during the war in order to become lieutenant-colonel of a regiment which came to be called the Rough Riders. He was elected as vice president under President McKinley in 1900 and succeeded to the presidency when McKinley was assassinated the following year. He was chiefly responsible for the construction of the *Panama Canal which was opened to shipping in 1914. His interest in naval affairs continued while he was in the White House and almost all his actions in regard to the navy were based on common sense and good judgement: one possible exception being his handling of the *Brownson case. In this the then Chief of the Bureau of Naval Personnel (Brownson) resigned when Roosevelt insisted on the appointment of a naval medical officer to command a hospital ship.

ROPE, the name given in the maritime world to all *cordage of over one inch in diameter, whether made from natural or man-made fibres or wire. The natural fibres used in rope-making are *hemp, *manila, *sisal, and *coir, each with its own particular characteristics and uses.

Hemp rope is made from the fibres of *Cannabis sativa*, a hard, smooth rope, pale straw in colour when new but often known as white rope when in this state. It is usually tarred to preserve it against deterioration when it gets wet. It was originally used for *hawsers, running *rigging, etc., but generally today its use is confined to the smaller ropes and lines, except in many yachts, where the white Italian hemp rope is considered the best natural fibre rope for *halyards and *sheets. Manila rope is made from the fibres of the wild banana, which gives it a good strength and spring. When made up into rope it is a golden brown in colour and is mainly used for such purposes as a boat's *falls, or in *tackles where considerable weights are liable to be lifted. It is the most dependable of the ropes made from natural fibres, but today is difficult to obtain as the source of supply is limited. Sisal rope is made from the fibres of the *Henniquin* plant which grows widely in Africa. Like hemp, it is a pale straw colour, but is frequently tarred to preserve it. It is a hairy rope, generally used in places where it is not subjected to great strain or the lifting of considerable weights. Coir rope, also known as *grass line, is made from the fibre of the coconut palm. It is a very rough rope, dark brown in colour, and weaker than the other natural fibre ropes, but has advantages in that it is lighter, more resilient, and floats on water. This last property makes it particularly suitable for use as *warps. Cotton is also occasionally used for rope in yachts, but is hard and difficult to handle when wet and is liable to mildew.

The process of rope-making is the same for all these fibres. Each fibre is generally about five feet in length and, in right-handed rope, known as the *'Z-twist', is spun right-handed to form yarns, sufficient overlapping fibres being used to form a continuous yarn. The spinning binds the fibres firmly together, the individual fibres being held in place by friction. The yarns are then gathered together and twisted left-handed into *strands; three strands (or four in the case of four-stranded, or *shroud-laid, rope) being laid up right-handed to form a *hawser-laid rope. The contrary twists of the strands and the rope ensures that it remains compact with no tendency to spread. The twist of the strand is known as the *foreturn, that of the rope, the *afterturn. In left-handed rope, known as the *'S-twist' (illustrated), each component of the rope is twisted in the opposite direction.

A rough and ready rule for finding the breaking strain of rope is to divide the square of its circumference in inches by three, the answer being in tons. Thus, the breaking strain in tons of 4-inch rope would be $\frac{16}{3}$ or $5\frac{1}{3}$ tons. A general rule with all rope is to divide the breaking strain by six in order to find the working load, a factor of safety of six to one.

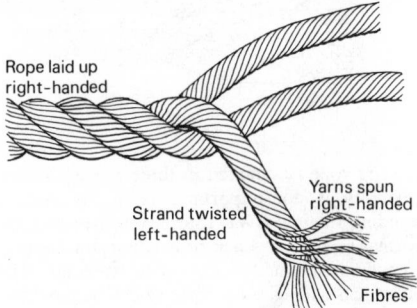

Right-handed hawser-laid rope

Synthetic rope, made from man-made fibres, is rapidly replacing natural rope, particularly in yachts, on account of its greater strength in relation to its size. The main fibres used are nylon, Terylene, and polythene, but when laid up into the normal three-stranded rope it is apt to have an unacceptable elasticity when under strain. This drawback, however, has been largely eliminated by laying up the yarns into braided rope. The strongest of the three is nylon rope. Other synthetic ropes made are Ulstron, which is pale green in colour and has the same degree of strength as Terylene rope, and Courlene, which is orange in colour and highly resistant to chafe. The great advantages of man-made fibre rope over natural fibre rope is that it does not absorb moisture, does not swell or lose part of its strength, as does natural fibre rope, and is not subject to rot.

The breaking strain of synthetic rope can be calculated, as in natural fibre ropes, by using the square of the circumference. In nylon rope, the breaking strain in tons is the square of the circumference, in Terylene it is 0·9 of the square of the circumference and in Courlene 0·7 of the square of the circumference.

Wire rope is made with a number of small wires which extend continuously throughout the length of the rope and give it its great strength. The small wires are twisted left-handed round a jute or wire core to form strands, and six strands are laid up right-handed round a hemp or jute heart to form the rope. The heart has two functions, acting as a cushion in which the strands bed themselves and can take up their natural position as the wire rope is bent and also as a lubricant by absorbing the oil with which wire rope is periodically dressed and forcing it between the individual wires when the rope is bent in the course of its use.

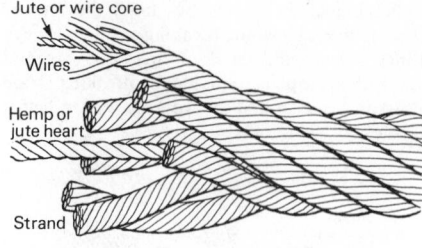

Jute or wire core

Wires

Hemp or jute heart

Strand

Wire rope

Wire rope is supplied in three grades. Where flexibility is not important, as in the case of standing rigging, SWR (Steel Wire Rope) is the normal type used. Lack of flexibility in SWR is compensated for by its added strength. The individual wires are of larger gauge than in other wire ropes and are wound round a steel wire core, seven wires per strand being used in the least flexible and 19 wires where a certain amount of flexibility is needed. In cases where considerable flexibility is required, as in wire hawsers, a certain loss of strength is unavoidable. FSWR (Flexible Steel Wire Rope) is supplied for these purposes, the individual wires being of medium gauge and wound round a large jute core. The number of wires used in each strand are 30 in very flexible wire, 24 in flexible wire, and 12 in less flexible. The third grade of wire rope is ESFSWR (Extra Special Flexible Steel Wire Rope) and this is supplied in cases where flexibility and strength are both necessities. The wire used is of small gauge wound round a hemp core, 61 wires per strand in extra flexible wire rope and 37, 24, and 19 wires in the less flexible grades. The term 'extra special' refers to the quality of steel used, which is of a higher grade then in FSWR and SWR, thus producing the extra strength.

As in the case of natural and man-made fibre ropes, the breaking strains of wire rope can be simply calculated by multiplying the square of the circumference in inches by factors, that for SWR being 2·75, for FSWR being 2, or 2·5 if the circumference of the wire rope is over $4\frac{1}{2}$ inches (114 mm), and for ESFSWR being 3·6, in each case the breaking strain being in tons.

In Great Britain the size of all rope is denoted by its circumference in inches, in the U.S.A. and most other countries the size is denoted by its diameter. See also ROGUE'S YARN.

ROPEWALK or **ROPEHOUSE**, a long building usually 300 to 400 yards in length, in which ropes are made by twisting *yarns into *strands and strands into *rope. The basis of the best natural rope is *hemp or *manila, though other fibres, such as cotton, *sisal, and *coir, have their uses. In the days before mechanization the process of rope-making in a ropewalk was first to *hackle the fibre by drawing it through hackle-boards, blocks studded with steel prongs, to separate the fibres and get them all lying straight. These fibres were then spun into strands by means of a spinning machine, the rope-maker making fast a sufficient number of fibres to three rotating hooks in the spinning machine and walking backwards with the fibres to keep the proper tension on them while an assistant worked the spinning machine. When the necessary number and length of strands had been spun they were then laid up into rope, the strands being attached to the spinning machine and fed through grooves in a 'top', a conical piece of wood with the grooves merging at the thin end. Again the rope-maker walked backwards down the ropewalk holding the top, and the strands emerged from the thin end of the 'top' laid up into rope.

Modern rope-making is, of course, all mechanized and the old hand ropewalks no longer exist; but the basic process of rope-making is still much as above. Man-made fibres are rapidly replacing natural fibres in all ropes.

ROSE, Sir ALEC RICHARD (1908–), British merchant and deep-sea yachtsman, was determined from an early age one day to sail his own boat round the world. After cruising from his home in Portsmouth, Hampshire, up and down the English Channel in a 27-ft converted ship's lifeboat, *Neptune's Daughter*, he bought *Lively Lady*, a 9-ton *cutter built in India in 1948, and sailed her in the 1964 single-handed transatlantic race, being placed fourth. His lifelong ambition was realized when in 1967–8 he sailed *Lively Lady* single-handed round the world from Portsmouth via the Cape of Good Hope, Melbourne, and Cape Horn back to Portsmouth in the short time of eleven months. He was given a knighthood for his feat and wrote an account of the voyage in *My Lively Lady* (1970).

ROSE BOX, the name given to the strainer at the end of the suction pipe of a *bilge pump to prevent solid material in the bilges being sucked up into the pump and choking it. It is also widely known, particularly in yachts, as a strum box.

ROSE LASHING, a *'tiddley' piece of *seizing by means of which the *eye of a rope is secured

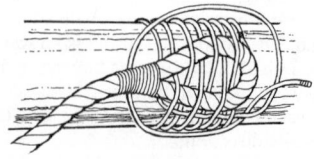

Rose lashing

to a *spar. The seizing is rove in the form of a cross lashing by being passed over and under the parts of the eye, the end being brought round the whole to finish it off.

ROSKILL, STEPHEN WENTWORTH (1903–), British naval officer, specialized in gunnery. Promoted to captain in 1944 he was senior British observer during the American atomic bomb tests at Bikini in 1946. He was appointed deputy director of Naval Intelligence in 1946 but was invalided two years later as a result of deafness caused by gunblast. In 1949 he was appointed official historian for the writing of the British naval history of the Second World War. In addition to the three volumes of official history, *The War at Sea* (1954–61), his works include *The Strategy of Sea Power* (1962), *The Art of Leadership* (1964), *Naval Policy between the Wars*, Vol. 1 (1968), *Hankey, Man of Secrets*, Vol. 1 (1970), Vol. 2 (1973).

ROSS, Sir JAMES CLARK (1800–62), was one of the most experienced of all the Royal Navy officers who explored the polar regions during the 19th century. He joined the navy in 1812 as a *midshipman under the command of his uncle Sir John *Ross, serving in the Baltic, the White Sea, and the North Sea during the last years of the Napoleonic War (1803–15). In 1818 he joined the first of a series of naval expeditions to the Arctic in search of the North-West passage with Sir John Ross in command of the *Isabella* and William Edward *Parry in command of the *Alexander*. During this and the four subsequent expeditions in which he served under Parry, Ross showed a special interest in magnetic observations, under the instruction of Sir Edward *Sabine, and in natural history. He also became skilled in the art of polar land travel, in navigating ships in ice, in combating *scurvy, and in maintaining the morale of his men. In 1827 Ross accompanied Parry in an attempt to reach the North pole from Spitsbergen, pulling boats and sledges across the ice. Between 1829 and 1832, Ross, now a commander, sailed once more with Sir John Ross on an expedition to find the North-West passage. It was on this voyage that he achieved fame by discovering the north *magnetic pole on the west side of Boothia Peninsula. In 1835–6, in command of H.M.S. *Cove*, Ross attempted the rescue of a number of British whaling ships beset in Davis Strait.

His crowning glory, however, was the Antarctic expedition of 1839–43. On this occasion the Admiralty put Ross in command of H.M. ships *Erebus* and *Terror* with instructions to carry out a magnetic survey in the far south. Ross penetrated, for the first time, the ice of the Ross Sea, discovered the Ross Ice Barrier, and charted the coast of that part of Antarctica which he claimed for Britain as Victoria Land. During a second season the James Ross Island group, off the northern tip of the Antarctic Peninsula, was discovered and also claimed for Britain. For these significant discoveries Ross received a knighthood. His last polar expedition was in 1848–9 when, with H.M.S. *Investigator* and *Enterprise*, he was sent to search for Sir John *Franklin.

He wrote a narrative of his 1839–43 voyage to Antarctica which was published in 1847 under the title *A Voyage of Discovery and Research to Southern and Antarctic Regions*.

ROSS, Sir JOHN (1777–1856), British rear admiral and Arctic explorer, was born at Inch, Wigtonshire. He made his first voyage to the Arctic in 1818 with the ships *Isabella* and *Alexander*, an account of which is given in his book *Voyage of Discovery for the purpose of exploring Baffin Bay*, published in 1819. Accompanying him on this voyage were several future Arctic explorers notably W. E. *Parry, J. C. *Ross (his nephew), and Edward *Sabine. Having reached Lancaster Sound on 30 August 1818 he refused to proceed any further west, insisting that his progress was barred by a chain of mountains, an opinion not shared by his colleagues. On his return the Admiralty refused him further funds and it was not until 1829 that, thanks to the patronage of a sheriff of London, Felix Booth, he was able to undertake a second voyage in the *paddle steamer *Victory*. After discovering and surveying the Boothia Peninsula and King William Island, his ship became ice-bound and he was obliged to endure four winters before being rescued in 1833. During this enforced stay his nephew J. C. Ross, who was his second-in-command, located the north magnetic pole on 31 May 1831. On his return to England he was knighted. He was British Consul at Stockholm between 1839 and 1846 and in 1850 he commanded a privately organized expedition to search for Sir John *Franklin. In addition to writing accounts of his voyages, he was a considerable naval historian and wrote a biography of Admiral Lord de Saumarez, published in 1838.

ROSSEL DE CERCY, AUGUSTE LOUIS, Marquis de (*fl.* 1775–1824), French naval officer, had the unusual distinction during his naval career of combining a command afloat with an appointment as an official war artist. He specialized in battle scenes of the War of American Independence (1775–82), the Revolutionary War (1793–1801), and the Napoleonic War (1803–15), and a collection of his pictures is to be found in the *Musée de la Marine in Paris. Though not of outstanding merit, they are nevertheless accurate interpretations of the naval battles of those wars.

The docks at Rotterdam

ROTTERDAM, a city and seaport of Holland on the banks of the River Maas. It was the birthplace of three Dutch admirals, de Witte, Kortanaer, and van Brakel, whose monuments are in the Groute Kerk. The construction of the 'New Waterway', opened in 1890, connecting Rotterdam with Hook of Holland, brought access to Rotterdam to the largest ships and from that date its development into what is today the greatest port of Europe, and indeed of the world, was extraordinarily rapid. In recent years its growth has been stimulated even faster by the construction of the new 'Europort', which is an extension of the original port down-river, and by the growth of container traffic which Rotterdam can handle quickly and efficiently. Part of its growth is due to the extensive system of inland canals which connect the Rhine to the Maas and which provide easy access to the port from most of the great manufacturing centres of western Europe. In addition to its importance as the world's largest and fastest growing seaport, it is also a large centre of shipbuilding and ship repair as well as a great industrial city in its own right. During the Second World War the port, like the city itself, was largely destroyed by bombing, and superb post-war planning and development

are responsible for its present pre-eminence. Today more than a quarter of all the seaborne goods that enter or leave the European Economic Community pass through Rotterdam.

ROUND, to, a verb, used in conjunction with an adverb, with a variety of maritime meanings. To round down a *tackle is to *overhaul it; to round up a tackle is to haul in on it before taking the strain. To round in is to haul in quickly, as on a weather *brace in a square-rigged sailing ship; to round to is to bring a sailing vessel up to the wind.

ROUND HOUSE, a name given to square or rectangular *cabins built on the *quarterdeck of large passenger ships and *East Indiamen in the 18th and 19th centuries, the *poop deck often forming the roof. These cabins were called round because one could walk round them; they corresponded closely to what was called the *coach in a warship. In some merchant ships, a round house for accommodation was placed on the upper deck abaft the mainmast. In the late 18th and early 19th centuries round houses (still square) were built in ships of the British Navy as lavatories for men confined in the sickbay.

ROUND OF A ROPE, the length of a single strand when it makes one complete turn round the circumference of the rope.

ROUND SEIZING, a *seizing used to lash two ropes together with a series of turns of small stuff with the end passing round the turns to finish it off. Two parts of the same rope can be secured by a round seizing to form an *eye.

ROUND SHIP, the generic name for the medieval ship, at least up to the 15th century, with the exception of the *galley and the *longship. The average proportion of length to *beam was two, or two and a half, to one and they were normally single-masted with a single square sail hoisted on a *yard. Within the generic term were sub-divisions, such as *cog, *dromon, etc., all of them basically of the typical round ship design. They were the standard ship for almost all sea purposes, being used as warships, as transports, and as cargo-carrying vessels.

ROUND TURN AND TWO HALF HITCHES, a knot widely used when making a boat or small vessel fast to a post or *bollard. It is made by taking a full turn round the post or bollard and finishing the knot off with two half hitches round the standing part of the rope. If there is likely to be much strain on the knot, a better one for the purpose is a *fisherman's bend, as a round turn and two half hitches is liable to jam when there is a heavy pull on it.

Round turn and two half hitches

ROUS, HENRY JOHN (1795–1877), British admiral, has a small niche in the temple of maritime fame when, in 1834, he brought home across the Atlantic the *frigate *Pique* which had run ashore and been much damaged on the Labrador coast. Under Rous's command, she made the voyage with a sprung foremast and lacking her *forefoot, *keel, and *rudder, a considerable feat of seamanship. During the whole of her passage she was making water at the rate of 23 inches an hour, which was kept in check by continual working of the *pumps throughout her passage. Rous retired from the navy in 1838 to devote the remainder of his life to horse-racing, and is remembered in this field from the race for the Rous Memorial Stakes run each year at the Royal Ascot meeting.

ROUSE OUT, to, the maritime term for turning out the hands on board ship in the morning, or calling the watch for duty on deck.

ROUSE-IN, to, to haul in any slack cable, or *slatch, which may lie on the bottom when a vessel lies to a single anchor. The reason for rousing-in such slack cable is that otherwise it might foul the anchor by becoming twisted round the shank or stock as the ship swings to wind or tide.

ROVER, another name occasionally used to describe a pirate or *freebooter. It comes from the Dutch word for pirate, *zee-rover*, literally sea-robber.

ROWLANDSON, THOMAS (1756–1827), British caricaturist, was one of the great geniuses of British art whose work covered a wide range of subjects. Born in Old Jewry, London, he studied in Paris for two years before going to the Royal Academy Schools in London. He began painting as a historical, landscape, and portrait painter, but quickly established himself as a caricaturist, specializing in a humorous commentary of social life in England around the turn of the 18th century. Some of the best of these were his satirical caricatures of the depravity of the

The Purser; aquatint by T. Rowlandson, 1799

human being, and his commentaries in this genre on lower-deck life in the British Navy of his period are among his best-known works. His quick sketches made on board, with their exuberance and sureness of line, express better than any words the quality of life as lived on the main or lower deck of a British man-of-war.

ROWLOCK, a U-shaped space cut in a boat's gunwale to take the *oars. When the boat is being used under sail, or secured alongside, the rowlocks are closed with *shutters. The term is often used, though wrongly, to describe the metal *crutches used for oars in smaller rowing boats. See also THOLE PINS.

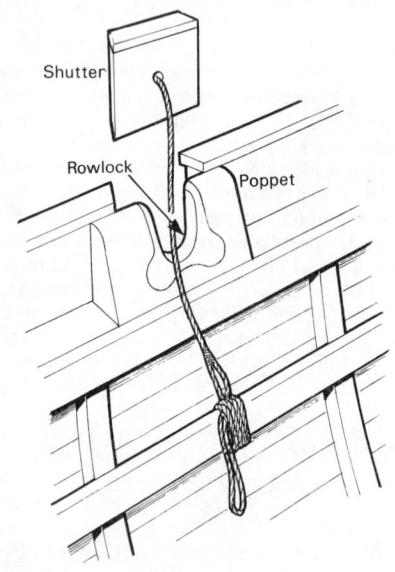

Shutter

Rowlock

Poppet

Rowlock

ROYAL, the name of the sail set next above the *topgallant-sail in a square-rigged ship, the fourth sail in ascending order from the deck, except where two topsails, upper and lower, are set, in which case it is the fifth sail in ascending order. The two clews are secured to the ends of the topgallant-yard. It is a light-weather sail, set only when the wind is steady and favourable, and was originally known as the topgallant-royal. For illus. see SAIL.

ROYAL CORINTHIAN YACHT CLUB, THE, was formed as the Corinthian Club in 1872 specifically for owners who sailed their own boat and did not employ professional skippers to do so for them. With 200 members and a clubhouse at Erith, Kent, the club held races for various classes of yachts on the Lower Thames. It received an Admiralty warrant to wear the *Blue Ensign on members' yachts in 1884, and

in 1893 was granted permission by Queen Victoria to be called the Royal Corinthian Yacht Club.

The following year a club room was secured at Burnham-on-Crouch, Essex, where yacht racing could be held on a deep-water river almost free from commercial traffic, and the club eventually relinquished its connections with the Thames and moved its headquarters to the River Crouch. Its present cube-style clubhouse at the eastern end of the Burnham anchorage was built in 1930. As the club became more involved in Solent racing and offshore events, a second clubhouse was obtained on the Parade at Cowes, Isle of Wight.

ROYAL CORK YACHT CLUB, THE, which claims to be the world's oldest yacht club, was founded by twenty-five members in 1720 as the Water Club of Cork, in southern Ireland. The members wore uniforms and made sailing excursions in their yachts under the command of an 'admiral' in the manner of naval manoeuvres, and engaged in mock battles. The Water Club, however, lapsed in 1765 and a group of its members then formed the Little Monkstown Club, which was later granted the title of the Royal Cork Yacht Club. Its present headquarters are at Crosshaven. Although it is now in the Republic of Ireland, or Eire, the prefix 'Royal' has nevertheless been retained.

ROYAL CRUISING CLUB, THE, was formed as the Cruising Club in 1880 at a time when there was no club in Britain devoted solely to yacht cruising. Following a series of articles on the new club's activities which appeared in *Hunt's Yachting Magazine*, membership grew rapidly as cruising yachtsmen found congenial supporters of the sport, and when *Hunt's* ceased publication in 1888 the club began to issue its own *Journal* to record accounts of members' cruises.

In 1902 permission was obtained to use the Royal prefix, and an Admiralty warrant was issued for members whose yachts were qualified to wear the *Blue Ensign. Membership was strictly limited to 300. In the years since the Second World War members of the R.C.C. have made many long distance voyages in their yachts, including cruises to Iceland, the Mediterranean, Australia and the Far East, the Antarctic, and around the world. Challenge cups are awarded for logs of each year's most outstanding cruises, which are published in the club's annual, *Roving Commissions*.

ROYAL DOCKYARDS, the generic name given to the naval dockyards of the Royal Navy, probably an abbreviation of Royal Naval Dockyard. In the early days of the British Navy there were five Royal dockyards in Britain, *Deptford, Woolwich, *Chatham, *Portsmouth, and *Plymouth. As the navy grew in size and complexity, the dockyards at Deptford and Woolwich were closed down, though Deptford remained as the principal victualling yard, and further naval dockyards in Britain were established at Sheerness, Haulbowline in south-west Ireland, and Rosyth. In the colonial era of British expansion, a number of naval (Royal) dockyards were constructed in other parts of the world, the principal ones being at * Gibraltar, * Malta, * Halifax, Bermuda, * Simonstown, Trincomalee, * Singapore, and * Hong Kong. The constitutional change from empire to commonwealth during the 20th century, in which the former colonial states have become independent nations, has resulted in the great majority of these overseas dockyards being handed over to new national ownership, and the only Royal dockyards outside British waters is that at Gibraltar. Inside British waters, the dockyards at Haulbowline and Sheerness have reverted to civilian use, and others may well follow.

ROYAL FISHES, see FISHES ROYAL.

ROYAL GEORGE, H.M.S., a ship's name used many times in the Royal Navy, and also in the British * East India Company. The first five ships of this name in the Royal Navy were all 1st * rates, the first four of 100 guns and the fifth of 120 guns. Not one of these ships was laid down under the name. The first was built as the *James Royal* in 1674, rebuilt as the *Victory* in 1695, and renamed *Royal George* in 1714. She was, however, named *Victory* again in 1715. The second was built as the *Royal Charles* in 1672 and rebuilt as the *Queen* in 1693, again rebuilt and renamed *Royal George* in 1715, but renamed *Royal Ann* in 1756.

The third was laid down as the *Royal Ann* but was renamed *Royal George* before being launched in 1756. This ship remained under the name throughout her career, which included the battle of * Quiberon Bay. This was the ship, flying the flag of Richard * Kempenfelt, which foundered at * Spithead in 1782, an event which has been commemorated in Cowper's poem 'The Loss of the *Royal George*', with its well-known opening lines 'Toll for the brave, the brave that are no more'. (See ROYAL GEORGE, LOSS OF THE.)

The fourth *Royal George* was laid down as the *Umpire*, but was renamed before being launched in 1788. She took part in Lord * Howe's action of the * Glorious First of June, was Lord Bridport's (see HOOD, Alexander) flagship in the action off Groix Island, 1795, and was Sir John Duckworth's flagship when he and his squadron forced the passage of the * Dardanelles under fire from the forts and castles in 1807. She was broken up in 1822. The fifth ship was laid down as the *Neptune*, but renamed *Royal George*

before her launch in 1827. She was fitted for a screw * propeller in 1854, in which year she proceeded to the Baltic to take part in the operations there during the Crimean War (1854–6). In 1860 her armament was reduced to 90 guns and in 1871 she was fitted as a hospital ship. She was broken up in 1875.

The Royal Navy has had a number of lesser ships named *Royal George*, one being a * Royal Yacht built in 1817 and paid off in 1843. She became a * receiving ship at Portsmouth, in which capacity she continued to serve until 1902, being finally broken up in 1905.

The East India Company also had three ships named *Royal George* between 1737 and 1825. The last of these ships was, in 1804, one of the squadron commanded by Captain Nathaniel * Dance which fought a successful action against Vice Admiral Linois in the Macassar Strait in February of that year.

ROYAL GEORGE, LOSS OF THE, is one of the best-known examples of the * capsizing of a ship with very heavy loss of life. H.M.S. * *Royal George* was a 1st * rate * ship of the line of 100 guns and on 29 August 1782 was lying at Spithead with almost her entire crew and a large number of wives and other women and children on board. She was being given a * Parliament heel to expose part of her side for the fitting of a cock below water. While she was heeled, she filled with water and sank very quickly, with a loss of about 900 lives, including that of Rear Admiral Richard * Kempenfelt, who was flying his flag on board.

The exact cause of the disaster is not known, but there are two possibilities; first, that she was heeled too far and the water entered the lower tier of * gunports, and second, that her * timbers were rotten and the ship's bottom, or part of it, dropped out while she was heeled. A court martial was assembled at Portsmouth on 9 September 1782 to try her survivors for negligence and after hearing both survivors and witnesses, found that the cause of the disaster was that part of the * frame of the ship gave way because of the decay of the timbers. But other evidence was given at the court martial that the officers on deck had become alarmed at the extent of the heel and had called the carpenter on deck to tell him to reduce it. Certainly her timbers were very much decayed, and equally certainly, water came in through the lower tier of gunports, but it is possible that a collapse of part of the frame was responsible for bringing the gunports below water, and not necessarily the extent of the heel.

The capsizing of so notable a ship has been commemorated in the poem by William Cowper with its well-known opening lines 'Toll for the brave, the brave that are no more'. Cowper, however, was no seaman and when he attributed the

Loss of the Royal George *at Spithead, 1782; early 19th-century engraving*

disaster to 'a land breeze (which) shook the shrouds', he was very far off beam.

Several attempts were made to raise the wreck but all were unsuccessful. Finally, in 1848, it was removed by the engineer Sir George Pasley, partly by being blown up with explosives and partly by being lifted. It was on this occasion that Augustus *Siebe was able to demonstrate the efficiency of his newly invented diving dress, receiving as a result a contract from the British Admiralty for the supply of diving dresses to the navy.

ROYAL MAIL LINE, a shipping company which ranks with the *Cunard Line and the *P & O as the oldest of Britain's great steamship companies. Like them it was formed to carry the mails, in this case to the West Indies. It was incorporated by Royal Charter in 1839 as the Royal Mail Steam Packet Company, the leading spirit in its formation being a traveller and writer on imperial affairs, James MacQueen. The mail service, Southampton–West Indies, was begun with a fleet of fourteen paddle steamships newly built for the company in 1842; in spite of excessive early losses to reefs and rocks the company prospered and in 1850 obtained a mail contract to Brazil. In 1869 this South American service was extended to the Argentine, which subsequently became the company's major route. In 1903 an ambitious young shipowner, Owen Philipps, was elected chairman, and in the following years by a spectacular series of acquisi-

tions made Royal Mail the centrepiece of the world's largest shipping group. However, in the slump of the early 1930s Philipps, now Lord Kylsant, over-reached himself and the group collapsed. The parent company was liquidated and Royal Mail Lines was formed in its place in 1932. In 1965 Royal Mail was absorbed into the Furness Withy shipping group; although still associated with its historic routes to South America, the company's ships are now integrated in the group's world-wide services.

ROYAL NAVAL AIR SERVICE, the first name given by the British Navy to its own air wing. It was formed unofficially in 1912 when the naval wing of the Royal Flying Corps, set up only a month previously, broke away to develop independently. Its first director was Captain (later Admiral Sir) Murray *Sueter and it was enthusiastically supported by the First Lord of the Admiralty, Winston *Churchill. It developed at a great rate under the impetus of the First World War (1914–18), operating a number of seaplane carriers and shore stations from which flew a great variety of aircraft. As the war progressed it came more and more into competition with the Royal Flying Corps of the army for the supply of aircraft, and it was to judge between these conflicting demands that a government committee was set up in 1917 under the chairmanship of General Smuts. The report recommended that the two organizations should be amalgamated to form a Royal Air Force under a separate Air Ministry, a course adopted by the government. The Royal Air Force came into being on 1 April 1918 and absorbed the whole of the Royal Naval Air Service, which at the time consisted of 103 airships, 2,949 aircraft, and 67,000 officers and men. See also AIRCRAFT CARRIER, NAVAL AVIATION, FLEET AIR ARM.

ROYAL OCEAN RACING CLUB, THE, the organizing authority for offshore racing in Britain, was formed in 1925 following a private race that year of some 635 miles from Ryde, Isle of Wight, round the Fastnet rock off the southern Irish coast and back to Plymouth. As the sport developed and more offshore races were organized, the club, which originated as the Ocean Racing Club, was granted Royal status in 1931 and received an Admiralty warrant for members with qualifying yachts to wear the *Blue Ensign.

At first the Fastnet race was held each year and attracted more and more entries, but in conjunction with the Cruising Club of America it became a biennial event so as to alternate with the C.C.A.'s organized biennial ocean race to Bermuda. Other offshore races were introduced in the R.O.R.C. programme as the sport attracted more yacht owners, and a new type of ocean-racing yacht was developed on both sides of the Atlantic. Yachts were divided by the rating rules of the club into three different classes, later increased to five after the Second World War in order to permit smaller boats to enter. From its headquarters off Piccadilly in London the R.O.R.C. regularly organizes nineteen or twenty offshore and ocean races during the season, attracting around 600 yachts to compete in them. See also RATING, YACHTING, Racing rules.

ROYAL SOVEREIGN, H.M.S., a ship's name used many times in the British Navy. The first ship of this name was a 1st *rate of 100 guns, built at Woolwich by Peter and Phineas *Pett. At the time of her launching, in October 1637, she was named Sovereign of the Seas and when the Commonwealth was established in 1649 there was a proposal to rename her Commonwealth but instead her name was shortened to Sovereign. Under this name she took part in the battle of *Kentish Knock during the First Dutch War (1652–4). It was not until she had been rebuilt at Chatham at the time of the Restoration in 1660 that she began to be known as the Royal Sovereign. Thereafter she saw plenty of action—the St. James's Day Fight in the Second Dutch War (1665–7); the battle of *Solebay (as flagship of Vice Admiral Sir Joseph Jordan); the first and second battles of the Schooneveld and the second battle of the *Texel in the Third Dutch War (1672–4), in the last two of which the Royal Sovereign served as

the flagship of Prince *Rupert, admiral of the fleet. After being again rebuilt at Chatham in 1684, this time with no alteration in her name, the Royal Sovereign served as the flagship of the commander-in-chief, Admiral the Earl of Torrington, at the battle of *Beachy Head. Two years later, in May 1692, as flagship of Vice Admiral Sir Ralph Delaval, she took part in the battle of *Barfleur. Her career ended when she was accidentally burnt at Chatham in January 1696.

The Royal Navy's third Royal Sovereign, a 1st rate of 100 guns, was launched at Plymouth in 1786. She was Vice Admiral Thomas *Graves's flagship in Lord *Howe's action of the *Glorious First of June, and a year later was the flagship of Vice Admiral William *Cornwallis when he and his squadron retreated from the French Brest fleet under Vice Admiral *Villaret de Joyeuse. During 1797–1800 the Royal Sovereign served as the flagship of Vice Admiral Alan Gardner in the Channel Fleet and was one of the ships involved in the mutiny at *Spithead in 1797. In 1804, as flagship of Rear Admiral Sir Richard Bickerton, the Royal Sovereign joined Vice Admiral Lord *Nelson in the *blockade of *Toulon. In 1805, after a refit, she joined Nelson off Cadiz and on 11 October Vice Admiral *Collingwood hoisted his flag in her as second-in-command. On the 21st the Royal Sovereign led the lee line into battle and was the first ship in action at *Trafalgar. In 1825 she was fitted to be a *receiving ship at Plymouth, her name being changed to Captain, and in 1841 she was finally broken up.

A *battleship of 25,750 tons launched at Portsmouth in 1915 was named Royal Sovereign. She joined the 1st Battle Squadron, *Grand Fleet, in May 1916 and served with it throughout the remainder of the First World War (1914–18), being present at the internment of the German *High Seas Fleet in November 1918. During the Second World War the Royal Sovereign served on the America and West Indies station and with the Eastern Fleet. After a refit in the U.S.A. in 1943 she was transferred to the U.S.S.R. in 1944, when she was renamed Archangel. In 1949 she was returned to the Royal Navy and broken up.

ROYAL THAMES YACHT CLUB, THE, one of the oldest and best-known of British yacht clubs. It owes its origin to a sailing match which was held on the Thames in 1749 from Greenwich to the Nore and back for a plate presented by the Prince of Wales. This sport of racing and sailing excursions under the command of a *commodore attracted owners of a number of small yachts who lived close to the Thames, and resulted in the formation in 1775 of the 'Cumberland Fleet' under the patronage of the Duke of

Cumberland. Members' yachts were permitted to wear the *White Ensign, though without the red cross of St. George, and sailing regattas were regularly held on the River Thames above Black-friars.

Following violent disagreements at the regatta held in 1823 to commemorate the coronation of George IV, some of the members made a breakaway group and formed the Thames Yacht Club, which became the forerunner of today's Royal Thames Yacht Club, which has club-houses in Knightsbridge, London, and at War-sash in Hampshire. See also THAMES MEASURE-MENT.

ROYAL YACHT SQUADRON, the premier yacht club of Britain. It was formed at Cowes, Isle of Wight, in 1815 by forty-two owners of yachts as the Yacht Club, and in 1820 became the Royal Yacht Club, the Prince Regent, later George IV, having joined it as a member in 1818. In 1833 its named was changed by royal command to the Royal Yacht Squadron. From its first registration the club adopted as its *ensign 'a white flag with the Union in the cor-ner', and in 1829 the Admiralty issued a warrant allowing members of the club to wear the White Ensign of the Royal Navy, a privilege it has exercised ever since.

ROYAL YACHTING ASSOCIATION, the controlling body in Britain for all matters con-cerning yachting. It was founded in 1875 as the Yacht Racing Association by a representative body of yachtsmen to control yacht racing and the design of racing yachts, with the authority to hold courts of appeal. One of the first rating rules under which yachts could race was initiated by Dixon *Kemp, the celebrated designer, who was the Association's first secretary. The rating rules were amended from time to time when it was found that designers were able to produce 'rule cheaters' under the earlier formulae.

In 1881 the Prince of Wales (later Edward VII) became its president, and the influence of the Y.R.A. spread rapidly to other countries. After the Second World War its activities expanded still further as yachting extended in all its branches, until it was involved in matters affect-ing yachtsmen outside yacht racing. H.R.H. Prince Philip became its new president and in 1952 its name was changed to Royal Yachting Association to become the national authority representing yachtsmen in the United Kingdom. It is financially supported by the yacht clubs, and general purposes committees have been set up to deal with such divers problems affecting yachts-men as the siting of oil refineries, power cables, bridges, and firing and bombing ranges, muni-cipal charges for moorings, river bed and fore-shore rights, and pollution of coastal waters. The

R.Y.A. has also been instrumental in forming the International Yacht Racing Centre in Portland Harbour and Weymouth Bay, where Olympic events as well as contests for a variety of sailing classes can be held in both sheltered and open water conditions. It is also affiliated to the Inter-national Yacht Racing Union (see YACHTING, Racing rules).

ROYAL YACHTS, vessels provided for the use of royalty for occasions of state, pleasure, etc. Such vessels are of very ancient origin, dating back long before the introduction of the word 'yacht'. An early example was the vessel presented by King Harold of Norway to King Athelstan, of which 'the head was wrought with gold'. Most European kings had their own private ships which they used on state occasions, and there are records in the 12th century of voyages made by Henry I and Henry II in their *esnekkas, which were the Royal yachts of the time.

In England the Royal yachts first came into real prominence with Charles II (1660–85). He was, perhaps, the first king of England to take an authoritative interest in the sea and the navy, and he had several yachts, both for state visits to the fleet and for purely pleasure sailing. The first was the *Mary*, presented to the king by the Dutch, a vessel of 100 tons, and she incidentally was responsible for the introduction of the Dutch word 'yacht' into the English language. Charles ordered several further vessels to be built as yachts, of which the best known were the *Katherine* (94 tons), *Anne* (100 tons), another *Katherine* (135 tons), *Bezan* (35 tons, presented by the Dutch), *Jamie* (27 tons), *Charles* (38 tons), another *Charles* (120 tons), *Henrietta* (104 tons), another *Henrietta* (162 tons), *Saudadoes* (86 tons), *Cleveland* (107 tons), *Queenborough* (29 tons), *Kitchen* (103 tons), another *Mary* (166 tons), *Fubbs* (148 tons), and *Isabella* (114 tons). Some of these served on occasions with the fleet during the Dutch wars as *advice boats; not all of them were in service at the same time.

The precedent set by Charles II was followed by succeeding monarchs, though not in such profusion. As the years went by the yachts got progressively larger; thus the *Royal Caroline* of 1749 had a *burthen of 232 tons, the *Augusta* of 1771 was 184 tons, the *Royal George* of 1817 was 330 tons. These yachts, and others of less tonnage, took the history of British Royal yachts up to the age of steam and the long reign of Queen Victoria (1837–1901).

The first British Royal yacht propelled by steam was the *Victoria and Albert I*, launched in 1843. She was fitted with paddle-wheels and sails, and had a *tonnage of 1,034. Victoria did not quite match her predecessor Charles II· in numbers of yachts, but like him she enjoyed the sea. Her yachts were the *Fairy* (1845) of 317 tons, the *Elfin* (1849) of 98 tons, the *Victoria and Albert II* (1855) of 2,470 tons, the *Alberta* (1863) of 370 tons, the *Osborne II* (1870) of 1,850 tons, and the *Victoria and Albert III* (1899) of 5,500 tons. All these were steam yachts, of which only the *Fairy* and the third *Victoria and Albert* were fitted with screw *propellers, all the remainder having paddle-wheels. Edward VII, although using the *Victoria and Albert III* as his principal Royal yacht, built the *Alexandra* (2,050 tons) in 1907, and the racing *cutter *Britannia* in 1893. The present British Royal yacht, H.M.Y. *Britannia*, of 5,769 tons, was launched in 1953.

The history of the Royal yachts of other nations follows that of Britain in general pattern. They can be said to represent the symbol of royalty at sea, gracious vessels specially designed to uphold the dignity and ceremonial associated with state visits by royalty to other nations. See also LIVADIA.

ROZHESTVENSKY, ZINOVI PETROVICH (1848–1909), Russian admiral, born in Moscow, is remembered for his remarkable display of dogged perseverance, drive, and organizational powers in bringing the heterogeneous and mainly obsolete Russian Baltic Fleet from Kronstadt to the Straits of *Tsushima during the Russo-Japanese War of 1904–5, a voyage which took from October 1904 to May 1905 and was performed in the face of extreme difficulties. The voyage, which was intended to regain for Russia naval dominance in Far Eastern waters during the war, was marked by a number of international incidents. The first of these was known as the 'Dogger Bank outrage', in which a British *trawler fleet, fishing peacefully at night on the *Dogger Bank, was suspected by the Russian fleet of concealing Japanese *torpedoboats and was fired on, causing some loss of life. The incident nearly led to a declaration of war by Britain. Later crises were caused by the fleet's refuelling and provisioning problems, which led to Rozhestvensky overstaying his welcome in a number of ports and anchorages. The difficulties of the voyage of these slow and ponderous ships were immense, but Rozhestvensky overcame them and led his ships into Japanese-controlled waters in his attempt to get them through to *Port Arthur.

Unhappily, after all the vicissitudes of this long voyage, neither the quality of the ships themselves nor the tactical leadership of their commander were a match for the Japanese fleet, and Admiral *Togo, its commander-in-chief, scored an annihilating victory at the battle of Tsushima, every Russian ship being either sunk or captured. Nevertheless, Rozhestvensky, who became a prisoner-of-war of the Japanese after

the disastrous action, gained wide sympathy for his personal bravery in the battle and his dignified and humble demeanour after his defeat.

RUBBER, a tool used by sailmakers to flatten the *seams of a sail after the canvas has been sewn.

RUBBING STRAKE, a piece of half-rounded timber or rubber running the length of a small vessel or *dinghy from bow to stern on either side just below the *gunwale to act as a permanent *fender and protect the side of the vessel when coming or lying alongside another vessel or *mole, etc.

RUDDER, the most efficient means of imparting direction to a ship or vessel under way. The rudder was the logical development of the older *steering oar and began to replace it in ships in the mid-13th century. Some of the seals of the Hanseatic League ports of this period show local *cogs with stern rudders, the earliest known record of this development.

Rudders in *dinghies and many other small vessels are usually hung from the *sternpost or *transom by means of *pintles, which engage in *gudgeons and allow lateral movement from side to side as required. In many yachts they are hung on a rudder stock which is led through the *counter, movement being imparted to the rudder by either a steering wheel or a *tiller. In larger vessels they are also hung on a rudder stock which enters the hull through a rudder port. A quadrant is fixed to the top of the rudder stock, known as the rudder head, and it is by means of the quadrant, with the assistance of a steering engine, that force is applied to turn the rudder as required to steer the ship. A balanced

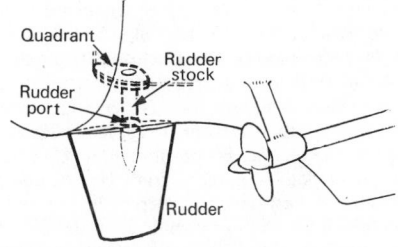

Balanced rudder

rudder is one that pivots on its central axis in order to distribute the thrust of the water on its surface. In the average steamship the rudder can be moved through an arc of 70°, 35° on either side of the fore-and-aft line of the ship, but in the very large *tankers of around 400,000 tons being built today, the arc of the rudder movement is increased to 80°, 40° each side, to give a greater measure of control when manoeuvring.

The effect on a ship of turning the rudder depends on the principle of mechanics that to every action there is an equal and opposite reaction. When turned at an angle to the ship's * course, the face of the rudder deflects the water in the direction in which it is turned, and the reaction of this force forces the ship's stern in the other direction, and thus the ship's head in the same direction as that in which the rudder is turned.

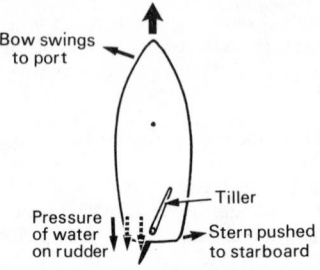

Shortly before the outbreak of the Second World War a new design of rudder for small motor craft was introduced by the British Navy. Known as the Kitchen rudder, it consisted of two curved plates working on a vertical axis, one each side of the * propeller. By movements controlled by the steering wheel they deflected the propeller stream to any desired angle so as to steer the vessel ahead or astern. Thus, when the plates were closed behind the propeller, the vessel would be moved astern by the thrust of the propeller stream on the plates, even though the motor continued to turn the propeller ahead. (For further illus. see COUNTER.)

RUGE, FRIEDRICH (1894–   ), German vice admiral, was born at Leipzig and served in the Imperial German Navy throughout the First World War (1914–18), his ship, Torpedoboat B.110, being part of the German * High Seas Fleet interned and subsequently * scuttled at * Scapa Flow after the war. He commanded a * motor torpedoboat from 1926 to 1928 and four years later, after his promotion, was in command of a flotilla of these craft. He became a recognized expert on minesweeping and in 1937 was appointed to command a squadron of * minesweepers. During the Second World War he was in charge of the minesweeping section of Naval Group West and was responsible for sweeping the path taken by the * Scharnhorst, Gneisenau, and Prinz Eugen during their dramatic escape through the Channel from Brest in 1942. His last active appointment during the war was as naval adviser to Field Marshal Erwin Rommel when the latter was made Inspector-General of the coast defences in the west.

After the war, on the re-creation of the Federal German Navy, he was recalled to active duty and in 1957 was made its Inspector-General with the rank of vice admiral, a post he held until 1961. Since his retirement he has devoted himself to writing, and is the author of many thoughtful books, of which the best known are *Decision in the Pacific* (1951), *Sea Warfare, 1939–45* (1952), *Sea Power and Security* (1955), *Politics and Strategy* (1967), and *Scapa Flow, 1919* (1969).

'RULE BRITANNIA', a famous naval song much sung and played in the British Navy from the date of its first performance in 1740 to the present day, and generally recognized today as the official march of the Royal Navy. It was written by James Thomson and first performed in the masque *Alfred* on 1 August 1740 in honour of the birth of the Princess Augusta. It was a favourite tune (but see also 'BRITONS, STRIKE HOME') played on board * ships of the line as they sailed into battle.

RULE OF THE ROAD, a set of thirty-one internationally agreed rules which govern the conduct of ships at sea in order to prevent collisions between them. They are compiled by the International Convention for Safety of Life at Sea and are known officially as the International Regulations for Preventing Collisions at Sea, or colloquially as the Rule of the Road.

The thirty-one rules are divided into six parts, which cover definitions, lights and shapes to be carried by vessels at night or day by which they can be recognized, sound signals and conduct in restricted visibility, steering and sailing rules to keep vessels apart when they are approaching each other, sound signals for vessels in sight of one another, and miscellaneous signals, such as * distress signals, etc.

Of the definitions laid down, the most important are those which define a power-driven vessel and a sailing vessel. Any form of mechanical propulsion, including oars, counts as a power-driven vessel; a sailing vessel is one propelled by

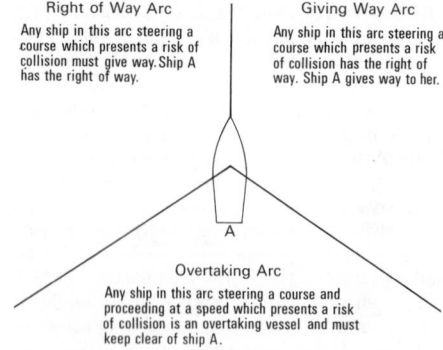

Rule of the road, powered vessels

sails only: a yacht with her sails spread but also using her auxiliary engine is a power-driven vessel.

The lights laid down to be carried under the Rule of the Road serve two purposes. The navigation (or steaming) lights carried by a ship are so designed and placed that any other ship sighting them can tell reasonably accurately the *course of the vessel carrying them. Other lights laid down by the Rule of the Road are designed to indicate the type of vessel and her actual employment, e.g., *trawlers and *drifters actually engaged in fishing carry distinguishing lights, as do vessels towing another, minesweepers, cable-laying vessels, etc. (For illustrations of navigation lights, see APPENDIX 3.)

Sound signals are used by ships in fog or restricted visibility. A power-driven vessel gives one prolonged blast every two minutes on her whistle or siren when she is making way through the water, and two prolonged blasts every two minutes if she is under way but stopped. If she has anchored, she rings her ship's bell rapidly for five seconds every two minutes. Sailing vessels sound one blast on their foghorn every minute if they are on the starboard *tack, two blasts on the port tack, and three blasts if running with the wind abaft the beam.

The most important group of rules are the steering and sailing rules, which lay down the procedure to be followed when ships approach each other and there is a danger of collision. Where this happens, the rules lay down which ship is to give way to the other. In a broad sense, vessels keep to the right when at sea. If, for example, two ships are approaching each other head on, both must alter course to starboard (or to the right) so that they pass each other port side to port side. Where a vessel is on the starboard hand of another, and steering a course which may result in a collision, she has the right of way and should maintain her course and speed, the other vessel giving way to her. Where a vessel is on the port hand of another, and her course, if she maintains it, may result in a collision, she is the giving way vessel and must alter course to avoid the other. But any ship overtaking another, i.e., approaching at any angle from two *points abaft the beam on either side, must keep clear. Also, generally speaking, all power-driven vessels must keep clear of all vessels under sail, although there are always circumstances (e.g., a sailing vessel approaching a very large tanker in narrow waters) where the sailing vessel will keep clear. The only rule to which this does not apply is the overtaking rule; a sailing vessel overtaking a power-driven vessel must keep clear of her. When a vessel has the duty of giving way to another under the rules, she normally does so by altering course to pass astern of the other, and should make a clear and significant alteration of course in plenty of time to indicate to the other vessel that she is taking the appropriate action.

The rules which govern vessels under sail are clear and precise. They lay down that when two sailing vessels approach each other with the wind on a different side, the vessel with the wind on the port side must give way to the other. When both have the wind on the same side, the vessel to *windward keeps clear of the vessel to *leeward.

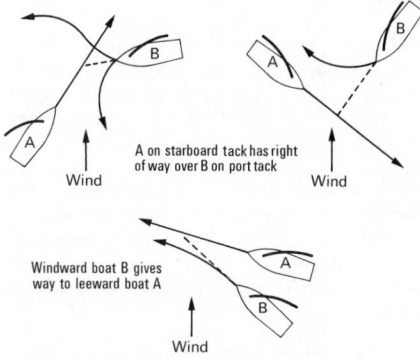

A on starboard tack has right of way over B on port tack

Windward boat B gives way to leeward boat A

Rule of the road, sailing vessels

When yachts are racing, however, they have additional rules which apply among themselves during the race, laid down by the International Yacht Racing Union. They fly a square racing flag at the masthead to indicate that they are racing and that these additional rules apply. For details of these racing rules, see YACHTING, Sail, Racing Rules. But the Rule of the Road overrides these special racing rules in cases where a racing yacht may be approaching another sailing vessel which is not herself engaged in a race and flies no racing flag.

The sailing and steering rules lay down that if a collision between two vessels appears possible, both vessels must take avoiding action even if such action involves a departure from the Rule of the Road on the part of one of them. This requirement is perhaps best summed up by the little verse which most seamen learn during the early years of their career:

> 'Here lies the body of Michael O'Day
> Who died maintaining the right of way;
> He was right, dead right, as he sailed along,
> But he's just as dead as if he'd been wrong'.

RUN, the shape of the after part of the underbody of a ship in relation to the resistance it engenders as she goes through the water. A clean run, an underbody shape at the after end of the *hull of a ship which slips easily through the water without creating excessive turbulence. It could be said to be the complement of *entry, which describes the shape of the forward end of a ship's underbody.

RUN FREE, to, the situation of a sailing vessel when the wind is either well abaft the beam and within a point or two of blowing from directly astern or blows directly from that direction. The term comes from the fact that with the wind from this direction, the * sheets of the sails are freed right away in order to present the maximum possible sail area as square as possible to the wind. See also BROACH TO, TO, and for illus. POINTS OF SAILING.

RUN THE EASTING DOWN, to, an expression referring to the long easterly passage from the Cape of Good Hope to Australia between the * latitudes of 40° and 50° S., in the area known as the * Roaring Forties. It originally referred to the big square-rigged ships on the Australian run which used the prevailing westerly gales which blew in this area to help them on their way, but no doubt many of the modern yachts engaged in offshore cruising or round-the-world races continue to run their easting down in this area of the Indian Ocean.

RUNCIMAN, WALTER, first Baron (1847–1937), British sailor, shipowner, and author, was born at Dunbar, Scotland. He ran away to sea as a boy of 12 and after serving in many ships gained his * master's certificate in 1871. He commanded the * barque *Althea* for four years and then became master of a steamship. In 1884, after twenty-five years at sea, he came ashore to start a shipping business, known as the Moor Line. It prospered for many years but had to be wound up after the First World War (1914–18) because of war losses. In 1924 he started a new shipping business and in 1935 acquired a controlling interest in the well-known Anchor Line. He wrote several books about the sea and his autobiography, *Before the Mast and After* (1924), was a considerable success. In his leisure time he was a keen yachtsman.

RUNNERS, the two preventer * backstays, led from the masthead to each * quarter of a sailing yacht, which support the mast when the wind blows from abaft the beam. On each occasion of going * about, or * gybing, the * lee runner is * overhauled to allow the * boom of the mainsail to swing over without restriction, the * weather runner being set up taut to take the strain on the mast. In many modern yachts, in which the boom swings inside the * counter of the vessel, a single standing backstay takes the place of the two runners. See also RIGGING.

RUNNING RIGGING, see RIGGING.

RUPERT, Prince Palatine (1618–82), was the third son of Elizabeth, Queen of Bohemia, and Frederick V, Elector Palatine, and thus a grand-son of James I of England. He achieved early fame as a cavalry commander, but also served arduously at sea. When, during the course of the English Civil War (1642–8), Charles I had at last been decisively defeated, Rupert and his brother Maurice (1620–52) did their best, with a handful of indifferent ships, to maintain the cause of the royalists at sea. After being driven from European waters by the Commonwealth admiral Robert * Blake, Rupert and Maurice, after a stay on the west coast of Africa, made a piratical cruise in the Caribbean during the course of which Maurice and his ship were lost.

Rupert went to France in 1653 and was in Germany thereafter until the restoration of Charles II in 1660, when he was invited by his cousin to return to England. In Charles's governing circle, Rupert was conspicuous for his interest in maritime and colonial affairs. He was one of the patentees of the Royal Africa Company, a commissioner for Tangier, and he later received a royal charter for the Hudson's Bay Company.

During the second maritime war with the Dutch (1665–7) Rupert was at sea in 1665 as admiral of the White at the battle of * Solebay with his cousin * James, Duke of York, then * Lord High Admiral of England.

In the following year he shared command of the English fleet with George * Monck, Duke of Albemarle, with whom, as a very young man, he had served as a soldier in the Low Countries. In the hard-fought * Four Days Battle of 1–4 June 1666 Rupert, who had originally been ordered on detached service, managed to join Monck for the final stages of the engagement when, with his squadron, he helped to prevent a tactical defeat from becoming a disaster. Rupert and Monck had their revenge on the Dutch the following month off * Orfordness, when they captured or destroyed twenty of de * Ruyter's ships at the cost of a single vessel of their own.

By the time of the outbreak of the Third Dutch War (1672–4) Rupert was a veteran who had experienced almost every kind of warfare by sea and land. In 1673 he fought two inconclusive engagements off Schooneveld and the * Texel, lack of success being due largely to the half-heartedness or incompetence of a French squadron which failed to conform with and support his movements. Rupert had no further service afloat, but he lived until 1682, for the most part at Windsor. He is buried in Henry VII's Chapel there.

He was a man of great versatility, his gifts including an ability in chemical experiments and in mezzotint engraving in which branch of art he showed himself to be of professional competence. As a sailor he met with little but misfortune in spite of sustained resolution in the face of adversity and an ability to infect others with his own courage.

RUSSELL, EDWARD, Earl of Orford (1653–1727), British admiral of the fleet, was a nephew of the Duke of Bedford and one of the first gentlemen officers of the British Navy bred to the sea as a permanent career. Details of his early service are lacking, but as a lieutenant in the *Rupert* he was present at the battle of *Solebay during the Third Dutch War (1672–4). He held a succession of commands and became an active supporter of William Prince of Orange whom he accompanied to England in 1688 on the abdication of James II. He was appointed Treasurer of the Navy in 1689 and later that year hoisted his flag as admiral of the Blue under the Earl of Torrington (see HERBERT, Arthur), whom, after much intrigue, he succeeded in 1691.

In 1692 in command of an Anglo-Dutch fleet of eighty-two ships, he engaged a French fleet of forty-five ships and gained a decisive victory at *Barfleur and La Hogue with the help of Sir George *Rooke. Nevertheless he was deemed not to have taken proper measures to complete the destruction of the enemy's fleet and was relieved of his command, but reinstated in November 1693. In 1694 he was appointed First Lord of the Admiralty, remaining as First Lord until 1699. In 1697 he was raised to the peerage as Earl of Orford and again held office as First Lord from November 1707 to September 1710 and from October 1714 to April 1717.

RUSSELL, JOHN SCOTT (1808–82), British engineer, became interested in the maritime side of engineering when he was consulted in 1834 as to the possibility of introducing steam navigation on the Edinburgh and Glasgow Canal. His studies of wave formation and hull resistance embraced a great many experiments, including tests both with models in a tank and with full-sized vessels on a canal. He attempted to translate what he called his 'wave system', or *wave line theory, to the design of ships, and was associated with I. K. *Brunel in the design of the *Great Eastern steamship in 1856 which was built on his principles, as also was the 50-ton racing yacht *Mosquito* which he designed in 1848 (see YACHTING). He also introduced the system of cellular *double bottoms for iron ships, pioneered many improvements in marine boilers and engines, and was concerned in the design of the *Warrior and *Black Prince*, the world's first *ironclad *battleships. He was also one of the founders of the British Institution of Naval Architects. Among the many books he wrote were *The Fleet of the Future* (1861) and *A Modern System of Naval Architecture* (1865).

RUSSELL, WILLIAM CLARK (1844–1911), American novelist, was born in New York and joined the British mercantile marine in 1858. Life on board ship, however, undermined his health although it provided him with much material for his subsequent successful literary career. His first novel, *John Holdsworth, Chief Mate* (1875), was well received and his next, *Wreck of the Grosvenor* (1877), was even more popular and established his reputation as a writer of sea stories. For the next thirty years novels flowed from his pen, twenty-two in all, and he has been described as 'the prose Homer of the great ocean'. He contributed to the *Daily Telegraph* under the pseudonym 'Seafarer' and was a zealous champion of the merchant seaman, for the improvement of whose conditions of service he did much valuable work.

RUTTER, from the French *routier*, itself from the Portuguese *roteiro*, a route or road, an early name for a book of sailing directions usually illustrated with views of ports and coastline seen from seaward. In 1483 a French sailor named Pierre Garcie wrote *Le Grand Routier et Pilotage*, a pilot book for the west coast of France, and a translation appeared in English, possibly the first of a long series of rutters which appeared over the next two centuries. A printed version appeared in 1521 with woodcut views to facilitate identification of the coast from seaward. There was also much information on tides and general navigational advice. In 1541 Richard Proude printed *The New Rutter of the Sea for the North Partes*, being sailing directions for the circumnavigation of the British Isles.

Rutter also referred to the English seaman's personal notebook in which he kept a record of courses, anchorages, etc.; such notebooks were usually handed down from father to son, being valuable for the local information they held. See also DERROTERRO.

RUYTER, MICHIEL ADRIENSZOON DE (1607–76), was the greatest of the Dutch admirals, a born leader, a fine seaman, and a man of exemplary character who shunned the public eye but whose courage became a legend. Born at Flushing, he went to sea in 1618 as a *boatswain's boy and on one occasion was wounded and captured in an action with a French *privateer but escaped and rejoined the merchant navy. In June 1641 he was made rear admiral of a fleet of fifteen ships sent to support Portugal against Spain and soon showed the qualities of courage and resolution which were to make him famous. In 1642 he rejoined the merchant service, but on the outbreak of the First Anglo-Dutch War (1652–4) he accepted naval service under the government of Zeeland. On 16 August 1652, while escorting a *convoy down Channel, he encountered and defeated an English fleet under Admiral Sir George *Ayscue off the Channel Islands, afterwards joining the main Dutch fleet under Admiral de *With and taking a prominent part in the battle of the *Kentish Knock. During the battle off Dungeness in November 1652, and at the three days battle off *Portland in February 1653, his squadron bore the brunt of the fighting. After the Dutch defeat off the North *Foreland in June he supported Marten *Tromp in his insistence that the Dutch fleet be rebuilt. In the final battle of the war, off *Scheveningen, his flagship *Lam* was so seriously damaged that she had to be towed home.

He was next employed in the Mediterranean on the supression of *piracy and in May 1659 was appointed lieutenant-admiral in command of a fleet sent to the Baltic to support the Danes against the Swedes. As a result of his defeat of the Swedish fleet, he was ennobled by the Danish king. From May 1661 to April 1663 he was again employed in the Mediterranean dealing with a resurgence of piracy. He returned there in May 1664, then made a cruise off the Guinea coast, followed by one to the West Indies, being still there on the outbreak of the Second Anglo-Dutch War (1665–7). He reached Delfzijl towing a number of *prizes and successfully evading the British squadrons sent out to cut him off from Holland, and was in command of the Dutch fleet at the *Four Days Battle of 1666, a notable Dutch victory; but, in the next engagement, on St. James's Day, the Dutch fleet was defeated, largely owing to Tromp's failure to support de Ruyter. The following year he carried out his most famous and daring raid on the English fleet in the Thames and the Medway, doing much damage, taking or destroying sixteen ships, and returning home with the pride of the English fleet, the *Royal Charles*, in tow.

When the Third Dutch War (1672–4) broke out, de Ruyter had to face the combined fleets of England and France, but at the battle of *Solebay in May 1672 he showed that he was undaunted by superior numbers. After two minor engagements in March and May 1673, he showed his real genius as an admiral at the battle of the *Texel on 11 August, achieving a tactical victory over the combined fleets under Prince *Rupert. Peace with England followed in February 1674, but the war with France continued, and when, on 16 August, Spain appealed for Dutch assistance, de Ruyter sailed to the Mediterranean with eighteen ships to recapture Messina from the French. On 8 January 1676, off Stromboli, he fought an indecisive battle with the French, then on 22 April, with the support of a small Spanish squadron, he defeated a French fleet under Admiral *Duquesne off the east coast of Sicily. He was severely wounded during the action and died seven days later. His body was brought back to Holland and he was buried in the Nieuwe Kerk in Amsterdam, a marble monument by Verhulst being erected over his tomb.

During his life, de Ruyter's name was one to conjure with. The greatest admiral of his time, he was a skilled naval tactician during the days when the handling of fleets was in its infancy, and to him the fleet formation of the *line of battle is at least partly due. He was also a man of undaunted courage, a stern disciplinarian, but much loved and respected by the crews of his ships. He is still regarded as the greatest and most skilful of the naval heroes of Holland.

P. Blok, *Life of Admiral de Ruyter* ('S-Gravenhage, 1933).

RYDER, ALBERT PINKHAM (1847–1917), American marine and landscape painter, was born at New Bedford, Mass. He studied art under W. E. Marshall at the National Academy, and among the many marine pictures he painted is the very well known series 'The Toilers of the Sea', a series frequently reproduced and widely popular. It is upon these that his fame as a marine artist chiefly rests, and they are certainly vivid pictures of varying sea types, full of movement.

S

S.I.N.S., the initial letters used to describe a ship's inertial *navigation system.

S.M.S., the prefix used before the name of a ship of the German Navy during the period of the Imperial Navy which came to an end with the abdication of Kaiser Wilhelm II in 1918. The initials stand for Seiner Majestät Schiff, the equivalent of the British H.M.S.

S.S., the prefix placed before the name of a ship to indicate that she is a merchant steamship. Originally the two letters stood for screw steamship, to distinguish her from a *paddle steamer, but with the disappearance of the paddle ship except in purely coastal waters, the designation came to be accepted as steamship.

SABINE, SIR EDWARD (1788–1883), British astronomer, accompanied many expeditions to Arctic waters as official astronomer, notably those of Sir John *Ross (1818) in search of the *North-West passage and, three years later, of Sir Edward *Parry. He was later responsible for the setting up, in many of the British possessions all round the globe, of a series of small observatories to observe and measure terrestrial magnetism.

SADDLE, a block of wood, or a wooden bracket, fixed to a *mast or *yard to support another spar attached to it. Thus, the *bowsprit of a sailing vessel has a saddle attached to it to support the heel of the *jib-boom, and a saddle on each lower yardarm supports the *studding-sail *boom in square-rigged ships.

SADRAS, BATTLE OF, was fought off the Coromandel coast of India on 29 April 1758, during the Seven Years War (1756–63) between British and French fleets commanded respectively by Vice Admiral George Pocock and Commodore the Comte d'Aché. Pocock sighted the enemy at about 9 a.m. when the latter was preparing to leave Port St. David roads. Contact, however, was not made until the afternoon, when the ships actually in the *line of battle were seven British to nine French, although one of the latter was no larger than a 36-gun *frigate; in addition, the French had another 74-gun ship and a frigate to *leeward of their line.

Although the French opened a long-range fire as the British approached, Pocock did not hoist the signal to engage until about 3 p.m., when he was within *half-musket shot of the French flagship. He was none too well supported by his rear ships (three captains were afterwards court-martialled) but this disadvantage was neutralized by similar derelictions of duty on the part of the enemy. Within an hour the French flagship had been driven out of the line, and about half an hour later the whole of the French line gave way, upon which Pocock ordered a *general chase. Owing to their damaged condition, however, the British ships could not overtake the retreating enemy.

SAG, to, (1) the tendency of the hull of a ship to settle *amidships when her weight is supported at *bow or *stern. Thus the hull of a ship in a long sea with her bow and stern taken on the crests of two succeeding waves and the wave hollow amidships undergoes a strain where the weight of the ship has less support from the water amidships than it has at bow and stern. It is the opposite of *hogging, which is the tendency of bow and stern to droop when a ship's hull is supported by a wave amidships and both ends are over the hollows of the waves. **(2)** A word also used by seamen to describe a *leeward drift. A ship is said to sag away to leeward when she makes excessive leeway.

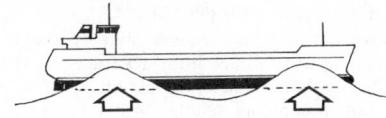

Sagging

SAIC, a small Greek trading *ketch of about 200–300 tons, of the 18th–19th centuries, without a *mizen topsail. It was possibly an original form of the word *caique.

SAIL, an assemblage of *cloths of canvas, Terylene, or other suitable material, cut to the necessary length and fashioned to a particular shape which is designed to catch the wind and use its force to give motion to a sailing vessel. The cloths are *seamed together with a double seam (see also PRICK, TO) and the *leech of the

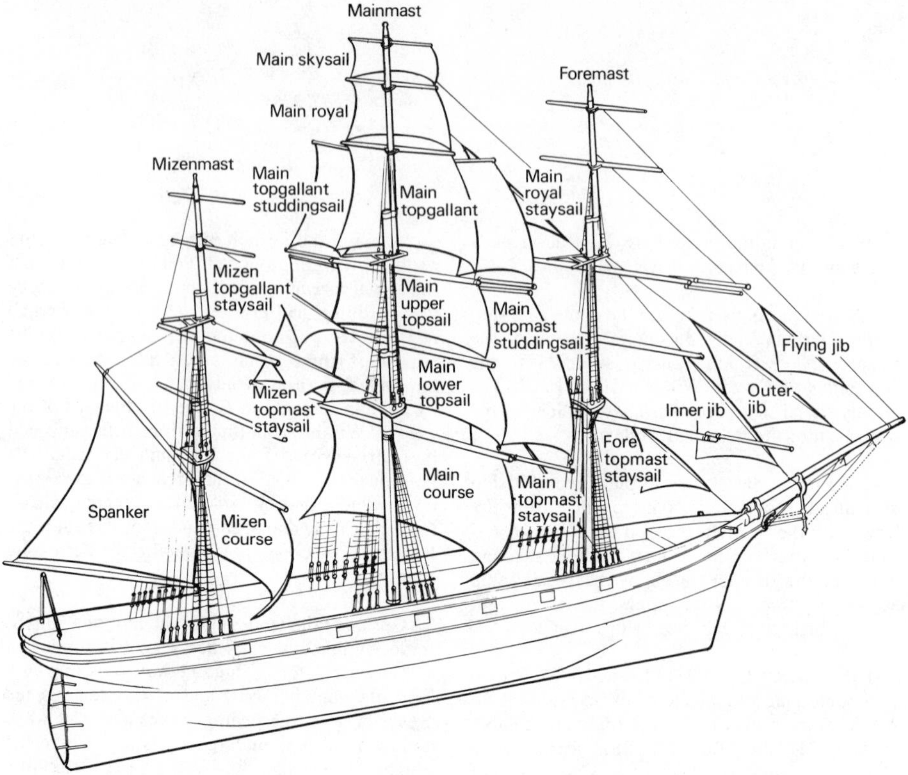

Diagram of a square-rigged ship with labelled sails:

Mainmast
Main skysail
Main royal
Mizenmast
Main topgallant studdingsail
Main topgallant
Foremast
Main royal staysail
Mizen topgallant staysail
Main upper topsail
Main topmast studdingsail
Main topmast staysail
Flying jib
Mizen topmast staysail
Main lower topsail
Main topmast staysail
Inner jib
Outer jib
Fore topmast staysail
Spanker
Mizen course
Main course
Main topmast staysail

sail shaped with *gores to give it the required aerodynamic curve.

Sails generally can be divided into two distinct types, those used in square-rigged ships which are set on horizontal *yards crossing the masts and those used in fore-and-aft rigged ships which are set from their *luffs on masts or *stays. There are areas where these two types of sail are used together, as with the *jibs, *staysails, and *spanker of a square-rigged ship or the occasional square sail set from a yard when running before the wind in a fore-and-aft rigged ship. The two exceptions to this general rule are *lateen sails and *lugsails which, though set on a yard, are generally accepted as fore-and-aft sails.

Square-rigged ships, setting all plain sail, have five square sails on each mast, though sometimes a sixth on the mainmast is included in this definition. Named in ascending order they are the *course, lower topsail, upper topsail, *topgallant, and *royal, the sixth sail on the mainmast being the *skysail. In fine settled weather, with the ship running with a wind abaft the beam, additional fine weather sails, known collectively as *kites, can be set to make the most of the wind. A short royal mast is fixed to the tops of the topgallant masts to set *moonrakers above

the royals and skysails, and *studdingsails (pron. stunsails) are set from booms rigged out from both yardarms of the topsail and topgallant yards of the fore- and mainmasts to extend temporarily the area of the topsails and topgallants. In older sailing days, the courses could also be enlarged by lacing a strip of canvas, known as a *bonnet, to the foot, but these went out of fashion at about the beginning of the 19th century. Only courses and topsails have *reef points, and a reef is taken in on the head of the sail, not on the foot as, in fore-and-aft sails. Square sails take their name from the mast on which they are set, as, for example, fore course, main lower topsail, mizen topgallant, etc.

Square sails are always cut from canvas, the

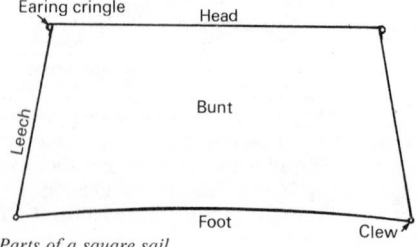

Parts of a square sail

Labels on diagram: Earing cringle, Head, Leech, Bunt, Foot, Clew

working sails being of heavy duty material and the kites of lighter canvas. All square-rigged ships used to number a sailmaker among the essential crew, since with passages lasting on occasions for four months or more continuously at sea and out of reach of shore support, it was important to be self-sufficient in the making and repairing of all working sails. The four sides of a square sail are the *head (top), *foot (bottom), and two *leeches (sides), which are differentiated by the terms *weather and *lee, according to the *bracing of the yards, or port and starboard. The two top corners are the earing cringles, the bottom corners are the clews, or clues, again differentiated by weather and lee or by port and starboard. The central part of a square sail, usually cut with a full belly to hold the wind, is known as the *bunt.

Fore-and-aft sails are either triangular in shape, such as a jib, staysail, *spinnaker, 'leg-o'-mutton', or *Bermuda mainsail, or four-sided, such as a *gaff mainsail or a lugsail. As in the case of square sails, they take their names from the mast or stay on which they are set.

The four sides of a gaff sail are the head (top), foot (bottom), luff (leading edge), and leech (trailing edge), the corners are the *throat (top, leading edge), *peak (top, trailing edge), tack (bottom, leading edge), and clew (bottom, trailing edge). Triangular sails have all their sides luff, leech, and foot, and as their corners tack, head, and clew. Only mainsails are reefed, either by

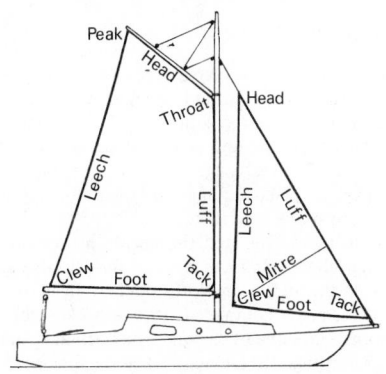

Parts of triangular and four-sided fore-and-aft sails

being rolled round the boom or with rows (up to three) of reef points sewn on to the sails with *crow's feet. On occasions a reefing jib was set in fore-and-aft rig, the luff of the sail being attached to a cylindrical spar so that the jib could be reduced in size by being rolled up round the spar, but this is a comparatively rare type of sail, and the usual practice, if a vessel is carrying too

much canvas forward, is to replace the jib set with a smaller one.

A gaff mainsail is frequently extended by setting a topsail above it to fill the area between the mast and the gaff. Two types of topsail can be set, a jib-headed topsail which extends from the *jaws of the gaff to the masthead, or a jackyard topsail which extends above the top of the mast to provide a greater area of sail in winds of light or moderate strength.

Until about 1950, all fore-and-aft sails were made of canvas, light or heavy according to the use of the sail in light or heavy winds. Since that date, man-made materials, such as Terylene, Dacron, etc., are much more widely used, particularly in yachts. The number of types of sail carried is also much greater so that the best use can be made of all the variations in wind strength likely to be encountered. Light winds naturally enable larger sails, such as *genoa jibs, *ghosters, and, when running with the wind abaft the beam, spinnakers to be set. These are invariably made of lightweight material, heavy canvas being used only for small storm sails such as jibs and staysails. The outfit of sails carried by a yacht is known collectively as her *wardrobe.

TO SET SAIL, strictly to hoist or loose the sails to give a vessel motion, but the term is frequently used of any ship when she departs on a voyage. TO MAKE SAIL, to spread additional sails to increase the speed of a sailing ship. TO SHORTEN SAIL, to take in or reef sails to reduce the speed of a ship. TO STRIKE SAIL, to lower it suddenly. Striking a topsail was in the old days a form of salute (see SALUTES AT SEA) which foreign ships would pay to men-of-war when meeting them in territorial waters of the nation to which the man-of-war belonged.

SAIL BURTON, the *purchase which extends from the heads of the topmasts to the deck in square-rigged ships and is used for hoisting sails aloft when it is required to *bend them on to the *yards. These sails are far too heavy, and the distance they have to be hoisted far too great, for them to be manhandled up the masts, hence the need for these purchases.

SAILING DIRECTIONS, publications of the British Hydrographic Department of the Navy, were first produced in 1828. They are usually known as 'Pilots' and are a source of original, worldwide information, almost entirely coastal, to supplement that included on *charts. Each covers a particular area of coast, such as the Channel Pilot (southern England and northern France), China Sea Pilot, Mediterranean Pilot, etc. A main source of original information was the 'Remark' Books which *masters, and later navigating officers, of H.M. ships were strictly enjoined to keep, and these remarks were co-ordinated and compiled in book form to cover various areas of seas and oceans. Modern additions come from a variety of sources, such as local announcements of new development, etc. After the issue of each *Sailing Directions*, periodical corrections were made by hydrographical notices issued to all ships until, in 1884, printed supplements to the *Sailing Directions* were issued at intervals of from one to three years. The content of the *Sailing Directions*, at one time full of historical and other details of general interest, is now more restricted to their particular navigational purpose. The British series of *Sailing Directions* is completed by the volume *Ocean Passages of the World*, the only one of the Pilots which is non-coastal. Similar publications are produced of course by the authorities of other nations which produce navigational charts.

SAILING THWART, a fore-and-aft *thwart running down the centre of some sailing/rowing boats, such as *gigs and *galleys used as ships' boats, to give support to the masts. Being essentially oared boats, though with the necessary fittings to ship masts and sail when required, such boats required this extra strengthening since they shipped two masts as against the more usual single mast of most other ships' boats.

SAILMAKER, ISAAC (*c*. 1633–1721), marine artist, was possibly of Dutch origin but is more usually thought of as the first of the great English marine painters. He was a pupil of George Feldorp, a German–Flemish artist who came to England as the Keeper of the Royal Pictures during the reign of Charles I (1625–49). It is known that Cromwell, during the Interregnum (1649–60), commissioned Sailmaker to paint a view of the English fleet before Mardyke during the First Dutch War (1652–4), and it is also known that he was the first artist to paint pictures of English naval battles, probably being commissioned to do so as a sort of official war artist. His pictures are very rare and their attribution to him is in some cases uncertain.

SAILMAKERS' STITCHING, the types of stitching used when making sails, awnings, and other canvas articles. Most modern sails are stitched by machine, which has advantages not only of speed but also of a closer stitch with a more even tension than can be achieved with hand sewing. There are some tasks, however, that cannot be done by machine, either because of the shape of the seam to be sewn or because a machine cannot be used, for example, to draw together the edges of a tear in a sail or awning. Man-made materials, now widely used for sails in yachts, are always best stitched by machine as hand sewing tends to tear the fabric.

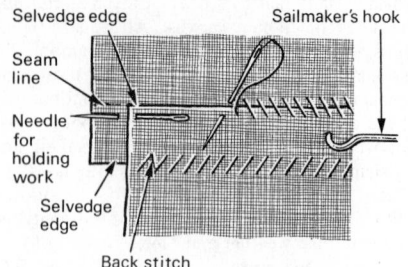

Flat sewing

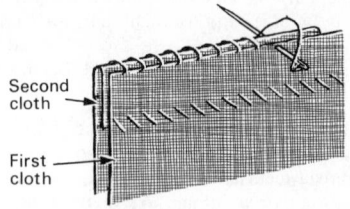

Round sewing

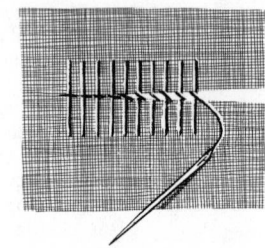

Sailmaker's darn

A sailmaker uses three types of stitch in his work, flat sewing, round sewing, and darning. Flat sewing is used to join two pieces of cloth or canvas where strength is not of paramount importance. The selvedge edge of one piece of material is placed along the seam line of the other, both are hooked on to a sailmaker's hook to keep them taut, and the needle passed down through the single cloth close to the selvedge and then up through both cloths, and so on until the whole seam is completed, with a back stitch to terminate the line of sewing. The normal spacing is three stitches to an inch. When the first seam is completed, the work is reversed and the selvedge of the other piece of cloth sewn to the seam line in the same way. The direction of sewing in flat sewing is always away from the hook.

Round sewing is used where greater strength is required, the stitches passing through four thicknesses of the cloth instead of two. There are two forms of round sewing, known as single last and double last. In single last, each cloth to be joined has its edge turned in about half an inch, the two are then placed together, held taut with a sailmaker's hook, and joined at the edge by passing the needle through all four parts about ⅛ inch from the edge and back over the top, making four stitches to the inch. In double last, the selvedge edge of one piece of cloth is placed level with the doubled edge of the other and the seam sewn as in the single last. The work is then reversed and the selvedge edge of the other piece is similarly stitched to the other, which is doubled at the seam line. In round sewing, the direction of sewing is always towards the hook.

Darning is used for the repair of small tears. The first stitch is made by bringing the needle up through the canvas about one inch from the side of the tear, down through the canvas a similar distance on the other side, then up through the tear and through the bight formed by the twine. Subsequent stitches are made by passing the needle through the tear, up through the canvas on one side, down on the other side leaving a small bight, and then up through the tear and the bight. This forms a locked stitch, each one being drawn taut as it is finished. The stitches are made close together to give greater strength. See also TABLE, TO, MONK'S SEAM.

SAILMAKER'S WHIPPING, a whipping used in cases where it is essential that it will not slip or come adrift, as in the ends of the *reef-points of a sail. It is made by unlaying the rope to be whipped for two or three inches and passing a bight of the whipping twine over the middle strand, leaving the two ends of the twine, one short and one long, and the bight hanging downwards. The rope is then laid up again and the turns of the whipping passed round the rope using the long end of the twine and working against the *lay of the rope and towards the end.

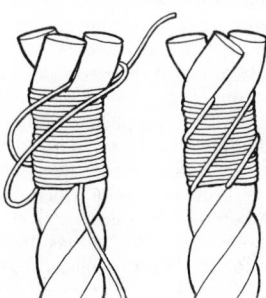

Sailmaker's whipping

When the whipping is long enough to take the bight, it is passed up outside the whipping, following the lay of the strand over which it was originally placed, and finally over the top of the same strand. The short end of the twine is now hauled taut, so that the bight is tightened, and is itself then brought up outside the whipping, again following the lay of the rope. The whipping is

completed by joining the two ends of the twine with a reef knot concealed in the middle of the rope. See also COMMON WHIPPING, WEST COUNTRY WHIPPING.

SAILORS' DRESS. The earliest reference to any sort of uniform dress for seamen appears to date from a few years after the Roman invasion of Britain (55 B.C.) with an order that the sails of *longboats in the Roman fleet were to be dyed blue to match the colour of the sea and that their crews were to wear clothing of the same colour to lessen the chances of the boats being seen by an enemy. Two thousand years later, the prevailing colour of all sea uniforms is still blue.

Of the general cut of the clothing worn, one of the earliest descriptions is that given by Geoffrey Chaucer to his 'shipman' in the *Canterbury Tales*, who was dressed 'all in a gowne of falding to the knee'. This gives a date of about 1380 for this knee-length gown, possibly the forerunner of the English seaman's petticoat trousers, which remained an article of his standard dress until as late as the beginning of the 19th century. There was a good functional reason for the longevity of this odd piece of maritime clothing in the protection it offered to the trousers of men working aloft on the *yards of square-rigged ships, and also when rowing in the boats of the fleet, where the petticoat gave good protection against rain and spray. As the years went by, the 'shipman's' gown became a canvas frock tucked in to breeches or trousers to form a blouse.

In general, the tendency to provide seamen with some sort of uniform clothing started in the fighting navies, and was only followed in merchant navies many years later. Thus, when men were hurriedly raised in England in 1587 and 1588 to man the ships that fought against the Spanish *Armada, they were all given a blue coat by Elizabeth I, and the blue coat did not appear in merchant ships, and then only in a few ships, until nearly a century later. James I, who followed Elizabeth on the English throne, was less generous to his seamen, writing to the *Lord High Admiral that 'it is not intended to clothe the men to make them handsome to run away'.

The elaborately illustrated title pages and cartouches with which the early mapmakers decorated their sea atlases provide much evidence about the contemporary dress of seamen. Those of the late 16th and early 17th centuries are virtually unanimous in showing seamen wearing very baggy breeches with woollen stockings, a thigh-length blouse or coat, and a tall, hairy hat, though one or two of the Dutch sea atlases show some of their seamen wearing long baggy trousers under an ankle-length coat. A 17th century journal kept by one of the English *buccaneers cruising in the Pacific Ocean records sighting another ship, and 'we knew her to be English because the seamen wore breeches'. The only other ships in the Pacific at that time would be those of Spain, which argues that the fashion for breeches as a rig for seamen had not yet spread to the Mediterranean.

Beyond this general overall fashion, which did not differ very greatly from the fashions worn on land except for the coat in place of the doublet, there was nothing that could be described as any sort of general uniform which differentiated the seaman from the landsman. But as, from the 16th century onwards, voyages got longer in search of new lands and new routes to the rich countries of the East, there was a tendency for ships' crews eventually to wear clothing similar in cut and colour because of the clothing carried on board, known as *slops, and sold to the crew by the *purser or *supercargo to replace items of clothing worn out during the voyage. These, if only

Seaman wearing petticoat-trousers; aquatint by D. Serres, 1777

for economic reasons, tended to be all of the same pattern and colour. A typical ship's slop chest of 1663, in accordance with a British Admiralty order, contained 'red caps, Monmouth caps [similar to a tam o' shanter], yarn stockings, Irish stockings, neat's-leather flat-heeled shoes, blue neckcloths, canvas suits and rugs'. Some forty years later the slop chest became much more elaborate, and an Admiralty order of 1706 stipulated that it should contain 'shrunk gray kersey jackets, lined with red cotton, with 15 brass buttons and two pockets of linen, the buttonholes stitched with gold-colour thread, at 10s6d. each; waistcoats of Welsh red, plain, unlined, with 18 brass buttons, the holes stitched with gold-colour thread, at 5s6d. each; red kersey breeches, lined with linen, with three leather pockets, and 13 white tin buttons, the buttonholes stitched with white thread, at the rate of 5s6d. each; red-flowered shag breeches, lined with linen, with three leather pockets and 14 brass buttons, the buttonholes stitched with gold-coloured thread, at the rate of 11s6d. each; striped shag breeches, lined with linen, with three leather pockets and 14 white tin buttons, the buttonholes stitched with white thread, at the rate of 10s6d. each'. Blue and white checked shirts and drawers; grey woollen stockings and gloves; shoes with round toes, brass buckles, and iron tongues; leather caps faced with red cotton and lined with white linen also figure in this list. It sounds like detailed uniform regulations, but in fact this was in no way a uniform, merely replacement clothing for any articles worn out, and seamen were in no way forced to buy it if they could cobble up anything else which would be serviceable.

Most seamen, both in navies and merchant navies, made their own clothes on board for few could afford recourse to the slop chest to any great extent out of their meagre pay. Worn out canvas sails provided the basic cloth for home-made clothing, and seamen very quickly discovered that a liberal application of tar made the canvas admirably weather resistant. Almost all seamen of all nations made themselves canvas hats with a brim and coated them with tar to form a waterproof headgear known as a tarpaulin, abbreviated into 'tar' as the universal synonym for a sailor. Canvas blouses and trousers were similarly treated with tar to become the more or less standard heavy-weather clothing of the seaman, giving the other well-known synonym of 'tarry-breeks' for a sailor. The tarpaulin hat and the tarred canvas blouse and trousers were the forerunners of the oilskin coat and sou'wester hat, introduced in the late 19th century. These were made of a very fine canvas impregnated with an oil-based preparation which gave it a glossy surface and made it completely waterproof. This type of oilskin suf-

Captain, Commander, Midshipman and Admiral; aquatint by J. Harris, 1848–9

fered from the defect that exposure to salt water eventually made it sticky and destroyed the waterproofing, and it has been largely displaced by modern types of PVC material which retain their waterproof quality until they are worn out.

Until uniforms were officially introduced few sailors, whether in a fighting or a merchant navy, originally owned more in the clothing line than the suit they stood up in when they first came on board. When it became too worn and ragged for further patching, a captain had the right to order a man to buy a replacement from the slop chest, and thus some of the outward decencies at least were preserved on board. There was no night clothing and in general men slept in the clothes they wore during the day. This shortage of clothing was frequently responsible for the diseases which ravaged so many crews of ships during the

16th to 18th centuries. A man who was forced to live in a suit wet from wind or spray because he had no dry clothes to change into had his resistance to *scurvy greatly reduced, and typhus-carrying lice throve and multiplied in the dirt inevitably engendered in a single and permanent suit of working clothes. In almost all ships, however, one afternoon a week was reserved for making and mending clothes, still the origin of the weekly 'make and mend', or half-day's rest on board ship.

The crews of ships engaged in polar exploration or voyages in search of the *North-East and *North-West passages were always better provided, mainly because such voyages were always of abnormally long duration. Fur-lined hats, coats, and trousers were issued as well as an additional supply of underclothing for adequate warmth. Most of these voyages were financed by official and relatively wealthy bodies, initially by the companies of merchant adventurers and later by geographical societies who were financially able to equip the men adequately for the hardships ahead.

Following the earlier fashion of baggy breeches and trousers, and spanning the last years of the petticoat-trousers, there was a period when striped waistcoats, shirts, and trousers, either red and white or blue and white, became a feature of the seaman's dress. They were accompanied by a straw hat. They originated in the main European navies and to some extent were copied in the merchant navies. Introduced in the last decade of the 18th century, these maritime fashions lasted until about 1820, when solid colours came back into favour. The straw hat, however, lasted a great deal longer and was worn by many seamen until the beginning of the 20th century, particularly in warmer climates.

Full uniforms as such were not introduced into navies until about the mid-18th century for officers and the mid-19th century for ratings. Merchant services were by now generally following the lead of their navies a few years later, though at first only in the better organized and larger shipping lines. Today, and for many years past, the prevailing colour of all marine uniforms is blue, and variations in cut and design are remarkably small as between the various seafaring nations of the world, both for officers and for ratings, and for navies and merchant navies.

ST. ELMO'S FIRE, the brush-like electric discharge which, under certain atmospheric conditions, takes place at the mastheads and yardarms of a ship. It is known by over fifty different names. In Graeco-Roman times it was attributed to *Castor and Pollux, whose heads were supposed to have been illumined by *Poseidon during a storm encountered when they were sailing on the first voyage of the *Argonauts. The name St. Elmo is by some believed to be a corruption of St. Erasmus, a martyr of c. 303 and a patron saint of Mediterranean sailors, but it has also been equated with St. Peter Gonzales (c. 1190–1246), a Dominican friar who accompanied Ferdinand III of Spain on his expedition against the Moors, and then devoted the remainder of his life in work to improve conditions of the seafaring people along the Spanish coasts. One of the earliest recorded uses of it appears in a vow invoking the aid of Pope Urban V (1362–70) which caused to appear 'the light of St. Elemi'. The many variations of the name include St. Ermyn, St. Telme, St. Helm, St. Ermo, St. Anselmo, etc.

In the Middle Ages the appearance of the phenomenon was greeted sometimes with joy, sometimes with dread. Italian mariners of the 15th and 16th centuries believed that the lights emanated from the body of Christ and gave them the name of Corposanto, of which again there are many derivatives, e.g., *Corposant, Cormazant, Comazant, Capra Saltante, Corbie's Aunt, etc. *Columbus, Vasco da *Gama, *Magellan, and *Dampier, to name but a few among the world's great navigators, all recorded encountering St. Elmo's Fire during their voyages. It is also occasionally seen on aircraft flying among thunder clouds and sometimes on prominent points like church spires ashore.

St. Elmo's Fire was regarded by most superstitious seamen as a favourable omen, foretelling the end of stormy weather, but it was also widely believed at one time that if the light from St. Elmo's Fire fell upon a man's face, he would die within 24 hours. Few of the older seamen would dare to look directly at the phenomenon when it appeared. This odd belief may have had its origin in a similar belief connected with the sighting of the *Flying Dutchman, or possibly vice-versa.

ST. LUCIA, one of the smaller islands in the Windward Islands group, was the scene of a naval action during the War of American Independence (1775–82) when it was captured from the French on 29 December 1778 by a British expeditionary force under the command of Rear Admiral the Hon. Samuel Barrington and Major-General James Grant, with about 12,000 troops. The British force anchored in the Grand Cul-de-Sac, on the west side of the island, on 13 December, and the troops were at once landed and occupied several key positions in the island. A French fleet of twelve *ships of the line, under the command of Vice Admiral the Comte d' *Estaing, reached St. Lucia two days later and unsuccessfully attacked the British ships as they lay at anchor. A second attack by the French was delivered the same afternoon but this also was beaten off.

Beyond landing about 9,000 troops on the island, d'Estaing was able to do nothing effective with his ships during the next fortnight, and the French troops had no success when they attacked the fortified posts which had been erected by the British. During the night of 28/29 December, d'Estaing re-embarked the troops and sailed for Martinique, leaving St. Lucia to its fate. The French governor of St. Lucia, finding that his position was now hopeless, capitulated on the following day.

ST. ROCH, a two-masted *gaff *schooner with an auxiliary engine, displacing 323 tons, was launched in April 1928, having been specially designed for Arctic service. In 1940–2, under the command of Staff Sergeant Henry A. Larsen of the Royal Canadian Mounted Police, she was the second ship to negotiate the *North-West passage from west to east and the first to navigate it in both directions. She is now on exhibition in the Maritime Museum at Vancouver, Canada.

ST. VINCENT, BATTLE OF, an action fought on 16 January 1780 during the War of American Independence (1776–82) between a British fleet of eighteen *ships of the line under the command of Admiral Sir George *Rodney, who was escorting a large *convoy carrying supplies for Gibraltar and Minorca, and a Spanish fleet of eleven sail of the line and two *frigates commanded by Admiral Don Juan de Langara. The Spanish fleet was sighted in the neighbourhood of Cape St. Vincent and Rodney made the signal for a *general chase, each ship to engage the Spanish warships as they came up by rotation, and also to take the *lee *gage in order to prevent the enemy's retreat into their own ports. The naval battle which ensued began at about 4 p.m. in weather that steadily deteriorated, and continued until 2 a.m. the following morning when all firing ceased. Of the Spanish fleet, only four ships of the line and the two frigates escaped. This action is sometimes referred to as the 'Moonlight Battle'. For the famous engagement of 1797 at the same locality, see CAPE ST. VINCENT, BATTLE OF.

ST. VINCENT, Earl of, see JERVIS, John.

SAINTS, The, a group of small islets in the West Indies, between Guadeloupe and Dominica, which gave their name to a naval battle, fought on 12 April 1782, the final sea battle of the War of American Independence (1775–82), between a British fleet commanded by Admiral Sir George *Rodney, with thirty-six *ships of the line, and a French fleet under the command of Vice Admiral the Comte de *Grasse with thirty ships of the line, which was escorting a French *convoy. Rodney had been home in England on sick leave and had returned to the West Indies in the latter part of February to resume the command of the fleet, bringing with him an additional seventeen ships of the line to reinforce it.

The action began at 7 a.m. with the fleets passing on opposite tacks. At 9.15 the wind veered four points, which enabled Rodney and five more ships to break through the French line, a movement which was also followed by the rear division of the fleet under the command of Rear Admiral Sir Samuel *Hood. The British thus gained the weather *gage, and the French endeavoured to reform their *line of battle on their leewardmost ships. The action ended at about sunset, and at 6.29 the French flagship *Ville de Paris* struck her colours to the *Barfleur*, Hood's flagship. Sixteen minutes later Rodney signalled the fleet to *bring to on the *port

*tack, and he remained stationary all night. Much to Hood's indignation Rodney did not pursue, and the disorganized French fleet got away to Cape François (Cape Haitien), where it joined up with its convoy and also with a squadron of nine Spanish ships of the line. Four other French ships were also captured during the battle, but of these five *prizes, only one (the ex-British *Ardent*) reached England, all the others foundering off Newfoundland in a gale on 16 September 1782.

Six days after the battle of the Saints, Hood was detached with ten sail of the line and two *frigates in pursuit of the flying French. He made for the Mona Passage, between Puerto Rico and Santo Domingo, and at daybreak on the 19th a small French squadron was seen. A *general chase resulted in the capture of two French ships of the line, a *frigate and an ex-British *sloop. A second enemy frigate escaped. This action took place about 12 miles south-east of the small island of Zacheo (Deseceo). Hood, in his report to Rodney, emphasized the fact that the main body of the retreating French fleet had only passed through the Mona Passage the day before he was in it, and implied that but for Rodney's inaction after the main action the defeat of the French fleet might well have been much more decisive.

The battle of the Saints is chiefly remembered for the introduction of the tactic of breaking the line of battle, throwing the enemy line into disorder by sailing through gaps between ships in the line, and engaging from the opposite side. It was a breakaway from the stereotyped form of naval battle in which lines of ships engaged each other at close range with negligible chances of a decisive result. Although on this occasion Rodney led his ships through a gap in the French line, it has been said that it was on the advice of his flag captain, Sir Charles *Douglas, that he did so. Nevertheless, the French line of battle was thrown into confusion and the tactic was adopted in the British Navy as a desirable addition to the *Fighting Instructions*. See also, for example, the British tactics at *Trafalgar, where the two lines led by Lord *Nelson and Admiral *Collingwood both broke the Franco-Spanish line.

SAKER, see GUNS, NAVAL.

SALAMIS, a Greek island in the Aegean Sea and the scene of a great naval battle fought between the fleets of Greece and Persia in 480 B.C. The Athenian leader Themistocles had drawn up his fleet in the bay of Eleusis, in which they were trapped by the Persians who closed the two channels leading into the bay. But the narrowness of these channels led to the Persian defeat, as they were not able to use their superiority in numbers in such restricted waters. Their ships were thrown into complete confusion as they advanced into the narrow channel, and a well-judged attack by *Cimon, second-in-command to Themistocles, threw them back in disorder. After several hours of fighting some 200 Persian ships had been sunk or burned, the Greek loss being about forty.

The Greek victory and destruction of the Persian fleet had a far-reaching effect in the war against the Persian invaders and led to the withdrawal of their land forces the next year and the abandonment for ever of the attempt to conquer Greece for the Persian Empire. Hence Salamis remained the outstanding example of Greek, and especially Athenian, sea power in preserving national independence, and played a part in Athenian history comparable to the defeat of the Spanish *Armada in that of England. The succeeding fifty years marked the height of Athenian political and cultural achievements, including the age of Pericles and the building of the Parthenon.

SALEM, a port on the Massachusetts coast of the U.S.A. and the home of the Peabody Museum of Salem, one of the oldest of the numerous maritime museums in the U.S.A., having been founded in 1799. It is housed in the East India Marine Hall. The collection is not limited to any period and it contains a fascinating collection of ship models, *figureheads, ship's carvings, tools, fishing gear, nautical instruments, weapons, dress, flags, paintings, engravings, and a very large number of photographs. The library contains 40,000 books. Also in Salem is a second maritime museum, the Salem Maritime National Historic Site, founded in 1938 and located in the Salem Custom House and also in Derby House. The collection amounts to some 1,000 exhibits.

SALINITY, the amount of salt held in suspension in seawater. Salinity varies from ocean to ocean, the salinity of the Atlantic being considerably higher than that of the Indian or Pacific Oceans. Maximum salinity in the Atlantic exists in two belts, of which one runs east and west across the North Atlantic between the latitudes of 20° and 30° N., and the other runs east from the coast of South America between 10° and 20° S. In general, the North Atlantic has a higher salinity than the South Atlantic. In the Indian Ocean, the areas of highest salinity are in the Arabian Sea and along a belt between the west coast of Australia and the east coast of South Africa. The Pacific is the least salty of the three, its only area of high salinity existing in a belt which extends westward from the American coast at the Tropic of Cancer as far as 160° E. longitude, where it turns southward towards the equator. In the South Pacific, the salinity diminishes steadily towards the higher latitudes.

The composition of the seawater in the English Channel per thousand parts by weight is: 964·74372 water, 27·05948 chloride of sodium, 0·76552 chloride of potassium, 3·66658 chloride of magnesium, 0·02929 bromide of magnesium, 2·29578 sulphate of magnesia, 1·40662 sulphate of lime, and 0·03301 carbonate of lime.

SALLEE PIRATES, Mediterranean *corsairs who operated from the port of Salli, in Morocco, from about the beginning of the 16th to the end of the 19th century, harassing Christian trade and making periodical piratical descents on the coast of Spain. Numerous British, Dutch, French, and Spanish expeditions were mounted against them, and although usually achieving temporary success, the *piracy always broke out again when the expeditions were withdrawn after their operations. See also BARBARY PIRATES.

SALLY PORT, (1) a large *port cut on each *quarter of a *fireship out of which officers and men made their escape into the boats towing alongside as soon as the fireship had *grappled an enemy ship and the powder train was fired. **(2)** The *entering port of a three-*decker warship during the days of sail. **(3)** A landing-place in Portsmouth Harbour which was reserved for the use of boats from men-of-war in the harbour. It was from this landing-place that Lord *Nelson was rowed out to H.M.S. *Victory* before sailing in September 1805 to join the British fleet off Cadiz and lead it to victory at *Trafalgar.

SALM, ADRIAEN VAN DER (d. 1720), Dutch marine artist of whose early life little is known. In 1686 he was living at Delft and while there painted some well known pictures of naval battles of the early years of the 18th century. In addition he made a number of pen and ink sketches of ships and shipping scenes which are of very considerable beauty and interest. A small collection of these may be seen in the British Museum.

SALMAGUNDI, a dish sometimes served at sea during the days of sail as a welcome change from salt meat. It consisted of slices of cured fish with onions, boiled together. Salted or cured fish was usually carried on board ships as an alternative victualling issue to salt beef or salt pork, usually at a rate of one pound of fish for one pound of beef or three-quarters of a pound of pork.

SALT HORSE, the seaman's slang name for the salted beef issued as victuals at sea until the introduction of refrigeration enabled fresh meat to be carried in ships. It was an expression more used in the days of sail than in the early days of steam, even though refrigeration still did not exist, as steam vessels made considerably shorter passages than sailing ships because of the limitations of fuel storage, and fresh meat would normally keep well on a short passage. The origin of the expression was of course the toughness of the beef as it came out of the cask. It was also known as salt junk, indicating the seaman's belief that any old meat was thrown into the casks for pickling in brine irrespective of the animal from which it was supposed to have come.

The term is also used in the British Navy to describe an officer who has not specialized in any professional branch of the navy.

SALT JUNK, see SALT HORSE.

SALUTES AT SEA, the recognized courtesies paid by ships at sea to the warships of all nations. They originally took two forms, the firing of guns and the striking of topsails, the latter when within the *territorial waters of the warship being saluted. Gun salutes were fired on every possible occasion and were often unlimited in extent, largely due to a predilection of naval officers of all nations for loud and prolonged noise, and it was not until 1675 that regulations were introduced in Britain, quickly followed by all other maritime nations, limiting the number of guns to be fired in salute. The immediate cause of the limitation was the need to stop the severe wastage of gunpowder, and Samuel *Pepys, Secretary of the British Admiralty, worked out a scale based on a minimum salute of three guns for the most junior rank of admiral, working up at two more guns for each step in rank until he reached nineteen guns for the admiral of the fleet. Two more guns were added for a salute to the monarch, and a royal or presidential salute still remains at twenty-one guns. The odd numbers were chosen for salutes because even numbers were always fired at naval funerals as a sign of mourning for the dead officer.

Merchant vessels which were armed, at this period a majority for reasons of self-defence against pirates and *privateers, saluted warships with their guns; those which were unarmed saluted by striking their topsails when meeting a man-of-war at sea. Gun salutes were always fired with the saluting ship's bows towards the ship being saluted in order to avoid any possibility that a salute might be construed as a hostile act, since muzzle-loading guns had to be shotted to make a satisfactory bang and they could only be fired broadside on to the ship's fore-and-aft line. A ship firing a salute bows-on to the ship saluted could not possibly hit her.

As the armed merchant ship went out of fashion and sail was gradually displaced by steam as a means of ship propulsion, a new means of saluting had to be devised to take the place of the guns or the struck topsails with which merchant vessels traditionally saluted warships. The new means evolved was by dipping the ensign, lowering it half way down the ensign staff and not rehoisting it until the warship had answered the salute. This is the current practice, and a merchant ship today dips her ensign when passing a warship of any nation on the high seas and keeps it dipped until the warship also dips her ensign in acknowledgement. As soon as it is rehoisted in the warship, the merchant vessel follows suit and the salute is complete. Yachts usually also fly the flag of a foreign country as a courtesy flag when in the waters of that country; it should be flown on the starboard side either from the *crosstrees or in the rigging.

Navies have a variety of salutes for officers of rank and ships of foreign nations, varying between gun salutes, guards and bands, guards without bands, bugle calls, and *piping the side, according to rank and circumstances.

SALVAGE, (1) a proportion of the value of ship or cargo paid by the owner or his insurance company to those by whose means they have been saved when in danger. The proportion is based on the labour and danger of saving the ship or cargo and the state of the prevailing weather. No salvage can however be claimed by the crew of a ship for their efforts in saving their own ship or its cargo.

(2) Underwater recovery of a ship and/or her contents. In recent years the great technological revolution in engineering practice has made possible the repair underwater of ships damaged by explosion or other means. A ship's *hull torn open by, for example, the explosion of a *mine or *torpedo can be patched either by steel plates riveted over the hole or by the construction of a metal blister over the damaged area, either of which will provide a sufficient measure of watertightness for ultimate salvage. Deck openings, such as funnels and *hatches, can be effectively sealed by divers working on the submerged hull, and a ship thus patched and sealed can have the water in her pumped out until she obtains sufficient positive buoyancy to bring her automatically to the surface.

Perhaps the greatest such feat of salvage was the raising of the larger part of the German *High Seas Fleet which scuttled itself at *Scapa Flow in June 1919, after the expiration of the period of armistice which brought the First World War (1914–18) to a close. Fifteen *battleships and *battle-cruisers and four light *cruisers were scuttled, as well as many *destroyers, of a total tonnage of 400,000 tons, and the great majority were subsequently raised by the salvage firm of Cox and Danks, to be towed away for breaking-up. The salvage operation extended over several years, as many of the larger ships had turned over while they were sinking and were lying on the sea bed with their bottoms upward. Of the fifty-one ships which sank that day, all but seven were later salvaged.

Many cases of the recovery of treasure from sunken ships are on record. In the early years of this century, before many of the problems of really deep diving had been solved, the more notable such cases were the recovery of silver bars to the value of £9,000 by a Spanish diver from the steamer *Skyro* off Cape Finisterre at a depth of 30 *fathoms, that of £70,000 from the Spanish mail ship *Alphonso XII* off Las Palmas, in the Grand Canary from a depth of 27 fathoms, and silver dollars worth £50,000 from the steamship *Hamilton Mitchell*, sunk on the Leuconna Reef, China, at a depth of 24 fathoms. These early recoveries of treasure are remarkable in view of the depth at which they were achieved at a period when there was much still to be learned of the behaviour of the human body when subjected to great pressure.

A considerably more valuable recovery was made between the years 1917 and 1924 when nearly £5,000,000 of gold bullion was brought up from the wreck of the *White Star *liner *Laurentic*, which had been sunk by a mine off the entrance to Lough Swilly, Northern Ireland, early in 1917. She lay in 19 fathoms of water, and during the course of salvage, over 5,000 individual dives were made.

Another spectacular recovery of gold was made in 1930–2 from the *P & O liner *Egypt*, which was sunk in 1922 off Ushant, in the Bay of Biscay, after a collision with a French ship. She lay at a depth of 65 fathoms, and at the time of the accident she was carrying about five tons of gold and ten tons of silver, worth a little over £1,000,000. See also DIVING, (3).

SAMPAN, the typical small and light boats of oriental waters and rivers. There are two types, the harbour sampan which usually has an awning over the centre and after part and is normally propelled by a single *scull over the stern, and the coastal sampan fitted with a single mast and *junk-type sail. The origin of the name is said to come from the Chinese *san*, thin, and *pan*, board, but some hold it to have a Malayan origin.

SAMPSON, WILLIAM THOMAS (1840–1902), American naval officer, commanded the North Atlantic Squadron during the Spanish–American War, 1898. He was born in Palmyra, N.Y., graduated from the Naval Academy in 1861, served with distinction during the American Civil War (1861–5), and was executive officer of the *monitor *Patapsco* when she was destroyed by a *mine in Charleston harbour. In 1886–90 he was superintendent of the Naval Academy. The action off Santiago, Cuba, in which the Spanish squadron under Admiral *Cervera was destroyed, opened a long and bitter controversy as to which of two

Raising the East German freighter Magdeburg, *sunk in the Thames, 1964*

Sampans at Canton

American * commodores was responsible for the victory, for Winfield S. * Schley, also present in the American squadron, was senior to Sampson. He had, however, been appointed to serve under Sampson, and there can be little doubt that it was to Sampson that the credit for the victory should go.

SAMSON POST, in the old days when * anchors were catted before being let go and on weighing, a samson post was a post erected temporarily on deck to take a * tackle with a sufficiently long lead for the whole crew to man the * fall. When all anchors had to be handled entirely by manpower, a large number of men were required on the tackles used in lifting and stowing. Today a samson post is a small derrick mast in a merchant ship to support the cargo booms. They are usually fitted in pairs and known colloquially as goalposts. See CAT, TO.

SAN DEMETRIO, an oil * tanker of 8,073 tons, laden with petrol, which was one of the ships in a * convoy attacked during the Second World War by the German * pocket-battleship *Admiral Scheer* on the evening of 5 November 1940. The convoy was being escorted by the * armed merchant cruiser * *Jervis Bay*, and after she had been

sunk in a very gallant action, the *Admiral Scheer* went for the convoy, which had meanwhile scattered. The *San Demetrio* was hit by a number of shells, set on fire, brought to a stop, and finally abandoned. The majority of her crew were rescued from their * lifeboats by the S.S. *Gloucester City*, a straggler from another convoy, but one boat, in charge of Second Officer Hawkins and containing Chief Engineer Charles Pollard and twelve other seamen and engineers, was not found. This lifeboat came across the burning *San Demetrio*, which was still afloat, the next morning and the men re-embarked in spite of the risk of imminent explosion of the cargo. Having extinguished the fires they managed to raise steam and get under way. The *San Demetrio* reached the coast of Ireland eight days later and thence, with the assistance of volunteers from the * destroyer H.M.S. *Arrow*, steamed on to the Clyde where the ship finally berthed on 19 November, an epic of courage, endurance, and ingenuity at sea.

SAN FRANCISCO, a major city of the state of California and the chief U.S. seaport on the Pacific coast. It was originally a Spanish missionary post, founded in 1776, of the Franciscan order. The town sprang into importance in 1848 with the discovery of gold in California, and within the year its population had risen from less than 1,000 to over 40,000. Ten years later the discovery of silver increased once more the rate of expansion. It has had a full maritime history, beginning with the host of adventurers attracted to it by the 1848 gold rush, and was notorious throughout the second half of the 19th century for its drinking dens and brothels designed to attract seamen into the hands of *crimps, of whom the port was reputed to have a greater number than any other port in the world. On several occasions during the early years of the city's growth fire and earthquake swept through the buildings, but the magnificent bay on which San Francisco is built is so fine a natural harbour that each time the city was rebuilt. The most disastrous earthquake and fire occurred in 1906 when much of the town was utterly destroyed and the losses amounted to several hundreds of millions of dollars. San Francisco, as well as being a great seaport, is also an important base of the U.S. Navy, with the main installation and dockyard on Mare Island in San Pablo Bay. It has a great shipbuilding and ship repairing industry. The *San Francisco Maritime Museum in the Maritime State Historical Park has one of the most important maritime collections on the Pacific coast of the U.S.A.

SAN FRANCISCO MARITIME MUSEUM, San Francisco, California, was opened in May 1951 and is housed in a building originally designed as a palace for the public in the Maritime State Historical Park. It is now one of the most important maritime collections on the west coast of the U.S.A.; the emphasis is not so much on ship models as on ships themselves preserved close alongside, of which the most interesting is the Scottish-built three-masted ship *Balclutha*, launched in 1886, and at one time employed in the Californian grain trade. Other ships preserved are the steam *schooner *Wapama*, the walking beam ferry boat *Eureka*, the three-masted lumber schooner *C. A. Thayer*, the *scow *Alma*, and the paddle-wheel *tug *Eppleton Hall*, which was British-built and crossed the Atlantic under her own steam in 1972 on her way to the museum. Also in the museum are *figureheads, bow and stern carvings, nameboards, *windlasses, *capstans, and *anchors. The library contains over 15,000 books, maps, plans, manuscripts, and log books, and there are some 25,000 photographs.

SAN JUAN, the capital city and principal seaport of Puerto Rico, lies on the north side of the island. It has a capacious harbour, landlocked except on the north. The present city was founded in 1520 when the original Spanish settlers moved from Caparra (now Pueblo Viejo)

to San Juan, and it has had a stormy history. In 1595 it was sacked by Sir Francis *Drake and in 1597 captured by Admiral George Clifford, Earl of Cumberland, but later abandoned as a result of an epidemic of yellow fever. In 1797 it was attacked by British troops under Sir Ralph Abercrombie, but the attack was beaten off. During the American–Spanish war of 1898 it was bombarded by an American fleet under Commodore W. T. *Sampson and blockaded by the American *cruiser *St. Paul*, but held out until the war ended.

SAN LUCAR, the seaport in southern Spain from which, in 1519, Ferdinand *Magellan set sail on his voyage around the world. Also in San Lucar is the palace of the Dukes of *Medina Sidonia, one of whom was the leader of the Spanish fleet in the great *Armada battle in 1588.

SAND-GLASS, the means of measuring the passage of time on board ship before the development of reliable everyday clocks suitable for the purpose. Basically a sand-glass consists of two vacuum globes connected by a narrow neck and sand runs from the top globe into the bottom one through the neck, emptying itself in a given interval of time. When all has run out, the sand-glass is reversed and the same process is repeated in the same interval of time. Sand-glasses were supplied for maritime use in four sizes, half-minute, half-hour, hour, and four-hour glasses, but the two most in use were the half-minute and half-hour. The former was used to estimate the speed of the ship with reference to the *log, by the measurement of the amount of line which would run out from a ship as she went through the water during the period of a half-minute glass emptying itself. The line was marked with knots spaced at intervals representing a speed of one nautical mile per hour (hence *knot as the unit of maritime speed). And with the more accurate earth measurement that came with the passage of years, the half-minute glass was changed to a 28-second glass to provide a more exact measurement of a ship's speed.

The half-hour sand-glass was the main means of measuring the passage of time on board ship, the ship's *bell being rung every time a half-hour glass emptied itself. A *watch on board amounted to eight half-hour glasses, or four hours. George *Shelvocke, in his *A Voyage Round the World* (1726), wrote: 'At the turning of every glass during the night we beat three ruffs on the drums.' Possibly there was no ship's bell fitted in his ship, the *Speedwell*.

SANDBAGGER, a type of broad, shallow, open or partly decked sailing boat which originated about 1850 in America, and in which movable ballast in the form of sandbags was used while racing. The vogue lasted, mainly around New York harbour and at New Orleans, only some thirty years, when the boats, generally of the *catboat type, were divided into four classes: 26–30 ft, 23–26 ft, 20–23 ft, and under 20 ft. They carried immense sail plans of mainsail and *jib, and agile crews of eight or more who shifted the sandbags on to the weather deck every time the boat *tacked. This type of spectacular racing, which usually carried wagers on results, disappeared during the 1880s with the advent of finer designs of yachts for racing, but it became a popular sport in Sydney harbour, New South Wales, where it lasted as a class until the 1960s.

SANDEFJORD SJØFARTSMUSEUM, Sandefjord, Norway, was opened in 1958. The museum owes much of its collection to Lars Christensen, Roald *Amundsen, and Helmer Hansen, and is designed to illustrate the maritime history of Sandefjord and the surrounding district. Exhibits range from the Gokstad era to the end of the 17th century, mainly *longships, and the sailing ship era up to the outbreak of the First World War (1914–18). The collection, originally housed in an old restored building, was transferred to a new building in 1965. One of the main exhibits of the later period is a reconstructed crew's *forecastle on board a sailing ship, and the object of the display is to show life at sea in those days. Also located at Sandefjord is the Christensen's Whaling Museum which contains a library of 2,000 books on the subject.

SANDWICH, Earl of, see MONTAGU, Edward.

SANSON, NICOLAS (1600–67), French cartographer, was geographer to both Louis XIII and Louis XIV, who prized his skill as a mapmaker so much that he was made a councillor of state. His principal maps were published between 1636 and 1653, and in 1692 they were collected by Hubert Jaillot and published in the *Atlas Nouveau*, one of the great maritime atlases of the period. His two younger sons, ADRIEN (d. 1708) and GUILLAUME (d. 1703) were both geographers to the king.

SANTA CRUZ, 1st Marquis of, see BAZAN, Alvaro de.

SANTA CRUZ, BATTLE OF, was fought on 20 April 1657 after Robert *Blake, who had been lying off *Cadiz in command of an English fleet of twenty-five ships, had learned that the Spanish plate fleet, with the annual consignment of treasure from America, had reached Santa Cruz, Tenerife. On arrival off Santa Cruz, Blake sent Richard Stayner, his rear admiral, into the harbour with twelve ships, where he attacked the Spanish *galleons lying under the fortifications.

Blake entered the harbour later with the rest of the fleet and engaged the shore defences. Before noon, five enemy ships had been taken and nine more were burnt or had blown up. Stayner then attacked the two remaining plate ships, and before 1 p.m. these also had been blown up.

At about 4 p.m. the English ships weighed and withdrew; but Stayner's own ship, the *Speaker*, which had over eight feet of water in her hold, had been so severely damaged that she was only kept afloat by nailing leather hides over several large holes in her hull between wind and water. She sailed at sunset, but had scarcely got clear of the harbour when all her masts went *by the board and she was taken in tow by the *Plymouth*. More than 600 men from the other ships were sent on board to assist in pumping her out, and by next day she was free of water and jury masts had been rigged. Blake sent the *Speaker* home escorted by the *Fairfax*; they arrived in London on 20 June when Stayner was knighted for his part in the battle. The total English loss was about 50 killed and 120 wounded, that of the Spaniards considerably larger.

SANTA CRUZ ISLANDS, BATTLE OF, a naval action fought in the Pacific in October 1942 during the Second World War. It came about when the Japanese Combined Fleet advanced southwards from its base in Truk Island, both to support the supreme effort being made by their army on *Guadalcanal Island to evict the Americans from Henderson Flying Field and to fly in naval aircraft as soon as this had been accomplished. The Combined Fleet, deployed in three widely separated groups and comprising four *battleships, eight heavy and two light *cruisers, four *aircraft carriers, and twenty-nine *destroyers, was confronted on 26 October 1942, to the northward of the Santa Cruz Islands, by two American carrier groups centred on the *Hornet* and *Enterprise* respectively, under the command of Rear Admiral Thomas C. *Kinkaid.

As usual, the objectives of air strikes launched by the Americans were the big Japanese fleet carriers *Shokaku* and *Zuikaku* of Vice Admiral *Nagumo's command. In company with the light carrier *Zuiho*, they had just launched their own first wave of strike aircraft when scouting planes from the *Enterprise* discovered and dive-bombed the *Zuiho*, driving her, crippled, out of action.

The main strikes from each side passed on opposite courses and briefly clashed as they flew towards their targets. The American carrier *Hornet*, hit by two *torpedoes, three 500-pound bombs, and two *kamikaze, was left a shattered and burning wreck. In reply, dive-bombers from the *Hornet* severely damaged the *Shokaku*, putting her out of action for nine months. They also hit the cruiser *Chikuma*.

A second strike wave from the Japanese carriers, attacking just when a *submarine torpedoed and sank the destroyer *Porter*, hit the carrier *Enterprise* with two bombs but did not vitally restrict her effectiveness as a carrier. Attempts by the cruiser *Northampton* to tow the *Hornet* to safety were ended when further Japanese strike planes succeeded in putting another torpedo into the carrier and hit her with another bomb. The *Hornet* was abandoned; eight American torpedoes failed to sink her and she was finally sunk by Japanese destroyers after the American task force had retired.

Although a superficial assessment of the outcome could give the victory to the Japanese on this occasion, the slaughter inflicted on their aircrews, who attacked with suicidal determination, left the Combined Fleet with less than 100 carrier planes to throw into the critical phase of the struggle for Guadalcanal.

SANTA MARIA, a *nao* (ship) of Galicia described as a *caravel of 100 tons in which, with a total crew of forty men, Christopher *Columbus, on 3 August 1492, sailed from Palos in company with the *Pinta* and *Niña* on a voyage to the westward in search of a new sea route to Japan and the east.

The ships reached the West Indies on 12 October 1492, a voyage hailed ever since as the first discovery of America. (But see also LEIF ERICSSON). The *Santa Maria* was wrecked on Christmas Eve, 1492, on a coral reef in Caracol Bay, Haiti, a fort being built ashore out of her timbers.

SANTANDER, one of the chief Spanish seaports, on the northern coast of Spain, with a magnificent harbour some three miles wide by four miles long. In 1753 it was made a *puerto habilitado*, a port with the privilege of trading with America.

The Emperor Charles V landed at Santander in 1522 when he arrived to take possession of the Spanish crown, and it was from Santander that Charles I of England embarked on his return in 1623 after his search for a wife. In 1808 the city was sacked by French forces under the command of Marshal Soult. Santander harbour was the scene, on 3 November 1893, of a catastrophe when the steamer *Cabo Machichaco*, loaded with 1,700 cases of dynamite, blew up alongside the quay.

SANUTO or **SANUDO, MARINO,** the elder (*c.* 1260–1338), Venetian geographer, is perhaps better known for his efforts to revive crusades against the Turkish provinces in the eastern Mediterranean, but the maps and charts he constructed in furtherance of this aim are of so high a standard that they can claim an important place in the development of marine cartography. They include a chart of the Mediterranean, the Black Sea, and western European coasts in the form of a *portulan, the remainder of the charts being of pre-portulan type. It is probable that Sanuto was much influenced by, and may well have copied, some of the work of the great portulan draughtsman Pietro *Vesconte.

SAOIRSE, an oceangoing yacht of 20 tons built for Conor *O'Brien at Baltimore, County Cork, in 1922 (the name being Erse for *Freedom* and pronounced *seershah*). For ocean cruising she was rigged as a *brigantine with square topsail and fore *course on the foremast and a *gunter *lugsail on the mainmast. Between 1922 and 1925 with this rig and a variety of crews, O'Brien sailed *Saoirse* round the world, and was the first to round Cape Horn in so small a yacht. This voyage was described in his book *Across Three Oceans*. After changing ownership in 1950 *Saoirse* was converted to normal *gaff *ketch rig and had an auxiliary engine installed.

SARATOGA, U.S.S., a name that has been carried by five ships of the U.S. Navy. The name represents the successful defeat of an attempted invasion from Canada in 1777. A *sloop *Saratoga*, built for the *Continental Navy, disappeared at sea in March 1781. The second *Saratoga* was the flagship of Thomas *Macdonough in the battle of *Lake Champlain, and a third vessel of the same name was in the Mexican War. The armoured *cruiser *New York*, of the Spanish–American War, was renamed *Saratoga* to become the fourth ship of the name. The fifth *Saratoga* was begun as a *battle-cruiser but completed as an *aircraft carrier. She was near San Diego at the time of the Japanese attack on *Pearl Harbor in 1941 and was in the expedition intended for the relief of Wake Island which left Hawaii in late December 1941 but was recalled. After outstanding service in the Pacific during the war, she was sunk as a trials ship in an atomic bomb test at Bikini on 25 July 1946.

SARGASSO SEA, an area of the North Atlantic east of the Bahama Islands and stretching approximately between 25° and 30° N. and 40° and 60° W. where a powerful eddy in the water causes the Sargasso weed (*Fucus natans*, originally named *sargaço* by the Portuguese) to collect in vast quantities and float on the surface. It is mentioned by Christopher *Columbus in his accounts of his voyages to the New World. This area of weed has given rise to many stories of ships trapped in it and unable to make their way out, a belief prevalent among many seamen of older days but finally disproved by Sir John Murray in the expedition of the *Michael Sars* in 1910 which proved that the surface was covered

Conor O'Brien's Saoirse *in 1923*

only in patches. It is said also to be the main breeding place of eels, the elvers swimming to Europe in the Gulf Stream.

SATURDAY NIGHT AT SEA, the night on which, at the evening meal, the toast 'Sweethearts and Wives' was traditionally drunk by British naval officers. It was a tradition of very long standing, though now probably fallen into relative oblivion. Henry *Teonge, writing in his diary on Saturday, 3 July 1675, on board H.M.S. *Assistance*, remarks: 'We end the day and week with drinking to our wives in punch-bowls.'

SAUMAREZ, JAMES, Lord de (1757–1836), British admiral, who came of a well-known Guernsey family, saw more varied active service during the course of a long life than most officers even of his own great era. He was made a lieutenant during the War of American Independence (1775–82); was present at the stubborn fight with the Dutch near the *Dogger Bank in 1781; served under Richard *Kempenfelt when he cap-

tured a French *convoy later the same year, and was one of the captains at Sir George *Rodney's great victory over de *Grasse in the West Indies in April 1782, when he commanded the *Russell*.

At the beginning of the war with Republican France in 1793, Saumarez was knighted for his capture of the *frigate *Réunion*, thirty-six guns, off Cherbourg, an encounter in which his own ship, the *Crescent*, suffered no casualties. He was commanding the 74-gun *Orion* when Lord Bridport (see HOOD, Alexander) defeated the French near *Brest in 1795, and he received the King's gold medal, along with other captains, for his brilliant part in Sir John *Jervis's victory off *Cape St. Vincent in February 1797.

Still in the *Orion* he took a leading part in the battle of the *Nile, on 1 August 1798, as Lord *Nelson's second-in-command. He used his initiative in taking his ship inshore of the French line, as did certain other captains. He was sent to *Gibraltar with the prizes, and in 1801, the year he received his flag, he was made a baronet.

Saumarez soon had a chance to show his quality as a flag officer, for in July 1801, after suffering a repulse off Algeciras when he lost the *Hannibal* to the fire of shore batteries, he refitted his squadron so speedily at Gibraltar that he was able to enjoy revenge in a night action during the course of which he captured a French *ship of the line and destroyed two Spanish three-deckers. The Spaniards, according to Captain Keats of the *Superb*, actually blew one another up in the confusion of the action.

Saumarez next commanded off Guernsey, and was later sent to the fleet blockading *Brest. An enlarged opportunity came in 1808, when he was made commander-in-chief of a force operating, during the ice-free months, in the Baltic, with his flag in the *Victory*. For five successive seasons his appearance in the northern area of war was of decisive consequence. He supported Sweden, who for much of the Napoleonic war was Britain's ally; he protected an enormous volume of trade; and he contained Denmark, which was within the French orbit. Saumarez's services were as much diplomatic as naval, a fact which was handsomely acknowledged by von Platen, the Swedish Foreign Minister. In the winter months the ships returned home to refit, or were used in support of Lord Wellington's armies, then fighting in Portugal and Spain.

After the war, Saumarez held the *Plymouth command from 1824 to 1827. He was made a peer in 1831. A man of attractive qualities and admirable judgement, he was eminently brave in battle, and was always willing to take a risk if possible advantage could justify it. He was, wrote Sir William Hotham, 'in his person tall and having the remains of a handsome man; rather formal and ceremonious in his manner, but without the least tincture of affectation or pride ... more than ordinarily attentive to his duty to God; but, with the meekness of Christianity, having the boldness of a lion whenever a sense of duty brings it into action'.

SAUNDERS, Sir CHARLES (1713–75), British admiral and, in the words of Dr. John Campbell (*Lives of the Admirals*, 1813) 'this brave and excellent officer', was a lieutenant in the *Centurion, Commodore George *Anson's ship in which he made his memorable voyage of circumnavigation in 1740–4, but before the start of the voyage was given command of the *brig *Tryal*, which accompanied the expedition. Anson appointed him to command one of the ships taken in *prize with the rank of *post-captain, and the Admiralty confirmed the rank when he returned to London with Anson's dispatches from Macao, announcing the capture of a Spanish treasure ship of immense value. He commanded the *Yarmouth* with great gallantry at the second battle of *Cape Finisterre in 1747 and in 1754 he was made treasurer of *Greenwich Hospital, a most lucrative post.

At the outbreak of the Seven Years War (1756–63) he was specially promoted rear admiral and was sent to the Mediterranean as second-in-command to Sir Edward *Hawke. But with Minorca, the only British base in the Mediterranean, irretrievably lost by the default of Admiral John *Byng, the task of regaining maritime control in those waters was an impossible one, and Hawke returned to England, leaving Saunders there as commander-in-chief.

With Anson firmly in control of the navy as First Lord of the Admiralty, Saunders's star remained in the ascendant and his great chance came when, in 1759, as a vice admiral, he was selected as naval commander-in-chief of the expedition designed to capture *Quebec, and later the whole of Canada, from the French. With 8,000 troops under the command of Major-General James Wolfe, he brought his fleet up the St. Lawrence River in a brilliant feat of navigation, the first large ships of war ever to have passed the notorious traverses of the river below Quebec. With much of his fleet lying off and above Quebec itself, he was able to support and supply the troops in their assault of the city and at the same time deny supplies and reinforcements to the French defenders. It has been said of him during this campaign that 'though he lacked the genius of Wolfe, his hand throughout was the surer of the two; and dazzling as was the final stroke by which Wolfe snatched victory from failure, the steadier flame of Saunders's exploit is worthy to burn beside it without loss of radiance for all time' (Sir Julian *Corbett, *England in the Seven Years War*, 1907).

In his subsequent career Saunders spent three years as commander-in-chief in the Mediterranean, though as the naval power of France had by then been shattered in those waters, there was little there to occupy him. In 1765 he was made a Lord of the Admiralty and in 1766 First Lord, being relieved at the end of that year by Sir Edward Hawke.

SAVANNAH, a U.S. vessel of 380 tons which has been claimed to have been the first steamship to cross the Atlantic Ocean. In 1819 she made a passage from Savannah to Liverpool in twenty-one days. She was originally a sailing vessel but was later fitted with a small auxiliary engine with detachable paddle-wheels which were unshipped and laid on deck when under sail. During her passage of the Atlantic she was in fact under power for only eight hours, all the remainder of the voyage being made under sail, and her claim to have been the first Atlantic-crossing steamship is not generally recognized. A later *Savannah* was the world's first merchant vessel powered by nuclear propulsion. Completed in 1958, she was built for demonstration purposes, but was never a success.

SAVE-ALL, a slang name given by seamen to a small additional sail or *bonnet which was sometimes set under a *studdingsail in a square-rigged ship in very fine weather with the wind *abaft the beam. It was also sometimes used to describe the bonnets proper, laced to the *courses, and also occasionally called by the slang term 'puff-ball'. There have been some references to this sail under the name *water sail, but this is an obviously wrong use of the term.

SAVO ISLAND, BATTLE OF, a naval action of the Second World War fought in the south-west Pacific on the night of 8/9 August 1942 between a combined force of Australian and U.S. *cruisers and *destroyers and a Japanese cruiser and destroyer force under the command of Rear Admiral Mikawa. The earlier discovery of Japanese preparations to build an airstrip on *Guadalcanal Island in the Solomons had called for an American amphibious attack, which was successfully carried out on 7 August, and during the following day supplies from the fleet of transports lying off the airstrip were unloaded. To guard against Japanese attack, the Australian–American force was divided into three divisions, each guarding one of the seaward approaches on either side of Savo Island by which the Japanese could appear.

The Japanese force of five heavy cruisers, two light cruisers, and a destroyer sailed from Rabaul and reached the area at 0100 on 9 August. They were not seen by two American destroyers which had been sent out to patrol the possible lines of advance and, steering south of Savo Island, fell on the southern division of the Australian–American force, sinking the heavy cruiser H.M.A.S. *Canberra* and damaging the other heavy cruiser U.S.S. *Chicago* with a *torpedo hit. There was virtually no return fire. Circling Savo Island, Mikawa's force then fell upon the northern division of three heavy cruisers and two destroyers, and sank all three cruisers, the U.S.S. *Vincennes*, *Quincy*, and *Astoria*, again with very little reply and receiving only minor damage. On its way back to Rabaul, Mikawa's force ran into one of the patrolling destroyers which was taken under gunfire and only escaped destruction by steaming into the cover of a heavy rainstorm.

But this shattering victory was not to go entirely unavenged. On its way back to Rabaul the Japanese squadron was intercepted by the U.S. *submarine *S.44* which sank the heavy cruiser *Kako* with a torpedo.

SAVOIA-AOSTA, Duca di, see ABRUZZI, Luigi.

SCAMPAVIA, a type of small warship of the kingdom of the two Sicilies (Naples and Sicily) during the Napoleonic War (1803–15). It was basically a large rowing boat or *galley of up to 150 feet in length, pulled by twenty *oars or

*sweeps a side, with each rower having his *bunk or sleeping place under his rowing bench. Scampavias were fitted in addition with a single mast one-third of the way from bow to stern on which was set an oversize *lateen sail, and occasionally a *jib was also set on a *boom. There was no forward *bulkhead, or *stemhead above deck level, and they were armed with a single long 6-pounder gun carried before the mast. When the gun was to be fired, the jib was *let fly. They were very fast in the water, whether sailing or pulling.

SCANDALIZE, to, a method of reducing sail in *fore-and-aft rig by hauling up the *tack and lowering the *peak of a sail. It was used by the older sailing *trawlers to reduce speed through the water when operating a trawl. Also the *yards in a square-rigged ship are said to be scandalized when they are not set square to the masts after the ship has anchored. Scandalizing the yards of a ship was a sign of mourning for a death on board.

SCANT, a term applied to the wind when it heads a square-rigged ship so that she can only just lay her *course with the *yards *braced very sharp up. It is a term very rarely heard today, having largely died out with the passing of the square-rigged ships.

SCANTLINGS, originally the dimensions of a *timber after it has been reduced to its standard size. It is now extended to cover the dimensions of all parts which go into the construction of a ship's hull, including her *frames, *stringers, girders, plates, etc. Rules governing these sizes, based on long experience and study, are published by *Lloyd's Register of Shipping, and most ships of any size built throughout the world are constructed to these Lloyd's rules.

SCAPA FLOW, a huge expanse of water in the Orkney Islands sheltered by the off-lying islands of Hoy, Flotta, South Ronaldsay, and Burray, and used by the British *Grand Fleet (1914–18) and Home Fleet (1939–45) as a main fleet anchorage during both world wars. It was from Scapa Flow that the Grand Fleet sailed in May 1916 for the battle of *Jutland. After the end of that war the German *High Seas Fleet was interned at Scapa Flow, and scuttled itself there on 21 June 1919. See also REUTER, Ludwig von.

'SCARBOROUGH WARNING', a nautical expression meaning to let anything on board go with a run without giving due warning. Thus a seaman, or a *stevedore when loading cargo, who lets go, for example, a *whip, *purchase, or a boat's *falls, with a run and without telling others to stand clear, is said to have given a

Scarborough warning. The term comes from an incident in English history, the surprise of Scarborough Castle by Stafford in 1557, when men encountered on the approach march were hanged without trial on suspicion of robbery. The poet and dramatist Thomas Heywood wrote of this:

'This term *Scarborow warning* grew, some say,
By hasty hanging for rank robbery theare,
Who that was met, but suspected in that way,
Straight he was truss'd, whatever he were.'

SCARF or **SCARPH,** the joining of two timbers by bevelling off the edges so that the same thickness is maintained throughout the length of the joint. In the construction of a wooden ship, the *stem and *sternposts are scarfed to the *keel. A scarf which embodies a step in the middle of the joint, so preventing the two parts from drawing apart, is called a lock scarf. It is a joint of great antiquity, having been used by the early Egyptian and Phoenician shipbuilders.

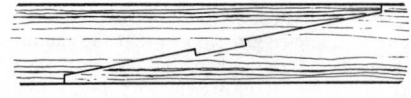

A scarfed spar

SCEND (pron. send), the quick upward motion when a ship is *pitching in a heavy sea. In its old meaning it was the opposite of pitching, the quick roll when a sea knocks a vessel off her *course, but this meaning has now died out. Scend of the sea, the surge of the sea as it runs into a harbour.

SCHARNHORST and **GNEISENAU,** sister warships of the German Navy in the two World Wars (1914–18 and 1939–45) which almost always operated together. In the First World War they were armoured *cruisers of 11,600 tons and at the outbreak of that war were the principal units of the German Far Eastern squadron commanded by Vice Admiral Graf von *Spee. On 1 November 1914, in company with the light cruisers *Nürnberg, Leipzig,* and *Dresden,* they were brought to battle by an ill-assorted British force commanded by Rear Admiral Sir Christopher *Cradock off *Coronel on the coast of Chile. After a decisive victory for the German squadron, von Spee took his ships round Cape Horn into the South Atlantic and on 8 December he was confronted by a superior force at anchor in the *Falkland Islands. After a long chase both the *Scharnhorst* and *Gneisenau* were sunk.

In the Second World War the *Scharnhorst* and *Gneisenau* were *battle-cruisers of 31,000 tons. Their first operation was in November 1939 when they attacked the British blockade line between Iceland and the Faeroe Islands, sinking the armed merchant cruiser *Rawalpindi.* In April 1940, while giving cover to the German invasion of Norway, they encountered the old British battle-cruiser *Renown* but used their superior speed to escape to the north. During the British evacuation of Narvik in June 1940 they sank the British *aircraft carrier *Glorious* and her two escorting *destroyers *Ardent* and *Acasta,* but the *Scharnhorst* was hit by a *torpedo from the *Acasta,* disabling her for six months. A few days later the *Gneisenau* was also hit by a torpedo from the British *submarine *Clyde,* joining her sister in dock.

They were ready for operations again in January 1941 and under the command of Vice Admiral Lütjens they both broke out into the Atlantic where, six weeks later, they encountered a *convoy which had dispersed and sank twenty-two merchant ships totalling 115,662 tons. For the next 11 months the two ships were at *Brest where they were subjected to continual bombing and aerial torpedo attacks by aircraft of the Royal Air Force, both being considerably damaged. French resistance networks played a vital part in providing news of these ships throughout their stay in French waters. Finally, to escape the bombing, they broke out from Brest in February 1942 bound for Germany. Commanded by Vice Admiral Ciliax they made their passage up Channel in a daring and well-planned operation and were nearly home in Germany when the *Scharnhorst* struck two *mines and the *Gneisenau* one. Both were docked for repairs in Kiel where they were again attacked from the air, the *Gneisenau* being so seriously damaged that she was never again operational. She was eventually towed to Gdynia where she was *scuttled in March 1945.

The *Scharnhorst* had completed repairs in January 1943 and was based in north Norway, taking part with the *Tirpitz* in the German attack on Spitsbergen in September. On the evening of Christmas Day, 1943, she was ordered to attack a British convoy making for north Russia but was driven off on the 26th by three British cruisers which chased her to the southward into the arms of the British *battleship *Duke of York.* After a battle fought almost entirely in darkness she was sunk by gunfire and torpedoes, nearly her whole crew being lost. See NORTH CAPE, BATTLE OF.

SCHEER, REINHARD (1863–1928), German admiral and commander-in-chief of the *High Seas Fleet at the battle of *Jutland, was born at Obernkirchen, Hesse-Nassau, son of a pastor and schoolmaster. Before he had seen a ship or the sea he resolved to be a sailor, attracted by a lavishly illustrated book on the German Navy. At the age of 15 he became a naval cadet, and on his earliest cruises saw something of the foundation of the German colonial empire in Africa and the Pacific. In 1888 he was decorated for leading a successful attack on a fortified native village near Dar-es-Salaam. On his return home in the same year he was appointed to the *torpedo school at a time when that weapon was the keystone of Germany's naval defence. Five years as a *torpedoboat captain followed and later he commanded the 1st Torpedoboat Flotilla. Still concerned with torpedo questions, he had a spell of duty at the German Admiralty, became Chief of Staff of the High Seas Fleet in 1909 with the rank of rear admiral, and, at the outbreak of the First World War (1914–18), was Vice Admiral commanding the Second Battle Squadron in that fleet. The squadron was composed of pre-*dreadnought *battleships, already semi-obsolete, and before the end of 1914 he was transferred to command of the Third Battle Squadron, the most powerful in the fleet. Finally, when the commander-in-chief of the High Seas Fleet fell ill in January 1916, he was appointed in his place.

Scheer was anxious that the fleet should have a more active part in operations than had been permitted in the past and hoped that by use of frequent sorties, air reconnaissance, and attacks, together with *mine and torpedo warfare, he might be able to cause the British *Grand Fleet losses which would equalize the opposing forces. He commanded the German fleet at the battle of *Jutland on 31 May 1916 but was worsted by the superior tactics of Sir John *Jellicoe, commander-in-chief of the Grand Fleet. When the two battle-fleets at last came into contact, Scheer found himself cut off from his bases by the British squadrons. Twice he attempted to find his way round the British line of battle only to find his path blocked by the presence of British battleships, and twice he was forced to extricate his fleet under cover of torpedo attacks and, on the second occasion, by a suicidal advance of his *battle-cruisers. It was only the mist and poor visibility in the North Sea that saved him at those moments from a shattering defeat. After nightfall he succeeded in passing behind the Grand Fleet, due largely to a breakdown in British signalling. It was the tactics of desperation, but it brought Scheer and his fleet safely home, and he was able to claim some credit for the action for having inflicted higher casualties on the Grand Fleet than his own fleet had suffered.

After the battle of Jutland, Scheer realized that there was no hope of the High Seas Fleet ever gaining a victory over the Grand Fleet and that only by unrestricted *submarine warfare would victory be possible. Unrestricted submarine warfare was in fact introduced in February 1917, and German defeat made inevitable by the entry of the U.S.A. into the war.

In August 1918 the ramshackle system of German naval high command, split between the Kaiser (who had said, 'I am the Naval High Command'), the Chief of his Naval Cabinet, the Ministry of Marine, and the Naval Staff, was at last overhauled and Scheer came ashore to a position roughly equivalent to that of the British First Sea Lord and Chief of the Naval Staff. There was little that he could do except order a vast expansion of the *U-boat building programme, which could not have produced significant results before the spring of 1920. He was succeeded as commander-in-chief of the High Seas Fleet by Admiral *Hipper, who had commanded the German battle-cruisers throughout the war with dash and skill, but neither Scheer nor Hipper could cope with the mutinies that broke out in October and November 1918. Nevertheless, as a fleet commander, trainer of men, and organizer, he is judged by many to have been one of the most efficient admirals of the First World War on either side though probably lacking that sense of tactical understanding which is one of the essential ingredients of the truly great admiral at sea.

SCHEPKE, JOACHIM (1912–41), German *submarine commander, was born at Flensburg, son of a naval officer. In the Second World War he commanded successively *U.3*, *U.19*, and *U.100*, and in all sank thirty-nine ships totalling 159,130 tons. His dashing and smart appearance, with his cap at a rakish angle, showed a temperament which was thoroughly at home in the early days of the submarine *'wolf packs'. On 21 September 1940, in an attack in company with other submarines, he himself sank seven ships of 50,340 tons within four hours from Convoy HX 72, and on 1 December 1940 he was awarded the Oakleaves to the Knight's Cross of the Iron Cross for his successes. On 15 March 1941 four *U-boats, including Schepke's and *Kretschmer's, attacked the forty-one ships of Convoy HX 112. Five merchant ships were sunk and two damaged, but on the night of 16 March *U.100*, coming in on the surface at full speed to attack, was rammed by the British *destroyer *Vanoc*. Schepke was still on the bridge and was last seen pinned into the ruins of the U-boat's superstructure as she sank. The *Vanoc* had located the almost invisible *U.100* at a range of 1,000 yards (900 m) by *radar, the first successful sighting by a radar of this type.

SCHETKY, JOHN CHRISTIAN (1778–1874), was marine painter to George IV, William IV, and Queen Victoria. Born at Ainslie's Close, Edinburgh, of Hungarian descent, he became a well-known figure in naval circles through his post as professor of drawing at the Royal Naval College, Portsmouth, from 1811 to 1836. His work shows the influence of the Van de *Veldes of whom he was a great admirer, yet it has a distinctive character which reveals his great knowledge of and affection for his subject. Among his best-known pictures are 'The Battle off Cape La Hogue', 'The Battle of Trafalgar', and 'The Sinking of the *Royal George*'. While at Portsmouth, he also designed a large number of *figureheads for British warships, but most of them were too intricate and detailed for the dock-yard carvers to copy.

SCHEVENINGEN, also known as the Texel, the last battle of the First Anglo-Dutch War (1652–4), was fought on 31 July 1653 between the English fleet commanded by George *Monck and that of the Dutch under Maerten *Tromp. Towards the end of July both fleets were at sea with about 100 ships each in the neighbourhood of the Texel, where a further force of twenty-seven ships and ten *fireships under Admiral de *With was being blockaded by Monck. The two main bodies sighted each other shortly before noon on 29 July. Tromp stood to the southward and was pursued, the leading English ship coming up with the Dutch rear at 5.00 p.m.; some of the heavier ships arrived on the scene an hour later but only about thirty ever got into action that evening. However, Tromp had effected his main purpose, which was to draw Monck away from the Texel and so enable de With to slip out. Next day a hard gale put a temporary stop to further fighting; in the afternoon, however, de With effected a junction with Tromp, which gave the Dutch a superiority of nearly thirty ships.

The weather moderated during the night, and at about 7.00 a.m. on the 31st the two fleets came to close action off Scheveningen. Tromp was killed by a musket ball about four hours later but his flag was kept flying, and Vice Admiral Jan *Evertsen took over command. The battle was continued with vigour until 1.00 p.m., but soon afterwards some of the Dutch ships began to give way, and by 8.00 p.m. all were in full flight. The survivors got into the Texel and other ports on the following day.

Casualties on both sides were heavy. The English had at least 250 killed and 700 wounded; the Dutch loss was even greater. In ships, the English lost the *Oak* which blew up after being attacked by a Dutch fireship; the *Hunter* fireship was also expended. The Dutch losses are unknown but Monck claimed to have accounted for between twenty and thirty ships of the Dutch fleet.

SCHICHAU, FERDINAND (1814–96), German shipbuilder, studied engineering in Berlin and England and set up an engineering work-shop in 1837 in Elbing which quickly grew in size. His first entry into shipbuilding was with the construction of *dredgers in 1841, of which he was the pioneer, but he quickly advanced into the naval field, specializing at first in building *torpedoboats and *destroyers for the Russian and German navies. In 1855 he built the *Borussia*, the first screw ship to be constructed in Germany. He introduced the *compound marine engine (1879) and later the *triple expansion engine (1881) into Germany and, in fact, built the first ships in Europe, excluding Great Britain, in which these forms of steam propulsion were used. With the Elbing yard capable of building only smaller ships, Schichau established a second yard at Danzig (now Gdansk) where he could build up to the largest size. The majority of the German fleet which followed the Navy Laws of Admiral von *Tirpitz, passed in 1898 and 1900, and which formed the *High Seas Fleet of the First World War (1914–18), were built at the Schichau yard at Danzig which under the direction of Schichau and his son-in-law Carl Ziese rivalled in size and excellence of production the finest shipyards in Great Britain.

SCHLEY, WINFIELD SCOTT (1839–1909), American naval officer, is remembered as one of the officers involved in the 'Sampson–Schley' controversy which followed the action against the Spanish fleet at Santiago, Cuba, in 1898. He graduated from the Naval Academy in 1860 and served with the Mississippi Squadron during the Civil War (1861–5). He was one of the two * commodores serving in the American squadron in the action at Santiago, and although senior to the other commodore, William *Sampson, had in fact been appointed to serve under his orders. The credit for the victory therefore is usually given to Sampson.

SCHNELLBOOT, the German *motor tor-pedoboat of the Second World War. See E-BOAT.

SCHNORKEL, the German name given to a tube attachment providing an air supply to a *submarine at *periscope depth. When a sub-marine dives she can no longer use her diesel engines since these depend on a constant supply of oxygen. When the Germans overran Holland during the Second World War they captured a half-completed Dutch submarine fitted with a tube which enabled the diesel engines to obtain air so long as the vessel did not go below peri-scope depth. The schnorkel is hinged at its lower end, and when not in use is folded down to lie flat along the submarine's casing. About nine inches in diameter, it can be brought to the vertical when the submarine dives and air can be sucked down it direct to the diesel engines so that they can be kept running with the submarine sub-merged. The tube is fitted with a flap valve at the top which prevents the entry of sea water in rough weather. This invention, which was not fitted to German *U-boats until the latter part of the war, enabled them to begin *U-boat operations in coastal waters around the British coasts since they no longer needed to surface to recharge their batteries. In the British Navy the schnorkel tube was given the name snort.

The name has also been given to the underwater swimming breathing tube which enables swimmers to remain beneath the surface for long periods and acts on the same principle as the submarine schnorkel.

SCHOKKER, a Dutch fishing vessel of the middle part of the Zuider Zee, usually from Enkhuizen, with a flat bottom, curved sides, a straight *stem raking at about 45 degrees, and narrow *leeboards. They are similar to a *hengst but are generally larger. Dating from the early part of the 18th century, the schokker was normally built of oak in sizes varying between 45 and 52 feet in length and 16 to 19 feet in beam. They were originally rigged with a *sprit mainsail and a *gaff mizen in addition to a forestaysail and a jib set flying on a *bowsprit. Later schokkers were built of steel and some have been converted or built as pleasure yachts.

SCHOONER (Du. *schooner*, Ger. *schouer*, Dan. *skonnert*, Sp. and Port. *escaña*) all possibly deriving from the Scottish verb 'to scon or scoon', to skip over water like a flat stone. An alternative source for the name is said to have come from a chance remark 'there she scoons' from a spectator at the launch of the first vessel of the type at Gloucester, Mass., in 1713, and there is some evidence that the type originated in North America and probably at Gloucester.

Whatever the origin of the name a schooner is a vessel rigged with *fore-and-aft sails on her two or more masts, and originally carried square topsails on the foremast, though later, with the advance in rig designs, these were changed to jib-headed or *jackyard-topsails. Today, the small schooner yachts normally set *Bermuda sails and thus have no topsails. Properly speaking, a schooner has two masts only, with the mainmast taller than the fore, but three-masted, four-masted, and five-masted schooners have been built, and one, the *Thomas W. Lawson*, had as many as seven. They were largely used in the coasting trade and also for fishing on the *Grand Banks off Newfoundland, their attraction to owners being that they required a smaller crew than a square-rigged vessel of comparable size.

SCHOUTEN, WILLEM CORNELISZ (*fl.* 1590–1618), Dutch *East India Company captain, sailed as pilot in the expedition under Jacob *le Maire in 1616 to discover a new way from the Atlantic to the Pacific Ocean. By sailing to the southward of the Magellan Strait, they discovered Staten Island, the strait which separates that island from Patagonia which they named after le Maire, and were the first Europeans to sight Cape Horn. The remainder of their voyage of discovery was less rewarding, and they found only a few small islands in the Tuamotu Archipelago and the Tabar Islands, near the coast of New Ireland. Schouten, according to Captain Burney, was 'a man well-experienced and very famous in navigation, as having already sailed three times to nearly all places in the East Indies as skipper, pilot and merchant, and still very eager of strange voyages and the visiting of new and unknown lands'.

SCHWATKA, FREDERICK (1849–92), American army lieutenant and explorer, was born at Galena, Illinois. He graduated from West Point Academy in 1871, and subsequently studied medicine and law. In 1878–80, in company with William H. Gilder, he led an expedition to King William Island in search of records of the ill-fated *Franklin expedition, during which he made the longest sledge journey on record, of 3,251 miles, and located some graves and wreckage from the Franklin expedition. His next expedition to the north in 1883–4 was spent in exploring the course of the Yukon River, Alaska. He resigned his army commission in 1885 to devote the rest of his life to exploring, writing, and lecturing.

SCIROCCO, an alternative spelling of the Mediterranean wind *sirocco.

SCOPE, the amount of *cable run out when a ship lies to a single *anchor. The minimum amount of cable to which a ship should lie is generally taken as three times the depth of water in which she is anchored, but conditions of wind and tide and the nature of the holding ground may call for up to double this amount. The scope of a ship's cable is approximately the radius of the circle through which she swings under the influence of the tide; approximate only because it is unlikely that her cable lies in a straight line stretched taut between anchor and ship.

SCORE, (1) the name given to the groove cut in the shell of a wooden *block in which the *strop is passed. Blocks are stropped with an *eye or hook at the top so that they can be used whenever necessary, and the score prevents the strop from slipping off the shell of the block. Similarly it is the groove cut round the body of a *deadeye for the same reason. **(2)** The space vacated in a rope when unlaying a strand in the course of making a *long splice is also known as a score.

SCORESBY, WILLIAM (1789–1857), Arctic explorer and physicist, was born at Cropton, Yorkshire, the son of a whaler. He made his first voyage to Greenland at the age of 11, and from 1810 to 1822 made annual visits there. In 1806 he was chief officer of the whaling ship *Resolution*, of which his father was in command, and which reached a *latitude of 81° 30′ N. He relieved his father in command of the ship in 1811, revisiting the Arctic regularly until 1822 when he decided to give up the life of a seaman to devote his time to scientific studies. He was ordained in 1825, becoming vicar of Bradford four years later. In 1856 he visited Australia in connection with research into terrestrial magnetism, on which he was then engaged, and of which he published an account in 1859, having previously published three other books describing his visits to the Arctic. The Antarctic research ship * *William Scoresby* was named after him.

SCOTCHMAN, (1) a piece of hide, or a wooden batten, secured to the *backstays or *shrouds of a sailing vessel so that any running rigging coming into contact with them should not be chafed. The name comes from the scotch, or notch, cut in the hide or batten along which is passed the line securing the scotchman to the backstays or shrouds so that it does not slip. **(2)** A strip of steel plating let into the wooden *forecastle deck of a ship in the wake of the *anchor *cables to protect the wood from damage by the chain links of the cable when the anchor is let go or weighed.

SCOTIA, a *barque-rigged auxiliary steam *whaler which accompanied the Scottish National Antarctic expedition led by W. S. *Bruce in 1902–4. She was originally the *Hekla*, built in Norway with a tonnage of about 400. On her return from the Antarctic she was employed as an ice patrol vessel in the North Atlantic, but was lost early in the First World War (1914–18) when she caught fire and ran ashore in the Scilly Isles. An earlier *Scotia*, built in 1861, was the last paddle steamer owned by the *Cunard Company for its transatlantic service.

SCOTT, the Revd. ALEXANDER JOHN (1768–1840), British naval chaplain, was appointed to H.M.S. * *Victory* in 1803, where he served as private secretary to Lord *Nelson. He was with him when he was shot on the quarterdeck of the *Victory* at the battle of *Trafalgar and he attended his dying chief in the *cockpit, receiving his last wishes. He refused to leave Nelson's body until it was brought to England and placed in its coffin to lie in the Painted Hall in Greenwich.

SCOTT, MICHAEL (1789–1835), British author, was born at Cowlain, Glasgow, and went to Jamaica in 1806. Four years later he settled in a business there which entailed his making

frequent sea voyages. He used these experiences as material when writing his book *Tom Cringle's Log* which was first serialized in *Blackwood's Magazine* in 1829–33. It is an amusing and vivid account of life in the Caribbean Islands during the early decades of the 19th century. He followed this with *The Cruise of the Midge*, also first serialized in Blackwood's in 1834–5, a story based on the capture of a shark which had swallowed a ship's papers and which played a vital part in a salvage lawsuit in 1799. Both were published in book form in 1836. Scott maintained a strict incognito in his writing career.

SCOTT, Sir PERCY (1853–1924), British admiral, was one of the most influential modern naval gunnery specialists and one of the earliest prophets of air power at sea. He joined the Royal Navy in 1866 and specialized in gunnery in 1878–9. In 1890 he was appointed commander of the gunnery school H.M.S. * *Excellent* and was instrumental in having it transferred from an old floating *ship of the line to dry land on Whale Island in *Portsmouth harbour. He was appointed captain of the *cruiser *Scylla* in the Mediterranean in 1896 and in the 1899 prize firings startled the navy with the unheard-of score of 80 per cent of hits to rounds fired with his 4·7-inch guns. The fleet average was 30 per cent. He repeated these astonishing results with his next command, the cruiser *Terrible* (1900–2). His main innovations were in the use of telescopic sights on the guns and also in keeping the sights on the target throughout the *roll of the ship instead of waiting to fire when the sights rolled on to the target. He devised, as aids to gun drill, the 'dotter', which simulated the ship's rolling, the 'loader' for loading practice, and the 'deflection teacher' which simulated a target's horizontal movement. By 1902 all these devices were being used throughout the fleet, and the standard of gunnery improved dramatically. In 1905 he was appointed to a new post at the Admiralty, Inspector of Target Practice, and raised the number of hits to rounds fired from 56 per cent to 81 per cent by 1907.

In 1908 Scott was promoted rear admiral and appointed in command of a cruiser *squadron attached to the Channel Fleet then commanded by Lord Charles *Beresford. He became involved in the violent quarrel between Beresford and the First Sea Lord, Sir John *Fisher, and the part he played in this finished his career afloat. He continued to work on his latest device for improving fleet gunnery, a *director sight mounted aloft in the foretop of *battleships from which all guns of the *broadside could be aimed and fired together. This proved to be his most important single contribution to gunnery. With the help of Admiral *Jellicoe, he succeeded against great opposition in having his director

Captain R. F. Scott writing his diary in the hut at Cape Evans, 1911

firing adopted by the Royal Navy in 1913 and by the time of the battle of *Jutland in 1916 nearly all the *Grand Fleet battleships had director gear. In this respect, both the German and U.S. Navies were behind the Royal Navy.

After the war, from his retirement, Scott launched a vigorous and picturesque attack on the heavy-gunned battleship, believing that *submarines and aircraft had rendered it obsolete. He ridiculed battleship building as a 'criminal, woeful, wicked, wanton, wilful waste of taxpayers' money ...' He had many supporters, but his point was not proved until the experiences of the Second World War vindicated his beliefs. Although his forthright views, bluntly and often contemptuously expressed, made him many enemies in the navy, he was a man of great dedication and vision in the modern naval field.

P. Padfield, *Aim Straight* (1966).

SCOTT, ROBERT FALCON (1868–1912), British naval officer and Antarctic explorer, was a native of Devonport and the descendant of three generations of sailors. He was coached for a cadetship in the Royal Navy at Stubbington House, Fareham, Hampshire, and at the age of 13 joined the training ship *Britannia*. Between 1883 and 1887 he served as *midshipman in the *Boadicea, Lion, Monarch,* and *Rover*. He was promoted lieutenant-commander in 1897, and in 1899 while serving in H.M.S. *Majestic* met Sir Clements *Markham, Secretary and afterwards President of the Royal Geographical Society, who recommended him to the command of the National Antarctic Expedition. On taking up his duties aboard the *Discovery*, Scott was promoted commander. The chief objective of this expedition was the scientific exploration of Victoria Land, in the New Zealand sector of Antarctica, discovered by Sir James Clark *Ross in 1841. The expedition sailed in August 1901 and, after discovering King Edward VII Land, wintered at Hut Point on Ross Island. During the two summer seasons of 1902–3 and 1903–4, several valuable sledging journeys were made. On one of these Scott, accompanied by Dr. E. A. Wilson and E. H. *Shackleton, reached a southern latitude of 82° 16′ 33″ on 30 December 1902, the most southerly point reached at that time. During this expedition Scott proved his capacity not only as a leader of men but as a keen observer of nature.

On his return to naval duties in England he was promoted captain and served successively in the *Victorious*, *Essex*, and *Bulwark*, and in September 1908 married the sculptress Kathleen Bruce. The following year, while serving as Naval Assistant to the Second Sea Lord of the Admiralty, he announced his intention of leading a new Antarctic expedition to continue the scientific work of the *Discovery* expedition and reaching the South pole. His ship, the *Terra Nova*, sailed in June 1910. On arrival in New Zealand, Scott heard that the Norwegian, Roald *Amundsen, was also planning to achieve the South pole. Determined not to change his plans, Scott established his winter quarters at Cape Evans and lost no time in laying supply depots, at the same time dispatching a northern party to Cape Adare in the *Terra Nova*. Scott set out for the pole on 1 November 1911. In spite of the failure of his motor transport, he succeeded in reaching the foot of the Beardmore Glacier using dogs and ponies. From this point he relied entirely on manhauling. On 4 January 1912 the last supporting party, led by Lieutenant E. R. G. R. *Evans, set up 'One Ton Depot' and left for base and Scott, accompanied by Dr. E. A. Wilson, Captain L. E. G. Oates, Lieutenant H. R. Bowers, and Petty Officer Edgar *Evans, pressed on across the Antarctic plateau to the pole which they reached on 18 January 1912, only to find that they had been forestalled by Amundsen's party. The return journey of over 800 miles was marked by a series of disasters, a combination of deteriorating weather, inadequate diet, and shortage of fuel. On 17 February Evans died after a severe fall. On 17 March Oates, badly frostbitten in the feet, and reluctant to be a hindrance to the others, voluntarily walked out of the tent to his death in a blizzard. A week later a final blizzard caught the remainder of the party only 11 miles from One Ton Depot and safety. Scott's body, along with those of Wilson and Bowers, were discovered in their tent by a search party from Cape Evans eight months later. Alongside them were their diaries, personal papers, and unique geological specimens.

S. Gwynn, *Captain Scott* (1929).

SCOTT, SAMUEL (*c.* 1702–72), British marine painter and etcher, of whose early years little is known, was working in London in the late 1720s, his sea pictures strongly resembling the style of the two Willem Van de *Veldes. In about 1730 he must have been commissioned by the British *East India Company to visit their settlements in India in company with George Lambert, a well-known landscape painter, for in 1731–2 the two artists collaborated in a series of views of these settlements, now in the Foreign and Commonwealth Office in London. Later Scott came under the influence of Canaletto, who was painting in London during the ten years 1746–55, and his many views of the River Thames and its bridges are strongly reminiscent of the style of that great master. Collections of Scott's pictures can be seen at the *National Maritime Museum, the Tate Gallery, and the Guildhall, all in London.

SCOTT-PAINE, HUBERT (1891–1954), British yachtsman, was born at Shoreham, Sussex, and was a pioneer from 1913 onwards in the design and construction of seaplanes and racing motor boats. In 1933 he established for Great Britain the world's speed record of over 100 m.p.h. on salt water for single-engined boats, and he continued to represent Britain in many international motor boat racing events in Europe until the outbreak of the Second World War. He was a founder-director of Imperial Airways, and chairman of the British Power Boat Company of Hythe, Southampton, as well as chairman of the Canadian Power Boat Company. His *motor torpedoboats (M.T.B.s), built at Hythe, were extensively used by the British Navy during the Second World War, while his air/sea rescue craft were claimed to have saved more than 10,000 airmen from the sea. He became an American citizen in 1948, and died at Greenwich, Connecticut.

'SCOUSE, the short name for *lobscouse.

SCOW, a large boat, very full in the *bilges and with a flat bottom, used as a *lighter or as a ferry to transport men a short distance at sea. They were either towed or pulled with oars. The term is used in the U.S.A. today to describe a small flat-bottomed racing yacht fitted with *bilge boards or retractable bilge keels.

SCREW, see PROPELLER.

SCREW SLIP, see CABLE STOPPERS.

SCRIMSHAW, the name given to the carving done by sailors of whaling ships on the jawbone or teeth of whales or the tusks of walrus. The origin of the word is not certain but the art was developed by the American whalemen of the early 19th century, and the word is believed to be derived from Admiral Scrimshaw, an expert in this work. Herman *Melville remarks of the whaler's crew in his *Moby Dick*: 'Some of them have little boxes of dentistical-looking implements specially intended for the skrimshandering business. But in general they toil with their jack-knives alone.'

SCUBA, the initial letters of self-contained underwater breathing apparatus, and another word widely used for the *aqualung apparatus and its derivatives. See also DIVING (3).

SCUD, to, in a sailing ship to run before a gale with reduced canvas, or under bare poles in the case of gales so strong that no sails could be left spread. It is apt to be a dangerous practice, with the risk of the vessel being *pooped.

SCULL, the name given to a light oar as used in a *dinghy, particularly of a size which can be pulled by a single rower with one in each hand.

SCULL, to, in its original meaning a method of giving a small boat headway by working a single oar to and fro over the stern of the boat, but this definition has now been extended to embrace one man working a pair of *sculls in a *dinghy or other light boat. See also YULOH.

SCULLER, the name given to a small river-boat which plied for hire on the River Thames in London during the 17th and 18th centuries, when the Thames was used as a main thorough-fare. It was rowed by a single man pulling a pair of oars. See also PAIR OF OARS.

An example of scrimshaw, showing the ship Mechanic *above the figures of Plenty and Justice*

SCUPPER, to, a word with the same meaning as to *scuttle, or deliberately to sink a ship by opening the seacocks in her hull or by blowing a hole in her side below the waterline. It has, presumably, the same general origin as scuttle, which is to make her sink until the sea comes in through her scuppers to finish her off.

SCUPPERS, draining holes cut through the *bulwarks of a ship on the *waterways to allow any water on deck to drain away down the ship's side. Scupper shutters are flaps fitted over the outboard side of the scuppers and hinged on the top so that the pressure of water inboard will swing them open while water pressure outside the ship will keep them firmly closed. See also FREEING PORTS.

SCURVY, a disease caused by a deficiency of vitamin C, was very prevalent at sea between the 16th and 19th centuries owing to the difficulty of preserving fresh fruit and vegetables. It usually became apparent after about six weeks on salt provisions. It became a common ailment when long voyages began in the 16th century and continued until passages were shortened in the age of steam, and canned vegetables became available. Since it enfeebled crews long before it killed them, it was responsible for many shipwrecks, particularly those of *East Indiamen. Its mani-festations were so various that no cause was discovered for a long time. The first symptoms were usually swellings on the gums and the fall-ing out of teeth, followed by blotches on the skin and a dull lethargy from which a man could be roused only at the danger of his life.

After the appalling casualties suffered on *Anson's voyage round the world in 1740–4, Dr. James *Lind published his *Treatise of the Scurvy* in 1753 in which he proved, by the first controlled dietetic experiment, that oranges and lemons were an effective cure; but it was not until 1795 that lemon juice was made a compul-sory issue in the Royal Navy. Scurvy was soon eradicated, only to reappear on the polar expedi-tions of the 19th century when lime juice was substituted for lemon; it is now known that limes have only half the antiscorbutic value of lemons and much less than blackcurrants. All British vessels were bound by law to carry lime juice, hence the American word 'limey' for a British immigrant or national. The true cause of scurvy was only found when vitamins were discovered in 1912. Lime juice was replaced by the issue of vitamin pills before the Second World War.

SCUTTLE, a circular *port cut in the side of a ship to admit light and air, consisting of a cir-cular metal frame with a thick disc of glass which is hinged on one side and which can be tightly secured to the ship's side by butterfly nuts. A deadlight, which is a metal plate hinged on the top and also secured by a butterfly nut at the bottom, is also fitted to scuttles. Its purpose is to prevent any light from inboard showing to seaward at night when a ship has to be darkened, as in time of war. Although many people call them portholes, the proper and more seamanlike name is scuttle.

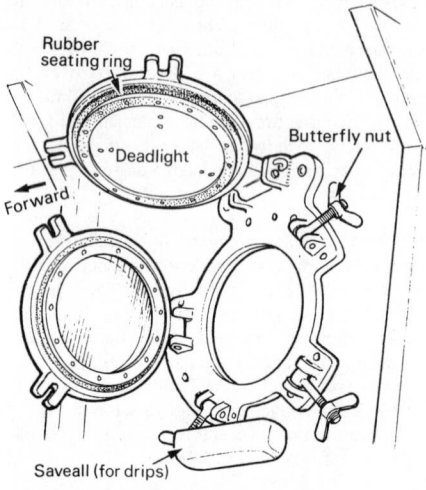

Scuttle

SCUTTLE, to, (1) deliberately to sink a ship by opening her seacocks or by blowing holes in her bottom with explosive charges so that she fills with water. A ship may be scuttled to avoid capture in wartime; it is not unknown for ships to be scuttled by unscrupulous owners to claim the insurance on them. The origin of the word, as in the synonymous verb to *scupper, presumably is to make her sink to the level of her *scuttles when the sea will pour in through them and finish her off. The most impressive act of mass scuttling occurred on 21 June 1919 when the German *High Seas Fleet, interned at *Scapa Flow, deliberately scuttled itself rather than face surrender. **(2)** A cask is said to be scuttled when its staves are stove in or broken.

SCUTTLE, or SCUTTLED, BUTT, a cask lashed in a convenient part of the ship to hold water for daily use before the days when ships were fitted with fresh-water tanks. All water in those days had to be carried on board in large casks and, in a long voyage, had to be used very sparingly to make it last out until the next opportunity of landing and refilling the casks. In order to prevent too much water being used, a scuttle butt had a square piece sawn out of its *bilge, the widest part of its curved side, so that no more than half a butt full was available daily. Hence its name.

SCYLLA and CHARYBDIS, the names of two navigational hazards in the Straits of Messina between which, according to the Greek legend, the fleet of *Odysseus, or the Latin legend that of Ulysses, passed after the capture of Troy. In the legend Scylla was a nymph seen bathing in the nude by the sea-god Glaucus who fell in love with her but whose advances she repelled. Glaucus appealed to Circe for a love potion but she, jealous of his affection for Scylla, gave him instead a poisonous mixture which, poured into the sea when she bathed, turned Scylla into a frightful monster, rooted to a rock on the Italian side of the Straits. Nevertheless she retained her lovely voice and whenever a ship passed she sang songs enticing the mariners on board to their destruction.

Charybdis was a dangerous whirlpool on the Sicilian side of the Straits opposite Scylla. She was said by legend originally to have been an avaricious woman who stole the oxen of Hercules and for this misdeed was punished by Zeus by being turned into a whirlpool. She was also said to swallow the sea three times a day and throw it up again, thus causing the whirlpool. Between Scylla on one side and Charybdis on the other, the unfortunate seamen of the time seemed to have little chance of survival.

SEA ANCHOR, anything that will hold a vessel's bow to the sea in heavy weather. Oars, *barricoes, or loose sails lashed together and veered from the bow on as long a line as possible will act as a satisfactory sea anchor to which a vessel can ride out a storm. Various forms of *drogue are often offered as sea anchors, but usually the vessel's own gear will prove as efficient a sea anchor as any. In very severe gales, such as typhoons, a ship's *anchor lowered to some depth on its cable has often been used to hold the ship's head to sea.

SEA BEGGARS, the name given during the second half of the 16th and early part of the 17th centuries to the independent Protestants who lived in what was later to be known as the Dutch Republic.

The Low Countries were at that time occupied by the forces of Spain with great severity and cruelty, and it was against the Spaniards that the Sea Beggars led a popular revolt. Their initial success was an amphibious attack against the Spaniards at Brill in 1572, and in the following year they defeated a Spanish squadron under the command of Admiral Bossu off the port of Hoorn in the Zuider Zee. Two of the great Dutch naval heroes, Admiral Jacob van *Heemskerk and Piet *Heyn, began their naval careers as Sea Beggars, and it was from these beginnings that the navy of Holland was established in the 17th century.

SEA FENCIBLES, a maritime militia raised in Britain for limited service, and for a definite period, as a defence against invasion during the Revolutionary (1793–1801) and Napoleonic (1803–15) Wars against France. They were made up mainly of fishermen and local residents in coastal areas, and service in the Sea Fencibles protected a man from *impressment into the navy. They were ranked junior to *marines and soldiers of the line regiments, but senior to yeomanry and volunteers. The force was first raised in 1798 and reached its peak in 1810 with a strength of 23,000 men.

'SEA OF SORE HEADS AND SORE HEARTS', the old square-rigged sailorman's term for the English Channel. That relatively narrow stretch of water, with its sandbanks and rocks, was often a nightmare for a full-rigged ship beating down Channel against the prevailing south-westerly wind, with the entire crew standing a *calashee watch.

SEA SONGS, the generic name given to songs either sung at sea by sailors in their leisure time, or songs sung ashore about the sea, which more often than not were never sung by seamen. They differ entirely from the *shanty, which was always a working song, and never sung on board except when required for an actual job of work.

The songs sung on board ship, known as *forebitters or fo'c'sle songs, were home-made songs which usually adopted the tune of an already existing song which was known by most men on board. The words could describe anything from a famous naval battle to a sailor's grouse about conditions on board his ship, could tell a story of an adventure ashore, usually amatory, or be rankly sentimental to start the seamen thinking of home and family life. One of the best-known of the British forebitters was 'The Limejuice Ship', a song which recalls both the Act of Parliament of 1795 which made a daily issue of lime juice to all seamen in the merchant navy compulsory as a preventive of *scurvy, and the Merchant Shipping Act of 1894 which laid down minimum scales of victuals in merchant ships and brought him other rights in the way of hours of employment, rates of pay, etc. The words of the song ran:

'Now if you want a merchant ship to sail the seas
    at large,
You'll not have any trouble if you have a good
    discharge,
Signed by the Board of Trade, and everything
    exact,
For there's nothin' done on a limejuice ship
    contrary to the Act.
So haul, boys, your weather mainbrace and ease
    away your lee,

Hoist jib and topsails, lads, an' let the ship go
    free,
Hurrah, boys, hurrah; we'll sing this jubilee,
"You can keep the navy, boys, a merchant ship
    for me."'

The other type of sea song, written, composed, and sung ashore, almost invariably tried to tell of the glories and delights of a life at sea, which the average sailor of the days of sail knew, only too well, painted a picture so false that he would have none of it. This was probably the reason why they were never adopted as part of the pattern of life on board. An early sea song was the aria 'Come away, fellow sailors, come away', which opens the second act of Henry Purcell's opera *Dido and Aeneas*, written in 1689, but the best known of them all was *'Heart of oak', written and sung by David Garrick in 1759 in the pantomime *Harlequin's Invasion*. This song was an exception in that it was played on board British warships, but not usually sung, when they were sailing into battle, as also was the song *'Britons Strike Home'.

The greatest writer of sea songs of this type was Charles *Dibdin, of which *'Tom Bowling' is probably the best known today. He wrote some hundreds of such songs which he made popular by singing himself. As he lived during the period of the great naval wars of the end of the 18th century, many of his songs had a considerable recruiting value at a time when the British Navy was desperate for men to sail the greatly increasing number of ships. Such a song was

'A sailor's life's the life for me,
    He takes his duty merrily;
    If winds can whistle, he can sing;
    Still faithful to his friend and King;
    He gets beloved by all his ship,
    And toasts his girl and drinks his flip.'

This was the sort of song which could paint a picture of life on board a British warship that might well tempt a young man into a *rendezvous, particularly when signing on to serve in the navy also brought with it the payment of a respectable *bounty.

The 19th century brought Gilbert and Sullivan's *H.M.S. Pinafore* with its quota of sea songs, immensely popular ashore but not sung on board, while perhaps the best known of the 20th century sea songs is John Ireland's setting of John *Masefield's haunting 'Sea Fever':

'I must down to the seas again, to the lonely sea
    and the sky,
And all I ask is a tall ship and a star to steer her
    by,
And the wheel's kick and the wind's song and
    the white sail's shaking
And a grey mist on the sea's face, and a grey
    dawn breaking.'

But here again, this was never a song which would be sung by sailors at sea. See also 'SPANISH LADIES'.

The most complete collection of sea songs is *Naval Songs and Ballads*, edited for the Navy Records Society by C. H. Firth in 1908; others are W. H. Whall, *Sea Songs and Shanties* (1920), C. Fox Smith, *Sea Songs and Ballads* (1923), and R. Palmer, *The Valiant Sailor* (1973).

SEABOAT, the name given in the Royal Navy to the ship's boats (*cutters or *whalers) which are suspended from *davits when at sea and not stowed inboard. They were used mainly for ship-to-ship communications at sea, but have been largely superseded in recent years by the use of a *jackstay rigged between ships when personnel and gear are to be passed from one to the other. When a seaboat is used for life-saving, as, for example, when picking up a man who has fallen overboard, it is invariably called a *lifeboat, and at the *pipe 'Away lifeboat's crew', the nearest men on deck man it whether detailed as its crew or not.

SEA-CARD, the old name for a *chart. Samuel *Pepys (*Diary*, 19 September 1666) bemoans the fact that, during the removal of his goods during the great fire of London, he lost, among other volumes, his book of cards. Fortunately they were found in a hamper later, and the total of his losses were 'but two little pictures of shipping and sea and a little gold frame for one of my sea-cards'. *Diary*, 22 September 1666.

SEA-CONNY or **SEACUNNY,** possibly a conjunction of the noun sea and the verb to *con, or from the Persian *sukkani* or Arabic *sukkan*, both meaning a *rudder, a name used as late as the early 19th century for a helmsman or quartermaster in a ship manned by Lascars.

SEAL FISHERY, the catching of seals for the use of their pelts, blubber, and meat. Like the whaling industry, with which it was at one time closely associated, sealing has been practised by man from earliest times. To this day there are still primitive shore hunters, like the Eskimo, who depend on the seal for their food, fuel, and clothing. Seals of commercial importance belong to all three families of the sub-order Pinnipedia—the Otariidae (eared seals), Odobaenidae (walrus), and the Phocidae (earless seals). The walrus is found only in the Arctic, but members of the other two families of seals are widely distributed in the world oceans, including some inland waters. The main concentrations of commercially important seals, however, are to be found in the North Atlantic and North Pacific Oceans, while in the Antarctic and sub-Antarctic

is a growing, but currently little exploited, seal population.

The North Atlantic seal fishery centres on two species in the main—the harp or Greenland seal (*Phoca groenlandica*), breeding in spring in the pack ice of the White Sea, the Norwegian Sea around Jan Mayen, and around Newfoundland, and the hood seal (*Cystophora cristata*), found mainly off east Greenland, Newfoundland, and the Davis Strait. The Russian White Sea ship-based fishery dates from 1898 and is now believed to be in decline. The hunting of harp and hood seals elsewhere in the Arctic dates from the 18th century after the pursuit of the Greenland whale became unprofitable. By the mid-19th century the Norwegians had the largest share of the industry and still send small ships to the 'West Ice' near Jan Mayen Island and to higher *latitudes of the north-east Atlantic. The New-foundland fishery began with coastal sealing and then from small ships out of Newfoundland in the late 18th century. In the early 19th century Scottish whalers began to participate in the New-foundland seal hunt before going north to the whaling grounds. Today the participating nations include Canada, Norway, Denmark on behalf of the Greenlanders, and the U.S.S.R. International control over the conservation of the seals is the responsibility of the International Commission for the North-west Atlantic Fisheries.

In the North Pacific the commercially profitable seals belong to the family of eared seals, the most valuable of which are the northern fur seals (*Callorhinus* species). They differ principally from the earless seals in possessing a permanent undercoat of short soft fur much sought after by furriers and costumiers. Their chief breeding grounds are the Pribilof Islands and Kommandorski Islands in the Bering Sea, and the Robben and Kuril Islands in the Sea of Okhotsk. Their migrations cover immense distances extending to California and Japan. This fishery was opened up by the voyage of Vitus *Bering in 1741. Subsequently enormous numbers were slaughtered both on their breeding islands and at sea so that by the end of the 19th century their numbers were seriously depleted. An international convention signed in 1911 at Washington by Great Britain, Japan, Russia, and the U.S.A. regulated the fishery so that today the Northern fur seal is commercially the most valuable in the world.

Sealing in the southern hemisphere has centred largely on the fur seals (*Arctocephalus* species) and the elephant seals (*Mirounga* species), the former chiefly valued for the skins and fur, the latter for their oil. During the 18th century fur seals were taken along the eastern coast of South America as far south as the Falkland Islands and then into the Pacific northwards to the Juan Fernandez and Galapagos islands. For the first fifty years of this trade the chief participating nations were the U.S.A. and Britain, the chief market for furs being Canton. Further stocks of fur seals were revealed at South Georgia when it was discovered by Captain *Cook in 1775. With the near extinction of the South American seal stocks, those of South Georgia were soon subjected to heavy exploitation. When these stocks in their turn began to dwindle the sealers were forced even further south in order to satisfy the demand. The discovery of the South Shetland Islands in 1819 by Captain William *Smith revealed even richer colonies and sealers from Argentina, the U.S.A., and Great Britain flocked to the area. It was this 'fur rush' which led to the first sighting of the Antarctic continent. By 1829 it was reported that not a single fur seal was to be seen in the South Shetlands. This was virtually the end of the trade in the South Atlantic though it was continued to a lesser extent at Tristan da Cunha, Gough Island, and on the coasts of south-west Africa. In the South Pacific the same sorry story was repeated among the islands of the Indian Ocean and Australasia. With the collapse of the fur seal industry the traders turned to exploiting the elephant seals which hauled up on the beaches of the sub-Antarctic islands to breed at regular seasons. By 1870 the hunting of this species, too, had become unprofitable. In recent years, as a result of a prolonged period of rigid protection by governments, the stocks of southern fur seals and elephant seals have slowly recovered their numbers but seem unlikely to rival commercially the northern industry in the immediate future.

SEAM, the narrow gap between the planks forming the sides and decks of vessels constructed of wood which is *caulked with *oakum and pitch to keep out the water. As wood swells when it is in contact with water, a narrow seam between the planks must be left to accommodate the expansion, and as the planks 'take up' when immersed, they compress the oakum and add to the watertightness.

SEAM, to, the work of the sailmaker when he joins together the *cloths from which a sail is made with a double seam. See also PRICK, TO, SAIL, TABLE, TO.

SEAMAN'S QUADRANT, often called the simple quadrant, was the earliest instrument used by navigators for measuring the *altitude of a heavenly body. It was in the form of a quarter circle of brass or wood with a plumb-line suspended, when the instrument was in use, from the centre of the circle of which the quadrant formed part. One radial edge of the instrument was fitted with two pins or sights by means of which the heavenly body, whose altitude was required, was sighted. This quadrant required two observers, one to bring the observed body into the line of the two pins and the other to note the position where the plumb-line crossed the arc of the instrument.

This seaman's quadrant was in use among the early Portuguese navigators during their voyages along the West African coast during the second half of the 15th century. Its first use appears to have been for measuring the altitude of the Pole Star (see POLARIS) as a means of finding the distance south of Lisbon or other port of departure. The arcs of these early quadrants were marked with the names of headlands and important coastal stations corresponding to the positions of the plumb-line when the pole star was observed.

With the introduction of tables of the sun's *declinations for navigational purposes, the navigator was able to express his *latitudes in degrees and minutes of arc north or south of the equator. From this time onwards, the arc of the seaman's quadrant was graduated in angular measurement so that altitudes could be read in angles.

This simple quadrant could not be used on board ship unless the sea was smooth and the air calm, and even in the most suitable conditions, its degree of accuracy of measured altitudes was coarse. But it was an instrument which could easily be manufactured by the navigator himself if the need arose, and by the use of a plumb-line to define the vertical, the quadrant could be used for measuring altitudes even when the horizon was obscured by darkness or fog, since altitudes were measured with it from a vertical base, and not a horizontal base as is the case in the later navigational instruments such as *Hadley's quadrant or a modern *sextant.

SEAMANSHIP, in its widest sense, is the whole art of taking a ship from one place to another at sea. It is an amalgam of all the arts of designing a ship and her motive power, whether sail, steam, or other means, of working her when at sea, and in harbour, and the science of navigation by which the way is found from her point of departure to her point of arrival. It thus embraces every aspect of a ship's life in port and her progress at sea.

Seamanship, however, has also a narrower meaning, divorced from a ship's design and engines, from her navigation, and from the other specialist skills which have their part in the smooth running of a ship. It is that department of a ship's being which is concerned with the rest of the daily management of the ship, her gear, boats, anchors and cables, rigging; her sails if she is a sailing vessel, and the watch kept at sea and in harbour. The old definition of a prime seaman was a man who could *hand, *reef, and *steer, and although the handing and reefing of sails is largely a thing of the past so far as ships are concerned, the same general definition holds good if the modern equivalents of handing and reefing are related to the steam or motor ship of today. It embodies a knowledge of knotting and splicing, of handling ropes and *hawsers, *blocks and *tackles, and it also embraces a knowledge of the weather and the means of competing with storms, of the *rule of the road, and of lights and their meanings. Every aspect of the day-to-day work of the ship, apart perhaps from the specialized skills of the navigator, the engineer, the electrician, the *radar operators and telegraphists, etc., are considered to be within this narrower meaning of the word.

Admiralty Manual of Seamanship, 3 vols (1964–72); D. Phillips-Birt, *History of Seamanship* (1971).

SEA-MARK, the seaman's name for any floating navigational mark, such as a *buoy or *lightship, as opposed to *landmark, which is a prominent mark on shore from which a navigational *compass *bearing can be obtained or which can be used as a *leading mark to indicate a safe channel. Because a sea-mark has to be *moored to the seabed and can drag its mooring, good navigators usually treat them with some caution when using them to *fix a ship's position. In olden days, marks set up ashore were known as sea-marks, not land-marks, and in its original charter *Trinity House was empowered to set up sea-marks ashore whenever necessary as an aid to navigation. Any person found destroying them was subject to a fine of £100, and if unable to pay, was to be outlawed. See also LEADING MARK.

SEA-PIE, a favourite dish for the crew on board in the old days of sailing vessels. Almost anything could go into a sea-pie, but the proper dish consisted of layers of meat, vegetables, and fish separated by crusts of bread or broken biscuit. By the number of layers it was known as a two- or three-decker.

SEARCHLIGHT, a high-powered light carried on warships at sea, usually mounted as high up as possible, and so fitted that it can be moved in elevation and *azimuth as required, and used at night for illumination and by day or night for visual signalling. The source of the light is normally a carbon arc reflected off a parabolic mirror to give a flat beam. The first operational searchlight, known as Mr. Wilde's 'electric light', was fitted in H.M.S. *Comet* in 1874. It was of 11,000 candlepower and could illuminate ships at a distance of one mile. It was superseded in 1880 by Gramme's lights of 20,000 candlepower, and when H.M.S. *Northampton* gave a night display with her new searchlight at St. Kitts in that year, Admiral McClintock, who flew his flag in her, wrote in his journal: 'Every animal, human or other, shouted and yelled after its kind. Natives referred to it as the Englishman's night sun.'

Searchlights were used at sea primarily in night actions, and as a means of signalling in *Morse code over comparatively long distances. Before the introduction of *radar, it was, along with *starshell, the only means of illuminating a target at night, though in doing so it revealed the user's presence to an enemy and gave him a target on which to range and fire. As a means of signalling between ships, it had the advantage of comparatively long range and did not necessarily indicate to an enemy, unless actually within sight, that the vessel using it was in the vicinity, as would a wireless signal.

Today, radar has almost completely replaced the searchlight as a means of target discovery at night, though it still has uses for illumination. It remains a valuable means of signalling by day and night though in this respect its use is almost entirely limited to purely naval occasions.

SEBASTOPOL, an important Russian seaport and naval base on the Black Sea coast, situated on an estuary which forms one of the finest and largest natural harbours in Europe. It was originally the location of a Greek colony, for a time became a tributary of Rome, and eventually was occupied by the Tartars. It was conquered by Russia in 1783 and made the chief naval station for the Black Sea. In 1854 during the Crimean War (1854–6) the town was bombarded by a combined British, French, and Turkish naval force and besieged from the land, but sustained the siege for eleven months before surrendering. An intensive naval dockyard and school of navigation add to its naval importance.

SECTIONS, drawings made during the design stages of a ship showing the positions of the *frames and their exact curvature in relation to the hull shape of the vessel. See also SHIPBUILDING.

SEEADLER, a German *armed merchant cruiser of the First World War (1914–18), notable for being a square-rigged ship, though with an auxiliary engine. She left Germany on 21 December 1916 under the command of Graf Felix von *Luckner, and cruised in the Atlantic and Pacific Oceans, sinking fourteen allied merchant vessels, of which eleven were sailing vessels, before being wrecked in the Society Islands. She was thus the last square-rigged ship to be used as a warship.

SEEL, to, an old seafaring term meaning to lurch over in a *roll, in connection with the motion of a sailing vessel at sea. Thus Sir Henry *Mainwaring, in his *Seaman's Dictionary* (1644), 'so that seeling is but a suddaine heeling, forced by the motion and force of the sea or wind'. The word is also used as a noun to describe a sudden or unexpected roll. Glanville, in his *Voyage to Cadiz* (1625), wrote: 'Our shipp did rolle more and fetch deeper and more dangerous Seeles than in the greatest storme.'

SEINE, a long shallow net often with a modified *cod-end used in fishing for surface fish. Where used for *ring netting, there is no cod-end and the seine is laid round a shoal of fish and then pursed at the bottom to prevent any fish from escaping below the net. It differs from a drift net in that the fish are caught within the net, and not by their gills in the meshes. In the days of the sailing navies, seine nets were always included among a ship's equipment as a means of providing additional fresh fish for the crew.

SEIZE, to, the operation of binding with small stuff as, for instance, one rope to another, or the end of a rope to its own part to form an eye. There are many varieties of *seizing according to the method of binding and the function which is to be served, such as flat or round seizing where the binding twine is passed in continuous turns, racking seizing where each turn is crossed between the two parts being seized, throat seizing where the seizing is passed with the turns crossing each other diagonally, etc. A seizing is always 'clapped on'.

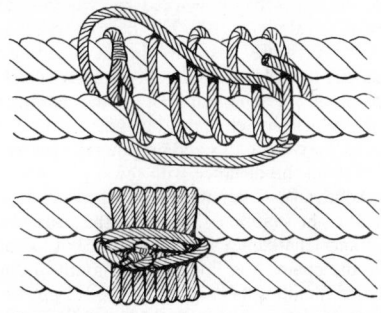

Racking seizing

SEIZING, (1) the cord or twine, generally known as small stuff, by which ropes are *seized to each other, **(2)** the name given to the finished product when the two parts have been seized together.

SELDEN, JOHN (1584–1654), English jurist, was the author of *Mare Clausum*, a work published in 1631 as a reply to the *Mare Liberum* of Grotius, who had argued that the so-called freedom of the sea, which his work preached, entitled Dutch fishermen to catch fish in waters off the English coast. The *Mare Clausum*, or

'closed sea', upheld the doctrine of the marine waters contiguous to the coastline of a country being solely under the dominion of that country. On its publication Charles I was so impressed by Selden's arguments that he ordered that a copy of the book should be retained in the Admiralty Court (see ADMIRALTY, HIGH COURT OF) in perpetuity.

SELF-RECORDING LOG, see LOG.

SELFRIDGE, THOMAS OLIVER (1836–1924), American naval officer, graduated from the Naval Academy in 1854. He was serving in the *sloop *Cumberland* at the time of the abandonment of the Norfolk Navy Yard during the American Civil War (1861–5) and was in command of the forward battery in the *Cumberland* when she was sunk by the Confederate ship *Virginia* (ex-*Merrimack*). He bore the brunt of the fire from the *Virginia* and saved himself only as the ship sank with her colours still flying. He commanded the *gunboat *Cairo* in the operations against Vicksburg when that vessel was destroyed by a *mine in December 1862, and after the surrender of the town he commanded a group of gunboats with the *Conestoga* as flagship. He assisted in the construction of the Red River dam and had a part in the successful escape of the gunboats after the erection of the dam. In the second attack on Fort Fisher he commanded a landing party of sailors and *marines which made a direct assault on the fort, and was commended for gallantry.

In 1878 he was in charge of a survey of the Isthmus of Darien and he also surveyed the Amazon and Madeira Rivers. His surveys of the Isthmus of Darien brought him an award of the Legion of Honour by France and commendation from the Royal Geographic Society of Belgium. He became a rear admiral in 1896 and retired in 1898.

SELF-STEERING GEAR, an arrangement by which a ship can be left to steer herself on a desired course for long periods. There are various types of self-steering gear, such as automatic gyroscopic pilots in large *liners and merchant ships in which the *course is set on a gyro compass and the rudder applied mechanically to bring the ship back to that course whenever the *lubber's line on the *binnacle moves away from it. In sailing vessels, particularly in ocean-going yachts, self-steering arrangements are usually based on a *vane mounted on the yacht's *counter. See, e.g., VANE SELF-STEERING GEAR.

SELKIRK, ALEXANDER (1676–1721), British seaman and the prototype of *Robinson Crusoe in Daniel *Defoe's story of the same name, was born in Lower Largo, Fife, Scotland,

and became a fisherman. In 1703 he volunteered as a member of the crew of the *privateer *Cinque Ports* for a voyage to the South Seas, the ship being commanded by Thomas Stradling and having William *Dampier on board as navigator. In 1705, after a violent disagreement with Stradling, Selkirk asked to be *marooned on the island of Juan Fernandez, and he was set ashore as the ship sailed away. He lived alone on the island, sustained by the vegetables and fruit which grew there in abundance and by the goats left there by the original Spanish discoverers, until 1709 when the privateers *Duke* and *Duchess*, commanded by Woodes *Rogers, called at Juan Fernandez during their circumnavigation of the world. It says something of the state of discontent which had existed in the *Cinque Ports* that when Selkirk saw Dampier on board the *Duke*—he accompanied that expedition as navigator—he asked to be set ashore again on Juan Fernandez, but was dissuaded. He was so good a seaman that Rogers put him in charge of one of the *prize ships captured by the *Duke* and *Duchess*.

After his return to England in 1711, Selkirk told the story of his years on Juan Fernandez to Richard Steele who wrote an account of it. It was this account which fell into the hands of Defoe and was used as the basis of his famous novel. Shortly after his return, Selkirk volunteered for service in the Royal Navy and at the time of his death was a *master's mate in H.M.S. *Weymouth*. There is a statue of him on the wall of the house in Lower Largo in which he is thought to have been born.

SELVAGEE, an untwisted skein of rope yarn *marled together to form a *strop. Selvagee strops are used for a variety of purposes on board ship, such as slings for heavy weights required to be hoisted by a *purchase or for securing masts and oars in ships' boats to prevent them rolling about in a seaway, etc.

SEMAPHORE, from the Greek *sema*, a sign, and *pherein*, to bear, a species of telegraph conveying signs by a machine having movable arms. The word itself was first introduced into Britain in 1816 when Admiral Sir Home *Popham's new signalling system was installed to replace the older telegraph invented by the Revd. Lord George Murray and first set up in 1796. Murray's system involved the use of six shutters working in a frame and operated by men hauling on ropes, and by opening or closing the shutters, sixty-three changes of appearance of the frame were possible. On these changes of appearance a code was evolved to cover any messages required to be sent. Murray's invention was accepted by the British Admiralty, whose first requirement was a telegraphic line from London to Deal, on the coast of Kent, with a branch to the naval base

at Sheerness. A chain of fifteen stations, each built on high ground and within visibility range of those on either side, was constructed and the first message from the Admiralty to Deal was passed on 27 January 1796. With a little practice the time for a message to leave the Admiralty in London and reach Deal, and acknowledgement of its receipt by Deal to be received back in the Admiralty, was reduced to two minutes. This success led to a requirement by the Admiralty for a similar telegraphic line to Portsmouth. Ten stations were found to be enough to cover the distance and this line was in operation by the end of 1796. In 1806 it was extended to Plymouth with the erection of twenty-two further stations, and it is recorded that the daily Admiralty time signal, transmitted at 1.00 p.m., could reach Plymouth and be acknowledged back to London within three minutes. Each station consisted of two rooms with the shutter frame on top and was equipped with 'an eight-guinea clock and two 12-guinea telescopes to be supplied by Messrs. Dollond'. The sole piece of furniture paid for by the Admiralty was 'a stove with an iron funnel pipe'.

One drawback of Murray's telegraph system was that it was entirely one-directional as the shutter frame had of course to be permanently fixed on the roof of the buildings. Popham's semaphore overcame this disadvantage, as the single post on which the movable arms were mounted could be revolved about its base and thus placed to be read from any direction. It was also more easily operated than Murray's shutters, the arms being worked by winches, and once a vocabulary code had been worked out, gave much more flexibility in the wording of messages and also considerably greater speed in transmission. Popham did not use the stations set up for Murray's telegraph but selected his own after extensive surveys and, in general, succeeded in covering the distance with fewer stations. On the Admiralty–Chatham line, opened on 3 July 1816, eight stations, including the Admiralty itself and Chatham Yard, were sufficient to complete the chain. The line to Portsmouth ran into initial difficulties as it could not be set up 'without interfering greatly with the tasteful ground of Mrs. Merrick, situated on the south-east end of Wimbledon Common or the park of the Right Hon. Earl Spencer to the eastward'.

In the end the objections by Lord Spencer were smoothed away and the line to Portsmouth established with fifteen stations, again including the Admiralty and Portsmouth Dockyard. It was opened for signals in 1823, and in 1825 an extension to Plymouth was authorized. It had reached the borders of Hampshire and Dorset before the Admiralty's money ran out in 1831, and there it stopped.

The buildings which housed Popham's semaphore were of three types; a four-storey tower built on to a single-storey bungalow, a two-storey house with a cupola on the roof, and a bungalow. Examples of these three types of building are still in existence, a tower building at Chatley Heath, Cobham, which still contains the original semaphore machinery; a five-storey building at Pewley Hill, Guildford, still known as Semaphore House, Semaphore Road; and bungalows at Holden Hill, Midhurst (now derelict and abandoned), Compton, Farringdon, and Farley Chamberlayne. Each station was manned by a half-pay naval lieutenant, who received an additional 3s. a day, and a naval signalman who was paid 2s. a day. The hours of signal activity were from 10.00 a.m. to 5.00 p.m. in summer and 10.00 a.m. to 3.00 p.m. in winter.

The days of Popham's semaphore as a long-distance signalling system began to be numbered in 1838 when Wheatstone's experiments in electric signalling had their first major success with signals made in London being read in Birmingham. Thenceforward the spread of the electric telegraph was rapid, and the last of Popham's naval signal stations, that at Portsmouth Dockyard, was closed in April 1849.

Popham's semaphore poles, however, did not die out with the closing of his long-distance system, for it was quickly recognized as an admirable method of short-distance communication for shore station-to-ship, and ship-to-ship messages. It became a universal code, widely used at sea by ships of all nations, either by means of a miniature Popham machine in which the arms were worked by chain and sprocket gear or by hand flags used as an extension of a signalman's arms. It still remains a simple, rapid, and reliable means of communication within visual range. See also SIGNALS AT SEA.

SEMI-DIAMETER, a correction which has to be applied to an *altitude observation of the sun or moon when measured by a *sextant. When a navigator takes a sun or moon sight, he normally brings the lower edge of it down to the horizon with his sextant and reads off the angle on the sextant scale. But the true altitude should be measured with the centre of the sun or moon brought to the horizon, and so a correction must be made to the angle read off the sextant to allow for half the diameter. In comparison with stars, which are so far distant from the earth that semi-diameter can be ignored, the sun and moon are relatively close, and there is an appreciable difference in the sextant angles measured from the lower edge and the centre. A table of semi-diameters is included in all editions of nautical tables.

SEMMES, RAPHAEL (1809–77), American and Confederate naval officer, is best remembered for his command of the *Sumter* and the *Alabama*, Confederate commerce-destroying *cruisers in the American Civil War (1861–5). Born in Charles County, Maryland, he became a *midshipman in the U.S. Navy in 1826 and studied law during leaves of absence from naval duties. He commanded the *brig *Somers* in the war with Mexico, served ashore with naval artillery at the bombardment of Vera Cruz in March 1847, and was with Scott's army in the capture of Mexico City. As a commander he resigned from the navy in February 1861 to take service with the Confederate States and went to sea as a commerce raider in the *Sumter*, a converted vessel. He cruised in the Caribbean and off the coast of Brazil before going to Gibraltar, capturing eighteen *prizes in all. With the *Sumter* blockaded in Gibraltar, Semmes laid up the vessel, discharged the crew, and ordered the officers back to the Confederate states. He became a captain in the Confederate Navy in 1862, and going to Liverpool, took command of the C.S.S. *Alabama*. This vessel sailed under British papers to the Azores, where she was armed and supplied. Commissioned on 24 August 1862, she began operations in the mid-Atlantic whaling area where Semmes captured and burned ten American ships. In the Gulf of Mexico he decoyed the U.S.S. *Hatteras* from the blockading squadron off Galveston, Texas, and on 11 January 1863 sank her after a 13-minute running fight in darkness. Semmes then took the *Alabama* to the West Indies, to the coast of Brazil, and the Atlantic coast of southern Africa. Rounding the Cape of Good Hope he sailed to Singapore and then returned to the Atlantic. In June 1864 he put into Cherbourg, France, having captured eighty-two merchant ships, but he had no means of selling what would otherwise have been valuable prizes.

Semmes asked permission for the *Alabama* to be repaired in the dockyard at Cherbourg but there were delays by the French government under pressure from the U.S.A. When the U.S.S. *Kearsarge (Captain *Winslow) appeared off Cherbourg, Semmes decided to fight although his vessel still needed repairs and was short of powder. On Sunday morning, 19 June 1864, the *Alabama* left Cherbourg and opened fire on the *Kearsarge*. Winslow held his fire until the range had closed to less than 1,000 yards and the two ships then fought while steaming in a series of tight circles. After about 70 minutes of fighting Semmes recognized that the *Alabama* was sinking, hauled down his colours, and sent a message of surrender as well as a request for help. The *Kearsarge* sent her boats but Semmes and about forty others from the *Alabama* were picked up by the British yacht *Deerhound* and other neutral vessels which landed the survivors in England and in France. After a rest in Switzerland Semmes returned to the Confederacy and was given command of the James River squadron with the rank of rear admiral. He was, however, forced to burn his ships when the Confederates evacuated the city of Richmond. He then formed a naval brigade with his men, but had to surrender with General Johnston's army at Greensboro, N.C. After the war Semmes was held for trial before a military commission but was released afterwards by Presidential order.

SENHOUSE SLIP, see CABLE STOPPERS.

SEPPINGS, Sir ROBERT (1767–1840), British naval architect, was apprenticed to the shipwright trade in the naval dockyard at Plymouth. He first came to notice in 1800 when he invented a device whereby, by means of wooden wedges, the whole bottom of a ship in *dry-dock became accessible for repair, the hull becoming suspended by the *shores when the wedges were knocked out. For this device the British Admiralty paid him £1,000 and made him master shipwright at Chatham. While there he introduced great improvements in the science of ship construction by the use of diagonal bracing to provide greater longitudinal strength, at the same time modifying the design of bow and stern to provide a cleaner *run of hull form and enabling ships to carry a more powerful armament. In 1813 he was made surveyor of the navy, holding the appointment until he retired in 1832.

SEPULCHRAL SHIPS, the name commonly given to ships used in connection with burial rites. The use of such ships is of very ancient origin. The Egyptian sun-god Osiris was said to have journeyed to the underworld in a golden *bark attended by the Hours, and in emulation, after embalming, Egyptian dead were often carried westward across lakes and canals towards the setting sun where it was thought lay the earthly paradise. Many of the pharaohs of Egypt used to have a decorated and fully stocked boat burned alongside them for their later journey to the underworld. In the Norse legend of Baldur, he was set afloat in his ship *Hringhorn* on a funeral pyre and, of course, there is ample evidence of the burial of Vikings in their *longships, many of them having been excavated in recent years. The Arthurian legends also tell of death ships, King Arthur being borne to Avalon in such a vessel. In Brittany, near the Pointe du Raz, there is the Baie de Trépassés where, according to a local legend, boats were summoned to convey the souls of drowned men to the Île au Sein, while in the Aleutian Islands boat-shaped coffins were used, and many of the North American Indian tribes buried their dead in *canoes raised up on poles, although the Cherokees and Chinooks sometimes buried them so at sea.

There are similar legends among the Solomon islanders, the Fijians, and the Maoris, and the Dyaks of Borneo used to place their dead in a canoe, together with some of the deceased's property, and set it adrift. In 1849, on the death of Thrien Thri, King of Cochin China, the boats used in his funeral procession were burned on his pyre.

SERANG, the Anglo-Indian name, from the Persian *sarhang*, commander, for a native *boatswain or the leader of a Lascar crew.

SERPENTINE, a small ship's hand-gun of the 15th and 16th centuries. It had a calibre of $1\frac{1}{2}$ inches and fired a $5\frac{1}{2}$-ounce shot with a charge of the same weight of 'cannon corn' powder. The maximum, or random, range was 1,300 paces. When the powder used was 'fine corn', the same quality as used in muskets, the charge was reduced by one-quarter. Serpentines were upper deck or 'castle' guns, i.e., fired into the *waist from the fore or after castle, and were used purely in an anti-personnel role. See also GUNS, NAVAL; ROBINET.

SERRES, DOMINIC (c. 1725–93), marine painter, was born at Auch, in Gascony, and was intended for the church but ran away to sea, eventually becoming the master of a French merchant vessel. The ship was captured by a British *frigate in 1752 and Serres was brought to England, where he decided to settle and to study art. This brought him into close contact with Charles *Brooking, a British marine painter of the Van de *Velde school, and Serres soon established a reputation as a painter of seascapes and naval battles, his practical experience of ships and the sea bringing to his work an authenticity which, in conjunction with a brilliance of colouring and design, made his pictures outstanding examples of the marine painter's art in the mid-18th century. He was elected an original member of the Royal Academy where he exhibited many fine paintings of naval actions.

His son, J. T. SERRES (1759–1825), was equally renowned as a marine artist but fell on evil days because of the extravagances of his wife, and died in a debtor's prison 'within the rules of the King's Bench'.

SERVE, orig. **SARVE, to,** the operation of winding *spunyarn close round a rope which has been *wormed and *parcelled, the serving being wound on with a serving board or *mallet to obtain maximum tension, with the turns made against the *lay of the rope. The purpose of worming, parcelling, and serving a rope is to make it impervious to water and thus to preserve it against rot. The expression was also used in the case of ships which, through age or weakness, had their hulls served round with *cables to hold them together. See also MARL, TO; POINT, TO.

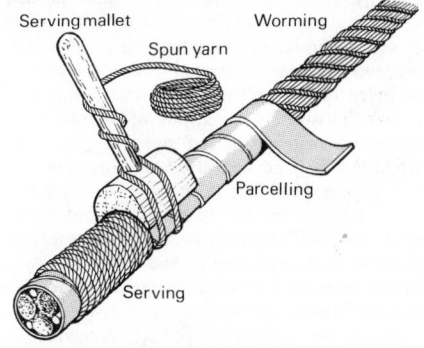

Worming, parcelling, and serving

SERVING MALLET, a wooden hand mallet used on board ships for passing a serving round a rope. The bottom of the mallet has a semicircular groove which fits round the rope and the *spunyarn, with which a serving is made, is led from the rope and a turn with it taken round the handle of the mallet. As the mallet is turned round the rope, the spunyarn renders round the mallet handle, by which means it can be kept taut and the serving applied with the maximum tightness. A board, with a similar groove at the bottom, is sometimes used instead of a mallet. See SERVE, TO.

SET, (1) the word used to denote the direction in which a current flows. It is also applied to the direction of the tide, e.g., 'the tide is setting to the southward', and also to the distance and direction in which a vessel is moved by the tide in relation to its desired *course and distance run. **(2)** It is a word also applied to sails in relation to their angle with the wind as, for example, in the set of a *jib or the set of a mainsail.

SET, to, a verb which when used in the maritime sense has many meanings. A current or tide sets in the direction in which it flows, a ship sets a *course when she is steadied down on it, a sail is set when it is hoisted and sheeted home to the wind. But to set sail, said of a ship when she departs on a voyage regardless of whether she uses sails or not. To set an *anchor watch, to detail a member of the crew of a ship to see that she does not drag her anchor when lying at anchor or *moored.

SETTEE, a two-masted ship of the Mediterranean, *lateen-rigged on both masts, which was often used as a transport for spare *galley crews. They were single-decked with a long, sharp bow, and belonged more to the eastern Mediterranean than to the western. Their dates are from the 16th to about the mid-19th century. Occasionally they were called balancelles, from the double lateen rig, and it was in a settee, or balancelle, that the fictional gun-running activities on behalf of the Carlist cause in Spain, described by Joseph *Conrad in his novel *The Arrow of Gold*, were performed.

SETTLE, to, a term used in connection with a *halyard after a sail has been hoisted. To settle a halyard is to ease it away slightly, and the term refers usually to a *peak halyard when a *gaff sail has been hoisted to an extent when there are wrinkles in the canvas at the *throat of the sail. Where these occur, they are the result of the peak of the sail having been hoisted too high, and the halyard is then settled until the wrinkles have disappeared.

SEVASTOPOL, see SEBASTOPOL.

SEVEN SEAS, a saying which really means all the waters which cover the earth and refers in fact to the seven oceans, the Arctic, Antarctic, North Atlantic, South Atlantic, North Pacific, South Pacific, and Indian.

'Which of our coming and departure heeds,
  As the seven seas should heed a pebble-cast.'
    Fitzgerald, *The Rubáiyát of Omar Khayyám*

SEVILLE, a seaport of Spain and chief city of Andalusia, is on the left bank of the Guadalquivir River, 54 miles from the Atlantic Ocean. It is a very ancient town, having been captured by Julius Caesar in 45 B.C., was a stronghold of the Vandals and Visigoths before being held by the Moors during their occupation of Spain from 712 to 1248, when it was finally restored to Christianity by Ferdinand VII. It was the discovery of America by Christopher *Columbus in 1492 that brought the growth of Seville as a seaport, as it became the starting point for many of the subsequent expeditions to colonize North and South America and to exploit trade with the new continents. In more recent years, with the increase in size of ships, the trade through the port fell off until, early in the 20th century, a ship canal from the Puerta de los Remedios to the Puerta del Verde eliminated a navigationally difficult stretch of the Guadalquivir. It now handles an extensive trade in mercury and other minerals, wine, citrus fruits, and cork.

In the great days of discovery of the 16th century, Seville was one of the principal centres for the study and teaching of navigation and of maritime cartography and early in that century Sebastian *Cabot was appointed Pilot Major, or chief examiner of all navigators and pilots, there.

SEW, to, an old maritime word which was used to describe a ship which had run ashore and had to await the next tide before refloating. She was said to be sewed by the difference between the level of the water and the flotation mark on her hull, e.g., she is sewed two feet if the level of the water is two feet below her normal flotation mark. The pronunciation of the word is *sue*.

SEXTANT, the modern navigational instrument for the measurement of vertical and horizontal angles at sea. It is an instrument of double reflection by means of two mirrors, and thus although its actual arc subtends an angle of 60° at the centre, it is capable of measuring angles up to 120°.

The sextant was developed in 1757 from the *quadrant, which could measure angles only up to 90°, following a suggestion of Captain John Campbell of the British Navy. The requirements for the additional 30° arose from the need of making lunar observations in order to discover a ship's *longitude, and even after the *chronometer had been perfected, by which longitude could be easily obtained and lunar observations made unnecessary, it was retained in use in preference to the quadrant as its additional measurement capability was still found to be of value in the measurement of horizontal angles.

The modern sextant employs the same optical principles as John *Hadley's quadrant, with a fixed mirror mounted on an arm of the sextant in line with the observer's telescope and parallel to the index bar when it is set at 0° on the sextant scale. This mirror is only half silvered, so that the horizon can be seen through the plain half and the reflected object seen in the silvered half. A second mirror is mounted on the index bar,

which is pivoted at the centre of the sextant, and as the index bar is swung, so this mirror swings with it. When a navigator takes an *altitude of a heavenly body, he holds the sextant perpendicular and swings the index bar along the arc of the sextant until he can see the object of his sight (sun, moon, or star) reflected from the mirror on the index bar, which has of course swung with the bar, on to the silvered half of the mirror on the sextant arm, and he can thus line it up on the horizon, which he can also see simultaneously through the plain half of the mirror. Once it is there, he reads off the altitude indicated by the position of the index bar on the arc of the sextant, which is graduated in degrees and minutes. A vernier on the index bar gives an accurate interpolation between the minutes.

A modern sextant in perfect adjustment is capable of an accuracy of better than half a minute of arc.

SHACKLE, a U-shaped iron closed with a pin across the jaws and used for securing such things as *halyards to sails, other parts of standing or running rigging where required, *anchors to their *cables, joining lengths of chain cable, etc.

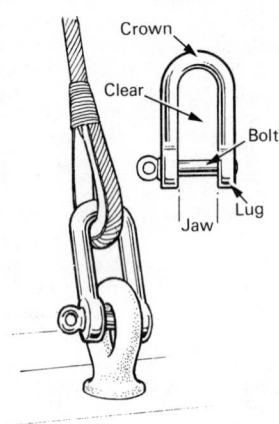

Shackle

Shackles used in the rigging normally have a threaded pin which is screwed into one of the jaws; those used to join lengths of cable are of two kinds. The older type of joining shackle is closed by a bolt flush with the lugs of the jaws which is kept in place by a tapered pin. This is driven into place with a hammer and punch and secured by means of a leaden pellet or ring which, when hammered in, expands into a socket cut round the inside of the hole. A more modern type of joining shackle is made in two parts with a fitted stud, the stud being kept in place by a steel pin which runs diagonally through the stud and both parts of the shackle. The advantage of

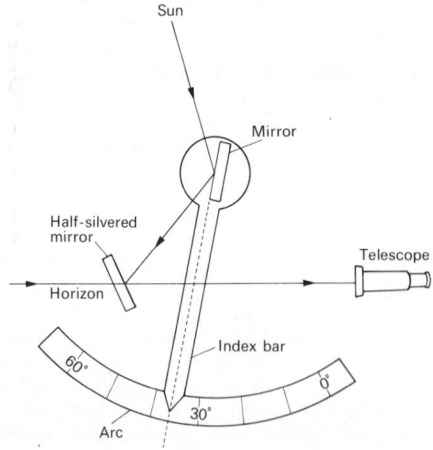

Path of light through sextant

this type of shackle is that it is the same size and shape as an ordinary link of the cable and so fits better into the snugs of the *cable-holder when veering or weighing.

A shackle is also the name given to a length of chain cable measuring 12½ fathoms, which is the amount of cable between each joining shackle. The length of a cable is eight shackles, 100 fathoms.

SHACKLETON, Sir ERNEST HENRY (1874–1922), British explorer, was born in Kilkee, southern Ireland, and educated at Dulwich College, London, but he left there at the age of 16 to join the merchant navy. He served before the mast in various sailing ships, finally becoming an officer in the *Union-Castle Line. Expressing an interest in polar exploration, he was appointed third lieutenant of the National Antarctic Expedition of 1901 under the command of Captain Robert Falcon *Scott and he accompanied Scott and Dr. E. A. Wilson on the first great south polar land journey, reaching a record southerly *latitude at that time of lat. 82° 7'. Invalided home after an attack of *scurvy, Shackleton made up his mind that he wanted to lead a private expedition of his own to the Antarctic, with the achievement of the South pole as its aim. In January 1908 he was made leader of the British National Expedition which reached Cape Royds in the *Nimrod*. The expedition accomplished some useful scientific work as well as climbing Mount Erebus, reaching the south magnetic pole, and finally scaling the Beardmore Glacier, attaining a point on the polar plateau only 100 miles from the pole. For these achievements Shackleton received a knighthood on his return home.

In 1914 he again sailed for the Antarctic in command of a party on board the *Endurance*, with the intention of crossing the continent of Antarctica from the Weddell to the Ross Seas. But after a combination of adverse circumstances, the *Endurance* was beset in the ice in the Weddell Sea, and was eventually crushed after drifting for nine months. Only Shackleton's superb natural gifts of leadership and organization enabled the expedition's members to survive. After drifting on ice-floes, they eventually took to the ship's boats and reached Elephant Island, in the South Shetland group, in April 1916. From Elephant Island Shackleton, leaving his second-in-command, Frank Wild, in charge, sailed in one of the boats, which he named *James Caird*, to South Georgia, 300 miles away, to seek help. After three unsuccessful attempts, the Elephant Island party was rescued with the help of the Chilean *tug *Yelcho*. In 1921 he sailed again to the Antarctic on board the *Quest*; he died on board, off South Georgia, of a heart attack.

M. and J. Fisher, *Shackleton* (1957).

SHADOW LINE, THE, a largely autobiographical novel by Joseph *Conrad, published in 1916 in which he recalls his experiences when in command of the *barque *Otago* from Bangkok to Singapore.

SHAKE, (1) the name given to a longitudinal crack in a mast or spar. **(2)** The staves of a cask after it has been taken to pieces; thus 'no great shakes' means something of little value. **(3)** The shivers of a sail when a sailing vessel is steered too close to the wind, a meaning which has given rise to the expression 'a brace of shakes' as very quickly or immediately, literally the time taken in which a sail shivers twice when too close to the wind.

'SHAKE A CLOTH IN THE WIND, to', a seaman's expression to indicate that a man is slightly intoxicated but not helplessly drunk.

SHAKE OUT A REEF, to, the expression used when enlarging a sail by casting off the *reef points and rehoisting it to spread a larger area to the wind.

SHAKINGS, the seaman's term to describe the ends of old rope and canvas to be unpicked for making *oakum.

SHALLOP, (1) a light, small vessel of about 25 tons, originally usually *schooner-rigged but later more frequently rigged with *lug sails, used for fishing. Being fast and weatherly, particularly with the lugsail rig, they were also frequently employed as tenders to men-of-war during the days of sailing navies. **(2)** A large, heavy, undecked boat with a single mast, *fore-and-aft rigged. In many cases in the 17th and 18th centuries when ships were driven ashore in storms, contemporary accounts mention the ship's carpenters building a shallop from the timber of the wrecked ship to enable some of the crew to sail to a nearby port to summon assistance. **(3)** A small French coastal *gunboat of the 18th and early 19th centuries, single-masted and armed with one gun. They were known as *chaloupes* and carried a crew of about forty men. **(4)** The term was also frequently used also to describe a *skiff rowed by one or two men.

SHAMAL, the name given to the prevailing wind from the north-west in the Persian Gulf.

SHAMROCK, the name of five racing yachts owned by Sir Thomas *Lipton for the five consecutive challenges, all unsuccessful, which he made for the *America*'s Cup in 1899, 1901, 1903, 1920, and 1930. The first *Shamrock*, a *cutter of 103 tons displacement spreading 13,400 sq ft of sail, was beaten by the American defender *Columbia. Shamrock II displaced 128 tons and spread 14,000 sq ft of canvas but was again beaten in three races by Columbia, though by very narrow margins. Shamrock III, of 139 tons, came up against the Reliance, designed on the skimming-dish principle with a *fin keel, and had little chance of success. She was the first of the series to have a wheel in place of a *tiller for steering. Shamrock IV, built in 1914, was half-way across the Atlantic when the First World War (1914–18) was declared. She continued her passage and was laid up in the U.S.A. until the races in 1920. With William Burton at the wheel, she won the first two out of five races but lost the Cup when the defending yacht Resolute beat her in the last three. The last Shamrock was built, like the American defender *Enterprise, to the *J-class rule. She was the first challenger to be built to Lloyd's *scantlings and also the first to set a *Bermuda mainsail. She was, however, no match for the Enterprise, which won every race with ease. She was the last of Lipton's yachts, her owner being 80 years old at the time of his last challenge; after his death she was bought and raced by Mr. T. O. M. *Sopwith.

SHAN, the name given to defects in wooden spars usually caused by knots in the wood when they contract and fall out, or to naval plank that had been sawn obliquely to the central axis of the tree. It is used mainly as an adjective, as 'a length of shan timber' or 'the timber is shan', but the word has now almost completely disappeared.

SHANGHAI, to, or to be shanghaied, said of a sailor when he is shipped against his will, usually under the influence of drink or drugs, as one of the crew of a ship. The practice of shanghai-ing was especially prevalent in the U.S.A. during the 19th century at a time when the reputations of many captains and their *'bucko' mates for ferocity in getting work out of their crews made normal recruitment unlikely. The sailors were delivered to the ships by *crimps, who ran the boarding houses in large ports in which seamen used to congregate, tempted there by women and drink, and who received payment from a ship's captain for every man they could ship aboard on the eve of sailing.

The term comes from the U.S.A., but its origin is obscure. It might possibly have arisen from the Australian word 'shanghai', meaning catapult, in that the unfortunate seamen were catapulted off to sea as soon as they were made insensible.

SHANK, that part of an *anchor which connects the arms to the anchor ring.

SHANNON, H.M.S., a name borne by eight ships of the Royal Navy between 1757 and 1922. The most famous was the *frigate, which mounted fifty-two guns, launched at Frindsbury in 1806. Commanded by Captain Philip Bowes Vere *Broke, she fought the epic battle with the U.S. frigate *Chesapeake of fifty guns, commanded by Captain James *Lawrence, off Boston on 1 June 1813. After a bitter and annihilating action which lasted only 15 minutes, the Chesapeake surrendered. Of her crew 61, including the captain, were killed or mortally wounded and 85 were more or less severely wounded. The Shannon had 33 killed, including her first lieutenant, and 50 wounded. Broke, himself severely wounded, received a baronetcy after this action. Later, in 1832, this Shannon became a *receiving ship at Sheerness and was renamed St. Lawrence in 1844. She was broken up at Chatham in 1859.

Another Shannon, a screw frigate launched at Portsmouth in 1855, added more glory to the name by the deeds of her Naval Brigade in India during the Mutiny in 1857–8. Her captain was William Peel who won the Victoria Cross for his courage and leadership in this campaign. The Royal Navy's last ship of the name was a 1st class armoured *cruiser launched at Chatham in 1906. She was present at the battle of *Jutland in 1916 and was sold for breaking up in 1922.

SHANTY or **CHANTEY,** old ships' songs sung on board to lighten the labour of working the ship. They were broadly divided into two classes, the *capstan shanties, designed to produce a continuous effort such as would be required from men heaving on the capstan bars, and *halyard shanties, where the accent was placed on occasional words or notes to encourage the men to pull together, as when *swaying up a spar. They all follow the same pattern, with short solo verses and rollicking choruses. Many of them have become famous as much for their tunes as for their words, such as 'Shenandoah', 'Rolling Home', 'Billy Boy', 'Bound for the Rio Grande', and perhaps best known of all, 'Blow the Man Down'. With the coming of steam to do much of the hard work of the ship, the shanty lost its purpose and was no longer used at sea, and by 1875 had disappeared in its proper context, being heard only as a turn in a concert-party or a sing-song.

The earliest known example of a true shanty, sung to co-ordinate the efforts of men working on the capstan bars, occurs in the Complaynt of Scotland, published about 1450, and 'Haul the Bowline' must be very nearly as old as in the earliest days of sail the *bowline was the most important rope in a ship. The words of many shanties often varied from ship to ship, sometimes to incorporate local personalities or to lengthen the words of a song: if the words ran out before a task was completed, a good shanty-man could improvise new words to keep the song going without a break. But though the words might differ, the tunes never varied.

Shanties were essentially merchant service songs, and were rarely heard in warships. The reason for this was that merchant ships were frequently undermanned so that the owners might make the more profit, and encouragement in the form of a shanty was necessary to make up for loss in numbers by proper co-ordination of the physical efforts put out by each man. Warships, on the other hand, were in comparison overmanned, the large number of men required to man the guns in battle being almost always available for the purely seamanship duties which required a heavy effort, such as weighing an anchor or swaying up a main * yard.

SHAPE, to, a verb frequently used in relation to the * course selected by the navigator for a ship to sail; e.g., 'a course was shaped to avoid some danger'; 'we will shape a course to reach such-and-such a destination'.

SHARP or **SHARPE, BARTHOLOMEW** (*c.* 1650–1688), * buccaneer, served under Henry * Morgan in the first piratical attack on Panama in 1671 and was a leader in the second in 1679. Having marched with his followers across the Isthmus of Panama, he seized a Spanish ship to cruise to the southward off the coasts of Peru and Chile. Later, while still in the Pacific, his buccaneering band broke up, some like William * Dampier returning to the Atlantic across the Panama Isthmus, the rest remaining with Sharp. On 29 July 1681 Sharp captured the Spanish ship *Rosario*, finding on board 'a Spanish manuscript of a prodigious value', a * derroterro, or atlas, of the South Seas. 'Also I took in this prize another jewell, viz., a young lady about 18 years of age, a very comely creature.' History does not relate the fate of the other 'jewell', but the book of Spanish charts undoubtedly saved Sharp's life. After a remarkable voyage to the West Indies round Cape Horn (he was the first Englishman to round it), Sharp made his way back to London, had his Spanish book of charts translated, and presented it to Charles II in time to receive an acquittal when tried on a charge of piracy. Charles made him a captain in the navy and he was appointed to command the * sloop *Bonetta*. But the call of a buccaneering life was too strong for him to resist. He deserted his ship, captured a small Dutch vessel off Ramsgate, and sailed back to the West Indies. He was last heard of as commander of a nest of pirates in the island of Anguilla.

SHARP UP, the description of a square-rigged ship with her sails trimmed up as near as possible to the wind and with her * yards * braced up as far fore-and-aft as the lee rigging will allow.

SHARPIE, a type of oyster * dredger which originated among the oystermen of New Haven, Connecticut, U.S.A., about 1830. Having a flat bottom with single * chines and a large wooden * centreboard, sharpies were built in sizes from 30 to 60 feet in length as oyster dredgers in Chesapeake Bay. They were developed later as flat-bottomed cruising yachts. The traditional colonial rig was a * ketch rig with jib-headed (* Bermuda) sails and no * headsails. The name came to be used during the decade preceding the Second World War to describe a class of small, hard-chine racing boat with a Bermudian * sloop rig which became very popular for racing in coastal waters at local regattas.

SHARPSHOOTER, a type of small work boat with a straight * stem, a * transom stern, and fixed * keel, from 25 to 28 feet (7·5–8·5 m) in length, native to the Bahamas, and thus often known as a Bahama sharpshooter to distinguish it from the small racing class of the same name. The sharply raked mast carries a jib-headed mainsail with sometimes a foresail on a long * bowsprit.

SHEAR, to, a ship is subject to the strain of shearing when its bow, midship section, and stern are poised on the crests of succeeding waves, with the portions of the hull between in the hollows between the waves. Shearing is similar to sagging (see SAG, TO) except that three wave crests are involved instead of two.

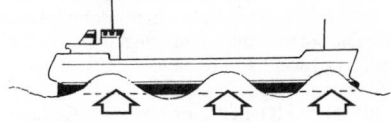

Shearing

SHEATHING, a covering of thin copper plates secured to the bottom of wooden ships to give protection against the activities of the *Teredo navalis*, a large wood-boring worm which exists in tropical seas. A mixture of tar and horsehair was laid between the sheathing and the bottom as an additional preservative for the wood. Although * junks were seen sheathed in eastern waters in the early part of the 17th century, it was not until 100 years later that the practice spread to Europe. It was more or less universal by 1780. In earlier years lead had been used for sheathing; earlier still deals or planks of fir had been used for this purpose. Neither proved satisfactory; the lead setting up a corrosive action with the iron bolts of the planking and also proving difficult to keep secured in position so that it did not peel off in a seaway, and the soft wood planks providing no barrier to the activities of the teredo worm.

Sheathing had another purpose as well as

defence against the teredo worm; it significantly improved the sailing qualities of ships by being more resistant to weed and barnacles than the bare wood of a ship's bottom.

SHEAVE, the revolving wheel in a *block. They are mostly made of *lignum vitae* or brass, sometimes a combination of the two, in which case the brass forms the bush of the sheave. The older name for a sheave is *shiver, and many seamen today spell sheave as shiv, using the same pronunciation.

SHEEPSHANK, a hitch made in a rope temporarily to shorten it. It consists of two long *bights in the rope and a half hitch over the end of each bight made in the standing part of the rope. A knotted sheepshank is formed by passing the two ends of the rope through the *eyes of the bights.

Sheepshank

SHEER, (1) the upward curve of the deck of a ship towards the bows and stern, with the lowest point of the upper deck level in the *waist. REVERSE SHEER, a downward curve of the deck level towards the bows and stern, the highest deck level amidships. Some cruising and ocean-racing yachts have been built to this principle chiefly in order to provide more head-room below the deck. **(2)** The angle which a ship takes to her *cable when lying to an *anchor, caused by the effects of wind and/or tide.

SHEER DRAUGHT, a drawing made during the design stages of a ship showing her outline in elevation, together with the spacing of her *frames. See also SHIPBUILDING.

SHEER LEGS or **SHEERS,** a temporary structure of two or three spars raised at an angle and lashed together at the point of intersection. With the aid of a *tackle secured to this point, sheers are used for lifting heavy weights on board ship where *derricks are not available. Their main original use was for lifting in and out the lower masts of square-rigged ships.

SHEER POLE, a horizontal steel rod fitted at the base of the *shrouds supporting a mast. It is attached (seized) to each shroud just above its rigging screw (see BOTTLESCREW) and serves to keep any turns out of the shrouds when they are being set up.

SHEER STRAKE, the top *strake, or plank, of a wooden vessel next below the *gunwale. It runs from *stem to *stern, level with the upper deck of the vessel. See also GARBOARD STRAKE, which is the bottom strake of such a vessel, next the *keel.

SHEET, a *purchase or single line used for trimming a sail to the wind. A square sail set on a *yard has two sheets, one to each *clew; fore-and-aft sails have only a single sheet to the clew.

SHEET ANCHOR, an additional anchor carried in the largest ships for security should the *bower anchors fail to hold the ship. Originally two additional anchors were carried, one at either *chesstree abaft the fore rigging, one anchor termed the sheet, the other the spare. The present practice in ships of any size is to carry the sheet anchor in its own *hawsepipe abaft the *starboard bower anchor, complete with its own cable and cable-holder and ready to let go at any moment. The term sheet anchor is also used as a synonym for security generally.

SHEET BEND, also sometimes known as a swab hitch, a hitch used to secure a rope's end through a small *eye, as, for example, in securing a boat's *lazy painter to the eye at the end of a *Jacob's ladder hanging from a lower *boom. It is a

Sheet bend

simple knot in which the end of the rope is threaded through the eye and the end led round the eye and underneath its own standing part so that it is jammed, or nipped, in the eye. The greater the pull on the rope, the tighter the nip. A double sheet bend is a similar knot but with the end of the rope led twice underneath the eye instead of once. A sheet bend is also sometimes used temporarily to join two ropes of approximately the same size, the end of one being passed through a bight in the other, round both parts of the other rope, and back underneath its own part.

The origin of the name presumably came from its original use as the means of bending a *sheet to the *clew of a small sail such as a *lugsail.

SHELL, the outer part or body of a *block inside which the sheave revolves. The shells of wooden blocks are *scored to hold the *strop with which they are bound (stropped) and which embrace the *eye or hook, at the top or bottom of the block.

SHELLBACK, a slang name given to an old sailor, in theory one who has been at sea for so long that there has been time for limpets or barnacles to grow on his back. It was originally employed in a slightly derogatory sense to indicate an old seaman who was old-fashioned and had failed to move with the times, but later became almost a term of affection as indicating an old seaman whose knowledge of seamanship was vast and who had much to teach the young-ster in his profession.

SHELVOCKE, GEORGE (1675–1742), British *privateer, was born at Deptford and entered the Royal Navy in about 1690, serving through the remainder of the War of the League of Augsburg (1689–97). He became a lieutenant in 1704, and in 1707 was made *purser of the *Monck*, a less honourable though more lucrative position than that of lieutenant. He came out of the navy in 1713 and fell into great poverty. In 1718 he approached a syndicate which was about to fit out two *privateers to operate against Spain and was offered command of the expedition with John Clipperton as his second-in-command. While the two vessels, the *Success* and *Speed-well*, were fitting out, Shelvocke took matters so much into his own hand that the syndicate of owners reversed the command structure, making Shelvocke second-in-command to Clipperton.

The two ships sailed with British *letters of marque, in February 1719, with Shelvocke secretly determined to give Clipperton the slip at the first opportunity. He succeeded in doing so at the Cape Verde Islands, and then proceeded on his own into the South Seas, acting much more as an out-and-out pirate than as a privateer. It was while the *Speedwell* was sailing through the Straits of le Maire that there occurred the well-known incident when Simon Hatley, second-in-command of the ship, shot a black *albatross which had been following the ship for several days, the action which gave Coleridge the theme for his 'Rime of the *Ancient Mariner'.

The *Speedwell* made her way to Juan Fernan-dez Island, capturing a number of *prizes on the way, and here she was lost probably through Shelvocke's carelessness. It was also here that the last vestiges of discipline on board broke down, the crew putting themselves under *Jamaica discipline, dividing up the plunder so far ac-quired into shares according to the rank held. Even then, Shelvocke was able to hide some of the plunder from the crew, which he then appro-priated to his own share.

From Juan Fernandez Shelvocke continued his piratical voyage in the Spanish ship *Sacra Familia* which had been captured, touching the coast of California where he claimed to have found gold, and bringing some on board which he subsequently lost in China. Had he managed to retain it until reaching England, the Califor-nian gold rush of 1848 might well have taken place more than a century earlier.

On his return to England in August 1722 Shelvocke was imprisoned, at the instance of the owners, but there was insufficient evidence to condemn him on a charge of *piracy. One of fraudulent conversion was then preferred, but before it could be heard Shelvocke escaped from the King's Bench Prison, it was thought by brib-ing a warder. He fled to France to escape the trial, but subsequently returned to England, dying at the home of his son in Lombard Street, London.

In 1726 Shelvocke published an entertaining but doubtful account of the expedition with the title *A Voyage Round the World*. A manuscript account, which Shelvocke presented to the Admiralty in 1724, is still in the Naval Library there. It is in a professional copyist's hand but contains many corrections made by Shelvocke himself.

SHERMAN, FORREST PERCIVAL (1896–1951), American admiral, was born in New Hampshire and saw service in the Mediterranean during the First World War (1914–18). After the war he specialized in naval aviation, becom-ing a pilot in 1922, and during the Second World War he commanded the *aircraft carrier *Wasp* in the Pacific, and was in her when she was sunk by the Japanese in the Solomon Islands area in September 1942. He was chief of staff to the commander of the air force of the Pacific Fleet and later deputy chief of staff to the commander-in-chief, returning to Washington in December 1945 to become deputy Chief of Naval Opera-tions.

Four years later he was made Chief of Naval Operations, but died in Naples, Italy, while on a military–diplomatic visit to Europe.

SHIFT, a term used at sea to denote a change in the direction of the wind. It is less positive than the terms *veer and *back, which indicate which way the wind is shifting. In a purely naval sense,

Roman merchant ship; engraving from a relief on a Pompeian tomb

and used as a verb, it indicates a change of clothing. 'Hands to shift into working rig', an order to change into working clothes.

SHIFTER, an old naval term for the cook's mate, one of whose chief duties was shifting, washing, and steeping the salted provisions stowed in casks in the ship's hold. The steeping, done to reduce the amount of salt acquired by the provisions during their long stowage in brine, was usually performed in a cask either on deck in the vicinity of the *galley or secured outboard over the ship's side.

'This day there came to the ship's side a monstrous great fish (I thinke it was a Gobarto) which put up his head to the steepe tubs where ye cooke was in shifting the victuals, whom I thought the fish would have carried away.' *The Second voyage to Benin ... with a ship called the Richard of Arundell*, Richard *Hakluyt, *Principal Navigations*, IV, p. 300.

SHIFTING-BOARDS, longitudinal wooden *bulkheads temporarily erected in the *holds of ships when a bulk cargo which is liable to shift in heavy seas, such as coal, grain, etc., is taken on board.

SHIP, from the Old English *scip*, the generic name for sea-going vessels, as opposed to *boats, originally personified as masculine but by the 16th century almost universally expressed as feminine. In strict maritime usage the word also signifies a particular type of vessel, one with a *bowsprit and three masts, each with topmast and *topgallant mast, and square-rigged on all three masts, but this narrow definition did not, even in the days of sail, invalidate the generic use of the term to encompass all types of sea-going vessels.

The genesis of the ship is lost in the mists of antiquity, beginning when man first thought to use a river or the sea as a means of conveying himself and his goods from one place or another, initially by means probably of a *raft loosely constructed of tree trunks, branches, or bundles of reeds. The need to acquire additional buoyancy and stowage space was first met by means of a hollowed-out tree trunk, and so by natural evolution this waterborne means of conveyance developed to the planked craft on an essential framework of *stem and *stern pieces fixed to a *keel, and with *ribs to support the two sides. This is, in its essentials, the basis on which ships are still constructed today.

The stages of development of the ship from the first tentative sea-going examples to the various types in use today relate more to development in the means of propulsion than to particular changes in the shipwright's art, the shape and purpose of a ship being limited more by its means of propulsion than by any other single consideration.

1. PROPULSION WITH OARS

(a) **The most ancient ship** of which present-day knowledge exists is the oared funeral ship of the Pharaoh Cheops (3969–3908 B.C.) which was preserved in a trench cut in the rock alongside his tomb. It had a length of 133 feet and a maximum beam of 26 feet, and over 600 individual pieces of wood, some of up to 75 feet in length, were used in her construction. It is unlikely that this particular vessel ever went to sea, or even ever floated on water, since she was constructed purely as a funeral ship for burial alongside her pharaoh, nor is it reasonable to assume that she was necessarily the first such ship to be built, but from the contemporary tomb paintings it is known that ships of similar design, though generally of smaller size, were in fact sea-going at that period. Their only means of propulsion at this early stage of development was by oars pulled by rowers. Such evidence as can be deduced from these paintings would appear to point to the fact that the early Egyptian ships were of a single, basic, one-purpose design, no difference being visible between the construction of a ship used for state purposes or pleasure, commerce or war. Illustrations of sea fights indicate that Egypt was not the only Mediterranean nation which deployed sea-going ships. The period covered by these single-design ships lasted approximately until 1000 B.C.

(b) **The war *galley.** The Phoenicians, whose empire grew around the Mediterranean between about 1000 B.C. and 250 B.C., were the people who gave the greatest impetus to ship development during these early years. Great traders and colonizers, they developed from the Egyptian model the war galley, rowed by disciplined banks of rowers, as *biremes, *triremes, etc., armed with, as a main weapon, a pointed *ram on the bow at or just below water level and carrying fighting men employed as archers and stone slingers. The galley, as a ship of war, lasted until about the year 1700 in the Mediterranean, but in more northern waters with a generally more tempestuous sea, it was superseded some 700 years earlier, the last examples in those seas being the Scandinavian *longships which, though not strictly galleys, relied on the oar as a main means of propulsion, but were fitted also with a short mast carrying a square sail on a *yard which could be braced for working to windward.

(c) **The purely merchant ship.** A further development by the Phoenicians from the original Egyptian model was the purely merchant ship, ranging from the relatively small broad-beamed *gaulus*, for local trade between Phoenicia and her adjacent neighbours and colonies (Egypt, Greece, Cyprus, etc.), and the great Tarshish-ships which traded to Spain and north-western Africa, venturing beyond the Straits of *Gibraltar into the Atlantic and reaching as far south as Mauretania and as far north as the tin-bearing Scilly Islands. According to Herodotus, a Phoenician fleet circumnavigated Africa in the 7th century B.C., taking three years on the voyage, which if true argues a surprising degree of constructive and navigational skill for those early days. In addition to oars, these ships carried a square sail on a single mast for running before the wind. Some of the larger ships carried in addition a *spritsail on a foremast heavily raked forward in the nature of a high-steeved bowsprit.

2. SAIL

By around the year A.D. 1000 sail was beginning to oust the oar as the prime means of ship propulsion in all but Mediterranean waters. The single square sail carried by some of the Mediterranean galleys to provide a period of rest to the rowers when the wind was fair, and also for the same reason by the Scandinavian longships, although in their case the yard could be braced for sailing to windward, was developed from one mast to two, and then to three, and from one sail per mast to two, three, or more. The invention during the 12th century of the *rudder, hung from the *sternpost, in place of the *steering oar

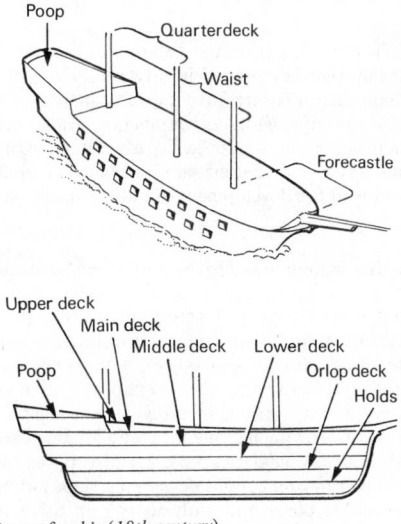

Parts of a ship (18th century)

Mediterranean ships in Venice c. 1500; detail of a painting by V. Carpaccio

which projected from the *starboard quarter of the ship (later developed into two steering oars, one on each quarter), gave a greater manoeuvrability to ships and, in conjunction with such modifications as longer keels, a greater length/beam ratio, and flatter sails, provided a great impetus in the development of more efficient sail plans.

(a) The sailing warship was relatively slow to develop as an exclusive type of ship, the general practice in the early days of sail being to hire merchant ships for this purpose in time of war. The introduction of gunpowder, with its obvious corollary of providing the warship with its own means of battle instead of being, as previously, a means of carrying fighting men who fought at sea with basically land weapons, led directly to the various seafaring nations developing ships purely for war purposes and with no role in times of peace. The first such ships were low-freeboard, wall-sided ships with guns mounted on *poop and *forecastle, but as guns developed in size and numbers, it became necessary for reasons of stability to mount them as low as possible in the ship, leading to a change in hull form to give an increase of *freeboard with a pronounced *tumble-home. High castles were erected at bow and stern to give a better field of fire for small anti-personnel guns and muskets, and also to provide a defence against boarders entering the ship by the *waist between the two castles. These ships, however, were poor performers when sailing on a wind, as the high forecastle resulted in their bows being blown down to *leeward.

In general, the largest warships built during these early years of their development were of about 500 tons, but in the early years of the 15th century some English shipwrights produced ships of twice this size. During the second half of the 16th century, again in England, the high forecastle was abandoned as a feature of warship

The Thames, *an East Indiaman of 1,424 tons; etching by E. W. Cooke, 1829*

building, resulting in a faster and more weatherly ship (see HAWKINS, Sir John). The English pattern was followed by the shipbuilders of other European nations, and the general design of sailing warship became universally similar, differing only in size and number of guns mounted.

During the 17th and 18th centuries, and the first few years of the 19th, there was virtually no significant advance in design in the sailing warship, ships merely increasing in overall size up to a final tonnage, by mid-19th century, of about 3,000, such ships carrying up to about 130 guns on three gundecks.

From the mid-18th century, most European nations had divided their principal warships into six *rates according to the number of guns they mounted. The first three rates, and occasionally the fourth, were recognized as *ships of the line, that is, ships with an armament powerful enough to lie in the *line of battle. Fifth and sixth rate ships were known as *frigates, with varying duties in war ranging from active participation in battles as signal repeating ships with the main fleets to *convoy escort duty. All these six rates of ships had the standard three masts, square-rigged on each mast. Subsidiary warship types, such as *brigs, *sloops, etc., proliferated in all navies for other war duties outside the scope of the main battle fleets.

(b) Merchant shipping. In the field of merchant shipping, design during the years of sail changed more rapidly than with warships. Originally, when time spent on a voyage was of little economic importance, the average sailing merchant ship had a length/beam ratio of about three to one, chiefly to provide the maximum carrying space available. The usual rig was simpler than in the warship, with often no more than two sails on each of two masts. The reason for this simplicity was that owners could not afford the size of crew carried in a warship and, with fewer working men on board, had need to simplify the essential daily tasks in working the ship.

Until about 1500, the average merchant ship was small, the *caravel of up to about 250 tons being a typical example. With the great discoveries in the 15th century of an all-sea route to the east and a new world to the west, and the consequent leap in trade which followed the opening of these new markets, the merchant ship made a substantial advance both in size and design, typified perhaps by the Spanish *carrack, of which the largest reached as much as 1,600 tons. It was the new trade to the east, where the immense profits of the early voyages attracted the attention of all European maritime nations, that was responsible for a further surge in development. *East India Companies were formed in all the principal seafaring nations to develop this trade, endowed in the main with peculiar powers of expansion and self-government by their sponsoring countries, and the promise of great profits led to a surge of ship development to take advantage of the vast opportunities which were offered by the East. *East Indiamen, as these ships were called, grew in size and design eventually to outstrip even the conventional warship, and they carried guns to an extent where they were able, with some degree of confidence, to defend themselves from the attacks of foreign warships. See, for example, DANCE, Sir Nathaniel, who in 1809, when bringing home a convoy of East Indiamen, outmanoeuvred and beat off the attack of a squadron of French warships in the Straits of Malacca.

With the continuing growth in trade during the 17th, 18th, and 19th centuries, and the consequent importance of time on voyage in relation to profits, the sailing merchant ship once again changed her design to improve her speed, mainly by increasing her length/beam ratio to five or six to one and by improving her rig through an increase in the number of sails carried on each mast. It was during the latter part of this period of increased competition that some owners increased the number of masts in their ships to four or five.

Even after the introduction of steam propulsion in ships, there remained for many years a profitable existence for merchant ships under sail. At first, the limitations of sufficient bunker space for long trans-ocean voyages made the steamship an uneconomic medium of transport except for relatively short voyages, and even after this disability had been overcome, certain trades and trade routes still offered advantages to the sailing merchant ship. The China tea trade and the Australian wool trade were examples in which the sailing ship not only held distinct advantages over the steamer but also stimulated the building of such magnificent ships as the *Lightning, *Cutty Sark, *Thermopylae, etc. This trade continued until, in 1869, the Suez Canal was opened, which so shortened the voyage to those places that the steam-driven merchant ship was able to capture the existing trade. The nitrate trade from South American nations on the Pacific coast remained in the hands of sailing ships until 1914, when, similarly, the opening of the *Panama Canal made it more profitable to use steamships. It was this South American trade which lifted the design of the sailing merchant ship to its highest peak of perfection. It was protected for so long a period by the inability of the steam-driven ship to use the Cape Horn route, and the competitive aspect of the trade encouraged the development of the great four-masted *barques and five-masted *schooners which were the epitome of grace and

power. Except in schooners, the fore-and-aft rig was never adopted in the larger sailing-ships except as a half-and-half measure in *barquentines and *brigantines. See also SAIL, RIG, RIGGING.

Today steam and diesel engine propulsion have, with one or two minor exceptions, completely ousted the use of sail for purposes of trade. At the time of writing (1976) between thirty and forty of the great sailing vessels remain in commission as sail training ships; some others are preserved as museum ships and memorials of the sailing era. One of the few types of sailing vessel still actively retained in trade is the sailing *barge, based on the River Thames and East Anglia in Britain, and used for local conveyance of goods.

Only one area remains where the use of sail is still predominant, that of pleasure sailing (see YACHTING, Sail), where the variety of rig and hull design can still present a stimulus to the art of the marine architect.

3. STEAM

The invention of the first efficient steam engine, patented by James Watt in 1769 and with subsequent improvements protected by patents of 1775, 1781, and 1782, was introduced into waterborne transport when the steam-propelled *Charlotte Dundas made her first appearance in 1802 on the Forth and Clyde Canal. Since that first introduction, steam propulsion made steady progress until it became ubiquitous in all spheres of maritime use.

(a) Warship design. In warship design, steam was slower to become adopted as the prime mover mainly because of the vulnerability to gunfire of paddle-wheels and their protective paddle-boxes, which until the invention of the *propeller were the only means of transforming the power of the engine to movement through the water. When, between 1840 and 1850, the propeller became established as in every way more efficient than paddle-wheels (see ALECTO, H.M.S., RATTLER, H.M.S.), most existing ships in all navies were lengthened and adapted to install a steam engine and propeller, although for many years steam was seen only as an auxiliary means of propulsion, with masts, yards, and sails being retained in all major warships. In many navies, among them particularly that of Great Britain, the addiction to masts and sails continued for years after they had become obsolete, mainly through a conservative resistance to change, and a belief that a true seaman could only be trained through the use of sail and the drills connected with it. It was not until the decade 1880–90 that sails finally disappeared from navies.

The Crimean War (1854–6), and particularly the burning of a Turkish squadron of wooden ships by the fire of Russian shells at *Sinope in November 1853, was responsible for the

H.M.S. Inflexible, *battleship launched in 1887; contemporary engraving*

H.M.S. Good Hope, *Cradock's flagship at the battle of Coronel, 1914*

introduction of iron as a material for naval ship-building, in either the form of iron plates bolted on to an existing wooden hull or iron construction from the keel up. Although the suitability of iron as a shipbuilding material had been demonstrated in the merchant vessel *Aaron Manby as early as 1820, the first warship to be built in iron, as opposed to iron plates on a wooden backing, was. H.M.S. *Warrior, built at Blackwall on the River Thames and launched in December 1860. She was a *battleship of 9,210 tons with a single expansion trunk engine of 5,270 i.h.p. driving a single centreline propeller.

This lead of building in iron was followed by all navies in the world, iron being replaced by steel in 1875–80. During the decade 1860–70, the compound steam engine was introduced, followed about ten years later by the triple expansion engine, which remained in favour as the ultimate development of the steam reciprocating engine until the introduction (1900–10) of the steam turbine.

Ships of all navies were divided into classes according to their function in war, ranging from *battleships of up to 45,000–50,000 tons (in 1937 the Japanese Navy built two exceptionally large battleships of 65,000 tons, the *Yamato* and the *Mushashi*), *aircraft carriers of similar or even greater tonnage, *cruisers, *destroyers, and *frigates. The battleship as a class of warship virtually disappeared from all navies after the end of the Second World War. *Submarines, with a very few exceptions, and minor war vessels now rely on the diesel engine or the gas turbine for their propulsion, and are thus included in section (4) under. See also NAVY.

(b) Merchant shipping generally made the transition from sail to steam and from wood to iron much more rapidly than warships, the vulnerability of paddle-wheels to gunfire not being an inhibiting factor. The first steamship to cross the Atlantic entirely under steam and without recourse to sails was the *Sirius, which made the passage in 1838; the first merchant vessel using iron for her hull was the *Aaron Manby* which in 1820 steamed from London to Paris and initiated a regular passenger service. The screw propeller, first tried out in 1838 in the 237-ton steamship *Archimedes*, proved so superior to the paddle-wheel that the engineer Isambard *Brunel incorporated it in place of paddle-wheels in his new iron ship, the *Great Britain, of 3,270 tons, which was laid down in 1839 and launched in 1845. Compound engines, with one high and one low pressure cylinder, were introduced by John Elder in 1854, and in 1874 Dr. A. C. Kirk fitted the first triple-expansion engine in the steamer *Propontis*. This first triple-expansion engine was not a success because the average pressure of steam generated by ships' boilers was only 40 lb

per square inch, but the introduction of forced or induced draught in ships' boilers raised the average pressure to 125 lb per square inch, at which level the triple-expansion engine proved both efficient and economical. At the turn of the 19th century the steam turbine was introduced by Sir Charles *Parsons and quickly made its mark as the most economical (in terms of conversion of engine power into propeller thrust) and efficient method of steam propulsion for ships.

The reliability and speed of steamships at sea, combined with the immense increase in world trade which followed the industrial revolution, had a big effect on the size of ships. Until 1850, the largest steamship built was the 3,270-ton *Great Britain*. In 1853 Brunel laid down the *Great Eastern*, originally named *Leviathan*, a vessel 688 feet long with a tonnage of 18,914 and engines to produce 11,000 horsepower. She was launched in 1858 but the world was not as yet ready for a ship of that size, and she proved a failure. Yet only thirty years later there were many ships of such size, mainly in the passenger-carrying trade, and during the first half of the 20th century the size of passenger *liners increased nearly fivefold. Today air travel has cut deeply into the viability of the seaborne passenger trade, and such liners as are built are normally of less than half the tonnage of those built during the great years of expansion.

In merchant shipping the trend has been exactly opposite, and it is only in comparatively recent years that tonnages have increased dramatically. Until 1945, the largest merchant vessels, including oil *tankers, were of around 50,000 tons; by 1970, a large bulk carrier ship averaged about 100,000–120,000 tons, while tankers of 275,000 tons were not uncommon. A Japanese tanker, *Nisseki Maru*, of 372,000 tons has been commissioned, while others of 800,000 tons are under construction or planned.

(c) Fishing vessels. Steam propulsion was introduced into fishing vessels towards the end of the 19th century, at first in the long-distance *trawlers, and only later into the smaller inshore fishing craft, such as *drifters. With the later development of the diesel engine, steam propulsion has virtually disappeared from the smaller fishing vessels and today is only found in the large *whale and fish factory ships.

(d) Yachting. Steam power became something in the nature of a status symbol in yachts in the mid-19th century, and continued to flourish for about seventy years until the diesel engine took over. The steam yacht was an expression of an owner's wealth and importance, not quite rivalling in size the official *royal yachts of reigning monarchs but often surpassing them in the luxury and magnificence of their internal decoration and fittings. See also YACHTING, Power.

The U.S. liner United States, *last holder of the Blue Riband of the Atlantic*

4. INTERNAL COMBUSTION ENGINE

(a) Naval vessels. The introduction, around the end of the 19th century, of the internal combustion petrol engine and, a few years later, the diesel engine had at first only a limited application to naval vessels. It solved a problem for the submarine where the need was for a compact engine to produce power for surface propulsion and to drive the electric motors as dynamos to recharge batteries. The earliest submarines were fitted with petrol-driven engines, always a possible source of danger from fire, until the development, around 1910, of the diesel engine provided a reliable substitute. During the First World War (1914–18), petrol engines were used in smaller war craft such as motor launches and coastal motor boats, and the only attempted use of the diesel in a large warship was in the British *minelayer/cruiser *Adventure*, launched in 1926. During the Second World War diesel and petrol engines were employed in a large variety of small craft, such as landing craft for amphibious operations, *motor torpedo and gun boats, etc., and since the war the gas turbine has been developed for use in fast patrol craft and some frigates.

(b) Merchant shipping. The greatest development of the diesel has been in the field of merchant shipping, where it has been found, when speed is not the prime consideration, to be the most economical means of propulsion. A great proportion of the world's tramp shipping uses diesel propulsion, and in other fields, such as cargo liners, *ferries, etc., the diesel has replaced the older steam engine.

(c) Fishing craft. Most modern fishing craft, except the large factory ships, are now powered by diesel engines.

(d) Yachts. The use of the petrol engine in yachts began during the first decade of the 20th century, almost entirely as small auxiliary engines in sailing yachts. Some small motor yachts were also built, particularly between the two world wars when several races were organized for powered yachts. The improvement during this same period of diesel engines led to their substitution in the larger powered yachts for steam propulsion, being more economical both in the space they occupied and in the engine-room complement required to run and maintain them. They are used either in direct drive to the propellers or in conjunction with electric drive. Since the end of the Second World War, power boat racing has been developed into a considerable sport, with a big increase in the number of craft now powered by petrol engines and, in some cases, by large outboard engines.

5. NUCLEAR POWER

Within the last ten or twelve years nuclear power has emerged as a means of ship propulsion. It is almost entirely restricted to naval use, mainly in submarines, where its almost unlimited endurance without the need of refuelling and its property of requiring no oxygen during combustion makes it an ideal means of submarine propulsion. Its use in the field of merchant shipping is inhibited both by the immense cost of installation and by the need for heavy shielding against radiation. In the U.S.A. an experimental merchant ship, the * Savannah, was constructed with nuclear propulsion but was not a success, while in the U.S.S.R. a large ice-breaker, the * Lenin, was built for use on the * North-East passage. Further nuclear ice-breakers for use in these waters are being constructed.

R. Lindsay, *History of Merchant Shipping*, 4 vols (1874); M. Vocino, *Ships Through the Ages* (Milan, 1951); B. Landström, *The Ship* (1961); E. H. H. Archibald, *The Wooden Fighting Ship* (1968); B. W. Bathe, *Seven Centuries of Sea Travel* (1972).

SHIP, THE, the title of a novel written by C. S. * Forester and published in 1943. It was based on the Second World War * cruiser action during the second battle of Sirte in the Mediterranean in 1942.

SHIP BROKER, an agent who acts for the owners or charterers of a ship in securing cargoes, clearances, and any other business, including insurance, connected with merchant shipping. He also negotiates the sale and purchase of merchant ships.

SHIP OF THE LINE, a warship of the days of sailing navies which carried a sufficiently large gun armament to lie in the line of battle. Until the time of the First Dutch War (1652–4), fleets of warships did not fight in formation, each ship sailing into battle with the purpose of finding an enemy vessel she could engage in single combat. The first attempt to make a fleet fight in formation was made by Robert * Blake at the battle of * Portland in 1653, but the * line of battle as such did not emerge until the Second Dutch War (1665–7), when fleets were more rigidly controlled by their admirals. And because a ship's guns of those days had no means of being trained, but could only fire through their * gunports at right angles to the fore-and-aft line of the ship, the line of battle had obviously to be in the line ahead formation, with each ship following in the track of her next ahead. This formation was rigidly laid down in the * Fighting Instructions issued to all admirals and captains of ships, and governed the conduct of all British ships in action.

Around the turn of the 17th century, in order to get a greater degree of regularity in naval shipbuilding and design, warships were rated according to the number of guns they carried. In the British Navy six * rates of ship were introduced, and of these ships of the first three rates were considered powerful enough to lie in the line of battle. They were therefore known generically as ships of the line. In some cases fourth rates, which were ships with from fifty to seventy guns, were included in the line of battle, depending on the composition of the enemy fleet, but they were not ships of the line in the generally accepted sense of the term. Fifth and sixth rates, generically known as * frigates, never fought in the line of battle, being stationed separately in battle with other duties than fighting. See also RATE.

SHIP STABILIZERS, equipment and/or fittings incorporated in the construction of a ship to dampen down rolling in a seaway in order to provide a steadier and more comfortable passage through the sea. Perhaps the earliest experiments in reducing a tendency to rolling can be found in the three ships designed by Sir William Petty in 1663–4, of which the *Experiment*, launched on 11 December 1664, was a double-keeled ship. 'It swims and looks finely, and I believe will do well,' wrote Samuel * Pepys in his *Diary* on the day of the launch. In fact, it didn't.

* Bilge keels, which are normally steel plate projections running fore and aft along each side of a ship's hull usually just below the turn of the bilge, are designed to take the weight of the ship on her launching * ways and in * dry-dock, but through the * athwartship resistance they create when the ship rolls they also act as a moderate roll damping or stabilizing device. They were first introduced with this in view in the design of the * *Great Eastern* in 1854 but are now a commonplace in the design of ships of any size. In addition, automatic stabilizers operated by gyroscopic control were incorporated in the design of large passenger * liners following their introduction by the shipbuilding firm of Denny–Brown during the 1930s. They have a naval significance in addition to a commercial one, as they produce a steadier gun platform for smaller warships when operating in a seaway. Gyro-operated stabilizers in large ships are retractable into compartments inside the hull below the waterline, and are thus stowed while the ship is in narrow waters or in port. They are extended for operation only when required at sea. The stabilizer is in the form of a pivoted fin or horizontal rudder like those used for effecting fore-and-aft trim in a * submarine; as the vessel begins to roll and thus deviate from the fixed plane of a gyroscope, the stabilizing mechanism comes into play and the angle of the fin is made to vary against the ship's tendency to roll.

In addition to some warships and most passenger liners, ship stabilizers are also fitted in some fishing vessels, particularly those which fish off the south-western coast of Africa where the average sea conditions normally produce excessive rolling. In many small craft, up to around 90 feet (27 m) in length, such as fishing *trawlers and motor yachts, only one stabilizer need be fitted, either to *port or *starboard as design dictates. In the smaller sizes these stabilizing fins are not retractable into the hull.

SHIPBUILDING. In the dawn of seafaring history man graduated from boats made of skins stretched over a cane framework and rafts made of papyrus reeds, and had learned to construct ships of planks hewn and fashioned from trees, which were at first fastened together with leather thongs, then with wooden pegs or *treenails, and later with iron spikes. The early Egyptians knew well how to dovetail and scarf timbers together and to render the *seams watertight with pitch or resin, camel hair, and teased rope; for trees tall enough to cut into long planks were not readily available and all the planks in the hull of an Egyptian ship had to be in short lengths. There were in consequence hundreds of scarfs and joints.

The Egyptian ships of the Eighteenth Dynasty (some 1 500 years B.C.) built for commerce were about 25 metres (82 ft) in length and some 5 metres (16½ ft) in breadth. A single mast amidships—sometimes formed of two poles lashed together at the top to form an A-type strut and arranged at the base to lower when not needed—carried a broad squaresail with, in addition to the long *yard at the head, a spar of the same length at the foot of the sail. By means of *sheets and *braces, clearly shown in ancient tomb reliefs illustrating contemporary ships, the yard could be braced round until the vessel was able to sail with the wind almost on the beam. With a fresh fair wind such ships would sail fast, making up to nine *knots. In calms or light head winds they could be propelled by from twelve to sixteen oars a side, the Egyptian rowers standing up to their work and facing the stern. A deep-laden merchant vessel would make up to three knots under oars alone, and for periods limited only by the stamina of the rowers. Steering of all ships of antiquity was by means of a long oar or paddle which was generally pivoted at the ship's stern quarter on the steerboard (or *starboard) side. In such merchantmen the Egyptians carried cargoes up and down the Nile, and on long coasting voyages down the east coast of Africa to trade with the Land of Punt, or modern Somalia.

Phoenician shipbuilding. After the Egyptians, the sea-minded Phoenicians put out in their ships from harbours on the coast of what is now known as Lebanon, and voyaged the length and breadth of the Mediterranean, venturing out beyond the Pillars of Hercules—the Straits of Gibraltar—into the Atlantic and along the western coasts of Europe to the shores of Britain, where their most sought-after commodity, tin, was to be traded. Although usually no larger than the Egyptian ships, for shipwrights had not yet learned how to construct much bigger wooden vessels with the necessary longitudinal strength to stay at sea in bad weather, the Phoenician ships were generally sturdier and safer at sea. They too carried a single squaresail on a mast amidships, which could be lowered and stowed inboard when the wind came ahead, and the oarsmen—as many as forty in some ships—would take over, working the long oars while seated on benches facing aft. By such sail- and oar-propelled ships before the birth of Christ was trade carried throughout the Mediterranean, and to accommodate this trade, harbours were built and cities grew up with access to the sea.

Roman shipbuilding. With the growth of the Roman Empire many more ships were needed, both for transporting military material and troops to the new outposts and for carrying cargoes, especially for transporting the immense quantities of corn from Egypt needed to feed Rome's populace. Fine engineers and accomplished imitators, the Romans built their own fleets improving on everything they had noted in the ships of neighbouring countries. The typical Roman merchant vessel was of a very different type from the early Egyptian, Phoenician, or Greek ships, being capacious, broad, full-bodied, and round-ended, much more heavily constructed with massive *frames and *stem and *sternpost, and capable of carrying as much as 400 tons of cargo. Known as a *corbita*, this type of freighter set on a mast amidships a single large squaresail with two triangular, or *raffee, topsails above the yard; and to help in steering, there was also an *artemon, a small squaresail, set on a forward-raking mast over the bows—like a well-*steeved *bowsprit of later centuries. The *corbita* was steered with two deep oars, one on each quarter, which in strong winds and high seas required as many as four men on each oar to control the vessel. In such sturdy ships the Romans carried out their commerce by sea, and during the first century A.D. were making regular seasonal voyages between Red Sea ports and the west coast of India.

The Norse longships. After them the Norsemen left their Scandinavian shores in their *longships to make epic voyages in the North Atlantic and down through the Bay of Biscay into the Mediterranean. Like the Phoenician ships the Vikings' vessels were long and slender, but lightly constructed and with little *draught so as to be easy to propel with oars when the wind failed, and to be able to make fast and long passages under a single squaresail when the winds served. Unlike the smooth-planked Mediterranean ships the Viking longboats were *clinker-built with overlapping strakes which were fastened together with leather thongs. The method of building ships with smooth, or *carvel, planking was not adopted in Western Europe for almost another 400 years. But another invention, slow in development, arrived towards the end of the 12th century when ships in Northern Europe began to be built with straight, instead of curved, sternposts, and it was found far more convenient to move the side steering oar and mount it on *gudgeons and *pintles on the sternpost. With what now came to be known as the *rudder, even the largest vessels of the day became more controllable.

Shipbuilding in the Middle Ages. Through the Middle Ages merchant ships followed a similar pattern with full-bodied round hulls (they were generally known as *'round ships'), the beam of some as much as half the length, carrying squaresails on one and, later, two masts, and still dependent on the tides and a fair slant of wind to make their destination, for they were too heavy to be propelled with oars. Fighting ships introduced the need for raised platforms at the bow and over the stern for the archers and slingers of stones and blazing pitch, and in time these raised additions became built as part of the hull and called the *forecastle (fo'c'sle) and aftercastle, later to become the *poop deck. With the introduction early in the 15th century of great guns which, because of their weight, had to be carried below the upper deck to shoot through gunports cut in the ship's sides, the vessel's topsides began to be given a distinct inward slope, or *tumble-home, to preserve stability while carrying more guns of a smaller size on the upper deck. To withstand the strains on the ship's structure of heavy guns firing, and the shocks delivered from broadsides in battle, fighting ships had to be especially strong, and all their main timbers securely locked and bolted together. The increasing size of merchant vessels and the weightier cargoes they carried also necessitated heavier construction to endure the wrenching strains on the hull labouring in a seaway, and the wringing strains when grounding in a swell.

Until late in the 16th century, when plans for constructing new ships began to be drawn up by the originators of the naval architect's profession, and a ship was planned on paper before the keel was laid, the trade of the shipwright had been a closely guarded one, handed down from father to son. Ships had been built through the centuries solely 'by eye' with the shipwright's own know-how using the rule-of-thumb methods

of tradition. But improvements in ship construction were introduced only slowly against deep-rooted suspicion and dogmatism. The wooden ships which *Nelson commanded at *Trafalgar were little better in their design and details of construction than had been the ships that *Howard, *Drake, and *Hawkins led out to meet the Spanish *Armada. But by the 1840s ships were reaching the ultimate size that could safely be built in timber, and there was already an embarrassing shortage of good shipbuilding timbers in Western Europe.

Introduction of iron. A new material for large ships was already a pressing need and the industrial revolution produced the answer through the increasing use of iron for the new steam engines, for industrial machinery and buildings, and for new bridges. With hulls manufactured of iron ships could safely be increased in length and still remain strong and rigid, while the methods of building them became more enlightened and scientific. At first, however, the few shipyards that turned over to working in iron copied all the methods they had long used in constructing wooden hulls, endeavouring to reproduce their individual parts in wrought iron or with castings. A fresh line of thinking with an engineer's approach to the problem was called for, and with the advent in 1843 of Isambard *Brunel's second steamship, the *Great Britain, of 3,270 tons gross and the first oceangoing iron screw ship, greatly improved methods of ship construction were shown to the shipping world. These innovations of Brunel's included iron *stringers of girder section running the full length of the vessel fore and aft and ensuring longitudinal strength, an inner as well as an outer bottom with cellular construction in between, bulkheads dividing the vessel into a number of watertight compartments, and great strength in all directions throughout the hull. Many owners and shipyards still baulked at the notion of having ships built entirely of iron ('Whoever heard of iron floating?' was a rallying cry of the doubters), but obvious advantages in strength, cargo-carrying capacity, and watertightness of iron ships induced some shipyards to adopt a form of composite construction. In this a skeleton of iron frames and fore-and-aft stringers, floor plates, *keelson, and cross bracing was covered with traditional wooden planks for bottom, topsides, and decks. Composite construction was adopted for many *clipper ships during the 1850s and 1860s, but later abandoned except for some large yachts.

Improvements in marine engines. Hand in hand with the ever-increasing size of merchant vessels and warships went steady improvements in methods of propulsion, both aloft in ships' spars, *rigging, and sail plans, and below decks in

Building the Great Eastern: *construction of the central compartment; engraving from the* Illustrated London News

power and efficiency in the engine room. The wasteful low-pressure engines of the 1820–50 period, when boiler pressures rose from 2 lb to only some 20 lb per square inch, were superseded by the more economical *compound engine in the 1860s, working at 60 lb pressure, and this in turn was eclipsed in the next decade by the *triple expansion engine, which used steam at 120 lb and more three times over before it was exhausted into the condenser for re-use in the boilers.

Introduction of steel. About the same time the introduction of the Siemens process which dramatically brought down the cost of manufacturing steel made it economical to build merchant vessels of steel. With its high tensile strength, the steel used in the plating and all other metal parts of the hull could be reduced by some 25 per cent. This resulted in an appreciable saving of weight which meant either a lower consumption of coal for a given speed in service, or in a passenger ship an extra knot or so of speed with the same engine power. One disadvantage in using mild steel in shipbuilding, however, is the rapidity with which it corrodes and rusts compared with wrought iron. Shipyards know well that from the moment the keel of a steel vessel is laid every part throughout will be steadily rusting, and

if for any reason building is held up for long periods, some form of rust inhibitor such as a red lead-based paint must be applied to prevent excessive wastage. And during the whole life of the ship in service scraping and painting has to be carried on whenever conditions allow. Modern treatment of steel plating before assembly and new synthetic rust-inhibiting compounds promise to minimize this bugbear of the steel-built ship, while the hoped-for reduction in the cost of producing corrosion-resistant light alloys would revolutionize building and maintenance problems in the shipping industry.

Launching. The launch of a big new ship is always a matter of concern for both the shipyard officials and for the naval architect responsible for the design. In the past grave problems have on occasion been met before a new vessel has slid into the water and floated at her designed marks, the classic case being that of Brunel's third and largest ship, the *Great Eastern*. A giant for her day in 1858, and not surpassed in tonnage for almost thirty years, she gave all concerned with her months of anxiety when she refused to move broadside down the launching ways at Millwall and her builders went into liquidation over her, until at last a number of hydraulic rams inched her into the waters of the Thames to begin her far from happy career as the world's biggest steam-ship. It is asserted that these months of anxiety and strenuous effort were the cause of her designer's death.

Launching techniques have improved enormously since that day, and it is unusual to encounter severe problems in launching at modern yards, even when they have built such monsters as super-tankers of 300,000 tons or more. Ships are normally launched stern first at the top of the tide—*l'heure de la mer*, as the French picturesquely call high water—with a series of heavy drag chains which are picked up in rotation as the vessel moves down the ways so that she will be checked and held as soon as she is fully afloat. The moment of possible crisis is just when the stern becomes waterborne and the weight of the forward half of the ship is still carried on the slipway. A ship has been known to stick at this point and refuse to be moved again, so that when the tide fell her stern became unsupported and her hull was badly strained. A successful launch which goes off so smoothly as to seem a matter of simple routine to the lay public is more often a moment of quiet relief to all those in charge.

The naval architect's part. Although ship draughts and preliminary drawings had been the work of naval architects for nearly three cen-turies, and many large ships had been built to plans already prepared by their designers, their work on the whole, like the shipwright's, was unscientific and generally followed specifications of shape and *scantlings which had been in use for generations. It was not until William *Froude's experiments with ship models in test tanks during the 1870s that naval architects were encouraged to approach the design of ships on a more critical basis. From then on naval architecture assumed a much greater importance in the design of the new and faster steamships and in improvements in the performance of sailing ships. No ship is built today without her design being meticulously prepared and an enormous number of calculations made concerning the strength of various parts of her hull, allowances for bending, *sagging, and *hogging when she is labouring in a seaway, the calculated weight or *displacement of the completed ship, the horsepower of the engines required for the service speed demanded, the carrying capacity of her cargo holds, and much else. Ships cost so much—some millions of pounds for the biggest oceangoing ships—that the owners cannot afford to take any chances before their ship is built.

In practice the ship designer, or naval architect, is first consulted and given the owners' exact requirements for their new ship. Anticipating the service conditions under which the vessel will

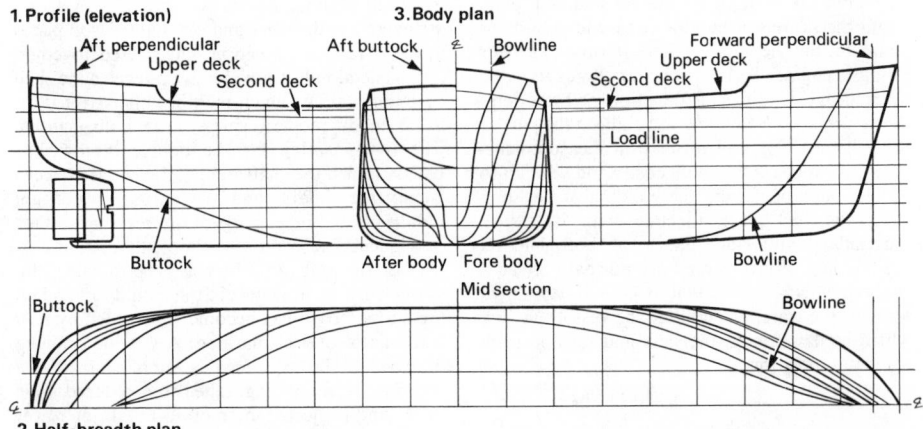

1. Profile (elevation)

Aft perpendicular
Upper deck
Second deck
Aft buttock
Bowline
3. Body plan
Forward perpendicular
Upper deck
Second deck
Load line

Buttock
After body | Fore body
Bowline

Mid section

Buttock
Bowline

2. Half-breadth plan

Simplified sheer draught plan for a medium size cargo vessel

have to work, as well as the general climatic conditions in the parts of the world where she will operate, he and his assistants will produce a preliminary outline drawing of the proposed vessel to a scale small enough to make the plan convenient to handle for discussion. This will be submitted to the owners with the designer's rough estimates of displacement, cargo capacity (or deadweight), horsepower of engines, fuel capacity and consumption at service speed, and other essentials. If the ship is of a normal design which has been based on preceding vessels of the same company and the design is approved, work on the detailed plans will go ahead. In the case of a vessel of unusual type, or a large and costly ship like a passenger liner, big tanker, or bulk carrier, the plans will be sent to one of the ship model test tanks which are available to shipbuilders in all the principal maritime countries.

At this establishment a large-scale model of the vessel, usually from 10 to 20 feet (3–6 m) in length, will be made in a malleable material such as wax using the electronic eye method to guide the blades of the cutters shaping the hull to exactly the lines on the designer's plan. The model will be submitted to a series of runs at various scale speeds and other tests under varying simulated sea conditions, until sufficient performance and behaviour data are collated by means of elaborate electronic recording devices. If during these tests it is found that some modification of the design is advisable—to achieve, say, a better speed or lower fuel consumption, or less tendency to pitch into a head sea—this can be carried out on the wax model using the same electronic monitor and scriving tool on the model. Any saving in fuel costs or improvement in behaviour of a vessel in heavy seas is well worth the relatively minor costs of such tank tests.

Architect's plans. The real work of the naval architect now begins on the drawing board. The first working drawing comprises three views of the vessel which are drawn to the same scale and presented at right angles one to another. Commonly referred to as the sheer draught, this drawing shows (1) the elevation or outline of the ship as viewed broadside on (the sheer plan), and (2) a half-breadth plan as viewed from above (half the breadth only as both sides of the ship are assumed to be identical), and (3) an end-on view called the body plan. This sheer draught will indicate the positions of the bulkheads and the main structural parts, the holds and machinery spaces, together with the run of the decks; and upon this key plan all subsequent plans will be based.

The construction plans are next to be drawn. The principal of these is the midship section, or body plan, which shows the system of construction together with the dimensions (the scantlings) of the principal parts of the hull and deck. On the side view, or elevation drawing, in many cases every individual steel plate forming the outer skin of the ship's hull will be shown and indicated by numbers. From these data detailed measurements of the numerous steel plates and angles and cross braces are sent to the steel makers, each member being dimensioned for its particular place in the ship and duly so marked by the steel worker.

Methods of construction. In the traditional methods of construction the exact shape of all the plates and other parts of the hull is obtained by having the lines on the plan projected full scale on to the mould loft floor. From these lines full-scale patterns or templates are made up and supplied to the steel workers. Each item when made is marked and numbered to correspond to its numbered position on the construction plan. From the same source also come the moulds or templates for the vessel's stem, sternpost, rudder fittings, engine beds, propeller brackets, and other heavy forgings. Production of these templates demands both care and skill on the part of the loftsmen, for any mistake in measurements here can lead to errors both costly and difficult to correct later on during the building of the ship. After the keel plate, together with its centre longitudinal and rider plate, has been laid on the building blocks, which are normally given a slight inclination of about one in thirty down towards the water to facilitate the vessel's launch when the day comes, the stem and sternpost are erected in position.

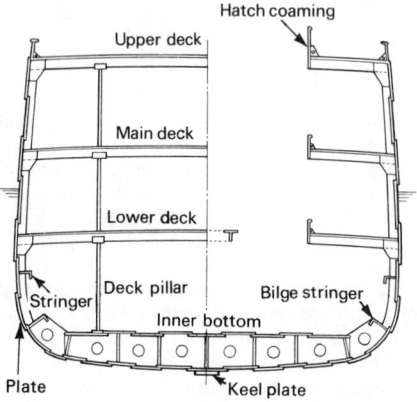

Mid section of a typical medium size general cargo vessel of traditional riveted construction (size of plates exaggerated for clarity)

The frames, the vessel's ribs, are next to be prepared. In the well-tried methods still in use in many shipyards throughout the world, this is accomplished by means of a scrive board which is made up with a full-size drawing showing the shape of each frame throughout the ship. From this all necessary measurements are taken for the men whose job it is to prepare the frames. The exact form of each frame is transferred from this drawing to the bending slabs (heavy plates drilled with small holes a few inches apart into which iron pegs can be inserted) and a length of light bar iron is bent between the pegs into the appropriate curve. The frame angle bar is then drawn from the furnace in a state of bright heat and quickly bent around the bar to the shape required. The reverse bar, together with its connecting floor plate, is prepared in a similar fashion and the whole assembly riveted together to form one complete frame. The completed frames are erected in their proper order across the keel plate, and after being adjusted into their correct position are secured by braces and wooden shores in a manner similar to scaffolding.

The hull plating. Beams for the various decks, stringers running fore and aft, and keelson plates are lowered into position and riveted together. The skeletal hull is now ready to receive the shell or outer plating, which may be either riveted or, as in many modern ships, welded throughout. The inner plating for the double bottom, the ballast tanks, the shaft tunnel, the between decks supporting pillars, and the various watertight bulkheads and other parts of the vessel are added in sequence according to the methods and custom of the shipyard. In many up-to-date shipyards work on drawings in the mould loft and on the scrive board has become superseded by new methods of optical marking. A $\frac{1}{10}$ scale drawing of parts to be fashioned is supplied from the drawing office, photographed to a reduced scale of $\frac{1}{100}$, and projected in an optical marking tower at full size on to the steel plate. The lines so marked on the plate enable the part to be cut or burnt out to the correct size. Many yards also use a plate-burning machine which reduces time and labour even more. A $\frac{1}{10}$ scale drawing is fixed to a table and an electronic eye (as in the ship testing tank model-making department) is made to follow the lines of the drawing while at the same time its movement controls from one to four flame jets (burning heads) which burn out to full size the exact shape of the plate on the drawing. Drawings down to $\frac{1}{100}$ scale can be used in this machine in the same manner. Computer control is also being increasingly introduced in modern shipyard production, thereby eliminating many drawings and even some of the naval architect's more laborious work. In time it is probable that computers will do away with the need to have a mould loft or even a $\frac{1}{10}$ scale drawing office and its staff.

Except in cargo vessels and coasters which normally have steel decks, some parts of the upper decks of any large ship are usually covered with wood. The planks traditionally may be of yellow pine for a passenger vessel, and teak for service in the tropics, laid with their seams running fore and aft. The planks vary from about $3\frac{1}{2}$ in. to $5\frac{1}{2}$ in. (89–144 mm) in width and from $2\frac{1}{2}$ in. to $3\frac{1}{2}$ in. (63–89 mm) in thickness, but new materials for ship's decks are being introduced from the plastics industry.

Internal fittings. With the hull completed the work of installing the fresh water and oil fuel systems, the air-conditioning and refrigeration plant, the water sprinkler system to conform with current fire risk regulations, and the general arrangement of plumbing throughout the vessel is put in hand before, or immediately after, the ship has been launched. Once afloat, however, the vessel is moved to her fitting-out berth where the engines and auxiliary machinery, and the boilers if she is a steamship, are lowered into position by the giant shipyard cranes. Among the jobs which help to make a modern ship such a complicated microcosm of machinery and technology is the fitting of the various telecommunication and electrical control systems throughout.

Each ship is built, whether of riveted or welded construction, to scantlings and methods which must conform to the classification rules of *Lloyd's, Bureau Veritas, or whatever registration society governs shipbuilding in the country of the shipyard. In many many modern passenger vessels and large freighters the built-up superstructure, such as the *bridge and cabins above the spar deck, are fabricated in aluminium alloy. This light-weight metal, whose density is a little over one-third that of mild steel (2,730 kg/m³ or 170 lb/cu. ft as against 7,860 kg/m³ or 490 lb/cu. ft) allows such a saving in weight where it most greatly affects the vessel's stability—high above the waterline—that its considerably higher cost is justified in certain types of ship.

Prefabrication. In modern shipbuilding the whole bridge unit and other deck structures are prefabricated, whether in steel or light alloy, and lowered into position as the ship is built. Prefabrication plays a major part in modernized yards in routine construction of ships of a similar type. This is especially so in the building of tankers, a type of vessel that lends itself to unit quantity production. Whole sections of the hull, such as the stem, *forefoot, and bow, are prefabricated in a series of erecting shops laid out on a rapid production plan adjacent to the building berth, and lifted into position by cranes capable of handling from 40 to 80 Mg (40 to 80 tons) apiece. Few yards in the world, however, have yet equalled the impressive degree of standardization and unit prefabrication that was introduced by the Kaiser Corporation in the U.S.A in the production of hundreds of *Liberty ships of some 7,000 Mg (7,000 tons) gross with completely standardized all-welded hulls and steam machinery during the Second World War. See also SHIP.

YACHTS

The design of yachts. Unlike merchant vessels whose sides for a long way amidships are usually straight and flat, the hulls of yachts usually follow a curve along their entire length. The art of the yacht designer, whether professional or amateur, has understandably therefore been likened to a form of sculpture on paper. Faced with a client's requirements, or the need to meet exacting *rating rules, the yacht designer, like the naval architect, begins by submitting preliminary drawings, and goes on to estimate roughly the yacht's displacement or total weight

in sailing trim, the weight of *ballast in the keel (in cast iron or lead) needed to give her the stability to stand up to the desired sail area, and the quantities of engine fuel and fresh water to be carried.

The completed plans which will be supplied to the yacht yard for building the vessel normally comprise the following:

(1) The lines plan. This is the equivalent of the merchant ship's sheer draught plan, and shows the yacht's hull form from three viewpoints at right angles to one another: the elevation, the half-breadth plan, and the body plan. Drawn usually to a scale from 1:24 to 1:12 (or 1:10 if metric) according to the size of the yacht, this plan shows accurately the curve of each cross-section (or frame station) in the body plan, and each of a series of level lines (or waterlines) spaced at regular intervals between the keel and the deck edge.

(2) Table of offsets. Often incorporated in the lines plan, this list of ordinates for all the curved lines and frame stations on the hull is used by the builder for shaping the moulds or patterns around which the hull will be built to the exact measurements on the drawing.

(3) General arrangement plan. This shows the layout of the accommodation below deck in both elevation and plan, together with a number of cross-sections (or half-sections) indicating how the interior arrangements are to be fitted in relation to the curved inside of the hull at various points.

(4) Construction plan. This gives details of all principal parts of the hull, ballast keel, decks, etc., with sizes and materials specified.

(5) Sail and rigging plan. An elevation view of the yacht afloat which gives positions and measurements of all the sails, the various sizes and types of standing rigging, and details of mast(s) and spars.

(6) Engine installation drawing, which may also include details of electrical installations, fuel and fresh water tanks, plumbing, deck winches and fittings, and individual ironwork for use by the yard engineers and foundry.

Traditional building methods. For many decades yachts were built by the methods which were traditional for contemporary wooden merchant vessels, *barges, and *smacks. The wood keel, of oak, elm, pitch pine, or other local timber, was laid on the slipway or on building blocks, and the wooden stem, sternpost, and stern frame bolted into place. The various frames (or ribs) were sawn to shape and erected in their respective positions along both sides of the keel from stem

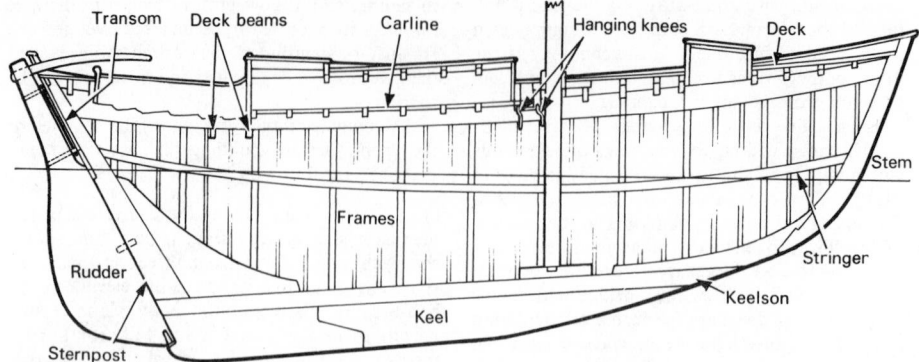

Profile construction of a typical wooden yacht

to stern, the lower ends of each pair being fastened to floor frames which were commonly oak crooks laid athwart the top of the keel. An inner keel, or keelson, was sometimes bolted on to the tops of the floor frames and running from the inside of the stem to the sternpost. Beam shelves, running from bow to stern and fastened to the inside of the head of every frame, carried the outboard ends of the deck beams which in turn were fastened to the shelves, often with a half-dovetail joint. Openings in the deck beams for hatches or skylights were joined by *carlines, square-sectioned lengths of timber to which the upright *coamings were fastened. At all junctions beneath the deck where the racking strains of hard sailing in heavy seas were greatest, oak crook *knees or wrought iron angle plates were bolted to give rigid strength.

The planking of the hull was fastened to the frames and floors with galvanized iron spikes, bronze bolts, or in the smaller yachts with cop-

per square-sectioned nails riveted over copper collars (or rooves) on the inside of every frame. The work of planking the vessels was started at the plank next the keel (the *garboard strake) on each side, and continued in sequence up to the turn of the *bilge, while other planks were fastened on from the deck edge (the sheer strake) downwards, until the final gap between the two sets of planks could be filled in with an exactly fitting shutter strake. Deck planks, traditionally of white pine or teak, were laid fore and aft usually following the curve of the wide *covering board at the yacht's side. The seams between the planks, cut in the form of a deep V, were caulked with cotton and payed with hot pitch. The seams of the hull planking were likewise caulked with cotton (teased rope or *oakum for the merchant vessels) and finished smooth and flush with a patent stopping mixture which never set hard enough to crack when the seams worked in a seaway.

Towards the end of the 19th century sawn frames were replaced in the smaller yachts by steam-bent timbers, and this has remained standard boatbuilding practice for wood-built yachts under about 14 m (45 ft) to today. In building a hull for steam-bent framing, after the keel is laid and stem and sternpost erected, moulds, or patterns, cut to the shape and measurements on the designer's plan to fit inside the planking and spaced at their appropriate stations throughout the vessel, are erected and on each side thin lengths of wood (called splines) are temporarily screwed to the edges of the moulds, running from bow to stern and spaced roughly 15 to 23 cm (6 to 9 in.) apart. Each frame-timber is then made pliable by heating in a steam box, and while still boiling hot is smartly bent into shape on the inside of the splines, with its lower end fitting into a check slot already cut in the side of the keel. When all the timbers are thus in place and temporarily fastened to the splines, the splines are removed one by one as the planks of the hull are laid in place, being fastened to the timbers by

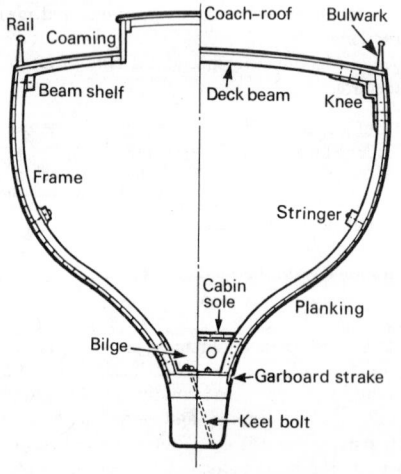

Sections through typical yacht of wooden construction

copper nails and rooves. Steam-bent timbering is suitable for either *carvel or *clinker (lapstrake) planking.

Modern developments. Developments in design and building techniques, together with the introduction of many new materials, have revolutionized yacht building since the Second World War. Water-resistant marine plywood, introduced during the war, opened up the possibilities for amateur builders to construct their own craft in back gardens, and numerous new designs were made available to yachtsmen to plank in plywood from small dinghies up to 12-m (40 ft) cruising yachts. Glass reinforced polyester resins (G.R.P.) enabled all kinds of small vessels, from dinghies to 18-m (60 ft) yachts and even larger fishing boats and harbour craft, to be produced from a mould, identical in size and form and in large numbers. G.R.P. production yachts in the United Kingdom, U.S.A., France, Denmark, Sweden, and other yacht-building countries far outnumber boats built of wood, while other methods of construction such as cold-moulded laminates fixed with resin glue over a mould have produced many lightweight dinghies and yachts for racing. Other successful racing yachts have been constructed on the foam sandwich principle, the hull being formed over a mould from two G.R.P. skins enclosing a centre core of polystyrene, balsa wood, or other very light material, the total weight being appreciably less than a similar hull of G.R.P. or wood.

Added to other amateur home-building techniques is the *ferrocement or ferroconcrete boat, in which a closely knit framework of small-diameter steel pipes and 8-mm ($\frac{1}{4}$ in.) diameter reinforcing rods, criss-crossed at close spacing and wired at every joint to several layers of small size steel welded mesh, forms a strong and resilient hull of any size from about 8 m (25 ft) in length to 32 m (100 ft) or more, which is rendered homogeneous and water-tight by impregnation throughout with a fine mortar. Large numbers of yachts, fishing boats, and harbour launches have been built in ferrocement in many parts of the world, and in China sampans are made of it. Aluminium alloy is sometimes used for the hulls of racing yachts where speed is more important than cost. The principles of construction are the same as for a similar vessel in steel, but the considerably lower density of light alloy enables more ballast weight to be carried in the keel, so that the yacht can meet one of the racing designer's most important objectives—a favourable ballast-to-weight ratio. Like ship designers and builders, yachtsmen would welcome with open arms a light alloy which could be produced as cheaply as steel.

F. H. af Chapman, *Architectura Navalis Mercatoria* (1768); J. Fincham, *History of Naval Architecture* (1851); J. Peake, *Rudiments of Naval Architecture* (1851); J. Scott Russell, *Modern Systems of Naval Architecture*, 3 vols (1865); W. H. White, *Manual of Naval Architecture* (1877); G. S. Baker, *Ship Designs*, 2 vols (1933); T. Harrison Butler, *Cruising Yachts, Design and Performance*, 3rd edn. (1947); K. C. Barnaby, *Basic Naval Architecture* (1963); C. J. Watts, *Practical Yacht Construction*, 3rd edn. (1947); M. Griffiths, *Man the Shipbuilder* (1973).

SHIP-MONEY FLEETS, the annual fleets sent out by Charles I between 1635 and 1641 to assert the English sovereignty of the *Narrow Seas which at that time were beset with pirates and with Dutch fishing *busses taking fish illegally from the English fishing grounds. These fleets got their name from the fact that they were financed by the levy of a tax known as ship-money. No English parliament was sitting at that period and the king levied the tax by his own decree. Such a tax had been levied previously, frequently during the 15th and 16th centuries and again as late as 1626 when a fleet had been fitted out during the war with Spain. The form of the tax was to assess each port and maritime town with a sum of money which the mayor was to raise in whatever method he thought best. Later, as the cost of succeeding fleets grew greater, the levy was made on all towns and parishes throughout the country.

These ship-money fleets achieved the object for which they were designed, clearing the English waters of the many pirates who were operating in them and policing the east coast herring fisheries so efficiently that almost all illegal fishing by the Dutch was stopped. But as the annual levy of ship-money grew, it became more and more difficult to collect as resistance to paying it spread. Parliament was recalled in November 1641 and in January of the following year the House of Lords declared ship-money to be illegal. This brought Charles I into a head-on collision with Parliament, and in the fleet fitted out in 1642 all captains with royalist sympathies were removed from their commands. It was a signal for the start of the English civil war.

SHIP'S BELL, see BELLS.

SHIPSHAPE, a word meaning in good and seamanlike order in reference to the condition of a ship. See also BRISTOL FASHION.

SHIP'S NUMBER, see SIGNAL LETTERS.

SHIVER, the word used by some older seamen to mean the *sheave of a *block. Today, many seamen still write sheave as shiv, using the same pronunciation.

SHIVER, to, the condition of the sails of a vessel when she is brought so close to the wind that it lifts the *luffs and makes them shiver.

'SHIVER MY TIMBERS', an expression of surprise or unbelief, as when a ship strikes a rock or shoal so hard that her timbers shiver. Although the saying has an obviously nautical origin, and is widely attributed to seamen by many writers of sea stories, it is unlikely that it was one much, if at all, used by seamen at sea or ashore.

SHMIDT, OTTO YULYEVICH (1891–1956), Russian Arctic explorer and administrator, was born at Mogilev and became a university teacher of mathematics. After taking part in the Soviet–German *Pamir* expedition of 1928, he became interested in the Arctic, and in 1929 led an expedition aboard the small *ice-breaker *Georgy Sedov* to set up a scientific station in Zemlya Frantsa-Josifa (Franz Josef Land). In 1930 he became director of the Arctic Research Institute, and led another exploratory expedition in the *Georgy Sedov*, visiting Zemlya Frantsa-Josifa and Severnaya Zemlya. An island discovered in the northern part of the Kara Sea was named Ostrov Shmidta in his honour. In 1932 he led an expedition aboard the *Sibiryakov*, which made the first traverse of the northern sea route in one season (see NORTH-EAST PASSAGE), and became the first head of the new government department, the Chief Administration of the Northern Sea Route (abbreviated to Glavsevmorput in Russian), set up to promote the development of the route. In this capacity in 1933 he led a party aboard the strengthened freighter *Chelyuskin*, which attempted to make the traverse in one season, just failed, and was crushed by the ice near Bering Strait early in 1934. He led the expedition which established a party of four men on the drifting ice at the North pole in 1937, and also led the party which brought them off the ice near the East Greenland coast in early 1938.

This was his last polar, and sea-faring, exploit. He ceased to be head of Glavsevmorput in 1939, but apparently left with honour at a time when many colleagues were disgraced and executed. He devoted the rest of his life to scientific studies.

SHOAL, a derivative of the word 'shallow', indicating a patch of water in the sea with a depth less than that of the surrounding water. They are the results of banks of sand, mud, or rock on the sea bed, and are usually marked, in pilotage waters, by buoys or other sea-marks.

SHOE, (1) a pair of triangular wooden boards which were occasionally fixed to the *palm of an *anchor to increase its holding power on the bottom. An anchor thus treated was said to be shod. (2) A block of wood with a hole in it which fitted the sharp bill of the anchor *flukes to protect the ship's side when the anchor was being

*fished. (3) A term occasionally used to describe a *false keel. (4) The projection of the *keel abaft the stern frame on which the spindle of the *rudder rests. (5) A plank on which the heels of the spars forming a *sheer-legs are placed.

SHOOT, to, a verb with more than one nautical meaning. A navigator is said to shoot the sun when he takes an *altitude of it with a *sextant. A sailing vessel shoots, or *fore-reaches, when she is *luffed into the wind and makes distance to windward. A fisherman, when using a *drift net or *ring net, shoots his nets when he lays them, but the word does not apply when fishing with a *trawl. When a naval gunlayer shoots very wide of his target at sea, he is said to be shooting the *compass.

SHORE, a stout wooden timber used to back up a *bulkhead in a ship when excessive pressure is applied to it from the other side, as with a flooded compartment. The name is also used on occasions to describe a long timber secured to a small vessel's side to hold her upright when she takes the ground, but this is more often known as a *leg.

SHORT, an adjective with many uses at sea. An *anchor *cable hove in short is one on which the anchor is nearly *up and down in preparation for the vessel's weighing it and getting under way. Short allowance, or *petty warrant, was a British naval expression to indicate that, because of the victuals on board running short, or because the ship was in *dockyard hands when seamen were not expected to need full daily rations, six men were to exist on the scale of victuals for four. An increase in the monthly rate of pay, known as short allowance money, was paid in compensation. (See also SIX-UPON-FOUR.) A *short splice is a means of splicing two ropes together by tucking the *strands over and under when the rope is not required to pass through a *block. Such a splice increases the circumference of the rope. (See also LONG SPLICE.) A short sea is one in which the distance between the wave crests is less than normal.

SHORT SPLICE, a method of *splicing two ropes together where the joined rope is not required to be rove through a *block. The ends of the two ropes are unlayed and then married together with the *strands of one rope alternating with the strands of the other. Each strand is then tucked over its adjacent strand and under the next, and the splice is completed when each strand has been tucked twice. If the joined rope is intended for heavy use a third tuck is often made to provide an extra strong join. A short splice increases the diameter of the rope along the length of the splice, which is the reason why it is never employed when the joined rope is required to be used through a block. See also LONG SPLICE.

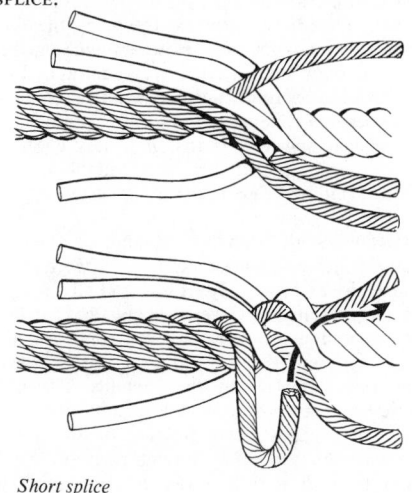

Short splice

SHORT STAY, see STAY.

SHORTEN IN, to, the operation of heaving in the *anchor *cable *short until the anchor is nearly *up and down.

SHOT, the name which applied to everything that was fired out of a naval gun except that which was filled with explosive, which was either a bomb or a shell. As Sir Henry *Mainwaring (*Seaman's Dictionary*, 1644) has it: 'There are many kinds of shot. That which flies farthest and pierces most is round shot; the next is crossbar, which is good for ropes and sails and masts, the other *langrel, which will not fly so far but is very good for the rigging and the like, and for men; so is *chain shot and *case shot, which is good to ply among men which stand naked (unprotected on deck) plying of their small shot.'

SHOVEL or **SHOVELL,** Sir CLOWDISLEY (1659–1707), English admiral, first went to sea in 1664 as a cabin-boy in the care of his kinsman, Sir Christopher *Myngs. After Myngs was killed during the Second Dutch War (1665–7), Shovel's career was forwarded by another relation, Sir John *Narborough, with whom he was probably serving at the battle of *Solebay during the Third Dutch War (1672–4).

Shovel followed Narborough to the Mediterranean in 1673. In 1676 he commanded the boats of the fleet in the operation to burn the ships in the *Barbary pirate stronghold of Tripoli and in 1677 he was promoted to *post-captain by Narborough and appointed in command of the *Sapphire.* For the next nine years he served in various ships continuously in opera-

tions against the Barbary pirates with notable success, returning at length to England in November 1686.

On the abdication of James II in 1688 he willingly transferred his allegiance to William III; after commanding the *Edgar* in the battle of *Bantry Bay, he was knighted and, as rear admiral of the *Blue, commanded a squadron in the Irish Sea during William III's campaign in Ireland.

In the battle of *Barfleur against a French fleet under the Comte de *Tourville, Shovel played a distinguished role in the victory; but sickness deprived him of a part in the subsequent destruction of the French ships by Sir George *Rooke at La Hogue. By the end of the war he had risen to admiral of the Blue and commanded the fleet in the Channel.

During the War of the Spanish Succession (1702–13), Shovel commanded a squadron in the fleet under Rooke and took a prominent part in the capture of *Gibraltar and the succeeding action off *Velez Malaga in 1704. In the following year he took over command of the fleet from Rooke as commander-in-chief, though by special commission the command was shared with the Earl of Peterborough during the latter's campaign to capture *Barcelona, the success of which was largely attributable to Shovel's conduct of the naval operations.

During 1707 the Mediterranean Fleet under Shovel operated with conspicuous skill in support of Prince Eugene's campaign in southern France which came near to capturing *Toulon and led to the *scuttling of the French fleet in that port. With that campaign at an end, Shovel sailed for home with the fleet in October 1707. Nearing the English Channel his flagship, the *Association*, and three other ships were swept in heavy weather by an unsuspected northerly current on to the Bishop and Clerk rocks off the Scilly Isles and were wrecked. Shovel, who was a very fat man, was washed overboard and floated to the shore, but was murdered by a local woman who smothered him in the sand as he lay semi-conscious on the beach. He was wearing a great emerald ring on his finger and it was for the possession of this that he was done to death. His body was later brought back to England and is buried in Westminster Abbey. The emerald ring was subsequently recovered and returned to his heirs.

'SHOW A LEG', the traditional call of the *boatswain's mates in a British warship when the hands are called to turn out in the morning. It arose from the old days when seamen, who were signed on for the duration of a ship's commission, were always refused shore leave when in harbour for fear that they would desert. Instead of shore leave, women, ostensibly wives, were allowed to live on board while the ship remained in harbour, and of course joined the men in their hammocks at night. When hands were called in the morning, the women were allowed to lie in, and the boatswain's mates, when they saw a hammock still occupied, would check the sex of the occupant by requiring him/her to show a leg over the edge of the hammock. If it was hairy, it was probably male, if hairless, probably female. The call remained in use for many years after the scandal of women living on board was finally abolished in the British Navy around 1840.

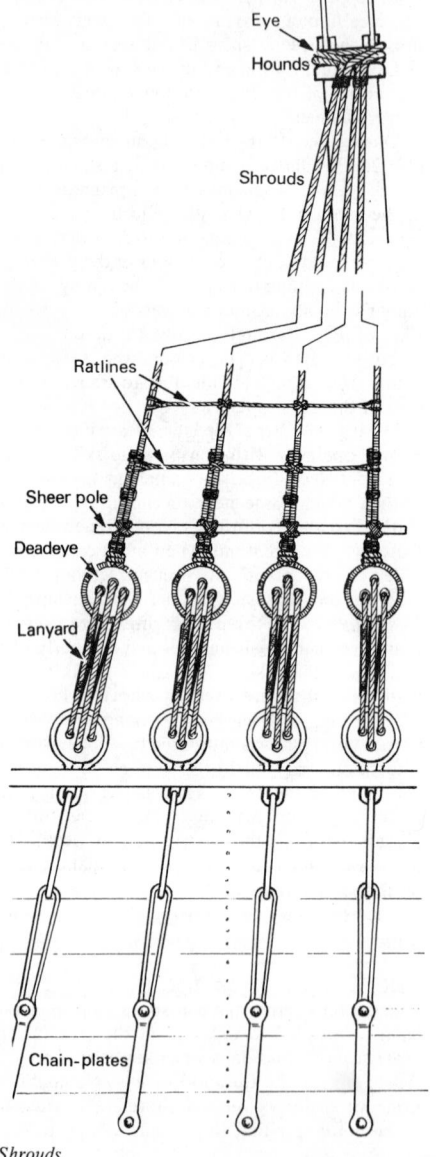

Shrouds

SHROUD-LAID ROPE, the name given to rope laid up with four *strands instead of the more usual three. In this case, the strands are laid up round a heart, or central strand, as the four strands would not bind close enough together and without a heart would leave a central hollow. Size for size, shroud-laid rope is not as strong as *hawser-laid rope having only three strands. Its advantage, however, is that it is less liable to stretch, and was therefore more suitable for use in the standing *rigging in sailing vessels.

SHROUDS, the standing *rigging of a sailing vessel which give a mast its lateral support, in the same way as *stays give it fore-and-aft support. In larger ships they were usually divided into pairs, or doubles, with an *eye spliced at the half-way point that slipped over the masthead and was supported by the *hounds. The ends were brought down to deck level and secured to the *chainplates on each side of the vessel abreast the mast, either through pairs of *deadeyes or with a turnbuckle, enabling them to be set up taut. Each mast had its shrouds, and in the larger sailing ships many pairs were used for each mast. Topmasts and *topgallant masts had their shrouds running to the edges of the *tops.
   In addition to these shrouds running from hounds or masthead to the deck, large sailing vessels had two other types of shroud, *Bentinck shrouds fixed on the *futtock staves of the lower rigging and extending to the opposite chain-plates, and futtock shrouds, which are those parts of the standing rigging between the futtock plates above the tops and the *catharpings below.
   Originally the rope used for shrouds was a finer quality of *hawser-laid rope, usually four-stranded and laid up from left to right. It was later replaced by wire rope, and in modern yacht design many mast shrouds are now made of solid bar mild steel, where its greater strength allows for a thinner shroud and consequently less windage when sailing. For illus. see RIGGING.

SHUTTER, a detachable portion of the *gunwale or *washstrake of a wooden boat fitted with *rowlocks for rowing. When removed, they provide space for an oar to be dropped into the rowlock. They were originally known as *poppets. For illus. see ROWLOCK.

SICKBAY, a compartment between decks in a large ship, in charge of the ship's doctor, which is used for the treatment of men sick or hurt, a combination of consulting room, dressing station, and hospital. It is normally fully equipped with the latest hospital equipment and a full supply of medicines and drugs. In smaller ships without a doctor or a sickbay, a medicine chest is usually carried, and men sick or injured have to rely on the skill of the captain, or perhaps some other officer with training in first aid, to diagnose and treat the ailment, often with only the aid of a medical handbook.

It was largely due to the efforts of Lord St. Vincent (see JERVIS, John), with the aid and encouragement of Andrew Baird, his fleet surgeon, that naval sickbays properly equipped and ventilated, and with hanging cots for men confined to bed, were instituted in major British warships. Before his reforms, naval sickbays were little more than a small area of the lower deck, with no ventilation and inadequate accommodation and sanitary arrangements, divided off from the rest of the deck by a canvas screen. The noise, smell, and lack of light and fresh air were hardly conducive to a return to health of the unfortunate men confined in them.

SIDELIGHTS, the red and green navigation lights which a vessel must display on either side when under way at night as a part of her *steaming lights. For details of all navigation lights, see APPENDIX 3.

SIDING, the width of the deck *beams which, in ship construction, are the transverse members of a ship's frames on which the decks are laid and supported.

SIEBE, AUGUSTUS (1788–1872), German inventor of the *diving suit, and widely known as the father of diving, was born in Saxony but as a young boy was taken by his parents to Berlin and apprenticed to a fine caster. His early interests were in modelling and chasing, but in 1812 he was called up for service in the Prussian Army and was wounded at the battle of Leipzig, in which he served as a lieutenant of artillery. When peace between Prussia and France was signed, he went to Kiel where he worked as a watchmaker, a profession he continued to follow when he came to London in 1814. His skill as a chaser brought him better employment in that art, and from that he went on to become a gunmaker. In 1820 he met C. A. Deane, who had invented an apparatus with which firemen could enter fires to extinguish them, and suggested to him that the apparatus could be adapted to enable men to work under water. He constructed an air pump and diving dress, now known as the open dress (see DIVING). He became quickly aware of the danger inherent in this dress, and followed it with the invention of the close diving helmet dress, by which the danger was removed. Through the succeeding years he made continued improvements to the helmet, introducing the inlet and outlet valves, the headpieces, and the regulating valve.

In 1848, when the engineer Sir George Pasley was engaged on removing the wreck of the *Royal George* at Spithead, Siebe was asked to demonstrate his diving suit, which was done with great success. This drew him to the attention of the British Admiralty, and after a further series of trials his dress was adapted for use in the Royal Navy.

Siebe had two sons, both of whom became experts in diving techniques and founded the firm of Siebe, Gorman and Co., one of the greatest names in the history of diving.

SIGHT, the term applied to a nautical astronomical *altitude observation of sun, moon, or star by means of which a ship's *position line can be worked out and drawn on a *chart when out of sight of land. A sight entails the simultaneous measurement of altitude, obtained with a *sextant, and of *Greenwich Mean Time (G.M.T.), obtained from a *chronometer. Many navigators when taking sights observe a rapid succession of altitudes of the observed heavenly body and the corresponding times. Each observation in this case is referred to as a shot (see SHOOT, TO). The purpose of this practice is to reduce or eliminate random errors of observation by taking as the sight the altitude and Greenwich Mean Time which correspond to the mean averages of the shots. See NAVIGATION, SEXTANT.

SIGNAL LETTERS, the four letters assigned to every ship as a means of identification, known for some reason as a ship's *number. They were hoisted using the alphabetical flags of the *International Code of Signals so that the ship could be easily identified by another ship or by coastguards, and thus reported to *Lloyd's and/or to her owners. This was the process known as 'making her number'. The allocation of these distinguishing letters is done on an international scale, each maritime nation being allocated blocks of letters from which they can assign individual groups for each ship registered in their country. In these modern days of wireless signalling, a ship's signal letters are no longer so necessary when she needs to make her identity known.

SIGNALS AT SEA. The description of the development of signalling at sea given here applies to the British Navy and is included as an example of the simultaneous development in other navies, which all followed on very similar lines.

Flag signalling. The first record of a system of communication between ship and ship in the British Navy other than by word of mouth or by message sent by boat is to be found in the *Instructions for the better ordering of the fleet in fighting* (1653) issued by the *generals-at-sea and admirals of the fleet—Robert *Blake, Richard *Deane, and George *Monck. This was a method of signalling by flags, and those used were only *ensign, *jack, a red flag, a blue flag, and a *pendant—with the addition that any of these flags could be used as a wheft, i.e., stopped (bunched up) at the head with the fly loose. The significance of each flag depended on where it was hoisted, but even when the variations so achieved the total number of meanings that could be signalled was small. By the end of the century, however, when Admiral *Russell issued the instructions that became the prototype of the so-called *Permanent Instructions* of later years, five more flags had been included—white; yellow; striped red and white, striped red, white, and blue; and the Genoese ensign (a red St. George's cross on a white ground). The Union flag (which was also the jack) was now included under that name and with the variation in hoisting positions, supplemented by the firing of particular numbers of guns, it was possible to make twenty-two manoeuvring signals for the purposes of battle tactics.

During the 18th century the number of signals that could be made by flags steadily increased, partly by adding to the variety of parti-coloured flags. Early in the century a code of *chasing signals was introduced for giving orders to individual ships for that purpose—the first signals in which *compass directions were included. From 1740 onwards many signals were added to the sailing and fighting instructions, so that by the end of the War of American Independence (1775–82) there were fifty-seven signals in the *Fighting Instructions* (general and additional) alone. During that war several officers, notably Sir Charles *Knowles, Richard *Kempenfelt, and Lord *Howe, investigated the problem of further increasing the scope of flag signalling and this was eventually achieved by including all requirements in a numbered code and specifying twenty-eight designs of flags (numbered 1 to 28) which could be used singly or in combination and could be hoisted in the most convenient position without affecting their signification. This system was first used in a main fleet during Lord Howe's final relief of *Gibraltar in 1782. Modifications in the early years of the Revolutionary War with France (1793–1801) resulted in the Admiralty issuing in 1799 the *Signal Book for the Ships of War* which remained in force with minor alterations for nearly thirty years.

In addition to signalling by flags, night and fog signals were developed as fully as the evident limitations allowed. From the 18th century to the middle of the 19th, night signals were based on arrangements of four lanterns or less, disposed in horizontal or vertical lines or in squares or triangles, sometimes supplemented by a mast-head light, either alone or with *rockets, *blue lights, or *false fires. Signals in fog could only be made by firing guns, significations being achieved

by number and timing—between groups of discharges and within each group.

The numerical signals of the 1799 *Signal Book* (about 300 were printed and there were plenty of blank spaces for manuscript additions) were supplemented in 1803 by a vocabulary signal book, known as Sir Home *Popham's *Telegraphic Signals or Marine Vocabulary*. For this a different set of numeral flags was introduced and each hoist, comprising three or four of these flags, denoted a word or phrase.

This system continued throughout the 19th century with a *General Signal Book* and a *Vocabulary Signal Book*, the only significant changes being that in the *General Signal Book* (which became the *Fleet Signal Book*) the signals were made with alphabetical flags instead of numerical and were normally limited to two flags, and the vocabulary signal hoists comprised three alphabetical flags.

This era also saw the introduction of an *International Code of Signals* based on a set of alphabetical flags and a code book in which the meanings of the various combinations of these flags were stated in the language of the ship concerned. Intended primarily for communication between merchant ships or between warships and merchant ships, it was also useful in peacetime between warships of different nations. The first advocate for such a code was Captain Frederick *Marryat, later the famous novelist, who devised one in 1817, but it was not until 1857 that the Board of Trade dealt with the matter officially. Some years later a revised code was introduced, and in 1897 there was a general agreement among all maritime nations to adopt it. See APPENDIX 2.

Though by the end of the 19th century the development of flag signalling was nearly complete, there had been in the meanwhile two important additions to signalling facilities, both derived from shore practice—the *semaphore and the *Morse code.

Telegraph or **semaphore** signals were developed both in England and in France in the last years of the 18th century. In England the original arrangement, designed and superintended by the Revd. Lord George Murray in 1796, was known as the shutter telegraph and comprised a vertical board with six large holes in its face, each of which could be opened, displaying the sky or a light, or closed. Distances between stations for passing signals along the required line depended on the lie of the land and were sometimes as much as eight miles. Four of these lines were set up: from the Admiralty to Portsmouth, Plymouth, Deal, and Yarmouth. As it was found before long that the line to Portsmouth could not carry all the signal traffic that was needed, a second line was constructed on a different principle. A tower was built for each station and on its summit was mounted a vertical spar carrying three hinged arms which could be worked by levers at the foot. It was from this that the sea-going semaphore was derived, being modified for use with only two arms, pivoted at the same point at the head of the pole. This system, which could be used with hand flags instead of the mechanical device, proved, within its limited range, the fastest form of communication between ships except for the well-known flag signals such as those for altering course. The use of the semaphore for sea service in the British Navy dates from 1866. Towards the end of the century a larger apparatus was installed at the masthead in some ships to increase the range, but this was heavier and slower and the introduction of signalling by * searchlight (see below) superseded it.

Use of the code devised by Samuel Morse to demonstrate his electric telegraph in Washington, U.S.A., in 1844, and thereafter adopted internationally, remained for some years confined to its original purpose; but in 1867 Captain (later Vice Admiral) Philip * Colomb conceived the idea that the dots and dashes could be used for short and long flashes from a lantern. His original code which the British Navy used for several years was not identical with Morse's but the latter was eventually adopted· with the addition of several special signs needed for naval purposes. This method widened the scope and eliminated the defects of the old system of night signalling. With steamships, too, the code could be used on their sirens for fog signalling.

The new method of night signalling employed in the first place an oil or candle lantern with a spring shutter. This was necessarily directional, but with the introduction of electricity, all-round signalling from a masthead flashing lamp became possible and of great value, even though it could not be used at sea in wartime for fear of being read by an enemy ship. With electricity available there were also searchlights and in 1897 Captain (later Admiral Sir Percy) * Scott devised a slatted shutter which could be fitted over a searchlight's face. This was originally intended for night signalling over long distances by the reflections in the sky, even with hills intervening, but it was soon realized that it could be used very effectively by day up to horizon distance between ships provided the light was accurately aimed, and from then on it was used extensively for long distance signalling.

Wireless telegraphy. The development of wireless telegraphy in the early years of the present century naturally had a profound effect on communications, not only from ship to ship but also from ship to shore and vice versa. At first strong electrical power and a long wavelength were needed to send signals to long distances. *Per*

contra it was thought that short-wave sets on low power would be particularly valuable for fleet work as it was assumed that they could not be detected by an enemy more than a few miles away. However it was found later that although the short waves died out on the surface, the transmissions included waves that inclined upwards and that these impinged on a layer in the atmosphere which reflected them downwards in such a way that after the first hundred miles or so the signals could again be received. Wireless telegraphy, therefore (also known as radio), though universally applicable to signalling at sea, carried with it the handicap that transmissions could always be detected by an enemy who might thereby be able to estimate the position of a transmitting ship by radio cross-bearings and perhaps interpret the signals by breaking their cyphers.

By the 1930s wireless had been extended to radio-telephony for tactical use in circumstances where enemy interception was not important.

Underwater signalling, by which communication can be established with * submarines, was in the early days of the 20th century achieved by the use of a Fessenden apparatus, by which sound waves through the water could be directed to the submarine over a distance of up to about a mile. Today, * sonar can be used, in which a supersonic beam can be transmitted to a considerably greater distance.

For non-naval signalling radio is the almost universal means used today, for communication between ship and ship and ship and shore. *The International Code of Signals* does, of course, still give ships of any nationality the opportunity of communicating with each other and with the shore, within visibility distance, in a limited number of phrases irrespective of the nationality of sender and receiver.

Sound and fog signals. Sound signals, made on a siren, steam whistle, or foghorn, are used to indicate a ship's movements to other vessels in the immediate vicinity, and a ship can indicate whether she is turning to * port or * starboard, is stopped, or is going astern by recognized numbers of blasts. Sound signals are also laid down by international regulations for use in fog, and are also used in some cases as recognition signals for * lightships, etc., when visibility is reduced by fog or mist. See also DISTRESS SIGNALS, INTERNATIONAL CODE OF SIGNALS, SIGNAL LETTERS.

SIGSBEE, CHARLES DWIGHT (1845–1923), American rear admiral, graduated from the Naval Academy in 1863. He served in the battle of * Mobile Bay and was Hydrographer of the U.S. Navy from 1893 to 1897, during which period he introduced new techniques in marine surveying. He commanded the *Maine* during the war with Spain in 1898, surviving her loss in

Havana Harbour, and then commanded the *St. Paul*, which was engaged by the Spanish *cruiser *Isabella II* off San Juan later the same year. He wrote two books, one of them an account of the sinking of the *Maine* and the other on deep sea sounding and dredging, published in 1880.

SILL, sometimes written as **CILL, (1)** the upper and lower framing, or lining, of a square *port cut in a ship's side, **(2)** the step at the bottom of the entrance of a *dry-dock and, by extension, the amount of water that a ship can draw (see DRAUGHT) if she is to be able to enter the dock over the sill.

SILVER OAR, the official badge in Britain of the High Court of Admiralty before which all maritime causes were judged. When the Admiralty Court was merged into the High Court during the 19th century, the silver oar became the badge of the Admiralty Marshal, an officer of the Court responsible for serving writs on the owners of vessels by fixing them to the mast, and for carrying out the sale of any ship ordered by the Court. While the High Court of Admiralty was an independent legal authority, the silver oar was carried before its judges during state processions in the nature of a verge, and it lay on the table before the judges while cases were being tried before the Court.

SIMONSTOWN, a South African naval base about 30 miles south of *Cape Town, on the western shore of False Bay, which was constructed during the early years of the 20th century as a main base for the British naval squadron then stationed in South African waters. Following the breakaway of South Africa from the British Commonwealth, its continued use by the British Navy was established under the terms of the Simonstown Agreement, signed by both countries. With the reduction of British naval commitments east of Suez following the Second World War, its use by British warships declined and has now altogether ceased. During the decade 1960–70 Simonstown was further developed as a submarine base for the South African Navy. A big expansion programme is currently in progress under which large areas of sea will be reclaimed and berthing facilities for ships will be doubled. Simonstown already has the biggest and best dry-dock between Europe and Singapore; the current expansion will also provide it with the largest and best equipped dockyard on this sea route.

SIMOON, the name given to the hot wind coming in off the desert, frequently laden with dust, which blows in the Red Sea. It is the Arabian name for the *sirocco, a similar hot southerly wind which blows in the Mediterranean.

SIMS, WILLIAM SOWDEN (1858–1936), American admiral, was one of the officers who played a considerable part in the improvement of gunnery in the United States fleet. Graduating from the Naval Academy in 1880, he served on the China station during the Sino-Japanese war and in 1900 was appointed gunnery officer of the new *battleship *Kentucky* serving on that station. There he met Percy *Scott, who was commanding the *cruiser H.M.S. *Terrible* and who was the greatest and most advanced expert in naval gunnery in the British Navy. Scott demonstrated to Sims his methods of training gunlayers and gun crews, and also his many training inventions by which systematic practice in gunlaying and loading had improved the standard of British gunnery to an extent where 80 per cent of the rounds fired hit the target. Sims, greatly impressed by these British techniques, made strong recommendations to the Navy Department that they be adopted for the U.S. Navy and then, believing that his recommendations were being ignored, followed with a letter addressed directly to President Theodore *Roosevelt. As a result he was appointed Inspector of Target Practice in the Navy Department in 1902, a post he held until 1909, during which time he was able to make sure that many of the British training practices were embodied in American gunnery methods. He followed this appointment as captain of the battleship *Minnesota* and then commanded the *destroyer *flotillas attached to the Atlantic Fleet, where he trained an excellent staff and made unquestioned progress in the development of new fighting doctrines.

Before the entry in 1917 of the U.S.A. in the First World War (1914–18) Sims was sent to London in April of that year to keep the Navy Department in Washington informed on British naval thought and practice and, when war was declared, to command the U.S. naval forces operating in European waters. Although his services in this appointment were undoubtedly valuable, Sims himself and some of his admirers later exaggerated his personal involvement in some of the major naval decisions of the war, a cause of criticism in U.S. naval circles. After the war he was appointed as head of the Naval War College.

'SINBAD THE SAILOR', the hero of the 291st tale of the great Persian–Arabian classic *A Thousand Nights and One Night*, better known perhaps as the *Arabian Night's Entertainments*. The story concerns the adventures of a wealthy citizen of Baghdad, known as 'the sailor' as a result of seven voyages which he undertook. Although parts of the tale are widely imaginative, such as the discovery of the Roc's egg, the valley of diamonds, and the Old Man of the Sea who had to be killed because he wouldn't get off the 'sailor's' back, much of it is based on the voyages and experiences of Persian and Indian navigators and has an origin in fact. The telling of this story occupied 25 of the 1,001 nights.

SINGAPORE, an island and city at the end of the Malay peninsular. The town dates from 1819 when Sir Stamford Raffles, recognizing its commercial and strategic value, founded a village on the island. The opening of the *Suez Canal in 1869, which greatly shortened the voyage from Europe to the East, gave a great impetus to its development as a port, so that the original harbour became inadequate and a new port, sheltered by the islands in the south, was developed at Keppel Harbour. It became a British naval base of importance between the two World Wars, with a considerable dockyard, but was overrun and captured by the Japanese in 1942 during the Second World War. In 1959 it became an independent state. The port, one of the greatest in South-East Asia, handles a huge entrepôt trade.

'SINGEING THE KING OF SPAIN'S BEARD', the contemporary English description given to the operation at *Cadiz in April 1587 in which Sir Francis *Drake, commanding a naval squadron, destroyed several Spanish ships and a vast quantity of stores which were being assembled for the invasion of England. The actual words were reported to have been said by Drake in jest after the exploit. See also ARMADA.

SINNET, written sometimes as synet, sennet, sennit, or sinnit, a flat woven cordage formed by plaiting an odd number, usually five or seven, rope yarns together to form a decorative pattern. Its original maritime uses were for chafing gear (see also BAGGYWRINKLE), *reef points, *gaskets, *earings, etc., but as such fancy work fell out of fashion at sea, its later uses were purely decorative. Various forms of sinnet were developed, of which the major ones were square plat, chain, and crown sinnet. The straw hats worn in hot weather by many sailors during the 19th and early 20th centuries were made of the fibres of palm leaves worked up in plat sinnet.

SINOPE, a small port on the southern (Turkish) coast of the Black Sea where, on 30 November 1853, a Turkish squadron of seven *frigates, two *corvettes, two transports, and two wooden steamers was set on fire in a few minutes, and destroyed by the shellfire from a Russian squadron of six ships of the line (*Tri Sviatitelia, Rotislav, Tcheswé, Paris, Empress Maria, Grand Duke Constantine*) under the command of Admiral Nakhimov. This action, which demonstrated the vulnerability of wooden ships to shellfire, was directly responsible for the introduction of iron as a building material for warships. See also IRONCLAD.

SIR LANCELOT, a famous British tea *clipper, was built by Robert *Steele of Greenock in 1865. She is stated by some authorities, notably Basil Lubbock, to have been the most beautiful of all the clipper ships.

SIRENS or **SIRENES,** the sea nymphs who charmed men so much with their melodious voices that all stopped their work to listen and ultimately died for want of food through their inability to proceed in their ships any further. Their names were Parthenope, Ligeia, and Leucosia, daughters of the muse Calliope, and they lived in a small island near Cape Pelorus in Sicily. The Sirens had been told by the oracle that as soon as any persons passed them by without being charmed by their songs, they themselves would perish. They prevailed in calling the attention of all sailors until *Odysseus, who had been warned of the power of their voices by Circe, prepared for his encounter with them by stopping the ears of his companions with wax and ordering that he himself should be tied to the mast of his ship, and that no attention should be paid to his commands, should he wish to stay and listen to the Sirens' song. His plan succeeded and the fatal coast was passed in safety. The Sirens were so disappointed by their failure that they threw themselves into the sea and perished. The place on the coast of Sicily where they destroyed themselves was afterwards called Sirenis.

SIRIUS, the name of the first ship to cross the Atlantic from Britain to America entirely under steam. She was a cross-Channel ship of 700 tons, with an engine developing 320 horsepower, and was chartered by the British and American Steam Navigation Company in 1838 when it became apparent that their own ship, the *British Queen*, would not be delivered in time from the builders to make the first Atlantic crossing. She left Cork, in Ireland, on 4 April 1838 with forty passengers on board, and reached New York on 22 April, having had to burn her cabin furniture, her spare yards, and even one mast *en route* to keep steam up in her boiler. Her passage had taken 18 days 10 hours, and her average speed was 6·7 knots. See also GREAT WESTERN, which arrived in New York a few hours later, having left Bristol four days after the *Sirius* had left Cork.

SIROCCO, sometimes spelled as **SCIROCCO,** the name of a hot southerly wind which blows across the Mediterranean after crossing the Sahara Desert. On occasions it can blow for days or weeks on end, usually during the summer months, bringing sand and acute discomfort with it. It is also often a precursor of a cyclonic storm. See also KHAMSIN, SIMOON.

SIRTE, a large gulf on the southern Mediterranean coast of Libya, lying between the port of Benghazi and Cape Masrata, and the scene of a *convoy battle of the Second World War between a British *cruiser and *destroyer force under the command of Rear Admiral Philip *Vian and an Italian force of a *battleship, cruisers, and destroyers commanded by Admiral Iachino. A supply convoy for the hard-pressed island of *Malta sailed from Alexandria on 20 March 1942 with the cruisers and destroyers escorting it, while the Italian ships sailed from *Taranto and Messina shortly after midnight on the 21st. The forces met north of the Gulf of Sirte at about 1500 on the 22nd, with the Italian force in such vast superiority that it seemed certain that the convoy must be destroyed. But by the use of smoke screens and persistent *torpedo attacks by the British destroyers as they came through the smoke and by gunfire from the cruisers in support of the destroyers, the Italian ships were at last driven off and forced to abandon the action. Throughout the action a rising gale was creating a heavy sea which made the work of the destroyers all the more difficult, but they achieved their object with great skill and gallantry, and two of the four vital supply ships of the convoy succeeded in reaching the Grand Harbour, *Valletta, the other two being sunk by German bombers just off the island of Malta. This battle of Sirte was one of the most brilliant smaller actions of the war, and it was very largely due to the great skill and determination with which Rear Admiral Vian handled his small force that defeat was staved off for the British.

SISAL, a fibre used in rope-making obtained from the leaves of *Agave sisalana*. It is a hard fibre, grown mainly in East Africa, Indonesia, and Cuba.

SISTER BLOCK, a block with two *sheaves in a single plane, one below the other. They were used for the running rigging of square-rigged ships and were fitted between the first pair of topmast *shrouds on each side and secured below the *catharpings. The topsail *lift was rove through the lower sheave and the *reef-tackle pendant through the upper. See RIGGING.

SIVERTSEN, KURT (1622–75), Norwegian–Danish naval commander, was born at Brevig, in Norway, and at the age of 15 joined the Dutch Navy as a cadet, serving under the famous Dutch admiral Cornelis *Tromp. After a few years he joined the Venetian Navy, at that time engaged in war with Turkey, and quickly rose in rank after securing many notable victories. He is best known for a brilliant exploit in the *Dardanelles in May 1654 when, with his ship alone, he broke through a line of Turkish *galleys, sinking

fifteen of them and setting many others on fire, with a loss to the Turks of over 5,000 men. This was followed by the full surrender of the Turks. On his return to Venice he was loaded with honours and made admiral-lieutenant. Many other countries now competed for his services, but he returned to Holland in 1661. The following year, on the offer of a title and a huge salary, he accepted command of the Danish fleet, being made Count Adelaer (Norwegian for eagle). In 1675 he commanded the fleet at the outbreak of hostilities against Sweden, but died suddenly in Copenhagen before any operations could take place.

'SIX ORIGINAL FRIGATES', the first ships authorized by Congress to form the U.S. Navy. They were laid down under the Act of Congress of 27 March 1794 which provided for a U.S. Navy, and their dimensions were fixed by three (John *Barry, Richard *Dale, Thomas *Truxton) of the six captains nominated by President Washington to command these *frigates. The six frigates were the *United States*, *Constitution*, *President*, *Chesapeake*, *Constellation*, and *Congress*.

SIX WATER GROG, a punishment in the British Navy often inflicted on seamen found guilty of neglect or drunkenness. It consisted of their daily tot of rum being diluted with six parts of water instead of the normal three. This form of punishment fell into disuse around the early years of the 20th century.

SIXPENNY OFFICE, an office set up within the *Navy Board in London in 1695 whereby the finances of the *Chatham Chest, and later of *Greenwich Hospital, were regularized. Each of these naval charities was, in its turn, financed by the deduction of sixpence monthly from the pay of every seaman, the Chatham Chest being absorbed by Greenwich Hospital when the latter was opened. The administrative work entailed by these deductions was performed by the Sixpenny Office, which remained in being until 1834 when the prevailing system of naval pensions was entirely reformed.

'SIX-UPON-FOUR', the general description given in the British Navy in sailing ship days for the issue of short allowance of victuals in cases where they began to run short, either because a voyage was unduly prolonged or because some had to be condemned as unfit for consumption. It involved six men being issued with the allowance for four, a ration of two-thirds of the full legal issue. Men under 'six-upon-four' received a short allowance increment to their daily pay equal to the value of the shortfall in their rations. See also PETTY WARRANT.

SJØFARTSMUSEET I GÖTEBORG, Göteborg, Sweden, a maritime museum which was founded and opened in 1913 and is housed in a building presented to the city by two Swedish benefactors. It depicts the maritime history of Sweden from the earliest times to the present day and contains a large collection of 600 model ships, a Gältaback boat of the 11th century, carvings, *figureheads, shipbuilders' models, nautical instruments, weapons, uniforms, *scrimshaw, medals, seals, and flags. Besides some 350 paintings there are 18,000 photographs and transparencies. The library contains over 8,000 books and 80,000 ship plans, together with maps, manuscripts, and archives.

SKATE, **U.S.S.,** the first *submarine to surface at the North pole, which she did on 17 March 1959 during a cruise under the polar ice-cap. Her sister ship, U.S.S. *Seadragon*, made the passage from the Atlantic to the Pacific via the *North-West passage (Lancaster Sound, Barrow and McClure Straits) in August 1960. The two ships later made a rendezvous at the North pole on 2 August 1962. Both are nuclear powered.

SKEET or **SKEAT,** a dipper with a long handle which was used to wet the sides and deck of a wooden ship in very hot weather to prevent the planking splitting or opening up in the heat of the sun. In small sailing vessels the skeet was also used to wet the sails in very light weather so that they might hold whatever breeze there might be. In larger sailing ships the sails were wetted for this purpose with the fire engine. It was a practice much used during the wars of the sailing navies when *chasing an enemy ship or in attempting to escape from a ship which was giving chase.

SKEG or **SKEGG,** the short length of *keel, normally tapered or cut to a step, which used to project aft beyond the *sternpost in early sailing vessels. Its purpose was to serve as a protection to the *rudder if the ship went aground and started to beat aft. The skeg did not last long as a shipbuilding practice as it was soon discovered that it was liable to snap off if the ship was beating aft when aground, that the cables of other ships were easily trapped between the skeg and the rudder as the ship swung to the tide, and that it held so much *dead water between skeg and rudder that ships fitted with them became sluggish under sail. They had gone completely out of shipbuilding fashion by about 1630. With the introduction of steam propulsion, however, the skeg came back as an extension of the *deadwood to prevent a ship's *propellers digging into the ground if she went ashore on a bank. In many modern racing yachts a skeg, in conjunction with a separate fin keel, is commonly fitted to protect the rudder.

SKIDS or **SKID-BOOMS,** the name given to the spare spars carried by a large sailing ship, usually stowed in the *waist and used as support for securing the ship's boats when at sea.

SKIFF, in its maritime sense, i.e., as a ship's working boat, a small *clinker-built boat pulling one or two pairs of oars and used for small errands around a ship when she is in harbour. It is not to be confused with the light pleasure boats used on inland waters and known generally as skiffs.

SKILLY, a poor broth, often served as an evening meal at sea in older days, made with oatmeal mixed with the water in which the salt meat had been boiled. It was often the basic food of naval prisoners-of-war and other prisoners kept in the prison *hulks during the 17th, 18th, and early 19th centuries.

SKILLYGALEE or **SKILLYGOLEE,** an oatmeal drink sweetened with sugar, which was often issued to seamen in British warships in place of cocoa up to the end of the Napoleonic War (1803–15). Later it was also a drink issued to stokers working in great heat in the stokeholds of British steam warships in the later 19th century. It was thought to protect them from stomach cramp.

SKIPJACK, a work-boat of the east coast of the U.S.A., *sloop-rigged with a jib-headed mainsail and a foresail set on a *bowsprit. They were hard-*chined boats with a large wooden *centreboard. A feature of the rig was the mast *raked some 25° aft to enable cargo to be hoisted on board by means of the main *halyards. Skipjacks were introduced in Chesapeake Bay in about 1860 and largely superseded the *sharpie.

SKIPPER, the captain or master of a ship, but particularly applicable to smaller vessels, whether merchant, fishing, or yacht, etc. The word was introduced in Britain in the late 14th century, probably from the Dutch *schipper*, captain, itself based on *schip*, ship.

'SKIPPER'S DAUGHTERS', a colloquial name for high waves when they break at sea with a white crest.

SKIRT, an additional strip of material sewn on to the *foot of a racing yacht's *spinnaker and/or large *genoa jib to increase their pulling power. Their form and function is similar to that of the older *bonnet, except that the skirt is a permanent addition and the bonnet was only temporary, being laced and not sewn.

SKRAM, PEDER (*c.* 1500–81), Danish naval
hero, commanded the Swedish fleet (then in alliance with the Danish King Christian III) in
1535 with great success against the Hanseatic
fleet of Christian II, blockading Copenhagen
and capturing an entire squadron from Lübeck.
Because of infirmity he resigned his post as
admiral after the war but in 1562 was persuaded
again to take command. He fought a successful
campaign against the Swedish fleet (now in opposition to Denmark) and virtually destroyed the
Hanseatic control of the Baltic. He was known
for his humanity in battle and earned for himself
the name of 'Denmark's dare-devil'.

SKYLIGHT, a glazed window frame, usually in
pairs, set at an angle in the deck of a ship to give
light and ventilation to a compartment below.
The glass is usually protected with brass rods.
Only smaller vessels use skylights.

Although once very common in yachts, skylights are difficult to keep watertight in bad
weather and have been largely superseded by
plastic hatches or transparent panels.

SKYSAIL, the name of the sail set next above the
* royal in a square-rigged ship, the sixth sail in
ascending order from the deck, its two tacks
secured to the ends of the * yard on which the
royal is set. Like the royal, it is a light-weather
sail, set only when the wind is steady and favourable. See also KITES, and for illus. SAIL.

SKYSCRAPER, the name given to a small triangular sail set above the * skysail in square-
rigged ships in very fine weather in order to get
the utmost advantage of every breath of wind. If
it were square it would be called a * moonsail.

SLAB LINE, a small rope attached by two
spans, or a * bridle, to the * foot of the main or
fore * course of a square-rigged ship and rove
through a * block on the lower * yard. Its purpose
was to truss up the foot of the sail to allow the
helmsman an uninterrupted view forward when
navigating in waters congested with other shipping.

SLACK WATER, the periods in the tidal curve
at the change of the tide when little or no stream
runs. When a tide flows, its maximum rate of
flow occurs during the two hours of mid-flow; as
it approaches high water the rate of flow slackens
until there is virtually no appreciable movement.
The same pattern occurs on the ebb. The period
of slack water is perhaps some 20 minutes or so
each side of high and low water. During this
period, at both high and low waters, the wind
frequently drops or changes direction, and it is
noticeable that bird life in and around estuaries
becomes quiet.

SLATCH, the slack parts of any rope or * cable
lying outside a ship, such as an anchor cable
lying on the bottom in a loose * bight, or the lee
running rigging slacked away too much, so that
it hangs loose. Slatch of the cable is * roused-in;
slatch of the rigging is hauled up.

'SLAUGHTER-HOUSE, THE', a slang name
given by British seamen in the days of the sailing
navies to the * waist of a * ship of the line, the
position where in battle a majority of the casualties might be expected to occur. This was probably because ships were usually * boarded in
the waist, with consequent hand-to-hand fighting,
or over the * poop, in which case the attackers
fired down with small arms on the men below in
the waist. It could also have been because, with a
greater concentration of men there, the waist was
an obvious target for marksmen stationed in the
* tops of enemy ships.

'SLEEVE', THE, the old name for the English
Channel extending from the * Downs in the east
to the * longitude of the Scilly Islands in the west.
The origin of the expression is obscure, possibly
from an association of the French *Manche*, English Channel, with *manchon*, a sleeve, or possibly
from the approximate shape of the Channel itself,
gradually tapering in the fashion of a sleeve with
its narrowest part, corresponding to a cuff, in the
Straits of * Dover.

SLINGS, in general, the ropes or chains attached
to any heavy article to hoist it. Boat slings are
made of strong rope or wire with hooks and
thimbles in the ends to hook into the stem, keel,
and stern bolts so that boats may be hoisted into
or out of a ship. BUTT SLINGS are used for hoisting casks, formed by passing a * strop round the
two ends of a cask and bringing the bight
through the end of the strop. YARD SLINGS are
the ropes or chains which support a * yard on the
mast. For illus. see YARD.

SLIP HOOK, a hinged hook of which the tongue
is held in place by a link which, when knocked
off, allows the hook to open. Small slip hooks
are used to secure the * gripes of * lifeboats
when hoisted at a ship's * davits so that they can
be quickly released when required. Large slip
hooks, known as Blake slips or Blake stoppers,
are used to hold the chain * cables before anchoring and to secure them when the * anchors are
* weighed. See CABLE STOPPERS.

SLIPPERY HITCH, a * bend or hitch used on
board ship to attach a rope to a ring or spar so
that, by a pull on the rope, the hitch comes free.
This is achieved by passing a * bight of the rope
under the other part so that when the strain is
taken the bight is jammed. A pull on the end of

the bight will clear it, and the bend is then dissolved. Hitches most often used in slippery form are sheet bends, clove hitches, and bowlines.

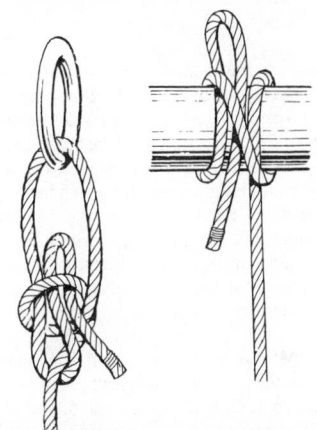

Slippery bowline and slippery clove hitch

SLIPWAY, a sloping foreshore in front of a shipyard on which ships are built. It is fitted with *keel blocks and launching *ways, and lined with cranes for handling shipbuilding material. A patent slipway is an inclined plane on the shore extending into the water, usually gravelled or made of concrete, and fitted with rails up which a small vessel, secured in a cradle, can be hauled for cleaning or repair.

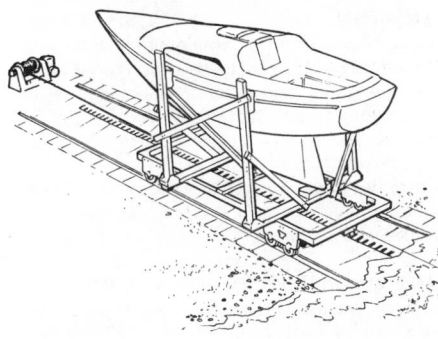

Patent slipway

SLOCUM, JOSHUA (1844–*c.* 1910), American sea captain, was born at Wilmot Township, Nova Scotia, and went to sea as a ship's cook at the age of 12 after running away from home. In 1869 he was *master of a trading *schooner on the coast of California and a year later commanded the *barque *Washington* in which, after a voyage to Australia, he sailed to set up a salmon fishery in Alaska. After an adventurous career as a merchant captain, which included building a steamer of 150 tons on the jungle coast of Manila,

Slocum became master and part-owner of the full-rigged ship *Northern Light*, 'the finest American sailing vessel afloat', and then purchased the small barque *Aquidneck* in which he made several voyages before she was lost in 1886 on a sandbank off the coast of Brazil. His second wife and two sons of his first, one of whom was still a small boy, were on board at the time of the wreck. From the wreckage of his ship Slocum completed a 35-ft *canoe which he had been building on board and, naming her *Liberdade*, brought his wife and two sons safely back to New York after a voyage of over 5,000 miles. On his arrival he began to write his first book, *Voyage of the Liberdade*, which was published in 1894. While he was writing it he was in 1892 offered another vessel by a friendly sea captain and discovered her to be lying under canvas some distance from the sea in a field at Fairhaven where she had been for the last seven years. She was the ruin of the 35-ft *sloop *Spray*. Slocum bought her, largely rebuilt her with oak which he felled, shaped, and treated himself, and in 1895 left Boston in her. His subsequent circumnavigation, by way of Gibraltar, the Magellan Straits, Australia, and South Africa, is believed to have been the first single-handed voyage round the world. Having little money he supported himself by lectures at his various ports of call, earning enough to keep his family and cover his expenses. He arrived back at Newport, Rhode Island, in 1898. He wrote a second book about his experiences entitled *Sailing Alone Around the World* (1900) which has become a classic of its kind through its simple, direct style, wit, and dry humour. In November 1909, at the age of 65, he set out on another lone voyage from Bristol, Rhode Island, but was never heard of again. It is thought that the *Spray* was either run down by a steamer in mid-ocean or struck a whale and sank, as she was too soundly built a boat and Slocum too experienced a mariner to have been lost from any other cause.

The *Liberdade*, in which Slocum and his family returned to New York after the wreck of the *Aquidneck*, is now preserved in the *Smithsonian Institution in Washington.

SLOOP, (1) a sailing vessel with a single mast, fore-and-aft rigged, setting, in western Europe, a single headsail. Its development, in respect of dates, etc., was parallel with that of the *cutter. In the U.S.A. the term sloop also embraces vessels setting two headsails, which in other parts of the world would be termed cutters. The U.S. cutter is the old-fashioned vessel of that designation which set its *jib, which was capable of being reefed, on a long *bowsprit. **(2)** A designation used during the Second World War to describe one of the smaller classes of anti-submarine *convoy escort vessels used during the battle of the *Atlantic. It was a resuscitation of the name of (3), an older navy class of ships, 17th–19th century, used mainly for auxiliary naval duties. Until the late 18th century the term was used somewhat indiscriminately to embrace any of the smaller naval vessels that did not fit specifically into a recognized class of minor warship, but by the beginning of the 19th century there were two accepted classes of sloop depending on the number of masts stepped, the ship sloop (three masts) and *brig sloop (two masts), both of them square-rigged on all masts. As a distinctive type of warship the sloop finally disappeared about 1888 although in some navies, including the British, a few were retained for sail-training purposes. Those in Britain were attached to the boys' training ships and continued in use until 1904. They were the last ships of the naval sailing era.

SLOPS, the name given to ready-made clothing carried in warships and issued to seamen on repayment against their pay when drawn. The name comes from the old English word *sloppe*, meaning breeches, and slop clothing originally referred only to the baggy trousers worn by seamen. Later it developed into a sort of unofficial uniform as the original clothing in which men joined their ships wore out. Slops were first officially issued in the Royal Navy in 1623 but the word did not appear in its naval usage until 1691 in a book written by Harry Maydman, a *purser in the British Navy. Slops were sold by pursers, who were allowed one shilling in the pound commission, and who opened their slop chests before the mast on certain days. Samuel Pepys refers to the business as one 'wherein the seaman is so much abused by the purser', as he continued to be until an official naval uniform for seamen was introduced in the navy in 1857. (See also SAILOR'S DRESS.)

SLUSH, originally the fat of the meat boiled on board in the coppers of naval ships which was the perquisite of the ship's cook. Usually he sold it to the *purser who made it into candles. It was later the name used for the grease with which masts and spars of sailing vessels were rubbed down after they had been scraped.

SLUYS, BATTLE OF, was fought between English and French fleets on 24 June 1340. Edward III commanded the English ships in person, having 250 vessels in his fleet, though many were very small and some no more than transports. The French ships, said to outnumber the English, were drawn up in defensive order in the harbour of Sluys, on the coast of Flanders, most of them lashed together in four lines to form a barrier against the English attack. Edward manoeuvred his ships so that they were to windward of the French and with the sun at their backs, and then attacked in a hand-to-hand battle, in which the French fleet was almost entirely destroyed with immense slaughter of men. Edward himself, it is said, was wounded in the battle.

SMACK, originally a *cutter or *ketch-rigged sailing vessel, normally from about 15 to 50 tons, used for inshore fishing. In older days it was often known as, and rigged as, a *hoy, and during the 18th and early 19th centuries in Britain they were sometimes used as tenders in the King's service, particularly in the *preventive (customs) service. Today, the word is frequently used as a generic term for all small fishing craft irrespective of whether they use sail or a small diesel engine for propulsion.

SMART MONEY, the old term for a wounds pension in the British Navy, which was issued according to rank and the extent of the wound. The term died out of use around the mid-19th century, probably when *Greenwich Hospital closed its wards and issued out-pensions in lieu of accommodation for naval pensioners.

'SMASHER', the colloquial term for a carronade in the British Navy during the period of their use from about 1785 to 1815. Firing a very heavy ball at very close range, they could do considerable damage against the wooden warships of the day, hence this name for them. See also GUNS, NAVAL.

SMEATON, JOHN (1724–92), British engineer, is best known for rebuilding the Eddystone *lighthouse in 1759. He also specialized in the design of canals and harbour works, and in this connection made many improvements in the diving bell (see DIVING, 2). He was, in addition, a keen astronomer and read papers on the subject before the Royal Society of London. In 1791 he published his *Narrative of the Building of the Eddystone Lighthouse*.

SMEETON, MILES R. (1906–   ), British soldier and yachtsman, made many long-distance cruises in his 46-ft (14 m) *ketch *Tzu Hang*, with his wife Beryl, his daughter Clio, and another companion. These cruises included a voyage from England to Vancouver via the Panama Canal and the Galapagos Islands in 1950–1, and from Vancouver across the Pacific to Australia and New Zealand in 1956. On her first attempt to round Cape Horn from west to east in 1957 *Tzu Hang* was up-ended *stern over *bows (pitchpoled) by giant seas, dismasted, and, after a jury rig had been erected by her crew, managed to make the port of Coronel in Chile. For this feat Miles and Beryl Smeeton and their crew, John *Guzzwell, were jointly awarded the Royal

Cruising Club's Seamanship medal. With repairs completed they set out again, but when off the Horn the yacht was again rolled over and saved only by superb seamanship.

After more cruises to the Mediterranean, the Arabian coast, South India, Seychelles Islands, and Durban, and the following year to Borneo, the Philippines, and Japan, Smeeton and his wife returned to the west coast of North America, and sailed to the Arctic circle. On a further voyage from England to the Pacific in 1968–9 they rounded Cape Horn once more, this time beating from east to west against strong winds and seas. Books written by Smeeton include *Once is Enough*, *A Taste of the Hills*, *A Change of Jungle*, *Sunrise to Windward*, *The Misty Islands*, and *Because the Horn is There*.

SMITH, Sir FRANCIS PETTIT (1808–74), British inventor, started life as a Kentish farmer but became engrossed in the construction of model boats and in methods of propelling them. In 1835 he constructed a model boat which was driven through the water by a *propeller actuated by a spring, and this was so successful that he became convinced of its superiority to the paddle-wheel universally used at that time.

Smith was unaware that contemporary steps in the same direction were being made by the Swedish engineer John *Ericsson and, in fact, his patent for his type of screw propulsion, taken out on 31 May 1836, predated Ericsson's different type by only six weeks. Thus Smith's improved model exhibited in that year can claim to have been the first of its kind.

With financial backing and some technical assistance, Smith now built a 10-ton vessel which was propelled by a six horsepower engine driving a wooden screw with two turns, later replaced by one with a single turn. So fitted, the little vessel made a successful voyage round the Kent coast in choppy weather. To satisfy Admiralty demands for experiments in a larger ship, a company was formed to build the 237-ton *Archimedes*, which in October 1839 achieved a speed of 10 knots and later made a successful cruise to the major ports of Britain, to Amsterdam, and to Oporto. Though the Admiralty sufficiently convinced to order their first screw-propelled *sloop, the *Rattler*, in 1841, it was not until she had easily overcome the paddle-driven *Alecto* in 1845 that Smith's screw was completely accepted and twenty more screw ships were ordered for the Royal Navy.

Smith received only meagre financial rewards for his invention and also was poorly paid as adviser to the Admiralty, a post he held until 1850. Thereafter, in spite of a pension of £200 and an unsuccessful effort to revert to farming in Guernsey when his patent expired in 1856, he was compelled to accept the post of curator of the Patent Office Museum in South Kensington which he held until his death. Some recognition of his services was, however, made by the knighthood conferred on him in 1871.

SMITH, WILLIAM (*fl.* 1819–20), a sealer of Blyth, Northumberland, discovered the South Shetland Islands when, during a trading voyage from the River Plate to Valparaiso in February 1819, his vessel was blown off course south of Cape Horn. He returned to the South Shetland Islands in October 1819 and took possession of them for Great Britain. In January 1820 he returned a second time in the expedition under the command of Edward *Bransfield, who carried out the first survey of the islands.

SMITH, Sir WILLIAM SIDNEY (1764–1840), British admiral, entered the Royal Navy in 1777 and soon attracted the notice of Sir George *Rodney, in two of whose battles (Cape *St. Vincent, 1780, and the *Saints, 1782) he did particularly well. Rodney made him a *post-captain at the age of 18, which was exceptional though not unparalleled. Between 1789 and 1791 Smith spent much time in the Baltic, where he was adviser to Gustavus III in the maritime war with Russia. Gustavus gave Smith an order of knighthood, a distinction which was approved by George III, so that from 1791 onwards Smith's contemporaries, who rarely liked him, referred to him ironically as 'the Swedish knight'.

When the Revolutionary War against France (1793–1801) broke out, Smith was in Turkey visiting his younger brother. He hastened home and was able to take part, as a volunteer, in the final stages of Lord *Hood's occupation of *Toulon. Charged with destroying the French ships in harbour on Hood's withdrawal, he failed, in the opinion of many good judges, to carry out his duty to the extent that should have been possible.

In April 1796 Smith was captured by the French near the mouth of the Seine, after serving in operations in the Channel and elsewhere. He was in prison for two years before he contrived to escape. He was next employed in the Mediterranean where, early in 1799, he had a brilliant success in amphibious operations at Acre, where he was engaged directly against Napoleon. He was promoted rear admiral in November 1805 and was sent again to the Mediterranean to serve under Lord *Collingwood. He always did well in partisan operations off the enemy coast but was never amenable to discipline and always found it hard to co-operate.

When Napoleon moved against Spain and Portugal, Smith escorted the Portuguese royal family to Brazil. Later, in January 1808, he was ordered to Rio de Janeiro as commander-in-chief of the squadron stationed off the coast of Brazil. It was not a wise appointment. While in South America Smith behaved so presumptuously towards the British ambassador, Lord Strangford, and was so outrageously indiscreet that he had to be recalled. He was more than two years ashore before he was appointed second-in-command of the Mediterranean Fleet where he served under Sir Edward * Pellew.

Smith had no further naval employment after 1814, but he interested himself in many causes, becoming President of the 'Knights Liberators and Anti-Piratical Society' whose object was to free the white slaves held in the Barbary States of North Africa. The last decades of his life were spent in France, where he felt that his personality was more appreciated than at home.

SMITHSONIAN INSTITUTION, U.S. NATIONAL MUSEUM, Washington, D.C. The marine artefacts of this famous museum are housed in the Museum of History and Technology opened in 1964. They illustrate American naval and merchant shipping history from the colonial era to the present day and include 75 warship and 170 merchant ship models, the * gunboat *Philadelphia* (1776), carvings, over 500 shipbuilder's models, tools, nautical instruments, flags of American shipping lines, and photographs.

Other maritime museums in Washington, are the Naval Gun Factory Museum, the Truxton-Decatur Naval Museum, the U.S. Coast Guard Museum, the U.S. Naval Historical Display Center, and the Old Navy Department Museum.

SMITING LINE, a small rope made fast to the under side of the * mizen yardarm at its lower end during the period when the normal rig of sailing ships was a * lateen mizen. When the mizen sail was furled, or * farthelled, this rope was led along the yard to the mizen peak with the sail and then down to the poop. The sail being stopped to the yard with ropeyarns, with the smiting line inside them, it could be set, or loosed, without striking down the yard simply by pulling on the smiting line and thus breaking the ropeyarns. 'SMITE THE MIZEN', the order to haul down on the smiting line.

SMOKE BOX, a canister containing phosphorus issued to allied merchant vessels during the First World War (1914–18) which, when released into the sea, produced a dense, heavy smoke behind which the ships might escape from an attacking submarine.

SMOKE SCREEN, a thick cloud of dense funnel smoke made by naval vessels to screen tactical movements from an enemy. The main means of its production was by decreasing the amount of air supplied to the combustion chambers of the boilers and by spraying in cold oil fuel. This causes only partial combustion of the oil fuel, and the result is a thick, heavy smoke which lies on the surface of the sea and takes a long time to clear. In small modern naval vessels which are not fitted with steam propulsion, smoke is made by chemical means and laid as a screen in the desired position.

SMOLLETT, TOBIAS GEORGE (1721–71), British novelist, was born at Dalquhum, Dumbartonshire, Scotland, and was educated at Glasgow University but had no means of support when he left the University. He enlisted as a surgeon's mate in H.M.S. *Chichester* and sailed for the West Indies in Sir Chaloner * Ogle's squadron sent out to reinforce Admiral Edward * Vernon during the War of the Austrian Succession (1739–48). He was present at the abortive attack on Cartagena in 1741 and had first-hand experience of the terrible conditions which existed in the hospital ships attached to the British fleet. He returned to London in 1744, where he had a practice as a surgeon, and began to write novels. His first was *The Adventures of Roderick Random* (1748), a book of considerable naval interest in which he drew upon his personal experiences at Cartagena and to which we owe today much of our knowledge of those conditions and of the general way of life of the British naval seaman of the day. It also introduced the well-known naval character of Lieutenant Tom Bowling.

Smollett was a considerable figure in 18th century English literature, both as a writer and as editor of the *Critical Review*, and is remembered today for the wit of his novels and for the light they throw on contemporary manners and on the political scene.

SMUGGLE, to, the operation of bringing goods into a country clandestinely to avoid the payment of duty. Smuggling has a very old history, largely connected with the sea as one of the main highways of trade between countries. During the Revolutionary and Napoleonic Wars (1793–1801 and 1803–15), when Britain was largely cut off from trade with much of Europe, smuggling, particularly in French brandies and lace, became almost an industry and the British government was forced to maintain a large fleet of fast sailing * cutters in the Channel, known as the preventive service, to attempt to cut off the smugglers before they could reach the shore to land their cargoes.

Today, all sea and air ports of any size have a customs office to deal with the import of all goods, and a preventive service at sea is no longer a necessity.

A Prussian snow; etching by E. W. Cooke, 1829

SMYTH, WILLIAM HENRY (1788–1865), British rear admiral, made surveys and scientific observations in the Mediterranean from 1813 to 1824 which were widely acclaimed as much in Mediterranean countries as in Britain.

His early naval service was spent largely in north European waters, with one voyage to the Pacific, providing him with opportunities to make several surveys and charts. Then, during the Napoleonic War (1803–15) the Hydrographer of the Navy, Thomas *Hurd, arranged his attachment in 1813 to the British flotillas operating in Sicily and in 1817 the *Aid*, renamed *Adventure* in 1821, was provided for his wide-ranging Mediterranean activities. Smyth collaborated with French, Austrian, and Neapolitan surveyors, scholars, and astronomers, and it is said that when in Egyptian waters he was offered Cleopatra's Needle by Mehemet Ali, as a present to George IV; but no opportunity occurred for its embarkation in the *Adventure*.

Admiralty appreciation of Smyth's work was shown in 1831 by an exceptional allowance of £500 for his finished drawings, a measure having also the object of encouraging officers to take up surveying. In fact several of Smyth's officers in the *Adventure* were ready pupils, and Thomas

*Graves, for one, carried on his Mediterranean work.

Smyth was made a Fellow of the Royal Society in 1826 and was a Doctor of Civil Law, besides receiving various foreign distinctions. He was a founder member of the Royal Geographical Society in 1830 and its President from 1849 to 1851.

SNATCH BLOCK, a *block with a single *sheave which has a hinged opening above the

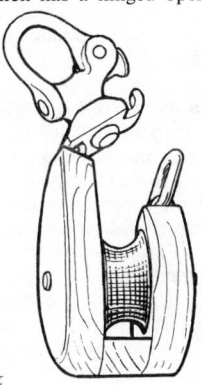

Snatch block

sheave to allow the *bight of a rope to be dropped in, thus saving the necessity of reeving the whole length of the rope through the block. It is also sometimes known as a notch-block.

SNOTTER, the name given to the fitting which holds the *heel of a *sprit close to the mast in a *spritsail-rigged barge. For illus. see SPRIT.

SNOW, a two-masted merchant vessel of the 16th–19th centuries, the largest two-masted ship of her period with a *tonnage of up to around 1,000 tons. She was rigged as a *brig, with square sails on both masts, but had a small try-sail mast stepped immediately abaft the main-mast from which a *trysail with a *boom was set, the *luff of the trysail being *hooped to this mast. In some cases this trysail mast was replaced by a *horse on the mainmast, to which the luff of the trysail was attached by rings. Snows were entirely European ships, not found in other parts of the world.

SNOWFLAKE, an artificial illuminant devised in 1941 for use at sea by anti-*submarine escorts in their operations against *U-boat attacks on *convoys. Snowflake ignited in contact with the air and produced a bright light for an appreciable period. Packed in a shellcase, it was fired from a gun, and provided a bright illumination over the surrounding sea. It was widely used in convoy operations until the introduction of efficient *radar in escort vessels and maritime air-craft solved the whole problem of visibility at night.

SNUB, to, the action of bringing a ship to a stop suddenly by letting go an *anchor with too much way on the ship. It is also the word used to describe the action of a ship when she *pitches while at anchor and the *cable tautens to such an extent that it holds the bows down at the top of the pitch. It is apt to occur when there is insuffi-cient *scope to the cable, and is easily corrected by *veering some more. A *hawser is also said to be snubbed when it is *checked suddenly while running out by taking a quick turn round a pair of *bollards.

SOCIETY FOR NAUTICAL RESEARCH, a learned society in Britain which publishes *The Mariner's Mirror,* a quarterly journal devoted to matters of the sea and ships. It was founded in 1910, mainly through the initiative of L. G. Carr Laughton, son of Sir John *Laughton, Morton Nance, and Sir Alan *Moore. In addition to publication of *The Mariner's Mirror,* the prin-cipal work of the Society has been the saving and restoration of H.M.S. *Victory* and its assistance in founding the *National Maritime Museum and the *Victory Museum.

SØFARTSSAMLINGERNE VED SVEND-BORGSUND, Troense, Isle of Tasinge, Den-mark, is a private *maritime museum opened in 1956 and housed in three buildings, one of which dates from 1790. It is designed to show the development of Danish shipping from 1850 to the present day, with special emphasis on *tramp steamers. It contains thirty ship models of sailing ships and a collection of 6,000 miniature ships of all types, as well as some half-models of yachts designed by Henry Rasmussen. The ship decorations include carvings and *figureheads. There are scale models of modern motorships, also some half-models, nautical instruments, medals, seals, and flags. The 500 pictures are mainly ship portraits and the library of 3,000 books is available to students.

'SOLDIER'S WIND', a name given to the wind when it blows on the *beam of a vessel under sail and therefore calls for no *tacking or *trimming of the sails. It is one which will take a sailing vessel there and back again without requiring much nautical ability.

SOLE, in some ships, and especially in yachts, the name given to the decks of the *cabin and *forecastle. It is also a name given to the bottom lining of the *bilge-ways and of the *rudder to bring it down to the level of the *false keel.

SOLEBAY, the older name for Southwold Bay, off the coast of Suffolk, England, and scene of the first battle of the Third Anglo-Dutch War (1672–4) which was fought on 28 May 1672 between an Anglo-French fleet of 98 ships under *James, Duke of York, and a Dutch fleet of seventy-five ships under Admiral de *Ruyter. After weighing from Solebay, where they were at anchor, with the wind from the east, the English ships stood north and the French south, the latter taking little part in the action. Being to *leeward, the English ships were only saved from destruction by the wind dropping before the Dutch *fireships could get among them. Later the wind freshened, *veering eight *points to the south, and the action became general and was hotly contested. The Duke of York was in the thick of the fight throughout, and on two oc-casions was obliged to shift his flag to other ships. A Dutch success was the destruction of the 100-gun *Royal James* by fireships; but in spite of this, the Dutch rear became demoralized and retired almost out of the action. This enabled the English ships to concentrate on the Dutch centre, which suffered severely. The battle ended at about 9 p.m. when the Dutch withdrew to the northward. Both sides claimed the victory; the result was perhaps more properly even. The Anglo-French fleet held the sea and captured a *prize; but the Dutch effected their main object, which was to prevent or delay the English fleet from crossing the North Sea and co-operating with the French in the Netherlands.

SOLE-PIECES, a name sometimes used to describe the * A-brackets which extend from the * sternpost of a steam or motor vessel and provide outboard support for the * propeller shafts where they extend beyond the hull of the vessel.

SOMERSCALES, THOMAS JAQUES (1842–1927), British marine artist, was born at Hull. He became a schoolmaster in the Royal Navy and was a self-taught artist, exhibiting at the Royal Academy in 1901. He was the painter of the picture 'Off Valparaiso', one of the best-known pictures of a full-rigged ship, which was purchased by the Chantrey Bequest and now hangs in the Tate Gallery, London.

SOMERVILLE, HENRY BOYLE TOWN-SHEND (1864–1936), British vice admiral, spent most of his naval service as a surveyor. He began in 1889 when as a lieutenant he joined H.M.S. * Dart in the New Hebrides, and some twenty-five years later he developed the ship * sounding gear that was to remain in use until * echo sounding was adopted in the 1930s. The lead was hauled forward to an * outrigger * boom by a wire sounding line led through appropriate * blocks to a steam winch on the quarterdeck. Beside the winch was an overside platform for the leadsman and a * davit with a block through which the depth line was rove from the lead and thence to a counterpoise weight towing astern. When the brake was taken off the winch the lead fell from the forward boom and reached bottom below the after platform where the leadsman read the depth on the lead line. The deeper the water, the slower had the ship's speed to be, but soundings of up to 25 * fathoms could be obtained without stopping the ship. In earlier arrangements the lead had to be reattached to the sounding line from which it was slipped at the forward boom for each sounding.

After the *Dart*, Somerville served in the *Penguin*, again in Australasia, and from 1897 to 1900 was in the * Egeria in British Columbia. After two years in home waters in the *Triton*, he did a strategic survey in the Persian Gulf, followed by three years from 1904 commanding the *Sealark* in the East Indies. A period in home waters included command of H.M.S. * Research, 1912–14, and during the First World War (1914–18) he had various general service appointments. Retiring in 1919, Somerville lived in Ireland until 1936 when he was murdered by I.R.A. gunmen apparently for advising young local men on how to join the British Navy. He wrote articles for *Blackwood's Magazine*, drawing on his personal experiences.

SOMERVILLE, Sir JAMES FOWNES (1882–1949), British admiral of the fleet, combined a talent for seamanship with a natural flair for technical matters and, having first qualified as a * torpedo officer, took wireless telegraphy for his speciality. It was as fleet wireless officer on the staff of Admiral Sir John * de Robeck that he served for the greater part of the First World War (1914–18) both through the * Dardanelles campaign and in the * Grand Fleet. As commander and captain, his sea service was in * battleships, and in 1933 he was promoted rear admiral. After serving at the Admiralty he commanded the * destroyer flotillas in the Mediterranean, in which post he was much involved in the naval activities and often delicate international relationships in connection with the Spanish Civil War.

Becoming commander-in-chief of the East Indies station in 1938 he had a recurrence of an illness suffered earlier in the year. It was diagnosed by naval doctors as pulmonary tuberculosis, and in spite of a contrary opinion by civilian specialists, Somerville was invalided out of the Royal Navy.

On the outbreak of the Second World War, Somerville busied himself in unofficial work in the development of technical devices, particularly * radar, and was largely responsible for speeding up the installation of effective surface warning radar in British warships. During the evacuation of the British Expeditionary Force from * Dunkirk in 1940, he volunteered his services in those difficult operations. He returned from Calais in the last ship to clear that port and subsequently at Dover took over control of operations at intervals to give the exhausted Admiral Sir Bertram Ramsay a chance of occasional rest.

At the end of June 1940 he was officially recalled to active service to command Force 'H', a powerful squadron based on Gibraltar; his first duty being the agonizing one of bombarding the French squadron at Mers-el-Kebir (Oran) when the French admiral refused to give satisfactory assurances with regard to the immobilization of his ships. Under Somerville's command, Force 'H' fought a number of * convoys through to Malta, beating off attacks by the Italian fleet. It carried out a successful bombardment of Genoa, and it was the torpedo-bombers from the * Ark Royal under Somerville's command which brought about the destruction of the German battleship * Bismarck in the Atlantic in 1941 by immobilizing her to enable the Home Fleet to catch and sink her.

On the entry of Japan into the war Somerville was given the unenviable task of assembling and commanding the exiguous Eastern Fleet in the Indian Ocean, a collection of veteran battleships and two ill-equipped * aircraft carriers. It could not in any way have challenged the Japanese Fast Carrier Striking Force which raided Ceylon in April 1942; it was fortunate, therefore, that the two fleets failed to discover one another. Not until January 1944 did the Eastern Fleet begin to become an effective force with the arrival of modernized battleships and properly equipped carriers; in April, May, and July it delivered successful air strikes on Sabang (Sumatra) and Sourabaya (Java). Somerville was relieved by Admiral *Fraser in August 1944 and he served as Head of the British Admiralty Mission in Washington until the end of 1945.

SON OF A GUN, a description given by the lower deck to children born on board ships of the British Navy during the period when the wives of seamen were allowed to live on board in harbour and, occasionally, at sea. As the gangways always had to be kept clear, the only place on board where women in labour could produce their children was in the spaces between the guns on the gundecks. Inevitably, any male child born on board was known as a 'son of a gun'. Such a birth gave rise to the saying: 'Begotten in the galley and born under a gun. Every hair a rope yarn, every tooth a marline spike, every finger a fishhook, and his blood right good Stockholm tar.'

SONAR, formerly known as *Asdic, the name being derived from the words SOund Navigation And Ranging and denoting an apparatus used in locating submerged *submarines. It comprises a transducer and a receiver attached to the hull of a ship or lowered to the required depth from a ship or a helicopter. The transducer, using the vibrating properties of quartz, emits pulses of high frequency sound which, passing through the water, are reflected by any solid object encountered. The accurate measurement of the time between the emission of a pulse and the arrival of the returning echo gives the range of the object. By using a narrow sweeping pulse beam, a bearing can also be obtained and in the case of a moving object, such as a submarine, observation of the Doppler effect, or change of note, gives an indication of the direction of movement. A British adaptation of sonar for *mine detection has proved most successful and the apparatus is now widely used by the fishing industry for the detection of shoals of fish. It is also the basis of all *echo-sounding equipment to find the depth of water under a ship.

SONGS, see SEA SONGS.

SOPWITH, Sir THOMAS OCTAVE MURDOCH (1888–   ), British industrialist and yachtsman, was president of the Hawker Siddeley group. His early interest was in aviation and he was among the first to obtain his pilot's licence in Britain. He designed aircraft during the First World War (1914–18), many of them famous in the history of the Royal Flying Corps and the *Royal Naval Air Service.

In 1910 he owned the 165-ton *schooner *Neva* and in 1912 the racing motorboat *Maple Leaf.* Between the two world wars he took to racing in sail, at first in the International 12-metre class with *Doris* (1926) and *Mouette* (1929), with the latter boat winning the Solent 12-metre championship. In 1932 he joined the big *J-class racing with *Shamrock V*, built as a challenger for the *America*'s Cup by Sir Thomas *Lipton, and later with *Endeavour* (1934) and *Endeavour II* (1937) with both of which he challenged for the *America*'s Cup, being unsuccessful with both challenges. He was president of the Council of the Yacht Racing Association (later the *Royal Yachting Association) from 1932 to 1935. In 1937 he built the 1,620-ton motor yacht *Philante* which was later to become the *royal yacht *Norge* of King Haakon of Norway.

'SOS', the internationally agreed wireless distress call made by a ship requiring assistance. It came into force on 1 July 1908. The three letters were chosen because they were easy to read and make in *Morse code (three dots, three dashes, three dots) and it did not stand for 'Save Our Souls', as many people thought. The first occasion on which it was used at sea was in August 1909 when the American steamer *Azoaahoe* was disabled with a broken propeller shaft.

SOUND, to (from the Anglo-Saxon *sond*, a messenger), the operation of ascertaining the depth of the sea in the vicinity of a ship. Until the wide adoption of *echo-sounding (see also SONAR) in most vessels of any size, the main method of finding the depth of water, for moderate depths up to about 15 *fathoms (27·4 m), was the *lead and line, the lead being *armed with tallow in order to provide information about the nature of the bottom.

For greater depths, the deep sea lead and line could measure depths of up to about 120 fathoms (220 m) with the ship either stopped or proceeding very slowly, greater depths being measured with a *sounding machine or, if the nature of the bottom was also required, with a Baillie rod. This consists essentially of two or three 20-lb (9 kg) weights at the end of a thin wire with a thin tube which penetrates the bottom, bringing up a core which provides information about the nature and surface structure of the seabed. Echo-sounding, of course, can measure the depth of the sea to any distance, providing a continuous trace of the variations of the seabed.

A whale, when it dives deep, is said to sound.

Sir T. O. M. Sopwith at the wheel of Shamrock V

SOUNDING, the name given to a depth of water obtained by a *lead and line, *sounding machine, or *echo-sounder, or by any other means. The figures on a maritime chart which indicate the depth of water are also known as soundings, and unless stated to the contrary are, in British charts, in *fathoms measured below the *chart datum. Eventually, all soundings on all charts will be indicated in metres. A ship in such a depth of water that the bottom can be reached with a deep sea lead is said to be *in soundings; where the bottom cannot be so reached, she is said to be *off, or out of, soundings. As a general rule, the 100-fathom (183 m) line on the chart is taken as the dividing line between in and off soundings.

SOUNDING MACHINE, a mechanical device invented by Lord Kelvin (see THOMSON, William) by which the depth of the sea can be measured. It consists of a drum of piano wire mounted on a framework secured to a ship's deck. A sinker is secured to the outboard end of the wire by a *shackle and the wire is led through a suitable *fairlead over the ship's side. When the brake on the drum is released, the wire runs out as the sinker falls through the water. A metal feeler is held by the person operating the machine hard up against the wire as it runs out, and when the sinker reaches the seabed, the wire slackens and this is instantly detected by the feeler. The length of wire which has run out is indicated on a scale of *fathoms on the sounding machine, and from this reading the approximate depth of water can be calculated, allowance being made for the speed of the ship through the water. For a more accurate measurement of depth a sounding tube is normally secured to the wire close to the sinker. This consists of a glass tube with one end closed. It is about 30 inches (762 mm) long and the inside is coated with a chemical composition which changes colour on contact with seawater. The tube is inserted in a brass protection case attached to the wire with its open end downwards. The air trapped in the tube is compressed into a smaller volume as the tube falls downwards through the water, and by the application of Boyle's Law (that the volume of a gas (air in this case) at constant temperature varies inversely as the pressure) the length of discoloured chemical is directly related to the depth to which the tube descended. The tube is then placed in a boxwood scale marked in fathoms, and the point on the tube where the discoloration due to seawater ends indicates the depth measured.

Lord Kelvin first demonstrated his sounding machine about a century ago in the Bay of Biscay, successfully measuring depths of over 2,000 fathoms (3·65 km).

SOUNDING ROD, the earliest aid to navigation in coastal waters, was a graduated rod by means of which the depth of water could be ascertained when the vessel was under way merely by feeling the bottom with the rod. Such a device is still commonly used by hydrographic surveyors when working in enclosed docks or in very shallow water.

SOUTH SEA BUBBLE, a series of financial hoaxes, or speculations in stocks of the South Sea Company which produced ruin for many investors in 1720. The company, founded by Robert Harley in 1711, was formed on the supposed possibility of vast trade with Spanish America, particularly in the Pacific, following the War of the Spanish Succession (1702–13), but the Treaty of Utrecht, signed after the war, in fact provided only very limited trade possibilities, restricted to no more than one ship per year. Nevertheless, with the King becoming governor of the company in 1718, popular confidence was enhanced and a wild boom was engendered in which the value of the stock, issued at £100, rose to over £1,000 in the summer of 1719. By the end of the year it had dropped to £124, and six months later was virtually valueless, and while a few holders of stock had made vast fortunes, the great majority had lost very heavily. Some holders fled the country because of their debts, many others committed suicide. A committee of inquiry found that three ministers of the crown had accepted bribes and speculated heavily in South Sea stock. The Chancellor of the Exchequer was sent to prison, the other two had their estates confiscated. The South Sea Company itself remained in existence until 1853, being mainly concerned, after selling its supposed trading right to Spain in 1750, with the Greenland whale fishery.

SOUTH SEAS, the old term for the *Pacific Ocean. It was given this name by Vasco Nuñez de *Balboa in 1513 when, after sighting the ocean from the top of a mountain range, he reached the coast near Panama and took possession of the 'Great South Sea' in the name of King Ferdinand of Spain. The expression occurs in most of the books of voyages at least up to the middle of the 18th century and embraced the whole of the Pacific Ocean, purely from the fact that the only means of reaching it from the west

was round Cape Horn or through the Magellan Straits, both of course far to the southward.

SOUTHAMPTON, a major seaport on the south coast of England, lying at the head of the estuary known as Southampton Water. Although it was a seaport from very early days, it only grew into real significance during the second half of the 19th century, partly through the building of the railway which connected it with London, partly through the growth in size of passenger *liners, but mainly because it has two high waters every *tide. There are two possible explanations of this unusual double high water; one being that the first high tide comes up the Solent while the second, two hours later, comes up *Spithead; the other that the tide, as it comes up Channel, gives Southampton its first high water in the normal way, while the second is caused by the tide hitting the *Cherbourg peninsula on the opposite side of the Channel and being deflected north to reach the English coast two hours later, thus causing the second high water. With a tidal rise of as much as 20 feet (6 m), this double high water at an interval of two hours is a tremendous asset in the working of any port.

Prosperity was assured to Southampton when the *Royal Mail and *Union-Castle steamship lines adopted it as their main English port, and the seal was set on this by the similar adoption by the *Cunard Line. This entailed the construction of new deep-water quays, basins, *dry-docks, and all the ancillary requirements of a great passenger port, including shipbuilding and ship-repairing. Since the end of the Second World War, Southampton has also been developed as a great oil port, with one of the largest refineries in Britain built at Fawley, on Southampton Water. It is also today a major container port.

SOUTHERN CROSS, a constellation in the form of a cross visible in the southern hemisphere. It is of no particular navigational significance, as is for example the northern constellation of *Ursa minor* which contains the Pole Star (see POLARIS), but it has acquired a sentimental interest among seamen since the first sight of it at sea is, to natives of the southern hemisphere, the sign that they are homeward bound, and similarly the last sight of the constellation by natives of the northern hemisphere indicates that they, too, are on the way home.

The Southern Cross is of more maritime interest, however, because it was a sign used in South American ports by the big full-rigged sailing ships in the late 19th and early 20th centuries after they had loaded nitrate, guano, or saltpetre that they were homeward bound. When the ship was loaded and ready to sail, the carpenter on board made a large wooden cross to which were fixed red and white lights in the shape of the constellation. This was hoisted to the mainmast head and was greeted by the well-known sea *shanty 'Hurrah, my boys, we're homeward bound'. When the shanty was finished, the ship's *bell in the ship next alongside was rung, and her crew cheered the departing vessel, and so in turn until all ships in harbour had cheered her. It was a representation of the Southern Cross that was hoisted because the homeward passage from these ports, irrespective of the ship's final destination, had to be to the southward to round Cape Horn.

SOUTHERN CROSS, the name of a *barque-rigged, steam auxiliary vessel of 521 tons which was built for G. E. Borchgrevink's British Antarctic expedition of 1898–1900. Later she was acquired by the Newfoundland Sealing Company for seal-hunting voyages, but was lost with all hands in 1914.

SOU'WESTER, see SAILORS' DRESS.

SOVEREIGN OF THE SEAS, American *clipper ship built in 1852 by Donald *Mackay of Boston for the Swallow Tail Line. She proved to be very fast on her trials and made a name for the speed of her voyages on the New York–California run. As a result of this reputation for speed she was chartered by James Baines of Liverpool for his Black Ball Line and was used in the Australian wool trade, setting a new record for the passage from London to Melbourne of sixty-five days. It was not until thirty years later that this record was beaten by the famous clipper *Thermopylae. Deeply impressed by this fine performance of the *Sovereign of the Seas*, Baines ordered four more clippers from Mackay, all of which were to become famous in the history of these great sailing ships, the *Lightning, Donald Mackay, James Baines*, and *Champion of the Seas*. All four were built in 1854.

SOVEREIGN OF THE SEAS, H.M.S., see ROYAL SOVEREIGN, H.M.S.

SPALES, the name given to the temporary cross *beams fixed to support and hold in position the *frames of a wooden vessel while still under construction. They are, of course, finally replaced by the permanent deck beams.

SPAN, (1) a rope or wire with each end secured between fixed points, which is used for hooking on the standing *block of a *tackle where no other convenient point is available. (2) The distance between the *port and *starboard *turn-buckles or *deadeyes of the *chain plates measured over the masthead of a sailing vessel is also known as the span of the rigging.

SPANISH BURTON, a *purchase in which two single *blocks are used, the upper block being fitted with a hook, *eye, or tail and its standing part forming the *strop of the lower block. The power gained is four times, but the lift is very limited in comparison with a normal purchase. A double Spanish burton has the same arrangement but employs a double block in addition to the two singles, increasing the power gained to six times.

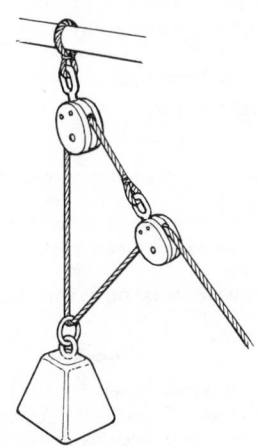

Single Spanish burton

'SPANISH LADIES', one of the oldest, and probably best known and best loved, songs of the sea. It was written and sung, it is thought, in 1694–5 when the British fleet under *Russell wintered at *Cadiz. Captain *Marryat, in his novel *Poor Jack*, gives the earliest complete version known but the song was an old one long before Marryat joined the British Navy. It has five verses and a chorus, and though there are many small differences in wording in the various versions, perhaps the best known runs as follows:

> Fare ye well and adieu to you, fair Spanish Ladies;
> Fare ye well and adieu to you, ladies of Spain,
> For we have got orders for to sail back to old England,
> But we hope in a short time for to see you again.

> *Chorus:* Then we'll rant and we'll roar like true British seamen,
> We'll rant and we'll roar all across the salt seas,
> Until we strike soundings in the Channel of old England;
> From Ushant to Scilly is thirty-five leagues.

> We hove the ship to with the wind at Sou'-West, my boys;
> We hove the ship to for to strike soundings clear.

We had forty-five fathom and a fine sandy bottom,
So we filled the main topsail and up Channel we steer.

(*Chorus*, as before)

The first land we made, 'twas the head called the Dodman,
Next Rame Head near Plymouth, Start, Portland, and Wight:
So we sailed by Beachy, by Fairlee, and Dungeness,
Where we bore right away for the South Foreland Light.

(*Chorus*)

The signal was made the Grand Fleet for to anchor,
All in the Downs the ships to be moored,
Let go your shank painter, stand by your cat stopper,
Haul up your clewgarnets, stick out tacks and sheets.

(*Chorus*)

Then let every man toss off a full bumper,
And let every man swig off a full bowl;
For we'll drink and be jolly and drown melancholy,
With a 'Here's a good health to each true-hearted soul.'

(*Chorus*)

See also SEA SONGS.

SPANISH MAIN, a term much used by writers of romantic stories of the sea to describe the Spanish possessions in America during the 16th, 17th, and 18th centuries, gained following the voyages of discovery by *Columbus and other Spanish navigators and conquistadors. In the strict and early meaning of the word it embraced that part of the mainland of the north-east coast of South America stretching from the Orinoco to the Isthmus of Panama and the former Spanish mainland possessions bordering on the Caribbean Sea and Gulf of Mexico. But by extension, particularly from the sense in which it was used by the *buccaneers of the late 17th and early 18th centuries, the term came to mean the Caribbean Sea itself. Thus the meaning changed completely; where originally in the 16th and early 17th centuries it referred to the main land, in the late 17th and 18th centuries it referred to the main sea.

SPANISH REEF, a method of reefing the topsails or *topgallant sails of a square-rigged ship by lowering the yard on to the *cap of the mast. It was, in British eyes in the days of sailing navies, thought to be a slovenly method of shortening

sail in a ship. Another form of Spanish reef, considered equally slovenly, was to shorten sail by tying a knot in the head of the *jibs.

SPANISH WINDLASS, a means of increasing the tautness of a *seizing by taking a couple of turns with the seizing round a short bar and then turning the bar with a *marline spike, held to it by a bight of the seizing and used as a lever. A Spanish windlass is used where maximum tautness is required, as in seizing together a couple of hawsers or binding a *strop tightly round a large *block and holding it taut while the neck is seized.

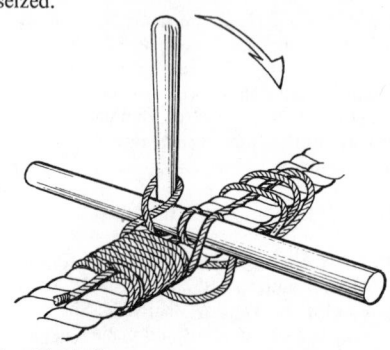

Spanish windlass

SPANKER, an additional sail hoisted on the *mizen-mast of sailing ships to take advantage of a following wind, was the name used for the final form of the *driver. It was originally regarded as a fair weather sail set in place of the mizen *course, but after about 1840 it became a standard sail set on the mizen, taking the place entirely of the mizen *course.

SPAR, a general term for any wooden support used in the rigging of a ship; it embraces all masts, *yards, *booms, *gaffs, etc.

SPAR BUOY, a *spar painted in a distinctive colour and moored from the bottom so as to float more or less upright as a navigational mark.

SPAR DECK, in its strict maritime meaning a temporary *deck laid in any part of a ship, the *beams across which it is laid being known as skid beams. But the term was often used to describe the *quarterdeck or *forecastle deck of a deep-waisted ship, possibly because in sailing ship days spare spars could be lashed to these decks as replacements for those damaged in use, rather than in the *waist of the ship. In modern usage, the term is sometimes employed to describe the upper deck of a flush-decked ship.

SPAR TORPEDO, an explosive charge, exploded by a contact pistol, fixed to the end of a long pole and carried over the bows of a small vessel for use against an enemy ship. They were developed during the American Civil War (1861–5) and the most notable example of their use was the sinking of the Confederate *ram *Albemarle* on 27 October 1864 by Lieutenant *Cushing, at Plymouth, North Carolina. They were rendered obsolete by the development of the locomotive *torpedo by Robert *Whitehead between 1870 and 1890.

SPARKMAN AND STEPHENS, see STEPHENS.

SPEAK, to, or **SPEAK A SHIP, to,** the act of communicating with a ship at sea. The term includes all methods of communication and does not necessarily mean that the ships are in sight of each other when communicating.

SPECKTIONEER, the name by which the chief harpooner in a whaling vessel was known, particularly when the vessel operated in Greenland waters. He was also responsible for directing the cutting operations in which the blubber was cleared from the whale. See also FLENSE, TO.

SPECTACLE IRON, two or three thimbles cast in a single mould so that two or three ropes may be hooked into it to lead in different directions.

SPEE, MAXIMILIAN JOHANNES MARIA HUBERTUS, Reichsgraf von (1861–1914), German vice admiral, was born at Copenhagen and in 1884 was a lieutenant in the *gunboat *Moewe* during the expedition which annexed German West Africa as a colony. In 1895, in the *Deutschland*, he was employed on similar colonial acquisitions in the South-West Pacific and on the China coast. He was with the German contingent in the Boxer Rebellion in China in 1900, and was promoted captain in 1905 with command of the *battleship *Wittelsbach*. When he was promoted rear admiral in 1912 he was appointed to command the East Asiatic Squadron, the most prized appointment in the German Navy, and still held that command at the outbreak of the First World War (1914–18). His squadron consisted of the two armoured *cruisers *Scharnhorst* and *Gneisenau* and the light cruisers *Emden*, *Leipzig*, and *Nürnberg*. Later the *Emden* was detached on an independent commerce-destruction cruise in the Indian Ocean and her place was taken by the light cruiser *Dresden*.

At the start of the war von Spee planned to attack British trade in the China Seas, but with Japan entering the war he switched his area of operations to the west coast of South America. During his squadron's passage there the *Nürnberg* cut the trans-Pacific cable at Fanning Island (7 September 1914) and the squadron shelled the French base at Papeete, Tahiti (22 September 1914). On arrival off the South American coast, von Spee met and defeated a British squadron which had rounded Cape Horn in search of him, sinking two old armoured cruisers (*Good Hope* and *Monmouth*) off the port of *Coronel. After the action he took his squadron round Cape Horn into the South Atlantic, proposing to attack Port Stanley in the *Falkland Islands and set up a German base there before returning to Germany. Two British *battle-cruisers were coaling in the port and, when von Spee's squadron was sighted, they put to sea and gave chase. Four out of five of the German squadron were sunk, including the *Scharnhorst* and *Gneisenau*, only the *Dresden* escaping. Von Spee's two sons were serving in the squadron, one in the *Gneisenau*, the other in the *Nürnberg*, and both, with their father, lost their lives in the action.

Always a strict disciplinarian, von Spee had had a model career in the German Navy, being promoted to his various ranks at the earliest opportunity. Had he returned to Germany after the battle of the Falkland Islands he would have been made commander-in-chief of the *High Seas Fleet by Admiral von *Tirpitz. The ships and squadrons he commanded were all superbly efficient, his reputation as a naval tactician was considerable, and he was especially admired for his chivalrous behaviour after battle.

SPENCER, the name given to a *trysail, laced to a *gaff and set on the after side of the fore- or mainmast of a square-rigged ship, much as a *spanker is set on a mizen-mast. They were introduced to take the place of the maintopmast and mizen staysails. R. H. *Dana, in his *Two Years Before the Mast*, talks about a spencer-mast (entry for 9 September 1834), but presumably means the mast on which the spencer was set; in the case of his ship, the *Pilgrim*, which was a *brig, the mainmast.

SPEND, to, a mast or yard, broken during bad weather, is said to be spent. But if broken in battle, it was 'shot by the board', or 'carried away by the board' if it was broken by the weight of other masts or yards bringing it down.

SPERMACETI, a form of liquid wax found in the head of the sperm whale (*Physeteridae*), which was used as a lubricating oil and industrial detergent. With the limitations now imposed on whale fishing, and the prohibition of imports of whale products into many countries, including Britain, substitutes for use in place of spermaceti have had to be found.

SPERRY, ELMER AMBROSE (1860–1930), U.S. inventor, is best known for his application of the gyroscopic principle in producing a *compass unaffected by iron or steel and always pointing to the true north pole. This gyroscopic compass underwent its first sea trials in 1907 and proved an immense boon to navigators. He is less well known for his invention of the high intensity carbon arc *searchlight, which he brought out in 1915 and which was adopted by all navies in the world. He also adapted the gyroscopic principle on which his compasses were based to the control of naval gunnery and, especially, to the guidance of *torpedoes, giving to them the important ability to run a straight course. Following these successes he produced in 1921 a gyroscopically controlled automatic steering gear for ships and, later, a gyroscopic stabilizer to counteract the pitch and roll in ships in a seaway.

SPEZIA, LA, a city in Italy in the province of Liguria, a seaport, and the chief naval base of Italy. Originally proposed as a naval base by Napoleon, it was not developed as such until 1861. The extensive *dockyard contains the chief naval *torpedo factory for the Italian Navy; a large gun foundry is also based in the dockyard. La Spezia was heavily bombed by allied air forces during the Second World War, but has since been largely rebuilt and modernized.

SPIDER, the name given to a metal outrigger to hold a *block clear of a mast or of a ship's side.

SPIDER BAND, a metal band with many *eyes welded to it, fitted around the mast of a square-rigged ship to which, in the later sailing ships, the *futtock shrouds are *shackled. It was also known as a futtock band. Also a metal band near the bottom of the mast in a fore-and-aft sailing vessels to which the *gooseneck of the main *boom is attached and which in *gaff-rigged vessels usually carries a number of *belaying pins to which the *halyards of the sail are *belayed.

SPILE, to, the operation of shaping the forward and after *timbers of a wooden vessel to take account of any *sheer in the design, and similarly the shaping of the *ribs of a steel vessel for the same purpose.

SPILL, to, the act of taking the wind out of a sail by bringing the vessel head to wind or by easing away the *sheet to an extent where the sail can hold no wind.

SPILLING LINES, the name given to ropes rove round the square sails in a square-rigged ship to keep them from blowing away when the tacks are eased off for the sails to be *clewed up, and to assist in *reefing and *furling. They are secured to the after side of the *yard and are led under

the sail and up to a *block on the forward side of the yard through which they are rove.

SPINDLER, ARNO (1880–1967), German rear admiral, served throughout the First World War (1914–18) in *U-boats and until his retirement in 1925 was considered a leading authority on submarine warfare. His reputation as a writer was established by the publication of the four volumes of his official history of the First World War U-boat campaign, *Der Handelskrieg mit U-Booten*, the fourth volume of which was produced during the Second World War and regarded as containing classified material. It was not released to the public until after the end of the war. The publication of a fifth and final volume, of which he had drawn up the first draft but which was completed by Professor *Hubatsch, was published, after his death, in 1967.

SPINNAKER, a three-cornered lightweight sail which is normally set forward of a yacht's mast with or without a boom to increase sail area with the wind aft of the beam. Its name is said to be derived from the 'spinxer', a word coined by yacht hands to describe the sail when it was first introduced aboard the yacht *Sphinx* during a race in the Solent in the 1870s. Since then many variations of the spinnaker have been tried out. At first the sail was shaped like a foresail, with only a moderate amount of flow or bulge in the belly of the canvas, but with the introduction of synthetic fibres for sail materials (e.g., Terylene, nylon, Dacron, etc.) more recent developments have produced spinnakers cut with a deep curve or *roach in the foot, and a great deal of flow in the belly of the sail. So full is this amount of flow in some sails that they quickly earned the name of parachute spinnakers. Designers and sailmakers have experimented with the effect of single or multiple large holes in the sail, following early parachute practice, which were designed to create a steady flow of air and prevent the wild gyrations that some spinnakers were prone to make when running before a freshening breeze.

Experiments continue in the handicap and offshore racing fleets to improve the effectiveness and handling qualities of spinnakers, some of which have appeared with cloths laid radially from the head with integral airfoil sections, as well as spinnakers with multi-cell sections which are claimed to give the sail increased 'lift' without extra weight. Racing spinnakers are noted for the variety and ingenuity of their coloured panels, making a colourful spectacle of any massed racing class.

Spinnaker was also the term bargees were wont to use to describe the jib topsail (usually of white canvas) which Thames *spritsail *barges set on their topmast forestays.

Morning Cloud III *under spinnaker*

SPIRKETTING, the name given to the extra thick *strake which used to be incorporated in the hull of a wooden ship to provide additional strength. It was fitted either at the outboard ends of the deck *beams or next above the *waterways.

SPITFIRE JIB, a small storm *jib made of very heavy canvas, used when the strength of the wind is such that the normal foresails in a small sailing vessel cannot be carried. It is almost entirely applicable to yachts; the larger sailing ships with several jibs being able to reduce their fore canvas in heavy weather by lowering one or more of their jibs.

SPITHEAD, a well-known and historical stretch of water in the east Solent lying off the British naval base of *Portsmouth. It is bounded on the north by the Spit Sand, on the east by the Horse and Dean Sand, on the south by the Sturbridge Shoal and the Motherbank, and on the west by the Ryde Middle Sand. It was the scene of the famous naval mutiny of 1797 when the British Channel Fleet refused to go to sea during the Revolutionary War against France (1793–1801) until the seamen's demands had been met. It was also the scene of an indecisive action between the English fleet and a French invasion fleet in 1545 and is the traditional anchorage where the British fleet is most frequently reviewed by the sovereign on great occasions. During the 17th and 18th century wars against Holland and France, Spithead was the fleet assembly point of many great battles and amphibious operations.

'SPITHEAD NIGHTINGALES', the British seaman's nickname on board a warship for *boatswain's mates. This of course came from their duty of *piping all orders with calls on their *pipes.

'SPITHEAD PHEASANT', the sailor's name for a kipper.

SPLICE, to, a method of joining two ropes or wires together by unlaying the strands at the two ends and tucking or relaying them according to the nature of the splice required. Ropes and wires are spliced together to join them permanently, but knotted when the join is temporary. Ropes can be joined by a *long splice when required to *reeve through a *block, a *short splice, or a *cut splice if it is required to incorporate an *eye at the point of junction. An eye required at the end of a rope or wire is produced by an *eye splice.

SPLICE THE MAIN BRACE, to, a traditional term in the British Navy for serving out an additional tot of rum or *grog to a ship's crew. The main *brace itself was a *purchase attached to the main lower *yard of a square-rigged ship to brace it round to the wind, but it probably has little to do with the saying beyond the fact that hauling on the main brace called for a maximum effort by the crew. In sailing ship days the main brace was spliced (in terms of drink) in very bad weather or after a period of severe exertion by the crew, more as a pick-me-up for the crew than for any other purpose. But with the introduction of steamships, with machines to take most of the harder labour out of seagoing, the main brace was spliced only on occasions of celebration or, occasionally, after battle. Now that, since 1970, rum is no longer issued in the British Navy, it is no longer possible to splice the main brace.

SPLICED, to get, the sailor's term for getting married. As two ropes or wires are joined permanently by being spliced, so also are a man and a woman when they get married.

SPLIT, orig. **SPALATO,** a city and seaport of Croatia, Yugoslavia, and the finest harbour in the Adriatic. The town was originally formed round the palace built there by the Roman emperor Diocletian in A.D. 300, and was frequently overrun by warfarers, particularly the Goths and Huns, being finally deserted by its inhabitants at the end of the 12th century. In 1105 it became a vassal state of Hungary and in 1327 a revolution brought it under the rule of Venice. It was occupied by France (1805–13) during the Napoleonic War (1803–15), becoming Austrian after the peace of 1815. After a brief occupation by Italy in 1918 it became Yugoslav in 1919. It is a principal base of the Yugoslav Navy, and is also a considerable port with a large trade in cement and marl.

SPOIL GROUND, an area of the seabed, marked by *buoys, on which sewage, spoil from dredging, and other rubbish may be deposited by *lighters or *hoppers specially equipped for the task, with bottom doors which open to allow the discharge underwater of the spoil they are carrying.

SPOKE, in any wheel a rod or bar extending outwards from the hub to support the rim, but in a ship's steering wheel a spoke is the extension beyond the rim which forms a handle by which the wheel is turned to angle the *rudder.

SPONSON, a platform formed on a ship's side either by an outboard bulge of the hull or by an indentation of the ship's side to form a flat surface on the deck level below. Sponsons were mainly associated with larger warships and were most often used to provide mountings for the secondary armament. Without a sponson the barrels of guns ranged along the ship's side would project beyond the line of the vessel's hull; when mounted in a ship with sponsons the barrels, when trained fore-and-aft, remain within the line of the hull. Modern warships, with the exception of most aircraft carriers, are very rarely built with sponsons today as normally the whole of their armament is mounted inboard.

In vessels propelled with paddle-wheels, the sponsons are those parts of the ship's structure which project beyond the ship's side forward and aft of each paddle-wheel and help to support the paddle boxes. There are thus four of them and they are level with the bottoms of the paddle boxes.

SPOON, to, an old maritime term meaning to * scud, or to run before a gale with reduced canvas or under bare poles. It passed out of use as a sea expression during the first half of the 18th century, but is sometimes to be seen in the works of maritime writers of the 16th and 17th centuries. Thus Samuel * Pepys, commenting on the St. James's Day battle against the Dutch, wrote in his diary for 3 August 1666: 'And more, that we might have spooned before the wind as well as they, and have overtaken their ships in the pursuite in all that while.'

SPRAGGE, Sir EDWARD (c. 1620–73), English admiral, began his career as a soldier. As a result of his royalist sympathies and active assistance in the restoration of Charles II in 1660 he was rewarded by being given the command of a naval ship. By the outbreak of the Second Anglo-Dutch War (1665–7) he was captain of H.M.S. * Triumph, commanding her with great dash at the battle of * Lowestoft. He was knighted after the battle and received rapid promotion to rear admiral and vice admiral following the courage and tenacity with which he fought his ships in the * Four Days Battle (June 1666) and the St. James's Day Fight (July 1666). In the following year he was port admiral at Sheerness when the Dutch fleet under de * Ruyter raided the * Medway.

He was appointed commander-in-chief in the Mediterranean after the war and fought a notable and successful action against the * Algerine pirates in * Bugia Bay, returning to England in 1672 in time to take part in the Third Dutch War (1672–4). He was always something of a 'fire-eater' in battle, as was Cornelis * Tromp in the Dutch fleet, and these two almost always singled each other out in battle to fight something of a personal duel with their ships. After taking part in three battles of the Third Dutch War, in which he and Tromp exulted in hammering each other whenever possible, he was promoted admiral and commanded the rear division of the English fleet at the battle of the * Texel in 1673. He again

sought out Cornelis Tromp, and these two fought a more or less private battle apart from the main fleet action. Spragge's flagship was so badly damaged in the early part of the battle that he took a boat to hoist his flag in another ship. She, too, became so damaged in the hottest gunfire of the fight that Spragge again took a boat to take over a third ship as his flagship, but the boat was sunk and Spragge was killed, Tromp losing his life in the same action.

SPRATT, Sir THOMAS ABEL BRIMAGE (1811–90), British vice admiral, spent his naval service almost entirely in the Mediterranean from 1832 to 1863. As a surveyor he served under Thomas * Graves and continued the work the latter had begun in what was then called the Grecian Archipelago, paying attention to the classical and geological history of the area. He published numerous reports and papers, the last being Travels and Researches in Crete in 1864. The naturalist, Edward Forbes, was sometimes a companion in his ship, H.M.S. Spitfire. Spratt was a Fellow of the Royal Geological, Zoological, and Geographical Societies, and also the Society of Antiquaries.

During the Crimean War (1854–6) it is said that the services of the Spitfire in the Black Sea were the admiration of the fleet, and she was an intelligence department in herself with surveys, sketches, and ground plans, often made under enemy fire. Spratt was specially promoted to captain in January 1855 and awarded a special honour at the end of the war.

SPREADERS, (1) metal or wooden struts placed in pairs * athwartships on a yacht's mast to spread the angle of the upper or masthead * shrouds, or side * stays. In the older * gaff rig, such spreaders were commonly known as * crosstrees (see illus.). **(2)** Metal bars fitted to the * bow of a square-rigged ship to give more spread to the * tacks of the fore * course.

SPRING, a rope or wire hawser led aft from the * bow or forward from the * stern of a ship and made fast to a * bollard ashore. They are known as a fore spring and a back spring respectively. In addition to preventing a ship from surging backwards or forwards when secured alongside, they enable a ship's bow or stern to be swung clear when leaving. By going ahead against a fore spring with the helm over, the stern swings outwards while the ship is held from moving ahead by the spring. Similarly, by going astern against a back spring with the helm over, the bow can be swung clear.

SPRING, to, the situation of a plank in the hull structure of a wooden vessel when one of its ends, or * butts, breaks loose of the copper nails or *treenails which secure it to the *timbers of a ship and, because of its shape bent to the curve of the hull, springs outwards and projects beyond the curve of the hull. Such a plank is said to be sprung. Similarly, the verb is used to describe the wooden mast or spar of a vessel when a crack develops by which the fibres are damaged, such a mast or spar then being sprung and needing to be *fished, or if very badly sprung, replaced.

SPRING A LEAK, to, to develop a break in the hull of a vessel through which seawater can enter. The term originated from the occasional tendency of the hull planking of a wooden vessel to *spring, or to break free of its fastenings at the vessel's *timbers at the butts (ends) of the plank, but now applies to any hole or break in a ship's hull, however made, by which the sea comes in.

SPRING STAYS, the name given to additional mast *stays carried on board warships in the days of the sailing navies to replace those shot away in battle. *Chain and bar shot were frequently used in action during those days specifically to sever the rigging of enemy ships, making it advisable to carry on board spare rigging of all descriptions.

SPRING TIDES, those *tides which rise highest and fall lowest from the mean tide level, as compared with *neap tides, which are those which rise lowest and fall highest. Spring tides occur when the pull of the moon and of the sun act in conjunction whether 0° or 180° apart; neaps when they act in opposition, either 90° or 270° apart. These conditions occur twice in each lunar month, so that there are two spring tides and two neap tides every twenty-nine days.

SPRIT, a long spar which stretches diagonally across a four-sided fore-and-aft sail to support the *peak, as in the typical *barge rig. Its heel or inboard end is held in a *snotter near the base of the mast. Although reliefs found at Thasos and dating from the 2nd century B.C. show that the sprit was known to the Greeks and Romans for

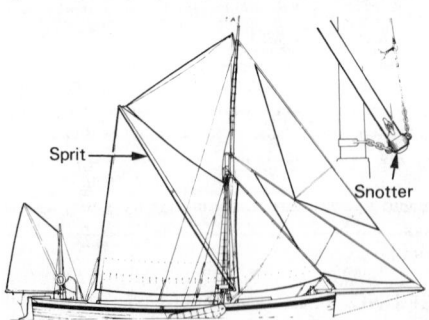

Thames barge with sprit

small boats, it was not introduced into western Europe for seagoing ships until the early 15th century, almost certainly by the Dutch, as a rig for smaller, coastal craft, proving much more weatherly than square-rig in the shoal and tidal waters off the Dutch coast. See SPRITSAIL (2).

SPRITSAIL, (1) a small square sail set on a *yard beneath the bowsprit in square-rigged ships, introduced at the beginning of the 16th century as a balancing sail to the *lateen mizen, which was the normal after canvas set in two- and three-masted ships. A spritsail topsail was a similar sail to the spritsail but set on a short mast, known as a spritsail topmast, stepped perpendicularly on the end of the bowsprit above the spritsail and sheeted to the yardarms of the spritsail. It was first introduced about 1600. Both these sails were superseded by the triangular *jibs and *staysails which were introduced in 1705 and performed the same balancing purpose more simply and efficiently. **(2)** A fore-and-aft four-sided sail set on a *sprit, as in the typical *barge rig. The top of the sprit supports the *peak of the sail, the bottom is held close to the mast in a *snotter just above deck level at the *tack of the sail. This type of spritsail is always loose-footed, i.e., it is not *laced to a *boom. For a short period a spritsail was set on the *mizen of a three-masted square-rigged ship, replacing the *lateen sail in about 1550 and itself being replaced by a *gaff sail about 100 years later.

SPRUANCE, RAYMOND AMES (1886–1969), American admiral, distinguished himself especially by his brilliant strategy and tactics in the battles of *Midway (1942) and the *Philippine Sea (1944). Born in Baltimore, Maryland, he was raised in Indiana and appointed to the Naval Academy from that State. Early in the First World War (1914–18) he served in the *battleship *Pennsylvania*, and later, in 1918, had special duty in London and in Edinburgh in connection with *director fire control installations. He completed the senior course of instruction at the Naval War College in May 1927, and after serving as executive officer of the battleship *Mississippi*, he was a member of the Naval War College staff from 1931 to 1933 and again from 1935 to 1938. After brief service in the Caribbean area, he took command of a *cruiser division as a rear admiral in September 1941. He served as second-in-command in task force operations in the Marshall Islands and at Wake Island in February 1942 and also took part in the Marcus Island operations in March.

In the battle of Midway, Spruance commanded a force of two *aircraft carriers, six cruisers, and nine *destroyers. His decisions had to be made on the basis of incomplete knowledge of the strength, disposition, and location of the enemy. He decided promptly and executed his intentions effectively while at the same time recognizing that Admiral *Yamamoto was attempting to draw him into a fight against a force of fast battleships and heavy cruisers.

Spruance served as chief of staff to Admiral *Nimitz from June 1942 and was designated deputy commander-in-chief of the Pacific Fleet in September of that year. In August 1943 he became Commander Central Pacific Force, and, in April 1944, Commander Fifth Fleet. He held the overall command in the occupation of the Gilbert Islands in November 1943 and in the invasion of the Marshall Islands in January 1944.

Spruance commanded the forces employed in the operations for the capture of Saipan, Guam, and Tinian, in the Mariana Islands, which included the battle of the Philippine Sea. Some critics have suggested that Spruance missed a great opportunity to destroy the Japanese fleet by failing to advance westward and bring on an engagement earlier, but he had the responsibility of supporting the troops ashore on Saipan and for the safety of the naval vessels and transports off that island and those waiting to assault Guam. The Japanese carriers lost 330 out of the 430 planes they carried and the Japanese high command recognized, as a result of the battle, that the war could no longer be won. Further successful operations under his command were those against Iwo Jima and Okinawa.

In November 1945, Spruance succeeded Nimitz as commander-in-chief of the Pacific Fleet. In March 1946 he became President of the Naval War College, retaining that post until his retirement on 1 July 1948. Afterwards, he served as ambassador to the Republic of the Philippines from 1952 to 1955.

E. P. Forrestel, *Admiral Raymond A. Spruance, USN* (Washington, 1966).

SPUNYARN, a small line made of two, three, or four yarns, not laid but loosely twisted. It has a variety of uses, on board ship, particularly for such purposes as *seizing, *serving, etc. It is also used in sailing vessels for *stopping sails, enabling them to be hoisted in stops (i.e., lightly secured with turns of spunyarn) and able to be broken out when required by a sharp pull on the *sheet.

SPURLING GATE, a cast iron fitting in the deck of a ship through which the *cable passes on the way down to the *chain locker.

SPURLING LINE, a line made fast to the rudder-head of a ship and brought up on either side to the position of the steering wheel. It operates the tell-tale by which the angle of the rudder is indicated to the *quartermaster at the wheel.

SQUADRON, from the Italian *squadrone*, a small number of warships which could comfortably be directed by a single flag officer. The term, in the British Navy, dates from 1588. Later, in the age of steam navies, it became the collective name for a small number of warships, usually eight, of the same type, down to the size of *cruisers. Smaller warships, such as *destroyers and submarines, were at that time similarly organized into *flotillas. More recently still all warships in most navies, even such ones as small as *minesweepers, are now organized into squadrons, the collective term flotilla having largely dropped out of use in naval organization.

SQUADRONAL COLOURS, an early method of subdividing the English fleet into *squadrons. It is said to have been inaugurated in the time of Elizabeth I; the earliest surviving instructions laying down the wearing of coloured flags to denote the three squadrons into which the fleet was divided are dated 1617. The admiral's squadron wore a red flag, the vice admiral's a white, and the rear admiral's a blue.

As fleets grew in size, and the three squadrons into which they were divided became correspondingly larger, it became impossible for one admiral to control the movements of his squadron efficiently from his position in the centre of it. In consequence, three admirals were, in theory, allocated to each squadron, a full admiral in command, a vice admiral as his second, and a rear admiral as third in command. Thus, the white squadron was commanded by an admiral of the White, with a vice admiral of the White and a rear admiral of the White as his second and third in command. The squadrons ranked in the order red, white, blue, and admirals took rank according to the colour of their squadron. Promotion of admirals also took place in this order, a rear admiral of the Blue on promotion becoming a rear admiral of the White as his first step in flag rank, and a rear admiral of the Red becoming a vice admiral of the Blue when he received promotion. Only in the red, or senior, squadron was this hierarchy not followed. There was no admiral of the Red since he was in overall command of the whole fleet and therefore, in theory, was the *admiral of the fleet.

The rank of admiral of the Red was introduced after the battle of *Trafalgar as a compliment to the British Navy for its successes in the Napoleonic War (1803–15) and as a means of rewarding the most successful admirals. It was not possible then to make promotions to the rank of admiral of the fleet since there was only one holder of this rank and he retained it for life.

In 1864 the organization of the British fleet into coloured squadrons was discarded, mainly because it had no further relevance in the age of steam warships. The red, or senior, ensign was allocated to the merchant navy of Britain, the Royal Navy adopting the white ensign, and the blue ensign being used by naval auxiliary vessels.

SQUALL, a sudden gust of wind of considerable strength. Squalls usually follow the passage of a *depression, when the barometer begins to rise from its lowest point. This is because the barometer gradient is almost always steeper in the wake of a depression than ahead of its centre. See METEOROLOGY.

SQUARE, the position of the *yards when a square-rigged ship is at anchor and set up in harbour trim. The yards are square by the *braces when they are at right-angles to the fore-and-aft line of the ship. They are square by the *lifts when they are horizontal.

SQUARE-BUTTED, the *yardarms of smaller square-rigged ships are said to be square-butted when they are cut to a thickness where they can have a sheave-hole cut in their ends without weakening them. These are used for *reeving the *braces.

SQUARE-RIG, see RIG.

SQUID, a development during the Second World War of the means of attacking a submerged *U-boat with *depth-charges. A great drawback of the conventional method of attack with these weapons was the means of delivery, dropping them over the stern of the attacking ship and firing them on each beam through depth-charge throwers. This entailed the attacking ship passing over the submerged U-boat and losing *sonar contact in the process. The squid was a three-barrelled mortar mounted on the quarterdeck which fired three full-sized depth-charges over the *bridge to fall ahead of the ship in a predetermined pattern. This method of attack enabled sonar contact with the U-boat to be held right up to the moment of explosion of the depth-charges.

STAGHORN, a metal bollard with horizontal arms forming the shape of a cross, fitted in big ships as a means of belaying larger hawsers.

STANCHIONS, the upright supports set along the side of the upper *deck of a ship which carry the guardrail or, in the case of smaller vessels, the wires which act as a guardrail. Longer stanchions are additionally used in large ships as the means of spreading an *awning over the deck in hot weather, and are also occasionally fitted to support a light deck above.

STANDING LUG, a sailing rig in which the forward end of the *yard carrying a *lugsail lies close along the mast so that the sail does not have to be lowered and dipped round the mast when the vessel goes *about. It includes the *gunter rig. See also MACARONI LUG.

Typical standing lug

STANDING PART, that part of the rope used in a *purchase of which the end is secured to the eye of the *block which does not move, known as the standing block. The part of the rope which is between the standing and the moving blocks is the running part, and the remainder, as it comes out of the purchase, is the hauling part. The whole of the rope is known as the *fall.

STANDING RIGGING, the fixed and permanent rigging of a ship. See RIGGING.

STANFIELD,   WILLIAM   CLARKSON (1793–1876), British marine artist, was born at Sunderland. He first served at sea in the merchant navy but was *impressed out of his ship into the Royal Navy, being invalided in 1818 after being disabled by a fall from the rigging. His captain at the time was Frederick *Marryat, who advised him to take up painting as a career. He later became a friend of Charles Dickens, for whom he painted some scenery. He was an early and important exponent of the naturalist school of British marine painting and has been referred to as the English Van de *Velde. He had the skill of producing a wonderful luminosity in his marine pictures, one of his best-known paintings, which now hangs in Admiralty House, Gibraltar, being of H.M.S. *Victory* being towed there after the battle of *Trafalgar. A small collection of his pictures is in the *National Maritime Museum at Greenwich.

STANLEY, OWEN (1811–50), British naval officer, joined the navy in 1826. He became a surveyor while serving in the *Adventure* in the Magellan Strait 1830–2; in 1834 he went to the *Mastiff* in the Mediterranean and two years later to the *Terror* during the 1836–7 Arctic expedition, where he was responsible for the astronomical and magnetic observations. In 1843–6, while in command of the *Britomart*, he assisted with the maintenance of the Port Essington colony in northern Australia and made a track survey of the Arafura Sea. He commanded the surveying ship *Rattlesnake* during her notable voyages in 1847–50 in the Torres Strait, the Louisade Archipelago, and on the eastern shores of New Guinea, T. H. Huxley being on board for his initiation as a naturalist. The surveying ship *Bramble* was in company and an account of the voyage was compiled in two volumes by the other naturalist carried, MacGillivray. Oswald *Brierly was also embarked as artist though Stanley was himself expert with water colours. Regrettably the constant anxiety of working in such dangerous waters, coupled with the news on his return to Sydney of the deaths of his father and brother, led Owen Stanley to end his own life. One monument to his dedicated work is the use of his name for the mountain range in New Guinea. He was a Fellow of the Royal Society and the Royal Astronomical Society.

A. Lubbock, *Owen Stanley, R.N.* (Melbourne, 1966).

STARBOARD, the right-hand side of a vessel as seen from aft. It is generally accepted to be a corruption of steer-board, the board or oar which projected into the sea from the starboard quarter of old vessels and by which they were steered before the invention of the hanging *rudder. See also LARBOARD, PORT, STEERING OAR. At night, a vessel under way at sea indicates her starboard side by carrying a green light on that side, visible from right ahead to two *points abaft the beam.

The starboard side of a ship used to be the side usually reserved for the captain; he used the starboard ladder when going ashore or returning to the ship, all others using the port ladder; the starboard side of the *poop deck or *quarterdeck was usually reserved for him when he came on deck for exercise; his cabin was normally on the starboard side of the ship. Today this distinction between the starboard and port side has largely died out except, perhaps, in some navies and the older and larger passenger steamship lines.

STARBOARD GYBE, a *fore-and-aft rigged sailing vessel is sometimes said to be on the *starboard *gybe, instead of on the *starboard tack, when the wind comes from abaft the beam on the starboard side.

STARBOARD TACK, the situation of a sailing vessel with her sails trimmed for a wind which comes over the *starboard side of the vessel. Although the verb 'to tack' postulates a vessel sailing *close-hauled, a vessel on any point of sailing is on the starboard tack if the wind comes over her starboard side. But see also STARBOARD GYBE.

'STARBOLINS', a name for the men of the *starboard *watch in a ship, as *'larbolins' was a name for the men of the *larboard, or *port, watch.

STARBUCK, the name of the chief mate of the *whaler *Pequod* in Herman *Melville's great tale of the sea *Moby Dick*, first published in 1851. See also AHAB, Captain.

STARGAZER, the name given to a small supplementary sail occasionally set in a square-rigged ship in very light weather to get the utmost out of a breeze. It was set above the *moonsail, which was set above the *skysail.

STARK, HAROLD RAYNSFORD (1880–1972), American admiral, was born in Pennsylvania and graduated from the Naval Academy in 1903. He was Chief of Naval Operations from 1 August 1939 to 12 March 1942, when he was succeeded by Admiral E. J. *King. Stark then served as Commander, Naval Forces in Europe, from 30 April 1942 to 15 August 1945, earning a considerable reputation for the conduct of operations in those waters, which included the amphibious assault on Normandy in June 1944, and for the close relations he fostered between British and American naval forces during joint operations.

STARSHELL, a shell containing a pyrotechnic flare suspended on a small parachute and fired to illuminate an enemy warship or fleet at night. They were fired at a high elevation with a fuse timed to burst the shell and release the flare in the air behind the enemy ship or fleet so that it would be silhouetted against the illumination which drifted down on its parachute, thus presenting a visible target to the gunlayers. One of the drawbacks of starshell was the relatively short time that elapsed between the release of the flare and its extinction when it reached the sea, another was the small area over which it spread its illumination. During the Second World War starshell were used to illuminate *U-boats attacking *convoys until superseded by the more efficient *snowflake, and were also used with great effect in the sinking in December 1943 of the German *battle-cruiser *Scharnhorst* by ships of the British Home Fleet. Modern seaborne *radar has now virtually ensured all-round visibility at sea even on the darkest of nights.

START, to, (1) the operation of easing away, as the *sheet of a sail, or a *hawser, by rendering it round a *bollard. A cask is started when it is topped or opened, a plank in the side of a wooden ship has started when it works loose. **(2)** An irregular punishment which was widespread on board ships of the British Navy during the days of sail in which the *master-at-arms and boatswain's mates of a ship were allowed to hit, or start, the seamen with canes or rope-ends to get them moving at their work. It was made illegal by Admiralty order in 1809, but some captains (fortunately very few) allowed the custom to continue in their ships and it was not until some years later that it was completely eradicated. See also 'THREE SISTERS'.

STATENS SJÖHISTORISKA MUSEUM, the national maritime museum of Sweden, housed in Stockholm. Though not as large as the maritime museum at *Gothenburg (Göteborg), it is an important museum which contains the Royal Swedish Navy's collection, which dates from 1752, and a mercantile marine section dating from 1913. Among the more important exhibits are models of ships designed and built by Frederik af *Chapman, Sweden's most famous naval architect, and the museum also contains the stern section of Gustav III's *schooner *Amphion* on board which he took the decision to engage the Russian fleet at Svensksund in July 1790. There are several models of *dockyards and a fine display of nautical instruments, implements, and uniforms.

Smaller maritime museums in Sweden can be found at the ports of Falsterbö, Gävle, Halmstad (Hallands Museum), Hälsingborg, Kalmar, Luleå (Norrbottens Museum), Malmö, Norrköping, Oskarshamn, Raa, Simrishamn (Österläns Museum), Skellefteå, Sundsvall, Torekov, Udevalla, Vaddö (Roslagens Museum), Västervik (Tjustbygdens Museum), and Växjö (Smålands Museum).

STATEROOM, the name often given in large *liners to the *cabins occupied by first-class passengers.

STATION BILL, a list showing the stations of all members of the crew of a ship for all evolutions required, such as entering or leaving harbour, fire drill, boat drill, and in warships, action stations. The station bill must by law be posted in various parts of the ship so that it can be seen by all on board.

STATION POINTER, a navigational instrument by which a ship's position on a *chart can be fixed in coastal waters by means of *horizontal sextant angles. In its simplest form a station pointer consists of a circular protractor of perspex about six inches in diameter which is fitted with three radial arms, each having a bevelled edge. The central arm is fixed at zero degrees on the protractor; the other two are pivoted at the axis of the protractor and each can be set to any angle relative to the fixed central arm. To use the station pointer, the navigator of the ship takes the horizontal sextant angles between three fixed points marked on the chart and sets these angles on the station pointer with the movable arms. When the station pointer thus set is laid on the chart so that the bevelled edges of the three arms correspond with the three fixed points marked on the chart, the ship's position is at the axis of the station pointer. As a navigational instrument, the station pointer is of most value to a hydrographic surveyor who needs to make frequent accurate fixes in coastal waters during the course of his survey.

The invention of the station pointer is attributed to Murdoch *Mackenzie, senior, the famous English hydrographic surveyor, who described it in his *Treatise on Maritim Surveying*, published in 1774. But a similar method of fixing a position, known to Dutch navigators as Snell's Fix, is attributed to the Dutch philosopher and surveyor Willebrord Snell (1591–1626), more commonly known as Snellius. His method, although based on horizontal angles between fixed positions on shore, required a tedious geometrical solution and for this reason was not widely used, though it is possible that the Snell's Fix gave Mackenzie the basic idea for his instrument.

An alternative means of solving the station pointer fix is by means of a piece of tracing paper on which the observed angles have been constructed from a common point. By laying the tracing paper on the navigation chart and setting it so that the arms of the angles are coincident each with the position on the chart of the three observed marks, the ship's position is pricked through the tracing paper on to the chart at the intersection of the arms of the angle.

STATIONAIRE, a steam yacht, manned by the Royal Navy, which used to be permanently stationed at some foreign ports for the exclusive use of the British ambassador accredited to the country. They were finally withdrawn under the naval economy measures of Admiral Sir John *Fisher when he was First Sea Lord, 1904–10.

STAVE, to, the operation of breaking in the planking of a boat or vessel in order to sink her, or to drive in the head of a cask, especially of spirits, to prevent the crew drinking it in the case of shipwreck. In the case of boats, the past tense of the verb is stove, in the case of casks, it is staved.

STAVE OFF, to, the operation of holding off a boat or small vessel with a spar to prevent her coming alongside too heavily, or of holding off another vessel when she is approaching so as to risk a collision. See also FEND OFF, TO.

STAVES, the component parts of a cask after it has been *knocked down. They are the curved wooden parts which form the barrel, *rabbeted at both ends to take the bottom and the top.

STAY, a part of the standing *rigging of a sailing vessel which supports a mast in the fore-and-aft line, forestays supporting it from forward and backstays from aft. They take their names from the masts they support, as forestay, fore topmast stay, fore topgallant-mast stay, etc.

STAY, a term used in connection with the position of a ship in relation to her anchor and cable. A cable is said to be at short stay when it is taut and leads down to the anchor at a steep angle; it is at long stay when it is taut and leads out to the anchor well away from the ship's bows, entering the water at an acute angle. See CATENARY.

STAY, to, the operation of bringing the head of a sailing vessel up to the wind in order to *tack, or go *about. It is a term used also to describe the inclination of a mast in relation to the perpendicular; a mast is stayed forward or *raked aft according to whether it inclines forward or aft.

STAYBAND, a metal ring fitted near the top of a mast, with projecting lugs to which are secured the *shrouds and *stays supporting the mast. It is the modern equivalent of the *hounds, which used to provide the support on which the top of the shrouds rested. See also RIGGING.

STAYS, the moment when, during the operation of *tacking, a sailing vessel is head to wind. If she hangs there, with her head not paying off on the opposite tack, she is said to be 'in stays'. If her head fails to pay off on the opposite tack but falls back on the original tack, she is said to have 'missed stays'.

STAYSAIL, a triangular fore-and-aft sail which is set by being *hanked to a *stay. They are set both in square-rigged and *fore-and-aft rigged ships, and take their names from the stay on which they are set, as fore staysail, fore topmast staysail, etc.

STEAMING LIGHTS, the compulsory white navigation lights carried on the masts of all vessels under way at sea by night by which their presence, and an indication of their *course, is made known to other vessels in the vicinity. For details of navigation lights, see APPENDIX 3.

STEELE, ROBERT (*fl.* 1840–70), Scottish shipbuilder of Greenock, was, during the 19th century, among the best known of the tea *clipper builders; among the famous ships he built were the *Taeping, *Ariel, *Sir Lancelot, and *Serica*.

STEER, to, to direct a vessel by means of a *steering oar, or by a *tiller or steering-wheel connected to a *rudder, so that she proceeds in the desired direction. Up to about the end of the first millennium A.D., all steering was achieved by means of the steering oar, usually projecting from the *starboard quarter of the vessel. It was a short step, taken in about the late 12th or early 13th century, to replace the steering oar with a rudder hung on the *sternpost of the ship and worked by a tiller attached to the rudder-head. This was very efficient until ships grew in size to the extent where the tiller had to be a relatively long spar in order to provide sufficient leverage to counteract the pressure of the water on the rudder when it was put over. In a gale of wind it could require several men to control the tiller of a large ship, even with the aid of *relieving tackles. The introduction of the steering-wheel in the late 17th century replaced the long tiller in larger ships and made easier the manual task of controlling the rudder. TO STEER SMALL, to keep a ship on her desired course with only small movements of the tiller or wheel. TO STEER LARGE, the opposite of to steer small, or in the case of a sailing vessel, to steer her so that she has the wind *free.

STEERAGE, a large space below deck, usually above the *propellers, which in some merchant ships was used for crew accommodation and in passenger ships during the 19th and early 20th centuries was reserved for those passengers who could not pay for a private *cabin. The sides were lined with wooden bunks, and often with one or more tiers of bunks running longitudinally in the space between the sides. In those days passengers were expected to bring their own bedclothes and also their own food, a large stove being erected on deck at which they could cook it. In the days of sailing ships carrying passengers the steerage was that part of the ship next below the *quarterdeck and immediately before the *bulkhead of the great *cabin.

STEERAGE WAY, a vessel has steerage way when she has sufficient headway for her *rudder to grip the water so that she will answer her *helm. A sailing vessel becalmed, or a steamship broken down, loses steerage way when it becomes impossible to hold her on *course.

STEERING OAR, the forerunner of the vertical *rudder hung on the *sternpost. Originally a single oar projecting over the quarter of the boat, usually on the *starboard (steerboard) side, it was multiplied in the larger vessels to two or three oars. A quarter gallery pierced for such steering oars gave the necessary pivotal support; examples of this technique being seen in Egyptian bas-reliefs of 3000 B.C. A somewhat later example from Egypt (2500 B.C.) shows a steering oar projecting over the *stern of a vessel, lashed to the *counter and secured to a vertical post in the sternsheets, and operated by a vertical *tiller dowelled into the *loom of the steering oar. Steering oars projecting from both quarters simultaneously were well known in Egypt by the 12th century B.C., an obvious improvement in directional control of a vessel. In some pictures of the Phoenician trading ships, steering oars are shown projecting on both quarters through the hull of the ship herself. Steering oars remained the only means of directing the course of a ship up to about the beginning of the 13th century A.D., when they were gradually replaced by the vertical *rudder hinged to the after end of the *sternpost.

STEEVE, the angle of the *bowsprit in relation to the horizontal. A high-steeved bowsprit, or one with a high steeve, is a bowsprit well cocked-up towards the vertical. In ancient single-masted sailing ships the bowsprit was always very high-steeved and in fact became the forerunner of the foremast when the two- and three-masted rig was adopted for ships.

STEFANSSON, VILHJALMUR (1879–1962), Canadian *Arctic explorer, commanded an overland expedition in 1908–12 in northern Canada to survey the coastal waters, and from 1913 to 1918 explored a great area north of Alaska and Canada, discovering the islands of Borden, Brock, Meighen, and Lougheed. He discovered also that, in these waters, man could live plentifully and healthily on the abundant indigenous seal life and became a great exponent of the development of the Arctic as one of the great meat-supplying areas of the world through cultivation of the seal and the musk ox. He became an adviser to the U.S. government during the Second World War on defence conditions in Alaska. He was also the author of many books describing life in these northern areas.

STEM, the foremost *timber or steel member forming the *bow of a vessel joined at the bottom to the *keel either by *scarfing (wood) or riveting (steel). In wooden vessels all the timber *strakes are *rabbeted to the stem, in steel ships the fore plates are riveted to it.

STEM, to, a seafaring term indicating that a vessel is holding her own, or making only slight headway, against a contrary *tidal stream or current. A vessel may require to do this if she is waiting for a *pilot, or for some other purpose in which she needs to remain stationary; it is unlikely in modern propulsion development that any steam or diesel vessel is so low-powered that she cannot overcome the strongest of tidal streams. It is, of course, a more common occurrence with sailing vessels when there is not sufficient strength in the wind to give them sufficient way to do more than stem the tidal stream.

STEP, a square framework of timber or steel built up and fixed to the *keelson of a ship to take the *heel of a mast. Masts are normally squared off at the heel, to fit securely into the square step so that they cannot twist or revolve. In some smaller craft, masts are stepped on the deck and not taken down through the deck to the keelson, and in such cases the deck is normally strengthened with an additional deck *beam to provide extra support. But see also TABERNACLE.

STEP A MAST, to, the operation of erecting a mast by fitting the *heel into the *step on the *keelson of a vessel and setting up all its standing rigging.

STEPHENS, OLIN JAMES (1908–   ), American naval architect and partner in the shipbuilding firm of Sparkman and Stephens, first became widely known when he designed and owned the *Dorade*, an advanced type of ocean racing *yawl in which he won the Transatlantic and *Fastnet races of 1931. With a waterline length of 50 feet (15·3 m) she embodied many novel features which became generally adopted for offshore racing/cruising yachts.

His skill as a helmsman and racing tactician brought him a place in the *afterguard in the *America*'s Cup defenders *Ranger*, of which he was co-designer, in 1937 and *Columbia*, which he designed, in 1958. He designed a large number of outstandingly successful racing yachts, including such well-known vessels as *Stormy Weather*, *Baruna*, *Vim*, *Bolero*, *Finisterre*, *Constellation* (an *America*'s Cup defender), *Deb*, *Roundabout*, and *Clarionet*.

For some years he was chairman of the International Technical Committee for offshore race rules and also the technical committee of the International Yacht Racing Union.

His brother RODERICK, born a year later, was also a naval architect and was first mate on board the *Dorade* in 1931 when she won the Transatlantic and Fastnet races, and skippered her two years later when she again won the Fastnet race. He was also skipper of his brother's *Stormy Weather* when she won the 1935 Transatlantic and Fastnet races. Again like his brother, he was a member of the afterguard of *Ranger*, of which he was Olin Stephens's co-designer, during the *America*'s Cup races of 1937 against the challenge of T. O. M. *Sopwith's *Endeavour II*. During the Second World War he was responsible for the design of the U.S. Army's *DUKW amphibious trucks and other aquatic projects.

STEPHENS, WILLIAM PICARD (1854–1946), American historian and yacht designer, was born in Philadelphia and his early exploits in sailing *canoes made him a leading member of the New York Canoe Club, and of the Humber Yawl Club in England. He contributed a regular yachting column to the magazine *Forest and Stream* from 1888 for many years, was editor of *Lloyd's Register of American Yachts* from 1897 to 1932, and official historian of the North American Yacht Racing Union and of the Cruising Club of America. He wrote *Traditions and Memories of American Yachting* (1942) and was co-author, with William M. Thompson and William U. Swan, of *The Yacht America*, a history of the *schooner which won the famous cup at Cowes in 1851.

The ocean racing yawl Dorade, *designed by O. Stephens*

The highly decorated stern of H.M.S. Naseby, 1655; detail of a model

STERN, the after end of a vessel, generally accepted as that part of the vessel built around the *sternpost, from the *counter up to the *taffrail.

STERN LIGHT, a navigation light carried by ships, also known as an overtaking light. For details of navigational lights, see APPENDIX 3.

STERNBOARD, a manoeuvre by a ship when she wishes to turn in narrow waters where there is insufficient room for her to turn normally while going ahead. If she goes astern with reversed *helm, her bows will continue to swing in the required direction of her original turn. It is the equivalent of backing and filling until the vessel is heading on her new *course. It was also a manoeuvre, though usually involuntary, in sailing ships when they were taken *aback while *tacking. But see also CLUBHAUL, TO.

STERN-CHASER, a gun, usually a long 9-pounder, fitted during the days of sailing navies in the stern of a *frigate or *cutter and used for firing directly astern.

When a ship was being *chased, she would hope to disable the vessel chasing her by carrying away some of her sails or rigging with a shot from her stern-chaser. See also BOW-CHASER; GUNS, NAVAL.

STERNPOST, the aftermost *timber, in a wooden vessel, or steel member in one built of steel, forming the *stern of a ship and joined to the *keel either by *scarfing (wood) or riveting (steel).

Originally the *rudder was hung on the after end of the sternpost, though today most ships of any size have a separate rudder post projecting vertically through the ship's *counter.

STERNSHEETS, that part of an open boat between the * stern and the after * thwart, usually fitted with seats to accommodate passengers. It is occasionally written as stern-sheets but the single word is the more correct usage. No doubt it was so named because the sheet was handled from this position when the boat was under sail.

STERNWALK, a roofed platform built around the stern of some large ships, particularly warships, up to about 1914, when they were largely discarded. They connected with the main * cabin and were fitted so that the admiral or captain could take the air without having to come on deck. They were the more modern version of the * gallery of the older sailing ships.

STERNWAY, the movement of a ship when she is going backwards in relation to the ground. In its most usual form the term is used to mean motion backwards through the water, either by the use of engines running astern or, in the case of a sailing vessel, by laying a sail * aback. But a ship lying stopped in the water and carried backwards by an adverse tide is also said to be carrying sternway even though she may not be making any movement through the water.

STERN-WHEELER, a steam vessel propelled by a single paddle-wheel mounted in the stern of the vessel and normally extending over the whole breadth of the stern. It was the initial form of the adaptation of steam power to the propulsion of ships on inland waters, but was quickly overtaken by the fitting of twin paddle-wheels, one on each side of the ship (see PADDLE STEAMER). The stern-wheeler was, however, retained for many years for work in rivers where its advantage over the propeller was that it could operate in waters so * shoal that, with a sternwheel, only an inch or two of water below the * keel was no bar to progression. Stern-wheelers were used extensively for police work in the Chinese rivers, in the form of river * gunboats, for some of the big excursion steamers on the Mississippi River in the U.S.A., and for freight and passenger services on rivers in India, Iraq, Australia, and the U.S.A. where shoals and rapids have to be negotiated.

STEVEDORE, a docker who is employed in the working of cargo in the * holds of a merchant ship when she is being loaded or unloaded in port.

STEVENS, JOHN COX (1785–1854), a pioneer figure in North American yachting, was brought up at Hoboken, New Jersey, one of four sons of Colonel John Stevens, all of whom were engaged in experiments and inventions in connection with steamboat services and early railroads. Separated from the city by the Hudson

River and unreliable ferries, each of the brothers used his own boat for transport, and John in particular found boat sailing and design an absorbing study. In 1809 he built a 20-ft sailing boat named *Diver*, and five years later had *Trouble*, a 56-ft two-masted * pirogue, built for pleasure sailing, the first real yacht in the U.S.A. His next yacht was *Double Trouble* (1820), an experimental but unsuccessful * catamaran with unsymmetrical hulls, and she was followed in 1832 by a 65-ft waterline * schooner, *Wave*, which in turn gave place in 1839 to *Onkahya*, a 91-ft schooner with a double-* bilge midship section and broad iron * keel. *Gimcrack*, a 49-ft waterline schooner, followed in 1844, and it was in this yacht's saloon that the * New York Yacht Club was formally organized in July of that year, Stevens becoming the first commodore.

Stevens next built a 92-ft waterline * sloop, *Maria* (1848), which was remarkable for her two * centreboards of iron plate weighted with lead, her streamlined mast, hollow main * boom, and hull planking sheathed on the outside with lead below the waterline. After her contemporary cod's-head–mackerel-tail form of hull had been lengthened into a longer and sharper bow she proved the fastest sloop in her day. Stevens led the syndicate of six yachtsmen who ordered from George Steers the 90-ft waterline schooner *America* in 1851 with which was won the * Royal Yacht Squadron's 100 guinea trophy for a race round the Isle of Wight, a trophy which later became known and famous as the *America*'s Cup. In the sixty-nine years of an active life his influence in encouraging other Americans to build and race fast yachts resulted in a national upsurge of the sport and the formation of many new yacht clubs wherever sailing races could be held.

STEWART, CHARLES (1778–1869), American naval officer, was born in Philadelphia and went to sea as a cabin boy in the merchant service at the age of 13. When the U.S. Navy was organized he became a lieutenant in 1798 and served initially in the * frigate * *United States* under John * Barry. In January 1800 he was given command of the * schooner *Experiment* in which he captured two armed French vessels and recaptured a number of American merchant vessels. He commanded the * brig *Siren* after serving as executive officer of the * *Constellation* in the Mediterranean. In December 1812 he was given command of the *Constellation* but she was tightly blockaded in Norfolk, Virginia, unable to put to sea, and in the summer of 1813 he was appointed instead to the * *Constitution* ('Old Ironsides') in which he captured the British frigate *Cyane* and the * sloop *Levant* near Madeira in 1815.

His service between 1815 and 1859 earned

him a special Act of Congress which created for him the title Senior Flag Officer. He was the senior officer on the Navy List at the outbreak of the Civil War (1861–5) and lamented the fact that he was not physically able to go to sea. He became a rear admiral on the retired list in 1862. He was the grandfather of the Irish statesman Charles Stewart Parnell.

STIFF, an adjective which, when applied to a ship, indicates that she returns quickly to the vertical when rolling in a heavy seaway and, when applied to a vessel under sail, is one that stands up well to her canvas. This is a function of the *metacentric height which has been built into the ship. It is an adjective which is also applied to the strength of the wind, a stiff breeze being one in which a sailing ship is just able to carry her full canvas; a little more and she would require to tie down a *reef.

STINKPOT, an earthenware pot, charged with gunpowder and other combustibles and fitted with a touch-hole and fuse, used mainly by *privateers during the 18th and early 19th centuries against an enemy ship when attempting to capture her by boarding. 'The fuses of the stink-pot being lighted, they are immediately thrown upon the deck of the enemy, where they burst and catch fire, producing an intolerable stench and smoke, and filling the deck with tumult and distraction. Amidst the confusion occasioned by this infernal apparatus the (boarding) detachment rush aboard sword in hand, under cover of the smoke, on their antagonist . . .' Falconer, *Marine Dictionary*, 1771. See also CLOSE-QUARTERS. A much-favoured alternative method of discharging them was to suspend them from the yardarms, cutting them adrift when the two ships came together and the yards projected over the vessel being attacked so that they fell on the enemy deck.

STIRRUPS, the name given to the short ropes which hang from the *yards of square-rigged sailing ships and support at intervals the *foot-ropes on which the *topmen stand when working on the sails aloft. The footropes themselves are known as *horses, hence the name stirrups. For illus. see YARD.

STOAK, to, the maritime equivalent of to choke in the sense of stopping the flow of water. Thus if dirt or a spillage of cargo gets into the *limber holes leading to the *bilge well so that the bilge water cannot run down to the well, they are said to be stoaked; the inlet of a pump is stoaked if it will not suck.

STOCK, the horizontal crosspiece of an Admiralty pattern or fisherman's *anchor, set at right-angles to the *arms of the anchor so that when hitting the bottom it will turn the anchor to bring the arms vertical, thus enabling the *flukes of the anchor to bite into the ground. Originally the anchor stock was fixed permanently in position, but later, for ease of stowage on board, was made to slide through a ring in the *shank of the anchor so that it would lie parallel to the shank when not in use. Most modern anchors no longer have stocks, instead the flukes are fitted with a tripping palm to force them into the ground; but the Danforth and Meon anchors have stocks at the base of the shank in addition to tripping palms. For illus. see ANCHOR.

STOCKHOLM, the capital city and a major seaport of Sweden on the eastern coast of the country with its outlet to the Baltic Sea. It is the home of the *Statens Sjöhistoriska Museum, the national maritime museum of Sweden, second only in size and interest among Swedish museums to that at *Gothenburg (Göteborg).

STOCKS, another name for *keel blocks, the line of blocks in a building berth on which the *keel of a ship is laid when being built. Thus, a vessel that is on the stocks is one in the course of construction.

STOKES, JOHN LORT (1812–85), British admiral, is best known for the survey of New Zealand coasts that he conducted in the *Acheron* from 1847 to 1851, having among his officers two future Hydrographers of the Navy in Richards and Frederick *Evans. Little had been done in this area since the days of Captain James *Cook. Stokes had the first ship with auxiliary steam power to work in these stormy waters. Previously he had spent from 1825 to 1843 entirely in the *Beagle*, under Robert *Fitzroy, from 1825 to 1830 in the Straits of Magellan and then from 1831 to 1836 on the world voyage with Charles Darwin embarked. The *Beagle* next sailed in 1837 for Australia's north-west coast under Wickham. When in 1840 Wickham was invalided, Stokes took command and his first work was a survey of the Gulf of Carpentaria; thereafter he completed the survey of Bass Strait before sailing for home in 1843.

Stokes was not employed afloat again after his New Zealand surveys but he surveyed the River Tamar in Devon. In 1845 he published *Discoveries in Australia during the voyage of H.M.S. Beagle in the years 1837–43*; and in 1856 he wrote a pamphlet entitled *Steam Communications with the Southern Colonies* which was published in the Royal Geographical Society's Journal.

STOP, to, the operation of securing, with a light turn of *spunyarn, a sail which may later be required. A sail neatly bunched or rolled up and secured with three or four light turns can be hoisted on its *halyards but will only operate as a sail when a sharp pull on the *sheet breaks it out of its stops so that it can be fully set. It is often useful, when a vessel is under sail, to have additional or substitute sails already hoisted in stops so that they can be brought into operation immediately when required.

STOPPER, the name given to a short length of rope secured at one end to hold temporarily parts of the running rigging of sailing ships with a stopper *hitch while the *fall is being *belayed. A stopper hitch is a *rolling hitch in which the second turn rides over the first. A chain stopper is a metal grab designed to hold a ship's anchor cable. See also CABLE STOPPERS, COMPRESSOR.

STOPPER KNOT, a name generally used for any knot in which the strands are tucked back, such as in a *Turk's head or *Matthew Walker knot, to form a knob at the end of the rope as a stop where, for example, the rope is threaded through an *eye or a *ringbolt, perhaps for use as a handrope. Strictly speaking, a stopper knot is another name for a single or double *wall knot.

STORCK, ABRAHAM (c.1635–c.1710), Dutch marine painter, was a native of Amsterdam. It is not known from whom he learned to paint but his style appears to indicate the influence of Ludolf *Bakhuysen. Many of his pictures are of shipping and boats on the rivers Amstel and Y, but he also painted scenes of naval action, and his picture of the *Four Days Battle between the English and Dutch fleets in 1666 is a magnificent painting full of life, colour, and movement. It now hangs in the *National Maritime Museum in *Greenwich. His ships are always finely drawn and painted and he was adept at the treatment of water to give lightness and movement to his compositions.

STORM, a wind whose average speed lies between 48 and 63 knots, i.e., force 10 and 11 on the *Beaufort Scale. The two types of storm recognized depend on the wind speed, from 48 to 55 knots being known as a storm, and from 56 to 63 knots as a violent storm. Winds blowing above 63 knots are classed as hurricanes. As with gales, the state of the sea gives an indication of the strength of the storm. When the waves are very high with long, overhanging crests, and the sea takes on a white appearance from the foam blown from them, a storm is in progress. In a violent storm the waves are so high that small and medium-sized ships are for a long time lost to view behind the waves, the sea is covered with long white patches of foam, the wave crests are blown into froth, and visibility is seriously affected by blown spray. See also TROPICAL STORMS.

STORM SIGNALS, distant signals in the form of black canvas cones hoisted at coastguard stations and other prominent places along the coast when a gale is forecast. When the point of the cone is up, a northerly gale is forecast, with the point downwards, the gale is expected from the south. These are known as north and south cones respectively. When an easterly gale is forecast a south cone is hoisted above a north; a north cone above a south warns of a westerly gale.

Storm cones were introduced in 1861 by Rear Admiral Robert *Fitzroy when he was superintendent of the meteorological department of the Board of Trade in London.

STOWAWAY, a person who hides himself on board a ship just before she sails in order to obtain a free passage to the ship's destination, to escape from a country by stealth, or to get to sea unobserved.

A stowaway, when discovered on board a ship, may be made to work his passage without pay and may also be turned over to the police in the port of arrival.

STRACHAN, Sir RICHARD JOHN (1760–1828), British admiral, saw much naval service all over the world. During the French Revolutionary War (1793–1801) he commanded a small *squadron of ships off the Normandy and Brittany coasts of France in 1795, inflicting heavy damage on French coasters which were carrying military stores to ports and garrisons along the French Biscay coast. At the start of the Napoleonic War (1803–15) he was in charge of the close *blockade of Cadiz under the overall orders of Lord *Nelson and in 1805, when commanding a squadron in the Bay of Biscay following the battle of *Trafalgar, fought a successful action off *Cape Finisterre against four ships of the French *van, which had escaped after the battle, capturing all four of them. One of them was the *Duguay-Trouin, taken into the Royal Navy as H.M.S. *Implacable. For this action he was promoted to rear admiral and received, in common with other officers and men who had fought at Trafalgar, the thanks of both Houses of Parliament. He was also awarded a pension of £1,000 a year and a baronetcy.

In 1809 Strachan commanded the fleet in the North Sea, and was thus naval commander-in-chief of the ill-fated Walcheren expedition, landing 30,000 troops under the command of the Earl of Chatham. The many hesitations, orders, and counter-orders which characterized this expedition were the basis of the well-known satirical lines:

'Great Chatham with his sabre drawn
Stood waiting for Sir Richard Strachan;
Sir Richard, longing to be at 'em,
Stood waiting for the Earl of Chatham.'

The Walcheren expedition was Strachan's last naval service, though he was made a vice admiral in 1810 and admiral in 1821.

STRAKE, the name given to each line of planking in a wooden vessel, or plating in a vessel built of steel, which runs the length of the ship's hull. The hull form therefore consists of rows of strakes from the *keel up to the top edge of the vessel's hull.

STRAND, a number of ropeyarns twisted together, ready to be laid up into a rope with other strands. Almost all rope used at sea is three-stranded, though where particular strength is required, four-stranded rope is occasionally used. A rope is said to be stranded when one of its strands is broken by too great a strain or worn too thin by chafing.

STRAND, to, a ship is stranded when she is driven ashore, or on to a shoal, by force of weather.

STRANGE, ALBERT (1856–1917), British yacht designer, was born at Gravesend, Kent, and grew up as a boy sailing in local fishing *bawleys, shrimpers, and work-boats. Although a love of boats and the sea attracted him, for a profession he chose art, and moved to Scarborough, Yorkshire, where he became director of the School of Art in 1883. He had long studied boat design, and pupils at the school who showed an interest in boats were treated to lessons in yacht design in addition to their art studies. Strange was an active member of the Royal Canoe Club (founded in 1866) and helped to found the Humber Yawl Club in 1883, for whose members he designed a series of canoe *yawls which were notable for the grace of their lines and their shapely canoe sterns. In time he developed this type into much larger yachts, up to 48 feet (14·7 m) in length, and became known in yacht designing circles as 'father of the yawl'. His yacht designs were in themselves works of art and from the 150 designs he produced many were reproduced in the yachting press, and greatly influenced the quality of current cruising yacht design for many years.

STRATUS, a type of cloud formation. See METEOROLOGY.

STRAY LINE, the name given to the length of line between the *log and the zero mark on the *log-line when measuring the speed of a vessel through the water before the days of more efficient mechanical means of measurement. This length of line was necessary so that the log could drift well astern and beyond the reach of any eddies caused by the motion of the ship before turning the sand-glass and beginning the actual measurement of the vessel's speed, thus achieving a more accurate assessment of speed. The glass was turned at the moment the zero mark passed, and the speed was indicated by the number of knots in the line which ran out while the glass emptied itself.

STREAM ANCHOR, an anchor carried as a spare in some of the larger ships, normally about one-third the weight of the *bower anchors and *sheet anchor, but larger than the *kedge. In many of the larger ships the stream anchor became a stern anchor with its own *hawsepipe in the stern of the ship. It had no permanent *cable but, if necessary to use it, one of the ship's wire *hawsers was shackled on as a cable. It was weighed by bringing the wire hawser to the after *capstan.

STREAM THE BUOY, to, to let the *anchor buoy fall into the sea from the after part of the ship before an anchor is let go. The reason for letting the buoy go from aft is to prevent the buoy-rope being fouled by the anchor or cable as it runs out. Patent *logs, *fog-buoys, and *sea-anchors are, like anchor buoys, said to be streamed when they are run out.

'STREIGHTS', THE, the old British naval name for the Mediterranean station. It originally referred only to the Straits of Gibraltar, but the meaning was extended to cover the whole Mediterranean when English fleets began operating in that sea during the 17th century. The name when used in this connection is now usually spelt Straits.

STRETCHER, (1) a piece of wood fixed *athwartships in the bottom of a pulling boat against which the rowers may brace their feet, **(2)** a short length of wood, notched at both ends, for spreading the *clews of a *hammock when sleeping in it.

STRIKE, to, the act of lowering the *colours of a warship in battle as an indication of surrender. A vessel also strikes *soundings when she can reach the bottom with a deep-sea *lead when coming in from sea. This is today generally accepted as the 100-*fathom contour, and a ship is *in soundings when she is inside this line.

STRIKE DOWN, to, the act of lowering a mast or *yard to the deck in a square-rigged ship, or of lowering heavy articles into the *hold of a ship. Thus *topgallant masts, topmasts, and yards are struck down when they are lowered to the deck (but see also HOUSE, TO, in the case of masts where they are lowered only sufficiently to lie alongside the mast next below them); casks are struck down into the *hold of a ship. When, in the days of sailing navies, guns were lowered to the lower gundeck in very rough weather to get the weight carried on board as low as possible in order to increase the *metacentric height of the ship, they were said to be struck down.

'STRINGBAG', the slang name for the *Swordfish aircraft with which the *Fleet Air Arm of the British Navy was largely equipped at the start of the Second World War.

STRINGER, the modern name for the older shelf-pieces, which were the fore-and-aft members of the structure of a ship's hull. There are deck stringers to give added strength to each deck in a ship, bilge stringers, and hold stringers, each designed to strengthen the frames in these particular localities by holding them firm in the fore-and-aft line. The *keelson, too, is in fact a stringer. See SHIPBUILDING.

STRIPPED TO THE GIRT-LINE, the condition of a sailing vessel when all the standing *rigging, *yards, topmasts, etc., have been stripped off the masts in the course of dismantling, so that the lower masts are mere poles standing upright without support.

STROP, a rope spliced into a circle for use around the shell of a *block so as to form an *eye at the bottom, or to form a sling for heavy articles which need to be hoisted with the aid of a *purchase, or *parbuckled to lift them up a slope. Strops are also frequently used to double round a rope or *hawser to form an eye into which a *tackle can be hooked in order to give a greater purchase.

STUDDINGSAIL, pronounced stunsail, an additional sail, set only in fine weather, with the wind abaft the beam, outside the square sails of a ship. They are set by extending the *yards with *booms, which are run out through a ring at the yardarm, to which the studding sails are *laced. Studdingsails were normally set on the *topgallant and topmast yards, the topmast studding-sail extending across the depth of two sails, the upper and lower topsails. Studdingsails were first introduced during the first half of the 16th century. For illus. see SAIL.

STURDEE, Sir FREDERICK DOVETON (1859–1925), British admiral of the fleet, joined the Royal Navy in 1871 and later qualified as a lieutenant in *gunnery and *torpedoes. He also achieved early distinction in command of *torpedoboats and by twice winning the Trench Gascoigne gold medal of the Royal United Service Institution, notably in 1894 for a study of naval tactics when the navy's interest in this vital art was largely moribund. As a commander in H.M.S. *Porpoise* in Australian waters, Sturdee's diplomatic handling of the dispute between Germany and the U.S.A. over Samoa (1899) gained him early promotion to captain. Service as assistant director of the Naval Intelligence Division, at that time the only naval staff in the Admiralty, and later in command of *cruisers, was followed by his appointment as chief of staff to Admiral Lord Charles *Beresford, commander-in-chief in the Mediterranean and subsequently of the Channel Fleet.

Attaining flag rank in 1908, Sturdee commanded the First Battle Squadron before becoming senior cruiser admiral in the Home Fleet. Shortly before the outbreak of the First World War (1914–18) he was appointed as chief of the Admiralty's recently fledged Naval War Staff. He had, however, no time to prove his talents in this testing appointment before the resignation of Prince Louis of Battenberg (see MOUNTBATTEN, Louis Alexander) in October 1914 compelled the First Lord, Winston *Churchill, to recall Lord *Fisher as First Sea Lord in his place. Fisher's anathema for an officer who had been among Beresford's strongest supporters was then resolved by appointing him to command the powerful force of two battle-cruisers that was hurriedly dispatched to the South Atlantic after the destruction of Rear Admiral *Cradock's squadron by the German East Asiatic Squadron off *Coronel.

Sturdee reached the *Falkland Islands on 7 December 1914, just 24 hours before Vice Admiral von *Spee, by attempting a raid on Port Stanley, gave him the opportunity to annihilate the only significant German naval force operating outside the North Sea. Sturdee was rewarded with command of the Fourth Battle Squadron in the *Grand Fleet, which he led at the battle of *Jutland, and where he remained until 1918, his devotion to the navy enabling him to serve loyally under Sir John *Jellicoe and Sir David *Beatty in spite of his antipathy for the former's rigid tactics and his resentment at being passed over by the latter for command of the Grand Fleet in 1916.

Sturdee ended his naval career as commander-in-chief at the *Nore (1918–21), after which he devoted his energies to the restoration of Lord *Nelson's flagship *Victory* to the condition she was in at the battle of *Trafalgar and to her preservation in dry-dock at Portsmouth. His outstanding merits were recognized by promotion to admiral of the fleet in 1921.

'S-TWIST', the description given by ropemakers to *rope which is laid up left-handed.

'S-twist' and 'Z-twist'

SUBMARINE, a vessel designed to operate below the surface of the sea. From the earliest time the cloak of invisibility acquired by a vessel able to navigate below the surface of the sea has acted as a spur to inventors, but there are few records of their achievements before the 16th century.

Between the years 1578 and 1763 some 17 designs of such craft have been chronicled, and among the early pioneers were men such as William Bourne, Cornelius van Drebbel, David *Bushnell, and Robert *Fulton, the work of the last two being specially noteworthy. With the introduction of metal for ship construction, further impetus was given to the design of such vessels, and in the latter half of the 19th century American and French engineers produced a number of models, none of them, however, sufficiently successful to attract serious attention. (But see also DAVID, a submarine which attacked and sank a warship during the American Civil War (1861–5)). At the turn of the century the invention of the internal combustion engine, coupled with that of the electric motor and the *Whitehead *torpedo, enabled real progress to be made with the design of an effective war vessel of this type.

The hull of a submarine must be circular in transverse section to withstand the pressure of water to which it is subject when submerged. It must be fitted with *ballast tanks to which water can be admitted to destroy her positive buoyancy when she wants to dive and from which it can be expelled by compressed air when she wants to surface. To control the depth when she is under way submerged, she needs horizontal rudders, and when dived she must have a propulsion system capable of operating without a supply of air. Until the advent of nuclear power, this could only be provided by electric motors powered by

batteries, the endurance of which was comparatively limited in relation to their weight. Lengthways the hull of the earlier submarines was cigar-shaped, but it has now been found that optimum results are attained with a teardrop design of hull.

Credit for the prototype of a submarine embodying the features listed above belongs to the Irish-born American J. P. Holland, whose design was accepted by the U.S. Navy. The first five submarines built in Britain were also based on his design. They displaced 105 tons on the surface and had surface and submerged speeds of $8\frac{1}{2}$ and 7 knots respectively. Their surface endurance was 500 miles at 7 knots using petrol driven engines. In Germany it was decided to await the perfection of the much safer diesel engine before embarking on the construction of the first of a long line of *U-boats (short for *Unterseeboot*) which were to play such an important part in the two World Wars.

On the outbreak of the First World War (1914–18) there were in existence some 400 submarines distributed among 16 navies, of which Britain and France accounted for about half the total. Britain entered the war with 74 submarines built and 31 building, Germany with 33 built and 28 building, but whereas most of the British boats were of a small, coastal type, the majority of those in the German Navy were overseas types ranging from 550 to 850 tons displacement. During the war both sides built a number of submarines of varying types which included minelayers, a role for which the submarine is specially suitable. German construction was far and away the largest and ranged from the coastal UB types of 125 to 250 tons to the cruiser types of 1,700 to 3,200 tons capable of crossing the Atlantic. The largest British submarines built during that period were the steam-driven *'K'-class, displacing 1,780 tons and with a surface speed of 21 knots which were designed to work with the fleet.

After the war, Britain and France each built a large cruiser-type submarine and experiments were also carried out with submarine monitors mounting a single 12-inch gun as well as with one from which an aircraft could be launched, but these developments were not followed up, except by Japan who favoured the carrying of an aircraft in her submarines.

The armament of submarines at this time included both guns and torpedoes, since they were prepared to operate both on the surface and submerged, being in fact submersibles rather than true submarines. Apart from increased range, improved habitability, and generally better engines and equipment, there was little change in the basic design of submarines between the two World Wars.

During the Second World War submarines

Bushnell's U.S.S. Turtle *attempting to attach a torpedo to H.M.S.* Eagle, *1776; oil painting by E. Tufnell*

played a much larger part than in the first. Germany repeated her offensive against shipping with even greater intensity, and operations now extended over the whole of the Atlantic, including the Caribbean and round the Cape into the Indian Ocean. The battle of the Atlantic, as it was called, became one of the most crucial of the whole war. British submarines waged an intensive and successful offensive in the Mediterranean against the enemy supply line between Italy and North Africa. U.S. submarines virtually swept the Pacific clear of Japanese shipping besides accounting for a large number of warships. Italian and Japanese submarines, though numerous, did not accomplish as much as they might have done, but the potential threat they offered had a decided influence on allied strategy. Mention should also be made of the miniature or midget type submarines manned by a crew of up to four which were used to attack ships in harbour. These proved themselves capable of penetrating even the most heavily defended ports.

But the greatest development in submarine construction had to await the end of the war. In 1944 Germany had begun to fit her U-boats with a *schnorkel or breathing tube which enabled them to use their diesel engines for charging their batteries while remaining at periscope depth. She also experimented with the development of a gas turbine using a mixture of diesel fuel and hydrogen peroxide, which would enable a submarine so fitted to attain a very high underwater speed for a limited period. The war ended before the experiment could be completed, though two experimental submarines to this design were built

in Britain after the war. In 1948 the U.S. Atomic Energy Commission awarded a contract to the Westinghouse Electrical Company to develop a nuclear propulsion plant suitable for installation in a submarine, and on 14 June 1952 the *keel of the first nuclear-powered submarine, U.S.S. *Nautilus*, was laid. The completion and successful trials of this vessel two years later meant that at long last the true submarine was a reality. The nuclear reactor fitted in vessels of this type is used to generate steam in much the same way as does the ordinary boiler, but with certain modifications to prevent injury to the personnel from radiation. Since the reactor functions without the use of oxygen from the air, the only factor limiting the time the submarine can remain submerged is the revitalization of the air to enable the crew to breathe. This is overcome by the installation of air purifying machinery which enables the vessel to remain submerged almost indefinitely. But a further most significant achievement is the ability it confers on a submarine to proceed submerged at or near her maximum speed also for an indefinite period. It was then found that by streamlining the hull and adopting a teardrop design, submerged speeds greatly in excess of anything previously attained were possible. Thus an entirely new factor was introduced into maritime warfare.

The arming of nuclear-powered submarines with intermediate ballistic missiles of the *Polaris and *Poseidon type capable of being fired while the vessel is submerged is one of the great engineering feats of this century. In addition to the U.S.A., Britain, France, and Russia have constructed vessels of this type. They displace about 6,000–7,000 tons and their role is primarily strategic. Smaller nuclear-powered submarines with functions akin to their conventionally powered predecessors have also been built by these four countries.

In the half century of its existence as a practical warship the submarine has developed from a coast defence vessel into a major warship capable of deterring the launching of a nuclear attack on her homeland and of mounting a potentially decisive attack on the seaborne commerce of an enemy. Because the means available for countering the threat posed by modern submarines are inadequate and imperfect, their existence imposes a large defensive effort on countries threatened by them. Further, the great advance made in recent years in methods of reconnoitring the surface of the sea means that a surface ship has very little chance of remaining unlocated for long. In any future conflict, therefore, submarines are likely to play a greater part than ever before; some thought has also been given to their employment commercially for the transport of vital commodities such as oil and food. Nevertheless the submarine still suffers from environmental limitations owing to her inability to extend her horizon beyond the limits of the range of her * sonar equipment. She also

has the disability that while she can receive wireless messages addressed to her while submerged, she cannot reply to them without raising an aerial and thus risking betraying her position.

Nuclear submarines, with their capability of remaining submerged for long periods over long voyages, need to employ a navigational system which fixes their position with great accuracy and without the need of coming periodically to the surface for the purpose of taking navigational observations of heavenly bodies. This is achieved by the inertial navigation system which gives a continuous reading of * latitude and * longitude. It was by this means that in 1959 the U.S. submarine *Skate* was able to navigate under the polar ice and surface at the North pole. Several nuclear submarines have made the passage from the Pacific to the Atlantic Oceans under the polar ice-cap with the aid of their inertial navigation systems. See NAVIGATION.

M. F. Sueter, *The Evolution of the Submarine Boat, Mine and Torpedo* (1908); D. Everitt, *The K Boats* (1963); W. Jameson, *The Most Formidable Thing* (1965); A. Hezlet, *The Submarine and Sea Power* (1967).

SUBMARINE LIBRARY AND MUSEUM, Groton, Connecticut, a library and museum devoted to the preservation of * submarine arte-

facts and memorabilia. Of particular interest in the collection are the papers of J. P. Holland, as also are the models illustrating the improvements made in the hull design of submarines from 1900 to the present time. An atomic reactor is on view as well as a number of relics of the Second World War. The library contains over 5,000 books, 800 plans, and 3,000 archives and manuscripts.

SUCKING THE MONKEY, a practice devised by British naval seamen in the 'West Indies during the War of American Independence (1775–82) of persuading native women, when they came on board warships, to bring with them fresh coconuts from which the milk had been emptied and replaced with rum. The resultant drunkenness on board remained an unexplained phenomenon for years.

SUCKLING, MAURICE (1728–78), British naval captain, commanded the *Dreadnought* in 1759 in a notable squadron action against a greatly superior French squadron in the West Indies. In 1770 he was appointed to command the *Raisonnable*, a third *rate *ship of the line captured from the French, and was approached by the Revd. Edmund Nelson with a request that he should take his son Horatio to sea and start him on a naval career. He was Horatio *Nelson's uncle, and wrote back: 'What has poor Horace done, who is so weak, that he above all the rest should be sent to rough it out at sea? But let him come; and the first time we go into action, a cannon-ball may knock off his head, and provide for him at once.' Thus it was that Horatio Nelson received his first appointment in the Royal Navy, being rated as *midshipman with seniority of 1 January 1771. Suckling was appointed to succeed Sir Hugh *Palliser as Comptroller of the Navy in 1775, a post of considerable influence, and he was able to further his nephew's career by ensuring that he got the best appointments for a rapid promotion, an act which Nelson amply repaid by earning through his own efforts the quick promotions which came his way.

SUE, EUGÈNE (1804–57), French author, was born in Paris, a godson of the Empress Josephine. He began his career as an assistant naval surgeon but left the navy in 1829 to devote himself to art and literature. Although better known for his novels of Paris, he wrote a *History of the French Navy* in five volumes which is not without merit. Among his novels was *Kernok the Pirate*, considered by many to be the prototype of the maritime novel.

SUETER, Sir MURRAY (1872–1960), British rear admiral, entered the Royal Navy through the training ship *Britannia* in 1886. In his subsequent career he showed himself to be a man

of vision and a patron of innovation, an early example being his interest in wireless telegraphy; in 1898 he gave the first lecture on the subject ever to be heard in the Naval Torpedo School, H.M.S. *Vernon*. In 1902–3 he was assistant to Captain Reginald *Bacon in introducing *submarines to the Royal Navy and was involved in an act of gallantry in saving life after a hydrogen explosion in the submarine *A.1*. He wrote *The Evolution of the Submarine Boat, Mine and Torpedo* (1908) which is generally accepted as a standard work on the subject. Sueter is best known, however, as a pioneer of British naval aviation and 'father' of the Royal Naval Air Service. He was Inspecting Captain of Airships, 1908–11, when the Admiralty envisaged lighter-than-air craft as the navy's air element, a phase which came to an end with the failure of the first British rigid airship in May 1911. In that year Sueter became the first director of the Air Department of the Admiralty, a post he held until 1915; during that time it can be said he created the Naval Air Service and was largely responsible for promoting the use of *torpedo-carrying aircraft. He also created the first anti-aircraft corps for London and an armoured car force which was manned by the Royal Naval Air Service in the early days of the First World War (1914–18).

Between 1915 and 1917 he was superintendent of Aircraft Construction and a member of the Joint War Air Committee. His inventive mind led him to contribute to the evolution of the tank, for which he received the thanks of the Army Council. From 1917 to 1918 he was in command of R.N.A.S. units in southern Italy.

This was his last appointment. His very outspoken views on what he considered the navy's lack of appreciation of the dominant role of the air in the future, views which he subsequently publicized in his book *Airmen or Noahs?*, barred him from selection for promotion to the flag list, though he retired in 1920 with the rank of rear admiral. From 1921 to 1945 he was Member of Parliament for Hertford and he was knighted in 1934.

SUEZ CANAL, the great ship canal, 100 miles long, which connects the Mediterranean with the Red Sea. It was begun in 1859 and officially opened ten years later in 1869. (See also LESSEPS, Ferdinand de.) Proposals for such a canal date back over 4,000 years, and during the Roman occupation of Egypt work was started in cutting a canal linking the River Nile with the Red Sea along the course of a previous small canal which had been in existence 700 years earlier. The Roman venture, however, never reached fruition.

The canal was blocked by the Egyptians during the short Arab–Israeli war of 1967 and remained closed until 1975. In the meantime the

U.S.S. Nautilus, *the first nuclear submarine, commissioned in 1954*

Ship passing down the Suez Canal from Port Said

development of bulk carriers and *tankers into vessels of immense *tonnage and size has lost the canal a significant proportion of the tonnage which formerly used it. It will need considerable widening and deepening (for which plans exist) before these very large ships can navigate it.

SUFFREN SAINT TROPEZ, PIERRE ANDRÉ DE (1729–88), French admiral, entered the French Navy in 1743 in the typical aristocratic way, as a *garde de la marine* (equivalent rank of a *midshipman) and membership of the Order of Malta. In 1747 he was taken prisoner by Admiral *Hawke in the Bay of Biscay but returned to France on the conclusion of the war in 1748, in which year he went to Malta to perform the symbolic cruise, or 'caravan', of the Order, a prior requirement for any of the high and lucrative posts in the Order of Malta. He was a lieutenant in the *Orphée* at the battle of *Minorca in 1756 at which Admiral *Byng was driven off and prevented from landing reinforcements on the island, but was again captured by the British in 1759 when the ship in which he was serving, the *Océan*, was taken off *Lagos by Admiral *Boscawen. On his return to France after the war he operated, in command of a *xebec, against the *Barbary pirates, later doing further 'caravans' which brought him promotion to the rank of commander in the Order of Malta. The French government then appointed him to the training squadron maintained in the Mediterranean to exercise officers in handling ships. With the outbreak of the War of American Independence (1775–82) he was with *Estaing in the operations off the coast of North America, and led the French line in the action against Admiral *Byron off Grenada.

In 1781 he commanded a squadron of five French ships destined to assist the Dutch in withstanding a possible British attack on the Cape of Good Hope and subsequently to join with another squadron at Mauritius and operate against the British fleet in the East Indies. He was able to damage the British squadron on its way to the Cape as it lay at anchor in the Cape Verde Islands, saved the Cape from capture, and on reaching Mauritius discovered that the French admiral, d'Orves, had died, leaving him in command of the fleet of eleven ships of the line.

The evidence of his campaign in Indian waters, and the result of the five actions he fought against the British admiral, Sir Edward *Hughes, shows Suffren as one of the most brilliant and aggressive of all French admirals. He was no believer in the normal French naval doctrine of engagement at long range, preferring to attack with all the vigour he could command, and although in all the five actions against Hughes his fleet was at a numerical disadvantage, he never lost a ship. Moreover, during the two years of this campaign, he maintained his fleet in first-class fighting order without the possession of any base at which to refit, a remarkable achievement in those eastern waters.

He returned to France at the end of the war, having been promoted to Bailli in the Order of Malta during his absence, and in 1788 was appointed to command the *Brest fleet. He died shortly before he could take up the command, officially from apoplexy but more probably as the result of a duel with the Prince de Mirepoix, whom he had offended by refusing to reinstate in the navy two of the Prince's relations who had been dismissed for misconduct.

He was unquestionably one of France's greatest admirals, and has been commemorated by several ships named after him.

SUHAILI, the name of the 12-ton *ketch yacht in which Robin *Knox-Johnson won *The Sunday Times* Golden Globe in the single-handed non-stop race round the world in 1968–9.

SULIVAN, Sir BARTHOLOMEW JAMES (1810–90), British vice admiral, was an outstanding proponent of the value of the surveying service to the fleet in military operations and also wrote, in 1859, on general naval service problems for improving officers' lists and promotions.

He first saw surveying work in H.M.S. *Beagle* under Robert *Fitzroy from 1831 on the South American station and he was with him again for the voyage with Darwin until 1836. Then, on the same station, Sulivan commanded H.M.S. *Philomel* from 1842 to 1846, during which he surveyed the Falkland Islands. It was from this ship, in 1845, that he first participated in a naval operation by leading a boat party to chart by night a position from which the fleet could bombard the forts of the obstreperous General Rosas on the River Parana. But his finest opportunity came with the Crimean War (1854–6) when in 1854 the Hydrographer of the Navy, Sir Francis *Beaufort, sent him in H.M.S. *Lightning* to join the Baltic Fleet which was to operate in narrow or shallow waters around the fortresses of Bomarsund, Sveaborg, and Kronstadt. Many surveys and charts were made with Sulivan making some remarkable personal contributions, which were recorded in the *Nautical Magazine* of the day. In the *National Maritime Museum there is a fine drawing by Sir Oswald *Brierly, showing the small paddle-wheeler *Lightning* leading the big ships of the fleet to Bomarsund. *Beaufort was indignant that, unlike Sir Thomas *Spratt in the Black Sea, Sulivan received not even a mention in dispatches. This work ended Sulivan's career afloat and from 1856 to 1865 he was naval professional member at the Board of Trade, a post he filled with much distinction.

SULLOM VOE, an immense deep-water anchorage in the Shetland Islands off the north coast of Scotland, for which development plans exist for making it into one of the largest oil ports in the world, capable of handling *tankers of up to 250,000 tons. The proposed development follows the discovery of the Brent oilfield during 1972 in the North Sea about 100 miles northeast of the Shetland Islands. During the First World War (1914–18) Sullom Voe was used as a naval anchorage for a *cruiser squadron, and during the Second World War it was again used as a base for flying-boats. See also ABERDEEN.

SUMNER'S POSITION LINE, a systemized method of finding a ship's position by means of a sight. The discovery which led to the introduction of the method was made in December 1837 by Captain Thomas H. Sumner, of Boston, U.S.A., who was approaching the south coast of Ireland on a passage from Charleston to Greenock. The weather had been overcast and foggy for some days, and Sumner had been unable to take any sights and was navigating on *dead reckoning. At 10.00 a.m. on 17 December the sun appeared through a break in the clouds, and Sumner took an observation of it before it clouded over again. Working out his sight, using his dead reckoning position, to get a longitude, he found that the position obtained placed him nine miles further east than he had expected. As he was not sure of the latitude of his dead reckoning position, he reworked his sight using a latitude 10 miles further north, and obtained a position 27 miles ENE. of the first. He then reworked his sight a third time, using a latitude yet another 10 miles north, and the position which resulted placed him a further 27 miles ENE. Discovering that these three positions all lay on a straight line running ENE., he realized that his ship must be on this line. He later developed this discovery into a means of fixing a ship's position accurately.

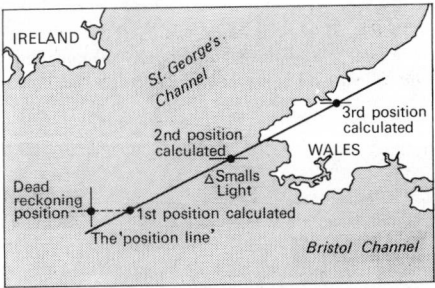

Sumner's position line, 17 December, 1837

A sight was worked out twice with different degrees of latitude, and the two positions obtained joined by a line drawn on the chart. Then, by plotting the course and distance run between the time of the sight and noon, the original position line was transferred to run through the new position on the chart and the point where it cut the latitude derived from a meridian *altitude must be the ship's actual position. This was bound to give a more accurate position than that obtained by transferring the longitude obtained from a sight for which a doubtful latitude had been used. Sumner described this method in a pamphlet which he published in Boston in 1843. See also MARCQ ST. HILAIRE METHOD, NAVIGATION.

'SUN OVER THE YARDARM, THE', a traditional maritime saying to indicate that it is time for a morning drink. It was generally assumed that in northern *latitudes the sun would show above the foreyard of a ship by 1100, which was approximately the time in many ships of the forenoon 'stand-easy', when many officers would slip below for their first drink of the day.

SUNBEAM, a 531-ton composite yacht owned by Lord *Brassey, designed by St. Clare J. Byrne, and launched in 1874. She was a three-masted topsail *schooner spreading 8,333 square feet of canvas, and was fitted with a 350-h.p. steam engine with a feathering propeller. In 1876–7 she made a voyage round the world, described in a Victorian best-selling travel book, *The Voyage in the 'Sunbeam'*, written by Lady Brassey. In the First World War (1914–18) she was initially used as a hospital ship in the eastern Mediterranean and was later presented by Lord Brassey to the Indian government for use as an auxiliary vessel. After the war she was sold to the Runciman family and was finally broken up in 1929.

'SUNDOWNER', a slang name for a bullying officer in a ship. The origin of the name comes from those captains who would only give shore leave to their crews up to the time of sunset.

SUPERB, H.M.S., a name not used for ships of the Royal Navy until the French 60-gun ship *Superbe* was taken by H.M.S. *Kent* in 1710 and added to the Royal Navy under the English version of her name. This ship saw much service with the Royal Navy, taking part in the destruction of the Spanish fleet off Cape Passaro in 1718, and the capture of *Louisburg in 1745. She was broken up in 1757. Another *Superb*, a 3rd *rate of seventy-four guns, was built at Deptford and launched in 1760. She was the flagship at Portsmouth from 1763 to 1770 and then took part, as his flagship, in the five actions of Sir Edward *Hughes against *Suffren in the East Indies in 1782–3, being finally wrecked at Telicherry in November 1783. The third *Superb*, a 3rd rate of seventy-four guns, was built on the Thames in 1798 and took part in the actions at Algeciras and in the Gut of Gibraltar in 1801; the *blockade of *Toulon, 1803–5; at San Domingo, in February 1806, as Vice Admiral Sir J. T. *Duckworth's flagship; and at the battle of *Copenhagen in 1807. Thereafter, until 1810, she flew the flag of Rear Admiral R. G. Keats in the Channel and Baltic and from 1813 served for two years on the Channel, Cape of Good Hope, and North America stations. She took part in the bombardment of Algiers in 1816 and was broken up in 1826. An 18,600-ton *battleship was launched for the Royal Navy in 1907 and named *Superb*. She served with the *Grand Fleet from 1914 to 1918, taking part in the battle of *Jut-

Lord Brassey's yacht Sunbeam; *illustration from* The Voyage in the 'Sunbeam', *1878*

land in 1916. After joining the Aegean Squadron at Mudros in October 1918 she became flagship of the commander-in-chief, Mediterranean Fleet, later that month. From November 1918 to January 1919 she took part in the operations in south Russia. After the war she was used as a gunnery training ship and was sold for breaking up at the end of 1922. The last *Superb* of the Royal Navy was a 9,000-ton *cruiser, launched in 1943 and sold for breaking up in 1960.

SUPERCARGO, an abbreviation of Cargo Superintendent, a representative of the ship's owner on board a merchant ship who looked after all commercial business in connection with the ship and her cargo during a voyage. In these modern days of high-speed wireless communication, with owners being in more or less permanent touch with their ship, the official, and the term, are almost entirely obsolete.

SUPERSTITIONS OF SAILORS. Although a great many of the old superstitions of seamen, which initially owed their origin to the desire of mariners of ancient times to guard themselves against the unknown dangers of the sea, have been forgotten or ignored by the sophisticated sailor of today, some linger on. In ancient days, for instance, it was the custom when a ship was *launched or about to sail on a long voyage to offer a libation to the gods of the sea by pouring wine upon the deck that good fortune should attend the ship. Today, when a ship is launched, a bottle of wine is still broken across her *bows as she is about to slide down the launching *ways into the sea for the first time, usually accompanied by a plea to 'bless this ship and all who sail in her'. That Friday is a day of ill-omen for a ship to start on a voyage is still widely believed among seamen, its origin lying in the fact that the Crucifixion took place on a Friday. Other days on which many seamen still consider it unlucky to start a voyage are the first Monday in April, believed to be the birthday of Cain and the day on which Abel was killed, the second Monday in August, thought to be the day on which Sodom and Gomorrah were destroyed, and 31 December, anniversary of the day on which Judas Iscariot hanged himself.

Flowers carried on board ship are thought by many sailors to be destined to form a wreath, either for a death on board or for the loss of the ship with all her company. This belief used to be very strongly held among the crews of *submarines. Priests, because of their black dress and their office of burying the dead, are thought by sailors to be unlucky passengers on board, as, for some reason, are women, an old belief being that the sea grows angry at the sight of a woman. This superstition was also strongly held by fishermen, and up to the end of the 19th century in the Firth of Forth a fisherman would refuse to go to sea if a bare-footed woman crossed his path while on his way to his boat. Yet many seamen used to believe that gales and high winds would subside if a naked woman appeared before them. It was for this reason that so many of the *figureheads of ships showed a woman with a naked breast.

Phantom ships, such as the *Flying Dutchman*, are the source of many superstitions of seamen, the general belief being that if such a ship is sighted the result will be shipwreck, or the death of any who set eyes on her. A variant belief is that a man sighting such a ship will be struck blind. *St. Elmo's Fire is equally a source of superstition, but of a more benevolent kind. It is held either to be a heaven-sent warning of an approaching storm, so that a ship can prepare herself for the ordeal, or to be a sign that the worst of a storm has passed. Only in one respect is St. Elmo's Fire feared by sailors. If the fire plays round the head or body of a man, he will die within 24 hours.

A very old superstition, fortunately now long abandoned, was that to be successful a warship's *keel must taste the blood of live persons during her launching. In the Mediterranean, when a *galley was launched, slaves were tied down on the *keel blocks so that as the galley gathered speed on her way into the sea, their bodies were crushed and their blood splashed the keel and hull of the galley. Captured prisoners-of-war were similarly used for the same purpose in the launching of Norse *longships.

Some superstitions still held by seamen defy analysis. To some the loss overboard of a bucket or a mop is an omen of misfortune, to others it is unlucky to repair a flag on the *quarterdeck of a ship or to hand a flag to a sailor between the rungs of a ladder. Black travelling bags bring misfortune, and to hear bells at sea is a sign of forthcoming death. It is also considered unlucky to wear the clothes of a sailor who has died at sea while the voyage is in progress; once it is over no calamity will follow such an action.

A very well-known superstition, which existed among many sailors certainly up to the early years of the 20th century, was that the possession of the caul of a new-born child was a sure prevention against death by drowning. Advertisements by sailors in newspapers for a caul were not uncommon, and the price offered was occasionally as much as £30.

In the Isle of Man, and among some other seafaring communities, possession of the feather of a wren was supposed to be a safeguard against death by shipwreck. The origin of this belief came from the tale of a beautiful mermaid who lured seamen to their death by singing to them in a voice so sweet that they had to follow. A knight-errant, in a desire to save the seamen, discovered a means of counteracting these siren charms but was foiled by the mermaid changing herself into a wren. As a penance for thus circumventing her just deserts, she was condemned to appear as a wren on New Year's Day every year. This legend unhappily led to a brisk demand among sailors for a tail or wing feather of a wren and a considerable slaughter of these attractive small birds followed, particularly on New Year's Day as the feather of a bird killed on that day was especially valued. The efficacy of the feather lasted only for one year, so that the slaughter became annual.

Another superstition of seamen, equally well known, is that to whistle in a calm will bring a wind, but to whistle on board when the wind is blowing is to bring a gale. Another belief is that a wind can also be brought by throwing the head of an old broom overboard in the direction from which the wind is desired.

SUPERSTRUCTURE, the constructions on board a ship which are above the level of the upper deck. It would include the whole of the *bridge structure and the deckhouses.

SURCOUF, ROBERT (1773–1827), French *privateer captain, was a native of St. Malo. Serving from the age of 13 in merchant ships, mostly engaged in the slave trade between Africa and Île de France (Mauritius), he became an officer in 1790. He got his first merchant ship command, the *Creole*, in 1794. Making a slaving voyage to Mozambique in spite of the new revolutionary law forbidding the slave trade, he narrowly escaped condemnation by the colonial Committee of Public Safety.

Moving on to command the 180-ton *Emilie*, he cruised as a privateer against British seaborne trade in spite of having been refused a *letter of marque and being licensed only to be defensively armed. In a series of bold attacks he made a number of captures in the Bay of Bengal, including the large *East Indiaman the *Triton*, only to have his prizes confiscated by the governor of the Île de France on account of the illegality of his actions. Returning to France, however, he fought and won his case in the courts there.

Between 1798 and 1800 he operated in the Bay of Bengal in command of the privateers *Clarisse* and *Confiance*, making numerous captures, again including a 1,200-ton East Indiaman, the *Kent*.

When war with Britain was resumed in 1803 after the brief Peace of Amiens, Surcouf was offered by Napoleon the rank of *post-captain; but he preferred the independence of a corsair. He fitted out and sent to sea a number of privateers from St. Malo and, in 1807, built for his own command the large, three-masted *Revenant* in which he made a notable cruise in the Indian Ocean.

The *Revenant* was commandeered by the governor of Mauritius, Decaen, after two cruises from that island. Surcouf returned to France where he was created a baron of the Empire. For the rest of the war he occupied himself in fitting out privateers under the command of his old shipmates.

SURF BOAT, a large open craft used mainly on beaches in Africa and India for landing passengers and goods where there is no deep water port and where the depth of water offshore is such that ships must lie a long way out. These craft are propelled by paddles and controlled by a steering oar over the stern, as the normal surf on African and Indian beaches is too heavy for craft under oars. But with the steady growth of ocean trade and the consequent *dredging of new ports to handle it, the need for surf boats is rapidly dying out even where they were most used.

SURGE, to, the operation of stopping the pull on a line or *hawser when it is being brought in round a *capstan or *winch by walking back on the hauling part so that the capstan or winch still revolves with the line or hawser rendering round it without coming in. It is a means of regulating the rate of pull with a capstan or winch turning at a constant speed. The word is also occasionally used as a noun to indicate the tapered part of the *whelps of a capstan where the *messenger was served when an *anchor was weighed by hand. A more common use of the word as a noun is to describe a *scend or exceptional run of the sea into a harbour.

SURVEYS AT SEA, the means by which all necessary data for the drawing of a *chart are obtained. Surveys at sea use the same basic framework as those on land, making use of the properties of a triangle to establish a number of marks in the area under survey which are positioned with accuracy relative to each other by triangulation. Out of sight of land, special methods of base measurement and *moored *beacons are used, and the *sextant replaces the theodolite. The major difference arises when filling in the detail. Ashore the plane table plots the visible detail. At sea there is no other way of delineating the seabed than by taking *soundings as prolifically as the changes in depth and the degree of accuracy required may demand. Working in ships and boats, a hydrographic surveyor needs seamanship of a high order as well as a knowledge of surveying principles. The work is therefore expedited when the captain and officers of a surveying ship execute the survey. The alternative (but seldom adopted) is to embark a team of engineers with the ship's captain acting at their behest always in so far as the safety of ship or boats allows.

Surf boats in Ghana, 1961

Maritime countries have commonly organized their surveying services within their navies, since the information to be obtained is often of national significance whether for military or commercial purposes. The 18th century voyages of exploration were most often naval expeditions under naval command, and it was a natural development when in 1809 the British Hydrographer of the Navy, Thomas *Hurd, obtained a naval ship for surveying in home waters and in 1816 proposed a corps of specialist naval officers, thereby constituting the Royal Navy's surveying service.

Since seamanship is one of the prime requirements, surveyors learn their art by experience on the surveying ground. Descriptions of the service expected of volunteers, who have always been attracted to the work, have always referred to the golden rule that each day's work must be recorded before the next begins, so that no gaps shall be left behind. Thus Hurd soon had to defend an excessive use of candles in surveying ships but, by the same token, got approval for specialist rates of pay.

Captain James *Cook taught George *Vancouver, and the chain has since continued unbroken. Only recently in British practice has a school ashore provided instruction and courses in the increasingly sophisticated modern methods.

As for the defence aspect, the precedent set by Cook's soundings in the St. Lawrence River prior to the capture of *Quebec has been followed in subsequent amphibious operations through the 19th century Chinese and Baltic wars and the 20th century wars culminating in the Normandy landings when beach gradients were measured by the surveyor Berncastle under cover of darkness.

Notable exceptions to the general rule of naval organizations have been the French Corps of Hydrographic Engineers and the U.S. Coast and Geodetics Survey with its responsibilities for U.S. home waters.

The development of methods may be followed in various British publications, e.g., Alexander *Dalrymple's *Essay on Nautical Surveying* (1771), Murdoch *Mackenzie's *Treatise on Maritim Surveying* (1774), Edward *Belcher's *Treatise on Nautical Surveying* (1835), William *Wharton's *Hydrographical Surveying* of 1882, and the *Admiralty Manuals* of 1938 and 1968. Belcher's was a remarkable compilation for one who spent such an active life at sea, while Wharton's came opportunely with the advance in scientific methods.

Cook in Newfoundland and Mackenzie in the Orkneys based their work on land triangulations and in Beaufort's day the home waters surveys used the Ordnance Survey triangulation. For fixing detail afloat the instrumental solution of the resection principle in the shape of the *station pointer was available from 1785. Angles by sextant and plotting by station pointer remain basic methods when modern electronic fixing is not available.

Much continued to be done by *compass and *log in the first half of the 19th century when the plotting of coastline was still a primary task in many parts of the world. Then, with the advent of steamships, a greater knowledge of offshore depths was necessary, but concurrently it became practicable for the surveyor to run lines of soundings in accordance with a prearranged design, usually at right-angles to the coast and normal to the bottom contours.

Meanwhile, in their worldwide activities, British ships constantly ran *meridian distances, carrying time by *chronometer to spread an accurate knowledge of *longitude until the method was superseded by the use of telegraph cables and then by wireless signals early in this century. Similarly, on passage or special cruises, they took deep sea soundings following the impetus given in 1853 when, in co-operation with the U.S. Navy, depths were obtained for the transatlantic cable. Deep sea cruises in the Pacific preceded the cable laying of 1901.

For coastal surveys, ships had steam *winches for heaving the *lead from 1880, a major improvement being the Somerville gear in 1913 which lasted until *echo-sounding, the most important advance in hydrographic surveying, was adopted in the early 1930s. Henry *Somerville was also concerned with the development of a ship's drift sweep, it having been appreciated in 1911 that the increasing *draught of modern vessels necessitated the discovery of pinnacle rocks which might not be located by sounding. *Asdic (*sonar) was to help the location of rocks and wrecks when it was developed after the end of the First World War (1914–18) in which also *taut wire measuring came into naval use. Originally used by cable ships, it still provides a method of base measurement at sea and gives accurate distances over the ground when running survey methods have to be adopted.

Next in importance to the introduction of echo-sounding has been the post Second World War development of *radar and *Loran and similar electronic position-finding methods. Concurrently there came the South African invention of the tellurometer giving electronic distances of great accuracy so that trilateration may be used instead of triangulation. In the oceans traditional methods of astro-fixing are now being replaced by satellite navigation.

Modern surveying continues to require intensive sounding by ship and boats, air photography having only provided limited assistance in special conditions. But ever more precise echo-sounding machines and sonar gear, coupled with electronic position fixing, allows work to proceed at speed and in all conditions of visibility.

U.S. Coast and Geodetic Survey (Washington, 1963); *Admiralty Manual of Hydrographic Surveying* (1968); G. S. Ritchie, *The Admiralty Chart* (1967); A. Day, *The Admiralty Hydrographic Service, 1793–1919* (1967).

SVAAP, the yacht in which William Albert Robinson sailed round the world in 1928–31. With two companions he left New York when he was 25, and sailed via the Panama Canal to the South Sea islands. In Tahiti his crew had to return to college and he shipped a young Polynesian fisherman, Etera, who stayed with him for the remainder of the circumnavigation. They sailed by way of the East Indies, Red Sea, Mediterranean, Gibraltar, and back to New York. *Svaap* (Sanskrit for dream) was a *Bermuda-rigged *ketch designed by John Alden of Boston. The voyage was described in Robinson's book *Deep Water and Shoal* (1932).

SVOLDE or **SWOLD, BATTLE OF,** was the most famous of the great sea fights of the Norsemen. *Olaf I of Norway had been with his fleet in the Baltic attempting to take possession of the estates of his wife Thyre and was returning to Norway when he was ambushed by the combined fleets of Denmark and Sweden. Deserted by the *longships of the Jomsborg Vikings, who were in the pay of his enemies, Olaf declined to flee, as he could easily have done, but turned to face his enemies. He lashed his eleven remaining longships together to form a floating fort and fought valiantly to the last against overwhelming odds. One by one his longships were taken and destroyed until only his own, the *Long Serpent* which had been in the centre of the 'fort', was left. When she too was overpowered, Olaf leapt into the sea with his shield and hauberk which carried him down. King Olaf is remembered in Norway as one of her greatest heroes, ranking in renown with Charlemagne of France and King Arthur of England.

SWALLOW, the name given to the space between the two sides of the shell of a *block in which the sheave is fitted.

'SWALLOW THE ANCHOR, to', a maritime term to indicate giving up, or retiring from, a life at sea and settling down to live ashore.

SWAY, to, the operation of hoisting the topmasts and *yards of a square-rigged sailing ship. They are swayed up by means of the *jeers. It is also the term used for taking the strain on a mast rope and lifting it sufficiently for the *fid to be removed before the mast is *struck down or *housed.

'SWAY AWAY ON ALL TOPROPES, to', a nautical expression indicating that a man will go to great lengths to get something done.

SWEAT, to, the means of getting the last bit of hoist, particularly in relation to *halyards, in order to get rid of any sign of slackness in the setting of a sail when it is hoisted by hand. A halyard is sweated up by taking a single turn round a *cleat, hauling the *standing part out from the mast horizontally while keeping tension on the end to prevent it slipping on the cleat. This raises the sail fractionally. The slack is then taken up round the cleat as the halyard is released so that the extra hoist gained is not lost. Today most of this hard labour in yachts is performed by hand winches.

SWEEP, a long, heavy oar carried in sailing vessels for use when the wind failed. In the days of sailing navies they were carried in the smallest class of *frigates and in all vessels below that rating; and until the general use of auxiliary engines, *smacks, *barges, and sailing yachts used to carry at least one sweep on board.

SWELL, a condition of the sea resulting from storms or high winds. It is the vertical movement of surface water in the form of waves or undulations retaining the motion imparted to it by the wind for a period after the wind has dropped, eventually dying out as the resistance of the surrounding water takes effect and slows the motion down. The length of a swell is proportional to the *fetch.

SWEYN I, known as 'Forkbeard', King of Denmark (d. 1014), was one of the Danish thorns that pricked deeply into the English flesh between A.D. 994 and 1014. He was a born leader and *buccaneer, and opened his career with an expedition against his father, Harold Bluetooth, who was killed during the fighting. He then led a large fleet of *longships against England and ravaged the land without mercy for six years. On his return to Denmark he repudiated his wife and married Sigrid, widow of the King of Sweden, one of the more bloodthirsty pagans of the time, who reckoned she had been insulted by King *Olaf I of Norway, who had refused to marry her unless she agreed to be baptized. At her instigation Sweyn and Olaf of Sweden went to war against the Norwegian Olaf, who fell in the great sea battle of *Svolde or Swold probably off the coast of Rügen, in the year 1000. From 1002 onwards Sweyn returned annually to England, systematically ravaging the land and exacting no less than £158,000 in ransoms during his campaigns. He was a great seaman, having learned the art from the Jomsborg Viking, Palnatoke.

SWIFTER, a 1½-inch or 2-inch rope with a *cut splice in the centre, a *thimble at one end, and *pointed at the other. Its purpose was to swift, or lash, together the ends of the *capstan bars when weighing an anchor by hand. The central cut splice was placed in the slot at the end of a capstan bar and the swifter passed from bar to bar, being secured to the end of each bar by means of two turns through the slot, the first inside and the second outside the standing part of the swifter. The purpose of the swifter was to provide extra accommodation for the men weighing the anchor, as the swifter could be manned as well as the bars. The foremost shrouds of each lower mast were also known as swifters.

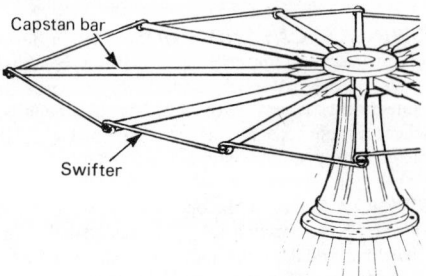

Capstan and bars, with a swifter fleeted

SWIFTSURE, H.M.S., a ship's name used by the Royal Navy since 1573, when a 400-ton ship of forty-one guns was launched at Deptford. She was one of the ships which fought against the Spanish *Armada in 1588 and in the following year she took part in the expedition to Corunna and Lisbon under Sir Francis *Drake and Sir John Norreys. In 1602 she was successively the flagship of Sir Amyas Preston on the Irish coast and of Sir William *Monson on the coast of Spain. After being rebuilt in 1607 she was renamed *Speedwell.* The Royal Navy's fifth *Swiftsure* was a 3rd *rate *ship of the line of seventy-four guns, launched at Buckler's Hard on the Beaulieu River in 1804, in time to take part, in 1805, in Lord *Nelson's pursuit of the combined fleets of France and Spain to the West Indies and back, and in the battle of *Trafalgar in October of that year. In 1903 a *battleship of 11,800 tons was launched for the Royal Navy on the Tyne and named *Swiftsure.* When the First World War (1914–18) broke out, she was serving as the flagship of Rear Admiral Richard Peirse, commander-in-chief in the East Indies, and in 1915 she became the flagship of Rear Admiral Stuart-Nicholson in the Eastern Mediterranean Squadron, taking part in the *Dardanelles operation. The Royal Navy's last *Swiftsure* was an 8,000-ton *cruiser launched in 1943. From November 1944 she served as flagship of the 4th Cruiser Squadron, British Pacific Fleet, until the end of the war against Japan, returning home in August 1946 to go into reserve. She later served for a time with the Home Fleet and was broken up in 1962.

SWIM, to, an old word used largely by seamen up to at least the start of the 17th century to describe the progress of a ship through the water. A ship would 'swimme well', or 'swimme ill', according to her speed under sail. Matthew Baker, the first English naval architect who drew the designs for Elizabeth I's warships, drew the underwater part of his ships in the form of a great fish to indicate that they would swim well under sail. Some of his original designs are preserved in the Pepys Library at Magdalene College, Cambridge.

'SWING A CAT, NO ROOM TO', a term widely used to describe a small or confined space. It originates from the days of corporal punishment at sea with the *cat-o'-nine-tails, where ample space was needed to swing it properly to produce the maximum effect.

SWING A SHIP, to, the operation of steadying a ship on a succession of *courses, usually on *cardinal and half-cardinal *compass headings, in order to ascertain the *deviations of the compass on those headings as a preliminary to compensating the effects on a magnetic compass of a ship's magnetic condition. It is not the compass that is adjusted in this operation; it is the ship's magnetic field at the compass position which is neutralized by placing correctors. These latter are in the form of permanently magnetized cylindrical bars and soft-iron correctors called Flinders bars and Kelvin spheres, so named in honour of Captain Matthew *Flinders, R.N., and Lord Kelvin (see THOMSON, William), whose investigations into the problems of ship magnetism led to the type of soft-iron correctors generally adopted.

The corrector magnets, which are housed in the *binnacle immediately below the compass, are designed and placed to neutralize the permanent magnetism of the ship due to what has been described as her hard-iron property; the Flinders bars and Kelvin spheres serve to neutralize the ship's 'soft-iron' property.

SWORDFISH, a type of aircraft of the *Fleet Air Arm used as a torpedo bomber in the Second World War. It was a biplane with fabric wings and body and with a single propeller, giving it a maximum speed of 90 knots when carrying one 18-inch *torpedo. Nevertheless, in spite of its slow speed and cumbersome build, it was a versatile aircraft admirably suited for operations from *aircraft carriers because of its slow stall-

ing speed which made landing-on a relatively simple operation. At the battle of *Taranto (11 November 1940) twenty-one Swordfish aircraft attacked the Italian battle fleet at anchor in harbour and sank three *battleships for the loss of two aircraft. In the action resulting in the loss of the German battleship *Bismarck, the success was entirely attributable to two torpedo hits delivered by Swordfish aircraft from the carrier *Ark Royal. But perhaps their best-known action was that against the *Scharnhorst, Gneisenau, and Prinz Eugen in the English Channel on 12 February 1942 which, though unsuccessful, was a naval epic of great gallantry against impossible odds. This antiquated but successful naval aircraft was affectionately known throughout the naval service as the 'stringbag'.

SYDNEY, the capital of New South Wales, Australia, and one of the great seaports of the world. It lies about six miles north of *Botany Bay, to which British convicts were to be transported after the loss of the American colonies, and was discovered by Captain Arthur *Phillip in 1788 when he led the *First Fleet of convicts to Australia. He decided that the magnificent harbour was a better site than Botany Bay, and he named the new settlement in honour of Viscount Sydney, Under-Secretary of State for Home Affairs. From these beginnings the city has grown at a great rate and, as an important centre of the wool and meat trade, the port has grown with it to become one of the major trading centres of the world. It is also a main base of the Royal Australian Navy, with extensive dockyards and shipbuilding yards.

SYNOPTIC CHART, a weather map on which the *isobars derived from a large number of weather station reports are drawn to provide a full picture of the position, shape, size, and depth of the various weather systems in the area covered by the chart. These charts are normally kept up to date in meteorological offices round the world and, by a comparison with previous charts of the same area, meteorologists can see the directions in which movements are taking place and thus predict the weather patterns in the immediate and near future. The distance apart of the isobars gives a basis for the prediction of wind strengths; the closer they are together, the stronger the wind is likely to be. Weather forecasts broadcast from meteorological offices are based on the information obtained from synoptic charts. See METEOROLOGY.

T

TABARLY, ERIC (1931–), French naval officer and yachtsman, is noted for his success in planning and sailing advanced type yachts in single-handed ocean races. His best-known yachts are the five which he named *Pen Duick*, winning in 1964 the single-handed Transatlantic race with *Pen Duick II*. He was the overall winner in 1967 of the *Royal Ocean Racing Club's Morgan Cup, The Channel, *Fastnet, and Plymouth–La Rochelle, and Benodet races, was second overall in the 1967 Sydney–Hobart race and second in the 1968 single-handed Transatlantic race. With *Pen Duick V* he finished first in the 1969 Transpacific race, organized by the Slocum Society, from San Francisco to Tokyo, sailing roughly 5,300 miles in just under forty days. Books he has written are *Lonely Victory* (1964) and *Pen Duick* (1971).

TABERNACLE, a wooden or metal trunk fixed to the deck of a sailing vessel to support a mast which has its heel at deck level and is not *stepped below decks. It is used in cases where it is necessary occasionally to lower the mast to deck level, as in inland waters for passing under bridges, etc. The mast is pivoted on a steel pin which passes through the top of the tabernacle, the forward side of the tabernacle being left open to allow the heel of the mast to swing forward as the mast is lowered aft. A slightly different fitting, known as a *lutchet but serving the same purpose, is used in *spritsail *barges and *wherries.

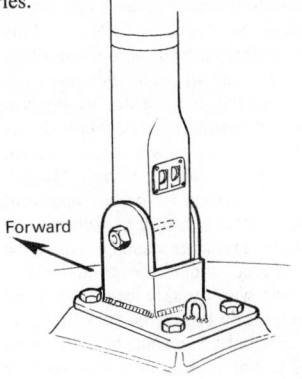

Forward

TABLE, to, the sailmaker's term for sewing *reef bands and *buntline bands on to sails to add additional strength to the sail where the reef points are fixed and to prevent chafe in a square sail where the buntline lies along the canvas. It is only the larger sails, particularly in square-rigged ships, that have these bands tabled on to them.

TABLING, the name given to an extra strip of canvas sewn around the edges of sails to reinforce them where the *boltrope is sewn on.

TACK, (1) a *board or *reach sailed in a sailing vessel with the wind kept on one side of the vessel. See also LEG, PORT TACK, STARBOARD TACK. **(2)** The name given to the lower forward corner of a fore-and-aft sail. For illus. see SAIL. **(3)** In square-rigged ships, it was the name of the rope used to hold in the *weather lower corners of *courses and *staysails when sailing *close-hauled. Also, when *studdingsails were set, it was the name given to the rope employed to haul out the lower outer *clew of the sail to the boom-end.

TACK, to, the operation of bringing a sailing vessel head to wind and across it so as to bring the wind on the opposite side of the vessel. During this manoeuvre the vessel is said to be in *stays, or staying, or coming about. When a sailing vessel wishes to make up to windward, she can only do so by tacking, crossing the wind continuously to make a series of *legs, of which the net distance gained is to windward.

TACKLE, pronounced taykle, a *purchase in which two or more *blocks are used in order to multiply the power exerted on a rope. The gain in power is equivalent to the number of parts which enter and leave the moving block of the tackle, depending on whether the tackle is rigged to *advantage or disadvantage. Tackles are employed for most lifting or moving jobs in a vessel, from *trimming the sails in a sailing vessel to shifting cargo in a merchant ship. They are of many varieties, depending partly on their particular purpose, e.g., a *luff tackle, and partly on the number and nature of the blocks used.

The clipper ship Taeping *with the* Ariel *in the Great China tea race; lithograph, 1866*

TACKLINE, a six-foot length of signal line with signal clips at each end. It is used, mainly in naval vessels, for inserting in a flag signal hoist to indicate a break in the signal, and that the flags below it form a new signal. All flags used in signals at sea have a clip at each end of the * hoist so that they can be clipped quickly to each other to form a particular signal; the clips on the tackline are of the same pattern and can be clipped equally quickly to signal flags when it is required to insert a break in the hoist.

TACTICAL DIAMETER, the distance a ship is displaced to port or starboard of her original line of advance after a turn of sixteen points (180°) under full helm at full speed.

TAEPING, one of the most successful British tea * clippers, was built in 1863 by Robert * Steele of Greenock alongside the equally famous *Serica*, each of about 770 tons gross. These two ships, with the *Ariel*, *Fiery Cross*, and *Taitsin*, raced home to London in 1866 with the first of the season's tea crop, the first three, the *Taeping*, *Serica*, and *Ariel*, arriving on the same tide in the Thames after a voyage of 16,000 miles which they accomplished in ninety-nine days.

TAFFRAIL, in strict definition, the after rail at the * stern of a ship, but formerly the curved wooden top of the stern of a sailing man-of-war or * East Indiaman, usually carved or otherwise decorated. It is a contraction of taffarel, the original name for this adornment. In its modern meaning it is often used to indicate the deck area right at the stern of a vessel.

'TAFFRAIL', the pseudonym under which Captain H. Taprell * Dorling wrote many books about the sea, mostly concerning the British

Navy. Among his best-known works were *Pincher Martin, O.D.*, a novel, and *Endless Story*, a history of * destroyers during the First World War (1914–18).

'TAKE A CAULK, to', a slang expression used by seamen meaning to sleep on deck, either legitimately during a * make and mend or when off * watch below, or illegitimately if the chances of discovery are slight. The probable origin of the expression is that the deck * seams of a ship, which are * caulked, are horizontal, the normal position of a man when he sleeps.

TALBOT, MARY ANNE (1778–1808), known as the 'British Amazon', was the youngest of sixteen illegitimate children of Lord William Talbot, later Earl Talbot, all by the same mother. As a girl Mary Anne was seduced by a captain in the army and, disguised in male dress as his footboy, accompanied him under the name of John Taylor to the West Indies when his regiment was posted there in 1792. Shortly after its arrival at St. Domingo, it was ordered back to take part in the Walcheren expedition, Mary Anne being enrolled in the regiment as a drummer-boy. She was in the siege of Valenciennes, being twice slightly wounded, but decided to desert when the town was captured, her captain having been killed. On her way to the coast she was driven by extremity to sign on in a French * lugger, which she later discovered to be operating as a * privateer. After a cruise of four months in the Channel, the privateer was sighted by the British Channel Fleet under the command of Lord * Howe and was quickly captured, Mary Anne being brought on board the flagship for questioning as a renegade. She was able to convince Lord Howe of her bona fides, and was sent by him to H.M.S. *Brunswick*, in which she served as a *powder-monkey to the *quarterdeck guns and later as principal cabin-boy to Captain Harvey, commanding the *Brunswick*. She was on board the ship at the battle in 1794 of the *Glorious First of June, and was wounded in the ankle and the thigh. She became an outpatient at *Haslar Hospital, and after her recovery served in the *bomb vessel *Vesuvius*, according to her account as a *midshipman though paid as a seaman. She and another midshipman were captured after an action with two French privateers and lodged in prison at Dunkirk, being exchanged after eighteen months. She was then employed on board an American merchant ship as second *mate, but after a voyage to New York and back, was taken by a *press gang as a likely recruit for the British Navy. Her only means of escaping this was by revealing her sex. She seems to have had a chequered career from then on, on one occasion nearly becoming a highwayman. She quickly spent the pay and *prize money due to her for the Glorious First of June, worked as a goldsmith's assistant for a time, became an actress in the Thespian Society, was in and out of prison for debt, and was a prostitute on the side.

Mary Anne Talbot wrote an account of her adventures which was first published in the second volume of Kirby's *Wonderful Museum of Remarkable Characters*. It was later separately published in 1809 as a pamphlet with the title *The Life and Surprising Adventures of Mary Anne Talbot*.

TALURIT SPLICING, a modern method of splicing wire rope when a *thimble or eye is required in the end. The end of the wire is threaded through a non-corrosive alloy ferrule of a size convenient for the wire and then threaded back to form a loop round the thimble. The ferrule is then gripped lightly in a hydraulic press while the wire is pulled through to make the loop the required size or to lie closely round the thimble. Further pressure is then exerted to make the metal of the ferrule flow round the strands of the wire thus holding each firmly in position, and the splice is complete.

A Talurit splice is as strong as a fully tucked eyesplice and is more economical in the use of wire rope. When making an eyesplice by hand, one foot of wire rope is needed for tucking for every inch of its circumference; the Talurit method uses only one inch of wire for the whole splice.

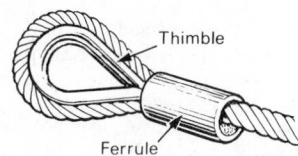

Talurit splicing

TAN, to, the means of preserving the life of canvas sails by dressing them with * cutch. The sails are immersed in a cutch solution for two or three hours, then hung over a spar to dry. The resultant colour is a rich deep red. When the sail is dry the cutch is fixed in the canvas by brushing into the sail, or immersing it in, a solution of one lb (0·453 kg) of bichromate to four gallons (18·18 l) of fresh water. This fixing process changes the colour of the sails from deep red to mahogany.

TANKER, a ship designed specifically to carry liquid cargoes, particularly oil, in bulk at sea. She is essentially a ship of the 20th century, as the growth of the use of oil for fuel on a large scale, calling for bulk carriage from the oil producing countries, dates from the first decade of the century with the development of the automobile and the flying machine.

The first ships specifically built as tankers were small, the largest carrying perhaps as much as 5,000 tons of oil, but the decision of the British Navy in 1912 to abandon coal as its boiler fuel in all ships and to switch to oil, a policy rapidly followed by all other modern navies, led to the design and building of larger tankers of up to 10,000–15,000 tons. The need for navies to build up large reserve stocks as a safeguard in the event of war stimulated the demand for tankers and a large number were built purely for this end, with no other possible cargo in view.

The immense growth in popularity of the automobile during the 20 years between the two World Wars, coupled with a big increase in the use of oil for steam generation both ashore and afloat, led to a large surge in tanker tonnage during these years, both in numbers and individual size. Size was largely dictated by the limitations imposed by the Suez Canal, the shortest route between the big producers in the Middle East and the immense market of western Europe, and the largest tankers built during this period rarely exceeded 25,000–30,000 tons.

The closure of the Suez Canal following the Anglo-French attack on Egypt in 1956 and again after the Arab–Israeli War of 1967, coupled at the same time with an immense new demand stimulated by the world-wide growth of all forms of mechanical transport on land, sea, and in the air, forced the birth of a new generation of supertankers, known generically as very large crude carriers (*V.L.C.C.) of 250,000–275,000 tons. Faced, by the closure of the Canal, with the much longer voyage round the Cape of Good Hope, these immense tankers provided the only economic means of bulk transport of oil by sea. Once they had proved themselves viable not only in economic transport but also in terms of safety at sea, even larger tankers, known as ultra large crude carriers (*U.L.C.C.) were built up to a tonnage of around 400,000. Even larger

A super-tanker of 250,000 tons

U.L.C.C. are in the course of design, plans existing for the construction of one in Japan of as much as 800,000 tons.

Basically a tanker consists of a number of separate oil containers built into the hull of a ship, each container, or tank, running the full width of the ship but separated from each other by a narrow athwartships compartment as a safety factor. Tankers are also built for the bulk transport of liquefied natural gas and, though on a much smaller scale, for the carriage of wine.

TAR, (1) the residue after distillation of the gum extracted from pine trees and used, among many other purposes, for the preservation of the standing rigging of a square-rigged ship and also for preserving hemp rope, which is liable to rot when wet. **(2)** An affectionate name for a sailor, derived from their habit in the days before the issue of official uniform of treating their canvas coats and hats with tar as a protection against the weather. It was a contraction of * tarpaulin.

TARANTO, BATTLE OF, an action of the Second World War, was fought in the Mediterranean on 11 November 1940 between aircraft of the British * aircraft carriers *Illustrious* and *Eagle* and the Italian battle fleet anchored in the harbour of Taranto.

The possibility of an attack by * Fleet Air Arm aircraft on the Italian fleet in harbour had long been considered, and on 11 November 1940, when air reconnaissance showed that five of the six Italian * battleships in commission were lying at anchor in Taranto, the commander-in-chief of the British Mediterranean Fleet, Admiral Sir Andrew * Cunningham, decided to launch the attack that night. It had been intended to use both H.M.S. *Illustrious* and H.M.S. *Eagle* as the two carriers from which the attack was to be launched, but the latter ship was in dock owing to defects and the *Illustrious* was the only carrier used, some of the *Eagle*'s aircraft being embarked on board the *Illustrious*. Proceeding to a position 180 miles south-east of Taranto, twenty-one aircraft were flown off in two waves from the flight deck of H.M.S. *Illustrious*, beginning at 2040, the first wave arriving over the target some two hours later. Complete surprise was achieved and while some aircraft illuminated the scene with flares, the * torpedo-armed * Swordfish dived to the attack. The new battleship *Littorio* and two older ones, *Conte di Cavour* and *Caio Duilio*, were torpedoed and sunk at their moorings for the loss of only two aircraft. By 0300 on 12 November all the remaining aircraft had been embarked. By this very successful operation British maritime power was re-established in the central Mediterranean. The Italian ships were later raised and refitted.

TARAWA, an *atoll of the Gilbert Island group in the western Pacific, was the scene of an amphibious action during the Second World War between U.S. amphibious assault forces and Japanese military defenders. The operation, which was the main episode in the recapture from the Japanese of the Gilbert Islands, took place between 20 and 23 November 1943. A simultaneous but smaller operation was the assault and capture of Butaritari Island of Makin atoll. This latter, fiercely defended by only 800 men, including 200 Korean labourers, against 6,507 U.S. soldiers, was captured in two days at the cost of 56 Americans killed and 131 wounded.

Tarawa, of which the principal island is Betio, was much more strongly fortified and was defended by 4,820 first-class Japanese troops supported by forty-one heavy guns and forty-two automatic weapons mounted in steel and concrete gun positions as well as in log pill-boxes. To assault it, 18,600 U.S. *marines of the 2nd Marine Division were brought to the island in a variety of troop transports, including tank landing ships, supported by a naval task force of three *battleships, five escort *aircraft carriers, three *cruisers, and fourteen *destroyers. The troops were put ashore in landing craft.

Before the assault the defences were softened up by air strikes from a supporting fast carrier group on 18 and 19 November and again at dawn on the 20th, the last air strike being followed by a systematic bombardment by battleships, cruisers, and destroyers before the first assault waves were landed. The defences were far from neutralized, however, and when unforeseen difficulties were encountered by the landing craft, very heavy casualties were suffered by the marines. By the evening 5,000 men were ashore, but it was not until noon on the 23rd that the whole island was occupied. The Japanese resisted almost to the last man, 4,690 dead being counted. Out of 146 prisoners taken, 129 were Korean labourers. American casualties amounted to nearly 1,000 killed and more than 2,000 wounded.

TARPAULIN, orig. **TARPAWLING,** in the old days canvas treated with *tar and cut up into clothing on board ship, but from about 1750 it has been the painted canvas used for covering the *hatches of cargo ships and for the protection of other gear on board ship, such as the reels on which wire rope is wound, which might suffer from seawater in rough weather.

TARPAULIN CAPTAIN, a captain of a British naval ship in the reigns of the Tudor and Stuart monarchs who had risen by promotion through service in the navy, as opposed to the courtiers who were appointed to posts of command by reason of their influence at Court and by no means because of any professional knowledge. There was always great bitterness between tarpaulin captains and what were known as 'gentlemen captains', for, as Sir Henry *Mainwaring wrote in his *Discourse on Pirates* (1617), the ability to command a ship with 'discretion and judgement, to manage, handle, content and command the company, both in fear and love (without which no Commander is absolute)' was beyond the capability of the gentleman captain. That the ships' crews also preferred to be commanded by a tarpaulin captain can be appreciated by the example of a dozen seamen at the funeral of Sir Christopher *Myngs, killed in 1666 during the Second Anglo-Dutch War (1665–7), who begged to be given a *fireship, a notoriously dangerous form of naval service, so that they could 'do that that shall show our memory of our dead commander and our revenge'. Myngs, of course, was a tarpaulin captain.

TARPAULIN MUSTER, a sailor's name for the pooling of the financial resources of a group of seamen for a run ashore.

TARRY-BREEKS, a North Country (England) name for a seaman, probably from the same origin as the name Tar, or Jack Tar, used familiarly to describe a sailor. This came from his habit of painting his canvas clothing with tar to keep out the wind and rain, and also from the fact that, in the period when pigtails were the fashionable hair style afloat, the seaman always dressed his pigtail with tar. In a sailor's song, popular in the 18th century, a girl whose mother wanted her to marry a rich husband sings:

> 'I know you'd have me wed a farmer
> And not give me my heart's delight.
> Mine's the lad whose tarry trousers
> Shine to me like diamonds bright.'

TARTAN, sometimes written as **TARTANE,** a small coasting vessel of the Mediterranean, possibly a development of the medieval tarette, which originated with the Arabs for use as a cargo-carrying vessel. Tartans were single-masted with a *lateen mainsail and a small foresail set on a *bowsprit. They carried a crew of about thirty men. Simultaneously there were in the Mediterranean fishing vessels known as tartanas; unlike the true tartan they had a flat bottom.

TASMAN, ABEL JANSZOON (*c.* 1603–59), Dutch navigator, was born at Lutjegast, Groningen, and was employed in the service of the Dutch *East India Company, becoming captain of one of the company's merchant ships. His reputation as a navigator came to the notice of Antony van Diemen, governor-general of the

Dutch East Indies, and in June 1639 he was given command of an exploring expedition to the north-western Pacific, to search for 'islands of gold and silver' supposed to exist to the eastward of Japan. As his chief pilot he had Matthew Quast on board, but beyond surveying the Bonin Islands, the two men discovered little beyond the emptiness of the Pacific Ocean in these northern latitudes.

For the next two years Tasman reverted to his mercantile command, mainly in trading voyages in the Indian Ocean, but in 1642 he was again selected by van Diemen to command an exploring expedition to the 'Great South Land' (Australia). Already several Dutch navigators had discovered various parts of the northern and western coasts of Australia, and van Diemen, who had ambitions to extend the Dutch colonial empire in the East Indies, planned an expedition to discover whether this land were part of the supposed great southern continent (*Terra Australis Incognita) or whether it were an island. With Frans Visscher as pilot, Tasman sailed in the ships *Heemskirk* and *Zeehaen* from Batavia to Mauritius, and then stretched away south and east to reach a latitude of 40° S., the area of the *roaring forties, when he steered due east, reaching land seven weeks later. He named this Antoonij van Diemen's Landt, in honour of the governor-general, the name being later changed to Tasmania, in honour of himself. He sailed on round the south of Tasmania, not realizing that it was an island separated from Australia, and set a course for the Solomon Islands which, if it succeeded, would prove that the Australian continent was not, in fact, a part of the great southern continent.

Eight days later he sighted high land ahead of him, which he named Staten Landt (now New Zealand), believing it to be the western extremity of the great continent of which the other Staten Landt, discovered and named by Lle Maire and *Schouten south of Tierra del Fuego, was the eastern extremity. He sailed along the west coast of New Zealand, mistaking the strait between the two islands, now Cook Strait, for a deep bay, and after rounding the northern end of North Island, which he named Cape Maria van Diemen, he sailed north-north-east, discovering several islands in the Tonga group and the eastern part of the Fiji archipelago, and finally returned to Batavia by the New Hebrides, Solomon Islands, and New Guinea after a voyage lasting ten months. He was thus the first man to make a circumnavigation of Australia and to prove that it was an island and not a part of the mythical southern continent.

His next voyage, also planned by van Diemen, was designed to discover whether New Guinea was a part of the Australian continent or was an island lying off its north coast, and whether van Diemen's Landt (Tasmania) was also a part of the Australian continent or was an island lying off its south coast. Still with Frans Visscher as his pilot, Tasman was given command of three ships, the *Limmen*, *Zeemeeuw*, and *Brak*, and sailed from Batavia in 1644. He sailed along the west coast of New Guinea, but either mistaking the Torres Strait for a bay or being unable to penetrate the mass of small islands or reefs which guard its western entrance, sheered south into the Gulf of Carpentaria of which he explored and surveyed the southern and western coasts with some accuracy. He then proceeded westward along the northern Australian coast, charting the coastline as far south as 22° S. before returning to Batavia. He was not well received on his return, having failed in both the main objectives of his voyage, but was reluctantly confirmed in the rank of commander, a rank which in fact he had already been using for some time.

In 1647 he was placed in command of a trading fleet to Siam, and the following year commanded a war fleet dispatched to operate against the Spaniards in the Philippine Islands in defence of Dutch interests in the East Indies. By now he had amassed a considerable fortune, and in 1653 retired from the Dutch East India Company to settle down and enjoy his wealth as one of the leading citizens of Batavia.

Tasman is generally considered to be the greatest of the Dutch navigators and explorers. Details of his voyages are published in the *Hakluyt Society's volume *Early Voyages to Terra Australis* (1859) and a biography of him is included in J. E. Heeres and others, *Tasman's Journal* (1898).

TASSAFARONGA, BATTLE OF, was a night action of the Second World War fought off *Guadalcanal in the south-west Pacific between an American force composed of the heavy cruisers *Minneapolis* (flag of Rear Admiral Carleton Wright), *Northampton*, *New Orleans*, and *Pensacola*, the light cruiser *Honolulu*, and six destroyers, and eight Japanese destroyers encountered as they were jettisoning buoyant drums containing supplies for their troops ashore on the night of 30 November 1942.

Following the repeated examples of Japanese superiority in night fighting, tactics had been worked out for this force by Rear Admiral Thomas *Kinkaid which would permit greater flexibility and initiative and make better use of the American *radar advantage. Kinkaid had been appointed elsewhere, however, and Wright had been only two days in command when the encounter took place. His opponent was the redoubtable Rear Admiral Tanaka who had brilliantly commanded the light forces responsible for the supply of Japanese troops on Guadalcanal since the beginning of the campaign.

The Americans were in their usual single line ahead with destroyers in van and rear when the enemy was detected by radar approaching on an opposite course. After an unjustifiable delay, permission was given for the American destroyers in the van to fire *torpedoes at the unsuspecting Japanese; but before they could reach their target the American cruisers opened gunfire on the nearest radar contact. This sank the destroyer *Takanami*, but alerted the remainder of Tanaka's ships which, recovering at once from their surprise, turned and launched their own torpedoes, avoiding at the same time those fired at them.

The *Minneapolis*, *New Orleans*, *Pensacola*, and *Northampton* were all torpedoed, the last-named sinking, the others only reaching Tulagi as a result of outstanding skill. Except for the *Takanami*, the Japanese retired unscathed.

TATTNALL, JOSIAH (1795–1871), American naval officer, entered the U.S. Navy in 1812. In June 1859, during the Second China War (1856–9), his flagship, the *Toeywan*, towed down the boats returning to the fleet with survivors of the British land attack on the Peiho forts; he is credited with the phrase 'blood is thicker than water' in conversation with the British commander-in-chief, Sir James Hope, the following day, when justifying his intervention.

In the American Civil War (1861–5) Tattnall joined the Confederate side and took over command of its naval forces after the action in Hampton Roads in which Franklin *Buchanan was wounded. His forces were, however, too small and too scattered ever to form a seagoing squadron.

TATTOO, a form of skin decoration, to which many sailors are said to be drawn, produced by the injection of coloured pigments into the skin. It was first revealed to the western world by Captain James *Cook in his journal of his first voyage of circumnavigation when describing the natives of Tahiti (entry for July 1764), ' "Tattow" as it is called in their language, this is done by inlaying the Colour of black under their skins in such a manner as to be indelible. Some have ill-design'd figures of men birds or dogs, the women generally have this figure Z simply on ever(y) joint of their fingers and toes. . . . As this is a painfull operation especially the tattowing thier buttocks it is perform'd but once in their life time.'

It was, however, prevalent among tribal people, particularly in the Pacific area, and the custom certainly pre-dated Cook's account by a great many years. According to Captain *Marryat, writing in 1830, the practice of tattooing was very common among sailors in the Royal Navy; French soldiers and criminals were also said to be great tattooers.

One of the able seamen on board the *Endeavour* during Cook's first voyage underwent this operation. He was Robert Stainsby and thus, perhaps, has the honour of inaugurating the long tradition of the tattooed sailor.

TAUNT, an old expression for a sailing ship with very high masts and narrow sails. Such a rig enabled a ship to point higher on a wind, but it was apt to wring, or twist, a ship's side because of the relatively narrow base for the shrouds supporting the masts. North European ships —German, Dutch, and Scandinavian—were usually very taunt during the sailing era; British ships used shorter masts and broader sails, and in general enjoyed a longer life, being subject to less strain through wringing. See also ALL-A-TAUNTO.

TAUT, the maritime word meaning tight, usually in relation to a sailing vessel's rigging or the hauling of ropes. Thus, a ship's rigging is taut when it is set up as hard as it will go; a rope is hauled taut when it is bar tight. A square-rigged ship sailing on a taut *bowline means that she is sailing as close to the wind as she will go, the bowlines on the weather *clews of the sails being hauled up taut as far forward as possible in order to *brace the yards round on the masts to form an acute angle in relation to the fore-and-aft line of the ship. The word is used for many similar meanings, as 'He's a taut hand', meaning 'he's a stern disciplinarian'; 'the ship is run on a taut string', meaning that she is a smart ship and well disciplined.

TAUT WIRE MEASUREMENT, a means developed in the British Navy during the First World War (1914–18) for providing an accurate measurement of the distance over the ground run by a ship. A reel of thin wire, some miles in length, was mounted on the stern of a ship, and when it was desired to start the measurement, a fire-bar or similar object was secured to the end and dropped overboard. As the ship steamed through the water the wire was pulled off the reel, with a friction bearing preventing it coming off too fast, by the speed of the ship through the water, and a dial on the reel recorded the amount which had run off. Taut wire measurement had a particular value in such naval operations as mine-laying, which needed exact navigational measurement to ensure that the mines were laid in the correct positions. A row of mines, for example, could be laid at the same distance apart by reading from the dial the actual distance run between the laying of each mine. A great advantage of this method was that it recorded the distance travelled by the ship over the ground and not through the water, which differs because of the effect of the tide on the ship.

Taut wire measurement also has a use in marine surveying where accurate distance over the ground run by a surveying vessel is an important function of the exact observation required in the making of a chart. This method of measurement of distance run at sea can only, of course, be used in comparatively shallow waters.

Captain Edward Teach; engraving, 1734

TEACH or **THATCH,** EDWARD (d. 1718), English pirate, was born in Bristol and is said to have served in a *privateer in the West Indies during the War of the Spanish Succession (1702–13) and to have turned pirate on the declaration of peace. In the course of his piracy he captured a large French merchant vessel in 1717, renamed her the *Queen Anne's Revenge*, and fitted her out as a warship of forty guns manned by local riff-raff. His captures and robberies with this ship were, it is said, shared by him with the governor of North Carolina who certainly provided him with many facilities for refitting and victualling his ship. In 1718, however, Teach's activities as a pirate so enraged the neighbouring governor of Virginia that he fitted out two *sloops, which were manned by men of the British Navy, and sent them to sea to hunt Teach down. On 22 November 1718 Lieutenant Robert Maynard, commanding the sloops, discovered and boarded Teach's ship, and after a short fight shot the pirate dead. His head was cut off and suspended from the end of the bowsprit while twelve of the fifteen pirates captured were immediately hanged from the various yardarms. Teach, whose real name was more probably Thatch, was widely known as 'Blackbeard' from his odd habit of tying up the ends of his long black beard with ribbons and curling them back over his ears.

TEGETTHOF, Baron WILHELM VON (1827–71), Austrian vice admiral, commanded the Austrian fleet at the battle of *Lissa (1866) in the Adriatic in which he inflicted a considerable defeat on a much larger and more modern Italian fleet. It was in this battle that his flagship, the *Ferdinand Maximilian*, rammed and sank the Italian flagship, the *Re d'Italia*. Tegetthof had a distinguished career in the Austrian Navy and commanded the Austro-Prussian squadron in the North Sea which, in 1864, drove off the blockading Danish squadron at Hamburg, even though, as at Lissa, he was seriously outnumbered in ships and guns. After his success at Lissa, the Austrian authorities decreed that there should always be an *ironclad in the Austrian fleet which bore his name. He died of dysentery which he had contracted in Mexico.

One effect of the battle of Lissa was a renewed belief in the value of the *ram as a naval weapon, and all warships of all nations of any size were constructed with heavy rams on their bows which served only to slow them down and make them peculiarly unwieldy. Against all reason, and particularly in the face of the development of the long range gun, rams continued to be fitted in battleships and heavy cruisers until the beginning of the 20th century, the belief in their effectiveness being fortified by one or two naval accidents during peacetime manoeuvres in which ships were sunk after being accidentally rammed. The best known of these accidents were the sinking of the H.M.S. *Vanguard by H.M.S. *Iron Duke in 1875 and of H.M.S. *Victoria by H.M.S. *Camperdown in 1893.

TELESCOPE, see GLASS.

TELLTALE. Originally the word referred only to a compass which the *master of a ship had in his cabin so that he could always know the direction in which his ship was heading. It was often fixed to hang face downwards from the deck beams so that he could read the ship's course while lying in his bunk. In these days of gyroscopic compasses, such a compass would be called a repeater, but the word telltale is used generally to indicate any mechanical contrivance which reproduces useful information, such as orders from the bridge of a ship for the operation of the main engines, or an indicator at the steering-wheel to tell the helmsman how many degrees of *helm he has on the rudder.

It is also a name used in yachts to describe the five-inch lengths of wool sewn at intervals just abaft the *luff of a sail to indicate the airflow.

***TEMERAIRE,* H.M.S.,** unquestionably one of the best-known names in the Royal Navy on account of Sir Henry *Newbolt's poem 'The

Fighting *Temeraire*' which immortalizes the Royal Navy's second ship of the name, the 98-gun 2nd *rate ship of the line which fought at *Trafalgar. She was named after her predecessor, a 74-gun French ship captured at *Lagos in 1759 by Admiral *Boscawen and added to the Royal Navy in 1760 under her own name. This ship served in the Royal Navy at Belleisle in 1761 and at Martinique and Havannah in 1762 and was sold in 1784. The second *Temeraire* was launched in 1798 at Chatham and was the second ship in the weather line at Trafalgar, next astern of H.M.S. *Victory*. During the battle she ran alongside the French *Redoutable*, and after pouring in a few broadsides from her port battery, took possession of her. The French *Fougueux*, coming up to assist the *Redoutable*, was received with a shattering broadside from the *Temeraire*'s starboard battery, drifted alongside out of control, and was quickly taken a prize. J. M. W. *Turner's famous picture of her, which was exhibited in the Royal Academy in 1839 and now hangs in the National Gallery in Trafalgar Square, London, shows her being towed up the river to be broken up at Rotherhithe after she had been sold out of the navy in 1838.

TENDER, a small vessel attached temporarily to a larger ship for general harbour duties such as collection of mails, delivery of fresh meat and vegetables, landing of seamen for short *liberty ashore, etc. A press tender was a small vessel under the command of a lieutenant which, in the days of *impressment in the British Navy, took on board volunteers or pressed men collected at a *rendezvous and delivered them to the *receiving ships in home ports. The men thus collected from the rendezvous were taken down in the tender's *hold which was then *battened down to prevent any chance of the men escaping. Conditions in press tenders were notoriously terrible and because of their filth and overcrowding were mainly responsible for the great incidence of typhus fever which decimated British fleets during the Revolutionary (1793–1801) and Napoleonic (1803–15) wars against France when the pressing of seamen was at its height.

TEONGE, the Revd. HENRY (*c.* 1621–90), English minister of religion, was the author of a diary of his experiences as chaplain in H.M. ships *Assistance* (1675–6), *Bristol* (1678–9), and *Royal Oak* (1679). Recognized as a minor classic of the sea, it gives a vivid view of life in the Royal Navy during the later years of Charles II, and has been compared with the more famous diary of Samuel * Pepys as an intensely human document full of fun and good humour. The best edition, transcribed and edited by G. E. Manwaring, was published in 1927.

TEREDO, a bivalve mollusc, family Teredinidae, commonly known as ship worms, and notorious for the damage they cause in the timbers of wooden ships, wooden piles in harbours, etc. They bore long cylindrical holes in the wood which they then inhabit, usually in such great numbers that only a thin film of wood exists between the holes. Some were said to be as much as three feet in length, with a diameter of nearly one inch. Species of teredo occur in all seas, but they are most prevalent in warmer waters. The attacks of the teredo worm on the hulls of wooden ships led to the almost universal habit of protection by copper *sheathing during the late 18th and early 19th centuries. It can now be controlled by anti-fouling preparations painted on a ship's underbody.

TERRA AUSTRALIS, on some early maps with the addition of INCOGNITA, unknown, was the name given to the great and unknown southern continent required by the classical Greek geographers, who knew that the earth was spherical, to balance the land mass which was known to exist north of the equator. For a period in the early Middle Ages the church's insistence that the earth was flat led to the complete eradication of all belief in a southern continent, but the great years of exploration in the 15th and early 16th centuries, confirming the spherical shape of the earth, brought the belief back into existence. Maps of that period showed Terra Australis as a vast continent centred on the South pole, and extending as far north as approximately latitude 60° S., and in the Pacific Ocean almost up to the equator. The rounding of the Cape of Good Hope by Bartholomew *Diaz in 1478 and of South America by Ferdinand *Magellan in 1520 stimulated the search for this unknown continent, which within a century was gradually reduced to two smaller continents, one of which is now known as Antarctica, the other as Australia.

Antarctica was not finally delineated as a continent until the early 20th century (see ANTARCTIC EXPLORATION), although Australia was shown to be one much earlier. The first explorers to reach the country were the Dutch. It was possibly first sighted by de *Torres, second in command of an expedition sent out by Philip III of Spain in 1605, of which de *Quiros was the admiral, but the first landing by white men on Australian soil was made by the crew of a small Dutch vessel, the *Duyfken*, which penetrated the Gulf of Carpentaria and sailed south as far as Cape Keerweer. Other Dutch ships followed and gradually the picture of the western coast of the continent was built up, being given the name of New Holland. In 1642 Abel *Tasman sailed from Batavia, the headquarters of the Dutch *East India Company, on a voyage which took him south of the continent and eventually across

Captain Scott's Terra Nova; *photograph by H. Ponting, 1912*

to the South Island of New Zealand. He named what is now known as Tasmania as Van Diemen's Land in honour of the then governor-general of the Dutch East Indies, but his voyage was later commemorated by changing the name of the island to Tasmania. He was the first navigator to prove that Australia was not a part of Terra Australis Incognita by circumnavigating it and thus proving that it was a separate island.

William *Dampier, the English navigator, sighted the shores of Australia in 1688 during the course of a buccaneering voyage with Captain Swan in the *Cygnet*; in the following year he was sent by the British Admiralty in the *Roebuck* on a part-privateering and part-exploring voyage to discover more of the new continent. He explored the west coast from Sharks Bay northward to Roebuck Bay, describing the aborigines he met there in words which later inspired Jonathan Swift in his description of the Yahoos in *Gulliver's Travels*.

Captain James *Cook, in the *Endeavour*, was given the subsidiary task in his first voyage of circumnavigation (1768–71) of investigating the existence of the great southern continent of Terra Australis Incognita. After he had observed the transit of Venus at Tahiti, the primary task of his voyage, Cook sailed south and reached the North Island of New Zealand on 7 October 1769. He sailed down the west coast, through the strait between the two islands which bears his name, and completely round South Island, thus proving it was not a northerly cape of the great southern continent, as had been thought. From New Zealand he sailed across to Australia and up the east coast, anchoring in *Botany Bay for water. Cook's second voyage of circumnavigation (1772–5), again designed to discover more of Terra Australis Incognita, finally proved conclusively that it did not exist. He made three penetrations of the Antarctic, and by sailing along the latitude of 60° S. for long stretches, encountering nothing but ice, demonstrated that no land existed in those waters and that Australia and New Zealand were islands, unconnected to any continent.

TERRA NOVA, a wooden three-masted *barque of 749 tons, was built in 1884 as 'the biggest whaling ship afloat', but was later better known as a polar expedition ship. She first served in the *Arctic with the Jackson–Harmsworth expedition of 1894–7, and then accompanied the *Morning* to the *Antarctic to relieve Captain Robert *Scott's *Discovery* expedition in 1903. She returned to the Antarctic in 1910 with Scott's second expedition of 1910–13, in which Scott and four companions died on the return journey from the South pole to their base camp. She was bought back by her original owners on her return home in 1913 and was used in the Newfoundland

*seal fishery and in coastal trading from 1914 to 1942. In September 1943 she sprang a leak off south-west Greenland and foundered.

TERRITORIAL WATERS, that area of sea adjacent to the coasts of nations which is under the full control of the nation concerned. A compromise between the claims of certain nations to exercise dominion over seas and oceans, and those of other nations which claimed that all areas of sea should be free to all ships, which was a point of argument, and even war, between nations during the 16th and 17th centuries, was found in a suggestion made in 1702 by Bynkershoek, in his book *De dominio maris*. He proposed that a nation should exercise dominion over the adjacent seas only to the extent that she could defend them from the shore, which was taken as the existing range of a cannon, and agreed to be three miles. This universally agreed limit remained in force until the mid-20th century, when certain nations unilaterally declared an extension to their territorial waters, mainly to protect their inshore fisheries. The generally accepted figure in recent years, though as yet without international agreement, is 12 miles, but with certain reservations for fishing rights within that limit where such fishing has been historically exercised. More recently still, some nations have claimed a big extension of territorial waters of up to 200 miles, either to protect prolific fishing grounds, as for example the cod fishing off Iceland, or for other reasons, such as the existence of oilfields under the seabed. A United Nations conference on the Law of the Sea is to discuss the extent of a new limit in 1976. See also MARE CLAUSUM.

TERROR, H.M.S., a *bomb *ketch of 326 tons launched in 1813. In company with H.M.S. *Erebus*, she formed part of Captain James C. *Ross's expeditition to the *Antarctic of 1839–43, and two years later she was fitted with a steam engine and screw propeller prior to sailing, again with the *Erebus*, on Sir John *Franklin's last polar expedition. She was abandoned in the ice in April 1848. Her name is always associated with that of the *Erebus* in the long story of *Arctic exploration.

TETHYS, the greatest of the Greek sea goddesses, was the wife of *Oceanus, and by legend the mother of the world's greatest rivers, including the Nile. She also had 3,000 daughters, known as the *Oceanides. By some, she has been identified with Thetis, who in fact was her granddaughter. Her name is frequently used poetically to express the sea itself.

TEXEL, The, scene of the last battle of the Third Dutch War (1672–4) which was fought off the Dutch coast on 11 August 1673 between an

The battle of the Texel; detail from the oil painting by A. Storck, 1673

Anglo-French fleet of eighty-one ships under the command of Prince *Rupert and a Dutch fleet of fifty-four ships commanded by Admiral de *Ruyter. The French ships formed a squadron by themselves and, possibly acting under secret orders from Louis XIV, appeared to be rather battle-shy and only opened fire if actually being attacked by a Dutch squadron. Although the fighting was hotly contested, fleet discipline was not always regarded by some flag officers as essential. Admirals Sir Edward *Spragge and Cornelis *Tromp, who had had many previous personal encounters, apparently thought that this was a proper occasion for another, irrespective of anything else. They withdrew from the main battle to conduct their own private war. The action, which had begun shortly after 7.00 a.m., was continued all day, when the Dutch then withdrew, having freed their ports from the allied blockade. Neither side lost any ship of importance though the casualties in men were heavy, especially among the English.

THAMES MEASUREMENT, generally abbreviated to T.M., a formula for the measurement of the tonnage of yachts, introduced in 1855 by the *Royal Thames Yacht Club to pro-

duce a fairer method of handicapping yachts for racing. Until that year the tonnage of yachts had been calculated by the *Builders Old Measurement formula, but some astute yacht designers had found a means of reducing a yacht's tonnage measurement, and thus increasing its handicap allowance, by shortening the keel as much as practicable. To prevent freak and unseaworthy yachts being built for the purpose of beating the race rules, and to introduce at the same time a more equitable means of handicapping yachts of widely differing sizes so that they could race against each other, the Thames Measurement rule was introduced. The new formula, still based on the Builders Old Measurement, was

$$\frac{(L - B) \times B \times \frac{1}{2}B}{94},$$

where L equals the length in feet taken from the forward side of the stem under the bowsprit and measured at deck level to the after side of the sternpost, and B equals the beam in feet measured to the outside of the hull planking.

This unit of Thames Measurement became adopted generally by British yachtsmen and is still used to indicate the tonnage of yachts listed in *Lloyd's Register of Yachts*. To a certain extent it is still used by some yacht builders in quoting approximately the cost of building a traditional cruising type of yacht—at so much per ton T.M.

THERMOPYLAE, a famous British tea *clipper built in 1868 by Hood of Aberdeen. Ship-rigged on three masts, she had a gross *tonnage of 991 tons and was a lifelong rival of the * *Cutty Sark*, the only ship seriously to contest the *Thermopylae*'s claim to be the fastest sailing clipper in the world. After the loss of the tea trade to steamships soon after the opening of the Suez Canal, the *Thermopylae* continued in the wool trade with Australia in her later years, and once made a record voyage by sailing from London to Melbourne in fifty-nine days. She ended her career as a training ship for Portuguese boys.

THETIS, one of the Greek sea deities, daughter of *Nereus and *Doris. She married *Peleus and by him became the mother of Achilles. Her name has been frequently used in many navies, particularly those of Britain, France, and Spain, as a ship's name. The last occasion of its use in Britain was for a submarine, which was accidentally sunk in 1938 in Liverpool Bay while on her trials, with considerable loss of life.

THIEVES' CAT, a *cat-o'-nine-tails with three knots in each of its tails, which was used in some navies in place of the ordinary cat-o'-nine-tails to punish seamen convicted of stealing from their messmates. In Britain its use was more prevalent in the army than in the navy, perhaps because most seamen in the British Navy had so few possessions worth stealing.

THIMBLE, a circular or heart-shaped ring, usually of iron or aluminium, grooved on the outside to receive a rope which is spliced round it to form an *eye. A thimble spliced into the *boltrope of a sail forms a *cringle.

THOLE PIN, a wooden pin fixed in the *gunwale of a boat to which, by means of a *grommet, an oar is held when rowing. A more usual method is to use two thole pins close together, with the oar between them when rowing. They form a substitute for a *crutch or a *rowlock.

THOMAS, GEORGE (1782–1850), a *master in the Royal Navy, was educated at the Bluecoat School and in 1796 went to sea in a South Seas *whaler. His ship was wrecked and he was for some four years marooned on an island, killing seals and curing their skins, until by chance a passing ship found and embarked him. Nearing home, a press gang boarded the ship and transferred Thomas to a *frigate where his mathematical education and skill with a sextant singled him out, eventually bringing him to the

notice of Thomas *Hurd, the Hydrographer of the Navy. The latter in 1809 had asked the Admiralty Board to provide a vessel for surveys of the east coast of England, and in 1810 Thomas took command of her, transferring in 1811 to H.M.S. *Investigator*, specially built in a matter of weeks at Deptford. There was already a master of the ship and it had to be established that he would take orders from Thomas, thus establishing the precedent that officers in charge of surveys would also command their ships. This first specially built naval surveying ship was directed in 1812 for operational surveys on the Dutch coast, and was armed with six carronades. But for the rest of her twenty-five years of life she worked always under Thomas on the coasts of both England and Scotland, but after 1825 principally in the Shetland and Orkney Islands.

Thomas then continued in H.M.S. *Mastiff* until his death ended his thirty-six years as a surveyor. From 1827 his son, F. W. L. THOMAS, was working under his orders and he later made surveys in the Firth of Forth.

THOMAS W. LAWSON, believed to be the largest *schooner ever built, was a ship of 5,000 gross tons with a waterline length of 385 feet. She had seven masts, each 193 feet high, and all her halyards, topping lifts, sheets, etc., were led to two large steam winches, one on the forecastle and the other on the after deckhouse. Built in Quincy, Massachusetts, in the last decade of the 19th century, she had a total crew of no more than sixteen hands, a result of employing auxiliary steam power in a sailing ship. She was lost in heavy weather off the Scilly Is. in 1907 with only one member of her crew surviving.

THOMSON, WILLIAM, first Baron Kelvin (1824–1907), British physicist, whose major scientific work lay in the sphere of electricity and submarine cables, nevertheless made a great impact on maritime affairs. In 1873 he undertook to write a series of articles on the mariner's compass for the magazine *Good Words*, but after writing the first of them realized that there were more problems concerned with the compass than he had originally thought. For the next five years he experimented and improved its capability and reliability, partly by reducing the weight of the compass card itself and increasing the time of its swing, but mainly in working out and laying down rules for compensation by which the temporary and permanent magnetism of an iron or steel ship could be easily counteracted. Through his research, the compass *binnacle was completely redesigned. It was only after the completion of this work that he was in a position to write the second article of his series, five years after the publication of the first.

His next most important contribution in the

maritime field was his *sounding apparatus, by which the depth of water up to 100 fathoms could be measured accurately by a ship proceeding at a speed of up to 16 knots. At the same time he produced a means of ocean sounding in deep water by the use of piano wire, an iron sinker, and a pressure gauge. Other maritime activities were his tide gauge, tidal harmonic analyser, tide predictor, and the compilation for simplifying *Sumner's method for determining the position of a ship at sea.

THORFINN KARLSEFNI (*fl.* 1002–7), Scandinavian explorer, was the leader of the main expedition in medieval times for the colonization of America. He came to Greenland in 1002, married the widow of Thorstein, son of *Eric the Red, and set forth with four ships and 160 men and women to settle *Vinland (probably northern Newfoundland), recently discovered by *Leif Ericsson. They made the coast of America at Helluland (country of flat stones—? Baffin Island), continued southward to Markland (land of trees—? Labrador), and eventually reached Vinland, where they landed and built huts in 1004. After internal quarrels and much fighting against the local Indians, the settlers decided to abandon Vinland and return with two ships, one of which was lost in the Irish Sea and the other, commanded by Thorfinn, reaching Greenland in safety in 1006.

THORNYCROFT, Sir JOHN (1862–1960), was the elder son of Sir JOHN ISAACS *Thornycroft, and followed his father as chairman and managing director of John I. Thornycroft & Company. During the First World War (1914–18) he assisted his brother, TOM I. *Thornycroft, in their firm's designs of fast naval craft, including destroyers and coastal motor boats (C.M.B.s), and in the Second World War he concentrated on motor torpedoboats and motor launches, with varied interests in the design of *depth-charge throwers and *torpedoes.

THORNYCROFT, Sir JOHN ISAACS (1843–1928), British marine engineer, was born into a family of sculptors. His father, however, was also an amateur engineer and it was in his workshop that John constructed a steam launch, the *Nautilus,* and acquired his lifelong interest in ship construction. After a period as a draughtsman with Palmer's Shipyard at Jarrow-on-Tyne, he went to Glasgow University where he studied under Sir William *Thomson (Lord Kelvin) and Professor Rankine. On graduating, he entered the drawing office of Randolph, Elder and Co. at their yard, which later became the famous Fairfield Yard.

In 1866, with the assistance of his father, John Thornycroft established a yard for construction of steam launches and torpedo craft at Chiswick, on the River Thames. His first small, high speed boat, the *Miranda,* with a 58 horsepower engine in a light steel hull, completed in 1871, achieved a speed of 16·4 knots. Two years later Thornycroft produced for Norway the first torpedoboat, the *Gitana,* which was armed with a *spar torpedo and, with a 458 horsepower engine, achieved 20·8 knots. This became the model for the epoch-making *Lightning* in 1877 which was equipped with a *Whitehead torpedo in a revolving tube.

A very large number of torpedoboats for various navies followed from Thornycroft's yard over the next fifteen years until, in 1892, the yard produced the *Daring* and *Decoy,* two of the first four experimental torpedoboat destroyers ordered by the British Admiralty. Thornycroft's were also pioneers in the design of water-tube boilers with which destroyers were from that time equipped.

Thornycroft, knighted in 1902, was a civilian member of the Admiralty design committee which recommended *Parsons *turbines for H.M.S. *Dreadnought.* With the increase in size of destroyers, the works were moved in 1906 from Chiswick to Woolston, Southampton. An important concept which Thornycroft had patented as long ago as 1877 was the single-stepped skimming hull which was adopted firstly for racing boats, later for seaplanes, and finally, in 1916, for the hulls of the first coastal motor boats in the First World War (1914–18).

THORNYCROFT, TOM ISAACS (1882–1955), British shipbuilder and yachtsman, was the second son of Sir John Isaacs *Thornycroft. He was an active yachtsman in both sail and power from the age of 14 and became well known in the field of progressive motor-boat hull design. In motor boats of his own designs he put up the fastest times in the London–Cowes motor-boat races six times between 1913 and 1923. He was also a keen and competent sailing man and in 1930, when he was 49, he won the Prince of Wales Cup in the 14-ft International dinghy class, a rare feat for a helmsman of his years. His design work was versatile and ranged from the hulls and engines for torpedo-launching coastal motor boats in the First World War (1914–18), to small racing yachts of the 18-ft Swallow and 5·5-metre classes in the 1950s.

THOROUGH FOOT, to, (1) a method of taking out a large number of turns in a rope after it has been unduly twisted. If the turns are left-handed, the rope is coiled down left-handed and the end dipped through the coil. If the coil is then hauled out, the turns will be taken out. If the turns are right-handed the rope is coiled down right-handed, and the same process will remove the turns. **(2)** A method of joining two ropes when they have an *eye spliced into their ends. The eye of rope A is passed through the eye of rope B and the bight of rope B passed through the eye.

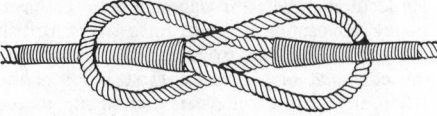

Thorough footing

THREE FIGURE METHOD, the description given to a method of graduating the card of a magnetic compass in degrees from 0° to 359°. The graduation starts at North, and continues in single degrees clockwise round the card until it again reaches North. In those cases where the number of degrees is less than 100, i.e., those with only one or two figures, the figure 0 is used as a prefix to bring them up to three figures. Thus, in this method, North would be read off the card as 000°, East as 090°, South as 180°, and West as 270°. This is the most usual method of compass graduation used in ships today, the other methods of division into *points or into *quadrants being now largely obsolescent.

THREE MILE LIMIT, the old limit of *territorial waters which nations bordering the seas claimed as their exclusive property. It was considered to be the maximum range of a shore-based gun in the days of muzzle-loading cannon, and thus the extent of the sea bordering a nation which could be effectively defended or commanded by gunfire from the shore line. The term has no relevance today, in face of many extended claims of territorial rights over adjacent seas, except in connection with national custom duties, goods subject to such duties being free of them beyond the three-mile limit at sea.

'THREE SHEETS IN THE WIND', a phrase, with a nautical derivation, meaning unsteadiness through drink. It implies that even if a man who has had too much to drink had three sheets with which to trim his sails, he would still be too incapacitated to steer a steady course.

'THREE SISTERS', the name given to a somewhat sinister, and wholly illegal, badge of office of a master-at-arms or a boatswain's mate in the British Navy, consisting of three rattans bound together with waxed twine. They were used indiscriminately on the backs of seamen in the practice known as *starting, to make the men move more quickly to their work. Always an unofficial punishment, it was rife throughout the British Navy throughout the 17th and 18th centuries, and generally accepted by officers and men alike as a custom that had grown up almost with the navy itself. Starting began in the earliest naval

days with a rope's end, later replaced by canes or rattans, and culminated in the 'three sisters', which was wielded entirely at the whim of the master-at-arms and the boatswain's mates. This unofficial punishment was prohibited by the Admiralty in 1809, but it was not until some years later that it was completely eradicated.

THROAT, the name given to the upper foremost corner of a four-sided fore-and-aft sail, and sometimes also to the jaws of a *gaff. For illus. see SAIL.

THROAT HALYARDS, those halyards used to hoist the *throat of a sail or the jaws of a *gaff.

THROAT SEIZINGS, the name given to those *seizings, put on with twine or spunyarn, which hold the hook and/or *thimble in the *strop which binds a block, and similarly the seizing with which two parts of a rope are bound together to form an *eye in the *bight.

THRUM, to. A sail or piece of canvas is thrummed by sewing short lengths of rope yarn to it by their *bights for use as a *collision mat. Smaller thrummed mats are sometimes used in the standing rigging of the larger sailing vessels to prevent chafe in those places where sails or parts of the running rigging may come in contact with it. See also BAGGYWRINKLE.

THUMB CLEAT, a small *cleat with a single arm, fixed near the end of a yardarm of a square-rigged ship to hold the topsail reef-*earings from slipping, or sometimes *seized to parts of the standing rigging to form a hook from which to suspend the *bight of a rope, for example, the *truss pendants on the lower masts. By looping them over a thumb cleat in the rigging, they are held secure and out of the way of other running rigging. Thumb cleats are also often fitted to the booms of sailing vessels as a means of securing the outhaul when the foot of the sail has been hauled out taut.

THUMB KNOT, another name for an overhand knot, which is no more than laying the end of a rope over its own part and bringing the end under and through the loop thus made. It is sometimes used in place of a figure-of-eight knot to prevent the end of a rope or *fall unreeving through a block, but most good seamen advise against its use because of its liability to jam.

THUROT, FRANÇOIS (1726–60), French privateer captain and one of the boldest and most accomplished French officers in this line of business, was born at Nuits, the son of a small innkeeper. He was very well educated by the Jesuits and apprenticed to a druggist, and when his indentures were completed, went to sea as a surgeon in a privateer in 1744, during the War of Austrian Succession (1739–48). The privateer was captured by the British and Thurot imprisoned, but he made his escape and for the rest of the war devoted himself to privateering. During the years of peace before the Seven Years War (1756–63) he lived for a time in London, and on the outbreak of war was given a commission in the French Navy and appointed to command the *frigate *Friponne*. His reputation as a privateer captain, however, was so outstanding that his ship was allowed mainly to act independently against British trade, and he captured a large number of *prizes in the North Sea and English Channel. In 1757 he was appointed to the larger 44-gun frigate *Maréchal de Belleisle* and given a regular squadron of six frigates and *sloops to command with the rank of commodore, though still operating a *guerre de course*. He was extraordinarily successful in the number of merchant ships he took as prizes, but on two occasions when, during 1756, he came up against single British frigates, he allowed himself to be beaten off although he commanded greatly superior strength.

In 1760 his force of six vessels, four frigates and two *sloops, was dispatched to Ireland, via the Faeroe Islands, with 1,300 troops on board for a descent on Carrickfergus and Belfast. The troops achieved little and, after they had been reembarked, Thurot was brought to action by three British frigates. He himself was killed in the action and the three frigates, to which his force had been reduced, were all captured. See also PASLEY, Sir Thomas.

Thurot had, and still has, a remarkable reputation in France as one of that country's greatest privateer captains, being often bracketed with so great a man as Jean *Bart. In Britain his reputation did not stand so high, partly because the guerre de course was not considered a main objective by British naval policy and partly because of his poor showing when confronted with warships. Nevertheless he was recognized in Britain as a man of great spirit and ability, brave, humane, and generous.

THURSFIELD, Sir JAMES (1840–1923), journalist and naval historian, was born at Kidderminster and educated at Merchant Taylors School and Oxford University, where he became a Fellow of Jesus College. He joined the staff of *The Times* as a leader-writer in 1881 and was sent to represent that newspaper at the naval manoeuvres of 1887, an event which wakened in him a lifelong interest in naval policy. This interest was greatly enhanced by the publication in 1890 of Captain A. T. *Mahan's *The Influence of Sea Power on History*, and he drew public attention to the importance of the doctrine it

preached. In collaboration with Sir George Clarke, he wrote a series of penetrating essays which was published in 1897, and in the same year he founded *The Times Literary Supplement*. He lectured widely throughout Britain on naval policy, advocating the need for a strong British Navy to maintain her overseas trade, and became the confidant of successive First Lords of the Admiralty during the years leading up to the First World War (1914–18). Among his publications were *Nelson and other Naval Studies* (1909) and *Naval Warfare* (1913). He was knighted in 1920. His only son, HENRY G. (1882–1963), was a rear admiral in the navy. He inherited much of his father's journalistic talent and after his retirement was naval correspondent of *The Times* from 1936 to 1952 and editor of *Brassey's Naval Annual* from 1936 to 1963. He was a councillor and vice-president of the *Navy Records Society and in 1951 edited *Five Naval Journals* for the Society.

THWART, the transverse wooden seat in a rowing boat on which the oarsman sits. Thwarts are normally supported by grown wooden *knees (i.e., grown so that the grain of the wood follows the curve of the knee), fitted to the *ribs of the two sides. In the larger ships' boats, such as *launches, *cutters, etc., they are additionally supported by hanging knees, fixed to the ribs above the level of the thwarts so that the thwart is held securely between a knee above it and one below it.

TICKET, the name given in the British merchant service to a certificate issued by the British Department of Trade as a result of examinations into an officer's competency and experience. It enables him to take a position on board a merchant ship in accordance with the limitations, if any, imposed by his ticket. There are various kinds of ticket based on degree of qualification, e.g., extra master's, master's, mate's, etc., and an officer cannot be promoted to a higher rank until he has passed the examination and received his ticket for that rank. Similar arrangements are in force with the national authorities of other maritime countries.

TIDAL ATLAS, collections of twelve charts covering the same area, each chart showing the direction of the tidal streams in the area for each hour while the tide rises or falls at a standard port, which in Great Britain is usually *Dover. The directions are shown by arrows, figures against the arrows indicating the speed in knots. Where only one figure is given, it indicates the rate at *springs; where two figures are given, the higher is the spring rate, the lower is the rate at *neaps. Tidal atlases are included in some *nautical almanacs, and many are published separately.

'TIDDLEY', the seaman's word for smart or neat. His shore-going uniform suit is tiddley if it is well pressed and brushed, *cheeses on deck are tiddley', *sinnet work is tiddley, and so on.

TIDE, the rise and fall of the sea as a result of the attraction of the sun and moon. The largest rise and fall of tide, known as *spring tides, occur when the sun and moon are in line and act together; the smallest rise and fall, known as *neap tides, when the sun and moon are in positions at right-angles to each other, thus exerting less combined attraction. In each case the influence of the moon upon the tides is two and a half times greater than that of the sun. The average level of the surface of the sea between high and low tide is known as the Mean Sea Level (M.S.L.).

Tides operate on a time period of 6 hours 20 minutes from high to low water or vice versa, and the total movement of the sea level between one high water and its succeeding one, a period of 12 hours 40 minutes, is known as the tidal oscillation. It follows that the true definition of high water is the highest level reached by the sea in one tidal oscillation, and of low water, the lowest level reached in one tidal oscillation. The direction of the tide is entirely vertical, the horizontal movement of the water as tides rise and fall being known as a tidal stream.

Inland seas, such as the Mediterranean and Baltic, are virtually tideless, the reason being that the entrances (Straits of Gibraltar for the Mediterranean and the Sound and Great Belt for the Baltic) are too narrow to allow the influx and outflow of sufficient tidal water within the duration of a tide to affect the level of the water within those seas by more than a few inches.

The heights of the tide at high and low water are measured above *chart datum, and their daily times and heights are predicted for selected ports around the world, known as standard ports, and published annually in *Tide Tables, produced by most national hydrographic authorities. These publications also include tables of tidal constants whereby the times of high and low water, with the height of the rise, can be easily ascertained for all intermediate ports. Tide Tables also enable a navigator to discover the actual height of the tide at any port at any time between high and low water.

TIDE TABLES, a publication, in three main parts, of the British Hydrographic Department of the Navy, giving predictions for the time and height of high and low water for every standard port in the world and tables of tidal constants for intermediate ports. Tide Tables was first produced in 1833, and since 1938 tidal predictions have been based on harmonic analysis of tidal flows. Tide Tables is published annually.

TIDE-RACE, a sharp acceleration in the speed of flow of a tide by reason of a break or fault in the bottom formation, where the depth of water rises or falls suddenly, as over rocky ledges below water.

TIDE-RIP, short waves or ripples caused by eddies made by a tide as it flows or ebbs over an uneven bottom, or at sea where two currents meet. Waves in a tide-rip do not break whereas in an *overfall they do, this being the principal difference between the two.

TIDE-RODE, the situation of a vessel lying at anchor when she is swung to her anchor by the force of the tide. It contrasts with wind-rode, when it is the force of the wind, irrespective of the tide, which swings her to her anchor.

TIDEWAY, a name given to a main *fairway in tidal waters, where the direction of ebb and flow of the tide is straight up and down the fairway.

TIDING OVER, an old expression to describe the method of working the tides, in the days of square-rigged ships, to make progress against a contrary wind, especially with reference to the English Channel where the prevailing wind, being south-westerly, is *foul for ships proceeding down Channel. It involved anchoring during the flood, or east-running tide, weighing anchor at high water and beating to windward, relying on the strength of the ebb or west-running tide to carry the ship in the required direction. When the tide turned, the ship anchored again until the next high water, when the process was repeated.

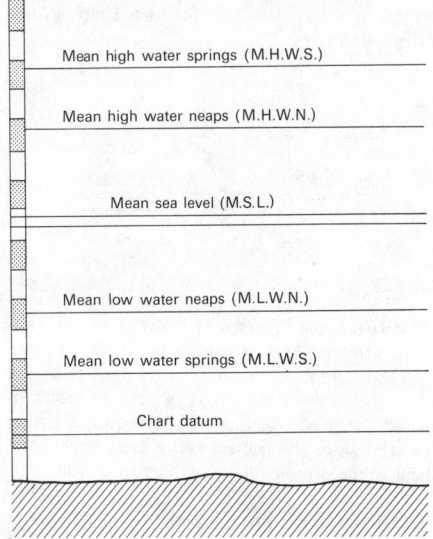

Mean high water springs (M.H.W.S.)

Mean high water neaps (M.H.W.N.)

Mean sea level (M.S.L.)

Mean low water neaps (M.L.W.N.)

Mean low water springs (M.L.W.S.)

Chart datum

Tidal ranges

TIER or **TYER**, see GASKET.

TIER, a regular row or layer of anything, such as a tier of casks in the *hold of a ship, a tier of *cable in the cable locker, a tier of guns on the gundeck of a sailing warship, etc. But CABLE-TIER, in the days of *hemp anchor cables, was the space left in the centre of the locker when the cable was coiled round the outside with the *fakes on top of each other. It is the name also given to a row of mooring buoys in a port for *barges or *lighters, or for a wharf or quay where barges can lie alongside three or four deep, with the inside barge secured to the wharf.

TIERCE, a regular measurement of maritime victuals in the old days of salt beef and pork in casks. A tierce of salt beef was 280 lb, a tierce of pork only 260 lb. In the early 19th century, when casks were made larger, the beef tierce was raised to 336 lb and the pork tierce to 300 lb. A tierce of port was one-third of a pipe or 42 gallons.

TILIKUM, the name of the dug-out *canoe in which Captain J. C. *Voss, with a companion, sailed round the world in 1901–4. The canoe was bought from a Vancouver Island Indian, decked over by Voss and her sides raised, and rigged with three masts, setting a *jib, *gaff foresail and mainsail, and a jib-headed *mizen, and is probably the smallest craft ever to have made a circumnavigation. She drew 24 inches aft and 22 inches forward. The *Tilikum* is now preserved in the Maritime Museum of British Columbia, Victoria.

TILLER, a wood or metal bar which fits into or round the head of the *rudder and by which the rudder is moved as required. Until the introduction of the steering-wheel in the late 17th century, all ships, no matter how large, were steered by a tiller, which grew in length and size so that it needed many more men to control it when sailing in a large ship in a high wind. (See also RELIEVING TACKLE.) Today, tillers are used only in small craft, wheel steering having been adopted for all vessels of any size. See also HELM.

TILLER HEAD, that part of a *tiller which is farthest away from the *rudder head and is thus the point of maximum moment.

TILLER ROPES, the lines, made of rope, hide, or chain, which lead from the *rudder head, or an extension fitted to it, to the barrel of the steering-wheel, whereby the rudder is moved as the wheel is put over. In large ships, the movement of the wheel does not operate the rudder direct, but activates a steering engine which puts the rudder over in accordance with the amount of movement of the wheel.

TILMAN, HAROLD WILLIAM (1898–   ), British explorer and deep-water sailor, has made long voyages to parts of the world not normally visited by shipping in his ex-Bristol Channel pilot *cutter *Mischief*. In 1955–6 he explored inlets along the Patagonian coast and in 1957–8 sailed round the African continent calling at little-known places. He cruised to the South Indian Ocean in 1959–60 and visited the Crozet and Kerguelen Islands, and between 1961 and 1964 was frequently in northern waters round Iceland, Greenland, Baffin Bay, and Lancaster Sound. Leaving *Mischief* in England during the winter of 1964–5 he sailed in the *schooner *Patanela* to Heard Island in latitude 53° S. in the South Indian Ocean, but in 1966–7 took his own yacht to the Antarctic, visiting the South Shetland Islands and South Georgia. He has written a number of books describing his cruises, including *Mischief among the Penguins*, *Mischief in Greenland*, *Mostly Mischief*, and *In Mischief's Wake*.

TILT, the name often given to a small boat's canvas *awning covering the sternsheets to give protection to passengers from the glare of the sun.

TIMBER HEADS, the prolongation of some of the *timbers in the hull of a wooden ship above the deck level so that they project above the *gunwale to serve as *bitts.

TIMBER HITCH, a method of securing a rope round a spar by taking the standing part of a rope round the spar with a *half hitch round itself and the end tucked three or four times round its own part. This forms a running, but self-jamming, eye.

Timber hitch

TIMBERS, the *frames or *ribs of a ship, connected to the *keel, which give a ship's hull both its shape and its strength. In wooden ships of any size, the timbers are made of several pieces of wood *scarfed together to the required shape. In steel ships the frames are of steel angle iron, bent to the desired shape by heat treatment.

TIMENOGUY, pronounced, and sometimes written, as timonoggy, originally a rope stretched taut between different parts of a sailing ship to prevent a *tack or *brace from fouling some projection, especially in the case of the fore-sheets and tacks fouling the *stocks of the *anchors when tacking. More recently it was a rope made fast in the *mizen rigging with a thimble in the end through which passed the hauling part of the main brace. The object was still to prevent fouling, particularly of the boat *davits.

TIMONEER, an old word occasionally used to describe the helmsman of a vessel. It is the anglicized version of the French *timonier*, helmsman, both being derivations of the older word *tymon*, a wooden staff, and thus a *tiller. As William *Falconer, in his poem *The Shipwreck* (1762), has it:

'The helm the attentive timoneer applies'.

The word remained in use throughout the 19th century perhaps used rather exotically by writers more than by seamen. G. C. Davies, writing in the magazine *Norfolk Broads* in 1884, talks about a boat's 'timoneer sitting with the tiller in one hand and the sheet in the other'.

TIRPITZ, ALFRED VON (1849–1930), German grand admiral, was Secretary of State of the German Ministry of Marine (Reichsmarineamt) from 1897 to 1916. He was born at Küstrin, Mark Brandenburg, the son and grandson of lawyers, and the 'von' before his name was an honour from the Kaiser, bestowed in 1900. At the age of 16 he joined the Prussian Navy, then at an early stage of its existence, its ships being mostly wooden sailing vessels with auxiliary steam engines and its officers a mixture of genuine naval officers, soldiers, merchant service officers, Dutchmen, Swedes, and Schleswig-Holsteiners. Greatly exceeded in strength by the French Navy, it accordingly spent the whole of the Franco-Prussian war closely *blockaded in its home ports. After that war Tirpitz did well in what then became the German Navy, though he was criticized from time to time because his self-discipline was not always sufficient to prevent his displaying to senior officers his conviction that he knew better than they did.

In 1879, however, he was given an excellent opportunity, being appointed to command the *torpedo *gunboat *Zieten* at a time when the torpedo was being developed by Caprivi, a general who was successively Chief of the Admiralty and Chancellor of the German Reich. Caprivi saw in the torpedo a counter to the vastly bigger fleets of *battleships belonging to Russia and France, with whom he feared Germany would be involved in a war on two fronts.

Tirpitz rose in rank in the German Navy with the growth of the torpedo arm. He received specially accelerated promotion to comman-

der—the only case in the whole history of the Imperial Navy—and was appointed inspector of the torpedo branch. By 1892 he was chief of staff to the supreme command of the navy, with the task of working out the tactics of the battle fleet. At this time the new battleships of steam and steel were virtually new weapons that had never fought in battle, and nobody was certain how they should be handled or what would happen in a fleet action. Tirpitz, who had already made a favourable impression on the Kaiser, produced two years later a memorandum outlining a plan for the growth of the fleet which both he and the Kaiser believed to be necessary for German expansion. In addition, he developed realistic tactical exercises for training, stressing that subordinate admirals should be able to handle their *squadrons independently when darkness or smoke might prevent the signals of the commander-in-chief from being understood. The fact that at the battle of *Jutland in 1916 the German battle fleet was handled much more flexibly than the British was one of the legacies of Tirpitz's work.

During 1896–7 Tirpitz was in command of the German squadron in the Far East and was responsible for the occupation of Tsingtao. In 1897 he was recalled to the appointment he was to occupy for the rest of his service career, Secretary of State of the Ministry of Marine. At once the Kaiser presented him with a complete scheme to double the German Navy within twenty years; this fleet would be so strong that Britain would not be able to challenge it without jeopardizing her position as the world's strongest naval power. This was the famous 'risk theory'. Together the German naval laws of 1898 and 1900, with the supplementary laws (*Novelle*) voted in 1906 and 1912, provided for a fleet of 41 battleships, 20 large *cruisers, and 40 light cruisers. To persuade the taxpayers to provide the vast sums of money necessary, Tirpitz embarked on a monster propaganda campaign through his ministry and the semi-official German Navy League, a body which eventually grew to be nearly 1,000,000 strong. The main point of the campaign was to stress the danger presented to Germany by the ruthless jealousy of Britain.

In the years immediately before 1914 Tirpitz was one of the most important people in Germany and came within measurable distance of being Chancellor of the Reich. But so clumsy was the organization of the naval command that when the First World War (1914–18) broke out, he was completely ignorant of the navy's war plan and was bitterly disappointed by the course of events in the war at sea. His advice was persistently neglected from the day in August 1914 when he urged his own appointment as commander-in-chief of the whole navy in order to put an end to a distribution of powers, by which he was

The German battleship Tirpitz *being attacked by the Fleet Air Arm in 1944; oil painting by C. Pears*

Secretary of State responsible for *matériel*, while the Chief of the Naval Staff looked after operations and the Chief of the Kaiser's Naval Cabinet dealt with personnel.

Once it was clear that the German surface fleet was not going to be risked in all-out battle, Tirpitz pressed unceasingly for unrestricted *submarine warfare. But on 12 March 1916 he lost patience with his powerlessness and resigned. He became involved with the extreme fringe of German nationalists until his death in 1930.

TIRPITZ, a 42,500-ton German *battleship, completed in 1941, and sister ship of the *Bismarck*. From January 1942 to November 1944 she served in Norwegian waters, where she constituted a permanent threat to the British *convoys to North Russia. Her operations were much curtailed by fuel shortage, but an inaccurate report of her appearance at sea on 5 July 1942 was responsible for an order to the British and American convoy *PQ 17 to scatter, which led to heavy loss among merchant ships. She was attacked during 1942 by the R.A.F. twice and by the *Fleet Air Arm once; in addition an unsuccessful attempt was made by British and Norwegians to attack her with *chariots. The

Tirpitz, for the first and last time, fired her heavy guns on 9 September 1943 during a bombardment of Barentsburg, Spitsbergen. On 22 September 1943 she was badly damaged by mines laid beneath her by two British midget *submarines (see X-CRAFT). Temporary repairs were finished on 3 April when she was attacked by aircraft of the Fleet Air Arm which, in less than a minute, put her out of action again and killed 300 of her crew. Again partially repaired, she was attacked by Russian bombers once and R.A.F. bombers three times, finally being sunk by the latter on 12 November 1944. In all these operations intelligence furnished by the Norwegian resistance played a great part.

TITANIC, R.M.S., a *White Star *liner of 46,328 tons, was the largest ship in the world when she was built. She struck an iceberg in the North Atlantic on her maiden voyage in 1912 and sank with the loss of 1,490 lives. Built to safety flotation standards higher than required by regulations then or now, and with sixteen watertight compartments, she was regarded as virtually unsinkable. She sailed on her maiden voyage from Southampton to New York on 10 April 1912. On the 14th, nearing the *Grand Banks, she received four warnings from ships of ice ahead, but the last one, describing a field right across her track, never reached the captain. As usual in clear weather she steamed on at her service speed of 22 knots throughout the evening. There are rumours, but no evidence, that she was out to break records; in fact she had insufficient coal aboard to try. At 11.40 p.m. the *crow's nest lookout reported an iceberg close ahead and the First Officer immediately ordered a full turn to port. The bows missed the iceberg, but an underwater spur of ice ripped an intermittent gash down her starboard side extending 300 feet and puncturing six forward compartments. She could not survive this damage, but the passengers were not told for fear of panic. Board of Trade regulations for *lifeboats had not kept pace with the increased size of ships, and while there were 2,201 persons aboard, the lifeboats could only hold 1,178. The boats were, however, lowered only partly filled with passengers who refused at first to believe the ship would or could sink.

*SOS wireless signals were sent, and rockets were fired when a light appeared on the horizon at about 1.00 a.m. on the 15th. But the light moved away and the nearest ship to receive the SOS, the *Cunard liner Carpathia, could not reach the scene before 4.00 a.m. The Titanic, after settling slowly by the bows, sank at 2.20 a.m. leaving 916 passengers and 673 crew to die in the icy water. The passengers who lost their lives included 106 women and 52 children,

nearly all from the third, or emigrant, class; the crew lost included all the engineer officers who were working below until the last moments. The Carpathia rescued 712 persons from the Titanic's boats.

Unprecedented shock and horror greeted the news, and two inquiries into the disaster found a scapegoat in the captain of the steamer *Californian, which they stated was the source of the light seen on the horizon at 1.00 a.m. The evidence is quite clear that the light could not have come from this ship. Captain Smith of the Titanic was not blamed as it was not normal practice for liners to reduce speed in clear weather. There is no reason to question this finding; it is likely that the iceberg had recently overturned and was showing a dark side; there was no wind or swell to create ripples around it. It was an accident, and blame is a product of hindsight and ignorance of the customs of the day. More important, the disaster led to new regulations requiring ships to carry sufficient lifeboats for all carried on board, a more southerly liner track across the Atlantic, and an ice patrol which continues to this day.

TIZARD, THOMAS HENRY (1839–1924), British naval captain, was one of the most distinguished surveying officers of his day. Entering the navy in 1854 and seeing war service in the Baltic, Tizard was on the China station from 1860 to 1867, becoming a *master in 1864. From 1868 to 1872 he was in the Newport,

commanded by George *Nares, in the Mediterranean and Red Sea.

During the *Challenger expedition of 1872–6 he served as senior surveyor to Nares and also worked as his navigating officer. In the following three years he compiled the narrative of the expedition as well as the oceanographic and hydrographic results, being highly complimented by Sir Wyville Thomson, the senior scientist. There followed twelve years' work in home waters in the Porcupine, Knight Errant, and in 1882 the new ship Triton. From 1891 to 1907 Tizard was Assistant Hydrographer of the Navy and his evidence to the 1905 Committee of Enquiry on the Hydrographic Department, which was reproduced in the subsequent report, was outstandingly useful. He served on the Joint Committee of the Royal and Geographical Societies for the National Antarctic Expedition of 1901–4, and was made a Fellow of the Royal Society in 1891, serving on its council from 1902 to 1904. He wrote a number of scientific papers and originated the table of chords of arc while a navigating lieutenant. In retirement he worked for many years as a reviser of the Hydrographic Office publications.

TJALK, a Dutch *barge-type vessel for the carriage of cargo, dating from the 17th century. It originally had the normal barge rig of *jib and *spritsail, but today is built of steel and fitted with a diesel engine. The design has been adapted for yachting purposes and a tjalk yacht (pavilijoen tjalk) closely resembles an enlarged *boeier.

TJOTTER, the smallest of the traditional Dutch types of small craft, much like a *boeier in rig but only 15 to 20 feet (4·6–6·1 m) in overall length. They are normally half-decked, and are popular for racing in inland waters.

TOGGLE, a strong wooden pin, in older days usually made of lignum vitae, occasionally still used through the *bight of a rope to hold it in position and for similar purposes. Its main use was during the days of sail, particularly in warships in battle, when toggles were fixed in the running parts of the topsail *sheets and in the *jeers, so that if the rope were shot away, the *yards might still be held aloft by the toggles. The typical duffle-coat, widely worn at sea, is buttoned by small toggles threaded through *beckets.

TOGO, Marquis HEIHACHIRO (1847–1934), Japanese admiral of the fleet, began his naval career as a volunteer in the earliest naval force organized in Japan following the opening of the country to foreign intercourse, the ships of the Lord of Satsuma. He was a member of a Samurai family of the Satsuma clan, but his first naval service was on shore in 1863 when the clash with the British Navy, known as the battle of Kagoshima Bay, occurred. Aged 16, the young Togo, with his father and two brothers, all armed in the still current Japanese fashion with two Samurai swords and a matchlock musket, served the primitive, stone-shotted guns in a fort.

His first active sea service came in 1867 when, during the civil war which followed the Meiji restoration, he served in the government *paddle steamer Kasuga in an indecisive fight with the rebel steamer Kaiyo. In 1869 he moved to Yokohama where, after attending school and a language academy to study English, he became a cadet in the naval training ship Ryojo. Selected to go to England for further education, he joined H.M.S. Worcester, the nautical training college at Greenhithe. On completion of a three-year course there he made a voyage to Melbourne and back in a square-rigged sailing ship before being appointed as one of the Japanese naval officers attending the construction of the two iron-hulled armour-clad ships Fuseo and Hiei which were being built in England for the Japanese Navy.

In January 1878 he joined the Hiei as a passenger when she sailed with a British crew for delivery at Yokohama. When she arrived there in May, he was appointed to her as a sub-lieutenant 1st Class. By his absence in England, Togo had fortunately avoided involvement in the Satsuma civil war in 1877, in which the rest of his family had inevitably served under their rebellious clan chieftain. By 1879 he had risen to the rank of lieutenant-commander and obtained his first command, the wooden warship Jingei. A reputation for great taciturnity, unusual in his countrymen, had by this time attached itself to his name and was to remain a notable feature all his life.

In command of the small warship Amagi in 1884, he was a witness, and learned much of current naval warfare as a result, of the French operations against the Chinese during the war in Annam, visiting Hankow, Indo-China, and Formosa. But it was as a captain, in command of the Elswick-built protected *cruiser Naniwa from 1892–5, that he spent the most active part of his career before achieving flag rank.

When the dispute with China over Korea arose in 1894, the Naniwa was first employed convoying troops to Chemulpo and, in July of that year, with two other cruisers of the Japanese Flying Squadron, took part in the destruction of two Chinese warships returning from convoying troops to Korea. Togo then became involved in an incident in which the British steamer Kowshing, carrying Chinese troops, was sunk by the Naniwa. The British master of the Kowshing had been prevented by the Chinese troops from obeying Togo's orders to follow the Naniwa into harbour. In the controversy which followed over the legal aspects of Togo's action, the British government came down on Togo's side and he was exonerated.

The *Naniwa* next took a prominent part in the destruction of the Chinese fleet in the battle of the Yalu, in the capture of Port Arthur and of Wei-hai-wei, and in the occupation of Formosa. Promoted to rear admiral in 1895, Togo commanded the Japanese main squadron in 1900 during the international operations in connection with the Boxer rising in China.

In 1904 Togo was appointed commander-in-chief of the Japanese Grand Fleet, a post he held throughout the war with Russia which followed, flying his flag in the battleship *Mikasa*. In the battle of 10 August 1904 in the Yellow Sea, the Russian Port Arthur * squadron was finally defeated after a hard-fought engagement in which the *Mikasa* suffered severe damage and many casualties.

The battle of * Tsushima in May 1905, for which Togo is best remembered and in which the Russian Baltic Fleet was annihilated, was a less hard-fought affair, though the *Mikasa* was again considerably damaged. The Russian fleet was largely untrained and inexperienced, was also handicapped by having in its charge a * convoy of auxiliaries, and their ships were some five knots slower than the Japanese, all of them considerable factors in the inevitable Japanese victory. It was the climax of the war at sea, however, and Togo emerged, alongside General Nogi, captor of Port Arthur, as a great national hero.

Admired almost as much in England, at that time Japan's ally, Togo received the almost unprecedented honour for a foreigner of the British Order of Merit in 1906. He was much fêted when he attended the coronation of George V in 1911 and the Naval Review at * Spithead of that year. At a dinner given by his old *Worcester* shipmates, he referred to England as his second mother country. He was similarly honoured in the U.S.A. where he was warmly welcomed by President Theodore * Roosevelt.

After the Emperor Meiji's death in 1912, Togo, by this time an admiral of the fleet, supervised the education of the Crown Prince until 1919 when the latter came of age. For another fifteen years he functioned as Japan's leading elder statesman and, when he died in 1934, was given an impressive State funeral attended by naval squadrons from Great Britain, France, Italy, and the U.S.A.

N. Ogasawara, *Life of Admiral Togo* (Tokyo, 1934).

TOLL, Baron EDUARD VASILYEVICH (1858–1902), Russian Arctic explorer, was born in Reval and studied geology. He explored Novosibirskiye Ostrova (New Siberian Islands)

in 1896 and again in 1898. In 1900 he led an Academy of Sciences expedition aboard the yacht *Zarya*, whose object was to complete the * North-East passage, making further studies of the region of Novosibirskiye Ostrova on the way. Toll himself and three companions were lost on a sledging trip, and the voyage did not continue beyond Novosibirskiye Ostrova, though valuable scientific observations were made.

'TOM BOWLING', the name of the most famous of Charles * Dibdin's sea songs, beginning, 'Here, a sheer hulk, lies poor Tom Bowling, The darling of our crew . . .' The original name is that of a naval character in * Smollet's *Roderick Random* but Dibdin modelled his Tom Bowling on his brother, Captain Thomas Dibdin. One of the verses of the song is engraved on Dibdin's tombstone.

TOM THUMB, the small open boat in which George * Bass and Matthew * Flinders made a coastal survey of part of the south-eastern coast of Australia in 1796.

The boat was said to be only eight feet in length, but as it carried Bass and Flinders, with their surveying instruments, and also Bass's boy servant as crew, this length would appear to be an underestimate.

TOMLINSON, HENRY MAJOR (1873–1958), British author, was born in Poplar, London, where as a boy he gained familiarity with ships through proximity to the London Docks and where he acquired a lifelong affection for the sea. In 1904 he took up journalism and his first assignment was to spend several weeks with the * trawlers fishing on the Dogger Bank in the North Sea. His next one took him on a voyage to Brazil on board the first British steamship to sail 2,000 miles up the River Amazon, which resulted in his first book, *The Sea and the Jungle*, published in 1912. During the First World War (1914–18) he was a war correspondent in Belgium and France, and it was this war which gave him the basis for his great novel *All Our Yesterdays*, published in 1930.

After the war he travelled widely and wrote many stories which later appeared in book form under the titles *Old Junk* (1918), *London River* (1921), and *Under the Red Ensign* (1926). His first novel, *Gallions Reach*, published in 1927, gained him the Femina Vie Heureuse prize; his last book, *The Trumpet Shall Sound*, published in 1957, was a description of a London family during the bombing of London in the Second World War.

TON, a measure of weight ashore, a measure of capacity at sea. The origin of the word in its maritime sense was the * tun, a large cask in which wine was transported, equivalent to two pipes, or four hogsheads, or 252 old wine gallons. The measurement of a ship in older days was by tunnage, or the number of tuns of wine she could carry in her holds. In ship measurement, a ton of oil fuel is 6·7 barrels, a ton of timber is 40 cubic feet in the rough and 50 when sawn. When calculating the gross *tonnage of a ship, one ton measurement is taken as 100 cubic feet capacity.

TONNAGE, originally the charge for the hire of a ship at so much a ton of her *burthen, and also a tax, first levied in 1303 by Edward I of England on all imports brought by ship into England, and a second tax, known as tunnage, levied in 1347 by Edward III, of three shillings on each *tun of wine imported.

It was from the first of these original meanings, the cost of the hire of a ship, that the word tonnage came into use as an alternative to burthen, meaning the capacity of the ship in the carriage of cargo. Although tonnage or burthen was still theoretically based on the number of tuns of wine that a ship could carry in her holds, it became necessary, both for taxation purposes and for calculating the harbour dues payable by a ship, to devise a rough and ready formula by which the tonnage or burthen could be quickly calculated. It was found, in the general design of ships of those early days, that the vessel's length in feet, multiplied by her maximum beam in feet, multiplied by the depth of her hold below the main deck in feet, with the product divided by 100, gave a reasonably accurate measurement of her tonnage, and this was the formula used for the measurement of warships as well as of merchant vessels.

In 1694, when a law was introduced in Britain requiring the marking of a waterline on merchant ships, both when light (in *ballast) and fully laden, this tonnage formula was officially adopted, though marginally amended to make the product of length, beam, and depth divisible by 94 instead of 100. This remained the standard of ship measurement until 1773, when more accurate limits of measurement were established. By an Act of Parliament passed in that year the length, for measurement purposes, was laid down to be along the *rabbet of the *keel from the fore side of the *stem beneath the *bowsprit to the after side of the *sternpost, and the formula became

$$\frac{(L - \frac{3}{5}B) \times B \times \frac{1}{2}B}{94},$$

the result giving the tonnage, L being the length and B being the maximum beam. This formula was known as the *Builders Old Measurement (B.O.M.) and remained in force until the advent of iron for shipbuilding and steam for propulsion revolutionized the design and shape of ships.

The B.O.M. served its purpose well for the typical bluff-bowed, full-bodied ship of the timber and sail era but had no relevance to the longer, finer hulls of the iron ship in which the ratio of length to beam increased from the average three to one to four, five, and even six to one. In place of the old B.O.M., the system was adopted of calculating the actual capacity of the ship's hull below the upper deck in cubic feet, and dividing the total capacity by 100, the resulting figure being taken as the ship's gross tonnage. But this figure did not, of course, bear very much resemblance to her cargo-carrying capacity, since it was calculated on the total hull space below her upper deck and made no allowance for spaces inside her hull set aside for such necessities as crew's quarters, ship's stores, fuel *bunkers, machinery spaces, etc. So a second calculation was made of the capacity in cubic feet of these necessary spaces and, still taking 100 cubic feet as equivalent to one ton, was deducted from the figure of her gross tonnage to give a net tonnage. Both these tonnages are known as register tonnages as they are entered on her certificate of registration. It is on the figure of a ship's net register tonnage that such charges as port and harbour dues, light and buoyage system dues, towage charges and salvage assessments, are normally levied.

Another tonnage measurement of merchant vessels is *deadweight tonnage, which is a measurement of the number of tons of cargo she can carry to trim her hull down to her allotted *Plimsoll marks. All these tonnages are based on cubic capacity divided by 100 and should not be confused with the *displacement, or actual weight in tons, of the ship herself, measured by the volume of water she displaces when afloat. Merchant ships are normally quoted by their gross or their deadweight tonnage, warships by their displacement tonnage. The tonnage of yachts is calculated by the *Thames Measurement rule.

TONNE, the metric ton of 1,000 kilograms, a measurement which, as a result of so many nations now adopting the metric system, is increasingly being used as the unit in the *displacement tonnage of ships. The metric ton (2,205 lb) varies from the avoirdupois ton (2,240 lb) by only 1·6 per cent, sufficiently close to the ton to be acceptable to shipowners and builders without large-scale re-registration, etc.

TOP, a platform at the masthead of a ship which, in the case of square-rigged ships, rests on the *trestle-trees and *crosstrees and whose main purpose is to extend the topmast *shrouds to give additional support to the topmast. In sailing ships of war they were used as fighting tops and manned by marines or soldiers with muskets; in later warships of the steam era they accommodated the *director firing system and were used for spotting the fall of shot. For illus. see RIGGING.

TOP-ARMOURS, cloths which in older days were hung around the *tops of fighting ships, partly for show, being painted red, and partly to hide men in the tops who, in battle, would act as musketeers or hurl fire-pots or *stinkpots on to the deck of an enemy preparatory to boarding.

TOP-CHAIN, the name given to the chain *slings used for the *yards of square-rigged warships in time of battle to prevent the yards from falling on deck if the rope slings were shot through. They were rigged additionally to the normal rope slings before a ship went into action.

TOPGALLANT MAST, the *mast in a square-rigged ship stepped next above the *topmast to form the third division of a complete mast, the uppermost of the three until the days when yet more sails, known as *kites, were piled upon the masts, when an additional temporary mast was rigged above the topgallant mast. The name is believed to be derived from the *garland round the original pole masts used as an additional support for the *yards. That part of the mast above the circular *top was naturally named top-mast, and when the third yard was added, the part of the mast above the garland was named top-garland, which in time became topgallant. Topgallant masts were always pole masts, in distinction to the made-up lower masts. For illus. see RIGGING.

TOPGALLANT SAIL, the sail set on the topgallant *yard in square-rigged ships, next above the *topsail, and normally the third sail in ascending order from the deck, except in those vessels which set two topsails, when of course it became fourth in ascending order. For illus. see SAIL.

TOPMARK, see BUOYS, BUOYAGE.

TOPMAST, in sailing vessels, that *mast next above the lower mast, the second division of a complete mast. (See also TOPGALLANT MAST.) Many of the larger warships in the steam era used to carry a topmast, but in general the practice today in most steam vessels is to step only a lower mast, although in the larger naval ships, of *cruiser size and above, a fitted topmast is included, which is either a continuation of one of the struts of the tripod lower mast or a separate mast stepped on the top. This is called a fitted topmast as it cannot normally be *housed or struck, and is thus a permanent fitting. For illus. see RIGGING.

TOPMEN or **YARDMEN,** seamen whose station in the *watch-bill, in the days of square-rigged sailing vessels, was on the *masts and *yards. They were the picked men of a ship's company, with the upper yardmen, those who worked on the *topsail and *topgallant sail yards, the aristocrats of the lower deck.

TOPPING-LIFT, a rope or flexible wire tackle by which the end of a spar is hoisted or lowered. In yachts a topping-lift is usually attached at or near the after end of the *boom, and takes the weight of the boom while the sail is being hoisted or stowed. Twin topping-lifts may sometimes be rigged so that when the sail is being set the lift on the lee side can be slacked away clear of the sail, while the weather lift takes the weight of the boom. It has been common practice in the U.S.A. for twin topping-lifts to be joined by one or two loops of light line which pass loosely beneath the boom. Known as lazyjacks, these lines prevent the sail from bellying out to leeward as it is being hoisted or lowered, a convenience for a short-handed crew.

TOPSAIL, the sail set, in square-rigged ships, on the topsail yard, next above the *course and the second in ascending order from the deck. In many of the square-rigged ships, two topsails were often set, a lower and an upper topsail. In the larger *fore-and-aft *gaff-rigged sailing vessels, a topsail was set above the mainsail, either in the form of a *jib-headed topsail, or set on a *jackyard. For illus. see SAIL.

TOPSIDES, (1) that part of the side of a ship which is above the main *wales. The term referred particularly to square-rigged sailing warships, where the main wales ran level with the bottom of the upper deck *gunports. In its modern meaning it usually refers to that portion of the ship's side which rises above the upper deck though the term is often loosely used to refer to the upper deck itself; 'I'm going top-sides': 'I'm going on the upper deck.' **(2)** The sides of yachts, above the *boot-topping, are also known as the topsides.

TORDENSKJOLD, PEDER (1691–1720), Danish admiral, was born Peder Wessel, tenth child of a Bergen alderman, and as a young boy ran away to sea. After several voyages to the West Indies he was appointed a second lieutenant in the Danish Navy and within a year was commanding the 4-gun *sloop *Ormen,* in which he operated successfully off the Swedish coast. Within a year he was promoted to command a 20-gun *frigate, in which his fine seamanship and audacity were given full play. With the Great Northern War in full swing, he found no lack of action among the fjords of Sweden in operations against Swedish frigates and troop *transports, and his fame as a brave and skilful commander began to spread. With the return of Charles XII to Sweden in 1715, Wessel did great execution among the Swedish shipping off the coast of Pomerania, and in the following year was ennobled by Frederick IV of Denmark under the title of Tordenskjold (Thundershield). He raised the siege by Charles XII of Fredrikshald in Norway by destroying the Swedish fleet of transports and supply ships, and was promoted captain. In 1717 he commanded a *squadron with the task of bringing to action and destroying the Swedish Gothenburg squadron, but disloyalty on the part of some of his officers prevented his achieving a decisive victory. Nevertheless, he was able to return to Denmark in 1718 with the news of the death of Charles XII, and was made a rear admiral by Frederick IV in the general rejoicing. His final claim to fame was the capture of the Swedish fortress of Marstrand and the final elimination of the Gothenburg squadron, partly by destruction and partly by capture. For this he was advanced to vice admiral. Shortly after the end of the Great Northern War he was killed in a duel. He is regarded in Denmark as a great naval hero, and, after Charles XII perhaps, the most heroic figure of the Great Northern War.

TORPEDO, a naval weapon used principally by light craft, submarines, and aircraft. The first weapon to which this name of an electric-shock-giving fish was applied was an explosive charge moored in the sea, which later became known as a sea *mine. The name followed the weapon when such explosive charges were attached to the end of spars projecting from the bows of small craft (the *spar torpedo), or were towed by a boat, the tow rope being carried out at an angle by a trawler fisherman's *otter board (the *Harvey torpedo). The spar torpedo was effectively used during the American Civil War (1861–5) by the Confederate submersible *H. L. Hunley* to sink the U.S.S. *Housatonic* in 1864 (see also 'DAVID'). It was still in use twenty years later when it played an important part in the defeat of a Chinese fleet by the French in the battle of the Min River.

Long before this, however, in 1865, the first steps had been taken to produce the self-propelled, buoyant missile which the name signifies today, when an Austrian captain named Luppis devised a clockwork-driven, boat-shaped craft guided by lines attached to its rudder. When this proved too crude for practical application, he turned to Robert *Whitehead, the English manager of a marine engine factory at Fiume. The result was the Luppis–Whitehead locomotive torpedo first produced in 1867, a spindle-shaped underwater missile driven by a compressed-air engine at six knots for a few

A Whitehead torpedo on board H.M.S. Thunderer; *engraving from the* Illustrated London News, *1878*

hundred yards and carrying an explosive charge of 18 pounds of dynamite in its head. Running depth was regulated by a hydrostatic valve and, in 1868, a balance chamber was incorporated in which a pendulum connected to horizontal rudders automatically corrected any fore-and-aft tilt.

The Austrian government declined to buy the exclusive rights of manufacture and Whitehead accepted an invitation in 1869 to bring to England the two torpedoes he had by that time developed—a 14-inch and a 16-inch diameter model. These were given extensive trials under Admiralty auspices at Sheerness, at the conclusion of which the government bought the rights of manufacture for £15,000.

The Royal Laboratory at Woolwich, which was entrusted with the task of development, concentrated at first on the 16-inch model which, driven by two contra-rotating propellers, had a range of 1,000 yards at 7 knots or 300 yards at $12\frac{1}{4}$ knots. It was one of these which had the distinction of being the first locomotive torpedo to be fired in action, launched from H.M.S. *Shah* in 1877 during her inconclusive action with the Peruvian *monitor *Huascar*.

By this time Whitehead torpedoes were being supplied to most navies and in 1878 they claimed their first victim when, during the Russo-Turkish War, a Turkish revenue *cutter was sunk by two Russian *torpedoboats, each of which obtained a hit. The first warship to be so sunk was the Chilean insurgent *battleship *Blanco Encalada* in 1891.

The directional reliability of the torpedo was

greatly improved by the introduction in 1878–9 of a gyro-controlled steering apparatus invented by L. Obry of Trieste. Another type of torpedo, invented in 1881 and used for some years for harbour defence, was the Brennan, in which motive power was supplied through two lines of piano wire wound in by a winch on the shore from two spools in the torpedo, thus revolving two contra-rotating propellers. By 1909 the standard Whitehead torpedo was an 18-inch weapon with a range of 2,000 yards at 35 knots or 4,000 yards at 29 knots.

The next development to improve the performance of the torpedo was the enrichment of the compressed air driving the engine. In British Whitehead torpedoes this took the form of a mixture of steam and gas resulting from water being evaporated and super-heated in a 'generator' by means of a jet burning shale oil. In the U.S. Navy the Bliss–Leavitt torpedo was propelled by a *turbine driven by steam generated by forcing a spray of water through an alcohol torch. By 1914, torpedoes were usually either 18 inches or 21 inches in diameter and about $17\frac{1}{2}$ or 22 feet respectively in length, with a range of 3,750 yards at 44 knots or 10,000 yards at 28 knots.

Except for improvements in performance, and refinements such as pre-set alteration of course after discharge and the adoption of magnetically actuated firing pistols for their warheads as an alternative for the more usual impact pistol, torpedoes remained much the same until the Second World War except for a very high-performance 24-inch weapon driven by liquid oxygen which the Japanese developed and used to good effect. During the war the Germans developed, for use by their *U-boats, an electrically driven and therefore trackless weapon incorporating an acoustic device which homed it on to the sound of a ship's propellers. This was the first of the generation of torpedoes in use today, many of which depend upon electronics for direction on to the target.

The U.S. Navy's standard anti-shipping torpedo for use by *submarines is a development of the 21-inch weapon in use at the end of the war, driven at extremely high speeds by machinery using hydrogen peroxide for its fuel. A number of homing torpedoes have been developed, particularly as anti-submarine weapons, modern types for launching from ships or submarines possessing passive or active homing systems or wire guidance in co-operation with electronic sensors. Miniaturization has enabled small, lightweight torpedoes to be devised for launching from helicopters or to be carried as anti-submarine missiles. Earlier models are electrically propelled; but in recent times types have been adopted employing machinery driven by either solid or liquid propellants.

TORPEDOBOAT, a naval vessel developed by most navies during the decade 1880–90 to take advantage of the *Whitehead *torpedo, by that time emerging from the development stage into a significant naval weapon. The world's first real torpedoboat was H.M.S. *Lightning*, launched in 1876 to carry *spar torpedoes, but modified in 1879 by the addition of two above-water tubes for the discharge of Whitehead torpedoes. Of 19 tons *displacement, she reached a speed of 19 *knots on her trials, and in 1880 was renamed Torpedoboat No. 1. Her success as a torpedoboat was such as to lead the British Admiralty to place an order for twelve more. They were intended for coast defence duties, the theory of the close *blockade of an enemy's coast, a legacy from the days of Lord *Nelson, still being the hub on which naval war strategy revolved.

The success of Torpedoboat No. 1 and her immediate followers inspired other navies to adopt the type; torpedoboats in large numbers were built for the navies of Russia, France, Holland, Italy, and Austria between 1881 and 1885, and in 1886 Chile, China, Greece, Spain, Portugal, Sweden, and Turkey followed suit.

The implied threat of so many torpedoboats in the hands of foreign navies to the naval supremacy of Britain acted as a spur on the British Admiralty, having produced the weapon, to try to discover the antidote. This took the shape, first, of producing a larger and faster vessel, carrying a 4-inch gun in addition to torpedo-tubes, to be known as a torpedoboat catcher. The first of these was H.M.S. *Rattlesnake*, launched in 1886, but she did not have a sufficient margin of speed to act as an efficient antidote. Further experiments in catchers were similarly unsuccessful, and it was not until 1893, when H.M.S. *Havock* and H.M.S. *Hornet* were launched as torpedoboat *destroyers, that the answer was found. With a displacement of 250 tons, a speed of 27 knots, and with an armament of four guns and three torpedo-tubes, they were not only too fast and powerful for any torpedoboat but at the same time usurped their function. H.M.S. *Havock* was, in fact, the world's first destroyer.

Nevertheless, most navies continued to build torpedoboats and they remained in the British Navy until the First World War (1914–18), the last class of them being built in 1908, known colloquially in the navy as 'oily wads'. In the German Navy, the name was retained to describe what by then most other navies had classed as destroyers.

A smaller type of torpedoboat produced towards the end of the First World War, and developed into a significant weapon during the Second, was the *motor torpedoboat, with an upper deck armament of torpedo-tubes and a very high speed. Today they are generally classed in most navies as fast patrol boats.

The classification of torpedoboat may have had a much earlier use, as according to a report in the *Standard* (29 December 1880), 'The first torpedoboat ever known (was) a very primitive model invented by Captain David *Bushnell of the Engineer Corps, U.S. Army, and launched in New York harbour in 1776.' However, most people would claim this as one of the earliest *submarines rather than the first torpedoboat.

TORRES, LUIS VAEZ DE (d. 1613), Portuguese navigator, was appointed second-in-command of the expedition under Pedro Fernandez de *Quiros which sailed in December 1605 from Callao and discovered the New Hebrides group of islands in April/May 1606. When the crew of the flagship forced Quiros to return home from Espiritu Santo, Torres continued to explore the south-west Pacific with his own ship, the 120-ton *San Pedro*, and a *launch.

On 18 July 1606 he reached the Louisiade Archipelago off the eastern tip of New Guinea; discovering a passage through the maze of reefs and shoals, he followed the south coast of New Guinea through the strait between the northern tip of Australia and the southern point of New Guinea that now bears his name and reached Ternate in the Molucca Islands, continuing thence to Manila in the Philippines. Unable there to find the means to return to Spain, he died in Manila, probably in 1613.

The Spanish authorities did not disclose this discovery by Torres—the reason, perhaps, why in 1644 Abel *Tasman was dispatched by the Dutch governor-general of the East Indies in command of an expedition to discover whether New Guinea was a part of the mainland of Australia—and it was not until 1792 that his letter describing his discoveries and passage of the strait was published. His name was given to the strait at the suggestion of the English geographer Alexander *Dalrymple.

TORRINGTON, Earl of, see BYNG, George; see also HERBERT, Arthur.

TORSION, a form of strain on a ship's hull caused when waves attempt to twist the forward end of a ship one way and the after end the opposite way.

TOUCHING, an old sailing term used in square-rigged ships to indicate that the ship was *on the wind, with the leading *leech of the sails just beginning to shiver, or 'touching' the wind.

TOULON, a main naval base and seaport on the south coast of France in the Mediterranean. Originally the Roman port of Telo Martius, it was successively sacked by Goths, Burgundians, Franks, and Saracens until finally conquered by

Charles of Anjou in 1259. A naval arsenal was established there by Henri IV, and the base was further strengthened and enlarged by Richelieu and Vauban. In 1792, after considerable disorders in the town, French royalists took control and opened the port to the British fleet, by whom it was occupied until 1793 when Napoleon, as an artillery colonel, made it untenable by capturing the forts which dominated the harbour. It is today the most important naval dockyard in France and the main base of the French Mediterranean fleet.

In 1744, during the War of the Austrian Succession (1739–48), a naval battle took place off the port between a British fleet of twenty-eight *ships of the line and a combined Franco-Spanish fleet of the same number. The British *van, commanded by Admiral Thomas *Mathews, attacked the main body of the enemy, severely damaging the Spanish flagship and capturing the 60-gun *Poder*, but Mathews was so poorly supported by his rear division, commanded by Vice Admiral Richard *Lestock, which in fact never entered the fight at all, that eventually he was forced to withdraw. The *Poder* was recaptured by the French but ultimately abandoned and burned. Although an indecisive and sorry affair, this battle had tremendous repercussions throughout the British Navy, ending in a long series of courts martial, in which several captains of ships were dismissed the navy, but in which also Lestock was acquitted and Mathews cashiered. This extraordinary result was based on a tactical technicality, Mathews being blamed for attacking the enemy before his leading ship was opposite the leading ship of the enemy, as laid down in the official *Fighting Instructions*. The effect of this verdict was to stifle the exercise of all initiative on the part of British admirals in battle, and condemned British fleets to fight ineffective and sterile battles for the next fifty years until the formal tactics laid down in the *Fighting Instructions* were successfully flouted by such admirals as Lords *Howe, *Hood, and *Nelson.

TOULOUSE, LOUIS ALEXANDRE DE BOURBON, Comte de (1678–1737), French admiral, was the third son of Louis XIV and Mme de Montespan. As a son of the reigning mistress, he was made admiral of France at the age of five. Nevertheless, he had a successful naval career and commanded the French fleet during the War of the Spanish Succession (1702–13). He had rather the better of the indecisive battle of *Velez Malaga against an English fleet commanded by Sir George *Rooke, though without remaining to reap the fruits of his success which thus went by default to Rooke. It was because of his withdrawal of his fleet after the battle that Gibraltar, captured a few days earlier, remained in British hands.

TOURVILLE, ANNE-HILARION DE CON-TENTIN, Comte de (1642–1701), admiral and marshal of France, first served with the * galleys of the Order of Malta against the * Barbary pirates. He was incorporated into the French Navy by Louis XIV, and during the Third Dutch War (1672–4) served at the battle of * Solebay in 1672, commanding the 50-gun ship *Page* in the French squadron which, allied to England, fought against the Dutch. He was similarly present at the battle of the * Texel in 1673. He then served in the Mediterranean under * Duquesne in the actions against the great de * Ruyter. By this time he had earned a reputation as a thorough seaman and is by many thought to be mainly responsible for the great work on naval tactics published later by the Abbé * Hoste, who was his secretary. He was a rear admiral in 1683 and vice admiral in 1689, and was appointed as commander-in-chief of the French Navy for the war against England. He had a fine opportunity of winning a signal victory against a weaker Anglo-Dutch fleet off * Beachy Head in 1690, but a too-cautious approach to the hazards of naval battle prevented him from risking his fleet in an all-out chase. He was himself unquestionably a man of great personal courage, but the weight of responsibility for the safety of his fleet outweighed his better naval judgement.

In 1692, when Louis XIV was committed to the exiled James II to land an army in England, Tourville found himself commanding in the Channel with a fleet greatly inferior to that of Britain, and suffered a considerable defeat at the battle of * Barfleur and the subsequent burning of French ships and transports at La Hogue. He had a chance in the following year to inflict immense damage on Britain when he had the great Smyrna * convoy at his mercy off the coast of Portugal, but by insisting on preserving his fleet in 'battle order', he allowed a substantial portion of the convoy to escape. Although never blamed by Louis XIV, of whom he was a great favourite, he did not serve again at sea.

TOVEY, JOHN, first Baron Tovey of Langton Matravers (1885–1971), British admiral of the fleet, joined the Royal Navy in 1900. By the outbreak of the First World War (1914–18) he had risen to the rank of lieutenant-commander and was serving as first lieutenant of the * destroyer *Faulknor* in the Harwich Force. In January 1915 he obtained his first command, the destroyer *Jackal*, transferring fifteen months later to the *Onslow* of the 13th Flotilla, attached to the Battle-cruiser Fleet. During the battle of * Jutland he distinguished himself in a gallant episode when he took the *Onslow* to within 8,000 yards of the German * battle-cruisers to attack them with * torpedoes. Enemy gunfire damaged his ship amidships, as a result of which only one

of her four torpedoes was launched, and it was not until the *Onslow* was retiring that Tovey discovered this fact. He returned to the attack, this time on the German * battleships and, in spite of a storm of enemy gunfire, launched his torpedoes and escaped destruction.

Promoted to commander on 30 June 1916 and to captain at the end of 1923, Tovey held shore appointments alternating with destroyer commands, including command of the 8th and 6th Destroyer Flotillas, followed by command of the battleship *Rodney*. He received his flag as a rear admiral in August 1935 and when the Second World War broke out, was second-in-command of the Mediterranean Fleet under Admiral Sir Andrew * Cunningham. On 18 October 1940 he was appointed Commander-in-Chief Home Fleet with the rank of admiral, an appointment he held until May 1943.

During that time the most important operations he conducted were the hunt and destruction of the battleship * *Bismarck* when she broke out into the Atlantic in May 1941, and the coverage of the Arctic convoys to Russia in 1941 and 1942. Tovey's well-planned dispositions enabled his forces promptly to locate and intercept the *Bismarck*, but the calamitous loss of the battle-cruiser * *Hood*, followed by a failure of his * cruisers to hold contact, led to a desperate hunt for the German battleship only successfully resolved at the eleventh hour when she was crippled by torpedo aircraft from the * aircraft carrier * *Ark Royal* and subsequently sunk by the guns and torpedoes of the Home Fleet.

In respect of the Arctic convoys, Tovey was in disagreement with, and overruled by, the First Sea Lord, Admiral Sir Dudley * Pound, in July 1942 when the latter ordered Convoy * PQ 17 to scatter under threat of attack by the German battleship * *Tirpitz*. Thus deprived of the protection of their close escorts, all but 11 of the 35 ships that had set out were sunk by air or * submarine attack.

Admiral Tovey became commander-in-chief at the * Nore in July 1943 and was promoted admiral of the fleet in October of that year. He was made a peer at the end of the war, but had no more naval service after March 1946.

TOW, to, the operation of hauling another vessel through the water by means of a towing * hawser made fast astern of the towing vessel (see also TUG) and in the bows of the vessel towed. When used as a noun, it signifies the vessel or vessels being towed.

TOWAGE, the charge made by a tug owner for towing another vessel. In the case of salvage at sea, it is the amount of the bargain struck between the * master of a * tug and the master of the ship requiring assistance in the form of a tow.

TRABACOLO or **TRABACCOLO,** a coasting vessel of medium size, of the 17th to 19th centuries, peculiar to the Adriatic and the waters around Italy. They were used mainly for trade but occasionally as transports for troops. Some had one mast, some two, and they were variously rigged according to the choice of the owner, but frequently with a *lateen rig.

TRACK, a strip of metal on a yacht's mast or boom to take slides fixed to the *luff or *foot of a sail. They were introduced to take the place of the mast hoops and lacing of the old-fashioned *gaff sails. With the introduction of the Bermudian form of mainsail for racing yachts during the 1920s, the luff was at first set on a taut stay running from masthead to deck. This was soon found unsatisfactory and a track composed of a strong strip of metal was screwed to a hardwood batten on the after side of the mast. The luff of the sail was attached to metal clips or slides which fitted over the track and slid up and down as the sail was hoisted or lowered. In strong wind conditions, however, this type of track proved inadequate to stand the strain on the luff, the clips tore away from the track or jammed and caused difficulty in lowering the sail. A stronger type of track on C-section, with more robust slides running inside the track, was introduced, and variations of this pattern in brass, bronze, light alloy, and nylon are used in Bermuda-rigged yachts throughout the world. In modern yachts the luff-rope without slides often feeds directly into the C-section track, which becomes known as the groove. Similar tracks and slides are often fitted to the boom to take the foot of the sail in place of lacing, while much heavier section tracks are employed on deck in many yachts for the sliding sheet leads.

TRADE WINDS, steady regular winds which blow in a belt between approximately 30° N. and 30° S. of the equator. They are caused by the action of the sun on and near the equator in heating the atmosphere and causing it to rise, the heavier air to north and south coming in to fill the vacuum thus caused. If the earth did not revolve, these winds would come directly from

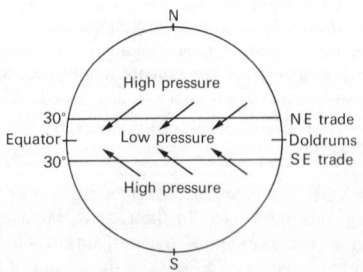

Trade winds

the south in the southern hemisphere and the north in the northern, but as the speed of revolution is greater at the equator than in higher latitudes these winds coming in are diverted towards the west. As a result, the trade winds in the southern hemisphere blow from the south-east, and in the northern from the north-east. They are known as trade winds from the great regularity with which they blow, thus assisting the ships which used to carry the trade around the world in the days before steam propulsion. See also PASSAT.

TRAFALGAR, BATTLE OF, was fought off Cape Trafalgar on the south-western coast of Spain on 21 October 1805, and was the last major fleet encounter of the classic days of sail except for *Navarino in 1827. It was the culmination of a campaign which was fought to prevent invasion of Great Britain by the Grand Army of Napoleon, which was encamped on the opposite shore of the Channel for that purpose. The campaign had in fact been won before the battle since Napoleon began to disperse his army during the late summer, turning it against continental enemies, but Trafalgar achieved the destruction of the main Franco-Spanish fleet, a fact which enabled Britain, for the ten remaining years of the Napoleonic War (1803–15), to dominate not only the Channel but the enemy-held Atlantic ports and the Mediterranean. Its effect was therefore both immediate and long-term, and Lord *Nelson, though he lost his life in the hour of far-reaching triumph, sacrificed it to good purpose.

Where his fleet was concerned, Napoleon thought like a soldier. His plans made no allowance for maritime conditions or for countermeasures by an enemy more formidable at sea than most of his opponents had proved to be by land.

In 1805, with the Spanish as well as the French Navy at his disposal, Napoleon proposed that his chosen admiral, the Comte de *Villeneuve, should elude Nelson's watch on Toulon and sail to the West Indies, releasing *squadrons at Cartagena and *Cadiz on his way. In the Caribbean he would be joined by other squadrons from French Atlantic ports. The combined fleet would then sail back to Europe in overwhelming force, defeat the fleet under Admiral William *Cornwallis which guarded the western approaches to the Channel, and secure the Straits of Dover for long enough to enable the Grand Army to cross.

Part of the plan succeeded. Villeneuve eluded Nelson twice. Once he was driven back to Toulon by stress of weather, but in April 1805 he got clear away, picked up some Spanish ships at Cadiz, and made a rendezvous in the West Indies. But that was the limit of his success. Nelson pursued him and Villeneuve, hearing the

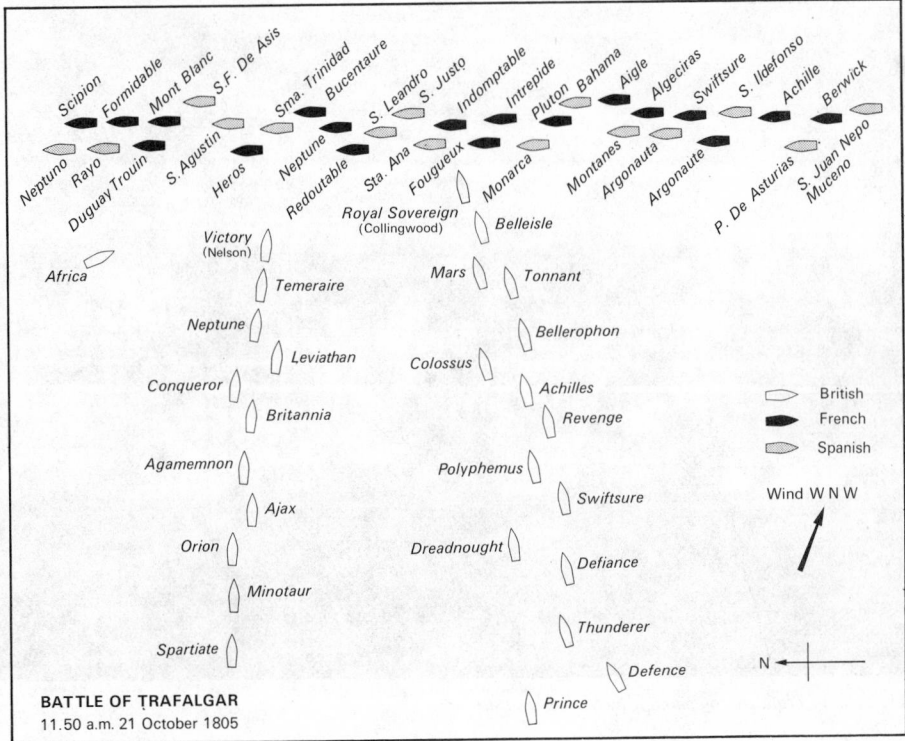

Scipion
Formidable
Mont Blanc
S. F. De Asis
Sma. Trinidad
Bucentaure
S. Leandro
S. Justo
Indomptable
Intrepide
Pluton
Bahama
Aigle
Algeciras
Swiftsure
S. Ildefonso
Achille
Berwick
Neptuno
Rayo
Duguay Trouin
S. Agustin
Heros
Neptune
Redoutable
Sta. Ana
Fougueux
Monarca
Montanes
Argonauta
Argonaute
P. De Asturias
S. Juan Nepo
Muceno

Africa
Victory
(Nelson)
Royal Sovereign
(Collingwood)
Belleisle
Temeraire
Mars
Tonnant
Neptune
Bellerophon
Leviathan
Colossus
Conqueror
Achilles
Britannia
Revenge

British
French
Spanish

Agamemnon
Polyphemus
Swiftsure
Wind W N W
Ajax
Orion
Dreadnought
Defiance
Minotaur
Thunderer
Spartiate
Defence
N
BATTLE OF TRAFALGAR
11.50 a.m. 21 October 1805
Prince

news of the British fleet's arrival in those waters, hastened back to Europe. He was engaged off *Cape Finisterre in July by Sir Robert *Calder, and later took his fleet to Cadiz, where it was *blockaded by Admiral *Collingwood.

Having missed Villeneuve in the West Indies, Nelson returned first to Gibraltar to make sure that the Mediterranean was safe, then went back to England, and finally resumed command of the fleet, off the Spanish coast, at the end of September. There he electrified his captains by a plan of attack in two columns, one under himself, the other under Collingwood, which would, he considered, bring on the 'pell-mell battle' he desired. Napoleon played into his hands by ordering his fleet to the Mediterranean. Villeneuve (under notice of suspension) ventured out, then, changing his mind, decided to return to Cadiz. Finally, he stood to face his great opponent.

Nelson's two-column attack involved extreme hazard for the leading ships in each line. During their approach they would be exposed to raking *broadsides long before they could make effective reply, but if they survived they could prevent the enemy *van from being able to support the centre until too late, confuse the Franco-Spanish order of sailing by breaking through the line, and prevent a return to port in any organized formation.

The strongest ships were placed at the head of each column. Nelson's own line was led by three three-decked ships, the *Victory, *Temeraire, and *Neptune. They did their work magnificently in spite of heavy casualties and damage. Collingwood's approach, in which he led in the *Royal Sovereign, was more oblique than Nelson's, though equally effective. Collingwood came under fire at least ten minutes before any later ships could support him. The action was begun at about three minutes before noon.

Once the Victory and succeeding ships could bring their broadsides to bear, the effect was devastating. Heavy fighting lasted about four hours. The Victory broke through the French line close to the *Bucentaure, the French flagship, and from that moment the crucial words of the memorandum which Nelson had circulated to his admirals and captains on 10 October were fulfilled. 'The whole impression of the British fleet,' he had written, 'must be to overpower from two or three ships ahead of their commander-in-chief (supposed to be in the centre) to the rear of the fleet.'

The enemy's combined fleet consisted of 33 *ships of the line (18 French and 15 Spanish), of which, during the course of the day, no less than 20 were at one time taken in *prize, or lowered their colours. This was the number on which

The battle of Trafalgar; oil painting by N. Pocock, 1806

Nelson had reckoned, though he did not live to see his hopes realized, for at about 1.15 p.m., while pacing the *quarterdeck with his flag-captain, Thomas Masterman *Hardy, he was mortally wounded by a shot from the French *Redoutable*, which had bravely grappled with the *Victory* and had at one stage tried to board her. Nelson was carried below, and lived only a few hours. The *Victory*'s log recorded: 'Partial firing continued until 4.30 when a victory having been reported to the Right Honourable Lord Viscount Nelson K.B and Commander-in-Chief, he then died of his wound.'

The weather deteriorated during the course of the day (it was blowing a full gale by midnight), the combatants were scattered, and of the prizes only four, one French and three Spanish, were brought to Gibraltar, the rest being sunk, driven ashore by storm, or recaptured. As soon as practicable, Hardy sent word to Collingwood that Nelson's wound was mortal, and before nightfall Collingwood assumed command of the fleet, at first from the *frigate *Euryalus* since the *Royal Sovereign* had been rendered temporarily unserviceable by battle damage.

Experts have debated the tactics of Trafalgar ever since, and under any other direction than Nelson's they could have proved disastrous. Led by him, his officers and men won the most complete sea victory of its era.

TRAIL-BOARD, a carved board fitted one on each side of the *stem of a square-rigged ship, which helped to support the *figurehead. In the older ships they were always richly carved and often gilded; later the carving became more simple and austere.

TRAIN, the name given to the after part of a wooden gun-carriage as used in sailing warships. It was to an *eyebolt in the train of the carriage that the *train-tackle was hooked during battle.

TRAINING SHIPS, vessels of various types used specifically for giving young aspirants to the sea an initial training to fit them for such a career. A majority of training ships are run for this purpose by national, or in some cases naval, authorities and many nations have adopted training in sail, rather than in power-driven ships, to produce the most efficient type of seaman. In some countries similar training schemes on a non-national basis, such as, for example, the Sail Training Association in Great Britain, exist to provide experience for leisure purposes, such as yacht racing or cruising.

Sail training ships vary from large four-masted *barques, such as those used by the U.S.S.R. for the training of seamen, to small *brigs, such as that used in Great Britain for the training of sea cadets. A majority of such sail

another port where a cargo, or part cargo, is awaiting transhipment. No doubt it was of the tramping trade that Rudyard *Kipling was thinking when he wrote:

'And where will you fetch it from, all you Big Steamers,
And where shall I write you when you are away?'
'We fetch it from Melbourne, Quebec, and Vancouver,
Address us at Hobart, Hong Kong, and Bombay.'

TRANE, or **TRAIN, OIL,** a former term for whale or seal oil.

TRANSOM, (1) the *athwartship *timbers bolted to the *sternpost of a ship to give her a flat stern. In the older square-rigged ships, particularly warships, they were usually rather heavier than other timbers in order to support the overhang of the stern and quarter *galleries. In modern vessels there is no overhang with a transom stern, and in consequence no need for the stern timbers to be heavier than any others. For illus. see SHIPBUILDING. **(2)** A name often given to the vane of a *cross-staff, that part which slides along the staff by means of a square socket cut in the centre of the vane. **(3)** The crosspiece of timber which connected the *cheeks of a wooden gun-carriage during the days of sailing navies.

TRANSPORT, a ship, either naval or hired, employed in the transport of troops or other persons to and from overseas, either for operations abroad in time of war or for the relief of garrisons serving abroad in time of peace. Until recent years, the transport service of many nations was a great and continuing operation, with large numbers of ships permanently employed. It was not without its hazards, certainly in wartime when the sinking of a transport with troops on board was always a desirable war objective, but also occasionally in peacetime, as when the naval transport *Birkenhead* was wrecked in Table Bay in 1852 with a loss of 454 officers and men of the 74th Highlanders. Today, the duties of such transport are almost entirely performed by aircraft.

TRAVELLER, (1) the ring of a lower *sheet *block, when *shackled to a *horse on the deck or *counter of a sailing vessel, and thus free to travel from side to side of the horse according to the direction in which the sail is trimmed, is usually known as a traveller. **(2)** A metal ring fitted to slide up and down a *spar or to run in and out on a *boom or *gaff to extend or draw in the tack or clew of a sail. Thus, a traveller is normally fitted to a long *bowsprit so that the

training authorities have adopted the square rig as most likely to produce self confidence and efficiency in the budding seaman.

TRAIN-TACKLE, a *tackle used during battle in the days of the muzzle-loading broadside guns of the wooden ships of war. It was hooked to an *eyebolt in the train of a wooden gun-carriage and to a *ringbolt in the deck, and used to prevent the gun from running out of the *port while it was being loaded and for running it in after firing for re-loading.

TRAMONTANA, the cold northerly wind of the Mediterranean, particularly around the coasts of Italy. It is the same wind that in other localities is called the *bora.

TRAMP, a cargo-carrying merchant vessel which does not work a regular route but carries general cargo to any destination as required, and may be diverted to any port to pick up available cargo. It is the modern trade version of the older merchant adventurer, who would load a cargo of goods and try to sell them at his various ports of call, usually buying other goods at those ports to sell at home on the conclusion of the voyage. The modern tramp does not sell her cargoes but merely delivers them at their various destinations, proceeding when empty in *ballast to tack of the jib can be hauled out when being set. **(3)** A metal ring, to which a hook is welded, by which a *lugsail is hoisted with a *halyard, a *strop around the *yard to which the sail is laced being attached to the hook and the ring sliding up the mast. **(4)** Another name for a *parrel, by which the yards in square-rigged ships are held close to the mast. **(5)** A rope about three feet in length with a *thimble spliced in one end, used to control the swing of a *topgallant yard during hoisting or lowering in a square-rigged ship. Two of these travellers were fixed on each *backstay, the thimbles travelling up and down them; the rope tails being secured to the ends of the topgallant yard to stop it swinging backwards and forwards while being *swayed up or *struck down at sea.

TRAVERSE BOARD, an old and approximate means of making out the *course made good by a ship during a *watch. It was a circular piece of wood marked out with all the *points of the compass and with eight holes bored in each. Eight small pegs were attached to the centre of the board, and each half hour one of the pegs was stuck into a hole on the compass point on which the ship had run during that half hour. At the end of the watch the mean course made good was calculated from the positions of the pegs.

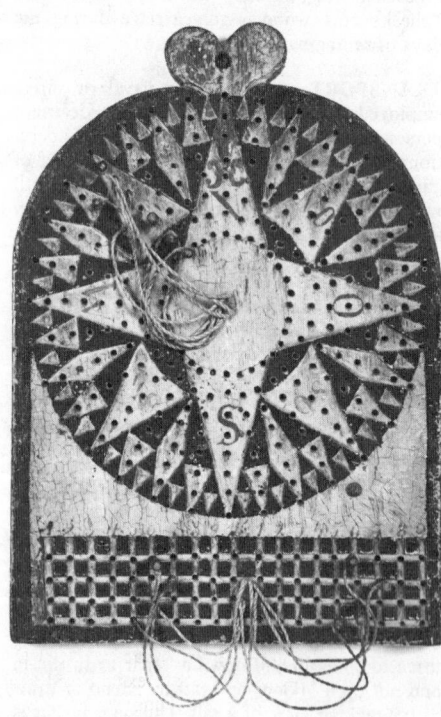

Traverse board; 16th century

TRAVERSE TABLE, a table, included in all books of navigational tables, which gives the measurement of the two sides of any right-angled triangle subtended by the hypotenuse. In navigational terms, it provides the navigator with the difference of *latitude and the *departure (from which he can find the change in his longitude) for any distance along a *rhumb-line *course steered by a ship, the course and distance forming the hypotenuse. This is essential information for the navigator when he needs to calculate his *dead reckoning position. Reversely, the navigator can discover from the traverse table, and without recourse to a chart, the distance and the rhumb-line course he would have to steer between two points of known latitude and longitude. The table gives difference of latitude and departure for each degree between 0° and 90°, and for a hypotenuse length from 0 usually to 600.

The table would appear to have taken its name from the *traverse board of older days by which the mean course steered by a ship during a four-hour *watch could be ascertained.

TRAWL, a large net in the form of a bag, with its mouth held open with *otter boards or a beam, which is towed by a trawler along the bottom of the sea, or at other desired depths, at the ends of *warps, to catch bottom-lying or pelagic fish. It is so designed that fish, once in the mouth of the trawl, are prevented from escaping by net baffles and are swept down to the *cod-end of the trawl. After a predetermined time the trawl is hauled by its warps to the surface and brought on board, the cod-end being hoisted above the fish deck of the trawler. When the cod-end is opened, the fish fall to the deck.

Modern deep-sea trawlers normally use trawls in which the otter-board method of spreading the trawl opening is used. These are large boards or metal plates, frequently also known as doors, either rectangular or oval, attached to each side of the trawl opening so that they remain vertical and angled outwards. The pressure of the water on their surfaces as they are towed along the bottom forces them outwards and keeps the opening spread taut. Many modern bottom trawls are now designed with an extra high vertical opening as well as a wide horizontal opening, and many fishermen consider this new design as the most efficient for bottom trawling.

A variation of the otter-board trawl is the semipelagic trawl, developed by Icelandic fishermen to catch fish, particularly cod, which normally lie in the water slightly above the bottom. In this type of trawl the otter boards are towed along the bottom with the trawl bag floating a short distance above them.

Before the development of the otter-board trawl, the beam trawl was the standard fishing

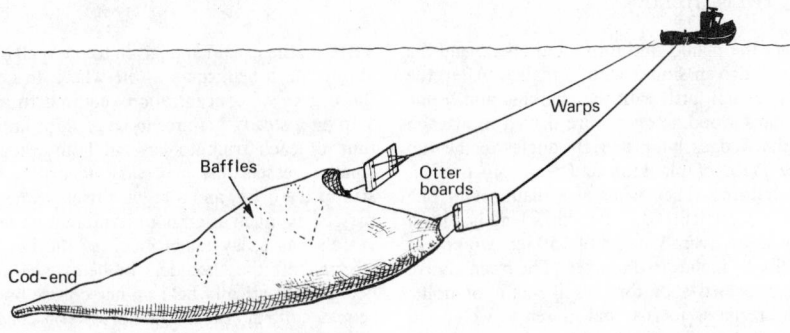

A trawl

gear for all deep-sea steam trawlers. Today, beam trawls are normally only used by the smaller fishing vessels. They vary in size according to the size of the fishing vessel and range up to a length of beam of about 39 feet (12 m). In this type of trawl the mouth is kept open by a wooden or metal beam along the top of the opening and mounted on guides, or skids, at each end, which travel easily along the sea bottom. They are frequently used in pairs, being towed one each side of the trawler. In some cases, particularly in Spain for the pareja fishing, a single trawl is towed by two trawlers, one on each warp, so that the mouth of the trawl is held open by each trawler acting in close co-operation with the other. This method of trawling is widely known as bull trawling. When used exclusively for bottom-lying flatfish, which often like to burrow slightly into the sand, some beam trawls are adapted to carry chains, known as tickler chains, in front of the opening of the trawl. As these chains drag along through the sand they disturb the fish which rise into the oncoming trawl.

In recent years trawling has been developed to cover the waters between the bottom and the surface in order to catch pelagic fish and crabs. The depth at which the trawl is towed is regulated by the length of the warps and the speed of towing: with long warps and a slow speed the trawl is on the bottom; as the warps are shortened and the speed of towing increased, the trawl rises. *Sonar equipment in the trawler indicates the depth at which the fish are swimming, and thus the depth at which the trawl should be towed.

Trawls are the most important type of fishing gear used in the commercial fisheries of northwest Europe, catching a greater weight of fish than any other method. Worldwide, trawls are second only to purse *seine nets in total catch.

TRAWL LINES, a method of fishing for cod on the *Grand Banks off Newfoundland which, in spite of its name, had nothing to do with trawling. A long line, buoyed at each end, was moored on the banks, and at short intervals along its length it carried smaller lines each with a baited hook. The trawl lines were laid by *dories which were carried in the Banks fishing *schooners which operated mainly out of Gloucester, Massachusetts.

TRAWLER, a fishing vessel specially designed to operate a *trawl for the catching of bottom-lying fish. Before the introduction of steam, and later diesel, propulsion and power, a sailing trawler could operate a trawl to a depth of 30–40 *fathoms, a modern steam or diesel-powered trawler can fish to a depth of 500 fathoms, and considerably greater depths than this have been fished experimentally with a trawl to try to discover new varieties of edible fish to satisfy a growing demand.

Modern trawlers, vessels up to 2,500–3,000 tons, are fitted with *sonar, which can indicate the presence of fish on the same principle as echo-sounding, and refrigerating machinery to preserve the catch so that they may remain longer on the fishing grounds.

A trawler may travel thousands of miles to reach the more distant fishing grounds from its home base, and remain there from four to five weeks, or until its holds are full. A new regulation generally in force among the world's trawler fleets requires daily communication with the home port, as many of the most prolific fishing grounds, particularly for cod and halibut, lie in cold and stormy waters, where a trawler can be in danger from ice forming on rigging and upper works and making her unstable. Daily communication insures that a search can be quickly mounted for any trawler that fails to make her daily report.

During the First and Second World Wars, large numbers of fishing trawlers were taken up by the belligerent powers and converted into *minesweepers, their crews having proved remarkably adaptable to minesweeping techniques and the trawlers ideally suited to this task.

TREENAILS, pronounced trennels, long cylindrical pins of oak which were used to secure the planks of a wooden ship's sides and bottom to her *timbers. Holes were bored with an auger through the planks and into the timbers, and the treenails driven home with a mallet. After the ends were cut flush with the planking and frame face, hard wood wedges were driven in at each end, the wedges lying at right angles to the run of the grain of planking and frame to prevent them splitting. They were of a diameter of one inch for every 100 feet of a ship's length; thus a ship with an overall length of 150 feet would use treenails $1\frac{1}{2}$ inches in diameter. 'The treenails are justly esteemed superior to spike-nails or bolts, which are liable to rust and loosen as well as to rot the timber; but it is necessary that the oak of which they are formed should be solid, close, and replete with gum, to prevent them from breaking and rotting in the ship's frame. They ought also to be well dried so as to fill their holes when they are swelled with moisture.' Thus Falconer, *Marine Dictionary* (1771).

TRENCHEMER or **TRENCH-THE-MER,** the name of the *dromon in which Richard I of England, known as Cœur de Lion, sailed to Acre for the third Crusade (1191–2). The dromon was no doubt named after her captain, Alan Trenchemer. In some accounts the vessel is described as a *galley.

TRESTLE-TREES, sometimes written tressel-trees, two short pieces of timber fixed horizontally fore-and-aft on each side of the lower masthead of a square-rigged vessel and used to support the topmast, the lower *crosstrees, and the *top. Smaller trestle-trees are similarly fitted to the topmast-head to support the topmast crosstrees and the *topgallant mast. For illus. see RIGGING.

TRIANA, RODRIGO DA, a sailor on board the *caravel *Niña, the first man to sight land on the voyage of Christopher *Columbus in 1492 which ended in the first discovery of America. He announced the sight of land at 2.00 a.m. in the morning of 12 October 1492.

TRIATIC STAY, in square-rigged ships, a *stay secured at each head of the fore- and main-*masts with *thimbles spliced into the *bight to which the stay *tackles were hooked. In its modern meaning it is a stay between the two masts of a ship to which the signal *halyards are bent.

TRICE UP, to, the operation of hauling up, generally in order to make something more secure, or to secure it in a more convenient position. In square-rigged ships, the order to trice up was to lift the *studdingsail boom-ends so that the *topmen could move out on the *yards in order to *reef or *furl the sail.

TRICK, the usual name given to the spell of duty allotted to a helmsman at the wheel. In general, the degree of concentration required to steer a ship on a steady *course in large ships limits the time of each trick to half an hour, though in smaller vessels this may vary according to the size of the crew, and a regular trick at the wheel may be as much as an hour. Automation in large vessels has today taken much of the burden of steering off the shoulders of helmsmen, a ship being automatically held on her course by gyroscopic control, except in narrow or congested waters where human control is essential.

TRIDENT, a three-pronged spear or sceptre, an attribute of the sea god *Poseidon or *Neptune. From this origin it has come to be accepted as a symbol of sovereignty over the seas, and the trident borne by Britannia is the symbol of Britain's sovereignty over the seas which surround her.

TRIESTE, an Italian seaport in the north-eastern corner of the Adriatic Sea. Originally the Roman outpost of Tergeste, ownership of the port passed through many hands until 1203, when it was captured by Venice. A series of conflicts with Venice ended in 1382 when Trieste put itself under the protection of Leopold III of Austria. This protection developed naturally over the years into possession, and except for two short periods (1797–1805 and 1809–13) during the Revolutionary and Napoleonic wars, Trieste remained as part of the Austrian empire, becoming its principal seaport and a main base of the Austrian Navy, subsidiary in this respect only to Pola (Pula). After the First World War (1914–18) it became for a time a free city and port until annexed by Italy. A similar attempt to make it a free city after the Second World War was a failure and it again became Italian. It has an extensive *dockyard and shipbuilding facilities, and a spacious area of docks, through which a flourishing trade flows. There is also in Trieste a famous natural history museum which contains examples of the fauna of the Adriatic Sea.

TRIM, the way in which a ship floats on the water, in relation to her fore-and-aft line, whether on an even *keel or down *by the head or by the stern. Most ships of any size have trimming tanks built into them, by which the vessel's trim can be adjusted as required by admitting or pumping out seawater acting as fore-and-aft *ballast. See also DRAG.

TRIM, to, (1) the act of flooding or emptying trimming tanks, known in a *submarine as auxiliary *ballast tanks, in order to adjust the *trim of a vessel so as to bring her to the required fore-and-aft line of flotation. (2) The act of setting the

sails of a sailing vessel by means of the * sheets in
fore-and-aft rig, or the * yards by means of the
* braces in square-rigged vessels, so that they lie
at the best angle to the fore-and-aft line to take
the fullest advantage of the wind.

TRIMARAN, a type of vessel with a central hull
and twin floats on either side, propelled normally
by sails or mechanical power. The form is a
development of the * catamaran, a twin-hulled
vessel. Trimarans have been largely developed
during the 20th century as yachts for ocean racing and cruising. Being of light construction and
with remarkable stability, they are faster than the
single-hulled yacht for any given sail area. See
also MULTI-HULL.

TRINITY HOUSE, originally a guild of 'ship-
men and mariners' of England set up by Henry
VIII in 1517, 'to the praise and honour of the
most glorious and individable Trinity ... in the
parish church of Deptford-Strond in our county
of Kent'. Its original purpose was to do all things
necessary for the 'relief, increase and augmenta-

The Trinity House vessel Siren *with buoys on board*

tion of the shipping of this our realm of England'.
Henry's daughter, Elizabeth I, extended the
duties of the guild to the erection of * sea-marks
since 'by the destroying and taking away of certain steeples, woods, and other marks standing
upon the main shores ... being as beacons and
marks of ancient time, divers ships have been
miscarried, perished, and lost in the sea ...'
Since then the Corporation of Trinity House
has been the body responsible in England for
the erection and maintenance of * lighthouses,
* lightships, * buoys, and other aids to navigation
within the waters surrounding English shores,
and is also the licensing authority for pilots.

In 1604 the members of Trinity House were
divided into Elder and Younger Brethren, of
whom the former are responsible for the discharge of the Corporation's practical duties and
also act as nautical assessors in the High Court,
Admiralty Division. They number thirteen, of
whom eleven are elected from the merchant service and two are appointed from the Royal Navy.
From time to time, persons of distinction are
admitted as honorary Elder Brethren. Younger
Brethren have no responsibility in the discharge
of the practical duties of Trinity House, but have
a vote in the election of a master and wardens.

TRIP AN ANCHOR, to, the operation of breaking out the * flukes of a ship's * anchor if they are
caught in any obstruction on the bottom which
prevents the anchor being weighed in the normal
way. When this happens, the anchor can be
tripped by being hauled up clear of the obstruction by the anchor * buoy-rope, which is always
made fast to the * crown of the anchor. This
buoy-rope is by some erroneously called a
* tripping line.

TRIPLE EXPANSION ENGINE, a further
development of the marine * reciprocating
engine, was introduced in ships during the
decade 1870–80 by adding a third cylinder to
the two-cylinder * compound engine. The third
cylinder was introduced between the high and
low pressure cylinders of the compound engine,
and its effect was to use the available steam three
times instead of twice as in the compound engine.
The steam was led first to a high pressure cylinder, the exhaust steam from that cylinder being
led into an intermediate pressure cylinder, and
then into a low pressure cylinder before being
converted by a * condenser back into boiler feed
water. It drove three pistons connected to the
same crankshaft to add to the power transmitted
to the propeller shaft, and was made possible by
improved designs of boilers to produce higher
steam pressures.

Shortly before the introduction of the marine
* turbine, a further development of the reciprocating engine took place by the addition of a

A Roman trireme; 18th century reconstruction

fourth stage in the expansion of the steam, and quadruple expansion engines were fitted in some ships, notably the four big German *liners (*Kaiser Wilhelm der Grosse*, etc.) built between 1897 and 1902. And even after the introduction of the turbine some ships were engined on the quadruple expansion principle, using three cylinders for the first three stages and a low pressure turbine for the fourth.

TRIPP, Sir HERBERT ALKER (1883–1954), British yachtsman, was an assistant commissioner of police whose greatest enthusiasms lay in sailing. He was a keen yachtsman for most of his life and wrote three delightful books on the subject, *Shoalwater and Fairway* (1924), *Suffolk Sea Borders* (1926), and *The Solent and Southern Waters* (1928). These were illustrated by him with a wealth of charming sketches and some of his paintings, particularly those which show shipping on a misty sea or in a calm, have a strength and beauty which can rank among the minor masterpieces of marine painting.

TRIPPING LINE, a small rope made fast to the *yardarm of a *topgallant *yard in a square-rigged sailing ship when it is being unrigged of the *lifts and *braces before being *struck down on deck. Its purpose was to hold one end of the yard so that it could be canted to the perpendicular before being lowered to the deck. Similarly, a tripping line was employed when lowering (striking) a topmast, being used to hoist the mast sufficiently to take its weight off the *fid to allow it to be withdrawn before lowering.

TRIREME, a war *galley of the Mediterranean propelled by three banks of oars. It is generally supposed that the rowers sat on three different levels, a supposition supported by some evidence that the lengths of the oars differed between the 14-ft oars pulled by the *thranites*, rowers in the upper bank, the 10-ft 6-in. oars pulled by the *zygites*, rowers in the middle bank, and the 7-ft 6-in. oars pulled by the *thalamites*, rowers in the lower bank. Galleys are, however, mentioned in ancient writings, with more banks of oars than three, in fact up to seventeen banks, but this cannot refer to banks of oars on different levels, and some other method of classification must have been adopted. It has been suggested that the banks were divided horizontally rather than vertically, and perhaps stepped with the lowest bank aft, a slightly higher bank amidships, and the highest bank in the forward end of the galley.

The trireme was the warship of pre-Christian Greek times. They were armed with a long *ram and sometimes carried a few archers and soldiers for boarding. They were credited with a speed of between eight and nine *knots, though only for a short period depending on the strength and stamina of the rowers.

Although galleys remained in operation as warships in the Mediterranean until the early 18th century, the trireme as such died out as a warship around A.D. 1200 when they began to be rigged as sailing vessels with two masts and *lateen sails, oars being used only in battle to provide extra mobility. At this stage of their development they rarely had more than a single bank of oars. See also BIREME.

TRITON, a sea deity of Greece and Rome, son of *Neptune by Amphitrite, or, according to some, by Celeno or Salacia. He was powerful among the sea deities and was said to be able to calm the ocean and abate storms at pleasure. His body above the waist was that of a man, and below the waist a dolphin, but he has also been represented with the fore-feet of a horse. He is generally depicted in the act of blowing a conch, or shell. The name has also been allocated to all sea deities who are half men and half fishes.

TRIUMPH, H.M.S., a 'great ship' of 1,100 tons, built in 1561, was the first ship of the name in the English Navy. In 1588, commanded by Sir Martin *Frobisher, she fought against the Spanish *Armada. The second *Triumph*, a 2nd *rate of 921 tons and forty-two guns, was built at Deptford in 1623. This ship had a long career of sixty-five years, being finally sold out of the navy to the Office of Ordnance in 1688. Ten of the seventeen battle honours which belong to the ship's name *Triumph* were added by this second holder of the name, all of them battles of the three Anglo-Dutch wars in the 17th century. A battleship, originally laid down for the Chilean government under the name *Libertad*, was launched in January 1903 and bought for the Royal Navy in December of that year, being renamed *Triumph*. She was on the China station at the outbreak of the First World War (1914–18) and continued to serve there until the beginning of 1915, when she left for Tenedos and took part in the operations in the *Dardanelles until she was sunk by the German submarine *U.7* off Gaba Tepe in May 1915. During the Second World War the name *Triumph* was borne by a submarine, launched in 1938.

TROLLE, HERLUP (1516–65), Danish naval hero, started life as a diplomat, being highly regarded by both Christian III and his successor on the throne, Frederick II of Denmark. In 1559, with no previous naval experience, he was appointed admiral and inspector of the fleet, and so efficiently did he perform his duties that in 1563 he became admiral-in-chief. In this year he put to sea in command of a fleet of twenty-seven ships of the line, encountering off the island of Öland a superior Swedish fleet of thirty-eight ships, which he at once attacked. After two days of battle the Swedish flagship *Makalos*, the largest ship of the line in northern waters, was captured, but blew up before she could be secured. The Swedish admiral, Jacob Bagge, was captured and his fleet driven into Stockholm. Later in the year Trolle fought another action against a Swedish fleet commanded by Klas Horn, an action which was indecisive. The following year was spent in building and equipping a new Danish fleet, which sailed in 1565 and again engaged a Swedish fleet

of superior force under Klas Horn off Fehmarn. The action was severe but indecisive, both fleets retiring to repair damage. Trolle was severely wounded in this action but refused to allow the surgeon of his ship to attend to his injuries until all other wounded men had been treated. His flagship reached Copenhagen safely, but Trolle died of his wounds seventeen days later.

TROMP, CORNELIS (1629–91), was the second son of Marten *Tromp and of a different calibre from his father, being gay, impetuous, and reckless. He was born at Rotterdam and at the age of 19 commanded a squadron employed in the Mediterranean subduing the *Barbary pirates. Between 1652 and 1653 he served in a fleet in the Mediterranean under van Galen and commanded the *Maan* in action with an English fleet off *Leghorn on 13 March 1653. On returning to Holland he was promoted to rear admiral. During the Second Anglo-Dutch War (1665–7) Tromp, now a vice admiral, took part in the battle of *Lowestoft in which the Dutch were defeated by an English fleet commanded by *James, Duke of York. Tromp next served under de *Ruyter and was present at the *Four Days Battle in 1666 which resulted in a Dutch victory. However, in the St. James's Day battle of 25 July of the same year off the North Foreland, his independent action and failure to support de Ruyter resulted in a Dutch defeat and cost Tromp his command. He was not reinstated until the middle of the Third Anglo-Dutch War (1672–4) when William of Orange became Stadtholder. During his first engagement off Schoonveld in 1673 he changed ship four times and is reported to have declared 'we have enjoyed ourselves like kings', and at the battle of the *Texel, which finally removed the threat of a seaborne invasion of his country, he engaged in a fierce duel with the *Royal Prince*, flagship of Sir Edward *Spragge, but failed to capture her as he intended.

After the end of the Third Anglo-Dutch War, Tromp was dispatched on a raiding cruise of the French west coast ports, and during the following year he visited England and was created a baronet by Charles II. In 1676 he was invited to take command of the Danish fleet in that country's war against Sweden, living up to his reputation and gaining a spirited victory off Öland. He died shortly after being appointed to command a Dutch fleet against the French.

TROMP, MARTEN HARPERTSZOON (1597–1653), Dutch admiral, was one of the Netherlands' most outstanding seamen, renowned for his skill and courage. Born at Den Briel, near Rotterdam, he went to sea at an early age with his father, Captain van der Tromp, and was present at Jacob van *Heemskerk's action in

*Gibraltar Bay on 25 April 1607. Two years later he was taken prisoner in an engagement with an English privateer in which his father was killed, and was held as a slave in North Africa. He escaped three years later, and for the next three years was engaged on the suppression of piracy in the Mediterranean. In 1622 he joined the navy as a lieutenant and two years later was promoted to captain. Relieved of his command a year or so later for his outspoken criticism of naval administration, he was recalled in 1637 and with the rank of lieutenant-admiral was employed in remedying the weaknesses and abuses from which the Dutch Navy was suffering. His solicitude for the officers and men earned him the name of 'Father' Tromp. On 18 September 1637, with a much inferior fleet, he forced a Spanish one under Don Oquendo to seek refuge in the *Downs until reinforcements arrived enabling him to defeat it.

On the outbreak of the First Anglo-Dutch War (1652–4), attributed in part to a misunderstanding between him and Robert *Blake over the salute due to English ships in their own waters, he was worsted in the skirmish off Dover on 19 May but in August, returning to look for his opponent, he heard that Blake was busy attacking the Dutch herring fleet in the North Sea. After a fruitless search, he returned home and was relieved of his command. However, after the defeat of the Dutch off the *Kentish Knock on 28 September, he was reinstated and while escorting a convoy down Channel, defeated Blake off Dungeness on 30 November. This victory gave rise to the unsubstantiated story of Tromp hoisting a broom to his masthead. Having escorted his convoy into the Bay of Biscay, he was returning with one homeward bound when, on 18 February 1653, off *Portland, he encountered an English fleet under Blake, William *Penn, and George *Monck. In a battle which lasted three days, Tromp was heavily defeated. Although thirsting for revenge, it was not until 2 June when, with a fleet of 98 ships, he encountered an English one of 100 ships under Monck and Richard *Deane off the North Foreland, that the opportunity occurred. Shortage of powder and shot, however, led to another defeat of the Dutch fleet. A blockade of Dutch ports by the English fleet followed, but on 24 July Tromp emerged from the Maas with eighty ships and by skilful tactics avoided action until joined by a fleet of twenty-five ships under de *With from the *Texel. A short, bloody, and decisive battle took place on 31 July against the English fleet under Monck, in which the Dutch were again defeated. Tromp was mortally wounded during the fight. He was given a state funeral and was buried in the Oudkerk at Delft, where a marble monument depicting his last fight was erected over his grave.

TROOPSHIP, a vessel used for the transport of troops, either operationally in wartime or for garrison duties in peacetime. Until the late 19th century they were naval vessels, often specially built, but later were liners hired from the major shipping lines for the purpose. See, e.g., QUEEN MARY, R.M.S; QUEEN ELIZABETH, R.M.S. Today almost all trooping in peacetime is done by aircraft.

TROPICAL STORMS, intense storms which occur in tropical and sub-tropical *latitudes in all oceans except the South Atlantic. They never occur on the equator itself, and very rarely within about eight degrees of the equator. They consist of fairly small but intense *depressions around which the wind circulates anti-clockwise in the northern hemisphere and clockwise in the southern, the normal directions for depressions in the two hemispheres, frequently at hurricane strength (64 knots and over on the *Beaufort Scale). This wind always causes very heavy seas, with torrential rain and driven spray reducing the visibility almost to nothing. Like all other depressions their rate of advance can be anything up to about 25 knots and in the same way there is an area of calm in the centre or eye of the storm. Because of their extreme intensity, with the area of storm concentrated in a small area, they can be immensely destructive. Their position can be estimated, as with all other depressions, by the application of *Buys Ballot Law.

The season for tropical storms in the northern hemisphere is June to November, with maximum frequency in August and September; in the southern hemisphere the normal season is from December to May, with February and March being the months of maximum frequency. An

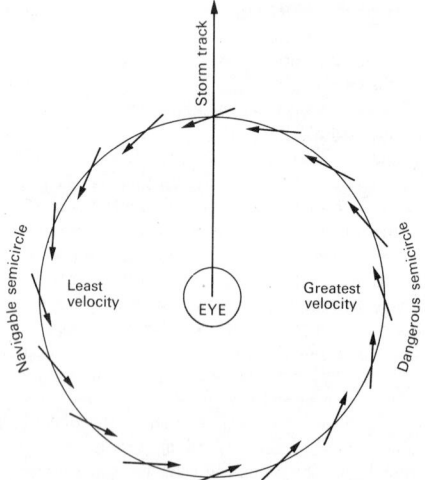

Tropical storm, northern hemisphere

exception to this general rule is the Arabian Sea, where tropical storms normally occur at the times of change of the monsoon, May and June, and October and November.

Tropical storms have different names in different oceans. They are known as hurricanes in the western North Atlantic, eastern North Pacific, and western South Pacific; as cyclones in the Arabian Sea, Bay of Bengal, south Indian Ocean, and in the vicinity of North-West Australia; and as typhoons in the western North Pacific. See also METEOROLOGY.

TROT, a multiple * mooring for small boats or yachts. The base mooring is laid in a straight line and from it individual moorings rise at intervals spaced to allow the boats room to swing with the tide. Trot moorings save considerable space in harbours, marinas, and congested anchorages, and are also more economical in * ground tackle.

Small vessels secured alongside each other are also said to be moored in a trot.

TROUBRIDGE, Sir THOMAS (1758–1807), British rear admiral, was one of Lord * Nelson's 'band of brothers' and greatly distinguished himself during the Revolutionary (1793–1801) and Napoleonic (1803–15) wars against France. Born in London, he entered the navy in 1773 and, together with Nelson, served in the East Indies in the * frigate *Seahorse*. In 1785 he returned to England in the *Sultan* as flag-captain to Admiral Sir Edward * Hughes. Appointed to command the frigate *Castor* in May 1794, he and his ship were captured by the French while escorting a * convoy, but he was liberated soon afterwards. On his return he was appointed to command the *Culloden*, a 3rd * rate * ship of the line, in which he led the line at the battle of * Cape St. Vincent, being commended for his courage and initiative by Admiral Sir John * Jervis. Subsequently he took part under Nelson's command in the abortive assault on Santa Cruz and, later, in the battle of the * Nile, in which the *Culloden* unfortunately grounded on a shoal near the entrance to Aboukir Bay. At Nelson's request, however, he was awarded the gold medal commemorating the victory. He was a Lord Commissioner of the Admiralty from 1801 to 1804 in which year he was promoted rear admiral, and a year later was appointed to command the eastern half of the East Indies Station. He hoisted his flag in the *Blenheim*, but on arrival the area of his command was changed to that of the Cape station. While on passage to take up this new appointment his ship was lost with all hands during a cyclone.

TRUCK, (1) a circular wooden cap fitted to the top of a vessel's mast and often furnished with one or two small sheaves through which are rove

signal * halyards for the hoisting of distinguishing flags, battle ensigns, commissioning pendants, etc. **(2)** Spherical pieces of wood with a hole drilled through the centre through which is rove the rope of the * parrel in the days when parrels were used in square-rigged ships to hold the yards close to the mast. Their purpose was to give more ease of movement to the yards when they were * braced to the wind. Similarly, the wooden balls which are threaded on the jaw-rope of a * gaff, and which serve to ease the gaff up and down the mast when the sail is hoisted or lowered, are also known as trucks. **(3)** The wooden wheels of the carriages on which the guns of a warship were mounted during the days of the sailing navies were also known as the trucks of the carriage.

TRUE, the direction of the North pole from any place on the earth's surface, or of any * course or * bearing in its relation to the North pole. The true direction of the North pole is an important function of all navigation, since all marine charts are drawn with their meridians of longitude passing through this pole, and as a result all courses and bearings laid down on the chart for navigational purposes must also relate to this pole.

There is, however, another north pole, known as the north magnetic pole, and it is to this pole, which is constantly changing its position, that a magnetic * compass points. Therefore, when using a magnetic compass for navigation, a correction must always be applied to any reading of the compass, whether it be a course or bearing, to relate it to the true North pole before it can be laid down on a chart. This difference is known as * variation, and since the position of the magnetic pole is constantly changing, so also does the amount of variation to be applied as a correction. See also DEVIATION.

TRUNDLE-HEAD, an old term which was applied to the lower drumhead of a * capstan when it was double and worked, through a single shaft, on an upper and lower deck. It is also sometimes used today to describe that part of a capstan which contains the holes in which the squared ends of the capstan bars are inserted, of which the correct name is the capstan head.

TRUSS, originally the * parrel of a * yard which bound it to its mast in a square-rigged ship, but the introduction of a metal goose-neck which centred and secured the yard well free of the mast made the original truss obsolete and itself took on the name of truss. It is hinged to allow both vertical and horizontal movement of the yard.

'TRUST-TO-GODS', a slang name used by seamen in sail to describe the small, light sails set above the *royals in square-rigged ships in the light winds. They were also sometimes known as 'Hope-in-Heavens'.

TRUXTON, THOMAS (1755–1822), American naval officer, was born at Jamaica, Long Island. He went to sea at the age of 12 and in 1771 was impressed into the British Navy, serving for a few months in H.M.S. *Prudent.* During the War of American Independence (1775–82) he commanded a number of *privateers, of which the *Independence* (1776), *Mars* (1777), and *St. James* (1781) are the best known and in which he had many successes against British trade. After the end of the war he continued his earlier career as a merchant captain, trading successfully as far afield as China.

When in 1794 the U.S. Congress authorized the building of the *'six original frigates', which were to become the foundation of the U.S. Navy, Truxton was the last of the six captains selected to command them, and was appointed to superintend the construction of the 36-gun *frigate *Constellation* at Baltimore. She was completed in 1798 and went to sea with Truxton in command and with John *Rodgers as his executive officer. It was the period of the 'Quasi War' with France and in February 1799 he had the distinction of capturing the French frigate *L'Insurgente* in a notable action. A year later he fought a night action against the 40-gun *La Vengeance*, but was unable to capture her when his mainmast went by the board. After the war Truxton was offered the command of a squadron of four frigates to be sent into the Mediterranean in 1802 for operations against the *Barbary pirates, but after a difference with the authorities over the appointment of a flag-captain to his ship, he sent in his resignation.

TRY, to, and old word used by seamen, but rarely found today, to describe the attempt by a sailing vessel during a severe storm to remain in the trough or hollow of the waves by reducing sail to a *mizen *topsail or *trysail, or even lying under *bare poles, although some sail was always preferable in order to hold the ship steady and prevent excessive rolling. Trying was virtually the same as *lying-to, except that slightly more forward motion was required to try to keep the vessel moving at the same rate as the sea.

TRY WORKS, the name given to the iron pots set in brickwork and used in older days for boiling the oil out of the blubber of whales. In the old *whaling days these would normally be set up either on the deck of a *whaler if out at sea or on shore if a suitable operating base was available. The process was called 'trying out' the oil. Today, the same process is done by more sophisticated methods on board a *whale factory ship.

TRYON, Sir GEORGE (1832–93), British vice admiral, is remembered chiefly for his tactical signal when commander-in-chief of the Mediterranean Fleet in 1893, by which he attempted to reverse the course of the fleet by turning the two lines inwards in succession, a manoeuvre of considerable danger as the two columns were only six *cables (1,200 yards) apart. The direct result was that the two leading ships collided, Tryon's flagship, H.M.S. *Victoria*, being sunk by H.M.S. *Camperdown*, a disaster in which Tryon and 358 officers and men were drowned.

This accident, in which he lost his life, clouded a naval career of hitherto great skill and enterprise. He held a series of appointments of importance, including those of commander of the *Warrior*, the first *ironclad *battleship in the world, when she first commissioned; private secretary to the First Lord of the Admiralty; and for two years Secretary of the Admiralty. His last appointment was that of commander-in-chief of the Mediterranean Fleet, and by constant drill and exercise he transformed the fleet from a collection of individual ships into a fleet trained to act as an integral whole. He can be said to have been the first British admiral of the Victorian period to begin training the navy for war, and his reputation as a tactician was prodigious. It was on his foundations of realistic training that subsequent admirals were able to build a navy which, no more than twenty years after his death, was the most skilled and efficient in the world.

TRYSAIL, (1) a small sail, normally triangular, which is set in a sailing vessel when heaving-to in a gale of wind. In smaller single-masted sailing vessels it is set on the main *halyards; when used for this purpose in square-rigged ships, it was usually set in place of the *mizen *topsail. **(2)** Fore-and-aft sails set with a *boom and *gaff on the fore- and mainmasts of a three-masted square-rigged ship. They are the same sails as the *spencer of a *brig, and although they are correctly called trysails in a three-masted ship, they are more often known as spencers in sailing vessels with two masts to bring them in line with the brig rig. **(3)** By some, the sails better known as *spankers are called trysails.

TSUSHIMA, BATTLE OF, a naval battle fought between the Russian and Japanese fleets in the Straits of Tsushima on 27 May 1905. The Russian fleet had left the Baltic in October 1904 under the command of Admiral *Rozhestvensky, and after a long and tedious voyage round South Africa, hampered and cluttered by a host of colliers and storeships, reached Japanese waters in late May 1905. The Japanese fleet, commanded by Admiral *Togo, lay in wait for them in the Tsushima Strait, and the two fleets met shortly after noon on 27 May. Togo led his *line of battle across the direction of the Russian advance, forcing them to give way, and concentrated his gunfire on each ship in succession, using at the same time his superior speed to force the Russian line still farther away from its original line of advance. For a time the issue of the action was in doubt, the Russian ships inflicting as much damage on the Japanese fleet as they themselves were receiving, but an attempt by Rozhestvensky to cut past the Japanese rear on his original course brought about a close range engagement in which the Russian battleships suffered severely. Rozhestvensky was wounded when his flagship *Suvarov* was driven out of the line and the command of the fleet devolved upon Vice Admiral Nebogatov, who perhaps lacked the tactical skill to extricate the Russian fleet from the enveloping manoeuvres of Togo's ships. As the day drew to a close, the Russian fleet disintegrated into hopeless confusion, and after night attacks by Togo's torpedoboats and a brief engagement the following morning, almost the entire Russian fleet had been sunk or captured.

Tsushima is notable as the first major battle fought by fleets of armoured battleships, and every maritime power studied it in great detail to try to form, from its results, a viable tactical doctrine for armoured fleet warfare at sea.

TUCK, the shape of the afterbody of a ship under the *stern or *counter, where the ends of the bottom planks or plates fit into the tuck-rail or tuck plate. The *frigates built of fir for the

British Navy towards the end of the Napoleonic War (1803–15) had flat, square *transoms and were known as square-tucked frigates.

TUCKER, SAMUEL (1747–1833), American naval officer, was born in Marblehead, Mass. He served in the Royal Navy in the *sloop *Royal George*. On the outbreak of the War of American Independence (1775–82) he served for a brief period in the Continental Army, but in January 1776 George Washington commissioned him in the 'fleet' which did so much to supply the Continental Army around Boston. Initially in command of the *Franklin*, he was transferred after a few months to a more powerful vessel, the *Hancock*. He was made a captain in the *Continental Navy, and in command of the *frigate *Boston* he sailed from Massachusetts Bay in February 1778 to carry John Adams to France where he was to serve as one of the commissioners to represent the U.S.A.

In company with the *Providence, Queen of France*, and *Ranger*, the *Boston* sailed for Charleston, S.C., where all four ships were lost with the surrender of that city on 10 May 1780. Tucker was exchanged for the captain of the *Thorn*, and became captain of that vessel as a *privateer, but was again captured, this time by the frigate *Hind*, off Prince Edward Island. He and his crew were given an open boat with orders under oath to go to Halifax and surrender as prisoners. Instead, breaking his oath, Tucker took his men and the open boat to Boston.

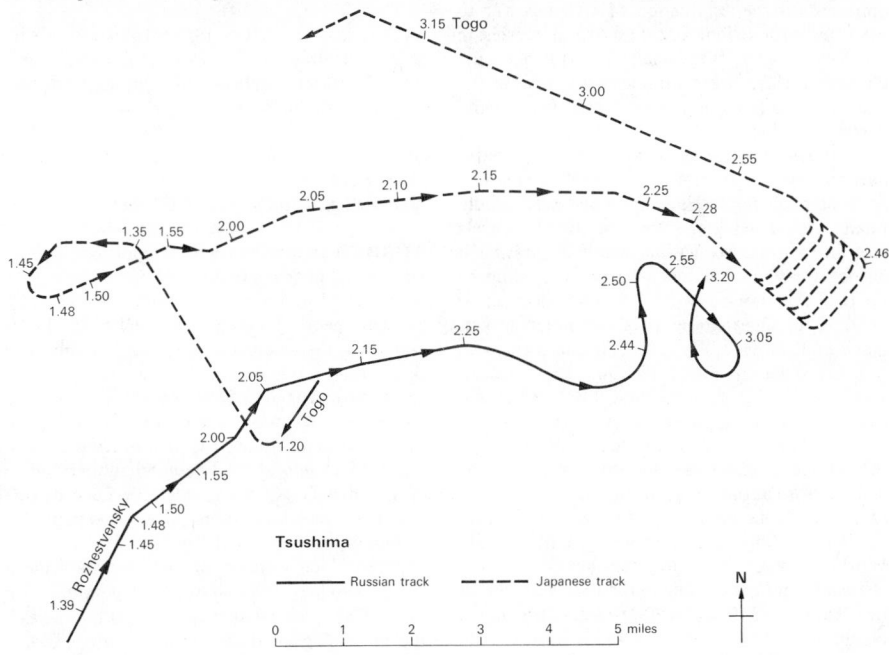

TUDGAY, the surname of a family of British marine painters of the 19th century who specialized in ship portraiture, frequently in collaboration with each other. The only member of the family of whom dates of birth and death are positively known is FREDERICK (1841–1921), and it would appear from the evidence of dated pictures that he was a younger relative of three brothers, I., J., and L. Tudgay. Their work is remarkable for the careful and exact delineation of the hull form of the ships they painted and for the meticulous accuracy of spars and rigging. Frederick Tudgay was commissioned by John Willis, shipowner of London, to paint a picture of a new ship he had ordered from John Linton, designer, and William Scott-Moncrieff, engineer, later to become famous as the *Cutty Sark*, and a copy of the original painting is exhibited on board the ship which is now preserved at *Greenwich. It was this picture by Frederick Tudgay which provided much of the evidence for the restoration of the famous ship to her original rig.

TUG, a relatively small and heavily built vessel of considerable engine power used for the towage of ships at sea or to assist in manoeuvring them in confined spaces, particularly when berthing or unberthing. They were known originally by the generic name of tug-boat, but the suffix was dropped very early on and the single word tug was in use at least by 1817, very shortly after the genesis of the type which, of course, did not appear until the application of steam power to maritime propulsion. The first steam vessels in the Royal Navy, the *Comet* and *Monkey*, purchased in 1822, were tugs used for towing the *ships of the line out of harbour when the wind was unfavourable.

Tugs generally can be divided into two groups, harbour or short-haul tugs, and oceangoing or long-haul tugs. Harbour tugs are usually fitted with a single screw or paddle-wheels (see PADDLE STEAMER), but are twin-screwed if needed for work beyond a harbour, developing up to 2,500 horsepower with a tonnage up to about 250. Oceangoing tugs are much larger, being built up to 2,000 tons *displacement with a horsepower of over 15,000. They are of specially long endurance and used either for ocean *salvage of ships disabled at sea and requiring a tow to a *dockyard for repair, or for the towage of ships, floating docks, etc., to far-distant destinations. Tugs of this kind were used to tow a large Admiralty floating dock from England to Singapore shortly before the Second World War and to bring the steamer *Great Britain* from Port Stanley in the Falkland Islands to Bristol in 1970 for restoration to her original condition.

A feature of the design of all tugs is the very pronounced overhang of the *counter. This is required to ensure that the towing *hawser, if it parts or falls slack into the water, cannot foul the tug's *propellers.

TUMBLE-HOME or **TUMBLING-HOME,** the amount by which the two sides of a ship are brought in towards the centreline after reaching their maximum beam. It is the opposite of *flare, in which the sides curve outwards. Wooden ships of the 15th to 18th centuries, and particularly wooden warships, were built with a very pronounced tumble-home, making the width of the upper deck considerably less than that of the main and lower decks. Warships had to have this tumble-home to accommodate the main and lower deck guns which were much larger than those mounted on the upper gundeck and needed more space for the gun crews to work them. An older term for tumbling-home was housing-in.

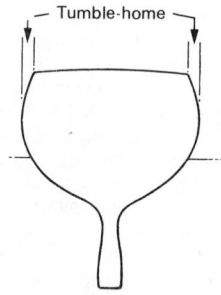

TUN, a large cask used for the transport of wine, with a capacity of two pipes, or four hogsheads, or 252 old wine gallons. In shipping terms it is the origin of the word *ton and was the normal means of measurement of the carrying capacity of a ship. The number of tuns of wine which a ship could stow in her *holds was the figure of her tunnage (*tonnage) or *burthen.

TURBINE, a marine rotary propulsion engine in which a jet of steam is directed on to blades set at an angle in a drum connected either direct or through gearing to the *propeller shaft. The action of the steam on the blades revolves the drum and by this means the drive is transmitted to the propellers. Turbine engines were invented by the Hon. Charles *Parsons in the last decade of the 19th century, and demonstrated in his small *Turbinia* at the Diamond Jubilee Review of the British Navy in 1897. Because of their simplicity and favourable power-to-weight ratio in comparison with the steam *reciprocating engines which were, until then, the only means of harnessing steam power, they were very quickly adopted by shipowners and by navies as the most efficient means of steam propulsion at sea.

TURBINIA, a yacht designed by Charles *Parsons in 1897, the first vessel in the world to be powered by steam *turbines. She was built specifically to demonstrate this new invention in marine motive power and made her first appearance at the British Naval Review held at Spithead in that year to celebrate the diamond jubilee of Queen Victoria, an international gathering of ships where she was certain to attract the maximum of attention and publicity. She produced a speed of 30 *knots, quite unheard of in those days, and her performance so impressed the various shipowners and naval authorities present that the introduction of the turbine as the motive power for ships of all sizes rapidly followed. She had three shafts, each carrying three *propellers, and each driven by a turbine.

'TURKEY', a name given by sailors in the British Navy to a member of the Royal Marine Light Infantry before their amalgamation with the Royal Marine Artillery to form the Royal Marines. The name came from the red tunics of their uniform.

TURK'S HEAD, an ornamental knot to provide a *stopper on the end of a rope. It is a continuation of a simple manrope knot by tucking the strands of the rope a second time. A running turk's head is formed by making the knot around the other part of the rope.

Turk's head

TURNBUCKLE, see BOTTLESCREW.

TURNER, JOSEPH MALLORD WILLIAM (1775–1851), British landscape artist, was born at Covent Garden, London, and studied at the Royal Academy School. He was at first a copyist and colourist, and worked as an engraver, but gradually broke away from this formal beginning and in 1792 began the first of his sketching tours, concentrating on landscapes and architectural views which he later worked up into watercolours. It was at this period that he first began to appreciate the interplay of light and space in the scenes he painted, and his first oil painting,

Self-portrait; oil painting by J. W. M. Turner, c. 1798

'Fishermen at Sea' which was exhibited in the Royal Academy in 1796, though in some ways influenced by the Dutch school of marine painting, showed a great originality in his use of atmosphere and light, and a distinct movement towards the Romantic school. This came out most strongly in his painting 'Shipwreck', exhibited in 1805 and now in the Tate Gallery, London. In the use he made of light and atmosphere, and the great luminosity which he was able to bring both to landscape and seascape, he blazed the way for the later Impressionists, and in some respects went further than they did in his leaning towards the abstract effects of light, atmosphere, and the elements.

Between 1827 and 1830 he contributed a number of drawings, which were engraved, in the series on ports of England, and his ship paintings, particularly that of H.M.S. *Temeraire being towed to her last berth, are famous. He was, as well as being the first of the Impressionists, the greatest of the English Romantics, and in many ways the greatest of all English landscape and seascape artists.

TURNER, RICHMOND KELLY (1885–1961), American admiral, successfully commanded a series of amphibious operations in the

Pacific from July 1942 to early 1945. He was born in Oregon, and graduated from the Naval Academy in 1908. After gunnery and ordnance assignments he specialized in naval aviation, and his knowledge helped him in the careful planning of his troop landings, especially in the early operations for the seizure of *Guadalcanal. At that period his force was under almost daily attacks and suffered many losses, his flagship, the *transport *McCawley*, being sunk in 1943.

Turner's middle name, Kelly, was used by his contemporaries, and he became known throughout the Pacific by that name. Always demanding high standards in his subordinates, Kelly Turner was a brilliant officer whose operations were carefully planned and well executed at all times.

TURTLE DECK, the upper deck of a vessel constructed with a pronounced curve from the centreline of the vessel down to the sides. Its purpose is to assist the flow of any seawater shipped over the bows down to the *scuppers. The early *torpedoboats and torpedoboat *destroyers all had pronounced turtle decks since, with very little *freeboard, they were apt to ship quantities of water over their bows when proceeding at speed. See also XEBEC.

TURTLE-BOAT, an American craft designed by Robert *Fulton for operations against British warships during the Anglo-American War of 1812. It was completely decked over and driven through the water by a screw *propeller worked by hand through a series of cranks inside the hull of the craft. Its weapon consisted of a number of floating charges towed astern, with their firing mechanism operated by long trigger *lanyards which were led into the turtle-boat. The method of attack was to swing the towed charges against the side of a British warship and explode them by a pull on the lanyard. With a freeboard of no more than six inches, it could be mistaken for a floating tree trunk or other object and thus, it was hoped, approach an enemy without causing suspicion. The turtle-boat was wrecked during a gale on the shores of Long Island after venturing out from New York, and was there discovered and destroyed by boats' crews from British warships before it could do any damage or its capabilities could be adequately tested.

TWICE LAID, (1) the name given to rope made from a selection of the best yarns from old rope which has been unlaid, **(2)** a sea dish made from salt fish left over from the previous day's rations and mashed up with potatoes or yams. It was not one of the most popular of dishes with seamen.

'TWO BLOCKS', a maritime term to describe a *purchase in which there is no more travel by reason of the moving *block having been hauled up to the standing block. By extension it has also come to mean a rope or wire which has been hauled to its maximum tautness. A similar term with the same meaning is 'chockablock'.

TWO YEARS BEFORE THE MAST, a classic book about the sea written by Richard Henry *Dana, Jnr., and published in 1840, in which he describes a voyage he undertook for health reasons to cure recurring eye trouble. The outward passage, from Boston to California, was made in the *brig *Pilgrim* and the return passage in the ship *Alert*. Dana served as a deckhand throughout the voyage, which lasted from August 1834 to September 1836. His book describes vividly the conditions under which American seamen served in merchant vessels in those days and did much to influence many needed reforms.

TYE, a single rope attached to the centre of the lower *yard, led through a *block on the masthead and secured to the *jeers, to transmit the pull of the jeers to the yard when it was being *swayed up to its position on the mast. They were used largely in merchant ships during the days of sail, the jeers in men-of-war having their upper blocks permanently secured to the masthead and thus not requiring a tye to transmit their power. In larger merchant ships with a very heavy lower yard, the tye was rove through a block on the yard and then led through two single blocks at the masthead, one on the forward side and one on the after side of the mast, the two falls being then secured to two jeers. The yard could then be swayed up by hauling both jeers together. Such an arrangement was necessary in the larger merchant vessels of the time since, carrying much smaller crews compared with men-of-war, they were always limited in available manpower for hoisting such heavy weights as a lower yard.

TYPHOON, see TROPICAL STORMS.

TYPHOON, the title of one of the best-known short stories of Joseph *Conrad. It was first serialized in the *Pall Mall Magazine* and published in book form under the title *Typhoon and Other Stories* in 1902. The story is regarded as a classic of sea literature and tells the story of Captain MacWhirr, who takes his ship through the eye of a typhoon because he is too unintelligent and unimaginative to heed the weather forecasts.

TYRWHITT, Sir REGINALD YORKE (1870–1951), British admiral of the fleet, was one of the most brilliant young captains in the Royal Navy during the years leading up to the First World War (1914–18), and on its outbreak was appointed to command the Harwich Force, a mixed force of light * cruisers and * destroyers based on Harwich, with the rank of * commodore. He was one of the young men selected by Admiral Sir John * Fisher, when he was First Sea Lord in 1904–10, for high command in the then coming war against Germany, and proved Fisher's judgement and confidence by the skill, courage, and initiative with which he led his force throughout the war.

Within three weeks of the declaration of war he had planned, in co-operation with Commodore Roger * Keyes, his first operation against the enemy, a raid on the German destroyer patrols which developed into the battle of the * Heligoland Bight, on 28 August 1914. In January 1915 the Harwich Force, in company with Admiral Sir David * Beatty's * battle-cruisers of the * Grand Fleet, was present at the battle of the * Dogger Bank. When the German battle-cruisers launched their bombardments of the English coast, Tyrwhitt was always ordered out with his force to attempt to cut them off and drive them north into the hands of the Grand Fleet, and on 25 April 1916 he fought a spirited action against four German battle-cruisers which had bombarded Lowestoft and prevented them from completing their planned programme with a bombardment of Yarmouth.

Although naval aviation was still in its infancy during the First World War, Tyrwhitt was one of the very few naval leaders who appreciated its potential and was the pioneer of sea–air co-operation. Under his direction a number of seaplane raids were launched on German targets ashore, in each case with the seaplanes escorted to their flying-off point by the Harwich Force and recovered at sea by them.

When information was received of the sailing of the German * High Seas Fleet on 30 May 1916 on their sortie which was to lead to the battle of * Jutland on the following day, Tyrwhitt led his force to sea from Harwich, only to be recalled by the Admiralty to counter the possibility that part of the German fleet might be detached to bombard ports in the English Channel or the Thames estuary. When at last he was permitted to sail, it was too late for him to reach the scene of the battle. At the close of the war he received the surrender of the German * U-boats, 150 of them being brought in to Harwich.

He was promoted rear admiral in 1919, vice admiral in 1925, admiral in 1929, and admiral of the fleet in 1934. His last active appointments were commander-in-chief on the China station (1927–9) and commander-in-chief at the * Nore (1930–3).

Tyrwhitt was a man of tremendous courage and a born leader at sea. His Harwich Force was recognized throughout the British fleet as the most efficient of all the detached squadrons, 'la belle force d'Harwich' as Admiral * Castex, the great French naval historian and strategist, used to call it. It spent more days at sea and suffered greater losses than any other British force during the war, but always more officers and men volunteered for service in it than the ships could accommodate.

A. Temple Patterson, *Tyrwhitt of the Harwich Force* (1973).

U

U.L.C.C., the initial letters of Ultra Large Crude Carrier, a code of letters to describe the huge oil *tankers, larger than the *V.L.C.C., currently being built. A tanker of 484,000 tons recently launched in Japan is the largest U.L.C.C. so far built, though tankers of over 500,000 tons are in the course of construction and still larger ones of up to 800,000 tons are being designed.

U.S. NAVAL ACADEMY MUSEUM, *Annapolis, Maryland, was founded in 1845 and opened in 1937. The collection is based on that presented by Henry H. Rogers and includes American and foreign ship models, yachts, *whalers, shipbuilders' models, weapons, medals, flags, paintings, and engravings. A reconstruction of the *schooner yacht *America is preserved in the Dewey Basin there.

U.S.S., United States Ship, the prefix placed before the name of a warship of the U.S. Navy.

U-BOAT, the German *unterseeboot*, or *submarine. During the Second World War the term·

was used to describe all submarines operating against the allied forces, Italian and Japanese as well as German, in contrast to the similar craft of the allies which were always called submarines. See also ATLANTIC, BATTLE OF THE; WOLF PACK.

ULLAGE, (1) the amount of wine or other liquor which has leaked from a cask, rendering the remainder of little worth and fit only to be thrown away. Damaged goods, particularly in relation to victuals, are commonly known on board ship as ullaged. **(2)** A lazy or cack-handed sailor who is of little use in a ship.

ULYSSES or **ULIXES,** see ODYSSEUS.

UMIAK, the Eskimo name for a *kayak when it is paddled by a woman. It is only a kayak when it has a male occupying the driving seat.

UNA RIG, a small sailing boat's rig consisting of a relatively large *gaff and *boom mainsail or *lugsail, set on a mast stepped very close to the boat's *stem, and carrying no headsails. This rig

A German U-boat of the Second World War

The Union-Castle liner Pendennis Castle *of 28,442 tons*

was common enough in lightly built up-river racing boats in the 19th century, and obtained its name in the United Kingdom from the $16\frac{1}{2}$-ft racing boat *Una* on which it was first tried in 1852. For generations it was the regular rig of the Cape Cod *catboats in the U.S.A.

UNDER BARE POLES, see BARE POLES.

UNDER WAY, the description of a ship which has movement through the water. The term is frequently written as under weigh. Theoretically, a ship is considered to be under weigh only when her anchor has been broken out of the bottom and she herself is still stationary in the water; she is under way as soon as she begins to move under her own power. However, the two terms have become virtually synonymous today, under weigh being a modern spelling distortion of an older term. As the *rudder of a ship is effective only when she is moving through the water, the importance of being under way is that the ship will then answer her *helm and thus becomes subject to the *rule of the road and at night must burn the correct *navigation lights.

UNDER-RUN, to, the operation of hauling a *hawser or *warp over a skiff or boat in order to clear it from an underwater obstruction. To under-run a *tackle is to separate all the moving parts so that none are crossing and the tackle is clear for use.

Under-running

UNDERWRITER, an insurer of ships and cargoes from loss and damage, the name coming from the insurer writing his name under the policy of insurance. The request for insurance is termed the offering of a 'risk', and in marine insurance the word risk is equivalent to the liability of the underwriter. Each underwriter of a marine insurance puts opposite his name the percentage of the total risk for which he accepts liability.

UNION-CASTLE LINE, a British shipping line well known for its lavender-hulled *liners on the Cape Town mail service, which was formed by the amalgamation of the Union Steam Ship Co. and the Castle Line of steamers in 1900.

The Union was the older company and had inaugurated the Cape Town mail service with the 530-ton steamer *Dane* in 1857; its leading spirit at the start had been Arthur Anderson, a founder of the * P & O Line. In 1872 Donald * Currie, a former employee of * Cunard who had built up a line of sailing ships with 'Castle' names trading around the Cape to the East, was asked by Cape merchants to provide competition for the Union Line; this he did with steamships and in 1876 a new mail contract was shared equally between the two lines, each providing alternate sailings for a weekly service. On the merger of the two in 1900 all ships took over the Castle Line colours in which they can still be seen. The Union-Castle Mail Steamship Co. was acquired by Owen Philipps in 1912 for his Royal Mail Shipping Group, but after the Group's collapse in 1931 became independent once more; in 1956 the Company merged with Clan Line to form the British & Commonwealth Shipping Group.

UNITED STATES, U.S.S., was one of the * 'six original frigates', and was built at Philadelphia and completed in 1798. She was the flagship of the senior officer afloat, John * Barry, during the naval war with France, and under the command of Stephen * Decatur, she captured the British * frigate *Macedonian* on 25 October 1812. She then served as flagship in the Mediterranean several times following the conclusion of peace in 1814. At the outbreak of the American Civil War (1861–5) the *United States*, then in poor repair, was out of commission at the Norfolk Yard, and after the evacuation of Norfolk by the Union Navy the Confederates acquired her and used her as a * receiving ship. When the Confederates evacuated the yard in 1862 they burned her.

The name *United States* has twice been assigned again in the U.S. Navy, first to a contemplated * battle-cruiser and later to a planned * aircraft carrier, but neither ship was built.

UNIVERSAL RULE, an international agreement on rating and construction introduced for racing yachts in 1923, under which a new method of measurement was laid down for certain classes of yachts designed for international racing, e.g., 23-metre (75 ft), 15-metre (49 ft), 12-metre (39 ft), etc. This new rule allowed designers to adopt certain variations in waterline length, beam, draught, etc., within each rate, the final measurement calculations equalling the rate. The purpose of the rule was to give individual yacht designers some scope to demonstrate their designing skills. The Universal Rule was superseded by the International Yacht Racing Union rating rules when that body was formed. See also OCEAN RATING COUNCIL, RATING, and YACHTING, Racing rules.

'UNREEVE HIS LIFELINE', to, a nautical expression to indicate a man who has died. It is used almost entirely in the past tense, 'Poor fellow, he's unrove his lifeline', 'Poor chap, he has died'.

UP AND DOWN, the situation of the * cable when it has been hove in sufficiently to bring the bows of the ship directly over her * anchor.

'UP FUNNEL, DOWN SCREW', the order given in British naval ships during the early days of steam propulsion when it was decided to furl the sails of a ship and proceed on the engine. In those early days, when no ship could carry on board enough fuel to work her engine for the whole of a passage, the engine was used only as an auxiliary means of propulsion when the wind failed. At the order, the boiler funnel was rigged on deck and the * propeller or screw lowered in its well until it was clear of the * hull and could be coupled to the engine shaft. For more detail of the operation, see BANJO.

UP HELLY AA, the name given to a festival which takes place annually on the last Friday in January at Lerwick, the capital of the Shetland Islands. It includes a torchlight procession in which a full-sized replica of a Viking * longship is carried by men dressed as Viking warriors. On the conclusion of the festival the boat is burned. The origin of the festival is not known but is clearly linked with ancient Norse customs.

UPHROE or **EUPHROE, (1)** from the Dutch *juffrouw*, maiden, the name given to a crowfoot * deadeye, a number of small lines spreading from a long wooden block and used to suspend an * awning when spread over a deck. It was applicable only to vessels with two or more masts, the uphroe being secured between two masts and the lines supporting the ridge of the awning. Why the Dutch word for maiden should provide the origin of this term is obscure, but there is no doubt that the Dutch word for deadeye is *juffer* or *juffrouw*. **(2)** Large mast timbers specially imported from Norway for use in the largest ships. The term dates from the 17th century, when the sizes of ships built, both for trade and war purposes, increased significantly. The word was used in Norway to describe a fir pole.

UPPER DECK, the highest of the continuous * decks which run the full length of a ship without a fall or interruption. It is the deck next above the main deck in those ships which have more than a single deck. In some very large passenger * liners, the decks are numbered, or designated by letters, instead of having names.

URCA, (1) a type of 16th century ship similar to a *galleon in rig but usually smaller and more lightly armed and used to carry military stores from place to place. The name was Spanish, and it was the Spanish by whom urcas were chiefly used in the Mediterranean. **(2)** A type of Spanish *fly-boat of the 17th and 18th centuries, flat-bottomed with a high *stern and wide *buttocks, of up to about 300 tons in size and armed with half a dozen or so guns according to size. Their *rig varied from square to *lateen according to individual taste. Though mainly designed for and used for the carriage of coastal trade, some were attached to the main fighting fleets for service as dispatch boats.

USHANT (Fr. Île d'Ouessant), an island lying off the north-western coast of France, about 40 miles west-north-west of Brest, and thus the most westerly point of France. It divides the entrance to the English Channel from the Bay of Biscay and was, especially in the days of sail, an important landmark for ships heading out of the English Channel to the south-west, whether bound for the Mediterranean, the West Indies, the Cape of Good Hope, or Cape Horn. It gave its name to a naval battle of the War of the Austrian Succession which was fought on 14 October 1747 about 200 miles west by south of Ushant between a British fleet commanded by Rear Admiral Sir Edward *Hawke with fourteen *ships of the line, against a French fleet under

the command of Commodore the Marquis de l'Etanduère which was escorting a large French *convoy. This convoy had been assembling for some weeks previously for the West Indies, and at the time of sailing comprised 252 vessels, escorted by nine ships of the line and some *frigates. Hawke had left Plymouth on 9 August to join the Western Squadron, but it was not until 7.00 a.m. on 14 October that he sighted his quarry. Etanduère ordered the merchantmen to make the best of their way under the care of one of his large ships and several frigates, while with the remaining eight ships of the escort he prepared to give battle.

At 10.00 a.m., Hawke made the signal for the *line of battle; but an hour later, finding that valuable time was being lost, he substituted for it that for a *general chase, and at 11.30 a.m. the leading British ships were in action, a running fight ensuing. The French fought well but were crushed by sheer weight of numbers, and by the evening six ships had been captured. In view of the mauled condition of the British ships, the convoy was not pursued; but the *Weazle*, four-teen guns, was victualled and dispatched to the West Indies to warn Commodore George Pocock of its approach, and thirty-eight vessels were ultimately captured.

A second battle between British and French fleets was fought off Ushant in July 1778. This was the action which led to the notorious courts martial of Admirals *Keppel and *Palliser.

V

V.L.C.C., the short title by which giant oil *tankers are generally known. It is taken from the initial letters of Very Large Crude Carrier.

VAIL, to, an old seafaring word meaning to lower sails in token of submission or salute. A foreign warship meeting another in her own territorial waters would lower, or vail, her *topgallants as a salute and acknowledgement that ownership of the waters through which she was sailing was represented by the other ship. A merchant ship would similarly vail her *topsails. See also SALUTES AT SEA.

VAKKA, a type of large canoe with an *outrigger, and paddled by several men, found in the Friendly Islands.

VALE, to, an old seafaring term for a ship dropping down a river before starting on a sea voyage. Thus a ship which had loaded a cargo in London would vale down the River Thames to the buoy of the *Nore before taking her departure for a sea voyage. The word probably takes its derivation in this sense from *vale*, farewell.

VALKYRIE, the name of three racing yachts owned by the Earl of Dunraven. The second of these, *Valkyrie II*, was a *cutter yacht designed by G. L. *Watson and built by Henderson in 1893 for a challenge for the *America's Cup that year. Of *composite construction, she had a *displacement of 93·6 tons and spread 10,270 sq ft of sail. Having returned from her unsuccessful attempt on the *America's Cup she was rammed and sunk in 1904 off the Holy Loch by the *Satanita*, another famous racing yacht, which had her bows stove in, during a race on the Clyde. She was followed by *Valkyrie III*, a slightly larger cutter yacht of 101·5 tons displacement with a sail area of 13,030 sq ft, designed by G. L. Watson in 1895 for Lord

Dunraven's second challenge for the *America*'s Cup. In the Cup series the *Defender*, the American 124-ft cutter, won the first two races and at the third *Valkyrie III* withdrew on crossing the starting line as a *protest. These races gave rise to accusations and much acrimony on both sides, Lord Dunraven accusing C. O. Iselin, co-owner of the *Defender*, of having taken on board extra *ballast during the night before the race. A long investigation could find no evidence of extra ballast being taken on board and Iselin and the crew of the *Defender* were completely exonerated.

VALLETTA, the capital city of the island of *Malta. It has one of the finest and best known natural harbours in the world, and was in early times used extensively by a variety of piratical nations as a base from which to attack Mediterranean seaborne trade. In the 16th century it became the headquarters of the Knights of St. John, and under their occupancy withstood a famous siege by the Turks. In 1798 it was captured from the Knights by Napoleon when on his way to Egypt, and two years later was taken by the British, whose colonial possession it became at the end of the Napoleonic War (1803–15). It was, because of its controlling position in the central Mediterranean, a natural base of considerable strategic value for the British Mediterranean Fleet, and was further fortified and developed to that end, with an extensive naval *dockyard built on the shores of two creeks in the Grand Harbour. During the Second World War it was extensively attacked from the air and huge damage done to the city and all the harbour works. Since that war Malta has become an independent nation, and the great harbour and dockyard is now mainly used for trade purposes and ship repairing.

VALPARAISO, the major seaport of Chile and the largest port on the South American Pacific coast, was founded in 1536 by the Spaniard Juan de Saavedra, and named after his birthplace in Spain; but the name (Valley of Paradise) is hardly appropriate either to the barren hills which surround the city on its landward side, much of the existing city itself, or the polluted waters of the harbour. It has had a stormy history, having been sacked and held to ransom by Sir Francis *Drake in 1578, Sir Richard *Hawkins in 1596, and by Olivier van *Noort in 1600. It was bombarded by a Spanish fleet in 1866 when much of the town was laid in ruins, and in 1891 was sacked by the Chileans themselves after the failure of an internal revolution. Serious earthquakes caused much damage in 1730, 1822, 1839, 1873, and 1906.

The port is a terminal and port of call for a number of steamship lines and is also the main operational base of the Chilean Navy.

VAN, the division of a *fleet of warships which leads the *line of battle. The word was originally *vant*, a corruption of the French *avant*, in front. As the usual mêlée in which ships fought each other regardless of any attempt at formation began to be replaced in the 17th century, the maritime nations organized their war fleets into three divisions, van, centre, and rear, the ships of each division flying a flag of the same colour so that it was easy in battle to recognize in which division a ship belonged. In the English Navy, ships of the van division flew the *White Ensign, ships of the centre division the *Red Ensign, and ships of the rear division the *Blue Ensign. See also SQUADRONAL COLOURS.

VAN DE STADT, ERICUS G. (1910–), Dutch yacht designer and builder, pioneered a form of lightweight hull for small class racers and offshore racing yachts, and is the designer and builder of numerous fast cruiser/racer yachts built in wood, glass reinforced plastic, and other materials. He was co-designer with Laurent *Giles of *Stormvogel*, a 73-ft (22 m) ocean-racing *ketch of 64 tons, which won the 1961 Fastnet race and other offshore events.

VAN DE VELDE, WILLEM, see VELDE, Willem van de.

VAN LOON, HENDRICK WILLEM (1882–1944), Dutch-American author, was born in Holland but emigrated to the U.S.A. where he was educated and graduated from Cornell University in 1905. In 1921 he obtained a Ph.D. at Munich while continuing to work as a journalist and author. In 1915 his third book, *The Golden Book of Dutch Navigators*, was published and this was followed in 1918 by *A Short History of Discovery*, which was well received. Among his later publications are *Van Loon's Geography* (1932) and *Ships and how they sailed the Seven Seas* (1935).

VANCOUVER, a city and seaport on the western coast of Canada, in the province of British Columbia. The city, named after George *Vancouver who made an extensive survey of Vancouver Sound in 1792, was established in 1880 on the mainland, on the southern side of Burrard Inlet. It was completely destroyed by fire in 1886 but was subsequently rebuilt, the original wooden buildings being replaced by stone and brick structures mainly designed in noble style to make the city worthy of its beautiful setting. Vancouver is the centre of the timber industry of British Columbia and is the chief Canadian port for trade with Japan, China, and Australia and carries on an extensive coastal trade with Alaska and the Yukon to the north and the U.S.A. to the south. Vancouver harbour

Lord Dunraven's yacht Valkyrie II; *lithograph by Currier and Ives*

is one of the finest natural harbours in the world, and the city is the home of a maritime museum at which, among many other notable exhibits, is preserved the auxiliary *schooner *St. Roch, the first vessel to navigate, in 1940–2, the *North-West passage in both directions.

VANCOUVER, GEORGE (1758–98), English navigator and explorer, began his career in the Royal Navy as a *midshipman when he served under Captain James *Cook in his second (1772–4) and third (1776–80) voyages of discovery. He subsequently served in the West Indies, taking part in Lord *Rodney's great victory over the French in the battle of the *Saints in 1782.

In 1791 Vancouver was appointed to command an expedition of discovery on the northwest coast of America and, on 1 April, he sailed in H.M.S. *Discovery, a new ship of 530 tons, accompanied by the Chatham of 135 tons commanded by Lieutenant Broughton. Proceeding by way of the Cape of Good Hope and the southwest coast of Australia, where he discovered and surveyed King George Sound, he continued on to Dusky Bay, New Zealand, which he was the first to explore and survey, and arrived at Tahiti on 30 December. The Chatham, which had lost touch in thick weather, rejoined there, having discovered Chatham Island en route.

After a stay of three weeks at Tahiti and a month at the Hawaiian Islands, the expedition sailed on to sight the Californian coast near Cape Mendocino on 18 April 1792 when the ships coasted northwards until reaching Juan de Fuca Strait. Passing through it, Vancouver entered and surveyed the island-studded sound beyond, a deep inlet of which he named Puget Sound after Lieutenant Peter Puget of the Discovery. Continuing his survey using the ships' boats, Vancouver discovered the insularity of the island that bears his name and, after extricating the Discovery when she grounded on submerged rocks at the northern end, he sailed down the west coast of the island to Nootka Sound where, in accordance with his instructions, he accepted the cession of the territory by the Spanish who had occupied it since 1789.

After the mid-winter months had been spent at Hawaii again, exploration of the American coast was resumed in April 1793, the stretch between 35° N. and 56° N. being surveyed before the end of the year. During Vancouver's third stay in Hawaii in January 1794, the Polynesian King Kamehameha formally ceded the island of Hawaii to the King of Great Britain; Vancouver accepted this, but the annexation appears never to have been officially ratified.

In March 1794, the Discovery and Chatham, having completed a survey of the other islands of the Hawaiian group, sailed north again to survey Cook's Inlet and Prince William Sound in Alaska, proving that the former was not a river estuary as had been surmised. Further surveys southwards down the coast were made to connect with the work of the preceding year, after which the expedition steered for home via Cape Horn, visiting Monterey for the second time, and Valparaiso, where it was necessary to stay from 25 March to 7 May 1795 to make repairs to the mainmast of the Discovery. Both ships finally reached the Thames in October 1795.

Though Vancouver lacked Cook's humanity and acquired a reputation for harsh and even brutal disciplinary methods, he was otherwise a worthy disciple of the great navigator. His surveys were of a very high standard; and though there was one short outbreak of *scurvy during the voyage, the expedition lost only six men, all killed in accidents, during the four years and nine months of its voyage.

B. Anderson, Surveyor of the Sea (Toronto, 1960).

VANDERBILT, HAROLD STIRLING (1884–1970), American businessman, author, and yachtsman, became a prominent figure in yacht racing and cruising circles around New York. He was at one time *commodore of the *New York Yacht Club, and a member of the Cruising Club of America and the Seawanhaka Corinthian, successfully defending the *America's Cup on three occasions, when he skippered Enterprise in 1930, Rainbow in 1934, and Ranger in the 1937 series. He was associated with William Kissam Vanderbilt, the railroad magnate, in the foundation of the Vanderbilt Marine Museum at Huntington, Long Island. Among the yachts he owned were Vara, 356-ton motor yacht, Vagrant, Prestige, and Ranger. He was the author of Enterprise, The Story of the Defence of the America's Cup (1931) as well as books on contract bridge.

VANE, (1) a narrow *pendant or strip of bunting mounted on a spindle and flown at the masthead of a sailing vessel to indicate to the helmsman the direction of the wind. In modern yachts the place of a vane is usually taken by the club *burgee or a racing flag, one of which is normally hoisted at the masthead when the yacht is under way. In square-rigged ships, where the helmsman was unable to see the mastheads because of the canvas spread, a small vane, known as a dog-vane, was attached to a pike and placed on the *weather side of the *quarterdeck so that he could judge the direction of the wind. The dog-vane usually consisted of thin strips of cork strung on a piece of twine and sometimes stuck round with feathers. (2) The sights of a *cross-staff, *back-staff, *quadrant, etc., by means of which *altitudes were measured, were also known as vanes.

VANE SELF-STEERING GEAR, a method by which the wind, acting on a rotatable * vane connected by linkage to a * rudder, can be set to steer a small sailing yacht on a given course. This principle of wind-vane operated gear was introduced about 1924 to enable model racing yachts to be controllable while running down wind. Known as the Braine gear, after the name of its inventor, it proved highly effective, and in the model-yacht-racing world quickly superseded the older hit-and-miss contrivances then in use with weights and springs.

When applied first to full-sized yachts about 1948, the gear comprised an upright metal or hardboard vane, like a small sail, mounted on a freely turning swivel plate. With the vane adjusted like a weathercock to the wind relative to the desired course, and connected by means of rods and linkage to a servo-tab on the yacht's rudder, or to a separate small rudder mounted right aft, the yacht is made to keep her course whether * close-hauled, or with wind abeam, or with a following wind.

These self-steering gears, which are manufactured in a variety of types and sizes, have been widely used in the long voyages offshore, the circumnavigations with minimal crews, and the solo voyages and ocean races of recent years.

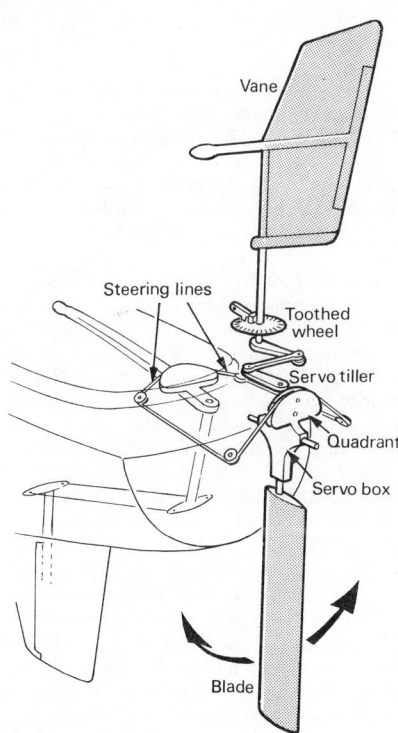

Vane
Steering lines
Toothed wheel
Servo tiller
Quadrant
Servo box
Blade

Vane self-steering gear of pendulum-servo type

VANGS, the ropes leading from the outer end of a * gaff of a * fore-and-aft sail to the rail of sailing vessels, one on each side, to steady the gaff and prevent the sail from sagging away to * leeward when sailing * close-hauled or * off the wind. They were used in square-rigged ships on the gaff of the * mizen, from which mast a gaff sail, known as a * spanker, was normally spread. The * sprit mainsail of * barges are also fitted with vangs. The * kicking-strap on the boom of a yacht is also often known as a vang.

VANGUARD, H.M.S., a ship's name used nine times in the British Royal Navy. The name dates back to 1586 when a * galleon-type ship of thirty-two guns was launched at Woolwich and given the name. She played a significant part in the campaign of the Spanish * Armada in 1588, was present at the taking of Fort Crozon, near Brest, in 1594, when she flew the flag of Martin * Frobisher, and of * Cadiz in 1596, when she was commanded by Sir Robert * Mansell, and was in Mansell's fleet, flying the flag of Sir Richard * Hawkins, in the operations against the Algerine pirates in 1620. She was twice taken to pieces and rebuilt, but reached the end of her useful life in 1630 after having taken part in the Duke of Buckingham's abortive attack on La Rochelle in 1627.

The second *Vanguard,* a ship of fifty-six guns with a complement of 390 men, was launched in 1631. She took part in most of the battles of the First (1652–4) and Second (1665–7) Dutch wars, numbering among her battle honours those of the * Kentish Knock and Dungeness in 1652, * Portland and the * Gabbard, as the flagship of George * Monck, one of the * generals-at-sea, and the * Texel in 1653 in the first war; and * Lowestoft in 1665, the * Four Days Battle and St. James's Day battle in 1666, in the second. She was scuttled in the River Medway at Chatham in 1667 to form a barrier to the Dutch fleet when Admiral de * Ruyter entered the river to burn and capture British ships.

The third *Vanguard,* a three-* decker of ninety guns, was built at Portsmouth under a reconstitution of the navy engineered by Samuel * Pepys and launched in 1678. She was in Edward * Russell's fleet at the battle of * Barfleur and its subsequent action when the French ships were burned at La Hogue in 1692. She was wrecked in the great gale of November 1703 but refloated and brought to Chatham, where she lay, neglected and rotting. The fourth ship of the name was a 3rd rate * ship of the line. She was with Admiral * Boscawen at the capture of * Louisburg, in Canada, in 1758, with Admiral * Saunders at the capture of * Quebec in 1759, and with Sir George * Rodney at the capture of Martinique in 1762. She was finally sold in 1774.

The fifth *Vanguard,* a 3rd rate of seventy-four

guns, was built at Deptford in 1787 and was Lord *Nelson's flagship at the battle of the *Nile in 1798. The seventh was a *battleship of 6,010 tons, launched in 1869 and lost during manoeuvres in the Irish Sea in 1875 when she was accidentally rammed by her sister ship, the *Iron Duke*. The eighth ship of the name was also a battleship, a *dreadnought of 19,250 tons launched in 1910. She was present at the battle of *Jutland in 1916 but in the following year blew up at *Scapa Flow when one of her *magazines overheated. The ninth ship of the name was also a battleship, completed shortly after the Second World War. She was broken up in 1960, and was the last battleship to serve in the British Navy.

VARENIUS, BERNHARDUS (1622–50), German geographer, was trained as a doctor of medicine but was attracted to the study of geography by the discoveries of such men as Abel *Tasman, Willem *Schouten, and other Dutch navigators. In 1650 he published *Geographia Generalis*, a work which was to have a profound influence on the study of geography, in which he laid down the general principles of the subject on a scientific basis. The third part of this great work deals with the actual surface of the earth, with relative positions of places, *longitude, *navigation, and globe- and map-making. He died at an early age of starvation, in those days a frequent end of poor scholars.

VARIATION, sometimes known as magnetic *declination, is the angle between the *bearing of the magnetic north pole and that of the true North pole at the position of the observer. It is named east or west according to whether the direction of the magnetic pole lies to the right or left respectively of the true pole, and is applied, together with *deviation, to any *course steered or bearing obtained with a magnetic *compass in order to obtain the true course or bearing. The amount of variation may increase or decrease slightly from year to year according to the movement of the magnetic pole, but on all *charts the amount of variation is given for the year of publication together with the annual rate of increase or decrease. The first nautical chart on which lines of equal variation, known as *isogonic lines, were drawn was produced by the astronomer Edmund *Halley in 1701.

In the time of Christopher *Columbus the amount of variation in western Europe was sufficiently small to escape notice, but it is said that during his first voyage to the west in 1492 Columbus noticed that the indication of north on his magnetic compass differed more and more from the true north the further west he went, a fact which caused him much alarm as he did not know the cause. For illus. see COMPASS ERROR.

VASA or *WASA*, a 64-gun wooden warship which was built to the order of Gustavus Adolphus of Sweden in the dockyard at Stockholm and sank at the outset of her maiden voyage on 10 August 1628. Attempts to raise the *Vasa* during the 17th century were unsuccessful, but the vessel was rediscovered in 1956. In April 1961 the almost complete wooden hull was brought to the surface from a depth of 110 feet. Over 16,000 objects, including carvings, textiles, leather, coins, equipment, and a number of skeletons of the unfortunate seamen who were drowned in the disaster, were recovered from the ship. She is now preserved at the *Vasa* Museum in Stockholm, the only surviving example of the complete hull of a 17th century warship.

Her raising from the mud into which she had sunk was an operation of great technical skill, particularly in the care which had to be taken to prevent the hull from breaking up when the wood dried. All woodwork had to be treated with a preservative as soon as it became exposed to the air, to prevent immediate decay.

VEER, to, (1) the operation of paying out a rope or *cable in a ship. The word is most usually applied to a vessel's *anchor cable, as there are many occasions when it is necessary to veer the cable, as for example when *mooring or unmooring, one of the two cables being veered while the other is shortened in. If a ship is lying to a single anchor and the weather deteriorates seriously, veering more cable frequently adds to her safety as, generally speaking, the greater the *scope of the cable, the greater the security. *Hawsers used in securing a ship to a *buoy or alongside a *quay are veered when they are paid out, but a *sheet is *eased or *checked when it is paid out, never veered. **(2)** Another form of the verb to *wear, when a sailing vessel brings her stern instead of her bows across the wind in order to sail on the other tack. It is not quite so old a term as to wear a ship, and is hardly ever used in this sense today. **(3)** The operation of the wind when it changes direction in a clockwise direction. A wind which veers is frequently a sign of settled weather in the northern hemisphere, of unsettled weather in the southern.

VEER AND HAUL, to, a means of obtaining an extra pull on a rope by alternately slackening it and hauling it on it three or four times in preparation for a heavy haul by giving the men hauling on it a sense of timing that will concentrate their force. In a full-rigged ship, when hauling the *bowlines on the *tacks of the sails, the order was normally 'veer and haul'. This expression in sailing ship days was also used to describe a change in direction of the wind in relation to the ship; it veered when it swung aft and hauled when it came forward. But see also VEER, TO (3).

VEGA, the name of the first vessel to circumnavigate Europe and Asia. She was built at Bremerhaven in 1872–3 as a *whaler for Arctic waters, constructed of oak with a greenheart iceskin. She was of 357 G.R.T., 299 net, and fully rigged as a *barque with a 60 horsepower auxiliary steam engine. On her successful voyage through the *North-East passage in 1878–9 she was commanded by Lieutenant L. Palander of the Royal Swedish Navy, the expedition being led by Professor N. A. E. *Nordenskiöld. The *Vega* returned for use as a whaler and sealer in 1880, but was crushed in the ice and sank off West Greenland, fortunately without loss of life, in 1903.

VELDE, WILLEM VAN DE (1610–93), one of the greatest of the Dutch marine artists, was born at Leiden. He started life as a seaman but very early earned a reputation as a painter of marine subjects, mainly in monochrome or grisaille. So great were his talents in this respect that the States General of Holland put a small ship at his disposal so that he could witness the sea battles of the First (1652–4) and Second (1665–7) Dutch wars and record them on canvas. He was invited to England by Charles II, arriving in London in 1672, and the king granted him a pension of £100 a year as a painter, which was continued after Charles's death in 1685 by James II. His son, also WILLEM (1633–1707), was also a marine artist of great repute, and in many respects even greater than his father. He was taught by his father and by Simon de *Vlieger. He too received £100 a year from Charles II but whereas his father's pension was given for 'taking and making draughts of seafights', that of the son was for 'putting the said draughts into colours for our own particular use'.

The two Van de Veldes are recognized as the greatest of the marine artists of the Dutch school, and their paintings and drawings, particularly those of the elder, are accepted as a historical archive of great value in ship architecture and rig of the period, and the tactics and manoeuvres of naval battles. The younger Willem's paintings are considered superior to his father's because of his sensitive feeling for light, atmosphere, and the sea. The main collections of both artists are in Buckingham Palace, Hampton Court, and the *National Maritime Museum at Greenwich, and there is also a good collection in Amsterdam.

VELEZ MALAGA, a naval battle of the War of the Spanish Succession (1702–13), was fought on 13 August 1704, about 25 miles south-east of Marbella, Spain, by an Anglo-Dutch fleet of fifty-one sail under Admiral Sir George *Rooke, against an approximately equal Franco-Spanish fleet, under Admiral the Comte de *Toulouse, which was supporting an attempt to recapture

*Gibraltar, which Rooke had taken a few days earlier. In addition, the Spanish had about twenty-four *galleys, but little use was made of them. The action lasted from 10.30 a.m. till 7.00 p.m. when the French and Spanish ships drew off and both fleets lay-to for the night repairing their considerable damage. Casualties were heavy: the British lost 695 killed and 1,663 wounded; the Dutch had 400 casualties; in the Franco-Spanish fleet there were 1,500 killed and more than 3,000 wounded. No ship on either side was taken, and the only loss during the action was a French *frigate and two Spanish galleys. It was this action which settled the fate of Gibraltar, for the Franco-Spanish ships, though by no means defeated, left the field of battle during the night, allowing Rooke to consolidate his occupation of Gibraltar.

VENICE (VENEZIA), a city and seaport of northern Italy at the head of the Adriatic Sea. The city, once the centre of an independent republic, has had a long and varied history. Originally it was a small settlement of fishermen who built their huts along the banks of the lagoons and probably dug deep ditches connecting with the lagoons in which they could moor up their boats; the origin, it is believed, of the present Venetian canal system. From a purely fishing village, Venice developed into a centre of the coasting trade, and as it grew gradually richer, atracted frequent attacks from Dalmatian pirates. It was as a result of these that the inhabitants built castellated houses for protection, and guarded the entries to the canals with chains, a description which occurs in Petrarch's (1304–74) account of his own house in Venice. The city became independent, largely through Byzantine influence, in 584, and the first doge, or head of state, was elected in 697. By 810 the new state was finally and firmly based on Rialto, the modern Venice, and as the most northerly seaport leading into the heart of Europe, grew rapidly in importance as the volume of Mediterranean trade handled through its port developed. This in turn attracted yet more frequent raids from the pirates of Dalmatia and led to the arming of Venetian ships and the birth of the Venetian Navy. The final defeat of the Dalmatian pirates came with the capture of the towns of Curzola and Lagosta in 1000 by the doge Pietro Orsielo II, a victory commemorated by the annual ceremony of the symbolic 'wedding of the sea' on Ascension Day (see also BUCENTAUR).

The first three Crusades brought immense wealth to Venice. Her fleet commanded the route to the Holy Land, and as her ships provided the transport of the Christian armies she was at the same time able to acquire valuable trading rights in the Levant. This sudden acquisition of wealth and trade attracted the envy of *Genoa, and the influence of Venice in the Levant was rudely shattered when the Emperor of Constantinople, urged on by the Genoese, not only expelled the 200,000 Venetians who had set up business in his city but also seized their goods. Venice declared war on the Empire but was defeated after a disastrous campaign. Yet the trade of Venice, by reason of the strategic importance of the port, continued to prosper, the losses of the war were soon recovered, and the fourth Crusade materially advanced the wealth of the republic. Constantinople was captured, through a diversion of the Crusade engineered by Venice in 1204, and the influence of the republic throughout the Levant was vastly increased. There followed the long wars against Genoa, brought finally to an end by the destruction of the Genoese fleet off Trepani (Sicily) in 1264. But although the victory fell to Venice, the rise of Turkish influence in the Levant resulted in another series of wars in defence of the Levantine trading rights, and in these Venice was finally defeated at sea off Curzola, in the Adriatic, in 1299. Further wars with Genoa developed and again the Venetian fleet was crushingly defeated at Sapienza in 1354, though the victorious Genoese were too exhausted after the battle to follow their victory with the capture of Venice.

The rivalry between the two Italian republics continued unabated and came to an end only with the final defeat of Genoa in 1380. The Genoan admiral, Luciano Doria, had defeated the Venetian admiral, Vettor *Pisani, at Pola (Pula) in 1379, and had followed up his victory with a close blockade of Venice, basing his victorious fleet at Chiogga. Pisani, recognizing the weakness of the Genoan position, in his turn set up a close blockade of Chiogga from the sea, and finally forced the Genoan fleet to surrender.

Although the victory of Chiogga left Venice the supreme maritime power in the Mediterranean, it forced her into another series of expensive and exhausting wars, this time on land. It was little use attracting most of the Mediterranean seaborne trade to Venice if there were no outlets for it, and so Venice was forced to acquire a hinterland whereby the trade could pass into Europe without being at the mercy of small kings, barons, and landowners who could levy duties on the goods as they passed through their borders. Although by these exhausting wars Venice eventually gained her hinterland, more trouble was now brewing in the east. Constantinople fell to the Turks in 1453, and a series of wars with Turkey to defend the Levantine trade were fought, all expensive and exhausting. Success in these wars came finally to Venice with the great victory at *Lepanto in 1571, but even before then the writing was on the wall. Bartholomew *Diaz had discovered a new all-sea route to India and China round the Cape of Good Hope, and the eastern trade, on which so much of the wealth of Venice depended, was about to fall into the hands of the Portuguese, Dutch, and English. The Venetian empire in the eastern Mediterranean began gradually to fall apart, but it was not until the advent of Napoleon that the end of the Venetian republic finally arrived. By the treaty of Campio Formio in 1797 Venice became a province of Austria. In 1866 the defeat of Austria by Prussia led to the incorporation of Venice in modern Italy.

The port of Venice lies at San Nicolo del Lido, connected directly with the sea by an entrance through the Lido itself. The opening of the *Suez Canal in 1869 brought a great increase in trade to the port, so that once again a large volume of eastern trade, upon which centuries earlier the wealth of Venice so largely depended, began to flow through its port. Modern docks, wharves, and cargo-handling facilities, allied to a vigorous seaborne tourist trade, keep Venice in the forefront of Mediterranean ports. The city is also the home of the Museo Storico Navale, an important maritime museum which illustrates the naval history of Venice.

One of the great features of Venice is the *gondola, a unique and traditional type of boat which plies for hire on the Venetian canals. It is a very ancient design, being first mentioned in 1094.

VERNE, JULES (1828–1905), French author, was born at Nantes, originally studied for the Bar, but went to Paris where he wrote the librettos for a couple of comic operas which had some small success. This inclined him towards writing as a career, and with the publication in a magazine of some stories of travel, he found his true *métier* in tales of travel with a background of scientific knowledge and invention, which proved immensely popular all through Europe. If *Around the World in Eighty Days* (1872) is his most famous book, his *Twenty Thousand Leagues under the Sea* (1869) runs it very close. In addition to his writing, Jules Verne was a keen and accomplished yachtsman.

VERNET, (CLAUDE) JOSEPH (1714–89), French marine painter, was born at Avignon. He came of an artistic family, his father and two uncles all being artists of the Avignon school. He was taught by his father and other local artists and soon showed a talent which earned him the patronage of a local nobleman who arranged for him to go to Rome to study. During a rough passage from Marseilles to Civita Vecchia he had himself tied to the mast so as better to observe the movement of the waves. As a result of this experience he decided to devote himself to marine painting. In Italy he earned his living at the start by painting coaches but soon made his reputation with his sea pictures and remained there until 1753 when, at the request of Madame de Pompadour, he returned to France. He excelled in painting pictures of storms at sea and was commissioned by Louis XV to paint twenty pictures of French ports, but was prevented from completing the four Channel ports by the outbreak of war with England. The sixteen which he did paint are now in the Louvre in Paris. He was a prolific painter, and examples of his pictures are to be found in most of the principal galleries of Europe.

VERNON, EDWARD (1684–1757), British admiral, was known throughout the British Navy as 'Old Grog' on account of the grogram boatcloak, or, according to some, breeches which he always wore on board. It was he who, in 1740, issued an order that the daily ration of rum issued to the seamen of the fleet was to be watered down in the proportion of three parts of water to one part of rum, and since that day watered down rum has always been known as grog.

Vernon was born in Westminster, London, and entered the navy in 1700 as a volunteer on board the *Shrewsbury*, flagship of Sir George *Rooke. He was promoted lieutenant two years later and appointed to the *Barfleur*, flagship of Sir Clowdisley *Shovel, being present at the capture of *Gibraltar in 1704 and at the subsequent battle of *Velez Malaga. He became a *postcaptain in 1706, serving in various commands at sea until the end of the War of the Spanish Succession (1702–13), and then came ashore. He was elected to Parliament in 1722 and took a prominent part in all naval debates, becoming a strong supporter of another war against Spain on account of the cruelties of the Spanish *guardacostas against Britain merchant seamen in the West Indies. The case of Captain *Jenkins, who was reputed to have had an ear cut off by the guarda-costas, was strongly supported by him in Parliament and proved to be the final argument which forced a reluctant British government to declare war against Spain in 1739.

As a result of a boastful speech in Parliament, he was given command of a *squadron of only six ships with instructions 'to destroy the Spanish settlements in the West Indies and distress their shipping by every method whatever'. It was hoped by the government that, with so tiny a force, Vernon would inevitably fail to achieve anything and thus be held up to ridicule, but he took his ships to the Spanish stronghold of *Porto Bello, on the Isthmus of Darien, captured the fort which guarded the entrance almost without loss, seized the town, and held it to ransom after destroying all warlike stores. The capture of Porto Bello aroused such vast enthusiasm in Britain that there was no course left open to the government but to send him a considerable reinforcement in ships and men for further operations against Spanish possessions.

His next operation was an attempt to capture the great port of Cartagena by an amphibious attack in 1741. This proved to be a disaster, partly because of an epidemic of yellow fever which ravaged both the crews of the ships and the soldiers ashore, but mainly because of the lack of initiative shown by the army commander, Major-General Wentworth, who refused to allow his men to advance against the town until all neighbouring forts had been silenced. Even after this had been done by parties of seamen landed from ships, the soldiers remained inactive. Vernon and Wentworth were not even on speaking terms, a fact which boded ill for any operation of this nature which called for combined naval and military tactics to achieve success. The attack on Cartagena had to be abandoned amid the vitriolic quarrels of the two leaders with nothing to show for it beyond a very heavy loss of life from disease. Tobias *Smollett was serving in the fleet as a surgeon's mate at Cartagena, and in his novel *Roderick Random* has left a vivid picture of conditions on board the British fleet.

Vernon was advanced to admiral in 1745 and appointed to command the North Sea Fleet. He was responsible for stopping supplies from France destined to nourish the attempt of Prince Charles Edward to regain the throne of Britain for the deposed Stuart line of kings. This was his last operational command, as he asked to be relieved when the Admiralty refused to grant him the status of a commander-in-chief. During the following year his name was removed from the list of flag officers as a result of the publication of a number of anonymous pamphlets highly critical of the Admiralty which, although he denied authorship, were known to have been written by him.

Vernon was a man of intemperate speech which made him many enemies, but for his time he was a most enlightened and far-seeing naval officer. He was one of the first admirals to practise his captains in naval manoeuvres and their ships' companies at gun drill. He also issued a number of additional instructions, for use in his fleet, to the official *Fighting Instructions*, by means of which he was able to produce an added flexibility in handling his fleet in battle. The majority of these additional instructions were accepted and added to, by all subsequent naval commanders of the British fleets.

D. Ford, *Admiral Vernon and the Navy* (1907).

VERRAZZANO, GIOVANNI DA (1485–1528), Florentine navigator, was born at the Castello Verrazzano in the Chianti district near Florence, Italy, a son of a noble family. At the

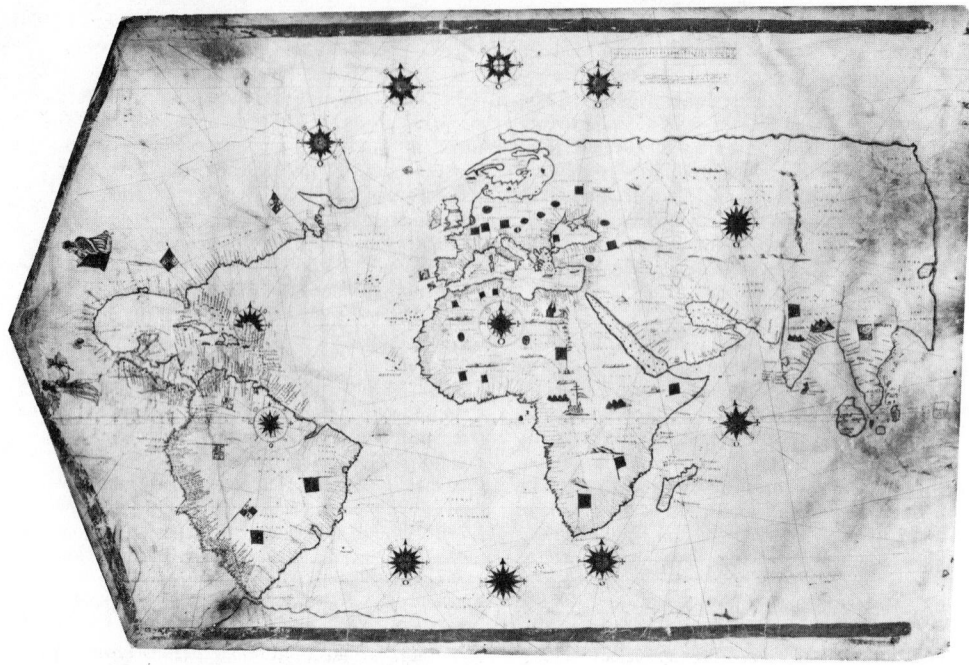

Girolamo da Verrazzano's planisphere

age of 21 or 22 he moved to Dieppe to take up a maritime career, and henceforward sailed in the service of France. During the next ten or twelve years he made a number of trading voyages to the Levant and appears to have met, and discussed navigation with, Ferdinand *Magellan before the latter's circumnavigation.

By 1523 he had interested François I in a project of exploration and discovery in the new world with the idea of discovering for France a new passage into the Pacific Ocean and thus access to the wealth of the Far East. The king lent him a ship of 100 tons, the *Dauphine*, and with financial backing from Florentine bankers, together with a second ship, the smaller *Normande*, Verrazzano sailed from Dieppe to Madeira as a jumping-off place for the Atlantic passage. Here the *Normande* left him to return to France, and the *Dauphine* went on by herself sailing along the northerly edge of the *trade winds belt. On board was Verrazzano's brother Girolamo, whose main task was to draw maps of new lands discovered. The *Dauphine* reached the American coast in the vicinity of the present Cape Fear in North Carolina and sailed north along the Carolina Outer Banks round Cape Hatteras and up to the present Kitty Hawk, mistaking the great extent of the Pamlico Sound, inside the Outer Banks, for the Pacific Ocean, and naming it the Sea of Verrazzano. He continued north and, encouraged by friendly Indians, entered New York Bay, probably anchoring in the narrows between Staten Island and the Long Island shore, the first known European to visit these waters. He continued northward, visiting Narragansett Bay, the site of the present Newport in Rhode Island, rounding Cape Cod, and finally reaching the Newfoundland coast, whence he took off for home, reaching Dieppe in July 1524.

Verrazzano was one of the first navigators to realize that America was a new continent, and not the outskirts of Asia, but he had difficulty in persuading either the king or the bankers to finance another voyage since he had brought back nothing of value from the new lands he had visited. But in 1527 he led a new expedition across the Atlantic, still in search of the mythical northern strait into the Pacific. Mutinous crews cut short his exploration, and all he achieved was a quick descent on Brazil and a return to France with a profitable cargo of logwood.

With the profits from the logwood, and the hope of more, Verrazzano set off from Dieppe on his third voyage in the spring of 1528. He had the intention of searching for the strait into the Pacific, south of his previous exploration, and reached America at the Florida coast hoping to find signs of a strait around the Isthmus of Darien. Instead, after reaching the Bahamas, he coasted down the Lower Antilles, anchoring probably off the coast of Guadeloupe. Here he and his brother took a boat with the intention of landing on the island, not knowing that instead of the friendly Indians they had encountered during their first voyage, the Antilles were inhabited by man-eating Caribs. As they drew near the shore Verrazzano stepped into the water and waded ashore, and was instantly cut up and eaten on the spot before the eyes of his horrified brother, who was unable to help.

Girolamo's original planisphere of the first voyage is in the * National Maritime Museum, Greenwich, London, with contemporary copies in the Vatican Library and Hispanic Society's Library in New York.

VERTEX, the two points on a * great circle which have the maximum * latitude north and south, each being antipodal to the other. The only great circle without vertices is the equator.

VERTICAL SEXTANT ANGLE, the angle in the vertical plane between the top of a * lighthouse, a hill-top, mountain peak, or other prominent feature, and the sea level below it read off on a * sextant. If the height of the top of the observed object is known, it is possible for the navigator of a ship to discover his distance off the object, either by trigonometry, or more easily by reference to the table included in most almanacs for this purpose. Vertical sextant angles are useful to the navigator who wants to keep a definite distance off a particular point. If the angle corresponding to the required distance is pre-set on the sextant, an occasional glance through the sextant at a suitable vertical object will indicate at once whether the ship is inside or outside the required distance.

VERY LIGHTS (pron. veery), coloured pyrotechnic lights fired from a pistol on board ship or from aircraft to indicate certain messages as from ship to ship, ship to aircraft, or aircraft to ship. They are in general confined to naval use for particular signals, such as a recognition signal during battle when a particular pattern of Very Lights (for example four green lights in a diamond shape) will indicate a friendly ship or aircraft, or as an executive signal for the start of a particular prearranged manoeuvre, etc. Ocean-going yachts used at one time often to carry Very Lights as distress signals in those cases where they did not carry * rockets or flares on board for this purpose, but they are very rarely used in yachts today as most offshore yachts have on board a distress 'pack' containing all necessary rockets or flares for immediate use in any emergency.

VESCONTE, PETRUS (*fl.* 1311–20), Genoese cartographer, was one of the earliest draughtsmen of * portulan charts. These charts were probably first developed towards the end of the 13th century, the earliest known one being the

Carta Pisana now housed in the Bibliothèque Nationale in Paris. In the early 14th century there were thriving cartographic workshops in both Venice and Genoa, the largest possibly being that of Petrus Vesconte at the latter place. There are five portulan charts existing today signed by Petrus Vesconte between 1311 and 1320 inclusive, while there are two more signed by Perrinus Vesconte, presumably another member of the family, in 1321 and 1327.

VESPUCCI, AMERIGO (1451–1512), a Florentine merchant-adventurer whose self-generated claims as an explorer and as the first white man to reach the mainland of America in June 1497 have been doubted owing to the impossible distances and positions quoted in the letters in which the claims were made. Nevertheless it is from the latin version of his name, *Americus*, that the New World takes its name.

Vespucci's letters described four voyages in all to the New World, the first a private venture, the second under the Spaniard Alonzo de Ojeda, and the last two in the service of King Manoel of Portugal. In 1505 he became a naturalized Spaniard. That his accounts of his voyages had a basis of truth and that he was an experienced navigator by that time is indicated by his appointment on 6 August 1508 as *piloto mayor*, or chief * pilot, of Spain, an office which he held until his death.

VIAN, Sir PHILIP (1894–1968), British admiral of the fleet, was one of the most successful tactical commanders of the Second World War. Much of his earlier life was spent in destroyers, including Mediterranean service under Admiral * Cunningham, whom he regarded as the pattern of a fighting leader.

When commanding H.M.S. * *Cossack* during the Second World War, he first came into the news in February 1940, when he boldly took his ship into Jössing Fjord, within Norwegian territorial waters, to investigate the German * tanker * *Altmark*, which was carrying in her hold 299 British merchant navy prisoners, who had been captured in the course of a cruise by the German * pocket-battleship * *Admiral Graf Spee*. These prisoners were rescued after a sharp fight, preceded by a welcome shout from the boarding-party: 'The Navy's here!'

In 1941 Vian played a vital part in the pursuit of the German * battleship * *Bismarck*. His * flotilla shadowed the enemy throughout the night of 26 May, delivering a series of * torpedo attacks and ensuring that the Commander-in-Chief, Home Fleet, with the *King George V* and *Rodney*, completed her destruction next day.

Later, Vian was sent to the Mediterranean as rear admiral commanding a * cruiser * squadron which was to be largely employed in fighting supplies through to * Malta. In the spring of

1942 Admiral Cunningham's fleet was severely overstretched. His battleships had been put out of action, and he had no alternative, if Malta were to survive, to sending Vian's cruisers and destroyers to face overwhelming surface and air opposition. Vian's first attempt at relief failed, but a second, which resulted in the battle of *Sirte in which heavy units of the Italian fleet were forced to retire, and supplies were brought to the Malta garrison, was a feat of arms which gained Vian a knighthood.

In later operations Vian was well equipped, and he made the most of his advantages. He commanded an *aircraft carrier force which supported landings on the mainland of Italy; he then returned home to prepare for the invasion of Normandy, the largest amphibious operation in which the Royal Navy had ever been concerned. He was appointed Eastern Task Force commander, to cover the British landings. His success was outstanding, and it led to his command of the British aircraft carrier force sent to the Far East for final operations against Japan.

After the war, Vian became Fifth Sea Lord, and later commanded the Home Fleet. His terse war memoir, *Action This Day* (1960), is characterized by generosity to those who served with him.

VIAUD, JULIEN, see LOTI, Pierre.

VICE ADMIRAL, the naval rank in all navies next below that of admiral, but see APPENDIX 1 for table of equivalent ranks. A vice admiral in all navies wears as insignia of rank one broad and two thinner rings of gold lace on his sleeves, and in Britain flies an admiral's flag defaced with one ball. The flags flown by vice admirals in other countries vary according to the designs adopted by the marine departments of their nation.

VICE ADMIRALTY COURT, a branch of the British High Court of Admiralty which in time of war was set up for convenience in various British colonies with power to adjudicate in Admiralty causes, and particularly in cases of condemnation in *prize. These courts stemmed from the judicial powers vested in the *Lord High Admiral and remained in operation until the Admiralty Court was merged with the High Court of Justice in 1864. See ADMIRALTY, HIGH COURT OF.

VICTORIA, H.M.S., a *battleship launched in 1887 which carried two of the heaviest guns ever designed for the British Navy. They were of 16·25-inch *calibre and each weighed 111 tons. They were so heavy that their muzzles drooped under the weight, and it was considered inadvisable to fire them with full charges. In 1893 she

H.M.S. Camperdown *in collision with H.M.S.* Victoria, *1893; contemporary coloured lithograph*

H.M.S. Victory, *famous as Nelson's flagship, leaving Spithead; oil painting by R. Dodd*

was the flagship of the British fleet in the Mediterranean, flying the flag of Vice Admiral Sir George *Tryon. She was rammed and sunk with heavy loss of life during fleet manoeuvres by H.M.S. *Camperdown* on 22 June 1893 as a result of a mistaken tactical signal hoisted by Tryon.

VICTORY, a novel by Joseph *Conrad published in 1915. In it Conrad returned to the scene of many of his earlier novels, the islands off the Malay peninsula.

VICTORY, H.M.S., probably the best known of all the Royal Navy's warships, was the flagship of Vice Admiral Lord *Nelson at the battle of *Trafalgar. She was the fifth and last of her name in the British Navy.

The first was a merchant ship of 800 tons, built in 1559 as the *Great Christopher*. She was bought for the English Navy in 1560 and renamed *Victory* in 1562, being rebuilt in 1586. During the campaign of the Spanish *Armada in 1588 she was the flagship of Sir John *Hawkins, serving in the *Lord High Admiral's (Lord *Howard of Effingham) squadron from Plymouth. The second *Victory* was a 2nd *rate *ship of the line of 807 tons and forty-two guns, built and launched at Deptford in 1620, but her

armament was increased to sixty guns during the course of a 'large repair' in 1645–6. During the First Anglo-Dutch War (1652–4) she was engaged in the battles of *Dover, the *Kentish Knock, and Dungeness in 1652 and those of *Portland, the *Gabbard, and *Scheveningen in 1653. After the restoration of Charles II in 1660, she was rebuilt and enlarged to a ship of 1,029 tons and eighty guns, and during the Second Anglo-Dutch War (1665–7) she was one of Prince *Rupert's detached squadron which rejoined the English fleet in time to take part in the fourth day's fighting of the *Four Days Battle in June 1666. She was the flagship of Sir Christopher *Myngs who was killed in the action. A month later, flying the flag of Vice Admiral Sir Edward *Spragge, she took part in the St. James's Day Fight. She was still going strong during the Third Anglo-Dutch War (1672–4) and fought in the battle of *Solebay in 1672 and the battles of Schooneveld and the *Texel in 1673. She was finally broken up in 1690.

The third and fourth ships of the name had no significant history; both were 1st rates of one hundred guns, the third took part in the battle of *Barfleur in 1692 and the fourth, which was in her day recognized as 'the finest ship in the world', was wrecked and lost with all hands on the Caskets, near the island of Alderney in the English Channel, in 1744 after becoming separated from the rest of the fleet in a gale.

The fifth H.M.S. *Victory*, Nelson's famous flagship, was laid down at Chatham in 1759 as a 1st rate ship of the line of 2,162 tons, mounting one hundred guns, but work was stopped on her after the end of the Seven Years War (1756–63) and she was not launched until 1765. During the years of peace very little work was done on her and she was not completed until 1778, during the War of American Independence (1775–82). Her first commission was as flagship of Admiral Augustus *Keppel and she flew his flag at the battle of *Ushant in that year. She saw much service, always as a flagship, both in the War of American Independence, in which, after Keppel, she flew the flag of Rear Admiral Richard *Kempenfelt, and in the Revolutionary War with France (1793–1801), in which she flew the flag of Lord *Howe when he commanded the Channel Fleet.

During the Napoleonic War (1803–15), she became Nelson's flagship in 1803 in the Mediterranean during his watch off *Toulon, carried him to the West Indies in his chase across the Atlantic after Admiral *Villeneuve, and took him from Portsmouth to join, and take command of, the fleet of Vice Admiral Cuthbert *Collingwood which was watching the combined Franco-Spanish fleet at *Cadiz in October 1805. Nelson was killed on the *quarterdeck of the *Victory* during the subsequent battle off Cape Trafalgar and, after some repairs at Gibraltar, the *Victory* brought Nelson's body home for his state funeral in St. Paul's cathedral.

She next served in the Baltic as the flagship of Admiral *Saumarez, and after various other service she was paid off into the *ordinary at Portsmouth in 1835. She was selected as the permanent, and stationary, flagship of the commander-in-chief at Portsmouth, lying at *moorings in the harbour and gradually deteriorating in condition over the years as she lay afloat.

Although she was always recognized as a historic ship, and particularly so by the closing years of the 19th and early years of the 20th centuries, no steps were taken to restore her to her Trafalgar condition beyond occasional repairs to her hull to keep her afloat. It was largely through the instigation of Sir Geoffrey *Callender, with the support of many influential friends and authorities, that a public appeal for funds was successfully launched to take the ship in hand and restore her in every respect to the condition in which she fought at Trafalgar. The British Admiralty made available a *dry-dock for her in Portsmouth Dockyard. She was docked and systematically repaired, restored, and re-rigged to her original state. On completion she was opened to the public, a permanent memorial

to Nelson, Trafalgar, and to the British Navy as a whole, and a notable place of pilgrimage to all lovers of ships and the sea. Alongside her as she lies in her permanent home in dry-dock is a small maritime musuem devoted to the age of Trafalgar known as the Victory Museum.

VICTORY SHIPS, a follow-on to the Second World War *Liberty ships, intended for post-war use to fill the immediate gap in overall tonnage left by the immense number of merchant ships sunk by *U-boats and other means during the Second World War. They were built to a less Spartan standard than the Liberty ships; the hull was lengthened and strengthened although remaining all-welded; a *forecastle was added; and *turbines replaced the Liberty ships' triple-expansion engines. The standard gross tonnage was 7,607 and top speed was 16 knots.

VICTUALLER, a merchant ship taken up for naval use to carry victuals during a long cruise or in time of war. In the days before there was any real knowledge of how to preserve food on board, victuallers were always required to supply a fleet when it was likely to be out for a long period. During the blockade of *Brest by Admirals *Hawke and *Boscawen in 1759–60, for example, a steady stream of victuallers was sailed from Plymouth to supply the fleet with the fresh food so necessary for the health of the seamen. Victuallers also formed part of the squadrons detached on long cruises; both Francis *Drake in 1577 and George *Anson in 1740 had victuallers accompanying them on the first stages of their voyages round the world. They were required because the ships of the squadrons had insufficient space on board to stow all the victuals required; in both cases the victuallers replenished the ships of the squadron when the Magellan Straits were reached, and being then empty were either sent home or broken up, in the latter case with the crews being taken on board the other ships of the squadron.

VICTUALLING BOARD, an autonomous subsidiary of the *Navy Board of Britain which, until 1832, was charged with the administration of the Royal Navy. The Victualling Board was responsible for the purchase, preservation, and distribution to ships of all naval victuals and slop clothing, entering into contracts with merchants for the supply of all articles of food and clothing required, and placing on board every ship, with an appointment by *warrant, a *purser to issue clothes and victuals and to keep all accounts. This wide responsibility opened the way, in the earlier years of its existence, to widespread peculation and dishonesty, both in regard to the actual weight and quality of the victuals supplied by the merchants to the commissioners of the Victualling Board and also in the daily issue of rations to seamen in the ships, where pursers usually reckoned 14 ounces to the pound, pocketing the difference (about 14 per cent). Complaints from captains of ships to the victualling commissioners were frequent and virulent, but rarely produced any improvement. 'In the case of pork,' ran a typical complaint, 'the cheeks, ears, feet and other offal of the hog were thrown in as part of the men's allowance, which among other things caused that frequent running-away of the seamen from the service, rather than to live upon bones and crag-ends, souse and hogs' feet, when they know the State allowed them better meat.' It was the same story with the flour, biscuit, butter, cheese, fish, and beer, particularly the last-named which was apt to hit seamen in their tenderest spot. But from about the mid-18th century most of the more blatant dishonesty had been removed and the Victualling Board, within the limits of the means of preservation of food then existing, did a reasonably satisfactory job.

In 1832 the Navy Board was amalgamated with the * Admiralty, and its subsidiary boards, including that of victualling, were abolished. All victualling for the fleet was put into the hands of a director of victualling who was a member of the Admiralty secretariat.

VIDAL, ALEXANDER THOMAS EMERIC (1792–1863), British vice admiral, and surveyor. He disproved the existence of the troublesome * vigia in the eastern Atlantic known as Aitkins's Rock, charted Vidal Bank, and surveyed the Azores.

VIGIA, a hydrographic term meaning a rock or shoal marked on a chart, usually by report of a ship's * master, but whose actual existence has not been yet proved by a hydrographic survey.

VIGO, a seaport and naval station in northwestern Spain, and a centre of the Spanish sardine fishery. Vigo Bay, at the top of which the seaport stands, is one of the finest natural anchorages in Europe, extending inland for 19 miles and well sheltered by low mountains and islands. A considerable shipbuilding industry is carried on there.

The port has been the scene of many attacks and battles. It was twice attacked by Sir Francis * Drake, in 1585 and 1589, but the most considerable action was in 1702, during the War of the Spanish Succession (1702–13), when a combined Anglo-Dutch fleet commanded by Sir George * Rooke destroyed a fleet of Spanish treasure * galleons which had been escorted into Vigo by a French fleet. Although the French and Spanish ships were protected by a * boom across the harbour mouth, with shore batteries erected

at either end and the French warships drawn up behind it, the boom was broken through by the English 80-gun ship *Torbay*. The French admiral, * Chateau-Renault, seeing that all was apparently lost, ordered his captains to burn their ships, but before this could be carried out ten of them, with eleven galleons, were taken by the attackers. Every other ship in the harbour was destroyed. Although some of the treasure brought by the galleons had already been landed, an enormous amount, said to be worth over £1,000,000, was captured. According to some accounts, an even larger amount was supposed to have been still on board the ships sunk during the battle, but although many attempts have been made by divers to search for it, none has yet been discovered.

VIKINGSKIPHUSET, Oslo, Norway, a small maritime museum, situated on the Bygdøy peninsula to the west of the city where the three famous Viking ships, the Osberg ship, the Gokstad ship, and the Tune ship, all from the 9th century, are housed in a special building. In addition to the three ships there are some Viking boats and other related items brought together in this important museum.

VILETTE-MURSAY, PHILIPPE DE VALOIS, Marquis de (1632–1707), French naval officer, was a grandson of Agrippa d'Aubigne and a cousin of Madame de Maintenon. His first service was in the French Army, but he subsequently transferred to the navy and by 1672 had reached the rank of captain. He was in the West Indies in the fleet commanded by Jean d'* Estrées, and later took part in the bombardment of the pirate headquarters of Algiers by a * squadron under Abraham * Duquesne in 1683. At the battle of * Barfleur in 1692 he made many attempts to drive off the British ships which were concentrating against the *Soleil Royale*, flagship of the Comte de * Tourville, but she was eventually driven ashore near Cherbourg and burned by the British. He also fought at Lagos under de Tourville in the following year. His memoirs, first published in 1844, contain an interesting and vivid account of his life in the navy of France over a span of twenty-five years.

VILKITSKIY, BORIS ANDREYEVICH (1885–1961), Russian rear admiral, explorer, and scientist, graduated at the naval academy at St. Petersburg (Leningrad) in 1903 and is credited with being the first to navigate the * North-East passage, an honour which, however, belongs to N. A. E. * Nordenskiöld. His first attempt, in which he employed the two * ice-breakers *Taimyr* and *Vaigach*, was unsuccessful, the ice-breakers being unable to break through the ice floes off Severnaya Zemlya, but on his second attempt in 1915 he got through from Vladivostok to Archangel without encountering any hold-ups and obtained much valuable hydrographic information. The strait separating the northernmost point of Eurasia (Cape Chelyuskin) from Severnaya Zemlya bears his name. See ARCTIC EXPLORATION.

VILLARET DE JOYEUSE, LOUIS THOMAS (1750–1812), French admiral, was born at Auch. On joining the French Navy, he served in Indian waters under the great French naval leader Pierre de *Suffren, having been earlier promoted captain for his gallantry in the siege of Pondicherry in 1778. In 1781 he was captured by the British after a fierce single ship action, was released in 1783, and in spite of his royalist sympathies, decided to continue service in the French Navy at the time of the revolution in 1792. After a short period in which he was actively engaged in the reorganization of the French fleet, he commanded the fleet in the battle of the *Glorious First of June. Becoming politically minded, he was appointed a member of the Council of the Ancients in 1796, but fell foul of its members a year later and was sentenced to deportation for royalist sympathies. However, he escaped arrest, lived in obscurity at Oleron, and on the formation of Napoleon's Consulate, was appointed to command the squadron which escorted a French Army to San Domingo in the West Indies in 1801. He was made captain-general of Martinique, but was forced to surrender the island to the British in 1809 after a heroic defence. On his return to France he was in temporary disfavour with Napoleon, but in 1811, with their differences healed, he was rewarded for his past services with the rank of lieutenant-general and an appointment as governor-general of Venice.

VILLENEUVE, PIERRE CHARLES JEAN BAPTISTE SILVESTRE, Comte de (1763–1806), French admiral, gained rapid promotion in the navy under the Republic, reaching the rank of captain in 1793 and rear admiral in 1796. In 1798 he commanded the rear division of the French fleet under Admiral *Brueys which had escorted Napoleon's army to Egypt and which was brought to action by Horatio *Nelson on 1 August 1798 and almost annihilated in the battle of the *Nile. Villeneuve's rear division was only lightly engaged during the action.

Early on 2 August, having seen the *van and centre of the anchored French fleet destroyed, Villeneuve set sail in his flagship, the *Guillaume Tell*, and escaped in company with the *Généreux* and two *frigates, the British ships being too shattered in the battle to pursue them. They were the only French ships of the whole fleet which escaped destruction or capture.

Villeneuve was later promoted and selected to command the French *Toulon squadron in November 1804, the role of which in Napoleon's 'grand design' was to cross the Atlantic to combine in the West Indies with squadrons from Brest, Ferrol, and Rochefort. The whole force was then to return in overwhelming strength to dominate the English Channel while Napoleon ferried his army across it to invade Britain.

The scheme broke down when Nelson pursued Villeneuve across the ocean, forcing him to return. Intercepted off Finisterre by a British squadron under Vice Admiral Sir Robert *Calder, he fought an indecisive action, losing two ships before seeking shelter in Ferrol. According to his instructions Villeneuve should now, in company with the ships already in Ferrol, have attempted to evade the *blockade and steered to join the squadron in Brest, but he had little confidence in Napoleon's plan, believing, incorrectly, that a superior British fleet lay between him and Brest, and convinced that his main duty was to preserve his fleet. It was on the strength of this conviction that when he led his ships out of Ferrol he turned south and took them to *Cadiz.

There his combined Franco-Spanish fleet was blockaded by an inferior British squadron commanded by Sir Cuthbert *Collingwood, who in October was reinforced when Nelson arrived from England to take over command. Convinced that his fleet, particularly in respect of the Spanish ships, was no match for the British veterans, Villeneuve refused to sail, as ordered, for the Mediterranean until induced to do so on 19 October 1805 by the news that a successor in command was on his way to Cadiz to relieve him. In the disastrous battle of *Trafalgar which resulted two days later, Villeneuve was taken prisoner and carried to England. He was released on parole, but met his death by stabbing with a dagger in a hotel at Rennes on 22 April 1806. Whether he was murdered or committed suicide has been argued by historians and others ever since, but as he left a farewell letter to his wife, suicide would seem to have been his most probable end.

VILLIERS, ALAN JOHN (1903–), British master mariner and marine author, was born in Melbourne, Australia. He went to sea at the age of 15 in the *barque *Rothesay Bay* and served altogether five years in square-rigged ships. He then tried his hand as a journalist in Australia and in 1931 became part owner of the four-masted barque *Parma* which twice won the grain race from Australia to England. In 1934 he purchased the Danish sail training ship *George Stage* and manned her with cadets, renaming her *Joseph Conrad* and sailing round the world to log 58,000 miles. He wrote an account of his experiences in the *Cruise of the Conrad* (1937). During the Second World War he served as an officer in the volunteer reserve of the British Navy and commanded a *squadron of landing craft during the invasions of Italy and Normandy. After the war he was master of the Outward Bound Sea School, Aberdovey, and in 1950 sailed with the Portuguese cod fishing fleet in the *schooner *Argus*. In 1956 he volunteered to sail a replica of the *Mayflower* to the U.S.A. to commemorate the voyage of the Pilgrim Fathers in 1620. He is a prolific author, and among his books are *Falmouth for Orders* (1929), *The Making of a Sailor* (1938), *The Coral Sea* (1950), *The Quest of the Schooner Argus* (1951), which gained him the Camoes Prize of Portugal, *The Way of a Ship* (1954), *The New Mayflower* (1959), and *The Battle of Trafalgar* (1965).

VINLAND, a region on the eastern coast of North America, reached by Norse navigators in the beginning of the 11th century and so named from the wild grapes found growing there. Vinland was the furthest westward exploration of the Norsemen during the great Scandinavian exodus of the 9th, 10th, and 11th centuries, when they, with Swedes and Danes, swarmed all over western Europe; the main direction taken by the Norsemen being westward, they reached Iceland in 874, Greenland in 985, and Vinland in 1000 or 1001. According to the Norse sagas, Biarni Heriulfsson, on a voyage from Iceland to Greenland during the early years of the Greenland colonization, was driven off his course and sighted new lands to the south-west. Fifteen years later *Leif Ericsson set out from Greenland to investigate these sightings, and landed progressively at Helluland (country of flat stones—probably Baffin Island), Markland (country of trees—probably Labrador), and Vinland (probably northern Newfoundland), naming each new land as he reached it. (See also THORFINN KARL-SEFNI.) He then returned to Greenland. A map, supposed to date from about 1440, and now in Yale University, shows Vinland as an island, with an outline curiously like that of Baffin Island. It was published, with a critical essay, in 1965, arousing tremendous discussion. In the opinion of some experts it shows the coasts of Iceland, Greenland, and Baffin Island (labelled Vinlandia) in far too accurate detail to be consistent with a date of 1440, and thus is held by many to be a forgery.

VIOL, VIOLL, or **VOYAL,** the old name for the large *messenger used to assist in *weighing an *anchor in cases where the anchor *cable was of too great a circumference conveniently to go round the barrel of a *capstan. See also NIPPERS. VIOL-BLOCK, a large single-sheaved block usually

lashed to the mainmast between decks through which the viol was rove when the anchor was weighed by means of the fore or *jeer capstan. When the main capstan was used the viol could be led direct to it without the use of a viol-block. For this method of weighing an anchor, see MESSENGER.

VIRGINIA, C.S.S., see MERRIMACK, U.S.S.

VIRGINIUS, an American steamer which was the centre of a notorious affair in October/November 1873. She sailed from Kingston, Jamaica, on 23 October 1873 with 103 passengers and 52 crew, ostensibly bound for Port Limon. Among the passengers were four chiefs of the Cuban rebellion. After leaving Jamaica the *Virginius* put into Haiti on the grounds of requiring repairs but in fact to embark arms and ammunition to sustain the rebellion. She then set sail for Cuba but was discovered and chased by the Spanish warship *Tornado* which boarded and captured her, with no international right to do so as she was still on the high seas. On 1 November she was brought into Santiago da Cuba by the *Tornado*.

The departmental governor of Santiago, Brigadier-General Burriel y Lynch, promptly imprisoned all on board declaring them to be pirates. Telegraphic communication to the outside world was cut and naval and military courts martial set up, sitting both day and night, to try the prisoners. The first four to be condemned and executed were the chiefs of the rebellion. Next to be condemned were thirty-seven members of the crew, including the captain, who was an American citizen, eight other Americans, and nineteen British subjects, mainly cooks, stewards, and firemen. They were marched from the gaol to the common slaughter-house of the town where, before a vast crowd, they were ranged on their knees facing a wall and shot in the back. The marksmanship of the 148 soldiers who formed the firing squad was so poor that it was seven minutes before the last victim died.

News of the impending butchery had reached Jamaica, however, and H.M.S. *Niobe*, commanded by Sir Lambton Loraine, Bt., was ordered to proceed to Santiago. She arrived at 9.30 a.m. on 8 November, by which time twelve more prisoners had been shot. Loraine went ashore and, with the British vice-consul, proceeded to Government House and demanded that all executions should cease. He received the reply that the prisoners were now in the power of Spain and, if sentenced to death, would inevitably be shot. Loraine replied that any more shedding of blood would be the signal for the *Niobe* to sink the Spanish warship lying nearest to her in the harbour.

No more executions took place. The *Virginius*

was surrendered to the U.S.A., but sank while under tow. The prisoners were released. The British government demanded and obtained from Spain a national recognition of the wrong done to her and compensation for the families of the British subjects who had been executed.

VISIT AND SEARCH, the right, enshrined in international law, by which a belligerent ship may stop and search any neutral merchant ship for contraband articles. Resistance to such a search amounts to a forfeiture of neutrality.

VITTORIA or *VICTORIA*, the first ship ever to complete a circumnavigation of the world. She was a * caravel of 85 tons and was the only ship of the five that set out which returned to Spain from Ferdinand * Magellan's voyage round the world of 1519–22, during the course of which the straits named after Magellan were discovered. Of the original 265 men who set out on the voyage in 1519, only 18 returned in the *Vittoria*. See also DEL CANO, Juan Sebastian.

VIVALDO, UGOLINO and SORLEONE DE (*fl.* 1291–1315), Genoese explorers, led the first known expeditions in search of a sea route from Europe to India. Ugolino was in command of an expedition of two * galleys which left Genoa in 1291 and sailed down the coast of Morocco as far as Cape Nun (28° 47′ N.), after which no more was heard of him. His son Sorleone undertook a series of voyages early in the 14th century in search of his father, but also disappeared. Nearly 150 years later a Genoese seaman, Antoniotto Uso di Mare, who sailed with * Cadamosto, reported meeting the last descendant of the survivors of Sorleone's voyage near the mouth of the Gambia River. According to his story one of the two galleys was wrecked in the Sea of Guinea, the other put ashore in Senegal where the crew were seized and held in captivity.

VLIEGER, SIMON JACOBSZ DE (*c.* 1600–53), Dutch marine artist, was born at Rotterdam and worked in the studios of the elder Willem Van de * Velde and Jan * Porcellis. He is said to have given the younger Willem Van de Velde his first lessons in painting, a suggestion which appears to be borne out by the monochrome style of painting which both adopted in their seascapes and which de Vlieger probably learned from Porcellis. Many of his paintings are remarkable for their silvery grey tones which harmonize so admirably with the seascape scene and which bring the feeling of quietness and repose suggested by his pictures. His work is generally considered to be among the most brilliant of the Dutch marine school.

VLISSINGEN, see FLUSHING.

VOJENNO-MARSKOI MOEZJEI, Leningrad, U.S.S.R., one of the most important naval museums in the world, was founded in 1709 but not opened to the public until 1946. It contains a fine collection of ship models dating from 1719 together with other relics illustrating Russian naval history from the earliest times to the present day. Connected with the museum is the * cruiser *Aurora* which played a prominent part in the Russian revolution of 1917 and which is moored near by. The thousand or more ship models, the majority of which are of warships, cover the period from the 16th century to the present day. The collection includes ship decorations from Russian and Swedish ships, archaeological finds, nautical instruments, nearly 5,000 weapons, uniforms, medals, seals, and flags. The paintings, drawings, and engravings number over 5,000 and the photographic collection contains 120,000 prints. The library, open to the public, contains several thousand books, maps, plans, and archives. Another Russian museum of some naval interest is the Central Museum of the Armed Forces of the U.S.S.R. (Centralnij Musej Vooruzhennijch Sd S.S.S.R.) in Moscow, which contains some 300,000 exhibits. Most of them, however, relate to the Red Army although a number of documents, photographs, flags, and pieces of equipment of naval significance are included in the collection.

VOLTURNO, S.S., a 3,518-ton cargo/emigrant steamer which was destroyed by fire in mid-Atlantic in 1913 in one of the more notorious disasters at sea. She was owned by the Royal Mail Line but was under charter to the Uranium Steamship Co. (British), and was sailing on the Rotterdam/Halifax/New York run when fire broke out in the forward * holds on 9 October 1913. The cargo included chemicals and other combustibles and she was soon blazing furiously. Emergency * SOS calls brought nine nearby ships to her aid but, because of a fierce gale and very heavy seas, they were unable to give assistance until the oil * tanker *Narragansett* spread oil from windward on the 10th to contain the breaking seas. Then * lifeboats from the * Cunard * liner *Carmania* and other ships rescued 521 people from the flames. The loss of life amounted to 136 passengers and crew, most of them in two lifeboats which had put off from the *Volturno* herself before the oil was spread. Both capsized in the heavy sea. After the *Volturno*'s loss British regulations were brought in to prevent passenger ships from carrying dangerous cargoes.

VORONIN, VLADIMIR IVANOVICH (1890–1952), Russian ice-breaker captain, commanded the *Georgiy Sedov* in the search for General Nobile in the Arctic in 1928, and on expeditions to Franz Josef Land in 1929 and 1930. In the

Sibiryakov in 1932 he made the first traverse of the northern sea route (see NORTH-EAST PASSAGE) in one season, and in the new ice-strengthened freighter *Chelyuskin* in 1933–4 he just failed to repeat the feat, the ship being crushed in the ice near Bering Strait. His later commands were the *Yermak*, 1934–8; *Josif Stalin*, the first Soviet-built ice-breaker, 1938–45; the whale factory ship *Slava* in the Antarctic, 1946–7; and again the *Josif Stalin*. In 1954 a new Finnish-built ice-breaker for Soviet use (5,360 tons *displacement, 9,750 h.p.) was named *Kapitan Voronin* in his honour.

VOSS, JOHN CLAUS (*c.* 1854–1922), Canadian sea captain and pioneer ocean navigator in small boats, spent many years at sea in square-rigged ships but was induced in 1897 to buy a 30-ft *sloop, *Xora*, and sail her with a companion some 6,000 miles on a treasure-seeking voyage to the Cocos Islands. No treasure was found, but during this cruise Voss learned how safe even such a small vessel could be at sea. Captain *Slocum's voyage around the world single-handed in the 36-ft *Spray* had caused widespread interest after its completion in 1895, and when a Canadian newspaper reporter six years later suggested to Voss that a fortune could be made from stories if between them they sailed round the world in a boat that was smaller than Slocum's *Spray*, Voss was attracted by the idea. Deciding on something much smaller and more fragile than the *Spray*, he fitted out in Victoria, British Columbia, an old Indian war *canoe, 38 feet (11·6 m) in length, 5 feet 6 inches (1·67 m) breadth at the deck, and 3 feet 9 inches (1·15 m) across the bottom, with only 2 feet (0·6 m) draught, and gave her a *schooner rig set on three short masts. In the *Tilikum*, as he named her, he set out from Victoria accompanied by his journalist friend. A severe gale in which the *Tilikum* rode to a *drogue or sea anchor which Voss had contrived proved enough ocean experience for the reporter, who left at the next port of call. Voss continued the voyage across the Pacific to Australia and New Zealand, across the Indian Ocean to the Cape, and thence by way of

The Tilikum *under sail; illustration from* The Venturesome Voyages of Captain Voss, *1913*

Pernambuco in Brazil to London after a combined sailing and lecture tour of some three and a quarter years. The *Tilikum* was shown at a marine exhibition at Earls Court, London, in 1905, while Voss continued to give lectures on the voyage and was elected a Fellow of the Royal Geographical Society.

After parting with his war canoe he next bought a tiny *yawl 19 feet (5·8 m) on the waterline, and called her *Sea Queen* (a smaller sister to Harry *Pidgeon's 34-ft (10·4 m) *Islander*). Sailing with a companion around the islands of Japan he rode out a typhoon, again using the sea anchor he advocated for small craft, when the yawl was turned completely over but survived. All three of these voyages are described in his book, *The Venturesome Voyages of Captain Voss*, which was first published in Japan in 1913. He died in reduced circumstances near San Francisco.

VOSTOK, a *sloop of the Imperial Russian Navy commanded by Captain Thaddeus von *Bellingshausen which, accompanied by the *Mirny*, circumnavigated the Antarctic continent in 1819–21 and made important surveys and discoveries in the region.

VOYAGE, a journey made at sea by a ship, but the word is generally held to include both the outward and homeward passages made by a ship. According to the traditional pattern of employment at sea, men used to be signed on for a voyage, i.e., they remained in the ship until she returned to her home port, where they were paid off; but this pattern is rapidly being superseded by continuity of service, whereby men join a ship or a shipping line more or less on a permanent career basis.

VOYAL, see VIOL.

VROOM, CORNELISZ, HENDRIKS (1566–1640), Dutch marine artist, was born at Haarlem. Most of his life was devoted to painting seascapes, and he is sometimes called the father of the Dutch school of marine painting. He travelled widely in Europe and was shipwrecked off the coast of Portugal where he resided for some time afterwards. During a visit to England the *Lord High Admiral, Lord *Howard of Effingham, commissioned him to design a series of tapestries depicting the defeat of the Spanish *Armada. These were unfortunately destroyed when the House of Lords caught fire in 1834, though they had previously been engraved by John *Pine, thus preserving this unique pictorial record of one of the great campaigns of the English Navy. The surviving examples of his paintings show him to have been a master of dramatic detail. He spent his later years in his native town of Haarlem.

W

WAFER, LIONEL (*c.* 1660–1705), *buccaneer, joined the band which included Bartholomew *Sharp, William *Dampier, and Basil *Ringrose as a surgeon in 1680. After the siege of Panama he sailed south with Sharp but quarrelled with him and returned across the Isthmus with Dampier. He was accidentally injured and cared for by the Indians, an experience which is the basis of his *Description of the Isthmus of America* (1699). He joined another band of buccaneers in 1686, returning to the Pacific in the *Batchelor's Delight*, in which he sailed back to Philadelphia and Jamestown, where he was fined and imprisoned for piracy, part of his fine being paid to the new College of William and Mary at Williamsburg. He returned to England in 1690 and on account of his book became an adviser to the disastrous Darien Scheme in which some 2,500 Scotsmen were induced to form a colony in the Isthmus as a 'general emporium for the commerce of all the world's nations'. They were virtually exterminated by the Spaniards, only a tiny handful escaping to return to their native land.

WAFT, WHEFT, or **WEFT,** a flag or ensign with its centre or its *fly stopped to the ensign staff. It used to be a signal indicating that a man had fallen overboard; when hung on the mainstay it was a signal of distress; and when hoisted at various mastheads had other meanings, such as recalling all boats, etc. When used today it is a request to the customs to come on board and release tobacco sealed under bond for issue to the crew.

WAFT, to, the old naval term meaning to *convoy; merchant ships in time of war were wafted from place to place by wafters, the equivalent of today's escort vessels.

WAGENAER, LUCAS JANSZOON (*c.* 1534–1605), Dutch seaman and cartographer, was born in Enchuysen. He went to sea at an early age, subsequently became a pilot, and later still a collector of maritime dues in Enchuysen. In 1582 he began the compilation of a pilot book for the coasts of western Europe; this finally developed into the *Spieghel der Zeevaerdt*, a manual of navigation, a pilot book, and a series of nautical charts for the navigation from the Zuiderzee along the continental coasts to Cadiz. It was published in two parts in 1584–5.

Lord *Howard of Effingham, *Lord High Admiral of England, was so impressed with the work that he commissioned Anthony Ashley to prepare an English translation which appeared in 1588 as *The *Mariner's Mirrour* and was widely used by British seamen for a century. Today it is a much prized book, copies being very rare.

WAGGONER, English corruption of the name of *Wagenaer, the great Dutch cartographer, used as a general term to indicate a sea atlas, so great an impact did the atlas *The *Mariner's Mirrour* containing Wagenaer's charts have upon the British seaman of the day. Greenvile *Collins's equally famous *Great Britain's Coasting Pilot*, published in 1693, was also generally known by English seamen as a waggoner in spite of its title. One of the loveliest and best known of these sea atlases is the manuscript *Waggoner of the Great South Sea*, drawn by William *Hack from a Spanish *derroterro captured by Bartholomew *Sharp during his *privateering voyage in the South Pacific, 1681–2, and now in the King's Library, British Museum.

WAIST, that part of the upper deck of a ship between the *forecastle and the *quarterdeck. In sailing ships, that part of the upper deck between the fore- and main-masts.

WAISTCLOTH, sometimes written **WASTECLOATH,** a decorative length of cloth which, during the 16th and 17th centuries, was hung on occasions of state and on royal anniversaries, along the sides of a warship between the *poop and the *forecastle.

WAISTER, the term in sailing ship days for a seaman employed in the waist of a ship for working ship, in which station there was no work on a mast or *yard and little to do beyond hauling on ropes or swabbing the deck. Hence, the name came to be used to describe an untrained or incompetent seaman or one who was worn out after many years of employment.

WALE, an extra thickness of wood bolted to the sides of a ship in positions where protection is needed. A wale running the full length of both sides of a ship just below the *gunwale is more often known as a *rubbing strake and it protects the hull from being damaged when a ship lies alongside a quay where the rise and fall of the tide may cause her to rub against the piers. It is a similar protection if another vessel bumps her while coming alongside. Sailing men-of-war had a wale fixed between each row of gunports similarly to prevent the port-lids being damaged when going alongside an enemy to carry her by boarding. The wale below the lower gunports was the channel-wale, those between the upper rows of gunports were main-wales. Shorter wales, known as chain-wales, were bolted to the ship's sides opposite the masts to carry the ends of the *shrouds (see RIGGING), the object here being to hold the shrouds clear of the gunwale to prevent them rubbing against the ship's side.

WALKER, FREDERICK JOHN (1897–1944), was one of the first officers in the Royal Navy to specialize in anti-submarine warfare in 1921, and in March 1941 he was appointed to H.M.S. *Stork* to command one of the regular escort groups then being formed. He brought his group to a high state of training and was rewarded by a notable victory over the *U-boats, sinking four of them when a *convoy from Gibraltar he was escorting was attacked in December 1941. His exploits in the *Stork* brought him a D.S.O. and bar and, in July 1942, promotion to captain, though he had been previously passed over for this promotion.

He achieved his greatest successes in command of H.M.S. *Starling*, leading the 2nd Escort Group as an independent support group in 1943 and 1944, his group accounting for six U-boats during a single mission.

WALKING BEAM ENGINE, a type of steam engine developed in America from the early pumping engines installed by James Watt in many Cornish mines, in which a beam is pivoted in the centre above a vertical cylinder and transmits the motion of the piston down to a crankshaft by a long connecting rod. This type of engine, used at first on land in mills and factories, was adapted for river steamboats from about 1830, and was to be seen on almost all the sidewheelers on the Mississippi, Ohio, and other western rivers as well as New York ferries and eastern seaboard coastal steamers until well into the present century.

With homespun ingenuity, to make local manufacture simple and to save top weight, the A-frames or entablature on which the beam was mounted in the vessel were almost entirely of wood, and the beam itself was made rigid by means of iron truss rods in the form of a flattened diamond. Owing to the height of these frames, the beam stood in full view above the upper deck of even the largest steamboats, and its movement as it rocked up and down turning the paddle-wheels earned it the Indians' description 'mill walkee on river'.

Because of the weight of this lofty structure and its effect on the vessel's stability, beam engines of this kind were seldom fitted to ocean-going ships. It was entirely American in conception and ideal for its purpose in smooth waters, but not to be found in quite the same form anywhere else in the world. In Europe its counterpart was the side lever engine with a pair of beams placed low down inside the ship. See also PADDLE STEAMER.

WALL KNOT, a *stopper knot on a rope to prevent anything passing beyond it. The rope is unlayed to a distance of four or five times the circumference of the rope and the individual strands tucked over the strand behind and under the strand in front. They are then each tucked again under the two strands in front and brought up to the centre. After each strand is hauled taut they are *whipped together close to the knot and the ends cut off.

Start of a wall knot

WALLIS, SAMUEL (1728–95), British naval captain, was a skilled navigator who made a well-known voyage of discovery round the world in 1766–8. Appointed to command H.M.S. *Dolphin*, he sailed from Plymouth in August 1766 in company with the *sloop *Swallow*, passing through the Magellan Straits into the Pacific in April 1767 when the two ships separated.

Wallis shaped a course to the north-west, discovering many new islands, of which one was Tahiti. After charting their positions, he returned home round the Cape of Good Hope, arriving in England in May 1768. His voyage was remarkable in its freedom from *scurvy, the scourge which in those days decimated crews during long voyages. His circumnavigation was the fore-runner of the three famous voyages of Captain James *Cook, who was equally successful in keeping scurvy at bay. It was only at Batavia, a notably fever-ridden place in this period, that Wallis, and after him Cook, suffered casualties in their crews.

An account of Wallis's circumnavigation was written by George Robertson, master of the *Dolphin*, and was published by the *Hakluyt Society in 1948.

WALT, an old term used of a ship when she was emptied of her *ballast so that she was not *stiff enough in the sea to carry a sail. Such a ship was said to be walt.

WALTER, RICHARD (*c.* 1716–85), British naval chaplain, entered Sidney Sussex College, Cambridge, and after obtaining his B.A. degree in 1740, joined H.M.S. *Centurion in which he accompanied Commodore *Anson during the first part of his voyage of circumnavigation (1740–4). He left the ship at Macao in November 1742 and returned to England in an *East Indiaman. In March 1745 he was appointed chaplain of Portsmouth Dockyard, a post he held until his death in 1785. In 1748 he published *A Voyage Round the World*, a well-known account of Anson's famous voyage, a work which went into several editions and is still considered the best and most accurate narrative. A claim put forward after his death that he was not the author of this work was satisfactorily refuted by his widow.

WARATAH, S.S., a cargo liner of 9,339 tons and probably the best-known example of a ship lost without trace. She was built in 1908 for the Blue Anchor Line and was employed on the Australia run via the Cape of Good Hope, carrying passengers, cargo, and emigrants. She had a service speed of 13 knots and was classed 100 A1 (see LLOYD'S REGISTER OF SHIPPING) at *Lloyd's. With cabin accommodation for 288 passengers, and a crew of 144, she also carried emigrants to Australia on the outward run in temporary berths between decks, returning with cargo on the homeward run. Her 17 lifeboats and three liferafts could accommodate 921 persons. She was not fitted with wireless, but this was not unusual in 1908.

She sailed from London on her second round voyage in April 1909, reached Australia where passengers and emigrants were landed, and sailed for home after loading 6,500 tons of cargo. Her first port of call was Durban where, after topping up her coal bunkers, she sailed for Cape Town on the evening of 26 July. Next day she overtook the S.S. *Clan MacIntyre*, which was steering the same course, and she was never seen or heard of again. On 28 July the *Clan MacIntyre* reported a gale of 'quite exceptional fierceness and power ... (with) tremendous sea', but she and other ships came through it safely. It was presumed

that this must have been the cause of the loss of the *Waratah* for there was no sign of her or her lifeboats, and neither wreckage nor any of the bodies of the 211 persons on board were found or washed ashore. Rumours that she lacked stability were brought forward at the official inquiry into her loss, but as no cargo stowage plan survived, they could not be substantiated. When last seen by the *Clan MacIntyre* she had no *list and was not *rolling unduly.

Her loss proved disastrous for the Blue Anchor Line, which was then bought by the *P & O Company.

WARDROBE, the name generally used to denote all the various sails carried on board a racing or cruising yacht. It ranges from the heavy weather sails, such as storm *jibs, storm staysails, etc., made of heavy duty canvas, to the light weather sails, such as *genoa and *yankee jibs, *spinnakers, *ghosters, etc., usually made of nylon, Terylene, or Dacron.

WARDROOM, the name which used to be given to the commissioned officers' mess in a British warship. The only commissioned officers who did not mess in the wardroom were the captain of the ship, who messed alone in his own apartments, and sub-lieutenants who, though commissioned, messed with *midshipmen in the *gunroom. Today, in all warships, all officers, whether commissioned or not, mess in the wardroom, with the exception of the captain who still normally messes alone.

WARM FRONT, the line, in a typical depression, where the cold air coming in to fill the low pressure area pushes the warm air up in a bulge. The front edge of the bulge, where the warm air has not yet been displaced by the cold, is the warm front. See DEPRESSION, METEOROLOGY.

WARM THE BELL, to, a phrase used in the British Navy to mean doing something unjustifiably or unnecessarily early. On board warships in the days of sail, time was measured by a half-hour sand-*glass. Each time the sand ran through, the glass was turned, usually by the *midshipman of the watch, and the appropriate number of bells struck. It was supposed, perhaps rightly, that if the glass was warmed the expansion of the neck would allow the sand to run through a little more quickly. Hence the idea that if midshipmen of night watches put the glass under their coats and grasped it tightly, eight bells, and the return to one's hammock, would come gratifyingly earlier than it should.

WARP, (1) a light *hawser used in the movement of a ship from one place to another by means of a *kedge anchor, a *capstan, or of men hauling on it. It is not a tow-rope, which involves the power of another ship. (2) The ropes or wires attached to a *trawl by which it is veered to the sea bottom and later hauled in by the trawler on completion of the fishing operations. (3) The ropes used for securing a ship alongside a quay, jetty, etc., or another ship. See also SPRINGS. (4) A warp of herrings, a packet of four. It is a term mainly confined to the east coasts of Britain which border the North Sea herring fishery.

WARP, to, the operation of moving a ship by means of warps from one position in a harbour or anchorage to another. It was also a term used in rigging lofts in the days of sail to mean the measurement and laying out of rigging before it was cut to the proper lengths. In this case the rigging was said to be warped before it was cut out.

WARREN, Sir JOHN BORLASE (1753–1822), British admiral, was commodore of a *frigate squadron off the coast of France in 1794 and was knighted in the same year after capturing three out of four French frigates which had done much damage to British trade during the Revolutionary War with France (1793–1801). In the following year he achieved what must be a record in frigate warfare, destroying or capturing 220 enemy ships and, incidentally, amassing a considerable fortune in *prize money. He was largely instrumental in defeating the French attempt to land an army in *Donegal Bay in Ireland in 1798, for which service he received the thanks of both the English and Irish parliaments.

He was promoted rear admiral in 1799 and vice admiral in 1805, hoisting his flag in the *Foudroyant and capturing in March 1806 the French 74-gun *Marengo* during the Napoleonic War (1803–15). In July 1810 he was promoted admiral and in 1813 became commander-in-chief on the North American station, this being his last naval appointment.

WARRIOR, H.M.S., was the first *ironclad ship built for the British Navy, a reply to the French armoured ship *Gloire*. She was originally classified as a steam *frigate of 9,210 tons and was launched at Blackwall on the River Thames in 1860, but was re-classified as a 3rd class armoured screw *battleship in 1887. She was armed with twenty-six 68-pounder muzzle loaders, ten 110-pounder, and four 70-pounder breech loaders. She had $4\frac{1}{2}$-in. iron armour with 18-in. teak backing and a full outfit of masts and sails. In 1904 she was renamed *Vernon III* and became part of the *Vernon* torpedo school at Portsmouth, continuing there until 1923, when she was removed from the Navy List and

presumably sold. In the 1960s she was discovered at Pembroke as '*C.77*', an oil fuel pier, where she is still in service.

The next ship of the name in the Royal Navy was an armoured *cruiser launched at Pembroke in 1903 and was serving with the 1st Cruiser Squadron in the Mediterranean when the First World War (1914–18) broke out. In December 1914 she joined the *Grand Fleet, based at *Scapa Flow, and was engaged in the battle of *Jutland on 31 May 1916. She was so severely damaged in the action that she had to be abandoned and sunk.

WARSPITE, H.M.S., a name which was given to one of the ships built by Elizabeth I. This first *Warspite*, or *Warspight*, was launched at Deptford in 1596 and was a 36-gun ship of 648 tons. In the year of her launch, commanded by Sir Walter *Raleigh, she took part in the expedition led by the Earl of Essex against Cadiz, and also in that to the Azores in the following year. In 1602 she was engaged in an expedition commanded by Admiral Sir Richard Leveson to the coast of Spain, and in 1627 was with the expedition of Admiral the Duke of Buckingham to the Île de Rhé. This was the end of her active service and in 1634 she became a hulk for harbour service.

Her successor, launched in 1666, saw a good deal of action before her name was changed to *Edinburgh* in 1715. She was present at the St. James's Day Fight during the Second Anglo-Dutch War (1665–7) in the month after she was launched and was also present at the battles of *Solebay, Schooneveld, and the *Texel in 1672 during the Third Dutch War (1672–4), and at *Barfleur in 1692. After being rebuilt in 1701–2 she took part in the battle of *Velez Malaga in 1704 during the War of Spanish Succession (1702–13). The third *Warspite*, launched in 1758 during the Seven Years War (1756–63), fought in Admiral *Boscawen's action off *Lagos, and in the battle of *Quiberon Bay, both in 1759, the 'year of victories'.

Another *Warspite* was a *battleship launched at Devonport in 1913, and she had the most glorious career of all the Royal Navy's ships of that name. In the First World War (1914–18) she fought at the battle of *Jutland, and in the Second World War saw varied service, mainly in the Mediterranean, which added no fewer than fourteen separate battle honours to her name. In 1947 she was sold, but, while being towed from Portsmouth to the Clyde for breaking up, she was driven ashore in Mount's Bay on the Cornish coast. It was not until 1956 that the work of dismantling and removing the remains of the *Warspite* was completed. The name has now been revived for one of the Royal Navy's nuclear *submarines.

WASHBOARD or **WASHSTRAKE,** a movable upper *strake which can be attached to the *gunwales of some open boats when under sail to keep out spray. The *coamings of the *cockpits of yachts are sometimes also known as washboards.

WASHINGTON, D.C., federal capital of the U.S.A. and home of the *Smithsonian Institution, which incorporates one of the best-known maritime collections in the U.S.A. There are five smaller maritime museums in Washington which illustrate particular aspects of the maritime history of the U.S.A.

WASHSTRAKE, see WASHBOARD.

WASSENAER, JACOB VAN, Lord of Obdam (1610–65), Dutch admiral, began his career as a soldier in the army of the United Provinces, commanding a troop of cavalry and taking part in various sieges, including that of Maastricht in 1623. When Marten *Tromp was killed at the battle of *Scheveningen in 1653, Wassenaer accepted the command of the Dutch fleet. He commanded the fleet during the war against Portugal in 1657 and, after a successful action in which he captured twenty-one Portuguese ships, returned to Holland to become embroiled in the war between Denmark and Sweden, in which Holland supported the Danish cause. In October 1658 he led the Dutch fleet into Danish waters and defeated the Swedish fleet commanded by Admiral Wrangel, which was blockading *Copenhagen, at the battle of the Sound.

He resigned in 1659 because of ill health, but on the outbreak of the Second Anglo-Dutch War (1665–7) was asked to resume command. He was early to sea with a fleet of 103 ships, capturing a valuable English convoy off Hamburg and, ten days later, appearing off the coast of Norfolk, where he fell in with the English fleet of 109 ships under the command of *James, Duke of York. The two fleets were engaged off *Lowestoft, where the two flagships, the English *Royal Charles* and the Dutch *Eendracht*, hotly engaged each other. At the height of the duel between these two ships the *Eendracht* blew up, only five men being saved out of her complement of 409. Wassenaer was not among the five. It was supposed that burning wads from her guns had ignited her powder, but a Dutch report stated that Wassenaer's Negro servant, in a fit of revenge for much hard treatment, flung a burning torch into the powder magazine and deliberately caused the explosion.

WATCH, (1) the division of the 24 hours of the seaman's day into periods of duty of 4 hours. Thus there should be six 4-hour watches in a day, but as this would entail ships' companies,

organized into two or three watches, keeping the same watches every day, the evening watch from 1600 to 2000 is divided into two 2-hour watches, known as the first and last dog watches. Starting at midnight, the names of the watches are Middle, Morning, Forenoon, Afternoon, First Dog, Last Dog, and First. See also BELLS. **(2)** The basis of the internal organization of a ship's company whereby men can obtain regular periods of rest although the work of the ship must go on day and night. The crew is divided either into two watches (*port and *starboard), with each watch alternating their periods of duty, or into three watches (usually red, white, and blue), so that every man gets two periods of rest to every one period of duty. The periods of duty correspond to the watches into which the seaman's day is divided.

WATCH, to, a navigational *buoy is said to be watching when it is floating in the correct position as marked on a *chart, and its light or other signal, if it has one, is in efficient working order. Other buoys are watching when they are carrying out the purpose for which they are intended, e.g., an *anchor buoy.

WATCH BUOY, a *buoy moored in the vicinity of a *lightship from which she can check her position to make sure that she has not shifted by *dragging. Since the positions of all lightships are marked on *charts and are widely used by navigators for *fixing the position of their ships by visual *bearings, it is of vital importance that the lightship should be exactly in the position indicated on the chart.

WATCH-BILL, a nominal list of officers and men on board a ship giving the *watches and stations to which each is quartered for all purposes on board. Thus any officer or man, on consulting the list, will know which watch he is in, to which *part of the ship he is allocated, his station for abandoning ship, for entering or leaving harbour, and for any other particular purpose on board. See also QUARTER-BILL.

WATER SAIL, a small sail spread in square-rigged ships in calm weather and a following wind to increase the area of canvas spread to the wind. There were two places where such sails could be spread, below the lower *studdingsail or below the boom of the *driver.

WATER-LAID ROPE, see CABLE-LAID ROPE.

WATERWAY, the outboard planks of a ship's deck, often hollowed to provide a shallow channel to carry off water on deck through the suppers. Larger ships often have a channel-iron along the outboard sides of the deck to serve the same purpose. See also DEVIL.

WATSON, CHARLES (1714–57), British vice admiral, was in his way one of the most brilliant, though one of the least known, of the 18th century British admirals. Appointed commander-in-chief in the East Indies, he proved himself a man of immense energy and performance, using his small squadron of warships, in co-operation with the native army of Robert Clive, to break the French hold on India. His naval campaigns, if small, were brilliantly conceived and executed, and culminated in Clive's victory at Plassey in 1757 by which India passed under the control of Britain in the form of its *East India Company. Without Watson's enthusiastic naval support and his determination to prevent all French movement in the seas around India, Plassey could never have been won. Watson died of fever two months after the battle, and with his death the British Navy lost one of its most far-seeing young admirals.

WATSON, GEORGE LENNOX (1851–1904), British naval architect, was born in Glasgow and started as a draughtsman in the shipyard of R. Napier and Son in 1867. While employed by A. and J. Inglis, shipbuilders, he designed and built himself a sailing boat which embodied some unusual ideas of his own, and followed her with a design for the 5-ton racing class. With two colleagues he built in a corner of the shipyard a second 5-tonner to his own design, *Vril*; launched in 1876 she was raced through three seasons with outstanding success in her class.

His first professional commission was a design for *Verve* of the 10-ton class for his friend Robert Wylie in 1877. For the next two seasons she repeated *Vril*'s success, but in 1879 his next 10-ton design, *Madge*, carried away all the prizes. In 1881 this boat was taken to the U.S.A. where her racing successes astonished the Americans in their broader and shallower yachts. In 1887 he was commissioned by Mr. James Bell to design a new challenger for the *America*'s *Cup. Named *Thistle*, this handsome 108-ft *cutter was narrowly beaten by the defender *Volunteer*. But his most famous yacht was the great *Britannia*, which he designed for the Prince of Wales (later Edward VII) in 1893, a 212-ton gaff cutter. He designed also the *Meteor*, the German Kaiser's great racing *schooner, and two more challengers for the *America*'s Cup, Lord Dunraven's *Valkyrie II* and Sir Thomas *Lipton's *Shamrock II*.

Watson designed more than 300 racing yachts, as well as cruising boats and some of the largest schooners and steam yachts in the country. His name was also perpetuated in the Watson-type of *lifeboat which he introduced for the Royal National Lifeboat Institution. All his creations were notable for their elegance of line and their seaworthiness.

WAVE, the oscillations of the sea caused by wind blowing along the surface and moving in the direction in which the wind blows. The water in a wave does not move forward in a horizontal direction but rises and falls below the surface, unless the force of the wind is enough to cause the crest of the wave to overbalance and break, when the water in the crest does move forward. The height of waves depend on the wind strength and the length of the *fetch, the distance that the wind has been blowing over the open sea; and the speed of waves depends on the wind strength, up to about a maximum speed of about 25 knots. The maximum height of a wave from trough to crest is about 45 feet (14 m), except perhaps in the centre of a hurricane, where greater heights have occasionally been recorded. A code of the sea state, in the same form as the *Beaufort Scale for winds, is:

Code	Description	Mean max. height of waves (feet)
0	glassy calm	0
1	calm (ripples)	0–1
2	smooth (wavelets)	1–2
3	slight	2–4
4	moderate	4–8
5	rough	8–13
6	very rough	13–20
7	high	20–30
8	very high	30–45
9	phenomenal	over 45

WAVE LINE THEORY, a theory explaining the pattern of waves caused by floating bodies when moving along the surface of the water. It was formulated by William *Froude after a series of experiments he carried out from 1868 onwards with models of ships in his private test tank near Torquay. Froude propounded the theory, later substantiated by Scott *Russell and other investigators in naval architecture, that when a floating body, such as a ship, moves through the water it creates a wave system around itself which is the complex result of varying pressures below the surface of the water. At the entrance of the body—in the case of a ship the bow—underwater pressures are set up which cause a heaping up of the water immediately ahead of and to each side of the vessel's bow. These bow waves are followed by alternate troughs and crests along the vessel's sides until this wave system meets round the stern, where reduced pressures—a partial suction, which can be intensified when the ship is propeller-driven—break up the waves, leaving a confused area of eddies and subsidiary waves in the wake of the vessel. From Froude's and Russell's observations was developed this theory of wave formation and pattern which has been used by naval architects and others connected with ship design ever since.

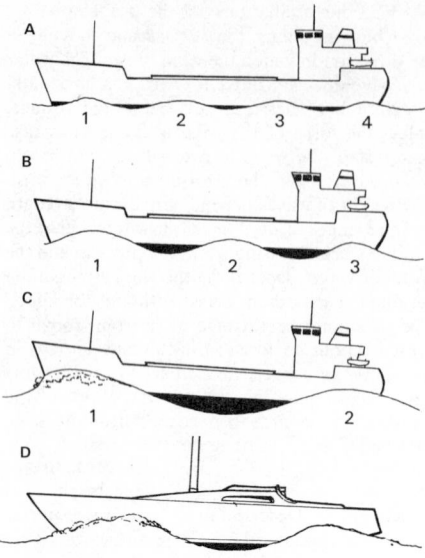

A Ship of 400 ft at speed of $(0·8\sqrt{L}) = 16·0$ *knots*
B Ship of 400 ft at speed of $(1·0\sqrt{L}) = 20·0$ *knots*
C Ship of 400 ft at speed of $(1·4\sqrt{L}) = 28·0$ *knots*
D Boat of 40 ft at maximum of $(1·4\sqrt{L}) = 8·5$ *knots*

Froude's experiments led to his discovery of the relative quantities of resistance to vessels of various forms when moving through water caused (*a*) by friction or drag, as a film of water is drawn along by the surface of the hull and forms eddies or local areas of disturbance in the water adjacent, and (*b*) at higher speeds by the formation of a pattern of waves which varies with the design of the hull and with the speed, and is called the vessel's wash. At very low speeds, a *knot or two, when no surface waves and only eddies are formed, almost the whole of the resistance to the ship's progress (some 90–95 per cent) is due to the drag on the hull, or skin friction. As the speed rises, however, and a wave at the bow begins to form, the relation of skin friction to wave-making resistance changes. At normal service speed for a conventional ship, expressed by the formula $0·8\sqrt{L}$ knots (where L is the ship's waterline length in feet), which gives, for example, a 400-ft ship a speed of 16 knots, the wave-making or wash accounts for some 40–50 per cent of the total resistance, according to the design of the hull and the state of the ship's bottom, whether clean and smooth or rusty and coated with weed and barnacles. At this relative speed the pattern of waves formed is shown roughly in diagram A in which there will be noted four distinct wave crests from bow to stern.

With an increase of speed to a value of, say, $1·0\sqrt{L}$ (or 20 knots for a 400-ft waterline ship)

the waves formed along the hull are considerably higher and their crests correspondingly farther apart, with one at the bow, a second roughly amidships and a third abreast the stern (diagram B, 1, 2, and 3). Such a wave pattern accounts for some 55–60 per cent of the total resistance, again according to the design and state of the hull. If speed is made to increase still further, both wave-forming resistance and surface drag begin to increase dramatically. The accompanying diagram shows, by a representative curve, this developing increase in resistance and the shaft horsepower needed to drive a normal vessel up to the theoretical maximum speed of $1·4\sqrt{L}$ knots: in the case of a 400-ft ship, 28 knots. If such a vessel had sufficiently powerful engines to reach that speed—for a conventional ship something of the order of 160,000 shaft horsepower would be needed, far more than any normal commercial vessel is likely to have available—the wave pattern would assume that shown in diagram C, where the bow wave and second wave crests are approximately the vessel's length apart. Under these conditions the ship's bow would be lifted by the pressure of the water passing under it, while the stern would squat or be drawn down until the after deck was awash, and the vessel would in effect be climbing a slope of water of her own making. So great is the resistance of this wave pattern that it is conceded to be impracticable, apart from being commercially uneconomic, to attain anything of the order of $1·4\sqrt{L}$ knots with a conventionally

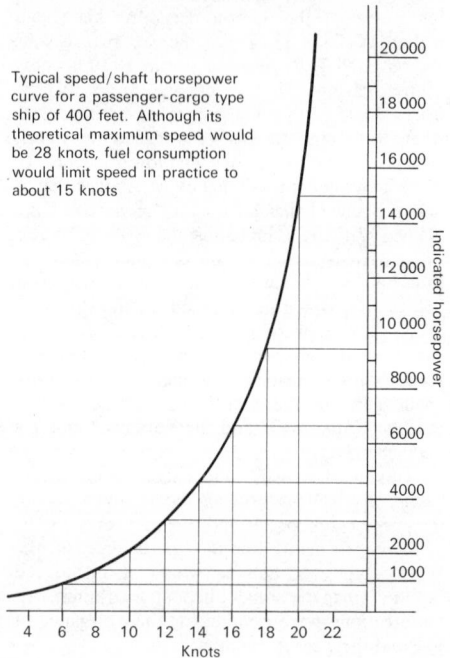

Typical speed/shaft horsepower curve for a passenger-cargo type ship of 400 feet. Although its theoretical maximum speed would be 28 knots, fuel consumption would limit speed in practice to about 15 knots

designed hull. If such speeds are demanded an entirely different design of hull is needed, with the fine entrance at the bow and broad flat stern of the naval *destroyer or the conventional speedboat, which reduces this tendency to squat and enables the vessel to run as level in a fore-and-aft lines as is practicable.

Sailing yachts of good racing design, when given the right conditions of a strong wind and a smooth sea, occasionally achieve this $1 \cdot 4\sqrt{L}$ relative speed, when the lee bow wave will rise almost to the rail, the lee deck amidships will be close to the bow wave's hollow or trough, and the stern will be awash on the lee quarter wave. This is the maximum theoretical speed of which the conventional single-hulled yacht is capable under sail power alone, the effective waterline length of the yacht, however, being increased by any over-hang at the bow and stern. Beyond this speed in any normal yacht, more sail area or a strengthen-ing wind will only cause her to heel farther over, presenting a curious shape of hull in the water and burying her lee deck, so that resistance rises sharply and her speed at once drops. Diagram D shows the wave formation of a conventional rac-ing yacht with an effective waterline length of 40 feet (12·2 m) sailing at her maximum speed $(1 \cdot 4\sqrt{L})$ of approximately 8·5 knots. These ratios, however, do not apply to multihull yachts (*catamarans, *trimarans, etc.), speedboats, or racing *dinghies designed for *planing. See also LAMINAR FLOW.

'WAVY NAVY', a colloquial term in the British Navy to describe officers and ratings of the reserves. The term comes from the wavy stripes of gold braid which used to be worn on their sleeves by reserve officers as indications of rank, but is no longer applicable since, in 1956, the wavy stripes were abolished and reserve officers now wear the same rank insignia on their sleeves as active service officers.

WAY, the movement of a ship through the water by means of her own power, or the force of the wind on her sails. But see also UNDER WAY.

WAYS, the parallel platforms of timber which incline gradually towards the water, one on each side of the *keel of a ship being built, and down which the cradle in which she is held slides when she is *launched. The fixed platforms are known as the ground ways, the sliding part as the sliding or launching ways, and the two together as a slipway.

WEAR, to, the operation of bringing a sailing vessel onto the other *tack by bringing the wind around the *stern, as opposed to tacking, when the wind is brought round the *bow. It has been suggested that the word originated from *veer, which has a similar meaning, but the term to

wear a ship is the earlier of the two. In the past tense, a ship is wore, not worn.

WEAR, to, a term used afloat in connection with the flying of flags. In nautical parlance a ship flies her national flag or ensign but wears a personal flag, such as an admiral's flag. In the past tense, a flag is worn, not wore as in the preceding entry.

WEATHER, in addition to its normal meteoro-logical meaning (for which see METEOROLOGY), weather is also used by seamen as an adjective applied to anything which lies to windward. Thus a ship is said to have the weather gage of another when she lies to windward; a ship under way has a weather side, which is that side which faces the wind; a vessel under sail has weather shrouds on her windward side; a coastline that lies to wind-ward of a ship is a weather shore. WEATHER HELM: a ship under sail carries weather *helm when the *tiller has to be held to windward, or the wheel put down to leeward, to make her keep a steady course. See also GRIPE, TO. A ship is said to be 'WEATHERLY' when she can steer closer to the wind than the average, thus gaining an advantage in manoeuvring or in making a pas-sage when the destination is to windward.

WEATHER LORE, the ability of the seaman to foretell the weather by the appearance of the sky, change of direction of winds, cloud formations, variation of atmospheric pressure, etc. It is often expressed in terms of jingles, of which perhaps the best known are:

Mackerel skies and mares' tails,
Make tall ships carry short sails.

When the wind shifts against the sun,
Trust it not for back it will run.
When the wind follows the sun,
Fine weather will never be done.

Although this is often true of the northern hemi-sphere, the reverse holds good in the southern.

If the wind is north-east three days without rain,
Eight days will go by before south again.

If woolly fleeces deck the heavenly way
Be sure no rain will mar a summer's day.

With the rain before the wind
Stays and topsails you must mind,
But with the wind before the rain
Your topsails you may set again.

When the sea-hog (porpoise) jumps,
Stand by at your pumps.

First rise after low
Foretells a stronger blow.

Seagull, seagull, sit on the sand,
It's never good weather when you're on the land.

The Jane *and the* Beaufoy *in Indian Cove, Tierra del Fuego; engraving from Weddell's* A Voyage toward the South Pole, *1825*

WEATHER SHIP, a vessel which occupies a station in the ocean and measures the various weather ingredients, such as barometric pressure, temperature, visibility, rainfall, force and direction of the upper wind, and the wind at sea level, etc., signalling them to a weather centre ashore which plots the information on a weather chart and uses it to predict the weather during the following 24–48 hours. Originally these vessels were small obsolescent warships, such as *frigates, *sloops, *cutters, etc., but today most weather ships are specially built for the purpose.

WEBBER, JOHN (c. 1750–93), British artist and draughtsman, was born in London, the son of a Swiss sculptor. He studied in Berne and Paris before entering the Royal Academy Schools in 1776. On Captain James *Cook's third voyage of discovery (1776–9), he took the place of William *Hodges as official draughtsman and on his return was employed by the British Admiralty to compile the official account of the voyage, which was published in 1784. He was well known as a landscape artist, and collections of the paintings he made on Cook's voyage are in Admiralty House and the *National Maritime Museum, both in London.

WEDDELL, JAMES (1787–1834), a former *master in the Royal Navy, was one of a number of British sealers active in Antarctic waters after

the conclusion of the Napoleonic wars. In 1820–1 he visited the South Shetland Islands and in 1822 sailed to and named the South Orkney Islands shortly after their discovery by Nathaniel *Palmer. In 1822–4, with the *brig *Jane* and the *cutter *Beaufoy*, he charted the South Shetland Islands and also part of the Weddell Sea, into which he penetrated as far south as latitude 74° 15′ S., longitude 34° 16′ W., a record at the time for this ice-choked region. He published an account of this voyage in *A Voyage towards the South Pole* (1825–7). See also DUMONT D'URVILLE, Jules-Sébastien-César.

WEDDING GARLAND, an 18th and 19th century custom in British warships of hoisting a garland of evergreens in the rigging of a warship when she entered harbour to indicate that she was out of discipline and women would be allowed on board. It was also hoisted on the day any member of the crew was married; if the captain, to the main topgallant stay, if a seaman, on the mast to which he was stationed in the watch-bill. The custom exists in the British Navy to the present day, and a garland is still hoisted on the day when a member of the ship's company is being married.

WELL, a vertical cylindrical trunk in a ship through which the suction pipes of the *bilge pumps pass, reaching right down into the lowest part of the *hull. Its object is to prevent *ballast or other objects from entering and choking the suction boxes of the pumps. In older wooden ships it was the trunk in which the ship's pump worked. It was the *carpenter's duty, particularly in warships after battle, continually to sound the well to make sure that the ship was not making water through damage to the hull. As the trunk led to the lowest portion of the hull, water inside the ship would naturally flow there and thus give a maximum reading of the amount inboard.

WELL DECK, the two spaces on the main deck of the older type of merchant ship, one between the *forecastle and the midships housing which supports the *bridge, the other between the latter and the *poop deck. Most modern merchant vessels are now built with the bridge right aft and an uninterrupted flush deck from the bridge to the *bows of the ship.

WELL FOUND, the description of a vessel which is adequately and fully equipped with all gear required for her efficient operation.

WELLES, GIDEON (1802–78), was the Secretary of the U.S. Navy in the cabinet of President Lincoln during the American Civil War (1861–5). He belonged to a Connecticut family which had emigrated to America in 1633. Although he had studied law, he spent his life as a newspaper editor and in politics, and it was his efforts in this field which brought about his appointment to the Lincoln cabinet. Although he was present at Lincoln's inaugural address, after the secession from the Union of the seven Confederate States, and heard the new President declare that the Union would hold all property belonging to it, Welles did nothing to organize the defence of the valuable Navy Yard at Norfolk, Virginia, or the revenue cutters, customs houses, lighthouse tenders, and other buildings within the seceding States, except those at Key West, Florida. His lack of activity did much to hamper the operations of the Union Navy throughout the war.

The main achievement of the Union Navy in the war was the blockade of the Confederate States, but Welles even disapproved of this and so expressed himself to Lincoln. Throughout the whole war period Welles avoided responsibility at all times, and was never on close terms with any of his colleagues. In particular, he did not care for the Assistant Secretary, G. V. Fox, although the latter was much more valuable in the Navy Department than his senior.

WEMYSS, ROSSLYN ERSKINE, 1st Baron Wester-Wemyss (1864–1933), British admiral of the fleet, was First Sea Lord at the time of

Germany's defeat in the First World War (1914–18). Born in London he entered the training ship H.M.S. *Britannia at the age of 13, at the same time as the Duke of York (later George V) and in 1879 joined the Bacchante in which the latter and his brother, the Duke of Clarence, made a world cruise. Service in the royal yachts, Osborne and Victoria and Albert, brought him accelerated promotion and in 1903 he became the first captain of the new Naval College at Osborne. In 1911 he was promoted rear admiral and in October 1912 hoisted his flag in the Orion in command of the 2nd Battle Squadron of the Home Fleet.

On the outbreak of war in 1914 he was commanding the 12th Cruiser Squadron, employed in protecting the transfer of Canadian troops to Britain; on its dispersal in February 1915, he became governor of Lemnos Island in the Mediterranean, the base from which the *Dardanelles operation was launched in April of that year, becoming second-in-command to Vice Admiral *de Robeck, the naval commander-in-chief, after Admiral Carden had been forced to retire because of ill health. In January 1916 he was appointed commander-in-chief in the East Indies and Egypt, and played an active part in the relief of Kut. He joined the Board of Admiralty as Deputy First Sea Lord in 1917, and on Sir John *Jellicoe's dismissal on 27 December of that year he took his place as First Sea Lord. After the end of the war he played a major part in drafting the naval clauses of the Treaty of Versailles, but his exclusion from the list of war honours awarded to the Services led him to tender his resignation, which was not accepted. When he left office in November 1919 he was promoted admiral of the fleet and raised to the peerage.

WERNER, BARTHOLOMAUS VON (1842–c. 1906), German naval officer, was born in Coblenz and joined the Prussian Navy in 1856. In command of the *corvette Ariadne, 1877–9, he concluded a treaty of friendship with the inhabitants of Samoa and the Marshall Islands, preventing the former from accepting the protection of any other power and by this means creating a valuable German sphere of influence in the Pacific Ocean.

He retired from the navy in 1887 with the rank of rear admiral and took up writing, choosing as his subjects descriptions of life on board ship and of the countries he had visited. His best-known works are Ein deutsches Kriegschiff in der Sudsee (1891), Deutsches Kreigschiffsleben und Seefahrtkunst (1891), Die Kampfmittel zur See (1892), Der Seekrieg, der Geschwaderdienst und die Bedeutung der Kriegswerften (1893), Der Kriegsmarine, ihr Personal und ihre Organisation (1894).

WEST COUNTRY WHIPPING, a method of *whipping the end of a rope by centring the whipping twine around the part of the rope to be whipped and half knotting it with an overhand knot at every half turn so that each consecutive knot is on the opposite side of the rope. The whipping is finished off with a *reef knot. See SAILMAKER'S WHIPPING, COMMON WHIPPING.

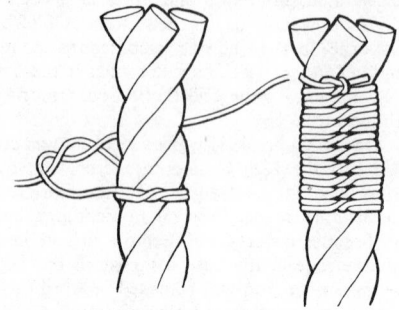

West country whipping

WESTALL, WILLIAM (1781–1850), British topographical painter and engraver, was born at Hartford and studied at the Royal Academy Schools. At the age of 18 he was chosen as the official draughtsman to sail with Captain Matthew *Flinders in H.M.S. *Investigator in his voyage to survey the coast of Australia. In 1803 he was shipwrecked off the north-east coast when returning home with Flinders in H.M.S. *Porpoise*, the *Investigator* having been condemned in Sydney as unseaworthy. He was rescued by a vessel bound for China and did not reach England until 1805. He then set out on a visit to Madeira, where he had a narrow escape from drowning, and thence to Jamaica, and on his return settled down to paint pictures from the sketches he had made during his travels.

Most of these were exhibited at the Royal Academy and the British Institute and today are recognized as a valuable and accurate record of the early Australian scene. In 1811 he was elected a member of the Old Water Colour Society and the following year was made A.R.A. During the latter part of his life he worked mainly on illustrations for topographical works, which form a remarkable collection of original drawings, aquatints, and lithographs of great distinction.

WESTON, Dame AGNES (1840–1918), religious and welfare worker and advocate of temperance, devoted her energies to working on behalf of sailors of the British Navy from 1872, when she met a Miss Wintz and in partnership with her raised funds to establish the Royal Sailors' Rests at Devonport, Portsmouth, and Chatham. In encouragement of Christian religion and temperance, she founded the journal *Ashore*

and Afloat and issued a monthly letter, both of which had a wide circulation among men of the British fleet. In 1918 she was created a Dame of the British Empire. 'Aggie' Weston, as she was known to many thousands of British naval ratings, was a much-loved figure in the Royal Navy, and her devoted work on behalf of seamen has a permanent memorial in the shape of the rest homes in British naval ports which are always open to seamen in need of rest and accommodation.

Her sailors' homes are still so well known and she herself so well remembered that when a new *frigate was named in 1940 after the town of Weston-super-Mare, a new generation of sailors gave the ship the nickname *Aggie-on-Horseback*.

'WET', a maritime term meaning stupid. 'Wet as a scrubber', extremely stupid.

WETTED SURFACE, that part of the hull of a vessel below the water level when she is upright in the water. It varies, of course, with the loading of the vessel. The wetted surface is an element of the calculations of a vessel's speed; the greater the wetted surface, the less the speed. In yachts and other sailing vessels, the wetted surface decreases momentarily as they *heel to the wind, thus allowing them to go faster. A further increase in speed derives from the large overhangs forward and aft, which become immersed as the yacht heels thus increasing her waterline length. For the relationship between speed and waterline length see HYDRODYNAMICS.

WHACK, the old seaman's term for his daily ration of victuals according to the scale laid down by the various national Merchant Shipping Acts in force at the time. The word signified the exact amount and no more. In Britain the Merchant Shipping Act of 1906 laid down, for the first time, a minimum scale which was adequate, and perhaps even generous, to maintain the health of merchant seamen. The weekly allowance was 3 lb bread, 4 lb biscuit, 3 lb salt beef, 2 lb salt pork, $2\frac{1}{4}$ lb preserved meat, $\frac{3}{4}$ lb fish, 6 lb potatoes, $\frac{1}{2}$ lb dried or compressed vegetables, 2 lb flour, 8 oz oatmeal, $1\frac{3}{4}$ oz tea, 4 oz coffee, $1\frac{1}{4}$ lb sugar, $\frac{1}{3}$ lb condensed milk, $\frac{1}{2}$ lb butter, 1 lb marmalade or jam, $\frac{1}{2}$ lb syrup or molasses, 4 oz suet. In general, American and Canadian ships were considered to be more generously victualled than the ships of other nations, British and French about average, and German and Scandinavian below the average. (1 oz = 2·83 gm, 1 lb = 0·454 kg.)

WHALE, (1) the largest mammal of the ocean, but see WHALING, **(2)** the code name given to the floating piers in a *Mulberry Harbour during the Second World War.

WHALE CATCHER, a tender to a * whale factory ship, used entirely for the * harpooning of whales. Each factory ship usually has from eight to ten catchers, whose only purpose is to locate and harpoon whales, using a harpoon gun mounted in the bows for the purpose. They are the modern descendant of the oar-propelled * whaleboats, and today are either steam or diesel engined of a size up to as much as 500 tons.

WHALE FACTORY SHIP, a large modern vessel of around 20,000 tons * displacement specifically designed to process whales as they are caught. She sails in company with a number of * whale catchers, which are smaller vessels carrying a * harpoon gun and usually fitted with * sonar; when these catchers kill a whale, they inflate it so that it floats, mark it with a small flag, and leave it for the whale factory ship to retrieve. The dead whale is hauled on board the factory ship up a sloping ramp at the stern on to the * flensing deck, where it is stripped of its blubber. All operations of extracting the whale oil, preserving the meat, etc., are carried out on board the whale factory ship, which is stored and equipped both to maintain its catchers and to remain on the whaling ground for the whole of a whaling season.

WHALEBOAT, the name given to an open boat, pointed at both ends so that it was convenient for beaching either * bow- or * stern-to, and used under oars. It had no * rudder and was steered by an oar over the stern. Of robust construction, they were used for a variety of coastal work which entailed the necessity of frequent beaching.

They were modelled on the original whaleboats carried by the old-fashioned whaling ships. The whaling ships, according to size, carried as many as six or eight whaleboats, each with its own well-trained crew and harpooner, and their particular shape gave them the speed required to get close enough to a whale, when it came up to the surface to * blow, for the harpoon to be launched by hand.

WHALER, (1) the generic and older name for ships of all types engaged in the whale fishery. It was originally the name used for the vessel, with its complement of * whaleboats, which sailed to catch whales with hand-launched * harpoons, until about 1865 when the harpoon gun was invented. The whaler's boats or tenders, each with its harpoon gun mounted in the bows, then themselves became known as whalers until the beginning of the 20th century, when they were powered with steam engines and became more widely known as whale catchers. Today there is no distinct type of vessel in the whaling industry specifically known as a whaler, although the term

remains as a loose description of vessels of all types engaged in the trade. It was, and still is, often used equally loosely to describe a man engaged in the whaling industry. **(2)** A warship's boat, usually fitted with oars and sails and taking its design from the original whaleboats used in whalers. In the British Navy a whaler * pulls five oars and is * yawl rigged with triangular * jib and * mizen and a * gunter mainsail.

WHALING, the general, overall term for the catching of whales, has been practised among primitive peoples since neolithic times, though then it would have involved nothing more than luring ashore shoals of the smaller cetaceans, such as dolphins or porpoises. To this day whaling of this type is carried on by fishermen in the Solomon Islands, the Faeroes, the Azores, and Newfoundland. The hunting of the larger species of cetaceans in European waters was practised by the Basques as early as the 10th century A.D., and reached its apogee in the 12th and 13th centuries. Their chief prey was the Atlantic Right whale (*Balaena glacialis*) known to the French as *Sarde* and to the Dutch and Scandinavians as *Nordkaper*. These were mostly * harpooned from small boats off-shore, towed to land, and cut up, the tongue being a particularly prized delicacy. By the 17th century the Biscay whale fishery had begun to decline, but long before this the Basques had extended their activities and by the second half of the 16th century had established a whale fishery off the Newfoundland banks.

These first long-distance whaling voyages in the North Atlantic were soon to be followed by the inauguration of an Arctic whale fishery occasioned by the discovery of Spitsbergen (Svalbard), or 'Greenland' as it was then called, by the Dutch explorer Willem * Barents in 1596. His reports of great multitudes of whales in the area at once attracted the Basques. Their local knowledge was employed on the first English whaling voyage to Spitsbergen fitted out in 1610 by the Muscovy Company, who engaged Basque harpooners to teach the English the art of catching and killing whales. Subsequently the monopoly which the Muscovy Company attempted to claim in this northern fishery was challenged by various interlopers, including the Dutch, as well as by British subjects themselves such as the Hull whalers, by Biscayans, and by Danes. By the middle of the 17th century the Dutch whale fishery was in the ascendant and that of the English in decline owing partly to the civil war in England, partly to the dispute between the monopolists and the interlopers. One of the best early descriptions of this 'Greenland' (Spitsbergen) whale fishery is that of Thomas Edge, a factor of the Muscovy Company at a time when the whales were abundant close to the shore.

Whaling in the early years of this fishery was

Whale fishing in the East Indies; engraving from India Orientalis *by T. de Bry, 1601*

carried out from ships of some 200 tons with a crew of about fifty. The whale was pursued in small boats (*pinnaces or *shallops), harpooned with a harping iron, and then lanced in the underbelly. The whale was then towed to the ship where it was laid across the stern. The blubber, after being peeled off with a hook attached to a crane or *capstan, was taken ashore where it was boiled or 'tryed out' in great vats. Each nation active in the trade at Spitsbergen had its own harbour where gear was stored and oil tryed out. One of the most famous was the Dutch whaling village of Smeerenburg ('Blubbertown'), which by 1633 was visited annually by over 1,000 whalers and included numerous shops, a bakehouse, and a church.

By the early years of the 18th century whales had become scarce in the waters off Spitsbergen and were being sought as far north as Davis Straits. Here the chief fishery was on Disco Island, where it was principally carried out by the Germans and Dutch. The latter were predominant until the middle of the 18th century when, encouraged by a system of bounties, a regular British Greenland whale fishery became established. (See also GREEN MEN.) Many seaports fitted out vessels for the trade, London, Hull, and Whitby being the most successful. The Greenland fishery was prosecuted with success for the first three decades of the 19th century after which, owing partly to the substitution of

coal gas for oil gas and partly to overfishing of the whale stocks, it went into a decline.

While the European countries were exploiting this Arctic whale fishery, an entirely independent fishery had grown up in the 18th century in Britain's North American colonies, prosecuted from such ports as Nantucket and New Bedford and from Newfoundland. From its beginnings in 1712, the Southern Whale Fishery, as it became known, was gradually extended southwards until by the mid-18th century it had reached the coasts of Brazil. The prey was the Sperm whale, or Cachalot (*Physeter catodon*), a toothed whale whose oil was considered superior to that of the Right whale. The southward advance of the American whalers was temporarily halted by the War of American Independence (1775–82), when the British made a determined effort to take this trade into their own hands. Aided by the bounty system, the new fishery prospered. The year 1787 saw the first British whaler round Cape Horn to pursue the whale into the Pacific. Here the Americans shortly followed, their former interest in the fishery having now begun to revive. In spite of the intervention of the Napoleonic Wars (1793–1815) the American trade continued to hold its own, expanding rapidly after the Anglo-U.S. War of 1812. By the 1820s American whalers were extending their range to all parts of the Pacific and Indian Oceans, reaching Japan in 1821 and Zanzibar and the Seychelles in 1828. During the 1840s American whalers were taking Right whales again in the North Pacific, off the coast of Kamchatka, and were sailing through Bering Strait into the Arctic Ocean. This prosperous Pacific whaling industry, based on San Francisco, received a major setback from the American Civil War (1861–5). A temporary post-war recovery was followed by a major disaster in 1871 when almost the entire North Pacific fleet of American whalers was crushed in the ice.

Modern whaling dates from the development of the harpoon gun by the Norwegian Sven Foyn in the 1860s and the introduction of steam-powered *whale catchers towards the end of the 19th century. For the first half of the 20th century the whaling industry was mainly concentrated in Antarctic waters. In 1904 a land-based station at South Georgia, operated by Norwegians under British licence, was established. The 1920s saw the introduction of floating *whale factory ships operating on the high seas and independent of the licensed shore bases. These factory ships were characterized by a ramp at the stern up which the whale carcasses were hauled for processing; an attendant fleet of small catchers could range far over the ocean spotting and catching whales.

During the inter-war years the rapid growth of the industry led to a marked decline in the stocks of whales and it became evident that restrictive measures were necessary. In 1937 an international agreement limited the duration of the season and set minimum sizes below which whales were not to be killed. In 1947 the International Whaling Commission was formed to give scientific advice to the industry and to attempt to regulate world whaling. These regulations have largely failed in their intention. The decline of the Blue whale (*Balaenoptera musculus*), largest and most valuable of the cetaceans, has been followed by that of the smaller Fin and Sei whales. Today only Japan and the U.S.S.R. send annual expeditions to the southern ocean. The decline of the Antarctic whaling industry, which once supplied over 75 per cent of the world catch, has led to the North Pacific taking the lead in production. Here, where Japan, the U.S.S.R., and the U.S.A. share a quota, there has been much uncertainty on how to allocate this quota between the competing nations.

During the present decade (1970–9) new attempts have been made to conserve the whale population of the oceans. In a conference held in Stockholm in 1972, agreement on a moratorium on the catching of all whales for a period of ten years was reached, though at the International Whaling Conference held a few months later, this agreement was rescinded except in the case of the rarer whales. A more promising line of attack has been adopted more recently by national

limitations on the uses to which whale products are put. The chief use today of whalemeat is in the production of pet foods, and both the U.S.A. and Britain have banned its import for this purpose, with other nations reputedly about to follow suit. Other uses for whale products are candles, soap, margarine, cosmetics, and, surprisingly, pencils. As these, however, amount to only a fraction of the whale products in comparison with the production of pet food, the economic pressure on the industry following the banning of the latter may be sufficient to curtail the killing of whales to an extent sufficient for the survival of all types of cetacean.

Further steps towards the conservation of whales were agreed at a 1975 meeting of the International Whaling Commission in London when reductions in the quotas of whale catching were agreed. Another proposal for a ten-year moratorium on all whale killing was not accepted but the catch allowed for 1975 was reduced from 37,300 to 32,450. In particular the permissible catch of Sperm whales has been reduced in the southern seas from 8,000 males and 5,000 females to 5,870 males and 4,870 females, and in

Whale carcass being stripped down into manageable sections on a South African whaler, 1970

936 WHARF

the North Pacific from 6,000 males and 4,000 females to 5,200 males and 3,100 females. The hunting of Fin and Sei whales, which have been particularly hard hit in the past years, is now prohibited except in one or two specified areas.
J. T. Jenkins, *A History of the Whale Fisheries* (1921); B. Lubbock, *The Arctic Whalers* (1937).

WHALING MUSEUMS, see NANTUCKET WHALING MUSEUM.

WHARF, (1) a projection built of wood or stone constructed along the banks of an anchorage or in a harbour to provide accommodation for ships to lie alongside for the loading or unloading of cargo, embarkation and disembarkation of passengers, etc. The word is virtually synonymous with *quay, though in general the latter is thought of as being built only in stone. **(2)** A term used in *hydrography to describe an underwater scar or rocky accretion, or even a sandbank, where the tides will throw up an *overfall or *race.

WHARFAGE, the charge made to a shipowner for the use of a *wharf by his ship.

WHARFINGER, the name given to a man who owns or has charge of a *wharf.

WHARTON, Sir WILLIAM JAMES LLOYD (1843–1905), British rear admiral, was Hydrographer of the Navy from 1884 to 1904, a term exceeded only by Sir Francis *Beaufort. Entering the navy in 1857, Wharton saw varied service, including three years in H.M.S. *Gannet* on the North America and West Indies station, this ship having surveying only as a secondary role.

In 1872, as a newly promoted commander, he turned to surveying and commanded H.M.S. *Shearwater* in the Mediterranean, including the Dardanelles, and on the Zanzibar coast, with a diversion to Rodriquez in 1874 with observers for a transit of Venus. He was later in H.M.S. *Fawn* on the east coast of Africa until, in 1878, he was ordered to the Sea of Marmara where the fleet needed charts on the conclusion of the Russo-Turkish war. From 1882 he was in H.M.S. *Sylvia* for surveys in Magellan Strait until ordered home in 1884 to succeed Sir Frederick *Evans as Hydrographer.

Wharton's abilities as a surveyor and his understanding of the subject were epitomized in his *Hydrographical Surveying*, published in 1882, which ran into four editions and was the textbook on surveying until the *Admiralty Manual* of 1938. His *General Instructions for Hydrographic Surveyors* also took account of the need for ever closer surveys to provide safety for steamships of increasing size and *draught. Under his direction there were always two or

three surveying ships in home waters and six or seven overseas, mainly in colonial waters, but with diversions for deep sea work in the Pacific in preparation for the telegraph cable laying of 1901. H.M.S. *Stork*'s surveys of the Zambezi River aided the transport of *gunboats to Matope where they were assembled to steam up the River Shire to Lake Nyasa, a project Wharton discussed with Livingstone's successor, Laws. The ships were old, and ships' companies inevitably suffered hardship, and the shortage of naval personnel made it necessary for Wharton to convince the Admiralty, not for the only time, that the surveying service was properly part of the navy.

Demands on the department grew inexorably and strained its resources as naval policy changed to meet the German naval expansion which began in 1900. The increasing demand for Admiralty charts led to new depots at Gibraltar, Malta, Hong Kong, Cape Town, and Sydney. One of Wharton's publications, *Ocean Passages for the World* issued in 1895, stimulated further voyaging by round-the-world yachtsmen and yet more work resulted from Marconi's invention of wireless in 1902. Some relief to the department's navigational responsibilities came with the setting up of the Navigation School at Portsmouth in 1903.

Wharton was concerned in the continuing exploration of Antarctica, being in 1901 a member of the committee for the British National Antarctic expedition under Captain R. F. *Scott in the *Discovery*. In 1903, when the ship was beset in ice, Wharton encouraged the Admiralty to take responsibility and was himself chairman of the Antarctic Relief Committee.

It is of present-day interest that Wharton in 1891 was asked to comment on a Channel Bridge and on Reed's Tubular Railway, a sort of tunnel lying on the bottom of the English Channel, to both of which he saw objections for navigational and defence reasons. He was made a fellow of the Royal Society in 1886 and was also a fellow of the Royal Geographical and Royal Astronomical Societies.

WHEELHOUSE, the deckhouse of a vessel within which the steering-wheel is fitted. In most large ships it forms part of the *bridge, in smaller vessels without a bridge, such as fishing *trawlers and *drifters, it is a separate compartment raised above deck level to provide all-round visibility to the helmsman.

WHELPS, the name given to the projections which stand out from the barrel of a *capstan or *winch to provide extra bite for a rope under strain than if the barrel were left smooth. They form an integral part of the barrel and project for a distance of about 1 or $1\frac{1}{2}$ inches.

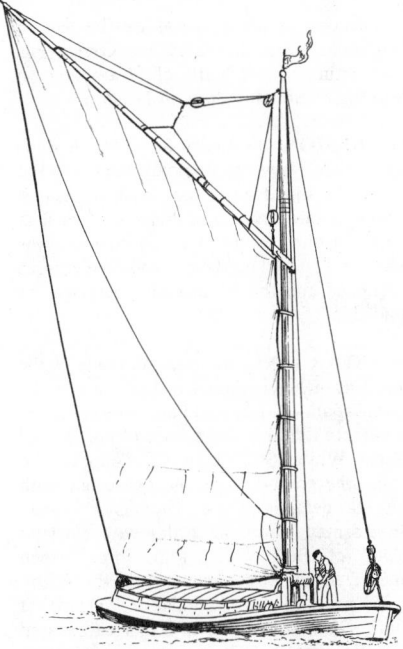

Norfolk wherry

WHERRY, (1) a decked sailing vessel of very shallow *draught used for the transport of small quantities of freight on the Norfolk Broads in England. They have a considerable *beam in relation to their length and are fitted with a single mast carrying a large loose-footed (i.e., without a *boom) *gaff mainsail and no headsails. The mast is normally *stepped with its heel on deck and supported in a *lutchet, similar to a *tabernacle, so that it can be lowered to the deck when passing under bridges, etc. **(2)** An open boat of the 17th and 18th centuries used for the carriage of passengers on the tidal reaches of the River Thames in England. They were propelled by oars, and varied in size from about 14 feet with a single rower, to about 25 feet with four rowers.

WHIP, the name given to a single rope rove through a single block and used for hoisting articles. Where greater power is required, another single block can be introduced to make a double whip, or another single whip can be applied to the fall of the first to form what is known as a whip-upon-whip.

WHIP, to, the operation of binding twine or yarn around the strands at the end of a rope or wire rope to prevent them from unlaying or fraying. The final result is known as a whipping, of which the *common whipping, *sailmaker's whipping, and *West Country whipping are in the most general use at sea.

WHIPPLE, ABRAHAM (1733–1819), American naval officer, was born in Providence, R.I. He went to sea as a boy and during the Seven Years War (1756–63) commanded the *privateer *Gamecock*, capturing twenty-three French merchant vessels in a period of six months. At the outbreak of the War of American Independence (1775–82) his native state of Rhode Island gave him command of two ships fitted out for the protection of commerce, and on the day he received his commission he captured an armed tender of the British *frigate *Rose*, the first *prize of war by an official American vessel.

Whipple commanded the ship *Columbus* in the fleet of Esek *Hopkins which sailed for the Bahamas in the spring of 1776. After this fleet failed to capture or destroy the frigate *Glasgow*, off Block Island, Whipple asked for a general court martial because of rumours that he had failed in his duty. The court absolved him of any blame. He was ranked 12th in the seniority list of *Continental Navy captains in 1776. In 1779, in the *Providence*, with two other Continental vessels under command, Whipple sighted a homeward-bound British *convoy and managed to capture ten merchantmen without alarming the escorting British men-of-war. Eight of the ten prizes reached American ports successfully. Later in 1779 he was the senior naval officer ordered to Charleston, S.C., in command of four Continental vessels. He was not responsible for the error in judgement involved in this misuse of naval vessels, which resulted in their loss when the British captured the city.

WHIPSTAFF, originally the name given to a wooden rod attached to a *yoke on the *rudder of a vessel, by which the vessel was steered. Its original purpose was to replace the *tiller, or rather to off-set it, so that with a *mizen-mast stepped right aft the rudder could still be moved from side to side. The whipstaff proper was a vertical lever attached by an eyebolt and *gooseneck to the forward end of the tiller of a sailing vessel. In all sailing vessels of any size, the tiller came in along the lower deck, and as ships began to have their sterns built high, so it became necessary to place the helmsman equally high so that he could see the sails and adjust the ship's *course accordingly. The whipstaff achieved this, being led up through slots in the decks to the helmsman's position. It had its fulcrum about one-fifth of the distance between the tiller and the helmsman's position, thus giving a gain in power of about four to one. As the helmsman pushed his end of the whipstaff over to one side, it acted through its fulcrum to push the tiller over in the opposite direction and the tiller movement was transmitted directly to the rudder. The maximum amount of helm which could be put on with a whipstaff was about five degrees either side of

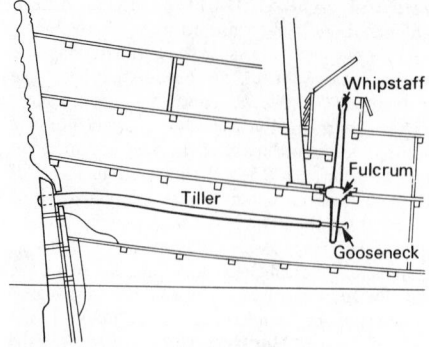

Whipstaff

centre. The end of the whipstaff came in about 1710 with the introduction of the steering-wheel, having lasted for about 250 years.

WHISKER POLE, a short bearing-out spar used in yachts and sailing *dinghies to bear out the *clew of the jib on the opposite side of the mainsail when running before the wind, thus obtaining some of the advantage which would be gained in a larger vessel when she sets a *spinnaker. See also GOOSE-WINGS.

WHISKERS, the name given to the short horizontal spars fitted to the *bowsprit of a large sailing vessel when it is extended by a *jib-boom, and used for spreading the guys in order to provide a wider base of support for the jib-boom.

WHISTLE, the older name for the *boatswain's pipe. It was originally the badge of the English *Lord High Admiral which he wore, heavily jewelled and suspended on a long gold or silver chain round his neck, in battle (as a sign of recognition) and on ceremonial occasions. When Lord Edward Howard, Lord High Admiral of England, was engaged against the French in *Brest roads in 1513, he wore a golden whistle on a chain of gold nobles. He led a boarding party to try to capture a French *galley but unfortunately his own ship drifted away as soon as he had sprung aboard the enemy and cut him off from his supporters. When he saw he was facing death he took off his chain and whistle and flung them into the sea in order that the insignia of a Lord High Admiral should not fall into the hands of an enemy.

WHITCOMBE, THOMAS (*c.* 1760–1824), British marine painter, was born in London. He was one of the most accomplished British artists in this genre, and his pictures show a mastery of medium and composition which have today made them into considerable collectors' pieces. His earlier pictures are considered to be his best. A small collection of his paintings can be seen in the *National Maritime Museum at Greenwich, and his picture of the battle of *Camperdown hangs in the National Gallery in London.

WHITE ENSIGN, the ensign flown by all ships of the British Navy. It originally denoted the vice admiral's squadron of the English fleet (see SQUADRONAL COLOURS). The division of the fleet into red, white, and blue squadrons was abolished in 1864 when the red and blue ensigns were dropped and the white ensign retained for all naval ships.

WHITE STAR LINE, the popular name of the Oceanic Steam Navigation Co. Ltd., one of the great transatlantic steamship lines. The company emerged from the financial failure of the famous Aberdeen White Star Line of *clippers to Australia, the goodwill and the house flag with its white star being bought by Thomas H. *Ismay in 1867. Ismay placed an order with Harland & Wolff of Belfast for four ships which revolutionized passenger comfort on the Atlantic; the first class accommodation, instead of being aft, was amidships with larger cabins and *scuttles than ever before, and a promenade deck was extended to the full width of the ship above, thus foreshadowing all future *liner design. When the first of the four, the S.S. *Oceanic*, sailed on her maiden voyage in 1871, she rendered all other Atlantic liners obsolete. The line continued to build up a great reputation for passenger comfort with larger and larger ships, and in 1911 the *Olympic*, of 45,324 tons, made a great public impact as the largest ship in the world. The next year her sister ship, the *Titanic*, made the most unhappy début of any liner when she sank after collision with an iceberg during her maiden voyage; a third giant sister ship, the *Britannic*, was sunk by a mine in the Aegean in 1916 during the First World War (1914–18). In spite of these and other losses, the line continued after the war, a rival to the *Cunard Line, and it was not until the financial slump of the early 1930s and the consequent failure of the Royal Mail group of companies, which had recently acquired White Star, that the British government forced a merger between Cunard and White Star in 1934. The two fleets merged as Cunard-White Star Ltd., but it was the effectual end of the White Star Line, and now even the name has been dropped by Cunard.

WHITEHEAD, ROBERT (1823–1905), British engineer and inventor of the locomotive *torpedo, spent most of his active career abroad and in 1856 was manager of the firm of Stabilimento Tecnico Fiumano at the then Austrian port of Fiume, now Rijeka. Invited by an Austrian, Captain Luppis, to improve his crude design for a torpedo which was, in effect, a small electric boat with an explosive bow steered from the shore by guidelines, Whitehead developed an entirely original design for an underwater, self-propelled missile with a secret depth-keeping device incorporating a 'balance chamber'.

Construction rights of Whitehead's torpedo were sold to Great Britain in 1870, and later to all the other leading naval powers. Under Whitehead's direction a branch of his factory in Fiume was established at Weymouth, England, in 1890 where considerable improvements in performance were added. Range and speed were greatly increased by using a mixture of steam and oil vapour with the original compressed air to give a 'hot' run instead of the original 'cold' run under compressed air only. A *course-holding ability was introduced by the use of a small gyroscope which controlled the vertical *rudder and held the torpedo on a fixed course, and the torpedo could be set to run at a predetermined depth by the introduction of a hydrostatic valve actuated by water pressure and linked to the horizontal rudders.

WHOODINGS, the planks in a wooden ship which are *rabbeted into the *stem are known as the whoodings. These refer only to those vessels large enough to need many planks to form a complete *strake, they would not refer to *dinghies and small craft where a single plank forms a strake. But see also HOOD ENDS.

WIDOWS' MEN, fictitious names entered in the *muster books of British warships so that their notional pay and the value of their rations could be used to swell the fund to provide pensions for the widows of men who died on board. Originally, money for such a purpose was raised by the old custom of *Dead Shares, but in 1733 the addition of widows' men to the muster books was made official at the rate of two men for every 100 borne on board. The practice lasted until 1829, when the payment of widows' pensions was organized on a more adequate and less haphazard basis.

WIGGINS, JOSEPH (1832–1905), British merchant seaman, first went to sea at the age of 13, became widely experienced, and was made Board of Trade examiner in seamanship for South Shields and Sunderland in 1869. He became interested in the possibility of finding a new route to Siberia by way of the Kara Sea and the rivers Ob and Yenisey. He undertook voyages to attempt this in 1874 and 1875, but it was not until 1876, in the *Thames*, that he was successful in ascending the Yenisey to a point 400 miles upstream. He made many more voyages into the Kara Sea over the next 20 years, and by them

helped to inaugurate a new sea route which has grown steadily in importance ever since.

WILD, FRANK (1874–1939), British Polar explorer, joined Captain R. F. *Scott's National Antarctic Expedition of 1901–4 after an initial career in the merchant navy and as a naval rating. It was during this expedition that he helped to lay the foundations of sledging techniques on the southern continent. In 1907 he returned to the Antarctic with E. H. *Shackleton in the *Nimrod* expedition and accompanied him up the Beardmore Glacier to within 100 miles of the South pole. He served in Mawson's Australasian Antarctic Expedition of 1911–14 and was in command of the western base in Queen Mary Land. In 1914 he sailed south again with Shackleton on the Imperial Trans-Antarctic Expedition and was left in charge of the ship's party on Elephant Island while his leader sailed to South Georgia to seek help. Wild's fifth and last Antarctic expedition was again with Shackleton in the *Quest* in 1921–2, taking over the command when Shackleton died on board off South Georgia. He spent the latter years of his life farming in South Africa.

WILKES, CHARLES (1798–1877), American rear admiral and Antarctic explorer of English parentage, joined the U.S. Navy as a *midshipman in 1818, after three years in the merchant service. He studied under Ferdinand Hassler, founder of the U.S. Coast and Geodetic Survey, and from 1826 to 1833 served in two surveying expeditions. He was appointed in 1834 as head of the recently established depot of charts and navigational instruments of the Navy Department, out of which were to grow the National Observatory and the Navy Hydrographic Office.

When, in 1836, Congress approved plans for a national expedition to the South Atlantic and South Pacific Oceans, to explore the islands and waters with a view to the promotion of the whale fishery and of commerce in general, Wilkes was sent to Europe to purchase the necessary scientific instruments. On his return he was promoted lieutenant and given the command of the expedition, which consisted of six ships, of which the senior was the *Vincennes*. The expedition sailed in 1838, and after a season of surveying and scientific studies in the Samoa group of islands, Wilkes set out on an Antarctic cruise with the object of sailing as far south as possible between the *longitudes of 160° E. and 45° E. Antarctic land was sighted on 19 January 1840, and in spite of adverse weather and ice conditions, and the poor state of his ships and crews, Wilkes sailed along the coast of the present Wilkes Land for a distance of 1,500 miles, sighting land at frequent intervals and naming the region, for the first time, the Antarctic Continent.

The expedition returned from this Antarctic cruise and spent most of 1841 in a long survey of the coast of western North America, finally returning to New York in June 1842, having accomplished a monumental task of surveying and scientific exploration. Far from being loaded with honours, however, Wilkes was brought to a court martial for having exceeded his authority. He was acquitted and spent the next few years writing up the official narrative of the expedition.

In 1861, at the start of the American Civil War, he was in command of the Federal *cruiser *San Jacinto* and figured in an international incident when he stopped the British mail steamer *Trent* in the Bahama Channel, north of Cuba, and removed two Confederate commissioners, James Mason and John Slidell. Although Confederate sympathizers in Britain hoped to use this incident to involve Great Britain against the U.S.A., the British government contented itself with a polite protest and a successful request for the release of the two men. The incident made Wilkes something of a naval hero to the American public, and in 1862, with the rank of acting rear admiral, he was placed in command of a special squadron to operate against Confederate commerce raiders in the West Indies and around the Bahamas. Although in this duty Wilkes accomplished as much as was to be expected from the small number of vessels placed under his command, he was court martialled again in 1864 and convicted of disobedience, disrespect, insubordination, and conduct unbecoming an officer. He was sentenced to be reprimanded and suspended from duty for three years, but the suspension was later reduced to one year and in 1866 he was placed on the retired list with the rank of rear admiral.

WILKINS, Sir GEORGE HUBERT (1888–1958), Australian polar explorer, was born at Mount Bryan East, South Australia. He served as second-in-command and photographer on Vilhjalmur *Stefansson's third expedition to the Canadian Arctic in 1913 but left it in 1917 to join the Australian Air Force, which was engaged in France during the First World War (1914–18), being seconded to the military historical section as an official photographer. In 1919 he was navigator of a Blackburn Kangaroo aircraft on a flight from England to Australia and in 1920–1 was appointed second-in-command and naturalist to the British Imperial Antarctic expedition under Sir Ernest *Shackleton. Between 1926 and 1928 he commanded an Arctic expedition sponsored by the *Detroit News*, during which, with Carl B. Eielson as co-pilot, he flew 2,100 miles across the Arctic from Point Barrow, Alaska, to Spitsbergen, a feat for which he was knighted. The following year he led the Hearst Antarctic expedition and in 1931 led an expedition in the conventionally powered *submarine *Nautilus* in an attempt to reach the North pole under the ice, but defects obliged the submarine to return after reaching a *latitude of 82° 15′ N. An account of the voyage is given in his book *Under the North Pole*. Between 1933 and 1939 he managed the four Lincoln Ellsworth Antarctic expeditions and between 1942 and 1952 he was consultant to the U.S. Army military planning division. After his death his ashes were scattered at the North pole from U.S.S. *Skate*.

WILKINSON, NORMAN (1878–1971), British marine painter, was the initiator of the principle of camouflage for warships during the First World War (1914–18), and was an official war artist in both World Wars. Born at Cambridge, he studied art in Paris. In 1915 he joined the Royal Naval Volunteer Reserve as a lieutenant-commander and saw service abroad and at home, painting a number of pictures of incidents connected with the *Dardanelles operations. He originated what was first known as *dazzle-painting for warships, later called camouflage, and in 1917 was lent to the U.S. Navy Department to organize a camouflage section for the American Navy. In 1923 he went to Canada and painted a number of pictures within the Arctic Circle. During the Second World War he was adviser on camouflage to the Air Ministry. He witnessed the allied landing in Normandy in June 1944 from H.M.S. *Jervis*, and he used the sketches made at the time to paint a historic picture of the operation which now hangs in the former Operations Room in H.M.S. *Dryad* (Southwick House), at the time used as headquarters for the launching of the invasion of Europe. He presented the sketches to H.M.S. *Dryad*, and his collection of fifty-four war pictures to the nation.

Wilkinson was a gifted painter of sea scenes, his bold use of colour and his vivid sense of light and atmosphere, particularly in his paintings of war scenes at sea, making his pictures notable examples of modern marine painting.

WILLIAM IV (1765–1837), King of Great Britain from 1830, was the third son of George III. As Prince William Henry (from 1789 as Duke of Clarence) he served in the Royal Navy from 1779 as *midshipman and lieutenant. He was made a *post-captain in 1786 and commanded the *frigate *Pegasus* in the West Indies. He was a close friend of John *Jervis and of Horatio *Nelson, who in a letter home wrote that ' ... His Royal Highness keeps up strict discipline in his ship ... she is one of the first-ordered frigates I have seen'. Prince William was promoted to rear admiral in 1790 but did not hold another active sea appointment, though continuing to receive nominal promotions and reaching the rank of admiral of the fleet in 1811. The office of *Lord High Admiral to which he was appointed in 1827, was specially revived for him, the Board of Admiralty being dissolved and a council of four officers appointed to advise him. Although this appointment was in theory nominal and designed as an honour to his social position, William was foolish enough to embark in the *Royal Sovereign* in 1828, hoist the Lord High Admiral's flag, and assume military command of the fleet during manoeuvres. Strong protests were made from several high authorities, including the king and the prime minister, and Prince William resigned his naval post.

Shortly afterwards he succeeded his brother, George IV, becoming known throughout the country, perhaps not surprisingly, as the 'Sailor King'.

WILLIAM SCORESBY, a vessel of 324 gross tons designed on the lines of a *whale catcher and used to carry out experiments in marking whales during the *Discovery* investigations. She was named after the Antarctic explorer. (See SCORESBY, William.)

WILLOUGHBY, Sir HUGH (d. 1554), British soldier and adventurer, comes into the maritime story with his voyage of 1553 in search of the *North-East passage. After a fairly successful military career, during which he was knighted, his thoughts turned to adventures at sea, of which, however, he had at the time no experience. Nevertheless in 1553 he was appointed captain-general of an expedition consisting of the ships *Bona Esperanza* (120 tons), *Edward Bonaventure* (160 tons), and *Bona Confidentia* (90 tons). The chief pilot of the squadron sailing in the *Edward Bonaventure* was Richard *Chancellor. The expedition sailed from London in May 1553, reached the Lofoten Islands, off the north Norwegian coast, in July, continuing their northward voyage three days later. After passing latitude 70° N. they encountered a gale in which the *Bonaventure* became separated from the other two ships. Willoughby sighted land in August but contrary winds kept his two ships at sea for another month, after which they were able to come to an anchor in the harbour of Arzinia in Lapland. 'Thus remaining in this haven the space of a weeke, seeing the yeare far spent, and also very evill wether, as frost, snow and haile, as though it had beene the deepe of winter, we thought best to winter there.' Lacking all the necessities for surviving Arctic conditions, all on board the ships perished. Willoughby's journal, from which the above is a quotation, was found later and showed that most of the company survived until January 1554.

An account of the voyage, and also the very full instructions under which the expedition was sent out, is included in Richard *Hakluyt's *Principal Voyages* (I, pp. 232–54).

WINCH, a small horizontal *capstan, driven by either steam or electricity, around the drum of which the hauling part of a *purchase is passed to provide power for hoisting, etc. In many yachts, smaller winches, turned by hand with a ratchet and pawl arrangement, are provided for *halyards, *sheets, and *runners, etc.

WIND, to, pronounced wind, an old nautical term to describe the act of *piping a call on a *boatswain's *whistle. When the whistle was the badge of office of the British *Lord High Admiral, the action of blowing a call was known as winding a call, and the word remained in use until the 18th century, although the equivalent expression, to pipe a call, was also widely used at this period and eventually took the place entirely of the older word.

WIND NAVIGATION, the means by which the early Mediterranean sailors found their way across the sea from port to port in the days before the introduction of the magnetic *compass. Certainly by the time of Homer, around 900 B.C., the Greek mariners used four winds which blew from the four quarters as their primary means of navigation. These winds were named Boreas, the wind from the north, Euros, the wind from the east, Notos, the wind from the south, and Zephuros, the wind from the west. Later, with increasingly long voyages across the Mediterranean being undertaken, four more winds, roughly bisecting the angles between the original four, were added, with one of the first four being moved to a new direction. The eight winds were now Boreas (north), Kaikias (north-east), Apeliotes (east), Euros (south-east), Notos (south), Lips (south-west), Zephuros (west), and Skiros (north-west).

There were various well-known ways in which it was possible to estimate the direction from which a wind was blowing when out of sight of land. The movement of the sun by day was reasonably well understood, and it was not difficult to make a fairly good guess at wind direction by relating it to the bearing of the sun. At night, the star *Polaris in the constellation of Ursa Minoris was well known to lie approximately due north, and this was another useful reference point from which to estimate the direction from which the wind was blowing. With this approximate knowledge the difficulties of navigation out of sight of land before the magnetic compass made its appearance were capable of a rough solution.

The Greek eight-wind system was adopted by the Italians, their winds having the names

Tramontana (north), Greco (north-east), Levante (east), Sirocco (south-east), Mezzodi (south), Garbino, which later became known as Africus or Affricone (south-west), Ponente (west), and Maestro (north-west). The system was later expanded to 12 winds, then 16, and finally to 32, to represent the 32 points of the *wind-rose. It has been claimed (B. Crescentio, *Nautica Mediterranea*, 1607) that it was the seamen of Amalfi who first introduced the 32-wind system, but it never became widely used.

The magnetic compass began to make its appearance in European waters during the 13th century. As it was far more accurate and reliable in providing navigators with the means of making voyages from port to port, it soon replaced the older wind system.

WINDJAMMER, a non-nautical name by which square-rigged sailing ships are frequently known.

WINDLASS, originally a small *capstan-like fitting, but on a horizontal shaft, in the fore part of a small vessel by which she rode to her anchor. It was also used sometimes for weighing an anchor if this could be done without recourse to the capstan. Like the old-time capstan, windlasses were fitted with bars to be worked by manpower, and had a pawl and ratchet gear to provide rotary motion to the spindle on which the windlass was mounted from an up and down motion of the bars.

The modern windlass takes the place in smaller vessels of the capstan and allied *cable-holders of a larger ship. Powered by steam or electricity, the motor drives a warping drum at each end of the horizontal shaft with, inboard of the drums, a pair of *gypsies for working the chain cables of the *bower anchors.

WINDLASS BITTS, the projecting timbers which were fitted to support the ends of the shaft of the old-fashioned windlass. They were also sometimes known as carrick bitts or carrick heads.

WIND-RODE, a vessel is said to be wind-rode when she is riding head to wind in spite of the influence of a tidal current which may be running across the wind or even dead to windward.

WIND-ROSE or **WIND-STAR,** the *compass of ancient seafarers before the introduction of the magnetic needle. Usually associated with the Phoenicians, the rose had eight points named for the prevailing winds which blew from the various countries round the Mediterranean. These were, in the Italian version of the wind-rose, Tramontana (north), Greco (north-east), Levante (east), Sirocco (south-east), Mezzodi (south), Garbino (south-west), Ponente (west), and Maestro (north-

west). It is to be assumed that mariners of those early ships were able to recognize these winds either by their characteristics of temperature, moisture content, etc., or else by association with sun, moon, or stars, otherwise it would be hardly possible to use a wind-rose for purposes of navigation with any degree of certitude. (See WIND NAVIGATION.)

WINDSAIL, a canvas funnel, the upper end of which is guyed to face the wind, used to ventilate a ship by deflecting the wind below decks, the funnel being led below through a hatchway.

WINDWARD, the weather side, or that from which the wind blows. It is the opposite side to *leeward. See also GAGE.

WINSLOW, JOHN ANCRUM (1811–73), American naval officer, commanded the *sloop *Kearsarge* when the Confederate commerce raider *Alabama* was sunk off Cherbourg in June 1864 during the American Civil War (1861–5). He was born in Wilmington, North Carolina, and became a midshipman in 1827. In the *Kearsarge*, Winslow patrolled the eastern Atlantic from the Azores to the English Channel during 1863 and early 1864. Learning that the *Alabama* was in Cherbourg, France, Winslow took the *Kearsarge* to that port and then spent five days outside the harbour hoping to engage her. The *Alabama* had spent a long period at sea and was in need of repair and her commanding officer, Captain *Semmes, had hoped to obtain French permission to have her docked and repaired. Pressure from the Federal States, however, induced the French government to follow strict neutrality, and permission to refit was refused. Semmes decided that there was nothing

Wind-rose from a 16th-century chart

that he could do but fight and took the *Alabama* out of harbour, heading for the *Kearsarge*. Winslow held his fire until the range had been reduced to 1,000 yards and in little more than an hour the *Alabama* was in a sinking condition and surrendered. Winslow's victory was universally acclaimed in the U.S.A. and he was promoted from captain to commodore to date from the day of the battle. He was promoted rear admiral in 1870 and Congress provided that he should be continued on active duty during his lifetime.

WINTER, JAN WILLEM DE (1750–1812), Dutch admiral, had reached the rank of lieutenant when, at the revolution of 1787, he was forced to flee to France for safety. He served with the French revolutionary army, and on his return to Holland in 1795 was given the task of reorganizing the Dutch Navy, being appointed vice admiral and commander-in-chief in 1796. In October 1797 he led it against a British fleet commanded by Admiral Adam *Duncan, and suffered an overwhelming defeat at the battle of *Camperdown. After the battle he was taken prisoner and brought to England, but was exchanged two months later.

He was next appointed ambassador in Paris, and later commanded a squadron in the Mediterranean engaged in suppressing the pirates of Tripoli. After the incorporation of Holland in the French empire, he was loaded with honours by Napoleon, and in 1811 was given command of the fleet which Napoleon had brought together at the Texel. But he was never able to exercise full command because of illness, and he died in Paris the following year.

WISHBONE, a divided spar whose two arms are pivoted together at the fore end and arched on either side in a roughly parabolic curve. The wishbone spar extends the *clew of the sail which is hoisted between the two arms, and the curves in the arms allow the sail to take up its natural flow without *girt or chafe. A wishbone can only be used in two-masted sailing vessels, such as a *schooner or a *ketch, as it is set on the forward mast and sheeted to the top of the after mast. It came briefly into fashion during the period 1920–40 but is very rarely seen today.

WITH, WITTE CORNELISZOON DE (1599–1651), Dutch admiral, was known as 'the bellicose' because of his fiery temperament. Born at Den Briel, he went to sea as a cabin boy in a merchant ship and in 1620 joined the navy, rising rapidly and being made a vice admiral òf Holland in 1637. He served for a time under Marten *Tromp, with whom he fell out but whom he succeeded after the latter's unsuccessful sortie at the start of the First Anglo-Dutch War (1652–4). On 28 September 1652, at the battle of the

*Kentish Knock, he fought a furious battle with the English fleet commanded by Robert *Blake in which the Dutch fleet had the worst of the encounter. He supported Tromp in his demand for the rebuilding of the Dutch fleet and played an important part in the battle off the *Texel on 31 July 1653. In 1658 he sailed as second-in-command to Jacob van *Wassenaer with a fleet dispatched to assist the Danes in their struggle with the Swedes. At the battle of the Sound on 29 October, in which the Swedish fleet was defeated, de With was wounded and died soon after. His body was taken home in a Swedish ship for burial.

WITMONT, HERMAN (c. 1605–83), Dutch marine artist, is believed to be the originator of the grisaille or monochrome style of painting of which the two Van de *Veldes became the outstanding practitioners. His drawings of ships, mostly in sepia, were always beautifully finished but in general suffer from a poor sense of composition. His picture of the battle of the *Gabbard hangs in the *National Maritime Museum at Greenwich; it is a typical example of 'penschilderij' or pen painting.

'WOBBLY EIGHT, the', the epithet used in the Royal Navy to describe the eight *battleships of the King Edward VII class which formed the 3rd Battle Squadron of the British *Grand Fleet in the First World War (1914–18). They were mixed armament ships, built and launched from 1904 onwards, and were the last class of battleship built in Britain before the *Dreadnought* introduced the all-big-gun type of capital ship. They earned their name because they were notoriously difficult to steer in shallow water or rough weather.

WOLF, ex-*Wachtfels* of the Hansa Line, served as a German *armed merchant raider during the First World War (1914–18). She was a vessel of 5,890 tons. Unlike other armed merchant raiders, her principal task was not to stop and sink enemy merchant ships by gunfire or by *scuttling but to lay *mines in places outside European waters through which allied trade was expected to pass. She began her minelaying career off the Cape of Good Hope and continued it off Karachi, after which she began to capture allied merchant ships, in part to replenish her own bunkers. Later she proceeded to Australasian waters and into the Pacific. A captured British *prize was equipped as an auxiliary minelayer and operated off Aden until she was intercepted and scuttled herself. At one time no less than 55 allied warships were searching for the *Wolf*. In all she sank 12 ships totalling 38,391 tons, while 15 more of 73,998 tons were accounted for by the mines which she laid. Having left Germany on 30 November 1916, she returned on 15 February 1918 after a voyage lasting 445 days.

WOLF PACK, the name given in the Second World War to the concentration of German *U-boats which operated together against the shipping of the allies. Although Admiral Karl *Dönitz was not the first man to use this concentration of U-boats—they had on occasions operated together during the First World War (1914–18)—he was the first to organize it as a valid operation of *submarine warfare, and achieved stupendous successes with it. The normal method of submarine operation had been to send a boat to patrol a specific area, waiting for enemy shipping to come into sight. Dönitz arranged for his U-boats to be continuously in wireless touch with the U-boat headquarters ashore and with each other, and although each group was distributed over a large area, the sighting of a *convoy by one of them was at once reported to headquarters, which informed the rest of the group so that a concentration of U-boats could be formed around the convoy to attack it with maximum intensity. The group was entirely controlled from Dönitz's headquarters ashore, which signalled to each individual U-boat the course she was to steer to bring her into contact with the convoy. The number of U-boats forming a wolf pack, eight, ten, or more, was normally sufficient to swamp the escort force of the average convoy.

The wolf pack, combined with surface attacks on convoys by night, was mainly responsible for the grievous loss of allied merchant shipping during the first three years of the war.

WOOLDING, the operation of binding a length of rope around a mast or spar to support it where it has been *fished. The rope used for this purpose is also called a woolding.

WORDEN, JOHN LORIMER (1818–97), American naval officer, is best known for his command of the *Monitor in her famous action with the Confederate *ironclad Virginia (ex-*Merrimack). He became a *midshipman in 1834 and early in the Civil War (1861–5) was captured and held prisoner for seven months by the Confederates. On 16 January 1862, he reported at Green Point, Long Island, to oversee the construction of the new ironclad Monitor, and to command her when commissioned. After a very rough passage from New York, Worden reached Hampton Roads on the night of 8 March 1862. During the action with the Virginia on the following day he was wounded in the face and nearly blinded. The battle earned him a vote of thanks from the Congress and he was made a captain in February 1863.

In January 1863, in command of the *monitor

Montauk, Worden bombarded Fort McAllister and also destroyed the Confederate *cruiser Nashville. He also took part in the attack made by Admiral *Dupont on Charleston Harbor in April 1863. Worden became a *commodore in 1868 and a rear admiral in 1872. He was Superintendent of the Naval Academy 1869–74 and commanded the European Squadron 1875–7.

WORM, to, the operation of passing a small rope spirally between the lays of a hemp cable, and similarly to pass codline between the lays of a rope, as a preparation for *parcelling and *serving. Rope is wormed, parcelled, and served to protect it against the wet, which is liable to rot it. See also CONTLINE, CUNTING.

WORSLEY, FRANK ARTHUR (1872–1943), British polar explorer, began his exploring career as *master of Sir Ernest *Shackleton's *Endurance during the Antarctic expedition of 1914–15, and was chosen as navigator of the James Caird during the dramatic and historic sixteen-day passage to South Georgia which led to the rescue of the marooned party on Elephant Island, an account of which is published in his book Endurance. Worsley made his second voyage to the Antarctic in 1921 as sailing master and hydrographer during Shackleton's last voyage in the *Quest. In 1925 he was joint leader with Grettir Algarsson of an expedition to Franz Josef Land, his narrative of which was published as Under Sail in the Frozen North.

WORTH, CLAUD (1864–1936), British cruising yachtsman, was an ophthalmic surgeon, with a practice in London, whose pioneer work on the squint in young children gave him an international reputation. As recreation he took to cruising in small yachts, and through his books Yacht Cruising (1910) and Yacht Navigation and Voyaging (1927) became a leading authority on the subject. His first venture was to convert, with two friends, an old ship's 22-ft boat which they named Ianthe and sail her, with home-made mast, spars, and sails, to the Thames in about 1886. In later years he made many cruises in a number of yachts which he owned, of which the four named Tern were among the most notable. The last yacht of this name was a 38-ton *cutter built to his own design in collaboration with Albert *Strange.

WRANGELL, Baron FERDINAND PETRO-VICH VON (1796–1870), Russian diplomat and explorer, was born at St. Petersburg (Leningrad) of Swedish parents. As a young man he made many expeditions to the Arctic during the years 1820–4 in search of lands reported to the north of the Siberian coast, but he failed to discover any. Later American and British expeditions showed that the object of his search must have been a group of islands off the Anadyr coast of Siberia in longitude 176° E., of which the largest was later named Wrangell Island. Between 1825 and 1827 he led a Russian voyage round the world. He held the post of Governor-General of Russian America (Alaska) from 1840 to 1849 and in 1867 opposed the sale of that territory to the U.S.A. He also served as minister of marine in Russia. See ARCTIC EXPLORATION.

WRECK, the hull of a ship which has become a total loss through stress of weather, stranding, collision, or any other cause, whether it lies on the bottom of the sea or on the shore. In maritime law, a vessel which is driven ashore is not a wreck if any man or domestic animal escapes death in her and is still alive on board when she strands. Where this occurs, her cargo is restored to the owners of it subject to the adequate recompense of those who may have salvaged it.

WRECK BUOY, a buoy, painted green with the letter W painted prominently on it in white, which is laid to mark the position of a wrecked ship and as a warning to navigators to keep clear. If the buoy is can shaped, it indicates that it is to be left to port when proceeding with the main flood stream, if conical to be left to starboard, and if spherical it may be left on either hand. If lit, it shows a green flashing light, one flash indicating that it may be left on either hand, two flashes on the port hand, and three flashes on the starboard hand. See APPENDIX 4.

WRECK VESSEL, a dumb vessel (i.e., without means of self-propulsion) painted green, with the word 'WRECK' in white letters painted on each side, which is *moored head and stern to mark the position of a wreck which may be a danger to navigation. It carries by day two green balls below one yardarm if it is to be left on the port hand when proceeding with the main flood stream, three green balls if to be left on the starboard hand, and two green balls below each yardarm if it may be passed on either side. At night the balls are replaced by green lights. In a fog a bell is sounded every 30 seconds, two

strokes if to be passed on the port hand, three if on the starboard hand, and four if it may be passed on either side.

WRIGHT, EDWARD (1558–1615), English mathematician, was a Fellow of Caius College, Cambridge. He applied his mathematical studies to *navigation and is best known, perhaps, for his publication of a table of meridional parts, the first of its kind. Later he went to sea and was disappointed with the rough and ready methods of navigation which he found in use there. This led him to write his book *Certaine Errors in Navigation Detected and Corrected*, which was published in 1599. In this book Wright made clear to the seaman the benefits to be gained by adopting *Mercator's method of constructing a chart. He described it in terms of a bladder blown up inside a cylinder and went on to show in simple terms how *rhumb lines could be drawn as straight lines on a chart compiled on Mercator's principle. *Certaine Errors in Navigation* included an important chart of the North Atlantic on the Mercator projection.

WYLLIE, WILLIAM LIONEL (1851–1931), British marine artist, was born in London and painted seascapes and coastal landscapes in which his treatment of light and atmosphere was the predominant feature, bringing to them a feeling of peace and quiet rather than of storm and shipwreck. Later in his life he played an important part in the restoration to her original condition of H.M.S. *Victory*, Lord *Nelson's flagship at the battle of *Trafalgar, and, somewhat uncharacteristically, painted an immense panorama, 36 feet long, of the battle as seen from the stern *gallery of the French *ship of the line *Neptune*.

His son HAROLD (1880–1973) was also born in London and became a marine painter, studying under his father. Again like his father he became interested in the restoration of historic ships and was largely responsible for the preservation of H.M.S. *Implacable and for the re-rigging of H.M.S. *Victory*. He was commissioned to paint murals of sea battles at various British naval establishments and there is a collection of his pictures at the Royal Naval Barracks at Chatham.

X

X-CRAFT, the official description of the British midget submarines of the Second World War. They were the conception of Admiral Sir Max *Horton in 1941, who wanted to see the development of submarines capable of attacking German capital ships inside their harbours. He turned his ideas over to Commander C. E. Varley to develop, and the first two prototype boats were ready for trials early in 1942. The trials were successful, and orders were placed in May 1942 for the first six operational boats.

X-craft were miniature submarines of 40 feet (12 m) in length and operated by a crew of four. As it was impossible within this overall length to handle a normal torpedo or to mount a tube through which to fire it, they carried instead two large detachable side charges each containing two tons of explosive fired by a time fuse. The method of attack was to proceed submerged into an enemy harbour and to dive beneath the selected target, detaching the two charges when directly under her hull. The X-craft were then to withdraw and, after a predetermined interval, the charges exploded blowing, it was hoped, a large hole in the bottom of the enemy ship.

These midget submarines were used on several occasions during the Second World War, the best remembered operation being their attack on 20 September 1943 on the German battleship *Tirpitz* as she lay at anchor in Kaa Fjord, on the northern tip of Norway. Six X-craft were detailed for the operation, each being towed submerged by a conventional submarine from their base in Scotland to the entrance of Alten Fjord, at the end of which lay Kaa Fjord. Only four of the X-craft arrived at Alten Fjord, one being lost when her tow parted, the other being scuttled when she had to jettison her charges because of air leaks. Of the four X-craft which proceeded in to the attack, two (X6 and X7) laid their charges beneath the *Tirpitz*, one (X5) was probably sunk by gunfire from the *Tirpitz* before she could make her attack, and one (X10) developed serious defects on the way in and was unable to remedy them in time to make her attack. She was the only one of the four which returned. The *Tirpitz* was seriously damaged by the attack but escaped possible complete destruction by swinging her bows away from the charges, having sighted one of the X-craft and recog-nized the danger before the charges were due to explode.

X-craft were also used with success in the Pacific, blowing a hole in the hull of the Japanese heavy cruiser *Takao* in Singapore harbour and also being used to cut telegraph cables on the sea-bed.

Other belligerent nations during the Second World War, notably Germany and Japan, also used midget submarines for operational purposes.

XEBEC, a small three-masted vessel of the 16th to 19th centuries used exclusively in the Mediter-ranean, similar in many respects to a *polacre but with a distinctive hull which had a pro-nounced overhanging bow and stern. They were greatly favoured by Mediterranean nations as *corsairs, and for this purpose were built with a narrow *floor to achieve a higher speed than their victims, but with a considerable beam in order to enable them to carry an extensive sail plan. They had pronounced *turtle decks to allow seas shipped when sailing to run down to the *scuppers, a feature of their construction being the provision of gratings from the centre-line of the ship to the sides, so that the crew could move easily and dry-shod while the water on the turtle deck ran down beneath the gratings. They had a rig which varied with the wind. In normal conditions they were square-rigged on the foremast and *lateen-rigged on the main and *mizen, but when the wind was fair extremely long square *yards were hoisted on the main in place of the lateen yards and immense square sails were spread. When sailing *close-hauled, a full lateen rig was substituted, but with over-length yards. In strong winds the overlength lateen yards were quickly replaced by normal length yards. When used as corsairs they carried a crew of 300–400 men and mounted up to twenty-four guns according to size. 'By the very complicated and inconvenient method of work-ing these vessels, it will be readily believed that one of their captains of Algiers acquainted the author, viz. That the crew of every Xebec has at least the labour of three *square-rigged* ships, wherein the standing sails are calculated to answer every situation of the wind' (Falconer, *Marine Dictionary*, 1771).

Y

YACHT, from the Dutch *jacht* (p.p. of *jachten*, to hurry, to hunt), originally 'a vessel of state, usually employed to convey princes, ambassadors or other great personages from one kingdom to another' (Falconer, *Marine Dictionary*, 1771); later any vessel propelled by either sail or power used for pleasure and not plying for hire. The word entered the English language in 1660, the year of the restoration of Charles II and the presentation to him by the States General of Holland of the *Mary* (100 tons, 8 guns) as a private pleasure vessel. There had been similar vessels long before this date, known as 'royal pleasure ships' or *esneccas, but the word 'yacht' was then unknown in relation to them. See also YACHTING.

YACHTING, the sport of racing or cruising in yachts under sail or power.

SAIL

Inshore racing. Although there are records of sailing races, or matches between two yachts, dating back to 1661, the sport of yacht racing did not begin to develop in a large way until the beginning of the 19th century. John Evelyn (Diary, 1 October 1661) was on board Charles II's yacht *Katherine* when the 1661 race was sailed on the Thames against the Duke of York's *Anne* over a course from Greenwich to Gravesend and back, and records that the King steered his yacht himself. Some records also exist of races in the 18th century organized by some of the clubs formed by members interested in sailing, particularly the Cork Harbour Water Club, later the *Royal Cork Yacht Club, founded in 1720, and the Cumberland Society, later the *Royal Thames Yacht Club, founded in 1775. Races were also sailed at Cowes, Isle of Wight, from 1780, but no yacht club was founded there until 1815.

The majority of yachts concerned in these early races were large vessels, mostly all square-rigged, and sailed by professional crews. The usual practice was for an owner to issue a challenge, backing his yacht against any others with a substantial stake, which was rarely less than £100 and often very much more. Other owners would match his stake, and so the race would be sailed, the first yacht home taking the stake

money. There was no form of handicap on size or sail area, and this was an encouragement to owners to build very large racing yachts, speed being closely related to size.

The first three decades of the 19th century saw the formation of many new yacht clubs around the coast of Britain, and most of them organized races for their members. Interest in the sport of yacht racing was slower to grow in other countries, with the possible exception of Holland; in the U.S.A., for example, the *New York Yacht Club was formed by nine local owners of yachts as late as 1844.

These early years of the 19th century saw racing yachts based very largely on the design of the revenue *cutters which, engaged in anti-smuggling duties, were in general the fastest vessels afloat. In addition to the hull design of the revenue cutters, racing owners also accepted their cutter *rig as being the most efficient. The rig consisted of a *jib set at the end of a long *bowsprit, a staysail, a *gaff mainsail laced to a *boom that extended several feet beyond the *counter, and upper and lower square topsails. Owners, however, quickly discovered that for their purpose it was unnecessary to build to the heavy *scantlings of the revenue cutters, and from about 1830 their yachts were built much lighter, though they still retained the typical revenue cutter design of a full forebody and a fine run aft. Since, in those years, there was still no system of handicapping, owners continued to build larger and larger in order to be able to spread a greater sail area. In 1830, for example, Joseph Weld's racing cutter *Alarm*, built at Lymington, had a measurement tonnage of 193. Other large yachts of the period were Lord Belfast's *brig *Waterwitch* of 381 tons and G. H. Ackers's *barque *Brilliant* of 493 tons.

The naval architect J. Scott *Russell drew attention in 1848 to the inefficiency of the standard yacht design of full forebody and fine run aft, known colloquially as the 'cod's head and mackerel tail' design, and produced an iron yacht, the *Mosquito*, with a long hollow bow and the maximum *beam well aft. She was a cutter of 50 tons, but the novelty of her design, in spite of her many successes in racing, aroused such acrimony and prejudice that only one other yacht was built to a similar design. It took the visit of

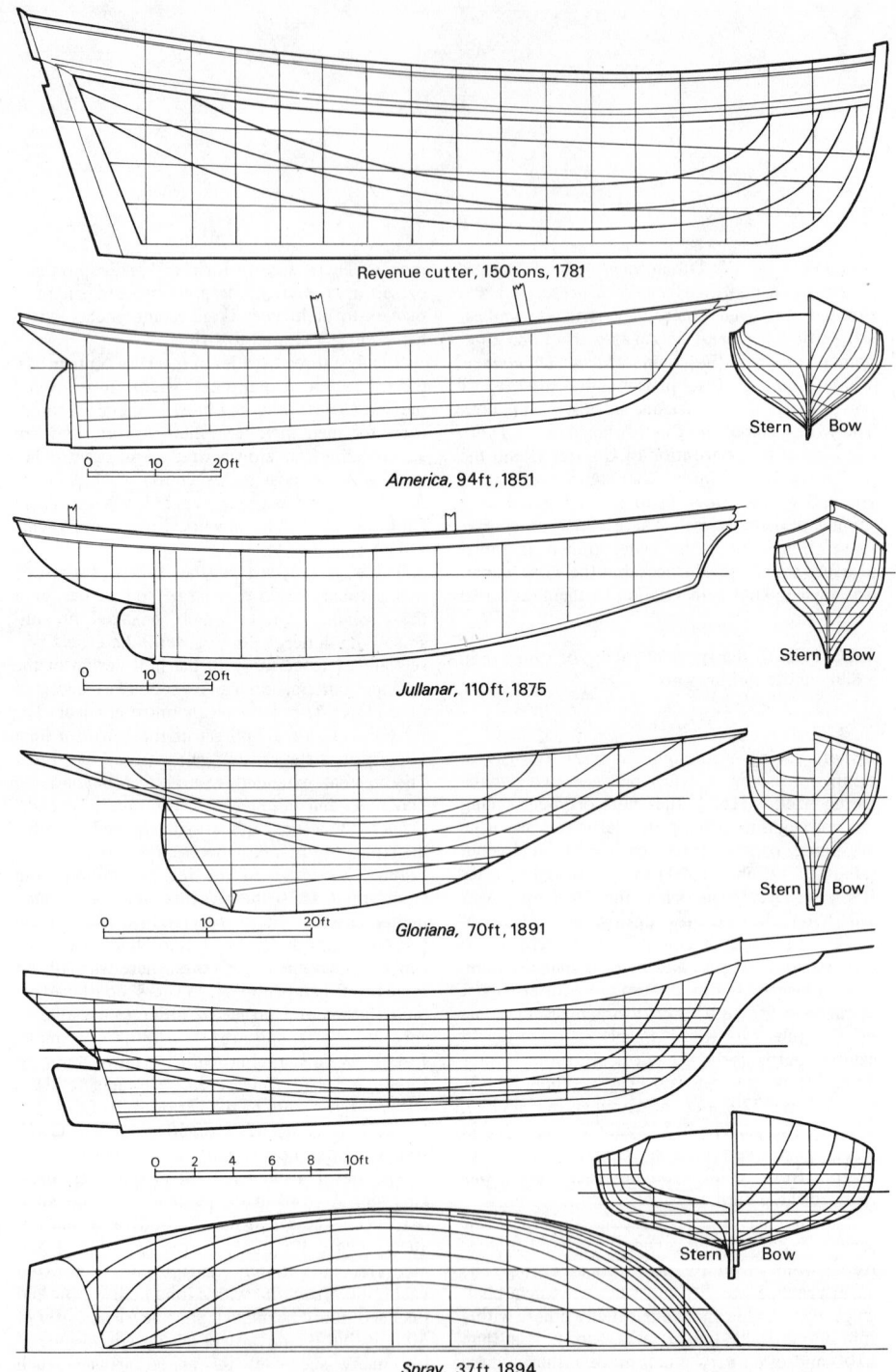

Revenue cutter, 150 tons, 1781

America, 94ft, 1851

Stern   Bow

Jullanar, 110ft, 1875

Stern   Bow

Gloriana, 70ft, 1891

Stern   Bow

Spray, 37ft, 1894

Stern   Bow

Evolution of yacht hulls

The Royal racing yacht Britannia, *built in 1893*

the yacht *America to Cowes in 1851 to convince the English owners that the old hull design
needed changing. The *America* was a *schooner
of 170 tons built in New York specially to race
in English waters during the year of the great
exhibition. She came in first in a race round the
Isle of Wight to win a cup presented by the
Royal Yacht Squadron, known ever since as the
*America's Cup, and to father what is, perhaps,
the best known series of races in the whole history of yachting. The novelty of her hull design
was enhanced by the cut of her sails, which were
of cotton and cut much flatter than the English
sails of flax cut to produce a greater bagginess.
For a time the *America's* success brought
schooners into fashion, but it did not last for
many years and the cutter soon came back into
favour in Britain although in the U.S.A. the
schooner has remained one of the most popular
of all yacht rigs.

A large number of yachts were built all over
the world during the next forty years, more particularly in Britain, where both racing and cruising increased vastly in popularity. Many notable
yachts were built, perhaps the most important

from the point of view of racing design being the
Jullanar, designed to his own ideas by E. H.
Bentall, an agricultural engineer of Maldon,
Essex. He built her himself on the Blackwater
River in 1875 to, in his own words, 'the longest
waterline, the smallest frictional surface, and the
shortest keel'. She proved phenomenally fast and
during her racing life won more races than any
other yacht. Her design was the direct forerunner
of such famous yachts as King Edward VII's
*Britannia, built in 1893, Lord Dunraven's two
*Valkyries, and the magnificent *Satanita*, built
for A. D. Clarke. In 1896 the Emperor of Germany had the huge cutter *Meteor II*, larger than
the *Britannia*, built on the Clyde to designs by G.
L. *Watson, who in 1900 also produced the
racing *yawl *Sybarita*, the same size as *Meteor
II*.

At almost exactly the same time Nathaniel
*Herreschoff was experimenting in the U.S.A.
with hull forms for racing yachts. In 1891 he
produced the *Gloriana*, which took America by
storm. She was a small boat with a waterline
length of 46 feet (14 m) but was completely
different in hull form to anything yet seen in

those waters. Built with very long overhangs at bow and stern, her forefoot was cut away to produce an entry that was almost a straight line from the stem to the bottom of the keel. It was a revolutionary design, and in every race in which she sailed that season there was never another yacht within striking distance of her. Herreschoff followed the *Gloriana* with the *Wasp* of an even more extreme design; a fin-keel type of boat with hard *bilges and a long narrow keel. Her racing successes stamped the Herreschoff design as an outstanding one for a purely racing yacht. He was commissioned to design and build racing boats for the big class, including a defender for the *America*'s Cup race of 1893, and of the two yachts he designed for that purpose, *Colonia* and *Vigilant*, the latter successfully defended the Cup against the challenge from Lord Dunraven's *Valkyrie II*.

There was in existence by this time a system of yacht measurement by which a time allowance was given to the smaller racing yachts in order to give them a reasonable chance of success when competing with the larger boats. These rules of measurement were calculated on the waterline length but did not include the beam measurement, and this had made it possible to produce racing machines which, though very fast, were virtually uninhabitable. These yachts were widely known as 'skimming dishes', having a very small *draught, a wide beam, and a deep fin keel, and their general undesirability as a function of healthy yacht design produced a demand for a new linear rule. An international conference was convened in London in 1906 by the British Yacht Racing Association, now the *Royal Yachting Association, and was attended by all countries interested in yacht racing, with the exception of the U.S.A. The conference adopted a new measurement rule which, as well as laying down minimum scantlings, included the beam measurement as a factor and thus penalized the 'skimming dish' type of yacht to an extent that made it unprofitable as a racer. To gain the maximum racing allowance under the new rule, new yachts were built that were not only habitable but also were excellent seaboats. This was the first of what were known as the 'metre' rules, and the new big racing class, which included such famous yachts as Sir Thomas *Lipton's *Shamrock, M. Kennedy's *White Heather II*, and Sir James Pender's *Brynhild*, were all constructed as 23-metre yachts. Other classes constructed to this rule were 15-metre, 12-metre, 8-metre, and 6-metre.

By 1911 the *Bermuda rig was beginning to be adopted for a few of the smaller racing and cruising yachts, particularly in the U.S.A. where research in *aerodynamics was demonstrating its improved efficiency over the gaff rig, but as yet the great majority of yachts, and all the big

yachts, still retained the gaff rig. The First World War (1914–18), which brought all yachting in the belligerent nations to a stop, effectively delayed any wider adoption of this rig. In 1921, in an attempt to restart the big class racing, George V, now the owner of *Britannia*, fitted her out for racing. His lead was followed by other owners, notably Sir Thomas Lipton with *Shamrock V*, J. Weld with *Lulworth*, Sir M. Singer with *Astra*, and the big schooner *Westward*. The big class restarted also in the U.S.A. in 1921. Lipton had already shown the way when his 1914 challenge for the *America*'s Cup, cut short by the war, was sailed in 1920. His yacht, *Shamrock IV*, was already in American waters, having crossed the Atlantic in 1914.

At a further international conference held in 1925 and this time joined by the U.S.A., a revised rating rule was agreed which gave yacht designers a certain amount of latitude in design in relation to beam, waterline length, and hull form while still remaining within the measurement rule. It was under this 1925 rule that the big *J-class racing yachts were built, in which the variation in waterline length, while still within the rule, could be from 75 to 87 feet (23–26·5 m), thus giving designers an opportunity of proving their individual skills. There were comparable latitudes in all the other international metre classes, within which designers could experiment with hull forms.

The big J-class yachts, perhaps the epitome of yachting design skills and beauty, lasted less than twenty years. By 1937 they were finished as a racing class, partly because the soaring costs of building, maintenance, and professional crews made them too heavy a financial burden for all except the wealthiest.

While it was the big racing yachts which naturally attracted most public attention, the sport grew amazingly in popularity in the years which preceded and followed the First World War. A large number of yacht clubs produced their own classes of small racing yachts designed under the linear rule of 1906, known colloquially as 'raters', as, for example, the '30-footers' which raced successfully for many years on the Clyde. France, Holland, Germany, the Scandinavian countries, and the U.S.A. also produced several classes of racing yachts, while on the other side of the world Australians and New Zealanders took to the sport in increasing numbers. International competition was provided at the big regattas, such as Cowes Week, Kiel Week, the Clyde fortnight, and many others, and also, from 1908, in the Olympic Games. Most of these international races were sailed in metre-class yachts, in which the existing rating rules had been accepted by the nations competing.

In addition to 'raters', many yacht clubs also introduced one-design classes, in which each

A modern ocean-racing yacht under spinnaker and big boy

boat in the class was built to exactly the same measurement and specification, including sails. They were introduced mainly as a test of a helmsman's individual racing skill, in which hull design had no place, but also partly to cater for the less wealthy yachtsmen who wanted to experience the excitement of racing. Most one-design classes were of small boats, some no larger than dinghies, but they filled a useful gap between the international metre classes and the other yachts which raced on handicap.

Racing yachts since the Second World War have seen the introduction of new materials and improved designs. Where mahogany or teak was, until about 1960, the prime material of which a yacht's hull was constructed, the introduction of materials such as marine plywood, glued laminates, and * fibre glass has subsequently revolutionized yacht building. Ferrocement, aluminium, and steel are also used for the hulls of racing yachts. As a result of aerodynamic research the traditional racing sail plan has

similarly changed, with the main driving power being transferred from the mainsail to the fore triangle. Another recent introduction into the racing scene is the * catamaran, a twin-hulled yacht developed from Polynesian and Malayan ancestors. It is considerably faster than the conventional design of racing yacht, capable of speeds of over 20 knots in favourable conditions. They have, because of the stiffness inherent in a design incorporating two widely spaced hulls rigidly connected with a central platform, their own particular handling characteristics which are unlike those of a conventional single-hull yacht.

It is not only in new materials for hull that recent advances have been made; sails and running rigging are today almost universally made from man-made materials, such as nylon or Terylene, instead of the traditional canvas and hemp, while mild-steel bars have replaced wire rope for the standing rigging in many racing and cruising yachts.

E. G. Martin's Jolie Brise, *ex-French pilot cutter built in 1912*

Offshore racing. Offshore racing and ocean racing has a long history. The first organized long distance race was sailed in December 1866 from Sandy Hook, U.S.A., to Cowes, England, and was contested by three schooners, the *Henrietta, Fleetwing,* and *Vesta.* It was held under New York Yacht Club rules for a prize of 30,000 dollars, and was won by the *Henrietta.* In 1869 a race was organized for schooners from Cherbourg, round the Nab Tower off the east corner of the Isle of Wight and back, for a trophy presented by Emperor Napoleon III. A second race across the Atlantic was held the following year from Queenstown, County Cork, to New York for the schooners *Dauntless* and *Cambria,* the *America's* Cup challenger of that year. Another offshore race was held in 1871 from Dover to Liverpool, while to celebrate Queen Victoria's jubilee in 1887 the Royal Thames Yacht Club staged a race round Great Britain and Ireland.

In 1897, in connection with the institution of Kiel Week as a comparable attraction to Cowes Week, and also in honour of Queen Victoria's diamond jubilee, the German emperor presented a trophy for a passage race from Dover to Kiel, an event which became an annual competition. The early organization of offshore racing, in fact, owes much to the German Kaiser who, at that time, and in the circumstances of the big programme of naval building which he was encouraging, was at pains to convince other countries that Germany was a truly maritime nation. During Kiel Week there were always a few offshore races for cruising yachts, and in 1905 he presented a trophy for a race across the Atlantic which attracted eight entries.

Following a transatlantic race from Sandy Hook to the Lizard in 1905, which the schooner *Atlantic* won from five other yachts in a record 12 days 4 hours, the first of the Bermuda races from New York to the island of Bermuda was held under the Cruising Club of America rules in 1906. Interrupted by the First World War, this race was resumed in 1923 and became a biennial event in 1926. The first *Fastnet race, from Cowes round the Fastnet rock off south-west Ireland to Plymouth, 605 miles, had been held the previous year with seven competing yachts and resulted in the formation of the Ocean Racing Club, to become the *Royal Ocean Racing Club six years later and the governing authority of offshore racing in Britain.

During the first few years of the club's existence competitors were mainly of a sturdy traditional cruising type, gaff cutter or yawl rigged with bowsprits, represented by such yachts as *Ilex*, a 20-ton yawl, *Altair*, a 14-ton cutter, *Penboch*, a 12-ton Breton-built cutter, and *Jolie Brise*, Commander E. G. *Martin's 44-ton ex-French pilot cutter. For the second Fastnet race in 1927 William *Fife designed and built a 50-ton racing Bermudian cutter, *Hallowe'en*, and from then on more yachts were specially designed and built for the coming R.O.R.C. events. With the arrival from America of Olin *Stephens's advanced ocean racer *Dorade*, a 58-ft (18 m) yawl, and her resounding win of the 1931 Fastnet and other races, designs for British yachts took on a new look and a faster, more sophisticated type of deep water racing yacht began to be developed.

Ocean racing was becoming a major part of the yachting scene following the end of the Second World War, largely taking the place of the defunct big class racers of pre-war years, and from about 1948 long distance races were being organized in many parts of the world. Among the principal more regular events are:

New York to Bermuda, 660 miles, every second year
California to Honolulu, 2,500 miles, every second year
Sydney to Hobart, 690 miles, every year
Sydney to Noumea, 1,100 miles, every second year
New Zealand to Australia, 1,500 miles, every year
Buenos Aires to Rio de Janeiro, 1,200 miles, every third year

But the best known and most prestigious ocean race is the Fastnet. It is sailed biennially, alternating with the New York to Bermuda race. As well as the Fastnet the R.O.R.C. programme each year now includes some nineteen or twenty offshore events in which several hundreds of yachts take part. In addition, through the efforts of Captain J. H. *Illingworth, Commodore of the R.O.R.C., the Junior Offshore Group was formed in 1950 for less costly yachts, which are limited to between 16 and 24 feet (5–7 m) in

waterline length and compete in races up to 250 miles. In the U.S.A., the Midget Ocean Racing Club meets a similar demand.

Of major importance in ocean racing today is the series of races which form the competition for the *Admiral's Cup. It was instituted in 1957 by the R.O.R.C. to foster the sport of ocean racing in countries other than Britain and the U.S.A., which had been the two most enthusiastic followers of the sport. It is sailed biennially between teams of three yachts selected by the participating countries and consists of two inshore races of 30 miles each, the R.O.R.C.'s Channel race of 215 miles, and the Fastnet race. Similarly, the international races for the *One Ton Cup were initiated by the Cercle de la Voile in Paris to further the sport of offshore racing.

In recent years, privately sponsored offshore races have become increasingly popular. The Transatlantic race from Britain to the U.S.A., first sailed in 1960, is a four-yearly event, and the Round Britain race is today's revival of the Royal Thames Yacht Club's race of 1887 to celebrate Queen Victoria's golden jubilee. The most ambitious of such privately sponsored races was the *Sunday Times* Golden Globe race for a single-handed non-stop race round the world. It was held in 1969 and was won by Robin *Knox-Johnston in his ketch *Suhaili* in a time of ten months and three days.

In order to provide a fair handicapping system to embrace offshore racing yachts of different size competing in the same race, a time correction factor is given to each yacht and applied to the elapsed time of completion of the course to produce a corrected time. This factor is based on measurements of the hull, sail area, spars, and other features taken by officials of each national racing authority. See also RATING.

Racing rules. All yachts race under a set of rules drawn up by the International Yacht Racing Union, in which each country is represented by its national authority. These racing rules, last revised in 1973, are based largely on the *Rule of the Road, internationally agreed to prevent the risk of collisions at sea, but differ from them in one or two respects applicable particularly in racing conditions. In cases where a strict application of the racing rules might present a risk of collision with another vessel which is, perhaps, proceeding through the area of the race, the Rule of the Road always takes precedence. And in offshore races where the race is continued at night the racing rules are suspended between the hours of sunset and sunrise in all cases where they may conflict with the Rule of the Road. When yachts are racing, they fly a square racing flag at the mainmast head to indicate to other vessels that they are engaged in the race and are sailing under the I.Y.R.U. rules.

There are seventy-eight racing rules and they cover every aspect of yacht racing, including organization, starting signals, rights of way during the race, and adjudication of *protests. A yacht engaged in a race is bound by the racing rules from the time of the preparatory gun or signal before the start of her race until she crosses the finishing line at the end of the race. To be eligible to race in any event under I.Y.R.U. rules a yacht must have on board, as the owner or his representative, a member of a yacht club recognized by the national authority. The rules also govern the provision of lifebelts, signal flares, dinghy, *dan buoy, and other safety gear for yachts engaged in offshore races.

The actual sailing rules embody in general the Rule of the Road as it affects sailing vessels. Thus a yacht on the starboard tack has the right of way over a yacht on the port tack, a yacht to windward keeps clear of a yacht to leeward, and an overtaking yacht keeps clear of the yacht being overtaken. When two yachts approach each other on the same tack, the yacht with the wind free gives way to the yacht close-hauled.

Where the I.Y.R.U. rules differ from the Rule of the Road is in their application to yachts in close company. The main object of the Rule of the Road is to keep vessels well apart so that there is no risk in collision but this is often not possible in highly competitive races where all the boats are set to sail the same course. So the I.Y.R.U. rules are designed not to keep the yachts apart but to govern their behaviour when in close company, indicating what additional duties or rights a yacht may have when in close competition with another.

If, during a race, one yacht is being overtaken to windward by another, she has the right under the racing rules to luff up to windward to try to prevent the overtaking yacht getting past, and she may luff right up until she is head to wind if she likes. The overtaking yacht may not continue her course if to do so would entail any risk of collision, but must also luff to keep clear. If, however, the overtaking yacht has established an overlap by having her mast abeam of her opponent, which the helmsman signifies by a hail of 'mast abeam', then the yacht being overtaken must allow a free passage, and if her helmsman attempts to luff, a protest may be lodged. And if during a race a yacht is being overtaken to leeward, the overtaking yacht must allow the yacht being overtaken plenty of room to keep clear. She may not luff up and crowd her opponent, and if she does so she will be disqualified if a protest is upheld by the race committee.

The I.Y.R.U. rules lay down procedures for rounding a mark of the course, where racing is likely to be at its closest with several yachts trying to round the mark more or less simultaneously. Here the overlap rule is brought into play to prevent yachts being 'squeezed' between the mark and the yacht or yachts rounding it. If a yacht approaching a mark has established an overlap on the yacht ahead of her, that yacht must give her room to round the mark and may not alter course towards the mark to force the yacht with the overlap to give way. Similarly, if the overlapped yacht has herself an overlap on the yacht next ahead, she too can claim room to round the mark. This is a rule which is on occasions difficult to interpret and enforce as an overtaking yacht may not claim room between the yacht ahead of her and the mark if the yacht ahead obviously cannot give her room because she herself is rounding it inside other yachts in the race.

Another rule governs the occasions when two yachts on the same tack are approaching an obstruction or a shallow patch with insufficient depth of water for the yachts to pass safely over it. If the helmsman of the yacht nearer the danger has insufficient room to *tack or *gybe without risk of a collision, he can oblige the other yacht to tack or gybe by calling 'water', but he must give the other yacht time to do so before he himself alters course away from the danger. But if the obstruction is a mark of the course, a yacht which has to tack to avoid it has no rights over a following yacht which is laying the mark correctly and she must keep clear.

Another I.Y.R.U. rule governs the rights of yachts at the start of a race. If a yacht is over the line when the starting gun is fired, she must return and recross the line before she can be considered as taking part in the race. And while she is doing so she loses all her rights under the I.Y.R.U. racing rules. She must keep clear of all the other yachts in the race, no matter what tack she may be on. Only when she has recovered the line and started correctly may she enjoy the rights under the racing rules.

A yacht which touches a mark of the course during a race must return and re-round the mark correctly (usually by going full circle around it). Failure to do so results in automatic disqualification. During the manoeuvre she forfeits her usual rights of way with regard to others in the race.

The final section of the I.Y.R.U. rules covers the procedures for judging protests. A yacht which protests against another during a race must fly a *burgee or some similar piece of material in her *shrouds, and after the race must deliver a written protest to the race committee setting out the grounds of the protest. The protest is heard as soon as possible after the end of the day's racing and judgement given.

Cruising. The non-competitive side of yachting, where an owner sails a yacht designed to accommodate himself and his crew in tolerable comfort for a voyage which may last overnight or extend over several months or years, is generally known as cruising. In the years before the First World War (1914–18) some of the more popular types of cruising yacht were conversions from pilot cutters and fishing *trawlers, well tried and strong vessels able to sail anywhere in the world, while several notable voyages, such as Captain Joshua *Slocum's single-handed voyage round the world in the *Spray* in 1895–8, and Captain J. C. *Voss's similar voyage in the *Tilikum*, 1901–4, gave a great impetus to the sport. Both these voyages were made in relatively small boats, the *Spray* having an overall length of 36 ft 9 in. (11 m) and a gross tonnage of nine tons, the *Tilikum* being even smaller, a dug-out canoe of red cedar with a tonnage less than a quarter of that of the *Spray*. Perhaps even more remarkable was the fact that both these voyages were achieved without any of the modern aids available to the cruising enthusiast today. Self-steering gear, radio direction finders and time signals, simplified navigational tables, purpose-built yachts, financial sponsorship, and modern food preservation techniques were all in the future when these voyages were made. Equally important in the birth of cruising as a sport were the writings of E. F. *Knight, who cruised in the Baltic in a 29-ft (9 m) converted ship's lifeboat, and R. T. *McMullen, whose cruises in British waters in small yachts opened the door for thousands of enthusiastic followers. All these had shown the possibilities of sailing very small yachts in safety over very long distances, and their examples inspired others to follow in their footsteps.

Before these pioneers had demonstrated what was possible of achievement in small yachts, most owners who wanted to make extended cruises in their yachts had built big; some very big indeed. Lord *Brassey's *Sunbeam*, which sailed round the world in 1876–7, was a three-masted auxiliary topsail schooner of 531 tons, and Lord Crawford's *Valhalla*, ship-rigged on three masts, had a tonnage of 1,490 and carried a professional crew of 100 men. These, however, were exceptions to the general rule, and few sailing cruisers were built above about 150 tons. As costs increased during the 20th century, the average size of cruising yachts became drastically smaller, and hulls were built in series to common designs. There was, however, still latitude in the successful series design for the individual owner to incorporate his own ideas of rig and accommodation below decks. A great advantage of series building was that production runs of the same design reduced the initial cost of purchase.

Traditional methods and materials of yacht building were largely superseded during the 1960s by new techniques, and the age-old shipwright's craft of building a vessel with selected woods became more of a rarity. Nowhere was this more in evidence than in yachts designed for cruising, and by 1972 more than 80 per cent of all new yachts and dinghies built in Britain, France, Holland, and the U.S.A. were of GRP moulded construction (see FIBRE GLASS).

The unprecedented growth of the sport of yachting since the Second World War has created many new conditions and new problems. Anchorages have become congested and rivers overcrowded as the masses have taken to boating in every form, and organized yacht harbours, or *marinas, have been, and still are being, built in America, Britain, and other countries where yachting is a popular sport.

One of the most notable aspects of yachting in recent years has been the immense growth of long-distance voyaging made practicable with the well-designed and properly equipped modern cruising yacht with her *self-steering gear. *Sopranino*, a lightly constructed 20-foot (6 m) sloop and forerunner of the Junior Offshore Group class, crossed the Atlantic with a crew of two in 1952, while *Borer Bee*, a 24-foot (7 m) plywood *chine sloop with *bilge keels, was sailed from Singapore, where her owner had built her, to England, via the Red Sea and Mediterranean, in 1958.

Some hundreds of yachts within the 25-ft to 40-ft (7·5 to 12 m) range have since crossed the Atlantic from Europe to the West Indies, while other voyages in yachts no bigger have been made between Europe and Australia and New Zealand, and from the U.S.A. to the Pacific islands and beyond. What were once regarded as astounding feats by small cruising yachts have become a way of life for many families making their home afloat in their well-found little ships.

POWER

With the adaptation of the steam engine as a means of ship propulsion during the first quarter of the 19th century, it was only to be expected that some yachtsmen should look to this new means of propulsion as an expression of their individuality. A steam yacht, as well as being more popular with ladies, who in general preferred the stately progression available with the steam engine to the hurly-burly of sail, and also being far more conducive to the lavish entertaining of the period, was an outward expression of wealth and leisure that appealed greatly to the rich owner of the 19th century. Most of the large steam yachts of that century were fitted out with extreme luxury, with heavy carving and panelling, thick carpeting, and large staterooms equipped with every conceivable convenience.

Like most innovations, the introduction of power in yachts had a difficult birth, and in May 1827 the Royal Yacht Club at Cowes (not yet renamed the *Royal Yacht Squadron) passed a resolution that 'the object of this Club is to promote seamanship to which the application of

The Turbinia, *built in 1897*

A modern power racing boat

steam is inimical, and any member applying steam to his yacht shall be disqualified hereby and shall cease to be a member'. Two years later, angry at what he considered an unreasonable ban on individual freedom, Thomas Assheton-Smith resigned from the club and built the 400-ton *Menai*, in which he installed a steam engine and paddle-wheels. She was the first steam yacht to be built in Britain. The first steam yacht built in the U.S.A. was the *North Star*, a large paddle yacht of 1,876 gross tons built for Commodore Cornelius Vanderbilt in 1853.

Early steam yachts were all paddlers, usually fitted with one or two oscillating or *walking beam engines and fire-tube boilers. With the introduction of the *propeller in the decade 1840–50, the power plant changed to the single-stage reciprocating engine, being replaced by the *compound engine in the 1860–70 period and by the *triple expansion engine about ten years later. Water-tube boilers began to be installed in some yachts around 1865, but it was not until Sir Alfred *Yarrow invented the three-drum type of water-tube boiler in 1889 that the older fire-tube boiler was finally discarded.

The first yacht to have *turbines fitted in her was the *Turbinia*, built by Sir Charles *Parsons in 1897 to demonstrate his new invention at the Naval Review held at Spithead to celebrate the diamond jubilee of Queen Victoria. She had three turbines giving direct drive to three propeller shafts, which each had three propellers mounted on them, and the three turbines developed a combined horsepower of 2,000. On the occasion of the Naval Review she achieved the remarkable speed, for that period, of over 30 *knots. But in general, except in the very largest yachts, the turbine proved unsuitable as a power plant, since to reach its maximum efficiency it needed to revolve at a rate too great to be used for direct drive to the propellers. Reduction gear was costly and noisy, and geared turbines, equally costly, gave poor manoeuvrability in small vessels. As a result, very few yachts, and those only the largest, adopted turbines in place of the triple expansion steam engine.

Steam had no rival as a reliable power in pleasure craft until about 1885, when launches fitted with an engine using naphtha gas in place of coal and water in the boiler appeared in numbers in British waters as well as in the U.S.A. Fires, however, were a frequent occurrence, and when a few years later the more compact, if noisy, internal combustion petrol (gasoline) engine was introduced for boat propulsion, the naphtha launch disappeared.

Impromptu racing had long taken place between privately owned steam launches and yachts, and while in Britain *Thornycroft and Yarrow were building fast launches, whose design later developed into these firms' naval

*torpedoboats and *destroyers, in America the *Herreschoff Company had introduced for wealthy businessmen living on Long Island Sound a series of lightly constructed steam yachts with small high-speed power plants capable of speeds up to 20 knots. As the petrol engine grew in power and reliability from the turn of the century, motor-boat racing became more popular and there was held in 1905 the first of the London-to-Cowes races which were to become an annual event until the outbreak of the First World War in 1914. The competing boats were still of the slender traditional round-*bilge type, but after the introduction of the Thornycroft torpedo-carrying *coastal motor boats during the war, a faster design of boat was evolved, and some phenomenal speeds were attained between the wars by power boats built and raced by H. *Scott-Paine and Sir Thomas *Sopwith.

Steady improvement in the power-to-weight ratio of high speed marine oil engines also enabled diesel-powered craft to compete in the principal racing events at sea, including the offshore races from Cowes to Torquay held annually from 1961. Reliability of modern power boats has made even longer courses practicable, and in the London to Monaco fourteen-stage race in 1972, eleven boats completed the 2,700-mile course out of twenty starters.

Outboard motors, compact portable power units which are clamped to the boat's stern, began to revolutionize the yachting scene with the sudden growth of boating sport from 1950. Ranging from easily carried units rated at 3 horsepower up to monster four-cylinder engines giving over 80 horsepower for racing boats, the outboard motor is found on all types of fun boat, small cabin cruiser, and mobile houseboat.

In some cases where boats are to be used in very shallow or weed-infested rivers a water jet propulsion unit is installed. In this an engine-driven impeller draws water through the bottom forward and ejects it in a powerful stream out at the stern. Gas turbine jets, introduced by a British company for fast naval motor gunboats, have also been a subject for experiment in private craft designed for water-speed record breaking.

D. Kemp, *Manual of Yacht and Boat Sailing*, 8th edn. (1895); Guest & Boulton, *Memorials of the Royal Yacht Squadron* (1903); Heckstall-Smith & Du Boulay, *The Complete Yachtsman* (1912); J. Slocum, *Sailing Alone Round the World* (Mariners Library, 1924); C. Worth, *Yacht Cruising* (1926); H. F. Speed, *Cruises in Small Yachts* (1926); M. Curry, *Racing Tactics* (1932); G. E. Hills, *The Sailing Rules in Yacht Racing* (1933); J. Irving, *Cruising and Ocean Racing* (1933); J. H. Illingworth, *Further Offshore* (1969); J. B. Atkins, *Further Memorials of the Royal Yacht Squadron* (1939); J. C. Voss, *The Venturesome Voyages of Captain Voss* (Mariners Library, 1949); E. C. Hiscock, *Cruising Under Sail*, 2nd edn. (1965); E. Hofman, *The Steam Yachts* (1970).

YAMAMOTO, ISOROKU (1884–1943), Japanese admiral, was born Isoroku Takano, the son of a village schoolmaster, but of Samurai descent. He entered the Naval Academy in 1900 where he spent the usual three years, followed by one year in a sail training ship. Appointed ensign in the *cruiser *Nisshin* at the beginning of the Russo-Japanese War, he took part in her in the battle of *Tsushima where he was wounded in the leg and hand, losing two fingers.

In accordance with a custom not unusual in Japan, he was in 1914 adopted by the Yamamotos, a prominent family of his home district, and took their name. In 1917 he was sent by the navy to the U.S.A. for a two-year course at Harvard.

A notable milestone in Yamamoto's career was his appointment in 1923 as executive officer of the new naval air training school at Kasumigaura where he became one of the minority among senior naval officers who encouraged naval aviation. He himself learned to fly and he became the chief proponent in Japan of the *aircraft carrier. Two years as Naval Attaché in Washington followed and, in 1930, after attending the London Naval Conference as a delegate, he was promoted rear admiral and appointed Commander of the First Air Fleet. Promoted to vice admiral in 1934, he headed the delegation to the London Naval Conference in that year, at which he rejected any further extension of the 5–5–3 ratio established by the Washington Treaty, and was instrumental in Japan's subsequent abrogation of the Treaty.

Yamamoto opposed Japanese alignment in 1938 with the Axis powers (Germany and Italy), or provocation of Britain or the U.S.A., whose far greater resources in manpower and *matériel* made them in his opinion too powerful to challenge. Accused as a result of pro-Americanism, he earned the hatred of the secret Black Dragon Society and it was partly to protect him from assassination at their hands that he was appointed commander-in-chief of the Combined Fleet in August 1939. Unable to deter the government from embarking on war, he decided that initial success, at least, could be assured by elimination of the U.S. Pacific Fleet and he secured approval for the surprise attack on *Pearl Harbor which opened the war against the U.S.A. in 1941.

The success of this surprise attack was minimized by the failure to eliminate American carrier strength; the raid on Tokyo by bombers launched from the carrier *Hornet* in April 1942 brought him to assent to the grandiose operation to capture Midway and the Aleutians, during which he hoped to be able to bring the U.S.

The Japanese battleship Yamato *of 65,000 tons*

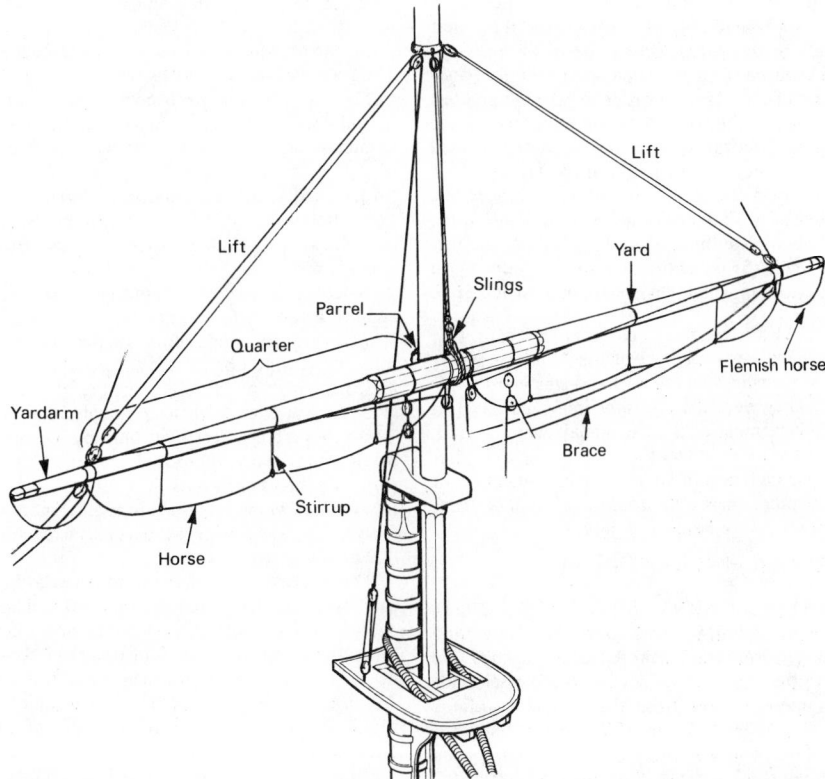

Yard

Pacific Fleet to action. In the fatal battle of * Midway which followed, two-thirds of his carrier strength was destroyed against the loss of a single carrier by the Americans.

Naval operations were thereafter concentrated in the south Pacific where Yamamoto deployed his fleet in support of the struggle for possession of * Guadalcanal and the Solomons. His strategic plans were repeatedly frustrated by the American ability to decode Japanese naval signals: the same fatal flaw led to his death in April 1943 when it enabled American fighters to ambush the aircraft in which he was travelling and shoot it down over Buin.

YAMATO, a battleship built by Japan which, with her sister ship *Musashi*, was the biggest * battleship ever built. Design work on these ships was begun in 1934 and they were laid down in 1937 under conditions of great secrecy, each building slip being concealed from public gaze behind a mile of sisal matting. The designed * displacement was 63,000 tons but on completion both ships were found to have an actual displacement of 65,000 tons. The main armament of nine 18·1-inch guns could fire a broadside of 28,800 lb (13,063 kg) to a maximum

range of 27 miles (43 km). Neither ship was ever in direct action with a U.S. or British battleship during the Second World War and thus never had the opportunity to try out their big guns against an enemy ship. The *Musashi* was sunk in October 1944 at the battle of * Leyte Gulf by U.S. carrier-borne aircraft after being hit by twenty torpedoes and thirty-three bombs; the *Yamato* was similarly sunk during the operation off Okinawa in April 1945 after being hit by ten torpedoes and twenty-three bombs.

YANKEE, a light-weather foresail used in yachts, set on the topmast stay with its * luff extending almost the whole length of the stay. It is similar to a * genoa but cut narrower, with its * leech not overlapping the * mainsail as does that of a genoa, and with its * clew higher than is normally the case with genoas. A yankee can be used in winds of up to about force 4 on the *Beaufort Scale. See also GHOSTER.

YARD, (1) a large wooden or metal spar crossing the * masts of a ship horizontally or diagonally, from which a sail is set. Yards crossing the masts of a square-rigged ship horizontally are supported from the mastheads by *slings and *lifts and are held to the mast by a *truss or *parrel. Square sails are laced by their *heads to the yards. By means of *braces, the yards can be turned at an angle to the fore-and-aft line of the vessel in order to take the greatest advantage of the wind direction in relation to the required *course of the vessel. When a yard crosses a mast diagonally, it is known as a *lateen yard and is not supported by braces but hoisted by a *halyard attached to a point on the yard about one-third of its length from the forward end. **(2)** A shortened form of the word *dockyard, in which vessels are built or repaired.

YARDARM, the outer quarters of a *yard, that part which lies outboard of the *lifts, on either side of the ship, i.e., the port and starboard yardarms. They were the positions in a square-rigged ship where most of the flag signals were hoisted, and in the older days of sail, when the disciplinary code on board included punishments of death by hanging, were the traditional points from which men were hanged on board.

YARDMEN, see TOPMEN.

YARNELL, HARRY ERVIN (1875–1959), American admiral, was born in Iowa and graduated from the Naval Academy in 1897. He was in the U.S.S. *Oregon* when that vessel made her famous voyage from the west coast of the U.S.A. to Key West in 1898 (see ROOSEVELT, Theodore); and was present in the action during the Spanish–American War of 1898 when the Spanish fleet was destroyed on 3 July off Santiago, Cuba. During the First World War (1914–18) he served on the staff of Admiral William *Sims in London. This was followed by duty in the office of the Chief of Naval Operations and an appointment on the staff of the Naval War College. He was the first commanding officer of the *aircraft carrier *Saratoga* when she commissioned in November 1927 and was Chief of the Bureau of Engineering in the Navy Department from 1928 to 1932. His last active service was as commander-in-chief of the Asiatic Fleet, October 1936 to July 1939, and during that period his reports to the Navy Department in Washington accurately forecast the occurrences in the Far East during the Japanese invasion of China in the years immediately preceding the Second World War.

YARROW, Sir ALFRED FERNANDEZ (1842–1932), British marine engineer, was the son of a Scottish father and a Jewish mother and was educated at University College School, London, where he soon showed a great aptitude for mechanics. At the age of 15 he was apprenticed to Ravenhill, Salkeld, and Co., marine engine builders, and during the next five years, in collaboration with his close friend James Hilditch,

he conducted many mechanical experiments and took out a number of patents.

In partnership with Hedley he established in 1866 a small marine works on the Isle of Dogs, Poplar, which was to become world famous, initially for the design and perfection of steam launches, of which some 350 were built in the next nine years. The invention of the *Whitehead torpedo led to the production of Yarrow's first *torpedoboat in 1876 for the Argentine Navy, to be followed by many others for the British, French, Greek, and Russian navies.

When the British Admiralty decided to acquire a new type of warship, the torpedoboat *destroyer, the construction of two of the first four experimental boats was entrusted to Yarrow and, launched in 1893, emerged as the *Havock* and *Hornet*, each with a speed of 27·3 knots. Two years later, a destroyer built by Yarrow for the Russian Navy, the *Sokol*, was the first such ship to achieve 30 knots. The Yarrow straight-tube boiler, which remained in use for more than forty years, was an integral part of the machinery of Yarrow destroyers.

The Yarrow works were transferred to Scotstoun, on the River Clyde, in 1907. Though Alfred Yarrow had retired from business before the outbreak of the First World War (1914–18) he collaborated with the then First Sea Lord, Admiral Sir John *Fisher, in developing the rapid construction of destroyers and of light-draught river *gunboats for the campaign in Mesopotamia (Iraq) in 1916–17. In recognition of his war services, Yarrow was made a baronet in 1916.

YAW, to, the effect on a ship's *course produced by a following wind or sea. With the vessel travelling through the water in the same direction as that in which the sea is running or the wind blowing, the effect of the *rudder is diminished and the vessel yaws away from the desired course. A good helmsman can often anticipate the moment when a vessel is most likely to yaw, and correct the tendency to do so by applying the requisite *helm to counteract it. The word is also used as a noun to denote the involuntary movement caused by wind or sea by which a ship deviates from her chosen course. A yaw can also be caused by unintelligent steering on the part of a helmsman.

YAWL, a type of rig of a small sailing boat or yacht, apparently an adaptation of the Dutch word *jol*, skiff. The true yawl rig consists of two masts, *cutter-rigged (in the English meaning of the term) on the foremast, with a small *mizenmast *stepped abaft the *rudder-head carrying a *spanker or driving sail. The term, however, refers more to the positions of the masts than the particular rig they carry, and thus a sailing boat with masts stepped as above but *sloop-rigged on the foremast would also be termed a yawl. The rig is very similar to that of a *ketch, the difference being the position in which the mizen is stepped. In a ketch, the mizen is stepped forward of the rudder-head; in a yawl it is stepped abaft it. Until about the mid-19th century, the term was also occasionally used for a ship's boat rowed by four or more oars, but this use of it is now obsolete.

'YELLOW ADMIRAL', a term used in Britain to denote a *post-captain promoted to rear admiral on retirement but without serving in that rank. The term dates from the days before 1864 when the British fleet was divided into red, white, and blue squadrons, and admirals took their rank from their *squadronal colour; thus, a rear admiral of the Blue was junior to a rear admiral of the White, who was junior to a rear admiral of the Red. A 'yellow admiral' therefore had no rank at all in the flag list.

The pressure to create 'yellow admirals' arose after the Napoleonic War (1803–15) when the list of post-captains was so large that the prospect of promotion was infinitely remote. Under the system of promotion then prevailing, every officer who had reached post-captain's rank was automatically promoted when his seniority brought him to the top of the list and a vacancy in the flag list occurred. It was to keep some movement in these lists that post-captains, on reaching the top by seniority, were promoted to flag rank and placed on the retired list on the following day, so that they did not automatically swell the rear-admirals' list.

These were the 'yellow admirals', and by their removal from the lists, ensured that those for whom future employment as admirals was envisaged had a reasonable chance of progressing up the list by seniority.

YELLOW JACK, the sailor's name for yellow fever, and also the slang name given to the quarantine flag in the *International Code of Signals, Q flag, which is coloured yellow. It was also the name often given to a naval pensioner in *Greenwich Hospital who was too fond of his liquor, such men being made to wear a particoloured coat in which yellow was the predominant colour so that the other pensioners might be warned that he was a man who might try to wheedle their daily ration of beer out of them.

YERMAK, the name of the first Russian polar *ice-breaker, a ship with a displacement of 10,000 tons and engines of 10,000 h.p. She was built at Newcastle, England, in 1898, for the Russian government at the instigation of Admiral S. O. Makarov (1848–1904), who intended to sail her direct to the North pole. Not unexpectedly, she proved unequal to this ambitious task but served for over sixty years in the waters to the north of Russia and Siberia on the Northern Sea Route. She was withdrawn from service in 1963 and handed over to a sea training school at Murmansk.

YEVGENOV, NIKOLAY IVANOVICH (1888–1964), Russian oceanographer, made his first voyage to Arctic waters, to whose study he devoted his life, as a young naval hydrographer in 1910. He was assistant to the leader of the hydrographic expedition which traversed the Northern Sea Route (see NORTH-EAST PASSAGE) north of Siberia, in 1914–15 in the *Taymyr* and *Vaygach*.

After the Russian revolution he made surveys of many regions off the north Siberian coast and was in charge of freight shipping into and out of the Kara Sea from 1925 to 1931, during which years he wrote the first Kara Sea Pilot. In 1933 he was appointed chief hydrographer of the commission which administered the Northern Sea Route, a position he held until 1938. He wrote a great many papers on many different aspects of oceanography, and became a recognized expert in the study of sea ice.

YOKE, a transverse board fitted to the top of a *rudder in a small boat instead of a *tiller, the rudder being moved by yoke lines attached to the ends of the yoke and operated by the helmsman. Yokes are mainly to be found in small boats which are pulled by oars; and very occasionally in small, open sailing craft where the position of a mizen or *jigger mast makes the operation of a tiller impossible.

YOKOHAMA, a major seaport of Japan on the western shore of Tokyo Bay and about 18 miles south of the capital city, of which it is the main port. Its growth started a year or two after Japan was opened to foreign traders in 1859, and has continued ever since. Ship repair and building facilities were developed to make Yokohama into one of the principal seaports of the world.

YOKOSUKA, a Japanese naval base in Tokyo Bay, approximately midway between Yokohama and Tokyo. The first shipyard was established there in 1865, converted three years later into a naval dockyard by the Japanese government. With the growth in importance of the Japanese Navy during the closing decades of the 19th century, the decision was taken in 1884 to convert Yokosuka into a first-class naval station and a principal naval base for the Japanese Navy.

YORK, JAMES, Duke of, see JAMES, Duke of York.

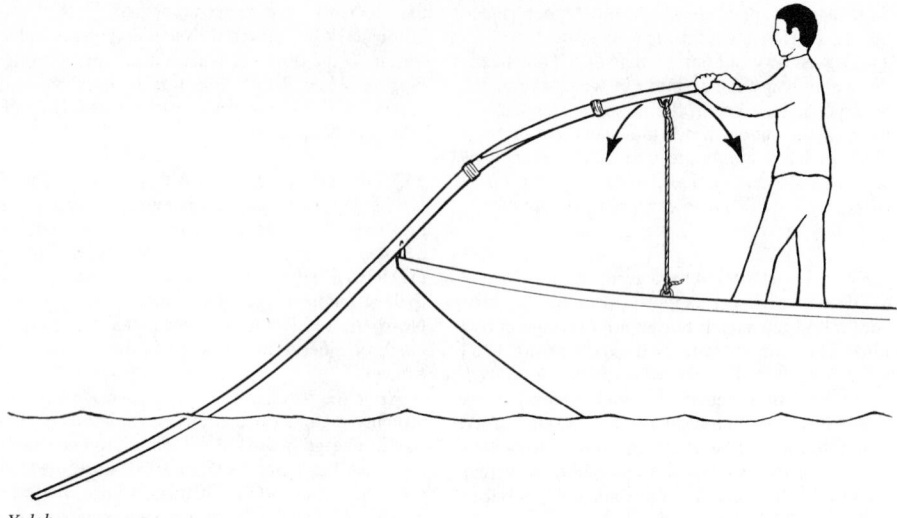

Yuloh

'YOUTH', one of the finest short stories of the sea, written by Joseph * Conrad and published, with other stories, in 1902. It is based on personal experience when Conrad was second mate of the *Palestine*, which caught fire and was abandoned off Java Head, the whole crew taking to the boats.

YULOH, a form of long * oar or * sweep used by Chinese boatmen over the stern to propel * sampans and the smaller * junks. It is usually made in two parts, either * scarfed and pegged or lashed together, giving the yuloh a distinct bow which causes the blade to be very whippy or flexible. It is mounted loosely over a peg on the boat's stern, and the forward or inboard end is attached to the deck by a length of line, allowing the end to be roughly waist high, while the outboard end with the blade enters the water at an angle of about 30 degrees. By alternately pushing and pulling the inboard end of the yuloh athwartships the sampan man or girl causes the blade to flex from side to side in the water with a fish's tail or * sculling action, and so drive the sampan forward.

Z

ZEEBRUGGE, a seaport on the coast of Belgium, connected to the inland port of Bruges by an eight-mile ship canal. It was the scene of a blocking operation by the Royal Navy during the First World War (1914–18), the objective being to stop German *destroyers and *U-boats based at Bruges from reaching the open sea. The operation, which was planned and directed by Vice Admiral Sir Roger *Keyes, took place on the night of 22/23 April 1918, three old *cruisers, *Thetis, Intrepid,* and *Iphigenia,* largely stripped and filled with concrete, attempting to sink themselves across the mouth of the canal. At the same time a diversionary attack on the detached mole was made by 200 seamen and 700 marines transported alongside in the old cruiser *Vindictive,* and two old *submarines filled with explosive were to force themselves under the bridge connecting the mole with the shore and blow themselves up.

Although the operation was most gallantly carried out—eight awards of the Victoria Cross were made—it was only of minimal success. The three blockships failed to reach their proper position and only partially impeded the fairway, and on the following day four German *torpedoboats successfully negotiated the obstacles and got safely to sea. A U-boat was equally successful on the 25th.

A simultaneous attempt to block the harbour entrance at Ostend, also connected by canal to Bruges, was a fiasco; the two blockships failing to find the entrance to the harbour because of the removal of a navigational buoy.

ZENITH, in nautical astronomy the point in the heavens immediately above an observer on the surface of the earth. A line through the centre of the earth and the observer on its surface points directly to his zenith. See NAVIGATION, Celestial.

ZENITH DISTANCE, the angle between an observer's *zenith and an observed celestial body subtended at the earth's centre. It is the complement of the true *altitude of a celestial body, and forms one side of the astronomical triangle, the basis of astronomical navigation at sea.

ZIMMERMANN TELEGRAM, an enciphered diplomatic telegram sent by Arthur Zimmermann, the Foreign Secretary of Germany, to Count von Bernstorff, the German Ambassador in Washington, on 16 January 1917 which was in the main responsible for the U.S.A. entering the First World War (1914–18) on the side of the allied powers. The telegram was dispatched by wireless and cable, read in England, and deciphered in *Room 40 O.B., in the British Admiralty. It announced the institution of unrestricted *submarine warfare on 1 February 1917 and, in the belief that this would be sufficient to bring the U.S.A. into the war, required von Bernstorff to approach the President of Mexico with a view to Mexico declaring war, in alliance with Japan, on the U.S.A. for the reconquest of the states of Texas, New Mexico, and Arizona, promising full German support. This, it was considered, would keep the U.S.A. sufficiently occupied to prevent her intervening in France. The telegram was passed by Britain to the U.S. Ambassador in London, who dispatched it to President Wilson.

The interception and deciphering of the Zimmermann telegram by the British Naval Intelligence Department was probably the greatest of the many coups which emerged from Room 40 O.B.

ZONE TIMES, the division of the world by meridians of *longitude into zones and sectors where the same time is kept, particularly in ships at sea. The sun crosses each meridian of longitude at its local noon; four minutes later it

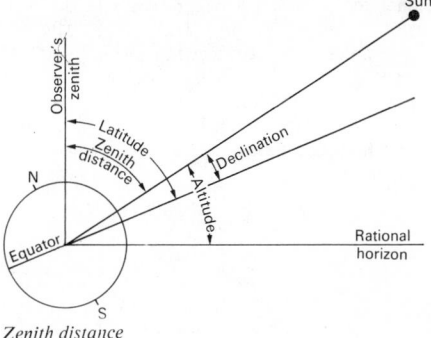

Zenith distance

A Zulu; contemporary model

reaches the next degree of longitude and crosses it also at its local noon. Without some agreed system of time, all clocks in the world would therefore show different times according to the longitude of the place where they are. The world therefore has been divided into zones of 15 degrees of longitude within which all clocks keep the same time. The sun takes one hour to cross 15 degrees of longitude, and so adjacent zones differ from each other by one hour. Zone times are measured east and west of the longitude of *Greenwich (0°), and are designated as plus or minus as to whether the zone difference must be added or subtracted to the local time to indicate the time at Greenwich. Zones east of Greenwich are therefore minus, and zones west are plus. The longitude of 180°, where Zones +12 and −12 meet, is known as the *international date line. Zone times were introduced in 1918.

'Z-TWIST', the description in the rope trade applied to *rope which is laid up right-handed. For illus. see s-TWIST.

ZUBIAN, H.M.S., a British *destroyer of the First World War (1914–18) constructed in 1917 out of the bow section of H.M.S. *Zulu,* whose stern had been blown off by a *mine, and the stern section of H.M.S. *Nubian,* whose bows had been severely damaged by a *torpedo. The joining of the two undamaged sections, and the composite name, were both the idea of Admiral Sir Reginald *Bacon, commanding the Dover Patrol in which the original ships were damaged.

ZULU, a type of fishing vessel peculiar to the north-east coastal ports of Scotland. It had a broad-beamed *carvel hull with a straight stem and a pointed stern with a pronounced rake, at times as much as 45°. These boats were rigged with a dipping *lug foresail and a standing lug mizen. They were introduced by a boat-builder named Cameron as an improvement on local types of fishing craft and were first produced during the Zulu War (1878–9), hence their name. The introduction of the internal combustion engine has rendered the type obsolete.

Appendix 1
EQUIVALENT RANKS

British	French	German	Italian
Admiral of the Fleet †	None	Grossadmiral	Grande Ammiraglio
Admiral	Amiral	Admiral	Ammiraglio (d'Armata)
Vice Admiral	Vice-amiral	Vizeadmiral	Ammiraglio di Squadra
Rear Admiral	Contre-amiral	Konteradmiral	Ammiraglio di Divisione or Contrammiraglio
Commodore	Chef d'Escadre	Kommodore	Commodoro
Captain	Capitaine de Vaisseau	Kapitän zur See	Capitano di Vascello
Commander	Capitaine de Frégate	{ Fregattenkapitän Korvettenkapitän	Capitano di Fregatta
Lieutenant-Commander	Capitaine de Corvette	Kapitänleutnant	Capitano di Corvetta
Lieutenant	Lieutenant de Vaisseau	Oberleutnant zur See	Tenente di Vascello
Sub-Lieutenant +	Enseigne de Vaisseau	Leutnant zur See	Sottotenente di Vascello
Midshipman	Aspirant	Fähnrich	Guardiamarina

Note Ranks in the United States Navy are the same as in the British Navy with the exception of † Fleet Admiral and + Lieutenant (j.g.)

Chief Petty Officer	Premier Maître	Oberbootman	Capo di prima classe
Petty Officer	Second Maître	Obermaat	Capo di Seconda classe
Leading Seaman	Quartier-maître or Matelot de 1ère classe	Obermatrose	secondo Capo
Able Seaman	Gabier breveté	Vollmatrose	Marinaio scelto
Ordinary Seaman	Matelot	Leichtmatrose	Marinaio
Boy	Mousse	Diener/Knabe	Mozzo

Royal Navy	British Army	Royal Air Force
Admiral of the Fleet	Field Marshal	Marshal of the Royal Air Force
Admiral	General	Air Chief Marshal
Vice Admiral	Lieutenant-General	Air Marshal
Rear Admiral	Major-General	Air Vice Marshal
Commodore	Brigadier	Air Commodore
Captain	Colonel	Group Captain
Commander	Lieutenant-Colonel	Wing Commander
Lieutenant-Commander	Major*	Squadron Leader
Lieutenant	Captain*	Flight Lieutenant
Sub-Lieutenant	Lieutenant*	Flying Officer
Midshipman	Second Lieutenant*	Pilot Officer

* Officers of the Royal Marines when embarked have an equivalent rank one grade higher.

Appendix 2
INTERNATIONAL CODE OF SIGNALS

A	Alpha	· —	I have a diver down; keep well clear at slow speed.
B	Bravo	— · · ·	I am taking in, or discharging, or carrying, dangerous goods.
C	Charlie	— · — ·	Yes (affirmative).
D	Delta	— · ·	Keep clear of me—I am manoeuvring with difficulty.
E	Echo	·	I am altering my course to starboard.
F	Foxtrot	· · — ·	I am disabled—communicate with me.
G	Golf	— — ·	I require a pilot. When made by fishing vessels operating in close proximity on the fishing grounds it means: 'I am hauling nets.'
H	Hotel	· · · ·	I have a pilot on board.
I	India	· ·	I am altering my course to port.
J	Juliett	· — — —	I am on fire and have dangerous cargo on board: keep well clear of me.
K	Kilo	— · —	I wish to communicate with you.
L	Lima	· — · ·	You should stop your vessel instantly.
M	Mike	— —	My vessel is stopped and making no way through the water.
N	November	— ·	No (negative).
O	Oscar	— — —	Man overboard.
P	Papa	· — — ·	In harbour hoisted at the foremast head, Blue Peter, 'All persons should report on board as the vessel is about to proceed to sea.' At sea, it may be used by fishing vessels to mean, 'My nets have come fast upon an obstruction.'
Q	Quebec	— — · —	My vessel is healthy and I request free pratique.
R	Romeo	· — ·	
S	Sierra	· · ·	My engines are going astern.
T	Tango	—	Keep clear of me; I am engaged in pair trawling.
U	Uniform	· · —	You are running into danger.
V	Victor	· · · —	I require assistance.
W	Whiskey	· — —	I require medical assistance.
X	Xray	— · · —	Stop carrying out your intentions and watch for my signals.
Y	Yankee	— · — —	I am dragging my anchor.
Z	Zulu	— — · ·	I require a tug. When made by fishing vessels operating in close proximity on the fishing grounds it means: 'I am shooting nets.'

1	· — — — —		6	— · · · ·
2	· · — — —		7	— — · · ·
3	· · · — —		8	— — — · ·
4	· · · · —		9	— — — — ·
5	· · · · ·		0	— — — — —

ALPHABETICAL FLAGS

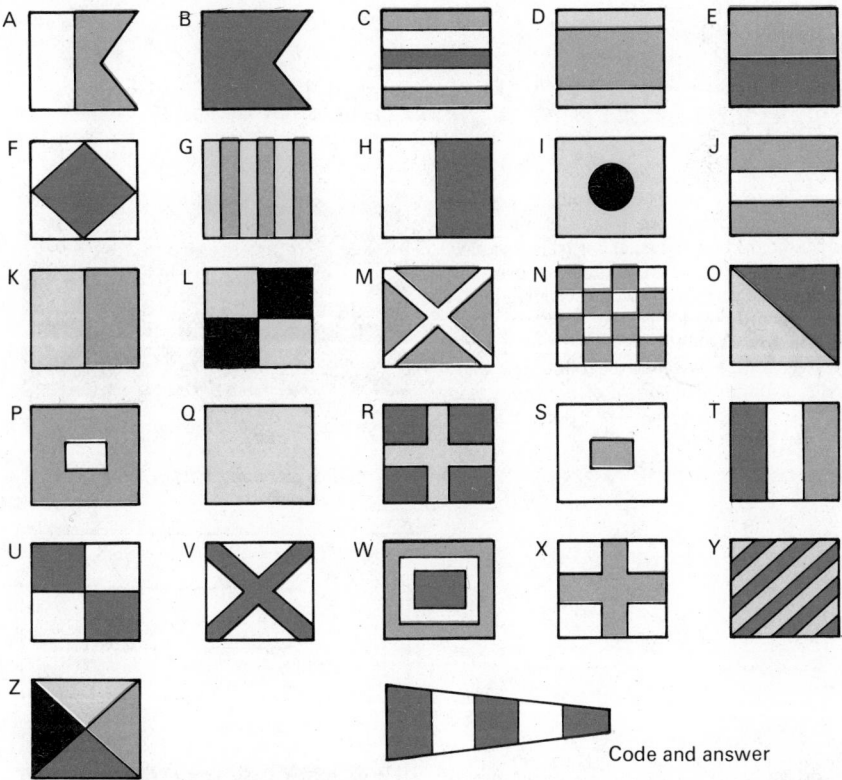

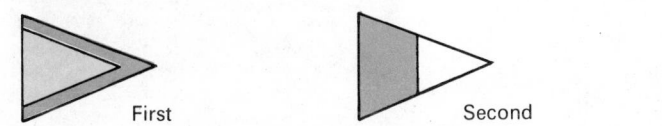

SUBSTITUTES

First   Second   Third

NUMERAL PENNANTS

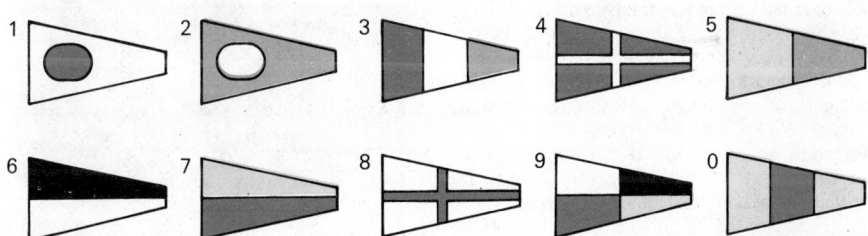

Appendix 3
RULE OF THE ROAD—Important Lights, Daymarks, and Fog Signals

A power-driven vessel under way at night, less than 150 feet in length, carries one white steaming light, port and starboard bow lights, and a white overtaking light (not visible in the illustrations). If over 150 feet in length, she carries two white steaming lights, port and starboard bow lights, and a white overtaking light. In low visibility, day or night, power-driven vessels under way sound the following signals (on whistle or siren) at intervals of not more than two minutes: if making way—one long blast; if stopped—two long blasts.

Power-driven vessel, over 150 feet in length, under way at night

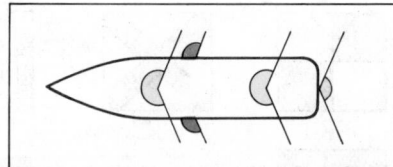

Arcs of visibility of lights

A power-driven vessel towing another vessel carries her bow lights, overtaking light and steaming light. If the length of tow is less than 600 feet an additional steaming light is carried; if the length of tow is more than 600 feet a third steaming light is carried. By day if the length of tow exceeds 600 feet a black diamond shape is carried. In low visibility, day or night, a vessel towing sounds one long followed by two short blasts on her siren or whistle at intervals of not more than one minute.

Vessel of over 150 feet towing another at night: length of tow is more than 600 feet

Vessels engaged in trawling show an all-round green light above an all-round white light, both visible two miles. They may carry in addition one steaming light, lower than and abaft the all-round green and white lights. When making way through the water they show bow lights and overtaking light. Drift net vessels show an all-round red light above an all-round white light. When making way through the water they show bow lights and overtaking light. If outlying gear extends more than 500 feet an additional all-round white light shows the direction of the gear. By day all fishing vessels show a black shape consisting of two cones point to point. If outlying gear extends more than 500 feet, a black cone, point upwards, indicates the direction of the gear.

Trawler trawling and making way, showing optional steaming light

A vessel under way at night, but not under command and stopped, hoists two all-round red lights, one above the other, visible two miles, and switches off all other navigation lights. If she is making way through the water she shows bow lights and overtaking light in addition. By day she hoists two black balls. In low visibility, day or night, she sounds one long blast followed by two short blasts at intervals of not more than one minute.

Vessel not under command and stopped, at night

A power-driven pilot-vessel on duty and under way carries bow lights, overtaking light and, at the mast-head, a white all-round light above a red all-round light, both visible three miles. She also shows one or more flare-ups at intervals not exceeding 10 minutes or an intermittent white light visible all round.

Power-driven pilot-vessel on duty and making way, at night

A sailing vessel under way at night carries bow lights and an overtaking light. In addition she may carry on the top of the foremast a red light above a green light, visible two miles and showing from ahead to two points abaft the beam. In low visibility, day or night, sailing vessels under way sound the following signals at intervals of not more than one minute: one blast—vessel on the starboard tack; two blasts—vessel on the port tack; three blasts—vessel running with the wind abaft the beam.

Sailing vessels under way at night, showing (left) optional fore masthead lights

A vessel of less than 150 feet, when at anchor, carries in the forepart a white all-round light visible two miles. If of 150 feet or more in length, she carried two white all-round lights, visible three miles: one near the bow, the other at or near the stern and 15 feet lower.

Vessel of less than 150 feet, anchored

A light-vessel when driven from her proper station shows by night a red fixed light at the bow and stern, and red and white flares shown simultaneously every 15 minutes. By day she shows two black balls, one forward and one aft, and the signal PC.

A light-vessel out of station at night

Appendix 4
BUOYS AND BUOYAGE

Port hand buoy
Top marks optional
1 to 4 red flashes or
2, 4 or 6 white flashes

Starboard hand buoy
Top marks optional
1, 3 or 5 white flashes

Landfall buoys
Shape in accordance
with rules for channel
marking, flashing light

Outer end   Inner end

Outer end   Inner end

Outer end   Inner end

Main channel to right

Channels of equal importance

Main channel to left

MIDDLE GROUND BUOYS AND SPARS
Light red or white and distinctive from port and starboard buoys

To be passed on

Outfall and spoilground buoy
Shape optional

Port hand
Green double
flashing

Either hand
Green single
occulting

Starboard hand
Green triple
flashing

WRECK BUOYS AND SPARS

To be passed on

Starboard hand, 3 strokes

Either hand, 4 strokes

Port hand, 2 strokes

WRECK VESSELS
In fog, bell sounds every 30 seconds. Green lights are hoisted in place of shapes at night.

The system of buoyage in E.E.C. waters may be radically changed during the late 1970s.

Appendix 5
EQUIVALENTS OF SOME COMMON
UNITS OF MEASUREMENT

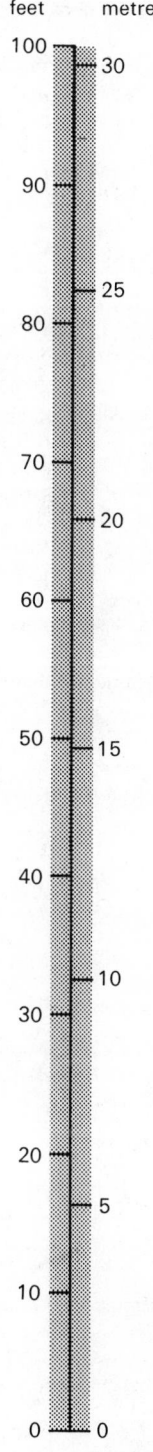

British to Metric

1 inch (in.) = 25·400 millimetres (mm)

1 foot (ft) = 0·305 metres (m)

1 yard (yd) = 0·914 metres (m)

1 fathom = 6 ft = 1·829 metres (m)

1 pound (lb) = 0·454 kilograms (kg)

1 ton = 1·016 tonnes

1 pint = 0·568 litres (l)

1 gallon = 4·546 litres (l)

Metric to British

1 centimetre (cm) = 0·394 inches (in.)

1 metre (m) = 39·370 inches (in.)

1 metre (m) = 3·281 feet (ft)

1 metre (m) = 1·094 yards (yd)

1 kilogram (kg) = 2·205 pounds (lb)

1 tonne (metric ton) = 2205 pounds (lb)

1 tonne = 0·984 tons

1 litre (l) = 1·760 pints

1 litre (l) = 0·220 gallons

1 nautical mile = 10 cables = 6,080 feet

1 nautical mile = 1 minute of latitude

Acknowledgements

Thanks are due to the following for permission to reproduce photographs on the pages indicated:

Ardea Photographics (Adrian Warren): 14; Beken of Cowes Ltd: 418, 566, 616, 823, 835, 949, 951, 952, 956 *top and bottom*; Bodleian Library: 330; Bord Fáilte: 219; British Library: 494, 783, 930; British Museum: 156, 280, 540, 619; Crown Copyright (1955): 160; Camera Press: 145, 254, 269, 468, 563, 794, 844, 935; J. Allan Cash: 724; Castle Museum, Norwich: 523 *top*; Central Press: 817; Guildhall Library: 241, 495; Imperial War Museum: 13, 285, 346, 395, 429, 441, 458, 515, 551, 565, 637, 666, 667, 714, 785 *bottom*, 900, 958; Kelvin Hughes Ltd: 582; Keystone Press Agency Ltd: 75, 165, 484; Kon-Tiki Museet: 456; Mansell Collection: 7, 19, 67, 115, 141, 154, 173, 179, 183, 184, 190, 223, 232, 298, 336, 348, 353, 385, 404, 437, 475, 480 *top*, 483, 511, 601, 613, 621, 628, 650, 658, 761, 782, 785 *top*, 791, 860, 943; Mystic Seaport Inc.: 763; National Maritime Museum: 60, 61, 66, 91, 204, 264, 277, 305, 328, 335, 386, 403, 415, 422, 447, 487, 492, 521, 522, 648, 649, 657, 664, 671, 678, 682, 694, 725, 728, 742, 743, 813, 834, 854, 864, 872, 884/5, 886, 904, 912, 913, 915; National Portrait Gallery: 356, 372, 591, 689, 717; Naval Library: 45, 158, 226, 525, 934; Novosti Press Agency: 413, 612, 665; Fred Olsen Line: 304: Universitets Oldsaksamling, Oslo: 497; Musée de la Marine, Paris: 577; Popperfoto: 217, 225, 243, 267, 329, 401, 609, 681, 748, 749, 787, 849, 855, 862; Radio Times Hulton Picture Library: 15, 21, 37, 57, 84, 101, 113, 195, 201, 202, 250 *top left*, 286, 309, 325, 351, 354, 398, 427, 435, 456, 504, 542, 550, 626, 641, 673, 715, 753, 780, 873, 890; Ronan Picture Library: 39, 250 *top right*, 250 *bottom*, 253, 316, 362, 367, 578, 579, 600, 677, 878; Ronan Picture Library and Royal Astronomical Society: 52; Vikingeskibshallen, Roskilde: 453; Royal National Lifeboat Institution: 480 *bottom*; Royal Scottish Museum: 964; Tate Gallery: 523 *bottom*, 897; Topix: 455; Trinity House Lighthouse Service: 889; Union-Castle: 901; U.S. Naval Academy Museum: 555; U.S. Naval Institute: 842; U.S. Navy Photo: 841; Victoria and Albert Museum: 345, 589.

The title-page illustration is by courtesy of the Mansell Collection.